W9-CVP-773

𝒫RESENTED

TO

_____

_____

_____

BY

_____

ON

_____

The STUDENT BIBLE

Notes by Philip Yancey and Tim Stafford

UPDATED
NASB
The Most Literal Is
Now More Readable

Updated New American Standard Bible

Zondervan Publishing House
Grand Rapids, Michigan 49530, USA

Contents

The Books of the Old Testament

The Books of the New Testament

Explanation and Abbreviations

EXPLANATION OF GENERAL FORMAT

FOOTNOTES are used only where the text especially requires them for clarification. Marginal notes and cross-references have been deleted from this edition.

PARAGRAPHS are designated by a paragraph symbol and bold face verse numbers or letters.

QUOTATION MARKS are used in the text in accordance with modern English usage.

"THOU," "THEE" AND "THY" are not used in this edition and have been rendered as "You" and "Your."

PERSONAL PRONOUNS are capitalized when pertaining to Deity.

ITALICS are used in the text to indicate words which are not found in the original Hebrew, Aramaic, or Greek but implied by it. Italics are used in the marginal notes to signify alternate readings for the text. Roman text in the marginal alternate readings is the same as italics in the Bible text.

SMALL CAPS in the New Testament are used in the text to indicate Old Testament quotations or obvious references to Old Testament texts. Variations of Old Testament wording are found in New Testament citations depending on whether the New Testament writer translated from a Hebrew text, used existing Greek or Aramaic translations, or paraphrased the material. It should be noted that modern rules for the indication of direct quotation were not used in biblical times; thus, the ancient writer would use exact quotations or references to quotation without specific indication of such.

ASTERISKS are used to mark verbs that are historical presents in the Greek which have been translated with an English past tense in order to conform to modern usage. The translators recognized that in some contexts the present tense seems more unexpected and unjustified to the English reader than a past tense would have been. But Greek authors frequently used the present tense for the sake of heightened vividness, thereby transporting their readers in imagination to the actual scene at the time of occurrence. However, the translators felt that it would be wise to change these historical presents to English past tenses.

ABBREVIATIONS AND SPECIAL MARKINGS

Aram = Aramaic

DSS = Dead Sea Scrolls

Gr = Greek translation of O.T. (Septuagint or LXX) or Greek text of N.T.

Heb = Hebrew text, usually Masoretic

Lat = Latin

M.T. = Masoretic text

Syr = Syriac

Lit = A literal translation

Or = An alternate translation justified by the Hebrew, Aramaic, or Greek

[ ] = In text, brackets indicate words probably not in the original writings

[ ] = In margin, brackets indicate references to a name, place or thing similar to, but not identical with that in the text

cf = compare

f, ff = following verse or verses

mg = Refers to a marginal reading on another verse

ms, mss = manuscript, manuscripts

v, vv = verse, verses

Why the Student Bible?

THE BIBLE IS THE MOST important book ever written—a gift to us from God himself. Styles and tastes change, but people all through history have recognized the Bible's uniqueness. They have treated it with special reverence, yet, strangely, even people who value the Bible often fail to read it. Most Americans believe the Bible to be from God. But Gallup polls reveal that only a small percentage of them can name basic Biblical facts, such as four of the Ten Commandments. Their Bibles sit somewhere on a shelf or coffee table, impressive to look at, but unread.

Christians we meet mention repeatedly their guilt about not reading the Bible consistently. They believe in the Bible. They expect to find help there. But they do not read the Bible nearly as often as they think they should.

Troubled by this reality, we began work on *The Student Bible.* Our aim: to produce an edition of the Bible that ordinary people could—and would—read on a regular, sustained basis. We used modern research techniques to try to find an answer to the question, "What keeps you from reading the Bible?" We discovered three main reasons. In developing this edition of the Bible, we worked hard to address those three reasons.

"I Get Discouraged"

Simple discouragement was the most common reason we heard for not reading the Bible. Many people we surveyed had tried to read the Bible regularly, but such experiments usually ended in failure.

The Bible is a big book. People who plan to read through the whole Bible starting with Genesis often get bogged down somewhere around Numbers or Deuteronomy. Fatigue sets in.

Other people never even start a reading plan. With busy schedules and limited confidence, they feel sure they'll fail such a project. Instead, they occasionally turn to familiar passages from the Gospel of John or the Psalms. They wouldn't know where to start venturing out into unfamiliar books.

We spent much time and research trying to find an answer to the discouragement problem. The result: the **3-Track Reading Plan**, which recognizes that people approach the Bible at different levels. All three "tracks" suggest reading one chapter a day—just 5 or 10 minutes, for most readers.

Track 1 requires a commitment of two weeks at a time, reading one chapter a day. By following it, a reader can encounter some of the most fundamental parts of the Bible. Pages 7-8 present two-week selections on Jesus and Paul, and a two-week sampling of the Old Testament. Pages 15-16 list a variety of further options depending on your personal interests. Just a few hours of investment can yield a solid introduction into the best of books.

Track 2 represents the next level of commitment. It takes six months, reading about one chapter a day. In Track 2 you will read at least one chapter from every book in the Bible. When you finish, you will have read the best-known, most-quoted, easiest-to-understand portions of the Bible.

Track 3 includes every word of the Bible. Reading about one chapter a day, you devote three years to reading the entire Bible.

We believe the 3-track plan offers a handy, realistic method for approaching the Bible. It builds in several levels of success to combat the discouragement that afflicts Bible readers. A complete description for the 3-track plan follows on the next pages. In addition, the How to Read section in the Introduction to each Bible book uses the icon above and describes how the 3-track plan fits into that book.

"I Can't Understand It"

Many readers grow up with very little exposure to the Bible. They may never have heard of Goliath or Abraham. Often they ask, "What is the point of reading about spears and chariots and village wells?"

Because it was written several thousand years ago, the Bible presents a culture gap. It mentions hard-to-pronounce names and refers to many outdated customs. For most readers, the Bible is the most ancient book in their library.

Most of us need some coaching on how to jump the 2,000-year gap back to when the Bible was written. *The Student Bible* addresses this problem with hundreds of additional notes scattered throughout the book. Each of these features is marked with a distinctive design element or icon.

Introductions: Each of the 66 books of the Bible is preceded by an Introduction that gives crucial background on the book and tells why it was written. By reading these Introductions, you'll gain a sense of how one particular book is different from, and yet fits together with, every other book in the Bible. In addition, you'll get clues to each book's contemporary relevance.

 Insights: Throughout *The Student Bible*, you'll find short articles marked with this "Insight" icon. Written in the style of a modern magazine article, Insights include important background information right in the Bible, near the passage they shed light on. They condense the material that, in our judgment, will most help you understand and find meaning in the Bible. At the end of each Insight, **Life Questions** help relate the passage to practical life situations.

Profiles: We have selected "100 People You Should Know" in the Bible. Profiles marked with this icon give background material to help introduce these people. In a few cases these Profiles are combined with Insights or are found in a book's Introduction; these, too, are marked with the Profiles icon. Each of these Profiles also features a **Life Question**.

Highlights: Much shorter notes, marked off from the text in this manner, appear frequently in *The Student Bible*. These explain confusing verses, point out interesting facts, and, in effect, highlight something in the passage that might get easily overlooked. They're designed to catch your attention and draw you to read the Bible more closely.

"I Can't Find It"

"I spend a lot of time just flipping through the Bible, looking for something," we were told again and again. Many Bible readers are searching for help on specific issues—but they don't know where to find it.

Everybody has heard of something in the Bible—the Ten Commandments, the Golden Rule, the story of Daniel in the lions' den. But how do you know where to look for them? The Bible is too large just to flip through on a random search.

To aid in such a search, this edition of *The Student Bible* has greatly expanded a section called "**Where to Find It.**" It appears at the back of this book, just before the maps section. You'll notice that the side of the book is marked with a tab that indicates this section's location. We hope this becomes the first place you turn when you want to find something in the Bible. The "Where to Find It" section includes the following features: a glossary of the proper names mentioned in the Bible notes; a list of miracles, parables, and other important Bible events and teachings; a guide to familiar psalms; a capsule history of the Old Testament kings and prophets. This is also where you'll find an index of the "100 People You Should Know" Profiles.

In addition to all these features, "Where to Find It" includes a Subject Guide. The Guide concentrates on major passages, not single verses. Whether you are looking for information about a familiar passage or are searching for help with a crucial life question, the Subject Guide should eliminate the "I can't find it" problem.

We hope these notes and features will help you learn some of the basic facts about the background and message of each book in the Bible. *The Student Bible* does not, of course, take the place of a Bible commentary or concordance. It is primarily a *reading* Bible. We believe that the habit of regular Bible reading is the best way for ordinary Christians to become familiar with the full breadth of God's Word.

In publishing *The Student Bible*, we are not trying to add to the Bible or to enliven it. The Bible speaks for itself. It is the most powerful book ever written, and it needs no help. We, its readers, are the ones who need help, and *The Student Bible* merely offers practical aids for the average reader. A good measure of our success will be whether this book helps you to read the Bible for yourself. That, after all, is our ultimate goal.

—*Philip Yancey and Tim Stafford*

3-Track Plan for Reading the Bible

O f all the reasons people mention for not reading the Bible, simple discouragement ranks highest. The Bible's length alone is imposing. More like a self-contained library than a book, it includes 66 different books, by several dozen authors. Little wonder people get confused and discouraged.

The following 3-Track Reading Plan helps break the Bible into more manageable portions. If you're new to the Bible, begin with Track 1, then proceed to Track 2, and finally—if you're ambitious—tackle Track 3. Your understanding and appreciation for the Bible should gradually increase.

All three tracks share one thing in common: They each assign usually one chapter a day. Reading an average Bible chapter should take only 5-10 minutes.

Note that the 3-track plan for each book is included within the Introduction to the book (see, for example, "How to Read Genesis," page 24). You can record your progress by checking off the boxes here or within each individual book.

TRACK 1: Introduction to the Bible

TIME COMMITMENT:
Two Weeks

GOAL:
To survey basic biblical foundations

T rack 1 is a place to begin reading the Bible. Three two-week reading courses take you quickly into passages of the Bible every Christian should know.

These were selected with two concerns in mind: first, they are frequently quoted or referred to. Second, they are relatively easy to read and understand. Track 1 is a sampler, designed to whet your appetite for more.

If you like Track 1, but feel unready to tackle Track 2, you can find more Track 1 courses on pages 15-16.

1. Two Weeks on the Life and Teachings of Jesus

☐ Day 1. LUKE 1: Preparing for Jesus' arrival

☐ Day 2. LUKE 2: The story of Jesus' birth

☐ Day 3. MARK 1: The beginning of Jesus' ministry

☐ Day 4. MARK 9: A day in the life of Jesus

☐ Day 5. MATTHEW 5: The Sermon on the Mount

☐ Day 6. MATTHEW 6: The Sermon on the Mount

☐ Day 7. LUKE 15: Parables of Jesus

☐ Day 8. JOHN 3: A conversation with Jesus

☐ Day 9. JOHN 14: Jesus' final instructions

☐ Day 10. JOHN 17: Jesus' prayer for his disciples

☐ Day 11. MATTHEW 26: Betrayal and arrest

☐ Day 12. MATTHEW 27: Jesus' execution on a cross

☐ Day 13. JOHN 20: Resurrection

☐ Day 14. LUKE 24: Jesus' appearance after resurrection

2. Two Weeks on the Life and Teachings of Paul

☐ Day 1.   ACTS 9: The conversion of Saul

☐ Day 2.   ACTS 16: Paul's Macedonian call and a jailbreak

☐ Day 3.   ACTS 17: Scenes from Paul's missionary journey

☐ Day 4.   ACTS 26: Paul tells his life story to a king

☐ Day 5.   ACTS 27: Shipwreck on the way to Rome

☐ Day 6.   ACTS 28: Paul's arrival in Rome

☐ Day 7.   ROMANS 3: Paul's theology in a nutshell

☐ Day 8.   ROMANS 7: Struggle with sin

☐ Day 9.   ROMANS 8: Life in the Spirit

☐ Day 10. 1 CORINTHIANS 13: Paul's description of love

☐ Day 11. 1 CORINTHIANS 15: Thoughts on the afterlife

☐ Day 12. GALATIANS 5: Freedom in Christ

☐ Day 13. EPHESIANS 3: Paul's summary of his mission

☐ Day 14. PHILIPPIANS 2: Imitating Christ

3. Two Weeks on the Old Testament

☐ Day 1.   GENESIS 1: The story of creation

☐ Day 2.   GENESIS 3: The origin of sin

☐ Day 3.   GENESIS 22: Abraham and Isaac

☐ Day 4.   EXODUS 3: Moses' encounter with God

☐ Day 5.   EXODUS 20: The gift of the Ten Commandments

☐ Day 6.   1 SAMUEL 17: David and Goliath

☐ Day 7.   2 SAMUEL 11: David and Bathsheba

☐ Day 8.   2 SAMUEL 12: Nathan's rebuke of the king

☐ Day 9.   1 KINGS 18: Elijah and the prophets of Baal

☐ Day 10. JOB 38: God's answer to Job

☐ Day 11. PSALM 51: A classic confession

☐ Day 12. ISAIAH 40: Words of comfort from God

☐ Day 13. DANIEL 6: Daniel and the lions

☐ Day 14. AMOS 4: A prophet's stern warning

TIME COMMITMENT:
Six Months

GOAL:
To gain an overview of the entire Bible

Track 2 includes 186 of the 1,189 chapters in the Bible. Many well-known parts of the Bible are not represented, and from some books (Leviticus, for example), you will read only a single chapter. These 186 chapters have been selected because they are understandable to the average reader without commentary. Taken together, they provide a good foundation of Bible understanding.

If you miss a few days, don't worry. Just resume reading when you can, about a chapter a day. In 180 total days, you will get an overview that includes something from every book in the Bible.

Track 2 recommends reading the Introduction to each book. You may also find it helpful to read the Insights that appear next to the assigned chapters.

GENESIS	☐ 1	☐ 2	☐ 3	☐ 4
	☐ 7	☐ 8	☐ 15	☐ 19
	☐ 22	☐ 27	☐ 28	☐ 37
	☐ 41	☐ 45		
EXODUS	☐ 3	☐ 10-11	☐ 14	☐ 20
	☐ 32			
LEVITICUS	☐ 26			
NUMBERS	☐ 11	☐ 14		
DEUTERONOMY	☐ 4	☐ 8	☐ 28	
JOSHUA	☐ 2	☐ 6	☐ 7	☐ 24
JUDGES	☐ 6	☐ 7	☐ 16	
RUTH	☐ 1			
1 SAMUEL	☐ 3	☐ 16	☐ 17	☐ 20
2 SAMUEL	☐ 6	☐ 11	☐ 12	
1 KINGS	☐ 3	☐ 8	☐ 17	☐ 18
2 KINGS	☐ 5	☐ 17	☐ 22	
1 CHRONICLES	☐ 17			
2 CHRONICLES	☐ 20	☐ 30	☐ 32	
EZRA	☐ 3			
NEHEMIAH	☐ 2	☐ 8		
ESTHER	☐ 4			
JOB	☐ 1-2	☐ 38	☐ 42	
PSALMS	☐ 19	☐ 23	☐ 27	☐ 51
	☐ 84	☐ 103	☐ 139	
PROVERBS	☐ 4	☐ 10	☐ The proverbs listed in "Verbal Dynamite" (page 703)	
ECCLESIASTES	☐ 3			
SONG OF SOLOMON	☐ 2			
ISAIAH	☐ 6	☐ 25	☐ 40	☐ 52
	☐ 53	☐ 55		
JEREMIAH	☐ 2	☐ 15	☐ 31	☐ 38
LAMENTATIONS	☐ 3			
EZEKIEL	☐ 1	☐ 2-3	☐ 4	☐ 37
DANIEL	☐ 1	☐ 3	☐ 5	☐ 6
HOSEA	☐ 2-3	☐ 11		
JOEL	☐ 2			
AMOS	☐ 4			
OBADIAH	☐ Obadiah			
JONAH	☐ 3-4			
MICAH	☐ 6			

NAHUM	☐ 1			
HABAKKUK	☐ 1			
ZEPHANIAH	☐ 3			
HAGGAI	☐ 1			
ZECHARIAH	☐ 8			
MALACHI	☐ 3			
MATTHEW	☐ 5	☐ 6	☐ 13	☐ 19
	☐ 26	☐ 27	☐ 28	
MARK	☐ 1	☐ 2	☐ 3	☐ 4
	☐ 5	☐ 6	☐ 7	☐ 8
	☐ 9	☐ 10	☐ 11	☐ 12
	☐ 13	☐ 14	☐ 15-16	
LUKE	☐ 1	☐ 2	☐ 10	☐ 12
	☐ 15	☐ 16	☐ 18	☐ 24
JOHN	☐ 3	☐ 6	☐ 10	☐ 14
	☐ 15	☐ 16	☐ 17	☐ 20
ACTS	☐ 1	☐ 2	☐ 5	☐ 9
	☐ 16	☐ 17	☐ 26	☐ 27
	☐ 28			
ROMANS	☐ 3	☐ 7	☐ 8	☐ 12
1 CORINTHIANS	☐ 13	☐ 15		
2 CORINTHIANS	☐ 4	☐ 12		
GALATIANS	☐ 3			
EPHESIANS	☐ 2	☐ 3		
PHILIPPIANS	☐ 2			
COLOSSIANS	☐ 1			
1 THESSALONIANS	☐ 3-4			
2 THESSALONIANS	☐ 2			
1 TIMOTHY	☐ 1			
2 TIMOTHY	☐ 2			
TITUS	☐ 2			
PHILEMON	☐ Philemon			
HEBREWS	☐ 2	☐ 11	☐ 12	
JAMES	☐ 1			
1 PETER	☐ 1			
2 PETER	☐ 1			
1 JOHN	☐ 3			
2 and 3 JOHN	☐ 2, 3 John			
JUDE	☐ Jude			
REVELATION	☐ 1	☐ 12	☐ 21	

TIME COMMITMENT:
Three Years

GOAL:
To read all the way through the Bible with understanding

Track 3 takes you completely through the Bible, reading every word. Other Bible-reading plans allot only a year for this project, requiring that at least 3 chapters be read each day. But many readers find such a pace to be unrealistic and discouraging. For this reason, Track 3 assigns usually only one chapter a day. (Some short chapters have been combined, so occasionally you will read two brief chapters in a day.) In all, the reading plan works out evenly to a three-year total.

The Track 3 plan alternates between the Old Testament and New Testament. This mixing provides variety and reduces the fatigue that may set in from reading long sections of the Old Testament.

GENESIS

☐1	☐2	☐3	☐4
☐5	☐6	☐7	☐8
☐9	☐10-11	☐12	☐13
☐14	☐15	☐16	☐17
☐18	☐19	☐20	☐21
☐22	☐23	☐24	☐25
☐26	☐27	☐28	☐29
☐30	☐31	☐32	☐33
☐34	☐35	☐36	☐37
☐38	☐39	☐40	☐41
☐42	☐43	☐44	☐45
☐46	☐47	☐48	☐49
☐50			

MATTHEW 1-9

☐1	☐2	☐3	☐4
☐5	☐6	☐7	☐8
☐9			

EXODUS

☐1	☐2	☐3	☐4
☐5	☐6	☐7	☐8
☐9	☐10-11	☐12	☐13
☐14	☐15	☐16	☐17
☐18	☐19	☐20	☐21
☐22	☐23	☐24	☐25
☐26	☐27	☐28	☐29
☐30	☐31	☐32	☐33
☐34	☐35	☐36	☐37
☐38	☐39	☐40	

MATTHEW 10-20

☐10	☐11	☐12	☐13
☐14	☐15	☐16	☐17
☐18	☐19	☐20	

LEVITICUS 1-14

☐1	☐2	☐3	☐4
☐5	☐6	☐7	☐8
☐9	☐10	☐11-12	☐13
☐14			

MATTHEW 21-28

☐21	☐22	☐23	☐24
☐25	☐26	☐27	☐28

LEVITICUS 15-27

☐15	☐16	☐17	☐18
☐19	☐20	☐21	☐22
☐23	☐24	☐25	☐26
☐27			

MARK 1-8

☐1	☐2	☐3	☐4
☐5	☐6	☐7	☐8

NUMBERS

☐1-2	☐3	☐4	☐5
☐6	☐7	☐8	☐9
☐10	☐11	☐12	☐13
☐14	☐15	☐16	☐17
☐18	☐19	☐20	☐21
☐22	☐23	☐24	☐25
☐26	☐27	☐28	☐29
☐30	☐31	☐32	☐33
☐34	☐35	☐36	

MARK 9-16

☐9	☐10	☐11	☐12
☐13	☐14	☐15-16	

DEUTERONOMY 1-17

☐1	☐2	☐3	☐4
☐5	☐6	☐7	☐8
☐9	☐10	☐11	☐12
☐13	☐14	☐15	☐16
☐17			

LUKE 1-8

☐1	☐2	☐3	☐4
☐5	☐6	☐7	☐8

DEUTERONOMY 18-34

☐18	☐19	☐20	☐21
☐22	☐23	☐24	☐25

☐ 26   ☐ 27   ☐ 28   ☐ 29
☐ 30   ☐ 31   ☐ 32   ☐ 33
☐ 34

LUKE 9-16

☐ 9   ☐ 10   ☐ 11   ☐ 12
☐ 13   ☐ 14   ☐ 15   ☐ 16

JOSHUA

☐ 1   ☐ 2   ☐ 3   ☐ 4
☐ 5   ☐ 6   ☐ 7   ☐ 8
☐ 9   ☐ 10   ☐ 11   ☐ 12-13
☐ 14-15   ☐ 16-17   ☐ 18   ☐ 19
☐ 20   ☐ 21   ☐ 22   ☐ 23
☐ 24

LUKE 17-24

☐ 17   ☐ 18   ☐ 19   ☐ 20
☐ 21   ☐ 22   ☐ 23   ☐ 24

JUDGES

☐ 1   ☐ 2   ☐ 3   ☐ 4
☐ 5   ☐ 6   ☐ 7   ☐ 8
☐ 9   ☐ 10   ☐ 11   ☐ 12
☐ 13   ☐ 14   ☐ 15   ☐ 16
☐ 17   ☐ 18   ☐ 19   ☐ 20
☐ 21

JOHN 1-7

☐ 1   ☐ 2   ☐ 3   ☐ 4
☐ 5   ☐ 6   ☐ 7

RUTH

☐ 1   ☐ 2   ☐ 3   ☐ 4

1 SAMUEL 1-15

☐ 1   ☐ 2   ☐ 3   ☐ 4
☐ 5   ☐ 6   ☐ 7   ☐ 8
☐ 9   ☐ 10   ☐ 11   ☐ 12
☐ 13   ☐ 14   ☐ 15

JOHN 8-14

☐ 8   ☐ 9   ☐ 10   ☐ 11
☐ 12   ☐ 13   ☐ 14

1 SAMUEL 16-31

☐ 16   ☐ 17   ☐ 18   ☐ 19
☐ 20   ☐ 21   ☐ 22   ☐ 23
☐ 24   ☐ 25   ☐ 26   ☐ 27
☐ 28   ☐ 29   ☐ 30   ☐ 31

JOHN 15-21

☐ 15   ☐ 16   ☐ 17   ☐ 18
☐ 19   ☐ 20   ☐ 21

2 SAMUEL

☐ 1   ☐ 2   ☐ 3   ☐ 4
☐ 5   ☐ 6   ☐ 7   ☐ 8
☐ 9   ☐ 10   ☐ 11   ☐ 12
☐ 13   ☐ 14   ☐ 15   ☐ 16
☐ 17   ☐ 18   ☐ 19   ☐ 20
☐ 21   ☐ 22   ☐ 23   ☐ 24

ACTS 1-7

☐ 1   ☐ 2   ☐ 3   ☐ 4
☐ 5   ☐ 6   ☐ 7

1 KINGS 1-11

☐ 1   ☐ 2   ☐ 3   ☐ 4-5
☐ 6   ☐ 7   ☐ 8   ☐ 9
☐ 10   ☐ 11

ACTS 8-14

☐ 8   ☐ 9   ☐ 10   ☐ 11
☐ 12   ☐ 13   ☐ 14

1 KINGS 12-22

☐ 12   ☐ 13   ☐ 14   ☐ 15
☐ 16   ☐ 17   ☐ 18   ☐ 19
☐ 20   ☐ 21   ☐ 22

ACTS 15-21

☐ 15   ☐ 16   ☐ 17   ☐ 18
☐ 19   ☐ 20   ☐ 21

2 KINGS

☐ 1   ☐ 2   ☐ 3   ☐ 4
☐ 5   ☐ 6   ☐ 7   ☐ 8
☐ 9   ☐ 10   ☐ 11   ☐ 12
☐ 13   ☐ 14   ☐ 15   ☐ 16
☐ 17   ☐ 18   ☐ 19   ☐ 20
☐ 21   ☐ 22   ☐ 23   ☐ 24
☐ 25

ACTS 22-28

☐ 22   ☐ 23   ☐ 24   ☐ 25
☐ 26   ☐ 27   ☐ 28

1 CHRONICLES 1-14

☐ 1-9   ☐ 10   ☐ 11   ☐ 12
☐ 13   ☐ 14

ROMANS 1-8

☐ 1   ☐ 2   ☐ 3   ☐ 4
☐ 5   ☐ 6   ☐ 7   ☐ 8

1 CHRONICLES 15-29

☐ 15   ☐ 16   ☐ 17   ☐ 18
☐ 19   ☐ 20   ☐ 21   ☐ 22
☐ 23-27   ☐ 28   ☐ 29

ROMANS 9-16

☐ 9   ☐ 10   ☐ 11   ☐ 12-13
☐ 14   ☐ 15-16

2 CHRONICLES 1-18

☐ 1   ☐ 2   ☐ 3   ☐ 4
☐ 5   ☐ 6   ☐ 7   ☐ 8
☐ 9   ☐ 10   ☐ 11   ☐ 12
☐ 13   ☐ 14   ☐ 15   ☐ 16-17
☐ 18

1 CORINTHIANS 1-9

☐ 1   ☐ 2   ☐ 3   ☐ 4-5
☐ 6   ☐ 7   ☐ 8-9

2 CHRONICLES 19-36

☐ 19   ☐ 20   ☐ 21   ☐ 22
☐ 23   ☐ 24   ☐ 25   ☐ 26-27
☐ 28   ☐ 29   ☐ 30   ☐ 31
☐ 32   ☐ 33   ☐ 34   ☐ 35
☐ 36

1 CORINTHIANS 10-16

☐ 10   ☐ 11   ☐ 12   ☐ 13
☐ 14   ☐ 15   ☐ 16

EZRA

☐ 1-2   ☐ 3   ☐ 4   ☐ 5
☐ 6   ☐ 7   ☐ 8   ☐ 9
☐ 10

NEHEMIAH

☐ 1   ☐ 2-3   ☐ 4   ☐ 5
☐ 6   ☐ 7   ☐ 8   ☐ 9
☐ 10   ☐ 11   ☐ 12   ☐ 13

2 CORINTHIANS

☐ 1   ☐ 2-3   ☐ 4   ☐ 5
☐ 6   ☐ 7   ☐ 8-9   ☐ 10
☐ 11   ☐ 12-13

ESTHER

☐ 1   ☐ 2   ☐ 3   ☐ 4
☐ 5   ☐ 6-7   ☐ 8   ☐ 9-10

JOB 1-21

☐ 1   ☐ 2   ☐ 3   ☐ 4
☐ 5   ☐ 6   ☐ 7   ☐ 8
☐ 9   ☐ 10   ☐ 11   ☐ 12
☐ 13   ☐ 14   ☐ 15   ☐ 16
☐ 17   ☐ 18   ☐ 19   ☐ 20
☐ 21

GALATIANS

☐ 1   ☐ 2   ☐ 3   ☐ 4
☐ 5-6

JOB 22-42

☐ 22   ☐ 23   ☐ 24   ☐ 25-26
☐ 27   ☐ 28   ☐ 29   ☐ 30
☐ 31   ☐ 32   ☐ 33   ☐ 34
☐ 35   ☐ 36   ☐ 37   ☐ 38
☐ 39   ☐ 40   ☐ 41   ☐ 42

EPHESIANS

☐ 1   ☐ 2   ☐ 3   ☐ 4
☐ 5   ☐ 6

PSALMS 1-40

☐ 1-2   ☐ 3-4   ☐ 5   ☐ 6
☐ 7   ☐ 8   ☐ 9   ☐ 10
☐ 11-12   ☐ 13-14   ☐ 15-16   ☐ 17
☐ 18   ☐ 19   ☐ 20-21   ☐ 22
☐ 23-24   ☐ 25   ☐ 26   ☐ 27
☐ 28-29   ☐ 30   ☐ 31   ☐ 32
☐ 33   ☐ 34   ☐ 35   ☐ 36
☐ 37   ☐ 38   ☐ 39   ☐ 40

PHILIPPIANS

☐ 1   ☐ 2   ☐ 3   ☐ 4

PSALMS 41-80

☐ 41   ☐ 42-43   ☐ 44   ☐ 45
☐ 46-47   ☐ 48   ☐ 49   ☐ 50
☐ 51   ☐ 52   ☐ 53-54   ☐ 55
☐ 56   ☐ 57   ☐ 58   ☐ 59
☐ 60-61   ☐ 62   ☐ 63-64   ☐ 65
☐ 66   ☐ 67   ☐ 68   ☐ 69
☐ 70   ☐ 71   ☐ 72   ☐ 73
☐ 74   ☐ 75   ☐ 76   ☐ 77
☐ 78   ☐ 79   ☐ 80

COLOSSIANS

☐ 1   ☐ 2   ☐ 3   ☐ 4

PSALMS 81-121

☐ 81	☐ 82	☐ 83	☐ 84
☐ 85	☐ 86	☐ 87	☐ 88
☐ 89	☐ 90	☐ 91	☐ 92-93
☐ 94	☐ 95	☐ 96	☐ 97
☐ 98-99	☐ 100-101	☐ 102	☐ 103
☐ 104	☐ 105	☐ 106	☐ 107
☐ 108	☐ 109	☐ 110-111	☐ 112
☐ 113	☐ 114	☐ 115	☐ 116-117
☐ 118	☐ 119.1-48	☐ 119.49-96	☐ 119.97-144
☐ 119.145-176		☐ 120-121	

1 THESSALONIANS

☐ 1-2	☐ 3-4	☐ 5

2 THESSALONIANS

☐ 1-2	☐ 3

PSALMS 122-150

☐ 122-123	☐ 124-125	☐ 126-128	☐ 129-130
☐ 131-132	☐ 133-134	☐ 135	☐ 136
☐ 137-138	☐ 139	☐ 140	☐ 141-142
☐ 143	☐ 144	☐ 145	☐ 146
☐ 147	☐ 148	☐ 149-150	

PROVERBS

☐ 1	☐ 2	☐ 3	☐ 4
☐ 5	☐ 6	☐ 7	☐ 8
☐ 9	☐ 10	☐ 11	☐ 12
☐ 13	☐ 14	☐ 15	☐ 16
☐ 17	☐ 18	☐ 19	☐ 20
☐ 21	☐ 22	☐ 23	☐ 24
☐ 25	☐ 26	☐ 27	☐ 28
☐ 29	☐ 30	☐ 31	

1 TIMOTHY

☐ 1-2	☐ 3-4	☐ 5	☐ 6

ECCLESIASTES

☐ 1	☐ 2	☐ 3	☐ 4
☐ 5	☐ 6	☐ 7	☐ 8
☐ 9	☐ 10	☐ 11	☐ 12

SONG OF SOLOMON

☐ 1	☐ 2	☐ 3	☐ 4
☐ 5	☐ 6	☐ 7	☐ 8

2 TIMOTHY

☐ 1	☐ 2	☐ 3	☐ 4

ISAIAH 1-36

☐ 1	☐ 2	☐ 3	☐ 4-5
☐ 6	☐ 7	☐ 8	☐ 9
☐ 10	☐ 11	☐ 12	☐ 13
☐ 14	☐ 15	☐ 16	☐ 17
☐ 18	☐ 19-20	☐ 21	☐ 22
☐ 23	☐ 24	☐ 25	☐ 26
☐ 27	☐ 28	☐ 29	☐ 30
☐ 31	☐ 32	☐ 33	☐ 34
☐ 35	☐ 36		

TITUS

☐ 1	☐ 2-3

ISAIAH 37-66

☐ 37	☐ 38-39	☐ 40	☐ 41
☐ 42	☐ 43	☐ 44	☐ 45
☐ 46	☐ 47	☐ 48	☐ 49
☐ 50	☐ 51	☐ 52	☐ 53
☐ 54	☐ 55	☐ 56	☐ 57
☐ 58	☐ 59	☐ 60	☐ 61
☐ 62	☐ 63	☐ 64	☐ 65
☐ 66			

PHILEMON

☐ Philemon

JEREMIAH 1-26

☐ 1	☐ 2	☐ 3	☐ 4
☐ 5	☐ 6	☐ 7	☐ 8
☐ 9	☐ 10	☐ 11	☐ 12
☐ 13	☐ 14	☐ 15	☐ 16
☐ 17	☐ 18	☐ 19	☐ 20
☐ 21	☐ 22	☐ 23	☐ 24
☐ 25	☐ 26		

HEBREWS 1-7

☐ 1	☐ 2	☐ 3-4	☐ 5-6
☐ 7			

JEREMIAH 27-52

☐ 27	☐ 28	☐ 29	☐ 30
☐ 31	☐ 32	☐ 33	☐ 34
☐ 35	☐ 36	☐ 37	☐ 38
☐ 39	☐ 40	☐ 41	☐ 42
☐ 43	☐ 44-45	☐ 46	☐ 47
☐ 48	☐ 49	☐ 50	☐ 51
☐ 52			

HEBREWS 8-13

☐ 8	☐ 9	☐ 10	☐ 11
☐ 12	☐ 13		

LAMENTATIONS

☐ 1 ☐ 2 ☐ 3 ☐ 4
☐ 5

EZEKIEL 1-24

☐ 1 ☐ 2-3 ☐ 4 ☐ 5
☐ 6 ☐ 7 ☐ 8 ☐ 9
☐ 10 ☐ 11 ☐ 12 ☐ 13
☐ 14 ☐ 15 ☐ 16 ☐ 17
☐ 18 ☐ 19 ☐ 20 ☐ 21
☐ 22 ☐ 23 ☐ 24

JAMES

☐ 1 ☐ 2 ☐ 3-4 ☐ 5

EZEKIEL 25-48

☐ 25 ☐ 26 ☐ 27 ☐ 28
☐ 29 ☐ 30 ☐ 31 ☐ 32
☐ 33 ☐ 34 ☐ 35 ☐ 36
☐ 37 ☐ 38 ☐ 39 ☐ 40
☐ 41 ☐ 42 ☐ 43 ☐ 44
☐ 45 ☐ 46 ☐ 47 ☐ 48

1 PETER

☐ 1 ☐ 2 ☐ 3 ☐ 4-5

DANIEL

☐ 1 ☐ 2 ☐ 3 ☐ 4
☐ 5 ☐ 6 ☐ 7 ☐ 8
☐ 9 ☐ 10 ☐ 11 ☐ 12

2 PETER

☐ 1 ☐ 2 ☐ 3

HOSEA

☐ 1 ☐ 2-3 ☐ 4 ☐ 5
☐ 6-7 ☐ 8 ☐ 9 ☐ 10
☐ 11-12 ☐ 13-14

1 JOHN

☐ 1-2 ☐ 3 ☐ 4 ☐ 5

JOEL

☐ 1 ☐ 2 ☐ 3

AMOS

☐ 1 ☐ 2 ☐ 3 ☐ 4

☐ 5 ☐ 6 ☐ 7 ☐ 8
☐ 9

OBADIAH

☐ Obadiah

JONAH

☐ 1-2 ☐ 3-4

2 and 3 JOHN

☐ 2 John, 3 John

MICAH

☐ 1 ☐ 2 ☐ 3 ☐ 4
☐ 5 ☐ 6 ☐ 7

NAHUM

☐ 1 ☐ 2 ☐ 3

JUDE

☐ Jude

HABAKKUK

☐ 1 ☐ 2 ☐ 3

ZEPHANIAH

☐ 1 ☐ 2 ☐ 3

REVELATION 1-7

☐ 1 ☐ 2 ☐ 3 ☐ 4-5
☐ 6 ☐ 7

HAGGAI

☐ 1 ☐ 2

REVELATION 8-14

☐ 8 ☐ 9 ☐ 10-11 ☐ 12
☐ 13 ☐ 14

ZECHARIAH

☐ 1 ☐ 2-3 ☐ 4-5 ☐ 6
☐ 7 ☐ 8 ☐ 9 ☐ 10
☐ 11 ☐ 12-13 ☐ 14

MALACHI

☐ 1 ☐ 2 ☐ 3-4

REVELATION 15-22

☐ 15-16 ☐ 17 ☐ 18 ☐ 19
☐ 20 ☐ 21 ☐ 22

TWO WEEKS ON BECOMING A CHRISTIAN

☐ Day 1. Genesis 3: The first sin creates a need.
☐ Day 2. Isaiah 52: Salvation prophesied.
☐ Day 3. Isaiah 53: The role of the suffering servant.
☐ Day 4. Luke 15: Three stories about God's love.
☐ Day 5. John 3: Jesus explains "born again."
☐ Day 6. John 10: The good shepherd.
☐ Day 7. Acts 8: Conversions spread outside the Jews.
☐ Day 8. Acts 26: Paul testifies of his conversion before a king.
☐ Day 9. Romans 3: God's provision for sin.
☐ Day 10. Romans 5: Peace with God.
☐ Day 11. Galatians 3: Salvation unavailable by obeying the law.
☐ Day 12. Ephesians 2: New life in Christ.
☐ Day 13. 1 Peter 1: Future rewards of salvation.
☐ Day 14. 2 Peter 1: Making your salvation sure.

TWO WEEKS ON PRAYERS OF THE BIBLE

☐ Day 1. Genesis 18: Abraham's plea for Sodom.
☐ Day 2. Exodus 15: Moses' song to the Lord.
☐ Day 3. Exodus 33: Moses meets with God.
☐ Day 4. 2 Samuel 7: David's response to God's promises.
☐ Day 5. 1 Kings 8: Solomon's dedication of the temple.
☐ Day 6. 2 Chronicles 20: Jehoshaphat prays for victory.
☐ Day 7. Ezra 9: Ezra's prayer for the people's sins.
☐ Day 8. Psalm 22: A cry to God for help.
☐ Day 9. Psalm 104: A prayer of praise.
☐ Day 10. Daniel 9: Daniel's prayer for the salvation of Jerusalem.
☐ Day 11. Habakkuk 3: A prophet's prayer of acceptance.
☐ Day 12. Matthew 6: The Lord's prayer.
☐ Day 13. John 17: Jesus' prayer for his disciples.
☐ Day 14. Colossians 1: Paul's prayer of thanksgiving.

TWO WEEKS ON THE HOLY SPIRIT

☐ Day 1. Judges 14: The Spirit gives Samson strength.
☐ Day 2. 1 Samuel 10: King Saul's experience.
☐ Day 3. Matthew 3:1–4:10: Role in Jesus' baptism and temptation.
☐ Day 4. John 14: Jesus promises the Spirit.
☐ Day 5. John 16: The work of the Spirit.
☐ Day 6. Acts 2: The Spirit comes at Pentecost.
☐ Day 7. Acts 10: The Spirit guides Peter to accept Gentiles.
☐ Day 8. Romans 8: Christians' victory in the Spirit.
☐ Day 9. 1 Corinthians 2: Wisdom from the Spirit.
☐ Day 10. 1 Corinthians 12: Gifts of the Spirit.
☐ Day 11. 1 Corinthians 14: Gifts of tongues and prophecy.
☐ Day 12. Galatians 5: Life in the Spirit.
☐ Day 13. Ephesians 4: Unity and gifts.
☐ Day 14. 1 John 4: Signs of the Spirit.

TWO WEEKS ON WOMEN OF THE BIBLE

☐ Day 1. Genesis 2: Eve, the first woman.
☐ Day 2. Genesis 18: Sarah laughs at God's promise.
☐ Day 3. Genesis 24: Rebekah's marriage to Isaac.
☐ Day 4. Genesis 27: Rebekah, the manipulative mother.
☐ Day 5. Judges 4: Deborah's leadership frees her people.
☐ Day 6. Ruth 1: Ruth and Naomi's deep friendship.
☐ Day 7. 1 Samuel 1: Hannah prays for a son.
☐ Day 8. 1 Kings 17: A poor widow and the prophet Elijah.
☐ Day 9. 1 Kings 21: Jezebel, an emblem of wickedness.
☐ Day 10. Esther 2: Esther is chosen as queen.
☐ Day 11. Esther 4: Esther's courage at the risk of death.

☐ Day 12. Luke 1: Mary and Elizabeth receive great news.
☐ Day 13. Luke 2: Mary gives birth to Jesus.
☐ Day 14. John 11: Mary and Martha and their brother's death.

TWO WEEKS ON MEN OF THE OLD TESTAMENT

☐ Day 1. Judges 6: God calls Gideon to rescue his people.
☐ Day 2. Judges 7: Gideon conquers his fears—and his enemies.
☐ Day 3. 1 Samuel 3: God calls young Samuel.
☐ Day 4. 1 Kings 3: Solomon is given wisdom.
☐ Day 5. 1 Kings 19: Elijah runs for his life.
☐ Day 6. 2 Kings 5: Elisha heals a powerful foreign general.
☐ Day 7. Isaiah 6: God calls the prophet Isaiah.
☐ Day 8. 2 Kings 18: King Hezekiah under military siege.
☐ Day 9. 2 Kings 19: Isaiah speaks God's word to King Hezekiah.
☐ Day 10. 2 Chronicles 34: Josiah sets his nation back on course.
☐ Day 11. Nehemiah 2: Nehemiah courageously begins rebuilding a wall.
☐ Day 12. Jeremiah 38: Jeremiah, in prison, refuses to change his message.
☐ Day 13. Daniel 1: Daniel risks his life in captivity.
☐ Day 14. Daniel 5: Daniel's word to a royal orgy.

TWO WEEKS ON SOCIAL JUSTICE

☐ Day 1. Exodus 3: God hears the cries of the slaves.
☐ Day 2. Leviticus 25: The year of jubilee, a time of economic revolution.
☐ Day 3. Ruth 2: A poor woman finds help.
☐ Day 4. 1 Kings 21: Elijah speaks to a land-grabbing, murderous king.
☐ Day 5. Nehemiah 5: Nehemiah demands justice for the poor.
☐ Day 6. Isaiah 5: Warning to fun-loving materialists.
☐ Day 7. Isaiah 58: Worship that God appreciates.
☐ Day 8. Jeremiah 34: Freedom for slaves.
☐ Day 9. Amos 2: Sins against God by his own people.
☐ Day 10. Amos 6: Warning to the complacent.
☐ Day 11. Micah 6: What the Lord requires.
☐ Day 12. Luke 3: John the Baptist tells how to prepare for Jesus.
☐ Day 13. Matthew 6: Jesus speaks on material things.
☐ Day 14. James 2: How to treat the rich and the poor.

TWO WEEKS ON GOD AND NATURE

☐ Day 1. Genesis 1: God creates the earth.
☐ Day 2. Genesis 2: God creates human beings.
☐ Day 3. Proverbs 8: Wisdom's view of creation.
☐ Day 4. Genesis 7: God preserves the species.
☐ Day 5. Job 38: The greatness of nature.
☐ Day 6. Job 39: The wildness of nature.
☐ Day 7. Job 40: God's mastery of nature.
☐ Day 8. Psalm 8: Praise for the Creator.
☐ Day 9. Psalm 98: Nature joins in the praise.
☐ Day 10. Psalm 104: God sustains the earth.
☐ Day 11. Isaiah 40: The ruler of all creation.
☐ Day 12. Romans 8: The "groanings" of our present state.
☐ Day 13. Isaiah 65: Preview of a restored earth.
☐ Day 14. Revelation 22: The end of history.

FURTHER TWO-WEEK COURSES FOR PERSONAL STUDY

Two weeks on Abraham, Isaac, and Jacob:
    Genesis 12, 13, 15, 17, 18, 19, 22, 24, 27, 28, 29, 31, 32, 33.
Two weeks on Moses and the exodus:
    Exodus 2, 3, 4, 7, 12, 14, 16, 19, 32; Numbers 14; Deuteronomy 1, 2, 4, 31.
Two weeks on David:
    1 Samuel 16, 17, 18, 20, 21, 22, 24; 2 Samuel 6, 7, 11, 12, 13, 15, 18.

Overview:
THE OLD TESTAMENT

The Five Books
The first five books of the Bible tell the origins of the Jewish race and culture.

GENESIS: The book of beginnings describes creation, the first rebellions against God, and God's choosing of Abraham and his offspring.

EXODUS: God rescued the Israelites from slavery in Egypt and led them to the Desert of Sinai. There, he gave Moses the laws to govern the new nation.

LEVITICUS: God set up laws for the Israelites, mostly regarding holiness and worship.

NUMBERS: Because of their rebellion and disobedience, the Israelites had to wander in a wilderness for 40 years before entering the promised land.

DEUTERONOMY: Just before his death, Moses made three emotional farewell speeches, recapping history and warning the Israelites against further mistakes.

History Books
The next 12 books continue the history of the Israelites. They moved into the land of Canaan and established a kingdom that lasted almost 500 years.

JOSHUA: After Moses' death, Joshua commanded the armies that conquered much of the territory in the promised land.

JUDGES: The new nation fell into a series of dismal failures. God raised up leaders called "judges."

RUTH: This story of love and loyalty between two widows shines out brightly in an otherwise dark period.

1 SAMUEL: Samuel became a transition leader between the time of the judges and that of the kings. He appointed Israel's first king, Saul. After his own failure, Saul tried violently to prevent God's king-elect David from taking the throne.

2 SAMUEL: David, a man after God's own heart, brought the nation together. But after committing adultery and murder, he was haunted by family and national crises.

1 KINGS: Solomon succeeded David, with mixed success. At his death, a civil war tore apart the nation. Successive kings were mostly bad, and the prophet Elijah had dramatic confrontations with King Ahab.

2 KINGS: This book continues the record of the rulers of the divided kingdom. None of the northern kings followed God consistently, and so Israel was finally destroyed by an invader. The South, Judah, lasted much longer, but finally Babylon conquered Judah and deported its citizens.

1 CHRONICLES: The book opens with the most complete genealogical record in the Bible, then adds many incidents from the life of David (often the same as those in 2 Samuel).

2 CHRONICLES: Often paralleling the books of Kings, this book records the history of the rulers of Judah, emphasizing the good kings.

EZRA: After being held captive in Babylon for decades, the Jews were allowed to return to their homeland. Ezra, a priest, emerged from one of the first waves of refugees.

NEHEMIAH: Nehemiah returned from the Babylonian captivity after the temple had been rebuilt. He concentrated on restoring the protective wall around Jerusalem and joined Ezra in leading a religious revival.

ESTHER: This story is set among captive Jews in Persia. A courageous Jewish queen foiled a plan to exterminate her people.

Books of Poetry

Almost one-third of the Old Testament was originally written in poetry. These books concentrate on questions about pain, God, life, and love.

JOB: The best man of his day suffers the greatest personal tragedy. The entire book deals with the question, "Why?"

PSALMS: These prayers and hymns cover the full range of human emotion; together, they represent a personal journal of how to relate to God. Some were also used in public worship services.

PROVERBS: The proverbs offer advice on every imaginable area of life. The style of wise living described here leads to a fulfilled life.

ECCLESIASTES: A life without God, "under the sun," leads to meaninglessness and despair, says the Teacher in a strikingly modern book.

SONG OF SOLOMON: This beautiful poem celebrates romantic and physical love.

Books of the Prophets

During the years when kings ruled Israel and Judah, God spoke through prophets. Though some prophets did predict future events, their primary role was to call God's people back to him.

ISAIAH: The most eloquent of the prophets, Isaiah analyzed the failures of all the nations around him and pointed to a future Messiah who would bring peace.

JEREMIAH: Jeremiah led an emotionally tortured life, yet held to his stern message. He spoke to Judah in the last decades before Babylon destroyed the nation.

LAMENTATIONS: All Jeremiah's warnings about Jerusalem came true, and Lamentations records five poems of sorrow for the fallen city.

EZEKIEL: Ezekiel spoke to the Jews who were captive in Babylon. He often used dramatic stories and "enacted parables" to make his points.

DANIEL: A captive in Babylon, Daniel rose to the office of prime minister. Despite intense political pressure, he lived a model life of integrity and left highly symbolic prophecies about the future.

HOSEA: By marrying a loose-living wife, Hosea lived out his message: that Israel had committed spiritual adultery against God.

JOEL: Beginning with a recent catastrophe in Judah (a locust plague), Joel foretold God's judgment on Judah.

AMOS: A country boy, Amos preached to Israel at the height of its prosperity. His grim warnings focused on materialism.

OBADIAH: Obadiah warned Edom, a nation bordering Judah.

JONAH: Jonah reluctantly went to Nineveh and found Israel's enemies responsive to God's message.

MICAH: Micah exposed corruption in every level of society, but closed with a promise of forgiveness and restoration.

NAHUM: Long after Jonah had stirred Nineveh to repentance, Nahum foretold the mighty city's total destruction.

HABAKKUK: Habakkuk addressed his book to God, not people. In a frank dialogue with God, he discussed problems of suffering and justice.

ZEPHANIAH: Zephaniah focused on the coming day of the Lord, which would purge Judah, resulting in a remnant used to bless the entire world.

HAGGAI: After returning from the Babylonian captivity, the Jews began rebuilding the temple of God. But before long they set aside that task to work on their own homes. Haggai reminded them to put God first.

ZECHARIAH: Writing around the same time as Haggai, Zechariah also urged the Jews to work on the temple. He used a more uplifting approach, describing how the temple would point to the coming Messiah.

MALACHI: The last Old Testament prophet, Malachi faced a nation that had grown indifferent. He sought to stir them from apathy.

Overview:
THE NEW TESTAMENT

History Books

The word *gospel* means "good news." Almost half of the New Testament consists of four accounts of the life of Jesus and the good news he brought to earth. Each of these four books, or Gospels, has a different focus and a different audience; taken together, they give a complete picture of Jesus' life and teaching. About a third of their pages are devoted to the events of his last week on earth, including the crucifixion and resurrection.

Acts continues the history into the period after Jesus left earth.

MATTHEW: Written to a Jewish audience, this Gospel links the Old and New Testaments. It presents Jesus as the Messiah and King promised in the Old Testament. Matthew emphasizes Jesus' authority and power.

MARK: Mark probably had pragmatic Roman readers in mind. His Gospel stresses action and gives a straightforward, blow-by-blow account of Jesus' work on earth.

LUKE: A doctor, Luke was also a fine writer. His Gospel provides many details of human interest, especially in Jesus' treatment of the poor and needy. A joyful tone characterizes Luke's book.

JOHN: John has a different, more reflective style than the other Gospels. Its author selected seven signs that pointed to Jesus as the Son of God and wove together everything else to underscore that point.

ACTS: Acts tells what happened to Jesus' followers after he left them. Peter and Paul soon emerged as leaders of the rapidly spreading church.

The Letters

The young church was nourished spiritually by apostles who set down their beliefs and messages in a series of letters. The first 13 such letters (Romans through Philemon) were written by the apostle Paul, who led the advance of Christianity to non-Jewish people.

Paul's Letters:

ROMANS: Written for a sophisticated audience, Romans sets forth theology in a logical, organized form.

1 CORINTHIANS: A very practical book, 1 Corinthians takes up the problems of a tumultuous church in Corinth: marriage, factions, immorality, public worship, and lawsuits.

2 CORINTHIANS: Paul wrote this follow-up letter to defend himself against a rebellion led by certain false apostles.

GALATIANS: A short version of the message of Romans, this book addresses legalism. It shows how Christ came to bring freedom, not bondage to a set of laws.

EPHESIANS: Although written in jail, this letter is Paul's most optimistic and encouraging. It tells of the advantages a believer has in Christ.

PHILIPPIANS: The church at Philippi ranked among Paul's favorites. This friendly letter stresses that joy can be found in any situation.

COLOSSIANS: Written to oppose certain cults, Colossians tells how faith in Christ is complete. Nothing needs to be added to what Christ did.

1 THESSALONIANS: Composed early in Paul's ministry, this letter gives a capsule history of one church, as well as Paul's direct advice about specific problems.

2 THESSALONIANS: Stronger in tone than his first letter to the Thessalonians, the sequel goes over the same topics, especially the church's questions about Christ's second coming.

1 TIMOTHY: As Paul neared the end of his life, he chose young men such as Timothy to carry on his work. His two letters to Timothy form a leadership manual for a young pastor.

2 TIMOTHY: Written just before Paul's death, 2 Timothy offers Paul's final words to his young assistant.

TITUS: Titus was left in Crete, a notoriously difficult place to nurture a church. Paul's letter gave practical advice on how to go about it.

PHILEMON: Paul urged Philemon, owner of runaway slave Onesimus, to forgive his slave and accept him as a brother in Christ.

Other Letters:

HEBREWS: No one knows who wrote Hebrews, but it probably first went to Christians in danger of slipping back into Judaism. It interprets the Old Testament, explaining many Jewish practices as symbols that prepared the way for Christ.

JAMES: James, a man of action, emphasized the right kind of behavior for a believer. Someone who calls himself or herself a Christian ought to act like it, James believed, and his letter spells out the specifics.

1 PETER: Early Christians often met violent opposition, and Peter's letter comforted and encouraged Christians who were being persecuted for their faith.

2 PETER: In contrast to Peter's first letter, this one focused on problems that sprang up from the inside. It warns against false teachers.

1 JOHN: John could fill simple words—*light, love, life*—with deep meaning, and in this letter, he elegantly explains basic truths about the Christian life.

2 JOHN: Warning against false teachers, John counseled churches on how to respond to them.

3 JOHN: Balancing 2 John, this companion letter mentions the need to be hospitable to true teachers.

JUDE: Jude gave a brief but fiery exposé of heretics.

REVELATION: A book of visions and symbols, Revelation is the only New Testament book that concentrates on prophecy. It completes the story, begun in Genesis, of the cosmic battle between good and evil being waged on earth. It ends with a picture of a new heaven and new earth.

THE
OLD
TESTAMENT

GENESIS

God at Work
Everything—literally everything—begins here

> Then God blessed the seventh day and sanctified it, because in it He rested from all His work which God had created and made. **2:3**

THE BIBLE BEGINS WITH WORDS that have become famous, "In the beginning God created." God, like an artist, fashioned a universe. How can we grasp the grandeur of this?

Michelangelo, perhaps the greatest artist in history, may help us to understand. He painted Rome's famous Sistine Chapel to retell Genesis' story of creation. His experience proves one thing: Creativity is work.

An Exhausting Effort

Michelangelo had 6,000 square feet of ceiling to cover—the size of four average house roofs. Anyone who has painted a ceiling with a paint roller has caught a hint of the physical difficulty of such a task. But Michelangelo's plan called for 300 separate, detailed portraits of men and women. For more than three years the 5'4" artist devoted all his labors to the exhausting strain of painting the vast overhead space with his tiny brushes.

Sometimes he painted standing on a huge scaffold, a paintbrush high over his head. Sometimes he sat, his nose inches from the ceiling. Sometimes he painted while lying on his back. His back, shoulders, neck, and arms cramped painfully.

In the long days of summer, he had light to paint 17 hours a day, taking food and a chamber pot with him on the 60-foot scaffold. For 30 days at a stretch he slept in his clothes, not even taking off his boots. Paint dribbled into his eyes so he could barely see. Freezing in the winter, sweating in the summer, he painted until at last the ceiling looked like a ceiling no more. He had transformed it into the creation drama, with creatures so real they seemed to breathe. Never before or since have paint and plaster been so changed.

The Miracle of Life

But, as Michelangelo knew very well, his work was a poor, dim image of what God had created. Over the plaster vault of the Sistine Chapel rose the immense dome of God's sky, breathtaking in its simple beauty. Mountains, seas, the continents—all these, and much more, are the creative work of God, the Master Artist.

God's world, so much bigger and more beautiful than Michelangelo's masterpiece, is the product of incomparably greater energy. As author Eugene Peterson has written, "The Bible begins with the announcement, 'In the beginning God created,' not 'sat majestic in the heavens' and not 'was filled with beauty and love.' He created. He did something." In the beginning, God went to work.

Genesis focuses attention on this creative, hardworking God. The word *God* appears 30 times in the 31 verses of chapter 1. He grabs our attention in action. Genesis is an account of his deeds, ringing splendidly with the magnificent effort of creation.

Mending Broken Pieces

Genesis also talks about the work of humankind—but the tone changes abruptly. God had barely finished creating the universe when human rebellion marred it, like a delinquent spraying graffiti on the Sistine Chapel. Chapters 3–11 of Genesis portray a series of disasters: Adam and Eve's rebellion, Cain's calculated murder of his brother, the worldwide wickedness leading to the great flood, and human arrogance at Babel.

God immediately began to mend the pieces his creatures had broken. He narrowed his scope from the whole universe to a single man—not a king or wealthy landowner, but a childless nomad, Abraham. Abraham, Sarah, Isaac, Rebekah, Jacob, Rachel, Joseph—the upward thrust from chapter 12 on came through God's work in these startlingly human individuals. They were far from perfect, yet God picked them up where they were and carried them forward. He promised them great things. He moved through them to restore his art. His creative activity did not stop on the seventh day.

Genesis and Revelation

Many people read the Old Testament as though it portrayed the "bad old days" before Jesus. But that's not an accurate picture. Actually, the first three chapters of Genesis link to the last book of the Bible, Revelation. They are like brackets of perfection around the sadness of life marred by sin, death, suffering, and hatred. In Genesis we learn that life didn't start out that way. In Revelation we find out it won't end that way either. But the Old and New Testaments take place between those brackets. Through Abraham, through Moses, ultimately in Jesus, God is hard at work to make things right.

How to Read Genesis

Genesis is one of the most enjoyable Old Testament books, full of memorable stories of people and events. It is a crucial book to know, for the rest of the Bible often refers back to it.

Genesis tells the story of many beginnings—the beginning of the universe, the beginning of sin, and perhaps most important, the beginning of God's work to restore a sinful humanity.

The book breaks into two major sections. The first 11 chapters take a big view. They give the origins of human society, including the familiar stories of Adam and Eve, Cain and Abel, Noah's ark, and the tower of Babel. Here, a few words carry great significance. You need to read slowly and reflectively, for what happens in a single line may echo off events for centuries to come. For instance, Adam and Eve's sin, because it was the first sin, became an emblem of disobedience against God.

Beginning at chapter 12, Genesis tells a different kind of story—that of a single family. The pace of the story slows to develop the personalities of Abraham, Isaac, Jacob, and Joseph. These fathers and sons are full of human faults and oddities. Do you recognize any of their traits in people you know?

Seeing their fully human personalities, try to understand what God's plans were for them as individuals—and through them, for the restoration of a whole world marred by sin.

PEOPLE YOU'LL MEET IN GENESIS

3-TRACK READING PLAN

For an explanation and complete listing of the 3-track reading plan, turn to page 7.

TRACK 1: *Two-Week Courses on the Bible*
The Track 1 reading program on the Old Testament includes three chapters from Genesis. See page 7 for a complete listing of this course.

TRACK 2: *An Overview of Genesis in 14 Days*
☐ Day 1. Read the Introduction to Genesis and chapter 1, the story of creation.
☐ Day 2. Read chapter 2, the story of Adam and Eve.
☐ Day 3. Read chapter 3, where sin enters a perfect world.
☐ Day 4. Read chapter 4, the story of Cain and Abel.
☐ Day 5. Read chapter 7, the story of Noah and the great flood.
☐ Day 6. Read chapter 8, the end of the great flood.
☐ Day 7. Read chapter 15, God's covenant with Abraham.
☐ Day 8. Read chapter 19, the destruction of Sodom and Gomorrah.
☐ Day 9. Read chapter 22, God's testing of Abraham.
☐ Day 10. Read chapter 27, in which Jacob cheats his brother Esau.
☐ Day 11. Read chapter 28, when Jacob, fleeing Esau, dreams about God.
☐ Day 12. Read chapter 37, the story of Joseph sold into slavery.

☐ Day 13. Read chapter 41, in which Joseph is raised to the highest position in Egypt.
☐ Day 14. Read chapter 45, in which Joseph reveals his identity to his brothers.

Now turn to page 9 for your next Track 2 reading project.

TRACK 3: *All of Genesis in 49 Days*
After you have read through Genesis, turn to pages 10–14 for your next Track 3 reading project.

☒1	☒2	☐3	☐4	☐5	☐6	☐7	☐8
☐9	☐10–11	☐12	☐13	☐14	☐15	☐16	☐17
☐18	☐19	☐20	☐21	☐22	☐23	☐24	☐25
☐26	☐27	☐28	☐29	☐30	☐31	☐32	☐33
☐34	☐35	☐36	☐37	☐38	☐39	☐40	☐41
☐42	☐43	☐44	☐45	☐46	☐47	☐48	☐49
☐50							

The Creation

1 In the beginning God created the heavens and the earth.

2 The earth was *a*formless and void, and darkness was over the surface of the deep, and the Spirit of God was *b*moving over the surface of the waters.

3 Then God said, "Let there be light"; and there was light.

4 God saw that the light was good; and God separated the light from the darkness.

5 God called the light day, and the darkness He called night. And there was evening and there was morning, one day.

6 ¶ Then God said, "Let there be an expanse in the midst of the waters, and let it separate the waters from the waters."

7 God made the *c*expanse, and separated the waters which were below the expanse from the waters which were above the expanse; and it was so.

8 God called the expanse heaven. And there was evening and there was morning, a second day.

9 ¶ Then God said, "Let the waters below the heavens be gathered into one place, and let the dry land appear"; and it was so.

10 God called the dry land earth, and the gathering of the waters He called seas; and God saw that it was good.

11 Then God said, "Let the earth sprout vegetation: plants yielding seed, *and* fruit trees on the earth bearing fruit after their kind with seed in them"; and it was so.

12 The earth brought forth vegetation, plants yielding seed after their kind, and trees bearing fruit with seed in them, after their kind; and God saw that it was good.

13 There was evening and there was morning, a third day.

14 ¶ Then God said, "Let there be lights in the expanse of the heavens to separate the day from the night, and let them be for signs and for seasons and for days and years;

15 and let them be for lights in the expanse of the heavens to give light on the earth"; and it was so.

16 God made the two great lights, the greater light to govern the day, and the lesser light to govern the night; He *made* the stars also.

17 God placed them in the expanse of the heavens to give light on the earth,

18 and to govern the day and the night, and to separate the light from the darkness; and God saw that it was good.

19 There was evening and there was morning, a fourth day.

20 ¶ Then God said, "Let the waters teem with swarms of living creatures, and let birds fly above the earth in the open expanse of the heavens."

21 God created the great sea monsters and every living creature that moves, with which the waters swarmed after their kind, and every winged bird after its kind; and God saw that it was good.

22 God blessed them, saying, "Be fruitful and multiply, and fill the waters in the seas, and let birds multiply on the earth."

23 There was evening and there was morning, a fifth day.

24 ¶ Then God said, "Let the earth bring forth living creatures after their kind: cattle and creeping things and beasts of the earth after their kind"; and it was so.

25 God made the beasts of the earth after their kind, and the cattle after their kind, and everything that creeps on the ground after its kind; and God saw that it was good.

26 ¶ Then God said, "Let Us make man in Our image, according to Our likeness; and let them rule over the fish of the sea and over the birds of

---

a Or *a waste and emptiness*   *b* Or *hovering*   *c* Or *firmament* the sky and over the cattle and over all the earth, and over every creeping thing that creeps on the earth."

27 God created man in His own image, in the image of God He created him; male and female He created them.

28 God blessed them; and God said to them, "Be fruitful and multiply, and fill the earth, and subdue it; and rule over the fish of the sea and over the birds of the sky and over every living thing that moves on the earth."

29 Then God said, "Behold, I have given you every plant yielding seed that is on the surface of all the earth, and every tree which has fruit yielding seed; it shall be food for you;

30 and to every beast of the earth and to every bird of the sky and to every thing that moves on the earth which has life, *I have given* every green plant for food"; and it was so.

31 God saw all that He had made, and behold, it was very good. And there was evening and there was morning, the sixth day.

The Creation of Man and Woman

2 Thus the heavens and the earth were completed, and all their hosts.

2 By the seventh day God completed His work which He had done, and He rested on the seventh day from all His work which He had done.

3 Then God blessed the seventh day and sanctified it, because in it He rested from all His work which God had created and made.

4 ¶ This is the account of the heavens and the earth when they were created, in the day that the LORD God made earth and heaven.

5 Now no shrub of the field was yet in the earth, and no plant of the field had yet sprouted, for the LORD God had not sent rain upon the earth, and there was no man to cultivate the ground.

1:31 God Takes Time

Why did God take "six days" to create? Why not make it all instantaneously—as he certainly could have? Genesis introduces God's normal way of working: through a process. Work that begins with a word may take time to complete. Similarly, Israel was freed from slavery overnight, but required forty years to reach the promised land. Christians are born anew in an instant, and, in a process that lasts a lifetime, God makes them new. The new heaven and new earth have been a long time coming, but God is in the process of making all things new.

---

6 But a mist used to rise from the earth and water the whole surface of the ground.

7 Then the LORD God formed man of dust from the ground, and breathed into his nostrils the breath of life; and man became a living being.

8 The LORD God planted a garden toward the east, in Eden; and there He placed the man whom He had formed.

9 Out of the ground the LORD God caused to grow every tree that is pleasing to the sight and good for food; the tree of life also in the midst of

---

ADAM AND EVE *First in Everything*

THEY WERE THE FIRST HUMAN beings on earth, part of God's original creation. As such, Adam and Eve set the standard for everything that followed. Their lives illustrate what God expects and loves from human beings—as well as what he loathes.

First ecologists. They were the first to name animals, the first to tend a garden, the first to be placed in charge of all the creatures. They took on the huge task of caring for earth and guiding its proper use.

First to form a relationship with God. Adam and Eve were made in God's image. He conversed with them and gave them responsibilities. When they failed God they felt ashamed and feared meeting him.

First married couple. God himself made the introductions and gave the first couple the delight of each other, body and soul. They also became the first parents, though their very first child (Cain) brought much pain as well as joy.

First to sin against God. They had only to follow directions, but they failed. In response they hid from God and blamed each other. "Think of all the squabbles Adam and Eve must have had in the course of their nine hundred years," wrote Martin Luther. "Eve would say, 'You ate the apple,' and Adam would retort, 'You gave it to me.'"

In the end, the first two human beings were banished from Eden and driven out into a world full of problems God had never intended for them to confront. In that, as in everything, these two led the way for all of us.

Life Questions: Are you ever in a position to set an example for others? What can you learn from Adam and Eve's experience?

the garden, and the tree of the knowledge of good and evil.

10 ¶ Now a river flowed out of Eden to water the garden; and from there it divided and became four rivers.

11 The name of the first is Pishon; it flows around the whole land of Havilah, where there is gold.

12 The gold of that land is good; the bdellium and the onyx stone are there.

13 The name of the second river is Gihon; it flows around the whole land of Cush.

14 The name of the third river is Tigris; it flows east of Assyria. And the fourth river is the Euphrates.

15 ¶ Then the LORD God took the man and put him into the garden of Eden to cultivate it and keep it.

16 The LORD God commanded the man, saying, "From any tree of the garden you may eat freely;

17 but from the tree of the knowledge of good and evil you shall not eat, for in the day that you eat from it you will surely die."

18 ¶ Then the LORD God said, "It is not good for the man to be alone; I will make him a helper *a*suitable for him."

19 Out of the ground the LORD God formed every beast of the field and every bird of the sky, and brought *them* to the man to see what he would call them; and whatever the man called a living creature, that was its name.

20 The man gave names to all the cattle, and to the birds of the sky, and to every beast of the field, but for *b*Adam there was not found a helper suitable for him.

21 So the LORD God caused a deep sleep to fall upon the man, and he slept; then He took one of his ribs and closed up the flesh at that place.

22 The LORD God *c*fashioned into a woman the rib which He had taken from the man, and brought her to the man.

23 The man said,

"This is now bone of my bones,
And flesh of my flesh;
She shall be called Woman,
Because she was taken out of Man."

2:23–25 The First Marriage

Adam joyfully recognized that he and Eve belonged together. As verse 24 suggests, this suitability is the basis for all marriages. This passage was quoted by Jesus (Matthew 19:5; Mark 10:7–8) and Paul (1 Corinthians 6:16; Ephesians 5:31) in their comments on sex and marriage.

24 For this reason a man shall leave his father and his mother, and be joined to his wife; and they shall become one flesh.

25 And the man and his wife were both naked and were not ashamed.

The Fall of Man

3 Now the serpent was more crafty than any beast of the field which the LORD God had made. And he said to the woman, "Indeed, has God said, 'You shall not eat from any tree of the garden'?"

2 The woman said to the serpent, "From the fruit of the trees of the garden we may eat;

3 but from the fruit of the tree which is in the middle of the garden, God has said, 'You shall not eat from it or touch it, or you will die.' "

4 The serpent said to the woman, "You surely will not die!

5 "For God knows that in the day you eat from it your eyes will be opened, and you will be like God, knowing good and evil."

6 When the woman saw that the tree was good for food, and that it was a delight to the eyes, and that the tree was desirable to make *one* wise, she took from its fruit and ate; and she gave also to her husband with her, and he ate.

7 Then the eyes of both of them were opened, and they knew that they were naked; and they sewed fig leaves together and made themselves loin coverings.

3:7 Sin and Shame

When Adam and Eve disobeyed God, they immediately became ashamed of their bodies and wanted to hide. Ever since, sinful human beings have been "hiding" from each other and from God.

God asked Adam and Eve three questions, typical of the questions he puts to anyone "in hiding": 1) Where are you? (And why are you hiding from me?) 2) Who told you that you were naked? (And why did you believe somebody else, not me?) 3) What is this you have done? (And are you ready to take responsibility for it?)

8 ¶ They heard the sound of the LORD God walking in the garden in the cool of the day, and the man and his wife hid themselves from the presence of the LORD God among the trees of the garden.

9 Then the LORD God called to the man, and said to him, "Where are you?"

10 He said, "I heard the sound of You in the garden, and I was afraid because I was naked; so I hid myself."

---

a Lit *corresponding to*   *b* Or *man*   *c* Lit *built*

11 And He said, "Who told you that you were naked? Have you eaten from the tree of which I commanded you not to eat?"

12 The man said, "The woman whom You gave *to be* with me, she gave me from the tree, and I ate."

13 Then the LORD God said to the woman, "What is this you have done?" And the woman said, "The serpent deceived me, and I ate."

14 The LORD God said to the serpent,

"Because you have done this,
Cursed are you more than all cattle,
And more than every beast of the field;
On your belly you will go,
And dust you will eat
All the days of your life;

15 And I will put enmity
Between you and the woman,
And between your seed and her seed;
He shall bruise you on the head,
And you shall bruise him on the heel."

16 To the woman He said,

"I will greatly multiply
Your pain in childbirth,
In pain you will bring forth children;
Yet your desire will be for your husband,
And he will rule over you."

17 Then to Adam He said, "Because you have listened to the voice of your wife, and have eaten from the tree about which I commanded you, saying, 'You shall not eat from it';

Cursed is the ground because of you;
In toil you will eat of it
All the days of your life.

18 "Both thorns and thistles it shall grow
for you;
And you will eat the plants of the
field;

19 By the sweat of your face
You will eat bread,
Till you return to the ground,
Because from it you were taken;

Where We Came From

Above all else, Genesis says this: God did it

THE BIOLOGY TEACHER DISPLAYS A chart showing six animals. At one end is an ape standing upright, its hands swinging below its knees. At the other end, a rather hairy, stooped man in skins. "These are the stages of human evolution," the teacher declares, "over a period of several million years."

One agonized student shoots up his hand. "I believe in the Bible," he stammers, "that God made the earth and that the first man was Adam."

The teacher lets him finish, then dismisses his view. "Everybody is free to have his own religious beliefs. But science has proven that evolution is a fact."

Scenes like this have thrown confusion over the first three chapters of the Bible. It's impossible to read about Adam and Eve without wondering how they fit in with the bones scientists proclaim as "earliest man."

> Then the LORD God formed man of dust from the ground, and breathed into his nostrils the breath of life; and man became a living being. 2:7

The Main Point

These differences stir up controversy, even court cases. Certainly they are important issues. It's unfortunate, though, that the debate over process diverts attention from the main truth Genesis teaches.

Above everything else, it proclaims this: God did it. We are not here by accident, nor are we here merely to please ourselves. We owe our very existence to God. Every helium atom, every spiral galaxy, every living creature exists because God wants it to. Genesis 1–3 is the artist's signature on the painting, saying, "This is mine."

God Made Us Good

Genesis 1–3 pays humanity its highest compliment. After making all the glories of the world, God topped off his work with man and woman. He put them in charge. Unlike the animals, they were like him, "in His own image." "Very good," he said to himself when he had finished. With humans he quit, satisfied.

Nobody, including God, has been satisfied with human beings since then. We were made good, but we disobeyed God right from the beginning. We've been suffering the consequences ever since. Genesis helps us understand why the universe is so flagrantly lovely, and yet so tragic. It is lovely because God made it. But it is tragic because he entrusted it to us—and we failed.

Life Questions: People say they can see God reflected in stars, forests, sunsets. What about people? How can you see God's artistry in them?

For you are dust,
And to dust you shall return."
20 ¶ Now the man called his wife's name
*a*Eve, because she was the mother of all *the* living.
21 The LORD God made garments of skin for
Adam and his wife, and clothed them.
22 ¶ Then the LORD God said, "Behold, the
man has become like one of Us, knowing good
and evil; and now, he might stretch out his hand,
and take also from the tree of life, and eat, and live
forever"—
23 therefore the LORD God sent him out from
the garden of Eden, to cultivate the ground from
which he was taken.
24 So He drove the man out; and at the east of
the garden of Eden He stationed the cherubim and
the flaming sword which turned every direction to
guard the way to the tree of life.

Cain and Abel

4 Now the man had relations with his wife Eve,
and she conceived and gave birth to Cain, and
she said, "I have gotten a manchild with *the help
of* the LORD."
2 Again, she gave birth to his brother Abel.
And Abel was a keeper of flocks, but Cain was a
tiller of the ground.
3 So it came about in the course of time that
Cain brought an offering to the LORD of the fruit
of the ground.
4 Abel, on his part also brought of the first-
lings of his flock and of their fat portions. And the
LORD had regard for Abel and for his offering;
5 but for Cain and for his offering He had no
regard. So Cain became very angry and his countenance fell.
6 Then the LORD said to Cain, "Why are you
angry? And why has your countenance fallen?

a I.e. living; or life

7 "If you do well, will not *your countenance* be
lifted up? And if you do not do well, sin is crouch-
ing at the door; and its desire is for you, but you
must master it."

4:4 Improper Offerings

*Why God preferred Abel's offering to Cain's is
uncertain; later in the Old Testament both
animal and agricultural offerings were
accepted by God. Quite possibly, Cain's problem
was his attitude. Cain certainly became
instantly angry with God when things did not
go his way.*

8 Cain told Abel his brother. And it came
about when they were in the field, that Cain rose
up against Abel his brother and killed him.
9 ¶ Then the LORD said to Cain, "Where is
Abel your brother?" And he said, "I do not know.
Am I my brother's keeper?"
10 He said, "What have you done? The voice of
your brother's blood is crying to Me from the
ground.
11 "Now you are cursed from the ground,
which has opened its mouth to receive your brother's blood from your hand.
12 "When you cultivate the ground, it will no
longer yield its strength to you; you will be a vagrant and a wanderer on the earth."
13 Cain said to the LORD, "My punishment is
too great to bear!
14 "Behold, You have driven me this day from
the face of the ground; and from Your face I will
be hidden, and I will be a vagrant and a wanderer
on the earth, and whoever finds me will kill me."

CAIN AND ABEL *Blood Brothers*

THEIR PARENTS HAD STARTED THE rebellion against God. Not much time passed before
Cain took sin to its logical conclusion. The first child on earth became the first murderer.
Cain and Abel were the first of many feuding siblings. After them came Isaac and Ishmael, Jacob and
Esau, Rachel and Leah, Joseph and his brothers. It's a theme song in Genesis (and in life): Blood kin
have a hard time getting along. They can make bitter rivals.
The Bible tells us little about Abel and a good deal about Cain. That makes sad sense because as
sinful humans we see more of ourselves in Cain than in Abel. Cain wears his emotions on his sleeve:
first murderous anger, then defensiveness and finally shame and fear. In response to Cain's great
crime, God both punishes and protects him. He must leave home to wander all his life, yet God also
provides him with a measure of protection, "the sign for Cain" (4:15).
Cain's children set the pattern for humanity as it has lived ever since, a mixture of good and bad.
On the one hand, as musicians, metalworkers and farmers, they helped civilize the earth. On the other
hand, Cain's problems got passed down to future generations. Where Cain felt shame for his crime and
punishment, his descendant Lamech would boast about his own murderous deed (Genesis 4:23–24).

Life Questions: Which of Cain's responses to God—anger, defensiveness, fear, shame—do you identify
with most easily?

15 So the LORD said to him, "Therefore whoever kills Cain, vengeance will be taken on him sevenfold." And the LORD appointed a sign for Cain, so that no one finding him would slay him.

16 ¶ Then Cain went out from the presence of the LORD, and settled in the land of Nod, east of Eden.

17 ¶ Cain had relations with his wife and she conceived, and gave birth to Enoch; and he built a city, and called the name of the city Enoch, after the name of his son.

18 Now to Enoch was born Irad, and Irad became the father of Mehujael, and Mehujael became the father of Methushael, and Methushael became the father of Lamech.

19 Lamech took to himself two wives: the name of the one was Adah, and the name of the other, Zillah.

20 Adah gave birth to Jabal; he was the father of those who dwell in tents and *have* livestock.

21 His brother's name was Jubal; he was the father of all those who play the lyre and pipe.

22 As for Zillah, she also gave birth to Tubal-cain, the forger of all implements of bronze and iron; and the sister of Tubal-cain was Naamah.

23 ¶ Lamech said to his wives,
"Adah and Zillah,
Listen to my voice,
You wives of Lamech,
Give heed to my speech,
For I have killed a man for
wounding me;
And a boy for striking me;
24 If Cain is avenged sevenfold,
Then Lamech seventy-sevenfold."

25 ¶ Adam had relations with his wife again; and she gave birth to a son, and named him Seth, for, *she said,* "God has appointed me another offspring in place of Abel, for Cain killed him."

26 To Seth, to him also a son was born; and he called his name Enosh. Then *men* began to call upon the name of the LORD.

Descendants of Adam

5 This is the book of the generations of Adam. In the day when God created man, He made him in the likeness of God.

2 He created them male and female, and He blessed them and named them *a*Man in the day when they were created.

3 ¶ When Adam had lived one hundred and thirty years, he *b*became the father of *a son* in his own likeness, according to his image, and named him Seth.

4 Then the days of Adam after he became the father of Seth were eight hundred years, and he had *other* sons and daughters.

5 So all the days that Adam lived were nine hundred and thirty years, and he died.

6 ¶ Seth lived one hundred and five years, and became the father of Enosh.

7 Then Seth lived eight hundred and seven years after he became the father of Enosh, and he had *other* sons and daughters.

8 So all the days of Seth were nine hundred and twelve years, and he died.

9 ¶ Enosh lived ninety years, and became the father of Kenan.

10 Then Enosh lived eight hundred and fifteen years after he became the father of Kenan, and he had *other* sons and daughters.

11 So all the days of Enosh were nine hundred and five years, and he died.

12 ¶ Kenan lived seventy years, and became the father of Mahalalel.

13 Then Kenan lived eight hundred and forty years after he became the father of Mahalalel, and he had *other* sons and daughters.

14 So all the days of Kenan were nine hundred and ten years, and he died.

15 ¶ Mahalalel lived sixty-five years, and became the father of Jared.

16 Then Mahalalel lived eight hundred and thirty years after he became the father of Jared, and he had *other* sons and daughters.

17 So all the days of Mahalalel were eight hundred and ninety-five years, and he died.

18 ¶ Jared lived one hundred and sixty-two years, and became the father of Enoch.

19 Then Jared lived eight hundred years after he became the father of Enoch, and he had *other* sons and daughters.

20 So all the days of Jared were nine hundred and sixty-two years, and he died.

21 ¶ Enoch lived sixty-five years, and became the father of Methuselah.

22 Then Enoch walked with God three hundred years after he became the father of Methuselah, and he had *other* sons and daughters.

23 So all the days of Enoch were three hundred and sixty-five years.

24 Enoch walked with God; and he was not, for God took him.

25 ¶ Methuselah lived one hundred and

5:24 The Man Who Did Not Die

All but one of the brief biographies in chapter 5 end with the words "and he died." We know very little about the exception, Enoch, except that he walked with God. Enoch did not die; he "was not, for God took him." Based on this evidence, Hebrews 11:5–6 commends Enoch as a man of faith, since "without faith it is impossible to please Him."

---

a Lit *Adam*   *b* Lit *begot,* and so throughout the ch

eighty-seven years, and became the father of Lamech.

26 Then Methuselah lived seven hundred and eighty-two years after he became the father of Lamech, and he had *other* sons and daughters.

27 So all the days of Methuselah were nine hundred and sixty-nine years, and he died.

28 ¶ Lamech lived one hundred and eighty-two years, and became the father of a son.

29 Now he called his name Noah, saying, "This one will give us rest from our work and from the toil of our hands *arising* from the ground which the LORD has cursed."

30 Then Lamech lived five hundred and ninety-five years after he became the father of Noah, and he had *other* sons and daughters.

31 So all the days of Lamech were seven hundred and seventy-seven years, and he died.

32 ¶ Noah was five hundred years old, and Noah became the father of Shem, Ham, and Japheth.

The Corruption of Mankind

6 Now it came about, when men began to multiply on the face of the land, and daughters were born to them,

2 that the sons of God saw that the daughters of men were beautiful; and they took wives for themselves, whomever they chose.

6:2 The Sons of God

This mysterious description may refer to the "sons of Seth," the line of God's people from Adam to Noah, or it may refer to angels, often called "sons of God" in the Old Testament. However you interpret it, the point is that evil behavior increased in the world, a fact that led to punishment by a flood.

3 Then the LORD said, "My Spirit shall not strive with man forever, because he also is flesh; nevertheless his days shall be one hundred and twenty years."

4 The Nephilim were on the earth in those days, and also afterward, when the sons of God came in to the daughters of men, and they bore *children* to them. Those were the mighty men who *were* of old, men of renown.

5 ¶ Then the LORD saw that the wickedness of man was great on the earth, and that every intent of the thoughts of his heart was only evil continually.

6 The LORD was sorry that He had made man on the earth, and He was grieved in His heart.

7 The LORD said, "I will blot out man whom I have created from the face of the land, from man to animals to creeping things and to birds of the sky; for I am sorry that I have made them."

8 But Noah found favor in the eyes of the LORD.

9 ¶ These are *the records of* the generations of Noah. Noah was a righteous man, blameless in his time; Noah walked with God.

10 Noah became the father of three sons: Shem, Ham, and Japheth.

11 ¶ Now the earth was corrupt in the sight of God, and the earth was filled with violence.

12 God looked on the earth, and behold, it was corrupt; for all flesh had corrupted their way upon the earth.

13 ¶ Then God said to Noah, "The end of all flesh has come before Me; for the earth is filled with violence because of them; and behold, I am about to destroy them with the earth.

14 "Make for yourself an ark of gopher wood; you shall make the ark with rooms, and shall cover it inside and out with pitch.

15 "This is how you shall make it: the length of the ark three hundred *a*cubits, its breadth fifty cubits, and its height thirty cubits.

16 "You shall make a window for the ark, and finish it to a cubit from the top; and set the door of the ark in the side of it; you shall make it with lower, second, and third decks.

17 "Behold, I, even I am bringing the flood of water upon the earth, to destroy all flesh in which is the breath of life, from under heaven; everything that is on the earth shall perish.

18 "But I will establish My covenant with you; and you shall enter the ark—you and your sons and your wife, and your sons' wives with you.

19 "And of every living thing of all flesh, you shall bring two of every *kind* into the ark, to keep *them* alive with you; they shall be male and female.

20 "Of the birds after their kind, and of the animals after their kind, of every creeping thing of the ground after its kind, two of every *kind* will come to you to keep *them* alive.

21 "As for you, take for yourself some of all food which is edible, and gather *it* to yourself; and it shall be for food for you and for them."

22 Thus Noah did; according to all that God had commanded him, so he did.

The Flood

7 Then the LORD said to Noah, "Enter the ark, you and all your household, for you *alone* I have seen *to be* righteous before Me in this time.

2 "You shall take with you of every clean animal by sevens, a male and his female; and of the animals that are not clean two, a male and his female;

3 also of the birds of the sky, by sevens, male and female, to keep offspring alive on the face of all the earth.

4 "For after seven more days, I will send rain

a I.e. One cubit equals approx 18 in.

on the earth forty days and forty nights; and I will blot out from the face of the land every living thing that I have made."

5 Noah did according to all that the LORD had commanded him.

6 ¶ Now Noah was six hundred years old when the flood of water came upon the earth.

7 Then Noah and his sons and his wife and his sons' wives with him entered the ark because of the water of the flood.

8 Of clean animals and animals that are not clean and birds and everything that creeps on the ground,

9 there went into the ark to Noah by twos, male and female, as God had commanded Noah.

10 It came about after the seven days, that the water of the flood came upon the earth.

11 In the six hundredth year of Noah's life, in the second month, on the seventeenth day of the month, on the same day all the fountains of the great deep burst open, and the floodgates of the sky were opened.

12 The rain fell upon the earth for forty days and forty nights.

13 ¶ On the very same day Noah and Shem and Ham and Japheth, the sons of Noah, and Noah's wife and the three wives of his sons with them, entered the ark,

14 they and every beast after its kind, and all the cattle after their kind, and every creeping thing that creeps on the earth after its kind, and every bird after its kind, all sorts of birds.

15 So they went into the ark to Noah, by twos of all flesh in which was the breath of life.

16 Those that entered, male and female of all flesh, entered as God had commanded him; and the LORD closed it behind him.

17 ¶ Then the flood came upon the earth for forty days, and the water increased and lifted up the ark, so that it rose above the earth.

18 The water prevailed and increased greatly upon the earth, and the ark floated on the surface of the water.

19 The water prevailed more and more upon the earth, so that all the high mountains everywhere under the heavens were covered.

20 The water prevailed fifteen cubits higher, and the mountains were covered.

21 All flesh that moved on the earth perished, birds and cattle and beasts and every swarming thing that swarms upon the earth, and all mankind;

22 of all that was on the dry land, all in whose nostrils was the breath of the spirit of life, died.

23 Thus He blotted out every living thing that was upon the face of the land, from man to animals to creeping things and to birds of the sky, and they were blotted out from the earth; and only Noah was left, together with those that were with him in the ark.

24 The water prevailed upon the earth one hundred and fifty days.

The Flood Subsides

8 But God remembered Noah and all the beasts and all the cattle that were with him in the ark; and God caused a wind to pass over the earth, and the water subsided.

2 Also the fountains of the deep and the floodgates of the sky were closed, and the rain from the sky was restrained;

3 and the water receded steadily from the earth, and at the end of one hundred and fifty days the water decreased.

4 In the seventh month, on the seventeenth day of the month, the ark rested upon the mountains of Ararat.

5 The water decreased steadily until the tenth month; in the tenth month, on the first day of the month, the tops of the mountains became visible.

6 ¶ Then it came about at the end of forty

NOAH *Starting Over*

THE PROBLEM WITH THE PLANET God made was not its geology, biology or meteorology. The problem centered, rather, in a single species: *Homo sapiens*. Sin, spreading like a disease, had taken over human thought and action. As a result God chose to blot out much of his creation and start all over again, using Noah for this new beginning.

Characteristically, Noah obeyed right away when God announced his plans. Noah "walked with God," says Genesis (6:9). He worked hard, building a gigantic, seaworthy structure and storing up food for hundreds of animals. Repeatedly the Bible says that Noah did "all that God had commanded him."

Noah and his family spent more than a year confined in the ark. When they emerged at last to step out on muddy ground, their first action was to worship God. Impressed, God made a new covenant with Noah, promising never again to destroy the earth. He urged Noah and his family to be fruitful and multiply, just as he had urged Adam and Eve in the beginning.

Did this new beginning work? The last we hear of Noah shows that sin had not been remedied. Noah got drunk, shamed himself in front of his sons, and cursed one of his grandsons (9:20–24). Not even a flood could solve the problem of sin, for it lived on inside the best of people, even Noah.

Life Questions: If you were given an assignment like Noah's, how would you respond?

days, that Noah opened the window of the ark which he had made;

7 and he sent out a raven, and it flew here and there until the water was dried up from the earth.

8 Then he sent out a dove from him, to see if the water was abated from the face of the land;

9 but the dove found no resting place for the sole of her foot, so she returned to him into the ark, for the water was on the surface of all the earth. Then he put out his hand and took her, and brought her into the ark to himself.

10 So he waited yet another seven days; and again he sent out the dove from the ark.

11 The dove came to him toward evening, and behold, in her beak was a freshly picked olive leaf. So Noah knew that the water was abated from the earth.

8:11 Peace Symbol

The dove with an olive branch stands as a symbol for peace, and the origin of that symbol traces back to this account of restored peace between God and his creation. The olive leaf carried by the dove told Noah that lower elevations (where olives grow) were above water and had sprouted new life.

12 Then he waited yet another seven days, and sent out the dove; but she did not return to him again.

13 ¶ Now it came about in the six hundred and first year, in the first *month,* on the first of the month, the water was dried up from the earth. Then Noah removed the covering of the ark, and looked, and behold, the surface of the ground was dried up.

14 In the second month, on the twenty-seventh day of the month, the earth was dry.

15 Then God spoke to Noah, saying,

16 "Go out of the ark, you and your wife and your sons and your sons' wives with you.

17 "Bring out with you every living thing of all flesh that is with you, birds and animals and every creeping thing that creeps on the earth, that they may breed abundantly on the earth, and be fruitful and multiply on the earth."

18 So Noah went out, and his sons and his wife and his sons' wives with him.

19 Every beast, every creeping thing, and every bird, everything that moves on the earth, went out by their families from the ark.

20 ¶ Then Noah built an altar to the LORD, and took of every clean animal and of every clean bird and offered burnt offerings on the altar.

21 The LORD smelled the soothing aroma; and the LORD said to Himself, "I will never again curse the ground on account of man, for the intent of man's heart is evil from his youth; and I will never again destroy every living thing, as I have done.

22 "While the earth remains,
Seedtime and harvest,
And cold and heat,
And summer and winter,
And day and night
Shall not cease."

Covenant of the Rainbow

9 And God blessed Noah and his sons and said to them, "Be fruitful and multiply, and fill the earth.

2 "The fear of you and the terror of you will be on every beast of the earth and on every bird of the sky; with everything that creeps on the ground, and all the fish of the sea, into your hand they are given.

3 "Every moving thing that is alive shall be food for you; I give all to you, as *I gave* the green plant.

4 "Only you shall not eat flesh with its life, *that is,* its blood.

9:4 Reverence for Life

In the Garden of Eden God had provided plants for humanity's food. Here, for the first time, he gave permission to add meat to their diet. Still, an animal was not to be eaten with "its life . . . its blood." Kosher dietary requirements kept by Orthodox Jews today derive partly from this statement. Leviticus 17:10–14 gives more detail.

The intent, many commentators believe, was to remind God's people to reverence life, including animal life. This passage makes clear, however, that human life has a special significance. Ironically, capital punishment derives its legitimacy from this. Murderers who destroy human life actually attack the image of God. Therefore God demands an accounting.

5 "Surely I will require your lifeblood; from every beast I will require it. And from *every* man, from every man's brother I will require the life of man.

6 "Whoever sheds man's blood,
By man his blood shall be shed,
For in the image of God
He made man.

7 "As for you, be fruitful and multiply;
Populate the earth abundantly and
multiply in it."

8 ¶ Then God spoke to Noah and to his sons with him, saying,

9 "Now behold, I Myself do establish My covenant with you, and with your descendants after you;

10 and with every living creature that is with you, the birds, the cattle, and every beast of the

earth with you; of all that comes out of the ark, even every beast of the earth.

11 "I establish My covenant with you; and all flesh shall never again be cut off by the water of the flood, neither shall there again be a flood to destroy the earth."

12 God said, "This is the sign of the covenant which I am making between Me and you and every living creature that is with you, for all successive generations;

9:12 The Reason for Rainbows

Throughout the Bible, God makes covenant agreements with the people he loves. This first recorded covenant was marked by an appropriate symbol—the rainbow. While later covenants applied specifically to the Israelites, this one extended—and still extends—to every living creature.

13 I set My bow in the cloud, and it shall be for a sign of a covenant between Me and the earth.

14 "It shall come about, when I bring a cloud over the earth, that the bow will be seen in the cloud,

15 and I will remember My covenant, which is between Me and you and every living creature of all flesh; and never again shall the water become a flood to destroy all flesh.

16 "When the bow is in the cloud, then I will look upon it, to remember the everlasting covenant between God and every living creature of all flesh that is on the earth."

17 And God said to Noah, "This is the sign of the covenant which I have established between Me and all flesh that is on the earth."

18 ¶ Now the sons of Noah who came out of the ark were Shem and Ham and Japheth; and Ham was the father of Canaan.

19 These three *were* the sons of Noah, and from these the whole earth was populated.

20 ¶ Then Noah began farming and planted a vineyard.

21 He drank of the wine and became drunk, and uncovered himself inside his tent.

22 Ham, the father of Canaan, saw the nakedness of his father, and told his two brothers outside.

23 But Shem and Japheth took a garment and laid it upon both their shoulders and walked backward and covered the nakedness of their father; and their faces were turned away, so that they did not see their father's nakedness.

24 When Noah awoke from his wine, he knew what his youngest son had done to him.

25 So he said,
"Cursed be Canaan;

[a]A servant of servants
He shall be to his brothers."

26 He also said,
"Blessed be the LORD,
The God of Shem;
And let Canaan be his servant.

27 "May God enlarge Japheth,
And let him dwell in the tents of Shem;
And let Canaan be his servant."

28 ¶ Noah lived three hundred and fifty years after the flood.

29 So all the days of Noah were nine hundred and fifty years, and he died.

Descendants of Noah

10 Now these are *the records of* the generations of Shem, Ham, and Japheth, the sons of Noah; and sons were born to them after the flood.

2 ¶ The sons of Japheth *were* Gomer and Magog and Madai and Javan and Tubal and Meshech and Tiras.

3 The sons of Gomer *were* Ashkenaz and Riphath and Togarmah.

4 The sons of Javan *were* Elishah and Tarshish, Kittim and Dodanim.

5 From these the coastlands of the nations were separated into their lands, every one according to his language, according to their families, into their nations.

6 ¶ The sons of Ham *were* Cush and Mizraim and Put and Canaan.

7 The sons of Cush *were* Seba and Havilah and Sabtah and Raamah and Sabteca; and the sons of Raamah *were* Sheba and Dedan.

8 Now Cush became the father of Nimrod; he became a mighty one on the earth.

9 He was a mighty hunter before the LORD; therefore it is said, "Like Nimrod a mighty hunter before the LORD."

10 The beginning of his kingdom was [b]Babel and Erech and Accad and Calneh, in the land of Shinar.

11 From that land he went forth into Assyria, and built Nineveh and Rehoboth-Ir and Calah,

12 and Resen between Nineveh and Calah; that is the great city.

13 Mizraim became the father of Ludim and Anamim and Lehabim and Naphtuhim

14 and Pathrusim and Casluhim (from which came the Philistines) and Caphtorim.

15 ¶ Canaan became the father of Sidon, his firstborn, and Heth

16 and the Jebusite and the Amorite and the Girgashite

17 and the Hivite and the Arkite and the Sinite

18 and the Arvadite and the Zemarite and the Hamathite; and afterward the families of the Canaanite were spread abroad.

19 The territory of the Canaanite extended from Sidon as you go toward Gerar, as far as Gaza;

---

[a] I.e. the lowest of servants   [b] Or *Babylon*

as you go toward Sodom and Gomorrah and Admah and Zeboiim, as far as Lasha.

20 These are the sons of Ham, according to their families, according to their languages, by their lands, by their nations.

21 ¶ Also to Shem, the father of all the children of Eber, *and* the older brother of Japheth, children were born.

22 The sons of Shem *were* Elam and Asshur and Arpachshad and Lud and Aram.

23 The sons of Aram *were* Uz and Hul and Gether and Mash.

24 Arpachshad became the father of Shelah; and Shelah became the father of Eber.

25 Two sons were born to Eber; the name of the one *was* Peleg, for in his days the earth was divided; and his brother's name *was* Joktan.

26 Joktan became the father of Almodad and Sheleph and Hazarmaveth and Jerah

27 and Hadoram and Uzal and Diklah

28 and Obal and Abimael and Sheba

29 and Ophir and Havilah and Jobab; all these were the sons of Joktan.

30 Now their settlement extended from Mesha as you go toward Sephar, the hill country of the east.

31 These are the sons of Shem, according to their families, according to their languages, by their lands, according to their nations.

32 ¶ These are the families of the sons of Noah, according to their genealogies, by their nations; and out of these the nations were separated on the earth after the flood.

Universal Language, Babel, Confusion

11 Now the whole earth used the same language and the same words.

2 It came about as they journeyed east, that they found a plain in the land of Shinar and settled there.

3 They said to one another, "Come, let us make bricks and burn *them* thoroughly." And they used brick for stone, and they used tar for mortar.

4 They said, "Come, let us build for ourselves a city, and a tower whose top *will reach* into heaven, and let us make for ourselves a name, otherwise we will be scattered abroad over the face of the whole earth."

5 The LORD came down to see the city and the tower which the sons of men had built.

6 The LORD said, "Behold, they are one people, and they all have the same language. And this is what they began to do, and now nothing which they purpose to do will be impossible for them.

7 "Come, let Us go down and there confuse their language, so that they will not understand one another's speech."

8 So the LORD scattered them abroad from there over the face of the whole earth; and they stopped building the city.

11:6 Human Ambition

People are ambitious—they want to succeed. Genesis portrays humans as so ambitious that they try to compete with, rather than serve, God. This was Adam and Eve's sin (3:5,22), and at Babel people were at it again, in a citywide effort. God frustrated their plans by confusing their language.

---

9 Therefore its name was called *a*Babel, because there the LORD confused the language of the whole earth; and from there the LORD scattered them abroad over the face of the whole earth.

Descendants of Shem

10 ¶ These are *the records of* the generations of Shem. Shem was one hundred years old, and became the father of Arpachshad two years after the flood;

11 and Shem lived five hundred years after he became the father of Arpachshad, and he had *other* sons and daughters.

12 ¶ Arpachshad lived thirty-five years, and became the father of Shelah;

13 and Arpachshad lived four hundred and three years after he became the father of Shelah, and he had *other* sons and daughters.

14 ¶ Shelah lived thirty years, and became the father of Eber;

15 and Shelah lived four hundred and three years after he became the father of Eber, and he had *other* sons and daughters.

16 ¶ Eber lived thirty-four years, and became the father of Peleg;

17 and Eber lived four hundred and thirty years after he became the father of Peleg, and he had *other* sons and daughters.

18 ¶ Peleg lived thirty years, and became the father of Reu;

19 and Peleg lived two hundred and nine years after he became the father of Reu, and he had *other* sons and daughters.

20 ¶ Reu lived thirty-two years, and became the father of Serug;

21 and Reu lived two hundred and seven years after he became the father of Serug, and he had *other* sons and daughters.

22 ¶ Serug lived thirty years, and became the father of Nahor;

23 and Serug lived two hundred years after he became the father of Nahor, and he had *other* sons and daughters.

---

a Or *Babylon;* cf Heb *balal,* confuse

24 ¶ Nahor lived twenty-nine years, and became the father of Terah;

25 and Nahor lived one hundred and nineteen years after he became the father of Terah, and he had *other* sons and daughters.

26 ¶ Terah lived seventy years, and became the father of Abram, Nahor and Haran.

27 ¶ Now these are *the records of* the generations of Terah. Terah became the father of Abram, Nahor and Haran; and Haran became the father of Lot.

28 Haran died in the presence of his father Terah in the land of his birth, in Ur of the Chaldeans.

29 Abram and Nahor took wives for themselves. The name of Abram's wife was Sarai; and the name of Nahor's wife was Milcah, the daughter of Haran, the father of Milcah and Iscah.

30 Sarai was barren; she had no child.

31 ¶ Terah took Abram his son, and Lot the son of Haran, his grandson, and Sarai his daughter-in-law, his son Abram's wife; and they went out together from Ur of the Chaldeans in order to enter the land of Canaan; and they went as far as Haran, and settled there.

32 The days of Terah were two hundred and five years; and Terah died in Haran.

Abram Journeys to Egypt

12 Now the LORD said to Abram,
   "Go forth from your country,
   And from your relatives

Abraham
God begins to rebuild

AFTER SCANNING CENTURIES, GENESIS CHANGES dramatically at chapter 12. Leaving the big picture of world history, it settles on one lonely individual—not a great king or a wealthy landowner, but a childless nomad, Abraham.

At God's call, Abraham had uprooted himself from civilization and begun wandering in the wilderness. With a few changes (cattle substituted for sheep, Conestoga wagons for tents), you could make a cowboy movie out of his life. Moving his flocks from place to place, fighting skirmishes and pitched battles with hostile local people, Abraham had to be tough to survive. But this hardly made him unique; lots of tough nomads wandered the Middle East. What made this particular wanderer so important?

> *"I will make you a great nation, And I will bless you ... And in you all the families of the earth will be blessed."*
> 12:2–3

God's New Way of Working

Abraham was important, first of all, simply because God chose him. Shortly after the destruction caused by the great flood, God picked Abraham as the foundation of a new humanity. On several remarkable occasions God spoke directly to him, promising to make his family great in the land he roamed. The promises were hard to believe: Abraham's wife was barren, Abraham was getting too old to have children, he owned no land and had no prospect of any. Nonetheless, God asked Abraham to trust him.

The second reason why Abraham matters follows from the first: When God spoke to him, Abraham listened. He was far from perfect. Sometimes he strayed from the path God put him on, lying and trying to make the promises work out in his own way. Yet in the decisive moments of life, he listened to God and obeyed. He was willing to sacrifice anything for God—even his only son. God put his brand on Abraham, the mark of circumcision. His descendants were to be forever known as "God's people."

Uncensored Truth

The life of Abraham is a fascinating story, true to life, full of bad moments as well as good. He was hardly a theologian; a more comprehensive understanding of God would have to wait for Moses. But Abraham's faith is the root of Judaism and, thus, of Christianity. In his encounters with God we get raw, uncensored truth; not religion invented by a philosopher, but religion as it really happens when God meets man.

No wonder the New Testament cites Abraham more than 80 times, and Paul tells Christians they are the true descendants of Abraham (Galatians 3:6–9). Abraham's life began to unfold the story of God's long-range plans. Two thousand years later, Abraham's descendant Jesus came to fulfill the promises made to Abraham and his descendants.

Life Questions: God asked Abraham to leave his home and family and go to a far-off foreign country. If you were in his place, how would you have responded? Has God ever asked anything hard or risky of you?

And from your father's house,
To the land which I will show you;
2 And I will make you a great nation,
And I will bless you,
And make your name great;
And so you shall be a blessing;
3 And I will bless those who bless you,
And the one who curses you I will curse.
And in you all the families of the earth
will be blessed."

4 ¶ So Abram went forth as the LORD had spoken to him; and Lot went with him. Now Abram was seventy-five years old when he departed from Haran.

5 Abram took Sarai his wife and Lot his nephew, and all their possessions which they had accumulated, and the persons which they had acquired in Haran, and they set out for the land of Canaan; thus they came to the land of Canaan.

6 Abram passed through the land as far as the site of Shechem, to the oak of Moreh. Now the Canaanite *was* then in the land.

7 The LORD appeared to Abram and said, "To your descendants I will give this land." So he built an altar there to the LORD who had appeared to him.

8 Then he proceeded from there to the mountain on the east of Bethel, and pitched his tent, with Bethel on the west and Ai on the east; and there he built an altar to the LORD and called upon the name of the LORD.

9 Abram journeyed on, continuing toward the *a*Negev.

10 ¶ Now there was a famine in the land; so Abram went down to Egypt to sojourn there, for the famine was severe in the land.

11 It came about when he came near to Egypt, that he said to Sarai his wife, "See now, I know that you are a beautiful woman;

12 and when the Egyptians see you, they will say, 'This is his wife'; and they will kill me, but they will let you live.

13 "Please say that you are my sister so that it may go well with me because of you, and that I may live on account of you."

14 It came about when Abram came into Egypt, the Egyptians saw that the woman was very beautiful.

15 Pharaoh's officials saw her and praised her to Pharaoh; and the woman was taken into Pharaoh's house.

16 Therefore he treated Abram well for her sake; and gave him sheep and oxen and donkeys and male and female servants and female donkeys and camels.

17 ¶ But the LORD struck Pharaoh and his house with great plagues because of Sarai, Abram's wife.

18 Then Pharaoh called Abram and said, "What is this you have done to me? Why did you not tell me that she was your wife?

19 "Why did you say, 'She is my sister,' so that I took her for my wife? Now then, here is your wife, take her and go."

20 Pharaoh commanded *his* men concerning him; and they escorted him away, with his wife and all that belonged to him.

Abram and Lot

13 So Abram went up from Egypt to the *a*Negev, he and his wife and all that belonged to him, and Lot with him.

2 ¶ Now Abram was very rich in livestock, in silver and in gold.

3 He went on his journeys from the *a*Negev as far as Bethel, to the place where his tent had been at the beginning, between Bethel and Ai,

13:3 On the Road

The main trade route through Canaan passed north to south through Shechem, Bethel, Hebron, and Beersheba. As Abraham and his children traveled, they naturally stopped in those places. These place-names crop up again and again in the story of God's work.

4 to the place of the altar which he had made there formerly; and there Abram called on the name of the LORD.

5 Now Lot, who went with Abram, also had flocks and herds and tents.

6 And the land could not sustain them while dwelling together, for their possessions were so great that they were not able to remain together.

7 And there was strife between the herdsmen of Abram's livestock and the herdsmen of Lot's livestock. Now the Canaanite and the Perizzite were dwelling then in the land.

8 ¶ So Abram said to Lot, "Please let there be no strife between you and me, nor between my herdsmen and your herdsmen, for we are brothers.

9 "Is not the whole land before you? Please

12:13 Abraham's Half-Truth

"A lie is an attempt to deceive," according to one definition, and by that standard Abraham was lying when he claimed Sarai was his sister. Yet he was telling half the truth, for she was his half sister (20:12). Abraham pulled this same trick years later and got caught again (chapter 20). On both occasions he had feared for his life, a situation in which half-truths are particularly appealing.

---

a I.e. South country

separate from me; if *to* the left, then I will go to the right; or if *to* the right, then I will go to the left."

10 Lot lifted up his eyes and saw all the valley of the Jordan, that it was well watered everywhere—*this was* before the LORD destroyed Sodom and Gomorrah—like the garden of the LORD, like the land of Egypt as you go to Zoar.

11 So Lot chose for himself all the valley of the Jordan, and Lot journeyed eastward. Thus they separated from each other.

12 Abram settled in the land of Canaan, while Lot settled in the cities of the valley, and moved his tents as far as Sodom.

13 Now the men of Sodom were wicked exceedingly and sinners against the LORD.

14 ¶ The LORD said to Abram, after Lot had separated from him, "Now lift up your eyes and look from the place where you are, northward and southward and eastward and westward;

15 for all the land which you see, I will give it to you and to your descendants forever.

16 "I will make your descendants as the dust of the earth, so that if anyone can number the dust of the earth, then your descendants can also be numbered.

17 "Arise, walk about the land through its length and breadth; for I will give it to you."

18 Then Abram moved his tent and came and dwelt by the oaks of Mamre, which are in Hebron, and there he built an altar to the LORD.

War of the Kings

14 And it came about in the days of Amraphel king of Shinar, Arioch king of Ellasar, Chedorlaomer king of Elam, and Tidal king of Goiim,

2 *that* they made war with Bera king of Sodom, and with Birsha king of Gomorrah, Shinab

king of Admah, and Shemeber king of Zeboiim, and the king of Bela (that is, Zoar).

3 All these came as allies to the valley of Siddim (that is, the Salt Sea).

4 Twelve years they had served Chedorlaomer, but the thirteenth year they rebelled.

5 In the fourteenth year Chedorlaomer and the kings that were with him, came and defeated the Rephaim in Ashteroth-karnaim and the Zuzim in Ham and the Emim in Shaveh-kiriathaim,

6 and the Horites in their Mount Seir, as far as El-paran, which is by the wilderness.

7 Then they turned back and came to En-mishpat (that is, Kadesh), and conquered all the country of the Amalekites, and also the Amorites, who lived in Hazazon-tamar.

8 And the king of Sodom and the king of Gomorrah and the king of Admah and the king of Zeboiim and the king of Bela (that is, Zoar) came out; and they arrayed for battle against them in the valley of Siddim,

9 against Chedorlaomer king of Elam and Tidal king of Goiim and Amraphel king of Shinar and Arioch king of Ellasar—four kings against five.

10 Now the valley of Siddim was full of tar pits; and the kings of Sodom and Gomorrah fled, and they fell into them. But those who survived fled to the hill country.

11 Then they took all the goods of Sodom and Gomorrah and all their food supply, and departed.

12 They also took Lot, Abram's nephew, and his possessions and departed, for he was living in Sodom.

13 ¶ Then a fugitive came and told Abram the

LOT *Different Pathways*

PEOPLE WHO GROW UP CLOSE together—neighbors, friends, cousins, even siblings—sometimes end up in very different places in life. Looking back, one wonders what made the difference.

Take Lot as an example. Abraham's nephew, he apparently latched on to his uncle after losing his own father. When God called Abraham to leave home and strike out for unknown territory, Lot packed up and joined Abraham on the long trip.

Abraham reciprocated with love. Even after the two men had separated to make better use of grazing lands, Abraham cared enough about his nephew to stage a daring raid to rescue Lot from kidnappers. Later, when God announced he would destroy Lot's adopted town of Sodom, Abraham pleaded with God to save it.

Though Lot started out close to Abraham, he ultimately chose a very different pathway. Abraham remained a nomad, following God all his days. Lot preferred the cushy surroundings of the city—despite Sodom's reputation as a center of immorality. Soon Lot grew attached.

Even when God sent angels warning him to escape the coming judgment, Lot had a hard time tearing himself away. He lost everything and ended up in a cave, engaged in drunken incest with his own daughters. In contrast, the more faithful Abraham became the father of God's chosen people and one of the great patriarchs of the Old Testament.

Life Questions: If someone offered you a comfortable, successful position in a morally questionable situation, would you accept? Why or why not?

Hebrew. Now he was living by the oaks of Mamre the Amorite, brother of Eshcol and brother of Aner, and these were allies with Abram.

14 When Abram heard that his relative had been taken captive, he led out his trained men, born in his house, three hundred and eighteen, and went in pursuit as far as Dan.

15 He divided his forces against them by night, he and his servants, and defeated them, and pursued them as far as Hobah, which is north of Damascus.

16 He brought back all the goods, and also brought back his relative Lot with his possessions, and also the women, and the people.

God's Promise to Abram

17 ¶ Then after his return from the defeat of Chedorlaomer and the kings who were with him, the king of Sodom went out to meet him at the valley of Shaveh (that is, the King's Valley).

18 And Melchizedek king of Salem brought out bread and wine; now he was a priest of God Most High.

19 He blessed him and said,
"Blessed be Abram of God Most High,
Possessor of heaven and earth;
20 And blessed be God Most High,
Who has delivered your enemies into
your hand."
He gave him a tenth of all.

14:20 Mystery Man

Melchizedek appeared to Abraham without warning, received tremendous honor, and then disappeared. Yet hundreds of years later he earned mention in Psalm 110, and hundreds of years after that in Hebrews 7:11–17. Melchizedek remains a mysterious figure, but he does set an important precedent for the Messiah: The same man can serve as both priest and king. (Jewish priests came from one tribe, and kings from another, different tribe.) Though Melchizedek did not have the proper family lineage, his spiritual power impressed Abraham, the father of Judaism.

21 The king of Sodom said to Abram, "Give the people to me and take the goods for yourself."

22 Abram said to the king of Sodom, "I have sworn to the LORD God Most High, possessor of heaven and earth,

23 that I will not take a thread or a sandal thong or anything that is yours, for fear you would say, 'I have made Abram rich.'

24 "I will take nothing except what the young men have eaten, and the share of the men who went with me, Aner, Eshcol, and Mamre; let them take their share."

Abram Promised a Son

15 After these things the word of the LORD came to Abram in a vision, saying,
"Do not fear, Abram,
I am a shield to you;
Your reward shall be very great."

2 Abram said, "O Lord GOD, what will You give me, since I am childless, and the heir of my house is Eliezer of Damascus?"

3 And Abram said, "Since You have given no offspring to me, one born in my house is my heir."

4 Then behold, the word of the LORD came to him, saying, "This man will not be your heir; but one who will come forth from your own body, he shall be your heir."

5 And He took him outside and said, "Now look toward the heavens, and count the stars, if you are able to count them." And He said to him, "So shall your descendants be."

6 Then he believed in the LORD; and He reckoned it to him as righteousness.

15:6 What God Looks For

God accepted Abraham not because he led a perfect life but because of his responsiveness to God's promises. This verse was quoted three times in the New Testament to demonstrate that salvation by faith was nothing new (Romans 4:3; Galatians 3:6; James 2:23). Even in the Old Testament, God looked for faith, not moral perfection.

7 And He said to him, "I am the LORD who brought you out of Ur of the Chaldeans, to give you this land to possess it."

8 He said, "O Lord GOD, how may I know that I will possess it?"

9 So He said to him, "Bring Me a three year old heifer, and a three year old female goat, and a three year old ram, and a turtledove, and a young pigeon."

10 Then he brought all these to Him and cut them in two, and laid each half opposite the other; but he did not cut the birds.

11 The birds of prey came down upon the carcasses, and Abram drove them away.

12 ¶ Now when the sun was going down, a deep sleep fell upon Abram; and behold, terror *and* great darkness fell upon him.

13 *God said* to Abram, "Know for certain that your descendants will be strangers in a land that is not theirs, where they will be enslaved and oppressed four hundred years.

14 "But I will also judge the nation whom they will serve, and afterward they will come out with many possessions.

15 "As for you, you shall go to your fathers in peace; you will be buried at a good old age.

16 "Then in the fourth generation they will return here, for the iniquity of the Amorite is not yet complete."

17 ¶ It came about when the sun had set, that it was very dark, and behold, *there appeared no* smoking oven and a flaming torch which passed between these pieces.

18 On that day the LORD made a covenant with Abram, saying,

"To your descendants I have given this
    land,
From the river of Egypt as far as the
    great river, the river Euphrates:

19 the Kenite and the Kenizzite and the Kadmonite

20 and the Hittite and the Perizzite and the Rephaim

21 and the Amorite and the Canaanite and the Girgashite and the Jebusite."

Sarai and Hagar

16 Now Sarai, Abram's wife had borne him no *children,* and she had an Egyptian maid whose name was Hagar.

2 So Sarai said to Abram, "Now behold, the LORD has prevented me from bearing *children.* Please go in to my maid; perhaps I will obtain children through her." And Abram listened to the voice of Sarai.

3 After Abram had lived ten years in the land of Canaan, Abram's wife Sarai took Hagar the Egyptian, her maid, and gave her to her husband Abram as his wife.

4 He went in to Hagar, and she conceived; and when she saw that she had conceived, her mistress was despised in her sight.

5 And Sarai said to Abram, "May the wrong done me be upon you. I gave my maid into your arms, but when she saw that she had conceived, I was despised in her sight. May the LORD judge between you and me."

6 But Abram said to Sarai, "Behold, your maid is in your power; do to her what is good in

16:2 A Substitute Wife

According to custom, a man could sleep with a servant and include her children in his household. Abraham was trying to get the children he and his wife longed for and to "help God out" in fulfilling his promise of a son. Abraham's way was not God's way, however, and Abraham's attempt led to considerable jealousy and sorrow. The same practice also led to trouble for Jacob's family (chapter 30).

your sight." So Sarai treated her harshly, and she fled from her presence.

7 ¶ Now the angel of the LORD found her by a spring of water in the wilderness, by the spring on the way to Shur.

8 He said, "Hagar, Sarai's maid, where have you come from and where are you going?" And she said, "I am fleeing from the presence of my mistress Sarai."

9 Then the angel of the LORD said to her, "Return to your mistress, and submit yourself to her authority."

10 Moreover, the angel of the LORD said to her, "I will greatly multiply your descendants so that they will be too many to count."

11 The angel of the LORD said to her further,
    "Behold, you are with child,
    And you will bear a son;

ISHMAEL *Second Best*

YOU MIGHT CALL ISHMAEL A mistake. His birth came about when Sarah and Abraham doubted God's promise to provide them a child in their old age. The two conspired to "help God out" by using an Egyptian servant, Hagar, as a substitute wife for Abraham. Then, when God fulfilled his promise and Sarah bore a son of her own, she cruelly drove the servant and her son out into the desert. Ishmael, the innocent victim of this scheming, suffered the consequences.

Yet God also blessed Ishmael. He "heard the lad crying" when Ishmael was nearly dying of thirst in the desert (21:17). God promised that Ishmael's descendants would comprise a great nation. The Bible records that Ishmael had twelve sons, and that "the Ishmaelites" were Israel's neighbors for centuries. In fact, Arabs today traditionally trace their lineage to Ishmael.

Ishmael apparently kept in contact with his original family; he attended Abraham's funeral, and his daughter would marry Abraham's grandson Esau. Yet his place in Abraham's "covenant" with God was lost. In a similar way, Ishmael's son-in-law Esau would enjoy the earthly blessings of success, even though God's greatest blessing was reserved for his brother Jacob. In the Bible's accounting, God's "covenant blessing" always matters more than earthly success.

Life Questions: Have you ever tried to "help God out" when you thought he couldn't possibly help you in the way you wanted? What was the result?

And you shall call his name *a*Ishmael,
Because the LORD has given heed to your
affliction.

12 "He will be a wild donkey of a man,
His hand *will be* against everyone,
And everyone's hand *will be* against him;
And he will live to the east of all his
brothers."

13 Then she called the name of the LORD who spoke to her, "You are a God who sees"; for she said, "Have I even remained alive here after seeing Him?"

14 Therefore the well was called *b*Beer-lahai-roi; behold, it is between Kadesh and Bered.

15 ¶ So Hagar bore Abram a son; and Abram called the name of his son, whom Hagar bore, Ishmael.

16 Abram was eighty-six years old when Hagar bore Ishmael to him.

Abraham and the Covenant of Circumcision

17 Now when Abram was ninety-nine years old, the LORD appeared to Abram and said to him,

"I am God Almighty;
Walk before Me, and be blameless.

2 "I will establish My covenant between Me
and you,
And I will multiply you exceedingly."

3 Abram fell on his face, and God talked with him, saying,

4 "As for Me, behold, My covenant is with
you,
And you will be the father of a multitude
of nations.

5 "No longer shall your name be called
*c*Abram,
But your name shall be *d*Abraham;
For I will make you the father of a
multitude of nations.

6 "I will make you exceedingly fruitful, and I will make nations of you, and kings will come forth from you.

7 "I will establish My covenant between Me and you and your descendants after you throughout their generations for an everlasting covenant, to be God to you and to your descendants after you.

8 "I will give to you and to your descendants after you, the land of your sojournings, all the land of Canaan, for an everlasting possession; and I will be their God."

9 ¶ God said further to Abraham, "Now as for you, you shall keep My covenant, you and your descendants after you throughout their generations.

10 "This is My covenant, which you shall keep, between Me and you and your descendants after

you: every male among you shall be circumcised.

11 "And you shall be circumcised in the flesh of your foreskin, and it shall be the sign of the covenant between Me and you.

12 "And every male among you who is eight days old shall be circumcised throughout your generations, a *servant* who is born in the house or who is bought with money from any foreigner, who is not of your descendants.

13 "A *servant* who is born in your house or who is bought with your money shall surely be circumcised; thus shall My covenant be in your flesh for an everlasting covenant.

14 "But an uncircumcised male who is not circumcised in the flesh of his foreskin, that person shall be cut off from his people; he has broken My covenant."

15 ¶ Then God said to Abraham, "As for Sarai your wife, you shall not call her name Sarai, but *e*Sarah *shall be* her name.

16 "I will bless her, and indeed I will give you a son by her. Then I will bless her, and she shall be *a mother of* nations; kings of peoples will come from her."

17 Then Abraham fell on his face and laughed, and said in his heart, "Will a child be born to a man one hundred years old? And will Sarah, who is ninety years old, bear *a child?*"

17:17 Laughing at God

Abraham was a man of faith, but his faith was less than 100 percent. Here, nearing the age of 100, he laughed heartily at God's promise that he would father a son, and he demonstrated his lack of belief by suggesting that God accept Ishmael as an adequate substitute. Some time later Sarah, his wife, shared in the "joke" (18:12).

18 And Abraham said to God, "Oh that Ishmael might live before You!"

19 But God said, "No, but Sarah your wife will bear you a son, and you shall call his name *f*Isaac; and I will establish My covenant with him for an everlasting covenant for his descendants after him.

20 "As for Ishmael, I have heard you; behold, I will bless him, and will make him fruitful and will multiply him exceedingly. He shall become the father of twelve princes, and I will make him a great nation.

21 "But My covenant I will establish with Isaac, whom Sarah will bear to you at this season next year."

22 When He finished talking with him, God went up from Abraham.

---

a I.e. God hears *b* I.e. the well of the living one who sees me *c* I.e. exalted father *d* I.e. father of a multitude
e I.e. princess *f* I.e. he laughs

23 ¶ Then Abraham took Ishmael his son, and all *the servants* who were born in his house and all who were bought with his money, every male among the men of Abraham's household, and circumcised the flesh of their foreskin in the very same day, as God had said to him.

24 Now Abraham was ninety-nine years old when he was circumcised in the flesh of his foreskin.

25 And Ishmael his son was thirteen years old when he was circumcised in the flesh of his foreskin.

26 In the very same day Abraham was circumcised, and Ishmael his son.

27 All the men of his household, who were born in the house or bought with money from a foreigner, were circumcised with him.

Birth of Isaac Promised

18 Now the LORD appeared to him by the oaks of Mamre, while he was sitting at the tent door in the heat of the day.

2 When he lifted up his eyes and looked, behold, three men were standing opposite him; and when he saw *them,* he ran from the tent door to meet them and bowed himself to the earth,

3 and said, "My lord, if now I have found favor in your sight, please do not pass your servant by.

4 "Please let a little water be brought and wash your feet, and rest yourselves under the tree;

5 and I will bring a piece of bread, that you may refresh yourselves; after that you may go on, since you have visited your servant." And they said, "So do, as you have said."

6 So Abraham hurried into the tent to Sarah, and said, "Quickly, prepare three measures of fine flour, knead *it* and make bread cakes."

7 Abraham also ran to the herd, and took a tender and choice calf and gave *it* to the servant, and he hurried to prepare it.

8 He took curds and milk and the calf which he had prepared, and placed *it* before them; and he was standing by them under the tree as they ate.

9 ¶ Then they said to him, "Where is Sarah your wife?" And he said, "There, in the tent."

10 He said, "I will surely return to you at this time next year; and behold, Sarah your wife will have a son." And Sarah was listening at the tent door, which was behind him.

11 Now Abraham and Sarah were old, advanced in age; Sarah was past childbearing.

12 Sarah laughed to herself, saying, "After I have become old, shall I have pleasure, my lord being old also?"

13 And the LORD said to Abraham, "Why did Sarah laugh, saying, 'Shall I indeed bear *a child,* when I am *so* old?'

14 "Is anything too difficult for the LORD? At the appointed time I will return to you, at this time next year, and Sarah will have a son."

15 Sarah denied *it* however, saying, "I did not laugh"; for she was afraid. And He said, "No, but you did laugh."

16 ¶ Then the men rose up from there, and looked down toward Sodom; and Abraham was walking with them to send them off.

17 The LORD said, "Shall I hide from Abraham what I am about to do,

18 since Abraham will surely become a great and mighty nation, and in him all the nations of the earth will be blessed?

19 "For I have chosen him, so that he may command his children and his household after him to keep the way of the LORD by doing righteousness and justice, so that the LORD may bring upon Abraham what He has spoken about him."

SARAH *Who's Laughing?*

SHE WAS BEAUTIFUL. SHE HAD a wonderful, wealthy husband. Sarah should have been content. Instead her life revolved around the one thing she lacked—a child. Although God had promised that her husband Abraham would father a great nation, as the decades passed Sarah remained childless. The odds of giving birth gradually dwindled. More descendants than the stars in the sky? God's promise seemed laughable as Sarah celebrated her ninetieth birthday.

A resourceful woman, Sarah came up with an alternate plan. She would use her servant Hagar as a surrogate mother. Obviously Sarah felt deep inner conflict about this decision, for when Abraham got Hagar pregnant, Sarah mistreated her and sent her away. Hagar returned, but Sarah's inner conflict persisted. She would ultimately drive both mother and son into the desert.

Meanwhile, God kept repeating the amazing promise that Sarah would become the mother of a nation. Once, Abraham fell face down and laughed incredulously at the notion. Sarah cackled too. But the joke turned on them both when old Sarah finally got pregnant. After all her years of waiting, her longings were fulfilled.

"God has made laughter for me," Sarah said when her son was born (21:6). It was a wonderful pun; in obedience to God (17:19), Abraham named his son Isaac, which means "he laughs" in Hebrew.

Life Questions: When a person has deep longings that seem impossible to fulfill, what should he or she do?

20 And the LORD said, "The outcry of Sodom and Gomorrah is indeed great, and their sin is exceedingly grave.

21 "I will go down now, and see if they have

18:18 The Gospel to Abraham

God predicted here (and in several other places) that all nations on earth would be blessed through Abraham. About two thousand years later the apostle Paul, seeing in this a prediction of God reaching out through Jews to non-Jews with the message of Christianity, wrote that God had "preached the gospel beforehand to Abraham" (Galatians 3:8).

done entirely according to its outcry, which has come to Me; and if not, I will know."

22 ¶ Then the men turned away from there and went toward Sodom, while Abraham was still standing before the LORD.

23 Abraham came near and said, "Will You indeed sweep away the righteous with the wicked?

24 "Suppose there are fifty righteous within the city; will You indeed sweep *it* away and not spare the place for the sake of the fifty righteous who are in it?

25 "Far be it from You to do such a thing, to slay the righteous with the wicked, so that the righteous and the wicked are *treated* alike. Far be it from You! Shall not the Judge of all the earth deal justly?"

26 So the LORD said, "If I find in Sodom fifty righteous within the city, then I will spare the whole place on their account."

27 And Abraham replied, "Now behold, I have ventured to speak to the Lord, although I am *but* dust and ashes.

28 "Suppose the fifty righteous are lacking five, will You destroy the whole city because of five?" And He said, "I will not destroy *it* if I find forty-five there."

29 He spoke to Him yet again and said, "Suppose forty are found there?" And He said, "I will not do *it* on account of the forty."

30 Then he said, "Oh may the Lord not be angry, and I shall speak; suppose thirty are found there?" And He said, "I will not do *it* if I find thirty there."

31 And he said, "Now behold, I have ventured to speak to the Lord; suppose twenty are found there?" And He said, "I will not destroy *it* on account of the twenty."

32 Then he said, "Oh may the Lord not be angry, and I shall speak only this once; suppose ten are found there?" And He said, "I will not destroy *it* on account of the ten."

33 As soon as He had finished speaking to Abraham the LORD departed, and Abraham returned to his place.

The Doom of Sodom

19 Now the two angels came to Sodom in the evening as Lot was sitting in the gate of Sodom. When Lot saw *them,* he rose to meet them and bowed down *with his* face to the ground.

19:1 A Man of Substance

The angels found Lot in the gateway to Sodom—a fact loaded with significance. Traditionally, city fathers gathered in the gateway to make important decisions. Lot's presence suggests that he had become "one of them" during his time in Sodom, which may explain why he struggled against leaving.

2 And he said, "Now behold, my lords, please turn aside into your servant's house, and spend the night, and wash your feet; then you may rise early and go on your way." They said however, "No, but we shall spend the night in the square."

3 Yet he urged them strongly, so they turned aside to him and entered his house; and he prepared a feast for them, and baked unleavened bread, and they ate.

4 Before they lay down, the men of the city, the men of Sodom, surrounded the house, both young and old, all the people from every quarter;

5 and they called to Lot and said to him, "Where are the men who came to you tonight? Bring them out to us that we may have relations with them."

6 But Lot went out to them at the doorway, and shut the door behind him,

7 and said, "Please, my brothers, do not act wickedly.

8 "Now behold, I have two daughters who have not had relations with man; please let me bring them out to you, and do to them whatever you like; only do nothing to these men, inasmuch as they have come under the shelter of my roof."

9 But they said, "Stand aside." Furthermore, they said, "This one came in as an alien, and already he is acting like a judge; now we will treat you worse than them." So they pressed hard against Lot and came near to break the door.

10 But the men reached out their hands and brought Lot into the house with them, and shut the door.

11 They struck the men who were at the doorway of the house with blindness, both small and great, so that they wearied *themselves trying* to find the doorway.

12 ¶ Then the *two* men said to Lot, "Whom else have you here? A son-in-law, and your sons, and your daughters, and whomever you have in the city, bring *them* out of the place;

13 for we are about to destroy this place, be-

cause their outcry has become so great before the LORD that the LORD has sent us to destroy it."

14 Lot went out and spoke to his sons-in-law, who were to marry his daughters, and said, "Up, get out of this place, for the LORD will destroy the city." But he appeared to his sons-in-law to be jesting.

15 ¶ When morning dawned, the angels urged Lot, saying, "Up, take your wife and your two daughters who are here, or you will be swept away in the punishment of the city."

16 But he hesitated. So the men seized his hand and the hand of his wife and the hands of his two daughters, for the compassion of the LORD *was* upon him; and they brought him out, and put him outside the city.

17 When they had brought them outside, one said, "Escape for your life! Do not look behind you, and do not stay anywhere in the valley; escape to the mountains, or you will be swept away."

a I.e. small

18 But Lot said to them, "Oh no, my lords!

19 "Now behold, your servant has found favor in your sight, and you have magnified your lovingkindness, which you have shown me by saving my life; but I cannot escape to the mountains, for the disaster will overtake me and I will die;

20 now behold, this town is near *enough* to flee to, and it is small. Please, let me escape there (is it not small?) that my life may be saved."

21 He said to him, "Behold, I grant you this request also, not to overthrow the town of which you have spoken.

22 "Hurry, escape there, for I cannot do anything until you arrive there." Therefore the name of the town was called *a*Zoar.

23 ¶ The sun had risen over the earth when Lot came to Zoar.

24 Then the LORD rained on Sodom and Gomorrah brimstone and fire from the LORD out of heaven,

A Catastrophe Sent from God

Sodom: a city that earned destruction

SHOULD A CATASTROPHE BE READ as a punishment from God? Do floods, famines, earthquakes come because God is angry? The Bible's answer is, "Sometimes, and sometimes not." In Genesis, several catastrophes seemed to "just happen"—they were not a punishment or a warning, though God used them to advance his plans. These included several famines such as the one that brought Joseph to power (chapter 41), a war (chapter 14), a rape (chapter 34).

But a few catastrophes God took full credit for—like the one at Sodom and Gomorrah. As usual, the Bible shows little or no interest in telling us the scientific facts about the destruction. Was it a volcanic eruption? The Bible doesn't say, and the area, now apparently at the bottom of the Dead Sea, cannot easily be investigated. The Bible stresses not how it happened, but why.

> "Whom else have you here? A son-in-law, and your sons, and your daughters, and whomever you have in the city, bring them out of the place; for we are about to destroy this place."
> 19:12–13

Gang Rape

Sodom was a wretched place. The whole town saw the coming of strangers as a chance for homosexual gang rape. Sexual violence was not the town's only problem. Ezekiel 16:49 says that Sodom had "arrogance, abundant food and careless ease, but she did not help the poor and needy." God would have let the city stand if Abraham could have located just ten righteous people. Apparently, ten such people did not exist. God's great patience finally ran out.

Years earlier, Abraham had refused to accept even a well-earned reward from the government of Sodom (14:21–24). He wanted nothing to do with such a society. But Lot had chosen the path of prosperity, the easy and successful life on the fertile plain near Sodom.

Lot had become a somebody there, a civic heavy who made important decisions in the city gateway. He was so entangled with life in Sodom he hesitated to leave until it was nearly too late. When Sodom went up in smoke, his hard-earned importance disappeared too. The shock was too great for him. Unable to start over, he ended up in a cave, too drunk to know that his two daughters were having sex with him. He is the perfect example of a man who, excessively tangled in a corrupt system, cannot bear to leave it behind.

Jesus did not let his followers think of Sodom simply as "those terrible people." He warned them that God would be even harder on those who saw Jesus' miracles, but ignored them (Matthew 11:24). God's patience has a limit.

Life Questions: Are any catastrophes of our time punishments from God? How would you know?

25 and He overthrew those cities, and all the valley, and all the inhabitants of the cities, and what grew on the ground.

26 But his wife, from behind him, looked *back,* and she became a pillar of salt.

19:26 Don't Look Back

Lot and his family found it hard to leave their adopted home of Sodom, despite its immorality. Angel messengers warned them to hurry, not even stopping to look back. When Lot's wife disobeyed, she turned into a pillar of salt—perhaps caught in volcanic explosions that engulfed Sodom. For this she became a symbol of indecision. Jesus urged his followers to remember her example when their time of trouble came (Luke 17:32).

27 ¶ Now Abraham arose early in the morning *and went* to the place where he had stood before the LORD;

28 and he looked down toward Sodom and Gomorrah, and toward all the land of the valley, and he saw, and behold, the smoke of the land ascended like the smoke of a furnace.

29 ¶ Thus it came about, when God destroyed the cities of the valley, that God remembered Abraham, and sent Lot out of the midst of the overthrow, when He overthrew the cities in which Lot lived.

Lot Is Debased

30 ¶ Lot went up from Zoar, and stayed in the mountains, and his two daughters with him; for he was afraid to stay in Zoar; and he stayed in a cave, he and his two daughters.

31 Then the firstborn said to the younger, "Our father is old, and there is not a man on earth to come in to us after the manner of the earth.

32 "Come, let us make our father drink wine, and let us lie with him that we may preserve our family through our father."

33 So they made their father drink wine that night, and the firstborn went in and lay with her father; and he did not know when she lay down or when she arose.

34 On the following day, the firstborn said to the younger, "Behold, I lay last night with my father; let us make him drink wine tonight also; then you go in and lie with him, that we may preserve our family through our father."

35 So they made their father drink wine that night also, and the younger arose and lay with him; and he did not know when she lay down or when she arose.

36 Thus both the daughters of Lot were with child by their father.

37 The firstborn bore a son, and called his name Moab; he is the father of the Moabites to this day.

38 As for the younger, she also bore a son, and called his name Ben-ammi; he is the father of the sons of Ammon to this day.

19:37 Family Quarrels

Lot's determination to enjoy life in Sodom ended tragically here, in drunken incest. The resulting sons founded the family-nations of Moab and Ammon, which for centuries fought with their distant relatives in Israel and tempted them to sin.

Abraham's Treachery

20 Now Abraham journeyed from there toward the land of the *ª*Negev, and settled between Kadesh and Shur; then he sojourned in Gerar.

2 Abraham said of Sarah his wife, "She is my sister." So Abimelech king of Gerar sent and took Sarah.

3 But God came to Abimelech in a dream of the night, and said to him, "Behold, you are a dead man because of the woman whom you have taken, for she is married."

4 Now Abimelech had not come near her; and he said, "Lord, will You slay a nation, even *though* blameless?

5 "Did he not himself say to me, 'She is my sister'? And she herself said, 'He is my brother.' In the integrity of my heart and the innocence of my hands I have done this."

6 Then God said to him in the dream, "Yes, I know that in the integrity of your heart you have done this, and I also kept you from sinning against Me; therefore I did not let you touch her.

7 "Now therefore, restore the man's wife, for he is a prophet, and he will pray for you and you will live. But if you do not restore *her,* know that you shall surely die, you and all who are yours."

8 ¶ So Abimelech arose early in the morning and called all his servants and told all these things in their hearing; and the men were greatly frightened.

9 Then Abimelech called Abraham and said to him, "What have you done to us? And how have I sinned against you, that you have brought on me and on my kingdom a great sin? You have done to me things that ought not to be done."

10 And Abimelech said to Abraham, "What have you encountered, that you have done this thing?"

ª I.e. South country

11 Abraham said, "Because I thought, surely there is no fear of God in this place, and they will kill me because of my wife.

12 "Besides, she actually is my sister, the daughter of my father, but not the daughter of my mother, and she became my wife;

13 and it came about, when God caused me to wander from my father's house, that I said to her, 'This is the kindness which you will show to me: everywhere we go, say of me, "He is my brother." ' "

14 Abimelech then took sheep and oxen and male and female servants, and gave them to Abraham, and restored his wife Sarah to him.

15 Abimelech said, "Behold, my land is before you; settle wherever you please."

16 To Sarah he said, "Behold, I have given your brother a thousand pieces of silver; behold, it is your vindication before all who are with you, and before all men you are cleared."

17 Abraham prayed to God, and God healed Abimelech and his wife and his maids, so that they bore *children*.

18 For the LORD had closed fast all the wombs of the household of Abimelech because of Sarah, Abraham's wife.

Isaac Is Born

21 Then the LORD took note of Sarah as He had said, and the LORD did for Sarah as He had promised.

2 So Sarah conceived and bore a son to Abraham in his old age, at the appointed time of which God had spoken to him.

3 Abraham called the name of his son who was born to him, whom Sarah bore to him, Isaac.

4 Then Abraham circumcised his son Isaac when he was eight days old, as God had commanded him.

5 Now Abraham was one hundred years old when his son Isaac was born to him.

6 Sarah said, "God has made laughter for me; everyone who hears will laugh with me."

7 And she said, "Who would have said to Abraham that Sarah would nurse children? Yet I have borne him a son in his old age."

8 ¶ The child grew and was weaned, and Abraham made a great feast on the day that Isaac was weaned.

Sarah Turns against Hagar

9 Now Sarah saw the son of Hagar the Egyptian, whom she had borne to Abraham, mocking.

10 Therefore she said to Abraham, "Drive out this maid and her son, for the son of this maid shall not be an heir with my son Isaac."

11 The matter distressed Abraham greatly because of his son.

12 But God said to Abraham, "Do not be distressed because of the lad and your maid; whatever Sarah tells you, listen to her, for through Isaac your descendants shall be named.

13 "And of the son of the maid I will make a nation also, because he is your descendant."

14 So Abraham rose early in the morning and took bread and a skin of water and gave *them* to Hagar, putting *them* on her shoulder, and *gave her* the boy, and sent her away. And she departed and wandered about in the wilderness of Beersheba.

15 ¶ When the water in the skin was used up, she left the boy under one of the bushes.

ISAAC *Ordinary People*

ISAAC SPENT HIS LIFE SURROUNDED by strong people. His father Abraham was a giant of faith who uprooted his family at God's call and moved to unknown territory. Isaac married a strong-willed woman, Rebekah, who dominated him and sometimes manipulated him to get her way. One of Isaac's sons, Jacob, grew up to become a major figure of the Old Testament, father of the twelve tribes of Israel.

For all that strength around him, Isaac was a rather ordinary, almost passive person. Maybe it was because his parents had dreamed of his birth for so long that they sheltered him, their only child. Maybe his personality formed in reaction to all those other, powerful figures. Regardless, the Bible portrays Isaac as a person who fit into other people's plans. Even when his father led him up a mountain to sacrifice him to God, Isaac did not protest or rebel (Genesis 22).

When famine drove Isaac to a foreign land, he lied about his relationship with Rebekah rather than risk a conflict with the local king. When his herdsmen bickered with other shepherds over water rights, Isaac simply moved on, avoiding a fight. In Isaac's old age, when his grown sons Jacob and Esau quarreled, Isaac seemed powerless to stop them. Instead of sorting out the details and resolving the feud, he sent Jacob away.

Despite his weaknesses, Isaac is counted among the three famous patriarchs of Old Testament faith: Abraham, Isaac and Jacob. In bringing blessings to the entire world, God uses all kinds—even quiet, ordinary people.

Life Questions: Think of an organization or cause you consider important. How many of those involved could be described as "ordinary people"? What do they contribute?

16 Then she went and sat down opposite him, about a bowshot away, for she said, "Do not let me see the boy die." And she sat opposite him, and lifted up her voice and wept.

17 God heard the lad crying; and the angel of God called to Hagar from heaven and said to her, "What is the matter with you, Hagar? Do not fear, for God has heard the voice of the lad where he is.

18 "Arise, lift up the lad, and hold him by the hand, for I will make a great nation of him."

19 Then God opened her eyes and she saw a well of water; and she went and filled the skin with water and gave the lad a drink.

20 ¶ God was with the lad, and he grew; and he lived in the wilderness and became an archer.

21 He lived in the wilderness of Paran, and his mother took a wife for him from the land of Egypt.

Covenant with Abimelech

22 ¶ Now it came about at that time that Abimelech and Phicol, the commander of his army, spoke to Abraham, saying, "God is with you in all that you do;

23 now therefore, swear to me here by God that you will not deal falsely with me or with my offspring or with my posterity, but according to the kindness that I have shown to you, you shall show to me and to the land in which you have sojourned."

24 Abraham said, "I swear it."

25 But Abraham complained to Abimelech because of the well of water which the servants of Abimelech had seized.

26 And Abimelech said, "I do not know who has done this thing; you did not tell me, nor did I hear of it until today."

27 ¶ Abraham took sheep and oxen and gave them to Abimelech, and the two of them made a covenant.

28 Then Abraham set seven ewe lambs of the flock by themselves.

29 Abimelech said to Abraham, "What do these seven ewe lambs mean, which you have set by themselves?"

30 He said, "You shall take these seven ewe lambs from my hand so that it may be a witness to me, that I dug this well."

31 Therefore he called that place Beersheba, because there the two of them took an oath.

32 So they made a covenant at Beersheba; and Abimelech and Phicol, the commander of his army, arose and returned to the land of the Philistines.

33 *Abraham* planted a tamarisk tree at Beersheba, and there he called on the name of the LORD, the Everlasting God.

34 And Abraham sojourned in the land of the Philistines for many days.

The Offering of Isaac

22 Now it came about after these things, that God tested Abraham, and said to him, "Abraham!" And he said, "Here I am."

2 He said, "Take now your son, your only son, whom you love, Isaac, and go to the land of Moriah, and offer him there as a burnt offering on one of the mountains of which I will tell you."

3 So Abraham rose early in the morning and saddled his donkey, and took two of his young men with him and Isaac his son; and he split wood for the burnt offering, and arose and went to the place of which God had told him.

4 On the third day Abraham raised his eyes and saw the place from a distance.

5 Abraham said to his young men, "Stay here with the donkey, and I and the lad will go over there; and we will worship and return to you."

6 Abraham took the wood of the burnt offering and laid it on Isaac his son, and he took in his hand the fire and the knife. So the two of them walked on together.

7 Isaac spoke to Abraham his father and said, "My father!" And he said, "Here I am, my son." And he said, "Behold, the fire and the wood, but where is the lamb for the burnt offering?"

8 Abraham said, "God will provide for Himself the lamb for the burnt offering, my son." So the two of them walked on together.

9 ¶ Then they came to the place of which God had told him; and Abraham built the altar there and arranged the wood, and bound his son Isaac and laid him on the altar, on top of the wood.

10 Abraham stretched out his hand and took the knife to slay his son.

11 But the angel of the LORD called to him from heaven and said, "Abraham, Abraham!" And he said, "Here I am."

12 He said, "Do not stretch out your hand against the lad, and do nothing to him; for now I know that you fear God, since you have not withheld your son, your only son, from Me."

13 Then Abraham raised his eyes and looked, and behold, behind *him* a ram caught in the thicket by his horns; and Abraham went and took the ram and offered him up for a burnt offering in the place of his son.

14 Abraham called the name of that place The LORD Will Provide, as it is said to this day, "In the mount of the LORD it will be provided."

15 ¶ Then the angel of the LORD called to Abraham a second time from heaven,

16 and said, "By Myself I have sworn, declares the LORD, because you have done this thing and have not withheld your son, your only son,

17 indeed I will greatly bless you, and I will greatly multiply your seed as the stars of the heavens and as the sand which is on the seashore; and your seed shall possess the gate of their enemies.

18 "In your seed all the nations of the earth shall be blessed, because you have obeyed My voice."

19 So Abraham returned to his young men, and they arose and went together to Beersheba; and Abraham lived at Beersheba.

20 ¶ Now it came about after these things, that it was told Abraham, saying, "Behold, Milcah also has borne children to your brother Nahor:

21 Uz his firstborn and Buz his brother and Kemuel the father of Aram

22 and Chesed and Hazo and Pildash and Jidlaph and Bethuel."

23 Bethuel became the father of Rebekah; these eight Milcah bore to Nahor, Abraham's brother.

24 His concubine, whose name was Reumah, also bore Tebah and Gaham and Tahash and Maacah.

Death and Burial of Sarah

23 Now Sarah lived one hundred and twenty-seven years; *these were* the years of the life of Sarah.

2 Sarah died in Kiriath-arba (that is, Hebron) in the land of Canaan; and Abraham went in to mourn for Sarah and to weep for her.

3 Then Abraham rose from before his dead, and spoke to the sons of Heth, saying,

4 "I am a stranger and a sojourner among you; give me a burial site among you that I may bury my dead out of my sight."

5 The sons of Heth answered Abraham, saying to him,

6 "Hear us, my lord, you are a mighty prince among us; bury your dead in the choicest of our graves; none of us will refuse you his grave for burying your dead."

7 So Abraham rose and bowed to the people of the land, the sons of Heth.

8 And he spoke with them, saying, "If it is your wish *for me* to bury my dead out of my sight, hear me, and approach Ephron the son of Zohar for me,

9 that he may give me the cave of Machpelah which he owns, which is at the end of his field; for the full price let him give it to me in your presence for a burial site."

10 Now Ephron was sitting among the sons of Heth; and Ephron the Hittite answered Abraham in the hearing of the sons of Heth; *even* of all who went in at the gate of his city, saying,

11 "No, my lord, hear me; I give you the field, and I give you the cave that is in it. In the presence

Promises, Promises

God promised to give Abraham all that he longed for . . . and more

HUMAN BEINGS HAVEN'T CHANGED MUCH in 4,000 years. The longing for children and the desire for land still surge up with surprising emotional power.

Consider the estimated six million American couples—one in seven would-be parents—who are unable to have children. For most of them, this brings deep anguish. Or think about the people who work double shifts, sacrificing their free time in order to own a home rather than rent.

> *"In your seed all the nations of the earth shall be blessed, because you have obeyed My voice."*
> 22:18

Abraham would have understood. When God wanted his attention, he promised him land and more sons than he could count. To a Babylonian emigrant, 75 years old and childless, owning nothing but his tents and animals, the promises sounded wonderful. In fact, they sounded impossible. Yet, because God himself was making the promise, Abraham "believed in the LORD, and He reckoned it to him as righteousness" (15:6).

For the God who had created the heavens and the earth, making good on the promises ought to have been a snap. But God did not make it easy for Abraham. Not until 25 years later, when Abraham was 100, did the promise of a son come true. Then, incredibly, God told Abraham to make a human sacrifice of his little boy. It was really asking too much.

Astonishingly, Abraham followed God's orders. And God gave him back his son.

Far from Fulfilled

When Abraham died, God's promises were far from fully realized. Abraham had only that one son to cling to. His only land was a burial plot. He still lived in a tent, and his only permanent structures were altars erected to worship the God who had made all those promises.

God, having promised him everything a man of that time could want, apparently wanted Abraham to think even bigger thoughts. He had slipped some words in along with the promises of offspring and land: "And in you all the families of the earth will be blessed " (12:3). God wanted to bless, not just Abraham, but the whole world. Thousands of years later, in the time of Jesus, the full meaning of those words became clear (see Galatians 3:6–9,16–18).

Life Questions: What kind of promises does God make today? What longings does he fulfill?

of the sons of my people I give it to you; bury your dead."

12 And Abraham bowed before the people of the land.

13 He spoke to Ephron in the hearing of the people of the land, saying, "If you will only please listen to me; I will give the price of the field, accept *it* from me that I may bury my dead there."

14 Then Ephron answered Abraham, saying to him,

15 "My lord, listen to me; a piece of land worth four hundred shekels of silver, what is that between me and you? So bury your dead."

23:15 Let's Make a Deal

This may be the oldest recorded business deal. The elaborate politeness sounds very much like bargaining in the Middle East today. Underneath the smooth words, shrewd negotiating is going on. The Hittites were probably reluctant to allow Abraham, an alien, to own property of any kind lest he gain a legal foothold in their country. Abraham zeroed in on Ephron, who stood to gain financially from the sale.

---

16 Abraham listened to Ephron; and Abraham weighed out for Ephron the silver which he had named in the hearing of the sons of Heth, four hundred shekels of silver, commercial standard.

17 ¶ So Ephron's field, which was in Machpelah, which faced Mamre, the field and cave which was in it, and all the trees which were in the field,

that were within all the confines of its border, were deeded over

18 to Abraham for a possession in the presence of the sons of Heth, before all who went in at the gate of his city.

19 After this, Abraham buried Sarah his wife in the cave of the field at Machpelah facing Mamre (that is, Hebron) in the land of Canaan.

20 So the field and the cave that is in it, were deeded over to Abraham for a burial site by the sons of Heth.

A Bride for Isaac

24 Now Abraham was old, advanced in age; and the LORD had blessed Abraham in every way.

2 Abraham said to his servant, the oldest of his household, who had charge of all that he owned, "Please place your hand under my thigh,

3 and I will make you swear by the LORD, the God of heaven and the God of earth, that you shall not take a wife for my son from the daughters of the Canaanites, among whom I live,

---

24:3 Marrying Foreigners

From this earliest period of Israelite history, there was an emphasis on not marrying foreigners. The reason had to do with religion, not race—in many cases foreigners were distant relatives. When foreigners were willing to worship Israel's God, they were welcomed (see the book of Ruth, for example).

REBEKAH *Forceful Woman*

"I'D RATHER BE A HAMMER than a nail," sang Paul Simon, meaning it's better to be an active force than to let others drive you. Rebekah followed that philosophy. When Abraham's servant asked for a drink of water, she took the initiative. "I will draw also for your camels until they have finished drinking," she said (24:19). And although camels require a lot of water, Rebekah didn't just walk to the well to draw it—she ran (v. 20).

When offered marriage to an unknown relative hundreds of miles' journey across dangerous wilderness, Rebekah grabbed the chance. Her family wanted time to adjust to the idea, but she got ready to leave the next day, never to see her home again.

Initiative is admirable, but an overdose can lead to trouble. Rebekah waited twenty years to have a child and then gave birth to twins. God told her that Jacob, the younger, would be God's chosen. In an attempt to manage Jacob's success, Rebekah pushed him into deceiving his father and stealing his brother's blessing. "Only obey my voice," she told him (27:13). Rebekah thought she could control everything, regardless of whether her actions pleased God.

The ploy worked as she predicted, but Rebekah had not foreseen the fury of Esau, Jacob's outwitted brother. Fearing for Jacob's life, she arranged to send him back to her childhood home. "Until your brother's anger against you subsides . . . Then I will send and get you from there" she told Jacob (27:45). For Rebekah, that time never came—she died without seeing her favorite child again.

Life Questions: When can initiative like Rebekah's be helpful? Under what conditions can it lead to trouble?

4 but you will go to my country and to my relatives, and take a wife for my son Isaac."

5 The servant said to him, "Suppose the woman is not willing to follow me to this land; should I take your son back to the land from where you came?"

6 Then Abraham said to him, "Beware that you do not take my son back there!

7 "The LORD, the God of heaven, who took me from my father's house and from the land of my birth, and who spoke to me and who swore to me, saying, 'To your descendants I will give this land,' He will send His angel before you, and you will take a wife for my son from there.

8 "But if the woman is not willing to follow you, then you will be free from this my oath; only do not take my son back there."

9 So the servant placed his hand under the thigh of Abraham his master, and swore to him concerning this matter.

10 ¶ Then the servant took ten camels from the camels of his master, and set out with a variety of good things of his master's in his hand; and he arose and went to Mesopotamia, to the city of Nahor.

11 He made the camels kneel down outside the city by the well of water at evening time, the time when women go out to draw water.

12 He said, "O LORD, the God of my master Abraham, please grant me success today, and show lovingkindness to my master Abraham.

13 "Behold, I am standing by the spring, and the daughters of the men of the city are coming out to draw water;

14 now may it be that the girl to whom I say, 'Please let down your jar so that I may drink,' and who answers, 'Drink, and I will water your camels also'—*may* she *be the one* whom You have appointed for Your servant Isaac; and by this I will know that You have shown lovingkindness to my master."

Rebekah Is Chosen

15 ¶ Before he had finished speaking, behold, Rebekah who was born to Bethuel the son of Milcah, the wife of Abraham's brother Nahor, came out with her jar on her shoulder.

16 The girl was very beautiful, a virgin, and no man had had relations with her; and she went down to the spring and filled her jar and came up.

17 Then the servant ran to meet her, and said, "Please let me drink a little water from your jar."

18 She said, "Drink, my lord"; and she quickly lowered her jar to her hand, and gave him a drink.

19 Now when she had finished giving him a drink, she said, "I will draw also for your camels until they have finished drinking."

20 So she quickly emptied her jar into the trough, and ran back to the well to draw, and she drew for all his camels.

21 Meanwhile, the man was gazing at her in silence, to know whether the LORD had made his journey successful or not.

22 ¶ When the camels had finished drinking, the man took a gold ring weighing a half-shekel and two bracelets for her wrists weighing ten shekels in gold,

23 and said, "Whose daughter are you? Please tell me, is there room for us to lodge in your father's house?"

24 She said to him, "I am the daughter of Bethuel, the son of Milcah, whom she bore to Nahor."

25 Again she said to him, "We have plenty of both straw and feed, and room to lodge in."

26 Then the man bowed low and worshiped the LORD.

27 He said, "Blessed be the LORD, the God of my master Abraham, who has not forsaken His lovingkindness and His truth toward my master; as for me, the LORD has guided me in the way to the house of my master's brothers."

28 ¶ Then the girl ran and told her mother's household about these things.

29 Now Rebekah had a brother whose name was Laban; and Laban ran outside to the man at the spring.

30 When he saw the ring and the bracelets on his sister's wrists, and when he heard the words of Rebekah his sister, saying, "This is what the man said to me," he went to the man; and behold, he was standing by the camels at the spring.

31 And he said, "Come in, blessed of the LORD! Why do you stand outside since I have prepared the house, and a place for the camels?"

32 So the man entered the house. Then Laban unloaded the camels, and he gave straw and feed to the camels, and water to wash his feet and the feet of the men who were with him.

33 But when *food* was set before him to eat, he said, "I will not eat until I have told my business." And he said, "Speak on."

34 So he said, "I am Abraham's servant.

35 "The LORD has greatly blessed my master, so that he has become rich; and He has given him flocks and herds, and silver and gold, and servants and maids, and camels and donkeys.

36 "Now Sarah my master's wife bore a son to my master in her old age, and he has given him all that he has.

37 "My master made me swear, saying, 'You shall not take a wife for my son from the daughters of the Canaanites, in whose land I live;

38 but you shall go to my father's house and to my relatives, and take a wife for my son.'

39 "I said to my master, 'Suppose the woman does not follow me.'

40 "He said to me, 'The LORD, before whom I have walked, will send His angel with you to make your journey successful, and you will take a wife for my son from my relatives and from my father's house;

41 then you will be free from my oath, when you come to my relatives; and if they do not give her to you, you will be free from my oath.'

42 ¶ "So I came today to the spring, and said, 'O LORD, the God of my master Abraham, if now You will make my journey on which I go successful;

43 behold, I am standing by the spring, and may it be that the maiden who comes out to draw, and to whom I say, "Please let me drink a little water from your jar";

44 and she will say to me, "You drink, and I will draw for your camels also"; let her be the woman whom the LORD has appointed for my master's son.'

45 ¶ "Before I had finished speaking in my heart, behold, Rebekah came out with her jar on her shoulder, and went down to the spring and drew, and I said to her, 'Please let me drink.'

46 "She quickly lowered her jar from her *shoulder*, and said, 'Drink, and I will water your camels also'; so I drank, and she watered the camels also.

47 "Then I asked her, and said, 'Whose daughter are you?' And she said, 'The daughter of Bethuel, Nahor's son, whom Milcah bore to him'; and I put the ring on her nose, and the bracelets on her wrists.

48 "And I bowed low and worshiped the LORD, and blessed the LORD, the God of my master Abraham, who had guided me in the right way to take the daughter of my master's kinsman for his son.

49 "So now if you are going to ^adeal kindly and truly with my master, tell me; and if not, let me know, that I may turn to the right hand or the left."

50 ¶ Then Laban and Bethuel replied, "The matter comes from the LORD; *so* we cannot speak to you bad or good.

51 "Here is Rebekah before you, take *her* and go, and let her be the wife of your master's son, as the LORD has spoken."

52 ¶ When Abraham's servant heard their words, he bowed himself to the ground before the LORD.

53 The servant brought out articles of silver and articles of gold, and garments, and gave them to Rebekah; he also gave precious things to her brother and to her mother.

54 Then he and the men who were with him ate and drank and spent the night. When they arose in the morning, he said, "Send me away to my master."

55 But her brother and her mother said, "Let the girl stay with us *a few* days, say ten; afterward she may go."

56 He said to them, "Do not delay me, since the LORD has prospered my way. Send me away that I may go to my master."

57 And they said, "We will call the girl and consult her wishes."

58 Then they called Rebekah and said to her, "Will you go with this man?" And she said, "I will go."

59 Thus they sent away their sister Rebekah and her nurse with Abraham's servant and his men.

60 They blessed Rebekah and said to her,
    "May you, our sister,
    Become thousands of ten thousands,
    And may your descendants possess
    The gate of those who hate them."

61 Then Rebekah arose with her maids, and they mounted the camels and followed the man. So the servant took Rebekah and departed.

Isaac Marries Rebekah

62 ¶ Now Isaac had come from going to Beer-lahai-roi; for he was living in the Negev.

63 Isaac went out to meditate in the field toward evening; and he lifted up his eyes and looked, and behold, camels were coming.

64 Rebekah lifted up her eyes, and when she saw Isaac she dismounted from the camel.

65 She said to the servant, "Who is that man walking in the field to meet us?" And the servant said, "He is my master." Then she took her veil and covered herself.

66 The servant told Isaac all the things that he had done.

67 Then Isaac brought her into his mother Sarah's tent, and he took Rebekah, and she became his wife, and he loved her; thus Isaac was comforted after his mother's death.

Abraham's Death

25 Now Abraham took another wife, whose name was Keturah.

2 She bore to him Zimran and Jokshan and Medan and Midian and Ishbak and Shuah.

3 Jokshan became the father of Sheba and Dedan. And the sons of Dedan were Asshurim and Letushim and Leummim.

4 The sons of Midian *were* Ephah and Epher and Hanoch and Abida and Eldaah. All these *were* the sons of Keturah.

5 Now Abraham gave all that he had to Isaac;

6 but to the sons of his concubines, Abraham gave gifts while he was still living, and sent them away from his son Isaac eastward, to the land of the east.

7 ¶ These are all the years of Abraham's life that he lived, one hundred and seventy-five years.

8 Abraham breathed his last and died in a ripe old age, an old man and satisfied *with life;* and he was gathered to his people.

9 Then his sons Isaac and Ishmael buried him in the cave of Machpelah, in the field of Ephron the son of Zohar the Hittite, facing Mamre,

---

^a Lit *show lovingkindness and truth*

10 the field which Abraham purchased from the sons of Heth; there Abraham was buried with Sarah his wife.

11 It came about after the death of Abraham, that God blessed his son Isaac; and Isaac lived by Beer-lahai-roi.

Descendants of Ishmael

12 ¶ Now these are the records of the generations of Ishmael, Abraham's son, whom Hagar the Egyptian, Sarah's maid, bore to Abraham;

13 and these are the names of the sons of Ishmael, by their names, in the order of their birth: Nebaioth, the firstborn of Ishmael, and Kedar and Adbeel and Mibsam

14 and Mishma and Dumah and Massa,

15 Hadad and Tema, Jetur, Naphish and Kedemah.

16 These are the sons of Ishmael and these are their names, by their villages, and by their camps; twelve princes according to their tribes.

17 These are the years of the life of Ishmael, one hundred and thirty-seven years; and he breathed his last and died, and was gathered to his people.

18 They settled from Havilah to Shur which is east of Egypt as one goes toward Assyria; he settled in defiance of all his relatives.

Isaac's Sons

19 ¶ Now these are the records of the generations of Isaac, Abraham's son: Abraham became the father of Isaac;

20 and Isaac was forty years old when he took Rebekah, the daughter of Bethuel the Aramean of Paddan-aram, the sister of Laban the Aramean, to be his wife.

21 Isaac prayed to the LORD on behalf of his wife, because she was barren; and the LORD answered him and Rebekah his wife conceived.

22 But the children struggled together within her; and she said, "If it is so, why then am I *this* way?" So she went to inquire of the LORD.

23 The LORD said to her,
"Two nations are in your womb;
And two peoples will be separated from your body;
And one people shall be stronger than the other;
And the older shall serve the younger."

24 When her days to be delivered were fulfilled, behold, there were twins in her womb.

25 Now the first came forth red, all over like a hairy garment; and they named him Esau.

26 Afterward his brother came forth with his hand holding on to Esau's heel, so his name was called *a*Jacob; and Isaac was sixty years old when she gave birth to them.

27 ¶ When the boys grew up, Esau became a skillful hunter, a man of the field, but Jacob was a peaceful man, living in tents.

28 Now Isaac loved Esau, because he had a taste for game, but Rebekah loved Jacob.

29 When Jacob had cooked stew, Esau came in from the field and he was famished;

30 and Esau said to Jacob, "Please let me have a swallow of that red stuff there, for I am famished." Therefore his name was called *b*Edom.

31 But Jacob said, "First sell me your birthright."

32 Esau said, "Behold, I am about to die; so of what *use* then is the birthright to me?"

33 And Jacob said, "First swear to me"; so he swore to him, and sold his birthright to Jacob.

25:33 No Sympathy for Esau

Esau's birthright, which he sold for a meal, was his inheritance as the firstborn son. He stood to be head of a large extended family and its property. Though his brother Jacob took advantage of him, the Bible gives Esau little sympathy for his role as victim: he "despised his birthright" (verse 34) by letting his hunger overwhelm his concern for things of lasting value. Because of this, he was later labeled "godless" (Hebrews 12:16).

34 Then Jacob gave Esau bread and lentil stew; and he ate and drank, and rose and went on his way. Thus Esau despised his birthright.

Isaac Settles in Gerar

26 Now there was a famine in the land, besides the previous famine that had occurred in the days of Abraham. So Isaac went to Gerar, to Abimelech king of the Philistines.

2 The LORD appeared to him and said, "Do not go down to Egypt; stay in the land of which I shall tell you.

3 "Sojourn in this land and I will be with you and bless you, for to you and to your descendants I will give all these lands, and I will establish the oath which I swore to your father Abraham.

4 "I will multiply your descendants as the stars of heaven, and will give your descendants all these lands; and by your descendants all the nations of the earth shall be blessed;

5 because Abraham obeyed Me and kept My charge, My commandments, My statutes and My laws."

6 ¶ So Isaac lived in Gerar.

7 When the men of the place asked about his wife, he said, "She is my sister," for he was afraid to say, "my wife," *thinking,* "the men of the place might kill me on account of Rebekah, for she is beautiful."

---

a I.e. one who takes by the heel or supplants   *b* I.e. red

8 It came about, when he had been there a long time, that Abimelech king of the Philistines looked out through a window, and saw, and behold, Isaac was caressing his wife Rebekah.

9 Then Abimelech called Isaac and said, "Behold, certainly she is your wife! How then did you say, 'She is my sister'?" And Isaac said to him, "Because I said, 'I might die on account of her.'"

10 Abimelech said, "What is this you have done to us? One of the people might easily have lain with your wife, and you would have brought guilt upon us."

11 So Abimelech charged all the people, saying, "He who touches this man or his wife shall surely be put to death."

12 ¶ Now Isaac sowed in that land and reaped in the same year a hundredfold. And the LORD blessed him,

13 and the man became rich, and continued to grow richer until he became very wealthy;

14 for he had possessions of flocks and herds and a great household, so that the Philistines envied him.

15 Now all the wells which his father's servants had dug in the days of Abraham his father, the Philistines stopped up by filling them with earth.

16 Then Abimelech said to Isaac, "Go away from us, for you are too powerful for us."

17 And Isaac departed from there and camped in the valley of Gerar, and settled there.

Quarrel over the Wells

18 ¶ Then Isaac dug again the wells of water which had been dug in the days of his father Abraham, for the Philistines had stopped them up after the death of Abraham; and he gave them the same names which his father had given them.

19 But when Isaac's servants dug in the valley and found there a well of flowing water,

20 the herdsmen of Gerar quarreled with the herdsmen of Isaac, saying, "The water is ours!" So he named the well Esek, because they contended with him.

21 Then they dug another well, and they quarreled over it too, so he named it Sitnah.

22 He moved away from there and dug another well, and they did not quarrel over it; so he named it Rehoboth, for he said, "At last the LORD has made room for us, and we will be fruitful in the land."

23 ¶ Then he went up from there to Beersheba.

24 The LORD appeared to him the same night and said,

"I am the God of your father Abraham;
Do not fear, for I am with you.
I will bless you, and multiply your
        descendants,
For the sake of My servant Abraham."

25 So he built an altar there and called upon the name of the LORD, and pitched his tent there; and there Isaac's servants dug a well.

Covenant with Abimelech

26 ¶ Then Abimelech came to him from Gerar with his adviser Ahuzzath and Phicol the commander of his army.

27 Isaac said to them, "Why have you come to me, since you hate me and have sent me away from you?"

28 They said, "We see plainly that the LORD has been with you; so we said, 'Let there now be an oath between us, even between you and us, and let us make a covenant with you,

29 that you will do us no harm, just as we have not touched you and have done to you nothing but good and have sent you away in peace. You are now the blessed of the LORD.'"

30 Then he made them a feast, and they ate and drank.

31 In the morning they arose early and exchanged oaths; then Isaac sent them away and they departed from him in peace.

32 Now it came about on the same day, that Isaac's servants came in and told him about the well which they had dug, and said to him, "We have found water."

33 So he called it Shibah; therefore the name of the city is Beersheba to this day.

34 ¶ When Esau was forty years old he married Judith the daughter of Beeri the Hittite, and Basemath the daughter of Elon the Hittite;

35 and they ᵃbrought grief to Isaac and Rebekah.

Jacob's Deception

27 Now it came about, when Isaac was old and his eyes were too dim to see, that he called his older son Esau and said to him, "My son." And he said to him, "Here I am."

2 Isaac said, "Behold now, I am old and I do not know the day of my death.

3 "Now then, please take your gear, your quiver and your bow, and go out to the field and hunt game for me;

4 and prepare a savory dish for me such as I love, and bring it to me that I may eat, so that my soul may bless you before I die."

5 ¶ Rebekah was listening while Isaac spoke to his son Esau. So when Esau went to the field to hunt for game to bring home,

6 Rebekah said to her son Jacob, "Behold, I heard your father speak to your brother Esau, saying,

7 'Bring me some game and prepare a savory dish for me, that I may eat, and bless you in the presence of the LORD before my death.'

8 "Now therefore, my son, listen to me as I command you.

9 "Go now to the flock and bring me two

ᵃ Lit were a bitterness of spirit to

Con Man in God's Family?

The Bible doesn't cover up Jacob's scheming

ASK PEOPLE WHY THEY DON'T go to church, and you'll often hear this answer: "There are too many hypocrites." It may be an excuse, but there's a troubling reality behind it. How can a religion with such high standards include so many people with such low standards?

Jacob's life poses the same question. The Bible does not mince words in describing his grasping, con-man character. He took advantage of his twin brother's impulsiveness to switch places with him in the family will (25:29–34). Later, seeing that his father Isaac still favored Esau, Jacob (with his mother) tricked the old man into blessing him in place of his brother. (A father's blessing was not merely symbolic. It had a permanent significance, like a swearing-in ceremony.)

> "He has supplanted me these two times. He took my birthright, and behold, now he has taken away my blessing."
> **27:36**

The Tricks Backfire

Dressed up in Esau's clothes and some fresh goatskins, Jacob flatly lied to his father and took the Lord's name in vain. Isaac, trusting his nose over his ears, fell for it (27:1–40). Yet the trick backfired. Jacob had to run for his life, and he spent 20 years in exile with his uncle. Uncle Laban gave Jacob a dose of his own medicine, planting an unwanted sister in his wedding bed and repeatedly changing his wages as head shepherd.

You might think Jacob would learn that tricks aren't nice. Yet Jacob didn't noticeably improve his ways. He made a poor husband, neglecting one of his wives and creating rivalry. He favored two sons, so that the neglected ones grew jealous to the point of murder. He certainly doesn't seem like choice material for a religious leader.

God Makes the Choice

But God chose Jacob. He was always making those kinds of choices, sometimes with no apparent reason at all. Often he went against the time-honored practice of letting the firstborn son be number one, as he did in choosing number-two sons Abel, Jacob, and Ephraim. In fact, an inspired prophecy marked Jacob as God's choice before he was even born—before he had done a single thing to merit the choice.

So God's choice did not necessarily depend on how a person behaved. God chose the one he wanted—it was as simple as that.

Is this fair? That's what the apostle Paul asked in Romans 9. He concluded that we have no right to find fault with God's choices, knowing as little as we do compared to his infinite understanding. And while we may never understand God's choices, we should note that all the "rejected" brothers of Genesis—Cain, Canaan, Ishmael, Reuben, Esau, and Manasseh—were treated more than fairly. Their offspring multiplied into nations under God's protection.

No One Excluded

For his chosen people, God had a much greater honor. Good or bad, they would be made a channel of blessing for the whole world. He told Abraham, right from the beginning, "in you all the families of the earth will be blessed" (12:3). By selecting a few, God planned to extend his blessings to all. And that is how it worked out: Abraham's small, fault-ridden family grew into a sizable, fault-ridden nation that brought forth, in the fullness of time, a faultless Jesus.

No wonder Paul wrote that we have no business questioning the wisdom of God. We may not see why he chose people like Jacob. But unquestionably, those choices worked for good—and the whole world became eligible to join the "chosen people." As Paul wrote, "You are all sons of God through faith in Christ Jesus. . . . There is neither Jew nor Greek, there is neither slave nor free man, there is neither male nor female, for you are all one in Christ Jesus. And If you belong to Christ, then you are Abraham's descendants" (Galatians 3:26–29). God has a habit of choosing flawed people to achieve great good. Who can say what he is doing with the hypocrites of our day?

Life Questions: Why do you think God chooses imperfect people like Jacob? Why did he choose you?

choice young goats from there, that I may prepare them *as* a savory dish for your father, such as he loves.

10 "Then you shall bring *it* to your father, that he may eat, so that he may bless you before his death."

11 Jacob answered his mother Rebekah, "Behold, Esau my brother is a hairy man and I am a smooth man.

12 "Perhaps my father will feel me, then I will be as a deceiver in his sight, and I will bring upon myself a curse and not a blessing."

13 But his mother said to him, "Your curse be on me, my son; only obey my voice, and go, get *them* for me."

14 So he went and got *them,* and brought *them* to his mother; and his mother made savory food such as his father loved.

15 Then Rebekah took the best garments of Esau her elder son, which were with her in the house, and put them on Jacob her younger son.

16 And she put the skins of the young goats on his hands and on the smooth part of his neck.

17 She also gave the savory food and the bread, which she had made, to her son Jacob.

18 ¶ Then he came to his father and said, "My father." And he said, "Here I am. Who are you, my son?"

19 Jacob said to his father, "I am Esau your firstborn; I have done as you told me. Get up, please, sit and eat of my game, that you may bless me."

20 Isaac said to his son, "How is it that you have *it* so quickly, my son?" And he said, "Because the LORD your God caused *it* to happen to me."

21 Then Isaac said to Jacob, "Please come close, that I may feel you, my son, whether you are really my son Esau or not."

22 So Jacob came close to Isaac his father, and he felt him and said, "The voice is the voice of Jacob, but the hands are the hands of Esau."

23 He did not recognize him, because his hands were hairy like his brother Esau's hands; so he blessed him.

24 And he said, "Are you really my son Esau?" And he said, "I am."

25 So he said, "Bring *it* to me, and I will eat of my son's game, that I may bless you." And he brought *it* to him, and he ate; he also brought him wine and he drank.

26 Then his father Isaac said to him, "Please come close and kiss me, my son."

27 So he came close and kissed him; and when he smelled the smell of his garments, he blessed him and said,

"See, the smell of my son
Is like the smell of a field which the
LORD has blessed;

28 Now may God give you of the dew of
heaven,
And of the fatness of the earth,

And an abundance of grain and new
wine;

29 May peoples serve you,
And nations bow down to you;

27:27 Sense of Smell

An old man, Isaac had lost his eyesight and apparently much of his sense of touch. He could still smell though, and thought he recognized his son by the scent of his clothes. In an age before deodorants and frequent laundering, people had distinctive scents.

Be master of your brothers,
And may your mother's sons bow down
to you.
Cursed be those who curse you,
And blessed be those who bless you."

The Stolen Blessing

30 ¶ Now it came about, as soon as Isaac had finished blessing Jacob, and Jacob had hardly gone out from the presence of Isaac his father, that Esau his brother came in from his hunting.

31 Then he also made savory food, and brought it to his father; and he said to his father, "Let my father arise and eat of his son's game, that you may bless me."

32 Isaac his father said to him, "Who are you?" And he said, "I am your son, your firstborn, Esau."

33 Then Isaac trembled violently, and said, "Who was he then that hunted game and brought *it* to me, so that I ate of all *of it* before you came, and blessed him? Yes, and he shall be blessed."

34 When Esau heard the words of his father, he cried out with an exceedingly great and bitter cry, and said to his father, "Bless me, *even* me also, O my father!"

35 And he said, "Your brother came deceitfully and has taken away your blessing."

36 Then he said, "Is he not rightly named Jacob, for he has supplanted me these two times? He took away my birthright, and behold, now he has taken away my blessing." And he said, "Have you not reserved a blessing for me?"

37 But Isaac replied to Esau, "Behold, I have made him your master, and all his relatives I have given to him as servants; and with grain and new wine I have sustained him. Now as for you then, what can I do, my son?"

38 Esau said to his father, "Do you have only one blessing, my father? Bless me, *even* me also, O my father." So Esau lifted his voice and wept.

39 ¶ Then Isaac his father answered and said to him,

"Behold, away from the fertility of the
earth shall be your dwelling,

And away from the dew of heaven from
    above.
40 "By your sword you shall live,
    And your brother you shall serve;
    But it shall come about when you
        become restless,
    That you will break his yoke from your
        neck."

41 ¶ So Esau bore a grudge against Jacob because of the blessing with which his father had
blessed him; and Esau said to himself, "The days
of mourning for my father are near; then I will kill
my brother Jacob."

42 Now when the words of her elder son Esau
were reported to Rebekah, she sent and called her
younger son Jacob, and said to him, "Behold your
brother Esau is consoling himself concerning you
by planning to kill you.

43 "Now therefore, my son, obey my voice, and
arise, flee to Haran, to my brother Laban!

44 "Stay with him a few days, until your brother's fury subsides,

45 until your brother's anger against you subsides and he forgets what you did to him. Then I
will send and get you from there. Why should I be
bereaved of you both in one day?"

46 ¶ Rebekah said to Isaac, "I am tired of living
because of the daughters of Heth; if Jacob takes a
wife from the daughters of Heth, like these, from
the daughters of the land, what good will my life
be to me?"

Jacob Is Sent Away

28 So Isaac called Jacob and blessed him and
charged him, and said to him, "You shall
not take a wife from the daughters of Canaan.

2 "Arise, go to Paddan-aram, to the house of
Bethuel your mother's father; and from there take
to yourself a wife from the daughters of Laban
your mother's brother.

3 "May God Almighty bless you and make you
fruitful and multiply you, that you may become a
company of peoples.

4 "May He also give you the blessing of Abraham, to you and to your descendants with you,
that you may possess the land of your sojournings,
which God gave to Abraham."

5 Then Isaac sent Jacob away, and he went to
Paddan-aram to Laban, son of Bethuel the Aramean, the brother of Rebekah, the mother of Jacob and Esau.

6 ¶ Now Esau saw that Isaac had blessed Jacob and sent him away to Paddan-aram to take
to himself a wife from there, *and that* when he
blessed him he charged him, saying, "You shall
not take a wife from the daughters of Canaan,"

7 and that Jacob had obeyed his father and his
mother and had gone to Paddan-aram.

8 So Esau saw that the daughters of Canaan
displeased his father Isaac;

9 and Esau went to Ishmael, and married, besides the wives that he had, Mahalath the daughter
of Ishmael, Abraham's son, the sister of Nebaioth.

Jacob's Dream

10 ¶ Then Jacob departed from Beersheba and
went toward Haran.

11 He came to a certain place and spent the
night there, because the sun had set; and he took
one of the stones of the place and put it under his
head, and lay down in that place.

12 He had a dream, and behold, a ladder was
set on the earth with its top reaching to heaven;
and behold, the angels of God were ascending and
descending on it.

13 And behold, the LORD stood above it and
said, "I am the LORD, the God of your father Abraham and the God of Isaac; the land on which you
lie, I will give it to you and to your descendants.

14 "Your descendants will also be like the dust
of the earth, and you will spread out to the west
and to the east and to the north and to the south;
and in you and in your descendants shall all the
families of the earth be blessed.

15 "Behold, I am with you and will keep you
wherever you go, and will bring you back to this
land; for I will not leave you until I have done
what I have promised you."

16 Then Jacob awoke from his sleep and said,
"Surely the LORD is in this place, and I did not
know it."

17 He was afraid and said, "How awesome is
this place! This is none other than the house of
God, and this is the gate of heaven."

18 ¶ So Jacob rose early in the morning, and
took the stone that he had put under his head and
set it up as a pillar and poured oil on its top.

19 He called the name of that place *a*Bethel;
however, previously the name of the city had
been Luz.

20 Then Jacob made a vow, saying, "If God will
be with me and will keep me on this journey that
I take, and will give me food to eat and garments
to wear,

21 and I return to my father's house in safety,
then the LORD will be my God.

28:12 A Stairway to Heaven

*God's grace: this is what Jacob found while
traveling alone in the desert. Through his own
greedy scheming he had won the family
birthright and then, ironically, had had to run
away from the family. Yet God came to him full
of promises, not the reproaches he deserved.
Jacob had not looked for God, but God looked
for him. Jacob's vision of a stairway to heaven
looked forward to Jesus, who himself is the
bridge between heaven and earth (John 1:51).*

---

a I.e. the house of God

The Women of Genesis

Despite their low status, they were anyone's equal

PARTNER SOUGHT FOR VAST CREATIVE endeavor. Global plans. Unlimited compensation. Immediate responsibilities include maintenance of large property, care and authority over all kinds of creatures—flying, walking, creeping, crawling. Object: teamwork and companionship. Female only. Contact Adam.

> The man said, "This is now bone of my bones, and flesh of my flesh; she shall be called Woman, because she was taken out of Man."
> 2:23

No woman after Eve got such an opportunity. After sin came into the picture, the original idea of marriage got twisted. " 'To love and to cherish' became 'to desire and to dominate,' " as author Derek Kidner put it. Throughout the Old Testament you catch only glimpses of the original spontaneous joy with which man greeted woman and regarded her as a partner. Granted, the people of God had a higher view of women than did their pagan neighbors. Still, women had value chiefly as seconds to men, whose children they bore, whose desires they fulfilled.

Yet the women of Genesis were no pushovers. They had strong characters, minds of their own. They exerted all the influence they were allowed, and then some.

The Joke Was on Her

Sarah, Abraham's partner, was caught laughing at God's astonishing promise (18:12–15). She thought she knew better than to expect babies at the age of 90. She later had the grace to admit the joke was on her (21:6). Though the New Testament commends her as an ideal submissive wife (1 Peter 3:5–6), she certainly expressed her views strongly to Abraham. Twice she had her rival Hagar driven out of their home and into the desert.

Hagar, though only a servant girl, showed backbone too. After her first expulsion from Abraham and Sarah's home she met God himself, who comforted her and sent her back to Abraham with promises of a great future. Later she showed strength of character by bringing up her son alone in the desert.

A Scheme that Backfired

Rebekah shows up in Chapter 24 as a young girl drawing water for a stranger's camels. By the next day you know she has a mind of her own—and enough courage to set off with a stranger for marriage in unknown territory. Her husband Isaac loved her, and so did her son Jacob. From her, it seems, Jacob got his strong, scheming personality. She initiated the plan to install him in family leadership, against the custom of firstborn sons—and against his father's will. Sadly for Rebekah, her scheme partly backfired, and she never saw Jacob again.

Rachel and Leah, sisters, fought for years over Jacob. Rachel had the looks, as well as a corner on her husband's love. Jacob neglected Leah, whom he hadn't wanted to marry in the first place. But to make up for that slight, God gave Leah children—four sons in a row. Rachel took each one like a fist to the face, which is probably what Leah intended. After a while, Jacob seemed to be just a tool in the struggle for dominance between two sisters, especially when Leah cooly informed him that she had hired his services for the night (30:16).

Who won? It's hard to say. Rachel held the love of Jacob to the end, her two sons most favored by him though last in line. But Leah's sons gained prominence of their own, especially Judah, who became the ancestor of kings—and Jesus. Leah would have enjoyed knowing that she, not Rachel, was great-great-great-grandmother to the King of kings.

Hardly Delicate Violets

In short, the women in Genesis were not delicate violets, but tough, pioneer women. One cannot approve of everything they did, by a long shot. But their toughness and courage demolish any theory that women are, by nature, weak. They used every advantage they had, fairly or unfairly—and did it skillfully. For instance, Rachel displayed classic chutzpah in facing down her father as he searched for some idols she had stolen. She sweetly claimed she couldn't stand up because she was having her period. In truth, she was sitting on the goods, knowing perfectly well even Laban lacked the nerve to try moving a woman in that condition (31:25–35).

They were a match for their men: in courage, in character, in independence, in determination, in orneriness. In that culture they were second-class citizens. But in real life these women were, as God intended, the equal of anybody.

Life Questions: Creative people often find ways to transcend the limits put on them. What do you feel hemmed in by? How can you achieve God's will despite obstacles?

22 "This stone, which I have set up as a pillar, will be God's house, and of all that You give me I will surely give a tenth to You."

Jacob Meets Rachel

29 Then Jacob [a]went on his journey, and came to the land of the sons of the east.

2 He looked, and saw a well in the field, and behold, three flocks of sheep were lying there beside it, for from that well they watered the flocks. Now the stone on the mouth of the well was large.

3 When all the flocks were gathered there, they would then roll the stone from the mouth of the well and water the sheep, and put the stone back in its place on the mouth of the well.

4 ¶ Jacob said to them, "My brothers, where are you from?" And they said, "We are from Haran."

5 He said to them, "Do you know Laban the son of Nahor?" And they said, "We know *him*."

6 And he said to them, "Is it well with him?" And they said, "It is well, and here is Rachel his daughter coming with the sheep."

7 He said, "Behold, it is still high day; it is not time for the livestock to be gathered. Water the sheep, and go, pasture them."

8 But they said, "We cannot, until all the flocks are gathered, and they roll the stone from the mouth of the well; then we water the sheep."

9 ¶ While he was still speaking with them, Rachel came with her father's sheep, for she was a shepherdess.

10 When Jacob saw Rachel the daughter of Laban his mother's brother, and the sheep of Laban his mother's brother, Jacob went up and rolled the stone from the mouth of the well and watered the flock of Laban his mother's brother.

11 Then Jacob kissed Rachel, and lifted his voice and wept.

[a] Lit *lifted up his feet*

12 Jacob told Rachel that he was a relative of her father and that he was Rebekah's son, and she ran and told her father.

13 ¶ So when Laban heard the news of Jacob his sister's son, he ran to meet him, and embraced him and kissed him and brought him to his house. Then he related to Laban all these things.

14 Laban said to him, "Surely you are my bone and my flesh." And he stayed with him a month.

15 ¶ Then Laban said to Jacob, "Because you are my relative, should you therefore serve me for nothing? Tell me, what shall your wages be?"

16 Now Laban had two daughters; the name of the older was Leah, and the name of the younger was Rachel.

17 And Leah's eyes were weak, but Rachel was beautiful of form and face.

18 Now Jacob loved Rachel, so he said, "I will serve you seven years for your younger daughter Rachel."

19 Laban said, "It is better that I give her to you than to give her to another man; stay with me."

20 So Jacob served seven years for Rachel and they seemed to him but a few days because of his love for her.

Laban's Treachery

21 ¶ Then Jacob said to Laban, "Give *me* my wife, for my time is completed, that I may go in to her."

22 Laban gathered all the men of the place and made a feast.

23 Now in the evening he took his daughter Leah, and brought her to him; and *Jacob* went in to her.

24 Laban also gave his maid Zilpah to his daughter Leah as a maid.

LABAN *Cheater*

HOW FITTING THAT JACOB, WHO had cheated his brother at least twice, fell into the hands of his uncle Laban, a notorious double-crosser. Deceit must have run in the family: Laban was brother to Rebekah, who had helped her son Jacob dupe his own father. Now Jacob learned how it felt to have the joke turned on him.

Laban won the first match by palming off his older daughter Leah on Jacob, who had just worked seven years to earn the beautiful Rachel. Throughout the rest of their working relationship, Jacob and Laban competed to outwit each other. Time and again Jacob accused Laban of changing his wages. Meanwhile Jacob schemed to get the biggest and best flock while tending Laban's animals.

Caught up in their wiles, neither man seemed to notice the obvious: Each trick damaged relationships. For example, deceit enabled Leah to share Rachel's husband, yet what did she really gain? For the rest of their lives the two quarreled miserably over Jacob's favor.

Jacob's flocks increased due to his cunning, but in the process Laban's sons grew hostile. Laban got cheap labor from Jacob, but Jacob so resented it that one day he left without warning, taking Laban's daughters with him. Laban never learned that, though cheating may get you what you want, it usually involves a heavy cost.

Life Questions: What is the best way to respond when someone tries to cheat you?

25 So it came about in the morning that, behold, it was Leah! And he said to Laban, "What is this you have done to me? Was it not for Rachel that I served with you? Why then have you deceived me?"

26 But Laban said, "It is not the practice in our place to marry off the younger before the firstborn.

27 "Complete the week of this one, and we will give you the other also for the service which you shall serve with me for another seven years."

28 Jacob did so and completed her week, and he gave him his daughter Rachel as his wife.

29 Laban also gave his maid Bilhah to his daughter Rachel as her maid.

30 So *Jacob* went in to Rachel also, and indeed he loved Rachel more than Leah, and he served with Laban for another seven years.

29:30 Playing Favorites

Throughout his life, Jacob's favoritism would cause problems in his family. He must have learned the habit from his own parents (see 25:28). Here, he favors one wife over the other. Later, he spoiled his son Joseph with favors, making his other sons so jealous they wanted to kill Joseph (see 37:4,18).

31 ¶ Now the LORD saw that Leah was unloved, and He opened her womb, but Rachel was barren.

32 Leah conceived and bore a son and named him Reuben, for she said, "Because the LORD has seen my affliction; surely now my husband will love me."

33 Then she conceived again and bore a son and said, "Because the LORD has heard that I am unloved, He has therefore given me this *son* also." So she named him Simeon.

34 She conceived again and bore a son and said, "Now this time my husband will become attached to me, because I have borne him three sons." Therefore he was named Levi.

35 And she conceived again and bore a son and said, "This time I will praise the LORD." Therefore she named him Judah. Then she stopped bearing.

The Sons of Jacob

30 Now when Rachel saw that she bore Jacob no children, she became jealous of her sister; and she said to Jacob, "Give me children, or else I die."

2 Then Jacob's anger burned against Rachel, and he said, "Am I in the place of God, who has withheld from you the fruit of the womb?"

3 She said, "Here is my maid Bilhah, go in to her that she may bear on my knees, that through her I too may have children."

4 So she gave him her maid Bilhah as a wife, and Jacob went in to her.

5 Bilhah conceived and bore Jacob a son.

6 Then Rachel said, "God has vindicated me, and has indeed heard my voice and has given me a son." Therefore she named him Dan.

7 Rachel's maid Bilhah conceived again and bore Jacob a second son.

8 So Rachel said, "With mighty wrestlings I have wrestled with my sister, *and* I have indeed prevailed." And she named him Naphtali.

9 ¶ When Leah saw that she had stopped bearing, she took her maid Zilpah and gave her to Jacob as a wife.

10 Leah's maid Zilpah bore Jacob a son.

11 Then Leah said, "How fortunate!" So she named him Gad.

12 Leah's maid Zilpah bore Jacob a second son.

13 Then Leah said, "Happy am I! For women will call me happy." So she named him Asher.

14 ¶ Now in the days of wheat harvest Reuben went and found mandrakes in the field, and brought them to his mother Leah. Then Rachel said to Leah, "Please give me some of your son's mandrakes."

15 But she said to her, "Is it a small matter for you to take my husband? And would you take my son's mandrakes also?" So Rachel said, "Therefore he may lie with you tonight in return for your son's mandrakes."

16 When Jacob came in from the field in the evening, then Leah went out to meet him and said, "You must come in to me, for I have surely hired you with my son's mandrakes." So he lay with her that night.

17 God gave heed to Leah, and she conceived and bore Jacob a fifth son.

18 Then Leah said, "God has given me my wages because I gave my maid to my husband." So she named him Issachar.

19 Leah conceived again and bore a sixth son to Jacob.

20 Then Leah said, "God has endowed me with a good gift; now my husband will dwell with me, because I have borne him six sons." So she named him Zebulun.

21 Afterward she bore a daughter and named her Dinah.

22 ¶ Then God remembered Rachel, and God gave heed to her and opened her womb.

23 So she conceived and bore a son and said, "God has taken away my reproach."

24 She named him Joseph, saying, "May the LORD give me another son."

Jacob Prospers

25 ¶ Now it came about when Rachel had borne Joseph, that Jacob said to Laban, "Send me away, that I may go to my own place and to my own country.

26 "Give *me* my wives and my children for

whom I have served you, and let me depart; for you yourself know my service which I have rendered you."

27 But Laban said to him, "If now ªit pleases you, *stay with me;* I have divined that the LORD has blessed me on your account."

28 He continued, "Name me your wages, and I will give it."

29 But he said to him, "You yourself know how I have served you and how your cattle have fared with me.

30 "For you had little before I came and it has increased to a multitude, and the LORD has blessed you wherever I turned. But now, when shall I provide for my own household also?"

31 So he said, "What shall I give you?" And Jacob said, "You shall not give me anything. If you will do this *one* thing for me, I will again pasture *and* keep your flock:

32 let me pass through your entire flock today, removing from there every speckled and spotted sheep and every black one among the lambs and the spotted and speckled among the goats; and *such* shall be my wages.

33 "So my honesty will answer for me later, when you come concerning my wages. Every one that is not speckled and spotted among the goats and black among the lambs, *if found* with me, will be considered stolen."

30:33 Misplaced Faith

In this classic encounter between two schemers, each trying to take advantage of the other, Jacob placed considerable faith in an animal-breeding trick. Many people have believed in similar methods over the centuries. Modern genetics indicates that Jacob's results had nothing to do with such techniques. God's intervening power increased Jacob's flocks, as Jacob himself acknowledged (31:7–9).

34 Laban said, "Good, let it be according to your word."

35 So he removed on that day the striped and spotted male goats and all the speckled and spotted female goats, every one with white in it, and all the black ones among the sheep, and gave them into the care of his sons.

36 And he put a *distance of* three days' journey between himself and Jacob, and Jacob fed the rest of Laban's flocks.

37 ¶ Then Jacob took fresh rods of poplar and almond and plane trees, and peeled white stripes in them, exposing the white which *was* in the rods.

38 He set the rods which he had peeled in front of the flocks in the gutters, *even* in the watering troughs, where the flocks came to drink; and they mated when they came to drink.

39 So the flocks mated by the rods, and the flocks brought forth striped, speckled, and spotted.

40 Jacob separated the lambs, and made the flocks face toward the striped and all the black in the flock of Laban; and he put his own herds apart, and did not put them with Laban's flock.

41 Moreover, whenever the stronger of the flock were mating, Jacob would place the rods in the sight of the flock in the gutters, so that they might mate by the rods;

42 but when the flock was feeble, he did not put *them* in; so the feebler were Laban's and the stronger Jacob's.

43 So the man became exceedingly prosperous, and had large flocks and female and male servants and camels and donkeys.

Jacob Leaves Secretly for Canaan

31 Now Jacob heard the words of Laban's sons, saying, "Jacob has taken away all that was our father's, and from what belonged to our father he has made all this wealth."

2 Jacob saw the ᵇattitude of Laban, and behold, it was not *friendly* toward him as formerly.

3 Then the LORD said to Jacob, "Return to the land of your fathers and to your relatives, and I will be with you."

4 So Jacob sent and called Rachel and Leah to his flock in the field,

5 and said to them, "I see your father's attitude, that it is not *friendly* toward me as formerly, but the God of my father has been with me.

6 "You know that I have served your father with all my strength.

7 "Yet your father has cheated me and changed my wages ten times; however, God did not allow him to hurt me.

8 "If he spoke thus, 'The speckled shall be your wages,' then all the flock brought forth speckled; and if he spoke thus, 'The striped shall be your wages,' then all the flock brought forth striped.

9 "Thus God has taken away your father's livestock and given *them* to me.

10 "And it came about at the time when the flock were mating that I lifted up my eyes and saw in a dream, and behold, the male goats which were mating *were* striped, speckled, and mottled.

11 "Then the angel of God said to me in the dream, 'Jacob,' and I said, 'Here I am.'

12 "He said, 'Lift up now your eyes and see *that* all the male goats which are mating are striped, speckled, and mottled; for I have seen all that Laban has been doing to you.

13 'I am the God *of* Bethel, where you anointed a pillar, where you made a vow to Me; now arise, leave this land, and return to the land of your birth.' "

ª Lit *I have found favor in your eyes*   ᵇ Lit *face*

14 Rachel and Leah said to him, "Do we still have any portion or inheritance in our father's house?

15 "Are we not reckoned by him as foreigners? For he has sold us, and has also entirely consumed our purchase price.

16 "Surely all the wealth which God has taken away from our father belongs to us and our children; now then, do whatever God has said to you."

17 ¶ Then Jacob arose and put his children and his wives upon camels;

18 and he drove away all his livestock and all his property which he had gathered, his acquired livestock which he had gathered in Paddan-aram, to go to the land of Canaan to his father Isaac.

19 When Laban had gone to shear his flock, then Rachel stole the household idols that were her father's.

20 And Jacob deceived Laban the Aramean by not telling him that he was fleeing.

21 So he fled with all that he had; and he arose and crossed the *Euphrates* River, and set his face toward the hill country of Gilead.

Laban Pursues Jacob

22 ¶ When it was told Laban on the third day that Jacob had fled,

23 then he took his kinsmen with him and pursued him *a distance of* seven days' journey, and he overtook him in the hill country of Gilead.

24 God came to Laban the Aramean in a dream of the night and said to him, "Be careful that you do not speak to Jacob either good or bad."

25 ¶ Laban caught up with Jacob. Now Jacob had pitched his tent in the hill country, and Laban with his kinsmen camped in the hill country of Gilead.

26 Then Laban said to Jacob, "What have you done by deceiving me and carrying away my daughters like captives of the sword?

27 "Why did you flee secretly and deceive me, and did not tell me so that I might have sent you away with joy and with songs, with timbrel and with lyre;

28 and did not allow me to kiss my sons and my daughters? Now you have done foolishly.

29 "It is in my power to do you harm, but the God of your father spoke to me last night, saying, 'Be careful not to speak either good or bad to Jacob.'

30 "Now you have indeed gone away because you longed greatly for your father's house; *but* why did you steal my gods?"

31 Then Jacob replied to Laban, "Because I was afraid, for I thought that you would take your daughters from me by force.

32 "The one with whom you find your gods shall not live; in the presence of our kinsmen point

RACHEL *Love and Grief*

JACOB ARRIVED PENNILESS AT HIS cousin Rachel's home, having traveled hundreds of miles on foot. To some he might appear a poor catch—a fugitive from his family, his character tainted with the grasping, scheming qualities that had created the problem. Rachel, however, could grasp and scheme quite well herself. In strength and cunning, Jacob had met his match.

In an age not known for romance, when young people often waited for their parents to arrange their marriages, Jacob fell profoundly in love with Rachel. He worked fourteen years to gain her (after being tricked into marrying her sister along the way). Clearly, to him, beautiful Rachel was worth the labor. He loved her from first sight to last breath.

Rachel knew what it was to be deeply loved, but she also knew piercing sorrow. More than anything she wanted children, and while her sister produced six sons for Jacob and two servants also bore him children, Rachel remained childless. Her rivalry with her sister Leah, told in Genesis 29 and 30, was profound and bitter. Finally Rachel gave birth to Joseph, her first son. Some years later she died in childbirth bearing Benjamin, her second. (Showing love even after her death, Jacob counted these two sons as his favorites.)

Rachel's fierce love for her children became an emblem for Israel. More than a thousand years after she lived, the prophet Jeremiah, mulling over the destruction of Israel, heard "lamentation and bitter weeping. Rachel is weeping for her children; she refuses to be comforted for her children, because they are no more" (Jeremiah 31:15). The same haunting poetry is quoted in Matthew 2:18 regarding the slaughter of babies by King Herod. Even today the phrase "Rachel weeping" serves as shorthand for the sufferings of the Jewish people.

Rachel was a strong woman whose loyalty to her husband and desire for children outweighed everything else. She and her sister became part of a traditional Jewish wedding blessing: "May the LORD make the woman who is coming into your home like Rachel and Leah, both of whom built the house of Israel" (Ruth 4:11).

Life Questions: Jacob longed for a wife. Rachel longed for children. What do you want more than anything else?

out what is yours among my belongings and take *it* for yourself." For Jacob did not know that Rachel had stolen them.

33 ¶ So Laban went into Jacob's tent and into Leah's tent and into the tent of the two maids, but he did not find *them.* Then he went out of Leah's tent and entered Rachel's tent.

34 Now Rachel had taken the household idols and put them in the camel's saddle, and she sat on them. And Laban felt through all the tent but did not find *them.*

35 She said to her father, "Let not my lord be angry that I cannot rise before you, for the manner of women is upon me." So he searched but did not find the household idols.

31:35 Household Gods

The "idols" Rachel had stolen from her father (verse 19) were small idols or "charms" supposed to protect the family from harm. They may also have served as something like a title deed for the family inheritance. Such idols continued to water down Israel's commitment to God for many generations to come.

36 ¶ Then Jacob became angry and contended with Laban; and Jacob said to Laban, "What is my transgression? What is my sin that you have hotly pursued me?

37 "Though you have felt through all my goods, what have you found of all your household goods? Set *it* here before my kinsmen and your kinsmen, that they may decide between us two.

38 "These twenty years I *have been* with you; your ewes and your female goats have not miscarried, nor have I eaten the rams of your flocks.

39 "That which was torn *of beasts* I did not bring to you; I bore the loss of it myself. You required it of my hand *whether* stolen by day or stolen by night.

40 "*Thus* I was: by day the heat consumed me and the frost by night, and my sleep fled from my eyes.

41 "These twenty years I have been in your house; I served you fourteen years for your two daughters and six years for your flock, and you changed my wages ten times.

42 "If the God of my father, the God of Abraham, and the fear of Isaac, had not been for me, surely now you would have sent me away empty-handed. God has seen my affliction and the toil of my hands, so He rendered judgment last night."

The Covenant of Mizpah

43 ¶ Then Laban replied to Jacob, "The daughters are my daughters, and the children are my

children, and the flocks are my flocks, and all that you see is mine. But what can I do this day to these my daughters or to their children whom they have borne?

44 "So now come, let us make a covenant, you and I, and let it be a witness between you and me."

45 Then Jacob took a stone and set it up *as a* pillar.

46 Jacob said to his kinsmen, "Gather stones." So they took stones and made a heap, and they ate there by the heap.

47 Now Laban called it *a*Jegar-sahadutha, but Jacob called it *b*Galeed.

48 Laban said, "This heap is a witness between you and me this day." Therefore it was named Galeed,

49 and *c*Mizpah, for he said, "May the LORD watch between you and me when we are absent one from the other.

50 "If you mistreat my daughters, or if you take wives besides my daughters, *although* no man is with us, see, God is witness between you and me."

51 Laban said to Jacob, "Behold this heap and behold the pillar which I have set between you and me.

52 "This heap is a witness, and the pillar is a witness, that I will not pass by this heap to you for harm, and you will not pass by this heap and this pillar to me, for harm.

53 "The God of Abraham and the God of Nahor, the God of their father, judge between us." So Jacob swore by the fear of his father Isaac.

54 Then Jacob offered a sacrifice on the mountain, and called his kinsmen to the meal; and they ate the meal and spent the night on the mountain.

55 Early in the morning Laban arose, and kissed his sons and his daughters and blessed them. Then Laban departed and returned to his place.

Jacob's Fear of Esau

32 Now as Jacob went on his way, the angels of God met him.

2 Jacob said when he saw them, "This is God's *d*camp." So he named that place *e*Mahanaim.

3 ¶ Then Jacob sent messengers before him to his brother Esau in the land of Seir, the country of Edom.

4 He also commanded them saying, "Thus you shall say to my lord Esau: 'Thus says your servant Jacob, "I have sojourned with Laban, and stayed until now;

5 I have oxen and donkeys *and* flocks and male and female servants; and I have sent to tell my lord, that I may find favor in your sight." ' "

6 ¶ The messengers returned to Jacob, saying, "We came to your brother Esau, and furthermore

---

a I.e. the heap of witness, in Aram   *b* I.e. the heap of witness, in Heb   *c* Lit *the Mizpah*; i.e. the watchtower   *d* Or company   *e* I.e. Two Camps, or Two Companies he is coming to meet you, and four hundred men are with him."

7 Then Jacob was greatly afraid and distressed; and he divided the people who were with him, and the flocks and the herds and the camels, into two companies;

8 for he said, "If Esau comes to the one company and attacks it, then the company which is left will escape."

9 ¶ Jacob said, "O God of my father Abraham and God of my father Isaac, O LORD, who said to me, 'Return to your country and to your relatives, and I will prosper you,'

10 I am unworthy of all the lovingkindness and of all the faithfulness which You have shown to Your servant; for with my staff *only* I crossed this Jordan, and now I have become two companies.

11 "Deliver me, I pray, from the hand of my brother, from the hand of Esau; for I fear him, that he will come and attack me *and* the mothers with the children.

12 "For You said, 'I will surely prosper you and make your descendants as the sand of the sea, which is too great to be numbered.'"

13 ¶ So he spent the night there. Then he selected from what he had with him a present for his brother Esau:

14 two hundred female goats and twenty male goats, two hundred ewes and twenty rams,

15 thirty milking camels and their colts, forty cows and ten bulls, twenty female donkeys and ten male donkeys.

16 He delivered *them* into the hand of his servants, every drove by itself, and said to his servants, "Pass on before me, and put a space between droves."

17 He commanded the one in front, saying, "When my brother Esau meets you and asks you, saying, 'To whom do you belong, and where are you going, and to whom do these *animals* in front of you belong?'

18 then you shall say, 'These belong to your servant Jacob; it is a present sent to my lord Esau. And behold, he also is behind us.'"

19 Then he commanded also the second and the third, and all those who followed the droves, saying, "After this manner you shall speak to Esau when you find him;

20 and you shall say, 'Behold, your servant Jacob also is behind us.'" For he said, "I will appease him with the present that goes before me. Then afterward I will see his face; perhaps he will accept me."

21 So the present passed on before him, while he himself spent that night in the camp.

22 ¶ Now he arose that same night and took his two wives and his two maids and his eleven children, and crossed the ford of the Jabbok.

23 He took them and sent them across the stream. And he sent across whatever he had.

Jacob Wrestles

24 Then Jacob was left alone, and a man wrestled with him until daybreak.

25 When he saw that he had not prevailed

32:24 Wrestling with God

This nighttime encounter, as strange as any in the Bible, sounds somewhat similar to Jacob's previous on-the-road encounter with God (28:12) in a dream. But this time God left Jacob evidence of his physical presence—a limp.

against him, he touched the socket of his thigh; so the socket of Jacob's thigh was dislocated while he wrestled with him.

26 Then he said, "Let me go, for the dawn is breaking." But he said, "I will not let you go unless you bless me."

27 So he said to him, "What is your name?" And he said, "Jacob."

28 He said, "Your name shall no longer be Jacob, but *a*Israel; for you have striven with God and with men and have prevailed."

29 Then Jacob asked him and said, "Please tell me your name." But he said, "Why is it that you ask my name?" And he blessed him there.

30 So Jacob named the place *b*Peniel, for *he* said, "I have seen God face to face, yet my life has been preserved."

31 Now the sun rose upon him just as he crossed over Penuel, and he was limping on his thigh.

32 Therefore, to this day the sons of Israel do not eat the sinew of the hip which is on the socket of the thigh, because he touched the socket of Jacob's thigh in the sinew of the hip.

Jacob Meets Esau

33 Then Jacob lifted his eyes and looked, and behold, Esau was coming, and four hundred men with him. So he divided the children among Leah and Rachel and the two maids.

2 He put the maids and their children in front, and Leah and her children next, and Rachel and Joseph last.

3 But he himself passed on ahead of them and bowed down to the ground seven times, until he came near to his brother.

4 ¶ Then Esau ran to meet him and embraced him, and fell on his neck and kissed him, and they wept.

5 He lifted his eyes and saw the women and the children, and said, "Who are these with you?" So he said, "The children whom God has graciously given your servant."

a I.e. he who strives with God; or God strives   *b* I.e. the face of God

6 Then the maids came near with their children, and they bowed down.

7 Leah likewise came near with her children, and they bowed down; and afterward Joseph came near with Rachel, and they bowed down.

8 And he said, "What do you mean by all this company which I have met?" And he said, "To find favor in the sight of my lord."

9 But Esau said, "I have plenty, my brother; let what you have be your own."

10 Jacob said, "No, please, if now I have found favor in your sight, then take my present from my hand, for I see your face as one sees the face of God, and you have received me favorably.

11 "Please take my gift which has been brought to you, because God has dealt graciously with me and because I have plenty." Thus he urged him and he took *it.*

12 ¶ Then Esau said, "Let us take our journey and go, and I will go before you."

13 But he said to him, "My lord knows that the children are frail and that the flocks and herds which are nursing are a care to me. And if they are driven hard one day, all the flocks will die.

14 "Please let my lord pass on before his servant, and I will proceed at my leisure, according to the pace of the cattle that are before me and according to the pace of the children, until I come to my lord at Seir."

15 ¶ Esau said, "Please let me leave with you some of the people who are with me." But he said,

ᵃ Lit *Why this?*   ᵇ I.e. booths

"ᵃWhat need is there? Let me find favor in the sight of my lord."

16 So Esau returned that day on his way to Seir.

33:15 Surface Reconciliation

On the surface, Jacob and Esau had reconciled. Underneath the niceties, however, mistrust continued, at least on Jacob's part. He did not want Esau to accompany him on his way, nor did he wish Esau to leave some of his men for "protection." He let his brother think he was on his way to Seir (verse 14), but turned north to Succoth as soon as Esau was out of sight.

17 Jacob journeyed to ᵇSuccoth, and built for himself a house and made booths for his livestock; therefore the place is named Succoth.

Jacob Settles in Shechem

18 ¶ Now Jacob came safely to the city of Shechem, which is in the land of Canaan, when he came from Paddan-aram, and camped before the city.

19 He bought the piece of land where he had pitched his tent from the hand of the sons of Hamor, Shechem's father, for one hundred pieces of money.

ESAU *Surprising Choice*

MANY PEOPLE FIND ESAU MORE attractive than his brother Jacob. Esau was an outdoorsman—rugged, impulsive, simple and unaffected. Jacob was the stay-at-home mama's boy who angled deceitfully for any personal advantage. He virtually stole his brother's inheritance from him.

Anyone can understand Esau's murderous feelings toward Jacob. As the oldest brother, Esau stood next in line to lead the family. Instead he became the lost brother, holding no significant place in God's plan.

Why God's surprising choice of the younger brother? The apostle Paul reflects on this question in Romans 9:10–18, pointing out that God's preference for Jacob began even before his birth. Again and again in history, God narrowed his focus to a single person in order to carry out his plan to save the world. God couldn't choose everyone—moreover, those individuals God did choose were not always the ones we admire. God makes his own judgments, Paul says, and God's people must bow before him even when they do not understand.

Yet in the stories recorded here, the reasons behind God's unexpected choice become clearer. Esau had major character flaws. At every crossroads he consistently followed his own desires, showing little spiritual sensitivity and no long-term vision. Jacob the grasper at least recognized that the family inheritance was precious; to Esau, momentary hunger mattered more (Genesis 27). And when it came to marriage, Esau chose the local women, even though they came from the wrong heritage and displeased his parents.

God seemed to hold no place in Esau's thinking. Jacob, however unattractively, set his sights higher. God channeled Jacob's passion and strong ambition toward divine purposes.

Life Questions: Do ordinary desires—for food, romance, peer approval, success—conflict with spiritual ambitions in your life? How can you deal with such conflicts?

20 Then he erected there an altar and called it [a]El-Elohe-Israel.

The Treachery of Jacob's Sons

34 Now Dinah the daughter of Leah, whom she had borne to Jacob, went out to visit the daughters of the land.

2 When Shechem the son of Hamor the Hivite, the prince of the land, saw her, he took her and lay with her by force.

3 He was deeply attracted to Dinah the daughter of Jacob, and he loved the girl and spoke tenderly to her.

4 So Shechem spoke to his father Hamor, saying, "Get me this young girl for a wife."

5 Now Jacob heard that he had defiled Dinah his daughter; but his sons were with his livestock in the field, so Jacob kept silent until they came in.

6 Then Hamor the father of Shechem went out to Jacob to speak with him.

7 Now the sons of Jacob came in from the field when they heard *it;* and the men were grieved, and they were very angry because he had done a disgraceful thing in Israel by lying with Jacob's daughter, for such a thing ought not to be done.

8 ¶ But Hamor spoke with them, saying, "The soul of my son Shechem longs for your daughter; please give her to him in marriage.

9 "Intermarry with us; give your daughters to us and take our daughters for yourselves.

10 "Thus you shall live with us, and the land shall be *open* before you; live and trade in it and acquire property in it."

11 Shechem also said to her father and to her brothers, "If I find favor in your sight, then I will give whatever you say to me.

12 "Ask me ever so much bridal payment and gift, and I will give according as you say to me; but give me the girl in marriage."

13 ¶ But Jacob's sons answered Shechem and his father Hamor with deceit, because he had defiled Dinah their sister.

14 They said to them, "We cannot do this thing, to give our sister to one who is uncircumcised, for that would be a disgrace to us.

15 "Only on this *condition* will we consent to you: if you will become like us, in that every male of you be circumcised,

16 then we will give our daughters to you, and we will take your daughters for ourselves, and we will live with you and become one people.

17 "But if you will not listen to us to be circumcised, then we will take our daughter and go."

18 ¶ Now their words seemed reasonable to Hamor and Shechem, Hamor's son.

19 The young man did not delay to do the thing, because he was delighted with Jacob's daughter. Now he was more respected than all the household of his father.

20 So Hamor and his son Shechem came to the gate of their city and spoke to the men of their city, saying,

21 "These men are friendly with us; therefore let them live in the land and trade in it, for behold, the land is large enough for them. Let us take their daughters in marriage, and give our daughters to them.

22 "Only on this *condition* will the men consent to us to live with us, to become one people: that every male among us be circumcised as they are circumcised.

23 "Will not their livestock and their property and all their animals be ours? Only let us consent to them, and they will live with us."

24 All who went out of the gate of his city listened to Hamor and to his son Shechem, and every male was circumcised, all who went out of the gate of his city.

25 ¶ Now it came about on the third day, when they were in pain, that two of Jacob's sons, Simeon and Levi, Dinah's brothers, each took his sword and came upon the city unawares, and killed every male.

26 They killed Hamor and his son Shechem with the edge of the sword, and took Dinah from Shechem's house, and went forth.

27 Jacob's sons came upon the slain and looted the city, because they had defiled their sister.

28 They took their flocks and their herds and their donkeys, and that which was in the city and that which was in the field;

29 and they captured and looted all their wealth and all their little ones and their wives, even all that *was* in the houses.

30 Then Jacob said to Simeon and Levi, "You have brought trouble on me by making me odious among the inhabitants of the land, among the Canaanites and the Perizzites; and my men being few in number, they will gather together against me and attack me and I will be destroyed, I and my household."

31 But they said, "Should he treat our sister as a harlot?"

Jacob Moves to Bethel

35 Then God said to Jacob, "Arise, go up to Bethel and live there, and make an altar there to God, who appeared to you when you fled from your brother Esau."

2 So Jacob said to his household and to all who were with him, "Put away the foreign gods which are among you, and purify yourselves and change your garments;

3 and let us arise and go up to Bethel, and I will make an altar there to God, who answered me in the day of my distress and has been with me wherever I have gone."

4 So they gave to Jacob all the foreign gods which they had and the rings which were in their

[a] I.e. God, the God of Israel

ears, and Jacob hid them under the oak which was near Shechem.

5 ¶ As they journeyed, there was a great terror upon the cities which were around them, and they did not pursue the sons of Jacob.

6 So Jacob came to Luz (that is, Bethel), which is in the land of Canaan, he and all the people who were with him.

7 He built an altar there, and called the place El-bethel, because there God had revealed Himself to him when he fled from his brother.

8 Now Deborah, Rebekah's nurse, died, and she was buried below Bethel under the oak; it was named ^aAllon-bacuth.

Jacob Is Named Israel

9 ¶ Then God appeared to Jacob again when he came from Paddan-aram, and He blessed him.

10 God said to him,
"Your name is Jacob;
You shall no longer be called Jacob,
But Israel shall be your name."
Thus He called him Israel.

11 God also said to him,
"I am God Almighty;
Be fruitful and multiply;
A nation and a company of nations shall
    come from you,
And kings shall come forth from you.

12 "The land which I gave to Abraham and
    Isaac,
I will give it to you,
And I will give the land to your
    descendants after you."

13 Then God went up from him in the place where He had spoken with him.

14 Jacob set up a pillar in the place where He had spoken with him, a pillar of stone, and he poured out a drink offering on it; he also poured oil on it.

15 So Jacob named the place where God had spoken with him, ^bBethel.

16 ¶ Then they journeyed from Bethel; and when there was still some distance to go to Ephrath, Rachel began to give birth and she suffered severe labor.

17 When she was in severe labor the midwife said to her, "Do not fear, for now you have another son."

18 It came about as her soul was departing (for she died), that she named him ^cBen-oni; but his father called him ^dBenjamin.

19 So Rachel died and was buried on the way to Ephrath (that is, Bethlehem).

20 Jacob set up a pillar over her grave; that is the pillar of Rachel's grave to this day.

21 Then Israel journeyed on and pitched his tent beyond the tower of Eder.

22 ¶ It came about while Israel was dwelling in that land, that Reuben went and lay with Bilhah his father's concubine, and Israel heard *of it*.

The Sons of Israel

¶ Now there were twelve sons of Jacob—

23 the sons of Leah: Reuben, Jacob's firstborn, then Simeon and Levi and Judah and Issachar and Zebulun;

35:22 A Sin that Lies Sleeping

This passage offers no indication that what Reuben did was wrong, let alone subject to punishment. Yet his deed was not forgotten. Decades later, when Jacob called his sons in for a final blessing, he brought up this sin (49:4) and predicted that leadership would pass from Reuben, the firstborn.

24 the sons of Rachel: Joseph and Benjamin;

25 and the sons of Bilhah, Rachel's maid: Dan and Naphtali;

26 and the sons of Zilpah, Leah's maid: Gad and Asher. These are the sons of Jacob who were born to him in Paddan-aram.

27 ¶ Jacob came to his father Isaac at Mamre of Kiriath-arba (that is, Hebron), where Abraham and Isaac had sojourned.

28 ¶ Now the days of Isaac were one hundred and eighty years.

29 Isaac breathed his last and died and was gathered to his people, an old man of ripe age; and his sons Esau and Jacob buried him.

Esau Moves

36 Now these are *the records of* the generations of Esau (that is, Edom).

2 ¶ Esau took his wives from the daughters of Canaan: Adah the daughter of Elon the Hittite, and Oholibamah the daughter of Anah and the granddaughter of Zibeon the Hivite;

3 also Basemath, Ishmael's daughter, the sister of Nebaioth.

4 Adah bore Eliphaz to Esau, and Basemath bore Reuel,

5 and Oholibamah bore Jeush and Jalam and Korah. These are the sons of Esau who were born to him in the land of Canaan.

6 ¶ Then Esau took his wives and his sons and his daughters and all his household, and his livestock and all his cattle and all his goods which he had acquired in the land of Canaan, and went to *another* land away from his brother Jacob.

7 For their property had become too great for them to live together, and the land where they sojourned could not sustain them because of their livestock.

---

^a I.e. oak of weeping   ^b I.e. the house of God   ^c I.e. the son of my sorrow   ^d I.e. the son of the right hand

8 So Esau lived in the hill country of Seir; Esau is Edom.

Descendants of Esau

9 ¶ These then are *the records of* the generations of Esau the father of the Edomites in the hill country of Seir.

10 These are the names of Esau's sons: Eliphaz the son of Esau's wife Adah, Reuel the son of Esau's wife Basemath.

11 The sons of Eliphaz were Teman, Omar, Zepho and Gatam and Kenaz.

12 Timna was a concubine of Esau's son Eliphaz and she bore Amalek to Eliphaz. These are the sons of Esau's wife Adah.

13 These are the sons of Reuel: Nahath and Zerah, Shammah and Mizzah. These were the sons of Esau's wife Basemath.

14 These were the sons of Esau's wife Oholibamah, the daughter of Anah and the granddaughter of Zibeon: she bore to Esau, Jeush and Jalam and Korah.

15 ¶ These are the chiefs of the sons of Esau. The sons of Eliphaz, the firstborn of Esau, are chief Teman, chief Omar, chief Zepho, chief Kenaz,

16 chief Korah, chief Gatam, chief Amalek. These are the chiefs descended from Eliphaz in the land of Edom; these are the sons of Adah.

17 These are the sons of Reuel, Esau's son: chief Nahath, chief Zerah, chief Shammah, chief Mizzah. These are the chiefs descended from Reuel in the land of Edom; these are the sons of Esau's wife Basemath.

18 These are the sons of Esau's wife Oholibamah: chief Jeush, chief Jalam, chief Korah. These are the chiefs descended from Esau's wife Oholibamah, the daughter of Anah.

19 These are the sons of Esau (that is, Edom), and these are their chiefs.

20 ¶ These are the sons of Seir the Horite, the inhabitants of the land: Lotan and Shobal and Zibeon and Anah,

21 and Dishon and Ezer and Dishan. These are the chiefs descended from the Horites, the sons of Seir in the land of Edom.

22 The sons of Lotan were Hori and Hemam; and Lotan's sister was Timna.

23 These are the sons of Shobal: Alvan and Manahath and Ebal, Shepho and Onam.

24 These are the sons of Zibeon: Aiah and Anah—he is the Anah who found the hot springs in the wilderness when he was pasturing the donkeys of his father Zibeon.

25 These are the children of Anah: Dishon, and Oholibamah, the daughter of Anah.

26 These are the sons of Dishon: Hemdan and Eshban and Ithran and Cheran.

27 These are the sons of Ezer: Bilhan and Zaavan and Akan.

28 These are the sons of Dishan: Uz and Aran.

29 These are the chiefs descended from the Horites: chief Lotan, chief Shobal, chief Zibeon, chief Anah,

30 chief Dishon, chief Ezer, chief Dishan. These are the chiefs descended from the Horites, according to their *various* chiefs in the land of Seir.

31 ¶ Now these are the kings who reigned in the land of Edom before any king reigned over the sons of Israel.

32 Bela the son of Beor reigned in Edom, and the name of his city was Dinhabah.

33 Then Bela died, and Jobab the son of Zerah of Bozrah became king in his place.

34 Then Jobab died, and Husham of the land of the Temanites became king in his place.

35 Then Husham died, and Hadad the son of Bedad, who defeated Midian in the field of Moab, became king in his place; and the name of his city was Avith.

36 Then Hadad died, and Samlah of Masrekah became king in his place.

37 Then Samlah died, and Shaul of Rehoboth on the *Euphrates* River became king in his place.

38 Then Shaul died, and Baal-hanan the son of Achbor became king in his place.

39 Then Baal-hanan the son of Achbor died, and Hadar became king in his place; and the name of his city was Pau; and his wife's name was Mehetabel, the daughter of Matred, daughter of Mezahab.

40 ¶ Now these are the names of the chiefs descended from Esau, according to their families *and* their localities, by their names: chief Timna, chief Alvah, chief Jetheth,

41 chief Oholibamah, chief Elah, chief Pinon,

42 chief Kenaz, chief Teman, chief Mibzar,

43 chief Magdiel, chief Iram. These are the chiefs of Edom (that is, Esau, the father of the Edomites), according to their habitations in the land of their possession.

Joseph's Dream

37 Now Jacob lived in the land where his father had sojourned, in the land of Canaan.

2 These are *the records of* the generations of Jacob.

¶ Joseph, when seventeen years of age, was pasturing the flock with his brothers while he was *still* a youth, along with the sons of Bilhah and the sons of Zilpah, his father's wives. And Joseph brought back a bad report about them to their father.

3 Now Israel loved Joseph more than all his sons, because he was the son of his old age; and he made him a *a*varicolored tunic.

4 His brothers saw that their father loved him more than all his brothers; and *so* they hated him and could not speak to him *b*on friendly terms.

---

a Or *full-length robe*   *b* Lit *in peace*

5 ¶ Then Joseph had a dream, and when he told it to his brothers, they hated him even more.
6 He said to them, "Please listen to this dream which I have had;
7 for behold, we were binding sheaves in the field, and lo, my sheaf rose up and also stood erect; and behold, your sheaves gathered around and bowed down to my sheaf."
8 Then his brothers said to him, "Are you actually going to reign over us? Or are you really going to rule over us?" So they hated him even more for his dreams and for his words.
9 ¶ Now he had still another dream, and related it to his brothers, and said, "Lo, I have had still another dream; and behold, the sun and the moon and eleven stars were bowing down to me."
10 He related *it* to his father and to his broth-

ers; and his father rebuked him and said to him, "What is this dream that you have had? Shall I and your mother and your brothers actually come to bow ourselves down before you to the ground?"

37:8 Big Mouth

God revealed Joseph's future by way of two dreams. Foolishly, Joseph told everything to his brothers, who hated him all the more. The spoiled, naive Joseph we meet here is a different character from the careful, prudent leader who would emerge from prison years later to lead Egypt.

Family Battles
The closer they are, the harder they fight

JOSEPH AND HIS BROTHERS FOUGHT bitterly—almost to the death. Nobody, it seems, can fight like brothers and sisters. Their very closeness seems to rub salt in their wounds.

Take a contemporary example: Esther Pauline Friedman came into this world 17 minutes before her sister Pauline Esther Friedman. The identical twins dressed alike, took the same classes, even shared the same purse, with one set of keys, one comb, one lipstick. They slept in the same twin bed. The first time they were separated, in fact, was after their double wedding.

The middle-aged Esther Pauline hooked a job replacing the original Ann Landers at the *Chicago Sun Times.* Two months later Pauline Esther started her own column with the *San Francisco Chronicle,* calling herself Abigail Van Buren. Ann sniffed to *Time* that her sister Abby's column was "very imitative." The feud was on. For eight years the two women who had dispensed advice to thousands could not resolve a petty family squabble.

Finally, the two were partially reconciled. They told journalists they were "very close." Yet bitter feelings lived on. Seventeen years after making up, Abby said about Ann, "If she looked old, if she needed a face-lift, believe me, it's because she needed it. I'm quite opposed to chopping myself up, but it was her right. Why not? When you cry a lot, it's got to show."

> They said to one another, "Here comes this dreamer. Now then, come and let us kill him."
> 37:19–20

A Father's Favorite

Joseph's story is the last of the brotherly battles of Genesis. Cain and Abel, Isaac and Ishmael, Jacob and Esau all quarreled. Joseph set his 11 brothers against him by telling his dream of their bowing down to him. He was his father's favorite and perhaps flaunted it. So when his brothers got a chance, they paid him back. They sold him as a slave to traveling merchants, who took him to Egypt. Never expecting to see him again, they cooked up a story that he had been killed by wild animals.

God had other plans. In Egypt, he gave Joseph the interpretation to several dreams. It was a ticket to prominence. Egyptians of that day were fascinated by dreams: Archaeologists have uncovered lengthy textbooks on dream interpretation. Joseph soon found himself at the top of Pharaoh's government.

But success was not enough. The Bible story goes on from there, for God wanted forgiveness within the family. A famine forced Joseph's brothers out of Palestine; they came to Egypt looking for food. Kneeling before Joseph—so Egyptian by now that they did not recognize him—they begged for the right to buy food.

A Strange Struggle

So began one of the strangest struggles of the Bible. Joseph could have made up with his brothers on the spot, welcoming them with open arms. Or he could have taken revenge, putting them to death. He did neither. He began a series of elaborate tests, demanding things from them, playing tricks on them, accusing them. For nearly two years he played these games. They brought confusion and fear to his brothers—and an admission of guilt.

11 His brothers were jealous of him, but his father kept the saying *in mind.*

12 ¶ Then his brothers went to pasture their father's flock in Shechem.

13 Israel said to Joseph, "Are not your brothers pasturing *the flock* in Shechem? Come, and I will send you to them." And he said to him, "I will go."

14 Then he said to him, "Go now and see about the welfare of your brothers and the welfare of the flock, and bring word back to me." So he sent him from the valley of Hebron, and he came to Shechem.

15 ¶ A man found him, and behold, he was wandering in the field; and the man asked him, "What are you looking for?"

16 He said, "I am looking for my brothers; please tell me where they are pasturing *the flock.*"

17 Then the man said, "They have moved from here; for I heard *them* say, 'Let us go to Dothan.'" So Joseph went after his brothers and found them at Dothan.

The Plot against Joseph

18 ¶ When they saw him from a distance and before he came close to them, they plotted against him to put him to death.

19 They said to one another, "Here comes this dreamer!

20 "Now then, come and let us kill him and throw him into one of the pits; and we will say, 'A wild beast devoured him.' Then let us see what will become of his dreams!"

21 But Reuben heard *this* and rescued him out of their hands and said, "Let us not take his life."

22 Reuben further said to them, "Shed no blood. Throw him into this pit that is in the wilderness, but do not lay hands on him"—that he might rescue him out of their hands, to restore him to his father.

23 So it came about, when Joseph reached his brothers, that they stripped Joseph of his tunic, the varicolored tunic that was on him;

24 and they took him and threw him into the pit. Now the pit was empty, without any water in it.

25 ¶ Then they sat down to eat a meal. And as they raised their eyes and looked, behold, a caravan of Ishmaelites was coming from Gilead, with their camels bearing aromatic gum and balm and myrrh, on their way to bring *them* down to Egypt.

26 Judah said to his brothers, "What profit is it for us to kill our brother and cover up his blood?

27 "Come and let us sell him to the Ishmaelites and not lay our hands on him, for he is our broth-

---

Twenty years had not erased the brothers' memory of Joseph. The moment their troubles began, their guilt surfaced. "Then they said to one another, 'Truly we are guilty concerning our brother, because we saw the distress of his soul when he pleaded with us, yet we would not listen; therefore this distress has come upon us'" (42:21). For Joseph, the drama brought tremendous emotional strain. Five times Genesis records that he broke into tears, once weeping so loudly that people in the next room heard him.

Joseph felt the strain of forgiveness. He wanted to reconcile with his brothers, whom he loved, but it was not easy. And until they had been pushed to the point of admitting and accepting their guilt, reconciliation could not occur. Their sins had planted deep-rooted bitterness, and only an emotionally wrenching struggle could pull it out.

Seeds of Bitterness

In this sense Joseph's story is the story of God and his people—the struggle to root out the sin that began in Genesis 3. Victory over sin does not happen automatically or easily. Ultimately, it demanded the death of God's Son.

Joseph's story points toward Jesus—a man God sent to save his people, one who was hated and betrayed by them just as Joseph was. But God's will to save conquers all. As Joseph told his brothers, "As for you, you meant evil against me, but God meant it for good in order to bring about this present result, to preserve many people alive" (50:20).

The Birth of a Nation

Joseph closes one chapter in the story of Israel. The children of Abraham were transformed from a chain of individuals to a nation. God did not choose Joseph over his brothers, as he did Abraham over Lot, Isaac over Ishmael, Jacob over Esau. The brothers' reconciliation opened the way for them to become one family of 12 tribes—a single nation.

But the story leads on. Prosperous and numerous though the 12 were to become, they still had no land. And so Genesis ends happily, but on a note of suspense: When will Joseph's bones go back to the land God promised? When will God's promises be fulfilled?

Life Questions: Have you ever fought hard with a person close to you, and then experienced reconciliation? What process did you go through?

er, our *own* flesh." And his brothers listened
to him.

28 Then some Midianite traders passed by, so
they pulled *him* up and lifted Joseph out of the pit,
and sold him to the Ishmaelites for twenty *shekels*
of silver. Thus they brought Joseph into Egypt.

29 ¶ Now Reuben returned to the pit, and behold, Joseph was not in the pit; so he tore his
garments.

30 He returned to his brothers and said, "The
boy is not *there;* as for me, where am I to go?"

31 So they took Joseph's tunic, and slaughtered
a male goat and dipped the tunic in the blood;

32 and they sent the varicolored tunic and
brought it to their father and said, "We found this;
please examine *it* to *see* whether it is your son's
tunic or not."

33 Then he examined it and said, "It is my
son's tunic. A wild beast has devoured him; Joseph has surely been torn to pieces!"

34 So Jacob tore his clothes, and put sackcloth
on his loins and mourned for his son many days.

35 Then all his sons and all his daughters arose
to comfort him, but he refused to be comforted.
And he said, "Surely I will go down to Sheol in
mourning for my son." So his father wept for him.

36 Meanwhile, the Midianites sold him in
Egypt to Potiphar, Pharaoh's officer, the captain
of the bodyguard.

Judah and Tamar

38 And it came about at that time, that Judah
departed from his brothers and visited a
certain Adullamite, whose name was Hirah.

2 Judah saw there a daughter of a certain Canaanite whose name was Shua; and he took her
and went in to her.

3 So she conceived and bore a son and he
named him Er.

4 Then she conceived again and bore a son
and named him Onan.

5 She bore still another son and named him
Shelah; and it was at Chezib that she bore him.

6 ¶ Now Judah took a wife for Er his firstborn, and her name *was* Tamar.

7 But Er, Judah's firstborn, was evil in the
sight of the LORD, so the LORD took his life.

8 Then Judah said to Onan, "Go in to your
brother's wife, and perform your duty as a
brother-in-law to her, and raise up offspring for
your brother."

9 Onan knew that the offspring would not be
his; so when he went in to his brother's wife, he
wasted his seed on the ground in order not to give
offspring to his brother.

10 But what he did was displeasing in the sight
of the LORD; so He took his life also.

11 Then Judah said to his daughter-in-law Tamar, "Remain a widow in your father's house until
my son Shelah grows up"; for he thought, "*I am*

afraid that he too may die like his brothers." So
Tamar went and lived in her father's house.

12 ¶ Now after a considerable time Shua's
daughter, the wife of Judah, died; and when the

38:8 A Brother's Duty

*Having children was so important in Old
Testament times that if a man died childless,
his brother was required to sleep with his
widow in order to produce a family for him.
(The regulations are found in Deuteronomy
25:5–10.)*

*Onan's sin was a deliberate refusal to treat
his brother's widow fairly by giving her
children. Family quarrels had split Jacob and
Esau and had sent Jacob's son Joseph into
slavery; now the next generation was carrying
on in the same way.*

---

time of mourning was ended, Judah went up to his
sheepshearers at Timnah, he and his friend Hirah
the Adullamite.

13 It was told to Tamar, "Behold, your father-
in-law is going up to Timnah to shear his sheep."

14 So she removed her widow's garments and
covered *herself* with a ᵃveil, and wrapped herself,
and sat in the gateway of Enaim, which is on the
road to Timnah; for she saw that Shelah had
grown up, and she had not been given to him as
a wife.

15 When Judah saw her, he thought she *was* a
harlot, for she had covered her face.

16 So he turned aside to her by the road, and
said, "Here now, let me come in to you"; for he
did not know that she was his daughter-in-law.
And she said, "What will you give me, that you
may come in to me?"

17 He said, therefore, "I will send you a young
goat from the flock." She said, moreover, "Will
you give a pledge until you send *it?*"

18 He said, "What pledge shall I give you?"
And she said, "Your seal and your cord, and your
staff that is in your hand." So he gave *them* to her
and went in to her, and she conceived by him.

19 Then she arose and departed, and removed
her veil and put on her widow's garments.

20 ¶ When Judah sent the young goat by his
friend the Adullamite, to receive the pledge from
the woman's hand, he did not find her.

21 He asked the men of her place, saying,
"Where is the temple prostitute who was by the
road at Enaim?" But they said, "There has been no
temple prostitute here."

22 So he returned to Judah, and said, "I did not
find her; and furthermore, the men of the place
said, 'There has been no temple prostitute here.' "

23 Then Judah said, "Let her keep them, other-

ᵃ Or *shawl*

wise we will become a laughingstock. After all, I sent this young goat, but you did not find her."

24 ¶ Now it was about three months later that Judah was informed, "Your daughter-in-law Tamar has played the harlot, and behold, she is also with child by harlotry." Then Judah said, "Bring her out and let her be burned!"

25 It was while she was being brought out that she sent to her father-in-law, saying, "I am with child by the man to whom these things belong." And she said, "Please examine and see, whose signet ring and cords and staff are these?"

26 Judah recognized *them,* and said, "She is more righteous than I, inasmuch as I did not give her to my son Shelah." And he did not have relations with her again.

27 ¶ It came about at the time she was giving birth, that behold, there were twins in her womb.

28 Moreover, it took place while she was giving birth, one put out a hand, and the midwife took and tied a scarlet *thread* on his hand, saying, "This one came out first."

29 But it came about as he drew back his hand, that behold, his brother came out. Then she said, "What a breach you have made for yourself!" So he was named *a*Perez.

30 Afterward his brother came out who had the scarlet *thread* on his hand; and he was named *b*Zerah.

Joseph's Success in Egypt

39 Now Joseph had been taken down to Egypt; and Potiphar, an Egyptian officer of Pharaoh, the captain of the bodyguard, bought him from the Ishmaelites, who had taken him down there.

2 The LORD was with Joseph, so he became a successful man. And he was in the house of his master, the Egyptian.

3 Now his master saw that the LORD was with him and *how* the LORD caused all that he did to prosper in his hand.

4 So Joseph found favor in his sight and became his personal servant; and he made him overseer over his house, and all that he owned he put in his charge.

5 It came about that from the time he made him overseer in his house and over all that he owned, the LORD blessed the Egyptian's house on account of Joseph; thus the LORD'S blessing was upon all that he owned, in the house and in the field.

6 So he left everything he owned in Joseph's charge; and with him *there* he did not concern himself with anything except the food which he ate.

¶ Now Joseph was handsome in form and appearance.

7 It came about after these events that his master's wife looked with desire at Joseph, and she said, "Lie with me."

8 But he refused and said to his master's wife, "Behold, with me *here,* my master does not concern himself with anything in the house, and he has put all that he owns in my charge.

9 "There is no one greater in this house than I, and he has withheld nothing from me except you, because you are his wife. How then could I do this great evil and sin against God?"

10 As she spoke to Joseph day after day, he did not listen to her to lie beside her *or* be with her.

11 Now it happened one day that he went into the house to do his work, and none of the men of the household was there inside.

12 She caught him by his garment, saying, "Lie with me!" And he left his garment in her hand and fled, and went outside.

13 When she saw that he had left his garment in her hand and had fled outside,

14 she called to the men of her household and said to them, "See, he has brought in a Hebrew to us to make sport of us; he came in to me to lie with me, and I screamed.

15 "When he heard that I raised my voice and *c*screamed, he left his garment beside me and fled and went outside."

16 So she left his garment beside her until his master came home.

17 Then she spoke to him with these words, "The Hebrew slave, whom you brought to us, came in to me to make sport of me;

18 and as I raised my voice and screamed, he left his garment beside me and fled outside."

Joseph Imprisoned

19 ¶ Now when his master heard the words of his wife, which she spoke to him, saying, "This is what your slave did to me," his anger burned.

20 So Joseph's master took him and put him into the jail, the place where the king's prisoners were confined; and he was there in the jail.

21 But the LORD was with Joseph and extended kindness to him, and gave him favor in the sight of the chief jailer.

22 The chief jailer committed to Joseph's charge all the prisoners who were in the jail; so that whatever was done there, he was responsible *for it.*

23 The chief jailer did not supervise anything under Joseph's charge because the LORD was with him; and whatever he did, the LORD made to prosper.

Joseph Interprets a Dream

40 Then it came about after these things, the cupbearer and the baker for the king of Egypt offended their lord, the king of Egypt.

2 Pharaoh was furious with his two officials, the chief cupbearer and the chief baker.

---

a I.e. a breach   *b* I.e. a dawning or brightness   *c* Lit *called out*

3 So he put them in confinement in the house of the captain of the bodyguard, in the jail, the *same* place where Joseph was imprisoned.

4 The captain of the bodyguard put Joseph in

40:2 Important Officials

When Joseph was thrown into prison on a false charge, his future seemed to vanish. Yet in prison he came into contact with men who would eventually help raise him to the highest post in the nation. The "chief baker" and "chief cupbearer" were important officials in Pharaoh's court.

charge of them, and he took care of them; and they were in confinement for some time.

5 Then the cupbearer and the baker for the king of Egypt, who were confined in jail, both had a dream the same night, each man with his *own* dream *and* each dream with its *own* interpretation.

6 When Joseph came to them in the morning and observed them, behold, they were dejected.

7 He asked Pharaoh's officials who were with him in confinement in his master's house, "Why are your faces so sad today?"

8 Then they said to him, "We have had a dream and there is no one to interpret it." Then Joseph said to them, "Do not interpretations belong to God? Tell *it* to me, please."

9 ¶ So the chief cupbearer told his dream to Joseph, and said to him, "In my dream, behold, *there was* a vine in front of me;

10 and on the vine *were* three branches. And as it was budding, its blossoms came out, *and* its clusters produced ripe grapes.

11 "Now Pharaoh's cup was in my hand; so I took the grapes and squeezed them into Pharaoh's cup, and I put the cup into Pharaoh's hand."

12 Then Joseph said to him, "This is the interpretation of it: the three branches are three days;

13 within three more days Pharaoh will ªlift up your head and restore you to your office; and you will put Pharaoh's cup into his hand according to your former custom when you were his cupbearer.

14 "Only keep me in mind when it goes well with you, and please do me a kindness by mentioning me to Pharaoh and get me out of this house.

15 "For I was in fact kidnapped from the land of the Hebrews, and even here I have done nothing that they should have put me into the dungeon."

16 ¶ When the chief baker saw that he had interpreted favorably, he said to Joseph, "I also *saw* in my dream, and behold, *there were* three baskets of white bread on my head;

17 and in the top basket *there were* some of all sorts of baked food for Pharaoh, and the birds were eating them out of the basket on my head."

18 Then Joseph answered and said, "This is its interpretation: the three baskets are three days;

19 within three more days Pharaoh will lift up your head from you and will hang you on a tree, and the birds will eat your flesh off you."

20 ¶ Thus it came about on the third day, *which was* Pharaoh's birthday, that he made a feast for all his servants; and he lifted up the head of the chief cupbearer and the head of the chief baker among his servants.

21 He restored the chief cupbearer to his office, and he put the cup into Pharaoh's hand;

22 but he hanged the chief baker, just as Joseph had interpreted to them.

23 Yet the chief cupbearer did not remember Joseph, but forgot him.

40:23—41:13 A Forgotten Man

Joseph had carefully prepared the way for his release from prison (verses 14–15). Everything worked according to plan except for one detail: the chief cupbearer forgot all about Joseph. Humanly speaking, Joseph was a forgotten man, stuck in prison with no hope of ever getting out. God alone remembered his existence.

Pharaoh's Dream

41 Now it happened at the end of two full years that Pharaoh had a dream, and behold, he was standing by the Nile.

2 And lo, from the Nile there came up seven cows, sleek and fat; and they grazed in the marsh grass.

3 Then behold, seven other cows came up after them from the Nile, ugly and gaunt, and they stood by the *other* cows on the bank of the Nile.

4 The ugly and gaunt cows ate up the seven sleek and fat cows. Then Pharaoh awoke.

5 He fell asleep and dreamed a second time; and behold, seven ears of grain came up on a single stalk, plump and good.

6 Then behold, seven ears, thin and scorched by the east wind, sprouted up after them.

7 The thin ears swallowed up the seven plump and full ears. Then Pharaoh awoke, and behold, *it was* a dream.

8 Now in the morning his spirit was troubled, so he sent and called for all the magicians of Egypt, and all its wise men. And Pharaoh told them his dreams, but there was no one who could interpret them to Pharaoh.

9 ¶ Then the chief cupbearer spoke to Phar-

ª Or possibly *forgive you*

aoh, saying, "I would make mention today of my *own* offenses.

10 "Pharaoh was furious with his servants, and he put me in confinement in the house of the captain of the bodyguard, *both* me and the chief baker.

11 "We had a dream on the same night, he and I; each of us dreamed according to the interpretation of his *own* dream.

12 "Now a Hebrew youth *was* with us there, a servant of the captain of the bodyguard, and we related *them* to him, and he interpreted our dreams for us. To each one he interpreted according to his *own* dream.

13 "And just as he interpreted for us, so it happened; he restored me in my office, but he hanged him."

Joseph Interprets

14 ¶ Then Pharaoh sent and called for Joseph, and they hurriedly brought him out of the dungeon; and when he had shaved himself and changed his clothes, he came to Pharaoh.

15 Pharaoh said to Joseph, "I have had a dream, but no one can interpret it; and I have heard it said about you, that when you hear a dream you can interpret it."

16 Joseph then answered Pharaoh, saying, "It is not in me; God will give Pharaoh a favorable answer."

17 So Pharaoh spoke to Joseph, "In my dream, behold, I was standing on the bank of the Nile;

18 and behold, seven cows, fat and sleek came up out of the Nile, and they grazed in the marsh grass.

19 "Lo, seven other cows came up after them, poor and very ugly and gaunt, such as I had never seen for ugliness in all the land of Egypt;

20 and the lean and ugly cows ate up the first seven fat cows.

21 "Yet when they had devoured them, it could not be detected that they had devoured them, for they were just as ugly as before. Then I awoke.

22 "I saw also in my dream, and behold, seven ears, full and good, came up on a single stalk;

23 and lo, seven ears, withered, thin, *and* scorched by the east wind, sprouted up after them;

24 and the thin ears swallowed the seven good ears. Then I told it to the magicians, but there was no one who could explain it to me."

25 ¶ Now Joseph said to Pharaoh, "Pharaoh's dreams are one *and the same;* God has told to Pharaoh what He is about to do.

26 "The seven good cows are seven years; and the seven good ears are seven years; the dreams are one *and the same.*

27 "The seven lean and ugly cows that came up after them are seven years, and the seven thin ears scorched by the east wind will be seven years of famine.

28 "It is as I have spoken to Pharaoh: God has shown to Pharaoh what He is about to do.

29 "Behold, seven years of great abundance are coming in all the land of Egypt;

30 and after them seven years of famine will come, and all the abundance will be forgotten in the land of Egypt, and the famine will ravage the land.

31 "So the abundance will be unknown in the land because of that subsequent famine; for it *will be* very severe.

32 "Now as for the repeating of the dream to Pharaoh twice, *it means* that the matter is determined by God, and God will quickly bring it about.

33 "Now let Pharaoh look for a man discerning and wise, and set him over the land of Egypt.

34 "Let Pharaoh take action to appoint overseers in charge of the land, and let him exact a fifth *of the produce* of the land of Egypt in the seven years of abundance.

35 "Then let them gather all the food of these good years that are coming, and store up the grain for food in the cities under Pharaoh's authority, and let them guard *it.*

36 "Let the food become as a reserve for the land for the seven years of famine which will occur in the land of Egypt, so that the land will not perish during the famine."

37 ¶ Now the proposal seemed good to Pharaoh and to all his servants.

Joseph Is Made a Ruler of Egypt

38 Then Pharaoh said to his servants, "Can we find a man like this, in whom is a divine spirit?"

39 So Pharaoh said to Joseph, "Since God has informed you of all this, there is no one so discerning and wise as you are.

40 "You shall be over my house, and according to your command all my people shall do homage; only in the throne I will be greater than you."

41 Pharaoh said to Joseph, "See, I have set you over all the land of Egypt."

42 Then Pharaoh took off his signet ring from his hand and put it on Joseph's hand, and clothed him in garments of fine linen and put the gold necklace around his neck.

43 He had him ride in his second chariot; and they proclaimed before him, "Bow the knee!" And he set him over all the land of Egypt.

44 Moreover, Pharaoh said to Joseph, "*Though* I am Pharaoh, yet without your permission no one shall raise his hand or foot in all the land of Egypt."

45 Then Pharaoh named Joseph *a*Zaphenath-paneah; and he gave him Asenath, the daughter of Potiphera priest of On, as his wife. And Joseph went forth over the land of Egypt.

46 ¶ Now Joseph was thirty years old when he *b*stood before Pharaoh, king of Egypt. And Jo-

---

a Probably Egyptian for "God speaks; he lives"   *b* Or *entered the service of* seph went out from the presence of Pharaoh and went through all the land of Egypt.

47 During the seven years of plenty the land brought forth abundantly.

41:45 Erasing Joseph's Past

Proud Egyptians did not care for Hebrews. In order that Joseph's ethnic past be erased as quickly as possible, Pharaoh gave Joseph an Egyptian name and married him into a prominent Egyptian family. Joseph gave his own sons Hebrew names, however, a practice that suggests he maintained his own identity.

48 So he gathered all the food of *these* seven years which occurred in the land of Egypt and placed the food in the cities; he placed in every city the food from its own surrounding fields.

49 Thus Joseph stored up grain in great abundance like the sand of the sea, until he stopped measuring *it,* for it was beyond measure.

The Sons of Joseph

50 ¶ Now before the year of famine came, two sons were born to Joseph, whom Asenath, the daughter of Potiphera priest of [a]On, bore to him.

51 Joseph named the firstborn [b]Manasseh, "For," *he said,* "God has made me forget all my trouble and all my father's household."

52 He named the second [c]Ephraim, "For," *he said,* "God has made me fruitful in the land of my affliction."

53 ¶ When the seven years of plenty which had been in the land of Egypt came to an end,

54 and the seven years of famine began to come, just as Joseph had said, then there was famine in all the lands, but in all the land of Egypt there was bread.

55 So when all the land of Egypt was famished, the people cried out to Pharaoh for bread; and Pharaoh said to all the Egyptians, "Go to Joseph; whatever he says to you, you shall do."

56 When the famine was *spread* over all the face of the earth, then Joseph opened all the storehouses, and sold to the Egyptians; and the famine was severe in the land of Egypt.

57 *The people of* all the earth came to Egypt to buy grain from Joseph, because the famine was severe in all the earth.

Joseph's Brothers Sent to Egypt

42 Now Jacob saw that there was grain in Egypt, and Jacob said to his sons, "Why are you staring at one another?"

2 He said, "Behold, I have heard that there is grain in Egypt; go down there and buy *some* for us from that place, so that we may live and not die."

3 Then ten brothers of Joseph went down to buy grain from Egypt.

4 But Jacob did not send Joseph's brother Benjamin with his brothers, for he said, "I am afraid that harm may befall him."

41:56 An Unusual Famine

Famine is common in the Middle East. There are records of two Egyptian famines so severe that starving people killed and ate each other. But it was rare for famine to affect both Egypt and Palestine at the same time, for they depended on totally different sources of water—Egypt on the Nile and Palestine on local rainfall.

5 So the sons of Israel came to buy grain among those who were coming, for the famine was in the land of Canaan *also.*

6 ¶ Now Joseph was the ruler over the land; he was the one who sold to all the people of the land. And Joseph's brothers came and bowed down to him with *their* faces to the ground.

7 When Joseph saw his brothers he recognized them, but he disguised himself to them and spoke to them harshly. And he said to them, "Where have you come from?" And they said, "From the land of Canaan, to buy food."

8 ¶ But Joseph had recognized his brothers, although they did not recognize him.

9 Joseph remembered the dreams which he had about them, and said to them, "You are spies; you have come to look at the undefended parts of our land."

10 Then they said to him, "No, my lord, but your servants have come to buy food.

11 "We are all sons of one man; we are honest men, your servants are not spies."

12 Yet he said to them, "No, but you have come to look at the undefended parts of our land!"

13 But they said, "Your servants are twelve brothers *in all,* the sons of one man in the land of Canaan; and behold, the youngest is with our father today, and one is no longer alive."

14 Joseph said to them, "It is as I said to you, you are spies;

15 by this you will be tested: by the life of Pharaoh, you shall not go from this place unless your youngest brother comes here!

16 "Send one of you that he may get your brother, while you remain confined, that your words may be tested, whether there is truth in you. But if not, by the life of Pharaoh, surely you are spies."

17 So he put them all together in prison for three days.

---

[a] Or *Heliopolis*   [b] I.e. making to forget   [c] I.e. fruitfulness

18 ¶ Now Joseph said to them on the third day, "Do this and live, for I fear God:

19 if you are honest men, let one of your brothers be confined in your prison; but as for *the rest of* you, go, carry grain for the famine of your households,

20 and bring your youngest brother to me, so your words may be verified, and you will not die." And they did so.

21 Then they said to one another, "Truly we are guilty concerning our brother, because we saw the distress of his soul when he pleaded with us, yet we would not listen; therefore this distress has come upon us."

22 Reuben answered them, saying, "Did I not tell you, 'Do not sin against the boy'; and you would not listen? Now comes the reckoning for his blood."

23 They did not know, however, that Joseph understood, for there was an interpreter between them.

24 He turned away from them and wept. But when he returned to them and spoke to them, he took Simeon from them and bound him before their eyes.

42:24 Joseph in Tears

Five times Genesis tells about Joseph weeping as he dealt with his brothers (43:30; 45:2,14–15; 50:17). They had sold him into slavery, and all those years had not erased his hurt and anger. Yet he loved his brothers, and wanted to be reconciled. He felt his conflicting emotions intensely: love versus anger, forgiveness versus bitterness.

25 Then Joseph gave orders to fill their bags with grain and to restore every man's money in his sack, and to give them provisions for the journey. And thus it was done for them.

26 ¶ So they loaded their donkeys with their grain and departed from there.

27 As one *of them* opened his sack to give his donkey fodder at the lodging place, he saw his money; and behold, it was in the mouth of his sack.

28 Then he said to his brothers, "My money has been returned, and behold, it is even in my sack." And their hearts sank, and they *turned* trembling to one another, saying, "What is this that God has done to us?"

Simeon Is Held Hostage

29 ¶ When they came to their father Jacob in the land of Canaan, they told him all that had happened to them, saying,

30 "The man, the lord of the land, spoke harshly with us, and took us for spies of the country.

31 "But we said to him, 'We are honest men; we are not spies.

32 'We are twelve brothers, sons of our father; one is no longer alive, and the youngest is with our father today in the land of Canaan.'

33 "The man, the lord of the land, said to us, 'By this I will know that you are honest men: leave one of your brothers with me and take *grain for* the famine of your households, and go.

34 'But bring your youngest brother to me that I may know that you are not spies, but honest men. I will give your brother to you, and you may trade in the land.' "

35 ¶ Now it came about as they were emptying their sacks, that behold, every man's bundle of money *was* in his sack; and when they and their father saw their bundles of money, they were dismayed.

36 Their father Jacob said to them, "You have bereaved me of my children: Joseph is no more, and Simeon is no more, and you would take Benjamin; all these things are against me."

37 Then Reuben spoke to his father, saying, "You may put my two sons to death if I do not bring him *back* to you; put him in my care, and I will return him to you."

38 But Jacob said, "My son shall not go down with you; for his brother is dead, and he alone is left. If harm should befall him on the journey you are taking, then you will bring my gray hair down to Sheol in sorrow."

The Return to Egypt

43 Now the famine was severe in the land.

2 So it came about when they had finished eating the grain which they had brought from Egypt, that their father said to them, "Go back, buy us a little food."

3 Judah spoke to him, however, saying, "The man solemnly warned us, 'You shall not see my face unless your brother is with you.'

4 "If you send our brother with us, we will go down and buy you food.

5 "But if you do not send *him,* we will not go down; for the man said to us, 'You will not see my face unless your brother is with you.' "

6 Then Israel said, "Why did you treat me so badly by telling the man whether you still had *another* brother?"

7 But they said, "The man questioned particularly about us and our relatives, saying, 'Is your father still alive? Have you *another* brother?' So we answered his questions. Could we possibly know that he would say, 'Bring your brother down'?"

8 Judah said to his father Israel, "Send the lad with me and we will arise and go, that we may live and not die, we as well as you and our little ones.

9 "I myself will be surety for him; you may hold me responsible for him. If I do not bring him *back* to you and set him before you, then let me bear the blame before you forever.

10 "For if we had not delayed, surely by now we could have returned twice."

11 ¶ Then their father Israel said to them, "If *it must be* so, then do this: take some of the best products of the land in your bags, and carry down to the man as a present, a little balm and a little honey, aromatic gum and myrrh, pistachio nuts and almonds.

43:11 The Perfect Gift

What kind of gift can you send to a man who has everything? Egypt was among the richest and most sophisticated countries in the world, and Israel (Jacob), a desert nomad. He wisely chose simple gifts of local produce—things that might not be available in Egypt.

12 "Take double *the* money in your hand, and take back in your hand the money that was returned in the mouth of your sacks; perhaps it was a mistake.

13 "Take your brother also, and arise, return to the man;

14 and may God Almighty grant you compassion in the sight of the man, so that he will release to you your other brother and Benjamin. And as for me, if I am bereaved of my children, I am bereaved."

15 So the men took this present, and they took double *the* money in their hand, and Benjamin; then they arose and went down to Egypt and stood before Joseph.

Joseph Sees Benjamin

16 ¶ When Joseph saw Benjamin with them, he said to his house steward, "Bring the men into the house, and slay an animal and make ready; for the men are to dine with me at noon."

17 So the man did as Joseph said, and brought the men to Joseph's house.

18 Now the men were afraid, because they were brought to Joseph's house; and they said, "*It is* because of the money that was returned in our sacks the first time that we are being brought in, that he may seek occasion against us and fall upon us, and take us for slaves with our donkeys."

19 So they came near to Joseph's house steward, and spoke to him at the entrance of the house,

20 and said, "Oh, my lord, we indeed came down the first time to buy food,

21 and it came about when we came to the lodging place, that we opened our sacks, and behold, each man's money was in the mouth of his sack, our money in full. So we have brought it back in our hand.

22 "We have also brought down other money in our hand to buy food; we do not know who put our money in our sacks."

23 He said, "*a*Be at ease, do not be afraid. Your God and the God of your father has given you treasure in your sacks; I had your money." Then he brought Simeon out to them.

24 Then the man brought the men into Joseph's house and gave them water, and they washed their feet; and he gave their donkeys fodder.

25 So they prepared the present for Joseph's coming at noon; for they had heard that they were to eat a meal there.

26 ¶ When Joseph came home, they brought into the house to him the present which was in their hand and bowed to the ground before him.

27 Then he asked them about their welfare, and said, "Is your old father well, of whom you spoke? Is he still alive?"

28 They said, "Your servant our father is well; he is still alive." They bowed down in homage.

29 As he lifted his eyes and saw his brother Benjamin, his mother's son, he said, "Is this your youngest brother, of whom you spoke to me?" And he said, "May God be gracious to you, my son."

30 Joseph hurried *out* for he was deeply stirred over his brother, and he sought *a place* to weep; and he entered his chamber and wept there.

31 Then he washed his face and came out; and he controlled himself and said, "Serve the meal."

32 So they served him by himself, and them by themselves, and the Egyptians who ate with him by themselves, because the Egyptians could not eat bread with the Hebrews, for that is loathsome to the Egyptians.

43:32 Prejudice

Despite his high rank, Joseph still fell victim to Egyptian prejudice: they would not eat at the same table with a Hebrew. Chapter 46 (verses 33–34) adds that Egyptians loathed shepherds—and Hebrews herded sheep.

33 Now they were seated before him, the first-born according to his birthright and the youngest according to his youth, and the men looked at one another in astonishment.

34 He took portions to them from his own table, but Benjamin's portion was five times as much as any of theirs. So they feasted and drank freely with him.

The Brothers Are Brought Back

44 Then he commanded his house steward, saying, "Fill the men's sacks with food, as

a Lit *Peace be to you*

much as they can carry, and put each man's money in the mouth of his sack.

2 "Put my cup, the silver cup, in the mouth of the sack of the youngest, and his money for the grain." And he did as Joseph had told *him.*

3 As soon as it was light, the men were sent away, they with their donkeys.

4 They had *just* gone out of the city, *and* were not far off, when Joseph said to his house steward, "Up, follow the men; and when you overtake them, say to them, 'Why have you repaid evil for good?

5 'Is not this the one from which my lord drinks and which he indeed uses for divination? You have done wrong in doing this.'"

6 ¶ So he overtook them and spoke these words to them.

7 They said to him, "Why does my lord speak such words as these? Far be it from your servants to do such a thing.

8 "Behold, the money which we found in the mouth of our sacks we have brought back to you from the land of Canaan. How then could we steal silver or gold from your lord's house?

9 "With whomever of your servants it is found, let him die, and we also will be my lord's slaves."

10 So he said, "Now let it also be according to your words; he with whom it is found shall be my slave, and *the rest of* you shall be innocent."

11 Then they hurried, each man lowered his sack to the ground, and each man opened his sack.

12 He searched, beginning with the oldest and ending with the youngest, and the cup was found in Benjamin's sack.

13 Then they tore their clothes, and when each man loaded his donkey, they returned to the city.

14 ¶ When Judah and his brothers came to Joseph's house, he was still there, and they fell to the ground before him.

15 Joseph said to them, "What is this deed that you have done? Do you not know that such a man as I can indeed practice divination?"

16 So Judah said, "What can we say to my lord? What can we speak? And how can we justify ourselves? God has found out the iniquity of your servants; behold, we are my lord's slaves, both we and the one in whose possession the cup has been found."

17 But he said, "Far be it from me to do this. The man in whose possession the cup has been found, he shall be my slave; but as for you, go up in peace to your father."

18 ¶ Then Judah approached him, and said, "Oh my lord, may your servant please speak a word in my lord's ears, and do not be angry with your servant; for you are equal to Pharaoh.

19 "My lord asked his servants, saying, 'Have you a father or a brother?'

20 "We said to my lord, 'We have an old father and a little child of *his* old age. Now his brother is dead, so he alone is left of his mother, and his father loves him.'

21 "Then you said to your servants, 'Bring him down to me that I may set my eyes on him.'

22 "But we said to my lord, 'The lad cannot leave his father, for if he should leave his father, his father would die.'

23 "You said to your servants, however, 'Unless your youngest brother comes down with you, you will not see my face again.'

24 "Thus it came about when we went up to your servant my father, we told him the words of my lord.

25 "Our father said, 'Go back, buy us a little food.'

26 "But we said, 'We cannot go down. If our youngest brother is with us, then we will go down; for we cannot see the man's face unless our youngest brother is with us.'

27 "Your servant my father said to us, 'You know that my wife bore me two sons;

28 and the one went out from me, and I said, "Surely he is torn in pieces," and I have not seen him since.

29 'If you take this one also from me, and harm befalls him, you will bring my gray hair down to Sheol in sorrow.'

30 "Now, therefore, when I come to your servant my father, and the lad is not with us, since his life is bound up in the lad's life,

31 when he sees that the lad is not *with us,* he will die. Thus your servants will bring the gray hair of your servant our father down to Sheol in sorrow.

32 "For your servant became surety for the lad to my father, saying, 'If I do not bring him *back* to you, then let me bear the blame before my father forever.'

33 "Now, therefore, please let your servant remain instead of the lad a slave to my lord, and let the lad go up with his brothers.

34 "For how shall I go up to my father if the lad is not with me—for fear that I see the evil that would overtake my father?"

Joseph Deals Kindly with His Brothers

45 Then Joseph could not control himself before all those who stood by him, and he cried, "Have everyone go out from me." So there was no man with him when Joseph made himself known to his brothers.

2 He wept so loudly that the Egyptians heard *it,* and the household of Pharaoh heard *of it.*

3 Then Joseph said to his brothers, "I am Joseph! Is my father still alive?" But his brothers could not answer him, for they were dismayed at his presence.

4 ¶ Then Joseph said to his brothers, "Please come closer to me." And they came closer. And he said, "I am your brother Joseph, whom you sold into Egypt.

5 "Now do not be grieved or angry with your-selves, because you sold me here, for God sent me before you to preserve life.

6 "For the famine *has been* in the land these

45:2 Weeping and Terror

This is one of the Bible's most intensely emotional scenes: it shows Joseph weeping so loudly people heard it in the next room, and Joseph's brothers speechless with terror and guilt. Though the moment ended with embraces and kissing (verses 14–15), years later the brothers were still afraid of revenge (50:15).

two years, and there are still five years in which there will be neither plowing nor harvesting.

7 "God sent me before you to preserve for you a remnant in the earth, and to keep you alive by a great deliverance.

8 "Now, therefore, it was not you who sent me here, but God; and He has made me a father to Pharaoh and lord of all his household and ruler over all the land of Egypt.

9 "Hurry and go up to my father, and say to him, 'Thus says your son Joseph, "God has made me lord of all Egypt; come down to me, do not delay.

10 "You shall live in the land of Goshen, and you shall be near me, you and your children and your children's children and your flocks and your herds and all that you have.

11 "There I will also provide for you, for there are still five years of famine *to come,* and you and your household and all that you have would be impoverished." '

12 "Behold, your eyes see, and the eyes of my brother Benjamin *see,* that it is my mouth which is speaking to you.

13 "Now you must tell my father of all my splendor in Egypt, and all that you have seen; and you must hurry and bring my father down here."

14 Then he fell on his brother Benjamin's neck and wept, and Benjamin wept on his neck.

15 He kissed all his brothers and wept on them, and afterward his brothers talked with him.

16 ¶ Now when the news was heard in Phar-aoh's house that Joseph's brothers had come, it pleased Pharaoh and his servants.

17 Then Pharaoh said to Joseph, "Say to your brothers, 'Do this: load your beasts and go to the land of Canaan,

18 and take your father and your households and come to me, and I will give you the best of the land of Egypt and you will eat the fat of the land.'

19 "Now you are ordered, 'Do this: take wagons from the land of Egypt for your little ones and for your wives, and bring your father and come.

20 'Do not concern yourselves with your goods, for the best of all the land of Egypt is yours.' "

21 ¶ Then the sons of Israel did so; and Joseph gave them wagons according to the command of Pharaoh, and gave them provisions for the jour-ney.

22 To each of them he gave changes of gar-ments, but to Benjamin he gave three hundred *pieces of* silver and five changes of garments.

23 To his father he sent as follows: ten donkeys loaded with the best things of Egypt, and ten fe-male donkeys loaded with grain and bread and sustenance for his father on the journey.

24 ¶ So he sent his brothers away, and as they departed, he said to them, "Do not quarrel on the journey."

25 Then they went up from Egypt, and came to the land of Canaan to their father Jacob.

26 They told him, saying, "Joseph is still alive, and indeed he is ruler over all the land of Egypt." But he was stunned, for he did not believe them.

27 When they told him all the words of Joseph that he had spoken to them, and when he saw the wagons that Joseph had sent to carry him, the spirit of their father Jacob revived.

28 Then Israel said, "It is enough; my son Jo-seph is still alive. I will go and see him before I die."

Jacob Moves to Egypt

46 So Israel set out with all that he had, and came to Beersheba, and offered sacrifices to the God of his father Isaac.

2 God spoke to Israel in visions of the night and said, "Jacob, Jacob." And he said, "Here I am."

3 He said, "I am God, the God of your father; do not be afraid to go down to Egypt, for I will make you a great nation there.

4 "I will go down with you to Egypt, and I will also surely bring you up again; and Joseph will close your eyes."

5 ¶ Then Jacob arose from Beersheba; and the sons of Israel carried their father Jacob and their little ones and their wives in the wagons which Pharaoh had sent to carry him.

6 They took their livestock and their property, which they had acquired in the land of Canaan, and came to Egypt, Jacob and all his descendants with him:

7 his sons and his grandsons with him, his daughters and his granddaughters, and all his descendants he brought with him to Egypt.

Those Who Came to Egypt

8 ¶ Now these are the names of the sons of Israel, Jacob and his sons, who went to Egypt: Reuben, Jacob's firstborn.

9 The sons of Reuben: Hanoch and Pallu and Hezron and Carmi.

10 The sons of Simeon: Jemuel and Jamin and

Ohad and Jachin and Zohar and Shaul the son of a Canaanite woman.

11 The sons of Levi: Gershon, Kohath, and Merari.

12 The sons of Judah: Er and Onan and Shelah and Perez and Zerah (but Er and Onan died in the land of Canaan). And the sons of Perez were Hezron and Hamul.

13 The sons of Issachar: Tola and Puvvah and Iob and Shimron.

14 The sons of Zebulun: Sered and Elon and Jahleel.

15 These are the sons of Leah, whom she bore to Jacob in Paddan-aram, with his daughter Dinah; all his sons and his daughters *numbered* thirty-three.

16 The sons of Gad: Ziphion and Haggi, Shuni and Ezbon, Eri and Arodi and Areli.

17 The sons of Asher: Imnah and Ishvah and Ishvi and Beriah and their sister Serah. And the sons of Beriah: Heber and Malchiel.

18 These are the sons of Zilpah, whom Laban gave to his daughter Leah; and she bore to Jacob these sixteen persons.

19 The sons of Jacob's wife Rachel: Joseph and Benjamin.

20 Now to Joseph in the land of Egypt were born Manasseh and Ephraim, whom Asenath, the daughter of Potiphera, priest of On, bore to him.

21 The sons of Benjamin: Bela and Becher and Ashbel, Gera and Naaman, Ehi and Rosh, Muppim and Huppim and Ard.

22 These are the sons of Rachel, who were born to Jacob; *there were* fourteen persons in all.

23 The sons of Dan: Hushim.

24 The sons of Naphtali: Jahzeel and Guni and Jezer and Shillem.

25 These are the sons of Bilhah, whom Laban gave to his daughter Rachel, and she bore these to Jacob; *there were* seven persons in all.

26 All the persons belonging to Jacob, who came to Egypt, his direct descendants, not including the wives of Jacob's sons, *were* sixty-six persons in all,

27 and the sons of Joseph, who were born to him in Egypt were two; all the persons of the house of Jacob, who came to Egypt, *were* seventy.

28 ¶ Now he sent Judah before him to Joseph, to point out *the way* before him to Goshen; and they came into the land of Goshen.

29 Joseph prepared his chariot and went up to Goshen to meet his father Israel; as soon as he appeared before him, he fell on his neck and wept on his neck a long time.

30 Then Israel said to Joseph, "Now let me die, since I have seen your face, that you are still alive."

31 Joseph said to his brothers and to his father's household, "I will go up and tell Pharaoh, and will say to him, 'My brothers and my father's

household, who *were* in the land of Canaan, have come to me;

32 and the men are shepherds, for they have been keepers of livestock; and they have brought their flocks and their herds and all that they have.'

33 "When Pharaoh calls you and says, 'What is your occupation?'

34 you shall say, 'Your servants have been keepers of livestock from our youth even until now, both we and our fathers,' that you may live in the land of Goshen; for every shepherd is loathsome to the Egyptians."

Jacob's Family Settles in Goshen

47 Then Joseph went in and told Pharaoh, and said, "My father and my brothers and their flocks and their herds and all that they have, have come out of the land of Canaan; and behold, they are in the land of Goshen."

2 He took five men from among his brothers and presented them to Pharaoh.

3 Then Pharaoh said to his brothers, "What is your occupation?" So they said to Pharaoh, "Your servants are shepherds, both we and our fathers."

4 They said to Pharaoh, "We have come to sojourn in the land, for there is no pasture for your servants' flocks, for the famine is severe in the land of Canaan. Now, therefore, please let your servants live in the land of Goshen."

5 Then Pharaoh said to Joseph, "Your father and your brothers have come to you.

6 "The land of Egypt is *a*at your disposal; settle your father and your brothers in the best of the land, let them live in the land of Goshen; and if you know any capable men among them, then put them in charge of my livestock."

7 ¶ Then Joseph brought his father Jacob and presented him to Pharaoh; and Jacob blessed Pharaoh.

8 Pharaoh said to Jacob, "How many years have you lived?"

9 So Jacob said to Pharaoh, "The years of my sojourning are one hundred and thirty; few and unpleasant have been the years of my life, nor have they attained the years that my fathers lived during the days of their sojourning."

10 And Jacob blessed Pharaoh, and went out from his presence.

11 So Joseph settled his father and his brothers and gave them a possession in the land of Egypt, in the best of the land, in the land of Rameses, as Pharaoh had ordered.

12 Joseph provided his father and his brothers and all his father's household with food, according to their little ones.

13 ¶ Now there was no food in all the land, because the famine was very severe, so that the land of Egypt and the land of Canaan languished because of the famine.

14 Joseph gathered all the money that was

a Lit *before you*

found in the land of Egypt and in the land of Canaan for the grain which they bought, and Joseph brought the money into Pharaoh's house.

15 When the money was all spent in the land of Egypt and in the land of Canaan, all the Egyptians came to Joseph and said, "Give us food, for why should we die in your presence? For *our* money is gone."

16 Then Joseph said, "Give up your livestock, and I will give you *food* for your livestock, since *your* money is gone."

17 So they brought their livestock to Joseph, and Joseph gave them food in exchange for the horses and the flocks and the herds and the donkeys; and he fed them with food in exchange for all their livestock that year.

18 When that year was ended, they came to him the next year and said to him, "We will not hide from my lord that our money is all spent, and the cattle are my lord's. There is nothing left for my lord except our bodies and our lands.

19 "Why should we die before your eyes, both we and our land? Buy us and our land for food, and we and our land will be slaves to Pharaoh. So give us seed, that we may live and not die, and that the land may not be desolate."

Result of the Famine

20 ¶ So Joseph bought all the land of Egypt for Pharaoh, for every Egyptian sold his field, because the famine was severe upon them. Thus the land became Pharaoh's.

21 As for the people, he removed them to the cities from one end of Egypt's border to the other.

22 Only the land of the priests he did not buy, for the priests had an allotment from Pharaoh, and they lived off the allotment which Pharaoh gave them. Therefore, they did not sell their land.

23 Then Joseph said to the people, "Behold, I have today bought you and your land for Pharaoh; now, *here* is seed for you, and you may sow the land.

24 "At the harvest you shall give a fifth to Pharaoh, and four-fifths shall be your own for seed of the field and for your food and for those of your households and as food for your little ones."

25 So they said, "You have saved our lives! Let us find favor in the sight of my lord, and we will be Pharaoh's slaves."

26 Joseph made it a statute concerning the land of Egypt *valid* to this day, that Pharaoh should have the fifth; only the land of the priests did not become Pharaoh's.

27 ¶ Now Israel lived in the land of Egypt, in Goshen, and they acquired property in it and were fruitful and became very numerous.

28 Jacob lived in the land of Egypt seventeen years; so the length of Jacob's life was one hundred and forty-seven years.

29 ¶ When the time for Israel to die drew near, he called his son Joseph and said to him, "Please, if I have found favor in your sight, place now your hand under my thigh and deal with me in kindness and [a]faithfulness. Please do not bury me in Egypt,

30 but when I lie down with my fathers, you shall carry me out of Egypt and bury me in their burial place." And he said, "I will do as you have said."

31 He said, "Swear to me." So he swore to him.

[a] Lit *truth*

JOSEPH   *School of Hard Knocks*

JOSEPH WAS A SPOILED BRAT, favored by his father over ten older brothers. He got the fancy clothes and preferential treatment and apparently thought he deserved them. When he had a dream of his brothers bowing down to him, he had the gall to tell them all about it.

What could make such a boy grow up? In Joseph's case, maturity came only through calamity. His resentful brothers threatened to kill him, then sold him to slave-traders. As a slave he resisted sexual temptation, and for his troubles was accused of rape and thrown into prison. Basically, the bottom fell out of Joseph's life.

Yet the man emerged with a wholly different character than the boy. Summoned before Pharaoh on a whim, Joseph the prisoner behaved with confidence and tact. Pharaoh gave him a huge government program to administer, and he carried out his tasks with tremendous skill.

Most remarkably, Joseph resisted the chance to get even. When his brothers fell into his hands, he struggled to forgive them rather than paying them back for their actions. In a time of famine, he saved his brothers—and his entire extended family—by bringing them down to Egypt to live with him.

Joseph's story shows how struggles and disappointments can turn out for good. They resulted in good for Joseph's family, who was able to escape a terrible famine. And they resulted in good for Joseph, who gained a whole new perspective on life. Looking back, he could see God at work even in all the trials he had experienced.

Life Questions: What struggles have you gone through? Can you see some positive effects on your personality as a result of these struggles?

Then Israel bowed *in worship* at the head of the bed.

Israel's Last Days

48 Now it came about after these things that Joseph was told, "Behold, your father is sick." So he took his two sons Manasseh and Ephraim with him.

2 When it was told to Jacob, "Behold, your son Joseph has come to you," Israel collected his strength and sat up in the bed.

3 Then Jacob said to Joseph, "God Almighty appeared to me at Luz in the land of Canaan and blessed me,

4 and He said to me, 'Behold, I will make you fruitful and numerous, and I will make you a company of peoples, and will give this land to your descendants after you for an everlasting possession.'

5 "Now your two sons, who were born to you in the land of Egypt before I came to you in Egypt, are mine; Ephraim and Manasseh shall be mine, as Reuben and Simeon are.

6 "But your offspring that have been born after them shall be yours; they shall be called by the names of their brothers in their inheritance.

7 "Now as for me, when I came from Paddan, Rachel died, to my sorrow, in the land of Canaan on the journey, when there was still some distance to go to Ephrath; and I buried her there on the way to Ephrath (that is, Bethlehem)."

8 ¶ When Israel saw Joseph's sons, he said, "Who are these?"

9 Joseph said to his father, "They are my sons, whom God has given me here." So he said, "Bring them to me, please, that I may bless them."

10 Now the eyes of Israel were *so* dim from age *that* he could not see. Then Joseph brought them close to him, and he kissed them and embraced them.

11 Israel said to Joseph, "I never expected to see your face, and behold, God has let me see your children as well."

12 Then Joseph took them from his knees, and bowed with his face to the ground.

13 Joseph took them both, Ephraim with his right hand toward Israel's left, and Manasseh with his left hand toward Israel's right, and brought them close to him.

14 But Israel stretched out his right hand and laid it on the head of Ephraim, who was the younger, and his left hand on Manasseh's head, crossing his hands, although Manasseh was the firstborn.

15 He blessed Joseph, and said,
"The God before whom my fathers
   Abraham and Isaac walked,
The God who has been my shepherd all
   my life to this day,
16 The angel who has redeemed me from all
   evil,

Bless the lads;
And may my name live on in them,
And the names of my fathers Abraham
   and Isaac;

48:14–20 The Younger Brother

Jacob gave his firstborn blessings to the younger of Joseph's boys, just as had been done for Isaac over Ishmael, for Jacob over Esau, and for Joseph over Reuben. In adopting both Manasseh and Ephraim as his own sons, Jacob was also giving Joseph's family a double share in the inheritance—these two grandsons would each receive a full share along with Jacob's other 11 sons. The "12 tribes" of Israel were the offspring of Jacob's sons; substituting Manasseh and Ephraim for Joseph made a total of 13.

And may they grow into a multitude in
   the midst of the earth."

17 ¶ When Joseph saw that his father laid his right hand on Ephraim's head, it displeased him; and he grasped his father's hand to remove it from Ephraim's head to Manasseh's head.

18 Joseph said to his father, "Not so, my father, for this one is the firstborn. Place your right hand on his head."

19 But his father refused and said, "I know, my son, I know; he also will become a people and he also will be great. However, his younger brother shall be greater than he, and his descendants shall become a multitude of nations."

20 He blessed them that day, saying,
"By you Israel will pronounce blessing,
   saying,
'May God make you like Ephraim and
   Manasseh!'"
Thus he put Ephraim before Manasseh.

21 Then Israel said to Joseph, "Behold, I am about to die, but God will be with you, and bring you back to the land of your fathers.

22 "I give you one portion more than your brothers, which I took from the hand of the Amorite with my sword and my bow."

Israel's Prophecy concerning His Sons

49 Then Jacob summoned his sons and said, "Assemble yourselves that I may tell you what will befall you in the days to come.

2 "Gather together and hear, O sons of
   Jacob;
And listen to Israel your father.

3 ¶ "Reuben, you are my firstborn;
My might and the beginning of my
   strength,
Preeminent in dignity and preeminent in
   power.

4 "Uncontrolled as water, you shall not have
preeminence,
Because you went up to your father's
bed;
Then you defiled *it*—he went up to my
couch.

5 ¶ "Simeon and Levi are brothers;
Their swords are implements of violence.
6 "Let my soul not enter into their council;
Let not my glory be united with their
assembly;
Because in their anger they slew men,
And in their self-will they lamed oxen.
7 "Cursed be their anger, for it is fierce;
And their wrath, for it is cruel.
I will disperse them in Jacob,
And scatter them in Israel.

8 ¶ "Judah, your brothers shall praise you;
Your hand shall be on the neck of your
enemies;
Your father's sons shall bow down to
you.
9 "Judah is a lion's whelp;
From the prey, my son, you have
gone up.
He couches, he lies down as a lion,
And as a lion, who dares rouse him up?
10 "The scepter shall not depart from Judah,
Nor the ruler's staff from between his
feet,
*a*Until Shiloh comes,
And to him *shall be* the obedience of the
peoples.
11 "He ties *his* foal to the vine,
And his donkey's colt to the choice vine;
He washes his garments in wine,
And his robes in the blood of grapes.
12 "His eyes are *b*dull from wine,
And his teeth *c*white from milk.

13 ¶ "Zebulun will dwell at the seashore;
And he *shall be* a haven for ships,
And his flank *shall be* toward Sidon.

14 ¶ "Issachar is a strong donkey,
Lying down between the sheepfolds.
15 "When he saw that a resting place was
good
And that the land was pleasant,
He bowed his shoulder to bear *burdens*,
And became a slave at forced labor.

16 ¶ "Dan shall judge his people,
As one of the tribes of Israel.
17 "Dan shall be a serpent in the way,
A horned snake in the path,
That bites the horse's heels,

So that his rider falls backward.
18 "For Your salvation I wait, O LORD.

19 ¶ "As for Gad, raiders shall raid him,
But he will raid *at* their heels.

20 ¶ "As for Asher, his food shall be rich,
And he will yield royal dainties.

21 ¶ "Naphtali is a doe let loose,
He gives beautiful words.

22 ¶ "Joseph is a fruitful *d*bough,
A fruitful bough by a spring;
Its *e*branches run over a wall.
23 "The archers bitterly attacked him,
And shot *at him* and harassed him;
24 But his bow remained firm,
And his arms were agile,
From the hands of the Mighty One of
Jacob
(From there is the Shepherd, the Stone of
Israel),
25 From the God of your father who helps
you,
And by the Almighty who blesses you
With blessings of heaven above,
Blessings of the deep that lies beneath,
Blessings of the breasts and of the womb.
26 "The blessings of your father
Have surpassed the blessings of my
ancestors
Up to the utmost bound of the
everlasting hills;
May they be on the head of Joseph,
And on the crown of the head of the one
distinguished among his brothers.

27 ¶ "Benjamin is a ravenous wolf;
In the morning he devours the prey,
And in the evening he divides the spoil."

28 ¶ All these are the twelve tribes of Israel, and
this is what their father said to them when he
blessed them. He blessed them, every one with the
blessing appropriate to him.
29 Then he charged them and said to them, "I
am about to be gathered to my people; bury me
with my fathers in the cave that is in the field of
Ephron the Hittite,
30 in the cave that is in the field of Machpelah,
which is before Mamre, in the land of Canaan,
which Abraham bought along with the field from
Ephron the Hittite for a burial site.
31 "There they buried Abraham and his wife
Sarah, there they buried Isaac and his wife Rebekah, and there I buried Leah—
32 the field and the cave that is in it, purchased
from the sons of Heth."
33 When Jacob finished charging his sons, he
drew his feet into the bed and breathed his last,
and was gathered to his people.

---

a Or *Until he comes to Shiloh*; or *Until he comes to whom it belongs*   *b* Or *darker than*   *c* Or *whiter than*   *d* Lit *son*
e Lit *daughters*

The Death of Israel

50 Then Joseph fell on his father's face, and wept over him and kissed him.

2 Joseph commanded his servants the physicians to embalm his father. So the physicians embalmed Israel.

3 Now forty days were required for it, for such is the period required for embalming. And the Egyptians wept for him seventy days.

50:3 An Egyptian Funeral

Joseph's political importance is underlined by this elaborate mummification procedure for his father. Jacob's mourning period was only two days shorter than that given for a pharaoh. All the elders of Pharaoh's household and all the elders of the land of Egypt went along for the funeral, a substantial journey (verse 7).

4 ¶ When the days of mourning for him were past, Joseph spoke to the household of Pharaoh, saying, "If now I have found favor in your sight, please speak to Pharaoh, saying,

5 'My father made me swear, saying, "Behold, I am about to die; in my grave which I dug for myself in the land of Canaan, there you shall bury me." Now therefore, please let me go up and bury my father; then I will return.' "

6 Pharaoh said, "Go up and bury your father, as he made you swear."

7 ¶ So Joseph went up to bury his father, and with him went up all the servants of Pharaoh, the elders of his household and all the elders of the land of Egypt,

8 and all the household of Joseph and his brothers and his father's household; they left only their little ones and their flocks and their herds in the land of Goshen.

9 There also went up with him both chariots and horsemen; and it was a very great company.

10 When they came to the threshing floor of Atad, which is beyond the Jordan, they lamented there with a very great and sorrowful lamentation; and he observed seven days mourning for his father.

11 Now when the inhabitants of the land, the Canaanites, saw the mourning at the threshing floor of Atad, they said, "This is a grievous mourning for the Egyptians." Therefore it was named Abel-mizraim, which is beyond the Jordan.

Burial at Machpelah

12 Thus his sons did for him as he had charged them;

13 for his sons carried him to the land of Canaan and buried him in the cave of the field of Machpelah before Mamre, which Abraham had bought along with the field for a burial site from Ephron the Hittite.

14 After he had buried his father, Joseph returned to Egypt, he and his brothers, and all who had gone up with him to bury his father.

15 ¶ When Joseph's brothers saw that their father was dead, they said, "What if Joseph bears a grudge against us and pays us back in full for all the wrong which we did to him!"

16 So they sent a *message* to Joseph, saying, "Your father charged before he died, saying,

17 'Thus you shall say to Joseph, "Please forgive, I beg you, the transgression of your brothers and their sin, for they did you wrong." ' And now, please forgive the transgression of the servants of the God of your father." And Joseph wept when they spoke to him.

18 Then his brothers also came and fell down before him and said, "Behold, we are your servants."

19 But Joseph said to them, "Do not be afraid, for am I in God's place?

50:19 You Intended Evil

Joseph's summation of his experience might apply to many human situations: You intended evil, but God intended good. Joseph's trust that God can bring good out of bad intentions enabled him finally to forgive his brothers, leaving judgment to God.

20 "As for you, you meant evil against me, *but* God meant it for good in order to bring about this present result, to preserve many people alive.

21 "So therefore, do not be afraid; I will provide for you and your little ones." So he comforted them and spoke kindly to them.

Death of Joseph

22 ¶ Now Joseph stayed in Egypt, he and his father's household, and Joseph lived one hundred and ten years.

23 Joseph saw the third generation of Ephraim's sons; also the sons of Machir, the son of Manasseh, were born on Joseph's knees.

24 Joseph said to his brothers, "I am about to die, but God will surely take care of you and bring you up from this land to the land which He promised on oath to Abraham, to Isaac and to Jacob."

25 Then Joseph made the sons of Israel swear, saying, "God will surely take care of you, and you shall carry my bones up from here."

26 So Joseph died at the age of one hundred and ten years; and he was embalmed and placed in a coffin in Egypt.

EXODUS

Free at Last
The slaves in Egypt get a liberator

NOTHING STIRS A NATION'S BLOOD like a liberator. The United States remembers two especially: Washington and Lincoln. George Washington led the original fight for independence. A century later Abraham Lincoln set three million people free when he signed the Emancipation Proclamation.

Other places, too, have liberators. India called a scrawny little man named Gandhi "Mahatma" (or "the great one") for leading his people to freedom. Poles honored Lech Walesa, the first freely elected head of state, for liberating Poland from Soviet communism. For the Israelites, one liberator named Moses accomplished what all these did—and more.

> The LORD said, "I have surely seen the affliction of My people who are in Egypt, and have given heed to their cry because of their taskmasters, for I am aware of their sufferings." 3:7

The Bible devotes one-eighth of its pages to the story of Moses' time (a bulk of material two-thirds the length of the entire New Testament). And when Jesus came as the great Liberator who set all humanity free, the New Testament reached back to Moses for a comparison (Hebrews 3:1–6).

Bondage in Egypt

The time was ripe for a liberator. Genesis closed with Jacob's family of 70 moving to Egypt. But in the opening scene of Exodus, 350 years later, hundreds of thousands of their ancestors were toiling on Pharaoh's huge construction projects—not as guests but as slaves.

One particularly ruthless pharaoh ordered the murder of all male Israelite babies, unwittingly setting the stage for one of the great ironies of history. Moses' parents hid him in a watertight basket among the grasses of a swamp. There, the tiny baby caught the eye of the pharaoh's daughter. The very edict intended to destroy the Israelites led to their deliverance.

Adopted into the palace, Moses got the benefit of a superb classical education. His Egyptian upbringing was balanced by Israelite nurture: In another striking irony, the pharaoh's daughter paid Moses' own mother to nurse him. The son of slaves, yet brought up in the seat of power, Moses prepared for his eventual goal of forging a nation out of a ragtag band of captives.

His career had to wait, though, for a period of humbling in the desert. Moses fled Egypt as a brash, self-confident man who liked to take matters into his own hands. Forty years later he reluctantly returned, with little besides a stick and a donkey.

Free at Last

The Israelites had endured nearly four centuries of oppression—almost twice as long as the history of America as a nation—before liberation. So far as we know, during those years they received no direct communication from heaven. Surely God must have seemed silent.

Moses faced a formidable challenge. Somehow he had to earn the trust of the slaves and inspire hope in them so that they could indeed throw off their chains. He had to prove that God had not forgotten them. When the time was right, God unleashed a spectacle of might and power that brought a cruel pharaoh to his knees—and convinced the Israelites that God really did care for them.

God used Moses in remarkable ways. He was the first person recorded in the Bible to work miracles. He met God in intimate ways granted no other human. He had a hand in the authorship of a good portion of the Old Testament. But in Jewish history he earned a place primarily as a liberator. He led the march from slavery to freedom, from Egypt to the promised land.

How to Read Exodus

Exodus divides neatly into two parts. The first 20 chapters, on the Israelites' flight from Egypt, read like an exciting novel. Movies based on the action here have strained Hollywood special-effects crews. Everything else in the Old Testament flows out of the events of the exodus—these 20 chapters simply cannot be missed.

As you read Exodus, look for important lessons that apply to your life. For example, study the life of Moses, one of a handful of truly great leaders in history. Chapter 18 shows Moses learning an important leadership principle, and chapters 32—35 include encounters and conversations with God that have no equal in the Bible.

Exodus contains much material about the nature of God. Search for each place where God makes an appearance. Exodus shows a greater proportion of miracles—direct supernatural acts of God—than any part of the Bible except the Gospels. Why were these miracles done? Can you see a pattern? What should the Israelites have learned from them? Did they?

The last 20 chapters mainly consist of laws and regulations, given at Mount Sinai, to govern the life of the nation. Read them to note the concerns and priorities important to God as he designs an entire culture.

The instructions are usually clustered in groups, encompassing every area of life:

1. Moral rules, such as the Ten Commandments
2. Civil and social rules, much like a criminal code
3. Religious and ceremonial rules for the Israelites.

See "A National Law Library," page 154, for more information on these laws.

The religious rituals with their many sacrifices and feasts seem strange to modern Westerners, but they were not at all unusual then. Also, they prepared the way for a Redeemer who was greater than Moses: Jesus Christ. You will need study books and commentaries to find all the symbols that apply to Jesus' life, as shown, for example, in the Passover. Fortunately, the Bible includes a brief but powerful commentary in Hebrews (see especially Hebrews 7—10). This book should be read alongside Exodus and the three books that follow.

PEOPLE YOU'LL MEET IN EXODUS

MOSES *(p. 84)*
JETHRO *(p. 104)*

3-TRACK READING PLAN

For an explanation and complete listing of the 3-track reading plan, turn to page 7.

TRACK 1:   *Two-Week Courses on the Bible*
The Track 1 reading program on the Old Testament includes two chapters from Exodus. See page 7 for a complete listing of this course.

TRACK 2:   *An Overview of Exodus in 5 Days*
☐ Day 1. Read the Introduction to Exodus and then chapter 3, God's call of Moses.
☐ Day 2. Read chapter 10 and the very brief chapter 11; they record three of the ten plagues against Egypt.
☐ Day 3. Read chapter 14, which contains the exciting story of crossing the Red Sea.
☐ Day 4. Read the Ten Commandments as recorded in chapter 20. (If you have time, chapter 19 gives the dramatic setting for these laws.)
☐ Day 5. Read chapter 32. It records the most striking example of what was to become a characteristic of the Israelites: mass rebellion.

Now turn to page 9 for your next Track 2 reading project.

TRACK 3:   *All of Exodus in 39 Days*
After you have read through Exodus, turn to pages 10—14 for your next Track 3 reading project.

☐1	☐2	☐3	☐4	☐5	☐6	☐7	☐8
☐9	☐10–11	☐12	☐13	☐14	☐15	☐16	☐17
☐18	☐19	☐20	☐21	☐22	☐23	☐24	☐25
☐26	☐27	☐28	☐29	☐30	☐31	☐32	☐33
☐34	☐35	☐36	☐37	☐38	☐39	☐40	

Israel Multiplies in Egypt

1 Now these are the names of the sons of Israel who came to Egypt with Jacob; they came each one with his household:

2 Reuben, Simeon, Levi and Judah;

3 Issachar, Zebulun and Benjamin;

4 Dan and Naphtali, Gad and Asher.

5 All the persons who came from the loins of Jacob were seventy in number, but Joseph was *already* in Egypt.

6 Joseph died, and all his brothers and all that generation.

7 But the sons of Israel were fruitful and increased greatly, and multiplied, and became exceedingly mighty, so that the land was filled with them.

8 ¶ Now a new king arose over Egypt, who did not know Joseph.

9 He said to his people, "Behold, the people of the sons of Israel are more and mightier than we.

10 "Come, let us deal wisely with them, or else they will multiply and in the event of war, they will also join themselves to those who hate us, and fight against us and depart from the land."

11 So they appointed taskmasters over them to afflict them with hard labor. And they built for Pharaoh storage cities, Pithom and Raamses.

12 But the more they afflicted them, the more they multiplied and the more they spread out, so that they were in dread of the sons of Israel.

13 The Egyptians compelled the sons of Israel to labor rigorously;

14 and they made their lives bitter with hard labor in mortar and bricks and at all *kinds* of labor in the field, all their labors which they rigorously imposed on them.

15 ¶ Then the king of Egypt spoke to the Hebrew midwives, one of whom was named Shiphrah and the other was named Puah;

16 and he said, "When you are helping the Hebrew women to give birth and see *them* upon the birthstool, if it is a son, then you shall put him to death; but if it is a daughter, then she shall live."

17 But the midwives feared God, and did not do as the king of Egypt had commanded them, but let the boys live.

18 So the king of Egypt called for the midwives and said to them, "Why have you done this thing, and let the boys live?"

19 The midwives said to Pharaoh, "Because the Hebrew women are not as the Egyptian women; for they are vigorous and give birth before the midwife can get to them."

20 So God was good to the midwives, and the people multiplied, and became very mighty.

21 Because the midwives feared God, He established households for them.

22 Then Pharaoh commanded all his people, saying, "Every son who is born [a]you are to cast into the Nile, and every daughter you are to keep alive."

The Birth of Moses

2 Now a man from the house of Levi went and married a daughter of Levi.

2 The woman conceived and bore a son; and when she saw that he was beautiful, she hid him for three months.

3 But when she could hide him no longer, she got him a [b]wicker basket and covered it over with tar and pitch. Then she put the child into it and set *it* among the reeds by the bank of the Nile.

4 His sister stood at a distance to find out what would happen to him.

5 ¶ The daughter of Pharaoh came down to bathe at the Nile, with her maidens walking alongside the Nile; and she saw the basket among the reeds and sent her maid, and she brought it *to her.*

6 When she opened *it,* she saw the child, and behold, *the* boy was crying. And she had pity on him and said, "This is one of the Hebrews' children."

7 Then his sister said to Pharaoh's daughter, "Shall I go and call a nurse for you from the Hebrew women that she may nurse the child for you?"

8 Pharaoh's daughter said to her, "Go *ahead.*" So the girl went and called the child's mother.

9 Then Pharaoh's daughter said to her, "Take this child away and nurse him for me and I will give *you* your wages." So the woman took the child and nursed him.

10 The child grew, and she brought him to Pharaoh's daughter and he became her son. And she named him Moses, and said, "Because I drew him out of the water."

11 ¶ Now it came about in those days, when Moses had grown up, that he went out to his brethren and looked on their hard labors; and he saw an Egyptian beating a Hebrew, one of his brethren.

12 So he looked this way and that, and when he saw there was no one *around,* he struck down the Egyptian and hid him in the sand.

1:16 New Tyrant in Town

Dictators often take out their wrath on a helpless minority: witness Hitler and the Jews or Saddam Hussein and the Kurds. At first pharaohs welcomed their Hebrew guests, and God used the peace and quiet of Egypt, far from the squabbling tribes of Canaan, to "grow" the people of Israel. But now the Israelites' very size and strength threatened the new pharaoh, who ruthlessly clamped down on them.

[a] Some versions insert *to the Hebrews*   [b] I.e. papyrus reeds

13 He went out the next day, and behold, two Hebrews were fighting with each other; and he said to the offender, "Why are you striking your companion?"

2:10 Selective History

Exodus illustrates how selective the Bible's history is. The first chapter, for example, skips over the name of the Egyptian pharaoh (leaving a riddle for scholars to argue over ever since), and yet identifies by name two Hebrew midwives (1:15). After compressing three-and-a-half centuries into a few verses, Exodus devotes chapters 3–40 to the events of a single year. In contrast to Genesis' large cast of characters, Exodus focuses on one main character, Moses.

---

14 But he said, "Who made you a prince or a judge over us? Are you intending to kill me as you killed the Egyptian?" Then Moses was afraid and said, "Surely the matter has become known."

Moses Escapes to Midian

15 When Pharaoh heard of this matter, he tried to kill Moses. But Moses fled from the presence of Pharaoh and settled in the land of Midian, and he sat down by a well.

16 ¶ Now the priest of Midian had seven daughters; and they came to draw water and filled the troughs to water their father's flock.

17 Then the shepherds came and drove them away, but Moses stood up and helped them and watered their flock.

18 When they came to Reuel their father, he said, "Why have you come *back* so soon today?"

19 So they said, "An Egyptian delivered us from the hand of the shepherds, and what is more, he even drew the water for us and watered the flock."

20 He said to his daughters, "Where is he then? Why is it that you have left the man behind? Invite him to have something to eat."

21 Moses was willing to dwell with the man, and he gave his daughter Zipporah to Moses.

22 Then she gave birth to a son, and he named him Gershom, for he said, "I have been a sojourner in a foreign land."

23 ¶ Now it came about in *the course of* those many days that the king of Egypt died. And the sons of Israel sighed because of the bondage, and they cried out; and their cry for help because of *their* bondage rose up to God.

24 So God heard their groaning; and God remembered His covenant with Abraham, Isaac, and Jacob.

25 God saw the sons of Israel, and God took notice *of them.*

The Burning Bush

3 Now Moses was pasturing the flock of Jethro his father-in-law, the priest of Midian; and he led the flock to the west side of the wilderness and came to Horeb, the mountain of God.

2 The angel of the LORD appeared to him in a blazing fire from the midst of a bush; and he looked, and behold, the bush was burning with fire, yet the bush was not consumed.

3 So Moses said, "I must turn aside now and see this marvelous sight, why the bush is not burned up."

4 When the LORD saw that he turned aside to look, God called to him from the midst of the bush and said, "Moses, Moses!" And he said, "Here I am."

5 Then He said, "Do not come near here; remove your sandals from your feet, for the place on which you are standing is holy ground."

6 He said also, "I am the God of your father, the God of Abraham, the God of Isaac, and the God of Jacob." Then Moses hid his face, for he was afraid to look at God.

7 ¶ The LORD said, "I have surely seen the affliction of My people who are in Egypt, and have given heed to their cry because of their taskmasters, for I am aware of their sufferings.

8 "So I have come down to deliver them from the power of the Egyptians, and to bring them up from that land to a good and spacious land, to a land flowing with milk and honey, to the place of the Canaanite and the Hittite and the Amorite and the Perizzite and the Hivite and the Jebusite.

9 "Now, behold, the cry of the sons of Israel has come to Me; furthermore, I have seen the oppression with which the Egyptians are oppressing them.

The Mission of Moses

10 "Therefore, come now, and I will send you to Pharaoh, so that you may bring My people, the sons of Israel, out of Egypt."

11 But Moses said to God, "Who am I, that I should go to Pharaoh, and that I should bring the sons of Israel out of Egypt?"

12 And He said, "Certainly I will be with you,

3:11–13 Who, Me?

Moses had big doubts about his ability to lead. He resisted God, bringing up his unworthiness (here) and lack of authority (verse 13), his fear of the people's distrust (4:1), his speech difficulties (4:10), and his sheer cowardice (4:13). The remainder of Exodus should give people with similar self-doubts great hope, for it traces Moses' personal development from this fumbling start to his emergence as one of history's most decisive and powerful leaders.

and this shall be the sign to you that it is I who have sent you: when you have brought the people out of Egypt, you shall worship God at this mountain."

13 ¶ Then Moses said to God, "Behold, I am going to the sons of Israel, and I will say to them, 'The God of your fathers has sent me to you.' Now they may say to me, 'What is His name?' What shall I say to them?"

14 God said to Moses, "*a*I AM WHO *a*I AM"; and He said, "Thus you shall say to the sons of Israel, '*a*I AM has sent me to you.'"

15 God, furthermore, said to Moses, "Thus you shall say to the sons of Israel, 'The LORD, the God of your fathers, the God of Abraham, the God of Isaac, and the God of Jacob, has sent me to you.' This is My name forever, and this is My memorial-name to all generations.

16 "Go and gather the elders of Israel together and say to them, 'The LORD, the God of your fathers, the God of Abraham, Isaac and Jacob, has appeared to me, saying, "I am indeed concerned about you and what has been done to you in Egypt.

17 "So I said, I will bring you up out of the affliction of Egypt to the land of the Canaanite and the Hittite and the Amorite and the Perizzite and the Hivite and the Jebusite, to a land flowing with milk and honey."'

18 "They will pay heed to what you say; and you with the elders of Israel will come to the king of Egypt and you will say to him, 'The LORD, the God of the Hebrews, has met with us. So now, please, let us go a three days' journey into the wilderness, that we may sacrifice to the LORD our God.'

19 "But I know that the king of Egypt will not permit you to go, except under compulsion.

20 "So I will stretch out My hand and strike Egypt with all My miracles which I shall do in the midst of it; and after that he will let you go.

21 "I will grant this people favor in the sight of the Egyptians; and it shall be that when you go, you will not go empty-handed.

22 "But every woman shall ask of her neighbor and the woman who lives in her house, articles of silver and articles of gold, and clothing; and you will put them on your sons and daughters. Thus you will plunder the Egyptians."

Moses Given Powers

4 Then Moses said, "What if they will not believe me or listen to what I say? For they may say, 'The LORD has not appeared to you.'"

2 The LORD said to him, "What is that in your hand?" And he said, "A staff."

3 Then He said, "Throw it on the ground." So he threw it on the ground, and it became a serpent; and Moses fled from it.

4 But the LORD said to Moses, "Stretch out your hand and grasp it by its tail"—so he

stretched out his hand and caught it, and it became a staff in his hand—

5 "that they may believe that the LORD, the God of their fathers, the God of Abraham, the God of Isaac, and the God of Jacob, has appeared to you."

6 ¶ The LORD furthermore said to him, "Now put your hand into your bosom." So he put his hand into his bosom, and when he took it out, behold, his hand was leprous like snow.

7 Then He said, "Put your hand into your bosom again." So he put his hand into his bosom again, and when he took it out of his bosom, behold, it was restored like *the rest of* his flesh.

8 "If they will not believe you or heed the witness of the first sign, they may believe the witness of the last sign.

9 "But if they will not believe even these two signs or heed what you say, then you shall take some water from the Nile and pour it on the dry ground; and the water which you take from the Nile will become blood on the dry ground."

10 ¶ Then Moses said to the LORD, "Please, Lord, I have never been eloquent, neither recently nor in time past, nor since You have spoken to Your servant; for I am slow of speech and slow of tongue."

11 The LORD said to him, "Who has made man's mouth? Or who makes *him* mute or deaf, or seeing or blind? Is it not I, the LORD?

12 "Now then go, and I, even I, will be with your mouth, and teach you what you are to say."

13 But he said, "Please, Lord, now send *the message* by whomever You will."

Aaron to Be Moses' Mouthpiece

14 Then the anger of the LORD burned against Moses, and He said, "Is there not your brother Aaron the Levite? I know that he speaks fluently. And moreover, behold, he is coming out to meet you; when he sees you, he will be glad in his heart.

15 "You are to speak to him and put the words in his mouth; and I, even I, will be with your mouth and his mouth, and I will teach you what you are to do.

16 "Moreover, he shall speak for you to the people; and he will be as a mouth for you and you will be as God to him.

17 "You shall take in your hand this staff, with which you shall perform the signs."

18 ¶ Then Moses departed and returned to Jethro his father-in-law and said to him, "Please, let me go, that I may return to my brethren who are in Egypt, and see if they are still alive." And Jethro said to Moses, "Go in peace."

19 Now the LORD said to Moses in Midian, "Go back to Egypt, for all the men who were seeking your life are dead."

20 So Moses took his wife and his sons and mounted them on a donkey, and returned to the

a Related to the name of God, YHWH, rendered LORD, which is derived from the verb HAYAH, *to be* land of Egypt. Moses also took the staff of God in his hand.

21 ¶ The LORD said to Moses, "When you go back to Egypt see that you perform before Pharaoh all the wonders which I have put in your power; but I will harden his heart so that he will not let the people go.

22 "Then you shall say to Pharaoh, 'Thus says the LORD, "Israel is My son, My firstborn.

23 "So I said to you, 'Let My son go that he may serve Me'; but you have refused to let him go. Behold, I will kill your son, your firstborn." ' "

24 ¶ Now it came about at the lodging place on the way that the LORD met him and sought to put him to death.

25 Then Zipporah took a flint and cut off her son's foreskin and threw it at Moses' feet, and she said, "You are indeed a bridegroom of blood to me."

26 So He let him alone. At that time she said, "*You are* a bridegroom of blood"—because of the circumcision.

27 ¶ Now the LORD said to Aaron, "Go to meet Moses in the wilderness." So he went and met him at the mountain of God and kissed him.

28 Moses told Aaron all the words of the LORD with which He had sent him, and all the signs that He had commanded him *to do.*

29 Then Moses and Aaron went and assembled all the elders of the sons of Israel;

30 and Aaron spoke all the words which the LORD had spoken to Moses. He then performed the signs in the sight of the people.

31 So the people believed; and when they heard that the LORD was concerned about the sons of Israel and that He had seen their affliction, then they bowed low and worshiped.

Israel's Labor Increased

5 And afterward Moses and Aaron came and said to Pharaoh, "Thus says the LORD, the God of Israel, 'Let My people go that they may celebrate a feast to Me in the wilderness.' "

2 But Pharaoh said, "Who is the LORD that I should obey His voice to let Israel go? I do not know the LORD, and besides, I will not let Israel go."

3 Then they said, "The God of the Hebrews has met with us. Please, let us go a three days' journey into the wilderness that we may sacrifice to the LORD our God, otherwise He will fall upon us with pestilence or with the sword."

4 But the king of Egypt said to them, "Moses and Aaron, why do you draw the people away from their work? Get *back* to your labors!"

5 Again Pharaoh said, "Look, the people of the land are now many, and you would have them cease from their labors!"

6 So the same day Pharaoh commanded the taskmasters over the people and their foremen, saying,

7 "You are no longer to give the people straw to make brick as previously; let them go and gather straw for themselves.

8 "But the quota of bricks which they were making previously, you shall impose on them; you are not to reduce any of it. Because they are lazy, therefore they cry out, 'Let us go and sacrifice to our God.'

9 "Let the labor be heavier on the men, and let them work at it so that they will pay no attention to false words."

10 ¶ So the taskmasters of the people and their foremen went out and spoke to the people, saying, "Thus says Pharaoh, 'I am not going to give you *any* straw.

5:10 Three Kinds of Bricks

Archaeologists digging up settlements from ancient Egypt have unearthed three kinds of sun-dried bricks—some made of good straw, some containing mere roots and bits of straw, and some with no straw—confirming this account of slave labor.

11 'You go *and* get straw for yourselves wherever you can find *it,* but none of your labor will be reduced.' "

12 So the people scattered through all the land of Egypt to gather stubble for straw.

13 The taskmasters pressed them, saying, "Complete your work quota, *your* daily amount, just as when you had straw."

14 Moreover, the foremen of the sons of Israel, whom Pharaoh's taskmasters had set over them, were beaten and were asked, "Why have you not completed your required amount either yesterday or today in making brick as previously?"

15 ¶ Then the foremen of the sons of Israel came and cried out to Pharaoh, saying, "Why do you deal this way with your servants?

16 "There is no straw given to your servants, yet they keep saying to us, 'Make bricks!' And behold, your servants are being beaten; but it is the fault of your *own* people."

17 But he said, "You are lazy, *very* lazy; therefore you say, 'Let us go *and* sacrifice to the LORD.'

18 "So go now *and* work; for you will be given no straw, yet you must deliver the quota of bricks."

19 The foremen of the sons of Israel saw that they were in trouble because they were told, "You must not reduce *your* daily amount of bricks."

20 When they left Pharaoh's presence, they met Moses and Aaron as they were waiting for them.

21 They said to them, "May the LORD look

upon you and judge *you,* for you have made *a*us odious in Pharaoh's sight and in the sight of his servants, to put a sword in their hand to kill us."

22 ¶ Then Moses returned to the LORD and said, "O Lord, why have You brought harm to this people? Why did You ever send me?

23 "Ever since I came to Pharaoh to speak in Your name, he has done harm to this people, and You have not delivered Your people at all."

God Promises Action

6 Then the LORD said to Moses, "Now you shall see what I will do to Pharaoh; for under compulsion he will let them go, and under compulsion he will drive them out of his land."

2 ¶ God spoke further to Moses and said to him, "I am the LORD;

3 and I appeared to Abraham, Isaac, and Jacob, as God Almighty, but *by* My name, *b*LORD, I did not make Myself known to them.

4 "I also established My covenant with them, to give them the land of Canaan, the land in which they sojourned.

5 "Furthermore I have heard the groaning of the sons of Israel, because the Egyptians are holding them in bondage, and I have remembered My covenant.

6 "Say, therefore, to the sons of Israel, 'I am the LORD, and I will bring you out from under the burdens of the Egyptians, and I will deliver you from their bondage. I will also redeem you with an outstretched arm and with great judgments.

6:6–9 Oppressed by Egypt

With Egypt at the peak of its power, Pharaoh used slaves to build massive monuments, enforcing his rule with an army of renowned charioteers and bowmen. Egyptian hieroglyphics pictured the word for foreigner as a bound man with blood flowing from a wound in his head; the Israelites felt the full weight of such oppression. For a while, the increasing cruelty of Egyptian taskmasters turned the Israelites against Moses and his campaign to free them. But this oppression also made them anxious to leave.

7 'Then I will take you for My people, and I will be your God; and you shall know that I am the LORD your God, who brought you out from under the burdens of the Egyptians.

8 'I will bring you to the land which I swore to give to Abraham, Isaac, and Jacob, and I will give it to you *for* a possession; I am the LORD.'"

9 So Moses spoke thus to the sons of Israel, but they did not listen to Moses on account of *their* despondency and cruel bondage.

10 ¶ Now the LORD spoke to Moses, saying,

11 "Go, tell Pharaoh king of Egypt to let the sons of Israel go out of his land."

12 But Moses spoke before the LORD, saying, "Behold, the sons of Israel have not listened to me; how then will Pharaoh listen to me, for I am unskilled in speech?"

13 Then the LORD spoke to Moses and to Aaron, and gave them a charge to the sons of Israel and to Pharaoh king of Egypt, to bring the sons of Israel out of the land of Egypt.

The Heads of Israel

14 ¶ These are the heads of their fathers' households. The sons of Reuben, Israel's firstborn: Hanoch and Pallu, Hezron and Carmi; these are the families of Reuben.

15 The sons of Simeon: Jemuel and Jamin and Ohad and Jachin and Zohar and Shaul the son of a Canaanite woman; these are the families of Simeon.

16 These are the names of the sons of Levi according to their generations: Gershon and Kohath and Merari; and the length of Levi's life was one hundred and thirty-seven years.

17 The sons of Gershon: Libni and Shimei, according to their families.

18 The sons of Kohath: Amram and Izhar and Hebron and Uzziel; and the length of Kohath's life was one hundred and thirty-three years.

19 The sons of Merari: Mahli and Mushi. These are the families of the Levites according to their generations.

20 Amram married his father's sister Jochebed, and she bore him Aaron and Moses; and the length of Amram's life was one hundred and thirty-seven years.

21 The sons of Izhar: Korah and Nepheg and Zichri.

22 The sons of Uzziel: Mishael and Elzaphan and Sithri.

23 Aaron married Elisheba, the daughter of Amminadab, the sister of Nahshon, and she bore him Nadab and Abihu, Eleazar and Ithamar.

24 The sons of Korah: Assir and Elkanah and Abiasaph; these are the families of the Korahites.

25 Aaron's son Eleazar married one of the daughters of Putiel, and she bore him Phinehas. These are the heads of the fathers' *households* of the Levites according to their families.

26 It was *the same* Aaron and Moses to whom the LORD said, "Bring out the sons of Israel from the land of Egypt according to their hosts."

27 They were the ones who spoke to Pharaoh king of Egypt about bringing out the sons of Israel from Egypt; it was *the same* Moses and Aaron.

28 ¶ Now it came about on the day when the LORD spoke to Moses in the land of Egypt,

29 that the LORD spoke to Moses, saying, "I am

---

a Lit *our savor to stink*   *b* Heb *YHWH,* usually rendered LORD the LORD; speak to Pharaoh king of Egypt all that I speak to you."

30 But Moses said before the LORD, "Behold, I am unskilled in speech; how then will Pharaoh listen to me?"

"I Will Stretch Out My Hand"

7 Then the LORD said to Moses, "See, I make you *as* God to Pharaoh, and your brother Aaron shall be your prophet.

2 "You shall speak all that I command you, and your brother Aaron shall speak to Pharaoh that he let the sons of Israel go out of his land.

3 "But I will harden Pharaoh's heart that I may multiply My signs and My wonders in the land of Egypt.

4 "When Pharaoh does not listen to you, then I will lay My hand on Egypt and bring out My hosts, My people the sons of Israel, from the land of Egypt by great judgments.

5 "The Egyptians shall know that I am the LORD, when I stretch out My hand on Egypt and bring out the sons of Israel from their midst."

6 So Moses and Aaron did *it;* as the LORD commanded them, thus they did.

7 Moses was eighty years old and Aaron eighty-three, when they spoke to Pharaoh.

Aaron's Rod Becomes a Serpent

8 ¶ Now the LORD spoke to Moses and Aaron, saying,

9 "When Pharaoh speaks to you, saying,

Day of the Locusts
The ten plagues proved a point for both Jews and Egyptians

LOCUSTS, OR GRASSHOPPERS, NORMALLY LIVE a solitary life, hopping from stalk to stalk and placidly munching on leaves and flowers. Then something happens—whether in response to climate, food supply, or crowded conditions—that triggers a change. The locusts grow restive, flush an ominous pink color, and begin to seek other locusts.

They become a plague. Great clattering hordes of them, millions strong, blacken the sky, shutting out sunlight. Groups of them fall to the ground like cluster bombs and disperse to destroy every sign of vegetation. Pesticide spraying may kill a few million, but the migratory swarm will barely notice such losses.

A single swarm crossing the Red Sea was once measured at 15 miles wide, three miles deep, and 100 miles long. Upon landing, the locusts consumed crops, leather, fences, and even tool handles, leaving behind total devastation over 2,000 square miles.

> "The Egyptians shall know that I am the LORD, when I stretch out My hand on Egypt and bring out the sons of Israel from their midst."
> 7:5

Why the Ten Plagues?

Exodus (7–12) depicts ten cataclysmic plagues on Egypt—including a locust swarm—in brief but graphic detail. The Bible does not concern itself with the question of how these natural phenomena occurred; it merely affirms that something supernatural took place. The miracles were an unprecedented display of God's power.

A nation was about to be born, and the Israelites' uprooting from Egypt called for such power. They had, after all, lived for centuries in Egypt. It would take a strong incentive indeed to motivate a massive, abrupt departure. And Egypt would not easily let thousands of valuable slaves walk away free.

Two Reputations at Stake

The ten plagues convincingly established Moses' authority. He had hesitated to accept a leadership role, doubting whether the other Israelites would trust him (4:1). But Moses' dramatic confrontations with Pharaoh dispelled all doubts. He and he alone could lead them to freedom.

Someone else's credibility was also at stake: that of God himself. In Egypt, religion centered around idolatry, with scores of gods—including even snakes and dung beetles—held up as objects of worship. Against that background, the plagues appear as God's open warfare against the false gods of Egypt. He said as much: "against all the gods of Egypt I will execute judgments" (12:12).

Exodus asserts more than a dozen times that the plagues were given so that Israel and Egypt would know the power of Israel's God. Evidently they worked. Egyptians became so convinced of God's power that they let thousands of slaves leave, with the wealth of Egypt showered upon them as farewell presents. The Israelites were so convinced that they left their home and history and marched out behind a single man toward a desert and a new life.

Life Questions: Do you know of any modern countries that treat minorities cruelly, like the Egyptians treated the Israelites? What would make such a government change its ways?

'Work a miracle,' then you shall say to Aaron, 'Take your staff and throw *it* down before Pharaoh, *that* it may become a serpent.' "

10 So Moses and Aaron came to Pharaoh, and thus they did just as the LORD had commanded; and Aaron threw his staff down before Pharaoh and his servants, and it became a serpent.

11 Then Pharaoh also called for *the* wise men and *the* sorcerers, and they also, the magicians of Egypt, did the same with their secret arts.

12 For each one threw down his staff and they turned into serpents. But Aaron's staff swallowed up their staffs.

13 Yet Pharaoh's heart was hardened, and he did not listen to them, as the LORD had said.

Water Is Turned to Blood

14 ¶ Then the LORD said to Moses, "Pharaoh's heart is stubborn; he refuses to let the people go.

15 "Go to Pharaoh in the morning as he is going out to the water, and station yourself to meet him on the bank of the Nile; and you shall take in your hand the staff that was turned into a serpent.

16 "You shall say to him, 'The LORD, the God of the Hebrews, sent me to you, saying, "Let My people go, that they may serve Me in the wilderness. But behold, you have not listened until now."

17 'Thus says the LORD, "By this you shall know that I am the LORD: behold, I will strike the water that is in the Nile with the staff that is in my hand, and it will be turned to blood.

18 "The fish that are in the Nile will die, and the Nile will become foul, and the Egyptians will find difficulty in drinking water from the Nile." ' "

19 Then the LORD said to Moses, "Say to Aaron, 'Take your staff and stretch out your hand over the waters of Egypt, over their rivers, over their streams, and over their pools, and over all their reservoirs of water, that they may become blood; and there will be blood throughout all the land of Egypt, both in *vessels of* wood and in *vessels of* stone.' "

20 ¶ So Moses and Aaron did even as the LORD had commanded. And he lifted up the staff and struck the water that *was* in the Nile, in the sight of Pharaoh and in the sight of his servants, and all the water that *was* in the Nile was turned to blood.

21 The fish that *were* in the Nile died, and the Nile became foul, so that the Egyptians could not drink water from the Nile. And the blood was through all the land of Egypt.

22 But the magicians of Egypt did the same with their secret arts; and Pharaoh's heart was hardened, and he did not listen to them, as the LORD had said.

23 Then Pharaoh turned and went into his house with no concern even for this.

24 So all the Egyptians dug around the Nile for water to drink, for they could not drink of the water of the Nile.

25 Seven days passed after the LORD had struck the Nile.

Frogs over the Land

8 Then the LORD said to Moses, "Go to Pharaoh and say to him, 'Thus says the LORD, "Let My people go, that they may serve Me.

2 "But if you refuse to let *them* go, behold, I will smite your whole territory with frogs.

3 "The Nile will swarm with frogs, which will come up and go into your house and into your bedroom and on your bed, and into the houses of your servants and on your people, and into your ovens and into your kneading bowls.

4 "So the frogs will come up on you and your people and all your servants." ' "

5 Then the LORD said to Moses, "Say to Aaron, 'Stretch out your hand with your staff over the rivers, over the streams and over the pools, and make frogs come up on the land of Egypt.' "

6 So Aaron stretched out his hand over the waters of Egypt, and the frogs came up and covered the land of Egypt.

7 The magicians did the same with their secret arts, making frogs come up on the land of Egypt.

8 ¶ Then Pharaoh called for Moses and Aaron and said, "Entreat the LORD that He remove the frogs from me and from my people; and I will let the people go, that they may sacrifice to the LORD."

9 Moses said to Pharaoh, "The honor is yours to tell me: when shall I entreat for you and your servants and your people, that the frogs be destroyed from you and your houses, *that* they may be left only in the Nile?"

10 ¶ Then he said, "Tomorrow." So he said, "*May it be* according to your word, that you may know that there is no one like the LORD our God.

11 "The frogs will depart from you and your houses and your servants and your people; they will be left only in the Nile."

12 Then Moses and Aaron went out from Pharaoh, and Moses cried to the LORD concerning the frogs which He had inflicted upon Pharaoh.

13 The LORD did according to the word of Moses, and the frogs died out of the houses, the courts, and the fields.

14 So they piled them in heaps, and the land became foul.

15 But when Pharaoh saw that there was relief, he hardened his heart and did not listen to them, as the LORD had said.

The Plague of Insects

16 ¶ Then the LORD said to Moses, "Say to Aaron, 'Stretch out your staff and strike the dust of the earth, that it may become ᵃgnats through all the land of Egypt.' "

ᵃ Or *lice*

17 They did so; and Aaron stretched out his hand with his staff, and struck the dust of the earth, and there were gnats on man and beast. All the dust of the earth became gnats through all the land of Egypt.

8:15 Pharaoh's Hard Heart

The Bible describes Pharaoh's stubbornness in three ways. Sometimes, as here, it says Pharaoh "hardened his heart," sometimes, God "hardened his heart" (10:1), and also, "Pharaoh's heart was hardened" (7:13). This is consistent with the Old Testament view: all of history was an act of God. Beyond that, the writers did not normally make clear distinctions on questions of who caused what.

18 The magicians tried with their secret arts to bring forth gnats, but they could not; so there were gnats on man and beast.

19 Then the magicians said to Pharaoh, "This is the finger of God." But Pharaoh's heart was hardened, and he did not listen to them, as the LORD had said.

20 ¶ Now the LORD said to Moses, "Rise early in the morning and present yourself before Pharaoh, as he comes out to the water, and say to him, 'Thus says the LORD, "Let My people go, that they may serve Me.

21 "For if you do not let My people go, behold, I will send swarms of insects on you and on your servants and on your people and into your houses; and the houses of the Egyptians will be full of swarms of insects, and also the ground on which they *dwell.*

22 "But on that day I will set apart the land of Goshen, where My people are living, so that no swarms of insects will be there, in order that you may know that I, the LORD, am in the midst of the land.

23 "I will *a*put a division between My people and your people. Tomorrow this sign will occur." ' "

24 Then the LORD did so. And there came great swarms of insects into the house of Pharaoh and the houses of his servants and the land was laid waste because of the swarms of insects in all the land of Egypt.

25 ¶ Pharaoh called for Moses and Aaron and said, "Go, sacrifice to your God within the land."

26 But Moses said, "It is not right to do so, for we will sacrifice to the LORD our God what is an abomination to the Egyptians. If we sacrifice what is an abomination to the Egyptians before their eyes, will they not then stone us?

27 "We must go a three days' journey into the wilderness and sacrifice to the LORD our God as He commands us."

28 Pharaoh said, "I will let you go, that you may sacrifice to the LORD your God in the wilderness; only you shall not go very far away. Make supplication for me."

29 Then Moses said, "Behold, I am going out from you, and I shall make supplication to the LORD that the swarms of insects may depart from Pharaoh, from his servants, and from his people tomorrow; only do not let Pharaoh deal deceitfully again in not letting the people go to sacrifice to the LORD."

30 ¶ So Moses went out from Pharaoh and made supplication to the LORD.

31 The LORD did as Moses asked, and removed the swarms of insects from Pharaoh, from his servants and from his people; not one remained.

32 But Pharaoh hardened his heart this time also, and he did not let the people go.

8:27 Oriental Bargaining

Those who have lived in the Middle East recognize in Moses' encounters with Pharaoh an example of high-level Oriental bargaining. As the pressure increased, Pharaoh kept raising his offers: from allowing sacrifices within Egypt (verse 25), to permitting sacrifices nearby in the wilderness (verse 28), to letting only the adult males go (10:11), to releasing all people but no flocks (10:24). Finally, with the tenth and final plague Pharaoh agreed to all Moses' demands (12:32).

Egyptian Cattle Die

9 Then the LORD said to Moses, "Go to Pharaoh and speak to him, 'Thus says the LORD, the God of the Hebrews, "Let My people go, that they may serve Me.

2 "For if you refuse to let *them* go and continue to hold them,

3 behold, the hand of the LORD will come *with* a very severe pestilence on your livestock which are in the field, on the horses, on the donkeys, on the camels, on the herds, and on the flocks.

4 "But the LORD will make a distinction between the livestock of Israel and the livestock of Egypt, so that nothing will die of all that belongs to the sons of Israel." ' "

5 The LORD set a definite time, saying, "Tomorrow the LORD will do this thing in the land."

6 So the LORD did this thing on the next day, and all the livestock of Egypt died; but of the livestock of the sons of Israel, not one died.

7 Pharaoh sent, and behold, there was not even one of the livestock of Israel dead. But the

a Lit *set a ransom*

heart of Pharaoh was hardened, and he did not let the people go.

The Plague of Boils

8 ¶ Then the LORD said to Moses and Aaron,

9:7 "Smart" Plagues

Like "smart bombs," targeted precisely, most of the plagues affected the Egyptians but not the Israelites—a miracle in itself. This fact should have convinced Pharaoh that he was contending against supernatural force, not just the caprice of nature. But it took ten plagues in all to persuade him to allow his main supply of cheap labor to walk away, and even then he had second thoughts and chased after them (14:5).

"Take for yourselves handfuls of soot from a kiln, and let Moses throw it toward the sky in the sight of Pharaoh.

9 "It will become fine dust over all the land of Egypt, and will become boils breaking out with sores on man and beast through all the land of Egypt."

10 So they took soot from a kiln, and stood before Pharaoh; and Moses threw it toward the sky, and it became boils breaking out with sores on man and beast.

11 The magicians could not stand before Moses because of the boils, for the boils were on the magicians as well as on all the Egyptians.

12 And the LORD hardened Pharaoh's heart, and he did not listen to them, just as the LORD had spoken to Moses.

13 ¶ Then the LORD said to Moses, "Rise up early in the morning and stand before Pharaoh and say to him, 'Thus says the LORD, the God of the Hebrews, "Let My people go, that they may serve Me.

14 "For this time I will send all My plagues on you and your servants and your people, so that you may know that there is no one like Me in all the earth.

15 "For *if by* now I had put forth My hand and struck you and your people with pestilence, you would then have been cut off from the earth.

16 "But, indeed, for this reason I have allowed you to remain, in order to show you My power and in order to proclaim My name through all the earth.

17 "Still you exalt yourself against My people by not letting them go.

The Plague of Hail

18 "Behold, about this time tomorrow, I will send a very heavy hail, such as has not been *seen* in Egypt from the day it was founded until now.

19 "Now therefore send, bring your livestock and whatever you have in the field to safety. Every man and beast that is found in the field and is not brought home, when the hail comes down on them, will die." ' "

20 The one among the servants of Pharaoh who feared the word of the LORD made his servants and his livestock flee into the houses;

21 but he who paid no regard to the word of the LORD left his servants and his livestock in the field.

22 ¶ Now the LORD said to Moses, "Stretch out your hand toward the sky, that hail may fall on all the land of Egypt, on man and on beast and on every plant of the field, throughout the land of Egypt."

23 Moses stretched out his staff toward the sky, and the LORD sent thunder and hail, and fire ran down to the earth. And the LORD rained hail on the land of Egypt.

24 So there was hail, and fire flashing continually in the midst of the hail, very severe, such as had not been in all the land of Egypt since it became a nation.

25 The hail struck all that was in the field through all the land of Egypt, both man and beast; the hail also struck every plant of the field and shattered every tree of the field.

26 Only in the land of Goshen, where the sons of Israel *were,* there was no hail.

27 ¶ Then Pharaoh sent for Moses and Aaron, and said to them, "I have sinned this time; the LORD is the righteous one, and I and my people are the wicked ones.

28 "Make supplication to the LORD, for there has been enough of God's thunder and hail; and I will let you go, and you shall stay no longer."

29 Moses said to him, "As soon as I go out of the city, I will spread out my hands to the LORD; the thunder will cease and there will be hail no longer, that you may know that the earth is the LORD'S.

30 "But as for you and your servants, I know that you do not yet fear the LORD God."

31 (Now the flax and the barley were ruined, for the barley was in the ear and the flax was in bud.

32 But the wheat and the spelt were not ruined, for they *ripen* late.)

33 So Moses went out of the city from Pharaoh, and spread out his hands to the LORD; and the thunder and the hail ceased, and rain no longer poured on the earth.

34 But when Pharaoh saw that the rain and the hail and the thunder had ceased, he sinned again and hardened his heart, he and his servants.

35 Pharaoh's heart was hardened, and he did not let the sons of Israel go, just as the LORD had spoken through Moses.

The Plague of Locusts

10 Then the LORD said to Moses, "Go to Pharaoh, for I have ªhardened his heart and the heart of his servants, that I may perform these signs of Mine among them,

2 and that you may tell in the hearing of your son, and of your grandson, how I made a mockery of the Egyptians and how I performed My signs among them, that you may know that I am the LORD."

3 ¶ Moses and Aaron went to Pharaoh and said to him, "Thus says the LORD, the God of the Hebrews, 'How long will you refuse to humble yourself before Me? Let My people go, that they may serve Me.

4 'For if you refuse to let My people go, behold, tomorrow I will bring locusts into your territory.

5 'They shall cover the surface of the land, so that no one will be able to see the land. They will also eat the rest of what has escaped—what is left to you from the hail—and they will eat every tree which sprouts for you out of the field.

6 'Then your houses shall be filled and the houses of all your servants and the houses of all the Egyptians, *something* which neither your fathers nor your grandfathers have seen, from the day that they came upon the earth until this day.' " And he turned and went out from Pharaoh.

7 Pharaoh's servants said to him, "How long will this man be a snare to us? Let the men go, that they may serve the LORD their God. Do you not realize that Egypt is destroyed?"

8 So Moses and Aaron were brought back to Pharaoh, and he said to them, "Go, serve the LORD your God! Who are the ones that are going?"

9 Moses said, "We shall go with our young and our old; with our sons and our daughters, with our flocks and our herds we shall go, for we must hold a feast to the LORD."

10 Then he said to them, "Thus may the LORD be with you, if ever I let you and your little ones go! Take heed, for evil is in your mind.

11 "Not so! Go now, the men *among you,* and serve the LORD, for that is what you desire." So they were driven out from Pharaoh's presence.

12 ¶ Then the LORD said to Moses, "Stretch out your hand over the land of Egypt for the locusts, that they may come up on the land of Egypt and eat every plant of the land, *even* all that the hail has left."

13 So Moses stretched out his staff over the land of Egypt, and the LORD directed an east wind on the land all that day and all that night; and when it was morning, the east wind brought the locusts.

14 The locusts came up over all the land of Egypt and settled in all the territory of Egypt; *they* were very numerous. There had never been so many locusts, nor would there be so *many* again.

15 For they covered the surface of the whole land, so that the land was darkened; and they ate every plant of the land and all the fruit of the trees that the hail had left. Thus nothing green was left on tree or plant of the field through all the land of Egypt.

16 Then Pharaoh hurriedly called for Moses and Aaron, and he said, "I have sinned against the LORD your God and against you.

17 "Now therefore, please forgive my sin only this once, and make supplication to the LORD your God, that He would only remove this death from me."

18 He went out from Pharaoh and made supplication to the LORD.

19 So the LORD shifted *the wind* to a very strong west wind which took up the locusts and drove them into the ᵇRed Sea; not one locust was left in all the territory of Egypt.

20 But the LORD hardened Pharaoh's heart, and he did not let the sons of Israel go.

Darkness over the Land

21 ¶ Then the LORD said to Moses, "Stretch out your hand toward the sky, that there may be darkness over the land of Egypt, even a darkness which may be felt."

10:21 Attack on False Gods

God used ten plagues as a form of warfare against the gods of Egypt (12:12). Some scholars see in each individual punishment an attack against a specific Egyptian idol. Thus they believe the plague on the Nile River opposed the Egyptians' river god, the plague of flies flouted worship of the sacred fly, the plague of darkness attacked the sun-god Ra, and the plague on livestock countered the sacred bull.

22 So Moses stretched out his hand toward the sky, and there was thick darkness in all the land of Egypt for three days.

23 They did not see one another, nor did anyone rise from his place for three days, but all the sons of Israel had light in their dwellings.

24 Then Pharaoh called to Moses, and said, "Go, serve the LORD; only let your flocks and your herds be detained. Even your little ones may go with you."

25 But Moses said, "You must also let us have sacrifices and burnt offerings, that we may sacrifice *them* to the LORD our God.

26 "Therefore, our livestock too shall go with us; not a hoof shall be left behind, for we shall take some of them to serve the LORD our God. And

---

ª Lit *made heavy*   ᵇ Lit *Sea of Reeds*

until we arrive there, we ourselves do not know with what we shall serve the LORD."

27 But the LORD hardened Pharaoh's heart, and he was not willing to let them go.

28 Then Pharaoh said to him, "Get away from me! Beware, do not see my face again, for in the day you see my face you shall die!"

29 Moses said, "You are right; I shall never see your face again!"

The Last Plague

11 Now the LORD said to Moses, "One more plague I will bring on Pharaoh and on Egypt; after that he will let you go from here. When he lets you go, he will surely drive you out from here completely.

2 "Speak now in the hearing of the people that each man ask from his neighbor and each woman

Independence Day
An unusual style of celebrating freedom

THE UNITED STATES CELEBRATES JULY 4 like no other day. The parades, the picnics, and the fireworks boisterously express national pride. We showed 'em, say the politicians in their speeches. With our own sweat and blood we created a nation. We're proud to be Americans.

> "There shall be a great cry in all the land of Egypt, such as there has not been before and such as shall never be again.'" 11:6

A Different Mood for the Jews

Our style of celebration—noisy and flag-waving and proud—captures something of the original spirit that led a young nation to declare independence. A similar spirit surges up in France on Bastille Day and in many other nations on their birthdays. But these celebrations bear a striking *unlikeness* to the Jewish independence day, a day called Passover.

The Jews trace their cultural birthday back to a dark, foreboding night—the Israelites' last in Egypt (Exodus 12). There are no blaring bands nor balloons nor fireworks to commemorate this event. Everything takes place inside a home, with a family or cluster of families gathered around a table. Participants taste morsels of food, pausing before each portion to hear Old Testament accounts of the history they are reliving. Their independence day resembles a worship service, not a party.

A Work of God Alone

More than anything else, the Jewish independence day expresses this one fact: God did it. No Israelite armies stood against the mighty Egyptians. Freedom came in the blackest night while Israelite families huddled around the Passover table, their bags packed, waiting for deliverance.

When God's time came, the Egyptian captors not only released the Israelites, but begged them to go and showered them with gold and riches. The Jews remember that event with humility and praise; there is no room for pride. Later, when Pharaoh changed his mind and set his chariots loose upon the fleeing tribes, God came through again. Israelites stood trembling like cowards, already second-guessing their freedom. But God destroyed the great Egyptian army.

For the children of Israel, independence from Egypt meant dependence on God. In fact, God came back to this event throughout the Bible as a way of describing himself: "I am the LORD your God, who brought you out of Egypt."

The pattern of dependence was to continue all through Exodus. When the wilderness wanderers ran out of water, God provided. When food supplies failed, God provided. When raiders attacked, God provided. Independence day merely set the tone for a national history that was an active movement of God.

Passover's New Meaning

Much later, Passover night would take on an even broader significance. During one particular Passover feast, as thousands of Jews were bringing their choice lambs to Jerusalem, one man was selected as the Passover Lamb for all humanity (1 Corinthians 5:7). The words "When I see the blood I will pass over you" (12:13) came to convey a whole new meaning.

Today, though Jewish people still celebrate Passover, most Christians do not. Rather, that ceremony has been incorporated into a new one called the Eucharist, or the Lord's Supper, with Christ representing the Passover lamb. Although much of the ceremony's content has changed, one thing has not. The Lord's Supper, too, memorializes a time of pain and of bloodshed, a time of freedom and deliverance. It, too, was God's act alone. He gets the credit.

Life Questions: Does your church's celebration of the Eucharist, or Lord's Supper, resemble the Jewish Passover described here? How are they similar or different?

from her neighbor for articles of silver and articles of gold."

3 The LORD gave the people favor in the sight of the Egyptians. Furthermore, the man Moses *himself* was greatly esteemed in the land of Egypt, *both* in the sight of Pharaoh's servants and in the sight of the people.

4 ¶ Moses said, "Thus says the LORD, 'About midnight I am going out into the midst of Egypt,

5 and all the firstborn in the land of Egypt shall die, from the firstborn of the Pharaoh who sits on his throne, even to the firstborn of the slave girl who is behind the millstones; all the firstborn of the cattle as well.

6 'Moreover, there shall be a great cry in all the land of Egypt, such as there has not been *before* and such as shall never be again.

7 'But against any of the sons of Israel a dog will not *even* bark, whether against man or beast, that you may understand how the LORD makes a distinction between Egypt and Israel.'

8 "All these your servants will come down to me and bow themselves before me, saying, 'Go out, you and all the people who follow you,' and after that I will go out." And he went out from Pharaoh in hot anger.

9 ¶ Then the LORD said to Moses, "Pharaoh will not listen to you, so that My wonders will be multiplied in the land of Egypt."

10 Moses and Aaron performed all these wonders before Pharaoh; yet the LORD hardened Pharaoh's heart, and he did not let the sons of Israel go out of his land.

The Passover Lamb

12 Now the LORD said to Moses and Aaron in the land of Egypt,

2 "This month shall be the beginning of months for you; it is to be the first month of the year to you.

3 "Speak to all the congregation of Israel, saying, 'On the tenth of this month they are each one to take a lamb for themselves, according to their fathers' households, a lamb for each household.

4 'Now if the household is too small for a lamb, then he and his neighbor nearest to his house are to take one according to the number of persons *in them*; according to what each man should eat, you are to divide the lamb.

5 'Your lamb shall be an unblemished male a year old; you may take it from the sheep or from the goats.

6 'You shall keep it until the fourteenth day of the same month, then the whole assembly of the congregation of Israel is to kill it at twilight.

7 'Moreover, they shall take some of the blood and put it on the two doorposts and on the lintel of the houses in which they eat it.

8 'They shall eat the flesh that *same* night, roasted with fire, and they shall eat it with unleavened bread and bitter herbs.

9 'Do not eat any of it raw or boiled at all with water, but rather roasted with fire, *both* its head and its legs along with its entrails.

10 'And you shall not leave any of it over until

12:8–11 Fast Food

God's instructions for the Passover stress the need for haste. Roasting over fire cooks meat faster than boiling, and (unlike frying or baking) requires no pan or oven. Likewise, bread without yeast doesn't need time to rise. The emphasis on speed indicated to the Israelites how terrible this plague would be, and how swiftly they had to flee from Egypt.

morning, but whatever is left of it until morning, you shall burn with fire.

11 'Now you shall eat it in this manner: *with* your loins girded, your sandals on your feet, and your staff in your hand; and you shall eat it in haste—it is the LORD'S Passover.

12 'For I will go through the land of Egypt on that night, and will strike down all the firstborn in the land of Egypt, both man and beast; and against all the gods of Egypt I will execute judgments—I am the LORD.

13 'The blood shall be a sign for you on the houses where you live; and when I see the blood I will pass over you, and no plague will befall you to destroy *you* when I strike the land of Egypt.

Feast of Unleavened Bread

14 ¶ 'Now this day will be a memorial to you, and you shall celebrate it *as* a feast to the LORD; throughout your generations you are to celebrate it *as* a permanent ordinance.

15 'Seven days you shall eat unleavened bread, but on the first day you shall remove leaven from your houses; for whoever eats anything leavened from the first day until the seventh day, that person shall be cut off from Israel.

16 'On the first day you shall have a holy assembly, and *another* holy assembly on the seventh day; no work at all shall be done on them, except what must be eaten by every person, that alone may be prepared by you.

17 'You shall also observe the *Feast of* Unleavened Bread, for on this very day I brought your hosts out of the land of Egypt; therefore you shall observe this day throughout your generations as a permanent ordinance.

18 'In the first *month*, on the fourteenth day of the month at evening, you shall eat unleavened bread, until the twenty-first day of the month at evening.

19 'Seven days there shall be no leaven found in your houses; for whoever eats what is leavened, that person shall be cut off from the congregation

of Israel, whether *he is* an alien or a native of the land.

20 'You shall not eat anything leavened; in all your dwellings you shall eat unleavened bread.' "

21 ¶ Then Moses called for all the elders of Israel and said to them, "Go and take for yourselves lambs according to your families, and slay the Passover *lamb.*

22 "You shall take a bunch of hyssop and dip it in the blood which is in the basin, and apply some of the blood that is in the basin to the lintel and the two doorposts; and none of you shall go outside the door of his house until morning.

A Memorial of Redemption

23 "For the LORD will pass through to smite the Egyptians; and when He sees the blood on the lintel and on the two doorposts, the LORD will pass over the door and will not allow the destroyer to come in to your houses to smite *you.*

24 "And you shall observe this event as an ordinance for you and your children forever.

25 "When you enter the land which the LORD will give you, as He has promised, you shall observe this rite.

26 "And when your children say to you, 'What does this rite mean to you?'

27 you shall say, 'It is a Passover sacrifice to the LORD who passed over the houses of the sons of Israel in Egypt when He smote the Egyptians, but spared our homes.' " And the people bowed low and worshiped.

28 ¶ Then the sons of Israel went and did *so;* just as the LORD had commanded Moses and Aaron, so they did.

29 ¶ Now it came about at midnight that the LORD struck all the firstborn in the land of Egypt, from the firstborn of Pharaoh who sat on his throne to the firstborn of the captive who was in the dungeon, and all the firstborn of cattle.

30 Pharaoh arose in the night, he and all his servants and all the Egyptians, and there was a great cry in Egypt, for there was no home where there was not someone dead.

31 Then he called for Moses and Aaron at night and said, "Rise up, get out from among my people, both you and the sons of Israel; and go, worship the LORD, as you have said.

32 "Take both your flocks and your herds, as you have said, and go, and bless me also."

Exodus of Israel

33 The Egyptians urged the people, to send them out of the land in haste, for they said, "We will all be dead."

34 So the people took their dough before it was leavened, *with* their kneading bowls bound up in the clothes on their shoulders.

35 ¶ Now the sons of Israel had done according to the word of Moses, for they had requested

from the Egyptians articles of silver and articles of gold, and clothing;

36 and the LORD had given the people favor in the sight of the Egyptians, so that they let them have their request. Thus they plundered the Egyptians.

37 ¶ Now the sons of Israel journeyed from Rameses to Succoth, about six hundred thousand men on foot, aside from children.

38 A mixed multitude also went up with them, along with flocks and herds, a very large number of livestock.

39 They baked the dough which they had brought out of Egypt into cakes of unleavened bread. For it had not become leavened, since they were driven out of Egypt and could not delay, nor had they prepared any provisions for themselves.

40 ¶ Now the time that the sons of Israel lived in Egypt was four hundred and thirty years.

41 And at the end of four hundred and thirty years, to the very day, all the hosts of the LORD went out from the land of Egypt.

Ordinance of the Passover

42 It is a night to be observed for the LORD for having brought them out from the land of Egypt; this night is for the LORD, to be observed by all the sons of Israel throughout their generations.

43 ¶ The LORD said to Moses and Aaron, "This is the ordinance of the Passover: no *ᵃforeigner is to eat of it;

44 but every man's slave purchased with money, after you have circumcised him, then he may eat of it.

45 "A sojourner or a hired servant shall not eat of it.

46 "It is to be eaten in a single house; you are not to bring forth any of the flesh outside of the house, nor are you to break any bone of it.

47 "All the congregation of Israel are to celebrate this.

48 "But if a stranger sojourns with you, and celebrates the Passover to the LORD, let all his males be circumcised, and then let him come near to celebrate it; and he shall be like a native of the land. But no uncircumcised person may eat of it.

49 "The same law shall apply to the native as to the stranger who sojourns among you."

50 ¶ Then all the sons of Israel did *so;* they did just as the LORD had commanded Moses and Aaron.

51 And on that same day the LORD brought the sons of Israel out of the land of Egypt by their hosts.

Consecration of the Firstborn

13 Then the LORD spoke to Moses, saying,
2 "Sanctify to Me every firstborn, the first offspring of every womb among the sons of Israel, both of man and beast; it belongs to Me."

ᵃ Lit *son of a stranger*

3 ¶ Moses said to the people, "Remember this day in which you went out from Egypt, from the house of slavery; for by a powerful hand the LORD brought you out from this place. And nothing leavened shall be eaten.

13:1 The Firstborn Principle

At the time of the Passover and the exodus from Egypt, God introduced an important principle: every firstborn male, including animals, was to be dedicated to him. Later, the Levites were established as a symbolic firstborn for all the people, with very precise accounting (Numbers 3:40–51).

4 "On this day in the month of Abib, you are about to go forth.

5 "It shall be when the LORD brings you to the land of the Canaanite, the Hittite, the Amorite, the Hivite and the Jebusite, which He swore to your fathers to give you, a land flowing with milk and honey, that you shall observe this rite in this month.

6 "For seven days you shall eat unleavened bread, and on the seventh day there shall be a feast to the LORD.

7 "Unleavened bread shall be eaten throughout the seven days; and nothing leavened shall be seen among you, nor shall any leaven be seen among you in all your borders.

8 "You shall tell your son on that day, saying, 'It is because of what the LORD did for me when I came out of Egypt.'

9 "And it shall serve as a sign to you on your hand, and as a reminder on your forehead, that the law of the LORD may be in your mouth; for with a powerful hand the LORD brought you out of Egypt.

10 "Therefore, you shall keep this ordinance at its appointed time from year to year.

11 ¶ "Now when the LORD brings you to the land of the Canaanite, as He swore to you and to your fathers, and gives it to you,

12 you shall devote to the LORD the first offspring of every womb, and the first offspring of every beast that you own; the males belong to the LORD.

13 "But every first offspring of a donkey you shall redeem with a lamb, but if you do not redeem *it,* then you shall break its neck; and every firstborn of man among your sons you shall redeem.

14 "And it shall be when your son asks you in time to come, saying, 'What is this?' then you shall say to him, 'With a powerful hand the LORD brought us out of Egypt, from the house of slavery.

15 'It came about, when Pharaoh was stubborn about letting us go, that the LORD killed every firstborn in the land of Egypt, both the firstborn of man and the firstborn of beast. Therefore, I sacrifice to the LORD the males, the first offspring of every womb, but every firstborn of my sons I redeem.'

16 "So it shall serve as a sign on your hand and as phylacteries on your forehead, for with a powerful hand the LORD brought us out of Egypt."

God Leads the People

17 ¶ Now when Pharaoh had let the people go, God did not lead them by the way of the land of the Philistines, even though it was near; for God said, "The people might change their minds when they see war, and return to Egypt."

18 Hence God led the people around by the way of the wilderness to the Red Sea; and the sons of Israel went up in martial array from the land of Egypt.

19 Moses took the bones of Joseph with him, for he had made the sons of Israel solemnly swear, saying, "God will surely take care of you, and you shall carry my bones from here with you."

20 Then they set out from Succoth and camped in Etham on the edge of the wilderness.

21 The LORD was going before them in a pillar of cloud by day to lead them on the way, and in a pillar of fire by night to give them light, that they might travel by day and by night.

22 He did not take away the pillar of cloud by day, nor the pillar of fire by night, from before the people.

Pharaoh in Pursuit

14 Now the LORD spoke to Moses, saying,
2 "Tell the sons of Israel to turn back and camp before Pi-hahiroth, between Migdol and the sea; you shall camp in front of Baal-zephon, opposite it, by the sea.

3 "For Pharaoh will say of the sons of Israel, 'They are wandering aimlessly in the land; the wilderness has shut them in.'

4 "Thus I will harden Pharaoh's heart, and he will chase after them; and I will be honored through Pharaoh and all his army, and the Egyptians will know that I am the LORD." And they did so.

5 ¶ When the king of Egypt was told that the people had fled, Pharaoh and his servants had a change of heart toward the people, and they said, "What is this we have done, that we have let Israel go from serving us?"

6 So he made his chariot ready and took his people with him;

7 and he took six hundred select chariots, and all the *other* chariots of Egypt with officers over all of them.

8 The LORD hardened the heart of Pharaoh, king of Egypt, and he chased after the sons of Israel as the sons of Israel were going out boldly.

9 Then the Egyptians chased after them *with*

all the horses *and* chariots of Pharaoh, his horsemen and his army, and they overtook them camping by the sea, beside Pi-hahiroth, in front of Baal-zephon.

10 ¶ As Pharaoh drew near, the sons of Israel looked, and behold, the Egyptians were marching after them, and they became very frightened; so the sons of Israel cried out to the LORD.

11 Then they said to Moses, "Is it because there were no graves in Egypt that you have taken us away to die in the wilderness? Why have you dealt with us in this way, bringing us out of Egypt?

12 "Is this not the word that we spoke to you in Egypt, saying, 'Leave us alone that we may serve the Egyptians'? For it would have been better for us to serve the Egyptians than to die in the wilderness."

The Sea Is Divided

13 But Moses said to the people, "Do not fear! Stand by and see the salvation of the LORD which He will accomplish for you today; for the Egyptians whom you have seen today, you will never see them again forever.

14 "The LORD will fight for you while you keep silent."

15 ¶ Then the LORD said to Moses, "Why are you crying out to Me? Tell the sons of Israel to go forward.

16 "As for you, lift up your staff and stretch out your hand over the sea and divide it, and the sons of Israel shall go through the midst of the sea on dry land.

17 "As for Me, behold, I will harden the hearts of the Egyptians so that they will go in after them; and I will be honored through Pharaoh and all his army, through his chariots and his horsemen.

18 "Then the Egyptians will know that I am the LORD, when I am honored through Pharaoh, through his chariots and his horsemen."

19 ¶ The angel of God, who had been going before the camp of Israel, moved and went behind them; and the pillar of cloud moved from before them and stood behind them.

20 So it came between the camp of Egypt and the camp of Israel; and there was the cloud along with the darkness, yet it gave light at night. Thus the one did not come near the other all night.

21 ¶ Then Moses stretched out his hand over the sea; and the LORD swept the sea *back* by a strong east wind all night and turned the sea into dry land, so the waters were divided.

22 The sons of Israel went through the midst of the sea on the dry land, and the waters *were like* a wall to them on their right hand and on their left.

23 Then the Egyptians took up the pursuit, and all Pharaoh's horses, his chariots and his horsemen went in after them into the midst of the sea.

24 At the morning watch, the LORD looked down on the army of the Egyptians through the pillar of fire and cloud and brought the army of the Egyptians into confusion.

25 He caused their chariot wheels to swerve, and He made them drive with difficulty; so the

14:21 Final Escape

Hemmed in by mountains, the sea, and the Egyptian army, the Israelites seemed doomed until God opened a highway through the sea. This miracle closed an important chapter in the Israelites' history. Never again would the powerful Egyptian empire rule over them; most of their future enemies swept in from the north and east.

Egyptians said, "Let us flee from Israel, for the LORD is fighting for them against the Egyptians."

26 ¶ Then the LORD said to Moses, "Stretch out your hand over the sea so that the waters may come back over the Egyptians, over their chariots and their horsemen."

27 So Moses stretched out his hand over the sea, and the sea returned to its normal state at daybreak, while the Egyptians were fleeing right into it; then the LORD overthrew the Egyptians in the midst of the sea.

28 The waters returned and covered the chariots and the horsemen, even Pharaoh's entire army that had gone into the sea after them; not even one of them remained.

29 But the sons of Israel walked on dry land through the midst of the sea, and the waters *were like* a wall to them on their right hand and on their left.

30 ¶ Thus the LORD saved Israel that day from the hand of the Egyptians, and Israel saw the Egyptians dead on the seashore.

31 When Israel saw the great power which the LORD had used against the Egyptians, the people feared the LORD, and they believed in the LORD and in His servant Moses.

The Song of Moses and Israel

15 Then Moses and the sons of Israel sang this song to the LORD, and said,
"I will sing to the LORD, for He is highly exalted;
The horse and its rider He has hurled into the sea.

2 "The LORD is my strength and song,
And He has become my salvation;
This is my God, and I will praise Him;
My father's God, and I will extol Him.

3 "The LORD is a warrior;
The LORD is His name.

4 "Pharaoh's chariots and his army He has cast into the sea;

And the choicest of his officers are
  drowned in the [a]Red Sea.
5 "The deeps cover them;
  They went down into the depths like a
    stone.

15:18 A Story for All Time

*Moses' song celebrates the event from which
this book gets its name: "the exodus" from
Egypt, when a band of slaves escaped from the
most powerful civilization on earth. The
psalmists never tired of celebrating that event
in song (see, for example, Psalms 78 and 105),
and the prophets later harked back to the days
of the exodus to stir the conscience of their
nation. The Israelites' liberation gave
inspiration to the slaves of the American South,
who often memorialized the exodus in their
spirituals.*

6 "Your right hand, O LORD, is majestic in
    power,
  Your right hand, O LORD, shatters the
    enemy.
7 "And in the greatness of Your excellence
  You overthrow those who rise up
    against You;
  You send forth Your burning anger, *and*
    it consumes them as chaff.
8 "At the blast of Your nostrils the waters
    were piled up,
  The flowing waters stood up like a heap;
  The deeps were congealed in the heart of
    the sea.
9 "The enemy said, 'I will pursue, I will
    overtake, I will divide the spoil;
  My desire shall be gratified against them;
  I will draw out my sword, my hand will
    destroy them.'
10 "You blew with Your wind, the sea
    covered them;
  They sank like lead in the mighty waters.
11 "Who is like You among the gods,
    O LORD?
  Who is like You, majestic in holiness,
  Awesome in praises, working wonders?
12 "You stretched out Your right hand,
  The earth swallowed them.
13 "In Your lovingkindness You have led the
    people whom You have redeemed;
  In Your strength You have guided *them*
    to Your holy habitation.
14 "The peoples have heard, they tremble;
  Anguish has gripped the inhabitants of
    Philistia.
15 "Then the chiefs of Edom were dismayed;

The leaders of Moab, trembling grips
  them;
All the inhabitants of Canaan have
  melted away.
16 "Terror and dread fall upon them;
  By the greatness of Your arm they are
    motionless as stone;
  Until Your people pass over, O LORD,
  Until the people pass over whom You
    have purchased.
17 "You will bring them and plant them in
    the mountain of Your inheritance,
  The place, O LORD, which You have
    made for Your dwelling,
  The sanctuary, O Lord, which Your
    hands have established.
18 "The LORD shall reign forever and ever."

19 ¶ For the horses of Pharaoh with his chariots and his horsemen went into the sea, and the
LORD brought back the waters of the sea on them,
but the sons of Israel walked on dry land through
the midst of the sea.

20 ¶ Miriam the prophetess, Aaron's sister,
took the timbrel in her hand, and all the women
went out after her with timbrels and with dancing.
21 Miriam answered them,
  "Sing to the LORD, for He is highly
    exalted;
  The horse and his rider He has hurled
    into the sea."

The LORD Provides Water

22 ¶ Then Moses led Israel from the Red Sea,
and they went out into the wilderness of Shur; and
they went three days in the wilderness and found
no water.
23 When they came to Marah, they could not
drink the waters of Marah, for they were bitter;
therefore it was named [b]Marah.
24 So the people grumbled at Moses, saying,
"What shall we drink?"
25 Then he cried out to the LORD, and the
LORD showed him a tree; and he threw *it* into the
waters, and the waters became sweet.
¶ There He made for them a statute and regulation, and there He tested them.
26 And He said, "If you will give earnest heed
to the voice of the LORD your God, and do what
is right in His sight, and give ear to His commandments, and keep all His statutes, I will put none of
the diseases on you which I have put on the Egyptians; for I, the LORD, am your healer."
27 ¶ Then they came to Elim where there *were*
twelve springs of water and seventy date palms,
and they camped there beside the waters.

The LORD Provides Manna

16 Then they set out from Elim, and all the
congregation of the sons of Israel came to
the wilderness of Sin, which is between Elim and

[a] Lit *Sea of Reeds*   [b] I.e. bitterness

Sinai, on the fifteenth day of the second month after their departure from the land of Egypt.

2 The whole congregation of the sons of Israel grumbled against Moses and Aaron in the wilderness.

3 The sons of Israel said to them, "Would that we had died by the LORD's hand in the land of Egypt, when we sat by the pots of meat, when we ate bread to the full; for you have brought us out into this wilderness to kill this whole assembly with hunger."

4 ¶ Then the LORD said to Moses, "Behold, I will rain bread from heaven for you; and the people shall go out and gather a day's portion every day, that I may test them, whether or not they will walk in My *a*instruction.

5 "On the sixth day, when they prepare what they bring in, it will be twice as much as they gather daily."

6 So Moses and Aaron said to all the sons of Israel, "At evening you will know that the LORD has brought you out of the land of Egypt;

7 and in the morning you will see the glory of the LORD, for He hears your grumblings against the LORD; and what are we, that you grumble against us?"

The LORD Provides Meat

8 Moses said, *"This will happen* when the LORD gives you meat to eat in the evening, and bread to the full in the morning; for the LORD hears your grumblings which you grumble against Him. And what are we? Your grumblings are not against us but against the LORD."

9 ¶ Then Moses said to Aaron, "Say to all the congregation of the sons of Israel, 'Come near before the LORD, for He has heard your grumblings.' "

10 It came about as Aaron spoke to the whole congregation of the sons of Israel, that they looked toward the wilderness, and behold, the glory of the LORD appeared in the cloud.

11 And the LORD spoke to Moses, saying,

12 "I have heard the grumblings of the sons of Israel; speak to them, saying, 'At twilight you shall eat meat, and in the morning you shall be filled with bread; and you shall know that I am the LORD your God.' "

13 ¶ So it came about at evening that the quails came up and covered the camp, and in the morning there was a layer of dew around the camp.

14 When the layer of dew evaporated, behold, on the surface of the wilderness there was a fine flake-like thing, fine as the frost on the ground.

15 When the sons of Israel saw *it,* they said to one another, "What is it?" For they did not know what it was. And Moses said to them, "It is the bread which the LORD has given you to eat.

16 "This is what the LORD has commanded, 'Gather of it every man as much as he should eat;

you shall take an omer apiece according to the number of persons each of you has in his tent.' "

17 The sons of Israel did so, and *some* gathered much and *some* little.

16:12–15 Food Supply

The word manna *means literally, "What is it?" recalling the Israelites' first reaction to it (verse 15). Manna is a clear example of the Israelites' enforced dependence on God; they had to rely on him every day for 40 years, just to survive. God's provision of manna made greed impossible: it could not be hoarded and was distributed with precise equity (verses 17–21).*

Quails, referred to here and in Numbers 11, still migrate across the Sinai peninsula, flying in great flocks between Europe and Arabia. Exhausted by their long flight, they roost on the ground or in low bushes at night, making capture easy.

18 When they measured it with an omer, he who had gathered much had no excess, and he who had gathered little had no lack; every man gathered as much as he should eat.

19 Moses said to them, "Let no man leave any of it until morning."

20 But they did not listen to Moses, and some left part of it until morning, and it bred worms and became foul; and Moses was angry with them.

21 They gathered it morning by morning, every man as much as he should eat; but when the sun grew hot, it would melt.

The Sabbath Observed

22 ¶ Now on the sixth day they gathered twice as much bread, two omers for each one. When all the leaders of the congregation came and told Moses,

23 then he said to them, "This is what the LORD meant: Tomorrow is a sabbath observance, a holy sabbath to the LORD. Bake what you will bake and boil what you will boil, and all that is left over put aside to be kept until morning."

24 So they put it aside until morning, as Moses had ordered, and it did not become foul nor was there any worm in it.

25 Moses said, "Eat it today, for today is a sabbath to the LORD; today you will not find it in the field.

26 "Six days you shall gather it, but on the seventh day, *the* sabbath, there will be none."

27 ¶ It came about on the seventh day that some of the people went out to gather, but they found none.

28 Then the LORD said to Moses, "How long

a Or *law*

do you refuse to keep My commandments and My ^ainstructions?

29 "See, the LORD has given you the sabbath; therefore He gives you bread for two days on the sixth day. Remain every man in his place; let no man go out of his place on the seventh day."

30 So the people rested on the seventh day.

31 ¶ The house of Israel named it manna, and it was like coriander seed, white, and its taste was like wafers with honey.

32 Then Moses said, "This is what the LORD has commanded, 'Let an omerful of it be kept throughout your generations, that they may see the bread that I fed you in the wilderness, when I brought you out of the land of Egypt.' "

33 Moses said to Aaron, "Take a jar and put an omerful of manna in it, and place it before the LORD to be kept throughout your generations."

34 As the LORD commanded Moses, so Aaron placed it before the Testimony, to be kept.

35 The sons of Israel ate the manna forty years, until they came to an inhabited land; they ate the manna until they came to the border of the land of Canaan.

36 (Now an omer is a tenth of an ephah.)

Water in the Rock

17 Then all the congregation of the sons of Israel journeyed by stages from the wilderness of Sin, according to the command of the LORD, and camped at Rephidim, and there was no water for the people to drink.

17:1 Change of Scenery

Unlike the Sahara and Saudi Arabian deserts, the Sinai peninsula is no dry, sandy wasteland. A high plateau in the north gives way to a broad belt of sandstone and sand, and then a tumbled mass of mountains (some reaching 9,000 feet) in the south. Herbs and acacia trees grow, and widely scattered springs permit some farming, although the Sinai cannot support a large population. Moses' 40-year stint as a shepherd here would have taught him much about wilderness survival.

2 Therefore the people quarreled with Moses and said, "Give us water that we may drink." And Moses said to them, "Why do you quarrel with me? Why do you test the LORD?"

3 But the people thirsted there for water; and they grumbled against Moses and said, "Why, now, have you brought us up from Egypt, to kill us and our children and our livestock with thirst?"

4 So Moses cried out to the LORD, saying, "What shall I do to this people? A little more and they will stone me."

5 Then the LORD said to Moses, "Pass before the people and take with you some of the elders of Israel; and take in your hand your staff with which you struck the Nile, and go.

6 "Behold, I will stand before you there on the rock at Horeb; and you shall strike the rock, and water will come out of it, that the people may drink." And Moses did so in the sight of the elders of Israel.

7 He named the place ^bMassah and ^cMeribah because of the quarrel of the sons of Israel, and because they tested the LORD, saying, "Is the LORD among us, or not?"

Amalek Fought

8 ¶ Then Amalek came and fought against Israel at Rephidim.

9 So Moses said to Joshua, "Choose men for us and go out, fight against Amalek. Tomorrow I will station myself on the top of the hill with the staff of God in my hand."

10 Joshua did as Moses told him, and fought against Amalek; and Moses, Aaron, and Hur went up to the top of the hill.

11 So it came about when Moses held his hand up, that Israel prevailed, and when he let his hand down, Amalek prevailed.

12 But Moses' hands were heavy. Then they took a stone and put it under him, and he sat on it; and Aaron and Hur supported his hands, one on one side and one on the other. Thus his hands were steady until the sun set.

13 So Joshua overwhelmed Amalek and his people with the edge of the sword.

14 ¶ Then the LORD said to Moses, "Write this in a book as a memorial and recite it to Joshua, that I will utterly blot out the memory of Amalek from under heaven."

17:14 First Writing

Civilization mastered the skill of writing at least as early as 3400 B.C., when a society near present-day Iraq introduced it, but this is the Bible's first mention of the practice. Moses' training in Egypt would have included writing on "paper" made from pulpy reeds of the papyrus plant. A basket fashioned out of such reeds had helped save Moses' life as an infant (2:3).

15 Moses built an altar and named it The LORD is My Banner;

16 and he said, "The LORD has sworn; the LORD will have war against Amalek from generation to generation."

^a Or *laws*   ^b I.e. test   ^c I.e. quarrel

Jethro, Moses' Father-in-law

18 Now Jethro, the priest of Midian, Moses' father-in-law, heard of all that God had done for Moses and for Israel His people, how the LORD had brought Israel out of Egypt.

2 Jethro, Moses' father-in-law, took Moses' wife Zipporah, after he had sent her away,

3 and her two sons, of whom one was named Gershom, for Moses said, "I have been a sojourner in a foreign land."

4 The other was named Eliezer, for *he said,* "The God of my father was my help, and delivered me from the sword of Pharaoh."

5 ¶ Then Jethro, Moses' father-in-law, came with his sons and his wife to Moses in the wilderness where he was camped, at the mount of God.

6 He sent word to Moses, "I, your father-in-law Jethro, am coming to you with your wife and her two sons with her."

7 Then Moses went out to meet his father-in-law, and he bowed down and kissed him; and they asked each other of their welfare and went into the tent.

8 Moses told his father-in-law all that the LORD had done to Pharaoh and to the Egyptians for Israel's sake, all the hardship that had befallen them on the journey, and *how* the LORD had delivered them.

9 Jethro rejoiced over all the goodness which the LORD had done to Israel, in delivering them from the hand of the Egyptians.

10 So Jethro said, "Blessed be the LORD who delivered you from the hand of the Egyptians and from the hand of Pharaoh, *and* who delivered the people from under the hand of the Egyptians.

11 "Now I know that the LORD is greater than all the gods; indeed, it was proven when they dealt proudly against the people."

12 Then Jethro, Moses' father-in-law, took a burnt offering and sacrifices for God, and Aaron came with all the elders of Israel to eat a meal with Moses' father-in-law before God.

13 ¶ It came about the next day that Moses sat to judge the people, and the people stood about Moses from the morning until the evening.

14 Now when Moses' father-in-law saw all that he was doing for the people, he said, "What is this thing that you are doing for the people? Why do you alone sit *as judge* and all the people stand about you from morning until evening?"

15 Moses said to his father-in-law, "Because the people come to me to inquire of God.

16 "When they have a dispute, it comes to me, and I judge between a man and his neighbor and make known the statutes of God and His laws."

Jethro Counsels Moses

17 Moses' father-in-law said to him, "The thing that you are doing is not good.

18 "You will surely wear out, both yourself and these people who are with you, for the task is too heavy for you; you cannot do it alone.

19 "Now listen to me: I will give you counsel, and God be with you. You be the people's representative before God, and you bring the disputes to God,

20 then teach them the statutes and the laws,

JETHRO *Advice from an In-Law*

A NEWLYWED HUSBAND CAN COUNT on one thing from his father-in-law: advice. He has, after all, married the woman his father-in-law has cared for from birth. And his father-in-law is older and more experienced than he. Under such conditions, advice is virtually inevitable.

After Moses led Israel out of Egypt, his father-in-law Jethro brought Moses' wife and children to join the rest of the Israelites. The old man stayed for a visit and observed Moses at work. Quickly he saw that the sheer volume of the work was overwhelming Moses. Jethro suggested that Moses appoint sub-officials to settle disputes, reserving only the most difficult cases for himself. Moses recognized this good advice, and acted on it.

Moses apparently liked and respected his father-in-law, and with good reason—Jethro took him in when he was running for his life after killing an Egyptian. And in addition to letting Moses marry his daughter, Jethro gave him a job. These men lived and worked together for forty years before God called Moses back to his people.

Jethro was, furthermore, a "priest of Midian." We don't know exactly how much of the true God Jethro knew before Moses came. Midianites, descended from Abraham, may have remembered "the God of Abraham, Isaac and Jacob." Surely Jethro and Moses talked often of their faith. After the Exodus, when Moses told Jethro how God had liberated the slaves from Pharaoh, Jethro acknowledged Moses' God as greater than all other gods.

Even so, Jethro did not accompany the Israelites on their journey to the promised land. He returned to his home, a believer in God remaining apart from God's chosen people.

Life Questions: Can you think of advice that proved especially helpful to you? What was it, and why was it beneficial?

and make known to them the way in which they are to walk and the work they are to do.

21 "Furthermore, you shall select out of all the people able men who fear God, men of truth, those who hate dishonest gain; and you shall place *these* over them *as* leaders of thousands, of hundreds, of fifties and of tens.

22 "Let them judge the people at all times; and let it be that every major dispute they will bring to you, but every minor dispute they themselves will judge. So it will be easier for you, and they will bear *the burden* with you.

23 "If you do this thing and God *so* commands you, then you will be able to endure, and all these people also will go to their place in peace."

24 ¶ So Moses listened to his father-in-law and did all that he had said.

25 Moses chose able men out of all Israel and made them heads over the people, leaders of thousands, of hundreds, of fifties and of tens.

26 They judged the people at all times; the difficult dispute they would bring to Moses, but every minor dispute they themselves would judge.

27 Then Moses bade his father-in-law farewell, and he went his way into his own land.

Moses on Sinai

19 In the third month after the sons of Israel had gone out of the land of Egypt, on that very day they came into the wilderness of Sinai.

2 When they set out from Rephidim, they came to the wilderness of Sinai and camped in the wilderness; and there Israel camped in front of the mountain.

3 Moses went up to God, and the LORD called to him from the mountain, saying, "Thus you shall say to the house of Jacob and tell the sons of Israel:

4 'You yourselves have seen what I did to the Egyptians, and *how* I bore you on eagles' wings, and brought you to Myself.

5 'Now then, if you will indeed obey My voice and keep My covenant, then you shall be My *a*own possession among all the peoples, for all the earth is Mine;

6 and you shall be to Me a kingdom of priests and a holy nation.' These are the words that you shall speak to the sons of Israel."

7 ¶ So Moses came and called the elders of the people, and set before them all these words which the LORD had commanded him.

8 All the people answered together and said, "All that the LORD has spoken we will do!" And Moses brought back the words of the people to the LORD.

9 The LORD said to Moses, "Behold, I will come to you in a thick cloud, so that the people may hear when I speak with you and may also believe in you forever." Then Moses told the words of the people to the LORD.

10 ¶ The LORD also said to Moses, "Go to the people and consecrate them today and tomorrow, and let them wash their garments;

11 and let them be ready for the third day, for

> ### 19:5 Book of the Covenant
> *The word* covenant *appears throughout the next portion of Exodus. Chapter 19 gives the dramatic setting, and chapters 20–23 contain the actual covenant, a treaty between God and the Israelites. Chapter 24 shows the covenant being confirmed. Another word for covenant is* testament, *and, in fact, the rest of the Old Testament builds on what took place in these six chapters. Centuries later, biblical writers would dust off the old word* covenant *and apply it to Jesus Christ (as in 1 Corinthians 11:25). He fulfilled and completed the reconciliation with God begun at Sinai.*

on the third day the LORD will come down on Mount Sinai in the sight of all the people.

12 "You shall set bounds for the people all around, saying, 'Beware that you do not go up on the mountain or touch the border of it; whoever touches the mountain shall surely be put to death.

13 'No hand shall touch him, but he shall surely be stoned or *b*shot through; whether beast or man, he shall not live.' When the ram's horn sounds a long blast, they shall come up to the mountain."

14 So Moses went down from the mountain to the people and consecrated the people, and they washed their garments.

15 He said to the people, "Be ready for the third day; do not go near a woman."

16 ¶ So it came about on the third day, when it was morning, that there were thunder and lightning flashes and a thick cloud upon the mountain and a very loud trumpet sound, so that all the people who *were* in the camp trembled.

17 And Moses brought the people out of the camp to meet God, and they stood at the foot of the mountain.

The LORD Visits Sinai

18 Now Mount Sinai *was* all in smoke because the LORD descended upon it in fire; and its smoke ascended like the smoke of a furnace, and the whole mountain quaked violently.

19 When the sound of the trumpet grew louder and louder, Moses spoke and God answered him with thunder.

20 The LORD came down on Mount Sinai, to the top of the mountain; and the LORD called Moses to the top of the mountain, and Moses went up.

a Or *special treasure*   *b* I.e. with arrows

21 Then the LORD spoke to Moses, "Go down, warn the people, so that they do not break through to the LORD to gaze, and many of them perish.

22 "Also let the priests who come near to the LORD consecrate themselves, or else the LORD will break out against them."

23 Moses said to the LORD, "The people cannot come up to Mount Sinai, for You warned us, saying, 'Set bounds about the mountain and consecrate it.' "

24 Then the LORD said to him, "Go down and come up *again*, you and Aaron with you; but do

a Or *besides Me*

not let the priests and the people break through to come up to the LORD, or He will break forth upon them."

25 So Moses went down to the people and told them.

The Ten Commandments

20 Then God spoke all these words, saying, 2 ¶ "I am the LORD your God, who brought you out of the land of Egypt, out of the house of slavery.

3 ¶ "You shall have no other gods *a*before Me.

The Covenant
What difference does a stone tablet make?

MANY SCHOLARS CALL THE NEXT few chapters the most pivotal section of the Old Testament. The Israelites, called before a trembling and smoking mountain by loud trumpet blasts, were about to receive something unique in all history: a stone document to be deposited in the most valuable piece of furniture in the nation, the ark of the covenant. What made a stone tablet so valuable? The "covenant" it summarized was sacred, signed by the finger of God himself.

"'Now then, if you will indeed obey My voice and keep My covenant, then you shall be My own possession among all the peoples.'" 19:5

And yet someone who simply turned to Exodus and started reading the contents of the covenant might have trouble understanding all the fuss. The covenant begins with the familiar Ten Commandments. It proceeds from there to rules on cursing parents and knocking out teeth, oddly mixed in with rules on interest rates and cooking young goats in their mothers' milk. What is so special, after all, about the laws and instructions described here?

Since we don't normally communicate on stone tablets today, the question "What made a stone tablet so valuable?" might better be rephrased, "What makes a piece of paper valuable?" Seen in that light, our society, like the Israelites', stakes an awful lot on certain pieces of paper. Take just three examples: a constitution, a birth certificate, and a marriage certificate.

Constitution

Resting in a helium-filled bronze case in the Library of Congress, the United States Constitution is arguably the most valuable single piece of paper in the entire country. At a moment's notice it can be lowered into a fireproof, shockproof safe. But dollars alone barely hint at the Constitution's value; its real importance comes to light in a marble building down the street, where the Supreme Court hears hundreds of legal cases.

Each case has climbed up from lower courts through an arduous, expensive process, and now only one decision remains. Whatever the Supreme Court decides will rule as the law of the land. The Supreme Court bases its decision on one final authority: the Constitution. If the nine members judge a law "constitutional," the law will stand. If not, it will be overturned.

For Israel, the covenant became their Constitution. Details of the law came out in three main places: here at Sinai (Exodus and Leviticus), during the wilderness wanderings (Numbers), and on the plains of Moab (Deuteronomy). The complete legal code, far longer than the U.S. Constitution, extended from the grand sweep of national policy to petty disputes of living together. God was shaping an entire culture for a group of homeless pilgrims. In all, 613 separate commands ordered their political, social, and spiritual lives. Other nations were haunted by the unpredictability of their gods. Who could tell what would anger or please them? But because of the covenant, Israelites knew exactly what God required and where they stood before him. They had a basis for trust and security as a nation.

Birth Certificate

This piece of paper, with its smudged baby footprint and fancy script, sits in a file drawer 99 per-

4 ¶ "You shall not make for yourself *a*an idol, or any likeness of what is in heaven above or on the earth beneath or in the water under the earth.

20:1–17 Long-lasting Laws

The Ten Commandments given here and in Deuteronomy 5 form a central core of morality, a major advance from other legal codes of the day. The phrase "Judeo-Christian ethics," heard often in U.S. courtrooms and legislative chambers, refers to the broad moral principles derived from laws outlined here and in the next three books.

5 "You shall not worship them or serve them; for I, the LORD your God, am a jealous God, visiting the iniquity of the fathers on the children, on the third and the fourth generations of those who hate Me,

6 but showing lovingkindness to thousands, to those who love Me and keep My commandments.

a Or a graven image

7 ¶ "You shall not take the name of the LORD your God in vain, for the LORD will not leave him unpunished who takes His name in vain.

8 ¶ "Remember the sabbath day, to keep it holy.

9 "Six days you shall labor and do all your work,

10 but the seventh day is a sabbath of the LORD your God; *in it* you shall not do any work, you or your son or your daughter, your male or your female servant or your cattle or your sojourner who stays with you.

11 "For in six days the LORD made the heavens and the earth, the sea and all that is in them, and rested on the seventh day; therefore the LORD blessed the sabbath day and made it holy.

12 ¶ "Honor your father and your mother, that your days may be prolonged in the land which the LORD your God gives you.

13 ¶ "You shall not murder.

14 ¶ "You shall not commit adultery.

15 ¶ "You shall not steal.

16 ¶ "You shall not bear false witness against your neighbor.

17 ¶ "You shall not covet your neighbor's house; you shall not covet your neighbor's wife or

---

cent of the time. But when you need it, you really need it. It can prove that a young-looking person deserves a driver's license or that an older person qualifies for Social Security payments. It establishes your rights as a United States citizen. A birth certificate is valuable indeed.

For Israel, the covenant established its birth as a nation. God said he had chosen the children of Israel as a treasured possession (19:5–6). He wanted a nation unlike any other, a model society centered around a commitment to him. He needed a pure people, kept separate.

The next few books of the Bible spell out the obligations, but also the rewards, of being God's chosen people, his "family." If they obeyed, the Israelites would live free from diseases, their crops would grow bountifully, their women would give birth to many children, their armies would prove victorious—in short, they would enjoy unprecedented national wealth and security (23:20–28). The covenant defined those benefits—all part of being born as the children of God.

Marriage Certificate

Marriage is far more than a piece of paper, surely. It involves love and trust, sexuality, the thousand details involved in two people sharing life together. But in the eyes of the law, marriage requires a piece of paper. The document makes formal and legal the most intimate, personal relationship human beings ever have.

Later, the prophets Hosea, Jeremiah, and Ezekiel would poignantly compare the covenant to marriage. They pointed out that Israel's treatment of God amounted to adultery, and they called the nation back to its original covenant. The laws listed in numbing detail are merely the formal expression of a love relationship between God and his people.

Pieces of paper define the boundaries of a relationship, but in no way can they express it adequately. You cannot get an adequate picture of life in the United States by reading the Constitution's dry prose, nor can you understand the mystery of marriage by studying a certificate in a county courthouse. In the same way, the laws and rules in the Book of the Covenant surely do not yield a complete picture of life in a nation bound to God. But the covenant, and the context in which it came, show much about what God desired from his followers.

Life Questions: Do you own any valuable papers that express a kind of "covenant"? If you drew up a covenant between yourself and God, what would it say?

his male servant or his female servant or his ox or his donkey or anything that belongs to your neighbor."

18 ¶ All the people perceived the thunder and the lightning flashes and the sound of the trumpet and the mountain smoking; and when the people saw *it,* they trembled and stood at a distance.

19 Then they said to Moses, "Speak to us yourself and we will listen; but let not God speak to us, or we will die."

20 Moses said to the people, "Do not be afraid; for God has come in order to test you, and in order that the fear of Him may remain with you, so that you may not sin."

21 So the people stood at a distance, while Moses approached the thick cloud where God *was.*

22 ¶ Then the LORD said to Moses, "Thus you shall say to the sons of Israel, 'You yourselves have seen that I have spoken to you from heaven.

23 'You shall not make *other gods* besides Me; gods of silver or gods of gold, you shall not make for yourselves.

24 'You shall make an altar of earth for Me, and you shall sacrifice on it your burnt offerings and your peace offerings, your sheep and your oxen; in every place where I cause My name to be remembered, I will come to you and bless you.

25 'If you make an altar of stone for Me, you shall not build it of cut stones, for if you wield your tool on it, you will profane it.

26 'And you shall not go up by steps to My altar, so that your nakedness will not be exposed on it.'

Ordinances for the People

21 "Now these are the ordinances which you are to set before them:

2 ¶ "If you buy a Hebrew slave, he shall serve for six years; but on the seventh he shall go out as a free man without payment.

3 "If he comes alone, he shall go out alone; if he is the husband of a wife, then his wife shall go out with him.

21:2 Slave Rights

Many of these laws set a new standard of morality: societies of that day oppressed aliens, mistreated slaves, exploited the poor, and awarded lost animals to their finder. The Israelites' rules governing slavery, for example, were enlightened for their time. Other ancient societies treated slaves as things rather than persons; Israelites were the first to honor them with formal rights. By beginning with laws protecting the lowest on the social scale, God was teaching the value of every human being.

4 "If his master gives him a wife, and she bears him sons or daughters, the wife and her children shall belong to her master, and he shall go out alone.

5 "But if the slave plainly says, 'I love my master, my wife and my children; I will not go out as a free man,'

6 then his master shall bring him to [a]God, then he shall bring him to the door or the doorpost. And his master shall pierce his ear with an awl; and he shall serve him permanently.

7 ¶ "If a man sells his daughter as a female slave, she is not to go free as the male slaves do.

8 "If she is displeasing in the eyes of her master who designated her for himself, then he shall let her be redeemed. He does not have authority to sell her to a foreign people because of his unfairness to her.

9 "If he designates her for his son, he shall deal with her according to the custom of daughters.

10 "If he takes to himself another woman, he may not reduce her food, her clothing, or her conjugal rights.

11 "If he will not do these three *things* for her, then she shall go out for nothing, without *payment of* money.

Personal Injuries

12 ¶ "He who strikes a man so that he dies shall surely be put to death.

13 "But if he did not lie in wait *for him,* but God let *him* fall into his hand, then I will appoint you a place to which he may flee.

14 "If, however, a man acts presumptuously toward his neighbor, so as to kill him craftily, you are to take him *even* from My altar, that he may die.

15 ¶ "He who strikes his father or his mother shall surely be put to death.

16 ¶ "He who kidnaps a man, whether he sells him or he is found in his possession, shall surely be put to death.

17 ¶ "He who curses his father or his mother shall surely be put to death.

18 ¶ "If men have a quarrel and one strikes the other with a stone or with *his* fist, and he does not die but remains in bed,

19 if he gets up and walks around outside on his staff, then he who struck him shall go unpunished; he shall only pay for his loss of time, and shall take care of him until he is completely healed.

20 ¶ "If a man strikes his male or female slave with a rod and he dies at his hand, he shall be punished.

21 "If, however, he survives a day or two, no vengeance shall be taken; for he is his property.

22 ¶ "If men struggle with each other and strike a woman with child so that she gives birth prematurely, yet there is no injury, he shall surely

---

[a] Or *the judges who acted in God's name*

be fined as the woman's husband may demand of him, and he shall pay as the judges *decide*.

23 "But if there is *any further* injury, then you shall appoint *as a penalty* life for life,

24 eye for eye, tooth for tooth, hand for hand, foot for foot,

25 burn for burn, wound for wound, bruise for bruise.

26 ¶ "If a man strikes the eye of his male or female slave, and destroys it, he shall let him go free on account of his eye.

27 "And if he knocks out a tooth of his male or female slave, he shall let him go free on account of his tooth.

28 ¶ "If an ox gores a man or a woman to death, the ox shall surely be stoned and its flesh shall not be eaten; but the owner of the ox shall go unpunished.

29 "If, however, an ox was previously in the habit of goring and its owner has been warned, yet he does not confine it and it kills a man or a woman, the ox shall be stoned and its owner also shall be put to death.

30 "If a ransom is demanded of him, then he shall give for the redemption of his life whatever is demanded of him.

31 "Whether it gores a son or a daughter, it shall be done to him according to the same rule.

32 "If the ox gores a male or female slave, the owner shall give his *or her* master thirty shekels of silver, and the ox shall be stoned.

33 ¶ "If a man opens a pit, or digs a pit and does not cover it over, and an ox or a donkey falls into it,

34 the owner of the pit shall make restitution; he shall give money to its owner, and the dead *animal* shall become his.

35 ¶ "If one man's ox hurts another's so that it dies, then they shall sell the live ox and divide its price equally; and also they shall divide the dead *ox*.

36 "Or *if* it is known that the ox was previously in the habit of goring, yet its owner has not confined it, he shall surely pay ox for ox, and the dead *animal* shall become his.

Property Rights

22 "If a man steals an ox or a sheep and slaughters it or sells it, he shall pay five oxen for the ox and four sheep for the sheep.

2 ¶ "If the thief is caught while breaking in and is struck so that he dies, there will be no bloodguiltiness on his account.

3 "*But* if the sun has risen on him, there will be bloodguiltiness on his account. He shall surely make restitution; if he owns nothing, then he shall be sold for his theft.

4 "If what he stole is actually found alive in his possession, whether an ox or a donkey or a sheep, he shall pay double.

5 ¶ "If a man lets a field or vineyard be grazed

bare and lets his animal loose so that it grazes in another man's field, he shall make restitution from the best of his own field and the best of his own vineyard.

6 ¶ "If a fire breaks out and spreads to thorn bushes, so that stacked grain or the standing grain or the field *itself* is consumed, he who started the fire shall surely make restitution.

7 ¶ "If a man gives his neighbor money or goods to keep *for him* and it is stolen from the man's house, if the thief is caught, he shall pay double.

8 "If the thief is not caught, then the owner of the house shall appear before the judges, *to* determine whether he laid his hands on his neighbor's property.

9 "For every breach of trust, *whether it is* for ox, for donkey, for sheep, for clothing, *or* for any lost thing about which one says, 'This is it,' the case of both parties shall come before the judges; he whom the judges condemn shall pay double to his neighbor.

22:9 Punishment by Restitution

In contrast to the punishments of other contemporary codes (such as Sumer and Babylonia), the penalties for wrongdoing described in the next few chapters emphasize punishments fitted to the crime. They stress restitution rather than vengeance. Modern courtrooms are once again practicing restitution—making the criminal serve society or "make good" to the victim.

10 ¶ "If a man gives his neighbor a donkey, an ox, a sheep, or any animal to keep *for him,* and it dies or is hurt or is driven away while no one is looking,

11 an oath before the LORD shall be made by the two of them that he has not laid hands on his neighbor's property; and its owner shall accept *it,* and he shall not make restitution.

12 "But if it is actually stolen from him, he shall make restitution to its owner.

13 "If it is all torn to pieces, let him bring it as evidence; he shall not make restitution for what has been torn to pieces.

14 ¶ "If a man borrows *anything* from his neighbor, and it is injured or dies while its owner is not with it, he shall make full restitution.

15 "If its owner is with it, he shall not make restitution; if it is hired, it came for its hire.

Sundry Laws

16 ¶ "If a man seduces a virgin who is not engaged, and lies with her, he must pay a dowry for her *to be* his wife.

17 "If her father absolutely refuses to give her to

him, he shall pay money equal to the dowry for virgins.

18 ¶ "You shall not allow a sorceress to live.

19 ¶ "Whoever lies with an animal shall surely be put to death.

20 ¶ "He who sacrifices to any god, other than to the LORD alone, shall be utterly destroyed.

21 ¶ "You shall not wrong a stranger or oppress him, for you were strangers in the land of Egypt.

22 "You shall not afflict any widow or orphan.

23 "If you afflict him at all, *and* if he does cry out to Me, I will surely hear his cry;

24 and My anger will be kindled, and I will kill you with the sword, and your wives shall become widows and your children fatherless.

25 ¶ "If you lend money to My people, to the poor among you, you are not to act as a creditor to him; you shall not charge him interest.

26 "If you ever take your neighbor's cloak as a pledge, you are to return it to him before the sun sets,

27 for that is his only covering; it is his cloak for his body. What else shall he sleep in? And it shall come about that when he cries out to Me, I will hear *him*, for I am gracious.

28 ¶ "You shall not curse God, nor curse a ruler of your people.

29 ¶ "You shall not delay *the offering from* your harvest and your vintage. The firstborn of your sons you shall give to Me.

30 "You shall do the same with your oxen *and* with your sheep. It shall be with its mother seven days; on the eighth day you shall give it to Me.

31 ¶ "You shall be holy men to Me, therefore you shall not eat *any* flesh torn to pieces in the field; you shall throw it to the dogs.

Sundry Laws

23 "You shall not bear a false report; do not join your hand with a wicked man to be a malicious witness.

2 "You shall not follow the masses in doing evil, nor shall you testify in a dispute so as to turn aside after a multitude in order to pervert *justice;*

3 nor shall you be partial to a poor man in his dispute.

4 ¶ "If you meet your enemy's ox or his donkey wandering away, you shall surely return it to him.

5 "If you see the donkey of one who hates you lying *helpless* under its load, you shall refrain from leaving it to him, you shall surely release *it* with him.

6 ¶ "You shall not pervert the justice *due* to your needy *brother* in his dispute.

7 "Keep far from a false charge, and do not kill the innocent or the righteous, for I will not acquit the guilty.

8 ¶ "You shall not take a bribe, for a bribe

blinds the clear-sighted and subverts the cause of the just.

9 ¶ "You shall not oppress a stranger, since you yourselves know the feelings of a stranger, for you *also* were strangers in the land of Egypt.

The Sabbath and Land

10 ¶ "You shall sow your land for six years and gather in its yield,

11 but *on* the seventh year you shall let it rest and lie fallow, so that the needy of your people may eat; and whatever they leave the beast of the field may eat. You are to do the same with your vineyard *and* your olive grove.

12 ¶ "Six days you are to do your work, but on the seventh day you shall cease *from labor* so that your ox and your donkey may rest, and the son of your female slave, as well as your stranger, may refresh themselves.

13 "Now concerning everything which I have said to you, be on your guard; and do not mention the name of other gods, nor let *them* be heard from your mouth.

Three National Feasts

14 ¶ "Three times a year you shall celebrate a feast to Me.

15 "You shall observe the Feast of Unleavened Bread; for seven days you are to eat unleavened bread, as I commanded you, at the appointed time in the month Abib, for in it you came out of Egypt. And none shall appear before Me empty-handed.

16 "Also *you shall observe* the Feast of the Harvest *of* the first fruits of your labors *from* what you sow in the field; also the Feast of the Ingathering at the end of the year when you gather in *the fruit of* your labors from the field.

17 "Three times a year all your males shall appear before the Lord GOD.

18 ¶ "You shall not offer the blood of My sacrifice with leavened bread; nor is the fat of My feast to remain overnight until morning.

19 ¶ "You shall bring the choice first fruits of your soil into the house of the LORD your God.

¶ "You are not to boil a young goat in the milk of its mother.

Conquest of the Land

20 ¶ "Behold, I am going to send an angel before you to guard you along the way and to bring you into the place which I have prepared.

21 "Be on your guard before him and obey his voice; do not be rebellious toward him, for he will not pardon your transgression, since My name is in him.

22 "But if you truly obey his voice and do all that I say, then I will be an enemy to your enemies and an adversary to your adversaries.

23 "For My angel will go before you and bring you in to *the land of* the Amorites, the Hittites, the

Perizzites, the Canaanites, the Hivites and the Jebusites; and I will completely destroy them.

24 "You shall not worship their gods, nor serve them, nor do according to their deeds; but you shall utterly overthrow them and break their *sacred* pillars in pieces.

25 "But you shall serve the LORD your God, and He will bless your bread and your water; and I will remove sickness from your midst.

26 "There shall be no one miscarrying or barren in your land; I will fulfill the number of your days.

27 "I will send My terror ahead of you, and throw into confusion all the people among whom you come, and I will make all your enemies turn *their* backs to you.

28 "I will send hornets ahead of you so that they will drive out the Hivites, the Canaanites, and the Hittites before you.

29 "I will not drive them out before you in a single year, that the land may not become desolate and the beasts of the field become too numerous for you.

30 "I will drive them out before you little by little, until you become fruitful and take possession of the land.

31 "I will fix your boundary from the Red Sea to the sea of the Philistines, and from the wilderness to the River *Euphrates;* for I will deliver the inhabitants of the land into your hand, and you will drive them out before you.

32 "You shall make no covenant with them or with their gods.

33 "They shall not live in your land, because they will make you sin against Me; for *if* you serve their gods, it will surely be a snare to you."

People Affirm Their Covenant with God

24 Then He said to Moses, "Come up to the LORD, you and Aaron, Nadab and Abihu and seventy of the elders of Israel, and you shall worship at a distance.

2 "Moses alone, however, shall come near to the LORD, but they shall not come near, nor shall the people come up with him."

3 ¶ Then Moses came and recounted to the people all the words of the LORD and all the ordinances; and all the people answered with one voice and said, "All the words which the LORD has spoken we will do!"

4 Moses wrote down all the words of the LORD. Then he arose early in the morning, and built an altar at the foot of the mountain with twelve pillars for the twelve tribes of Israel.

5 He sent young men of the sons of Israel, and they offered burnt offerings and sacrificed young bulls as peace offerings to the LORD.

6 Moses took half of the blood and put *it* in basins, and the *other* half of the blood he sprinkled on the altar.

7 Then he took the book of the covenant and read *it* in the hearing of the people; and they said, "All that the LORD has spoken we will do, and we will be obedient!"

8 So Moses took the blood and sprinkled *it* on the people, and said, "Behold the blood of the covenant, which the LORD has made with you in accordance with all these words."

24:8 Covenant Blood

This chapter depicts one of the most important transactions in Israel's history. Since Aaron and his sons had not yet been named or consecrated, Moses served as priest for the dramatic personal encounter with God. A unique sacrifice formally set Israel apart as the people of God and laid the foundation for all the sacrifices to follow.

The New Testament applies the very phraseology from this solemn ceremony to the new covenant made possible by Christ's sacrifice. The phrase "blood of the covenant" appears six times in the New Testament, in each case referring to the death of Christ. Jesus himself used the phrase at the Last Supper (Matthew 26:28), and it became a part of the ceremony of the Lord's Supper.

9 ¶ Then Moses went up with Aaron, Nadab and Abihu, and seventy of the elders of Israel,

10 and they saw the God of Israel; and under His feet there appeared to be a pavement of sapphire, as clear as the sky itself.

11 Yet He did not stretch out His hand against the nobles of the sons of Israel; and they saw God, and they ate and drank.

12 ¶ Now the LORD said to Moses, "Come up to Me on the mountain and remain there, and I will give you the stone tablets with the law and the commandment which I have written for their instruction."

13 So Moses arose with Joshua his servant, and Moses went up to the mountain of God.

14 But to the elders he said, "Wait here for us until we return to you. And behold, Aaron and Hur are with you; whoever has a legal matter, let him approach them."

15 Then Moses went up to the mountain, and the cloud covered the mountain.

16 The glory of the LORD rested on Mount Sinai, and the cloud covered it for six days; and on the seventh day He called to Moses from the midst of the cloud.

17 And to the eyes of the sons of Israel the appearance of the glory of the LORD was like a consuming fire on the mountain top.

18 Moses entered the midst of the cloud as he

went up to the mountain; and Moses was on the mountain forty days and forty nights.

Offerings for the Sanctuary

25 Then the LORD spoke to Moses, saying, 2 "Tell the sons of Israel to raise a contribution for Me; from every man whose heart moves him you shall raise My contribution.

3 "This is the contribution which you are to raise from them: gold, silver and bronze,

4 blue, purple and scarlet *material*, fine linen, goat *hair*,

5 rams' skins dyed red, porpoise skins, acacia wood,

6 oil for lighting, spices for the anointing oil and for the fragrant incense,

7 onyx stones and setting stones for the ephod and for the breastpiece.

8 "Let them construct a sanctuary for Me, that I may dwell among them.

9 "According to all that I am going to show you, *as* the pattern of the tabernacle and the pattern of all its furniture, just so you shall construct *it.*

When God Was Obvious
Few atheists, but many rebels

WHY DOESN'T GOD INTERVENE MORE? Why doesn't he directly feed the hungry, heal all the sick, and stop all wars? If God really exists, at the least why doesn't he make himself more obvious?

People who ask such questions often assume that if God ever did spectacularly reveal himself, all doubts would vanish. Everyone would line up to believe in him.

> *To the sons of Israel the glory of the LORD was like a consuming fire on the mountain top.*
> **24:17**

Astonishing Reactions

Exodus tells of a time when God made himself perfectly obvious. The plagues on Egypt revealed his mighty power. An enormous miracle at the Red Sea provided sensational deliverance. A recurring miracle supplied food for the Israelites every morning. And, if questions about God's existence arose, doubters needed only to look to the ever-present glory cloud or pillar of fire. It must have been hard to be an atheist in those days.

Yet every instance of God's faithfulness seemed to summon up astonishing human *un*faithfulness. The same Israelites who had watched God crush a pharaoh quaked at the first sign of Egyptian chariots. Three days after a miraculous escape across the Red Sea they were grumbling to Moses and God about water supplies.

A month or so later, when hunger pangs began to gnaw at them, they bitterly complained, "Would that we had died by the LORD's hand in the land of Egypt, when we sat by the pots of meat, when we ate bread to the full; for you have brought us out into this wilderness to kill this whole assembly with hunger" (16:3). God responded with a provision of manna (that would continue for 40 years) and quail, but the Israelites were soon grousing about the water supplies again.

The Great Rebellion

Exodus 32 shows the Israelites at their worst. People who had eaten manna for breakfast, who had just solemnly agreed to keep every word of the covenant, who were at that moment standing beside a mountain stormy with the Lord's presence—those very people proceeded to melt down their gold jewelry and flagrantly flout the first commandment.

"Obstinate," God called the Israelites as he burned in anger against them. Only Moses' eloquent appeal saved their lives.

The history of the Israelites should nail a coffin lid on the notion that impressive displays of God's power will guarantee faith. (Jesus would later say, "If they do not listen to Moses and the Prophets, they will not be persuaded even if someone rises from the dead," Luke 16:31.) People who had everyday proof of God demonstrated only one thing: the monotonous consistency of human nature.

The offenders would pay for their acts by wandering 40 years in a desolate wilderness while a new, untainted generation grew up to replace them. But a pattern was beginning to emerge: If the Israelites failed God in the shadow of Mount Sinai, how would they possibly withstand the seduction of new cultures in the promised land? The next generation, too, would fail God, as would all their descendants. The old covenant, as Paul would so convincingly argue in the book of Galatians, succeeded mainly by proving undeniably the need for a new one.

Life Questions: Do you ever have doubts about God's existence? What would it take to completely convince you?

Ark of the Covenant

10 ¶ "They shall construct an ark of acacia wood two and a half cubits long, and one and a half cubits wide, and one and a half cubits high.

11 "You shall overlay it with pure gold, inside and out you shall overlay it, and you shall make a gold molding around it.

12 "You shall cast four gold rings for it and fasten them on its four feet, and two rings shall be on one side of it and two rings on the other side of it.

13 "You shall make poles of acacia wood and overlay them with gold.

14 "You shall put the poles into the rings on the sides of the ark, to carry the ark with them.

15 "The poles shall remain in the rings of the ark; they shall not be removed from it.

16 "You shall put into the ark the testimony which I shall give you.

17 ¶ "You shall make a *a*mercy seat of pure gold, two and a half cubits long and one and a half cubits wide.

18 "You shall make two cherubim of gold, make them of hammered work at the two ends of the mercy seat.

19 "Make one cherub at one end and one cherub at the other end; you shall make the cherubim *of one piece* with the mercy seat at its two ends.

20 "The cherubim shall have *their* wings spread upward, covering the mercy seat with their wings and facing one another; the faces of the cherubim are to be *turned* toward the mercy seat.

21 "You shall put the mercy seat on top of the ark, and in the ark you shall put the testimony which I will give to you.

22 "There I will meet with you; and from above the mercy seat, from between the two cherubim which are upon the ark of the testimony, I will speak to you about all that I will give you in commandment for the sons of Israel.

The Table of Showbread

23 ¶ "You shall make a table of acacia wood, two cubits long and one cubit wide and one and a half cubits high.

24 "You shall overlay it with pure gold and make a gold border around it.

25 "You shall make for it a rim of a handbreadth around *it;* and you shall make a gold border for the rim around it.

26 "You shall make four gold rings for it and put rings on the four corners which are on its four feet.

27 "The rings shall be close to the rim as holders for the poles to carry the table.

28 "You shall make the poles of acacia wood and overlay them with gold, so that with them the table may be carried.

29 "You shall make its dishes and its pans and its jars and its bowls with which to pour drink offerings; you shall make them of pure gold.

30 "You shall set the bread of the Presence on the table before Me at all times.

The Golden Lampstand

31 ¶ "Then you shall make a lampstand of pure gold. The lampstand *and* its base and its shaft are to be made of hammered work; its cups, its bulbs and its flowers shall be *of one piece* with it.

32 "Six branches shall go out from its sides; three branches of the lampstand from its one side and three branches of the lampstand from its other side.

33 "Three cups *shall be* shaped like almond *blossoms* in the one branch, a *b*bulb and a flower, and three cups shaped like almond *blossoms* in the other branch, a bulb and a flower—so for six branches going out from the lampstand;

34 and in the lampstand four cups shaped like almond *blossoms,* its bulbs and its flowers.

35 "A bulb shall be under the *first* pair of branches *coming* out of it, and a bulb under the *second* pair of branches *coming* out of it, and a bulb under the *third* pair of branches *coming* out of it, for the six branches coming out of the lampstand.

36 "Their bulbs and their branches *shall be of one piece* with it; all of it shall be one piece of hammered work of pure gold.

37 "Then you shall make its lamps seven *in number;* and they shall mount its lamps so as to shed light on the space in front of it.

38 "Its snuffers and their trays *shall be* of pure gold.

39 "It shall be made from a talent of pure gold, with all these utensils.

40 "See that you make *them* after the pattern for them, which was shown to you on the mountain.

Curtains of Linen

26 "Moreover you shall make the tabernacle with ten curtains of fine twisted linen and *c*blue and purple and scarlet *material;* you shall make them with cherubim, the work of a skillful workman.

---

a Lit *propitiatory,* and so through v 22   *b* Or *calyx*   *c* Or *violet*

2 "The length of each curtain shall be twenty-eight cubits, and the width of each curtain four cubits; all the curtains shall have the same measurements.

3 "Five curtains shall be joined to one another, and *the other* five curtains *shall be* joined to one another.

4 "You shall make loops of blue on the edge of the outermost curtain in the *first* set, and likewise you shall make *them* on the edge of the curtain that is outermost in the second set.

5 "You shall make fifty loops in the one curtain, and you shall make fifty loops on the edge of the curtain that is in the second set; the loops shall be opposite each other.

6 "You shall make fifty clasps of gold, and join the curtains to one another with the clasps so that the *ª*tabernacle will be a unit.

Curtains of Goats' Hair

7 ¶ "Then you shall make curtains of goats' *hair* for a tent over the tabernacle; you shall make eleven curtains in all.

8 "The length of each curtain *shall be* thirty cubits, and the width of each curtain four cubits; the eleven curtains shall have the same measurements.

9 "You shall join five curtains by themselves and *the other* six curtains by themselves, and you shall double over the sixth curtain at the front of the tent.

10 "You shall make fifty loops on the edge of the curtain that is outermost in the *first* set, and fifty loops on the edge of the curtain *that is outermost in* the second set.

11 ¶ "You shall make fifty clasps of *ᵇ*bronze, and you shall put the clasps into the loops and join the tent together so that it will be a unit.

12 "The overlapping part that is left over in the curtains of the tent, the half curtain that is left over, shall lap over the back of the tabernacle.

13 "The cubit on one side and the cubit on the other, of what is left over in the length of the curtains of the tent, shall lap over the sides of the tabernacle on one side and on the other, to cover it.

14 "You shall make a covering for the tent of rams' skins dyed red and a covering of porpoise skins above.

Boards and Sockets

15 ¶ "Then you shall make the boards for the tabernacle of acacia wood, standing upright.

16 "Ten cubits *shall be* the length of each board and one and a half cubits the width of each board.

17 "*There shall be* two tenons for each board, fitted to one another; thus you shall do for all the boards of the tabernacle.

18 "You shall make the boards for the tabernacle: twenty boards for the south side.

19 "You shall make forty *ᶜ*sockets of silver under the twenty boards, two sockets under one board for its two tenons and two sockets under another board for its two tenons;

20 and for the second side of the tabernacle, on the north side, twenty boards,

21 and their forty sockets of silver; two sockets under one board and two sockets under another board.

22 "For the rear of the tabernacle, to the west, you shall make six boards.

23 "You shall make two boards for the corners of the tabernacle at the rear.

24 "They shall be double beneath, and together they shall be complete to its top to the first ring; thus it shall be with both of them: they shall form the two corners.

25 "There shall be eight boards with their sockets of silver, sixteen sockets; two sockets under one board and two sockets under another board.

26 ¶ "Then you shall make bars of acacia wood, five for the boards of one side of the tabernacle,

27 and five bars for the boards of the other side of the tabernacle, and five bars for the boards of the side of the tabernacle for the rear *side* to the west.

28 "The middle bar in the center of the boards shall pass through from end to end.

29 "You shall overlay the boards with gold and make their rings of gold *as* holders for the bars; and you shall overlay the bars with gold.

30 "Then you shall erect the tabernacle according to its plan which you have been shown in the mountain.

The Veil and Screen

31 ¶ "You shall make a veil of blue and purple and scarlet *material* and fine twisted linen; it shall be made with cherubim, the work of a skillful workman.

32 "You shall hang it on four pillars of acacia overlaid with gold, their hooks *also being of* gold, on four sockets of silver.

33 "You shall hang up the veil under the clasps, and shall bring in the ark of the testimony there within the veil; and the veil shall serve for you as a partition between the holy place and the holy of holies.

34 "You shall put the mercy seat on the ark of the testimony in the holy of holies.

35 "You shall set the table outside the veil, and the lampstand opposite the table on the side of the tabernacle toward the south; and you shall put the table on the north side.

36 ¶ "You shall make a screen for the doorway of the tent of blue and purple and scarlet *material* and fine twisted linen, the work of a weaver.

37 "You shall make five pillars of acacia for the screen and overlay them with gold, their hooks

---

ª Or *dwelling place,* and so throughout the ch   *ᵇ* Or *copper*   *ᶜ* Or *bases also being of* gold; and you shall cast five sockets of bronze for them.

The Bronze Altar

27 "And you shall make the altar of acacia wood, five cubits long and five cubits wide;

26:33 A Torn Curtain

The thick curtain described here separated the holy place from the holy of holies. Anyone who ventured beyond that curtain would die. The New Testament, however, records that at Jesus' crucifixion the curtain tore in two, from top to bottom. The tearing symbolized what Christ had accomplished: he broke down the separation between God and humanity (Matthew 27:51; Hebrews 10:20).

---

the altar shall be square, and its height shall be three cubits.

2 "You shall make its horns on its four corners; its horns shall be of one piece with it, and you shall overlay it with bronze.

3 "You shall make its pails for removing its ashes, and its shovels and its basins and its forks and its firepans; you shall make all its utensils of bronze.

4 "You shall make for it a grating of network of bronze, and on the net you shall make four bronze rings at its four corners.

5 "You shall put it beneath, under the ledge of the altar, so that the net will reach halfway up the altar.

6 "You shall make poles for the altar, poles of acacia wood, and overlay them with bronze.

7 "Its poles shall be inserted into the rings, so that the poles shall be on the two sides of the altar when it is carried.

8 "You shall make it hollow with planks; as it was shown to you in the mountain, so they shall make *it.*

Court of the Tabernacle

9 ¶ "You shall make the court of the tabernacle. On the south side *there shall be* hangings for the court of fine twisted linen one hundred cubits long for one side;

10 and its pillars *shall be* twenty, with their twenty sockets of bronze; the hooks of the pillars and their bands *shall be* of silver.

11 "Likewise for the north side in length *there shall be* hangings one hundred *cubits* long, and its twenty pillars with their twenty sockets of bronze; the hooks of the pillars and their bands *shall be* of silver.

12 "*For* the width of the court on the west side

shall be hangings of fifty cubits *with* their ten pillars and their ten sockets.

13 "The width of the court on the east side *shall be* fifty cubits.

14 "The hangings for the *one* side *of the gate shall be* fifteen cubits *with* their three pillars and their three sockets.

15 "And for the other side *shall be* hangings of fifteen cubits *with* their three pillars and their three sockets.

16 "For the gate of the court *there shall be* a screen of twenty cubits, of blue and purple and scarlet *material* and fine twisted linen, the work of a weaver, *with* their four pillars and their four sockets.

17 "All the pillars around the court shall be furnished with silver bands *with* their hooks of silver and their sockets of bronze.

18 "The length of the court *shall be* one hundred cubits, and the width fifty throughout, and the height five cubits of fine twisted linen, and their sockets of bronze.

19 "All the utensils of the tabernacle *used* in all its service, and all its pegs, and all the pegs of the court, *shall be* of bronze.

20 ¶ "You shall charge the sons of Israel, that they bring you clear oil of beaten olives for the light, to make a lamp burn continually.

21 "In the tent of meeting, outside the veil which is before the testimony, Aaron and his sons shall keep it in order from evening to morning before the Lord; *it shall be* a perpetual statute throughout their generations for the sons of Israel.

Garments of the Priests

28 "Then bring near to yourself Aaron your brother, and his sons with him, from among the sons of Israel, to minister as priest to Me—Aaron, Nadab and Abihu, Eleazar and Ithamar, Aaron's sons.

2 "You shall make holy garments for Aaron your brother, for glory and for beauty.

3 "You shall speak to all the skillful persons whom I have endowed with the spirit of wisdom, that they make Aaron's garments to consecrate him, that he may minister as priest to Me.

4 "These are the garments which they shall make: a ᵃbreastpiece and an ephod and a robe and a tunic of checkered work, a turban and a sash, and they shall make holy garments for Aaron your brother and his sons, that he may minister as priest to Me.

5 "They shall take the gold and the blue and the purple and the scarlet *material* and the fine linen.

6 ¶ "They shall also make the ephod of gold, of blue and purple *and* scarlet *material* and fine twisted linen, the work of the skillful workman.

7 "It shall have two shoulder pieces joined to its two ends, that it may be joined.

ᵃ Or pouch

8 "The skillfully woven band, which is on it, shall be like its workmanship, of the same material: of gold, of blue and purple and scarlet *material* and fine twisted linen.

9 "You shall take two onyx stones and engrave on them the names of the sons of Israel,

10 six of their names on the one stone and the names of the remaining six on the other stone, according to their birth.

11 "As a jeweler engraves a signet, you shall engrave the two stones according to the names of the sons of Israel; you shall set them in filigree *settings* of gold.

12 "You shall put the two stones on the shoulder pieces of the ephod, *as* stones of memorial for the sons of Israel, and Aaron shall bear their names before the LORD on his two shoulders for a memorial.

13 "You shall make filigree *settings* of gold,

14 and two chains of pure gold; you shall make them of twisted cordage work, and you shall put the corded chains on the filigree *settings*.

15 ¶ "You shall make a breastpiece of judgment, the work of a skillful workman; like the work of the ephod you shall make it: of gold, of blue and purple and scarlet *material* and fine twisted linen you shall make it.

16 "It shall be square *and* folded double, a span in length and a span in width.

17 "You shall mount on it four rows of stones; the first row *shall be* a row of ruby, topaz and emerald;

18 and the second row a turquoise, a sapphire and a diamond;

19 and the third row a jacinth, an agate and an amethyst;

20 and the fourth row a beryl and an onyx and a jasper; they shall be set in gold filigree.

21 "The stones shall be according to the names of the sons of Israel: twelve, according to their names; they shall be *like* the engravings of a seal, each according to his name for the twelve tribes.

22 "You shall make on the breastpiece chains of twisted cordage work in pure gold.

23 "You shall make on the breastpiece two rings of gold, and shall put the two rings on the two ends of the breastpiece.

24 "You shall put the two cords of gold on the two rings at the ends of the breastpiece.

25 "You shall put the *other* two ends of the two cords on the two filigree *settings*, and put them on the shoulder pieces of the ephod, at the front of it.

26 "You shall make two rings of gold and shall place them on the two ends of the breastpiece, on the edge of it, which is toward the inner side of the ephod.

27 "You shall make two rings of gold and put them on the bottom of the two shoulder pieces of the ephod, on the front of it close to the place where it is joined, above the skillfully woven band of the ephod.

28 "They shall bind the breastpiece by its rings to the rings of the ephod with a blue cord, so that it will be on the skillfully woven band of the ephod, and that the breastpiece will not come loose from the ephod.

29 "Aaron shall carry the names of the sons of Israel in the breastpiece of judgment over his heart when he enters the holy place, for a memorial before the LORD continually.

30 "You shall put in the breastpiece of judgment the *a*Urim and the Thummim, and they shall be over Aaron's heart when he goes in before the LORD; and Aaron shall carry the judgment of the sons of Israel over his heart before the LORD continually.

31 ¶ "You shall make the robe of the ephod all of blue.

32 "There shall be an opening at its top in the middle of it; around its opening there shall be a binding of woven work, as like the opening of a coat of mail, so that it will not be torn.

33 "You shall make on its hem pomegranates of blue and purple and scarlet *material*, all around on its hem, and bells of gold between them all around:

34 a golden bell and a pomegranate, a golden bell and a pomegranate, all around on the hem of the robe.

35 "It shall be on Aaron when he ministers; and its tinkling shall be heard when he enters and leaves the holy place before the LORD, so that he will not die.

36 ¶ "You shall also make a plate of pure gold and shall engrave on it, like the engravings of a seal, 'Holy to the LORD.'

37 "You shall fasten it on a blue cord, and it shall be on the turban; it shall be at the front of the turban.

38 "It shall be on Aaron's forehead, and Aaron shall take away the iniquity of the holy things which the sons of Israel consecrate, with regard to all their holy gifts; and it shall always be on his forehead, that they may be accepted before the LORD.

39 ¶ "You shall weave the tunic of checkered work of fine linen, and shall make a turban of fine linen, and you shall make a sash, the work of a weaver.

40 ¶ "For Aaron's sons you shall make tunics; you shall also make sashes for them, and you shall make caps for them, for glory and for beauty.

41 "You shall put them on Aaron your brother and on his sons with him; and you shall anoint them and ordain them and consecrate them, that they may serve Me as priests.

42 "You shall make for them linen breeches to cover *their* bare flesh; they shall reach from the loins even to the thighs.

a I.e. lights and perfections

43 "They shall be on Aaron and on his sons when they enter the tent of meeting, or when they approach the altar to minister in the holy place, so that they do not incur guilt and die. It *shall be* a statute forever to him and to his descendants after him.

Consecration of the Priests

29 "Now this is what you shall do to them to consecrate them to minister as priests to Me: take one young bull and two rams without blemish,

2 and unleavened bread and unleavened cakes mixed with oil, and unleavened wafers spread with oil; you shall make them of fine wheat flour.

3 "You shall put them in one basket, and present them in the basket along with the bull and the two rams.

4 "Then you shall bring Aaron and his sons to the doorway of the tent of meeting and wash them with water.

5 "You shall take the garments, and put on Aaron the tunic and the robe of the ephod and the ephod and the breastpiece, and gird him with the skillfully woven band of the ephod;

6 and you shall set the turban on his head and put the holy crown on the turban.

7 "Then you shall take the anointing oil and pour it on his head and anoint him.

8 "You shall bring his sons and put tunics on them.

9 "You shall gird them with sashes, Aaron and his sons, and bind caps on them, and they shall have the priesthood by a perpetual statute. So you shall ordain Aaron and his sons.

The Sacrifices

10 ¶ "Then you shall bring the bull before the tent of meeting, and Aaron and his sons shall lay their hands on the head of the bull.

11 "You shall slaughter the bull before the LORD at the doorway of the tent of meeting.

12 "You shall take some of the blood of the bull and put *it* on the horns of the altar with your finger; and you shall pour out all the blood at the base of the altar.

13 "You shall take all the fat that covers the entrails and the lobe of the liver, and the two kidneys and the fat that is on them, and offer them up in smoke on the altar.

14 "But the flesh of the bull and its hide and its refuse, you shall burn with fire outside the camp; it is a sin offering.

15 ¶ "You shall also take the one ram, and Aaron and his sons shall lay their hands on the head of the ram;

16 and you shall slaughter the ram and shall take its blood and sprinkle it around on the altar.

17 "Then you shall cut the ram into its pieces, and wash its entrails and its legs, and put *them* with its pieces and its head.

18 "You shall offer up in smoke the whole ram on the altar; it is a burnt offering to the LORD: it is a soothing aroma, an offering by fire to the LORD.

19 ¶ "Then you shall take the other ram, and Aaron and his sons shall lay their hands on the head of the ram.

20 "You shall slaughter the ram, and take some of its blood and put *it* on the lobe of Aaron's right ear and on the lobes of his sons' right ears and on the thumbs of their right hands and on the big toes of their right feet, and sprinkle the *rest of the* blood around on the altar.

29:20 The Whole Body

As part of their purification, the priests daubed blood on their ears (which hear God's laws), their hands (which do his will), and their toes (which were prepared to follow in his steps).

21 "Then you shall take some of the blood that is on the altar and some of the anointing oil, and sprinkle *it* on Aaron and on his garments and on his sons and on his sons' garments with him; so he and his garments shall be consecrated, as well as his sons and his sons' garments with him.

22 ¶ "You shall also take the fat from the ram and the fat tail, and the fat that covers the entrails and the lobe of the liver, and the two kidneys and the fat that is on them and the right thigh (for it is a ram of ordination),

23 and one cake of bread and one cake of bread *mixed with* oil and one wafer from the basket of unleavened bread which is *set* before the LORD;

24 and you shall put all these in the hands of Aaron and in the hands of his sons, and shall wave them as a wave offering before the LORD.

25 "You shall take them from their hands, and offer them up in smoke on the altar on the burnt offering for a soothing aroma before the LORD; it is an offering by fire to the LORD.

26 ¶ "Then you shall take the breast of Aaron's ram of ordination, and wave it as a wave offering before the LORD; and it shall be your portion.

27 "You shall consecrate the breast of the wave offering and the thigh of the heave offering which was waved and which was offered from the ram of ordination, from the one which was for Aaron and from the one which was for his sons.

28 "It shall be for Aaron and his sons as *their* portion forever from the sons of Israel, for it is a heave offering; and it shall be a heave offering from the sons of Israel from the sacrifices of their peace offerings, *even* their heave offering to the LORD.

29 ¶ "The holy garments of Aaron shall be for

his sons after him, that in them they may be anointed and ordained.

30 "For seven days the one of his sons who is priest in his stead shall put them on when he enters the tent of meeting to minister in the holy place.

Food of the Priests

31 ¶ "You shall take the ram of ordination and boil its flesh in a holy place.

32 "Aaron and his sons shall eat the flesh of the ram and the bread that is in the basket, at the doorway of the tent of meeting.

33 "Thus they shall eat those things by which atonement was made at their ordination *and* consecration; but a layman shall not eat *them*, because they are holy.

34 "If any of the flesh of ordination or any of the bread remains until morning, then you shall burn the remainder with fire; it shall not be eaten, because it is holy.

35 ¶ "Thus you shall do to Aaron and to his sons, according to all that I have commanded you; you shall ordain them through seven days.

36 "Each day you shall offer a bull as a sin offering for atonement, and you shall purify the altar when you make atonement for it, and you shall anoint it to consecrate it.

37 "For seven days you shall make atonement for the altar and consecrate it; then the altar shall be most holy, *and* whatever touches the altar shall be holy.

38 ¶ "Now this is what you shall offer on the altar: two one year old lambs each day, continuously.

39 "The one lamb you shall offer in the morning and the other lamb you shall offer at twilight;

40 and there *shall be* one-tenth *of an ephah* of fine flour mixed with one-fourth of a hin of beaten oil, and one-fourth of a hin of wine for a drink offering with one lamb.

41 "The other lamb you shall offer at twilight, and shall offer with it the same grain offering and the same drink offering as in the morning, for a soothing aroma, an offering by fire to the LORD.

42 "It shall be a continual burnt offering throughout your generations at the doorway of the tent of meeting before the LORD, where I will meet with you, to speak to you there.

43 "I will meet there with the sons of Israel, and it shall be consecrated by My glory.

44 "I will consecrate the tent of meeting and the altar; I will also consecrate Aaron and his sons to minister as priests to Me.

45 "I will dwell among the sons of Israel and will be their God.

46 "They shall know that I am the LORD their God who brought them out of the land of Egypt, that I might dwell among them; I am the LORD their God.

The Altar of Incense

30 "Moreover, you shall make an altar as a place for burning incense; you shall make it of acacia wood.

2 "Its length *shall be* a cubit, and its width a cubit, it shall be square, and its height *shall be* two cubits; its horns *shall be* of one piece with it.

3 "You shall overlay it with pure gold, its top and its sides all around, and its horns; and you shall make a gold molding all around for it.

4 "You shall make two gold rings for it under its molding; you shall make *them* on its two side walls—on opposite sides—and they shall be holders for poles with which to carry it.

5 "You shall make the poles of acacia wood and overlay them with gold.

6 "You shall put this altar in front of the veil that is near the ark of the testimony, in front of the mercy seat that is over *the ark of* the testimony, where I will meet with you.

7 "Aaron shall burn fragrant incense on it; he shall burn it every morning when he trims the lamps.

8 "When Aaron trims the lamps at twilight, he shall burn incense. *There shall be* perpetual incense before the LORD throughout your generations.

9 "You shall not offer any strange incense on this altar, or burnt offering or meal offering; and you shall not pour out a drink offering on it.

10 "Aaron shall make atonement on its horns once a year; he shall make atonement on it with the blood of the sin offering of atonement once a year throughout your generations. It is most holy to the LORD."

30:10 Jewish Holy Days

Orthodox Jews still faithfully honor the Day of Atonement described here, the holy day of Yom Kippur. But the New Testament book of Hebrews reinterprets this period of time as a copy, or shadow, of the real thing to come in Jesus Christ. What a high priest accomplished, through elaborate ceremony, once a year on the Day of Atonement, Christ did once for all (Hebrews 8–9). As a consequence, all of us—not just a purified priest—can confidently "enter the Most Holy Place."

11 ¶ The LORD also spoke to Moses, saying,

12 "When you take a census of the sons of Israel to number them, then each one of them shall give a ransom for himself to the LORD, when you number them, so that there will be no plague among them when you number them.

13 "This is what everyone who is numbered shall give: half a shekel according to the shekel of the sanctuary (the shekel is twenty gerahs), half a shekel as a contribution to the LORD.

14 "Everyone who is numbered, from twenty years old and over, shall give the contribution to the LORD.

15 "The rich shall not pay more and the poor shall not pay less than the half shekel, when you give the contribution to the LORD to make atonement for yourselves.

16 "You shall take the atonement money from the sons of Israel and shall give it for the service of the tent of meeting, that it may be a memorial for the sons of Israel before the LORD, to make atonement for yourselves."

17 ¶ The LORD spoke to Moses, saying,

18 "You shall also make a laver of bronze, with its base of bronze, for washing; and you shall put it between the tent of meeting and the altar, and you shall put water in it.

19 "Aaron and his sons shall wash their hands and their feet from it;

20 when they enter the tent of meeting, they shall wash with water, so that they will not die; or when they approach the altar to minister, by offering up in smoke a fire *sacrifice* to the LORD.

21 "So they shall wash their hands and their feet, so that they will not die; and it shall be a perpetual statute for them, for Aaron and his descendants throughout their generations."

The Anointing Oil

22 ¶ Moreover, the LORD spoke to Moses, saying,

23 "Take also for yourself the finest of spices: of flowing myrrh five hundred *shekels,* and of fragrant cinnamon half as much, two hundred and fifty, and of fragrant cane two hundred and fifty,

24 and of cassia five hundred, according to the shekel of the sanctuary, and of olive oil a hin.

25 "You shall make of these a holy anointing oil, a perfume mixture, the work of a perfumer; it shall be a holy anointing oil.

26 "With it you shall anoint the tent of meeting and the ark of the testimony,

27 and the table and all its utensils, and the lampstand and its utensils, and the altar of incense,

28 and the altar of burnt offering and all its utensils, and the laver and its stand.

29 "You shall also consecrate them, that they may be most holy; whatever touches them shall be holy.

30 "You shall anoint Aaron and his sons, and consecrate them, that they may minister as priests to Me.

31 "You shall speak to the sons of Israel, saying, 'This shall be a holy anointing oil to Me throughout your generations.

32 'It shall not be poured on anyone's body, nor shall you make *any* like it in the same proportions; it is holy, *and* it shall be holy to you.

33 'Whoever shall mix *any* like it or whoever puts any of it on a layman shall be cut off from his people.' "

The Incense

34 ¶ Then the LORD said to Moses, "Take for yourself spices, stacte and onycha and galbanum, spices with pure frankincense; there shall be an equal part of each.

35 "With it you shall make incense, a perfume, the work of a perfumer, salted, pure, *and* holy.

36 "You shall beat some of it very fine, and put part of it before the testimony in the tent of meeting where I will meet with you; it shall be most holy to you.

37 "The incense which you shall make, you shall not make in the same proportions for yourselves; it shall be holy to you for the LORD.

38 "Whoever shall make *any* like it, to use as perfume, shall be cut off from his people."

The Skilled Craftsmen

31 Now the LORD spoke to Moses, saying,

2 "See, I have called by name Bezalel, the son of Uri, the son of Hur, of the tribe of Judah.

3 "I have filled him with the Spirit of God in wisdom, in understanding, in knowledge, and in all *kinds of* craftsmanship,

4 to make artistic designs for work in gold, in silver, and in bronze,

5 and in the cutting of stones for settings, and in the carving of wood, that he may work in all *kinds of* craftsmanship.

6 "And behold, I Myself have appointed with him Oholiab, the son of Ahisamach, of the tribe of Dan; and in the hearts of all who are skillful I have put skill, that they may make all that I have commanded you:

7 the tent of meeting, and the ark of testimony, and the mercy seat upon it, and all the furniture of the tent,

8 the table also and its utensils, and the pure *gold* lampstand with all its utensils, and the altar of incense,

9 the altar of burnt offering also with all its utensils, and the laver and its stand,

10 the woven garments as well, and the holy garments for Aaron the priest, and the garments of his sons, *with which* to carry on their priesthood;

11 the anointing oil also, and the fragrant incense for the holy place, they are to make *them* according to all that I have commanded you."

The Sign of the Sabbath

12 ¶ The LORD spoke to Moses, saying,

13 "But as for you, speak to the sons of Israel, saying, 'You shall surely observe My sabbaths; for *this* is a sign between Me and you throughout your generations, that you may know that I am the LORD who sanctifies you.

14 'Therefore you are to observe the sabbath,

for it is holy to you. Everyone who profanes it shall surely be put to death; for whoever does any work on it, that person shall be cut off from among his people.

15 'For six days work may be done, but on the seventh day there is a sabbath of complete rest, holy to the LORD; whoever does any work on the sabbath day shall surely be put to death.

16 'So the sons of Israel shall observe the sabbath, to celebrate the sabbath throughout their generations as a perpetual covenant.'

17 "It is a sign between Me and the sons of Israel forever; for in six days the LORD made heaven and earth, but on the seventh day He ceased *from labor*, and was refreshed."

18 ¶ When He had finished speaking with him upon Mount Sinai, He gave Moses the two tablets of the testimony, tablets of stone, written by the finger of God.

The Golden Calf

32 Now when the people saw that Moses delayed to come down from the mountain, the people assembled about Aaron and said to him, "Come, make us a god who will go before us; as for this Moses, the man who brought us up from the land of Egypt, we do not know what has become of him."

2 Aaron said to them, "Tear off the gold rings which are in the ears of your wives, your sons, and your daughters, and bring *them* to me."

3 Then all the people tore off the gold rings which were in their ears and brought *them* to Aaron.

4 He took *this* from their hand, and fashioned it with a graving tool and made it into a molten calf; and they said, "This is your god, O Israel, who brought you up from the land of Egypt."

5 Now when Aaron saw *this*, he built an altar

32:4–8 Recent Discovery

Not until 1990 did archaeologists unearth the first golden calf in Palestine, and, to their surprise, it stood only a few inches tall. Contrary to popular depictions in movies and historical books, Aaron's solid gold calf too may have been very small, but elevated on a pedestal for visual emphasis. Undoubtedly the Israelites knew of the bull-god Apis, one of Egypt's important gods.

Moses stayed on Mount Sinai for nearly six weeks (24:18), which helps explain the Israelites' panicky behavior. Had Moses died or run away? Would he ever come back? Nevertheless, by flagrantly breaking the second commandment they failed their first test under the new covenant with God.

before it; and Aaron made a proclamation and said, "Tomorrow *shall be* a feast to the LORD."

6 So the next day they rose early and offered burnt offerings, and brought peace offerings; and the people sat down to eat and to drink, and rose up to play.

7 ¶ Then the LORD spoke to Moses, "Go down at once, for your people, whom you brought up from the land of Egypt, have corrupted *themselves*.

8 "They have quickly turned aside from the way which I commanded them. They have made for themselves a molten calf, and have worshiped it and have sacrificed to it and said, 'This is your god, O Israel, who brought you up from the land of Egypt!'"

9 The LORD said to Moses, "I have seen this people, and behold, they are an obstinate people.

10 "Now then let Me alone, that My anger may burn against them and that I may destroy them; and I will make of you a great nation."

Moses' Entreaty

11 ¶ Then Moses entreated the LORD his God, and said, "O LORD, why does Your anger burn against Your people whom You have brought out from the land of Egypt with great power and with a mighty hand?

12 "Why should the Egyptians speak, saying, 'With evil *intent* He brought them out to kill them in the mountains and to destroy them from the face of the earth'? Turn from Your burning anger and change Your mind about *doing* harm to Your people.

13 "Remember Abraham, Isaac, and Israel, Your servants to whom You swore by Yourself, and said to them, 'I will multiply your descendants as the stars of the heavens, and all this land of which I have spoken I will give to your descendants, and they shall inherit *it* forever.'"

14 So the LORD changed His mind about the harm which He said He would do to His people.

15 ¶ Then Moses turned and went down from the mountain with the two tablets of the testimony in his hand, tablets which were written on both sides; they were written on one *side* and the other.

16 The tablets were God's work, and the writing was God's writing engraved on the tablets.

17 Now when Joshua heard the sound of the people as they shouted, he said to Moses, "There is a sound of war in the camp."

18 But he said,

"It is not the sound of the cry of triumph,
Nor is it the sound of the cry of defeat;
But the sound of singing I hear."

Moses' Anger

19 It came about, as soon as Moses came near the camp, that he saw the calf and *the* dancing;

and Moses' anger burned, and he threw the tablets from his hands and shattered them at the foot of the mountain.

20 He took the calf which they had made and burned *it* with fire, and ground it to powder, and scattered it over the surface of the water and made the sons of Israel drink *it*.

21 ¶ Then Moses said to Aaron, "What did this people do to you, that you have brought *such* great sin upon them?"

22 Aaron said, "Do not let the anger of my lord burn; you know the people yourself, that they are prone to evil.

23 "For they said to me, 'Make a god for us who will go before us; for this Moses, the man who brought us up from the land of Egypt, we do not know what has become of him.'

24 "I said to them, 'Whoever has any gold, let them tear it off.' So they gave *it* to me, and I threw it into the fire, and out came this calf."

25 ¶ Now when Moses saw that the people were out of control—for Aaron had let them get out of control to be a derision among their enemies—

26 then Moses stood in the gate of the camp, and said, "Whoever is for the LORD, *come* to me!" And all the sons of Levi gathered together to him.

27 He said to them, "Thus says the LORD, the God of Israel, 'Every man *of you* put his sword upon his thigh, and go back and forth from gate to gate in the camp, and kill every man his brother, and every man his friend, and every man his neighbor.'"

28 So the sons of Levi did as Moses instructed, and about three thousand men of the people fell that day.

29 Then Moses said, "Dedicate yourselves today to the LORD—for every man has been against his son and against his brother—in order that He may bestow a blessing upon you today."

30 ¶ On the next day Moses said to the people, "You yourselves have committed a great sin; and now I am going up to the LORD, perhaps I can make atonement for your sin."

31 Then Moses returned to the LORD, and said, "Alas, this people has committed a great sin, and they have made a god of gold for themselves.

32 "But now, if You will, forgive their sin—and if not, please blot me out from Your book which You have written!"

33 The LORD said to Moses, "Whoever has sinned against Me, I will blot him out of My book.

34 "But go now, lead the people where I told you. Behold, My angel shall go before you; nevertheless in the day when I punish, I will punish them for their sin."

35 Then the LORD smote the people, because of what they did with the calf which Aaron had made.

The Journey Resumed

33 Then the LORD spoke to Moses, "Depart, go up from here, you and the people whom you have brought up from the land of Egypt, to the land of which I swore to Abraham, Isaac, and Jacob, saying, 'To your descendants I will give it.'

2 "I will send an angel before you and I will drive out the Canaanite, the Amorite, the Hittite, the Perizzite, the Hivite and the Jebusite.

3 "*Go up* to a land flowing with milk and honey; for I will not go up in your midst, because you are an obstinate people, and I might destroy you on the way."

33:3 Why the Israelites?

This remarkable scene shows Moses pleading with God not to abandon the Israelites, his chosen people. Eventually, God did agree to lead them on (verse 17). Why were the children of Israel chosen? Why not some other race? When the Bible touches on the question at all, it gives no comprehensive answer. Usually, the reply boils down to something like this, "I will be gracious to whom I will be gracious" (verse 19). God reserves the right to choose whomever he wants. But Exodus makes one thing clear. Israelites were not chosen because of their bravery or impressiveness or even faithfulness. Their selection was an act of God's pure grace; no one else can take the credit.

4 ¶ When the people heard this sad word, they went into mourning, and none of them put on his ornaments.

5 For the LORD had said to Moses, "Say to the sons of Israel, 'You are an obstinate people; should I go up in your midst for one moment, I would destroy you. Now therefore, put off your ornaments from you, that I may know what I shall do with you.'"

6 So the sons of Israel stripped themselves of their ornaments, from Mount Horeb *onward*.

7 ¶ Now Moses used to take the tent and pitch it outside the camp, a good distance from the camp, and he called it the tent of meeting. And everyone who sought the LORD would go out to the tent of meeting which was outside the camp.

8 And it came about, whenever Moses went out to the tent, that all the people would arise and stand, each at the entrance of his tent, and gaze after Moses until he entered the tent.

9 Whenever Moses entered the tent, the pillar of cloud would descend and stand at the entrance of the tent; and the LORD would speak with Moses.

10 When all the people saw the pillar of cloud standing at the entrance of the tent, all the people would arise and worship, each at the entrance of his tent.

11 Thus the LORD used to speak to Moses face

to face, just as a man speaks to his friend. When Moses returned to the camp, his servant Joshua, the son of Nun, a young man, would not depart from the tent.

Moses Intercedes

12 ¶ Then Moses said to the LORD, "See, You say to me, 'Bring up this people!' But You Yourself have not let me know whom You will send with me. Moreover, You have said, 'I have known you by name, and you have also found favor in My sight.'

13 "Now therefore, I pray You, if I have found favor in Your sight, let me know Your ways that I may know You, so that I may find favor in Your sight. Consider too, that this nation is Your people."

14 And He said, "My presence shall go *with you,* and I will give you rest."

15 Then he said to Him, "If Your presence does not go *with us,* do not lead us up from here.

16 "For how then can it be known that I have found favor in Your sight, I and Your people? Is it not by Your going with us, so that we, I and Your people, may be distinguished from all the *other* people who are upon the face of the earth?"

17 ¶ The LORD said to Moses, "I will also do this thing of which you have spoken; for you have found favor in My sight and I have known you by name."

18 Then Moses said, "I pray You, show me Your glory!"

19 And He said, "I Myself will make all My goodness pass before you, and will proclaim the name of the LORD before you; and I will be gracious to whom I will be gracious, and will show compassion on whom I will show compassion."

20 But He said, "You cannot see My face, for no man can see Me and live!"

21 Then the LORD said, "Behold, there is a place by Me, and you shall stand *there* on the rock;

22 and it will come about, while My glory is passing by, that I will put you in the cleft of the rock and cover you with My hand until I have passed by.

23 "Then I will take My hand away and you shall see My back, but My face shall not be seen."

The Two Tablets Replaced

34 Now the LORD said to Moses, "Cut out for yourself two stone tablets like the former ones, and I will write on the tablets the words that were on the former tablets which you shattered.

2 "So be ready by morning, and come up in the morning to Mount Sinai, and present yourself there to Me on the top of the mountain.

3 "No man is to come up with you, nor let any man be seen anywhere on the mountain; even the flocks and the herds may not graze in front of that mountain."

---

4 So he cut out two stone tablets like the former ones, and Moses rose up early in the morning and went up to Mount Sinai, as the LORD had commanded him, and he took two stone tablets in his hand.

5 The LORD descended in the cloud and stood there with him as he called upon the name of the LORD.

6 Then the LORD passed by in front of him and proclaimed, "The LORD, the LORD God, compassionate and gracious, slow to anger, and abounding in lovingkindness and truth;

34:6–7 Capsule Description

The self-description of God found in these two verses became for the Jews a profound summary of God's nature. The Old Testament quotes or alludes to this passage more than any other.

7 who keeps lovingkindness for thousands, who forgives iniquity, transgression and sin; yet He will by no means leave *the guilty* unpunished, visiting the iniquity of fathers on the children and on the grandchildren to the third and fourth generations."

8 Moses made haste to bow low toward the earth and worship.

9 He said, "If now I have found favor in Your sight, O Lord, I pray, let the Lord go along in our midst, even though the people are so obstinate, and pardon our iniquity and our sin, and take us as Your own possession."

The Covenant Renewed

10 ¶ Then God said, "Behold, I am going to make a covenant. Before all your people I will perform miracles which have not been produced in all the earth nor among any of the nations; and all the people among whom you live will see the working of the LORD, for it is a fearful thing that I am going to perform with you.

11 ¶ "Be sure to observe what I am commanding you this day: behold, I am going to drive out the Amorite before you, and the Canaanite, the Hittite, the Perizzite, the Hivite and the Jebusite.

12 "Watch yourself that you make no covenant with the inhabitants of the land into which you are going, or it will become a snare in your midst.

13 "But *rather,* you are to tear down their altars and smash their *sacred* pillars and cut down their *a*Asherim

14 —for you shall not worship any other god, for the LORD, whose name is Jealous, is a jealous God—

15 otherwise you might make a covenant with the inhabitants of the land and they would play

---

a I.e. wooden symbols of a female deity

the harlot with their gods and sacrifice to their gods, and someone might invite you to eat of his sacrifice,

16 and you might take some of his daughters for your sons, and his daughters might play the harlot with their gods and cause your sons *also* to play the harlot with their gods.

17 "You shall make for yourself no molten gods.

18 ¶ "You shall observe the Feast of Unleavened Bread. For seven days you are to eat unleavened bread, as I commanded you, at the appointed time in the month of Abib, for in the month of Abib you came out of Egypt.

19 ¶ "The first offspring from every womb belongs to Me, and all your male livestock, the first offspring from cattle and sheep.

20 "You shall redeem with a lamb the first offspring from a donkey; and if you do not redeem *it*, then you shall break its neck. You shall redeem all the firstborn of your sons. None shall appear before Me empty-handed.

21 ¶ "You shall work six days, but on the seventh day you shall rest; *even* during plowing time and harvest you shall rest.

22 "You shall celebrate the Feast of Weeks, *that is*, the first fruits of the wheat harvest, and the Feast of Ingathering at the turn of the year.

23 "Three times a year all your males are to appear before the Lord GOD, the God of Israel.

24 "For I will drive out nations before you and enlarge your borders, and no man shall covet your land when you go up three times a year to appear before the LORD your God.

25 ¶ "You shall not offer the blood of My sacrifice with leavened bread, nor is the sacrifice of the Feast of the Passover to be left over until morning.

26 ¶ "You shall bring the very first of the first fruits of your soil into the house of the LORD your God.

¶ "You shall not boil a young goat in its mother's milk."

27 ¶ Then the LORD said to Moses, "Write down these words, for in accordance with these words I have made a covenant with you and with Israel."

28 So he was there with the LORD forty days and forty nights; he did not eat bread or drink water. And he wrote on the tablets the words of the covenant, the Ten Commandments.

Moses' Face Shines

29 ¶ It came about when Moses was coming down from Mount Sinai (and the two tablets of the testimony *were* in Moses' hand as he was coming down from the mountain), that Moses did not know that the skin of his face shone because of his speaking with Him.

30 So when Aaron and all the sons of Israel saw Moses, behold, the skin of his face shone, and they were afraid to come near him.

31 Then Moses called to them, and Aaron and all the rulers in the congregation returned to him; and Moses spoke to them.

32 Afterward all the sons of Israel came near, and he commanded them *to do* everything that the LORD had spoken to him on Mount Sinai.

33 When Moses had finished speaking with them, he put a veil over his face.

34 But whenever Moses went in before the LORD to speak with Him, he would take off the veil until he came out; and whenever he came out and spoke to the sons of Israel what he had been commanded,

35 the sons of Israel would see the face of Moses, that the skin of Moses' face shone. So Moses would replace the veil over his face until he went in to speak with Him.

The Sabbath Emphasized

35 Then Moses assembled all the congregation of the sons of Israel, and said to them, "These are the things that the LORD has commanded *you* to do:

2 ¶ "For six days work may be done, but on the seventh day you shall have a holy *day*, a sabbath of complete rest to the LORD; whoever does any work on it shall be put to death.

3 "You shall not kindle a fire in any of your dwellings on the sabbath day."

4 ¶ Moses spoke to all the congregation of the sons of Israel, saying, "This is the thing which the LORD has commanded, saying,

5 'Take from among you a contribution to the LORD; whoever is of a willing heart, let him bring it as the LORD'S contribution: gold, silver, and bronze,

6 and blue, purple and scarlet *material,* fine linen, goats' *hair*,

7 and rams' skins dyed red, and porpoise skins, and acacia wood,

8 and oil for lighting, and spices for the anointing oil, and for the fragrant incense,

9 and onyx stones and setting stones for the ephod and for the breastpiece.

Tabernacle Workmen

10 ¶ 'Let every skillful man among you come, and make all that the LORD has commanded:

11 the tabernacle, its tent and its covering, its hooks and its boards, its bars, its pillars, and its sockets;

12 the ark and its poles, the mercy seat, and the curtain of the screen;

13 the table and its poles, and all its utensils, and the bread of the *a*Presence;

14 the lampstand also for the light and its utensils and its lamps and the oil for the light;

15 and the altar of incense and its poles, and

---

a Lit *Face*

the anointing oil and the fragrant incense, and the screen for the doorway at the entrance of the tabernacle;

16 the altar of burnt offering with its bronze grating, its poles, and all its utensils, the basin and its stand;

17 the hangings of the court, its pillars and its

sockets, and the screen for the gate of the court;

18 the pegs of the tabernacle and the pegs of the court and their cords;

19 the woven garments for ministering in the holy place, the holy garments for Aaron the priest and the garments of his sons, to minister as priests.' "

A Portable Cathedral
An unlikely sight in the desert

IN A.D. 1144 A GREAT building began to take shape in a village in northwest France. Enthusiasm for the project soon spread across the entire country, and volunteer workers streamed to the site. Working together, the people managed to construct one of the most beautiful buildings in the world, the magnificent cathedral at Chartres.

Fifty years later, after a terrible fire, the villagers of France rebuilt their cathedral from scratch. Today, tourists throng to marvel at what was splendidly fashioned to the glory of God so long ago.

Everyone whose heart stirred him and everyone whose spirit moved him came and brought the LORD's contribution for the work of the tent of meeting.
35:21

Inspired Builders

A work of art took shape in similar fashion thousands of years earlier than Chartres, and the last chapters of Exodus provide a wealth of details. In a hostile desert landscape, a tribe of just-liberated slaves built something of exquisite beauty: a portable cathedral, or tabernacle.

God directed the project personally, specially endowing the craftsmen with skill (31:1–6) and elaborating right down to the color choice of woven yarns, the precise length of curtains and wooden frames, and the design of gold filigree. The people of Israel joined together in a flurry of activity, carefully following God's pattern. A ton of gold went into the project, as well as nearly four tons of silver and stockpiles of precious gems and rare woods.

God Moves In

After describing the tabernacle construction in great detail, the Bible devotes just five verses, the last five in Exodus, to its culmination. In a matter-of-fact tone, those sentences record a remarkable event.

Throughout the book of Exodus God had been progressively revealing himself to Moses: once in a burning bush, once in a mysterious appearance beside a rock, once on a trembling mountain, and often in a cloud-covered Tent of Meeting. God's presence caused such fear and awe that the people of Israel begged that he not speak to them directly (20:19). When Moses had come down from Mount Sinai after meeting with God, he glowed as if radioactive, and everyone was too frightened to go near him (34:30).

Yet, on the day the tabernacle was completed, this same God moved in. His glory filled the new tabernacle. God took up residence with his people.

A Visible Reminder

From then on, whenever the Israelites marched or camped, their portable cathedral stayed in the exact center of the camp, with their tents and personal belongings radiating out from the holy of holies and ark of the covenant. The tabernacle gave them a visible reminder of God's central place. Each day priests performed functions of sacrifice and worship there.

The story of the tabernacle, which takes up one-third of Exodus, reveals much about the character of God. He can never be taken lightly—the rituals here and in the next three books show that God must be approached with care and reverence. He cannot be experienced directly, in his fullness, by ordinary people; a holy God is simply too overwhelming. Even Moses, Exodus says, could not look on God's face and live (33:20).

And yet, amazingly, that same God who seemed so distant came near. Despite the huge gulf separating God and humanity—a gulf that all the rules on holiness and purification only hint at—God allowed personal access to himself. He made himself available.

Life Questions: Where does God "live" now?

Gifts Received

20 ¶ Then all the congregation of the sons of Israel departed from Moses' presence.

21 Everyone whose heart stirred him and everyone whose spirit moved him came *and* brought the LORD'S contribution for the work of the tent of meeting and for all its service and for the holy garments.

22 Then all whose hearts moved them, both men and women, came *and* brought brooches and earrings and signet rings and bracelets, all articles of gold; so *did* every man who presented an offering of gold to the LORD.

23 Every man, who had in his possession blue and purple and scarlet *material* and fine linen and goats' *hair* and rams' skins dyed red and porpoise skins, brought them.

24 Everyone who could make a contribution of silver and bronze brought the LORD'S contribution; and every man who had in his possession acacia wood for any work of the service brought it.

25 All the skilled women spun with their hands, and brought what they had spun, *in* blue and purple *and* scarlet *material* and *in* fine linen.

26 All the women whose heart stirred with a skill spun the goats' *hair.*

27 The rulers brought the onyx stones and the stones for setting for the ephod and for the breastpiece;

28 and the spice and the oil for the light and for the anointing oil and for the fragrant incense.

29 The Israelites, all the men and women, whose heart moved them to bring *material* for all the work, which the LORD had commanded through Moses to be done, brought a freewill offering to the LORD.

30 ¶ Then Moses said to the sons of Israel, "See, the LORD has called by name Bezalel the son of Uri, the son of Hur, of the tribe of Judah.

31 "And He has filled him with the Spirit of God, in wisdom, in understanding and in knowledge and in all craftsmanship;

32 to make designs for working in gold and in silver and in bronze,

33 and in the cutting of stones for settings and in the carving of wood, so as to perform in every inventive work.

34 "He also has put in his heart to teach, both he and Oholiab, the son of Ahisamach, of the tribe of Dan.

35 "He has filled them with skill to perform every work of an engraver and of a designer and of an embroiderer, in blue and in purple *and* in scarlet *material,* and in fine linen, and of a weaver, as performers of every work and makers of designs.

The Tabernacle Underwritten

36 "Now Bezalel and Oholiab, and every skillful person in whom the LORD has put skill and understanding to know how to perform all the work in the construction of the sanctuary, shall perform in accordance with all that the LORD has commanded."

2 ¶ Then Moses called Bezalel and Oholiab and every skillful person in whom the LORD had put skill, everyone whose heart stirred him, to come to the work to perform it.

3 They received from Moses all the contributions which the sons of Israel had brought to perform the work in the construction of the sanctuary. And they still *continued* bringing to him freewill offerings every morning.

4 And all the skillful men who were performing all the work of the sanctuary came, each from the work which he was performing,

5 and they said to Moses, "The people are bringing much more than enough for the construction work which the LORD commanded *us* to perform."

6 So Moses issued a command, and a proclamation was circulated throughout the camp, saying, "Let no man or woman any longer perform work for the contributions of the sanctuary." Thus the people were restrained from bringing *any* more.

7 For the material they had was sufficient and more than enough for all the work, to perform it.

Construction Proceeds

8 ¶ All the skillful men among those who were performing the work made the tabernacle with ten curtains; of fine twisted linen and blue and purple and scarlet *material,* with cherubim, the work of a skillful workman, Bezalel made them.

36:8–38 Enthusiastic Givers

Some commentators estimate that descriptions of the tabernacle make up the largest single subject covered in the Bible. When the time came for construction, the Israelites pitched in with such enthusiasm that they had to be restrained from bringing more offerings (verse 5). Those who could not afford material gifts donated time and labor.

9 The length of each curtain was twenty-eight cubits and the width of each curtain four cubits; all the curtains had the same measurements.

10 He joined five curtains to one another and *the other* five curtains he joined to one another.

11 He made loops of blue on the edge of the outermost curtain in the first set; he did likewise on the edge of the curtain that was outermost in the second set.

12 He made fifty loops in the one curtain and he made fifty loops on the edge of the curtain that was in the second set; the loops were opposite each other.

13 He made fifty clasps of gold and joined the curtains to one another with the clasps, so the tabernacle was a unit.

14 ¶ Then he made curtains of goats' *hair* for a tent over the tabernacle; he made eleven curtains in all.

15 The length of each curtain *was* thirty cubits and four cubits the width of each curtain; the eleven curtains had the same measurements.

16 He joined five curtains by themselves and *the other* six curtains by themselves.

17 Moreover, he made fifty loops on the edge of the curtain that was outermost in the *first* set, and he made fifty loops on the edge of the curtain *that was outermost in* the second set.

18 He made fifty clasps of bronze to join the tent together so that it would be a unit.

19 He made a covering for the tent of rams' skins dyed red, and a covering of porpoise skins above.

20 ¶ Then he made the boards for the tabernacle of acacia wood, standing upright.

21 Ten cubits *was* the length of each board and one and a half cubits the width of each board.

22 *There were* two tenons for each board, fitted to one another; thus he did for all the boards of the tabernacle.

23 He made the boards for the tabernacle: twenty boards for the south side;

24 and he made forty sockets of silver under the twenty boards; two sockets under one board for its two tenons and two sockets under another board for its two tenons.

25 Then for the second side of the tabernacle, on the north side, he made twenty boards,

26 and their forty sockets of silver; two sockets under one board and two sockets under another board.

27 For the rear of the tabernacle, to the west, he made six boards.

28 He made two boards for the corners of the tabernacle at the rear.

29 They were double beneath, and together they were complete to its top to the first ring; thus he did with both of them for the two corners.

30 There were eight boards with their sockets of silver, sixteen sockets, two under every board.

31 ¶ Then he made bars of acacia wood, five for the boards of one side of the tabernacle,

32 and five bars for the boards of the other side of the tabernacle, and five bars for the boards of the tabernacle for the rear *side* to the west.

33 He made the middle bar to pass through in the center of the boards from end to end.

34 He overlaid the boards with gold and made their rings of gold *as* holders for the bars, and overlaid the bars with gold.

35 ¶ Moreover, he made the veil of blue and purple and scarlet *material,* and fine twisted linen; he made it with cherubim, the work of a skillful workman.

36 He made four pillars of acacia for it, and overlaid them with gold, with their hooks of gold; and he cast four sockets of silver for them.

37 He made a screen for the doorway of the tent, of blue and purple and scarlet *material,* and fine twisted linen, the work of a weaver;

38 and *he made* its five pillars with their hooks, and he overlaid their tops and their bands with gold; but their five sockets were of bronze.

Construction Continues

37 Now Bezalel made the ark of acacia wood; its length was two and a half cubits, and its width one and a half cubits, and its height one and a half cubits;

37:1 Sacred Furniture

In contrast to the elaborate worship sites of the pagans, the Hebrews' tabernacle was sparsely furnished and decorated. Obviously God did not need a place to live. Rather, the furnishings mentioned in this passage—only six pieces—had a specific purpose in showing the proper way for human beings to approach God.

2 and he overlaid it with pure gold inside and out, and made a gold molding for it all around.

3 He cast four rings of gold for it on its four feet; even two rings on one side of it, and two rings on the other side of it.

4 He made poles of acacia wood and overlaid them with gold.

5 He put the poles into the rings on the sides of the ark, to carry it.

6 He made a mercy seat of pure gold, two and a half cubits long and one and a half cubits wide.

7 He made two cherubim of gold; he made them of hammered work at the two ends of the mercy seat;

8 one cherub at the one end and one cherub at the other end; he made the cherubim *of one piece* with the mercy seat at the two ends.

9 The cherubim had *their* wings spread upward, covering the mercy seat with their wings, with their faces toward each other; the faces of the cherubim were toward the mercy seat.

10 ¶ Then he made the table of acacia wood, two cubits long and a cubit wide and one and a half cubits high.

11 He overlaid it with pure gold, and made a gold molding for it all around.

12 He made a rim for it of a handbreadth all around, and made a gold molding for its rim all around.

13 He cast four gold rings for it and put the rings on the four corners that were on its four feet.

14 Close by the rim were the rings, the holders for the poles to carry the table.

15 He made the poles of acacia wood and overlaid them with gold, to carry the table.

16 He made the utensils which were on the table, its dishes and its pans and its bowls and its jars, with which to pour out drink offerings, of pure gold.

17 ¶ Then he made the lampstand of pure gold. He made the lampstand of hammered work, its base and its shaft; its cups, its bulbs and its flowers were *of one piece* with it.

18 There were six branches going out of its sides; three branches of the lampstand from the one side of it and three branches of the lampstand from the other side of it;

19 three cups shaped like almond *blossoms,* a bulb and a flower in one branch, and three cups shaped like almond *blossoms,* a bulb and a flower in the other branch—so for the six branches going out of the lampstand.

20 In the lampstand *there were* four cups shaped like almond *blossoms,* its bulbs and its flowers;

21 and a bulb was under the *first* pair of branches *coming* out of it, and a bulb under the *second* pair of branches *coming* out of it, and a bulb under the *third* pair of branches *coming* out of it, for the six branches coming out of the lampstand.

22 Their bulbs and their branches were *of one piece* with it; the whole of it *was* a single hammered work of pure gold.

23 He made its seven lamps with its snuffers and its trays of pure gold.

24 He made it and all its utensils from a talent of pure gold.

25 ¶ Then he made the altar of incense of acacia wood: a cubit long and a cubit wide, square, and two cubits high; its horns were *of one piece* with it.

26 He overlaid it with pure gold, its top and its sides all around, and its horns; and he made a gold molding for it all around.

27 He made two golden rings for it under its molding, on its two sides—on opposite sides—as holders for poles with which to carry it.

28 He made the poles of acacia wood and overlaid them with gold.

29 And he made the holy anointing oil and the pure, fragrant incense of spices, the work of a perfumer.

The Tabernacle Completed

38 Then he made the altar of burnt offering of acacia wood, five cubits long, and five cubits wide, square, and three cubits high.

2 He made its horns on its four corners, its horns being *of one piece* with it, and he overlaid it with bronze.

3 He made all the utensils of the altar, the pails and the shovels and the basins, the flesh hooks and the firepans; he made all its utensils of bronze.

4 He made for the altar a grating of bronze network beneath, under its ledge, reaching halfway up.

5 He cast four rings on the four ends of the bronze grating *as* holders for the poles.

6 He made the poles of acacia wood and overlaid them with bronze.

7 He inserted the poles into the rings on the sides of the altar, with which to carry it. He made it hollow with planks.

8 ¶ Moreover, he made the laver of bronze with its base of bronze, from the mirrors of the serving women who served at the doorway of the tent of meeting.

9 ¶ Then he made the court: for the south side the hangings of the court were of fine twisted linen, one hundred cubits;

38:9–13 Tabernacle Layout

Unlike a church or synagogue, neither the tabernacle nor temple functioned as a gathering place for public meetings. Worshipers entered a large, open courtyard area to present their offerings and sacrifices. After receiving the offerings, the priests approached the holy place, which contained some of the sacred furniture. Only the high priest could go further, into the holy of holies where the ark of the covenant stayed, and he did so only once a year, on the Day of Atonement.

10 their twenty pillars, and their twenty sockets, *made* of bronze; the hooks of the pillars and their bands *were* of silver.

11 For the north side *there were* one hundred cubits; their twenty pillars and their twenty sockets *were* of bronze, the hooks of the pillars and their bands *were* of silver.

12 For the west side *there were* hangings of fifty cubits *with* their ten pillars and their ten sockets; the hooks of the pillars and their bands *were* of silver.

13 For the east side fifty cubits.

14 The hangings for the *one* side *of the gate* were fifteen cubits, *with* their three pillars and their three sockets,

15 and so for the other side. On both sides of the gate of the court *were* hangings of fifteen cubits, *with* their three pillars and their three sockets.

16 All the hangings of the court all around *were* of fine twisted linen.

17 The sockets for the pillars *were* of bronze, the hooks of the pillars and their bands, of silver; and the overlaying of their tops, of silver, and all the pillars of the court were furnished with silver bands.

18 The screen of the gate of the court was the work of the weaver, of blue and purple and scarlet *material* and fine twisted linen. And the length *was* twenty cubits and the height *was* five cubits, corresponding to the hangings of the court.

19 Their four pillars and their four sockets *were* of bronze; their hooks *were* of silver, and the overlaying of their tops and their bands *were* of silver.

20 All the pegs of the tabernacle and of the court all around *were* of bronze.

The Cost of the Tabernacle

21 ¶ This is the number of the things for the tabernacle, the tabernacle of the testimony, as they were numbered according to the command of Moses, for the service of the Levites, by the hand of Ithamar the son of Aaron the priest.

22 Now Bezalel the son of Uri, the son of Hur, of the tribe of Judah, made all that the LORD had commanded Moses.

23 With him *was* Oholiab the son of Ahisamach, of the tribe of Dan, an engraver and a skillful workman and a weaver in blue and in purple and in scarlet *material,* and fine linen.

24 ¶ All the gold that was used for the work, in all the work of the sanctuary, even the gold of the wave offering, was 29 talents and 730 shekels, according to the shekel of the sanctuary.

25 The silver of those of the congregation who were numbered was 100 talents and 1,775 shekels, according to the shekel of the sanctuary;

26 a beka a head (*that is,* half a shekel according to the shekel of the sanctuary), for each one who passed over to those who were numbered, from twenty years old and upward, for 603,550 men.

27 The hundred talents of silver were for casting the sockets of the sanctuary and the sockets of the veil; one hundred sockets for the hundred talents, a talent for a socket.

28 Of the 1,775 *shekels,* he made hooks for the pillars and overlaid their tops and made bands for them.

29 The bronze of the wave offering was 70 talents and 2,400 shekels.

30 With it he made the sockets to the doorway of the tent of meeting, and the bronze altar and its bronze grating, and all the utensils of the altar,

31 and the sockets of the court all around and the sockets of the gate of the court, and all the pegs of the tabernacle and all the pegs of the court all around.

The Priestly Garments

39 Moreover, from the blue and purple and scarlet *material,* they made finely woven garments for ministering in the holy place as well as the holy garments which were for Aaron, just as the LORD had commanded Moses.

2 ¶ He made the ephod of gold, *and* of blue and purple and scarlet *material,* and fine twisted linen.

3 Then they hammered out gold sheets and cut *them* into threads to be woven in *with* the blue and the purple and the scarlet *material,* and the fine linen, the work of a skillful workman.

4 They made attaching shoulder pieces for the ephod; it was attached at its two *upper* ends.

5 The skillfully woven band which was on it was like its workmanship, of the same material: of gold *and* of blue and purple and scarlet *material,* and fine twisted linen, just as the LORD had commanded Moses.

6 ¶ They made the onyx stones, set in gold filigree *settings;* they were engraved *like* the engravings of a signet, according to the names of the sons of Israel.

7 And he placed them on the shoulder pieces of the ephod, *as* memorial stones for the sons of Israel, just as the LORD had commanded Moses.

8 ¶ He made the breastpiece, the work of a skillful workman, like the workmanship of the ephod: of gold *and* of blue and purple and scarlet *material* and fine twisted linen.

9 It was square; they made the breastpiece folded double, a span long and a span wide when folded double.

10 And they mounted four rows of stones on it. The first row *was* a row of ruby, topaz, and emerald;

11 and the second row, a turquoise, a sapphire and a diamond;

12 and the third row, a jacinth, an agate, and an amethyst;

13 and the fourth row, a beryl, an onyx, and a jasper. They were set in gold filigree *settings* when they were mounted.

14 The stones were corresponding to the names of the sons of Israel; they were twelve, corresponding to their names, *engraved with* the engravings of a signet, each with its name for the twelve tribes.

15 They made on the breastpiece chains like cords, of twisted cordage work in pure gold.

16 They made two gold filigree *settings* and two gold rings, and put the two rings on the two ends of the breastpiece.

17 Then they put the two gold cords in the two rings at the ends of the breastpiece.

18 They put the *other* two ends of the two cords on the two filigree *settings,* and put them on the shoulder pieces of the ephod at the front of it.

19 They made two gold rings and placed *them* on the two ends of the breastpiece, on its inner edge which was next to the ephod.

20 Furthermore, they made two gold rings and placed them on the bottom of the two shoulder pieces of the ephod, on the front of it, close to the place where it joined, above the woven band of the ephod.

21 They bound the breastpiece by its rings to

the rings of the ephod with a blue cord, so that it would be on the woven band of the ephod, and that the breastpiece would not come loose from the ephod, just as the LORD had commanded Moses.

22 ¶ Then he made the robe of the ephod of woven work, all of blue;

23 and the opening of the robe was *at the top* in the center, as the opening of a coat of mail, with a binding all around its opening, so that it would not be torn.

24 They made pomegranates of blue and purple and scarlet *material and* twisted *linen* on the hem of the robe.

25 They also made bells of pure gold, and put the bells between the pomegranates all around on the hem of the robe,

26 alternating a bell and a pomegranate all around on the hem of the robe for the service, just as the LORD had commanded Moses.

27 ¶ They made the tunics of finely woven linen for Aaron and his sons,

28 and the turban of fine linen, and the decorated caps of fine linen, and the linen breeches of fine twisted linen,

29 and the sash of fine twisted linen, and blue and purple and scarlet *material,* the work of the weaver, just as the LORD had commanded Moses.

30 ¶ They made the plate of the holy crown of pure gold, and inscribed it like the engravings of a signet, "Holy to the LORD."

31 They fastened a blue cord to it, to fasten it on the turban above, just as the LORD had commanded Moses.

32 ¶ Thus all the work of the tabernacle of the tent of meeting was completed; and the sons of Israel did according to all that the LORD had commanded Moses; so they did.

33 They brought the tabernacle to Moses, the tent and all its *a*furnishings: its clasps, its boards, its bars, and its pillars and its sockets;

34 and the covering of rams' skins dyed red, and the covering of porpoise skins, and the screening veil;

35 the ark of the testimony and its poles and the mercy seat;

36 the table, all its utensils, and the bread of the Presence;

37 the pure *gold* lampstand, with its arrangement of lamps and all its utensils, and the oil for the light;

38 and the gold altar, and the anointing oil and the fragrant incense, and the veil for the doorway of the tent;

39 the bronze altar and its bronze grating, its poles and all its utensils, the laver and its stand;

40 the hangings for the court, its pillars and its sockets, and the screen for the gate of the court, its cords and its pegs and all the equipment for the service of the tabernacle, for the tent of meeting;

41 the woven garments for ministering in the holy place and the holy garments for Aaron the priest and the garments of his sons, to minister as priests.

42 So the sons of Israel did all the work according to all that the LORD had commanded Moses.

43 And Moses examined all the work and behold, they had done it; just as the LORD had commanded, this they had done. So Moses blessed them.

The Tabernacle Erected

40 Then the LORD spoke to Moses, saying, 2 "On the first day of the first month you shall set up the tabernacle of the tent of meeting.

3 "You shall place the ark of the testimony there, and you shall screen the ark with the veil.

4 "You shall bring in the table and arrange what belongs on it; and you shall bring in the lampstand and mount its lamps.

5 "Moreover, you shall set the gold altar of incense before the ark of the testimony, and set up the veil for the doorway to the tabernacle.

6 "You shall set the altar of burnt offering in front of the doorway of the tabernacle of the tent of meeting.

7 "You shall set the laver between the tent of meeting and the altar and put water in it.

8 "You shall set up the court all around and hang up the veil for the gateway of the court.

9 "Then you shall take the anointing oil and anoint the tabernacle and all that is in it, and shall consecrate it and all its furnishings; and it shall be holy.

10 "You shall anoint the altar of burnt offering and all its utensils, and consecrate the altar, and the altar shall be most holy.

11 "You shall anoint the laver and its stand, and consecrate it.

39:32 Following Orders

The last few chapters of Exodus repeat almost verbatim what has gone before; they simply record that the Israelites followed all of God's prior instructions for building the tabernacle. The phrase "did according to all that the LORD had commanded" resonates like a drumbeat through this section. A people not known for following orders took the tabernacle project very seriously. It became for them not just a symbol, but the actual reality of God living in their midst. The tabernacle was the focal point of worship for 300 years, until the temple was built. Later, the apostle Paul used this imagery when he called believers God's "temple," or dwelling place.

---

a Or *utensils*

12 "Then you shall bring Aaron and his sons to the doorway of the tent of meeting and wash them with water.

13 "You shall put the holy garments on Aaron and anoint him and consecrate him, that he may minister as a priest to Me.

14 "You shall bring his sons and put tunics on them;

15 and you shall anoint them even as you have anointed their father, that they may minister as priests to Me; and their anointing will qualify them for a perpetual priesthood throughout their generations."

16 Thus Moses did; according to all that the LORD had commanded him, so he did.

17 ¶ Now in the first month of the second year, on the first *day* of the month, the tabernacle was erected.

18 Moses erected the tabernacle and laid its sockets, and set up its boards, and inserted its bars and erected its pillars.

19 He spread the tent over the tabernacle and put the covering of the tent on top of it, just as the LORD had commanded Moses.

20 Then he took the testimony and put *it* into the ark, and attached the poles to the ark, and put the mercy seat on top of the ark.

21 He brought the ark into the tabernacle, and set up a veil for the screen, and screened off the ark of the testimony, just as the LORD had commanded Moses.

22 Then he put the table in the tent of meeting on the north side of the tabernacle, outside the veil.

23 He set the arrangement of bread in order on it before the LORD, just as the LORD had commanded Moses.

24 Then he placed the lampstand in the tent of meeting, opposite the table, on the south side of the tabernacle.

25 He lighted the lamps before the LORD, just as the LORD had commanded Moses.

26 Then he placed the gold altar in the tent of meeting in front of the veil;

27 and he burned fragrant incense on it, just as the LORD had commanded Moses.

28 Then he set up the veil for the doorway of the tabernacle.

29 He set the altar of burnt offering *before* the doorway of the tabernacle of the tent of meeting, and offered on it the burnt offering and the meal offering, just as the LORD had commanded Moses.

30 He placed the laver between the tent of meeting and the altar and put water in it for washing.

31 From it Moses and Aaron and his sons washed their hands and their feet.

32 When they entered the tent of meeting, and when they approached the altar, they washed, just as the LORD had commanded Moses.

33 He erected the court all around the tabernacle and the altar, and hung up the veil for the gateway of the court. Thus Moses finished the work.

The Glory of the LORD

34 ¶ Then the cloud covered the tent of meeting, and the glory of the LORD filled the tabernacle.

35 Moses was not able to enter the tent of meeting because the cloud had settled on it, and the glory of the LORD filled the tabernacle.

36 Throughout all their journeys whenever the cloud was taken up from over the tabernacle, the sons of Israel would set out;

37 but if the cloud was not taken up, then they did not set out until the day when it was taken up.

38 For throughout all their journeys, the cloud of the LORD was on the tabernacle by day, and there was fire in it by night, in the sight of all the house of Israel.

LEVITICUS

Living with Fire
Dangerous material more powerful than the atom

L EVITICUS SEEMS MIGHTY STRANGE TO the modern world. Unlike most of the Bible, it has few personalities and stories, and no poetry. Instead, it is crammed full of detailed rules and procedures.

Its painstaking ritual is, however, strikingly similar to the procedures surrounding nuclear technology. The specialized clothing, the concern for purification, the precise handling of crucial materials—both nuclear workers and Old Testament priests share these. This similarity gives an important clue to understanding Leviticus.

> "'Moreover, I will make My dwelling among you, and My soul will not reject you. I will also walk among you and be your God, and you shall be My people'"
> 26:11-12

Cleaning Up a Nuclear Spill

At the Hanford plutonium separation plant in eastern Washington, plutonium and U-235 are kept in a special high-security vault, in brass cans wrapped three times in plastic. To move the radioactive material, specially trained handlers don white protection overalls and special breather masks. They never touch the materials except through a sealed "glove box."

If an accident occurs, such as a small fire ignited by the "hot" material, the entire area must be cleansed through laborious scrubbing with soap and water. Carefully trained workers dispose of the dirty water in a specially protected toxic waste area. Anyone contaminated must also be "cleansed" from the exposure. In extreme cases, she or he must stay away from other people for months.

These rigid rules grew out of hard experience. For decades no one knew the dangers of radioactivity. Workers who used radioactive materials to hand-paint the first "glow in the dark" watches licked their paintbrushes to get a fine tip; their supervisors said they would gain sex appeal. Instead, they got cancer. The introduction of nuclear weapons and nuclear power plants increased the amount of radioactive material being handled. Gradually scientists realized: If you are going to use the atom, you must adopt procedures to fit its power.

The Intimate Presence of God

Leviticus reads something like a training manual for atomic plant workers. Its "dangerous material," however, is more powerful than the atom. Leviticus gives exhaustive detail on how to live with God.

A pamphlet on "how to survive a nuclear accident" may be dull if read on vacation, but it's gripping if read in a vibrating nuclear reactor. Similarly, Leviticus is dull if you do not realize the wonderful news behind it: God, the Creator of the universe, has entered the life of a small and insignificant tribe. The Israelites could not merely fit this God into their lives. They needed to restructure their lives—food, sex, economics—to fit with his. It was essential not just for priests, but for everyone.

Ignoring the operations manual could be deadly. It was for Aaron's two sons (chapter 10).

Free from Contamination

Today, because of Jesus Christ, we don't live in the world of Leviticus. Jesus' perfect self-sacrifice made the daily sacrifice of animals unnecessary. He replaced the high priest as our representative before God. Jesus cleanses the real source of contamination, our sinful nature. Leviticus was meant to teach people some basic truths about God, and when their lessons were complete, they could go on to bigger and better things. (The New Testament book of Hebrews spells out this graduation.)

Yet we need to be reminded of the principles Leviticus taught. It tells us that God was then, as he is today, "a consuming fire" (Hebrews 12:29). He has taught us how to live with that fire, not because we deserved to know, but because he wanted our company. We dare not treat him lightly.

How to Read Leviticus

Many well-intentioned readers, determined to read the Bible from beginning to end, bog down in Leviticus. It's a lawbook, a procedural manual for getting along with a holy and powerful God. Sheer detail can bore you, especially if you miss the point behind it.

When you read the Bible, careful attention to detail is usually a key to understanding. In Leviticus, however, you will get more from looking at the big picture than from studying the details. Some laws we simply don't understand. But Leviticus as a whole shows what kind of people God wanted the Israelites to be. As you read, keep your mind on the big picture. Pay special attention to the explanatory notes. Try to imagine how these laws affected everyday life. Keep asking yourself: How would these laws make the Israelites different from other people—and why were those differences important to God?

3-TRACK READING PLAN

For an explanation and complete listing of the 3-track reading plan, turn to page 7.

TRACK 1:   *Two-Week Courses on the Bible*
See page 8 for information on these courses.

TRACK 2:   *An Overview of Leviticus in 1 Day*
☐ Day 1. Read the Introduction to Leviticus and chapter 26, which summarizes the purpose of God's laws. Scan through the sectional headings of the book to get an idea of what subjects it covers.

Now turn to page 9 for your next Track 2 reading project.

TRACK 3:   *All of Leviticus in 26 Days*
After you have read through Leviticus, turn to pages 10–14 for your next Track 3 reading project.

☐1   ☐2   ☐3   ☐4   ☐5   ☐6   ☐7   ☐8
☐9   ☐10   ☐11–12 ☐13   ☐14   ☐15   ☐16   ☐17
☐18   ☐19   ☐20   ☐21   ☐22   ☐23   ☐24   ☐25
☐26   ☐27

The Law of Burnt Offerings

1 Then the LORD called to Moses and spoke to him from the tent of meeting, saying,

2 "Speak to the sons of Israel and say to them, 'When any man of you brings an offering to the LORD, you shall bring your offering of animals from the herd or the flock.

3 'If his offering is a burnt offering from the herd, he shall offer it, a male without defect; he shall offer it at the doorway of the tent of meeting, that he may be accepted before the LORD.

4 'He shall lay his hand on the head of the burnt offering, that it may be accepted for him to make atonement on his behalf.

5 'He shall slay the young bull before the LORD; and Aaron's sons the priests shall offer up the blood and sprinkle the blood around on the altar that is at the doorway of the tent of meeting.

6 'He shall then skin the burnt offering and cut it into its pieces.

7 'The sons of Aaron the priest shall put fire on the altar and arrange wood on the fire.

8 'Then Aaron's sons the priests shall arrange the pieces, the head and the suet over the wood which is on the fire that is on the altar.

9 'Its entrails, however, and its legs he shall wash with water. And the priest shall offer up in smoke all of it on the altar for a burnt offering, an offering by fire of a soothing aroma to the LORD.

10 ¶ 'But if his offering is from the flock, of the sheep or of the goats, for a burnt offering, he shall offer it a male without defect.

11 'He shall slay it on the side of the altar north-

1:13 Original Holocaust

The word "holocaust," which simply means "burnt whole," derives from the Israelite practice of offering up the entire animal, including legs, head, and inner parts. Later the word stood for a great devastation, especially by fire. After World War II, Jews began referring to Hitler's mass destruction of their race in gas chambers and ovens as "The Holocaust."

ward before the LORD, and Aaron's sons the priests shall sprinkle its blood around on the altar.

12 'He shall then cut it into its pieces with its head and its suet, and the priest shall arrange them on the wood which is on the fire that is on the altar.

13 'The entrails, however, and the legs he shall wash with water. And the priest shall offer all of it, and offer it up in smoke on the altar; it is a burnt offering, an offering by fire of a soothing aroma to the LORD.

14 ¶ 'But if his offering to the LORD is a burnt offering of birds, then he shall bring his offering from the turtledoves or from young pigeons.

15 'The priest shall bring it to the altar, and wring off its head and offer it up in smoke on the altar; and its blood is to be drained out on the side of the altar.

16 'He shall also take away its crop with its feathers and cast it beside the altar eastward, to the place of the ashes.

17 'Then he shall tear it by its wings, *but* shall not sever *it*. And the priest shall offer it up in smoke on the altar on the wood which is on the fire; it is a burnt offering, an offering by fire of a soothing aroma to the LORD.

The Law of Grain Offerings

2 'Now when anyone presents a grain offering as an offering to the LORD, his offering shall be of fine flour, and he shall pour oil on it and put frankincense on it.

2 'He shall then bring it to Aaron's sons the priests; and shall take from it his handful of its fine flour and of its oil with all of its frankincense. And the priest shall offer *it* up in smoke *as* its memorial portion on the altar, an offering by fire of a soothing aroma to the LORD.

3 'The remainder of the grain offering belongs to Aaron and his sons: a thing most holy, of the offerings to the LORD by fire.

4 ¶ 'Now when you bring an offering of a grain offering baked in an oven, *it shall be* unleavened cakes of fine flour mixed with oil, or unleavened wafers spread with oil.

5 'If your offering is a grain offering *made* on the griddle, *it shall be* of fine flour, unleavened, mixed with oil;

6 you shall break it into bits and pour oil on it; it is a grain offering.

7 'Now if your offering is a grain offering *made* in a pan, it shall be made of fine flour with oil.

8 'When you bring in the grain offering which is made of these things to the LORD, it shall be presented to the priest and he shall bring it to the altar.

9 'The priest then shall take up from the grain offering its memorial portion, and shall offer *it* up in smoke on the altar *as* an offering by fire of a soothing aroma to the LORD.

10 'The remainder of the grain offering belongs to Aaron and his sons: a thing most holy of the offerings to the LORD by fire.

11 ¶ 'No grain offering, which you bring to the LORD, shall be made with leaven, for you shall not offer up in smoke any leaven or any honey as an offering by fire to the LORD.

12 'As an offering of first fruits you shall bring them to the LORD, but they shall not ascend for a soothing aroma on the altar.

13 'Every grain offering of yours, moreover, you shall season with salt, so that the salt of the covenant of your God shall not be lacking from your grain offering; with all your offerings you shall offer salt.

14 ¶ 'Also if you bring a grain offering of early ripened things to the LORD, you shall bring fresh heads of grain roasted in the fire, grits of new growth, for the grain offering of your early ripened things.

15 'You shall then put oil on it and lay incense on it; it is a grain offering.

16 'The priest shall offer up in smoke its memorial portion, part of its grits and its oil with all its incense as an offering by fire to the LORD.

The Law of Peace Offerings

3 'Now if his offering is a sacrifice of peace offerings, if he is going to offer out of the herd, whether male or female, he shall offer it without defect before the LORD.

2 'He shall lay his hand on the head of his offering and slay it at the doorway of the tent of meeting, and Aaron's sons the priests shall sprinkle the blood around on the altar.

3 'From the sacrifice of the peace offerings he shall present an offering by fire to the LORD, the fat that covers the entrails and all the fat that is on the entrails,

4 and the two kidneys with the fat that is on them, which is on the loins, and the lobe of the liver, which he shall remove with the kidneys.

5 'Then Aaron's sons shall offer *it* up in smoke on the altar on the burnt offering, which is on the wood that is on the fire; it is an offering by fire of a soothing aroma to the LORD.

6 'But if his offering for a sacrifice of peace offerings to the LORD is from the flock, he shall offer it, male or female, without defect.

7 'If he is going to offer a lamb for his offering, then he shall offer it before the LORD,

8 and he shall lay his hand on the head of his offering and slay it before the tent of meeting, and Aaron's sons shall sprinkle its blood around on the altar.

9 'From the sacrifice of peace offerings he shall bring as an offering by fire to the LORD, its fat, the entire fat tail which he shall remove close to the backbone, and the fat that covers the entrails and all the fat that is on the entrails,

10 and the two kidneys with the fat that is on

them, which is on the loins, and the lobe of the liver, which he shall remove with the kidneys.

11 'Then the priest shall offer *it* up in smoke on the altar *as* food, an offering by fire to the LORD.

12 ¶ 'Moreover, if his offering is a goat, then he shall offer it before the LORD,

13 and he shall lay his hand on its head and slay it before the tent of meeting, and the sons of Aaron shall sprinkle its blood around on the altar.

14 'From it he shall present his offering as an offering by fire to the LORD, the fat that covers the entrails and all the fat that is on the entrails,

15 and the two kidneys with the fat that is on them, which is on the loins, and the lobe of the liver, which he shall remove with the kidneys.

16 'The priest shall offer them up in smoke on the altar *as* food, an offering by fire for a soothing aroma; all fat is the LORD'S.

17 'It is a perpetual statute throughout your generations in all your dwellings: you shall not eat any fat or any blood.'"

The Law of Sin Offerings

4 Then the LORD spoke to Moses, saying, 2 "Speak to the sons of Israel, saying, 'If a person sins unintentionally in any of the things which the LORD has commanded not to be done, and commits any of them,

3 if the anointed priest sins so as to bring guilt on the people, then let him offer to the LORD a bull without defect as a sin offering for the sin he has committed.

4:3 The One for the Many

For his sin, a priest had to sacrifice one bull— the same sacrifice required for a sin by the whole community (verses 13–14). The two sins were, in a sense, equal, for the high priest represented the whole community before God. The belief that a single purified individual can stand up for a nation prepared the way for Jesus, whose sinless obedience stands before God in our place.

4 'He shall bring the bull to the doorway of the tent of meeting before the LORD, and he shall lay his hand on the head of the bull and slay the bull before the LORD.

5 'Then the anointed priest is to take some of the blood of the bull and bring it to the tent of meeting,

6 and the priest shall dip his finger in the blood and sprinkle some of the blood seven times before the LORD, in front of the veil of the sanctuary.

7 'The priest shall also put some of the blood on the horns of the altar of fragrant incense which is before the LORD in the tent of meeting; and all the blood of the bull he shall pour out at the base

of the altar of burnt offering which is at the doorway of the tent of meeting.

8 'He shall remove from it all the fat of the bull of the sin offering: the fat that covers the entrails, and all the fat which is on the entrails,

9 and the two kidneys with the fat that is on them, which is on the loins, and the lobe of the liver, which he shall remove with the kidneys

10 (just as it is removed from the ox of the sacrifice of peace offerings), and the priest is to offer them up in smoke on the altar of burnt offering.

11 'But the hide of the bull and all its flesh with its head and its legs and its entrails and its refuse,

12 that is, all *the rest of* the bull, he is to bring out to a clean place outside the camp where the ashes are poured out, and burn it on wood with fire; where the ashes are poured out it shall be burned.

13 ¶ 'Now if the whole congregation of Israel commits error and the matter escapes the notice of the assembly, and they commit any of the things which the LORD has commanded not to be done, and they become guilty;

4:13 Ignorance Isn't Bliss

"I didn't know the speed limit had dropped to 30, officer. How can you give me a ticket?" Under the law, ignorance provides no excuse. This chapter and the next cover many instances of unintentional sin. Although held accountable for such wrongdoing, the Israelites could overcome their guilt by offering the prescribed sacrifices.

14 when the sin which they have committed becomes known, then the assembly shall offer a bull of the herd for a sin offering and bring it before the tent of meeting.

15 'Then the elders of the congregation shall lay their hands on the head of the bull before the LORD, and the bull shall be slain before the LORD.

16 'Then the anointed priest is to bring some of the blood of the bull to the tent of meeting;

17 and the priest shall dip his finger in the blood and sprinkle *it* seven times before the LORD, in front of the veil.

18 'He shall put some of the blood on the horns of the altar which is before the LORD in the tent of meeting; and all the blood he shall pour out at the base of the altar of burnt offering which is at the doorway of the tent of meeting.

19 'He shall remove all its fat from it and offer it up in smoke on the altar.

20 'He shall also do with the bull just as he did with the bull of the sin offering; thus he shall do with it. So the priest shall make atonement for them, and they will be forgiven.

21 'Then he is to bring out the bull to *a place*

outside the camp and burn it as he burned the first bull; it is the sin offering for the assembly.

22 ¶ 'When a leader sins and unintentionally does any one of all the things which the LORD his God has commanded not to be done, and he becomes guilty,

23 if his sin which he has committed is made known to him, he shall bring for his offering a goat, a male without defect.

24 'He shall lay his hand on the head of the male goat and slay it in the place where they slay the burnt offering before the LORD; it is a sin offering.

25 'Then the priest is to take some of the blood of the sin offering with his finger and put it on the horns of the altar of burnt offering; and *the rest of* its blood he shall pour out at the base of the altar of burnt offering.

26 'All its fat he shall offer up in smoke on the altar as *in the case of* the fat of the sacrifice of peace offerings. Thus the priest shall make atonement for him in regard to his sin, and he will be forgiven.

27 ¶ 'Now if anyone of the common people sins unintentionally in doing any of the things which the LORD has commanded not to be done, and becomes guilty,

28 if his sin which he has committed is made known to him, then he shall bring for his offering a goat, a female without defect, for his sin which he has committed.

29 'He shall lay his hand on the head of the sin offering and slay the sin offering at the place of the burnt offering.

30 'The priest shall take some of its blood with his finger and put it on the horns of the altar of burnt offering; and all *the rest of* its blood he shall pour out at the base of the altar.

31 'Then he shall remove all its fat, just as the fat was removed from the sacrifice of peace offerings; and the priest shall offer it up in smoke on the altar for a soothing aroma to the LORD. Thus the priest shall make atonement for him, and he will be forgiven.

32 ¶ 'But if he brings a lamb as his offering for a sin offering, he shall bring it, a female without defect.

33 'He shall lay his hand on the head of the sin offering and slay it for a sin offering in the place where they slay the burnt offering.

34 'The priest is to take some of the blood of the sin offering with his finger and put it on the horns of the altar of burnt offering, and all *the rest of* its blood he shall pour out at the base of the altar.

35 'Then he shall remove all its fat, just as the fat of the lamb is removed from the sacrifice of the peace offerings, and the priest shall offer them up in smoke on the altar, on the offerings by fire to the LORD. Thus the priest shall make atonement

for him in regard to his sin which he has committed, and he will be forgiven.

The Law of Guilt Offerings

5 'Now if a person sins after he hears a public adjuration *to testify* when he is a witness, whether he has seen or *otherwise* known, if he does not tell *it*, then he will bear his guilt.

2 'Or if a person touches any unclean thing, whether a carcass of an unclean beast or the carcass of unclean cattle or a carcass of unclean swarming things, though it is hidden from him and he is unclean, then he will be guilty.

3 'Or if he touches human uncleanness, of whatever *sort* his uncleanness *may* be with which he becomes unclean, and it is hidden from him, and then he comes to know *it,* he will be guilty.

4 'Or if a person swears thoughtlessly with his lips to do evil or to do good, in whatever matter a man may speak thoughtlessly with an oath, and it is hidden from him, and then he comes to know *it,* he will be guilty in one of these.

5 'So it shall be when he becomes guilty in one of these, that he shall confess that in which he has sinned.

6 'He shall also bring his guilt offering to the LORD for his sin which he has committed, a female from the flock, a lamb or a goat as a sin offering. So the priest shall make atonement on his behalf for his sin.

7 ¶ 'But if he cannot afford a lamb, then he shall bring to the LORD his guilt offering for that in which he has sinned, two turtledoves or two young pigeons, one for a sin offering and the other for a burnt offering.

8 'He shall bring them to the priest, who shall offer first that which is for the sin offering and shall nip its head at the front of its neck, but he shall not sever *it.*

9 'He shall also sprinkle some of the blood of the sin offering on the side of the altar, while the rest of the blood shall be drained out at the base of the altar: it is a sin offering.

10 'The second he shall then prepare as a burnt offering according to the ordinance. So the priest shall make atonement on his behalf for his sin which he has committed, and it will be forgiven him.

11 ¶ 'But if his means are insufficient for two turtledoves or two young pigeons, then for his offering for that which he has sinned, he shall bring the tenth of an ᵃephah of fine flour for a sin offering; he shall not put oil on it or place incense on it, for it is a sin offering.

12 'He shall bring it to the priest, and the priest shall take his handful of it as its memorial portion and offer *it* up in smoke on the altar, with the offerings of the LORD by fire: it is a sin offering.

13 'So the priest shall make atonement for him concerning his sin which he has committed from

---

ᵃ I.e. Approx one bu

one of these, and it will be forgiven him; then *the rest* shall become the priest's, like the grain offering.'"

14 ¶ Then the LORD spoke to Moses, saying,

15 "If a person acts unfaithfully and sins unintentionally against the LORD'S holy things, then he shall bring his guilt offering to the LORD: a ram without defect from the flock, according to your valuation in silver by shekels, in *terms of* the shekel of the sanctuary, for a guilt offering.

16 "He shall make restitution for that which he has sinned against the holy thing, and shall add to it a fifth part of it and give it to the priest. The

priest shall then make atonement for him with the ram of the guilt offering, and it will be forgiven him.

17 ¶ "Now if a person sins and does any of the things which the LORD has commanded not to be done, though he was unaware, still he is guilty and shall bear his punishment.

18 "He is then to bring to the priest a ram without defect from the flock, according to your valuation, for a guilt offering. So the priest shall make atonement for him concerning his error in which he sinned unintentionally and did not know *it*, and it will be forgiven him.

The Reason for Sacrifice

Justice: Someone has to pay

WHEN YOU COMMIT A CRIME, you don't get off in court just by saying "Sorry, I'll try not to do it again." Justice requires that you pay for what you did.

The Israelites, therefore, could not just march into God's presence to fellowship with him. They had to bring sacrifices to pay, or "atone," for their inadequacies.

These sacrifices cost dearly. To subsistence farmers, a bull or goat represented a sizable contribution. Very poor people could give less—a pair of doves, or some flour. But, in all cases, a person would feel the cost, cost in terms of something he had worked for, something grown on his own farm.

> "'Thus the priest shall make atonement for him in regard to his sin which he has committed, and he will be forgiven.'"
> 4:35

Up in Smoke

A good portion of the national economy went up in smoke each year: hundreds of animals and a lot of manpower to gather wood, keep the fire lit, and offer sacrifices. Since the Tent of Meeting stood at the center of the camp, the smell of the two-a-day sacrifices always hung over the Israelites. They rarely could afford meat, but every day they smelled the aroma of barbecue dedicated to God.

Offerings fell into three broad types. The guilt and sin offerings were usually offered first: they cleansed people from sin. Then came the burnt offerings, in which whole animals were burnt to ashes. Made at least twice a day, these sacrifices evidently expressed complete dedication to God. The final sacrifice was the fellowship offering, essentially a family meal shared in the presence of God. (The grain offerings were usually given along with one of the other offerings.)

The sequence of the offerings—forgiveness of sins, then total dedication, then fellowship—shows that their goal was fellowship with God. To reach that goal, forgiveness of sin and complete dedication to God were necessary.

Leviticus, however, does not explain this underlying philosophy; it reads more like an instruction manual on how to make sacrifices exactly the way God wanted. The exactness helped produce a proper attitude. You couldn't approach God carelessly. You had to be very careful to do just what he said, to obey him in every detail.

Can an Animal Really Pay?

The whole scene—with its concern for blood, priests, ritual—is strange to modern people. Just how can killing a goat make things right between God and people? Is the sacrifice of an animal really enough to "pay for" our mistakes? We may forget that throughout history, people have intuitively felt that sacrifice was needed to satisfy God. Many religions around the world still sacrifice today.

For us these sacrifices seem outmoded primarily because one great sacrifice—that of God's own Son—outdid them all. The animal sacrifices were not enough, ultimately, to pay for human sin. They prepared the way for a sacrifice that was.

The cost of an animal was substantial, but the true cost, even for us, is infinitely greater. Yet we don't have to pay the cost. Jesus paid it all.

Life Questions: Do you think of God as requiring sacrifice? How does the picture of God in Leviticus fit with your ideas about God?

19 "It is a guilt offering; he was certainly guilty before the LORD."

Guilt Offering

6 Then the LORD spoke to Moses, saying, 2 "When a person sins and acts unfaithfully against the LORD, and deceives his companion in regard to a deposit or a security entrusted to him, or through robbery, or if he has extorted from his companion,

3 or has found what was lost and lied about it and sworn falsely, so that he sins in regard to any one of the things a man may do;

4 then it shall be, when he sins and becomes guilty, that he shall restore what he took by robbery or what he got by extortion, or the deposit which was entrusted to him or the lost thing which he found,

5 or anything about which he swore falsely; he shall make restitution for it in full and add to it one-fifth more. He shall give it to the one to whom it belongs on the day he presents his guilt offering.

6:5–7 Double Jeopardy

An Israelite who committed a crime against another person (such as stealing) had two parties to reckon with. First, the offender had to make full restitution, along with a 20 percent penalty, to the person cheated. Second, he or she had to bring a special offering to God. A crime against another person also counted as a sin against God.

6 "Then he shall bring to the priest his guilt offering to the LORD, a ram without defect from the flock, according to your valuation, for a guilt offering,

7 and the priest shall make atonement for him before the LORD, and he will be forgiven for any one of the things which he may have done to incur guilt."

The Priest's Part in the Offerings

8 ¶ Then the LORD spoke to Moses, saying,

9 "Command Aaron and his sons, saying, 'This is the law for the burnt offering: the burnt offering itself shall remain on the hearth on the altar all night until the morning, and the fire on the altar is to be kept burning on it.

10 'The priest is to put on his linen robe, and he shall put on undergarments next to his flesh; and he shall take up the ashes to which the fire reduces the burnt offering on the altar and place them beside the altar.

11 'Then he shall take off his garments and put on other garments, and carry the ashes outside the camp to a clean place.

12 'The fire on the altar shall be kept burning on it. It shall not go out, but the priest shall burn wood on it every morning; and he shall lay out the burnt offering on it, and offer up in smoke the fat portions of the peace offerings on it.

13 'Fire shall be kept burning continually on the altar; it is not to go out.

14 ¶ 'Now this is the law of the grain offering: the sons of Aaron shall present it before the LORD in front of the altar.

15 'Then one of them shall lift up from it a handful of the fine flour of the grain offering, with its oil and all the incense that is on the grain offering, and he shall offer it up in smoke on the altar, a soothing aroma, as its memorial offering to the LORD.

16 'What is left of it Aaron and his sons are to eat. It shall be eaten as unleavened cakes in a holy place; they are to eat it in the court of the tent of meeting.

17 'It shall not be baked with leaven. I have given it as their share from My offerings by fire; it is most holy, like the sin offering and the guilt offering.

18 'Every male among the sons of Aaron may eat it; it is a permanent ordinance throughout your generations, from the offerings by fire to the LORD. Whoever touches them will become consecrated.'"

19 ¶ Then the LORD spoke to Moses, saying,

20 "This is the offering which Aaron and his sons are to present to the LORD on the day when he is anointed; the tenth of an ephah of fine flour as a regular grain offering, half of it in the morning and half of it in the evening.

21 "It shall be prepared with oil on a griddle. When it is well stirred, you shall bring it. You shall present the grain offering in baked pieces as a soothing aroma to the LORD.

22 "The anointed priest who will be in his place among his sons shall offer it. By a permanent ordinance it shall be entirely offered up in smoke to the LORD.

23 "So every grain offering of the priest shall be burned entirely. It shall not be eaten."

24 ¶ Then the LORD spoke to Moses, saying,

25 "Speak to Aaron and to his sons, saying, 'This is the law of the sin offering: in the place where the burnt offering is slain the sin offering shall be slain before the LORD; it is most holy.

26 'The priest who offers it for sin shall eat it. It shall be eaten in a holy place, in the court of the tent of meeting.

27 'Anyone who touches its flesh will become consecrated; and when any of its blood splashes on a garment, in a holy place you shall wash what was splashed on.

28 'Also the earthenware vessel in which it was boiled shall be broken; and if it was boiled in a bronze vessel, then it shall be scoured and rinsed in water.

29 'Every male among the priests may eat of it; it is most holy.

30 'But no sin offering of which any of the blood is brought into the tent of meeting to make atonement in the holy place shall be eaten; it shall be burned with fire.

The Priest's Part in the Offerings

7 'Now this is the law of the guilt offering; it is most holy.

2 'In the place where they slay the burnt offering they are to slay the guilt offering, and he shall sprinkle its blood around on the altar.

3 'Then he shall offer from it all its fat: the fat tail and the fat that covers the entrails,

4 and the two kidneys with the fat that is on them, which is on the loins, and the lobe on the liver he shall remove with the kidneys.

5 'The priest shall offer them up in smoke on the altar as an offering by fire to the LORD; it is a guilt offering.

6 'Every male among the priests may eat of it. It shall be eaten in a holy place; it is most holy.

7 'The guilt offering is like the sin offering, there is one law for them; the priest who makes atonement with it shall have it.

8 'Also the priest who presents any man's burnt offering, that priest shall have for himself the skin of the burnt offering which he has presented.

9 'Likewise, every grain offering that is baked in the oven and everything prepared in a pan or on a griddle shall belong to the priest who presents it.

10 'Every grain offering, mixed with oil or dry, shall belong to all the sons of Aaron, to all alike.

11 ¶ 'Now this is the law of the sacrifice of peace offerings which shall be presented to the LORD.

12 'If he offers it by way of thanksgiving, then along with the sacrifice of thanksgiving he shall offer unleavened cakes mixed with oil, and unleavened wafers spread with oil, and cakes of well stirred fine flour mixed with oil.

13 'With the sacrifice of his peace offerings for thanksgiving, he shall present his offering with cakes of leavened bread.

14 'Of this he shall present one of every offering as a contribution to the LORD; it shall belong to the priest who sprinkles the blood of the peace offerings.

15 ¶ 'Now as for the flesh of the sacrifice of his thanksgiving peace offerings, it shall be eaten on the day of his offering; he shall not leave any of it over until morning.

16 'But if the sacrifice of his offering is a votive or a freewill offering, it shall be eaten on the day that he offers his sacrifice, and on the next day what is left of it may be eaten;

17 but what is left over from the flesh of the

sacrifice on the third day shall be burned with fire.

18 'So if any of the flesh of the sacrifice of his peace offerings should *ever* be eaten on the third day, he who offers it will not be accepted, *and* it will not be reckoned to his *benefit*. It shall be an offensive thing, and the person who eats of it will bear his *own* iniquity.

19 ¶ 'Also the flesh that touches anything unclean shall not be eaten; it shall be burned with fire. As for *other* flesh, anyone who is clean may eat *such* flesh.

20 'But the person who eats the flesh of the sacrifice of peace offerings which belong to the LORD, in his uncleanness, that person shall be cut off from his people.

21 'When anyone touches anything unclean, whether human uncleanness, or an unclean animal, or any unclean ᵃdetestable thing, and eats of the flesh of the sacrifice of peace offerings which belong to the LORD, that person shall be cut off from his people.' "

22 ¶ Then the LORD spoke to Moses, saying,

23 "Speak to the sons of Israel, saying, 'You shall not eat any fat *from* an ox, a sheep or a goat.

24 'Also the fat of *an animal* which dies and the fat of an animal torn *by beasts* may be put to any other use, but you must certainly not eat it.

25 'For whoever eats the fat of the animal from which an offering by fire is offered to the LORD, even the person who eats shall be cut off from his people.

26 'You are not to eat any blood, either of bird or animal, in any of your dwellings.

27 'Any person who eats any blood, even that person shall be cut off from his people.' "

28 ¶ Then the LORD spoke to Moses, saying,

29 "Speak to the sons of Israel, saying, 'He who offers the sacrifice of his peace offerings to the LORD shall bring his offering to the LORD from the sacrifice of his peace offerings.

30 'His own hands are to bring offerings by fire to the LORD. He shall bring the fat with the breast, that the breast may be presented as a wave offering before the LORD.

31 'The priest shall offer up the fat in smoke on the altar, but the breast shall belong to Aaron and his sons.

32 'You shall give the right thigh to the priest as a contribution from the sacrifices of your peace offerings.

33 'The one among the sons of Aaron who offers the blood of the peace offerings and the fat, the right thigh shall be his as *his* portion.

34 'For I have taken the breast of the wave offering and the thigh of the contribution from the sons of Israel from the sacrifices of their peace offerings, and have given them to Aaron the priest and to his sons as *their* due forever from the sons of Israel.

35 ¶ 'This is that which is consecrated to Aaron

ᵃ Some mss read *swarming thing*

and that which is consecrated to his sons from the offerings by fire to the LORD, in that day when he presented them to serve as priests to the LORD.

36 'These the LORD had commanded to be given them from the sons of Israel in the day that He anointed them. It is *their* due forever throughout their generations.' "

37 ¶ This is the law of the burnt offering, the grain offering and the sin offering and the guilt offering and the ordination offering and the sacrifice of peace offerings,

38 which the LORD commanded Moses at Mount Sinai in the day that He commanded the sons of Israel to present their offerings to the LORD in the wilderness of Sinai.

The Consecration of Aaron and His Sons

8 Then the LORD spoke to Moses, saying, 2 "Take Aaron and his sons with him, and the garments and the anointing oil and the bull of the sin offering, and the two rams and the basket of unleavened bread,

3 and assemble all the congregation at the doorway of the tent of meeting."

4 So Moses did just as the LORD commanded him. When the congregation was assembled at the doorway of the tent of meeting,

5 Moses said to the congregation, "This is the thing which the LORD has commanded to do."

6 ¶ Then Moses had Aaron and his sons come near and washed them with water.

7 He put the tunic on him and girded him with the sash, and clothed him with the robe and put the ephod on him; and he girded him with the artistic band of the ephod, with which he tied *it* to him.

8 He then placed the breastpiece on him, and in the breastpiece he put *a*the Urim and the Thummim.

9 He also placed the turban on his head, and on the turban, at its front, he placed the golden plate, the holy crown, just as the LORD had commanded Moses.

10 ¶ Moses then took the anointing oil and anointed the tabernacle and all that was in it, and consecrated them.

11 He sprinkled some of it on the altar seven times and anointed the altar and all its utensils, and the basin and its stand, to consecrate them.

12 Then he poured some of the anointing oil on Aaron's head and anointed him, to consecrate him.

13 Next Moses had Aaron's sons come near and clothed them with tunics, and girded them with sashes and bound caps on them, just as the LORD had commanded Moses.

14 ¶ Then he brought the bull of the sin offering, and Aaron and his sons laid their hands on the head of the bull of the sin offering.

15 Next Moses slaughtered *it* and took the blood and with his finger put *some of it* around on the horns of the altar, and purified the altar. Then he poured out *the rest of* the blood at the base of the altar and consecrated it, to make atonement for it.

16 He also took all the fat that was on the entrails and the lobe of the liver, and the two kidneys and their fat; and Moses offered it up in smoke on the altar.

17 But the bull and its hide and its flesh and its refuse he burned in the fire outside the camp, just as the LORD had commanded Moses.

18 ¶ Then he presented the ram of the burnt offering, and Aaron and his sons laid their hands on the head of the ram.

19 Moses slaughtered *it* and sprinkled the blood around on the altar.

20 When he had cut the ram into its pieces, Moses offered up the head and the pieces and the suet in smoke.

21 After he had washed the entrails and the legs with water, Moses offered up the whole ram in smoke on the altar. It was a burnt offering for a soothing aroma; it was an offering by fire to the LORD, just as the LORD had commanded Moses.

22 ¶ Then he presented the second ram, the ram of *b*ordination, and Aaron and his sons laid their hands on the head of the ram.

23 Moses slaughtered *it* and took some of its blood and put it on the lobe of Aaron's right ear,

---

a I.e. the lights and perfections   *b* Lit *filling,* and so throughout the ch and on the thumb of his right hand and on the big toe of his right foot.

24 He also had Aaron's sons come near; and Moses put some of the blood on the lobe of their right ear, and on the thumb of their right hand and on the big toe of their right foot. Moses then sprinkled *the rest of* the blood around on the altar.

25 He took the fat, and the fat tail, and all the fat that was on the entrails, and the lobe of the liver and the two kidneys and their fat and the right thigh.

26 From the basket of unleavened bread that was before the LORD, he took one unleavened cake and one cake of bread *mixed with* oil and one wafer, and placed *them* on the portions of fat and on the right thigh.

27 He then put all *these* on the hands of Aaron and on the hands of his sons and presented them as a wave offering before the LORD.

28 Then Moses took them from their hands and offered them up in smoke on the altar with the burnt offering. They were an ordination offering for a soothing aroma; it was an offering by fire to the LORD.

29 Moses also took the breast and presented it for a wave offering before the LORD; it was Moses' portion of the ram of ordination, just as the LORD had commanded Moses.

30 ¶ So Moses took some of the anointing oil and some of the blood which was on the altar and sprinkled it on Aaron, on his garments, on his sons, and on the garments of his sons with him; and he consecrated Aaron, his garments, and his sons, and the garments of his sons with him.

31 ¶ Then Moses said to Aaron and to his sons, "Boil the flesh at the doorway of the tent of meeting, and eat it there together with the bread which is in the basket of the ordination offering, just as I commanded, saying, 'Aaron and his sons shall eat it.'

32 "The remainder of the flesh and of the bread you shall burn in the fire.

33 "You shall not go outside the doorway of the tent of meeting for seven days, until the day that the period of your ordination is fulfilled; for he will ordain you through seven days.

34 "The LORD has commanded to do as has been done this day, to make atonement on your behalf.

35 "At the doorway of the tent of meeting, moreover, you shall remain day and night for seven days and keep the charge of the LORD, so that you will not die, for so I have been commanded."

36 Thus Aaron and his sons did all the things which the LORD had commanded through Moses.

Aaron Offers Sacrifices

9 Now it came about on the eighth day that Moses called Aaron and his sons and the elders of Israel;

2 and he said to Aaron, "Take for yourself a calf, a bull, for a sin offering and a ram for a burnt offering, *both* without defect, and offer *them* before the LORD.

3 "Then to the sons of Israel you shall speak, saying, 'Take a male goat for a sin offering, and a calf and a lamb, both one year old, without defect, for a burnt offering,

4 and an ox and a ram for peace offerings, to sacrifice before the LORD, and a grain offering mixed with oil; for today the LORD will appear to you.' "

5 So they took what Moses had commanded to the front of the tent of meeting, and the whole congregation came near and stood before the LORD.

6 Moses said, "This is the thing which the LORD has commanded you to do, that the glory of the LORD may appear to you."

7 Moses then said to Aaron, "Come near to the altar and offer your sin offering and your burnt offering, that you may make atonement for yourself and for the people; then make the offering for the people, that you may make atonement for them, just as the LORD has commanded."

8 ¶ So Aaron came near to the altar and slaughtered the calf of the sin offering which was for himself.

9 Aaron's sons presented the blood to him; and he dipped his finger in the blood and put *some* on the horns of the altar, and poured out *the rest of* the blood at the base of the altar.

10 The fat and the kidneys and the lobe of the liver of the sin offering, he then offered up in smoke on the altar just as the LORD had commanded Moses.

11 The flesh and the skin, however, he burned with fire outside the camp.

12 ¶ Then he slaughtered the burnt offering; and Aaron's sons handed the blood to him and he sprinkled it around on the altar.

13 They handed the burnt offering to him in pieces, with the head, and he offered *them* up in smoke on the altar.

14 He also washed the entrails and the legs, and offered *them* up in smoke with the burnt offering on the altar.

15 ¶ Then he presented the people's offering, and took the goat of the sin offering which was for the people, and slaughtered it and offered it for sin, like the first.

16 He also presented the burnt offering, and offered it according to the ordinance.

17 Next he presented the grain offering, and filled his hand with some of it and offered *it* up in smoke on the altar, besides the burnt offering of the morning.

18 ¶ Then he slaughtered the ox and the ram, the sacrifice of peace offerings which was for the people; and Aaron's sons handed the blood to him and he sprinkled it around on the altar.

19 As for the portions of fat from the ox and

from the ram, the fat tail, and the *fat* covering, and the kidneys and the lobe of the liver,

20 they now placed the portions of fat on the breasts; and he offered them up in smoke on the altar.

21 But the breasts and the right thigh Aaron presented as a wave offering before the LORD, just as Moses had commanded.

22 ¶ Then Aaron lifted up his hands toward the people and blessed them, and he stepped down after making the sin offering and the burnt offering and the peace offerings.

23 Moses and Aaron went into the tent of meeting. When they came out and blessed the people, the glory of the LORD appeared to all the people.

9:23 The Glory of the Lord

Israelites were familiar with the brilliant glory of the Lord, but they had seen it only from a distance, on Mount Sinai. Even from that distance it had frightened them (Exodus 19:16–22). Now this glory had come to the Tent of Meeting itself, in the camp's center. They were indeed "close to God."

24 Then fire came out from before the LORD and consumed the burnt offering and the portions of fat on the altar; and when all the people saw *it*, they shouted and fell on their faces.

The Sin of Nadab and Abihu

10 Now Nadab and Abihu, the sons of Aaron, took their respective firepans, and after putting fire in them, placed incense on it and offered strange fire before the LORD, which He had not commanded them.

2 And fire came out from the presence of the LORD and consumed them, and they died before the LORD.

3 Then Moses said to Aaron, "It is what the LORD spoke, saying,

10:2 Fatal Error

At first Aaron and his sons did everything according to God's instructions, and God honored them (8:36; 9:24). But in very short order some of the first official priests got careless about following God's explicit orders. The severe punishment sent out a strong message to other priests: they were there to carry out God's plan, not their own.

'By those who come near Me I will be
    treated as holy,
And before all the people I will be
    honored.' "
So Aaron, therefore, kept silent.

4 ¶ Moses called also to Mishael and Elzaphan, the sons of Aaron's uncle Uzziel, and said to them, "Come forward, carry your relatives away from the front of the sanctuary to the outside of the camp."

5 So they came forward and carried them still in their tunics to the outside of the camp, as Moses had said.

6 Then Moses said to Aaron and to his sons Eleazar and Ithamar, "Do not [a]uncover your heads nor tear your clothes, so that you will not die and that He will not become wrathful against all the congregation. But your kinsmen, the whole house of Israel, shall bewail the burning which the LORD has brought about.

7 "You shall not even go out from the doorway of the tent of meeting, or you will die; for the LORD'S anointing oil is upon you." So they did according to the word of Moses.

8 ¶ The LORD then spoke to Aaron, saying,

9 "Do not drink wine or strong drink, neither you nor your sons with you, when you come into the tent of meeting, so that you will not die—it is a perpetual statute throughout your generations—

10 and so as to make a distinction between the holy and the profane, and between the unclean and the clean,

11 and so as to teach the sons of Israel all the statutes which the LORD has spoken to them through Moses."

12 ¶ Then Moses spoke to Aaron, and to his surviving sons, Eleazar and Ithamar, "Take the grain offering that is left over from the LORD'S offerings by fire and eat it unleavened beside the altar, for it is most holy.

13 "You shall eat it, moreover, in a holy place, because it is your due and your sons' due out of the LORD'S offerings by fire; for thus I have been commanded.

14 "The breast of the wave offering, however, and the thigh of the offering you may eat in a clean place, you and your sons and your daughters with you; for they have been given as your due and your sons' due out of the sacrifices of the peace offerings of the sons of Israel.

15 "The thigh offered by lifting up and the breast offered by waving they shall bring along with the offerings by fire of the portions of fat, to present as a wave offering before the LORD; so it shall be a thing perpetually due you and your sons with you, just as the LORD has commanded."

16 ¶ But Moses searched carefully for the goat of the sin offering, and behold, it had been burned

---

a Lit *unbind*

up! So he was angry with Aaron's surviving sons Eleazar and Ithamar, saying,

17 "Why did you not eat the sin offering at the holy place? For it is most holy, and He gave it to you to bear away the guilt of the congregation, to make atonement for them before the LORD.

18 "Behold, since its blood had not been brought inside, into the sanctuary, you should certainly have eaten it in the sanctuary, just as I commanded."

19 But Aaron spoke to Moses, "Behold, this very day they presented their sin offering and their burnt offering before the LORD. When things like these happened to me, if I had eaten a sin offering today, would it have been good in the sight of the LORD?"

20 When Moses heard that, it seemed good in his sight.

Laws about Animals for Food

11 The LORD spoke again to Moses and to Aaron, saying to them,

2 "Speak to the sons of Israel, saying, 'These are the creatures which you may eat from all the animals that are on the earth.

3 'Whatever divides a hoof, thus making split hoofs, and chews the cud, among the animals, that you may eat.

4 'Nevertheless, you are not to eat of these, among those which chew the cud, or among those which divide the hoof: the camel, for though it chews cud, it does not divide the hoof, it is unclean to you.

5 'Likewise, the shaphan, for though it chews cud, it does not divide the hoof, it is unclean to you;

An Invisible Danger
Taking precautions: like a surgeon preparing to operate

FOR MANY YEARS SURGERY REMAINED a desperate last resort for the hopelessly ill. Surgeons knew nothing about germs. Without washing, they would don operating garb, usually an old coat caked with blood and pus from numerous operations. They would pick up the scalpel, wiped clean with an old rag after the last operation, and go to work. Half of those operated on died.

> [You must] make a distinction between the unclean and the clean.
> 11:47

One pioneer after another stumbled on the correct sterile techniques. But each was scorned and humiliated by fellow doctors. Professor Ignaz Semmelweis, for one, discovered that making doctors wash their hands could dramatically cut the death rate in maternity wards. Yet his colleagues opposed Semmelweis strenuously, and though he argued for handwashing throughout his life, he died without seeing his ideas take hold.

Why So Slow?

Why were doctors so slow to adopt sterile techniques? The answer is simple: Germs had not yet been discovered. Doctors could not see—and reformers like Semmelweis could not give them—any reason why washing hands should make a difference.

Then Louis Pasteur discovered micro-organisms under his microscope. Sterile procedures began to make sense: they made war on germs. Even so, each reform, from rubber gloves to gauze masks, was accepted only grudgingly and with considerable opposition. It was as though doctors had a hard time remembering that something invisible could be so devastating. Fifty years of constant education and reform were necessary before "sterile technique" became a routine part of surgery, and germs became "real" to most medical minds.

Why All the Rules?

As germs are to a surgeon, "uncleanness" is to Leviticus. Chapters 11–15 describe elaborate precautions—what animals to avoid and how to treat "unclean" skin disease, mildewed clothing or walls, and bodily emissions.

Scholars point out that many clean and unclean rules have good health habits behind them, such as the rule to quarantine a person with an infectious disease or the rule against eating pork (which carries many parasites).

Others say that dietary laws were meant to keep the Israelites apart from their neighbors. Pigs were prominent in Canaanite worship; therefore the Israelites were not to eat pigs. A different dietary standard would keep the two groups from mixing socially, for a meal was always part of Middle Eastern hospitality.

Still other scholars suggest that the uncleanness rules simply fit into what Israelites intuitively thought proper. God was reinforcing a natural sense of repulsion toward creeping insects, scavenger birds, bodily emissions, and skin diseases.

6 the rabbit also, for though it chews cud, it does not divide the hoof, it is unclean to you;

7 and the pig, for though it divides the hoof, thus making a split hoof, it does not chew cud, it is unclean to you.

8 'You shall not eat of their flesh nor touch their carcasses; they are unclean to you.

9 ¶ 'These you may eat, whatever is in the water: all that have fins and scales, those in the water, in the seas or in the rivers, you may eat.

10 'But whatever is in the seas and in the rivers that does not have fins and scales among all the teeming life of the water, and among all the living creatures that are in the water, they are detestable things to you,

11 and they shall be *abhorrent to you; you may not eat of their flesh, and their carcasses you shall detest.

12 'Whatever in the water does not have fins and scales is abhorrent to you.

Avoid the Unclean

13 ¶ 'These, moreover, you shall detest among the birds; they are abhorrent, not to be eaten: the eagle and the vulture and the buzzard,

Lit detestable things

14 and the kite and the falcon in its kind,

15 every raven in its kind,

16 and the ostrich and the owl and the sea gull and the hawk in its kind,

17 and the little owl and the cormorant and the great owl,

18 and the white owl and the pelican and the carrion vulture,

19 and the stork, the heron in its kinds, and the hoopoe, and the bat.

20 ¶ 'All the winged insects that walk on *all* fours are detestable to you.

21 'Yet these you may eat among all the winged insects which walk on *all* fours: those which have above their feet jointed legs with which to jump on the earth.

22 'These of them you may eat: the locust in its kinds, and the devastating locust in its kinds, and the cricket in its kinds, and the grasshopper in its kinds.

23 'But all other winged insects which are four-footed are detestable to you.

24 ¶ 'By these, moreover, you will be made unclean: whoever touches their carcasses becomes unclean until evening,

---

The Habit of Carefulness

All these explanations have merit, but the underlying basis of clean and unclean was religious. Being unclean was not dangerous or wrong. In fact, you could hardly avoid it. Practically everyone became "unclean" from time to time. But you could not worship God in the Tent of Meeting while you were unclean, nor bring anything unclean into the presence of God. His holiness would destroy it—and you (Leviticus 15:31).

So Leviticus trains God's people to watch their lives as carefully as surgeons watch their sterile techniques. They must develop the habit of carefulness, even about something they cannot see or feel. They must think about preparing themselves for God, not just do whatever "feels right."

It was not a question of how they felt about God, any more than a surgeon's concern is how he "feels" about germs. Clear, absolute standards laid out what could be acceptable to a God who is perfectly clean, absolute, unchanging. Just as surgeons had to struggle to take germs seriously, so God's people must learn to "purify themselves" for God.

Touching the Unclean

The uncleanness rules of Leviticus are outmoded because of Jesus' declaration that all things are clean (Mark 7:19; see also Acts 10:9–16). But the lessons behind these rules remain valid. God still may not be approached carelessly. Each person must examine his or her life, to be certain that God's purity is not violated.

Until Jesus' day, the slow spread of uncleanness seemed irreversible. You could avoid it, but you could not get rid of it. Contact with anything unclean made you unclean yourself. Naturally, certain diseases, notably leprosy, were twice cursed: they were both dangerous and unclean. You kept away from leprosy, absolutely.

Then Jesus touched a man with leprosy, and he became clean. Jesus touched a woman suffering from internal bleeding, and she was healed. For the first time, cleanness rather than uncleanness spread. The rules of Leviticus tell how to avoid uncleanness. Contact with Jesus, however, changes the unclean to clean.

Life Questions: Suppose sin were visible—small green spots that break out on the skin. Do you think it would help people to take sin more seriously?

25 and whoever picks up any of their carcasses shall wash his clothes and be unclean until evening.

26 'Concerning all the animals which divide the hoof but do not make a split *hoof,* or which do not chew cud, they are unclean to you: whoever touches them becomes unclean.

27 'Also whatever walks on its paws, among all the creatures that walk on *all* fours, are unclean to you; whoever touches their carcasses becomes unclean until evening,

28 and the one who picks up their carcasses shall wash his clothes and be unclean until evening; they are unclean to you.

29 ¶ 'Now these are to you the unclean among the swarming things which swarm on the earth: the mole, and the mouse, and the great lizard in its kinds,

30 and the gecko, and the crocodile, and the lizard, and the sand reptile, and the chameleon.

31 'These are to you the unclean among all the swarming things; whoever touches them when they are dead becomes unclean until evening.

32 'Also anything on which one of them may fall when they are dead becomes unclean, including any wooden article, or clothing, or a skin, or a sack—any article of which use is made—it shall be put in the water and be unclean until evening, then it becomes clean.

33 'As for any earthenware vessel into which one of them may fall, whatever is in it becomes unclean and you shall break the vessel.

34 'Any of the food which may be eaten, on which water comes, shall become unclean, and any liquid which may be drunk in every vessel shall become unclean.

35 'Everything, moreover, on which part of their carcass may fall becomes unclean; an oven or a *a*stove shall be smashed; they are unclean and shall continue as unclean to you.

36 'Nevertheless a spring or a cistern collecting water shall be clean, though the one who touches their carcass shall be unclean.

37 'If a part of their carcass falls on any seed for sowing which is to be sown, it is clean.

38 'Though if water is put on the seed and a part of their carcass falls on it, it is unclean to you.

39 ¶ 'Also if one of the animals dies which you have for food, the one who touches its carcass becomes unclean until evening.

40 'He too, who eats some of its carcass shall wash his clothes and be unclean until evening, and the one who picks up its carcass shall wash his clothes and be unclean until evening.

41 ¶ 'Now every swarming thing that swarms on the earth is detestable, not to be eaten.

42 'Whatever crawls on its belly, and whatever walks on *all* fours, whatever has many feet, in respect to every swarming thing that swarms on the earth, you shall not eat them, for they are detestable.

43 'Do not render yourselves detestable through any of the swarming things that swarm; and you shall not make yourselves unclean with them so that you become unclean.

44 'For I am the LORD your God. Consecrate yourselves therefore, and be holy, for I am holy. And you shall not make yourselves unclean with any of the swarming things that swarm on the earth.

45 'For I am the LORD who brought you up from the land of Egypt to be your God; thus you shall be holy, for I am holy.'"

46 ¶ This is the law regarding the animal and the bird, and every living thing that moves in the waters and everything that swarms on the earth,

47 to make a distinction between the unclean and the clean, and between the edible creature and the creature which is not to be eaten.

11:47 Of Scallops and Rabbits

Scholars have long puzzled over the seemingly arbitrary division between "clean" and "unclean" foods. Why permit the eating of certain fish but not shrimp, and cows but not pigs? "An Invisible Danger" on page 142 discusses some of the theories that have been proposed. Probably the best explanation is that God was indeed being arbitrary, in order to form a nation different from any other (see 20:26). In Acts 10 God shows there is nothing intrinsically wrong with the animals labeled "unclean" in Leviticus.

Laws of Motherhood

12 Then the LORD spoke to Moses, saying, 2 "Speak to the sons of Israel, saying:

¶ 'When a woman gives birth and bears a male *child,* then she shall be unclean for seven days, as in the days of her menstruation she shall be unclean.

3 'On the eighth day the flesh of his foreskin shall be circumcised.

4 'Then she shall remain in the blood of *her* purification for thirty-three days; she shall not touch any consecrated thing, nor enter the sanctuary until the days of her purification are completed.

5 'But if she bears a female *child,* then she shall be unclean for two weeks, as in her menstruation; and she shall remain in the blood of *her* purification for sixty-six days.

---

a Lit *hearth for supporting (two) pots*

6 ¶ 'When the days of her purification are completed, for a son or for a daughter, she shall bring to the priest at the doorway of the tent of meeting a one year old lamb for a burnt offering and a young pigeon or a turtledove for a sin offering.

7 'Then he shall offer it before the LORD and make atonement for her, and she shall be cleansed from the flow of her blood. This is the law for her who bears *a child, whether* a male or a female.

8 'But if she cannot afford a lamb, then she shall take two turtledoves or two young pigeons, the one for a burnt offering and the other for a sin offering; and the priest shall make atonement for her, and she will be clean.' "

12:8 For Poor People

This alternate offering enabled poor women to live up to their duty to God. Mary offered such a sacrifice after Jesus' birth (see Luke 2:24)— an indication that Jesus' family was not well-off.

The Test for Leprosy

13 Then the LORD spoke to Moses and to Aaron, saying,

2 "When a man has on the skin of his body a swelling or a scab or a bright spot, and it becomes *a* an infection of leprosy on the skin of his body, then he shall be brought to Aaron the priest or to one of his sons the priests.

3 "The priest shall look at the mark on the skin of the body, and if the hair in the infection has turned white and the infection appears to be deeper than the skin of his body, it is an infection of leprosy; when the priest has looked at him, he shall pronounce him unclean.

4 "But if the bright spot is white on the skin of his body, and it does not appear to be deeper than the skin, and the hair on it has not turned white, then the priest shall isolate *him who has* the infection for seven days.

5 "The priest shall look at him on the seventh day, and if in his eyes the infection has not changed *and* the infection has not spread on the skin, then the priest shall isolate him for seven more days.

6 "The priest shall look at him again on the seventh day, and if the infection has faded and the mark has not spread on the skin, then the priest shall pronounce him clean; it is *only* a scab. And he shall wash his clothes and be clean.

7 ¶ "But if the scab spreads farther on the skin after he has shown himself to the priest for his cleansing, he shall appear again to the priest.

8 "The priest shall look, and if the scab has spread on the skin, then the priest shall pronounce him unclean; it is leprosy.

9 ¶ "When the infection of leprosy is on a man, then he shall be brought to the priest.

10 "The priest shall then look, and if there is a white swelling in the skin, and it has turned the hair white, and there is quick raw flesh in the swelling,

11 it is a chronic leprosy on the skin of his body, and the priest shall pronounce him unclean; he shall not isolate him, for he is unclean.

12 "If the leprosy breaks out farther on the skin, and the leprosy covers all the skin of *him who has* the infection from his head even to his feet, as far as the priest can see,

13 then the priest shall look, and behold, *if* the leprosy has covered all his body, he shall pronounce clean *him who has* the infection; it has all turned white *and* he is clean.

14 "But whenever raw flesh appears on him, he shall be unclean.

15 "The priest shall look at the raw flesh, and he shall pronounce him unclean; the raw flesh is unclean, it is leprosy.

16 "Or if the raw flesh turns again and is changed to white, then he shall come to the priest,

17 and the priest shall look at him, and behold, *if* the infection has turned to white, then the priest shall pronounce clean *him who has* the infection; he is clean.

18 ¶ "When the body has a boil on its skin and it is healed,

19 and in the place of the boil there is a white swelling or a reddish-white, bright spot, then it shall be shown to the priest;

20 and the priest shall look, and behold, *if* it appears to be lower than the skin, and the hair on it has turned white, then the priest shall pronounce him unclean; it is the infection of leprosy, it has broken out in the boil.

21 "But if the priest looks at it, and behold, there are no white hairs in it and it is not lower than the skin and is faded, then the priest shall isolate him for seven days;

22 and if it spreads farther on the skin, then the priest shall pronounce him unclean; it is an infection.

23 "But if the bright spot remains in its place and does not spread, it is *only* the scar of the boil; and the priest shall pronounce him clean.

24 ¶ "Or if the body sustains in its skin a burn by fire, and the raw *flesh* of the burn becomes a bright spot, reddish-white, or white,

25 then the priest shall look at it. And if the hair in the bright spot has turned white and it appears to be deeper than the skin, it is leprosy; it has broken out in the burn. Therefore, the priest

---

a Lit *a mark, stroke,* and so throughout the ch

shall pronounce him unclean; it is an infection of leprosy.

26 "But if the priest looks at it, and indeed, there is no white hair in the bright spot and it is no deeper than the skin, but is dim, then the priest shall isolate him for seven days;

27 and the priest shall look at him on the seventh day. If it spreads farther in the skin, then the priest shall pronounce him unclean; it is an infection of leprosy.

28 "But if the bright spot remains in its place and has not spread in the skin, but is dim, it is the swelling from the burn; and the priest shall pronounce him clean, for it is *only* the scar of the burn.

29 ¶ "Now if a man or woman has an infection on the head or on the beard,

30 then the priest shall look at the infection, and if it appears to be deeper than the skin and there is thin yellowish hair in it, then the priest shall pronounce him unclean; it is a scale, it is leprosy of the head or of the beard.

31 "But if the priest looks at the infection of the scale, and indeed, it appears to be no deeper than the skin and there is no black hair in it, then the priest shall isolate *the person* with the scaly infection for seven days.

32 "On the seventh day the priest shall look at the infection, and if the scale has not spread and no yellowish hair has grown in it, and the appearance of the scale is no deeper than the skin,

33 then he shall shave himself, but he shall not shave the scale; and the priest shall isolate *the person* with the scale seven more days.

34 "Then on the seventh day the priest shall look at the scale, and if the scale has not spread in the skin and it appears to be no deeper than the skin, the priest shall pronounce him clean; and he shall wash his clothes and be clean.

35 "But if the scale spreads farther in the skin after his cleansing,

36 then the priest shall look at him, and if the scale has spread in the skin, the priest need not seek for the yellowish hair; he is unclean.

37 "If in his sight the scale has remained, however, and black hair has grown in it, the scale has healed, he is clean; and the priest shall pronounce him clean.

38 ¶ "When a man or a woman has bright spots on the skin of the body, *even* white bright spots,

39 then the priest shall look, and if the bright spots on the skin of their bodies are a faint white, it is eczema that has broken out on the skin; he is clean.

40 ¶ "Now if a man loses the hair of his head, he is bald; he is clean.

41 "If his head becomes bald at the front and sides, he is bald on the forehead; he is clean.

42 "But if on the bald head or the bald forehead, there occurs a reddish-white infection, it is leprosy breaking out on his bald head or on his bald forehead.

43 "Then the priest shall look at him; and if the swelling of the infection is reddish-white on his bald head or on his bald forehead, like the appearance of leprosy in the skin of the body,

44 he is a leprous man, he is unclean. The priest shall surely pronounce him unclean; his infection is on his head.

45 ¶ "As for the leper who has the infection, his clothes shall be torn, and the hair of his head shall be uncovered, and he shall cover his mustache and cry, 'Unclean! Unclean!'

46 "He shall remain unclean all the days during which he has the infection; he is unclean. He shall live alone; his dwelling shall be outside the camp.

47 ¶ "When a garment has a mark of leprosy in it, whether it is a wool garment or a linen garment,

48 whether in warp or woof, of linen or of wool, whether in leather or in any article made of leather,

49 if the mark is greenish or reddish in the garment or in the leather, or in the warp or in the woof, or in any article of leather, it is a leprous mark and shall be shown to the priest.

50 "Then the priest shall look at the mark and shall quarantine the article with the mark for seven days.

51 "He shall then look at the mark on the seventh day; if the mark has spread in the garment, whether in the warp or in the woof, or in the leather, whatever the purpose for which the leather is used, the mark is a leprous malignancy, it is unclean.

52 "So he shall burn the garment, whether the warp or the woof, in wool or in linen, or any article of leather in which the mark occurs, for it is a leprous malignancy; it shall be burned in the fire.

53 ¶ "But if the priest shall look, and indeed the mark has not spread in the garment, either in the warp or in the woof, or in any article of leather,

54 then the priest shall order them to wash the thing in which the mark occurs and he shall quarantine it for seven more days.

55 "After the article with the mark has been washed, the priest shall again look, and if the mark has not changed its appearance, even though the mark has not spread, it is unclean; you shall burn it in the fire, whether an eating away has produced bareness on the top or on the front of it.

56 ¶ "Then if the priest looks, and if the mark has faded after it has been washed, then he shall tear it out of the garment or out of the leather, whether from the warp or from the woof;

57 and if it appears again in the garment,

whether in the warp or in the woof, or in any article of leather, it is an outbreak; the article with the mark shall be burned in the fire.

58 "The garment, whether the warp or the woof, or any article of leather from which the mark has departed when you washed it, it shall then be washed a second time and will be clean."

59 ¶ This is the law for the mark of leprosy in a garment of wool or linen, whether in the warp or in the woof, or in any article of leather, for pronouncing it clean or unclean.

Law of Cleansing a Leper

14 Then the LORD spoke to Moses, saying, 2 "This shall be the law of the leper in the day of his cleansing. Now he shall be brought to the priest,

3 and the priest shall go out to the outside of the camp. Thus the priest shall look, and if the infection of leprosy has been healed in the leper,

4 then the priest shall give orders to take two live clean birds and cedar wood and a scarlet string and hyssop for the one who is to be cleansed.

5 "The priest shall also give orders to slay the one bird in an earthenware vessel over running water.

6 "As for the live bird, he shall take it together with the cedar wood and the scarlet string and the hyssop, and shall dip them and the live bird in the blood of the bird that was slain over the running water.

7 "He shall then sprinkle seven times the one who is to be cleansed from the leprosy and shall pronounce him clean, and shall let the live bird go free over the open field.

14:7 A Bird Set Free

It is difficult to assign definite symbolic meaning to all the details in this ceremony for the cleansing of skin diseases. Many scholars suggest that the bird that was killed represented purification by sacrifice, while the bird set free represented new liberty after a long quarantine. When Jesus healed a man with leprosy (Matthew 8:4), he told him to follow these instructions.

8 "The one to be cleansed shall then wash his clothes and shave off all his hair and bathe in water and be clean. Now afterward, he may enter the camp, but he shall stay outside his tent for seven days.

9 "It will be on the seventh day that he shall shave off all his hair: he shall shave his head and his beard and his eyebrows, even all his hair, He

shall then wash his clothes and bathe his body in water and be clean.

10 ¶ "Now on the eighth day he is to take two male lambs without defect, and a yearling ewe lamb without defect, and three-tenths *of an ephah* of fine flour mixed with oil for a grain offering, and one ªlog of oil;

11 and the priest who pronounces him clean shall present the man to be cleansed and the aforesaid before the LORD at the doorway of the tent of meeting.

12 "Then the priest shall take the one male lamb and bring it for a guilt offering, with the log of oil, and present them as a wave offering before the LORD.

13 "Next he shall slaughter the male lamb in the place where they slaughter the sin offering and the burnt offering, at the place of the sanctuary—for the guilt offering, like the sin offering, belongs to the priest; it is most holy.

14 "The priest shall then take some of the blood of the guilt offering, and the priest shall put *it* on the lobe of the right ear of the one to be cleansed, and on the thumb of his right hand and on the big toe of his right foot.

15 "The priest shall also take some of the log of oil, and pour *it* into his left palm;

16 the priest shall then dip his right-hand finger into the oil that is in his left palm, and with his finger sprinkle some of the oil seven times before the LORD.

17 "Of the remaining oil which is in his palm, the priest shall put some on the right ear lobe of the one to be cleansed, and on the thumb of his right hand, and on the big toe of his right foot, on the blood of the guilt offering;

18 while the rest of the oil that is in the priest's palm, he shall put on the head of the one to be cleansed. So the priest shall make atonement on his behalf before the LORD.

19 "The priest shall next offer the sin offering and make atonement for the one to be cleansed from his uncleanness. Then afterward, he shall slaughter the burnt offering.

20 "The priest shall offer up the burnt offering and the grain offering on the altar. Thus the priest shall make atonement for him, and he will be clean.

21 ¶ "But if he is poor and his means are insufficient, then he is to take one male lamb for a guilt offering as a wave offering to make atonement for him, and one-tenth *of an ephah* of fine flour mixed with oil for a grain offering, and a log of oil,

22 and two turtledoves or two young pigeons which are within his means, the one shall be a sin offering and the other a burnt offering.

23 "Then the eighth day he shall bring them for his cleansing to the priest, at the doorway of the tent of meeting, before the LORD.

24 "The priest shall take the lamb of the guilt

ª I.e. Approx one pt

offering and the log of oil, and the priest shall offer them for a wave offering before the LORD.

25 "Next he shall slaughter the lamb of the guilt offering; and the priest is to take some of the blood of the guilt offering and put *it* on the lobe of the right ear of the one to be cleansed and on the thumb of his right hand and on the big toe of his right foot.

26 "The priest shall also pour some of the oil into his left palm;

27 and with his right-hand finger the priest shall sprinkle some of the oil that is in his left palm seven times before the LORD.

28 "The priest shall then put some of the oil that is in his palm on the lobe of the right ear of the one to be cleansed, and on the thumb of his right hand and on the big toe of his right foot, on the place of the blood of the guilt offering.

29 "Moreover, the rest of the oil that is in the priest's palm he shall put on the head of the one to be cleansed, to make atonement on his behalf before the LORD.

30 "He shall then offer one of the turtledoves or young pigeons, which are within his means.

31 "*He shall offer* what he can afford, the one for a sin offering and the other for a burnt offering, together with the grain offering. So the priest shall make atonement before the LORD on behalf of the one to be cleansed.

32 "This is the law *for him* in whom there is an infection of leprosy, whose means are limited for his cleansing."

Cleansing a Leprous House

33 ¶ The LORD further spoke to Moses and to Aaron, saying:

34 ¶ "When you enter the land of Canaan, which I give you for a possession, and I put a mark of leprosy on a house in the land of your possession,

35 then the one who owns the house shall come and tell the priest, saying, '*Something* like a mark *of leprosy* has become visible to me in the house.'

36 "The priest shall then command that they empty the house before the priest goes in to look at the mark, so that everything in the house need not become unclean; and afterward the priest shall go in to look at the house.

37 "So he shall look at the mark, and if the mark on the walls of the house has greenish or reddish depressions and appears deeper than the surface,

38 then the priest shall come out of the house, to the doorway, and quarantine the house for seven days.

39 "The priest shall return on the seventh day and make an inspection. If the mark has indeed spread in the walls of the house,

40 then the priest shall order them to tear out the stones with the mark in them and throw them away at an unclean place outside the city.

41 "He shall have the house scraped all around inside, and they shall dump the plaster that they scrape off at an unclean place outside the city.

42 "Then they shall take other stones and replace *those* stones, and he shall take other plaster and replaster the house.

43 ¶ "If, however, the mark breaks out again in the house after he has torn out the stones and scraped the house, and after it has been replastered,

44 then the priest shall come in and make an inspection. If he sees that the mark has indeed spread in the house, it is a malignant mark in the house; it is unclean.

45 "He shall therefore tear down the house, its stones, and its timbers, and all the plaster of the house, and he shall take *them* outside the city to an unclean place.

46 "Moreover, whoever goes into the house during the time that he has quarantined it, becomes unclean until evening.

47 "Likewise, whoever lies down in the house shall wash his clothes, and whoever eats in the house shall wash his clothes.

48 ¶ "If, on the other hand, the priest comes in and makes an inspection and the mark has not indeed spread in the house after the house has been replastered, then the priest shall pronounce the house clean because the mark has not reappeared.

49 "To cleanse the house then, he shall take two birds and cedar wood and a scarlet string and hyssop,

50 and he shall slaughter the one bird in an earthenware vessel over running water.

51 "Then he shall take the cedar wood and the hyssop and the scarlet string, with the live bird, and dip them in the blood of the slain bird as well as in the running water, and sprinkle the house seven times.

52 "He shall thus cleanse the house with the blood of the bird and with the running water, along with the live bird and with the cedar wood and with the hyssop and with the scarlet string.

53 "However, he shall let the live bird go free outside the city into the open field. So he shall make atonement for the house, and it will be clean."

54 ¶ This is the law for any mark of leprosy—even for a scale,

55 and for the leprous garment or house,

56 and for a swelling, and for a scab, and for a bright spot—

57 to teach when they are unclean and when they are clean. This is the law of leprosy.

Cleansing Unhealthiness

15 The LORD also spoke to Moses and to Aaron, saying,

2 "Speak to the sons of Israel, and say to them,

'When any man has a discharge from his body, his discharge is unclean.

3 'This, moreover, shall be his uncleanness in his discharge: it is his uncleanness whether his

15:2 Sex Rules

Some of the rules regarding sex and bodily discharges mystify modern readers, but the Israelites took for granted that God had dominion over the most private aspects of their lives. The Bible does not provide a detailed rationale for these regulations. Some relate to health and hygiene: following the rules would help the Israelites avoid the venereal diseases that plagued their neighbors. Also, pagan religions commonly employed temple prostitutes, and God clearly intended for the Israelites to keep worship and sex separate.

body allows its discharge to flow or whether his body obstructs its discharge.

4 'Every bed on which the person with the discharge lies becomes unclean, and everything on which he sits becomes unclean.

5 'Anyone, moreover, who touches his bed shall wash his clothes and bathe in water and be unclean until evening;

6 and whoever sits on the thing on which the man with the discharge has been sitting, shall wash his clothes and bathe in water and be unclean until evening.

7 'Also whoever touches the person with the discharge shall wash his clothes and bathe in water and be unclean until evening.

8 'Or if the man with the discharge spits on one who is clean, he too shall wash his clothes and bathe in water and be unclean until evening.

9 'Every saddle on which the person with the discharge rides becomes unclean.

10 'Whoever then touches any of the things which were under him shall be unclean until evening, and he who carries them shall wash his clothes and bathe in water and be unclean until evening.

11 'Likewise, whomever the one with the discharge touches without having rinsed his hands in water shall wash his clothes and bathe in water and be unclean until evening.

12 'However, an earthenware vessel which the person with the discharge touches shall be broken, and every wooden vessel shall be rinsed in water.

13 ¶ 'Now when the man with the discharge becomes cleansed from his discharge, then he shall count off for himself seven days for his cleansing; he shall then wash his clothes and bathe his body in running water and will become clean.

14 'Then on the eighth day he shall take for himself two turtledoves or two young pigeons,

and come before the LORD to the doorway of the tent of meeting and give them to the priest;

15 and the priest shall offer them, one for a sin offering and the other for a burnt offering. So the priest shall make atonement on his behalf before the LORD because of his discharge.

16 ¶ 'Now if a man has a seminal emission, he shall bathe all his body in water and be unclean until evening.

17 'As for any garment or any leather on which there is seminal emission, it shall be washed with water and be unclean until evening.

18 'If a man lies with a woman so that there is a seminal emission, they shall both bathe in water and be unclean until evening.

19 ¶ 'When a woman has a discharge, if her discharge in her body is blood, she shall continue in her menstrual impurity for seven days; and whoever touches her shall be unclean until evening.

20 'Everything also on which she lies during her menstrual impurity shall be unclean, and everything on which she sits shall be unclean.

21 'Anyone who touches her bed shall wash his clothes and bathe in water and be unclean until evening.

22 'Whoever touches any thing on which she sits shall wash his clothes and bathe in water and be unclean until evening.

23 'Whether it be on the bed or on the thing on which she is sitting, when he touches it, he shall be unclean until evening.

24 'If a man actually lies with her so that her menstrual impurity is on him, he shall be unclean seven days, and every bed on which he lies shall be unclean.

25 ¶ 'Now if a woman has a discharge of her blood many days, not at the period of her menstrual impurity, or if she has a discharge beyond that period, all the days of her impure discharge she shall continue as though in her menstrual impurity; she is unclean.

26 'Any bed on which she lies all the days of her discharge shall be to her like her bed at menstruation; and every thing on which she sits shall be unclean, like her uncleanness at that time.

27 'Likewise, whoever touches them shall be unclean and shall wash his clothes and bathe in water and be unclean until evening.

28 'When she becomes clean from her discharge, she shall count off for herself seven days; and afterward she will be clean.

29 'Then on the eighth day she shall take for herself two turtledoves or two young pigeons and bring them in to the priest, to the doorway of the tent of meeting.

30 'The priest shall offer the one for a sin offering and the other for a burnt offering. So the priest shall make atonement on her behalf before the LORD because of her impure discharge.'

31 ¶ "Thus you shall keep the sons of Israel

separated from their uncleanness, so that they will not die in their uncleanness by their defiling My tabernacle that is among them."

32 This is the law for the one with a discharge, and for the man who has a seminal emission so that he is unclean by it,

33 and for the woman who is ill because of menstrual impurity, and for the one who has a discharge, whether a male or a female, or a man who lies with an unclean woman.

Law of Atonement

16 Now the LORD spoke to Moses after the death of the two sons of Aaron, when they had approached the presence of the LORD and died.

2 The LORD said to Moses:

¶ "Tell your brother Aaron that he shall not enter at any time into the holy place inside the veil, before the [a]mercy seat which is on the ark, or he will die; for I will appear in the cloud over the mercy seat.

3 "Aaron shall enter the holy place with this: with a bull for a sin offering and a ram for a burnt offering.

4 "He shall put on the holy linen tunic, and the linen undergarments shall be next to his body, and he shall be girded with the linen sash and attired with the linen turban (these are holy garments). Then he shall bathe his body in water and put them on.

5 "He shall take from the congregation of the sons of Israel two male goats for a sin offering and one ram for a burnt offering.

6 "Then Aaron shall offer the bull for the sin offering which is for himself, that he may make atonement for himself and for his household.

7 "He shall take the two goats and present them before the LORD at the doorway of the tent of meeting.

8 "Aaron shall cast lots for the two goats, one lot for the LORD and the other lot for the [b]scapegoat.

9 "Then Aaron shall offer the goat on which the lot for the LORD fell, and make it a sin offering.

10 "But the goat on which the lot for the scapegoat fell shall be presented alive before the LORD, to make atonement upon it, to send it into the wilderness as the scapegoat.

11 ¶ "Then Aaron shall offer the bull of the sin offering which is for himself and make atonement for himself and for his household, and he shall slaughter the bull of the sin offering which is for himself.

12 "He shall take a firepan full of coals of fire from upon the altar before the LORD and two handfuls of finely ground sweet incense, and bring it inside the veil.

13 "He shall put the incense on the fire before the LORD, that the cloud of incense may cover the

mercy seat that is on the ark of the testimony, otherwise he will die.

14 "Moreover, he shall take some of the blood of the bull and sprinkle it with his finger on the mercy seat on the east side; also in front of the mercy seat he shall sprinkle some of the blood with his finger seven times.

15 ¶ "Then he shall slaughter the goat of the sin offering which is for the people, and bring its blood inside the veil and do with its blood as he did with the blood of the bull, and sprinkle it on the mercy seat and in front of the mercy seat.

16 "He shall make atonement for the holy place, because of the impurities of the sons of Israel and because of their transgressions in regard to all their sins; and thus he shall do for the tent of meeting which abides with them in the midst of their impurities.

17 "When he goes in to make atonement in the holy place, no one shall be in the tent of meeting until he comes out, that he may make atonement for himself and for his household and for all the assembly of Israel.

18 "Then he shall go out to the altar that is before the LORD and make atonement for it, and shall take some of the blood of the bull and of the blood of the goat and put it on the horns of the altar on all sides.

19 "With his finger he shall sprinkle some of the blood on it seven times and cleanse it, and from the impurities of the sons of Israel consecrate it.

20 ¶ "When he finishes atoning for the holy place and the tent of meeting and the altar, he shall offer the live goat.

16:20 Scapegoat

The English word scapegoat (escape goat) was formed to capture the essence of this crucial ceremony in which a goat symbolically carried all the sins of Israel into the desert. Today the word is applied to anyone who takes the blame for something other people did.

21 "Then Aaron shall lay both of his hands on the head of the live goat, and confess over it all the iniquities of the sons of Israel and all their transgressions in regard to all their sins; and he shall lay them on the head of the goat and send it away into the wilderness by the hand of a man who stands in readiness.

22 "The goat shall bear on itself all their iniquities to a solitary land; and he shall release the goat in the wilderness.

23 ¶ "Then Aaron shall come into the tent of meeting and take off the linen garments which he put on when he went into the holy place, and shall leave them there.

---

[a] Lit propitiatory   [b] Lit goat of removal, or else a name: Azazel

24 "He shall bathe his body with water in a holy place and put on his clothes, and come forth and offer his burnt offering and the burnt offering of the people and make atonement for himself and for the people.

25 "Then he shall offer up in smoke the fat of the sin offering on the altar.

26 "The one who released the goat as the scapegoat shall wash his clothes and bathe his body with water; then afterward he shall come into the camp.

27 "But the bull of the sin offering and the goat of the sin offering, whose blood was brought in to make atonement in the holy place, shall be taken outside the camp, and they shall burn their hides, their flesh, and their refuse in the fire.

28 "Then the one who burns them shall wash his clothes and bathe his body with water, then afterward he shall come into the camp.

An Annual Atonement

29 ¶ "*This* shall be a permanent statute for you: in the seventh month, on the tenth day of the month, you shall humble your souls and not do any work, whether the native, or the alien who sojourns among you;

30 for it is on this day that atonement shall be made for you to cleanse you; you will be clean from all your sins before the LORD.

31 "It is to be a sabbath of solemn rest for you, that you may humble your souls; it is a permanent statute.

32 "So the priest who is anointed and ordained to serve as priest in his father's place shall make atonement: he shall thus put on the linen garments, the holy garments,

33 and make atonement for the holy sanctuary, and he shall make atonement for the tent of meeting and for the altar. He shall also make atonement for the priests and for all the people of the assembly.

34 "Now you shall have this as a permanent statute, to make atonement for the sons of Israel for all their sins once every year." And just as the LORD had commanded Moses, *so* he did.

Blood for Atonement

17 Then the LORD spoke to Moses, saying,

2 "Speak to Aaron and to his sons and to all the sons of Israel and say to them, 'This is what the LORD has commanded, saying,

3 "Any man from the house of Israel who slaughters an ox or a lamb or a goat in the camp, or who slaughters it outside the camp,

4 and has not brought it to the doorway of the tent of meeting to present *it* as an offering to the LORD before the tabernacle of the LORD, bloodguiltiness is to be reckoned to that man. He has shed blood and that man shall be cut off from among his people.

5 "The reason is so that the sons of Israel may bring their sacrifices which they were sacrificing in the open field, that they may bring them in to the LORD, at the doorway of the tent of meeting to the priest, and sacrifice them as sacrifices of peace offerings to the LORD.

6 "The priest shall sprinkle the blood on the altar of the LORD at the doorway of the tent of meeting, and offer up the fat in smoke as a soothing aroma to the LORD.

7 "They shall no longer sacrifice their sacrifices to the goat demons with which they play the harlot. This shall be a permanent statute to them throughout their generations." '

8 ¶ "Then you shall say to them, 'Any man from the house of Israel, or from the aliens who sojourn among them, who offers a burnt offering or sacrifice,

9 and does not bring it to the doorway of the tent of meeting to offer it to the LORD, that man also shall be cut off from his people.

10 ¶ 'And any man from the house of Israel, or from the aliens who sojourn among them, who eats any blood, I will set My face against that person who eats blood and will cut him off from among his people.

17:10 Kosher

To this day many Jews avoid meat unless it has been carefully drained of blood. Blood, which represented the life of living creatures, was to make atonement for, or to "cover up," sins. Thus Jesus' blood, signifying his death, has special significance to Christians. It is the blood of the ultimate sacrifice for sin.

The first Christians debated how much of the law should be required of non-Jews who became Christians (Acts 15). Of the four requirements they settled on, two were "kosher."

11 'For the life of the flesh is in the blood, and I have given it to you on the altar to make atonement for your souls; for it is the blood by reason of the life that makes atonement.'

12 "Therefore I said to the sons of Israel, 'No person among you may eat blood, nor may any alien who sojourns among you eat blood.'

13 "So when any man from the sons of Israel, or from the aliens who sojourn among them, in hunting catches a beast or a bird which may be eaten, he shall pour out its blood and cover it with earth.

14 ¶ "For *as for the* life of all flesh, its blood is *identified* with its life. Therefore I said to the sons of Israel, 'You are not to eat the blood of any flesh, for the life of all flesh is its blood; whoever eats it shall be cut off.'

15 "When any person eats *an animal* which dies or is torn *by beasts,* whether he is a native or an alien, he shall wash his clothes and bathe in water,

and remain unclean until evening; then he will become clean.

16 "But if he does not wash *them* or bathe his body, then he shall bear his guilt."

Laws on Immoral Relations

18 Then the LORD spoke to Moses, saying, 2 "Speak to the sons of Israel and say to them, 'I am the LORD your God.

3 'You shall not do what is done in the land of Egypt where you lived, nor are you to do what is done in the land of Canaan where I am bringing you; you shall not walk in their statutes.

4 'You are to perform My judgments and keep My statutes, to live in accord with them; I am the LORD your God.

5 'So you shall keep My statutes and My judgments, by which a man may live if he does them; I am the LORD.

6 ¶ 'None of you shall approach any blood relative of his to uncover nakedness; I am the LORD.

7 'You shall not uncover the nakedness of your father, that is, the nakedness of your mother. She is your mother; you are not to uncover her nakedness.

8 'You shall not uncover the nakedness of your father's wife; it is your father's nakedness.

9 'The nakedness of your sister, *either* your father's daughter or your mother's daughter, whether born at home or born outside, their nakedness you shall not uncover.

10 'The nakedness of your son's daughter or your daughter's daughter, their nakedness you shall not uncover; for their nakedness is yours.

11 'The nakedness of your father's wife's daughter, born to your father, she is your sister, you shall not uncover her nakedness.

12 'You shall not uncover the nakedness of your father's sister; she is your father's blood relative.

13 'You shall not uncover the nakedness of your mother's sister, for she is your mother's blood relative.

14 'You shall not uncover the nakedness of your father's brother; you shall not approach his wife, she is your aunt.

15 'You shall not uncover the nakedness of your daughter-in-law; she is your son's wife, you shall not uncover her nakedness.

16 'You shall not uncover the nakedness of your brother's wife; it is your brother's nakedness.

17 'You shall not uncover the nakedness of a woman and of her daughter, nor shall you take her son's daughter or her daughter's daughter, to uncover her nakedness; they are blood relatives. It is lewdness.

18 'You shall not marry a woman in addition to her sister as a rival while she is alive, to uncover her nakedness.

19 ¶ 'Also you shall not approach a woman to uncover her nakedness during her menstrual impurity.

20 'You shall not have intercourse with your neighbor's wife, to be defiled with her.

21 'You shall not give any of your offspring to offer them to Molech, nor shall you profane the name of your God; I am the LORD.

18:21 Child Sacrifice and Sex

This warning against child sacrifice (repeated and expanded in 20:1–5) seems out of place in the middle of a chapter on rules about sex. Yet, for the Israelites, there was a connection. Their neighbors, who sacrificed their children as a part of their religion, also practiced temple prostitution as a way of worship. To them, sex was a way to get in touch with their gods. God's warnings against various sexual practices begin and end with warnings to behave differently from these neighbors (verses 3,24).

22 'You shall not lie with a male as one lies with a female; it is an abomination.

23 'Also you shall not have intercourse with any animal to be defiled with it, nor shall any woman stand before an animal to mate with it; it is a perversion.

24 ¶ 'Do not defile yourselves by any of these things; for by all these the nations which I am casting out before you have become defiled.

25 'For the land has become defiled, therefore I have brought its punishment upon it, so the land has spewed out its inhabitants.

26 'But as for you, you are to keep My statutes and My judgments and shall not do any of these abominations, *neither* the native, nor the alien who sojourns among you

27 (for the men of the land who have been before you have done all these abominations, and the land has become defiled);

28 so that the land will not spew you out, should you defile it, as it has spewed out the nation which has been before you.

29 'For whoever does any of these abominations, those persons who do *so* shall be cut off from among their people.

30 'Thus you are to keep My charge, that you do not practice any of the abominable customs which have been practiced before you, so as not to defile yourselves with them; I am the LORD your God.' "

Idolatry Forbidden

19 Then the LORD spoke to Moses, saying: 2 ¶ "Speak to all the congregation of the sons of Israel and say to them, 'You shall be holy, for I the LORD your God am holy.

3 'Every one of you shall reverence his mother

and his father, and you shall keep My sabbaths; I am the LORD your God.

4 'Do not turn to idols or make for yourselves molten gods; I am the LORD your God.

5 ¶ 'Now when you offer a sacrifice of peace offerings to the LORD, you shall offer it so that you may be accepted.

6 'It shall be eaten the same day you offer *it*, and the next day; but what remains until the third day shall be burned with fire.

7 'So if it is eaten at all on the third day, it is an offense; it will not be accepted.

8 'Everyone who eats it will bear his iniquity, for he has profaned the holy thing of the LORD; and that person shall be cut off from his people.

Sundry Laws

9 ¶ 'Now when you reap the harvest of your land, you shall not reap to the very corners of your field, nor shall you gather the gleanings of your harvest.

19:9 A Form of Welfare

God's law was persistently concerned with the welfare of the poor. Everyday farming was to be done in such a way that poor and foreign people could fend for themselves. The reasons for such care are given: we are to imitate the holy character of God (verse 2), who cares for the poor, and to love our neighbor as ourselves (verse 18).

10 'Nor shall you glean your vineyard, nor shall you gather the fallen fruit of your vineyard; you shall leave them for the needy and for the stranger. I am the LORD your God.

11 ¶ 'You shall not steal, nor deal falsely, nor lie to one another.

12 'You shall not swear falsely by My name, so as to profane the name of your God; I am the LORD.

13 ¶ 'You shall not oppress your neighbor, nor rob *him*. The wages of a hired man are not to remain with you all night until morning.

14 'You shall not curse a deaf man, nor place a stumbling block before the blind, but you shall revere your God; I am the LORD.

15 ¶ 'You shall do no injustice in judgment; you shall not be partial to the poor nor defer to the great, but you are to judge your neighbor fairly.

16 'You shall not go about as a slanderer among your people, and you are not to act against the life of your neighbor; I am the LORD.

17 ¶ 'You shall not hate your fellow countryman in your heart; you may surely reprove your neighbor, but shall not incur sin because of him.

18 'You shall not take vengeance, nor bear any grudge against the sons of your people, but you shall love your neighbor as yourself; I am the LORD.

19 ¶ 'You are to keep My statutes. You shall not breed together two kinds of your cattle; you shall not sow your field with two kinds of seed, nor wear a garment upon you of two kinds of material mixed together.

20 ¶ 'Now if a man lies carnally with a woman who is a slave acquired for *another* man, but who has in no way been redeemed nor given her freedom, there shall be punishment; they shall not, *however*, be put to death, because she was not free.

21 'He shall bring his guilt offering to the LORD to the doorway of the tent of meeting, a ram for a guilt offering.

22 'The priest shall also make atonement for him with the ram of the guilt offering before the LORD for his sin which he has committed, and the sin which he has committed will be forgiven him.

23 ¶ 'When you enter the land and plant all kinds of trees for food, then you shall count their fruit as forbidden. Three years it shall be forbidden to you; *it* shall not be eaten.

24 'But in the fourth year all its fruit shall be holy, an offering of praise to the LORD.

25 'In the fifth year you are to eat of its fruit, that its yield may increase for you; I am the LORD your God.

26 ¶ 'You shall not eat *anything* with the blood, nor practice divination or soothsaying.

27 'You shall not round off the side-growth of your heads nor harm the edges of your beard.

28 'You shall not make any cuts in your body for the dead nor make any tattoo marks on yourselves: I am the LORD.

29 ¶ 'Do not profane your daughter by making her a harlot, so that the land will not fall to harlotry and the land become full of lewdness.

30 'You shall keep My sabbaths and revere My sanctuary; I am the LORD.

31 ¶ 'Do not turn to mediums or spiritists; do not seek them out to be defiled by them. I am the LORD your God.

32 ¶ 'You shall rise up before the grayheaded and honor the aged, and you shall revere your God; I am the LORD.

33 ¶ 'When a stranger resides with you in your land, you shall not do him wrong.

34 'The stranger who resides with you shall be to you as the native among you, and you shall love him as yourself, for you were aliens in the land of Egypt; I am the LORD your God.

35 ¶ 'You shall do no wrong in judgment, in measurement of weight, or capacity.

36 'You shall have just balances, just weights, a just *ª*ephah, and a just *ᵇ*hin; I am the LORD your God, who brought you out from the land of Egypt.

37 'You shall thus observe all My statutes and all My ordinances and do them; I am the LORD.'"

ª I.e. Approx one bu   *ᵇ* I.e. Approx one gal.

On Human Sacrifice and Immoralities

20 Then the LORD spoke to Moses, saying, 2 "You shall also say to the sons of Israel: ¶ 'Any man from the sons of Israel or from the aliens sojourning in Israel who gives any of his offspring to Molech, shall surely be put to death; the people of the land shall stone him with stones.

3 'I will also set My face against that man and will cut him off from among his people, because he has given some of his offspring to Molech, so as to defile My sanctuary and to profane My holy name.

4 'If the people of the land, however, should ever disregard that man when he gives any of his

A National Law Library
Setting Israel apart from its neighbors

THE LAWS OF THE UNITED States would fill a library. Elaborate indexes guide lawyers where to look when dealing with a particular issue. No one person can know even a fraction of all the federal, state, and local laws.

If the Old Testament laws recorded in Leviticus (and Exodus, Numbers, and Deuteronomy) seem dull and long-winded, keep them in perspective. These—just over 600 in all—were the entire set of laws for a nation, as far as we know. Their most striking feature, to a lawyer, is brevity and simplicity. You don't have to go to law school to understand them.

The laws are listed in no particular order. A law against witchcraft is followed by a law against improper haircuts, which is followed by a law against tattoos, which in turn is followed by a law against making your daughter into a prostitute. This mixing reveals an important feature of Old Testament thinking. Life is not analyzed in separate components, but seen as a whole.

For the Israelites, separation of church and state did not exist. Every aspect of life—politics, family life, diet, economics—concerned God. Even the Ten Commandments (in Exodus 20) show this, for they include laws regarding our relationship to both God and our neighbor. The two cannot be separated.

> *"You are to be holy to Me, for I the LORD am holy; and I have set you apart from the peoples to be Mine.'"* 20:26

Remarkable Features

In comparison with laws from other countries at that time, the Old Testament made a considerable advance. (Indeed, these laws have greatly influenced laws for our day.) Some of the remarkable features:

People were more important than property. For instance, there was never a death penalty for a crime against someone's property. Also, slaves were treated as human beings, not property. This was not true of many other legal codes of that time.

There was no class system. In many ancient countries, a noble was treated far differently from a commoner. Not so in Israel: Everybody stood on the same level before the law. Even a foreigner had clearly defined rights.

The punishment fit the crime. No "cruel and unusual punishment" was allowed. "Eye for eye" (Leviticus 24:20) ensured that no privileged character was "let off" for a crime, while at the same time it limited revenge.

Sexuality mattered. In most countries, the law cared little whether you slept with your neighbor's wife. In Israel, sexual immorality got stern treatment.

The poor and weak had protection. Specific provisions protected their rights from the powerful and wealthy. "Welfare" offered them a way to stay alive, such as the right to "glean the fields." In 19:9,13–14,32–33, God gave protection to various groups that could not defend themselves.

Attitudes, as well as actions, mattered. For instance, Leviticus 19:18 contains the famous law to "love your neighbor as yourself." Living up to the letter of the law was not enough. The law aimed to develop loving relationships.

Designed to Be Different

While we do not understand the reasons for some of the laws (many may have been designed simply to keep the Israelites "different" from their pagan neighbors), their overall impact is clear. These rules were intended to form a nation of compassionate, consistent, fair-minded people. They insisted that each person act positively and lovingly toward his or her neighbor—and particularly toward those in need. The reason? God lived with them. Since he is both just and merciful, his people must be too.

Life Questions: Everybody has a code to live by. Does your personal rulebook show as much concern for the poor and defenseless as that of Leviticus?

offspring to Molech, so as not to put him to death, 5 then I Myself will set My face against that man and against his family, and I will cut off from among their people both him and all those who play the harlot after him, by playing the harlot after Molech.

6 ¶ 'As for the person who turns to mediums and to spiritists, to play the harlot after them, I will also set My face against that person and will cut him off from among his people.

7 'You shall consecrate yourselves therefore and be holy, for I am the LORD your God.

20:7–8 The Bottom Line

These verses, along with verse 26, sum up the underlying reason for many of the laws outlined in Leviticus: God wanted the Israelites to be different. The New Testament makes clear that some of these regulations—eating forbidden animals, touching unclean persons— do not apply for all time. But at this moment, as God's people entered their new land, God wanted them to stand out from the nations around them (verses 22–24). Sadly, before long the Israelites were mimicking almost all the practices of their pagan neighbors.

8 'You shall keep My statutes and practice them; I am the LORD who sanctifies you.

9 ¶ 'If *there is* anyone who curses his father or his mother, he shall surely be put to death; he has cursed his father or his mother, his bloodguiltiness is upon him.

10 ¶ 'If *there is* a man who commits adultery with another man's wife, one who commits adultery with his friend's wife, the adulterer and the adulteress shall surely be put to death.

11 'If *there is* a man who lies with his father's wife, he has uncovered his father's nakedness; both of them shall surely be put to death, their bloodguiltiness is upon them.

12 'If *there is* a man who lies with his daughter-in-law, both of them shall surely be put to death; they have committed incest, their bloodguiltiness is upon them.

13 'If *there is* a man who lies with a male as those who lie with a woman, both of them have committed a detestable act; they shall surely be put to death. Their bloodguiltiness is upon them.

14 'If *there is* a man who marries a woman and her mother, it is immorality; both he and they shall be burned with fire, so that there will be no immorality in your midst.

15 'If *there is* a man who lies with an animal, he shall surely be put to death; you shall also kill the animal.

16 'If *there is* a woman who approaches any animal to mate with it, you shall kill the woman

and the animal; they shall surely be put to death. Their bloodguiltiness is upon them.

17 ¶ 'If *there is* a man who takes his sister, his father's daughter or his mother's daughter, so that he sees her nakedness and she sees his nakedness, it is a disgrace; and they shall be cut off in the sight of the sons of their people. He has uncovered his sister's nakedness; he bears his guilt.

18 'If *there is* a man who lies with a menstruous woman and uncovers her nakedness, he has laid bare her flow, and she has exposed the flow of her blood; thus both of them shall be cut off from among their people.

19 'You shall also not uncover the nakedness of your mother's sister or of your father's sister, for such a one has made naked his blood relative; they will bear their guilt.

20 'If *there is* a man who lies with his uncle's wife he has uncovered his uncle's nakedness; they will bear their sin. They will die childless.

21 'If *there is* a man who takes his brother's wife, it is abhorrent; he has uncovered his brother's nakedness. They will be childless.

22 ¶ 'You are therefore to keep all My statutes and all My ordinances and do them, so that the land to which I am bringing you to live will not spew you out.

23 'Moreover, you shall not follow the customs of the nation which I will drive out before you, for they did all these things, and therefore I have abhorred them.

24 'Hence I have said to you, "You are to possess their land, and I Myself will give it to you to possess it, a land flowing with milk and honey." I am the LORD your God, who has separated you from the peoples.

25 'You are therefore to make a distinction between the clean animal and the unclean, and between the unclean bird and the clean; and you shall not make yourselves detestable by animal or by bird or by anything that creeps on the ground, which I have separated for you as unclean.

26 'Thus you are to be holy to Me, for I the LORD am holy; and I have set you apart from the peoples to be Mine.

27 ¶ 'Now a man or a woman who is a medium or a spiritist shall surely be put to death. They shall be stoned with stones, their bloodguiltiness is upon them.' "

Regulations concerning Priests

21 Then the LORD said to Moses, "Speak to the priests, the sons of Aaron, and say to them: ¶ 'No one shall defile himself for a *dead* person among his people,

2 except for his relatives who are nearest to him, his mother and his father and his son and his daughter and his brother,

3 also for his virgin sister, who is near to him because she has had no husband; for her he may defile himself.

4 'He shall not defile himself as a relative by marriage among his people, and so profane himself.

5 'They shall not make any baldness on their heads, nor shave off the edges of their beards, nor make any cuts in their flesh.

6 'They shall be holy to their God and not profane the name of their God, for they present the offerings by fire to the LORD, the food of their God; so they shall be holy.

7 'They shall not take a woman who is profaned by harlotry, nor shall they take a woman divorced from her husband; for he is holy to his God.

8 'You shall consecrate him, therefore, for he offers the food of your God; he shall be holy to you; for I the LORD, who sanctifies you, am holy.

9 'Also the daughter of any priest, if she profanes herself by harlotry, she profanes her father; she shall be burned with fire.

10 ¶ 'The priest who is the highest among his brothers, on whose head the anointing oil has been poured and who has been consecrated to wear the garments, shall not uncover his head nor tear his clothes;

11 nor shall he approach any dead person, nor defile himself *even* for his father or his mother;

12 nor shall he go out of the sanctuary nor profane the sanctuary of his God, for the consecration of the anointing oil of his God is on him; I am the LORD.

13 'He shall take a wife in her virginity.

14 'A widow, or a divorced woman, or one who is profaned by harlotry, these he may not take; but rather he is to marry a virgin of his own people,

15 so that he will not profane his offspring among his people; for I am the LORD who sanctifies him.' "

16 ¶ Then the LORD spoke to Moses, saying,

17 "Speak to Aaron, saying, 'No man of your offspring throughout their generations who has a defect shall approach to offer the food of his God.

18 'For no one who has a defect shall approach: a blind man, or a lame man, or he who has a disfigured *face,* or any deformed *limb,*

19 or a man who has a broken foot or broken hand,

20 or a hunchback or a dwarf, or *one who has* a defect in his eye or eczema or scabs or crushed testicles.

21 'No man among the descendants of Aaron the priest who has a defect is to come near to offer the LORD'S offerings by fire; *since* he has a defect, he shall not come near to offer the food of his God.

22 'He may eat the food of his God, *both* of the most holy and of the holy,

23 only he shall not go in to the veil or come near the altar because he has a defect, so that he will not profane My sanctuaries. For I am the LORD who sanctifies them.' "

24 So Moses spoke to Aaron and to his sons and to all the sons of Israel.

Sundry Rules for Priests

22 Then the LORD spoke to Moses, saying,
2 "Tell Aaron and his sons to be careful with the holy *gifts* of the sons of Israel, which they dedicate to Me, so as not to profane My holy name; I am the LORD.

3 "Say to them, 'If any man among all your descendants throughout your generations approaches the holy *gifts* which the sons of Israel dedicate to the LORD, while he has an uncleanness, that person shall be cut off from before Me; I am the LORD.

4 'No man of the descendants of Aaron, who is a leper or who has a discharge, may eat of the holy *gifts* until he is clean. And if one touches anything made unclean by a corpse or if a man has a seminal emission,

5 or if a man touches any teeming things by which he is made unclean, or any man by whom he is made unclean, whatever his uncleanness;

6 a person who touches any such shall be unclean until evening, and shall not eat of the holy *gifts* unless he has bathed his body in water.

7 'But when the sun sets, he will be clean, and afterward he shall eat of the holy *gifts,* for it is his food.

8 'He shall not eat *an animal* which dies or is torn *by beasts,* becoming unclean by it; I am the LORD.

9 'They shall therefore keep My charge, so that they will not bear sin because of it and die thereby because they profane it; I am the LORD who sanctifies them.

10 ¶ 'No [a]layman, however, is to eat the holy *gift;* a sojourner with the priest or a hired man shall not eat of the holy *gift.*

11 'But if a priest buys a slave as *his* property with his money, that one may eat of it, and those who are born in his house may eat of his food.

12 'If a priest's daughter is married to a layman, she shall not eat of the offering of the *gifts.*

13 'But if a priest's daughter becomes a widow or divorced, and has no child and returns to her father's house as in her youth, she shall eat of her father's food; but no layman shall eat of it.

14 'But if a man eats a holy *gift* unintentionally, then he shall add to it a fifth of it and shall give the holy *gift* to the priest.

15 'They shall not profane the holy *gifts* of the sons of Israel which they offer to the LORD,

16 and *so* cause them to bear punishment for guilt by eating their holy *gifts;* for I am the LORD who sanctifies them.' "

---

[a] Lit *stranger*

Flawless Animals for Sacrifice

17 ¶ Then the LORD spoke to Moses, saying,

18 "Speak to Aaron and to his sons and to all the sons of Israel and say to them, 'Any man of the house of Israel or of the aliens in Israel who presents his offering, whether it is any of their votive or any of their freewill offerings, which they present to the LORD for a burnt offering—

19 for you to be accepted—*it must be* a male without defect from the cattle, the sheep, or the goats.

22:19 The Very Best for God

For the Israelite farmers, a farm animal represented a considerable contribution. It would have been tempting to cull out their weakest animals. Instead, they were commanded to give their very best. Similarly, at every harvest they were to bring their very first fruits to the Lord (23:10). These practices reminded them again and again of God's place in their lives.

---

20 'Whatever has a defect, you shall not offer, for it will not be accepted for you.

21 'When a man offers a sacrifice of peace offerings to the LORD to fulfill a special vow or for a freewill offering, of the herd or of the flock, it must be perfect to be accepted; there shall be no defect in it.

22 'Those *that are* blind or fractured or maimed or having a running sore or eczema or scabs, you shall not offer to the LORD, nor make of them an offering by fire on the altar to the LORD.

23 'In respect to an ox or a lamb which has an overgrown or stunted *member,* you may present it for a freewill offering, but for a vow it will not be accepted.

24 'Also anything *with its testicles* bruised or crushed or torn or cut, you shall not offer to the LORD, or sacrifice in your land,

25 nor shall you accept any such from the hand of a foreigner for offering as the food of your God; for their corruption is in them, they have a defect, they shall not be accepted for you.' "

26 ¶ Then the LORD spoke to Moses, saying,

27 "When an ox or a sheep or a goat is born, it shall remain seven days with its mother, and from the eighth day on it shall be accepted as a sacrifice of an offering by fire to the LORD.

28 "But, *whether* it is an ox or a sheep, you shall not kill *both* it and its young in one day.

29 "When you sacrifice a sacrifice of thanksgiving to the LORD, you shall sacrifice it so that you may be accepted.

30 "It shall be eaten on the same day, you shall leave none of it until morning; I am the LORD.

31 "So you shall keep My commandments, and do them; I am the LORD.

32 ¶ "You shall not profane My holy name, but I will be sanctified among the sons of Israel; I am the LORD who sanctifies you,

33 who brought you out from the land of Egypt, to be your God; I am the LORD."

Laws of Religious Festivals

23 The LORD spoke again to Moses, saying,

2 "Speak to the sons of Israel and say to them, 'The LORD'S appointed times which you shall proclaim as holy convocations—My appointed times are these:

3 ¶ 'For six days work may be done, but on the seventh day there is a sabbath of complete rest, a holy convocation. You shall not do any work; it is a sabbath to the LORD in all your dwellings.

4 ¶ 'These are the appointed times of the LORD, holy convocations which you shall proclaim at the times appointed for them.

5 'In the first month, on the fourteenth day of the month at twilight is the LORD'S Passover.

6 'Then on the fifteenth day of the same month there is the Feast of Unleavened Bread to the LORD; for seven days you shall eat unleavened bread.

7 'On the first day you shall have a holy convocation; you shall not do any laborious work.

8 'But for seven days you shall present an offering by fire to the LORD. On the seventh day is a holy convocation; you shall not do any laborious work.' "

9 ¶ Then the LORD spoke to Moses, saying,

10 "Speak to the sons of Israel and say to them, 'When you enter the land which I am going to give to you and reap its harvest, then you shall bring in the sheaf of the first fruits of your harvest to the priest.

11 'He shall wave the sheaf before the LORD for you to be accepted; on the day after the sabbath the priest shall wave it.

12 'Now on the day when you wave the sheaf, you shall offer a male lamb one year old without defect for a burnt offering to the LORD.

13 'Its grain offering shall then be two-tenths *of an ephah* of fine flour mixed with oil, an offering by fire to the LORD *for* a soothing aroma, with its drink offering, a fourth of a ᵃhin of wine.

14 'Until this same day, until you have brought in the offering of your God, you shall eat neither bread nor roasted grain nor new growth. It is to be a perpetual statute throughout your generations in all your dwelling places.

15 ¶ 'You shall also count for yourselves from the day after the sabbath, from the day when you brought in the sheaf of the wave offering; there shall be seven complete sabbaths.

ᵃ I.e. Approx one gal.

16 'You shall count fifty days to the day after the seventh sabbath; then you shall present a new grain offering to the LORD.

17 'You shall bring in from your dwelling places two *loaves* of bread for a wave offering, made of two-tenths *of an ephah;* they shall be of a fine flour, baked with leaven as first fruits to the LORD.

18 'Along with the bread you shall present seven one year old male lambs without defect, and a bull of the herd and two rams; they are to be a burnt offering to the LORD, with their grain offering and their drink offerings, an offering by fire of a soothing aroma to the LORD.

19 'You shall also offer one male goat for a sin offering and two male lambs one year old for a sacrifice of peace offerings.

20 'The priest shall then wave them with the bread of the first fruits for a wave offering with two lambs before the LORD; they are to be holy to the LORD for the priest.

21 'On this same day you shall make a proclamation as well; you are to have a holy convocation. You shall do no laborious work. It is to be a perpetual statute in all your dwelling places throughout your generations.

22 ¶ 'When you reap the harvest of your land, moreover, you shall not reap to the very corners of your field nor gather the gleaning of your harvest; you are to leave them for the needy and the alien. I am the LORD your God.' "

23 ¶ Again the LORD spoke to Moses, saying,

24 "Speak to the sons of Israel, saying, 'In the seventh month on the first of the month you shall

In Celebration of God
Jewish holidays focused on one thing

> "'Rejoice before the LORD your God for seven days.'"
> 23:40

ANTHROPOLOGISTS STUDYING REMOTE TRIBES ROUTINELY describe their feast days, for these show the people's common values. What would stand out to an anthropologist studying the United States? Undoubtedly he would notice that our celebration of Christmas, Thanksgiving, and the Fourth of July emphasize family, food, and gifts—the more the better.

What about the Israelites? Leviticus describes five feasts, all focusing on God. Each was marked by special sacrifices to God and a sacred assembly in the Tent of Meeting where God had "pitched his tent." Rather than giving gifts to each other, the Israelites gave gifts to God.

Sometimes they rejoiced: During the Feast of Tabernacles everyone camped out to "rejoice before the LORD" for a solid week (23:40). On other occasions, such as the Day of Atonement, they were sober and solemn (chapter 16, 23:26–32). But always their orientation was God-directed.

God over Money

Nobody worked on Israelite feast days, but their "days off" had a different motive than ours. An Israelite farmer never got a paid holiday. In fact, a holiday could cost him—it might fall on a day perfect for harvesting. But God took priority over work. The weekly Sabbath day reinforced the same idea. You had to stop working to worship.

God mattered more than wealth. This fundamental belief showed itself even more in the sabbath year and in the Year of Jubilee (chapter 25). Every seventh year, people did not farm at all. They lived off whatever the land produced by itself, and dedicated themselves to God. This would be like our closing all businesses and factories for a year.

After 49 years—seven sabbath years—the Year of Jubilee came. This time, people went for two years straight without planting. All land bought or sold during the previous 49 years went back to its original family ownership. Since the land had originally been equally distributed, this meant that no family would ever become either totally destitute or overwhelmingly rich. Any Israelites who had sold themselves as slaves would also be freed in that year.

Prosperity Came from God

Hard work and the resulting abundance were never scorned in Israel. But prosperity always came ultimately from God, not from hard work or clever dealings alone. The feasts and Sabbaths, set aside as special days, helped people remember and praise the God who had given them so much.

So far as we know, no Year of Jubilee was ever actually practiced. Some of the feasts were forgotten for long periods of time. But such failure is not surprising. After all, think what we have done to the holy day of Christmas! The feast days described in Leviticus give us a good idea of what God wanted Israel to be. Sadly, reality did not often match the ideal.

Life Questions: If someone examined the way you spend your holidays and weekends, what would he or she conclude about your priorities?

have a rest, a reminder by blowing *of trumpets,* a holy convocation.

25 'You shall not do any laborious work, but you shall present an offering by fire to the LORD.' "

The Day of Atonement

26 ¶ The LORD spoke to Moses, saying,

27 "On exactly the tenth day of this seventh month is the day of atonement; it shall be a holy convocation for you, and you shall humble your souls and present an offering by fire to the LORD.

28 "You shall not do any work on this same day, for it is a day of atonement, to make atonement on your behalf before the LORD your God.

29 "If there is any person who will not humble himself on this same day, he shall be cut off from his people.

30 "As for any person who does any work on this same day, that person I will destroy from among his people.

31 "You shall do no work at all. It is to be a perpetual statute throughout your generations in all your dwelling places.

32 "It is to be a sabbath of complete rest to you, and you shall humble your souls; on the ninth of the month at evening, from evening until evening you shall keep your sabbath."

33 ¶ Again the LORD spoke to Moses, saying,

34 "Speak to the sons of Israel, saying, 'On the fifteenth of this seventh month is the Feast of Booths for seven days to the LORD.

35 'On the first day is a holy convocation; you shall do no laborious work of any kind.

36 'For seven days you shall present an offering by fire to the LORD. On the eighth day you shall have a holy convocation and present an offering by fire to the LORD; it is an assembly. You shall do no laborious work.

37 ¶ 'These are the appointed times of the LORD which you shall proclaim as holy convocations, to present offerings by fire to the LORD— burnt offerings and grain offerings, sacrifices and drink offerings, *each* day's matter on its own day—

38 besides *those of* the sabbaths of the LORD, and besides your gifts and besides all your votive and freewill offerings, which you give to the LORD.

39 ¶ 'On exactly the fifteenth day of the seventh month, when you have gathered in the crops of the land, you shall celebrate the feast of the LORD for seven days, with a rest on the first day and a rest on the eighth day.

40 'Now on the first day you shall take for yourselves the foliage of beautiful trees, palm branches and boughs of leafy trees and willows of the brook, and you shall rejoice before the LORD your God for seven days.

41 'You shall thus celebrate it *as* a feast to the LORD for seven days in the year. It *shall be* a perpetual statute throughout your generations; you shall celebrate it in the seventh month.

42 'You shall live in booths for seven days; all the native-born in Israel shall live in booths,

43 so that your generations may know that I had the sons of Israel live in booths when I

23:40 Seven Days of Rejoicing

Though the worship of God was a serious business, it was also joyful. Every year, for instance, the Israelites were to hold this week-long campout and celebration, filled with rejoicing.

brought them out from the land of Egypt. I am the LORD your God.' "

44 So Moses declared to the sons of Israel the appointed times of the LORD.

The Lamp and the Bread of the Sanctuary

24 Then the LORD spoke to Moses, saying, 2 "Command the sons of Israel that they bring to you clear oil from beaten olives for the light, to make a lamp burn continually.

3 "Outside the veil of testimony in the tent of meeting, Aaron shall keep it in order from evening to morning before the LORD continually; *it shall be* a perpetual statute throughout your generations.

4 "He shall keep the lamps in order on the pure *gold* lampstand before the LORD continually.

5 ¶ "Then you shall take fine flour and bake twelve cakes with it; two-tenths *of an ephah* shall be *in* each cake.

6 "You shall set them *in* two rows, six *to* a row, on the pure *gold* table before the LORD.

7 "You shall put pure frankincense on each row that it may be a memorial portion for the bread, *even* an offering by fire to the LORD.

8 "Every sabbath day he shall set it in order before the LORD continually; it is an everlasting covenant for the sons of Israel.

9 "It shall be for Aaron and his sons, and they shall eat it in a holy place; for it is most holy to him from the LORD'S offerings by fire, *his* portion forever."

10 ¶ Now the son of an Israelite woman, whose father was an Egyptian, went out among the sons of Israel; and the Israelite woman's son and a man of Israel struggled with each other in the camp.

11 The son of the Israelite woman blasphemed the Name and cursed. So they brought him to Moses. (Now his mother's name was Shelomith, the daughter of Dibri, of the tribe of Dan.)

12 They put him in custody so that the command of the LORD might be made clear to them.

13 ¶ Then the LORD spoke to Moses, saying,

14 "Bring the one who has cursed outside the camp, and let all who heard him lay their hands on his head; then let all the congregation stone him.

15 "You shall speak to the sons of Israel, saying, 'If anyone curses his God, then he will bear his sin.

16 'Moreover, the one who blasphemes the name of the LORD shall surely be put to death; all the congregation shall certainly stone him. The alien as well as the native, when he blasphemes the Name, shall be put to death.

"An Eye for an Eye"

17 ¶ 'If a man takes the life of any human being, he shall surely be put to death.

18 'The one who takes the life of an animal shall make it good, life for life.

19 'If a man injures his neighbor, just as he has done, so it shall be done to him:

20 fracture for fracture, eye for eye, tooth for tooth; just as he has injured a man, so it shall be inflicted on him.

24:20 An Eye for an Eye

Jesus, speaking of this law in Matthew 5:38, told his followers not to resist evil people. Apparently people had been taking "an eye for an eye" as a basis for private vengeance—as some do today. The law's original intent, however, was to set a standard for punishment in court. It limited vengeance and made certain that both rich and poor, native and foreigner, would pay the same price for their crimes.

21 'Thus the one who kills an animal shall make it good, but the one who kills a man shall be put to death.

22 'There shall be one standard for you; it shall be for the stranger as well as the native, for I am the LORD your God.' "

23 Then Moses spoke to the sons of Israel, and they brought the one who had cursed outside the camp and stoned him with stones. Thus the sons of Israel did, just as the LORD had commanded Moses.

The Sabbatic Year and Year of Jubilee

25 The LORD then spoke to Moses at Mount Sinai, saying,

2 "Speak to the sons of Israel and say to them, 'When you come into the land which I shall give you, then the land shall have a sabbath to the LORD.

3 'Six years you shall sow your field, and six years you shall prune your vineyard and gather in its crop,

4 but during the seventh year the land shall have a sabbath rest, a sabbath to the LORD; you shall not sow your field nor prune your vineyard.

5 'Your harvest's ᵃaftergrowth you shall not reap, and your grapes of untrimmed vines you shall not gather; the land shall have a sabbatical year.

6 'All of you shall have the sabbath *products* of the land for food; yourself, and your male and female slaves, and your hired man and your foreign resident, those who live as aliens with you.

7 'Even your cattle and the animals that are in your land shall have all its crops to eat.

8 ¶ 'You are also to count off seven sabbaths of years for yourself, seven times seven years, so that you have the time of the seven sabbaths of years, *namely,* forty-nine years.

9 'You shall then sound a ram's horn abroad on the tenth day of the seventh month; on the day of atonement you shall sound a horn all through your land.

10 'You shall thus consecrate the fiftieth year and proclaim ᵇa release through the land to all its inhabitants. It shall be a jubilee for you, and each of you shall return to his own property, and each of you shall return to his family.

11 'You shall have the fiftieth year as a jubilee; you shall not sow, nor reap its aftergrowth, nor gather in *from* its untrimmed vines.

12 'For it is a jubilee; it shall be holy to you. You shall eat its crops out of the field.

13 ¶ 'On this year of jubilee each of you shall return to his own property.

14 'If you make a sale, moreover, to your friend or buy from your friend's hand, you shall not wrong one another.

15 'Corresponding to the number of years after the jubilee, you shall buy from your friend; he is to sell to you according to the number of years of crops.

16 'In proportion to the extent of the years you shall increase its price, and in proportion to the fewness of the years you shall diminish its price, for *it is* a number of crops he is selling to you.

17 'So you shall not wrong one another, but you shall fear your God; for I am the LORD your God.

18 ¶ 'You shall thus observe My statutes and keep My judgments, so as to carry them out, that you may live securely on the land.

19 'Then the land will yield its produce, so that you can eat your fill and live securely on it.

20 'But if you say, "What are we going to eat on the seventh year if we do not sow or gather in our crops?"

21 then I will so order My blessing for you in the sixth year that it will bring forth the crop for three years.

22 'When you are sowing the eighth year, you can still eat old things from the crop, eating *the old* until the ninth year when its crop comes in.

The Law of Redemption

23 ¶ 'The land, moreover, shall not be sold permanently, for the land is Mine; for you are *but* aliens and sojourners with Me.

ᵃ Lit *growth from spilled kernels*   ᵇ Or *liberty*

24 'Thus for every piece of your property, you are to provide for the redemption of the land.

25 ¶ 'If a fellow countryman of yours becomes so poor he has to sell part of his property, then his nearest kinsman is to come and buy back what his relative has sold.

26 'Or in case a man has no kinsman, but so recovers his means as to find sufficient for its redemption,

27 then he shall calculate the years since its sale and refund the balance to the man to whom he sold it, and so return to his property.

28 'But if he has not found sufficient means to get it back for himself, then what he has sold shall remain in the hands of its purchaser until the year of jubilee; but at the jubilee it shall revert, that he may return to his property.

25:28 Property Rights

God's law provided for a kind of redistribution of wealth every 50 years, when all land would revert to its original owners. The tendency for the rich to buy up all the property (which originally had been divided equally among families) was reversed in the Year of Jubilee. In essence, you could not sell your land—only lease it out.

29 ¶ 'Likewise, if a man sells a dwelling house in a walled city, then his redemption right remains valid until a full year from its sale; his right of redemption lasts a full year.

30 'But if it is not bought back for him within the space of a full year, then the house that is in the walled city passes permanently to its purchaser throughout his generations; it does not revert in the jubilee.

31 'The houses of the villages, however, which have no surrounding wall shall be considered as open fields; they have redemption rights and revert in the jubilee.

32 'As for cities of the Levites, the Levites have a permanent right of redemption for the houses of the cities which are their possession.

33 'What, therefore, belongs to the Levites may be redeemed and a house sale in the city of this possession reverts in the jubilee, for the houses of the cities of the Levites are their possession among the sons of Israel.

34 'But pasture fields of their cities shall not be sold, for that is their perpetual possession.

Of Poor Countrymen

35 ¶ 'Now in case a countryman of yours becomes poor and his means with regard to you falter, then you are to sustain him, like a stranger or a sojourner, that he may live with you.

36 'Do not take usurious interest from him, but revere your God, that your countryman may live with you.

37 'You shall not give him your silver at interest, nor your food for gain.

38 'I am the LORD your God, who brought you out of the land of Egypt to give you the land of Canaan *and* to be your God.

39 ¶ 'If a countryman of yours becomes so poor with regard to you that he sells himself to you, you shall not subject him to a slave's service.

40 'He shall be with you as a hired man, as if he were a sojourner; he shall serve with you until the year of jubilee.

41 'He shall then go out from you, he and his sons with him, and shall go back to his family, that he may return to the property of his forefathers.

42 'For they are My servants whom I brought out from the land of Egypt; they are not to be sold *in* a slave sale.

43 'You shall not rule over him with severity, but are to revere your God.

44 'As for your male and female slaves whom you may have—you may acquire male and female slaves from the pagan nations that are around you.

45 'Then, too, *it is* out of the sons of the sojourners who live as aliens among you that you may gain acquisition, and out of their families who are with you, whom they will have produced in your land; they also may become your possession.

46 'You may even bequeath them to your sons after you, to receive as a possession; you can use them as permanent slaves. But in respect to your countrymen, the sons of Israel, you shall not rule with severity over one another.

Of Redeeming a Poor Man

47 ¶ 'Now if the means of a stranger or of a sojourner with you becomes sufficient, and a countryman of yours becomes so poor with regard to him as to sell himself to a stranger who is sojourning with you, or to the descendants of a stranger's family,

48 then he shall have redemption right after he has been sold. One of his brothers may redeem him,

49 or his uncle, or his uncle's son, may redeem him, or one of his blood relatives from his family may redeem him; or if he prospers, he may redeem himself.

50 'He then with his purchaser shall calculate from the year when he sold himself to him up to the year of jubilee; and the price of his sale shall correspond to the number of years. *It is* like the days of a hired man *that* he shall be with him.

51 'If there are still many years, he shall refund part of his purchase price in proportion to them for his own redemption;

52 and if few years remain until the year of jubilee, he shall so calculate with him. In propor-

tion to his years he is to refund *the amount for* his redemption.

53 'Like a man hired year by year he shall be with him; he shall not rule over him with severity in your sight.

54 'Even if he is not redeemed by these *means,* he shall still go out in the year of jubilee, he and his sons with him.

55 'For the sons of Israel are My servants; they are My servants whom I brought out from the land of Egypt. I am the LORD your God.

Blessings of Obedience

26 'You shall not make for yourselves idols, nor shall you set up for yourselves an image or a *sacred* pillar, nor shall you place a figured stone in your land to bow down to it; for I am the LORD your God.

2 'You shall keep My sabbaths and reverence My sanctuary; I am the LORD.

3 'If you walk in My statutes and keep My commandments so as to carry them out,

4 then I shall give you rains in their season, so that the land will yield its produce and the trees of the field will bear their fruit.

5 'Indeed, your threshing will last for you until grape gathering, and grape gathering will last until sowing time. You will thus eat your food to the full and live securely in your land.

6 'I shall also grant peace in the land, so that you may lie down with no one making *you* tremble. I shall also eliminate harmful beasts from the land, and no sword will pass through your land.

7 'But you will chase your enemies and they will fall before you by the sword;

8 five of you will chase a hundred, and a hundred of you will chase ten thousand, and your enemies will fall before you by the sword.

9 'So I will turn toward you and make you fruitful and multiply you, and I will confirm My covenant with you.

10 'You will eat the old supply and clear out the old because of the new.

11 'Moreover, I will make My dwelling among you, and My soul will not reject you.

12 'I will also walk among you and be your God, and you shall be My people.

13 'I am the LORD your God, who brought you out of the land of Egypt so that *you* would not be their slaves, and I broke the bars of your yoke and made you walk erect.

Penalties of Disobedience

14 ¶ 'But if you do not obey Me and do not carry out all these commandments,

15 if, instead, you reject My statutes, and if your soul abhors My ordinances so as not to carry out all My commandments, *and* so break My covenant,

16 I, in turn, will do this to you: I will appoint over you a sudden terror, consumption and fever that will waste away the eyes and cause the soul to pine away; also, you will sow your seed uselessly, for your enemies will eat it up.

17 'I will set My face against you so that you will be struck down before your enemies; and those who hate you will rule over you, and you will flee when no one is pursuing you.

18 'If also after these things you do not obey Me, then I will punish you seven times more for your sins.

19 'I will also break down your pride of power; I will also make your sky like iron and your earth like bronze.

20 'Your strength will be spent uselessly, for your land will not yield its produce and the trees of the land will not yield their fruit.

21 ¶ 'If then, you act with hostility against Me and are unwilling to obey Me, I will increase the plague on you seven times according to your sins.

22 'I will let loose among you the beasts of the field, which will bereave you of your children and destroy your cattle and reduce your number so that your roads lie deserted.

23 ¶ 'And if by these things you are not turned to Me, but act with hostility against Me,

24 then I will act with hostility against you; and I, even I, will strike you seven times for your sins.

25 'I will also bring upon you a sword which will execute vengeance for the covenant; and when you gather together into your cities, I will send pestilence among you, so that you shall be delivered into enemy hands.

26 'When I break your staff of bread, ten women will bake your bread in one oven, and they will bring back your bread [a]in rationed amounts, so that you will eat and not be satisfied.

27 ¶ 'Yet if in spite of this you do not obey Me, but act with hostility against Me,

28 then I will act with wrathful hostility against you, and I, even I, will punish you seven times for your sins.

29 'Further, you will eat the flesh of your sons and the flesh of your daughters you will eat.

30 'I then will destroy your high places, and cut down your incense altars, and heap your remains on the remains of your idols, for My soul shall abhor you.

31 'I will lay waste your cities as well and will make your sanctuaries desolate, and I will not smell your soothing aromas.

32 'I will make the land desolate so that your enemies who settle in it will be appalled over it.

33 'You, however, I will scatter among the nations and will draw out a sword after you, as your land becomes desolate and your cities become waste.

34 ¶ 'Then the land will enjoy its sabbaths all the days of the desolation, while you are in your

---

[a] Lit *by weight*

enemies' land; then the land will rest and enjoy its sabbaths.

35 'All the days of *its* desolation it will observe the rest which it did not observe on your sabbaths, while you were living on it.

26:34 Revenge of the Land

There is little evidence that the Israelites ever followed the rules on sabbath years and Jubilee. Nevertheless, as ominously foretold here, the land eventually did get its rest. For 70 years the Babylonians held the Israelites hostage, far away from their homeland. And the land had rest.

36 'As for those of you who may be left, I will also bring weakness into their hearts in the lands of their enemies. And the sound of a driven leaf will chase them, and even when no one is pursuing they will flee as though from the sword, and they will fall.

37 'They will therefore stumble over each other as if *running* from the sword, although no one is pursuing; and you will have *no strength* to stand up before your enemies.

38 'But you will perish among the nations, and your enemies' land will consume you.

39 'So those of you who may be left will rot away because of their iniquity in the lands of your enemies; and also because of the iniquities of their forefathers they will rot away with them.

40 ¶ 'If they confess their iniquity and the iniquity of their forefathers, in their unfaithfulness which they committed against Me, and also in their acting with hostility against Me—

41 I also was acting with hostility against them, to bring them into the land of their enemies—or if their uncircumcised heart becomes humbled so that they then make amends for their iniquity,

26:41 Uncircumcised Hearts

Circumcision was the ritual that made a man into a Jew, so to speak. But this reference to uncircumcised hearts shows that, right from the beginning, the inward attitude, as well as the physical operation, was crucial. Six hundred years later Jeremiah accused the Israelites of being uncircumcised of heart (Jeremiah 9:26); another 600 years after him Stephen made the same complaint (Acts 7:51). On this basis Paul wrote, "For he is not a Jew who is one outwardly . . . he is a Jew who is one inwardly; and circumcision is that which is of the heart, by the Spirit" (Romans 2:28–29). Leviticus offered more than a legal system; these laws appealed to a person's relationship with God.

42 then I will remember My covenant with Jacob, and I will remember also My covenant with Isaac, and My covenant with Abraham as well, and I will remember the land.

43 'For the land will be abandoned by them, and will make up for its sabbaths while it is made desolate without them. They, meanwhile, will be making amends for their iniquity, because they rejected My ordinances and their soul abhorred My statutes.

44 'Yet in spite of this, when they are in the land of their enemies, I will not reject them, nor will I so abhor them as to destroy them, breaking My covenant with them; for I am the LORD their God.

45 'But I will remember for them the covenant with their ancestors, whom I brought out of the land of Egypt in the sight of the nations, that I might be their God. I am the LORD.' "

46 ¶ These are the statutes and ordinances and laws which the LORD established between Himself and the sons of Israel through Moses at Mount Sinai.

Rules concerning Valuations

27 Again, the LORD spoke to Moses, saying, 2 "Speak to the sons of Israel and say to them, 'When a man makes a difficult vow, he *shall be valued* according to your valuation of persons belonging to the LORD.

3 'If your valuation is of the male from twenty years even to sixty years old, then your valuation shall be fifty shekels of silver, after the shekel of the sanctuary.

4 'Or if it is a female, then your valuation shall be thirty shekels.

5 'If it be from five years even to twenty years old then your valuation for the male shall be twenty shekels and for the female ten shekels.

6 'But if *they are* from a month even up to five years old, then your valuation shall be five shekels of silver for the male, and for the female your valuation shall be three shekels of silver.

7 'If *they are* from sixty years old and upward, if it is a male, then your valuation shall be fifteen shekels, and for the female ten shekels.

8 'But if he is poorer than your valuation, then he shall be placed before the priest and the priest shall value him; according to the means of the one who vowed, the priest shall value him.

9 ¶ 'Now if it is an animal of the kind which men can present as an offering to the LORD, any such that one gives to the LORD shall be holy.

10 'He shall not replace it or exchange it, a good for a bad, or a bad for a good; or if he does exchange animal for animal, then both it and its substitute shall become holy.

11 'If, however, it is any unclean animal of the kind which men do not present as an offering to the LORD, then he shall place the animal before the priest.

12 'The priest shall value it as either good or bad; as you, the priest, value it, so it shall be.

13 'But if he should ever *wish to* redeem it, then he shall add one-fifth of it to your valuation.

14 ¶ 'Now if a man consecrates his house as holy to the LORD, then the priest shall value it as either good or bad; as the priest values it, so it shall stand.

15 'Yet if the one who consecrates it should *wish to* redeem his house, then he shall add one-fifth of your valuation price to it, so that it may be his.

16 ¶ 'Again, if a man consecrates to the LORD part of the fields of his own property, then your valuation shall be proportionate to the seed needed for it: a homer of barley seed at fifty shekels of silver.

17 'If he consecrates his field as of the year of jubilee, according to your valuation it shall stand.

18 'If he consecrates his field after the jubilee, however, then the priest shall calculate the price for him proportionate to the years that are left until the year of jubilee; and it shall be deducted from your valuation.

19 'If the one who consecrates it should ever wish to redeem the field, then he shall add one-fifth of your valuation price to it, so that it may pass to him.

20 'Yet if he will not redeem the field, but has sold the field to another man, it may no longer be redeemed;

21 and when it reverts in the jubilee, the field shall be holy to the LORD, like a field set apart; it shall be for the priest as his property.

22 'Or if he consecrates to the LORD a field which he has bought, which is not a part of the field of his own property,

23 then the priest shall calculate for him the amount of your valuation up to the year of jubilee;

and he shall on that day give your valuation as holy to the LORD.

24 'In the year of jubilee the field shall return to the one from whom he bought it, to whom the possession of the land belongs.

25 'Every valuation of yours, moreover, shall be after the shekel of the sanctuary. The shekel shall be twenty gerahs.

26 ¶ 'However, a firstborn among animals, which as a firstborn belongs to the LORD, no man may consecrate it; whether ox or sheep, it is the LORD'S.

27 'But if *it is* among the unclean animals, then he shall redeem it according to your valuation and add to it one-fifth of it; and if it is not redeemed, then it shall be sold according to your valuation.

28 ¶ 'Nevertheless, anything which a man ᵃsets apart to the LORD out of all that he has, of man or animal or of the fields of his own property, shall not be sold or redeemed. Anything devoted to destruction is most holy to the LORD.

29 'No one who may have been set apart among men shall be ransomed; he shall surely be put to death.

30 ¶ 'Thus all the tithe of the land, of the seed of the land or of the fruit of the tree, is the LORD'S; it is holy to the LORD.

31 'If, therefore, a man wishes to redeem part of his tithe, he shall add to it one-fifth of it.

32 'For every tenth part of herd or flock, whatever passes under the rod, the tenth one shall be holy to the LORD.

33 'He is not to be concerned whether *it is* good or bad, nor shall he exchange it; or if he does exchange it, then both it and its substitute shall become holy. It shall not be redeemed.' "

34 ¶ These are the commandments which the LORD commanded Moses for the sons of Israel at Mount Sinai.

ᵃ Lit *anything devoted*; or *banned*

NUMBERS

Forty Years of Misery
A joyous adventure comes to a tragic end

A S NUMBERS OPENS, THE ISRAELITES are gearing up for a great adventure. Free at last from the chains of slavery, they are headed for the promised land. Yet the book that begins with a bang ends with a whimper. Weeks, months, and then years in a hostile desert have seemed to melt the spirit of adventure. The Israelites act like people who have lost their moorings. In relentless detail, Numbers records a whole sequence of grumblings and rebellions.

> *Now the people became like those who complain of adversity in the hearing of the Lord; and when the Lord heard it, His anger was kindled. 11:1*

Forty-Year Detour

Stomachs complained first, as the Israelites began to long for the spices of Egypt. Soon, the great mob of people simply unraveled. At least ten times they lashed out in despair or rose up in open rebellion. They plotted against their leaders and denounced God. Revolt spread to the priests, to the top military scouts, to Moses' family, and finally to Moses himself.

The original Hebrew title of this book was not "Numbers" but rather "In the desert," and this cryptic phrase expresses a little of the Israelites' futility. Surrounded by hostile nations, they had to march under the broiling sun in a desert plagued by snakes, scorpions, and drought. Even today, visitors to the Sinai Desert marvel that an entire nation wandered that ground for so long.

A march through the desert should have taken about two weeks. Instead, it took almost 40 years. Numbers spans the years of wandering and ends where the trek began: at the very spot (Kadesh) where the Israelites' faith had failed. Of the many thousands who left Egypt, only two adults, Joshua and Caleb, would make it into the promised land.

A Different Kind of History

Most ancient histories sound very different from this book. They tell of heroic exploits by mighty warriors and unblemished leaders. With an almost numbing monotony, Numbers presents a far more realistic picture. It shows the early symptoms, the full progression, and the tragic end of grumbling and unbelief.

The Israelites lost faith not only in themselves, but in their God. Because of that, a whole generation of them lies buried in the peninsula known as Sinai.

References to the "desert wanderings" crop up again and again in the Bible. The period of rebellion left an indelible mark on the Jewish people. Exactly what went wrong? The book of Numbers is given to tell us. The apostle Paul points out that these failures "happened to them as an example, and they were written for our instruction, upon whom the ends of the ages have come. Therefore let him who thinks he stands take heed that he does not fall." (1 Corinthians 10:11–12).

How to Read Numbers

P eople who read straight through Numbers very often come away confused or discouraged. The book begins with a long description of a census and proceeds into lists of laws and rituals. These were the official records of a nation, and each word had great significance for the Israelites. (Imagine how our Yellow Pages or Congressional Record would appear to people 3,000 years from now.)

Yet, unlike Leviticus, Numbers does not consist mainly of these long descriptions. Rather, it focuses on stories, with laws and rituals sprinkled in at various points. The stories are exciting, and some, such as the story of Balaam, are quite remarkable.

The action in Numbers takes place in three different settings: (1) Chapters 1–14 begin in the same place Exodus ended: at the foot of Mount Sinai. (2) Chapters 15–19 cover a period of 37 years, the time of the desert wanderings. Moses' summary in chapter 33 lists 42 stops in the desert, but Numbers details very few of them. (3) Chapters 20–36 concern a whole new generation of Israelites, who were making final preparations before the invasion.

As you read Numbers, it will help to have a major theme in mind, such as grumbling and rebellion. Work through the book, looking at examples of this problem. Major outbreaks occur in chapters 11, 12, 13, 14, 16, 20, and 21–at least ten incidents in all. Notice the cause of each rebellion, and also God's response. Can you see parallels to the Israelites' experience in your own life?

Numbers also offers insight into the leadership of Moses by showing his response to each crisis. One illustration of his prominence: Over 80 times the book says that "the LORD said to Moses." Look for the qualities, both positive and negative, that made him an effective leader.

Other parts of the Bible often refer to Numbers. Some of the historical psalms, such as Psalms 78, 105, and 136, recast these events in poetry.

PEOPLE YOU'LL MEET IN NUMBERS

MIRIAM *(p. 182)*
AARON *(p. 183)*
BALAAM *(p. 195)*

3-TRACK READING PLAN

For an explanation and complete listing of the 3-track reading plan, turn to page 7.

TRACK 1: *Two-Week Courses on the Bible*
See page 7 for information on these courses.

TRACK 2: *An Overview of Numbers in 2 Days*
□ Day 1. Read the Introduction to Numbers and then chapter 11, which shows a typical Israelite response to hardship.
□ Day 2. Read chapter 14, the hinge chapter of Numbers.

Now turn to page 9 for your next Track 2 reading project.

TRACK 3: *All of Numbers in 35 Days*
After you have read through Numbers, turn to pages 10–14 for your next Track 3 reading project.

□1–2	□3	□4	□5	□6	□7	□8	□9
□10	□11	□12	□13	□14	□15	□16	□17
□18	□19	□20	□21	□22	□23	□24	□25
□26	□27	□28	□29	□30	□31	□32	□33
□34	□35	□36					

The Census of Israel's Warriors

1 Then the LORD spoke to Moses in the wilderness of Sinai, in the tent of meeting, on the first of the second month, in the second year after they had come out of the land of Egypt, saying,

2 "Take a ᵃcensus of all the congregation of the sons of Israel, by their families, by their fathers' households, according to the number of names, every male, head by head

3 from twenty years old and upward, whoever *is able to* go out to war in Israel, you and Aaron shall ᵇnumber them by their armies.

4 "With you, moreover, there shall be a man of each tribe, each one head of his father's household.

5 "These then are the names of the men who shall stand with you: of Reuben, Elizur the son of Shedeur;

6 of Simeon, Shelumiel the son of Zurishaddai;

7 of Judah, Nahshon the son of Amminadab;

8 of Issachar, Nethanel the son of Zuar;

9 of Zebulun, Eliab the son of Helon;

10 of the sons of Joseph: of Ephraim, Elishama the son of Ammihud; of Manasseh, Gamaliel the son of Pedahzur;

11 of Benjamin, Abidan the son of Gideoni;

12 of Dan, Ahiezer the son of Ammishaddai;

13 of Asher, Pagiel the son of Ochran;

14 of Gad, Eliasaph the son of Deuel;

15 of Naphtali, Ahira the son of Enan.

16 "These are they who were called of the congregation, the leaders of their fathers' tribes; they were the heads of ᶜdivisions of Israel."

17 ¶ So Moses and Aaron took these men who had been designated by name,

18 and they assembled all the congregation together on the first of the second month. Then they registered by ancestry in their families, by their fathers' households, according to the number of names, from twenty years old and upward, head by head,

19 just as the LORD had commanded Moses. So he numbered them in the wilderness of Sinai.

20 ¶ Now the sons of Reuben, Israel's firstborn, their genealogical registration by their families, by their fathers' households, according to the number of names, head by head, every male from twenty years old and upward, whoever *was able to* go out to war,

21 their numbered men of the tribe of Reuben *were* 46,500.

22 ¶ Of the sons of Simeon, their genealogical registration by their families, by their fathers' households, their numbered men, according to the number of names, head by head, every male from twenty years old and upward, whoever *was able to* go out to war,

23 their numbered men of the tribe of Simeon *were* 59,300.

24 ¶ Of the sons of Gad, their genealogical registration by their families, by their fathers' households, according to the number of names, from twenty years old and upward, whoever *was able to* go out to war,

25 their numbered men of the tribe of Gad *were* 45,650.

26 ¶ Of the sons of Judah, their genealogical registration by their families, by their fathers' households, according to the number of names, from twenty years old and upward, whoever *was able to* go out to war,

27 their numbered men of the tribe of Judah *were* 74,600.

28 ¶ Of the sons of Issachar, their genealogical registration by their families, by their fathers' households, according to the number of names, from twenty years old and upward, whoever *was able to* go out to war,

29 their numbered men of the tribe of Issachar *were* 54,400.

30 ¶ Of the sons of Zebulun, their genealogical registration by their families, by their fathers' households, according to the number of names, from twenty years old and upward, whoever *was able to* go out to war,

31 their numbered men of the tribe of Zebulun *were* 57,400.

32 ¶ Of the sons of Joseph, *namely,* of the sons of Ephraim, their genealogical registration by their families, by their fathers' households, according to the number of names, from twenty years old and upward, whoever *was able to* go out to war,

1:32 Two for One

Although Joseph was only one of the twelve brothers who formed the tribes of Israel, his father Israel (Jacob) had adopted Joseph's two sons, Ephraim and Manasseh, as his own (see Genesis 48:5–6). Thus Joseph got a double share of the family inheritance, and there are really thirteen tribes of Israel.

The tribe of Levi were often treated separately, however, because of their special role in worship. This census, for example, taken primarily to prepare a roster for military purposes, excluded the tribe of Levi. As caretakers of God's tabernacle, Levites were ineligible for the draft.

33 their numbered men of the tribe of Ephraim *were* 40,500.

34 ¶ Of the sons of Manasseh, their genealogical registration by their families, by their fathers' households, according to the number of names,

---

ᵃ Lit *sum*   ᵇ Lit *muster,* and so throughout the ch   ᶜ Lit *thousands*; or *clans* from twenty years old and upward, whoever *was able to* go out to war,

35 their numbered men of the tribe of Manasseh *were* 32,200.

36 ¶ Of the sons of Benjamin, their genealogical registration by their families, by their fathers' households, according to the number of names, from twenty years old and upward, whoever *was able to* go out to war,

37 their numbered men of the tribe of Benjamin *were* 35,400.

38 ¶ Of the sons of Dan, their genealogical registration by their families, by their fathers' households, according to the number of names, from twenty years old and upward, whoever *was able to* go out to war,

39 their numbered men of the tribe of Dan *were* 62,700.

40 ¶ Of the sons of Asher, their genealogical registration by their families, by their fathers' households, according to the number of names, from twenty years old and upward, whoever *was able to* go out to war,

41 their numbered men of the tribe of Asher *were* 41,500.

42 ¶ Of the sons of Naphtali, their genealogical registration by their families, by their fathers' households, according to the number of names, from twenty years old and upward, whoever *was able to* go out to war,

43 their numbered men of the tribe of Naphtali *were* 53,400.

44 ¶ These are the ones who were numbered, whom Moses and Aaron numbered, with the leaders of Israel, twelve men, each of whom was of his father's household.

45 So all the numbered men of the sons of Israel by their fathers' households, from twenty years old and upward, whoever *was able to* go out to war in Israel,

46 even all the numbered men were 603,550.

Levites Exempted

47 ¶ The Levites, however, were not numbered among them by their fathers' tribe.

48 For the LORD had spoken to Moses, saying,

49 "Only the tribe of Levi you shall not number, nor shall you take their census among the sons of Israel.

50 "But you shall appoint the Levites over the ᵃtabernacle of the testimony, and over all its furnishings and over all that belongs to it. They shall carry the tabernacle and all its furnishings, and they shall take care of it; they shall also camp around the tabernacle.

51 "So when the tabernacle is to set out, the Levites shall take it down; and when the tabernacle encamps, the Levites shall set it up. But the ᵇlayman who comes near shall be put to death.

52 "The sons of Israel shall camp, each man by his own camp, and each man by his own standard, according to their armies.

53 "But the Levites shall camp around the tabernacle of the testimony, so that there will be no wrath on the congregation of the sons of Israel. So the Levites shall keep charge of the tabernacle of the testimony."

54 Thus the sons of Israel did; according to all which the LORD had commanded Moses, so they did.

Arrangement of the Camps

2 Now the LORD spoke to Moses and to Aaron, saying,

2 "The sons of Israel shall camp, each by his own standard, with the banners of their fathers' households; they shall camp around the tent of meeting at a distance.

2:2 A Place for Everyone

The Israelites did not wander through the wilderness as an undisciplined mob. On the contrary, each tribe had an assigned place to camp. At the center of their camp was the tent of meeting (the tabernacle)—a visual reminder, each time they pitched their tents, of what should be at the center of their lives.

3 "Now those who camp on the east side toward the sunrise *shall be* of the standard of the camp of Judah, by their armies, and the leader of the sons of Judah: Nahshon the son of Amminadab,

4 and his army, even their numbered men, 74,600.

5 "Those who camp next to him *shall be* the tribe of Issachar, and the leader of the sons of Issachar: Nethanel the son of Zuar,

6 and his army, even their numbered men, 54,400.

7 "*Then comes* the tribe of Zebulun, and the leader of the sons of Zebulun: Eliab the son of Helon,

8 and his army, even his numbered men, 57,400.

9 "The total of the numbered men of the camp of Judah: 186,400, by their armies. They shall set out first.

10 ¶ "On the south side *shall be* the standard of the camp of Reuben by their armies, and the leader of the sons of Reuben: Elizur the son of Shedeur,

11 and his army, even their numbered men, 46,500.

12 "Those who camp next to him *shall be* the tribe of Simeon, and the leader of the sons of Simeon: Shelumiel the son of Zurishaddai,

---

ᵃ Lit *dwelling place,* and so throughout the ch   ᵇ Lit *stranger*

13 and his army, even their numbered men, 59,300.

14 "Then *comes* the tribe of Gad, and the leader of the sons of Gad: Eliasaph the son of Deuel,

15 and his army, even their numbered men, 45,650.

16 "The total of the numbered men of the camp of Reuben: 151,450 by their armies. And they shall set out second.

17 ¶ "Then the tent of meeting shall set out *with* the camp of the Levites in the midst of the camps; just as they camp, so they shall set out, every man in his place by their standards.

18 ¶ "On the west side *shall be* the standard of the camp of Ephraim by their armies, and the leader of the sons of Ephraim *shall be* Elishama the son of Ammihud,

19 and his army, even their numbered men, 40,500.

20 "Next to him *shall be* the tribe of Manasseh, and the leader of the sons of Manasseh: Gamaliel the son of Pedahzur,

21 and his army, even their numbered men, 32,200.

22 "Then *comes* the tribe of Benjamin, and the leader of the sons of Benjamin: Abidan the son of Gideoni,

23 and his army, even their numbered men, 35,400.

24 "The total of the numbered men of the camp of Ephraim: 108,100, by their armies. And they shall set out third.

25 ¶ "On the north side *shall be* the standard of the camp of Dan by their armies, and the leader of the sons of Dan: Ahiezer the son of Ammishaddai,

26 and his army, even their numbered men, 62,700.

27 "Those who camp next to him *shall be* the tribe of Asher, and the leader of the sons of Asher: Pagiel the son of Ochran,

28 and his army, even their numbered men, 41,500.

29 "Then *comes* the tribe of Naphtali, and the leader of the sons of Naphtali: Ahira the son of Enan,

30 and his army, even their numbered men, 53,400.

31 "The total of the numbered men of the camp of Dan *was* 157,600. They shall set out last by their standards."

32 ¶ These are the numbered men of the sons of Israel by their fathers' households; the total of the numbered men of the camps by their armies, 603,550.

33 The Levites, however, were not numbered among the sons of Israel, just as the LORD had commanded Moses.

34 Thus the sons of Israel did; according to all that the LORD commanded Moses, so they camped by their standards, and so they set out, every one by his family according to his father's household.

Levites to Be Priesthood

3 Now these are *the records of* the generations of Aaron and Moses at the time when the LORD spoke with Moses on Mount Sinai.

2:32 How Many Israelites?

Debate has raged among scholars about the vast numbers of Israelites reported in the censuses of Numbers. Could two-and-a-half million people (counting women and children) have left Egypt in one day and then survived for 40 years in a desolate wilderness? Those who defend the large numbers point out that climatic conditions might have been very different in those days when, for example, Egypt was the granary of the world. (Also, the Bible gives many indications of God's miraculous supply of food and water.) Opposing scholars note that the Hebrews had different means of counting, and that the word translated "thousand" could have other meanings, resulting in much smaller figures. Regardless, both positions admit to a very large band of people wandering around a wilderness for a very long time.

2 These then are the names of the sons of Aaron: Nadab the firstborn, and Abihu, Eleazar and Ithamar.

3 These are the names of the sons of Aaron, the anointed priests, whom he ordained to serve as priests.

4 But Nadab and Abihu died before the LORD when they offered strange fire before the LORD in the wilderness of Sinai; and they had no children. So Eleazar and Ithamar served as priests in the lifetime of their father Aaron.

5 ¶ Then the LORD spoke to Moses, saying,

6 "Bring the tribe of Levi near and set them before Aaron the priest, that they may serve him.

7 "They shall perform the duties for him and for the whole congregation before the tent of meeting, to do the service of the tabernacle.

8 "They shall also keep all the furnishings of the tent of meeting, along with the duties of the sons of Israel, to do the service of the tabernacle.

9 "You shall thus give the Levites to Aaron and to his sons; they are wholly given to him from among the sons of Israel.

10 "So you shall appoint Aaron and his sons that they may keep their priesthood, but the layman who comes near shall be put to death."

11 ¶ Again the LORD spoke to Moses, saying,

12 "Now, behold, I have taken the Levites from among the sons of Israel instead of every firstborn, the first issue of the womb among the sons of Israel. So the Levites shall be Mine.

13 "For all the firstborn are Mine; on the day that I struck down all the firstborn in the land of

Egypt, I sanctified to Myself all the firstborn in Israel, from man to beast. They shall be Mine; I am the LORD."

14 ¶ Then the LORD spoke to Moses in the wilderness of Sinai, saying,

15 "Number the sons of Levi by their fathers' households, by their families; every male from a month old and upward you shall number."

16 So Moses numbered them according to the word of the LORD, just as he had been commanded.

17 These then are the sons of Levi by their names: Gershon and Kohath and Merari.

18 These are the names of the sons of Gershon by their families: Libni and Shimei;

19 and the sons of Kohath by their families: Amram and Izhar, Hebron and Uzziel;

20 and the sons of Merari by their families: Mahli and Mushi. These are the families of the Levites according to their fathers' households.

21 ¶ Of Gershon was the family of the Libnites and the family of the Shimeites; these were the families of the Gershonites.

22 Their numbered men, in the numbering of every male from a month old and upward, even their numbered men were 7,500.

23 The families of the Gershonites were to camp behind the tabernacle westward,

24 and the leader of the fathers' households of the Gershonites was Eliasaph the son of Lael.

Duties of the Priests

25 Now the duties of the sons of Gershon in the tent of meeting involved the tabernacle and the tent, its covering, and the screen for the doorway of the tent of meeting,

26 and the hangings of the court, and the screen for the doorway of the court which is around the tabernacle and the altar, and its cords, according to all the service concerning them.

27 ¶ Of Kohath was the family of the Amramites and the family of the Izharites and the family of the Hebronites and the family of the Uzzielites; these were the families of the Kohathites.

28 In the numbering of every male from a month old and upward, there were 8,600, performing the duties of the sanctuary.

29 The families of the sons of Kohath were to camp on the southward side of the tabernacle,

30 and the leader of the fathers' households of the Kohathite families was Elizaphan the son of Uzziel.

31 Now their duties involved the ark, the table, the lampstand, the altars, and the utensils of the sanctuary with which they minister, and the screen, and all the service concerning them;

32 and Eleazar the son of Aaron the priest was the chief of the leaders of Levi, and had the oversight of those who perform the duties of the sanctuary.

33 ¶ Of Merari was the family of the Mahlites

and the family of the Mushites; these were the families of Merari.

34 Their numbered men in the numbering of every male from a month old and upward, were 6,200.

35 The leader of the fathers' households of the families of Merari was Zuriel the son of Abihail. They were to camp on the northward side of the tabernacle.

36 Now the appointed duties of the sons of Merari involved the frames of the tabernacle, its bars, its pillars, its sockets, all its equipment, and the service concerning them,

37 and the pillars around the court with their sockets and their pegs and their cords.

38 ¶ Now those who were to camp before the tabernacle eastward, before the tent of meeting toward the sunrise, are Moses and Aaron and his sons, performing the duties of the sanctuary for the obligation of the sons of Israel; but the layman coming near was to be put to death.

39 All the numbered men of the Levites, whom Moses and Aaron numbered at the command of the LORD by their families, every male from a month old and upward, were 22,000.

Firstborn Redeemed

40 ¶ Then the LORD said to Moses, "Number every firstborn male of the sons of Israel from a month old and upward, and make a list of their names.

41 "You shall take the Levites for Me, I am the LORD, instead of all the firstborn among the sons of Israel, and the cattle of the Levites instead of all the firstborn among the cattle of the sons of Israel."

42 So Moses numbered all the firstborn among the sons of Israel, just as the LORD had commanded him;

43 and all the firstborn males by the number of names from a month old and upward, for their numbered men were 22,273.

44 ¶ Then the LORD spoke to Moses, saying,

45 "Take the Levites instead of all the firstborn among the sons of Israel and the cattle of the

3:45 Designated Firstborn

At the first Passover (Exodus 13:2) God established the firstborn principle, which held that every firstborn male, human or animal, must be dedicated to him. Here, in careful accounting, the Levites are accepted as "designated firstborn" offerings to God. Just as a "designated hitter" in baseball is appointed to bat in place of the pitcher, so here a whole tribe is named to take the place of firstborn members from every family.

Levites. And the Levites shall be Mine; I am the LORD.

46 "For the ransom of the 273 of the firstborn of the sons of Israel who are in excess beyond the Levites,

47 you shall take five shekels apiece, per head; you shall take *them* in terms of the shekel of the sanctuary (the shekel is twenty ᵃgerahs),

48 and give the money, the ransom of those who are in excess among them, to Aaron and to his sons."

49 So Moses took the ransom money from those who were in excess, beyond those ransomed by the Levites;

50 from the firstborn of the sons of Israel he took the money in terms of the shekel of the sanctuary, 1,365.

51 Then Moses gave the ransom money to Aaron and to his sons, at the command of the LORD, just as the LORD had commanded Moses.

Duties of the Kohathites

4 Then the LORD spoke to Moses and to Aaron, saying,

2 "Take a census of the descendants of Kohath from among the sons of Levi, by their families, by their fathers' households,

3 from thirty years and upward, even to fifty years old, all who enter the service to do the work in the tent of meeting.

4 "This is the work of the descendants of Kohath in the tent of meeting, *concerning* the most holy things.

5 ¶ "When the camp sets out, Aaron and his sons shall go in and they shall take down the veil of the screen and cover the ark of the testimony with it;

6 and they shall lay a covering of porpoise skin on it, and shall spread over *it* a cloth of pure blue, and shall insert its poles.

7 "Over the table of the bread of the Presence they shall also spread a cloth of blue and put on it the dishes and the pans and the sacrificial bowls and the jars for the drink offering, and the continual bread shall be on it.

8 "They shall spread over them a cloth of scarlet *material*, and cover the same with a covering of porpoise skin, and they shall insert its poles.

9 "Then they shall take a blue cloth and cover the lampstand for the light, along with its lamps and its snuffers, and its trays and all its oil vessels, by which they serve it;

10 and they shall put it and all its utensils in a covering of porpoise skin, and shall put it on the carrying bars.

11 "Over the golden altar they shall spread a blue cloth and cover it with a covering of porpoise skin, and shall insert its poles;

12 and they shall take all the utensils of service, with which they serve in the sanctuary, and put

them in a blue cloth and cover them with a covering of porpoise skin, and put them on the carrying bars.

13 "Then they shall take away the ashes from the altar, and spread a purple cloth over it.

14 "They shall also put on it all its utensils by which they serve in connection with it: the fire-pans, the forks and shovels and the basins, all the utensils of the altar; and they shall spread a cover of porpoise skin over it and insert its poles.

15 "When Aaron and his sons have finished covering the holy *objects* and all the furnishings of the sanctuary, when the camp is to set out, after that the sons of Kohath shall come to carry *them*, so that they will not touch the holy *objects* and die. These are the things in the tent of meeting which the sons of Kohath are to carry.

4:15 Touch and Die

The precise instructions for moving the holy things reflected the awe and respect that were due God alone. Years later, King David's men flagrantly ignored these instructions and one man, Uzza, died as a result (see "Why Did Uzza Die?" page 465). Earlier in Numbers, two of Aaron's sons had died while trying out their own version of worship, ignoring God's directions (3:4, also Leviticus 10:1–5). In the Bible, these drastic punishments tend to occur as God's people enter a new phase of their history (see Joshua 7; 2 Samuel 6:7; Acts 5:1–11). There is no compromising God's holiness.

16 ¶ "The responsibility of Eleazar the son of Aaron the priest is the oil for the light and the fragrant incense and the continual grain offering and the anointing oil—the responsibility of all the tabernacle and of all that is in it, with the sanctuary and its furnishings."

17 ¶ Then the LORD spoke to Moses and to Aaron, saying,

18 "Do not let the tribe of the families of the Kohathites be cut off from among the Levites.

19 "But do this to them that they may live and not die when they approach the most holy *objects*: Aaron and his sons shall go in and assign each of them to his work and to his load;

20 but they shall not go in to see the holy *objects* even for a moment, or they will die."

Duties of the Gershonites

21 ¶ Then the LORD spoke to Moses, saying,

22 "Take a census of the sons of Gershon also, by their fathers' households, by their families;

23 from thirty years and upward to fifty years old, you shall number them; all who enter to per-

---

ᵃ I.e. A gerah equals approx one-fortieth oz

form the service to do the work in the tent of meeting.

24 "This is the service of the families of the Gershonites, in serving and in carrying:

25 they shall carry the curtains of the tabernacle and the tent of meeting *with* its covering and the covering of porpoise skin that is on top of it, and the screen for the doorway of the tent of meeting,

26 and the hangings of the court, and the screen for the doorway of the gate of the court which is around the tabernacle and the altar, and their cords and all the equipment for their service; and all that is to be done, they shall perform.

27 "All the service of the sons of the Gershonites, in all their loads and in all their work, shall be *performed* at the command of Aaron and his sons; and you shall assign to them as a duty all their loads.

28 "This is the service of the families of the sons of the Gershonites in the tent of meeting, and their duties *shall be* under the direction of Ithamar the son of Aaron the priest.

Duties of the Merarites

29 ¶ *"As for* the sons of Merari, you shall number them by their families, by their fathers' households;

30 from thirty years and upward even to fifty years old, you shall number them, everyone who enters the service to do the work of the tent of meeting.

31 "Now this is the duty of their loads, for all their service in the tent of meeting: the boards of the tabernacle and its bars and its pillars and its sockets,

32 and the pillars around the court and their sockets and their pegs and their cords, with all their equipment and with all their service; and you shall assign *each man* by name the items he is to carry.

33 "This is the service of the families of the sons of Merari, according to all their service in the tent of meeting, under the direction of Ithamar the son of Aaron the priest."

34 ¶ So Moses and Aaron and the leaders of the congregation numbered the sons of the Kohathites by their families and by their fathers' households,

35 from thirty years and upward even to fifty years old, everyone who entered the service for work in the tent of meeting.

36 Their numbered men by their families were 2,750.

37 These are the numbered men of the Kohathite families, everyone who was serving in the tent of meeting, whom Moses and Aaron numbered according to the commandment of the LORD through Moses.

38 ¶ The numbered men of the sons of Gershon by their families and by their fathers' households,

39 from thirty years and upward even to fifty years old, everyone who entered the service for work in the tent of meeting.

40 Their numbered men by their families, by their fathers' households, were 2,630.

41 These are the numbered men of the families of the sons of Gershon, everyone who was serving in the tent of meeting, whom Moses and Aaron numbered according to the commandment of the LORD.

42 ¶ The numbered men of the families of the sons of Merari by their families, by their fathers' households,

43 from thirty years and upward even to fifty years old, everyone who entered the service for work in the tent of meeting.

44 Their numbered men by their families were 3,200.

45 These are the numbered men of the families of the sons of Merari, whom Moses and Aaron numbered according to the commandment of the LORD through Moses.

46 ¶ All the numbered men of the Levites, whom Moses and Aaron and the leaders of Israel numbered, by their families and by their fathers' households,

47 from thirty years and upward even to fifty years old, everyone who could enter to do the work of service and the work of carrying in the tent of meeting.

48 Their numbered men were 8,580.

49 According to the commandment of the LORD through Moses, they were numbered, everyone by his serving or carrying; thus *these were* his numbered men, just as the LORD had commanded Moses.

On Defilement

5 Then the LORD spoke to Moses, saying,

2 "Command the sons of Israel that they send away from the camp every leper and everyone having a discharge and everyone who is unclean because of a *dead* person.

3 "You shall send away both male and female; you shall send them outside the camp so that they will not defile their camp where I dwell in their midst."

4 The sons of Israel did so and sent them outside the camp; just as the LORD had spoken to Moses, thus the sons of Israel did.

5 ¶ Then the LORD spoke to Moses, saying,

6 "Speak to the sons of Israel, 'When a man or woman commits any of the sins of mankind, acting unfaithfully against the LORD, and that person is guilty,

7 then he shall confess his sins which he has committed, and he shall make restitution in full for his wrong and add to it one-fifth of it, and give *it* to him whom he has wronged.

8 'But if the man has no *a*relative to whom restitution may be made for the wrong, the restitution which is made for the wrong *must go* to the LORD for the priest, besides the ram of atonement, by which atonement is made for him.

9 'Also every contribution pertaining to all the holy *gifts* of the sons of Israel, which they offer to the priest, shall be his.

10 'So every man's holy *gifts* shall be his; whatever any man gives to the priest, it becomes his.' "

The Adultery Test

11 ¶ Then the LORD spoke to Moses, saying,

12 "Speak to the sons of Israel and say to them, 'If any man's wife goes astray and is unfaithful to him,

13 and a man has intercourse with her and it is hidden from the eyes of her husband and she is undetected, although she has defiled herself, and there is no witness against her and she has not been caught in the act,

14 if a spirit of jealousy comes over him and he is jealous of his wife when she has defiled herself, or if a spirit of jealousy comes over him and he is jealous of his wife when she has not defiled herself,

15 the man shall then bring his wife to the priest, and shall bring *as* an offering for her one-tenth of an ephah of barley meal; he shall not pour oil on it nor put frankincense on it, for it is a grain offering of jealousy, a grain offering of memorial, a reminder of iniquity.

16 ¶ 'Then the priest shall bring her near and have her stand before the LORD,

5:16 Test for Adultery

The strange test for adultery described here resembles other "trials by ordeal" common then in the Middle East. Presumably, either the emotional reactions of the guilty woman would give her away physiologically (much as a lie detector may), or God would reveal true results through the outcome of the ordeal. The public trial may have helped to clear the reputation of wives who had been falsely accused by their husbands. There is no biblical record of the procedure actually being used, and the trial described is the only one like it in the Bible.

17 and the priest shall take holy water in an earthenware vessel; and he shall take some of the dust that is on the floor of the tabernacle and put *it* into the water.

18 'The priest shall then have the woman stand before the LORD and let *the hair of* the woman's head go loose, and place the grain offering of memorial in her hands, which is the grain offering of

jealousy, and in the hand of the priest is to be the water of bitterness that brings a curse.

19 'The priest shall have her take an oath and shall say to the woman, "If no man has lain with you and if you have not gone astray into uncleanness, *being* under *the authority of* your husband, be immune to this water of bitterness that brings a curse;

20 if you, however, have gone astray, *being* under *the authority of* your husband, and if you have defiled yourself and a man other than your husband has had intercourse with you"

21 (then the priest shall have the woman swear with the oath of the curse, and the priest shall say to the woman), "the LORD make you a curse and an oath among your people by the LORD'S making your thigh waste away and your abdomen swell;

22 and this water that brings a curse shall go into your stomach, and make your abdomen swell and your thigh waste away." And the woman shall say, "Amen. Amen."

23 ¶ 'The priest shall then write these curses on a scroll, and he shall wash them off into the water of bitterness.

24 'Then he shall make the woman drink the water of bitterness that brings a curse, so that the water which brings a curse will go into her and *cause* bitterness.

25 'The priest shall take the grain offering of jealousy from the woman's hand, and he shall wave the grain offering before the LORD and bring it to the altar;

26 and the priest shall take a handful of the grain offering as its memorial offering and offer *it* up in smoke on the altar, and afterward he shall make the woman drink the water.

27 'When he has made her drink the water, then it shall come about, if she has defiled herself and has been unfaithful to her husband, that the water which brings a curse will go into her and *cause* bitterness, and her abdomen will swell and her thigh will waste away, and the woman will become a curse among her people.

28 'But if the woman has not defiled herself and is clean, she will then be free and conceive children.

29 ¶ 'This is the law of jealousy: when a wife, *being* under *the authority of* her husband, goes astray and defiles herself,

30 or when a spirit of jealousy comes over a man and he is jealous of his wife, he shall then make the woman stand before the LORD, and the priest shall apply all this law to her.

31 'Moreover, the man will be free from guilt, but that woman shall bear her guilt.' "

Law of the Nazirites

6 Again the LORD spoke to Moses, saying,

2 "Speak to the sons of Israel and say to them, 'When a man or woman makes a special

---

a Lit *redeemer*

vow, the vow of a ^{a}Nazirite, to dedicate himself to the Lord,

3 he shall abstain from wine and strong drink; he shall drink no vinegar, whether made from wine or strong drink, nor shall he drink any grape juice nor eat fresh or dried grapes.

4 'All the days of his ^{b}separation he shall not eat anything that is produced by the grape vine, from *the* seeds even to *the* skin.

5 ¶ 'All the days of his vow of separation no razor shall pass over his head. He shall be holy until the days are fulfilled for which he separated himself to the Lord; he shall let the locks of hair on his head grow long.

6 ¶ 'All the days of his separation to the Lord he shall not go near to a dead person.

6:6 Types of Uncleanness

In its emphasis on purity, Numbers lists three types of unclean persons: victims of certain diseases, people with a discharge of any kind (including sexual ones), and those in contact with dead bodies. Besides offering obvious health benefits, these rules served to draw a sharp contrast between the Israelites and those who practiced other religions: Egyptians who virtually worshiped the dead, and Phoenicians and others who made sex an important part of religious rites.

An unclean person went into a period of quarantine (5:1–4). When Miriam got leprosy, she was kept away from camp for seven days (12:15). Soldiers, too, went through the same cleansing ritual if they had killed anyone or touched anyone who had died (31:19).

7 'He shall not make himself unclean for his father or for his mother, for his brother or for his sister, when they die, because his separation to God is on his head.

8 'All the days of his separation he is holy to the Lord.

9 ¶ 'But if a man dies very suddenly beside him and he defiles his dedicated head *of hair,* then he shall shave his head on the day when he becomes clean; he shall shave it on the seventh day.

10 'Then on the eighth day he shall bring two turtledoves or two young pigeons to the priest, to the doorway of the tent of meeting.

11 'The priest shall offer one for a sin offering and *the* other for a burnt offering, and make atonement for him concerning his sin because of the *dead* person. And that same day he shall consecrate his head,

12 and shall dedicate to the Lord his days as a Nazirite, and shall bring a male lamb a year old for a guilt offering; but the former days will be void because his separation was defiled.

13 ¶ 'Now this is the law of the Nazirite when the days of his separation are fulfilled, he shall bring the offering to the doorway of the tent of meeting.

14 'He shall present his offering to the Lord: one male lamb a year old without defect for a burnt offering and one ewe-lamb a year old without defect for a sin offering and one ram without defect for a peace offering,

15 and a basket of unleavened cakes of fine flour mixed with oil and unleavened wafers spread with oil, along with their grain offering and their drink offering.

16 'Then the priest shall present *them* before the Lord and shall offer his sin offering and his burnt offering.

17 'He shall also offer the ram for a sacrifice of peace offerings to the Lord, together with the basket of unleavened cakes; the priest shall likewise offer its grain offering and its drink offering.

18 'The Nazirite shall then shave his dedicated head *of hair* at the doorway of the tent of meeting, and take the dedicated hair of his head and put *it* on the fire which is under the sacrifice of peace offerings.

6:18 Well-known Nazirites

Samson and John the Baptist are two of the most famous Nazirites in the Bible. The apostle Paul took a Nazirite vow in Jerusalem (Acts 21:21–29) to demonstrate his conformity to Jewish law.

19 'The priest shall take the ram's shoulder *when it has been* boiled, and one unleavened cake out of the basket and one unleavened wafer, and shall put *them* on the hands of the Nazirite after he has shaved his dedicated *hair.*

20 'Then the priest shall wave them for a wave offering before the Lord. It is holy for the priest, together with the breast offered by waving and the thigh offered by lifting up; and afterward the Nazirite may drink wine.'

21 ¶ 'This is the law of the Nazirite who vows his offering to the Lord according to his separation, in addition to what *else* he can afford; according to his vow which he takes, so he shall do according to the law of his separation."

Aaron's Benediction

22 ¶ Then the Lord spoke to Moses, saying,

23 "Speak to Aaron and to his sons, saying, 'Thus you shall bless the sons of Israel. You shall say to them:

24 ¶ The Lord bless you, and keep you;

25 ¶ The Lord make His face shine on you, And be gracious to you;

---

^{a} I.e. one separated ^{b} Or *living as a Nazirite,* and so through v 21

26 ¶ The LORD lift up His countenance on you,
  And give you peace.'
27 "So they shall invoke My name on the sons of Israel, and I *then* will bless them."

Offerings of the Leaders

7 Now on the day that Moses had finished setting up the tabernacle, he anointed it and consecrated it with all its furnishings and the altar and all its utensils; he anointed them and consecrated them also.

2 Then the leaders of Israel, the heads of their fathers' households, made an offering (they were the leaders of the tribes; they were the ones who were over the numbered men).

3 When they brought their offering before the LORD, six covered carts and twelve oxen, a cart for *every* two of the leaders and an ox for each one, then they presented them before the tabernacle.

4 Then the LORD spoke to Moses, saying,

5 "Accept *these things* from them, that they may be used in the service of the tent of meeting, and you shall give them to the Levites, *to* each man according to his service."

6 So Moses took the carts and the oxen and gave them to the Levites.

7 Two carts and four oxen he gave to the sons of Gershon, according to their service,

8 and four carts and eight oxen he gave to the sons of Merari, according to their service, under the direction of Ithamar the son of Aaron the priest.

9 But he did not give *any* to the sons of Kohath because theirs *was* the service of the holy *objects, which* they carried on the shoulder.

10 ¶ The leaders offered the dedication *offering* for the altar when it was anointed, so the leaders offered their offering before the altar.

11 Then the LORD said to Moses, "Let them present their offering, one leader each day, for the dedication of the altar."

12 ¶ Now the one who presented his offering on the first day was Nahshon the son of Amminadab, of the tribe of Judah;

13 and his offering *was* one silver [a]dish whose weight *was* one hundred and thirty *shekels,* one silver bowl of seventy shekels, according to [b]the shekel of the sanctuary, both of them full of fine flour mixed with oil for a grain offering;

14 one gold pan of ten *shekels,* full of incense;

15 one bull, one ram, one male lamb one year old, for a burnt offering;

16 one male goat for a sin offering;

17 and for the sacrifice of peace offerings, two oxen, five rams, five male goats, five male lambs one year old. This *was* the offering of Nahshon the son of Amminadab.

18 ¶ On the second day Nethanel the son of Zuar, leader of Issachar, presented *an offering;*

19 he presented as his offering one silver dish whose weight *was* one hundred and thirty *shekels,* one silver bowl of seventy shekels, according to the shekel of the sanctuary, both of them full of fine flour mixed with oil for a grain offering;

20 one gold pan of ten *shekels,* full of incense;

21 one bull, one ram, one male lamb one year old, for a burnt offering;

22 one male goat for a sin offering;

23 and for the sacrifice of peace offerings, two oxen, five rams, five male goats, five male lambs one year old. This *was* the offering of Nethanel the son of Zuar.

24 ¶ On the third day *it was* Eliab the son of Helon, leader of the sons of Zebulun;

25 his offering *was* one silver dish whose weight *was* one hundred and thirty *shekels,* one silver bowl of seventy shekels, according to the shekel of the sanctuary, both of them full of fine flour mixed with oil for a grain offering;

26 one gold pan of ten *shekels,* full of incense;

27 one young bull, one ram, one male lamb one year old, for a burnt offering;

28 one male goat for a sin offering;

29 and for the sacrifice of peace offerings, two oxen, five rams, five male goats, five male lambs one year old. This *was* the offering of Eliab the son of Helon.

30 ¶ On the fourth day *it was* Elizur the son of Shedeur, leader of the sons of Reuben;

31 his offering *was* one silver dish whose weight *was* one hundred and thirty *shekels,* one silver bowl of seventy shekels, according to the shekel of the sanctuary, both of them full of fine flour mixed with oil for a grain offering;

32 one gold pan of ten *shekels,* full of incense;

33 one bull, one ram, one male lamb one year old, for a burnt offering;

34 one male goat for a sin offering;

35 and for the sacrifice of peace offerings, two oxen, five rams, five male goats, five male lambs one year old. This *was* the offering of Elizur the son of Shedeur.

36 ¶ On the fifth day *it was* Shelumiel the son of Zurishaddai, leader of the children of Simeon;

37 his offering *was* one silver dish whose weight *was* one hundred and thirty *shekels,* one silver bowl of seventy shekels, according to the shekel of the sanctuary, both of them full of fine flour mixed with oil for a grain offering;

38 one gold pan of ten *shekels,* full of incense;

39 one bull, one ram, one male lamb one year old, for a burnt offering;

40 one male goat for a sin offering;

41 and for the sacrifice of peace offerings, two oxen, five rams, five male goats, five male lambs one year old. This *was* the offering of Shelumiel the son of Zurishaddai.

42 ¶ On the sixth day *it was* Eliasaph the son of Deuel, leader of the sons of Gad;

---

[a] Or *platter,* and so through v 85   [b] I.e. Approx one-half oz, and so through v 86

43 his offering *was* one silver dish whose weight *was* one hundred and thirty *shekels,* one silver bowl of seventy shekels, according to the shekel of the sanctuary, both of them full of fine flour mixed with oil for a grain offering;

44 one gold pan of ten *shekels,* full of incense;

45 one bull, one ram, one male lamb one year old, for a burnt offering;

46 one male goat for a sin offering;

47 and for the sacrifice of peace offerings, two oxen, five rams, five male goats, five male lambs one year old. This *was* the offering of Eliasaph the son of Deuel.

48 ¶ On the seventh day *it was* Elishama the son of Ammihud, leader of the sons of Ephraim;

49 his offering *was* one silver dish whose weight *was* one hundred and thirty *shekels,* one silver bowl of seventy shekels, according to the shekel of the sanctuary, both of them full of fine flour mixed with oil for a grain offering;

50 one gold pan of ten *shekels,* full of incense;

51 one bull, one ram, one male lamb one year old, for a burnt offering;

52 one male goat for a sin offering;

53 and for the sacrifice of peace offerings, two oxen, five rams, five male goats, five male lambs one year old. This *was* the offering of Elishama the son of Ammihud.

54 ¶ On the eighth day *it was* Gamaliel the son of Pedahzur, leader of the sons of Manasseh;

55 his offering *was* one silver dish whose weight *was* one hundred and thirty *shekels,* one silver bowl of seventy shekels, according to the shekel of the sanctuary, both of them full of fine flour mixed with oil for a grain offering;

7:55 Gold and Silver Dishes

The plates and bowls used in Israelite worship have a history of their own. Some of these originals, perhaps all, were lost during the dark years of the judges. David produced more, which his son Solomon installed in the temple (2 Chronicles 5:1); all were taken as captured goods when the Babylonians destroyed Jerusalem (2 Kings 25:15). At last they were returned to Jerusalem when the Persian king Cyrus let the Jews return (Ezra 1:9–10).

56 one gold pan of ten *shekels,* full of incense;

57 one bull, one ram, one male lamb one year old, for a burnt offering;

58 one male goat for a sin offering;

59 and for the sacrifice of peace offerings, two oxen, five rams, five male goats, five male lambs one year old. This *was* the offering of Gamaliel the son of Pedahzur.

60 ¶ On the ninth day *it was* Abidan the son of Gideoni, leader of the sons of Benjamin;

61 his offering *was* one silver dish whose weight *was* one hundred and thirty *shekels,* one silver bowl of seventy shekels, according to the shekel of the sanctuary, both of them full of fine flour mixed with oil for a grain offering;

62 one gold pan of ten *shekels,* full of incense;

63 one bull, one ram, one male lamb one year old, for a burnt offering;

64 one male goat for a sin offering;

65 and for the sacrifice of peace offerings, two oxen, five rams, five male goats, five male lambs one year old. This *was* the offering of Abidan the son of Gideoni.

66 ¶ On the tenth day *it was* Ahiezer the son of Ammishaddai, leader of the sons of Dan;

67 his offering *was* one silver dish whose weight *was* one hundred and thirty *shekels,* one silver bowl of seventy shekels, according to the shekel of the sanctuary, both of them full of fine flour mixed with oil for a grain offering;

68 one gold pan of ten *shekels,* full of incense;

69 one bull, one ram, one male lamb one year old, for a burnt offering;

70 one male goat for a sin offering;

71 and for the sacrifice of peace offerings, two oxen, five rams, five male goats, five male lambs one year old. This *was* the offering of Ahiezer the son of Ammishaddai.

72 ¶ On the eleventh day *it was* Pagiel the son of Ochran, leader of the sons of Asher;

73 his offering *was* one silver dish whose weight *was* one hundred and thirty *shekels,* one silver bowl of seventy shekels, according to the shekel of the sanctuary, both of them full of fine flour mixed with oil for a grain offering;

74 one gold pan of ten *shekels,* full of incense;

75 one bull, one ram, one male lamb one year old, for a burnt offering;

76 one male goat for a sin offering;

77 and for the sacrifice of peace offerings, two oxen, five rams, five male goats, five male lambs one year old. This *was* the offering of Pagiel the son of Ochran.

78 ¶ On the twelfth day *it was* Ahira the son of Enan, leader of the sons of Naphtali;

79 his offering *was* one silver dish whose weight *was* one hundred and thirty *shekels,* one silver bowl of seventy shekels, according to the shekel of the sanctuary, both of them full of fine flour mixed with oil for a grain offering;

80 one gold pan of ten *shekels,* full of incense;

81 one bull, one ram, one male lamb one year old, for a burnt offering;

82 one male goat for a sin offering;

83 and for the sacrifice of peace offerings, two oxen, five rams, five male goats, five male lambs one year old. This *was* the offering of Ahira the son of Enan.

84 ¶ This *was* the dedication *offering* for the altar from the leaders of Israel when it was anoint-

ed: twelve silver dishes, twelve silver bowls, twelve gold pans,

85 each silver dish *weighing* one hundred and thirty *shekels* and each bowl seventy; all the silver of the utensils *was* 2,400 *shekels*, according to the shekel of the sanctuary;

86 the twelve gold pans, full of incense, *weighing* ten *shekels* apiece, according to the *shekel* of the sanctuary, all the gold of the pans 120 *shekels;*

87 all the oxen for the burnt offering twelve bulls, *all* the rams twelve, the male lambs one year old with their grain offering twelve, and the male goats for a sin offering twelve;

88 and all the oxen for the sacrifice of peace offerings 24 bulls, *all* the rams 60, the male goats 60, the male lambs one year old 60. This *was* the dedication *offering* for the altar after it was anointed.

89 ¶ Now when Moses went into the tent of meeting to speak with Him, he heard the voice speaking to him from above the mercy seat that was on the ark of the testimony, from between the two cherubim, so He spoke to him.

The Seven Lamps

8 Then the LORD spoke to Moses, saying, 2 "Speak to Aaron and say to him, 'When

8:1 The Lord said to Moses . . .

Numbers emphasizes time and again—over 150 times—that God spoke directly to Moses, and through him to the people of Israel. When Moses' leadership was challenged, God insisted that his communication with Moses was unique (12:6–8).

you mount the lamps, the seven lamps will give light in the front of the lampstand.' "

3 Aaron therefore did so; he mounted its lamps at the front of the lampstand, just as the LORD had commanded Moses.

4 Now this was the workmanship of the lampstand, hammered work of gold; from its base to its flowers it was hammered work; according to the

National Reminders
Built-in object lessons for the Israelites

ALTHOUGH PARTS OF NUMBERS MAY seem strange to a modern reader, it clearly expresses two of the Israelites' chief values: purity and holiness. They had to become pure before they could approach God. And they were called to demonstrate God's holiness before other nations. The need for purity and holiness was reflected in what the Israelites ate and wore, and how they acted each day.

"Aaron then shall present the Levites before the LORD as a wave offering from the sons of Israel, that they may qualify to perform the service of the LORD."
8:11

Visual Reminders

God set aside certain groups of people as a visual reminder of purity and holiness. The Levites, who somewhat parallel the full-time clergy of our day, took care of formal religious duties (chapters 3, 4, 8). One of their clans packed up the holy objects for moving, while other clans carried the tabernacle curtains and covers and structural parts.

Numbers describes a second group: the Nazirites (chapter 6). These ordinary laypeople dedicated themselves to an extra regimen of purity. They drank no wine and let their hair grow long. Much as Amish people do today, they stood out from the majority in their dress and style.

Holiness was not left to special groups, though. Every Israelite participated in the daily offerings, sacrifices, and occasional festivals. When a family brought a whole bull and saw it skinned, butchered, and then burned on the altar, they were forced to reflect. Sin was serious, and a great gulf was fixed between them and God. In some way, either through story, ritual, or visual symbol, Numbers expresses that separateness on almost every page. In approaching God, the Israelites had to use great care.

Bridging the Gulf

The style of life described in this book differs from our own era of casual dress, informal worship, and talk of "friendship" with God. Later, the New Testament would spell out a God who is our Father, who can be approached at any time, who is interested in the personal details of our individual lives. But Numbers serves as an important background to that kind of relationship. It shows graphically just how great was the gulf between people and God, and helps us fully appreciate all that Jesus Christ did in providing a way across that gulf.

Life Questions: Words like *holiness* and *purity* are not heard in many churches today. Do you think we take God for granted and approach him too casually?

pattern which the LORD had showed Moses, so he made the lampstand.

Cleansing the Levites

5 ¶ Again the LORD spoke to Moses, saying,

6 "Take the Levites from among the sons of Israel and cleanse them.

7 "Thus you shall do to them, for their cleansing: *sprinkle* purifying water on them, and let them use a razor over their whole body and wash their clothes, and they will be clean.

8 "Then let them take a bull with its grain offering, fine flour mixed with oil; and a second bull you shall take for a sin offering.

9 "So you shall present the Levites before the tent of meeting. You shall also assemble the whole congregation of the sons of Israel,

10 and present the Levites before the LORD; and the sons of Israel shall lay their hands on the Levites.

11 "Aaron then shall present the Levites before the LORD as a wave offering from the sons of Israel, that they may qualify to perform the service of the LORD.

12 "Now the Levites shall lay their hands on the heads of the bulls; then offer the one for a sin offering and the other for a burnt offering to the LORD, to make atonement for the Levites.

13 "You shall have the Levites stand before Aaron and before his sons so as to present them as a wave offering to the LORD.

14 ¶ "Thus you shall separate the Levites from among the sons of Israel, and the Levites shall be Mine.

15 "Then after that the Levites may go in to serve the tent of meeting. But you shall cleanse them and present them as a wave offering;

16 for they are wholly given to Me from among the sons of Israel. I have taken them for Myself instead of every first issue of the womb, the firstborn of all the sons of Israel.

17 "For every firstborn among the sons of Israel is Mine, among the men and among the animals; on the day that I struck down all the firstborn in the land of Egypt I sanctified them for Myself.

18 "But I have taken the Levites instead of every firstborn among the sons of Israel.

19 "I have given the Levites as a gift to Aaron and to his sons from among the sons of Israel, to perform the service of the sons of Israel at the tent of meeting and to make atonement on behalf of the sons of Israel, so that there will be no plague among the sons of Israel by their coming near to the sanctuary."

20 ¶ Thus did Moses and Aaron and all the congregation of the sons of Israel to the Levites; according to all that the LORD had commanded Moses concerning the Levites, so the sons of Israel did to them.

21 The Levites, too, purified themselves from sin and washed their clothes; and Aaron presented them as a wave offering before the LORD. Aaron also made atonement for them to cleanse them.

22 Then after that the Levites went in to perform their service in the tent of meeting before Aaron and before his sons; just as the LORD had commanded Moses concerning the Levites, so they did to them.

Retirement

23 ¶ Now the LORD spoke to Moses, saying,

24 "This is what *applies* to the Levites: from twenty-five years old and upward they shall enter to perform service in the work of the tent of meeting.

25 "But at the age of fifty years they shall retire from service in the work and not work any more.

26 "They may, however, assist their brothers in the tent of meeting, to keep an obligation, but they *themselves* shall do no work. Thus you shall deal with the Levites concerning their obligations."

The Passover

9 Thus the LORD spoke to Moses in the wilderness of Sinai, in the first month of the second year after they had come out of the land of Egypt, saying,

2 "Now, let the sons of Israel observe the Passover at its appointed time.

3 "On the fourteenth day of this month, at twilight, you shall observe it at its appointed time; you shall observe it according to all its statutes and according to all its ordinances."

4 So Moses told the sons of Israel to observe the Passover.

5 They observed the Passover in the first *month,* on the fourteenth day of the month, at twilight, in the wilderness of Sinai; according to all that the LORD had commanded Moses, so the sons of Israel did.

6 But there were *some* men who were unclean because of *the* dead person, so that they could not observe Passover on that day; so they came before Moses and Aaron on that day.

7 Those men said to him, "*Though* we are unclean because of *the* dead person, why are we restrained from presenting the offering of the LORD at its appointed time among the sons of Israel?"

8 Moses therefore said to them, "Wait, and I will listen to what the LORD will command concerning you."

9 ¶ Then the LORD spoke to Moses, saying,

10 "Speak to the sons of Israel, saying, 'If any one of you or of your generations becomes unclean because of a *dead* person, or is on a distant journey, he may, however, observe the Passover to the LORD.

11 'In the second month on the fourteenth day at twilight, they shall observe it; they shall eat it with unleavened bread and bitter herbs.

12 'They shall leave none of it until morning,

nor break a bone of it; according to all the statute of the Passover they shall observe it.

13 'But the man who is clean and is not on a journey, and yet neglects to observe the Passover, that person shall then be cut off from his people, for he did not present the offering of the LORD at its appointed time. That man will bear his sin.

14 'If an alien sojourns among you and observes the Passover to the LORD, according to the statute of the Passover and according to its ordinance, so he shall do; you shall have one statute, both for the alien and for the native of the land.'"

The Cloud on the Tabernacle

15 ¶ Now on the day that the tabernacle was erected the cloud covered the tabernacle, the tent of the testimony, and in the evening it was like the appearance of fire over the tabernacle, until morning.

16 So it was continuously; the cloud would cover it *by day,* and the appearance of fire by night.

17 Whenever the cloud was lifted from over the tent, afterward the sons of Israel would then set out; and in the place where the cloud settled down, there the sons of Israel would camp.

18 At the command of the LORD the sons of Israel would set out, and at the command of the LORD they would camp; as long as the cloud settled over the tabernacle, they remained camped.

19 Even when the cloud lingered over the tabernacle for many days, the sons of Israel would keep the LORD's charge and not set out.

20 If sometimes the cloud remained a few days over the tabernacle, according to the command of the LORD they remained camped. Then according to the command of the LORD they set out.

21 If sometimes the cloud remained from evening until morning, when the cloud was lifted in the morning, they would move out; or *if it remained* in the daytime and at night, whenever the cloud was lifted, they would set out.

22 Whether it was two days or a month or a year that the cloud lingered over the tabernacle, staying above it, the sons of Israel remained camped and did not set out; but when it was lifted, they did set out.

23 At the command of the LORD they camped, and at the command of the LORD they set out; they

kept the LORD's charge, according to the command of the LORD through Moses.

The Silver Trumpets

10 The LORD spoke further to Moses, saying, 2 "Make yourself two trumpets of silver, of hammered work you shall make them; and you shall use them for summoning the congregation and for having the camps set out.

3 "When both are blown, all the congregation shall gather themselves to you at the doorway of the tent of meeting.

4 "Yet if *only* one is blown, then the leaders, the heads of the divisions of Israel, shall assemble before you.

5 "But when you blow an alarm, the camps that are pitched on the east side shall set out.

6 "When you blow an alarm the second time, the camps that are pitched on the south side shall set out; an alarm is to be blown for them to set out.

7 "When convening the assembly, however, you shall blow without sounding an alarm.

8 "The priestly sons of Aaron, moreover, shall blow the trumpets; and this shall be for you a perpetual statute throughout your generations.

9 "When you go to war in your land against the adversary who attacks you, then you shall sound an alarm with the trumpets, that you may be remembered before the LORD your God, and be saved from your enemies.

10 "Also in the day of your gladness and in your appointed feasts, and on the first *days* of your months, you shall blow the trumpets over your burnt offerings, and over the sacrifices of your peace offerings; and they shall be as a reminder of you before your God. I am the LORD your God."

The Tribes Leave Sinai

11 ¶ Now in the second year, in the second month, on the twentieth of the month, the cloud was lifted from over the tabernacle of the testimony;

12 and the sons of Israel set out on their journeys from the wilderness of Sinai. Then the cloud settled down in the wilderness of Paran.

13 So they moved out for the first time according to the commandment of the LORD through Moses.

14 The standard of the camp of the sons of Judah, according to their armies, set out first, with Nahshon the son of Amminadab, over its army,

15 and Nethanel the son of Zuar, over the tribal army of the sons of Issachar;

16 and Eliab the son of Helon over the tribal army of the sons of Zebulun.

17 ¶ Then the tabernacle was taken down; and the sons of Gershon and the sons of Merari, who were carrying the tabernacle, set out.

18 Next the standard of the camp of Reuben,

9:22 Unmistakable Guidance

This passage describes a remarkable fact of the desert experience: the Israelites knew exactly whether and how far God wanted them to move each day. Although they disobeyed God in almost every other way, they usually followed his specific guidance on location.

according to their armies, set out with Elizur the son of Shedeur, over its army,

19 and Shelumiel the son of Zurishaddai over the tribal army of the sons of Simeon,

20 and Eliasaph the son of Deuel was over the tribal army of the sons of Gad.

21 ¶ Then the Kohathites set out, carrying the holy *objects;* and the tabernacle was set up before their arrival.

22 Next the standard of the camp of the sons of Ephraim, according to their armies, was set out, with Elishama the son of Ammihud over its army,

23 and Gamaliel the son of Pedahzur over the tribal army of the sons of Manasseh;

24 and Abidan the son of Gideoni over the tribal army of the sons of Benjamin.

25 ¶ Then the standard of the camp of the sons of Dan, according to their armies, *which formed* the rear guard for all the camps, set out, with Ahiezer the son of Ammishaddai over its army,

26 and Pagiel the son of Ochran over the tribal army of the sons of Asher;

27 and Ahira the son of Enan over the tribal army of the sons of Naphtali.

28 This was the order of march of the sons of Israel by their armies as they set out.

29 ¶ Then Moses said to Hobab the son of Reuel the Midianite, Moses' father-in-law, "We are setting out to the place of which the LORD said, 'I will give it to you'; come with us and we will do you good, for the LORD has promised good concerning Israel."

30 But he said to him, "I will not come, but rather will go to my *own* land and relatives."

31 Then he said, "Please do not leave us, inasmuch as you know where we should camp in the wilderness, and you will be as eyes for us.

32 "So it will be, if you go with us, that whatever good the LORD does for us, we will do for you."

33 ¶ Thus they set out from the mount of the LORD three days' journey, with the ark of the covenant of the LORD journeying in front of them for the three days, to seek out a resting place for them.

34 The cloud of the LORD was over them by day when they set out from the camp.

35 ¶ Then it came about when the ark set out that Moses said,

"Rise up, O LORD!
And let Your enemies be scattered,
And let those who hate You flee
    [a]before You."

36 When it came to rest, he said,
"Return, O LORD,
To the myriad thousands of Israel."

The People Complain

11 Now the people became like those who complain of adversity in the hearing of the LORD; and when the LORD heard *it,* His anger was kindled, and the fire of the LORD burned among them

and consumed *some* of the outskirts of the camp.

2 The people therefore cried out to Moses, and Moses prayed to the LORD and the fire died out.

10:36 Famous Prayers

Moses' prayer is still repeated in Jewish services when the scroll of the law is removed from its container. Another prayer from Numbers, the blessing of 6:24–26, is quoted both in Jewish and Christian services. In ancient thought, a person's name stood for his character, including all his virtues and powers, and the benediction in 6:27 showed God "putting his name on" the Israelites.

3 So the name of that place was called [b]Taberah, because the fire of the LORD burned among them.

4 ¶ The rabble who were among them had greedy desires; and also the sons of Israel wept again and said, "Who will give us meat to eat?

5 "We remember the fish which we used to eat free in Egypt, the cucumbers and the melons and the leeks and the onions and the garlic,

6 but now our [c]appetite is gone. There is nothing at all to look at except this manna."

7 ¶ Now the manna was like coriander seed, and its appearance like that of bdellium.

8 The people would go about and gather *it* and grind *it* between two millstones or beat *it* in the mortar, and boil *it* in the pot and make cakes with it; and its taste was as the taste of cakes baked with oil.

9 When the dew fell on the camp at night, the manna would fall with it.

The Complaint of Moses

10 ¶ Now Moses heard the people weeping throughout their families, each man at the doorway of his tent; and the anger of the LORD was kindled greatly, and Moses was displeased.

11 So Moses said to the LORD, "Why have You [d]been so hard on Your servant? And why have I not found favor in Your sight, that You have laid the burden of all this people on me?

12 "Was it I who conceived all this people? Was it I who brought them forth, that You should say to me, 'Carry them in your bosom as a nurse carries a nursing infant, to the land which You swore to their fathers'?

13 "Where am I to get meat to give to all this people? For they weep before me, saying, 'Give us meat that we may eat!'

14 "I alone am not able to carry all this people, because it is too burdensome for me.

15 "So if You are going to deal thus with me,

---

[a] Or *from Your presence*   [b] I.e. *burning*   [c] Lit *soul is dried up*   [d] Lit *dealt ill with*

please kill me at once, if I have found favor in Your sight, and do not let me see my wretchedness."

Seventy Elders to Assist

16 ¶ The LORD therefore said to Moses, "Gather for Me seventy men from the elders of Israel, whom you know to be the elders of the people and their officers and bring them to the tent of meeting, and let them take their stand there with you. 17 "Then I will come down and speak with you there, and I will take of the Spirit who is upon you, and will put *Him* upon them; and they shall bear the burden of the people with you, so that you will not bear *it* all alone.

18 "Say to the people, 'Consecrate yourselves for tomorrow, and you shall eat meat; for you have wept in the ears of the LORD, saying, "Oh that someone would give us meat to eat! For we were well-off in Egypt." Therefore the LORD will give you meat and you shall eat.

19 'You shall eat, not one day, nor two days, nor five days, nor ten days, nor twenty days, 20 but a whole month, until it comes out of your nostrils and becomes loathsome to you; because you have rejected the LORD who is among you and have wept before Him, saying, "Why did we ever leave Egypt?" ' "

21 But Moses said, "The people, among whom I am, are 600,000 on foot; yet You have said, 'I will give them meat, so that they may eat for a whole month.'

22 "Should flocks and herds be slaughtered for them, to be sufficient for them? Or should all the fish of the sea be gathered together for them, to be sufficient for them?"

23 The LORD said to Moses, "Is the LORD's power limited? Now you shall see whether My word will come true for you or not."

24 ¶ So Moses went out and told the people the words of the LORD. Also, he gathered seventy men of the elders of the people, and stationed them around the tent.

25 Then the LORD came down in the cloud and spoke to him; and He took of the Spirit who was upon him and placed *Him* upon the seventy elders. And when the Spirit rested upon them, they prophesied. But they did not do *it* again.

26 ¶ But two men had remained in the camp; the name of one was Eldad and the name of the other Medad. And the Spirit rested upon them (now they were among those who had been registered, but had not gone out to the tent), and they prophesied in the camp.

27 So a young man ran and told Moses and said, "Eldad and Medad are prophesying in the camp."

28 Then Joshua the son of Nun, the attendant of Moses from his youth, said, "Moses, my lord, restrain them."

29 But Moses said to him, "Are you jealous for my sake? Would that all the LORD's people were prophets, that the LORD would put His Spirit upon them!"

30 Then Moses returned to the camp, *both* he and the elders of Israel.

11:29 Burdens of Leadership

In this striking conversation with God, Moses confessed the terrible burden involved in leading a whining, complaining band of "rabble." Although his patience neared the breaking point, he still showed mercy toward rivals. His response to other prophets here resembles Jesus' attitude toward other workers (Mark 9:38–41), as well as Paul's (Philippians 1:18).

The Quail and the Plague

31 ¶ Now there went forth a wind from the LORD and it brought quail from the sea, and let *them* fall beside the camp, about a day's journey on this side and a day's journey on the other side, all around the camp and about two cubits *deep* on the surface of the ground.

32 The people spent all day and all night and all the next day, and gathered the quail (he who gathered least gathered ten homers) and they spread *them* out for themselves all around the camp.

33 While the meat was still between their teeth, before it was chewed, the anger of the LORD was kindled against the people, and the LORD struck the people with a very severe plague.

34 So the name of that place was called ᵃKibroth-hattaavah, because there they buried the people who had been greedy.

35 From Kibroth-hattaavah the people set out for Hazeroth, and they remained at Hazeroth.

The Murmuring of Miriam and Aaron

12 Then Miriam and Aaron spoke against Moses because of the Cushite woman whom he had married (for he had married a Cushite woman);

2 and they said, "Has the LORD indeed spoken only through Moses? Has He not spoken through us as well?" And the LORD heard it.

3 (Now the man Moses was very humble, more than any man who was on the face of the earth.)

4 Suddenly the LORD said to Moses and Aaron and to Miriam, "You three come out to the tent of meeting." So the three of them came out.

5 Then the LORD came down in a pillar of cloud and stood at the doorway of the tent, and

---

ᵃ I.e. the graves of greediness

He called Aaron and Miriam. When they had both come forward,

6 He said,
"Hear now My words:
If there is a prophet among you,
I, the LORD, shall make Myself known to
him in a vision.
I shall speak with him in a dream.

12:2 Family Jealousy

Miriam, Moses' older sister, had helped save his life when he was a baby (Exodus 2:7). But she and her brother Aaron felt some sibling rivalry for their kid brother. Irked by his foreign wife, they began undercutting his leadership by asking whether he had a monopoly on God's will.

Moses apparently did not defend himself, but God came to his defense with scathing words that made clear their special relationship. Hebrews 3:1–6 refers to God's homage to Moses, showing that as close as Moses was to God, Jesus deserved even more honor.

7 "Not so, with My servant Moses,
He is faithful in all My household;
8 With him I speak mouth to mouth,
Even openly, and not in dark sayings,
And he beholds the form of the LORD.
Why then were you not afraid
To speak against My servant, against
Moses?"

9 ¶ So the anger of the LORD burned against them and He departed.

10 But when the cloud had withdrawn from over the tent, behold, Miriam *was* leprous, as *white as* snow. As Aaron turned toward Miriam, behold, she *was* leprous.

11 Then Aaron said to Moses, "Oh, my lord, I beg you, do not account *this* sin to us, in which we have acted foolishly and in which we have sinned. 12 "Oh, do not let her be like one dead, whose flesh is half eaten away when he comes from his mother's womb!"

13 Moses cried out to the LORD, saying, "O God, heal her, I pray!"

14 But the LORD said to Moses, "If her father had but spit in her face, would she not bear her shame for seven days? Let her be shut up for seven days outside the camp, and afterward she may be received again."

15 So Miriam was shut up outside the camp for seven days, and the people did not move on until Miriam was received again. 16 ¶ Afterward, however, the people moved out from Hazeroth and camped in the wilderness of Paran.

Spies View the Land

13 Then the LORD spoke to Moses saying, 2 "Send out for yourself men so that they may spy out the land of Canaan, which I am going to give to the sons of Israel; you shall send a man from each of their fathers' tribes, every one a leader among them."

3 So Moses sent them from the wilderness of Paran at the command of the LORD, all of them men who were heads of the sons of Israel. 4 These then *were* their names: from the tribe of Reuben, Shammua the son of Zaccur; 5 from the tribe of Simeon, Shaphat the son of Hori; 6 from the tribe of Judah, Caleb the son of Jephunneh; 7 from the tribe of Issachar, Igal the son of Joseph; 8 from the tribe of Ephraim, Hoshea the son of Nun; 9 from the tribe of Benjamin, Palti the son of Raphu;

MIRIAM *Jealous Sister*

AMONG LIFE'S MOST DIFFICULT TASKS is enjoying the success of a brother or sister who outdoes you. Certainly Moses' sister Miriam found it difficult.

At Moses' birth she was the hero, watching over her baby brother and cleverly jumping in to outwit Pharaoh's daughter (Exodus 2:7). She took the spotlight again when the Israelites crossed the Red Sea, leading the women in a wild song of triumph (Exodus 15:20). As a prophetess, she played an important leadership role alongside Moses, who carried the chief responsibilities.

Then jealousy crept in. Miriam and her brother Aaron, another strong leader, began to grumble. They objected to Moses' wife, a foreigner, and they felt they ought to have equal spiritual status with Moses. "Has the LORD indeed spoken only through Moses?" they asked. "Has He not spoken through us as well?" (12:2).

In essence, God responded with a fierce "How dare you?" He singled out Miriam, apparently the leader of the two, for punishment. He would not tolerate jealousy among the leaders of his people—especially jealousy aimed at the humble man whom he had chosen.

Life Questions: What makes you jealous? How can you best handle those feelings?

10 from the tribe of Zebulun, Gaddiel the son of Sodi;

11 from the tribe of Joseph, from the tribe of Manasseh, Gaddi the son of Susi;

12 from the tribe of Dan, Ammiel the son of Gemalli;

13 from the tribe of Asher, Sethur the son of Michael;

14 from the tribe of Naphtali, Nahbi the son of Vophsi;

15 from the tribe of Gad, Geuel the son of Machi.

16 These are the names of the men whom Moses sent to spy out the land; but Moses called Hoshea the son of Nun, Joshua.

17 ¶ When Moses sent them to spy out the land of Canaan, he said to them, "Go up there into the *Negev; then go up into the hill country.

18 "See what the land is like, and whether the people who live in it are strong or weak, whether they are few or many.

19 "How is the land in which they live, is it good or bad? And how are the cities in which they live, are *they* like *open* camps or with fortifications?

20 "How is the land, is it fat or lean? Are there trees in it or not? Make an effort then to get some of the fruit of the land." Now the time was the time of the first ripe grapes.

21 ¶ So they went up and spied out the land from the wilderness of Zin as far as Rehob, at Lebo-hamath.

22 When they had gone up into the Negev, they came to Hebron where Ahiman, Sheshai and Talmai, the descendants of Anak were. (Now He-

bron was built seven years before Zoan in Egypt.)

23 ¶ Then they came to the valley of *Eshcol and from there cut down a branch with a single cluster of grapes; and they carried it on a pole between two *men*, with some of the pomegranates and the figs.

24 That place was called the valley of Eshcol, because of the cluster which the sons of Israel cut down from there.

The Spies' Reports

25 ¶ When they returned from spying out the land, at the end of forty days,

26 they proceeded to come to Moses and Aaron and to all the congregation of the sons of Israel in the wilderness of Paran, at Kadesh; and they brought back word to them and to all the congregation and showed them the fruit of the land.

27 Thus they told him, and said, "We went in to the land where you sent us; and it certainly does flow with milk and honey, and this is its fruit.

28 "Nevertheless, the people who live in the land are strong, and the cities are fortified *and* very large; and moreover, we saw the descendants of Anak there.

29 "Amalek is living in the land of the Negev and the Hittites and the Jebusites and the Amorites are living in the hill country, and the Canaanites are living by the sea and by the side of the Jordan."

30 ¶ Then Caleb quieted the people before Moses and said, "We should by all means go up and take possession of it, for we will surely overcome it."

*I.e. South country, and so throughout the ch   *I.e. cluster

---

AARON *Working Together ... and Apart*

EXODUS 1 INTRODUCES US TO one of the Bible's most famous families: two devout parents from the tribe of Levi and their children Aaron, Miriam and Moses. Surprisingly it was Moses, the younger brother, who got the Bible's star assignments, while the elder Aaron gained fame mainly as a substitute. For example, when God called Moses to free Israel from slavery, Moses shook like a coward. In response, God proposed teamwork. Moses' older brother Aaron would join Moses and make up for his weaknesses (Exodus 4:10–16).

The two worked side by side confronting Pharaoh, leading the Israelites out of Egypt, and calming the ornery people they were supposed to lead. Aaron's gifts in public speaking made up for Moses' stumbling speech, and so Aaron often accompanied Moses to meetings and did the talking. When God gave Moses the Law governing the new nation of Israel, Aaron and his sons were appointed priests. They and only they could lead in worship at the newly built tabernacle in the center of the camp (28:1).

Twice, however, Aaron thwarted teamwork, with disastrous results. While Moses was meeting with God on Mount Sinai, the people grew restless. Aaron came up with the idea of fashioning a golden idol for them to worship (chapter 32). On another occasion, Aaron and his sister openly carped about Moses' foreign-born wife and conspired to challenge his leadership (Numbers 12). Each time, God grew very angry at Aaron.

Aaron was an effective team player, but when he tried to go out on his own he got into trouble.

Life Questions: On what "teams" do you participate? What role do you usually play—starring or substitute?

31 But the men who had gone up with him said, "We are not able to go up against the people, for they are too strong for us."

32 So they gave out to the sons of Israel a bad report of the land which they had spied out, saying, "The land through which we have gone, in spying it out, is a land that devours its inhabitants; and all the people whom we saw in it are men of *great* size.

33 "There also we saw the Nephilim (the sons of Anak are part of the Nephilim); and we became like grasshoppers in our own sight, and so we were in their sight."

The People Rebel

14 Then all the congregation lifted up their voices and cried, and the people wept that night.

14:1 The Worst Rebellion

Chapter 14 records the tragic watershed of Numbers. Despite numerous proofs of God's power on their behalf, the Israelites cowered at the spies' report from Canaan. Fear led to open rebellion, and the nation plotted mutiny against Moses. At the very border of the promised land, theirs for the taking, they lost faith and turned away. In the face of such rebellion, God decided to wait for a whole new generation of Israelites; the original slaves would not cross into the promised land. All of them over the age of 20—except for Caleb and Joshua—were destined to fall as carcasses in the wilderness.

2 All the sons of Israel grumbled against Moses and Aaron; and the whole congregation said to them, "Would that we had died in the land of Egypt! Or would that we had died in this wilderness!

3 "Why is the LORD bringing us into this land, to fall by the sword? Our wives and our little ones will become plunder; would it not be better for us to return to Egypt?"

4 So they said to one another, "Let us appoint a leader and return to Egypt."

5 ¶ Then Moses and Aaron fell on their faces in the presence of all the assembly of the congregation of the sons of Israel.

6 Joshua the son of Nun and Caleb the son of Jephunneh, of those who had spied out the land, tore their clothes;

7 and they spoke to all the congregation of the sons of Israel, saying, "The land which we passed through to spy out is an exceedingly good land.

8 "If the LORD is pleased with us, then He will bring us into this land and give it to us—a land which flows with milk and honey.

9 "Only do not rebel against the LORD; and do not fear the people of the land, for they will be our prey. Their protection has been removed from them, and the LORD is with us; do not fear them."

10 But all the congregation said to stone them with stones. Then the glory of the LORD appeared in the tent of meeting to all the sons of Israel.

Moses Pleads for the People

11 ¶ The LORD said to Moses, "How long will this people spurn Me? And how long will they not believe in Me, despite all the signs which I have performed in their midst?

12 "I will smite them with pestilence and dispossess them, and I will make you into a nation greater and mightier than they."

13 ¶ But Moses said to the LORD, "Then the Egyptians will hear of it, for by Your strength You brought up this people from their midst,

14 and they will tell *it* to the inhabitants of this land. They have heard that You, O LORD, are in the midst of this people, for You, O LORD, are seen eye to eye, while Your cloud stands over them; and You go before them in a pillar of cloud by day and in a pillar of fire by night.

15 "Now if You slay this people as one man, then the nations who have heard of Your fame will say,

16 'Because the LORD could not bring this people into the land which He promised them by oath, therefore He slaughtered them in the wilderness.'

17 "But now, I pray, let the power of the Lord be great, just as You have declared,

18 'The LORD is slow to anger and abundant in lovingkindness, forgiving iniquity and transgression; but He will by no means clear *the guilty,* visiting the iniquity of the fathers on the children to the third and the fourth *generations.*'

19 "Pardon, I pray, the iniquity of this people according to the greatness of Your lovingkindness, just as You also have forgiven this people, from Egypt even until now."

The LORD Pardons and Rebukes

20 ¶ So the LORD said, "I have pardoned *them* according to your word;

21 but indeed, as I live, all the earth will be filled with the glory of the LORD.

22 "Surely all the men who have seen My glory and My signs which I performed in Egypt and in the wilderness, yet have put Me to the test these ten times and have not listened to My voice,

23 shall by no means see the land which I swore to their fathers, nor shall any of those who spurned Me see it.

24 "But My servant Caleb, because he has had a different spirit and has followed Me fully, I will bring into the land which he entered, and his descendants shall take possession of it.

25 "Now the Amalekites and the Canaanites live

in the valleys; turn tomorrow and set out to the wilderness by the way of the Red Sea."

26 ¶ The LORD spoke to Moses and Aaron, saying,

27 "How long *shall I bear* with this evil congregation who are grumbling against Me? I have heard the complaints of the sons of Israel, which they are making against Me.

28 "Say to them, 'As I live,' says the LORD, 'just as you have spoken in My hearing, so I will surely do to you;

29 your corpses will fall in this wilderness, even all your numbered men, according to your complete number from twenty years old and upward, who have grumbled against Me.

30 'Surely you shall not come into the land in which I swore to settle you, except Caleb the son of Jephunneh and Joshua the son of Nun.

31 'Your children, however, whom you said would become a prey—I will bring them in, and they will know the land which you have rejected.

32 'But as for you, your corpses will fall in this wilderness.

33 'Your sons shall be shepherds for forty years in the wilderness, and they will suffer *for* your unfaithfulness, until your corpses lie in the wilderness.

34 'According to the number of days which you spied out the land, forty days, for every day you shall bear your guilt a year, *even* forty years, and you will know My opposition.

35 'I, the LORD, have spoken, surely this I will do to all this evil congregation who are gathered together against Me. In this wilderness they shall be destroyed, and there they will die.' "

36 ¶ As for the men whom Moses sent to spy out the land and who returned and made all the congregation grumble against him by bringing out a bad report concerning the land,

37 even those men who brought out the very bad report of the land died by a plague before the LORD.

38 But Joshua the son of Nun and Caleb the son of Jephunneh remained alive out of those men who went to spy out the land.

Israel Repulsed

39 ¶ When Moses spoke these words to all the sons of Israel, the people mourned greatly.

40 In the morning, however, they rose up early and went up to the ridge of the hill country, saying, "Here we are; we have indeed sinned, but we will go up to the place which the LORD has promised."

41 But Moses said, "Why then are you transgressing the commandment of the LORD, when it will not succeed?

42 "Do not go up, or you will be struck down before your enemies, for the LORD is not among you.

43 "For the Amalekites and the Canaanites will be there in front of you, and you will fall by the sword, inasmuch as you have turned back from following the LORD. And the LORD will not be with you."

14:39 Imperfect Timing

When the Israelites heard how God would punish them for disobeying, they suddenly found the courage to go up and fight. God sought obedience, though, not courage, and obedience meant following directions immediately. Though Moses warned the Israelites that their courage came too late, and that God would not support them, they went anyway—and were soundly beaten.

44 But they went up heedlessly to the ridge of the hill country; neither the ark of the covenant of the LORD nor Moses left the camp.

45 Then the Amalekites and the Canaanites who lived in that hill country came down, and struck them and beat them down as far as Hormah.

Laws for Canaan

15 Now the LORD spoke to Moses, saying,

2 "Speak to the sons of Israel and say to them, 'When you enter the land where you are to live, which I am giving you,

3 then make an offering by fire to the LORD, a burnt offering or a sacrifice to fulfill a special vow, or as a freewill offering or in your appointed times, to make a soothing aroma to the LORD, from the herd or from the flock.

4 'The one who presents his offering shall present to the LORD a grain offering of one-tenth *of an ephah* of fine flour mixed with one-fourth of a ªhin of oil,

5 and you shall prepare wine for the drink offering, one-fourth of a hin, with the burnt offering or for the sacrifice, for each lamb.

6 'Or for a ram you shall prepare as a grain offering two-tenths *of an ephah* of fine flour mixed with one-third of a hin of oil;

7 and for the drink offering you shall offer one-third of a hin of wine as a soothing aroma to the LORD.

8 'When you prepare a bull as a burnt offering or a sacrifice, to fulfill a special vow, or for peace offerings to the LORD,

9 then you shall offer with the bull a grain offering of three-tenths *of an ephah* of fine flour mixed with one-half a hin of oil;

10 and you shall offer as the drink offering one-half a hin of wine as an offering by fire, as a soothing aroma to the LORD.

ª I.e. Approx one gal., and so through v 10

11 ¶ 'Thus it shall be done for each ox, or for each ram, or for each of the male lambs, or of the goats.

12 'According to the number that you prepare, so you shall do for everyone according to their number.

13 'All who are native shall do these things in this manner, in presenting an offering by fire, as a soothing aroma to the LORD.

Law of the Sojourner

14 'If an alien sojourns with you, or one who may be among you throughout your generations, and he *wishes to* make an offering by fire, as a soothing aroma to the LORD, just as you do so he shall do.

15 '*As for* the assembly, there shall be one statute for you and for the alien who sojourns *with you,* a perpetual statute throughout your generations; as you are, so shall the alien be before the LORD.

16 'There is to be one law and one ordinance for you and for the alien who sojourns with you.' "

17 ¶ Then the LORD spoke to Moses, saying,

18 "Speak to the sons of Israel and say to them, 'When you enter the land where I bring you,

19 then it shall be, that when you eat of the food of the land, you shall lift up an offering to the LORD.

20 'Of the first of your ᵃdough you shall lift up a cake as an offering; as the offering of the threshing floor, so you shall lift it up.

21 'From the first of your ᵃdough you shall give to the LORD an offering throughout your generations.

22 ¶ 'But when you unwittingly fail and do not observe all these commandments, which the LORD has spoken to Moses,

23 *even* all that the LORD has commanded you through Moses, from the day when the LORD gave commandment and onward throughout your generations,

24 then it shall be, if it is done unintentionally, without the knowledge of the congregation, that all the congregation shall offer one bull for a burnt offering, as a soothing aroma to the LORD, with its grain offering and its drink offering, according to the ordinance, and one male goat for a sin offering.

25 'Then the priest shall make atonement for all the congregation of the sons of Israel, and they will be forgiven; for it was an error, and they have brought their offering, an offering by fire to the LORD, and their sin offering before the LORD, for their error.

26 'So all the congregation of the sons of Israel will be forgiven, with the alien who sojourns among them, for *it happened* to all the people through error.

27 ¶ 'Also if one person sins unintentionally, then he shall offer a one year old female goat for a sin offering.

28 'The priest shall make atonement before the LORD for the person who goes astray when he sins unintentionally, making atonement for him that he may be forgiven.

29 'You shall have one law for him who does *anything* unintentionally, for him who is native among the sons of Israel and for the alien who sojourns among them.

30 'But the person who does *anything* defiantly, whether he is native or an alien, that one is blaspheming the LORD; and that person shall be cut off from among his people.

31 'Because he has despised the word of the LORD and has broken His commandment, that person shall be completely cut off; his guilt *will be* on him.' "

Sabbath-breaking Punished

32 ¶ Now while the sons of Israel were in the wilderness, they found a man gathering wood on the sabbath day.

33 Those who found him gathering wood brought him to Moses and Aaron and to all the congregation;

34 and they put him in custody because it had not been declared what should be done to him.

35 Then the LORD said to Moses, "The man shall surely be put to death; all the congregation shall stone him with stones outside the camp."

36 So all the congregation brought him outside the camp and stoned him to death with stones, just as the LORD had commanded Moses.

37 ¶ The LORD also spoke to Moses, saying,

38 "Speak to the sons of Israel, and tell them that they shall make for themselves tassels on the corners of their garments throughout their generations, and that they shall put on the tassel of each corner a cord of blue.

15:38 A Safeguard Against Lust

The Israelites had large reminders of God—such as the pillar of fire—and small ones: they wore tassels and blue cords on the corners of clothing to remind them of the Lord's commands. God specifically mentions this practice as a safeguard against lust—a reminder impossible to avoid for one tempted to adultery.

39 "It shall be a tassel for you to look at and remember all the commandments of the LORD, so as to do them and not follow after your own heart and your own eyes, after which you played the harlot,

ᵃ Or *coarse meal*

40 so that you may remember to do all My commandments and be holy to your God.

41 "I am the LORD your God who brought you out from the land of Egypt to be your God; I am the LORD your God."

Korah's Rebellion

16 Now Korah the son of Izhar, the son of Kohath, the son of Levi, with Dathan and Abiram, the sons of Eliab, and On the son of Peleth, sons of Reuben, took *action,*

2 and they rose up before Moses, together with some of the sons of Israel, two hundred and fifty leaders of the congregation, chosen in the assembly, men of renown.

3 They assembled together against Moses and Aaron, and said to them, "You have gone far enough, for all the congregation are holy, every one of them, and the LORD is in their midst; so why do you exalt yourselves above the assembly of the LORD?"

16:3 Open Revolt

Two hundred and fifty well-known council members, led by Korah, Dathan, and Abiram, rebelled against Moses' leadership. They apparently wanted more people recognized as priests. But in a dramatic test, Moses showed that he was the leader God had chosen.

This rebellion and a second one immediately afterwards (verse 41) are the only two major events that the Bible mentions during the Israelites' 37 years of wandering in the wilderness. Deuteronomy, however (2:7; 8:4; 29:5–6), indicates the people were well cared for.

4 ¶ When Moses heard *this,* he fell on his face;

5 and he spoke to Korah and all his company, saying, "Tomorrow morning the LORD will show who is His, and who is holy, and will bring *him* near to Himself; even the one whom He will choose, He will bring near to Himself.

6 "Do this: take censers for yourselves, Korah and all your company,

7 and put fire in them, and lay incense upon them in the presence of the LORD tomorrow; and the man whom the LORD chooses *shall be* the one who is holy. You have gone far enough, you sons of Levi!"

8 ¶ Then Moses said to Korah, "Hear now, you sons of Levi,

9 is it not enough for you that the God of Israel has separated you from the *rest of* the congregation of Israel, to bring you near to Himself, to do the service of the tabernacle of the LORD, and to stand before the congregation to minister to them;

10 and that He has brought you near, *Korah,*

and all your brothers, sons of Levi, with you? And are you seeking for the priesthood also?

11 "Therefore you and all your company are gathered together against the LORD; but as for Aaron, who is he that you grumble against him?"

12 ¶ Then Moses sent a summons to Dathan and Abiram, the sons of Eliab; but they said, "We will not come up.

13 "Is it not enough that you have brought us up out of a land flowing with milk and honey to have us die in the wilderness, but you would also lord it over us?

14 "Indeed, you have not brought us into a land flowing with milk and honey, nor have you given us an inheritance of fields and vineyards. Would you put out the eyes of these men? We will not come up!"

15 ¶ Then Moses became very angry and said to the LORD, "Do not regard their offering! I have not taken a single donkey from them, nor have I done harm to any of them."

16 Moses said to Korah, "You and all your company be present before the LORD tomorrow, both you and they along with Aaron.

17 "Each of you take his firepan and put incense on it, and each of you bring his censer before the LORD, two hundred and fifty firepans; also you and Aaron *shall* each *bring* his firepan."

18 So they each took his *own* censer and put fire on it, and laid incense on it; and they stood at the doorway of the tent of meeting, with Moses and Aaron.

19 Thus Korah assembled all the congregation against them at the doorway of the tent of meeting. And the glory of the LORD appeared to all the congregation.

20 ¶ Then the LORD spoke to Moses and Aaron, saying,

21 "Separate yourselves from among this congregation, that I may consume them instantly."

22 But they fell on their faces and said, "O God, God of the spirits of all flesh, when one man sins, will You be angry with the entire congregation?"

23 ¶ Then the LORD spoke to Moses, saying,

24 "Speak to the congregation, saying, 'Get back from around the dwellings of Korah, Dathan and Abiram.' "

25 ¶ Then Moses arose and went to Dathan and Abiram, with the elders of Israel following him,

26 and he spoke to the congregation, saying, "Depart now from the tents of these wicked men, and touch nothing that belongs to them, or you will be swept away in all their sin."

27 So they got back from around the dwellings of Korah, Dathan and Abiram; and Dathan and Abiram came out *and* stood at the doorway of their tents, along with their wives and their sons and their little ones.

28 Moses said, "By this you shall know that the

LORD has sent me to do all these deeds; for this is not my doing.

29 "If these men die the death of all men or if they suffer the fate of all men, *then* the LORD has not sent me.

30 "But if the LORD brings about an entirely new thing and the ground opens its mouth and swallows them up with all that is theirs, and they descend alive into Sheol, then you will understand that these men have spurned the LORD."

31 ¶ As he finished speaking all these words, the ground that was under them split open;

32 and the earth opened its mouth and swallowed them up, and their households, and all the men who belonged to Korah with *their* possessions.

33 So they and all that belonged to them went down alive to Sheol; and the earth closed over them, and they perished from the midst of the assembly.

34 All Israel who *were* around them fled at their outcry, for they said, "The earth may swallow us up!"

35 Fire also came forth from the LORD and consumed the two hundred and fifty men who were offering the incense.

36 ¶ Then the LORD spoke to Moses, saying,

37 "Say to Eleazar, the son of Aaron the priest, that he shall take up the censers out of the midst of the blaze, for they are holy; and you scatter the burning coals abroad.

38 "As for the censers of these men who have sinned at the cost of their lives, let them be made into hammered sheets for a plating of the altar, since they did present them before the LORD and they are holy; and they shall be for a sign to the sons of Israel."

39 So Eleazar the priest took the bronze censers which the men who were burned had offered, and they hammered them out as a plating for the altar,

40 as a reminder to the sons of Israel that no layman who is not of the descendants of Aaron should come near to burn incense before the LORD; so that he will not become like Korah and his company—just as the LORD had spoken to him through Moses.

Murmuring and Plague

41 ¶ But on the next day all the congregation of the sons of Israel grumbled against Moses and Aaron, saying, "You are the ones who have caused the death of the LORD'S people."

42 It came about, however, when the congregation had assembled against Moses and Aaron, that they turned toward the tent of meeting, and behold, the cloud covered it and the glory of the LORD appeared.

43 Then Moses and Aaron came to the front of the tent of meeting,

44 and the LORD spoke to Moses, saying,

45 "Get away from among this congregation, that I may consume them instantly." Then they fell on their faces.

46 Moses said to Aaron, "Take your censer and put in it fire from the altar, and lay incense *on it;* then bring it quickly to the congregation and make atonement for them, for wrath has gone forth from the LORD, the plague has begun!"

47 Then Aaron took *it* as Moses had spoken, and ran into the midst of the assembly, for behold, the plague had begun among the people. So he put *on* the incense and made atonement for the people.

48 He took his stand between the dead and the living, so that the plague was checked.

49 But those who died by the plague were 14,700, besides those who died on account of Korah.

50 Then Aaron returned to Moses at the doorway of the tent of meeting, for the plague had been checked.

Aaron's Rod Buds

17 Then the LORD spoke to Moses, saying,

2 "Speak to the sons of Israel, and get from them a rod for each father's household: twelve rods, from all their leaders according to their fathers' households. You shall write each name on his rod,

3 and write Aaron's name on the rod of Levi; for there is one rod for the head *of each* of their fathers' households.

4 "You shall then deposit them in the tent of meeting in front of the testimony, where I meet with you.

5 "It will come about that the rod of the man whom I choose will sprout. Thus I will lessen from upon Myself the grumblings of the sons of Israel, who are grumbling against you."

6 Moses therefore spoke to the sons of Israel, and all their leaders gave him a rod apiece, for each leader according to their fathers' households, twelve rods, with the rod of Aaron among their rods.

7 So Moses deposited the rods before LORD in the tent of the testimony.

8 ¶ Now on the next day Moses went into the tent of the testimony; and behold, the rod of Aaron for the house of Levi had sprouted and put forth buds and produced blossoms, and it bore ripe almonds.

9 Moses then brought out all the rods from the presence of the LORD to all the sons of Israel; and they looked, and each man took his rod.

10 But the LORD said to Moses, "Put back the rod of Aaron before the testimony to be kept as a sign against the rebels, that you may put an end to their grumblings against Me, so that they will not die."

11 Thus Moses did; just as the LORD had commanded him, so he did.

12 ¶ Then the sons of Israel spoke to Moses, saying, "Behold, we perish, we are dying, we are all dying!

13 "Everyone who comes near, who comes near to the tabernacle of the LORD, must die. Are we to perish completely?"

17:10 What's in the Ark

The ark of the covenant was the holiest sign of God's presence. In or near it were placed a few highly significant mementos of the journey to the promised land: the stone tablets of the Law of Moses (Exodus 25:16), a jar of the miraculous manna (Exodus 16:33–34), and Aaron's sprouted staff. As a visible proof that God had chosen Aaron to be priest, the miraculous staff could help deter future rebellions.

Duties of Levites

18 So the LORD said to Aaron, "You and your sons and your father's household with you shall bear the guilt in connection with the sanctuary, and you and your sons with you shall bear the guilt in connection with your priesthood.

2 "But bring with you also your brothers, the tribe of Levi, the tribe of your father, that they may be joined with you and serve you, while you and your sons with you are before the tent of the testimony.

3 "And they shall thus attend to your obligation and the obligation of all the tent, but they shall not come near to the furnishings of the sanctuary and the altar, or both they and you will die.

4 "They shall be joined with you and attend to the obligations of the tent of meeting, for all the service of the tent; but an outsider may not come near you.

5 "So you shall attend to the obligations of the sanctuary and the obligations of the altar, so that there will no longer be wrath on the sons of Israel.

6 "Behold, I Myself have taken your fellow Levites from among the sons of Israel; they are a gift to you, dedicated to the LORD, to perform the service for the tent of meeting.

7 "But you and your sons with you shall attend to your priesthood for everything concerning the altar and inside the veil, and you are to perform service. I am giving you the priesthood as a bestowed service, but the outsider who comes near shall be put to death."

The Priests' Portion

8 ¶ Then the LORD spoke to Aaron, "Now behold, I Myself have given you charge of My offerings, even all the holy gifts of the sons of Israel I have given them to you as a portion and to your sons as a perpetual allotment.

9 "This shall be yours from the most holy *gifts reserved* from the fire; every offering of theirs, even every grain offering and every sin offering and every guilt offering, which they shall render to Me, shall be most holy for you and for your sons.

10 "As the most holy *gifts* you shall eat it; every male shall eat it. It shall be holy to you.

11 "This also is yours, the offering of their gift, even all the wave offerings of the sons of Israel; I have given them to you and to your sons and daughters with you as a perpetual allotment. Everyone of your household who is clean may eat it.

12 "All the best of the fresh oil and all the best of the fresh wine and of the grain, the first fruits of those which they give to the LORD, I give them to you.

13 "The first ripe fruits of all that is in their land, which they bring to the LORD, shall be yours; everyone of your household who is clean may eat it.

14 "Every devoted thing in Israel shall be yours.

15 "Every first issue of the womb of all flesh, whether man or animal, which they offer to the LORD, shall be yours; nevertheless the firstborn of man you shall surely redeem, and the firstborn of unclean animals you shall redeem.

16 "As to their redemption price, from a month old you shall redeem them, by your valuation, five ªshekels in silver, according to the shekel of the sanctuary, which is twenty gerahs.

17 "But the firstborn of an ox or the firstborn of a sheep or the firstborn of a goat, you shall not redeem; they are holy. You shall sprinkle their blood on the altar and shall offer up their fat in smoke *as* an offering by fire, for a soothing aroma to the LORD.

18 "Their meat shall be yours; it shall be yours like the breast of a wave offering and like the right thigh.

19 "All the offerings of the holy *gifts,* which the sons of Israel offer to the LORD, I have given to you and your sons and your daughters with you, as a perpetual allotment. It is an everlasting covenant of salt before the LORD to you and your descendants with you."

20 Then the LORD said to Aaron, "You shall have no inheritance in their land nor own any portion among them; I am your portion and your inheritance among the sons of Israel.

21 ¶ "To the sons of Levi, behold, I have given all the tithe in Israel for an inheritance, in return for their service which they perform, the service of the tent of meeting.

22 "The sons of Israel shall not come near the tent of meeting again, or they will bear sin and die.

23 "Only the Levites shall perform the service of the tent of meeting, and they shall bear their iniquity; it shall be a perpetual statute throughout

___
ª I.e. A shekel equals approx one-half oz

your generations, and among the sons of Israel they shall have no inheritance.

24 "For the tithe of the sons of Israel, which they offer as an offering to the LORD, I have given to the

18:20 No Land for Levites

The tribe of Levites got special privileges, but in contrast to the wealthy priestly caste of, say, Egypt, they received no land. God himself was their share and inheritance. For food, they relied largely on offerings from other tribes. Thus the physical survival of "full-time ministers" depended on how faithful the other Israelites were.

Levites for an inheritance; therefore I have said concerning them, 'They shall have no inheritance among the sons of Israel.' "

25 ¶ Then the LORD spoke to Moses, saying,

26 "Moreover, you shall speak to the Levites and say to them, 'When you take from the sons of Israel the tithe which I have given you from them for your inheritance, then you shall present an offering from it to the LORD, a tithe of the tithe.

27 'Your offering shall be reckoned to you as the grain from the threshing floor or the full produce from the wine vat.

28 'So you shall also present an offering to the LORD from your tithes, which you receive from the sons of Israel; and from it you shall give the LORD's offering to Aaron the priest.

29 'Out of all your gifts you shall present every offering due to the LORD, from all the best of them, the sacred part from them.'

30 "You shall say to them, 'When you have offered from it the best of it, then *the rest* shall be reckoned to the Levites as the product of the threshing floor, and as the product of the wine vat.

31 'You may eat it anywhere, you and your households, for it is your compensation in return for your service in the tent of meeting.

32 'You will bear no sin by reason of it when you have offered the best of it. But you shall not profane the sacred gifts of the sons of Israel, or you will die.' "

Ordinance of the Red Heifer

19 Then the LORD spoke to Moses and Aaron, saying,

2 "This is the statute of the law which the LORD has commanded, saying, 'Speak to the sons of Israel that they bring you an unblemished red heifer in which is no defect *and* on which a yoke has never been placed.

3 'You shall give it to Eleazar the priest, and it shall be brought outside the camp and be slaughtered in his presence.

4 'Next Eleazar the priest shall take some of its blood with his finger and sprinkle some of its

blood toward the front of the tent of meeting seven times.

5 'Then the heifer shall be burned in his sight; its hide and its flesh and its blood, with its refuse, shall be burned.

6 'The priest shall take cedar wood and hyssop and scarlet *material* and cast it into the midst of the burning heifer.

7 'The priest shall then wash his clothes and bathe his body in water, and afterward come into the camp, but the priest shall be unclean until evening.

8 'The one who burns it shall also wash his clothes in water and bathe his body in water, and shall be unclean until evening.

9 'Now a man who is clean shall gather up the ashes of the heifer and deposit them outside the camp in a clean place, and the congregation of the sons of Israel shall keep it as water to remove impurity; it is purification from sin.

10 'The one who gathers the ashes of the heifer shall wash his clothes and be unclean until evening; and it shall be a perpetual statute to the sons of Israel and to the alien who sojourns among them.

11 ¶ 'The one who touches the corpse of any person shall be unclean for seven days.

12 'That one shall purify himself from uncleanness with the water on the third day and on the seventh day, *and then* he will be clean; but if he does not purify himself on the third day and on the seventh day, he will not be clean.

13 'Anyone who touches a corpse, the body of a man who has died, and does not purify himself, defiles the tabernacle of the LORD; and that person shall be cut off from Israel. Because the water for impurity was not sprinkled on him, he shall be unclean; his uncleanness is still on him.

14 ¶ 'This is the law when a man dies in a tent: everyone who comes into the tent and everyone who is in the tent shall be unclean for seven days.

15 'Every open vessel, which has no covering tied down on it, shall be unclean.

16 'Also, anyone who in the open field touches one who has been slain with a sword or who has died *naturally*, or a human bone or a grave, shall be unclean for seven days.

17 'Then for the unclean *person* they shall take some of the ashes of the burnt purification from sin and flowing water shall be added to them in a vessel.

18 'A clean person shall take hyssop and dip *it* in the water, and sprinkle *it* on the tent and on all the furnishings and on the persons who were there, and on the one who touched the bone or the one slain or the one dying *naturally* or the grave.

19 'Then the clean *person* shall sprinkle on the unclean on the third day and on the seventh day; and on the seventh day he shall purify him from uncleanness, and he shall wash his clothes and

bathe *himself* in water and shall be clean by evening.

20 ¶ 'But the man who is unclean and does not purify himself from uncleanness, that person shall be cut off from the midst of the assembly, because he has defiled the sanctuary of the LORD; the water for impurity has not been sprinkled on him, he is unclean.

21 'So it shall be a perpetual statute for them. And he who sprinkles the water for impurity shall wash his clothes, and he who touches the water for impurity shall be unclean until evening.

22 'Furthermore, anything that the unclean *person* touches shall be unclean; and the person who touches *it* shall be unclean until evening.' "

Death of Miriam

20 Then the sons of Israel, the whole congregation, came to the wilderness of Zin in the first month; and the people stayed at Kadesh. Now Miriam died there and was buried there.

2 ¶ There was no water for the congregation, and they assembled themselves against Moses and Aaron.

3 The people thus contended with Moses and spoke, saying, "If only we had perished when our brothers perished before the LORD!

4 "Why then have you brought the LORD's assembly into this wilderness, for us and our beasts to die here?

5 "Why have you made us come up from Egypt, to bring us in to this wretched place? It is not a place of grain or figs or vines or pomegranates, nor is there water to drink."

6 Then Moses and Aaron came in from the presence of the assembly to the doorway of the tent of meeting and fell on their faces. Then the glory of the LORD appeared to them;

7 and the LORD spoke to Moses, saying,

The Water of Meribah

8 "Take the rod; and you and your brother Aaron assemble the congregation and speak to the rock before their eyes, that it may yield its water. You shall thus bring forth water for them out of the rock and let the congregation and their beasts drink."

9 ¶ So Moses took the rod from before the LORD, just as He had commanded him;

10 and Moses and Aaron gathered the assembly before the rock. And he said to them, "Listen now, you rebels; shall we bring forth water for you out of this rock?"

11 Then Moses lifted up his hand and struck the rock twice with his rod; and water came forth abundantly, and the congregation and their beasts drank.

12 But the LORD said to Moses and Aaron, "Because you have not believed Me, to treat Me as holy in the sight of the sons of Israel, therefore you shall not bring this assembly into the land which I have given them."

13 Those *were* the waters of ªMeribah, because the sons of Israel contended with the LORD, and He proved Himself holy among them.

20:12 Moses' Sin

After so many displays of loyalty and courage, Moses faltered. Numbers does not specify exactly what Moses did that upset God. Was it striking the rock rather than speaking to it as God commanded? Regardless, Moses lashed out angrily against the Israelites and was faulted for his lack of trust in God. In Deuteronomy, God describes the sin as "breaking faith" with him and tells Moses that he "did not treat Me as holy in the midst of the sons of Israel" (32:51).

The scene at Meribah brought a tragic end to a great man's career: Moses, footsore and weary, was told he too would die in the wilderness, before the Israelites crossed into the promised land. Deuteronomy 3:23–27 adds a postscript: Moses pleaded with God to reverse the punishment, and, when that failed, he threw the blame back on the Israelites.

14 ¶ From Kadesh Moses then sent messengers to the king of Edom: "Thus your brother Israel has said, 'You know all the hardship that has befallen us;

15 that our fathers went down to Egypt, and we stayed in Egypt a long time, and the Egyptians treated us and our fathers badly.

16 'But when we cried out to the LORD, He heard our voice and sent an angel and brought us out from Egypt; now behold, we are at Kadesh, a town on the edge of your territory.

17 'Please let us pass through your land. We will not pass through field or through vineyard; we will not even drink water from a well. We will go along the king's highway, not turning to the right or left, until we pass through your territory.' "

18 ¶ Edom, however, said to him, "You shall not pass through us, or I will come out with the sword against you."

19 Again, the sons of Israel said to him, "We will go up by the highway, and if I and my livestock do drink any of your water, then I will pay its price. Let me only pass through on my feet, nothing *else*."

20 But he said, "You shall not pass through." And Edom came out against him with a heavy force and with a strong hand.

21 Thus Edom refused to allow Israel to pass through his territory; so Israel turned away from him.

22 ¶ Now when they set out from Kadesh, the

ª I.e. contention

sons of Israel, the whole congregation, came to Mount Hor.

Death of Aaron

23 Then the LORD spoke to Moses and Aaron

20:21 Blood Feud

Israel asked politely for the right to pass through Edom, offering to pay for water rights. Since the Edomites were distant relatives, descendants of Jacob's brother Esau, Israel expected a favorable response. Instead, Edom's refusal meant a long, hard detour. Moses warned the Israelites not to hate the Edomites, their kin (Deuteronomy 23:7–8). But for the rest of biblical history, there were wars and hatred between the two nations.

at Mount Hor by the border of the land of Edom, saying,

24 "Aaron will be gathered to his people; for he shall not enter the land which I have given to the sons of Israel, because you rebelled against My command at the waters of Meribah.

25 "Take Aaron and his son Eleazar and bring them up to Mount Hor;

26 and strip Aaron of his garments and put them on his son Eleazar. So Aaron will be gathered *to his people,* and will die there."

27 So Moses did just as the LORD had commanded, and they went up to Mount Hor in the sight of all the congregation.

28 After Moses had stripped Aaron of his garments and put them on his son Eleazar, Aaron died there on the mountain top. Then Moses and Eleazar came down from the mountain.

29 When all the congregation saw that Aaron had died, all the house of Israel wept for Aaron thirty days.

Arad Conquered

21 When the Canaanite, the king of Arad, who lived in the ªNegev, heard that Israel was coming by the way of ᵇAtharim, then he fought against Israel and took some of them captive.

2 So Israel made a vow to the LORD and said, "If You will indeed deliver this people into my hand, then I will utterly destroy their cities."

3 The LORD heard the voice of Israel and delivered up the Canaanites; then they utterly destroyed them and their cities. Thus the name of the place was called ᶜHormah.

4 ¶ Then they set out from Mount Hor by the way of the Red Sea, to go around the land of Edom; and the people became impatient because of the journey.

5 The people spoke against God and Moses, "Why have you brought us up out of Egypt to die in the wilderness? For there is no food and no water, and we loathe this miserable food."

The Bronze Serpent

6 The LORD sent fiery serpents among the people and they bit the people, so that many people of Israel died.

7 So the people came to Moses and said, "We have sinned, because we have spoken against the LORD and you; intercede with the LORD, that He may remove the serpents from us." And Moses interceded for the people.

8 Then the LORD said to Moses, "Make a fiery *serpent,* and set it on a standard; and it shall come about, that everyone who is bitten, when he looks at it, he will live."

9 And Moses made a bronze serpent and set it on the standard; and it came about, that if a serpent bit any man, when he looked to the bronze serpent, he lived.

21:9 Bronze Serpent

Jesus chose this incident as one of the examples from Old Testament history that illustrates his own person and work (John 3:14). Through the serpent and through Jesus, God provided a way of escape that required only faith from the people. In typical style, the Israelites corrupted the meaning by keeping the bronze serpent as an idol to worship. Centuries later, King Hezekiah destroyed this image (2 Kings 18:4).

10 ¶ Now the sons of Israel moved out and camped in Oboth.

11 They journeyed from Oboth and camped at Iyeabarim, in the wilderness which is opposite Moab, to the east.

12 From there they set out and camped in ᵈWadi Zered.

13 From there they journeyed and camped on the other side of the Arnon, which is in the wilderness that comes out of the border of the Amorites, for the Arnon is the border of Moab, between Moab and the Amorites.

14 Therefore it is said in the Book of the Wars of the LORD,

"Waheb in Suphah,
    And the wadis of the Arnon,
15 And the slope of the wadis
    That extends to the site of Ar,
    And leans to the border of Moab."

16 ¶ From there *they continued* to Beer, that is

ª I.e. South country   ᵇ Or *the spies*   ᶜ I.e. a devoted thing; or Destruction   ᵈ I.e. a dry ravine except during rainy season the well where the LORD said to Moses, "Assemble the people, that I may give them water."

17 ¶ Then Israel sang this song:
"Spring up, O well! Sing to it!

21:14 Out of Print

This quotation comes from a book no longer in existence. The Bible makes many mentions of such vanished books. Joshua 10:13 and 2 Samuel 1:18, for example, name the book of Jashar. There are references to the works of various prophets or seers (Gad, Ahijah, Shemaiah) and many references to royal annals such as the book of the kings of Israel (1 Chronicles 9:1). Israel must have had a sizable library.

18 "The well, which the leaders sank,
Which the nobles of the people dug,
With the scepter *and* with their staffs."
And from the wilderness *they continued* to Mattanah,
19 and from Mattanah to Nahaliel, and from Nahaliel to Bamoth,
20 and from Bamoth to the valley that is in the land of Moab, at the top of Pisgah which overlooks the wasteland.

Two Victories

21 ¶ Then Israel sent messengers to Sihon, king of the Amorites, saying,
22 "Let me pass through your land. We will not turn off into field or vineyard; we will not drink water from wells. We will go by the king's highway until we have passed through your border."
23 But Sihon would not permit Israel to pass through his border. So Sihon gathered all his people and went out against Israel in the wilderness, and came to Jahaz and fought against Israel.
24 Then Israel struck him with the edge of the sword, and took possession of his land from the Arnon to the Jabbok, as far as the sons of Ammon; for the border of the sons of Ammon *was* Jazer.
25 Israel took all these cities and Israel lived in all the cities of the Amorites, in Heshbon, and in all her villages.
26 For Heshbon was the city of Sihon, king of the Amorites, who had fought against the former king of Moab and had taken all his land out of his hand, as far as the Arnon.
27 Therefore those who use proverbs say,
"Come to Heshbon! Let it be built!
So let the city of Sihon be established.
28 "For a fire went forth from Heshbon,
A flame from the town of Sihon;
It devoured Ar of Moab,
The dominant heights of the Arnon.

29 "Woe to you, O Moab!
You are ruined, O people of Chemosh!
He has given his sons as fugitives,
And his daughters into captivity,
To an Amorite king, Sihon.
30 "But we have cast them down,
Heshbon is ruined as far as Dibon,
Then we have laid waste even to Nophah,
Which *reaches* to Medeba."

31 ¶ Thus Israel lived in the land of the Amorites.
32 Moses sent to spy out Jazer, and they captured its villages and dispossessed the Amorites who *were* there.
33 ¶ Then they turned and went up by the way of Bashan, and Og the king of Bashan went out with all his people, for battle at Edrei.
34 But the LORD said to Moses, "Do not fear him, for I have given him into your hand, and all his people and his land; and you shall do to him as you did to Sihon, king of the Amorites, who lived at Heshbon."
35 So they killed him and his sons and all his people, until there was no remnant left him; and they possessed his land.

Balak Sends for Balaam

22 Then the sons of Israel journeyed, and camped in the plains of Moab beyond the Jordan *opposite* Jericho.
2 ¶ Now Balak the son of Zippor saw all that Israel had done to the Amorites.
3 So Moab was in great fear because of the people, for they were numerous; and Moab was in dread of the sons of Israel.
4 Moab said to the elders of Midian, "Now this horde will lick up all that is around us, as the ox licks up the grass of the field." And Balak the son of Zippor was king of Moab at that time.
5 So he sent messengers to Balaam the son of Beor, at Pethor, which is near the [a]River, *in* the land of the sons of his people, to call him, saying, "Behold, a people came out of Egypt; behold, they cover the surface of the land, and they are living opposite me.
6 "Now, therefore, please come, curse this people for me since they are too mighty for me; perhaps I may be able to defeat them and drive them out of the land. For I know that he whom you bless is blessed, and he whom you curse is cursed."
7 ¶ So the elders of Moab and the elders of Midian departed with the *fees for* divination in their hand; and they came to Balaam and repeated Balak's words to him.
8 He said to them, "Spend the night here, and I will bring word back to you as the LORD may speak to me." And the leaders of Moab stayed with Balaam.

---

[a] I.e. Euphrates

9 Then God came to Balaam and said, "Who are these men with you?"

10 Balaam said to God, "Balak the son of Zippor, king of Moab, has sent *word* to me,

11 'Behold, there is a people who came out of Egypt and they cover the surface of the land; now come, curse them for me; perhaps I may be able to fight against them and drive them out.' "

12 God said to Balaam, "Do not go with them; you shall not curse the people, for they are blessed."

13 So Balaam arose in the morning and said to Balak's leaders, "Go back to your land, for the LORD has refused to let me go with you."

14 The leaders of Moab arose and went to Balak and said, "Balaam refused to come with us."

15 ¶ Then Balak again sent leaders, more numerous and more distinguished than the former.

16 They came to Balaam and said to him, "Thus says Balak the son of Zippor, 'Let nothing, I beg you, hinder you from coming to me;

17 for I will indeed honor you richly, and I will do whatever you say to me. Please come then, curse this people for me.' "

18 Balaam replied to the servants of Balak, "Though Balak were to give me his house full of silver and gold, I could not do anything, either small or great, contrary to the command of the LORD my God.

19 "Now please, you also stay here tonight, and I will find out what else the LORD will speak to me."

20 God came to Balaam at night and said to him, "If the men have come to call you, rise up *and* go with them; but only the word which I speak to you shall you do."

21 ¶ So Balaam arose in the morning, and saddled his donkey and went with the leaders of Moab.

The Angel and Balaam

22 But God was angry because he was going, and the angel of the LORD took his stand in the way as an adversary against him. Now he was riding on his donkey and his two servants were with him.

23 When the donkey saw the angel of the LORD standing in the way with his drawn sword in his hand, the donkey turned off from the way and went into the field; but Balaam struck the donkey to turn her back into the way.

24 Then the angel of the LORD stood in a narrow path of the vineyards, *with* a wall on this side and a wall on that side.

25 When the donkey saw the angel of the LORD, she pressed herself to the wall and pressed Balaam's foot against the wall, so he struck her again.

26 The angel of the LORD went further, and stood in a narrow place where there was no way to turn to the right hand or the left.

27 When the donkey saw the angel of the LORD, she lay down under Balaam; so Balaam was angry and struck the donkey with his stick.

28 And the LORD opened the mouth of the donkey, and she said to Balaam, "What have I done to you, that you have struck me these three times?"

29 Then Balaam said to the donkey, "Because you have made a mockery of me! If there had been a sword in my hand, I would have killed you by now."

30 The donkey said to Balaam, "Am I not your donkey on which you have ridden all your life to this day? Have I ever been accustomed to do so to you?" And he said, "No."

31 ¶ Then the LORD opened the eyes of Balaam, and he saw the angel of the LORD standing in the way with his drawn sword in his hand; and he bowed all the way to the ground.

32 The angel of the LORD said to him, "Why have you struck your donkey these three times? Behold, I have come out as an adversary, because your way was contrary to me.

33 "But the donkey saw me and turned aside from me these three times. If she had not turned aside from me, I would surely have killed you just now, and let her live."

34 Balaam said to the angel of the LORD, "I have sinned, for I did not know that you were standing in the way against me. Now then, if it is displeasing to you, I will turn back."

35 But the angel of the LORD said to Balaam, "Go with the men, but you shall speak only the word which I tell you." So Balaam went along with the leaders of Balak.

36 ¶ When Balak heard that Balaam was coming, he went out to meet him at the city of Moab, which is on the Arnon border, at the extreme end of the border.

37 Then Balak said to Balaam, "Did I not urgently send to you to call you? Why did you not come to me? Am I really unable to honor you?"

38 So Balaam said to Balak, "Behold, I have come now to you! Am I able to speak anything at all? The word that God puts in my mouth, that I shall speak."

39 And Balaam went with Balak, and they came to Kiriath-huzoth.

40 Balak sacrificed oxen and sheep, and sent *some* to Balaam and the leaders who were with him.

41 ¶ Then it came about in the morning that Balak took Balaam and brought him up to the high places of Baal, and he saw from there a portion of the people.

The Prophecies of Balaam

23 Then Balaam said to Balak, "Build seven altars for me here, and prepare seven bulls and seven rams for me here."

2 Balak did just as Balaam had spoken, and

Balak and Balaam offered up a bull and a ram on each altar.

3 Then Balaam said to Balak, "Stand beside your burnt offering, and I will go; perhaps the LORD will come to meet me, and whatever He shows me I will tell you." So he went to a bare hill.

4 ¶ Now God met Balaam, and he said to Him, "I have set up the seven altars, and I have offered up a bull and a ram on each altar."

5 Then the LORD put a word in Balaam's mouth and said, "Return to Balak, and you shall speak thus."

6 So he returned to him, and behold, he was standing beside his burnt offering, he and all the leaders of Moab.

7 He took up his ªdiscourse and said,
"From Aram Balak has brought me,
Moab's king from the mountains of the East,
'Come curse Jacob for me,
And come, denounce Israel!'
8 "How shall I curse whom God has not cursed?
And how can I denounce whom the LORD has not denounced?

ª Lit *parable*

Whose Side Is Balaam On?

A balky prophet, a talking donkey, and a furious king

NUMBERS 22–24 CONTAINS ONE OF the most bizarre stories in the entire Bible. It features a donkey speaking fluent Hebrew and showing more insight than a prophet. One man is at the center of the story, the mysterious character named Balaam.

Balaam was evidently a professional magician of a nomadic clan somewhat like the gypsies. He had an impressive reputation: Nearby kings alarmed by the Israelites hired him to work magic and get the gods on their side.

> Balak said to Balaam, "What have you done to me? I took you to curse my enemies, but behold, you have actually blessed them!" 23:11

Prophet for Hire

Numbers gives enough detail to paint a colorful, dramatic story, but even so, Balaam is cloaked in a fog of mystery. Clearly, God chose to speak through him—he communicated directly to Balaam seven times. Just as clearly, Balaam proved a reluctant prophet, subject to ambition and a handsome bribe. Even his own donkey rebuked him, in the only biblical account of an animal speaking. An angel gave not Balaam, but the donkey, high praise.

Balaam appeared at a solemn occasion designed to curse the Israelites, but instead he pronounced blessings on them and curses on their enemies. He gave four stirring messages, far different in content from what his employer wanted to hear.

"How shall I curse whom God has not cursed?" Balaam asked (23:8). His magnificent prophecies shine out from scenes of comic irony. Balaam grew bolder and bolder, changing from a sorcerer into a prophet with backbone.

Prophet or Traitor?

Numbers 22–24 presents Balaam as an apparent convert. Tragically, the changes in him were only temporary. Balaam next appears in Numbers 31:8, the slain victim of an Israelite raid. Outright condemnations in 2 Peter 2:15, Jude 11, and Revelation 2:14 indicate that Balaam quickly returned to his treacherous ways. Having failed to manipulate the Israelites' God for his purposes, he resorted to manipulating the Israelites themselves. He convinced other nations to seduce them with sex and the worship of false gods. His actions led to the deaths of 24,000 people (25:9).

Some have called Balaam the Judas of the Old Testament, and certain parallels do emerge. Both men came close enough to truth to appear sincere and faithful. For a time, both seemed to serve the true God. But, motivated by ambition and greed, they renounced God and turned against him, with catastrophic results.

Part of a Bigger Battle

Seven books of the Bible refer to Balaam. The importance given to his story implies that it stood as a key event in the Israelites' relationship to pagan cultures. The Israelites were about to enter a land where magic and sorcery were used as national weapons. In a stroke of irony, God selected a spokesman who was both magician and pagan. Through him God rebuked those nations and their false gods.

Life Questions: Have you ever been used by God despite your own reluctance?

9 "As I see him from the top of the rocks,
And I look at him from the hills;
Behold, a people *who* dwells apart,
And will not be reckoned among the
nations.
10 "Who can count the dust of Jacob,
Or number the fourth part of Israel?
Let me die the death of the upright,
And let my end be like his!"

11 ¶ Then Balak said to Balaam, "What have
you done to me? I took you to curse my enemies,
but behold, you have actually blessed them!"

12 He replied, "Must I not be careful to speak
what the LORD puts in my mouth?"

13 ¶ Then Balak said to him, "Please come
with me to another place from where you may see
them, although you will only see the extreme end
of them and will not see all of them; and curse
them for me from there."

14 So he took him to the field of Zophim, to
the top of Pisgah, and built seven altars and offered a bull and a ram on *each* altar.

15 And he said to Balak, "Stand here beside
your burnt offering while I myself meet *the LORD*
over there."

16 Then the LORD met Balaam and put a word
in his mouth and said, "Return to Balak, and thus
you shall speak."

17 He came to him, and behold, he was standing beside his burnt offering, and the leaders of
Moab with him. And Balak said to him, "What
has the LORD spoken?"

18 Then he took up his [a]discourse and said,
"Arise, O Balak, and hear;
Give ear to me, O son of Zippor!
19 "God is not a man, that He should lie,
Nor a son of man, that He should
repent;
Has He said, and will He not do it?
Or has He spoken, and will He not make
it good?
20 "Behold, I have received *a command* to
bless;
When He has blessed, then I cannot
revoke it.
21 "He has not observed misfortune in Jacob;
Nor has He seen trouble in Israel;
The LORD his God is with him,
And the shout of a king is among them.
22 "God brings them out of Egypt,
He is for him like the horns of the
wild ox.
23 "For there is no omen against Jacob,
Nor is there any divination against Israel;
At the proper time it shall be said to
Jacob
And to Israel, what God has done!
24 "Behold, a people rises like a lioness,
And as a lion it lifts itself;

It will not lie down until it devours the
prey,
And drinks the blood of the slain."

25 ¶ Then Balak said to Balaam, "Do not curse
them at all nor bless them at all!"

26 But Balaam replied to Balak, "Did I not tell
you, 'Whatever the LORD speaks, that I must do'?"

27 ¶ Then Balak said to Balaam, "Please come,
I will take you to another place; perhaps it will be
agreeable with God that you curse them for me
from there."

28 So Balak took Balaam to the top of Peor
which overlooks the wasteland.

29 Balaam said to Balak, "Build seven altars for
me here and prepare seven bulls and seven rams
for me here."

30 Balak did just as Balaam had said, and offered up a bull and a ram on *each* altar.

The Prophecy from Peor

24 When Balaam saw that it pleased the LORD
to bless Israel, he did not go as at other
times to seek omens but he set his face toward the
wilderness.

2 And Balaam lifted up his eyes and saw Israel
camping tribe by tribe; and the Spirit of God came
upon him.

3 He took up his discourse and said,
"The oracle of Balaam the son of Beor,
And the oracle of the man whose eye is
opened;
4 The oracle of him who hears the words
of God,
Who sees the vision of the Almighty,
Falling down, yet having his eyes
uncovered;
5 How fair are your tents, O Jacob,
Your dwellings, O Israel!
6 "Like valleys that stretch out,
Like gardens beside the river,
Like aloes planted by the LORD,
Like cedars beside the waters.
7 "Water will flow from his buckets,
And his seed *will be* by many waters,
And his king shall be higher than Agag,
And his kingdom shall be exalted.
8 "God brings him out of Egypt,
He is for him like the horns of the
wild ox.
He will devour the nations *who are* his
adversaries,
And will crush their bones in pieces,
And shatter *them* with his arrows.
9 "He couches, he lies down as a lion,
And as a lion, who dares rouse him?
Blessed is everyone who blesses you,
And cursed is everyone who curses you."

10 ¶ Then Balak's anger burned against Balaam, and he struck his hands together; and Balak

---

[a] Lit *parable*

said to Balaam, "I called you to curse my enemies, but behold, you have persisted in blessing them these three times!

11 "Therefore, flee to your place now. I said I would honor you greatly, but behold, the LORD has held you back from honor."

12 Balaam said to Balak, "Did I not tell your messengers whom you had sent to me, saying,

13 'Though Balak were to give me his house full of silver and gold, I could not do anything contrary to the command of the LORD, either good or bad, of my own accord. What the LORD speaks, that I will speak'?

14 "And now, behold, I am going to my people; come, *and* I will advise you what this people will do to your people in the days to come."

15 ¶ He took up his discourse and said,
"The oracle of Balaam the son of Beor,
And the oracle of the man whose eye is
    opened,
16 The oracle of him who hears the words
    of God,
And knows the knowledge of the Most
    High,
Who sees the vision of the Almighty,
Falling down, yet having his eyes
    uncovered.
17 "I see him, but not now;
I behold him, but not near;
A star shall come forth from Jacob,
A scepter shall rise from Israel,
And shall crush through the forehead of
    Moab,
And tear down all the sons of ᵃSheth.

24:17 Balaam's Prophecy

This prediction delivered by Balaam came true during the reign of King David, who crushed the nations of Moab and Edom (2 Samuel 8:2,14).

18 "Edom shall be a possession,
Seir, its enemies, also will be a
    possession,
While Israel performs valiantly.
19 "One from Jacob shall have dominion,
And will destroy the remnant from the
    city."
20 ¶ And he looked at Amalek and took up his discourse and said,
"Amalek was the first of the nations,
But his end *shall be* destruction."
21 ¶ And he looked at the Kenite, and took up his discourse and said,
"Your dwelling place is enduring,
And your nest is set in the cliff.

22 "Nevertheless Kain will be consumed;
How long will Asshur keep you captive?"
23 ¶ Then he took up his discourse and said,
"Alas, who can live except God has
    ordained it?
24 "But ships *shall come* from the coast of
    Kittim,
And they shall afflict Asshur and will
    afflict Eber;
So they also *will come* to destruction."
25 ¶ Then Balaam arose and departed and returned to his place, and Balak also went his way.

The Sin of Peor

25 While Israel remained at Shittim, the people began to play the harlot with the daughters of Moab.

25:1 Sexual Seduction

Militarily, Israel was doing well. Their enemies were terrified (22:3), and the man summoned to put a curse on Israel had instead spoken God's blessing (24:8–9). But the Israelites were vulnerable to sexual temptation. Moabite women offered sexual favors, then invited the foreigners to local religious services. (Numbers 31:16 reports that Balaam suggested the tactic.) It is an old method of subverting God's people, and it still works.

2 For they invited the people to the sacrifices of their gods, and the people ate and bowed down to their gods.

3 So Israel joined themselves to Baal of Peor, and the LORD was angry against Israel.

4 The LORD said to Moses, "Take all the leaders of the people and execute them in broad daylight before the LORD, so that the fierce anger of the LORD may turn away from Israel."

5 So Moses said to the judges of Israel, "Each of you slay his men who have joined themselves to Baal of Peor."

6 ¶ Then behold, one of the sons of Israel came and brought to his relatives a Midianite woman, in the sight of Moses and in the sight of all the congregation of the sons of Israel, while they were weeping at the doorway of the tent of meeting.

7 When Phinehas the son of Eleazar, the son of Aaron the priest, saw it, he arose from the midst of the congregation and took a spear in his hand,

8 and he went after the man of Israel into the tent and pierced both of them through, the man of Israel and the woman, through the body. So the plague on the sons of Israel was checked.

9 Those who died by the plague were 24,000.

ᵃ I.e. tumult

The Zeal of Phinehas

10 ¶ Then the LORD spoke to Moses, saying,

11 "Phinehas the son of Eleazar, the son of Aaron the priest, has turned away My wrath from the sons of Israel in that he was jealous with My jealousy among them, so that I did not destroy the sons of Israel in My jealousy.

12 "Therefore say, 'Behold, I give him My covenant of peace;

13 and it shall be for him and his descendants after him, a covenant of a perpetual priesthood, because he was jealous for his God and made atonement for the sons of Israel.'"

14 ¶ Now the name of the slain man of Israel who was slain with the Midianite woman, was Zimri the son of Salu, a leader of a father's household among the Simeonites.

15 The name of the Midianite woman who was slain was Cozbi the daughter of Zur, who was head of the people of a father's household in Midian.

16 ¶ Then the LORD spoke to Moses, saying,

17 "Be hostile to the Midianites and strike them;

18 for they have been hostile to you with their tricks, with which they have deceived you in the affair of Peor and in the affair of Cozbi, the daughter of the leader of Midian, their sister who was slain on the day of the plague because of Peor."

Census of a New Generation

26 Then it came about after the plague, that the LORD spoke to Moses and to Eleazar the son of Aaron the priest, saying,

2 "Take a census of all the congregation of the sons of Israel from twenty years old and upward, by their fathers' households, whoever is able to go out to war in Israel."

3 So Moses and Eleazar the priest spoke with them in the plains of Moab by the Jordan at Jericho, saying,

4 "Take a census of the people from twenty years old and upward, as the LORD has commanded Moses."

¶ Now the sons of Israel who came out of the land of Egypt were:

5 ¶ Reuben, Israel's firstborn, the sons of Reuben: of Hanoch, the family of the Hanochites; of Pallu, the family of the Palluites;

6 of Hezron, the family of the Hezronites; of Carmi, the family of the Carmites.

7 These are the families of the Reubenites, and those who were numbered of them were 43,730.

8 The son of Pallu: Eliab.

9 The sons of Eliab: Nemuel and Dathan and Abiram. These are the Dathan and Abiram who were called by the congregation, who contended against Moses and against Aaron in the company of Korah, when they contended against the LORD,

10 and the earth opened its mouth and swallowed them up along with Korah, when that company died, when the fire devoured 250 men, so that they became a warning.

11 The sons of Korah, however, did not die.

12 ¶ The sons of Simeon according to their families: of Nemuel, the family of the Nemuelites; of Jamin, the family of the Jaminites; of Jachin, the family of the Jachinites;

13 of Zerah, the family of the Zerahites; of Shaul, the family of the Shaulites.

14 These are the families of the Simeonites, 22,200.

15 ¶ The sons of Gad according to their families: of Zephon, the family of the Zephonites; of Haggi, the family of the Haggites; of Shuni, the family of the Shunites;

16 of Ozni, the family of the Oznites; of Eri, the family of the Erites;

17 of Arod, the family of the Arodites; of Areli, the family of the Arelites.

18 These are the families of the sons of Gad according to those who were numbered of them, 40,500.

19 ¶ The sons of Judah were Er and Onan, but Er and Onan died in the land of Canaan.

20 The sons of Judah according to their families were: of Shelah, the family of the Shelanites; of Perez, the family of the Perezites; of Zerah, the family of the Zerahites.

21 The sons of Perez were: of Hezron, the family of the Hezronites; of Hamul, the family of the Hamulites.

22 These are the families of Judah according to those who were numbered of them, 76,500.

23 ¶ The sons of Issachar according to their families: of Tola, the family of the Tolaites; of Puvah, the family of the Punites;

24 of Jashub, the family of the Jashubites; of Shimron, the family of the Shimronites.

25 These are the families of Issachar according to those who were numbered of them, 64,300.

26 ¶ The sons of Zebulun according to their families: of Sered, the family of the Seredites; of Elon, the family of the Elonites; of Jahleel, the family of the Jahleelites.

27 These are the families of the Zebulunites according to those who were numbered of them, 60,500.

28 ¶ The sons of Joseph according to their families: Manasseh and Ephraim.

29 The sons of Manasseh: of Machir, the family of the Machirites; and Machir became the father of Gilead: of Gilead, the family of the Gileadites.

30 These are the sons of Gilead: of Iezer, the family of the Iezerites; of Helek, the family of the Helekites;

31 and of Asriel, the family of the Asrielites; and of Shechem, the family of the Shechemites;

32 and of Shemida, the family of the Shemidaites; and of Hepher, the family of the Hepherites.

33 Now Zelophehad the son of Hepher had no sons, but only daughters; and the names of the

daughters of Zelophehad were Mahlah, Noah, Hoglah, Milcah and Tirzah.

34 These are the families of Manasseh; and those who were numbered of them were 52,700.

35 ¶ These are the sons of Ephraim according to their families: of Shuthelah, the family of the Shuthelahites; of Becher, the family of the Becherites; of Tahan, the family of the Tahanites.

36 These are the sons of Shuthelah: of Eran, the family of the Eranites.

37 These are the families of the sons of Ephraim according to those who were numbered of them, 32,500. These are the sons of Joseph according to their families.

38 ¶ The sons of Benjamin according to their families: of Bela, the family of the Belaites; of Ashbel, the family of the Ashbelites; of Ahiram, the family of the Ahiramites;

39 of Shephupham, the family of the Shuphamites; of Hupham, the family of the Huphamites.

40 The sons of Bela were Ard and Naaman: *of Ard,* the family of the Ardites; of Naaman, the family of the Naamites.

41 These are the sons of Benjamin according to their families; and those who were numbered of them were 45,600.

42 ¶ These are the sons of Dan according to their families: of Shuham, the family of the Shuhamites. These are the families of Dan according to their families.

43 All the families of the Shuhamites, according to those who were numbered of them, were 64,400.

44 ¶ The sons of Asher according to their families: of Imnah, the family of the Imnites; of Ishvi, the family of the Ishvites; of Beriah, the family of the Beriites.

45 Of the sons of Beriah: of Heber, the family of the Heberites; of Malchiel, the family of the Malchielites.

46 The name of the daughter of Asher *was* Serah.

47 These are the families of the sons of Asher according to those who were numbered of them, 53,400.

48 ¶ The sons of Naphtali according to their families: of Jahzeel, the family of the Jahzeelites; of Guni, the family of the Gunites;

49 of Jezer, the family of the Jezerites; of Shillem, the family of the Shillemites.

50 These are the families of Naphtali according to their families; and those who were numbered of them were 45,400.

51 ¶ These are those who were numbered of the sons of Israel, 601,730.

52 ¶ Then the LORD spoke to Moses, saying,

53 "Among these the land shall be divided for an inheritance according to the number of names.

54 "To the larger *group* you shall increase their inheritance, and to the smaller *group* you shall diminish their inheritance; each shall be given their inheritance according to those who were numbered of them.

55 "But the land shall be divided by lot. They

26:51 Recount

The two censuses in Numbers (chapter 1 and here) stand like bookends, marking the hopeful beginning and tragic end of the vast numbers of Israelites heading toward freedom. After 40 years, the totals were nearly the same—600,000 men—but only two of the original pilgrims would cross the Jordan River. The nation renewed itself like a human body, which looks the same but replaces all its cells every few years.

shall receive their inheritance according to the names of the tribes of their fathers.

56 "According to the selection by lot, their inheritance shall be divided between the larger and the smaller *groups.*"

57 ¶ These are those who were numbered of the Levites according to their families: of Gershon, the family of the Gershonites; of Kohath, the family of the Kohathites; of Merari, the family of the Merarites.

58 These are the families of Levi: the family of the Libnites, the family of the Hebronites, the family of the Mahlites, the family of the Mushites, the family of the Korahites. Kohath became the father of Amram.

59 The name of Amram's wife was Jochebed, the daughter of Levi, who was born to Levi in Egypt; and she bore to Amram: Aaron and Moses and their sister Miriam.

60 To Aaron were born Nadab and Abihu, Eleazar and Ithamar.

61 But Nadab and Abihu died when they offered strange fire before the LORD.

62 Those who were numbered of them were 23,000, every male from a month old and upward, for they were not numbered among the sons of Israel since no inheritance was given to them among the sons of Israel.

63 ¶ These are those who were numbered by Moses and Eleazar the priest, who numbered the sons of Israel in the plains of Moab by the Jordan at Jericho.

64 But among these there was not a man of those who were numbered by Moses and Aaron the priest, who numbered the sons of Israel in the wilderness of Sinai.

65 For the LORD had said of them, "They shall surely die in the wilderness." And not a man was left of them, except Caleb the son of Jephunneh and Joshua the son of Nun.

A Law of Inheritance

27 Then the daughters of Zelophehad, the son of Hepher, the son of Gilead, the son of Machir, the son of Manasseh, of the families of Manasseh the son of Joseph, came near; and these are the names of his daughters: Mahlah, Noah and Hoglah and Milcah and Tirzah.

2 They stood before Moses and before Eleazar the priest and before the leaders and all the congregation, at the doorway of the tent of meeting, saying,

3 "Our father died in the wilderness, yet he was not among the company of those who gathered themselves together against the LORD in the company of Korah; but he died in his own sin, and he had no sons.

4 "Why should the name of our father be withdrawn from among his family because he had no son? Give us a possession among our father's brothers."

5 So Moses brought their case before the LORD.

6 ¶ Then the LORD spoke to Moses, saying,

7 "The daughters of Zelophehad are right in *their* statements. You shall surely give them a hereditary possession among their father's brothers, and you shall transfer the inheritance of their father to them.

8 "Further, you shall speak to the sons of Israel, saying, 'If a man dies and has no son, then you shall transfer his inheritance to his daughter.

9 'If he has no daughter, then you shall give his inheritance to his brothers.

10 'If he has no brothers, then you shall give his inheritance to his father's brothers.

11 'If his father has no brothers, then you shall give his inheritance to his nearest relative in his own family, and he shall possess it; and it shall be a statutory ordinance to the sons of Israel, just as the LORD commanded Moses.' "

12 ¶ Then the LORD said to Moses, "Go up to this mountain of Abarim, and see the land which I have given to the sons of Israel.

13 "When you have seen it, you too will be gathered to your people, as Aaron your brother was;

14 for in the wilderness of Zin, during the strife of the congregation, you rebelled against My command to treat Me as holy before their eyes at the water." (These are the waters of Meribah of Kadesh in the wilderness of Zin.)

Joshua to Succeed Moses

15 ¶ Then Moses spoke to the LORD, saying,

16 "May the LORD, the God of the spirits of all flesh, appoint a man over the congregation,

17 who will go out and come in before them, and who will lead them out and bring them in, so that the congregation of the LORD will not be like sheep which have no shepherd."

18 So the LORD said to Moses, "Take Joshua the son of Nun, a man in whom is the Spirit, and lay your hand on him;

19 and have him stand before Eleazar the priest and before all the congregation, and commission him in their sight.

27:14 Moses Stayed Out

Because Moses had disobeyed God (the scene is described in 20:1–13), he was not allowed to enter the promised land. In this account he seems to accept his punishment without complaint, quietly turning over his leadership to Joshua. But in his great final speech, recorded in Deuteronomy, he bitterly raised the topic three times (Deuteronomy 1:37, 3:23–27, 4:21–24). The punishment was not forever; Moses did "get in" hundreds of years after his death, in the company of Jesus (Mark 9:4).

20 "You shall put some of your authority on him, in order that all the congregation of the sons of Israel may obey *him*.

21 "Moreover, he shall stand before Eleazar the priest, who shall inquire for him by the judgment of the Urim before the LORD. At his command they shall go out and at his command they shall come in, *both* he and the sons of Israel with him, even all the congregation."

22 Moses did just as the LORD commanded him; and he took Joshua and set him before Eleazar the priest and before all the congregation.

23 Then he laid his hands on him and commissioned him, just as the LORD had spoken through Moses.

Laws for Offerings

28 Then the LORD spoke to Moses, saying,

2 "Command the sons of Israel and say to them, 'You shall be careful to present My offering, My food for My offerings by fire, of a soothing aroma to Me, at their appointed time.'

3 "You shall say to them, 'This is the offering by fire which you shall offer to the LORD: two male lambs one year old without defect *as* a continual burnt offering every day.

4 'You shall offer the one lamb in the morning and the other lamb you shall offer at twilight;

5 also a tenth of an ephah of fine flour for a grain offering, mixed with a fourth of a hin of beaten oil.

6 'It is a continual burnt offering which was ordained in Mount Sinai as a soothing aroma, an offering by fire to the LORD.

7 'Then the drink offering with it *shall be* a fourth of a hin for each lamb, in the holy place you shall pour out a drink offering of strong drink to the LORD.

8 'The other lamb you shall offer at twilight; as the grain offering of the morning and as its drink

offering, you shall offer it, an offering by fire, a soothing aroma to the LORD.

9 ¶ 'Then on the sabbath day two male lambs one year old without defect, and two-tenths *of an ephah* of fine flour mixed with oil as a grain offering, and its drink offering:

10 'This is the burnt offering of every sabbath in addition to the continual burnt offering and its drink offering.

11 ¶ 'Then at the beginning of each of your months you shall present a burnt offering to the LORD: two bulls and one ram, seven male lambs one year old without defect;

12 and three-tenths *of an ephah* of fine flour mixed with oil for a grain offering, for each bull; and two-tenths of fine flour mixed with oil for a grain offering, for the one ram;

13 and a tenth *of an ephah* of fine flour mixed with oil for a grain offering for each lamb, for a burnt offering of a soothing aroma, an offering by fire to the LORD.

14 'Their drink offerings shall be half a hin of wine for a bull and a third of a hin for the ram and a fourth of a hin for a lamb; this is the burnt offering of each month throughout the months of the year.

15 'And one male goat for a sin offering to the LORD; it shall be offered with its drink offering in addition to the continual burnt offering.

16 ¶ 'Then on the fourteenth day of the first month shall be the LORD'S Passover.

17 'On the fifteenth day of this month *shall be* a feast, unleavened bread *shall be* eaten for seven days.

18 'On the first day *shall be* a holy convocation; you shall do no laborious work.

19 'You shall present an offering by fire, a burnt offering to the LORD: two bulls and one ram and seven male lambs one year old, having them without defect.

20 'For their grain offering, you shall offer fine flour mixed with oil: three-tenths *of an ephah* for a bull and two-tenths for the ram.

21 'A tenth *of an ephah* you shall offer for each of the seven lambs;

22 and one male goat for a sin offering to make atonement for you.

23 'You shall present these besides the burnt offering of the morning, which is for a continual burnt offering.

24 'After this manner you shall present daily, for seven days, the food of the offering by fire, of a soothing aroma to the LORD; it shall be presented with its drink offering in addition to the continual burnt offering.

25 'On the seventh day you shall have a holy convocation; you shall do no laborious work.

26 ¶ 'Also on the day of the first fruits, when you present a new grain offering to the LORD in your *Feast of* Weeks, you shall have a holy convocation; you shall do no laborious work.

27 'You shall offer a burnt offering for a soothing aroma to the LORD: two young bulls, one ram, seven male lambs one year old;

28 and their grain offering, fine flour mixed with oil: three-tenths *of an ephah* for each bull, two-tenths for the one ram,

29 a tenth for each of the seven lambs;

30 *also* one male goat to make atonement for you.

31 'Besides the continual burnt offering and its grain offering, you shall present *them* with their drink offerings. They shall be without defect.

Offerings of the Seventh Month

29 'Now in the seventh month, on the first day of the month, you shall also have a holy convocation; you shall do no laborious work. It will be to you a day for blowing trumpets.

29:1 Interruptions of the Story

Numbers periodically interrupts its history with lists of rules or rituals, such as in this section, chapters 28–30. Usually, they relate to what appears just before or afterward. The instructions here were not new, but God saw a need to review them just as the nation was about to enter the promised land.

2 'You shall offer a burnt offering as a soothing aroma to the LORD: one bull, one ram, *and* seven male lambs one year old without defect;

3 also their grain offering, fine flour mixed with oil: three-tenths *of an ephah* for the bull, two-tenths for the ram,

4 and one-tenth for each of the seven lambs.

5 'Offer one male goat for a sin offering, to make atonement for you,

6 besides the burnt offering of the new moon and its grain offering, and the continual burnt offering and its grain offering, and their drink offerings, according to their ordinance, for a soothing aroma, an offering by fire to the LORD.

7 ¶ 'Then on the tenth day of this seventh month you shall have a holy convocation, and you shall humble yourselves; you shall not do any work.

8 'You shall present a burnt offering to the LORD *as* a soothing aroma: one bull, one ram, seven male lambs one year old, having them without defect;

9 and their grain offering, fine flour mixed with oil: three-tenths *of an ephah* for the bull, two-tenths for the one ram,

10 a tenth for each of the seven lambs;

11 one male goat for a sin offering, besides the sin offering of atonement and the continual burnt offering and its grain offering, and their drink offerings.

12 ¶ 'Then on the fifteenth day of the seventh

month you shall have a holy convocation; you shall do no laborious work, and you shall observe a feast to the LORD for seven days.

13 'You shall present a burnt offering, an offering by fire as a soothing aroma to the LORD: thirteen bulls, two rams, fourteen male lambs one year old, which are without defect;

14 and their grain offering, fine flour mixed with oil: three-tenths *of an ephah* for each of the thirteen bulls, two-tenths for each of the two rams,

15 and a tenth for each of the fourteen lambs;

16 and one male goat for a sin offering, besides the continual burnt offering, its grain offering and its drink offering.

17 ¶ 'Then on the second day: twelve bulls, two rams, fourteen male lambs one year old without defect;

18 and their grain offering and their drink offerings for the bulls, for the rams and for the lambs, by their number according to the ordinance;

19 and one male goat for a sin offering, besides the continual burnt offering and its grain offering, and their drink offerings.

20 ¶ 'Then on the third day: eleven bulls, two rams, fourteen male lambs one year old without defect;

21 and their grain offering and their drink offerings for the bulls, for the rams and for the lambs, by their number according to the ordinance;

22 and one male goat for a sin offering, besides the continual burnt offering and its grain offering and its drink offering.

23 ¶ 'Then on the fourth day: ten bulls, two rams, fourteen male lambs one year old without defect;

24 their grain offering and their drink offerings for the bulls, for the rams and for the lambs, by their number according to the ordinance;

25 and one male goat for a sin offering, besides the continual burnt offering, its grain offering and its drink offering.

26 ¶ 'Then on the fifth day: nine bulls, two rams, fourteen male lambs one year old without defect;

27 and their grain offering and their drink offerings for the bulls, for the rams and for the lambs, by their number according to the ordinance;

28 and one male goat for a sin offering, besides the continual burnt offering and its grain offering and its drink offering.

29 ¶ 'Then on the sixth day: eight bulls, two rams, fourteen male lambs one year old without defect;

30 and their grain offering and their drink offerings for the bulls, for the rams and for the lambs, by their number according to the ordinance;

31 and one male goat for a sin offering, besides

the continual burnt offering, its grain offering and its drink offerings.

32 ¶ 'Then on the seventh day: seven bulls, two rams, fourteen male lambs one year old without defect;

33 and their grain offering and their drink offerings for the bulls, for the rams and for the lambs, by their number according to the ordinance;

34 and one male goat for a sin offering, besides the continual burnt offering, its grain offering and its drink offering.

35 ¶ 'On the eighth day you shall have a solemn assembly; you shall do no laborious work.

36 'But you shall present a burnt offering, an offering by fire, as a soothing aroma to the LORD: one bull, one ram, seven male lambs one year old without defect;

37 their grain offering and their drink offerings for the bull, for the ram and for the lambs, by their number according to the ordinance;

38 and one male goat for a sin offering, besides the continual burnt offering and its grain offering and its drink offering.

39 ¶ 'You shall present these to the LORD at your appointed times, besides your votive offerings and your freewill offerings, for your burnt offerings and for your grain offerings and for your drink offerings and for your peace offerings.' "

40 Moses spoke to the sons of Israel in accordance with all that the LORD had commanded Moses.

The Law of Vows

30 Then Moses spoke to the heads of the tribes of the sons of Israel, saying, "This is the word which the LORD has commanded.

2 "If a man makes a vow to the LORD, or takes an oath to bind himself with a binding obligation, he shall not violate his word; he shall do according to all that proceeds out of his mouth.

3 ¶ "Also if a woman makes a vow to the LORD, and binds herself by an obligation in her father's house in her youth,

4 and her father hears her vow and her obligation by which she has bound herself, and her father says nothing to her, then all her vows shall stand and every obligation by which she has bound herself shall stand.

5 "But if her father should forbid her on the day he hears *of it*, none of her vows or her obligations by which she has bound herself shall stand; and the LORD will forgive her because her father had forbidden her.

6 ¶ "However, if she should marry while under her vows or the rash statement of her lips by which she has bound herself,

7 and her husband hears of it and says nothing to her on the day he hears *it*, then her vows shall stand and her obligations by which she has bound herself shall stand.

8 "But if on the day her husband hears *of it*, he forbids her, then he shall annul her vow which she is under and the rash statement of her lips by which she has bound herself; and the LORD will forgive her.

9 ¶ "But the vow of a widow or of a divorced woman, everything by which she has bound herself, shall stand against her.

10 "However, if she vowed in her husband's house, or bound herself by an obligation with an oath,

11 and her husband heard *it*, but said nothing to her *and* did not forbid her, then all her vows shall stand and every obligation by which she bound herself shall stand.

12 "But if her husband indeed annuls them on the day he hears *them,* then whatever proceeds out of her lips concerning her vows or concerning the obligation of herself shall not stand; her husband has annulled them, and the LORD will forgive her.

13 ¶ "Every vow and every binding oath to humble herself, her husband may confirm it or her husband may annul it.

14 "But if her husband indeed says nothing to her from day to day, then he confirms all her vows or all her obligations which are on her; he has confirmed them, because he said nothing to her on the day he heard them.

15 "But if he indeed annuls them after he has heard them, then he shall bear her guilt."

16 ¶ These are the statutes which the LORD commanded Moses, *as* between a man and his wife, *and as* between a father and his daughter, *while she is* in her youth in her father's house.

The Slaughter of Midian

31 Then the LORD spoke to Moses, saying,
2 "Take full vengeance for the sons of Israel on the Midianites; afterward you will be gathered to your people."

3 Moses spoke to the people, saying, "Arm men from among you for the war, that they may go against Midian to execute the LORD's vengeance on Midian.

4 "A thousand from each tribe of all the tribes of Israel you shall send to the war."

5 So there were furnished from the thousands of Israel, a thousand from each tribe, twelve thousand armed for war.

6 Moses sent them, a thousand from each tribe, to the war, and Phinehas the son of Eleazar the priest, to the war with them, and the holy vessels and the trumpets for the alarm in his hand.

7 So they made war against Midian, just as LORD had commanded Moses, and they killed every male.

8 They killed the kings of Midian along with the *rest of* their slain: Evi and Rekem and Zur and Hur and Reba, the five kings of Midian; they also killed Balaam the son of Beor with the sword.

9 The sons of Israel captured the women of Midian and their little ones; and all their cattle and all their flocks and all their goods they plundered.

10 Then they burned all their cities where they lived and all their camps with fire.

11 They took all the spoil and all the prey, both of man and of beast.

12 They brought the captives and the prey and the spoil to Moses, and to Eleazar the priest and to the congregation of the sons of Israel, to the camp at the plains of Moab, which are by the Jordan *opposite* Jericho.

13 ¶ Moses and Eleazar the priest and all the leaders of the congregation went out to meet them outside the camp.

14 Moses was angry with the officers of the army, the captains of thousands and the captains of hundreds, who had come from service in the war.

15 And Moses said to them, "Have you spared all the women?

16 "Behold, these caused the sons of Israel, through the counsel of Balaam, to trespass against the LORD in the matter of Peor, so the plague was among the congregation of the LORD.

17 "Now therefore, kill every male among the little ones, and kill every woman who has known man intimately.

18 "But all the girls who have not known man intimately, spare for yourselves.

19 "And you, camp outside the camp seven days; whoever has killed any person and whoever has touched any slain, purify yourselves, you and your captives, on the third day and on the seventh day.

31:19–24 Acts of War

Many readers struggle with the harsh warfare policies God demanded of the Israelites. Numbers 35:34 summarizes one basic reason why policies were so strict: so that the land itself, set apart by God, would not become defiled (see "Is a War Ever Holy?" page 262). Even so, this passage shows that killing was not taken lightly—even war heroes had to go through the process of purification.

20 "You shall purify for yourselves every garment and every article of leather and all the work of goats' *hair,* and all articles of wood."

21 ¶ Then Eleazar the priest said to the men of war who had gone to battle, "This is the statute of the law which the LORD has commanded Moses:

22 only the gold and the silver, the bronze, the iron, the tin and the lead,

23 everything that can stand the fire, you shall pass through the fire, and it shall be clean, but it shall be purified with water for impurity. But whatever cannot stand the fire you shall pass through the water.

24 "And you shall wash your clothes on the seventh day and be clean, and afterward you may enter the camp."

Division of the Booty

25 ¶ Then the LORD spoke to Moses, saying,

26 "You and Eleazar the priest and the heads of the fathers' *households* of the congregation take a count of the booty that was captured, both of man and of animal;

27 and divide the booty between the warriors who went out to battle and all the congregation.

28 "Levy a tax for the LORD from the men of war who went out to battle, one in five hundred of the persons and of the cattle and of the donkeys and of the sheep;

29 take it from their half and give it to Eleazar the priest, as an offering to the LORD.

30 "From the sons of Israel's half, you shall take one drawn out of every fifty of the persons, of the cattle, of the donkeys and of the sheep, from all the animals, and give them to the Levites who keep charge of the tabernacle of the LORD."

31 Moses and Eleazar the priest did just as the LORD had commanded Moses.

32 ¶ Now the booty that remained from the spoil which the men of war had plundered was 675,000 sheep,

33 and 72,000 cattle,

34 and 61,000 donkeys,

35 and of human beings, of the women who had not known man intimately, all the persons were 32,000.

36 ¶ The half, the portion of those who went out to war, was *as follows:* the number of sheep was 337,500,

37 and the LORD's levy of the sheep was 675;

38 and the cattle were 36,000, from which the LORD's levy was 72;

39 and the donkeys were 30,500, from which the LORD's levy was 61;

40 and the human beings were 16,000, from whom the LORD's levy was 32 persons.

41 Moses gave the levy *which was* the LORD's offering to Eleazar the priest, just as the LORD had commanded Moses.

42 ¶ As for the sons of Israel's half, which Moses separated from the men who had gone to war—

43 now the congregation's half was 337,500 sheep,

44 and 36,000 cattle,

45 and 30,500 donkeys,

46 and the human beings were 16,000—

47 and from the sons of Israel's half, Moses took one drawn out of every fifty, both of man and of animals, and gave them to the Levites, who kept charge of the tabernacle of the LORD, just as the LORD had commanded Moses.

48 ¶ Then the officers who were over the thousands of the army, the captains of thousands and the captains of hundreds, approached Moses,

49 and they said to Moses, "Your servants have taken a census of men of war who are in our charge, and no man of us is missing.

50 "So we have brought as an offering to the LORD what each man found, articles of gold, armlets and bracelets, signet rings, earrings and necklaces, to make atonement for ourselves before the LORD."

51 Moses and Eleazar the priest took the gold from them, all kinds of wrought articles.

52 All the gold of the offering which they offered up to the LORD, from the captains of thousands and the captains of hundreds, was 16,750 shekels.

53 The men of war had taken booty, every man for himself.

54 So Moses and Eleazar the priest took the gold from the captains of thousands and of hundreds, and brought it to the tent of meeting as a memorial for the sons of Israel before the LORD.

Reuben and Gad Settle in Gilead

32 Now the sons of Reuben and the sons of Gad had an exceedingly large number of livestock. So when they saw the land of Jazer and the land of Gilead, that it was indeed a place suitable for livestock,

2 the sons of Gad and the sons of Reuben came and spoke to Moses and to Eleazar the priest and to the leaders of the congregation, saying,

3 "Ataroth, Dibon, Jazer, Nimrah, Heshbon, Elealeh, Sebam, Nebo and Beon,

4 the land which the LORD conquered before the congregation of Israel, is a land for livestock, and your servants have livestock."

5 They said, "If we have found favor in your sight, let this land be given to your servants as a possession; do not take us across the Jordan."

6 ¶ But Moses said to the sons of Gad and to the sons of Reuben, "Shall your brothers go to war while you yourselves sit here?

7 "Now why are you discouraging the sons of Israel from crossing over into the land which the LORD has given them?

8 "This is what your fathers did when I sent them from Kadesh-barnea to see the land.

9 "For when they went up to the valley of Eshcol and saw the land, they discouraged the sons of Israel so that they did not go into the land which the LORD had given them.

10 "So the LORD's anger burned in that day, and He swore, saying,

11 'None of the men who came up from Egypt, from twenty years old and upward, shall see the land which I swore to Abraham, to Isaac and to Jacob; for they did not follow Me fully,

12 except Caleb the son of Jephunneh the Kenizzite and Joshua the son of Nun, for they have followed the LORD fully.'

13 "So the LORD'S anger burned against Israel, and He made them wander in the wilderness forty years, until the entire generation of those who had done evil in the sight of the LORD was destroyed.

14 "Now behold, you have risen up in your fathers' place, a brood of sinful men, to add still more to the burning anger of the LORD against Israel.

15 "For if you turn away from following Him, He will once more abandon them in the wilderness, and you will destroy all these people."

16 ¶ Then they came near to him and said, "We will build here sheepfolds for our livestock and cities for our little ones;

17 but we ourselves will be armed ready *to go* before the sons of Israel, until we have brought them to their place, while our little ones live in the fortified cities because of the inhabitants of the land.

18 "We will not return to our homes until every one of the sons of Israel has possessed his inheritance.

19 "For we will not have an inheritance with them on the other side of the Jordan and beyond, because our inheritance has fallen to us on this side of the Jordan toward the east."

20 ¶ So Moses said to them, "If you will do this, if you will arm yourselves before the LORD for the war,

21 and all of you armed men cross over the Jordan before the LORD until He has driven His enemies out from before Him,

22 and the land is subdued before the LORD, then afterward you shall return and be free of obligation toward the LORD and toward Israel, and this land shall be yours for a possession before the LORD.

32:22 Trouble Ahead

According to Joshua 22:1–6, the two and a half tribes did keep their promise to fight with the others. The land they chose was appealing, with parklike scenery, wide pastures, and lush forests. However, their settlement proved troublesome. With no natural borders, the land was open to enemy attack and easy infiltration.

23 "But if you will not do so, behold, you have sinned against the LORD, and be sure your sin will find you out.

24 "Build yourselves cities for your little ones, and sheepfolds for your sheep, and do what you have promised."

25 ¶ The sons of Gad and the sons of Reuben spoke to Moses, saying, "Your servants will do just as my lord commands.

26 "Our little ones, our wives, our livestock and all our cattle shall remain there in the cities of Gilead;

27 while your servants, everyone who is armed for war, will cross over in the presence of the LORD to battle, just as my lord says."

28 ¶ So Moses gave command concerning them to Eleazar the priest, and to Joshua the son of Nun, and to the heads of the fathers' *households* of the tribes of the sons of Israel.

29 Moses said to them, "If the sons of Gad and the sons of Reuben, everyone who is armed for battle, will cross with you over the Jordan in the presence of the LORD, and the land is subdued before you, then you shall give them the land of Gilead for a possession;

30 but if they will not cross over with you armed, they shall have possessions among you in the land of Canaan."

31 The sons of Gad and the sons of Reuben answered, saying, "As the LORD has said to your servants, so we will do.

32 "We ourselves will cross over armed in the presence of the LORD into the land of Canaan, and the possession of our inheritance *shall remain* with us across the Jordan."

33 ¶ So Moses gave to them, to the sons of Gad and to the sons of Reuben and to the half-tribe of Joseph's son Manasseh, the kingdom of Sihon, king of the Amorites and the kingdom of Og, the king of Bashan, the land with its cities with *their* territories, the cities of the surrounding land.

34 The sons of Gad built Dibon and Ataroth and Aroer,

35 and Atroth-shophan and Jazer and Jogbehah,

36 and Beth-nimrah and Beth-haran as fortified cities, and sheepfolds for sheep.

37 The sons of Reuben built Heshbon and Elealeh and Kiriathaim,

38 and Nebo and Baal-meon—*their* names being changed—and Sibmah, and they gave *other* names to the cities which they built.

39 The sons of Machir the son of Manasseh went to Gilead and took it, and dispossessed the Amorites who were in it.

40 So Moses gave Gilead to Machir the son of Manasseh, and he lived in it.

41 Jair the son of Manasseh went and took its towns, and called them Havvoth-jair.

42 Nobah went and took Kenath and its villages, and called it Nobah after his own name.

Review of the Journey from Egypt to Jordan

33 These are the journeys of the sons of Israel, by which they came out from the land of Egypt by their armies, under the leadership of Moses and Aaron.

2 Moses recorded their starting places according to their journeys by the command of the

LORD, and these are their journeys according to their starting places.

3 They journeyed from Rameses in the first month, on the fifteenth day of the first month; on the next day after the Passover the sons of Israel started out boldly in the sight of all the Egyptians,

4 while the Egyptians were burying all their firstborn whom the LORD had struck down among them. The LORD had also executed judgments on their gods.

5 ¶ Then the sons of Israel journeyed from Rameses and camped in Succoth.

6 They journeyed from Succoth and camped in Etham, which is on the edge of the wilderness.

7 They journeyed from Etham and turned back to Pi-hahiroth, which faces Baal-zephon, and they camped before Migdol.

8 They journeyed from before Hahiroth and passed through the midst of the sea into the wilderness; and they went three days' journey in the wilderness of Etham and camped at Marah.

9 They journeyed from Marah and came to Elim; and in Elim there were twelve springs of water and seventy palm trees, and they camped there.

10 They journeyed from Elim and camped by the Red Sea.

11 They journeyed from the Red Sea and camped in the wilderness of Sin.

12 They journeyed from the wilderness of Sin and camped at Dophkah.

13 They journeyed from Dophkah and camped at Alush.

14 They journeyed from Alush and camped at Rephidim; now it was there that the people had no water to drink.

15 They journeyed from Rephidim and camped in the wilderness of Sinai.

16 They journeyed from the wilderness of Sinai and camped at Kibroth-hattaavah.

17 ¶ They journeyed from Kibroth-hattaavah and camped at Hazeroth.

18 They journeyed from Hazeroth and camped at Rithmah.

19 They journeyed from Rithmah and camped at Rimmon-perez.

20 They journeyed from Rimmon-perez and camped at Libnah.

21 They journeyed from Libnah and camped at Rissah.

22 They journeyed from Rissah and camped in Kehelathah.

23 They journeyed from Kehelathah and camped at Mount Shepher.

24 They journeyed from Mount Shepher and camped at Haradah.

25 They journeyed from Haradah and camped at Makheloth.

26 They journeyed from Makheloth and camped at Tahath.

27 They journeyed from Tahath and camped at Terah.

28 They journeyed from Terah and camped at Mithkah.

29 They journeyed from Mithkah and camped at Hashmonah.

30 They journeyed from Hashmonah and camped at Moseroth.

31 They journeyed from Moseroth and camped at Bene-jaakan.

32 They journeyed from Bene-jaakan and camped at Hor-haggidgad.

33 They journeyed from Hor-haggidgad and camped at Jotbathah.

34 They journeyed from Jotbathah and camped at Abronah.

35 They journeyed from Abronah and camped at Ezion-geber.

36 They journeyed from Ezion-geber and camped in the wilderness of Zin, that is, Kadesh.

37 They journeyed from Kadesh and camped at Mount Hor, at the edge of the land of Edom.

38 ¶ Then Aaron the priest went up to Mount Hor at the command of the LORD, and died there in the fortieth year after the sons of Israel had come from the land of Egypt, on the first *day* in the fifth month.

39 Aaron was one hundred twenty-three years old when he died on Mount Hor.

40 ¶ Now the Canaanite, the king of Arad who lived in the Negev in the land of Canaan, heard of the coming of the sons of Israel.

41 ¶ Then they journeyed from Mount Hor and camped at Zalmonah.

42 They journeyed from Zalmonah and camped at Punon.

43 They journeyed from Punon and camped at Oboth.

44 They journeyed from Oboth and camped at Iye-abarim, at the border of Moab.

45 They journeyed from Iyim and camped at Dibon-gad.

46 They journeyed from Dibon-gad and camped at Almon-diblathaim.

47 They journeyed from Almon-diblathaim and camped in the mountains of Abarim, before Nebo.

48 They journeyed from the mountains of Abarim and camped in the plains of Moab by the Jordan *opposite* Jericho.

49 They camped by the Jordan, from Beth-jeshimoth as far as Abel-shittim in the plains of Moab.

Law of Possessing the Land

50 ¶ Then the LORD spoke to Moses in the plains of Moab by the Jordan *opposite* Jericho, saying,

51 "Speak to the sons of Israel and say to them, 'When you cross over the Jordan into the land of Canaan,

52 then you shall drive out all the inhabitants of the land from before you, and destroy all their figured stones, and destroy all their molten images and demolish all their high places;

33:50–56 Final Warnings

Just before the dramatic crossing into the promised land, God gave a clear statement of his priorities and a warning of what would happen if the Israelites failed to obey. His words would one day come back to haunt them, for they failed to carry out fully any of his orders.

53 and you shall take possession of the land and live in it, for I have given the land to you to possess it.

54 'You shall inherit the land by lot according to your families; to the larger you shall give more inheritance, and to the smaller you shall give less inheritance. Wherever the lot falls to anyone, that shall be his. You shall inherit according to the tribes of your fathers.

55 'But if you do not drive out the inhabitants of the land from before you, then it shall come about that those whom you let remain of them *will become* as pricks in your eyes and as thorns in your sides, and they will trouble you in the land in which you live.

56 'And as I plan to do to them, so I will do to you.' "

Instruction for Apportioning Canaan

34 Then the LORD spoke to Moses, saying, 2 "Command the sons of Israel and say to them, 'When you enter the land of Canaan, this is the land that shall fall to you as an inheritance, *even the* land of Canaan according to its borders.

3 'Your southern sector shall extend from the wilderness of Zin along the side of Edom, and your southern border shall extend from the end of the Salt Sea eastward.

4 'Then your border shall turn *direction* from the south to the ascent of Akrabbim and continue to Zin, and its [a]termination shall be to the south of Kadesh-barnea; and it shall reach Hazaraddar and continue to Azmon.

5 'The border shall turn *direction* from Azmon to the brook of Egypt, and its termination shall be at the sea.

6 ¶ 'As for the western border, you shall have the Great Sea, that is, *its* coastline; this shall be your west border.

7 ¶ 'And this shall be your north border: you shall draw your *border* line from the Great Sea to Mount Hor.

8 'You shall draw a line from Mount Hor to the Lebo-hamath, and the termination of the border shall be at Zedad;

9 and the border shall proceed to Ziphron, and its termination shall be at Hazar-enan. This shall be your north border.

10 ¶ 'For your eastern border you shall also draw a line from Hazar-enan to Shepham,

11 and the border shall go down from Shepham to Riblah on the east side of Ain; and the border shall go down and reach to the [b]slope on the east side of the Sea of Chinnereth.

12 'And the border shall go down to the Jordan and its termination shall be at the Salt Sea. This shall be your land according to its borders all around.' "

13 ¶ So Moses commanded the sons of Israel, saying, "This is the land that you are to apportion by lot among you as a possession, which the LORD has commanded to give to the nine and a half tribes.

14 "For the tribe of the sons of Reuben have received *theirs* according to their fathers' households, and the tribe of the sons of Gad according to their fathers' households, and the half-tribe of Manasseh have received their possession.

15 "The two and a half tribes have received their possession across the Jordan opposite Jericho, eastward toward the sunrising."

16 ¶ Then the LORD spoke to Moses, saying,

17 "These are the names of the men who shall apportion the land to you for inheritance: Eleazar the priest and Joshua the son of Nun.

18 "You shall take one leader of every tribe to apportion the land for inheritance.

19 "These are the names of the men: of the tribe of Judah, Caleb the son of Jephunneh.

20 "Of the tribe of the sons of Simeon, Samuel the son of Ammihud.

21 "Of the tribe of Benjamin, Elidad the son of Chislon.

22 "Of the tribe of the sons of Dan a leader, Bukki the son of Jogli.

23 "Of the sons of Joseph: of the tribe of the sons of Manasseh a leader, Hanniel the son of Ephod.

24 "Of the tribe of the sons of Ephraim a leader, Kemuel the son of Shiphtan.

25 "Of the tribe of the sons of Zebulun a leader, Elizaphan the son of Parnach.

26 "Of the tribe of the sons of Issachar a leader, Paltiel the son of Azzan.

27 "Of the tribe of the sons of Asher a leader, Ahihud the son of Shelomi.

28 "Of the tribe of the sons of Naphtali a leader, Pedahel the son of Ammihud."

29 These are those whom the LORD commanded to apportion the inheritance to the sons of Israel in the land of Canaan.

---

[a] Lit *goings out,* and so throughout the ch   [b] Lit *shoulder*

Cities for the Levites

35 Now the LORD spoke to Moses in the plains of Moab by the Jordan *opposite* Jericho, saying,

2 "Command the sons of Israel that they give to the Levites from the inheritance of their possession cities to live in; and you shall give to the Levites pasture lands around the cities.

3 "The cities shall be theirs to live in; and their pasture lands shall be for their cattle and for their herds and for all their beasts.

4 ¶ "The pasture lands of the cities which you shall give to the Levites *shall extend* from the wall of the city outward a thousand cubits around.

5 "You shall also measure outside the city on the east side two thousand cubits, and on the south side two thousand cubits, and on the west side two thousand cubits, and on the north side two thousand cubits, with the city in the center. This shall become theirs as pasture lands for the cities.

Cities of Refuge

6 "The cities which you shall give to the Levites *shall be* the six cities of refuge, which you shall give for the manslayer to flee to; and in addition to them you shall give forty-two cities.

35:6 Controlling Blood Feuds

Even today some nomadic tribes still follow the principles of blood feuds. If a person is responsible, even accidentally, for another's death, a relative of the victim can in turn kill either the murderer or, as a substitute, one of the murderer's relatives. The cities of refuge put a control on this practice, making allowance for "involuntary manslaughter." The congregation judged whether the killing was accidental or intentional (verse 24).

7 "All the cities which you shall give to the Levites *shall be* forty-eight cities, together with their pasture lands.

8 "As for the cities which you shall give from the possession of the sons of Israel, you shall take more from the larger and you shall take less from the smaller; each shall give some of his cities to the Levites in proportion to his possession which he inherits."

9 ¶ Then the LORD spoke to Moses, saying,

10 "Speak to the sons of Israel and say to them, 'When you cross the Jordan into the land of Canaan,

11 then you shall select for yourselves cities to be your cities of refuge, that the manslayer who has killed any person unintentionally may flee there.

12 'The cities shall be to you as a refuge from the avenger, so that the manslayer will not die until he stands before the congregation for trial.

13 'The cities which you are to give shall be your six cities of refuge.

14 'You shall give three cities across the Jordan and three cities in the land of Canaan; they are to be cities of refuge.

15 'These six cities shall be for refuge for the sons of Israel, and for the alien and for the sojourner among them; that anyone who kills a person unintentionally may flee there.

16 ¶ 'But if he struck him down with an iron object, so that he died, he is a murderer; the murderer shall surely be put to death.

17 'If he struck him down with a stone in the hand, by which he will die, and *as a result* he died, he is a murderer; the murderer shall surely be put to death.

18 'Or if he struck him with a wooden object in the hand, by which he might die, and *as a result* he died, he is a murderer; the murderer shall surely be put to death.

19 'The blood avenger himself shall put the murderer to death; he shall put him to death when he meets him.

20 'If he pushed him of hatred, or threw something at him lying in wait and *as a result* he died,

21 or if he struck him down with his hand in enmity, and *as a result* he died, the one who struck him shall surely be put to death, he is a murderer; the blood avenger shall put the murderer to death when he meets him.

22 ¶ 'But if he pushed him suddenly without enmity, or threw something at him without lying in wait,

23 or with any deadly object of stone, and without seeing it dropped on him so that he died, while he was not his enemy nor seeking his injury,

24 then the congregation shall judge between the slayer and the blood avenger according to these ordinances.

25 'The congregation shall deliver the manslayer from the hand of the blood avenger, and the congregation shall restore him to his city of refuge to which he fled; and he shall live in it until the death of the high priest who was anointed with the holy oil.

26 'But if the manslayer at any time goes beyond the border of his city of refuge to which he may flee,

27 and the blood avenger finds him outside the border of his city of refuge, and the blood avenger kills the manslayer, he will not be guilty of blood

28 because he should have remained in his city of refuge until the death of the high priest. But after the death of the high priest the manslayer shall return to the land of his possession.

29 ¶ 'These things shall be for a statutory ordinance to you throughout your generations in all your dwellings.

30 ¶ 'If anyone kills a person, the murderer shall be put to death at the evidence of witnesses,

but no person shall be put to death on the testimony of one witness.

31 'Moreover, you shall not take ransom for the life of a murderer who is guilty of death, but he shall surely be put to death.

32 'You shall not take ransom for him who has fled to his city of refuge, that he may return to live in the land before the death of the priest.

33 'So you shall not pollute the land in which you are; for blood pollutes the land and no expiation can be made for the land for the blood that is shed on it, except by the blood of him who shed it.

34 'You shall not defile the land in which you live, in the midst of which I dwell; for I the LORD am dwelling in the midst of the sons of Israel.' "

Inheritance by Marriage

36 And the heads of the fathers' *households* of the family of the sons of Gilead, the son of Machir, the son of Manasseh, of the families of the sons of Joseph, came near and spoke before Moses and before the leaders, the heads of the fathers' *households* of the sons of Israel,

2 and they said, "The LORD commanded my lord to give the land by lot to the sons of Israel as an inheritance, and my lord was commanded by the LORD to give the inheritance of Zelophehad our brother to his daughters.

3 "But if they marry one of the sons of the *other* tribes of the sons of Israel, their inheritance will be withdrawn from the inheritance of our fathers and will be added to the inheritance of the tribe to which they belong; thus it will be withdrawn from our allotted inheritance.

4 "When the jubilee of the sons of Israel comes, then their inheritance will be added to the inheritance of the tribe to which they belong; so their inheritance will be withdrawn from the inheritance of the tribe of our fathers."

5 ¶ Then Moses commanded the sons of Israel according to the word of the LORD, saying, "The tribe of the sons of Joseph are right in *their* statements.

6 "This is what the LORD has commanded concerning the daughters of Zelophehad, saying, 'Let them marry whom they wish; only they must marry within the family of the tribe of their father.'

7 "Thus no inheritance of the sons of Israel shall be transferred from tribe to tribe, for the sons of Israel shall each hold to the inheritance of the tribe of his fathers.

8 "Every daughter who comes into possession of an inheritance of any tribe of the sons of Israel shall be wife to one of the family of the tribe of her father, so that the sons of Israel each may possess the inheritance of his fathers.

9 "Thus no inheritance shall be transferred from one tribe to another tribe, for the tribes of the sons of Israel shall each hold to his own inheritance."

10 ¶ Just as the LORD had commanded Moses, so the daughters of Zelophehad did:

11 Mahlah, Tirzah, Hoglah, Milcah and Noah, the daughters of Zelophehad married their uncles' sons.

12 They married *those* from the families of the sons of Manasseh the son of Joseph, and their inheritance remained with the tribe of the family of their father.

13 ¶ These are the commandments and the ordinances which the LORD commanded to the sons of Israel through Moses in the plains of Moab by the Jordan *opposite* Jericho.

DEUTERONOMY

A Personal Plea
Moses' last chance with the people he loved

POLITICIANS GET THIS ADVICE: "WHEN you deliver a speech, make it seem as if you're having a personal talk in a small room with each one of your listeners." No one took that advice better than Franklin Delano Roosevelt—unless, perhaps, you consider Moses' speeches in Deuteronomy.

When Roosevelt became president of the United States in 1932, he faced a national crisis greater than any since the Civil War. Fifteen million people were unemployed in the Great Depression (a 25 percent unemployment rate), and two million of those wandered around the country, homeless, searching for work and food. In addition, war in Europe was not far away.

> "But from there you will seek the LORD your God, and you will find Him if you search for Him with all your heart and all your soul." 4:29

Fireside Chats

To combat the mood of despair, Roosevelt turned to a powerful new communications weapon: radio. The very first week of his presidency he gave his first "fireside chat" from a homey setting in the White House, and a series of such chats helped him pull the nation through its hard times.

Warm and personal in tone, the book of Deuteronomy resembles just such a fireside chat, delivered by the great leader Moses to his people, the Israelites. He, too, led a nation through dangerous times, and at the end of his life he had many parting words. This book is Moses' State of the Union address, personal diary, and tearful swan song all combined into one.

Poised on the Edge

For their length and emotional power, these speeches have no equal in the Bible. Moses passionately went over and over the same ground, occasionally lashing out, but more often showing the anguish and love of a doting parent. An undercurrent of sadness runs through the speeches: Moses knew he would not join in the triumph of entering Canaan. God had revealed that Moses would die before then.

In Exodus, Moses was marked by a quick temper and a reluctance to speak. His humility and eloquence as seen in Deuteronomy show how far he had come in 40 years.

Deep in his soul, Moses felt that the entire history of the Israelites depended on what happened next. Poised on the banks of the Jordan River, they were about to enter the promised land and face the most crucial test of their lives. How would they react to the new land? Would they keep their covenant with God or reject it for the more immediate pleasures around them?

Desert-bred, the Israelites knew little about the seductions of other cultures: the sensuality, the exotic religions, the glittering wealth. They had spent their lives in near-isolation, sheltered from civilization. Now they were marching into a land full of enticements.

Three Speeches

Moses' first great speech, in chapters 1–3, reviewed God's dealings with Israel. Moses recalled Israel's history through his own eyes, mentioning such details as the irrigation system in Egypt, the abrupt departure, the fearsome desert with its snakes and scorpions, and the amazing miracles of God. He filled the account with personal reflections, like an aging father telling his children what to remember after he is gone.

The longest speech, chapters 4–26, went over the moral and civil code the Israelites had agreed to keep. Even here, a personal tone came through. Moses did not list laws as in a textbook; he discussed and amplified and preached them. Along with the laws, he included reminders, object lessons, personal outbursts. In chapters 27–33 Moses gave a final summing up, a farewell charge from an old man facing certain death. As clearly as he could, he presented the choices facing the Israelites. He would not be with them as they chose their future. They were on their own; they held their destiny in their own hands.

How to Read Deuteronomy

Early in this century archaeologists began turning up samples of Near Eastern treaties. These "suzerainty treaties" set down in official form the relationship between a powerful king (suzerain) and the people he ruled over. Such treaties shed new light on the book of Deuteronomy, which seems to follow very closely the pattern of such a treaty. Typically, a treaty with a powerful king consisted of the following elements:

1. *A preamble identifying the parties of the treaty,* such as a king and a small cluster of tribes who want his protection.

2. *A capsule history describing previous relations between the two parties.*

3. *Rules defining each party's obligations.* The king may swear to defend some tribes with his armies in return for allegiance, taxes, and a percentage of produce.

4. *Witnesses to the treaties,* including, in many cases, a list of gods.

5. *Curses and blessings specifying what will take place if one of the parties breaks the treaty.* The king may promise the people prosperity and peace if they keep the terms, but invasion, deportation, or death if they break them.

Read Deuteronomy as an example of a treaty between a king and his people. *Treaty* is another word for the one we have been using—*covenant*—to describe the formal agreement between God and the Israelites. With a little work, you can identify various portions of Deuteronomy that parallel the five elements above.

Chapters 1–11 and 27–34 contain the best summary of Moses' speeches to the Israelites. He holds back no emotion as he retells the story of his life. Almost all the action he describes repeats what we've heard before (see Exodus 12–20; 32–34; Numbers 11–17; 20–24), but Deuteronomy provides a much more personal account.

Unlike other ancient books, the Bible gives major emphasis to "nobodies"—poor people, aliens, widows, orphans, the sick. Many of the laws relating to them repeat laws from the three preceding books. But Deuteronomy gives hidden insights into why God has such special concern for nobodies and why the Israelites should also. It also gives intriguing ideas on how such concern can be translated into actual political and economic policies. As you go through the book, mark each passage that relates to such people.

The New Testament quotes Deuteronomy more often than almost any other Old Testament book. Twenty-one of the 27 New Testament books allude to Deuteronomy; some scholars count 90 different citations. Jesus himself drew from it during his temptation (Matthew 4).

3-TRACK READING PLAN

For an explanation and complete listing of the 3-track reading plan, turn to page 7.

TRACK 1: **Two-Week Courses on the Bible**
See page 7 for information on these courses.

TRACK 2: **An Overview of Deuteronomy in 3 Days**
☐ Day 1. Read the Introduction to Deuteronomy and then chapter 4, part of Moses' first emotional speech.
☐ Day 2. Read chapter 8; here, Moses reveals his fears about how success may have a harmful effect on the Israelites.
☐ Day 3. Read chapter 28, which, in vivid, shocking language, sets out before the Israelites the choice between obedience and disobedience.

Now turn to page 9 for your next Track 2 reading project.

TRACK 3: **All of Deuteronomy in 34 Days**
After you have read through Deuteronomy, turn to pages 10–14 for your next Track 3 reading project.

☐1	☐2	☐3	☐4	☐5	☐6	☐7	☐8
☐9	☐10	☐11	☐12	☐13	☐14	☐15	☐16
☐17	☐18	☐19	☐20	☐21	☐22	☐23	☐24
☐25	☐26	☐27	☐28	☐29	☐30	☐31	☐32
☐33	☐34						

Israel's History after the Exodus

1 These are the words which Moses spoke to all Israel across the Jordan in the wilderness, in the Arabah opposite Suph, between Paran and Tophel and Laban and Hazeroth and Dizahab.

2 It is eleven days' *journey* from Horeb by the way of Mount Seir to Kadesh-barnea.

3 In the fortieth year, on the first *day* of the eleventh month, Moses spoke to the children of Israel, according to all that the LORD had commanded him *to give* to them,

4 after he had defeated Sihon the king of the Amorites, who lived in Heshbon, and Og the king of Bashan, who lived in Ashtaroth and Edrei.

5 Across the Jordan in the land of Moab, Moses undertook to expound this law, saying,

6 ¶ "The LORD our God spoke to us at Horeb, saying, 'You have stayed long enough at this mountain.

7 'Turn and set your journey, and go to the hill country of the Amorites, and to all their neighbors in the Arabah, in the hill country and in the lowland and in the *a*Negev and by the seacoast, the land of the Canaanites, and Lebanon, as far as the great river, the river Euphrates.

8 'See, I have placed the land before you; go in and possess the land which the LORD swore to give to your fathers, to Abraham, to Isaac, and to Jacob, to them and their descendants after them.'

9 ¶ "I spoke to you at that time, saying, 'I am not able to bear *the burden* of you alone.

10 'The LORD your God has multiplied you, and behold, you are this day like the stars of heaven in number.

11 'May the LORD, the God of your fathers, increase you a thousand-fold more than you are and bless you, just as He has promised you!

12 'How can I alone bear the load and burden of you and your strife?

13 'Choose wise and discerning and experienced men from your tribes, and I will appoint them as your heads.'

14 "You answered me and said, 'The thing which you have said to do is good.'

15 "So I took the heads of your tribes, wise and experienced men, and appointed them heads over you, leaders of thousands and of hundreds, of fifties and of tens, and officers for your tribes.

16 ¶ "Then I charged your judges at that time, saying, 'Hear *the cases* between your fellow countrymen, and judge righteously between a man and his fellow countryman, or the alien who is with him.

17 'You shall not show partiality in judgment; you shall hear the small and the great alike. You shall not fear man, for the judgment is God's. The case that is too hard for you, you shall bring to me, and I will hear it.'

18 "I commanded you at that time all the things that you should do.

19 ¶ "Then we set out from Horeb, and went through all that great and terrible wilderness which you saw on the way to the hill country of the Amorites, just as the LORD our God had commanded us; and we came to Kadesh-barnea.

20 "I said to you, 'You have come to the hill country of the Amorites which the LORD our God is about to give us.

21 'See, the LORD your God has placed the land before you; go up, take possession, as the LORD, the God of your fathers, has spoken to you. Do not fear or be dismayed.'

22 ¶ "Then all of you approached me and said, 'Let us send men before us, that they may search out the land for us, and bring back to us word of the way by which we should go up and the cities which we shall enter.'

23 "The thing pleased me and I took twelve of your men, one man for each tribe.

24 "They turned and went up into the hill country, and came to the valley of Eshcol and spied it out.

25 "Then they took *some* of the fruit of the land in their hands and brought it down to us; and they brought us back a report and said, 'It is a good land which the LORD our God is about to give us.'

26 ¶ "Yet you were not willing to go up, but rebelled against the command of the LORD your God;

27 and you grumbled in your tents and said, 'Because the LORD hates us, He has brought us out of the land of Egypt to deliver us into the hand of the Amorites to destroy us.

28 'Where can we go up? Our brethren have made our hearts melt, saying, "The people are bigger and taller than we; the cities are large and fortified to heaven. And besides, we saw the sons of the Anakim there." '

29 "Then I said to you, 'Do not be shocked, nor fear them.

30 'The LORD your God who goes before you will Himself fight on your behalf, just as He did for you in Egypt before your eyes,

31 and in the wilderness where you saw how the LORD your God carried you, just as a man carries his son, in all the way which you have walked until you came to this place.'

32 "But for all this, you did not trust the LORD your God,

33 who goes before you on *your* way, to seek out a place for you to encamp, in fire by night and cloud by day, to show you the way in which you should go.

34 ¶ "Then the LORD heard the sound of your words, and He was angry and took an oath, saying,

35 'Not one of these men, this evil generation,

---

a I.e. South country

shall see the good land which I swore to give your fathers,

36 except Caleb the son of Jephunneh; he shall see it, and to him and to his sons I will give the land on which he has set foot, because he has followed the LORD fully.'

37 "The LORD was angry with me also on your account, saying, 'Not even you shall enter there.

1:37 Distributing Blame

God forbade Moses to enter the promised land because of the incident reported in Numbers 20. In his farewell speech, Moses could not resist expressing his own resentment at the Israelites' part in provoking his punishment. In this verse and in 3:26 and 4:21, he turned the blame back on his countrymen.

---

38 'Joshua the son of Nun, who stands before you, he shall enter there; encourage him, for he will cause Israel to inherit it.

39 'Moreover, your little ones who you said would become a prey, and your sons, who this day have no knowledge of good or evil, shall enter there, and I will give it to them and they shall possess it.

40 'But as for you, turn around and set out for the wilderness by the way to the Red Sea.'

41 ¶ "Then you said to me, 'We have sinned against the LORD; we will indeed go up and fight, just as the LORD our God commanded us.' And every man of you girded on his weapons of war, and regarded it as easy to go up into the hill country.

42 "And the LORD said to me, 'Say to them, "Do not go up nor fight, for I am not among you; otherwise you will be defeated before your enemies."'

43 "So I spoke to you, but you would not listen. Instead you rebelled against the command of the LORD, and acted presumptuously and went up into the hill country.

44 "The Amorites who lived in that hill country came out against you and chased you as bees do, and crushed you from Seir to Hormah.

45 "Then you returned and wept before the LORD; but the LORD did not listen to your voice nor give ear to you.

46 "So you remained in Kadesh many days, the days that you spent *there*.

Wanderings in the Wilderness

2 "Then we turned and set out for the wilderness by the way to the Red Sea, as the LORD spoke to me, and circled Mount Seir for many days.

2 "And the LORD spoke to me, saying,

3 'You have circled this mountain long enough. *Now* turn north,

4 and command the people, saying, "You will pass through the territory of your brothers the sons of Esau who live in Seir; and they will be afraid of you. So be very careful;

5 do not provoke them, for I will not give you any of their land, even *as little as* a footstep because I have given Mount Seir to Esau as a possession.

6 "You shall buy food from them with money so that you may eat, and you shall also purchase water from them with money so that you may drink.

7 "For the LORD your God has blessed you in all that you have done; He has known your wanderings through this great wilderness. These forty years the LORD your God has been with you; you have not lacked a thing." '

8 ¶ "So we passed beyond our brothers the sons of Esau, who live in Seir, away from the Arabah road, away from Elath and from Eziongeber. And we turned and passed through by the way of the wilderness of Moab.

9 "Then the LORD said to me, 'Do not harass Moab, nor provoke them to war, for I will not give you any of their land as a possession, because I have given Ar to the sons of Lot as a possession.

10 (The Emim lived there formerly, a people as great, numerous, and tall as the Anakim.

11 Like the Anakim, they are also regarded as Rephaim, but the Moabites call them Emim.

12 The Horites formerly lived in Seir, but the sons of Esau dispossessed them and destroyed them from before them and settled in their place, just as Israel did to the land of their possession which the LORD gave to them.)

13 'Now arise and cross over the brook Zered yourselves.' So we crossed over the brook Zered.

14 "Now the time that it took for us to come from Kadesh-barnea until we crossed over the brook Zered was thirty-eight years, until all the generation of the men of war perished from within the camp, as the LORD had sworn to them.

2:14 Children of the Wilderness

As he reviewed the Israelites' history, Moses recalled with bitterness the series of rebellions leading to the 40-year punishment in "that great and terrible wilderness" (1:19). Actually, of course, the people listening to him had been mere children when the decisive rebellions occurred (1:39); their parents were the ones forbidden to enter the promised land. Except for Joshua, Caleb, and Moses' own family, all those listening to Moses had grown up in the wilderness.

---

15 "Moreover the hand of the LORD was against them, to destroy them from within the camp until they all perished.

16 ¶ "So it came about when all the men of war had finally perished from among the people,

17 that the LORD spoke to me, saying,

18 'Today you shall cross over Ar, the border of Moab.

19 'When you come opposite the sons of Ammon, do not harass them nor provoke them, for I will not give you any of the land of the sons of Ammon as a possession, because I have given it to the sons of Lot as a possession.'

20 (It is also regarded as the land of the Rephaim, for Rephaim formerly lived in it, but the Ammonites call them Zamzummin,

21 a people as great, numerous, and tall as the Anakim, but the LORD destroyed them before them. And they dispossessed them and settled in their place,

22 just as He did for the sons of Esau, who live in Seir, when He destroyed the Horites from before them; they dispossessed them and settled in their place even to this day.

23 And the Avvim, who lived in villages as far as Gaza, the ªCaphtorim who came from ᵇCaphtor, destroyed them and lived in their place.)

24 'Arise, set out, and pass through the valley of Arnon. Look! I have given Sihon the Amorite, king of Heshbon, and his land into your hand; begin to take possession and contend with him in battle.

25 'This day I will begin to put the dread and fear of you upon the peoples everywhere under the heavens, who, when they hear the report of you, will tremble and be in anguish because of you.'

26 ¶ "So I sent messengers from the wilderness of Kedemoth to Sihon king of Heshbon with words of peace, saying,

27 'Let me pass through your land, I will travel only on the highway; I will not turn aside to the right or to the left.

28 'You will sell me food for money so that I may eat, and give me water for money so that I may drink, only let me pass through on foot,

29 just as the sons of Esau who live in Seir and the Moabites who live in Ar did for me, until I cross over the Jordan into the land which the LORD our God is giving to us.'

30 "But Sihon king of Heshbon was not willing for us to pass through his land; for the LORD your God hardened his spirit and made his heart obstinate, in order to deliver him into your hand, as he is today.

31 "The LORD said to me, 'See, I have begun to deliver Sihon and his land over to you. Begin to occupy, that you may possess his land.'

32 ¶ "Then Sihon with all his people came out to meet us in battle at Jahaz.

33 "The LORD our God delivered him over to us,

and we defeated him with his sons and all his people.

34 "So we captured all his cities at that time and utterly destroyed the men, women and children of every city. We left no survivor.

35 "We took only the animals as our booty and the spoil of the cities which we had captured.

36 "From Aroer which is on the edge of the valley of Arnon and from the city which is in the valley, even to Gilead, there was no city that was too high for us; the LORD our God delivered all over to us.

37 "Only you did not go near to the land of the sons of Ammon, all along the river Jabbok and the cities of the hill country, and wherever the LORD our God had commanded us.

Conquests Recounted

3 "Then we turned and went up the road to Bashan, and Og, king of Bashan, with all his people came out to meet us in battle at Edrei.

2 "But the LORD said to me, 'Do not fear him, for I have delivered him and all his people and his land into your hand; and you shall do to him just as you did to Sihon king of the Amorites, who lived at Heshbon.'

3 "So the LORD our God delivered Og also, king of Bashan, with all his people into our hand, and we smote them until no survivor was left.

4 "We captured all his cities at that time; there was not a city which we did not take from them: sixty cities, all the region of Argob, the kingdom of Og in Bashan.

5 "All these were cities fortified with high walls, gates and bars, besides a great many unwalled towns.

6 "We utterly destroyed them, as we did to Sihon king of Heshbon, utterly destroying the men, women and children of every city.

7 "But all the animals and the spoil of the cities we took as our booty.

8 ¶ "Thus we took the land at that time from the hand of the two kings of the Amorites who were beyond the Jordan, from the valley of Arnon to Mount Hermon

9 (Sidonians call Hermon Sirion, and the Amorites call it Senir):

10 all the cities of the plateau and all Gilead and all Bashan, as far as Salecah and Edrei, cities of the kingdom of Og in Bashan.

11 (For only Og king of Bashan was left of the remnant of the Rephaim. Behold, his bedstead was an iron bedstead; it is in Rabbah of the sons of Ammon. Its length was nine cubits and its width four cubits by ordinary cubit.)

12 ¶ "So we took possession of this land at that time. From Aroer, which is by the valley of Arnon, and half the hill country of Gilead and its cities I gave to the Reubenites and to the Gadites.

13 "The rest of Gilead and all Bashan, the king-

ª I.e. Philistines   ᵇ I.e. Crete

dom of Og, I gave to the half-tribe of Manasseh, all the region of Argob (concerning all Bashan, it is called the land of Rephaim.

14 Jair the son of Manasseh took all the region of Argob as far as the border of the Geshurites and the Maacathites, and called it, *that is,* Bashan, after his own name, Havvoth-jair, *as it is* to this day.)

15 "To Machir I gave Gilead.

16 "To the Reubenites and to the Gadites I gave from Gilead even as far as the valley of Arnon, the middle of the valley as a border and as far as the river Jabbok, the border of the sons of Ammon;

17 the Arabah also, with the Jordan as *a* border, from ᵃChinnereth even as far as the sea of the Arabah, the Salt Sea, at the foot of the slopes of Pisgah on the east.

18 ¶ "Then I commanded you at that time, saying, 'The LORD your God has given you this land to possess it; all you valiant men shall cross over armed before your brothers, the sons of Israel.

19 'But your wives and your little ones and your livestock (I know that you have much livestock) shall remain in your cities which I have given you,

20 until the LORD gives rest to your fellow countrymen as to you, and they also possess the land which the LORD your God will give them beyond the Jordan. Then you may return every man to his possession which I have given you.'

21 "I commanded Joshua at that time, saying, 'Your eyes have seen all that the LORD your God has done to these two kings; so the LORD shall do to all the kingdoms into which you are about to cross.

22 'Do not fear them, for the LORD your God is the one fighting for you.'

23 ¶ "I also pleaded with the LORD at that time, saying,

24 'O Lord GOD, You have begun to show Your servant Your greatness and Your strong hand; for what god is there in heaven or on earth who can do such works and mighty acts as Yours?

25 'Let me, I pray, cross over and see the fair land that is beyond the Jordan, that good hill country and Lebanon.'

26 "But the LORD was angry with me on your account, and would not listen to me; and the LORD said to me, 'Enough! Speak to Me no more of this matter.

27 'Go up to the top of Pisgah and lift up your eyes to the west and north and south and east, and see *it* with your eyes, for you shall not cross over this Jordan.

28 'But charge Joshua and encourage him and strengthen him, for he shall go across at the head of this people, and he will give them as an inheritance the land which you will see.'

29 "So we remained in the valley opposite Beth-peor.

ᵃ I.e. the Sea of Galilee

Israel Urged to Obey God's Law

4 "Now, O Israel, listen to the statutes and the judgments which I am teaching you to perform, so that you may live and go in and take possession of the land which the LORD, the God of your fathers, is giving you.

2 "You shall not add to the word which I am commanding you, nor take away from it, that you may keep the commandments of the LORD your God which I command you.

4:2 Do Not Add

People usually remember they are not supposed to "drop" one of God's commands, but it is more subtly tempting to add commands. Religious people of Jesus' time, for example, invented elaborate rules on how far you could walk on the Sabbath. Such "legalism" may seem holy, but goes against God's directions.

3 "Your eyes have seen what the LORD has done in the case of Baal-peor, for all the men who followed Baal-peor, the LORD your God has destroyed them from among you.

4 "But you who held fast to the LORD your God are alive today, every one of you.

5 ¶ "See, I have taught you statutes and judgments just as the LORD my God commanded me, that you should do thus in the land where you are entering to possess it.

6 "So keep and do *them,* for that is your wisdom and your understanding in the sight of the peoples who will hear all these statutes and say, 'Surely this great nation is a wise and understanding people.'

4:6 Old Testament Evangelism

As he explained various laws to the Israelites, Moses often appealed to their unique calling as a nation. God had chosen them as a "kingdom of priests" and a "treasured possession." This passage describes yet another benefit to keeping the law: what today we would call evangelism. The purity of the Israelites would serve as an example to the nations around them, who would then be attracted to the true God.

7 "For what great nation is there that has a god so near to it as is the LORD our God whenever we call on Him?

8 "Or what great nation is there that has stat-

utes and judgments as righteous as this whole law which I am setting before you today?

9 ¶ "Only give heed to yourself and keep your soul diligently, so that you do not forget the things which your eyes have seen and they do not depart from your heart all the days of your life; but make them known to your sons and your grandsons.

10 "*Remember* the day you stood before the LORD your God at Horeb, when the LORD said to me, 'Assemble the people to Me, that I may let them hear My words so they may learn to *a*fear Me all the days they live on the earth, and that they may teach their children.'

11 "You came near and stood at the foot of the mountain, and the mountain burned with fire to the *very* heart of the heavens: darkness, cloud and thick gloom.

12 "Then the LORD spoke to you from the midst of the fire; you heard the sound of words, but you saw no form—only a voice.

13 "So He declared to you His covenant which He commanded you to perform, *that is,* the Ten Commandments; and He wrote them on two tablets of stone.

14 "The LORD commanded me at that time to teach you statutes and judgments, that you might perform them in the land where you are going over to possess it.

15 ¶ "So watch yourselves carefully, since you did not see any form on the day the LORD spoke to you at Horeb from the midst of the fire,

16 so that you do not act corruptly and make a graven image for yourselves in the form of any figure, the likeness of male or female,

17 the likeness of any animal that is on the earth, the likeness of any winged bird that flies in the sky,

18 the likeness of anything that creeps on the ground, the likeness of any fish that is in the water below the earth.

19 "And *beware* not to lift up your eyes to heaven and see the sun and the moon and the stars, all the host of heaven, and be drawn away and worship them and serve them, those which the LORD your God has allotted to all the peoples under the whole heaven.

20 "But the LORD has taken you and brought you out of the iron furnace, from Egypt, to be a people for His own possession, as today.

21 ¶ "Now the LORD was angry with me on your account, and swore that I would not cross the Jordan, and that I would not enter the good land which the LORD your God is giving you as an inheritance.

22 "For I will die in this land, I shall not cross the Jordan, but you shall cross and take possession of this good land.

23 "So watch yourselves, that you do not forget the covenant of the LORD your God which He made with you, and make for yourselves a graven

image in the form of anything *against* which the LORD your God has commanded you.

24 "For the LORD your God is a consuming fire, a jealous God.

25 ¶ "When you become the father of children and children's children and have remained long in the land, and act corruptly, and make an idol in the form of anything, and do that which is evil in the sight of the LORD your God *so as* to provoke Him to anger,

26 I call heaven and earth to witness against you today, that you will surely perish quickly from the land where you are going over the Jordan to possess it. You shall not live long on it, but will be utterly destroyed.

27 "The LORD will scatter you among the peoples, and you will be left few in number among the nations where the LORD drives you.

28 "There you will serve gods, the work of man's hands, wood and stone, which neither see nor hear nor eat nor smell.

29 "But from there you will seek the LORD your God, and you will find *Him* if you search for Him with all your heart and all your soul.

30 "When you are in distress and all these things have come upon you, in the latter days you will return to the LORD your God and listen to His voice.

31 "For the LORD your God is a compassionate God; He will not fail you nor destroy you nor forget the covenant with your fathers which He swore to them.

32 ¶ "Indeed, ask now concerning the former days which were before you, since the day that God created man on the earth, and *inquire* from one end of the heavens to the other. Has *anything* been done like this great thing, or has *anything* been heard like it?

33 "Has *any* people heard the voice of God speaking from the midst of the fire, as you have heard *it,* and survived?

34 "Or has a god tried to go to take for himself a nation from within *another* nation by trials, by signs and wonders and by war and by a mighty hand and by an outstretched arm and by great terrors, as the LORD your God did for you in Egypt before your eyes?

35 "To you it was shown that you might know that the LORD, He is God; there is no other besides Him.

36 "Out of the heavens He let you hear His voice to discipline you; and on earth He let you see His great fire, and you heard His words from the midst of the fire.

37 "Because He loved your fathers, therefore He chose their descendants after them. And He personally brought you from Egypt by His great power,

38 driving out from before you nations greater

---

a Or *reverence*

and mightier than you, to bring you in *and* to give you their land for an inheritance, as it is today.

39 "Know therefore today, and take it to your heart, that the LORD, He is God in heaven above and on the earth below; there is no other.

4:35 Experience Teaches

Chapter 4 follows a typical pattern in Deuteronomy: Moses begins with the Israelites' experience and then shows how the laws of the covenant relate directly to that experience. In this chapter, he vividly reminds them of their own encounters with God, especially at Mount Sinai. How did God reveal himself to them? "You did not see any form ," Moses concludes (verse 15); therefore, idols made with human hands would insult and devalue such a God. Then he describes the unique privilege the Israelites have: to know personally the God who created the universe.

40 "So you shall keep His statutes and His commandments which I am giving you today, that it may go well with you and with your children after you, and that you may live long on the land which the LORD your God is giving you for all time."

41 ¶ Then Moses set apart three cities across the Jordan to the east,

42 that a manslayer might flee there, who unintentionally slew his neighbor without having enmity toward him in time past; and by fleeing to one of these cities he might live:

43 Bezer in the wilderness on the plateau for the Reubenites, and Ramoth in Gilead for the Gadites, and Golan in Bashan for the Manassites.

44 ¶ Now this is the law which Moses set before the sons of Israel;

45 these are the testimonies and the statutes and the ordinances which Moses spoke to the sons of Israel, when they came out from Egypt,

46 across the Jordan, in the valley opposite Beth-peor, in the land of Sihon king of the Amorites who lived at Heshbon, whom Moses and the sons of Israel defeated when they came out from Egypt.

47 They took possession of his land and the land of Og king of Bashan, the two kings of the Amorites, *who were* across the Jordan to the east,

48 from Aroer, which is on the edge of the valley of Arnon, even as far as Mount Sion (that is, Hermon),

49 with all the Arabah across the Jordan to the east, even as far as the sea of the Arabah, at the foot of the slopes of Pisgah.

The Ten Commandments Repeated

5 Then Moses summoned all Israel and said to them:

¶ "Hear, O Israel, the statutes and the ordinances which I am speaking today in your hearing, that you may learn them and observe them carefully.

2 "The LORD our God made a covenant with us at Horeb.

3 "The LORD did not make this covenant with our fathers, but with us, *with* all those of us alive here today.

4 "The LORD spoke to you face to face at the mountain from the midst of the fire,

5 *while* I was standing between the LORD and you at that time, to declare to you the word of the LORD; for you were afraid because of the fire and did not go up the mountain. He said,

6 ¶ 'I am the LORD your God who brought you out of the land of Egypt, out of the house of slavery.

7 ¶ 'You shall have no other gods before Me.

8 ¶ 'You shall not make for yourself an idol, *or* any likeness *of* what is in heaven above or on the earth beneath or in the water under the earth.

9 'You shall not worship them or serve them; for I, the LORD your God, am a jealous God, visiting the iniquity of the fathers on the children, and on the third and the fourth *generations* of those who hate Me,

10 but showing lovingkindness to thousands, to those who love Me and keep My commandments.

11 ¶ 'You shall not take the name of the LORD your God in vain, for the LORD will not leave him unpunished who takes His name in vain.

12 ¶ 'Observe the sabbath day to keep it holy, as the LORD your God commanded you.

13 'Six days you shall labor and do all your work,

14 but the seventh day is a sabbath of the LORD your God; *in it* you shall not do any work, you or your son or your daughter or your male servant or your female servant or your ox or your donkey or any of your cattle or your sojourner who stays with you, so that your male servant and your female servant may rest as well as you.

15 'You shall remember that you were a slave in the land of Egypt, and the LORD your God brought you out of there by a mighty hand and by an outstretched arm; therefore the LORD your God commanded you to observe the sabbath day.

16 ¶ 'Honor your father and your mother, as the LORD your God has commanded you, that your days may be prolonged and that it may go well with you on the land which the LORD your God gives you.

17 ¶ 'You shall not murder.

18 ¶ 'You shall not commit adultery.

19 ¶ 'You shall not steal.

20 ¶ 'You shall not bear false witness against your neighbor.

21 ¶ 'You shall not covet your neighbor's wife, and you shall not desire your neighbor's house, his field or his male servant or his female servant,

his ox or his donkey or anything that belongs to your neighbor.'

Moses Interceded

22 ¶ "These words the LORD spoke to all your assembly at the mountain from the midst of the fire, *of* the cloud and *of* the thick gloom, with a great voice, and He added no more. He wrote them on two tablets of stone and gave them to me.

23 "And when you heard the voice from the midst of the darkness, while the mountain was burning with fire, you came near to me, all the heads of your tribes and your elders.

24 "You said, 'Behold, the LORD our God has shown us His glory and His greatness, and we have heard His voice from the midst of the fire; we have seen today that God speaks with man, yet he lives.

25 'Now then why should we die? For this great fire will consume us; if we hear the voice of the LORD our God any longer, then we will die.

26 'For who is there of all flesh who has heard the voice of the living God speaking from the midst of the fire, as we *have*, and lived?

27 'Go near and hear all that the LORD our God says; then speak to us all that the LORD our God speaks to you, and we will hear and do *it*.'

28 ¶ "The LORD heard the voice of your words when you spoke to me, and the LORD said to me, 'I have heard the voice of the words of this people which they have spoken to you. They have done well in all that they have spoken.

29 'Oh that they had such a heart in them, that they would fear Me and keep all My commandments always, that it may be well with them and with their sons forever!

30 'Go, say to them, "Return to your tents."

31 'But as for you, stand here by Me, that I may speak to you all the commandments and the statutes and the judgments which you shall teach them, that they may observe *them* in the land which I give them to possess.'

32 "So you shall observe to do just as the LORD your God has commanded you; you shall not turn aside to the right or to the left.

33 "You shall walk in all the way which the LORD your God has commanded you, that you may live and that it may be well with you, and that you may prolong *your* days in the land which you will possess.

Obey God and Prosper

6 "Now this is the commandment, the statutes and the judgments which the LORD your God has commanded *me* to teach you, that you might do *them* in the land where you are going over to possess it,

2 so that you and your son and your grandson might fear the LORD your God, to keep all His statutes and His commandments which I com-

mand you, all the days of your life, and that your days may be prolonged.

3 "O Israel, you should listen and be careful to do *it*, that it may be well with you and that you may multiply greatly, just as the LORD, the God of your fathers, has promised you, *in* a land flowing with milk and honey.

4 ¶ "Hear, O Israel! The LORD is our God, the LORD is one!

6:4 Most Quoted Verses

These six verses (4–9) may well be the most quoted portion in the entire Bible. Known as the Shema, they are recited every morning and every evening by orthodox Jews—and have been for hundreds of years. They graphically emphasize the importance of God's laws to the Israelites.

5 "You shall love the LORD your God with all your heart and with all your soul and with all your might.

6 "These words, which I am commanding you today, shall be on your heart.

7 You shall teach them diligently to your sons and shall talk of them when you sit in your house and when you walk by the way and when you lie down and when you rise up.

8 "You shall bind them as a sign on your hand and they shall be as frontals on your forehead.

9 "You shall write them on the doorposts of your house and on your gates.

10 ¶ "Then it shall come about when the LORD your God brings you into the land which He swore to your fathers, Abraham, Isaac and Jacob, to give you, great and splendid cities which you did not build,

11 and houses full of all good things which you did not fill, and hewn cisterns which you did not dig, vineyards and olive trees which you did not plant, and you eat and are satisfied,

12 then watch yourself, that you do not forget the LORD who brought you from the land of Egypt, out of the house of slavery.

13 "You shall [a]fear *only* the LORD your God; and you shall worship Him and swear by His name.

14 "You shall not follow other gods, any of the gods of the peoples who surround you,

15 for the LORD your God in the midst of you is a jealous God; otherwise the anger of the LORD your God will be kindled against you, and He will wipe you off the face of the earth.

16 ¶ "You shall not put the LORD your God to the test, as you tested *Him* at Massah.

17 "You should diligently keep the commandments of the LORD your God, and His testimonies

---

[a] Or *reverence*

and His statutes which He has commanded you.

18 "You shall do what is right and good in the sight of the LORD, that it may be well with you and that you may go in and possess the good land which the LORD swore to *give* your fathers,

19 by driving out all your enemies from before you, as the LORD has spoken.

20 ¶ "When your son asks you in time to come, saying, 'What *do* the testimonies and the statutes and the judgments *mean* which the LORD our God commanded you?'

21 then you shall say to your son, 'We were slaves to Pharaoh in Egypt, and the LORD brought us from Egypt with a mighty hand.

22 'Moreover, the LORD showed great and distressing signs and wonders before our eyes against Egypt, Pharaoh and all his household;

23 He brought us out from there in order to bring us in, to give us the land which He had sworn to our fathers.'

24 "So the LORD commanded us to observe all these statutes, to fear the LORD our God for our good always and for our survival, as *it is* today.

25 "It will be righteousness for us if we are careful to observe all this commandment before the LORD our God, just as He commanded us.

Warnings

7 "When the LORD your God brings you into the land where you are entering to possess it, and clears away many nations before you, the Hittites and the Girgashites and the Amorites and the Canaanites and the Perizzites and the Hivites and the Jebusites, seven nations greater and stronger than you,

2 and when the LORD your God delivers them before you and you defeat them, then you shall utterly destroy them. You shall make no covenant with them and show no favor to them.

3 "Furthermore, you shall not intermarry with them; you shall not give your daughters to their sons, nor shall you take their daughters for your sons.

4 "For they will turn your sons away from following Me to serve other gods; then the anger of the LORD will be kindled against you and He will quickly destroy you.

5 "But thus you shall do to them: you shall tear down their altars, and smash their *sacred* pillars, and hew down their [a]Asherim, and burn their graven images with fire.

6 "For you are a holy people to the LORD your God; the LORD your God has chosen you to be a people for His own possession out of all the peoples who are on the face of the earth.

7 ¶ "The LORD did not set His love on you nor choose you because you were more in number than any of the peoples, for you were the fewest of all peoples,

8 but because the LORD loved you and kept the oath which He swore to your forefathers, the LORD brought you out by a mighty hand and redeemed you from the house of slavery, from the hand of Pharaoh king of Egypt.

7:7 Why the Israelites?

Deuteronomy makes clear that God chose Israel out of pure grace. He did not select them for their impressiveness (this verse), their goodness (9:5), or their faithfulness (9:24). Rather, he chose them because he loved them, and he had made absolute promises to their ancestors. Deuteronomy promises the new land to the Israelites 69 times.

9 "Know therefore that the LORD your God, He is God, the faithful God, who keeps His covenant and His lovingkindness to a thousandth generation with those who love Him and keep His commandments;

10 but repays those who hate Him to their faces, to destroy them; He will not delay with him who hates Him, He will repay him to his face.

11 "Therefore, you shall keep the commandment and the statutes and the judgments which I am commanding you today, to do them.

Promises of God

12 ¶ "Then it shall come about, because you listen to these judgments and keep and do them, that the LORD your God will keep with you His covenant and His lovingkindness which He swore to your forefathers.

13 "He will love you and bless you and multiply you; He will also bless the fruit of your womb and the fruit of your ground, your grain and your new wine and your oil, the increase of your herd and the young of your flock, in the land which He swore to your forefathers to give you.

14 "You shall be blessed above all peoples; there will be no male or female barren among you or among your cattle.

15 "The LORD will remove from you all sickness; and He will not put on you any of the harmful diseases of Egypt which you have known, but He will lay them on all who hate you.

16 "You shall consume all the peoples whom the LORD your God will deliver to you; your eye shall not pity them, nor shall you serve their gods, for that *would be* a snare to you.

17 ¶ "If you should say in your heart, 'These nations are greater than I; how can I dispossess them?'

18 you shall not be afraid of them; you shall

---

[a] I.e. wooden symbols of a female deity

well remember what the LORD your God did to Pharaoh and to all Egypt:

19 the great trials which your eyes saw and the signs and the wonders and the mighty hand and the outstretched arm by which the LORD your God brought you out. So shall the LORD your God do to all the peoples of whom you are afraid.

20 "Moreover, the LORD your God will send the hornet against them, until those who are left and hide themselves from you perish.

21 "You shall not dread them, for the LORD your God is in your midst, a great and awesome God.

22 "The LORD your God will clear away these nations before you little by little; you will not be able to put an end to them quickly, for the wild beasts would grow too numerous for you.

23 "But the LORD your God will deliver them before you, and will throw them into great confusion until they are destroyed.

24 "He will deliver their kings into your hand so that you will make their name perish from under heaven; no man will be able to stand before you until you have destroyed them.

25 "The graven images of their gods you are to burn with fire; you shall not covet the silver or the gold that is on them, nor take it for yourselves, or you will be snared by it, for it is an abomination to the LORD your God.

26 "You shall not bring an abomination into your house, and like it come under the ban; you shall utterly detest it and you shall utterly abhor it, for it is something banned.

God's Gracious Dealings

8 "All the commandments that I am commanding you today you shall be careful to do, that you may live and multiply, and go in and possess the land which the LORD swore *to give* to your forefathers.

2 "You shall remember all the way which the LORD your God has led you in the wilderness these forty years, that He might humble you, testing you, to know what was in your heart, whether you would keep His commandments or not.

3 "He humbled you and let you be hungry, and fed you with manna which you did not know, nor did your fathers know, that He might make you

8:3 Words for the Devil

When tempted by Satan (Luke 4:1–13), Jesus responded with three separate quotations from Deuteronomy: this verse, and Deuteronomy 6:13,16. In the wilderness, Israelites had learned that God would provide all they needed. Jesus, also in the wilderness, quoted Scripture to forcefully remind Satan of that lesson.

understand that man does not live by bread alone, but man lives by everything that proceeds out of the mouth of the LORD.

4 "Your clothing did not wear out on you, nor did your foot swell these forty years.

5 "Thus you are to know in your heart that the LORD your God was disciplining you just as a man disciplines his son.

6 "Therefore, you shall keep the commandments of the LORD your God, to walk in His ways and to fear Him.

7 "For the LORD your God is bringing you into a good land, a land of brooks of water, of fountains and springs, flowing forth in valleys and hills;

8 a land of wheat and barley, of vines and fig trees and pomegranates, a land of olive oil and honey;

9 a land where you will eat food without scarcity, in which you will not lack anything; a land whose stones are iron, and out of whose hills you can dig copper.

10 "When you have eaten and are satisfied, you shall bless the LORD your God for the good land which He has given you.

11 ¶ "Beware that you do not forget the LORD your God by not keeping His commandments and His ordinances and His statutes which I am commanding you today;

12 otherwise, when you have eaten and are satisfied, and have built good houses and lived *in them,*

13 and when your herds and your flocks multiply, and your silver and gold multiply, and all that you have multiplies,

14 then your heart will become proud and you will forget the LORD your God who brought you out from the land of Egypt, out of the house of slavery.

15 "He led you through the great and terrible wilderness, *with its* fiery serpents and scorpions and thirsty ground where there was no water; He brought water for you out of the rock of flint.

16 "In the wilderness He fed you manna which your fathers did not know, that He might humble you and that He might test you, to do good for you in the end.

17 "Otherwise, you may say in your heart, 'My power and the strength of my hand made me this wealth.'

18 "But you shall remember the LORD your God, for it is He who is giving you power to make wealth, that He may confirm His covenant which He swore to your fathers, as *it is* this day.

19 "It shall come about if you ever forget the LORD your God and go after other gods and serve them and worship them, I testify against you today that you will surely perish.

20 "Like the nations that the LORD makes to perish before you, so you shall perish; because you would not listen to the voice of the LORD your God.

Israel Provoked God

9 "Hear, O Israel! You are crossing over the Jordan today to go in to dispossess nations greater and mightier than you, great cities fortified to heaven,

2 a people great and tall, the sons of the Anakim, whom you know and of whom you have heard *it said,* 'Who can stand before the sons of Anak?'

3 "Know therefore today that it is the LORD your God who is crossing over before you as a consuming fire. He will destroy them and He will subdue them before you, so that you may drive them out and destroy them quickly, just as the LORD has spoken to you.

4 ¶ "Do not say in your heart when the LORD your God has driven them out before you, 'Because of my righteousness the LORD has brought me in to possess this land,' but *it is* because of the wickedness of these nations *that* the LORD is dispossessing them before you.

9:4 Reasons for Warfare

Commands for the Israelites to utterly destroy other nations have caused modern readers of the Old Testament much concern. This passage reveals that God was acting not because of the Israelites' superior moral character, but because of the inhabitants' own wickedness. Chapter 20:16–18 gives yet another rationale for the wars: to keep Israel free from contamination by other nations. The Israelites never followed these commands completely, and their nation was ultimately weakened and destroyed precisely because of such contamination. (See "Is a War Ever Holy?" page 262, for further details.)

5 "It is not for your righteousness or for the uprightness of your heart that you are going to possess their land, but *it is* because of the wickedness of these nations *that* the LORD your God is driving them out before you, in order to confirm the oath which the LORD swore to your fathers, to Abraham, Isaac and Jacob.

6 ¶ "Know, then, *it is* not because of your righteousness *that* the LORD your God is giving you this good land to possess, for you are a stubborn people.

7 "Remember, do not forget how you provoked the LORD your God to wrath in the wilderness; from the day that you left the land of Egypt until you arrived at this place, you have been rebellious against the LORD.

8 "Even at Horeb you provoked the LORD to wrath, and the LORD was so angry with you that He would have destroyed you.

9 "When I went up to the mountain to receive the tablets of stone, the tablets of the covenant which the LORD had made with you, then I remained on the mountain forty days and nights; I neither ate bread nor drank water.

10 "The LORD gave me the two tablets of stone written by the finger of God; and on them *were* all the words which the LORD had spoken with you at the mountain from the midst of the fire on the day of the assembly.

11 "It came about at the end of forty days and nights that the LORD gave me the two tablets of stone, the tablets of the covenant.

12 "Then the LORD said to me, 'Arise, go down from here quickly, for your people whom you brought out of Egypt have acted corruptly. They have quickly turned aside from the way which I commanded them; they have made a molten image for themselves.'

13 "The LORD spoke further to me, saying, 'I have seen this people, and indeed, it is a stubborn people.

14 'Let Me alone, that I may destroy them and blot out their name from under heaven; and I will make of you a nation mightier and greater than they.'

15 ¶ "So I turned and came down from the mountain while the mountain was burning with fire, and the two tablets of the covenant were in my two hands.

16 "And I saw that you had indeed sinned against the LORD your God. You had made for yourselves a molten calf; you had turned aside quickly from the way which the LORD had commanded you.

17 "I took hold of the two tablets and threw them from my hands and smashed them before your eyes.

18 "I fell down before the LORD, as at the first, forty days and nights; I neither ate bread nor drank water, because of all your sin which you had committed in doing what was evil in the sight of the LORD to provoke Him to anger.

19 "For I was afraid of the anger and hot displeasure with which the LORD was wrathful against you in order to destroy you, but the LORD listened to me that time also.

20 "The LORD was angry enough with Aaron to destroy him; so I also prayed for Aaron at the same time.

21 "I took your sinful *thing,* the calf which you had made, and burned it with fire and crushed it, grinding it very small until it was as fine as dust; and I threw its dust into the brook that came down from the mountain.

22 ¶ "Again at Taberah and at Massah and at Kibroth-hattaavah you provoked the LORD to wrath.

23 "When the LORD sent you from Kadeshbarnea, saying, 'Go up and possess the land which I have given you,' then you rebelled against the command of the LORD your God; you neither believed Him nor listened to His voice.

24 "You have been rebellious against the LORD from the day I knew you.

25 ¶ "So I fell down before the LORD the forty days and nights, which I did because the LORD had said He would destroy you.

26 "I prayed to the LORD and said, 'O Lord GOD, do not destroy Your people, even Your inheritance, whom You have redeemed through Your greatness, whom You have brought out of Egypt with a mighty hand.

27 'Remember Your servants, Abraham, Isaac, and Jacob; do not look at the stubbornness of this people or at their wickedness or their sin.

28 'Otherwise the land from which You brought us may say, "Because the LORD was not able to bring them into the land which He had promised them and because He hated them He has brought them out to slay them in the wilderness."

29 'Yet they are Your people, even Your inheritance, whom You have brought out by Your great power and Your outstretched arm.'

The Tablets Rewritten

10 "At that time the LORD said to me, 'Cut out for yourself two tablets of stone like the former ones, and come up to Me on the mountain, and make an ark of wood for yourself.

2 'I will write on the tablets the words that

Healthier, Wealthier, and Wiser
Do only good things happen to good people?

DO CHRISTIANS HAVE CAR ACCIDENTS? Do they get cancer? Are they ever fired from their jobs? The answer to all three questions is, of course, yes. But that answer causes big problems for some new Christians. Doesn't the Bible promise that God will look out for and protect his followers? How can such bad things occur?

People puzzled by such questions often refer to Old Testament books where God clearly promised success and protection to the Israelites. In Deuteronomy, Moses spelled out God's promises in complete detail. Israelite wives would have many babies. All the crops—grain, grapes, olive trees—would produce bountifully. Cattle and sheep would multiply. And Moses even included this extraordinary promise: "The LORD will remove from you all sickness" (7:15).

A Special Arrangement

For the Israelites to receive these benefits, God asked only one thing in return: follow the covenant agreement first set forth in the book of Exodus. Deuteronomy repeats much of the covenant and affirms, "The LORD did not make this covenant with our fathers, but with us, with all those of us alive here today" (5:3).

And when your herds and your flocks multiply, and your silver and gold multiply, and all that you have multiplies, then your heart will become proud and you will forget the LORD your God who brought you out from the land of Egypt, out of the house of slavery. 8:13–14

God had a unique relationship with the band of refugees who had been roaming the Sinai for 40 years (10:15; 14:2). Moses, for one, could not seem to get over the arrangement. "Inquire from one end of the heavens to the other," he said. "Has anything been done like this great thing, or has anything been heard like it? Or has a god tried to go to take for himself a nation from within another nation . . . as . . . the LORD your God did for you in Egypt before your eyes?" (4:32,34).

Moses promised that good things would come the Israelites' way if they merely held up their end of the covenant. *If*, he said—underscoring that small but very crucial word. Threads of doubt and anxiety run all through the book. Will the Israelites stick to the terms of the covenant? Will they obey?

Dangers of Success

Moses seemed to fear the coming prosperity even more than the rigors of the desert, and he voiced those fears in chapter 8. In the promised land, a lush country of streams and fruit trees and valuable resources, the Israelites might forget God and begin to take credit for their own success. That, at least, was the danger, and the reason Moses kept urging, "Remember!" Remember the days of slavery in Egypt, and God's acts in liberating you. Remember the trials of the vast and desolate desert, and God's faithfulness there. Remember your special calling as a treasured possession of God. Do not forget, as a prosperous nation, what you learned as refugees in the Sinai.

God predicted bluntly, "For when I bring them into the land flowing with milk and honey, which I swore to their fathers, and they have eaten and are satisfied and become prosperous, then they will turn to other gods and serve them, and spurn Me and break My covenant" (31:20).

As the books following Deuteronomy record, all that God and Moses feared came true. The were on the former tablets which you shattered, and you shall put them in the ark.'

3 "So I made an ark of acacia wood and cut out two tablets of stone like the former ones, and went up on the mountain with the two tablets in my hand.

4 "He wrote on the tablets, like the former writing, the Ten Commandments which the LORD had spoken to you on the mountain from the midst of the fire on the day of the assembly; and the LORD gave them to me.

5 "Then I turned and came down from the mountain and put the tablets in the ark which I had made; and there they are, as the LORD commanded me."

6 ¶ (Now the sons of Israel set out from Beeroth Bene-jaakan to Moserah. There Aaron died and there he was buried and Eleazar his son ministered as priest in his place.

7 From there they set out to Gudgodah, and from Gudgodah to Jotbathah, a land of brooks of water.

8 At that time the LORD set apart the tribe of Levi to carry the ark of the covenant of the LORD, to stand before the LORD to serve Him and to bless in His name until this day.

9 Therefore, Levi does not have a portion or inheritance with his brothers; the LORD is his inheritance, just as the LORD your God spoke to him.)

10 ¶ "I, moreover, stayed on the mountain forty days and forty nights like the first time, and the LORD listened to me that time also; the LORD was not willing to destroy you.

11 "Then the LORD said to me, 'Arise, proceed on your journey ahead of the people, that they may go in and possess the land which I swore to their fathers to give them.'

12 ¶ "Now, Israel, what does the LORD your God require from you, but to fear the LORD your God, to walk in all His ways and love Him, and to serve the LORD your God with all your heart and with all your soul,

10:12 More Than a Feeling

Twelve times Deuteronomy says we are to love God. In fact, Jesus was quoting Deuteronomy 6:5 when he gave the most important commandment as "Love the Lord your God with all your heart" (Mark 12:30). How can we love when we don't feel loving? In the Bible, love is more than a feeling; it is a decision to serve another person's interest. Only through God's help can this decision be made with "all your heart."

13 *and* to keep the LORD's commandments and His statutes which I am commanding you today for your good?

14 "Behold, to the LORD your God belong heaven and the highest heavens, the earth and all that is in it.

15 "Yet on your fathers did the LORD set His affection to love them, and He chose their descendants after them, *even* you above all peoples, as *it is* this day.

16 "So circumcise your heart, and stiffen your neck no longer.

17 "For the LORD your God is the God of gods and the Lord of lords, the great, the mighty, and

---

covenant was irreparably broken. Ultimately, the Israelites received not wealth and happiness but slavery and suffering.

A Message for Us Today

The promises of Deuteronomy were given to a particular people, the Israelites, in a special covenant relationship—a covenant that God prophesied would be broken. The formula was simple: "Do good, get rewarded; do evil, get punished." But Christians of today cannot simply turn to those flagrant promises of wealth and prosperity and apply them directly. Rather, we must look at this book in light of the new covenant introduced by Jesus Christ and spelled out in the New Testament.

When Jesus came, he promised certain rewards for Christians, but he also predicted poverty, rejection, and even persecution. Rewards on this earth cannot be reduced to such a simple "Do good, get rewarded; do evil, get punished" formula. (See Hebrews 11 and "What Is True Faith?" page 1272.) Jesus' disciples proved faithful to him, and yet most of them lived through poverty and persecution and died martyrs' deaths. For them, full rewards had to wait until heaven.

Deuteronomy may offer a clue to why God does not exempt his followers from every bad thing in life. Ironically, prosperity and health may make it harder to depend on God. Moses' fears came true: The Israelites proved least faithful to God after they moved into the prosperity of the promised land. In the desert, at least, they had been forced to lean on God just for daily survival. But after a very short time in Canaan, they forgot about him. There is a grave danger in finally getting what you want.

Life Questions: When do you think most about God: when things are going well or when you are in trouble?

the awesome God who does not show partiality nor take a bribe.

18 "He executes justice for the orphan and the widow, and shows His love for the alien by giving him food and clothing.

19 "So show your love for the alien, for you were aliens in the land of Egypt.

20 "You shall fear the LORD your God; you shall serve Him and cling to Him, and you shall swear by His name.

21 "He is your praise and He is your God, who has done these great and awesome things for you which your eyes have seen.

22 "Your fathers went down to Egypt seventy persons *in all,* and now the LORD your God has made you as numerous as the stars of heaven.

Rewards of Obedience

11 "You shall therefore love the LORD your God, and always keep His charge, His statutes, His ordinances, and His commandments.

2 "Know this day that I *am* not *speaking* with your sons who have not known and who have not seen the *a*discipline of the LORD your God—His greatness, His mighty hand and His outstretched arm,

3 and His signs and His works which He did in the midst of Egypt to Pharaoh the king of Egypt and to all his land;

4 and what He did to Egypt's army, to its horses and its chariots, when He made the water of the Red Sea to engulf them while they were pursuing you, and the LORD completely destroyed them;

5 and what He did to you in the wilderness until you came to this place;

6 and what He did to Dathan and Abiram, the sons of Eliab, the son of Reuben, when the earth opened its mouth and swallowed them, their households, their tents, and every living thing that followed them, among all Israel—

7 but your own eyes have seen all the great work of the LORD which He did.

8 ¶ "You shall therefore keep every commandment which I am commanding you today, so that you may be strong and go in and possess the land into which you are about to cross to possess it;

9 so that you may prolong *your* days on the land which the LORD swore to your fathers to give to them and to their descendants, a land flowing with milk and honey.

10 "For the land, into which you are entering to possess it, is not like the land of Egypt from which you came, where you used to sow your seed and water it with your *b*foot like a vegetable garden.

11 "But the land into which you are about to cross to possess it, a land of hills and valleys, drinks water from the rain of heaven,

12 a land for which the LORD your God cares;

the eyes of the LORD your God are always on it, from the beginning even to the end of the year.

13 ¶ "It shall come about, if you listen obediently to my commandments which I am commanding you today, to love the LORD your God and to serve Him with all your heart and all your soul,

14 that He will give the rain for your land in its season, the *c*early and late rain, that you may gather in your grain and your new wine and your oil.

15 "He will give grass in your fields for your cattle, and you will eat and be satisfied.

16 "Beware that your hearts are not deceived, and that you do not turn away and serve other gods and worship them.

17 "Or the anger of the LORD will be kindled against you, and He will shut up the heavens so that there will be no rain and the ground will not yield its fruit; and you will perish quickly from the good land which the LORD is giving you.

18 ¶ "You shall therefore impress these words of mine on your heart and on your soul; and you shall bind them as a sign on your hand, and they shall be as frontals on your forehead.

11:18 Laws on the Head

Many commentators, both Jewish and Christian, read these sentences figuratively. But strict Jews take them literally. They wear handwritten portions of the Old Testament (including Deuteronomy 6:4–9 and 11:18–20) in a small box strapped to their foreheads, and they also mount them in a box beside the door to their homes. The boxes are called "phylacteries." Jesus referred to the practice (Matthew 23:5), commenting that it could become a showy way of expressing spiritual pride.

19 "You shall teach them to your sons, talking of them when you sit in your house and when you walk along the road and when you lie down and when you rise up.

20 "You shall write them on the doorposts of your house and on your gates,

21 so that your days and the days of your sons may be multiplied on the land which the LORD swore to your fathers to give them, as long as the heavens *remain* above the earth.

22 "For if you are careful to keep all this commandment which I am commanding you to do, to love the LORD your God, to walk in all His ways and hold fast to Him,

23 then the LORD will drive out all these nations from before you, and you will dispossess nations greater and mightier than you.

a Or *instruction*   *b* I.e. probably a treadmill   *c* I.e. autumn

24 "Every place on which the sole of your foot treads shall be yours; your border will be from the wilderness to Lebanon, *and* from the river, the river Euphrates, as far as *a*the western sea.

25 "No man will be able to stand before you; the LORD your God will lay the dread of you and the fear of you on all the land on which you set foot, as He has spoken to you.

26 ¶ "See, I am setting before you today a blessing and a curse:

27 the blessing, if you listen to the commandments of the LORD your God, which I am commanding you today;

28 and the curse, if you do not listen to the commandments of the LORD your God, but turn aside from the way which I am commanding you today, by following other gods which you have not known.

29 ¶ "It shall come about, when the LORD your God brings you into the land where you are entering to possess it, that you shall place the blessing on Mount Gerizim and the curse on Mount Ebal.

30 "Are they not across the Jordan, west of the way toward the sunset, in the land of the Canaanites who live in the Arabah, opposite Gilgal, beside the oaks of Moreh?

31 "For you are about to cross the Jordan to go in to possess the land which the LORD your God is giving you, and you shall possess it and live in it,

32 and you shall be careful to do all the statutes and the judgments which I am setting before you today.

Laws of the Sanctuary

12 "These are the statutes and the judgments which you shall carefully observe in the land which the LORD, the God of your fathers, has given you to possess as long as you live on the earth.

2 "You shall utterly destroy all the places where the nations whom you shall dispossess serve their gods, on the high mountains and on the hills and under every green tree.

3 "You shall tear down their altars and smash their *sacred* pillars and burn their *b*Asherim with fire, and you shall cut down the engraved images of their gods and obliterate their name from that place.

4 "You shall not act like this toward the LORD your God.

5 "But you shall seek *the* LORD at the place which the LORD your God will choose from all your tribes, to establish His name there for His dwelling, and there you shall come.

6 "There you shall bring your burnt offerings, your sacrifices, your tithes, the contribution of your hand, your votive offerings, your freewill offerings, and the firstborn of your herd and of your flock.

7 "There also you and your households shall eat before the LORD your God, and rejoice in all your undertakings in which the LORD your God has blessed you.

8 ¶ "You shall not do at all what we are doing

12:2 Historic Discovery

The Israelites did not fully follow these instructions on destroying the "high places," which were centers of idol worship. But hundreds of years after this scene with Moses, a dramatic event took place. In the midst of a temple renovation, workers came across an old scroll containing the Book of the Law. Discovery of the book had an electrifying effect on the nation. When King Josiah heard it read, he wept and tore his robes, then called for all the elders to hear the words. The event ushered in a sweeping spiritual revival that included a campaign against idolatry and the "high places." Many scholars believe Deuteronomy was the book that stirred a kingdom (see 2 Kings 22–23 for the full account).

---

here today, every man *doing* whatever is right in his own eyes;

9 for you have not as yet come to the resting place and the inheritance which the LORD your God is giving you.

10 "When you cross the Jordan and live in the land which the LORD your God is giving you to inherit, and He gives you rest from all your enemies around *you* so that you live in security,

11 then it shall come about that the place in which the LORD your God will choose for His name to dwell, there you shall bring all that I command you: your burnt offerings and your sacrifices, your tithes and the contribution of your hand, and all your choice votive offerings which you will vow to the LORD.

12 "And you shall rejoice before the LORD your God, you and your sons and daughters, your male and female servants, and the Levite who is within your gates, since he has no portion or inheritance with you.

13 ¶ "Be careful that you do not offer your burnt offerings in every *cultic* place you see,

14 but in the place which the LORD chooses in one of your tribes, there you shall offer your burnt offerings, and there you shall do all that I command you.

15 ¶ "However, you may slaughter and eat meat within any of your gates, whatever you desire, according to the blessing of the LORD your God which He has given you; the unclean and the

---

a I.e. the Mediterranean   *b* I.e. wooden symbols of a female deity clean may eat of it, as of the gazelle and the deer.

16 "Only you shall not eat the blood; you are to pour it out on the ground like water.

17 "You are not allowed to eat within your gates the tithe of your grain or new wine or oil, or the firstborn of your herd or flock, or any of your votive offerings which you vow, or your freewill offerings, or the contribution of your hand.

18 "But you shall eat them before the LORD your God in the place which the LORD your God will choose, you and your son and daughter, and your male and female servants, and the Levite who is within your gates; and you shall rejoice before the LORD your God in all your undertakings.

19 "Be careful that you do not forsake the Levite as long as you live in your land.

20 ¶ "When the LORD your God extends your border as He has promised you, and you say, 'I

Who Needs Laws?
Love makes the difference in this rulebook

DEUTERONOMY REPEATS VERBATIM MANY OF the laws given in Exodus, Leviticus, and Numbers. Yet it is far from a rulebook. A different spirit pervades it: the spirit of love. The rules in Deuteronomy read more like a guide on "How to Have a Successful Family" than, say, an automobile maintenance manual. To keep up a car you need only follow the rules. To maintain a close personal relationship you need more—you need love.

> "Be careful to listen to all these words which I command you, so that it may be well with you and your sons after you forever, for you will be doing what is good and right in the sight of the LORD your God." 12:28

What Makes Deuteronomy Different

Deuteronomy focuses on motives: *why* people should obey laws. The preceding three books barely mentioned the love of God for his people, but Deuteronomy again and again refers to it (see 4:37; 7:7–8; 10:15; 23:5). The author portrays God as a father with his children, as a mother who gives them life, as an eagle hovering over its young.

In return, God asks for obedience based on love, not on a sense of duty. At least 15 times in the book Moses tells the Israelites to love God and cling to him. God wants not just an outward conformity, but an obedience that comes from the heart. (Later, in summing up the Old Testament, Jesus quoted the first and greatest commandment from Deuteronomy: "Love the Lord your God with all your heart and with all your soul, and with all your mind" [Matthew 22:37; Deuteronomy 6:5].)

Restating the Negatives

Deuteronomy also hints at why laws are needed in the first place. Moses stated the principle directly, "The LORD commanded us to observe all these statutes, to fear the LORD our God for our good always and for our survival, as it is today" (6:24). In other words, the laws were given for the Israelites' own good.

Most of the Ten Commandments were given in a negative form, "You shall not." But each of these negative statements protects a privileged relationship between two people or a person and God. For example, "Do not murder" could be restated, "Human life is sacred and has enormous worth. Respect such life as the image of God, and defend it." Other commandments protect marriage, private property, honesty, and the day set aside to worship God.

Never Forget

Moses could not have emphasized the laws more strongly. "These words, which I am commanding you today, shall be on your heart," he said. "You shall teach them diligently to your sons and shall talk of them when you sit in your house and when you walk by the way and when you lie down and when you rise up" (6:6–7).

Moses wanted to make sure the Israelites would not possibly forget the laws. He instructed the priests to gather the whole nation together to hear them read aloud every seven years (31:9–13). Any king of Israel was required, as one of his first acts, to write out the laws by hand (17:18–19).

One last visual reminder served to impress the laws on the Israelites' minds. The priests wrote them in bold letters on stones covered with plaster. As the tribes marched across the Jordan River into the new land, they passed between the writing-covered stones (27:1–8).

No one in Israel could plead ignorance of what God required of them—his rules were carved in stone. As history would prove, obeying the rules was another matter.

Life Questions: Read over the Ten Commandments in Deuteronomy 5. How do they help us? What "rights" are they protecting?

will eat meat,' because you desire to eat meat, *then* you may eat meat, whatever you desire.

21 "If the place which the LORD your God chooses to put His name is too far from you, then you may slaughter of your herd and flock which the LORD has given you, as I have commanded you; and you may eat within your gates whatever you desire.

22 "Just as a gazelle or a deer is eaten, so you will eat it; the unclean and the clean alike may eat of it.

23 "Only be sure not to eat the blood, for the blood is the life, and you shall not eat the life with the flesh.

24 "You shall not eat it; you shall pour it out on the ground like water.

25 "You shall not eat it, so that it may be well with you and your sons after you, for you will be doing what is right in the sight of the LORD.

26 "Only your holy things which you may have and your votive offerings, you shall take and go to the place which the LORD chooses.

27 "And you shall offer your burnt offerings, the flesh and the blood, on the altar of the LORD your God; and the blood of your sacrifices shall be poured out on the altar of the LORD your God, and you shall eat the flesh.

28 ¶ "Be careful to listen to all these words which I command you, so that it may be well with you and your sons after you forever, for you will be doing what is good and right in the sight of the LORD your God.

29 ¶ "When the LORD your God cuts off before you the nations which you are going in to dispossess, and you dispossess them and dwell in their land,

30 beware that you are not ensnared to follow them, after they are destroyed before you, and that you do not inquire after their gods, saying, 'How do these nations serve their gods, that I also may do likewise?'

31 "You shall not behave thus toward the LORD your God, for every abominable act which the LORD hates they have done for their gods; for they even burn their sons and daughters in the fire to their gods.

32 ¶ "Whatever I command you, you shall be careful to do; you shall not add to nor take away from it.

Shun Idolatry

13 "If a prophet or a dreamer of dreams arises among you and gives you a sign or a wonder,

2 and the sign or the wonder comes true, concerning which he spoke to you, saying, 'Let us go after other gods (whom you have not known) and let us serve them,'

3 you shall not listen to the words of that prophet or that dreamer of dreams; for the LORD your God is testing you to find out if you love the LORD your God with all your heart and with all your soul.

4 "You shall follow the LORD your God and fear Him; and you shall keep His commandments,

13:1–5 Testing Prophets

Lots of people—cult members as well as Christians—claim that God has spoken to them. How do you evaluate those claims? Deuteronomy offers two tests. First, a prediction made in God's name must in fact come true (18:21–22). The second test, given here, matters just as much. If a prediction does come true, but the prophet tries to lead people to worship some other god, that prophet should be rejected.

listen to His voice, serve Him, and cling to Him.

5 "But that prophet or that dreamer of dreams shall be put to death, because he has counseled rebellion against the LORD your God who brought you from the land of Egypt and redeemed you from the house of slavery, to seduce you from the way in which the LORD your God commanded you to walk. So you shall purge the evil from among you.

6 ¶ "If your brother, your mother's son, or your son or daughter, or the wife you cherish, or your friend who is as your own soul, entice you secretly, saying, 'Let us go and serve other gods' (whom neither you nor your fathers have known,

7 of the gods of the peoples who are around you, near you or far from you, from one end of the earth to the other end),

8 you shall not yield to him or listen to him; and your eye shall not pity him, nor shall you spare or conceal him.

9 "But you shall surely kill him; your hand shall be first against him to put him to death, and afterwards the hand of all the people.

10 "So you shall stone him to death because he has sought to seduce you from the LORD your God who brought you out from the land of Egypt, out of the house of slavery.

11 "Then all Israel will hear and be afraid, and will never again do such a wicked thing among you.

12 ¶ "If you hear in one of your cities, which the LORD your God is giving you to live in, *anyone* saying *that*

13 some worthless men have gone out from among you and have seduced the inhabitants of their city, saying, 'Let us go and serve other gods' (whom you have not known),

14 then you shall investigate and search out and inquire thoroughly. If it is true *and* the matter established that this abomination has been done among you,

15 you shall surely strike the inhabitants of that

city with the edge of the sword, utterly destroying it and all that is in it and its cattle with the edge of the sword.

16 "Then you shall gather all its booty into the middle of its open square and burn the city and all its booty with fire as a whole burnt offering to the LORD your God; and it shall be a ruin forever. It shall never be rebuilt.

17 "Nothing from that which is put under the ban shall cling to your hand, in order that the LORD may turn from His burning anger and show mercy to you, and have compassion on you and make you increase, just as He has sworn to your fathers,

18 if you will listen to the voice of the LORD your God, keeping all His commandments which I am commanding you today, and doing what is right in the sight of the LORD your God.

Clean and Unclean Animals

14 "You are the sons of the LORD your God; you shall not cut yourselves nor shave your forehead for the sake of the dead.

2 "For you are a holy people to the LORD your God, and the LORD has chosen you to be a people for His own possession out of all the peoples who are on the face of the earth.

3 ¶ "You shall not eat any detestable thing.

4 "These are the animals which you may eat: the ox, the sheep, the goat,

5 the deer, the gazelle, the roebuck, the wild goat, the ibex, the antelope and the mountain sheep.

6 "Any animal that divides the hoof and has the hoof split in two *and* chews the cud, among the animals, that you may eat.

7 "Nevertheless, you are not to eat of these among those which chew the cud, or among those that divide the hoof in two: the camel and the rabbit and the shaphan, for though they chew the cud, they do not divide the hoof; they are unclean for you.

8 "The pig, because it divides the hoof but *does* not *chew* the cud, it is unclean for you. You shall not eat any of their flesh nor touch their carcasses.

9 ¶ "These you may eat of all that are in water: anything that has fins and scales you may eat,

10 but anything that does not have fins and scales you shall not eat; it is unclean for you.

11 ¶ "You may eat any clean bird.

12 "But these are the ones which you shall not eat: the eagle and the vulture and the buzzard,

13 and the red kite, the falcon, and the kite in their kinds,

14 and every raven in its kind,

15 and the ostrich, the owl, the sea gull, and the hawk in their kinds,

16 the little owl, the great owl, the white owl,

17 the pelican, the carrion vulture, the cormorant,

18 the stork, and the heron in their kinds, and the hoopoe and the bat.

19 "And all the teeming life with wings are unclean to you; they shall not be eaten.

20 "You may eat any clean bird.

21 ¶ "You shall not eat anything which dies of *itself.* You may give it to the alien who is in your town, so that he may eat it, or you may sell it to a foreigner, for you are a holy people to the LORD your God. You shall not boil a young goat in its mother's milk.

22 ¶ "You shall surely tithe all the produce from what you sow, which comes out of the field every year.

23 "You shall eat in the presence of the LORD your God, at the place where He chooses to establish His name, the tithe of your grain, your new wine, your oil, and the firstborn of your herd and your flock, so that you may learn to fear the LORD your God always.

24 "If the distance is so great for you that you are not able to bring *the tithe,* since the place where the LORD your God chooses to set His name is too far away from you when the LORD your God blesses you,

25 then you shall exchange *it* for money, and bind the money in your hand and go to the place which the LORD your God chooses.

26 "You may spend the money for whatever your heart desires: for oxen, or sheep, or wine, or strong drink, or whatever your heart desires; and there you shall eat in the presence of the LORD your God and rejoice, you and your household.

27 "Also you shall not neglect the Levite who is in your town, for he has no portion or inheritance among you.

28 ¶ "At the end of every third year you shall bring out all the tithe of your produce in that year, and shall deposit *it* in your town.

14:28–29 Tithe to the Poor

Each year the Israelites presented a tithe of produce as an offering to God. Every third year the tithe would be distributed to needy people. God accepted the gifts to these people as an offering to himself. The principle behind this practice was later powerfully expressed in a parable by Jesus (Matthew 25:31–46), who said, "Truly I say to you, to the extent that you did it to one of these brothers of Mine, even the least of them, you did it to Me."

29 "The Levite, because he has no portion or inheritance among you, and the alien, the orphan and the widow who are in your town, shall come and eat and be satisfied, in order that the LORD your God may bless you in all the work of your hand which you do.

The Sabbatic Year

15 "At the end of *every* seven years you shall *a*grant a remission *of debts.*

2 "This is the manner of remission: every creditor shall release what he has loaned to his neighbor; he shall not exact it of his neighbor and his brother, because the LORD's remission has been proclaimed.

3 "From a foreigner you may exact *it,* but your hand shall release whatever of yours is with your brother.

4 "However, there will be no poor among you, since the LORD will surely bless you in the land which the LORD your God is giving you as an inheritance to possess,

5 if only you listen obediently to the voice of the LORD your God, to observe carefully all this commandment which I am commanding you today.

6 "For the LORD your God will bless you as He has promised you, and you will lend to many nations, but you will not borrow; and you will rule over many nations, but they will not rule over you.

7 ¶ "If there is a poor man with you, one of your brothers, in any of your towns in your land which the LORD your God is giving you, you shall not harden your heart, nor close your hand from your poor brother;

8 but you shall freely open your hand to him, and shall generously lend him sufficient for his need *in* whatever he lacks.

9 "Beware that there is no base thought in your heart, saying, 'The seventh year, the year of remission, is near,' and your eye is hostile toward your poor brother, and you give him nothing; then he may cry to the LORD against you, and it will be a sin in you.

10 "You shall generously give to him, and your heart shall not be grieved when you give to him, because for this thing the LORD your God will bless you in all your work and in all your undertakings.

11 "For the poor will never cease *to be* in the land; therefore I command you, saying, 'You shall freely open your hand to your brother, to your needy and poor in your land.'

12 ¶ "If your kinsman, a Hebrew man or woman, is sold to you, then he shall serve you six years, but in the seventh year you shall set him free.

13 "When you set him free, you shall not send him away empty-handed.

14 "You shall furnish him liberally from your flock and from your threshing floor and from your wine vat; you shall give to him as the LORD your God has blessed you.

15 "You shall remember that you were a slave in the land of Egypt, and the LORD your God redeemed you; therefore I command you this today.

16 "It shall come about if he says to you, 'I will

not go out from you,' because he loves you and your household, since he fares well with you;

17 then you shall take an awl and pierce it through his ear into the door, and he shall be your

15:11 Any Poor People?

At first glance, this verse seems to contradict verse 4, which says there should be no poor people in Israel. Moses knew the difference between what should happen and what will happen. God's blessings in the promised land ought to have eliminated poverty—if the Israelites had obeyed completely. But since some people always fall short, poverty remains a problem. (Jesus confirmed this in a passing remark in Matthew 26:11.) As a result, in our time as in Moses', generosity is essential.

servant forever. Also you shall do likewise to your maidservant.

18 ¶ "It shall not seem hard to you when you set him free, for he has given you six years *with* double the service of a hired man; so the LORD your God will bless you in whatever you do.

19 ¶ "You shall consecrate to the LORD your God all the firstborn males that are born of your herd and of your flock; you shall not work with the firstborn of your herd, nor shear the firstborn of your flock.

20 "You and your household shall eat it every year before the LORD your God in the place which the LORD chooses.

21 "But if it has any defect, *such as* lameness or blindness, *or* any serious defect, you shall not sacrifice it to the LORD your God.

22 "You shall eat it within your gates; the unclean and the clean alike *may eat it,* as a gazelle or a deer.

23 "Only you shall not eat its blood; you are to pour it out on the ground like water.

The Feasts of Passover, of Weeks, and of Booths

16 "Observe the month of Abib and celebrate the Passover to the LORD your God, for in the month of Abib the LORD your God brought you out of Egypt by night.

2 "You shall sacrifice the Passover to the LORD your God from the flock and the herd, in the place where the LORD chooses to establish His name.

3 "You shall not eat leavened bread with it; seven days you shall eat with it unleavened bread, the bread of affliction (for you came out of the land of Egypt in haste), so that you may remember all the days of your life the day when you came out of the land of Egypt.

4 "For seven days no leaven shall be seen with

---

a Lit *make a release*

you in all your territory, and none of the flesh which you sacrifice on the evening of the first day shall remain overnight until morning.

5 "You are not allowed to sacrifice the Passover in any of your towns which the LORD your God is giving you;

6 but at the place where the LORD your God chooses to establish His name, you shall sacrifice the Passover in the evening at sunset, at the time that you came out of Egypt.

7 "You shall cook and eat *it* in the place which the LORD your God chooses. In the morning you are to return to your tents.

8 "Six days you shall eat unleavened bread, and on the seventh day there shall be a solemn assembly to the LORD your God; you shall do no work *on it.*

9 ¶ "You shall count seven weeks for yourself; you shall begin to count seven weeks from the time you begin to put the sickle to the standing grain.

10 "Then you shall celebrate the Feast of Weeks to the LORD your God with a tribute of a freewill offering of your hand, which you shall give just as the LORD your God blesses you;

11 and you shall rejoice before the LORD your God, you and your son and your daughter and your male and female servants and the Levite who is in your town, and the stranger and the orphan and the widow who are in your midst, in the place where the LORD your God chooses to establish His name.

12 "You shall remember that you were a slave in Egypt, and you shall be careful to observe these statutes.

13 ¶ "You shall celebrate the Feast of Booths seven days after you have gathered in from your threshing floor and your wine vat;

14 and you shall rejoice in your feast, you and your son and your daughter and your male and female servants and the Levite and the stranger and the orphan and the widow who are in your towns.

15 "Seven days you shall celebrate a feast to the LORD your God in the place which the LORD chooses, because the LORD your God will bless you in all your produce and in all the work of your hands, so that you will be altogether joyful.

16 ¶ "Three times in a year all your males shall appear before the LORD your God in the place which He chooses, at the Feast of Unleavened Bread and at the Feast of Weeks and at the Feast of Booths, and they shall not appear before the LORD empty-handed.

17 "Every man shall give as he is able, according to the blessing of the LORD your God which He has given you.

18 ¶ "You shall appoint for yourself judges and officers in all your towns which the LORD your God is giving you, according to your tribes, and

they shall judge the people with righteous judgment.

19 "You shall not distort justice; you shall not be partial, and you shall not take a bribe, for a bribe blinds the eyes of the wise and perverts the words of the righteous.

20 "Justice, *and only* justice, you shall pursue, that you may live and possess the land which the LORD your God is giving you.

21 ¶ "You shall not plant for yourself an Asherah of any kind of tree beside the altar of the LORD your God, which you shall make for yourself.

22 "You shall not set up for yourself a *sacred* pillar which the LORD your God hates.

Administration of Justice

17 "You shall not sacrifice to the LORD your God an ox or a sheep which has a blemish *or* any defect, for that is a detestable thing to the LORD your God.

2 ¶ "If there is found in your midst, in any of your towns, which the LORD your God is giving you, a man or a woman who does what is evil in the sight of the LORD your God, by transgressing His covenant,

3 and has gone and served other gods and worshiped them, or the sun or the moon or any of the heavenly host, which I have not commanded,

4 and if it is told you and you have heard of it, then you shall inquire thoroughly. Behold, if it is true and the thing certain that this detestable thing has been done in Israel,

5 then you shall bring out that man or that woman who has done this evil deed to your gates, *that is,* the man or the woman, and you shall stone them to death.

6 "On the evidence of two witnesses or three witnesses, he who is to die shall be put to death; he shall not be put to death on the evidence of one witness.

7 "The hand of the witnesses shall be first against him to put him to death, and afterward the hand of all the people. So you shall purge the evil from your midst.

8 ¶ "If any case is too difficult for you to decide, between one kind of homicide or another, between one kind of lawsuit or another, and between one kind of assault or another, being cases of dispute in your courts, then you shall arise and go up to the place which the LORD your God chooses.

9 "So you shall come to the Levitical priest or the judge who is *in office* in those days, and you shall inquire *of them* and they will declare to you the verdict in the case.

10 "You shall do according to the terms of the verdict which they declare to you from that place which the LORD chooses; and you shall be careful to observe according to all that they teach you.

11 "According to the terms of the law which they teach you, and according to the verdict which

they tell you, you shall do; you shall not turn aside from the word which they declare to you, to the right or the left.

12 "The man who acts presumptuously by not listening to the priest who stands there to serve the LORD your God, nor to the judge, that man shall die; thus you shall purge the evil from Israel.

13 "Then all the people will hear and be afraid, and will not act presumptuously again.

14 ¶ "When you enter the land which the LORD your God gives you, and you possess it and live in it, and you say, 'I will set a king over me like all the nations who are around me,'

15 you shall surely set a king over you whom the LORD your God chooses, *one* from among your countrymen you shall set as king over yourselves; you may not put a foreigner over yourselves who is not your countryman.

17:15 Prescription for a King

Until now, the Bible has not mentioned the possibility of an Israelite king. But here, long before the nation actually got a king, God lays down his prescription for a good one. The list of qualities hardly fits the normal image of a king—or the kind of person the Israelites' descendants usually got.

16 "Moreover, he shall not multiply horses for himself, nor shall he cause the people to return to Egypt to multiply horses, since the LORD has said to you, 'You shall never again return that way.'

17 "He shall not multiply wives for himself, or else his heart will turn away; nor shall he greatly increase silver and gold for himself.

18 ¶ "Now it shall come about when he sits on the throne of his kingdom, he shall write for himself a copy of this law on a scroll in the presence of the Levitical priests.

19 "It shall be with him and he shall read it all the days of his life, that he may learn to fear the LORD his God, by carefully observing all the words of this law and these statutes,

20 that his heart may not be lifted up above his countrymen and that he may not turn aside from the commandment, to the right or the left, so that he and his sons may continue long in his kingdom in the midst of Israel.

Portion of the Levites

18 "The Levitical priests, the whole tribe of Levi, shall have no portion or inheritance with Israel; they shall eat the LORD's offerings by fire and His portion.

2 "They shall have no inheritance among their countrymen; the LORD is their inheritance, as He promised them.

3 ¶ "Now this shall be the priests' due from the people, from those who offer a sacrifice, either an ox or a sheep, of which they shall give to the priest the shoulder and the two cheeks and the stomach.

4 "You shall give him the first fruits of your grain, your new wine, and your oil, and the first shearing of your sheep.

5 "For the LORD your God has chosen him and his sons from all your tribes, to stand and serve in the name of the LORD forever.

6 ¶ "Now if a Levite comes from any of your towns throughout Israel where he resides, and comes whenever he desires to the place which the LORD chooses,

7 then he shall serve in the name of the LORD his God, like all his fellow Levites who stand there before the LORD.

8 "They shall eat equal portions, except *what they receive* from the sale of their fathers' *estates.*

Spiritism Forbidden

9 ¶ "When you enter the land which the LORD your God gives you, you shall not learn to imitate the detestable things of those nations.

18:9–13 "Detestable Things"

This brief paragraph gives a preview of some of the "detestable things" the Israelites would encounter in the promised land. Child sacrifice was a common part of worship in Canaan. God had already stated that the Israelites' invasion was a form of punishment on the Canaanites for these kinds of practices (9:4).

10 "There shall not be found among you anyone who makes his son or his daughter pass through the fire, one who uses divination, one who practices witchcraft, or one who interprets omens, or a sorcerer,

11 or one who casts a spell, or a medium, or a spiritist, or one who calls up the dead.

12 "For whoever does these things is detestable to the LORD; and because of these detestable things the LORD your God will drive them out before you.

13 "You shall be blameless before the LORD your God.

14 "For those nations, which you shall dispossess, listen to those who practice witchcraft and to diviners, but as for you, the LORD your God has not allowed you *to do* so.

15 ¶ "The LORD your God will raise up for you a prophet like me from among you, from your countrymen, you shall listen to him.

16 "This is according to all that you asked of the LORD your God in Horeb on the day of the assembly, saying, 'Let me not hear again the voice of the LORD my God, let me not see this great fire anymore, or I will die.'

17 "The LORD said to me, 'They have spoken well.

18 'I will raise up a prophet from among their countrymen like you, and I will put My words in his mouth, and he shall speak to them all that I command him.

19 'It shall come about that whoever will not listen to My words which he shall speak in My name, I Myself will require *it* of him.

20 'But the prophet who speaks a word presumptuously in My name which I have not commanded him to speak, or which he speaks in the name of other gods, that prophet shall die.'

21 "You may say in your heart, 'How will we know the word which the LORD has not spoken?'

22 "When a prophet speaks in the name of the LORD, if the thing does not come about or come true, that is the thing which the LORD has not spoken. The prophet has spoken it presumptuously; you shall not be afraid of him.

Cities of Refuge

19 "When the LORD your God cuts off the nations, whose land the LORD your God gives you, and you dispossess them and settle in their cities and in their houses,

2 you shall set aside three cities for yourself in the midst of your land, which the LORD your God gives you to possess.

3 "You shall prepare the roads for yourself, and divide into three parts the territory of your land which the LORD your God will give you as a possession, so that any manslayer may flee there.

4 ¶ "Now this is the case of the manslayer who may flee there and live: when he kills his friend unintentionally, not hating him previously—

5 as when *a man* goes into the forest with his friend to cut wood, and his hand swings the axe to cut down the tree, and the iron *head* slips off the handle and strikes his friend so that he dies—he may flee to one of these cities and live;

6 otherwise the avenger of blood might pursue the manslayer in the heat of his anger, and overtake him, because the way is long, and take his life, though he was not deserving of death, since he had not hated him previously.

7 "Therefore, I command you, saying, 'You shall set aside three cities for yourself.'

8 ¶ "If the LORD your God enlarges your territory, just as He has sworn to your fathers, and gives you all the land which He promised to give your fathers—

9 if you carefully observe all this commandment which I command you today, to love the LORD your God, and to walk in His ways always—then you shall add three more cities for yourself, besides these three.

10 "So innocent blood will not be shed in the midst of your land which the LORD your God gives

you as an inheritance, and bloodguiltiness be on you.

11 ¶ "But if there is a man who hates his neighbor and lies in wait for him and rises up against him and strikes him so that he dies, and he flees to one of these cities,

12 then the elders of his city shall send and take him from there and deliver him into the hand of the avenger of blood, that he may die.

13 "You shall not pity him, but you shall purge the blood of the innocent from Israel, that it may go well with you.

Laws of Landmark and Testimony

14 ¶ "You shall not move your neighbor's boundary mark, which the ancestors have set, in your inheritance which you will inherit in the land that the LORD your God gives you to possess.

15 ¶ "A single witness shall not rise up against a man on account of any iniquity or any sin which he has committed; on the evidence of two or three witnesses a matter shall be confirmed.

16 "If a malicious witness rises up against a man to accuse him of wrongdoing,

17 then both the men who have the dispute shall stand before the LORD, before the priests and the judges who will be *in office* in those days.

18 "The judges shall investigate thoroughly, and if the witness is a false witness *and* he has accused his brother falsely,

19 then you shall do to him just as he had intended to do to his brother. Thus you shall purge the evil from among you.

20 "The rest will hear and be afraid, and will never again do such an evil thing among you.

21 "Thus you shall not show pity: life for life, eye for eye, tooth for tooth, hand for hand, foot for foot.

Laws of Warfare

20 "When you go out to battle against your enemies and see horses and chariots *and* people more numerous than you, do not be afraid of them; for the LORD your God, who brought you up from the land of Egypt, is with you.

2 "When you are approaching the battle, the priest shall come near and speak to the people.

3 "He shall say to them, 'Hear, O Israel, you are approaching the battle against your enemies today. Do not be fainthearted. Do not be afraid, or panic, or tremble before them,

4 for the LORD your God is the one who goes with you, to fight for you against your enemies, to save you.'

5 "The officers also shall speak to the people, saying, 'Who is the man that has built a new house and has not dedicated it? Let him depart and return to his house, otherwise he might die in the battle and another man would dedicate it.

6 'Who is the man that has planted a vineyard and has not begun to use its fruit? Let him depart

and return to his house, otherwise he might die in the battle and another man would begin to use its fruit.

7 'And who is the man that is engaged to a woman and has not married her? Let him depart and return to his house, otherwise he might die in the battle and another man would marry her.'

20:5 Uncommon Military Rules

The Israelites gained a reputation as fierce and bloody fighters. Yet Moses' instructions in this chapter defied normal military practice. Soldiers with new homes, new vineyards, and new fiancées—or even just plain scared soldiers—got exemptions from fighting. And before attacking any city, the army was to make a peace offer.

8 "Then the officers shall speak further to the people and say, 'Who is the man that is afraid and fainthearted? Let him depart and return to his house, so that he might not make his brothers' hearts melt like his heart.'

9 "When the officers have finished speaking to the people, they shall appoint commanders of armies at the head of the people.

10 ¶ "When you approach a city to fight against it, you shall offer it terms of peace.

11 "If it agrees to make peace with you and opens to you, then all the people who are found in it shall become your forced labor and shall serve you.

12 "However, if it does not make peace with you, but makes war against you, then you shall besiege it.

13 "When the LORD your God gives it into your hand, you shall strike all the men in it with the edge of the sword.

14 "Only the women and the children and the animals and all that is in the city, all its spoil, you shall take as booty for yourself; and you shall use the spoil of your enemies which the LORD your God has given you.

15 "Thus you shall do to all the cities that are very far from you, which are not of the cities of these nations nearby.

16 "Only in the cities of these peoples that the LORD your God is giving you as an inheritance, you shall not leave alive anything that breathes.

17 "But you shall utterly destroy them, the Hittite and the Amorite, the Canaanite and the Perizzite, the Hivite and the Jebusite, as the LORD your God has commanded you,

18 so that they may not teach you to do according to all their detestable things which they have done for their gods, so that you would sin against the LORD your God.

19 ¶ "When you besiege a city a long time, to make war against it in order to capture it, you shall not destroy its trees by swinging an axe against them; for you may eat from them, and you shall not cut them down. For is the tree of the field a man, that it should be besieged by you?

20 "Only the trees which you know are not fruit trees you shall destroy and cut down, that you may construct siegeworks against the city that is making war with you until it falls.

Expiation of a Crime

21 "If a slain person is found lying in the open country in the land which the LORD your God gives you to possess, *and* it is not known who has struck him,

2 then your elders and your judges shall go out and measure *the distance* to the cities which are around the slain one.

3 "It shall be that the city which is nearest to the slain man, that is, the elders of that city, shall take a heifer of the herd, which has not been worked and which has not pulled in a yoke;

4 and the elders of that city shall bring the heifer down to a valley with running water, which has not been plowed or sown, and shall break the heifer's neck there in the valley.

5 "Then the priests, the sons of Levi, shall come near, for the LORD your God has chosen them to serve Him and to bless in the name of the LORD; and every dispute and every assault shall be settled by them.

6 "All the elders of that city which is nearest to the slain man shall wash their hands over the heifer whose neck was broken in the valley;

7 and they shall answer and say, 'Our hands did not shed this blood, nor did our eyes see *it*.

8 '[a]Forgive Your people Israel whom You have redeemed, O LORD, and do not place the guilt of innocent blood in the midst of Your people Israel.' And the bloodguiltiness shall be forgiven them.

9 "So you shall remove the guilt of innocent blood from your midst, when you do what is right in the eyes of the LORD.

Domestic Relations

10 ¶ "When you go out to battle against your enemies, and the LORD your God delivers them into your hands and you take them away captive,

11 and see among the captives a beautiful woman, and have a desire for her and would take her as a wife for yourself,

12 then you shall bring her home to your house, and she shall shave her head and trim her nails.

13 "She shall also remove the clothes of her captivity and shall remain in your house, and mourn her father and mother a full month; and after that

---

[a] Lit *Cover over, atone for*

you may go in to her and be her husband and she shall be your wife.

14 "It shall be, if you are not pleased with her, then you shall let her go wherever she wishes; but you shall certainly not sell her for money, you shall not mistreat her, because you have humbled her.

15 ¶ "If a man has two wives, the one loved and the other unloved, and *both* the loved and the unloved have borne him sons, if the firstborn son belongs to the unloved,

16 then it shall be in the day he wills what he has to his sons, he cannot make the son of the loved the firstborn before the son of the unloved, who is the firstborn.

17 "But he shall acknowledge the firstborn, the son of the unloved, by giving him a double portion of all that he has, for he is the beginning of his strength; to him belongs the right of the firstborn.

18 ¶ "If any man has a stubborn and rebellious son who will not obey his father or his mother, and when they chastise him, he will not even listen to them,

19 then his father and mother shall seize him, and bring him out to the elders of his city at the gateway of his hometown.

20 "They shall say to the elders of his city, 'This son of ours is stubborn and rebellious, he will not obey us, he is a glutton and a drunkard.'

21 "Then all the men of his city shall stone him to death; so you shall remove the evil from your midst, and all Israel will hear *of it* and fear.

22 ¶ "If a man has committed a sin worthy of death and he is put to death, and you hang him on a tree,

23 his corpse shall not hang all night on the tree, but you shall surely bury him on the same day (for he who is hanged is accursed of God), so that you do not defile your land which the LORD your God gives you as an inheritance.

Sundry Laws

22 "You shall not see your countryman's ox or his sheep straying away, and pay no attention to them; you shall certainly bring them back to your countryman.

2 "If your countryman is not near you, or if you do not know him, then you shall bring it

22:1–7 Respect for Nature

The laws in Deuteronomy demonstrate God's concern that nature be treated with respect. In his instructions on war, Moses ordered those who laid siege to a city to choose carefully which trees to cut down (20:19). God's concern for the weak and helpless extended into the animal kingdom, for the law protected oxen, donkeys, and even birds (22:1–7).

home to your house, and it shall remain with you until your countryman looks for it; then you shall restore it to him.

3 "Thus you shall do with his donkey, and you shall do the same with his garment, and you shall do likewise with anything lost by your countryman, which he has lost and you have found. You are not allowed to neglect *them*.

4 "You shall not see your countryman's donkey or his ox fallen down on the way, and pay no attention to them; you shall certainly help him to raise *them* up.

5 ¶ "A woman shall not wear man's clothing, nor shall a man put on a woman's clothing; for whoever does these things is an abomination to the LORD your God.

6 ¶ "If you happen to come upon a bird's nest along the way, in any tree or on the ground, with young ones or eggs, and the mother sitting on the young or on the eggs, you shall not take the mother with the young;

7 you shall certainly let the mother go, but the young you may take for yourself, in order that it may be well with you and that you may prolong your days.

8 ¶ "When you build a new house, you shall make a parapet for your roof, so that you will not bring bloodguilt on your house if anyone falls from it.

9 ¶ "You shall not sow your vineyard with two kinds of seed, or all the produce of the seed which you have sown and the increase of the vineyard will become defiled.

10 ¶ "You shall not plow with an ox and a donkey together.

11 ¶ "You shall not wear a material mixed of wool and linen together.

12 ¶ "You shall make yourself tassels on the four corners of your garment with which you cover yourself.

Laws on Morality

13 ¶ "If any man takes a wife and goes in to her and *then* turns against her,

14 and charges her with shameful deeds and publicly defames her, and says, 'I took this woman, *but* when I came near her, I did not find her a virgin,'

15 then the girl's father and her mother shall take and bring out the *evidence* of the girl's virginity to the elders of the city at the gate.

16 "The girl's father shall say to the elders, 'I gave my daughter to this man for a wife, but he turned against her;

17 and behold, he has charged her with shameful deeds, saying, "I did not find your daughter a virgin." But this is the evidence of my daughter's virginity.' And they shall spread the garment before the elders of the city.

18 "So the elders of that city shall take the man and chastise him,

19 and they shall fine him a hundred *shekels* of silver and give it to the girl's father, because he publicly defamed a virgin of Israel. And she shall remain his wife; he cannot divorce her all his days.

20 ¶ "But if this charge is true, that the girl was not found a virgin,

21 then they shall bring out the girl to the doorway of her father's house, and the men of her city shall stone her to death because she has committed an act of folly in Israel by playing the harlot in her father's house; thus you shall purge the evil from among you.

22 ¶ "If a man is found lying with a married woman, then both of them shall die, the man who lay with the woman, and the woman; thus you shall purge the evil from Israel.

23 ¶ "If there is a girl who is a virgin engaged to a man, and *another* man finds her in the city and lies with her,

24 then you shall bring them both out to the gate of that city and you shall stone them to death; the girl, because she did not cry out in the city, and the man, because he has violated his neighbor's wife. Thus you shall purge the evil from among you.

25 ¶ "But if in the field the man finds the girl who is engaged, and the man forces her and lies with her, then only the man who lies with her shall die.

26 "But you shall do nothing to the girl; there is no sin in the girl worthy of death, for just as a man rises against his neighbor and murders him, so is this case.

27 "When he found her in the field, the engaged girl cried out, but there was no one to save her.

28 ¶ "If a man finds a girl who is a virgin, who is not engaged, and seizes her and lies with her and they are discovered,

29 then the man who lay with her shall give to the girl's father fifty *shekels* of silver, and she shall become his wife because he has violated her; he cannot divorce her all his days.

30 ¶ "A man shall not take his father's wife so that he will not uncover his father's skirt.

Persons Excluded from the Assembly

23 "No one who is emasculated or has his male organ cut off shall enter the assembly of the LORD.

2 "No one of illegitimate birth shall enter the assembly of the LORD; none of his *descendants,* even to the tenth generation, shall enter the assembly of the LORD.

3 "No Ammonite or Moabite shall enter the assembly of the LORD; none of their *descendants,* even to the tenth generation, shall ever enter the assembly of the LORD,

4 because they did not meet you with food and water on the way when you came out of Egypt, and because they hired against you Balaam

the son of Beor from Pethor of Mesopotamia, to curse you.

5 "Nevertheless, the LORD your God was not willing to listen to Balaam, but the LORD your God turned the curse into a blessing for you because the LORD your God loves you.

6 "You shall never seek their peace or their prosperity all your days.

7 ¶ "You shall not detest an Edomite, for he is your brother; you shall not detest an Egyptian, because you were an alien in his land.

8 "The sons of the third generation who are born to them may enter the assembly of the LORD.

9 ¶ "When you go out as an army against your enemies, you shall keep yourself from every evil thing.

10 "If there is among you any man who is unclean because of a nocturnal emission, then he must go outside the camp; he may not reenter the camp.

11 "But it shall be when evening approaches, he shall bathe himself with water, and at sundown he may reenter the camp.

12 ¶ "You shall also have a place outside the camp and go out there,

13 and you shall have a spade among your tools, and it shall be when you sit down outside, you shall dig with it and shall turn to cover up your excrement.

14 "Since the LORD your God walks in the midst of your camp to deliver you and to defeat your enemies before you, therefore your camp must be holy; and He must not see anything indecent among you or He will turn away from you.

15 ¶ "You shall not hand over to his master a slave who has escaped from his master to you.

16 "He shall live with you in your midst, in the place which he shall choose in one of your towns where it pleases him; you shall not mistreat him.

17 ¶ "None of the daughters of Israel shall be a cult prostitute, nor shall any of the sons of Israel be a cult prostitute.

18 "You shall not bring the hire of a harlot or the wages of a ªdog into the house of the LORD your God for any votive offering, for both of these are an abomination to the LORD your God.

19 ¶ "You shall not charge interest to your countrymen: interest on money, food, *or* anything that may be loaned at interest.

20 "You may charge interest to a foreigner, but to your countrymen you shall not charge interest, so that the LORD your God may bless you in all that you undertake in the land which you are about to enter to possess.

21 ¶ "When you make a vow to the LORD your God, you shall not delay to pay it, for it would be sin in you, and the LORD your God will surely require it of you.

22 "However, if you refrain from vowing, it would not be sin in you.

ª I.e. male prostitute, sodomite

23 "You shall be careful to perform what goes out from your lips, just as you have voluntarily vowed to the LORD your God, what you have promised.

24 ¶ "When you enter your neighbor's vineyard, then you may eat grapes until you are fully satisfied, but you shall not put any in your basket.

25 ¶ "When you enter your neighbor's standing grain, then you may pluck the heads with your hand, but you shall not wield a sickle in your neighbor's standing grain.

Law of Divorce

24 "When a man takes a wife and marries her, and it happens that she finds no favor in his eyes because he has found some indecency in her, and he writes her a certificate of divorce and puts *it* in her hand and sends her out from his house,

2 and she leaves his house and goes and becomes another man's *wife*,

3 and if the latter husband turns against her and writes her a certificate of divorce and puts *it* in her hand and sends her out of his house, or if the latter husband dies who took her to be his wife,

4 *then* her former husband who sent her away is not allowed to take her again to be his wife, since she has been defiled; for that is an abomination before the LORD, and you shall not bring sin on the land which the LORD your God gives you as an inheritance.

5 ¶ "When a man takes a new wife, he shall not go out with the army nor be charged with any duty; he shall be free at home one year and shall give happiness to his wife whom he has taken.

Sundry Laws

6 ¶ "No one shall take a handmill or an upper millstone in pledge, for he would be taking a life in pledge.

7 ¶ "If a man is caught kidnapping any of his countrymen of the sons of Israel, and he deals with him violently or sells him, then that thief shall

die; so you shall purge the evil from among you.

8 ¶ "Be careful against an infection of leprosy, that you diligently observe and do according to all that the Levitical priests teach you; as I have commanded them, so you shall be careful to do.

9 "Remember what the LORD your God did to Miriam on the way as you came out of Egypt.

10 ¶ "When you make your neighbor a loan of any sort, you shall not enter his house to take his pledge.

11 "You shall remain outside, and the man to whom you make the loan shall bring the pledge out to you.

12 "If he is a poor man, you shall not sleep with his pledge.

13 "When the sun goes down you shall surely return the pledge to him, that he may sleep in his cloak and bless you; and it will be righteousness for you before the LORD your God.

14 ¶ "You shall not oppress a hired servant *who is* poor and needy, whether *he is* one of your countrymen or one of your aliens who is in your land in your towns.

15 "You shall give him his wages on his day before the sun sets, for he is poor and sets his heart on it; so that he will not cry against you to the LORD and it become sin in you.

16 ¶ "Fathers shall not be put to death for *their* sons, nor shall sons be put to death for *their* fathers; everyone shall be put to death for his own sin.

17 ¶ "You shall not pervert the justice due an alien *or* [a]an orphan, nor take a widow's garment in pledge.

18 "But you shall remember that you were a slave in Egypt, and that the LORD your God redeemed you from there; therefore I am commanding you to do this thing.

19 ¶ "When you reap your harvest in your field and have forgotten a sheaf in the field, you shall not go back to get it; it shall be for the alien, for the orphan, and for the widow, in order that the LORD your God may bless you in all the work of your hands.

20 "When you beat your olive tree, you shall not

24:6 Respect People, Not Money

Old Testament laws contained many provisions to protect people from exploitation. Israelites could not charge each other interest for loans (Exodus 22:25). And Deuteronomy set limits on the "collateral," or pledge, that secured a loan. Here, the lender could not accept a millstone, for that would threaten the debtor's livelihood. Verses 10–13 show further safeguards. The debtor was allowed to keep everything necessary for living. And the lender could not even enter the debtor's house to get his pledge.

24:19 Don't Forget the Poor

Chapter 24 contains some of the regulations expressly designed to protect the poor. One, called gleaning, is still practiced today in a modern form. Certain religious organizations in America contract with farmers to harvest their "wasted" or abandoned crops in order to feed the poor. God's laws built a concern for the poor into the Israelites' daily routine.

[a] Or the fatherless

go over the boughs again; it shall be for the alien, for the orphan, and for the widow.

21 ¶ "When you gather the grapes of your vineyard, you shall not go over it again; it shall be for the alien, for the orphan, and for the widow.

22 "You shall remember that you were a slave in the land of Egypt; therefore I am commanding you to do this thing.

Sundry Laws

25 "If there is a dispute between men and they go to court, and the judges decide their case, and they justify the righteous and condemn the wicked,

2 then it shall be if the wicked man deserves to be beaten, the judge shall then make him lie down and be beaten in his presence with the number of stripes according to his guilt.

3 "He may beat him forty times *but* no more, so that he does not beat him with many more stripes than these and your brother is not degraded in your eyes.

4 ¶ "You shall not muzzle the ox while he is threshing.

5 ¶ "When brothers live together and one of them dies and has no son, the wife of the deceased shall not be *married* outside *the family* to a strange man. Her husband's brother shall go in to her and take her to himself as wife and perform the duty of a husband's brother to her.

6 "It shall be that the firstborn whom she bears shall assume the name of his dead brother, so that his name will not be blotted out from Israel.

7 "But if the man does not desire to take his brother's wife, then his brother's wife shall go up to the gate to the elders and say, 'My husband's brother refuses to establish a name for his brother in Israel; he is not willing to perform the duty of a husband's brother to me.'

8 "Then the elders of his city shall summon him and speak to him. And *if* he persists and says, 'I do not desire to take her,'

9 then his brother's wife shall come to him in the sight of the elders, and pull his sandal off his foot and spit in his face; and she shall declare, 'Thus it is done to the man who does not build up his brother's house.'

10 "In Israel his name shall be called, 'The house of him whose sandal is removed.'

11 ¶ "If *two* men, a man and his countryman, are struggling together, and the wife of one comes near to deliver her husband from the hand of the one who is striking him, and puts out her hand and seizes his genitals,

12 then you shall cut off her hand; you shall not show pity.

13 ¶ "You shall not have in your bag differing weights, a large and a small.

14 "You shall not have in your house differing measures, a large and a small.

15 "You shall have a full and just weight; you shall have a full and just measure, that your days may be prolonged in the land which the LORD your God gives you.

16 "For everyone who does these things, everyone who acts unjustly is an abomination to the LORD your God.

17 ¶ "Remember what Amalek did to you along the way when you came out from Egypt,

18 how he met you along the way and attacked among you all the stragglers at your rear when you were faint and weary; and he did not *a*fear God.

19 "Therefore it shall come about when the LORD your God has given you rest from all your surrounding enemies, in the land which the LORD your God gives you as an inheritance to possess, you shall blot out the memory of Amalek from under heaven; you must not forget.

Offering First Fruits

26 "Then it shall be, when you enter the land which the LORD your God gives you as an inheritance, and you possess it and live in it,

2 that you shall take some of the first of all the produce of the ground which you bring in from your land that the LORD your God gives you, and you shall put *it* in a basket and go to the place where the LORD your God chooses to establish His name.

3 "You shall go to the priest who is in office at that time and say to him, 'I declare this day to the LORD my God that I have entered the land which the LORD swore to our fathers to give us.'

4 "Then the priest shall take the basket from your hand and set it down before the altar of the LORD your God.

5 "You shall answer and say before the LORD your God, 'My father was a wandering Aramean, and he went down to Egypt and sojourned there, few in number; but there he became a great, mighty and populous nation.

6 'And the Egyptians treated us harshly and afflicted us, and imposed hard labor on us.

7 'Then we cried to the LORD, the God of our fathers, and the LORD heard our voice and saw our affliction and our toil and our oppression;

8 and the LORD brought us out of Egypt with a mighty hand and an outstretched arm and with great terror and with signs and wonders;

9 and He has brought us to this place and has given us this land, a land flowing with milk and honey.

10 'Now behold, I have brought the first of the produce of the ground which You, O LORD have given me.' And you shall set it down before the LORD your God, and worship before the LORD your God;

11 and you and the Levite and the alien who is among you shall rejoice in all the good which the

---

a Or *reverence*

LORD your God has given you and your household.

12 ¶ "When you have finished paying all the tithe of your increase in the third year, the year of tithing, then you shall give it to the Levite, to the stranger, to the orphan and to the widow, that they may eat in your towns and be satisfied.

13 "You shall say before the LORD your God, 'I have removed the sacred *portion* from *my* house, and also have given it to the Levite and the alien, the orphan and the widow, according to all Your commandments which You have commanded me; I have not transgressed or forgotten any of Your commandments.

14 'I have not eaten of it while mourning, nor have I removed any of it while I was unclean, nor offered any of it to the dead. I have listened to the voice of the LORD my God; I have done according to all that You have commanded me.

15 'Look down from Your holy habitation, from heaven, and bless Your people Israel, and the ground which You have given us, a land flowing with milk and honey, as You swore to our fathers.'

16 ¶ "This day the LORD your God commands you to do these statutes and ordinances. You shall therefore be careful to do them with all your heart and with all your soul.

26:16 Law of the Heart

The Old Testament gives many rules and regulations. Deuteronomy makes clear, however, that the law was meant to penetrate a person's heart. Unless the law becomes part of a person's inner attitudes, it will probably make no difference.

17 "You have today declared the LORD to be your God, and that you would walk in His ways and keep His statutes, His commandments and His ordinances, and listen to His voice.

18 "The LORD has today declared you to be His people, a treasured possession, as He promised you, and that you should keep all His commandments;

19 and that He will set you high above all nations which He has made, for praise, fame, and honor; and that you shall be a consecrated people to the LORD your God, as He has spoken."

The Curses of Mount Ebal

27 Then Moses and the elders of Israel charged the people, saying, "Keep all the commandments which I command you today.

2 "So it shall be on the day when you cross the Jordan to the land which the LORD your God gives you, that you shall set up for yourself large stones and coat them with lime

3 and write on them all the words of this law, when you cross over, so that you may enter the land which the LORD your God gives you, a land flowing with milk and honey, as the LORD, the God of your fathers, promised you.

4 "So it shall be when you cross the Jordan, you shall set up on Mount Ebal, these stones, as I am commanding you today, and you shall coat them with lime.

5 "Moreover, you shall build there an altar to the LORD your God, an altar of stones; you shall not wield an iron *tool* on them.

6 "You shall build the altar of the LORD your God of uncut stones, and you shall offer on it burnt offerings to the LORD your God;

7 and you shall sacrifice peace offerings and eat there, and rejoice before the LORD your God.

8 "You shall write on the stones all the words of this law very distinctly."

9 ¶ Then Moses and the Levitical priests spoke to all Israel, saying, "Be silent and listen, O Israel! This day you have become a people for the LORD your God.

10 "You shall therefore obey the LORD your God, and do His commandments and His statutes which I command you today."

11 ¶ Moses also charged the people on that day, saying,

12 "When you cross the Jordan, these shall stand on Mount Gerizim to bless the people: Simeon, Levi, Judah, Issachar, Joseph, and Benjamin.

27:12–26 A Task for Joshua

Joshua carried out Moses' instructions for these blessings and curses, as recorded in Joshua 8:31–35. Mount Ebal had special significance for the Israelites, who believed that Abraham first worshiped God near here after receiving the original promise of the land (Genesis 15).

13 "For the curse, these shall stand on Mount Ebal: Reuben, Gad, Asher, Zebulun, Dan, and Naphtali.

14 "The Levites shall then answer and say to all the men of Israel with a loud voice,

15 ¶ 'Cursed is the man who makes an idol or a molten image, an abomination to the LORD, the work of the hands of the craftsman, and sets *it* up in secret.' And all the people shall answer and say, 'Amen.'

16 ¶ 'Cursed is he who dishonors his father or mother.' And all the people shall say, 'Amen.'

17 ¶ 'Cursed is he who moves his neighbor's boundary mark.' And all the people shall say, 'Amen.'

18 ¶ 'Cursed is he who misleads a blind *person* on the road.' And all the people shall say, 'Amen.'

19 ¶ 'Cursed is he who distorts the justice due an alien, orphan, and widow.' And all the people shall say, 'Amen.'

20 ¶ 'Cursed is he who lies with his father's

wife, because he has uncovered his father's skirt.' And all the people shall say, 'Amen.'

21 ¶ 'Cursed is he who lies with any animal.' And all the people shall say, 'Amen.'

22 ¶ 'Cursed is he who lies with his sister, the daughter of his father or of his mother.' And all the people shall say, 'Amen.'

23 ¶ 'Cursed is he who lies with his mother-in-law.' And all the people shall say, 'Amen.'

24 ¶ 'Cursed is he who strikes his neighbor in secret.' And all the people shall say, 'Amen.'

25 ¶ 'Cursed is he who accepts a bribe to strike down an innocent person.' And all the people shall say, 'Amen.'

26 ¶ 'Cursed is he who does not confirm the words of this law by doing them.' And all the people shall say, 'Amen.'

Blessings at Gerizim

28 "Now it shall be, if you diligently obey the LORD your God, being careful to do all His commandments which I command you today, the LORD your God will set you high above all the nations of the earth.

2 "All these blessings will come upon you and overtake you if you obey the LORD your God:

3 ¶ "Blessed *shall* you *be* in the city, and blessed *shall* you *be* in the country.

4 ¶ "Blessed *shall be* the offspring of your body and the produce of your ground and the offspring of your beasts, the increase of your herd and the young of your flock.

5 ¶ "Blessed *shall be* your basket and your kneading bowl.

6 ¶ "Blessed *shall* you *be* when you come in, and blessed *shall* you *be* when you go out.

7 ¶ "The LORD shall cause your enemies who rise up against you to be defeated before you; they will come out against you one way and will flee before you seven ways.

8 "The LORD will command the blessing upon you in your barns and in all that you put your hand to, and He will bless you in the land which the LORD your God gives you.

9 "The LORD will establish you as a holy people to Himself, as He swore to you, if you keep the commandments of the LORD your God and walk in His ways.

10 "So all the peoples of the earth will see that you are called by the name of the LORD, and they will be afraid of you.

11 "The LORD will make you abound in prosperity, in the offspring of your body and in the offspring of your beast and in the produce of your ground, in the land which the LORD swore to your fathers to give you.

12 "The LORD will open for you His good storehouse, the heavens, to give rain to your land in its season and to bless all the work of your hand; and

you shall lend to many nations, but you shall not borrow.

13 "The LORD will make you the head and not the tail, and you only will be above, and you will not be underneath, if you listen to the commandments of the LORD your God, which I charge you today, to observe *them* carefully,

14 and do not turn aside from any of the words which I command you today, to the right or to the left, to go after other gods to serve them.

Consequences of Disobedience

15 ¶ "But it shall come about, if you do not obey the LORD your God, to observe to do all His commandments and His statutes with which I charge you today, that all these curses will come upon you and overtake you:

16 ¶ "Cursed *shall* you *be* in the city, and cursed *shall* you *be* in the country.

17 ¶ "Cursed *shall be* your basket and your kneading bowl.

18 ¶ "Cursed *shall be* the offspring of your body and the produce of your ground, the increase of your herd and the young of your flock.

19 ¶ "Cursed *shall* you *be* when you come in, and cursed *shall* you *be* when you go out.

20 ¶ "The LORD will send upon you curses, confusion, and rebuke, in all you undertake to do, until you are destroyed and until you perish quickly, on account of the evil of your deeds, because you have forsaken Me.

21 "The LORD will make the pestilence cling to you until He has consumed you from the land where you are entering to possess it.

22 "The LORD will smite you with consumption and with fever and with inflammation and with fiery heat and with ªthe sword and with blight and with mildew, and they will pursue you until you perish.

23 "The heaven which is over your head shall be bronze, and the earth which is under you, iron.

24 "The LORD will make the rain of your land powder and dust; from heaven it shall come down on you until you are destroyed.

25 ¶ "The LORD shall cause you to be defeated before your enemies; you will go out one way against them, but you will flee seven ways before them, and you will be *an example of* terror to all the kingdoms of the earth.

26 "Your carcasses will be food to all birds of the sky and to the beasts of the earth, and there will be no one to frighten *them* away.

27 ¶ "The LORD will smite you with the boils of Egypt and with tumors and with the scab and with the itch, from which you cannot be healed.

28 "The LORD will smite you with madness and with blindness and with bewilderment of heart;

29 and you will grope at noon, as the blind man gropes in darkness, and you will not prosper

ª Another reading is *drought*

in your ways; but you shall only be oppressed and robbed continually, with none to save you.

30 "You shall betroth a wife, but another man will violate her; you shall build a house, but you will not live in it; you shall plant a vineyard, but you will not use its fruit.

31 "Your ox shall be slaughtered before your eyes, but you will not eat of it; your donkey shall be torn away from you, and will not be restored to you; your sheep shall be given to your enemies, and you will have none to save you.

32 "Your sons and your daughters shall be given to another people, while your eyes look on and yearn for them continually; but there will be nothing you can do.

33 "A people whom you do not know shall eat up the produce of your ground and all your labors, and you will never be anything but oppressed and crushed continually.

34 "You shall be driven mad by the sight of what you see.

35 "The LORD will strike you on the knees and legs with sore boils, from which you cannot be healed, from the sole of your foot to the crown of your head.

36 "The LORD will bring you and your king, whom you set over you, to a nation which neither you nor your fathers have known, and there you shall serve other gods, wood and stone.

28:36–37 Scattered Abroad

Moses warned that if the Israelites failed to obey God's law, they would be uprooted from the new land and scattered all over the earth. At least three times in history this kind of dispersion of Jews (called Diaspora) took place on a massive scale. Assyria, Babylon, and finally the Roman empire invaded the homeland of the Jews and scattered them far abroad.

37 "You shall become a horror, a proverb, and a taunt among all the people where the LORD drives you.

38 ¶ "You shall bring out much seed to the field but you will gather in little, for the locust will consume it.

39 "You shall plant and cultivate vineyards, but you will neither drink of the wine nor gather *the* grapes, for the worm will devour them.

40 "You shall have olive trees throughout your territory but you will not anoint yourself with the oil, for your olives will drop off.

41 "You shall have sons and daughters but they will not be yours, for they will go into captivity.

42 "The cricket shall possess all your trees and the produce of your ground.

43 "The alien who is among you shall rise above

you higher and higher, but you will go down lower and lower.

44 "He shall lend to you, but you will not lend to him; he shall be the head, and you will be the tail.

45 ¶ "So all these curses shall come on you and pursue you and overtake you until you are destroyed, because you would not obey the LORD your God by keeping His commandments and His statutes which He commanded you.

46 "They shall become a sign and a wonder on you and your descendants forever.

47 ¶ "Because you did not serve the LORD your God with joy and a glad heart, for the abundance of all things;

48 therefore you shall serve your enemies whom the LORD will send against you, in hunger, in thirst, in nakedness, and in the lack of all things; and He will put an iron yoke on your neck until He has destroyed you.

49 ¶ "The LORD will bring a nation against you from afar, from the end of the earth, as the eagle swoops down, a nation whose language you shall not understand,

50 a nation of fierce countenance who will have no respect for the old, nor show favor to the young.

51 "Moreover, it shall eat the offspring of your herd and the produce of your ground until you are destroyed, who also leaves you no grain, new wine, or oil, nor the increase of your herd or the young of your flock until they have caused you to perish.

52 "It shall besiege you in all your towns until your high and fortified walls in which you trusted come down throughout your land, and it shall besiege you in all your towns throughout your land which the LORD your God has given you.

53 "Then you shall eat the offspring of your own body, the flesh of your sons and of your daughters whom the LORD your God has given you, during the siege and the distress by which your enemy will oppress you.

54 "The man who is refined and very delicate among you shall be hostile toward his brother and toward the wife he cherishes and toward the rest of his children who remain,

55 so that he will not give *even* one of them any of the flesh of his children which he will eat, since he has nothing *else* left, during the siege and the distress by which your enemy will oppress you in all your towns.

56 "The refined and delicate woman among you, who would not venture to set the sole of her foot on the ground for delicateness and refinement, shall be hostile toward the husband she cherishes and toward her son and daughter,

57 and toward her afterbirth which issues from between her legs and toward her children whom she bears; for she will eat them secretly for lack of anything *else,* during the siege and the distress by

which your enemy will oppress you in your towns.

58 ¶ "If you are not careful to observe all the words of this law which are written in this book, to fear this honored and awesome name, the LORD your God,

59 then the LORD will bring extraordinary plagues on you and your descendants, even severe and lasting plagues, and miserable and chronic sicknesses.

60 "He will bring back on you all the diseases of Egypt of which you were afraid, and they will cling to you.

61 "Also every sickness and every plague which, not written in the book of this law, the LORD will bring on you until you are destroyed.

62 "Then you shall be left few in number, whereas you were as numerous as the stars of heaven, because you did not obey the LORD your God.

63 "It shall come about that as the LORD delighted over you to prosper you, and multiply you, so the LORD will delight over you to make you perish and destroy you; and you will be torn from the land where you are entering to possess it.

64 "Moreover, the LORD will scatter you among all peoples, from one end of the earth to the other end of the earth; and there you shall serve other gods, wood and stone, which you or your fathers have not known.

65 "Among those nations you shall find no rest, and there will be no resting place for the sole of your foot; but there the LORD will give you a trembling heart, failing of eyes, and despair of soul.

66 "So your life shall hang in doubt before you; and you will be in dread night and day, and shall have no assurance of your life.

67 "In the morning you shall say, 'Would that it were evening!' And at evening you shall say, 'Would that it were morning!' because of the dread of your heart which you dread, and for the sight of your eyes which you will see.

68 "The LORD will bring you back to Egypt in ships, by the way about which I spoke to you, 'You will never see it again!' And there you will offer yourselves for sale to your enemies as male and female slaves, but there will be no buyer."

The Covenant in Moab

29 These are the words of the covenant which the LORD commanded Moses to make with the sons of Israel in the land of Moab, besides the covenant which He had made with them at Horeb.

2 ¶ And Moses summoned all Israel and said to them, "You have seen all that the LORD did before your eyes in the land of Egypt to Pharaoh and all his servants and all his land;

3 the great trials which your eyes have seen, those great signs and wonders.

4 "Yet to this day the LORD has not given you a heart to know, nor eyes to see, nor ears to hear.

5 "I have led you forty years in the wilderness;

your clothes have not worn out on you, and your sandal has not worn out on your foot.

6 "You have not eaten bread, nor have you drunk wine or strong drink, in order that you might know that I am the LORD your God.

29:5–6 Miracles in the Wilderness

The Sinai peninsula was a harsh place, and the Bible records the Israelites' problems with food and water supplies. But, as these two verses show, God cared for his people there, giving them daily food and drink and even making sure their clothes did not wear out.

7 "When you reached this place, Sihon the king of Heshbon and Og the king of Bashan came out to meet us for battle, but we defeated them;

8 and we took their land and gave it as an inheritance to the Reubenites, the Gadites, and the half-tribe of the Manassites.

9 "So keep the words of this covenant to do them, that you may prosper in all that you do.

10 ¶ "You stand today, all of you, before LORD your God: your chiefs, your tribes, your elders and your officers, *even* all the men of Israel,

11 your little ones, your wives, and the alien who is within your camps, from the one who chops your wood to the one who draws your water,

12 that you may enter into the covenant with the LORD your God, and into His oath which the LORD your God is making with you today,

13 in order that He may establish you today as His people and that He may be your God, just as He spoke to you and as He swore to your fathers, to Abraham, Isaac, and Jacob.

14 ¶ "Now not with you alone am I making this covenant and this oath,

15 but both with those who stand here with us today in the presence of the LORD our God and with those who are not with us here today

16 (for you know how we lived in the land of Egypt, and how we came through the midst of the nations through which you passed;

17 moreover, you have seen their abominations and their idols *of* wood, stone, silver, and gold, which *they had* with them);

18 so that there will not be among you a man or woman, or family or tribe, whose heart turns away today from the LORD our God, to go and serve the gods of those nations; that there will not be among you a root bearing poisonous fruit and wormwood.

19 "It shall be when he hears the words of this curse, that he will boast, saying, 'I have peace though I walk in the stubbornness of my heart in order to destroy the watered *land* with the dry.'

20 "The LORD shall never be willing to forgive him, but rather the anger of the LORD and His

jealousy will burn against that man, and every curse which is written in this book will rest on him, and the LORD will blot out his name from under heaven.

21 "Then the LORD will single him out for adversity from all the tribes of Israel, according to all the curses of the covenant which are written in this book of the law.

22 ¶ "Now the generation to come, your sons who rise up after you and the foreigner who comes from a distant land, when they see the plagues of the land and the diseases with which the LORD has afflicted it, will say,

23 'All its land is brimstone and salt, a burning waste, unsown and unproductive, and no grass grows in it, like the overthrow of Sodom and Gomorrah, Admah and Zeboiim, which the LORD overthrew in His anger and in His wrath.'

24 "All the nations will say, 'Why has the LORD done thus to this land? Why this great outburst of anger?'

25 "Then men will say, 'Because they forsook the covenant of the LORD, the God of their fathers, which He made with them when He brought them out of the land of Egypt.

26 'They went and served other gods and wor-

A Scent of Doom
All were jubilant, except one man

OLD HABITS DIE HARD. DEUTERONOMY underscores that lesson, and a more contemporary character shows that people have not changed much. In 1901 Bill Miner got out of San Quentin Prison, where he had served 33 years in all. It was his third stint, and both previous times he had barely sniffed free air before landing in jail again.

Miner was a Wild West legend. He had robbed his first stagecoach at 16. He is credited with first using the line that has played on thousands of Westerns: "Hands up!" Stagecoach passengers called him the Gentleman Bandit because he never shot anyone and he spoke respectfully, using "Sir" and "Ma'am."

When Bill Miner emerged from prison at age 58, his long hair had turned gray and most of his friends had either died or disappeared. Stepping into a new century, he had a new lease on life. No stagecoaches were left to rob: The Wells Fargo company had sold their horses and invested in something he had never seen, steam trains.

> "Because you did not serve the LORD your God with joy and a glad heart, for the abundance of all things; therefore you shall serve your enemies whom the LORD will send against you, in hunger, in thirst, in nakedness, and in the lack of all things." 28:47–48

A Hint of Doom

Miner tried various odd jobs, but most work seemed degrading and boring to a former stagecoach robber. The old restlessness returned. One afternoon, in a Seattle theater, he watched the movie The Great Train Robbery, and discovered a new career, or at least a new twist on an old one. The Gentleman Bandit, at age 60, became The Gray Fox. He went on to mastermind six train robberies, and probably more, until the Mounties tracked him down in British Columbia.

Three separate times Bill Miner had a chance for a new start. The last time, he had entered a new city, in a new century, with no one around to remind him of his reputation. Yet inevitably he went back to the familiar ways of crime. His life had the scent of doom about it.

The last chapters of Deuteronomy show the Israelites facing a situation much like that met by Bill Miner or any prisoner who emerges into freedom after many years. Four decades in the Desert of Sinai had served as a kind of imprisonment, or probation period. And then the long-awaited day of freedom arrived.

Everyone in the Israelite camp was jubilant—all but one man, Moses. He could see past the joy. When he spoke to the crowd, he spoke with an air of doom. He knew his people too well to think that geography would change their old ways.

Moses Pulls out the Stops

For 40 years Moses had led the cranky assortment of tribes. He had listened to their grumbling, endured their gossip, and survived their insurrections. Now he had one last chance to warn them not to repeat their ways.

You cannot read the last chapters of Deuteronomy without detecting a doleful sense of fatalism in Moses' words. The Israelites' settling down into a life of quiet obedience was about as likely as Bill Miner's becoming a banker. They had failed far too often; they were doomed to fail again.

Moses pulled out all the stops. He orchestrated a dramatic object lesson that would live in their memories forever. It actually took place after Moses' death, as recorded in Joshua 8:30–35. Represenshiped them, gods whom they have not known and whom He had not allotted to them.

27 'Therefore, the anger of the LORD burned against that land, to bring upon it every curse which is written in this book;

29:24–29 God's Secrets

"I don't understand why God is doing this," people say. But God hasn't told us everything. Our finite minds could not possibly grasp some things, and other information is simply unnecessary or unhelpful for us to know. What God has told us (in his law, for instance) he intends for us to obey.

---

28 and the LORD uprooted them from their land in anger and in fury and in great wrath, and cast them into another land, as *it is* this day.'

29 ¶ "The secret things belong to the LORD our God, but the things revealed belong to us and to our sons forever, that we may observe all the words of this law.

Restoration Promised

30 "So it shall be when all of these things have come upon you, the blessing and the curse which I have set before you, and you call *them* to mind in all nations where the LORD your God has banished you,

2 and you return to the LORD your God and obey Him with all your heart and soul according to all that I command you today, you and your sons,

3 then the LORD your God will restore you from captivity, and have compassion on you, and will gather you again from all the peoples where the LORD your God has scattered you.

4 "If your outcasts are at the ends of the earth, from there the LORD your God will gather you, and from there He will bring you back.

5 "The LORD your God will bring you into the land which your fathers possessed, and you shall possess it; and He will prosper you and multiply you more than your fathers.

6 ¶ "Moreover the LORD your God will circumcise your heart and the heart of your descendants, to love the LORD your God with all your heart and with all your soul, so that you may live.

7 "The LORD your God will inflict all these curses on your enemies and on those who hate you, who persecuted you.

8 "And you shall again obey the LORD, and observe all His commandments which I command you today.

9 "Then the LORD your God will prosper you abundantly in all the work of your hand, in the offspring of your body and in the offspring of your cattle and in the produce of your ground, for the LORD will again rejoice over you for good, just as He rejoiced over your fathers;

10 if you obey the LORD your God to keep His commandments and His statutes which are written in this book of the law, if you turn to the LORD your God with all your heart and soul.

---

tatives from all the tribes climbed two mountains, with a narrow valley in between. These designated speakers shouted out curses and blessings on the Israelites (see 11:26–32; 27–28). As they entered the new land, their ears rang with the dissonance of wonderful blessings and horrific curses.

Future Terrors

Moses starkly summarized the future of the Jewish race. They would, he said, have "a trembling heart, failing of eyes, and despair of soul. So your life shall hang in doubt before you; and you will be in dread night and day, and shall have no assurance of your life. In the morning you shall say, 'Would that it were evening!' And at evening you shall say, 'Would that it were morning!' because of the dread of your heart which you dread, and for the sight of your eyes which you will see" (28:65–67). His descriptions of their future are unmatched for their horror.

Just in case the Israelites didn't get the message, Moses taught them a song given him by God (chapter 32). It became a kind of national anthem, memorized by everyone and sung as they marched into Canaan. But the song is like no other national anthem. It has virtually no words of encouragement or hope, only doom.

Moses knew that even the promised land would not change his people's ingrained habits of disobeying God. They would fail in the promised land, just as they had failed in the desert. He concluded his farewell speech to the people with these words, "For it is not an idle word for you—it is your life" (32:47). And then on that same day he ascended a mountain to die. He had been forbidden by God to cross into Canaan because of his own disobedience.

This sad final scene may have made the strongest impression of all. No one could get away with rebellion against God—not even Moses, "whom the LORD knew face to face" (34:10).

Life Questions: Why do you think the Bible includes accounts of big failures like this? Have you ever experienced a repeated failure: a sin or problem that keeps returning, no matter what you do?

11 ¶ "For this commandment which I command you today is not too difficult for you, nor is it out of reach.

12 "It is not in heaven, that you should say, 'Who will go up to heaven for us to get it for us and make us hear it, that we may observe it?'

13 "Nor is it beyond the sea, that you should say, 'Who will cross the sea for us to get it for us and make us hear it, that we may observe it?'

14 "But the word is very near you, in your mouth and in your heart, that you may observe it.

30:14 Keep It Simple

Sometimes people make a relationship with God sound impossibly difficult. Moses emphasizes its simplicity. You don't have to swim oceans or ascend into heaven; you just have to understand, believe, and obey the word God has given. In a famous New Testament passage, the apostle Paul applied this lesson to confessing faith in Jesus Christ (Romans 10:6–10).

Choose Life

15 ¶ "See, I have set before you today life and prosperity, and death and adversity;

16 in that I command you today to love the LORD your God, to walk in His ways and to keep His commandments and His statutes and His judgments, that you may live and multiply, and that the LORD your God may bless you in the land where you are entering to possess it.

17 "But if your heart turns away and you will not obey, but are drawn away and worship other gods and serve them,

18 I declare to you today that you shall surely perish. You will not prolong *your* days in the land where you are crossing the Jordan to enter and possess it.

19 "I call heaven and earth to witness against you today, that I have set before you life and death, the blessing and the curse. So choose life in order that you may live, you and your descendants,

20 by loving the LORD your God, by obeying His voice, and by holding fast to Him; for this is your life and the length of your days, that you may live in the land which the LORD swore to your fathers, to Abraham, Isaac, and Jacob, to give them."

Moses' Last Counsel

31 So Moses went and spoke these words to all Israel.

2 And he said to them, "I am a hundred and twenty years old today; I am no longer able to come and go, and the LORD has said to me, 'You shall not cross this Jordan.'

3 "It is the LORD your God who will cross ahead of you; He will destroy these nations before you, and you shall dispossess them. Joshua is the one who will cross ahead of you, just as the LORD has spoken.

4 "The LORD will do to them just as He did to Sihon and Og, the kings of the Amorites, and to their land, when He destroyed them.

5 "The LORD will deliver them up before you, and you shall do to them according to all the commandments which I have commanded you.

6 "Be strong and courageous, do not be afraid or tremble at them, for the LORD your God is the one who goes with you. He will not fail you or forsake you."

7 ¶ Then Moses called to Joshua and said to him in the sight of all Israel, "Be strong and courageous, for you shall go with this people into the land which the LORD has sworn to their fathers to give them, and you shall give it to them as an inheritance.

8 "The LORD is the one who goes ahead of you; He will be with you. He will not fail you or forsake you. Do not fear or be dismayed."

9 ¶ So Moses wrote this law and gave it to the priests, the sons of Levi who carried the ark of the covenant of the LORD, and to all the elders of Israel.

10 Then Moses commanded them, saying, "At the end of *every* seven years, at the time of the year of remission of debts, at the Feast of Booths,

11 when all Israel comes to appear before the LORD your God at the place which He will choose, you shall read this law in front of all Israel in their hearing.

12 "Assemble the people, the men and the women and children and the alien who is in your town, so that they may hear and learn and fear the LORD your God, and be careful to observe all the words of this law.

13 "Their children, who have not known, will hear and learn to fear the LORD your God, as long as you live on the land which you are about to cross the Jordan to possess."

Israel Will Fall Away

14 ¶ Then the LORD said to Moses, "Behold, the time for you to die is near; call Joshua, and present yourselves at the tent of meeting, that I may commission him." So Moses and Joshua went and presented themselves at the tent of meeting.

15 The LORD appeared in the tent in a pillar of cloud, and the pillar of cloud stood at the doorway of the tent.

16 The LORD said to Moses, "Behold, you are about to lie down with your fathers; and this people will arise and play the harlot with the strange gods of the land, into the midst of which they are going, and will forsake Me and break My covenant which I have made with them.

17 "Then My anger will be kindled against them in that day, and I will forsake them and hide My

face from them, and they will be consumed, and many evils and troubles will come upon them; so that they will say in that day, 'Is it not because our God is not among us that these evils have come upon us?'

18 "But I will surely hide My face in that day because of all the evil which they will do, for they will turn to other gods.

19 ¶ "Now therefore, write this song for yourselves, and teach it to the sons of Israel; put it on their lips, so that this song may be a witness for Me against the sons of Israel.

20 "For when I bring them into the land flowing with milk and honey, which I swore to their fathers, and they have eaten and are satisfied and become prosperous, then they will turn to other gods and serve them, and spurn Me and break My covenant.

21 "Then it shall come about, when many evils and troubles have come upon them, that this song will testify before them as a witness (for it shall not be forgotten from the lips of their descendants); for I know their intent which they are developing today, before I have brought them into the land which I swore."

22 So Moses wrote this song the same day, and taught it to the sons of Israel.

Joshua Is Commissioned

23 ¶ Then He commissioned Joshua the son of Nun, and said, "Be strong and courageous, for you shall bring the sons of Israel into the land which I swore to them, and I will be with you."

24 ¶ It came about, when Moses finished writing the words of this law in a book until they were complete,

25 that Moses commanded the Levites who carried the ark of the covenant of the LORD, saying,

26 "Take this book of the law and place it beside the ark of the covenant of the LORD your God, that it may remain there as a witness against you.

27 "For I know your rebellion and your stubbornness; behold, while I am still alive with you today, you have been rebellious against the LORD; how much more, then, after my death?

28 "Assemble to me all the elders of your tribes and your officers, that I may speak these words in their hearing and call the heavens and the earth to witness against them.

29 "For I know that after my death you will act corruptly and turn from the way which I have commanded you; and evil will befall you in the latter days, for you will do that which is evil in the sight of the LORD, provoking Him to anger with the work of your hands."

30 ¶ Then Moses spoke in the hearing of all the assembly of Israel the words of this song, until they were complete:

The Song of Moses

32 "Give ear, O heavens, and let me speak;
And let the earth hear the words of my mouth.
2 "Let my teaching drop as the rain,
My speech distill as the dew,
As the droplets on the fresh grass
And as the showers on the herb.
3 "For I proclaim the name of the LORD;
Ascribe greatness to our God!
4 "The Rock! His work is perfect,
For all His ways are just;
A God of faithfulness and without injustice,
Righteous and upright is He.
5 "They have acted corruptly toward Him,
They are not His children, because of their defect;
But are a perverse and crooked generation.
6 "Do you thus repay the LORD,
O foolish and unwise people?
Is not He your Father who has bought you?
He has made you and established you.
7 "Remember the days of old,
Consider the years of all generations.
Ask your father, and he will inform you,
Your elders, and they will tell you.
8 "When the Most High gave the nations their inheritance,
When He separated the sons of man,
He set the boundaries of the peoples
According to the number of the sons of Israel.
9 "For the LORD'S portion is His people;
Jacob is the allotment of His inheritance.
10 "He found him in a desert land,
And in the howling waste of a wilderness;
He encircled him, He cared for him,
He guarded him as the pupil of His eye.
11 "Like an eagle that stirs up its nest,
That hovers over its young,
He spread His wings and caught them,
He carried them on His pinions.
12 "The LORD alone guided him,

32:11 Mixed Emotions

The tender words of the song in this chapter express God's true love for Israel. And yet the song contains words of dreadful realism as well. God knew the Israelites would fail him, and this song would "testify before them as a witness" when they turned away from him (31:21). Indeed, the apostle Paul quoted from this in his agonizing account of Jewish rejection of Jesus (Romans 10:19).

And there was no foreign god with him.
13 "He made him ride on the high places of
　　the earth,
　And he ate the produce of the field;
　And He made him suck honey from the
　　rock,
　And oil from the flinty rock,
14 Curds of cows, and milk of the flock,
　With fat of lambs,
　And rams, the breed of Bashan, and
　　goats,
　With the finest of the wheat—
　And of the blood of grapes you drank
　　wine.

15 ¶ "But [a]Jeshurun grew fat and kicked—
　You are grown fat, thick, and sleek—
　Then he forsook God who made him,
　And scorned the Rock of his salvation.
16 "They made Him jealous with strange
　　gods;
　With abominations they provoked Him
　　to anger.
17 "They sacrificed to demons who were not
　　God,
　To gods whom they have not known,
　New *gods* who came lately,
　Whom your fathers did not dread.
18 "You neglected the Rock who begot you,
　And forgot the God who gave you birth.

19 ¶ "The LORD saw *this,* and spurned *them*
　Because of the provocation of His sons
　　and daughters.
20 "Then He said, 'I will hide My face from
　　them,
　I will see what their end *shall be;*
　For they are a perverse generation,
　Sons in whom is no faithfulness.
21 'They have made Me jealous with *what* is
　　not God;
　They have provoked Me to anger with
　　their idols.
　So I will make them jealous with *those*
　　who are not a people;
　I will provoke them to anger with a
　　foolish nation,
22 For a fire is kindled in My anger,
　And burns to the lowest part of Sheol,
　And consumes the earth with its yield,
　And sets on fire the foundations of the
　　mountains.
23 ¶ 'I will heap misfortunes on them;
　I will use My arrows on them.
24 '*They will be* wasted by famine, and
　　consumed by plague
　And bitter destruction;
　And the teeth of beasts I will send upon
　　them,

With the venom of crawling things of the
　　dust.
25 'Outside the sword will bereave,
　And inside terror—
　Both young man and virgin,
　The nursling with the man of gray hair.
26 'I would have said, "I will cut them to
　　pieces,
　I will remove the memory of them
　　from men,"
27 Had I not feared the provocation by the
　　enemy,
　That their adversaries would misjudge,
　That they would say, "Our hand is
　　triumphant,
　And the LORD has not done all this." '

28 ¶ "For they are a nation lacking in
　　counsel,
　And there is no understanding in them.
29 "Would that they were wise, that they
　　understood this,
　That they would discern their future!
30 "How could one chase a thousand,
　And two put ten thousand to flight,
　Unless their Rock had sold them,
　And the LORD had given them up?
31 "Indeed their rock is not like our Rock,
　Even our enemies themselves judge this.
32 "For their vine is from the vine of Sodom,
　And from the fields of Gomorrah;
　Their grapes are grapes of poison,
　Their clusters, bitter.
33 "Their wine is the venom of serpents,
　And the deadly poison of cobras.

34 ¶ 'Is it not laid up in store with Me,
　Sealed up in My treasuries?
35 'Vengeance is Mine, and retribution,
　In due time their foot will slip;
　For the day of their calamity is near,
　And the impending things are hastening
　　upon them.'

32:35 God's Vengeance

*The New Testament quotes this verse twice, in
two very different ways. The apostle Paul
emphasized that because vengeance is God's
business, not ours, we should never seek
revenge (Romans 12:19). But the author of
Hebrews also cited these words to highlight the
seriousness of rejecting God, who will certainly
judge his people (Hebrews 10:30).*

36 "For the LORD will vindicate His people,
　And will have compassion on His
　　servants,
　When He sees that *their* strength is gone,

---

[a] I.e. Israel

And there is none *remaining*, bond or
free.
37 "And He will say, 'Where are their gods,
The rock in which they sought refuge?
38 'Who ate the fat of their sacrifices,
And drank the wine of their drink
offering?
Let them rise up and help you,
Let them be your hiding place!
39 'See now that I, I am He,
And there is no god besides Me;
It is I who put to death and give life.
I have wounded and it is I who heal,
And there is no one who can deliver
from My hand.
40 'Indeed, I lift up My hand to heaven,
And say, as I live forever,
41 If I sharpen My flashing sword,
And My hand takes hold on justice,
I will render vengeance on My
adversaries,
And I will repay those who hate Me.
42 'I will make My arrows drunk with blood,
And My sword will devour flesh,
With the blood of the slain and the
captives,
From the long-haired leaders of the
enemy.'
43 "Rejoice, O nations, *with* His people;
For He will avenge the blood of His
servants,
And will render vengeance on His
adversaries,
And will atone for His land *and* His
people."

44 ¶ Then Moses came and spoke all the words
of this song in the hearing of the people, he, with
Joshua the son of Nun.
45 When Moses had finished speaking all these
words to all Israel,
46 he said to them, "Take to your heart all the
words with which I am warning you today, which
you shall command your sons to observe carefully, *even* all the words of this law.
47 "For it is not an idle word for you; indeed it
is your life. And by this word you will prolong
your days in the land, which you are about to
cross the Jordan to possess."
48 ¶ The LORD spoke to Moses that very same
day, saying,
49 "Go up to this mountain of the Abarim,
Mount Nebo, which is in the land of Moab opposite Jericho, and look at the land of Canaan, which
I am giving to the sons of Israel for a possession.
50 "Then die on the mountain where you ascend, and be gathered to your people, as Aaron
your brother died on Mount Hor and was gathered to his people,
51 because you broke faith with Me in the
midst of the sons of Israel at the waters of
Meribah-kadesh, in the wilderness of Zin, because

you did not treat Me as holy in the midst of the
sons of Israel.
52 "For you shall see the land at a distance, but
you shall not go there, into the land which I am
giving the sons of Israel."

The Blessing of Moses

33 Now this is the blessing with which Moses
the man of God blessed the sons of Israel
before his death.

33:1–29 Dying Words

*Just before he died, Moses gave a final word to
the Israelites, most of whom had lived their
entire adult lives under his leadership. Now
they would no longer have him to lean on. As
they prepared to enter the promised land
without him, he bequeathed to them something
more valuable than money, stronger than
power, deeper than learning: a blessing. Tribe
by tribe, Moses spoke of God's personal care
and salvation for the people of Israel.*

2 He said,
"The LORD came from Sinai,
And dawned on them from Seir;
He shone forth from Mount Paran,
And He came from the midst of ten
thousand holy ones;
At His right hand there was flashing
lightning for them.
3 "Indeed, He loves the people;
All Your holy ones are in Your hand,
And they followed in Your steps;
Everyone receives of Your words.
4 "Moses charged us with a law,
A possession for the assembly of Jacob.
5 "And He was king in Jeshurun,
When the heads of the people were
gathered,
The tribes of Israel together.

6 ¶ "May Reuben live and not die,
Nor his men be few."

7 ¶ And this regarding Judah; so he said,
"Hear, O LORD, the voice of Judah,
And bring him to his people.
With his hands he contended for them,
And may You be a help against his
adversaries."

8 ¶ Of Levi he said,
"*Let* Your Thummim and Your Urim
belong to Your godly man,
Whom You proved at Massah,
With whom You contended at the waters
of Meribah;
9 Who said of his father and his mother,
'I did not consider them';

And he did not acknowledge his
brothers,
Nor did he regard his own sons,
For they observed Your word,
And kept Your covenant.
10 "They shall teach Your ordinances to
Jacob,
And Your law to Israel.
They shall put incense before You,
And whole burnt offerings on Your altar.
11 "O LORD, bless his substance,
And accept the work of his hands;
Shatter the loins of those who rise up
against him,
And those who hate him, so that they
will not rise *again*."

12 ¶ Of Benjamin he said,
"May the beloved of the LORD dwell in
security by Him,
Who shields him all the day,
And he dwells between His shoulders."

13 ¶ Of Joseph he said,
"Blessed of the LORD *be* his land,
With the choice things of heaven, with
the dew,
And from the deep lying beneath,
14 And with the choice yield of the sun,
And with the choice produce of the
months.
15 "And with the best things of the ancient
mountains,
And with the choice things of the
everlasting hills,
16 And with the choice things of the earth
and its fullness,
And the favor of Him who dwelt in the
bush.
Let it come to the head of Joseph,
And to the crown of the head of the one
distinguished among his brothers.
17 "As the firstborn of his ox, majesty is his,
And his horns are the horns of the
wild ox;
With them he will push the peoples,
All at once, *to* the ends of the earth.
And those are the ten thousands of
Ephraim,
And those are the thousands of
Manasseh."

18 ¶ Of Zebulun he said,
"Rejoice, Zebulun, in your going forth,
And, Issachar, in your tents.
19 "They will call peoples *to* the mountain;
There they will offer righteous sacrifices;
For they will draw out the abundance of
the seas,
And the hidden treasures of the sand."

20 ¶ Of Gad he said,

"Blessed is the one who enlarges Gad;
He lies down as a lion,
And tears the arm, also the crown of the
head.
21 "Then he provided the first *part* for
himself,
For there the ruler's portion was
reserved;
And he came *with* the leaders of the
people;
He executed the justice of the LORD,
And His ordinances with Israel."

22 ¶ Of Dan he said,
"Dan is a lion's whelp,
That leaps forth from Bashan."

23 ¶ Of Naphtali he said,
"O Naphtali, satisfied with favor,
And full of the blessing of the LORD,
Take possession of the sea and the
south."

24 ¶ Of Asher he said,
"More blessed than sons is Asher;
May he be favored by his brothers,
And may he dip his foot in oil.
25 "Your locks will be iron and bronze,
And according to your days, so will your
leisurely walk be.

26 ¶ "There is none like the God of
[a]Jeshurun,
Who rides the heavens to your help,
And through the skies in His majesty.
27 "The eternal God is a dwelling place,
And underneath are the everlasting arms;
And He drove out the enemy from
before you,
And said, 'Destroy!'
28 "So Israel dwells in security,
The fountain of Jacob secluded,
In a land of grain and new wine;
His heavens also drop down dew.
29 "Blessed are you, O Israel;
Who is like you, a people saved by the
LORD,
Who is the shield of your help
And the sword of your majesty!
So your enemies will cringe before you,
And you will tread upon their high
places."

The Death of Moses

34 Now Moses went up from the plains of
Moab to Mount Nebo, to the top of Pisgah,
which is opposite Jericho. And the LORD showed
him all the land, Gilead as far as Dan,
2 and all Naphtali and the land of Ephraim
and Manasseh, and all the land of Judah as far as
the [b]western sea,

[a] I.e. Israel   [b] I.e. Mediterranean Sea

3 and the Negev and the plain in the valley of Jericho, the city of palm trees, as far as Zoar.

4 Then the LORD said to him, "This is the land which I swore to Abraham, Isaac, and Jacob, saying, 'I will give it to your descendants'; I have let you see *it* with your eyes, but you shall not go over there."

5 So Moses the servant of the LORD died there in the land of Moab, according to the word of the LORD.

6 And He buried him in the valley in the land of Moab, opposite Beth-peor; but no man knows his burial place to this day.

7 Although Moses was one hundred and twenty years old when he died, his eye was not dim, nor his vigor abated.

8 So the sons of Israel wept for Moses in the plains of Moab thirty days; then the days of weeping *and* mourning for Moses came to an end.

9 ¶ Now Joshua the son of Nun was filled with the spirit of wisdom, for Moses had laid his hands on him; and the sons of Israel listened to him and did as the LORD had commanded Moses.

10 Since that time no prophet has risen in Israel like Moses, whom the LORD knew face to face,

11 for all the signs and wonders which the LORD sent him to perform in the land of Egypt against Pharaoh, all his servants, and all his land,

34:5 Moses Gets a Preview

To his great disappointment, Moses could not lead his people into the new land, for reasons mentioned in 32:48–52. But God allowed him a final look over all the promised land. And, in a very unexpected way, Moses did realize his dream of setting foot in the promised land. Over a thousand years later, he returned with the prophet Elijah and visited with Jesus on the Mount of Transfiguration (Matthew 17; Mark 9; Luke 9).

12 and for all the mighty power and for all the great terror which Moses performed in the sight of all Israel.

JOSHUA

The Difference 40 Years Can Make
They faced overwhelming odds with renewed hope

O N THE SURFACE, NOT MUCH had changed in 40 years. The band of refugees amassing beside the Jordan River greatly resembled a similar horde from four decades before. They had panicked once. Would they again?

> *"Do not tremble or be dismayed, for the LORD your God is with you wherever you go." 1:9*

The Israelites still faced overwhelming odds. They had no chariots or even horses. They had only primitive arms, an untested new leader, and long-delayed marching orders from God.

A New Spirit, a New Leader

Yet, in another sense, everything had changed. Older Israelites with fearful, slave mentalities had died off in the desert—all the older generation except Joshua and Caleb, two legendary warriors. The new generation had decided to trust God, no matter what. In stark contrast to the spies in Numbers (13:31–33), Joshua's scouts brought back this report, "Surely the LORD has given all the land into our hands; moreover, all the inhabitants of the land have melted away before us" (2:24).

The book of Joshua contains not a word about rebellion against a leader or grumbling against God. It is a good news book, a welcome relief from the discouraging tone of Numbers and the fatalism of Deuteronomy. What a difference 40 years had made!

As newly appointed leader of the Israelites, Joshua took on two main tasks. First, he was to direct a military campaign to take control of the land God had promised. Then, he would parcel out the conquered land among all the tribes.

Learning to Follow Instructions

Once inside Canaan, the Israelites followed God's instructions precisely, even when doing so must have strained their faith to new limits. The residents of Jericho had shut themselves behind stone walls, awaiting the onslaught of the feared Israelites. But how did the Israelites spend their first week in Canaan? They built a stone monument to God, performed circumcision rituals, and held a Passover celebration. No conquering army had ever behaved in such a manner.

Everything in Joshua seems hand-picked to strike home the point that God was really in charge. Covering a period of approximately seven years, Joshua's 24 chapters devote only a few sentences to some extensive military campaigns (see chapters 10–11). But key events, such as the fall of Jericho, get detailed coverage, underscoring that the Israelites succeeded when they relied on God, not on military might. The few negative stories (such as the battle of Ai and the trick of the Gibeonites) show what happened when the Israelites did not seek God's will.

A Book of Hope

The Bible does not give history for its own sake. Rather, it presents practical and spiritual lessons. Fortunately, Joshua's lessons are overwhelmingly positive ones. Guided by God, the nation of Israel met with unprecedented success. In fact, the book concludes that "not one of the good promises which the LORD had made to the house of Israel failed; all came to pass" (21:45).

The book of Joshua gives a fresh breeze of hope. Writers of hymns and spirituals have often gone back to it to try to recapture the spirit of success that swept over God's people those first few years in the new land. It *can* work: people can follow God. Joshua shows how.

How to Read Joshua

Phrases in the first paragraph of Joshua hint at the tone to follow. "I will not fail you or forsake you," God promised. "Every place on which the sole of your foot treads, I have given it to you." "Be careful to do according to all that is written in [the law] . . . then you will have success."

Often the Israelites offer examples of what *not* to do. Already the books of Exodus, Numbers, and Deuteronomy have given negative examples, and the historical books to follow will describe further failures in lurid detail. But the Old Testament does offer a few bright spots of hope, the book of Joshua being one of the brightest.

(The "good news" character of Joshua causes some people to compare it to the New Testament books of Ephesians and Philippians, which share its success-and-triumph tone. You may want to read one of those New Testament books along with Joshua.)

Fast-paced battle action appears in chapters 1–11, "the book of war." The latter chapters, "the book of distribution," mostly concern the parceling out of the land.

You can casually read about the military campaigns of Joshua, but to truly appreciate them you must study a map or Bible atlas. Joshua is a very geographical book. Place-names appear in every chapter, describing the military progress and also the division of the land among the tribes of Israel.

As you read Joshua, keep two major themes in mind: Joshua's leadership and God's direct involvement in history. Study Joshua's life as an example of leadership. What were the reasons behind his few failures, such as those recorded in chapters 7 and 9? You may also want to refer to the background passages on his life in Exodus (17,24,32,33) and Numbers (11,13,26). What lesson did Joshua learn at each of these key moments?

PEOPLE YOU'LL MEET IN JOSHUA

RAHAB *(p. 256)*
JOSHUA *(p. 276)*

3-TRACK READING PLAN

For an explanation and complete listing of the 3-track reading plan, turn to page 7.

TRACK 1: *Two-Week Courses on the Bible*
See page 7 for information on these courses.

TRACK 2: *An Overview of Joshua in 4 Days*
☐ Day 1. Read the Introduction to Joshua and then chapter 2, the story of Rahab and the spies.
☐ Day 2. Read the story of Jericho in chapter 6; the Israelites practiced very unorthodox military tactics, but learned to rely on God.
☐ Day 3. Success at Jericho immediately preceded a great failure; read about it in chapter 7.
☐ Day 4. Read chapter 24, part of Joshua's stirring farewell speech to the nation he led so well.

Now turn to page 9 for your next Track 2 reading project.

TRACK 3: *All of Joshua in 21 Days*
After you have read through Joshua, turn to pages 10–14 for your next Track 3 reading project.

☐1   ☐2   ☐3   ☐4   ☐5   ☐6   ☐7   ☐8
☐9   ☐10   ☐11   ☐12–13   ☐14–15   ☐16–17   ☐18   ☐19
☐20   ☐21   ☐22   ☐23   ☐24

God's Charge to Joshua

1 Now it came about after the death of Moses the servant of the LORD, that the LORD spoke to Joshua the son of Nun, Moses' [a]servant, saying,

2 "Moses My servant is dead; now therefore arise, cross this Jordan, you and all this people, to the land which I am giving to them, to the sons of Israel.

3 "Every place on which the sole of your foot treads, I have given it to you, just as I spoke to Moses.

4 "From the wilderness and this Lebanon, even as far as the great river, the river Euphrates, all the land of the Hittites, and as far as the Great Sea toward the setting of the sun will be your territory.

5 "No man will *be able to* stand before you all the days of your life. Just as I have been with Moses, I will be with you; I will not fail you or forsake you.

6 "Be strong and courageous, for you shall give this people possession of the land which I swore to their fathers to give them.

7 "Only be strong and very courageous; be careful to do according to all the law which Moses My servant commanded you; do not turn from it to the right or to the left, so that you may have success wherever you go.

8 "This book of the law shall not depart from your mouth, but you shall meditate on it day and night, so that you may be careful to do according to all that is written in it; for then you will make your way prosperous, and then you will have success.

1:8 Secret of Success

Three times in this short speech God urged Joshua to "be strong and courageous." Joshua must have quaked at the prospect of taking over for a great man like Moses. But God promised him the resources he needed: God's own presence (verse 5) and the Book of the Law, which Joshua was to lean on every day.

9 "Have I not commanded you? Be strong and courageous! Do not tremble or be dismayed, for the LORD your God is with you wherever you go."

Joshua Assumes Command

10 ¶ Then Joshua commanded the officers of the people, saying,

11 "Pass through the midst of the camp and command the people, saying, 'Prepare provisions for yourselves, for within three days you are to cross this Jordan, to go in to possess the land which the LORD your God is giving you, to possess it.'"

12 ¶ To the Reubenites and to the Gadites and to the half-tribe of Manasseh, Joshua said,

13 "Remember the word which Moses the servant of the LORD commanded you, saying, 'The LORD your God gives you rest and will give you this land.'

14 "Your wives, your little ones, and your cattle shall remain in the land which Moses gave you beyond the Jordan, but you shall cross before your brothers in battle array, all your valiant warriors, and shall help them,

15 until the LORD gives your brothers rest, as *He gives* you, and they also possess the land which the LORD your God is giving them. Then you shall return to your own land, and possess that which Moses the servant of the LORD gave you beyond the Jordan toward the sunrise."

16 ¶ They answered Joshua, saying, "All that you have commanded us we will do, and wherever you send us we will go.

17 "Just as we obeyed Moses in all things, so we will obey you; only may the LORD your God be with you as He was with Moses.

18 "Anyone who rebels against your command and does not obey your words in all that you command him, shall be put to death; only be strong and courageous."

Rahab Shelters Spies

2 Then Joshua the son of Nun sent two men as spies secretly from Shittim, saying, "Go, view the land, especially Jericho." So they went and came into the house of a harlot whose name was Rahab, and lodged there.

2 It was told the king of Jericho, saying, "Behold, men from the sons of Israel have come here tonight to search out the land."

3 And the king of Jericho sent *word* to Rahab, saying, "Bring out the men who have come to you, who have entered your house, for they have come to search out all the land."

4 But the woman had taken the two men and hidden them, and she said, "Yes, the men came to me, but I did not know where they were from.

5 "It came about when *it was time* to shut the gate at dark, that the men went out; I do not know where the men went. Pursue them quickly, for you will overtake them."

6 But she had brought them up to the roof and hidden them in the stalks of flax which she had laid in order on the roof.

7 So the men pursued them on the road to the Jordan to the fords; and as soon as those who were pursuing them had gone out, they shut the gate.

8 ¶ Now before they lay down, she came up to them on the roof,

9 and said to the men, "I know that the LORD has given you the land, and that the terror of you has fallen on us, and that all the inhabitants of the land have melted away before you.

---

[a] Or *minister*

10 "For we have heard how the LORD dried up the water of the Red Sea before you when you came out of Egypt, and what you did to the two kings of the Amorites who were beyond the Jordan, to Sihon and Og, whom you utterly destroyed.

11 "When we heard *it,* our hearts melted and no courage remained in any man any longer because of you; for the LORD your God, He is God in heaven above and on earth beneath.

12 "Now therefore, please swear to me by the LORD, since I have dealt kindly with you, that you also will deal kindly with my father's household, and give me a pledge of truth,

2:12 Rahab's Future

References to Rahab elsewhere in the Bible show that she gained a unique place in Jewish history. She and her family alone survived the battle of Jericho. By marrying a man named Salmon (possibly a relative of the hero Caleb), she became a direct ancestor of Jesus Christ (Matthew 1:5). The authors of James (2:25) and Hebrews (11:31) hold up Rahab as an example of faith.

13 and spare my father and my mother and my brothers and my sisters, with all who belong to them, and deliver our *a*lives from death."

14 So the men said to her, "Our life for yours if you do not tell this business of ours; and it shall come about when the LORD gives us the land that we will deal kindly and faithfully with you."

The Promise to Rahab

15 ¶ Then she let them down by a rope through the window, for her house was on the city wall, so that she was living on the wall.

16 She said to them, "Go to the hill country, so that the pursuers will not happen upon you, and hide yourselves there for three days until the pursuers return. Then afterward you may go on your way."

17 The men said to her, "We *shall be* free from this oath to you which you have made us swear,

18 unless, when we come into the land, you tie this cord of scarlet thread in the window through which you let us down, and gather to yourself into the house your father and your mother and your brothers and all your father's household.

19 "It shall come about that anyone who goes out of the doors of your house into the street, his blood *shall be* on his own head, and we *shall be* free; but anyone who is with you in the house, his blood *shall be* on our head if a hand is *laid* on him.

20 "But if you tell this business of ours, then we

shall be free from the oath which you have made us swear."

21 She said, "According to your words, so be it." So she sent them away, and they departed; and she tied the scarlet cord in the window.

22 ¶ They departed and came to the hill country, and remained there for three days until the pursuers returned. Now the pursuers had sought *them* all along the road, but had not found *them.*

23 Then the two men returned and came down from the hill country and crossed over and came to Joshua the son of Nun, and they related to him all that had happened to them.

24 They said to Joshua, "Surely the LORD has given all the land into our hands; moreover, all the inhabitants of the land have melted away before us."

Israel Crosses the Jordan

3 Then Joshua rose early in the morning; and he and all the sons of Israel set out from Shittim and came to the Jordan, and they lodged there before they crossed.

2 At the end of three days the officers went through the midst of the camp;

3 and they commanded the people, saying, "When you see the ark of the covenant of the LORD your God with the Levitical priests carrying it, then you shall set out from your place and go after it.

4 "However, there shall be between you and it a distance of about 2,000 cubits by measure. Do not come near it, that you may know the way by which you shall go, for you have not passed this way before."

5 ¶ Then Joshua said to the people, "Consecrate yourselves, for tomorrow the LORD will do wonders among you."

6 And Joshua spoke to the priests, saying, "Take up the ark of the covenant and cross over ahead of the people." So they took up the ark of the covenant and went ahead of the people.

7 ¶ Now the LORD said to Joshua, "This day I will begin to exalt you in the sight of all Israel, that they may know that just as I have been with Moses, I will be with you.

8 "You shall, moreover, command the priests who are carrying the ark of the covenant, saying, 'When you come to the edge of the waters of the Jordan, you shall stand *still* in the Jordan.' "

9 Then Joshua said to the sons of Israel, "Come here, and hear the words of the LORD your God."

10 Joshua said, "By this you shall know that the living God is among you, and that He will assuredly dispossess from before you the Canaanite, the Hittite, the Hivite, the Perizzite, the Girgashite, the Amorite, and the Jebusite.

11 "Behold, the ark of the covenant of the Lord

a Lit *souls*

of all the earth is crossing over ahead of you into the Jordan.

12 "Now then, take for yourselves twelve men from the tribes of Israel, one man for each tribe.

13 "It shall come about when the soles of the feet of the priests who carry the ark of the LORD, the Lord of all the earth, rest in the waters of the Jordan, the waters of the Jordan will be cut off, *and* the waters which are flowing down from above will stand in one heap."

14 ¶ So when the people set out from their tents to cross the Jordan with the priests carrying the ark of the covenant before the people,

15 and when those who carried the ark came into the Jordan, and the feet of the priests carrying the ark were dipped in the edge of the water (for the Jordan overflows all its banks all the days of harvest),

16 the waters which were flowing down from above stood *and* rose up in one heap, a great distance away at Adam, the city that is beside Zarethan; and those which were flowing down toward the sea of the Arabah, the Salt Sea, were completely cut off. So the people crossed opposite Jericho.

3:16 Stopping the Jordan River

A 1927 earthquake caused the 40-foot clay banks of the Jordan River to collapse, totally damming the Jordan for 21 hours. Whatever means God used to allow the Israelites to cross, this miracle in Joshua achieved a similar result during the river's swollen flood stage. The miracle echoed the crossing of the Red Sea 40 years before, helping to establish Joshua as a worthy successor to Moses. Joshua and the Israelites crossed at a location very close to where Jesus was later baptized.

17 And the priests who carried the ark of the covenant of the LORD stood firm on dry ground in the middle of the Jordan while all Israel crossed on dry ground, until all the nation had finished crossing the Jordan.

Memorial Stones from Jordan

4 Now when all the nation had finished crossing the Jordan, the LORD spoke to Joshua, saying,

2 "Take for yourselves twelve men from the people, one man from each tribe,

3 and command them, saying, 'Take up for yourselves twelve stones from here out of the middle of the Jordan, from the place where the priests' feet are standing firm, and carry them over with you and lay them down in the lodging place where you will lodge tonight.'"

4 So Joshua called the twelve men whom he had appointed from the sons of Israel, one man from each tribe;

5 and Joshua said to them, "Cross again to the ark of the LORD your God into the middle of the Jordan, and each of you take up a stone on his shoulder, according to the number of the tribes of the sons of Israel.

6 "Let this be a sign among you, so that when your children ask later, saying, 'What do these stones mean to you?'

7 then you shall say to them, 'Because the waters of the Jordan were cut off before the ark of the covenant of the LORD; when it crossed the Jordan, the waters of the Jordan were cut off.' So these stones shall become a memorial to the sons of Israel forever."

8 ¶ Thus the sons of Israel did as Joshua commanded, and took up twelve stones from the middle of the Jordan, just as the LORD spoke to Joshua, according to the number of the tribes of the sons of Israel; and they carried them over with them to the lodging place and put them down there.

9 Then Joshua set up twelve stones in the middle of the Jordan at the place where the feet of the priests who carried the ark of the covenant were standing, and they are there to this day.

10 For the priests who carried the ark were standing in the middle of the Jordan until everything was completed that the LORD had commanded Joshua to speak to the people, according to all that Moses had commanded Joshua. And the people hurried and crossed;

11 and when all the people had finished crossing, the ark of the LORD and the priests crossed before the people.

12 The sons of Reuben and the sons of Gad and the half-tribe of Manasseh crossed over in battle array before the sons of Israel, just as Moses had spoken to them;

13 about 40,000 equipped for war, crossed for battle before the LORD to the desert plains of Jericho.

14 ¶ On that day the LORD exalted Joshua in the sight of all Israel; so that they [a]revered him, just as they had revered Moses all the days of his life.

15 ¶ Now the LORD said to Joshua,

16 "Command the priests who carry the ark of the testimony that they come up from the Jordan."

17 So Joshua commanded the priests, saying, "Come up from the Jordan."

18 It came about when the priests who carried the ark of the covenant of the LORD had come up from the middle of the Jordan, and the soles of the priests' feet were lifted up to the dry ground, that the waters of the Jordan returned to their place, and went over all its banks as before.

19 ¶ Now the people came up from the Jordan

---

[a] Or *feared*

on the tenth of the first month and camped at Gilgal on the eastern edge of Jericho.

20 Those twelve stones which they had taken from the Jordan, Joshua set up at Gilgal.

21 He said to the sons of Israel, "When your children ask their fathers in time to come, saying, 'What are these stones?'

22 then you shall inform your children, saying, 'Israel crossed this Jordan on dry ground.'

23 "For the LORD your God dried up the waters of the Jordan before you until you had crossed, just as the LORD your God had done to the Red Sea, which He dried up before us until we had crossed;

24 that all the peoples of the earth may know that the hand of the LORD is mighty, so that you may fear the LORD your God forever."

Israel Is Circumcised

5 Now it came about when all the kings of the Amorites who *were* beyond the Jordan to the west, and all the kings of the Canaanites who *were* by the sea, heard how the LORD had dried up the waters of the Jordan before the sons of Israel until they had crossed, that their hearts melted, and there was no spirit in them any longer because of the sons of Israel.

2 ¶ At that time the LORD said to Joshua, "Make for yourself flint knives and circumcise again the sons of Israel the second time."

3 So Joshua made himself flint knives and circumcised the sons of Israel at *a*Gibeath-haaraloth.

4 This is the reason why Joshua circumcised them: all the people who came out of Egypt who were males, all the men of war, died in the wilderness along the way after they came out of Egypt.

5 For all the people who came out were circumcised, but all the people who were born in the wilderness along the way as they came out of Egypt had not been circumcised.

6 For the sons of Israel walked forty years in the wilderness, until all the nation, *that is*, the men of war who came out of Egypt, perished because they did not listen to the voice of the LORD, to whom the LORD had sworn that He would not let them see the land which the LORD had sworn to their fathers to give us, a land flowing with milk and honey.

7 Their children whom He raised up in their place, Joshua circumcised; for they were uncircumcised, because they had not circumcised them along the way.

8 ¶ Now when they had finished circumcising all the nation, they remained in their places in the camp until they were healed.

9 Then the LORD said to Joshua, "Today I have rolled away the reproach of Egypt from you." So the name of that place is called *b*Gilgal to this day.

10 ¶ While the sons of Israel camped at Gilgal they observed the Passover on the evening of the fourteenth day of the month on the desert plains of Jericho.

11 On the day after the Passover, on that very day, they ate some of the produce of the land, unleavened cakes and parched *grain*.

12 The manna ceased on the day after they had eaten some of the produce of the land, so that the sons of Israel no longer had manna, but they ate some of the yield of the land of Canaan during that year.

5:12 No More Free Lunch

For 40 years God had provided manna, a miraculous food that appeared like dew on the ground every night. In the desert, manna had been necessary for survival. In Palestine, however, the free food stopped. Israelites would be able to grow or gather adequate food for themselves.

13 ¶ Now it came about when Joshua was by Jericho, that he lifted up his eyes and looked, and behold, a man was standing opposite him with his sword drawn in his hand, and Joshua went to him and said to him, "Are you for us or for our adversaries?"

14 He said, "No; rather I indeed come now *as* captain of the host of the LORD." And Joshua fell on his face to the earth, and bowed down, and said to him, "What has my lord to say to his servant?"

15 The captain of the LORD'S host said to Joshua, "Remove your sandals from your feet, for the place where you are standing is holy." And Joshua did so.

The Conquest of Jericho

6 Now Jericho was tightly shut because of the sons of Israel; no one went out and no one came in.

2 The LORD said to Joshua, "See, I have given Jericho into your hand, with its king *and* the valiant warriors.

3 "You shall march around the city, all the men of war circling the city once. You shall do so for six days.

4 "Also seven priests shall carry seven trumpets of rams' horns before the ark; then on the seventh day you shall march around the city seven times, and the priests shall blow the trumpets.

5 "It shall be that when they make a long blast with the ram's horn, and when you hear the sound of the trumpet, all the people shall shout with a great shout; and the wall of the city will fall down flat, and the people will go up every man straight ahead."

---

a I.e. the hill of the foreskins   *b* I.e. rolling

6 ¶ So Joshua the son of Nun called the priests and said to them, "Take up the ark of the covenant, and let seven priests carry seven trumpets of rams' horns before the ark of the LORD."

7 Then he said to the people, "Go forward, and march around the city, and let the armed men go on before the ark of the LORD."

8 And it was so, that when Joshua had spoken to the people, the seven priests carrying the seven trumpets of rams' horns before the LORD went forward and blew the trumpets; and the ark of the covenant of the LORD followed them.

9 The armed men went before the priests who blew the trumpets, and the rear guard came after the ark, while they continued to blow the trumpets.

10 But Joshua commanded the people, saying, "You shall not shout nor let your voice be heard nor let a word proceed out of your mouth, until the day I tell you, 'Shout!' Then you shall shout!"

11 So he had the ark of the LORD taken around the city, circling it once; then they came into the camp and spent the night in the camp.

12 ¶ Now Joshua rose early in the morning, and the priests took up the ark of the LORD.

13 The seven priests carrying the seven trumpets of rams' horns before the ark of the LORD went on continually, and blew the trumpets; and the armed men went before them and the rear guard came after the ark of the LORD, while they continued to blow the trumpets.

14 Thus the second day they marched around the city once and returned to the camp; they did so for six days.

15 ¶ Then on the seventh day they rose early at the dawning of the day and marched around the city in the same manner seven times; only on that day they marched around the city seven times.

16 At the seventh time, when the priests blew the trumpets, Joshua said to the people, "Shout! For the LORD has given you the city.

17 "The city shall be under the ban, it and all that is in it belongs to the LORD; only Rahab the harlot and all who are with her in the house shall live, because she hid the messengers whom we sent.

18 "But as for you, only keep yourselves from the things under the ban, so that you do not covet them and take some of the things under the ban, and make the camp of Israel accursed and bring trouble on it.

19 "But all the silver and gold and articles of bronze and iron are holy to the LORD; they shall go into the treasury of the LORD."

20 So the people shouted, and priests blew the trumpets; and when the people heard the sound of the trumpet, the people shouted with a great shout and the wall fell down flat, so that the people went up into the city, every man straight ahead, and they took the city.

21 They utterly destroyed everything in the city, both man and woman, young and old, and ox and sheep and donkey, with the edge of the sword.

22 ¶ Joshua said to the two men who had spied out the land, "Go into the harlot's house and bring the woman and all she has out of there, as you have sworn to her."

23 So the young men who were spies went in and brought out Rahab and her father and her mother and her brothers and all she had; they also brought out all her relatives and placed them outside the camp of Israel.

24 They burned the city with fire, and all that was in it. Only the silver and gold, and articles of bronze and iron, they put into the treasury of the *a*house of the LORD.

25 However, Rahab the harlot and her father's household and all she had, Joshua spared; and she has lived in the midst of Israel to this day, for she

a I.e. tabernacle

RAHAB *A Prostitute's Faith*

PEOPLE WHO STUDY THE BIBLE are often surprised to find a prostitute held up as an example of faith. In two separate places the New Testament commends the prostitute named Rahab. The writers pass over both her profession and the lie that she told the king of Jericho (2:4–5). Her vision is what they admire. Rahab saw things differently than every one else in her community, and she gambled her future on that vision.

Word of the Israelites' amazing successes had spread. According to Rahab, the residents of Jericho had 'melted away' at the news of Israel's triumphs over Egypt and other nations. Yet the people of Jericho determined all the more to dig in and fight. Rahab took the opposite course: She decided to join the opposition. Concluding that Israel's God was the real God, she chose to switch to his side.

Perhaps her social position—a prostitute living on the margins of society—made it easier for Rahab to take a stand against her own people. (Centuries later people on the margins of respectability often accepted Jesus, too.) Regardless, because she risked her neck to save the Israelite spies, they made sure that she and her entire family survived the assault.

Life Questions: Do you know anyone with real vision? If so, what do they see that others don't?

hid the messengers whom Joshua sent to spy out Jericho.

26 ¶ Then Joshua made them take an oath at that time, saying, "Cursed before the LORD is the man who rises up and builds this city Jericho; with *the loss of* his firstborn he shall lay its foundation, and with *the loss of* his youngest son he shall set up its gates."

6:26 Cursed City

Joshua's curse was fulfilled literally when a man attempted to rebuild the city of Jericho in the days of King Ahab (see 1 Kings 16:34).

27 So the LORD was with Joshua, and his fame was in all the land.

Israel Is Defeated at Ai

7 But the sons of Israel acted unfaithfully in regard to the things under the ban, for Achan, the son of Carmi, the son of Zabdi, the son of Zerah, from the tribe of Judah, took some of the things under the ban, therefore the anger of the LORD burned against the sons of Israel.

2 ¶ Now Joshua sent men from Jericho to Ai, which is near Beth-aven, east of Bethel, and said to them, "Go up and spy out the land." So the men went up and spied out Ai.

3 They returned to Joshua and said to him, "Do not let all the people go up; *only* about two or three thousand men need go up to Ai; do not make all the people toil up there, for they are few."

4 So about three thousand men from the people went up there, but they fled from the men of Ai.

5 The men of Ai struck down about thirty-six of their men, and pursued them from the gate as far as Shebarim and struck them down on the descent, so the hearts of the people melted and became as water.

6 ¶ Then Joshua tore his clothes and fell to the earth on his face before the ark of the LORD until the evening, *both* he and the elders of Israel; and they put dust on their heads.

7 Joshua said, "Alas, O Lord GOD, why did You ever bring this people over the Jordan, *only* to deliver us into the hand of the Amorites, to destroy us? If only we had been willing to dwell beyond the Jordan!

8 "O Lord, what can I say since Israel has turned *their* back before their enemies?

9 "For the Canaanites and all the inhabitants of the land will hear of it, and they will surround us and cut off our name from the earth. And what will You do for Your great name?"

10 ¶ So the LORD said to Joshua, "Rise up! Why is it that you have fallen on your face?

11 "Israel has sinned, and they have also transgressed My covenant which I commanded them.

And they have even taken some of the things under the ban and have both stolen and deceived. Moreover, they have also put *them* among their own things.

7:7 A Crisis of Confidence

Ai stood near the original location where God had promised the land to Abraham hundreds of years before (Genesis 12:8). Military defeat here, coming so quickly after a great victory at Jericho, caused even Joshua to tremble. Without God's protection, the Israelites were militarily vulnerable—trapped without possibility of escape across the flooding Jordan River.

The trouble at Ai came because of a single man who had greedily disobeyed God's battle commands. His punishment was drastic. Evidently the fledgling nation (like the fledgling church of Acts 5:1–10) needed a strong lesson in the consequences of taking God's word lightly.

12 "Therefore the sons of Israel cannot stand before their enemies; they turn *their* backs before their enemies, for they have become accursed. I will not be with you anymore unless you destroy the things under the ban from your midst.

13 "Rise up! Consecrate the people and say, 'Consecrate yourselves for tomorrow, for thus the LORD, the God of Israel, has said, "There are things under the ban in your midst, O Israel. You cannot stand before your enemies until you have removed the things under the ban from your midst."

14 'In the morning then you shall come near by your tribes. And it shall be that the tribe which the LORD takes *by lot* shall come near by families, and the family which the LORD takes shall come near by households, and the household which the LORD takes shall come near man by man.

15 'It shall be that the one who is taken with the things under the ban shall be burned with fire, he and all that belongs to him, because he has transgressed the covenant of the LORD, and because he has committed a disgraceful thing in Israel.' "

The Sin of Achan

16 ¶ So Joshua arose early in the morning and brought Israel near by tribes, and the tribe of Judah was taken.

17 He brought the family of Judah near, and he took the family of the Zerahites; and he brought the family of the Zerahites near man by man, and Zabdi was taken.

18 He brought his household near man by man; and Achan, son of Carmi, son of Zabdi, son of Zerah, from the tribe of Judah, was taken.

19 Then Joshua said to Achan, "My son, I im-

plore you, give glory to the LORD, the God of Israel, and give praise to Him; and tell me now what you have done. Do not hide it from me."

20 So Achan answered Joshua and said, "Truly, I have sinned against the LORD, the God of Israel, and this is what I did:

21 when I saw among the spoil a beautiful mantle from Shinar and two hundred shekels of silver and a bar of gold fifty shekels in weight, then I coveted them and took them; and behold, they are concealed in the earth inside my tent with the silver underneath it."

22 ¶ So Joshua sent messengers, and they ran to the tent; and behold, it was concealed in his tent with the silver underneath it.

23 They took them from inside the tent and brought them to Joshua and to all the sons of Israel, and they poured them out before the LORD.

24 Then Joshua and all Israel with him, took Achan the son of Zerah, the silver, the mantle, the bar of gold, his sons, his daughters, his oxen, his donkeys, his sheep, his tent and all that belonged to him; and they brought them up to the valley of ªAchor.

25 Joshua said, "Why have you troubled us? The LORD will trouble you this day." And all Israel stoned them with stones; and they burned them with fire after they had stoned them with stones.

26 They raised over him a great heap of stones that stands to this day, and the LORD turned from the fierceness of His anger. Therefore the name of that place has been called the valley of ªAchor to this day.

The Conquest of Ai

8 Now the LORD said to Joshua, "Do not fear or be dismayed. Take all the people of war with you and arise, go up to Ai; see, I have given into your hand the king of Ai, his people, his city, and his land.

2 "You shall do to Ai and its king just as you did to Jericho and its king; you shall take only its spoil and its cattle as plunder for yourselves. Set an ambush for the city behind it."

8:2 War Strategy

Joshua used expert military strategy against Israel's many enemies in Canaan. His assignment as one of the original spies had given Joshua valuable knowledge of the topography of the land. Israelite armies entered the middle of Canaan, splitting the country in two and intersecting strategic trade routes. His "flying column" formations, night marches, ambush tactics rather than long sieges, and destruction of key cities showed awareness of advanced military techniques.

3 ¶ So Joshua rose with all the people of war to go up to Ai; and Joshua chose 30,000 men, valiant warriors, and sent them out at night.

4 He commanded them, saying, "See, you are going to ambush the city from behind it. Do not go very far from the city, but all of you be ready.

5 "Then I and all the people who are with me will approach the city. And when they come out to meet us as at the first, we will flee before them.

6 "They will come out after us until we have drawn them away from the city, for they will say, '*They* are fleeing before us as at the first.' So we will flee before them.

7 "And you shall rise from *your* ambush and take possession of the city, for the LORD your God will deliver it into your hand.

8 "Then it will be when you have seized the city, that you shall set the city on fire. You shall do *it* according to the word of the LORD. See, I have commanded you."

9 So Joshua sent them away, and they went to the place of ambush and remained between Bethel and Ai, on the west side of Ai; but Joshua spent that night among the people.

10 ¶ Now Joshua rose early in the morning and mustered the people, and he went up with the elders of Israel before the people to Ai.

11 Then all the people of war who *were* with him went up and drew near and arrived in front of the city, and camped on the north side of Ai. Now *there was* a valley between him and Ai.

12 And he took about 5,000 men and set them in ambush between Bethel and Ai, on the west side of the city.

13 So they stationed the people, all the army that was on the north side of the city, and its rear guard on the west side of the city, and Joshua spent that night in the midst of the valley.

14 It came about when the king of Ai saw *it,* that the men of the city hurried and rose up early and went out to meet Israel in battle, he and all his people at the appointed place before the desert plain. But he did not know that *there was* an ambush against him behind the city.

15 Joshua and all Israel pretended to be beaten before them, and fled by the way of the wilderness.

16 And all the people who were in the city were called together to pursue them, and they pursued Joshua and were drawn away from the city.

17 So not a man was left in Ai or Bethel who had not gone out after Israel, and they left the city unguarded and pursued Israel.

18 ¶ Then the LORD said to Joshua, "Stretch out the javelin that is in your hand toward Ai, for I will give it into your hand." So Joshua stretched out the javelin that was in his hand toward the city.

19 The *men in* ambush rose quickly from their place, and when he had stretched out his hand,

ª I.e. trouble

they ran and entered the city and captured it, and they quickly set the city on fire.

20 When the men of Ai turned back and looked, behold, the smoke of the city ascended to the sky, and they had no place to flee this way or that, for the people who had been fleeing to the wilderness turned against the pursuers.

21 When Joshua and all Israel saw that the *men in* ambush had captured the city and that the smoke of the city ascended, they turned back and slew the men of Ai.

22 The others came out from the city to encounter them, so that they were *trapped* in the midst of Israel, some on this side and some on that side; and they slew them until no one was left of those who survived or escaped.

23 But they took alive the king of Ai and brought him to Joshua.

24 ¶ Now when Israel had finished killing all the inhabitants of Ai in the field in the wilderness where they pursued them, and all of them were fallen by the edge of the sword until they were destroyed, then all Israel returned to Ai and struck it with the edge of the sword.

25 All who fell that day, both men and women, were 12,000—all the people of Ai.

26 For Joshua did not withdraw his hand with which he stretched out the javelin until he had utterly destroyed all the inhabitants of Ai.

27 Israel took only the cattle and the spoil of that city as plunder for themselves, according to the word of the LORD which He had commanded Joshua.

28 So Joshua burned Ai and made it a heap forever, a desolation until this day.

29 He hanged the king of Ai on a tree until evening; and at sunset Joshua gave command and they took his body down from the tree and threw it at the entrance of the city gate, and raised over it a great heap of stones *that stands* to this day.

30 ¶ Then Joshua built an altar to the LORD, the God of Israel, in Mount Ebal,

31 just as Moses the servant of the LORD had commanded the sons of Israel, as it is written in the book of the law of Moses, an altar of uncut stones on which no man had wielded an iron *tool;* and they offered burnt offerings on it to the LORD, and sacrificed peace offerings.

32 He wrote there on the stones a copy of the law of Moses, which he had written, in the presence of the sons of Israel.

33 All Israel with their elders and officers and their judges were standing on both sides of the ark before the Levitical priests who carried the ark of the covenant of the LORD, the stranger as well as the native. Half of them *stood* in front of Mount Gerizim and half of them in front of Mount Ebal, just as Moses the servant of the LORD had given command at first to bless the people of Israel.

34 Then afterward he read all the words of the law, the blessing and the curse, according to all that is written in the book of the law.

35 There was not a word of all that Moses had commanded which Joshua did not read before all the assembly of Israel with the women and the little ones and the strangers who were living among them.

Guile of the Gibeonites

9 Now it came about when all the kings who were beyond the Jordan, in the hill country and in the lowland and on all the coast of the Great Sea toward Lebanon, the Hittite and the Amorite, the Canaanite, the Perizzite, the Hivite and the Jebusite, heard of it,

2 that they gathered themselves together with one accord to fight with Joshua and with Israel.

3 ¶ When the inhabitants of Gibeon heard what Joshua had done to Jericho and to Ai,

4 they also acted craftily and set out as envoys, and took worn-out sacks on their donkeys, and wineskins worn-out and torn and mended,

5 and worn-out and patched sandals on their feet, and worn-out clothes on themselves; and all the bread of their provision was dry *and* had become crumbled.

6 They went to Joshua to the camp at Gilgal and said to him and to the men of Israel, "We have come from a far country; now therefore, make a covenant with us."

7 The men of Israel said to the Hivites, "Perhaps you are living within our land; how then shall we make a covenant with you?"

8 But they said to Joshua, "We are your servants." Then Joshua said to them, "Who are you and where do you come from?"

9 They said to him, "Your servants have come from a very far country because of the fame of the LORD your God; for we have heard the report of Him and all that He did in Egypt,

10 and all that He did to the two kings of the Amorites who were beyond the Jordan, to Sihon king of Heshbon and to Og king of Bashan who was at Ashtaroth.

8:30–34 Blessings and Curses

The scene in this section, which describes the carrying out of Moses' instructions in Deuteronomy 27–28, was a profoundly symbolic event in the history of the Israelites. It elaborately portrayed what would happen if they obeyed the covenant, and if they disobeyed. The two mountains, Ebal and Gerizim, formed a natural amphitheater ideal for such a public ceremony. From their peaks much of the promised land could be seen. (Mount Gerizim eventually became the seat of worship for the Samaritans, which helps explain Jesus' conversation in John 4.)

11 "So our elders and all the inhabitants of our country spoke to us, saying, 'Take provisions in your hand for the journey, and go to meet them and say to them, "We are your servants; now then, make a covenant with us." '

12 "This our bread *was* warm *when* we took it for our provisions out of our houses on the day that we left to come to you; but now behold, it is dry and has become crumbled.

13 "These wineskins which we filled were new, and behold, they are torn; and these our clothes and our sandals are worn out because of the very long journey."

14 So the men *of Israel* took some of their provisions, and did not ask for the counsel of the LORD.

9:14 Tricked!

The Gibeonites saved themselves by performing an elaborate deception on the Israelite soldiers, acting as if they had come from far away. The Israelites tried to check their story, but neglected the most important test of all: they "did not ask for the counsel of the LORD." Throughout Joshua, God shows that he is in charge and that following him is the only way to victory.

The Gibeonites' trick saved their lives, but they were forced to become servants. Some of them later converted to Judaism. The book of Nehemiah includes Gibeonites (sometimes called Hivites) among those who helped rebuild the walls of Jerusalem. And at least one of King David's "mighty men" was a Gibeonite. (See also the incident recorded in 2 Samuel 21:1–14.) Even so, the Gibeonites often caused trouble for Israel.

15 Joshua made peace with them and made a covenant with them, to let them live; and the leaders of the congregation swore *an oath* to them.

16 ¶ It came about at the end of three days after they had made a covenant with them, that they heard that they were neighbors and that they were living within their land.

17 Then the sons of Israel set out and came to their cities on the third day. Now their cities *were* Gibeon and Chephirah and Beeroth and Kiriath-jearim.

18 The sons of Israel did not strike them because the leaders of the congregation had sworn to them by the LORD the God of Israel. And the whole congregation grumbled against the leaders.

19 But all the leaders said to the whole congregation, "We have sworn to them by the LORD, the God of Israel, and now we cannot touch them.

20 "This we will do to them, even let them live, so that wrath will not be upon us for the oath which we swore to them."

21 The leaders said to them, "Let them live." So they became hewers of wood and drawers of water for the whole congregation, just as the leaders had spoken to them.

22 ¶ Then Joshua called for them and spoke to them, saying, "Why have you deceived us, saying, 'We are very far from you,' when you are living within our land?

23 "Now therefore, you are cursed, and you shall never cease being slaves, both hewers of wood and drawers of water for the house of my God."

24 So they answered Joshua and said, "Because it was certainly told your servants that the LORD your God had commanded His servant Moses to give you all the land, and to destroy all the inhabitants of the land before you; therefore we feared greatly for our lives because of you, and have done this thing.

25 "Now behold, we are in your hands; do as it seems good and right in your sight to do to us."

26 Thus he did to them, and delivered them from the hands of the sons of Israel, and they did not kill them.

27 But Joshua made them that day hewers of wood and drawers of water for the congregation and for the altar of the LORD, to this day, in the place which He would choose.

Five Kings Attack Gibeon

10 Now it came about when Adoni-zedek king of Jerusalem heard that Joshua had captured Ai, and had utterly destroyed it (just as he had done to Jericho and its king, so he had done to Ai and its king), and that the inhabitants of Gibeon had made peace with Israel and were within their land,

2 that he feared greatly, because Gibeon *was* a great city, like one of the royal cities, and because it was greater than Ai, and all its men *were* mighty.

3 Therefore Adoni-zedek king of Jerusalem sent *word* to Hoham king of Hebron and to Piram king of Jarmuth and to Japhia king of Lachish and to Debir king of Eglon, saying,

4 "Come up to me and help me, and let us attack Gibeon, for it has made peace with Joshua and with the sons of Israel."

5 So the five kings of the Amorites, the king of Jerusalem, the king of Hebron, the king of Jarmuth, the king of Lachish, *and* the king of Eglon, gathered together and went up, they with all their armies, and camped by Gibeon and fought against it.

6 ¶ Then the men of Gibeon sent *word* to Joshua to the camp at Gilgal, saying, "Do not abandon your servants; come up to us quickly and save us and help us, for all the kings of the Amorites that live in the hill country have assembled against us."

7 So Joshua went up from Gilgal, he and all the people of war with him and all the valiant warriors.

8 The LORD said to Joshua, "Do not fear them, for I have given them into your hands; not one of them shall stand before you."

9 So Joshua came upon them suddenly by marching all night from Gilgal.

10 And the LORD confounded them before Israel, and He slew them with a great slaughter at Gibeon, and pursued them by the way of the ascent of Beth-horon and struck them as far as Azekah and Makkedah.

11 As they fled from before Israel, *while* they were at the descent of Beth-horon, the LORD threw large stones from heaven on them as far as Azekah, and they died; *there were* more who died from the hailstones than those whom the sons of Israel killed with the sword.

12 ¶ Then Joshua spoke to the LORD in the day when the LORD delivered up the Amorites before the sons of Israel, and he said in the sight of Israel,

> "O sun, stand still at Gibeon,
> And O moon in the valley of Aijalon."

13 So the sun stood still, and the moon
> stopped,
> Until the nation avenged themselves of
> their enemies.

Is it not written in the book of Jashar? And the sun stopped in the middle of the sky and did not hasten to go *down* for about a whole day.

14 There was no day like that before it or after it, when the LORD listened to the voice of a man; for the LORD fought for Israel.

15 ¶ Then Joshua and all Israel with him returned to the camp to Gilgal.

Victory at Makkedah

16 ¶ Now these five kings had fled and hidden themselves in the cave at Makkedah.

17 It was told Joshua, saying, "The five kings have been found hidden in the cave at Makkedah."

18 Joshua said, "Roll large stones against the mouth of the cave, and assign men by it to guard them,

19 but do not stay *there* yourselves; pursue your enemies and attack them in the rear. Do not allow them to enter their cities, for the LORD your God has delivered them into your hand."

20 It came about when Joshua and the sons of Israel had finished slaying them with a very great slaughter, until they were destroyed, and the survivors *who* remained of them had entered the fortified cities,

21 that all the people returned to the camp to Joshua at Makkedah in peace. No one uttered a word against any of the sons of Israel.

22 ¶ Then Joshua said, "Open the mouth of the cave and bring these five kings out to me from the cave."

23 They did so, and brought these five kings out to him from the cave: the king of Jerusalem, the king of Hebron, the king of Jarmuth, the king of Lachish, *and* the king of Eglon.

24 When they brought these kings out to Joshua, Joshua called for all the men of Israel, and said to the chiefs of the men of war who had gone with him, "Come near, put your feet on the necks of these kings." So they came near and put their feet on their necks.

10:24 Act of Humiliation

This act—stepping on a neck—was the ultimate way to humiliate a king. It expressed utter, enforced submission. Egyptian and Assyrian sculptures frequently portrayed this custom.

25 Joshua then said to them, "Do not fear or be dismayed! Be strong and courageous, for thus the LORD will do to all your enemies with whom you fight."

26 So afterward Joshua struck them and put them to death, and he hanged them on five trees; and they hung on the trees until evening.

27 It came about at sunset that Joshua gave a command, and they took them down from the trees and threw them into the cave where they had hidden themselves, and put large stones over the mouth of the cave, to this very day.

28 ¶ Now Joshua captured Makkedah on that day, and struck it and its king with the edge of the sword; he utterly destroyed it and every [a]person who was in it. He left no survivor. Thus he did to the king of Makkedah just as he had done to the king of Jericho.

Joshua's Conquest of Southern Palestine

29 ¶ Then Joshua and all Israel with him passed on from Makkedah to Libnah, and fought against Libnah.

30 The LORD gave it also with its king into the hands of Israel, and he struck it and every person who *was* in it with the edge of the sword. He left no survivor in it. Thus he did to its king just as he had done to the king of Jericho.

31 ¶ And Joshua and all Israel with him passed on from Libnah to Lachish, and they camped by it and fought against it.

32 The LORD gave Lachish into the hands of Israel; and he captured it on the second day, and struck it and every person who *was* in it with the edge of the sword, according to all that he had done to Libnah.

33 ¶ Then Horam king of Gezer came up to help Lachish, and Joshua defeated him and his people until he had left him no survivor.

---

[a] Lit *soul,* and so throughout the ch

34 ¶ And Joshua and all Israel with him passed on from Lachish to Eglon, and they camped by it and fought against it.

35 They captured it on that day and struck it with the edge of the sword; and he utterly destroyed that day every person who *was* in it, according to all that he had done to Lachish.

36 ¶ Then Joshua and all Israel with him went up from Eglon to Hebron, and they fought against it.

37 They captured it and struck it and its king and all its cities and all the persons who *were* in it with the edge of the sword. He left no survivor, according to all that he had done to Eglon. And he utterly destroyed it and every person who *was* in it.

Is a War Ever Holy?
Why did God order a ruthless military campaign?

HOLY WAR. IRONICALLY, THE TERM applies to the most vicious, bloody wars. And often, far too often, Christians have been at the heart of such holy wars.

There is something irrational and even repulsive about a holy war. It harnesses all the best energies of religion for one of the ugliest acts of human nature. And yet anyone who reads the Bible cannot ignore the holy wars in the Old Testament.

Whole books have been written about the problem, and no brief article can begin to cover the issues. But modern readers need some background to help understand why a fierce holy war is presented in such a good light.

> The LORD said to Joshua, "Do not be afraid because of them, for tomorrow at this time I will deliver all of them slain before Israel."
> 11:6

A Land Promised to the Israelites

The Israelites' fighting style fit the harsh pattern of warfare in that day. Contemporary Egyptian and Assyrian reports boasted of mass executions, torture, and the systematic razing of cities. But God's involvement raises unique questions. He personally ordered the destruction of seven Canaanite nations, with no survivors. Why?

The Old Testament makes clear that the Canaanites were not being uprooted on a sudden whim. God had promised the land to the Israelites over 400 years before Joshua. He had called one man, Abraham, to found a nation of chosen people. He repeated those promises often (Genesis 12:1–3; 15:5–18; 17:2–8; 26:3,23–24; 28:13–14) and finally called the Israelites out of Egypt to take over the promised land. Almost from the beginning Canaan was a vital part of God's plan.

Delayed Punishment

Israel's inheritance, however, meant kicking out the Canaanites. How could innocent people simply be pushed aside, or killed? In answer to this question, the Bible makes clear that the Canaanites were *not* "innocent." Through their long history of sin, they had forfeited their right to the land.

Four hundred years before Joshua, God had told Abraham that his descendants would not occupy the land until the sin of its inhabitants had reached its full measure (Genesis 15:16). Later, just days before the onset of Joshua's campaign, Moses stated, "It is not for your righteousness or for the uprightness of your heart that you are going to possess their land, but it is because of the wickedness of these nations that the LORD your God is driving them out before you" (Deuteronomy 9:5).

Historians have uncovered plenty of evidence of this wickedness. Canaanite temples featured prostitutes, orgies, and human sacrifice. Relics and plaques of exaggerated sex organs hint at the morality that characterized Canaan.

Canaanite gods, such as Baal and his wife Anath, delighted in butchery and sadism. Archaeologists have found great numbers of jars containing the tiny bones of children sacrificed to Baal. Families seeking good luck in a new home practiced "foundation sacrifice." They would kill one of their children and seal the body in the mortar of the wall. In many ways, Canaan had become like Sodom and Gomorrah. The Bible records that God has patience with decadent societies for a time, but judgment inevitably follows. For Sodom and Gomorrah it took the form of fire and brimstone. For Canaan it came through Joshua's conquering armies. Later, God let his own chosen people be ravaged by invaders as punishment for their sins. The judgment pronounced on Canaan seems severe, but no more severe than what was later inflicted on Israel itself.

The Contamination Problem

The Israelites could not simply settle down as new neighbors among existing Canaanite cities.

38 ¶ Then Joshua and all Israel with him returned to Debir, and they fought against it.

39 He captured it and its king and all its cities, and they struck them with the edge of the sword, and utterly destroyed every person *who was* in it. He left no survivor. Just as he had done to Hebron, so he did to Debir and its king, as he had also done to Libnah and its king.

40 ¶ Thus Joshua struck all the land, the hill country and the *a*Negev and the lowland and the slopes and all their kings. He left no survivor, but he utterly destroyed all who breathed, just as the LORD, the God of Israel, had commanded.

41 Joshua struck them from Kadesh-barnea even as far as Gaza, and all the country of Goshen even as far as Gibeon.

42 Joshua captured all these kings and their lands at one time, because the LORD, the God of Israel, fought for Israel.

43 So Joshua and all Israel with him returned to the camp at Gilgal.

a I.e. South country   *b* I.e. Sea of Galilee

Northern Palestine Taken

11 Then it came about, when Jabin king of Hazor heard *of it*, that he sent to Jobab king of Madon and to the king of Shimron and to the king of Achshaph,

2 and to the kings who were of the north in the hill country, and in the Arabah—south of *b*Chinneroth and in the lowland and on the heights of Dor on the west—

3 to the Canaanite on the east and on the west, and the Amorite and the Hittite and the Perizzite and the Jebusite in the hill country, and the Hivite at the foot of Hermon in the land of Mizpeh.

4 They came out, they and all their armies with them, *as* many people as the sand that is on the seashore, with very many horses and chariots.

5 So all of these kings having agreed to meet, came and encamped together at the waters of Merom, to fight against Israel.

From the time when the tribes had made a golden calf while Moses was receiving the Ten Commandments (Exodus 32), Israelites had shown a fatal weakness to infection from outside. They seemed particularly susceptible to sins of sex and idolatry, Canaan's national specialties.

Israel's later history offers a negative proof of why God commanded utter destruction of Canaanites. The damning phrase in Joshua, "the sons of Israel did not dispossess the Geshurites or the Maacathites," hints at trouble to come, and the very next book, Judges, tells of the devastating results. The Israelites slid to one of their lowest levels because they had not fulfilled the original mission of cleansing the land of impure elements.

A Struggle beyond Nations

Looking back at this period of time, we tend to see the battles of Joshua as national or racial struggles: the Israelites versus the people of Canaan. But the Bible presents the warfare as a wider struggle: one between those who followed God and those who opposed him.

When God judged groups, as he judged the world in Noah's day or as he judged Sodom and Gomorrah, those few who remained faithful to him found a way of escape. And in Joshua one bright story shines out: the story of Rahab, a non-Israelite. A typical Canaanite who worked as a professional prostitute, she nevertheless learned to fear and then trust the God of Israel. She escaped the fall of Jericho. Furthermore, she went on to marry a leading Israelite and become one of the ancestors of the Messiah himself, Jesus.

Rahab claimed that others in her city of Jericho had quaked in fear for 40 years, waiting for the judgment of the God of Israel (2:9–11). Yet only she took the further step of seeking help. If others in Canaan had repented and turned to God, they might well have escaped punishment, as Rahab did.

Holy Wars Today

One fact about "holy war" is very clear. We cannot argue from a war specifically commanded by God in Joshua to any national situation today. In the Old Testament, God was dealing primarily with one particular nation, the Israelites, for a stated purpose. When the Messiah finally emerged out of that nation, everything changed.

Jesus' followers all lived in the same territory captured by Joshua, the "promised" land." But four times, in his very last words, Jesus commanded his disciples to go out, away from Jerusalem, into all the world. Go, he told them, not as conquering armies but rather as bearers of the good news that applies to all people, all races, all nations.

Anyone who looks to the book of Joshua for a rationalization of a holy war must also look ahead to Jesus. Although on a holy crusade, he chose against violent means. In fact, he chose suffering and death. Nothing in the New Testament gives consolation to a religious warrior.

(For a longer discussion of this topic, see *The Goodness of God*, by John Wenham.)

Life Questions: What arguments have you heard Christians use for or against wars?

6 ¶ Then the LORD said to Joshua, "Do not be afraid because of them, for tomorrow at this time I will deliver all of them slain before Israel; you shall hamstring their horses and burn their chariots with fire."

7 So Joshua and all the people of war with him came upon them suddenly by the waters of Merom, and attacked them.

8 The LORD delivered them into the hand of Israel, so that they defeated them, and pursued them as far as Great Sidon and Misrephoth-maim and the valley of Mizpeh to the east; and they struck them until no survivor was left to them.

9 Joshua did to them as the LORD had told him; he hamstrung their horses and burned their chariots with fire.

11:9 Advanced Weaponry

If a guerrilla band in Central America captured an F-16 fighter, what could they do with it? Probably nothing, unless they had trained pilots. The Israelites faced a similar situation. War-horses and chariots were advanced weapons of war that the Israelites would not master for hundreds more years. Joshua probably crippled the captured horses to ensure they would not fall into enemy hands again. Militarily and economically, the Israelites were up against people more sophisticated than they.

10 ¶ Then Joshua turned back at that time, and captured Hazor and struck its king with the sword; for Hazor formerly was the head of all these kingdoms.

11 They struck every person who was in it with the edge of the sword, utterly destroying *them;* there was no one left who breathed. And he burned Hazor with fire.

12 Joshua captured all the cities of these kings, and all their kings, and he struck them with the edge of the sword, *and* utterly destroyed them; just as Moses the servant of the LORD had commanded.

13 However, Israel did not burn any cities that stood on their mounds, except Hazor alone, *which* Joshua burned.

14 All the spoil of these cities and the cattle, the sons of Israel took as their plunder; but they struck every man with the edge of the sword, until they had destroyed them. They left no one who breathed.

15 Just as the LORD had commanded Moses his servant, so Moses commanded Joshua, and so Joshua did; he left nothing undone of all that the LORD had commanded Moses.

16 ¶ Thus Joshua took all that land: the hill country and all the Negev, all that land of Goshen, the lowland, the Arabah, the hill country of Israel and its lowland

17 from Mount Halak, that rises toward Seir, even as far as Baal-gad in the valley of Lebanon at the foot of Mount Hermon. And he captured all their kings and struck them down and put them to death.

18 Joshua waged war a long time with all these kings.

19 There was not a city which made peace with the sons of Israel except the Hivites living in Gibeon; they took them all in battle.

20 For it was of the LORD to harden their hearts, to meet Israel in battle in order that he might utterly destroy them, that they might receive no mercy, but that he might destroy them, just as the LORD had commanded Moses.

21 ¶ Then Joshua came at that time and cut off the Anakim from the hill country, from Hebron, from Debir, from Anab and from all the hill country of Judah and from all the hill country of Israel. Joshua utterly destroyed them with their cities.

22 There were no Anakim left in the land of the sons of Israel; only in Gaza, in Gath, and in Ashdod some remained.

23 So Joshua took the whole land, according to all that the LORD had spoken to Moses, and Joshua gave it for an inheritance to Israel according to their divisions by their tribes. Thus the land had rest from war.

11:23 Two Accounts of Warfare

Judges 1 summarizes the incidents recorded in Joshua, but from a different point of view. Joshua presents the campaign as highly successful; Judges shows that many military goals were never achieved. One possible explanation: Joshua presented the wars as a series of raids on territory and did not include the "mopping up" and settlement process. Judges shows that, after they divided up the land, the Israelites proved far less successful in the second phase of conquest.

Kings Defeated by Israel

12 Now these are the kings of the land whom the sons of Israel defeated, and whose land they possessed beyond the Jordan toward the sunrise, from the valley of the Arnon as far as Mount Hermon, and all the Arabah to the east:

2 Sihon king of the Amorites, who lived in Heshbon, *and* ruled from Aroer, which is on the edge of the valley of the Arnon, both the middle of the valley and half of Gilead, even as far as the brook Jabbok, the border of the sons of Ammon;

3 and the Arabah as far as the Sea of *a*Chin-

a I.e. Galilee

neroth toward the east, and as far as the sea of the Arabah, *even* the Salt Sea, eastward toward Beth-jeshimoth, and on the south, at the foot of the slopes of Pisgah;

4 and the territory of Og king of Bashan, one of the remnant of Rephaim, who lived at Ashtaroth and at Edrei,

5 and ruled over Mount Hermon and Salecah and all Bashan, as far as the border of the Geshurites and the Maacathites, and half of Gilead, *as far as* the border of Sihon king of Heshbon.

6 Moses the servant of the LORD and the sons of Israel defeated them; and Moses the servant of the LORD gave it to the Reubenites and the Gadites and the half-tribe of Manasseh as a possession.

7 ¶ Now these are the kings of the land whom Joshua and the sons of Israel defeated beyond the Jordan toward the west, from Baal-gad in the valley of Lebanon even as far as Mount Halak, which rises toward Seir; and Joshua gave it to the tribes of Israel as a possession according to their divisions,

8 in the hill country, in the lowland, in the Arabah, on the slopes, and in the wilderness, and in the Negev; the Hittite, the Amorite and the Canaanite, the Perizzite, the Hivite and the Jebusite:

9 the king of Jericho, one; the king of Ai, which is beside Bethel, one;

10 the king of Jerusalem, one; the king of Hebron, one;

11 the king of Jarmuth, one; the king of Lachish, one;

12 the king of Eglon, one; the king of Gezer, one;

13 the king of Debir, one; the king of Geder, one;

14 the king of Hormah, one; the king of Arad, one;

15 the king of Libnah, one; the king of Adullam, one;

16 the king of Makkedah, one; the king of Bethel, one;

17 the king of Tappuah, one; the king of Hepher, one;

18 the king of Aphek, one; the king of Lasharon, one;

19 the king of Madon, one; the king of Hazor, one;

20 the king of Shimron-meron, one; the king of Achshaph, one;

21 the king of Taanach, one; the king of Megiddo, one;

22 the king of Kedesh, one; the king of Jokneam in Carmel, one;

23 the king of Dor in the heights of Dor, one; the king of Goiim in Gilgal, one;

24 the king of Tirzah, one: in all, thirty-one kings.

Canaan Divided among the Tribes

13 Now Joshua was old *and* advanced in years when the LORD said to him, "You are old *and* advanced in years, and very much of the land remains to be possessed.

13:1 Dividing Up the Land

Chapter 13 introduces an abrupt transition. The rest of Joshua tells about what happened five to seven years after the crossing of the Jordan. Chapters 13–22 give a kind of land-title record for the new nation. Genesis 48–49 and Deuteronomy 33 provide background material. For example, Reuben's tribe forfeited the right to first choice because of a sexual sin, and Simeon and Levi lost their rights because of their violent past.

2 "This is the land that remains: all the regions *of* the Philistines and all *those of* the Geshurites;

3 from the Shihor which is east of Egypt, even as far as the border of Ekron to the north (it is counted as Canaanite); the five lords of the Philistines: the Gazite, the Ashdodite, the Ashkelonite, the Gittite, the Ekronite; and the Avvite

4 to the south, all the land of the Canaanite, and Mearah that belongs to the Sidonians, as far as Aphek, to the border of the Amorite;

5 and the land of the Gebalite, and all of Lebanon, toward the east, from Baal-gad below Mount Hermon as far as Lebo-hamath.

6 "All the inhabitants of the hill country from Lebanon as far as Misrephoth-maim, all the Sidonians, I will drive them out from before the sons of Israel; only allot it to Israel for an inheritance as I have commanded you.

7 "Now therefore, apportion this land for an inheritance to the nine tribes and the half-tribe of Manasseh."

8 ¶ With the other half-tribe, the Reubenites and the Gadites received their inheritance which Moses gave them beyond the Jordan to the east, just as Moses the servant of the LORD gave to them;

9 from Aroer, which is on the edge of the valley of the Arnon, with the city which is in the middle of the valley, and all the plain of Medeba, as far as Dibon;

10 and all the cities of Sihon king of the Amorites, who reigned in Heshbon, as far as the border of the sons of Ammon;

11 and Gilead, and the territory of the Geshurites and Maacathites, and all Mount Hermon, and all Bashan as far as Salecah;

12 all the kingdom of Og in Bashan, who reigned in Ashtaroth and in Edrei (he alone was left of the remnant of the Rephaim); for Moses struck them and dispossessed them.

13 But the sons of Israel did not dispossess the

Geshurites or the Maacathites; for Geshur and Maacath live among Israel until this day.

14 Only to the tribe of Levi he did not give an inheritance; the offerings by fire to the LORD, the God of Israel, are their inheritance, as He spoke to him.

15 ¶ So Moses gave *an inheritance* to the tribe of the sons of Reuben according to their families.

16 Their territory was from Aroer, which is on the edge of the valley of the Arnon, with the city which is in the middle of the valley and all the plain by Medeba;

17 Heshbon, and all its cities which are on the plain: Dibon and Bamoth-baal and Beth-baal-meon,

18 and Jahaz and Kedemoth and Mephaath,

19 and Kiriathaim and Sibmah and Zereth-shahar on the hill of the valley,

20 and Beth-peor and the slopes of Pisgah and Beth-jeshimoth,

21 even all the cities of the plain and all the kingdom of Sihon king of the Amorites who reigned in Heshbon, whom Moses struck with the chiefs of Midian, Evi and Rekem and Zur and Hur and Reba, the princes of Sihon, who lived in the land.

22 The sons of Israel also killed Balaam the son of Beor, the diviner, with the sword among *the rest of* their slain.

23 The border of the sons of Reuben was the Jordan. This was the inheritance of the sons of Reuben according to their families, the cities and their villages.

24 ¶ Moses also gave *an inheritance* to the tribe of Gad, to the sons of Gad, according to their families.

25 Their territory was Jazer, and all the cities of Gilead, and half the land of the sons of Ammon, as far as Aroer which is before Rabbah;

26 and from Heshbon as far as Ramath-mizpeh and Betonim, and from Mahanaim as far as the border of Debir;

27 and in the valley, Beth-haram and Beth-nimrah and Succoth and Zaphon, the rest of the kingdom of Sihon king of Heshbon, with the Jordan as a border, as far as the *lower* end of the Sea of Chinnereth beyond the Jordan to the east.

28 This is the inheritance of the sons of Gad according to their families, the cities and their villages.

29 ¶ Moses also gave *an inheritance* to the half-tribe of Manasseh; and it was for the half-tribe of the sons of Manasseh according to their families.

30 Their territory was from Mahanaim, all Bashan, all the kingdom of Og king of Bashan, and all the towns of Jair, which are in Bashan, sixty cities;

31 also half of Gilead, with Ashtaroth and Edrei, the cities of the kingdom of Og in Bashan, *were* for the sons of Machir the son of Manasseh,

for half of the sons of Machir according to their families.

32 ¶ These are *the territories* which Moses apportioned for an inheritance in the plains of Moab, beyond the Jordan at Jericho to the east.

33 But to the tribe of Levi, Moses did not give an inheritance; the LORD, the God of Israel, is their inheritance, as He had promised to them.

Caleb's Request

14 Now these are *the territories* which the sons of Israel inherited in the land of Canaan, which Eleazar the priest, and Joshua the son of Nun, and the heads of the households of the tribes of the sons of Israel apportioned to them for an inheritance,

2 by the lot of their inheritance, as the LORD commanded through Moses, for the nine tribes and the half-tribe.

3 For Moses had given the inheritance of the two tribes and the half-tribe beyond the Jordan; but he did not give an inheritance to the Levites among them.

4 For the sons of Joseph were two tribes, Manasseh and Ephraim, and they did not give a portion to the Levites in the land, except cities to live in, with their pasture lands for their livestock and for their property.

5 Thus the sons of Israel did just as the LORD had commanded Moses, and they divided the land.

6 ¶ Then the sons of Judah drew near to Joshua in Gilgal, and Caleb the son of Jephunneh the Kenizzite said to him, "You know the word which the LORD spoke to Moses the man of God concerning you and me in Kadesh-barnea.

7 "I was forty years old when Moses the servant of the LORD sent me from Kadesh-barnea to spy out the land, and I brought word back to him as *it was* in my heart.

8 "Nevertheless my brethren who went up with me made the heart of the people melt with fear; but I followed the LORD my God fully.

9 "So Moses swore on that day, saying, 'Surely the land on which your foot has trodden will be an inheritance to you and to your children forever, because you have followed the LORD my God fully.'

10 "Now behold, the LORD has let me live, just as He spoke, these forty-five years, from the time that the LORD spoke this word to Moses, when Israel walked in the wilderness; and now behold, I am eighty-five years old today.

11 "I am still as strong today as I was in the day Moses sent me; as my strength was then, so my strength is now, for war and for going out and coming in.

12 "Now then, give me this hill country about which the LORD spoke on that day, for you heard on that day that Anakim *were* there, with great fortified cities; perhaps the LORD will be with me,

and I will drive them out as the LORD has spoken."

13 ¶ So Joshua blessed him and gave Hebron to Caleb the son of Jephunneh for an inheritance.

14 Therefore, Hebron became the inheritance

14:10 Seven-Year Fight

Just how long did the capture of Palestine take? The book of Joshua doesn't say, but a little arithmetic shows that the fighting had been going on for about seven years. Caleb was 40 when Moses first sent him to explore the land (verse 7). Israel spent 38 years in the desert after that (Deuteronomy 2:14), making Caleb 78 when they finally invaded. Since he had now reached 85, the last seven years of Caleb's life must have been spent fighting. He was one of the two oldest Israelites; all others of his generation had died in the desert.

of Caleb the son of Jephunneh the Kenizzite until this day, because he followed the LORD God of Israel fully.

15 Now the name of Hebron was formerly Kiriath-arba; *for Arba* was the greatest man among the Anakim. Then the land had rest from war.

Territory of Judah

15 Now the lot for the tribe of the sons of Judah according to their families reached the border of Edom, southward to the wilderness of Zin at the extreme south.

2 Their south border was from the lower end of the Salt Sea, from the bay that turns to the south.

3 Then it proceeded southward to the ascent of Akrabbim and continued to Zin, then went up by the south of Kadesh-barnea and continued to Hezron, and went up to Addar and turned about to Karka.

4 It continued to Azmon and proceeded to the brook of Egypt, and the border ended at the sea. This shall be your south border.

5 The east border *was* the Salt Sea, as far as the mouth of the Jordan. And the border of the north side was from the bay of the sea at the mouth of the Jordan.

6 Then the border went up to Beth-hoglah, and continued on the north of Beth-arabah, and the border went up to the stone of Bohan the son of Reuben.

7 The border went up to Debir from the valley of Achor, and turned northward toward Gilgal which is opposite the ascent of Adummim, which is on the south of the valley; and the border continued to the waters of En-shemesh and it ended at En-rogel.

8 Then the border went up the valley of Ben-hinnom to the slope of the Jebusite on the south

(that is, Jerusalem); and the border went up to the top of the mountain which is before the valley of Hinnom to the west, which is at the end of the valley of Rephaim toward the north.

9 From the top of the mountain the border curved to the spring of the waters of Nephtoah and proceeded to the cities of Mount Ephron, then the border curved to Baalah (that is, Kiriath-jearim).

10 The border turned about from Baalah westward to Mount Seir, and continued to the slope of Mount Jearim on the north (that is, Chesalon), and went down to Beth-shemesh and continued through Timnah.

11 The border proceeded to the side of Ekron northward. Then the border curved to Shikkeron and continued to Mount Baalah and proceeded to Jabneel, and the border ended at the sea.

12 The west border *was* at the Great Sea, even *its* coastline. This is the border around the sons of Judah according to their families.

13 ¶ Now he gave to Caleb the son of Jephunneh a portion among the sons of Judah, according to the command of the LORD to Joshua, *namely,* Kiriath-arba, *Arba being* the father of Anak (that is, Hebron).

14 Caleb drove out from there the three sons of Anak: Sheshai and Ahiman and Talmai, the children of Anak.

15 Then he went up from there against the inhabitants of Debir; now the name of Debir formerly was Kiriath-sepher.

16 And Caleb said, "The one who attacks Kiriath-sepher and captures it, I will give him Achsah my daughter as a wife."

17 Othniel the son of Kenaz, the brother of Caleb, captured it; so he gave him Achsah his daughter as a wife.

18 It came about that when she came *to him,* she persuaded him to ask her father for a field. So she alighted from the donkey, and Caleb said to her, "What do you want?"

19 Then she said, "Give me a blessing; since you have given me the land of the Negev, give me also springs of water." So he gave her the upper springs and the lower springs.

20 ¶ This is the inheritance of the tribe of the sons of Judah according to their families.

21 ¶ Now the cities at the extremity of the tribe of the sons of Judah toward the border of Edom in the south were Kabzeel and Eder and Jagur,

22 and Kinah and Dimonah and Adadah,

23 and Kedesh and Hazor and Ithnan,

24 Ziph and Telem and Bealoth,

25 and Hazor-hadattah and Kerioth-hezron (that is, Hazor),

26 Amam and Shema and Moladah,

27 and Hazar-gaddah and Heshmon and Beth-pelet,

28 and Hazar-shual and Beersheba and Biziothiah,

29 Baalah and Iim and Ezem,

30 and Eltolad and Chesil and Hormah,

31 and Ziklag and Madmannah and Sansannah,

32 and Lebaoth and Shilhim and Ain and Rimmon; in all, twenty-nine cities with their villages.

33 ¶ In the lowland: Eshtaol and Zorah and Ashnah,

34 and Zanoah and En-gannim, Tappuah and Enam,

35 Jarmuth and Adullam, Socoh and Azekah,

36 and Shaaraim and Adithaim and Gederah and Gederothaim; fourteen cities with their villages.

37 ¶ Zenan and Hadashah and Migdal-gad,

38 and Dilean and Mizpeh and Joktheel,

39 Lachish and Bozkath and Eglon,

40 and Cabbon and Lahmas and Chitlish,

41 and Gederoth, Beth-dagon and Naamah and Makkedah; sixteen cities with their villages.

42 ¶ Libnah and Ether and Ashan,

43 and Iphtah and Ashnah and Nezib,

44 and Keilah and Achzib and Mareshah; nine cities with their villages.

45 ¶ Ekron, with its towns and its villages;

46 from Ekron even to the sea, all that were by the side of Ashdod, with their villages.

47 ¶ Ashdod, its towns and its villages; Gaza, its towns and its villages; as far as the brook of Egypt and the Great Sea, even *its* coastline.

48 ¶ In the hill country: Shamir and Jattir and Socoh,

49 and Dannah and Kiriath-sannah (that is, Debir),

50 and Anab and Eshtemoh and Anim,

51 and Goshen and Holon and Giloh; eleven cities with their villages.

52 ¶ Arab and Dumah and Eshan,

53 and Janum and Beth-tappuah and Aphekah,

54 and Humtah and Kiriath-arba (that is, Hebron), and Zior; nine cities with their villages.

55 ¶ Maon, Carmel and Ziph and Juttah,

56 and Jezreel and Jokdeam and Zanoah,

57 Kain, Gibeah and Timnah; ten cities with their villages.

58 ¶ Halhul, Beth-zur and Gedor,

59 and Maarath and Beth-anoth and Eltekon; six cities with their villages.

60 ¶ Kiriath-baal (that is, Kiriath-jearim), and Rabbah; two cities with their villages.

61 ¶ In the wilderness: Beth-arabah, Middin and Secacah,

62 and Nibshan and the City of Salt and En-gedi; six cities with their villages.

63 ¶ Now as for the Jebusites, the inhabitants of Jerusalem, the sons of Judah could not drive them out; so the Jebusites live with the sons of Judah at Jerusalem until this day.

Territory of Ephraim

16 Then the lot for the sons of Joseph went from the Jordan at Jericho to the waters of Jericho on the east into the wilderness, going up from Jericho through the hill country to Bethel.

15:63 Hints of Failure

In several key places (13:2–7; 16:10; 23:4) and in Judges 1, the Bible indicates that pockets of Canaanites remained in the land. The Israelites "could not drive them out." The unconquered tribes became thorns in Israel's side.

2 It went from Bethel to Luz, and continued to the border of the Archites at Ataroth.

3 It went down westward to the territory of the Japhletites, as far as the territory of lower Beth-horon even to Gezer, and it ended at the sea.

4 ¶ The sons of Joseph, Manasseh and Ephraim, received their inheritance.

5 Now *this* was the territory of the sons of Ephraim according to their families: the border of their inheritance eastward was Ataroth-addar, as far as upper Beth-horon.

6 Then the border went westward at Michmethath on the north, and the border turned about eastward to Taanath-shiloh and continued *beyond* it to the east of Janoah.

7 It went down from Janoah to Ataroth and to Naarah, then reached Jericho and came out at the Jordan.

8 From Tappuah the border continued westward to the brook of Kanah, and it ended at the sea. This is the inheritance of the tribe of the sons of Ephraim according to their families,

9 *together* with the cities which were set apart for the sons of Ephraim in the midst of the inheritance of the sons of Manasseh, all the cities with their villages.

10 But they did not drive out the Canaanites who lived in Gezer, so the Canaanites live in the midst of Ephraim to this day, and they became forced laborers.

Territory of Manasseh

17 Now *this* was the lot for the tribe of Manasseh, for he was the firstborn of Joseph. To Machir the firstborn of Manasseh, the father of Gilead, were allotted Gilead and Bashan, because he was a man of war.

2 So *the lot* was *made* for the rest of the sons of Manasseh according to their families: for the sons of Abiezer and for the sons of Helek and for the sons of Asriel and for the sons of Shechem and for the sons of Hepher and for the sons of Shemida; these *were* the male descendants of Manasseh the son of Joseph according to their families.

3 ¶ However, Zelophehad, the son of Hepher,

the son of Gilead, the son of Machir, the son of Manasseh, had no sons, only daughters; and these are the names of his daughters: Mahlah and Noah, Hoglah, Milcah and Tirzah.

4 They came near before Eleazar the priest and before Joshua the son of Nun and before the leaders, saying, "The LORD commanded Moses to give us an inheritance among our brothers." So according to the command of the LORD he gave them an inheritance among their father's brothers.

17:4 Daughters' Rights

See Numbers 27:1–11 and Numbers 36 for the historical context to these women's appeal.

5 Thus there fell ten portions to Manasseh, besides the land of Gilead and Bashan, which is beyond the Jordan,

6 because the daughters of Manasseh received an inheritance among his sons. And the land of Gilead belonged to the rest of the sons of Manasseh.

7 ¶ The border of Manasseh ran from Asher to Michmethath which was east of Shechem; then the border went southward to the inhabitants of En-tappuah.

8 The land of Tappuah belonged to Manasseh, but Tappuah on the border of Manasseh *belonged* to the sons of Ephraim.

9 The border went down to the brook of Kanah, southward of the brook (these cities *belonged* to Ephraim among the cities of Manasseh), and the border of Manasseh *was* on the north side of the brook and it ended at the sea.

10 The south side *belonged* to Ephraim and the north side to Manasseh, and the sea was their border; and they reached to Asher on the north and to Issachar on the east.

11 In Issachar and in Asher, Manasseh had Beth-shean and its towns and Ibleam and its towns, and the inhabitants of Dor and its towns, and the inhabitants of En-dor and its towns, and the inhabitants of Taanach and its towns, and the inhabitants of Megiddo and its towns, the third is Napheth.

12 But the sons of Manasseh could not take possession of these cities, because the Canaanites persisted in living in that land.

13 It came about when the sons of Israel became strong, they put the Canaanites to forced labor, but they did not drive them out completely.

14 ¶ Then the sons of Joseph spoke to Joshua, saying, "Why have you given me only one lot and one portion for an inheritance, since I am a numerous people whom the LORD has thus far blessed?"

15 Joshua said to them, "If you are a numerous people, go up to the forest and clear a place for yourself there in the land of the Perizzites and of the Rephaim, since the hill country of Ephraim is too narrow for you."

16 The sons of Joseph said, "The hill country is not enough for us, and all the Canaanites who live in the valley land have chariots of iron, both those who are in Beth-shean and its towns and those who are in the valley of Jezreel."

17 Joshua spoke to the house of Joseph, to Ephraim and Manasseh, saying, "You are a numerous people and have great power; you shall not have one lot *only*,

18 but the hill country shall be yours. For though it is a forest, you shall clear it, and to its farthest borders it shall be yours; for you shall drive out the Canaanites, even though they have chariots of iron *and* though they are strong."

Rest of the Land Divided

18 Then the whole congregation of the sons of Israel assembled themselves at Shiloh, and set up the tent of meeting there; and the land was subdued before them.

2 ¶ There remained among the sons of Israel seven tribes who had not divided their inheritance.

3 So Joshua said to the sons of Israel, "How long will you put off entering to take possession of the land which the LORD, the God of your fathers, has given you?

18:3 Missing an Opportunity

Such verses as 17:13 and 18:3 imply that the Israelites could have driven out the Canaanites, but chose not to. They were using the Canaanites for forced labor and demanding tribute from them—perhaps they learned to rely too comfortably on these services. Also, some tribes balked at campaigns simply because of fear (17:16).

4 "Provide for yourselves three men from each tribe that I may send them, and that they may arise and walk through the land and write a description of it according to their inheritance; then they shall return to me.

5 "They shall divide it into seven portions; Judah shall stay in its territory on the south, and the house of Joseph shall stay in their territory on the north.

6 "You shall describe the land in seven divisions, and bring *the description* here to me. I will cast lots for you here before the LORD our God.

7 "For the Levites have no portion among you, because the priesthood of the LORD is their inheritance. Gad and Reuben and the half-tribe of Manasseh also have received their inheritance eastward beyond the Jordan, which Moses the servant of the LORD gave them."

8 ¶ Then the men arose and went, and Joshua commanded those who went to describe the land, saying, "Go and walk through the land and describe it, and return to me; then I will cast lots for you here before the LORD in Shiloh."

9 So the men went and passed through the land, and described it by cities in seven divisions in a book; and they came to Joshua to the camp at Shiloh.

10 And Joshua cast lots for them in Shiloh before the LORD, and there Joshua divided the land to the sons of Israel according to their divisions.

The Territory of Benjamin

11 ¶ Now the lot of the tribe of the sons of Benjamin came up according to their families, and the territory of their lot lay between the sons of Judah and the sons of Joseph.

12 Their border on the north side was from the Jordan, then the border went up to the side of Jericho on the north, and went up through the hill country westward, and *a*it ended at the wilderness of Beth-aven.

13 From there the border continued to Luz, to the side of Luz (that is, Bethel) southward; and the border went down to Ataroth-addar, near the hill which *lies* on the south of lower Beth-horon.

14 The border extended *from there* and turned round on the west side southward, from the hill which *lies* before Beth-horon southward; and *a*it ended at Kiriath-baal (that is, Kiriath-jearim), a city of the sons of Judah. This *was* the west side.

15 Then the south side *was* from the edge of Kiriath-jearim, and the border went westward and went to the fountain of the waters of Nephtoah.

16 The border went down to the edge of the hill which is in the valley of Ben-hinnom, which is in the valley of Rephaim northward; and it went down to the valley of Hinnom, to the slope of the Jebusite southward, and went down to En-rogel.

17 It extended northward and went to En-shemesh and went to Geliloth, which is opposite the ascent of Adummim, and it went down to the stone of Bohan the son of Reuben.

18 It continued to the side in front of the Arabah northward and went down to the Arabah.

19 The border continued to the side of Beth-hoglah northward; and the *b*border ended at the north bay of the Salt Sea, at the south end of the Jordan. This *was* the south border.

20 Moreover, the Jordan was its border on the east side. This *was* the inheritance of the sons of Benjamin, according to their families *and* according to its borders all around.

21 ¶ Now the cities of the tribe of the sons of Benjamin according to their families were Jericho and Beth-hoglah and Emek-keziz,

22 and Beth-arabah and Zemaraim and Bethel,

23 and Avvim and Parah and Ophrah,

24 and Chephar-ammoni and Ophni and Geba; twelve cities with their villages.

25 Gibeon and Ramah and Beeroth,

26 and Mizpeh and Chephirah and Mozah,

27 and Rekem and Irpeel and Taralah,

28 and Zelah, Haeleph and the Jebusite (that is, Jerusalem), Gibeah, Kiriath; fourteen cities with their villages. This is the inheritance of the sons of Benjamin according to their families.

Territory of Simeon

19 Then the second lot fell to Simeon, to the tribe of the sons of Simeon according to their families, and their inheritance was in the midst of the inheritance of the sons of Judah.

2 So they had as their inheritance Beersheba or Sheba and Moladah,

3 and Hazar-shual and Balah and Ezem,

4 and Eltolad and Bethul and Hormah,

5 and Ziklag and Beth-marcaboth and Hazar-susah,

6 and Beth-lebaoth and Sharuhen; thirteen cities with their villages;

7 Ain, Rimmon and Ether and Ashan; four cities with their villages;

8 and all the villages which *were* around these cities as far as Baalath-beer, Ramah of the Negev. This *was* the inheritance of the tribe of the sons of Simeon according to their families.

9 The inheritance of the sons of Simeon *was taken* from the portion of the sons of Judah, for the share of the sons of Judah was too large for them; so the sons of Simeon received *an* inheritance in the midst of Judah's inheritance.

Territory of Zebulun

10 ¶ Now the third lot came up for the sons of Zebulun according to their families. And the territory of their inheritance was as far as Sarid.

11 Then their border went up to the west and to Maralah, it then touched Dabbesheth and reached to the brook that is before Jokneam.

12 Then it turned from Sarid to the east toward the sunrise as far as the border of Chisloth-tabor, and it proceeded to Daberath and up to Japhia.

13 From there it continued eastward toward the sunrise to Gath-hepher, to Eth-kazin, and it proceeded to Rimmon which stretches to Neah.

14 The border circled around it on the north to Hannathon, and it ended at the valley of Iphtahel.

15 *Included* also *were* Kattah and Nahalal and Shimron and Idalah and Bethlehem; twelve cities with their villages.

16 This *was* the inheritance of the sons of Zebulun according to their families, these cities with their villages.

Territory of Issachar

17 ¶ The fourth lot fell to Issachar, to the sons of Issachar according to their families.

---

a Lit *the goings out of it were*   *b* Lit *goings out of the border were*

18 Their territory was to Jezreel and *included* Chesulloth and Shunem,

19 and Hapharaim and Shion and Anaharath,

20 and Rabbith and Kishion and Ebez,

21 and Remeth and En-gannim and En-haddah and Beth-pazzez.

22 The border reached to Tabor and Shahazumah and Beth-shemesh, and their border ended at the Jordan; sixteen cities with their villages.

23 This *was* the inheritance of the tribe of the sons of Issachar according to their families, the cities with their villages.

Territory of Asher

24 ¶ Now the fifth lot fell to the tribe of the sons of Asher according to their families.

25 Their territory was Helkath and Hali and Beten and Achshaph,

26 and Allammelech and Amad and Mishal; and it reached to Carmel on the west and to Shihor-libnath.

27 It turned toward the east to Beth-dagon and reached to Zebulun, and to the valley of Iphtahel northward to Beth-emek and Neiel; then it proceeded on north to Cabul,

28 and Ebron and Rehob and Hammon and Kanah, as far as Great Sidon.

29 The border turned to Ramah and to the fortified city of Tyre; then the border turned to Hosah, and it ended at the sea by the region of Achzib.

30 *Included* also *were* Ummah, and Aphek and Rehob; twenty-two cities with their villages.

31 This *was* the inheritance of the tribe of the sons of Asher according to their families, these cities with their villages.

Territory of Naphtali

32 ¶ The sixth lot fell to the sons of Naphtali; to the sons of Naphtali according to their families.

33 Their border was from Heleph, from the oak in Zaanannim and Adami-nekeb and Jabneel, as far as Lakkum, and it ended at the Jordan.

34 Then the border turned westward to Aznoth-tabor and proceeded from there to Hukkok; and it reached to Zebulun on the south and touched Asher on the west, and to Judah at the Jordan toward the east.

35 The fortified cities *were* Ziddim, Zer and Hammath, Rakkath and Chinnereth,

36 and Adamah and Ramah and Hazor,

37 and Kedesh and Edrei and En-hazor,

38 and Yiron and Migdal-el, Horem and Beth-anath and Beth-shemesh; nineteen cities with their villages.

39 This *was* the inheritance of the tribe of the sons of Naphtali according to their families, the cities with their villages.

Territory of Dan

40 ¶ The seventh lot fell to the tribe of the sons of Dan according to their families.

41 The territory of their inheritance was Zorah and Eshtaol and Ir-shemesh,

42 and Shaalabbin and Aijalon and Ithlah,

43 and Elon and Timnah and Ekron,

44 and Eltekeh and Gibbethon and Baalath,

45 and Jehud and Bene-berak and Gath-rimmon,

46 and Me-jarkon and Rakkon, with the territory over against Joppa.

47 The territory of the sons of Dan proceeded beyond them; for the sons of Dan went up and fought with Leshem and captured it. Then they struck it with the edge of the sword and possessed it and settled in it; and they called Leshem Dan after the name of Dan their father.

48 This *was* the inheritance of the tribe of the sons of Dan according to their families, these cities with their villages.

49 ¶ When they finished apportioning the land for inheritance by its borders, the sons of Israel gave an inheritance in their midst to Joshua the son of Nun.

50 In accordance with the command of the LORD they gave him the city for which he asked, Timnath-serah in the hill country of Ephraim. So he built the city and settled in it.

51 ¶ These are the inheritances which Eleazar the priest, and Joshua the son of Nun, and the heads of the households of the tribes of the sons of Israel distributed by lot in Shiloh before the LORD at the doorway of the tent of meeting. So they finished dividing the land.

Six Cities of Refuge

20 Then the LORD spoke to Joshua, saying, 2 "Speak to the sons of Israel, saying, 'Designate the cities of refuge, of which I spoke to you through Moses,

20:2 Cities of Refuge

The cities of refuge were designed to aid a person who caused an accidental death or "involuntary manslaughter." They provided a sanctuary from revenge. They did not, however, shelter a person who had committed a premeditated, intentional murder. (See Numbers 35:6 and Deuteronomy 4:41–43; 19:1–21.)

3 that the manslayer who kills any person unintentionally, without premeditation, may flee there, and they shall become your refuge from the avenger of blood.

4 'He shall flee to one of these cities, and shall stand at the entrance of the gate of the city and

state his case in the hearing of the elders of that city; and they shall take him into the city to them and give him a place, so that he may dwell among them.

5 'Now if the avenger of blood pursues him, then they shall not deliver the manslayer into his hand, because he struck his neighbor without premeditation and did not hate him beforehand.

6 'He shall dwell in that city until he stands before the congregation for judgment, until the death of the one who is high priest in those days. Then the manslayer shall return to his own city and to his own house, to the city from which he fled.'"

7 ¶ So they set apart Kedesh in Galilee in the hill country of Naphtali and Shechem in the hill country of Ephraim, and Kiriath-arba (that is, Hebron) in the hill country of Judah.

8 Beyond the Jordan east of Jericho, they designated Bezer in the wilderness on the plain from the tribe of Reuben, and Ramoth in Gilead from the tribe of Gad, and Golan in Bashan from the tribe of Manasseh.

9 These were the appointed cities for all the sons of Israel and for the stranger who sojourns among them, that whoever kills any person unintentionally may flee there, and not die by the hand of the avenger of blood until he stands before the congregation.

Forty-eight Cities of the Levites

21 Then the heads of households of the Levites approached Eleazar the priest, and Joshua the son of Nun, and the heads of households of the tribes of the sons of Israel.

2 They spoke to them at Shiloh in the land of Canaan, saying, "The LORD commanded through Moses to give us cities to live in, with their pasture lands for our cattle."

3 So the sons of Israel gave the Levites from their inheritance these cities with their pasture lands, according to the command of the LORD.

4 Then the lot came out for the families of the Kohathites. And the sons of Aaron the priest, who were of the Levites, received thirteen cities by lot from the tribe of Judah and from the tribe of the Simeonites and from the tribe of Benjamin.

5 ¶ The rest of the sons of Kohath received ten cities by lot from the families of the tribe of Ephraim and from the tribe of Dan and from the half-tribe of Manasseh.

6 ¶ The sons of Gershon received thirteen cities by lot from the families of the tribe of Issachar and from the tribe of Asher and from the tribe of Naphtali and from the half-tribe of Manasseh in Bashan.

7 ¶ The sons of Merari according to their families received twelve cities from the tribe of Reuben and from the tribe of Gad and from the tribe of Zebulun.

8 ¶ Now the sons of Israel gave by lot to the Levites these cities with their pasture lands, as the LORD had commanded through Moses.

9 ¶ They gave these cities which are *here* mentioned by name from the tribe of the sons of Judah and from the tribe of the sons of Simeon;

21:8 Towns for the Levites

As part of their calling to serve God, the Levites got no land in Canaan. Rather, they received 48 towns scattered in the other tribes' lands—four towns from each tribe. This forced them to depend not on their inheritance of the land, but on God (see Numbers 18:20). It dispersed the priests among all the people and enabled them to instruct the tribes in the law and to lead worship.

10 and they were for the sons of Aaron, one of the families of the Kohathites, of the sons of Levi, for the lot was theirs first.

11 Thus they gave them Kiriath-arba, *Arba being* the father of Anak (that is, Hebron), in the hill country of Judah, with its surrounding pasture lands.

12 But the fields of the city and its villages they gave to Caleb the son of Jephunneh as his possession.

13 ¶ So to the sons of Aaron the priest they gave Hebron, the city of refuge for the manslayer, with its pasture lands, and Libnah with its pasture lands,

14 and Jattir with its pasture lands and Eshtemoa with its pasture lands,

15 and Holon with its pasture lands and Debir with its pasture lands,

16 and Ain with its pasture lands and Juttah with its pasture lands *and* Beth-shemesh with its pasture lands; nine cities from these two tribes.

17 From the tribe of Benjamin, Gibeon with its pasture lands, Geba with its pasture lands,

18 Anathoth with its pasture lands and Almon with its pasture lands; four cities.

19 All the cities of the sons of Aaron, the priests, were thirteen cities with their pasture lands.

20 ¶ Then the cities from the tribe of Ephraim were allotted to the families of the sons of Kohath, the Levites, *even to* the rest of the sons of Kohath.

21 They gave them Shechem, the city of refuge for the manslayer, with its pasture lands, in the hill country of Ephraim, and Gezer with its pasture lands,

22 and Kibzaim with its pasture lands and Beth-horon with its pasture lands; four cities.

23 From the tribe of Dan, Elteke with its pasture lands, Gibbethon with its pasture lands,

24 Aijalon with its pasture lands, Gathrimmon with its pasture lands; four cities.

25 From the half-tribe of Manasseh, *they allot-*

ted Taanach with its pasture lands and Gath-rimmon with its pasture lands; two cities.

26 All the cities with their pasture lands for the families of the rest of the sons of Kohath were ten.

27 ¶ To the sons of Gershon, one of the families of the Levites, from the half-tribe of Manasseh, *they gave* Golan in Bashan, the city of refuge for the manslayer, with its pasture lands, and Be-eshterah with its pasture lands; two cities.

28 From the tribe of Issachar, *they gave* Kishi-on with its pasture lands, Daberath with its pasture lands,

29 Jarmuth with its pasture lands, En-gannim with its pasture lands; four cities.

30 From the tribe of Asher, *they gave* Mishal with its pasture lands, Abdon with its pasture lands,

31 Helkath with its pasture lands and Rehob with its pasture lands; four cities.

32 From the tribe of Naphtali, *they gave* Ke-desh in Galilee, the city of refuge for the man-slayer, with its pasture lands and Hammoth-dor with its pasture lands and Kartan with its pasture lands; three cities.

33 All the cities of the Gershonites according to their families were thirteen cities with their pasture lands.

34 ¶ To the families of the sons of Merari, the rest of the Levites, *they gave* from the tribe of Zebulun, Jokneam with its pasture lands and Kar-tah with its pasture lands.

35 Dimnah with its pasture lands, Nahalal with its pasture lands; four cities.

36 From the tribe of Reuben, *they gave* Bezer with its pasture lands and Jahaz with its pasture lands,

37 Kedemoth with its pasture lands and Meph-aath with its pasture lands; four cities.

38 From the tribe of Gad, *they gave* Ramoth in Gilead, the city of refuge for the manslayer, with its pasture lands and Mahanaim with its pasture lands,

39 Heshbon with its pasture lands, Jazer with its pasture lands; four cities in all.

40 All *these were* the cities of the sons of Merari according to their families, the rest of the families of the Levites; and their lot was twelve cities.

41 ¶ All the cities of the Levites in the midst of the possession of the sons of Israel were forty-eight cities with their pasture lands.

42 These cities each had its surrounding pasture lands; thus *it was* with all these cities.

43 ¶ So the LORD gave Israel all the land which He had sworn to give to their fathers, and they possessed it and lived in it.

44 And the LORD gave them rest on every side, according to all that He had sworn to their fathers, and no one of all their enemies stood before them; the LORD gave all their enemies into their hand.

45 Not one of the good promises which the LORD had made to the house of Israel failed; all came to pass.

Tribes beyond Jordan Return

22 Then Joshua summoned the Reubenites and the Gadites and the half-tribe of Manasseh,

2 and said to them, "You have kept all that Moses the servant of the LORD commanded you, and have listened to my voice in all that I commanded you.

3 "You have not forsaken your brothers these many days to this day, but have kept the charge of the commandment of the LORD your God.

4 "And now the LORD your God has given rest to your brothers, as He spoke to them; therefore turn now and go to your tents, to the land of your possession, which Moses the servant of the LORD gave you beyond the Jordan.

5 "Only be very careful to observe the commandment and the law which Moses the servant of the LORD commanded you, to love the LORD your God and walk in all His ways and keep His commandments and hold fast to Him and serve Him with all your heart and with all your soul."

6 So Joshua blessed them and sent them away, and they went to their tents.

7 ¶ Now to the one half-tribe of Manasseh Moses had given *a possession* in Bashan, but to the other half Joshua gave *a possession* among their brothers westward beyond the Jordan. So when Joshua sent them away to their tents, he blessed them,

8 and said to them, "Return to your tents with great riches and with very much livestock, with silver, gold, bronze, iron, and with very many clothes; divide the spoil of your enemies with your brothers."

9 The sons of Reuben and the sons of Gad and the half-tribe of Manasseh returned *home* and departed from the sons of Israel at Shiloh which is in the land of Canaan, to go to the land of Gilead, to the land of their possession which they had possessed, according to the command of the LORD through Moses.

The Offensive Altar

10 ¶ When they came to the region of the Jordan which is in the land of Canaan, the sons of Reuben and the sons of Gad and the half-tribe of Manasseh built an altar there by the Jordan, a large altar in appearance.

11 And the sons of Israel heard *it* said, "Behold, the sons of Reuben and the sons of Gad and the half-tribe of Manasseh have built an altar at the frontier of the land of Canaan, in the region of the Jordan, on the side *belonging to* the sons of Israel."

12 When the sons of Israel heard *of it,* the whole congregation of the sons of Israel gathered themselves at Shiloh to go up against them in war.

13 ¶ Then the sons of Israel sent to the sons of Reuben and to the sons of Gad and to the half-tribe of Manasseh, into the land of Gilead, Phinehas the son of Eleazar the priest,

22:10–30 Explosive Quarrel

Chapter 22 records a misunderstanding that could have led to civil war. Several Israelite tribes built a large altar. This inflamed the other tribes. Weren't the builders grossly violating God's law by erecting an altar, a function only priests should perform? Were these tribes so soon abandoning the rules of worship Moses and Joshua had laid down? Or, perhaps, had they provocatively built their altar on the western side of the Jordan River to stake a claim to others' land? The western tribes soon learned the truth: the easterners had built not an altar, but a monument to commemorate their national unity with the western tribes. A civil war was averted after some heated exchanges. The incident reveals the intensity of religious feeling in the new nation.

14 and with him ten chiefs, one chief for each father's household from each of the tribes of Israel; and each one of them *was* the head of his father's household among the thousands of Israel.

15 They came to the sons of Reuben and to the sons of Gad and to the half-tribe of Manasseh, to the land of Gilead, and they spoke with them saying,

16 "Thus says the whole congregation of the LORD, 'What is this unfaithful act which you have committed against the God of Israel, turning away from following the LORD this day, by building yourselves an altar, to rebel against the LORD this day?

17 'Is not the iniquity of Peor enough for us, from which we have not cleansed ourselves to this day, although a plague came on the congregation of the LORD,

18 that you must turn away this day from following the LORD? If you rebel against the LORD today, He will be angry with the whole congregation of Israel tomorrow.

19 'If, however, the land of your possession is unclean, then cross into the land of the possession of the LORD, where the LORD'S tabernacle stands, and take possession among us. Only do not rebel against the LORD, or rebel against us by building an altar for yourselves, besides the altar of the LORD our God.

20 'Did not Achan the son of Zerah act unfaithfully in the things under the ban, and wrath fall on all the congregation of Israel? And that man did not perish alone in his iniquity.' "

21 ¶ Then the sons of Reuben and the sons of Gad and the half-tribe of Manasseh answered and spoke to the heads of the families of Israel.

22 "The Mighty One, God, the LORD, the Mighty One, God, the LORD! He knows, and may Israel itself know. If *it was* in rebellion, or if in an unfaithful act against the LORD do not save us this day!

23 "If we have built us an altar to turn away from following the LORD, or if to offer a burnt offering or grain offering on it, or if to offer sacrifices of peace offerings on it, may the LORD Himself require it.

24 "But truly we have done this out of concern, for a reason, saying, 'In time to come your sons may say to our sons, "What have you to do with the LORD, the God of Israel?

25 "For the LORD has made the Jordan a border between us and you, *you* sons of Reuben and sons of Gad; you have no portion in the LORD." So your sons may make our sons stop fearing the LORD.'

26 ¶ "Therefore we said, 'Let us build an altar, not for burnt offering or for sacrifice;

27 rather it shall be a witness between us and you and between our generations after us, that we are to perform the service of the LORD before Him with our burnt offerings, and with our sacrifices and with our peace offerings, so that your sons will not say to our sons in time to come, "You have no portion in the LORD." '

28 "Therefore we said, 'It shall also come about if they say *this* to us or to our generations in time to come, then we shall say, "See the copy of the altar of the LORD which our fathers made, not for burnt offering or for sacrifice; rather it is a witness between us and you." '

29 "Far be it from us that we should rebel against the LORD and turn away from following the LORD this day, by building an altar for burnt offering, for grain offering or for sacrifice, besides the altar of the LORD our God which is before His [a]tabernacle."

30 ¶ So when Phinehas the priest and the leaders of the congregation, even the heads of the families of Israel who *were* with him, heard the words which the sons of Reuben and the sons of Gad and the sons of Manasseh spoke, it pleased them.

31 And Phinehas the son of Eleazar the priest said to the sons of Reuben and to the sons of Gad and to the sons of Manasseh, "Today we know that the LORD is in our midst, because you have not committed this unfaithful act against the LORD; now you have delivered the sons of Israel from the hand of the LORD."

32 ¶ Then Phinehas the son of Eleazar the priest and the leaders returned from the sons of Reuben and from the sons of Gad, from the land of Gilead to the land of Canaan, to the sons of Israel, and brought back word to them.

[a] Lit *dwelling place*

33 The word pleased the sons of Israel, and the sons of Israel blessed God; and they did not speak of going up against them in war to destroy the land in which the sons of Reuben and the sons of Gad were living.

34 The sons of Reuben and the sons of Gad called the altar *Witness;* "For," *they said,* "it is a witness between us that the LORD is God."

Joshua's Farewell Address

23 Now it came about after many days, when the LORD had given rest to Israel from all their enemies on every side, and Joshua was old, advanced in years,

2 that Joshua called for all Israel, for their elders and their heads and their judges and their officers, and said to them, "I am old, advanced in years.

3 "And you have seen all that the LORD your God has done to all these nations because of you, for the LORD your God is He who has been fighting for you.

4 "See, I have apportioned to you these nations which remain as an inheritance for your tribes, with all the nations which I have cut off, from the Jordan even to the Great Sea toward the setting of the sun.

5 "The LORD your God, He will thrust them out from before you and drive them from before you; and you will possess their land, just as the LORD your God promised you.

6 "Be very firm, then, to keep and do all that is written in the book of the law of Moses, so that you may not turn aside from it to the right hand or to the left,

7 so that you will not associate with these nations, these which remain among you, or mention the name of their gods, or make *anyone* swear *by them,* or serve them, or bow down to them.

8 "But you are to cling to the LORD your God, as you have done to this day.

9 "For the LORD has driven out great and strong nations from before you; and as for you, no man has stood before you to this day.

10 "One of your men puts to flight a thousand, for the LORD your God is He who fights for you, just as He promised you.

11 "So take diligent heed to yourselves to love the LORD your God.

12 "For if you ever go back and cling to the rest of these nations, these which remain among you, and intermarry with them, so that you associate with them and they with you,

13 know with certainty that the LORD your God will not continue to drive these nations out from before you; but they will be a snare and a trap to you, and a whip on your sides and thorns in your eyes, until you perish from off this good land which the LORD your God has given you.

14 ¶ "Now behold, today I am going the way of all the earth, and you know in all your hearts and in all your souls that not one word of all the good words which the LORD your God spoke concerning you has failed; all have been fulfilled for you, not one of them has failed.

15 "It shall come about that just as all the good words which the LORD your God spoke to you have come upon you, so the LORD will bring upon you all the threats, until He has destroyed you from off this good land which the LORD your God has given you.

16 "When you transgress the covenant of the LORD your God, which He commanded you, and go and serve other gods and bow down to them, then the anger of the LORD will burn against you, and you will perish quickly from off the good land which He has given you."

Joshua Reviews Israel's History

24 Then Joshua gathered all the tribes of Israel to Shechem, and called for the elders of Israel and for their heads and their judges and their officers; and they presented themselves before God.

2 Joshua said to all the people, "Thus says the LORD, the God of Israel, 'From ancient times your fathers lived beyond the *a*River, *namely,* Terah, the father of Abraham and the father of Nahor, and they served other gods.

24:2 Joshua's Farewell

Joshua's final speech has many similarities to the much longer speeches given by Moses in Deuteronomy. Both follow the pattern of a treaty between a ruler and his people. Joshua used the occasion to renew the covenant between God and the Israelites (verses 25–27). For more details, see the description of "suzerainty treaties" in "How to Read Deuteronomy," page 211.

3 'Then I took your father Abraham from beyond the *a*River, and led him through all the land of Canaan, and multiplied his descendants and gave him Isaac.

4 'To Isaac I gave Jacob and Esau, and to Esau I gave Mount Seir to possess it; but Jacob and his sons went down to Egypt.

5 'Then I sent Moses and Aaron, and I plagued Egypt by what I did in its midst; and afterward I brought you out.

6 'I brought your fathers out of Egypt, and you came to the sea; and Egypt pursued your fathers with chariots and horsemen to the Red Sea.

7 'But when they cried out to the LORD, He put darkness between you and the Egyptians, and brought the sea upon them and covered them; and

a I.e. Euphrates

Filling Moses' Shoes
Joshua could follow orders as well as give them

Israel served the LORD all the days of Joshua.
24:31

LIKE ALL THE ISRAELITES, JOSHUA began in humble surroundings. He was born a slave in Egypt and followed Moses across the Red Sea to freedom. He first appears in the Bible as a military commander. Soon after escaping from Egypt, the Israelites confronted a new enemy, and Moses turned to Joshua to lead their very first battle (Exodus 17:9–15).

A month later, when Moses climbed craggy Mount Sinai to meet with God, Joshua was at his side He first reported to Moses the strange sounds coming from the camp, sounds that turned out to be the Israelites' great spiritual rebellion (Exodus 32:17). Joshua rose to become Moses' trusted number-two man, an aide who served him at almost every major crisis. Moses changed his name from Hoshea, which meant "help," or "salvation," to Joshua, meaning "The LORD saves." (The Greek form of Joshua is *Jesus*.)

Becoming Number One

On the verge of entering Canaan, Moses turned to Joshua again, choosing him as one of 12 spies sent to collect information about the land. Ten came back frightened, with predictions of doom. Only Joshua and Caleb had faith that God would keep his promises to the Israelites despite the military odds.

Joshua learned about the hazards of leadership from that spy trip: on his return, thousands of angry Israelites called for his public stoning (Numbers 14). But he stood firm, and God rewarded him. Of all the Israelites who left Egypt, only he and Caleb were allowed to enter the promised land—not even Moses had that honor. As Moses' death neared, God and Moses made Joshua their uncontested choice for a new leader for Israel. It was time for number two to become number one.

Joshua made a remarkably smooth transition into leadership. In fact, Joshua's life had many parallels to that of Moses. The miracle of crossing the Jordan River poignantly replayed Moses' crossing of the Red Sea. Moses encountered God directly at the burning bush; Joshua met God's special representative, the "commander of the army of the LORD," and likewise took off his shoes at the meeting (5:13–15).

Both Moses and Joshua wrote the law onto stones: Moses creating a permanent record for Israel, and Joshua erecting a monument for the nation to pass by on the way into the new land (8:32). Both leaders pleaded with God on behalf of their people. And both ended their terms with stirring speeches that reviewed history and challenged the people toward a critical choice.

Well-rounded Leader

Moses, who grew up in the courts of Pharaoh, obviously received a better education than Joshua. He showed a philosophical bent. Joshua, on the other hand, was action-oriented and pragmatic, a perfect military man. He had the rare combination of knowing how to follow orders as well as how to give them.

The Bible, never guilty of glossing over its heroes' flaws, reveals some of Joshua's mistakes. In one incident in the desert, he was rash (Numbers 11:26–30). During the first battle of Ai and the treaty negotiations with the Gibeonites, he acted impulsively, without first seeking God's advice. And, faced with his first major defeat at Ai, he uncharacteristically dissolved in fright, earning God's stern rebuke: "Rise up! Why is it that you have fallen on your face?" (7:6–12).

Apart from these few incidents, Joshua's life was marked by unusual faith and obedience. Joshua never let the press of military action interfere with worship and the renewal of the covenant. When he divided up the land (an immense bureaucratic burden that takes up the last half of this book), he did so with wisdom and fairness, selecting his own portion only after all others had chosen.

The Bible records this simple legacy: "Israel served the LORD all the days of Joshua" (24:31). History would show how rarely that occurred in the life of a troublesome nation.

Life Questions: Often when a popular leader—a pastor, a politician, a teacher—retires from office, something slips. What made Joshua such an effective replacement?

your own eyes saw what I did in Egypt. And you lived in the wilderness for a long time.

8 'Then I brought you into the land of the Amorites who lived beyond the Jordan, and they fought with you; and I gave them into your hand, and you took possession of their land when I destroyed them before you.

9 'Then Balak the son of Zippor, king of Moab, arose and fought against Israel, and he sent and summoned Balaam the son of Beor to curse you.

10 'But I was not willing to listen to Balaam. So he had to bless you, and I delivered you from his hand.

11 'You crossed the Jordan and came to Jericho; and the citizens of Jericho fought against you, *and* the Amorite and the Perizzite and the Canaanite and the Hittite and the Girgashite, the Hivite and the Jebusite. Thus I gave them into your hand.

12 'Then I sent the hornet before you and it drove out the two kings of the Amorites from before you, *but* not by your sword or your bow.

13 'I gave you a land on which you had not labored, and cities which you had not built, and you have lived in them; you are eating of vineyards and olive groves which you did not plant.'

"We Will Serve the LORD"

14 ¶ "Now, therefore, fear the LORD and serve Him in sincerity and truth; and put away the gods which your fathers served beyond the River and in Egypt, and serve the LORD.

15 "If it is disagreeable in your sight to serve the LORD, choose for yourselves today whom you will serve: whether the gods which your fathers served which were beyond the River, or the gods of the Amorites in whose land you are living; but as for me and my house, we will serve the LORD."

24:15 Free Choice

After all God had done for them, the Israelites still faced a fundamental choice. They could worship the gods their ancestors had served in Egypt or Mesopotamia, they could follow the religious practices of the new land they had entered—or they could follow the God who had freed them from slavery. The choice seems obvious, and Joshua knew exactly which direction he and his family would take. But as the book of Judges shows, many of the Israelites exercised their free will to enslave themselves to foreign gods.

16 ¶ The people answered and said, "Far be it from us that we should forsake the LORD to serve other gods;

17 for the LORD our God is He who brought us and our fathers up out of the land of Egypt, from the house of bondage, and who did these great signs in our sight and preserved us through all the way in which we went and among all the peoples through whose midst we passed.

18 "The LORD drove out from before us all the peoples, even the Amorites who lived in the land. We also will serve the LORD, for He is our God."

19 ¶ Then Joshua said to the people, "You will not be able to serve the LORD, for He is a holy God. He is a jealous God; He will not forgive your transgression or your sins.

20 "If you forsake the LORD and serve foreign gods, then He will turn and do you harm and consume you after He has done good to you."

21 The people said to Joshua, "No, but we will serve the LORD."

22 Joshua said to the people, "You are witnesses against yourselves that you have chosen for yourselves the LORD, to serve Him." And they said, "We are witnesses."

23 "Now therefore, put away the foreign gods which are in your midst, and incline your hearts to the LORD, the God of Israel."

24 The people said to Joshua, "We will serve the LORD our God and we will obey His voice."

25 So Joshua made a covenant with the people that day, and made for them a statute and an ordinance in Shechem.

26 And Joshua wrote these words in the book of the law of God; and he took a large stone and set it up there under the oak that was by the sanctuary of the LORD.

24:26 Monuments

The Israelites established at least seven memorials to remind future generations of what God had done for them. (Other stone monuments are described in chapters 4,7,8,10,22.) Even if people forgot their debt to God, the land would speak its own story.

27 Joshua said to all the people, "Behold, this stone shall be for a witness against us, for it has heard all the words of the LORD which He spoke to us; thus it shall be for a witness against you, so that you do not deny your God."

28 Then Joshua dismissed the people, each to his inheritance.

Joshua's Death and Burial

29 ¶ It came about after these things that Joshua the son of Nun, the servant of the LORD, died, being one hundred and ten years old.

30 And they buried him in the territory of his inheritance in Timnath-serah, which is in the hill country of Ephraim, on the north of Mount Gaash.

31 ¶ Israel served the LORD all the days of Josh-

ua and all the days of the elders who survived
Joshua, and had known all the deeds of the LORD
which He had done for Israel.

32 ¶ Now they buried the bones of Joseph,
which the sons of Israel brought up from Egypt, at
Shechem, in the piece of ground which Jacob had
bought from the sons of Hamor the father of Shechem for one hundred pieces of money; and they
became the inheritance of Joseph's sons.

33 And Eleazar the son of Aaron died; and they
buried him at Gibeah of Phinehas his son, which
was given him in the hill country of Ephraim.

JUDGES

Freedom Fighters
These "judges" took up arms to defend their homeland

THE "JUDGES" OF THIS BOOK might be called guerrillas or freedom fighters today. These men (and one woman) were renowned not for court cases, but for their military campaigns against foreign invaders. Like all military leaders, they sometimes settled disputes; the book of Judges, however, is preoccupied not with legal matters, but with the excitement of fighting for freedom.

Israel's judges certainly did not stick to "the rules of proper warfare." Judge Ehud tricked his opponent into a private conference; behind closed doors he pulled out a knife and plunged it into the enemy king's belly (3:12–30). Judge Gideon won a surprise victory in the middle of the night. His small band so confused the occupying army with noise and lights that the enemy soldiers stabbed each other and fled in the darkness (chapter 7). Samson never led an army; his battle tricks have been compared to the pranks of an overgrown juvenile delinquent (chapters 14–16).

> When the LORD raised up judges for them, the LORD was with the judge and delivered them from the hand of their enemies all the days of the judge. 2:18

Most of the time the Israelites hid in the hills while their enemies, with superior weapons, controlled the plains. (Chariots, like tanks, were devastating in level country, but almost useless in muddy or rugged terrain.) Outnumbered, the Israelites relied on ambushes and sneak attacks. They knew every gully, for they were fighting for their homeland. Strategy made up for lack of strength.

Ugliest Stories of the Bible

As a book about early Jewish military heroes, Judges inspires and fascinates. But you can't make the whole book fit that description. If you read strictly looking for heroes, you'd have to ignore half of Judges—and you would miss its most important point about God's work with Israel.

For one thing, Judges' "heroes" were badly flawed. Samson was pitifully vulnerable to his lust for women. Gideon won a battle, then led the nation into idolatry. Jephthah, a former outlaw, apparently knew very little about the God he was supposed to serve.

Add to this the "non-heroic" material: Abimelech, Gideon's son, who slaughtered 70 half brothers so he could be named king; Jephthah and Gideon, who massacred fellow Israelites who had failed to support them; and the sad characters of the last five chapters of Judges. These contain some of the ugliest stories in the Bible—tales of homosexual assault, idolatry, civil war, thievery, rape, and murder. The book of Judges runs downhill, from bad to worse. You may end up wondering what such material is doing in the Bible.

Every picture has shadows; every suspenseful novel has chapters that look truly dark. In the story of God and his people, Judges is that kind of chapter. Heroes appear sporadically, but humanity remains terribly unheroic.

Enthusiasm Fades

God wanted better things for his people than he got in Judges. He had rescued Israel from slavery in Egypt. He had given them a rich land and presented them with a grand system of worship and government centering on him. He would be no distant God in the heavens—he would live with them.

But after some initial enthusiasm, the Israelites didn't continue the way God had pointed. Instead, they learned to live with the sophisticated people they found as their neighbors—people whose faults included worshiping idols through sex orgies and child sacrifice.

The Israelites held the mountains, but the foreign-held valleys, cutting through the land, separated the tribes. Soon each group of isolated Israelites began operating independently. The next generation lost its sense of national identity. The people worshiped the idol Baal alongside the Lord. Though descended from 12 brothers, they spent more time fighting each other than the foreign oppressors.

They violated virtually every moral standard. The last verse of Judges sums it up: "Everyone did what was right in his own eyes." What was right in their eyes, wasn't.

The Secret of Their Survival

The foreign invasions were no accident, Judges says: They came from God just as surely as the heroic rescuers did. A pattern developed. God allowed suffering as a consequence of the Israelites' disobedience. When things grew really terrible, their attention would turn back to God. He would respond by sending a judge to rescue them. But soon they would fail again. This pattern repeated itself time and again. The Israelites always forgot their need for God, and the dreary cycle ground on.

The secret of Israel's survival was not, then, military heroes or guerrilla tactics. It was the persistent, unwearied love of God himself. Though they forgot him, he did not forget them. He gave innumerable new beginnings. Again and again he sent "judges" to rescue them. He would not let them go. God is the real hero of Judges.

How to Read Judges

You can read Judges as a collection of heroic stories, the most famous of which are Gideon's and Samson's. But together the tales tell a less heroic story.

Read Judges, therefore, on two levels at once. On one level focus on the new beginning God repeatedly offered by sending a judge to rescue Israel. These are character stories with great fascination. You can gain a great deal by studying the strengths and weaknesses of the individual judges.

On another level, read of the deterioration of a nation that quickly forgot what God had done for it. This will help you understand why, in the next stage of Israel's history, God gave the Israelites a king. For background on this change of government, read "The First King," page 325. Another interesting study is the book of Ruth, a lovely story from the time of Judges that shows a softer, more hopeful side.

PEOPLE YOU'LL MEET IN JUDGES

DEBORAH *(p. 284)*
GIDEON *(p. 287)*
SAMSON *(p. 297)*

3-TRACK READING PLAN

For an explanation and complete listing of the 3-track reading plan, turn to page 7.

TRACK 1: *Two-Week Courses on the Bible*
See page 7 for information on these courses.

TRACK 2: *An Overview of Judges in 3 Days*
☐ Day 1. Read the Introduction to Judges and chapter 6, in which God calls Gideon to lead a guerrilla army.
☐ Day 2. Read chapter 7, Gideon's victory in battle.
☐ Day 3. Read chapter 16, the story of Samson and Delilah, and Samson's death.

Now turn to page 9 for your next Track 2 reading project.

TRACK 3: *All of Judges in 21 Days*
After you have read through Judges, turn to pages 10–14 for your next Track 3 reading project.

☐1   ☐2   ☐3   ☐4   ☐5   ☐6   ☐7   ☐8
☐9   ☐10   ☐11   ☐12   ☐13   ☐14   ☐15   ☐16
☐17   ☐18   ☐19   ☐20   ☐21

Jerusalem Is Captured

1 Now it came about after the death of Joshua that the sons of Israel inquired of the LORD, saying, "Who shall go up first for us against the Canaanites, to fight against them?"

2 The LORD said, "Judah shall go up; behold, I have given the land into his hand."

3 Then Judah said to Simeon his brother, "Come up with me into the territory allotted me, that we may fight against the Canaanites; and I in turn will go with you into the territory allotted you." So Simeon went with him.

4 Judah went up, and the LORD gave the Canaanites and the Perizzites into their hands, and they defeated ten thousand men at Bezek.

5 They found Adoni-bezek in Bezek and fought against him, and they defeated the Canaanites and the Perizzites.

6 But Adoni-bezek fled; and they pursued him and caught him and cut off his thumbs and big toes.

7 Adoni-bezek said, "Seventy kings with their thumbs and their big toes cut off used to gather up *scraps* under my table; as I have done, so God has repaid me." So they brought him to Jerusalem and he died there.

1:7 Thumbs and Big Toes

A person lacking thumbs and big toes could not grip a weapon or run quickly. So cutting off those appendages guaranteed that a captured enemy would never fight again.

8 ¶ Then the sons of Judah fought against Jerusalem and captured it and struck it with the edge of the sword and set the city on fire.

9 Afterward the sons of Judah went down to fight against the Canaanites living in the hill country and in the *a*Negev and in the lowland.

10 So Judah went against the Canaanites who lived in Hebron (now the name of Hebron formerly *was* Kiriath-arba); and they struck Sheshai and Ahiman and Talmai.

Capture of Other Cities

11 ¶ Then from there he went against the inhabitants of Debir (now the name of Debir formerly *was* Kiriath-sepher).

12 And Caleb said, "The one who attacks Kiriath-sepher and captures it, I will even give him my daughter Achsah for a wife."

13 Othniel the son of Kenaz, Caleb's younger brother, captured it; so he gave him his daughter Achsah for a wife.

14 Then it came about when she came *to him,* that she persuaded him to ask her father for a field. Then she alighted from her donkey, and Caleb said to her, "What do you want?"

15 She said to him, "Give me a blessing, since you have given me the land of the *a*Negev, give me also springs of water." So Caleb gave her the upper springs and the lower springs.

16 ¶ The descendants of the Kenite, Moses' father-in-law, went up from the city of palms with the sons of Judah, to the wilderness of Judah which is in the south of Arad; and they went and lived with the people.

17 Then Judah went with Simeon his brother, and they struck the Canaanites living in Zephath, and utterly destroyed it. So the name of the city was called Hormah.

18 And Judah took Gaza with its territory and Ashkelon with its territory and Ekron with its territory.

19 Now the LORD was with Judah, and they took possession of the hill country; but they could not drive out the inhabitants of the valley because they had iron chariots.

1:19 Military Setbacks

Why did the Israelites fail to take all the territory allotted them? One reason was stubborn military opposition. The Israelites had never developed the sophistication to use chariots, the equivalent of modern-day tanks. Israel controlled the hills where chariots were unwieldy, but could not win the plains. The Israelites also failed to conquer Jerusalem (verse 21); its mountainous setting made that city almost impregnable.

20 Then they gave Hebron to Caleb, as Moses had promised; and he drove out from there the three sons of Anak.

21 But the sons of Benjamin did not drive out the Jebusites who lived in Jerusalem; so the Jebusites have lived with the sons of Benjamin in Jerusalem to this day.

22 ¶ Likewise the house of Joseph went up against Bethel, and the LORD was with them.

23 The house of Joseph spied out Bethel (now the name of the city was formerly Luz).

24 The spies saw a man coming out of the city and they said to him, "Please show us the entrance to the city and we will treat you kindly."

25 So he showed them the entrance to the city, and they struck the city with the edge of the sword, but they let the man and all his family go free.

26 The man went into the land of the Hittites and built a city and named it Luz which is its name to this day.

---

a I.e. South country

Places Not Conquered

27 ¶ But Manasseh did not take possession of Beth-shean and its villages, or Taanach and its villages, or the inhabitants of Dor and its villages, or the inhabitants of Ibleam and its villages, or the inhabitants of Megiddo and its villages; so the Canaanites persisted in living in that land.

28 It came about when Israel became strong, that they put the Canaanites to forced labor, but they did not drive them out completely.

29 ¶ Ephraim did not drive out the Canaanites who were living in Gezer; so the Canaanites lived in Gezer among them.

30 ¶ Zebulun did not drive out the inhabitants of Kitron, or the inhabitants of ᵃNahalol; so the Canaanites lived among them and became subject to forced labor.

31 ¶ Asher did not drive out the inhabitants of Acco, or the inhabitants of Sidon, or of Ahlab, or of Achzib, or of Helbah, or of Aphik, or of Rehob.

32 So the Asherites lived among the Canaanites, the inhabitants of the land; for they did not drive them out.

33 ¶ Naphtali did not drive out the inhabitants of Beth-shemesh, or the inhabitants of Beth-anath, but lived among the Canaanites, the inhabitants of the land; and the inhabitants of Beth-shemesh and Beth-anath became forced labor for them.

34 ¶ Then the Amorites forced the sons of Dan into the hill country, for they did not allow them to come down to the valley;

35 yet the Amorites persisted in living in Mount Heres, in Aijalon and in Shaalbim; but when the power of the house of Joseph grew strong, they became forced labor.

36 The border of the Amorites ran from the ascent of Akrabbim, from Sela and upward.

Israel Rebuked

2 Now the angel of the LORD came up from Gilgal to Bochim. And he said, "I brought you up out of Egypt and led you into the land which I have sworn to your fathers; and I said, 'I will never break My covenant with you,

2 and as for you, you shall make no covenant with the inhabitants of this land; you shall tear down their altars.' But you have not obeyed Me; what is this you have done?

3 "Therefore I also said, 'I will not drive them out before you; but they will ᵇbecome as thorns in your sides and their gods will be a snare to you.'"

4 When the angel of the LORD spoke these words to all the sons of Israel, the people lifted up their voices and wept.

5 So they named that place ᶜBochim; and there they sacrificed to the LORD.

Joshua Dies

6 ¶ When Joshua had dismissed the people, the sons of Israel went each to his inheritance to possess the land.

7 The people served the LORD all the days of Joshua, and all the days of the elders who survived Joshua, who had seen all the great work of the LORD which He had done for Israel.

8 Then Joshua the son of Nun, the servant of the LORD, died at the age of one hundred and ten.

9 And they buried him in the territory of his inheritance in Timnath-heres, in the hill country of Ephraim, north of Mount Gaash.

10 All that generation also were gathered to their fathers; and there arose another generation after them who did not know the LORD, nor yet the work which He had done for Israel.

Israel Serves Baals

11 ¶ Then the sons of Israel did evil in the sight of the LORD and ᵈserved the Baals,

12 and they forsook the LORD, the God of their fathers, who had brought them out of the land of Egypt, and followed other gods from *among* the gods of the peoples who were around them, and bowed themselves down to them; thus they provoked the LORD to anger.

13 So they forsook the LORD and served Baal and the Ashtaroth.

2:13 Fertility Gods

Israel's neighbors worshiped Baal and Ashtaroth, male and female gods of fertility. Followers practiced ritual sex at the shrines, believing that sex with sacred prostitutes led to good crops and many children. Sometimes, too, worshipers sacrificed their children to the gods. The Israelites' attraction to these foreign religions continued for most of their history as a nation.

14 The anger of the LORD burned against Israel, and He gave them into the hands of plunderers who plundered them; and He sold them into the hands of their enemies around *them,* so that they could no longer stand before their enemies.

15 Wherever they went, the hand of the LORD was against them for evil, as the LORD had spoken and as the LORD had sworn to them, so that they were severely distressed.

16 ¶ Then the LORD raised up judges who delivered them from the hands of those who plundered them.

17 Yet they did not listen to their judges, for they played the harlot after other gods and bowed themselves down to them. They turned aside quickly from the way in which their fathers had

---

ᵃ Perhaps same as *Nahalal*   ᵇ Some ancient mss read *be adversaries, and*   ᶜ I.e. weepers   ᵈ Or *worshiped* walked in obeying the commandments of the LORD; they did not do as *their fathers.*

18 When the LORD raised up judges for them, the LORD was with the judge and delivered them from the hand of their enemies all the days of the judge; for the LORD was moved to pity by their groaning because of those who oppressed and afflicted them.

19 But it came about when the judge died, that they would turn back and act more corruptly than their fathers, in following other gods to serve them and bow down to them; they did not abandon their practices or their stubborn ways.

20 So the anger of the LORD burned against Israel, and He said, "Because this nation has transgressed My covenant which I commanded their fathers and has not listened to My voice,

21 I also will no longer drive out before them any of the nations which Joshua left when he died,

22 in order to test Israel by them, whether they will keep the way of the LORD to walk in it as their fathers did, or not."

23 So the LORD allowed those nations to remain, not driving them out quickly; and He did not give them into the hand of Joshua.

Idolatry Leads to Servitude

3 Now these are the nations which the LORD left, to test Israel by them (*that is,* all who had not experienced any of the wars of Canaan;

2 only in order that the generations of the sons of Israel might be taught war, those who had not experienced it formerly).

3 *These nations are:* the five lords of the Philistines and all the Canaanites and the Sidonians and the Hivites who lived in Mount Lebanon, from Mount Baal-hermon as far as Lebo-hamath.

4 They were for testing Israel, to find out if they would obey the commandments of the LORD, which He had commanded their fathers through Moses.

5 The sons of Israel lived among the Canaanites, the Hittites, the Amorites, the Perizzites, the Hivites, and the Jebusites;

6 and they took their daughters for themselves as wives, and gave their own daughters to their sons, and served their gods.

7 ¶ The sons of Israel did what was evil in the sight of the LORD, and forgot the LORD their God and served the Baals and the *a* Asheroth.

8 Then the anger of the LORD was kindled against Israel, so that He sold them into the hands of Cushan-rishathaim king of Mesopotamia; and the sons of Israel served Cushan-rishathaim eight years.

The First Judge Delivers Israel

9 When the sons of Israel cried to the LORD, the LORD raised up a deliverer for the sons of Israel to deliver them, Othniel the son of Kenaz, Caleb's younger brother.

10 The Spirit of the LORD came upon him, and he judged Israel. When he went out to war, the

3:6 Intermarriage

This passage shows why the Old Testament opposed mixed marriages, which were common in the period of the judges. Ethnic differences were not the main issue. In fact, during the period of the judges Ruth, a non-Jew, married into a Jewish family with full acceptance (see the book of Ruth). But Ruth had accepted the God of Israel. When mixed marriages meant mixed religions, they diluted faith in God.

LORD gave Cushan-rishathaim king of Mesopotamia into his hand, so that he prevailed over Cushan-rishathaim.

11 Then the land had rest forty years. And Othniel the son of Kenaz died.

12 ¶ Now the sons of Israel again did evil in the sight of the LORD. So the LORD strengthened Eglon the king of Moab against Israel, because they had done evil in the sight of the LORD.

13 And he gathered to himself the sons of Ammon and Amalek; and he went and defeated Israel, and they possessed the city of the palm trees.

14 The sons of Israel served Eglon the king of Moab eighteen years.

Ehud Delivers from Moab

15 ¶ But when the sons of Israel cried to the LORD, the LORD raised up a deliverer for them, Ehud the son of Gera, the Benjamite, a left-handed man. And the sons of Israel sent tribute by him to Eglon the king of Moab.

16 Ehud made himself a sword which had two edges, a cubit in length, and he bound it on his right thigh under his cloak.

17 He presented the tribute to Eglon king of Moab. Now Eglon was a very fat man.

18 It came about when he had finished presenting the tribute, that he sent away the people who had carried the tribute.

19 But he himself turned back from the idols which were at Gilgal, and said, "I have a secret message for you, O king." And he said, "Keep silence." And all who attended him left him.

20 Ehud came to him while he was sitting alone in his cool roof chamber. And Ehud said, "I have a message from God for you." And he arose from his seat.

21 Ehud stretched out his left hand, took the sword from his right thigh and thrust it into his belly.

---

a I.e. wooden symbol of a female deity

22 The handle also went in after the blade, and the fat closed over the blade, for he did not draw the sword out of his belly; and the refuse came out.

23 Then Ehud went out into the vestibule and shut the doors of the roof chamber behind him, and locked *them*.

24 ¶ When he had gone out, his servants came and looked, and behold, the doors of the roof chamber were locked; and they said, "He is only relieving himself in the cool room."

25 They waited until they became anxious; but behold, he did not open the doors of the roof chamber. Therefore they took the key and opened them, and behold, their master had fallen to the floor dead.

26 ¶ Now Ehud escaped while they were delaying, and he passed by the idols and escaped to Seirah.

27 It came about when he had arrived, that he blew the trumpet in the hill country of Ephraim; and the sons of Israel went down with him from the hill country, and he *was* in front of them.

28 He said to them, "Pursue *them*, for the LORD has given your enemies the Moabites into your hands." So they went down after him and seized the fords of the Jordan opposite Moab, and did not allow anyone to cross.

29 They struck down at that time about ten thousand Moabites, all robust and valiant men; and no one escaped.

30 So Moab was subdued that day under the hand of Israel. And the land was undisturbed for eighty years.

Shamgar Delivers from Philistines

31 ¶ After him came Shamgar the son of Anath, who struck down six hundred Philistines with an oxgoad; and he also saved Israel.

Deborah and Barak Deliver from Canaanites

4 Then the sons of Israel again did evil in the sight of the LORD, after Ehud died.

2 And the LORD sold them into the hand of Jabin king of Canaan, who reigned in Hazor; and the commander of his army was Sisera, who lived in Harosheth-hagoyim.

3 The sons of Israel cried to the LORD; for he had nine hundred iron chariots, and he oppressed the sons of Israel severely for twenty years.

4 ¶ Now Deborah, a prophetess, the wife of Lappidoth, was judging Israel at that time.

5 She used to sit under the palm tree of Deborah between Ramah and Bethel in the hill country of Ephraim; and the sons of Israel came up to her for judgment.

6 Now she sent and summoned Barak the son of Abinoam from Kedesh-naphtali, and said to him, "Behold, the LORD, the God of Israel, has commanded, 'Go and march to Mount Tabor, and take with you ten thousand men from the sons of Naphtali and from the sons of Zebulun.

7 'I will draw out to you Sisera, the commander of Jabin's army, with his chariots and his many *troops* to the river Kishon, and I will give him into your hand.'"

8 Then Barak said to her, "If you will go with me, then I will go; but if you will not go with me, I will not go."

9 She said, "I will surely go with you; nevertheless, the honor shall not be yours on the journey that you are about to take, for the LORD will

---

DEBORAH *Multi-talented Woman*

WOMEN OFTEN GET OVERLOOKED IN the Old Testament, but Deborah is one spectacular exception. As a military leader, poet, prophet and judge, she used her talents to inspire Israel during a dark time.

Deborah won her fame leading a desperate nation to victory. With Israel under the thumb of a cruel foreign ruler, she gave orders for Barak to lead a revolt. He refused to go unless brave Deborah accompanied him to battle. With her giving the orders, Israel's ten thousand troops routed a better-equipped enemy. Deborah's triumph led to forty years of peace.

It is hard to think of an area in which Deborah did not excel. She was a mother and wife. Her wisdom was so renowned that people brought their disputes to her as she sat under a large palm tree, the palm tree of Deborah. As a prophet, she had the ability to understand God's message and relay it to his people. When she sent Barak into battle, she stated it this way: "The LORD, the God of Israel, has commanded . . ." (4:6).

Finally, Deborah was an accomplished poet, as chapter 5 demonstrates. One of the oldest and most expressive poems in the Bible, it was sung as a duet by Barak and Deborah, but the words give Deborah proper credit (5:7).

Throughout the Bible we can hardly find a more well-rounded leader, male or female, than Deborah.

Life Questions: In what areas could you strengthen your talents to become more well-rounded?

sell Sisera into the hands of a woman." Then Deborah arose and went with Barak to Kedesh.

10 Barak called Zebulun and Naphtali together to Kedesh, and ten thousand men went up with him; Deborah also went up with him.

11 ¶ Now Heber the Kenite had separated himself from the Kenites, from the sons of Hobab the father-in-law of Moses, and had pitched his tent as far away as the oak in Zaanannim, which is near Kedesh.

12 ¶ Then they told Sisera that Barak the son of Abinoam had gone up to Mount Tabor.

13 Sisera called together all his chariots, nine hundred iron chariots, and all the people who *were* with him, from Harosheth-hagoyim to the river Kishon.

14 Deborah said to Barak, "Arise! For this is the day in which the LORD has given Sisera into your hands; *a*behold, the LORD has gone out before you." So Barak went down from Mount Tabor with ten thousand men following him.

15 The LORD routed Sisera and all *his* chariots and all *his* army with the edge of the sword before Barak; and Sisera alighted from *his* chariot and fled away on foot.

16 But Barak pursued the chariots and the army as far as Harosheth-hagoyim, and all the army of Sisera fell by the edge of the sword; not even one was left.

17 ¶ Now Sisera fled away on foot to the tent of Jael the wife of Heber the Kenite, for *there was* peace between Jabin the king of Hazor and the house of Heber the Kenite.

18 Jael went out to meet Sisera, and said to him, "Turn aside, my master, turn aside to me! Do not be afraid." And he turned aside to her into the tent, and she covered him with a rug.

19 He said to her, "Please give me a little water to drink, for I am thirsty." So she opened a *b*bottle of milk and gave him a drink; then she covered him.

20 He said to her, "Stand in the doorway of the tent, and it shall be if anyone comes and inquires of you, and says, 'Is there anyone here?' that you shall say, 'No.'"

21 But Jael, Heber's wife, took a tent peg and seized a hammer in her hand, and went secretly to him and drove the peg into his temple, and it went through into the ground; for he was sound asleep and exhausted. So he died.

22 And behold, as Barak pursued Sisera, Jael came out to meet him and said to him, "Come, and I will show you the man whom you are seeking." And he entered with her, and behold Sisera was lying dead with the tent peg in his temple.

23 ¶ So God subdued on that day Jabin the king of Canaan before the sons of Israel.

24 The hand of the sons of Israel pressed heavier and heavier upon Jabin the king of Canaan, until they had destroyed Jabin the king of Canaan.

The Song of Deborah and Barak

5 Then Deborah and Barak the son of Abinoam sang on that day, saying,

2 "That the leaders led in Israel,
That the people volunteered,
Bless the LORD!

3 "Hear, O kings; give ear, O rulers!
I—to the LORD, I will sing,
I will sing praise to the LORD, the God of Israel.

4 "LORD, when You went out from Seir,
When You marched from the field of Edom,
The earth quaked, the heavens also dripped,
Even the clouds dripped water.

5 "The mountains quaked at the presence of the LORD,
This Sinai, at the presence of the LORD, the God of Israel.

6 ¶ "In the days of Shamgar the son of Anath,
In the days of Jael, the highways were deserted,
And travelers went by roundabout ways.

7 "The peasantry ceased, they ceased in Israel,
Until I, Deborah, arose,
Until I arose, a mother in Israel.

8 "New gods were chosen;
Then war *was* in the gates.
Not a shield or a spear was seen
Among forty thousand in Israel.

9 "My heart *goes out* to the commanders of Israel,
The volunteers among the people;
Bless the LORD!

10 "You who ride on white donkeys,
You who sit on *rich* carpets,
And you who travel on the road—sing!

11 "At the sound of those who divide *flocks*
among the watering places,
There they shall recount the righteous deeds of the LORD,
The righteous deeds for His peasantry in Israel.
Then the people of the LORD went down to the gates.

12 ¶ "Awake, awake, Deborah;
Awake, awake, sing a song!
Arise, Barak, and take away your captives, O son of Abinoam.

13 "Then survivors came down to the nobles;
The people of the LORD came down to me as warriors.

14 "From Ephraim those whose root is in Amalek *came down,*

Following you, Benjamin, with your
   peoples;
From Machir commanders came down,
And from Zebulun those who wield the
   staff of office.
15 "And the princes of Issachar *were* with
   Deborah;
As *was* Issachar, so *was* Barak;
Into the valley they rushed at his heels;
Among the divisions of Reuben
There were great resolves of heart.
16 "Why did you sit among the *a*sheepfolds,
To hear the piping for the flocks?
Among the divisions of Reuben
There were great searchings of heart.
17 "Gilead remained across the Jordan;
And why did Dan stay in ships?
Asher sat at the seashore,
And remained by its landings.
18 "Zebulun *was* a people who despised their
   lives *even* to death,
And Naphtali also, on the high places of
   the field.

19 ¶ "The kings came *and* fought;
Then fought the kings of Canaan
At Taanach near the waters of Megiddo;
They took no plunder in silver.
20 "The stars fought from heaven,
From their courses they fought against
   Sisera.
21 "The torrent of Kishon swept them away,
The ancient torrent, the torrent Kishon.
O my soul, march on with strength.
22 "Then the horses' hoofs beat
From the dashing, the dashing of his
   valiant steeds.
23 'Curse Meroz,' said the angel of the LORD,
'Utterly curse its inhabitants;
Because they did not come to the help of
   the LORD,
To the help of the LORD against the
   warriors.'

24 ¶ "Most blessed of women is Jael,
The wife of Heber the Kenite;
Most blessed is she of women in the tent.
25 "He asked for water *and* she gave him
   milk;
In a magnificent bowl she brought him
   curds.
26 "She reached out her hand for the tent
   peg,
And her right hand for the workmen's
   hammer.
Then she struck Sisera, she smashed his
   head;
And she shattered and pierced his
   temple.
27 "Between her feet he bowed, he fell, he
   lay;

Between her feet he bowed, he fell;
Where he bowed, there he fell dead.

28 ¶ "Out of the window she looked and
   lamented,
The mother of Sisera through the lattice,
'Why does his chariot delay in coming?
Why do the hoofbeats of his chariots
   tarry?'
29 "Her wise princesses would answer her,
Indeed she repeats her words to herself,
30 'Are they not finding, are they not
   dividing the spoil?
A maiden, two maidens for every
   warrior;
To Sisera a spoil of dyed work,
A spoil of dyed work embroidered,
Dyed work of double embroidery on the
   neck of the spoiler?'
31 "Thus let all Your enemies perish,
   O LORD;
But let those who love Him be like the
   rising of the sun in its might."
And the land was undisturbed for forty years.

Israel Oppressed by Midian

6 Then the sons of Israel did what was evil in the
sight of the LORD; and the LORD gave them
into the hands of Midian seven years.
2 The power of Midian prevailed against Israel. Because of Midian the sons of Israel made for
themselves the dens which were in the mountains
and the caves and the strongholds.
3 For it was when Israel had sown, that the
Midianites would come up with the Amalekites
and the sons of the east and go against them.
4 So they would camp against them and destroy the produce of the earth as far as Gaza, and
leave no sustenance in Israel as well as no sheep,
ox, or donkey.
5 For they would come up with their livestock
and their tents, they would come in like locusts for
number, both they and their camels were innumerable; and they came into the land to devastate it.
6 So Israel was brought very low because of
Midian, and the sons of Israel cried to the LORD.

6:5 Camel Power

*This is the earliest mention in the Bible of
camels used for military purposes. Midianite
marauders let the Israelites raise their crops,
then swept in and took everything when the
crops were ripe. With no effective defense, the
Israelites hid out in caves and other remote
spots.*

---

a Or *saddlebags*

7 ¶ Now it came about when the sons of Israel cried to the LORD on account of Midian,

8 that the LORD sent a prophet to the sons of Israel, and he said to them, "Thus says the LORD, the God of Israel, 'It was I who brought you up from Egypt and brought you out from the house of slavery.

9 'I delivered you from the hands of the Egyptians and from the hands of all your oppressors, and dispossessed them before you and gave you their land,

10 and I said to you, "I am the LORD your God; you shall not fear the gods of the Amorites in whose land you live. But you have not obeyed Me." ' "

Gideon Is Visited

11 ¶ Then the angel of the LORD came and sat under the oak that was in Ophrah, which belonged to Joash the Abiezrite as his son Gideon was beating out wheat in the wine press in order to save it from the Midianites.

12 The angel of the LORD appeared to him and said to him, "The LORD is with you, O valiant warrior."

13 Then Gideon said to him, "O my lord, if the LORD is with us, why then has all this happened to us? And where are all His miracles which our fathers told us about, saying, 'Did not the LORD bring us up from Egypt?' But now the LORD has abandoned us and given us into the hand of Midian."

14 The LORD looked at him and said, "Go in this your strength and deliver Israel from the hand of Midian. Have I not sent you?"

15 He said to Him, "O Lord, how shall I deliv-

Unlikely Leaders
God drew out Gideon's hidden potential

> The LORD said to him, "Peace to you, do not fear; you shall not die."
> 6:23

GIDEON MADE AN UNLIKELY FIGHTER—HESITANT and fearful. We first meet him as he furtively threshed wheat in a winepress. To thresh wheat openly was to invite the occupying Midianite army to confiscate it. The Midianites dominated Israel so thoroughly that Israelites could rarely harvest crops; some lived in caves.

Gideon was planning no heroics until the angel of the Lord came to him with a battle commission. "Who, me?" Gideon seemed to ask, trembling.

In view of the facts, his doubts were justified. His family and village worshiped Baal, not the Lord. He himself was subject to paralyzing fears, even on the eve of battle. Gideon kept demanding miraculous proof that God really was with him—and one miracle was not enough.

At the same time, God seemed to make Gideon's job more formidable. He reduced his army from 32,000 to a pitiful 300. If an army so outnumbered were to win, that would prove beyond a doubt that God was in charge.

God knew Gideon's potential and patiently brought Gideon to the point of courage. He encouraged him, directed him, transformed him. Overnight Gideon became a strong and decisive general. He used noise and lights for scare tactics, enabling his small band to scatter the enemy. Thorough mopping-up operations followed. The little army devastated the scattered Midianites, and Gideon, triumphant, brought in an era of freedom. Perhaps no one was as surprised as he.

Cast-off Material

The selection of Gideon shows a pattern. At a time when women were regarded as second-class citizens (see 9:54; 19:24), God chose Deborah to lead. Jephthah, another judge, had been a social outcast, the leader of a gang of outlaws, before God chose him to lead.

And the pattern is found not only in Judges. Throughout the Bible, God used cast-off material. Israel was not chosen because of its great size or sophistication. (In fact, archaeologists report a drop in the culture of a city after the Israelites captured it.) God did not seek the most capable people, nor the most naturally "good." He chose a small, weak slave tribe, uncultured, with a short memory for his kindness to them. Time and again the Israelites proved themselves faulty. So did their leaders. With this unlikely material God did great things so the world could see that the glory was his and his alone.

Paul took up this theme when he wrote, over a thousand years later, "For consider your calling, brethren, that there were not many wise according to the flesh, not many mighty, not many noble; but God has chosen the foolish things of the world to shame the wise, and God has chosen the weak things of the world to shame the things which are strong. . . . so that, just as it is written: 'LET HIM WHO BOASTS, BOAST IN THE LORD' " (1 Corinthians 1:26–31).

Life Questions: Do you picture yourself as a leader? Why or why not? What would God have to change to make you a leader?

er Israel? Behold, my family is the least in Manasseh, and I am the youngest in my father's house."

16 But the LORD said to him, "Surely I will be with you, and you shall defeat Midian as one man."

17 So Gideon said to Him, "If now I have found favor in Your sight, then show me a sign that it is You who speak with me.

18 "Please do not depart from here, until I come *back* to You, and bring out my offering and lay it before You." And He said, "I will remain until you return."

19 ¶ Then Gideon went in and prepared a young goat and unleavened bread from an *a*ephah of flour; he put the meat in a basket and the broth in a pot, and brought *them* out to him under the oak and presented *them*.

20 The angel of God said to him, "Take the meat and the unleavened bread and lay them on this rock, and pour out the broth." And he did so.

21 Then the angel of the LORD put out the end of the staff that was in his hand and touched the meat and the unleavened bread; and fire sprang up from the rock and consumed the meat and the unleavened bread. Then the angel of the LORD vanished from his sight.

22 When Gideon saw that he was the angel of the LORD, he said, "Alas, O Lord GOD! For now I have seen the angel of the LORD face to face."

23 The LORD said to him, "Peace to you, do not fear; you shall not die."

24 Then Gideon built an altar there to the LORD and named it The LORD is Peace. To this day it is still in Ophrah of the Abiezrites.

25 ¶ Now on the same night the LORD said to him, "Take your father's bull and a second bull seven years old, and pull down the altar of Baal which belongs to your father, and cut down the *b*Asherah that is beside it;

26 and build an altar to the LORD your God on the top of this stronghold in an orderly manner, and take a second bull and offer a burnt offering with the wood of the Asherah which you shall cut down."

27 Then Gideon took ten men of his servants and did as the LORD had spoken to him; and because he was too afraid of his father's household and the men of the city to do it by day, he did it by night.

The Altar of Baal Destroyed

28 ¶ When the men of the city arose early in the morning, behold, the altar of Baal was torn down, and the Asherah which was beside it was cut down, and the second bull was offered on the altar which had been built.

29 They said to one another, "Who did this thing?" And when they searched about and inquired, they said, "Gideon the son of Joash did this thing."

30 Then the men of the city said to Joash, "Bring out your son, that he may die, for he has torn down the altar of Baal, and indeed, he has cut down the Asherah which was beside it."

6:30 Topsy-turvy

Israel had turned God's commands upside down. According to Deuteronomy 13:6–10, those who worshiped idols should be stoned. But here Israelites were ready to execute Gideon for destroying their idols.

31 But Joash said to all who stood against him, "Will you contend for Baal, or will you deliver him? Whoever will plead for him shall be put to death by morning. If he is a god, let him contend for himself, because someone has torn down his altar."

32 Therefore on that day he named him Jerubbaal, that is to say, "Let Baal contend against him," because he had torn down his altar.

33 ¶ Then all the Midianites and the Amalekites and the sons of the east assembled themselves; and they crossed over and camped in the valley of Jezreel.

34 So the Spirit of the LORD came upon Gideon; and he blew a trumpet, and the Abiezrites were called together to follow him.

35 He sent messengers throughout Manasseh, and they also were called together to follow him; and he sent messengers to Asher, Zebulun, and Naphtali, and they came up to meet them.

Sign of the Fleece

36 ¶ Then Gideon said to God, "If You will deliver Israel through me, as You have spoken,

37 behold, I will put a fleece of wool on the threshing floor. If there is dew on the fleece only, and it is dry on all the ground, then I will know that You will deliver Israel through me, as You have spoken."

6:37 Putting Out a Fleece

How much proof of God's will does one person need? Though the angel of the Lord had assured Gideon of success, he took fright and wanted to double-check, then triple-check, by asking for miracles. In some circles today, "putting out a fleece" has come to mean asking God to do something unusual to confirm his guidance. However, Gideon's action seems more like a lack of faith than a model of seeking God's guidance.

---

a I.e. Approx one bu   *b* I.e. wooden symbol of a female deity, also vv 26, 28, 30

38 And it was so. When he arose early the next morning and squeezed the fleece, he drained the dew from the fleece, a bowl full of water.

39 Then Gideon said to God, "Do not let Your anger burn against me that I may speak once more; please let me make a test once more with the fleece, let it now be dry only on the fleece, and let there be dew on all the ground."

40 God did so that night; for it was dry only on the fleece, and dew was on all the ground.

Gideon's 300 Chosen Men

7 Then Jerubbaal (that is, Gideon) and all the people who were with him, rose early and camped beside the spring of Harod; and the camp of Midian was on the north side of them by the hill of Moreh in the valley.

2 ¶ The LORD said to Gideon, "The people who are with you are too many for Me to give Midian into their hands, for Israel would become boastful, saying, 'My own power has delivered me.'

3 "Now therefore come, proclaim in the hearing of the people, saying, 'Whoever is afraid and trembling, let him return and depart from Mount Gilead.' " So 22,000 people returned, but 10,000 remained.

4 ¶ Then the LORD said to Gideon, "The people are still too many; bring them down to the water and I will test them for you there. Therefore it shall be that he of whom I say to you, 'This one shall go with you,' he shall go with you; but everyone of whom I say to you, 'This one shall not go with you,' he shall not go."

5 So he brought the people down to the water. And the LORD said to Gideon, "You shall separate everyone who laps the water with his tongue as a dog laps, as well as everyone who kneels to drink."

6 Now the number of those who lapped, putting their hand to their mouth, was 300 men; but all the rest of the people kneeled to drink water.

7 The LORD said to Gideon, "I will deliver you with the 300 men who lapped and will give the Midianites into your hands; so let all the *other* people go, each man to his home."

8 So the 300 men took the people's provisions and their trumpets into their hands. And Gideon sent all the *other* men of Israel, each to his tent, but retained the 300 men; and the camp of Midian was below him in the valley.

9 ¶ Now the same night it came about that the LORD said to him, "Arise, go down against the camp, for I have given it into your hands.

10 "But if you are afraid to go down, go with Purah your servant down to the camp,

11 and you will hear what they say; and afterward your hands will be strengthened that you may go down against the camp." So he went with Purah his servant down to the outposts of the army that was in the camp.

12 Now the Midianites and the Amalekites and all the sons of the east were lying in the valley as numerous as locusts; and their camels were without number, as numerous as the sand on the seashore.

13 When Gideon came, behold, a man was relating a dream to his friend. And he said, "Behold, I had a dream; a loaf of barley bread was tumbling into the camp of Midian, and it came to the tent and struck it so that it fell, and turned it upside down so that the tent lay flat."

14 His friend replied, "This is nothing less than the sword of Gideon the son of Joash, a man of Israel; God has given Midian and all the camp into his hand."

15 ¶ When Gideon heard the account of the dream and its interpretation, he bowed in worship. He returned to the camp of Israel and said, "Arise, for the LORD has given the camp of Midian into your hands."

16 He divided the 300 men into three companies, and he put trumpets and empty pitchers into the hands of all of them, with torches inside the pitchers.

17 He said to them, "Look at me and do likewise. And behold, when I come to the outskirts of the camp, do as I do.

18 "When I and all who are with me blow the trumpet, then you also blow the trumpets all around the camp and say, 'For the LORD and for Gideon.' "

Confusion of the Enemy

19 ¶ So Gideon and the hundred men who were with him came to the outskirts of the camp at the beginning of the middle watch, when they had just posted the watch; and they blew the trumpets and smashed the pitchers that were in their hands.

20 When the three companies blew the trumpets and broke the pitchers, they held the torches in their left hands and the trumpets in their right hands for blowing, and cried, "A sword for the LORD and for Gideon!"

21 Each stood in his place around the camp; and all the *a*army ran, crying out as they fled.

22 When they blew 300 trumpets, the LORD set the sword of one against another even throughout the whole army; and the army fled as far as Bethshittah toward Zererah, as far as the edge of Abelmeholah, by Tabbath.

23 The men of Israel were summoned from Naphtali and Asher and all Manasseh, and they pursued Midian.

24 ¶ Gideon sent messengers throughout all the hill country of Ephraim, saying, "Come down against Midian and take the waters before them, as far as Beth-barah and the Jordan." So all the men of Ephraim were summoned and they took the waters as far as Beth-barah and the Jordan.

---

a Or *camp*

25 They captured the two leaders of Midian, Oreb and Zeeb, and they killed Oreb at the rock of Oreb, and they killed Zeeb at the wine press of Zeeb, while they pursued Midian; and they brought the heads of Oreb and Zeeb to Gideon from across the Jordan.

Zebah and Zalmunna Routed

8 Then the men of Ephraim said to him, "What is this thing you have done to us, not calling us when you went to fight against Midian?" And they contended with him vigorously.

2 But he said to them, "What have I done now in comparison with you? Is not the gleaning of the grapes of Ephraim better than the vintage of Abiezer?

3 "God has given the leaders of Midian, Oreb and Zeeb into your hands; and what was I able to do in comparison with you?" Then their anger toward him subsided when he said that.

4 ¶ Then Gideon and the 300 men who were with him came to the Jordan and crossed over, weary yet pursuing.

5 He said to the men of Succoth, "Please give loaves of bread to the people who are following me, for they are weary, and I am pursuing Zebah and Zalmunna, the kings of Midian."

6 The leaders of Succoth said, "Are the hands of Zebah and Zalmunna already in your hands, that we should give bread to your army?"

7 Gideon said, "All right, when the LORD has given Zebah and Zalmunna into my hand, then I will thrash your bodies with the thorns of the wilderness and with briers."

8 He went up from there to Penuel and spoke similarly to them; and the men of Penuel answered him just as the men of Succoth had answered.

9 So he spoke also to the men of Penuel, saying, "When I return safely, I will tear down this tower."

10 ¶ Now Zebah and Zalmunna were in Karkor, and their armies with them, about 15,000 men, all who were left of the entire army of the sons of the east; for the fallen were 120,000 swordsmen.

11 Gideon went up by the way of those who lived in tents on the east of Nobah and Jogbehah, and attacked the camp when the camp was unsuspecting.

12 When Zebah and Zalmunna fled, he pursued them and captured the two kings of Midian, Zebah and Zalmunna, and routed the whole army.

13 ¶ Then Gideon the son of Joash returned from the battle by the ascent of Heres.

14 And he captured a youth from Succoth and questioned him. Then the youth wrote down for him the princes of Succoth and its elders, seventy-seven men.

15 He came to the men of Succoth and said, "Behold Zebah and Zalmunna, concerning whom you taunted me, saying, 'Are the hands of Zebah and Zalmunna already in your hand, that we should give bread to your men who are weary?'"

16 He took the elders of the city, and thorns of

the wilderness and briers, and he disciplined the men of Succoth with them.

17 He tore down the tower of Penuel and killed the men of the city.

18 ¶ Then he said to Zebah and Zalmunna, "What kind of men were they whom you killed at Tabor?" And they said, "They were like you, each one resembling the son of a king."

19 He said, "They were my brothers, the sons of my mother. As the LORD lives, if only you had let them live, I would not kill you."

20 So he said to Jether his firstborn, "Rise, kill them." But the youth did not draw his sword, for he was afraid, because he was still a youth.

21 Then Zebah and Zalmunna said, "Rise yourself, and fall on us; for as the man, so is his strength." So Gideon arose and killed Zebah and Zalmunna, and took the crescent ornaments which were on their camels' necks.

22 ¶ Then the men of Israel said to Gideon, "Rule over us, both you and your son, also your son's son, for you have delivered us from the hand of Midian."

23 But Gideon said to them, "I will not rule over you, nor shall my son rule over you; the LORD shall rule over you."

24 Yet Gideon said to them, "I would request of you, that each of you give me an earring from

his spoil." (For they had gold earrings, because they were Ishmaelites.)

25 They said, "We will surely give *them*." So they spread out a garment, and every one of them threw an earring there from his spoil.

26 The weight of the gold earrings that he requested was 1,700 *shekels* of gold, besides the crescent ornaments and the pendants and the purple robes which *were* on the kings of Midian, and besides the neck bands that *were* on their camels' necks.

27 Gideon made it into an ephod, and placed it in his city, Ophrah, and all Israel played the harlot with it there, so that it became a snare to Gideon and his household.

Forty Years of Peace

28 So Midian was subdued before the sons of Israel, and they did not lift up their heads anymore. And the land was undisturbed for forty years in the days of Gideon.

29 ¶ Then Jerubbaal the son of Joash went and lived in his own house.

30 Now Gideon had seventy sons who were his direct descendants, for he had many wives.

31 His concubine who was in Shechem also bore him a son, and he named him Abimelech.

32 And Gideon the son of Joash died at a ripe old age and was buried in the tomb of his father Joash, in Ophrah of the Abiezrites.

33 ¶ Then it came about, as soon as Gideon was dead, that the sons of Israel again played the harlot with the Baals, and made Baal-berith their god.

34 Thus the sons of Israel did not remember the LORD their God, who had delivered them from the hands of all their enemies on every side;

35 nor did they show kindness to the household of Jerubbaal (*that is,* Gideon) in accord with all the good that he had done to Israel.

Abimelech's Conspiracy

9 And Abimelech the son of Jerubbaal went to Shechem to his mother's relatives, and spoke to them and to the whole clan of the household of his mother's father, saying,

2 "Speak, now, in the hearing of all the leaders of Shechem, 'Which is better for you, that seventy men, all the sons of Jerubbaal, rule over you, or that one man rule over you?' Also, remember that I am your bone and your flesh."

3 And his mother's relatives spoke all these words on his behalf in the hearing of all the leaders of Shechem; and they were inclined to follow Abimelech, for they said, "He is our relative."

4 They gave him seventy *pieces* of silver from the house of Baal-berith with which Abimelech hired worthless and reckless fellows, and they followed him.

5 Then he went to his father's house at Ophrah and killed his brothers the sons of Jerubbaal, seventy men, on one stone. But Jotham the youngest son of Jerubbaal was left, for he hid himself.

6 All the men of Shechem and all *a*Bethmillo assembled together, and they went and made Abimelech king, by the oak of the pillar which was in Shechem.

7 ¶ Now when they told Jotham, he went and stood on the top of Mount Gerizim, and lifted his voice and called out. Thus he said to them, "Listen to me, O men of Shechem, that God may listen to you.

8 "Once the trees went forth to anoint a king over them, and they said to the olive tree, 'Reign over us!'

9 "But the olive tree said to them, 'Shall I leave my fatness with which God and men are honored, and go to wave over the trees?'

10 "Then the trees said to the fig tree, 'You come, reign over us!'

11 "But the fig tree said to them, 'Shall I leave my sweetness and my good fruit, and go to wave over the trees?'

12 "Then the trees said to the vine, 'You come, reign over us!'

13 "But the vine said to them, 'Shall I leave my new wine, which cheers God and men, and go to wave over the trees?'

14 "Finally all the trees said to the bramble, 'You come, reign over us!'

15 "The bramble said to the trees, 'If in truth you are anointing me as king over you, come and take refuge in my shade; but if not, may fire come out from the bramble and consume the cedars of Lebanon.'

16 ¶ "Now therefore, if you have dealt in truth and integrity in making Abimelech king, and if you have dealt well with Jerubbaal and his house, and have dealt with him as he deserved—

17 for my father fought for you and risked his life and delivered you from the hand of Midian;

18 but you have risen against my father's house today and have killed his sons, seventy men, on one stone, and have made Abimelech, the son of his maidservant, king over the men of Shechem, because he is your relative—

19 if then you have dealt in truth and integrity with Jerubbaal and his house this day, rejoice in Abimelech, and let him also rejoice in you.

20 "But if not, let fire come out from Abimelech and consume the men of Shechem and Bethmillo; and let fire come out from the men of Shechem and from Beth-millo, and consume Abimelech."

21 Then Jotham escaped and fled, and went to Beer and remained there because of Abimelech his brother.

a Or *the house of Millo*

Shechem and Abimelech Fall

22 ¶ Now Abimelech ruled over Israel three years.

23 Then God sent an evil spirit between Abimelech and the men of Shechem; and the men of Shechem dealt treacherously with Abimelech,

9:23 Evil Spirit

The "evil spirit" God sent was not necessarily a supernatural being. "Spirit" means literally "wind" or "breath" in the Bible, and this comment might be translated, "God sent an ill wind." Perhaps an attitude of bitterness or distrust grew up between Abimelech and the people of Shechem. Characteristically, the Bible attributes this development to God, though human causes were probably involved as well.

24 so that the violence done to the seventy sons of Jerubbaal might come, and their blood might be laid on Abimelech their brother, who killed them, and on the men of Shechem, who strengthened his hands to kill his brothers.

25 The men of Shechem set men in ambush against him on the tops of the mountains, and they robbed all who might pass by them along the road; and it was told to Abimelech.

26 ¶ Now Gaal the son of Ebed came with his relatives, and crossed over into Shechem; and the men of Shechem put their trust in him.

27 They went out into the field and gathered *the grapes of* their vineyards and trod *them,* and held a festival; and they went into the house of their god, and ate and drank and cursed Abimelech.

28 Then Gaal the son of Ebed said, "Who is Abimelech, and who is Shechem, that we should serve him? Is he not the son of Jerubbaal, and *is* Zebul *not* his lieutenant? Serve the men of Hamor the father of Shechem; but why should we serve him?

29 "Would, therefore, that this people were under my authority! Then I would remove Abimelech." And he said to Abimelech, "Increase your army and come out."

30 ¶ When Zebul the ruler of the city heard the words of Gaal the son of Ebed, his anger burned.

31 He sent messengers to Abimelech deceitfully, saying, "Behold, Gaal the son of Ebed and his relatives have come to Shechem; and behold, they are stirring up the city against you.

32 "Now therefore, arise by night, you and the people who are with you, and lie in wait in the field.

33 "In the morning, as soon as the sun is up, you shall rise early and rush upon the city; and behold, when he and the people who are with him come out against you, you shall do to them whatever you can."

34 ¶ So Abimelech and all the people who *were* with him arose by night and lay in wait against Shechem in four companies.

35 Now Gaal the son of Ebed went out and stood in the entrance of the city gate; and Abimelech and the people who *were* with him arose from the ambush.

36 When Gaal saw the people, he said to Zebul, "Look, people are coming down from the tops of the mountains." But Zebul said to him, "You are seeing the shadow of the mountains as *if they were* men."

37 Gaal spoke again and said, "Behold, people are coming down from the highest part of the land, and one company comes by the way of the diviners' oak."

38 Then Zebul said to him, "Where is your boasting now with which you said, 'Who is Abimelech that we should serve him?' Is this not the people whom you despised? Go out now and fight with them!"

39 So Gaal went out before the leaders of Shechem and fought with Abimelech.

40 Abimelech chased him, and he fled before him; and many fell wounded up to the entrance of the gate.

41 Then Abimelech remained at Arumah, but Zebul drove out Gaal and his relatives so that they could not remain in Shechem.

42 ¶ Now it came about the next day, that the people went out to the field, and it was told to Abimelech.

43 So he took his people and divided them into three companies, and lay in wait in the field; when he looked and saw the people coming out from the city, he arose against them and slew them.

44 Then Abimelech and the company who was with him dashed forward and stood in the entrance of the city gate; the other two companies then dashed against all who *were* in the field and slew them.

45 Abimelech fought against the city all that day, and he captured the city and killed the people who *were* in it; then he razed the city and sowed it with salt.

46 ¶ When all the leaders of the tower of Shechem heard of *it,* they entered the inner chamber of the temple of El-berith.

47 It was told Abimelech that all the leaders of the tower of Shechem were gathered together.

48 So Abimelech went up to Mount Zalmon, he and all the people who *were* with him; and Abimelech took an axe in his hand and cut down a branch from the trees, and lifted it and laid *it* on his shoulder. Then he said to the people who *were* with him, "What you have seen me do, hurry *and* do likewise."

49 All the people also cut down each one his branch and followed Abimelech, and put *them* on the inner chamber and set the inner chamber on fire over those *inside,* so that all the men of the

tower of Shechem also died, about a thousand men and women.

50 ¶ Then Abimelech went to Thebez, and he camped against Thebez and captured it.

51 But there was a strong tower in the center of the city, and all the men and women with all the leaders of the city fled there and shut themselves in; and they went up on the roof of the tower.

52 So Abimelech came to the tower and fought against it, and approached the entrance of the tower to burn it with fire.

53 But a certain woman threw an upper millstone on Abimelech's head, crushing his skull.

54 Then he called quickly to the young man, his armor bearer, and said to him, "Draw your sword and kill me, so that it will not be said of me, 'A woman slew him.' " So the young man pierced him through, and he died.

9:54 Sexist Attitudes

Abimelech preferred dying immediately to having it said that a woman killed him. Sexist attitudes clearly prevailed in the time of the judges, but nevertheless women made their marks, both good and bad. Here and in the story of Jael (4:21), women used domestic implements to kill dangerous men. (Grinding grain with millstones and setting up tents with pegs were traditionally considered "women's work.") Deborah, a judge and general, and Delilah, who seduced Samson, used their wits for good and evil, respectively.

55 When the men of Israel saw that Abimelech was dead, each departed to his home.

56 Thus God repaid the wickedness of Abimelech, which he had done to his father in killing his seventy brothers.

57 Also God returned all the wickedness of the men of Shechem on their heads, and the curse of Jotham the son of Jerubbaal came upon them.

Oppression of Philistines and Ammonites

10 Now after Abimelech died, Tola the son of Puah, the son of Dodo, a man of Issachar, arose to save Israel; and he lived in Shamir in the hill country of Ephraim.

2 He judged Israel twenty-three years. Then he died and was buried in Shamir.

3 ¶ After him, Jair the Gileadite arose and judged Israel twenty-two years.

4 He had thirty sons who rode on thirty donkeys, and they had thirty cities in the land of Gilead that are called Havvoth-jair to this day.

5 And Jair died and was buried in Kamon.

6 ¶ Then the sons of Israel again did evil in the sight of the LORD, served the Baals and the Ashtaroth, the gods of Aram, the gods of Sidon, the gods of Moab, the gods of the sons of Ammon,

and the gods of the Philistines; thus they forsook the LORD and did not serve Him.

7 The anger of the LORD burned against Israel, and He sold them into the hands of the Philistines and into the hands of the sons of Ammon.

8 They afflicted and crushed the sons of Israel that year; for eighteen years they *afflicted* all the sons of Israel who were beyond the Jordan in Gilead in the land of the Amorites.

9 The sons of Ammon crossed the Jordan to fight also against Judah, Benjamin, and the house of Ephraim, so that Israel was greatly distressed.

10 ¶ Then the sons of Israel cried out to the LORD, saying, "We have sinned against You, for indeed, we have forsaken our God and served the Baals."

11 The LORD said to the sons of Israel, "*Did I not deliver you* from the Egyptians, the Amorites, the sons of Ammon, and the Philistines?

12 "Also when the Sidonians, the Amalekites and the Maonites oppressed you, you cried out to Me, and I delivered you from their hands.

13 "Yet you have forsaken Me and served other gods; therefore I will no longer deliver you.

14 "Go and cry out to the gods which you have chosen; let them deliver you in the time of your distress."

15 The sons of Israel said to the LORD, "We have sinned, do to us whatever seems good to You; only please deliver us this day."

16 So they put away the foreign gods from among them and served the LORD; and He could bear the misery of Israel no longer.

17 ¶ Then the sons of Ammon were summoned and they camped in Gilead. And the sons of Israel gathered together and camped in Mizpah.

18 The people, the leaders of Gilead, said to one another, "Who is the man who will begin to fight against the sons of Ammon? He shall become head over all the inhabitants of Gilead."

Jephthah the Ninth Judge

11 Now Jephthah the Gileadite was a valiant warrior, but he was the son of a harlot. And Gilead was the father of Jephthah.

2 Gilead's wife bore him sons; and when his wife's sons grew up, they drove Jephthah out and said to him, "You shall not have an inheritance in our father's house, for you are the son of another woman."

3 So Jephthah fled from his brothers and lived in the land of Tob; and worthless fellows gathered themselves about Jephthah, and they went out with him.

4 ¶ It came about after a while that the sons of Ammon fought against Israel.

5 When the sons of Ammon fought against Israel, the elders of Gilead went to get Jephthah from the land of Tob;

6 and they said to Jephthah, "Come and be

our chief that we may fight against the sons of Ammon."

7 Then Jephthah said to the elders of Gilead, "Did you not hate me and drive me from my

11:6 A Man Like David

Jephthah, like King David to come, was an outlaw who gained leadership experience at the head of a small band of adventurers. Israel turned to him when they needed military leadership, as they later would turn to David. Yet Jephthah's reputation never equaled David's, and the reason must have had something to do with his lack of wisdom. His rash vow to God (verse 31) and his harsh answer to a complaint (12:3) each had destructive results.

father's house? So why have you come to me now when you are in trouble?"

8 The elders of Gilead said to Jephthah, "For this reason we have now returned to you, that you may go with us and fight with the sons of Ammon and become head over all the inhabitants of Gilead."

9 So Jephthah said to the elders of Gilead, "If you take me back to fight against the sons of Ammon and the LORD gives them up to me, will I become your head?"

10 The elders of Gilead said to Jephthah, "The LORD is witness between us; surely we will do as you have said."

11 Then Jephthah went with the elders of Gilead, and the people made him head and chief over them; and Jephthah spoke all his words before the LORD at Mizpah.

12 ¶ Now Jephthah sent messengers to the king of the sons of Ammon, saying, "What is between you and me, that you have come to me to fight against my land?"

13 The king of the sons of Ammon said to the messengers of Jephthah, "Because Israel took away my land when they came up from Egypt, from the Arnon as far as the Jabbok and the Jordan; therefore, return them peaceably now."

14 But Jephthah sent messengers again to the king of the sons of Ammon,

15 and they said to him, "Thus says Jephthah, 'Israel did not take away the land of Moab nor the land of the sons of Ammon.

16 'For when they came up from Egypt, and Israel went through the wilderness to the Red Sea and came to Kadesh,

17 then Israel sent messengers to the king of Edom, saying, "Please let us pass through your land," but the king of Edom would not listen. And they also sent to the king of Moab, but he would not consent. So Israel remained at Kadesh.

18 'Then they went through the wilderness and around the land of Edom and the land of Moab, and came to the east side of the land of Moab, and they camped beyond the Arnon; but they did not enter the territory of Moab, for the Arnon *was* the border of Moab.

19 'And Israel sent messengers to Sihon king of the Amorites, the king of Heshbon, and Israel said to him, "Please let us pass through your land to our place."

20 'But Sihon did not trust Israel to pass through his territory; so Sihon gathered all his people and camped in Jahaz and fought with Israel.

21 'The LORD, the God of Israel, gave Sihon and all his people into the hand of Israel, and they defeated them; so Israel possessed all the land of the Amorites, the inhabitants of that country.

22 'So they possessed all the territory of the Amorites, from the Arnon as far as the Jabbok, and from the wilderness as far as the Jordan.

23 'Since now the LORD, the God of Israel, drove out the Amorites from before His people Israel, are you then to possess it?

24 'Do you not possess what Chemosh your god gives you to possess? So whatever the LORD our God has driven out before us, we will possess it.

25 'Now are you any better than Balak the son of Zippor, king of Moab? Did he ever strive with Israel, or did he ever fight against them?

26 'While Israel lived in Heshbon and its villages, and in Aroer and its villages, and in all the cities that are on the banks of the Arnon, three hundred years, why did you not recover them within that time?

27 'I therefore have not sinned against you, but you are doing me wrong by making war against me; may the LORD, the Judge, judge today between the sons of Israel and the sons of Ammon.'"

28 But the king of the sons of Ammon disregarded the message which Jephthah sent him.

Jephthah's Tragic Vow

29 ¶ Now the Spirit of the LORD came upon Jephthah, so that he passed through Gilead and Manasseh; then he passed through Mizpah of Gilead, and from Mizpah of Gilead he went on to the sons of Ammon.

30 Jephthah made a vow to the LORD and said, "If You will indeed give the sons of Ammon into my hand,

31 then it shall be that whatever comes out of the doors of my house to meet me when I return in peace from the sons of Ammon, it shall be the LORD'S, and I will offer it up as a burnt offering."

32 So Jephthah crossed over to the sons of Ammon to fight against them; and the LORD gave them into his hand.

33 He struck them with a very great slaughter from Aroer to the entrance of Minnith, twenty cities, and as far as Abel-keramim. So the sons of

Ammon were subdued before the sons of Israel.

34 ¶ When Jephthah came to his house at Mizpah, behold, his daughter was coming out to meet him with tambourines and with dancing. Now she was his one *and* only child; besides her he had no son or daughter.

35 When he saw her, he tore his clothes and said, "Alas, my daughter! You have brought me very low, and you are among those who trouble me; for I have given my word to the LORD, and I cannot take *it* back."

36 So she said to him, "My father, you have given your word to the LORD; do to me as you have said, since the LORD has avenged you of your enemies, the sons of Ammon."

37 She said to her father, "Let this thing be done for me; let me alone two months, that I may go to the mountains and weep because of my virginity, I and my companions."

38 Then he said, "Go." So he sent her away for two months; and she left with her companions, and wept on the mountains because of her virginity.

39 At the end of two months she returned to her father, who did to her according to the vow which he had made; and she had no relations with a man. Thus it became a custom in Israel,

40 that the daughters of Israel went yearly to commemorate the daughter of Jephthah the Gileadite four days in the year.

Jephthah and His Successors

12 Then the men of Ephraim were summoned, and they crossed to Zaphon and said to Jephthah, "Why did you cross over to fight against the sons of Ammon without calling us to go with you? We will burn your house down on you."

12:1 A Soft Answer

"A gentle answer turns away wrath," says Proverbs 15:1. Compare Jephthah's answer to the men of Ephraim with Gideon's softer response to the same complaint in Judges 8:1–3. In Gideon's case, anger subsided. In this, civil war resulted, and 42,000 Israelites died.

2 Jephthah said to them, "I and my people were at great strife with the sons of Ammon; when I called you, you did not deliver me from their hand.

3 "When I saw that you would not deliver *me*, I took my life in my hands and crossed over against the sons of Ammon, and the LORD gave them into my hand. Why then have you come up to me this day to fight against me?"

4 Then Jephthah gathered all the men of Gilead and fought Ephraim; and the men of Gilead defeated Ephraim, because they said, "You are

fugitives of Ephraim, O Gileadites, in the midst of Ephraim *and* in the midst of Manasseh."

5 The Gileadites captured the fords of the Jordan opposite Ephraim. And it happened when *any of* the fugitives of Ephraim said, "Let me cross over," the men of Gilead would say to him, "Are you an Ephraimite?" If he said, "No,"

6 then they would say to him, "Say now, 'Shibboleth.'" But he said, "Sibboleth," for he could not pronounce it correctly. Then they seized him and slew him at the fords of the Jordan. Thus there fell at that time 42,000 of Ephraim.

7 ¶ Jephthah judged Israel six years. Then Jephthah the Gileadite died and was buried in *one of* the cities of Gilead.

8 ¶ Now Ibzan of Bethlehem judged Israel after him.

9 He had thirty sons, and thirty daughters *whom* he gave in marriage outside *the family,* and he brought in thirty daughters from outside for his sons. And he judged Israel seven years.

10 Then Ibzan died and was buried in Bethlehem.

11 ¶ Now Elon the Zebulunite judged Israel after him; and he judged Israel ten years.

12 Then Elon the Zebulunite died and was buried at Aijalon in the land of Zebulun.

13 ¶ Now Abdon the son of Hillel the Pirathonite judged Israel after him.

14 He had forty sons and thirty grandsons who rode on seventy donkeys; and he judged Israel eight years.

15 Then Abdon the son of Hillel the Pirathonite died and was buried at Pirathon in the land of Ephraim, in the hill country of the Amalekites.

Philistines Oppress Again

13 Now the sons of Israel again did evil in the sight of the LORD, so that the LORD gave them into the hands of the Philistines forty years.

2 ¶ There was a certain man of Zorah, of the family of the Danites, whose name was Manoah; and his wife was barren and had borne no *children.*

3 Then the angel of the LORD appeared to the woman and said to her, "Behold now, you are barren and have borne no *children,* but you shall conceive and give birth to a son.

4 "Now therefore, be careful not to drink wine or strong drink, nor eat any unclean thing.

5 "For behold, you shall conceive and give birth to a son, and no razor shall come upon his head, for the boy shall be a Nazirite to God from the womb; and he shall begin to deliver Israel from the hands of the Philistines."

6 Then the woman came and told her husband, saying, "A man of God came to me and his appearance was like the appearance of the angel of God, very awesome. And I did not ask him where he *came* from, nor did he tell me his name.

7 "But he said to me, 'Behold, you shall con-

ceive and give birth to a son, and now you shall not drink wine or strong drink nor eat any unclean thing, for the boy shall be a Nazirite to God from the womb to the day of his death.' "

8 ¶ Then Manoah entreated the LORD and said, "O Lord, please let the man of God whom You have sent come to us again that he may teach us what to do for the boy who is to be born."

9 God listened to the voice of Manoah; and the angel of God came again to the woman as she was sitting in the field, but Manoah her husband was not with her.

10 So the woman ran quickly and told her husband, "Behold, the man who came the *other* day has appeared to me."

11 Then Manoah arose and followed his wife, and when he came to the man he said to him, "Are you the man who spoke to the woman?" And he said, "I am."

12 Manoah said, "Now when your words come *to pass*, what shall be the boy's mode of life and his vocation?"

13 So the angel of the LORD said to Manoah, "Let the woman pay attention to all that I said.

14 "She should not eat anything that comes from the vine nor drink wine or strong drink, nor eat any unclean thing; let her observe all that I commanded."

15 ¶ Then Manoah said to the angel of the LORD, "Please let us detain you so that we may prepare a young goat for you."

16 The angel of the LORD said to Manoah, "Though you detain me, I will not eat your food, but if you prepare a burnt offering, *then* offer it to the LORD." For Manoah did not know that he was the angel of the LORD.

17 Manoah said to the angel of the LORD, "What is your name, so that when your words come *to pass*, we may honor you?"

18 But the angel of the LORD said to him, "Why do you ask my name, seeing it is *a*wonderful?"

19 So Manoah took the young goat with the grain offering and offered it on the rock to the LORD, and He performed wonders while Manoah and his wife looked on.

20 For it came about when the flame went up from the altar toward heaven, that the angel of the LORD ascended in the flame of the altar. When Manoah and his wife saw *this*, they fell on their faces to the ground.

21 ¶ Now the angel of the LORD did not appear to Manoah or his wife again. Then Manoah knew that he was the angel of the LORD.

22 So Manoah said to his wife, "We will surely die, for we have seen God."

23 But his wife said to him, "If the LORD had desired to kill us, He would not have accepted a burnt offering and a grain offering from our hands, nor would He have shown us all these things, nor would He have let us hear *things* like this at this time."

24 ¶ Then the woman gave birth to a son and named him Samson; and the child grew up and the LORD blessed him.

25 And the Spirit of the LORD began to stir him in *b*Mahaneh-dan, between Zorah and Eshtaol.

Samson's Marriage

14 Then Samson went down to Timnah and saw a woman in Timnah, *one* of the daughters of the Philistines.

14:1 The First Sign of Trouble

Timnah was only four miles across the valley from Samson's hometown. Apparently, the Philistines and Israelites moved freely back and forth, and not all Israelites opposed the Philistines (see 15:11). Samson, making the short stroll, was attracted to a young Philistine woman. His lack of concern for differences of religion and his lack of submission to his parents were ominous signs pointing toward Samson's future troubles.

2 So he came back and told his father and mother, "I saw a woman in Timnah, *one* of the daughters of the Philistines; now therefore, get her for me as a wife."

3 Then his father and his mother said to him, "Is there no woman among the daughters of your relatives, or among all our people, that you go to take a wife from the uncircumcised Philistines?" But Samson said to his father, "Get her for me, for she looks good to me."

4 However, his father and mother did not know that it was of the LORD, for He was seeking an occasion against the Philistines. Now at that time the Philistines were ruling over Israel.

5 ¶ Then Samson went down to Timnah with his father and mother, and came as far as the vineyards of Timnah; and behold, a young lion *came* roaring toward him.

6 The Spirit of the LORD came upon him mightily, so that he tore him as one tears a young goat though he had nothing in his hand; but he did not tell his father or mother what he had done.

7 So he went down and talked to the woman; and she looked good to Samson.

8 When he returned later to take her, he turned aside to look at the carcass of the lion; and behold, a swarm of bees and honey were in the body of the lion.

9 So he scraped the honey into his hands and went on, eating as he went. When he came to his father and mother, he gave *some* to them and they

a I.e. incomprehensible   *b* I.e. the camp of Dan

ate *it;* but he did not tell them that he had scraped the honey out of the body of the lion.

10 ¶ Then his father went down to the woman; and Samson made a feast there, for the young men customarily did this.

11 When they saw him, they brought thirty companions to be with him.

Samson's Riddle

12 Then Samson said to them, "Let me now propound a riddle to you; if you will indeed tell it to me within the seven days of the feast, and find it out, then I will give you thirty linen wraps and thirty changes of clothes.

13 "But if you are unable to tell me, then you shall give me thirty linen wraps and thirty changes of clothes." And they said to him, "Propound your riddle, that we may hear it."

14 So he said to them,

"Out of the eater came something to eat,

And out of the strong came something sweet."

But they could not tell the riddle in three days.

15 ¶ Then it came about on the fourth day that they said to Samson's wife, "Entice your husband, so that he will tell us the riddle, or we will burn you and your father's house with fire. Have you invited us to impoverish us? Is this not *so?*"

16 Samson's wife wept before him and said, "You only hate me, and you do not love me; you have propounded a riddle to the sons of my people, and have not told *it* to me." And he said to her, "Behold, I have not told *it* to my father or mother; so should I tell you?"

17 However she wept before him seven days while their feast lasted. And on the seventh day he told her because she pressed him so hard. She then told the riddle to the sons of her people.

18 So the men of the city said to him on the seventh day before the sun went down,

Samson: A Weakness for Women

The strongest man of his generation never lived up to his promise

> *"I saw a woman. . . one of the daughters of the Philistines. . . now therefore, get her for me as a wife."* 14:2

SAMSON, THE STRONGEST MAN OF his generation, was tragically unable to control his lust. When he saw an attractive woman, he wanted her. He first fell for a young woman he saw in a Philistine village just across the valley from his home. His parents tried to dissuade him, since her religion and culture were unacceptable, but he would not listen. Desire was his only rule. The marriage ended in a matter of days and resulted in dozens of deaths.

The famous Delilah was at least the third woman who dallied with Samson, according to Judges. She, like his first love, was a Philistine living near his home. Where thousands of men had failed to overcome Samson, a wheedling woman succeeded. Thanks to her, he was captured, blinded, and set to work pushing a grinding machine. His final triumph was ironically fitting: Blind and bound, brought out like a freak for a hooting crowd's amusement, he destroyed himself while wreaking vengeance on the crowd. At his death, as throughout his life, it was hard to say who suffered most from Samson's hot temper: the Philistines or Samson.

Needed: A Leader

When you think of what God meant Samson to be, his life appears particularly tragic. Israel desperately needed a strong, confident leader, for the Philistines were moving in as masters, and many Israelites were willing to let them. God intended Samson for great things. Of all the judges, only Samson was announced by an angel before he was born (13:3). He was assigned to that special class of people known as Nazirites (described in Numbers 6), whose lives were specially devoted to God. Nazirites never drank wine, went near a dead body, or cut their hair.

Samson never lived up to his promise. Rule 3 was probably the only part of the Nazirite vow he kept—it required little self-discipline to let hair grow.

Despite all of Samson's weaknesses, God used him. He is mentioned in the Bible "Hall of Fame" (Hebrews 11:32) as a hero of faith along with Gideon, Barak, and Jephthah, all from Judges. Barely conscious of what it meant to live for God, and given to fits of lust and temper, Samson still had great physical strength, which came supernaturally from God. With it, he pushed back the Philistines—more by accident than by intention—and kept Israel intact.

Samson seems like a train whose engineer has fallen out of the cab, an oversized accident smashing into everything it meets. But for God, there are no accidents. He used the tragedy of Samson's life for good.

Life Questions: Which might best be said of you: "Oh, what he/she might have been!" or "He/she made the best of his/her abilities"?

"What is sweeter than honey?
And what is stronger than a lion?"
And he said to them,
"If you had not plowed with my heifer,
You would not have found out my
riddle."

19 Then the Spirit of the LORD came upon him mightily, and he went down to Ashkelon and killed thirty of them and took their spoil and gave the changes *of clothes* to those who told the riddle. And his anger burned, and he went up to his father's house.

20 But Samson's wife was *given* to his companion who had been his friend.

Samson Burns Philistine Crops

15 But after a while, in the time of wheat harvest, Samson visited his wife with a young goat, and said, "I will go in to my wife in *her* room." But her father did not let him enter.

2 Her father said, "I really thought that you hated her intensely; so I gave her to your companion. Is not her younger sister more beautiful than she? Please let her be yours instead."

3 Samson then said to them, "This time I shall be blameless in regard to the Philistines when I do them harm."

4 Samson went and caught three hundred foxes, and took torches, and turned *the foxes* tail to tail and put one torch in the middle between two tails.

5 When he had set fire to the torches, he released the foxes into the standing grain of the Philistines, thus burning up both the shocks and the standing grain, along with the vineyards *and* groves.

6 Then the Philistines said, "Who did this?" And they said, "Samson, the son-in-law of the Timnite, because he took his wife and gave her to his companion." So the Philistines came up and burned her and her father with fire.

7 Samson said to them, "Since you act like this, I will surely take revenge on you, but after that I will quit."

8 He struck them ruthlessly with a great slaughter; and he went down and lived in the cleft of the rock of Etam.

9 ¶ Then the Philistines went up and camped in Judah, and spread out in Lehi.

10 The men of Judah said, "Why have you come up against us?" And they said, "We have come up to bind Samson in order to do to him as he did to us."

11 Then 3,000 men of Judah went down to the cleft of the rock of Etam and said to Samson, "Do you not know that the Philistines are rulers over us? What then is this that you have done to us?" And he said to them, "As they did to me, so I have done to them."

12 They said to him, "We have come down to bind you so that we may give you into the hands of the Philistines." And Samson said to them, "Swear to me that you will not kill me."

13 So they said to him, "No, but we will bind you fast and give you into their hands; yet surely we will not kill you." Then they bound him with two new ropes and brought him up from the rock.

14 ¶ When he came to Lehi, the Philistines shouted as they met him. And the Spirit of the LORD came upon him mightily so that the ropes that were on his arms were as flax that is burned with fire, and his bonds dropped from his hands.

15:14 The Spirit and Samson

Four times (see also 13:25; 14:6,19) Judges comments that "the Spirit of the LORD" came on Samson. The same comment is made of other judges, though less frequently. But the Spirit only gave Samson great strength, as far as we can see; fruit of the Spirit like love and self-control seem lacking from his life.

15 He found a fresh jawbone of a donkey, so he reached out and took it and killed a thousand men with it.

16 Then Samson said,
"With the jawbone of a donkey,
Heaps upon heaps,
With the jawbone of a donkey
I have killed a thousand men."

17 When he had finished speaking, he threw the jawbone from his hand; and he named that place ªRamath-lehi.

18 Then he became very thirsty, and he called to the LORD and said, "You have given this great deliverance by the hand of Your servant, and now shall I die of thirst and fall into the hands of the uncircumcised?"

19 But God split the hollow place that is in Lehi so that water came out of it. When he drank, his strength returned and he revived. Therefore he named it En-hakkore, which is in Lehi to this day.

20 So he judged Israel twenty years in the days of the Philistines.

Samson's Weakness

16 Now Samson went to Gaza and saw a harlot there, and went in to her.

2 *When it was told* to the Gazites, saying, "Samson has come here," they surrounded *the place* and lay in wait for him all night at the gate of the city. And they kept silent all night, saying, "*Let us wait* until the morning light, then we will kill him."

3 Now Samson lay until midnight, and at midnight he arose and took hold of the doors of the city gate and the two posts and pulled them up

ª I.e. the high place of the jawbone

along with the bars; then he put them on his shoulders and carried them up to the top of the mountain which is opposite Hebron.

4 ¶ After this it came about that he loved a woman in the valley of Sorek, whose name was Delilah.

5 The lords of the Philistines came up to her and said to her, "Entice him, and see where his great strength *lies* and how we may overpower him that we may bind him to afflict him. Then we will each give you eleven hundred *pieces* of silver."

6 So Delilah said to Samson, "Please tell me where your great strength is and how you may be bound to afflict you."

7 Samson said to her, "If they bind me with seven fresh cords that have not been dried, then I will become weak and be like any *other* man."

8 Then the lords of the Philistines brought up to her seven fresh cords that had not been dried, and she bound him with them.

9 Now she had *men* lying in wait in an inner room. And she said to him, "The Philistines are upon you, Samson!" But he snapped the cords as a string of tow snaps when it touches fire. So his strength was not discovered.

10 ¶ Then Delilah said to Samson, "Behold, you have deceived me and told me lies; now please tell me how you may be bound."

11 He said to her, "If they bind me tightly with new ropes which have not been used, then I will become weak and be like any *other* man."

12 So Delilah took new ropes and bound him with them and said to him, "The Philistines are upon you, Samson!" For the *men* were lying in wait in the inner room. But he snapped the ropes from his arms like a thread.

13 ¶ Then Delilah said to Samson, "Up to now you have deceived me and told me lies; tell me how you may be bound." And he said to her, "If you weave the seven locks of my hair with the web *a*[and fasten it with a pin, then I will become weak and be like any other man."

14 So while he slept, Delilah took the seven locks of his hair and wove them into the web]. And she fastened *it* with the pin and said to him, "The Philistines are upon you, Samson!" But he awoke from his sleep and pulled out the pin of the loom and the web.

Delilah Extracts His Secret

15 ¶ Then she said to him, "How can you say, 'I love you,' when your heart is not with me? You have deceived me these three times and have not told me where your great strength is."

16 It came about when she pressed him daily with her words and urged him, that his soul was annoyed to death.

17 So he told her all *that was* in his heart and said to her, "A razor has never come on my head, for I have been a Nazirite to God from my moth-

er's womb. If I am shaved, then my strength will leave me and I will become weak and be like any *other* man."

18 ¶ When Delilah saw that he had told her all *that was* in his heart, she sent and called the lords of the Philistines, saying, "Come up once more, for he has told me all *that is* in his heart." Then the lords of the Philistines came up to her and brought the money in their hands.

19 She made him sleep on her knees, and called for a man and had him shave off the seven locks of his hair. Then she began to afflict him, and his strength left him.

20 She said, "The Philistines are upon you, Samson!" And he awoke from his sleep and said, "I will go out as at other times and shake myself free." But he did not know that the LORD had departed from him.

21 Then the Philistines seized him and gouged out his eyes; and they brought him down to Gaza and bound him with bronze chains, and he was a grinder in the prison.

22 However, the hair of his head began to grow again after it was shaved off.

23 ¶ Now the lords of the Philistines assembled to offer a great sacrifice to Dagon their god, and to rejoice, for they said,

"Our god has given Samson our enemy into our hands."

24 When the people saw him, they praised their god, for they said,

"Our god has given our enemy into our hands,
Even the destroyer of our country,
Who has slain many of us."

25 It so happened when they were in high spirits, that they said, "Call for Samson, that he may amuse us." So they called for Samson from the prison, and he entertained them. And they made him stand between the pillars.

26 Then Samson said to the boy who was holding his hand, "Let me feel the pillars on which the house rests, that I may lean against them."

27 Now the house was full of men and women, and all the lords of the Philistines were there. And about 3,000 men and women were on the roof looking on while Samson was amusing *them*.

Samson Is Avenged

28 ¶ Then Samson called to the LORD and said, "O Lord GOD, please remember me and please strengthen me just this time, O God, that I may at once be avenged of the Philistines for my two eyes."

29 Samson grasped the two middle pillars on which the house rested, and braced himself against them, the one with his right hand and the other with his left.

30 And Samson said, "Let me die with the Philistines!" And he bent with all his might so that the

---

a The passage in brackets is found in Gr but not in any Heb mss house fell on the lords and all the people who were in it. So the dead whom he killed at his death were more than those whom he killed in his life.

31 Then his brothers and all his father's house-hold came down, took him, brought him up and buried him between Zorah and Eshtaol in the tomb of Manoah his father. Thus he had judged Israel twenty years.

Micah's Idolatry

17 Now there was a man of the hill country of Ephraim whose name was Micah.

2 He said to his mother, "The eleven hundred *pieces* of silver which were taken from you, about which you uttered a curse in my hearing, behold, the silver is with me; I took it." And his mother said, "Blessed be my son by the LORD."

3 He then returned the eleven hundred *pieces* of silver to his mother, and his mother said, "I wholly dedicate the silver from my hand to the LORD for my son to make a graven image and a molten image; now therefore, I will return them to you."

16:30 Bring the House Down

Archaeologists have excavated temples from Samson's period. Typically, wooden pillars were set close together to support a roof, which sometimes included a covered area for spectators. Quite possibly this structure was already creaking under the weight of 3,000 people, who would have crowded to one side to see Samson perform. Samson managed to push the pillars off their stone bases, and the roof collapsed.

Hanging by a Thread

Theft, rape, murder, idolatry: Israel was destroying itself

A TIME COMES WHEN YOU can no longer blame your problems on other people. In the comic strip character Pogo's immortal words, "We have met the enemy, and he is us."

So it is at the end of Judges. The camera zooms in for a close-up, focusing on internal violence. Foreign enemies are no longer in view: The enemy is Israel itself.

> *In those days there was no king in Israel; every man did what was right in his own eyes. 17:6*

They make ugly portraits, these last five chapters. Pointless and violent, they begin with a son stealing from his mother and end with parents agreeing to let their daughters be kidnapped. In between are homosexual and heterosexual gang rape, murder, idolatry, armed robbery, mass slaughter. No enemy does all this: Israelites do it to each other. Clearly, the exalted nation of Israel, God's chosen people, has lost all sense of direction.

Who Can Rescue Them Now?

The first 16 chapters of Judges tell of repeated enemy invasions that moved Israel to call out to God. Hearing his people, God would send a freedom fighter to save them.

In the last five chapters, by contrast, God sends no freedom fighters. No military leader could rescue them from themselves. These chapters instead repeat the solemn words: "In those days there was no king in Israel; every man did what was right in his own eyes."

"Every man did what was right in his own eyes" may not sound very negative in our era, which places high value on individualism and personal freedom. But God prizes something more: unity. He wants his people united in love for him and each other. God's law had bound his people to a common worship in the tabernacle and to a common standard of caring for each other. For this the Israelites substituted do-as-you-please religion and a fractured society, where each family or group fought for its own rights alone. The result? These chapters tell the dismal story.

Israel's Worst Enemy

By the end of Judges, Israelites are reduced to fighting themselves. They have adopted their enemies' customs. They worship idols. They are sexually immoral. They lack respect for parents. They cannot remember the pattern of life God had set out. It is hard to say, by the end of Judges, why God should save Israel from their enemies. It is hard to say whether Israelites are the least bit different from their enemies. Israel has become, in fact, its own worst enemy.

Only one glimmer of hope appears: the Israelites' shock at the Benjamites' gang rape. They can still get together to punish such outrages, and they still consult the Lord about them. But they are a far cry from the hopeful people Joshua led into the promised land.

Life Questions: Do your troubles come more from your circumstances or from your own internal weaknesses? What kind of help do you need from God?

4 So when he returned the silver to his mother, his mother took two hundred *pieces* of silver and gave them to the silversmith who made them into a graven image and a molten image, and they were in the house of Micah.

5 And the man Micah had a *a*shrine and he made an ephod and household idols and consecrated one of his sons, that he might become his priest.

6 In those days there was no king in Israel; every man did what was right in his own eyes.

17:6 A State of Anarchy

Four times the final chapters of Judges mention there was "no king." Twice Judges adds that "every man did what was right in his own eyes." This editorial remark was probably made later, after the monarchy had begun under Saul and David; a king unified the nation. Some problems of this period are evident in verse 5: idolatry and the installation of a priest who did not come from the priestly family. The story that follows shows one group of Israelites raiding another, as though they were enemies, not relatives.

7 ¶ Now there was a young man from Bethlehem in Judah, of the family of Judah, who was a Levite; and he was staying there.

8 Then the man departed from the city, from Bethlehem in Judah, to stay wherever he might find *a place;* and as he made his journey, he came to the hill country of Ephraim to the house of Micah.

9 Micah said to him, "Where do you come from?" And he said to him, "I am a Levite from Bethlehem in Judah, and I am going to stay wherever I may find *a place.*"

10 Micah then said to him, "Dwell with me and be a father and a priest to me, and I will give you ten *pieces* of silver a year, a suit of clothes, and your maintenance." So the Levite went *in.*

11 The Levite agreed to live with the man, and the young man became to him like one of his sons.

12 So Micah consecrated the Levite, and the young man became his priest and lived in the house of Micah.

13 Then Micah said, "Now I know that the LORD will prosper me, seeing I have a Levite as priest."

Danites Seek Territory

18 In those days there was no king of Israel; and in those days the tribe of the Danites was seeking an inheritance for themselves to live in, for until that day an inheritance had not been allotted to them as a possession among the tribes of Israel.

2 So the sons of Dan sent from their family five men out of their whole number, valiant men from Zorah and Eshtaol, to spy out the land and to search it; and they said to them, "Go, search the land." And they came to the hill country of Ephraim, to the house of Micah, and lodged there.

3 When they were near the house of Micah, they recognized the voice of the young man, the Levite; and they turned aside there and said to him, "Who brought you here? And what are you doing in this *place?* And what do you have here?"

4 He said to them, "Thus and so has Micah done to me, and he has hired me and I have become his priest."

5 They said to him, "Inquire of God, please, that we may know whether our way on which we are going will be prosperous."

6 The priest said to them, "Go in peace; your way in which you are going has the LORD'S approval."

7 ¶ Then the five men departed and came to Laish and saw the people who were in it living in security, after the manner of the Sidonians, quiet and secure; for there was no ruler humiliating *them* for anything in the land, and they were far from the Sidonians and had no dealings with anyone.

8 When they came back to their brothers at Zorah and Eshtaol, their brothers said to them, "What *do* you *report?*"

9 They said, "Arise, and let us go up against them; for we have seen the land, and behold, it is very good. And will you sit still? Do not delay to go, to enter, to possess the land.

10 "When you enter, you will come to a secure people with a spacious land; for God has given it into your hand, a place where there is no lack of anything that is on the earth."

11 ¶ Then from the family of the Danites, from Zorah and from Eshtaol, six hundred men armed with weapons of war set out.

12 They went up and camped at Kiriath-jearim in Judah. Therefore they called that place *b*Mahaneh-dan to this day; behold, it is west of Kiriath-jearim.

13 They passed from there to the hill country of Ephraim and came to the house of Micah.

Danites Take Micah's Idols

14 ¶ Then the five men who went to spy out the country of Laish said to their kinsmen, "Do you know that there are in these houses an ephod and *c*household idols and a graven image and a molten image? Now therefore, consider what you should do."

15 They turned aside there and came to the house of the young man, the Levite, to the house of Micah, and asked him of his welfare.

---

a Lit *house of gods*   *b* I.e. the camp of Dan   *c* Heb *teraphim*

16 The six hundred men armed with their weapons of war, who were of the sons of Dan, stood by the entrance of the gate.

17 Now the five men who went to spy out the land went up *and* entered there, *and* took the graven image and the ephod and household idols and the molten image, while the priest stood by the entrance of the gate with the six hundred men armed with weapons of war.

18 When these went into Micah's house and took the graven image, the ephod and household idols and the molten image, the priest said to them, "What are you doing?"

19 They said to him, "Be silent, put your hand over your mouth and come with us, and be to us a father and a priest. Is it better for you to be a priest to the house of one man, or to be priest to a tribe and a family in Israel?"

20 The priest's heart was glad, and he took the ephod and household idols and the graven image and went among the people.

21 ¶ Then they turned and departed, and put the little ones and the livestock and the valuables in front of them.

22 When they had gone some distance from the house of Micah, the men who *were* in the houses near Micah's house assembled and overtook the sons of Dan.

23 They cried to the sons of Dan, who turned around and said to Micah, "What is *the matter* with you, that you have assembled together?"

24 He said, "You have taken away my gods which I made, and the priest, and have gone away, and what do I have besides? So how can you say to me, 'What is *the matter* with you?' "

18:24 Sad Commentary

Micah's outraged cry offers a sad commentary on the state of Israel. Even though his stolen gods were obviously unable to protect themselves, let alone him, Micah knew no other refuge. Anarchy ruled, as did idolatry.

25 The sons of Dan said to him, "Do not let your voice be heard among us, or else fierce men will fall upon you and you will lose your life, with the lives of your household."

26 So the sons of Dan went on their way; and when Micah saw that they were too strong for him, he turned and went back to his house.

27 ¶ Then they took what Micah had made and the priest who had belonged to him, and came to Laish, to a people quiet and secure, and struck them with the edge of the sword; and they burned the city with fire.

28 And there was no one to deliver *them*, because it was far from Sidon and they had no deal-

ings with anyone, and it was in the valley which is near Beth-rehob. And they rebuilt the city and lived in it.

29 They called the name of the city Dan, after the name of Dan their father who was born in Israel; however, the name of the city formerly was Laish.

30 The sons of Dan set up for themselves the graven image; and Jonathan, the son of Gershom, the son of *ª*Manasseh, he and his sons were priests to the tribe of the Danites until the day of the captivity of the land.

31 So they set up for themselves Micah's graven image which he had made, all the time that the house of God was at Shiloh.

A Levite's Concubine Degraded

19 Now it came about in those days, when there was no king in Israel, that there was a certain Levite staying in the remote part of the hill country of Ephraim, who took a concubine for himself from Bethlehem in Judah.

2 But his concubine played the harlot against him, and she went away from him to her father's house in Bethlehem in Judah, and was there for a period of four months.

3 Then her husband arose and went after her to speak tenderly to her in order to bring her back, taking with him his servant and a pair of donkeys. So she brought him into her father's house, and when the girl's father saw him, he was glad to meet him.

4 His father-in-law, the girl's father, detained him; and he remained with him three days. So they ate and drank and lodged there.

5 Now on the fourth day they got up early in the morning, and he prepared to go; and the girl's father said to his son-in-law, "Sustain yourself with a piece of bread, and afterward you may go."

6 So both of them sat down and ate and drank together; and the girl's father said to the man, "Please be willing to spend the night, and let your heart be merry."

7 Then the man arose to go, but his father-in-law urged him so that he spent the night there again.

8 On the fifth day he arose to go early in the morning, and the girl's father said, "Please sustain yourself, and wait until afternoon"; so both of them ate.

9 When the man arose to go along with his concubine and servant, his father-in-law, the girl's father, said to him, "Behold now, the day has drawn to a close; please spend the night. Lo, the day is coming to an end; spend the night here that your heart may be merry. Then tomorrow you may arise early for your journey so that you may go home."

10 ¶ But the man was not willing to spend the night, so he arose and departed and came to *a*

---

*ª Some ancient versions read *Moses*

place opposite Jebus (that is, Jerusalem). And there were with him a pair of saddled donkeys; his concubine also was with him.

11 When they *were* near Jebus, the day was almost gone; and the servant said to his master, "Please come, and let us turn aside into this city of the Jebusites and spend the night in it."

12 However, his master said to him, "We will not turn aside into the city of foreigners who are not of the sons of Israel; but we will go on as far as Gibeah."

13 He said to his servant, "Come and let us approach one of these places; and we will spend the night in Gibeah or Ramah."

14 So they passed along and went their way, and the sun set on them near Gibeah which belongs to Benjamin.

15 They turned aside there in order to enter *and* lodge in Gibeah. When they entered, they sat down in the open square of the city, for no one took them into *his* house to spend the night.

19:15 A Breach of Hospitality

In the ancient Middle East, people took hospitality very seriously. When the Levite sat down in the city square of an Israelite city, he expected the townspeople (his relatives) to offer him a place to stay. But only an old man from his home area offered the Levite lodging—the locals were inhospitable, an ominous sign.

The old man obviously took hospitality seriously. Unfortunately, he took women much less seriously. In fact, he urged the hostile mob to rape his daughter and his guest's concubine as a substitute for the guest himself. His response was nearly identical to Lot's on the eve of Sodom's destruction (Genesis 19:6–8). The story suggests that Israel had become as bad as Sodom.

16 ¶ Then behold, an old man was coming out of the field from his work at evening. Now the man was from the hill country of Ephraim, and he was staying in Gibeah, but the men of the place were Benjamites.

17 And he lifted up his eyes and saw the traveler in the open square of the city; and the old man said, "Where are you going, and where do you come from?"

18 He said to him, "We are passing from Bethlehem in Judah to the remote part of the hill country of Ephraim, *for* I am from there, and I went to Bethlehem in Judah. But I am *now* going to my house, and no man will take me into his house.

19 "Yet there is both straw and fodder for our donkeys, and also bread and wine for me, your maidservant, and the young man who is with your servants; there is no lack of anything."

20 The old man said, "Peace to you. Only let me *take care of* all your needs; however, do not spend the night in the open square."

21 So he took him into his house and gave the donkeys fodder, and they washed their feet and ate and drank.

22 ¶ While they were celebrating, behold, the men of the city, certain worthless fellows, surrounded the house, pounding the door; and they spoke to the owner of the house, the old man, saying, "Bring out the man who came into your house that we may have relations with him."

23 Then the man, the owner of the house, went out to them and said to them, "No, my fellows, please do not act so wickedly; since this man has come into my house, do not commit this act of folly.

24 "Here is my virgin daughter and his concubine. Please let me bring them out that you may ravish them and do to them whatever you wish. But do not commit such an act of folly against this man."

25 But the men would not listen to him. So the man seized his concubine and brought *her* out to them; and they raped her and abused her all night until morning, then let her go at the approach of dawn.

26 As the day began to dawn, the woman came and fell down at the doorway of the man's house where her master was, until *full* daylight.

27 ¶ When her master arose in the morning and opened the doors of the house and went out to go on his way, then behold, his concubine was lying at the doorway of the house with her hands on the threshold.

28 He said to her, "Get up and let us go," but there was no answer. Then he placed her on the donkey; and the man arose and went to his home.

29 When he entered his house, he took a knife and laid hold of his concubine and cut her in twelve pieces, limb by limb, and sent her throughout the territory of Israel.

30 All who saw *it* said, "Nothing like this *ever* happened or been seen from the day when the sons of Israel came up from the land of Egypt to this day. Consider it, take counsel and speak up!"

Resolve to Punish the Guilty

20 Then all the sons of Israel from Dan to Beersheba, including the land of Gilead, came out, and the congregation assembled as one man to the LORD at Mizpah.

2 The chiefs of all the people, *even* of all the tribes of Israel, took their stand in the assembly of the people of God, 400,000 foot soldiers who drew the sword.

3 (Now the sons of Benjamin heard that the sons of Israel had gone up to Mizpah.) And the sons of Israel said, "Tell *us*, how did this wickedness take place?"

4 So the Levite, the husband of the woman

who was murdered, answered and said, "I came with my concubine to spend the night at Gibeah which belongs to Benjamin.

5 "But the men of Gibeah rose up against me and surrounded the house at night because of me. They intended to kill me; instead, they ravished my concubine so that she died.

6 "And I took hold of my concubine and cut her in pieces and sent her throughout the land of Israel's inheritance; for they have committed a lewd and disgraceful act in Israel.

7 "Behold, all you sons of Israel, give your advice and counsel here."

8 ¶ Then all the people arose as one man, saying, "Not one of us will go to his tent, nor will any of us return to his house.

9 "But now this is the thing which we will do to Gibeah; *we will go up* against it by lot.

10 "And we will take 10 men out of 100 throughout the tribes of Israel, and 100 out of 1,000, and 1,000 out of 10,000 to supply food for the people, that when they come to Gibeah of Benjamin, they may punish *them* for all the disgraceful acts that they have committed in Israel."

11 Thus all the men of Israel were gathered against the city, united as one man.

12 ¶ Then the tribes of Israel sent men through the entire tribe of Benjamin, saying, "What is this wickedness that has taken place among you?

13 "Now then, deliver up the men, the *a*worthless fellows in Gibeah, that we may put them to death and remove *this* wickedness from Israel." But the sons of Benjamin would not listen to the voice of their brothers, the sons of Israel.

14 The sons of Benjamin gathered from the cities to Gibeah, to go out to battle against the sons of Israel.

15 From the cities on that day the sons of Benjamin were numbered, 26,000 men who draw the sword, besides the inhabitants of Gibeah who were numbered, 700 choice men.

16 Out of all these people 700 choice men were left-handed; each one could sling a stone at a hair and not miss.

17 ¶ Then the men of Israel besides Benjamin were numbered, 400,000 men who draw the sword; all these were men of war.

Civil War, Benjamin Defeated

18 ¶ Now the sons of Israel arose, went up to Bethel, and inquired of God and said, "Who shall go up first for us to battle against the sons of Benjamin?" Then the LORD said, "Judah *shall go up* first."

19 ¶ So the sons of Israel arose in the morning and camped against Gibeah.

20 The men of Israel went out to battle against Benjamin, and the men of Israel arrayed for battle against them at Gibeah.

21 Then the sons of Benjamin came out of Gib-

eah and felled to the ground on that day 22,000 men of Israel.

22 But the people, the men of Israel, encouraged themselves and arrayed for battle again in the place where they had arrayed themselves the first day.

23 The sons of Israel went up and wept before the LORD until evening, and inquired of the LORD, saying, "Shall we again draw near for battle against the sons of my brother Benjamin?" And the LORD said, "Go up against him."

24 ¶ Then the sons of Israel came against the sons of Benjamin the second day.

25 Benjamin went out against them from Gibeah the second day and felled to the ground again 18,000 men of the sons of Israel; all these drew the sword.

26 Then all the sons of Israel and all the people went up and came to Bethel and wept; thus they remained there before the LORD and fasted that day until evening. And they offered burnt offerings and peace offerings before the LORD.

27 The sons of Israel inquired of the LORD (for the ark of the covenant of God *was* there in those days,

28 and Phinehas the son of Eleazar, Aaron's son, stood before it to *minister* in those days), saying, "Shall I yet again go out to battle against the sons of my brother Benjamin, or shall I cease?" And the LORD said, "Go up, for tomorrow I will deliver them into your hand."

29 ¶ So Israel set men in ambush around Gibeah.

30 The sons of Israel went up against the sons of Benjamin on the third day and arrayed themselves against Gibeah as at other times.

31 The sons of Benjamin went out against the people and were drawn away from the city, and they began to strike and kill some of the people as at other times, on the highways, one of which goes up to Bethel and the other to Gibeah, *and* in the field, about thirty men of Israel.

32 The sons of Benjamin said, "They are struck down before us, as at the first." But the sons of Israel said, "Let us flee that we may draw them away from the city to the highways."

33 Then all the men of Israel arose from their place and arrayed themselves at Baal-tamar; and the men of Israel in ambush broke out of their place, even out of Maareh-geba.

34 When ten thousand choice men from all Israel came against Gibeah, the battle became fierce; but Benjamin did not know that disaster was close to them.

35 And the LORD struck Benjamin before Israel, so that the sons of Israel destroyed 25,100 men of Benjamin that day, all who draw the sword.

36 ¶ So the sons of Benjamin saw that they were defeated. When the men of Israel gave ground to Benjamin because they relied on the

men in ambush whom they had set against Gibeah,

37 the men in ambush hurried and rushed against Gibeah; the men in ambush also deployed and struck all the city with the edge of the sword.

38 Now the appointed sign between the men of Israel and the men in ambush was that they would make a great cloud of smoke rise from the city.

39 Then the men of Israel turned in the battle, and Benjamin began to strike and kill about thirty men of Israel, for they said, "Surely they are defeated before us, as in the first battle."

40 But when the cloud began to rise from the city in a column of smoke, Benjamin looked behind them; and behold, the whole city was going up *in smoke* to heaven.

41 Then the men of Israel turned, and the men of Benjamin were terrified; for they saw that disaster was close to them.

42 Therefore, they turned their backs before the men of Israel toward the direction of the wilderness, but the battle overtook them while those who came out of the cities destroyed them in the midst of them.

43 They surrounded Benjamin, pursued them without rest *and* trod them down opposite Gibeah toward the east.

44 Thus 18,000 men of Benjamin fell; all these were valiant warriors.

45 The rest turned and fled toward the wilderness to the rock of Rimmon, but they caught 5,000 of them on the highways and overtook them at Gidom and killed 2,000 of them.

46 So all of Benjamin who fell that day were 25,000 men who draw the sword; all these were valiant warriors.

47 But 600 men turned and fled toward the wilderness to the rock of Rimmon, and they remained at the rock of Rimmon four months.

48 The men of Israel then turned back against the sons of Benjamin and struck them with the edge of the sword, both the entire city with the cattle and all that they found; they also set on fire all the cities which they found.

Mourning Lost Tribe

21 Now the men of Israel had sworn in Mizpah, saying, "None of us shall give his daughter to Benjamin in marriage."

2 So the people came to Bethel and sat there before God until evening, and lifted up their voices and wept bitterly.

3 They said, "Why, O LORD, God of Israel, has this come about in Israel, so that one tribe should be *missing* today in Israel?"

4 It came about the next day that the people arose early and built an altar there and offered burnt offerings and peace offerings.

5 ¶ Then the sons of Israel said, "Who is there among all the tribes of Israel who did not come up in the assembly to the LORD?" For they had taken a great oath concerning him who did not come up to the LORD at Mizpah, saying, "He shall surely be put to death."

6 And the sons of Israel were sorry for their brother Benjamin and said, "One tribe is cut off from Israel today.

7 "What shall we do for wives for those who are left, since we have sworn by the LORD not to give them any of our daughters in marriage?"

Provision for Their Survival

8 ¶ And they said, "What one is there of the tribes of Israel who did not come up to the LORD at Mizpah?" And behold, no one had come to the camp from Jabesh-gilead to the assembly.

9 For when the people were numbered, behold, not one of the inhabitants of Jabesh-gilead was there.

10 And the congregation sent 12,000 of the valiant warriors there, and commanded them, saying, "Go and strike the inhabitants of Jabesh-gilead with the edge of the sword, with the women and the little ones.

11 "This is the thing that you shall do: you shall utterly destroy every man and every woman who has lain with a man."

12 And they found among the inhabitants of Jabesh-gilead 400 young virgins who had not known a man by lying with him; and they brought them to the camp at Shiloh, which is in the land of Canaan.

13 ¶ Then the whole congregation sent *word* and spoke to the sons of Benjamin who were at the rock of Rimmon, and proclaimed peace to them.

14 Benjamin returned at that time, and they gave them the women whom they had kept alive from the women of Jabesh-gilead; yet they were not enough for them.

15 And the people were sorry for Benjamin because the LORD had made a breach in the tribes of Israel.

16 ¶ Then the elders of the congregation said, "What shall we do for wives for those who are left, since the women are destroyed out of Benjamin?"

17 They said, "*There must be* an inheritance for the survivors of Benjamin, so that a tribe will not be blotted out from Israel.

18 "But we cannot give them wives of our daughters." For the sons of Israel had sworn, saying, "Cursed is he who gives a wife to Benjamin."

19 ¶ So they said, "Behold, there is a feast of the LORD from year to year in Shiloh, which is on the north side of Bethel, on the east side of the highway that goes up from Bethel to Shechem, and on the south side of Lebonah."

20 And they commanded the sons of Benjamin, saying, "Go and lie in wait in the vineyards,

21 and watch; and behold, if the daughters of Shiloh come out to take part in the dances, then

you shall come out of the vineyards and each of you shall catch his wife from the daughters of Shiloh, and go to the land of Benjamin. 22 "It shall come about, when their fathers or their brothers come to complain to us, that we shall say to them, 'Give them to us voluntarily, because we did not take for each man *of Benjamin* a wife in battle, nor did you give *them* to them, *else* you would now be guilty.'"

23 The sons of Benjamin did so, and took wives according to their number from those who danced, whom they carried away. And they went and returned to their inheritance and rebuilt the cities and lived in them.

24 The sons of Israel departed from there at that time, every man to his tribe and family, and each one of them went out from there to his inheritance.

25 ¶ In those days there was no king in Israel; everyone did what was right in his own eyes.

Ruth

A Rare Bond of Love
Ruth and Naomi lost everything, except their care for each other

RUTH AND NAOMI WERE UNLIKELY friends: a generation apart, one young and strong, the other past middle age. Stranger still, one was the other's mother-in-law and came from a completely different ethnic and religious background. Who would have put them together?

They had lost everything when their husbands died. With no man to rely on, their lives were at risk in those rough times. No one else would come to their defense: They had only each other.

> *"Where you go, I will go, and where you lodge, I will lodge. Your people shall be my people, and your God, my God. . . . May the* Lord *do to me, and worse, if anything but death parts you and me." 1:16–17*

The Woman's Initiative

The book of Ruth is not "two women against the world." Rather, it shows the women taking initiative to find, by God's help, a man who would care for them.

A woman's initiative rarely gets so direct as in Ruth. At her mother-in-law's direction Ruth located where Boaz, a relative, was camping out. She waited until dark, then crept to his feet and lay down. When Boaz woke and found her, he didn't have to be told what was on her mind. She wanted him for a husband. Flattered, he didn't let another sun set before making the legal arrangements for marriage.

Society the way God had designed it encouraged men like Boaz to help the needy. For instance, by Old Testament law a farmer had to leave some of his grain behind so that poor people like Ruth could harvest it. And, also by law, a helpless widow had to be taken into the home of her husband's family. This was the law by which Boaz claimed Ruth (4:1–12).

God's Invisible Presence

Behind the eloquent story of Ruth looms an invisible helper—God. He didn't intervene in the events, so far as the story tells. But nobody in Ruth doubted that life proceeded under God's direction. It was the Lord by whom Ruth swore when declaring her love to Naomi (1:17), and the Lord whom Naomi credited for bringing Ruth to Boaz's field (2:20). God's law brought Boaz and Ruth into marriage. Finally, the Lord gave them a son, in whom mother, father, and "grandmother" found deep satisfaction.

The last verses of Ruth show, furthermore, that God's plan extended beyond Ruth and Naomi's personal problems. Ruth was a member of the despised Moabites—enemies of Israel. Yet God not only accepted her into his family, but also used her to produce Israel's greatest king. Ruth's great-grandson turned out to be David. To anyone who thought that God's love was for Israelites only, Ruth's life made a striking contradiction.

How to Read Ruth

Ruth, brief enough to read in 15 minutes, is a delight. The German poet Goethe called it "the loveliest complete work on a small scale." But because Ruth's author didn't hammer his points home, it is possible to overlook his deeper meaning. As you read, concentrate on the loving bond between Ruth and Naomi. This love, which thrived in suffering, is the root of the book. It offers hope for other people in hard circumstances.

The author of Ruth assumed that readers understood the cultural and historical background of Ruth's time. You may wish to read about it for deeper understanding.

Deuteronomy 25:5–10 describes the background on marriage for a widow with a member of her husband's family, the "close relative." Leviticus 25:23–28 gives background on a poor person's property. The Introduction to Judges offers historical perspective, for the book of Judges is an overview of the brutal times Ruth lived in.

PEOPLE YOU'LL MEET IN RUTH

RUTH *(p. 310)*

3-TRACK READING PLAN

For an explanation and complete listing of the 3-track reading plan, turn to page 7.

TRACK 1: *Two-Week Courses on the Bible*
See page 8 for information on these courses.

TRACK 2: *An Overview of Ruth in 1 Day*
☐ Day 1. Read the Introduction to Ruth and chapter 1, which describes an unusual friendship developing under the unkindest of conditions.
Now turn to page 9 for your next Track 2 reading project.

TRACK 3: *All of Ruth in 4 Days*
After you have read through Ruth, turn to pages 10–14 for your next Track 3 reading project.
☐1 ☐2 ☐3 ☐4

Naomi Widowed

1 Now it came about in the days when the judges governed, that there was a famine in the land. And a certain man of Bethlehem in Judah went to sojourn in the land of Moab with his wife and his two sons.

2 The name of the man *was* Elimelech, and the name of his wife, Naomi; and the names of his two sons *were* Mahlon and Chilion, Ephrathites of Bethlehem in Judah. Now they entered the land of Moab and remained there.

3 Then Elimelech, Naomi's husband, died; and she was left with her two sons.

4 They took for themselves Moabite women *as* wives; the name of the one was Orpah and the name of the other Ruth. And they lived there about ten years.

5 Then both Mahlon and Chilion also died, and the woman was bereft of her two children and her husband.

6 ¶ Then she arose with her daughters-in-law that she might return from the land of Moab, for she had heard in the land of Moab that the LORD had visited His people in giving them food.

7 So she departed from the place where she was, and her two daughters-in-law with her; and they went on the way to return to the land of Judah.

8 And Naomi said to her two daughters-in-law, "Go, return each of you to her mother's house. May the LORD deal kindly with you as you have dealt with the dead and with me.

9 "May the LORD grant that you may find rest, each in the house of her husband." Then she kissed them, and they lifted up their voices and wept.

10 And they said to her, "*No*, but we will surely return with you to your people."

11 But Naomi said, "Return, my daughters. Why should you go with me? Have I yet sons in my womb, that they may be your husbands?

12 "Return, my daughters! Go, for I am too old to have a husband. If I said I have hope, if I should even have a husband tonight and also bear sons,

13 would you therefore wait until they were grown? Would you therefore refrain from marrying? No, my daughters; for it is harder for me than for you, for the hand of the LORD has gone forth against me."

Ruth's Loyalty

14 And they lifted up their voices and wept again; and Orpah kissed her mother-in-law, but Ruth clung to her.

15 ¶ Then she said, "Behold, your sister-in-law has gone back to her people and her gods; return after your sister-in-law."

16 But Ruth said, "Do not urge me to leave you *or* turn back from following you; for where you go, I will go, and where you lodge, I will lodge.

Your people *shall be* my people, and your God, my God.

17 "Where you die, I will die, and there I will be buried. Thus may the LORD do to me, and worse, if *anything but* death parts you and me."

18 When she saw that she was determined to go with her, she said no more to her.

19 ¶ So they both went until they came to Bethlehem. And when they had come to Bethlehem, all the city was stirred because of them, and the women said, "Is this Naomi?"

20 She said to them, "Do not call me *a*Naomi; call me *b*Mara, for the Almighty has dealt very bitterly with me.

21 "I went out full, but the LORD has brought me back empty. Why do you call me Naomi, since the LORD has witnessed against me and the Almighty has afflicted me?"

22 ¶ So Naomi returned, and with her Ruth the Moabitess, her daughter-in-law, who returned from the land of Moab. And they came to Bethlehem at the beginning of barley harvest.

1:22 The Worst of Times

The author stresses that Ruth was a Moabitess, a fact that would have greatly impressed the original readers. Moab and Israel were bitter enemies, and Ruth took a risk by emigrating to a land that might treat her as a despised foreigner. This story of family love and loyalty took place during the time of the judges, when murder, immorality, and general anarchy prevailed.

Ruth Gleans in Boaz' Field

2 Now Naomi had a kinsman of her husband, a man of great wealth, of the family of Elimelech, whose name was Boaz.

2 And Ruth the Moabitess said to Naomi, "Please let me go to the field and glean among the ears of grain after one in whose sight I may find favor." And she said to her, "Go, my daughter."

3 So she departed and went and gleaned in the field after the reapers; and she happened to come to the portion of the field belonging to Boaz, who was of the family of Elimelech.

4 Now behold, Boaz came from Bethlehem and said to the reapers, "May the LORD be with you." And they said to him, "May the LORD bless you."

5 Then Boaz said to his servant who was in charge of the reapers, "Whose young woman is this?"

6 The servant in charge of the reapers replied, "She is the young Moabite woman who returned with Naomi from the land of Moab.

7 "And she said, 'Please let me glean and gath-er after the reapers among the sheaves.' Thus she came and has remained from the morning until now; she has been sitting in the house for a little while."

2:3 Caring for the Poor

In the Old Testament God used several welfare programs to help poor people. One, reflected in this passage, was the command to leave some of the harvest in the field for the poor to gather. Poor people didn't beg for handouts, but worked for what they got. (Leviticus 19:9–10 and Deuteronomy 24:19–22 give the directions.)

Gleaning was humiliating and sometimes dangerous work. Ruth, a single woman and a foreigner, showed courage by working in the fields, and her diligence soon attracted the foreman's attention.

8 ¶ Then Boaz said to Ruth, "Listen carefully, my daughter. Do not go to glean in another field; furthermore, do not go on from this one, but stay here with my maids.

9 "Let your eyes be on the field which they reap, and go after them. Indeed, I have commanded the servants not to touch you. When you are thirsty, go to the water jars and drink from what the servants draw."

10 Then she fell on her face, bowing to the ground and said to him, "Why have I found favor in your sight that you should take notice of me, since I am a foreigner?"

11 Boaz replied to her, "All that you have done for your mother-in-law after the death of your husband has been fully reported to me, and how you left your father and your mother and the land of your birth, and came to a people that you did not previously know.

12 "May the LORD reward your work, and your wages be full from the LORD, the God of Israel, under whose wings you have come to seek refuge."

13 Then she said, "I have found favor in your sight, my lord, for you have comforted me and indeed have spoken kindly to your maidservant, though I am not like one of your maidservants."

14 ¶ At mealtime Boaz said to her, "Come here, that you may eat of the bread and dip your piece of bread in the vinegar." So she sat beside the reapers; and he served her roasted grain, and she ate and was satisfied and had some left.

15 When she rose to glean, Boaz commanded his servants, saying, "Let her glean even among the sheaves, and do not insult her.

16 "Also you shall purposely pull out for her

---

a I.e. pleasant *b* I.e. bitter

some grain from the bundles and leave *it* that she may glean, and do not rebuke her."

17 ¶ So she gleaned in the field until evening. Then she beat out what she had gleaned, and it was about an ephah of barley.

18 She took *it* up and went into the city, and her mother-in-law saw what she had gleaned. She also took *it* out and gave Naomi what she had left after she was satisfied.

19 Her mother-in-law then said to her, "Where did you glean today and where did you work? May he who took notice of you be blessed." So she told her mother-in-law with whom she had worked and said, "The name of the man with whom I worked today is Boaz."

20 Naomi said to her daughter-in-law, "May he be blessed of the LORD who has not withdrawn his kindness to the living and to the dead." Again Naomi said to her, "The man is our relative, he is one of our closest relatives."

21 Then Ruth the Moabitess said, "Furthermore, he said to me, 'You should stay close to my servants until they have finished all my harvest.'"

22 Naomi said to Ruth her daughter-in-law, "It is good, my daughter, that you go out with his maids, so that *others* do not fall upon you in another field."

23 So she stayed close by the maids of Boaz in order to glean until the end of the barley harvest and the wheat harvest. And she lived with her mother-in-law.

Boaz Will Redeem Ruth

3 Then Naomi her mother-in-law said to her, "My daughter, shall I not seek security for you, that it may be well with you?

2 "Now is not Boaz our kinsman, with whose

maids you were? Behold, he winnows barley at the threshing floor tonight.

3 "Wash yourself therefore, and anoint yourself and put on your *best* clothes, and go down to the threshing floor; *but* do not make yourself known to the man until he has finished eating and drinking.

4 "It shall be when he lies down, that you shall notice the place where he lies, and you shall go and uncover his feet and lie down; then he will tell you what you shall do."

5 She said to her, "All that you say I will do."

6 ¶ So she went down to the threshing floor and did according to all that her mother-in-law had commanded her.

7 When Boaz had eaten and drunk and his heart was merry, he went to lie down at the end of the heap of grain; and she came secretly, and uncovered his feet and lay down.

8 It happened in the middle of the night that the man was startled and bent forward; and behold, a woman was lying at his feet.

9 He said, "Who are you?" And she answered, "I am Ruth your maid. So spread your covering over your maid, for you are a *a*close relative."

10 Then he said, "May you be blessed of the LORD, my daughter. You have shown your last kindness to be better than the first by not going after young men, whether poor or rich.

11 "Now, my daughter, do not fear. I will do for you whatever you ask, for all my people in the city know that you are a woman of excellence.

12 "Now it is true I am a close relative; however, there is a relative closer than I.

13 "Remain this night, and when morning comes, if he will redeem you, good; let him redeem you. But if he does not wish to redeem you,

---

a Or *redeemer*

RUTH *Character Counts*

SHE ARRIVED IN ISRAEL PENNILESS, a foreigner and a widow, with her mother-in-law as her only friend. Considering that her home country Moab was often at war with Israel, and that the two nations worshiped different gods, the immigrant named Ruth hardly figured to thrive in Israel. Yet she went to work without delay.

Even though she was a foreigner, Ruth showed herself a model Israelite woman: modest, hardworking and deeply loyal to those she loved. (Her speech to Naomi is one of the world's great love poems [1:16–17]). Ruth never complained about hardship; rather, she responded with gratitude when anyone showed kindness to her. In the end she proved that character counts more than circumstances.

As this gem of a love story recounts, Ruth caught the eye of a very good man. The two married, began a new life together and had a son. Ultimately, through that son, Ruth the refugee became an ancestor of Israel's greatest king.

Ruth's life makes a lovely story in itself, but it has a larger significance. She contradicts a common assumption about the God of the Old Testament—that only members of one special tribe could be his chosen people. Ruth was fully accepted among God's people because she chose to follow the true God, despite her foreign background. Anyone could join in worshiping God, just as Ruth did.

Life Questions: Do you find it hard to accept and admire those who come from outside your group? What "qualifications" do you set up?

then I will redeem you, as the LORD lives. Lie down until morning."

14 ¶ So she lay at his feet until morning and rose before one could recognize another; and he said, "Let it not be known that the woman came to the threshing floor."

15 Again he said, "Give me the cloak that is on you and hold it." So she held it, and he measured six *measures* of barley and laid *it* on her. Then she went into the city.

16 When she came to her mother-in-law, she said, "How did it go, my daughter?" And she told her all that the man had done for her.

17 She said, "These six *measures* of barley he gave to me, for he said, 'Do not go to your mother-in-law empty-handed.'"

18 Then she said, "Wait, my daughter, until you know how the matter turns out; for the man will not rest until he has settled it today."

The Marriage of Ruth

4 Now Boaz went up to the gate and sat down there, and behold, the close relative of whom Boaz spoke was passing by, so he said, "Turn aside, friend, sit down here." And he turned aside and sat down.

4:1 Expensive Bride

In order to marry Ruth, Boaz had to go through a complicated legal procedure at the town gate, a public gathering place. The laws were designed to keep property in the family and to protect family members who might have suffered financial or other setbacks. As a distant relative, Boaz could purchase, or "redeem," Naomi's family property, but only after a closer relative had declined. Along with the property, Boaz acquired marriage rights to Ruth, Naomi's relative.

2 He took ten men of the elders of the city and said, "Sit down here." So they sat down.

3 Then he said to the closest relative, "Naomi, who has come back from the land of Moab, has to sell the piece of land which belonged to our brother Elimelech.

4 "So I thought to inform you, saying, 'Buy *it* before those who are sitting *here,* and before the elders of my people. If you will redeem *it,* redeem *it;* but if not, tell me that I may know; for there is no one but you to redeem *it,* and I am after you.'" And he said, "I will redeem *it.*"

5 Then Boaz said, "On the day you buy the field from the hand of Naomi, you must also acquire Ruth the Moabitess, the widow of the deceased, in order to raise up the name of the deceased on his inheritance."

6 The closest relative said, "I cannot redeem *it* for myself, because I would jeopardize my own inheritance. Redeem *it* for yourself; you *may have* my right of redemption, for I cannot redeem *it.*"

7 ¶ Now this was *the custom* in former times in Israel concerning the redemption and the exchange *of land* to confirm any matter: a man removed his sandal and gave it to another; and this was the *manner of* attestation in Israel.

8 So the closest relative said to Boaz, "Buy *it* for yourself." And he removed his sandal.

9 Then Boaz said to the elders and all the people, "You are witnesses today that I have bought from the hand of Naomi all that belonged to Elimelech and all that belonged to Chilion and Mahlon.

10 "Moreover, I have acquired Ruth the Moabitess, the widow of Mahlon, to be my wife in order to raise up the name of the deceased on his inheritance, so that the name of the deceased will not be cut off from his brothers or from the court of his *birth* place; you are witnesses today."

11 All the people who were in the court, and the elders, said, "*We are* witnesses. May the LORD make the woman who is coming into your home like Rachel and Leah, both of whom built the house of Israel; and may you achieve wealth in Ephrathah and become famous in Bethlehem.

12 "Moreover, may your house be like the house of Perez whom Tamar bore to Judah, through the offspring which the LORD will give you by this young woman."

13 ¶ So Boaz took Ruth, and she became his wife, and he went in to her. And the LORD enabled her to conceive, and she gave birth to a son.

14 Then the women said to Naomi, "Blessed is the LORD who has not left you without a redeemer today, and may his name become famous in Israel.

15 "May he also be to you a restorer of life and a sustainer of your old age; for your daughter-in-law, who loves you and is better to you than seven sons, has given birth to him."

The Line of David Began Here

16 Then Naomi took the child and laid him in her lap, and became his nurse.

17 The neighbor women gave him a name, saying, "A son has been born to Naomi!" So they named him Obed. He is the father of Jesse, the father of David.

18 ¶ Now these are the generations of Perez: to Perez was born Hezron,

19 and to Hezron was born Ram, and to Ram, Amminadab,

20 and to Amminadab was born Nahshon, and to Nahshon, Salmon,

21 and to Salmon was born Boaz, and to Boaz, Obed,

22 and to Obed was born Jesse, and to Jesse, David.

1 SAMUEL

What Leadership Requires
Israel, fighting for survival, needed a leader

> *"For not by might
> shall a man prevail.
> Those who contend
> with the LORD will be
> shattered."*
> 2:9–10

NO COUNTRY, NO ORGANIZATION, NO family is great without great leadership. But how do you get it? Israel was forced to ask that question during a critical, do-or-die period. Three men rose to the highest power: Samuel, Saul, and David. All were attractive, powerful figures who commanded admiration and respect. Two, David and Samuel, made very successful leaders. The other, Saul, had a promising beginning but ended as a failure.

Fighting for Survival

Israel was fighting for survival. The Philistines had migrated to the region about the same time Israel had escaped from Egypt. Now, from their cities near the Mediterranean coast, they were gradually pushing deeper into the mountains of Israel. They had superior weapons—chariots, in particular. Though less populous than Israel, they were apparently better organized.

Israel had neither central administration nor a regular army. A loose confederation of 12 tribes, Israelites called on each other for help only in emergencies. Occasional inspired leaders—"judges"—took charge of military defense when necessary. The nation had worked that way for well over 100 years, and the tribes seemed too independent to change. But the Philistines were pressing them. A crisis of leadership—a crisis testing the very existence of Israel—was building.

Why Begin with Hannah?

Surprisingly, 1 Samuel opens not with a battle or even with the leadership crisis, but with a very private family problem. Two bitterly jealous wives had a long-standing quarrel, one taunting the other because of her infertility. Hannah, the childless woman, turned to God in desperation, praying and promising to dedicate a son to him. The result was a little boy named Samuel.

Hannah kept her vow to God, and Samuel grew into one of the greatest leaders Israel had ever known. He had a triple role: He served as a prophet who could discern God's will, as a priest who led Israel to worship, and as a military leader. He chose, under God's direction, Israel's first two kings. Samuel's strong personality undergirds the entire book of 1 Samuel, even though he officially retired at the end of chapter 15.

Why begin 1 Samuel with Hannah? Hannah's struggles are Israel's, in miniature. Her frustration forced her to look to God, and as a result her son Samuel served in the tabernacle instead of following in his father's footsteps as a farmer. Hannah's story shows that from bitter pain may come great promise, if that pain leads you to God. The Israelites, who were going to experience a great many more troubles in their history, needed Hannah's example.

God Chooses His Own Leaders

Hannah's story also reminds us that God's leaders don't necessarily come through regulation channels. Ordinarily, Eli's corrupt sons would have carried on national leadership. But God wanted no part of them. Instead, he blessed a woman who had turned to him in her troubles, and he blessed her son as long as that son trusted in him for help. God chose a leader to suit himself, a leader who listened to him. "The LORD declares . . . 'for those who honor Me I will honor, and those who despise Me will be lightly esteemed' " (2:30).

Samuel never forgot that lesson. He anointed Saul as the first king, and then, when Saul failed to honor God, stripped him of his authority. Passing over many impressive men, Samuel chose David, a young shepherd, to replace Saul. Under David, Israel would be transformed into a wealthy, secure kingdom. Was this because David had such natural leadership qualities? First Samuel suggests a different perspective: David succeeded because God chose him for the job, and because David persistently turned to God for his direction. The best leadership, ultimately, belongs to God.

How to Read 1 Samuel

Some of the stories of 1 Samuel—David and Goliath, for instance—are justly famous as great adventures. But you should read for more than excitement. Look for insights into the character required for leadership. Samuel and David were great leaders. Saul, on the other hand, was a miserable failure.

These men led Israel during a crucial, bloody period. Israel had been dominated by a foreign power and, partly because of this, was changing its government to a monarchy. This change in governmental institutions, along with tribal tensions, form the background for the book. A good commentary can help explain this, but you can get much of it for yourself by asking, as you read, three questions: What are the most important national problems facing Israel? What kind of leadership is needed? How do these three leaders (and numerous smaller figures) respond to these needs?

PEOPLE YOU'LL MEET IN 1 SAMUEL

HANNAH *(p. 315)*	SAMUEL *(p. 321)*	JONATHAN *(p. 336)*
ELI *(p. 317)*	SAUL *(p. 330)*	ABIGAIL *(p. 343)*

3-TRACK READING PLAN

For an explanation and complete listing of the 3-track reading plan, turn to page 7.

TRACK 1: **Two-Week Courses on the Bible**
The Track 1 reading program includes one chapter from 1 Samuel. See page 8 for a complete listing of this course.

TRACK 2: **An Overview of 1 Samuel in 4 Days**
☐ Day 1. Read the Introduction to 1 Samuel and chapter 3, God's call of Samuel when he was very young.
☐ Day 2. Read chapter 16 to see how God chose David, and why.
☐ Day 3. Read chapter 17 for the exciting story of David's victory over Goliath, noting the qualities David showed.
☐ Day 4. Read chapter 20 for a glimpse of a model friendship between David and Jonathan.

Now turn to page 9 for your next Track 2 reading project.

TRACK 3: **All of 1 Samuel in 31 Days**
After you have read through 1 Samuel, turn to pages 10–14 for your next Track 3 reading project.

☐1	☐2	☐3	☐4	☐5	☐6	☐7	☐8
☐9	☐10	☐11	☐12	☐13	☐14	☐15	☐16
☐17	☐18	☐19	☐20	☐21	☐22	☐23	☐24
☐25	☐26	☐27	☐28	☐29	☐30	☐31	

Elkanah and His Wives

1 Now there was a certain man from Ramathaim-zophim from the hill country of Ephraim, and his name was Elkanah the son of Jeroham, the son of Elihu, the son of Tohu, the son of Zuph, an Ephraimite.

2 He had two wives: the name of one was Hannah and the name of the other Peninnah; and Peninnah had children, but Hannah had no children.

3 ¶ Now this man would go up from his city yearly to worship and to sacrifice to the LORD of hosts in Shiloh. And the two sons of Eli, Hophni and Phinehas, were priests to the LORD there.

4 When the day came that Elkanah sacrificed, he would give portions to Peninnah his wife and to all her sons and her daughters;

5 but to Hannah he would give a double portion, for he loved Hannah, but the LORD had closed her womb.

6 Her rival, however, would provoke her bitterly to irritate her, because the LORD had closed her womb.

7 It happened year after year, as often as she went up to the house of the LORD, she would provoke her; so she wept and would not eat.

8 Then Elkanah her husband said to her, "Hannah, why do you weep and why do you not eat and why is your heart sad? Am I not better to you than ten sons?"

9 ¶ Then Hannah rose after eating and drinking in Shiloh. Now Eli the priest was sitting on the seat by the doorpost of the temple of the LORD.

10 She, greatly distressed, prayed to the LORD and wept bitterly.

11 She made a vow and said, "O LORD of hosts, if You will indeed look on the affliction of Your maidservant and remember me, and not forget Your maidservant, but will give Your maidservant a son, then I will give him to the LORD all the days of his life, and a razor shall never come on his head."

12 ¶ Now it came about, as she continued praying before the LORD, that Eli was watching her mouth.

13 As for Hannah, she was speaking in her heart, only her lips were moving, but her voice was not heard. So Eli thought she was drunk.

14 Then Eli said to her, "How long will you make yourself drunk? Put away your wine from you."

15 But Hannah replied, "No, my lord, I am a woman oppressed in spirit; I have drunk neither wine nor strong drink, but I have poured out my soul before the LORD.

16 "Do not consider your maidservant as a worthless woman, for I have spoken until now out of my great concern and provocation."

17 Then Eli answered and said, "Go in peace; and may the God of Israel grant your petition that you have asked of Him."

18 She said, "Let your maidservant find favor in your sight." So the woman went her way and ate, and her face was no longer *sad*.

1:13 Sad, Not Drunk

Eli's mistaken assumption suggests that people sometimes came to the tabernacle drunk. Perhaps in these troubled times drunkenness was more common than heartfelt prayer. Hannah prayed with great anguish because she had no children. She is one of several barren women in the Bible whom God helped; others include Sarah (Genesis 11:30), Rebekah (Genesis 25:21), Rachel (Genesis 29:31), and Elizabeth (Luke 1:7).

Samuel Is Born to Hannah

19 ¶ Then they arose early in the morning and worshiped before the LORD, and returned again to their house in Ramah. And Elkanah had relations with Hannah his wife, and the LORD remembered her.

20 It came about in due time, after Hannah had conceived, that she gave birth to a son; and she named him Samuel, *saying*, "Because I have asked him of the LORD."

21 ¶ Then the man Elkanah went up with all his household to offer to the LORD the yearly sacrifice and *pay* his vow.

22 But Hannah did not go up, for she said to her husband, "*I will not go up* until the child is weaned; then I will bring him, that he may appear before the LORD and stay there forever."

23 Elkanah her husband said to her, "Do what seems best to you. Remain until you have weaned him; only may the LORD confirm His word." So the woman remained and nursed her son until she weaned him.

24 Now when she had weaned him, she took him up with her, with a three-year-old bull and one ephah of flour and a jug of wine, and brought him to the house of the LORD in Shiloh, although the child was young.

25 Then they slaughtered the bull, and brought the boy to Eli.

26 She said, "Oh, my lord! As your soul lives, my lord, I am the woman who stood here beside you, praying to the LORD.

27 "For this boy I prayed, and the LORD has given me my petition which I asked of Him.

28 "So I have also ᵃdedicated him to the LORD; as long as he lives he is ᵃdedicated to the LORD." And he worshiped the LORD there.

ᵃ Lit *lent*

Hannah's Song of Thanksgiving

2 Then Hannah prayed and said,
"My heart exults in the LORD;
My horn is exalted in the LORD,
My mouth speaks boldly against my
    enemies,
Because I rejoice in Your salvation.
2 "There is no one holy like the LORD,
Indeed, there is no one besides You,
Nor is there any rock like our God.
3 "Boast no more so very proudly,
Do not let arrogance come out of your
    mouth;
For the LORD is a God of knowledge,
And with Him actions are weighed.
4 "The bows of the mighty are shattered,
But the feeble gird on strength.
5 "Those who were full hire themselves out
    for bread,
But those who were hungry cease *to*
    hunger.
Even the barren gives birth to seven,
But she who has many children
    languishes.
6 "The LORD kills and makes alive;
He brings down to Sheol and raises up.
7 "The LORD makes poor and rich;
He brings low, He also exalts.
8 "He raises the poor from the dust,
He lifts the needy from the ash heap
To make them sit with nobles,
And inherit a seat of honor;
For the pillars of the earth are the
    LORD's,
And He set the world on them.
9 "He keeps the feet of His godly ones,
But the wicked ones are silenced in
    darkness;
For not by might shall a man prevail.

10 "Those who contend with the LORD will
    be shattered;
Against them He will thunder in the
    heavens,
The LORD will judge the ends of the
    earth;
And He will give strength to His king,
And will exalt the horn of His anointed."
11 ¶ Then Elkanah went to his home at Ramah. But the boy ministered to the LORD before Eli the priest.

The Sin of Eli's Sons

12 ¶ Now the sons of Eli were ᵃworthless men; they did not know the LORD
13 and the custom of the priests with the people. When any man was offering a sacrifice, the priest's servant would come while the meat was boiling, with a three-pronged fork in his hand.
14 Then he would thrust it into the pan, or kettle, or caldron, or pot; all that the fork brought up the priest would take for himself. Thus they did in Shiloh to all the Israelites who came there.
15 Also, before they burned the fat, the priest's servant would come and say to the man who was sacrificing, "Give the priest meat for roasting, as he will not take boiled meat from you, only raw."
16 If the man said to him, "They must surely burn the fat first, and then take as much as you desire," then he would say, "No, but you shall give *it to me* now; and if not, I will take it by force."
17 Thus the sin of the young men was very great before the LORD, for the men despised the offering of the LORD.

Samuel before the LORD as a Boy

18 ¶ Now Samuel was ministering before the LORD, *as* a boy wearing a linen ephod.
19 And his mother would make him a little robe and bring it to him from year to year when

a Lit *sons of Belial*

HANNAH *Deepest Longing*

OTHER WOMEN MIGHT ENVY HANNAH. She had, at least, a kind husband who obviously loved her. Yet for Hannah, one deep, unfulfilled longing made life miserable. Hannah wanted a child. (It hardly helped that a rival wife, Peninnah, brought the subject up at every opportunity.)

The longing for children may be the strongest in life. Today, infertile couples spend thousands of dollars in search of a medical remedy. For Hannah, who had no such recourse, her longing outweighed every blessing. Hannah wept, felt bitter and poured out her woes to God.

When God answered Hannah's prayer and gave her a son, Samuel, she poured out her joy to God as well. Remarkably, for a woman who had waited so long for a son, she took Samuel to God's tabernacle as soon as he reached an appropriate age. There she placed him in the priest's care.

Hannah certainly loved her child and never forgot him. Every year she made a garment for him—a huge expenditure in an age when cloth and even thread had to be made by hand. Yet she did not cling to her blessing any more than she had clung to her woes. She gave both to God.

Life Questions: Is some unfulfilled longing making you miserable? How can you take it to God?

she would come up with her husband to offer the yearly sacrifice.

20 Then Eli would bless Elkanah and his wife and say, "May the LORD give you children from this woman in place of the one she dedicated to the LORD." And they went to their own home.

21 ¶ The LORD visited Hannah; and she conceived and gave birth to three sons and two daughters. And the boy Samuel grew before the LORD.

Eli Rebukes His Sons

22 ¶ Now Eli was very old; and he heard all that his sons were doing to all Israel, and how they lay with the women who served at the doorway of the tent of meeting.

23 He said to them, "Why do you do such things, the evil things that I hear from all these people?

24 "No, my sons; for the report is not good which I hear the LORD'S people circulating.

25 "If one man sins against another, God will mediate for him; but if a man sins against the LORD, who can intercede for him?" But they would not listen to the voice of their father, for the LORD desired to put them to death.

2:25 God in Charge

Eli's sons disobeyed, the Bible says, because God wanted to put them to death. Does this mean that God took away their free choice? To Old Testament writers this "contradiction" seemed less troubling than to us. To them every event occurred only because, ultimately, God let it. Within his overall control people acted freely. In this case, Eli's sons were free to obey or disobey. The author wants us to know, however, that their disobedience was not beyond God's power: He planned to judge their evil activities.

26 ¶ Now the boy Samuel was growing in stature and in favor both with the LORD and with men.

27 ¶ Then a man of God came to Eli and said to him, "Thus says the LORD, 'Did I *not* indeed reveal Myself to the house of your father when they were in Egypt *in bondage* to Pharaoh's house?

28 'Did I *not* choose them from all the tribes of Israel to be My priests, to go up to My altar, to burn incense, to carry an ephod before Me; and did I *not* give to the house of your father all the fire *offerings* of the sons of Israel?

29 'Why do you kick at My sacrifice and at My offering which I have commanded *in My* dwelling, and honor your sons above Me, by making yourselves fat with the choicest of every offering of My people Israel?'

30 "Therefore the LORD God of Israel declares, 'I did indeed say that your house and the house of your father should walk before Me forever'; but now the LORD declares, 'Far be it from Me—for those who honor Me I will honor, and those who despise Me will be lightly esteemed.

2:30 Bad News for Eli

For Eli, this pronouncement came as bad news. He was held responsible for his sons' disgraceful behavior in the tabernacle. Eli rebuked them (3:13) but, as the priest in charge of the tabernacle, it was his job to stop any abuse there.

31 'Behold, the days are coming when I will break your strength and the strength of your father's house so that there will not be an old man in your house.

32 'You will see the distress of *My* dwelling, in *spite of* all the good that I do for Israel; and an old man will not be in your house forever.

33 'Yet I will not cut off every man of yours from My altar so that your eyes will fail *from weeping* and your soul grieve, and all the increase of your house will die in the prime of life.

34 'This will be the sign to you which will come concerning your two sons, Hophni and Phinehas: on the same day both of them will die.

35 'But I will raise up for Myself a faithful priest who will do according to what is in My heart and in My soul; and I will build him an enduring house, and he will walk before My anointed always.

36 'Everyone who is left in your house will come and bow down to him for a piece of silver or a loaf of bread and say, "Please assign me to one of the priest's offices so that I may eat a piece of bread." ' "

The Prophetic Call to Samuel

3 Now the boy Samuel was ministering to the LORD before Eli. And word from the LORD was rare in those days, visions were infrequent.

2 ¶ It happened at that time as Eli was lying down in his place (now his eyesight had begun to grow dim *and* he could not see *well*),

3 and the lamp of God had not yet gone out, and Samuel was lying down in the temple of the LORD where the ark of God *was*,

4 that the LORD called Samuel; and he said, "Here I am."

5 Then he ran to Eli and said, "Here I am, for you called me." But he said, "I did not call, lie down again." So he went and lay down.

6 The LORD called yet again, "Samuel!" So Samuel arose and went to Eli and said, "Here I am, for you called me." But he answered, "I did not call, my son, lie down again."

7 Now Samuel did not yet know the LORD,

nor had the word of the LORD yet been revealed to him.

8 So the LORD called Samuel again for the third time. And he arose and went to Eli and said, "Here I am, for you called me." Then Eli discerned that the LORD was calling the boy.

9 And Eli said to Samuel, "Go lie down, and it shall be if He calls you, that you shall say, 'Speak, LORD, for Your servant is listening.'" So Samuel went and lay down in his place.

10 ¶ Then the LORD came and stood and called as at other times, "Samuel! Samuel!" And Samuel said, "Speak, for Your servant is listening."

11 The LORD said to Samuel, "Behold, I am about to do a thing in Israel at which both ears of everyone who hears it will tingle.

12 "In that day I will carry out against Eli all that I have spoken concerning his house, from beginning to end.

13 "For I have told him that I am about to judge his house forever for the iniquity which he knew, because his sons brought a curse on themselves and he did not rebuke them.

14 "Therefore I have sworn to the house of Eli that the iniquity of Eli's house shall not be atoned for by sacrifice or offering forever."

15 ¶ So Samuel lay down until morning. Then he opened the doors of the house of the LORD. But Samuel was afraid to tell the vision to Eli.

16 Then Eli called Samuel and said, "Samuel, my son." And he said, "Here I am."

17 He said, "What is the word that He spoke to you? Please do not hide it from me. May God do so to you, and more also, if you hide anything from me of all the words that He spoke to you."

18 So Samuel told him everything and hid nothing from him. And he said, "It is the LORD; let Him do what seems good to Him."

19 ¶ Thus Samuel grew and the LORD was with him and let none of his words fail.

20 All Israel from Dan even to Beersheba knew that Samuel was confirmed as a prophet of the LORD.

21 And the LORD appeared again at Shiloh, because the LORD revealed Himself to Samuel at Shiloh by the word of the LORD.

3:19 Still a Boy

While still a boy, Samuel heard God speak. He delivered God's message even though it rebuked Eli, the man who had raised him from childhood. This was one indication that Samuel was a genuine prophet, for false prophets usually delivered only good news. Samuel's message agreed with the prophecy given earlier by a man of God (2:27–36), confirming that God had indeed spoken to him.

Philistines Take the Ark in Victory

4 Thus the word of Samuel came to all Israel. Now Israel went out to meet the Philistines in battle and camped beside Ebenezer while the Philistines camped in Aphek.

2 The Philistines drew up in battle array to meet Israel. When the battle spread, Israel was defeated before the Philistines who killed about four thousand men on the battlefield.

3 When the people came into the camp, the elders of Israel said, "Why has the LORD defeated us today before the Philistines? Let us take to ourselves from Shiloh the ark of the covenant of the LORD, that it may come among us and deliver us from the power of our enemies."

4 So the people sent to Shiloh, and from there they carried the ark of the covenant of the LORD of hosts who sits *above* the cherubim; and the two

ELI *An End and a Beginning*

ELI'S SONS ARE THE WORST example of stereotypically rebellious "preacher's kids." They greedily grabbed from the offerings people brought to the tabernacle, and slept with the female assistants. Though they followed their father into a career as priests, they played God's tent of worship like carnival barkers, bringing contempt on the worship service.

Eli knew about his sons' antics. He talked to them and scolded them, yet he never took firm action. According to the Bible, he honored his sons more than God. As a result, God brought judgment on Eli and his family. Not only would his sons die, but his whole family line would also lose the right to serve as priests.

This tragic message came from the lips of a little boy, Samuel, who had been brought to the tabernacle for Eli to raise. While Eli's biological sons were being cursed, God blessed Eli's foster child. In the same tabernacle that Eli's sons had dishonored, a boy learned to hear God's word from the old, worn-down priest.

Samuel would go on to be the greatest leader Israel had known since Joshua. Although Eli's family legacy died out, through Samuel his best qualities lived on.

Life Questions: Often from the ruins of one era, a new one springs to life. Can you see this cycle of decay and revival in any of the families you know? In your own life?

sons of Eli, Hophni and Phinehas, *were* there with the ark of the covenant of God.

5 ¶ As the ark of the covenant of the LORD came into the camp, all Israel shouted with a great shout, so that the earth resounded.

6 When the Philistines heard the noise of the shout, they said, "What *does* the noise of this great shout in the camp of the Hebrews *mean?*" Then they understood that the ark of the LORD had come into the camp.

7 The Philistines were afraid, for they said, "God has come into the camp." And they said, "Woe to us! For nothing like this has happened before.

8 "Woe to us! Who shall deliver us from the hand of these mighty gods? These are the gods who smote the Egyptians with all *kinds of* plagues in the wilderness.

9 "Take courage and be men, O Philistines, or you will become slaves to the Hebrews, as they have been slaves to you; therefore, be men and fight."

10 ¶ So the Philistines fought and Israel was defeated, and every man fled to his tent; and the slaughter was very great, for there fell of Israel thirty thousand foot soldiers.

11 And the ark of God was taken; and the two sons of Eli, Hophni and Phinehas, died.

12 ¶ Now a man of Benjamin ran from the battle line and came to Shiloh the same day with his clothes torn and dust on his head.

4:12 The End of Shiloh

The Philistine victory may have led to Shiloh's capture, for the next time we encounter Eli's family, they have moved as a group to Nob. Several Bible passages mention Shiloh's destruction as a punishment for sin (Jeremiah 7:12,14; 26:6,9; Psalm 78:60). If Shiloh did fall at this time, its capture must have added greatly to Israel's general sense of despair, for the city was an important site for worship.

13 When he came, behold, Eli was sitting on *his* seat by the road eagerly watching, because his heart was trembling for the ark of God. So the man came to tell *it* in the city, and all the city cried out.

14 When Eli heard the noise of the outcry, he said, "What *does* the noise of this commotion *mean?*" Then the man came hurriedly and told Eli.

15 Now Eli was ninety-eight years old, and his eyes were set so that he could not see.

16 The man said to Eli, "I am the one who came from the battle line. Indeed, I escaped from the battle line today." And he said, "How did things go, my son?"

17 Then the one who brought the news replied, "Israel has fled before the Philistines and there has also been a great slaughter among the people, and your two sons also, Hophni and Phinehas, are dead, and the ark of God has been taken."

18 When he mentioned the ark of God, Eli fell off the seat backward beside the gate, and his neck was broken and he died, for he was old and heavy. Thus he judged Israel forty years.

19 ¶ Now his daughter-in-law, Phinehas's wife, was pregnant and about to give birth; and when she heard the news that the ark of God was taken and that her father-in-law and her husband had died, she kneeled down and gave birth, for her pains came upon her.

20 And about the time of her death the women who stood by her said to her, "Do not be afraid, for you have given birth to a son." But she did not answer or pay attention.

21 And she called the boy [a]Ichabod, saying, "The glory has departed from Israel," because the ark of God was taken and because of her father-in-law and her husband.

22 She said, "The glory has departed from Israel, for the ark of God was taken."

Capture of the Ark Provokes God

5 Now the Philistines took the ark of God and brought it from Ebenezer to Ashdod.

2 Then the Philistines took the ark of God and brought it to the house of Dagon and set it by Dagon.

3 When the Ashdodites arose early the next morning, behold, Dagon had fallen on his face to the ground before the ark of the LORD. So they took Dagon and set him in his place again.

4 But when they arose early the next morning, behold, Dagon had fallen on his face to the ground before the ark of the LORD. And the head of Dagon and both the palms of his hands *were* cut off on the threshold; only the trunk of Dagon was left to him.

5 Therefore neither the priests of Dagon nor all who enter Dagon's house tread on the threshold of Dagon in Ashdod to this day.

6 ¶ Now the hand of the LORD was heavy on the Ashdodites, and He ravaged them and smote them with tumors, both Ashdod and its territories.

7 When the men of Ashdod saw that it was so, they said, "The ark of the God of Israel must not remain with us, for His hand is severe on us and on Dagon our god."

8 So they sent and gathered all the lords of the Philistines to them and said, "What shall we do with the ark of the God of Israel?" And they said, "Let the ark of the God of Israel be brought around to Gath." And they brought the ark of the God of Israel *around.*

[a] I.e. No glory

9 After they had brought it around, the hand of the LORD was against the city with very great confusion; and He smote the men of the city, both young and old, so that tumors broke out on them.

10 So they sent the ark of God to Ekron. And as the ark of God came to Ekron the Ekronites cried out, saying, "They have brought the ark of the God of Israel around to us, to kill us and our people."

11 They sent therefore and gathered all the lords of the Philistines and said, "Send away the ark of the God of Israel, and let it return to its own place, so that it will not kill us and our people." For there was a deadly confusion throughout the city; the hand of God was very heavy there.

12 And the men who did not die were smitten with tumors and the cry of the city went up to heaven.

The Ark Returned to Israel

6 Now the ark of the LORD had been in the country of the Philistines seven months.

2 And the Philistines called for the priests and the diviners, saying, "What shall we do with the ark of the LORD? Tell us how we shall send it to its place."

3 They said, "If you send away the ark of the God of Israel, do not send it empty; but you shall surely return to Him a guilt offering. Then you will be healed and it will be known to you why His hand is not removed from you."

4 Then they said, "What shall be the guilt offering which we shall return to Him?" And they said, "Five golden tumors and five golden mice *according to* the number of the lords of the Philistines, for one plague was on all of you and on your lords.

5 "So you shall make likenesses of your tumors and likenesses of your mice that ravage the land, and you shall give glory to the God of Israel; perhaps He will ease His hand from you, your gods, and your land.

6 "Why then do you harden your hearts as the Egyptians and Pharaoh hardened their hearts?

6:5 Magic

The Philistine strategy shows traditional magical thinking, still common in some occult or voodoo rites. By sending gold models of the tumors and rats out of the country, the Philistines hoped to send the originals out of the country too. This is similar to the voodoo practice of sticking pins into wax models of one's enemies.

The Israelites, instead of looking for a magical technique, appealed to the overwhelming power of a personal God, who could not be manipulated with magic.

When He had severely dealt with them, did they not allow the people to go, and they departed?

7 "Now therefore, take and prepare a new cart and two milch cows on which there has never been a yoke; and hitch the cows to the cart and take their calves home, away from them.

8 "Take the ark of the LORD and place it on the cart; and put the articles of gold which you return to Him as a guilt offering in a box by its side. Then send it away that it may go.

9 "Watch, if it goes up by the way of its own territory to Beth-shemesh, then He has done us this great evil. But if not, then we will know that it was not His hand that struck us; it happened to us by chance."

10 ¶ Then the men did so, and took two milch cows and hitched them to the cart, and shut up their calves at home.

11 They put the ark of the LORD on the cart, and the box with the golden mice and the likenesses of their tumors.

12 And the cows took the straight way in the direction of Beth-shemesh; they went along the highway, lowing as they went, and did not turn aside to the right or to the left. And the lords of the Philistines followed them to the border of Beth-shemesh.

13 ¶ Now *the people of* Beth-shemesh were reaping their wheat harvest in the valley, and they raised their eyes and saw the ark and were glad to see *it.*

14 The cart came into the field of Joshua the Beth-shemite and stood there where there *was* a large stone; and they split the wood of the cart and offered the cows as a burnt offering to the LORD.

15 The Levites took down the ark of the LORD and the box that was with it, in which were the articles of gold, and put them on the large stone; and the men of Beth-shemesh offered burnt offerings and sacrificed sacrifices that day to the LORD.

16 When the five lords of the Philistines saw it, they returned to Ekron that day.

17 ¶ These are the golden tumors which the Philistines returned for a guilt offering to the LORD: one for Ashdod, one for Gaza, one for Ashkelon, one for Gath, one for Ekron;

18 and the golden mice, *according* to the number of all the cities of the Philistines belonging to the five lords, both of fortified cities and of country villages. The large stone on which they set the ark of the LORD *is a witness* to this day in the field of Joshua the Beth-shemite.

19 ¶ He struck down some of the men of Beth-shemesh because they had looked into the ark of the LORD. He struck down of all the people, 50,070 men, and the people mourned because the LORD had struck the people with a great slaughter.

20 The men of Beth-shemesh said, "Who is able to stand before the LORD, this holy God? And to whom shall He go up from us?"

21 So they sent messengers to the inhabitants

of Kiriath-jearim, saying, "The Philistines have brought back the ark of the LORD; come down and take it up to you."

Deliverance from the Philistines

7 And the men of Kiriath-jearim came and took the ark of the LORD and brought it into the house of Abinadab on the hill, and consecrated Eleazar his son to keep the ark of the LORD.

2 From the day that the ark remained at Kiriath-jearim, the time was long, for it was twenty years; and all the house of Israel lamented after the LORD.

3 ¶ Then Samuel spoke to all the house of Israel, saying, "If you return to the LORD with all your heart, remove the foreign gods and the Ashtaroth from among you and direct your hearts to the LORD and serve Him alone; and He will deliver you from the hand of the Philistines."

4 So the sons of Israel removed the Baals and the Ashtaroth and served the LORD alone.

5 ¶ Then Samuel said, "Gather all Israel to Mizpah and I will pray to the LORD for you."

6 They gathered to Mizpah, and drew water and poured it out before the LORD, and fasted on that day and said there, "We have sinned against the LORD." And Samuel judged the sons of Israel at Mizpah.

7 ¶ Now when the Philistines heard that the sons of Israel had gathered to Mizpah, the lords of the Philistines went up against Israel. And when the sons of Israel heard it, they were afraid of the Philistines.

8 Then the sons of Israel said to Samuel, "Do not cease to cry to the LORD our God for us, that He may save us from the hand of the Philistines."

9 Samuel took a suckling lamb and offered it for a whole burnt offering to the LORD; and Samuel cried to the LORD for Israel and the LORD answered him.

10 Now Samuel was offering up the burnt offering, and the Philistines drew near to battle against Israel. But the LORD thundered with a great thunder on that day against the Philistines and confused them, so that they were routed before Israel.

11 The men of Israel went out of Mizpah and pursued the Philistines, and struck them down as far as below Beth-car.

12 ¶ Then Samuel took a stone and set it between Mizpah and Shen, and named it ᵃEbenezer, saying, "Thus far the LORD has helped us."

13 So the Philistines were subdued and they did not come anymore within the border of Israel. And the hand of the LORD was against the Philistines all the days of Samuel.

14 The cities which the Philistines had taken from Israel were restored to Israel, from Ekron even to Gath; and Israel delivered their territory from the hand of the Philistines. So there was peace between Israel and the Amorites.

Samuel's Ministry

15 ¶ Now Samuel judged Israel all the days of his life.

16 He used to go annually on circuit to Bethel and Gilgal and Mizpah, and he judged Israel in all these places.

17 Then his return was to Ramah, for his house was there, and there he judged Israel; and he built there an altar to the LORD.

Israel Demands a King

8 And it came about when Samuel was old that he appointed his sons judges over Israel.

2 Now the name of his firstborn was Joel, and the name of his second, Abijah; they were judging in Beersheba.

3 His sons, however, did not walk in his ways, but turned aside after dishonest gain and took bribes and perverted justice.

4 ¶ Then all the elders of Israel gathered together and came to Samuel at Ramah;

5 and they said to him, "Behold, you have grown old, and your sons do not walk in your ways. Now appoint a king for us to judge us like all the nations."

8:5 Why Not a King?

Considering the disorganized state of the Israelite nation, their request for a new form of government—a monarchy—seems understandable. A king would centralize power, making the nation more efficient in defending itself. However, both Samuel and God opposed the idea, particularly because of the Israelites' motive: They wanted "a king . . . to judge us like all the nations." Israel was supposed to be different from the other nations. Whatever the form of their government, they were to trust in God as their leader.

6 But the thing was displeasing in the sight of Samuel when they said, "Give us a king to judge us." And Samuel prayed to the LORD.

7 The LORD said to Samuel, "Listen to the voice of the people in regard to all that they say to you, for they have not rejected you, but they have rejected Me from being king over them.

8 "Like all the deeds which they have done since the day that I brought them up from Egypt even to this day—in that they have forsaken Me and served other gods—so they are doing to you also.

9 "Now then, listen to their voice; however,

ᵃ I.e. The stone of help

you shall solemnly warn them and tell them of the *procedure of the king who will reign over them."

Warning concerning a King

10 ¶ So Samuel spoke all the words of the LORD to the people who had asked of him a king.

11 He said, "This will be the procedure of the king who will reign over you: he will take your sons and place *them* for himself in his chariots and among his horsemen and they will run before his chariots.

12 "He will appoint for himself commanders of thousands and of fifties, and *some* to do his plowing and to reap his harvest and to make his weapons of war and equipment for his chariots.

13 "He will also take your daughters for perfumers and cooks and bakers.

14 "He will take the best of your fields and your vineyards and your olive groves and give *them* to his servants.

15 "He will take a tenth of your seed and of your vineyards and give to his officers and to his servants.

16 "He will also take your male servants and your female servants and your best young men and your donkeys and use *them* for his work.

17 "He will take a tenth of your flocks, and you yourselves will become his servants.

18 "Then you will cry out in that day because of your king whom you have chosen for yourselves, but the LORD will not answer you in that day."

19 ¶ Nevertheless, the people refused to listen

a Lit *custom*

to the voice of Samuel, and they said, "No, but there shall be a king over us,

20 that we also may be like all the nations, that our king may judge us and go out before us and fight our battles."

21 Now after Samuel had heard all the words of the people, he repeated them in the LORD's hearing.

22 The LORD said to Samuel, "Listen to their voice and appoint them a king." So Samuel said to the men of Israel, "Go every man to his city."

Saul's Search

9 Now there was a man of Benjamin whose name was Kish the son of Abiel, the son of Zeror, the son of Becorath, the son of Aphiah, the son of a Benjamite, a mighty man of valor.

2 He had a son whose name was Saul, a choice and handsome *man,* and there was not a more handsome person than he among the sons of Israel; from his shoulders and up he was taller than any of the people.

3 ¶ Now the donkeys of Kish, Saul's father, were lost. So Kish said to his son Saul, "Take now with you one of the servants, and arise, go search for the donkeys."

4 He passed through the hill country of Ephraim and passed through the land of Shalishah, but they did not find *them.* Then they passed through the land of Shaalim, but *they were* not *there.* Then he passed through the land of the Benjamites, but they did not find *them.*

5 ¶ When they came to the land of Zuph, Saul

SAMUEL *Faithful Leadership*

TIMES OF CRISIS REQUIRE EXCEPTIONAL leadership. That's why George Washington made so great a President. In order to survive, the fledgling United States needed his flawless reputation, his decisive leadership and his wide-ranging talents.

Samuel, similarly, ruled during a difficult transition. The last judge in Israel, Eli, had failed, and Philistine armies were pressing in. With everything in flux, the Israelites needed someone worthy of their trust. Samuel was the leader for the times. He oversaw the change from a loose tribal federation to a monarchy. He anointed Israel's first two kings, wrote down the rules kings were to live by and then deposed one king, Saul, who did not measure up. Samuel ended his long career without a single black mark on his record, and the entire country mourned his death.

Samuel showed remarkable versatility. A lifelong judge, he settled disputes in a regular circuit of Israelite towns. He also gained fame as a prophet, alert to hear God's word and quick to proclaim it clearly—especially when God entrusted him with key information about the future. Finally, he functioned as a priest, presenting sacrifices and prayers on behalf of God's people. He considered prayer one of his basic duties as a leader (12:23).

Like any good leader, Samuel sometimes had to bring bad news. When he was just a boy, he heard God's message of judgment against his foster father Eli (3:11–14). Samuel also gave stern warnings about a king's potential abuses of power, abuses he later had to denounce in Saul. Yet the nation remembered him more for his positive contributions. Taking over the helm when the nation was near disaster, Samuel steered the course faithfully until he could deliver leadership to David, a young man who would become Israel's greatest king.

Life Questions: What leader do you respect most? What qualities does he or she show?

said to his servant who was with him, "Come, and let us return, or else my father will cease *to be concerned* about the donkeys and will become anxious for us."

9:3 A Donkey Hunt

Saul, hunting for donkeys, certainly was not looking for a chance to become king. He was so politically unaware he didn't even know about the great man Samuel. Similarly, Samuel was a small boy when God called him (chapter 3), and David was anointed king while tending sheep (16:11–13). The leaders God appoints are not necessarily those seeking power.

6 He said to him, "Behold now, there is a man of God in this city, and the man is held in honor; all that he says surely comes true. Now let us go there, perhaps he can tell us about our journey on which we have set out."

7 Then Saul said to his servant, "But behold, if we go, what shall we bring the man? For the bread is gone from our sack and there is no present to bring to the man of God. What do we have?"

8 The servant answered Saul again and said, "Behold, I have in my hand a fourth of a shekel of silver; I will give *it* to the man of God and he will tell us our way."

9 (Formerly in Israel, when a man went to inquire of God, he used to say, "Come, and let us go to the seer"; for *he who is called* a prophet now was formerly called a seer.)

10 Then Saul said to his servant, "Well said; come, let us go." So they went to the city where the man of God was.

11 ¶ As they went up the slope to the city, they found young women going out to draw water and said to them, "Is the seer here?"

12 They answered them and said, "He is; see, *he is* ahead of you. Hurry now, for he has come into the city today, for the people have a sacrifice on the high place today.

13 "As soon as you enter the city you will find him before he goes up to the high place to eat, for the people will not eat until he comes, because he must bless the sacrifice; afterward those who are invited will eat. Now therefore, go up for you will find him at once."

14 So they went up to the city. As they came into the city, behold, Samuel was coming out toward them to go up to the high place.

God's Choice for King

15 ¶ Now a day before Saul's coming, the LORD had revealed *this* to Samuel saying,

16 "About this time tomorrow I will send you a man from the land of Benjamin, and you shall anoint him to be prince over My people Israel; and he will deliver My people from the hand of the Philistines. For I have regarded My people, because their cry has come to Me."

17 When Samuel saw Saul, the LORD said to him, "Behold, the man of whom I spoke to you! This one shall rule over My people."

18 Then Saul approached Samuel in the gate and said, "Please tell me where the seer's house is."

19 Samuel answered Saul and said, "I am the seer. Go up before me to the high place, for you shall eat with me today; and in the morning I will let you go, and will tell you all that is on your mind.

20 "As for your donkeys which were lost three days ago, do not set your mind on them, for they have been found. And for whom is all that is desirable in Israel? Is it not for you and for all your father's household?"

21 Saul replied, "Am I not a Benjamite, of the smallest of the tribes of Israel, and my family the least of all the families of the tribe of Benjamin? Why then do you speak to me in this way?"

22 ¶ Then Samuel took Saul and his servant and brought them into the hall and gave them a place at the head of those who were invited, who were about thirty men.

23 Samuel said to the cook, "Bring the portion that I gave you, concerning which I said to you, 'Set it aside.' "

24 Then the cook took up the leg with what was on it and set *it* before Saul. And *Samuel* said, "Here is what has been reserved! Set *it* before you *and* eat, because it has been kept for you until the appointed time, since I said I have invited the people." So Saul ate with Samuel that day.

25 ¶ When they came down from the high place into the city, *Samuel* spoke with Saul on the ªroof.

26 And they arose early; and at daybreak Samuel called to Saul on the roof, saying, "Get up, that I may send you away." So Saul arose, and both he and Samuel went out into the street.

27 As they were going down to the edge of the city, Samuel said to Saul, "Say to the servant that he might go ahead of us and pass on, but you remain standing now, that I may proclaim the word of God to you."

Saul among Prophets

10 Then Samuel took the flask of oil, poured it on his head, kissed him and said, "Has not the LORD anointed you a ruler over His inheritance?

2 "When you go from me today, then you will find two men close to Rachel's tomb in the territory of Benjamin at Zelzah; and they will say to you, 'The donkeys which you went to look for have

---

ª Gr adds *and they spread a bed for Saul on the roof and he slept* been found. Now behold, your father has ceased to be concerned about the donkeys and is anxious for you, saying, "What shall I do about my son?" '

3 "Then you will go on further from there, and you will come as far as the oak of Tabor, and there three men going up to God at Bethel will meet you, one carrying three young goats, another carrying three loaves of bread, and another carrying a jug of wine;

4 and they will greet you and give you two *loaves* of bread, which you will accept from their hand.

5 "Afterward you will come to the hill of God where the Philistine garrison is; and it shall be as soon as you have come there to the city, that you will meet a group of prophets coming down from the high place with harp, tambourine, flute, and a lyre before them, and they will be prophesying.

10:5 Musical Prophets

This is one of the earliest references to prophets in the Bible. Under the kings, prophets became much more significant, possibly because they so often spoke out against the kings. The description of the prophets' musical procession is intriguing, though we can only guess what exactly they were doing. Unquestionably, the Spirit's powerful effect on Saul made a startling change in him (verse 11).

6 "Then the Spirit of the LORD will come upon you mightily, and you shall prophesy with them and be changed into another man.

7 "It shall be when these signs come to you, do for yourself what the occasion requires, for God is with you.

8 "And you shall go down before me to Gilgal; and behold, I will come down to you to offer burnt offerings and sacrifice peace offerings. You shall wait seven days until I come to you and show you what you should do."

9 ¶ Then it happened when he turned his back to leave Samuel, God changed his heart; and all those signs came about on that day.

10 When they came to the hill there, behold, a group of prophets met him; and the Spirit of God came upon him mightily, so that he prophesied among them.

11 It came about, when all who knew him previously saw that he prophesied now with the prophets, that the people said to one another, "What has happened to the son of Kish? Is Saul also among the prophets?"

12 A man there said, "Now, who is their father?" Therefore it became a proverb: "Is Saul also among the prophets?"

13 When he had finished prophesying, he came to the high place.

14 ¶ Now Saul's uncle said to him and his servant, "Where did you go?" And he said, "To look for the donkeys. When we saw that they could not be found, we went to Samuel."

15 Saul's uncle said, "Please tell me what Samuel said to you."

16 So Saul said to his uncle, "He told us plainly that the donkeys had been found." But he did not tell him about the matter of the kingdom which Samuel had mentioned.

Saul Publicly Chosen King

17 ¶ Thereafter Samuel called the people together to the LORD at Mizpah;

18 and he said to the sons of Israel, "Thus says the LORD, the God of Israel, 'I brought Israel up from Egypt, and I delivered you from the hand of the Egyptians and from the power of all the kingdoms that were oppressing you.'

19 "But you have today rejected your God, who delivers you from all your calamities and your distresses; yet you have said, 'No, but set a king over us!' Now therefore, present yourselves before the LORD by your tribes and by your clans."

20 ¶ Thus Samuel brought all the tribes of Israel near, and the tribe of Benjamin was taken by lot.

21 Then he brought the tribe of Benjamin near by its families, and the Matrite family was taken. And Saul the son of Kish was taken; but when they looked for him, he could not be found.

22 Therefore they inquired further of the LORD, "Has the man come here yet?" So the LORD said, "Behold, he is hiding himself by the baggage."

23 So they ran and took him from there, and when he stood among the people, he was taller than any of the people from his shoulders upward.

24 Samuel said to all the people, "Do you see him whom the LORD has chosen? Surely there is no one like him among all the people." So all the people shouted and said, "*Long* live the king!"

25 ¶ Then Samuel told the people the ordinances of the kingdom, and wrote *them* in the book and placed *it* before the LORD. And Samuel sent all the people away, each one to his house.

10:25 Limits on the King

Though Samuel reluctantly designated Saul as the first king, he insisted on safeguards. Much as the United States government rests on a document, the Constitution, so Saul's kingship was defined and limited by certain rules, which Samuel wrote down and placed in the tabernacle as a permanent record.

26 Saul also went to his house at Gibeah; and the valiant *men* whose hearts God had touched went with him.

27 But certain worthless men said, "How can

this one deliver us?" And they despised him and did not bring him any present. But he kept silent.

Saul Defeats the Ammonites

11 Now Nahash the Ammonite came up and besieged Jabesh-gilead; and all the men of Jabesh said to Nahash, "Make a covenant with us and we will serve you."

2 But Nahash the Ammonite said to them, "I will make *it* with you on this condition, that I will gouge out the right eye of every one of you, thus I will make it a reproach on all Israel."

3 The elders of Jabesh said to him, "Let us alone for seven days, that we may send messengers throughout the territory of Israel. Then, if there is no one to deliver us, we will come out to you."

4 Then the messengers came to Gibeah of Saul and spoke these words in the hearing of the people, and all the people lifted up their voices and wept.

5 ¶ Now behold, Saul was coming from the field behind the oxen, and he said, "What is *the matter* with the people that they weep?" So they related to him the words of the men of Jabesh.

6 Then the Spirit of God came upon Saul mightily when he heard these words, and he became very angry.

7 He took a yoke of oxen and cut them in pieces, and sent *them* throughout the territory of Israel by the hand of messengers, saying, "Whoever does not come out after Saul and after Samuel, so shall it be done to his oxen." Then the dread of the LORD fell on the people, and they came out as one man.

8 He numbered them in Bezek; and the sons of Israel were 300,000, and the men of Judah 30,000.

9 They said to the messengers who had come, "Thus you shall say to the men of Jabesh-gilead, 'Tomorrow, by the time the sun is hot, you will have deliverance.'" So the messengers went and told the men of Jabesh; and they were glad.

10 Then the men of Jabesh said, "Tomorrow we will come out to you, and you may do to us whatever seems good to you."

11 The next morning Saul put the people in three companies; and they came into the midst of the camp at the morning watch and struck down the Ammonites until the heat of the day. Those who survived were scattered, so that no two of them were left together.

12 ¶ Then the people said to Samuel, "Who is he that said, 'Shall Saul reign over us?' Bring the men, that we may put them to death."

13 But Saul said, "Not a man shall be put to death this day, for today the LORD has accomplished deliverance in Israel."

14 ¶ Then Samuel said to the people, "Come and let us go to Gilgal and renew the kingdom there."

15 So all the people went to Gilgal, and there they made Saul king before the LORD in Gilgal. There they also offered sacrifices of peace offerings before the LORD; and there Saul and all the men of Israel rejoiced greatly.

Samuel Addresses Israel

12 Then Samuel said to all Israel, "Behold, I have listened to your voice in all that you said to me and I have appointed a king over you.

2 "Now, here is the king walking before you, but I am old and gray, and behold my sons are with you. And I have walked before you from my youth even to this day.

3 "Here I am; bear witness against me before the LORD and His anointed. Whose ox have I taken, or whose donkey have I taken, or whom have I defrauded? Whom have I oppressed, or from whose hand have I taken a bribe to blind my eyes with it? I will restore *it* to you."

4 They said, "You have not defrauded us or oppressed us or taken anything from any man's hand."

12:4 Accuse Me!

Unlike some political and religious leaders who get caught in financial scandals, Samuel considered himself publicly accountable. He began his farewell speech by offering an opportunity for anyone to stand up and testify that he, Samuel, had been dishonest or had taken advantage of his leadership position. Before going on, he asked those present to witness aloud to his honesty.

5 He said to them, "The LORD is witness against you, and His anointed is witness this day that you have found nothing in my hand." And they said, "*He is* witness."

6 ¶ Then Samuel said to the people, "It is the LORD who appointed Moses and Aaron and who brought your fathers up from the land of Egypt.

7 "So now, take your stand, that I may plead with you before the LORD concerning all the righteous acts of the LORD which He did for you and your fathers.

8 "When Jacob went into Egypt and your fathers cried out to the LORD, then the LORD sent Moses and Aaron who brought your fathers out of Egypt and settled them in this place.

9 "But they forgot the LORD their God, so He sold them into the hand of Sisera, captain of the army of Hazor, and into the hand of the Philistines and into the hand of the king of Moab, and they fought against them.

10 "They cried out to the LORD and said, 'We have sinned because we have forsaken the LORD

The First King

Every other nation had one—why not Israel?

"Then both you and also the king who reigns over you will follow the LORD your God. If you will not listen to the voice of the LORD . . . then the hand of the LORD will be against you."
12:14–15

MAKING A SINGLE NATION OUT of a dozen tribes was not easy. Unity came hard for Israel; it also came hard for the United States. U.S. history may shed light on 1 Samuel's story.

Most people think George Washington was the first president of the United States, but that honor actually belongs to Samuel Huntington. He never achieved fame because the states he presided over weren't united. They had no Constitution, only Articles of Confederation that made them 13 independent nations loosely linked together.

Congress under Siege

Two years after Huntington took office, on June 21, 1783, 500 unpaid federal soldiers laid siege to Congress in Philadelphia, breaking windows and shouting threats because Congress, which was supposed to pay them, had no money. The jealously independent states had given them none. Driven out of town by the soldiers, Congress became nomadic, meeting in Princeton, Annapolis, Trenton, and New York City. That same June, George Washington wrote, "It is yet to be decided whether the Revolution must ultimately be considered a blessing or a curse."

Troubles continued. In Shays's Rebellion, 1,500 hostile farmers surrounded courtrooms, refusing to let courts meet. The army should have quickly dispersed them, but the national army consisted of only 700 men. Shays's Rebellion made obvious the need for a stronger central government. The next year a constitutional convention met in Philadelphia to hammer out the document that still unifies Americans. Washington was elected president.

Why Israel Needed a King

The 12 tribes of Israel, like the 13 states, were a nation in name only. They had no central government at all. Since conquering Palestine, they had worked together only during emergencies, when inspired "judges"—military heroes like Gideon, Deborah, and Samson—came forward to lead them into battle.

In Samuel's time, though, the Philistines' military threat wouldn't go away. Israel needed superior leadership, but Samuel was an old man. His sons made unappealing successors. What could be done? Looking around them, the tribes noticed that virtually every other country had a king. A king offered two advantages: first, he provided central government; second, since his sons would normally succeed a king, the nation did not have a crisis of leadership every time its leader got old. So the leaders of Israel asked Samuel to appoint a king (8:4–5).

Against God's Will

The idea seems to have been popular with everyone except Samuel and God. Samuel may have been displeased that he and his sons were being rejected. God had a deeper objection: Israel was rejecting his leadership. God told Samuel to warn the elders that a king would oppress his own citizens. Samuel warned of the military draft, of high taxation, of the king's power to make people into slaves (8:10–18).

Was God against a king? Some scholars see the monarchy as a marvelous example of God's use of a choice made against his will. God counseled Israel against the very institution that ultimately produced King David, and through him Jesus, King of kings.

Others suggest that God only opposed the motive behind the request. (Deuteronomy 17:14–20 had assumed that the Israelites would eventually want and get a king.) The key is the phrase the elders used: "that we also may be like all the nations" (8:20). God did not want them to be like all the other nations.

The King Was a Servant

Yet God gave in to their request, bad motives and all. He not only allowed the Israelites a king, he picked out their man. He accepted the monarchy on condition that Israel still consider the Lord as its ultimate ruler (12:14).

Apparently, Israel's king didn't answer to a parliament or court system, but he did answer to God. In short order the first king, Saul, was rejected because he disobeyed God. God rebuked and punished his replacement, David. Most nations' kings held absolute power. In Israel only God was absolute, and the king was his servant.

Life Questions: Have you ever seen God take a bad request made with bad motives and use it for his own purposes?

and have served the Baals and the Ashtaroth; but now deliver us from the hands of our enemies, and we will serve You.'

11 "Then the LORD sent Jerubbaal and *a*Bedan and Jephthah and Samuel, and delivered you from the hands of your enemies all around, so that you lived in security.

The King Confirmed

12 "When you saw that Nahash the king of the sons of Ammon came against you, you said to me, 'No, but a king shall reign over us,' although the LORD your God *was* your king.

13 "Now therefore, here is the king whom you have chosen, whom you have asked for, and behold, the LORD has set a king over you.

14 "If you will fear the LORD and serve Him, and listen to His voice and not rebel against the command of the LORD, then both you and also the king who reigns over you will follow the LORD your God.

15 "If you will not listen to the voice of the LORD, but rebel against the command of the LORD, then the hand of the LORD will be against you, *as it was* against your fathers.

16 "Even now, take your stand and see this great thing which the LORD will do before your eyes.

17 "Is it not the wheat harvest today? I will call to the LORD, that He may send thunder and rain. Then you will know and see that your wickedness is great which you have done in the sight of the LORD by asking for yourselves a king."

18 So Samuel called to the LORD, and the LORD sent thunder and rain that day; and all the people greatly feared the LORD and Samuel.

19 ¶ Then all the people said to Samuel, "Pray for your servants to the LORD your God, so that we may not die, for we have added to all our sins this evil by asking for ourselves a king."

20 Samuel said to the people, "Do not fear. You have committed all this evil, yet do not turn aside from following the LORD, but serve the LORD with all your heart.

21 "You must not turn aside, for *then you would go* after futile things which can not profit or deliver, because they are futile.

22 "For the LORD will not abandon His people on account of His great name, because the LORD has been pleased to make you a people for Himself.

23 "Moreover, as for me, far be it from me that I should sin against the LORD by ceasing to pray for you; but I will instruct you in the good and right way.

24 "Only *b*fear the LORD and serve Him in truth with all your heart; for consider what great things He has done for you.

25 "But if you still do wickedly, both you and your king will be swept away."

War with the Philistines

13 Saul was *thirty* years old when he began to reign, and he reigned *forty* two years over Israel.

2 ¶ Now Saul chose for himself 3,000 men of Israel, of which 2,000 were with Saul in Michmash and in the hill country of Bethel, while 1,000 were with Jonathan at Gibeah of Benjamin. But he sent away the rest of the people, each to his tent.

3 Jonathan smote the garrison of the Philistines that was in Geba, and the Philistines heard of *it.* Then Saul blew the trumpet throughout the land, saying, "Let the Hebrews hear."

4 All Israel heard the news that Saul had smitten the garrison of the Philistines, and also that Israel had become odious to the Philistines. The people were then summoned to Saul at Gilgal.

5 ¶ Now the Philistines assembled to fight with Israel, 30,000 chariots and 6,000 horsemen, and people like the sand which is on the seashore in abundance; and they came up and camped in Michmash, east of Beth-aven.

6 When the men of Israel saw that they were in a strait (for the people were hard-pressed), then the people hid themselves in caves, in thickets, in cliffs, in cellars, and in pits.

7 Also *some of* the Hebrews crossed the Jordan into the land of Gad and Gilead. But as for Saul, he *was* still in Gilgal, and all the people followed him trembling.

8 ¶ Now he waited seven days, according to the appointed time set by Samuel, but Samuel did not come to Gilgal; and the people were scattering from him.

9 So Saul said, "Bring to me the burnt offering and the peace offerings." And he offered the burnt offering.

10 As soon as he finished offering the burnt offering, behold, Samuel came; and Saul went out to meet him *and* to greet him.

11 But Samuel said, "What have you done?" And Saul said, "Because I saw that the people were scattering from me, and that you did not come within the appointed days, and that the Philistines were assembling at Michmash,

12 therefore I said, 'Now the Philistines will come down against me at Gilgal, and I have not asked the favor of the LORD.' So I forced myself and offered the burnt offering."

13 Samuel said to Saul, "You have acted foolishly; you have not kept the commandment of the LORD your God, which He commanded you, for now the LORD would have established your kingdom over Israel forever.

14 "But now your kingdom shall not endure. The LORD has sought out for Himself a man after His own heart, and the LORD has appointed him as ruler over His people, because you have not kept what the LORD commanded you."

a Gr and Syr read *Barak*　　*b* Or *reverence*

15 ¶ Then Samuel arose and went up from Gilgal to Gibeah of Benjamin. And Saul numbered the people who were present with him, about six hundred men.

16 Now Saul and his son Jonathan and the people who were present with them were staying in Geba of Benjamin while the Philistines camped at Michmash.

17 And the raiders came from the camp of the Philistines in three companies: one company turned toward Ophrah, to the land of Shual,

18 and another company turned toward Bethhoron, and another company turned toward the border which overlooks the valley of Zeboim toward the wilderness.

19 ¶ Now no blacksmith could be found in all the land of Israel, for the Philistines said, "Otherwise the Hebrews will make swords or spears."

13:19 Military Dominance

Samuel's leadership had kept the Philistines from occupying Israel (see 7:13). However, nobody could question the Philistines' military dominance. They had outposts in several central Israelite towns (10:5; 13:3) and, most important, kept a monopoly on iron weapons by outlawing local blacksmiths. Only the royal family of Israel possessed a sword or a spear (verse 22), presumably weapons that had been smuggled in and hidden.

20 So all Israel went down to the Philistines, each to sharpen his plowshare, his mattock, his axe, and his hoe.

21 The charge was two-thirds of a shekel for the plowshares, the mattocks, the forks, and the axes, and to fix the hoes.

22 So it came about on the day of battle that neither sword nor spear was found in the hands of any of the people who *were* with Saul and Jonathan, but they were found with Saul and his son Jonathan.

23 And the garrison of the Philistines went out to the pass of Michmash.

Jonathan's Victory

14 Now the day came that Jonathan, the son of Saul, said to the young man who was carrying his armor, "Come and let us cross over to the Philistines' garrison that is on the other side." But he did not tell his father.

2 Saul was staying in the outskirts of Gibeah under the pomegranate tree which is in Migron. And the people who *were* with him *were* about six hundred men,

3 and Ahijah, the son of Ahitub, Ichabod's brother, the son of Phinehas, the son of Eli, the priest of the LORD at Shiloh, was wearing an ephod. And the people did not know that Jonathan had gone.

4 Between the passes by which Jonathan sought to cross over to the Philistines' garrison, there was a sharp crag on the one side and a sharp crag on the other side, and the name of the one was Bozez, and the name of the other Seneh.

5 The one crag rose on the north opposite Michmash, and the other on the south opposite Geba.

6 ¶ Then Jonathan said to the young man who was carrying his armor, "Come and let us cross over to the garrison of these uncircumcised; perhaps the LORD will work for us, for the LORD is not restrained to save by many or by few."

7 His armor bearer said to him, "Do all that is in your heart; turn yourself, *and* here I am with you according to your desire."

8 Then Jonathan said, "Behold, we will cross over to the men and reveal ourselves to them.

9 "If they say to us, 'Wait until we come to you'; then we will stand in our place and not go up to them.

10 "But if they say, 'Come up to us,' then we will go up, for the LORD has given them into our hands; and this shall be the sign to us."

11 When both of them revealed themselves to the garrison of the Philistines, the Philistines said, "Behold, Hebrews are coming out of the holes where they have hidden themselves."

12 So the men of the garrison hailed Jonathan and his armor bearer and said, "Come up to us and we will tell you something." And Jonathan said to his armor bearer, "Come up after me, for the LORD has given them into the hands of Israel."

13 Then Jonathan climbed up on his hands and feet, with his armor bearer behind him; and they fell before Jonathan, and his armor bearer put some to death after him.

14 That first slaughter which Jonathan and his armor bearer made was about twenty men within about half a furrow in an acre of land.

15 And there was a trembling in the camp, in the field, and among all the people. Even the garrison and the raiders trembled, and the earth quaked so that it became a *a*great trembling.

16 ¶ Now Saul's watchmen in Gibeah of Benjamin looked, and behold, the multitude melted away; and they went here and *there.*

17 Saul said to the people who *were* with him, "Number now and see who has gone from us." And when they had numbered, behold, Jonathan and his armor bearer were not *there.*

18 Then Saul said to Ahijah, "Bring the ark of God here." For the ark of God was at that time with the sons of Israel.

19 While Saul talked to the priest, the commotion in the camp of the Philistines continued and

a Lit *trembling of God*

increased; so Saul said to the priest, "Withdraw your hand."

20 Then Saul and all the people who *were* with him rallied and came to the battle; and behold, every man's sword was against his fellow, *and there was* very great confusion.

21 Now the Hebrews *who* were with the Philistines previously, who went up with them all around in the camp, even they also *turned* to be with the Israelites who *were* with Saul and Jonathan.

22 When all the men of Israel who had hidden themselves in the hill country of Ephraim heard that the Philistines had fled, even they also pursued them closely in the battle.

23 So the LORD delivered Israel that day, and the battle spread beyond Beth-aven.

Saul's Foolish Order

24 ¶ Now the men of Israel were hard-pressed on that day, for Saul had put the people under oath, saying, "Cursed be the man who eats food before evening, and until I have avenged myself on my enemies." So none of the people tasted food.

14:24 Big Ego

Saul's problems surface here in two ways. First, he impulsively pronounced a curse (a very solemn vow) without thinking it through. This rash vow made his hungry army less effective, and led to trouble for his own son. Second, Saul apparently saw the battle as a personal vendetta in which he was avenging himself on his enemies. A wiser leader would have understood that God's honor and the security of his people were the issues.

25 All *the people of* the land entered the forest, and there was honey on the ground.

26 When the people entered the forest, behold, *there was* a flow of honey; but no man put his hand to his mouth, for the people feared the oath.

27 But Jonathan had not heard when his father put the people under oath; therefore, he put out the end of the staff that *was* in his hand and dipped it in the honeycomb, and put his hand to his mouth, and his eyes brightened.

28 Then one of the people said, "Your father strictly put the people under oath, saying, 'Cursed be the man who eats food today.' " And the people were weary.

29 Then Jonathan said, "My father has troubled the land. See now, how my eyes have brightened because I tasted a little of this honey.

30 "How much more, if only the people had eaten freely today of the spoil of their enemies which they found! For now the slaughter among the Philistines has not been great."

31 ¶ They struck among the Philistines that day from Michmash to Aijalon. And the people were very weary.

32 The people rushed greedily upon the spoil, and took sheep and oxen and calves, and slew *them* on the ground; and the people ate *them* with the blood.

33 Then they told Saul, saying, "Behold, the people are sinning against the LORD by eating with the blood." And he said, "You have acted treacherously; roll a great stone to me today."

34 Saul said, "Disperse yourselves among the people and say to them, 'Each one of you bring me his ox or his sheep, and slaughter *it* here and eat; and do not sin against the LORD by eating with the blood.' " So all the people that night brought each one his ox with him and slaughtered *it* there.

35 And Saul built an altar to the LORD; it was the first altar that he built to the LORD.

36 ¶ Then Saul said, "Let us go down after the Philistines by night and take spoil among them until the morning light, and let us not leave a man of them." And they said, "Do whatever seems good to you." So the priest said, "Let us draw near to God here."

37 Saul inquired of God, "Shall I go down after the Philistines? Will You give them into the hand of Israel?" But He did not answer him on that day.

38 Saul said, "Draw near here, all you chiefs of the people, and investigate and see how this sin has happened today.

39 "For as the LORD lives, who delivers Israel, though it is in Jonathan my son, he shall surely die." But not one of all the people answered him.

40 Then he said to all Israel, "You shall be on one side and I and Jonathan my son will be on the other side." And the people said to Saul, "Do what seems good to you."

41 Therefore, Saul said to the LORD, the God of Israel, "Give a perfect *lot*." And Jonathan and Saul were taken, but the people escaped.

42 Saul said, "Cast *lots* between me and Jonathan my son." And Jonathan was taken.

43 ¶ Then Saul said to Jonathan, "Tell me what you have done." So Jonathan told him and said, "I indeed tasted a little honey with the end of the staff that was in my hand. Here I am, I must die!"

44 Saul said, "May God do this *to me* and more also, for you shall surely die, Jonathan."

45 But the people said to Saul, "Must Jonathan die, who has brought about this great deliverance in Israel? Far from it! As the LORD lives, not one hair of his head shall fall to the ground, for he has worked with God this day." So the people rescued Jonathan and he did not die.

46 Then Saul went up from pursuing the Philistines, and the Philistines went to their own place.

Constant Warfare

47 ¶ Now when Saul had taken the kingdom

over Israel, he fought against all his enemies on every side, against Moab, the sons of Ammon, Edom, the kings of Zobah, and the Philistines; and wherever he turned, he inflicted punishment.

48 He acted valiantly and defeated the Amalekites, and delivered Israel from the hands of those who plundered them.

49 ¶ Now the sons of Saul were Jonathan and Ishvi and Malchi-shua; and the names of his two daughters *were these:* the name of the firstborn Merab and the name of the younger Michal.

50 The name of Saul's wife was Ahinoam the daughter of Ahimaaz. And the name of the captain of his army was Abner the son of Ner, Saul's uncle.

51 Kish *was* the father of Saul, and Ner the father of Abner *was* the son of Abiel.

52 ¶ Now the war against the Philistines was severe all the days of Saul; and when Saul saw any mighty man or any valiant man, he attached him to his staff.

Saul's Disobedience

15 Then Samuel said to Saul, "The LORD sent me to anoint you as king over His people, over Israel; now therefore, listen to the words of the LORD.

2 "Thus says the LORD of hosts, 'I will punish Amalek *for* what he did to Israel, how he set himself against him on the way while he was coming up from Egypt.

15:2 Old Enemies

The Israelites had first encountered the Amalekites, a semi-nomadic group of pitiless raiders, on their way out of Egypt. Due to the Amalekites' unprovoked attack, Moses had declared that God wanted Amalek wiped out (Exodus 17:8–16; Deuteronomy 25:17–19). The hostility continued. Typically, the Amalekites would sweep into unprotected towns and villages on the edge of the southern desert, killing and looting, leaving the survivors without food. Though Samuel's order to Saul is hard to understand, knowing the Amalekites' reputation makes it easier to sympathize with. For a more general explanation of holy war, see "Is a War Ever Holy?" page 262.

3 'Now go and strike Amalek and utterly destroy all that he has, and do not spare him; but put to death both man and woman, child and infant, ox and sheep, camel and donkey.' "

4 ¶ Then Saul summoned the people and numbered them in Telaim, 200,000 foot soldiers and 10,000 men of Judah.

5 Saul came to the city of Amalek and set an ambush in the valley.

6 Saul said to the Kenites, "Go, depart, go down from among the Amalekites, so that I do not destroy you with them; for you showed kindness to all the sons of Israel when they came up from Egypt." So the Kenites departed from among the Amalekites.

7 So Saul defeated the Amalekites, from Havilah as you go to Shur, which is east of Egypt.

8 He captured Agag the king of the Amalekites alive, and utterly destroyed all the people with the edge of the sword.

9 But Saul and the people spared Agag and the best of the sheep, the oxen, the fatlings, the lambs, and all that was good, and were not willing to destroy them utterly; but everything despised and worthless, that they utterly destroyed.

Samuel Rebukes Saul

10 ¶ Then the word of the LORD came to Samuel, saying,

11 "I regret that I have made Saul king, for he has turned back from following Me and has not carried out My commands." And Samuel was distressed and cried out to the LORD all night.

12 Samuel rose early in the morning to meet Saul; and it was told Samuel, saying, "Saul came to Carmel, and behold, he set up a monument for himself, then turned and proceeded on down to Gilgal."

13 Samuel came to Saul, and Saul said to him, "Blessed are you of the LORD! I have carried out the command of the LORD."

14 But Samuel said, "What then is this bleating of the sheep in my ears, and the lowing of the oxen which I hear?"

15 Saul said, "They have brought them from the Amalekites, for the people spared the best of the sheep and oxen, to sacrifice to the LORD your God; but the rest we have utterly destroyed."

16 Then Samuel said to Saul, "Wait, and let me tell you what the LORD said to me last night." And he said to him, "Speak!"

17 ¶ Samuel said, "Is it not true, though you were little in your own eyes, you were *made* the head of the tribes of Israel? And the LORD anointed you king over Israel,

18 and the LORD sent you on a mission, and said, 'Go and utterly destroy the sinners, the Amalekites, and fight against them until they are exterminated.'

19 "Why then did you not obey the voice of the LORD, but rushed upon the spoil and did what was evil in the sight of the LORD?"

20 ¶ Then Saul said to Samuel, "I did obey the voice of the LORD, and went on the mission on which the LORD sent me, and have brought back Agag the king of Amalek, and have utterly destroyed the Amalekites.

21 "But the people took *some* of the spoil, sheep and oxen, the choicest of the things devoted to destruction, to sacrifice to the LORD your God at Gilgal."

Why Saul Was Rejected

A leader who failed under pressure

SAUL HAD EVERYTHING GOING FOR him. Tall and handsome, he struck people with his appearance. God chose him as the first king in the history of Israel. Soon after he was secretly anointed, God's Spirit came on him—an encounter with God that affected his entire personality.

"Because you have rejected the word of the Lord, He has also rejected you from being king."
15:23

Almost immediately Saul led a successful rescue operation, saving the people of a besieged city from mutilation. He was then publicly crowned king, even though he himself did no politicking for the office. (In fact, he hid during the selection.) He wisely refrained from allowing his opponents to be punished. Instead, he united all 12 tribes behind him, even though he himself came from a small, minority tribe.

Saul chose the best young men to serve in his army. One of them, David, was not only a skilled general, but also a loyal follower who would never oppose Saul—even when he had good reason. David married Saul's daughter, and Saul's oldest son, Jonathan, became David's best friend. This should have cemented an alliance, sealing Saul's success.

Deterioration under Pressure

Yet Saul's life went tragically wrong. The first sign of trouble, as 1 Samuel tells the story, came not long after he became king. While preparing for a campaign against the Philistines, Saul grew impatient. Samuel, scheduled to lead in the proper spiritual preparation for battle, was seven days late. Saul's men began to desert, and Saul decided he could wait no longer. He himself began to make the religious sacrifices that Samuel, as priest, was supposed to make. Just then Samuel arrived. He blasted Saul (13:13–14). Saul's hastiness, insignificant though it may seem, showed an inner weakness: his willingness to compromise God's directions under pressure.

The battle came soon afterwards, and Israel won miraculously. But in the victory Saul acted sometimes indecisively, sometimes rashly. He could not decide to attack. Then he made a boastful vow that disrupted the Israelite army, allowing the Philistines to escape.

Attempted Murder

Sometime later Saul compromised again in a high-pressure situation, not following the precise instructions God had given for a military campaign (15:3). Again, Samuel caught him in the act. This time he accused Saul of rebelling against God. Samuel's words must have rung in Saul's head the rest of his life: "Because you have rejected the word of the Lord, He has also rejected you from being king" (15:23).

Without God's and Samuel's support, Saul lost his sense of confidence. An evil spirit began to torment him. Instead of building an alliance with David, Saul drove David away, causing him to run for his life in the desert. Eventually fear reduced Saul to a quivering, helpless jellyfish, incapable of leadership. In that condition he and his army lost a historic battle to the Philistines, allowing them to regain control. In the battle, both Saul and Jonathan were killed.

Why Saul Failed

The book of 1 Samuel doesn't psychoanalyze Saul; it merely reports what happened. The facts do point to a moral, though. Saul had begun with all the opportunity in the world. He only lacked, it seems, a strong compulsion to obey God no matter what. Under pressure he bent the rules. He lost God's backing. He grew fearful, rash, and jealous.

Saul's poor leadership left Israel worse off than at the beginning. The kingdom David inherited from Saul was again under Philistine military domination, and it was divided between north and south. Saul shows the unique tragedy of a poor leader. He fails not just himself. Inevitably he drags others down with him.

Life Questions: When you are put in the role of leader, how do you respond to pressure? Are Saul's weaknesses your weaknesses?

22 Samuel said,
"Has the LORD as much delight in burnt
   offerings and sacrifices
As in obeying the voice of the LORD?
Behold, to obey is better than sacrifice,
And to heed than the fat of rams.
23 "For rebellion is as the sin of divination,
And insubordination is as iniquity and
   idolatry.
Because you have rejected the word of
   the LORD,
He has also rejected you from *being*
   king."

24 ¶ Then Saul said to Samuel, "I have sinned; I have indeed transgressed the command of the LORD and your words, because I feared the people and listened to their voice.
25 "Now therefore, please pardon my sin and return with me, that I may worship the LORD."
26 But Samuel said to Saul, "I will not return with you; for you have rejected the word of the LORD, and the LORD has rejected you from being king over Israel."
27 As Samuel turned to go, *Saul* seized the edge of his robe, and it tore.
28 So Samuel said to him, "The LORD has torn the kingdom of Israel from you today and has given it to your neighbor, who is better than you.
29 "Also the Glory of Israel will not lie or change His mind; for He is not a man that He should change His mind."
30 Then he said, "I have sinned; *but* please honor me now before the elders of my people and before Israel, and go back with me, that I may worship the LORD your God."
31 So Samuel went back following Saul, and Saul worshiped the LORD.
32 ¶ Then Samuel said, "Bring me Agag, the king of the Amalekites." And Agag came to him cheerfully. And Agag said, "Surely the bitterness of death is past."
33 But Samuel said, "As your sword has made women childless, so shall your mother be childless among women." And Samuel hewed Agag to pieces before the LORD at Gilgal.
34 ¶ Then Samuel went to Ramah, but Saul went up to his house at Gibeah of Saul.
35 Samuel did not see Saul again until the day of his death; for Samuel grieved over Saul. And the LORD regretted that He had made Saul king over Israel.

Samuel Goes to Bethlehem

16 Now the LORD said to Samuel, "How long will you grieve over Saul, since I have rejected him from being king over Israel? Fill your horn with oil and go; I will send you to Jesse the Bethlehemite, for I have selected a king for Myself among his sons."
2 But Samuel said, "How can I go? When Saul hears *of it*, he will kill me." And the LORD said,

"Take a heifer with you and say, 'I have come to sacrifice to the LORD.'
3 "You shall invite Jesse to the sacrifice, and I will show you what you shall do; and you shall anoint for Me the one whom I designate to you."
4 So Samuel did what the LORD said, and came to Bethlehem. And the elders of the city came trembling to meet him and said, "Do you come in peace?"
5 He said, "In peace; I have come to sacrifice to the LORD. Consecrate yourselves and come with me to the sacrifice." He also consecrated Jesse and his sons and invited them to the sacrifice.
6 ¶ When they entered, he looked at Eliab and thought, "Surely the LORD'S anointed is before Him."
7 But the LORD said to Samuel, "Do not look at his appearance or at the height of his stature, because I have rejected him; for God *sees* not as man sees, for man looks at the outward appearance, but the LORD looks at the heart."

16:7 What God Values

What qualified David to be king? Apparently he did not make an overpowering first impression, but God valued hidden qualities far more. Throughout his life David would demonstrate that he loved and trusted God with all his heart, as the law in Deuteronomy 6:4–6 demanded.

8 Then Jesse called Abinadab and made him pass before Samuel. And he said, "The LORD has not chosen this one either."
9 Next Jesse made Shammah pass by. And he said, "The LORD has not chosen this one either."
10 Thus Jesse made seven of his sons pass before Samuel. But Samuel said to Jesse, "The LORD has not chosen these."
11 And Samuel said to Jesse, "Are these all the children?" And he said, "There remains yet the youngest, and behold, he is tending the sheep." Then Samuel said to Jesse, "Send and bring him; for we will not sit down until he comes here."

David Anointed

12 So he sent and brought him in. Now he was ruddy, with beautiful eyes and a handsome appearance. And the LORD said, "Arise, anoint him; for this is he."
13 Then Samuel took the horn of oil and anointed him in the midst of his brothers; and the Spirit of the LORD came mightily upon David from that day forward. And Samuel arose and went to Ramah.
14 ¶ Now the Spirit of the LORD departed from Saul, and an evil spirit from the LORD terrorized him.

15 Saul's servants then said to him, "Behold now, an evil spirit from God is terrorizing you.

16 "Let our lord now command your servants who are before you. Let them seek a man who is a skillful player on the harp; and it shall come about when the evil spirit from God is on you, that he shall play *the harp* with his hand, and you will be well."

17 So Saul said to his servants, "Provide for me now a man who can play well and bring *him* to me."

18 Then one of the young men said, "Behold, I have seen a son of Jesse the Bethlehemite who is a skillful musician, a mighty man of valor, a warrior, one prudent in speech, and a handsome man; and the LORD is with him."

19 So Saul sent messengers to Jesse and said, "Send me your son David who is with the flock."

20 Jesse took a donkey *loaded with* bread and a jug of wine and a young goat, and sent *them* to Saul by David his son.

21 Then David came to Saul and attended him; and Saul loved him greatly, and he became his armor bearer.

22 Saul sent to Jesse, saying, "Let David now stand before me, for he has found favor in my sight."

23 So it came about whenever the *evil* spirit from God came to Saul, David would take the harp and play *it* with his hand; and Saul would be refreshed and be well, and the evil spirit would depart from him.

Goliath's Challenge

17 Now the Philistines gathered their armies for battle; and they were gathered at Socoh which belongs to Judah, and they camped between Socoh and Azekah, in Ephes-dammim.

2 Saul and the men of Israel were gathered and camped in the valley of Elah, and drew up in battle array to encounter the Philistines.

3 The Philistines stood on the mountain on one side while Israel stood on the mountain on the other side, with the valley between them.

4 Then a champion came out from the armies of the Philistines named Goliath, from Gath, whose height was six [a]cubits and a span.

5 *He had* a bronze helmet on his head, and he was clothed with scale-armor which weighed five thousand shekels of bronze.

6 *He* also *had* bronze [b]greaves on his legs and a bronze javelin *slung* between his shoulders.

7 The shaft of his spear was like a weaver's beam, and the head of his spear *weighed* six hundred shekels of iron; his shield-carrier also walked before him.

8 He stood and shouted to the ranks of Israel and said to them, "Why do you come out to draw up in battle array? Am I not the Philistine and you

servants of Saul? Choose a man for yourselves and let him come down to me.

9 "If he is able to fight with me and kill me, then we will become your servants; but if I prevail

17:4 Everyone Watched Goliath

Wars in ancient times were sometimes decided by "representative combat": champions from each side would fight, and the results of their combat would determine the battle's result. People believed the outcome of the fight was controlled by the warriors' gods more than by the two sides' military strength.

Saul lacked confidence in God's support. His terror demoralized the Israelite army. David, by contrast, was as confident in his God as Goliath was scornful of God's people.

against him and kill him, then you shall become our servants and serve us."

10 Again the Philistine said, "I defy the ranks of Israel this day; give me a man that we may fight together."

11 When Saul and all Israel heard these words of the Philistine, they were dismayed and greatly afraid.

12 ¶ Now David was the son of the Ephrathite of Bethlehem in Judah, whose name was Jesse, and he had eight sons. And Jesse was old in the days of Saul, advanced *in years* among men.

13 The three older sons of Jesse had gone after Saul to the battle. And the names of his three sons who went to the battle were Eliab the firstborn, and the second to him Abinadab, and the third Shammah.

14 David was the youngest. Now the three oldest followed Saul,

15 but David went back and forth from Saul to tend his father's flock at Bethlehem.

16 The Philistine came forward morning and evening for forty days and took his stand.

17 ¶ Then Jesse said to David his son, "Take now for your brothers an ephah of this roasted grain and these ten loaves and run to the camp to your brothers.

18 "Bring also these ten cuts of cheese to the commander of *their* thousand, and look into the welfare of your brothers, and bring back news of them.

19 "For Saul and they and all the men of Israel are in the valley of Elah, fighting with the Philistines."

David Accepts the Challenge

20 ¶ So David arose early in the morning and left the flock with a keeper and took *the supplies* and went as Jesse had commanded him. And he

---

[a] I.e. One cubit equals approx 18 in.   [b] Or *shin guards*

came to the circle of the camp while the army was going out in battle array shouting the war cry.

21 Israel and the Philistines drew up in battle array, army against army.

22 Then David left his baggage in the care of the baggage keeper, and ran to the battle line and entered in order to greet his brothers.

23 As he was talking with them, behold, the champion, the Philistine from Gath named Goliath, was coming up from the army of the Philistines, and he spoke these same words; and David heard *them*.

24 ¶ When all the men of Israel saw the man, they fled from him and were greatly afraid.

25 The men of Israel said, "Have you seen this man who is coming up? Surely he is coming up to defy Israel. And it will be that the king will enrich the man who kills him with great riches and will give him his daughter and make his father's house *a*free in Israel."

26 ¶ Then David spoke to the men who were standing by him, saying, "What will be done for the man who kills this Philistine and takes away the reproach from Israel? For who is this uncircumcised Philistine, that he should taunt the armies of the living God?"

27 The people answered him in accord with this word, saying, "Thus it will be done for the man who kills him."

28 ¶ Now Eliab his oldest brother heard when he spoke to the men; and Eliab's anger burned against David and he said, "Why have you come down? And with whom have you left those few sheep in the wilderness? I know your insolence and the wickedness of your heart; for you have come down in order to see the battle."

29 But David said, "What have I done now? Was it not just a question?"

30 Then he turned away from him to another and said the same thing; and the people answered the same thing as before.

David Kills Goliath

31 ¶ When the words which David spoke were heard, they told *them* to Saul, and he sent for him.

32 David said to Saul, "Let no man's heart fail on account of him; your servant will go and fight with this Philistine."

33 Then Saul said to David, "You are not able to go against this Philistine to fight with him; for you are *but* a youth while he has been a warrior from his youth."

34 But David said to Saul, "Your servant was tending his father's sheep. When a lion or a bear came and took a lamb from the flock,

35 I went out after him and attacked him, and rescued *it* from his mouth; and when he rose up against me, I seized *him* by his beard and struck him and killed him.

36 "Your servant has killed both the lion and the bear; and this uncircumcised Philistine will be like one of them, since he has taunted the armies of the living God."

37 And David said, "The LORD who delivered me from the paw of the lion and from the paw of the bear, He will deliver me from the hand of this Philistine." And Saul said to David, "Go, and may the LORD be with you."

38 Then Saul clothed David with his garments and put a bronze helmet on his head, and he clothed him with armor.

39 David girded his sword over his armor and tried to walk, for he had not tested *them*. So David said to Saul, "I cannot go with these, for I have not tested *them*." And David took them off.

40 He took his stick in his hand and chose for himself five smooth stones from the brook, and put them in the shepherd's bag which he had, even in *his* pouch, and his sling was in his hand; and he approached the Philistine.

17:40 Deadly Rocks

The "five smooth stones" that David took from the stream were each probably bigger than a baseball. Someone skilled with a sling could hurl them at close to 100 miles per hour.

41 ¶ Then the Philistine came on and approached David, with the shield-bearer in front of him.

42 When the Philistine looked and saw David, he disdained him; for he was *but* a youth, and ruddy, with a handsome appearance.

43 The Philistine said to David, "Am I a dog, that you come to me with sticks?" And the Philistine cursed David by his gods.

44 The Philistine also said to David, "Come to me, and I will give your flesh to the birds of the sky and the beasts of the field."

45 Then David said to the Philistine, "You come to me with a sword, a spear, and a javelin, but I come to you in the name of the LORD of hosts, the God of the armies of Israel, whom you have taunted.

46 "This day the LORD will deliver you up into my hands, and I will strike you down and remove your head from you. And I will give the dead bodies of the army of the Philistines this day to the birds of the sky and the wild beasts of the earth, that all the earth may know that there is a God in Israel,

47 and that all this assembly may know that the LORD does not deliver by sword or by spear; for the battle is the LORD's and He will give you into our hands."

48 ¶ Then it happened when the Philistine rose and came and drew near to meet David, that Da-

---

a I.e. free from taxes and public service

vid ran quickly toward the battle line to meet the Philistine.

49 And David put his hand into his bag and took from it a stone and slung *it*, and struck the Philistine on his forehead. And the stone sank into his forehead, so that he fell on his face to the ground.

50 ¶ Thus David prevailed over the Philistine with a sling and a stone, and he struck the Philistine and killed him; but there was no sword in David's hand.

51 Then David ran and stood over the Philistine and took his sword and drew it out of its sheath and killed him, and cut off his head with it. When the Philistines saw that their champion was dead, they fled.

52 The men of Israel and Judah arose and shouted and pursued the Philistines as far as the valley, and to the gates of Ekron. And the slain Philistines lay along the way to Shaaraim, even to Gath and Ekron.

53 The sons of Israel returned from chasing the Philistines and plundered their camps.

54 Then David took the Philistine's head and brought it to Jerusalem, but he put his weapons in his tent.

55 ¶ Now when Saul saw David going out against the Philistine, he said to Abner the commander of the army, "Abner, whose son is this young man?" And Abner said, "By your life, O king, I do not know."

56 The king said, "You inquire whose son the youth is."

57 So when David returned from killing the Philistine, Abner took him and brought him before Saul with the Philistine's head in his hand.

58 Saul said to him, "Whose son are you, young man?" And David answered, "*I am* the son of your servant Jesse the Bethlehemite."

Jonathan and David

18 Now it came about when he had finished speaking to Saul, that the soul of Jonathan was knit to the soul of David, and Jonathan loved him as himself.

2 Saul took him that day and did not let him return to his father's house.

3 Then Jonathan made a covenant with David because he loved him as himself.

4 Jonathan stripped himself of the robe that was on him and gave it to David, with his armor, including his sword and his bow and his belt.

5 So David went out wherever Saul sent him, *and* prospered; and Saul set him over the men of war. And it was pleasing in the sight of all the people and also in the sight of Saul's servants.

6 ¶ It happened as they were coming, when David returned from killing the Philistine, that the women came out of all the cities of Israel, singing and dancing, to meet King Saul, with tambourines, with joy and with *a*musical instruments.

7 The women sang as they played, and said,
"Saul has slain his thousands,
And David his ten thousands."

8 Then Saul became very angry, for this saying displeased him; and he said, "They have ascribed to David ten thousands, but to me they have ascribed thousands. Now what more can he have but the kingdom?"

9 Saul looked at David with suspicion from that day on.

Saul Turns against David

10 ¶ Now it came about on the next day that an evil spirit from God came mightily upon Saul, and he raved in the midst of the house, while David was playing *the harp* with his hand, as usual; and a spear *was* in Saul's hand.

11 Saul hurled the spear for he thought, "I will pin David to the wall." But David escaped from his presence twice.

12 ¶ Now Saul was afraid of David, for the LORD was with him but had departed from Saul.

13 Therefore Saul removed him from his presence and appointed him as his commander of a thousand; and he went out and came in before the people.

14 David was prospering in all his ways for the LORD *was* with him.

15 When Saul saw that he was prospering greatly, he dreaded him.

16 But all Israel and Judah loved David, and he went out and came in before them.

17 ¶ Then Saul said to David, "Here is my older daughter Merab; I will give her to you as a wife, only be a valiant man for me and fight the LORD'S battles." For Saul thought, "My hand shall not be against him, but let the hand of the Philistines be against him."

18 But David said to Saul, "Who am I, and what is my life *or* my father's family in Israel, that I should be the king's son-in-law?"

19 So it came about at the time when Merab, Saul's daughter, should have been given to David, that she was given to Adriel the Meholathite for a wife.

David Marries Saul's Daughter

20 ¶ Now Michal, Saul's daughter, loved David. When they told Saul, the thing was agreeable to him.

21 Saul thought, "I will give her to him that she may become a snare to him, and that the hand of the Philistines may be against him." Therefore Saul said to David, "For a second time you may be my son-in-law today."

22 Then Saul commanded his servants, "Speak to David secretly, saying, 'Behold, the king de-

---

a I.e. triangles; or three-stringed instruments

lights in you, and all his servants love you; now therefore, become the king's son-in-law.'"

23 So Saul's servants spoke these words to David. But David said, "Is it trivial in your sight to become the king's son-in-law, since I am a poor man and lightly esteemed?"

24 The servants of Saul reported to him according to these words *which* David spoke.

25 Saul then said, "Thus you shall say to David, 'The king does not desire any dowry except a hundred foreskins of the Philistines, to take vengeance on the king's enemies.'" Now Saul planned to make David fall by the hand of the Philistines.

26 When his servants told David these words, it pleased David to become the king's son-in-law. Before the days had expired

27 David rose up and went, he and his men, and struck down two hundred men among the Philistines. Then David brought their foreskins, and they gave them in full number to the king, that he might become the king's son-in-law. So Saul gave him Michal his daughter for a wife.

18:27 "Scalps"

This bloody prize, something like the scalps that native Americans and white settlers collected in battles, proved that David's battle claims were not exaggerated. Foreskins would come from Philistines, since other tribes of the area, like Israel, practiced circumcision.

28 When Saul saw and knew that the LORD was with David, and *that* Michal, Saul's daughter, loved him,

29 then Saul was even more afraid of David. Thus Saul was David's enemy continually.

30 ¶ Then the commanders of the Philistines went out *to battle,* and it happened as often as they went out, that David behaved himself more wisely than all the servants of Saul. So his name was highly esteemed.

David Protected from Saul

19 Now Saul told Jonathan his son and all his servants to put David to death. But Jonathan, Saul's son, greatly delighted in David.

2 So Jonathan told David saying, "Saul my father is seeking to put you to death. Now therefore, please be on guard in the morning, and stay in a secret place and hide yourself.

3 "I will go out and stand beside my father in the field where you are, and I will speak with my father about you; if I find out anything, then I will tell you."

4 Then Jonathan spoke well of David to Saul his father and said to him, "Do not let the king sin against his servant David, since he has not sinned

against you, and since his deeds *have been* very beneficial to you.

5 "For he took his life in his hand and struck the Philistine, and the LORD brought about a great deliverance for all Israel; you saw *it* and rejoiced. Why then will you sin against innocent blood by putting David to death without a cause?"

6 Saul listened to the voice of Jonathan, and Saul vowed, "As the LORD lives, he shall not be put to death."

7 Then Jonathan called David, and Jonathan told him all these words. And Jonathan brought David to Saul, and he was in his presence as formerly.

8 ¶ When there was war again, David went out and fought with the Philistines and defeated them with great slaughter, so that they fled before him.

9 Now there was an evil spirit from the LORD on Saul as he was sitting in his house with his spear in his hand, and David was playing *the harp* with *his* hand.

10 Saul tried to pin David to the wall with the spear, but he slipped away out of Saul's presence, so that he stuck the spear into the wall. And David fled and escaped that night.

11 ¶ Then Saul sent messengers to David's house to watch him, in order to put him to death in the morning. But Michal, David's wife, told him, saying, "If you do not save your life tonight, tomorrow you will be put to death."

12 So Michal let David down through a window, and he went out and fled and escaped.

13 Michal took the household idol and laid *it* on the bed, and put a quilt of goats' *hair* at its head, and covered *it* with clothes.

14 When Saul sent messengers to take David, she said, "He is sick."

15 Then Saul sent messengers to see David, saying, "Bring him up to me on his bed, that I may put him to death."

16 When the messengers entered, behold, the household idol *was* on the bed with the quilt of goats' *hair* at its head.

17 So Saul said to Michal, "Why have you deceived me like this and let my enemy go, so that he has escaped?" And Michal said to Saul, "He said to me, 'Let me go! Why should I put you to death?'"

18 ¶ Now David fled and escaped and came to Samuel at Ramah, and told him all that Saul had done to him. And he and Samuel went and stayed in Naioth.

19 It was told Saul, saying, "Behold, David is at Naioth in Ramah."

20 Then Saul sent messengers to take David, but when they saw the company of the prophets prophesying, with Samuel standing *and* presiding over them, the Spirit of God came upon the messengers of Saul; and they also prophesied.

21 When it was told Saul, he sent other mes-

sengers, and they also prophesied. So Saul sent messengers again the third time, and they also prophesied.

22 Then he himself went to Ramah and came as far as the large well that is in Secu; and he asked and said, "Where are Samuel and David?" And *someone* said, "Behold, they are at Naioth in Ramah."

23 He proceeded there to Naioth in Ramah; and the Spirit of God came upon him also, so that he went along prophesying continually until he came to Naioth in Ramah.

19:23 Out of Control

Prophets are usually pictured as somber figures. First Samuel reveals a different side: prophecy accompanying ecstatic worship. Saul had met a musical band of such prophets soon after he was anointed king (10:5–11). Now that he was planning evil, however, meeting the Spirit of God made him utterly lose control.

24 He also stripped off his clothes, and he too prophesied before Samuel and lay down naked all that day and all that night. Therefore they say, "Is Saul also among the prophets?"

David and Jonathan Covenant

20 Then David fled from Naioth in Ramah, and came and said to Jonathan, "What have I done? What is my iniquity? And what is my sin before your father, that he is seeking my life?"

2 He said to him, "Far from it, you shall not die. Behold, my father does nothing either great or small without disclosing it to me. So why should my father hide this thing from me? It is not so!"

3 Yet David vowed again, saying, "Your father knows well that I have found favor in your sight, and he has said, 'Do not let Jonathan know this, or he will be grieved.' But truly as the LORD lives and as your soul lives, there is hardly a step between me and death."

4 Then Jonathan said to David, "Whatever you say, I will do for you."

5 So David said to Jonathan, "Behold, tomorrow is the new moon, and I ought to sit down to eat with the king. But let me go, that I may hide myself in the field until the third evening.

6 "If your father misses me at all, then say, 'David earnestly asked *leave* of me to run to Bethlehem his city, because it is the yearly sacrifice there for the whole family.'

7 "If he says, 'It is good,' your servant *will be* safe; but if he is very angry, know that he has decided on evil.

8 "Therefore deal kindly with your servant, for you have brought your servant into a covenant of the LORD with you. But if there is iniquity in me, put me to death yourself; for why then should you bring me to your father?"

9 Jonathan said, "Far be it from you! For if I should indeed learn that evil has been decided by my father to come upon you, then would I not tell you about it?"

10 Then David said to Jonathan, "Who will tell me if your father answers you harshly?"

11 Jonathan said to David, "Come, and let us go out into the field." So both of them went out to the field.

12 ¶ Then Jonathan said to David, "The LORD, the God of Israel, *be witness!* When I have sound-

JONATHAN *Friends First*

JEALOUS FRIENDS SOMETIMES FORCE US to choose. "Who is your best friend?" they demand, when we'd prefer not to rank them. Jonathan faced that kind of loyalty dilemma with his father, who grew insanely jealous of his son's friendship with David.

Palace intrigues in those days resembled the plot of a Shakespearean play. Insecure and guilt-ridden over past misdeeds, Saul feared that young David would take away his crown. (Indeed, Samuel had secretly anointed David as Israel's future king, but David fought bravely in Saul's service and never tried to usurp the throne.)

Though Jonathan tried to stay loyal to both father and friend, his father made it impossible. Soon Jonathan realized that Saul would kill David if he caught him. Once, in a blind rage, Saul hurled a spear at his own son for standing up for David (20:32–33).

One major factor further complicated Jonathan's choice: As Saul's son, he stood next in line for the throne. By siding with David, he would ultimately harm himself. Even so, at the risk of his own neck, Jonathan chose to help David escape. He told David he would happily follow his friend as his number-two man (23:17).

Tragically, the two friends never got the chance to rule together. In a battle against the Philistines, Jonathan fought at his father's side and was killed (31:2). David, mourning his dearest friend, sang a poignant song in tribute (2 Samuel 1:17–27). Their loyalty and love make for one of the most beautiful stories of friendship ever told.

Life Questions: What friend is most loyal to you? What does that loyalty mean to you?

ed out my father about this time tomorrow, *or* the third day, behold, if there is good *feeling* toward David, shall I not then send to you and make it known to you?

13 "If it please my father *to do* you harm, may the LORD do so to Jonathan and more also, if I do not make it known to you and send you away, that you may go in safety. And may the LORD be with you as He has been with my father.

14 "If I am still alive, will you not show me the lovingkindness of the LORD, that I may not die?

15 "You shall not cut off your lovingkindness from my house forever, not even when the LORD cuts off every one of the enemies of David from the face of the earth."

16 So Jonathan made a *covenant* with the house of David, *saying,* "May the LORD require *it* at the hands of David's enemies."

17 Jonathan made David vow again because of his love for him, because he loved him as he loved his own life.

18 ¶ Then Jonathan said to him, "Tomorrow is the new moon, and you will be missed because your seat will be empty.

19 "When you have stayed for three days, you shall go down quickly and come to the place where you hid yourself on that eventful day, and you shall remain by the stone Ezel.

20 "I will shoot three arrows to the side, as though I shot at a target.

21 "And behold, I will send the lad, *saying,* 'Go, find the arrows.' If I specifically say to the lad, 'Behold, the arrows are on this side of you, get them,' then come; for there is safety for you and no harm, as the LORD lives.

22 "But if I say to the youth, 'Behold, the arrows are beyond you,' go, for the LORD has sent you away.

23 "As for the agreement of which you and I have spoken, behold, the LORD is between you and me forever."

24 ¶ So David hid in the field; and when the new moon came, the king sat down to eat food.

25 The king sat on his seat as usual, the seat by the wall; then Jonathan rose up and Abner sat down by Saul's side, but David's place was empty.

26 Nevertheless Saul did not speak anything that day, for he thought, "It is an accident, he is not clean, surely *he is* not clean."

27 It came about the next day, the second *day* of the new moon, that David's place was empty; so Saul said to Jonathan his son, "Why has the son of Jesse not come to the meal, either yesterday or today?"

28 Jonathan then answered Saul, "David earnestly asked leave of me *to go* to Bethlehem,

29 for he said, 'Please let me go, since our family has a sacrifice in the city, and my brother has commanded me to attend. And now, if I have found favor in your sight, please let me get away

that I may see my brothers.' For this reason he has not come to the king's table."

Saul Is Angry with Jonathan

30 ¶ Then Saul's anger burned against Jonathan and he said to him, "You son of a perverse, rebellious woman! Do I not know that you are choosing the son of Jesse to your own shame and to the shame of your mother's nakedness?

31 "For as long as the son of Jesse lives on the earth, neither you nor your kingdom will be established. Therefore now, send and bring him to me, for he must surely die."

32 But Jonathan answered Saul his father and said to him, "Why should he be put to death? What has he done?"

33 Then Saul hurled his spear at him to strike him down; so Jonathan knew that his father had decided to put David to death.

34 Then Jonathan arose from the table in fierce anger, and did not eat food on the second day of the new moon, for he was grieved over David because his father had dishonored him.

35 ¶ Now it came about in the morning that Jonathan went out into the field for the appointment with David, and a little lad *was* with him.

36 He said to his lad, "Run, find now the arrows which I am about to shoot." As the lad was running, he shot an arrow past him.

37 When the lad reached the place of the arrow which Jonathan had shot, Jonathan called after the lad and said, "Is not the arrow beyond you?"

38 And Jonathan called after the lad, "Hurry, be quick, do not stay!" And Jonathan's lad picked up the arrow and came to his master.

39 But the lad was not aware of anything; only Jonathan and David knew about the matter.

40 Then Jonathan gave his weapons to his lad and said to him, "Go, bring *them* to the city."

41 When the lad was gone, David rose from the south side and fell on his face to the ground, and bowed three times. And they kissed each other and wept together, but David *wept* the more.

42 Jonathan said to David, "Go in safety, inasmuch as we have sworn to each other in the name of the LORD, saying, 'The LORD will be between me and you, and between my descendants and your descendants forever.'" Then he rose and departed, while Jonathan went into the city.

David Takes Consecrated Bread

21 Then David came to Nob to Ahimelech the priest; and Ahimelech came trembling to meet David and said to him, "Why are you alone and no one with you?"

2 David said to Ahimelech the priest, "The king has commissioned me with a matter and has said to me, 'Let no one know anything about the matter on which I am sending you and with which I have commissioned you; and I have directed the young men to a certain place.'

3 "Now therefore, what do you have on hand? Give me five loaves of bread, or whatever can be found."

4 The priest answered David and said, "There is no ordinary bread on hand, but there is consecrated bread; if only the young men have kept themselves from women."

21:4 Disobeying the Law

David was desperate when he reached Nob. He did not even have food. He lied about his situation. Then he ate consecrated bread that was supposed to be reserved for the priests. (A thousand years later Jesus raised the issue of the consecrated bread, suggesting that keeping the ritual laws mattered less than David's survival [Matthew 12:3–4].)

David later admitted that he had been wrong to go to Nob and endanger the priests. Saul, suspicious of their involvement, slaughtered them (22:17–18).

5 David answered the priest and said to him, "Surely women have been kept from us as previously when I set out and the vessels of the young men were holy, though it was an ordinary journey; how much more then today will their vessels *be holy?*"

6 So the priest gave him consecrated *bread;* for there was no bread there but the bread of the Presence which was removed from before the LORD, in order to put hot bread *in its place* when it was taken away.

7 ¶ Now one of the servants of Saul was there that day, detained before the LORD; and his name was Doeg the Edomite, the chief of Saul's shepherds.

8 ¶ David said to Ahimelech, "Now is there not a spear or a sword on hand? For I brought neither my sword nor my weapons with me, because the king's matter was urgent."

9 Then the priest said, "The sword of Goliath the Philistine, whom you killed in the valley of Elah, behold, it is wrapped in a cloth behind the ephod; if you would take it for yourself, take *it.* For there is no other except it here." And David said, "There is none like it; give it to me."

10 ¶ Then David arose and fled that day from Saul, and went to Achish king of Gath.

11 But the servants of Achish said to him, "Is this not David the king of the land? Did they not sing of this one as they danced, saying,

'Saul has slain his thousands,
And David his ten thousands'?"

12 David took these words to heart and greatly feared Achish king of Gath.

13 So he disguised his sanity before them, and acted insanely in their hands, and scribbled on the doors of the gate, and let his saliva run down into his beard.

14 Then Achish said to his servants, "Behold, you see the man behaving as a madman. Why do you bring him to me?

15 "Do I lack madmen, that you have brought this one to act the madman in my presence? Shall this one come into my house?"

The Priests Slain at Nob

22 So David departed from there and escaped to the cave of Adullam; and when his brothers and all his father's household heard *of it,* they went down there to him.

2 Everyone who was in distress, and everyone who was in debt, and everyone who was discontented gathered to him; and he became captain over them. Now there were about four hundred men with him.

3 ¶ And David went from there to Mizpah of Moab; and he said to the king of Moab, "Please let my father and my mother come *and stay* with you until I know what God will do for me."

22:3 Long-lost Relatives

Afraid that Saul would hold his family hostage, David took his parents to the neighboring kingdom of Moab for safekeeping. Why Moab? Possibly because he had distant relatives there. His great-grandmother, Ruth, had come from Moab.

4 Then he left them with the king of Moab; and they stayed with him all the time that David was in the stronghold.

5 The prophet Gad said to David, "Do not stay in the stronghold; depart, and go into the land of Judah." So David departed and went into the forest of Hereth.

6 ¶ Then Saul heard that David and the men who were with him had been discovered. Now Saul was sitting in Gibeah, under the tamarisk tree on the height with his spear in his hand, and all his servants were standing around him.

7 Saul said to his servants who stood around him, "Hear now, O Benjamites! Will the son of Jesse also give to all of you fields and vineyards? Will he make you all commanders of thousands and commanders of hundreds?

8 "For all of you have conspired against me so that there is no one who discloses to me when my son makes *a covenant* with the son of Jesse, and there is none of you who is sorry for me or discloses to me that my son has stirred up my servant against me to lie in ambush, as *it is* this day."

9 Then Doeg the Edomite, who was standing by the servants of Saul, said, "I saw the son of Jesse coming to Nob, to Ahimelech the son of Ahitub.

10 "He inquired of the LORD for him, gave him

provisions, and gave him the sword of Goliath the Philistine."

11 ¶ Then the king sent someone to summon Ahimelech the priest, the son of Ahitub, and all his father's household, the priests who were in Nob; and all of them came to the king.

12 Saul said, "Listen now, son of Ahitub." And he answered, "Here I am, my lord."

13 Saul then said to him, "Why have you and the son of Jesse conspired against me, in that you have given him bread and a sword and have inquired of God for him, so that he would rise up against me by lying in ambush as *it is* this day?"

14 ¶ Then Ahimelech answered the king and said, "And who among all your servants is as faithful as David, even the king's son-in-law, who is captain over your guard, and is honored in your house?

15 "Did I *just* begin to inquire of God for him today? Far be it from me! Do not let the king impute anything to his servant *or* to any of the household of my father, for your servant knows nothing at all of this whole affair."

16 But the king said, "You shall surely die, Ahimelech, you and all your father's household!"

17 And the king said to the guards who were attending him, "Turn around and put the priests of the LORD to death, because their hand also is with David and because they knew that he was fleeing and did not reveal it to me." But the servants of the king were not willing to put forth their hands to attack the priests of the LORD.

18 Then the king said to Doeg, "You turn around and attack the priests." And Doeg the Edomite turned around and attacked the priests, and he killed that day eighty-five men who wore the linen ephod.

19 And he struck Nob the city of the priests with the edge of the sword, both men and women, children and infants; also oxen, donkeys, and sheep *he struck* with the edge of the sword.

20 ¶ But one son of Ahimelech the son of Ahitub, named Abiathar, escaped and fled after David.

21 Abiathar told David that Saul had killed the priests of the LORD.

22 Then David said to Abiathar, "I knew on that day, when Doeg the Edomite was there, that he would surely tell Saul. I have brought about *the death* of every person in your father's household.

23 "Stay with me; do not be afraid, for he who seeks my life seeks your life, for you are safe with me."

David Delivers Keilah

23 Then they told David, saying, "Behold, the Philistines are fighting against Keilah and are plundering the threshing floors."

2 So David inquired of the LORD, saying, "Shall I go and attack these Philistines?" And the LORD said to David, "Go and attack the Philistines and deliver Keilah."

3 But David's men said to him, "Behold, we are afraid here in Judah. How much more then if we go to Keilah against the ranks of the Philistines?"

4 Then David inquired of the LORD once more. And the LORD answered him and said, "Arise, go down to Keilah, for I will give the Philistines into your hand."

5 So David and his men went to Keilah and fought with the Philistines; and he led away their livestock and struck them with a great slaughter. Thus David delivered the inhabitants of Keilah.

6 ¶ Now it came about, when Abiathar the son of Ahimelech fled to David at Keilah, *that* he came down *with* an ephod in his hand.

7 When it was told Saul that David had come to Keilah, Saul said, "God has delivered him into my hand, for he shut himself in by entering a city with double gates and bars."

8 So Saul summoned all the people for war, to go down to Keilah to besiege David and his men.

9 Now David knew that Saul was plotting evil against him; so he said to Abiathar the priest, "Bring the ephod here."

10 Then David said, "O LORD God of Israel, Your servant has heard for certain that Saul is seeking to come to Keilah to destroy the city on my account.

11 "Will the men of Keilah surrender me into his hand? Will Saul come down just as Your servant has heard? O LORD God of Israel, I pray, tell Your servant." And the LORD said, "He will come down."

12 Then David said, "Will the men of Keilah surrender me and my men into the hand of Saul?" And the LORD said, "They will surrender you."

13 Then David and his men, about six hundred, arose and departed from Keilah, and they went wherever they could go. When it was told Saul that David had escaped from Keilah, he gave up the pursuit.

14 David stayed in the wilderness in the strongholds, and remained in the hill country in the wilderness of Ziph. And Saul sought him every day, but God did not deliver him into his hand.

Saul Pursues David

15 ¶ Now David became aware that Saul had come out to seek his life while David was in the wilderness of Ziph at Horesh.

16 And Jonathan, Saul's son, arose and went to David at Horesh, and [a]encouraged him in God.

17 Thus he said to him, "Do not be afraid, because the hand of Saul my father will not find you, and you will be king over Israel and I will be next to you; and Saul my father knows that also."

18 So the two of them made a covenant before

[a] Lit *strengthened his hand*

the LORD; and David stayed at Horesh while Jonathan went to his house.

19 ¶ Then Ziphites came up to Saul at Gibeah, saying, "Is David not hiding with us in the strongholds at Horesh, on the hill of Hachilah, which is on the south of [a]Jeshimon?

23:16 Final Farewell

This last, secret meeting between Jonathan and David reveals the essence of their friendship. They had grown to love each other despite Saul's (Jonathan's father's) hatred for David. Now, when David was desperate, Jonathan sought him out and "encouraged him in God." Jonathan expected to become David's right-hand man when David became king, but Jonathan's death soon put an end to that dream (see 31:2).

20 "Now then, O king, come down according to all the desire of your soul to do so; and our part *shall be* to surrender him into the king's hand."

21 Saul said, "May you be blessed of the LORD, for you have had compassion on me.

22 "Go now, make more sure, and investigate and see his place where his haunt is, *and* who has seen him there; for I am told that he is very cunning.

23 "So look, and learn about all the hiding places where he hides himself and return to me with certainty, and I will go with you; and if he is in the land, I will search him out among all the thousands of Judah."

24 ¶ Then they arose and went to Ziph before Saul. Now David and his men were in the wilderness of Maon, in the Arabah to the south of Jeshimon.

25 When Saul and his men went to seek *him,* they told David, and he came down to the rock and stayed in the wilderness of Maon. And when Saul heard *it,* he pursued David in the wilderness of Maon.

26 Saul went on one side of the mountain, and David and his men on the other side of the mountain; and David was hurrying to get away from Saul, for Saul and his men were surrounding David and his men to seize them.

27 But a messenger came to Saul, saying, "Hurry and come, for the Philistines have made a raid on the land."

28 So Saul returned from pursuing David and went to meet the Philistines; therefore they called that place the Rock of Escape.

29 David went up from there and stayed in the strongholds of Engedi.

[a] Or *the desert*

David Spares Saul's Life

24 Now when Saul returned from pursuing the Philistines, he was told, saying, "Behold, David is in the wilderness of Engedi."

2 Then Saul took three thousand chosen men from all Israel and went to seek David and his men in front of the Rocks of the Wild Goats.

3 He came to the sheepfolds on the way, where *was* a cave; and Saul went in to relieve himself. Now David and his men were sitting in the inner recesses of the cave.

4 The men of David said to him, "Behold, *this is* the day of which the LORD said to you, 'Behold; I am about to give your enemy into your hand, and you shall do to him as it seems good to you.' " Then David arose and cut off the edge of Saul's robe secretly.

5 It came about afterward that David's conscience bothered him because he had cut off the edge of Saul's *robe.*

24:5 David's Bad Conscience

David's conscience troubled him after he cut off part of Saul's robe. Why? Possibly because, to people of that day, a man looked ridiculous with his clothes cut short. See 2 Samuel 10:4–5 for a case where cutting a garment was a deliberate insult that led to war.

6 So he said to his men, "Far be it from me because of the LORD that I should do this thing to my lord, the LORD'S anointed, to stretch out my hand against him, since he is the LORD'S anointed."

7 David persuaded his men with *these* words and did not allow them to rise up against Saul. And Saul arose, left the cave, and went on *his* way.

8 ¶ Now afterward David arose and went out of the cave and called after Saul, saying, "My lord the king!" And when Saul looked behind him, David bowed with his face to the ground and prostrated himself.

9 David said to Saul, "Why do you listen to the words of men, saying, 'Behold, David seeks to harm you'?

10 "Behold, this day your eyes have seen that the LORD had given you today into my hand in the cave, and some said to kill you, but *my eye* had pity on you; and I said, 'I will not stretch out my hand against my lord, for he is the LORD'S anointed.'

11 "Now, my father, see! Indeed, see the edge of your robe in my hand! For in that I cut off the edge of your robe and did not kill you, know and perceive that there is no evil or rebellion in my

hands, and I have not sinned against you, though you are lying in wait for my life to take it.

12 "May the LORD judge between you and me, and may the LORD avenge me on you; but my hand shall not be against you.

13 "As the proverb of the ancients says, 'Out of the wicked comes forth wickedness'; but my hand shall not be against you.

14 "After whom has the king of Israel come out? Whom are you pursuing? A dead dog, a single flea?

15 "The LORD therefore be judge and decide between you and me; and may He see and plead my cause and deliver me from your hand."

16 ¶ When David had finished speaking these words to Saul, Saul said, "Is this your voice, my son David?" Then Saul lifted up his voice and wept.

A Sense of God's Timing
Two leaders locked in a death struggle—with one refusing to fight

> "I have not sinned against you, though you are lying in wait for my life to take it. May the LORD judge between you and me."
> 24:11–12

IN THE WINTER OF 1777, America had two armies. One lived in comfortable homes in Philadelphia. The other camped in the snow in the hills to the northwest, at a place called Valley Forge. One showed impeccable discipline. The other tried desperately to keep its untrained recruits from deserting. One was supplied by ship with every luxury. The other fought frostbite because its soldiers had no boots.

In sum, one army had everything it could want to weather a cold winter and a war, while the other hung by a thread. Who could have thought, seeing the two, that within three years the army with nothing would defeat the army with everything?

The impoverished American army could never go head-on against the crack British forces. But it could always outwait them. George Washington's army had the support of the American people, while the British army, for all its strength, was far from home. The British had to win decisively, putting an end to the rebellion. The Americans merely had to survive and outlast them.

Washington was a military genius not at battle tactics, but at a more fundamental necessity: encouraging his men to fight on. One-quarter of them died of cold and disease that bitter winter at Valley Forge. Only his personal strength held the miserable army together. That was the key to victory.

Two Kings in Israel

David and his followers lived in a similar situation. Saul was the right and proper king, living in luxury. David had been secretly anointed as his replacement, but he lived in the desert, scrabbling to survive. Saul had a professional army, David a small band composed of family members and an assortment of outlaws.

Twice Saul accidentally fell into David's hands, but David refused to kill him. He felt that would violate God's will. He would not use his sword to become king. He fought not to win but to survive.

Survival was not easy. You can read between the lines of chapters 21–31 and see a great drama unfolding. Saul is clearly deteriorating. Can David hold on long enough to outlast him?

At first David ran from one place to another, alone and completely vulnerable. Then, when 400 outlaws gathered around him, the local people turned him in twice (23:19; 26:1). Perhaps they feared that Saul would slaughter them the way he had the Nob priests (22:6–23).

David survived and managed to keep his army intact. He even built popular support by providing military protection to his neighbors. But eventually he saw that his position was impossible. "Now I will perish one day by the hand of Saul," he said (27:1). He left Israel and became, with his army, a hired soldier for one of the Philistine kings.

Sooner or later David's double-agent act would have been found out. In fact, when the Philistines planned a major military effort against Israel, David barely escaped having to fight his own people.

Time on His Side

Throughout his desert period, David's position was desperate. David had one precious asset only: God had promised he would be king. David believed this promise even when his situation looked very bad. He would wait for God's timing.

A sense of timing, people say, is essential to leadership. You must know when to act boldly and when to wait patiently; when to bend and when to stand firm. David had that critical sense of timing because he trusted God's control of events.

Life Questions: What makes you impatient? What can you learn about patience from David's life?

17 He said to David, "You are more righteous than I; for you have dealt well with me, while I have dealt wickedly with you.

18 "You have declared today that you have done good to me, that the LORD delivered me into your hand and yet you did not kill me.

19 "For if a man finds his enemy, will he let him go away safely? May the LORD therefore reward you with good in return for what you have done to me this day.

20 "Now, behold, I know that you will surely be king, and that the kingdom of Israel will be established in your hand.

21 "So now swear to me by the LORD that you will not cut off my descendants after me and that you will not destroy my name from my father's household."

24:21 The Survival of a Family

Slaughtering the rival's entire family was normal practice when one would-be king won out over another. Such action tended to lessen the probability that the rival family would compete for the throne again. Jonathan, David's closest friend, is asking David not to follow that course when he becomes king. Because of their relationship, David let Jonathan's son Mephibosheth live (2 Samuel 9).

22 David swore to Saul. And Saul went to his home, but David and his men went up to the stronghold.

Samuel's Death

25 Then Samuel died; and all Israel gathered together and mourned for him, and buried him at his house in Ramah. And David arose and went down to the wilderness of Paran.

Nabal and Abigail

2 ¶ Now *there was* a man in Maon whose business was in Carmel; and the man was very rich, and he had three thousand sheep and a thousand goats. And it came about while he was shearing his sheep in Carmel

3 (now the man's name was Nabal, and his wife's name was Abigail. And the woman was intelligent and beautiful in appearance, but the man was harsh and evil in *his* dealings, and he was a Calebite),

4 that David heard in the wilderness that Nabal was shearing his sheep.

5 So David sent ten young men; and David said to the young men, "Go up to Carmel, visit Nabal and greet him in my name;

6 and thus you shall say, 'Have a long life, peace be to you, and peace be to your house, and peace be to all that you have.

7 'Now I have heard that you have shearers;

now your shepherds have been with us and we have not insulted them, nor have they missed anything all the days they were in Carmel.

8 'Ask your young men and they will tell you. Therefore let *my* young men find favor in your eyes, for we have come on a festive day. Please give whatever you find at hand to your servants and to your son David.' "

9 ¶ When David's young men came, they spoke to Nabal according to all these words in David's name; then they waited.

10 But Nabal answered David's servants and said, "Who is David? And who is the son of Jesse? There are many servants today who are each breaking away from his master.

11 "Shall I then take my bread and my water and my meat that I have slaughtered for my shearers, and give it to men whose origin I do not know?"

12 So David's young men retraced their way and went back; and they came and told him according to all these words.

13 David said to his men, "Each *of you* gird on his sword." So each man girded on his sword. And David also girded on his sword, and about four hundred men went up behind David while two hundred stayed with the baggage.

14 ¶ But one of the young men told Abigail, Nabal's wife, saying, "Behold, David sent messengers from the wilderness to greet our master, and he scorned them.

15 "Yet the men were very good to us, and we were not insulted, nor did we miss anything as long as we went about with them, while we were in the fields.

16 "They were a wall to us both by night and by day, all the time we were with them tending the sheep.

17 "Now therefore, know and consider what you should do, for evil is plotted against our master and against all his household; and he is such a worthless man that no one can speak to him."

Abigail Intercedes

18 ¶ Then Abigail hurried and took two hundred *loaves* of bread and two jugs of wine and five sheep already prepared and five measures of roasted grain and a hundred clusters of raisins and two hundred cakes of figs, and loaded *them* on donkeys.

19 She said to her young men, "Go on before me; behold, I am coming after you." But she did not tell her husband Nabal.

20 It came about as she was riding on her donkey and coming down by the hidden part of the mountain, that behold, David and his men were coming down toward her; so she met them.

21 Now David had said, "Surely in vain I have guarded all that this *man* has in the wilderness, so that nothing was missed of all that belonged to him; and he has returned me evil for good.

22 "May God do so to the enemies of David, and more also, if by morning I leave *as much as* one male of any who belong to him."

23 ¶ When Abigail saw David, she hurried and dismounted from her donkey, and fell on her face before David and bowed herself to the ground.

24 She fell at his feet and said, "On me alone, my lord, be the blame. And please let your maidservant speak to you, and listen to the words of your maidservant.

25 "Please do not let my lord pay attention to this worthless man, Nabal, for as his name is, so is he. Nabal is his name and folly is with him; but I your maidservant did not see the young men of my lord whom you sent.

26 ¶ "Now therefore, my lord, as the LORD lives, and as your soul lives, since the LORD has restrained you from shedding blood, and from avenging yourself by your own hand, now then let your enemies and those who seek evil against my lord, be as Nabal.

27 "Now let this gift which your maidservant has brought to my lord be given to the young men who accompany my lord.

28 "Please forgive the transgression of your maidservant; for the LORD will certainly make for my lord an enduring house, because my lord is fighting the battles of the LORD, and evil will not be found in you all your days.

29 "Should anyone rise up to pursue you and to seek your life, then the life of my lord shall be bound in the bundle of the living with the LORD your God; but the lives of your enemies He will sling out as from the hollow of a sling.

30 "And when the LORD does for my lord according to all the good that He has spoken concerning you, and appoints you ruler over Israel,

31 this will not cause grief or a troubled heart to my lord, both by having shed blood without cause and by my lord having avenged himself. When the LORD deals well with my lord, then remember your maidservant."

32 ¶ Then David said to Abigail, "Blessed be the LORD God of Israel, who sent you this day to meet me,

33 and blessed be your discernment, and blessed be you, who have kept me this day from bloodshed and from avenging myself by my own hand.

34 "Nevertheless, as the LORD God of Israel lives, who has restrained me from harming you, unless you had come quickly to meet me, surely there would not have been left to Nabal until the morning light *as much as* one male."

35 So David received from her hand what she had brought him and said to her, "Go up to your house in peace. See, I have listened to you and granted your request."

36 ¶ Then Abigail came to Nabal, and behold, he was holding a feast in his house, like the feast of a king. And Nabal's heart was merry within him, for he was very drunk; so she did not tell him anything at all until the morning light.

37 But in the morning, when the wine had gone out of Nabal, his wife told him these things, and his heart died within him so that he became *as* a stone.

38 About ten days later, the LORD struck Nabal and he died.

David Marries Abigail

39 ¶ When David heard that Nabal was dead, he said, "Blessed be the LORD, who has pleaded the cause of my reproach from the hand of Nabal and has kept back His servant from evil. The LORD has also returned the evildoing of Nabal on his

ABIGAIL *Beauty and Brains*

ABIGAIL WAS NOT A MAIN player in the history of Israel, but as this story shows, she had an instinctive skill for diplomacy and peace-making. A woman of beauty and brains, Abigail could defuse a dangerous situation between hot-headed men.

It is hard to imagine such a shrewd woman choosing marriage to Nabal, and indeed in those days parents, not lovers, arranged the marriages. Nabal was rich, which probably influenced Abigail's parents. She, however, knew her husband as a fool, and this incident characteristically portrays him as rude, drunk and stupid.

Though Abigail may have been trapped in a bad marriage, she was hardly helpless. When her husband mistreated David, Abigail rushed to take decisive action. She saved the day for her people as well as for David, who had lost his temper and was about to take vengeance he would doubtless regret.

A man of passion, David could lose his temper, but he also had the courage to back down when challenged with good sense. He thanked Abigail warmly and made a mental note about this remarkable woman. When her husband died a short time later, David asked the widow to be his wife. Without hesitation, without tears or mourning, Abigail agreed.

Though David was still an outlaw, Abigail sensed that a great future awaited him. As a result of her wise decisions, she became forever linked to Israel's greatest king.

Life Questions: What can you learn from Abigail's style of dealing with hot-tempered people?

own head." Then David sent a proposal to Abigail, to take her as his wife.

40 When the servants of David came to Abigail at Carmel, they spoke to her, saying, "David has sent us to you to take you as his wife."

41 She arose and bowed with her face to the ground and said, "Behold, your maidservant is a maid to wash the feet of my lord's servants."

42 Then Abigail quickly arose, and rode on a donkey, with her five maidens who attended her; and she followed the messengers of David and became his wife.

43 ¶ David had also taken Ahinoam of Jezreel, and they both became his wives.

44 ¶ Now Saul had given Michal his daughter, David's wife, to Palti the son of Laish, who was from Gallim.

David Again Spares Saul

26 Then the Ziphites came to Saul at Gibeah, saying, "Is not David hiding on the hill of Hachilah, *which is* before ªJeshimon?"

2 So Saul arose and went down to the wilderness of Ziph, having with him three thousand chosen men of Israel, to search for David in the wilderness of Ziph.

3 Saul camped in the hill of Hachilah, which is before ªJeshimon, beside the road, and David was staying in the wilderness. When he saw that Saul came after him into the wilderness,

4 David sent out spies, and he knew that Saul was definitely coming.

5 David then arose and came to the place where Saul had camped. And David saw the place where Saul lay, and Abner the son of Ner, the commander of his army; and Saul was lying in the circle of the camp, and the people were camped around him.

6 ¶ Then David said to Ahimelech the Hittite and to Abishai the son of Zeruiah, Joab's brother, saying, "Who will go down with me to Saul in the camp?" And Abishai said, "I will go down with you."

7 So David and Abishai came to the people by night, and behold, Saul lay sleeping inside the circle of the camp with his spear stuck in the ground at his head; and Abner and the people were lying around him.

8 Then Abishai said to David, "Today God has delivered your enemy into your hand; now therefore, please let me strike him with the spear to the ground with one stroke, and I will not strike him the second time."

9 But David said to Abishai, "Do not destroy him, for who can stretch out his hand against the LORD's anointed and be without guilt?"

10 David also said, "As the LORD lives, surely the LORD will strike him, or his day will come that he dies, or he will go down into battle and perish.

11 "The LORD forbid that I should stretch out my hand against the LORD's anointed; but now please take the spear that is at his head and the jug of water, and let us go."

12 So David took the spear and the jug of water from *beside* Saul's head, and they went away, but no one saw or knew *it,* nor did any awake, for they were all asleep, because a sound sleep from the LORD had fallen on them.

13 ¶ Then David crossed over to the other side and stood on top of the mountain at a distance *with* a large area between them.

14 David called to the people and to Abner the son of Ner, saying, "Will you not answer, Abner?" Then Abner replied, "Who are you who calls to the king?"

15 So David said to Abner, "Are you not a man? And who is like you in Israel? Why then have you not guarded your lord the king? For one of the people came to destroy the king your lord.

16 "This thing that you have done is not good. As the LORD lives, *all* of you must surely die, because you did not guard your lord, the LORD's anointed. And now, see where the king's spear is and the jug of water that was at his head."

17 ¶ Then Saul recognized David's voice and said, "Is this your voice, my son David?" And David said, "It is my voice, my lord the king."

18 He also said, "Why then is my lord pursuing his servant? For what have I done? Or what evil is in my hand?

19 "Now therefore, please let my lord the king listen to the words of his servant. If the LORD has stirred you up against me, let Him accept an offering; but if it is men, cursed are they before the LORD, for they have driven me out today so that I would have no attachment with the inheritance of the LORD, saying, 'Go, serve other gods.'

20 "Now then, do not let my blood fall to the ground away from the presence of the LORD; for the king of Israel has come out to search for a single flea, just as one hunts a partridge in the mountains."

21 ¶ Then Saul said, "I have sinned. Return, my son David, for I will not harm you again because my life was precious in your sight this day. Behold, I have played the fool and have committed a serious error."

22 David replied, "Behold the spear of the king! Now let one of the young men come over and take it.

23 "The LORD will repay each man *for* his righteousness and his faithfulness; for the LORD delivered you into *my* hand today, but I refused to stretch out my hand against the LORD's anointed.

24 "Now behold, as your life was highly valued in my sight this day, so may my life be highly valued in the sight of the LORD, and may He deliver me from all distress."

25 Then Saul said to David, "Blessed are you, my son David; you will both accomplish much

ª Or *the desert*

and surely prevail." So David went on his way, and Saul returned to his place.

David Flees to the Philistines

27 Then David said to himself, "Now I will perish one day by the hand of Saul. There is nothing better for me than to escape into the land of the Philistines. Saul then will despair of searching for me anymore in all the territory of Israel, and I will escape from his hand."

2 So David arose and crossed over, he and the six hundred men who were with him, to Achish the son of Maoch, king of Gath.

3 And David lived with Achish at Gath, he and his men, each with his household, *even* David with his two wives, Ahinoam the Jezreelitess, and Abigail the Carmelitess, Nabal's widow.

4 Now it was told Saul that David had fled to Gath, so he no longer searched for him.

5 ¶ Then David said to Achish, "If now I have found favor in your sight, let them give me a place in one of the cities in the country, that I may live there; for why should your servant live in the royal city with you?"

6 So Achish gave him Ziklag that day; therefore Ziklag has belonged to the kings of Judah to this day.

7 The number of days that David lived in the country of the Philistines was a year and four months.

8 ¶ Now David and his men went up and raided the Geshurites and the Girzites and the Amalekites; for they were the inhabitants of the land from ancient times, as you come to Shur even as far as the land of Egypt.

27:8 David's Double Game

The Philistines accepted David because they thought he would fight against his own people. Had they known that he retained his Israelite loyalty, they would never have trusted him. So David had to pretend that he was raiding the Israelites, while actually he raided Israel's nomadic enemies. To keep his game secret, he took no prisoners, for it might be noticed that none of them were Israelites.

9 David attacked the land and did not leave a man or a woman alive, and he took away the sheep, the cattle, the donkeys, the camels, and the clothing. Then he returned and came to Achish.

10 Now Achish said, "Where have you made a raid today?" And David said, "Against the ᵃNegev of Judah and against the Negev of the Jerahmeelites and against the Negev of the Kenites."

11 David did not leave a man or a woman alive to bring to Gath, saying, "Otherwise they will tell

ᵃ I.e. South country

about us, saying, 'So has David done and so *has been* his practice all the time he has lived in the country of the Philistines.' "

12 So Achish believed David, saying, "He has surely made himself odious among his people Israel; therefore he will become my servant forever."

Saul and the Spirit Medium

28 Now it came about in those days that the Philistines gathered their armed camps for war, to fight against Israel. And Achish said to David, "Know assuredly that you will go out with me in the camp, you and your men."

2 David said to Achish, "Very well, you shall know what your servant can do." So Achish said to David, "Very well, I will make you my bodyguard for life."

3 ¶ Now Samuel was dead, and all Israel had lamented him and buried him in Ramah, his own city. And Saul had removed from the land those who were mediums and spiritists.

4 So the Philistines gathered together and came and camped in Shunem; and Saul gathered all Israel together and they camped in Gilboa.

28:4 Battle Strategy

For their massive assault from Shunem, the Philistines tried a new tactic. They had fought previous battles in the mountains, rough terrain where their chariots were next to useless. Now they chose strategically important level ground that Israel had to defend. The Valley of Jezreel is the only part of Palestine where you can go from west to east without crossing mountains. A Philistine victory here would cut Israel in half.

5 When Saul saw the camp of the Philistines, he was afraid and his heart trembled greatly.

6 When Saul inquired of the LORD, the LORD did not answer him, either by dreams or by Urim or by prophets.

7 Then Saul said to his servants, "Seek for me a woman who is a medium, that I may go to her and inquire of her." And his servants said to him, "Behold, there is a woman who is a medium at En-dor."

8 ¶ Then Saul disguised himself by putting on other clothes, and went, he and two men with him, and they came to the woman by night; and he said, "Conjure up for me, please, and bring up for me whom I shall name to you."

9 But the woman said to him, "Behold, you know what Saul has done, how he has cut off those who are mediums and spiritists from the land. Why are you then laying a snare for my life to bring about my death?"

10 Saul vowed to her by the LORD, saying, "As the LORD lives, no punishment shall come upon you for this thing."

11 Then the woman said, "Whom shall I bring up for you?" And he said, "Bring up Samuel for me."

12 When the woman saw Samuel, she cried out with a loud voice; and the woman spoke to Saul, saying, "Why have you deceived me? For you are Saul."

28:12 The Witch of Endor

Consulting a medium or spiritist was forbidden (Leviticus 20:6,27; Deuteronomy 18:10–12), as Saul knew well. Earlier, he had banned mediums in the kingdom. But through his disobedience Saul had lost contact with God, and was desperate to know the future. Whether Samuel actually appeared or whether the woman faked it, the results were the same: Saul left more fearful than when he came.

13 The king said to her, "Do not be afraid; but what do you see?" And the woman said to Saul, "I see a divine being coming up out of the earth."

14 He said to her, "What is his form?" And she said, "An old man is coming up, and he is wrapped with a robe." And Saul knew that it was Samuel, and he bowed with his face to the ground and did homage.

15 ¶ Then Samuel said to Saul, "Why have you disturbed me by bringing me up?" And Saul answered, "I am greatly distressed; for the Philistines are waging war against me, and God has departed from me and no longer answers me, either through prophets or by dreams; therefore I have called you, that you may make known to me what I should do."

16 Samuel said, "Why then do you ask me, since the LORD has departed from you and has become your adversary?

17 "The LORD has done accordingly as He spoke through me; for the LORD has torn the kingdom out of your hand and given it to your neighbor, to David.

18 "As you did not obey the LORD and did not execute His fierce wrath on Amalek, so the LORD has done this thing to you this day.

19 "Moreover the LORD will also give over Israel along with you into the hands of the Philistines, therefore tomorrow you and your sons will be with me. Indeed the LORD will give over the army of Israel into the hands of the Philistines!"

20 ¶ Then Saul immediately fell full length upon the ground and was very afraid because of the words of Samuel; also there was no strength in him, for he had eaten no food all day and all night.

21 The woman came to Saul and saw that he was terrified, and said to him, "Behold, your maidservant has obeyed you, and I have taken my life in my hand and have listened to your words which you spoke to me.

22 "So now also, please listen to the voice of your maidservant, and let me set a piece of bread before you that *you may* eat and have strength when you go on *your* way."

23 But he refused and said, "I will not eat." However, his servants together with the woman urged him, and he listened to them. So he arose from the ground and sat on the bed.

24 The woman had a fattened calf in the house, and she quickly slaughtered it; and she took flour, kneaded it and baked unleavened bread from it.

25 She brought *it* before Saul and his servants, and they ate. Then they arose and went away that night.

The Philistines Mistrust David

29 Now the Philistines gathered together all their armies to Aphek, while the Israelites were camping by the spring which is in Jezreel.

2 And the lords of the Philistines were proceeding on by hundreds and by thousands, and David and his men were proceeding on in the rear with Achish.

3 Then the commanders of the Philistines said, "What *are* these Hebrews *doing here?*" And Achish said to the commanders of the Philistines, "Is this not David, the servant of Saul the king of Israel, who has been with me these days, or *rather* these years, and I have found no fault in him from the day he deserted *to me* to this day?"

4 But the commanders of the Philistines were angry with him, and the commanders of the Philistines said to him, "Make the man go back, that he may return to his place where you have assigned him, and do not let him go down to battle with us, or in the battle he may become an adversary to us. For with what could this *man* make himself acceptable to his lord? *Would it* not *be* with the heads of these men?

5 "Is this not David, of whom they sing in the dances, saying,

'Saul has slain his thousands,
And David his ten thousands'?"

6 ¶ Then Achish called David and said to him, "*As* the LORD lives, you *have been* upright, and your going out and your coming in with me in the army are pleasing in my sight; for I have not found evil in you from the day of your coming to me to this day. Nevertheless, you are not pleasing in the sight of the lords.

7 "Now therefore return and go in peace, that you may not displease the lords of the Philistines."

8 David said to Achish, "But what have I done? And what have you found in your servant from the day when I came before you to this day, that I may not go and fight against the enemies of my lord the king?"

9 But Achish replied to David, "I know that

you are pleasing in my sight, like an angel of God; nevertheless the commanders of the Philistines have said, 'He must not go up with us to the battle.'

29:8 Faking It

For the sake of survival, David had become a mercenary in the Philistine army. But he had not yet fought against his own people, and it is doubtful that he would have done so. Now, dismissed from service because he wasn't trusted in the upcoming battle, David acted distressed. Was he genuinely upset? It's quite possible he had hoped to turn the tables against the Philistines by attacking them from behind their own lines. The Philistine commanders made a shrewd move in sending him off.

10 "Now then arise early in the morning with the servants of your lord who have come with you, and as soon as you have arisen early in the morning and have light, depart."

11 So David arose early, he and his men, to depart in the morning to return to the land of the Philistines. And the Philistines went up to Jezreel.

David's Victory over the Amalekites

30 Then it happened when David and his men came to Ziklag on the third day, that the Amalekites had made a raid on the Negev and on Ziklag, and had overthrown Ziklag and burned it with fire;

2 and they took captive the women *and all* who were in it, both small and great, without killing anyone, and carried *them* off and went their way.

3 When David and his men came to the city, behold, it was burned with fire, and their wives and their sons and their daughters had been taken captive.

4 Then David and the people who were with him lifted their voices and wept until there was no strength in them to weep.

5 Now David's two wives had been taken captive, Ahinoam the Jezreelitess and Abigail the widow of Nabal the Carmelite.

6 Moreover David was greatly distressed because the people spoke of stoning him, for all the people were embittered, each one because of his sons and his daughters. But David strengthened himself in the LORD his God.

7 ¶ Then David said to Abiathar the priest, the son of Ahimelech, "Please bring me the ephod." So Abiathar brought the ephod to David.

8 David inquired of the LORD, saying, "Shall I pursue this band? Shall I overtake them?" And He said to him, "Pursue, for you will surely overtake them, and you will surely rescue *all*."

9 So David went, he and the six hundred men who were with him, and came to the brook Besor, *where* those left behind remained.

10 But David pursued, he and four hundred men, for two hundred who were too exhausted to cross the brook Besor remained *behind*.

11 ¶ Now they found an Egyptian in the field and brought him to David, and gave him bread and he ate, and they provided him water to drink.

12 They gave him a piece of fig cake and two clusters of raisins, and he ate; then his spirit revived. For he had not eaten bread or drunk water for three days and three nights.

13 David said to him, "To whom do you belong? And where are you from?" And he said, "I am a young man of Egypt, a servant of an Amalekite; and my master left me behind when I fell sick three days ago.

14 "We made a raid on the Negev of the Cherethites, and on that which belongs to Judah, and on the Negev of Caleb, and we burned Ziklag with fire."

15 Then David said to him, "Will you bring me down to this band?" And he said, "Swear to me by God that you will not kill me or deliver me into the hands of my master, and I will bring you down to this band."

16 ¶ When he had brought him down, behold, they were spread over all the land, eating and drinking and dancing because of all the great spoil that they had taken from the land of the Philistines and from the land of Judah.

17 David slaughtered them from the twilight until the evening of the next day; and not a man of them escaped, except four hundred young men who rode on camels and fled.

18 So David recovered all that the Amalekites had taken, and rescued his two wives.

19 But nothing of theirs was missing, whether small or great, sons or daughters, spoil or anything that they had taken for themselves; David brought *it* all back.

20 So David had captured all the sheep and the cattle *which the people* drove ahead of the *other* livestock, and they said, "This is David's spoil."

The Spoils Are Divided

21 ¶ When David came to the two hundred men who were too exhausted to follow David, who had also been left at the brook Besor, and they went out to meet David and to meet the people who were with him, then David approached the people and greeted them.

22 Then all the wicked and worthless men among those who went with David said, "Because they did not go with us, we will not give them any of the spoil that we have recovered, except to every man his wife and his children, that they may lead *them* away and depart."

23 Then David said, "You must not do so, my brothers, with what the LORD has given us, who

has kept us and delivered into our hand the band that came against us.

24 "And who will listen to you in this matter? For as his share is who goes down to the battle, so shall his share be who stays by the baggage; they shall share alike."

25 So it has been from that day forward, that he made it a statute and an ordinance for Israel to this day.

26 ¶ Now when David came to Ziklag, he sent *some* of the spoil to the elders of Judah, to his friends, saying, "Behold, a gift for you from the spoil of the enemies of the LORD:

27 to those who were in Bethel, and to those who were in Ramoth of the Negev, and to those who were in Jattir,

28 and to those who were in Aroer, and to those who were in Siphmoth, and to those who were in Eshtemoa,

29 and to those who were in Racal, and to those who were in the cities of the Jerahmeelites, and to those who were in the cities of the Kenites,

30 and to those who were in Hormah, and to those who were in Bor-ashan, and to those who were in Athach,

31 and to those who were in Hebron, and to all the places where David himself and his men were accustomed to go."

Saul and His Sons Slain

31 Now the Philistines were fighting against Israel, and the men of Israel fled from before the Philistines and fell slain on Mount Gilboa.

2 The Philistines overtook Saul and his sons; and the Philistines killed Jonathan and Abinadab and Malchi-shua the sons of Saul.

3 The battle went heavily against Saul, and the archers hit him; and he was badly wounded by the archers.

4 Then Saul said to his armor bearer, "Draw your sword and pierce me through with it, otherwise these uncircumcised will come and pierce me through and make sport of me." But his armor

bearer would not, for he was greatly afraid. So Saul took his sword and fell on it.

5 When his armor bearer saw that Saul was dead, he also fell on his sword and died with him.

6 Thus Saul died with his three sons, his armor bearer, and all his men on that day together.

7 ¶ When the men of Israel who were on the other side of the valley, with those who were beyond the Jordan, saw that the men of Israel had fled and that Saul and his sons were dead, they abandoned the cities and fled; then the Philistines came and lived in them.

8 ¶ It came about on the next day when the Philistines came to strip the slain, that they found Saul and his three sons fallen on Mount Gilboa.

9 They cut off his head and stripped off his weapons, and sent *them* throughout the land of the Philistines, to carry the good news to the house of their idols and to the people.

10 They put his weapons in the temple of Ashtaroth, and they fastened his body to the wall of Beth-shan.

11 Now when the inhabitants of Jabesh-gilead heard what the Philistines had done to Saul,

31:11 Loyal Friends in Death

Saul's first military action as king had been the rescue of Jabesh-gilead (chapter 11). Through all these years its citizens had not forgotten. When they heard of the disgraceful display of Saul's and his sons' bodies, they undertook a dangerous night mission to steal the bodies and give them proper burial.

12 all the valiant men rose and walked all night, and took the body of Saul and the bodies of his sons from the wall of Beth-shan, and they came to Jabesh and burned them there.

13 They took their bones and buried them under the tamarisk tree at Jabesh, and fasted seven days.

2 SAMUEL

The Life of King David
From herding sheep to ruling a nation

> "'I took you from
> the pasture, from
> following the sheep,
> to be ruler over My
> people Israel.'" 7:8

THE BIBLE IS FILLED WITH strong personalities, but none leads David in the parade. His life was a whirlwind, from which striking images flash. We see him playing his harp, writing poems, fighting battles, faking insanity, dancing jubilantly in praise of God. We watch his tear-streaked face when he learns of his closest friend's death. We see him on his rooftop, gazing down lustfully on Bathsheba's bath. We see Nathan point his finger at him, accusing him of adultery and murder. We hear David's guilty, anguished voice crying to God for the life of his infant child. We see David's bowed head as he stumbles out of Jerusalem, pursued by his murderous son.

David survived the crises of a dozen lives. Somehow he always bounced back. Somehow he maintained a passionate trust in God. First and Second Samuel don't paint him as a flawless character, nor as a perfect model of strength and courage. David had striking weaknesses. Yet he appeals to us as he did to the Israelites: He was completely, passionately alive. Whatever he did, right or wrong, he did with his whole heart. In his love for God, he held nothing back.

Healing the Wounds of War

While 1 Samuel tells of David's youth and his long exile, 2 Samuel focuses on David as king, leading, uniting, inspiring his people. His time in the desert was over. Different qualities of leadership were required in a king.

David inherited a country in tatters. His fellow southerners recognized him as the new king. But Saul's son, backed by a powerful general, launched a civil war for the throne. Ugly infighting followed: intrigue, murder, and treachery.

Even after David's rivals were eliminated, peace was uneasy. Unless David could heal the wounds of war, resentment might smolder in the hearts of the northerners. David's decisive action showed wisdom and firmness. He justly punished murderers who expected his gratitude. He showed respect for his enemies by mourning their deaths. From his first day in office David behaved as the king of all the people, not just his loyal followers. The northern tribes soon came over to him, submitting to his leadership (5:1–3).

David's next move was to capture Jerusalem. People said it couldn't be done; mountainous Jerusalem was impregnable. David did it, and made Jerusalem his new political and religious capital. Located on the border between north and south, Jerusalem symbolized a new national unity based on trust in God.

That was just the beginning. David led the unified tribes to do what they had barely dreamed of: They defeated the dreaded Philistines once and for all. Almost overnight the tiny, threatened nation of Israel became safe. Secure borders encouraged expanded trade, and Israel boomed. (David's son Solomon reaped most of the wealth from this.) Naturally, David's popularity increased.

A Murderer and an Adulterer

But David's reign held ironic tragedies, too. Second Samuel makes no effort to hide them. David could lead a nation but not his own children. His ineffective parenting nearly destroyed all he had done, when his heartless son Absalom led a rebellion. Second Samuel portrays David without retouching his blemishes: He was a murderer and an adulterer and a leader capable of cruelty.

Nevertheless, he was Israel's greatest king. Even at his lowest points, his great strength of character showed. He was never vengeful with his enemies. He took full responsibility for his mistakes. He managed to remember that he had started out as a mere shepherd. He held power only by the grace of God—and he believed that God had every right to take power away.

Through his love for God and his sense of astonished gratefulness for what God had done for him, David became a living embodiment of the Israel God wanted. Like all truly great leaders, he made his country thrive not just by what he did, but by who he was.

How to Read 2 Samuel

Second Samuel continues, without a break, the story begun in 1 Samuel—the two were originally one book. The difference is that David, who once sought only to survive, now seeks to unify a badly divided country. His greater responsibilities put extra stress on his leadership qualities. You can study his life with leadership in mind. You can also study chapters 11–20 to see the cancerous effects of a leader's private sins and poor family leadership.

Chapters 21–24 seem to be an appendix, bringing in other important events and facts of David's reign. Much of 2 Samuel's story is also told in 1 Chronicles 11–21, often word for word the same.

PEOPLE YOU'LL MEET IN 2 SAMUEL

DAVID (p. 349)
ABNER (p. 353)
NATHAN (p. 357)

BATHSHEBA (p. 361)
ABSALOM (p. 366)

3-TRACK READING PLAN

For an explanation and complete listing of the 3-track reading plan, turn to page 7.

TRACK 1:   **Two-Week Courses on the Bible**
The Track 1 reading program on the Old Testament includes two chapters from 2 Samuel. See page 8 for a complete listing of this course.

TRACK 2:   **An Overview of 2 Samuel in 3 Days**
☐ Day 1. Read the Introduction to 2 Samuel and chapter 6, in which the ark of the covenant was brought to Jerusalem and David danced before the Lord.
☐ Day 2. Read chapter 11, in which David's adultery with Bathsheba led to murder.
☐ Day 3. Read chapter 12 for the dramatic account of the prophet Nathan coming to confront David.

Now turn to page 9 for your next Track 2 reading project.

TRACK 3:   **All of 2 Samuel in 24 Days**
After you have read through 2 Samuel, turn to pages 10–14 for your next Track 3 reading project.

☐1   ☐2   ☐3   ☐4   ☐5   ☐6   ☐7   ☐8
☐9   ☐10   ☐11   ☐12   ☐13   ☐14   ☐15   ☐16
☐17   ☐18   ☐19   ☐20   ☐21   ☐22   ☐23   ☐24

David Learns of Saul's Death

1 Now it came about after the death of Saul, when David had returned from the slaughter of the Amalekites, that David remained two days in Ziklag.

2 On the third day, behold, a man came out of the camp from Saul, with his clothes torn and dust on his head. And it came about when he came to David that he fell to the ground and prostrated himself.

3 Then David said to him, "From where do you come?" And he said to him, "I have escaped from the camp of Israel."

4 David said to him, "How did things go? Please tell me." And he said, "The people have fled from the battle, and also many of the people have fallen and are dead; and Saul and Jonathan his son are dead also."

5 So David said to the young man who told him, "How do you know that Saul and his son Jonathan are dead?"

6 The young man who told him said, "By chance I happened to be on Mount Gilboa, and behold, Saul was leaning on his spear. And behold, the chariots and the horsemen pursued him closely.

7 "When he looked behind him, he saw me and called to me. And I said, 'Here I am.'

8 "He said to me, 'Who are you?' And I answered him, 'I am an Amalekite.'

9 "Then he said to me, 'Please stand beside me and kill me, for agony has seized me because my life still lingers in me.'

10 "So I stood beside him and killed him, because I knew that he could not live after he had fallen. And I took the crown which *was* on his head and the bracelet which *was* on his arm, and I have brought them here to my lord."

11 ¶ Then David took hold of his clothes and tore them, and *so* also *did* all the men who *were* with him.

12 They mourned and wept and fasted until evening for Saul and his son Jonathan and for the people of the LORD and the house of Israel, because they had fallen by the sword.

13 David said to the young man who told him, "Where are you from?" And he answered, "I am the son of an alien, an Amalekite."

14 Then David said to him, "How is it you were not afraid to stretch out your hand to destroy the LORD'S anointed?"

15 And David called one of the young men and said, "Go, cut him down." So he struck him and he died.

16 David said to him, "Your blood is on your head, for your mouth has testified against you, saying, 'I have killed the LORD'S anointed.'"

David's Dirge for Saul and Jonathan

17 ¶ Then David chanted with this lament over Saul and Jonathan his son,

18 and he told *them* to teach the sons of Judah *the song of* the bow; behold, it is written in the book of Jashar.

19 "Your beauty, O Israel, is slain on your high places!
How have the mighty fallen!
20 "Tell *it* not in Gath,
Proclaim it not in the streets of Ashkelon,
Or the daughters of the Philistines will rejoice,
The daughters of the uncircumcised will exult.
21 "O mountains of Gilboa,
Let not dew or rain be on you, nor fields of offerings;
For there the shield of the mighty was defiled,
The shield of Saul, not anointed with oil.
22 "From the blood of the slain, from the fat of the mighty,
The bow of Jonathan did not turn back,
And the sword of Saul did not return empty.
23 "Saul and Jonathan, beloved and pleasant in their life,
And in their death they were not parted;
They were swifter than eagles,
They were stronger than lions.
24 "O daughters of Israel, weep over Saul,
Who clothed you luxuriously in scarlet,
Who put ornaments of gold on your apparel.
25 "How have the mighty fallen in the midst of the battle!
Jonathan is slain on your high places.
26 "I am distressed for you, my brother Jonathan;
You have been very pleasant to me.
Your love to me was more wonderful Than the love of women.
27 "How have the mighty fallen,
And the weapons of war perished!"

David Made King over Judah

2 Then it came about afterwards that David inquired of the LORD, saying, "Shall I go up to one of the cities of Judah?" And the LORD said to him, "Go up." So David said, "Where shall I go up?" And He said, "To Hebron."

2 So David went up there, and his two wives also, Ahinoam the Jezreelitess and Abigail the widow of Nabal the Carmelite.

3 And David brought up his men who *were* with him, each with his household; and they lived in the cities of Hebron.

4 Then the men of Judah came and there anointed David king over the house of Judah.

¶ And they told David, saying, "It was the men of Jabesh-gilead who buried Saul."

5 David sent messengers to the men of

Jabesh-gilead, and said to them, "May you be blessed of the LORD because you have shown this kindness to Saul your lord, and have buried him.

2:5 Potential Rivals

For their own security, dictators try to eliminate all competitors. In the ancient world, rulers did the same: A new king customarily killed the former king's relatives, since they were potential rivals. Not David! He executed the man who claimed to have killed his old enemy King Saul (1:14–15), he sang a painful lament over Saul's and Jonathan's deaths, and he blessed the people of Jabesh-gilead for their kindness in giving Saul a decent burial. David never abandoned his love for Saul's family.

6 "Now may the LORD show lovingkindness and truth to you; and I also will show this goodness to you, because you have done this thing.

7 "Now therefore, let your hands be strong and be valiant; for Saul your lord is dead, and also the house of Judah has anointed me king over them."

Ish-bosheth Made King over Israel

8 ¶ But Abner the son of Ner, commander of Saul's army, had taken *a*Ish-bosheth the son of Saul and brought him over to Mahanaim.

9 He made him king over Gilead, over the Ashurites, over Jezreel, over Ephraim, and over Benjamin, even over all Israel.

10 Ish-bosheth, Saul's son, was forty years old when he became king over Israel, and he was king for two years. The house of Judah, however, followed David.

11 The time that David was king in Hebron over the house of Judah was seven years and six months.

Civil War

12 ¶ Now Abner the son of Ner, went out from Mahanaim to Gibeon with the servants of Ish-bosheth the son of Saul.

13 And Joab the son of Zeruiah and the servants of David went out and met them by the pool of Gibeon; and they sat down, one on the one side of the pool and the other on the other side of the pool.

14 Then Abner said to Joab, "Now let the young men arise and *b*hold a contest before us." And Joab said, "Let them arise."

15 So they arose and went over by count, twelve for Benjamin and Ish-bosheth the son of Saul, and twelve of the servants of David.

16 Each one of them seized his opponent by the head and *thrust* his sword in his opponent's side; so they fell down together. Therefore that

place was called *c*Helkath-hazzurim, which is in Gibeon.

17 That day the battle was very severe, and Abner and the men of Israel were beaten before the servants of David.

18 ¶ Now the three sons of Zeruiah were there, Joab and Abishai and Asahel; and Asahel *was as* swift-footed as one of the gazelles which is in the field.

19 Asahel pursued Abner and did not turn to the right or to the left from following Abner.

20 Then Abner looked behind him and said, "Is that you, Asahel?" And he answered, "It is I."

21 So Abner said to him, "Turn to your right or to your left, and take hold of one of the young men for yourself, and take for yourself his spoil." But Asahel was not willing to turn aside from following him.

22 Abner repeated again to Asahel, "Turn aside from following me. Why should I strike you to the ground? How then could I lift up my face to your brother Joab?"

23 However, he refused to turn aside; therefore Abner struck him in the belly with the butt end of the spear, so that the spear came out at his back. And he fell there and died on the spot. And it came about that all who came to the place where Asahel had fallen and died, stood still.

24 ¶ But Joab and Abishai pursued Abner, and when the sun was going down, they came to the hill of Ammah, which is in front of Giah by the way of the wilderness of Gibeon.

25 The sons of Benjamin gathered together behind Abner and became one band, and they stood on the top of a certain hill.

26 Then Abner called to Joab and said, "Shall the sword devour forever? Do you not know that it will be bitter in the end? How long will you refrain from telling the people to turn back from following their brothers?"

27 Joab said, "As God lives, if you had not spoken, surely then the people would have gone away in the morning, each from following his brother."

28 So Joab blew the trumpet; and all the people halted and pursued Israel no longer, nor did they continue to fight anymore.

29 Abner and his men then went through the Arabah all that night; so they crossed the Jordan, walked all morning, and came to Mahanaim.

30 ¶ Then Joab returned from following Abner; when he had gathered all the people together, nineteen of David's servants besides Asahel were missing.

31 But the servants of David had struck down many of Benjamin and Abner's men, *so that* three hundred and sixty men died.

32 And they took up Asahel and buried him in his father's tomb which was in Bethlehem. Then

---

a I.e. man of shame; cf 1 Chr 8:33, *Eshbaal*   *b* Lit *make sport*   *c* I.e. the field of sword-edges

Joab and his men went all night until the day dawned at Hebron.

The House of David Strengthened

3 Now there was a long war between the house of Saul and the house of David; and David grew steadily stronger, but the house of Saul grew weaker continually.

2 ¶ Sons were born to David at Hebron: his firstborn was Amnon, by Ahinoam the Jezreelitess;

3 and his second, Chileab, by Abigail the widow of Nabal the Carmelite; and the third, Absalom the son of Maacah, the daughter of Talmai, king of Geshur;

4 and the fourth, Adonijah the son of Haggith; and the fifth, Shephatiah the son of Abital;

5 and the sixth, Ithream, by David's wife Eglah. These were born to David at Hebron.

Abner Joins David

6 ¶ It came about while there was war between the house of Saul and the house of David that Abner was making himself strong in the house of Saul.

7 Now Saul had a concubine whose name was Rizpah, the daughter of Aiah; and Ish-bosheth said to Abner, "Why have you gone in to my father's concubine?"

8 Then Abner was very angry over the words of Ish-bosheth and said, "Am I a dog's head that belongs to Judah? Today I show kindness to the house of Saul your father, to his brothers and to his friends, and have not delivered you into the hands of David; and yet today you charge me with a guilt concerning the woman.

9 "May God do so to Abner, and more also, if as the LORD has sworn to David, I do not accomplish this for him,

10 to transfer the kingdom from the house of Saul and to establish the throne of David over

---

3:7 Women in Politics

In David's time, women were political symbols. Abner's sleeping with Saul's concubine would have suggested that he had his eyes on becoming king himself. Later, when Absalom drove his father David out of Jerusalem, he slept with David's concubines in public, demonstrating to all eyes that he had taken over from his father (16:22).

David sometimes may have married for political benefit. One wife, Absalom's mother (verse 3), was a princess from a neighboring country; the marriage undoubtedly promoted good foreign relations. David's request that Michal be returned to him (though she had remarried, verses 14–16) made political sense: an alliance with Saul's daughter would tie Saul's family to the palace.

Israel and over Judah, from Dan even to Beersheba."

11 And he could no longer answer Abner a word, because he was afraid of him.

12 ¶ Then Abner sent messengers to David in his place, saying, "Whose is the land? Make your covenant with me, and behold, my hand shall be with you to bring all Israel over to you."

13 He said, "Good! I will make a covenant with you, but I demand one thing of you, namely, you shall not see my face unless you first bring Michal, Saul's daughter, when you come to see me."

ABNER *On the Wrong Side*

WAR IS NEVER PRETTY, AND neither are most of the soldiers who fight it. Famous generals such as Rommel, Sherman, Lee or Patton do not always stand for great causes or great morals. They earn respect for their ability to lead men into battle, to kill and to triumph.

Abner was a fine general who fought most of his life for a bad king. Though he introduced David to King Saul (1 Samuel 17:55–58) and commanded David during his early campaigns, Abner ultimately followed Saul's orders and fought against David. During the years when David's band of outlaws was roaming the hills, Abner led the hunt to track them down. Along the way he and David won mutual respect as honorable enemies.

Even after Saul died, Abner remained loyal to the forces arrayed against David. He installed Saul's son as king and fought a long civil war against David's side. Abner died not from battle but from treachery. Joab, David's general, had never forgiven Abner for killing his brother. When Abner finally came to make peace with David, Joab saw his opportunity for revenge. Pretending to conference with Abner, he stuck a knife in him (3:27).

David denounced this act of treachery and gave his former enemy a state funeral. Abner, he said, was a "prince and a great man" (3:38). Israel would need more such soldiers, people who combined war-making skill with loyalty to their king.

Life Questions: Can you think of any sincere men or women today who are passionately fighting on the wrong side of an important cause?

14 So David sent messengers to Ish-bosheth, Saul's son, saying, "Give me my wife Michal, to whom I was betrothed for a hundred foreskins of the Philistines."

15 Ish-bosheth sent and took her from *her* husband, from Paltiel the son of Laish.

16 But her husband went with her, weeping as he went, and followed her as far as Bahurim. Then Abner said to him, "Go, return." So he returned.

17 ¶ Now Abner had consultation with the elders of Israel, saying, "In times past you were seeking for David to be king over you.

18 "Now then, do *it!* For the LORD has spoken of David, saying, 'By the hand of My servant David I will save My people Israel from the hand of the Philistines and from the hand of all their enemies.'"

19 Abner also spoke in the hearing of Benjamin; and in addition Abner went to speak in the hearing of David in Hebron all that seemed good to Israel and to the whole house of Benjamin.

20 ¶ Then Abner and twenty men with him came to David at Hebron. And David made a feast for Abner and the men who were with him.

21 Abner said to David, "Let me arise and go and gather all Israel to my lord the king, that they may make a covenant with you, and that you may be king over all that your soul desires." So David sent Abner away, and he went in peace.

22 ¶ And behold, the servants of David and Joab came from a raid and brought much spoil with them; but Abner was not with David in Hebron, for he had sent him away, and he had gone in peace.

23 When Joab and all the army that was with him arrived, they told Joab, saying, "Abner the son of Ner came to the king, and he has sent him away, and he has gone in peace."

24 Then Joab came to the king and said, "What have you done? Behold, Abner came to you; why then have you sent him away and he is already gone?

25 "You know Abner the son of Ner, that he came to deceive you and to learn of your going out and coming in and to find out all that you are doing."

Joab Murders Abner

26 ¶ When Joab came out from David, he sent messengers after Abner, and they brought him back from the well of Sirah; but David did not know *it*.

27 So when Abner returned to Hebron, Joab took him aside into the middle of the gate to speak with him privately, and there he struck him in the belly so that he died on account of the blood of Asahel his brother.

28 Afterward when David heard it, he said, "I and my kingdom are innocent before the LORD forever of the blood of Abner the son of Ner.

29 "May it fall on the head of Joab and on all his father's house; and may there not fail from the house of Joab one who has a discharge, or who is a leper, or who takes hold of a distaff, or who falls by the sword, or who lacks bread."

30 So Joab and Abishai his brother killed Abner because he had put their brother Asahel to death in the battle at Gibeon.

3:30 Easy on Joab

Though General Douglas MacArthur had been popular and effective during World War II, he opposed the President's Korean War policy, and finally Harry Truman fired him. David faced a similar dilemma, but made a different decision. After David had made peace with Abner, a former enemy, David's commander Joab tricked and murdered Abner. This undercut David's policy of bringing harmony to a divided land. Although David cursed Joab, he didn't punish him or strip away his power. Why not? Perhaps he needed Joab's abilities, and feared what Joab might do if alienated. Many years later, when David lay dying, he instructed Solomon to punish Joab for the crime (1 Kings 2:5–6).

David Mourns Abner

31 ¶ Then David said to Joab and to all the people who were with him, "Tear your clothes and gird on sackcloth and lament before Abner." And King David walked behind the bier.

32 Thus they buried Abner in Hebron; and the king lifted up his voice and wept at the grave of Abner, and all the people wept.

33 The king chanted a *lament* for Abner and said,

"Should Abner die as a fool dies?
34 "Your hands were not bound, nor your
        feet put in fetters;
    As one falls before the wicked, you have
        fallen."

And all the people wept again over him.

35 Then all the people came to persuade David to eat bread while it was still day; but David vowed, saying, "May God do so to me, and more also, if I taste bread or anything else before the sun goes down."

36 Now all the people took note *of it*, and it pleased them, just as everything the king did pleased all the people.

37 So all the people and all Israel understood that day that it had not been *the will* of the king to put Abner the son of Ner to death.

38 Then the king said to his servants, "Do you not know that a prince and a great man has fallen this day in Israel?

39 "I am weak today, though anointed king; and these men the sons of Zeruiah are too difficult for

me. May the LORD repay the evildoer according to his evil."

Ish-bosheth Murdered

4 Now when Ish-bosheth, Saul's son, heard that Abner had died in Hebron, he lost courage, and all Israel was disturbed.

2 Saul's son *had* two men who were commanders of bands: the name of the one was Baanah and the name of the other Rechab, sons of Rimmon the Beerothite, of the sons of Benjamin (for Beeroth is also considered *part* of Benjamin,

3 and the Beerothites fled to Gittaim and have been aliens there until this day).

4 ¶ Now Jonathan, Saul's son, had a son crippled in his feet. He was five years old when the report of Saul and Jonathan came from Jezreel, and his nurse took him up and fled. And it happened that in her hurry to flee, he fell and became lame. And his name was Mephibosheth.

5 ¶ So the sons of Rimmon the Beerothite, Rechab and Baanah, departed and came to the house of Ish-bosheth in the heat of the day while he was taking his midday rest.

6 They came to the middle of the house as if to get wheat, and they struck him in the belly; and Rechab and Baanah his brother escaped.

7 Now when they came into the house, as he was lying on his bed in his bedroom, they struck him and killed him and beheaded him. And they took his head and traveled by way of the Arabah all night.

8 Then they brought the head of Ish-bosheth to David at Hebron and said to the king, "Behold, the head of Ish-bosheth the son of Saul, your enemy, who sought your life; thus the LORD has given my lord the king vengeance this day on Saul and his descendants."

9 ¶ David answered Rechab and Baanah his brother, sons of Rimmon the Beerothite, and said to them, "As the LORD lives, who has redeemed my life from all distress,

10 when one told me, saying, 'Behold, Saul is dead,' and thought he was bringing good news, I seized him and killed him in Ziklag, which was the reward I gave him for *his* news.

11 "How much more, when wicked men have killed a righteous man in his own house on his bed, shall I not now require his blood from your hand and destroy you from the earth?"

12 Then David commanded the young men, and they killed them and cut off their hands and feet and hung them up beside the pool in Hebron. But they took the head of Ish-bosheth and buried it in the grave of Abner in Hebron.

David King over All Israel

5 Then all the tribes of Israel came to David at Hebron and said, "Behold, we are your bone and your flesh.

2 "Previously, when Saul was king over us, you were the one who led Israel out and in. And the LORD said to you, 'You will shepherd My people Israel, and you will be a ruler over Israel.'"

3 So all the elders of Israel came to the king at Hebron, and King David made a covenant with them before the LORD at Hebron; then they anointed David king over Israel.

4 David was thirty years old when he became king, *and* he reigned forty years.

5 At Hebron he reigned over Judah seven years and six months, and in Jerusalem he reigned thirty-three years over all Israel and Judah.

6 ¶ Now the king and his men went to Jerusalem against the Jebusites, the inhabitants of the land, and they said to David, "You shall not come in here, but the blind and lame will turn you away"; thinking, "David cannot enter here."

5:6 Choosing a Capital

In trying to unify the northern and southern tribes, David wanted a capital that offended neither side. He found it in Jerusalem, on the border between North and South and belonging to neither. Its choice can be compared to the U.S. capital that, Washington, D.C., a compromise between North and South.

7 Nevertheless, David captured the stronghold of Zion, that is the city of David.

8 David said on that day, "Whoever would strike the Jebusites, let him reach the lame and the blind, who are hated by David's soul, through the water tunnel." Therefore they say, "The blind or the lame shall not come into the house."

9 So David lived in the stronghold and called it the city of David. And David built all around from the [a]Millo and inward.

10 David became greater and greater, for the LORD God of hosts was with him.

11 ¶ Then Hiram king of Tyre sent messengers to David with cedar trees and carpenters and stonemasons; and they built a house for David.

12 And David realized that the LORD had established him as king over Israel, and that He had exalted his kingdom for the sake of His people Israel.

13 ¶ Meanwhile David took more concubines and wives from Jerusalem, after he came from Hebron; and more sons and daughters were born to David.

14 Now these are the names of those who were born to him in Jerusalem: Shammua, Shobab, Nathan, Solomon,

15 Ibhar, Elishua, Nepheg, Japhia,

16 Elishama, Eliada and Eliphelet.

[a] I.e. citadel

War with the Philistines

17 ¶ When the Philistines heard that they had anointed David king over Israel, all the Philistines went up to seek out David; and when David heard *of it,* he went down to the stronghold.

18 Now the Philistines came and spread themselves out in the valley of Rephaim.

19 Then David inquired of the LORD, saying, "Shall I go up against the Philistines? Will You give them into my hand?" And the LORD said to David, "Go up, for I will certainly give the Philistines into your hand."

5:19 Seeking Guidance

Most ancient kings sought signs from God. David went well beyond that practice, regularly asking God for guidance about military and governmental decisions. David's faith wasn't impersonal; he had a close, practical, and deep relationship with God.

20 So David came to Baal-perazim and defeated them there; and he said, "The LORD has broken through my enemies before me like the breakthrough of waters." Therefore he named that place *ª*Baal-perazim.

21 They abandoned their idols there, so David and his men carried them away.

22 ¶ Now the Philistines came up once again and spread themselves out in the valley of Rephaim.

23 When David inquired of the LORD, He said, "You shall not go *directly* up; circle around behind them and come at them in front of the *ᵇ*balsam trees.

24 "It shall be, when you hear the sound of marching in the tops of the *ᵇ*balsam trees, then you shall act promptly, for then the LORD will have gone out before you to strike the army of the Philistines."

25 Then David did so, just as the LORD had commanded him, and struck down the Philistines from Geba as far as Gezer.

Peril in Moving the Ark

6 Now David again gathered all the chosen men of Israel, thirty thousand.

2 And David arose and went with all the people who were with him to Baale-judah, to bring up from there the ark of God which is called by the Name, the very name of the LORD of hosts who is enthroned *above* the cherubim.

3 They placed the ark of God on a new cart that they might bring it from the house of Abinadab which was on the hill; and Uzzah and Ahio, the sons of Abinadab, were leading the new cart.

4 So they brought it with the ark of God from the house of Abinadab, which was on the hill; and Ahio was walking ahead of the ark.

5 Meanwhile, David and all the house of Israel were celebrating before the LORD with all kinds of *instruments made of* fir wood, and with lyres, harps, tambourines, castanets and cymbals.

6 ¶ But when they came to the threshing floor of Nacon, Uzzah reached out toward the ark of God and took hold of it, for the oxen nearly upset *it.*

7 And the anger of the LORD burned against Uzzah, and God struck him down there for his irreverence; and he died there by the ark of God.

8 David became angry because of the LORD's outburst against Uzzah, and that place is called *ᶜ*Perez-uzzah to this day.

9 So David was afraid of the LORD that day; and he said, "How can the ark of the LORD come to me?"

10 And David was unwilling to move the ark of the LORD into the city of David with him; but David took it aside to the house of Obed-edom the Gittite.

11 Thus the ark of the LORD remained in the house of Obed-edom the Gittite three months, and the LORD blessed Obed-edom and all his household.

The Ark Is Brought to Jerusalem

12 ¶ Now it was told King David, saying, "The LORD has blessed the house of Obed-edom and all that belongs to him, on account of the ark of God." David went and brought up the ark of God from the house of Obed-edom into the city of David with gladness.

13 And so it was, that when the bearers of the ark of the LORD had gone six paces, he sacrificed an ox and a fatling.

14 And David was dancing before the LORD with all *his* might, and David was wearing a linen ephod.

15 So David and all the house of Israel were bringing up the ark of the LORD with shouting and the sound of the trumpet.

16 ¶ Then it happened *as* the ark of the LORD came into the city of David that Michal the daughter of Saul looked out of the window and saw King David leaping and dancing before the LORD; and she despised him in her heart.

17 ¶ So they brought in the ark of the LORD and set it in its place inside the tent which David had pitched for it; and David offered burnt offerings and peace offerings before the LORD.

18 When David had finished offering the burnt offering and the peace offering, he blessed the people in the name of the LORD of hosts.

19 Further, he distributed to all the people, to all the multitude of Israel, both to men and women, a cake of bread and one of dates and one of

---

ª I.e. the master of breakthrough   *ᵇ* Or *baka-shrubs*   *ᶜ* I.e. the breakthrough of Uzzah raisins to each one. Then all the people departed each to his house.

20 ¶ But when David returned to bless his household, Michal the daughter of Saul came out to meet David and said, "How the king of Israel distinguished himself today! He uncovered himself today in the eyes of his servants' maids as one of the foolish ones shamelessly uncovers himself!"

21 So David said to Michal, "*It was* before the LORD, who chose me above your father and above all his house, to appoint me ruler over the people of the LORD, over Israel; therefore I will celebrate before the LORD.

22 "I will be more lightly esteemed than this and will be humble in my own eyes, but with the maids of whom you have spoken, with them I will be distinguished."

23 Michal the daughter of Saul had no child to the day of her death.

David Plans to Build a Temple

7 Now it came about when the king lived in his house, and the LORD had given him rest on every side from all his enemies,

2 that the king said to Nathan the prophet, "See now, I dwell in a house of cedar, but the ark of God dwells within tent curtains."

3 Nathan said to the king, "Go, do all that is in your mind, for the LORD is with you."

4 ¶ But in the same night the word of the LORD came to Nathan, saying,

5 "Go and say to My servant David, 'Thus says the LORD, "Are you the one who should build Me a house to dwell in?

6 "For I have not dwelt in a house since the day I brought up the sons of Israel from Egypt, even to this day; but I have been moving about in a tent, even in a tabernacle.

7 "Wherever I have gone with all the sons of Israel, did I speak a word with one of the tribes of Israel, which I commanded to shepherd My people Israel, saying, 'Why have you not built Me a house of cedar?' " '

God's Covenant with David

8 "Now therefore, thus you shall say to My servant David, 'Thus says the LORD of hosts, "I took you from the pasture, from following the sheep, to be ruler over My people Israel.

9 "I have been with you wherever you have gone and have cut off all your enemies from before you; and I will make you a great name, like the names of the great men who are on the earth.

10 "I will also appoint a place for My people Israel and will plant them, that they may live in their own place and not be disturbed again, nor will the wicked afflict them any more as formerly,

11 even from the day that I commanded judges to be over My people Israel; and I will give you rest from all your enemies. The LORD also declares to you that the LORD will make a house for you.

12 "When your days are complete and you lie down with your fathers, I will raise up your descendant after you, who will come forth from you, and I will establish his kingdom.

13 "He shall build a house for My name, and I will establish the throne of his kingdom forever.

14 "I will be a father to him and he will be a son

NATHAN *The King's Conscience*

"LET YOUR CONSCIENCE BE YOUR guide." That's good advice only if your conscience doesn't cheat. Most people find ways to soothe their consciences by rationalizing whatever they want to do. That's why it's best to check with trustworthy people for advice.

Ancient rulers had an additional problem. Since few people had the courage to contradict an all-powerful king, such kings tended to get favorable advice even if they were doing something dead wrong. As one Roman senator said to Tiberius Caesar, "But if you speak first no one will want to refute you, and if you speak last, we will not want to have spoken against your position."

Only a few brave souls dared to be different. The prophet Nathan, for example, told the king the truth, pleasant or not. Nathan burst David's bubble by informing him that God did not want him to build the temple (7:5–16). He also spoke up to remind David of his neglected promise to crown Solomon as his successor (1 Kings 1:24–30).

Most memorably, Nathan accused David of sinning against God by committing adultery with Bathsheba and murdering her husband (2 Samuel 12). Nathan did so artfully, trapping the king with a powerful story that aroused the king's fury—until Nathan drove home the point. Nathan could have died for bringing this message, but it was a measure of David's character that he listened to Nathan even when his own conscience had gone numb. When David repented, Nathan stood beside him, assuring him of God's forgiveness.

Nathan was a true prophet. Though Biblical prophets sometimes predicted the future (as Nathan did in describing the punishments David would suffer) they were best known for telling the truth—especially the unpleasant truth that no one wanted to hear.

Life Questions: Who helps your conscience? Who can you count on to tell you the unpleasant truth about yourself?

to Me; when he commits iniquity, I will correct him with the rod of men and the strokes of the sons of men,

15 but My lovingkindness shall not depart from him, as I took *it* away from Saul, whom I removed from before you.

16 "Your house and your kingdom shall endure before Me forever; your throne shall be established forever." ' "

7:16 God's Great Promise

The Lord's promise to "establish David's throne forever" suggested that Israel would never lack the leadership they needed. This promise was one of a series of covenants between God and his people—with Abraham (Genesis 12), with Moses at Sinai (Exodus 20), and now with David. The New Testament sees this promise fulfilled in Jesus, a son of David, and King of kings forever (Luke 1:32–33).

17 In accordance with all these words and all this vision, so Nathan spoke to David.

David's Prayer

18 ¶ Then David the king went in and sat before the LORD, and he said, "Who am I, O Lord GOD, and what is my house, that You have brought me this far?

19 "And yet this was insignificant in Your eyes, O Lord GOD, for You have spoken also of the house of Your servant concerning the distant future. And this is the custom of man, O Lord GOD.

20 "Again what more can David say to You? For You know Your servant, O Lord GOD!

21 "For the sake of Your word, and according to Your own heart, You have done all this greatness to let Your servant know.

22 "For this reason You are great, O Lord GOD; for there is none like You, and there is no God besides You, according to all that we have heard with our ears.

23 "And what one nation on the earth is like Your people Israel, whom God went to redeem for Himself as a people and to make a name for Himself, and to do a great thing for You and awesome things for Your land, before Your people whom You have redeemed for Yourself from Egypt, *from* nations and their gods?

24 "For You have established for Yourself Your people Israel as Your own people forever, and You, O LORD, have become their God.

25 "Now therefore, O LORD God, the word that You have spoken concerning Your servant and his house, confirm *it* forever, and do as You have spoken,

26 that Your name may be magnified forever,

by saying, 'The LORD of hosts is God over Israel'; and may the house of Your servant David be established before You.

27 "For You, O LORD of hosts, the God of Israel, have made a revelation to Your servant, saying, 'I will build you a house'; therefore Your servant has found courage to pray this prayer to You.

28 "Now, O Lord GOD, You are God, and Your words are truth, and You have promised this good thing to Your servant.

29 "Now therefore, may it please You to bless the house of Your servant, that it may continue forever before You. For You, O Lord GOD, have spoken; and with Your blessing may the house of Your servant be blessed forever."

David's Triumphs

8 Now after this it came about that David defeated the Philistines and subdued them; and David took control of the chief city from the hand of the Philistines.

2 ¶ He defeated Moab, and measured them with the line, making them lie down on the ground; and he measured two lines to put to death and one full line to keep alive. And the Moabites became servants to David, bringing tribute.

3 ¶ Then David defeated Hadadezer, the son of Rehob king of Zobah, as he went to restore his rule at the *a*River.

4 David captured from him 1,700 horsemen and 20,000 foot soldiers; and David hamstrung the chariot horses, but reserved *enough* of them for 100 chariots.

8:4 Not Ready for Chariots

Chariots were as great an innovation in weaponry as were guns centuries later. However, chariots required trained charioteers. Since David hamstrung all but 100 chariot horses, he may have lacked such trained personnel. Israel could defend the mountains, where chariots were of little use, but they were not ready to take on big armies on the surrounding plains.

5 When the Arameans of Damascus came to help Hadadezer, king of Zobah, David killed 22,000 Arameans.

6 Then David put garrisons among the Arameans of Damascus, and the Arameans became servants to David, bringing tribute. And the LORD helped David wherever he went.

7 David took the shields of gold which were carried by the servants of Hadadezer and brought them to Jerusalem.

8 From Betah and from Berothai, cities of

---

a I.e. Euphrates

Hadadezer, King David took a very large amount of bronze.

9 ¶ Now when Toi king of Hamath heard that David had defeated all the army of Hadadezer,

10 Toi sent Joram his son to King David to greet him and bless him, because he had fought against Hadadezer and defeated him; for Hadadezer had been at war with Toi. And *Joram* brought with him articles of silver, of gold and of bronze.

11 King David also dedicated these to the LORD, with the silver and gold that he had dedicated from all the nations which he had subdued:

12 from ᵃAram and Moab and the sons of Ammon and the Philistines and Amalek, and from the spoil of Hadadezer, son of Rehob, king of Zobah.

13 ¶ So David made a name *for himself* when he returned from killing 18,000 ᵃArameans in the Valley of Salt.

14 He put garrisons in Edom. In all Edom he put garrisons, and all the Edomites became servants to David. And the LORD helped David wherever he went.

15 ¶ So David reigned over all Israel; and David administered justice and righteousness for all his people.

16 Joab the son of Zeruiah *was* over the army, and Jehoshaphat the son of Ahilud *was* recorder.

17 Zadok the son of Ahitub and Ahimelech the son of Abiathar *were* priests, and Seraiah *was* secretary.

18 Benaiah the son of Jehoiada was over the Cherethites and the Pelethites; and David's sons were chief ministers.

David's Kindness to Mephibosheth

9 Then David said, "Is there yet anyone left of the house of Saul, that I may show him kindness for Jonathan's sake?"

2 Now there was a servant of the house of Saul whose name was Ziba, and they called him to David; and the king said to him, "Are you Ziba?" And he said, "I am your servant."

3 The king said, "Is there not yet anyone of the house of Saul to whom I may show the kindness of God?" And Ziba said to the king, "There is still a son of Jonathan who is crippled in both feet."

4 So the king said to him, "Where is he?" And Ziba said to the king, "Behold, he is in the house of Machir the son of Ammiel in Lo-debar."

5 Then King David sent and brought him from the house of Machir the son of Ammiel, from Lo-debar.

6 Mephibosheth, the son of Jonathan the son of Saul, came to David and fell on his face and prostrated himself. And David said, "Mephibosheth." And he said, "Here is your servant!"

7 David said to him, "Do not fear, for I will surely show kindness to you for the sake of your father Jonathan, and will restore to you all the land of your grandfather Saul; and you shall eat at my table regularly."

9:7 Saul's Lame Grandson

Although Saul had been David's worst enemy, David consistently showed kindness and generosity to his family. In other kingdoms of that day, Mephibosheth would have been killed. David sought him out, restored his land, and welcomed him as a permanent guest at the royal table—a considerable honor. Later, when Mephibosheth suspiciously failed to join David in fleeing from Absalom's insurrection, David gave him the benefit of the doubt (19:24–30).

8 Again he prostrated himself and said, "What is your servant, that you should regard a dead dog like me?"

9 ¶ Then the king called Saul's servant Ziba and said to him, "All that belonged to Saul and to all his house I have given to your master's grandson.

10 "You and your sons and your servants shall cultivate the land for him, and you shall bring in *the produce* so that your master's grandson may have food; nevertheless Mephibosheth your master's grandson shall eat at my table regularly." Now Ziba had fifteen sons and twenty servants.

11 Then Ziba said to the king, "According to all that my lord the king commands his servant so your servant will do." So Mephibosheth ate at David's table as one of the king's sons.

12 Mephibosheth had a young son whose name was Mica. And all who lived in the house of Ziba were servants to Mephibosheth.

13 So Mephibosheth lived in Jerusalem, for he ate at the king's table regularly. Now he was lame in both feet.

Ammon and Aram Defeated

10 Now it happened afterwards that the king of the Ammonites died, and Hanun his son became king in his place.

2 Then David said, "I will show kindness to Hanun the son of Nahash, just as his father showed kindness to me." So David sent some of his servants to console him concerning his father. But when David's servants came to the land of the Ammonites,

3 the princes of the Ammonites said to Hanun their lord, "Do you think that David is honoring your father because he has sent consolers to you? Has David not sent his servants to you in order to search the city, to spy it out and overthrow it?"

4 So Hanun took David's servants and shaved

ᵃSome mss read *Edom*

off half of their beards, and cut off their garments in the middle as far as their hips, and sent them away.

5 When they told *it* to David, he sent to meet them, for the men were greatly humiliated. And the king said, "Stay at Jericho until your beards grow, and *then* return."

6 ¶ Now when the sons of Ammon saw that they had become odious to David, the sons of Ammon sent and hired the Arameans of Beth-rehob and the Arameans of Zobah, 20,000 foot soldiers, and the king of Maacah with 1,000 men, and the men of Tob with 12,000 men.

7 When David heard *of it*, he sent Joab and all the army, the mighty men.

8 The sons of Ammon came out and drew up in battle array at the entrance of the city, while the Arameans of Zobah and of Rehob and the men of Tob and Maacah *were* by themselves in the field.

9 ¶ Now when Joab saw that the battle was set against him in front and in the rear, he selected from all the choice men of Israel, and arrayed *them* against the Arameans.

10 But the remainder of the people he placed in the hand of Abishai his brother, and he arrayed *them* against the sons of Ammon.

11 He said, "If the Arameans are too strong for me, then you shall help me, but if the sons of Ammon are too strong for you, then I will come to help you.

12 "Be strong, and let us show ourselves courageous for the sake of our people and for the cities of our God; and may the LORD do what is good in His sight."

13 So Joab and the people who were with him drew near to the battle against the Arameans, and they fled before him.

14 When the sons of Ammon saw that the Arameans fled, they *also* fled before Abishai and entered the city. Then Joab returned from *fighting* against the sons of Ammon and came to Jerusalem.

15 ¶ When the Arameans saw that they had been defeated by Israel, they gathered themselves together.

16 And Hadadezer sent and brought out the Arameans who were beyond the *ª*River, and they came to Helam; and Shobach the commander of the army of Hadadezer led them.

17 Now when it was told David, he gathered all Israel together and crossed the Jordan, and came to Helam. And the Arameans arrayed themselves to meet David and fought against him.

18 But the Arameans fled before Israel, and David killed 700 charioteers of the Arameans and 40,000 horsemen and struck down Shobach the commander of their army, and he died there.

19 When all the kings, servants of Hadadezer, saw that they were defeated by Israel, they made

peace with Israel and served them. So the Arameans feared to help the sons of Ammon anymore.

Bathsheba, David's Great Sin

11 Then it happened in the spring, at the time when kings go out *to battle,* that David sent Joab and his servants with him and all Israel, and they destroyed the sons of Ammon and besieged Rabbah. But David stayed at Jerusalem.

2 ¶ Now when evening came David arose from his bed and walked around on the roof of the king's house, and from the roof he saw a woman bathing; and the woman was very beautiful in appearance.

3 So David sent and inquired about the woman. And one said, "Is this not Bathsheba, the daughter of Eliam, the wife of Uriah the Hittite?"

4 David sent messengers and took her, and when she came to him, he lay with her; and when she had purified herself from her uncleanness, she returned to her house.

5 The woman conceived; and she sent and told David, and said, "I am pregnant."

6 ¶ Then David sent to Joab, *saying,* "Send me Uriah the Hittite." So Joab sent Uriah to David.

7 When Uriah came to him, David asked concerning the welfare of Joab and the people and the state of the war.

8 Then David said to Uriah, "Go down to your house, and wash your feet." And Uriah went out of the king's house, and a present from the king was sent out after him.

9 But Uriah slept at the door of the king's house with all the servants of his lord, and did not go down to his house.

10 Now when they told David, saying, "Uriah did not go down to his house," David said to Uriah, "Have you not come from a journey? Why did you not go down to your house?"

11 Uriah said to David, "The ark and Israel and Judah are staying in temporary shelters, and my lord Joab and the servants of my lord are camping in the open field. Shall I then go to my house to eat and to drink and to lie with my wife? By your life and the life of your soul, I will not do this thing."

11:11 A Military Hero

Israelite soldiers had no sexual relations while they were preparing for battle. (See, for instance, 1 Samuel 21:5.) Uriah refused to sleep with Bathsheba because he remembered duty before pleasure. He is mentioned (in 23:39) as one of the thirty, a group of leading warriors under David.

ª I.e. Euphrates

12 Then David said to Uriah, "Stay here today also, and tomorrow I will let you go." So Uriah remained in Jerusalem that day and the next.

13 Now David called him, and he ate and drank before him, and he made him drunk; and in the evening he went out to lie on his bed with his lord's servants, but he did not go down to his house.

14 ¶ Now in the morning David wrote a letter to Joab and sent *it* by the hand of Uriah.

15 He had written in the letter, saying, "Place Uriah in the front line of the fiercest battle and withdraw from him, so that he may be struck down and die."

16 So it was as Joab kept watch on the city, that he put Uriah at the place where he knew there *were* valiant men.

17 The men of the city went out and fought against Joab, and some of the people among David's servants fell; and Uriah the Hittite also died.

18 Then Joab sent and reported to David all the events of the war.

19 He charged the messenger, saying, "When you have finished telling all the events of the war to the king,

20 and if it happens that the king's wrath rises and he says to you, 'Why did you go so near to the city to fight? Did you not know that they would shoot from the wall?

21 'Who struck down Abimelech the son of Jerubbesheth? Did not a woman throw an upper millstone on him from the wall so that he died at Thebez? Why did you go so near the wall?'—then you shall say, 'Your servant Uriah the Hittite is dead also.' "

22 ¶ So the messenger departed and came and reported to David all that Joab had sent him *to tell.*

23 The messenger said to David, "The men prevailed against us and came out against us in the field, but we pressed them as far as the entrance of the gate.

24 "Moreover, the archers shot at your servants from the wall; so some of the king's servants are dead, and your servant Uriah the Hittite is also dead."

25 Then David said to the messenger, "Thus you shall say to Joab, 'Do not let this thing displease you, for the sword devours one as well as another; make your battle against the city stronger and overthrow it'; and *so* encourage him."

26 ¶ Now when the wife of Uriah heard that Uriah her husband was dead, she mourned for her husband.

27 When the *time of* mourning was over, David sent and brought her to his house and she became his wife; then she bore him a son. But the thing that David had done was evil in the sight of the LORD.

Nathan Rebukes David

12 Then the LORD sent Nathan to David. And he came to him and said,
"There were two men in one city, the one
   rich and the other poor.
2 "The rich man had a great many flocks
   and herds.
3 "But the poor man had nothing except
   one little ewe lamb
Which he bought and nourished;
And it grew up together with him and
   his children.

BATHSHEBA *Only Following Orders*

AFTER WORLD WAR II, NAZI soldiers made a classic defense for their war crimes: "We were only following orders." Then and ever since courts have struck down that defense. A person who knowingly does wrong is responsible, regardless of the circumstances.

Still, many people feel sympathy for the person who commits a crime under pressure or coercion. Perhaps Bathsheba fits this category. She could hardly help being beautiful, and in all probability she was bathing quite innocently when she caught David's eye (houses then had no bathrooms). To complicate matters, the king—not just anybody—summoned her to sleep with him. The king's word was law, and had Bathsheba refused him she might have expected severe penalties—perhaps even death.

Certainly, Bathsheba suffered for what she did. She lost her husband and her child. Did she join with David in his repentance? The Bible does not say. After bearing another child, Solomon, she received no further mention in Scripture until the very end of David's life, when she supported Solomon's bid for the throne. The one really notable thing Bathsheba accomplished in life was the wrong thing—her affair with the king.

The way the Bible tells the story, David bore the chief responsibility for this national scandal. He initiated the adultery, followed it up with murder, and suffered the consequences throughout the rest of his life. When we consider how the repercussions of David's actions affected the entire nation, however, we can see why "I was only following orders" is no defense. Although Bathsheba was in some ways a victim, her failure to resist a sinful situation made David's sin possible.

Life Questions: Are there any situations in which you are tempted to "just go along" with sin because of pressure?

It would eat of his bread and drink of
his cup and lie in his bosom,
And was like a daughter to him.
4 "Now a traveler came to the rich man,
And he was unwilling to take from his
own flock or his own herd,
To prepare for the wayfarer who had
come to him;
Rather he took the poor man's ewe lamb
and prepared it for the man who
had come to him."

5 Then David's anger burned greatly against
the man, and he said to Nathan, "As the LORD
lives, surely the man who has done this deserves to
die.
6 "He must make restitution for the lamb four-
fold, because he did this thing and had no compassion."

7 ¶ Nathan then said to David, "You are the
man! Thus says the LORD God of Israel, 'It is I who
anointed you king over Israel and it is I who delivered you from the hand of Saul.
8 'I also gave you your master's house and
your master's wives into your care, and I gave you
the house of Israel and Judah; and if that had been
too little, I would have added to you many more
things like these!
9 'Why have you despised the word of the
LORD by doing evil in His sight? You have struck
down Uriah the Hittite with the sword, have taken
his wife to be your wife, and have killed him with
the sword of the sons of Ammon.

Adultery and Murder
The king could do as he pleased—or so he thought

AN ANCIENT AND ENDURING TRADITION teaches that the
people on top make the rules—they don't have to live by them. Lots of
leaders in history have followed this course, taking the women they
wanted, the money they wanted, the privileges they wanted.

Nobody, therefore, challenged David's right to sleep with another man's
wife. David saw Bathsheba, lusted for her, and sent for her. As far as we know,
neither his servants nor Bathsheba lodged a protest. Only when she got pregnant did a problem arise. Then David, who had had no thought of marrying
Bathsheba, found himself in a jam. He called her husband, Uriah, home on
leave from the army, hoping that Uriah would sleep with his wife and later be
unable to prove the child belonged to another father.

Uriah's single-minded devotion to duty spoiled David's plan. David
rewarded Uriah with murder. Again, not a word of protest was filed: What the
king wanted the king got, no questions asked. The murder of Uriah took other
good men with him, but David showed no regrets. He was at his worst: cold as iron, arrogant in his
power.

> David's anger
> burned greatly
> against the man,
> and he said to
> Nathan, "As the
> LORD lives, surely
> the man who has
> done this deserves
> to die!" ... Nathan
> then said to David,
> "You are the man!"
> 12:5,7

After a mourning period, Bathsheba came into his house and he married her. A good many people must have known what had happened—the servants knew, at any rate—but the Bible doesn't report
that any of them were displeased. It only says, "The thing that David had done was evil in the sight of
the LORD" (11:27).

Who Will Challenge the King?

Who would have the courage—or the authority—to challenge the king? In most nations, no one.
But Israel had this distinctive: its ultimate king was not David, but God. And God had his spokesmen,
the prophets. He sent Nathan to David.

Nathan cleverly captivated David with a heartrending story about a rich man who had abused his
power. He offered the case to David, the highest judge in Israel. David knew exactly how to judge such
a case: The man deserved death! When he said so, Nathan turned David's own judgment around: "You
are the man!"

In this dramatic scene David's greatness showed itself. He could easily have had Nathan killed. Or
he could have laughed and shown him out of the palace. Instead, "David said to Nathan, 'I have
sinned against the LORD'" (12:13). David recognized that God was the true king of Israel.

Nathan's confrontation with David set the standard for centuries of conflict between kings and
prophets. Time and again an Old Testament prophet went to the palace—sometimes risking his life—
and told the king that God would punish him for what he was doing. The kings, rich and powerful by
birth, did not have to listen. In fact, they rarely did. David was a great king partly because he did not
act with the normal pride of a king. When confronted with the truth, he repented.

Life Questions: What determines your choices? Your own desires? Or your understanding of God's will?
Think of some recent decisions you have made and apply this question to them.

10 'Now therefore, the sword shall never depart from your house, because you have despised Me and have taken the wife of Uriah the Hittite to be your wife.'

11 "Thus says the LORD, 'Behold, I will raise up evil against you from your own household; I will even take your wives before your eyes and give *them* to your companion, and he will lie with your wives in broad daylight.

12 'Indeed you did it secretly, but I will do this thing before all Israel, and under the sun.' "

13 Then David said to Nathan, "I have sinned against the LORD." And Nathan said to David, "The LORD also has taken away your sin; you shall not die.

12:13 David's Finest Moment

David, who possessed absolute power, could have had Nathan killed for his daring public confrontation. Or, he could have laughed him off and thrown him out of the palace. But David knew Nathan spoke for God, and in what may have been the greatest moment of his life, he admitted, "I have sinned against the LORD." David showed what made him a man after God's own heart; though he was king, he humbled himself before the King of kings.

14 "However, because by this deed you have given occasion to the enemies of the LORD to blaspheme, the child also that is born to you shall surely die."

15 So Nathan went to his house.

Loss of a Child

¶ Then the LORD struck the child that Uriah's widow bore to David, so that he was *very* sick.

16 David therefore inquired of God for the child; and David fasted and went and lay all night on the ground.

17 The elders of his household stood beside him in order to raise him up from the ground, but he was unwilling and would not eat food with them.

18 Then it happened on the seventh day that the child died. And the servants of David were afraid to tell him that the child was dead, for they said, "Behold, while the child was *still* alive, we spoke to him and he did not listen to our voice. How then can we tell him that the child is dead, since he might do *himself* harm!"

19 But when David saw that his servants were whispering together, David perceived that the child was dead; so David said to his servants, "Is the child dead?" And they said, "He is dead."

20 So David arose from the ground, washed, anointed *himself*, and changed his clothes; and he

came into the house of the LORD and worshiped. Then he came to his own house, and when he requested, they set food before him and he ate.

21 ¶ Then his servants said to him, "What is this thing that you have done? While the child was alive, you fasted and wept; but when the child died, you arose and ate food."

22 He said, "While the child was *still* alive, I fasted and wept; for I said, 'Who knows, the LORD may be gracious to me, that the child may live.'

23 "But now he has died; why should I fast? Can I bring him back again? I will go to him, but he will not return to me."

Solomon Born

24 ¶ Then David comforted his wife Bathsheba, and went in to her and lay with her; and she gave birth to a son, and he named him Solomon. Now the LORD loved him

25 and sent *word* through Nathan the prophet, and he named him *a*Jedidiah for the LORD'S sake.

War Again

26 ¶ Now Joab fought against Rabbah of the sons of Ammon and captured the royal city.

27 Joab sent messengers to David and said, "I have fought against Rabbah, I have even captured the city of waters.

28 "Now therefore, gather the rest of the people together and camp against the city and capture it, or I will capture the city myself and it will be named after me."

29 So David gathered all the people and went to Rabbah, fought against it and captured it.

30 Then he took the crown of their king from his head; and its weight *was* a talent of gold, and *in it was* a precious stone; and it was *placed* on David's head. And he brought out the spoil of the city in great amounts.

31 He also brought out the people who were in it, and set *them* under saws, sharp iron instruments, and iron axes, and made them pass through the brickkiln. And thus he did to all the cities of the sons of Ammon. Then David and all the people returned *to* Jerusalem.

Amnon and Tamar

13 Now it was after this that Absalom the son of David had a beautiful sister whose name was Tamar, and Amnon the son of David loved her.

2 Amnon was so frustrated because of his sister Tamar that he made himself ill, for she was a virgin, and it seemed hard to Amnon to do anything to her.

3 But Amnon had a friend whose name was Jonadab, the son of Shimeah, David's brother; and Jonadab was a very shrewd man.

4 He said to him, "O son of the king, why are you so depressed morning after morning? Will

---

a I.e. beloved of the LORD

you not tell me?" Then Amnon said to him, "I am in love with Tamar, the sister of my brother Absalom."

5 Jonadab then said to him, "Lie down on your bed and pretend to be ill; when your father comes to see you, say to him, 'Please let my sister Tamar come and give me *some* food to eat, and let her prepare the food in my sight, that I may see *it* and eat from her hand.' "

6 So Amnon lay down and pretended to be ill; when the king came to see him, Amnon said to the king, "Please let my sister Tamar come and make me a couple of cakes in my sight, that I may eat from her hand."

7 ¶ Then David sent to the house for Tamar, saying, "Go now to your brother Amnon's house, and prepare food for him."

8 So Tamar went to her brother Amnon's house, and he was lying down. And she took dough, kneaded *it*, made cakes in his sight, and baked the cakes.

9 She took the pan and dished *them* out before him, but he refused to eat. And Amnon said, "Have everyone go out from me." So everyone went out from him.

10 Then Amnon said to Tamar, "Bring the food into the bedroom, that I may eat from your hand." So Tamar took the cakes which she had made and brought them into the bedroom to her brother Amnon.

11 When she brought *them* to him to eat, he took hold of her and said to her, "Come, lie with me, my sister."

12 But she answered him, "No, my brother, do not violate me, for such a thing is not done in Israel; do not do this disgraceful thing!

13 "As for me, where could I get rid of my reproach? And as for you, you will be like one of the fools in Israel. Now therefore, please speak to the king, for he will not withhold me from you."

14 However, he would not listen to her; since he was stronger than she, he violated her and lay with her.

15 ¶ Then Amnon hated her with a very great hatred; for the hatred with which he hated her was greater than the love with which he had loved her. And Amnon said to her, "Get up, go away!"

16 But she said to him, "No, because this wrong in sending me away is greater than the other that you have done to me!" Yet he would not listen to her.

17 Then he called his young man who attended him and said, "Now throw this woman out of my *presence,* and lock the door behind her."

18 Now she had on a long-sleeved garment; for in this manner the virgin daughters of the king dressed themselves in robes. Then his attendant took her out and locked the door behind her.

19 Tamar put ashes on her head and tore her long-sleeved garment which *was* on her; and she put her hand on her head and went away, crying aloud as she went.

20 ¶ Then Absalom her brother said to her, "Has Amnon your brother been with you? But now keep silent, my sister, he is your brother; do not take this matter to heart." So Tamar remained and was desolate in her brother Absalom's house.

21 Now when King David heard of all these matters, he was very angry.

22 But Absalom did not speak to Amnon either good or bad; for Absalom hated Amnon because he had violated his sister Tamar.

23 ¶ Now it came about after two full years that Absalom had sheepshearers in Baal-hazor, which is near Ephraim, and Absalom invited all the king's sons.

Absalom Avenges Tamar

24 Absalom came to the king and said, "Behold now, your servant has sheepshearers; please let the king and his servants go with your servant."

25 But the king said to Absalom, "No, my son, we should not all go, for we will be burdensome to you." Although he urged him, he would not go, but blessed him.

26 Then Absalom said, "If not, please let my brother Amnon go with us." And the king said to him, "Why should he go with you?"

27 But when Absalom urged him, he let Amnon and all the king's sons go with him.

28 ¶ Absalom commanded his servants, saying, "See now, when Amnon's heart is merry with wine, and when I say to you, 'Strike Amnon,' then put him to death. Do not fear; have not I myself commanded you? Be courageous and be valiant."

29 The servants of Absalom did to Amnon just as Absalom had commanded. Then all the king's sons arose and each mounted his mule and fled.

13:29 Vicious Children

What went wrong with David's children? Amnon raped his sister Tamar. Absalom killed Amnon in revenge. Ultimately Absalom plotted a coup against his father, driving David from Jerusalem. All through these events—rape, murder, rebellion—David failed to discipline his children. According to the law they deserved severe punishment, but David let them off with hardly a word. Perhaps his own guilt over Bathsheba had undercut his sense of moral authority.

30 ¶ Now it was while they were on the way that the report came to David, saying, "Absalom has struck down all the king's sons, and not one of them is left."

31 Then the king arose, tore his clothes and lay on the ground; and all his servants were standing by with clothes torn.

32 Jonadab, the son of Shimeah, David's brother, responded, "Do not let my lord suppose they have put to death all the young men, the king's sons, for Amnon alone is dead; because by the intent of Absalom this has been determined since the day that he violated his sister Tamar.

33 "Now therefore, do not let my lord the king take the report to heart, namely, 'all the king's sons are dead,' for only Amnon is dead."

34 ¶ Now Absalom had fled. And the young man who was the watchman raised his eyes and looked, and behold, many people were coming from the road behind him by the side of the mountain.

35 Jonadab said to the king, "Behold, the king's sons have come; according to your servant's word, so it happened."

36 As soon as he had finished speaking, behold, the king's sons came and lifted their voices and wept; and also the king and all his servants wept very bitterly.

37 ¶ Now Absalom fled and went to Talmai the son of Ammihud, the king of Geshur. And *David* mourned for his son every day.

38 So Absalom had fled and gone to Geshur, and was there three years.

13:38 A Refuge with His Family

Absalom ran to Geshur, a neighboring kingdom, probably because his mother was a daughter of Geshur's king. He could be assured of safety there.

39 *The heart of* King David longed to go out to Absalom; for he was comforted concerning Amnon, since he was dead.

The Woman of Tekoa

14 Now Joab the son of Zeruiah perceived that the king's heart *was inclined* toward Absalom.

2 So Joab sent to Tekoa and brought a wise woman from there and said to her, "Please pretend to be a mourner, and put on mourning garments now, and do not anoint yourself with oil, but be like a woman who has been mourning for the dead many days;

3 then go to the king and speak to him in this manner." So Joab put the words in her mouth.

4 ¶ Now when the woman of Tekoa [a]spoke to the king, she fell on her face to the ground and prostrated herself and said, "Help, O king."

5 The king said to her, "What is your trouble?" And she answered, "Truly I am a widow, for my husband is dead.

6 "Your maidservant had two sons, but the two of them struggled together in the field, and there

was no [b]one to separate them, so one struck the other and killed him.

7 "Now behold, the whole family has risen against your maidservant, and they say, 'Hand over the one who struck his brother, that we may put him to death for the life of his brother whom he killed, and destroy the heir also.' Thus they will extinguish my coal which is left, so as to leave my husband neither name nor remnant on the face of the earth."

8 ¶ Then the king said to the woman, "Go to your house, and I will give orders concerning you."

9 The woman of Tekoa said to the king, "O my lord, the king, the iniquity is on me and my father's house, but the king and his throne are guiltless."

10 So the king said, "Whoever speaks to you, bring him to me, and he will not touch you anymore."

11 Then she said, "Please let the king remember the LORD your God, *so that* the avenger of blood will not continue to destroy, otherwise they will destroy my son." And he said, "As the LORD lives, not one hair of your son shall fall to the ground."

12 ¶ Then the woman said, "Please let your maidservant speak a word to my lord the king." And he said, "Speak."

13 The woman said, "Why then have you planned such a thing against the people of God? For in speaking this word the king is as one who is guilty, *in that* the king does not bring back his banished one.

14 "For we will surely die and are like water spilled on the ground which cannot be gathered up again. Yet God does not take away life, but plans ways so that the banished one will not be cast out from him.

15 "Now the reason I have come to speak this word to my lord the king is that the people have made me afraid; so your maidservant said, 'Let me now speak to the king, perhaps the king will perform the request of his maidservant.

16 'For the king will hear and deliver his maidservant from the hand of the man who would destroy both me and my son from the inheritance of God.'

17 "Then your maidservant said, 'Please let the word of my lord the king be comforting, for as the angel of God, so is my lord the king to discern good and evil. And may the LORD your God be with you.'"

18 ¶ Then the king answered and said to the woman, "Please do not hide anything from me that I am about to ask you." And the woman said, "Let my lord the king please speak."

19 So the king said, "Is the hand of Joab with you in all this?" And the woman replied, "As your

---

[a] Many mss and ancient versions read *came*   [b] Lit *deliverer between*

soul lives, my lord the king, no one can turn to the right or to the left from anything that my lord the king has spoken. Indeed, it was your servant Joab who commanded me, and it was he who put all these words in the mouth of your maidservant;

20 in order to change the appearance of things your servant Joab has done this thing. But my lord is wise, like the wisdom of the angel of God, to know all that is in the earth."

Absalom Is Recalled

21 ¶ Then the king said to Joab, "Behold now, I will surely do this thing; go therefore, bring back the young man Absalom."

22 Joab fell on his face to the ground, prostrated himself and blessed the king; then Joab said, "Today your servant knows that I have found favor in your sight, O my lord, the king, in that the king has performed the request of his servant."

23 So Joab arose and went to Geshur and brought Absalom to Jerusalem.

24 However the king said, "Let him turn to his own house, and let him not see my face." So Absalom turned to his own house and did not see the king's face.

25 ¶ Now in all Israel was no one as handsome as Absalom, so highly praised; from the sole of his foot to the crown of his head there was no defect in him.

26 When he cut the hair of his head (and it was at the end of every year that he cut *it*, for it was heavy on him so he cut it), he weighed the hair of his head at 200 shekels by the king's weight.

27 To Absalom there were born three sons, and one daughter whose name was Tamar; she was a woman of beautiful appearance.

a Lit *portion*

28 ¶ Now Absalom lived two full years in Jerusalem, and did not see the king's face.

29 Then Absalom sent for Joab, to send him to the king, but he would not come to him. So he sent again a second time, but he would not come.

30 Therefore he said to his servants, "See, Joab's *a*field is next to mine, and he has barley there; go and set it on fire." So Absalom's servants set the field on fire.

31 Then Joab arose, came to Absalom at his house and said to him, "Why have your servants set my *a*field on fire?"

32 Absalom answered Joab, "Behold, I sent for you, saying, 'Come here, that I may send you to the king, to say, "Why have I come from Geshur? It would be better for me still to be there." ' Now therefore, let me see the king's face, and if there is iniquity in me, let him put me to death."

33 So when Joab came to the king and told him, he called for Absalom. Thus he came to the king and prostrated himself on his face to the ground before the king, and the king kissed Absalom.

Absalom's Conspiracy

15 Now it came about after this that Absalom provided for himself a chariot and horses and fifty men as runners before him.

2 Absalom used to rise early and stand beside the way to the gate; and when any man had a suit to come to the king for judgment, Absalom would call to him and say, "From what city are you?" And he would say, "Your servant is from one of the tribes of Israel."

3 Then Absalom would say to him, "See, your

ABSALOM *All That Glitters*

HE WAS THE MOST HANDSOME man of his day, a royal prince with plenty of charisma thrown in for good measure. When people had needs, Absalom seemed to care: In this way he "stole away the hearts of the men of Israel" (15:6). We first meet him sheltering his sister after she had been raped (13:20). Two years later, Absalom got murderous revenge in defense of his sister's honor. Unlike his father David, he refused to let such a crime go unpunished.

Nevertheless, Absalom's glittering surface did not reveal a golden heart. As time went on it became clear that Absalom cared mainly for himself. Absalom was a tragic figure, a symbol of David's failures as a parent. For five years father and son did not speak to one another, and this simmering family feud only hardened Absalom further.

Absalom tended to act like a spoiled brat, whether getting Joab's attention by burning his barley field, or gaining the honor he thought he deserved by driving his own father out of town. Like many egotists, however, Absalom overestimated his strength and popularity.

During the bloody revolt one of David's advisers, pretending to have switched to Absalom's side, shrewdly advised a delay. David gained time to assemble his own seasoned fighters, who quickly put down Absalom's uprising. The king's son died as vainly as he had lived: While escaping on a mule, he caught his long, handsome hair in a tree and was killed by Joab and his men.

Life Questions: If someone is good-looking, gifted or naturally likable, how can such a person guard against egotism?

claims are good and right, but no man listens to you on the part of the king."

4 Moreover, Absalom would say, "Oh that one would appoint me judge in the land, then every man who has any suit or cause could come to me and I would give him justice."

5 And when a man came near to prostrate himself before him, he would put out his hand and take hold of him and kiss him.

6 In this manner Absalom dealt with all Israel who came to the king for judgment; so Absalom stole away the hearts of the men of Israel.

7 ¶ Now it came about at the end of *a*forty years that Absalom said to the king, "Please let me go and pay my vow which I have vowed to the LORD, in Hebron.

8 "For your servant vowed a vow while I was living at Geshur in Aram, saying, 'If the LORD shall indeed bring me back to Jerusalem, then I will serve the LORD.' "

9 The king said to him, "Go in peace." So he arose and went to Hebron.

10 But Absalom sent spies throughout all the tribes of Israel, saying, "As soon as you hear the sound of the trumpet, then you shall say, 'Absalom is king in Hebron.' "

11 Then two hundred men went with Absalom from Jerusalem, who were invited and went innocently, and they did not know anything.

12 And Absalom sent for Ahithophel the Gilonite, David's counselor, from his city Giloh, while he was offering the sacrifices. And the conspiracy was strong, for the people increased continually with Absalom.

David Flees Jerusalem

13 ¶ Then a messenger came to David, saying, "The hearts of the men of Israel are with Absalom."

14 David said to all his servants who were with him at Jerusalem, "Arise and let us flee, for *otherwise* none of us will escape from Absalom. Go in haste, or he will overtake us quickly and bring down calamity on us and strike the city with the edge of the sword."

15 Then the king's servants said to the king, "Behold, your servants *are ready to do* whatever my lord the king chooses."

16 So the king went out and all his household with him. But the king left ten concubines to keep the house.

17 The king went out and all the people with him, and they stopped at the last house.

18 Now all his servants passed on beside him, all the Cherethites, all the Pelethites and all the Gittites, six hundred men who had come with him from Gath, passed on before the king.

19 ¶ Then the king said to Ittai the Gittite, "Why will you also go with us? Return and remain with the king, for you are a foreigner and also an exile; *return* to your own place.

20 "You came *only* yesterday, and shall I today make you wander with us, while I go where I will? Return and take back your brothers; mercy and truth be with you."

21 But Ittai answered the king and said, "As the LORD lives, and as my lord the king lives, surely wherever my lord the king may be, whether for death or for life, there also your servant will be."

22 Therefore David said to Ittai, "Go and pass over." So Ittai the Gittite passed over with all his men and all the little ones who *were* with him.

15:22 Mercenaries

David's army included more than just loyal Israelites; he had added mercenaries (hired soldiers). The Gittites came from the Philistine city of Gath. David had probably recruited them during his stay there (1 Samuel 27:2), and they had loyally followed him ever since.

23 While all the country was weeping with a loud voice, all the people passed over. The king also passed over the brook Kidron, and all the people passed over toward the way of the wilderness.

24 ¶ Now behold, Zadok also *came,* and all the Levites with him carrying the ark of the covenant of God. And they set down the ark of God, and Abiathar came up until all the people had finished passing from the city.

25 The king said to Zadok, "Return the ark of God to the city. If I find favor in the sight of the LORD, then He will bring me back again and show me both it and His habitation.

26 "But if He should say thus, 'I have no delight in you,' behold, here I am, let Him do to me as seems good to Him."

27 The king said also to Zadok the priest, "Are you *not* a seer? Return to the city in peace and your two sons with you, your son Ahimaaz and Jonathan the son of Abiathar.

28 "See, I am going to wait at the fords of the wilderness until word comes from you to inform me."

29 Therefore Zadok and Abiathar returned the ark of God to Jerusalem and remained there.

30 ¶ And David went up the ascent of the *Mount of* Olives, and wept as he went, and his head was covered and he walked barefoot. Then all the people who were with him each covered his head and went up weeping as they went.

31 Now someone told David, saying, "Ahithophel is among the conspirators with Absalom." And David said, "O LORD, I pray, make the counsel of Ahithophel foolishness."

---

a Some ancient versions render *four*

32 ¶ It happened as David was coming to the summit, where God was worshiped, that behold, Hushai the Archite met him with his coat torn and dust on his head.

33 David said to him, "If you pass over with me, then you will be a burden to me.

34 "But if you return to the city, and say to Absalom, 'I will be your servant, O king; as I have been your father's servant in time past, so I will now be your servant,' then you can thwart the counsel of Ahithophel for me.

35 "Are not Zadok and Abiathar the priests with you there? So it shall be that whatever you hear from the king's house, you shall report to Zadok and Abiathar the priests.

36 "Behold their two sons are with them there, Ahimaaz, Zadok's son and Jonathan, Abiathar's son; and by them you shall send me everything that you hear."

37 So Hushai, David's friend, came into the city, and Absalom came into Jerusalem.

Ziba, a False Servant

16 Now when David had passed a little beyond the summit, behold, Ziba the servant of Mephibosheth met him with a couple of saddled donkeys, and on them *were* two hundred loaves of bread, a hundred clusters of raisins, a hundred summer fruits, and a jug of wine.

2 The king said to Ziba, "Why do you have these?" And Ziba said, "The donkeys are for the king's household to ride, and the bread and summer fruit for the young men to eat, and the wine, for whoever is faint in the wilderness to drink."

3 Then the king said, "And where is your master's son?" And Ziba said to the king, "Behold, he is staying in Jerusalem, for he said, 'Today the house of Israel will restore the kingdom of my father to me.' "

4 So the king said to Ziba, "Behold, all that belongs to Mephibosheth is yours." And Ziba said, "I prostrate myself; let me find favor in your sight, O my lord, the king!"

David Is Cursed

5 ¶ When King David came to Bahurim, behold, there came out from there a man of the family of the house of Saul whose name was Shimei, the son of Gera; he came out cursing continually as he came.

6 He threw stones at David and at all the servants of King David; and all the people and all the mighty men were at his right hand and at his left.

7 Thus Shimei said when he cursed, "Get out, get out, you man of bloodshed, and worthless fellow!

8 "The LORD has returned upon you all the bloodshed of the house of Saul, in whose place you have reigned; and the LORD has given the kingdom into the hand of your son Absalom. And behold, you are *taken* in your own evil, for you are a man of bloodshed!"

9 ¶ Then Abishai the son of Zeruiah said to the king, "Why should this dead dog curse my lord the king? Let me go over now and cut off his head."

10 But the king said, "What have I to do with you, O sons of Zeruiah? If he curses, and if the LORD has told him, 'Curse David,' then who shall say, 'Why have you done so?' "

11 Then David said to Abishai and to all his servants, "Behold, my son who came out from me seeks my life; how much more now this Benjamite? Let him alone and let him curse, for the LORD has told him.

12 "Perhaps the LORD will look on my affliction and return good to me instead of his cursing this day."

13 So David and his men went on the way; and Shimei went along on the hillside parallel with him and as he went he cursed and cast stones and threw dust at him.

14 The king and all the people who were with him arrived weary and he refreshed himself there.

Absalom Enters Jerusalem

15 ¶ Then Absalom and all the people, the men of Israel, entered Jerusalem, and Ahithophel with him.

16 Now it came about when Hushai the Archite, David's friend, came to Absalom, that Hushai said to Absalom, "*Long* live the king! *Long* live the king!"

17 Absalom said to Hushai, "Is this your loyalty to your friend? Why did you not go with your friend?"

18 Then Hushai said to Absalom, "No! For whom the LORD, this people, and all the men of Israel have chosen, his I will be, and with him I will remain.

19 "Besides, whom should I serve? *Should I* not *serve* in the presence of his son? As I have served in your father's presence, so I will be in your presence."

20 ¶ Then Absalom said to Ahithophel, "Give your advice. What shall we do?"

21 Ahithophel said to Absalom, "Go in to your father's concubines, whom he has left to keep the house; then all Israel will hear that you have made yourself odious to your father. The hands of all who are with you will also be strengthened."

22 So they pitched a tent for Absalom on the roof, and Absalom went in to his father's concubines in the sight of all Israel.

23 The advice of Ahithophel, which he gave in those days, *was* as if one inquired of the word of God; so was all the advice of Ahithophel *regarded* by both David and Absalom.

Hushai's Counsel

17 Furthermore, Ahithophel said to Absalom, "Please let me choose 12,000 men that I may arise and pursue David tonight.

16:22 No Way Back

Absalom publicly slept with his father's concubines for political reasons. It made clear his claim to the throne (see 3:6 for a similar case) and was extremely offensive to David. Israelites who had held back their allegiance, thinking that father and son would reconcile their differences, knew now that the breach was permanent. They had to take sides.

2 "I will come upon him while he is weary and exhausted and terrify him, so that all the people who are with him will flee. Then I will strike down the king alone,

3 and I will bring back all the people to you. The return of everyone depends on the man you seek; *then* all the people will be at peace."

4 So the plan pleased Absalom and all the elders of Israel.

5 ¶ Then Absalom said, "Now call Hushai the Archite also, and let us hear what he has to say."

6 When Hushai had come to Absalom, Absalom said to him, "Ahithophel has spoken thus. Shall we carry out his plan? If not, you speak."

7 So Hushai said to Absalom, "This time the advice that Ahithophel has given is not good."

8 Moreover, Hushai said, "You know your father and his men, that they are mighty men and they are fierce, like a bear robbed of her cubs in the field. And your father is an expert in warfare, and will not spend the night with the people.

9 "Behold, he has now hidden himself in one of the caves or in another place; and it will be when he falls on them at the first attack, that whoever hears *it* will say, 'There has been a slaughter among the people who follow Absalom.'

10 "And even the one who is valiant, whose heart is like the heart of a lion, will completely lose heart; for all Israel knows that your father is a mighty man and those who are with him are valiant men.

11 "But I counsel that all Israel be surely gathered to you, from Dan even to Beersheba, as the sand that is by the sea in abundance, and that you personally go into battle.

12 "So we shall come to him in one of the places where he can be found, and we will fall on him as the dew falls on the ground; and of him and of all the men who are with him, not even one will be left.

13 "If he withdraws into a city, then all Israel shall bring ropes to that city, and we will drag it into the valley until not even a small stone is found there."

14 Then Absalom and all the men of Israel said, "The counsel of Hushai the Archite is better than the counsel of Ahithophel." For the LORD had ordained to thwart the good counsel of Ahithophel, so that the LORD might bring calamity on Absalom.

Hushai's Warning Saves David

15 ¶ Then Hushai said to Zadok and to Abiathar the priests, "This is what Ahithophel counseled Absalom and the elders of Israel, and this is what I have counseled.

16 "Now therefore, send quickly and tell David, saying, 'Do not spend the night at the fords of the wilderness, but by all means cross over, or else the king and all the people who are with him will be destroyed.'"

17 Now Jonathan and Ahimaaz were staying at En-rogel, and a maidservant would go and tell them, and they would go and tell King David, for they could not be seen entering the city.

18 But a lad did see them and told Absalom; so the two of them departed quickly and came to the house of a man in Bahurim, who had a well in his courtyard, and they went down into it.

19 And the woman took a covering and spread it over the well's mouth and scattered grain on it, so that nothing was known.

20 Then Absalom's servants came to the woman at the house and said, "Where are Ahimaaz and Jonathan?" And the woman said to them, "They have crossed the brook of water." And when they searched and could not find *them,* they returned to Jerusalem.

17:11 Flattering Advice

Hushai, one of David's top advisers, slipped into Absalom's camp pretending to have deserted David. He deliberately gave bad advice, cleverly phrasing it to flatter Absalom. Hushai suggested that if Absalom delayed his pursuit of David, Absalom (who had never fought in battle) could gather a gigantic army to lead. Absalom fell for it, and the delay gave David enough time to consolidate his support.

21 ¶ It came about after they had departed that they came up out of the well and went and told King David; and they said to David, "Arise and cross over the water quickly for thus Ahithophel has counseled against you."

22 Then David and all the people who *were* with him arose and crossed the Jordan; and by dawn not even one remained who had not crossed the Jordan.

23 ¶ Now when Ahithophel saw that his counsel was not followed, he saddled *his* donkey and

arose and went to his home, to his city, and set his house in order, and strangled himself; thus he died and was buried in the grave of his father.

24 ¶ Then David came to Mahanaim. And Absalom crossed the Jordan, he and all the men of Israel with him.

25 Absalom set Amasa over the army in place of Joab. Now Amasa was the son of a man whose name was Ithra the Israelite, who went in to Abigail the daughter of Nahash, sister of Zeruiah, Joab's mother.

26 And Israel and Absalom camped in the land of Gilead.

27 ¶ Now when David had come to Mahanaim, Shobi the son of Nahash from Rabbah of the sons of Ammon, Machir the son of Ammiel from Lo-debar, and Barzillai the Gileadite from Rogelim,

28 brought beds, basins, pottery, wheat, barley, flour, parched *grain,* beans, lentils, parched *seeds,*

29 honey, curds, sheep, and cheese of the herd, for David and for the people who *were* with him, to eat; for they said, "The people are hungry and weary and thirsty in the wilderness."

Absalom Slain

18 Then David numbered the people who were with him and set over them commanders of thousands and commanders of hundreds.

2 David sent the people out, one third under the command of Joab, one third under the command of Abishai the son of Zeruiah, Joab's brother, and one third under the command of Ittai the Gittite. And the king said to the people, "I myself will surely go out with you also."

3 But the people said, "You should not go out; for if we indeed flee, they will not care about us; even if half of us die, they will not care about us. But you are worth ten thousand of us; therefore now it is better that you *be ready* to help us from the city."

4 Then the king said to them, "Whatever seems best to you I will do." So the king stood beside the gate, and all the people went out by hundreds and thousands.

5 The king charged Joab and Abishai and Ittai, saying, "*Deal* gently for my sake with the young man Absalom." And all the people heard when the king charged all the commanders concerning Absalom.

6 ¶ Then the people went out into the field against Israel, and the battle took place in the forest of Ephraim.

7 The people of Israel were defeated there before the servants of David, and the slaughter there that day was great, 20,000 men.

8 For the battle there was spread over the whole countryside, and the forest devoured more people that day than the sword devoured.

9 ¶ Now Absalom happened to meet the servants of David. For Absalom was riding on *his* mule, and the mule went under the thick branches of a great oak. And his head caught fast in the oak, so he was left hanging between heaven and earth, while the mule that was under him kept going.

10 When a certain man saw *it,* he told Joab and said, "Behold, I saw Absalom hanging in an oak."

11 Then Joab said to the man who had told him, "Now behold, you saw *him!* Why then did you not strike him there to the ground? And I would have given you ten *pieces* of silver and a belt."

12 The man said to Joab, "Even if I should receive a thousand *pieces of* silver in my hand, I would not put out my hand against the king's son; for in our hearing the king charged you and Abishai and Ittai, saying, 'Protect for me the young man Absalom!'

13 "Otherwise, if I had dealt treacherously against his life (and there is nothing hidden from the king), then you yourself would have stood aloof."

14 Then Joab said, "I will not waste time here with you." So he took three spears in his hand and thrust them through the heart of Absalom while he was yet alive in the midst of the oak.

15 And ten young men who carried Joab's armor gathered around and struck Absalom and killed him.

16 ¶ Then Joab blew the trumpet, and the people returned from pursuing Israel, for Joab restrained the people.

17 They took Absalom and cast him into a deep pit in the forest and erected over him a very great heap of stones. And all Israel fled, each to his tent.

18 Now Absalom in his lifetime had taken and set up for himself a pillar which is in the King's Valley, for he said, "I have no son to preserve my name." So he named the pillar after his own name, and it is called Absalom's Monument to this day.

David Is Grief-stricken

19 ¶ Then Ahimaaz the son of Zadok said, "Please let me run and bring the king news that the LORD has freed him from the hand of his enemies."

20 But Joab said to him, "You are not the man to carry news this day, but you shall carry news another day; however, you shall carry no news today because the king's son is dead."

21 Then Joab said to the Cushite, "Go, tell the king what you have seen." So the Cushite bowed to Joab and ran.

22 Now Ahimaaz the son of Zadok said once more to Joab, "But whatever happens, please let me also run after the Cushite." And Joab said, "Why would you run, my son, since you will have no reward for going?"

23 "But whatever happens," *he said,* "I will run." So he said to him, "Run." Then Ahimaaz ran by way of the plain and passed up the Cushite.

Sin As a Cancer
First David, then his family, then a nation

SINS: MANY PEOPLE THINK OF them as parking tickets. If you get too many, the cops may track you down or give your car "the boot." However, one or two here and there won't make a big difference.

The Bible views sins more as cancer cells. One or two here and there do make a difference— often the difference between life and death. Because cancer cells grow, multiply, and take over, major surgery may be needed to save your life.

> "O my son Absalom, my son, my son Absalom! Would I had died instead of you, O Absalom, my son, my son!"
> 18:33

Second Samuel 11–20 reads like a history of a spreading cancer. In the beginning, David was on top of the world—and so was Israel. The civil war was over, the land was at peace, and Israel was entering an era of unprecedented prosperity. God had promised to ensure David's descendants a continuous reign forever. What more could David hope for? The rest of life appeared as one long celebration.

The Cancer Grows

That celebration never began. One night David caught a glimpse of Bathsheba's beautiful, naked body and impulsively sent for her. The cover-up required a murder. Nobody could deny it was an ugly business: Even David admitted it when Nathan confronted him. However, it was soon over. He repented. He married Bathsheba. He did not intend to fall to that temptation again.

But the consequences of the sin were far from over. Unknown to David, cancer was growing in his own household. David's oldest son Amnon had an eye for women too. He tricked his half sister Tamar into his bedroom, then raped her. Afterwards, filled with disgust, he threw her out.

David was furious. But, maybe because he felt his own sin had robbed him of moral authority, he did nothing to punish his son. According to the law (Leviticus 18:9,29), Amnon deserved exile, but he got off free. David apparently wanted the matter forgotten.

A Cold-blooded Character

It merely disappeared from view. Absalom waited two full years to avenge his sister's rape. Then he murdered Amnon in cold blood. Again David was long on regret, short on punishment. He wept over Amnon's death but perhaps recognized his own responsibility for it. After three years David let Absalom return to Jerusalem unpunished; two years later, when Absalom angrily demanded either a murder trial or full acceptance back into the palace (14:32), David kissed and made up completely.

Again the cancer disappeared from view. But it was not gone; it grew. Now an arrogant Absalom started a program of public relations designed to make him look better than his aging father. At the end of four years, having become quite popular, he set his coup in motion. Taken completely by surprise, David was driven out of Jerusalem, into the desert.

The shock seemed to awaken David. Though dazed and weeping as he left the city, he had enough sense to make some clever plans. When the battle came at last, David's army won, and Absalom was captured and killed.

Weeping for His Son

For David the king, Absalom's defeat was a great triumph. For David the father, it was a horrible tragedy. The worst thing that can happen to a father had happened to him. His own son had tried to kill him, and in trying, had been killed. David could not stop weeping over his son's death until Joab, his general, warned him that he was insulting the troops who had fought for him.

David pulled himself together. Piece by piece, he put his kingdom back in order. He sent conciliatory words to the rebellious leaders of his own tribe. He rewarded his supporters. He took no revenge on any rebel faction, but showed remarkable fairness. A second rebellion broke out but was soon put down. The cancer seemed finally to have run its course.

Yet it had not. David had no more trouble with rebellion in his lifetime, but after his death Solomon killed a brother who he thought was scheming for the throne (1 Kings 2:25). After Solomon's reign, the old tribal tensions rose again, and the North and the South, which David had so carefully knit together, split for good (1 Kings 12). Such may be the consequences when a leader sins. His cancer not only poisons him; it grows to affect all those he leads—and it undermines his work.

Life Questions: Many people will, at some point, see their well-run lives disintegrate. What enables someone to pick up the pieces, as David did?

24 ¶ Now David was sitting between the two gates; and the watchman went up to the roof of the gate by the wall, and raised his eyes and looked, and behold, a man running by himself.

25 The watchman called and told the king. And the king said, "If he is by himself there is good news in his mouth." And he came nearer and nearer.

26 Then the watchman saw another man running; and the watchman called to the gatekeeper and said, "Behold, *another* man running by himself." And the king said, "This one also is bringing good news."

27 The watchman said, "I think the running of the first one is like the running of Ahimaaz the son of Zadok." And the king said, "This is a good man and comes with good news."

28 ¶ Ahimaaz called and said to the king, "ᵃAll is well." And he prostrated himself before the king with his face to the ground. And he said, "Blessed is the LORD your God, who has delivered up the men who lifted their hands against my lord the king."

29 The king said, "Is it well with the young man Absalom?" And Ahimaaz answered, "When Joab sent the king's servant, and your servant, I saw a great tumult, but I did not know what *it was.*"

30 Then the king said, "Turn aside and stand here." So he turned aside and stood still.

31 ¶ Behold, the Cushite arrived, and the Cushite said, "Let my lord the king receive good news, for the LORD has freed you this day from the hand of all those who rose up against you."

32 Then the king said to the Cushite, "Is it well with the young man Absalom?" And the Cushite answered, "Let the enemies of my lord the king, and all who rise up against you for evil, be as that young man!"

33 ¶ The king was deeply moved and went up to the chamber over the gate and wept. And thus he said as he walked, "O my son Absalom, my son, my son Absalom! Would I had died instead of you, O Absalom, my son, my son!"

18:33 Absalom, Absalom!

David's cry is one of the most poignant in all literature. Yet here again, David's love for his children collided with his effectiveness as a leader. He wept so excessively over Absalom that it demoralized the troops who had just risked their necks for the king (19:3).

Joab Reproves David's Lament

19 Then it was told Joab, "Behold, the king is weeping and mourns for Absalom."

2 The victory that day was turned to mourning for all the people, for the people heard *it* said that day, "The king is grieved for his son."

3 So the people went by stealth into the city that day, as people who are humiliated steal away when they flee in battle.

4 The king covered his face and cried out with a loud voice, "O my son Absalom, O Absalom, my son, my son!"

5 Then Joab came into the house to the king and said, "Today you have covered with shame the faces of all your servants, who today have saved your life and the lives of your sons and daughters, the lives of your wives, and the lives of your concubines,

6 by loving those who hate you, and by hating those who love you. For you have shown today that princes and servants are nothing to you; for I know this day that if Absalom were alive and all of us were dead today, then you would be pleased.

7 "Now therefore arise, go out and speak kindly to your servants, for I swear by the LORD, if you do not go out, surely not a man will pass the night with you, and this will be worse for you than all the evil that has come upon you from your youth until now."

David Restored as King

8 So the king arose and sat in the gate. When they told all the people, saying, "Behold, the king is sitting in the gate," then all the people came before the king.

¶ Now Israel had fled, each to his tent.

9 All the people were quarreling throughout all the tribes of Israel, saying, "The king delivered us from the hand of our enemies and saved us from the hand of the Philistines, but now he has fled out of the land from Absalom.

10 "However, Absalom, whom we anointed over us, has died in battle. Now then, why are you silent about bringing the king back?"

11 ¶ Then King David sent to Zadok and Abiathar the priests, saying, "Speak to the elders of Judah, saying, 'Why are you the last to bring the king back to his house, since the word of all Israel has come to the king, *even* to his house?

12 'You are my brothers; you are my bone and my flesh. Why then should you be the last to bring back the king?'

13 "Say to Amasa, 'Are you not my bone and my flesh? May God do so to me, and more also, if you will not be commander of the army before me continually in place of Joab.'"

14 Thus he turned the hearts of all the men of Judah as one man, so that they sent *word* to the king, *saying,* "Return, you and all your servants."

15 The king then returned and came as far as the Jordan. And Judah came to Gilgal in order to go to meet the king, to bring the king across the Jordan.

ᵃ Lit *Peace*

16 ¶ Then Shimei the son of Gera, the Benjamite who was from Bahurim, hurried and came down with the men of Judah to meet King David.

17 There were a thousand men of Benjamin with him, with Ziba the servant of the house of Saul, and his fifteen sons and his twenty servants with him; and they rushed to the Jordan before the king.

18 Then they kept crossing the ford to bring over the king's household, and to do what was good in his sight. And Shimei the son of Gera fell down before the king as he was about to cross the Jordan.

19 So he said to the king, "Let not my lord consider me guilty, nor remember what your servant did wrong on the day when my lord the king came out from Jerusalem, so that the king would take *it* to heart.

20 "For your servant knows that I have sinned; therefore behold, I have come today, the first of all the house of Joseph to go down to meet my lord the king."

21 But Abishai the son of Zeruiah said, "Should not Shimei be put to death for this, because he cursed the LORD's anointed?"

22 David then said, "What have I to do with you, O sons of Zeruiah, that you should this day be an adversary to me? Should any man be put to death in Israel today? For do I not know that I am king over Israel today?"

23 The king said to Shimei, "You shall not die." Thus the king swore to him.

24 ¶ Then Mephibosheth the ᵃson of Saul came down to meet the king; and he had neither cared for his feet, nor trimmed his mustache, nor washed his clothes, from the day the king departed until the day he came *home* in peace.

25 It was when he came from Jerusalem to meet the king, that the king said to him, "Why did you not go with me, Mephibosheth?"

26 So he answered, "O my lord, the king, my servant deceived me; for your servant said, 'I will saddle a donkey for myself that I may ride on it and go with the king,' because your servant is lame.

27 "Moreover, he has slandered your servant to my lord the king; but my lord the king is like the angel of God, therefore do what is good in your sight.

28 "For all my father's household was nothing but dead men before my lord the king; yet you set your servant among those who ate at your own table. What right do I have yet that I should complain anymore to the king?"

29 So the king said to him, "Why do you still speak of your affairs? I have decided, 'You and Ziba shall divide the land.'"

30 Mephibosheth said to the king, "Let him even take it all, since my lord the king has come safely to his own house."

31 ¶ Now Barzillai the Gileadite had come down from Rogelim; and he went on to the Jordan with the king to escort him over the Jordan.

32 Now Barzillai was very old, being eighty years old; and he had sustained the king while he stayed at Mahanaim, for he was a very great man.

33 The king said to Barzillai, "You cross over with me and I will sustain you in Jerusalem with me."

34 But Barzillai said to the king, "How long have I yet to live, that I should go up with the king to Jerusalem?

35 "I am now eighty years old. Can I distinguish between good and bad? Or can your servant taste what I eat or what I drink? Or can I hear anymore the voice of singing men and women? Why then should your servant be an added burden to my lord the king?

36 "Your servant would merely cross over the Jordan with the king. Why should the king compensate me *with* this reward?

37 "Please let your servant return, that I may die in my own city near the grave of my father and my mother. However, here is your servant Chimham, let him cross over with my lord the king, and do for him what is good in your sight."

38 The king answered, "Chimham shall cross over with me, and I will do for him what is good in your sight; and whatever you require of me, I will do for you."

39 All the people crossed over the Jordan and the king crossed too. The king then kissed Barzillai and blessed him, and he returned to his place.

40 ¶ Now the king went on to Gilgal, and Chimham went on with him; and all the people of Judah and also half the people of Israel accompanied the king.

41 And behold, all the men of Israel came to

19:24 The "Traitor's" Story

Mephibosheth's servant Ziba had told David that Mephibosheth was a traitor with dreams that he, as Saul's grandson, would be made king (16:1–4). Hearing this, David had given Ziba all of Mephibosheth's property.

Now we hear Mephibosheth's side of the story. He claimed that Ziba had betrayed him, presumably by taking his donkey so he, a cripple, could not follow David. More convincing than his words was his appearance. He had not washed himself or trimmed his mustache. He looked as though he had been mourning, not grooming himself for the throne.

Did David believe him? Perhaps not completely. He ordered Ziba to give back half, but not all, of the property.

ᵃ I.e. grandson

the king and said to the king, "Why had our brothers the men of Judah stolen you away, and brought the king and his household and all David's men with him over the Jordan?"

42 Then all the men of Judah answered the men of Israel, "Because the king is a close relative to us. Why then are you angry about this matter? Have we eaten at all at the king's *expense,* or has anything been taken for us?"

43 But the men of Israel answered the men of Judah and said, "We have ten parts in the king, therefore we also have more *claim* on David than you. Why then did you treat us with contempt? Was it not our advice first to bring back our king?" Yet the words of the men of Judah were harsher than the words of the men of Israel.

Sheba's Revolt

20 Now a worthless fellow happened to be there whose name was Sheba, the son of Bichri, a Benjamite; and he blew the trumpet and said,

"We have no portion in David,
 Nor do we have inheritance in the son of
   Jesse;
 Every man to his tents, O Israel!"

2 So all the men of Israel withdrew from following David *and* followed Sheba the son of Bichri; but the men of Judah remained steadfast to their king, from the Jordan even to Jerusalem.

20:2 North Versus South

Ethnic tension crackled between North ("Israel") and South ("Judah"). Saul came from the tribe of Benjamin in the north; David was a southerner. David worked hard to heal these divisions, but this rebellion shows that many in the north remained dissatisfied. David and his son Solomon managed to keep the two regions together, but after Solomon's death they broke apart for good.

3 ¶ Then David came to his house at Jerusalem, and the king took the ten women, the concubines whom he had left to keep the house, and placed them under guard and provided them with sustenance, but did not go in to them. So they were shut up until the day of their death, living as widows.

4 ¶ Then the king said to Amasa, "Call out the men of Judah for me within three days, and be present here yourself."

5 So Amasa went to call out *the men of* Judah, but he delayed longer than the set time which he had appointed him.

6 And David said to Abishai, "Now Sheba the son of Bichri will do us more harm than Absalom; take your lord's servants and pursue him, so that he does not find for himself fortified cities and escape from our sight."

7 So Joab's men went out after him, along with the Cherethites and the Pelethites and all the mighty men; and they went out from Jerusalem to pursue Sheba the son of Bichri.

8 When they were at the large stone which is in Gibeon, Amasa came to meet them. Now Joab was dressed in his military attire, and over it was a belt with a sword in its sheath fastened at his waist; and as he went forward, it fell out.

9 Joab said to Amasa, "Is it well with you, my brother?" And Joab took Amasa by the beard with his right hand to kiss him.

Amasa Murdered

10 But Amasa was not on guard against the sword which was in Joab's hand so he struck him in the belly with it and poured out his inward parts on the ground, and did not *strike* him again, and he died. Then Joab and Abishai his brother pursued Sheba the son of Bichri.

11 Now there stood by him one of Joab's young men, and said, "Whoever favors Joab and whoever is for David, *let him* follow Joab."

12 But Amasa lay wallowing in *his* blood in the middle of the highway. And when the man saw that all the people stood still, he removed Amasa from the highway into the field and threw a garment over him when he saw that everyone who came by him stood still.

Revolt Put Down

13 As soon as he was removed from the highway, all the men passed on after Joab to pursue Sheba the son of Bichri.

14 ¶ Now he went through all the tribes of Israel to Abel, even Beth-maacah, and all the Berites; and they were gathered together and also went after him.

15 They came and besieged him in Abel Bethmaacah, and they cast up a siege ramp against the city, and it stood by the rampart; and all the people who were with Joab were wreaking destruction in order to topple the wall.

16 Then a wise woman called from the city, "Hear, hear! Please tell Joab, 'Come here that I may speak with you.'"

17 So he approached her, and the woman said, "Are you Joab?" And he answered, "I am." Then she said to him, "Listen to the words of your maidservant." And he answered, "I am listening."

18 Then she spoke, saying, "Formerly they used to say, 'They will surely ask *advice* at Abel,' and thus they ended *the dispute.*

19 "I am of those who are peaceable *and* faithful in Israel. You are seeking to destroy a city, even a mother in Israel. Why would you swallow up the inheritance of the LORD?"

20 Joab replied, "Far be it, far be it from me that I should swallow up or destroy!

21 "Such is not the case. But a man from the hill country of Ephraim, Sheba the son of Bichri by name, has lifted up his hand against King David. Only hand him over, and I will depart from the city." And the woman said to Joab, "Behold, his head will be thrown to you over the wall."

22 Then the woman wisely came to all the people. And they cut off the head of Sheba the son of Bichri and threw it to Joab. So he blew the trumpet, and they were dispersed from the city, each to his tent. Joab also returned to the king at Jerusalem.

23 ¶ Now Joab was over the whole army of Israel, and Benaiah the son of Jehoiada was over the Cherethites and the Pelethites;

24 and Adoram was over the forced labor, and Jehoshaphat the son of Ahilud was the recorder;

25 and Sheva was scribe, and Zadok and Abiathar were priests;

26 and Ira the Jairite was also a priest to David.

Gibeonite Revenge

21 Now there was a famine in the days of David for three years, year after year; and David sought the presence of the LORD. And the LORD said, "It is for Saul and his bloody house, because he put the Gibeonites to death."

2 So the king called the Gibeonites and spoke to them (now the Gibeonites were not of the sons of Israel but of the remnant of the Amorites, and the sons of Israel made a covenant with them, but Saul had sought to kill them in his zeal for the sons of Israel and Judah).

3 Thus David said to the Gibeonites, "What should I do for you? And how can I make atonement that you may bless the inheritance of the LORD?"

4 Then the Gibeonites said to him, "We have no *concern* of silver or gold with Saul or his house, nor is it for us to put any man to death in Israel." And he said, "I will do for you whatever you say."

5 So they said to the king, "The man who consumed us and who planned to exterminate us from remaining within any border of Israel,

6 let seven men from his sons be given to us, and we will hang them before the LORD in Gibeah of Saul, the chosen of the LORD." And the king said, "I will give *them*."

7 ¶ But the king spared Mephibosheth, the son of Jonathan the son of Saul, because of the oath of the LORD which was between them, between David and Saul's son Jonathan.

8 So the king took the two sons of Rizpah the daughter of Aiah, Armoni and Mephibosheth whom she had borne to Saul, and the five sons of Merab the daughter of Saul, whom she had borne to Adriel the son of Barzillai the Meholathite.

9 Then he gave them into the hands of the Gibeonites, and they hanged them in the mountain before the LORD, so that the seven of them fell together; and they were put to death in the first days of harvest at the beginning of barley harvest.

10 ¶ And Rizpah the daughter of Aiah took sackcloth and spread it for herself on the rock, from the beginning of harvest until it rained on

21:6 Needless Deaths

Is there any excuse for David's agreeing to the execution of Saul's descendants? Perhaps. One must remember that David had certain legal responsibilities as king of Israel. Having offered compensation to the Gibeonites for their mistreatment under Saul, he may have been under legal obligation to cooperate with their demand for blood. In Old Testament times, a family was considered responsible for the crimes of any individual in his family. By modern standards, however, these executions seem needless and cruel.

them from the sky; and she allowed neither the birds of the sky to rest on them by day nor the beasts of the field by night.

11 When it was told David what Rizpah the daughter of Aiah, the concubine of Saul, had done,

12 then David went and took the bones of Saul and the bones of Jonathan his son from the men of Jabesh-gilead, who had stolen them from the open square of Beth-shan, where the Philistines had hanged them on the day the Philistines struck down Saul in Gilboa.

13 He brought up the bones of Saul and the bones of Jonathan his son from there, and they gathered the bones of those who had been hanged.

14 They buried the bones of Saul and Jonathan his son in the country of Benjamin in Zela, in the grave of Kish his father; thus they did all that the king commanded, and after that God was moved by prayer for the land.

15 ¶ Now when the Philistines were at war again with Israel, David went down and his servants with him; and as they fought against the Philistines, David became weary.

16 Then Ishbi-benob, who was among the descendants of the giant, the weight of whose spear was three hundred *shekels* of bronze in weight, was girded with a new *sword*, and he intended to kill David.

17 But Abishai the son of Zeruiah helped him, and struck the Philistine and killed him. Then the men of David swore to him, saying, "You shall not go out again with us to battle, so that you do not extinguish the lamp of Israel."

18 ¶ Now it came about after this that there was war again with the Philistines at Gob; then Sibbecai the Hushathite struck down Saph, who was among the descendants of the giant.

19 There was war with the Philistines again at Gob, and Elhanan the son of Jaare-oregim the

Bethlehemite killed Goliath the Gittite, the shaft of whose spear was like a weaver's beam.

20 There was war at Gath again, where there was a man of *great* stature who had six fingers on each hand and six toes on each foot, twenty-four in number; and he also had been born to the giant.

21 When he defied Israel, Jonathan the son of Shimei, David's brother, struck him down.

22 These four were born to the giant in Gath, and they fell by the hand of David and by the hand of his servants.

David's Psalm of Deliverance

22 And David spoke the words of this song to the LORD in the day that the LORD delivered him from the hand of all his enemies and from the hand of Saul.

22:1 David's Psalms

This song of praise was included in the book of Psalms as Psalm 18. Many psalms are credited to David, and some have titles suggesting the events that inspired them. You can read these as a spiritual and emotional commentary on key events in David's life:

Psalm 3. *When he fled from his son Absalom (2 Samuel 15:13)*

Psalm 18. *When the Lord delivered him from his enemies and Saul (1 Samuel 19–31)*

Psalm 51. *After Nathan confronted David over Bathsheba (2 Samuel 12)*

Psalm 52. *When Doeg turned in the high priest for helping David (1 Samuel 22:9–10)*

Psalm 54. *When the Ziphites told Saul that David was hiding in their territory (1 Samuel 23:19–20; 26:1–25)*

Psalm 56. *When the Philistines seized David in Gath (1 Samuel 21:10–15)*

Psalm 57. *When David fled from Saul into the cave (1 Samuel 22:1–2)*

Psalm 59. *When Saul sent men to watch David's house in order to kill him (1 Samuel 19:11)*

Psalm 60. *After an important battle*

Psalm 63. *When he was in the Desert of Judah*

Psalm 142. *When he was in the cave, hiding from Saul*

---

2 He said,
"The LORD is my rock and my fortress
    and my deliverer;
3 My God, my rock, in whom I take
    refuge,
My shield and the horn of my salvation,
    my stronghold and my refuge;
My savior, You save me from violence.
4 "I call upon the LORD, who is worthy to
    be praised,
And I am saved from my enemies.
5 "For the waves of death encompassed me;

The torrents of destruction
    overwhelmed me;
6 The cords of Sheol surrounded me;
The snares of death confronted me.
7 "In my distress I called upon the LORD,
Yes, I cried to my God;
And from His temple He heard my
    voice,
And my cry for help *came* into His ears.
8 "Then the earth shook and quaked,
The foundations of heaven were
    trembling
And were shaken, because He was angry.
9 "Smoke went up out of His nostrils,
Fire from His mouth devoured;
Coals were kindled by it.
10 "He bowed the heavens also, and came
    down
With thick darkness under His feet.
11 "And He rode on a cherub and flew;
And He appeared on the wings of the
    wind.
12 "And He made darkness canopies around
    Him,
A mass of waters, thick clouds of the sky.
13 "From the brightness before Him
Coals of fire were kindled.
14 "The LORD thundered from heaven,
And the Most High uttered His voice.
15 "And He sent out arrows, and scattered
    them,
Lightning, and routed them.
16 "Then the channels of the sea appeared,
The foundations of the world were laid
    bare
By the rebuke of the LORD,
At the blast of the breath of His nostrils.
17 "He sent from on high, He took me;
He drew me out of many waters.
18 "He delivered me from my strong enemy,
From those who hated me, for they were
    too strong for me.
19 "They confronted me in the day of my
    calamity,
But the LORD was my support.
20 "He also brought me forth into a broad
    place;
He rescued me, because He delighted
    in me.
21 "The LORD has rewarded me according to
    my righteousness;
According to the cleanness of my hands
He has recompensed me.
22 "For I have kept the ways of the LORD,
And have not acted wickedly against my
    God.
23 "For all His ordinances *were* before me,
And *as for* His statutes, I did not depart
    from them.
24 "I was also blameless toward Him,
And I kept myself from my iniquity.

25 "Therefore the LORD has recompensed me
according to my righteousness,
According to my cleanness before His
eyes.
26 "With the kind You show Yourself kind,
With the blameless You show Yourself
blameless;
27 With the pure You show Yourself pure,
And with the perverted You show
Yourself astute.
28 "And You save an afflicted people;
But Your eyes are on the haughty *whom*
You abase.
29 "For You are my lamp, O LORD;
And the LORD illumines my darkness.
30 "For by You I can *a*run upon a troop;
By my God I can leap over a wall.
31 "As for God, His way is blameless;
The word of the LORD is tested;
He is a shield to all who take refuge in
Him.
32 "For who is God, besides the LORD?
And who is a rock, besides our God?
33 "God is my strong fortress;
And He sets the blameless in His way.
34 "He makes my feet like hinds' *feet*,
And sets me on my high places.
35 "He trains my hands for battle,
So that my arms can bend a bow of
bronze.
36 "You have also given me the shield of
Your salvation,
And Your help makes me great.
37 "You enlarge my steps under me,
And my feet have not slipped.
38 "I pursued my enemies and destroyed
them,
And I did not turn back until they were
consumed.
39 "And I have devoured them and shattered
them, so that they did not rise;
And they fell under my feet.
40 "For You have girded me with strength
for battle;
You have subdued under me those who
rose up against me.
41 "You have also made my enemies turn
their backs to me,
And I destroyed those who hated me.
42 "They looked, but there was none to save;
Even to the LORD, but He did not answer
them.
43 "Then I pulverized them as the dust of
the earth;
I crushed *and* stamped them as the mire
of the streets.
44 "You have also delivered me from the
contentions of my people;
You have kept me as head of the nations;

A people whom I have not known
serve me.
45 "Foreigners pretend obedience to me;
As soon as they hear, they obey me.
46 "Foreigners lose heart,
And come trembling out of their
fortresses.
47 "The LORD lives, and blessed be my rock;
And exalted be God, the rock of my
salvation,
48 The God who executes vengeance for me,
And brings down peoples under me,
49 Who also brings me out from my
enemies;
You even lift me above those who rise up
against me;
You rescue me from the violent man.
50 "Therefore I will give thanks to You,
O LORD, among the nations,
And I will sing praises to Your name.
51 "*He* is a tower of *b*deliverance to His
king,
And shows lovingkindness to His
anointed,
To David and his descendants forever."

David's Last Song

23 Now these are the last words of David.
David the son of Jesse declares,
The man who was raised on high
declares,
The anointed of the God of Jacob,
And the sweet psalmist of Israel,

23:1 Final Words

People hold on to a loved one's last words, for they sometimes sum up his or her life. This, David's final poem, shows David's deep concern to be a king who pleases God. He insists that a leader in tune with God will always be a blessing to God's people, and recalls God's promise that his descendants will always rule. A memorial to David's "mighty men" follows this psalm, honoring those who fought alongside him with unusual courage. Uriah the Hittite, whom David had murdered, makes the list. The vindictive Joab does not.

2 "The Spirit of the LORD spoke by me,
And His word was on my tongue.
3 "The God of Israel said,
The Rock of Israel spoke to me,
'He who rules over men righteously,
Who rules in the fear of God,
4 Is as the light of the morning *when* the
sun rises,
A morning without clouds,

*a*Or *crush a troop*   *b*I.e. victories; lit *salvation*

When the tender grass *springs* out of the
earth,
Through sunshine after rain.'
5 "Truly is not my house so with God?
For He has made an everlasting covenant
with me,
Ordered in all things, and secured;
For all my salvation and all *my* desire,
Will He not indeed make *it* grow?
6 "But the worthless, every one of them will
be thrust away like thorns,
Because they cannot be taken in hand;
7 But the man who touches them
Must be armed with iron and the shaft of
a spear,
And they will be completely burned with
fire in *their* place."

His Mighty Men

8 ¶ These are the names of the mighty men
whom David had: Josheb-basshebeth a Tah-
chemonite, chief of the captains, he was *called*
Adino the Eznite, because of eight hundred slain
by him at one time;

9 and after him was Eleazar the son of Dodo
the Ahohite, one of the three mighty men with
David when they defied the Philistines who were
gathered there to battle and the men of Israel had
withdrawn.

10 He arose and struck the Philistines until his
hand was weary and clung to the sword, and the
LORD brought about a great victory that day; and
the people returned after him only to strip *the
slain.*

11 ¶ Now after him was Shammah the son of
Agee a Hararite. And the Philistines were gathered
into a troop where there was a plot of ground full
of lentils, and the people fled from the Philistines.

12 But he took his stand in the midst of the
plot, defended it and struck the Philistines; and
the LORD brought about a great victory.

13 ¶ Then three of the thirty chief men went
down and came to David in the harvest time to the
cave of Adullam, while the troop of the Philistines
was camping in the valley of Rephaim.

14 David was then in the stronghold, while the
garrison of the Philistines was then in Bethlehem.

15 David had a craving and said, "Oh that
someone would give me water to drink from the
well of Bethlehem which is by the gate!"

16 So the three mighty men broke through the
camp of the Philistines, and drew water from the
well of Bethlehem which was by the gate, and took
it and brought *it* to David. Nevertheless he would
not drink it, but poured it out to the LORD;

17 and he said, "Be it far from me, O LORD,
that I should do this. *Shall I drink* the blood of the
men who went in *jeopardy* of their lives?" Therefore he would not drink it. These things the three
mighty men did.

18 ¶ Abishai, the brother of Joab, the son of

Zeruiah, was chief of the thirty. And he swung his
spear against three hundred and killed *them,* and
had a name as well as the three.

19 He was most honored of the thirty, therefore he became their commander; however, he did
not attain to the three.

20 ¶ Then Benaiah the son of Jehoiada, the son
of a valiant man of Kabzeel, who had done mighty
deeds, killed the two *sons of* Ariel of Moab. He also
went down and killed a lion in the middle of a pit
on a snowy day.

21 He killed an Egyptian, an impressive man.
Now the Egyptian *had* a spear in his hand, but he
went down to him with a club and snatched the
spear from the Egyptian's hand and killed him
with his own spear.

22 These *things* Benaiah the son of Jehoiada
did, and had a name as well as the three mighty
men.

23 He was honored among the thirty, but he
did not attain to the three. And David appointed
him over his guard.

24 ¶ Asahel the brother of Joab was among the
thirty; Elhanan the son of Dodo of Bethlehem,

25 Shammah the Harodite, Elika the Harodite,

26 Helez the Paltite, Ira the son of Ikkesh the
Tekoite,

27 Abiezer the Anathothite, Mebunnai the Hushathite,

28 Zalmon the Ahohite, Maharai the Netophathite,

29 Heleb the son of Baanah the Netophathite,
Ittai the son of Ribai of Gibeah of the sons of
Benjamin,

30 Benaiah a Pirathonite, Hiddai of the brooks
of Gaash,

31 Abi-albon the Arbathite, Azmaveth the Bar-
humite,

32 Eliahba the Shaalbonite, the sons of Jashen,
Jonathan,

33 Shammah the Hararite, Ahiam the son of
Sharar the Ararite,

34 Eliphelet the son of Ahasbai, the son of the
Maacathite, Eliam the son of Ahithophel the Gilonite,

35 Hezro the Carmelite, Paarai the Arbite,

36 Igal the son of Nathan of Zobah, Bani the
Gadite,

37 Zelek the Ammonite, Naharai the Beerothite, armor bearers of Joab the son of Zeruiah,

38 Ira the Ithrite, Gareb the Ithrite,

39 Uriah the Hittite; thirty-seven in all.

The Census Taken

24 Now again the anger of the LORD burned
against Israel, and it incited David against
them to say, "Go, number Israel and Judah."

2 The king said to Joab the commander of the
army who was with him, "Go about now through
all the tribes of Israel, from Dan to Beersheba, and

register the people, that I may know the number of the people."

3 But Joab said to the king, "Now may the LORD your God add to the people a hundred times

24:1 Satan or the Lord?

In a parallel account, 1 Chronicles 21:1 says that Satan moved David to take a census. Who was it—Satan or the Lord? One explanation is that both are true. The Lord, as the ultimate power, allowed the census, and as is typical in the Old Testament, he gets full credit here. The Chronicles version is more concerned about being precise: Because the census was clearly evil (David confessed it as a sin, verse 10), Satan was more directly responsible. As is so often true of evil, people (and Satan) meant it for evil, but God used it for his own purposes.

as many as they are, while the eyes of my lord the king *still* see; but why does my lord the king delight in this thing?"

4 Nevertheless, the king's word prevailed against Joab and against the commanders of the army. So Joab and the commanders of the army went out from the presence of the king to register the people of Israel.

5 They crossed the Jordan and camped in Aroer, on the right side of the city that is in the middle of the valley of Gad and toward Jazer.

6 Then they came to Gilead and to *a*the land of Tahtim-hodshi, and they came to Dan-jaan and around to Sidon,

7 and came to the fortress of Tyre and to all the cities of the Hivites and of the Canaanites, and they went out to the south of Judah, *to* Beersheba.

8 So when they had gone about through the whole land, they came to Jerusalem at the end of nine months and twenty days.

9 And Joab gave the number of the registration of the people to the king; and there were in Israel eight hundred thousand valiant men who drew the sword, and the men of Judah were five hundred thousand men.

10 ¶ Now David's heart troubled him after he had numbered the people. So David said to the LORD, "I have sinned greatly in what I have done. But now, O LORD, please take away the iniquity of Your servant, for I have acted very foolishly."

11 When David arose in the morning, the word of the LORD came to the prophet Gad, David's seer, saying,

12 "Go and speak to David, 'Thus the LORD says, "I am offering you three things; choose for yourself one of them, which I will do to you."'"

13 So Gad came to David and told him, and said to him, "Shall seven years of famine come to

you in your land? Or will you flee three months before your foes while they pursue you? Or shall there be three days' pestilence in your land? Now consider and see what answer I shall return to Him who sent me."

14 Then David said to Gad, "I am in great distress. Let us now fall into the hand of the LORD for His mercies are great, but do not let me fall into the hand of man."

Pestilence Sent

15 ¶ So the LORD sent a pestilence upon Israel from the morning until the appointed time, and seventy thousand men of the people from Dan to Beersheba died.

16 When the angel stretched out his hand toward Jerusalem to destroy it, the LORD relented from the calamity and said to the angel who destroyed the people, "It is enough! Now relax your hand!" And the angel of the LORD was by the threshing floor of Araunah the Jebusite.

17 Then David spoke to the LORD when he saw the angel who was striking down the people, and said, "Behold, it is I who have sinned, and it is I who have done wrong; but these sheep, what have they done? Please let Your hand be against me and against my father's house."

David Builds an Altar

18 ¶ So Gad came to David that day and said to him, "Go up, erect an altar to the LORD on the threshing floor of Araunah the Jebusite."

19 David went up according to the word of Gad, just as the LORD had commanded.

20 Araunah looked down and saw the king and his servants crossing over toward him; and Araunah went out and bowed his face to the ground before the king.

24:24 The Cost of True Worship

David's response is timeless: He sees that worship which costs nothing is not true worship at all. It is typical of David that even after falling into sin, he was not blinded to spiritual concerns. Feeling guilty already, he might have thought "one more compromise" would make no difference. Instead he stuck to his principle.

21 Then Araunah said, "Why has my lord the king come to his servant?" And David said, "To buy the threshing floor from you, in order to build an altar to the LORD, that the plague may be held back from the people."

22 Araunah said to David, "Let my lord the king take and offer up what is good in his sight.

---

a Or Kadesh in the land of the Hittite

Look, the oxen for the burnt offering, the threshing sledges and the yokes of the oxen for the
wood.

23 "Everything, O king, Araunah gives to the
king." And Araunah said to the king, "May the
LORD your God accept you."

24 However, the king said to Araunah, "No,
but I will surely buy *it* from you for a price, for I
will not offer burnt offerings to the LORD my God
which cost me nothing." So David bought the
threshing floor and the oxen for fifty shekels of
silver.

25 David built there an altar to the LORD and
offered burnt offerings and peace offerings. Thus
the LORD was moved by prayer for the land, and
the plague was held back from Israel.

1 KINGS

The Man Who Had Everything
The richest, wisest, most successful person of his time

> "But if you or your sons indeed turn away from following Me, and do not keep My commandments and My statutes which I have set before you, and go and serve other gods and worship them, then I will cut off Israel from the land which I have given them, and the house which I have consecrated for My name."
> 9:6–7

THE FIRST HALF OF 1 KINGS describes a man who got life handed to him on a silver platter. The son of King David and Queen Bathsheba, young Solomon grew up in the royal palace. Early on, he astounded others with his talent for song writing and natural history. He composed 1,005 songs and spun off 3,000 proverbs (a sampling of which were collected in the Biblical book of Proverbs).

Solomon became king of Israel and received from God the special gift of wisdom. He was called the wisest man in the world, and kings and queens traveled hundreds of miles to meet him. They went away dazzled by the genius of Israel's king and by the prosperity of his nation.

The Best Years Ever

Israel reached its Golden Age under King Solomon, a time forever remembered with nostalgia by Jews. Almost all the promised land lay in Israel's hands, and the nation was at peace. Literature and culture flourished. Of the people, the Bible records simply that "they were eating and drinking and rejoicing" (4:20). "The king made silver as common as stones in Jerusalem " (10:27).

Of all Solomon's accomplishments, one stands out above the others. He built the temple of God, the finest building in the world of that day. Almost 200,000 men labored for seven years to complete it.

Despite the successes of Solomon's reign, however, later in his life the king had a dramatic downturn. His fall eventually brought the kingdom crashing down around him, and the second half of 1 Kings describes the grim process of dismemberment.

What Went Wrong?

How did it happen? How could the liveliest, wealthiest, most contented nation of its day slide so disastrously in one generation?

As 1 Kings tells it, Solomon seemed unable to control his excesses. Reared in a palace, he loved luxury. When Israel launched its first maritime expeditions, he used them to gather such exotica as gold, ivory, apes, peacocks, and silver. He plated the floor of the temple with gold, wastefully gilded over fine cedar and precious ivory, and fashioned militarily useless shields out of gold. First Kings describes the seven-year construction of the temple in elaborate detail. But then it pointedly notes that the construction of Solomon's palace—twice the temple's size—took 13 years (7:1).

Solomon showed similar extravagance in his love life. First, he married the daughter of the Egyptian pharaoh (perhaps indicating he was relying on military alliances, not on God, for the defense of his country). Then, disobeying God's specific orders, he married the princesses of Moab, Ammon, Edom, Sidon, and other nations. Seven hundred wives in all, and 300 concubines! The entire complexion of the court changed. It became un-Jewish, foreign. To please his wives, Solomon took a final, terrible step: He built altars to all their gods. The one who had built the Israelites' greatest monument to God had fallen to worshiping idols.

Rumblings of Discontent in the Land

To pay for the building projects, Solomon instituted Israel's first national taxation system. He drafted workers for employment and kept them as virtual slaves. When bills mounted, he went so far as to cede certain northern towns in the promised land to another king (9:10–14). Resentment opened up between Israel's North and South.

But the gulf separating Israel from God was even more dangerous. Previously, the people of Israel had looked to God as their leader. Now, however, the focus shifted from God in heaven to the king in Jerusalem. Solomon had even made himself the unofficial religious leader of the country, and when he slid badly, the nation soon followed.

Solomon started out with every advantage of wealth, power, and wisdom. But 1 Kings gives this tragic conclusion: "Solomon did what was evil in the sight of the Lord, and did not follow the Lord fully, as David his father had done" (11:6).

Solomon seemed obsessed with a desire to outdo anyone who had ever lived. Along the way, he failed to make God the center of his life. He achieved lasting fame in history, but as a negative example. Jesus Christ himself rendered the final verdict on Solomon and his striving for glory when he pointed to a lily growing wild in the field. "Not even Solomon in all his glory," he said, "clothed himself like one of these" (Matthew 6:29).

How to Read 1 Kings

First and Second Kings were originally one book: The same Hebrew scroll contained both. Hebrew, having no vowels, is a very compact language, and when the book of Kings was translated into the wordier Greek and Latin, more space was needed. Translators arbitrarily split Kings. The two books, however, should be read as one.

First Kings divides neatly almost in half, with mostly good news in the first half. It tells of Israel's Golden Age, when King Solomon brought peace and prosperity to the nation. But he also sowed the seed for the calamities to follow. Chapter 12 marks the beginning of a civil war that ruptured Israel into two nations: Israel in the North and Judah in the South. The rest of 1, 2 Kings describes, ruler by ruler, the reigns of 19 kings in the North and 19 kings and one queen in the South.

Another book, 2 Chronicles, covers the exact same historical period as 1, 2 Kings. In some cases, 2 Chronicles adds more detail, so if a story interests you, read the parallel account there. These books of history form the background for 17 other books of the Bible: the Prophets. Famous prophets such as Isaiah, Jeremiah, Hosea, and Amos preached during the time of Kings.

Keeping 39 rulers straight can seem hopeless, especially since the books jump back and forth between two countries. Remember:

> Israel was the Northern Kingdom, with its capital in Samaria. Its kings were all unfaithful to God.
> Judah was the Southern Kingdom, with its capital in Jerusalem. Almost half of its rulers remained somewhat faithful to God; the others proved disobedient.

On pages 1417–1425, you will find a lineup of all the rulers, tracing the rise and fall of both the Northern and Southern Kingdoms. Use this handy reference as you read the history. You may find it helpful to underline the various rulers' names, using different colored marking pens (for example, red for Judah and blue for Israel). Add a star by those kings cited as doing "what was right in the sight of the Lord." First Kings mentions two such kings: Asa and Jehoshaphat. By marking the kings and queen with some visual scheme, you can quickly refer back to them when you read references to them in the books of the prophets.

PEOPLE YOU'LL MEET IN 1 KINGS

SOLOMON *(p. 381)*
ABIATHAR *(p. 386)*
JEROBOAM *(p. 398)*

ELIJAH *(p. 406)*
AHAB *(p. 413)*

3-TRACK READING PLAN

For an explanation and complete listing of the 3-track reading plan, turn to page 7.

TRACK 1: **Two-Week Courses on the Bible**
The Track 1 reading program on the Old Testament includes one chapter from 1 Kings. See page 8 for a complete listing of this course.

David in Old Age

1 Now King David was old, advanced in age; and they covered him with clothes, but he could not keep warm.

2 So his servants said to him, "Let them seek a young virgin for my lord the king, and let her attend the king and become his nurse; and let her lie in your bosom, that my lord the king may keep warm."

3 So they searched for a beautiful girl throughout all the territory of Israel, and found Abishag the Shunammite, and brought her to the king.

4 The girl was very beautiful; and she became the king's nurse and served him, but the king did not cohabit with her.

5 ¶ Now Adonijah the son of Haggith exalted himself, saying, "I will be king." So he prepared for himself chariots and horsemen with fifty men to run before him.

6 His father had never crossed him at any time by asking, "Why have you done so?" And he was also a very handsome man, and he was born after Absalom.

7 He had conferred with Joab the son of Zeruiah and with Abiathar the priest; and following Adonijah they helped him.

8 But Zadok the priest, Benaiah the son of Jehoiada, Nathan the prophet, Shimei, Rei, and the mighty men who belonged to David, were not with Adonijah.

9 ¶ Adonijah sacrificed sheep and oxen and fatlings by the ᵃstone of Zoheleth, which is beside En-rogel; and he invited all his brothers, the king's sons, and all the men of Judah, the king's servants.

10 But he did not invite Nathan the prophet, Benaiah, the mighty men, and Solomon his brother.

Nathan and Bathsheba

11 ¶ Then Nathan spoke to Bathsheba the mother of Solomon, saying, "Have you not heard that Adonijah the son of Haggith has become king, and David our lord does not know *it*?

12 "So now come, please let me give you counsel and save your life and the life of your son Solomon.

13 "Go at once to King David and say to him, 'Have you not, my lord, O king, sworn to your maidservant, saying, "Surely Solomon your son shall be king after me, and he shall sit on my throne"? Why then has Adonijah become king?'

14 "Behold, while you are still there speaking with the king, I will come in after you and confirm your words."

15 ¶ So Bathsheba went in to the king in the bedroom. Now the king was very old, and Abishag the Shunammite was ministering to the king.

16 Then Bathsheba bowed and prostrated herself before the king. And the king said, "What do you wish?"

17 She said to him, "My lord, you swore to your maidservant by the LORD your God, *saying*, 'Surely your son Solomon shall be king after me and he shall sit on my throne.'

18 "Now, behold, Adonijah is king; and now, my lord the king, you do not know *it*.

19 "He has sacrificed oxen and fatlings and sheep in abundance, and has invited all the sons of the king and Abiathar the priest and Joab the commander of the army, but he has not invited Solomon your servant.

20 "As for you now, my lord the king, the eyes of all Israel are on you, to tell them who shall sit on the throne of my lord the king after him.

21 "Otherwise it will come about, as soon as my lord the king sleeps with his fathers, that I and my son Solomon will be considered offenders."

22 ¶ Behold, while she was still speaking with the king, Nathan the prophet came in.

23 They told the king, saying, "Here is Nathan the prophet." And when he came in before the

ᵃ Or *Gliding* or *Serpent Stone*

king, he prostrated himself before the king with his face to the ground.

24 Then Nathan said, "My lord the king, have you said, 'Adonijah shall be king after me, and he shall sit on my throne'?

25 "For he has gone down today and has sacrificed oxen and fatlings and sheep in abundance, and has invited all the king's sons and the commanders of the army and Abiathar the priest, and behold, they are eating and drinking before him; and they say, 'Long live King Adonijah!'

26 "But me, even me your servant, and Zadok the priest and Benaiah the son of Jehoiada and your servant Solomon, he has not invited.

27 "Has this thing been done by my lord the king, and you have not shown to your servants who should sit on the throne of my lord the king after him?"

28 ¶ Then King David said, "Call Bathsheba to me." And she came into the king's presence and stood before the king.

29 The king vowed and said, "As the LORD lives, who has redeemed my life from all distress,

30 surely as I vowed to you by the LORD the God of Israel, saying, 'Your son Solomon shall be king after me, and he shall sit on my throne in my place'; I will indeed do so this day."

31 Then Bathsheba bowed with her face to the ground, and prostrated herself before the king and said, "May my lord King David live forever."

32 ¶ Then King David said, "Call to me Zadok the priest, Nathan the prophet, and Benaiah the son of Jehoiada." And they came into the king's presence.

33 The king said to them, "Take with you the servants of your lord, and have my son Solomon ride on my own mule, and bring him down to Gihon.

34 "Let Zadok the priest and Nathan the prophet anoint him there as king over Israel, and blow the trumpet and say, 'Long live King Solomon!'

35 "Then you shall come up after him, and he shall come and sit on my throne and be king in my place; for I have appointed him to be ruler over Israel and Judah."

36 Benaiah the son of Jehoiada answered the king and said, "Amen! Thus may the LORD, the God of my lord the king, say.

37 "As the LORD has been with my lord the king, so may He be with Solomon, and make his throne greater than the throne of my lord King David!"

Solomon Anointed King

38 ¶ So Zadok the priest, Nathan the prophet, Benaiah the son of Jehoiada, the Cherethites, and the Pelethites went down and had Solomon ride on King David's mule, and brought him to Gihon.

39 Zadok the priest then took the horn of oil from the tent and anointed Solomon. Then they blew the trumpet, and all the people said, "Long live King Solomon!"

40 All the people went up after him, and the people were playing on flutes and rejoicing with great joy, so that the earth shook at their noise.

41 ¶ Now Adonijah and all the guests who were with him heard it as they finished eating. When Joab heard the sound of the trumpet, he said, "Why is the city making such an uproar?"

42 While he was still speaking, behold, Jonathan the son of Abiathar the priest came. Then Adonijah said, "Come in, for you are a valiant man and bring good news."

43 But Jonathan replied to Adonijah, "No! Our lord King David has made Solomon king.

44 "The king has also sent with him Zadok the priest, Nathan the prophet, Benaiah the son of Jehoiada, the Cherethites, and the Pelethites; and they have made him ride on the king's mule.

45 "Zadok the priest and Nathan the prophet have anointed him king in Gihon, and they have come up from there rejoicing, so that the city is in an uproar. This is the noise which you have heard.

46 "Besides, Solomon has even taken his seat on the throne of the kingdom.

47 "Moreover, the king's servants came to bless our lord King David, saying, 'May your God make the name of Solomon better than your name and his throne greater than your throne!' And the king bowed himself on the bed.

48 "The king has also said thus, 'Blessed be the LORD, the God of Israel, who has granted one to sit on my throne today while my own eyes see it.' "

49 ¶ Then all the guests of Adonijah were terrified; and they arose and each went on his way.

50 And Adonijah was afraid of Solomon, and he arose, went and took hold of the horns of the altar.

51 Now it was told Solomon, saying, "Behold, Adonijah is afraid of King Solomon, for behold, he has taken hold of the horns of the altar, saying, 'Let King Solomon swear to me today that he will not put his servant to death with the sword.' "

52 Solomon said, "If he is a worthy man, not one of his hairs will fall to the ground; but if wickedness is found in him, he will die."

53 So King Solomon sent, and they brought him down from the altar. And he came and prostrated himself before King Solomon, and Solomon said to him, "Go to your house."

David's Charge to Solomon

2 As David's time to die drew near, he charged Solomon his son, saying,

2 "I am going the way of all the earth. Be strong, therefore, and show yourself a man.

3 "Keep the charge of the LORD your God, to walk in His ways, to keep His statutes, His commandments, His ordinances, and His testimonies, according to what is written in the Law of Moses, that you may succeed in all that you do and wherever you turn,

4 so that the LORD may carry out His promise which He spoke concerning me, saying, 'If your sons are careful of their way, to walk before Me in [a]truth with all their heart and with all their soul, you shall not lack a man on the throne of Israel.'

5 ¶ "Now you also know what Joab the son of Zeruiah did to me, what he did to the two commanders of the armies of Israel, to Abner the son of Ner, and to Amasa the son of Jether, whom he killed; he also shed the blood of war in peace. And he put the blood of war on his belt about his waist, and on his sandals on his feet.

2:5 Paying Back Joab

For the background to David's comments about Joab, see 2 Samuel 3:17–30; 20:4–11.

6 "So act according to your wisdom, and do not let his gray hair go down to Sheol in peace.

7 "But show kindness to the sons of Barzillai the Gileadite, and let them be among those who eat at your table; for they assisted me when I fled from Absalom your brother.

8 "Behold, there is with you Shimei the son of Gera the Benjamite, of Bahurim; now it was he who cursed me with a violent curse on the day I went to Mahanaim. But when he came down to me at the Jordan, I swore to him by the LORD, saying, 'I will not put you to death with the sword.'

9 "Now therefore, do not let him go unpunished, for you are a wise man; and you will know what you ought to do to him, and you will bring his gray hair down to Sheol with blood."

Death of David

10 ¶ Then David slept with his fathers and was buried in the city of David.

11 The days that David reigned over Israel *were* forty years: seven years he reigned in Hebron and thirty-three years he reigned in Jerusalem.

12 And Solomon sat on the throne of David his father, and his kingdom was firmly established.

13 ¶ Now Adonijah the son of Haggith came to Bathsheba the mother of Solomon. And she said, "Do you come peacefully?" And he said, "Peacefully."

14 Then he said, "I have something *to say* to you." And she said, "Speak."

15 So he said, "You know that the kingdom was mine and that all Israel expected me to be king; however, the kingdom has turned about and become my brother's, for it was his from the LORD.

16 "Now I am making one request of you; do not [b]refuse me." And she said to him, "Speak."

17 Then he said, "Please speak to Solomon the king, for he will not refuse you, that he may give me Abishag the Shunammite as a wife."

18 Bathsheba said, "Very well; I will speak to the king for you."

Adonijah Executed

19 ¶ So Bathsheba went to King Solomon to speak to him for Adonijah. And the king arose to meet her, bowed before her, and sat on his throne; then he had a throne set for the king's mother, and she sat on his right.

20 Then she said, "I am making one small request of you; do not refuse me." And the king said to her, "Ask, my mother, for I will not refuse you."

21 So she said, "Let Abishag the Shunammite be given to Adonijah your brother as a wife."

22 King Solomon answered and said to his mother, "And why are you asking Abishag the Shunammite for Adonijah? Ask for him also the kingdom—for he is my older brother—even for him, for Abiathar the priest, and for Joab the son of Zeruiah!"

23 Then King Solomon swore by the LORD, saying, "May God do so to me and more also, if Adonijah has not spoken this word against his own life.

24 " Now therefore, as the LORD lives, who has established me and set me on the throne of David my father and who has made me a house as He promised, surely Adonijah shall be put to death today."

25 So King Solomon sent Benaiah the son of Jehoiada; and he fell upon him so that he died.

2:17 After More than a Wife?

Solomon had a rather harsh response (verse 23) to Adonijah's request to marry King David's companion. But asking for her may have been Adonijah's veiled attempt to regain the throne lost to Solomon. In the ancient Middle East, a person who married any of the late king's wives or concubines publicly claimed the rights of the former king (see 2 Samuel 12:8 and 16:21–22 for examples). Adonijah might have been cunningly hatching another conspiracy; Solomon, at least, seemed to think so.

26 ¶ Then to Abiathar the priest the king said, "Go to Anathoth to your own field, for you deserve to die; but I will not put you to death at this time, because you carried the ark of the Lord GOD before my father David, and because you were afflicted in everything with which my father was afflicted."

27 So Solomon dismissed Abiathar from being priest to the LORD, in order to fulfill the word of the LORD, which He had spoken concerning the house of Eli in Shiloh.

---

[a] Or *faithfulness* [b] Lit *turn away my face*

Joab Executed

28 ¶ Now the news came to Joab, for Joab had followed Adonijah, although he had not followed Absalom. And Joab fled to the tent of the LORD and took hold of the horns of the altar.

29 It was told King Solomon that Joab had fled to the tent of the LORD, and behold, he is beside the altar. Then Solomon sent Benaiah the son of Jehoiada, saying, "Go, fall upon him."

30 So Benaiah came to the tent of the LORD and said to him, "Thus the king has said, 'Come out.' " But he said, "No, for I will die here." And Benaiah brought the king word again, saying, "Thus spoke Joab, and thus he answered me."

31 The king said to him, "Do as he has spoken and fall upon him and bury him, that you may remove from me and from my father's house the blood which Joab shed without cause.

32 "The LORD will return his blood on his own head, because he fell upon two men more righteous and better than he and killed them with the sword, while my father David did not know it: Abner the son of Ner, commander of the army of Israel, and Amasa the son of Jether, commander of the army of Judah.

33 "So shall their blood return on the head of Joab and on the head of his descendants forever; but to David and his descendants and his house and his throne, may there be peace from the LORD forever."

34 Then Benaiah the son of Jehoiada went up and fell upon him and put him to death, and he was buried at his own house in the wilderness.

35 The king appointed Benaiah the son of Jehoiada over the army in his place, and the king appointed Zadok the priest in the place of Abiathar.

Shimei Executed

36 ¶ Now the king sent and called for Shimei and said to him, "Build for yourself a house in Jerusalem and live there, and do not go out from there to any place.

37 "For on the day you go out and cross over the brook Kidron, you will know for certain that you shall surely die; your blood shall be on your own head."

38 Shimei then said to the king, "The word is good. As my lord the king has said, so your servant will do." So Shimei lived in Jerusalem many days.

39 ¶ But it came about at the end of three years, that two of the servants of Shimei ran away to Achish son of Maacah, king of Gath. And they told Shimei, saying, "Behold, your servants are in Gath."

40 Then Shimei arose and saddled his donkey, and went to Gath to Achish to look for his servants. And Shimei went and brought his servants from Gath.

41 It was told Solomon that Shimei had gone from Jerusalem to Gath, and had returned.

42 So the king sent and called for Shimei and said to him, "Did I not make you swear by the LORD and solemnly warn you, saying, 'You will know for certain that on the day you depart and go anywhere, you shall surely die'? And you said to me, 'The word which I have heard is good.'

43 "Why then have you not kept the oath of the LORD, and the command which I have laid on you?"

ABIATHAR *Outlaw Priest*

GENERATIONS BEFORE, A PROPHET HAD predicted that Israel's chief family of priests would be destroyed (1 Samuel 2:31–36). Abiathar witnessed the horrible fulfillment of that prediction. All the men in his extended family—85 in all—were lined up and slaughtered. Abiathar's whole village—women, children, babies, even animals—perished, all because they were suspected of helping David escape from King Saul (1 Samuel 22:18).

Abiathar somehow got away and straggled into David's outlaw camp, the lone survivor bearing news of the massacre. He brought with him the ephod: the priest's garment containing the Urim and Thummim, sacred objects used to determine God's will.

From that day on David relied on Abiathar and his ephod to gain direction from God. Somewhat like Friar Tuck in Robin Hood's band, Abiathar became official priest to the outlaw band. When King Saul died and David and his guerrilla army finally came to power, David made Abiathar the nation's high priest in the new sanctuary at Jerusalem.

Abiathar's harrowing moments did not end even after he joined the power structure. When David's son Absalom led a rebellion, Abiathar remained loyal to David, returning to the conquered city as a spy (2 Samuel 15:24–29). When David grew old and feeble, Abiathar backed the wrong son to succeed the king. The aging priest might have been executed—others were—but Solomon showed mercy and banished him instead. Abiathar thus ended his career as he began: as an outcast (1 Kings 2:26).

Life Questions: Do you know anyone like Abiathar, someone who has suffered stunning losses? How can you—or someone else—be like David to him or her?

44 The king also said to Shimei, "You know all the evil which you acknowledge in your heart, which you did to my father David; therefore the LORD shall return your evil on your own head.

45 "But King Solomon shall be blessed, and the throne of David shall be established before the LORD forever."

46 So the king commanded Benaiah the son of Jehoiada, and he went out and fell upon him so that he died.

¶ Thus the kingdom was established in the hands of Solomon.

2:46 Wise Yet Ruthless

Chapters 2 and 3 show conflicting personality traits in Solomon. In the power struggles of chapter 2 he proved more ruthless than his father David had ever been. This tendency stirred up resentment among the northern tribes of Israel and eventually led to civil war. But chapter 3 shows Solomon could also be faithful, wise, and even humble. Tragically, he gave in to his darker side more and more as his reign wore on.

Solomon's Rule Consolidated

3 Then Solomon formed a marriage alliance with Pharaoh king of Egypt, and took Pharaoh's daughter and brought her to the city of David until he had finished building his own house and the house of the LORD and the wall around Jerusalem.

2 The people were still sacrificing on the high places, because there was no house built for the name of the LORD until those days.

3 ¶ Now Solomon loved the LORD, walking in the statutes of his father David, except he sacrificed and burned incense on the high places.

4 The king went to Gibeon to sacrifice there, for that was the great high place; Solomon offered a thousand burnt offerings on that altar.

5 In Gibeon the LORD appeared to Solomon in a dream at night; and God said, "Ask what *you wish* me to give you."

Solomon's Prayer

6 Then Solomon said, "You have shown great lovingkindness to Your servant David my father, according as he walked before You in ªtruth and righteousness and uprightness of heart toward You; and You have reserved for him this great lovingkindness, that You have given him a son to sit on his throne, as *it is* this day.

7 "Now, O LORD my God, You have made Your servant king in place of my father David, yet I am but a little child; I do not know how to go out or come in.

8 "Your servant is in the midst of Your people which You have chosen, a great people who are too many to be numbered or counted.

9 "So give Your servant an understanding heart to judge Your people to discern between good and evil. For who is able to judge this great people of Yours?"

3:9 Solomon's Wish

By requesting the wisdom to be a good king, Solomon showed that he possessed much wisdom already. Pleased at Solomon's unselfish request, God gave Solomon even more. Unfortunately, the humility displayed in this scene did not stay with Solomon throughout his career.

God's Answer

10 ¶ It was pleasing in the sight of the Lord that Solomon had asked this thing.

11 God said to him, "Because you have asked this thing and have not asked for yourself long life, nor have asked riches for yourself, nor have you asked for the life of your enemies, but have asked for yourself discernment to understand justice,

12 behold, I have done according to your words. Behold, I have given you a wise and discerning heart, so that there has been no one like you before you, nor shall one like you arise after you.

13 "I have also given you what you have not asked, both riches and honor, so that there will not be any among the kings like you all your days.

14 "If you walk in My ways, keeping My statutes and commandments, as your father David walked, then I will prolong your days."

15 ¶ Then Solomon awoke, and behold, it was a dream. And he came to Jerusalem and stood before the ark of the covenant of the Lord, and offered burnt offerings and made peace offerings, and made a feast for all his servants.

Solomon Wisely Judges

16 ¶ Then two women who were harlots came to the king and stood before him.

17 The one woman said, "Oh, my lord, this woman and I live in the same house; and I gave birth to a child while she *was* in the house.

18 "It happened on the third day after I gave birth, that this woman also gave birth to a child, and we were together. There was no stranger with us in the house, only the two of us in the house.

19 "This woman's son died in the night, because she lay on it.

20 "So she arose in the middle of the night and took my son from beside me while your maidser-

ª Or *faithfulness*

vant slept, and laid him in her bosom, and laid her dead son in my bosom.

21 "When I rose in the morning to nurse my son, behold, he was dead; but when I looked at him carefully in the morning, behold, he was not my son, whom I had borne."

22 Then the other woman said, "No! For the living one is my son, and the dead one is your son." But the first woman said, "No! For the dead one is your son, and the living one is my son." Thus they spoke before the king.

23 ¶ Then the king said, "The one says, 'This is my son who is living, and your son is the dead one'; and the other says, 'No! For your son is the dead one, and my son is the living one.'"

24 The king said, "Get me a sword." So they brought a sword before the king.

25 The king said, "Divide the living child in two, and give half to the one and half to the other."

26 Then the woman whose child was the living one spoke to the king, for she was deeply stirred over her son and said, "Oh, my lord, give her the living child, and by no means kill him." But the other said, "He shall be neither mine nor yours; divide him!"

27 Then the king said, "Give the first woman the living child, and by no means kill him. She is his mother."

28 When all Israel heard of the judgment which the king had handed down, they feared the king, for they saw that the wisdom of God was in him to administer justice.

Solomon's Officials

4 Now King Solomon was king over all Israel. 2 These were his officials: Azariah the son of Zadok was the priest;

3 Elihoreph and Ahijah, the sons of Shisha were secretaries; Jehoshaphat the son of Ahilud was the recorder;

4 and Benaiah the son of Jehoiada was over the army; and Zadok and Abiathar were priests;

5 and Azariah the son of Nathan was over the deputies; and Zabud the son of Nathan, a priest, was the king's friend;

6 and Ahishar was over the household; and Adoniram the son of Abda was over the men subject to forced labor.

7 ¶ Solomon had twelve deputies over all Israel, who provided for the king and his household; each man had to provide for a month in the year.

8 These are their names: Ben-hur, in the hill country of Ephraim;

9 Ben-deker in Makaz and Shaalbim and Beth-shemesh and Elonbeth-hanan;

10 Ben-hesed, in Arubboth (Socoh was his and all the land of Hepher);

11 Ben-abinadab, in all the height of Dor (Taphath the daughter of Solomon was his wife);

12 Baana the son of Ahilud, in Taanach and Megiddo, and all Beth-shean which is beside Zarethan below Jezreel, from Beth-shean to Abelmeholah as far as the other side of Jokmeam;

13 Ben-geber, in Ramoth-gilead (the towns of Jair, the son of Manasseh, which are in Gilead were his: the region of Argob, which is in Bashan, sixty great cities with walls and bronze bars were his);

14 Ahinadab the son of Iddo, in Mahanaim;

15 Ahimaaz, in Naphtali (he also married Basemath the daughter of Solomon);

16 Baana the son of Hushai, in Asher and Bealoth;

17 Jehoshaphat the son of Paruah, in Issachar;

18 Shimei the son of Ela, in Benjamin;

19 Geber the son of Uri, in the land of Gilead, the country of Sihon king of the Amorites and of Og king of Bashan; and he was the only deputy who was in the land.

Solomon's Power, Wealth and Wisdom

20 ¶ Judah and Israel were as numerous as the sand that is on the seashore in abundance; they were eating and drinking and rejoicing.

21 ¶ Now Solomon ruled over all the kingdoms from the ªRiver to the land of the Philistines and to the border of Egypt; they brought tribute and served Solomon all the days of his life.

4:21 How Large Was Israel?

Under the reigns of David and Solomon, Israel stretched from the border of Egypt to the border of Babylonia. It was approximately three times the size of the modern nation of Israel, encompassing land that now belongs to Jordan, Syria, and Lebanon.

22 ¶ Solomon's provision for one day was thirty ᵇkors of fine flour and sixty kors of meal,

23 ten fat oxen, twenty pasture-fed oxen, a hundred sheep besides deer, gazelles, roebucks, and fattened fowl.

24 For he had dominion over everything west of the River, from Tiphsah even to Gaza, over all the kings west of the River; and he had peace on all sides around about him.

25 So Judah and Israel lived in safety, every man under his vine and his fig tree, from Dan even to Beersheba, all the days of Solomon.

26 Solomon had ᶜ40,000 stalls of horses for his chariots, and 12,000 horsemen.

27 Those deputies provided for King Solomon and all who came to King Solomon's table, each in his month; they left nothing lacking.

28 They also brought barley and straw for the

ª I.e. Euphrates   ᵇ I.e. One kor equals approx 10 bu   ᶜ One ms reads *4000*, cf 2 Chr 9:25

horses and swift steeds to the place where it should be, each according to his charge.

29 ¶ Now God gave Solomon wisdom and very great discernment and breadth of mind, like the sand that is on the seashore.

30 Solomon's wisdom surpassed the wisdom of all the sons of the east and all the wisdom of Egypt.

31 For he was wiser than all men, than Ethan the Ezrahite, Heman, Calcol and Darda, the sons of Mahol; and his fame was *known* in all the surrounding nations.

32 He also spoke 3,000 proverbs, and his songs were 1,005.

33 He spoke of trees, from the cedar that is in Lebanon even to the hyssop that grows on the wall; he spoke also of animals and birds and creeping things and fish.

34 Men came from all peoples to hear the wisdom of Solomon, from all the kings of the earth who had heard of his wisdom.

Alliance with King Hiram

5 Now Hiram king of Tyre sent his servants to Solomon, when he heard that they had anointed him king in place of his father, for Hiram had always been a friend of David.

2 Then Solomon sent *word* to Hiram, saying,

3 "You know that David my father was unable to build a house for the name of the LORD his God because of the wars which surrounded him, until the LORD put them under the soles of his feet.

4 "But now the LORD my God has given me rest on every side; there is neither adversary nor misfortune.

5 "Behold, I intend to build a house for the name of the LORD my God, as the LORD spoke to David my father, saying, 'Your son, whom I will set on your throne in your place, he will build the house for My name.'

6 "Now therefore, command that they cut for me cedars from Lebanon, and my servants will be with your servants; and I will give you wages for your servants according to all that you say, for you know that there is no one among us who knows how to cut timber like the Sidonians."

7 ¶ When Hiram heard the words of Solomon, he rejoiced greatly and said, "Blessed be the LORD today, who has given to David a wise son over this great people."

8 So Hiram sent *word* to Solomon, saying, "I have heard *the message* which you have sent me; I will do what you desire concerning the cedar and cypress timber.

9 "My servants will bring *them* down from Lebanon to the sea; and I will make them into rafts *to go* by sea to the place where you direct me, and I will have them broken up there, and you shall carry *them* away. Then you shall accomplish my desire by giving food to my household."

10 So Hiram gave Solomon as much as he desired of the cedar and cypress timber.

11 Solomon then gave Hiram 20,000 kors of wheat as food for his household, and twenty kors of beaten oil; thus Solomon would give Hiram year by year.

12 The LORD gave wisdom to Solomon, just as He promised him; and there was peace between Hiram and Solomon, and the two of them made a covenant.

Conscription of Laborers

13 ¶ Now King Solomon levied forced laborers from all Israel; and the forced laborers numbered 30,000 men.

14 He sent them to Lebanon, 10,000 a month in relays; they were in Lebanon a month *and* two months at home. And Adoniram *was* over the forced laborers.

15 Now Solomon had 70,000 transporters, and 80,000 hewers *of stone* in the mountains,

16 besides Solomon's 3,300 chief deputies who *were* over the project *and* who ruled over the people who were doing the work.

17 Then the king commanded, and they quarried great stones, costly stones, to lay the foundation of the house with cut stones.

18 So Solomon's builders and Hiram's builders and the Gebalites cut them, and prepared the timbers and the stones to build the house.

The Building of the Temple

6 Now it came about in the four hundred and eightieth year after the sons of Israel came out of the land of Egypt, in the fourth year of Solomon's reign over Israel, in the month of Ziv which is the second month, that he began to build the house of the LORD.

2 As for the house which King Solomon built for the LORD, its length *was* sixty *ª*cubits and its width twenty *cubits* and its height thirty cubits.

3 The porch in front of the nave of the house *was* twenty cubits in length, corresponding to the width of the house, *and* its depth along the front of the house *was* ten cubits.

4 Also for the house he made windows with *artistic* frames.

5 Against the wall of the house he built stories encompassing the walls of the house around both the nave and the inner sanctuary; thus he made side chambers all around.

6 The lowest story *was* five cubits wide, and the middle *was* six cubits wide, and the third *was* seven cubits wide; for on the outside he made offsets *in the wall* of the house all around in order that *the beams* would not be inserted in the walls of the house.

7 ¶ The house, while it was being built, was built of stone prepared at the quarry, and there

---

ª I.e. One cubit equals approx 18 in.

was neither hammer nor axe nor any iron tool heard in the house while it was being built.

8 ¶ The doorway for the [a]lowest side chamber *was* on the right side of the house; and they

6:3 History of the Temple

The Bible describes the temple architecture in some detail, though, notably, it does not record detailed instructions from God—in contrast to the very specific commands given for the tabernacle. Solomon's temple lasted about 380 years, occasionally falling into disrepair. Destroyed by Babylon's King Nebuchadnezzar, it was partially rebuilt under the leadership of Ezra and Nehemiah, and then reconstructed by King Herod in Jesus' day. Jesus walked in the temple on "Solomon's Porch." The early church met on the temple grounds, Peter preached there, and Ananias and Sapphira probably died there (Acts 5). Currently the temple site is occupied by a Muslim mosque.

would go up by winding stairs to the middle *story*, and from the middle to the third.

9 So he built the house and finished it; and he covered the house with beams and planks of cedar.

10 He also built the stories against the whole house, each five cubits high; and they were fastened to the house with timbers of cedar.

11 ¶ Now the word of the LORD came to Solomon saying,

12 "*Concerning* this house which you are building, if you will walk in My statutes and execute My ordinances and keep all My commandments by walking in them, then I will carry out My word with you which I spoke to David your father.

13 "I will dwell among the sons of Israel, and will not forsake My people Israel."

14 ¶ So Solomon built the house and finished it.

15 Then he built the walls of the house on the inside with boards of cedar; from the floor of the house to the ceiling he overlaid *the walls* on the inside with wood, and he overlaid the floor of the house with boards of cypress.

16 He built twenty cubits on the rear part of the house with boards of cedar from the floor to the ceiling; he built *them* for it on the inside as an inner sanctuary, *even* as the most holy place.

17 The house, that is, the nave in front of *the inner sanctuary,* was forty cubits *long.*

18 There was cedar on the house within, carved *in the shape* of gourds and open flowers; all was cedar, there was no stone seen.

19 Then he prepared an inner sanctuary within

the house in order to place there the ark of the covenant of the LORD.

20 The inner sanctuary *was* twenty cubits in length, twenty cubits in width, and twenty cubits in height, and he overlaid it with pure gold. He also overlaid the altar with cedar.

21 So Solomon overlaid the inside of the house with pure gold. And he drew chains of gold across the front of the inner sanctuary, and he overlaid it with gold.

22 He overlaid the whole house with gold, until all the house was finished. Also the whole altar which was by the inner sanctuary he overlaid with gold.

23 ¶ Also in the inner sanctuary he made two cherubim of olive wood, each ten cubits high.

24 Five cubits *was* the one wing of the cherub and five cubits the other wing of the cherub; from the end of one wing to the end of the other wing *were* ten cubits.

25 The other cherub *was* ten cubits; both the cherubim were of the same measure and the same form.

26 The height of the one cherub *was* ten cubits, and so *was* the other cherub.

27 He placed the cherubim in the midst of the inner house, and the wings of the cherubim were spread out, so that the wing of the one was touching the *one* wall, and the wing of the other cherub was touching the other wall. So their wings were touching each other in the center of the house.

28 He also overlaid the cherubim with gold.

29 ¶ Then he carved all the walls of the house round about with carved engravings of cherubim, palm trees, and open flowers, inner and outer *sanctuaries.*

30 He overlaid the floor of the house with gold, inner and outer *sanctuaries.*

31 ¶ For the entrance of the inner sanctuary he made doors of olive wood, the lintel *and* five-sided doorposts.

32 So *he made* two doors of olive wood, and he carved on them carvings of cherubim, palm trees, and open flowers, and overlaid them with gold; and he spread the gold on the cherubim and on the palm trees.

33 ¶ So also he made for the entrance of the nave four-sided doorposts of olive wood

34 and two doors of cypress wood; the two leaves of the one door turned on pivots, and the two leaves of the other door turned on pivots.

35 He carved *on it* cherubim, palm trees, and open flowers; and he overlaid *them* with gold evenly applied on the engraved work.

36 He built the inner court with three rows of cut stone and a row of cedar beams.

37 ¶ In the fourth year the foundation of the house of the LORD was laid, in the month of Ziv.

38 In the eleventh year, in the month of Bul, which is the eighth month, the house was finished

---

[a] So with Gr and versions; M.T. *middle*

throughout all its parts and according to all its plans. So he was seven years in building it.

Solomon's Palace

7 Now Solomon was building his own house thirteen years, and he finished all his house.

7:1 Prosperity under Solomon

The magnificent temple and palace built by Solomon came to symbolize Israel's Golden Age. Solomon built many leading cities, assuming control of vital trade routes. He fortified Jerusalem, the capital, with a wall so thick that parts of it still stand. He modernized the Israelite army with 12,000 horses and the first chariot brigades, and made shrewd alliances with neighboring countries.

2 He built the house of the forest of Lebanon; its length was 100 ᵃcubits and its width 50 cubits and its height 30 cubits, on four rows of cedar pillars with cedar beams on the pillars.

3 It was paneled with cedar above the side chambers which were on the 45 pillars, 15 in each row.

4 *There were artistic window* frames in three rows, and window was opposite window in three ranks.

5 All the doorways and doorposts *had* squared *artistic* frames, and window was opposite window in three ranks.

6 ¶ Then he made the hall of pillars; its length was 50 cubits and its width 30 cubits, and a porch *was* in front of them and pillars and a threshold in front of them.

7 ¶ He made the hall of the throne where he was to judge, the hall of judgment, and it was paneled with cedar from floor to floor.

8 ¶ His house where he was to live, the other court inward from the hall, was of the same workmanship. He also made a house like this hall for Pharaoh's daughter, whom Solomon had married.

9 ¶ All these were of costly stones, of stone cut according to measure, sawed with saws, inside and outside; even from the foundation to the coping, and so on the outside to the great court.

10 ¶ The foundation was of costly stones, *even* large stones, stones of ten cubits and stones of eight cubits.

11 And above were costly stones, stone cut according to measure, and cedar.

12 So the great court all around *had* three rows of cut stone and a row of cedar beams even as the inner court of the house of the LORD, and the porch of the house.

Hiram's Work in the Temple

13 ¶ Now King Solomon sent and brought Hiram from Tyre.

14 He was a widow's son from the tribe of Naphtali, and his father was a man of Tyre, a worker in bronze; and he was filled with wisdom and understanding and skill for doing any work in bronze. So he came to King Solomon and performed all his work.

15 ¶ He fashioned the two pillars of bronze; eighteen cubits was the height of one pillar, and a line of twelve cubits measured the circumference of both.

16 He also made two capitals of molten bronze to set on the tops of the pillars; the height of the one capital was five cubits and the height of the other capital was five cubits.

17 *There were* nets of network and twisted threads of chainwork for the capitals which were on the top of the pillars; seven for the one capital and seven for the other capital.

18 So he made the pillars, and two rows around on the one network to cover the capitals which were on the top of the pomegranates; and so he did for the other capital.

19 The capitals which *were* on the top of the pillars in the porch were of lily design, four cubits.

20 *There were* capitals on the two pillars, even above *and* close to the rounded projection which was beside the network; and the pomegranates *numbered* two hundred in rows around both capitals.

21 Thus he set up the pillars at the porch of the nave; and he set up the right pillar and named it ᵇJachin, and he set up the left pillar and named it ᶜBoaz.

22 On the top of the pillars was lily design. So the work of the pillars was finished.

23 ¶ Now he made the sea of cast *metal* ten cubits from brim to brim, circular in form, and its height was five cubits, and thirty cubits in circumference.

24 Under its brim gourds went around encircling it ten to a cubit, completely surrounding the sea; the gourds were in two rows, cast with the rest.

25 It stood on twelve oxen, three facing north, three facing west, three facing south, and three facing east; and the sea *was set* on top of them, and all their rear parts *turned* inward.

26 It was a handbreadth thick, and its brim was made like the brim of a cup, *as* a lily blossom; it could hold two thousand baths.

27 ¶ Then he made the ten stands of bronze; the length of each stand was four cubits and its width four cubits and its height three cubits.

28 This was the design of the stands: they had borders, even borders between the ᵈframes,

29 and on the borders which were between the

ᵃ I.e. One cubit equals approx 18 in.   ᵇ I.e. he shall establish   ᶜ I.e. in it is strength   ᵈ Or *crossbars*

[a]frames *were* lions, oxen and cherubim; and on the [a]frames there *was* a pedestal above, and beneath the lions and oxen *were* wreaths of hanging work.

30 Now each stand had four bronze wheels with bronze axles, and its four feet had supports; beneath the basin *were* cast supports with wreaths at each side.

31 Its opening inside the crown at the top *was* a cubit, and its opening *was* round like the design of a pedestal, a cubit and a half; and also on its opening *there were* engravings, and their borders were square, not round.

32 The four wheels *were* underneath the borders, and the axles of the wheels *were* on the stand. And the height of a wheel *was* a cubit and a half.

33 The workmanship of the wheels *was* like the workmanship of a chariot wheel. Their axles, their rims, their spokes, and their hubs *were* all cast.

34 Now *there were* four supports at the four corners of each stand; its supports *were* part of the stand itself.

35 On the top of the stand *there was* a circular form half a cubit high, and on the top of the stand its stays and its borders *were* part of it.

36 He engraved on the plates of its stays and on its borders, cherubim, lions and palm trees, according to the clear space on each, with wreaths *all* around.

37 He made the ten stands like this: all of them had one casting, one measure and one form.

38 ¶ He made ten basins of bronze, one basin held forty baths; each basin *was* four cubits, *and* on each of the ten stands *was* one basin.

39 Then he set the stands, five on the right side of the house and five on the left side of the house; and he set the sea *of cast metal* on the right side of the house eastward toward the south.

40 ¶ Now Hiram made the basins and the shovels and the bowls. So Hiram finished doing all the work which he performed for King Solomon *in* the house of the LORD:

41 the two pillars and the *two* bowls of the capitals which *were* on the top of the two pillars, and the two networks to cover the two bowls of the capitals which *were* on the top of the pillars;

42 and the four hundred pomegranates for the two networks, two rows of pomegranates for each network to cover the two bowls of the capitals which *were* on the tops of the pillars;

43 and the ten stands with the ten basins on the stands;

44 and the one sea and the twelve oxen under the sea;

45 and the pails and the shovels and the bowls; even all these utensils which Hiram made for King Solomon *in* the house of the LORD *were* of polished bronze.

46 In the plain of the Jordan the king cast them, in the clay ground between Succoth and Zarethan.

47 Solomon left all the utensils *unweighed,* because *they were* too many; the weight of the bronze could not be ascertained.

48 ¶ Solomon made all the furniture which *was in* the house of the LORD: the golden altar and the golden table on which *was* the bread of the Presence;

49 and the lampstands, five on the right side and five on the left, in front of the inner sanctuary, of pure gold; and the flowers and the lamps and the tongs, of gold;

50 and the cups and the snuffers and the bowls and the spoons and the firepans, of pure gold; and the hinges both for the doors of the inner house, the most holy place, *and* for the doors of the house, *that is,* of the nave, of gold.

51 ¶ Thus all the work that King Solomon performed *in* the house of the LORD was finished. And Solomon brought in the things dedicated by his father David, the silver and the gold and the utensils, *and* he put them in the treasuries of the house of the LORD.

The Ark Brought into the Temple

8 Then Solomon assembled the elders of Israel and all the heads of the tribes, the leaders of the fathers' *households* of the sons of Israel, to King Solomon in Jerusalem, to bring up the ark of the covenant of the LORD from the city of David, which is Zion.

2 All the men of Israel assembled themselves to King Solomon at the feast, in the month Ethanim, which is the seventh month.

3 Then all the elders of Israel came, and the priests took up the ark.

4 They brought up the ark of the LORD and the tent of meeting and all the holy utensils, which were in the tent, and the priests and the Levites brought them up.

5 And King Solomon and all the congregation of Israel, who were assembled to him, were with him before the ark, sacrificing so many sheep and oxen they could not be counted or numbered.

6 Then the priests brought the ark of the covenant of the LORD to its place, into the inner sanctuary of the house, to the most holy place, under the wings of the cherubim.

7 For the cherubim spread *their* wings over the place of the ark, and the cherubim made a covering over the ark and its poles from above.

8 But the poles were so long that the ends of the poles could be seen from the holy place before the inner sanctuary, but they could not be seen outside; they are there to this day.

9 There was nothing in the ark except the two tablets of stone which Moses put there at Horeb, where the LORD made a covenant with the sons of Israel, when they came out of the land of Egypt.

---

[a] Or *crossbars*

10 It happened that when the priests came from the holy place, the cloud filled the house of the LORD,

11 so that the priests could not stand to minister because of the cloud, for the glory of the LORD filled the house of the LORD.

8:11 Off-limits for People

Much of the temple stayed off-limits to the general public; only priests went in. Not even priests ventured into the Most Holy Place, except on very special occasions. Solomon had not intended the building for humans—he wanted a place suitable for God to dwell. And on the memorable day described here, the awesome glory of the Lord did indeed fill the temple.

Solomon Addresses the People

12 ¶ Then Solomon said,
"The LORD has said that He would dwell
    in the thick cloud.
13 "I have surely built You a lofty house,
    A place for Your dwelling forever."
14 ¶ Then the king faced about and blessed all the assembly of Israel, while all the assembly of Israel was standing.

15 He said, "Blessed be the LORD, the God of Israel, who spoke with His mouth to my father David and has fulfilled *it* with His hand, saying,

16 'Since the day that I brought My people Israel from Egypt, I did not choose a city out of all the tribes of Israel *in which* to build a house that My name might be there, but I chose David to be over My people Israel.'

17 "Now it was in the heart of my father David to build a house for the name of the LORD, the God of Israel.

18 "But the LORD said to my father David, 'Because it was in your heart to build a house for My name, you did well that it was in your heart.

19 'Nevertheless you shall not build the house, but your son who will be born to you, he will build the house for My name.'

20 "Now the LORD has fulfilled His word which He spoke; for I have risen in place of my father David and sit on the throne of Israel, as the LORD promised, and have built the house for the name of the LORD, the God of Israel.

21 "There I have set a place for the ark, in which is the covenant of the LORD, which He made with our fathers when He brought them from the land of Egypt."

The Prayer of Dedication

22 ¶ Then Solomon stood before the altar of the LORD in the presence of all the assembly of Israel and spread out his hands toward heaven.

23 He said, "O LORD, the God of Israel, there is no God like You in heaven above or on earth beneath, keeping covenant and *showing* lovingkindness to Your servants who walk before You with all their heart,

24 who have kept with Your servant, my father David, that which You have promised him; indeed, You have spoken with Your mouth and have fulfilled it with Your hand as it is this day.

25 "Now therefore, O LORD, the God of Israel, keep with Your servant David my father that which You have promised him, saying, 'You shall not lack a man to sit on the throne of Israel, if only your sons take heed to their way to walk before Me as you have walked.'

26 "Now therefore, O God of Israel, let Your word, I pray, be confirmed which You have spoken to Your servant, my father David.

27 ¶ "But will God indeed dwell on the earth? Behold, heaven and the highest heaven cannot contain You, how much less this house which I have built!

8:27 Where God Dwells

King Solomon was at his most eloquent in the great speech and prayer of chapter 8. He made it clear that the Lord of the universe could not fully dwell in a building. Nevertheless, God's presence, or his "Name," would indeed live there. For that reason, Solomon began the practice of praying toward Jerusalem, a practice still followed by many Jews today (verse 29).

28 "Yet have regard to the prayer of Your servant and to his supplication, O LORD my God, to listen to the cry and to the prayer which Your servant prays before You today;

29 that Your eyes may be open toward this house night and day, toward the place of which You have said, 'My name shall be there,' to listen to the prayer which Your servant shall pray toward this place.

30 "Listen to the supplication of Your servant and of Your people Israel, when they pray toward this place; hear in heaven Your dwelling place; hear and forgive.

31 ¶ "If a man sins against his neighbor and is made to take an oath, and he comes *and* takes an oath before Your altar in this house,

32 then hear in heaven and act and judge Your servants, condemning the wicked by bringing his way on his own head and justifying the righteous by giving him according to his righteousness.

33 ¶ "When Your people Israel are defeated before an enemy, because they have sinned against You, if they turn to You again and confess Your name and pray and make supplication to You in this house,

34 then hear in heaven, and forgive the sin of

Your people Israel, and bring them back to the land which You gave to their fathers.

35 ¶ "When the heavens are shut up and there is no rain, because they have sinned against You, and they pray toward this place and confess Your name and turn from their sin when You afflict them,

36 then hear in heaven and forgive the sin of Your servants and of Your people Israel, indeed, teach them the good way in which they should walk. And send rain on Your land, which You have given Your people for an inheritance.

37 ¶ "If there is famine in the land, if there is pestilence, if there is blight or mildew, locust or grasshopper, if their enemy besieges them in the land of their cities, whatever plague, whatever sickness there is,

38 whatever prayer or supplication is made by any man or by all Your people Israel, each knowing the affliction of his own heart, and spreading his hands toward this house;

39 then hear in heaven Your dwelling place, and forgive and act and render to each according to all his ways, whose heart You know, for You alone know the hearts of all the sons of men,

40 that they may ᵃfear You all the days that they live in the land which You have given to our fathers.

41 ¶ "Also concerning the foreigner who is not of Your people Israel, when he comes from a far country for Your name's sake

42 (for they will hear of Your great name and Your mighty hand, and of Your outstretched arm); when he comes and prays toward this house,

43 hear in heaven Your dwelling place, and do according to all for which the foreigner calls to You, in order that all the peoples of the earth may know Your name, to ᵇfear You, as do Your people Israel, and that they may know that this house which I have built is called by Your name.

44 ¶ "When Your people go out to battle against their enemy, by whatever way You shall send them, and they pray to the LORD toward the city which You have chosen and the house which I have built for Your name,

45 then hear in heaven their prayer and their supplication, and maintain their cause.

46 ¶ "When they sin against You (for there is no man who does not sin) and You are angry with them and deliver them to an enemy, so that they take them away captive to the land of the enemy, far off or near;

47 if they take thought in the land where they have been taken captive, and repent and make supplication to You in the land of those who have taken them captive, saying, 'We have sinned and have committed iniquity, we have acted wickedly';

48 if they return to You with all their heart and with all their soul in the land of their enemies who

have taken them captive, and pray to You toward their land which You have given to their fathers, the city which You have chosen, and the house which I have built for Your name;

49 then hear their prayer and their supplication in heaven Your dwelling place, and maintain their cause,

50 and forgive Your people who have sinned against You and all their transgressions which they have transgressed against You, and make them objects of compassion before those who have taken them captive, that they may have compassion on them

51 (for they are Your people and Your inheritance which You have brought forth from Egypt, from the midst of the iron furnace),

52 that Your eyes may be open to the supplication of Your servant and to the supplication of Your people Israel, to listen to them whenever they call to You.

53 "For You have separated them from all the peoples of the earth as Your inheritance, as You spoke through Moses Your servant, when You brought our fathers forth from Egypt, O Lord GOD."

Solomon's Benediction

54 ¶ When Solomon had finished praying this entire prayer and supplication to the LORD, he arose from before the altar of the LORD, from kneeling on his knees with his hands spread toward heaven.

55 And he stood and blessed all the assembly of Israel with a loud voice, saying:

56 ¶ "Blessed be the LORD, who has given rest to His people Israel, according to all that He promised; not one word has failed of all His good promise, which He promised through Moses His servant.

57 "May the LORD our God be with us, as He was with our fathers; may He not leave us or forsake us,

58 that He may incline our hearts to Himself, to walk in all His ways and to keep His commandments and His statutes and His ordinances, which He commanded our fathers.

59 "And may these words of mine, with which I have made supplication before the LORD, be near to the LORD our God day and night, that He may maintain the cause of His servant and the cause of His people Israel, as each day requires,

60 so that all the peoples of the earth may know that the LORD is God; there is no one else.

61 "Let your heart therefore be wholly devoted to the LORD our God, to walk in His statutes and to keep His commandments, as at this day."

Dedicatory Sacrifices

62 ¶ Now the king and all Israel with him offered sacrifice before the LORD.

ᵃOr revere   ᵇOr reverence

63 Solomon offered for the sacrifice of peace offerings, which he offered to the LORD, 22,000 oxen and 120,000 sheep. So the king and all the sons of Israel dedicated the house of the LORD.

64 On the same day the king consecrated the middle of the court that *was* before the house of the LORD, because there he offered the burnt offering and the grain offering and the fat of the peace offerings; for the bronze altar that *was* before the LORD *was* too small to hold the burnt offering and the grain offering and the fat of the peace offerings.

65 ¶ So Solomon observed the feast at that time, and all Israel with him, a great assembly from the entrance of Hamath to the brook of Egypt, before the LORD our God, for seven days and seven *more* days, *even* fourteen days.

66 On the eighth day he sent the people away and they blessed the king. Then they went to their tents joyful and glad of heart for all the goodness that the LORD had shown to David His servant and to Israel His people.

God's Promise and Warning

9 Now it came about when Solomon had finished building the house of the LORD, and the king's house, and all that Solomon desired to do,

2 that the LORD appeared to Solomon a second time, as He had appeared to him at Gibeon.

3 The LORD said to him, "I have heard your prayer and your supplication, which you have made before Me; I have consecrated this house which you have built by putting My name there forever, and My eyes and My heart will be there perpetually.

4 "As for you, if you will walk before Me as your father David walked, in integrity of heart and uprightness, doing according to all that I have commanded you *and* will keep My statutes and My ordinances,

5 then I will establish the throne of your kingdom over Israel forever, just as I promised to your father David, saying, 'You shall not lack a man on the throne of Israel.'

6 ¶ "But if you or your sons indeed turn away from following Me, and do not keep My commandments and My statutes which I have set before you, and go and serve other gods and worship them,

7 then I will cut off Israel from the land which I have given them, and the house which I have consecrated for My name, I will cast out of My sight. So Israel will become a proverb and a byword among all peoples.

8 "And this house will become a heap of ruins; everyone who passes by will be astonished and hiss and say, 'Why has the LORD done thus to this land and to this house?'

9 "And they will say, 'Because they forsook the LORD their God, who brought their fathers out of the land of Egypt, and adopted other gods and worshiped them and served them, therefore the LORD has brought all this adversity on them.' "

Cities Given to Hiram

10 ¶ It came about at the end of twenty years in which Solomon had built the two houses, the house of the LORD and the king's house

11 (Hiram king of Tyre had supplied Solomon with cedar and cypress timber and gold according to all his desire), then King Solomon gave Hiram twenty cities in the land of Galilee.

12 So Hiram came out from Tyre to see the cities which Solomon had given him, and they did not please him.

13 He said, "What are these cities which you have given me, my brother?" So they were called the land of ªCabul to this day.

> ### 9:13 Good-for-nothing Towns
> *Solomon gave away part of God's promised land to a foreigner, an act that may have stirred up the resentment of northern tribes against the South. King Hiram, unimpressed with the 20 Galilean towns Solomon gave him as payment for services, called them "Cabul" (good-for-nothing). Interestingly, Jesus chose this very area as the early focal point of his ministry on earth.*

14 And Hiram sent to the king 120 talents of gold.

15 ¶ Now this is the account of the forced labor which King Solomon levied to build the house of the LORD, his own house, the ᵇMillo, the wall of Jerusalem, Hazor, Megiddo, and Gezer.

16 *For* Pharaoh king of Egypt had gone up and captured Gezer and burned it with fire, and killed the Canaanites who lived in the city, and had given it *as* a dowry to his daughter, Solomon's wife.

17 So Solomon rebuilt Gezer and the lower Beth-horon

18 and Baalath and Tamar in the wilderness, in the land *of Judah,*

19 and all the storage cities which Solomon had, even the cities for his chariots and the cities for his horsemen, and all that it pleased Solomon to build in Jerusalem, in Lebanon, and in all the land under his rule.

20 *As for* all the people who were left of the Amorites, the Hittites, the Perizzites, the Hivites and the Jebusites, who were not of the sons of Israel,

21 their descendants who were left after them in the land whom the sons of Israel were unable to destroy utterly, from them Solomon levied forced laborers, even to this day.

ª I.e. as good as nothing   ᵇ I.e. citadel

22 But Solomon did not make slaves of the sons of Israel; for they were men of war, his servants, his princes, his captains, his chariot commanders, and his horsemen.

23 ¶ These *were* the chief officers who *were* over Solomon's work, five hundred and fifty, who ruled over the people doing the work.

24 ¶ As soon as Pharaoh's daughter came up from the city of David to her house which *Solomon* had built for her, then he built the Millo.

25 ¶ Now three times in a year Solomon offered burnt offerings and peace offerings on the altar which he built to the LORD, burning incense with them *on the altar* which *was* before the LORD. So he finished the house.

26 ¶ King Solomon also built a fleet of ships in Ezion-geber, which is near Eloth on the shore of the Red Sea, in the land of Edom.

27 And Hiram sent his servants with the fleet, sailors who knew the sea, along with the servants of Solomon.

28 They went to Ophir and took four hundred and twenty talents of gold from there, and brought *it* to King Solomon.

The Queen of Sheba

10 Now when the queen of Sheba heard about the fame of Solomon concerning the name of the LORD, she came to test him with difficult questions.

2 So she came to Jerusalem with a very large retinue, with camels carrying spices and very much gold and precious stones. When she came to Solomon, she spoke with him about all that was in her heart.

3 Solomon answered all her questions; nothing was hidden from the king which he did not explain to her.

4 When the queen of Sheba perceived all the wisdom of Solomon, the house that he had built,

5 the food of his table, the seating of his servants, the attendance of his waiters and their attire, his cupbearers, and his stairway by which he went up to the house of the LORD, there was no more spirit in her.

6 Then she said to the king, "It was a true report which I heard in my own land about your words and your wisdom.

7 "Nevertheless I did not believe the reports, until I came and my eyes had seen it. And behold, the half was not told me. You exceed *in* wisdom and prosperity the report which I heard.

8 "How blessed are your men, how blessed are these your servants who stand before you continually *and* hear your wisdom.

9 "Blessed be the LORD your God who delighted in you to set you on the throne of Israel; because the LORD loved Israel forever, therefore He made you king, to do justice and righteousness."

10 She gave the king a hundred and twenty talents of gold, and a very great *amount* of spices and precious stones. Never again did such abundance of spices come in as that which the queen of Sheba gave King Solomon.

11 ¶ Also the ships of Hiram, which brought gold from Ophir, brought in from Ophir a very great *number of* almug trees and precious stones.

12 The king made of the almug trees supports for the house of the LORD and for the king's house, also lyres and harps for the singers; such almug trees have not come in *again* nor have they been seen to this day.

13 ¶ King Solomon gave to the queen of Sheba all her desire which she requested, besides what he gave her according to his royal bounty. Then she turned and went to her own land together with her servants.

Wealth, Splendor and Wisdom

14 ¶ Now the weight of gold which came in to Solomon in one year was 666 talents of gold,

10:14 A King of Excess

This passage (10:14–29) graphically illustrates how far Solomon had strayed from God's ideal. The book of Deuteronomy cites Moses' forthright warnings about what kind of king should rule over Israel (Deuteronomy 17:14–20). Solomon defied those warnings by acquiring huge numbers of horses, getting involved in foreign trade, taking many wives, and accumulating silver and gold.

15 besides *that* from the traders and the ᵃwares of the merchants and all the kings of the Arabs and the governors of the country.

16 King Solomon made 200 large shields of beaten gold, using 600 *shekels of* gold on each large shield.

17 *He* made 300 shields of beaten gold, using three minas of gold on each shield, and the king put them in the house of the forest of Lebanon.

18 Moreover, the king made a great throne of ivory and overlaid it with refined gold.

19 *There were* six steps to the throne and a round top to the throne at its rear, and arms on each side of the seat, and two lions standing beside the arms.

20 Twelve lions were standing there on the six steps on the one side and on the other; nothing like *it* was made for any other kingdom.

21 All King Solomon's drinking vessels *were* of gold, and all the vessels of the house of the forest of Lebanon *were* of pure gold. None was of silver; it was not considered ᵇvaluable in the days of Solomon.

22 For the king had at sea the ships of Tarshish

ᵃ Or *traffic*   ᵇ Lit *anything*

with the ships of Hiram; once every three years the ships of Tarshish came bringing gold and silver, ivory and apes and peacocks.

23 ¶ So King Solomon became greater than all the kings of the earth in riches and in wisdom.

24 All the earth was seeking the presence of Solomon, to hear his wisdom which God had put in his heart.

25 They brought every man his gift, articles of silver and gold, garments, weapons, spices, horses, and mules, so much year by year.

26 ¶ Now Solomon gathered chariots and horsemen; and he had 1,400 chariots and 12,000 horsemen, and he stationed them in the chariot cities and with the king in Jerusalem.

27 The king made silver *as common* as stones in Jerusalem, and he made cedars as plentiful as sycamore trees that are in the *a*lowland.

28 Also Solomon's import of horses was from Egypt and Kue, *and* the king's merchants procured *them* from Kue for a price.

29 A chariot was imported from Egypt for 600 *shekels* of silver, and a horse for 150; and by the same means they exported them to all the kings of the Hittites and to the kings of the Arameans.

Solomon Turns from God

11 Now King Solomon loved many foreign women along with the daughter of Pharaoh: Moabite, Ammonite, Edomite, Sidonian, and Hittite women,

2 from the nations concerning which the LORD had said to the sons of Israel, "You shall not associate with them, nor shall they associate with you, *for* they will surely turn your heart away after their gods." Solomon held fast to these in love.

3 He had seven hundred wives, princesses, and three hundred concubines, and his wives turned his heart away.

11:3 So Many Women

Solomon's 700 wives were foreigners who worshiped other gods and had different standards of right and wrong. He probably married them as part of treaty arrangements with surrounding nations; a royal marriage was supposed to cement a bond between peoples. These marriages violated God's law (Deuteronomy 7:3–4; 17:17) and ultimately led Solomon away from God. Because of his wives' religions, he built shrines and encouraged pagan worship right in Jerusalem.

4 For when Solomon was old, his wives turned his heart away after other gods; and his heart was not *b*wholly devoted to the LORD his God, as the heart of David his father *had been.*

5 For Solomon went after Ashtoreth the goddess of the Sidonians and after Milcom the detestable idol of the Ammonites.

6 Solomon did what was evil in the sight of the LORD, and did not follow the LORD fully, as David his father *had done.*

7 Then Solomon built a high place for Chemosh the detestable idol of Moab, on the mountain which is east of Jerusalem, and for Molech the detestable idol of the sons of Ammon.

8 Thus also he did for all his foreign wives, who burned incense and sacrificed to their gods.

9 ¶ Now the LORD was angry with Solomon because his heart was turned away from the LORD, the God of Israel, who had appeared to him twice,

10 and had commanded him concerning this thing, that he should not go after other gods; but he did not observe what the LORD had commanded.

11 So the LORD said to Solomon, "Because you have done this, and you have not kept My covenant and My statutes, which I have commanded you, I will surely tear the kingdom from you, and will give it to your servant.

12 "Nevertheless I will not do it in your days for the sake of your father David, *but* I will tear it out of the hand of your son.

13 "However, I will not tear away all the kingdom, *but* I will give one tribe to your son for the sake of My servant David and for the sake of Jerusalem which I have chosen."

God Raises Adversaries

14 ¶ Then the LORD raised up an adversary to Solomon, Hadad the Edomite; he was of the royal line in Edom.

15 For it came about, when David was in Edom, and Joab the commander of the army had gone up to bury the slain, and had struck down every male in Edom

16 (for Joab and all Israel stayed there six months, until he had cut off every male in Edom),

17 that Hadad fled to Egypt, he and certain Edomites of his father's servants with him, while Hadad *was* a young boy.

18 They arose from Midian and came to Paran; and they took men with them from Paran and came to Egypt, to Pharaoh king of Egypt, who gave him a house and assigned him food and gave him land.

19 Now Hadad found great favor before Pharaoh, so that he gave him in marriage the sister of his own wife, the sister of Tahpenes the queen.

20 The sister of Tahpenes bore his son Genubath, whom Tahpenes weaned in Pharaoh's house; and Genubath was in Pharaoh's house among the sons of Pharaoh.

21 But when Hadad heard in Egypt that David slept with his fathers and that Joab the commander of the army was dead, Hadad said to Pharaoh,

---

a Heb *Shephelah*　　*b* Lit *complete with*

"Send me away, that I may go to my own country."

22 Then Pharaoh said to him, "But what have you lacked with me, that behold, you are seeking to go to your own country?" And he answered, "Nothing; nevertheless you must surely let me go."

23 ¶ God also raised up *another* adversary to him, Rezon the son of Eliada, who had fled from his lord Hadadezer king of Zobah.

24 He gathered men to himself and became leader of a marauding band, after David slew them of *Zobah;* and they went to Damascus and stayed there, and reigned in Damascus.

25 So he was an adversary to Israel all the days of Solomon, along with the evil that Hadad *did;* and he abhorred Israel and reigned over Aram.

26 ¶ Then Jeroboam the son of Nebat, an Ephraimite of Zeredah, Solomon's servant, whose mother's name was Zeruah, a widow, also rebelled against the king.

27 Now this was the reason why he rebelled against the king: Solomon built the Millo, *and* closed up the breach of the city of his father David.

28 Now the man Jeroboam was a valiant warrior, and when Solomon saw that the young man was industrious, he appointed him over all the forced labor of the house of Joseph.

29 It came about at that time, when Jeroboam went out of Jerusalem, that the prophet Ahijah the Shilonite found him on the road. Now Ahijah had clothed himself with a new cloak; and both of them were alone in the field.

30 Then Ahijah took hold of the new cloak which was on him and tore it into twelve pieces.

31 He said to Jeroboam, "Take for yourself ten pieces; for thus says the LORD, the God of Israel, 'Behold, I will tear the kingdom out of the hand of Solomon and give you ten tribes

32 (but he will have one tribe, for the sake of My servant David and for the sake of Jerusalem, the city which I have chosen from all the tribes of Israel),

33 because they have forsaken Me, and have worshiped Ashtoreth the goddess of the Sidonians, Chemosh the god of Moab, and Milcom the god of the sons of Ammon; and they have not walked in My ways, doing what is right in My sight and *observing* My statutes and My ordinances, as his father David *did*.

34 'Nevertheless I will not take the whole kingdom out of his hand, but I will make him ruler all the days of his life, for the sake of My servant David whom I chose, who observed My commandments and My statutes;

35 but I will take the kingdom from his son's hand and give it to you, *even* ten tribes.

36 'But to his son I will give one tribe, that My servant David may have a lamp always before Me in Jerusalem, the city where I have chosen for Myself to put My name.

37 'I will take you, and you shall reign over whatever you desire, and you shall be king over Israel.

38 'Then it will be, that if you listen to all that I command you and walk in My ways, and do

JEROBOAM *Blown Opportunity*

POLITICIANS WHO RUN ON A platform of reform often, when they attain power, act depressingly like the corrupt leaders they have just replaced. Such is the story of Jeroboam, a decent man who had a unique chance to stop Israel's slide into corruption.

Jeroboam came to power by the back door. On his way out of Jerusalem, where he worked as a top official for King Solomon, Jeroboam met a prophet named Ahijah. The prophet took off the cloak he was wearing and ripped the brand-new garment into twelve pieces. Then he handed ten pieces to Jeroboam and delivered the message behind the object lesson: Because of King Solomon's failures, God would rip the kingdom of Israel apart. The bureaucrat Jeroboam would soon inherit leadership over ten of the twelve tribes.

This dramatic prophecy launched a fierce struggle for power. At first, fearing for his life, Jeroboam fled the country. Years later he came back from exile to make peace with Solomon's son, but found the son stupidly harsher than the old man. (See "Rehoboam: a Fool's Answer," p. 472.) The fed-up northern tribes rebelled, and Jeroboam became king of a new nation. God's people were irrevocably split into two camps.

Jeroboam's rule may have begun with God's approval, but the bureaucrat who would be king never lived up to God's call. Fearing that his citizens would gradually be won back to the south—they had to travel to Jerusalem to worship in the temple—Jeroboam made a clever but terrible choice. He started his own, competing religion in the north.

By outward standards the new religion succeeded, enduring as long as Israel did. God, however, who had brought Jeroboam to power, reacted with outrage. He predicted and then carried out the total destruction of Jeroboam's family (15:27–30).

Life Questions: Do you find it easier to criticize leaders than to lead? How do you usually respond when you're placed in a leadership position?

what is right in My sight by observing My statutes and My commandments, as My servant David did, then I will be with you and build you an enduring house as I built for David, and I will give Israel to you.

39 'Thus I will afflict the descendants of David for this, but not always.'"

40 Solomon sought therefore to put Jeroboam to death; but Jeroboam arose and fled to Egypt to Shishak king of Egypt, and he was in Egypt until the death of Solomon.

The Death of Solomon

41 ¶ Now the rest of the acts of Solomon and whatever he did, and his wisdom, are they not written in the book of the acts of Solomon?

11:41 Using Other Sources

The author makes liberal use of other historical records, most of which have not survived. This verse refers to "the book of the acts of Solomon." Elsewhere, 1 Kings relies on accounts of the kings of Judah (22:45) or of Israel (15:31). In all, the two books of Kings make 34 references to other sources.

42 Thus the time that Solomon reigned in Jerusalem over all Israel was forty years.

43 And Solomon slept with his fathers and was buried in the city of his father David, and his son Rehoboam reigned in his place.

King Rehoboam Acts Foolishly

12 Then Rehoboam went to Shechem, for all Israel had come to Shechem to make him king.

2 Now when Jeroboam the son of Nebat heard *of it,* he was living in Egypt (for he was yet in Egypt, where he had fled from the presence of King Solomon).

3 Then they sent and called him, and Jeroboam and all the assembly of Israel came and spoke to Rehoboam, saying,

4 "Your father made our yoke hard; now therefore lighten the hard service of your father and his heavy yoke which he put on us, and we will serve you."

5 Then he said to them, "Depart for three days, then return to me." So the people departed.

6 ¶ King Rehoboam consulted with the elders who had served his father Solomon while he was still alive, saying, "How do you counsel *me* to answer this people?"

7 Then they spoke to him, saying, "If you will be a servant to this people today, and will serve them and grant them their petition, and speak good words to them, then they will be your servants forever."

8 But he forsook the counsel of the elders

which they had given him, and consulted with the young men who grew up with him and served him.

9 So he said to them, "What counsel do you give that we may answer this people who have spoken to me, saying, 'Lighten the yoke which your father put on us'?"

10 The young men who grew up with him spoke to him, saying, "Thus you shall say to this people who spoke to you, saying, 'Your father made our yoke heavy, now you make it lighter for us!' But you shall speak to them, 'My little finger is thicker than my father's loins!

11 'Whereas my father loaded you with a heavy yoke, I will add to your yoke; my father disciplined you with whips, but I will discipline you with scorpions.'"

12 ¶ Then Jeroboam and all the people came to Rehoboam on the third day as the king had directed, saying, "Return to me on the third day."

13 The king answered the people harshly, for he forsook the advice of the elders which they had given him,

14 and he spoke to them according to the advice of the young men, saying, "My father made your yoke heavy, but I will add to your yoke; my father disciplined you with whips, but I will discipline you with scorpions."

15 So the king did not listen to the people; for it was a turn of *events* from the LORD, that He might establish His word, which the LORD spoke through Ahijah the Shilonite to Jeroboam the son of Nebat.

The Kingdom Divided
Jeroboam Rules Israel

16 ¶ When all Israel *saw* that the king did not listen to them, the people answered the king, saying,

"What portion do we have in David?
We have no inheritance in the son of Jesse;
To your tents, O Israel!
Now look after your own house, David!"

So Israel departed to their tents.

17 But as for the sons of Israel who lived in the cities of Judah, Rehoboam reigned over them.

18 Then King Rehoboam sent Adoram, who was over the forced labor, and all Israel stoned him to death. And King Rehoboam made haste to mount his chariot to flee to Jerusalem.

19 So Israel has been in rebellion against the house of David to this day.

20 ¶ It came about when all Israel heard that Jeroboam had returned, that they sent and called him to the assembly and made him king over all Israel. None but the tribe of Judah followed the house of David.

21 ¶ Now when Rehoboam had come to Jerusalem, he assembled all the house of Judah and the tribe of Benjamin, 180,000 chosen men who were

warriors, to fight against the house of Israel to restore the kingdom to Rehoboam the son of Solomon.

22 But the word of God came to Shemaiah the man of God, saying,

23 "Speak to Rehoboam the son of Solomon, king of Judah, and to all the house of Judah and Benjamin and to the rest of the people, saying,

24 'Thus says the LORD, "You must not go up and fight against your relatives the sons of Israel; return every man to his house, for this thing has come from Me." ' " So they listened to the word of the LORD, and returned and went *their way* according to the word of the LORD.

Jeroboam's Idolatry

25 ¶ Then Jeroboam built Shechem in the hill country of Ephraim, and lived there. And he went out from there and built Penuel.

26 Jeroboam said in his heart, "Now the kingdom will return to the house of David.

27 "If this people go up to offer sacrifices in the house of the LORD at Jerusalem, then the heart of this people will return to their lord, *even* to Rehoboam king of Judah; and they will kill me and return to Rehoboam king of Judah."

28 So the king consulted, and made two golden calves, and he said to them, "It is too much for you to go up to Jerusalem; behold your gods, O Israel, that brought you up from the land of Egypt."

29 He set one in Bethel, and the other he put in Dan.

30 Now this thing became a sin, for the people went *to worship* before the one as far as Dan.

31 And he made houses on high places, and made priests from among all the people who were not of the sons of Levi.

32 Jeroboam instituted a feast in the eighth month on the fifteenth day of the month, like the feast which is in Judah, and he went up to the altar; thus he did in Bethel, sacrificing to the calves which he had made. And he stationed in Bethel the priests of the high places which he had made.

33 Then he went up to the altar which he had made in Bethel on the fifteenth day in the eighth month, even in the month which he had devised in his own heart; and he instituted a feast for the sons of Israel and went up to the altar to burn incense.

Jeroboam Warned, Stricken

13 Now behold, there came a man of God from Judah to Bethel by the word of the LORD, while Jeroboam was standing by the altar to burn incense.

2 He cried against the altar by the word of the LORD, and said, "O altar, altar, thus says the LORD, 'Behold, a son shall be born to the house of David, Josiah by name; and on you he shall sacrifice the

priests of the high places who burn incense on you, and human bones shall be burned on you.' "

3 Then he gave a sign the same day, saying, "This is the sign which the LORD has spoken, 'Behold, the altar shall be split apart and the ashes which are on it shall be poured out.' "

4 Now when the king heard the saying of the man of God, which he cried against the altar in Bethel, Jeroboam stretched out his hand from the altar, saying, "Seize him." But his hand which he stretched out against him dried up, so that he could not draw it back to himself.

5 The altar also was split apart and the ashes were poured out from the altar, according to the sign which the man of God had given by the word of the LORD.

6 The king said to the man of God, "Please aentreat the LORD your God, and pray for me, that my hand may be restored to me." So the man of God bentreated the LORD, and the king's hand was restored to him, and it became as it was before.

7 Then the king said to the man of God, "Come home with me and refresh yourself, and I will give you a reward."

13:7–10 Standing Up to the King

Afraid that temple worship in Jerusalem would lure his northern supporters back to the South, Jeroboam lifted a page from Israel's past (Exodus 32:1–4) and put up two golden calves for worship (see 12:32). An anonymous man of God prophesied against this idol worship in the strongest terms.

Jeroboam's offer of a gift to the prophet reflects the kings' tendencies to keep "court prophets," paid to tell the kings what they wanted to hear. The anonymous man of God would have nothing to do with Jeroboam's hospitality. He had come to protest Jeroboam's new religion, and would not be bought.

8 But the man of God said to the king, "If you were to give me half your house I would not go with you, nor would I eat bread or drink water in this place.

9 "For so it was commanded me by the word of the LORD, saying, 'You shall eat no bread, nor drink water, nor return by the way which you came.' "

10 So he went another way and did not return by the way which he came to Bethel.

The Disobedient Prophet

11 ¶ Now an old prophet was living in Bethel; and his sons came and told him all the deeds which the man of God had done that day in Beth-

---

a Lit *soften the face of*   b Lit *softened the face of*

el; the words which he had spoken to the king, these also they related to their father.

12 Their father said to them, "Which way did he go?" Now his sons had seen the way which the man of God who came from Judah had gone.

13 Then he said to his sons, "Saddle the donkey for me." So they saddled the donkey for him and he rode away on it.

14 So he went after the man of God and found him sitting under an oak; and he said to him, "Are you the man of God who came from Judah?" And he said, "I am."

15 Then he said to him, "Come home with me and eat bread."

16 He said, "I cannot return with you, nor go with you, nor will I eat bread or drink water with you in this place.

17 "For a command *came* to me by the word of the LORD, 'You shall eat no bread, nor drink water there; do not return by going the way which you came.'"

18 He said to him, "I also am a prophet like you, and an angel spoke to me by the word of the LORD, saying, 'Bring him back with you to your house, that he may eat bread and drink water.'" *But* he lied to him.

19 So he went back with him, and ate bread in his house and drank water.

20 ¶ Now it came about, as they were sitting down at the table, that the word of the LORD came to the prophet who had brought him back;

21 and he cried to the man of God who came from Judah, saying, "Thus says the LORD, 'Because you have disobeyed the command of the LORD, and have not observed the commandment which the LORD your God commanded you,

22 but have returned and eaten bread and drunk water in the place of which He said to you, "Eat no bread and drink no water"; your body shall not come to the grave of your fathers.'"

23 It came about after he had eaten bread and after he had drunk, that he saddled the donkey for him, for the prophet whom he had brought back.

24 Now when he had gone, a lion met him on the way and killed him, and his body was thrown on the road, with the donkey standing beside it; the lion also was standing beside the body.

25 And behold, men passed by and saw the body thrown on the road, and the lion standing beside the body; so they came and told *it* in the city where the old prophet lived.

26 ¶ Now when the prophet who brought him back from the way heard *it*, he said, "It is the man of God, who disobeyed the command of the LORD; therefore the LORD has given him to the lion, which has torn him and killed him, according to the word of the LORD which He spoke to him."

27 Then he spoke to his sons, saying, "Saddle the donkey for me." And they saddled *it*.

28 He went and found his body thrown on the road with the donkey and the lion standing beside

the body; the lion had not eaten the body nor torn the donkey.

29 So the prophet took up the body of the man of God and laid it on the donkey and brought it back, and he came to the city of the old prophet to mourn and to bury him.

30 He laid his body in his own grave, and they mourned over him, *saying*, "Alas, my brother!"

31 After he had buried him, he spoke to his sons, saying, "When I die, bury me in the grave in which the man of God is buried; lay my bones beside his bones.

32 "For the thing shall surely come to pass which he cried by the word of the LORD against the altar in Bethel and against all the houses of the high places which are in the cities of Samaria."

33 ¶ After this event Jeroboam did not return from his evil way, but again he made priests of the high places from among all the people; any who would, he ordained, to be priests of the high places.

34 This event became sin to the house of Jeroboam, even to blot *it* out and destroy *it* from off the face of the earth.

Ahijah Prophesies against the King

14 At that time Abijah the son of Jeroboam became sick.

2 Jeroboam said to his wife, "Arise now, and disguise yourself so that they will not know that you are the wife of Jeroboam, and go to Shiloh; behold, Ahijah the prophet is there, who spoke concerning me *that I would be* king over this people.

3 "Take ten loaves with you, *some* cakes and a jar of honey, and go to him. He will tell you what will happen to the boy."

4 ¶ Jeroboam's wife did so, and arose and went to Shiloh, and came to the house of Ahijah. Now Ahijah could not see, for his eyes were dim because of his age.

5 Now the LORD had said to Ahijah, "Behold, the wife of Jeroboam is coming to inquire of you concerning her son, for he is sick. You shall say thus and thus to her, for it will be when she arrives that she will pretend to be another woman."

6 ¶ When Ahijah heard the sound of her feet coming in the doorway, he said, "Come in, wife of Jeroboam, why do you pretend to be another woman? For I am sent to you *with* a harsh *message.*

7 "Go, say to Jeroboam, 'Thus says the LORD God of Israel, "Because I exalted you from among the people and made you leader over My people Israel,

8 and tore the kingdom away from the house of David and gave it to you—yet you have not been like My servant David, who kept My commandments and who followed Me with all his heart, to do only that which was right in My sight;

9 you also have done more evil than all who

The Nation Splits Apart

A rebellion leads to civil war

CHAPTER 12 OF 1 KINGS MARKS a decisive turning point in the nation of Israel. For 120 years Saul, David, and Solomon had consolidated power, expanded borders, and built a strong government. But immediately after Solomon's death everything began to unravel. Simmering hostility in the North boiled over at last, and the northern tribes seceded to form their own nation.

> There was war . . . continually.
> 14:30

Two Nations out of One

Ten tribes joined together under Jeroboam to form a nation in the North called Israel. Only two tribes, Judah and Benjamin, remained loyal to Solomon's heir in Jerusalem. These southerners took on the name Judah and made Jerusalem, home of the temple, their capital. From that time forward, the united nation of Israel ceased to exist.

The northern rebellion brought a terrible civil war to Israel, a war that dragged on for 50 years. Despite a peace treaty, war kept breaking out.

The book of Kings records the histories of both nations. Action shifts back and forth between Israel in the North and Judah in the South. The effect resembles an account of America during Civil War years, first describing events in the North and then shifting to what was simultaneously taking place in the South.

This book does not attempt to give a full history of both nations. Rather, it focuses on their kings and queens. As guardian of the covenant with God, the king or queen came to symbolize the spiritual health of the nation. As that monarch went, so went the nation. Each ruler gets a capsule summary and usually a one-sentence rating. He or she either performed like David, who "did what was right in the sight of the LORD," or like the northern king Jeroboam, who "caused Israel to " sin.

The North: A Perpetual Slide Downward

Ironically, the northern tribes seceded as part of a reform movement, to correct some of the excesses of Solomon's reign. But starting with the first king, Jeroboam, no king of Israel did what was right in God's eyes. The books of 1, 2 Kings condemn all the northern kings.

Northern kings brought idolatry into their religion and corruption into their politics. They adopted all the oppressive ways that had sparked the original rebellion: harsh taxation, repression of prophets, abuse of power. Of 19 northern kings, eight either were murdered or committed suicide. One king, Zimri, lasted only seven days.

The worst rulers, King Ahab and Queen Jezebel, introduced the terrible practice of Baal worship (see "Why All the Fuss about Idols?" page 437). Israel hit its spiritual low point, and Ahab replaced Jeroboam as a symbol of evil. Kings to follow were called "Ahabs" much as a ruthless tyrant today is compared with Hitler. Israel's future destruction became certain; after Ahab and Jezebel, the nation was merely marking time.

The South: A Surprising Twist

While Israel—which began as a reform movement—slid toward disaster, the two tribes in the South, Judah, proved more faithful to God. They produced at least a handful of good kings. Even when other nations took advantage of Judah's weakness and plundered Jerusalem, the nation still held together.

Idolatry plagued Judah also, but not to the same extent as in the North. The temple remained a powerful symbol of worship of the true God. And every few generations a sincere, committed king arose to sweep away his predecessors' dangerous practices. The authors pointedly note that these good kings usually outlived the bad rulers.

Within 250 years the Northern Kingdom, Israel, was obliterated. Judah survived another 135 years before likewise falling to foreign invaders. In a sense, their fate was sealed from the time of the original secession. The prophet Isaiah would remember the schism as the worst disaster that had befallen his people (Isaiah 7:17).

Life Questions: Have you seen rebellion lead to "civil war" in families? Churches? Schools? When you don't like what the leaders are doing, are there alternatives to outright rebellion?

were before you, and have gone and made for yourself other gods and molten images to provoke Me to anger, and have cast Me behind your back—

10 therefore behold, I am bringing calamity on the house of Jeroboam, and will cut off from Jeroboam every male person, both bond and free in Israel, and I will make a clean sweep of the house of Jeroboam, as one sweeps away dung until it is all gone.

11 "Anyone belonging to Jeroboam who dies in the city the dogs will eat. And he who dies in the field the birds of the heavens will eat; for the LORD has spoken it." '

12 "Now you, arise, go to your house. When your feet enter the city the child will die.

13 "All Israel shall mourn for him and bury him, for he alone of Jeroboam's *family* will come to the grave, because in him something good was found toward the LORD God of Israel in the house of Jeroboam.

14 "Moreover, the LORD will raise up for Himself a king over Israel who will cut off the house of Jeroboam this day and from now on.

15 ¶ "For the LORD will strike Israel, as a reed is shaken in the water; and He will uproot Israel from this good land which He gave to their fathers, and will scatter them beyond the *Euphrates* River, because they have made their *ª*Asherim, provoking the LORD to anger.

16 "He will give up Israel on account of the sins of Jeroboam, which he committed and with which he made Israel to sin."

17 ¶ Then Jeroboam's wife arose and departed and came to Tirzah. As she was entering the threshold of the house, the child died.

18 All Israel buried him and mourned for him, according to the word of the LORD which He spoke through His servant Ahijah the prophet.

19 ¶ Now the rest of the acts of Jeroboam, how he made war and how he reigned, behold, they are written in the Book of the Chronicles of the Kings of Israel.

20 The time that Jeroboam reigned *was* twenty-two years; and he slept with his fathers, and Nadab his son reigned in his place.

Rehoboam Misleads Judah

21 ¶ Now Rehoboam the son of Solomon reigned in Judah. Rehoboam was forty-one years old when he became king, and he reigned seventeen years in Jerusalem, the city which the LORD had chosen from all the tribes of Israel to put His name there. And his mother's name was Naamah the Ammonitess.

22 Judah did evil in the sight of the LORD, and they provoked Him to jealousy more than all that their fathers had done, with the sins which they committed.

23 For they also built for themselves high places and *sacred* pillars and Asherim on every high hill and beneath every luxuriant tree.

24 There were also male cult prostitutes in the land. They did according to all the abominations

14:23 Notorious Asherim Poles

Introduced in the reign of Rehoboam, Asherim poles became a regular feature of Judah's landscape for hundreds of years. They were dedicated to a mother-goddess and often erected alongside altars on the high places devoted to God. They came to represent Judah's slide into idolatry. When judging the failures of various kings, the authors often comment, "the high places were not taken away."

of the nations which the LORD dispossessed before the sons of Israel.

25 ¶ Now it happened in the fifth year of King Rehoboam, that Shishak the king of Egypt came up against Jerusalem.

26 He took away the treasures of the house of the LORD and the treasures of the king's house, and he took everything, even taking all the shields of gold which Solomon had made.

27 So King Rehoboam made shields of bronze in their place, and committed them to the care of the commanders of the *ᵇ*guard who guarded the doorway of the king's house.

28 Then it happened as often as the king entered the house of the LORD, that the *ᶜ*guards would carry them and would bring them back into the guards' room.

29 ¶ Now the rest of the acts of Rehoboam and all that he did, are they not written in the Book of the Chronicles of the Kings of Judah?

30 There was war between Rehoboam and Jeroboam continually.

31 And Rehoboam slept with his fathers and was buried with his fathers in the city of David; and his mother's name was Naamah the Ammonitess. And Abijam his son became king in his place.

Abijam Reigns over Judah

15 Now in the eighteenth year of King Jeroboam, the son of Nebat, Abijam became king over Judah.

2 He reigned three years in Jerusalem; and his mother's name was Maacah the daughter of Abishalom.

3 He walked in all the sins of his father which he had committed before him; and his heart was not wholly devoted to the LORD his God, like the heart of his father David.

4 But for David's sake the LORD his God gave

ª I.e. wooden symbols of a female deity   *ᵇ* Lit *runner*   *ᶜ* Lit *runners* him a lamp in Jerusalem, to raise up his son after him and to establish Jerusalem;

5 because David did what was right in the sight of the LORD, and had not turned aside from anything that He commanded him all the days of his life, except in the case of Uriah the Hittite.

6 There was war between Rehoboam and Jeroboam all the days of his life.

7 ¶ Now the rest of the acts of Abijam and all that he did, are they not written in the Book of the Chronicles of the Kings of Judah? And there was war between Abijam and Jeroboam.

Asa Succeeds Abijam

8 And Abijam slept with his fathers and they buried him in the city of David; and Asa his son became king in his place.

9 ¶ So in the twentieth year of Jeroboam the king of Israel, Asa began to reign as king of Judah.

10 He reigned forty-one years in Jerusalem; and his mother's name was Maacah the daughter of Abishalom.

11 Asa did what was right in the sight of the LORD, like David his father.

12 He also put away the male cult prostitutes from the land and removed all the idols which his fathers had made.

13 He also removed Maacah his mother from *being* queen mother, because she had made a horrid image as an Asherah; and Asa cut down her horrid image and burned *it* at the brook Kidron.

14 But the high places were not taken away; nevertheless the heart of Asa was wholly devoted to the LORD all his days.

15 He brought into the house of the LORD the dedicated things of his father and his own dedicated things: silver and gold and utensils.

16 ¶ Now there was war between Asa and Baasha king of Israel all their days.

17 Baasha king of Israel went up against Judah and fortified Ramah in order to prevent *anyone* from going out or coming in to Asa king of Judah.

18 Then Asa took all the silver and the gold which were left in the treasuries of the house of the LORD and the treasuries of the king's house, and delivered them into the hand of his servants. And King Asa sent them to Ben-hadad the son of Tabrimmon, the son of Hezion, king of Aram, who lived in Damascus, saying,

19 "*Let there be* a treaty between you and me, *as* between my father and your father. Behold, I have sent you a present of silver and gold; go, break your treaty with Baasha king of Israel so that he will withdraw from me."

20 So Ben-hadad listened to King Asa and sent the commanders of his armies against the cities of Israel, and conquered Ijon, Dan, Abel-beth-maacah and all Chinneroth, besides all the land of Naphtali.

21 When Baasha heard *of it*, he ceased fortifying Ramah and remained in Tirzah.

22 Then King Asa made a proclamation to all Judah—none was exempt—and they carried away the stones of Ramah and its timber with which Baasha had built. And King Asa built with them Geba of Benjamin and Mizpah.

Jehoshaphat Succeeds Asa

23 ¶ Now the rest of all the acts of Asa and all his might and all that he did and the cities which he built, are they not written in the Book of the Chronicles of the Kings of Judah? But in the time of his old age he was diseased in his feet.

24 And Asa slept with his fathers and was buried with his fathers in the city of David his father; and Jehoshaphat his son reigned in his place.

Nadab, then Baasha, Rules over Israel

25 ¶ Now Nadab the son of Jeroboam became king over Israel in the second year of Asa king of Judah, and he reigned over Israel two years.

26 He did evil in the sight of the LORD, and walked in the way of his father and in his sin which he made Israel sin.

27 Then Baasha the son of Ahijah of the house of Issachar conspired against him, and Baasha struck him down at Gibbethon, which belonged to the Philistines, while Nadab and all Israel were laying siege to Gibbethon.

28 ¶ So Baasha killed him in the third year of Asa king of Judah and reigned in his place.

29 It came about as soon as he was king, he struck down all the household of Jeroboam. He did not leave to Jeroboam any persons alive, until he had destroyed them, according to the word of the LORD, which He spoke by His servant Ahijah the Shilonite,

30 *and* because of the sins of Jeroboam which he sinned, and which he made Israel sin, because of his provocation with which he provoked the LORD God of Israel to anger.

31 ¶ Now the rest of the acts of Nadab and all that he did, are they not written in the Book of the Chronicles of the Kings of Israel?

War with Judah

32 There was war between Asa and Baasha king of Israel all their days.

33 ¶ In the third year of Asa king of Judah, Baasha the son of Ahijah became king over all Israel at Tirzah, *and reigned* twenty-four years.

34 He did evil in the sight of the LORD, and walked in the way of Jeroboam and in his sin which he made Israel sin.

Prophecy against Baasha

16 Now the word of the LORD came to Jehu the son of Hanani against Baasha, saying,

2 "Inasmuch as I exalted you from the dust and made you leader over My people Israel, and you have walked in the way of Jeroboam and have

made My people Israel sin, provoking Me to anger with their sins,

3 behold, I will consume Baasha and his house, and I will make your house like the house of Jeroboam the son of Nebat.

4 "Anyone of Baasha who dies in the city the dogs will eat, and anyone of his who dies in the field the birds of the heavens will eat."

5 ¶ Now the rest of the acts of Baasha and what he did and his might, are they not written in the Book of the Chronicles of the Kings of Israel?

The Israelite Kings

6 And Baasha slept with his fathers and was buried in Tirzah, and Elah his son became king in his place.

7 Moreover, the word of the LORD through the prophet Jehu the son of Hanani also came against Baasha and his household, both because of all the evil which he did in the sight of the LORD, provoking Him to anger with the work of his hands, in being like the house of Jeroboam, and because he struck it.

8 ¶ In the twenty-sixth year of Asa king of Judah, Elah the son of Baasha became king over Israel at Tirzah, *and reigned* two years.

9 His servant Zimri, commander of half his chariots, conspired against him. Now he *was* at Tirzah drinking himself drunk in the house of Arza, who *was* over the household at Tirzah.

10 Then Zimri went in and struck him and put him to death in the twenty-seventh year of Asa king of Judah, and became king in his place.

11 It came about when he became king, as soon as he sat on his throne, that he killed all the household of Baasha; he did not leave a single male, neither of his relatives nor of his friends.

12 ¶ Thus Zimri destroyed all the household of Baasha, according to the word of the LORD, which He spoke against Baasha through Jehu the prophet,

13 for all the sins of Baasha and the sins of Elah his son, which they sinned and which they made Israel sin, provoking the LORD God of Israel to anger with their idols.

14 Now the rest of the acts of Elah and all that he did, are they not written in the Book of the Chronicles of the Kings of Israel?

15 ¶ In the twenty-seventh year of Asa king of Judah, Zimri reigned seven days at Tirzah. Now the people were camped against Gibbethon, which belonged to the Philistines.

16 The people who were camped heard it said, "Zimri has conspired and has also struck down the king." Therefore all Israel made Omri, the commander of the army, king over Israel that day in the camp.

17 Then Omri and all Israel with him went up from Gibbethon and besieged Tirzah.

18 When Zimri saw that the city was taken, he went into the citadel of the king's house and

burned the king's house over him with fire, and died,

19 because of his sins which he sinned, doing evil in the sight of the LORD, walking in the way of Jeroboam, and in his sin which he did, making Israel sin.

20 Now the rest of the acts of Zimri and his conspiracy which he carried out, are they not written in the Book of the Chronicles of the Kings of Israel?

21 ¶ Then the people of Israel were divided into two parts: half of the people followed Tibni the son of Ginath, to make him king; the *other* half followed Omri.

16:21–28 A Strong, Weak King

King Omri gets a grand total of eight verses in 1 Kings, even though secular historians regard him as one of Israel's most powerful kings. After his firm rule, Israel was called Omriland in Assyrian records. He built the capital city of Samaria in a location that guarded all routes north and south. Yet he also started the religious heresies that led to his nation's extinction. Politically shrewd, he married off his son to a neighboring king's daughter (Jezebel). The books of 1, 2 Kings, however, are concerned with the rulers' spiritual health, and Omri scored very poorly.

22 But the people who followed Omri prevailed over the people who followed Tibni the son of Ginath. And Tibni died and Omri became king.

23 In the thirty-first year of Asa king of Judah, Omri became king over Israel *and reigned* twelve years; he reigned six years at Tirzah.

24 He bought the hill Samaria from Shemer for two talents of silver; and he built on the hill, and named the city which he built Samaria, after the name of Shemer, the owner of the hill.

25 ¶ Omri did evil in the sight of the LORD, and acted more wickedly than all who *were* before him.

26 For he walked in all the way of Jeroboam the son of Nebat and in his sins which he made Israel sin, provoking the LORD God of Israel with their idols.

27 Now the rest of the acts of Omri which he did and his might which he showed, are they not written in the Book of the Chronicles of the Kings of Israel?

28 So Omri slept with his fathers and was buried in Samaria; and Ahab his son became king in his place.

29 ¶ Now Ahab the son of Omri became king over Israel in the thirty-eighth year of Asa king of Judah, and Ahab the son of Omri reigned over Israel in Samaria twenty-two years.

30 Ahab the son of Omri did evil in the sight of the LORD more than all who were before him.

31 ¶ It came about, as though it had been a trivial thing for him to walk in the sins of Jeroboam the son of Nebat, that he married Jezebel the daughter of Ethbaal king of the Sidonians, and went to serve Baal and worshiped him.

32 So he erected an altar for Baal in the house of Baal which he built in Samaria.

33 Ahab also made the ^aAsherah. Thus Ahab did more to provoke the LORD God of Israel than all the kings of Israel who were before him.

34 In his days Hiel the Bethelite built Jericho; he laid its foundations with the *loss of* Abiram his firstborn, and set up its gates with the *loss of* his youngest son Segub, according to the word of the LORD, which He spoke by Joshua the son of Nun.

16:34 A Curse from Joshua

Joshua 6:26 records the solemn pronouncement of what would happen to anyone who attempted to rebuild Jericho. The curse had tragic consequences for Hiel.

Elijah Predicts Drought

17 Now Elijah the Tishbite, who was of the settlers of Gilead, said to Ahab, "As the LORD, the God of Israel lives, before whom I stand, surely there shall be neither dew nor rain these years, except by my word."

2 The word of the LORD came to him, saying,

3 "Go away from here and turn eastward, and hide yourself by the brook Cherith, which is east of the Jordan.

4 "It shall be that you will drink of the brook,

^a I.e. wooden symbol of a female deity

and I have commanded the ravens to provide for you there."

5 So he went and did according to the word of the LORD, for he went and lived by the brook Cherith, which is east of the Jordan.

6 The ravens brought him bread and meat in the morning and bread and meat in the evening, and he would drink from the brook.

7 It happened after a while that the brook dried up, because there was no rain in the land.

8 ¶ Then the word of the LORD came to him, saying,

9 "Arise, go to Zarephath, which belongs to Sidon, and stay there; behold, I have commanded a widow there to provide for you."

10 So he arose and went to Zarephath, and when he came to the gate of the city, behold, a widow was there gathering sticks; and he called to her and said, "Please get me a little water in a jar, that I may drink."

11 As she was going to get *it*, he called to her and said, "Please bring me a piece of bread in your hand."

12 But she said, "As the LORD your God lives, I have no bread, only a handful of flour in the bowl and a little oil in the jar; and behold, I am gathering a few sticks that I may go in and prepare for me and my son, that we may eat it and die."

13 Then Elijah said to her, "Do not fear; go, do as you have said, but make me a little bread cake from it first and bring *it* out to me, and afterward you may make *one* for yourself and for your son.

14 "For thus says the LORD God of Israel, 'The bowl of flour shall not be exhausted, nor shall the jar of oil be empty, until the day that the LORD sends rain on the face of the earth.' "

15 So she went and did according to the word of Elijah, and she and he and her household ate for *many* days.

ELIJAH *Miracle Worker*

WHEN WE SPEAK OF MIRACLES in the Bible, three names stand out: Moses, Elijah and Jesus. Those three, in fact, are the ones who met on the Mount of Transfiguration to talk about Jesus' departure from earth (Luke 9:30–31). In their lifetimes, all three saw the power—and also the limitations—of miracles.

First and Second Kings record eight amazing miracles God worked through Elijah. Some, like his contest with the prophets of Baal (1 Kings 18:16–39), were performed before a large audience. Others, like his restoration of the widow's son (17:17–24), were more private. Ironically, Elijah's experience shows the limits of miracles in encouraging faith. Right after his greatest miracle—the contest with Baal—Elijah grew depressed and afraid. It was then that God revealed his presence not through demonstrations of power, but in "a gentle blowing" (19:12).

The prophet Malachi predicted that a visit by Elijah would precede the Messiah's arrival—a prediction Jesus said that John the Baptist fulfilled (Matthew 17:9–13). All the Jews of Jesus' day—including Jesus—held Elijah in highest esteem. Even today during certain holidays Orthodox Jews leave a place at the table for Elijah, worker of wonders.

Life Questions: Have you ever witnessed a miracle? If so, how did it affect you?

16 The bowl of flour was not exhausted nor did the jar of oil become empty, according to the word of the LORD which He spoke through Elijah.

17:12–16 Down to the Last Meal

Elijah's unusual sources of food demanded the utmost faith in God. First, he was fed by ravens. Then, when his water supply gave out, God ordered Elijah to a very unlikely place: the home of a famished, poverty-stricken widow. The widow, not even an Israelite, lived in Jezebel's home territory, a dangerous place for a hunted prophet. Yet the widow at Zarephath showed enough faith in the prophet and his God to use up her last meager resources. The result proved her faith was well-founded. Jesus referred to this story as an example of God's reaching out to Gentiles (Luke 4:25–26).

Elijah Raises the Widow's Son

17 ¶ Now it came about after these things that the son of the woman, the mistress of the house, became sick; and his sickness was so severe that there was no breath left in him.

18 So she said to Elijah, "What do I have to do with you, O man of God? You have come to me to bring my iniquity to remembrance and to put my son to death!"

19 He said to her, "Give me your son." Then he took him from her bosom and carried him up to the upper room where he was living, and laid him on his own bed.

20 He called to the LORD and said, "O LORD my God, have You also brought calamity to the widow with whom I am staying, by causing her son to die?"

21 Then he stretched himself upon the child three times, and called to the LORD and said, "O LORD my God, I pray You, let this child's life return to him."

22 The LORD heard the voice of Elijah, and the life of the child returned to him and he revived.

23 Elijah took the child and brought him down from the upper room into the house and gave him to his mother; and Elijah said, "See, your son is alive."

24 Then the woman said to Elijah, "Now I know that you are a man of God and that the word of the LORD in your mouth is truth."

Obadiah Meets Elijah

18 Now it happened *after* many days that the word of the LORD came to Elijah in the third year, saying, "Go, show yourself to Ahab, and I will send rain on the face of the earth."

2 So Elijah went to show himself to Ahab. Now the famine *was* severe in Samaria.

3 Ahab called Obadiah who *was* over the household. (Now Obadiah [a]feared the LORD greatly;

4 for when Jezebel destroyed the prophets of the LORD, Obadiah took a hundred prophets and hid them by fifties in a cave, and provided them with bread and water.)

5 Then Ahab said to Obadiah, "Go through the land to all the springs of water and to all the valleys; perhaps we will find grass and keep the horses and mules alive, and not have to kill some of the cattle."

6 So they divided the land between them to survey it; Ahab went one way by himself and Obadiah went another way by himself.

7 ¶ Now as Obadiah was on the way, behold, Elijah met him, and he recognized him and fell on his face and said, "Is this you, Elijah my master?"

8 He said to him, "It is I. Go, say to your master, 'Behold, Elijah *is here.*'"

9 He said, "What sin have I committed, that you are giving your servant into the hand of Ahab to put me to death?

10 "As the LORD your God lives, there is no nation or kingdom where my master has not sent to search for you; and when they said, 'He is not *here*,' he made the kingdom or nation swear that they could not find you.

11 "And now you are saying, 'Go, say to your master, "Behold, Elijah *is here.*"'

12 "It will come about when I leave you that the Spirit of the LORD will carry you where I do not know; so when I come and tell Ahab and he cannot find you, he will kill me, although *I* your servant have feared the LORD from my youth.

13 "Has it not been told to my master what I did when Jezebel killed the prophets of the LORD, that I hid a hundred prophets of the LORD by fifties in a cave, and provided them with bread and water?

14 "And now you are saying, 'Go, say to your master, "Behold, Elijah *is here*"'; he will then kill me."

15 Elijah said, "As the LORD of hosts lives, before whom I stand, I will surely show myself to him today."

16 So Obadiah went to meet Ahab and told him; and Ahab went to meet Elijah.

17 ¶ When Ahab saw Elijah, Ahab said to him, "Is this you, you troubler of Israel?"

18 He said, "I have not troubled Israel, but you and your father's house *have*, because you have forsaken the commandments of the LORD and you have followed the Baals.

19 "Now then send *and* gather to me all Israel at Mount Carmel, *together* with 450 prophets of Baal and 400 prophets of the Asherah, who eat at Jezebel's table."

[a] Or *revered*

The Contest
One lone prophet against a thousand priests

> Elijah came near to all the people and said, "How long will you hesitate between two opinions? If the LORD is God, follow Him; but if Baal, follow him." 18:21

FEW SCENES IN THE BIBLE are more dramatic than this one. The forces of evil and the forces of good collided head on. In books like J.R.R. Tolkien's *Lord of the Rings* or television shows such as the "Star Trek" series, mythmakers dream up cosmic confrontations. But the incident in 1 Kings 18 is no myth. On that day, a bedraggled desert prophet single-handedly took on a king and nearly a thousand powerful priests.

Elijah had made a grand entrance three years before. Like a wild, startling apparition, he came out of nowhere to stalk the terraced streets of affluent Samaria. Clothed in black camel's hair, he made a striking contrast to the priests of Baal in their white linen robes and high-pointed bonnets. He had a simple, unpopular message of doom: "There shall be neither dew nor rain these years, except by my word" (17:1). It was a direct affront to followers of Baal, who believed their god could control the weather.

Having delivered his message, Elijah disappeared. For three years he was the most wanted fugitive in Israel, for he alone had the power to bring rain. And then, in the scene reported in chapter 18, the prophet Elijah returned to Samaria.

Elijah's Contest

Israel was at a crossroads. Other kings had introduced idolatry into Israelite religion, but King Ahab and the notorious Queen Jezebel were going much further. They wanted to wipe out all worship of the true God.

The prophet Elijah proved a worthy adversary. His very name meant "The LORD is my God." He proposed a showdown, the ultimate contest to prove who was the true God. First Kings presents the scene in full color, complete with the priests' desperate contortions and Elijah's mocking, taunting commentary. In the final analysis, it was no contest at all. God unleashed a spectacular display of raw power.

Elijah was one of the most colorful of all Israel's prophets. He suffered from bouts of depression and self-doubt, but during times of crisis he showed amazing courage. The Mount Carmel showdown was merely one sign of the high drama going on. Elijah lived during one of the greatest outbreaks of miracles in biblical history. God was sounding a final warning to Israel.

Israel's Real Heroes

The author of the book of 1 Kings starts out by recording the history of God's anointed leaders. But as the rulers and then priests grow more and more corrupt, this book trains the spotlight on prophets like Elijah. They emerge as Israel's real heroes.

The prophets were not, to Israel, merely preachers or poets. They were channels of God's power, through word and deed. They served on the front line of the struggle between good and evil. Over time, the prophets' significance overtook and even surpassed that of kings. Kings came and went, but the message of the prophets endured.

Voices in the Desert

Whether they served in the government or wandered in occasionally from the desert, the true prophets remained accountable only to God. They decried other, "false," prophets, employed by the king, who generally told the king whatever he wished to hear.

Not all prophets left written messages (Elijah and Elisha, for example, did not). But those prophetic writings that did survive form 17 books of the Old Testament, most of them stemming from the time period described in 1 and 2 Kings.

The prophets told of a God who worked in history to accomplish his will in the world. Sometimes he seemed silent. Sometimes he worked slowly and mysteriously. But occasionally God did step in directly, spectacularly, with a display of power. And when he did, a prophet was usually right in the middle of things—like Elijah on Mount Carmel.

Life Questions: Who serves the role of "prophet" today?

God or Baal on Mount Carmel

20 ¶ So Ahab sent *a message* among all the sons of Israel and brought the prophets together at Mount Carmel.

21 Elijah came near to all the people and said, "How long *will* you hesitate between two opinions? If the LORD is God, follow Him; but if Baal, follow him." But the people did not answer him a word.

22 Then Elijah said to the people, "I alone am left a prophet of the LORD, but Baal's prophets are 450 men.

23 "Now let them give us two oxen; and let them choose one ox for themselves and cut it up, and place it on the wood, but put no fire *under it;* and I will prepare the other ox and lay it on the wood, and I will not put a fire *under it.*

24 "Then you call on the name of your god, and I will call on the name of the LORD, and the God who answers by fire, He is God." And all the people said, "*a*That is a good idea."

25 ¶ So Elijah said to the prophets of Baal, "Choose one ox for yourselves and prepare it first for you are many, and call on the name of your god, but put no fire *under it.*"

26 Then they took the ox which was given them and they prepared it and called on the name of Baal from morning until noon saying, "O Baal, answer us." But there was no voice and no one answered. And they leaped about the altar which they made.

27 It came about at noon, that Elijah mocked them and said, "Call out with a loud voice, for he is a god; either he is occupied or gone aside, or is on a journey, or perhaps he is asleep and needs to be awakened."

28 So they cried with a loud voice and cut themselves according to their custom with swords and lances until the blood gushed out on them.

29 When midday was past, they raved until the time of the offering of the *evening* sacrifice; but there was no voice, no one answered, and no one paid attention.

30 ¶ Then Elijah said to all the people, "Come near to me." So all the people came near to him. And he repaired the altar of the LORD which had been torn down.

31 Elijah took twelve stones according to the number of the tribes of the sons of Jacob, to whom the word of the LORD had come, saying, "Israel shall be your name."

32 So with the stones he built an altar in the name of the LORD, and he made a trench around the altar, large enough to hold two measures of seed.

33 Then he arranged the wood and cut the ox in pieces and laid *it* on the wood.

34 And he said, "Fill four pitchers with water and pour *it* on the burnt offering and on the wood." And he said, "Do it a second time," and they did it a second time. And he said, "Do it a third time," and they did it a third time.

35 The water flowed around the altar and he also filled the trench with water.

18:33 Elijah Rubs It In

Elijah designed the contest to expose Baal, the alleged god of weather, who was often depicted carrying a thunderbolt. Elijah doused his own altar with 12 large jars of water—a precious commodity after three years of drought—before calling on God. Fire from heaven burned up the sacrifice, the wood, the stones, the dust, and even licked up the water in the trench.

Elijah's Prayer

36 At the time of the offering of the *evening* sacrifice, Elijah the prophet came near and said, "O LORD, the God of Abraham, Isaac and Israel, today let it be known that You are God in Israel and that I am Your servant and I have done all these things at Your word.

37 "Answer me, O LORD, answer me, that this people may know that You, O LORD, are God, and *that* You have turned their heart back again."

38 Then the fire of the LORD fell and consumed the burnt offering and the wood and the stones and the dust, and licked up the water that was in the trench.

39 When all the people saw it, they fell on their faces; and they said, "The LORD, He is God; the LORD, He is God."

40 Then Elijah said to them, "Seize the prophets of Baal; do not let one of them escape." So they seized them; and Elijah brought them down to the brook Kishon, and slew them there.

41 ¶ Now Elijah said to Ahab, "Go up, eat and drink; for there is the sound of the roar of a *heavy* shower."

42 So Ahab went up to eat and drink. But Elijah went up to the top of Carmel; and he crouched down on the earth and put his face between his knees.

43 He said to his servant, "Go up now, look toward the sea." So he went up and looked and said, "There is nothing." And he said, "Go back" seven times.

44 It came about at the seventh *time,* that he said, "Behold, a cloud as small as a man's hand is coming up from the sea." And he said, "Go up, say to Ahab, 'Prepare *your chariot* and go down, so that the *heavy* shower does not stop you.'"

45 In a little while the sky grew black with clouds and wind, and there was a heavy shower. And Ahab rode and went to Jezreel.

a Lit *The matter is good*

46 Then the hand of the LORD was on Elijah, and he girded up his loins and outran Ahab to Jezreel.

Elijah Flees from Jezebel

19 Now Ahab told Jezebel all that Elijah had done, and how he had killed all the prophets with the sword.

2 Then Jezebel sent a messenger to Elijah, saying, "So may the gods do to me and even more, if I do not make your *a*life as the life of one of them by tomorrow about this time."

3 And he was afraid and arose and ran for his *a*life and came to Beersheba, which belongs to Judah, and left his servant there.

19:3 Wicked Queen Jezebel

Queen Jezebel's reputation was such that Elijah ran from her in fear even after God had triumphantly displayed his power on Mount Carmel. The Roman historian Josephus records her family history. Her father, who had served as high priest in a pagan temple in Tyre, murdered the king and ruled there for 32 years. His reign was characterized by murderous idolatries and a reckless contempt for human rights.

Jezebel followed in her father's footsteps. Married to Ahab as part of a political alliance, she installed 950 prophets of Baal and ordered the wholesale slaughter of any prophets of God who opposed her. Ahab fell under her sway. Alone, he could be brave, chivalrous, and even conscientious. But his weakness and Jezebel's influence led him to become the most wicked king of Israel.

4 But he himself went a day's journey into the wilderness, and came and sat down under a juniper tree; and he requested for himself that he might die, and said, "It is enough; now, O LORD, take my *a*life, for I am not better than my fathers."

5 He lay down and slept under a juniper tree; and behold, there was an angel touching him, and he said to him, "Arise, eat."

6 Then he looked and behold, there was at his head a bread cake *baked on* hot stones, and a jar of water. So he ate and drank and lay down again.

7 The angel of the LORD came again a second time and touched him and said, "Arise, eat, because the journey is too great for you."

8 So he arose and ate and drank, and went in the strength of that food forty days and forty nights to Horeb, the mountain of God.

Elijah at Horeb

9 ¶ Then he came there to a cave and lodged there; and behold, the word of the LORD *came* to him, and He said to him, "What are you doing here, Elijah?"

10 He said, "I have been very zealous for the LORD, the God of hosts; for the sons of Israel have forsaken Your covenant, torn down Your altars and killed Your prophets with the sword. And I alone am left; and they seek my life, to take it away."

11 ¶ So He said, "Go forth and stand on the mountain before the LORD." And behold, the LORD was passing by! And a great and strong wind was rending the mountains and breaking in pieces the rocks before the LORD; *but* the LORD *was* not in the wind. And after the wind an earthquake, *but* the LORD *was* not in the earthquake.

12 After the earthquake a fire, *but* the LORD *was* not in the fire; and after the fire a sound of a gentle blowing.

13 When Elijah heard *it,* he wrapped his face in his mantle and went out and stood in the entrance of the cave. And behold, a voice *came* to him and said, "What are you doing here, Elijah?"

14 Then he said, "I have been very zealous for the LORD, the God of hosts; for the sons of Israel have forsaken Your covenant, torn down Your altars and killed Your prophets with the sword. And I alone am left; and they seek my life, to take it away."

15 ¶ The LORD said to him, "Go, return on your way to the wilderness of Damascus, and when you have arrived, you shall anoint Hazael king over Aram;

16 and Jehu the son of Nimshi you shall anoint king over Israel; and Elisha the son of Shaphat of Abel-meholah you shall anoint as prophet in your place.

17 "It shall come about, the one who escapes from the sword of Hazael, Jehu shall put to death, and the one who escapes from the sword of Jehu, Elisha shall put to death.

18 "Yet I will leave 7,000 in Israel, all the knees that have not bowed to Baal and every mouth that has not kissed him."

19 ¶ So he departed from there and found Elisha the son of Shaphat, while he was plowing with twelve pairs *of oxen* before him, and he with the twelfth. And Elijah passed over to him and threw his mantle on him.

20 He left the oxen and ran after Elijah and said, "Please let me kiss my father and my mother, then I will follow you." And he said to him, "Go back again, for what have I done to you?"

21 So he returned from following him, and took the pair of oxen and sacrificed them and boiled their flesh with the implements of the oxen, and gave *it* to the people and they ate. Then he arose and followed Elijah and ministered to him.

a Lit *soul*

War with Aram

20 Now Ben-hadad king of Aram gathered all his army, and there *were* thirty-two kings with him, and horses and chariots. And he went up and besieged Samaria and fought against it.

2 Then he sent messengers to the city to Ahab king of Israel and said to him, "Thus says Ben-hadad,

3 'Your silver and your gold are mine; your most beautiful wives and children are also mine.'"

4 The king of Israel replied, "It is according to your word, my lord, O king; I am yours, and all that I have."

5 Then the messengers returned and said, "Thus says Ben-hadad, 'Surely, I sent to you saying, "You shall give me your silver and your gold and your wives and your children,"

6 but about this time tomorrow I will send my servants to you, and they will search your house and the houses of your servants; and whatever is desirable in your eyes, they will take in their hand and carry away.'"

7 ¶ Then the king of Israel called all the elders of the land and said, "Please observe and see how this man is looking for trouble; for he sent to me for my wives and my children and my silver and my gold, and I did not refuse him."

8 All the elders and all the people said to him, "Do not listen or consent."

9 So he said to the messengers of Ben-hadad, "Tell my lord the king, 'All that you sent for to your servant at the first I will do, but this thing I cannot do.'" And the messengers departed and brought him word again.

10 Ben-hadad sent to him and said, "May the gods do so to me and more also, if the dust of Samaria will suffice for handfuls for all the people who follow me."

11 Then the king of Israel replied, "Tell *him,* 'Let not him who girds on *his armor* boast like him who takes *it* off.'"

12 When *Ben-hadad* heard this message, as he was drinking with the kings in the temporary shelters, he said to his servants, "Station *yourselves.*" So they stationed *themselves* against the city.

Ahab Victorious

13 ¶ Now behold, a prophet approached Ahab king of Israel and said, "Thus says the LORD, 'Have you seen all this great multitude? Behold, I will deliver them into your hand today, and you shall know that I am the LORD.'"

14 Ahab said, "By whom?" So he said, "Thus says the LORD, 'By the young men of the rulers of the provinces.'" Then he said, "Who shall begin the battle?" And he answered, "You."

15 Then he mustered the young men of the rulers of the provinces, and there were 232; and after them he mustered all the people, *even* all the sons of Israel, 7,000.

16 ¶ They went out at noon, while Ben-hadad was drinking himself drunk in the temporary shelters with the thirty-two kings who helped him.

17 The young men of the rulers of the provinces went out first; and Ben-hadad sent out and they told him, saying, "Men have come out from Samaria."

18 Then he said, "If they have come out for peace, take them alive; or if they have come out for war, take them alive."

19 ¶ So these went out from the city, the young men of the rulers of the provinces, and the army which followed them.

20 They killed each his man; and the Arameans fled and Israel pursued them, and Ben-hadad king of Aram escaped on a horse with horsemen.

21 The king of Israel went out and struck the horses and chariots, and killed the Arameans with a great slaughter.

22 ¶ Then the prophet came near to the king of Israel and said to him, "Go, strengthen yourself and observe and see what you have to do; for at the turn of the year the king of Aram will come up against you."

23 ¶ Now the servants of the king of Aram said to him, "Their gods are gods of the mountains, therefore they were stronger than we; but rather let us fight against them in the plain, *and* surely we will be stronger than they.

24 "Do this thing: remove the kings, each from his place, and put captains in their place,

25 and muster an army like the army that you have lost, horse for horse, and chariot for chariot. Then we will fight against them in the plain, and surely we will be stronger than they." And he listened to their voice and did so.

Another Aramean War

26 ¶ At the turn of the year, Ben-hadad mustered the Arameans and went up to Aphek to fight against Israel.

27 The sons of Israel were mustered and were provisioned and went to meet them; and the sons of Israel camped before them like two little flocks of goats, but the Arameans filled the country.

28 Then a man of God came near and spoke to the king of Israel and said, "Thus says the LORD, 'Because the Arameans have said, "The LORD is a god of *the* mountains, but He is not a god of *the* valleys," therefore I will give all this great multitude into your hand, and you shall know that I am the LORD.'"

29 So they camped one over against the other seven days. And on the seventh day the battle was joined, and the sons of Israel killed *of* the Arameans 100,000 foot soldiers in one day.

30 But the rest fled to Aphek into the city, and the wall fell on 27,000 men who were left. And Ben-hadad fled and came into the city into an inner chamber.

31 ¶ His servants said to him, "Behold now, we have heard that the kings of the house of Israel are

merciful kings, please let us put sackcloth on our loins and ropes on our heads, and go out to the king of Israel; perhaps he will save your life."

32 So they girded sackcloth on their loins and *put* ropes on their heads, and came to the king of Israel and said, "Your servant Ben-hadad says, 'Please let me live.' " And he said, "Is he still alive? He is my brother."

33 Now the men took this as an omen, and quickly catching his word said, "Your brother Ben-hadad." Then he said, "Go, bring him." Then Ben-hadad came out to him, and he took him up into the chariot.

34 *Ben-hadad* said to him, "The cities which my father took from your father I will restore, and you shall make streets for yourself in Damascus, as my father made in Samaria." *Ahab said,* "And I will let you go with this covenant." So he made a covenant with him and let him go.

35 ¶ Now a certain man of the sons of the prophets said to another by the word of the LORD, "Please strike me." But the man refused to strike him.

36 Then he said to him, "Because you have not listened to the voice of the LORD, behold, as soon as you have departed from me, a lion will kill you." And as soon as he had departed from him a lion found him and killed him.

37 Then he found another man and said, "Please strike me." And the man struck him, wounding him.

38 So the prophet departed and waited for the king by the way, and disguised himself with a bandage over his eyes.

39 As the king passed by, he cried to the king and said, "Your servant went out into the midst of the battle; and behold, a man turned aside and brought a man to me and said, 'Guard this man; if for any reason he is missing, then your life shall be for his life, or else you shall pay a talent of silver.'

40 "While your servant was busy here and there, he was gone." And the king of Israel said to him, "So shall your judgment be; you yourself have decided *it.*"

41 Then he hastily took the bandage away from his eyes, and the king of Israel recognized him that he was of the prophets.

42 He said to him, "Thus says the LORD, 'Because you have let go out of *your* hand the man whom I had devoted to destruction, therefore your life shall go for his life, and your people for his people.' "

43 So the king of Israel went to his house sullen and vexed, and came to Samaria.

Ahab Covets Naboth's Vineyard

21 Now it came about after these things that Naboth the Jezreelite had a vineyard which *was* in Jezreel beside the palace of Ahab king of Samaria.

2 Ahab spoke to Naboth, saying, "Give me your vineyard, that I may have it for a vegetable garden because it is close beside my house, and I will give you a better vineyard than it in its

21:1 A Stolen Vineyard

The incident of Naboth's vineyard shows the selective way in which Old Testament authors wove history together. In one sense, the theft was a minor incident in King Ahab's reign. Yet 1 Kings devotes more space to it than to the entire reigns of some kings. It showed the kings' abuse of power and disrespect for God's covenant. Every Israelite had the right to possess a piece of the promised land—not even a king could legally usurp that right. In fact, selling the land would break a law God gave Moses (Leviticus 25:23–31). Ahab's greed and Jezebel's intrigue led to murder and ultimately spelled doom for the kingdom.

place; if you like, I will give you the price of it in money."

3 But Naboth said to Ahab, "The LORD forbid me that I should give you the inheritance of my fathers."

4 So Ahab came into his house sullen and vexed because of the word which Naboth the Jezreelite had spoken to him; for he said, "I will not give you the inheritance of my fathers." And he lay down on his bed and turned away his face and ate no food.

5 ¶ But Jezebel his wife came to him and said to him, "How is it that your spirit is so sullen that you are not eating food?"

6 So he said to her, "Because I spoke to Naboth the Jezreelite and said to him, 'Give me your vineyard for money; or else, if it pleases you, I will give you a vineyard in its place.' But he said, 'I will not give you my vineyard.' "

7 Jezebel his wife said to him, "Do you now reign over Israel? Arise, eat bread, and let your heart be joyful; I will give you the vineyard of Naboth the Jezreelite."

8 ¶ So she wrote letters in Ahab's name and sealed them with his seal, and sent letters to the elders and to the nobles who were living with Naboth in his city.

9 Now she wrote in the letters, saying, "Proclaim a fast and seat Naboth at the head of the people;

10 and seat two worthless men before him, and let them testify against him, saying, 'You cursed God and the king.' Then take him out and stone him to death."

Jezebel's Plot

11 ¶ So the men of his city, the elders and the

nobles who lived in his city, did as Jezebel had sent *word* to them, just as it was written in the letters which she had sent them.

12 They proclaimed a fast and seated Naboth at the head of the people.

13 Then the two worthless men came in and sat before him; and the worthless men testified against him, even against Naboth, before the people, saying, "Naboth cursed God and the king." So they took him outside the city and stoned him to death with stones.

14 Then they sent *word* to Jezebel, saying, "Naboth has been stoned and is dead."

15 ¶ When Jezebel heard that Naboth had been stoned and was dead, Jezebel said to Ahab, "Arise, take possession of the vineyard of Naboth, the Jezreelite, which he refused to give you for money; for Naboth is not alive, but dead."

16 When Ahab heard that Naboth was dead, Ahab arose to go down to the vineyard of Naboth the Jezreelite, to take possession of it.

17 ¶ Then the word of the LORD came to Elijah the Tishbite, saying,

18 "Arise, go down to meet Ahab king of Israel, who is in Samaria; behold, he is in the vineyard of Naboth where he has gone down to take possession of it.

19 "You shall speak to him, saying, 'Thus says the LORD, "Have you murdered and also taken possession?" ' And you shall speak to him, saying, 'Thus says the LORD, "In the place where the dogs licked up the blood of Naboth the dogs will lick up your blood, even yours." ' "

20 ¶ Ahab said to Elijah, "Have you found me, O my enemy?" And he answered, "I have found *you*, because you have sold yourself to do evil in the sight of the LORD.

21 "Behold, I will bring evil upon you, and will utterly sweep you away, and will cut off from Ahab every male, both bond and free in Israel;

22 and I will make your house like the house of Jeroboam the son of Nebat, and like the house of Baasha the son of Ahijah, because of the provocation with which you have provoked *Me* to anger, and *because* you have made Israel sin.

23 "Of Jezebel also has the LORD spoken, saying, 'The dogs will eat Jezebel in the district of Jezreel.'

24 "The one belonging to Ahab, who dies in the city, the dogs will eat, and the one who dies in the field the birds of heaven will eat."

25 ¶ Surely there was no one like Ahab who sold himself to do evil in the sight of the LORD, because Jezebel his wife incited him.

26 He acted very abominably in following idols, according to all that the Amorites had done, whom the LORD cast out before the sons of Israel.

27 ¶ It came about when Ahab heard these words, that he tore his clothes and put on sackcloth and fasted, and he lay in sackcloth and went about despondently.

28 Then the word of the LORD came to Elijah the Tishbite, saying,

29 "Do you see how Ahab has humbled himself before Me? Because he has humbled himself before Me, I will not bring the evil in his days, *but* I will bring the evil upon his house in his son's days."

Ahab's Third Campaign against Aram

22 Three years passed without war between Aram and Israel.

2 In the third year Jehoshaphat the king of Judah came down to the king of Israel.

3 Now the king of Israel said to his servants, "Do you know that Ramoth-gilead belongs to us,

AHAB *Worst King Yet*

IMAGINE THE UPROAR IF A U.S. president suddenly decided to demolish all church buildings and replace every Christian pastor with a Hindu priest. Something like that happened in King Ahab's day. True, Ahab inherited a bad situation: a divided kingdom in which religious faith was in free fall. Yet somehow he made it worse, doing "evil in the sight of the LORD more than all who were before him" (16:30).

The Bible lays much of the blame for Ahab's performance on a bad marriage. To forge a political alliance he married Jezebel, the daughter of a neighboring king. When she brought along her idols of Baal, Ahab joined in, building a temple to Baal right in his capital. Jezebel then tried to hunt down and destroy all remnants of true Israelite faith, replacing God's prophets with her own imported substitutes.

While Ahab may seem like the passive partner in crime, he bore his share of responsibility as well. The prophet Elijah might have been his salvation; Ahab saw him instead as an enemy and a troublemaker (18:17; 21:20). Time after time Ahab rejected good and godly advice.

By secular standards of prosperity and military strength, Ahab achieved success. He built a fine palace inlaid with ivory. (Archaeologists have found ivory plaques from homes of this period.) He drove back invaders from Syria. From the Bible's point of view, however, these achievements meant nothing compared to his failures of faith and morality. As a traitor to God, Ahab was the worst king yet.

Life Questions: In today's world, how do political leaders affect a country's overall moral and spiritual climate? Should they do more?

and we are still doing nothing to take it out of the hand of the king of Aram?"

4 And he said to Jehoshaphat, "Will you go with me to battle at Ramoth-gilead?" And Jehoshaphat said to the king of Israel, "I am as you are, my people as your people, my horses as your horses."

22:4 Unholy Alliance

After years of warfare, peace was finally arranged between Israel and Judah. Ironically, it joined Israel's worst king, Ahab, with one of Judah's best, King Jehoshaphat. The unholy alliance with Ahab led to a fateful battle against Aram that almost cost Jehoshaphat his life (verses 29–33). Judah's king spurned later offers of cooperation (verse 49), but his son married King Ahab's daughter. This unwise marriage exposed Judah to the evil practices of the North and ultimately led to a royal bloodbath.

5 ¶ Moreover, Jehoshaphat said to the king of Israel, "Please inquire first for the word of the LORD."

6 Then the king of Israel gathered the prophets together, about four hundred men, and said to them, "Shall I go against Ramoth-gilead to battle or shall I refrain?" And they said, "Go up, for the Lord will give *it* into the hand of the king."

7 But Jehoshaphat said, "Is there not yet a prophet of the LORD here that we may inquire of him?"

8 The king of Israel said to Jehoshaphat, "There is yet one man by whom we may inquire of the LORD, but I hate him, because he does not prophesy good concerning me, but evil. *He is* Micaiah son of Imlah." But Jehoshaphat said, "Let not the king say so."

9 Then the king of Israel called an officer and said, "Bring quickly Micaiah son of Imlah."

10 Now the king of Israel and Jehoshaphat king of Judah were sitting each on his throne, arrayed in *their* robes, at the threshing floor at the entrance of the gate of Samaria; and all the prophets were prophesying before them.

11 Then Zedekiah the son of Chenaanah made horns of iron for himself and said, "Thus says the LORD, 'With these you will gore the Arameans until they are consumed.'"

12 All the prophets were prophesying thus, saying, "Go up to Ramoth-gilead and prosper, for the LORD will give *it* into the hand of the king."

Micaiah Predicts Defeat

13 ¶ Then the messenger who went to summon Micaiah spoke to him saying, "Behold now, the words of the prophets are uniformly favorable

to the king. Please let your word be like the word of one of them, and speak favorably."

14 But Micaiah said, "As the LORD lives, what the LORD says to me, that I shall speak."

15 ¶ When he came to the king, the king said to him, "Micaiah, shall we go to Ramoth-gilead to battle, or shall we refrain?" And he answered him, "Go up and succeed, and the LORD will give *it* into the hand of the king."

16 Then the king said to him, "How many times must I adjure you to speak to me nothing but the truth in the name of the LORD?"

17 So he said,
"I saw all Israel
Scattered on the mountains,
Like sheep which have no shepherd.
And the LORD said, 'These have no master.
Let each of them return to his house in peace.'"

18 Then the king of Israel said to Jehoshaphat, "Did I not tell you that he would not prophesy good concerning me, but evil?"

19 ¶ Micaiah said, "Therefore, hear the word of the LORD. I saw the LORD sitting on His throne, and all the host of heaven standing by Him on His right and on His left.

20 "The LORD said, 'Who will entice Ahab to go up and fall at Ramoth-gilead?' And one said this while another said that.

21 "Then a spirit came forward and stood before the LORD and said, 'I will entice him.'

22 "The LORD said to him, 'How?' And he said, 'I will go out and be a deceiving spirit in the mouth of all his prophets.' Then He said, 'You are to entice *him* and also prevail. Go and do so.'

23 "Now therefore, behold, the LORD has put a deceiving spirit in the mouth of all these your prophets; and the LORD has proclaimed disaster against you."

24 ¶ Then Zedekiah the son of Chenaanah came near and struck Micaiah on the cheek and said, "How did the Spirit of the LORD pass from me to speak to you?"

25 Micaiah said, "Behold, you shall see on that day when you enter an inner room to hide yourself."

26 Then the king of Israel said, "Take Micaiah and return him to Amon the governor of the city and to Joash the king's son;

27 and say, 'Thus says the king, "Put this man in prison and feed him sparingly with bread and water until I return safely."'"

28 Micaiah said, "If you indeed return safely the LORD has not spoken by me." And he said, "Listen, all you people."

Defeat and Death of Ahab

29 ¶ So the king of Israel and Jehoshaphat king of Judah went up against Ramoth-gilead.

30 The king of Israel said to Jehoshaphat, "I

will disguise myself and go into the battle, but you put on your robes." So the king of Israel disguised himself and went into the battle.

31 Now the king of Aram had commanded the thirty-two captains of his chariots, saying, "Do not fight with small or great, but with the king of Israel alone."

32 So when the captains of the chariots saw Jehoshaphat, they said, "Surely it is the king of Israel," and they turned aside to fight against him, and Jehoshaphat cried out.

33 When the captains of the chariots saw that it was not the king of Israel, they turned back from pursuing him.

34 ¶ Now a certain man drew his bow at random and struck the king of Israel in a joint of the armor. So he said to the driver of his chariot, "Turn around and take me out of the fight; for I am severely wounded."

35 The battle raged that day, and the king was propped up in his chariot in front of the Arameans, and died at evening, and the blood from the wound ran into the bottom of the chariot.

36 Then a cry passed throughout the army close to sunset, saying, "Every man to his city and every man to his country."

37 ¶ So the king died and was brought to Samaria, and they buried the king in Samaria.

38 They washed the chariot by the pool of Samaria, and the dogs licked up his blood (now the harlots bathed themselves *there*), according to the word of the LORD which He spoke.

39 Now the rest of the acts of Ahab and all that he did and the ivory house which he built and all the cities which he built, are they not written in the Book of the Chronicles of the Kings of Israel?

40 So Ahab slept with his fathers, and Ahaziah his son became king in his place.

The New Rulers

41 ¶ Now Jehoshaphat the son of Asa became king over Judah in the fourth year of Ahab king of Israel.

42 Jehoshaphat was thirty-five years old when he became king, and he reigned twenty-five years in Jerusalem. And his mother's name was Azubah the daughter of Shilhi.

43 He walked in all the way of Asa his father; he did not turn aside from it, doing right in the sight of the LORD. However, the high places were not taken away; the people still sacrificed and burnt incense on the high places.

44 Jehoshaphat also made peace with the king of Israel.

45 ¶ Now the rest of the acts of Jehoshaphat, and his might which he showed and how he warred, are they not written in the Book of the Chronicles of the Kings of Judah?

46 The remnant of the sodomites who remained in the days of his father Asa, he expelled from the land.

47 ¶ Now there was no king in Edom; a deputy was king.

48 Jehoshaphat made ships of Tarshish to go to Ophir for gold, but they did not go for the ships were broken at Ezion-geber.

49 Then Ahaziah the son of Ahab said to Jehoshaphat, "Let my servants go with your servants in the ships." But Jehoshaphat was not willing.

50 And Jehoshaphat slept with his fathers and was buried with his fathers in the city of his father David, and Jehoram his son became king in his place.

51 ¶ Ahaziah the son of Ahab became king over Israel in Samaria in the seventeenth year of Jehoshaphat king of Judah, and he reigned two years over Israel.

52 He did evil in the sight of the LORD and walked in the way of his father and in the way of his mother and in the way of Jeroboam the son of Nebat, who caused Israel to sin.

53 So he served Baal and worshiped him and provoked the LORD God of Israel to anger, according to all that his father had done.

2 KINGS

The Great Wars of Israel
The promised land turns into a bloody battlefield

T HE BOOK OF 2 KINGS TELLS of dark days in the promised land. First, the Northern Kingdom, Israel, fell to outside invaders. Then Judah, the Southern Kingdom, was conquered. To appreciate what those two events meant in Jewish history, consider our century's two great wars.

In 1918 the bloodiest war of all time came to an end. The entire planet had chosen sides. In all, nine million soldiers died. Survivors thought nothing could ever again match The Great War's ferocity and destruction. "The war to end all wars," they called it.

Yet, in a mere 20 years, a man named Adolf Hitler brought war again. In World War II, global violence stretched from London in the West to Japan in the East. The war finally closed with a blinding mushroom cloud, an ominous portent for the future.

> The LORD said, "I will remove Judah also from My sight, as I have removed Israel. And I will cast off Jerusalem, this city which I have chosen, and the temple of which I said, 'My name shall be there.'" 23:27

Two Large Blots in History

No matter what else happens, the 20th century has been permanently stained by those two large blots: World War I and World War II. Everything else—art, literature, advances in science and medicine—fades into the background.

As 2 Kings tells it, something very similar occurred in the Biblical nation of Israel. Two large blots spread across the land: successive invasions by foreign giants. In the long, turbulent history of the Jews, these two invasions stand out as the Great Wars, overshadowing nearly everything else.

Israel Falls First

The kingdom had already split into two—1 Kings tells that story. Its sequel, 2 Kings, describes ever-increasing tragedy.

From the very first chapters you can sense the pending crisis in the North. Not one northern king followed the ways of God. National politics slipped into an endless cycle of intrigue and bloody revolt. Meanwhile, Elijah and Elisha intensified their attacks on the kings, and miracles broke out with unusual frequency.

Assyria's campaigns—the "World War I" in Israel's history—are reported in 2 Kings 15–18. Other records of the period tell of vicious fighting. Samaria, Israel's capital, made one final heroic stand against a two-year siege. Finally, the starving survivors surrendered, and the people of Israel were carried away into captivity.

Only two Israelite tribes remained in the promised land, holding out in the tiny Southern Kingdom of Judah. Ultimately, King Sennacherib of Assyria turned against Judah also, penetrating all the way to the gates of Jerusalem. Contemporary accounts record that he leveled 46 walled cities and carried away 200,150 people, young and old, along with all their horses, mules, cattle, and possessions. He scornfully dismissed King Hezekiah as "a bird in a cage."

A Brief Comeback

Could the tiny nation of Judah survive such an onslaught? Somehow the "caged bird" (Hezekiah) made a remarkable comeback, and Judah did survive for another 135 years. Still, Judah did not learn from the dramatic object lesson of Israel's destruction in the North. Most of the kings who followed Hezekiah failed dismally to obey God. Another foreign invader, Babylon, finally leveled Jerusalem in the "World War II" of that era.

The book of Kings ends with a bleak picture: refugees picking through the rubble of Jerusalem, and the Israelites enslaved by foreign powers. The temple itself, God's house, lay in ruins, its treasures carted off to Babylon. When the dust settled around 600 B.C., the Israelites were scattered across the earth, not to be reunited as an independent nation for 25 centuries.

All along, prophets had given eloquent warnings of what would happen to a nation that turned its back on God. But nothing makes a bigger impact than the object lesson of history itself. Ever since, Jews have looked back on their history and seen two indelible stains. Those were the dark days of Assyria and Babylon, when everything came apart.

How to Read 2 Kings

The first eight chapters of 2 Kings, full of excitement and adventure, read easily. They focus on the last days of the prophet Elijah and on the long life of his successor Elisha. But beginning with chapter 9, the book can become very confusing. It switches back and forth between two histories: that of Israel in the North and Judah in the South.

Israel was strong initially, with 10 of the 12 tribes united there. But it proved less faithful to God and was ultimately destroyed by Assyria. Chapters 18–25 cover the period after the Assyrian invasion, when only Judah existed.

Use the boldface sectional headings in this Bible for orientation: They clearly mark whether a king or queen ruled over Judah or Israel. Also, a lineup of all the rulers appears on pages 1417–1425, giving an overview of the history of each country.

One important reason for studying the books of Kings and Chronicles is that they give historical background on the prophets. Elijah and Elisha appeared at a crucial turning point in the history of the Northern Kingdom, just as Ahab was changing the official religion from worship of God to worship of Baal. Other prophets, who wrote books of the Bible, were also active during this time.

Amos and Hosea concentrated their work in the Northern Kingdom of Israel. The following prophets lived and preached in the Southern Kingdom of Judah: Obadiah, Joel, Isaiah, Micah, Nahum, Zephaniah, Jeremiah, and Habakkuk. More prophets came later, when the Israelites were still captive in Babylon or after they had returned to their homeland. The How to Read section of each book of the prophets gives a brief summary of when and where each author worked (see An Overview of the Bible, pages 17–20, for a list of the books of the prophets).

Second Kings, like its companion books, makes brief and sweeping judgments of each king or queen. As you read, look for what pleased God and what displeased him. The 39 rulers comprise a fine study of leadership of all kinds, from the inspiring to the degenerate.

PEOPLE YOU'LL MEET IN 2 KINGS

ELISHA *(p. 420)*
JEZEBEL *(p. 429)*
JOSIAH *(p. 445)*
ZEDEKIAH *(p. 448)*

3-TRACK READING PLAN

For an explanation and complete listing of the 3-track reading plan, turn to page 7.

TRACK 1: **Two-Week Courses on the Bible**
See page 7 for information on these courses.

TRACK 2: **An Overview of 2 Kings in 3 Days**
☐ Day 1. Read the Introduction to 2 Kings and then chapter 5 on Elisha's miracle of healing an enemy from Aram.
☐ Day 2. Read chapter 17, which gives a final summary of the decline and utter devastation of the Northern Kingdom of Israel.
☐ Day 3. One of the high points in 2 Kings occurred during the reign of the boy-king Josiah. Read about the beginning of his reforms in chapter 22 and the first three verses of chapter 23.

Now turn to page 9 for your next Track 2 reading project.

TRACK 3: **All of 2 Kings in 25 Days**
After you have read through 2 Kings, turn to pages 10–14 for your next Track 3 reading project.

☐1 ☐2 ☐3 ☐4 ☐5 ☐6 ☐7 ☐8
☐9 ☐10 ☐11 ☐12 ☐13 ☐14 ☐15 ☐16
☐17 ☐18 ☐19 ☐20 ☐21 ☐22 ☐23 ☐24
☐25

Ahaziah's Messengers Meet Elijah

1 Now Moab rebelled against Israel after the death of Ahab.

2 And Ahaziah fell through the lattice in his upper chamber which *was* in Samaria, and became ill. So he sent messengers and said to them, "Go, inquire of Baal-zebub, the god of Ekron, whether I will recover from this sickness."

3 But the angel of the LORD said to Elijah the Tishbite, "Arise, go up to meet the messengers of the king of Samaria and say to them, 'Is it because there is no God in Israel *that* you are going to inquire of Baal-zebub, the god of Ekron?'

4 "Now therefore thus says the LORD, 'You shall not come down from the bed where you have gone up, but you shall surely die.'" Then Elijah departed.

5 ¶ When the messengers returned to him he said to them, "Why have you returned?"

6 They said to him, "A man came up to meet us and said to us, 'Go, return to the king who sent you and say to him, "Thus says the LORD, 'Is it because there is no God in Israel *that* you are sending to inquire of Baal-zebub, the god of Ekron? Therefore you shall not come down from the bed where you have gone up, but shall surely die.'"'"

7 He said to them, "What kind of man was he who came up to meet you and spoke these words to you?"

8 They answered him, "*He was* a hairy man with a leather girdle bound about his loins." And he said, "It is Elijah the Tishbite."

9 ¶ Then *the king* sent to him a captain of fifty with his fifty. And he went up to him, and behold, he was sitting on the top of the hill. And he said to him, "O man of God, the king says, 'Come down.'"

10 Elijah replied to the captain of fifty, "If I am a man of God, let fire come down from heaven and consume you and your fifty." Then fire came down from heaven and consumed him and his fifty.

11 ¶ So he again sent to him another captain of fifty with his fifty. And he said to him, "O man of God, thus says the king, 'Come down quickly.'"

12 Elijah replied to them, "If I am a man of God, let fire come down from heaven and consume you and your fifty." Then the fire of God came down from heaven and consumed him and his fifty.

13 ¶ So he again sent the captain of a third fifty with his fifty. When the third captain of fifty went up, he came and bowed down on his knees before Elijah, and begged him and said to him, "O man of God, please let my life and the lives of these fifty servants of yours be precious in your sight.

14 "Behold fire came down from heaven and consumed the first two captains of fifty with their fifties; but now let my life be precious in your sight."

15 The angel of the LORD said to Elijah, "Go down with him; do not be afraid of him." So he arose and went down with him to the king.

16 Then he said to him, "Thus says the LORD, 'Because you have sent messengers to inquire of Baal-zebub, the god of Ekron—is it because there is no God in Israel to inquire of His word?—therefore you shall not come down from the bed where you have gone up, but shall surely die.'"

Jehoram Reigns over Israel

17 ¶ So Ahaziah died according to the word of the LORD which Elijah had spoken. And because he had no son, Jehoram became king in his place in the second year of Jehoram the son of Jehoshaphat, king of Judah.

18 Now the rest of the acts of Ahaziah which he did, are they not written in the Book of the Chronicles of the Kings of Israel?

Elijah Taken to Heaven

2 And it came about when the LORD was about to take up Elijah by a whirlwind to heaven, that Elijah went with Elisha from Gilgal.

2 Elijah said to Elisha, "Stay here please, for the LORD has sent me as far as Bethel." But Elisha said, "As the LORD lives and as you yourself live, I will not leave you." So they went down to Bethel.

3 Then the sons of the prophets who *were at* Bethel came out to Elisha and said to him, "Do you know that the LORD will take away your master from over you today?" And he said, "Yes, I know; be still."

4 ¶ Elijah said to him, "Elisha, please stay here, for the LORD has sent me to Jericho." But he said, "As the LORD lives, and as you yourself live, I will not leave you." So they came to Jericho.

5 The sons of the prophets who *were* at Jericho approached Elisha and said to him, "Do you

know that the LORD will take away your master from over you today?" And he answered, "Yes, I know; be still."

6 Then Elijah said to him, "Please stay here, for the LORD has sent me to the Jordan." And he said, "As the LORD lives, and as you yourself live, I will not leave you." So the two of them went on.

7 ¶ Now fifty men of the sons of the prophets went and stood opposite *them* at a distance, while the two of them stood by the Jordan.

8 Elijah took his mantle and folded it together and struck the waters, and they were divided here and there, so that the two of them crossed over on dry ground.

9 ¶ When they had crossed over, Elijah said to Elisha, "Ask what I shall do for you before I am taken from you." And Elisha said, "Please, let a double portion of your spirit be upon me."

10 He said, "You have asked a hard thing. *Nevertheless,* if you see me when I am taken from you, it shall be so for you; but if not, it shall not be *so.*"

11 As they were going along and talking, behold, *there appeared* a chariot of fire and horses of fire which separated the two of them. And Elijah went up by a whirlwind to heaven.

12 Elisha saw *it* and cried out, "My father, my father, the chariots of Israel and its horsemen!" And he saw Elijah no more. Then he took hold of his own clothes and tore them in two pieces.

13 He also took up the mantle of Elijah that fell from him and returned and stood by the bank of the Jordan.

14 He took the mantle of Elijah that fell from him and struck the waters and said, "Where is the LORD, the God of Elijah?" And when he also had struck the waters, they were divided here and there; and Elisha crossed over.

Elisha Succeeds Elijah

15 ¶ Now when the sons of the prophets who *were* at Jericho opposite *him* saw him, they said, "The spirit of Elijah rests on Elisha." And they came to meet him and bowed themselves to the ground before him.

2:12 An Obscure Compliment

Elisha's last words to Elijah were obviously a compliment, but what did they mean? Most likely they referred to Elijah's power, indicating he was worth more to the nation of Israel than a company of chariots and horsemen. Interestingly, a king of Israel said these exact words to Elisha himself as he lay dying (13:14).

16 They said to him, "Behold now, there are with your servants fifty strong men, please let them go and search for your master; perhaps the Spirit of the LORD has taken him up and cast him

on some mountain or into some valley." And he said, "You shall not send."

17 But when they urged him until he was ashamed, he said, "Send." They sent therefore fifty men; and they searched three days but did not find him.

18 They returned to him while he was staying at Jericho; and he said to them, "Did I not say to you, 'Do not go'?"

19 ¶ Then the men of the city said to Elisha, "Behold now, the situation of this city is pleasant, as my lord sees; but the water is bad and the land is unfruitful."

20 He said, "Bring me a new jar, and put salt in it." So they brought *it* to him.

21 He went out to the spring of water and threw salt in it and said, "Thus says the LORD, 'I have purified these waters; there shall not be from there death or unfruitfulness any longer.' "

22 So the waters have been purified to this day, according to the word of Elisha which he spoke.

23 ¶ Then he went up from there to Bethel; and as he was going up by the way, young lads came out from the city and mocked him and said to him, "Go up, you baldhead; go up, you baldhead!"

2:23 Background on the Bears

At first reading, the brief account in these three verses is very troubling. A prophet calling on bears to maul children? But, in this instance, historical background and a precise translation help cast the event in a different light. Bethel was a hotbed of Baal worship, and its residents were engaged in a life-and-death struggle with the true prophets of God. When the youths called out, "Go up, you baldhead!" they were likely referring to what had just happened to the prophet Elijah—they were calling for Elisha to vanish into the sky, or in other words, to die. Furthermore, the word translated youths usually refers to young people in their late teens. In actuality, a large gang of teenagers was threatening a prophet's life. Elisha cursed them, but there is no indication he actually called for a bear attack.

24 When he looked behind him and saw them, he cursed them in the name of the LORD. Then two female bears came out of the woods and tore up forty-two lads of their number.

25 He went from there to Mount Carmel, and from there he returned to Samaria.

Jehoram Meets Moab Rebellion

3 Now Jehoram the son of Ahab became king over Israel at Samaria in the eighteenth year of Jehoshaphat king of Judah, and reigned twelve years.

2 He did evil in the sight of the LORD, though

not like his father and his mother; for he put away the *sacred* pillar of Baal which his father had made.

3 Nevertheless, he clung to the sins of Jeroboam the son of Nebat, which he made Israel sin; he did not depart from them.

4 ¶ Now Mesha king of Moab was a sheep breeder, and used to pay the king of Israel 100,000 lambs and the wool of 100,000 rams.

5 But when Ahab died, the king of Moab rebelled against the king of Israel.

6 And King Jehoram went out of Samaria at that time and mustered all Israel.

7 Then he went and sent *word* to Jehoshaphat the king of Judah, saying, "The king of Moab has rebelled against me. Will you go with me to fight against Moab?" And he said, "I will go up; I am as

Replacing a Legend
Who could follow the great Elijah?

WHEN A PROPHET LIKE Elijah leaves the scene, who will dare to take his place? As time came to choose a successor, Elijah looked to find someone out of a different mold. He settled on his most faithful companion, a farmer named Elisha.

Similar Names but Different Styles

The slight variance in the two men's names expresses their difference in style. Elijah, whose name meant "The LORD is my God," dueled a king and the priests of Baal in dramatic confrontations of power. He lived apart from the people and preached judgment and the need for repentance.

> *When they had crossed over, Elijah said to Elisha, "Ask what I shall do for you before I am taken from you." And Elisha said, "Please, let a double portion of your spirit be upon me." 2:9*

Elisha ("God is salvation") shifted the emphasis. He lived among people, preferring the poor and outcast, and stressed life, hope, and God's grace. All social classes had access to Elisha, from lowly widows to foreign kings. His colorful life included work as a spy, a miracle worker, an adviser to the king, a leader of a school of prophets, and an anointer of revolutionaries.

Elisha traveled widely, and his bald head and wooden walking staff became his trademarks. News of his miracles spread, making him a famous national figure for 50 years. As Elisha lay on his deathbed, the distraught king of Israel knelt beside him, asking for one last word of advice.

Serving the People and the Kingdom

Elisha's exploits fall roughly into two categories, and the Bible seems to group them that way. One set of stories concerns people with evident needs. Elisha showed a deep sensitivity for the suffering and distressed, and sometimes helped them in miraculous ways: providing food, healing diseases, even raising a young boy from the dead. He dealt far more gently with the poor and downtrodden than with kings and generals.

Another group of stories relates to the nation. Israel was reeling from the corruption brought in during King Ahab's reign (see page 1419). Politically, Israel was at the mercy of the neighboring state of Aram (the area known today as Syria), which launched periodic raids across the border.

Sometimes Elisha helped out Israel's army, using his special insight to detect bands of raiders. Twice, miracles he predicted allowed Israel's army to break out of an impossible situation and rout the enemy. Yet he refused to become a "court prophet" serving the king's whims. On at least one occasion, he blatantly insulted a king of Israel (3:13–14). Another time, he anointed a general to overthrow the king in an outright revolution.

A Dying Breed

Incidents from Elisha's life—the healing of Naaman, the chariots of fire, the widow's oil—have become among the most familiar of Old Testament stories. In a sense, Elijah and Elisha represent the last of a breed. Prophets who followed them relied less on spectacular displays and more on the power of verbal messages from God.

Elijah and Elisha used both words and dramatic events to convey their message. Everyone knew their power, especially the kings who sometimes sought them out for advice and other times tried to kill them. In a great irony, the kings and political leaders—who thought themselves the center of history at the time—all faded away. Meanwhile the stories and words of Israel's prophets live on, expressing a message as forceful today as ever.

Life Questions: Elijah and Elisha show how God uses quite different personalities to get his message across. From the description above, which of the two prophets do you more closely identify with?

you are, my people as your people, my horses as your horses."

8 He said, "Which way shall we go up?" And he answered, "The way of the wilderness of Edom."

9 ¶ So the king of Israel went with the king of Judah and the king of Edom; and they made a circuit of seven days' journey, and there was no water for the army or for the cattle that followed them.

10 Then the king of Israel said, "Alas! For the LORD has called these three kings to give them into the hand of Moab."

11 But Jehoshaphat said, "Is there not a prophet of the LORD here, that we may inquire of the LORD by him?" And one of the king of Israel's servants answered and said, "Elisha the son of Shaphat is here, who used to pour water on the hands of Elijah."

12 Jehoshaphat said, "The word of the LORD is with him." So the king of Israel and Jehoshaphat and the king of Edom went down to him.

13 ¶ Now Elisha said to the king of Israel, "What do I have to do with you? Go to the prophets of your father and to the prophets of your mother." And the king of Israel said to him, "No, for the LORD has called these three kings together to give them into the hand of Moab."

14 Elisha said, "As the LORD of hosts lives, before whom I stand, were it not that I regard the presence of Jehoshaphat the king of Judah, I would not look at you nor see you.

15 "But now bring me a minstrel." And it came about, when the minstrel played, that the hand of the LORD came upon him.

16 He said, "Thus says the LORD, 'Make this valley full of trenches.'

17 "For thus says the LORD, 'You shall not see wind nor shall you see rain; yet that valley shall be filled with water, so that you shall drink, both you and your cattle and your beasts.

18 'This is but a slight thing in the sight of the LORD; He will also give the Moabites into your hand.

19 'Then you shall strike every fortified city and every choice city, and fell every good tree and stop all springs of water, and mar every good piece of land with stones.' "

20 It happened in the morning about the time of offering the sacrifice, that behold, water came by the way of Edom, and the country was filled with water.

21 ¶ Now all the Moabites heard that the kings had come up to fight against them. And all who were able to put on armor and older were summoned and stood on the border.

22 They rose early in the morning, and the sun shone on the water, and the Moabites saw the water opposite *them* as red as blood.

23 Then they said, "This is blood; the kings have surely fought together, and they have slain

one another. Now therefore, Moab, to the spoil!"

24 But when they came to the camp of Israel, the Israelites arose and struck the Moabites, so that they fled before them; and they went forward into the land, slaughtering the Moabites.

25 Thus they destroyed the cities; and each one threw a stone on every piece of good land and filled it. So they stopped all the springs of water and felled all the good trees, until in Kir-haraseth *only* they left its stones; however, the slingers went about *it* and struck it.

26 When the king of Moab saw that the battle was too fierce for him, he took with him 700 men who drew swords, to break through to the king of Edom; but they could not.

27 Then he took his oldest son who was to reign in his place, and offered him as a burnt offering on the wall. And there came great wrath against Israel, and they departed from him and returned to their own land.

The Widow's Oil

4 Now a certain woman of the wives of the sons of the prophets cried out to Elisha, "Your servant my husband is dead, and you know that your servant feared the LORD; and the creditor has come to take my two children to be his slaves."

2 Elisha said to her, "What shall I do for you? Tell me, what do you have in the house?" And she said, "Your maidservant has nothing in the house except a jar of oil."

3 Then he said, "Go, borrow vessels at large for yourself from all your neighbors, *even* empty vessels; do not get a few.

4 "And you shall go in and shut the door behind you and your sons, and pour out into all these vessels, and you shall set aside what is full."

5 So she went from him and shut the door behind her and her sons; they were bringing *the vessels* to her and she poured.

6 When the vessels were full, she said to her son, "Bring me another vessel." And he said to her, "There is not one vessel more." And the oil stopped.

7 Then she came and told the man of God. And he said, "Go, sell the oil and pay your debt, and you *and* your sons can live on the rest."

The Shunammite Woman

8 ¶ Now there came a day when Elisha passed over to Shunem, where there was a prominent woman, and she persuaded him to eat food. And so it was, as often as he passed by, he turned in there to eat food.

9 She said to her husband, "Behold now, I perceive that this is a holy man of God passing by us continually.

10 "Please, let us make a little walled upper chamber and let us set a bed for him there, and a table and a chair and a lampstand; and it shall be, when he comes to us, *that* he can turn in there."

11 ¶ One day he came there and turned in to the upper chamber and rested.

12 Then he said to Gehazi his servant, "Call this Shunammite." And when he had called her, she stood before him.

4:8 Elisha's Miracles

Elisha had asked for a double portion of Elijah's spirit (2:9), and the Bible pointedly records about twice as many miracles performed by Elisha. Many of these miracles, especially those in chapter 4, have great similarities to the miracles Jesus himself would later perform; they show God caring for the needs of ordinary people. Although Elisha was very famous in his own time, his name appears only once outside the book of Kings (Luke 4:27). In contrast, Elijah is often mentioned, and John the Baptist is frequently compared to him.

13 He said to him, "Say now to her, 'Behold, you have been careful for us with all this care; what can I do for you? Would you be spoken for to the king or to the captain of the army?' " And she answered, "I live among my own people."

14 So he said, "What then is to be done for her?" And Gehazi answered, "Truly she has no son and her husband is old."

15 He said, "Call her." When he had called her, she stood in the doorway.

16 Then he said, "At this season next year you will embrace a son." And she said, "No, my lord, O man of God, do not lie to your maidservant."

17 ¶ The woman conceived and bore a son at that season the next year, as Elisha had said to her.

The Shunammite's Son

18 ¶ When the child was grown, the day came that he went out to his father to the reapers.

19 He said to his father, "My head, my head." And he said to his servant, "Carry him to his mother."

20 When he had taken him and brought him to his mother, he sat on her lap until noon, and *then* died.

21 She went up and laid him on the bed of the man of God, and shut *the door* behind him and went out.

22 Then she called to her husband and said, "Please send me one of the servants and one of the donkeys, that I may run to the man of God and return."

23 He said, "Why will you go to him today? It is neither new moon nor sabbath." And she said, "*It will be* well."

24 Then she saddled a donkey and said to her servant, "Drive and go forward; do not slow down the pace for me unless I tell you."

25 So she went and came to the man of God to Mount Carmel.

¶ When the man of God saw her at a distance, he said to Gehazi his servant, "Behold, there is the Shunammite.

26 "Please run now to meet her and say to her, 'Is it well with you? Is it well with your husband? Is it well with the child?' " And she answered, "It is well."

27 When she came to the man of God to the hill, she caught hold of his feet. And Gehazi came near to push her away; but the man of God said, "Let her alone, for her soul is troubled within her; and the LORD has hidden it from me and has not told me."

28 Then she said, "Did I ask for a son from my lord? Did I not say, 'Do not deceive me'?"

29 ¶ Then he said to Gehazi, "Gird up your loins and take my staff in your hand, and go your way; if you meet any man, do not salute him, and if anyone salutes you, do not answer him; and lay my staff on the lad's face."

30 The mother of the lad said, "As the LORD lives and as you yourself live, I will not leave you." And he arose and followed her.

31 Then Gehazi passed on before them and laid the staff on the lad's face, but there was no sound or response. So he returned to meet him and told him, "The lad has not awakened."

32 ¶ When Elisha came into the house, behold the lad was dead and laid on his bed.

33 So he entered and shut the door behind them both and prayed to the LORD.

34 And he went up and lay on the child, and put his mouth on his mouth and his eyes on his eyes and his hands on his hands, and he stretched himself on him; and the flesh of the child became warm.

35 Then he returned and walked in the house once back and forth, and went up and stretched himself on him; and the lad sneezed seven times and the lad opened his eyes.

36 He called Gehazi and said, "Call this Shunammite." So he called her. And when she came in to him, he said, "Take up your son."

37 Then she went in and fell at his feet and bowed herself to the ground, and she took up her son and went out.

The Poisonous Stew

38 ¶ When Elisha returned to Gilgal, *there was* a famine in the land. As the sons of the prophets were sitting before him, he said to his servant, "Put on the large pot and boil stew for the sons of the prophets."

39 Then one went out into the field to gather herbs, and found a wild vine and gathered from it his lap full of wild gourds, and came and sliced them into the pot of stew, for they did not know *what they were.*

40 So they poured *it* out for the men to eat.

And as they were eating of the stew, they cried out and said, "O man of God, there is death in the pot." And they were unable to eat.

41 But he said, "Now bring meal." He threw it into the pot and said, "Pour *it* out for the people that they may eat." Then there was no harm in the pot.

42 ¶ Now a man came from Baal-shalishah, and brought the man of God bread of the first fruits, twenty loaves of barley and fresh ears of grain in his sack. And he said, "Give *them* to the people that they may eat."

43 His attendant said, "What, will I set this before a hundred men?" But he said, "Give *them* to the people that they may eat, for thus says the LORD, 'They shall eat and have *some* left over.'"

44 So he set *it* before them, and they ate and had *some* left over, according to the word of the LORD.

Naaman Is Healed

5 Now Naaman, captain of the army of the king of Aram, was a great man with his master, and highly respected, because by him the LORD had given victory to Aram. The man was also a valiant warrior, *but he was* a leper.

2 Now the Arameans had gone out in bands and had taken captive a little girl from the land of Israel; and she waited on Naaman's wife.

3 She said to her mistress, "I wish that my master were with the prophet who is in Samaria! Then he would cure him of his leprosy."

5:3 A Captive's Compassion

She had been captured in a raid, taken to a foreign country, and made a slave. Yet instead of bitterness, she showed compassion toward her master. She wanted him healed, and she believed her God would do it. God used this girl's tragedy to heal and convert her enemy—a wonderful example of love reaching out.

4 Naaman went in and told his master, saying, "Thus and thus spoke the girl who is from the land of Israel."

5 Then the king of Aram said, "Go now, and I will send a letter to the king of Israel." He departed and took with him ten talents of silver and six thousand *shekels* of gold and ten changes of clothes.

6 ¶ He brought the letter to the king of Israel, saying, "And now as this letter comes to you, behold, I have sent Naaman my servant to you, that you may cure him of his leprosy."

7 When the king of Israel read the letter, he tore his clothes and said, "Am I God, to kill and to make alive, that this man is sending *word* to me to cure a man of his leprosy? But consider now, and see how he is seeking a quarrel against me."

8 ¶ It happened when Elisha the man of God heard that the king of Israel had torn his clothes, that he sent *word* to the king, saying, "Why have you torn your clothes? Now let him come to me, and he shall know that there is a prophet in Israel."

9 So Naaman came with his horses and his chariots and stood at the doorway of the house of Elisha.

10 Elisha sent a messenger to him, saying, "Go and wash in the Jordan seven times, and your flesh will be restored to you and *you will* be clean."

5:10–16 Harder on the Rich

Elisha's treatment of the general Naaman here, and of the king of Israel elsewhere, contrasts sharply with his mild manner around the poor and oppressed. Elisha's prescribed cure obviously offended Naaman's pride. And Elisha pointedly refused to accept payment from the wealthy general, who was used to paying his way. In this incident, and in another (8:7–15), Elisha was serving the kingdom of Aram, an enemy of Israel.

11 But Naaman was furious and went away and said, "Behold, I thought, 'He will surely come out to me and stand and call on the name of the LORD his God, and wave his hand over the place and cure the leper.'

12 "Are not Abanah and Pharpar, the rivers of Damascus, better than all the waters of Israel? Could I not wash in them and be clean?" So he turned and went away in a rage.

13 Then his servants came near and spoke to him and said, "My father, had the prophet told you *to do some* great thing, would you not have done *it*? How much more *then*, when he says to you, 'Wash, and be clean'?"

14 So he went down and dipped *himself* seven times in the Jordan, according to the word of the man of God; and his flesh was restored like the flesh of a little child and he was clean.

Gehazi's Greed

15 ¶ When he returned to the man of God with all his company, and came and stood before him, he said, "Behold now, I know that there is no God in all the earth, but in Israel; so please take a present from your servant now."

16 But he said, "As the LORD lives, before whom I stand, I will take nothing." And he urged him to take *it*, but he refused.

17 Naaman said, "If not, please let your servant at least be given two mules' load of earth; for your servant will no longer offer burnt offering nor will he sacrifice to other gods, but to the LORD.

18 "In this matter may the LORD pardon your servant: when my master goes into the house of

Rimmon to worship there, and he leans on my hand and I bow myself in the house of Rimmon, when I bow myself in the house of Rimmon, the LORD pardon your servant in this matter."

19 He said to him, "Go in peace." So he departed from him some distance.

20 ¶ But Gehazi, the servant of Elisha the man of God, thought, "Behold, my master has spared this Naaman the Aramean, by not receiving from his hands what he brought. As the LORD lives, I will run after him and take something from him."

21 So Gehazi pursued Naaman. When Naaman saw one running after him, he came down from the chariot to meet him and said, "Is all well?"

22 He said, "All is well. My master has sent me, saying, 'Behold, just now two young men of the sons of the prophets have come to me from the hill country of Ephraim. Please give them a talent of silver and two changes of clothes.'"

23 Naaman said, "Be pleased to take two talents." And he urged him, and bound two talents of silver in two bags with two changes of clothes and gave them to two of his servants; and they carried *them* before him.

24 When he came to the hill, he took them from their hand and deposited them in the house, and he sent the men away, and they departed.

25 But he went in and stood before his master. And Elisha said to him, "Where have you been, Gehazi?" And he said, "Your servant went nowhere."

26 ¶ Then he said to him, "Did not my heart go *with you,* when the man turned from his chariot to meet you? Is it a time to receive money and to receive clothes and olive groves and vineyards and sheep and oxen and male and female servants?

27 "Therefore, the leprosy of Naaman shall cling to you and to your descendants forever." So he went out from his presence a leper *as white* as snow.

The Axe Head Recovered

6 Now the sons of the prophets said to Elisha, "Behold now, the place before you where we are living is too limited for us.

2 "Please let us go to the Jordan and each of us take from there a beam, and let us make a place there for ourselves where we may live." So he said, "Go."

3 Then one said, "Please be willing to go with your servants." And he answered, "I shall go."

4 So he went with them; and when they came to the Jordan, they cut down trees.

5 But as one was felling a beam, the axe head fell into the water; and he cried out and said, "Alas, my master! For it was borrowed."

6 Then the man of God said, "Where did it fall?" And when he showed him the place, he cut

off a stick and threw *it* in there, and made the iron float.

7 He said, "Take it up for yourself." So he put out his hand and took it.

The Arameans Plot to Capture Elisha

8 ¶ Now the king of Aram was warring against Israel; and he counseled with his servants saying, "In such and such a place shall be my camp."

9 The man of God sent *word* to the king of Israel saying, "Beware that you do not pass this place, for the Arameans are coming down there."

10 The king of Israel sent to the place about which the man of God had told him; thus he warned him, so that he guarded himself there, more than once or twice.

11 ¶ Now the heart of the king of Aram was enraged over this thing; and he called his servants and said to them, "Will you tell me which of us is for the king of Israel?"

12 One of his servants said, "No, my lord, O king; but Elisha, the prophet who is in Israel, tells the king of Israel the words that you speak in your bedroom."

13 So he said, "Go and see where he is, that I may send and take him." And it was told him, saying, "Behold, he is in Dothan."

14 He sent horses and chariots and a great army there, and they came by night and surrounded the city.

15 ¶ Now when the attendant of the man of God had risen early and gone out, behold, an army with horses and chariots was circling the city. And his servant said to him, "Alas, my master! What shall we do?"

16 So he answered, "Do not fear, for those who are with us are more than those who are with them."

17 Then Elisha prayed and said, "O LORD, I pray, open his eyes that he may see." And the LORD opened the servant's eyes and he saw; and behold, the mountain was full of horses and chariots of fire all around Elisha.

6:17 Chariots of Fire

Surrounded by an army, Elisha's servant cried, "What shall we do?" But when Elisha prayed, the servant could suddenly see that God's forces, invisible to everyone else, far outnumbered the enemy. The story offers a rare glimpse of the "invisible world" of supernatural forces. God has resources to help that we cannot see.

18 When they came down to him, Elisha prayed to the LORD and said, "Strike this people with blindness, I pray." So He struck them with blindness according to the word of Elisha.

19 Then Elisha said to them, "This is not the way, nor is this the city; follow me and I will bring you to the man whom you seek." And he brought them to Samaria.

20 ¶ When they had come into Samaria, Elisha said, "O LORD, open the eyes of these *men,* that they may see." So the LORD opened their eyes and they saw; and behold, they were in the midst of Samaria.

21 Then the king of Israel when he saw them, said to Elisha, "My father, shall I kill them? Shall I kill them?"

22 He answered, "You shall not kill *them.* Would you kill those you have taken captive with your sword and with your bow? Set bread and water before them, that they may eat and drink and go to their master."

23 So he prepared a great feast for them; and when they had eaten and drunk he sent them away, and they went to their master. And the marauding bands of Arameans did not come again into the land of Israel.

The Siege of Samaria—Cannibalism

24 ¶ Now it came about after this, that Benhadad king of Aram gathered all his army and went up and besieged Samaria.

25 There was a great famine in Samaria; and behold, they besieged it, until a donkey's head was sold for eighty *shekels* of silver, and a fourth of a ªkab of dove's dung for five *shekels* of silver.

26 As the king of Israel was passing by on the wall a woman cried out to him, saying, "Help, my lord, O king!"

27 He said, "If the LORD does not help you, from where shall I help you? From the threshing floor, or from the wine press?"

28 And the king said to her, "What is the matter with you?" And she answered, "This woman said to me, 'Give your son that we may eat him today, and we will eat my son tomorrow.'

29 "So we boiled my son and ate him; and I said to her on the next day, 'Give your son, that we may eat him'; but she has hidden her son."

30 When the king heard the words of the woman, he tore his clothes—now he was passing by on the wall—and the people looked, and behold, he had sackcloth beneath on his body.

31 Then he said, "May God do so to me and more also, if the head of Elisha the son of Shaphat remains on him today."

32 ¶ Now Elisha was sitting in his house, and the elders were sitting with him. And *the king* sent a man from his presence; but before the messenger came to him, he said to the elders, "Do you see how this son of a murderer has sent to take away my head? Look, when the messenger comes, shut the door and hold the door shut against him. Is not the sound of his master's feet behind him?"

33 While he was still talking with them, behold,

the messenger came down to him and he said, "Behold, this evil is from the LORD; why should I wait for the LORD any longer?"

Elisha Promises Food

7 Then Elisha said, "Listen to the word of the LORD; thus says the LORD, 'Tomorrow about

this time a measure of fine flour will be *sold* for a shekel, and two measures of barley for a shekel, in the gate of Samaria.' "

2 The royal officer on whose hand the king was leaning answered the man of God and said, "Behold, if the LORD should make windows in heaven, could this thing be?" Then he said, "Behold, you will see it with your own eyes, but you will not eat of it."

Four Lepers Relate Arameans' Flight

3 ¶ Now there were four leprous men at the entrance of the gate; and they said to one another, "Why do we sit here until we die?

4 "If we say, 'We will enter the city,' then the famine is in the city and we will die there; and if we sit here, we die also. Now therefore come, and let us go over to the camp of the Arameans. If they spare us, we will live; and if they kill us, we will but die."

5 They arose at twilight to go to the camp of the Arameans; when they came to the outskirts of the camp of the Arameans, behold, there was no one there.

6 For the Lord had caused the army of the Arameans to hear a sound of chariots and a sound of horses, *even* the sound of a great army, so that they said to one another, "Behold, the king of Israel has hired against us the kings of the Hittites and the kings of the Egyptians, to come upon us."

7 Therefore they arose and fled in the twilight, and left their tents and their horses and their donkeys, *even* the camp just as it was, and fled for their life.

8 When these lepers came to the outskirts of the camp, they entered one tent and ate and drank, and carried from there silver and gold and clothes, and went and hid *them;* and they returned

ª I.e. One kab equals approx 2 qts

and entered another tent and carried from there *also,* and went and hid *them.*

9 ¶ Then they said to one another, "We are not doing right. This day is a day of good news, but we are keeping silent; if we wait until morning light, punishment will overtake us. Now therefore come, let us go and tell the king's household."

10 So they came and called to the gatekeepers of the city, and they told them, saying, "We came to the camp of the Arameans, and behold, there was no one there, nor the voice of man, only the horses tied and the donkeys tied, and the tents just as they were."

11 The gatekeepers called and told *it* within the king's household.

12 Then the king arose in the night and said to his servants, "I will now tell you what the Arameans have done to us. They know that we are hungry; therefore they have gone from the camp to hide themselves in the field, saying, 'When they come out of the city, we will capture them alive and get into the city.'"

13 One of his servants said, "Please, let some *men* take five of the horses which remain, which are left in the city. Behold, they *will be in any case* like all the multitude of Israel who are left in it; behold, they *will be in any case* like all the multitude of Israel who have already perished, so let us send and see."

14 They took therefore two chariots with horses, and the king sent after the army of the Arameans, saying, "Go and see."

The Promise Fulfilled

15 They went after them to the Jordan, and behold, all the way was full of clothes and equipment which the Arameans had thrown away in their haste. Then the messengers returned and told the king.

16 ¶ So the people went out and plundered the camp of the Arameans. Then a measure of fine flour *was sold* for a shekel and two measures of barley for a shekel, according to the word of the LORD.

17 Now the king appointed the royal officer on whose hand he leaned to have charge of the gate; but the people trampled on him at the gate, and he died just as the man of God had said, who spoke when the king came down to him.

18 It happened just as the man of God had spoken to the king, saying, "Two measures of barley for a shekel and a measure of fine flour for a shekel, will be *sold* tomorrow about this time at the gate of Samaria."

19 Then the royal officer answered the man of God and said, "Now behold, if the LORD should make windows in heaven, could such a thing be?" And he said, "Behold, you will see it with your own eyes, but you will not eat of it."

20 And so it happened to him, for the people trampled on him at the gate and he died.

Jehoram Restores the Shunammite's Land

8 Now Elisha spoke to the woman whose son he had restored to life, saying, "Arise and go with your household, and sojourn wherever you can sojourn; for the LORD has called for a famine, and it will even come on the land for seven years."

2 So the woman arose and did according to the word of the man of God, and she went with her household and sojourned in the land of the Philistines seven years.

3 At the end of seven years, the woman returned from the land of the Philistines; and she went out to appeal to the king for her house and for her field.

4 Now the king was talking with Gehazi, the servant of the man of God, saying, "Please relate to me all the great things that Elisha has done."

5 As he was relating to the king how he had restored to life the one who was dead, behold, the woman whose son he had restored to life appealed to the king for her house and for her field. And Gehazi said, "My lord, O king, this is the woman and this is her son, whom Elisha restored to life."

6 When the king asked the woman, she related *it* to him. So the king appointed for her a certain officer, saying, "Restore all that was hers and all the produce of the field from the day that she left the land even until now."

Elisha Predicts Evil from Hazael

7 ¶ Then Elisha came to Damascus. Now Ben-hadad king of Aram was sick, and it was told him, saying, "The man of God has come here."

8 The king said to Hazael, "Take a gift in your hand and go to meet the man of God, and inquire of the LORD by him, saying, 'Will I recover from this sickness?'"

9 So Hazael went to meet him and took a gift in his hand, even every kind of good thing of Damascus, forty camels' loads; and he came and stood before him and said, "Your son Ben-hadad king of Aram has sent me to you, saying, 'Will I recover from this sickness?'"

10 Then Elisha said to him, "Go, say to him, 'You will surely recover,' but the LORD has shown me that he will certainly die."

11 He fixed his gaze steadily *on him* until he was ashamed, and the man of God wept.

12 Hazael said, "Why does my lord weep?" Then he answered, "Because I know the evil that you will do to the sons of Israel: their strongholds you will set on fire, and their young men you will kill with the sword, and their little ones you will dash in pieces, and their women with child you will rip up."

13 Then Hazael said, "But what is your servant, *who is but* a dog, that he should do this great thing?" And Elisha answered, "The LORD has shown me that you will be king over Aram."

14 So he departed from Elisha and returned to his master, who said to him, "What did Elisha say

to you?" And he answered, "He told me that you would surely recover."

15 On the following day, he took the cover and dipped it in water and spread it on his face, so that he died. And Hazael became king in his place.

Another Jehoram Reigns in Judah

16 ¶ Now in the fifth year of Joram the son of Ahab king of Israel, Jehoshaphat being then the king of Judah, Jehoram the son of Jehoshaphat king of Judah became king.

8:16 Two Kings, One Name

It's difficult enough to keep 39 rulers straight. When two of them from neighboring countries have the same name, the plot thickens. Joram, a son of Ahab, ruled Israel at the same time Jehoram (sometimes spelled Joram also) took over Judah's throne. Both were wicked. Jehoram's marriage to Ahab's daughter ushered in a terrible period in Judah's history. (2 Chronicles 21 gives much more detail on this king.) In addition, both Judah and Israel had a king named Ahaziah.

17 He was thirty-two years old when he became king, and he reigned eight years in Jerusalem.

18 He walked in the way of the kings of Israel, just as the house of Ahab had done, for the daughter of Ahab became his wife; and he did evil in the sight of the LORD.

19 However, the LORD was not willing to destroy Judah, for the sake of David His servant, since He had promised him to give a lamp to him through his sons always.

20 ¶ In his days Edom revolted from under the hand of Judah, and made a king over themselves.

21 Then Joram crossed over to Zair, and all his chariots with him. And he arose by night and struck the Edomites who had surrounded him and the captains of the chariots; but *his* army fled to their tents.

22 So Edom revolted against Judah to this day. Then Libnah revolted at the same time.

23 The rest of the acts of Joram and all that he did, are they not written in the Book of the Chronicles of the Kings of Judah?

Ahaziah Succeeds Jehoram in Judah

24 So Joram slept with his fathers and was buried with his fathers in the city of David; and Ahaziah his son became king in his place.

25 ¶ In the twelfth year of Joram the son of Ahab king of Israel, Ahaziah the son of Jehoram king of Judah began to reign.

26 Ahaziah *was* twenty-two years old when he became king, and he reigned one year in Jerusa-

lem. And his mother's name *was* Athaliah the granddaughter of Omri king of Israel.

27 He walked in the way of the house of Ahab and did evil in the sight of the LORD, like the house of Ahab *had done,* because he was a son-in-law of the house of Ahab.

8:27 Political Marriages

Ahab shrewdly arranged marriages to cement alliances with Israel's neighbors. His wife Jezebel, for example, hailed from Phoenicia, which thus became an ally of Israel. Ahab also married off his daughter to the king of Judah, bringing peace to the two warring neighbors. Later, when Jehu revolted and slaughtered all of Ahab's family members, he aroused the ire of those allies and threw Israel's foreign policy into disarray.

28 ¶ Then he went with Joram the son of Ahab to war against Hazael king of Aram at Ramoth-gilead, and the Arameans wounded Joram.

29 So King Joram returned to be healed in Jezreel of the wounds which the Arameans had inflicted on him at Ramah when he fought against Hazael king of Aram. Then Ahaziah the son of Jehoram king of Judah went down to see Joram the son of Ahab in Jezreel because he was sick.

Jehu Reigns over Israel

9 Now Elisha the prophet called one of the sons of the prophets and said to him, "Gird up your loins, and take this flask of oil in your hand and go to Ramoth-gilead.

2 "When you arrive there, search out Jehu the son of Jehoshaphat the son of Nimshi, and go in and bid him arise from among his brothers, and bring him to an inner room.

3 "Then take the flask of oil and pour it on his head and say, 'Thus says the LORD, "I have anointed you king over Israel." ' Then open the door and flee and do not wait."

4 ¶ So the young man, the servant of the prophet, went to Ramoth-gilead.

5 When he came, behold, the captains of the army were sitting, and he said, "I have a word for you, O captain." And Jehu said, "For which *one* of us?" And he said, "For you, O captain."

6 He arose and went into the house, and he poured the oil on his head and said to him, "Thus says the LORD, the God of Israel, 'I have anointed you king over the people of the LORD, *even* over Israel.

7 'You shall strike the house of Ahab your master, that I may avenge the blood of My servants the prophets, and the blood of all the servants of the LORD, at the hand of Jezebel.

8 'For the whole house of Ahab shall perish,

and I will cut off from Ahab every male person both bond and free in Israel.

9 'I will make the house of Ahab like the house of Jeroboam the son of Nebat, and like the house of Baasha the son of Ahijah.

10 'The dogs shall eat Jezebel in the territory of Jezreel, and none shall bury *her*.' " Then he opened the door and fled.

11 ¶ Now Jehu came out to the servants of his master, and one said to him, "Is all well? Why did this mad fellow come to you?" And he said to them, "You know *very well* the man and his talk."

12 They said, "It is a lie, tell us now." And he said, "Thus and thus he said to me, 'Thus says the LORD, "I have anointed you king over Israel." ' "

13 Then they hurried and each man took his garment and placed it under him on the bare steps, and blew the trumpet, saying, "Jehu is king!"

Jehoram (Joram) Is Assassinated

14 ¶ So Jehu the son of Jehoshaphat the son of Nimshi conspired against Joram. Now Joram with all Israel was defending Ramoth-gilead against Hazael king of Aram,

15 but King [a]Joram had returned to Jezreel to be healed of the wounds which the Arameans had inflicted on him when he fought with Hazael king of Aram. So Jehu said, "If this is your mind, *then* let no one escape *or* leave the city to go tell *it* in Jezreel."

16 Then Jehu rode in a chariot and went to Jezreel, for Joram was lying there. Ahaziah king of Judah had come down to see Joram.

17 ¶ Now the watchman was standing on the tower in Jezreel and he saw the company of Jehu as he came, and said, "I see a company." And Joram said, "Take a horseman and send him to meet them and let him say, 'Is it peace?' "

18 So a horseman went to meet him and said, "Thus says the king, 'Is it peace?' " And Jehu said, "What have you to do with peace? Turn behind me." And the watchman reported, "The messenger came to them, but he did not return."

19 Then he sent out a second horseman, who came to them and said, "Thus says the king, 'Is it peace?' " And Jehu answered, "What have you to do with peace? Turn behind me."

20 The watchman reported, "He came even to them, and he did not return; and the driving is like the driving of Jehu the son of Nimshi, for he drives furiously."

21 ¶ Then Joram said, "Get ready." And they made his chariot ready. Joram king of Israel and Ahaziah king of Judah went out, each in his chariot, and they went out to meet Jehu and found him in the property of Naboth the Jezreelite.

22 When Joram saw Jehu, he said, "Is it peace, Jehu?" And he answered, "What peace, so long as

the harlotries of your mother Jezebel and her witchcrafts are so many?"

23 So Joram reined about and fled and said to Ahaziah, "*There is* treachery, O Ahaziah!"

24 And Jehu drew his bow with his full strength and shot Joram between his arms; and the arrow went through his heart and he sank in his chariot.

25 Then *Jehu* said to Bidkar his officer, "Take *him* up and cast him into the [b]property of the field of Naboth the Jezreelite, for I remember when you and I were riding together after Ahab his father, that the LORD laid this oracle against him:

26 'Surely I have seen yesterday the blood of Naboth and the blood of his sons,' says the LORD, 'and I will repay you in this [b]property,' says the LORD. Now then, take and cast him into the property, according to the word of the LORD."

Jehu Assassinates Ahaziah

27 ¶ When Ahaziah the king of Judah saw *this*, he fled by the way of the garden house. And Jehu pursued him and said, "Shoot him too, in the chariot." *So they shot him* at the ascent of Gur, which is at Ibleam. But he fled to Megiddo and died there.

28 Then his servants carried him in a chariot to Jerusalem and buried him in his grave with his fathers in the city of David.

29 ¶ Now in the eleventh year of Joram, the son of Ahab, Ahaziah became king over Judah.

30 ¶ When Jehu came to Jezreel, Jezebel heard *of it*, and she painted her eyes and adorned her head and looked out the window.

31 As Jehu entered the gate, she said, "Is it well, Zimri, your master's murderer?"

32 Then he lifted up his face to the window and said, "Who is on my side? Who?" And two or three officials looked down at him.

Jezebel Is Slain

33 He said, "Throw her down." So they threw her down, and some of her blood was sprinkled on the wall and on the horses, and he trampled her under foot.

34 When he came in, he ate and drank; and he said, "See now to this cursed woman and bury her, for she is a king's daughter."

35 They went to bury her, but they found nothing more of her than the skull and the feet and the palms of her hands.

36 Therefore they returned and told him. And he said, "This is the word of the LORD, which He spoke by His servant Elijah the Tishbite, saying, 'In the property of Jezreel the dogs shall eat the flesh of Jezebel;

37 and the corpse of Jezebel will be as dung on the face of the field in the property of Jezreel, so they cannot say, "This is Jezebel." ' "

[a] Heb *Jehoram*   [b] Lit *portion*

Judgment upon Ahab's House

10 Now Ahab had seventy sons in Samaria. And Jehu wrote letters and sent *them* to Samaria, to the rulers of Jezreel, the elders, and to the guardians of *the children of* Ahab, saying,

2 "Now, when this letter comes to you, since your master's sons are with you, as well as the chariots and horses and a fortified city and the weapons,

3 select the best and *a*fittest of your master's sons, and set *him* on his father's throne, and fight for your master's house."

4 But they feared greatly and said, "Behold, the two kings did not stand before him; how then can we stand?"

5 And the one who *was* over the household, and he who *was* over the city, the elders, and the guardians of *the children,* sent *word* to Jehu, saying, "We are your servants, all that you say to us we will do, we will not make any man king; do what is good in your sight."

6 Then he wrote a letter to them a second time saying, "If you are on my side, and you will listen to my voice, take the heads of the men, your master's sons, and come to me at Jezreel tomorrow about this time." Now the king's sons, seventy persons, *were* with the great men of the city, *who* were rearing them.

7 When the letter came to them, they took the king's sons and slaughtered *them,* seventy persons, and put their heads in baskets, and sent *them* to him at Jezreel.

8 When the messenger came and told him, saying, "They have brought the heads of the king's sons," he said, "Put them in two heaps at the entrance of the gate until morning."

9 Now in the morning he went out and stood and said to all the people, "You are innocent; behold, I conspired against my master and killed him, but who killed all these?

10 "Know then that there shall fall to the earth nothing of the word of the LORD, which the LORD spoke concerning the house of Ahab, for the LORD has done what He spoke through His servant Elijah."

11 So Jehu killed all who remained of the house of Ahab in Jezreel, and all his great men and his acquaintances and his priests, until he left him without a survivor.

12 ¶ Then he arose and departed and went to Samaria. On the way while he was at *b*Beth-eked of the shepherds,

13 Jehu met the relatives of Ahaziah king of Judah and said, "Who are you?" And they answered, "We are the relatives of Ahaziah; and we have come down to greet the sons of the king and the sons of the queen mother."

14 He said, "Take them alive." So they took them alive and killed them at the pit of Beth-eked, forty-two men; and he left none of them.

15 ¶ Now when he had departed from there, he

a Lit *most upright*   *b* I.e. house of binding

JEZEBEL   *Wild and Wicked*

JEZEBEL WAS SUCH A REMARKABLE woman that her name came to define a type of person. "An impudent, shameless or abandoned woman," says the dictionary listing for jezebel. No modern jezebel ever exceeded the original, however. The proud, determined daughter of a king, Jezebel set out single-handedly to force Israel into paganism—and she nearly succeeded.

She came from Sidon on the Mediterranean coast, where her father reigned over the Phoenicians. Her royal wedding to Ahab, king of Israel, cemented an alliance between the two kingdoms. Other Israelite kings, such as Solomon, had also flouted God's law by marrying foreign wives. Typically, these women brought their religion with them (which explains why God forbade foreign marriage in the first place).

Jezebel went far beyond other foreign wives, however. Not content to worship Baal by herself, she insisted that all Israelites worship with her. She convinced Ahab to build a temple for Baal in the capital, and imported hundreds of foreign priests to work in that temple. She set out to exterminate the worship of Israel's God, killing anyone who stood in her way.

Only one man dared to oppose Jezebel publicly: the prophet Elijah. Yet even his amazing triumph on Mount Carmel (1 Kings 18) failed to faze her. God's unmistakable display of power only made her want to kill Elijah, not convert.

Jezebel died as she lived, cutting a memorable figure. When her luck ran out, she didn't beg for mercy. Like a Hollywood vamp she dressed up for the showdown and waited at the window to taunt the man who had come to deal with her. A woman who inspired no loyalty, she was tossed out the window by her own servants. As Elijah had prophesied (1 Kings 21:23), the town dogs devoured her body.

Life Questions: Some people say it doesn't matter what you believe, as long as you believe it with all your heart. What would Jezebel say to this? What would Elijah?

met Jehonadab the son of Rechab *coming* to meet him; and he greeted him and said to him, "Is your heart right, as my heart is with your heart?" And Jehonadab answered, "It is." *Jehu said,* "If it is,

give *me* your hand." And he gave him his hand, and he took him up to him into the chariot.

16 He said, "Come with me and see my zeal for the LORD." So he made him ride in his chariot.

17 When he came to Samaria, he killed all who remained to Ahab in Samaria, until he had destroyed him, according to the word of the LORD which He spoke to Elijah.

Jehu Destroys Baal Worshipers

18 ¶ Then Jehu gathered all the people and said to them, "Ahab served Baal a little; Jehu will serve him much.

19 "Now, summon all the prophets of Baal, all his worshipers and all his priests; let no one be missing, for I have a great sacrifice for Baal; whoever is missing shall not live." But Jehu did it in cunning, so that he might destroy the worshipers of Baal.

20 And Jehu said, "Sanctify a solemn assembly for Baal." And they proclaimed *it.*

21 Then Jehu sent throughout Israel and all the worshipers of Baal came, so that there was not a man left who did not come. And when they went into the house of Baal, the house of Baal was filled from one end to the other.

22 He said to the one who *was* in charge of the wardrobe, "Bring out garments for all the worshipers of Baal." So he brought out garments for them.

23 Jehu went into the house of Baal with Jehonadab the son of Rechab; and he said to the worshipers of Baal, "Search and see that there is here with you none of the servants of the LORD, but only the worshipers of Baal."

24 Then they went in to offer sacrifices and burnt offerings.

¶ Now Jehu had stationed for himself eighty men outside, and he had said, "The one who per-

mits any of the men whom I bring into your hands to escape shall give up his life in exchange."

25 ¶ Then it came about, as soon as he had finished offering the burnt offering, that Jehu said to the guard and to the royal officers, "Go in, kill them; let none come out." And they killed them with the edge of the sword; and the guard and the royal officers threw *them* out, and went to the inner room of the house of Baal.

26 They brought out the *sacred* pillars of the house of Baal and burned them.

27 They also broke down the *sacred* pillar of Baal and broke down the house of Baal, and made it a latrine to this day.

28 ¶ Thus Jehu eradicated Baal out of Israel.

29 However, *as for* the sins of Jeroboam the son of Nebat, which he made Israel sin, from these Jehu did not depart, *even* the golden calves that *were* at Bethel and that *were* at Dan.

30 The LORD said to Jehu, "Because you have done well in executing what is right in My eyes, *and* have done to the house of Ahab according to all that *was* in My heart, your sons of the fourth generation shall sit on the throne of Israel."

31 But Jehu was not careful to walk in the law of the LORD, the God of Israel, with all his heart; he did not depart from the sins of Jeroboam, which he made Israel sin.

32 ¶ In those days the LORD began to cut off *portions* from Israel; and Hazael defeated them throughout the territory of Israel:

33 from the Jordan eastward, all the land of Gilead, the Gadites and the Reubenites and the Manassites, from Aroer, which is by the valley of the Arnon, even Gilead and Bashan.

Jehoahaz Succeeds Jehu

34 Now the rest of the acts of Jehu and all that he did and all his might, are they not written in the Book of the Chronicles of the Kings of Israel?

35 And Jehu slept with his fathers, and they buried him in Samaria. And Jehoahaz his son became king in his place.

36 Now the time which Jehu reigned over Israel in Samaria *was* twenty-eight years.

Athaliah Queen of Judah

11 When Athaliah the mother of Ahaziah saw that her son was dead, she rose and destroyed all the royal offspring.

2 But Jehosheba, the daughter of King Joram, sister of Ahaziah, took Joash the son of Ahaziah and stole him from among the king's sons who were being put to death, and placed him and his nurse in the bedroom. So they hid him from Athaliah, and he was not put to death.

3 So he was hidden with her in the house of the LORD six years, while Athaliah was reigning over the land.

4 ¶ Now in the seventh year Jehoiada sent and brought the captains of hundreds of the Carites

and of the *a*guard, and brought them to him in the house of the LORD. Then he made a covenant with them and put them under oath in the house of the LORD, and showed them the king's son.

11:2 Preserving the Royal Line

Queen Athaliah came within one baby of wiping out the royal line descending from King David. The prophets predicted that Jesus the Messiah would come from David's line, so in a sense the entire future of God's plan rested with the family's success in hiding Joash and returning him to the throne.

5 He commanded them, saying, "This is the thing that you shall do: one third of you, who come in on the sabbath and keep watch over the king's house

6 (one third also *shall be* at the gate Sur, and one third at the gate behind the *a*guards), shall keep watch over the house for defense.

7 "Two parts of you, *even* all who go out on the sabbath, shall also keep watch over the house of the LORD for the king.

8 "Then you shall surround the king, each with his weapons in his hand; and whoever comes within the ranks shall be put to death. And be with the king when he goes out and when he comes in."

9 ¶ So the captains of hundreds did according to all that Jehoiada the priest commanded. And each one of them took his men who were to come in on the sabbath, with those who were to go out on the sabbath, and came to Jehoiada the priest.

10 The priest gave to the captains of hundreds the spears and shields that *had been* King David's, which *were* in the house of the LORD.

11 The guards stood each with his weapons in his hand, from the right side of the house to the left side of the house, by the altar and by the house, around the king.

12 Then he brought the king's son out and put the crown on him and *gave him* the testimony; and they made him king and anointed him, and they clapped their hands and said, "*Long* live the king!"

13 ¶ When Athaliah heard the noise of the guard *and of* the people, she came to the people in the house of the LORD.

14 She looked and behold, the king was standing by the pillar, according to the custom, with the captains and the trumpeters beside the king; and all the people of the land rejoiced and blew trumpets. Then Athaliah tore her clothes and cried, "Treason! Treason!"

15 And Jehoiada the priest commanded the captains of hundreds who were appointed over the army and said to them, "Bring her out between the ranks, and whoever follows her put to death with the sword." For the priest said, "Let her not be put to death in the house of the LORD."

16 So they seized her, and when she arrived at the horses' entrance of the king's house, she was put to death there.

17 ¶ Then Jehoiada made a covenant between the LORD and the king and the people, that they would be the LORD's people, also between the king and the people.

18 All the people of the land went to the house of Baal, and tore it down; his altars and his images they broke in pieces thoroughly, and killed Mattan the priest of Baal before the altars. And the priest appointed officers over the house of the LORD.

19 He took the captains of hundreds and the Carites and the guards and all the people of the land; and they brought the king down from the house of the LORD, and came by the way of the gate of the guards to the king's house. And he sat on the throne of the kings.

20 So all the people of the land rejoiced and the city was quiet. For they had put Athaliah to death with the sword at the king's house.

21 ¶ Jehoash was seven years old when he became king.

Joash (Jehoash) Reigns over Judah

12 In the seventh year of Jehu, Jehoash became king, and he reigned forty years in Jerusalem; and his mother's name was Zibiah of Beersheba.

2 Jehoash did right in the sight of the LORD all his days in which Jehoiada the priest instructed him.

3 Only the high places were not taken away; the people still sacrificed and burned incense on the high places.

The Temple to Be Repaired

4 ¶ Then Jehoash said to the priests, "All the money of the sacred things which is brought into the house of the LORD, in current money, *both* the money of each man's assessment *and* all the money which any man's heart prompts him to bring into the house of the LORD,

5 let the priests take it for themselves, each from his acquaintance; and they shall repair the *b*damages of the house wherever any damage may be found."

6 ¶ But it came about that in the twenty-third year of King Jehoash the priests had not repaired the damages of the house.

7 Then King Jehoash called for Jehoiada the priest, and for the *other* priests and said to them, "Why do you not repair the damages of the house? Now therefore take no *more* money from your acquaintances, but pay it for the damages of the house."

a Lit *runners*   *b* Lit *breaches,* and so through v 12

8 So the priests agreed that they would take no *more* money from the people, nor repair the damages of the house.

9 ¶ But Jehoiada the priest took a chest and bored a hole in its lid and put it beside the altar, on the right side as one comes into the house of the LORD; and the priests who guarded the threshold put in it all the money which was brought into the house of the LORD.

10 When they saw that there was much money in the chest, the king's scribe and the high priest came up and tied *it* in bags and counted the money which was found in the house of the LORD.

11 They gave the money which was weighed out into the hands of those who did the work, who had the oversight of the house of the LORD; and they paid it out to the carpenters and the builders who worked on the house of the LORD;

12 and to the masons and the stonecutters, and for buying timber and hewn stone to repair the damages to the house of the LORD, and for all that was laid out for the house to repair it.

13 But there were not made for the house of the LORD silver cups, snuffers, bowls, trumpets, any vessels of gold, or vessels of silver from the money which was brought into the house of the LORD;

14 for they gave that to those who did the work, and with it they repaired the house of the LORD.

15 Moreover, they did not require an accounting from the men into whose hand they gave the money to pay to those who did the work, for they dealt faithfully.

16 The money from the guilt offerings and the money from the sin offerings was not brought into the house of the LORD; it was for the priests.

17 ¶ Then Hazael king of Aram went up and fought against Gath and captured it, and Hazael set his face to go up to Jerusalem.

18 Jehoash king of Judah took all the sacred things that Jehoshaphat and Jehoram and Ahaziah, his fathers, kings of Judah, had dedicated, and his own sacred things and all the gold that was found among the treasuries of the house of the LORD and of the king's house, and sent *them* to Hazael king of Aram. Then he went away from Jerusalem.

Joash (Jehoash) Succeeded by Amaziah in Judah

19 ¶ Now the rest of the acts of Joash and all that he did, are they not written in the Book of the Chronicles of the Kings of Judah?

20 His servants arose and made a conspiracy and struck down Joash at the house of Millo *as he was* going down to Silla.

21 For Jozacar the son of Shimeath and Jehozabad the son of Shomer, his servants, struck *him*

and he died; and they buried him with his fathers in the city of David, and Amaziah his son became king in his place.

Kings of Israel: Jehoahaz and Jehoash

13 In the twenty-third year of Joash the son of Ahaziah, king of Judah, Jehoahaz the son of Jehu became king over Israel at Samaria, *and he reigned* seventeen years.

2 He did evil in the sight of the LORD, and followed the sins of Jeroboam the son of Nebat, with which he made Israel sin; he did not turn from them.

3 So the anger of the LORD was kindled against Israel, and He gave them continually into the hand of Hazael king of Aram, and into the hand of Ben-hadad the son of Hazael.

4 Then Jehoahaz entreated the favor of the LORD, and the LORD listened to him; for He saw the oppression of Israel, how the king of Aram oppressed them.

13:4 Turnaround

Like so many kings of Israel, Jehoahaz started out doing "evil in the sight of the LORD." Unlike so many kings of Israel, he repented. God, never eager to punish and always willing to relent, accepted his change of heart. Unfortunately, Jehoahaz's repentance didn't rub off. The Israelites continued their idol worship, in direct disobedience of God's command.

5 The LORD gave Israel a ªdeliverer, so that they escaped from under the hand of the Arameans; and the sons of Israel lived in their tents as formerly.

6 Nevertheless they did not turn away from the sins of the house of Jeroboam, with which he made Israel sin, but walked in them; and the Asherah also remained standing in Samaria.

7 For he left to Jehoahaz of the army not more than fifty horsemen and ten chariots and 10,000 footmen, for the king of Aram had destroyed them and made them like the dust at threshing.

8 Now the rest of the acts of Jehoahaz, and all that he did and his might, are they not written in the Book of the Chronicles of the Kings of Israel?

9 And Jehoahaz slept with his fathers, and they buried him in Samaria; and Joash his son became king in his place.

10 ¶ In the thirty-seventh year of Joash king of Judah, Jehoash the son of Jehoahaz became king over Israel in Samaria, *and reigned* sixteen years.

11 He did evil in the sight of the LORD; he did not turn away from all the sins of Jeroboam the

ª Or *savior*

son of Nebat, with which he made Israel sin, but he walked in them.

12 Now the rest of the acts of Joash and all that he did and his might with which he fought against Amaziah king of Judah, are they not written in the Book of the Chronicles of the Kings of Israel?

13 So Joash slept with his fathers, and Jeroboam sat on his throne; and Joash was buried in Samaria with the kings of Israel.

Death of Elisha

14 ¶ When Elisha became sick with the illness of which he was to die, Joash the king of Israel came down to him and wept over him and said, "My father, my father, the chariots of Israel and its horsemen!"

15 Elisha said to him, "Take a bow and arrows." So he took a bow and arrows.

16 Then he said to the king of Israel, "Put your hand on the bow." And he put his hand *on it,* then Elisha laid his hands on the king's hands.

17 He said, "Open the window toward the east," and he opened *it.* Then Elisha said, "Shoot!" And he shot. And he said, "The LORD'S arrow of victory, even the arrow of victory over Aram; for you will defeat the Arameans at Aphek until you have destroyed *them.*"

18 Then he said, "Take the arrows," and he took them. And he said to the king of Israel, "Strike the ground," and he struck *it* three times and stopped.

19 So the man of God was angry with him and said, "You should have struck five or six times, then you would have struck Aram until you would have destroyed it. But now you shall strike Aram *only* three times."

20 ¶ Elisha died, and they buried him. Now the bands of the Moabites would invade the land in the spring of the year.

13:20 Troublesome Neighbors

Moab and Aram (Syria) often make an appearance in the books of 1, 2 Kings. They were small kingdoms much like Judah and Israel. Sometimes they fought against Israel or Judah, and sometimes they joined together in alliances to oppose a larger threat. On the world scene, constant threats came from Egypt and Assyria. Assyria cut a huge swath through history before its empire declined. Later, Babylon became the giant of the region.

21 As they were burying a man, behold, they saw a marauding band; and they cast the man into the grave of Elisha. And when the man touched the bones of Elisha he revived and stood up on his feet.

22 ¶ Now Hazael king of Aram had oppressed Israel all the days of Jehoahaz.

23 But the LORD was gracious to them and had compassion on them and turned to them because of His covenant with Abraham, Isaac, and Jacob, and would not destroy them or cast them from His presence until now.

24 ¶ When Hazael king of Aram died, Benhadad his son became king in his place.

25 Then Jehoash the son of Jehoahaz took again from the hand of Ben-hadad the son of Hazael the cities which he had taken in war from the hand of Jehoahaz his father. Three times Joash defeated him and recovered the cities of Israel.

Amaziah Reigns over Judah

14 In the second year of Joash son of Joahaz king of Israel, Amaziah the son of Joash king of Judah became king.

2 He was twenty-five years old when he became king, and he reigned twenty-nine years in Jerusalem. And his mother's name was Jehoaddin of Jerusalem.

3 He did right in the sight of the LORD, yet not like David his father; he did according to all that Joash his father had done.

4 Only the high places were not taken away; the people still sacrificed and burned incense on the high places.

5 Now it came about, as soon as the kingdom was firmly in his hand, that he killed his servants who had slain the king his father.

6 But the sons of the slayers he did not put to death, according to what is written in the book of the Law of Moses, as the LORD commanded, saying, "The fathers shall not be put to death for the sons, nor the sons be put to death for the fathers; but each shall be put to death for his own sin."

7 ¶ He killed *of* Edom in the Valley of Salt 10,000 and took Sela by war, and named it Joktheel to this day.

8 ¶ Then Amaziah sent messengers to Jehoash, the son of Jehoahaz son of Jehu, king of Israel, saying, "Come, let us face each other."

9 Jehoash king of Israel sent to Amaziah king of Judah, saying, "The thorn bush which was in Lebanon sent to the cedar which was in Lebanon, saying, 'Give your daughter to my son in marriage.' But there passed by a wild beast that was in Lebanon, and trampled the thorn bush.

10 "You have indeed defeated Edom, and your heart has become proud. Enjoy your glory and stay at home; for why should you provoke trouble so that you, even you, would fall, and Judah with you?"

11 ¶ But Amaziah would not listen. So Jehoash king of Israel went up; and he and Amaziah king of Judah faced each other at Beth-shemesh, which belongs to Judah.

12 Judah was defeated by Israel, and they fled each to his tent.

13 Then Jehoash king of Israel captured Amaziah king of Judah, the son of Jehoash the son of

Ahaziah, at Beth-shemesh, and came to Jerusalem and tore down the wall of Jerusalem from the Gate of Ephraim to the Corner Gate, 400 cubits.

14 He took all the gold and silver and all the utensils which were found in the house of the LORD, and in the treasuries of the king's house, the hostages also, and returned to Samaria.

Jeroboam II Succeeds Jehoash in Israel

15 ¶ Now the rest of the acts of Jehoash which he did, and his might and how he fought with Amaziah king of Judah, are they not written in the Book of the Chronicles of the Kings of Israel?

16 So Jehoash slept with his fathers and was buried in Samaria with the kings of Israel; and Jeroboam his son became king in his place.

Azariah (Uzziah) Succeeds Amaziah in Judah

17 ¶ Amaziah the son of Joash king of Judah lived fifteen years after the death of Jehoash son of Jehoahaz king of Israel.

18 Now the rest of the acts of Amaziah, are they not written in the Book of the Chronicles of the Kings of Judah?

19 They conspired against him in Jerusalem, and he fled to Lachish; but they sent after him to Lachish and killed him there.

20 Then they brought him on horses and he was buried at Jerusalem with his fathers in the city of David.

21 All the people of Judah took Azariah, who was sixteen years old, and made him king in the place of his father Amaziah.

22 He built Elath and restored it to Judah after the king slept with his fathers.

23 ¶ In the fifteenth year of Amaziah the son of Joash king of Judah, Jeroboam the son of Joash king of Israel became king in Samaria, and reigned forty-one years.

24 He did evil in the sight of the LORD; he did not depart from all the sins of Jeroboam the son of Nebat, which he made Israel sin.

25 He restored the border of Israel from the entrance of Hamath as far as the Sea of the Arabah, according to the word of the LORD, the God of Israel, which He spoke through His servant Jonah the son of Amittai, the prophet, who was of Gath-hepher.

26 For the LORD saw the affliction of Israel, which was very bitter; for there was neither bond nor free, nor was there any helper for Israel.

27 The LORD did not say that He would blot out the name of Israel from under heaven, but He saved them by the hand of Jeroboam the son of Joash.

Zechariah Reigns over Israel

28 ¶ Now the rest of the acts of Jeroboam and all that he did and his might, how he fought and how he recovered for Israel, Damascus and Hamath, which had belonged to Judah, are they not written in the Book of the Chronicles of the Kings of Israel?

29 And Jeroboam slept with his fathers, even with the kings of Israel, and Zechariah his son became king in his place.

Series of Kings: Azariah (Uzziah) over Judah

15 In the twenty-seventh year of Jeroboam king of Israel, Azariah son of Amaziah king of Judah became king.

2 He was sixteen years old when he became king, and he reigned fifty-two years in Jerusalem; and his mother's name was Jecoliah of Jerusalem.

3 He did right in the sight of the LORD, according to all that his father Amaziah had done.

4 Only the high places were not taken away; the people still sacrificed and burned incense on the high places.

5 The LORD struck the king, so that he was a leper to the day of his death. And he lived in a separate house, while Jotham the king's son was over the household, judging the people of the land.

6 Now the rest of the acts of Azariah and all that he did, are they not written in the Book of the Chronicles of the Kings of Judah?

7 And Azariah slept with his fathers, and they buried him with his fathers in the city of David, and Jotham his son became king in his place.

Zechariah over Israel

8 ¶ In the thirty-eighth year of Azariah king of Judah, Zechariah the son of Jeroboam became king over Israel in Samaria for six months.

9 He did evil in the sight of the LORD, as his fathers had done; he did not depart from the sins of Jeroboam the son of Nebat, which he made Israel sin.

10 Then Shallum the son of Jabesh conspired against him and struck him before the people and killed him, and reigned in his place.

11 Now the rest of the acts of Zechariah, behold they are written in the Book of the Chronicles of the Kings of Israel.

12 This is the word of the LORD which He spoke to Jehu, saying, "Your sons to the fourth generation shall sit on the throne of Israel." And so it was.

13 ¶ Shallum son of Jabesh became king in the thirty-ninth year of Uzziah king of Judah, and he reigned one month in Samaria.

14 Then Menahem son of Gadi went up from Tirzah and came to Samaria, and struck Shallum son of Jabesh in Samaria, and killed him and became king in his place.

15 Now the rest of the acts of Shallum and his conspiracy which he made, behold they are written in the Book of the Chronicles of the Kings of Israel.

16 Then Menahem struck Tiphsah and all who were in it and its borders from Tirzah, because they did not open *to him;* therefore he struck *it* and ripped up all its women who were with child.

Menahem over Israel

17 ¶ In the thirty-ninth year of Azariah king of Judah, Menahem son of Gadi became king over Israel *and reigned* ten years in Samaria.

18 He did evil in the sight of the LORD; he did not depart all his days from the sins of Jeroboam the son of Nebat, which he made Israel sin.

19 ¶ Pul, king of Assyria, came against the land, and Menahem gave Pul a thousand talents of silver so that his hand might be with him to strengthen the kingdom under his rule.

20 Then Menahem exacted the money from Israel, even from all the mighty men of wealth, from each man fifty shekels of silver to pay the king of Assyria. So the king of Assyria returned and did not remain there in the land.

21 Now the rest of the acts of Menahem and all that he did, are they not written in the Book of the Chronicles of the Kings of Israel?

22 And Menahem slept with his fathers, and Pekahiah his son became king in his place.

Pekahiah over Israel

23 ¶ In the fiftieth year of Azariah king of Judah, Pekahiah son of Menahem became king over Israel in Samaria, *and reigned* two years.

24 He did evil in the sight of the LORD; he did not depart from the sins of Jeroboam son of Nebat, which he made Israel sin.

25 Then Pekah son of Remaliah, his officer, conspired against him and struck him in Samaria, in the castle of the king's house with Argob and Arieh; and with him were fifty men of the Gileadites, and he killed him and became king in his place.

26 Now the rest of the acts of Pekahiah and all that he did, behold they are written in the Book of the Chronicles of the Kings of Israel.

Pekah over Israel

27 ¶ In the fifty-second year of Azariah king of Judah, Pekah son of Remaliah became king over Israel in Samaria, *and reigned* twenty years.

28 He did evil in the sight of the LORD; he did not depart from the sins of Jeroboam son of Nebat, which he made Israel sin.

29 ¶ In the days of Pekah king of Israel, Tiglath-pileser king of Assyria came and captured Ijon and Abel-beth-maacah and Janoah and Kedesh and Hazor and Gilead and Galilee, all the land of Naphtali; and he carried them captive to Assyria.

30 And Hoshea the son of Elah made a conspiracy against Pekah the son of Remaliah, and struck him and put him to death and became king in his place, in the twentieth year of Jotham the son of Uzziah.

31 Now the rest of the acts of Pekah and all that he did, behold, they are written in the Book of the Chronicles of the Kings of Israel.

Jotham over Judah

32 ¶ In the second year of Pekah the son of Remaliah king of Israel, Jotham the son of Uzziah king of Judah became king.

33 He was twenty-five years old when he became king, and he reigned sixteen years in Jerusalem; and his mother's name *was* Jerusha the daughter of Zadok.

34 He did what was right in the sight of the LORD; he did according to all that his father Uzziah had done.

35 Only the high places were not taken away; the people still sacrificed and burned incense on the high places. He built the upper gate of the house of the LORD.

36 Now the rest of the acts of Jotham and all that he did, are they not written in the Book of the Chronicles of the Kings of Judah?

37 In those days the LORD began to send Rezin king of Aram and Pekah the son of Remaliah against Judah.

38 And Jotham slept with his fathers, and he was buried with his fathers in the city of David his father; and Ahaz his son became king in his place.

Ahaz Reigns over Judah

16 In the seventeenth year of Pekah the son of Remaliah, Ahaz the son of Jotham, king of Judah, became king.

2 Ahaz *was* twenty years old when he became king, and he reigned sixteen years in Jerusalem; and he did not do what was right in the sight of the LORD his God, as his father David *had done.*

3 But he walked in the way of the kings of Israel, and even made his son pass through the

fire, according to the abominations of the nations whom the LORD had driven out from before the sons of Israel.

4 He sacrificed and burned incense on the high places and on the hills and under every green tree.

16:1 Ahaz's Fateful Decisions

King Ahaz figured large in the histories of Israel and Judah. When Israel threatened his kingdom of Judah, he purchased military aid from Assyria. In response, Assyria obliterated Israel and made Judah a virtual puppet. Worse, Ahaz copied the pagan religions of his conquered territories, even to the extent of sacrificing his son in the fire.

5 ¶ Then Rezin king of Aram and Pekah son of Remaliah, king of Israel, came up to Jerusalem to *wage* war; and they besieged Ahaz, but could not overcome him.

6 At that time Rezin king of Aram recovered Elath for Aram, and cleared the Judeans out of Elath entirely; and the Arameans came to Elath and have lived there to this day.

Ahaz Seeks Help of Aram

7 ¶ So Ahaz sent messengers to Tiglath-pileser king of Assyria, saying, "I am your servant and your son; come up and deliver me from the hand of the king of Aram and from the hand of the king of Israel, who are rising up against me."

8 Ahaz took the silver and gold that was found in the house of the LORD and in the treasuries of the king's house, and sent a present to the king of Assyria.

9 So the king of Assyria listened to him; and the king of Assyria went up against Damascus and captured it, and carried *the people of* it away into exile to Kir, and put Rezin to death.

Damascus Falls

10 ¶ Now King Ahaz went to Damascus to meet Tiglath-pileser king of Assyria, and saw the altar which *was* at Damascus; and King Ahaz sent to Urijah the priest the pattern of the altar and its model, according to all its workmanship.

11 So Urijah the priest built an altar; according to all that King Ahaz had sent from Damascus, thus Urijah the priest made *it*, before the coming of King Ahaz from Damascus.

12 When the king came from Damascus, the king saw the altar; then the king approached the altar and went up to it,

13 and burned his burnt offering and his meal offering, and poured his drink offering and sprinkled the blood of his peace offerings on the altar.

14 The bronze altar, which *was* before the LORD, he brought from the front of the house,

from between *his* altar and the house of the LORD, and he put it on the north side of *his* altar.

15 Then King Ahaz commanded Urijah the priest, saying, "Upon the great altar burn the morning burnt offering and the evening meal offering and the king's burnt offering and his meal offering, with the burnt offering of all the people of the land and their meal offering and their drink offerings; and sprinkle on it all the blood of the burnt offering and all the blood of the sacrifice. But the bronze altar shall be for me to inquire *by*."

16 So Urijah the priest did according to all that King Ahaz commanded.

17 ¶ Then King Ahaz cut off the borders of the stands, and removed the laver from them; he also took down the sea from the bronze oxen which were under it and put it on a pavement of stone.

18 The covered way for the sabbath which they had built in the house, and the outer entry of the king, he removed from the house of the LORD because of the king of Assyria.

Hezekiah Reigns over Judah

19 Now the rest of the acts of Ahaz which he did, are they not written in the Book of the Chronicles of the Kings of Judah?

20 So Ahaz slept with his fathers, and was buried with his fathers in the city of David; and his son Hezekiah reigned in his place.

Hoshea Reigns over Israel

17 In the twelfth year of Ahaz king of Judah, Hoshea the son of Elah became king over Israel in Samaria, *and reigned* nine years.

2 He did evil in the sight of the LORD, only not as the kings of Israel who were before him.

3 Shalmaneser king of Assyria came up against him, and Hoshea became his servant and paid him tribute.

4 But the king of Assyria found conspiracy in Hoshea, who had sent messengers to So king of Egypt and had offered no tribute to the king of Assyria, as *he had done* year by year; so the king of Assyria shut him up and bound him in prison.

5 ¶ Then the king of Assyria invaded the whole land and went up to Samaria and besieged it three years.

Israel Captive

6 In the ninth year of Hoshea, the king of Assyria captured Samaria and carried Israel away into exile to Assyria, and settled them in Halah and Habor, *on* the river of Gozan, and in the cities of the Medes.

Why Israel Fell

7 ¶ Now *this* came about because the sons of Israel had sinned against the LORD their God, who had brought them up from the land of Egypt from

Why All the Fuss about Idols?
The strange practice that led to a kingdom's fall

YOU CANNOT READ VERY FAR in the Old Testament without encountering idols, for idolatry ranks as perhaps the most common topic in the Bible. A nagging question haunts these pages: Why did the Israelites keep deserting the God who had delivered them from Egypt for the sake of carved tree trunks and bronze statues? What was the big attraction?

Idolatry seems especially strange to us in modern times. Today, idols may show up as exotic props in a movie, but does anyone truly believe in them anymore? Why do they merit so much attention in the Old Testament?

Responses to Idols Today

Actually, idols still thrive in such places as Africa and Asia, and their effect on the people there sheds light on Old Testament idolatry. In India, for example, each city and village has its own favorite god—over 1,000 different gods are worshiped. Portable idols stand on street corners of the major cities.

For devout Hindus, idolatry adds a dimension of magic to life. Hindus believe the gods control all events, including such disasters as monsoons, floods, diseases, and traffic accidents. These powerful gods must be kept happy at all costs.

But what pleases a god depends on the god's character, and gods can be fearsome and violent. Some Indians worship idols in the form of a snake; others worship the smallpox goddess. The largest city in India, Calcutta, has adopted the murderous goddess Kali, who wears a garland of gruesome heads around her waist. Devotion to such gods can easily lead to a paralyzing fear. If Kali isn't kept happy, her followers believe, she will cruelly punish them.

Other Hindus, less devout, take a different approach. They treat their gods almost as good-luck charms. A taxi driver mounts a tiny statue of a monkey god on the dashboard of his car, occasionally draping it with flowers for decoration. If you ask, he'll say he prays to the god for safety—but you know about the traffic in India, he adds with a laugh.

A Good-Luck Charm or an Evil Cult

Idolatry had similar effects on the ancient Israelites. Some Israelites took the same spirit as the Indian taxi driver: Maybe an idol will help you out, maybe not, but why not play along? They drifted carelessly from god to god, adopting the religion of whatever group seemed to be having the most success with its agriculture or armies.

No attitude could be further from that demanded by the true God. He had chosen the Israelites as a kingdom of priests, a treasured possession set apart for him. As Lord of the universe, he wanted not a casual faith, but total allegiance. He was not a good-luck charm.

Far too often, however, idols in Israel took on a more sinister form, resembling the evil goddess of Calcutta. Legends about Baal, for example, celebrated his drunkenness and debauchery. Followers worshiped him by having sex in the temple with prostitutes or even by sacrificing human babies.

Worshiping Baal meant a complete rejection of God's special relationship with the Israelites—a crime very much like adultery, as the prophets often pointed out. Baal worship could not possibly coexist with the worship of God.

What Was the Appeal?

Why did Baal and the other idols prove so appealing to the Israelites? Like peasants gawking at big-city life, the Israelites moved from 40 years of wilderness wanderings into a land of cities and more advanced technology. They had been landless nomads and shepherds. When they settled down to a new occupation of farming, they looked to a Canaanite god, Baal, as a possible means of guaranteeing good crops. In other words, they sought a shortcut through magic.

Similarly, when a mighty army threatened their borders, they smuggled in a few of that army's favorite idols, hedging their bets in case their own religion did not bring them military success. Idols became a phantom source of power, an alternative place to invest faith and hope.

Idolatry made such inroads into Israel and Judah that God had to tear apart both kingdoms in order to root it out. Second Kings clearly blames idolatry as the chief sin leading to both nations' collapse. History records that the punishment ultimately worked. After the Assyrian and Babylonian invasions, never again did the Israelites dabble in idolatry.

Life Questions: Idolatry need not involve images of wood or stone; it's possible to worship such things as money, another person, or fame. What are some "idols" you might be tempted to worship?

under the hand of Pharaoh, king of Egypt, and they had *a*feared other gods

8 and walked in the customs of the nations whom the LORD had driven out before the sons of Israel, and *in the customs* of the kings of Israel which they had introduced.

9 The sons of Israel did things secretly which were not right against the LORD their God. Moreover, they built for themselves high places in all their towns, from watchtower to fortified city.

10 They set for themselves *sacred* pillars and *b*Asherim on every high hill and under every green tree,

11 and there they burned incense on all the high places as the nations *did* which the LORD had carried away to exile before them; and they did evil things provoking the LORD.

12 They served idols, concerning which the LORD had said to them, "You shall not do this thing."

13 Yet the LORD warned Israel and Judah through all His prophets *and* every seer, saying, "Turn from your evil ways and keep My commandments, My statutes according to all the law which I commanded your fathers, and which I sent to you through My servants the prophets."

14 However, they did not listen, but stiffened their neck like their fathers, who did not believe in the LORD their God.

15 They rejected His statutes and His covenant which He made with their fathers and His warnings with which He warned them. And they followed vanity and became vain, and *went* after the nations which surrounded them, concerning which the LORD had commanded them not to do like them.

16 They forsook all the commandments of the LORD their God and made for themselves molten images, *even* two calves, and made an Asherah and worshiped all the host of heaven and served Baal.

17 Then they made their sons and their daughters pass through the fire, and practiced divination and enchantments, and sold themselves to do evil in the sight of the LORD, provoking Him.

18 So the LORD was very angry with Israel and removed them from His sight; none was left except the tribe of Judah.

19 ¶ Also Judah did not keep the commandments of the LORD their God, but walked in the customs which Israel had introduced.

20 The LORD rejected all the descendants of Israel and afflicted them and gave them into the hand of plunderers, until He had cast them out of His sight.

21 ¶ When He had torn Israel from the house of David, they made Jeroboam the son of Nebat king. Then Jeroboam drove Israel away from fol-lowing the LORD and made them commit a great sin.

22 The sons of Israel walked in all the sins of Jeroboam which he did; they did not depart from them

17:17 A Higher Standard

To the casual eye, it seemed unfair. God let the Assyrians, a much crueler people, conquer Israel and take the whole nation into exile. Why? Israel was judged by a higher standard, on the basis of the great advantages God had given them. As Jesus would say hundreds of years later, "From everyone who has been given much, much will be required" (Luke 12:48).

A hair-raising list of Israel's sins (verses 7–23) shows why they deserved judgment: they adopted their neighbors' fertility religion, even offering their own children as human sacrifices. Assyria lacked Israel's advantages, but they would be judged too—which explains why the powerful nation of Assyria no longer exists.

23 until the LORD removed Israel from His sight, as He spoke through all His servants the prophets. So Israel was carried away into exile from their own land to Assyria until this day.

Cities of Israel Filled with Strangers

24 ¶ The king of Assyria brought *men* from Babylon and from Cuthah and from Avva and from Hamath and Sephar-vaim, and settled *them* in the cities of Samaria in place of the sons of Israel. So they possessed Samaria and lived in its cities.

25 At the beginning of their living there, they

17:24 Scorched-Earth Policy

In early wars Assyrian conquerors followed a cruel policy of genocide. They exterminated their enemies and destroyed their land and property. But in later years they adopted a new technique: deporting their victims to Assyria and other countries and replacing them with foreigners from other conquered territories. In this way, they disrupted cultures and made sure the conquered peoples would never regroup and rise up as a new threat. This verse shows the origin of Samaritans, a group that still existed in New Testament times and, in fact, can still be found in modern Israel. They combined their own religions with some reverence for the true God.

---

a Lit *revered*, and so throughout the ch   *b* I.e. wooden symbols of a female deity did not fear the LORD; therefore the LORD sent lions among them which killed some of them.

26 So they spoke to the king of Assyria, saying, "The nations whom you have carried away into exile in the cities of Samaria do not know the custom of the god of the land; so he has sent lions among them, and behold, they kill them because they do not know the custom of the god of the land."

27 ¶ Then the king of Assyria commanded, saying, "Take there one of the priests whom you carried away into exile and let him go and live there; and let him teach them the custom of the god of the land."

28 So one of the priests whom they had carried away into exile from Samaria came and lived at Bethel, and taught them how they should fear the LORD.

29 ¶ But every nation still made gods of its own and put them in the houses of the high places which the people of Samaria had made, every nation in their cities in which they lived.

30 The men of Babylon made Succoth-benoth, the men of Cuth made Nergal, the men of Hamath made Ashima,

31 and the Avvites made Nibhaz and Tartak; and the Sepharvites burned their children in the fire to Adrammelech and Anammelech the gods of Sepharvaim.

32 They also feared the LORD and appointed from among themselves priests of the high places, who acted for them in the houses of the high places.

33 They feared the LORD and served their own gods according to the custom of the nations from among whom they had been carried away into exile.

34 ¶ To this day they do according to the earlier customs: they do not fear the LORD, nor do they follow their statutes or their ordinances or the law, or the commandments which the LORD commanded the sons of Jacob, whom He named Israel;

35 with whom the LORD made a covenant and commanded them, saying, "You shall not fear other gods, nor bow down yourselves to them nor serve them nor sacrifice to them.

36 "But the LORD, who brought you up from the land of Egypt with great power and with an outstretched arm, Him you shall fear, and to Him you shall bow yourselves down, and to Him you shall sacrifice.

37 "The statutes and the ordinances and the law and the commandment which He wrote for you, you shall observe to do forever; and you shall not fear other gods.

38 "The covenant that I have made with you, you shall not forget, nor shall you fear other gods.

39 "But the LORD your God you shall fear; and

He will deliver you from the hand of all your enemies."

40 However, they did not listen, but they did according to their earlier custom.

41 So while these nations feared the LORD, they also served their idols; their children likewise and their grandchildren, as their fathers did, so they do to this day.

Hezekiah Reigns over Judah

18 Now it came about in the third year of Hoshea, the son of Elah king of Israel, that Hezekiah the son of Ahaz king of Judah became king.

2 He was twenty-five years old when he became king, and he reigned twenty-nine years in Jerusalem; and his mother's name was Abi the daughter of Zechariah.

3 He did right in the sight of the LORD, according to all that his father David had done.

4 He removed the high places and broke down the *sacred* pillars and cut down the [a]Asherah. He also broke in pieces the bronze serpent that Moses had made, for until those days the sons of Israel burned incense to it; and it was called [b]Nehushtan.

5 He trusted in the LORD, the God of Israel; so that after him there was none like him among all the kings of Judah, nor *among those* who were before him.

6 For he clung to the LORD; he did not depart from following Him, but kept His commandments, which the LORD had commanded Moses.

Hezekiah Victorious

7 And the LORD was with him; wherever he went he prospered. And he rebelled against the king of Assyria and did not serve him.

8 He defeated the Philistines as far as Gaza and its territory, from watchtower to fortified city.

9 ¶ Now in the fourth year of King Hezekiah, which was the seventh year of Hoshea son of Elah king of Israel, Shalmaneser king of Assyria came up against Samaria and besieged it.

10 At the end of three years they captured it; in the sixth year of Hezekiah, which was the ninth year of Hoshea king of Israel, Samaria was captured.

11 Then the king of Assyria carried Israel away into exile to Assyria, and put them in Halah and on the Habor, the river of Gozan, and in the cities of the Medes,

12 because they did not obey the voice of the LORD their God, but transgressed His covenant, *even* all that Moses the servant of the LORD commanded; they would neither listen nor do *it*.

Invasion of Judah

13 ¶ Now in the fourteenth year of King Heze-

---

[a] I.e. a wooden symbol of a female deity   [b] I.e. a piece of bronze

kiah, Sennacherib king of Assyria came up against all the fortified cities of Judah and seized them.

14 Then Hezekiah king of Judah sent to the king of Assyria at Lachish, saying, "I have done wrong. Withdraw from me; whatever you impose on me I will bear." So the king of Assyria required of Hezekiah king of Judah three hundred talents of silver and thirty talents of gold.

15 Hezekiah gave *him* all the silver which was found in the house of the LORD, and in the treasuries of the king's house.

16 At that time Hezekiah cut off *the gold from* the doors of the temple of the LORD, and *from* the doorposts which Hezekiah king of Judah had overlaid, and gave it to the king of Assyria.

18:16 King of Contradictions

Overall, Hezekiah made a good king, trusting in God. But his life contained a mixture of wisdom and folly, vice and virtue. On the good side, Hezekiah "trusted in the LORD" (verse 5), cleansed Judah from idol worship, and won independence from the powerful nations around. When he prayed for healing, he was granted an unprecedented extension of his life (20:1–11).

On the bad side, Hezekiah foolishly tried to bribe the Assyrians with gold stripped from the temple. Later, when representatives from Babylon came (20:13), he boastfully showed them all his treasures. And when the prophet Isaiah warned that Babylon would come back to take those treasures and more, Hezekiah blithely contented himself that there would be "peace and truth in my days" (20:19).

17 ¶ Then the king of Assyria sent Tartan and Rab-saris and Rabshakeh from Lachish to King Hezekiah with a large army to Jerusalem. So they went up and came to Jerusalem. And when they went up, they came and stood by the conduit of the upper pool, which is on the highway of the *a*fuller's field.

18 When they called to the king, Eliakim the son of Hilkiah, who was over the household, and Shebnah the scribe and Joah the son of Asaph the recorder, came out to them.

19 ¶ Then Rabshakeh said to them, "Say now to Hezekiah, 'Thus says the great king, the king of Assyria, "What is this confidence that you have?

20 "You say (but *they are* only empty words), '*I have* counsel and strength for the war.' Now on whom do you rely, that you have rebelled against me?

21 "Now behold, you rely on the staff of this crushed reed, *even* on Egypt; on which if a man leans, it will go into his hand and pierce it. So is Pharaoh king of Egypt to all who rely on him.

22 "But if you say to me, 'We trust in the LORD our God,' is it not He whose high places and whose altars Hezekiah has taken away, and has said to Judah and to Jerusalem, 'You shall worship before this altar in Jerusalem'?

23 "Now therefore, come, make a bargain with my master the king of Assyria, and I will give you two thousand horses, if you are able on your part to set riders on them.

24 "How then can you repulse one official of the least of my master's servants, and rely on Egypt for chariots and for horsemen?

25 "Have I now come up without the LORD's approval against this place to destroy it? The LORD said to me, 'Go up against this land and destroy it.' " ' "

26 ¶ Then Eliakim the son of Hilkiah, and Shebnah and Joah, said to Rabshakeh, "Speak now to your servants in Aramaic, for we understand *it;* and do not speak with us in Judean in the hearing of the people who are on the wall."

27 But Rabshakeh said to them, "Has my master sent me only to your master and to you to speak these words, *and* not to the men who sit on the wall, *doomed* to eat their own dung and drink their own urine with you?"

28 ¶ Then Rabshakeh stood and cried with a loud voice in Judean, saying, "Hear the word of the great king, the king of Assyria.

29 "Thus says the king, 'Do not let Hezekiah deceive you, for he will not be able to deliver you from my hand;

30 nor let Hezekiah make you trust in the LORD, saying, "The LORD will surely deliver us, and this city will not be given into the hand of the king of Assyria."

31 'Do not listen to Hezekiah, for thus says the king of Assyria, "Make your peace with me and come out to me, and eat each of his vine and each of his fig tree and drink each of the waters of his own cistern,

32 until I come and take you away to a land like your own land, a land of grain and new wine, a land of bread and vineyards, a land of olive trees and honey, that you may live and not die." But do not listen to Hezekiah when he misleads you, saying, "The LORD will deliver us."

33 'Has any one of the gods of the nations delivered his land from the hand of the king of Assyria?

34 'Where are the gods of Hamath and Arpad? Where are the gods of Sepharvaim, Hena and Ivvah? Have they delivered Samaria from my hand?

35 'Who among all the gods of the lands have delivered their land from my hand, that the LORD should deliver Jerusalem from my hand?' "

36 ¶ But the people were silent and answered him not a word, for the king's commandment was, "Do not answer him."

37 Then Eliakim the son of Hilkiah, who was

over the household, and Shebna the scribe and Joah the son of Asaph, the recorder, came to Hezekiah with their clothes torn and told him the words of Rabshakeh.

Isaiah Encourages Hezekiah

19 And when King Hezekiah heard *it*, he tore his clothes, covered himself with sackcloth and entered the house of the LORD.

2 Then he sent Eliakim who was over the household with Shebna the scribe and the elders of the priests, covered with sackcloth, to Isaiah the prophet the son of Amoz.

3 They said to him, "Thus says Hezekiah, 'This day is a day of distress, rebuke, and rejection; for children have come to birth and there is no strength to *deliver.*

4 'Perhaps the LORD your God will hear all the words of Rabshakeh, whom his master the king of Assyria has sent to reproach the living God, and will rebuke the words which the LORD your God has heard. Therefore, offer a prayer for the remnant that is left.' "

5 So the servants of King Hezekiah came to Isaiah.

6 Isaiah said to them, "Thus you shall say to your master, 'Thus says the LORD, "Do not be afraid because of the words that you have heard, with which the servants of the king of Assyria have blasphemed Me.

7 "Behold, I will put a spirit in him so that he will hear a rumor and return to his own land. And I will make him fall by the sword in his own land." ' "

Sennacherib Defies God

8 ¶ Then Rabshakeh returned and found the king of Assyria fighting against Libnah, for he had heard that the king had left Lachish.

9 When he heard *them* say concerning Tirhakah king of Cush, "Behold, he has come out to fight against you," he sent messengers again to Hezekiah saying,

10 "Thus you shall say to Hezekiah king of Judah, 'Do not let your God in whom you trust deceive you saying, "Jerusalem will not be given into the hand of the king of Assyria."

11 'Behold, you have heard what the kings of Assyria have done to all the lands, destroying them completely. So will you be spared?

12 'Did the gods of those nations which my fathers destroyed deliver them, *even* Gozan and Haran and Rezeph and the sons of Eden who *were* in Telassar?

13 'Where is the king of Hamath, the king of Arpad, the king of the city of Sepharvaim, and *of* Hena and Ivvah?' "

Hezekiah's Prayer

14 ¶ Then Hezekiah took the letter from the hand of the messengers and read it, and he went up to the house of the LORD and spread it out before the LORD.

15 Hezekiah prayed before the LORD and said, "O LORD, the God of Israel, who are enthroned *above* the cherubim, You are the God, You alone, of all the kingdoms of the earth. You have made heaven and earth.

16 "Incline Your ear, O LORD, and hear; open Your eyes, O LORD, and see; and listen to the words of Sennacherib, which he has sent to reproach the living God.

17 "Truly, O LORD, the kings of Assyria have devastated the nations and their lands

18 and have cast their gods into the fire, for they were not gods but the work of men's hands, wood and stone. So they have destroyed them.

19 "Now, O LORD our God, I pray, deliver us from his hand that all the kingdoms of the earth may know that You alone, O LORD, are God."

God's Answer through Isaiah

20 ¶ Then Isaiah the son of Amoz sent to Hezekiah saying, "Thus says the LORD, the God of Israel, 'Because you have prayed to Me about Sennacherib king of Assyria, I have heard *you.*'

21 "This is the word that the LORD has spoken against him:

'She has despised you and mocked you,
The virgin daughter of Zion;
She has shaken *her* head behind you,
The daughter of Jerusalem!
22 'Whom have you reproached and
        blasphemed?
And against whom have you raised *your*
        voice,
And haughtily lifted up your eyes?
Against the Holy One of Israel!
23 'Through your messengers you have
        reproached the Lord,
And you have said, "With my many
        chariots
I came up to the heights of the
        mountains,
To the remotest parts of Lebanon;
And I cut down its tall cedars *and* its
        choice cypresses.
And I entered its farthest lodging place,
        its thickest forest.
24 "I dug *wells* and drank foreign waters,
And with the sole of my feet I dried up
All the rivers of Egypt."

25 ¶ 'Have you not heard?
Long ago I did it;
From ancient times I planned it.
Now I have brought it to pass,
That you should turn fortified cities into
        ruinous heaps.
26 'Therefore their inhabitants were short of
        strength,
They were dismayed and put to shame;

They were as the vegetation of the field
and as the green herb,
As grass on the housetops is scorched
before it is grown up.
27 'But I know your sitting down,
And your going out and your coming in,
And your raging against Me.
28 'Because of your raging against Me,
And because your arrogance has come
up to My ears,
Therefore I will put My hook in your
nose,
And My bridle in your lips,
And I will turn you back by the way
which you came.
29 ¶ 'Then this shall be the sign for you: you
will eat this year what grows of itself, in the second
year what springs from the same, and in the third
year sow, reap, plant vineyards, and eat their fruit.
30 'The surviving remnant of the house of Judah will again take root downward and bear fruit
upward.
31 'For out of Jerusalem will go forth a remnant, and out of Mount Zion survivors. The zeal
of ªthe LORD will perform this.

19:31 Deliverance for Jerusalem

*Jerusalem appeared to be a doomed city
during the dark days of Assyria's siege. But two
things happened to fulfill this prophecy. First, a
great plague struck the Assyrians (verse 35), a
plague also recorded by the historian
Herodotus. Later, the murder of Assyria's
leader brought internal chaos to that country,
canceling out the Assyrian threat. The
miraculous deliverance convinced some
Israelites that Jerusalem, God's city, was
indestructible—a belief that would later be
proven false.*

32 ¶ 'Therefore thus says the LORD concerning
the king of Assyria, "He will not come to this city
or shoot an arrow there; and he will not come
before it with a shield or throw up a siege ramp
against it.
33 "By the way that he came, by the same he will
return, and he shall not come to this city," ' declares the LORD.
34 'For I will defend this city to save it for My
own sake and for My servant David's sake.' "
35 ¶ Then it happened that night that the angel
of the LORD went out and struck 185,000 in the
camp of the Assyrians; and when men rose early
in the morning, behold, all of them were dead.
36 So Sennacherib king of Assyria departed
and returned *home*, and lived at Nineveh.
37 It came about as he was worshiping in the

ª Some ancient mss read *the* LORD *of hosts*

house of Nisroch his god, that Adrammelech and
Sharezer killed him with the sword; and they escaped into the land of Ararat. And Esarhaddon his
son became king in his place.

Hezekiah's Illness and Recovery

20 In those days Hezekiah became mortally ill.
And Isaiah the prophet the son of Amoz
came to him and said to him, "Thus says the
LORD, 'Set your house in order, for you shall die
and not live.' "
2 Then he turned his face to the wall and
prayed to the LORD, saying,
3 "Remember now, O LORD, I beseech You,
how I have walked before You in truth and with
a whole heart and have done what is good in Your
sight." And Hezekiah wept bitterly.
4 Before Isaiah had gone out of the middle
court, the word of the LORD came to him, saying,
5 "Return and say to Hezekiah the leader of
My people, 'Thus says the LORD, the God of your
father David, "I have heard your prayer, I have
seen your tears; behold, I will heal you. On the
third day you shall go up to the house of the LORD.
6 "I will add fifteen years to your life, and I will
deliver you and this city from the hand of the king
of Assyria; and I will defend this city for My own
sake and for My servant David's sake." ' "
7 Then Isaiah said, "Take a cake of figs." And
they took and laid *it* on the boil, and he recovered.
8 ¶ Now Hezekiah said to Isaiah, "What will
be the sign that the LORD will heal me, and that I
shall go up to the house of the LORD the third
day?"
9 Isaiah said, "This shall be the sign to you
from the LORD, that the LORD will do the thing
that He has spoken: shall the shadow go forward
ten steps or go back ten steps?"
10 So Hezekiah answered, "It is easy for the
shadow to decline ten steps; no, but let the shadow
turn backward ten steps."
11 Isaiah the prophet cried to the LORD, and
He brought the shadow on the stairway back ten
steps by which it had gone down on the stairway
of Ahaz.

Hezekiah Shows Babylon His Treasures

12 ¶ At that time Berodach-baladan a son of
Baladan, king of Babylon, sent letters and a
present to Hezekiah, for he heard that Hezekiah
had been sick.
13 Hezekiah listened to them, and showed
them all his treasure house, the silver and the gold
and the spices and the precious oil and the house
of his armor and all that was found in his treasuries. There was nothing in his house nor in all his
dominion that Hezekiah did not show them.
14 Then Isaiah the prophet came to King Hezekiah and said to him, "What did these men say,
and from where have they come to you?" And

Hezekiah said, "They have come from a far country, from Babylon."

15 He said, "What have they seen in your house?" So Hezekiah answered, "They have seen all that is in my house; there is nothing among my treasuries that I have not shown them."

16 ¶ Then Isaiah said to Hezekiah, "Hear the word of the LORD.

17 'Behold, the days are coming when all that is in your house, and all that your fathers have laid up in store to this day will be carried to Babylon; nothing shall be left,' says the LORD.

18 'Some of your sons who shall issue from you, whom you will beget, will be taken away; and they will become officials in the palace of the king of Babylon.'"

19 Then Hezekiah said to Isaiah, "The word of the LORD which you have spoken is good." For he thought, "Is it not so, if there will be peace and truth in my days?"

20 ¶ Now the rest of the acts of Hezekiah and all his might, and how he made the pool and the conduit and brought water into the city, are they not written in the Book of the Chronicles of the Kings of Judah?

20:20 A Lifeline Tunnel

The tunnel, one of Hezekiah's major accomplishments, can still be seen in modern Jerusalem. In ancient days, Jerusalem had no source of water within its walls, making it vulnerable to an extended siege. Hezekiah undertook a tremendous engineering feat to bring water from a spring to a reservoir inside Jerusalem. In the late 1800s some boys swimming in the pool of Siloam happened upon a carved record, dating from Hezekiah's time, of how the tunnel had been dug. The marks of pickaxes are still clearly visible.

21 So Hezekiah slept with his fathers, and Manasseh his son became king in his place.

Manasseh Succeeds Hezekiah

21 Manasseh was twelve years old when he became king, and he reigned fifty-five years in Jerusalem; and his mother's name was Hephzibah.

2 He did evil in the sight of the LORD, according to the abominations of the nations whom the LORD dispossessed before the sons of Israel.

3 For he rebuilt the high places which Hezekiah his father had destroyed; and he erected altars for Baal and made an Asherah, as Ahab king of Israel had done, and worshiped all the host of heaven and served them.

4 He built altars in the house of the LORD, of which the LORD had said, "In Jerusalem I will put My name."

5 For he built altars for all the host of heaven in the two courts of the house of the LORD.

6 He made his son pass through the fire, practiced witchcraft and used divination, and dealt with mediums and spiritists. He did much evil in the sight of the LORD provoking *Him to anger*.

7 Then he set the carved image of Asherah that he had made, in the house of which the LORD said to David and to his son Solomon, "In this house and in Jerusalem, which I have chosen from all the tribes of Israel, I will put My name forever.

8 "And I will not make the feet of Israel wander anymore from the land which I gave their fathers, if only they will observe to do according to all that I have commanded them, and according to all the law that My servant Moses commanded them."

9 But they did not listen, and Manasseh seduced them to do evil more than the nations whom the LORD destroyed before the sons of Israel.

The King's Idolatries Rebuked

10 ¶ Now the LORD spoke through His servants the prophets, saying,

11 "Because Manasseh king of Judah has done these abominations, having done wickedly more than all the Amorites did who *were* before him, and has also made Judah sin with his idols;

12 therefore thus says the LORD, the God of Israel, 'Behold, I am bringing *such* calamity on Jerusalem and Judah, that whoever hears of it, both his ears will tingle.

13 'I will stretch over Jerusalem the line of Samaria and the plummet of the house of Ahab, and I will wipe Jerusalem as one wipes a dish, wiping it and turning it upside down.

14 'I will abandon the remnant of My inheritance and deliver them into the hand of their enemies, and they will become as plunder and spoil to all their enemies;

15 because they have done evil in My sight, and have been provoking Me to anger since the day their fathers came from Egypt, even to this day.'"

16 ¶ Moreover, Manasseh shed very much innocent blood until he had filled Jerusalem from one end to another; besides his sin with which he made Judah sin, in doing evil in the sight of the LORD.

17 Now the rest of the acts of Manasseh and all that he did and his sin which he committed, are they not written in the Book of the Chronicles of the Kings of Judah?

18 And Manasseh slept with his fathers and was buried in the garden of his own house, in the garden of Uzza, and Amon his son became king in his place.

Amon Succeeds Manasseh

19 ¶ Amon was twenty-two years old when he became king, and he reigned two years in Jerusa-

lem; and his mother's name *was* Meshullemeth the daughter of Haruz of Jotbah.

20 He did evil in the sight of the LORD, as Manasseh his father had done.

21 For he walked in all the way that his father had walked, and served the idols that his father had served and worshiped them.

22 So he forsook the LORD, the God of his fathers, and did not walk in the way of the LORD.

23 The servants of Amon conspired against him and killed the king in his own house.

24 Then the people of the land killed all those who had conspired against King Amon, and the people of the land made Josiah his son king in his place.

25 Now the rest of the acts of Amon which he did, are they not written in the Book of the Chronicles of the Kings of Judah?

26 He was buried in his grave in the garden of Uzza, and Josiah his son became king in his place.

Josiah Succeeds Amon

22 Josiah was eight years old when he became king, and he reigned thirty-one years in Jerusalem; and his mother's name *was* Jedidah the daughter of Adaiah of Bozkath.

2 He did right in the sight of the LORD and walked in all the way of his father David, nor did he turn aside to the right or to the left.

3 ¶ Now in the eighteenth year of King Josiah, the king sent Shaphan, the son of Azaliah the son of Meshullam the scribe, to the house of the LORD saying,

4 "Go up to Hilkiah the high priest that he may count the money brought in to the house of the LORD which the doorkeepers have gathered from the people.

5 "Let them deliver it into the hand of the workmen who have the oversight of the house of the LORD, and let them give it to the workmen who are in the house of the LORD to repair the damages of the house,

6 to the carpenters and the builders and the masons and for buying timber and hewn stone to repair the house.

7 "Only no accounting shall be made with them for the money delivered into their hands, for they deal faithfully."

The Lost Book

8 ¶ Then Hilkiah the high priest said to Shaphan the scribe, "I have found the book of the law in the house of the LORD." And Hilkiah gave the book to Shaphan who read it.

9 Shaphan the scribe came to the king and brought back word to the king and said, "Your servants have emptied out the money that was found in the house, and have delivered it into the hand of the workmen who have the oversight of the house of the LORD."

10 Moreover, Shaphan the scribe told the king

saying, "Hilkiah the priest has given me a book." And Shaphan read it in the presence of the king.

11 ¶ When the king heard the words of the book of the law, he tore his clothes.

22:11 Dramatic Discovery

Most scholars believe the book of the law referred to was Deuteronomy—or at least a portion of that book. The find, confirmed by a prophetess, resulted in the most thoroughgoing religious reform Judah had ever seen.

12 Then the king commanded Hilkiah the priest, Ahikam the son of Shaphan, Achbor the son of Micaiah, Shaphan the scribe, and Asaiah the king's servant saying,

13 "Go, inquire of the LORD for me and the people and all Judah concerning the words of this book that has been found, for great is the wrath of the LORD that burns against us, because our fathers have not listened to the words of this book, to do according to all that is written concerning us."

Huldah Predicts

14 ¶ So Hilkiah the priest, Ahikam, Achbor, Shaphan, and Asaiah went to Huldah the prophetess, the wife of Shallum the son of Tikvah, the son of Harhas, keeper of the wardrobe (now she lived in Jerusalem in the Second Quarter); and they spoke to her.

15 She said to them, "Thus says the LORD God of Israel, 'Tell the man who sent you to me,

16 thus says the LORD, "Behold, I bring evil on this place and on its inhabitants, *even* all the words of the book which the king of Judah has read.

17 "Because they have forsaken Me and have burned incense to other gods that they might provoke Me to anger with all the work of their hands, therefore My wrath burns against this place, and it shall not be quenched." '

18 "But to the king of Judah who sent you to inquire of the LORD thus shall you say to him, 'Thus says the LORD God of Israel, "*Regarding* the words which you have heard,

19 because your heart was tender and you humbled yourself before the LORD when you heard what I spoke against this place and against its inhabitants that they should become a desolation and a curse, and you have torn your clothes and wept before Me, I truly have heard you," declares the LORD.

20 "Therefore, behold, I will gather you to your fathers, and you will be gathered to your grave in peace, and your eyes will not see all the evil which I will bring on this place." ' " So they brought back word to the king.

Josiah's Covenant

23 Then the king sent, and they gathered to him all the elders of Judah and of Jerusalem.

2 The king went up to the house of the LORD and all the men of Judah and all the inhabitants of Jerusalem with him, and the priests and the prophets and all the people, both small and great; and he read in their hearing all the words of the book of the covenant which was found in the house of the LORD.

3 The king stood by the pillar and made a covenant before the LORD, to walk after the LORD, and to keep His commandments and His testimonies and His statutes with all *his* heart and all *his* soul, to carry out the words of this covenant that were written in this book. And all the people entered into the covenant.

Reforms under Josiah

4 ¶ Then the king commanded Hilkiah the high priest and the priests of the second order and the doorkeepers, to bring out of the temple of the LORD all the vessels that were made for Baal, for *a*Asherah, and for all the host of heaven; and he burned them outside Jerusalem in the fields of the Kidron, and carried their ashes to Bethel.

5 He did away with the idolatrous priests whom the kings of Judah had appointed to burn incense in the high places in the cities of Judah and in the surrounding area of Jerusalem, also those who burned incense to Baal, to the sun and to the moon and to the constellations and to all the host of heaven.

6 He brought out the Asherah from the house of the LORD outside Jerusalem to the brook Kidron, and burned it at the brook Kidron, and ground *it* to dust, and threw its dust on the graves of the common people.

7 He also broke down the houses of the *male* cult prostitutes which *were* in the house of the LORD, where the women were weaving hangings for the Asherah.

8 Then he brought all the priests from the cities of Judah, and defiled the high places where the priests had burned incense, from Geba to Beersheba; and he broke down the high places of the gates which *were* at the entrance of the gate of Joshua the governor of the city, which *were* on one's left at the city gate.

9 Nevertheless the priests of the high places did not go up to the altar of the LORD in Jerusalem, but they ate unleavened bread among their brothers.

10 He also defiled *b*Topheth, which is in the valley of the son of Hinnom, that no man might make his son or his daughter pass through the fire for Molech.

11 He did away with the horses which the kings of Judah had given to the sun, at the entrance of the house of the LORD, by the chamber of Nathan-melech the official, which *was* in the precincts; and he burned the chariots of the sun with fire.

12 The altars which *were* on the roof, the upper chamber of Ahaz, which the kings of Judah had made, and the altars which Manasseh had made in

---

a I.e. a wooden symbol of a female deity, and so throughout the ch   *b* I.e. place of burning

JOSIAH   *Last Gasp*

JOSIAH CAME TO THE THRONE when his father, at age 24, fell to assassins. Josiah himself was a mere child of eight when he was abruptly called to fill a king's shoes. By the time he reached 16, however, the boy-king had begun to find himself.

God's holy city of Jerusalem and his chosen people, the Israelites, had sunk to historic lows. The temple featured idols, male shrine prostitutes, and carved horses dedicated to sun worshipers. In a nearby valley, people burned their children in sacrifice to the god Molech. Other pagan shrines dotted the hilltops around Jerusalem and throughout the land of Judah.

During the long slide away from God, all sacred records had disappeared. The God of Abraham, Isaac and Jacob was just a faint memory.

Perhaps Josiah had heard about his great-grandfather Hezekiah, who while king had purified the temple and restored the Passover celebration. In his youth Josiah set reforms like Hezekiah's in motion again. Then, in the process of cleaning out the temple, priests discovered an old book of Scripture. Josiah took its message to heart, spurred on by his fear of God's judgment against those who failed to obey his law.

Josiah sent to a prophetess, Huldah, for advice. (Both Jeremiah and Zephaniah were prophesying at the time, but Huldah got the call.) The nation would indeed be punished, Huldah confirmed, but because of Josiah's humility the calamity would not occur in his lifetime (22:15–20). Her words came true. After Josiah's tragic death at the age of 39, Judah went quickly downhill to total destruction. Josiah was the Israelites' last, great gasp.

Life Questions: When you see immorality all around you, what can you do to change it?

the two courts of the house of the LORD, the king broke down; and he *a*smashed them there and threw their dust into the brook Kidron.

13 The high places which *were* before Jerusalem, which *were* on the right of the mount of destruction which Solomon the king of Israel had built for Ashtoreth the abomination of the Sidonians, and for Chemosh the abomination of Moab, and for Milcom the abomination of the sons of Ammon, the king defiled.

14 He broke in pieces the *sacred* pillars and cut down the Asherim and filled their places with human bones.

15 ¶ Furthermore, the altar that *was* at Bethel *and* the high place which Jeroboam the son of Nebat, who made Israel sin, had made, even that altar and the high place he broke down. Then he demolished its stones, ground them to dust, and burned the Asherah.

16 Now when Josiah turned, he saw the graves that *were* there on the mountain, and he sent and took the bones from the graves and burned *them* on the altar and defiled it according to the word of the LORD which the man of God proclaimed, who proclaimed these things.

17 Then he said, "What is this monument that I see?" And the men of the city told him, "It is the grave of the man of God who came from Judah and proclaimed these things which you have done against the altar of Bethel."

18 He said, "Let him alone; let no one disturb his bones." So they left his bones undisturbed with the bones of the prophet who came from Samaria.

19 Josiah also removed all the houses of the high places which *were* in the cities of Samaria, which the kings of Israel had made provoking the LORD; and he did to them just as he had done in Bethel.

20 All the priests of the high places who *were* there he slaughtered on the altars and burned human bones on them; then he returned to Jerusalem.

Passover Reinstituted

21 ¶ Then the king commanded all the people saying, "Celebrate the Passover to the LORD your God as it is written in this book of the covenant."

22 Surely such a Passover had not been celebrated from the days of the judges who judged Israel, nor in all the days of the kings of Israel and of the kings of Judah.

23 But in the eighteenth year of King Josiah, this Passover was observed to the LORD in Jerusalem.

24 ¶ Moreover, Josiah removed the mediums and the spiritists and the teraphim and the idols and all the abominations that were seen in the land of Judah and in Jerusalem, that he might confirm the words of the law which were written

in the book that Hilkiah the priest found in the house of the LORD.

25 Before him there was no king like him who turned to the LORD with all his heart and with all his soul and with all his might, according to all the law of Moses; nor did any like him arise after him.

26 ¶ However, the LORD did not turn from the fierceness of His great wrath with which His anger burned against Judah, because of all the provocations with which Manasseh had provoked Him.

23:26–28 Too Little Too Late

Josiah became king when he was only eight, and at the age of 26 led a dramatic reform movement. Yet for all this wise king accomplished, the Lord still determined to punish Judah, as verse 26 tells us. Evil had become so deeply ingrained that the best efforts of one good king could not root it out. In fact, as soon as Josiah died, Judah reverted to their previous form.

27 The LORD said, "I will remove Judah also from My sight, as I have removed Israel. And I will cast off Jerusalem, this city which I have chosen, and the temple of which I said, 'My name shall be there.' "

Jehoahaz Succeeds Josiah

28 ¶ Now the rest of the acts of Josiah and all that he did, are they not written in the Book of the Chronicles of the Kings of Judah?

29 In his days Pharaoh Neco king of Egypt went up to the king of Assyria to the river Euphrates. And King Josiah went to meet him, and when *Pharaoh Neco* saw him he killed him at Megiddo.

30 His servants drove his body in a chariot from Megiddo, and brought him to Jerusalem and buried him in his own tomb. Then the people of the land took Jehoahaz the son of Josiah and anointed him and made him king in place of his father.

31 ¶ Jehoahaz was twenty-three years old when he became king, and he reigned three months in Jerusalem; and his mother's name was Hamutal the daughter of Jeremiah of Libnah.

32 He did evil in the sight of the LORD, according to all that his fathers had done.

33 Pharaoh Neco imprisoned him at Riblah in the land of Hamath, that he might not reign in Jerusalem; and he imposed on the land a fine of one hundred talents of silver and a talent of gold.

Jehoiakim Made King by Pharaoh

34 Pharaoh Neco made Eliakim the son of Josiah king in the place of Josiah his father, and changed his name to Jehoiakim. But he took Jeho-

a Or *ran from there*

ahaz away and brought *him* to Egypt, and he died there.

35 So Jehoiakim gave the silver and gold to Pharaoh, but he taxed the land in order to give the money at the command of Pharaoh. He exacted the silver and gold from the people of the land, each according to his valuation, to give it to Pharaoh Neco.

36 ¶ Jehoiakim was twenty-five years old when he became king, and he reigned eleven years in Jerusalem; and his mother's name *was* Zebidah the daughter of Pedaiah of Rumah.

37 He did evil in the sight of the LORD, according to all that his fathers had done.

Babylon Controls Jehoiakim

24 In his days Nebuchadnezzar king of Babylon came up, and Jehoiakim became his servant *for* three years; then he turned and rebelled against him.

24:1 Jeremiah's Influence

The last two chapters, which closely parallel material in Jeremiah 52, reveal the influence of that prophet on the book of Kings. Some scholars have concluded that he wrote this historical record.

---

2 The LORD sent against him bands of Chaldeans, bands of Arameans, bands of Moabites, and bands of Ammonites. So He sent them against Judah to destroy it, according to the word of the LORD which He had spoken through His servants the prophets.

3 Surely at the command of the LORD it came upon Judah, to remove *them* from His sight because of the sins of Manasseh, according to all that he had done,

4 and also for the innocent blood which he shed, for he filled Jerusalem with innocent blood; and the LORD would not forgive.

5 Now the rest of the acts of Jehoiakim and all that he did, are they not written in the Book of the Chronicles of the Kings of Judah?

Jehoiachin Reigns

6 So Jehoiakim slept with his fathers, and Jehoiachin his son became king in his place.

7 The king of Egypt did not come out of his land again, for the king of Babylon had taken all that belonged to the king of Egypt from the brook of Egypt to the river Euphrates.

8 ¶ Jehoiachin was eighteen years old when he became king, and he reigned three months in Jerusalem; and his mother's name *was* Nehushta the daughter of Elnathan of Jerusalem.

9 He did evil in the sight of the LORD, according to all that his father had done.

Deportation to Babylon

10 ¶ At that time the servants of Nebuchadnezzar king of Babylon went up to Jerusalem, and the city came under siege.

11 And Nebuchadnezzar the king of Babylon came to the city, while his servants were besieging it.

12 Jehoiachin the king of Judah went out to the king of Babylon, he and his mother and his servants and his captains and his officials. So the king of Babylon took him captive in the eighth year of his reign.

13 He carried out from there all the treasures of the house of the LORD, and the treasures of the king's house, and cut in pieces all the vessels of gold which Solomon king of Israel had made in the temple of the LORD, just as the LORD had said.

14 Then he led away into exile all Jerusalem and all the captains and all the mighty men of valor, ten thousand captives, and all the craftsmen and the smiths. None remained except the poorest people of the land.

15 ¶ So he led Jehoiachin away into exile to Babylon; also the king's mother and the king's wives and his officials and the leading men of the land, he led away into exile from Jerusalem to Babylon.

16 All the men of valor, seven thousand, and the craftsmen and the smiths, one thousand, all strong and fit for war, and these the king of Babylon brought into exile to Babylon.

Zedekiah Made King

17 Then the king of Babylon made his uncle Mattaniah king in his place, and changed his name to Zedekiah.

18 ¶ Zedekiah was twenty-one years old when he became king, and he reigned eleven years in Jerusalem; and his mother's name was Hamutal the daughter of Jeremiah of Libnah.

19 He did evil in the sight of the LORD, according to all that Jehoiakim had done.

20 For through the anger of the LORD *this* came about in Jerusalem and Judah until He cast them out from His presence. And Zedekiah rebelled against the king of Babylon.

Nebuchadnezzar Besieges Jerusalem

25 Now in the ninth year of his reign, on the tenth day of the tenth month, Nebuchadnezzar king of Babylon came, he and all his army, against Jerusalem, camped against it and built a siege wall all around it.

2 So the city was under siege until the eleventh year of King Zedekiah.

3 On the ninth day of the *fourth* month the famine was so severe in the city that there was no food for the people of the land.

4 Then the city was broken into, and all the men of war *fled* by night by way of the gate between the two walls beside the king's garden,

though the Chaldeans were all around the city. And they went by way of the Arabah.

5 But the army of the Chaldeans pursued the king and overtook him in the plains of Jericho and all his army was scattered from him.

6 Then they captured the king and brought him to the king of Babylon at Riblah, and he passed sentence on him.

7 They slaughtered the sons of Zedekiah before his eyes, then put out the eyes of Zedekiah and bound him with bronze fetters and brought him to Babylon.

Jerusalem Burned and Plundered

8 ¶ Now on the seventh day of the fifth month, which was the nineteenth year of King Nebuchadnezzar, king of Babylon, Nebuzaradan the captain of the guard, a servant of the king of Babylon, came to Jerusalem.

9 He burned the house of the LORD, the king's house, and all the houses of Jerusalem; even every great house he burned with fire.

10 So all the army of the Chaldeans who *were with* the captain of the guard broke down the walls around Jerusalem.

11 Then the rest of the people who were left in the city and the deserters who had deserted to the king of Babylon and the rest of the people, Nebuzaradan the captain of the guard carried away into exile.

12 But the captain of the guard left some of the poorest of the land to be vinedressers and plowmen.

13 ¶ Now the bronze pillars which were in the house of the LORD, and the stands and the bronze sea which were in the house of the LORD, the Chaldeans broke in pieces and carried the bronze to Babylon.

14 They took away the pots, the shovels, the snuffers, the spoons, and all the bronze vessels which were used in *temple* service.

15 The captain of the guard also took away the firepans and the basins, what was fine gold and what was fine silver.

16 The two pillars, the one sea, and the stands which Solomon had made for the house of the LORD—the bronze of all these vessels was beyond weight.

17 The height of the one pillar was eighteen cubits, and a bronze capital was on it; the height of the capital was three cubits, with a network and pomegranates on the capital all around, all of bronze. And the second pillar was like these with network.

18 ¶ Then the captain of the guard took Seraiah the chief priest and Zephaniah the second priest, with the three officers of the temple.

19 From the city he took one official who was overseer of the men of war, and five of the king's advisers who were found in the city; and the scribe of the captain of the army who mustered the people of the land; and sixty men of the people of the land who were found in the city.

20 Nebuzaradan the captain of the guard took them and brought them to the king of Babylon at Riblah.

21 Then the king of Babylon struck them down and put them to death at Riblah in the land of Hamath. So Judah was led away into exile from its land.

Gedaliah Made Governor

22 ¶ Now *as for* the people who were left in the land of Judah, whom Nebuchadnezzar king of Babylon had left, he appointed Gedaliah the son of Ahikam, the son of Shaphan over them.

ZEDEKIAH *The Bitter End*

FOR A VERY LONG TIME the kingdom of Judah had been sliding downhill. Good kings like Hezekiah and Josiah managed to stop the decline temporarily, but as soon as they passed from the scene, immorality and idolatry surged back. Prophets warned again and again of God's judgment, but few heeded them.

Fittingly, Judah endured its bitter end under the weak leadership of Zedekiah, a puppet king put on the throne by Judah's captor, the Babylonian King Nebuchadnezzar. Zedekiah personified all that was wrong with Judah. He took an oath of loyalty to Babylon, then spent his eleven-year reign cheating on it.

The great prophet Jeremiah lived during this same time, offering a strong counterpoint to Zedekiah's weakness. Zedekiah could never make up his mind whether to treat Jeremiah as a prophet of truth or as a trouble-making traitor. When Jeremiah warned against Zedekiah's policies, the king had him beaten and imprisoned. At the same time, he kept bringing Jeremiah in for secret consultations, usually ignoring his advice.

Judah paid cruelly for Zedekiah's poor leadership. Responding to his rebellion, the Babylonians put Jerusalem under a two-year siege, then utterly wrecked the city. They treated Zedekiah as a traitor, executing his sons while he watched, then putting out his eyes so that their deaths would be his last visual memory. Judah's final king was led off to Babylon, blind and in chains.

Life Questions: Under pressure, are you confident or indecisive? What do you need to gain confidence?

23 When all the captains of the forces, they and *their* men, heard that the king of Babylon had appointed Gedaliah *governor,* they came to Gedaliah to Mizpah, namely, Ishmael the son of Nethaniah, and Johanan the son of Kareah, and Seraiah

25:22 A Kingdom Disappears

Judah's final rebellion against mighty Babylon failed, resulting in an 18-month siege and the destruction of Jerusalem. Survivors were taken away in what became known as the "Babylonian captivity," a tragic moment in Jewish history. God spelled out the reasons for this disaster in 2 Kings 21:10–16.

the son of Tanhumeth the Netophathite, and Jaazaniah the son of the Maacathite, they and their men.

24 Gedaliah swore to them and their men and said to them, "Do not be afraid of the servants of the Chaldeans; live in the land and serve the king of Babylon, and it will be well with you."

25 ¶ But it came about in the seventh month, that Ishmael the son of Nethaniah, the son of Elishama, of the royal family, came with ten men and struck Gedaliah down so that he died along with the Jews and the Chaldeans who were with him at Mizpah.

26 Then all the people, both small and great, and the captains of the forces arose and went to Egypt; for they were afraid of the Chaldeans.

27 ¶ Now it came about in the thirty-seventh year of the exile of Jehoiachin king of Judah, in the twelfth month, on the twenty-seventh *day* of the month, that Evil-merodach king of Babylon, in the year that he became king, released Jehoiachin king of Judah from prison;

28 and he spoke kindly to him and set his throne above the throne of the kings who *were* with him in Babylon.

29 Jehoiachin changed his prison clothes and had his meals in the king's presence regularly all the days of his life;

30 and for his allowance, a regular allowance was given him by the king, a portion for each day, all the days of his life.

1 CHRONICLES

A Family Record
These facts reminded Israelites of their place in God's plan

> *"And what one nation in the earth is like Your people Israel, whom God went to redeem for Himself?" 17:21*

I N PIONEER DAYS, MANY AMERICAN families prized a huge black family Bible. Often the only book in the house, it served for more than reading. It was also the family memory bank. Every important event—a marriage, a birth, a death—was recorded on its flyleaves. The Bible was passed down from generation to generation, and through it, a family kept track of its past.

The book of 1 Chronicles is something like that—a record of Israel's family history, and particularly of David, Israel's greatest king. In fact, at first glance, 1 Chronicles looks like a rehash of David's life as told in 2 Samuel and 1 Kings. Some of the most dramatic episodes in David's life—his clash with Goliath, his sin with Bathsheba—don't make it into this account. But David's organization of the temple is told in great detail, and long lists and genealogies fill over half the book.

Because of that, few people read 1 Chronicles. Most of us are more interested in personalities than in institutions and genealogies.

David's Lasting Impact

First Chronicles, however, is far more interested in David's lasting accomplishments than in his ups and downs as an individual. The nation he led was more than a collection of inspired individuals. It was founded on God's unshakable promises to the children of Abraham. He had promised to be with them. He had promised to provide leadership. He had promised to make them a blessing to the world. These promises took shape in enduring institutions—the temple and the monarchy, most notably.

Why a List of Names?

The first nine chapters of 1 Chronicles trace the genealogy of Israel back to Adam. The author brings together more family records than you'll find anywhere else in the Bible. These records helped the Israelites remember their position as members in God's chosen family. God had given them unique ways to follow and worship him. First Chronicles reminded the Israelites—as it reminds us—of how different their family was meant to be.

How to Read 1 Chronicles

F ew will enjoy reading 1 Chronicles' many lists and genealogies straight through. You should approach them more like a puzzle. Don't get lost in the hundreds of names. Instead, try to understand how the different parts of 1 Chronicles fit together. For each section ask, "Why was this included? What did it mean to the original audience—to the Israelites who had returned from exile in Babylon? How did it encourage them as they made a new beginning?"

First Chronicles divides cleanly into two parts. The first nine chapters are mainly lists of names. In these, the Israelites read their family tree and discovered their heritage. Chapters 10 to 29 tell David's story, focusing on the legacy he left behind for future generations—especially the temple. David, a founding father of Israel, transformed the nation in a way that lasted hundreds of years.

PEOPLE YOU'LL MEET IN 1 CHRONICLES

JOAB, ABSHAI AND ASAHEL *(p. 462)*

3-TRACK READING PLAN

For an explanation and complete listing of the 3-track reading plan, turn to page 7.

TRACK 1: *Two-Week Courses on the Bible*
See page 7 for information on these courses.

TRACK 2: *An Overview of 1 Chronicles in 1 Day*
☐ Day 1. Read the Introduction to 1 Chronicles and chapter 17, which describes God's promise to David and David's prayerful response.
Now turn to page 9 for your next Track 2 reading project.

TRACK 3: *All of 1 Chronicles in 17 Days*
You should only skim chapters 1–9 and 23–27, which contain lists and genealogies. After you have skimmed and read 1 Chronicles, turn to pages 10–14 for your next Track 3 reading project.

☐1–9 ☐10 ☐11 ☐12 ☐13 ☐14 ☐15 ☐16
☐17 ☐18 ☐19 ☐20 ☐21 ☐22 ☐23–27 ☐28
☐29

Genealogy from Adam

1 Adam, Seth, Enosh,
2 Kenan, Mahalalel, Jared,
3 Enoch, Methuselah, Lamech,
4 Noah, Shem, Ham and Japheth.
5 ¶ The sons of Japheth *were* Gomer, Magog, Madai, Javan, Tubal, Meshech and Tiras.
6 The sons of Gomer *were* Ashkenaz, Diphath, and Togarmah.
7 The sons of Javan *were* Elishah, Tarshish, Kittim and Rodanim.
8 ¶ The sons of Ham *were* Cush, Mizraim, Put, and Canaan.
9 The sons of Cush *were* Seba, Havilah, Sabta, Raama and Sabteca; and the sons of Raamah *were* Sheba and Dedan.
10 Cush became the father of Nimrod; he began to be a mighty one in the earth.
11 ¶ Mizraim became the father of the people of Lud, Anam, Lehab, Naphtuh,
12 Pathrus, Casluh, from which the Philistines came, and Caphtor.
13 ¶ Canaan became the father of Sidon, his firstborn, Heth,
14 and the Jebusites, the Amorites, the Girgashites,
15 the Hivites, the Arkites, the Sinites,
16 the Arvadites, the Zemarites and the Hamathites.
17 ¶ The sons of Shem *were* Elam, Asshur, Arpachshad, Lud, Aram, Uz, Hul, Gether and Meshech.
18 Arpachshad became the father of Shelah and Shelah became the father of Eber.

19 Two sons were born to Eber, the name of the one was Peleg, for in his days the earth was divided, and his brother's name was Joktan.
20 Joktan became the father of Almodad, Sheleph, Hazarmaveth, Jerah,
21 Hadoram, Uzal, Diklah,
22 Ebal, Abimael, Sheba,
23 Ophir, Havilah and Jobab; all these *were* the sons of Joktan.
24 ¶ Shem, Arpachshad, Shelah,
25 Eber, Peleg, Reu,
26 Serug, Nahor, Terah,
27 Abram, that is Abraham.

Descendants of Abraham

28 ¶ The sons of Abraham *were* Isaac and Ishmael.
29 These are their genealogies: the firstborn of Ishmael *was* Nebaioth, then Kedar, Adbeel, Mibsam,

1:28 Compressed History

The books of 1 and 2 Chronicles, focusing on the kings of the recent past, do not pretend to give a complete history of the Israelites. But by recording individuals' names all the way back to Adam, the books underscore that God has kept his hand on this line of people from the very beginning. The Gospels complete the list begun here: Matthew traces Jesus' lineage back to Abraham, and Luke traces it back to Adam.

30 Mishma, Dumah, Massa, Hadad, Tema,
31 Jetur, Naphish and Kedemah; these *were* the sons of Ishmael.

32 The sons of Keturah, Abraham's concubine, *whom* she bore, *were* Zimran, Jokshan, Medan, Midian, Ishbak and Shuah. And the sons of Jokshan *were* Sheba and Dedan.

33 The sons of Midian were Ephah, Epher, Hanoch, Abida and Eldaah. All these were the sons of Keturah.

34 ¶ Abraham became the father of Isaac. The sons of Isaac *were* Esau and Israel.

35 The sons of Esau *were* Eliphaz, Reuel, Jeush, Jalam and Korah.

36 The sons of Eliphaz *were* Teman, Omar, Zephi, Gatam, Kenaz, Timna and Amalek.

37 The sons of Reuel *were* Nahath, Zerah, Shammah and Mizzah.

38 The sons of Seir *were* Lotan, Shobal, Zibeon, Anah, Dishon, Ezer and Dishan.

39 The sons of Lotan *were* Hori and Homam; and Lotan's sister *was* Timna.

40 The sons of Shobal *were* Alian, Manahath, Ebal, Shephi and Onam. And the sons of Zibeon *were* Aiah and Anah.

41 The son of Anah *was* Dishon. And the sons of Dishon *were* Hamran, Eshban, Ithran and Cheran.

42 The sons of Ezer *were* Bilhan, Zaavan and Jaakan. The sons of Dishan *were* Uz and Aran.

43 ¶ Now these are the kings who reigned in the land of Edom before any king of the sons of Israel reigned. Bela was the son of Beor, and the name of his city was Dinhabah.

44 When Bela died, Jobab the son of Zerah of Bozrah became king in his place.

45 When Jobab died, Husham of the land of the Temanites became king in his place.

46 When Husham died, Hadad the son of Bedad, who defeated Midian in the field of Moab, became king in his place; and the name of his city *was* Avith.

47 When Hadad died, Samlah of Masrekah became king in his place.

48 When Samlah died, Shaul of Rehoboth by the River became king in his place.

49 When Shaul died, Baal-hanan the son of Achbor became king in his place.

50 When Baal-hanan died, Hadad became king in his place; and the name of his city was Pai, and his wife's name was Mehetabel, the daughter of Matred, the daughter of Mezahab.

51 Then Hadad died.

¶ Now the chiefs of Edom were: chief Timna, chief Aliah, chief Jetheth,

52 chief Oholibamah, chief Elah, chief Pinon,
53 chief Kenaz, chief Teman, chief Mibzar,
54 chief Magdiel, chief Iram. These *were* the chiefs of Edom.

Genealogy: Twelve Sons of Jacob (Israel)

2 These are the sons of Israel: Reuben, Simeon, Levi, Judah, Issachar, Zebulun,

2 Dan, Joseph, Benjamin, Naphtali, Gad and Asher.

3 ¶ The sons of Judah *were* Er, Onan and Shelah; *these* three were born to him by Bath-shua the Canaanitess. And Er, Judah's firstborn, was wicked in the sight of the LORD, so He put him to death.

4 Tamar his daughter-in-law bore him Perez and Zerah. Judah had five sons in all.

5 ¶ The sons of Perez *were* Hezron and Hamul.

6 The sons of Zerah *were* Zimri, Ethan, Heman, Calcol and Dara; five of them in all.

7 The son of Carmi *was* Achar, the troubler of Israel, who violated the ban.

8 The son of Ethan *was* Azariah.

Genealogy of David

9 ¶ Now the sons of Hezron, who were born to him *were* Jerahmeel, Ram and Chelubai.

10 Ram became the father of Amminadab, and Amminadab became the father of Nahshon, leader of the sons of Judah;

11 Nahshon became the father of Salma, Salma became the father of Boaz,

12 Boaz became the father of Obed, and Obed became the father of Jesse;

13 and Jesse became the father of Eliab his firstborn, then Abinadab the second, Shimea the third,

14 Nethanel the fourth, Raddai the fifth,

15 Ozem the sixth, David the seventh;

16 and their sisters *were* Zeruiah and Abigail. And the three sons of Zeruiah *were* Abshai, Joab and Asahel.

17 Abigail bore Amasa, and the father of Amasa was Jether the Ishmaelite.

18 ¶ Now Caleb the son of Hezron had sons by Azubah *his* wife, and by Jerioth; and these were her sons: Jesher, Shobab, and Ardon.

19 When Azubah died, Caleb married Ephrath, who bore him Hur.

20 Hur became the father of Uri, and Uri became the father of Bezalel.

21 ¶ Afterward Hezron went in to the daughter of Machir the father of Gilead, whom he married when he was sixty years old; and she bore him Segub.

22 Segub became the father of Jair, who had twenty-three cities in the land of Gilead.

23 But Geshur and Aram took the towns of Jair from them, with Kenath and its villages, *even* sixty cities. All these were the sons of Machir, the father of Gilead.

24 After the death of Hezron in Caleb-ephrathah, Abijah, Hezron's wife, bore him Ashhur the father of Tekoa.

25 ¶ Now the sons of Jerahmeel the firstborn

of Hezron *were* Ram the firstborn, then Bunah, Oren, Ozem *and* Ahijah.

26 Jerahmeel had another wife, whose name was Atarah; she was the mother of Onam.

27 The sons of Ram, the firstborn of Jerahmeel, were Maaz, Jamin and Eker.

28 The sons of Onam were Shammai and Jada. And the sons of Shammai *were* Nadab and Abishur.

29 The name of Abishur's wife *was* Abihail, and she bore him Ahban and Molid.

30 The sons of Nadab *were* Seled and Appaim, and Seled died without sons.

31 The son of Appaim *was* Ishi. And the son of Ishi *was* Sheshan. And the son of Sheshan *was* Ahlai.

32 The sons of Jada the brother of Shammai *were* Jether and Jonathan, and Jether died without sons.

33 The sons of Jonathan *were* Peleth and Zaza. These were the sons of Jerahmeel.

34 Now Sheshan had no sons, only daughters. And Sheshan had an Egyptian servant whose name was Jarha.

35 Sheshan gave his daughter to Jarha his servant in marriage, and she bore him Attai.

36 Attai became the father of Nathan, and Nathan became the father of Zabad,

37 and Zabad became the father of Ephlal, and Ephlal became the father of Obed,

38 and Obed became the father of Jehu, and Jehu became the father of Azariah,

39 and Azariah became the father of Helez, and Helez became the father of Eleasah,

40 and Eleasah became the father of Sismai, and Sismai became the father of Shallum,

41 and Shallum became the father of Jekamiah, and Jekamiah became the father of Elishama.

42 ¶ Now the sons of Caleb, the brother of Jerahmeel, *were* Mesha his firstborn, who was the father of Ziph; and his son was Mareshah, the father of Hebron.

43 The sons of Hebron *were* Korah and Tappuah and Rekem and Shema.

44 Shema became the father of Raham, the father of Jorkeam; and Rekem became the father of Shammai.

45 The son of Shammai was Maon, and Maon *was* the father of Bethzur.

46 Ephah, Caleb's concubine, bore Haran, Moza and Gazez; and Haran became the father of Gazez.

47 The sons of Jahdai *were* Regem, Jotham, Geshan, Pelet, Ephah and Shaaph.

48 Maacah, Caleb's concubine, bore Sheber and Tirhanah.

49 She also bore Shaaph the father of Madmannah, Sheva the father of Machbena and the father of Gibea; and the daughter of Caleb *was* Achsah.

50 These were the sons of Caleb.

¶ The sons of Hur, the firstborn of Ephrathah, *were* Shobal the father of Kiriath-jearim,

51 Salma the father of Bethlehem *and* Hareph the father of Beth-gader.

52 Shobal the father of Kiriath-jearim had sons: Haroeh, half of the Manahathites,

53 and the families of Kiriath-jearim: the Ithrites, the Puthites, the Shumathites and the Mishraites; from these came the Zorathites and the Eshtaolites.

54 The sons of Salma *were* Bethlehem and the Netophathites, Atroth-beth-joab and half of the Manahathites, the Zorites.

55 The families of scribes who lived at Jabez *were* the Tirathites, the Shimeathites *and* the Sucathites. Those are the Kenites who came from Hammath, the father of the house of Rechab.

Family of David

3 Now these were the sons of David who were born to him in Hebron: the firstborn *was* Amnon, by Ahinoam the Jezreelitess; the second *was* Daniel, by Abigail the Carmelitess;

2 the third *was* Absalom the son of Maacah, the daughter of Talmai king of Geshur; the fourth *was* Adonijah the son of Haggith;

3 the fifth *was* Shephatiah, by Abital; the sixth *was* Ithream, by his wife Eglah.

4 Six were born to him in Hebron, and there he reigned seven years and six months. And in Jerusalem he reigned thirty-three years.

5 These were born to him in Jerusalem: Shimea, Shobab, Nathan and Solomon, four, by Bathshua the daughter of Ammiel;

3:5 Why the Cleanup?

Names like Bathsheba, Absalom, and Tamar all bring to mind unsavory scenes from David's life (see 2 Samuel 11—18). The author certainly would have known about these stories, but chose to omit them. Writing to dispirited refugees, he wanted to inspire them with a model of what the nation could become, not remind them of how it had failed in the past.

6 and Ibhar, Elishama, Eliphelet,

7 Nogah, Nepheg and Japhia,

8 Elishama, Eliada and Eliphelet, nine.

9 All *these were* the sons of David, besides the sons of the concubines; and Tamar *was* their sister.

10 ¶ Now Solomon's son *was* Rehoboam, Abijah *was* his son, Asa his son, Jehoshaphat his son,

11 Joram his son, Ahaziah his son, Joash his son,

12 Amaziah his son, Azariah his son, Jotham his son,

13 Ahaz his son, Hezekiah his son, Manasseh his son,

14 Amon his son, Josiah his son.

15 The sons of Josiah *were* Johanan the first-born, and the second *was* Jehoiakim, the third Zedekiah, the fourth Shallum.

16 The sons of Jehoiakim *were* Jeconiah his son, Zedekiah his son.

17 The sons of Jeconiah, the prisoner, *were* Shealtiel his son,

3:17 The Royal Line

Chronicles was written to people who no longer had a king. However, as this section reminds us, they still knew the royal line. God's promise to provide them with kingly leadership forever still held. They could expect a son of David to someday become king again. This is one reason why the New Testament takes the trouble to show that Jesus was descended from David. He was that King.

18 and Malchiram, Pedaiah, Shenazzar, Jekamiah, Hoshama and Nedabiah.

19 The sons of Pedaiah *were* Zerubbabel and Shimei. And the sons of Zerubbabel *were* Meshullam and Hananiah, and Shelomith *was* their sister;

20 and Hashubah, Ohel, Berechiah, Hasadiah and Jushab-hesed, five.

21 The sons of Hananiah *were* Pelatiah and Jeshaiah, the sons of Rephaiah, the sons of Arnan, the sons of Obadiah, the sons of Shecaniah.

22 The ᵃdescendants of Shecaniah *were* Shemaiah, and the sons of Shemaiah: Hattush, Igal, Bariah, Neariah and Shaphat, six.

23 The sons of Neariah *were* Elioenai, Hizkiah and Azrikam, three.

24 The sons of Elioenai *were* Hodaviah, Eliashib, Pelaiah, Akkub, Johanan, Delaiah and Anani, seven.

Line of Hur, Asher

4 The sons of Judah *were* Perez, Hezron, Carmi, Hur and Shobal.

2 Reaiah the son of Shobal became the father of Jahath, and Jahath became the father of Ahumai and Lahad. These *were* the families of the Zorathites.

3 These *were* the sons of Etam: Jezreel, Ishma and Idbash; and the name of their sister *was* Hazzelelponi.

4 Penuel *was* the father of Gedor, and Ezer the father of Hushah. These *were* the sons of Hur, the firstborn of Ephrathah, the father of Bethlehem.

5 Ashhur, the father of Tekoa, had two wives, Helah and Naarah.

6 Naarah bore him Ahuzzam, Hepher, Temeni and Haahashtari. These were the sons of Naarah.

ᵃ Lit *sons*

7 The sons of Helah *were* Zereth, Izhar and Ethnan.

8 Koz became the father of Anub and Zobebah, and the families of Aharhel the son of Harum.

9 Jabez was more honorable than his brothers, and his mother named him Jabez saying, "Because I bore *him* with pain."

10 Now Jabez called on the God of Israel, saying, "Oh that You would bless me indeed and enlarge my border, and that Your hand might be with me, and that You would keep *me* from harm that *it* may not pain me!" And God granted him what he requested.

11 ¶ Chelub the brother of Shuhah became the father of Mehir, who was the father of Eshton.

12 Eshton became the father of Beth-rapha and Paseah, and Tehinnah the father of Ir-nahash. These are the men of Recah.

13 ¶ Now the sons of Kenaz *were* Othniel and Seraiah. And the sons of Othniel *were* Hathath and Meonothai.

14 Meonothai became the father of Ophrah, and Seraiah became the father of Joab the father of Ge-harashim, for they were craftsmen.

15 The sons of Caleb the son of Jephunneh *were* Iru, Elah and Naam; and the son of Elah *was* Kenaz.

16 The sons of Jehallelel *were* Ziph and Ziphah, Tiria and Asarel.

17 The sons of Ezrah *were* Jether, Mered, Epher and Jalon. (And these are the sons of Bithia the daughter of Pharaoh, whom Mered took) and she conceived *and bore* Miriam, Shammai and Ishbah the father of Eshtemoa.

18 His Jewish wife bore Jered the father of Gedor, and Heber the father of Soco, and Jekuthiel the father of Zanoah.

19 The sons of the wife of Hodiah, the sister of Naham, *were* the fathers of Keilah the Garmite and Eshtemoa the Maacathite.

20 The sons of Shimon *were* Amnon and Rinnah, Benhanan and Tilon. And the sons of Ishi *were* Zoheth and Ben-zoheth.

21 The sons of Shelah the son of Judah *were* Er the father of Lecah and Laadah the father of Mareshah, and the families of the house of the linen workers at Beth-ashbea;

22 and Jokim, the men of Cozeba, Joash, Saraph, who ruled in Moab, and Jashubi-lehem. And the records are ancient.

23 These were the potters and the inhabitants of Netaim and Gederah; they lived there with the king for his work.

Descendants of Simeon

24 ¶ The sons of Simeon *were* Nemuel and Jamin, Jarib, Zerah, Shaul;

25 Shallum his son, Mibsam his son, Mishma his son.

26 The sons of Mishma *were* Hammuel his son, Zaccur his son, Shimei his son.

27 Now Shimei had sixteen sons and six daughters; but his brothers did not have many sons, nor did all their family multiply like the sons of Judah.

28 They lived at Beersheba, Moladah and Hazar-shual,

29 at Bilhah, Ezem, Tolad,

30 Bethuel, Hormah, Ziklag,

31 Beth-marcaboth, Hazar-susim, Beth-biri and Shaaraim. These *were* their cities until the reign of David.

32 Their villages *were* Etam, Ain, Rimmon, Tochen and Ashan, five cities;

33 and all their villages that *were* around the same cities as far as Baal. These *were* their settlements, and they have their genealogy.

34 ¶ Meshobab and Jamlech and Joshah the son of Amaziah,

35 and Joel and Jehu the son of Joshibiah, the son of Seraiah, the son of Asiel,

36 and Elioenai, Jaakobah, Jeshohaiah, Asaiah, Adiel, Jesimiel, Benaiah,

37 Ziza the son of Shiphi, the son of Allon, the son of Jedaiah, the son of Shimri, the son of Shemaiah;

38 these mentioned by name *were* leaders in their families; and their fathers' houses increased greatly.

39 They went to the entrance of Gedor, even to the east side of the valley, to seek pasture for their flocks.

40 They found rich and good pasture, and the land was broad and quiet and peaceful; for those who lived there formerly *were* Hamites.

41 These, recorded by name, came in the days of Hezekiah king of Judah, and attacked their tents and the Meunites who were found there, and destroyed them utterly to this day, and lived in their place, because there was pasture there for their flocks.

42 From them, from the sons of Simeon, five hundred men went to Mount Seir, with Pelatiah, Neariah, Rephaiah and Uzziel, the sons of Ishi, as their leaders.

43 They destroyed the remnant of the Amalekites who escaped, and have lived there to this day.

Genealogy from Reuben

5 Now the sons of Reuben the firstborn of Israel (for he was the firstborn, but because he defiled his father's bed, his birthright was given to the sons of Joseph the son of Israel; so that he is not enrolled in the genealogy according to the birthright.

2 Though Judah prevailed over his brothers, and from him *came* the leader, yet the birthright belonged to Joseph),

3 the sons of Reuben the firstborn of Israel *were* Hanoch and Pallu, Hezron and Carmi.

4 The sons of Joel *were* Shemaiah his son, Gog his son, Shimei his son,

5 Micah his son, Reaiah his son, Baal his son,

6 Beerah his son, whom Tilgath-pilneser king of Assyria carried away into exile; he was leader of the Reubenites.

7 His kinsmen by their families, in the genealogy of their generations, *were* Jeiel the chief, then Zechariah

8 and Bela the son of Azaz, the son of Shema, the son of Joel, who lived in Aroer, even to Nebo and Baal-meon.

9 To the east he settled as far as the entrance of the wilderness from the river Euphrates, because their cattle had increased in the land of Gilead.

10 In the days of Saul they made war with the Hagrites, who fell by their hand, so that they occupied their tents throughout all the land east of Gilead.

11 ¶ Now the sons of Gad lived opposite them in the land of Bashan as far as Salecah.

12 Joel *was* the chief and Shapham the second, then Janai and Shaphat in Bashan.

13 Their kinsmen of their fathers' households *were* Michael, Meshullam, Sheba, Jorai, Jacan, Zia and Eber, seven.

14 These *were* the sons of Abihail, the son of Huri, the son of Jaroah, the son of Gilead, the son of Michael, the son of Jeshishai, the son of Jahdo, the son of Buz;

15 Ahi the son of Abdiel, the son of Guni, *was* head of their fathers' households.

16 They lived in Gilead, in Bashan and in its towns, and in all the pasture lands of Sharon, as far as their borders.

17 All of these were enrolled in the genealogies in the days of Jotham king of Judah and in the days of Jeroboam king of Israel.

18 ¶ The sons of Reuben and the Gadites and the half-tribe of Manasseh, *consisting* of valiant men, men who bore shield and sword and shot with bow and *were* skillful in battle, *were* 44,760, who went to war.

19 They made war against the Hagrites, Jetur, Naphish and Nodab.

20 They were helped against them, and the Hagrites and all who *were* with them were given into their hand; for they cried out to God in the battle, and He answered their prayers because they trusted in Him.

21 They took away their cattle: their 50,000 camels, 250,000 sheep, 2,000 donkeys; and 100,000 men.

22 For many fell slain, because the war *was* of God. And they settled in their place until the exile.

23 ¶ Now the sons of the half-tribe of Manasseh lived in the land; from Bashan to Baal-hermon and Senir and Mount Hermon they were numerous.

24 These were the heads of their fathers' house-

holds, even Epher, Ishi, Eliel, Azriel, Jeremiah, Hodaviah and Jahdiel, mighty men of valor, famous men, heads of their fathers' households.

25 ¶ But they acted treacherously against the God of their fathers and played the harlot after the gods of the peoples of the land, whom God had destroyed before them.

26 So the God of Israel stirred up the spirit of Pul, king of Assyria, even the spirit of Tilgathpilneser king of Assyria, and he carried them away into exile, namely the Reubenites, the Gadites and the half-tribe of Manasseh, and brought them to Halah, Habor, Hara and to the river of Gozan, to this day.

Genealogy: The Priestly Line

6 The sons of Levi were Gershon, Kohath and Merari.

6:1 Key People

First Chronicles 1–9 form the Bible's most complete genealogical record. These chapters emphasize the two tribes most crucial to God's plans: Judahites, the tribe that David and all the later kings of Judah came from, and Levites, who had responsibility to lead Israel in worship.

It's possible that the Levite priest named Ezra wrote the two books of Chronicles, for they date from his time period. Jewish refugees had returned from exile in Babylon, and leaders like Ezra were trying to inspire the exiles to reestablish their proud nation and rebuild the temple.

2 The sons of Kohath were Amram, Izhar, Hebron and Uzziel.

3 The children of Amram were Aaron, Moses and Miriam. And the sons of Aaron were Nadab, Abihu, Eleazar and Ithamar.

4 Eleazar became the father of Phinehas, *and* Phinehas became the father of Abishua,

5 and Abishua became the father of Bukki, and Bukki became the father of Uzzi,

6 and Uzzi became the father of Zerahiah, and Zerahiah became the father of Meraioth,

7 Meraioth became the father of Amariah, and Amariah became the father of Ahitub,

8 and Ahitub became the father of Zadok, and Zadok became the father of Ahimaaz,

9 and Ahimaaz became the father of Azariah, and Azariah became the father of Johanan,

10 and Johanan became the father of Azariah (it was he who served as the priest in the house which Solomon built in Jerusalem),

11 and Azariah became the father of Amariah, and Amariah became the father of Ahitub,

12 and Ahitub became the father of Zadok, and Zadok became the father of Shallum,

13 and Shallum became the father of Hilkiah, and Hilkiah became the father of Azariah,

14 and Azariah became the father of Seraiah, and Seraiah became the father of Jehozadak;

15 and Jehozadak went *along* when the LORD carried Judah and Jerusalem away into exile by Nebuchadnezzar.

16 ¶ The sons of Levi were Gershom, Kohath and Merari.

17 These are the names of the sons of Gershom: Libni and Shimei.

18 The sons of Kohath were Amram, Izhar, Hebron and Uzziel.

19 The sons of Merari were Mahli and Mushi. And these are the families of the Levites according to their fathers' *households.*

20 Of Gershom: Libni his son, Jahath his son, Zimmah his son,

21 Joah his son, Iddo his son, Zerah his son, Jeatherai his son.

22 The sons of Kohath were Amminadab his son, Korah his son, Assir his son,

23 Elkanah his son, Ebiasaph his son and Assir his son,

24 Tahath his son, Uriel his son, Uzziah his son and Shaul his son.

25 The sons of Elkanah were Amasai and Ahimoth.

26 *As for* Elkanah, the sons of Elkanah were Zophai his son and Nahath his son,

27 Eliab his son, Jeroham his son, Elkanah his son.

28 The sons of Samuel were Joel the firstborn, and Abijah the second.

29 The sons of Merari were Mahli, Libni his son, Shimei his son, Uzzah his son,

30 Shimea his son, Haggiah his son, Asaiah his son.

31 ¶ Now these are those whom David appointed over the service of song in the house of the LORD, after the ark rested *there.*

6:31 And Now, the Choir . . .

The author of 1 Chronicles had a special fondness for musicians. Several times he mentions David's role in establishing guilds of musicians for temple worship, and here he even records their ancestry.

32 They ministered with song before the tabernacle of the tent of meeting, until Solomon had built the house of the LORD in Jerusalem; and they served in their office according to their order.

33 These are those who served with their sons: From the sons of the Kohathites were Heman the singer, the son of Joel, the son of Samuel,

34 the son of Elkanah, the son of Jeroham, the son of Eliel, the son of Toah,

35 the son of Zuph, the son of Elkanah, the son of Mahath, the son of Amasai,

36 the son of Elkanah, the son of Joel, the son of Azariah, the son of Zephaniah,

37 the son of Tahath, the son of Assir, the son of Ebiasaph, the son of Korah,

38 the son of Izhar, the son of Kohath, the son of Levi, the son of Israel.

39 *Heman's* brother Asaph stood at his right hand, even Asaph the son of Berechiah, the son of Shimea,

40 the son of Michael, the son of Baaseiah, the son of Malchijah,

41 the son of Ethni, the son of Zerah, the son of Adaiah,

42 the son of Ethan, the son of Zimmah, the son of Shimei,

43 the son of Jahath, the son of Gershom, the son of Levi.

44 On the left hand *were* their kinsmen the sons of Merari: Ethan the son of Kishi, the son of Abdi, the son of Malluch,

45 the son of Hashabiah, the son of Amaziah, the son of Hilkiah,

46 the son of Amzi, the son of Bani, the son of Shemer,

47 the son of Mahli, the son of Mushi, the son of Merari, the son of Levi.

48 Their kinsmen the Levites were appointed for all the service of the tabernacle of the house of God.

49 ¶ But Aaron and his sons offered on the altar of burnt offering and on the altar of incense, for all the work of the most holy place, and to make atonement for Israel, according to all that Moses the servant of God had commanded.

50 These are the sons of Aaron: Eleazar his son, Phinehas his son, Abishua his son,

51 Bukki his son, Uzzi his son, Zerahiah his son,

52 Meraioth his son, Amariah his son, Ahitub his son,

53 Zadok his son, Ahimaaz his son.

54 ¶ Now these are their settlements according to their camps within their borders. To the sons of Aaron of the families of the Kohathites (for theirs was the *first* lot),

55 to them they gave Hebron in the land of Judah and its pasture lands around it;

56 but the fields of the city and its villages, they gave to Caleb the son of Jephunneh.

57 To the sons of Aaron they gave the *following* cities of refuge: Hebron, Libnah also with its pasture lands, Jattir, Eshtemoa with its pasture lands,

58 Hilen with its pasture lands, Debir with its pasture lands,

59 Ashan with its pasture lands and Beth-shemesh with its pasture lands;

60 and from the tribe of Benjamin: Geba with its pasture lands, Allemeth with its pasture lands, and Anathoth with its pasture lands. All their cit-

ies throughout their families were thirteen cities.

61 ¶ Then to the rest of the sons of Kohath *were given* by lot, from the family of the tribe, from the half-tribe, the half of Manasseh, ten cities.

62 To the sons of Gershom, according to their families, *were given* from the tribe of Issachar and from the tribe of Asher, the tribe of Naphtali, and the tribe of Manasseh, thirteen cities in Bashan.

63 To the sons of Merari *were given* by lot, according to their families, from the tribe of Reuben, the tribe of Gad and the tribe of Zebulun, twelve cities.

64 So the sons of Israel gave to the Levites the cities with their pasture lands.

65 They gave by lot from the tribe of the sons of Judah, the tribe of the sons of Simeon and the tribe of the sons of Benjamin, these cities which are mentioned by name.

66 ¶ Now some of the families of the sons of Kohath had cities of their territory from the tribe of Ephraim.

67 They gave to them the *following* cities of refuge: Shechem in the hill country of Ephraim with its pasture lands, Gezer also with its pasture lands,

68 Jokmeam with its pasture lands, Beth-horon with its pasture lands,

69 Aijalon with its pasture lands and Gath-rimmon with its pasture lands;

70 and from the half-tribe of Manasseh: Aner with its pasture lands and Bileam with its pasture lands, for the rest of the family of the sons of Kohath.

71 ¶ To the sons of Gershom *were given,* from the family of the half-tribe of Manasseh: Golan in Bashan with its pasture lands and Ashtaroth with its pasture lands;

72 and from the tribe of Issachar: Kedesh with its pasture lands, Daberath with its pasture lands

73 and Ramoth with its pasture lands, Anem with its pasture lands;

74 and from the tribe of Asher: Mashal with its pasture lands, Abdon with its pasture lands,

75 Hukok with its pasture lands and Rehob with its pasture lands;

76 and from the tribe of Naphtali: Kedesh in Galilee with its pasture lands, Hammon with its pasture lands and Kiriathaim with its pasture lands.

77 ¶ To the rest of *the Levites,* the sons of Merari, *were given,* from the tribe of Zebulun: Rimmono with its pasture lands, Tabor with its pasture lands;

78 and beyond the Jordan at Jericho, on the east side of the Jordan, *were given them,* from the tribe of Reuben: Bezer in the wilderness with its pasture lands, Jahzah with its pasture lands,

79 Kedemoth with its pasture lands and Mephaath with its pasture lands;

80 and from the tribe of Gad: Ramoth in Gile-

ad with its pasture lands, Mahanaim with its pasture lands,

81 Heshbon with its pasture lands and Jazer with its pasture lands.

Genealogy from Issachar

7 Now the sons of Issachar were four: Tola, Puah, Jashub and Shimron.

2 The sons of Tola were Uzzi, Rephaiah, Jeriel, Jahmai, Ibsam and Samuel, heads of their fathers' households. The sons of Tola were mighty men of valor in their generations; their number in the days of David was 22,600.

3 The son of Uzzi was Izrahiah. And the sons of Izrahiah were Michael, Obadiah, Joel, Isshiah; all five of them were chief men.

4 With them by their generations according to their fathers' households were 36,000 troops of the army for war, for they had many wives and sons.

5 Their relatives among all the families of Issachar were mighty men of valor, enrolled by genealogy, in all 87,000.

Descendants of Benjamin

6 ¶ The sons of Benjamin were three: Bela and Becher and Jediael.

7 The sons of Bela were five: Ezbon, Uzzi, Uzziel, Jerimoth and Iri. They were heads of fathers' households, mighty men of valor, and were 22,034 enrolled by genealogy.

8 The sons of Becher were Zemirah, Joash, Eliezer, Elioenai, Omri, Jeremoth, Abijah, Anathoth and Alemeth. All these were the sons of Becher.

9 They were enrolled by genealogy, according to their generations, heads of their fathers' households, 20,200 mighty men of valor.

10 The son of Jediael was Bilhan. And the sons of Bilhan were Jeush, Benjamin, Ehud, Chenaanah, Zethan, Tarshish and Ahishahar.

11 All these were sons of Jediael, according to the heads of their fathers' households, 17,200 mighty men of valor, who were ready to go out with the army to war.

12 Shuppim and Huppim were the sons of Ir; Hushim was the son of Aher.

Sons of Naphtali

13 ¶ The sons of Naphtali were Jahziel, Guni, Jezer, and Shallum, the sons of Bilhah.

Descendants of Manasseh

14 ¶ The sons of Manasseh were Asriel, whom his Aramean concubine bore; she bore Machir the father of Gilead.

15 Machir took a wife for Huppim and Shuppim, whose sister's name was Maacah. And the name of the second was Zelophehad, and Zelophehad had daughters.

16 Maacah the wife of Machir bore a son, and she named him Peresh; and the name of his brother was Sheresh, and his sons were Ulam and Rakem.

17 The son of Ulam was Bedan. These were the sons of Gilead the son of Machir, the son of Manasseh.

7:14 Joseph's Heirs

Joseph, Jacob's son, by rights deserved to have one of the "twelve tribes of Israel" named after him. Instead, Joseph passed that honor to his own sons Ephraim and Manasseh, whose offspring settled one of the largest tracts of land in Palestine and then competed with each other for prestige and influence. Their mention here is significant, for these tribes lived in the Northern Kingdom of Israel; wounds had healed, and the southern leaders in Jerusalem were now beginning to welcome back their estranged relatives.

18 His sister Hammolecheth bore Ishhod and Abiezer and Mahlah.

19 The sons of Shemida were Ahian and Shechem and Likhi and Aniam.

Descendants of Ephraim

20 ¶ The sons of Ephraim were Shuthelah and Bered his son, Tahath his son, Eleadah his son, Tahath his son,

21 Zabad his son, Shuthelah his son, and Ezer and Elead whom the men of Gath who were born in the land killed, because they came down to take their livestock.

22 Their father Ephraim mourned many days, and his relatives came to comfort him.

23 Then he went in to his wife, and she conceived and bore a son, and he named him Beriah, because misfortune had come upon his house.

24 His daughter was Sheerah, who built lower and upper Beth-horon, also Uzzen-sheerah.

25 Rephah was his son along with Resheph, Telah his son, Tahan his son,

26 Ladan his son, Ammihud his son, Elishama his son,

27 Non his son and Joshua his son.

28 ¶ Their possessions and settlements were Bethel with its towns, and to the east Naaran, and to the west Gezer with its towns, and Shechem with its towns as far as Ayyah with its towns,

29 and along the borders of the sons of Manasseh, Beth-shean with its towns, Taanach with its towns, Megiddo with its towns, Dor with its towns. In these lived the sons of Joseph the son of Israel.

Descendants of Asher

30 ¶ The sons of Asher were Imnah, Ishvah, Ishvi and Beriah, and Serah their sister.

31 The sons of Beriah *were* Heber and Malchiel, who was the father of Birzaith.

32 Heber became the father of Japhlet, Shomer and Hotham, and Shua their sister.

33 The sons of Japhlet *were* Pasach, Bimhal and Ashvath. These were the sons of Japhlet.

34 The sons of Shemer *were* Ahi and Rohgah, Jehubbah and Aram.

35 The sons of his brother Helem *were* Zophah, Imna, Shelesh and Amal.

36 The sons of Zophah *were* Suah, Harnepher, Shual, Beri and Imrah,

37 Bezer, Hod, Shamma, Shilshah, Ithran and Beera.

38 The sons of Jether *were* Jephunneh, Pispa and Ara.

39 The sons of Ulla *were* Arah, Hanniel and Rizia.

40 All these *were* the sons of Asher, heads of the fathers' houses, choice and mighty men of valor, heads of the princes. And the number of them enrolled by genealogy for service in war was 26,000 men.

Genealogy from Benjamin

8 And Benjamin became the father of Bela his firstborn, Ashbel the second, Aharah the third,

8:1 Dynasty Rejected

Saul, Israel's first king, came from the tribe of Benjamin. Normally a royal dynasty would have followed him, descending from that same tribe. After Saul's dismal performance, however, God turned instead to the tribe of Judah and selected David, who became one of the ancestors of Jesus the Messiah.

2 Nohah the fourth and Rapha the fifth.

3 Bela had sons: Addar, Gera, Abihud,

4 Abishua, Naaman, Ahoah,

5 Gera, Shephuphan and Huram.

6 These are the sons of Ehud: these are the heads of fathers' *households* of the inhabitants of Geba, and they carried them into exile to Manahath,

7 namely, Naaman, Ahijah and Gera—he carried them into exile; and he became the father of Uzza and Ahihud.

8 Shaharaim became the father of children in the country of Moab after he had sent away Hushim and Baara his wives.

9 By Hodesh his wife he became the father of Jobab, Zibia, Mesha, Malcam,

10 Jeuz, Sachia, Mirmah. These were his sons, heads of fathers' *households*.

11 By Hushim he became the father of Abitub and Elpaal.

12 The sons of Elpaal *were* Eber, Misham, and Shemed, who built Ono and Lod, with its towns;

13 and Beriah and Shema, who were heads of fathers' *households* of the inhabitants of Aijalon, who put to flight the inhabitants of Gath;

14 and Ahio, Shashak and Jeremoth.

15 Zebadiah, Arad, Eder,

16 Michael, Ishpah and Joha *were* the sons of Beriah.

17 Zebadiah, Meshullam, Hizki, Heber,

18 Ishmerai, Izliah and Jobab *were* the sons of Elpaal.

19 Jakim, Zichri, Zabdi,

20 Elienai, Zillethai, Eliel,

21 Adaiah, Beraiah and Shimrath *were* the sons of Shimei.

22 Ishpan, Eber, Eliel,

23 Abdon, Zichri, Hanan,

24 Hananiah, Elam, Anthothijah,

25 Iphdeiah and Penuel *were* the sons of Shashak.

26 Shamsherai, Shehariah, Athaliah,

27 Jaareshiah, Elijah and Zichri *were* the sons of Jeroham.

28 These were heads of the fathers' *households* according to their generations, chief men who lived in Jerusalem.

29 ¶ Now in Gibeon, *Jeiel,* the father of Gibeon lived, and his wife's name was Maacah;

30 and his firstborn son *was* Abdon, then Zur, Kish, Baal, Nadab,

31 Gedor, Ahio and Zecher.

32 Mikloth became the father of Shimeah. And they also lived with their relatives in Jerusalem opposite their *other* relatives.

Genealogy from King Saul

33 Ner became the father of Kish, and Kish became the father of Saul, and Saul became the father of Jonathan, Malchi-shua, Abinadab and Eshbaal.

34 The son of Jonathan *was* Merib-baal, and Merib-baal became the father of Micah.

35 The sons of Micah *were* Pithon, Melech, Tarea and Ahaz.

36 Ahaz became the father of Jehoaddah, and Jehoaddah became the father of Alemeth, Azmaveth and Zimri; and Zimri became the father of Moza.

37 Moza became the father of Binea; Raphah *was* his son, Eleasah his son, Azel his son.

38 Azel had six sons, and these *were* their names: Azrikam, Bocheru, Ishmael, Sheariah, Obadiah and Hanan. All these *were* the sons of Azel.

39 The sons of Eshek his brother *were* Ulam his firstborn, Jeush the second and Eliphelet the third.

40 The sons of Ulam were mighty men of valor, archers, and had many sons and grandsons, 150 *of them.* All these *were* of the sons of Benjamin.

People of Jerusalem

9 So all Israel was enrolled by genealogies; and behold, they are written in the Book of the Kings of Israel. And Judah was carried away into exile to Babylon for their unfaithfulness.

9:1 The Source of Genealogies

The author of 1 Chronicles acknowledges that he relied on older documents for his information. In 1 and 2 Chronicles (originally one book) approximately 14 sources are named. During the Israelites' exile in Babylon, historical records had been lost and family information forgotten (see Ezra 2:59). First Chronicles condenses the most important of the genealogical information. It was meant to help the Israelites reestablish their identity as God's people.

2 ¶ Now the first who lived in their possessions in their cities *were* Israel, the priests, the Levites and the temple servants.

9:2–34 After the Exile

While most of 1 Chronicles deals with the time of David, this short section (2–34) jumps ahead 500 years to the time when a small portion of Israel had returned from exile. (See the books of Ezra, Nehemiah, Haggai, and Zechariah for more information about these returned exiles.)

3 Some of the sons of Judah, of the sons of Benjamin and of the sons of Ephraim and Manasseh lived in Jerusalem:

4 Uthai the son of Ammihud, the son of Omri, the son of Imri, the son of Bani, from the sons of Perez the son of Judah.

5 From the Shilonites *were* Asaiah the firstborn and his sons.

6 From the sons of Zerah *were* Jeuel and their relatives, 690 *of them.*

7 From the sons of Benjamin *were* Sallu the son of Meshullam, the son of Hodaviah, the son of Hassenuah,

8 and Ibneiah the son of Jeroham, and Elah the son of Uzzi, the son of Michri, and Meshullam the son of Shephatiah, the son of Reuel, the son of Ibnijah;

9 and their relatives according to their generations, 956. All these *were* heads of fathers' *households* according to their fathers' houses.

10 ¶ From the priests *were* Jedaiah, Jehoiarib, Jachin,

11 and Azariah the son of Hilkiah, the son of Meshullam, the son of Zadok, the son of Mera-

ioth, the son of Ahitub, the chief officer of the house of God;

12 and Adaiah the son of Jeroham, the son of Pashhur, the son of Malchijah, and Maasai the son of Adiel, the son of Jahzerah, the son of Meshullam, the son of Meshillemith, the son of Immer;

13 and their relatives, heads of their fathers' households, 1,760 very able men for the work of the service of the house of God.

14 ¶ Of the Levites *were* Shemaiah the son of Hasshub, the son of Azrikam, the son of Hashabiah, of the sons of Merari;

15 and Bakbakkar, Heresh and Galal and Mattaniah the son of Mica, the son of Zichri, the son of Asaph,

16 and Obadiah the son of Shemaiah, the son of Galal, the son of Jeduthun, and Berechiah the son of Asa, the son of Elkanah, who lived in the villages of the Netophathites.

17 ¶ Now the gatekeepers *were* Shallum and Akkub and Talmon and Ahiman and their relatives (Shallum the chief

18 *being stationed* until now at the king's gate to the east). These *were* the gatekeepers for the camp of the sons of Levi.

19 Shallum the son of Kore, the son of Ebiasaph, the son of Korah, and his relatives of his father's house, the Korahites, *were* over the work of the service, keepers of the thresholds of the tent; and their fathers had been over the camp of the LORD, keepers of the entrance.

20 Phinehas the son of Eleazar was ruler over them previously, *and* the LORD was with him.

21 Zechariah the son of Meshelemiah was gatekeeper of the entrance of the tent of meeting.

22 All these who were chosen to be gatekeepers at the thresholds were 212. These were enrolled by genealogy in their villages, whom David and Samuel the seer appointed in their office of trust.

23 So they and their sons had charge of the gates of the house of the LORD, *even* the house of the tent, as guards.

24 The gatekeepers were on the four sides, to the east, west, north and south.

25 Their relatives in their villages were to come in every seven days from time to time *to be* with them;

26 for the four chief gatekeepers who *were* Levites, were in an office of trust, and were over the chambers and over the treasuries in the house of God.

27 They spent the night around the house of God, because the watch was committed to them; and they *were* in charge of opening *it* morning by morning.

28 ¶ Now some of them had charge of the utensils of service, for they counted them when they brought them in and when they took them out.

29 Some of them also were appointed over the furniture and over all the utensils of the sanctuary

and over the fine flour and the wine and the oil and the frankincense and the spices.

30 Some of the sons of the priests prepared the mixing of the spices.

31 Mattithiah, one of the Levites, who was the firstborn of Shallum the Korahite, had the responsibility over the things which were baked in pans.

32 Some of their relatives of the sons of the Kohathites *were* over the showbread to prepare it every sabbath.

33 ¶ Now these are the singers, heads of fathers' *households* of the Levites, *who lived* in the chambers *of the temple* free *from other service;* for they were engaged in their work day and night.

34 These were heads of fathers' *households* of the Levites according to their generations, chief men, who lived in Jerusalem.

Ancestry and Descendants of Saul

35 ¶ In Gibeon Jeiel the father of Gibeon lived, and his wife's name was Maacah,

36 and his firstborn son *was* Abdon, then Zur, Kish, Baal, Ner, Nadab,

37 Gedor, Ahio, Zechariah and Mikloth.

38 Mikloth became the father of Shimeam. And they also lived with their relatives in Jerusalem opposite their *other* relatives.

39 Ner became the father of Kish, and Kish became the father of Saul, and Saul became the father of Jonathan, Malchi-shua, Abinadab and Eshbaal.

40 The son of Jonathan *was* Merib-baal; and Merib-baal became the father of Micah.

41 The sons of Micah *were* Pithon, Melech, Tahrea *and Ahaz.*

42 Ahaz became the father of Jarah, and Jarah became the father of Alemeth, Azmaveth and Zimri; and Zimri became the father of Moza,

43 and Moza became the father of Binea and Rephaiah his son, Eleasah his son, Azel his son.

44 Azel had six sons whose names are these: Azrikam, Bocheru and Ishmael and Sheariah and Obadiah and Hanan. These were the sons of Azel.

Defeat and Death of Saul and His Sons

10 Now the Philistines fought against Israel; and the men of Israel fled before the Philistines and fell slain on Mount Gilboa.

2 The Philistines closely pursued Saul and his sons, and the Philistines struck down Jonathan, Abinadab and Malchi-shua, the sons of Saul.

3 The battle became heavy against Saul, and the archers overtook him; and he was wounded by the archers.

4 Then Saul said to his armor bearer, "Draw your sword and thrust me through with it, otherwise these uncircumcised will come and abuse me." But his armor bearer would not, for he was greatly afraid. Therefore Saul took his sword and fell on it.

5 When his armor bearer saw that Saul was dead, he likewise fell on his sword and died.

6 Thus Saul died with his three sons, and all *those* of his house died together.

7 ¶ When all the men of Israel who were in the valley saw that they had fled, and that Saul and his sons were dead, they forsook their cities and fled; and the Philistines came and lived in them.

8 ¶ It came about the next day, when the Philistines came to strip the slain, that they found Saul and his sons fallen on Mount Gilboa.

9 So they stripped him and took his head and his armor and sent *messengers* around the land of the Philistines to carry the good news to their idols and to the people.

10 They put his armor in the house of their gods and fastened his head in the house of Dagon.

Jabesh-gilead's Tribute to Saul

11 When all Jabesh-gilead heard all that the Philistines had done to Saul,

12 all the valiant men arose and took away the body of Saul and the bodies of his sons and brought them to Jabesh, and they buried their bones under the oak in Jabesh, and fasted seven days.

13 ¶ So Saul died for his trespass which he committed against the LORD, because of the word of the LORD which he did not keep; and also because he asked counsel of a medium, making inquiry *of it,*

10:13 Moral of the Story

First Chronicles covers much the same history as 1 Samuel, but with a distinctive approach. First Samuel gives more details about Saul's failures, while 1 Chronicles primarily concerns itself with drawing moral lessons from them. For example, 1 Samuel 28 tells the background to Saul's consulting a medium; 1 Chronicles merely alludes to it (most original readers would know the story well) and connects that act of disobedience to Saul's death.

14 and did not inquire of the LORD. Therefore He killed him and turned the kingdom to David the son of Jesse.

David Made King over All Israel

11 Then all Israel gathered to David at Hebron and said, "Behold, we are your bone and your flesh.

2 "In times past, even when Saul was king, you *were* the one who led out and brought in Israel; and the LORD your God said to you, 'You shall shepherd My people Israel, and you shall be prince over My people Israel.'"

3 So all the elders of Israel came to the king at Hebron, and David made a covenant with them in Hebron before the LORD; and they anointed David king over Israel, according to the word of the LORD through Samuel.

Jerusalem, Capital City

4 ¶ Then David and all Israel went to Jerusalem (that is, Jebus); and the Jebusites, the inhabitants of the land, *were* there.

5 The inhabitants of Jebus said to David, "You shall not enter here." Nevertheless David captured the stronghold of Zion (that is, the city of David).

6 Now David had said, "Whoever strikes down a Jebusite first shall be chief and commander." Joab the son of Zeruiah went up first, so he became chief.

7 Then David dwelt in the stronghold; therefore it was called the city of David.

8 He built the city all around, from the *a*Millo even to the surrounding area; and Joab repaired the rest of the city.

9 David became greater and greater, for the LORD of hosts *was* with him.

a I.e. citadel

David's Mighty Men

10 ¶ Now these are the heads of the mighty men whom David had, who gave him strong support in his kingdom, together with all Israel, to make him king, according to the word of the LORD concerning Israel.

11 These *constitute* the list of the mighty men whom David had: Jashobeam, the son of a Hachmonite, the chief of the thirty; he lifted up his spear against three hundred whom he killed at one time.

12 ¶ After him was Eleazar the son of Dodo, the Ahohite, who *was* one of the three mighty men.

13 He was with David at Pasdammim when the Philistines were gathered together there to battle, and there was a plot of ground full of barley; and the people fled before the Philistines.

14 They took their stand in the midst of the plot and defended it, and struck down the Philistines; and the LORD saved them by a great victory.

15 ¶ Now three of the thirty chief men went down to the rock to David, into the cave of Adullam, while the army of the Philistines was camping in the valley of Rephaim.

JOAB, ABSHAI AND ASAHEL *Bloody Brothers*

WAR IS ALWAYS BRUTAL, AND hand-to-hand combat especially so. Allow one instant of pity as you look into your enemy's eyes, and he may stick a knife in your gut. A good warrior must be ruthless, and by that criterion Joab, Abshai and Asahel excelled. They lived violent lives, and at least two of the three died violent deaths.

Relatives of David, the brothers joined up with the future king while he was an outlaw hiding from King Saul. In a famous incident from those days, Abshai and David crept into the enemy camp at night and caught Saul fast asleep. Abshai wanted to kill Saul then and there, but David stopped him. That incident set a pattern: Several times Abshai impulsively sought to slaughter someone, only to be restrained by David.

The three brothers held to a strict code of revenge. When Asahel died in battle, the remaining brothers plotted revenge. The opportunity came some time later, when Saul's chief of the army called a truce to talk peace. Joab pretended to greet Abner and then, in an unguarded moment, stabbed him in the stomach.

David disapproved of the brothers' violent tactics, but he needed such strong and loyal soldiers. Joab proved his mettle by leading David's armies in a rout of powerful enemies. From that point on, Joab's brilliant soldiering became indispensable. David even trusted Joab with his sins: The two collaborated to murder Bathsheba's husband after David's adulterous affair. Significantly, David repented but Joab showed no interest in God or morality. He cared only about winning at war.

The bloody brothers had a fierce loyalty to David, and yet his inability to control them cost him dearly. When David's son Absalom led a rebellion, Joab and Abshai crushed the revolt. Joab caught the rebel son and dispatched him in cold blood, against David's explicit orders to let Absalom live.

Later, when David turned over the army to another general (perhaps because of the disobeyed order), Joab tricked and murdered his new rival. David never seemed capable of controlling Joab.

There is nothing pretty about these brothers and their careers in war. And as their commander-in-chief, David was inevitably drawn into their way of life. That may explain why God said to David, "You shall not build a house for My name because you are a man of war and have shed blood" (1 Chronicles 28:3).

Life Questions: Have you ever felt yourself being drawn in to another person's way of life, even when you disapprove? What can you do to escape?

16 David was then in the stronghold, while the garrison of the Philistines *was* then in Bethlehem.

17 David had a craving and said, "Oh that someone would give me water to drink from the well of Bethlehem, which is by the gate!"

18 So the three broke through the camp of the Philistines and drew water from the well of Bethlehem which *was* by the gate, and took *it* and brought *it* to David; nevertheless David would not drink it, but poured it out to the LORD;

19 and he said, "Be it far from me before my God that I should do this. Shall I drink the blood of these men *who went* at the risk of their lives? For at the risk of their lives they brought it." Therefore he would not drink it. These things the three mighty men did.

20 ¶ As for Abshai the brother of Joab, he was chief of the thirty, and he swung his spear against three hundred and killed them; and he had a name as well as the thirty.

21 Of the three in the second *rank* he was the most honored and became their commander; however, he did not attain to the *first* three.

22 ¶ Benaiah the son of Jehoiada, the son of a valiant man of Kabzeel, mighty in deeds, struck down the two *sons of* Ariel of Moab. He also went down and killed a lion inside a pit on a snowy day.

23 He killed an Egyptian, a man of *great* stature five cubits tall. Now in the Egyptian's hand *was* a spear like a weaver's beam, but he went down to him with a club and snatched the spear from the Egyptian's hand and killed him with his own spear.

24 These *things* Benaiah the son of Jehoiada did, and had a name as well as the three mighty men.

25 Behold, he was honored among the thirty, but he did not attain to the three; and David appointed him over his guard.

26 ¶ Now the mighty men of the armies *were* Asahel the brother of Joab, Elhanan the son of Dodo of Bethlehem,

27 Shammoth the Harorite, Helez the Pelonite,

28 Ira the son of Ikkesh the Tekoite, Abiezer the Anathothite,

29 Sibbecai the Hushathite, Ilai the Ahohite,

30 Maharai the Netophathite, Heled the son of Baanah the Netophathite,

31 Ithai the son of Ribai of Gibeah of the sons of Benjamin, Benaiah the Pirathonite,

32 Hurai of the brooks of Gaash, Abiel the Arbathite,

33 Azmaveth the Baharumite, Eliahba the Shaalbonite,

34 the sons of Hashem the Gizonite, Jonathan the son of Shagee the Hararite,

35 Ahiam the son of Sacar the Hararite, Eliphal the son of Ur,

36 Hepher the Mecherathite, Ahijah the Pelonite,

37 Hezro the Carmelite, Naarai the son of Ezbai,

38 Joel the brother of Nathan, Mibhar the son of Hagri,

39 Zelek the Ammonite, Naharai the Berothite, the armor bearer of Joab the son of Zeruiah,

40 Ira the Ithrite, Gareb the Ithrite,

41 Uriah the Hittite, Zabad the son of Ahlai,

42 Adina the son of Shiza the Reubenite, a chief of the Reubenites, and thirty with him,

43 Hanan the son of Maacah and Joshaphat the Mithnite,

44 Uzzia the Ashterathite, Shama and Jeiel the sons of Hotham the Aroerite,

45 Jediael the son of Shimri and Joha his brother, the Tizite,

46 Eliel the Mahavite and Jeribai and Joshaviah, the sons of Elnaam, and Ithmah the Moabite,

47 Eliel and Obed and Jaasiel the Mezobaite.

David's Supporters in Ziklag

12 Now these are the ones who came to David at Ziklag, while he was still restricted because of Saul the son of Kish; and they were among the mighty men who helped *him* in war.

2 They were equipped with bows, using both the right hand and the left *to sling* stones and *to shoot* arrows from the bow; *they were* Saul's kinsmen from Benjamin.

12:2 Accent on Unity

Chronicles bends over backwards to emphasize the need for unity of "all Israel," an important theme for a nation riven by tribalism and civil war. Here the author points out that even Saul's own kinsmen joined David's revolt. Later in the chapter (verses 23–38) he takes pains to mention compatriots from every tribe of Israel.

3 The chief was Ahiezer, then Joash, the sons of Shemaah the Gibeathite; and Jeziel and Pelet, the sons of Azmaveth, and Beracah and Jehu the Anathothite,

4 and Ishmaiah the Gibeonite, a mighty man among the thirty, and over the thirty. Then Jeremiah, Jahaziel, Johanan, Jozabad the Gederathite,

5 Eluzai, Jerimoth, Bealiah, Shemariah, Shephatiah the Haruphite,

6 Elkanah, Isshiah, Azarel, Joezer, Jashobeam, the Korahites,

7 and Joelah and Zebadiah, the sons of Jeroham of Gedor.

8 ¶ From the Gadites there came over to David in the stronghold in the wilderness, mighty men of valor, men trained for war, who could handle shield and spear, and whose faces were like the faces of lions, and *they were* as swift as the gazelles on the mountains.

9 Ezer *was* the first, Obadiah the second, Eliab the third,

10 Mishmannah the fourth, Jeremiah the fifth,

11 Attai the sixth, Eliel the seventh,

12 Johanan the eighth, Elzabad the ninth,

13 Jeremiah the tenth, Machbannai the eleventh.

14 These of the sons of Gad were captains of the army; he who was least was equal to a hundred and the greatest to a thousand.

15 These are the ones who crossed the Jordan in the first month when it was overflowing all its banks and they put to flight all those in the valleys, both to the east and to the west.

16 ¶ Then some of the sons of Benjamin and Judah came to the stronghold to David.

17 David went out to meet them, and said to them, "If you come peacefully to me to help me, my heart shall be united with you; but if to betray me to my adversaries, since there is no wrong in my hands, may the God of our fathers look on *it* and decide."

18 Then the Spirit came upon Amasai, who was the chief of the thirty, *and he said,*

"*We* are yours, O David,
And with you, O son of Jesse!
Peace, peace to you,
And peace to him who helps you;
Indeed, your God helps you!"

Then David received them and made them captains of the band.

19 ¶ From Manasseh also some defected to David when he was about to go to battle with the Philistines against Saul. But they did not help them, for the lords of the Philistines after consultation sent him away, saying, "At *the cost of* our heads he may defect to his master Saul."

20 As he went to Ziklag there defected to him from Manasseh: Adnah, Jozabad, Jediael, Michael, Jozabad, Elihu and Zillethai, captains of thousands who belonged to Manasseh.

21 They helped David against the band of raiders, for they were all mighty men of valor, and were captains in the army.

22 For day by day *men* came to David to help him, until there was a great army like the army of God.

Supporters Gathered at Hebron

23 ¶ Now these are the numbers of the divisions equipped for war, who came to David at Hebron, to turn the kingdom of Saul to him, according to the word of the LORD.

24 The sons of Judah who bore shield and spear *were* 6,800, equipped for war.

25 Of the sons of Simeon, mighty men of valor for war, 7,100.

26 Of the sons of Levi 4,600.

27 Now Jehoiada was the leader of *the house of* Aaron, and with him were 3,700,

28 also Zadok, a young man mighty of valor, and of his father's house twenty-two captains.

29 Of the sons of Benjamin, Saul's kinsmen, 3,000; for until now the greatest part of them had kept their allegiance to the house of Saul.

30 Of the sons of Ephraim 20,800, mighty men of valor, famous men in their fathers' households.

31 Of the half-tribe of Manasseh 18,000, who were designated by name to come and make David king.

32 Of the sons of Issachar, men who understood the times, with knowledge of what Israel should do, their chiefs *were* two hundred; and all their kinsmen *were* at their command.

33 Of Zebulun, there were 50,000 who went out in the army, who could draw up in battle formation with all kinds of weapons of war and helped *David* with an undivided heart.

34 Of Naphtali *there were* 1,000 captains, and with them 37,000 with shield and spear.

35 Of the Danites who could draw up in battle formation, *there were* 28,600.

36 Of Asher *there were* 40,000 who went out in the army to draw up in battle formation.

37 From the other side of the Jordan, of the Reubenites and the Gadites and of the half-tribe of Manasseh, *there were* 120,000 with all *kinds* of weapons of war for the battle.

38 ¶ All these, being men of war who could draw up in battle formation, came to Hebron with a perfect heart to make David king over all Israel; and all the rest also of Israel were of one mind to make David king.

39 They were there with David three days, eating and drinking, for their kinsmen had prepared for them.

40 Moreover those who were near to them, *even* as far as Issachar and Zebulun and Naphtali, brought food on donkeys, camels, mules and on oxen, great quantities of flour cakes, fig cakes and bunches of raisins, wine, oil, oxen and sheep. There was joy indeed in Israel.

Peril in Transporting the Ark

13 Then David consulted with the captains of the thousands and the hundreds, even with every leader.

2 David said to all the assembly of Israel, "If it seems good to you, and if it is from the LORD our God, let us send everywhere to our kinsmen who remain in all the land of Israel, also to the priests and Levites who are with them in their cities with pasture lands, that they may meet with us;

3 and let us bring back the ark of our God to us, for we did not seek it in the days of Saul."

4 Then all the assembly said that they would do so, for the thing was right in the eyes of all the people.

5 ¶ So David assembled all Israel together, from the Shihor of Egypt even to the entrance of Hamath, to bring the ark of God from Kiriath-jearim.

6 David and all Israel went up to Baalah, *that is*, to Kiriath-jearim, which belongs to Judah, to bring up from there the ark of God, the LORD who is enthroned *above* the cherubim, where His name is called.

7 They carried the ark of God on a new cart from the house of Abinadab, and Uzza and Ahio drove the cart.

8 David and all Israel were celebrating before God with all *their* might, even with songs and with lyres, harps, tambourines, cymbals and with trumpets.

9 ¶ When they came to the threshing floor of Chidon, Uzza put out his hand to hold the ark, because the oxen nearly upset *it*.

13:9 Why Did Uzza Die?

People who read of Uzza's death in 2 Samuel 6:6–7 have often puzzled over why he died for trying to keep God's ark from tipping over. In 1 Chronicles the reason is clearer. David explained (15:13) that the Lord had been angry at them for moving the ark in a way disobedient to God's law.

Numbers 4:14–15 and Exodus 37:5 specify that Levites were to carry the ark with poles—and never touch it, on pain of death. Uzza and his brother, non-Levites, were carrying it on an oxcart—the same vehicle the Philistines had used (1 Samuel 6:7). When the oxen stumbled and Uzza stepped in to catch the ark, that was the final straw. Uzza's death resulted from prolonged (though possibly well-intentioned) disobedience to God's direction. God had told them how to honor the ark, a sign of his presence. Their sloppiness revealed a lack of concern for God's honor.

10 The anger of the LORD burned against Uzza, so He struck him down because he put out his hand to the ark; and he died there before God.

11 Then David became angry because of the LORD'S outburst against Uzza; and he called that place ªPerez-uzza to this day.

12 David was afraid of God that day, saying, "How can I bring the ark of God *home* to me?"

13 So David did not take the ark with him to the city of David, but took it aside to the house of Obed-edom the Gittite.

14 Thus the ark of God remained with the family of Obed-edom in his house three months; and the LORD blessed the family of Obed-edom with all that he had.

David's Family Enlarged

14 Now Hiram king of Tyre sent messengers to David with cedar trees, masons and carpenters, to build a house for him.

2 And David realized that the LORD had established him as king over Israel, *and* that his kingdom was highly exalted, for the sake of His people Israel.

3 ¶ Then David took more wives at Jerusalem, and David became the father of more sons and daughters.

4 These are the names of the children born *to him* in Jerusalem: Shammua, Shobab, Nathan, Solomon,

5 Ibhar, Elishua, Elpelet,

6 Nogah, Nepheg, Japhia,

7 Elishama, Beeliada and Eliphelet.

Philistines Defeated

8 ¶ When the Philistines heard that David had been anointed king over all Israel, all the Philistines went up in search of David; and David heard of it and went out against them.

9 Now the Philistines had come and made a raid in the valley of Rephaim.

10 David inquired of God, saying, "Shall I go up against the Philistines? And will You give them into my hand?" Then the LORD said to him, "Go up, for I will give them into your hand."

11 So they came up to Baal-perazim, and David defeated them there; and David said, "God has broken through my enemies by my hand, like the breakthrough of waters." Therefore they named that place ᵇBaal-perazim.

12 They abandoned their gods there; so David gave the order and they were burned with fire.

13 ¶ The Philistines made yet another raid in the valley.

14 David inquired again of God, and God said to him, "You shall not go up after them; circle around behind them and come at them in front of the balsam trees.

15 "It shall be when you hear the sound of marching in the tops of the balsam trees, then you shall go out to battle, for God will have gone out before you to strike the army of the Philistines."

16 David did just as God had commanded him, and they struck down the army of the Philistines from Gibeon even as far as Gezer.

17 Then the fame of David went out into all the lands; and the LORD brought the fear of him on all the nations.

Plans to Move the Ark to Jerusalem

15 Now *David* built houses for himself in the city of David; and he prepared a place for the ark of God and pitched a tent for it.

2 Then David said, "No one is to carry the ark of God but the Levites; for the LORD chose them

ª I.e. the breakthrough of Uzza   ᵇ I.e. the master of breakthrough to carry the ark of God and to minister to Him forever."

3 And David assembled all Israel at Jerusalem to bring up the ark of the LORD to its place which he had prepared for it.

15:3 Red-letter Day

Much of Chronicles summarizes and interprets history that is covered more fully in the books of Samuel. But this chapter contains mostly new material, reflecting a central concern of the author. David's bringing the ark to Jerusalem had been a landmark event, signifying the renewed presence of God in the nation (see also Psalm 132). The Chronicler yearned for a similar spirit of renewal among the people of his own time.

4 David gathered together the sons of Aaron and the Levites:

5 of the sons of Kohath, Uriel the chief, and 120 of his relatives;

6 of the sons of Merari, Asaiah the chief, and 220 of his relatives;

7 of the sons of Gershom, Joel the chief, and 130 of his relatives;

8 of the sons of Elizaphan, Shemaiah the chief, and 200 of his relatives;

9 of the sons of Hebron, Eliel the chief, and 80 of his relatives;

10 of the sons of Uzziel, Amminadab the chief, and 112 of his relatives.

11 ¶ Then David called for Zadok and Abiathar the priests, and for the Levites, for Uriel, Asaiah, Joel, Shemaiah, Eliel and Amminadab,

12 and said to them, "You are the heads of the fathers' *households* of the Levites; consecrate yourselves both you and your relatives, that you may bring up the ark of the LORD God of Israel to *the place* that I have prepared for it.

13 "Because you did not *carry it* at the first, the LORD our God made an outburst on us, for we did not seek Him according to the ordinance."

14 So the priests and the Levites consecrated themselves to bring up the ark of the LORD God of Israel.

15 The sons of the Levites carried the ark of God on their shoulders with the poles thereon, as Moses had commanded according to the word of the LORD.

16 ¶ Then David spoke to the chiefs of the Levites to appoint their relatives the singers, with instruments of music, harps, lyres, loud-sounding cymbals, to raise sounds of joy.

17 So the Levites appointed Heman the son of Joel, and from his relatives, Asaph the son of Berechiah; and from the sons of Merari their relatives, Ethan the son of Kushaiah,

18 and with them their relatives of the second rank, Zechariah, Ben, Jaaziel, Shemiramoth, Jehiel, Unni, Eliab, Benaiah, Maaseiah, Mattithiah, Eliphelehu, Mikneiah, Obed-edom and Jeiel, the gatekeepers.

19 So the singers, Heman, Asaph and Ethan *were appointed* to sound aloud cymbals of bronze;

20 and Zechariah, Aziel, Shemiramoth, Jehiel, Unni, Eliab, Maaseiah and Benaiah, with harps *tuned* to alamoth;

21 and Mattithiah, Eliphelehu, Mikneiah, Obed-edom, Jeiel and Azaziah, to lead with lyres tuned to the sheminith.

22 Chenaniah, chief of the Levites, was *in charge of* the singing; he gave instruction in singing because he was skillful.

23 Berechiah and Elkanah were gatekeepers for the ark.

24 Shebaniah, Joshaphat, Nethanel, Amasai, Zechariah, Benaiah and Eliezer, the priests, blew the trumpets before the ark of God. Obed-edom and Jehiah also *were* gatekeepers for the ark.

25 ¶ So *it was* David, with the elders of Israel and the captains over thousands, who went to bring up the ark of the covenant of the LORD from the house of Obed-edom with joy.

26 Because God was helping the Levites who were carrying the ark of the covenant of the LORD, they sacrificed seven bulls and seven rams.

27 Now David was clothed with a robe of fine linen with all the Levites who were carrying the ark, and the singers and Chenaniah the leader of the singing *with* the singers. David also wore an ephod of linen.

28 Thus all Israel brought up the ark of the covenant of the LORD with shouting, and with sound of the horn, with trumpets, with loud-sounding cymbals, with harps and lyres.

29 ¶ It happened when the ark of the covenant of the LORD came to the city of David, that Michal the daughter of Saul looked out of the window and saw King David leaping and celebrating; and she despised him in her heart.

A Tent for the Ark

16 And they brought in the ark of God and placed it inside the tent which David had pitched for it, and they offered burnt offerings and peace offerings before God.

2 When David had finished offering the burnt offering and the peace offerings, he blessed the people in the name of the LORD.

3 He distributed to everyone of Israel, both man and woman, to everyone a loaf of bread and a portion *of meat* and a raisin cake.

4 ¶ He appointed some of the Levites *as* ministers before the ark of the LORD, even to celebrate and to thank and praise the LORD God of Israel:

5 Asaph the chief, and second to him Zechariah, *then* Jeiel, Shemiramoth, Jehiel, Mattithiah, Eliab, Benaiah, Obed-edom and Jeiel, with musi-

cal instruments, harps, lyres; also Asaph *played* loud-sounding cymbals,

6 and Benaiah and Jahaziel the priests *blew* trumpets continually before the ark of the covenant of God.

7 ¶ Then on that day David first assigned Asaph and his relatives to give thanks to the LORD.

Psalm of Thanksgiving

8 Oh give thanks to the LORD, call upon
    His name;
Make known His deeds among the
    peoples.
9 Sing to Him, sing praises to Him;
    ᵃSpeak of all His wonders.
10 Glory in His holy name;
Let the heart of those who seek the LORD
    be glad.
11 Seek the LORD and His strength;
Seek His face continually.
12 Remember His wonderful deeds which
    He has done,
His marvels and the judgments from His
    mouth,
13 O seed of Israel His servant,
Sons of Jacob, His chosen ones!
14 He is the LORD our God;
His judgments are in all the earth.
15 Remember His covenant forever,
The word which He commanded to a
    thousand generations,
16 *The covenant* which He made with
    Abraham,
And His oath to Isaac.
17 He also confirmed it to Jacob for a
    statute,
To Israel as an everlasting covenant,
18 Saying, "To you I will give the land of
    Canaan,
As the portion of your inheritance."
19 When they were only a few in number,
Very few, and strangers in it,
20 And they wandered about from nation to
    nation,
And from *one* kingdom to another
    people,
21 He permitted no man to oppress them,
And He reproved kings for their sakes,
    saying,
22 "Do not touch My anointed ones,
And do My prophets no harm."
23 Sing to the LORD, all the earth;
Proclaim good tidings of His salvation
    from day to day.
24 Tell of His glory among the nations,
His wonderful deeds among all the
    peoples.
25 For great is the LORD, and greatly to be
    praised;
He also is to be feared above all gods.

26 For all the gods of the peoples are idols,
But the LORD made the heavens.
27 Splendor and majesty are before Him,
Strength and joy are in His place.
28 Ascribe to the LORD, O families of the
    peoples,
Ascribe to the LORD glory and strength.
29 Ascribe to the LORD the glory due His
    name;
Bring an offering, and come before Him;
Worship the LORD in holy array.
30 Tremble before Him, all the earth;
Indeed, the world is firmly established, it
    will not be moved.
31 Let the heavens be glad, and let the earth
    rejoice;
And let them say among the nations,
    "The LORD reigns."
32 Let the sea roar, and all it contains;
Let the field exult, and all that is in it.
33 Then the trees of the forest will sing for
    joy before the LORD;
For He is coming to judge the earth.
34 O give thanks to the LORD, for *He is*
    good;
For His lovingkindness is everlasting.
35 Then say, "Save us, O God of our
    salvation,
And gather us and deliver us from the
    nations,
To give thanks to Your holy name,
And glory in Your praise."
36 Blessed be the LORD, the God of Israel,
From everlasting even to everlasting.
Then all the people said, "Amen," and praised the
LORD.

Worship before the Ark

37 ¶ So he left Asaph and his relatives there before the ark of the covenant of the LORD to minister before the ark continually, as every day's work required;

38 and Obed-edom with his 68 relatives; Obed-edom, also the son of Jeduthun, and Hosah as gatekeepers.

39 *He left* Zadok the priest and his relatives the priests before the tabernacle of the LORD in the high place which *was* at Gibeon,

40 to offer burnt offerings to the LORD on the altar of burnt offering continually morning and evening, even according to all that is written in the law of the LORD, which He commanded Israel.

41 With them *were* Heman and Jeduthun, and the rest who were chosen, who were designated by name, to give thanks to the LORD, because His lovingkindness is everlasting.

42 And with them *were* Heman and Jeduthun *with* trumpets and cymbals for those who should sound aloud, and *with* instruments *for* the songs of God, and the sons of Jeduthun for the gate.

ᵃ Or *Meditate on*

43 ¶ Then all the people departed each to his house, and David returned to bless his household.

God's Covenant with David

17 And it came about, when David dwelt in his house, that David said to Nathan the prophet, "Behold, I am dwelling in a house of cedar, but the ark of the covenant of the LORD is under curtains."

2 Then Nathan said to David, "Do all that is in your heart, for God is with you."

3 ¶ It came about the same night that the word of God came to Nathan, saying,

4 "Go and tell David My servant, 'Thus says the LORD, "You shall not build a house for Me to dwell in;

5 for I have not dwelt in a house since the day that I brought up Israel to this day, but I have gone from tent to tent and from *one* dwelling place *to another*.

6 "In all places where I have walked with all Israel, have I spoken a word with any of the judges of Israel, whom I commanded to shepherd My people, saying, 'Why have you not built for Me a house of cedar?' " '

7 "Now, therefore, thus shall you say to My servant David, 'Thus says the LORD of hosts, "I took you from the pasture, from following the sheep, to be leader over My people Israel.

16:39 Two Tabernacles

For a number of years, Israel had two tabernacles. David had constructed a new tent for the ark of the covenant when it came to Jerusalem. Yet the old tent, dating from Moses' time, still stood at Gibeon, five miles away. Sacrifices were offered at both locations. When the temple was built under David's son Solomon, worship was centralized at Jerusalem.

Hope in a Time of Sorrow
A people starting over need to know God's promises

FIRST CHRONICLES WAS WRITTEN FOR Israelites living centuries after David. In those years Israel had gone through tremendous sorrow. None of the kings who followed David had matched him. Israel had deteriorated until God let Babylon capture and destroy Jerusalem, carrying its population into exile.

> "Who am I, O LORD God, and what is my house that You have brought me this far?" 17:16

After half a century as captives, a small proportion of the Israelites returned to their former home. They had lost, in those beaten-down years, their own sense of identity. They were no longer self-governing. They had no king to follow in David's footsteps. Their relatives were scattered all over the Middle East. Chronicles was written to help them get in touch with what Israel had once been and could become again.

After devoting nine chapters to genealogies, 1 Chronicles tells the life of David. In keeping with its goal of encouragement, Chronicles leaves out stories of David's personal sin and failure. Nor does it tell of David's life before he became king. Instead it concentrates on the accomplishments David left behind for future generations.

The Importance of Worship

David emphasized worship as the foundation of Israel. As soon as he conquered Jerusalem, he brought the ark of the covenant there. He made preparations to build the temple and organized the priests and Levites to serve there. He established large corps of musicians to praise God. In response, God promised that a line of leaders would descend from him (17:10–14).

David's days were the high point of Israelite history: prosperous, secure, and, above all, devoted to God. How could the returned exiles recapture that grandeur? What resources could they use to begin again? First Chronicles emphasizes a legacy they still possessed. They had Jerusalem, and they had a new temple built on the site of the old one. They had the priests and Levites, so essential to proper worship. In short, they had the resources necessary to rise again, to be God's people in God's land.

Most important, they had God. They could find strength in worshiping him, as David always had. God had made them great before; he could make them great again, and provide a new leader in David's line. A sorrowful people could start over on the old foundations—foundations that depended on an unchanging God and his unchanging choice of them.

Life Questions: If you were to suffer great personal and material loss, as the Israelites did, what would you cling to?

8 "I have been with you wherever you have gone, and have cut off all your enemies from before you; and I will make you a name like the name of the great ones who are in the earth.

9 "I will appoint a place for My people Israel, and will plant them, so that they may dwell in their own place and not be moved again; and the wicked will not waste them anymore as formerly,

10 even from the day that I commanded judges *to be* over My people Israel. And I will subdue all your enemies.

¶ Moreover, I tell you that the LORD will build a house for you.

11 "When your days are fulfilled that you must go *to be* with your fathers, that I will set up *one of* your descendants after you, who will be of your sons; and I will establish his kingdom.

12 "He shall build for Me a house, and I will establish his throne forever.

13 "I will be his father and he shall be My son; and I will not take My lovingkindness away from him, as I took it from him who was before you.

14 "But I will settle him in My house and in My kingdom forever, and his throne shall be established forever." ' "

15 According to all these words and according to all this vision, so Nathan spoke to David.

David's Prayer in Response

16 ¶ Then David the king went in and sat before the LORD and said, "Who am I, O LORD God, and what is my house that You have brought me this far?

17:16 Rare Trait

King David possessed in abundance that rarest of qualities in a powerful ruler: humility. Ever mindful of his modest background, he credited God's grace, not his own merit, for his success. David could have taken offense at Nathan's message; after all, God was rejecting his offer to build a temple. Instead, David accepted the news with meekness and thanksgiving.

---

17 "This was a small thing in Your eyes, O God; but You have spoken of Your servant's house for a great while to come, and have regarded me according to the standard of a man of high degree, O LORD God.

18 "What more can David still *say* to You concerning the honor *bestowed* on Your servant? For You know Your servant.

19 "O LORD, for Your servant's sake, and according to Your own heart, You have wrought all this greatness, to make known all these great things.

20 "O LORD, there is none like You, nor is there any God besides You, according to all that we have heard with our ears.

21 "And what one nation in the earth is like Your people Israel, whom God went to redeem for Himself *as* a people, to make You a name by great and terrible things, in driving out nations from before Your people, whom You redeemed out of Egypt?

22 "For Your people Israel You made Your own people forever, and You, O LORD, became their God.

23 ¶ "Now, O LORD, let the word that You have spoken concerning Your servant and concerning his house be established forever, and do as You have spoken.

24 "Let Your name be established and magnified forever, saying, 'The LORD of hosts is the God of Israel, *even* a God to Israel; and the house of David Your servant is established before You.'

25 "For You, O my God, have revealed to Your servant that You will build for him a house; therefore Your servant has found *courage* to pray before You.

26 "Now, O LORD, You are God, and have promised this good thing to Your servant.

27 "And now it has pleased You to bless the house of Your servant, that it may continue forever before You; for You, O LORD, have blessed, and it is blessed forever."

David's Kingdom Strengthened

18 Now after this it came about that David defeated the Philistines and subdued them and took Gath and its towns from the hand of the Philistines.

2 He defeated Moab, and the Moabites became servants to David, bringing tribute.

3 ¶ David also defeated Hadadezer king of Zobah *as far as* Hamath, as he went to establish his rule to the Euphrates River.

4 David took from him 1,000 chariots and 7,000 horsemen and 20,000 foot soldiers, and David hamstrung all the chariot horses, but reserved *enough* of them for 100 chariots.

5 ¶ When the Arameans of Damascus came to help Hadadezer king of Zobah, David killed 22,000 men of the Arameans.

6 Then David put *garrisons* among the Arameans of Damascus; and the Arameans became servants to David, bringing tribute. And the LORD helped David wherever he went.

7 David took the shields of gold which were carried by the servants of Hadadezer and brought them to Jerusalem.

8 Also from Tibhath and from Cun, cities of Hadadezer, David took a very large amount of bronze, with which Solomon made the bronze sea and the pillars and the bronze utensils.

9 ¶ Now when Tou king of Hamath heard that David had defeated all the army of Hadadezer king of Zobah,

10 he sent Hadoram his son to King David to greet him and to bless him, because he had fought

against Hadadezer and had defeated him; for Hadadezer had been at war with Tou. And *Hadoram brought* all kinds of articles of gold and silver and bronze.

11 King David also dedicated these to the LORD with the silver and the gold which he had carried away from all the nations: from Edom, Moab, the sons of Ammon, the Philistines, and from Amalek.

12 ¶ Moreover Abishai the son of Zeruiah defeated 18,000 Edomites in the Valley of Salt.

13 Then he put garrisons in Edom, and all the Edomites became servants to David. And the LORD helped David wherever he went.

14 ¶ So David reigned over all Israel; and he administered justice and righteousness for all his people.

15 Joab the son of Zeruiah *was* over the army, and Jehoshaphat the son of Ahilud *was* recorder;

16 and Zadok the son of Ahitub and Abimelech the son of Abiathar *were* priests, and Shavsha *was* secretary;

17 and Benaiah the son of Jehoiada *was* over the Cherethites and the Pelethites, and the sons of David *were* chiefs at the king's side.

David's Messengers Abused

19 Now it came about after this, that Nahash the king of the sons of Ammon died, and his son became king in his place.

2 Then David said, "I will show kindness to Hanun the son of Nahash, because his father showed kindness to me." So David sent messengers to console him concerning his father. And David's servants came into the land of the sons of Ammon to Hanun to console him.

3 But the princes of the sons of Ammon said to Hanun, "Do you think that David is honoring your father, in that he has sent comforters to you? Have not his servants come to you to search and to overthrow and to spy out the land?"

4 So Hanun took David's servants and shaved them and cut off their garments in the middle as far as their hips, and sent them away.

19:4 Comedy of Errors

Wars start for the oddest reasons. One modern war in Central America erupted after a poorly refereed soccer match. In this instance the king of Ammon misjudged the motives of a funeral delegation, and David felt obliged to respond to an insult that today seems more humorous than humiliating. The resulting war crushed one of Israel's peskiest enemies, the Ammonites, offspring of the incestuous relations between Lot and his daughter (Genesis 19).

5 Then *certain persons* went and told David about the men. And he sent to meet them, for the men were greatly humiliated. And the king said, "Stay at Jericho until your beards grow, and *then* return."

6 ¶ When the sons of Ammon saw that they had made themselves odious to David, Hanun and the sons of Ammon sent 1,000 talents of silver to hire for themselves chariots and horsemen from Mesopotamia, from Aram-maacah and from Zobah.

7 So they hired for themselves 32,000 chariots, and the king of Maacah and his people, who came and camped before Medeba. And the sons of Ammon gathered together from their cities and came to battle.

8 When David heard *of it*, he sent Joab and all the army, the mighty men.

9 The sons of Ammon came out and drew up in battle array at the entrance of the city, and the kings who had come were by themselves in the field.

Ammon and Aram Defeated

10 ¶ Now when Joab saw that the battle was set against him in front and in the rear, he selected from all the choice men of Israel and they arrayed themselves against the Arameans.

11 But the remainder of the people he placed in the hand of Abshai his brother; and they arrayed themselves against the sons of Ammon.

12 He said, "If the Arameans are too strong for me, then you shall help me; but if the sons of Ammon are too strong for you, then I will help you.

13 "Be strong, and let us show ourselves courageous for the sake of our people and for the cities of our God; and may the LORD do what is good in His sight."

14 So Joab and the people who were with him drew near to the battle against the Arameans, and they fled before him.

15 When the sons of Ammon saw that the Arameans fled, they also fled before Abshai his brother and entered the city. Then Joab came to Jerusalem.

16 ¶ When the Arameans saw that they had been defeated by Israel, they sent messengers and brought out the Arameans who were beyond the [a]River, with Shophach the commander of the army of Hadadezer leading them.

17 When it was told David, he gathered all Israel together and crossed the Jordan, and came upon them and drew up in formation against them. And when David drew up in battle array against the Arameans, they fought against him.

18 The Arameans fled before Israel, and David killed of the Arameans 7,000 charioteers and 40,000 foot soldiers, and put to death Shophach the commander of the army.

[a] I.e. Euphrates

19 So when the servants of Hadadezer saw that they were defeated by Israel, they made peace with David and served him. Thus the Arameans were not willing to help the sons of Ammon anymore.

War with Philistine Giants

20 Then it happened in the spring, at the time when kings go out *to battle*, that Joab led out the army and ravaged the land of the sons of Ammon, and came and besieged Rabbah. But David stayed at Jerusalem. And Joab struck Rabbah and overthrew it.

2 David took the crown of their king from his head, and he found it to weigh a talent of gold, and there was a precious stone in it; and it was placed on David's head. And he brought out the spoil of the city, a very great amount.

3 He brought out the people who *were* in it, and cut *them* with saws and with sharp instruments and with axes. And thus David did to all the cities of the sons of Ammon. Then David and all the people returned *to* Jerusalem.

4 ¶ Now it came about after this, that war broke out at Gezer with the Philistines; then Sibbecai the Hushathite killed Sippai, one of the descendants of the giants, and they were subdued.

5 And there was war with the Philistines again, and Elhanan the son of Jair killed Lahmi the brother of Goliath the Gittite, the shaft of whose spear *was* like a weaver's beam.

6 Again there was war at Gath, where there was a man of *great* stature who had twenty-four fingers and toes, six *fingers on each hand* and six *toes on each foot;* and he also was descended from the giants.

7 When he taunted Israel, Jonathan the son of Shimea, David's brother, killed him.

8 These were descended from the giants in Gath, and they fell by the hand of David and by the hand of his servants.

Census Brings Pestilence

21 Then Satan stood up against Israel and moved David to number Israel.

2 So David said to Joab and to the princes of the people, "Go, number Israel from Beersheba even to Dan, and bring me *word* that I may know their number."

3 Joab said, "May the LORD add to His people a hundred times as many as they are! But, my lord the king, are they not all my lord's servants? Why does my lord seek this thing? Why should he be a cause of guilt to Israel?"

4 Nevertheless, the king's word prevailed against Joab. Therefore, Joab departed and went throughout all Israel, and came to Jerusalem.

5 Joab gave the number of the census of *all* the people to David. And all Israel were 1,100,000 men who drew the sword; and Judah *was* 470,000 men who drew the sword.

6 But he did not number Levi and Benjamin among them, for the king's command was abhorrent to Joab.

7 ¶ God was displeased with this thing, so He struck Israel.

21:7 Act of Pride

Taking a census was not in itself immoral— God commanded it in the book of Numbers (chapters 1,26). This census, however, came out of David's desire to survey his kingdom, now at peace, in order to glory in its size and its potential military strength. God wanted him to continue relying on divine help and guidance, not on national pride. Even Joab, a top general, sensed the grievous mistake (verse 3). For more details, see "Satan or the Lord?" page 379.

8 David said to God, "I have sinned greatly, in that I have done this thing. But now, please take away the iniquity of Your servant, for I have done very foolishly."

9 ¶ The LORD spoke to Gad, David's seer, saying,

10 "Go and speak to David, saying, 'Thus says the LORD, "I offer you three things; choose for yourself one of them, which I will do to you." ' "

11 So Gad came to David and said to him, "Thus says the LORD, 'Take for yourself

12 either three years of famine, or three months to be swept away before your foes, while the sword of your enemies overtakes *you,* or else three days of the sword of the LORD, even pestilence in the land, and the angel of the LORD destroying throughout all the territory of Israel.' Now, therefore, consider what answer I shall return to Him who sent me."

13 David said to Gad, "I am in great distress; please let me fall into the hand of the LORD, for His mercies are very great. But do not let me fall into the hand of man."

14 ¶ So the LORD sent a pestilence on Israel; 70,000 men of Israel fell.

15 And God sent an angel to Jerusalem to destroy it; but as he was about to destroy *it,* the LORD saw and was sorry over the calamity, and said to the destroying angel, "It is enough; now relax your hand." And the angel of the LORD was standing by the threshing floor of Ornan the Jebusite.

16 Then David lifted up his eyes and saw the angel of the LORD standing between earth and heaven, with his drawn sword in his hand stretched out over Jerusalem. Then David and the elders, covered with sackcloth, fell on their faces.

17 David said to God, "Is it not I who commanded to count the people? Indeed, I am the one who has sinned and done very wickedly, but these sheep, what have they done? O LORD my God, please let Your hand be against me and my fa-

ther's household, but not against Your people that they should be plagued."

David's Altar

18 ¶ Then the angel of the LORD commanded Gad to say to David, that David should go up and build an altar to the LORD on the threshing floor of Ornan the Jebusite.

19 So David went up at the word of Gad, which he spoke in the name of the LORD.

20 Now Ornan turned back and saw the angel, and his four sons *who were* with him hid themselves. And Ornan was threshing wheat.

21 As David came to Ornan, Ornan looked and saw David, and went out from the threshing floor and prostrated himself before David with his face to the ground.

22 Then David said to Ornan, "Give me the site of *this* threshing floor, that I may build on it an altar to the LORD; for the full price you shall give it to me, that the plague may be restrained from the people."

23 Ornan said to David, "Take *it* for yourself; and let my lord the king do what is good in his sight. See, I will give the oxen for burnt offerings and the threshing sledges for wood and the wheat for the grain offering; I will give *it* all."

24 But King David said to Ornan, "No, but I will surely buy *it* for the full price; for I will not take what is yours for the LORD, or offer a burnt offering which costs me nothing."

25 So David gave Ornan 600 shekels of gold by weight for the site.

26 Then David built an altar to the LORD there and offered burnt offerings and peace offerings. And he called to the LORD and He answered him with fire from heaven on the altar of burnt offering.

27 The LORD commanded the angel, and he put his sword back in its sheath.

28 ¶ At that time, when David saw that the LORD had answered him on the threshing floor of Ornan the Jebusite, he offered sacrifice there.

29 For the tabernacle of the LORD, which Moses had made in the wilderness, and the altar of burnt offering *were* in the high place at Gibeon at that time.

30 But David could not go before it to inquire of God, for he was terrified by the sword of the angel of the LORD.

David Prepares for Temple Building

22 Then David said, "This is the house of the LORD God, and this is the altar of burnt offering for Israel."

2 ¶ So David gave orders to gather the foreigners who were in the land of Israel, and he set stonecutters to hew out stones to build the house of God.

3 David prepared large quantities of iron to

make the nails for the doors of the gates and for the clamps, and more bronze than could be weighed;

4 and timbers of cedar logs beyond number, for the Sidonians and Tyrians brought large quantities of cedar timber to David.

5 David said, "My son Solomon is young and inexperienced, and the house that is to be built for the LORD shall be exceedingly magnificent, famous and glorious throughout all lands. *Therefore* now I will make preparation for it." So David made ample preparations before his death.

Solomon Charged with the Task

6 ¶ Then he called for his son Solomon, and charged him to build a house for the LORD God of Israel.

7 David said to Solomon, "My son, I had intended to build a house to the name of the LORD my God.

8 "But the word of the LORD came to me, saying, 'You have shed much blood and have waged great wars; you shall not build a house to My name, because you have shed *so* much blood on the earth before Me.

22:8 A Man of Blood

David explained to Solomon that the Lord had not allowed him to build the temple because of his life of bloodshed. This does not suggest that David had been wrong to lead Israel in battle. God had directed him to conduct at least some of the wars. Nonetheless, war and bloodshed, even when necessary, fall short of God's ideal. He wanted the temple built by a man of peace.

9 'Behold, a son will be born to you, who shall be a man of rest; and I will give him rest from all his enemies on every side; for his name shall be ªSolomon, and I will give peace and quiet to Israel in his days.

10 'He shall build a house for My name, and he shall be My son and I will be his father; and I will establish the throne of his kingdom over Israel forever.'

11 "Now, my son, the LORD be with you that you may be successful, and build the house of the LORD your God just as He has spoken concerning you.

12 "Only the LORD give you discretion and understanding, and give you charge over Israel, so that you may keep the law of the LORD your God.

13 "Then you will prosper, if you are careful to observe the statutes and the ordinances which the LORD commanded Moses concerning Israel. Be strong and courageous, do not fear nor be dismayed.

ª I.e. peaceful

14 "Now behold, with great pains I have prepared for the house of the LORD 100,000 talents of gold and 1,000,000 talents of silver, and bronze and iron beyond weight, for they are in great quantity; also timber and stone I have prepared, and you may add to them.

15 "Moreover, there are many workmen with you, stonecutters and masons of stone and carpenters, and all men who are skillful in every kind of work.

16 "Of the gold, the silver and the bronze and the iron there is no limit. Arise and work, and may the LORD be with you."

17 ¶ David also commanded all the leaders of Israel to help his son Solomon, *saying,*

18 "Is not the LORD your God with you? And has He not given you rest on every side? For He has given the inhabitants of the land into my hand, and the land is subdued before the LORD and before His people.

19 "Now set your heart and your soul to seek the LORD your God; arise, therefore, and build the sanctuary of the LORD God, so that you may bring the ark of the covenant of the LORD and the holy vessels of God into the house that is to be built for the name of the LORD."

Solomon Reigns

23 Now when David reached old age, he made his son Solomon king over Israel.

2 And he gathered together all the leaders of Israel with the priests and the Levites.

Offices of the Levites

3 The Levites were numbered from thirty years old and upward, and their number by census of men was 38,000.

4 Of these, 24,000 were to oversee the work of the house of the LORD; and 6,000 *were* officers and judges,

5 and 4,000 *were* gatekeepers, and 4,000 *were* praising the LORD with the instruments which David made for giving praise.

6 David divided them into divisions according to the sons of Levi: Gershon, Kohath, and Merari.

23:6 Keeping the Temple

Ever since the time of Moses, the Levites had been in charge of carrying and caring for the tabernacle—the portable tent where God was worshiped. But now that the ark had been placed permanently in Jerusalem, and a temple was to be built, the Levites needed new duties and organization. Chapters 23–26 describe those duties in detail.

Gershonites

7 ¶ Of the Gershonites *were* Ladan and Shimei.

8 The sons of Ladan *were* Jehiel the first and Zetham and Joel, three.

9 The sons of Shimei *were* Shelomoth and Haziel and Haran, three. These were the heads of the fathers' *households* of Ladan.

10 The sons of Shimei *were* Jahath, Zina, Jeush and Beriah. These four *were* the sons of Shimei.

11 Jahath was the first and Zizah the second; but Jeush and Beriah did not have many sons, so they became a father's household, one class.

Kohathites

12 ¶ The sons of Kohath were four: Amram, Izhar, Hebron and Uzziel.

13 The sons of Amram were Aaron and Moses. And Aaron was set apart to sanctify him as most holy, he and his sons forever, to burn incense before the LORD, to minister to Him and to bless in His name forever.

14 But *as for* Moses the man of God, his sons were named among the tribe of Levi.

15 The sons of Moses *were* Gershom and Eliezer.

16 The son of Gershom *was* Shebuel the chief.

17 The son of Eliezer was Rehabiah the chief; and Eliezer had no other sons, but the sons of Rehabiah were very many.

18 The son of Izhar was Shelomith the chief.

19 The sons of Hebron *were* Jeriah the first, Amariah the second, Jahaziel the third and Jekameam the fourth.

20 The sons of Uzziel *were* Micah the first and Isshiah the second.

Merarites

21 ¶ The sons of Merari were Mahli and Mushi. The sons of Mahli *were* Eleazar and Kish.

22 Eleazar died and had no sons, but daughters only, so their brothers, the sons of Kish, took them *as wives.*

23 The sons of Mushi *were* three: Mahli, Eder and Jeremoth.

Duties Revised

24 ¶ These were the sons of Levi according to their fathers' households, *even* the heads of the fathers' *households* of those of them who were counted, in the number of names by their census, doing the work for the service of the house of the LORD, from twenty years old and upward.

25 For David said, "The LORD God of Israel has given rest to His people, and He dwells in Jerusalem forever.

26 "Also, the Levites will no longer need to carry the tabernacle and all its utensils for its service."

27 For by the last words of David the sons of Levi *were* numbered from twenty years old and upward.

28 For their office is to assist the sons of Aaron with the service of the house of the LORD, in the courts and in the chambers and in the purifying of all holy things, even the work of the service of the house of God,

29 and with the showbread, and the fine flour for a grain offering, and unleavened wafers, or *what is baked in* the pan or what is well-mixed, and all measures of volume and size.

23:29 Little People

The best way to get volunteers is to guarantee them adequate credit, and 1 Chronicles leaves no volunteer in nation-building overlooked. After focusing on King David for several chapters, the book turns attention to those who performed menial tasks: bailiffs, bureaucrats, bread-bakers, weight-checkers, custodians, accountants, musicians, guards, a recording secretary.

30 They are to stand every morning to thank and to praise the LORD, and likewise at evening,

31 and to offer all burnt offerings to the LORD, on the sabbaths, the new moons and the fixed festivals in the number *set* by the ordinance concerning them, continually before the LORD.

32 Thus they are to keep charge of the tent of meeting, and charge of the holy place, and charge of the sons of Aaron their relatives, for the service of the house of the LORD.

Divisions of Levites

24 Now the divisions of the descendants of Aaron *were these*: the sons of Aaron *were* Nadab, Abihu, Eleazar and Ithamar.

2 But Nadab and Abihu died before their father and had no sons. So Eleazar and Ithamar served as priests.

3 David, with Zadok of the sons of Eleazar and Ahimelech of the sons of Ithamar, divided them according to their offices for their ministry.

4 Since more chief men were found from the descendants of Eleazar than the descendants of Ithamar, they divided them thus: *there were* sixteen heads of fathers' households of the descendants of Eleazar and eight of the descendants of Ithamar, according to their fathers' households.

5 Thus they were divided by lot, the one as the other; for they were officers of the sanctuary and officers of God, both from the descendants of Eleazar and the descendants of Ithamar.

6 Shemaiah, the son of Nethanel the scribe, from the Levites, recorded them in the presence of the king, the princes, Zadok the priest, Ahimelech the son of Abiathar, and the heads of the fathers' *households* of the priests and of the Levites; one father's household taken for Eleazar and one taken for Ithamar.

7 ¶ Now the first lot came out for Jehoiarib, the second for Jedaiah,

8 the third for Harim, the fourth for Seorim,

9 the fifth for Malchijah, the sixth for Mijamin,

10 the seventh for Hakkoz, the eighth for Abijah,

11 the ninth for Jeshua, the tenth for Shecaniah,

12 the eleventh for Eliashib, the twelfth for Jakim,

13 the thirteenth for Huppah, the fourteenth for Jeshebeab,

14 the fifteenth for Bilgah, the sixteenth for Immer,

15 the seventeenth for Hezir, the eighteenth for Happizzez,

16 the nineteenth for Pethahiah, the twentieth for Jehezkel,

17 the twenty-first for Jachin, the twenty-second for Gamul,

18 the twenty-third for Delaiah, the twenty-fourth for Maaziah.

19 These were their offices for their ministry when *they* came in to the house of the LORD according to the ordinance *given* to them through Aaron their father, just as the LORD God of Israel had commanded him.

20 ¶ Now for the rest of the sons of Levi: of the sons of Amram, Shubael; of the sons of Shubael, Jehdeiah.

21 Of Rehabiah: of the sons of Rehabiah, Isshiah the first.

22 Of the Izharites, Shelomoth; of the sons of Shelomoth, Jahath.

23 The sons *of Hebron:* Jeriah *the first,* Amariah the second, Jahaziel the third, Jekameam the fourth.

24 *Of* the sons of Uzziel, Micah; of the sons of Micah, Shamir.

25 The brother of Micah, Isshiah; of the sons of Isshiah, Zechariah.

26 The sons of Merari, Mahli and Mushi; the sons of Jaaziah, Beno.

27 The sons of Merari: by Jaaziah *were* Beno, Shoham, Zaccur and Ibri.

28 By Mahli: Eleazar, who had no sons.

29 By Kish: the sons of Kish, Jerahmeel.

30 The sons of Mushi: Mahli, Eder and Jerimoth. These *were* the sons of the Levites according to their fathers' households.

31 These also cast lots just as their relatives the sons of Aaron in the presence of David the king, Zadok, Ahimelech, and the heads of the fathers' *households* of the priests and of the Levites—the head of fathers' *households* as well as those of his younger brother.

Number and Services of Musicians

25 Moreover, David and the commanders of the army set apart for the service *some of*

the sons of Asaph and of Heman and of Jeduthun, who *were* to prophesy with lyres, harps and cymbals; and the number of those who performed their service was:

25:1 Church and State

Israel, a theocracy ruled by God through a king, had no "separation of church and state." David even consulted with his military commanders for such decisions as appointing prophets and musicians for worship.

2 Of the sons of Asaph: Zaccur, Joseph, Nethaniah and Asharelah; the sons of Asaph *were* under the direction of Asaph, who prophesied under the direction of the king.

3 Of Jeduthun, the sons of Jeduthun: Gedaliah, Zeri, Jeshaiah, Shimei, Hashabiah and Mattithiah, six, under the direction of their father Jeduthun with the harp, who prophesied in giving thanks and praising the LORD.

4 Of Heman, the sons of Heman: Bukkiah, Mattaniah, Uzziel, Shebuel and Jerimoth, Hananiah, Hanani, Eliathah, Giddalti and Romamti-ezer, Joshbekashah, Mallothi, Hothir, Mahazioth.

5 All these *were* the sons of Heman the king's seer to exalt him according to the words of God, for God gave fourteen sons and three daughters to Heman.

6 All these were under the direction of their father to sing in the house of the LORD, with cymbals, harps and lyres, for the service of the house of God. Asaph, Jeduthun and Heman *were* under the direction of the king.

7 Their number who were trained in singing to the LORD, with their *a*relatives, all who were skillful, *was* 288.

Divisions of Musicians

8 They cast lots for their duties, all alike, the small as well as the great, the teacher *as well* as the pupil.

9 ¶ Now the first lot came out for Asaph to Joseph, the second for Gedaliah, he with his relatives and sons *were* twelve;

10 the third to Zaccur, his sons and his relatives, twelve;

11 the fourth to Izri, his sons and his relatives, twelve;

12 the fifth to Nethaniah, his sons and his relatives, twelve;

13 the sixth to Bukkiah, his sons and his relatives, twelve;

14 the seventh to Jesharelah, his sons and his relatives, twelve;

15 the eighth to Jeshaiah, his sons and his relatives, twelve;

16 the ninth to Mattaniah, his sons and his relatives, twelve;

17 the tenth to Shimei, his sons and his relatives, twelve;

18 the eleventh to Azarel, his sons and his relatives, twelve;

19 the twelfth to Hashabiah, his sons and his relatives, twelve;

20 for the thirteenth, Shubael, his sons and his relatives, twelve;

21 for the fourteenth, Mattithiah, his sons and his relatives, twelve;

22 for the fifteenth to Jeremoth, his sons and his relatives, twelve;

23 for the sixteenth to Hananiah, his sons and his relatives, twelve;

24 for the seventeenth to Joshbekashah, his sons and his relatives, twelve;

25 for the eighteenth to Hanani, his sons and his relatives, twelve;

26 for the nineteenth to Mallothi, his sons and his relatives, twelve;

27 for the twentieth to Eliathah, his sons and his relatives, twelve;

28 for the twenty-first to Hothir, his sons and his relatives, twelve;

29 for the twenty-second to Giddalti, his sons and his relatives, twelve;

30 for the twenty-third to Mahazioth, his sons and his relatives, twelve;

31 for the twenty-fourth to Romamti-ezer, his sons and his relatives, twelve.

Divisions of the Gatekeepers

26 For the divisions of the gatekeepers *there were* of the Korahites, Meshelemiah the son of Kore, of the sons of Asaph.

26:1-12 Major Enterprise

To aid in worship, David appointed 4,000 gatekeepers, or temple guards, and 4,000 musicians (23:3–4). The numbers give some indication of the importance attached to worship in national life. David was preparing his nation for the day when his son Solomon would build the temple.

2 Meshelemiah had sons: Zechariah the firstborn, Jediael the second, Zebadiah the third, Jathniel the fourth,

3 Elam the fifth, Johanan the sixth, Eliehoenai the seventh.

4 Obed-edom had sons: Shemaiah the firstborn, Jehozabad the second, Joah the third, Sacar the fourth, Nethanel the fifth,

5 Ammiel the sixth, Issachar the seventh *and*

a Lit *brothers*, and so throughout the ch

Peullethai the eighth; God had indeed blessed him.

6 Also to his son Shemaiah sons were born who ruled over the house of their father, for they were mighty men of valor.

7 The sons of Shemaiah *were* Othni, Rephael, Obed and Elzabad, whose brothers, Elihu and Semachiah, were valiant men.

8 All these *were* of the sons of Obed-edom; they and their sons and their relatives *were* able men with strength for the service, 62 from Obed-edom.

9 Meshelemiah had sons and relatives, 18 valiant men.

10 Also Hosah, *one* of the sons of Merari had sons: Shimri the first (although he was not the firstborn, his father made him first),

11 Hilkiah the second, Tebaliah the third, Zechariah the fourth; all the sons and relatives of Hosah *were* 13.

12 ¶ To these divisions of the gatekeepers, the chief men, *were given* duties like their relatives to minister in the house of the LORD.

13 They cast lots, the small and the great alike, according to their fathers' households, for every gate.

14 The lot to the east fell to Shelemiah. Then they cast lots *for* his son Zechariah, a counselor with insight, and his lot came out to the north.

15 For Obed-edom *it fell* to the south, and to his sons went the storehouse.

16 For Shuppim and Hosah *it was* to the west, by the gate of Shallecheth, on the ascending highway. Guard corresponded to guard.

17 On the east there were six Levites, on the north four daily, on the south four daily, and at the storehouse two by two.

18 At the [a]Parbar on the west *there were* four at the highway and two at the Parbar.

19 These were the divisions of the gatekeepers of the sons of Korah and of the sons of Merari.

Keepers of the Treasure

20 ¶ [b]The Levites, their relatives, had charge of the treasures of the house of God and of the treasures of the dedicated gifts.

21 The sons of Ladan, the sons of the Gershonites belonging to Ladan, *namely*, the Jehielites, *were* the heads of the fathers' *households*, belonging to Ladan the Gershonite.

22 ¶ The sons of Jehieli, Zetham and Joel his brother, had charge of the treasures of the house of the LORD.

23 As for the Amramites, the Izharites, the Hebronites and the Uzzielites,

24 Shebuel the son of Gershom, the son of Moses, was officer over the treasures.

25 His relatives by Eliezer *were* Rehabiah his son, Jeshaiah his son, Joram his son, Zichri his son and Shelomoth his son.

26 This Shelomoth and his relatives had charge of all the treasures of the dedicated gifts which King David and the heads of the fathers' *households*, the commanders of thousands and hundreds, and the commanders of the army, had dedicated.

27 They dedicated part of the spoil won in battles to repair the house of the LORD.

28 And all that Samuel the seer had dedicated and Saul the son of Kish, Abner the son of Ner and Joab the son of Zeruiah, everyone who had dedicated *anything, all of this* was in the care of Shelomoth and his relatives.

Outside Duties

29 ¶ As for the Izharites, Chenaniah and his sons were *assigned* to outside duties for Israel, as officers and judges.

30 As for the Hebronites, Hashabiah and his relatives, 1,700 capable men, had charge of the affairs of Israel west of the Jordan, for all the work of the LORD and the service of the king.

31 As for the Hebronites, Jerijah the chief (these Hebronites were investigated according to their genealogies and fathers' *households*, in the fortieth year of David's reign, and men of outstanding capability were found among them at Jazer of Gilead)

32 and his relatives, capable men, *were* 2,700 in number, heads of fathers' *households*. And King David made them overseers of the Reubenites, the Gadites and the half-tribe of the Manassites concerning all the affairs of God and of the king.

Commanders of the Army

27 Now *this is* the enumeration of the sons of Israel, the heads of fathers' *households*, the commanders of thousands and of hundreds, and their officers who served the king in all the affairs of the divisions which came in and went out month by month throughout all the months of the year, each division *numbering* 24,000:

2 ¶ Jashobeam the son of Zabdiel [c]had charge of the first division for the first month; and in his division *were* 24,000.

3 *He was* from the sons of Perez, *and was* chief of all the commanders of the army for the first month.

4 Dodai the Ahohite and his division had charge of the division for the second month, Mikloth *being* the chief officer; and in his division *were* 24,000.

5 The third commander of the army for the third month *was* Benaiah, the son of Jehoiada the priest, *as* chief; and in his division *were* 24,000.

6 This Benaiah *was* the mighty man of the thirty, and had charge of thirty; and over his division was Ammizabad his son.

7 The fourth for the fourth month *was* Asahel

---

[a] Possibly *court* or *colonnade*   [b] So Gr; Heb *As for the Levites, Ahijah had*   [c] Lit *was over,* and so throughout the ch

the brother of Joab, and Zebadiah his son after him; and in his division *were* 24,000.

8 The fifth for the fifth month *was* the commander Shamhuth the Izrahite; and in his division *were* 24,000.

9 The sixth for the sixth month *was* Ira the son of Ikkesh the Tekoite; and in his division *were* 24,000.

10 The seventh for the seventh month *was* Helez the Pelonite of the sons of Ephraim; and in his division *were* 24,000.

11 The eighth for the eighth month *was* Sibbecai the Hushathite of the Zerahites; and in his division *were* 24,000.

12 The ninth for the ninth month *was* Abiezer the Anathothite of the Benjamites; and in his division *were* 24,000.

13 The tenth for the tenth month *was* Maharai the Netophathite of the Zerahites; and in his division *were* 24,000.

14 The eleventh for the eleventh month *was* Benaiah the Pirathonite of the sons of Ephraim; and in his division *were* 24,000.

15 The twelfth for the twelfth month *was* Heldai the Netophathite of Othniel; and in his division *were* 24,000.

Chief Officers of the Tribes

16 ¶ Now in charge of the tribes of Israel: chief officer for the Reubenites was Eliezer the son of Zichri; for the Simeonites, Shephatiah the son of Maacah;

17 for Levi, Hashabiah the son of Kemuel; for Aaron, Zadok;

18 for Judah, Elihu, *one* of David's brothers; for Issachar, Omri the son of Michael;

19 for Zebulun, Ishmaiah the son of Obadiah; for Naphtali, Jeremoth the son of Azriel;

20 for the sons of Ephraim, Hoshea the son of Azaziah; for the half-tribe of Manasseh, Joel the son of Pedaiah;

21 for the half-tribe of Manasseh in Gilead, Iddo the son of Zechariah; for Benjamin, Jaasiel the son of Abner;

22 for Dan, Azarel the son of Jeroham. These *were* the princes of the tribes of Israel.

23 But David did not count those twenty years of age and under, because the LORD had said He would multiply Israel as the stars of heaven.

24 Joab the son of Zeruiah had begun to count *them,* but did not finish; and because of this, wrath came upon Israel, and the number was not included in the account of the chronicles of King David.

Various Overseers

25 ¶ Now Azmaveth the son of Adiel had charge of the king's storehouses. And Jonathan the son of Uzziah had charge of the storehouses in the country, in the cities, in the villages and in the towers.

26 Ezri the son of Chelub had charge of the agricultural workers who tilled the soil.

27 Shimei the Ramathite had charge of the vineyards; and Zabdi the Shiphmite had charge of the produce of the vineyards *stored* in the wine cellars.

28 Baal-hanan the Gederite had charge of the olive and sycamore trees in the ᵃShephelah; and Joash had charge of the stores of oil.

29 Shitrai the Sharonite had charge of the cattle which were grazing in Sharon; and Shaphat the son of Adlai had charge of the cattle in the valleys.

30 Obil the Ishmaelite had charge of the camels; and Jehdeiah the Meronothite had charge of the donkeys.

31 Jaziz the Hagrite had charge of the flocks. All these were overseers of the property which belonged to King David.

Counselors

32 ¶ Also Jonathan, David's uncle, *was* a counselor, a man of understanding, and a scribe; and Jehiel the son of Hachmoni tutored the king's sons.

33 Ahithophel *was* counselor to the king; and Hushai the Archite *was* the king's friend.

34 Jehoiada the son of Benaiah, and Abiathar succeeded Ahithophel; and Joab was the commander of the king's army.

David's Address about the Temple

28 Now David assembled at Jerusalem all the officials of Israel, the princes of the tribes, and the commanders of the divisions that served the king, and the commanders of thousands, and the commanders of hundreds, and the overseers of all the property and livestock belonging to the king and his sons, with the officials and the mighty men, even all the valiant men.

2 Then King David rose to his feet and said, "Listen to me, my brethren and my people; I *had* ᵇintended to build a ᶜpermanent home for the ark of the covenant of the LORD and for the footstool of our God. So I had made preparations to build *it.*

3 "But God said to me, 'You shall not build a house for My name because you are a man of war and have shed blood.'

4 "Yet, the LORD, the God of Israel, chose me from all the house of my father to be king over Israel forever. For He has chosen Judah to be a leader; and in the house of Judah, my father's house, and among the sons of my father He took pleasure in me to make *me* king over all Israel.

5 "Of all my sons (for the LORD has given me many sons), He has chosen my son Solomon to sit

---

ᵃ Or *lowlands*   ᵇ Lit *in my heart*   ᶜ Lit *house of rest* on the throne of the kingdom of the LORD over Israel.

6 "He said to me, 'Your son Solomon is the one who shall build My house and My courts; for I have chosen him to be a son to Me, and I will be a father to him.

7 'I will establish his kingdom forever if he resolutely performs My commandments and My ordinances, as is done now.'

8 "So now, in the sight of all Israel, the assembly of the LORD, and in the hearing of our God, observe and seek after all the commandments of the LORD your God so that you may possess the good land and bequeath it to your sons after you forever.

9 ¶ "As for you, my son Solomon, know the God of your father, and serve Him with a whole heart and a willing mind; for the LORD searches all hearts, and understands every intent of the thoughts. If you seek Him, He will let you find Him; but if you forsake Him, He will reject you forever.

28:9 Conditional Promise

God's promise to David of unending descendants on the throne was so important to Israel that it was reported, in different forms, several times. (See chapter 17, for instance.) Sometimes it read as though God would bless a line of successful kings regardless of their behavior. Here, though, David explained that God's favor would depend on Solomon's devotion to God.

10 "Consider now, for the LORD has chosen you to build a house for the sanctuary; be courageous and act."

11 ¶ Then David gave to his son Solomon the plan of the porch *of the temple*, its buildings, its storehouses, its upper rooms, its inner rooms and the room for the mercy seat;

12 and the plan of all that he had in mind, for the courts of the house of the LORD, and for all the surrounding rooms, for the storehouses of the house of God and for the storehouses of the dedicated things;

13 also for the divisions of the priests and the Levites and for all the work of the service of the house of the LORD and for all the utensils of service in the house of the LORD;

14 for the golden *utensils,* the weight of gold for all utensils for every kind of service; for the silver utensils, the weight *of silver* for all utensils for every kind of service;

15 and the weight *of gold* for the golden lampstands and their golden lamps, with the weight of each lampstand and its lamps; and *the weight of silver* for the silver lampstands, with the weight of each lampstand and its lamps according to the use of each lampstand;

16 and the gold by weight for the tables of showbread, for each table; and silver for the silver tables;

17 and the forks, the basins, and the pitchers of pure gold; and for the golden bowls with the weight for each bowl; and for the silver bowls with the weight for each bowl;

18 and for the altar of incense refined gold by weight; and gold for the model of the chariot, *even* the cherubim that spread out *their wings* and covered the ark of the covenant of the LORD.

19 ¶ "All *this,*" said David, "the LORD made me understand in writing by His hand upon me, all the details of this pattern."

20 ¶ Then David said to his son Solomon, "Be strong and courageous, and act; do not fear nor be dismayed, for the LORD God, my God, is with you. He will not fail you nor forsake you until all the work for the service of the house of the LORD is finished.

21 "Now behold, *there are* the divisions of the priests and the Levites for all the service of the house of God, and every willing man of any skill will be with you in all the work for all kinds of service. The officials also and all the people will be entirely at your command."

Offerings for the Temple

29 Then King David said to the entire assembly, "My son Solomon, whom alone God has chosen, is still young and inexperienced and the work is great; for the temple is not for man, but for the LORD God.

2 "Now with all my ability I have provided for the house of my God the gold for the *things of* gold, and the silver for the *things of* silver, and the bronze for the *things of* bronze, the iron for the *things of* iron, and wood for the *things of* wood, onyx stones and inlaid *stones,* stones of antimony and stones of various colors, and all kinds of precious stones and alabaster in abundance.

3 "Moreover, in my delight in the house of my God, the treasure I have of gold and silver, I give to the house of my God, over and above all that I have already provided for the holy ᵃtemple,

4 namely, 3,000 talents of gold, of the gold of Ophir, and 7,000 talents of refined silver, to overlay the walls of the buildings;

5 of gold for the *things of* gold and of silver for the *things of* silver, that is, for all the work done by the craftsmen. Who then is willing to consecrate himself this day to the LORD?"

6 ¶ Then the rulers of the fathers' *households,* and the princes of the tribes of Israel, and the commanders of thousands and of hundreds, with

ᵃ Lit *house*

the overseers over the king's work, offered willingly;

7 and for the service for the house of God they gave 5,000 talents and 10,000 darics of gold, and 10,000 talents of silver, and 18,000 talents of brass, and 100,000 talents of iron.

8 Whoever possessed *precious* stones gave them to the treasury of the house of the LORD, in care of Jehiel the Gershonite.

9 Then the people rejoiced because they had offered so willingly, for they made their offering to the LORD with a whole heart, and King David also rejoiced greatly.

David's Prayer

10 ¶ So David blessed the LORD in the sight of all the assembly; and David said, "Blessed are You, O LORD God of Israel our father, forever and ever.

29:10 David's Great Prayer

David's prayer at the beginning of temple construction shows why he was a man after God's own heart. Despite all his achievements, he was deeply humble. He wanted glory to go to God, not himself. This passage would have reminded the original readers of Chronicles, back from exile and without a king, that David's greatest concern was for the temple, where his people could worship and serve God. They, his descendants, did not need a king to carry on David's deepest concerns.

11 "Yours, O LORD, is the greatness and the power and the glory and the victory and the majesty, indeed everything that is in the heavens and the earth; Yours is the dominion, O LORD, and You exalt Yourself as head over all.

12 "Both riches and honor *come* from You, and You rule over all, and in Your hand is power and might; and it lies in Your hand to make great and to strengthen everyone.

13 "Now therefore, our God, we thank You, and praise Your glorious name.

14 ¶ "But who am I and who are my people that we should be able to offer as generously as this? For all things come from You, and from Your hand we have given You.

15 "For we are sojourners before You, and tenants, as all our fathers were; our days on the earth are like a shadow, and there is no hope.

16 "O LORD our God, all this abundance that we have provided to build You a house for Your holy name, it is from Your hand, and all is Yours.

17 "Since I know, O my God, that You try the heart and delight in uprightness, I, in the integrity of my heart, have willingly offered all these *things;* so now with joy I have seen Your people, who

are present here, make *their* offerings willingly to You.

18 "O LORD, the God of Abraham, Isaac and Israel, our fathers, preserve this forever in the intentions of the heart of Your people, and direct their heart to You;

19 and give to my son Solomon a perfect heart to keep Your commandments, Your testimonies and Your statutes, and to do *them* all, and to build the temple, for which I have made provision."

20 ¶ Then David said to all the assembly, "Now bless the LORD your God." And all the assembly blessed the LORD, the God of their fathers, and bowed low and did homage to the LORD and to the king.

Sacrifices

21 On the next day they made sacrifices to the LORD and offered burnt offerings to the LORD, 1,000 bulls, 1,000 rams *and* 1,000 lambs, with their drink offerings and sacrifices in abundance for all Israel.

22 So they ate and drank that day before the LORD with great gladness.

Solomon Again Made King

¶ And they made Solomon the son of David king a second time, and they anointed *him* as ruler for the LORD and Zadok as priest.

23 Then Solomon sat on the throne of the LORD as king instead of David his father; and he prospered, and all Israel obeyed him.

24 All the officials, the mighty men, and also all the sons of King David pledged allegiance to King Solomon.

29:24 A Second Coronation

Assuming that his readers were familiar with the family quarrels told of in 1 Kings 1, the author refers to this coronation as the "second time" (verse 22). The first coronation happened when David learned that Solomon's older brother had been conspiring to become king. David immediately called for a private coronation (1 Kings 1:32–40). Only later did this public ceremony occur, when the rebellious brother swore his loyalty. Typically, 1 Chronicles leaves out the nasty politics and emphasizes the positive result.

25 The LORD highly exalted Solomon in the sight of all Israel, and bestowed on him royal majesty which had not been on any king before him in Israel.

26 ¶ Now David the son of Jesse reigned over all Israel.

27 The period which he reigned over Israel *was*

forty years; he reigned in Hebron seven years and in Jerusalem thirty-three *years*.

Death of David

28 Then he died in a ripe old age, full of days, riches and honor; and his son Solomon reigned in his place.

29 Now the acts of King David, from first to last, are written in the chronicles of Samuel the seer, in the chronicles of Nathan the prophet and in the chronicles of Gad the seer,

30 with all his reign, his power, and the circumstances which came on him, on Israel, and on all the kingdoms of the lands.

2 CHRONICLES

A Time for Hope
Restoring pride to a group of refugees

I N THE EARLY 1960s, A wave of feeling known as "black pride" swept across America. It started when African-American leaders realized that far more than legal rights had been repressed for 200 years. Everything about the African-American culture, from hair texture to history, had taken a back seat to that of the white majority.

Over time, a dramatic rediscovery of the African-American heritage occurred. Textbook publishers issued new editions that for the first time included the stories of African-Americans: a soldier who rowed George Washington across the Delaware, a scientist who perfected the process of blood transfusion, an educator who founded colleges for African-Americans.

"Black pride" reminded all Americans that a minority race had made giant contributions in many fields. People encountered a heritage they had known little about. Heroes were uncovered. African-Americans everywhere began to see the past in a new light.

Need for a Pep Talk

There was a time when the Israelites, too, desperately needed a new look at the past. Their ancestors had also been torn from home, beaten, and dragged off in chains to serve as slaves in a foreign country. In Babylon, a new generation grew up knowing little of the Israelite past: the covenant with God, the promised line of kings, the magnificent temple in Jerusalem.

When captive Israelites were finally allowed to return home, they found a pile of rubble. In Israel's Golden Age, people had traveled thousands of miles to view the majesty of Jerusalem and its temple. But to the refugees' horror, not one stone of the temple remained standing. The carved beams had all been hacked to pieces, the gold and ivory stripped away, and the furniture auctioned off or destroyed.

Outside the capital, whole villages had disappeared. Vital religious customs had gone uncelebrated for 70 years. Jewish culture was in danger of leaking away.

The book of Chronicles was written to those refugees who returned. For that dispirited group of people, the author recounted the glory days of Israel. He wanted to restore pride in the Israelite past and bring hope to their future.

History in a New Light

Chronicles (both 1 and 2) thus retells history, starting all the way at the beginning, with Adam. Most of the characters are familiar, but Chronicles tells old stories in a new light. Its author isn't just reciting facts. He is delivering a word of bright hope, a pep talk, to just-freed refugees.

Some accuse Chronicles of being a "whitewashed" history, especially in comparison to the Bible's other history books. True, the book barely mentions the Israelites' great failures—it says nothing of David's or Solomon's mistakes, for instance. Presumably, the refugees had heard plenty about the dark side of their nation's recent past: The books of Samuel and Kings, which ruthlessly exposed those failures, had been around for years.

Similarly, Chronicles ignores the chaotic Northern Kingdom of Israel, and the civil war Judah waged against it. Nothing remained of the ten scattered tribes of the North, and the book wastes little space on them. Instead, Chronicles reaches higher, seeking to restore pride in the original ideals of the nation.

A Distant Hope

The good kings of Judah, eight in all, dominate the story: Over two-thirds of 2 Chronicles is devoted to their reigns. Chronicles focuses on God's special relationship with the Israelites, recalling the covenant that had brought about their Golden Age. It reviews the religious reforms led by each king, and, above all, highlights the temple, the house where God's presence came to rest. If God had lived among them in the past, couldn't he do so again?

How to Read 2 Chronicles

You will recognize many of the stories in 2 Chronicles—about half of it closely follows other Bible passages. The author freely admits he has relied on the books of Moses, Samuel, and Kings. He also quotes from Judges, Jeremiah, Psalms, Isaiah, and Lamentations, as well as many books that have been lost to history.

But 2 Chronicles does not merely repeat. It weaves together stories and facts for a specific purpose: a Jewish philosophy of history. Chronicles sheds new light on that history by highlighting rare moments of peace and prosperity. Worship of the true God had made Israel strong. As you read, notice how 2 Chronicles underscores that fact by stressing the temple and the priests.

For comparison, you may want to read companion passages in the book of Kings (for a list, see "A Lineup of Rulers," pages 1417–1425). Read side by side, the two accounts clearly reveal the distinct purpose behind the book of Chronicles.

Look past all the names and events for the few kings who did right. (See "The Great Reformers," page 498) What made them successful? What lessons about faith can we learn from them?

PEOPLE YOU'LL MEET IN 2 CHRONICLES

REHOBOAM *(p. 491)*
ATHALIAH *(p. 501)*
HEZEKIAH *(p. 507)*

3-TRACK READING PLAN

For an explanation and complete listing of the 3-track reading plan, turn to page 7.

TRACK 1: *Two-Week Courses on the Bible*
See page 7 for information on these courses.

TRACK 2: *An Overview of 2 Chronicles in 3 Days*
☐ Day 1. Read the Introduction to 2 Chronicles and then chapter 20. It tells of a high point when King Jehoshaphat brought the whole nation together in prayer.
☐ Day 2. Hezekiah had an eventful life, with soaring highs and deep lows. Read about a national high point in chapter 30.
☐ Day 3. Hezekiah lived in treacherous times. Read of his close scrape with disaster in chapter 32.

Now turn to page 9 for your next Track 2 reading project.

TRACK 3: *All of 2 Chronicles in 34 Days*
After you have read through 2 Chronicles, turn to pages 10–14 for your next Track 3 reading project.

☐1	☐2	☐3	☐4	☐5	☐6	☐7	☐8
☐9	☐10	☐11	☐12	☐13	☐14	☐15	☐16–17
☐18	☐19	☐20	☐21	☐22	☐23	☐24	☐25
☐26–27	☐28	☐29	☐30	☐31	☐32	☐33	☐34
☐35	☐36						

Solomon Worships at Gibeon

1 Now Solomon the son of David established himself securely over his kingdom, and the LORD his God *was* with him and exalted him greatly.

2 ¶ Solomon spoke to all Israel, to the commanders of thousands and of hundreds and to the judges and to every leader in all Israel, the heads of the fathers' *households*.

3 Then Solomon and all the assembly with him went to the high place which was at Gibeon, for God's tent of meeting was there, which Moses the servant of the LORD had made in the wilderness.

4 However, David had brought up the ark of God from Kiriath-jearim to the place he had prepared for it, for he had pitched a tent for it in Jerusalem.

5 Now the bronze altar, which Bezalel the son of Uri, the son of Hur, had made, was there before the tabernacle of the LORD, and Solomon and the assembly sought it out.

6 Solomon went up there before the LORD to the bronze altar which *was* at the tent of meeting, and offered a thousand burnt offerings on it.

7 ¶ In that night God appeared to Solomon and said to him, "Ask what I shall give you."

Solomon's Prayer for Wisdom

8 Solomon said to God, "You have dealt with my father David with great lovingkindness, and have made me king in his place.

9 "Now, O LORD God, Your promise to my father David is fulfilled, for You have made me king over a people as numerous as the dust of the earth.

10 "Give me now wisdom and knowledge, that I may go out and come in before this people, for who can rule this great people of Yours?"

11 God said to Solomon, "Because you had this in mind, and did not ask for riches, wealth or honor, or the life of those who hate you, nor have you even asked for long life, but you have asked for yourself wisdom and knowledge that you may rule My people over whom I have made you king,

12 wisdom and knowledge have been granted to you. And I will give you riches and wealth and honor, such as none of the kings who were before you has possessed nor those who will come after you."

13 So Solomon went from the high place which was at Gibeon, from the tent of meeting, to Jerusalem, and he reigned over Israel.

Solomon's Wealth

14 ¶ Solomon amassed chariots and horsemen. He had 1,400 chariots and 12,000 horsemen, and he stationed them in the chariot cities and with the king at Jerusalem.

15 The king made silver and gold as plentiful in Jerusalem as stones, and he made cedars as plentiful as sycamores in the lowland.

16 Solomon's horses were imported from Egypt and from Kue; the king's traders procured them from Kue for a price.

17 They imported chariots from Egypt for 600 *shekels* of silver apiece and horses for 150 apiece, and by the same means they exported them to all the kings of the Hittites and the kings of Aram.

Solomon Will Build a Temple and Palace

2 Now Solomon decided to build a house for the name of the LORD and a royal palace for himself.

2 So Solomon assigned 70,000 men to carry loads and 80,000 men to quarry *stone* in the mountains and 3,600 to supervise them.

2:2 Solomon's Forced Labor

King Solomon drafted laborers for his construction projects much like an army drafts soldiers. His policy of forced labor sowed dissension in the kingdom, especially among resentful northern tribes. In keeping with its morale-building purpose, 2 Chronicles has little bad to say about Solomon. The author mentions Solomon's wealth (1:14; 9:22–25) without comment, although such excess defied the rules for kings (Deuteronomy 17:15–17). Chronicles also omits reference to Solomon's palace, which Kings had pointedly described as exceeding even the temple in its splendor.

3 ¶ Then Solomon sent *word* to Huram the king of Tyre, saying, "As you dealt with David my father and sent him cedars to build him a house to dwell in, so do for me.

4 "Behold, I am about to build a house for the name of the LORD my God, dedicating it to Him, to burn fragrant incense before Him and *to set out* the showbread continually, and to offer burnt offerings morning and evening, on sabbaths and on new moons and on the appointed feasts of the LORD our God, this *being required* forever in Israel.

5 "The house which I am about to build *will be* great, for greater is our God than all the gods.

6 "But who is able to build a house for Him, for the heavens and the highest heavens cannot contain Him? So who am I, that I should build a house for Him, except to *a*burn *incense* before Him?

7 "Now send me a skilled man to work in gold, silver, brass and iron, and in purple, crimson and violet *fabrics,* and who knows how to make engravings, to *work* with the skilled men whom I

a Lit *offer up in smoke*

have in Judah and Jerusalem, whom David my father provided.

8 "Send me also cedar, cypress and algum timber from Lebanon, for I know that your servants know how to cut timber of Lebanon; and indeed my servants *will work* with your servants,

9 to prepare timber in abundance for me, for the house which I am about to build *will be* great and wonderful.

10 "Now behold, I will give to your servants, the woodsmen who cut the timber, 20,000 ᵃkors of crushed wheat and 20,000 kors of barley, and 20,000 baths of wine and 20,000 baths of oil."

Huram to Assist

11 ¶ Then Huram, king of Tyre, answered in a letter sent to Solomon: "Because the LORD loves His people, He has made you king over them."

12 Then Huram continued, "Blessed be the LORD, the God of Israel, who has made heaven and earth, who has given King David a wise son, endowed with discretion and understanding, who will build a house for the LORD and a royal palace for himself.

13 ¶ "Now I am sending Huram-abi, a skilled man, endowed with understanding,

14 the son of a Danite woman and a Tyrian father, who knows how to work in gold, silver, bronze, iron, stone and wood, *and* in purple, violet, linen and crimson fabrics, and *who knows how* to make all kinds of engravings and to execute any design which may be assigned to him, *to work* with your skilled men and with those of my lord David your father.

15 "Now then, let my lord send to his servants wheat and barley, oil and wine, of which he has spoken.

16 "We will cut whatever timber you need from Lebanon and bring it to you on rafts by sea to Joppa, so that you may carry it up to Jerusalem."

17 ¶ Solomon numbered all the aliens who *were* in the land of Israel, following the census which his father David had taken; and 153,600 were found.

18 He appointed 70,000 of them to carry loads and 80,000 to quarry *stones* in the mountains and 3,600 supervisors to make the people work.

The Temple Construction in Jerusalem

3 Then Solomon began to build the house of the LORD in Jerusalem on Mount Moriah, where *the* LORD had appeared to his father David, at the place that David had prepared on the threshing floor of Ornan the Jebusite.

2 He began to build on the second *day* in the second month of the fourth year of his reign.

Dimensions and Materials of the Temple

3 Now these are the foundations which Solomon laid for building the house of God. The length in ᵇcubits, according to the old standard *was* sixty cubits, and the width twenty cubits.

4 The porch which was in front of the house was as long as the width of the house, twenty cubits, and the height 120; and inside he overlaid it with pure gold.

5 He overlaid the main room with cypress wood and overlaid it with fine gold, and ornamented it with palm trees and chains.

6 Further, he adorned the house with precious stones; and the gold was gold from Parvaim.

7 He also overlaid the house with gold—the beams, the thresholds and its walls and its doors; and he carved cherubim on the walls.

8 ¶ Now he made the room of the holy of holies: its length across the width of the house *was* twenty cubits, and its width *was* twenty cubits; and he overlaid it with fine gold, *amounting* to 600 talents.

9 The weight of the nails was fifty shekels of gold. He also overlaid the upper rooms with gold.

10 ¶ Then he made two sculptured cherubim in the room of the holy of holies and overlaid them with gold.

11 The wingspan of the cherubim *was* twenty cubits; the wing of one, of five cubits, touched the wall of the house, and *its* other wing, of five cubits, touched the wing of the other cherub.

12 The wing of the other cherub, of five cubits, touched the wall of the house; and *its* other wing of five cubits was attached to the wing of the first cherub.

13 The wings of these cherubim extended twenty cubits, and they stood on their feet facing the *main* room.

14 He made the veil of violet, purple, crimson and fine linen, and he worked cherubim on it.

3:14 A Temporary Separation

Just as it had in the tabernacle, a curtain in the temple separated the holy place and the holy of holies. The curtain symbolized the distance between God and people. Even priests were forbidden to go beyond that curtain into the presence of God, except on the Day of Atonement. When Jesus died on the cross, this temple curtain miraculously ripped in two. That event also had symbolic meaning: Christ had opened up the way to God (Hebrews 9:7–12).

15 ¶ He also made two pillars for the front of the house, thirty-five cubits high, and the capital on the top of each *was* five cubits.

16 He made chains in the inner sanctuary and placed *them* on the tops of the pillars; and he made one hundred pomegranates and placed *them* on the chains.

ᵃ I.e. One kor equals approx 10 bu   ᵇ I.e. One cubit equals approx 18 in.

17 He erected the pillars in front of the temple, one on the right and the other on the left, and named the one on the right Jachin and the one on the left Boaz.

Furnishings of the Temple

4 Then he made a bronze altar, twenty cubits in length and twenty cubits in width and ten cubits in height.

2 Also he made the cast *metal* sea, ten cubits from brim to brim, circular in form, and its height *was* five cubits and its circumference thirty cubits.

3 Now figures like oxen *were* under it *and* all around it, ten cubits, entirely encircling the sea. The oxen *were* in two rows, cast in one piece.

4 It stood on twelve oxen, three facing the north, three facing west, three facing south and three facing east; and the sea *was set* on top of them and all their hindquarters turned inwards.

5 It was a handbreadth thick, and its brim was made like the brim of a cup, *like* a lily blossom; it could hold 3,000 baths.

6 He also made ten basins in which to wash, and he set five on the right side and five on the left to rinse things for the burnt offering; but the sea *was* for the priests to wash in.

7 ¶ Then he made the ten golden lampstands in the way prescribed for them and he set them in the temple, five on the right side and five on the left.

8 He also made ten tables and placed them in the temple, five on the right side and five on the left. And he made one hundred golden bowls.

9 Then he made the court of the priests and the great court and doors for the court, and overlaid their doors with bronze.

10 He set the sea on the right side *of the house* toward the southeast.

11 ¶ Huram also made the pails, the shovels and the bowls. So Huram finished doing the work which he performed for King Solomon in the house of God:

12 the two pillars, the bowls and the two capitals on top of the pillars, and the two networks to cover the two bowls of the capitals which were on top of the pillars,

13 and the four hundred pomegranates for the two networks, two rows of pomegranates for each network to cover the two bowls of the capitals which were on the pillars.

14 He also made the stands and he made the basins on the stands,

15 *and* the one sea with the twelve oxen under it.

16 The pails, the shovels, the forks and all its utensils, Huram-abi made of polished bronze for King Solomon for the house of the LORD.

17 On the plain of the Jordan the king cast them in the clay ground between Succoth and Zeredah.

18 Thus Solomon made all these utensils in great quantities, for the weight of the bronze could not be found out.

19 ¶ Solomon also made all the things that *were* in the house of God: even the golden altar, the tables with the bread of the Presence on them,

20 the lampstands with their lamps of pure gold, to burn in front of the inner sanctuary in the way prescribed;

21 the flowers, the lamps, and the tongs of gold, of purest gold;

22 and the snuffers, the bowls, the spoons and the firepans of pure gold; and the entrance of the house, its inner doors for the holy of holies and the doors of the house, *that is*, of the nave, of gold.

The Ark Is Brought into the Temple

5 Thus all the work that Solomon performed for the house of the LORD was finished. And Solomon brought in the things that David his father had dedicated, even the silver and the gold and all the utensils, *and* put *them* in the treasuries of the house of God.

2 ¶ Then Solomon assembled to Jerusalem the elders of Israel and all the heads of the tribes, the leaders of the fathers' *households* of the sons of Israel, to bring up the ark of the covenant of the LORD out of the city of David, which is Zion.

3 All the men of Israel assembled themselves to the king at the feast, that is *in* the seventh month.

4 Then all the elders of Israel came, and the Levites took up the ark.

5 They brought up the ark and the tent of meeting and all the holy utensils which *were* in the tent; the Levitical priests brought them up.

6 And King Solomon and all the congregation of Israel who were assembled with him before the ark, were sacrificing so many sheep and oxen that they could not be counted or numbered.

7 Then the priests brought the ark of the covenant of the LORD to its place, into the inner sanctuary of the house, to the holy of holies, under the wings of the cherubim.

8 For the cherubim spread their wings over the place of the ark, so that the cherubim made a covering over the ark and its poles.

9 The poles were so long that the ends of the poles of the ark could be seen in front of the inner sanctuary, but they could not be seen outside; and they are there to this day.

10 There was nothing in the ark except the two tablets which Moses put *there* at Horeb, where the LORD made a covenant with the sons of Israel, when they came out of Egypt.

The Glory of God Fills the Temple

11 ¶ When the priests came forth from the holy place (for all the priests who were present had sanctified themselves, without regard to divisions),

12 and all the Levitical singers, Asaph, Heman,

Jeduthun, and their sons and kinsmen, clothed in fine linen, with cymbals, harps and lyres, standing east of the altar, and with them one hundred and twenty priests blowing trumpets

13 in unison when the trumpeters and the singers were to make themselves heard with one voice to praise and to glorify the LORD, and when they lifted up their voice accompanied by trumpets and cymbals and instruments of music, and when they praised the LORD *saying*, "*He* indeed is good for His lovingkindness is everlasting," then the house, the house of the LORD, was filled with a cloud,

5:10 Proof of the Covenant

Until the invasion by Babylon, the Israelites possessed a visible reminder of God's treaty, or "covenant," with them. It stayed in the most sacred piece of furniture in Israel, the ark. But the ark was lost during the Babylonian captivity— and has never been found.

14 so that the priests could not stand to minister because of the cloud, for the glory of the LORD filled the house of God.

Solomon's Dedication

6 Then Solomon said,
"The LORD has said that He would dwell
in the thick cloud.

2 "I have built You a lofty house,
And a place for Your dwelling forever."

3 ¶ Then the king faced about and blessed all the assembly of Israel, while all the assembly of Israel was standing.

4 He said, "Blessed be the LORD, the God of Israel, who spoke with His mouth to my father David and has fulfilled *it* with His hands, saying,

5 'Since the day that I brought My people from the land of Egypt, I did not choose a city out of all the tribes of Israel *in which* to build a house that My name might be there, nor did I choose any man for a leader over My people Israel;

6 but I have chosen Jerusalem that My name might be there, and I have chosen David to be over My people Israel.'

7 "Now it was in the heart of my father David to build a house for the name of the LORD, the God of Israel.

8 "But the LORD said to my father David, 'Because it was in your heart to build a house for My name, you did well that it was in your heart.

9 'Nevertheless you shall not build the house, but your son who will be born to you, he shall build the house for My name.'

10 "Now the LORD has fulfilled His word which He spoke; for I have risen in the place of my father David and sit on the throne of Israel, as the LORD

promised, and have built the house for the name of the LORD, the God of Israel.

11 "There I have set the ark in which is the covenant of the LORD, which He made with the sons of Israel."

Solomon's Prayer of Dedication

12 ¶ Then he stood before the altar of the LORD in the presence of all the assembly of Israel and spread out his hands.

13 Now Solomon had made a bronze platform, five cubits long, five cubits wide and three cubits high, and had set it in the midst of the court; and he stood on it, knelt on his knees in the presence of all the assembly of Israel and spread out his hands toward heaven.

14 He said, "O LORD, the God of Israel, there is no god like You in heaven or on earth, keeping covenant and *showing* lovingkindness to Your servants who walk before You with all their heart;

6:14 Solomon's Peak

This chapter records Solomon's high point as a leader and hints at his lost potential. Thanks to David's conquests, Israel was at peace, and prosperous. Solomon's splendid prayer reveals the depth of his wisdom and spiritual sensitivity. But from this point on, Solomon, potentially the greatest of all Israel's rulers, slid toward selfishness and overindulgence. His failings led the nation into immorality and eventual civil war.

15 who has kept with Your servant David, my father, that which You have promised him; indeed You have spoken with Your mouth and have fulfilled it with Your hand, as it is this day.

16 "Now therefore, O LORD, the God of Israel, keep with Your servant David, my father, that which You have promised him, saying, 'You shall not lack a man to sit on the throne of Israel, if only your sons take heed to their way, to walk in My law as you have walked before Me.'

17 "Now therefore, O LORD, the God of Israel, let Your word be confirmed which You have spoken to Your servant David.

18 ¶ "But will God indeed dwell with mankind on the earth? Behold, heaven and the highest heaven cannot contain You; how much less this house which I have built.

19 "Yet have regard to the prayer of Your servant and to his supplication, O LORD my God, to listen to the cry and to the prayer which Your servant prays before You;

20 that Your eye may be open toward this house day and night, toward the place of which You have said that *You would* put Your name there, to listen to the prayer which Your servant shall pray toward this place.

21 "Listen to the supplications of Your servant and of Your people Israel when they pray toward this place; hear from Your dwelling place, from heaven; hear and forgive.

22 ¶ "If a man sins against his neighbor and is made to take an oath, and he comes *and* takes an oath before Your altar in this house,

23 then hear from heaven and act and judge Your servants, punishing the wicked by bringing his way on his own head and justifying the righteous by giving him according to his righteousness.

24 ¶ "If Your people Israel are defeated before an enemy because they have sinned against You, and they return *to You* and confess Your name, and pray and make supplication before You in this house,

25 then hear from heaven and forgive the sin of Your people Israel, and bring them back to the land which You have given to them and to their fathers.

26 ¶ "When the heavens are shut up and there is no rain because they have sinned against You, and they pray toward this place and confess Your name, and turn from their sin when You afflict them;

27 then hear in heaven and forgive the sin of Your servants and Your people Israel, indeed, teach them the good way in which they should walk. And send rain on Your land which You have given to Your people for an inheritance.

28 ¶ "If there is famine in the land, if there is pestilence, if there is blight or mildew, if there is locust or grasshopper, if their enemies besiege them in the land of their cities, whatever plague or whatever sickness *there is,*

29 whatever prayer or supplication is made by any man or by all Your people Israel, each knowing his own affliction and his own pain, and spreading his hands toward this house,

30 then hear from heaven Your dwelling place, and forgive, and render to each according to all his ways, whose heart You know for You alone know the hearts of the sons of men,

31 that they may *a*fear You, to walk in Your ways as long as they live in the land which You have given to our fathers.

32 ¶ "Also concerning the foreigner who is not from Your people Israel, when he comes from a far country for Your great name's sake and Your mighty hand and Your outstretched arm, when they come and pray toward this house,

33 then hear from heaven, from Your dwelling place, and do according to all for which the foreigner calls to You, in order that all the peoples of the earth may know Your name, and *a*fear You as *do* Your people Israel, and that they may know that this house which I have built is called by Your name.

34 ¶ "When Your people go out to battle

against their enemies, by whatever way You shall send them, and they pray to You toward this city which You have chosen and the house which I have built for Your name,

35 then hear from heaven their prayer and their supplication, and maintain their cause.

36 ¶ "When they sin against You (for there is no man who does not sin) and You are angry with them and deliver them to an enemy, so that they take them away captive to a land far off or near,

37 if they take thought in the land where they are taken captive, and repent and make supplication to You in the land of their captivity, saying, 'We have sinned, we have committed iniquity and have acted wickedly';

38 if they return to You with all their heart and with all their soul in the land of their captivity, where they have been taken captive, and pray toward their land which You have given to their fathers and the city which You have chosen, and toward the house which I have built for Your name,

39 then hear from heaven, from Your dwelling place, their prayer and supplications, and maintain their cause and forgive Your people who have sinned against You.

40 ¶ "Now, O my God, I pray, let Your eyes be open and Your ears attentive to the prayer *offered* in this place.

41 ¶ "Now therefore arise, O LORD God, to Your resting place, You and the ark of Your might; let Your priests, O LORD God, be clothed with salvation and let Your godly ones rejoice in what is good.

42 ¶ "O LORD God, do not turn away the face of Your anointed; remember *Your* lovingkindness to Your servant David."

The Shekinah Glory

7 Now when Solomon had finished praying, fire came down from heaven and consumed the burnt offering and the sacrifices, and the glory of the LORD filled the house.

2 The priests could not enter into the house of

7:1 A High-Water Mark

Solomon's prayer in chapter 6 and God's response in chapter 7 marked a high point in Israel's existence as a nation. United, the Israelites gathered before the gleaming new temple. They saw fire come down from heaven and the glory of the Lord fill the temple. Later, when this building was destroyed, Ezra led a drive to build a new temple. But the dramatic scene of God's glory coming down was never duplicated.

a Or *reverence*

the LORD because the glory of the LORD filled the LORD's house.

3 All the sons of Israel, seeing the fire come down and the glory of the LORD upon the house, bowed down on the pavement with their faces to the ground, and they worshiped and gave praise to the LORD, *saying*, "Truly He is good, truly His lovingkindness is everlasting."

Sacrifices Offered

4 ¶ Then the king and all the people offered sacrifice before the LORD.

5 King Solomon offered a sacrifice of 22,000 oxen and 120,000 sheep. Thus the king and all the people dedicated the house of God.

6 The priests stood at their posts, and the Levites also, with the instruments of music to the LORD, which King David had made for giving praise to the LORD—"for His lovingkindness is everlasting"—whenever he gave praise by their means, while the priests on the other side blew trumpets; and all Israel was standing.

7 ¶ Then Solomon consecrated the middle of the court that *was* before the house of the LORD, for there he offered the burnt offerings and the fat of the peace offerings because the bronze altar which Solomon had made was not able to contain the burnt offering, the grain offering and the fat.

The Feast of Dedication

8 ¶ So Solomon observed the feast at that time for seven days, and all Israel with him, a very great assembly *who came* from the entrance of Hamath to the brook of Egypt.

9 On the eighth day they held a solemn assembly, for the dedication of the altar they observed seven days and the feast seven days.

10 Then on the twenty-third day of the seventh month he sent the people to their tents, rejoicing and happy of heart because of the goodness that the LORD had shown to David and to Solomon and to His people Israel.

God's Promise and Warning

11 ¶ Thus Solomon finished the house of the LORD and the king's palace, and successfully completed all that he had planned on doing in the house of the LORD and in his palace.

12 ¶ Then the LORD appeared to Solomon at night and said to him, "I have heard your prayer and have chosen this place for Myself as a house of sacrifice.

13 "If I shut up the heavens so that there is no rain, or if I command the locust to devour the land, or if I send pestilence among My people,

14 and My people who are called by My name humble themselves and pray and seek My face and turn from their wicked ways, then I will hear from heaven, will forgive their sin and will heal their land.

15 "Now My eyes will be open and My ears attentive to the prayer *offered* in this place.

16 "For now I have chosen and consecrated this house that My name may be there forever, and My eyes and My heart will be there perpetually.

17 "As for you, if you walk before Me as your father David walked, even to do according to all that I have commanded you, and will keep My statutes and My ordinances,

18 then I will establish your royal throne as I covenanted with your father David, saying, 'You shall not lack a man *to be* ruler in Israel.'

19 ¶ "But if you turn away and forsake My statutes and My commandments which I have set before you, and go and serve other gods and worship them,

20 then I will uproot you from My land which I have given you, and this house which I have consecrated for My name I will cast out of My sight and I will make it a proverb and a byword among all peoples.

21 "As for this house, which was exalted, everyone who passes by it will be astonished and say, 'Why has the LORD done thus to this land and to this house?'

22 "And they will say, 'Because they forsook the LORD, the God of their fathers who brought them from the land of Egypt, and they adopted other gods and worshiped them and served them; therefore He has brought all this adversity on them.'"

Solomon's Activities and Accomplishments

8 Now it came about at the end of the twenty years in which Solomon had built the house of the LORD and his own house

2 that he built the cities which Huram had given to him, and settled the sons of Israel there.

3 ¶ Then Solomon went to Hamath-zobah and captured it.

4 He built Tadmor in the wilderness and all the storage cities which he had built in Hamath.

5 He also built upper Beth-horon and lower Beth-horon, fortified cities *with* walls, gates and bars;

6 and Baalath and all the storage cities that Solomon had, and all the cities for his chariots and cities for his horsemen, and all that it pleased Solomon to build in Jerusalem, in Lebanon, and in all the land under his rule.

7 ¶ All of the people who were left of the Hittites, the Amorites, the Perizzites, the Hivites and the Jebusites, who were not of Israel,

8 *namely,* from their descendants who were left after them in the land whom the sons of Israel had not destroyed, them Solomon raised as forced laborers to this day.

9 But Solomon did not make slaves for his work from the sons of Israel; they were men of war, his chief captains and commanders of his chariots and his horsemen.

10 These were the chief officers of King Solo-

mon, two hundred and fifty who ruled over the people.

11 ¶ Then Solomon brought Pharaoh's daughter up from the city of David to the house which he had built for her, for he said, "My wife shall not dwell in the house of David king of Israel, because the places are holy where the ark of the LORD has entered."

8:11 Inconsistent Ethics

Solomon scrupulously kept Pharaoh's daughter, a Gentile foreigner, apart from the Israelite sacred places. Yet as the book of Kings shows, he eventually allowed his foreign wives to bring in their own idols, which had a disastrous effect on Israel.

12 ¶ Then Solomon offered burnt offerings to the LORD on the altar of the LORD which he had built before the porch;

13 and *did so* according to the daily rule, offering *them* up according to the commandment of Moses, for the sabbaths, the new moons and the three annual feasts—the Feast of Unleavened Bread, the Feast of Weeks and the Feast of Booths.

14 ¶ Now according to the ordinance of his father David, he appointed the divisions of the priests for their service, and the Levites for their duties of praise and ministering before the priests according to the daily rule, and the gatekeepers by their divisions at every gate; for David the man of God had so commanded.

15 And they did not depart from the commandment of the king to the priests and Levites in any manner or concerning the storehouses.

16 ¶ Thus all the work of Solomon was carried out from the day of the foundation of the house of the LORD, and until it was finished. So the house of the LORD was completed.

17 ¶ Then Solomon went to Ezion-geber and to Eloth on the seashore in the land of Edom.

18 And Huram by his servants sent him ships and servants who knew the sea; and they went with Solomon's servants to Ophir, and took from there four hundred and fifty talents of gold and brought them to King Solomon.

Visit of the Queen of Sheba

9 Now when the queen of Sheba heard of the fame of Solomon, she came to Jerusalem to test Solomon with difficult questions. She had a very large retinue, with camels carrying spices and a large amount of gold and precious stones; and when she came to Solomon, she spoke with him about all that was on her heart.

2 Solomon answered all her questions; nothing was hidden from Solomon which he did not explain to her.

3 When the queen of Sheba had seen the wis-

dom of Solomon, the house which he had built,

4 the food at his table, the seating of his servants, the attendance of his ministers and their attire, his cupbearers and their attire, and his stairway by which he went up to the house of the LORD, she was breathless.

5 Then she said to the king, "It was a true report which I heard in my own land about your words and your wisdom.

6 "Nevertheless I did not believe their reports until I came and my eyes had seen it. And behold, the half of the greatness of your wisdom was not told me. You surpass the report that I heard.

7 "How blessed are your men, how blessed are these your servants who stand before you continually and hear your wisdom.

8 "Blessed be the LORD your God who delighted in you, setting you on His throne as king for the LORD your God; because your God loved Israel establishing them forever, therefore He made you king over them, to do justice and righteousness."

9 Then she gave the king one hundred and twenty talents of gold and a very great *amount of* spices and precious stones; there had never been spice like that which the queen of Sheba gave to King Solomon.

10 ¶ The servants of Huram and the servants of Solomon who brought gold from Ophir, also brought algum trees and precious stones.

11 From the algum trees the king made steps for the house of the LORD and for the king's palace, and lyres and harps for the singers; and none like that was seen before in the land of Judah.

12 ¶ King Solomon gave to the queen of Sheba all her desire which she requested besides *a return for* what she had brought to the king. Then she turned and went to her own land with her servants.

9:12 An Unfounded Rumor

The Queen of Sheba has mistakenly gone down in legend as one of Solomon's lovers. The king had 700 wives and 300 concubines, but the Queen of Sheba was not among them.

The queen's personal visit from hundreds of miles away shows Jerusalem's reputation as the sumptuous showpiece of the Middle East. She was probably on a high-level diplomatic mission. Solomon's kingdom represented a huge threat to her land, which previously had held a trade monopoly over the land route through Israel.

Solomon financed his building projects through iron and copper-smelting industries. He traded these products to Arabia and Africa for gold, silver, ivory, and exotic animals. Evidently, he and the queen reached an agreement.

Solomon's Wealth and Power

13 ¶ Now the weight of gold which came to Solomon in one year was 666 talents of gold,

14 besides that which the traders and merchants brought; and all the kings of Arabia and the governors of the country brought gold and silver to Solomon.

15 King Solomon made 200 large shields of beaten gold, using 600 *shekels of* beaten gold on each large shield.

16 *He made* 300 shields of beaten gold, using three hundred shekels of gold on each shield, and the king put them in the house of the forest of Lebanon.

17 ¶ Moreover, the king made a great throne of ivory and overlaid it with pure gold.

18 *There were* six steps to the throne and a footstool in gold attached to the throne, and arms on each side of the seat, and two lions standing beside the arms.

19 Twelve lions were standing there on the six steps on the one side and on the other; nothing like *it* was made for any *other* kingdom.

20 All King Solomon's drinking vessels *were* of gold, and all the vessels of the house of the forest of Lebanon *were* of pure gold; silver was not considered valuable in the days of Solomon.

21 For the king had ships which went to Tarshish with the servants of Huram; once every three years the ships of Tarshish came bringing gold and silver, ivory and apes and peacocks.

22 ¶ So King Solomon became greater than all the kings of the earth in riches and wisdom.

23 And all the kings of the earth were seeking the presence of Solomon, to hear his wisdom which God had put in his heart.

24 They brought every man his gift, articles of silver and gold, garments, weapons, spices, horses and mules, so much year by year.

25 ¶ Now Solomon had 4,000 stalls for horses and chariots and 12,000 horsemen, and he stationed them in the chariot cities and with the king in Jerusalem.

26 He was the ruler over all the kings from the Euphrates River even to the land of the Philistines, and as far as the border of Egypt.

27 The king made silver *as common* as stones in Jerusalem, and he made cedars as plentiful as sycamore trees that are in the lowland.

28 And they were bringing horses for Solomon from Egypt and from all countries.

29 ¶ Now the rest of the acts of Solomon, from first to last, are they not written in the records of Nathan the prophet, and in the prophecy of Ahijah the Shilonite, and in the visions of Iddo the seer concerning Jeroboam the son of Nebat?

30 Solomon reigned forty years in Jerusalem over all Israel.

Death of Solomon

31 And Solomon slept with his fathers and was buried in the city of his father David; and his son Rehoboam reigned in his place.

Rehoboam's Reign of Folly

10 Then Rehoboam went to Shechem, for all Israel had come to Shechem to make him king.

2 When Jeroboam the son of Nebat heard *of* it (for he was in Egypt where he had fled from the presence of King Solomon), Jeroboam returned from Egypt.

3 So they sent and summoned him. When Jeroboam and all Israel came, they spoke to Rehoboam, saying,

4 "Your father made our yoke hard; now therefore lighten the hard service of your father and his heavy yoke which he put on us, and we will serve you."

5 He said to them, "Return to me again in three days." So the people departed.

6 ¶ Then King Rehoboam consulted with the elders who had served his father Solomon while he was still alive, saying, "How do you counsel *me* to answer this people?"

7 They spoke to him, saying, "If you will be kind to this people and please them and speak good words to them, then they will be your servants forever."

8 But he forsook the counsel of the elders which they had given him, and consulted with the young men who grew up with him and served him.

9 So he said to them, "What counsel do you give that we may answer this people, who have spoken to me, saying, 'Lighten the yoke which your father put on us'?"

10 The young men who grew up with him spoke to him, saying, "Thus you shall say to the people who spoke to you, saying, 'Your father made our yoke heavy, but you make it lighter for us.' Thus you shall say to them, 'My little finger is thicker than my father's loins!

11 'Whereas my father loaded you with a heavy yoke, I will add to your yoke; my father disciplined you with whips, but I *will discipline you* with scorpions.' "

12 ¶ So Jeroboam and all the people came to Rehoboam on the third day as the king had directed, saying, "Return to me on the third day."

13 The king answered them harshly, and King Rehoboam forsook the counsel of the elders.

14 He spoke to them according to the advice of the young men, saying, "My father made your yoke heavy, but I will add to it; my father disciplined you with whips, but I *will discipline you* with scorpions."

15 So the king did not listen to the people, for it was a turn *of events* from God that the LORD might establish His word, which He spoke through Ahijah the Shilonite to Jeroboam the son of Nebat.

16 ¶ When all Israel *saw* that the king did not listen to them the people answered the king, saying,

"What portion do we have in David?
    We have no inheritance in the son of Jesse.
Every man to your tents, O Israel;
    Now look after your own house, David."

So all Israel departed to their tents.

17 But as for the sons of Israel who lived in the cities of Judah, Rehoboam reigned over them.

18 Then King Rehoboam sent Hadoram, who was over the forced labor, and the sons of Israel stoned him to death. And King Rehoboam made haste to mount his chariot to flee to Jerusalem.

19 So Israel has been in rebellion against the house of David to this day.

10:19 Unified Front

Second Chronicles pays little attention to the rebellion of the ten northern tribes against the two tribes in Judah. As the book of Kings shows, the two kingdoms existed side by side, and the North, Israel, often achieved more power than the South. But Chronicles, written to survivors in the South, virtually ignores the history of the North. In fact, in several places it uses the word Israel to refer to the South, Judah.

Rehoboam Reigns over Judah and Builds Cities

11 Now when Rehoboam had come to Jerusalem, he assembled the house of Judah and Benjamin, 180,000 chosen men who were warriors, to fight against Israel to restore the kingdom to Rehoboam.

2 But the word of the LORD came to Shemaiah the man of God, saying,

3 "Speak to Rehoboam the son of Solomon, king of Judah, and to all Israel in Judah and Benjamin, saying,

4 'Thus says the LORD, "You shall not go up or fight against your relatives; return every man to his house, for this thing is from Me." ' " So they listened to the words of the LORD and returned from going against Jeroboam.

5 ¶ Rehoboam lived in Jerusalem and built cities for defense in Judah.

6 Thus he built Bethlehem, Etam, Tekoa,

7 Beth-zur, Soco, Adullam,

8 Gath, Mareshah, Ziph,

9 Adoraim, Lachish, Azekah,

10 Zorah, Aijalon and Hebron, which are fortified cities in Judah and in Benjamin.

11 He also strengthened the fortresses and put officers in them and stores of food, oil and wine.

12 *He put* shields and spears in every city and strengthened them greatly. So he held Judah and Benjamin.

13 ¶ Moreover, the priests and the Levites who were in all Israel stood with him from all their districts.

Jeroboam Appoints False Priests

14 For the Levites left their pasture lands and their property and came to Judah and Jerusalem, for Jeroboam and his sons had excluded them from serving as priests to the LORD.

15 He set up priests of his own for the high places, for the satyrs and for the calves which he had made.

16 Those from all the tribes of Israel who set their hearts on seeking the LORD God of Israel

---

REHOBOAM *A Fool's Answer*

HIS FATHER SOLOMON HAD ASKED God for wisdom as his reign began (1:10). Evidently the wisdom did not get passed down in the family DNA.

At a coronation ceremony, the northern tribes of Israel were ready to swear allegiance to Rehoboam. They asked only that the new king ease Solomon's harsh taxation and forced labor policies. Rehoboam wisely asked for three days to think about it, and wisely consulted a number of counselors. But then he foolishly followed the very worst advice of some young men he had grown up with. "My father disciplined you with whips," he told the Israelites. "but I will discipline you with scorpions" (10:14).

This harsh answer resulted in armed rebellion, the tragic split of Israel into two countries and a "family fight" that continued on and off as long as both nations survived. The twelve tribes of Israel, named for twelve brothers, broke into two warring factions. One man's misplaced bravado caused it all.

Rehoboam was not always so foolish. At times he listened to the right counselors. Yet in general he showed little interest in the godliness that would have strengthened his kingdom: "He did evil because he did not set his heart to seek the LORD" (12:14). By the Bible's standard, that made him the biggest fool.

Life Questions: When pressed, do you tend to harden your position, or listen carefully to the other side? What can help you avoid a belligerent response?

followed them to Jerusalem, to sacrifice to the LORD God of their fathers.

17 They strengthened the kingdom of Judah and supported Rehoboam the son of Solomon for three years, for they walked in the way of David and Solomon for three years.

Rehoboam's Family

18 ¶ Then Rehoboam took as a wife Mahalath the daughter of Jerimoth the son of David *and of* Abihail the daughter of Eliab the son of Jesse,

19 and she bore him sons: Jeush, Shemariah and Zaham.

20 After her he took Maacah the daughter of Absalom, and she bore him Abijah, Attai, Ziza and Shelomith.

21 Rehoboam loved Maacah the daughter of Absalom more than all his *other* wives and concubines. For he had taken eighteen wives and sixty concubines and fathered twenty-eight sons and sixty daughters.

22 Rehoboam appointed Abijah the son of Maacah as head and leader among his brothers, for he *intended* to make him king.

23 He acted wisely and distributed some of his sons through all the territories of Judah and Benjamin to all the fortified cities, and he gave them food in abundance. And he sought many wives *for them.*

Shishak of Egypt Invades Judah

12 When the kingdom of Rehoboam was established and strong, he and all Israel with him forsook the law of the LORD.

2 And it came about in King Rehoboam's fifth year, because they had been unfaithful to the LORD, that Shishak king of Egypt came up against Jerusalem

3 with 1,200 chariots and 60,000 horsemen. And the people who came with him from Egypt were without number: the Lubim, the Sukkiim and the Ethiopians.

4 He captured the fortified cities of Judah and came as far as Jerusalem.

5 Then Shemaiah the prophet came to Rehoboam and the princes of Judah who had gathered at Jerusalem because of Shishak, and he said to them, "Thus says the LORD, 'You have forsaken Me, so I also have forsaken you to Shishak.'"

6 So the princes of Israel and the king humbled themselves and said, "The LORD is righteous."

7 ¶ When the LORD saw that they humbled themselves, the word of the LORD came to Shemaiah, saying, "They have humbled themselves *so I* will not destroy them, but I will grant them some *measure* of deliverance, and My wrath shall not be poured out on Jerusalem by means of Shishak.

8 "But they will become his slaves so that they may learn *the difference between* My service and the service of the kingdoms of the countries."

Plunder Impoverishes Judah

9 ¶ So Shishak king of Egypt came up against Jerusalem, and took the treasures of the house of the LORD and the treasures of the king's palace. He took everything; he even took the golden shields which Solomon had made.

10 Then King Rehoboam made shields of bronze in their place and committed them to the care of the commanders of the guard who guarded the door of the king's house.

11 As often as the king entered the house of the LORD, the guards came and carried them and *then* brought them back into the guards' room.

12 And when he humbled himself, the anger of the LORD turned away from him, so as not to destroy *him* completely; and also conditions were good in Judah.

13 ¶ So King Rehoboam strengthened himself in Jerusalem and reigned. Now Rehoboam was forty-one years old when he began to reign, and he reigned seventeen years in Jerusalem, the city which the LORD had chosen from all the tribes of Israel, to put His name there. And his mother's name was Naamah the Ammonitess.

14 He did evil because he did not set his heart to seek the LORD.

15 ¶ Now the acts of Rehoboam, from first to last, are they not written in the records of Shemaiah the prophet and of Iddo the seer, according to genealogical enrollment? And *there were* wars between Rehoboam and Jeroboam continually.

16 And Rehoboam slept with his fathers and was buried in the city of David; and his son Abijah became king in his place.

Abijah Succeeds Rehoboam

13 In the eighteenth year of King Jeroboam, Abijah became king over Judah.

2 He reigned three years in Jerusalem; and his mother's name was Micaiah the daughter of Uriel of Gibeah.

¶ Now there was war between Abijah and Jeroboam.

3 Abijah began the battle with an army of valiant warriors, 400,000 chosen men, while Jeroboam drew up in battle formation against him with 800,000 chosen men *who were* valiant warriors.

Civil War

4 ¶ Then Abijah stood on Mount Zemaraim, which is in the hill country of Ephraim, and said, "Listen to me, Jeroboam and all Israel:

5 "Do you not know that the LORD God of Israel gave the rule over Israel forever to David and his sons by a covenant of salt?

6 "Yet Jeroboam the son of Nebat, the servant of Solomon the son of David, rose up and rebelled against his master,

7 and worthless men gathered about him, scoundrels, who proved too strong for Rehoboam,

the son of Solomon, when he was young and timid and could not hold his own against them.

8 ¶ "So now you intend to resist the kingdom of the LORD through the sons of David, being a

---

13:4 A Brighter Outlook

Typically, Chronicles paints a rosy picture of Judah's kings. The account of Abijam in Kings, for example, tells nothing of this speech and dismisses his reign as wicked (1 Kings 15:1–8).

---

great multitude and *having* with you the golden calves which Jeroboam made for gods for you.

9 "Have you not driven out the priests of the LORD, the sons of Aaron and the Levites, and made for yourselves priests like the peoples of *other* lands? Whoever comes to consecrate himself with a young bull and seven rams, even he may become a priest of *what are* no gods.

10 "But as for us, the LORD is our God, and we have not forsaken Him; and the sons of Aaron are ministering to the LORD as priests, and the Levites attend to their work.

11 "Every morning and evening they burn to the LORD burnt offerings and fragrant incense, and the showbread is *set* on the clean table, and the golden lampstand with its lamps is *ready* to light every evening; for we keep the charge of the LORD our God, but you have forsaken Him.

12 "Now behold, God is with us at *our* head and His priests with the signal trumpets to sound the alarm against you. O sons of Israel, do not fight against the LORD God of your fathers, for you will not succeed."

13 ¶ But Jeroboam had set an ambush to come from the rear, so that *Israel* was in front of Judah and the ambush was behind them.

14 When Judah turned around, behold, they were attacked both front and rear; so they cried to the LORD, and the priests blew the trumpets.

15 Then the men of Judah raised a war cry, and when the men of Judah raised the war cry, then it was that God routed Jeroboam and all Israel before Abijah and Judah.

16 When the sons of Israel fled before Judah, God gave them into their hand.

17 Abijah and his people defeated them with a great slaughter, so that 500,000 chosen men of Israel fell slain.

18 Thus the sons of Israel were subdued at that time, and the sons of Judah conquered because they trusted in the LORD, the God of their fathers.

19 Abijah pursued Jeroboam and captured from him *several* cities, Bethel with its villages, Jeshanah with its villages and Ephron with its villages.

---

a I.e. wooden symbols of a female deity

Death of Jeroboam

20 Jeroboam did not again recover strength in the days of Abijah; and the LORD struck him and he died.

21 ¶ But Abijah became powerful; and took fourteen wives to himself, and became the father of twenty-two sons and sixteen daughters.

22 Now the rest of the acts of Abijah, and his ways and his words are written in the treatise of the prophet Iddo.

Asa Succeeds Abijah in Judah

14 So Abijah slept with his fathers, and they buried him in the city of David, and his son Asa became king in his place. The land was undisturbed for ten years during his days.

2 ¶ Asa did good and right in the sight of the LORD his God,

3 for he removed the foreign altars and high places, tore down the *sacred* pillars, cut down the ᵃAsherim,

4 and commanded Judah to seek the LORD God of their fathers and to observe the law and the commandment.

5 He also removed the high places and the incense altars from all the cities of Judah. And the kingdom was undisturbed under him.

6 He built fortified cities in Judah, since the land was undisturbed, and there was no one at war with him during those years, because the LORD had given him rest.

7 For he said to Judah, "Let us build these cities and surround *them* with walls and towers, gates and bars. The land is still ours because we have sought the LORD our God; we have sought Him, and He has given us rest on every side." So they built and prospered.

8 Now Asa had an army of 300,000 from Judah, bearing large shields and spears, and 280,000 from Benjamin, bearing shields and wielding bows; all of them were valiant warriors.

9 ¶ Now Zerah the Ethiopian came out against them with an army of a million men and 300 chariots, and he came to Mareshah.

10 So Asa went out to meet him, and they drew up in battle formation in the valley of Zephathah at Mareshah.

11 Then Asa called to the LORD his God and said, "LORD, there is no one besides You to help *in the battle* between the powerful and those who have no strength; so help us, O LORD our God, for we trust in You, and in Your name have come against this multitude. O LORD, You are our God; let not man prevail against You."

12 So the LORD routed the Ethiopians before Asa and before Judah, and the Ethiopians fled.

13 Asa and the people who *were* with him pursued them as far as Gerar; and so many Ethiopians fell that they could not recover, for they were shat-

tered before the Lord and before His army. And they carried away very much plunder.

14 They destroyed all the cities around Gerar, for the dread of the Lord had fallen on them; and they despoiled all the cities, for there was much plunder in them.

15 They also struck down those who owned livestock, and they carried away large numbers of sheep and camels. Then they returned to Jerusalem.

The Prophet Azariah Warns Asa

15 Now the Spirit of God came on Azariah the son of Oded,

2 and he went out to meet Asa and said to him, "Listen to me, Asa, and all Judah and Benjamin: the Lord is with you when you are with Him. And if you seek Him, He will let you find Him; but if you forsake Him, He will forsake you.

3 "For many days Israel was without the true God and without a teaching priest and without law.

4 "But in their distress they turned to the Lord God of Israel, and they sought Him, and He let them find Him.

5 "In those times there was no peace to him who went out or to him who came in, for many disturbances afflicted all the inhabitants of the lands.

6 "Nation was crushed by nation, and city by city, for God troubled them with every kind of distress.

7 "But you, be strong and do not lose courage, for there is reward for your work."

Asa's Reforms

8 ¶ Now when Asa heard these words and the prophecy which Azariah the son of Oded the prophet spoke, he took courage and removed the abominable idols from all the land of Judah and Benjamin and from the cities which he had captured in the hill country of Ephraim. He then restored the altar of the Lord which was in front of the porch of the Lord.

9 He gathered all Judah and Benjamin and those from Ephraim, Manasseh and Simeon who resided with them, for many defected to him from Israel when they saw that the Lord his God was with him.

10 So they assembled at Jerusalem in the third month of the fifteenth year of Asa's reign.

11 They sacrificed to the Lord that day 700 oxen and 7,000 sheep from the spoil they had brought.

12 They entered into the covenant to seek the Lord God of their fathers with all their heart and soul;

13 and whoever would not seek the Lord God of Israel should be put to death, whether small or great, man or woman.

14 Moreover, they made an oath to the Lord with a loud voice, with shouting, with trumpets and with horns.

15 All Judah rejoiced concerning the oath, for they had sworn with their whole heart and had

15:9–15 Northern Visitors

For the first 50 years after Jeroboam's rebellion, Israel and Judah fought a civil war. Judah was badly outnumbered, but had one great rallying point: God's temple in the city of Jerusalem. Many of the kings of Israel had built idols on "high places" as alternative worship sites to discourage their citizens from making the pilgrimage to Jerusalem. But when a southern king such as Asa launched a religious revival, members of the northern tribes would sometimes come over to Jerusalem.

sought Him earnestly, and He let them find Him. So the Lord gave them rest on every side.

16 ¶ He also removed Maacah, the mother of King Asa, from the *position of* queen mother, because she had made a horrid image as an Asherah, and Asa cut down her horrid image, crushed *it* and burned *it* at the brook Kidron.

17 But the high places were not removed from Israel; nevertheless Asa's heart was blameless all his days.

18 He brought into the house of God the dedicated things of his father and his own dedicated things: silver and gold and utensils.

19 And there was no more war until the thirty-fifth year of Asa's reign.

Asa Wars against Baasha

16 In the thirty-sixth year of Asa's reign Baasha king of Israel came up against Judah and fortified Ramah in order to prevent *anyone* from going out or coming in to Asa king of Judah.

2 Then Asa brought out silver and gold from the treasuries of the house of the Lord and the king's house, and sent them to Ben-hadad king of Aram, who lived in Damascus, saying,

3 "*Let there be* a treaty between you and me, *as* between my father and your father. Behold, I have sent you silver and gold; go, break your treaty with Baasha king of Israel so that he will withdraw from me."

4 So Ben-hadad listened to King Asa and sent the commanders of his armies against the cities of Israel, and they conquered Ijon, Dan, Abel-maim and all the store cities of Naphtali.

5 When Baasha heard *of it*, he ceased fortifying Ramah and stopped his work.

6 Then King Asa brought all Judah, and they carried away the stones of Ramah and its timber with which Baasha had been building, and with them he fortified Geba and Mizpah.

Asa Imprisons the Prophet

7 ¶ At that time Hanani the seer came to Asa king of Judah and said to him, "Because you have relied on the king of Aram and have not relied on the LORD your God, therefore the army of the king of Aram has escaped out of your hand.

8 "Were not the Ethiopians and the Lubim an immense army with very many chariots and horsemen? Yet because you relied on the LORD, He delivered them into your hand.

9 "For the eyes of the LORD move to and fro throughout the earth that He may strongly support those whose heart is completely His. You have acted foolishly in this. Indeed, from now on you will surely have wars."

10 Then Asa was angry with the seer and put him in prison, for he was enraged at him for this. And Asa oppressed some of the people at the same time.

11 ¶ Now, the acts of Asa from first to last, behold, they are written in the Book of the Kings of Judah and Israel.

12 In the thirty-ninth year of his reign Asa became diseased in his feet. His disease was severe, yet even in his disease he did not seek the LORD, but the physicians.

16:12 Bad Medical Advice

King Asa suffered from a serious foot disease, which some scholars think was dropsy. The Bible criticizes his consultations with physicians because in those days "physicians" were pagan healers who used rituals that conflicted with the law of God.

13 So Asa slept with his fathers, having died in the forty-first year of his reign.

14 They buried him in his own tomb which he had cut out for himself in the city of David, and they laid him in the resting place which he had filled with spices of various kinds blended by the perfumers' art; and they made a very great fire for him.

Jehoshaphat Succeeds Asa

17 Jehoshaphat his son then became king in his place, and made his position over Israel firm.

2 He placed troops in all the fortified cities of Judah, and set garrisons in the land of Judah and in the cities of Ephraim which Asa his father had captured.

His Good Reign

3 The LORD was with Jehoshaphat because he followed the example of his father David's earlier days and did not seek the Baals,

4 but sought the God of his father, followed His commandments, and did not act as Israel did.

5 So the LORD established the kingdom in his control, and all Judah brought tribute to Jehoshaphat, and he had great riches and honor.

6 He took great pride in the ways of the LORD and again removed the high places and the Asherim from Judah.

7 ¶ Then in the third year of his reign he sent his officials, Ben-hail, Obadiah, Zechariah, Nethanel and Micaiah, to teach in the cities of Judah;

8 and with them the Levites, Shemaiah, Nethaniah, Zebadiah, Asahel, Shemiramoth, Jehonathan, Adonijah, Tobijah and Tobadonijah, the Levites; and with them Elishama and Jehoram, the priests.

9 They taught in Judah, *having* the book of the law of the LORD with them; and they went throughout all the cities of Judah and taught among the people.

10 ¶ Now the dread of the LORD was on all the kingdoms of the lands which *were* around Judah, so that they did not make war against Jehoshaphat.

11 Some of the Philistines brought gifts and silver as tribute to Jehoshaphat; the Arabians also brought him flocks, 7,700 rams and 7,700 male goats.

12 So Jehoshaphat grew greater and greater, and he built fortresses and store cities in Judah.

13 He had large supplies in the cities of Judah, and warriors, valiant men, in Jerusalem.

14 This was their muster according to their fathers' households: of Judah, commanders of thousands, Adnah *was* the commander, and with him 300,000 valiant warriors;

15 and next to him *was* Johanan the commander, and with him 280,000;

16 and next to him Amasiah the son of Zichri, who volunteered for the LORD, and with him 200,000 valiant warriors;

17 and of Benjamin, Eliada a valiant warrior, and with him 200,000 armed with bow and shield;

18 and next to him Jehozabad, and with him 180,000 equipped for war.

19 These are they who served the king, apart from those whom the king put in the fortified cities through all Judah.

Jehoshaphat Allies with Ahab

18 Now Jehoshaphat had great riches and honor; and he allied himself by marriage with Ahab.

2 Some years later he went down to *visit* Ahab at Samaria. And Ahab slaughtered many sheep and oxen for him and the people who were with him, and induced him to go up against Ramoth-gilead.

3 Ahab king of Israel said to Jehoshaphat king of Judah, "Will you go with me *against* Ramoth-gilead?" And he said to him, "I am as you are, and

my people as your people, and *we will be* with you in the battle."

4 ¶ Moreover, Jehoshaphat said to the king of Israel, "Please inquire first for the word of the LORD."

5 Then the king of Israel assembled the prophets, four hundred men, and said to them, "Shall we go against Ramoth-gilead to battle, or shall I refrain?" And they said, "Go up, for God will give *it* into the hand of the king."

6 But Jehoshaphat said, "Is there not yet a prophet of the LORD here that we may inquire of him?"

18:6 A True or False Prophet?

Looking back from a modern perspective, it is difficult to imagine the confusion that surrounded ancient prophets. Which ones were true prophets and which were false? In this case, 400 prophets all insisted God said one thing; only one bold man contradicted them. King Jehoshaphat sensed a falseness in the 400 and insisted on listening to the true prophet. Yet, unaccountably, he failed to heed Micaiah's warning. The decision nearly cost him his life. See Deuteronomy 18:17–22 for advice on distinguishing true prophets from false.

7 The king of Israel said to Jehoshaphat, "There is yet one man by whom we may inquire of the LORD, but I hate him, for he never prophesies good concerning me but always evil. He is Micaiah, son of Imla." But Jehoshaphat said, "Let not the king say so."

Ahab's False Prophets Assure Victory

8 Then the king of Israel called an officer and said, "Bring quickly Micaiah, Imla's son."

9 Now the king of Israel and Jehoshaphat the king of Judah were sitting each on his throne, arrayed in *their* robes, and *they* were sitting at the threshing floor at the entrance of the gate of Samaria; and all the prophets were prophesying before them.

10 Zedekiah the son of Chenaanah made horns of iron for himself and said, "Thus says the LORD, 'With these you shall gore the Arameans until they are consumed.' "

11 All the prophets were prophesying thus, saying, "Go up to Ramoth-gilead and succeed, for the LORD will give *it* into the hand of the king."

Micaiah Brings Word from God

12 ¶ Then the messenger who went to summon Micaiah spoke to him saying, "Behold, the words of the prophets are uniformly favorable to the king. So please let your word be like one of them and speak favorably."

13 But Micaiah said, "As the LORD lives, what my God says, that I will speak."

14 ¶ When he came to the king, the king said to him, "Micaiah, shall we go to Ramoth-gilead to battle, or shall I refrain?" He said, "Go up and succeed, for they will be given into your hand."

15 Then the king said to him, "How many times must I adjure you to speak to me nothing but the truth in the name of the LORD?"

16 So he said,
"I saw all Israel
Scattered on the mountains,
Like sheep which have no shepherd;
And the LORD said,
'These have no master.
Let each of them return to his house in peace.' "

17 Then the king of Israel said to Jehoshaphat, "Did I not tell you that he would not prophesy good concerning me, but evil?"

18 ¶ Micaiah said, "Therefore, hear the word of the LORD. I saw the LORD sitting on His throne, and all the host of heaven standing on His right and on His left.

19 "The LORD said, 'Who will entice Ahab king of Israel to go up and fall at Ramoth-gilead?' And one said this while another said that.

20 "Then a spirit came forward and stood before the LORD and said, 'I will entice him.' And the LORD said to him, 'How?'

21 "He said, 'I will go and be a deceiving spirit in the mouth of all his prophets.' Then He said, 'You are to entice *him* and prevail also. Go and do so.'

22 "Now therefore, behold, the LORD has put a deceiving spirit in the mouth of these your prophets, for the LORD has proclaimed disaster against you."

23 ¶ Then Zedekiah the son of Chenaanah came near and struck Micaiah on the cheek and said, "How did the Spirit of the LORD pass from me to speak to you?"

24 Micaiah said, "Behold, you will see on that day when you enter an inner room to hide yourself."

25 Then the king of Israel said, "Take Micaiah and return him to Amon the governor of the city and to Joash the king's son;

26 and say, 'Thus says the king, "Put this *man* in prison and feed him sparingly with bread and water until I return safely." ' "

27 Micaiah said, "If you indeed return safely, the LORD has not spoken by me." And he said, "Listen, all you people."

Ahab's Defeat and Death

28 ¶ So the king of Israel and Jehoshaphat king of Judah went up against Ramoth-gilead.

29 The king of Israel said to Jehoshaphat, "I will disguise myself and go into battle, but you put

on your robes." So the king of Israel disguised himself, and they went into battle.

30 Now the king of Aram had commanded the captains of his chariots, saying, "Do not fight with small or great, but with the king of Israel alone."

31 So when the captains of the chariots saw Jehoshaphat, they said, "It is the king of Israel," and they turned aside to fight against him. But Jehoshaphat cried out, and the LORD helped him, and God diverted them from him.

32 When the captains of the chariots saw that it was not the king of Israel, they turned back from pursuing him.

33 A certain man drew his bow at random and struck the king of Israel in a joint of the armor. So he said to the driver of the chariot, "Turn around and take me out of the fight, for I am severely wounded."

34 The battle raged that day, and the king of Israel propped himself up in his chariot in front of the Arameans until the evening; and at sunset he died.

Jehu Rebukes Jehoshaphat

19 Then Jehoshaphat the king of Judah returned in safety to his house in Jerusalem.

2 Jehu the son of Hanani the seer went out to meet him and said to King Jehoshaphat, "Should you help the wicked and love those who hate the LORD and so *bring* wrath on yourself from the LORD?

3 "But there is *some* good in you, for you have removed the Asheroth from the land and you have set your heart to seek God."

4 ¶ So Jehoshaphat lived in Jerusalem and went out again among the people from Beersheba to the hill country of Ephraim and brought them back to the LORD, the God of their fathers.

Reforms Instituted

5 He appointed judges in the land in all the fortified cities of Judah, city by city.

6 He said to the judges, "Consider what you are doing, for you do not judge for man but for the LORD who is with you when you render judgment.

7 "Now then let the fear of the LORD be upon you; be very careful what you do, for the LORD our God will have no part in unrighteousness or partiality or the taking of a bribe."

8 ¶ In Jerusalem also Jehoshaphat appointed some of the Levites and priests, and some of the heads of the fathers' *households* of Israel, for the judgment of the LORD and to judge disputes among the inhabitants of Jerusalem.

9 Then he charged them saying, "Thus you shall do in the fear of the LORD, faithfully and wholeheartedly.

10 "Whenever any dispute comes to you from your brethren who live in their cities, between blood and blood, between law and command-

ment, statutes and ordinances, you shall warn them so that they may not be guilty before the LORD, and wrath may *not* come on you and your brethren. Thus you shall do and you will not be guilty.

11 "Behold, Amariah the chief priest will be over you in all that pertains to the LORD, and Zebadiah the son of Ishmael, the ruler of the house of Judah, in all that pertains to the king. Also the Levites shall be officers before you. Act resolutely, and the LORD be with the upright."

Judah Invaded

20 Now it came about after this that the sons of Moab and the sons of Ammon, together with some of the Meunites, came to make war against Jehoshaphat.

2 Then some came and reported to Jehoshaphat, saying, "A great multitude is coming against you from beyond the sea, out of Aram and behold, they are in Hazazon-tamar (that is Engedi)."

3 Jehoshaphat was afraid and turned his attention to seek the LORD, and proclaimed a fast throughout all Judah.

4 So Judah gathered together to seek help from the LORD; they even came from all the cities of Judah to seek the LORD.

Jehoshaphat's Prayer

5 ¶ Then Jehoshaphat stood in the assembly of Judah and Jerusalem, in the house of the LORD before the new court,

6 and he said, "O LORD, the God of our fathers, are You not God in the heavens? And are You not ruler over all the kingdoms of the nations? Power and might are in Your hand so that no one can stand against You.

20:6 A Model Prayer

Second Chronicles contains two great prayers: Solomon's in chapter 6 and King Jehoshaphat's here. Commentators often point to this as a model prayer. Jehoshaphat began with adoration of God, reminded him of his promises, set forth a problem, and asked for help. Confident, Jehoshaphat thanked God for the answer even before it came.

7 "Did You not, O our God, drive out the inhabitants of this land before Your people Israel and give it to the descendants of Abraham Your friend forever?

8 "They have lived in it, and have built You a sanctuary there for Your name, saying,

9 'Should evil come upon us, the sword, *or* judgment, or pestilence, or famine, we will stand before this house and before You (for Your name is in this house) and cry to You in our distress, and You will hear and deliver *us*.'

10 "Now behold, the sons of Ammon and Moab and Mount Seir, whom You did not let Israel invade when they came out of the land of Egypt (they turned aside from them and did not destroy them),

11 see *how* they are rewarding us by coming to drive us out from Your possession which You have given us as an inheritance.

12 "O our God, will You not judge them? For we are powerless before this great multitude who are coming against us; nor do we know what to do, but our eyes are on You."

13 ¶ All Judah was standing before the LORD, with their infants, their wives and their children.

Jahaziel Answers the Prayer

14 Then in the midst of the assembly the Spirit of the LORD came upon Jahaziel the son of Zecha-riah, the son of Benaiah, the son of Jeiel, the son of Mattaniah, the Levite of the sons of Asaph;

15 and he said, "Listen, all Judah and the inhabitants of Jerusalem and King Jehoshaphat: thus says the LORD to you, 'Do not fear or be dismayed because of this great multitude, for the battle is not yours but God's.

16 'Tomorrow go down against them. Behold, they will come up by the ascent of Ziz, and you will find them at the end of the valley in front of the wilderness of Jeruel.

17 'You *need* not fight in this *battle*; station yourselves, stand and see the salvation of the LORD on your behalf, O Judah and Jerusalem.' Do not fear or be dismayed; tomorrow go out to face them, for the LORD is with you."

18 ¶ Jehoshaphat bowed his head with *his* face to the ground, and all Judah and the inhabitants of

---

The Great Reformers
Profiles in courage: the heroic kings of Judah

IN 1954 UNITED STATES SENATOR John F. Kennedy knew he would spend at least six months flat on his back. Surgeons were about to begin work on him to correct an old war injury. How could he best spend his time?

Kennedy decided to use those "idle" hours to research the most courageous individuals in American history. The idea for a book was born. *Profiles in Courage* went on to win the Pulitzer Prize and become a best seller. Kennedy's study of courageous people inspired the young senator to model his own life after them.

> "The LORD is with you when you are with Him. And if you seek Him, He will let you find Him; but if you forsake Him, He will forsake you." 15:2

Courage in Judah

The book of 2 Chronicles can be seen as a kind of "profiles in courage" for the nation of Judah. The vast majority of kings flunked the courage test. But a few exceptions did stand out, and 2 Chronicles dwells on them.

This book records a form of courage different from what John Kennedy had in mind. Judah was drifting further and further away from the worship of the true God. It took great courage to fight against that trend and call for a return to the law of Moses. Therefore these kings excelled not so much because of military or political strength, but because of their faithfulness to God. All the great reformers described here took over in difficult times. They helped stop, at least temporarily, their nation's tragic slide away from God.

Asa: Cleaning Up the Land (chapters 14–16)

Asa inherited a country full of crime and anarchy. He led a wildfire revival, with the whole nation uniting behind him in a huge celebration in Jerusalem. Yet Asa became cocky in his later years—he jailed a prophet of God and lived out his last days plagued by war and by disease. He did much good, but fell short of the kind of courage that endures a national crisis.

Jehoshaphat: The Organizer (chapters 17–20)

Where Asa inspired the nation, Jehoshaphat organized it. He had an outstanding domestic policy: He educated his citizens in the Book of the Law and built up a national court system and large army. Curiously, Jehoshaphat's wise judgment failed to carry over into foreign policy, for he made foolish alliances with neighboring Israel's very worst king, Ahab.

Joash: Refurbishing the Temple (chapters 23–24)

Joash stepped onto the throne as a boy of seven. He reigned 40 years and accomplished much

Jerusalem fell down before the LORD, worshiping the LORD.

19 The Levites, from the sons of the Kohathites and of the sons of the Korahites, stood up to praise the LORD God of Israel, with a very loud voice.

Enemies Destroy Themselves

20 ¶ They rose early in the morning and went out to the wilderness of Tekoa; and when they went out, Jehoshaphat stood and said, "Listen to me, O Judah and inhabitants of Jerusalem, put your trust in the LORD your God and you will be established. Put your trust in His prophets and succeed."

21 When he had consulted with the people, he appointed those who sang to the LORD and those who praised *Him* in holy attire, as they went out before the army and said, "Give thanks to the LORD, for His lovingkindness is everlasting."

22 When they began singing and praising, the LORD set ambushes against the sons of Ammon, Moab and Mount Seir, who had come against Judah; so they were routed.

23 For the sons of Ammon and Moab rose up against the inhabitants of Mount Seir destroying *them* completely; and when they had finished with the inhabitants of Seir, they helped to destroy one another.

24 ¶ When Judah came to the lookout of the wilderness, they looked toward the multitude, and behold, they *were* corpses lying on the ground, and no one had escaped.

25 When Jehoshaphat and his people came to take their spoil, they found much among them, *including* goods, garments and valuable things which they took for themselves, more than they could carry. And they were three days taking the spoil because there was so much.

Triumphant Return to Jerusalem

26 Then on the fourth day they assembled in the valley of Beracah, for there they blessed the LORD. Therefore they have named that place "The Valley of *a*Beracah" until today.

27 Every man of Judah and Jerusalem returned with Jehoshaphat at their head, returning to Jerusalem with joy, for the LORD had made them to rejoice over their enemies.

28 They came to Jerusalem with harps, lyres and trumpets to the house of the LORD.

29 And the dread of God was on all the kingdoms of the lands when they heard that the LORD had fought against the enemies of Israel.

30 So the kingdom of Jehoshaphat was at peace, for his God gave him rest on all sides.

31 ¶ Now Jehoshaphat reigned over Judah. He *was* thirty-five years old when he became king, and he reigned in Jerusalem twenty-five years.

a I.e. blessing

---

good. Second Chronicles focuses mainly on his repairs of the temple, which he tried to restore to former glory.

Jehoiada: Strength behind the Throne (chapters 23–24)

King Joash hardly deserves a compliment without the mention of a priest named Jehoiada. He hid the boy Joash from a murderous queen and led the dramatic revolt against her. When Jehoiada died at a very old age, the nation gave him the extraordinary honor of a burial place alongside kings. After Jehoiada's death, everything went downhill. The boy king who had shown such promise murdered Jehoiada's son, a deed that went down as one of the great crimes of Israelite history. It became clear that the real strength of the kingdom had come from the old priest, not the young king.

Hezekiah: A Day to Remember (chapters 29–32)

Second Chronicles gives more space to the reign of Hezekiah than to that of any other reformer. He sponsored a great religious festival, an idea that first met with scorn and ridicule. But the nation did come together in a remarkable scene of happiness and unity. "There was great joy in Jerusalem," the Bible says, "because there was nothing like this in Jerusalem since the days of Solomon son of David, king of Israel " (30:26).

Josiah: The Complete Reformer (chapters 34–35)

Josiah was perhaps the most reform-conscious of all Judah's kings. When the Book of the Law (probably Deuteronomy) was discovered, Josiah realized just how far his kingdom had strayed from God's ideal. He tore his robes and wept, and led Judah back toward God. A foolish military campaign brought about Josiah's death and ruined the chances for permanent change in Judah. Known as "the good king Josiah," he was mourned by the whole nation. The prophet Jeremiah composed songs, or laments, in his memory.

Life Questions: These kings demonstrate that one person's faith can affect a great many others. Think of strong leaders you know up close. What makes them effective at inspiring and motivating others?

And his mother's name *was* Azubah the daughter of Shilhi.

32 He walked in the way of his father Asa and did not depart from it, doing right in the sight of the LORD.

33 The high places, however, were not removed; the people had not yet directed their hearts to the God of their fathers.

34 ¶ Now the rest of the acts of Jehoshaphat, first to last, behold, they are written in the annals of Jehu the son of Hanani, which is recorded in the Book of the Kings of Israel.

Alliance Displeases God

35 ¶ After this Jehoshaphat king of Judah allied himself with Ahaziah king of Israel. He acted wickedly in so doing.

36 So he allied himself with him to make ships to go to Tarshish, and they made the ships in Ezion-geber.

37 Then Eliezer the son of Dodavahu of Mareshah prophesied against Jehoshaphat saying, "Because you have allied yourself with Ahaziah, the LORD has destroyed your works." So the ships were broken and could not go to Tarshish.

Jehoram Succeeds Jehoshaphat in Judah

21 Then Jehoshaphat slept with his fathers and was buried with his fathers in the city of David, and Jehoram his son became king in his place.

2 He had brothers, the sons of Jehoshaphat: Azariah, Jehiel, Zechariah, Azaryahu, Michael and Shephatiah. All these *were* the sons of Jehoshaphat king of Israel.

3 Their father gave them many gifts of silver, gold and precious things, with fortified cities in Judah, but he gave the kingdom to Jehoram because he was the firstborn.

4 ¶ Now when Jehoram had taken over the kingdom of his father and made himself secure, he killed all his brothers with the sword, and some of the rulers of Israel also.

5 Jehoram *was* thirty-two years old when he became king, and he reigned eight years in Jerusalem.

6 He walked in the way of the kings of Israel, just as the house of Ahab did (for Ahab's daughter was his wife), and he did evil in the sight of the LORD.

7 Yet the LORD was not willing to destroy the house of David because of the covenant which He had made with David, and since He had promised to give a lamp to him and his sons forever.

Revolt against Judah

8 ¶ In his days Edom revolted ᵃagainst the rule of Judah and set up a king over themselves.

9 Then Jehoram crossed over with his commanders and all his chariots with him. And he

arose by night and struck down the Edomites who were surrounding him and the commanders of the chariots.

21:6 Married Despots

After the benign reign of Jehoshaphat, Judah got one of its worst kings ever, Jehoram. His marriage to Athaliah, daughter of a despised pagan king, undoubtedly stirred up revolt. To eliminate rivals, Jehoram promptly killed off his brothers, along with the "princes of Israel" (possibly leaders of the revolt). Later, Athaliah would become Judah's only reigning queen— and commit even greater atrocities (22:10).

10 So Edom revolted ᵃagainst Judah to this day. Then Libnah revolted at the same time against his rule, because he had forsaken the LORD God of his fathers.

11 Moreover, he made high places in the mountains of Judah, and caused the inhabitants of Jerusalem to play the harlot and led Judah astray.

12 ¶ Then a letter came to him from Elijah the prophet saying, "Thus says the LORD God of your father David, 'Because you have not walked in the ways of Jehoshaphat your father and the ways of Asa king of Judah,

13 but have walked in the way of the kings of Israel, and have caused Judah and the inhabitants of Jerusalem to play the harlot as the house of Ahab played the harlot, and you have also killed your brothers, your own family, who were better than you,

14 behold, the LORD is going to strike your people, your sons, your wives and all your possessions with a great calamity;

15 and you will suffer severe sickness, a disease of your bowels, until your bowels come out because of the sickness, day by day.'"

16 ¶ Then the LORD stirred up against Jehoram the spirit of the Philistines and the Arabs who bordered the Ethiopians;

17 and they came against Judah and invaded it, and carried away all the possessions found in the king's house together with his sons and his wives, so that no son was left to him except Jehoahaz, the youngest of his sons.

18 ¶ So after all this the LORD smote him in his bowels with an incurable sickness.

19 Now it came about in the course of time, at the end of two years, that his bowels came out because of his sickness and he died in great pain. And his people made no fire for him like the fire for his fathers.

20 He was thirty-two years old when he became king, and he reigned in Jerusalem eight years; and he departed with no one's regret, and

ᵃ Lit *from under the hand of*

they buried him in the city of David, but not in the tombs of the kings.

Ahaziah Succeeds Jehoram in Judah

22 Then the inhabitants of Jerusalem made Ahaziah, his youngest son, king in his place, for the band of men who came with the Arabs to the camp had slain all the older *sons*. So Ahaziah the son of Jehoram king of Judah began to reign.

2 Ahaziah *was* twenty-two years old when he became king, and he reigned one year in Jerusalem. And his mother's name was Athaliah, the granddaughter of Omri.

3 He also walked in the ways of the house of Ahab, for his mother was his counselor to do wickedly.

4 He did evil in the sight of the LORD like the house of Ahab, for they were his counselors after the death of his father, to his destruction.

Ahaziah Allies with Jehoram of Israel

5 He also walked according to their counsel, and went with Jehoram the son of Ahab king of Israel to wage war against Hazael king of Aram at Ramoth-gilead. But the Arameans wounded Joram.

6 So he returned to be healed in Jezreel of the wounds which they had inflicted on him at Ramah, when he fought against Hazael king of Aram. And Ahaziah, the son of Jehoram king of Judah, went down to see Jehoram the son of Ahab in Jezreel, because he was sick.

7 ¶ Now the destruction of Ahaziah was from God, in that he went to Joram. For when he came, he went out with Jehoram against Jehu the son of Nimshi, whom the LORD had anointed to cut off the house of Ahab.

Jehu Murders Princes of Judah

8 It came about when Jehu was executing judgment on the house of Ahab, he found the princes of Judah and the sons of Ahaziah's brothers ministering to Ahaziah, and slew them.

9 He also sought Ahaziah, and they caught him while he was hiding in Samaria; they brought him to Jehu, put him to death and buried him. For they said, "He is the son of Jehoshaphat, who sought the LORD with all his heart." So there was no one of the house of Ahaziah to retain the power of the kingdom.

10 ¶ Now when Athaliah the mother of Ahaziah saw that her son was dead, she rose and destroyed all the royal offspring of the house of Judah.

11 But Jehoshabeath the king's daughter took Joash the son of Ahaziah, and stole him from among the king's sons who were being put to death, and placed him and his nurse in the bedroom. So Jehoshabeath, the daughter of King Jehoram, the wife of Jehoiada the priest (for she was the sister of Ahaziah), hid him from Athaliah so that she would not put him to death.

12 He was hidden with them in the house of God six years while Athaliah reigned over the land.

Jehoiada Sets Joash on the Throne of Judah

23 Now in the seventh year Jehoiada strengthened himself, and took captains of hundreds: Azariah the son of Jeroham, Ishmael the son of Johanan, Azariah the son of Obed, Maaseiah the son of Adaiah, and Elishaphat the son of Zichri, *and they entered* into a covenant with him.

2 They went throughout Judah and gathered the Levites from all the cities of Judah, and the heads of the fathers' *households* of Israel, and they came to Jerusalem.

3 Then all the assembly made a covenant with the king in the house of God. And Jehoiada said

ATHALIAH   *Live by the Sword . . .*

IN OLD TESTAMENT TIMES AMBITIOUS women usually exerted themselves through their husbands. Athaliah's wicked mother Jezebel, for example, dominated her husband Ahab, king of Israel.

Athaliah took another route, preferring to go it alone. She reigned eight years as queen to King Jehoram and a year as Queen Mother with their son Ahaziah. But when Ahaziah died a violent death, Mother decided to take charge for herself. Ruthless as Lady Macbeth, Athaliah had all potential rivals—including her own children and grandchildren—put to death. She reigned alone for six years, secure in the throne since she had eliminated all opposition.

Then appeared, in a scene as dramatic as any in the Bible, a royal heir she had overlooked. The seven-year-old boy Joash—her grandson—had been hidden in the temple all those years. This boy was now brought out and displayed on the temple steps. When Athaliah heard the tumultuous response, she went to see what the commotion was about. A revolution was underway. Rebels captured her and put her to death, and not a single person came to her defense.

Life Questions: Which type of people do you think are more likely to cause trouble: "loners," or people who have many friends and allies? Why?

to them, "Behold, the king's son shall reign, as the LORD has spoken concerning the sons of David.

4 "This is the thing which you shall do: one third of you, of the priests and Levites who come in on the sabbath, *shall be* gatekeepers,

5 and one third *shall be* at the king's house, and a third at the Gate of the Foundation; and all the people *shall be* in the courts of the house of the LORD.

6 "But let no one enter the house of the LORD except the priests and the ministering Levites; they may enter, for they are holy. And let all the people keep the charge of the LORD.

7 "The Levites will surround the king, each man with his weapons in his hand; and whoever enters the house, let him be killed. Thus be with the king when he comes in and when he goes out."

23:7 The Priests Take up Arms

Athaliah, daughter of Jezebel, introduced Baal worship to Judah and very nearly destroyed the entire royal line of David. Conditions in Judah got so bad that a priest, Jehoiada, took the extraordinary step of arming the Levites for a palace coup. They placed the rightful heir, Joash, on the throne.

8 ¶ So the Levites and all Judah did according to all that Jehoiada the priest commanded. And each one of them took his men who were to come in on the sabbath, with those who were to go out on the sabbath, for Jehoiada the priest did not dismiss *any of* the divisions.

9 Then Jehoiada the priest gave to the captains of hundreds the spears and the large and small shields which had been King David's, which were in the house of God.

10 He stationed all the people, each man with his weapon in his hand, from the right side of the house to the left side of the house, by the altar and by the house, around the king.

11 Then they brought out the king's son and put the crown on him, and *gave him* the testimony and made him king. And Jehoiada and his sons anointed him and said, "*Long* live the king!"

Athaliah Murdered

12 ¶ When Athaliah heard the noise of the people running and praising the king, she came into the house of the LORD to the people.

13 She looked, and behold, the king was standing by his pillar at the entrance, and the captains and the trumpeters *were* beside the king. And all the people of the land rejoiced and blew trumpets, the singers with *their* musical instruments leading the praise. Then Athaliah tore her clothes and said, "Treason! Treason!"

14 Jehoiada the priest brought out the captains of hundreds who were appointed over the army

and said to them, "Bring her out between the ranks; and whoever follows her, put to death with the sword." For the priest said, "Let her not be put to death in the house of the LORD."

15 So they seized her, and when she arrived at the entrance of the Horse Gate of the king's house, they put her to death there.

Reforms Carried Out

16 ¶ Then Jehoiada made a covenant between himself and all the people and the king, that they would be the LORD'S people.

17 And all the people went to the house of Baal and tore it down, and they broke in pieces his altars and his images, and killed Mattan the priest of Baal before the altars.

18 Moreover, Jehoiada placed the offices of the house of the LORD under the authority of the Levitical priests, whom David had assigned over the house of the LORD, to offer the burnt offerings of the LORD, as it is written in the law of Moses— with rejoicing and singing according to the order of David.

19 He stationed the gatekeepers of the house of the LORD, so that no one would enter *who was* in any way unclean.

20 He took the captains of hundreds, the nobles, the rulers of the people and all the people of the land, and brought the king down from the house of the LORD, and came through the upper gate to the king's house. And they placed the king upon the royal throne.

21 So all of the people of the land rejoiced and the city was quiet. For they had put Athaliah to death with the sword.

Young Joash Influenced by Jehoiada

24 Joash *was* seven years old when he became king, and he reigned forty years in Jerusalem; and his mother's name *was* Zibiah from Beersheba.

2 Joash did what was right in the sight of the LORD all the days of Jehoiada the priest.

3 Jehoiada took two wives for him, and he became the father of sons and daughters.

Faithless Priests

4 ¶ Now it came about after this that Joash decided to restore the house of the LORD.

5 He gathered the priests and Levites and said to them, "Go out to the cities of Judah and collect money from all Israel to repair the house of your God annually, and you shall do the matter quickly." But the Levites did not act quickly.

6 So the king summoned Jehoiada the chief *priest* and said to him, "Why have you not required the Levites to bring in from Judah and from Jerusalem the levy *fixed by* Moses the servant of the LORD on the congregation of Israel for the tent of the testimony?"

7 For the sons of the wicked Athaliah had

broken into the house of God and even used the holy things of the house of the LORD for the Baals.

Temple Repaired

8 ¶ So the king commanded, and they made a chest and set it outside by the gate of the house of the LORD.

9 They made a proclamation in Judah and Jerusalem to bring to the LORD the levy *fixed by* Moses the servant of God on Israel in the wilderness.

10 All the officers and all the people rejoiced and brought in their levies and dropped *them* into the chest until they had finished.

11 It came about whenever the chest was brought in to the king's officer by the Levites, and when they saw that there was much money, then the king's scribe and the chief priest's officer would come, empty the chest, take it, and return it to its place. Thus they did daily and collected much money.

12 The king and Jehoiada gave it to those who did the work of the service of the house of the LORD; and they hired masons and carpenters to restore the house of the LORD, and also workers in iron and bronze to repair the house of the LORD.

13 So the workmen labored, and the repair work progressed in their hands, and they restored the house of God according to its specifications and strengthened it.

14 When they had finished, they brought the rest of the money before the king and Jehoiada; and it was made into utensils for the house of the LORD, utensils for the service and the burnt offering, and pans and utensils of gold and silver. And they offered burnt offerings in the house of the LORD continually all the days of Jehoiada.

15 ¶ Now when Jehoiada reached a ripe old age he died; he was one hundred and thirty years old at his death.

16 They buried him in the city of David among the kings, because he had done well in Israel and to God and His house.

17 ¶ But after the death of Jehoiada the officials of Judah came and bowed down to the king, and the king listened to them.

18 They abandoned the house of the LORD, the God of their fathers, and served the *a*Asherim and the idols; so wrath came upon Judah and Jerusalem for this their guilt.

19 Yet He sent prophets to them to bring them back to the LORD; though they testified against them, they would not listen.

Joash Murders Son of Jehoiada

20 ¶ Then the Spirit of God came on Zechariah the son of Jehoiada the priest; and he stood above the people and said to them, "Thus God has said, 'Why do you transgress the commandments of

the LORD and do not prosper? Because you have forsaken the LORD, He has also forsaken you.'"

21 So they conspired against him and at the command of the king they stoned him to death in the court of the house of the LORD.

24:21 An Infamous Murder

Joash showed promise in his early years as king. But, like many other kings, he could not tolerate the damning words of one of God's prophets. The murder carried out on his order brought in enemy armies, inspired a conspiracy against Joash, and destroyed his reputation forever. Jesus may have been speaking of this incident when he alluded to a murder hundreds of years later (Luke 11:51; Matthew 23:35).

22 Thus Joash the king did not remember the kindness which his father Jehoiada had shown him, but he murdered his son. And as he died he said, "May the LORD see and avenge!"

Aram Invades and Defeats Judah

23 ¶ Now it happened at the turn of the year that the army of the Arameans came up against him; and they came to Judah and Jerusalem, destroyed all the officials of the people from among the people, and sent all their spoil to the king of Damascus.

24 Indeed the army of the Arameans came with a small number of men; yet the LORD delivered a very great army into their hands, because they had forsaken the LORD, the God of their fathers. Thus they executed judgment on Joash.

25 ¶ When they had departed from him (for they left him very sick), his own servants conspired against him because of the blood of the son of Jehoiada the priest, and murdered him on his bed. So he died, and they buried him in the city of David, but they did not bury him in the tombs of the kings.

26 Now these are those who conspired against him: Zabad the son of Shimeath the Ammonitess, and Jehozabad the son of Shimrith the Moabitess.

27 As to his sons and the many oracles against him and the rebuilding of the house of God, behold, they are written in the treatise of the Book of the Kings. Then Amaziah his son became king in his place.

Amaziah Succeeds Joash in Judah

25 Amaziah was twenty-five years old when he became king, and he reigned twenty-nine years in Jerusalem. And his mother's name was Jehoaddan of Jerusalem.

2 He did right in the sight of the LORD, yet not with a whole heart.

---

a I.e. wooden symbols of a female deity

3 Now it came about as soon as the kingdom was firmly in his grasp, that he killed his servants who had slain his father the king.

4 However, he did not put their children to death, but *did* as it is written in the law in the book of Moses, which the LORD commanded, saying, "Fathers shall not be put to death for sons, nor sons be put to death for fathers, but each shall be put to death for his own sin."

Amaziah Defeats Edomites

5 ¶ Moreover, Amaziah assembled Judah and appointed them according to *their* fathers' households under commanders of thousands and commanders of hundreds throughout Judah and Benjamin; and he took a census of those from twenty years old and upward and found them to be 300,000 choice men, *able* to go to war *and* handle spear and shield.

6 He hired also 100,000 valiant warriors out of Israel for one hundred talents of silver.

7 But a man of God came to him saying, "O king, do not let the army of Israel go with you, for the LORD is not with Israel *nor with* any of the sons of Ephraim.

8 "But if you do go, do *it*, be strong for the battle; *yet* God will bring you down before the enemy, for God has power to help and to bring down."

9 Amaziah said to the man of God, "But what *shall we* do for the hundred talents which I have given to the troops of Israel?" And the man of God answered, "The LORD has much more to give you than this."

10 Then Amaziah dismissed them, the troops which came to him from Ephraim, to go home; so their anger burned against Judah and they returned home in fierce anger.

11 ¶ Now Amaziah strengthened himself and led his people forth, and went to the Valley of Salt and struck down 10,000 of the sons of Seir.

12 The sons of Judah also captured 10,000 alive and brought them to the top of the cliff and threw them down from the top of the cliff, so that they were all dashed to pieces.

13 But the troops whom Amaziah sent back from going with him to battle, raided the cities of Judah, from Samaria to Beth-horon, and struck down 3,000 of them and plundered much spoil.

Amaziah Rebuked for Idolatry

14 ¶ Now after Amaziah came from slaughtering the Edomites, he brought the gods of the sons of Seir, set them up as his gods, bowed down before them and burned incense to them.

15 Then the anger of the LORD burned against Amaziah, and He sent him a prophet who said to him, "Why have you sought the gods of the people who have not delivered their own people from your hand?"

16 As he was talking with him, the king said to him, "Have we appointed you a royal counselor? Stop! Why should you be struck down?" Then the prophet stopped and said, "I know that God has planned to destroy you, because you have done this and have not listened to my counsel."

Amaziah Defeated by Joash of Israel

17 ¶ Then Amaziah king of Judah took counsel and sent to Joash the son of Jehoahaz the son of Jehu, the king of Israel, saying, "Come, let us face each other."

18 Joash the king of Israel sent to Amaziah king of Judah, saying, "The thorn bush which was in Lebanon sent to the cedar which was in Lebanon, saying, 'Give your daughter to my son in marriage.' But there passed by a wild beast that was in Lebanon and trampled the thorn bush.

19 "You said, 'Behold, you have defeated Edom.' And your heart has become proud in boasting. Now stay at home; for why should you provoke trouble so that you, even you, would fall and Judah with you?"

20 ¶ But Amaziah would not listen, for it was from God, that He might deliver them into the hand *of Joash* because they had sought the gods of Edom.

21 So Joash king of Israel went up, and he and Amaziah king of Judah faced each other at Beth-shemesh, which belonged to Judah.

22 Judah was defeated by Israel, and they fled each to his tent.

23 Then Joash king of Israel captured Amaziah king of Judah, the son of Joash the son of Jehoahaz, at Beth-shemesh, and brought him to Jerusalem and tore down the wall of Jerusalem from the Gate of Ephraim to the Corner Gate, 400 cubits.

24 *He took* all the gold and silver and all the utensils which were found in the house of God with Obed-edom, and the treasures of the king's house, the hostages also, and returned to Samaria.

25 ¶ And Amaziah, the son of Joash king of Judah, lived fifteen years after the death of Joash, son of Jehoahaz, king of Israel.

26 Now the rest of the acts of Amaziah, from first to last, behold, are they not written in the Book of the Kings of Judah and Israel?

27 From the time that Amaziah turned away from following the LORD they conspired against him in Jerusalem, and he fled to Lachish; but they sent after him to Lachish and killed him there.

28 Then they brought him on horses and buried him with his fathers in the city of Judah.

Uzziah Succeeds Amaziah in Judah

26 And all the people of Judah took Uzziah, who *was* sixteen years old, and made him king in the place of his father Amaziah.

2 He built Eloth and restored it to Judah after the king slept with his fathers.

3 Uzziah was sixteen years old when he became king, and he reigned fifty-two years in Jeru-

salem; and his mother's name was Jechiliah of Jerusalem.

4 He did right in the sight of the LORD according to all that his father Amaziah had done.

5 He continued to seek God in the days of Zechariah, who had understanding through the vision of God; and as long as he sought the LORD, God prospered him.

Uzziah Succeeds in War

6 ¶ Now he went out and warred against the Philistines, and broke down the wall of Gath and the wall of Jabneh and the wall of Ashdod; and he built cities in *the area of* Ashdod and among the Philistines.

7 God helped him against the Philistines, and against the Arabians who lived in Gur-baal, and the Meunites.

8 The Ammonites also gave tribute to Uzziah, and his fame extended to the border of Egypt, for he became very strong.

9 Moreover, Uzziah built towers in Jerusalem at the Corner Gate and at the Valley Gate and at the corner buttress and fortified them.

10 He built towers in the wilderness and hewed many cisterns, for he had much livestock, both in the lowland and in the plain. *He also had* plowmen and vinedressers in the hill country and the fertile fields, for he loved the soil.

11 Moreover, Uzziah had an army ready for battle, which entered combat by divisions according to the number of their muster, prepared by Jeiel the scribe and Maaseiah the official, under the direction of Hananiah, one of the king's officers.

12 The total number of the heads of the households, of valiant warriors, was 2,600.

13 Under their direction was an elite army of 307,500, who could wage war with great power, to help the king against the enemy.

14 Moreover, Uzziah prepared for all the army shields, spears, helmets, body armor, bows and sling stones.

15 In Jerusalem he made engines *of war* invented by skillful men to be on the towers and on the corners for the purpose of shooting arrows and great stones. Hence his fame spread afar, for he was marvelously helped until he *was* strong.

Pride Is Uzziah's Undoing

16 ¶ But when he became strong, his heart was so proud that he acted corruptly, and he was unfaithful to the LORD his God, for he entered the temple of the LORD to burn incense on the altar of incense.

17 Then Azariah the priest entered after him and with him eighty priests of the LORD, valiant men.

18 They opposed Uzziah the king and said to him, "It is not for you, Uzziah, to burn incense to the LORD, but for the priests, the sons of Aaron who are consecrated to burn incense. Get out of the sanctuary, for you have been unfaithful and will have no honor from the LORD God."

26:16 A King's Pride

Archaeological discoveries have verified the prosperity of Judah during Uzziah's reign. However, like many of Judah's kings, he fell victim to the sin of pride. He usurped the role of the priests and suffered ever after from a contagious skin disease.

19 But Uzziah, with a censer in his hand for burning incense, was enraged; and while he was enraged with the priests, the leprosy broke out on his forehead before the priests in the house of the LORD, beside the altar of incense.

20 Azariah the chief priest and all the priests looked at him, and behold, he *was* leprous on his forehead; and they hurried him out of there, and he himself also hastened to get out because the LORD had smitten him.

21 King Uzziah was a leper to the day of his death; and he lived in a separate house, being a leper, for he was cut off from the house of the LORD. And Jotham his son *was* over the king's house judging the people of the land.

22 ¶ Now the rest of the acts of Uzziah, first to last, the prophet Isaiah, the son of Amoz, has written.

23 So Uzziah slept with his fathers, and they buried him with his fathers in the field of the grave which belonged to the kings, for they said, "He is a leper." And Jotham his son became king in his place.

Jotham Succeeds Uzziah in Judah

27 Jotham was twenty-five years old when he became king, and he reigned sixteen years in Jerusalem. And his mother's name was Jerushah the daughter of Zadok.

2 He did right in the sight of the LORD, according to all that his father Uzziah had done; however he did not enter the temple of the LORD. But the people continued acting corruptly.

3 He built the upper gate of the house of the LORD, and he built extensively the wall of Ophel.

4 Moreover, he built cities in the hill country of Judah, and he built fortresses and towers on the wooded *hills.*

5 He fought also with the king of the Ammonites and prevailed over them so that the Ammonites gave him during that year one hundred talents of silver, ten thousand [a]kors of wheat and ten thousand of barley. The Ammonites also paid

---

[a] I.e. One kor equals approx 10 bu

him this *amount* in the second and in the third year.

6 So Jotham became mighty because he ordered his ways before the LORD his God.

7 Now the rest of the acts of Jotham, even all his wars and his acts, behold, they are written in the Book of the Kings of Israel and Judah.

8 He was twenty-five years old when he became king, and he reigned sixteen years in Jerusalem.

9 And Jotham slept with his fathers, and they buried him in the city of David; and Ahaz his son became king in his place.

Ahaz Succeeds Jotham in Judah

28 Ahaz *was* twenty years old when he became king, and he reigned sixteen years in Jerusalem; and he did not do right in the sight of the LORD as David his father *had done*.

2 But he walked in the ways of the kings of Israel; he also made molten images for the Baals.

3 Moreover, he burned incense in the valley of Ben-hinnom and burned his sons in fire, according to the abominations of the nations whom the LORD had driven out before the sons of Israel.

4 He sacrificed and burned incense on the high places, on the hills and under every green tree.

Judah Is Invaded

5 ¶ Wherefore, the LORD his God delivered him into the hand of the king of Aram; and they defeated him and carried away from him a great number of captives and brought *them* to Damascus. And he was also delivered into the hand of the king of Israel, who inflicted him with heavy casualties.

6 For Pekah the son of Remaliah slew in Judah 120,000 in one day, all valiant men, because they had forsaken the LORD God of their fathers.

7 And Zichri, a mighty man of Ephraim, slew Maaseiah the king's son and Azrikam the ruler of the house and Elkanah the second to the king.

8 ¶ The sons of Israel carried away captive of their brethren 200,000 women, sons and daughters; and they took also a great deal of spoil from them, and brought the spoil to Samaria.

9 But a prophet of the LORD was there, whose name *was* Oded; and he went out to meet the army which came to Samaria and said to them, "Behold, because the LORD, the God of your fathers, was angry with Judah, He has delivered them into your hand, and you have slain them in a rage *which* has even reached heaven.

10 "Now you are proposing to subjugate for yourselves the people of Judah and Jerusalem for male and female slaves. Surely, *do* you not *have* transgressions of your own against the LORD your God?

11 "Now therefore, listen to me and return the

captives whom you captured from your brothers, for the burning anger of the LORD is against you."

12 Then some of the heads of the sons of Ephraim—Azariah the son of Johanan, Berechiah the son of Meshillemoth, Jehizkiah the son of

28:9 Limits of a Just War

Advocates of a "just war" theory sometimes cite the fascinating story in this chapter. God sanctioned Israel's attack on Judah, but the invaders from the North went too far. They slaughtered many civilians and carried away others as captives. A prophet rebuked Israel's army for their crimes committed "in a rage which has even reached to heaven." The Israelites had fought a war with a just end—carrying out God's punishment—but used cruel and unjust means in waging it.

The prophet convinced the Israelites to give up plunder and prisoners and make restitution. They fed the prisoners from Judah, gave them clothes, sandals, and medicine, and put them on donkeys to return home. This scene is one of the few in 2 Chronicles that shows the Northern Kingdom in a favorable light.

Shallum, and Amasa the son of Hadlai—arose against those who were coming from the battle,

13 and said to them, "You must not bring the captives in here, for you are proposing *to bring* upon us guilt against the LORD adding to our sins and our guilt; for our guilt is great so that *His* burning anger is against Israel."

14 So the armed men left the captives and the spoil before the officers and all the assembly.

15 Then the men who were designated by name arose, took the captives, and they clothed all their naked ones from the spoil; and they gave them clothes and sandals, fed them and gave them drink, anointed them *with oil,* led all their feeble ones on donkeys, and brought them to Jericho, the city of palm trees, to their brothers; then they returned to Samaria.

Compromise with Assyria

16 ¶ At that time King Ahaz sent to the [a]kings of Assyria for help.

17 For again the Edomites had come and attacked Judah and carried away captives.

18 The Philistines also had invaded the cities of the lowland and of the Negev of Judah, and had taken Beth-shemesh, Aijalon, Gederoth, and Soco with its villages, Timnah with its villages, and Gimzo with its villages, and they settled there.

19 For the LORD humbled Judah because of Ahaz king of Israel, for he had brought about a lack of restraint in Judah and was very unfaithful to the LORD.

[a] Ancient versions read *king*

20 So Tilgath-pilneser king of Assyria came against him and afflicted him instead of strengthening him.

21 Although Ahaz took a portion out of the house of the LORD and out of the palace of the king and of the princes, and gave it to the king of Assyria, it did not help him.

22 ¶ Now in the time of his distress this same King Ahaz became yet more unfaithful to the LORD.

23 For he sacrificed to the gods of Damascus which had defeated him, and said, "Because the gods of the kings of Aram helped them, I will sacrifice to them that they may help me." But they became the downfall of him and all Israel.

24 Moreover, when Ahaz gathered together the utensils of the house of God, he cut the utensils of the house of God in pieces; and he closed the doors of the house of the LORD and made altars for himself in every corner of Jerusalem.

25 In every city of Judah he made high places to burn incense to other gods, and provoked the LORD, the God of his fathers, to anger.

26 Now the rest of his acts and all his ways, from first to last, behold, they are written in the Book of the Kings of Judah and Israel.

27 So Ahaz slept with his fathers, and they buried him in the city, in Jerusalem, for they did not bring him into the tombs of the kings of Israel; and Hezekiah his son reigned in his place.

Hezekiah Succeeds Ahaz in Judah

29 Hezekiah became king when he was twenty-five years old; and he reigned twenty-nine years in Jerusalem. And his mother's name was Abijah, the daughter of Zechariah.

2 He did right in the sight of the LORD, according to all that his father David had done.

3 ¶ In the first year of his reign, in the first month, he opened the doors of the house of the LORD and repaired them.

4 He brought in the priests and the Levites and gathered them into the square on the east.

Reforms Begun

5 Then he said to them, "Listen to me, O Levites. Consecrate yourselves now, and consecrate the house of the LORD, the God of your fathers, and carry the uncleanness out from the holy place.

6 "For our fathers have been unfaithful and have done evil in the sight of the LORD our God, and have forsaken Him and turned their faces away from the dwelling place of the LORD, and have turned their backs.

7 "They have also shut the doors of the porch

HEZEKIAH *Cleaning House*

HIS OWN FATHER HAD CLOSED the temple in Jerusalem, imported a pagan altar from Damascus and erected shrines to other gods on every street corner. Inheriting the throne as a young man, Hezekiah saw that his nation was hurtling toward disaster. He watched as the great power of Assyria invaded his sister nation Israel, demolishing its cities and sending its citizens into exile.

Unlike other kings, Hezekiah did not scurry around seeking political alliances to bolster his strength. He listened carefully to the prophet Isaiah and looked instead for God's protection. To reverse the course of his nation, he began by cleaning out God's house—the temple in Jerusalem.

When he began this task, priests and Levites who had been assigned to coordinate temple worship had dwindled away, demoralized. Hezekiah rallied them like an army and gave them marching orders: Clean up yourselves and clean up the temple. It took more than two weeks for them to dump all the idolatrous materials into a nearby ravine and to reconsecrate the temple. Worship recommenced: regular sacrifices to God, singing of the temple music written by David, even a dramatic restaging of the long-neglected Passover festival.

In these policies Hezekiah showed courage and initiative. He took risks, raising dust and probably raising hackles. Even Moses' bronze snake had to go—people were now worshiping it! (2 Kings 18:4). Hezekiah embarked on these reforms out of deep personal commitment. "Every work which he began in the service of the house of God in law and in commandment, seeking his God, he did with all his heart and prospered" (31:21).

When the powerful Assyrians camped at his gate, sneering at his God and threatening to destroy him, Hezekiah knew where to turn—to God. The prophet Isaiah prayed with Hezekiah, and Judah was miraculously saved. Later, when Hezekiah himself was close to death, God also answered his prayers for healing, extending his life by 15 years.

Hezekiah had some flaws, but overall he went down as one of the finest rulers in the Old Testament. "So that after him there was none like him among all the kings of Judah, nor among those who were before him. For he clung to the LORD; he did not depart from following Him, but kept His commandments, which the LORD had commanded Moses" (2 Kings 18:5–6).

Life Questions: Where do you think house cleaning most needs to occur? In your life? In your church? Among your friends? In your city, state or nation?

and put out the lamps, and have not burned incense or offered burnt offerings in the holy place to the God of Israel.

8 "Therefore the wrath of the LORD was against Judah and Jerusalem, and He has made them an object of terror, of horror, and of hissing, as you see with your own eyes.

9 "For behold, our fathers have fallen by the sword, and our sons and our daughters and our wives are in captivity for this.

10 "Now it is in my heart to make a covenant with the LORD God of Israel, that His burning anger may turn away from us.

11 "My sons, do not be negligent now, for the LORD has chosen you to stand before Him, to minister to Him, and to be His ministers and burn incense."

12 ¶ Then the Levites arose: Mahath, the son of Amasai and Joel the son of Azariah, from the sons of the Kohathites; and from the sons of Merari, Kish the son of Abdi and Azariah the son of Jehallelel; and from the Gershonites, Joah the son of Zimmah and Eden the son of Joah;

13 and from the sons of Elizaphan, Shimri and Jeiel; and from the sons of Asaph, Zechariah and Mattaniah;

14 and from the sons of Heman, Jehiel and Shimei; and from the sons of Jeduthun, Shemaiah and Uzziel.

15 They assembled their brothers, consecrated themselves, and went in to cleanse the house of the LORD, according to the commandment of the king by the words of the LORD.

16 So the priests went in to the inner part of the house of the LORD to cleanse it, and every unclean thing which they found in the temple of the LORD they brought out to the court of the house of the LORD. Then the Levites received it to carry out to the Kidron valley.

17 Now they began the consecration on the first day of the first month, and on the eighth day of the month they entered the porch of the LORD. Then they consecrated the house of the LORD in eight days, and finished on the sixteenth day of the first month.

18 Then they went in to King Hezekiah and said, "We have cleansed the whole house of the LORD, the altar of burnt offering with all of its utensils, and the table of showbread with all of its utensils.

19 "Moreover, all the utensils which King Ahaz had discarded during his reign in his unfaithfulness, we have prepared and consecrated; and behold, they are before the altar of the LORD."

Hezekiah Restores Temple Worship

20 ¶ Then King Hezekiah arose early and assembled the princes of the city and went up to the house of the LORD.

21 They brought seven bulls, seven rams, seven lambs and seven male goats for a sin offering for the kingdom, the sanctuary, and Judah. And he ordered the priests, the sons of Aaron, to offer them on the altar of the LORD.

22 So they slaughtered the bulls, and the priests took the blood and sprinkled it on the altar. They also slaughtered the rams and sprinkled the blood on the altar; they slaughtered the lambs also and sprinkled the blood on the altar.

23 Then they brought the male goats of the sin offering before the king and the assembly, and they laid their hands on them.

24 The priests slaughtered them and purged the altar with their blood to atone for all Israel, for the king ordered the burnt offering and the sin offering for all Israel.

25 ¶ He then stationed the Levites in the house of the LORD with cymbals, with harps and with lyres, according to the command of David and of Gad the king's seer, and of Nathan the prophet; for the command was from the LORD through His prophets.

26 The Levites stood with the musical instruments of David, and the priests with the trumpets.

27 Then Hezekiah gave the order to offer the burnt offering on the altar. When the burnt offering began, the song to the LORD also began with the trumpets, accompanied by the instruments of David, king of Israel.

28 While the whole assembly worshiped, the singers also sang and the trumpets sounded; all this continued until the burnt offering was finished.

29 ¶ Now at the completion of the burnt offerings, the king and all who were present with him bowed down and worshiped.

30 Moreover, King Hezekiah and the officials ordered the Levites to sing praises to the LORD with the words of David and Asaph the seer. So they sang praises with joy, and bowed down and worshiped.

31 ¶ Then Hezekiah said, "Now that you have consecrated yourselves to the LORD, come near and bring sacrifices and thank offerings to the house of the LORD." And the assembly brought sacrifices and thank offerings, and all those who were willing brought burnt offerings.

32 The number of the burnt offerings which the assembly brought was 70 bulls, 100 rams, and 200 lambs; all these were for a burnt offering to the LORD.

33 The consecrated things were 600 bulls and 3,000 sheep.

34 But the priests were too few, so that they were unable to skin all the burnt offerings; therefore their brothers the Levites helped them until the work was completed and until the other priests had consecrated themselves. For the Levites were more conscientious to consecrate themselves than the priests.

35 There were also many burnt offerings with the fat of the peace offerings and with the libations

for the burnt offerings. Thus the service of the house of the LORD was established *again.*

36 Then Hezekiah and all the people rejoiced over what God had prepared for the people, because the thing came about suddenly.

All Israel Invited to the Passover

30 Now Hezekiah sent to all Israel and Judah and wrote letters also to Ephraim and Manasseh, that they should come to the house of the LORD at Jerusalem to celebrate the Passover to the LORD God of Israel.

30:1 Delayed Passover

By moving the Passover date back one month, Hezekiah allowed extra time for priests to prepare and for pilgrims to make travel plans. Pointedly, Hezekiah invited tribes from the ravaged Northern Kingdom. For the first time in 200 years, the entire nation celebrated a religious festival together.

2 For the king and his princes and all the assembly in Jerusalem had decided to celebrate the Passover in the second month,

3 since they could not celebrate it at that time, because the priests had not consecrated themselves in sufficient numbers, nor had the people been gathered to Jerusalem.

4 Thus the thing was right in the sight of the king and all the assembly.

5 So they established a decree to circulate a proclamation throughout all Israel from Beersheba even to Dan, that they should come to celebrate the Passover to the LORD God of Israel at Jerusalem. For they had not celebrated *it* in great numbers as it was prescribed.

6 The couriers went throughout all Israel and Judah with the letters from the hand of the king and his princes, even according to the command of the king, saying, "O sons of Israel, return to the LORD God of Abraham, Isaac and Israel, that He may return to the remnant of you who escaped *and* are left from the hand of the kings of Assyria.

7 "Do not be like your fathers and your brothers, who were unfaithful to the LORD God of their fathers, so that He made them a horror, as you see.

8 "Now do not stiffen your neck like your fathers, but yield to the LORD and enter His sanctuary which He has consecrated forever, and serve the LORD your God, that His burning anger may turn away from you.

9 "For if you return to the LORD, your brothers and your sons *will find* compassion before those who led them captive and will return to this land. For the LORD your God is gracious and compassionate, and will not turn *His* face away from you if you return to Him."

10 ¶ So the couriers passed from city to city

through the country of Ephraim and Manasseh, and as far as Zebulun, but they laughed them to scorn and mocked them.

11 Nevertheless some men of Asher, Manasseh and Zebulun humbled themselves and came to Jerusalem.

12 The hand of God was also on Judah to give them one heart to do what the king and the princes commanded by the word of the LORD.

Passover Reinstituted

13 ¶ Now many people were gathered at Jerusalem to celebrate the Feast of Unleavened Bread in the second month, a very large assembly.

14 They arose and removed the altars which *were* in Jerusalem; they also removed all the incense altars and cast *them* into the brook Kidron.

15 Then they slaughtered the Passover *lambs* on the fourteenth of the second month. And the priests and Levites were ashamed of themselves, and consecrated themselves and brought burnt offerings to the house of the LORD.

16 They stood at their stations after their custom, according to the law of Moses the man of God; the priests sprinkled the blood *which they received* from the hand of the Levites.

17 For *there were* many in the assembly who had not consecrated themselves; therefore, the Levites *were* over the slaughter of the Passover *lambs* for everyone who *was* unclean, in order to consecrate *them* to the LORD.

18 For a multitude of the people, *even* many from Ephraim and Manasseh, Issachar and Zebulun, had not purified themselves, yet they ate the Passover otherwise than prescribed. For Hezekiah prayed for them, saying, "May the good LORD pardon

19 everyone who prepares his heart to seek God, the LORD God of his fathers, though not according to the purification *rules* of the sanctuary."

20 So the LORD heard Hezekiah and healed the people.

21 The sons of Israel present in Jerusalem celebrated the Feast of Unleavened Bread *for* seven days with great joy, and the Levites and the priests praised the LORD day after day with loud instruments to the LORD.

22 Then Hezekiah spoke encouragingly to all the Levites who showed good insight *in the things* of the LORD. So they ate for the appointed seven days, sacrificing peace offerings and giving thanks to the LORD God of their fathers.

23 ¶ Then the whole assembly decided to celebrate *the feast* another seven days, so they celebrated the seven days with joy.

24 For Hezekiah king of Judah had contributed to the assembly 1,000 bulls and 7,000 sheep, and the princes had contributed to the assembly 1,000 bulls and 10,000 sheep; and a large number of priests consecrated themselves.

25 All the assembly of Judah rejoiced, with the priests and the Levites and all the assembly that came from Israel, both the sojourners who came from the land of Israel and those living in Judah.

26 So there was great joy in Jerusalem, because there was nothing like this in Jerusalem since the days of Solomon the son of David, king of Israel.

27 Then the Levitical priests arose and blessed the people; and their voice was heard and their prayer came to His holy dwelling place, to heaven.

Idols Are Destroyed

31 Now when all this was finished, all Israel who were present went out to the cities of Judah, broke the pillars in pieces, cut down the [a]Asherim and pulled down the high places and the altars throughout all Judah and Benjamin, as well as in Ephraim and Manasseh, until they had destroyed them all. Then all the sons of Israel returned to their cities, each to his possession.

2 ¶ And Hezekiah appointed the divisions of the priests and the Levites by their divisions, each according to his service, both the priests and the Levites, for burnt offerings and for peace offerings, to minister and to give thanks and to praise in the gates of the camp of the LORD.

Reforms Continued

3 He also appointed the king's portion of his goods for the burnt offerings, namely, for the morning and evening burnt offerings, and the burnt offerings for the sabbaths and for the new moons and for the fixed festivals, as it is written in the law of the LORD.

4 Also he commanded the people who lived in Jerusalem to give the portion due to the priests and the Levites, that they might devote themselves to the law of the LORD.

5 As soon as the order spread, the sons of Israel provided in abundance the first fruits of grain, new wine, oil, honey and of all the produce of the field; and they brought in abundantly the tithe of all.

6 The sons of Israel and Judah who lived in the cities of Judah also brought in the tithe of oxen and sheep, and the tithe of sacred gifts which were consecrated to the LORD their God, and placed them in heaps.

7 In the third month they began to make the heaps, and finished them by the seventh month.

8 When Hezekiah and the rulers came and saw the heaps, they blessed the LORD and His people Israel.

9 Then Hezekiah questioned the priests and the Levites concerning the heaps.

10 Azariah the chief priest of the house of Zadok said to him, "Since the contributions began to be brought into the house of the LORD, we have had enough to eat with plenty left over, for the

LORD has blessed His people, and this great quantity is left over."

11 ¶ Then Hezekiah commanded them to prepare rooms in the house of the LORD, and they prepared them.

12 They faithfully brought in the contributions and the tithes and the consecrated things; and Conaniah the Levite was the officer in charge of them and his brother Shimei was second.

13 Jehiel, Azaziah, Nahath, Asahel, Jerimoth, Jozabad, Eliel, Ismachiah, Mahath and Benaiah were overseers under the authority of Conaniah and Shimei his brother by the appointment of King Hezekiah, and Azariah was the chief officer of the house of God.

14 Kore the son of Imnah the Levite, the keeper of the eastern gate, was over the freewill offerings of God, to apportion the contributions for the LORD and the most holy things.

15 Under his authority were Eden, Miniamin, Jeshua, Shemaiah, Amariah and Shecaniah in the cities of the priests, to distribute faithfully their portions to their brothers by divisions, whether great or small,

16 without regard to their genealogical enrollment, to the males from thirty years old and upward—everyone who entered the house of the LORD for his daily obligations—for their work in their duties according to their divisions;

17 as well as the priests who were enrolled genealogically according to their fathers' households, and the Levites from twenty years old and upwards, by their duties and their divisions.

18 The genealogical enrollment included all their little children, their wives, their sons and their daughters, for the whole assembly, for they consecrated themselves faithfully in holiness.

19 Also for the sons of Aaron the priests who were in the pasture lands of their cities, or in each and every city, there were men who were designated by name to distribute portions to every male among the priests and to everyone genealogically enrolled among the Levites.

20 ¶ Thus Hezekiah did throughout all Judah; and he did what was good, right and true before the LORD his God.

21 Every work which he began in the service of the house of God in law and in commandment, seeking his God, he did with all his heart and prospered.

Sennacherib Invades Judah

32 After these acts of faithfulness Sennacherib king of Assyria came and invaded Judah and besieged the fortified cities, and thought to break into them for himself.

2 Now when Hezekiah saw that Sennacherib had come and that he intended to make war on Jerusalem,

3 he decided with his officers and his warriors

---

[a] I.e. wooden symbols of a female deity

to cut off the *supply of* water from the springs which *were* outside the city, and they helped him.

4 So many people assembled and stopped up all the springs and the stream which flowed through the region, saying, "Why should the kings of Assyria come and find abundant water?"

5 And he took courage and rebuilt all the wall that had been broken down and erected towers on it, and *built* another outside wall and strengthened the Millo *in* the city of David, and made weapons and shields in great number.

6 He appointed military officers over the people and gathered them to him in the square at the city gate, and spoke encouragingly to them, saying,

7 "Be strong and courageous, do not fear or be dismayed because of the king of Assyria nor because of all the horde that is with him; for the one with us is greater than the one with him.

8 "With him is *only* an arm of flesh, but with us is the LORD our God to help us and to fight our battles." And the people relied on the words of Hezekiah king of Judah.

Sennacherib Undermines Hezekiah

9 ¶ After this Sennacherib king of Assyria sent his servants to Jerusalem while he *was* besieging Lachish with all his forces with him, against Hezekiah king of Judah and against all Judah who *were* at Jerusalem, saying,

Lessons from the Battlefield

What made Judah win some wars and lose others?

NO KING OF JUDAH HAD a wholly peaceful reign. As a result, much of the action in 2 Chronicles takes place on a battlefield. And, in a nutshell, here is the book's philosophy of war: "Humble yourself and rely totally on God—regardless of the odds against you. If you rely on your own military might or that of powerful neighbors, you will lose."

> "Do not fear or be dismayed because of the king of Assyria nor because of all the horde that is with him; for the one with us is greater than the one with him." 32:7

Listening to the Prophets

Chapter 12, for example, tells of a grave crisis facing Judah's very first king. Five years into Rehoboam's reign, a huge military machine from Egypt rolled in with chariots and battering rams. Surrounded, Rehoboam wanted a word of hope from a prophet. Instead, he got a rebuke: "Thus says the LORD , 'You have forsaken Me, so I also have forsaken you to Shishak' " (12:5).

God was using the armies of Egypt to punish Judah for its errors. This first invasion set a pattern: Whenever an immoral king corrupted the nation, God sent an invading army as punishment.

Often the kings of Judah ignored their prophets' hard advice. But in this first case, King Rehoboam repented and humbled himself, saving his country from even greater devastation.

A Wrong Way and a Right Way

Few kings had the faith to believe in God alone at moments of great peril. Even the best of them reached into the royal treasury and purchased help from neighboring nations. When they did, Judah usually ended up weaker than before. But 2 Chronicles concentrates on the good moments, when kings turned to God.

King Jehoshaphat was a textbook example of the proper response. He called the entire nation together in a giant prayer meeting (20:4–28). When the time came for battle, he sent a choir in front of his army to sing praises to God. Judah's enemies all turned on each other and Jehoshaphat's armies marched home victorious.

Hezekiah's Faith

Perhaps the greatest single example of a king following his prophet's advice occurred during the reign of Hezekiah. The Bible reports the incident in three places: 2 Chronicles 32, 2 Kings 18–19, and Isaiah 36–37. At the time, Judah's situation looked hopeless. Mighty Assyria had taken 27 cities and villages in Judah and was now laying siege to Jerusalem.

Hezekiah showed his true moral strength by joining together with the prophet Isaiah to humble himself in prayer. God granted a miracle that drove off the Assyrian army.

Second Chronicles stressed incidents like these as a lesson to its first readers, who had inherited a land in ruins. Looking back over their history, they could see what had gone wrong: The nation had forgotten to rely on God. To rebuild their nation they would have to relearn the simple faith that had brought them victory in the past.

Life Questions: What does it mean to trust God completely today?

10 "Thus says Sennacherib king of Assyria, 'On what are you trusting that you are remaining in Jerusalem under siege?

11 'Is not Hezekiah misleading you to give yourselves over to die by hunger and by thirst, saying, "The LORD our God will deliver us from the hand of the king of Assyria"?

12 'Has not the same Hezekiah taken away His high places and His altars, and said to Judah and Jerusalem, "You shall worship before one altar, and on it you shall burn incense"?

13 'Do you not know what I and my fathers have done to all the peoples of the lands? Were the gods of the nations of the lands able at all to deliver their land from my hand?

14 'Who *was there* among all the gods of those nations which my fathers utterly destroyed who could deliver his people out of my hand, that your God should be able to deliver you from my hand?

15 'Now therefore, do not let Hezekiah deceive you or mislead you like this, and do not believe him, for no god of any nation or kingdom was able to deliver his people from my hand or from the hand of my fathers. How much less will your God deliver you from my hand?' "

16 ¶ His servants spoke further against the LORD God and against His servant Hezekiah.

17 He also wrote letters to insult the LORD God of Israel, and to speak against Him, saying, "As the gods of the nations of the lands have not delivered their people from my hand, so the God of Hezekiah will not deliver His people from my hand."

18 They called this out with a loud voice in the language of Judah to the people of Jerusalem who were on the wall, to frighten and terrify them, so that they might take the city.

19 They spoke of the God of Jerusalem as of the gods of the peoples of the earth, the work of men's hands.

Hezekiah's Prayer Is Answered

20 ¶ But King Hezekiah and Isaiah the prophet, the son of Amoz, prayed about this and cried out to heaven.

21 And the LORD sent an angel who destroyed every mighty warrior, commander and officer in the camp of the king of Assyria. So he returned in shame to his own land. And when he had entered the temple of his god, some of his own children killed him there with the sword.

22 So the LORD saved Hezekiah and the inhabitants of Jerusalem from the hand of Sennacherib the king of Assyria and from the hand of all *others*, and guided them on every side.

23 And many were bringing gifts to the LORD at Jerusalem and choice presents to Hezekiah king of Judah, so that he was exalted in the sight of all nations thereafter.

24 ¶ In those days Hezekiah became mortally ill; and he prayed to the LORD, and the LORD spoke to him and gave him a sign.

25 But Hezekiah gave no return for the benefit he received, because his heart was proud; therefore wrath came on him and on Judah and Jerusalem.

32:1–21 Invasion

Sennacherib's campaign is well-documented, for he kept scrupulous records of his military ventures. Invading Palestine in 701 B.C., his armies captured 46 cities in Judah and then laid siege to Jerusalem. The Bible includes three different accounts of this major event: here, in 2 Kings 18, and in Isaiah 36.

26 However, Hezekiah humbled the pride of his heart, both he and the inhabitants of Jerusalem, so that the wrath of the LORD did not come on them in the days of Hezekiah.

27 ¶ Now Hezekiah had immense riches and honor; and he made for himself treasuries for silver, gold, precious stones, spices, shields and all kinds of valuable articles,

28 storehouses also for the produce of grain, wine and oil, pens for all kinds of cattle and sheepfolds for the flocks.

29 He made cities for himself and acquired flocks and herds in abundance, for God had given him very great wealth.

30 It was Hezekiah who stopped the upper outlet of the waters of Gihon and directed them to the west side of the city of David. And Hezekiah prospered in all that he did.

31 Even *in the matter of* the envoys of the rulers of Babylon, who sent to him to inquire of the wonder that had happened in the land, God left him *alone only* to test him, that He might know all that was in his heart.

32 ¶ Now the rest of the acts of Hezekiah and his deeds of devotion, behold, they are written in the vision of Isaiah the prophet, the son of Amoz, in the Book of the Kings of Judah and Israel.

33 So Hezekiah slept with his fathers, and they buried him in the upper section of the tombs of the sons of David; and all Judah and the inhabitants of Jerusalem honored him at his death. And his son Manasseh became king in his place.

Manasseh Succeeds Hezekiah in Judah

33 Manasseh was twelve years old when he became king, and he reigned fifty-five years in Jerusalem.

2 He did evil in the sight of the LORD according to the abominations of the nations whom the LORD dispossessed before the sons of Israel.

3 For he rebuilt the high places which Hezekiah his father had broken down; he also erected

altars for the Baals and made *a*Asherim, and worshiped all the host of heaven and served them.

4 He built altars in the house of the LORD of which the LORD had said, "My name shall be in Jerusalem forever."

5 For he built altars for all the host of heaven in the two courts of the house of the LORD.

6 He made his sons pass through the fire in the valley of Ben-hinnom; and he practiced witchcraft, used divination, practiced sorcery and dealt with mediums and spiritists. He did much evil in the sight of the LORD, provoking Him *to anger.*

7 Then he put the carved image of the idol which he had made in the house of God, of which God had said to David and to Solomon his son, "In this house and in Jerusalem, which I have chosen from all the tribes of Israel, I will put My name forever;

8 and I will not again remove the foot of Israel from the land which I have appointed for your fathers, if only they will observe to do all that I have commanded them according to all the law, the statutes and the ordinances *given* through Moses."

9 Thus Manasseh misled Judah and the inhabitants of Jerusalem to do more evil than the nations whom the LORD destroyed before the sons of Israel.

Manasseh's Idolatry Rebuked

10 ¶ The LORD spoke to Manasseh and his people, but they paid no attention.

11 Therefore the LORD brought the commanders of the army of the king of Assyria against them, and they captured Manasseh with *b*hooks, bound him with bronze *chains* and took him to Babylon.

12 When he was in distress, he entreated the LORD his God and humbled himself greatly before the God of his fathers.

13 When he prayed to Him, He was moved by his entreaty and heard his supplication, and brought him again to Jerusalem to his kingdom. Then Manasseh knew that the LORD *was* God.

33:13 A Tardy Change of Mind

Unlike the other history books, Chronicles records great moments of faith, even when they have no lasting consequences for the nation as a whole. Second Chronicles characteristically adds a new perspective on the reign of Manasseh, one of Judah's worst kings. While acknowledging his weaknesses, it adds this account of his amazing turnabout late in life. This brief episode gave an object lesson to the nation on what happens when even a wicked king repents.

14 ¶ Now after this he built the outer wall of the city of David on the west side of Gihon, in the valley, even to the entrance of the Fish Gate; and he encircled the Ophel *with it* and made it very high. Then he put army commanders in all the fortified cities of Judah.

15 He also removed the foreign gods and the idol from the house of the LORD, as well as all the altars which he had built on the mountain of the house of the LORD and in Jerusalem, and he threw *them* outside the city.

16 He set up the altar of the LORD and sacrificed peace offerings and thank offerings on it; and he ordered Judah to serve the LORD God of Israel.

17 Nevertheless the people still sacrificed in the high places, *although* only to the LORD their God.

18 ¶ Now the rest of the acts of Manasseh even his prayer to his God, and the words of the seers who spoke to him in the name of the LORD God of Israel, behold, they are among the records of the kings of Israel.

19 His prayer also and *how God* was entreated by him, and all his sin, his unfaithfulness, and the sites on which he built high places and erected the Asherim and the carved images, before he humbled himself, behold, they are written in the records of the Hozai.

20 So Manasseh slept with his fathers, and they buried him in his own house. And Amon his son became king in his place.

Amon Becomes King in Judah

21 ¶ Amon *was* twenty-two years old when he became king, and he reigned two years in Jerusalem.

22 He did evil in the sight of the LORD as Manasseh his father had done, and Amon sacrificed to all the carved images which his father Manasseh had made, and he served them.

23 Moreover, he did not humble himself before the LORD as his father Manasseh had done, but Amon multiplied guilt.

24 Finally his servants conspired against him and put him to death in his own house.

25 But the people of the land killed all the conspirators against King Amon, and the people of the land made Josiah his son king in his place.

Josiah Succeeds Amon in Judah

34 Josiah *was* eight years old when he became king, and he reigned thirty-one years in Jerusalem.

2 He did right in the sight of the LORD, and walked in the ways of his father David and did not turn aside to the right or to the left.

3 For in the eighth year of his reign while he was still a youth, he began to seek the God of his father David; and in the twelfth year he began to purge Judah and Jerusalem of the high places, the

a I.e. wooden symbols of a female deity   *b* I.e. thongs put through the nose

Asherim, the carved images and the molten images.

4 They tore down the altars of the Baals in his presence, and the incense altars that were high above them he chopped down; also the Asherim, the carved images and the molten images he broke in pieces and ground to powder and scattered *it* on the graves of those who had sacrificed to them.

5 Then he burned the bones of the priests on their altars and purged Judah and Jerusalem.

6 In the cities of Manasseh, Ephraim, Simeon, even as far as Naphtali, in their surrounding ruins,

7 he also tore down the altars and beat the Asherim and the carved images into powder, and chopped down all the incense altars throughout the land of Israel. Then he returned to Jerusalem.

Josiah Repairs the Temple

8 ¶ Now in the eighteenth year of his reign, when he had purged the land and the house, he sent Shaphan the son of Azaliah, and Maaseiah an official of the city, and Joah the son of Joahaz the recorder, to repair the house of the LORD his God.

9 They came to Hilkiah the high priest and delivered the money that was brought into the house of God, which the Levites, the doorkeepers, had collected from Manasseh and Ephraim, and from all the remnant of Israel, and from all Judah and Benjamin and the inhabitants of Jerusalem.

10 Then they gave *it* into the hands of the workmen who had the oversight of the house of the LORD, and the workmen who were working in the house of the LORD used it to restore and repair the house.

11 They in turn gave *it* to the carpenters and to the builders to buy quarried stone and timber for couplings and to make beams for the houses which the kings of Judah had let go to ruin.

12 The men did the work faithfully with foremen over them to supervise: Jahath and Obadiah, the Levites of the sons of Merari, Zechariah and Meshullam of the sons of the Kohathites, and the Levites, all who were skillful with musical instruments.

13 *They were* also over the burden bearers, and supervised all the workmen from job to job; and *some* of the Levites *were* scribes and officials and gatekeepers.

Hilkiah Discovers Lost Book of the Law

14 ¶ When they were bringing out the money which had been brought into the house of the LORD, Hilkiah the priest found the book of the law of the LORD *given* by Moses.

15 Hilkiah responded and said to Shaphan the scribe, "I have found the book of the law in the house of the LORD." And Hilkiah gave the book to Shaphan.

16 Then Shaphan brought the book to the king and reported further word to the king, saying,

"Everything that was entrusted to your servants they are doing.

17 "They have also emptied out the money which was found in the house of the LORD, and have delivered it into the hands of the supervisors and the workmen."

18 Moreover, Shaphan the scribe told the king saying, "Hilkiah the priest gave me a book." And Shaphan read from it in the presence of the king.

19 ¶ When the king heard the words of the law, he tore his clothes.

20 Then the king commanded Hilkiah, Ahikam the son of Shaphan, Abdon the son of Micah, Shaphan the scribe, and Asaiah the king's servant, saying,

21 "Go, inquire of the LORD for me and for those who are left in Israel and in Judah, concerning the words of the book which has been found; for great is the wrath of the LORD which is poured out on us because our fathers have not observed the word of the LORD, to do according to all that is written in this book."

Huldah, the Prophetess, Speaks

22 ¶ So Hilkiah and *those* whom the king had told went to Huldah the prophetess, the wife of Shallum the son of Tokhath, the son of Hasrah, the keeper of the wardrobe (now she lived in Jerusalem in the Second Quarter); and they spoke to her regarding this.

23 She said to them, "Thus says the LORD, the God of Israel, 'Tell the man who sent you to Me,

24 thus says the LORD, "Behold, I am bringing evil on this place and on its inhabitants, *even* all the curses written in the book which they have read in the presence of the king of Judah.

25 "Because they have forsaken Me and have burned incense to other gods, that they might provoke Me to anger with all the works of their hands; therefore My wrath will be poured out on this place and it shall not be quenched." '

26 "But to the king of Judah who sent you to inquire of the LORD, thus you will say to him, 'Thus says the LORD God of Israel *regarding* the words which you have heard,

27 "Because your heart was tender and you humbled yourself before God when you heard His words against this place and against its inhabitants, and *because* you humbled yourself before Me, tore your clothes and wept before Me, I truly have heard you," declares the LORD.

28 "Behold, I will gather you to your fathers and you shall be gathered to your grave in peace, so your eyes will not see all the evil which I will bring on this place and on its inhabitants." ' " And they brought back word to the king.

29 ¶ Then the king sent and gathered all the elders of Judah and Jerusalem.

30 The king went up to the house of the LORD and all the men of Judah, the inhabitants of Jerusalem, the priests, the Levites and all the people,

from the greatest to the least; and he read in their hearing all the words of the book of the covenant which was found in the house of the LORD.

Josiah's Good Reign

31 Then the king stood in his place and made a covenant before the LORD to walk after the LORD, and to keep His commandments and His testimonies and His statutes with all his heart and with all his soul, to perform the words of the covenant written in this book.

32 Moreover, he made all who were present in Jerusalem and Benjamin to stand with him. So the inhabitants of Jerusalem did according to the covenant of God, the God of their fathers.

33 Josiah removed all the abominations from all the lands belonging to the sons of Israel, and made all who were present in Israel to serve the LORD their God. Throughout his lifetime they did not turn from following the LORD God of their fathers.

The Passover Observed Again

35 Then Josiah celebrated the Passover to the LORD in Jerusalem, and they slaughtered the Passover animals on the fourteenth day of the first month.

2 He set the priests in their offices and encouraged them in the service of the house of the LORD.

3 He also said to the Levites who taught all Israel and who were holy to the LORD, "Put the holy ark in the house which Solomon the son of David king of Israel built; it will be a burden on your shoulders no longer. Now serve the LORD your God and His people Israel.

4 "Prepare yourselves by your fathers' households in your divisions, according to the writing of David king of Israel and according to the writing of his son Solomon.

5 "Moreover, stand in the holy place according to the sections of the fathers' households of your brethren the lay people, and according to the Levites, by division of a father's household.

6 "Now slaughter the Passover animals, sanctify yourselves and prepare for your brethren to do according to the word of the LORD by Moses."

7 ¶ Josiah contributed to the lay people, to all who were present, flocks of lambs and young goats, all for the Passover offerings, numbering 30,000 plus 3,000 bulls; these were from the king's possessions.

8 His officers also contributed a freewill offering to the people, the priests and the Levites. Hilkiah and Zechariah and Jehiel, the officials of the house of God, gave to the priests for the Passover offerings 2,600 from the flocks and 300 bulls.

9 Conaniah also, and Shemaiah and Nethanel, his brothers, and Hashabiah and Jeiel and Jozabad, the officers of the Levites, contributed to the Levites for the Passover offerings 5,000 from the flocks and 500 bulls.

10 ¶ So the service was prepared, and the priests stood at their stations and the Levites by their divisions according to the king's command.

11 They slaughtered the Passover animals, and while the priests sprinkled the blood received from their hand, the Levites skinned them.

12 Then they removed the burnt offerings that they might give them to the sections of the fathers' households of the lay people to present to the LORD, as it is written in the book of Moses. They did this also with the bulls.

13 So they roasted the Passover animals on the fire according to the ordinance, and they boiled the holy things in pots, in kettles, in pans, and carried them speedily to all the lay people.

14 Afterwards they prepared for themselves and for the priests, because the priests, the sons of Aaron, were offering the burnt offerings and the fat until night; therefore the Levites prepared for themselves and for the priests, the sons of Aaron.

15 The singers, the sons of Asaph, were also at their stations according to the command of David, Asaph, Heman, and Jeduthun the king's seer; and the gatekeepers at each gate did not have to depart from their service, because the Levites their brethren prepared for them.

16 ¶ So all the service of the LORD was prepared on that day to celebrate the Passover, and to offer burnt offerings on the altar of the LORD according to the command of King Josiah.

17 Thus the sons of Israel who were present celebrated the Passover at that time, and the Feast of Unleavened Bread seven days.

18 There had not been celebrated a Passover like it in Israel since the days of Samuel the prophet; nor had any of the kings of Israel celebrated such a Passover as Josiah did with the priests, the Levites, all Judah and Israel who were present, and the inhabitants of Jerusalem.

19 In the eighteenth year of Josiah's reign this Passover was celebrated.

Josiah Dies in Battle

20 ¶ After all this, when Josiah had set the temple in order, Neco king of Egypt came up to make war at Carchemish on the Euphrates, and Josiah went out to engage him.

21 But Neco sent messengers to him, saying, "What have we to do with each other, O King of Judah? I am not coming against you today but against the house with which I am at war, and God has ordered me to hurry. Stop for your own sake from interfering with God who is with me, so that He will not destroy you."

22 However, Josiah would not turn away from him, but disguised himself in order to make war with him; nor did he listen to the words of Neco

from the mouth of God, but came to make war on the plain of Megiddo.

23 The archers shot King Josiah, and the king said to his servants, "Take me away, for I am badly wounded."

35:22 A Bloody Battlefield

Some historians estimate that the valley of Megiddo has seen more fighting and bloodshed than any other spot on earth. Sitting astride the chief north-south trade route in Canaan, it has great strategic significance. The book of Revelation records that the last battle of the age, Armageddon, will take place here (Revelation 16:16).

24 So his servants took him out of the chariot and carried him in the second chariot which he had, and brought him to Jerusalem where he died and was buried in the tombs of his fathers. All Judah and Jerusalem mourned for Josiah.

25 Then Jeremiah chanted a lament for Josiah. And all the male and female singers speak about Josiah in their lamentations to this day. And they made them an ordinance in Israel; behold, they are also written in the Lamentations.

26 Now the rest of the acts of Josiah and his deeds of devotion as written in the law of the LORD,

27 and his acts, first to last, behold, they are written in the Book of the Kings of Israel and Judah.

Jehoahaz, Jehoiakim, then Jehoiachin Rule

36 Then the people of the land took *a*Joahaz the son of Josiah, and made him king in place of his father in Jerusalem.

2 Joahaz was twenty-three years old when he became king, and he reigned three months in Jerusalem.

3 Then the king of Egypt deposed him at Jerusalem, and imposed on the land a fine of one hundred talents of silver and one talent of gold.

4 The king of Egypt made Eliakim his brother king over Judah and Jerusalem, and changed his name to Jehoiakim. But Neco took Joahaz his brother and brought him to Egypt.

5 ¶ Jehoiakim was twenty-five years old when he became king, and he reigned eleven years in Jerusalem; and he did evil in the sight of the LORD his God.

6 Nebuchadnezzar king of Babylon came up against him and bound him with bronze *chains* to take him to Babylon.

7 Nebuchadnezzar also brought *some* of the articles of the house of the LORD to Babylon and put them in his temple at Babylon.

a I.e. short form of Jehoahaz

8 Now the rest of the acts of Jehoiakim and the abominations which he did, and what was found against him, behold, they are written in the Book of the Kings of Israel and Judah. And Jehoiachin his son became king in his place.

9 ¶ Jehoiachin was eight years old when he became king, and he reigned three months and ten days in Jerusalem, and he did evil in the sight of the LORD.

Captivity in Babylon Begun

10 At the turn of the year King Nebuchadnezzar sent and brought him to Babylon with the valuable articles of the house of the LORD, and he made his kinsman Zedekiah king over Judah and Jerusalem.

Zedekiah Rules in Judah

11 ¶ Zedekiah was twenty-one years old when he became king, and he reigned eleven years in Jerusalem.

12 He did evil in the sight of the LORD his God; he did not humble himself before Jeremiah the prophet who spoke for the LORD.

13 He also rebelled against King Nebuchadnezzar who had made him swear *allegiance* by God. But he stiffened his neck and hardened his heart against turning to the LORD God of Israel.

14 Furthermore, all the officials of the priests and the people were very unfaithful *following* all the abominations of the nations; and they defiled the house of the LORD which He had sanctified in Jerusalem.

15 ¶ The LORD, the God of their fathers, sent *word* to them again and again by His messengers, because He had compassion on His people and on His dwelling place;

16 but they *continually* mocked the messengers of God, despised His words and scoffed at His prophets, until the wrath of the LORD arose against His people, until there was no remedy.

17 Therefore He brought up against them the king of the Chaldeans who slew their young men

36:19 Between the Temples

For about 70 years the Jews had no temple. The first local synagogues probably developed during this time, as gathering places where Jews could hear readings from the Old Testament and offer prayers. The last few verses of Chronicles hint that a more hopeful time is coming when the temple will be rebuilt. These verses are repeated at the beginning of Ezra. Most scholars believe Chronicles, Ezra, and Nehemiah were originally connected in one book.

with the sword in the house of their sanctuary, and had no compassion on young man or virgin, old man or infirm; He gave *them* all into his hand.

18 All the articles of the house of God, great and small, and the treasures of the house of the LORD, and the treasures of the king and of his officers, he brought *them* all to Babylon.

19 Then they burned the house of God and broke down the wall of Jerusalem, and burned all its fortified buildings with fire and destroyed all its valuable articles.

20 Those who had escaped from the sword he carried away to Babylon; and they were servants to him and to his sons until the rule of the kingdom of Persia,

21 to fulfill the word of the LORD by the mouth of Jeremiah, until the land had enjoyed its sab-

baths. All the days of its desolation it kept sabbath until seventy years were complete.

Cyrus Permits Return

22 ¶ Now in the first year of Cyrus king of Persia—in order to fulfill the word of the LORD by the mouth of Jeremiah—the LORD stirred up the spirit of Cyrus king of Persia, so that he sent a proclamation throughout his kingdom, and also *put it* in writing, saying,

23 "Thus says Cyrus king of Persia, 'The LORD, the God of heaven, has given me all the kingdoms of the earth, and He has appointed me to build Him a house in Jerusalem, which is in Judah. Whoever there is among you of all His people, may the LORD his God be with him, and let him go up!' "

EZRA

Beginning Again
For the exiles from Babylon, news almost too good to be true

EZRA BEGINS WITH EXILES RETURNING to a ruined city—a brush-covered ghost town burned and pillaged nearly 50 years before by an overpowering Babylonian army. Would Jerusalem now have a new beginning?

Psalm 126 captures the returning exiles' feelings: "We were like those who dream. Then our mouth was filled with laughter and our tongue with joyful shouting." The Persian empire had conquered mighty Babylon and, under the emperor Cyrus, offered all Jews a chance to return to their land. It was too good to believe.

> Yet many of the priests and Levites and heads of fathers' households, the old men who had seen the first temple, wept with a loud voice . . . while many shouted aloud. 3:12

A New Start with God

One poet in exile had written, "If I forget you, O Jerusalem, may my right hand forget her skill" (Psalm 137:5). These returned exiles were the minority who, decades afterwards, had not forgotten. They treasured their spiritual heritage more than the houses and businesses they had built in Babylon. They wanted to live and worship in the place God had given his people. Any sacrifice was worth this opportunity. Their first impulse when they arrived was to rebuild the temple, God's home.

The tolerant Persians (whose official policy was to encourage the local religion in every area they governed) had even brought out the silver and gold temple articles, carefully preserved in a Babylonian temple as though waiting on God's timing. When the returned exiles laid the foundation to the new temple, the sound of their shouting (and noisy weeping) could be heard from far away (3:13). The temple, after all, was the place where they would meet God. It symbolized a new start with him.

The Problems of Beginning Again

God had opened the way, but the exiles needed determination to follow it. The book of Ezra divides into three parts, each one dealing with an obstacle that arose. The first part tells how, immediately after the return of the exiles, their neighbors in the surrounding countryside became hostile. After their deceptive offer of "help" was turned down, these neighbors began a campaign of opposition. They managed to stop further progress on the temple.

The temple lay in ruins for nearly 20 more years, until the prophets Haggai and Zechariah (whose messages are recorded in the books named after them) again stirred up interest in building. This "second push" is described in chapters 5 and 6. When opposition arose this time, the Jews managed to push through—again with the assistance of a Persian king.

Another problem preoccupies the final four chapters. Ezra, the man after whom this book is named, actually arrived in Jerusalem during this period, 80 years after the first party. The temple had by then been up for half a century. But the "new beginning" stood in severe jeopardy again. The Jews had begun to mingle (and compromise their faith) with the hostile people around them. Ezra's leadership, which came from deep Biblical faith and genuine sorrow over sin, forced a radical, painful solution.

Ezra Leads Up to Jesus

The book of Ezra introduces an entirely new period in Israel's history—a period in which they became more like a church than a nation. Israelites before the exile had given much of their energy to fighting enemy armies. Now they focused on fighting sin and spiritual compromise.

The minority who returned could build a temple only with the permission of a foreign government in Persia. They had lost political independence, yet they clung to their religion, especially to the Old

Testament Scriptures and temple worship. They feared repeating the mistakes that had sent them into exile. True, they did flirt with spiritual compromise. Yet when God's prophets spoke, people responded.

As those who had chosen a ruined Jerusalem over a prosperous Babylon, the returned Jews looked to God instead of to government for help. Still they dreamed, more than ever, of the powerful Messiah the prophets promised. This dream, and their strong determination to obey the law of God, continued right up until the time of Jesus, about 450 years after Ezra's last words.

How to Read Ezra

T he book of Ezra describes several highly emotional events. Yet it reads like a historical report, citing official documents, letters, and lists written over an 80-year span. You are often left to imagine for yourself the feelings of the returning exiles. The book can, therefore, seem confusing and dry unless you take time to imagine how the scenes must have looked and to reflect on how people must have felt.

The three distinct periods Ezra deals with all have the same theme: a new beginning for God's people. In each situation God gave opportunity and the outside world threatened it. God's people drifted back and forth in their response. Carefully take note of the "messages" from both God and the world, and how the Israelites responded. Examine Ezra's model, as an unwavering man of the law as well as of deep personal faith.

To understand how Ezra fits into Israel's long-term pattern of response to God and the world, read some historical background. Articles on "Ezra," "Haggai" or "Israel, History of" in a Bible dictionary may offer the best summary. The short book of Haggai zeroes in on the crucial months described in Ezra 5:1–2 and makes a valuable companion to any study of Ezra.

PEOPLE YOU'LL MEET IN EZRA

ARTAXERXES *(p. 525)*
EZRA *(p. 526)*

3-TRACK READING PLAN

For an explanation and complete listing of the 3-track reading plan, turn to page 7.

TRACK 1: *Two-Week Courses on the Bible*
See page 7 for information on these courses.

TRACK 2: *An Overview of Ezra in 1 Day*
☐ Day 1. Read the Introduction to Ezra and chapter 3 for the emotional story of how the returned exiles laid the foundation for the new temple.

Now turn to page 9 for your next Track 2 reading project.

TRACK 3: *All of Ezra in 9 Days*
After you have read through Ezra, turn to pages 10–14 for your next Track 3 reading project.

☐1–2   ☐3   ☐4   ☐5   ☐6   ☐7   ☐8   ☐9
☐10

Cyrus's Proclamation

1 Now in the first year of Cyrus king of Persia, in order to fulfill the word of the LORD by the mouth of Jeremiah, the LORD stirred up the spirit of Cyrus king of Persia, so that he sent a proclamation throughout all his kingdom, and also *put it* in writing, saying:

2 ¶ "Thus says Cyrus king of Persia, 'The LORD, the God of heaven, has given me all the kingdoms of the earth and He has appointed me to build Him a house in Jerusalem, which is in Judah.

1:2 Prediction Fulfilled

The fulfilled prophecy was probably Jeremiah 29:10, God's promise to bring Israel back to Jerusalem after 70 years. Additionally, Isaiah 44:28 and 45:1,13 had named Cyrus of Persia as God's agent to see Jerusalem and the temple rebuilt. This is not evidence that Cyrus worshiped Israel's God. He had a policy of religious toleration and contributed to the rebuilding of several nations' temples.

3 'Whoever there is among you of all His people, may his God be with him! Let him go up to Jerusalem which is in Judah and rebuild the house of the LORD, the God of Israel; He is the God who is in Jerusalem.

4 'Every survivor, at whatever place he may live, let the men of that place support him with silver and gold, with goods and cattle, together with a freewill offering for the house of God which is in Jerusalem.'"

Holy Vessels Restored

5 ¶ Then the heads of fathers' *households* of Judah and Benjamin and the priests and the Levites arose, even everyone whose spirit God had stirred to go up and rebuild the house of the LORD which is in Jerusalem.

6 All those about them encouraged them with articles of silver, with gold, with goods, with cattle and with valuables, aside from all that was given as a freewill offering.

7 Also King Cyrus brought out the articles of the house of the LORD, which Nebuchadnezzar had carried away from Jerusalem and put in the house of his gods;

8 and Cyrus, king of Persia, had them brought out by the hand of Mithredath the treasurer, and he counted them out to Sheshbazzar, the prince of Judah.

9 Now this *was* their number: 30 gold dishes, 1,000 silver dishes, 29 duplicates;

10 30 gold bowls, 410 silver bowls of a second *kind and* 1,000 other articles.

11 All the articles of gold and silver *numbered* 5,400. Sheshbazzar brought them all up with the exiles who went up from Babylon to Jerusalem.

Number of Those Returning

2 Now these are the people of the province who came up out of the captivity of the exiles whom Nebuchadnezzar the king of Babylon had carried away to Babylon, and returned to Jerusalem and Judah, each to his city.

2:1 A People Preserved

Lists of names, whether in the Bible or the telephone book, make dull reading. But the way these names are grouped reveals God's care for the people of Israel. They had not lost track of their Israelite identity during two generations in Babylon. They knew their family record, and they could place themselves according to Israelite families, Israelite towns, and Israelite religious duties in the temple. Like the temple articles, carefully stored in readiness (1:7), these were a people preserved to serve God again.

2 These came with Zerubbabel, Jeshua, Nehemiah, Seraiah, Reelaiah, Mordecai, Bilshan, Mispar, Bigvai, Rehum *and* Baanah.

¶ The number of the men of the people of Israel:

3 the sons of Parosh, 2,172;

4 the sons of Shephatiah, 372;

5 the sons of Arah, 775;

6 the sons of Pahath-moab of the sons of Jeshua *and* Joab, 2,812;

7 the sons of Elam, 1,254;

8 the sons of Zattu, 945;

9 the sons of Zaccai, 760;

10 the sons of Bani, 642;

11 the sons of Bebai, 623;

12 the sons of Azgad, 1,222;

13 the sons of Adonikam, 666;

14 the sons of Bigvai, 2,056;

15 the sons of Adin, 454;

16 the sons of Ater of Hezekiah, 98;

17 the sons of Bezai, 323;

18 the sons of Jorah, 112;

19 the sons of Hashum, 223;

20 the sons of Gibbar, 95;

21 the men of Bethlehem, 123;

22 the men of Netophah, 56;

23 the men of Anathoth, 128;

24 the sons of Azmaveth, 42;

25 the sons of Kiriath-arim, Chephirah and Beeroth, 743;

26 the sons of Ramah and Geba, 621;

27 the men of Michmas, 122;

28 the men of Bethel and Ai, 223;

29 the sons of Nebo, 52;

30 the sons of Magbish, 156;

31 the sons of the other Elam, 1,254;

32 the sons of Harim, 320;

33 the sons of Lod, Hadid and Ono, 725;

34 the men of Jericho, 345;

35 the sons of Senaah, 3,630.

Priests Returning

36 ¶ The priests: the sons of Jedaiah of the house of Jeshua, 973;

37 the sons of Immer, 1,052;

38 the sons of Pashhur, 1,247;

39 the sons of Harim, 1,017.

Levites Returning

40 ¶ The Levites: the sons of Jeshua and Kadmiel, of the sons of Hodaviah, 74.

41 The singers: the sons of Asaph, 128.

42 The sons of the gatekeepers: the sons of Shallum, the sons of Ater, the sons of Talmon, the sons of Akkub, the sons of Hatita, the sons of Shobai, in all 139.

43 ¶ The temple servants: the sons of Ziha, the sons of Hasupha, the sons of Tabbaoth,

44 the sons of Keros, the sons of Siaha, the sons of Padon,

45 the sons of Lebanah, the sons of Hagabah, the sons of Akkub,

46 the sons of Hagab, the sons of Shalmai, the sons of Hanan,

47 the sons of Giddel, the sons of Gahar, the sons of Reaiah,

48 the sons of Rezin, the sons of Nekoda, the sons of Gazzam,

49 the sons of Uzza, the sons of Paseah, the sons of Besai,

50 the sons of Asnah, the sons of Meunim, the sons of Nephisim,

51 the sons of Bakbuk, the sons of Hakupha, the sons of Harhur,

52 the sons of Bazluth, the sons of Mehida, the sons of Harsha,

53 the sons of Barkos, the sons of Sisera, the sons of Temah,

54 the sons of Neziah, the sons of Hatipha.

55 ¶ The sons of Solomon's servants: the sons of Sotai, the sons of Hassophereth, the sons of Peruda,

56 the sons of Jaalah, the sons of Darkon, the sons of Giddel,

57 the sons of Shephatiah, the sons of Hattil, the sons of Pochereth-hazzebaim, the sons of Ami.

58 ¶ All the temple servants and the sons of Solomon's servants were 392.

59 ¶ Now these are those who came up from Tel-melah, Tel-harsha, Cherub, Addan *and* Immer, but they were not able to give evidence of their fathers' households and their descendants, whether they were of Israel:

60 the sons of Delaiah, the sons of Tobiah, the sons of Nekoda, 652.

Priests Removed

61 Of the sons of the priests: the sons of Habaiah, the sons of Hakkoz, the sons of Barzillai, who took a wife from the daughters of Barzillai the Gileadite, and he was called by their name.

62 These searched *among* their ancestral registration, but they could not be located; therefore they were considered unclean *and excluded* from the priesthood.

63 The governor said to them that they should not eat from the most holy things until a priest stood up with Urim and Thummim.

2:63 The Need for Guidance

The Urim and Thummim were probably something like dice. Priests in the Old Testament used them to determine God's will. Until the Urim and Thummim could be employed, the families whose records were lost (verse 62) had no way to establish themselves as genuine priests. For a people determined to follow God's word precisely, this mattered tremendously. God had said that only Aaron's descendants could touch the holy things in the sanctuary, on pain of death (Numbers 18:1–7).

64 ¶ The whole assembly numbered 42,360,

65 besides their male and female servants who numbered 7,337; and they had 200 singing men and women.

66 Their horses were 736; their mules, 245;

67 their camels, 435; *their* donkeys, 6,720.

68 ¶ Some of the heads of fathers' *households,* when they arrived at the house of the LORD which is in Jerusalem, offered willingly for the house of God to restore it on its foundation.

69 According to their ability they gave to the treasury for the work 61,000 gold drachmas and 5,000 silver minas and 100 priestly garments.

70 ¶ Now the priests and the Levites, some of the people, the singers, the gatekeepers and the temple servants lived in their cities, and all Israel in their cities.

Altar and Sacrifices Restored

3 Now when the seventh month came, and the sons of Israel *were* in the cities, the people gathered together as one man to Jerusalem.

2 Then Jeshua the son of Jozadak and his brothers the priests, and Zerubbabel the son of Shealtiel and his brothers arose and built the altar of the God of Israel to offer burnt offerings on it, as it is written in the law of Moses, the man of God.

3 So they set up the altar on its foundation, for they were terrified because of the peoples of the lands; and they offered burnt offerings on it to the LORD, burnt offerings morning and evening.

4 They celebrated the Feast of [a]Booths, as it is written, and *offered* the fixed number of burnt offerings daily, according to the ordinance, as each day required;

5 and afterward *there was* a continual burnt offering, also for the new moons and for all the fixed festivals of the LORD that were consecrated, and from everyone who offered a freewill offering to the LORD.

6 From the first day of the seventh month they began to offer burnt offerings to the LORD, but the foundation of the temple of the LORD had not been laid.

7 Then they gave money to the masons and carpenters, and food, drink and oil to the Sidonians and to the Tyrians, to bring cedar wood from Lebanon to the sea at Joppa, according to the permission they had from Cyrus king of Persia.

Temple Restoration Begun

8 ¶ Now in the second year of their coming to the house of God at Jerusalem in the second month, Zerubbabel the son of Shealtiel and Jeshua the son of Jozadak and the rest of their brothers the priests and the Levites, and all who came from the captivity to Jerusalem, began *the work* and appointed the Levites from twenty years and older to oversee the work of the house of the LORD.

9 Then Jeshua *with* his sons and brothers stood united *with* Kadmiel and his sons, the sons of Judah *and* the sons of Henadad *with* their sons and brothers the Levites, to oversee the workmen in the temple of God.

10 ¶ Now when the builders had laid the foundation of the temple of the LORD, the priests stood in their apparel with trumpets, and the Levites, the sons of Asaph, with cymbals, to praise the LORD according to the directions of King David of Israel.

11 They sang, praising and giving thanks to the LORD, *saying*, "For He is good, for His lovingkindness is upon Israel forever." And all the people shouted with a great shout when they praised the LORD because the foundation of the house of the LORD was laid.

12 Yet many of the priests and Levites and heads of fathers' *households*, the old men who had seen the first temple, wept with a loud voice when the foundation of this house was laid before their eyes, while many shouted aloud for joy,

13 so that the people could not distinguish the sound of the shout of joy from the sound of the weeping of the people, for the people shouted with a loud shout, and the sound was heard far away.

Adversaries Hinder the Work

4 Now when the enemies of Judah and Benjamin heard that the people of the exile were building a temple to the LORD God of Israel,

2 they approached Zerubbabel and the heads of fathers' *households*, and said to them, "Let us

build with you, for we, like you, seek your God; and we have been sacrificing to Him since the days of Esarhaddon king of Assyria, who brought us up here."

4:1 How to Stop God's Work

Chapter 4 describes three different strategies used to hinder God's people: 1) Offer help that will lead to compromises or even a complete takeover of the project by unbelievers (verses 1–3). 2) Discourage, frighten, and frustrate God's people (verses 4–5). 3) Use official power to force them to stop (verses 23–24). Now as then, governments and opposition groups use these strategies to stop the work of believers.

3 But Zerubbabel and Jeshua and the rest of the heads of fathers' *households* of Israel said to them, "You have nothing in common with us in building a house to our God; but we ourselves will together build to the LORD God of Israel, as King Cyrus, the king of Persia has commanded us."

4 ¶ Then the people of the land discouraged the people of Judah, and frightened them from building,

5 and hired counselors against them to frustrate their counsel all the days of Cyrus king of Persia, even until the reign of Darius king of Persia.

6 ¶ Now in the reign of [b]Ahasuerus, in the beginning of his reign, they wrote an accusation against the inhabitants of Judah and Jerusalem.

4:6–23 A Flash Forward

This section is a glance forward in history. The Israelites would continue to feel opposition from their neighbors even long after the temple was successfully completed. The quarrel described here, during Ahasuerus' and Artaxerxes' reigns, was not over the temple but the defensive wall to be built around Jerusalem—a wall Nehemiah, with Ezra's help, completed years later.

7 ¶ And in the days of Artaxerxes, Bishlam, Mithredath, Tabeel and the rest of his colleagues wrote to Artaxerxes king of Persia; and the text of the letter was written in Aramaic and translated *from* Aramaic.

The Letter to King Artaxerxes

8 Rehum the commander and Shimshai the scribe wrote a letter against Jerusalem to King Artaxerxes, as follows—

9 then *wrote* Rehum the commander and

---

[a] Or *Tabernacles*   [b] Or *Xerxes*; Heb *Ahash-verosh*

Shimshai the scribe and the rest of their colleagues, the judges and the lesser governors, the officials, the secretaries, the men of Erech, the Babylonians, the men of Susa, that is, the Elamites,

10 and the rest of the nations which the great and honorable Osnappar deported and settled in the city of Samaria, and in the rest of the region beyond the *River. Now

11 this is the copy of the letter which they sent to him:

¶ "To King Artaxerxes: Your servants, the men in the region beyond the River, and now

12 let it be known to the king that the Jews who came up from you have come to us at Jerusalem; they are rebuilding the rebellious and evil city and are finishing the walls and repairing the foundations.

13 "Now let it be known to the king, that if that city is rebuilt and the walls are finished, they will not pay tribute, custom or toll, and it will damage the revenue of the kings.

14 "Now because we are in the service of the palace, and it is not fitting for us to see the king's dishonor, therefore we have sent and informed the king,

15 so that a search may be made in the record books of your fathers. And you will discover in the record books and learn that that city is a rebellious city and damaging to kings and provinces, and that they have incited revolt within it in past days; therefore that city was laid waste.

16 "We inform the king that if that city is rebuilt and the walls finished, as a result you will have no possession in *the province* beyond the River."

The King Replies and Work Stops

17 ¶ *Then* the king sent an answer to Rehum the commander, to Shimshai the scribe, and to the rest of their colleagues who live in Samaria and in the rest of *the provinces* beyond the River: "Peace. And now

18 the document which you sent to us has been translated and read before me.

19 "A decree has been issued by me, and a search has been made and it has been discovered that that city has risen up against the kings in past days, that rebellion and revolt have been perpetrated in it,

20 that mighty kings have ruled over Jerusalem, governing all *the provinces* beyond the River, and that tribute, custom and toll were paid to them.

21 "So, now issue a decree to make these men stop *work*, that this city may not be rebuilt until a decree is issued by me.

22 "Beware of being negligent in carrying out this *matter;* why should damage increase to the detriment of the kings?"

23 ¶ Then as soon as the copy of King Artaxerxes' document was read before Rehum and

Shimshai the scribe and their colleagues, they went in haste to Jerusalem to the Jews and stopped them by force of arms.

24 ¶ Then work on the house of God in Jerusalem ceased, and it was stopped until the second year of the reign of Darius king of Persia.

Temple Work Resumed

5 When the prophets, Haggai the prophet and Zechariah the son of Iddo, prophesied to the Jews who were in Judah and Jerusalem in the name of the God of Israel, who was over them,

2 then Zerubbabel the son of Shealtiel and Jeshua the son of Jozadak arose and began to rebuild the house of God which is in Jerusalem; and the prophets of God were with them supporting them.

3 ¶ At that time Tattenai, the governor of *the province* beyond the River, and Shethar-bozenai and their colleagues came to them and spoke to them thus, "Who issued you a decree to rebuild this *btemple and to finish this structure?"

4 Then we told them accordingly what the names of the men were who were reconstructing this building.

5 But the eye of their God was on the elders of the Jews, and they did not stop them until a report could come to Darius, and then a written reply be returned concerning it.

Adversaries Write to Darius

6 ¶ *This is* the copy of the letter which Tattenai, the governor of *the province* beyond the River, and Shethar-bozenai and his colleagues the officials, who were beyond the River, sent to Darius the king.

7 They sent a report to him in which it was written thus: "To Darius the king, all peace.

8 "Let it be known to the king that we have gone to the province of Judah, to the house of the great God, which is being built with huge stones, and beams are being laid in the walls; and this work is going on with great care and is succeeding in their hands.

9 "Then we asked those elders and said to them thus, 'Who issued you a decree to rebuild this temple and to finish this structure?'

10 "We also asked them their names so as to inform you, and that we might write down the names of the men who were at their head.

11 "Thus they answered us, saying, 'We are the servants of the God of heaven and earth and are rebuilding the temple that was built many years ago, which a great king of Israel built and finished.

12 'But because our fathers had provoked the God of heaven to wrath, He gave them into the hand of Nebuchadnezzar king of Babylon, the Chaldean, *who* destroyed this temple and deported the people to Babylon.

13 'However, in the first year of Cyrus king of

---

a I.e. Euphrates River, and so throughout the ch   *b* Lit *house,* and so in vv 9, 11, 12

Babylon, King Cyrus issued a decree to rebuild this house of God.

14 'Also the gold and silver utensils of the house of God which Nebuchadnezzar had taken from the temple in Jerusalem, and brought them to the temple of Babylon, these King Cyrus took from the temple of Babylon and they were given to one whose name was Sheshbazzar, whom he had appointed governor.

15 'He said to him, "Take these utensils, go *and* deposit them in the temple in Jerusalem and let the house of God be rebuilt in its place."

16 'Then that Sheshbazzar came *and* laid the foundations of the house of God in Jerusalem; and from then until now it has been under construction and it is not *yet* completed.'

17 "Now if it pleases the king, let a search be conducted in the king's treasure house, which is there in Babylon, if it be that a decree was issued by King Cyrus to rebuild this house of God at Jerusalem; and let the king send to us his decision concerning this *matter*."

Darius Finds Cyrus's Decree

6 Then King Darius issued a decree, and search was made in the [a]archives, where the treasures were stored in Babylon.

2 In [b]Ecbatana in the fortress, which is in the province of Media, a scroll was found and there was written in it as follows: "Memorandum—

3 "In the first year of King Cyrus, Cyrus the king issued a decree: 'Concerning the house of God at Jerusalem, let the temple, the place where sacrifices are offered, be rebuilt and let its foundations be retained, its height being 60 cubits and its width 60 cubits;

6:2 The Ring of Truth

In a made-up legend, there is no need for insignificant, divergent details. All the loose ends tie up neatly. Real life, however, is messier. Ezra records a typical example: a document was searched for in Babylon, but it unexpectedly turned up in remote Ecbatana, where (history records) Cyrus spent the summer of his first year as king. Such details suggest that Ezra is based on accurate and detailed historical sources.

4 with three layers of huge stones and one layer of timbers. And let the cost be paid from the royal treasury.

5 'Also let the gold and silver utensils of the house of God, which Nebuchadnezzar took from the temple in Jerusalem and brought to Babylon, be returned and brought to their places in the temple in Jerusalem; and you shall put *them* in the house of God.'

6 ¶ "Now *therefore*, Tattenai, governor of *the province* beyond the River, Shethar-bozenai and your colleagues, the officials of *the provinces* beyond the River, keep away from there.

7 "Leave this work on the house of God alone; let the governor of the Jews and the elders of the Jews rebuild this house of God on its site.

8 "Moreover, I issue a decree concerning what you are to do for these elders of Judah in the rebuilding of this house of God: the full cost is to be paid to these people from the royal treasury out of the taxes of *the provinces* beyond the River, and that without delay.

9 "Whatever is needed, both young bulls, rams, and lambs for a burnt offering to the God of heaven, and wheat, salt, wine and anointing oil, as the priests in Jerusalem request, *it* is to be given to them daily without fail,

10 that they may offer [c]acceptable sacrifices to the God of heaven and pray for the life of the king and his sons.

11 "And I issued a decree that any man who violates this edict, a timber shall be drawn from his house and he shall be impaled on it and his house shall be made a refuse heap on account of this.

6:11 Ironic Outcome

Governor Tattenai had written the central government in order to harass the Jews who sought to rebuild the temple (5:7–17). As it turned out, his strategy backfired. He and his local government were ordered to pay all the Jews' expenses or be impaled on their own roof beams.

12 "May the God who has caused His name to dwell there overthrow any king or people who attempts to change *it*, so as to destroy this house of God in Jerusalem. I, Darius, have issued *this* decree, let *it* be carried out with all diligence!"

The Temple Completed and Dedicated

13 ¶ Then Tattenai, the governor of *the province* beyond the River, Shethar-bozenai and their colleagues carried out *the decree* with all diligence, just as King Darius had sent.

14 And the elders of the Jews were successful in building through the prophesying of Haggai the prophet and Zechariah the son of Iddo. And they finished building according to the command of the God of Israel and the decree of Cyrus, Darius, and Artaxerxes king of Persia.

15 This temple was completed on the third day

---

[a] Lit *house of the books*   [b] Aram *Achmetha*   [c] Lit *pleasing*; or *sweet-smelling sacrifices*

of the month Adar; it was the sixth year of the reign of King Darius.

16 ¶ And the sons of Israel, the priests, the Levites and the rest of the exiles, celebrated the dedication of this house of God with joy.

17 They offered for the dedication of this temple of God 100 bulls, 200 rams, 400 lambs, and as a sin offering for all Israel 12 male goats, corresponding to the number of the tribes of Israel.

18 Then they appointed the priests to their divisions and the Levites in their orders for the service of God in Jerusalem, as it is written in the book of Moses.

The Passover Observed

19 ¶ The exiles observed the Passover on the fourteenth of the first month.

20 For the priests and the Levites had purified themselves together; all of them were pure. Then they slaughtered the Passover *lamb* for all the exiles, both for their brothers the priests and for themselves.

21 The sons of Israel who returned from exile and all those who had separated themselves from the impurity of the nations of the land to *join* them, to seek the LORD God of Israel, ate *the Passover*.

22 And they observed the Feast of Unleavened Bread seven days with joy, for the LORD had caused them to rejoice, and had turned the heart of the king of Assyria toward them to encourage them in the work of the house of God, the God of Israel.

Ezra Journeys from Babylon to Jerusalem

7 Now after these things, in the reign of Artaxerxes king of Persia, *there went up* Ezra son of Seraiah, son of Azariah, son of Hilkiah,

2 son of Shallum, son of Zadok, son of Ahitub,

3 son of Amariah, son of Azariah, son of Meraioth,

4 son of Zerahiah, son of Uzzi, son of Bukki,

5 son of Abishua, son of Phinehas, son of Eleazar, son of Aaron the chief priest.

6 This Ezra went up from Babylon, and he was a scribe skilled in the law of Moses, which the LORD God of Israel had given; and the king granted him all he requested because the hand of the LORD his God *was* upon him.

7 Some of the sons of Israel and some of the priests, the Levites, the singers, the gatekeepers and the temple servants went up to Jerusalem in the seventh year of King Artaxerxes.

8 ¶ He came to Jerusalem in the fifth month, which was in the seventh year of the king.

9 For on the first of the first month he began to go up from Babylon; and on the first of the fifth month he came to Jerusalem, because the good hand of his God *was* upon him.

10 For Ezra had set his heart to study the law of the LORD and to practice *it*, and to teach *His* statutes and ordinances in Israel.

King's Decree on Behalf of Ezra

11 ¶ Now this is the copy of the decree which King Artaxerxes gave to Ezra the priest, the scribe, learned in the words of the commandments of the LORD and His statutes to Israel:

12 "Artaxerxes, king of kings, to Ezra the priest, the scribe of the law of the God of heaven, perfect *peace*. And now

13 I have issued a decree that any of the people of Israel and their priests and the Levites in my kingdom who are willing to go to Jerusalem, may go with you.

ARTAXERXES *Friendly Foreigner*

THROUGHOUT HISTORY, STRONG GOVERNMENTS HAVE had a love-hate relationship with religion. Some encourage faith and try to manipulate it for political gain. Others, such as Communist China or Albania, pass harsh laws against religion and persecute the faithful. Only rarely does a totalitarian regime let religion go its own way.

After domination by the brutal regimes of Assyria and Babylon, the Persian Empire must have seemed like a relief to the Jews. They especially welcomed the Persians' tolerant, even friendly attitude toward other nations' religions. Not only did Persia's King Artaxerxes allow Ezra to return to Jerusalem, he wrote a remarkable letter of support for Ezra's mission.

Other despots, like the Pharaoh of Egypt, saw Israel's God as a threat to their unrestricted power. Artaxerxes apparently hoped to win God's favor. He provided material support, safe passage to Jews wanting to return to their land and freedom from taxation for all temple employees. In effect, this secular regime subsidized Judaism.

Later, Artaxerxes encouraged Nehemiah to go to Jerusalem for a potentially risky task: rebuilding the walls of the city so it could be militarily defended (Nehemiah 2:1–9). As one of his top officials, Nehemiah had evidently given Artaxerxes assurance that a strong Israelite nation would not cause trouble.

Life Questions: Is it good for churches to receive help—financial or otherwise—as the Jews did from Artaxerxes? What would be the dangers in such an approach?

14 "Forasmuch as you are sent by the king and his seven counselors to inquire concerning Judah and Jerusalem according to the law of your God which is in your hand,

15 and to bring the silver and gold, which the king and his counselors have freely offered to the God of Israel, whose dwelling is in Jerusalem,

16 with all the silver and gold which you find in the whole province of Babylon, along with the freewill offering of the people and of the priests, who offered willingly for the house of their God which is in Jerusalem;

17 with this money, therefore, you shall dili-

gently buy bulls, rams and lambs, with their grain offerings and their drink offerings and offer them on the altar of the house of your God which is in Jerusalem.

18 "Whatever seems good to you and to your brothers to do with the rest of the silver and gold, you may do according to the will of your God.

19 "Also the utensils which are given to you for the service of the house of your God, deliver in full before the God of Jerusalem.

20 "The rest of the needs for the house of your God, for which you may have occasion to provide, provide *for it* from the royal treasury.

Ezra, a Man of the Heart
He applied God's word to himself before preaching it to others

EZRA KNEW HOW TO GET things done. He had the political savvy to win a Persian king's support for the trip back to Jerusalem, the salesmanship to convince Jewish family leaders to go along, and the organizational know-how to mount the long, complicated, and dangerous expedition. (There were no Holiday Inns.)

At the same time, Ezra was a priest who depended on God. He set aside days for fasting and prayer. He knew and lived by the Old Testament law, but used it as a path to a profound relationship with God. When he studied Scripture, he applied it to himself before applying it to others (7:10).

> *While Ezra was praying and making confession, weeping and prostrating himself before the house of God, a very large assembly, men, women and children, gathered to him from Israel.*
> **10:1**

A Strong Negative Reaction

Ezra's party got to Jerusalem 80 years after the first exiles had returned. Yet within four months the Jewish leaders were asking this latecomer for advice on the most sensitive matters.

They told Ezra that Israelites were marrying their idolatrous neighbors. At the news, Ezra completely lost his composure, tore his clothes, and sat down stunned (9:3). His grief-filled prayer of repentance inspired a large crowd to join him in bitter weeping. Then and there they resolved to break up the marriages. The women and children were to be sent away. Ezra, a practical man even in his emotional condition, put the machinery into operation and saw it done.

Why did Ezra react so negatively to these marriages? How could he allow children to be sent away from their fathers, families split? Some people see proof that he was racially oriented, bound to exclude non-Jews from Israel.

But racial purity was not Ezra's worry. Non-Jews like Rahab and Ruth, who converted to Judaism, had long been accepted into Israel. Ezra 6:21 suggests that outsiders who sought the Lord were still welcomed. Ezra's concern was that intermarriage represented a compromised faith that threatened the future existence of Israel.

Tossing Away One Last Chance

Marriage in those days was more than a personal matter. It created a political and religious alliance between two families. These mixed marriages were tying Israelites to other faiths—for Israel's neighbors worshiped idols, an act God hated. Ezra knew that his God must hold the only place in his people's hearts. They must be a special people with a sense of their unique destiny. The law told them not to intermarry (Exodus 34:15–16; Deuteronomy 7:3–6). (In a related situation Paul instructed Christians not to be "bound together with unbelievers" [2 Corinthians 6:14], though he told Christians already married to non-Christians not to divorce [1 Corinthians 7:12–16].)

Ezra's prayer shows that petty technicalities of the law were far from his mind. His concerns involved the heart. He saw his people falling into the same pattern of compromise that had led God to give them up to the Babylonians years before. Had they learned nothing from their long exile? They were tossing away one last remarkable chance to start over.

Life Questions: Ezra saw intermarriage as a compromise in people's faith. Do people today make other compromises that have the same impact on their faith?

21 ¶ "I, even I, King Artaxerxes, issue a decree to all the treasurers who are *in the provinces* beyond the River, that whatever Ezra the priest, the scribe of the law of the God of heaven, may require of you, it shall be done diligently,

22 *even* up to 100 talents of silver, 100 kors of wheat, 100 baths of wine, 100 baths of oil, and salt as needed.

23 "Whatever is commanded by the God of heaven, let it be done with zeal for the house of the God of heaven, so that there will not be wrath against the kingdom of the king and his sons.

24 "We also inform you that it is not allowed to impose tax, tribute or toll *on* any of the priests, Levites, singers, doorkeepers, Nethinim or servants of this house of God.

25 ¶ "You, Ezra, according to the wisdom of your God which is in your hand, appoint magistrates and judges that they may judge all the people who are in *the province* beyond the River, *even* all those who know the laws of your God; and you may teach anyone who is ignorant *of them.*

26 "Whoever will not observe the law of your God and the law of the king, let judgment be executed upon him strictly, whether for death or for banishment or for confiscation of goods or for imprisonment."

The King's Kindness

27 ¶ Blessed be the LORD, the God of our fathers, who has put *such a thing* as this in the king's heart, to adorn the house of the LORD which is in Jerusalem,

28 and has extended lovingkindness to me before the king and his counselors and before all the king's mighty princes. Thus I was strengthened according to the hand of the LORD my God upon me, and I gathered leading men from Israel to go up with me.

People Who Went with Ezra

8 Now these are the heads of their fathers' households and the genealogical enrollment of those who went up with me from Babylon in the reign of King Artaxerxes:

2 of the sons of Phinehas, Gershom; of the sons of Ithamar, Daniel; of the sons of David, Hattush;

3 of the sons of Shecaniah *who was* of the sons of Parosh, Zechariah and with him 150 males *who were in* the genealogical list;

4 of the sons of Pahath-moab, Eliehoenai the son of Zerahiah and 200 males with him;

5 of the sons of Zattu, Shecaniah, the son of Jahaziel and 300 males with him;

6 and of the sons of Adin, Ebed the son of Jonathan and 50 males with him;

7 and of the sons of Elam, Jeshaiah the son of Athaliah and 70 males with him;

8 and of the sons of Shephatiah, Zebadiah the son of Michael and 80 males with him;

9 of the sons of Joab, Obadiah the son of Jehiel and 218 males with him;

10 and of the sons of Bani, Shelomith, the son of Josiphiah and 160 males with him;

11 and of the sons of Bebai, Zechariah the son of Bebai and 28 males with him;

12 and of the sons of Azgad, Johanan the son of Hakkatan and 110 males with him;

13 and of the sons of Adonikam, the last ones, these being their names, Eliphelet, Jeuel and Shemaiah, and 60 males with them;

14 and of the sons of Bigvai, Uthai and Zabbud, and 70 males with them.

Ezra Sends for Levites

15 ¶ Now I assembled them at the river that runs to Ahava, where we camped for three days; and when I observed the people and the priests, I did not find any Levites there.

16 So I sent for Eliezer, Ariel, Shemaiah, Elnathan, Jarib, Elnathan, Nathan, Zechariah and Meshullam, leading men, and for Joiarib and Elnathan, teachers.

17 I sent them to Iddo the leading man at the place Casiphia; and I told them what to say to Iddo *and* his brothers, the temple servants at the place Casiphia, *that is,* to bring ministers to us for the house of our God.

18 According to the good hand of our God upon us they brought us a man of insight of the sons of Mahli, the son of Levi, the son of Israel, namely Sherebiah, and his sons and brothers, 18 men;

19 and Hashabiah and Jeshaiah of the sons of Merari, with his brothers and their sons, 20 men;

20 and 220 of the temple servants, whom David and the princes had given for the service of the Levites, all of them designated by name.

Protection of God Invoked

21 ¶ Then I proclaimed a fast there at the river of Ahava, that we might humble ourselves before our God to seek from Him a safe journey for us, our little ones, and all our possessions.

22 For I was ashamed to request from the king troops and horsemen to protect us from the enemy on the way, because we had said to the king, "The hand of our God is favorably disposed to all those who seek Him, but His power and His anger are against all those who forsake Him."

23 So we fasted and sought our God concerning this *matter,* and He listened to our entreaty.

24 ¶ Then I set apart twelve of the leading priests, Sherebiah, Hashabiah, and with them ten of their brothers;

25 and I weighed out to them the silver, the gold and the utensils, the offering for the house of our God which the king and his counselors and his princes and all Israel present *there* had offered.

26 Thus I weighed into their hands 650 talents

of silver, and silver utensils *worth* 100 talents, *and* 100 gold talents,

27 and 20 gold bowls *worth* 1,000 darics, and two utensils of fine shiny bronze, precious as gold.

8:22 Risk of Faith

Like gold shipments in the old Wild West, Ezra's consignment of treasure made for a dangerous journey through lawless Palestine. A military escort would surely have helped. But, having told the king that God would protect the settlers, Ezra was ashamed to ask for help that would seem to contradict his statement. His faith on the line, he determined to rely on prayer rather than soldiers.

28 Then I said to them, "You are holy to the LORD, and the utensils are holy; and the silver and the gold are a freewill offering to the LORD God of your fathers.

29 "Watch and keep *them* until you weigh *them* before the leading priests, the Levites and the heads of the fathers' *households* of Israel at Jerusalem, *in* the chambers of the house of the LORD."

30 So the priests and the Levites accepted the weighed out silver and gold and the utensils, to bring *them* to Jerusalem to the house of our God.

31 ¶ Then we journeyed from the river Ahava on the twelfth of the first month to go to Jerusalem; and the hand of our God was over us, and He delivered us from the hand of the enemy and the ambushes by the way.

32 Thus we came to Jerusalem and remained there three days.

Treasure Placed in the Temple

33 On the fourth day the silver and the gold and the utensils were weighed out in the house of our God into the hand of Meremoth the son of Uriah the priest, and with him *was* Eleazar the son of Phinehas; and with them *were* the Levites, Jozabad the son of Jeshua and Noadiah the son of Binnui.

34 Everything *was* numbered and weighed, and all the weight was recorded at that time.

35 ¶ The exiles who had come from the captivity offered burnt offerings to the God of Israel: 12 bulls for all Israel, 96 rams, 77 lambs, 12 male goats for a sin offering, all as a burnt offering to the LORD.

36 Then they delivered the king's edicts to the king's satraps and to the governors *in the* provinces beyond the River, and they supported the people and the house of God.

Mixed Marriages

9 Now when these things had been completed, the princes approached me, saying, "The people of Israel and the priests and the Levites have not separated themselves from the peoples of the lands, according to their abominations, *those* of the Canaanites, the Hittites, the Perizzites, the Jebusites, the Ammonites, the Moabites, the Egyptians and the Amorites.

2 "For they have taken some of their daughters *as wives* for themselves and for their sons, so that the holy race has intermingled with the peoples of the lands; indeed, the hands of the princes and the rulers have been foremost in this unfaithfulness."

3 When I heard about this matter, I tore my garment and my robe, and pulled some of the hair from my head and my beard, and sat down appalled.

4 Then everyone who trembled at the words of the God of Israel on account of the unfaithfulness of the exiles gathered to me, and I sat appalled until the evening offering.

Prayer of Confession

5 ¶ But at the evening offering I arose from my humiliation, even with my garment and my robe torn, and I fell on my knees and stretched out my hands to the LORD my God;

6 and I said, "O my God, I am ashamed and embarrassed to lift up my face to You, my God, for our iniquities have risen above our heads and our guilt has grown even to the heavens.

7 "Since the days of our fathers to this day we *have been* in great guilt, and on account of our iniquities we, our kings *and* our priests have been given into the hand of the kings of the lands, to the sword, to captivity and to plunder and to open shame, as *it is* this day.

8 "But now for a brief moment grace has been *shown* from the LORD our God, to leave us an escaped remnant and to give us a peg in His holy place, that our God may enlighten our eyes and grant us a little reviving in our bondage.

9 "For we are slaves; yet in our bondage our God has not forsaken us, but has extended lovingkindness to us in the sight of the kings of Persia, to give us reviving to raise up the house of our God, to restore its ruins and to give us a wall in Judah and Jerusalem.

10 ¶ "Now, our God, what shall we say after this? For we have forsaken Your commandments,

11 which You have commanded by Your servants the prophets, saying, 'The land which you are entering to possess is an unclean land with the uncleanness of the peoples of the lands, with their abominations which have filled it from end to end *and* with their impurity.

12 'So now do not give your daughters to their sons nor take their daughters to your sons, and never seek their peace or their prosperity, that you may be strong and eat the good *things* of the land and leave *it* as an inheritance to your sons forever.'

13 "After all that has come upon us for our evil deeds and our great guilt, since You our God have

requited *us* less than our iniquities *deserve,* and have given us an escaped remnant as this,

14 shall we again break Your commandments and intermarry with the peoples who commit these abominations? Would You not be angry with us to the point of destruction, until there is no remnant nor any who escape?

15 "O LORD God of Israel, You are righteous, for we have been left an escaped remnant, as *it is* this day; behold, we are before You in our guilt, for no one can stand before You because of this."

Reconciliation with God

10 Now while Ezra was praying and making confession, weeping and prostrating himself before the house of God, a very large assembly, men, women and children, gathered to him from Israel; for the people wept bitterly.

10:1 Unprecedented Response

Ezra's grief over Israel's spiritual compromise was similar to that of many prophets. But the people's response to Ezra was unprecedented. Pre-exile prophets like Amos or Jeremiah never saw such heartfelt repentance. Evidently the exile really had purified Israel.

2 Shecaniah the son of Jehiel, one of the sons of Elam, said to Ezra, "We have been unfaithful to our God and have married foreign women from the peoples of the land; yet now there is hope for Israel in spite of this.

3 "So now let us make a covenant with our God to put away all the wives and their children, according to the counsel of ªmy lord and of those who tremble at the commandment of our God; and let it be done according to the law.

4 "Arise! For *this* matter is your responsibility, but we will be with you; be courageous and act."

5 ¶ Then Ezra rose and made the leading priests, the Levites and all Israel, take oath that they would do according to this proposal; so they took the oath.

6 Then Ezra rose from before the house of God and went into the chamber of Jehohanan the son of Eliashib. Although he went there, he did not eat bread nor drink water, for he was mourning over the unfaithfulness of the exiles.

7 They made a proclamation throughout Judah and Jerusalem to all the exiles, that they should assemble at Jerusalem,

8 and that whoever would not come within three days, according to the counsel of the leaders and the elders, all his possessions should be forfeited and he himself excluded from the assembly of the exiles.

9 ¶ So all the men of Judah and Benjamin assembled at Jerusalem within the three days. It was the ninth month on the twentieth of the month, and all the people sat in the open square *before* the house of God, trembling because of this matter and the heavy rain.

10 Then Ezra the priest stood up and said to them, "You have been unfaithful and have married foreign wives adding to the guilt of Israel.

11 "Now therefore, make confession to the LORD God of your fathers and do His will; and separate yourselves from the peoples of the land and from the foreign wives."

12 Then all the assembly replied with a loud voice, "That's right! As you have said, so it is our duty to do.

13 "But there are many people; it is the rainy season and we are not able to stand in the open. Nor *can* the task *be done* in one or two days, for we have transgressed greatly in this matter.

14 "Let our leaders represent the whole assembly and let all those in our cities who have married foreign wives come at appointed times, together with the elders and judges of each city, until the fierce anger of our God on account of this matter is turned away from us."

15 Only Jonathan the son of Asahel and Jahzeiah the son of Tikvah opposed this, with Meshullam and Shabbethai the Levite supporting them.

16 ¶ But the exiles did so. And Ezra the priest selected men *who were* heads of fathers' *households* for *each of* their father's households, all of them by name. So they convened on the first day of the tenth month to investigate the matter.

17 They finished *investigating* all the men who had married foreign wives by the first day of the first month.

10:17 Corrupt Leaders

The problem Ezra had evidently expected to solve in a day (verse 13) took, in fact, two months to sort out. Intermarriage must have been more widespread than he realized. The list of those involved shows that the priests and Levites, who were the religious leaders, had a higher proportion of intermarriage than the rest of the people.

List of Offenders

18 ¶ Among the sons of the priests who had married foreign wives were found of the sons of Jeshua the son of Jozadak, and his brothers: Maaseiah, Eliezer, Jarib and Gedaliah.

19 They pledged to put away their wives, and being guilty, *they offered* a ram of the flock for their offense.

20 Of the sons of Immer *there were* Hanani and Zebadiah;

ª Or *the Lord*

21 and of the sons of Harim: Maaseiah, Elijah, Shemaiah, Jehiel and Uzziah;

22 and of the sons of Pashhur: Elioenai, Maaseiah, Ishmael, Nethanel, Jozabad and Elasah.

23 ¶ Of Levites there were Jozabad, Shimei, Kelaiah (that is, Kelita), Pethahiah, Judah and Eliezer.

24 ¶ Of the singers there was Eliashib; and of the gatekeepers: Shallum, Telem and Uri.

25 ¶ Of Israel, of the sons of Parosh there were Ramiah, Izziah, Malchijah, Mijamin, Eleazar, Malchijah and Benaiah;

26 and of the sons of Elam: Mattaniah, Zechariah, Jehiel, Abdi, Jeremoth and Elijah;

27 and of the sons of Zattu: Elioenai, Eliashib, Mattaniah, Jeremoth, Zabad and Aziza;

28 and of the sons of Bebai: Jehohanan, Hananiah, Zabbai and Athlai;

29 and of the sons of Bani: Meshullam, Malluch and Adaiah, Jashub, Sheal and Jeremoth;

30 and of the sons of Pahath-moab: Adna, Chelal, Benaiah, Maaseiah, Mattaniah, Bezalel, Binnui and Manasseh;

31 and of the sons of Harim: Eliezer, Isshijah, Malchijah, Shemaiah, Shimeon,

32 Benjamin, Malluch and Shemariah;

33 of the sons of Hashum: Mattenai, Mattattah, Zabad, Eliphelet, Jeremai, Manasseh and Shimei;

34 of the sons of Bani: Maadai, Amram, Uel,

35 Benaiah, Bedeiah, Cheluhi,

36 Vaniah, Meremoth, Eliashib,

37 Mattaniah, Mattenai, Jaasu,

38 Bani, Binnui, Shimei,

39 Shelemiah, Nathan, Adaiah,

40 Machnadebai, Shashai, Sharai,

41 Azarel, Shelemiah, Shemariah,

42 Shallum, Amariah and Joseph.

43 Of the sons of Nebo there were Jeiel, Mattithiah, Zabad, Zebina, Jaddai, Joel and Benaiah.

44 All these had married foreign wives, and some of them had wives by whom they had children.

NEHEMIAH

A Man of Action
He set out to build a wall, but left an enduring legacy of leadership

I N THE BOOK OF NEHEMIAH we peek inside the personal memoirs of a great leader. You can't mistake his style. He was an organizer, a pragmatic leader. That, no doubt, is why he had made his way to a top position in the Persian empire, one of the grandest in the history of the world.

> *"Do not be afraid of them; remember the Lord who is great and awesome, and fight." 4:14*

Yet his heart was elsewhere—in Jerusalem, a small, troublesome place far from the center of power. When he heard of the difficulties his people were experiencing there, he took his career—and probably his life—in his hands and spoke to the king about it. Shortly thereafter he was touring, by night, the broken-down walls of a city he probably had never seen before.

Nearly 100 years had passed since his people had returned to Jerusalem from exile. Though the temple had been rebuilt, the city was barely occupied. More Jews lived in the outlying villages and towns than in the holy city. They mixed with all kinds of foreigners. They were in danger of losing their identity. Why? Partly because the city lacked a wall.

What's in a Wall?

Compared to many concerns, building a wall may not seem terribly important. But think of it this way—what if the border between Mexico and the United States was wide open, so that anyone could cross and live on either side at will? One thing is certain: The distinction between Mexico and Texas would soon dissolve.

For lack of a wall the Jews were facing assimilation into the culture of their neighbors. In those days a city without a wall was easy pickings for any robber band. Jews, concerned for security, had scattered among other nationalities in small villages outside Jerusalem. There they were intermarrying and gradually losing their own language, culture and—most important—their own religion. A wall would give them a chance to make Jerusalem a truly Jewish city, keeping it safe and controlling who came and went.

Waiting for a Leader

What had kept them from doing anything about the broken-down wall for nearly 100 years? One obstacle was local resistance: powerful politicians were determined to keep the Jews down. Perhaps another reason was the lack of a leader like Nehemiah. In his memoirs, which fill most of this book, he shows remarkable qualities of leadership: impassioned speech, prayer, organization, resolve, trust in God, quick and determined response to problems, unselfishness. Perhaps his years in the Persian court had been preparing him. Organizing a difficult building project and handling fierce opposition seemed to come easily to him.

Nehemiah was more than a good business manager. He was a man of God. He did not act without prayer, and he did not pray without acting. His prayers punctuate the book. He recognized God's role in all that happened and never forgot to give Him credit. He was not looking for earthly status—if he had been, he never would have left Persia.

How to Read Nehemiah

Nehemiah's personality is the outstanding quality of the book that bears his name. No other Biblical character gives such clear information about how to "practice the presence of God" while carrying a leadership role. As you read, take note of the qualities that made Nehemiah successful as a leader and man of God. You may also wish to contrast his leadership with Ezra's. They worked in tandem but had very different styles. Nehemiah was an activist, Ezra a student; Nehemiah was outspoken, Ezra more withdrawn. Yet both faced similar problems and had similar success—and the two worked smoothly together.

The books of Ezra and Nehemiah both tell how the disgraced and chastened Jews returned from exile to rebuild their country. As history, Nehemiah includes some long lists of different family groups, as well as a detailed description of who built which parts of the Jerusalem wall. Unless you are an advanced student, you should skim these lists mainly to get an understanding of why they were kept. Concentrate more on how the Israelites had been transformed and purified by exile, making them ready to meet new challenges when they returned home.

PEOPLE YOU'LL MEET IN NEHEMIAH

NEHEMIAH *(p. 531)*

3-TRACK READING PLAN

For an explanation and complete listing of the 3-track reading plan, turn to page 7.

TRACK 1: *Two-Week Courses on the Bible*
See page 7 for information on these courses.

TRACK 2: *An Overview of Nehemiah in 2 Days*
☐ Day 1. Read the Introduction to Nehemiah and chapter 2, which tells how Nehemiah began his work on the wall.
☐ Day 2. Read chapter 8, showing the power of God's Word read aloud.
Now turn to page 9 for your next Track 2 reading project.

TRACK 3: *All of Nehemiah in 12 Days*
After you have read through Nehemiah, turn to pages 10–14 for your next Track 3 reading project.

☐1 ☐2–3 ☐4 ☐5 ☐6 ☐7 ☐8 ☐9
☐10 ☐11 ☐12 ☐13

Nehemiah's Grief for the Exiles

1 The words of Nehemiah the son of Hacaliah.
¶ Now it happened in the month Chislev, *in* the twentieth year, while I was in Susa the *a*capitol,

2 that Hanani, one of my brothers, and some men from Judah came; and I asked them concerning the Jews who had escaped *and* had survived the captivity, and about Jerusalem.

3 They said to me, "The remnant there in the province who survived the captivity are in great distress and reproach, and the wall of Jerusalem is broken down and its gates are burned with fire."

4 ¶ When I heard these words, I sat down and wept and mourned for days; and I was fasting and praying before the God of heaven.

5 I said, "I beseech You, O LORD God of heaven, the great and awesome God, who preserves the covenant and lovingkindness for those who love Him and keep His commandments,

6 let Your ear now be attentive and Your eyes open to hear the prayer of Your servant which I am praying before You now, day and night, on behalf of the sons of Israel Your servants, confessing the sins of the sons of Israel which we have sinned against You; I and my father's house have sinned.

7 "We have acted very corruptly against You and have not kept the commandments, nor the

a Or *palace* or *citadel*

statutes, nor the ordinances which You commanded Your servant Moses.

8 "Remember the word which You commanded Your servant Moses, saying, 'If you are unfaithful I will scatter you among the peoples;

9 but *if* you return to Me and keep My commandments and do them, though those of you who have been scattered were in the most remote part of the heavens, I will gather them from there and will bring them to the place where I have chosen to cause My name to dwell.'

10 "They are Your servants and Your people whom You redeemed by Your great power and by Your strong hand.

11 "O Lord, I beseech You, may Your ear be attentive to the prayer of Your servant and the prayer of Your servants who delight to revere Your name, and make Your servant successful today and grant him compassion before this man."

¶ Now I was the cupbearer to the king.

Nehemiah's Prayer Answered

2 And it came about in the month Nisan, in the twentieth year of King Artaxerxes, that wine *was* before him, and I took up the wine and gave it to the king. Now I had not been sad in his presence.

2 So the king said to me, "Why is your face sad though you are not sick? This is nothing but sadness of heart." Then I was very much afraid.

3 I said to the king, "Let the king live forever. Why should my face not be sad when the city, the place of my fathers' tombs, lies desolate and its gates have been consumed by fire?"

4 Then the king said to me, "What would you request?" So I prayed to the God of heaven.

2:4 The "Arrow Prayer"

Nehemiah characteristically prayed to God while he went about his duties. He even "shot an arrow" to God, silently asking him for help in the middle of this crucial conversation with the king. He spontaneously inserted prayers as he wrote his memoirs. Some other examples: 1:5–11; 4:4–5; 5:19; 6:9,14; 13:14,22,31.

5 I said to the king, "If it please the king, and if your servant has found favor before you, send me to Judah, to the city of my fathers' tombs, that I may rebuild it."

6 Then the king said to me, the queen sitting beside him, "How long will your journey be, and when will you return?" So it pleased the king to send me, and I gave him a definite time.

7 And I said to the king, "If it please the king, let letters be given me for the governors *of the provinces* beyond the River, that they may allow me to pass through until I come to Judah,

8 and a letter to Asaph the keeper of the king's forest, that he may give me timber to make beams for the gates of the fortress which is by the *a*temple, for the wall of the city and for the house to which I will go." And the king granted *them* to me because the good hand of my God *was* on me.

9 ¶ Then I came to the governors *of the provinces* beyond the River and gave them the king's letters. Now the king had sent with me officers of the army and horsemen.

10 When Sanballat the Horonite and Tobiah the Ammonite official heard *about it,* it was very displeasing to them that someone had come to seek the welfare of the sons of Israel.

2:10 Powerful Opponents

Both Sanballat and Tobiah were influential local politicians. Sanballat's family governed Samaria and had managed to marry into the high priest's family (see 13:28). Tobiah, an official in Ammon (a small country east of Judah), had family ties and influence among the top Jewish families (see 6:17–19; 13:4–5). There is some evidence both men were from Jewish backgrounds, though they preferred the political status quo in which Jewish identity was diluted.

Nehemiah Inspects Jerusalem's Walls

11 ¶ So I came to Jerusalem and was there three days.

12 And I arose in the night, I and a few men with me. I did not tell anyone what my God was putting into my mind to do for Jerusalem and there was no animal with me except the animal on which I was riding.

13 So I went out at night by the Valley Gate in the direction of the Dragon's Well and *on* to the Refuse Gate, inspecting the walls of Jerusalem which were broken down and its gates which were consumed by fire.

14 Then I passed on to the Fountain Gate and the King's Pool, but there was no place for my mount to pass.

15 So I went up at night by the ravine and inspected the wall. Then I entered the Valley Gate again and returned.

16 The officials did not know where I had gone or what I had done; nor had I as yet told the Jews, the priests, the nobles, the officials or the rest who did the work.

17 ¶ Then I said to them, "You see the bad situation we are in, that Jerusalem is desolate and its gates burned by fire. Come, let us rebuild the

a Lit *house*

wall of Jerusalem so that we will no longer be a reproach."

18 I told them how the hand of my God had been favorable to me and also about the king's words which he had spoken to me. Then they said, "Let us arise and build." So they put their hands to the good *work.*

19 But when Sanballat the Horonite and Tobiah the Ammonite official, and Geshem the Arab heard *it,* they mocked us and despised us and said, "What is this thing you are doing? Are you rebelling against the king?"

20 So I answered them and said to them, "The God of heaven will give us success; therefore we His servants will arise and build, but you have no portion, right or memorial in Jerusalem."

Builders of the Walls

3 Then Eliashib the high priest arose with his brothers the priests and built the Sheep Gate; they consecrated it and hung its doors. They consecrated the wall to the Tower of the Hundred *and* the Tower of Hananel.

3:1–32 Lasting Credit

Archaeologists love this chapter for its valuable clues to the design of ancient Jerusalem. Other readers may find these details less inspiring, but they do give evidence of Nehemiah's organizational genius. Somehow he motivated skilled craftsmen to work alongside ordinary laborers, and he even got children to pitch in. For added motivation, he assigned families repair projects just outside their own homes. This chapter, like a brass plaque listing "Important Contributors," assured that they would receive lasting credit for their efforts.

2 Next to him the men of Jericho built, and next to them Zaccur the son of Imri built.

3 ¶ Now the sons of Hassenaah built the Fish Gate; they laid its beams and hung its doors with its bolts and bars.

4 Next to them Meremoth the son of Uriah the son of Hakkoz made repairs. And next to him Meshullam the son of Berechiah the son of Meshezabel made repairs. And next to him Zadok the son of Baana *also* made repairs.

5 Moreover, next to him the Tekoites made repairs, but their nobles did not support the work of their masters.

6 ¶ Joiada the son of Paseah and Meshullam the son of Besodeiah repaired the Old Gate; they laid its beams and hung its doors with its bolts and its bars.

7 Next to them Melatiah the Gibeonite and Jadon the Meronothite, the men of Gibeon and of Mizpah, also made repairs for the official seat of the governor *of the province* beyond the River.

8 Next to him Uzziel the son of Harhaiah of the goldsmiths made repairs. And next to him Hananiah, one of the perfumers, made repairs, and they restored Jerusalem as far as the Broad Wall.

9 Next to them Rephaiah the son of Hur, the official of half the district of Jerusalem, made repairs.

10 Next to them Jedaiah the son of Harumaph made repairs opposite his house. And next to him Hattush the son of Hashabneiah made repairs.

11 Malchijah the son of Harim and Hasshub the son of Pahath-moab repaired another section and the Tower of Furnaces.

12 Next to him Shallum the son of Hallohesh, the official of half the district of Jerusalem, made repairs, he and his daughters.

13 ¶ Hanun and the inhabitants of Zanoah repaired the Valley Gate. They built it and hung its doors with its bolts and its bars, and a thousand cubits of the wall to the Refuse Gate.

14 ¶ Malchijah the son of Rechab, the official of the district of Beth-haccherem repaired the Refuse Gate. He built it and hung its doors with its bolts and its bars.

15 ¶ Shallum the son of Col-hozeh, the official of the district of Mizpah, repaired the Fountain Gate. He built it, covered it and hung its doors with its bolts and its bars, and the wall of the Pool of Shelah at the king's garden as far as the steps that descend from the city of David.

16 After him Nehemiah the son of Azbuk, official of half the district of Beth-zur, made repairs as far as *a point* opposite the tombs of David, and as far as the artificial pool and the house of the mighty men.

17 After him the Levites carried out repairs *under* Rehum the son of Bani. Next to him Hashabiah, the official of half the district of Keilah, carried out repairs for his district.

18 After him their brothers carried out repairs *under* Bavvai the son of Henadad, official of *the other* half of the district of Keilah.

19 Next to him Ezer the son of Jeshua, the official of Mizpah, repaired another section in front of the ascent of the armory at the Angle.

20 After him Baruch the son of Zabbai zealously repaired another section, from the Angle to the doorway of the house of Eliashib the high priest.

21 After him Meremoth the son of Uriah the son of Hakkoz repaired another section, from the doorway of Eliashib's house even as far as the end of his house.

22 After him the priests, the men of the ᵃvalley, carried out repairs.

23 After them Benjamin and Hasshub carried out repairs in front of their house. After them

---

Azariah the son of Maaseiah, son of Ananiah, carried out repairs beside his house.

24 After him Binnui the son of Henadad repaired another section, from the house of Azariah as far as the Angle and as far as the corner.

25 Palal the son of Uzai *made repairs* in front of the Angle and the tower projecting from the upper house of the king, which is by the court of the guard. After him Pedaiah the son of Parosh *made repairs.*

26 The temple servants living in Ophel *made repairs* as far as the front of the Water Gate toward the east and the projecting tower.

27 After them the Tekoites repaired another section in front of the great projecting tower and as far as the wall of Ophel.

28 ¶ Above the Horse Gate the priests carried out repairs, each in front of his house.

29 After them Zadok the son of Immer carried out repairs in front of his house. And after him Shemaiah the son of Shecaniah, the keeper of the East Gate, carried out repairs.

30 After him Hananiah the son of Shelemiah, and Hanun the sixth son of Zalaph, repaired another section. After him Meshullam the son of Berechiah carried out repairs in front of his own quarters.

31 After him Malchijah, one of the goldsmiths, carried out repairs as far as the house of the temple servants and of the merchants, in front of the Inspection Gate and as far as the upper room of the corner.

32 Between the upper room of the corner and the Sheep Gate the goldsmiths and the merchants carried out repairs.

Work Is Ridiculed

4 Now it came about that when Sanballat heard that we were rebuilding the wall, he became furious and very angry and mocked the Jews.

2 He spoke in the presence of his brothers and the wealthy *men* of Samaria and said, "What are these feeble Jews doing? Are they going to restore *it* for themselves? Can they offer sacrifices? Can they finish in a day? Can they revive the stones from the dusty rubble even the burned ones?"

3 Now Tobiah the Ammonite *was* near him and he said, "Even what they are building—if a fox should jump on *it,* he would break their stone wall down!"

4 ¶ Hear, O our God, how we are despised! Return their reproach on their own heads and give them up for plunder in a land of captivity.

5 Do not forgive their iniquity and let not their sin be blotted out before You, for they have demoralized the builders.

6 ¶ So we built the wall and the whole wall was joined together to half its *height,* for the people had a mind to work.

7 ¶ Now when Sanballat, Tobiah, the Arabs, the Ammonites and the Ashdodites heard that the repair of the walls of Jerusalem went on, *and* that the breaches began to be closed, they were very angry.

8 All of them conspired together to come *and* fight against Jerusalem and to cause a disturbance in it.

Discouragement Overcome

9 But we prayed to our God, and because of them we set up a guard against them day and night.

4:9 Praise the Lord and Fight

Nehemiah felt no difficulty combining prayer and action, as this verse shows: "We prayed to our God and . . . set up a guard." Verse 14 gives another unembarrassed combination of spiritual and military tactics: "Remember the Lord . . . and fight."

10 ¶ Thus in Judah it was said,
"The strength of the burden bearers is
failing,
Yet there is much rubbish;
And we ourselves are unable
To rebuild the wall."

11 Our enemies said, "They will not know or see until we come among them, kill them and put a stop to the work."

12 When the Jews who lived near them came and told us ten times, "They will come up against us from every place where you may turn,"

13 then I stationed *men* in the lowest parts of the space behind the wall, the exposed places, and I stationed the people in families with their swords, spears and bows.

14 When I saw *their fear,* I rose and spoke to the nobles, the officials and the rest of the people: "Do not be afraid of them; remember the Lord who is great and awesome, and fight for your brothers, your sons, your daughters, your wives and your houses."

15 ¶ When our enemies heard that it was known to us, and that God had frustrated their plan, then all of us returned to the wall, each one to his work.

16 From that day on, half of my servants carried on the work while half of them held the spears, the shields, the bows and the breastplates; and the captains *were* behind the whole house of Judah.

17 Those who were rebuilding the wall and those who carried burdens took *their* load with one hand doing the work and the other holding a weapon.

18 As for the builders, each *wore* his sword girded at his side as he built, while the trumpeter *stood* near me.

19 I said to the nobles, the officials and the rest of the people, "The work is great and extensive, and we are separated on the wall far from one another.

20 "At whatever place you hear the sound of the trumpet, rally to us there. Our God will fight for us."

21 ¶ So we carried on the work with half of them holding spears from dawn until the stars appeared.

22 At that time I also said to the people, "Let each man with his servant spend the night within Jerusalem so that they may be a guard for us by night and a laborer by day."

23 So neither I, my brothers, my servants, nor the men of the guard who followed me, none of us removed our clothes, each *took* his weapon *even to* the water.

Usury Abolished

5 Now there was a great outcry of the people and of their wives against their Jewish brothers.

2 For there were those who said, "We, our sons and our daughters are many; therefore let us get grain that we may eat and live."

3 There were others who said, "We are mortgaging our fields, our vineyards and our houses that we might get grain because of the famine."

4 Also there were those who said, "We have borrowed money for the king's tax *on* our fields and our vineyards.

5 "Now our flesh is like the flesh of our brothers, our children like their children. Yet behold, we are forcing our sons and our daughters to be slaves, and some of our daughters are forced into bondage *already,* and we are helpless because our fields and vineyards belong to others."

6 ¶ Then I was very angry when I had heard their outcry and these words.

7 I consulted with myself and contended with the nobles and the rulers and said to them, "You are exacting usury, each from his brother!" Therefore, I held a great assembly against them.

8 I said to them, "We according to our ability have redeemed our Jewish brothers who were sold to the nations; now would you even sell your brothers that they may be sold to us?" Then they were silent and could not find a word *to say.*

9 Again I said, "The thing which you are doing is not good; should you not walk in the fear of our God because of the reproach of the nations, our enemies?

10 "And likewise I, my brothers and my servants are lending them money and grain. Please, let us leave off this usury.

11 "Please, give back to them this very day their fields, their vineyards, their olive groves and their houses, also the hundredth *part* of the money and

of the grain, the new wine and the oil that you are exacting from them."

12 Then they said, "We will give *it* back and will require nothing from them; we will do exactly as you say." So I called the priests and took an oath from them that they would do according to this promise.

13 I also shook out the front of my garment and said, "Thus may God shake out every man from his house and from his possessions who does not fulfill this promise; even thus may he be shaken out and emptied." And all the assembly said, "Amen!" And they praised the LORD. Then the people did according to this promise.

Nehemiah's Example

14 ¶ Moreover, from the day that I was appointed to be their governor in the land of Judah, from the twentieth year to the thirty-second year of King Artaxerxes, *for* twelve years, neither I nor my kinsmen have eaten the governor's food *allowance.*

5:14 Politician Without Greed

Nehemiah faced a daunting task similar to that confronting many leaders of developing countries today. The land was devastated, with all wealth concentrated in the hands of a few powerful families. Jews were mortgaging their property and even selling their children into slavery in order to raise money to pay taxes. Nehemiah, who apparently came from wealth, could have profited further from his political position. Instead, he set a sterling example of generosity and self-sacrifice that made a profound impression on his oppressed countrymen.

15 But the former governors who were before me laid burdens on the people and took from them bread and wine besides forty shekels of silver; even their servants domineered the people. But I did not do so because of the fear of God.

16 I also ᵃapplied myself to the work on this wall; we did not buy any land, and all my servants were gathered there for the work.

17 Moreover, *there were* at my table one hundred and fifty Jews and officials, besides those who came to us from the nations that were around us.

18 Now that which was prepared for each day was one ox *and* six choice sheep, also birds were prepared for me; and once in ten days all sorts of wine *were furnished* in abundance. Yet for all this I did not demand the governor's food *allowance,* because the servitude was heavy on this people.

19 Remember me, O my God, for good, *according to* all that I have done for this people.

ᵃ Or *held fast*

The Enemy's Plot

6 Now when it was reported to Sanballat, Tobiah, to Geshem the Arab and to the rest of our enemies that I had rebuilt the wall, and *that* no breach remained in it, although at that time I had not set up the doors in the gates,

2 then Sanballat and Geshem sent *a message* to me, saying, "Come, let us meet together at ᵃChephirim in the plain of Ono." But they were planning to harm me.

3 So I sent messengers to them, saying, "I am doing a great work and I cannot come down. Why should the work stop while I leave it and come down to you?"

4 They sent *messages* to me four times in this manner, and I answered them in the same way.

5 Then Sanballat sent his servant to me in the same manner a fifth time with an open letter in his hand.

6:5 Psychological Warfare

After fending off ridicule and threats of violence from his enemies (chapter 4), Nehemiah suddenly faced a new scare tactic. The author points out that this accusatory letter came "open," or open to public view. Ordinarily, letters were rolled up, tied, sealed with wax, and delivered in a silk bag to guarantee privacy. Opponents were doubtless trying to intimidate Nehemiah by openly spreading rumors to arouse the suspicion of his Persian overseers. As usual, he was not easily intimidated.

6 In it was written, "It is reported among the nations, and Gashmu says, that you and the Jews are planning to rebel; therefore you are rebuilding the wall. And you are to be their king, according to these reports.

7 "You have also appointed prophets to proclaim in Jerusalem concerning you, 'A king is in Judah!' And now it will be reported to the king according to these reports. So come now, let us take counsel together."

8 Then I sent *a message* to him saying, "Such things as you are saying have not been done, but you are inventing them in your own mind."

9 For all of them were *trying* to frighten us, thinking, "They will become discouraged with the work and it will not be done." But now, O God, strengthen my hands.

10 ¶ When I entered the house of Shemaiah the son of Delaiah, son of Mehetabel, who was confined at home, he said, "Let us meet together in the house of God, within the temple, and let us close the doors of the temple, for they are coming

to kill you, and they are coming to kill you at night."

11 But I said, "Should a man like me flee? And could one such as I go into the temple to save his life? I will not go in."

12 Then I perceived that surely God had not sent him, but he uttered *his* prophecy against me because Tobiah and Sanballat had hired him.

13 He was hired for this reason, that I might become frightened and act accordingly and sin, so that they might have an evil report in order that they could reproach me.

14 Remember, O my God, Tobiah and Sanballat according to these works of theirs, and also Noadiah the prophetess and the rest of the prophets who were *trying* to frighten me.

The Wall Is Finished

15 ¶ So the wall was completed on the twenty-fifth of *the month* Elul, in fifty-two days.

16 When all our enemies heard *of it,* and all the nations surrounding us saw *it,* they lost their confidence; for they recognized that this work had been accomplished with the help of our God.

17 Also in those days many letters went from the nobles of Judah to Tobiah, and Tobiah's *letters* came to them.

18 For many in Judah were bound by oath to him because he was the son-in-law of Shecaniah the son of Arah, and his son Jehohanan had married the daughter of Meshullam the son of Berechiah.

19 Moreover, they were speaking about his good deeds in my presence and reported my words to him. Then Tobiah sent letters to frighten me.

Census of First Returned Exiles

7 Now when the wall was rebuilt and I had set up the doors, and the gatekeepers and the singers and the Levites were appointed,

2 then I put Hanani my brother, and Hananiah the commander of the fortress, in charge of Jerusalem, for he was a faithful man and feared God more than many.

3 Then I said to them, "Do not let the gates of Jerusalem be opened until the sun is hot, and while they are standing *guard,* let them shut and bolt the doors. Also appoint guards from the inhabitants of Jerusalem, each at his post, and each in front of his own house."

4 Now the city was large and spacious, but the people in it were few and the houses were not built.

5 ¶ Then my God put it into my heart to assemble the nobles, the officials and the people to be enrolled by genealogies. Then I found the book of the genealogy of those who came up first in which I found the following record:

6 ¶ These are the people of the province who

ᵃ Another reading is, one of *the villages*

came up from the captivity of the exiles whom Nebuchadnezzar the king of Babylon had carried away, and who returned to Jerusalem and Judah, each to his city,

7:6 Remembering Our Past

Because their cultural identity was threatened, the Jews in Ezra and Nehemiah kept careful track of their roots. All Jews wanted to trace their family lineage back to Abraham's grandson Israel (Jacob) in order to prove their Jewishness. In addition, descendants of Levi the priest and David the king took great pains to establish their heritage. The process had been vastly complicated by Nebuchadnezzar's burning of Jerusalem, which destroyed many records (see verses 61,64). This list (verses 8–73) almost exactly repeats the one found in Ezra 2.

7 who came with Zerubbabel, Jeshua, Nehemiah, Azariah, Raamiah, Nahamani, Mordecai, Bilshan, Mispereth, Bigvai, Nehum, Baanah.

¶ The number of men of the people of Israel:
8 the sons of Parosh, 2,172;
9 the sons of Shephatiah, 372;
10 the sons of Arah, 652;
11 the sons of Pahath-moab of the sons of Jeshua and Joab, 2,818;
12 the sons of Elam, 1,254;
13 the sons of Zattu, 845;
14 the sons of Zaccai, 760;
15 the sons of Binnui, 648;
16 the sons of Bebai, 628;
17 the sons of Azgad, 2,322;
18 the sons of Adonikam, 667;
19 the sons of Bigvai, 2,067;
20 the sons of Adin, 655;
21 the sons of Ater, of Hezekiah, 98;
22 the sons of Hashum, 328;
23 the sons of Bezai, 324;
24 the sons of Hariph, 112;
25 the sons of Gibeon, 95;
26 the men of Bethlehem and Netophah, 188;
27 the men of Anathoth, 128;
28 the men of Beth-azmaveth, 42;
29 the men of Kiriath-jearim, Chephirah and Beeroth, 743;
30 the men of Ramah and Geba, 621;
31 the men of Michmas, 122;
32 the men of Bethel and Ai, 123;
33 the men of the other Nebo, 52;
34 the sons of the other Elam, 1,254;
35 the men of Harim, 320;
36 the men of Jericho, 345;
37 the sons of Lod, Hadid and Ono, 721;
38 the men of Senaah, 3,930.
39 ¶ The priests: the sons of Jedaiah of the house of Jeshua, 973;

40 the sons of Immer, 1,052;
41 the sons of Pashhur, 1,247;
42 the sons of Harim, 1,017.
43 ¶ The Levites: the sons of Jeshua, of Kadmiel, of the sons of Hodevah, 74.
44 The singers: the sons of Asaph, 148.
45 The gatekeepers: the sons of Shallum, the sons of Ater, the sons of Talmon, the sons of Akkub, the sons of Hatita, the sons of Shobai, 138.
46 ¶ The temple servants: the sons of Ziha, the sons of Hasupha, the sons of Tabbaoth,
47 the sons of Keros, the sons of Sia, the sons of Padon,
48 the sons of Lebana, the sons of Hagaba, the sons of Shalmai,
49 the sons of Hanan, the sons of Giddel, the sons of Gahar,
50 the sons of Reaiah, the sons of Rezin, the sons of Nekoda,
51 the sons of Gazzam, the sons of Uzza, the sons of Paseah,
52 the sons of Besai, the sons of Meunim, the sons of Nephushesim,
53 the sons of Bakbuk, the sons of Hakupha, the sons of Harhur,
54 the sons of Bazlith, the sons of Mehida, the sons of Harsha,
55 the sons of Barkos, the sons of Sisera, the sons of Temah,
56 the sons of Neziah, the sons of Hatipha.
57 ¶ The sons of Solomon's servants: the sons of Sotai, the sons of Sophereth, the sons of Perida,
58 the sons of Jaala, the sons of Darkon, the sons of Giddel,
59 the sons of Shephatiah, the sons of Hattil, the sons of Pochereth-hazzebaim, the sons of Amon.
60 ¶ All the temple servants and the sons of Solomon's servants *were* 392.
61 ¶ These *were* they who came up from Telmelah, Tel-harsha, Cherub, Addon and Immer; but they could not show their fathers' houses or their descendants, whether they were of Israel:
62 the sons of Delaiah, the sons of Tobiah, the sons of Nekoda, 642.
63 Of the priests: the sons of Hobaiah, the sons of Hakkoz, the sons of Barzillai, who took a wife of the daughters of Barzillai, the Gileadite, and was named after them.
64 These searched *among* their ancestral registration, but it could not be located; therefore they were considered unclean *and excluded* from the priesthood.
65 The governor said to them that they should not eat from the most holy things until a priest arose with Urim and Thummim.

Total of People and Gifts

66 ¶ The whole assembly together *was* 42,360,
67 besides their male and their female servants,

of whom *there were* 7,337; and they had 245 male and female singers.

68 Their horses were 736; their mules, 245;

69 *their* camels, 435; *their* donkeys, 6,720.

70 ¶ Some from among the heads of fathers' *households* gave to the work. The governor gave to the treasury 1,000 gold drachmas, 50 basins, 530 priests' garments.

71 Some of the heads of fathers' *households* gave into the treasury of the work 20,000 gold drachmas and 2,200 silver minas.

72 That which the rest of the people gave was 20,000 gold drachmas and 2,000 silver minas and 67 priests' garments.

73 ¶ Now the priests, the Levites, the gatekeepers, the singers, some of the people, the temple servants and all Israel, lived in their cities.

¶ And when the seventh month came, the sons of Israel *were* in their cities.

Ezra Reads the Law

8 And all the people gathered as one man at the square which was in front of the Water Gate, and they asked Ezra the scribe to bring the book

A People of the Book
Ezra stood on a wooden platform, reading from a simple scroll

PICTURE IT: A VAST, HUSHED crowd watching as Ezra ascends a newly built platform in the square. As he opens the book, they stand up. They praise God, hands lifted high; then they bow down, faces in the dirt. Ezra begins to read. His helpers circulate in the crowd, explaining and interpreting what God's Word says. The people listen attentively. And then a strange sound begins to rise, spreading through the multitude. It is the sound of weeping.

> Ezra the priest brought the law before the assembly... He read from it... from early morning until midday.
> 8:2–3

The law Ezra read was very ancient, but that day marked something new. The Jews were becoming, in a way they had never been before, a people of the book. They were being rebuilt, with material as strong as the stones in their newly built city wall.

Throughout their history, they had drawn strength from two sources besides the law. One was the temple, where they worshiped God. It was a magnificently beautiful building in which they met God. The other was their leadership—first Moses, then Joshua, then the judges, and finally David and his offspring, the kings.

The Disappointing Reality

But these realities had not saved them from disgrace. The temple? For all its splendor it had become a meaningless symbol to most Jews. They had even put idols in it. God had finally allowed the Babylonians to burn the temple down.

After the exile the Jews had made rebuilding the temple their first priority (see Ezra 1–6). But it was no longer an automatic insurance policy. They could never again see the building as a substitute for real devotion to God.

Their leaders? Not one king, over hundreds of years, had come close to matching God's ideal. Most kings had been scoundrels—descendants of David in name only. After the exile, Israel had no king of its own. The Israelites were under the thumb of a Persian, who was determined to keep all power himself.

The Power of the Word

They turned to another source of power: the Word of God. The great gathering of chapter 8 stands in contrast to temples and kings. The splendor of jewels and crowns is replaced by a single man atop a wooden platform, reading from a simple scroll. Yet the words he reads, carefully explained to all, show their power in the way they affect those who hear them. The people are moved to praise God, to weep over their sins, to change their behavior, and to make renewed promises to God.

From this time on, the Jews were known as the people of the book. They lived under foreign domination, so their political leadership became secondary. Their temple, while important, was never again a guarantee of God's presence. Increasingly they studied God's law and tried to obey it. A new kind of leader emerged, following Ezra—the scribe, a student of Scripture. The nation we see at the end of Nehemiah looks very much like the nation we find, after 400 years of Scriptural silence, when Jesus appears. Israelites found their unique strength neither in government nor in worship rituals, but in reverence for God's written Word.

Life Questions: Can you point to ways in which God's Word has been powerful in your life? How has it changed you?

of the law of Moses which the LORD had given to Israel.

2 Then Ezra the priest brought the law before the assembly of men, women and all who *could* listen with understanding, on the first day of the seventh month.

3 He read from it before the square which was in front of the Water Gate from early morning until midday, in the presence of men and women, those who could understand; and all the people were attentive to the book of the law.

4 Ezra the scribe stood at a wooden podium which they had made for the purpose. And beside him stood Mattithiah, Shema, Anaiah, Uriah, Hilkiah, and Maaseiah on his right hand; and Pedaiah, Mishael, Malchijah, Hashum, Hashbaddanah, Zechariah *and* Meshullam on his left hand.

5 Ezra opened the book in the sight of all the people for he was standing above all the people; and when he opened it, all the people stood up.

6 Then Ezra blessed the LORD the great God. And all the people answered, "Amen, Amen!" while lifting up their hands; then they bowed low and worshiped the LORD with *their* faces to the ground.

7 Also Jeshua, Bani, Sherebiah, Jamin, Akkub, Shabbethai, Hodiah, Maaseiah, Kelita, Azariah, Jozabad, Hanan, Pelaiah, the Levites, explained the law to the people while the people *remained* in their place.

8 They read from the book, from the law of God, translating to give the sense so that they understood the reading.

"This Day Is Holy"

9 ¶ Then Nehemiah, who was the governor, and Ezra the priest *and* scribe, and the Levites who taught the people said to all the people, "This day is holy to the LORD your God; do not mourn or weep." For all the people were weeping when they heard the words of the law.

8:9 The Joy of the Lord

People sometimes think of the Old Testament as gloomy. Here, however (verses 9–12), Israel's leaders urged the people to stop weeping. Sadness, they said, did not suit a sacred day. As they discovered the next day, the law they mourned over commanded not weeping, but an eight-day celebration and campout.

---

10 Then he said to them, "Go, eat of the fat, drink of the sweet, and send portions to him who has nothing prepared; for this day is holy to our Lord. Do not be grieved, for the joy of the LORD is your strength."

11 So the Levites calmed all the people, saying, "Be still, for the day is holy; do not be grieved."

12 All the people went away to eat, to drink, to send portions and to celebrate a great festival, because they understood the words which had been made known to them.

Feast of Booths Restored

13 ¶ Then on the second day the heads of fathers' *households* of all the people, the priests and the Levites were gathered to Ezra the scribe that they might gain insight into the words of the law.

14 They found written in the law how the LORD had commanded through Moses that the sons of Israel should live in booths during the feast of the seventh month.

15 So they proclaimed and circulated a proclamation in all their cities and in Jerusalem, saying, "Go out to the hills, and bring olive branches and wild olive branches, myrtle branches, palm branches and branches of *other* leafy trees, to make booths, as it is written."

16 So the people went out and brought *them* and made booths for themselves, each on his roof, and in their courts and in the courts of the house of God, and in the square at the Water Gate and in the square at the Gate of Ephraim.

17 The entire assembly of those who had returned from the captivity made booths and lived in them. The sons of Israel had indeed not done so from the days of Joshua the son of Nun to that day. And there was great rejoicing.

18 He read from the book of the law of God daily, from the first day to the last day. And they celebrated the feast seven days, and on the eighth day *there was* a solemn assembly according to the ordinance.

The People Confess Their Sin

9 Now on the twenty-fourth day of this month the sons of Israel assembled with fasting, in sackcloth and with dirt upon them.

2 The descendants of Israel separated themselves from all foreigners, and stood and confessed their sins and the iniquities of their fathers.

3 While they stood in their place, they read from the book of the law of the LORD their God for a fourth of the day; and for *another* fourth they confessed and worshiped the LORD their God.

4 Now on the Levites' platform stood Jeshua, Bani, Kadmiel, Shebaniah, Bunni, Sherebiah, Bani *and* Chenani, and they cried with a loud voice to the LORD their God.

5 ¶ Then the Levites, Jeshua, Kadmiel, Bani, Hashabneiah, Sherebiah, Hodiah, Shebaniah *and* Pethahiah, said, "Arise, bless the LORD your God forever and ever!

O may Your glorious name be blessed
And exalted above all blessing and praise!

6 "You alone are the LORD.
You have made the heavens,
The heaven of heavens with all their host,
The earth and all that is on it,

The seas and all that is in them.
You give life to all of them
And the heavenly host bows down
  before You.

9:6 Stained-Glass Prayer

In cathedrals of medieval Europe, stained-glass windows served a dual purpose: 1) the artists designed them as aids to the worship of God; and 2) for a nonliterate society, scenes depicted in glass made it easier to learn biblical history. Old Testament Jews prohibited all images, but often their prayers served a similar purpose: they expressed worship and reminded the listeners of their providential past. This beautiful example reviews essential lessons from all of human history—an important guide for a people beginning a new life.

7 "You are the LORD God,
  Who chose Abram
  And brought him out from Ur of the
    Chaldees,
  And gave him the name Abraham.
8 "You found his heart faithful before You,
  And made a covenant with him
  To give *him* the land of the Canaanite,
  Of the Hittite and the Amorite,
  Of the Perizzite, the Jebusite and the
    Girgashite—
  To give *it* to his descendants.
  And You have fulfilled Your promise,
  For You are righteous.

9 ¶ "You saw the affliction of our fathers
    in Egypt,
  And heard their cry by the Red Sea.
10 "Then You performed signs and wonders
    against Pharaoh,
  Against all his servants and all the people
    of his land;
  For You knew that they acted arrogantly
    toward them,
  And made a name for Yourself as *it is*
    this day.
11 "You divided the sea before them,
  So they passed through the midst of the
    sea on dry ground;
  And their pursuers You hurled into the
    depths,
  Like a stone into raging waters.
12 "And with a pillar of cloud You led them
    by day,
  And with a pillar of fire by night
  To light for them the way
  In which they were to go.
13 "Then You came down on Mount Sinai,
  And spoke with them from heaven;

You gave them just ordinances and true
    laws,
  Good statutes and commandments.
14 "So You made known to them Your holy
    sabbath,
  And laid down for them commandments,
    statutes and law,
  Through Your servant Moses.
15 "You provided bread from heaven for
    them for their hunger,
  You brought forth water from a rock for
    them for their thirst,
  And You told them to enter in order to
    possess
  The land which You swore to give them.

16 ¶ "But they, our fathers, acted arrogantly;
  They ^abecame stubborn and would not
    listen to Your commandments.
17 "They refused to listen,
  And did not remember Your wondrous
    deeds which You had performed
    among them;
  So they became stubborn and appointed
    a leader to return to their slavery in
    Egypt.
  But You are a God of forgiveness,
  Gracious and compassionate,
  Slow to anger and abounding in
    lovingkindness;
  And You did not forsake them.
18 "Even when they made for themselves
  A calf of molten metal
  And said, 'This is your God
  Who brought you up from Egypt,'
  And committed great ^bblasphemies,
19 You, in Your great compassion,
  Did not forsake them in the wilderness;
  The pillar of cloud did not leave them by
    day,
  To guide them on their way,
  Nor the pillar of fire by night, to light for
    them the way in which they were
    to go.
20 "You gave Your good Spirit to instruct
    them,
  Your manna You did not withhold from
    their mouth,
  And You gave them water for their thirst.
21 "Indeed, forty years You provided for
    them in the wilderness *and* they
    were not in want;
  Their clothes did not wear out, nor did
    their feet swell.
22 "You also gave them kingdoms and
    peoples,
  And allotted *them* to them as a
    boundary.
  They took possession of the land of
    Sihon the king of Heshbon

---

^a Lit *stiffened their neck*; so also v 17   ^b Lit *acts of contempt*

And the land of Og the king of Bashan.

23 "You made their sons numerous as the
    stars of heaven,
And You brought them into the land
Which You had told their fathers to
    enter and possess.

24 "So their sons entered and possessed the
    land.
And You subdued before them the
    inhabitants of the land, the
    Canaanites,
And You gave them into their hand, with
    their kings and the peoples of the
    land,
To do with them as they desired.

25 "They captured fortified cities and a fertile
    land.
They took possession of houses full of
    every good thing,
Hewn cisterns, vineyards, olive groves,
Fruit trees in abundance.
So they ate, were filled and grew fat,
And reveled in Your great goodness.

26 ¶ "But they became disobedient and
    rebelled against You,
And cast Your law behind their backs
And killed Your prophets who had
    admonished them
So that they might return to You,
And they committed great *a*blasphemies.

27 "Therefore You delivered them into the
    hand of their oppressors who
    oppressed them,
But when they cried to You in the time
    of their distress,
You heard from heaven, and according
    to Your great compassion
You gave them deliverers who delivered
    them from the hand of their
    oppressors.

28 "But as soon as they had rest, they did
    evil again before You;
Therefore You abandoned them to the
    hand of their enemies, so that they
    ruled over them.
When they cried again to You, You
    heard from heaven,
And many times You rescued them
    according to Your compassion,

29 And admonished them in order to turn
    them back to Your law.
Yet they acted arrogantly and did not
    listen to Your commandments but
    sinned against Your ordinances,
By which if a man observes them he shall
    live.
And they turned a stubborn shoulder
    and stiffened their neck, and would
    not listen.

30 "However, You bore with them for many
    years,
And admonished them by Your Spirit
    through Your prophets,
Yet they would not give ear.
Therefore You gave them into the hand
    of the peoples of the lands.

31 "Nevertheless, in Your great compassion
    You did not make an end of them
    or forsake them,
For You are a gracious and
    compassionate God.

32 ¶ "Now therefore, our God, the great, the
    mighty, and the awesome God, who
    keeps covenant and lovingkindness,
Do not let all the hardship seem
    insignificant before You,
Which has come upon us, our kings, our
    princes, our priests, our prophets,
    our fathers and on all Your people,
From the days of the kings of Assyria to
    this day.

33 "However, You are just in all that has
    come upon us;
For You have dealt faithfully, but we
    have acted wickedly.

34 "For our kings, our leaders, our priests
    and our fathers have not kept
    Your law
Or paid attention to Your
    commandments and Your
    admonitions with which You have
    admonished them.

35 "But they, in their own kingdom,
With Your great goodness which You
    gave them,
With the broad and rich land which You
    set before them,
Did not serve You or turn from their evil
    deeds.

36 "Behold, we are slaves today,
And as to the land which You gave to
    our fathers to eat of its fruit and its
    bounty,
Behold, we are slaves in it.

37 "Its abundant produce is for the kings
Whom You have set over us because of
    our sins;
They also rule over our bodies
And over our cattle as they please,
So we are in great distress.

A Covenant Results

38 ¶ "Now because of all this
We are making an agreement in writing;
And on the sealed document *are the
    names of* our leaders, our Levites
    and our priests."

---

a Lit *acts of contempt*

Signers of the Document

10 Now on the sealed document *were the names of:* Nehemiah the governor, the son of Hacaliah, and Zedekiah,

2 Seraiah, Azariah, Jeremiah,

3 Pashhur, Amariah, Malchijah,

4 Hattush, Shebaniah, Malluch,

5 Harim, Meremoth, Obadiah,

6 Daniel, Ginnethon, Baruch,

7 Meshullam, Abijah, Mijamin,

8 Maaziah, Bilgai, Shemaiah. These *were* the priests.

9 And the Levites: Jeshua the son of Azaniah, Binnui of the sons of Henadad, Kadmiel;

10 also their brothers Shebaniah, Hodiah, Kelita, Pelaiah, Hanan,

11 Mica, Rehob, Hashabiah,

12 Zaccur, Sherebiah, Shebaniah,

13 Hodiah, Bani, Beninu.

14 The leaders of the people: Parosh, Pahathmoab, Elam, Zattu, Bani,

15 Bunni, Azgad, Bebai,

16 Adonijah, Bigvai, Adin,

17 Ater, Hezekiah, Azzur,

18 Hodiah, Hashum, Bezai,

19 Hariph, Anathoth, Nebai,

20 Magpiash, Meshullam, Hezir,

21 Meshezabel, Zadok, Jaddua,

22 Pelatiah, Hanan, Anaiah,

23 Hoshea, Hananiah, Hasshub,

24 Hallohesh, Pilha, Shobek,

25 Rehum, Hashabnah, Maaseiah,

26 Ahiah, Hanan, Anan,

27 Malluch, Harim, Baanah.

Obligations of the Document

28 ¶ Now the rest of the people, the priests, the Levites, the gatekeepers, the singers, the temple servants and all those who had separated themselves from the peoples of the lands to the law of God, their wives, their sons and their daughters, all those who had knowledge and understanding,

29 are joining with their kinsmen, their nobles, and are taking on themselves a curse and an oath to walk in God's law, which was given through Moses, God's servant, and to keep and to observe all the commandments of GOD our Lord, and His ordinances and His statutes;

30 and that we will not give our daughters to the peoples of the land or take their daughters for our sons.

31 As for the peoples of the land who bring wares or any grain on the sabbath day to sell, we will not buy from them on the sabbath or a holy day; and we will forego *the crops* the seventh year and the exaction of every debt.

32 ¶ We also placed ourselves under obligation to contribute yearly one third of a shekel for the service of the house of our God:

33 for the showbread, for the continual grain offering, for the continual burnt offering, the sabbaths, the new moon, for the appointed times, for the holy things and for the sin offerings to make atonement for Israel, and all the work of the house of our God.

10:31 A Year of Freedom

According to God's law, Jews were supposed to take every seventh day—the Sabbath—off from work. Not only that, but every seventh year was a holiday from farming and a time when all debts were canceled (see Leviticus 25:1–7; Deuteronomy 15:1–11). But these rules for the seventh year were seldom if ever followed; "business as usual" generally prevailed.

34 ¶ Likewise we cast lots for the supply of wood *among* the priests, the Levites and the people so that they might bring it to the house of our God, according to our fathers' households, at fixed times annually, to burn on the altar of the LORD our God, as it is written in the law;

35 and that they might bring the first fruits of our ground and the first fruits of all the fruit of every tree to the house of the LORD annually,

36 and bring to the house of our God the firstborn of our sons and of our cattle, and the firstborn of our herds and our flocks as it is written in the law, for the priests who are ministering in the house of our God.

37 We will also bring the first of our dough, our contributions, the fruit of every tree, the new wine and the oil to the priests at the chambers of the house of our God, and the tithe of our ground to the Levites, for the Levites are they who receive the tithes in all the rural towns.

38 The priest, the son of Aaron, shall be with the Levites when the Levites receive tithes, and the Levites shall bring up the tenth of the tithes to the house of our God, to the chambers of the storehouse.

39 For the sons of Israel and the sons of Levi shall bring the contribution of the grain, the new wine and the oil to the chambers; there are the utensils of the sanctuary, the priests who are ministering, the gatekeepers and the singers. Thus we will not neglect the house of our God.

Time Passes
Heads of Provinces

11 Now the leaders of the people lived in Jerusalem, but the rest of the people cast lots to bring one out of ten to live in Jerusalem, the holy city, while nine-tenths *remained* in the *other* cities.

2 And the people blessed all the men who volunteered to live in Jerusalem.

3 ¶ Now these are the heads of the provinces

who lived in Jerusalem, but in the cities of Judah each lived on his own property in their cities—the Israelites, the priests, the Levites, the temple servants and the descendants of Solomon's servants.

4 Some of the sons of Judah and some of the sons of Benjamin lived in Jerusalem. From the sons of Judah: Athaiah the son of Uzziah, the son

11:1 City Fright

The 1990 U.S. census revealed that for the first time a majority of Americans lived in cities having more than a million in population. Worldwide, people are flocking to mega-cities such as Tokyo, London, and Mexico City. Not so in Nehemiah's day. The Israelites had learned that big cities like Jerusalem made prime targets for invading armies. In order to repopulate the city, leaders had to resort to a lottery system. (Characteristically, Nehemiah made sure the new settlers got proper credit.)

of Zechariah, the son of Amariah, the son of Shephatiah, the son of Mahalalel, of the sons of Perez;

5 and Maaseiah the son of Baruch, the son of Col-hozeh, the son of Hazaiah, the son of Adaiah, the son of Joiarib, the son of Zechariah, the son of the Shilonite.

6 All the sons of Perez who lived in Jerusalem were 468 able men.

7 ¶ Now these are the sons of Benjamin: Sallu the son of Meshullam, the son of Joed, the son of Pedaiah, the son of Kolaiah, the son of Maaseiah, the son of Ithiel, the son of Jeshaiah;

8 and after him Gabbai *and* Sallai, 928.

9 Joel the son of Zichri was their overseer, and Judah the son of Hassenuah was second in command of the city.

10 ¶ From the priests: Jedaiah the son of Joiarib, Jachin,

11 Seraiah the son of Hilkiah, the son of Meshullam, the son of Zadok, the son of Meraioth, the son of Ahitub, the leader of the house of God,

12 and their [a]kinsmen who performed the work of the temple, 822; and Adaiah the son of Jeroham, the son of Pelaliah, the son of Amzi, the son of Zechariah, the son of Pashhur, the son of Malchijah,

13 and his kinsmen, heads of fathers' *households*, 242; and Amashsai the son of Azarel, the son of Ahzai, the son of Meshillemoth, the son of Immer,

14 and their brothers, valiant warriors, 128. And their overseer was Zabdiel, the son of Haggedolim.

15 ¶ Now from the Levites: Shemaiah the son of Hasshub, the son of Azrikam, the son of Hashabiah, the son of Bunni;

16 and Shabbethai and Jozabad, from the leaders of the Levites, who were in charge of the outside work of the house of God;

17 and Mattaniah the son of Mica, the son of Zabdi, the son of Asaph, who was the leader in beginning the thanksgiving at prayer, and Bakbukiah, the second among his brethren; and Abda the son of Shammua, the son of Galal, the son of Jeduthun.

18 All the Levites in the holy city *were* 284.

19 ¶ Also the gatekeepers, Akkub, Talmon and their brethren who kept watch at the gates, *were* 172.

Outside Jerusalem

20 The rest of Israel, of the priests *and* of the Levites, *were* in all the cities of Judah, each on his own inheritance.

21 But the temple servants were living in Ophel, and Ziha and Gishpa were in charge of the temple servants.

22 ¶ Now the overseer of the Levites in Jerusalem was Uzzi the son of Bani, the son of Hashabiah, the son of Mattaniah, the son of Mica, from the sons of Asaph, who were the singers for the service of the house of God.

23 For *there was* a commandment from the king concerning them and a firm regulation for the song leaders day by day.

24 Pethahiah the son of Meshezabel, of the sons of Zerah the son of Judah, was the king's representative in all matters concerning the people.

25 ¶ Now as for the villages with their fields, some of the sons of Judah lived in Kiriath-arba and its [b]towns, in Dibon and its towns, and in Jekabzeel and its villages,

26 and in Jeshua, in Moladah and Beth-pelet,

27 and in Hazar-shual, in Beersheba and its towns,

28 and in Ziklag, in Meconah and in its towns,

29 and in En-rimmon, in Zorah and in Jarmuth,

30 Zanoah, Adullam, and their villages, Lachish and its fields, Azekah and its towns. So they encamped from Beersheba as far as the valley of Hinnom.

31 The sons of Benjamin also *lived* from Geba onward, at Michmash and Aija, at Bethel and its towns,

32 at Anathoth, Nob, Ananiah,

33 Hazor, Ramah, Gittaim,

34 Hadid, Zeboim, Neballat,

35 Lod and Ono, the valley of craftsmen.

36 From the Levites, *some* divisions in Judah belonged to Benjamin.

---

[a] Lit *brothers,* and so throughout the ch   [b] Lit *daughters,* and so throughout the ch

Priests and Levites Who Returned to Jerusalem with Zerubbabel

12 Now these are the priests and the Levites who came up with Zerubbabel the son of Shealtiel, and Jeshua: Seraiah, Jeremiah, Ezra,

2 Amariah, Malluch, Hattush,

3 Shecaniah, Rehum, Meremoth,

4 Iddo, Ginnethoi, Abijah,

5 Mijamin, Maadiah, Bilgah,

6 Shemaiah and Joiarib, Jedaiah,

7 Sallu, Amok, Hilkiah and Jedaiah. These were the heads of the priests and their kinsmen in the days of Jeshua.

8 ¶ The Levites *were* Jeshua, Binnui, Kadmiel, Sherebiah, Judah, *and* Mattaniah *who was* in charge of the songs of thanksgiving, he and his brothers.

9 Also Bakbukiah and Unni, their brothers, stood opposite them in *their* service divisions.

10 Jeshua became the father of Joiakim, and Joiakim became the father of Eliashib, and Eliashib became the father of Joiada,

11 and Joiada became the father of Jonathan, and Jonathan became the father of Jaddua.

12 ¶ Now in the days of Joiakim, the priests, the heads of fathers' *households* were: of Seraiah, Meraiah; of Jeremiah, Hananiah;

13 of Ezra, Meshullam; of Amariah, Jehohanan;

14 of Malluchi, Jonathan; of Shebaniah, Joseph;

15 of Harim, Adna; of Meraioth, Helkai;

16 of Iddo, Zechariah; of Ginnethon, Meshullam;

17 of Abijah, Zichri; of Miniamin, of Moadiah, Piltai;

18 of Bilgah, Shammua; of Shemaiah, Jehonathan;

19 of Joiarib, Mattenai; of Jedaiah, Uzzi;

20 of Sallai, Kallai; of Amok, Eber;

21 of Hilkiah, Hashabiah; of Jedaiah, Nethanel.

The Chief Levites

22 ¶ As for the Levites, the heads of fathers' *households* were registered in the days of Eliashib, Joiada, and Johanan and Jaddua; so *were* the priests in the reign of Darius the Persian.

23 The sons of Levi, the heads of fathers' *households*, were registered in the Book of the Chronicles up to the days of Johanan the son of Eliashib.

24 The heads of the Levites *were* Hashabiah, Sherebiah and Jeshua the son of Kadmiel, with their brothers opposite them, to praise *and* give thanks, as prescribed by David the man of God, division corresponding to division.

25 Mattaniah, Bakbukiah, Obadiah, Meshullam, Talmon *and* Akkub *were* gatekeepers keeping watch at the storehouses of the gates.

26 These *served* in the days of Joiakim the son of Jeshua, the son of Jozadak, and in the days of Nehemiah the governor and of Ezra the priest *and* scribe.

Dedication of the Wall

27 ¶ Now at the dedication of the wall of Jerusalem they sought out the Levites from all their places, to bring them to Jerusalem so that they might celebrate the dedication with gladness, with hymns of thanksgiving and with songs *to the accompaniment* of cymbals, harps and lyres.

12:27 Victory Party

Ezra, a religious leader, tried for a decade to get the wall rebuilt. Nehemiah, more pragmatic and action-oriented, managed to get the job done in 52 days (6:15). When the huge task was finished, he orchestrated a giant celebration featuring two choirs that circled the wall in opposite directions. Ezra led one of the choirs; Nehemiah, in an act of humility, brought up the rear of the other. When they met in the middle, near the temple area, they held a worship service such as Jerusalem had not seen in more than a century.

28 So the sons of the singers were assembled from the district around Jerusalem, and from the villages of the Netophathites,

29 from Beth-gilgal and from *their* fields in Geba and Azmaveth, for the singers had built themselves villages around Jerusalem.

30 The priests and the Levites purified themselves; they also purified the people, the gates and the wall.

Procedures for the Temple

31 ¶ Then I had the leaders of Judah come up on top of the wall, and I appointed two great choirs, the first proceeding to the right on top of the wall toward the Refuse Gate.

32 Hoshaiah and half of the leaders of Judah followed them,

33 with Azariah, Ezra, Meshullam,

34 Judah, Benjamin, Shemaiah, Jeremiah,

35 and some of the sons of the priests with trumpets; *and* Zechariah the son of Jonathan, the son of Shemaiah, the son of Mattaniah, the son of Micaiah, the son of Zaccur, the son of Asaph,

36 and his kinsmen, Shemaiah, Azarel, Milalai, Gilalai, Maai, Nethanel, Judah *and* Hanani, with the musical instruments of David the man of God. And Ezra the scribe went before them.

37 At the Fountain Gate they went directly up the steps of the city of David by the stairway of the wall above the house of David to the Water Gate on the east.

38 ¶ The second choir proceeded to the left, while I followed them with half of the people on

the wall, above the Tower of Furnaces, to the Broad Wall,

39 and above the Gate of Ephraim, by the Old Gate, by the Fish Gate, the Tower of Hananel and the Tower of the Hundred, as far as the Sheep Gate; and they stopped at the Gate of the Guard.

40 Then the two choirs took their stand in the house of God. So did I and half of the officials with me;

41 and the priests, Eliakim, Maaseiah, Miniamin, Micaiah, Elioenai, Zechariah and Hananiah, with the trumpets;

42 and Maaseiah, Shemaiah, Eleazar, Uzzi, Jehohanan, Malchijah, Elam and Ezer. And the singers sang, with Jezrahiah *their* leader,

43 and on that day they offered great sacrifices and rejoiced because God had given them great joy, even the women and children rejoiced, so that the joy of Jerusalem was heard from afar.

44 ¶ On that day men were also appointed over the chambers for the stores, the contributions, the first fruits and the tithes, to gather into them from the fields of the cities the portions required by the law for the priests and Levites; for Judah rejoiced over the priests and Levites who served.

45 For they performed the worship of their God and the service of purification, together with the singers and the gatekeepers in accordance with the command of David *and* of his son Solomon.

46 For in the days of David and Asaph, in ancient times, *there were* leaders of the singers, songs of praise and hymns of thanksgiving to God.

47 So all Israel in the days of Zerubbabel and Nehemiah gave the portions due the singers and the gatekeepers as each day required, and set apart the consecrated *portion* for the Levites, and the Levites set apart the consecrated *portion* for the sons of Aaron.

Foreigners Excluded

13 On that day they read aloud from the book of Moses in the hearing of the people; and there was found written in it that no Ammonite or Moabite should ever enter the assembly of God,

2 because they did not meet the sons of Israel with bread and water, but hired Balaam against them to curse them. However, our God turned the curse into a blessing.

3 So when they heard the law, they excluded all foreigners from Israel.

Tobiah Expelled and the Temple Cleansed

4 ¶ Now prior to this, Eliashib the priest, who was appointed over the chambers of the house of our God, being related to Tobiah,

5 had prepared a large room for him, where formerly they put the grain offerings, the frankincense, the utensils and the tithes of grain, wine and oil prescribed for the Levites, the singers and the gatekeepers, and the contributions for the priests.

6 But during all this *time* I was not in Jerusalem, for in the thirty-second year of Artaxerxes king of Babylon I had gone to the king. After some time, however, I asked leave from the king,

7 and I came to Jerusalem and learned about the evil that Eliashib had done for Tobiah, by preparing a room for him in the courts of the house of God.

8 It was very displeasing to me, so I threw all of Tobiah's household goods out of the room.

9 Then I gave an order and they cleansed the rooms; and I returned there the utensils of the house of God with the grain offerings and the frankincense.

Tithes Restored

10 ¶ I also discovered that the portions of the Levites had not been given *them,* so that the Levites and the singers who performed the service had gone away, each to his own field.

11 So I reprimanded the officials and said, "Why is the house of God forsaken?" Then I gathered them together and restored them to their posts.

12 All Judah then brought the tithe of the grain, wine and oil into the storehouses.

13 In charge of the storehouses I appointed Shelemiah the priest, Zadok the scribe, and Pedaiah of the Levites, and in addition to them was Hanan the son of Zaccur, the son of Mattaniah; for they were considered reliable, and it was their task to distribute to their kinsmen.

14 Remember me for this, O my God, and do not blot out my loyal deeds which I have performed for the house of my God and its services.

Sabbath Restored

15 ¶ In those days I saw in Judah some who were treading wine presses on the sabbath, and bringing in sacks of grain and loading *them* on donkeys, as well as wine, grapes, figs and all kinds of loads, and they brought *them* into Jerusalem on the sabbath day. So I admonished *them* on the day they sold food.

16 Also men of Tyre were living there *who* imported fish and all kinds of merchandise, and sold *them* to the sons of Judah on the sabbath, even in Jerusalem.

17 Then I reprimanded the nobles of Judah and said to them, "What is this evil thing you are doing, by profaning the sabbath day?

18 "Did not your fathers do the same, so that our God brought on us and on this city all this trouble? Yet you are adding to the wrath on Israel by profaning the sabbath."

19 ¶ It came about that just as it grew dark at the gates of Jerusalem before the sabbath, I commanded that the doors should be shut and that they should not open them until after the sabbath. Then I stationed some of my servants at the gates *so that* no load would enter on the sabbath day.

20 Once or twice the traders and merchants of

every kind of merchandise spent the night outside Jerusalem.

21 Then I warned them and said to them, "Why do you spend the night in front of the wall?

13:19 Never-ending Task

Fairy tales end, "and they lived happily ever after," but real life never does. Pointedly, Nehemiah's book does not close with the triumph of chapter 12, but with a preview of the continuing hassles of leadership. Old problems recurred, new problems sprang up, and Nehemiah tackled both kinds with courage and wisdom.

If you do so again, I will use force against you." From that time on they did not come on the sabbath.

22 And I commanded the Levites that they should purify themselves and come as gatekeepers to sanctify the sabbath day. *For* this also remember me, O my God, and have compassion on me according to the greatness of Your lovingkindness.

Mixed Marriages Forbidden

23 ¶ In those days I also saw that the Jews had married women from Ashdod, Ammon *and* Moab.

24 As for their children, half spoke in the language of Ashdod, and none of them was able to speak the language of Judah, but the language of his own people.

25 So I contended with them and cursed them and struck some of them and pulled out their hair, and made them swear by God, "You shall not give your daughters to their sons, nor take of their daughters for your sons or for yourselves.

26 "Did not Solomon king of Israel sin regarding these things? Yet among the many nations there was no king like him, and he was loved by his God, and God made him king over all Israel; nevertheless the foreign women caused even him to sin.

27 "Do we then hear about you that you have committed all this great evil by acting unfaithfully against our God by marrying foreign women?"

28 Even one of the sons of Joiada, the son of Eliashib the high priest, was a son-in-law of Sanballat the Horonite, so I drove him away from me.

29 Remember them, O my God, because they have defiled the priesthood and the covenant of the priesthood and the Levites.

30 ¶ Thus I purified them from everything foreign and appointed duties for the priests and the Levites, each in his task,

31 and *I* arranged for the supply of wood at appointed times and for the first fruits. Remember me, O my God, for good.

ESTHER

A Profile of Courage
Heroes act while others stand and watch

> "I will go in to the king, which is not according to the law; and if I perish, I perish." 4:16

WHAT MAKES A HERO? ASK one, and you may find a surprising nonchalance: "I'm sure other people would have done exactly the same thing," they say. "I was just in the right place at the right time."

People become heroes because they take quick action at that "right time," while others stand watching in horror. The true hero recognizes the crisis and moves to meet it. This kind of courage made Esther great—worthy of a book in the Bible.

A Queen Risks Her Life

By the "accident" of her beauty and the "accident" of the former queen's dismissal, Esther found herself queen of one of the greatest powers of the world. Then, when all seemed smooth, her crucial moment came.

This moment has been echoed many times since. As a successful racial minority in the Persian empire, Esther's people, the Jews, had not melted into their surroundings. Others were jealous of their success and separatism. A vengeful prime minister, Haman, made up his mind to destroy them. He issued an edict of government-sponsored genocide.

Would Queen Esther intervene? Doing so would risk her life. And what difference could she make? She was a powerless sex partner to a king who strongly preferred women who never interfered with his wishes. She came only when he called, and he had not called her for a month. And yet she alone, of all the Jews, had access to the king.

Esther's cousin Mordecai reminded her of her unique place. "Who knows whether you have not attained royalty for such a time as this?" Esther responded with action. Her courageous words are a classic statement of heroism: "I will go in to the king, which is not according to the law; and if I perish, I perish" (4:16).

Coincidence or Plan?

The book of Esther shows, though indirectly, God's heroic concern for the Jews. The story runs on a series of extraordinary coincidences. Esther just "happened" to be chosen as the new queen. The king just "happened" to be unable to sleep, and, when he picked up some reading, just "happened" across an account of a good deed Esther's cousin Mordecai had done. The evil Haman just "happened" along at that crucial moment. These coincidences, along with Esther's courage, tilted terrible events toward the Jews' favor.

Were these really mere coincidences? Or was God behind them? The book of Esther doesn't say directly: God is not mentioned even once, and sometimes seems deliberately left out. But believing readers, whether Jews or Christians, can have no doubt. All of life is under God's command. Nothing just happens. These "coincidences" were part of God's plan to save the Jews.

God protected his people because he loved them—because he had chosen them from the beginning. Even their enemies knew the "luck" of the Jews. (See Esther 6:13, for instance.) Esther's story is another chapter in the amazing story of God's perpetual love for the Jews. Though sometimes far from his will, this tiny, often hated minority has survived and thrived down the centuries.

From Haman to Hitler, vindictive leaders have hated the Jews. Yet while no other group has been so hated, no other group has shown the Jews' ability to overcome adversity. Nor can any other ethnic group alive today point to such continuity with their ancestors. They have endured as a unique and great people. How? Esther shows that God's exquisite timing—combined with the courage of individuals who "happened" to be in the right place at the right time—made his chosen people prosper.

How to Read Esther

Esther makes such suspenseful reading that most people will find it hard to quit. As in a detective story, every detail folds into another. You don't know, from one page to the next, how the drama will turn out.

The essence of Esther lies in its characters. Study Esther, Mordecai, Haman, and King Ahasuerus. What kind of people were they? What were their ambitions? What were their strengths and weaknesses? What crucial moment showed the true character of each? What do you learn from them that can help you rise to the challenge when you are "the right person at the right place at the right time"?

Knowing the historical setting for Esther's story can enrich your study. A good commentary or Bible dictionary (under "Esther") will illuminate many of the details that make Esther such a convincing historical document.

PEOPLE YOU'LL MEET IN ESTHER

ESTHER *(p. 548)*
MORDECAI *(p. 552)*

3-TRACK READING PLAN

For an explanation and complete listing of the 3-track reading plan, turn to page 7.

TRACK 1: *Two-Week Courses on the Bible*
See page 7 for information on these courses.

TRACK 2: *An Overview of Esther in 1 Day*
☐ Day 1. Read the Introduction to Esther and chapter 4, in which Esther learns that her people are in dire straits and decides to take action.

Now turn to page 9 for your next Track 2 reading project.

TRACK 3: *All of Esther in 8 Days*
After you have read through Esther, turn to pages 10–14 for your next Track 3 reading project.
☐1   ☐2   ☐3   ☐4   ☐5   ☐6–7   ☐8   ☐9–10

The Banquets of the King

1 Now it took place in the days of Ahasuerus, the Ahasuerus who reigned from India to Ethiopia over 127 provinces,

2 in those days as King Ahasuerus sat on his royal throne which *was* at the citadel in Susa,

3 in the third year of his reign he gave a banquet for all his princes and attendants, the army *officers* of Persia and Media, the nobles and the princes of his provinces being in his presence.

4 And he displayed the riches of his royal glory and the splendor of his great majesty for many days, 180 days.

5 ¶ When these days were completed, the king gave a banquet lasting seven days for all the people who were present at the citadel in Susa, from the greatest to the least, in the court of the garden of the king's palace.

6 *There were hangings of* fine white and violet linen held by cords of fine purple linen on silver rings and marble columns, *and* couches of gold and silver on a mosaic pavement of porphyry, marble, mother-of-pearl and precious stones.

7 Drinks were served in golden vessels of various kinds, and the royal wine was plentiful according to the king's bounty.

8 The drinking was *done* according to the law, there was no compulsion, for so the king had

1:7 The Influence of Wine

Other historical sources bear out the accuracy of this verse. Greek historian Herodotus wrote that the Persians "are very fond of wine, and drink it in large quantities . . . It is also their general practice to deliberate upon affairs of weight when they are drunk . . . Sometimes, however, they are sober at their first deliberation, but in this case they always reconsider the matter under the influence of wine."

given orders to each official of his household that he should do according to the desires of each person.

9 Queen Vashti also gave a banquet for the women in the palace which belonged to King Ahasuerus.

Queen Vashti's Refusal

10 ¶ On the seventh day, when the heart of the king was merry with wine, he commanded Mehuman, Biztha, Harbona, Bigtha, Abagtha, Zethar and Carkas, the seven eunuchs who served in the presence of King Ahasuerus,

11 to bring Queen Vashti before the king with *her* royal crown in order to display her beauty to the people and the princes, for she was beautiful.

12 But Queen Vashti refused to come at the king's command delivered by the eunuchs. Then the king became very angry and his wrath burned within him.

13 ¶ Then the king said to the wise men who understood the times—for it was the custom of the king so *to speak* before all who knew law and justice

14 and were close to him: Carshena, Shethar, Admatha, Tarshish, Meres, Marsena and Memucan, the seven princes of Persia and Media who had access to the king's presence and sat in the first place in the kingdom—

15 "According to law, what is to be done with Queen Vashti, because she did not obey the command of King Ahasuerus *delivered* by the eunuchs?"

16 In the presence of the king and the princes, Memucan said, "Queen Vashti has wronged not only the king but *also* all the princes and all the peoples who are in all the provinces of King Ahasuerus.

17 "For the queen's conduct will become known to all the women causing them to look with contempt on their husbands by saying, 'King Ahasuerus commanded Queen Vashti to be brought in to his presence, but she did not come.'

18 "This day the ladies of Persia and Media who have heard of the queen's conduct will speak in *the same way* to all the king's princes, and there will be plenty of contempt and anger.

19 "If it pleases the king, let a royal edict be issued by him and let it be written in the laws of Persia and Media so that it cannot be repealed, that Vashti may no longer come into the presence of King Ahasuerus, and let the king give her royal position to another who is more worthy than she.

20 "When the king's edict which he will make is heard throughout all his kingdom, great as it is, then all women will give honor to their husbands, great and small."

21 ¶ *This* word pleased the king and the princes, and the king did as Memucan proposed.

22 So he sent letters to all the king's provinces, to each province according to its script and to every people according to their language, that every man should be the master in his own house and the one who speaks in the language of his own people.

Vashti's Successor Sought

2 After these things when the anger of King Ahasuerus had subsided, he remembered Vashti and what she had done and what had been decreed against her.

2 Then the king's attendants, who served him, said, "Let beautiful young virgins be sought for the king.

3 "Let the king appoint overseers in all the provinces of his kingdom that they may gather every beautiful young virgin to the citadel of Susa, to the harem, into the custody of Hegai, the king's eunuch, who is in charge of the women; and let their cosmetics be given *them*.

4 "Then let the young lady who pleases the king be queen in place of Vashti." And the matter pleased the king, and he did accordingly.

5 ¶ *Now* there was at the citadel in Susa a Jew whose name was Mordecai, the son of Jair, the son of Shimei, the son of Kish, a Benjamite,

6 who had been taken into exile from Jerusalem with the captives who had been exiled with Jeconiah king of Judah, whom Nebuchadnezzar the king of Babylon had exiled.

2:6 Those Who Stayed Behind

Ezra and Nehemiah, the books preceding Esther, tell the inspiring story of Jews returning to Jerusalem after years of captivity. Actually, only 50,000 Jews came back to their plundered land, however. Many more—among them Mordecai's family—stayed behind, and some of these prospered. The story of Esther takes place in that foreign setting, ruled by the Persian empire. Modern-day communities of Jews in Iraq and Iran have descended from these ancient exiles.

7 He was bringing up Hadassah, that is Esther, his uncle's daughter, for she had no father or mother. Now the young lady was beautiful of form and face, and when her father and her mother died, Mordecai took her as his own daughter.

Esther Finds Favor

8 ¶ So it came about when the command and decree of the king were heard and many young ladies were gathered to the citadel of Susa into the custody of Hegai, that Esther was taken to the king's palace into the custody of Hegai, who was in charge of the women.

9 Now the young lady pleased him and found favor with him. So he quickly provided her with

her cosmetics and food, gave her seven choice maids from the king's palace and transferred her and her maids to the best place in the harem.

10 Esther did not make known her people or her kindred, for Mordecai had instructed her that she should not make *them* known.

11 Every day Mordecai walked back and forth in front of the court of the harem to learn how Esther was and how she fared.

12 ¶ Now when the turn of each young lady came to go in to King Ahasuerus, after the end of her twelve months under the regulations for the women—for the days of their beautification were completed as follows: six months with oil of myrrh and six months with spices and the cosmetics for women—

13 the young lady would go in to the king in this way: anything that she desired was given her to take with her from the harem to the king's palace.

14 In the evening she would go in and in the morning she would return to the second harem, to the custody of Shaashgaz, the king's eunuch who was in charge of the concubines. She would not again go in to the king unless the king delighted in her and she was summoned by name.

15 ¶ Now when the turn of Esther, the daughter of Abihail the uncle of Mordecai who had taken her as his daughter, came to go in to the king, she did not request anything except what Hegai, the king's eunuch who was in charge of the women, advised. And Esther found favor in the eyes of all who saw her.

16 So Esther was taken to King Ahasuerus to his royal palace in the tenth month which is the month Tebeth, in the seventh year of his reign.

2:16 Off at War

Between Queen Vashti's dismissal (chapter 1) and Esther's acceptance as the new queen, four years passed. Why did Ahasuerus wait so long? Historians say that during these four years he was off fighting, unsuccessfully trying to conquer Greece. The six-month conference described in chapter 1 was, most likely, a consultation to prepare the invasion.

Esther Becomes Queen

17 ¶ The king loved Esther more than all the women, and she found favor and kindness with him more than all the virgins, so that he set the royal crown on her head and made her queen instead of Vashti.

18 Then the king gave a great banquet, Esther's banquet, for all his princes and his servants; he also made a holiday for the provinces and gave gifts according to the king's bounty.

19 ¶ When the virgins were gathered together the second time, then Mordecai was sitting at the king's gate.

20 Esther had not yet made known her kindred or her people, even as Mordecai had commanded her; for Esther did what Mordecai told her as she had done when under his care.

Mordecai Saves the King

21 In those days, while Mordecai was sitting at the king's gate, Bigthan and Teresh, two of the king's officials from those who guarded the door, became angry and sought to lay hands on King Ahasuerus.

22 But the plot became known to Mordecai and he told Queen Esther, and Esther informed the king in Mordecai's name.

23 Now when the plot was investigated and found *to be so,* they were both hanged on a ᵃgallows; and it was written in the Book of the Chronicles in the king's presence.

Haman's Plot against the Jews

3 After these events King Ahasuerus promoted Haman, the son of Hammedatha the Agagite, and advanced him and established his authority over all the princes who *were* with him.

2 All the king's servants who were at the king's gate bowed down and paid homage to Haman; for so the king had commanded concerning him. But Mordecai neither bowed down nor paid homage.

3 Then the king's servants who were at the king's gate said to Mordecai, "Why are you transgressing the king's command?"

4 Now it was when they had spoken daily to him and he would not listen to them, that they told Haman to see whether Mordecai's reason would stand; for he had told them that he was a Jew.

5 When Haman saw that Mordecai neither bowed down nor paid homage to him, Haman was filled with rage.

6 But he disdained to lay hands on Mordecai alone, for they had told him *who* the people of Mordecai *were;* therefore Haman sought to destroy all the Jews, the people of Mordecai, who *were* throughout the whole kingdom of Ahasuerus.

7 ¶ In the first month, which is the month Nisan, in the twelfth year of King Ahasuerus, Pur, that is the lot, was cast before Haman from day to day and from month *to month,* until the twelfth month, that is the month Adar.

8 Then Haman said to King Ahasuerus, "There is a certain people scattered and dispersed among the peoples in all the provinces of your kingdom; their laws are different from *those* of all *other* people and they do not observe the king's

---

ᵃ Lit *tree*

laws, so it is not in the king's interest to let them remain.

9 "If it is pleasing to the king, let it be decreed that they be destroyed, and I will pay ten thousand talents of silver into the hands of those who carry on the *king's* business, to put into the king's treasuries."

10 Then the king took his signet ring from his hand and gave it to Haman, the son of Hammedatha the Agagite, the enemy of the Jews.

11 The king said to Haman, "The silver is yours, and the people *also,* to do with them as you please."

12 ¶ Then the king's scribes were summoned on the thirteenth day of the first month, and it was written just as Haman commanded to the king's satraps, to the governors who were over each province and to the princes of each people, each province according to its script, each people according to its language, being written in the name of King Ahasuerus and sealed with the king's signet ring.

13 Letters were sent by couriers to all the king's provinces to destroy, to kill and to annihilate all the Jews, both young and old, women and children, in one day, the thirteenth *day* of the twelfth month, which is the month Adar, and to seize their possessions as plunder.

14 A copy of the edict to be issued as law in every province was published to all the peoples so that they should be ready for this day.

15 The couriers went out impelled by the king's command while the decree was issued at the citadel in Susa; and while the king and Haman sat down to drink, the city of Susa was in confusion.

Esther Learns of Haman's Plot

4 When Mordecai learned all that had been done, he tore his clothes, put on sackcloth and

3:13 Pony Express

Persia boasted one of the first efficient communication systems. The king kept men and horses stationed a day's journey apart on all major highways. Each messenger rode for a day and relayed the message on to the next station. "Nothing mortal travels so fast as these Persian messengers," wrote the historian Herodotus. Their efficiency made it essential for Mordecai and Esther to overturn the king's edict as soon as possible.

ashes, and went out into the midst of the city and wailed loudly and bitterly.

2 He went as far as the king's gate, for no one was to enter the king's gate clothed in sackcloth.

3 In each and every province where the command and decree of the king came, there was great mourning among the Jews, with fasting, weeping and wailing; and many lay on sackcloth and ashes.

4 ¶ Then Esther's maidens and her eunuchs came and told her, and the queen writhed in great anguish. And she sent garments to clothe Mordecai that he might remove his sackcloth from him, but he did not accept *them.*

5 Then Esther summoned Hathach from the king's eunuchs, whom the king had appointed to attend her, and ordered him *to go* to Mordecai to learn what this *was* and why it *was.*

MORDECAI *Standing Tall*

HIS FAMILY HAD COME TO Persia as virtual slaves, captives of Jerusalem's last stand against the Babylonians. Yet even in enemy territory Mordecai succeeded in business. His relative, Esther, found more success; she was selected from all the beautiful women in the land as King Ahasuerus's queen.

With his connections inside the palace, Mordecai probably had high ambitions. He would have to hide his background, though, and he strongly advised Esther to keep her Jewish heritage a secret as well.

Yet when a crisis came Mordecai stood tall, showing extraordinary courage. The king had named the evil Haman his second-in-command, and everyone bowed before him—everyone except Mordecai, who stayed on his feet. His motive? Perhaps he knew of Haman's character, and of his hatred for Jews.

When Haman set out to annihilate all Jews in the empire, Mordecai urged Esther to "come out" completely, even at the risk of her life. Clearly, loyalty to their people came before success or safety.

Mordecai's stand and Esther's courage led to a dramatic turnaround for the whole community of Jewish exiles. King Ahasuerus rewarded Mordecai with a high position in his court. More importantly, his own community honored him because he was "one who sought the good of his people and one who spoke for the welfare of his whole nation" (10:3).

The feast of Purim, still celebrated by Jews today, commemorates these amazing events. Against history's dark background of anti-Semitism, Mordecai's triumph shines.

Life Questions: Whom do you speak up for? For what group would you willingly risk your life or your reputation?

6 So Hathach went out to Mordecai to the city square in front of the king's gate.

7 Mordecai told him all that had happened to him, and the exact amount of money that Haman had promised to pay to the king's treasuries for the destruction of the Jews.

8 He also gave him a copy of the text of the edict which had been issued in Susa for their destruction, that he might show Esther and inform her, and to order her to go in to the king to implore his favor and to plead with him for her people.

9 ¶ Hathach came back and related Mordecai's words to Esther.

10 Then Esther spoke to Hathach and ordered him *to reply* to Mordecai:

11 "All the king's servants and the people of the king's provinces know that for any man or woman who comes to the king to the inner court who is not summoned, he has but one law, that he be put to death, unless the king holds out to him the golden scepter so that he may live. And I have not been summoned to come to the king for these thirty days."

12 They related Esther's words to Mordecai.

13 ¶ Then Mordecai told *them* to reply to Esther, "Do not imagine that you in the king's palace can escape any more than all the Jews.

4:13 One Safe Jew?

Esther, ensconced in the safety and luxury of the palace, was possibly the only Jew in Persia who had not heard of the extermination plans. Most likely she would have been spared, but, as Mordecai warned, the king might just as easily turn against her. Mordecai had a sophisticated view of God's providence that never lapsed into fatalism. He believed that God would somehow preserve his people; yet he also knew that God might accomplish that goal through the courageous actions of people like himself and Esther.

14 "For if you remain silent at this time, relief and deliverance will arise for the Jews from another place and you and your father's house will perish. And who knows whether you have not attained royalty for such a time as this?"

Esther Plans to Intercede

15 Then Esther told *them* to reply to Mordecai,

16 "Go, assemble all the Jews who are found in Susa, and fast for me; do not eat or drink for three days, night or day. I and my maidens also will fast in the same way. And thus I will go in to the king, which is not according to the law; and if I perish, I perish."

17 So Mordecai went away and did just as Esther had commanded him.

Esther Plans a Banquet

5 Now it came about on the third day that Esther put on her royal robes and stood in the inner court of the king's palace in front of the king's rooms, and the king was sitting on his royal throne in the throne room, opposite the entrance to the palace.

2 When the king saw Esther the queen standing in the court, she obtained favor in his sight; and the king extended to Esther the golden scepter which *was* in his hand. So Esther came near and touched the top of the scepter.

3 Then the king said to her, "What is *troubling* you, Queen Esther? And what is your request? Even to half of the kingdom it shall be given to you."

4 Esther said, "If it pleases the king, may the king and Haman come this day to the banquet that I have prepared for him."

5 ¶ Then the king said, "Bring Haman quickly that we may do as Esther desires." So the king and Haman came to the banquet which Esther had prepared.

6 As they drank their wine at the banquet, the king said to Esther, "What is your petition, for it shall be granted to you. And what is your request? Even to half of the kingdom it shall be done."

7 So Esther replied, "My petition and my request is:

8 if I have found favor in the sight of the king, and if it pleases the king to grant my petition and do what I request, may the king and Haman come to the banquet which I will prepare for them, and tomorrow I will do as the king says."

Haman's Pride

9 ¶ Then Haman went out that day glad and pleased of heart; but when Haman saw Mordecai in the king's gate and that he did not stand up or tremble before him, Haman was filled with anger against Mordecai.

10 Haman controlled himself, however, went to his house and sent for his friends and his wife Zeresh.

11 Then Haman recounted to them the glory of his riches, and the number of his sons, and every *instance* where the king had magnified him and how he had promoted him above the princes and servants of the king.

12 Haman also said, "Even Esther the queen let no one but me come with the king to the banquet which she had prepared; and tomorrow also I am invited by her with the king.

13 "Yet all of this does not satisfy me every time I see Mordecai the Jew sitting at the king's gate."

14 Then Zeresh his wife and all his friends said to him, "Have a gallows fifty cubits high made and in the morning ask the king to have Mordecai hanged on it; then go joyfully with the king to the banquet." And the advice pleased Haman, so he had the gallows made.

The King Plans to Honor Mordecai

6 During that night the king could not sleep so he gave an order to bring the book of records, the chronicles, and they were read before the king.

6:1 Ahasuerus: A Wild Man

Other historical sources portray Ahasuerus as a dangerously impulsive king. When a bridge he had ordered built was destroyed in a storm, he commanded that the sea receive 300 lashes, and then had the bridge builders beheaded. When one of his loyal subjects contributed a huge sum toward a military expedition, Ahasuerus was so enraptured that he returned the money, along with a handsome gift of his own. But when the same man asked Ahasuerus to let just one of his sons go free from the draft, Ahasuerus, enraged, ordered the son cut into two and the army to march between the pieces.

2 It was found written what Mordecai had reported concerning Bigthana and Teresh, two of the king's eunuchs who were doorkeepers, that they had sought to lay hands on King Ahasuerus.
3 The king said, "What honor or dignity has been bestowed on Mordecai for this?" Then the king's servants who attended him said, "Nothing has been done for him."
4 So the king said, "Who is in the court?" Now Haman had just entered the outer court of the king's palace in order to speak to the king about hanging Mordecai on the gallows which he had prepared for him.
5 The king's servants said to him, "Behold, Haman is standing in the court." And the king said, "Let him come in."
6 So Haman came in and the king said to him, "What is to be done for the man whom the king desires to honor?" And Haman said to himself, "Whom would the king desire to honor more than me?"
7 Then Haman said to the king, "For the man whom the king desires to honor,
8 let them bring a royal robe which the king has worn, and the horse on which the king has ridden, and on whose head a royal crown has been placed;
9 and let the robe and the horse be handed over to one of the king's most noble princes and let them array the man whom the king desires to honor and lead him on horseback through the city square, and proclaim before him, 'Thus it shall be done to the man whom the king desires to honor.'"

Haman Must Honor Mordecai

10 ¶ Then the king said to Haman, "Take quickly the robes and the horse as you have said, and do so for Mordecai the Jew, who is sitting at the king's gate; do not fall short in anything of all that you have said."
11 So Haman took the robe and the horse, and arrayed Mordecai, and led him *on horseback* through the city square, and proclaimed before him, "Thus it shall be done to the man whom the king desires to honor."
12 ¶ Then Mordecai returned to the king's gate. But Haman hurried home, mourning, with *his* head covered.
13 Haman recounted to Zeresh his wife and all his friends everything that had happened to him. Then his wise men and Zeresh his wife said to him, "If Mordecai, before whom you have begun to fall, is of Jewish origin, you will not overcome him, but will surely fall before him."
14 ¶ While they were still talking with him, the king's eunuchs arrived and hastily brought Haman to the banquet which Esther had prepared.

Esther's Plea

7 Now the king and Haman came to drink *wine* with Esther the queen.

7:1 Subtle Approach

Esther knew well the perils of standing up to autocratic Ahasuerus: she had gotten her job because of the king's furious response to a queen's brashness (1:12–2:7). Esther's "banquet plot" shows that she had mastered the wiles necessary to soften the king. She grew increasingly bold and more direct, finally convincing the king to issue another decree, countering the one against the Jews—a rare turnabout for a Persian ruler (8:8).

2 And the king said to Esther on the second day also as they drank their wine at the banquet, "What is your petition, Queen Esther? It shall be granted you. And what is your request? Even to half of the kingdom it shall be done."
3 Then Queen Esther replied, "If I have found favor in your sight, O king, and if it pleases the king, let my life be given me as my petition, and my people as my request;
4 for we have been sold, I and my people, to be destroyed, to be killed and to be annihilated. Now if we had only been sold as slaves, men and women, I would have remained silent, for the trouble would not be commensurate with the annoyance to the king."
5 Then King Ahasuerus asked Queen Esther, "Who is he, and where is he, who would presume to do thus?"
6 Esther said, "A foe and an enemy is this wicked Haman!" Then Haman became terrified before the king and queen.

Haman Is Hanged

7 The king arose in his anger from drinking wine *and went* into the palace garden; but Haman stayed to beg for his life from Queen Esther, for he saw that harm had been determined against him by the king.

8 Now when the king returned from the palace garden into the place where they were drinking wine, Haman was falling on the couch where Esther was. Then the king said, "Will he even assault the queen with me in the house?" As the word went out of the king's mouth, they covered Haman's face.

9 Then Harbonah, one of the eunuchs who *were* before the king said, "Behold indeed, the gallows standing at Haman's house fifty cubits high, which Haman made for Mordecai who spoke good on behalf of the king!" And the king said, "Hang him on it."

10 So they hanged Haman on the gallows which he had prepared for Mordecai, and the king's anger subsided.

Mordecai Promoted

8 On that day King Ahasuerus gave the house of Haman, the enemy of the Jews, to Queen Esther; and Mordecai came before the king, for Esther had disclosed what he was to her.

2 The king took off his signet ring which he had taken away from Haman, and gave it to Mordecai. And Esther set Mordecai over the house of Haman.

3 ¶ Then Esther spoke again to the king, fell at his feet, wept and implored him to avert the evil *scheme* of Haman the Agagite and his plot which he had devised against the Jews.

4 The king extended the golden scepter to Esther. So Esther arose and stood before the king.

5 Then she said, "If it pleases the king and if I have found favor before him and the matter *seems* proper to the king and I am pleasing in his sight, let it be written to revoke the letters devised by Haman, the son of Hammedatha the Agagite, which he wrote to destroy the Jews who are in all the king's provinces.

6 "For how can I endure to see the calamity which will befall my people, and how can I endure to see the destruction of my kindred?"

7 So King Ahasuerus said to Queen Esther and to Mordecai the Jew, "Behold, I have given the house of Haman to Esther, and him they have hanged on the gallows because he had stretched out his hands against the Jews.

The King's Decree Avenges the Jews

8 "Now you write to the Jews as you see fit, in the king's name, and seal *it* with the king's signet ring; for a decree which is written in the name of the king and sealed with the king's signet ring may not be revoked."

9 ¶ So the king's scribes were called at that time in the third month (that is, the month Sivan), on the twenty-third day; and it was written according to all that Mordecai commanded to the Jews, the satraps, the governors and the princes of the provinces which *extended* from India to Ethiopia, 127 provinces, to every province according to its script, and to every people according to their language as well as to the Jews according to their script and their language.

10 He wrote in the name of King Ahasuerus, and sealed it with the king's signet ring, and sent letters by couriers on horses, riding on steeds sired by the royal stud.

11 In them the king granted the Jews who were in each and every city *the right* to assemble and to defend their lives, to destroy, to kill and to annihilate the entire army of any people or province which might attack them, including children and women, and to plunder their spoil,

8:11–17 What about God?

Why is God's name not mentioned in Esther—especially in obvious places like this one? Scholars suggest several answers to this riddle. Some, reading between the lines, suggest that Esther and Mordecai were not outstanding examples of faith. They were even willing to hide Esther's Jewish background. Esther showed no reluctance to be married to a pagan king and become part of his harem. Most critically, she and Mordecai (along with all the other Jews in Esther) had chosen not to return to Jerusalem with the first wave of Jews nearly half a century before. (The story of that return is told in Ezra 1–6.) Those who stayed in Persia presumably cared more about their finances than about God's plans for the Jews to return to Jerusalem from exile. Perhaps because of this, Esther is told as a secular story, to illustrate God's care over even "secularized" Jews.

12 on one day in all the provinces of King Ahasuerus, the thirteenth *day* of the twelfth month (that is, the month Adar).

13 A copy of the edict to be issued as law in each and every province was published to all the peoples, so that the Jews would be ready for this day to avenge themselves on their enemies.

14 The couriers, hastened and impelled by the king's command, went out, riding on the royal steeds; and the decree was given out at the citadel in Susa.

15 ¶ Then Mordecai went out from the presence of the king in royal robes of blue and white, with a large crown of gold and a garment of fine linen and purple; and the city of Susa shouted and rejoiced.

16 For the Jews there was light and gladness and joy and honor.

17 In each and every province and in each and

every city, wherever the king's commandment and his decree arrived, there was gladness and joy for the Jews, a feast and a holiday. And many among the peoples of the land became Jews, for the dread of the Jews had fallen on them.

The Jews Destroy Their Enemies

9 Now in the twelfth month (that is, the month Adar), on the thirteenth day when the king's command and edict were about to be executed, on the day when the enemies of the Jews hoped to gain the mastery over them, it was turned to the contrary so that the Jews themselves gained the mastery over those who hated them.

2 The Jews assembled in their cities throughout all the provinces of King Ahasuerus to lay hands on those who sought their harm; and no one could stand before them, for the dread of them had fallen on all the peoples.

3 Even all the princes of the provinces, the satraps, the governors and those who were doing the king's business assisted the Jews, because the dread of Mordecai had fallen on them.

4 Indeed, Mordecai was great in the king's house, and his fame spread throughout all the provinces; for the man Mordecai became greater and greater.

5 Thus the Jews struck all their enemies with the sword, killing and destroying; and they did what they pleased to those who hated them.

6 At the citadel in Susa the Jews killed and destroyed five hundred men,

7 and Parshandatha, Dalphon, Aspatha,

8 Poratha, Adalia, Aridatha,

9 Parmashta, Arisai, Aridai and Vaizatha,

10 the ten sons of Haman the son of Hammedatha, the Jews' enemy; but they did not lay their hands on the plunder.

11 ¶ On that day the number of those who were killed at the citadel in Susa was reported to the king.

12 The king said to Queen Esther, "The Jews have killed and destroyed five hundred men and the ten sons of Haman at the citadel in Susa. What then have they done in the rest of the king's provinces! Now what is your petition? It shall even be granted you. And what is your further request? It shall also be done."

13 Then said Esther, "If it pleases the king, let tomorrow also be granted to the Jews who are in Susa to do according to the edict of today; and let Haman's ten sons be hanged on the gallows."

14 So the king commanded that it should be done so; and an edict was issued in Susa, and Haman's ten sons were hanged.

15 The Jews who were in Susa assembled also on the fourteenth day of the month Adar and killed three hundred men in Susa, but they did not lay their hands on the plunder.

16 ¶ Now the rest of the Jews who *were* in the king's provinces assembled, to defend their lives and rid themselves of their enemies, and kill 75,000 of those who hated them; but they did not lay their hands on the plunder.

17 *This was done* on the thirteenth day of the month Adar, and on the fourteenth day they rested and made it a day of feasting and rejoicing.

18 ¶ But the Jews who were in Susa assembled on the thirteenth and the fourteenth of the same month, and they rested on the fifteenth day and made it a day of feasting and rejoicing.

19 Therefore the Jews of the rural areas, who live in the rural towns, make the fourteenth day of the month Adar *a* holiday for rejoicing and feasting and sending portions *of food* to one another.

9:19 A Day to Remember

Just as Christians retell the Christmas story each December, acting it out in church plays and manger scenes, the Jews commemorate great moments from their history. Jewish families read the book of Esther aloud on the day of Purim. The festival got its name from the casting of lots (like dice) against the Jews (3:7), a gamble that eventually backfired against Haman. The author explains the origin of celebrating Purim on two different days; even today, Jews observe Purim on the 14th everywhere except in Jerusalem, which schedules it on the 15th.

The Feast of Purim Instituted

20 ¶ Then Mordecai recorded these events, and he sent letters to all the Jews who were in all the provinces of King Ahasuerus, both near and far,

21 obliging them to celebrate the fourteenth day of the month Adar, and the fifteenth day of the same month, annually,

22 because on those days the Jews rid themselves of their enemies, and *it was a* month which was turned for them from sorrow into gladness and from mourning into a holiday; that they should make them days of feasting and rejoicing and sending portions *of food* to one another and gifts to the poor.

23 ¶ Thus the Jews undertook what they had started to do, and what Mordecai had written to them.

24 For Haman the son of Hammedatha, the Agagite, the adversary of all the Jews, had schemed against the Jews to destroy them and had cast Pur, that is the lot, to disturb them and destroy them.

25 But when it came to the king's attention, he commanded by letter that his wicked scheme which he had devised against the Jews, should return on his own head and that he and his sons should be hanged on the gallows.

26 Therefore they called these days Purim after the name of Pur. And because of the instructions

in this letter, both what they had seen in this regard and what had happened to them,

27 the Jews established and made a custom for themselves and for their descendants and for all those who allied themselves with them, so that they would not fail to celebrate these two days according to their regulation and according to their appointed time annually.

28 So these days were to be remembered and celebrated throughout every generation, every family, every province and every city; and these days of Purim were not to fail from among the Jews, or their memory fade from their descendants.

10:2 Is Esther Accurate?

Because of the many coincidences in Esther, some have considered it "just a story," having little or no historical validity. Yet as archaeologists have learned more about ancient Persian history, the details of Esther have proven remarkably reliable. Certainly the book presents itself as history: Here the author confidently asserts that readers can check the facts in the historical records. These records are lost—but evidently they were known to the early readers of Esther.

29 ¶ Then Queen Esther, daughter of Abihail, with Mordecai the Jew, wrote with full authority to confirm this second letter about Purim.

30 He sent letters to all the Jews, to the 127 provinces of the kingdom of Ahasuerus, *namely,* words of peace and truth,

31 to establish these days of Purim at their appointed times, just as Mordecai the Jew and Queen Esther had established for them, and just as they had established for themselves and for their descendants with instructions for their times of fasting and their lamentations.

32 The command of Esther established these customs for Purim, and it was written in the book.

Mordecai's Greatness

10 Now King Ahasuerus laid a tribute on the land and on the coastlands of the sea.

2 And all the accomplishments of his authority and strength, and the full account of the greatness of Mordecai to which the king advanced him, are they not written in the Book of the Chronicles of the Kings of Media and Persia?

3 For Mordecai the Jew was second *only* to King Ahasuerus, and great among the Jews and in favor with his many kinsmen, one who sought the good of his people and one who spoke for the welfare of his whole nation.

JOB

When Bad Things Happened to a Good Person
Nobody suffered more; nobody deserved it less

H OW COULD IT HAPPEN? ALL at once the world came crashing down on a
single innocent man, a man named Job. It was the ultimate in unfairness.
First, raiders stole his belongings and slaughtered his servants. Then
fire from the sky burned up his sheep, and a mighty wind destroyed his house
and killed his sons and daughters. Finally, Job came down with a horrible,
painful disease. *What did I do to deserve such suffering?*, he wailed.

> "Have you considered My servant Job?
> For there is no one like him on the earth, a blameless and upright man, fearing God and turning away from evil." 1:8

A Cosmic Contest

The book of Job reads like a detective story in which the readers know
far more than the central characters. The very first chapter answers
Job's main question: He had done nothing to deserve such suffering. We, the readers, know
that, but nobody tells Job and his friends.

Unknown to him, Job was involved in a cosmic test, a contest proposed in heaven but staged on
earth. In this extreme test of faith, the best man on earth suffered the worst calamities. Satan had
claimed that people like Job love God only because of the good things he provides. Remove those
good things, Satan challenged, and Job's faith would melt away along with his riches and health.

God's reputation was on the line. Would Job continue to trust him, even while his life was falling
apart? This is the crucial question of the book: Would Job turn against God?

Job's wife mocked him, "Do you still hold fast your integrity? Curse God and die!" (2:9). His friends
were even more cruel: They argued that Job was being punished, that he fully deserved the tragedies
crashing into his life. For his part, Job struggled to do what seemed impossible: to keep on believing in
a loving, fair God even though all the evidence pointed against such a God.

Job on Trial

It helps to think of this book as a courtroom drama, full of long, eloquent speeches. For most of the
book, Job sits in the defendant's chair listening to his friends' harangues. He knows no airtight refuta-
tions; what they say about suffering as punishment seems to make sense. Yet he also knows, deep in
his soul, that they are wrong. He does not deserve the treatment he is getting. There has to be some
other explanation.

Like all grieving persons, Job went through emotional cycles. He whined, exploded, cajoled, and
collapsed into self-pity. He agreed with his friends, then shifted positions and contradicted himself. And
occasionally he came up with a statement of brilliant hope.

Mainly, Job asked for one thing: an appearance by the one Person who could explain his miserable
fate. He wanted to meet God himself, face to face. Eventually Job got his wish; God did show up in person. And when God finally spoke, no one—not Job, nor any of his friends—was prepared for what he
had to say.

When We Feel Like Job

Sooner or later we all find ourselves in a position somewhat like Job's. Our world seems to crumble.
Nothing makes sense any more. God seems distant and silent.

At such moments of great crisis, each one of us is put on trial. In a sense we become actors in a
contest like the one Job went through. This book records every step in that process with unflinching
honesty. Job's life stands as an example to every person who must go through great suffering.

How to Read Job

The book of Job is regarded as one of the world's truly great literary masterpieces. It contains some of the finest, most expressive poetry in the Bible. Yet first-time readers of Job can easily get lost because the complete "story line" is found in the first two chapters and the last one. Everything in between consists of a series of speeches.

The boldface sectional headings and the phrases that follow, such as "then Job continued his discourse" and "Then Eliphaz the Temanite answered," serve as markers or signposts throughout the book. Rather than reading large sections of the book, read one entire speech by Job, or a speech by Job and a rebuttal from one of his friends.

It may help if you try to summarize the statement behind each speech in one sentence and write that sentence in the margin (for example, "Job protests that he's innocent"). Speakers of that day impressed their audience more by eloquence than by rigorous logic, so the speeches may seem flowery. The issues Job and his friends address, however, are life-and-death ones.

As you read the speeches of Job's friends, remember that their views do not necessarily reflect God's. The book of Job merely records the friends' viewpoints; it does not endorse them.

PEOPLE YOU'LL MEET IN JOB

JOB *(p. 558)*

3-TRACK READING PLAN

For an explanation and complete listing of the 3-track reading plan, turn to page 7.

TRACK 1: *Two-Week Courses on the Bible*
The Track 1 reading program on the Old Testament includes one chapter from Job. See page 8 for a complete listing of this course.

TRACK 2: *An Overview of Job in 3 Days*
☐ Day 1. Read the Introduction to Job and then two short chapters, 1 and 2, which give background for the entire book.
☐ Day 2. Read chapter 38, which opens God's great speech to Job.
☐ Day 3. Read chapter 42, completing the "plot" of Job.

Now turn to page 9 for your next Track 2 reading project.

TRACK 3: *All of Job in 41 Days*
After you have read through Job, turn to pages 10–14 for your next Track 3 reading project.

☐1 ☐2 ☐3 ☐4 ☐5 ☐6 ☐7 ☐8
☐9 ☐10 ☐11 ☐12 ☐13 ☐14 ☐15 ☐16
☐17 ☐18 ☐19 ☐20 ☐21 ☐22 ☐23 ☐24
☐25–26 ☐27 ☐28 ☐29 ☐30 ☐31 ☐32 ☐33
☐34 ☐35 ☐36 ☐37 ☐38 ☐39 ☐40 ☐41
☐42

Job's Character and Wealth

1 There was a man in the land of Uz whose name was Job; and that man was blameless, upright, fearing God and turning away from evil.

2 Seven sons and three daughters were born to him.

3 His possessions also were 7,000 sheep, 3,000 camels, 500 yoke of oxen, 500 female donkeys, and very many servants; and that man was the greatest of all the men of the east.

4 His sons used to go and hold a feast in the house of each one on his day, and they would send and invite their three sisters to eat and drink with them.

5 When the days of feasting had completed their cycle, Job would send and consecrate them, rising up early in the morning and offering burnt offerings *according to* the number of them all; for Job said, "Perhaps my sons have sinned and cursed God in their hearts." Thus Job did continually.

6 ¶ Now there was a day when the sons of God came to present themselves before the LORD, and *a*Satan also came among them.

7 The LORD said to Satan, "From where do you come?" Then Satan answered the LORD and said, "From roaming about on the earth and walking around on it."

8 The LORD said to Satan, "Have you considered My servant Job? For there is no one like him on the earth, a blameless and upright man, fearing God and turning away from evil."

9 Then Satan answered the LORD, "Does Job fear God for nothing?

10 "Have You not made a hedge about him and his house and all that he has, on every side? You have blessed the work of his hands, and his possessions have increased in the land.

11 "But put forth Your hand now and touch all that he has; he will surely curse You to Your face."

12 Then the LORD said to Satan, "Behold, all that he has is in your power, only do not put forth your hand on him." So Satan departed from the presence of the LORD.

1:12—2:6 The Extent of Satan's Power

Job's portrayal of Satan echoes the story in Genesis 3: Satan has supernatural power to oppress people, but is restrained by God. As John Newton said, "Satan can only go to the end of his chain." The Bible records at least one other instance where Satan specifically asked permission to attack an individual: Luke 22:31–32.

Satan Allowed to Test Job

13 ¶ Now on the day when his sons and his daughters were eating and drinking wine in their oldest brother's house,

14 a messenger came to Job and said, "The oxen were plowing and the donkeys feeding beside them,

15 and the Sabeans attacked and took them. They also slew the servants with the edge of the sword, and I alone have escaped to tell you."

16 While he was still speaking, another also came and said, "The fire of God fell from heaven and burned up the sheep and the servants and consumed them, and I alone have escaped to tell you."

17 While he was still speaking, another also came and said, "The Chaldeans formed three bands and made a raid on the camels and took them and slew the servants with the edge of the sword, and I alone have escaped to tell you."

18 While he was still speaking, another also came and said, "Your sons and your daughters were eating and drinking wine in their oldest brother's house,

19 and behold, a great wind came from across the wilderness and struck the four corners of the house, and it fell on the young people and they died, and I alone have escaped to tell you."

20 ¶ Then Job arose and tore his robe and shaved his head, and he fell to the ground and worshiped.

21 He said,

"Naked I came from my mother's womb,
And naked I shall return there.
The LORD gave and the LORD has taken away.
Blessed be the name of the LORD."

22 ¶ Through all this Job did not sin nor did he blame God.

Job Loses His Health

2 Again there was a day when the sons of God came to present themselves before the LORD, and Satan also came among them to present himself before the LORD.

2 The LORD said to Satan, "Where have you come from?" Then Satan answered the LORD and said, "From roaming about on the earth and walking around on it."

3 The LORD said to Satan, "Have you considered My servant Job? For there is no one like him on the earth, a blameless and upright man fearing God and turning away from evil. And he still holds fast his integrity, although you incited Me against him to ruin him without cause."

4 Satan answered the LORD and said, "Skin for skin! Yes, all that a man has he will give for his life.

5 "However, put forth Your hand now, and

---

a I.e. the adversary, and so throughout chs 1 and 2

touch his bone and his flesh; he will curse You to Your face."

6 So the LORD said to Satan, "Behold, he is in your power, only spare his life."

7 ¶ Then Satan went out from the presence of the LORD and smote Job with sore boils from the sole of his foot to the crown of his head.

8 And he took a potsherd to scrape himself while he was sitting among the ashes.

9 ¶ Then his wife said to him, "Do you still hold fast your integrity? Curse God and die!"

10 But he said to her, "You speak as one of the foolish women speaks. Shall we indeed accept good from God and not accept adversity?" In all this Job did not sin with his lips.

11 ¶ Now when Job's three friends heard of all this adversity that had come upon him, they came each one from his own place, Eliphaz the Temanite, Bildad the Shuhite and Zophar the Naamathite; and they made an appointment together to come to sympathize with him and comfort him.

12 When they lifted up their eyes at a distance and did not recognize him, they raised their voices and wept. And each of them tore his robe and they threw dust over their heads toward the sky.

13 Then they sat down on the ground with him for seven days and seven nights with no one speaking a word to him, for they saw that *his* pain was very great.

2:13 Keeping Quiet

The term "Job's comforter" has come to describe how not to act around a suffering person. These three friends proved of scant help to Job and were dismissed by God himself in the end. This verse, though, reveals the depth of their feeling for Job: They sat with him for a full week in shared, silent grief. As it turned out, compassionate silence was the most profound help they imparted to Job—a good lesson to remember for anyone who works with suffering people.

Job's Lament

3 Afterward Job opened his mouth and cursed the day of his *birth.*

2 And Job said,

3 "Let the day perish on which I was to be born,
 And the night *which* said, 'A boy is conceived.'

4 "May that day be darkness;
 Let not God above care for it,
 Nor light shine on it.

5 "Let darkness and black gloom claim it;
 Let a cloud settle on it;
 Let the blackness of the day terrify it.

6 "*As for* that night, let darkness seize it;

Let it not rejoice among the days of the year;
 Let it not come into the number of the months.

7 "Behold, let that night be barren;
 Let no joyful shout enter it.

8 "Let those curse it who curse the day,
 Who are prepared to rouse Leviathan.

9 "Let the stars of its twilight be darkened;
 Let it wait for light but have none,
 And let it not see the breaking dawn;

10 Because it did not shut the opening of
 my *mother's* womb,
 Or hide trouble from my eyes.

11 ¶ "Why did I not die at birth,
 Come forth from the womb and expire?

12 "Why did the knees receive me,
 And why the breasts, that I should suck?

13 "For now I would have lain down and
 been quiet;
 I would have slept then, I would have
 been at rest,

14 With kings and *with* counselors of the
 earth,
 Who rebuilt ruins for themselves;

15 Or with princes who had gold,
 Who were filling their houses *with* silver.

16 "Or like a miscarriage which is discarded,
 I would not be,
 As infants that never saw light.

17 "There the wicked cease from raging,
 And there the weary are at rest.

18 "The prisoners are at ease together;
 They do not hear the voice of the
 taskmaster.

19 "The small and the great are there,
 And the slave is free from his master.

20 ¶ "Why is light given to him who suffers,
 And life to the bitter of soul,

21 Who long for death, but there is none,
 And dig for it more than for hidden
 treasures,

22 Who rejoice greatly,
 And exult when they find the grave?

23 "*Why is light given* to a man whose way is
 hidden,
 And whom God has hedged in?

24 "For my groaning comes at the sight of
 my food,
 And my cries pour out like water.

25 "For what I fear comes upon me,
 And what I dread befalls me.

26 "I am not at ease, nor am I quiet,
 And I am not at rest, but turmoil
 comes."

Eliphaz: Innocent Do Not Suffer

4 Then Eliphaz the Temanite answered,
2 "If one ventures a word with you, will
 you become impatient?

But who can refrain from speaking?

3 "Behold you have admonished many,
And you have strengthened weak hands.

4 "Your words have helped the tottering to
stand,
And you have strengthened feeble knees.

5 "But now it has come to you, and you are
impatient;
It touches you, and you are dismayed.

6 "Is not your ᵃfear of God your
confidence,
And the integrity of your ways your
hope?

7 ¶ "Remember now, who ever perished
being innocent?
Or where were the upright destroyed?

8 "According to what I have seen, those
who plow iniquity
And those who sow trouble harvest it.

9 "By the breath of God they perish,
And by the blast of His anger they come
to an end.

10 "The roaring of the lion and the voice of
the fierce lion,
And the teeth of the young lions are
broken.

11 "The lion perishes for lack of prey,
And the whelps of the lioness are
scattered.

12 ¶ "Now a word was brought to me
stealthily,
And my ear received a whisper of it.

13 "Amid disquieting thoughts from the
visions of the night,
When deep sleep falls on men,

4:13 Appealing to a Vision

*The book of Job includes parallels to most
modern-day responses to people in pain. To
impress the other listeners with his religious
authority, Eliphaz appealed to a mysterious
vision in which a "spirit" restated Eliphaz's own
line of argument. In the next chapter, he hints
that Job should turn to God for a miracle
(5:8–10).*

14 Dread came upon me, and trembling,
And made all my bones shake.

15 "Then a ᵇspirit passed by my face;
The hair of my flesh bristled up.

16 "It stood still, but I could not discern its
appearance;
A form was before my eyes;
There was silence, then I heard a voice:

17 'Can mankind be just before God?
Can a man be pure before his Maker?

18 'He puts no trust even in His servants;
And against His angels He charges error.

19 'How much more those who dwell in
houses of clay,
Whose foundation is in the dust,
Who are crushed before the moth!

20 'Between morning and evening they are
broken in pieces;
Unobserved, they perish forever.

21 'Is not their tent-cord plucked up within
them?
They die, yet without wisdom.'

God Is Just

5 "Call now, is there anyone who will
answer you?
And to which of the holy ones will you
turn?

2 "For anger slays the foolish man,
And jealousy kills the simple.

3 "I have seen the foolish taking root,
And I cursed his abode immediately.

4 "His sons are far from safety,
They are even ᶜoppressed in the gate,
And there is no deliverer.

5 "His harvest the hungry devour
And take it to a place of thorns,
And the schemer is eager for their
wealth.

6 "For affliction does not come from the
dust,
Nor does trouble sprout from the
ground,

7 For man is born for trouble,
As sparks fly upward.

8 ¶ "But as for me, I would seek God,
And I would place my cause before God;

9 Who does great and unsearchable things,
Wonders without number.

10 "He gives rain on the earth
And sends water on the fields,

11 So that He sets on high those who are
lowly,
And those who mourn are lifted to
safety.

12 "He frustrates the plotting of the shrewd,
So that their hands cannot attain success.

13 "He captures the wise by their own
shrewdness,
And the advice of the cunning is quickly
thwarted.

14 "By day they meet with darkness,
And grope at noon as in the night.

15 "But He saves from the sword of their
mouth,
And the poor from the hand of the
mighty.

16 "So the helpless has hope,

ᵃ Or reverence   ᵇ Or breath passed over   ᶜ Lit crushed

And unrighteousness must shut its
mouth.

17 ¶ "Behold, how happy is the man whom
God reproves,
So do not despise the discipline of the
Almighty.

5:17 Pain as Punishment

Job's friends sound so pious and eloquent that it's easy to accept their words as all-encompassing truth. Some Christians have quoted this verse like a proverb, applying it indiscriminately to instances of suffering. In reality, Eliphaz was dead wrong in his theory that God was disciplining Job. God had already held up Job as a model of goodness (1:9).

18 "For He inflicts pain, and gives relief;
He wounds, and His hands *also* heal.
19 "From six troubles He will deliver you,
Even in seven evil will not touch you.
20 "In famine He will redeem you from
death,
And in war from the power of the sword.
21 "You will be hidden from the scourge of
the tongue,
And you will not be afraid of violence
when it comes.
22 "You will laugh at violence and famine,
And you will not be afraid of wild beasts.
23 "For you will be in league with the stones
of the field,
And the beasts of the field will be at
peace with you.
24 "You will know that your tent is secure,
For you will visit your abode and fear no
loss.
25 "You will know also that your
descendants will be many,
And your offspring as the grass of the
earth.
26 "You will come to the grave in full vigor,
Like the stacking of grain in its season.
27 "Behold this; we have investigated it, *and*
so it is.
Hear it, and know for yourself."

Job's Friends Are No Help

6 Then Job answered,
2 "Oh that my grief were actually weighed
And laid in the balances together with
my calamity!
3 "For then it would be heavier than the
sand of the seas;
Therefore my words have been rash.
4 "For the arrows of the Almighty are
within me,
Their poison my spirit drinks;

The terrors of God are arrayed
against me.
5 "Does the wild donkey bray over *his*
grass,
Or does the ox low over his fodder?
6 "Can something tasteless be eaten without
salt,
Or is there any taste in the white of
an egg?
7 "My soul refuses to touch *them*;
They are like loathsome food to me.

8 ¶ "Oh that my request might come to
pass,
And that God would grant my longing!
9 "Would that God were willing to
crush me,
That He would loose His hand and cut
me off!

6:9 Why Keep on Living?

Job steadfastly refused to curse God, but he did curse the day he was born. In this speech he asked for a quick death, realizing he could not hold out trusting in God forever. If he died soon, at least he would die still believing. His speeches contain some of the most profound expressions of pain and despair in all of literature.

10 "But it is still my consolation,
And I rejoice in unsparing pain,
That I have not denied the words of the
Holy One.
11 "What is my strength, that I should wait?
And what is my end, that I should
endure?
12 "Is my strength the strength of stones,
Or is my flesh bronze?
13 "Is it that my help is not within me,
And that deliverance is driven from me?

14 ¶ "For the despairing man *there should
be* kindness from his friend;
So that he does not forsake the fear of
the Almighty.
15 "My brothers have acted deceitfully like a
wadi,
Like the torrents of wadis which vanish,
16 Which are turbid because of ice
And into which the snow melts.
17 "When they become waterless, they are
silent,
When it is hot, they vanish from their
place.
18 "The paths of their course wind along,
They go up into nothing and perish.
19 "The caravans of Tema looked,

The travelers of Sheba hoped for them.
20 "They were disappointed for they had
trusted,
They came there and were confounded.
21 "Indeed, you have now become such,
You see a terror and are afraid.
22 "Have I said, 'Give me *something*,'
Or, 'Offer a bribe for me from your
wealth,'
23 Or, 'Deliver me from the hand of the
adversary,'

Or, 'Redeem me from the hand of the
tyrants'?

24 ¶ "Teach me, and I will be silent;
And show me how I have erred.
25 "How painful are honest words!
But what does your argument prove?
26 "Do you intend to reprove *my* words,
When the words of one in despair belong
to the wind?
27 "You would even cast *lots* for the orphans
And barter over your friend.

What Not to Say to a Hurting Person
Job's friends only made it worse

> "Indeed, you have
> now become such.
> You see a terror and
> are afraid." 6:21

YOU ARE SITTING IN A hospital room, where the faint smell of antiseptic lingers and the sound of lowered voices rustles all around you. The medical prognosis of your friend is bleak. You've listened to your friend's anger and despair, and a jumble of other emotions. Now it's your turn to reply. Everyone in the room waits for your response.

What do you say to a suffering person? The book of Job gives page after page of examples. Job's three friends, finding him in despair, filled the air with high-sounding advice. But unfortunately they offer models of what *not* to say. Their main argument only made Job feel worse, and at the end God dismissed them all with a scowl.

Who Were Job's Friends?

This book gives few details on time and place, but it presents Job as a very wealthy "sheik" of the Middle East. His three friends, from neighboring lands, were also prosperous and well respected. When they first saw Job, they wept aloud and sat with him on the ground, silent, for seven days and nights, overcome with grief (2:12-13).

After Job finally broke the silence, each friend delivered a flowery speech on Job's dilemma. There are three cycles of speeches in all, with Eliphaz, Bildad, and Zophar taking turns, allowing Job to respond to each. Eliphaz, who led off, had strong and noble ideas. Bildad was briefer and slightly less sympathetic. Zophar (who did not speak in the third cycle) showed passion and fire.

The friends seemed to crescendo in emotional intensity. In the first cycle (chapters 4–14), they showed hope of winning Job over to their point of view. In the second cycle (chapters 15–21), the speeches grew more severe and threatening. And by the time of the concluding speeches (chapters 22–25), Job's friends were making direct accusations against him.

A Flawed Theory about Suffering

Job's friends believed in a God of love and fairness; their arguments started from that fact. Surely a just God would not allow an *innocent* man to suffer so much, they reasoned. Most of their comments boil down to one simple theory: Job must have committed some great crime for which God was punishing him. All three believed that good people prosper and bad people suffer; therefore, suffering must betray some hidden sin.

"Lo, God will not reject a man of integrity, nor will He support the evildoers," they said to Job (8:20). Repent, they admonished him, and God will forgive and restore you. Their words got this response from Job: "But you smear with lies; you are all worthless physicians." (13:4). Job also believed in a loving God, but he knew he was innocent.

When God finally made his appearance, he dismissed the three friends in one sentence to Eliphaz, "My wrath is kindled against you and against your two friends, because you have not spoken of Me what is right as My servant Job has" (42:7).

Although the Bible elsewhere gives examples of suffering that resulted from a person's sin, Job clearly shows that such a theory cannot be applied in every case. (For a related discussion, see "Healthier, Wealthier, and Wiser," page 222.) It is not for us to try to reason out the specific cause of a person's suffering; God reserves that knowledge for himself.

Life Questions: What is the most "unfair" thing that has ever happened to you? How did it affect the way you thought about God?

28 "Now please look at me,
  And *see* if I lie to your face.
29 "Desist now, let there be no injustice;
  Even desist, my righteousness is yet in it.
30 "Is there injustice on my tongue?
  Cannot my palate discern calamities?

Job's Life Seems Futile

7 "Is not man forced to labor on earth,
  And *are not* his days like the days of a
    hired man?
2 "As a slave who pants for the shade,
  And as a hired man who eagerly waits
    for his wages,
3 So am I allotted months of vanity,
  And nights of trouble are appointed me.
4 "When I lie down I say,
  'When shall I arise?'
  But the night continues,
  And I am continually tossing until dawn.
5 "My flesh is clothed with worms and a
    crust of dirt,
  My skin hardens and runs.
6 "My days are swifter than a weaver's
    shuttle,
  And come to an end without hope.

7 ¶ "Remember that my life is *but* breath;
  My eye will not again see good.
8 "The eye of him who sees me will behold
    me no longer;
  Your eyes *will be* on me, but I will
    not be.
9 "When a cloud vanishes, it is gone,
  So he who goes down to Sheol does not
    come up.
10 "He will not return again to his house,
  Nor will his place know him anymore.

11 ¶ "Therefore I will not restrain my
    mouth;
  I will speak in the anguish of my spirit,
  I will complain in the bitterness of my
    soul.
12 "Am I the sea, or the sea monster,
  That You set a guard over me?
13 "If I say, 'My bed will comfort me,
  My couch will ease my complaint,'
14 Then You frighten me with dreams
  And terrify me by visions;
15 So that my soul would choose
    suffocation,
  Death rather than my pains.
16 "I waste away; I will not live forever.
  Leave me alone, for my days are *but* a
    breath.
17 "What is man that You magnify him,
  And that You are concerned about him,
18 That You examine him every morning
  And try him every moment?
19 "Will You never turn Your gaze away
    from me,

Nor let me alone until I swallow my
    spittle?
20 "Have I sinned? What have I done
    to You,
  O watcher of men?
  Why have You set me as Your target,
  So that I am a burden to myself?
21 "Why then do You not pardon my
    transgression
  And take away my iniquity?
  For now I will lie down in the dust;
  And You will seek me, but I will not be."

Bildad Says God Rewards the Good

8 Then Bildad the Shuhite answered,
2 "How long will you say these things,
  And the words of your mouth be a
    mighty wind?
3 "Does God pervert justice?
  Or does the Almighty pervert what is
    right?
4 "If your sons sinned against Him,
  Then He delivered them into the power
    of their transgression.

8:4 A Mixture of True and False

*Although God rejected the overall force of their
arguments, Job's three friends said some
things that were totally false and others that
were true. In this case, Bildad appealed to
common sense, ("Lo, God will not reject a man
of integrity," verse 20), implying that Job
sinned to deserve his suffering. But God
specifically had called Job "blameless and
upright" (2:3). Elsewhere, a statement by
Eliphaz (5:11–13) is quoted approvingly in the
New Testament (1 Corinthians 3:19).*

5 "If you would seek God
  And implore the compassion of the
    Almighty,
6 If you are pure and upright,
  Surely now He would rouse Himself
    for you
  And restore your righteous estate.
7 "Though your beginning was insignificant,
  Yet your end will increase greatly.

8 ¶ "Please inquire of past generations,
  And consider the things searched out by
    their fathers.
9 "For we are *only* of yesterday and know
    nothing,
  Because our days on earth are as a
    shadow.
10 "Will they not teach you *and* tell you,
  And bring forth words from their minds?
11 ¶ "Can the papyrus grow up without a
    marsh?

Can the rushes grow without water?
12 "While it is still green *and* not cut down,
Yet it withers before any *other* plant.
13 "So are the paths of all who forget God;
And the hope of the godless will perish,
14 Whose confidence is fragile,
And whose trust a spider's web.
15 "He trusts in his house, but it does not
stand;
He holds fast to it, but it does not
endure.
16 "He thrives before the sun,
And his shoots spread out over his
garden.
17 "His roots wrap around a rock pile,
He grasps a house of stones.
18 "If he is removed from his place,
Then it will deny him, *saying*, 'I never
saw you.'
19 "Behold, this is the joy of His way;
And out of the dust others will spring.
20 "Lo, God will not reject *a man of*
integrity,
Nor will He support the evildoers.
21 "He will yet fill your mouth with laughter
And your lips with shouting.
22 "Those who hate you will be clothed with
shame,
And the tent of the wicked will be no
longer."

Job Says There Is No Arbitrator between God and Man

9 Then Job answered,
2 "In truth I know that this is so;
But how can a man be in the right
before God?
3 "If one wished to dispute with Him,
He could not answer Him once in a
thousand *times.*
4 "Wise in heart and mighty in strength,
Who has defied Him without harm?
5 "*It is God* who removes the mountains,
they know not *how,*

9:4 Arms Too Short

A gospel musical based on the book of Job took the title "Arms Too Short to Box with God." From the beginning Job knew he didn't stand a chance in a dispute with God. Moreover, he wasn't sure what to dispute—much of the time Job demonstrated a better grasp of theology than his friends. (For example, his words in this chapter bear striking resemblance to what God says at the end of the book.) But good insights did not relieve Job's sense of being abandoned by God. His crisis of faith was more personal than intellectual.

When He overturns them in His anger;
6 Who shakes the earth out of its place,
And its pillars tremble;
7 Who commands the sun not to shine,
And sets a seal upon the stars;
8 Who alone stretches out the heavens
And tramples down the waves of the sea;
9 Who makes the Bear, Orion and the
Pleiades,
And the chambers of the south;
10 Who does great things, unfathomable,
And wondrous works without number.
11 "Were He to pass by me, I would not see
Him;
Were He to move past *me*, I would not
perceive Him.
12 "Were He to snatch away, who could
restrain Him?
Who could say to Him, 'What are You
doing?'
13 ¶ "God will not turn back His anger;
Beneath Him crouch the helpers of
Rahab.
14 "How then can I answer Him,
And choose my words before Him?
15 "For though I were right, I could not
answer;
I would have to implore the mercy of my
judge.
16 "If I called and He answered me,
I could not believe that He was listening
to my voice.
17 "For He bruises me with a tempest
And multiplies my wounds without
cause.
18 "He will not allow me to get my breath,
But saturates me with bitterness.
19 "If *it is a matter* of power, behold, *He is*
the strong one!
And if *it is a matter* of justice, who can
summon Him?
20 "Though I am righteous, my mouth will
condemn me;
Though I am guiltless, He will declare
me guilty.
21 "I am guiltless;
I do not take notice of myself;
I despise my life.
22 "It is *all* one; therefore I say,
'He destroys the guiltless and the wicked.'
23 "If the scourge kills suddenly,
He mocks the despair of the innocent.
24 "The earth is given into the hand of the
wicked;
He covers the faces of its judges.
If *it is* not *He*, then who is it?
25 ¶ "Now my days are swifter than a
runner;
They flee away, they see no good.
26 "They slip by like reed boats,

Like an eagle that swoops on its prey.

27 "Though I say, 'I will forget my
complaint,
I will leave off my *sad* countenance and
be cheerful,'

28 I am afraid of all my pains,
I know that You will not acquit me.

29 "I am accounted wicked,
Why then should I toil in vain?

30 "If I should wash myself with snow
And cleanse my hands with lye,

31 Yet You would plunge me into the pit,
And my own clothes would abhor me.

32 "For *He is* not a man as I am that I may
answer Him,
That we may go to court together.

33 "There is no umpire between us,
Who may lay his hand upon us both.

9:33–35 Looking for an Arbitrator

*Job recognized the enormous gulf between God
and people. He poignantly asked for an
arbitrator "who may lay his hand upon us
both." A few such comments of Job, expressing
great longing for an advocate, found their full
realization in Jesus, who was called the "one
mediator also between God and men"
(1 Timothy 2:5).*

34 "Let Him remove His rod from me,
And let not dread of Him terrify me.

35 "*Then* I would speak and not fear Him;
But I am not like that in myself.

Job Despairs of God's Dealings

10 "I loathe my own life;
I will give full vent to my complaint;
I will speak in the bitterness of my soul.

2 "I will say to God, 'Do not condemn me;
Let me know why You contend with me.

3 'Is it right for You indeed to oppress,
To reject the labor of Your hands,
And to look favorably on the schemes of
the wicked?

4 'Have You eyes of flesh?
Or do You see as a man sees?

5 'Are Your days as the days of a mortal,
Or Your years as man's years,

6 That You should seek for my guilt
And search after my sin?

7 'According to Your knowledge I am
indeed not guilty,
Yet there is no deliverance from Your
hand.

8 ¶ 'Your hands fashioned and made me
altogether,
And would You destroy me?

9 'Remember now, that You have made me
as clay;
And would You turn me into dust again?

10 'Did You not pour me out like milk

10:8 Fond Memories

*Author Joseph Bayly, who watched three of his
sons die in their youth, said, "Don't forget in the
darkness what you've learned in the light." Job
lived by this same principle. Even though he
could not understand God at the moment, he
never belittled the blessings he had already
received. In a fit of anger, a divorcée might say,
"Oh, I never really loved him anyway"; Job
never once turned his back on God in that way.*

And curdle me like cheese;

11 Clothe me with skin and flesh,
And knit me together with bones and
sinews?

12 'You have granted me life and
lovingkindness;
And Your care has preserved my spirit.

13 'Yet these things You have concealed in
Your heart;
I know that this is within You:

14 If I sin, then You would take note of me,
And would not acquit me of my guilt.

15 'If I am wicked, woe to me!
And if I am righteous, I dare not lift up
my head.
I am sated with disgrace and conscious
of my misery.

16 'Should *my head* be lifted up, You would
hunt me like a lion;
And again You would show Your power
against me.

17 'You renew Your witnesses against me
And increase Your anger toward me;
Hardship after hardship is with me.

18 ¶ 'Why then have You brought me out
of the womb?
Would that I had died and no eye had
seen me!

19 'I should have been as though I had not
been,
Carried from womb to tomb.'

20 "Would He not let my few days alone?
Withdraw from me that I may have a
little cheer

21 Before I go—and I shall not return—
To the land of darkness and deep
shadow,

22 The land of utter gloom as darkness
itself,
Of deep shadow without order,
And which shines as the darkness."

Zophar Rebukes Job

11 Then Zophar the Naamathite answered,
2 "Shall a multitude of words go
unanswered,
And a talkative man be acquitted?
3 "Shall your boasts silence men?
And shall you scoff and none rebuke?
4 "For you have said, 'My teaching is pure,
And I am innocent in your eyes.'
5 "But would that God might speak,
And open His lips against you,
6 And show you the secrets of wisdom!
For sound wisdom has two sides.
Know then that God forgets a part of
your iniquity.

7 ¶ "Can you discover the depths of God?
Can you discover the limits of the
Almighty?
8 "*They are* high as the heavens, what can
you do?
Deeper than Sheol, what can you know?
9 "Its measure is longer than the earth
And broader than the sea.
10 "If He passes by or shuts up,
Or calls an assembly, who can restrain
Him?
11 "For He knows false men,
And He sees iniquity without
investigating.
12 "An idiot will become intelligent
When the foal of a wild donkey is born
a man.

13 ¶ "If you would direct your heart right
And spread out your hand to Him,
14 If iniquity is in your hand, put it far
away,
And do not let wickedness dwell in your
tents;

11:14 Unfair Accusation

*Zophar, the least tactful of the three friends,
made direct accusations against Job, repeating
the common refrain that Job was being
punished for some sin. In a speech recorded in
chapter 12, Job agreed in principle that God
rewards the righteous and punishes the
wicked. But in his own case he knew he was
innocent. No matter how convincing their
arguments, he had to protest against them.*

15 "Then, indeed, you could lift up your face
without *moral* defect,
And you would be steadfast and not fear.
16 "For you would forget *your* trouble,
As waters that have passed by, you
would remember *it*.
17 "Your life would be brighter than
noonday;

Darkness would be like the morning.
18 "Then you would trust, because there is
hope;
And you would look around and rest
securely.
19 "You would lie down and none would
disturb *you*,
And many would entreat your favor.
20 "But the eyes of the wicked will fail,
And there will be no escape for them;
And their hope is to breathe their last."

Job Chides His Accusers

12 Then Job responded,
2 "Truly then you are the people,
And with you wisdom will die!
3 "But I have intelligence as well as you;
I am not inferior to you.
And who does not know such things as
these?
4 "I am a joke to my friends,
The one who called on God and He
answered him;
The just *and* blameless *man* is a joke.
5 "He who is at ease holds calamity in
contempt,
As prepared for those whose feet slip.

12:5 Contempt, not Sympathy

*After his release from a Siberian prison,
Alexander Solzhenitsyn gained overnight fame
as a novelist. One day he was summoned to the
opulent office of an admiring Soviet official. In
those comfortable surroundings, the agony of
the Soviet prison camps seemed very far away.
"It is impossible for a man who is warm to
understand one who is cold," he concluded. Job
accused his friends—and even God—of the
same lack of sympathy. His complaint against
God would be answered finally by the
Incarnation, when God voluntarily subjected
himself to cold, hunger, and every other
human misfortune.*

6 "The tents of the destroyers prosper,
And those who provoke God are secure,
Whom God brings into their power.
7 ¶ "But now ask the beasts, and let them
teach you;
And the birds of the heavens, and let
them tell you.
8 "Or speak to the earth, and let it teach
you;
And let the fish of the sea declare to you.
9 "Who among all these does not know
That the hand of the LORD has done this,
10 In whose hand is the life of every living
thing,
And the breath of all mankind?

11 "Does not the ear test words,
  As the palate tastes its food?
12 "Wisdom is with aged men,
  With long life is understanding.

Job Speaks of the Power of God

13 ¶ "With Him are wisdom and might;
  To Him belong counsel and
    understanding.
14 "Behold, He tears down, and it cannot be
    rebuilt;
  He imprisons a man, and there can be
    no release.
15 "Behold, He restrains the waters, and they
    dry up;
  And He sends them out, and they
    inundate the earth.
16 "With Him are strength and sound
    wisdom,
  The misled and the misleader belong to
    Him.
17 "He makes counselors walk barefoot
  And makes fools of judges.
18 "He loosens the bond of kings
  And binds their loins with a girdle.
19 "He makes priests walk barefoot
  And overthrows the secure ones.
20 "He deprives the trusted ones of speech
  And takes away the discernment of the
    elders.
21 "He pours contempt on nobles
  And loosens the belt of the strong.
22 "He reveals mysteries from the darkness
  And brings the deep darkness into light.
23 "He makes the nations great, then
    destroys them;
  He enlarges the nations, then leads them
    away.
24 "He deprives of intelligence the chiefs of
    the earth's people
  And makes them wander in a pathless
    waste.
25 "They grope in darkness with no light,
  And He makes them stagger like a
    drunken man.

Job Says His Friends' Proverbs Are Ashes

13 "Behold, my eye has seen all *this*,
  My ear has heard and understood it.
2 "What you know I also know;
  I am not inferior to you.

3 ¶ "But I would speak to the Almighty,
  And I desire to argue with God.
4 "But you smear with lies;
  You are all worthless physicians.
5 "O that you would be completely silent,
  And that it would become your wisdom!
6 "Please hear my argument
  And listen to the contentions of my lips.
7 "Will you speak what is unjust for God,
  And speak what is deceitful for Him?

8 "Will you show partiality for Him?
  Will you contend for God?
9 "Will it be well when He examines you?
  Or will you deceive Him as one deceives
    a man?
10 "He will surely reprove you
  If you secretly show partiality.
11 "Will not His majesty terrify you,
  And the dread of Him fall on you?
12 "Your memorable sayings are proverbs of
    ashes,
  Your defenses are defenses of clay.

Job Is Sure He Will Be Vindicated

13 ¶ "Be silent before me so that I may
    speak;
  Then let come on me what may.
14 "Why should I take my flesh in my teeth
  And put my life in my hands?
15 "Though He slay me,
  I will hope in Him.
  Nevertheless I will argue my ways before
    Him.

13:15 A Desperate Hope

*This statement more than any other shows the
depth of Job's faith, and the reason he made
good on God's challenge against Satan. He
valued his faith in God even above his own life.
He asked only for a "day in court," a chance to
confront God personally and hear an
explanation.*

16 "This also will be my salvation,
  For a godless man may not come before
    His presence.
17 "Listen carefully to my speech,
  And let my declaration *fill* your ears.
18 "Behold now, I have prepared my case;
  I know that I will be vindicated.
19 "Who will contend with me?
  For then I would be silent and die.

20 ¶ "Only two things do not do to me,
  Then I will not hide from Your face:
21 Remove Your hand from me,
  And let not the dread of You terrify me.
22 "Then call, and I will answer;
  Or let me speak, then reply to me.
23 "How many are my iniquities and sins?
  Make known to me my rebellion and my
    sin.
24 "Why do You hide Your face
  And consider me Your enemy?
25 "Will You cause a driven leaf to tremble?
  Or will You pursue the dry chaff?
26 "For You write bitter things against me
  And make me to inherit the iniquities of
    my youth.

27 "You put my feet in the stocks
   And watch all my paths;
   You set a limit for the soles of my feet,
28 While I am decaying like a rotten thing,
   Like a garment that is moth-eaten.

Job Speaks of the Finality of Death

14 "Man, who is born of woman,
   Is short-lived and full of turmoil.
2 "Like a flower he comes forth and withers.
   He also flees like a shadow and does not
      remain.
3 "You also open Your eyes on him
   And bring him into judgment with
      Yourself.
4 "Who can make the clean out of the
      unclean?
   No one!
5 "Since his days are determined,
   The number of his months is with You;
   And his limits You have set so that he
      cannot pass.
6 "Turn Your gaze from him that he may
      rest,
   Until he fulfills his day like a hired man.

7 ¶ "For there is hope for a tree,
   When it is cut down, that it will sprout
      again,
   And its shoots will not fail.
8 "Though its roots grow old in the ground
   And its stump dies in the dry soil,
9 At the scent of water it will flourish
   And put forth sprigs like a plant.
10 "But man dies and lies prostrate.
   Man expires, and where is he?
11 "As water evaporates from the sea,
   And a river becomes parched and
      dried up,
12 So man lies down and does not rise.
   Until the heavens are no longer,
   He will not awake nor be aroused out of
      his sleep.

13 ¶ "Oh that You would hide me in Sheol,
   That You would conceal me until Your
      wrath returns to You,
   That You would set a limit for me and
      remember me!
14 "If a man dies, will he live again?
   All the days of my struggle I will wait
   Until my change comes.
15 "You will call, and I will answer You;
   You will long for the work of Your
      hands.
16 "For now You number my steps,
   You do not observe my sin.
17 "My transgression is sealed up in a bag,
   And You wrap up my iniquity.

18 ¶ "But the falling mountain crumbles
      away,
   And the rock moves from its place;

19 Water wears away stones,
   Its torrents wash away the dust of the
      earth;
   So You destroy man's hope.
20 "You forever overpower him and he
      departs;
   You change his appearance and send him
      away.
21 "His sons achieve honor, but he does not
      know it;
   Or they become insignificant, but he
      does not perceive it.
22 "But his body pains him,
   And he mourns only for himself."

Eliphaz Says Job Presumes Much

15 Then Eliphaz the Temanite responded,
2 "Should a wise man answer with
      windy knowledge
   And fill himself with the east wind?
3 "Should he argue with useless talk,
   Or with words which are not profitable?
4 "Indeed, you do away with reverence
   And hinder meditation before God.

15:4 A Shocking Lack of Piety

*Job minced no words in his complaints against
God. As a result, his friends criticized him for
undermining piety and hindering devotion to
God. Notably, in his summing-up speech God
did not condemn Job's varying moods; he
instead dismissed the pious words of Job's
friends.*

*Counselors know that repressed feelings of
anger or disappointment don't just disappear;
they usually fester inside, and grow even more
toxic. Job expressed his feeling openly, much to
his friends' dismay.*

5 "For your guilt teaches your mouth,
   And you choose the language of the
      crafty.
6 "Your own mouth condemns you, and
      not I;
   And your own lips testify against you.

7 ¶ "Were you the first man to be born,
   Or were you brought forth before the
      hills?
8 "Do you hear the secret counsel of God,
   And limit wisdom to yourself?
9 "What do you know that we do not
      know?
   What do you understand that we do not?
10 "Both the gray-haired and the aged are
      among us,
   Older than your father.
11 "Are the consolations of God too small
      for you,
   Even the word spoken gently with you?

12 "Why does your heart carry you away?
And why do your eyes flash,

13 That you should turn your spirit against God
And allow *such* words to go out of your mouth?

14 "What is man, that he should be pure,
Or he who is born of a woman, that he should be righteous?

15 "Behold, He puts no trust in His holy ones,
And the heavens are not pure in His sight;

16 How much less one who is detestable and corrupt,
Man, who drinks iniquity like water!

What Eliphaz Has Seen of Life

17 ¶ "I will tell you, listen to me;
And what I have seen I will also declare;

18 What wise men have told,
And have not concealed from their fathers,

19 To whom alone the land was given,
And no alien passed among them.

20 "The wicked man writhes in pain all *his* days,
And numbered are the years stored up for the ruthless.

21 "Sounds of terror are in his ears;
While at peace the destroyer comes upon him.

22 "He does not believe that he will return from darkness,
And he is destined for the sword.

23 "He wanders about for food, saying, 'Where is it?'
He knows that a day of darkness is at hand.

24 "Distress and anguish terrify him,
They overpower him like a king ready for the attack,

25 Because he has stretched out his hand against God
And conducts himself arrogantly against the Almighty.

26 "He rushes headlong at Him
With his massive shield.

27 "For he has covered his face with his fat
And made his thighs heavy with flesh.

28 "He has lived in desolate cities,
In houses no one would inhabit,
Which are destined to become ruins.

29 "He will not become rich, nor will his wealth endure;
And his grain will not bend down to the ground.

30 "He will not escape from darkness;
The flame will wither his shoots,
And by the breath of His mouth he will go away.

31 "Let him not trust in emptiness, deceiving himself;
For emptiness will be his reward.

32 "It will be accomplished before his time,
And his palm branch will not be green.

33 "He will drop off his unripe grape like the vine,
And will cast off his flower like the olive tree.

34 "For the company of the godless is barren,
And fire consumes the tents of the corrupt.

35 "They conceive mischief and bring forth iniquity,
And their mind prepares deception."

Job Says Friends Are Sorry Comforters

16 Then Job answered,
2 "I have heard many such things;
Sorry comforters are you all.

3 "Is there *no* limit to windy words?
Or what plagues you that you answer?

4 "I too could speak like you,
If I were in your place.
I could compose words against you
And shake my head at you.

5 "I could strengthen you with my mouth,
And the solace of my lips could lessen *your pain.*

Job Says God Shattered Him

6 ¶ "If I speak, my pain is not lessened,
And if I hold back, what has left me?

7 "But now He has exhausted me;
You have laid waste all my company.

8 "You have shriveled me up,
It has become a witness;
And my leanness rises up against me,
It testifies to my face.

9 "His anger has torn me and hunted me down,
He has gnashed at me with His teeth;
My adversary glares at me.

16:9 When God Seems Angry

In his trauma, Job could not help feeling that he was the object of God's anger. Many people who undergo great pain feel the same. In Job's case, however, we know that God was not angry with him. God had held him up before Satan as a "man, fearing God and turning away from evil" (1:8).

10 "They have gaped at me with their mouth,
They have slapped me on the cheek with contempt;
They have massed themselves against me.

11 "God hands me over to ruffians

And tosses me into the hands of the
wicked.
12 "I was at ease, but He shattered me,
And He has grasped me by the neck and
shaken me to pieces;
He has also set me up as His target.
13 "His arrows surround me.
Without mercy He splits my kidneys
open;
He pours out my gall on the ground.
14 "He breaks through me with breach after
breach;
He runs at me like a warrior.
15 "I have sewed sackcloth over my skin
And thrust my horn in the dust.
16 "My face is flushed from weeping,
And deep darkness is on my eyelids,
17 Although there is no violence in my
hands,
And my prayer is pure.

18 ¶ "O earth, do not cover my blood,
And let there be no *resting* place for my
cry.
19 "Even now, behold, my witness is in
heaven,
And my advocate is on high.
20 "My friends are my scoffers;
My eye weeps to God.
21 "O that a man might plead with God
As a man with his neighbor!
22 "For when a few years are past,
I shall go the way of no return.

Job Says He Has Become a Byword

17 "My spirit is broken, my days are
extinguished,
The grave is *ready* for me.
2 "Surely mockers are with me,
And my eye gazes on their provocation.

3 ¶ "Lay down, now, a pledge for me with
Yourself;
Who is there that will be my guarantor?
4 "For You have kept their heart from
understanding,
Therefore You will not exalt *them*.
5 "He who informs against friends for a
share *of the spoil*,
The eyes of his children also will
languish.

6 ¶ "But He has made me a byword of the
people,
And I am one at whom men spit.
7 "My eye has also grown dim because of
grief,
And all my members are as a shadow.
8 "The upright will be appalled at this,
And the innocent will stir up himself
against the godless.
9 "Nevertheless the righteous will hold to
his way,

And he who has clean hands will grow
stronger and stronger.
10 "But come again all of you now,
For I do not find a wise man among
you.
11 "My days are past, my plans are torn
apart,
Even the wishes of my heart.
12 "They make night into day, *saying*,
'The light is near,' in the presence of
darkness.

17:12–16 A Wrong Time for Cheer

*Falsely cheerful advice can actually make a
suffering person even more discouraged. Job's
sentiments here are echoed in a verse from
Proverbs: "Like one who takes off a garment on
a cold day, or like vinegar on soda, is he who
sings songs to a troubled heart" (25:20).*

13 "If I look for Sheol as my home,
I make my bed in the darkness;
14 If I call to the pit, 'You are my father';
To the worm, 'my mother and my sister';
15 Where now is my hope?
And who regards my hope?
16 "Will it go down with me to Sheol?
Shall we together go down into the
dust?"

Bildad Speaks of the Wicked

18 Then Bildad the Shuhite responded,
2 "How long will you hunt for words?
Show understanding and then we can
talk.
3 "Why are we regarded as beasts,
As stupid in your eyes?
4 "O you who tear yourself in your anger—
For your sake is the earth to be
abandoned,
Or the rock to be moved from its place?

5 ¶ "Indeed, the light of the wicked goes
out,
And the flame of his fire gives no light.
6 "The light in his tent is darkened,
And his lamp goes out above him.
7 "His vigorous stride is shortened,
And his own scheme brings him down.
8 "For he is thrown into the net by his own
feet,
And he steps on the webbing.
9 "A snare seizes *him* by the heel,
And a trap snaps shut on him.
10 "A noose for him is hidden in the ground,
And a trap for him on the path.
11 "All around terrors frighten him,
And harry him at every step.
12 "His strength is famished,

And calamity is ready at his side.

13 "His skin is devoured by disease,
The firstborn of death devours his limbs.

14 "He is torn from the security of his tent,

And they march him before the king of terrors.

15 "There dwells in his tent nothing of his;
Brimstone is scattered on his habitation.

16 "His roots are dried below,
And his branch is cut off above.

17 "Memory of him perishes from the earth,
And he has no name abroad.

18 "He is driven from light into darkness,
And chased from the inhabited world.

19 "He has no offspring or posterity among his people,
Nor any survivor where he sojourned.

20 "Those in the west are appalled at his fate,
And those in the east are seized with horror.

21 "Surely such are the dwellings of the wicked,
And this is the place of him who does not know God."

Job Feels Insulted

19 Then Job responded,
2 "How long will you torment me
And crush me with words?

3 "These ten times you have insulted me;
You are not ashamed to wrong me.

4 "Even if I have truly erred,
My error lodges with me.

5 "If indeed you vaunt yourselves against me
And prove my disgrace to me,

6 Know then that God has wronged me
And has closed His net around me.

Everything Is against Him

7 ¶ "Behold, I cry, 'Violence!' but I get no answer;
I shout for help, but there is no justice.

8 "He has walled up my way so that I cannot pass,
And He has put darkness on my paths.

9 "He has stripped my honor from me
And removed the crown from my head.

10 "He breaks me down on every side, and I am gone;
And He has uprooted my hope like a tree.

11 "He has also kindled His anger against me
And considered me as His enemy.

12 "His troops come together,
And build up their way against me
And camp around my tent.

13 ¶ "He has removed my brothers far from me,
And my acquaintances are completely estranged from me.

14 "My relatives have failed,
And my intimate friends have forgotten me.

15 "Those who live in my house and my maids consider me a stranger.
I am a foreigner in their sight.

16 "I call to my servant, but he does not answer;
I have to implore him with my mouth.

17 "My breath is offensive to my wife,
And I am loathsome to my own brothers.

18 "Even young children despise me;
I rise up and they speak against me.

19 "All my associates abhor me,
And those I love have turned against me.

20 "My bone clings to my skin and my flesh,
And I have escaped *only* by the skin of my teeth.

21 "Pity me, pity me, O you my friends,
For the hand of God has struck me.

22 "Why do you persecute me as God *does*,
And are not satisfied with my flesh?

Job Says, "My Redeemer Lives"

23 ¶ "Oh that my words were written!
Oh that they were inscribed in a book!

24 "That with an iron stylus and lead
They were engraved in the rock forever!

25 "As for me, I know that my Redeemer lives,
And at the last He will take His stand on the earth.

26 "Even after my skin is destroyed,

Yet from my flesh I shall see God;
27 Whom I myself shall behold,
And whom my eyes will see and not
another.
My heart faints within me!
28 "If you say, 'How shall we persecute him?'
And 'What pretext for a case against him
can we find?'
29 *Then* be afraid of the sword for
yourselves,
For wrath *brings* the punishment of the
sword,
So that you may know there is
judgment.'"

Zophar Says, "The Triumph of the Wicked Is Short"

20 Then Zophar the Naamathite answered,
2 "Therefore my disquieting thoughts
make me respond,
Even because of my inward agitation.
3 "I listened to the reproof which
insults me,
And the spirit of my understanding
makes me answer.
4 "Do you know this from of old,
From the establishment of man on earth,
5 That the triumphing of the wicked is
short,
And the joy of the godless momentary?
6 "Though his loftiness reaches the heavens,
And his head touches the clouds,
7 He perishes forever like his refuse;
Those who have seen him will say,
'Where is he?'
8 "He flies away like a dream, and they
cannot find him;
Even like a vision of the night he is
chased away.
9 "The eye which saw him sees him no
longer,
And his place no longer beholds him.
10 "His sons favor the poor,
And his hands give back his wealth.
11 "His bones are full of his youthful vigor,
But it lies down with him in the dust.
12 ¶ "Though evil is sweet in his mouth
And he hides it under his tongue,
13 *Though* he desires it and will not let
it go,
But holds it in his mouth,
14 *Yet* his food in his stomach is changed
To the venom of cobras within him.
15 "He swallows riches,
But will vomit them up;
God will expel them from his belly.
16 "He sucks the poison of cobras;
The viper's tongue slays him.
17 "He does not look at the streams,
The rivers flowing with honey and curds.
18 "He returns what he has attained

And cannot swallow *it*;
As to the riches of his trading,
He cannot even enjoy *them*.
19 "For he has oppressed *and* forsaken the
poor;
He has seized a house which he has not
built.
20 ¶ "Because he knew no quiet within him,
He does not retain anything he desires.
21 "Nothing remains for him to devour,
Therefore his prosperity does not endure.
22 "In the fullness of his plenty he will be
cramped;
The hand of everyone who suffers will
come *against* him.
23 "When he fills his belly,
God will send His fierce anger on him
And will rain *it* on him while he is
eating.
24 "He may flee from the iron weapon,
But the bronze bow will pierce him.
25 "It is drawn forth and comes out of his
back,
Even the glittering point from his gall.
Terrors come upon him,
26 Complete darkness is held in reserve for
his treasures,
And unfanned fire will devour him;
It will consume the survivor in his tent.
27 "The heavens will reveal his iniquity,
And the earth will rise up against him.
28 "The increase of his house will depart;
His possessions will flow away in the day
of His anger.
29 "This is the wicked man's portion from
God,
Even the heritage decreed to him by
God."

Job Says God Will Deal with the Wicked

21 Then Job answered,
2 "Listen carefully to my speech,
And let this be your *way of* consolation.
3 "Bear with me that I may speak;
Then after I have spoken, you may
mock.
4 "As for me, is my complaint to man?
And why should I not be impatient?
5 "Look at me, and be astonished,
And put *your* hand over *your* mouth.
6 "Even when I remember, I am disturbed,
And horror takes hold of my flesh.
7 "Why do the wicked *still* live,
Continue on, also become very powerful?
8 "Their descendants are established with
them in their sight,
And their offspring before their eyes,
9 Their houses are safe from fear,
And the rod of God is not on them.
10 "His ox mates without fail;
His cow calves and does not abort.

11 "They send forth their little ones like the flock,
And their children skip about.
12 "They sing to the timbrel and harp

21:7–15 Wicked People Prosper

In most of his speeches Job accepted the general principle that evil people suffer punishment in this life. But in this speech he began to question that theory. He cited examples of wicked people who lived comfortable, successful lives. His meandering thoughts proved so convincing to him that he concluded his friends' advice was nonsense (verse 34).

And rejoice at the sound of the flute.
13 "They spend their days in prosperity,
And suddenly they go down to Sheol.
14 "They say to God, 'Depart from us!
We do not even desire the knowledge of Your ways.
15 'Who is the Almighty, that we should serve Him,
And what would we gain if we entreat Him?'
16 "Behold, their prosperity is not in their hand;
The counsel of the wicked is far from me.
17 ¶ "How often is the lamp of the wicked put out,
Or does their calamity fall on them?
Does God apportion destruction in His anger?
18 "Are they as straw before the wind,
And like chaff which the storm carries away?
19 "*You say*, 'God stores away a man's iniquity for his sons.'
Let God repay him so that he may know *it*.
20 "Let his own eyes see his decay,
And let him drink of the wrath of the Almighty.
21 "For what does he care for his household [a]after him,
When the number of his months is cut off?
22 "Can anyone teach God knowledge,
In that He judges those on high?
23 "One dies in his full strength,
Being wholly at ease and satisfied;
24 His sides are filled out with fat,
And the marrow of his bones is moist,
25 While another dies with a bitter soul,

Never even tasting *anything* good.
26 "Together they lie down in the dust,
And worms cover them.
27 ¶ "Behold, I know your thoughts,
And the plans by which you would wrong me.
28 "For you say, 'Where is the house of the nobleman,
And where is the tent, the dwelling places of the wicked?'
29 "Have you not asked wayfaring men,
And do you not recognize their witness?
30 "For the wicked is reserved for the day of calamity;
They will be led forth at the day of fury.
31 "Who will confront him with his actions,
And who will repay him for what he has done?
32 "While he is carried to the grave,
Men will keep watch over *his* tomb.
33 "The clods of the valley will gently cover him;
Moreover, all men will follow after him,
While countless ones *go* before him.
34 "How then will you vainly comfort me,
For your answers remain *full of* falsehood?"

Eliphaz Accuses and Exhorts Job

22 Then Eliphaz the Temanite responded,
2 "Can a vigorous man be of use to God,
Or a wise man be useful to himself?
3 "Is there any pleasure to the Almighty if you are righteous,
Or profit if you make your ways perfect?
4 "Is it because of your reverence that He reproves you,
That He enters into judgment against you?
5 "Is not your wickedness great,
And your iniquities without end?
6 "For you have taken pledges of your brothers without cause,
And stripped men naked.
7 "To the weary you have given no water to drink,

22:6 The Attacks Get Personal

Unable to convince Job through philosophizing, Eliphaz shifted to more personal attacks against Job's behavior. These arguments were perhaps the unkindest of all, and Job specifically refuted each one in his closing speech (chapters 29–31).

[a] I.e. after he dies

And from the hungry you have withheld
bread.
8 "But the earth belongs to the mighty man,
And the honorable man dwells in it.
9 "You have sent widows away empty,
And the strength of the orphans has been
crushed.
10 "Therefore snares surround you,
And sudden dread terrifies you,
11 Or darkness, so that you cannot see,
And an abundance of water covers you.
12 ¶ "Is not God *in* the height of heaven?
Look also at the distant stars, how high
they are!
13 "You say, 'What does God know?
Can He judge through the thick
darkness?
14 'Clouds are a hiding place for Him, so
that He cannot see;
And He walks on the vault of heaven.'
15 "Will you keep to the ancient path
Which wicked men have trod,
16 Who were snatched away before their
time,
Whose foundations were washed away by
a river?
17 "They said to God, 'Depart from us!'
And 'What can the Almighty do to
them?'
18 "Yet He filled their houses with good
things;
But the counsel of the wicked is far
from me.
19 "The righteous see and are glad,
And the innocent mock them,
20 *Saying*, 'Truly our adversaries are cut off,
And their abundance the fire has
consumed.'
21 ¶ "Yield now and be at peace with Him;
Thereby good will come to you.
22 "Please receive instruction from His
mouth
And establish His words in your heart.
23 "If you return to the Almighty, you will
be restored;
If you remove unrighteousness far from
your tent,
24 And place *your* gold in the dust,
And *the gold of* Ophir among the stones
of the brooks,
25 Then the Almighty will be your gold
And choice silver to you.
26 "For then you will delight in the Almighty
And lift up your face to God.
27 "You will pray to Him, and He will hear
you;
And you will pay your vows.
28 "You will also decree a thing, and it will
be established for you;
And light will shine on your ways.

29 "When you are cast down, you will speak
with confidence,
And the humble person He will save.
30 "He will deliver one who is not innocent,
And he will be delivered through the
cleanness of your hands."

Job Says He Longs for God

23 Then Job replied,
2 "Even today my complaint is
rebellion;
His hand is heavy despite my groaning.
3 "Oh that I knew where I might find Him,
That I might come to His seat!
4 "I would present *my* case before Him
And fill my mouth with arguments.
5 "I would learn the words *which* He would
answer,
And perceive what He would say to me.
6 "Would He contend with me by the
greatness of *His* power?
No, surely He would pay attention
to me.
7 "There the upright would reason with
Him;
And I would be delivered forever from
my Judge.
8 ¶ "Behold, I go forward but He is not
there,
And backward, but I cannot perceive
Him;
9 When He acts on the left, I cannot
behold *Him*;
He turns on the right, I cannot see Him.
10 "But He knows the way I take;
When He has tried me, I shall come
forth as gold.
11 "My foot has held fast to His path;
I have kept His way and not turned
aside.
12 "I have not departed from the command
of His lips;
I have treasured the words of His mouth
more than my necessary food.
13 "But He is unique and who can turn
Him?
And *what* His soul desires, that He does.

23:13 Unstable Ground

*Job's friends hammered away at consistent
themes whereas Job, like most people in pain,
found himself shifting back and forth, unsure
what to believe. In the first paragraph of
chapter 23, he is ready to take God on; in the
second, he wonders if he'll ever find God to
state his case; in the third, he trembles to think
what might happen if he actually does locate
God!*

14 "For He performs what is appointed
    for me,
And many such *decrees* are with Him.
15 "Therefore, I would be dismayed at His
    presence;
When I consider, I am terrified of Him.
16 "*It is* God *who* has made my heart faint,
And the Almighty *who* has dismayed me,
17 But I am not silenced by the darkness,
Nor deep gloom *which* covers me.

Job Says God Seems to Ignore Wrongs

24 "Why are times not stored up by the
    Almighty,
And why do those who know Him not
    see His days?
2 "Some remove the landmarks;
They seize and devour flocks.
3 "They drive away the donkeys of the
    orphans;
They take the widow's ox for a pledge.
4 "They push the needy aside from the
    road;
The poor of the land are made to hide
    themselves altogether.
5 "Behold, as wild donkeys in the wilderness
They go forth seeking food in their
    activity,
As bread for *their* children in the desert.
6 "They harvest their fodder in the field
And glean the vineyard of the wicked.
7 "They spend the night naked, without
    clothing,
And have no covering against the cold.
8 "They are wet with the mountain rains
And hug the rock for want of a shelter.
9 "Others snatch the orphan from the
    breast,
And against the poor they take a pledge.
10 "They cause *the poor* to go about naked
    without clothing,
And they take away the sheaves from the
    hungry.
11 "Within the walls they produce oil;
They tread wine presses but thirst.
12 "From the city men groan,
And the souls of the wounded cry out;
Yet God does not pay attention to folly.

13 ¶ "Others have been with those who
    rebel against the light;
They do not want to know its ways
Nor abide in its paths.
14 "The murderer arises at dawn;
He kills the poor and the needy,
And at night he is as a thief.
15 "The eye of the adulterer waits for the
    twilight,
Saying, 'No eye will see me.'
And he disguises his face.
16 "In the dark they dig into houses,
They shut themselves up by day;

They do not know the light.
17 "For the morning is the same to him as
    thick darkness,
For he is familiar with the terrors of
    thick darkness.

18 ¶ "They are insignificant on the surface
    of the water;
Their portion is cursed on the earth.
They do not turn toward the vineyards.
19 "Drought and heat consume the snow
    waters,
So does Sheol *those who* have sinned.
20 "A mother will forget him;
The worm feeds sweetly till he is no
    longer remembered.
And wickedness will be broken like a
    tree.
21 "He wrongs the barren woman
And does no good for the widow.
22 "But He drags off the valiant by His
    power;
He rises, but no one has assurance of
    life.
23 "He provides them with security, and they
    are supported;
And His eyes are on their ways.
24 "They are exalted a little while, then they
    are gone;
Moreover, they are brought low and like
    everything gathered up;
Even like the heads of grain they are cut
    off.
25 "Now if it is not so, who can prove me a
    liar,
And make my speech worthless?"

Bildad Says Man Is Inferior

25 Then Bildad the Shuhite answered,
2 "Dominion and awe belong to Him

25:1–6 Where Is God?

In the speech recorded in chapters 23–24, Job movingly described the feeling of God's absence at his time of greatest need. God must also seem absent to the poor, the fatherless, and all those suffering without relief, he said. Bildad replied with the shortest speech in the book (chapter 25). He questioned whether any person ("that maggot . . . that worm") had the right to challenge God so boldly.

Who establishes peace in His heights.
3 "Is there any number to His troops?
And upon whom does His light not rise?
4 "How then can a man be just with God?
Or how can he be clean who is born of
    woman?
5 "If even the moon has no brightness

And the stars are not pure in His sight,
6 How much less man, *that* maggot,
And the son of man, *that* worm!"

Job Rebukes Bildad

26 Then Job responded,
2 "What a help you are to the weak!
How you have saved the arm without
strength!
3 "What counsel you have given to *one*
without wisdom!
What helpful insight you have
abundantly provided!
4 "To whom have you uttered words?
And whose spirit was expressed
through you?

The Greatness of God

5 ¶ "The departed spirits tremble
Under the waters and their inhabitants.
6 "Naked is Sheol before Him,
And *a*Abaddon has no covering.

26:6–14 A Faint Whisper of God

*The book of Job contains some of the best
nature poetry ever written; it frequently cites
nature as one of the proofs of God's existence.
Job himself never denied God's power. All the
wonders of nature, he said, are "the fringes of
His ways," a faint whisper of God. His
complaint was not about power, but about
justice. How could a God so powerful treat him
so unfairly?*

7 "He stretches out the north over empty
space
And hangs the earth on nothing.
8 "He wraps up the waters in His clouds,
And the cloud does not burst under
them.
9 "He obscures the face of the full moon
And spreads His cloud over it.
10 "He has inscribed a circle on the surface
of the waters
At the boundary of light and darkness.
11 "The pillars of heaven tremble
And are amazed at His rebuke.
12 "He quieted the sea with His power,
And by His understanding He shattered
Rahab.
13 "By His breath the heavens are cleared;
His hand has pierced the fleeing serpent.
14 "Behold, these are the fringes of His ways;
And how faint a word we hear of Him!
But His mighty thunder, who can
understand?"

a I.e. place of destruction

Job Affirms His Righteousness

27 Then Job continued his discourse and said,
2 "As God lives, who has taken away
my right,
And the Almighty, who has embittered
my soul,
3 For as long as life is in me,
And the breath of God is in my nostrils,
4 My lips certainly will not speak unjustly,
Nor will my tongue mutter deceit.
5 "Far be it from me that I should declare
you right;
Till I die I will not put away my integrity
from me.
6 "I hold fast my righteousness and will not
let it go.
My heart does not reproach any of my
days.

The State of the Godless

7 ¶ "May my enemy be as the wicked
And my opponent as the unjust.
8 "For what is the hope of the godless when
he is cut off,
When God requires his life?
9 "Will God hear his cry
When distress comes upon him?
10 "Will he take delight in the Almighty?
Will he call on God at all times?
11 "I will instruct you in the power of God;
What is with the Almighty I will not
conceal.
12 "Behold, all of you have seen *it*;
Why then do you act foolishly?

13 ¶ "This is the portion of a wicked man
from God,
And the inheritance *which* tyrants receive
from the Almighty.
14 "Though his sons are many, they are
destined for the sword;
And his descendants will not be satisfied
with bread.
15 "His survivors will be buried because of
the plague,
And their widows will not be able to
weep.
16 "Though he piles up silver like dust
And prepares garments as *plentiful as* the
clay,
17 He may prepare *it*, but the just will
wear *it*
And the innocent will divide the silver.
18 "He has built his house like the spider's
web,
Or as a hut *which* the watchman has
made.
19 "He lies down rich, but never again;
He opens his eyes, and it is no longer.
20 "Terrors overtake him like a flood;

A tempest steals him away in the night.

21 "The east wind carries him away, and he
is gone,
For it whirls him away from his place.

22 "For it will hurl at him without sparing;
He will surely try to flee from its power.

23 "*Men* will clap their hands at him
And will hiss him from his place.

Job Tells of Earth's Treasures

28 "Surely there is a *a*mine for silver
And a place where they refine gold.

28:1 A Poem on Wisdom

*In the midst of one of his most beautiful
speeches, Job included a self-contained poem
on wisdom. It uses the analogy of mining
precious metals to make the point that wisdom
cannot be found by any amount of searching
(verses 1–19). God alone knows where it
dwells. In the rest of the poem, Job admitted
some things were beyond his understanding,
then lapsed into a reminiscence of what life
was like before his time of trials.*

2 "Iron is taken from the dust,
And copper is smelted from rock.

3 "*Man* puts an end to darkness,
And to the farthest limit he searches out
The rock in gloom and deep shadow.

4 "He sinks a shaft far from habitation,
Forgotten by the foot;
They hang and swing to and fro far from
men.

5 "The earth, from it comes food,
And underneath it is turned up as fire.

6 "Its rocks are the source of sapphires,
And its dust *contains* gold.

7 "The path no bird of prey knows,
Nor has the falcon's eye caught sight
of it.

8 "The proud beasts have not trodden it,
Nor has the *fierce* lion passed over it.

9 "He puts his hand on the flint;
He overturns the mountains at the base.

10 "He hews out channels through the rocks,
And his eye sees anything precious.

11 "He dams up the streams from flowing,
And what is hidden he brings out to the
light.

The Search for Wisdom Is Harder

12 ¶ "But where can wisdom be found?
And where is the place of understanding?

13 "Man does not know its value,
Nor is it found in the land of the living.

14 "The deep says, 'It is not in me';

And the sea says, 'It is not with me.'

15 "Pure gold cannot be given in exchange
for it,
Nor can silver be weighed as its price.

16 "It cannot be valued in the gold of Ophir,
In precious onyx, or sapphire.

17 "Gold or glass cannot equal it,
Nor can it be exchanged for articles of
fine gold.

18 "Coral and crystal are not to be
mentioned;
And the acquisition of wisdom is above
that of pearls.

19 "The topaz of Ethiopia cannot equal it,
Nor can it be valued in pure gold.

20 "Where then does wisdom come from?
And where is the place of understanding?

21 "Thus it is hidden from the eyes of all
living
And concealed from the birds of the sky.

22 "*b*Abaddon and Death say,
'With our ears we have heard a report
of it.'

23 ¶ "God understands its way,
And He knows its place.

24 "For He looks to the ends of the earth
And sees everything under the heavens.

25 "When He imparted weight to the wind
And meted out the waters by measure,

26 When He set a limit for the rain
And a course for the thunderbolt,

27 Then He saw it and declared it;
He established it and also searched it out.

28 "And to man He said, 'Behold, the fear of
the Lord, that is wisdom;
And to depart from evil is
understanding.' "

Job's Past Was Glorious

29 And Job again took up his discourse and
said,

2 "Oh that I were as in months gone by,
As in the days when God watched
over me;

3 When His lamp shone over my head,
And by His light I walked through
darkness;

4 As I was in *c*the prime of my days,
When the friendship of God *was* over
my tent;

5 When the Almighty was yet with me,
And my children were around me;

6 When my steps were bathed in butter,
And the rock poured out for me streams
of oil!

7 "When I went out to the gate of the city,
When I took my seat in the square,

8 The young men saw me and hid
themselves,

---

a Or *source*   *b* I.e. Destruction   *c* Lit *the days of my autumn*

And the old men arose *and* stood.
9 "The princes stopped talking
And put *their* hands on their mouths;
10 The voice of the nobles was hushed,
And their tongue stuck to their palate.
11 "For when the ear heard, it called me
blessed,
And when the eye saw, it gave witness
of me,

29:11 The Good Old Days

Tenderly, Job reminisces about the "months gone by" (verse 2), before his trials began. Job could think of no reason why he might "deserve" such treatment—the point of the book of Job exactly. His recollections of life in those days refute his friends' accusations against him. He had shown concern for the poor and oppressed—a fact that must have increased his puzzlement over the unfair treatment he was receiving.

12 Because I delivered the poor who cried
for help,
And the orphan who had no helper.
13 "The blessing of the one ready to perish
came upon me,
And I made the widow's heart sing for
joy.
14 "I put on righteousness, and it
clothed me;
My justice was like a robe and a turban.
15 "I was eyes to the blind
And feet to the lame.
16 "I was a father to the needy,
And I investigated the case which I did
not know.
17 "I broke the jaws of the wicked
And snatched the prey from his teeth.
18 "Then I thought, 'I shall die in my nest,
And I shall multiply *my* days as the sand.
19 'My root is spread out to the waters,
And dew lies all night on my branch.
20 'My glory is *ever* new with me,
And my bow is renewed in my hand.'
21 ¶ "To me they listened and waited,
And kept silent for my counsel.
22 "After my words they did not speak again,
And my speech dropped on them.
23 "They waited for me as for the rain,
And opened their mouth as for the
spring rain.
24 "I smiled on them when they did not
believe,
And the light of my face they did not
cast down.
25 "I chose a way for them and sat as chief,

And dwelt as a king among the troops,
As one who comforted the mourners.

Job's Present State Is Humiliating

30 "But now those younger than I mock me,
Whose fathers I disdained to put with
the dogs of my flock.
2 "Indeed, what *good was* the strength of
their hands to me?
Vigor had perished from them.
3 "From want and famine they are gaunt
Who gnaw the dry ground by night in
waste and desolation,
4 Who pluck ᵃmallow by the bushes,
And whose food is the root of the broom
shrub.
5 "They are driven from the community;
They shout against them as *against* a
thief,
6 So that they dwell in dreadful valleys,
In holes of the earth and of the rocks.
7 "Among the bushes they cry out;
Under the nettles they are gathered
together.
8 "Fools, even those without a name,
They were scourged from the land.
9 ¶ "And now I have become their taunt,
I have even become a byword to them.
10 "They abhor me *and* stand aloof from me,
And they do not refrain from spitting at
my face.
11 "Because He has loosed His bowstring
and afflicted me,
They have cast off the bridle before me.
12 "On the right hand their brood arises;
They thrust aside my feet and build up
against me their ways of destruction.
13 "They break up my path,
They profit from my destruction;
No one restrains them.
14 "As *through* a wide breach they come,
Amid the tempest they roll on.
15 "Terrors are turned against me;
They pursue my honor as the wind,
And my prosperity has passed away like
a cloud.
16 ¶ "And now my soul is poured out
within me;
Days of affliction have seized me.
17 "At night it pierces my bones within me,
And my gnawing *pains* take no rest.
18 "By a great force my garment is distorted;
It binds me about as the collar of my
coat.
19 "He has cast me into the mire,
And I have become like dust and ashes.
20 "I cry out to You for help, but You do
not answer me;

ᵃ I.e. plant of the salt marshes

I stand up, and You turn Your attention
    against me.
21 "You have become cruel to me;
    With the might of Your hand You
        persecute me.
22 "You lift me up to the wind *and* cause me
        to ride;
    And You dissolve me in a storm.
23 "For I know that You will bring me to
        death
    And to the house of meeting for all
        living.

24 ¶ "Yet does not one in a heap of ruins
        stretch out *his* hand,
    Or in his disaster therefore cry out for
        help?
25 "Have I not wept for the one whose life is
        hard?
    Was not my soul grieved for the needy?
26 "When I expected good, then evil came;
    When I waited for light, then darkness
        came.
27 "I am seething within and cannot relax;
    Days of affliction confront me.
28 "I go about mourning without comfort;

I stand up in the assembly *and* cry out
    for help.
29 "I have become a brother to jackals
    And a companion of ostriches.
30 "My skin turns black on me,
    And my bones burn with fever.
31 "Therefore my harp is turned to
        mourning,
    And my flute to the sound of those who
        weep.

Job Asserts His Integrity

31 "I have made a covenant with my eyes;
    How then could I gaze at a virgin?
2 "And what is the portion of God from above
    Or the heritage of the Almighty from on
        high?
3 "Is it not calamity to the unjust
    And disaster to those who work iniquity?
4 "Does He not see my ways
    And number all my steps?

5 ¶ "If I have walked with falsehood,
    And my foot has hastened after deceit,
6 Let Him weigh me with accurate scales,
    And let God know my integrity.

A Silent Friend Decides to Speak Up
Elihu, out of nowhere, proposes new ideas about suffering

> "Indeed, there was no one who refuted Job, not one of you who answered his words." 32:12

UP TO THIS POINT IN Job, the action has revolved around Job and his three friends. The debate among them, growing ever more heated, finally breaks off. They have reached a standoff. Job will not admit to any sin deserving of terrible punishment, and his three friends will not back down from their ideas about suffering.

Suddenly, a new voice is heard. Elihu, a young man, has been listening in silence all this time. He can restrain himself no longer. He flares up, first at Job for being so self-righteous and then at the three friends for not coming up with an answer to Job's questions. He refutes all four of them, turning their own words against them.

Is Elihu Right?

Elihu is shocked at Job's vigorous self-defense. Surely God cannot be unjust, he insists. Submit to the pain, even if you don't understand it. Don't blame God; praise him. God has shown too much of his wisdom and perfection, especially in nature, for anyone to doubt him.

Elihu offers a new explanation for Job's pain. Perhaps, he suggests, God gave suffering to Job not as punishment but as a purifying influence. God can use suffering to improve a person, if it is received in the right spirit.

Where did Elihu come from? Who is he? Are his theories right? Mystery surrounds the man. His speeches stand alone, and no one responds to them. As a result, the book of Job gives no clue on whether Elihu expressed a worthy point of view.

Some readers believe Elihu forms a bridge between the flawed theories of Job's three friends and God's own speech. Perhaps his speeches prepare the way for God's. Others see him as repeating the same fine-sounding, but not-quite-true, advice of Job's three friends.

When God does make an entrance, he dismisses Job's friends and has some mild criticism for Job. But he ignores Elihu entirely. Elihu remains a mysterious figure.

Life Questions: Do Elihu's arguments sound familiar? What do you think of friends who have similar thoughts about others who suffer?

7 "If my step has turned from the way,
  Or my heart followed my eyes,
  Or if any spot has stuck to my hands,
8 Let me sow and another eat,
  And let my crops be uprooted.

31:1 Binding Oaths

This chapter, Job's final line of defense, is
written in a form that had legal significance to
his hearers. Job was solemnly swearing his
innocence in response to a whole series of
accusations. He called down curses on himself
if he could be proved wrong. The oaths were
somewhat like our modern custom of swearing
on the Bible "to tell the truth, the whole truth
and nothing but the truth." Job's oaths
impressed his three friends and effectively
ended the debate. Then a new character, Elihu,
joined in.

9 ¶ "If my heart has been enticed by a
  woman,
  Or I have lurked at my neighbor's
  doorway,
10 May my wife grind for another,
  And let others kneel down over her.
11 "For that would be a lustful crime;
  Moreover, it would be an iniquity
  punishable by judges.
12 "For it would be fire that consumes to
  Abaddon,
  And would uproot all my increase.
13 ¶ "If I have despised the claim of my
  male or female slaves
  When they filed a complaint against me,
14 What then could I do when God arises?
  And when He calls me to account, what
  will I answer Him?
15 "Did not He who made me in the womb
  make him,
  And the same one fashion us in the
  womb?
16 ¶ "If I have kept the poor from their
  desire,
  Or have caused the eyes of the widow to
  fail,
17 Or have eaten my morsel alone,
  And the orphan has not shared it—
18 (But from my youth he grew up with me
  as with a father,
  And from infancy I guided her),
19 If I have seen anyone perish for lack of
  clothing,
  Or that the needy had no covering,
20 If his loins have not thanked me,
  And if he has not been warmed with the
  fleece of my sheep,

21 If I have lifted up my hand against the
  orphan,
  Because I saw I had support in the gate,
22 Let my shoulder fall from the socket,

31:16 A Habit of Trust

This chapter gives insights into Job's life of
spiritual discipline. He had developed the habit
of obeying God. Now, with all the props
knocked out, he still turned to God for strength,
even though God seemed utterly absent. It was
as if he had a resource bank of trust in God:
The trust he had accumulated in more
comfortable times helped him survive his time
of hardship.

  And my arm be broken off at the elbow.
23 "For calamity from God is a terror to me,
  And because of His majesty I can do
  nothing.
24 ¶ "If I have put my confidence in gold,
  And called fine gold my trust,
25 If I have gloated because my wealth was
  great,
  And because my hand had secured so
  much;
26 If I have looked at the sun when it shone
  Or the moon going in splendor,
27 And my heart became secretly enticed,
  And my hand threw a kiss from my
  mouth,
28 That too would have been an iniquity
  calling for judgment,
  For I would have denied God above.
29 ¶ "Have I rejoiced at the extinction of
  my enemy,
  Or exulted when evil befell him?
30 "No, I have not allowed my mouth to sin
  By asking for his life in a curse.
31 "Have the men of my tent not said,
  'Who can find one who has not been
  satisfied with his meat'?
32 "The alien has not lodged outside,
  For I have opened my doors to the
  traveler.
33 "Have I covered my transgressions like
  Adam,
  By hiding my iniquity in my bosom,
34 Because I feared the great multitude,
  And the contempt of families
  terrified me,
  And kept silent and did not go out of
  doors?
35 "Oh that I had one to hear me!
  Behold, here is my signature;
  Let the Almighty answer me!
  And the indictment which my adversary
  has written,

36 Surely I would carry it on my shoulder,
  I would bind it to myself like a crown.
37 "I would declare to Him the number of
    my steps;
  Like a prince I would approach Him.

38 ¶ "If my land cries out against me,
  And its furrows weep together;
39 If I have eaten its fruit without money,
  Or have caused its owners to lose their
    lives,
40 Let briars grow instead of wheat,
  And stinkweed instead of barley."
The words of Job are ended.

Elihu in Anger Rebukes Job

32 Then these three men ceased answering
Job, because he was righteous in his own
eyes.
2 But the anger of Elihu the son of Barachel
the Buzite, of the family of Ram burned; against
Job his anger burned because he justified himself
before God.
3 And his anger burned against his three
friends because they had found no answer, and yet
had condemned Job.
4 Now Elihu had waited to speak to Job because they were years older than he.
5 And when Elihu saw that there was no answer in the mouth of the three men his anger
burned.

6 ¶ So Elihu the son of Barachel the Buzite
spoke out and said,
  "I am young in years and you are old;
  Therefore I was shy and afraid to tell you
    what I think.
7 "I thought age should speak,
  And increased years should teach
    wisdom.
8 "But it is a spirit in man,
  And the breath of the Almighty gives
    them understanding.
9 "The abundant *in years* may not be wise,
  Nor may elders understand justice.
10 "So I say, 'Listen to me,
  I too will tell what I think.'

11 ¶ "Behold, I waited for your words,
  I listened to your reasonings,
  While you pondered what to say.
12 "I even paid close attention to you;
  Indeed, there was no one who
    refuted Job,
  Not one of you who answered his words.
13 "Do not say,
  'We have found wisdom;
  God will rout him, not man.'
14 "For he has not arranged *his* words
    against me,
  Nor will I reply to him with your
    arguments.

15 ¶ "They are dismayed, they no longer
    answer;
  Words have failed them.
16 "Shall I wait, because they do not speak,
  Because they stop *and* no longer answer?
17 "I too will answer my share,
  I also will tell my opinion.
18 "For I am full of words;
  The spirit within me constrains me.
19 "Behold, my belly is like unvented wine,
  Like new wineskins it is about to burst.
20 "Let me speak that I may get relief;
  Let me open my lips and answer.
21 "Let me now be partial to no one,
  Nor flatter *any* man.
22 "For I do not know how to flatter,
  Else my Maker would soon take me
    away.

Elihu Claims to Speak for God

33 "However now, Job, please hear my
    speech,
  And listen to all my words.
2 "Behold now, I open my mouth,
  My tongue in my mouth speaks.
3 "My words are *from* the uprightness of
    my heart,
  And my lips speak knowledge sincerely.
4 "The Spirit of God has made me,
  And the breath of the Almighty gives me
    life.
5 "Refute me if you can;
  Array yourselves before me, take your
    stand.
6 "Behold, I belong to God like you;
  I too have been formed out of the clay.
7 "Behold, no fear of me should terrify you,
  Nor should my pressure weigh heavily
    on you.

8 ¶ "Surely you have spoken in my
    hearing,
  And I have heard the sound of *your*
    words:
9 'I am pure, without transgression;
  I am innocent and there is no guilt
    in me.
10 'Behold, He invents pretexts against me;
  He counts me as His enemy.
11 'He puts my feet in the stocks;
  He watches all my paths.'
12 "Behold, let me tell you, you are not right
    in this,
  For God is greater than man.

13 ¶ "Why do you complain against Him
  That He does not give an account of all
    His doings?
14 "Indeed God speaks once,
  Or twice, *yet* no one notices it.
15 "In a dream, a vision of the night,

When sound sleep falls on men,
While they slumber in their beds,
16 Then He opens the ears of men,
And seals their instruction,
17 That He may turn man aside *from his*
conduct,
And keep man from pride;
18 He keeps back his soul from the pit,
And his life from passing over into
Sheol.

19 ¶ "Man is also chastened with pain on
his bed,
And with unceasing complaint in his
bones;

33:19 Kinder, Gentler Friend

*Evidently, Elihu had sat in silence throughout
the discussions to this point (in deference to the
other speakers' age, as he explains). That fact
alone shows his calmer nature: he refused to
jump into very heated arguments. Although
Elihu introduces some new ideas, he also
follows the general line of reasoning—"You're
being punished for your sins, Job" (see verses
17–22)—that God corrects in the end.*

20 So that his life loathes bread,
And his soul favorite food.
21 "His flesh wastes away from sight,
And his bones which were not seen stick
out.
22 "Then his soul draws near to the pit,
And his life to those who bring death.

23 ¶ "If there is an angel *as* mediator for
him,
One out of a thousand,
To remind a man what is right for him,
24 Then let him be gracious to him, and
say,
'Deliver him from going down to the pit,
I have found a ransom';
25 Let his flesh become fresher than in
youth,
Let him return to the days of his
youthful vigor;
26 Then he will pray to God, and He will
accept him,
That he may see His face with joy,
And He may restore His righteousness to
man.
27 "He will sing to men and say,
'I have sinned and perverted what is
right,
And it is not proper for me.
28 'He has redeemed my soul from going to
the pit,
And my life shall see the light.'

29 ¶ "Behold, God does all these oftentimes
with men,
30 To bring back his soul from the pit,
That he may be enlightened with the
light of life.

33:30 Pain as a Warning

*Elihu did not defend Job as innocent. But his
arguments shifted the emphasis of suffering
from punishment to warning. Perhaps, he
suggested, God allows a man to suffer in order
"to bring back his soul from the pit." Primarily,
however, Elihu defended God's actions. "Surely,
God will not act wickedly . . . the Almighty will
not pervert justice" (34:12).*

31 "Pay attention, O Job, listen to me;
Keep silent, and let me speak.
32 "*Then* if you have anything to say,
answer me;
Speak, for I desire to justify you.
33 "If not, listen to me;
Keep silent, and I will teach you
wisdom."

Elihu Vindicates God's Justice

34 Then Elihu continued and said,
2 "Hear my words, you wise men,
And listen to me, you who know.
3 "For the ear tests words
As the palate tastes food.
4 "Let us choose for ourselves what is right;
Let us know among ourselves what is
good.
5 "For Job has said, 'I am righteous,
But God has taken away my right;
6 Should I lie concerning my right?
My wound is incurable, *though I am*
without transgression.'
7 "What man is like Job,
Who drinks up derision like water,
8 Who goes in company with the workers
of iniquity,
And walks with wicked men?
9 "For he has said, 'It profits a man nothing
When he is pleased with God.'

10 ¶ "Therefore, listen to me, you men of
understanding.
Far be it from God to do wickedness,
And from the Almighty to do wrong.
11 "For He pays a man according to his
work,
And makes him find it according to his
way.
12 "Surely, God will not act wickedly,
And the Almighty will not pervert justice.
13 "Who gave Him authority over the earth?

And who has laid *on Him* the whole
    world?
14 "If He should determine to do so,
    If He should gather to Himself His spirit
      and His breath,
15 All flesh would perish together,
    And man would return to dust.

16 ¶ "But if *you have* understanding, hear
    this;
    Listen to the sound of my words.
17 "Shall one who hates justice rule?
    And will you condemn the righteous
      mighty One,
18 Who says to a king, 'Worthless one,'
    To nobles, 'Wicked ones';
19 Who shows no partiality to princes
    Nor regards the rich above the poor,
    For they all are the work of His hands?
20 "In a moment they die, and at midnight
    People are shaken and pass away,
    And the mighty are taken away without a
      hand.

21 ¶ "For His eyes are upon the ways of a
    man,
    And He sees all his steps.
22 "There is no darkness or deep shadow
    Where the workers of iniquity may hide
      themselves.
23 "For He does not *need to* consider a man
    further,
    That he should go before God in
      judgment.
24 "He breaks in pieces mighty men without
    inquiry,
    And sets others in their place.
25 "Therefore He knows their works,
    And He overthrows *them* in the night,
    And they are crushed.
26 "He strikes them like the wicked
    In a public place,
27 Because they turned aside from following
    Him,
    And had no regard for any of His ways;
28 So that they caused the cry of the poor
    to come to Him,
    And that He might hear the cry of the
      afflicted—
29 When He keeps quiet, who then can
    condemn?
    And when He hides His face, who then
      can behold Him,
    That is, in regard to both nation
      and man?—
30 So that godless men would not rule
    Nor be snares of the people.

31 ¶ "For has anyone said to God,
    'I have borne *chastisement;*
    I will not offend *anymore;*
32 Teach me what I do not see;
    If I have done iniquity,

I will not do it again'?
33 "Shall He recompense on your terms,
    because you have rejected *it?*
    For you must choose, and not I;
    Therefore declare what you know.
34 "Men of understanding will say to me,
    And a wise man who hears me,
35 'Job speaks without knowledge,
    And his words are without wisdom.
36 'Job ought to be tried to the limit,
    Because he answers like wicked men.
37 'For he adds rebellion to his sin;
    He claps his hands among us,
    And multiplies his words against God.'"

Elihu Sharply Reproves Job

35 Then Elihu continued and said,
2 "Do you think this is according to
    justice?
    Do you say, 'My righteousness is more
      than God's'?
3 "For you say, 'What advantage will it be
    to You?
    What profit will I have, more than if I
      had sinned?'
4 "I will answer you,
    And your friends with you.
5 "Look at the heavens and see;
    And behold the clouds—they are higher
      than you.
6 "If you have sinned, what do you
    accomplish against Him?
    And if your transgressions are many,
      what do you do to Him?
7 "If you are righteous, what do you give to
    Him,
    Or what does He receive from your
      hand?
8 "Your wickedness is for a man like
    yourself,
    And your righteousness is for a son
      of man.

9 ¶ "Because of the multitude of
    oppressions they cry out;
    They cry for help because of the arm of
      the mighty.
10 "But no one says, 'Where is God my
    Maker,
    Who gives songs in the night,
11 Who teaches us more than the beasts of
    the earth
    And makes us wiser than the birds of the
      heavens?'
12 "There they cry out, but He does not
    answer
    Because of the pride of evil men.
13 "Surely God will not listen to an
    empty *cry,*
    Nor will the Almighty regard it.
14 "How much less when you say you do not
    behold Him,

The case is before Him, and you must
wait for Him!

15 "And now, because He has not visited in
His anger,

Nor has He acknowledged transgression
well,

16 So Job opens his mouth emptily;
He multiplies words without knowledge."

Elihu Speaks of God's Dealings with Men

36 Then Elihu continued and said,
2 "Wait for me a little, and I will
show you
That there is yet more to be said in
God's behalf.

3 "I will fetch my knowledge from afar,
And I will ascribe righteousness to my
Maker.

4 "For truly my words are not false;
One who is perfect in knowledge is with
you.

5 "Behold, God is mighty but does not
despise *any*;
He is mighty in strength of
understanding.

6 "He does not keep the wicked alive,
But gives justice to the afflicted.

7 "He does not withdraw His eyes from the
righteous;
But with kings on the throne
He has seated them forever, and they are
exalted.

8 "And if they are bound in fetters,
And are caught in the cords of affliction,

9 Then He declares to them their work
And their transgressions, that they have
magnified themselves.

10 "He opens their ear to instruction,
And commands that they return from
evil.

11 "If they hear and serve *Him*,
They will end their days in prosperity
And their years in pleasures.

12 "But if they do not hear, they shall perish
by the sword
And they will die without knowledge.

13 "But the godless in heart lay up anger;
They do not cry for help when He binds
them.

14 "They die in youth,
And their life *perishes* among the cult
prostitutes.

15 "He delivers the afflicted in their affliction,
And opens their ear in *time of*
oppression.

16 "Then indeed, He enticed you from the
mouth of distress,
Instead of it, a broad place with no
constraint;
And that which was set on your table
was full of fatness.

17 ¶ "But you were full of judgment on the
wicked;
Judgment and justice take hold *of you*.

18 "*Beware* that wrath does not entice you to
scoffing;
And do not let the greatness of the
ransom turn you aside.

19 "Will your riches keep you from distress,
Or all the forces of *your* strength?

20 "Do not long for the night,
When people vanish in their place.

21 "Be careful, do not turn to evil,
For you have preferred this to affliction.

22 "Behold, God is exalted in His power;
Who is a teacher like Him?

23 "Who has appointed Him His way,
And who has said, 'You have done
wrong'?

24 ¶ "Remember that you should exalt His
work,
Of which men have sung.

25 "All men have seen it;
Man beholds from afar.

26 "Behold, God is exalted, and we do not
know *Him;*
The number of His years is unsearchable.

27 "For He draws up the drops of water,
They distill rain from the mist,

28 Which the clouds pour down,
They drip upon man abundantly.

29 "Can anyone understand the spreading of
the clouds,
The thundering of His pavilion?

30 "Behold, He spreads His lightning about
Him,
And He covers the depths of the sea.

31 "For by these He judges peoples;
He gives food in abundance.

32 "He covers *His* hands with the lightning,
And commands it to strike the mark.

33 "Its noise declares His presence;
The cattle also, concerning what is
coming up.

Elihu Says God Is Back of the Storm

37 "At this also my heart trembles,
And leaps from its place.

2 "Listen closely to the thunder of His
voice,
And the rumbling that goes out from His
mouth.

3 "Under the whole heaven He lets it loose,
And His lightning to the ends of the
earth.

4 "After it, a voice roars;
He thunders with His majestic voice,
And He does not restrain the lightnings
when His voice is heard.

5 "God thunders with His voice wondrously,
Doing great things which we cannot
comprehend.

6 "For to the snow He says, 'Fall on the
earth,'
And to the downpour and the rain, 'Be
strong.'

7 "He seals the hand of every man,
That all men may know His work.

37:7 The Message of a Blizzard

*Anyone who has lived in a northern city can
identify with Elihu's comment about a
snowstorm. A blizzard "seals the hand of every
man," as schools, businesses, and buses shut
down. It's a reminder, says Elihu, of God's
undeniable power.*

8 "Then the beast goes into its lair
And remains in its den.

9 "Out of the south comes the storm,
And out of the north the cold.

10 "From the breath of God ice is made,
And the expanse of the waters is frozen.

11 "Also with moisture He loads the thick
cloud;
He disperses the cloud of His lightning.

12 "It changes direction, turning around by
His guidance,
That it may do whatever He
commands it
On the face of the inhabited earth.

13 "Whether for correction, or for His world,
Or for lovingkindness, He causes it to
happen.

14 ¶ "Listen to this, O Job,
Stand and consider the wonders of God.

15 "Do you know how God establishes them,
And makes the lightning of His cloud to
shine?

16 "Do you know about the layers of the
thick clouds,
The wonders of one perfect in
knowledge,

17 You whose garments are hot,
When the land is still because of the
south wind?

18 "Can you, with Him, spread out the skies,
Strong as a molten mirror?

19 "Teach us what we shall say to Him;
We cannot arrange *our case* because of
darkness.

20 "Shall it be told Him that I would speak?
Or should a man say that he would be
swallowed up?

21 ¶ "Now men do not see the light which
is bright in the skies;
But the wind has passed and cleared
them.

22 "Out of the north comes golden *splendor*;
Around God is awesome majesty.

23 "The Almighty—we cannot find Him;
He is exalted in power
And He will not do violence to justice
and abundant righteousness.

24 "Therefore men fear Him;
He does not regard any who are wise of
heart."

God Speaks Now to Job

38 Then the LORD answered Job out of the
whirlwind and said,

2 "Who is this that darkens counsel
By words without knowledge?

3 "Now gird up your loins like a man,
And I will ask you, and you instruct Me!

4 "Where were you when I laid the
foundation of the earth?
Tell *Me*, if you have understanding,

5 Who set its measurements? Since you
know.
Or who stretched the line on it?

6 "On what were its bases sunk?
Or who laid its cornerstone,

7 When the morning stars sang together
And all the sons of God shouted for joy?

8 ¶ "Or *who* enclosed the sea with doors
When, bursting forth, it went out from
the womb;

9 When I made a cloud its garment
And thick darkness its swaddling band,

10 And I placed boundaries on it
And set a bolt and doors,

11 And I said, 'Thus far you shall come, but
no farther;
And here shall your proud waves stop'?

God's Mighty Power

12 ¶ "Have you ever in your life
commanded the morning,
And caused the dawn to know its place,

13 That it might take hold of the ends of
the earth,
And the wicked be shaken out of it?

14 "It is changed like clay *under* the seal;
And they stand forth like a garment.
15 "From the wicked their light is withheld,
And the uplifted arm is broken.

16 ¶ "Have you entered into the springs of
the sea
Or walked in the recesses of the deep?
17 "Have the gates of death been revealed to
you,
Or have you seen the gates of deep
darkness?
18 "Have you understood the expanse of the
earth?
Tell *Me*, if you know all this.

19 ¶ "Where is the way to the dwelling of
light?
And darkness, where is its place,

20 That you may take it to its territory
And that you may discern the paths to
its home?
21 "You know, for you were born then,
And the number of your days is great!
22 "Have you entered the storehouses of the
snow,

38:21 God Pulls Out the Stops

God is not above using sarcasm, as this barb directed at Job clearly shows. His entire speech stresses the vast difference between a God of all creation and one puny man like Job. "Do you have an arm like God?" he asks (40:9).

What Job Teaches about Suffering
The problem of pain and the book of Job

"WHY ME?" ALMOST EVERYONE ASKS this question when terrible suffering strikes. An automobile accident, a diagnosis of cancer, a long-term disease like arthritis—each of these raises intense questions about why God allows pain.

Over the centuries, suffering Christians have gained help and comfort from studying the book of Job. The book gives no compact theory of why good people suffer. Nevertheless, the following insights into the problem of suffering do come out of the book of Job.

"He delivers the afflicted in their affliction, and opens their ear in time of oppression."
36:15

Principles from Job

1. *Some suffering is caused by Satan.* Chapters 1 and 2 make the important distinction that God did not cause Job's problems. He allowed them, but Satan actually caused the pain.

2. *God is all-powerful and good.* Nowhere does the book of Job suggest that God lacks power or goodness. Some people say that God is weak and powerless to prevent human suffering. Others, called deists, assume he runs the world at a distance, without personal involvement. But in Job, God's power is never questioned; only his fairness. And in his final summation speech, God used splendid illustrations from nature to prove his power.

3. *Suffering doesn't always come as a result of sin.* The Bible supports the general principle that a man reaps what he sows, even in this life (Galatians 6:7; see Psalms 1:3; 37:25). But other people have no right to apply that *general* principle to a *particular* person. Job's friends tried with all their persuasive power. However, when God rendered the final verdict, he said simply, "You have not spoken of Me what is right, as My servant Job has" (42:7). The Old Testament includes other examples of people who suffered through no fault of their own, such as Abel (Genesis 4) and Uriah (2 Samuel 11). And Jesus spoke out against the notion that suffering implies sin (see John 9:1–5 and Luke 13:1–5).

4. *God will reward and punish fairly in a final judgment after death.* Job's friends, along with most Old Testament folk, did not have a clearly formed belief in an afterlife. Therefore, they expected that God's fairness—his approval or disapproval of people—had to be shown in this life. Other parts of the Bible teach that God will reward and punish fairly after death.

5. *God does not condemn doubt and despair.* God did not condemn Job's anguished responses, only his ignorance. Job did not take his pain meekly; he cried out in anguish to God. His strong remarks scandalized his friends (see, for example, 15:1–16), but not God. Ironically, despite his bitter speeches, Job earned God's praise, while his pious friends were soundly rebuked.

6. *No one person has all the facts about suffering.* Neither Job nor his friends had enough facts. Job concluded God was unfair, treating him like an enemy. His friends maintained that God opposed Job because of his sin. All of them later learned they had been viewing the situation from a very limited

Or have you seen the storehouses of the
  hail,
23 Which I have reserved for the time of
  distress,
  For the day of war and battle?
24 "Where is the way that the light is
  divided,
  Or the east wind scattered on the earth?

25 ¶ "Who has cleft a channel for the flood,
  Or a way for the thunderbolt,
26 To bring rain on a land without people,
  On a desert without a man in it,
27 To satisfy the waste and desolate land
  And to make the seeds of grass to
  sprout?
28 "Has the rain a father?
  Or who has begotten the drops of dew?
29 "From whose womb has come the ice?
  And the frost of heaven, who has given it
  birth?
30 "Water becomes hard like stone,
  And the surface of the deep is
  imprisoned.

31 ¶ "Can you bind the chains of the
  Pleiades,
  Or loose the cords of Orion?
32 "Can you lead forth a constellation in its
  season,
  And guide the Bear with her satellites?

33 "Do you know the ordinances of the
  heavens,
  Or fix their rule over the earth?

34 ¶ "Can you lift up your voice to the
  clouds,
  So that an abundance of water will
  cover you?
35 "Can you send forth lightnings that they
  may go
  And say to you, 'Here we are'?
36 "Who has put wisdom in the innermost
  being
  Or given understanding to the mind?
37 "Who can count the clouds by wisdom,
  Or tip the water jars of the heavens,
38 When the dust hardens into a mass
  And the clods stick together?

39 ¶ "Can you hunt the prey for the lion,
  Or satisfy the appetite of the young lions,
40 When they crouch in *their* dens
  And lie in wait in *their* lair?
41 "Who prepares for the raven its
  nourishment
  When its young cry to God
  And wander about without food?

God Speaks of Nature and Its Beings

39 "Do you know the time the mountain
  goats give birth?

---

perspective, blind to the real struggle being waged in heaven.

7. *God is never totally silent.* Elihu made that point convincingly, reminding Job of dreams, visions, past blessings, even the daily works of God in nature (chapter 33). God also appealed to nature as giving evidence of his wisdom and power. Although he may seem silent, some evidence of him can be found. One contemporary author expressed that truth this way, "Remember in the darkness what you have learned in the light."

8. *Well-intentioned advice can sometimes do more harm than good.* Job's friends were classic examples of people who let their pride and sense of being right interfere with their compassion. They repeated pious phrases and argued theology with Job. His response: "O that you would be completely silent, and that it would become your wisdom!" (13:5).

9. *God asks for faith.* God refocused the central issue from the *cause* of Job's suffering to his *response.* Mysteriously, God never gave an explanation for the problem of suffering. He did not even inform Job of the reason behind it: the contest recorded in chapters 1 and 2. He concentrated instead on Job's response. The real issue at stake was Job's faith—whether he would continue to trust God even when everything went wrong.

10. *Suffering can be used for a higher good.* In Job's case, God used a time of very great pain to win an important, even cosmic, victory over Satan. Looking backward, but only looking backward, we can see the "advantage" Job gained by continuing to trust God. Job is often cited as an Old Testament picture of Jesus Christ, who lived a perfectly innocent life but endured great pain and death. The terrible event of Christ's death was also transformed into a great victory.

Thousands of years later, Job's questions have not gone away. People who suffer still find themselves borrowing Job's own words as they cry out against God's seeming lack of concern. But Job affirms that God is not deaf to our cries and is in control of this world no matter how it looks. God did not answer all Job's questions, but his very appearance caused Job's doubts to melt away. Job learned that God cared about him and that God rules the world. It was enough.

Life Questions: Do these principles from Job match up with what you have heard about suffering from other Christians?

Do you observe the calving of the deer?
2 "Can you count the months they fulfill,
Or do you know the time they give birth?
3 "They kneel down, they bring forth their young,
They get rid of their labor pains.
4 "Their offspring become strong, they grow up in the open field;
They leave and do not return to them.

5 ¶ "Who sent out the wild donkey free?
And who loosed the bonds of the swift donkey,
6 To whom I gave the wilderness for a home
And the salt land for his dwelling place?
7 "He scorns the tumult of the city,
The shoutings of the driver he does not hear.
8 "He explores the mountains for his pasture

God Speaks to Job
At last, Job gets what he demanded

IN THE SPAN OF A few days Job experienced more tragedy than most people encounter in a lifetime. He scratched himself with shards of pottery and mourned the day he was born. He could not even suffer with dignity; he had to endure his wife's taunts and his friends' ramblings. Nothing anyone said helped him.

> "Will the fault-finder contend with the Almighty? Let him who reproves God answer it."
> 40:2

Through it all, Job steadfastly refused to turn his back on God. He had only one request. He wanted to hear from God in person. He wanted an explanation straight from the Source.

At last Job got his wish. God answered Job with a speech often quoted for its majesty and beauty. In a touch of irony, God made his entrance just as Elihu was explaining why Job could not expect a direct answer from him.

Not the Expected Message

Job had saved up a long list of questions, but it was God who asked the questions, not Job. "Gird up your loins like a man," he began. "I will ask you, and you instruct Me."

Author Frederick Buechner sums up what follows: "God doesn't explain. He explodes. He asks Job who he thinks he is anyway. He says that to try to explain the kind of things Job wants explained would be like trying to explain Einstein to a little-neck clam." God did not need Job's or anyone else's advice on how to run the world.

God's reply resembled a nature lesson more than an explanation of the problem of suffering. He pointed out, one by one, all the creations that gave him greatest pride. In short, God asked Job, "Do you want to try running the universe for a while? Go ahead, try designing an ostrich, or a mountain goat, or even a snowflake."

Astonishingly, the question of suffering itself did not even come up. Yet somehow Job seemed satisfied—humiliated, actually. "Therefore I have declared that which I did not understand," he confessed, "things too wonderful for me, which I did not know" (42:3).

Job Passes the Test

Job had endured his terrible sufferings in the dark. When he needed God most, God had stayed silent. And that was exactly the point of the contest begun at the beginning of the book, back in chapter 1. Satan had promised God that Job would "surely curse You to Your face." He lost the challenge. Despite everything that happened, Job did not curse God. He clung to his belief in a just God, even when everything in his experience seemed to contradict it.

God had some words of correction for Job. No one, not Job and especially not his friends, had the evidence needed to make judgments about how he runs the world. But mainly, God had praise for Job. He called him "My servant," and, in an ironic twist, told the three friends to go to Job and ask for his mercy (42:7–8). Much later, in the book of Ezekiel (14:14), God included Job in a list of the finest human examples of righteousness.

The book of Job ends on a note of surprise. Job's friends, who had spouted all the right pieties and clichés, ask for forgiveness. Job, who had raged and cried out, is given twice as much as he ever had before. "And Job died, an old man and full of days" (42:17).

Life Questions: In Job's place, what kind of answer would you have wanted from God? Does God's reply to Job surprise you?

And searches after every green thing.
9 "Will the wild ox consent to serve you,
  Or will he spend the night at your
    manger?

39:9 The Wildness of Animals

God seems to take special delight in animals with a streak of wildness: mountain goats, lions, wild donkeys, hawks, wild oxen. They serve as reminders that people are not as fully in control of the world as they might think.

10 "Can you bind the wild ox in a furrow
    with ropes,
  Or will he harrow the valleys after you?
11 "Will you trust him because his strength
    is great
  And leave your labor to him?
12 "Will you have faith in him that he will
    return your grain
  And gather *it from* your threshing floor?

13 ¶ "The ostriches' wings flap joyously
  With the pinion and plumage of *a*love,
14 For she abandons her eggs to the earth
  And warms them in the dust,
15 And she forgets that a foot may crush
    them,
  Or that a wild beast may trample them.
16 "She treats her young cruelly, as if *they*
    were not hers;
  Though her labor be in vain, *she* is
    unconcerned;
17 Because God has made her forget
    wisdom,
  And has not given her a share of
    understanding.
18 "When she lifts herself on high,
  She laughs at the horse and his rider.

19 ¶ "Do you give the horse *his* might?
  Do you clothe his neck with a mane?
20 "Do you make him leap like the locust?
  His majestic snorting is terrible.
21 "He paws in the valley, and rejoices in *his*
    strength;
  He goes out to meet the weapons.
22 "He laughs at fear and is not dismayed;
  And he does not turn back from the
    sword.
23 "The quiver rattles against him,
  The flashing spear and javelin.
24 "With shaking and rage he races over the
    ground,
  And he does not stand still at the voice
    of the trumpet.
25 "As often as the trumpet *sounds* he
    says, 'Aha!'

And he scents the battle from afar,
  And the thunder of the captains and the
    war cry.

26 ¶ "Is it by your understanding that the
    hawk soars,
  Stretching his wings toward the south?
27 "Is it at your command that the eagle
    mounts up
  And makes his nest on high?
28 "On the cliff he dwells and lodges,
  Upon the rocky crag, an inaccessible
    place.
29 "From there he spies out food;
  His eyes see *it* from afar.
30 "His young ones also suck up blood;
  And where the slain are, there is he."

Job: What Can I Say?

40 Then the LORD said to Job,
2 "Will the faultfinder contend with the
    Almighty?
  Let him who reproves God answer it."

3 ¶ Then Job answered the LORD and said,
4 "Behold, I am insignificant; what can I
    reply to You?
  I lay my hand on my mouth.
5 "Once I have spoken, and I will not
    answer;
  Even twice, and I will add nothing
    more."

God Questions Job

6 ¶ Then the LORD answered Job out of the
    storm and said,
7 "Now gird up your loins like a man;
  I will ask you, and you instruct Me.
8 "Will you really annul My judgment?
  Will you condemn Me that you may be
    justified?
9 "Or do you have an arm like God,
  And can you thunder with a voice
    like His?

10 ¶ "Adorn yourself with eminence and
    dignity,
  And clothe yourself with honor and
    majesty.
11 "Pour out the overflowings of your anger,
  And look on everyone who is proud, and
    make him low.
12 "Look on everyone who is proud, *and*
    humble him,
  And tread down the wicked where they
    stand.
13 "Hide them in the dust together;
  Bind them in the hidden *place.*
14 "Then I will also confess to you,
  That your own right hand can save you.

a Or *a stork*

God's Power Shown in Creatures

15 ¶ "Behold now, ªBehemoth, which I
    made as well as you;
    He eats grass like an ox.

40:15 Behemoth and Leviathan?

No one is quite sure what is meant by these two words, so the English Bible leaves them untranslated. The Behemoth resembles a hippopotamus or elephant. The Leviathan (41:1) has some features of a crocodile and some of a dragon. In other places, the Bible refers to the Leviathan as either a whale-like creature (Psalm 104:26) or a serpent or monster of the sea (Isaiah 27:1). God used the Leviathan as a symbol of something powerful and uncontrollable. Job got the message: If you can't take on one of God's fearsome creatures, don't attempt to take on God.

16 "Behold now, his strength in his loins
    And his power in the muscles of his
      belly.
17 "He bends his tail like a cedar;
    The sinews of his thighs are knit
      together.
18 "His bones are tubes of bronze;
    His limbs are like bars of iron.

19 ¶ "He is the first of the ways of God;
    Let his maker bring near his sword.
20 "Surely the mountains bring him food,
    And all the beasts of the field play there.
21 "Under the lotus plants he lies down,
    In the covert of the reeds and the marsh.
22 "The lotus plants cover him with shade;
    The willows of the brook surround him.
23 "If a river rages, he is not alarmed;
    He is confident, though the Jordan
      rushes to his mouth.
24 "Can anyone capture him when he is on
      watch,
    With barbs can anyone pierce *his* nose?

God's Power Shown in Creatures

41 "Can you draw out ᵇLeviathan with a
      fishhook?
    Or press down his tongue with a cord?
2 "Can you put a rope in his nose
    Or pierce his jaw with a hook?
3 "Will he make many supplications to you,
    Or will he speak to you soft words?
4 "Will he make a covenant with you?
    Will you take him for a servant forever?
5 "Will you play with him as with a bird,
    Or will you bind him for your maidens?
6 "Will the traders bargain over him?

Will they divide him among the
    merchants?
7 "Can you fill his skin with harpoons,
    Or his head with fishing spears?
8 "Lay your hand on him;
    Remember the battle; you will not do it
      again!
9 "Behold, your expectation is false;
    Will you be laid low even at the sight
      of him?
10 "No one is so fierce that he dares to
      arouse him;
    Who then is he that can stand
      before Me?
11 "Who has given to Me that I should
      repay *him*?
    Whatever is under the whole heaven is
      Mine.

12 ¶ "I will not keep silence concerning his
      limbs,
    Or his mighty strength, or his orderly
      frame.
13 "Who can strip off his outer armor?
    Who can come within his double mail?
14 "Who can open the doors of his face?
    Around his teeth there is terror.
15 "*His* strong scales are *his* pride,
    Shut up *as with* a tight seal.
16 "One is so near to another
    That no air can come between them.
17 "They are joined one to another;
    They clasp each other and cannot be
      separated.
18 "His sneezes flash forth light,
    And his eyes are like the eyelids of the
      morning.
19 "Out of his mouth go burning torches;
    Sparks of fire leap forth.
20 "Out of his nostrils smoke goes forth
    As *from* a boiling pot and *burning*
      rushes.
21 "His breath kindles coals,
    And a flame goes forth from his mouth.
22 "In his neck lodges strength,
    And dismay leaps before him.
23 "The folds of his flesh are joined together,
    Firm on him and immovable.
24 "His heart is as hard as a stone,
    Even as hard as a lower millstone.
25 "When he raises himself up, the mighty
      fear;
    Because of the crashing they are
      bewildered.
26 "The sword that reaches him cannot avail,
    Nor the spear, the dart or the javelin.
27 "He regards iron as straw,
    Bronze as rotten wood.
28 "The arrow cannot make him flee;

ª Or *the hippopotamus*   ᵇ Or *the crocodile*

Slingstones are turned into stubble for
him.
29 "Clubs are regarded as stubble;
He laughs at the rattling of the javelin.
30 "His underparts are *like* sharp potsherds;
He spreads out *like* a threshing sledge on
the mire.
31 "He makes the depths boil like a pot;
He makes the sea like a jar of ointment.
32 "Behind him he makes a wake to shine;
One would think the deep to be
gray-haired.
33 "Nothing on earth is like him,
One made without fear.
34 "He looks on everything that is high;
He is king over all the sons of pride."

Job's Confession

42 Then Job answered the LORD and said,
2 "I know that You can do all things,
And that no purpose of Yours can be
thwarted.

42:2–5 A Visit for All Time

A personal visit from God utterly silenced all Job's questions about unfairness. Once he saw God, he had nothing more to say. Few people in history have had such a direct, visible encounter with God, but the book of Job foreshadows a time when God paid a much longer personal visit to earth. In Jesus, God came not in power and majesty, but in poverty and pain. Job stands as the clearest Old Testament example of unfairness: an upright man who suffered greatly. Jesus stands as the New Testament example: a perfect man who suffered even more. Both hint at a happy ending after all.

3 'Who is this that hides counsel without
knowledge?'
"Therefore I have declared that which I
did not understand,
Things too wonderful for me, which I
did not know."
4 'Hear, now, and I will speak;
I will ask You, and You instruct me.'
5 "I have heard of You by the hearing of
the ear;
But now my eye sees You;
6 Therefore I retract,
And I repent in dust and ashes."

God Displeased with Job's Friends

7 ¶ It came about after the LORD had spoken these words to Job, that the LORD said to Eliphaz the Temanite, "My wrath is kindled against you and against your two friends, because you have not spoken of Me what is right as My servant Job has.
8 "Now therefore, take for yourselves seven bulls and seven rams, and go to My servant Job, and offer up a burnt offering for yourselves, and My servant Job will pray for you. For I will accept him so that I may not do with you *according to your* folly, because you have not spoken of Me what is right, as My servant Job has."
9 So Eliphaz the Temanite and Bildad the Shuhite *and* Zophar the Naamathite went and did as the LORD told them; and the LORD accepted Job.

God Restores Job's Fortunes

10 ¶ The LORD restored the fortunes of Job when he prayed for his friends, and the LORD increased all that Job had twofold.

42:10 Seeing in the Dark

Significantly, Job spoke his contrite words (verse 6) before any of his losses had been restored, while still sitting in a pile of ashes, naked and covered with sores. Because he had seen God, he had learned to believe God even in the midst of suffering, with no certainty of relief.

11 Then all his brothers and all his sisters and all who had known him before came to him, and they ate bread with him in his house; and they consoled him and comforted him for all the adversities that the LORD had brought on him. And each one gave him one piece of money, and each a ring of gold.
12 The LORD blessed the latter *days* of Job more than his beginning; and he had 14,000 sheep and 6,000 camels and 1,000 yoke of oxen and 1,000 female donkeys.
13 He had seven sons and three daughters.
14 He named the first Jemimah, and the second Keziah, and the third Keren-happuch.
15 In all the land no women were found so fair as Job's daughters; and their father gave them inheritance among their brothers.
16 After this, Job lived 140 years, and saw his sons and his grandsons, four generations.
17 And Job died, an old man and full of days.

PSALMS

Cries from the Heart
Songs for sorrow as well as joy

> You are my hiding place; You preserve me from trouble; You surround me with songs of deliverance. 32:7

HERE AT THE VERY CENTER of the Bible are songs, rising up like a tune from its heart. They capture the innermost thoughts and prayers of Old Testament people—and they still speak directly to our needs.

For every emotion and mood you can find a psalm to match. The psalms wrestle with the deepest sorrow and ask God the hardest questions about suffering and injustice. Their voice is refreshingly spontaneous. They do not tip flowery compliments toward God; they cry out to him, or shout for joy before him.

After you read these poems, you can't think of the Old Testament as dry and rule-bound. Nor is the Old Testament God distant and impersonal. In almost every psalm you find the presence of God, not as a philosophical principle, but as an active, strong, and loving ruler—a God who makes a difference in life.

How Did the Psalms Come Together?

While almost half of the psalms are credited to David, at least one was written 500 years after his birth. A number of poets and writers contributed, and about a third of the psalms are completely anonymous.

How did the psalms come together? They seem to have been compiled as a hymnbook for use in temple worship. Some psalms were written from an individual's experiences, but were adapted for congregational use. Directions for musicians were added, along with a few verses to widen the psalms' meaning to everybody.

The psalms show tremendous variation, reflecting the many personalities who contributed their poems and prayers over several centuries. Yet readers have found an inner consistency in the whole book, so they can move from one psalm to the next without being particularly aware that one poem is centuries older than another. Some have called the psalms a Bible within the Bible—different books telling a single story.

Others have compared the book of Psalms to a beautiful cathedral built over centuries. Each wing and each window show the individual genius of its designers, yet all the parts are somehow harmonious. This harmony comes not merely from a common sense of style, but from unity of purpose: The whole cathedral is made for the worship of one and the same God. Just so, the psalms reflect, in a hundred moods and experiences, the never-changing reality of a strong and loving God who cares for his people.

The Presence of Real Enemies

God is not the only reality in the psalms. Equally persistent are enemies who sneer and hurt and plot violence. They, too, appear in nearly every psalm. For the psalmists, faith in God was a struggle against powerful forces that often seemed more real than God.

The psalm writers frequently asked, "Where are you, God? Why don't you help me?" Despite their love for God, they often felt abandoned, misused, betrayed. They found no guarantee of safety in their closeness to God. The joy and praise that saturate these prayers came not from an absence of problems, but from a deep conviction that a great God would overcome them.

Jesus, dying on the cross, twice expressed himself in the words of psalms (22:1 and 31:5), and his disciples, in trying to explain his life, quoted from Psalms more than any other book. They appear to have meditated on the psalms often as they considered the meaning of Jesus' life. In the psalms they could see that even the best men—even David, the great king—suffer agony and feel abandoned.

Living by faith is not easy. It was not for David; it was not for Jesus either. These powerful poems of praise and worship, some of the most beautiful ever written, offer no magical formulas to make troubles go away. Yet, while real-life questions, struggles, and discouragements have a strong voice in these poems, more powerful still is the voice of joy and security in the strength and fortress of Israel: the Lord himself.

How to Read Psalms

The best way to read the psalms is also the most common way: to make these ancient prayers your own and speak them directly to God. So many of the poems catch such deep human feelings that you can't help being moved by them.

But not all the psalms seem attractive. Some sound harsh, self-congratulatory, or boring. You will not find it easy to pray these until you understand them.

And there are so many psalms! This is the longest book in the Bible. To compensate, many people read only selected psalms, skimming over the others. But then they miss the deeper messages found there, including the messages that the New Testament writers saw when they quoted Psalms more than any other Old Testament book. The richest lessons from Psalms may come from particularly difficult poems you must read again and again until you begin to see what the author had in mind.

The original Hebrew of these poems probably used no rhyme or strict rhythm as traditional English poems do. Instead, the psalmists wrote with parallelism, following one thought by a "rhyming" thought or by its opposite. (For more on this, see "Hebrew Poetry," page 696.) Fortunately, this kind of poetry can be translated into almost any language without loss.

Readers may be confused by the psalms' frequent change of voice. In a single poem the psalmist may talk to God, then talk about him, and then return to talking to him, all in rapid succession. This would be strange English prose, but was common in Hebrew poetry.

Because so many of the psalm titles refer to David, you may find it helpful to refer to his life story. It is found in 1 Samuel 16—31, the whole book of 2 Samuel, and the first two chapters of 1 Kings. However, most of the psalms can make perfect sense without reference to any outside information. They merely ask—and reward—time and close attention. Read and reread them. They grow richer with careful study.

PEOPLE YOU'LL MEET IN PSALMS

MELCHIZEDEK *(p. 666)*

3-TRACK READING PLAN

For an explanation and complete listing of the 3-track reading plan, turn to page 7.

TRACK 1: *Two-Week Courses on the Bible*
The Track 1 reading program on the Old Testament includes one chapter from Psalms. See page 8 for a complete listing of this course.

TRACK 2: *An Overview of Psalms in 7 Days*
☐ Day 1. Read the Introduction to Psalms and Psalm 19: Perfect Harmony.
☐ Day 2. Read Psalm 23: The Shepherd Song.
☐ Day 3. Read Psalm 27: Confidence in Trouble.
☐ Day 4. Read Psalm 51: The Great Confession.
☐ Day 5. Read Psalm 84: The Delight of Worshiping God.
☐ Day 6. Read Psalm 103: God's Benefits.
☐ Day 7. Read Psalm 139: God's Care.

Now turn to page 9 for your next Track 2 reading project.

TRACK 3: *All of Psalms in Two Two-Month Periods (122 days)*
After you have read through Psalms, turn to pages 10–14 for your next Track 3 reading project.

Part I ☐1–2 ☐3–4 ☐5 ☐6 ☐7 ☐8 ☐9 ☐10 ☐11–12 ☐13–14
☐15–16 ☐17 ☐18 ☐19 ☐20–21 ☐22 ☐23–24 ☐25 ☐26 ☐27
☐28–29 ☐30 ☐31 ☐32 ☐33 ☐34 ☐35 ☐36 ☐37 ☐38
☐39 ☐40 ☐41 ☐42–43 ☐44 ☐45 ☐46–47 ☐48 ☐49 ☐50
☐51 ☐52 ☐53–54 ☐55 ☐56 ☐57 ☐58 ☐59 ☐60–61 ☐62
☐63–64 ☐65 ☐66 ☐67 ☐68 ☐69 ☐70 ☐71 ☐72 ☐73
☐74 ☐75

Part II	□76	□77	□78	□79	□80	□81	□82	□83	□84	□85	□86
	□87	□88	□89	□90	□91	□92–93	□94	□95	□96	□97	
	□98–99	□100–101	□102	□103	□104	□105	□106	□107	□108		
	□109	□110–111	□112–113	□114	□115	□116–117	□118				
	□119.1–48	□119.49–96	□119.97–144	□119.145–176	□120–121						
	□122–123	□124–125	□126–128	□129–130	□131–132	□133–134					
	□135	□136	□137–138	□139	□140	□141–142	□143	□144			
	□145	□146	□147	□148	□149–150						

The following expressions occur often in the Psalms:

Selah May mean *Pause, Crescendo* or *Musical Interlude*
Maskil Possibly *Contemplative,* or *Didactic,* or *Skillful Psalm*
Mikhtam Possibly *Epigrammatic Poem,* or *Atonement Psalm*
Sheol The nether world

BOOK 1

Psalm 1

The Righteous and the Wicked Contrasted.

1 ¶ How blessed is the man who does not
  walk in the counsel of the wicked,
  Nor stand in the path of sinners,
  Nor sit in the seat of scoffers!
2 But his delight is in the law of the LORD,
  And in His law he meditates day and
    night.
3 He will be like a tree *firmly* planted by
    streams of water,
  Which yields its fruit in its season
  And its leaf does not wither;
  And in whatever he does, he prospers.

4 ¶ The wicked are not so,
  But they are like chaff which the wind
    drives away.

1:4 Blowing in the Wind

The opposite of "a tree firmly planted by streams" (verse 3) should be a tree withered by drought—and so it is in Jeremiah 17:5–8, which paints a similar contrast between good and bad people. This image of the wicked as "chaff," however, is far more absolute—for chaff, utterly worthless even for a fire, disappears in the wind. God's judgment day is what finally makes the wicked seem like chaff.

5 Therefore the wicked will not stand in
    the judgment,
  Nor sinners in the assembly of the
    righteous.
6 For the LORD knows the way of the
    righteous,
  But the way of the wicked will perish.

Psalm 2

The Reign of the LORD's Anointed.

1 ¶ Why are the nations in an uproar
  And the peoples devising a vain thing?
2 The kings of the earth take their stand
  And the rulers take counsel together
  Against the LORD and against His
    ᵃAnointed, saying,

2:2 The Messiah in the Psalms

Israelite kings and priests were anointed with oil when they took office. The "Anointed" probably originally meant "king." It came, however, to stand for more. The Hebrew word is masiah, which became Messiah and translated into Greek as Christos or Christ. This psalm was understood in the New Testament as referring to Jesus—for no Old Testament king ever gained the control of the nations implied here. You can find quotations in Acts 4:25–26; 13:33; Hebrews 1:5; 5:5; and Revelation 2:27; 12:5; and 19:15.

3 "Let us tear their fetters apart
  And cast away their cords from us!"

4 ¶ He who ᵇsits in the heavens laughs,
  The Lord scoffs at them.
5 Then He will speak to them in His anger
  And terrify them in His fury, saying,
6 "But as for Me, I have installed My King
  Upon Zion, My holy mountain."

7 ¶ "I will surely tell of the decree of the
    LORD:
  He said to Me, 'You are My Son,
  Today I have begotten You.
8 'Ask of Me, and I will surely give the
    nations as Your inheritance,

ᵃ Or *Messiah* ᵇ Or *is enthroned*

And the *very* ends of the earth as Your
possession.
9 'You shall [a]break them with a rod of
iron,
You shall shatter them like
earthenware.' "
10 ¶ Now therefore, O kings, show
discernment;
Take warning, O [b]judges of the earth.
11 Worship the Lord with reverence
And rejoice with trembling.
12 Do homage to the Son, that He not
become angry, and you perish *in* the
way,
For His wrath may [c]soon be kindled.
How blessed are all who take refuge in
Him!

Psalm 3

Morning Prayer of Trust in God.

A Psalm of David, when he fled
from Absalom his son.

1 ¶ O Lord, how my adversaries have
increased!
Many are rising up against me.
2 Many are saying of my soul,
"There is no deliverance for him in God."
[d]Selah.

3 ¶ But You, O Lord, are a shield
about me,
My glory, and the One who lifts my
head.
4 I was crying to the Lord with my voice,
And He answered me from His holy
mountain.   Selah.
5 I lay down and slept;
I awoke, for the Lord sustains me.
6 I will not be afraid of ten thousands of
people
Who have set themselves against me
round about.

7 ¶ Arise, O Lord; save me, O my God!
For You have smitten all my enemies on
the cheek;
You have shattered the teeth of the
wicked.
8 Salvation belongs to the Lord;
Your blessing *be* upon Your people!
Selah.

Psalm 4

Evening Prayer of Trust in God.

For the choir director; on stringed instruments.
A Psalm of David.

1 ¶ Answer me when I call, O God of my
righteousness!

You have relieved me in my distress;
Be gracious to me and hear my prayer.

2 ¶ O sons of men, how long will my
honor become a reproach?
How long will you love what is worthless
and aim at deception?   Selah.
3 But know that the Lord has set apart the
godly man for Himself;
The Lord hears when I call to Him.

4 ¶ Tremble, and do not sin;
Meditate in your heart upon your bed,
and be still.   Selah.

4:4 Angry Inside

*Is anger sinful? No, though it can certainly lead
to sin. This prayer depicts anger springing from
anxiety, which proves especially troublesome
on sleepless nights. The psalm suggests that,
rather than venting your worry in outbursts
against others, you should examine your own
heart. Paul applied this verse to another
situation: difficult personal relationships
(Ephesians 4:26).*

5 Offer the sacrifices of righteousness,
And trust in the Lord.

6 ¶ Many are saying, "Who will show us
any good?"
Lift up the light of Your countenance
upon us, O Lord!
7 You have put gladness in my heart,
More than when their grain and new
wine abound.
8 In peace I will both lie down and sleep,
For You alone, O Lord, make me to
dwell in safety.

Psalm 5

Prayer for Protection from the Wicked.

For the choir director; for flute accompaniment.
A Psalm of David.

1 ¶ Give ear to my words, O Lord,
Consider my [e]groaning.
2 Heed the sound of my cry for help, my
King and my God,
For to You I pray.
3 In the morning, O Lord, You will hear
my voice;
In the morning I will order *my prayer* to
You and *eagerly* watch.

4 ¶ For You are not a God who takes
pleasure in wickedness;
No evil dwells with You.

[a] Another reading is *rule*   [b] Or *leaders*   [c] Or *quickly, suddenly, easily*   [d] *Selah* may mean: *Pause, Crescendo* or
Musical interlude   [e] Or *meditation*

5 The boastful shall not stand before Your
eyes;
You hate all who do iniquity.
6 You destroy those who speak falsehood;
The LORD abhors the man of bloodshed
and deceit.
7 But as for me, by Your abundant
lovingkindness I will enter Your
house,
At Your holy temple I will bow in
reverence for You.

8 ¶ O LORD, lead me in Your righteousness
because of my foes;
Make Your way straight before me.
9 There is nothing reliable in what they
say;
Their inward part is destruction *itself*.
Their throat is an open grave;
They flatter with their tongue.

5:9 Evil Everywhere

*Renowned for their beautiful pictures of God's
love, the psalms present equally heartfelt
portraits of evil. They often describe people
who deeply deserve God's punishment. In
Romans 3:10–18, Paul quotes from a number
of different psalms like this one, making his
case that evil infects all people, everywhere.*

10 Hold them guilty, O God;
By their own devices let them fall!
In the multitude of their transgressions
thrust them out,
For they are rebellious against You.
11 ¶ But let all who take refuge in You be
glad,
Let them ever sing for joy;
And may You shelter them,
That those who love Your name may
exult in You.
12 For it is You who blesses the righteous
man, O LORD,
You surround him with favor as with a
shield.

Psalm 6

Prayer for Mercy in Time of Trouble.

For the choir director; with stringed instruments,
upon an eight-string lyre. A Psalm of David.

1 ¶ O LORD, do not rebuke me in Your
anger,
Nor chasten me in Your wrath.
2 Be gracious to me, O LORD, for I *am*
pining away;

Heal me, O LORD, for my bones are
dismayed.
3 And my soul is greatly dismayed;
But You, O LORD—how long?

4 ¶ Return, O LORD, rescue my [a]soul;
Save me because of Your lovingkindness.
5 For there is no [b]mention of You in
death;
In Sheol who will give You thanks?

6 ¶ I am weary with my sighing;
Every night I make my bed swim,
I dissolve my couch with my tears.
7 My eye has wasted away with grief;
It has become old because of all my
adversaries.

8 ¶ Depart from me, all you who do
iniquity,
For the LORD has heard the voice of my
weeping.
9 The LORD has heard my supplication,
The LORD receives my prayer.
10 All my enemies will be ashamed and
greatly dismayed;
They shall turn back, they will suddenly
be ashamed.

Psalm 7

The LORD Implored to Defend the Psalmist
against the Wicked.

A [c]Shiggaion of David, which he sang to the
LORD concerning Cush, a Benjamite.

1 ¶ O LORD my God, in You I have taken
refuge;
Save me from all those who pursue me,
and deliver me,
2 Or he will tear my soul like a lion,
Dragging me away, while there is none to
deliver.

3 ¶ O LORD my God, if I have done this,
If there is injustice in my hands,
4 If I have rewarded evil to my friend,
Or have plundered him who without
cause was my adversary,
5 Let the enemy pursue my soul and
overtake *it*;
And let him trample my life down to the
ground
And lay my glory in the dust.   Selah.

6 ¶ Arise, O LORD, in Your anger;
Lift up Yourself against the rage of my
adversaries,
And arouse Yourself for me; You have
appointed judgment.
7 Let the assembly of the peoples
encompass You,
And over them return on high.

[a] Or *life*   [b] Or *remembrance*   [c] I.e. Dithyrambic rhythm; or wild passionate song

8 The LORD judges the peoples;
　Vindicate me, O LORD, according to my
　　righteousness and my integrity that
　　is in me.
9 O let the evil of the wicked come to an
　　end, but establish the righteous;
　For the righteous God tries the hearts
　　and [a]minds.
10 My shield is with God,
　Who saves the upright in heart.
11 God is a righteous judge,
　And a God who has indignation
　　every day.

12 ¶ If a man does not repent, He will
　　sharpen His sword;
　He has bent His bow and made it ready.
13 He has also prepared for Himself deadly
　　weapons;
　He makes His arrows fiery shafts.
14 Behold, he travails with wickedness,
　And he conceives mischief and brings
　　forth falsehood.
15 He has dug a pit and hollowed it out,
　And has fallen into the hole which he
　　made.
16 His mischief will return upon his own
　　head,
　And his violence will descend upon [b]his
　　own pate.

17 ¶ I will give thanks to the LORD
　　according to His righteousness
　And will sing praise to the name of the
　　LORD Most High.

Psalm 8

The LORD's Glory and Man's Dignity.

For the choir director; on the Gittith.
A Psalm of David.

1 ¶ O LORD, our Lord,
　How majestic is Your name in all the
　　earth,
　Who have displayed Your splendor
　　above the heavens!
2 From the mouth of infants and nursing
　　babes You have established strength
　Because of Your adversaries,
　To make the enemy and the revengeful
　　cease.
3 ¶ When I consider Your heavens, the
　　work of Your fingers,
　The moon and the stars, which You have
　　ordained;
4 What is man that You take thought of
　　him,
　And the son of man that You care
　　for him?

5 Yet You have made him a little lower
　　than God,
　And You crown him with glory and
　　majesty!

8:2 Children's Power

*An almighty God needs no great powers to
back him. He shuts up his enemies through
little children and their spontaneous praise.
That is exactly what happened in Jesus' time
(Matthew 21:16).*

6 You make him to rule over the works of
　　Your hands;
　You have put all things under his feet,
7 All sheep and oxen,
　And also the beasts of the field,
8 The birds of the heavens and the fish of
　　the sea,
　Whatever passes through the paths of the
　　seas.

9 ¶ O LORD, our Lord,
　How majestic is Your name in all the
　　earth!

Psalm 9

A Psalm of Thanksgiving for God's Justice.

For the choir director; on [c]Muth-labben.
A Psalm of David.

1 ¶ I will give thanks to the LORD with all
　　my heart;
　I will tell of all Your wonders.
2 I will be glad and exult in You;
　I will sing praise to Your name, O Most
　　High.

3 ¶ When my enemies turn back,
　They stumble and perish before You.
4 For You have maintained my just cause;
　You have sat on the throne judging
　　righteously.
5 You have rebuked the nations, You have
　　destroyed the wicked;
　You have blotted out their name forever
　　and ever.
6 The enemy has come to an end in
　　perpetual ruins,
　And You have uprooted the cities;
　The very memory of them has perished.

7 ¶ But the LORD [d]abides forever;
　He has established His throne for
　　judgment,
8 And He will judge the world in
　　righteousness;

---

[a] Lit *kidneys,* figurative for inner man　　[b] I.e. the crown of his own head　　[c] I.e. "Death to the Son"　　[d] Or *sits*
as king

He will execute judgment for the peoples
with equity.
9 The LORD also will be a stronghold for
the oppressed,
A stronghold in times of trouble;
10 And those who know Your name will put
their trust in You,
For You, O LORD, have not forsaken
those who seek You.

11 ¶ Sing praises to the LORD, who dwells in
Zion;
Declare among the peoples His deeds.
12 For He who ᵃrequires blood remembers
them;
He does not forget the cry of the
afflicted.
13 Be gracious to me, O LORD;
See my affliction from those who
hate me,
You who lift me up from the gates of
death,
14 That I may tell of all Your praises,
That in the gates of the daughter of Zion
I may rejoice in Your salvation.
15 The nations have sunk down in the pit
which they have made;
In the net which they hid, their own foot
has been caught.
16 The LORD has made Himself known;
He has executed judgment.
In the work of his own hands the wicked
is snared.   Higgaion Selah.

17 ¶ The wicked will return to Sheol,
Even all the nations who forget God.
18 For the needy will not always be
forgotten,
Nor the hope of the afflicted perish
forever.
19 Arise, O LORD, do not let man prevail;
Let the nations be judged before You.
20 Put them in fear, O LORD;
Let the nations know that they are but
men.   Selah.

Psalm 10

A Prayer for the Overthrow of the Wicked.

1 ¶ Why do You stand afar off, O LORD?
Why do You hide *Yourself* in times of
trouble?
2 In pride the wicked hotly pursue the
afflicted;
Let them be caught in the plots which
they have devised.
3 ¶ For the wicked boasts of his heart's
desire,

And ᵇthe greedy man curses *and* spurns
the LORD.
4 The wicked, in the haughtiness of his
countenance, does not seek *Him*.
All his thoughts are, "There is no God."

5 ¶ His ways prosper at all times;
Your judgments are on high, out of his
sight;
As for all his adversaries, he snorts at
them.
6 He says to himself, "I will not be moved;
Throughout all generations I will not be
in adversity."
7 His mouth is full of curses and deceit
and oppression;
Under his tongue is mischief and
wickedness.
8 He sits in the lurking places of the
villages;
In the hiding places he kills the innocent;
His eyes stealthily watch for the
unfortunate.
9 He lurks in a hiding place as a lion in his
lair;
He lurks to catch the afflicted;
He catches the afflicted when he draws
him into his net.
10 He crouches, he bows down,
And the unfortunate fall ᶜby his mighty
ones.
11 He says to himself, "God has forgotten;
He has hidden His face; He will never
see it."

12 ¶ Arise, O LORD; O God, lift up Your
hand.
Do not forget the afflicted.
13 Why has the wicked spurned God?
He has said to himself, "You will not
require *it*."
14 You have seen *it,* for You have beheld
mischief and vexation to take it into
Your hand.
The unfortunate commits *himself* to You;
You have been the helper of the orphan.
15 Break the arm of the wicked and the
evildoer,
Seek out his wickedness until You find
none.

16 ¶ The LORD is King forever and ever;
Nations have perished from His land.
17 O LORD, You have heard the desire of
the ᵈhumble;
You will strengthen their heart, You will
incline Your ear
18 To ᵉvindicate the orphan and the
oppressed,
So that man who is of the earth will no
longer cause terror.

ᵃ I.e. avenges bloodshed   ᵇ Or *blesses the greedy man*   ᶜ Or *into his claws*   ᵈ Or *afflicted*   ᵉ Lit *judge*

Psalm 11

The LORD a Refuge and Defense.

For the choir director. *A Psalm* of David.

1 ¶ In the LORD I take refuge;
   How can you say to my soul, "Flee *as* a
      bird to your mountain;
2 For, behold, the wicked bend the bow,
   They make ready their arrow upon the
      string
   To shoot in darkness at the upright in
      heart.
3 If the foundations are destroyed,
   What can the righteous do?"

4 ¶ The LORD is in His holy temple; the
      LORD's throne is in heaven;
   His eyes behold, His eyelids test the sons
      of men.
5 The LORD tests the righteous and the
      wicked,
   And the one who loves violence His soul
      hates.
6 Upon the wicked He will rain *a*snares;
   Fire and brimstone and burning wind
      will be the portion of their cup.
7 For the LORD is righteous, He loves
      righteousness;
   The upright will behold His face.

Psalm 12

God, a Helper against the Treacherous.

For the choir director; upon an eight-stringed lyre.
A Psalm of David.

1 ¶ Help, LORD, for the godly man ceases
      to be,
   For the faithful disappear from among
      the sons of men.
2 They speak falsehood to one another;
   With flattering lips and with a double
      heart they speak.
3 May the LORD cut off all flattering lips,
   The tongue that speaks great things;
4 Who have said, "With our tongue we
      will prevail;
   Our lips are our own; who is lord
      over us?"

12:4 Who Owns Your Lips?

*Repeatedly the Bible stresses that talk can do
tremendous good or evil. One key distinctive is
suggested here: Wicked people use words to
build themselves up over others. They insist
that no one has the right to tell them what to
say.*

5 "Because of the devastation of the
      afflicted, because of the groaning of
      the needy,
   Now I will arise," says the LORD; "I will
      set him in the safety for which he
      longs."

6 ¶ The words of the LORD are pure words;
   As silver tried in a furnace on the earth,
      refined seven times.
7 You, O LORD, will keep them;
   You will preserve him from this
      generation forever.
8 The wicked strut about on every side
   When *b*vileness is exalted among the
      sons of men.

Psalm 13

Prayer for Help in Trouble.

For the choir director. A Psalm of David.

1 ¶ How long, O LORD? Will You forget
      me forever?
   How long will You hide Your face
      from me?
2 How long shall I take counsel in my
      soul,
   Having sorrow in my heart all the day?
   How long will my enemy be exalted
      over me?

3 ¶ Consider *and* answer me, O LORD my
      God;
   Enlighten my eyes, or I will sleep the
      sleep of death,
4 And my enemy will say, "I have
      overcome him,"
   And my adversaries will rejoice when I
      am shaken.

5 ¶ But I have trusted in Your
      lovingkindness;
   My heart shall rejoice in Your salvation.
6 I will sing to the LORD,
   Because He has dealt bountifully
      with me.

Psalm 14

Folly and Wickedness of Men.

For the choir director. *A Psalm* of David.

1 ¶ The fool has said in his heart, "There is
      no God."
   They are corrupt, they have committed
      abominable deeds;
   There is no one who does good.
2 The LORD has looked down from heaven
      upon the sons of men
   To see if there are any who understand,
   Who seek after God.

---

a Or *coals of fire*   *b* Or *worthlessness*

3 They have all turned aside, together they
    have become corrupt;
There is no one who does good, not
    even one.

14:3 Who Seeks God?

Though David was called a "man after God's own heart," he is credited with this chilling assessment of humankind—including himself. In God's eyes, nobody—not even David—is good. Paul quoted this in a crucial New Testament passage, Romans 3:10–12.

4 ¶ Do all the workers of wickedness not
    know,
Who eat up my people *as* they eat bread,
And do not call upon the Lord?
5 There they are in great dread,
For God is with the righteous generation.
6 You would put to shame the counsel of
    the afflicted,
But the LORD is his refuge.

7 ¶ Oh, that the salvation of Israel would
    come out of Zion!
When the LORD *ª*restores His captive
    people,
Jacob will rejoice, Israel will be glad.

Psalm 15

Description of a Citizen of Zion.

A Psalm of David.

1 ¶ O LORD, who may abide in Your tent?
Who may dwell on Your holy hill?
2 He who walks with integrity, and works
    righteousness,
And speaks truth in his heart.
3 He does not slander with his tongue,
Nor does evil to his neighbor,
Nor takes up a reproach against his
    friend;
4 In whose eyes a reprobate is despised,
But who honors those who fear the
    LORD;
He swears to his own hurt and does not
    change;
5 He does not put out his money *b*at
    interest,
Nor does he take a bribe against the
    innocent.
He who does these things will never be
    shaken.

Psalm 16

The LORD the Psalmist's Portion in Life and Deliverer in Death.

A *c*Mikhtam of David.

1 ¶ Preserve me, O God, for I take refuge
    in You.
2 I said to the LORD, "You are my Lord;
I have no good besides You."
3 As for the saints who are in the earth,
They are the majestic ones in whom is all
    my delight.
4 The sorrows of those who have bartered
    for another *god* will be multiplied;
I shall not pour out their drink offerings
    of blood,
Nor will I take their names upon my lips.

5 ¶ The LORD is the portion of my
    inheritance and my cup;
You support my lot.
6 The lines have fallen to me in pleasant
    places;
Indeed, my heritage is beautiful to me.

7 ¶ I will bless the LORD who has
    counseled me;
Indeed, my mind instructs me in the
    night.
8 I have set the LORD continually
    before me;
Because He is at my right hand, I will
    not be shaken.
9 Therefore my heart is glad and my glory
    rejoices;
My flesh also will dwell securely.

16:9–11 Resurrection!

In this confident, happy psalm, David rejoices that the life God gives cannot be canceled by the grave. Generally, the Old Testament offers little insight into life after death, but here David's faith carries him to a deeper understanding. The apostles Peter and Paul understood this psalm as prophesying Jesus' resurrection (see Acts 2:25–28; 13:35–37). Because of Jesus' resurrection, David and all God's people would come to new life in him.

10 For You will not abandon my soul to
    Sheol;
Nor will You allow Your Holy One to
    *d*undergo decay.
11 You will make known to me the path of
    life;
In Your presence is fullness of joy;

ª Or *restores the fortunes of His people*   *b* I.e. to a fellow Israelite   *c* Possibly *Epigrammatic Poem* or *Atonement Psalm*
d Or *see corruption* or *the pit*

In Your right hand there are pleasures
forever.

Psalm 17

Prayer for Protection against Oppressors.

A Prayer of David.

1 ¶ Hear a just cause, O LORD, give heed
to my cry;
Give ear to my prayer, which is not from
deceitful lips.
2 Let my judgment come forth from Your
presence;
Let Your eyes look with equity.
3 You have tried my heart;
You have visited *me* by night;
You have tested me and You find
*a*nothing;
I have purposed that my mouth will not
transgress.
4 As for the deeds of men, by the word of
Your lips
I have kept from the paths of the violent.
5 My steps have held fast to Your paths.
My feet have not slipped.

6 ¶ I have called upon You, for You will
answer me, O God;
Incline Your ear to me, hear my speech.
7 Wondrously show Your lovingkindness,
O Savior of those who take refuge at
Your right hand
From those who rise up *against them.*
8 Keep me as *b*the apple of the eye;
Hide me in the shadow of Your wings
9 From the wicked who despoil me,
My deadly enemies who surround me.
10 They have closed their unfeeling *heart,*
With their mouth they speak proudly.
11 They have now surrounded us in our
steps;
They set their eyes to cast *us* down to the
ground.
12 He is like a lion that is eager to tear,
And as a young lion lurking in hiding
places.
13 ¶ Arise, O LORD, confront him, bring
him low;
Deliver my soul from the wicked with
Your sword,

a Or *no evil device in me; My mouth*   *b* Lit *the pupil, the daughter of the eye*

Life after Death
When you die, will it all be over?

WHAT HAPPENS TO YOU AFTER you die? People have always
wanted an answer to that question, and the psalmists were no different.
They lived in an age without effective medicine, in an age when wars
were fought hand-to-hand. Dead bodies were a familiar reality. Yet death,
however familiar, remained mysterious and frightening to them.

*For You will not
abandon my soul to
Sheol; nor will You
allow Your Holy One
to undergo decay.
16:10*

Israelites called the dark and shadowy place where dead people go "Sheol."
When you got there, your life seemed thoroughly finished. The psalmists
emphatically did not want to go there, and they asked God, when praying for his help, what possible
good there might be in death. "Will Your wonders be made known in the darkness? And Your righteousness in the land of forgetfulness?" (Psalm 88:12). Sheol was the great leveler: it meant the end of
plans, of worship, of a relationship with God (Psalms 30:9; 88:5; 146:4). The dead were found there,
not the living.

God's Power over Death

Yet some psalms also hint at a happier view. They hold such a strong view of God's authority that
they show—vaguely, but unmistakably—God's power over the grave. For instance, God is *in* Sheol
(Psalm 139:8). He—and only he—can redeem a person from there (49:7–9,15). God will not let his "Holy
One" see decay—a claim that both Peter and Paul saw as a clear prediction of Jesus' resurrection from
the dead (Psalm 16:10, quoted in Acts 2:27; 13:35).

What did they expect life after death to be like, if God's power redeemed someone from Sheol?
You won't find a clearly defined picture of heaven here—only hints. The psalmists' thoughts center on
God's face and his presence. For God is the only unchangeable reality: Wherever you are, in life or in
death, he will be there. He is the ultimate reward to those who love him.

The expectation of God's face shows through in Psalms 16:8–11; 17:15; 49:15; 73:23–26. But for
a clearer perspective on life after death, you must read, in the Old Testament, Isaiah 26:19 and Daniel
12:1–3, and in the New Testament, 2 Corinthians 5:1–10, among many other passages.

Life Questions: Describe what you believe happens after you die. Is this a frightening or an encouraging picture to you?

14 From men with Your hand, O LORD,
From men of the world, whose portion is
in *this* life,
And whose belly You fill with Your
treasure;
They are satisfied with children,
And leave their abundance to their babes.
15 As for me, I shall behold Your face in
righteousness;
I will be satisfied with Your likeness
when I awake.

17:15 The Face of God

While the psalms often ask God to provide "refuge" in a time of trouble, they also look forward to seeing His face—a goal that is valuable only to someone who deeply loves God. To see God's face is to see and know him personally, deeply, and without the clouds of mystery that so often make faith difficult.

Psalm 18

The LORD Praised for Giving Deliverance.

For the choir director. *A Psalm* of David the servant of the LORD, who spoke to the LORD the words of this song in the day that the LORD delivered him from the hand of all his enemies and from the hand of Saul. And he said,

1 ¶ "I love You, O LORD, my strength."
2 The LORD is my rock and my fortress
and my deliverer,
My God, my rock, in whom I take
refuge;
My shield and the horn of my salvation,
my stronghold.
3 I call upon the LORD, who is worthy to
be praised,
And I am saved from my enemies.
4 ¶ The cords of death encompassed me,
And the torrents of *a*ungodliness
terrified me.
5 The cords of Sheol surrounded me;
The snares of death confronted me.
6 In my distress I called upon the LORD,
And cried to my God for help;
He heard my voice out of His temple,
And my cry for help before Him came
into His ears.
7 ¶ Then the earth shook and quaked;
And the foundations of the mountains
were trembling
And were shaken, because He was angry.
8 Smoke went up out of His nostrils,
And fire from His mouth devoured;
Coals were kindled by it.

9 He bowed the heavens also, and came
down
With thick darkness under His feet.
10 He rode upon a cherub and flew;
And He sped upon the wings of the
wind.
11 He made darkness His hiding place, His
canopy around Him,
Darkness of waters, thick clouds of the
skies.
12 From the brightness before Him passed
His thick clouds,
Hailstones and coals of fire.
13 The LORD also thundered in the heavens,
And the Most High uttered His voice,
Hailstones and coals of fire.
14 He sent out His arrows, and scattered
them,
And lightning flashes in abundance, and
routed them.
15 Then the channels of water appeared,
And the foundations of the world were
laid bare
At Your rebuke, O LORD,
At the blast of the breath of Your
nostrils.
16 ¶ He sent from on high, He took me;
He drew me out of many waters.
17 He delivered me from my strong enemy,
And from those who hated me, for they
were too mighty for me.
18 They confronted me in the day of my
calamity,
But the LORD was my stay.
19 He brought me forth also into a broad
place;
He rescued me, because He delighted
in me.
20 ¶ The LORD has rewarded me according
to my righteousness;
According to the cleanness of my hands
He has recompensed me.
21 For I have kept the ways of the LORD,
And have not wickedly departed from
my God.
22 For all His ordinances were before me,
And I did not put away His statutes
from me.
23 I was also *b*blameless with Him,
And I kept myself from my iniquity.
24 Therefore the LORD has recompensed me
according to my righteousness,
According to the cleanness of my hands
in His eyes.
25 ¶ With the kind You show Yourself kind;
With the blameless You show Yourself
blameless;
26 With the pure You show Yourself pure,

---

a Or *destruction*; Heb *Belial*   *b* Lit *complete*; or *having integrity*; or *perfect*

And with the crooked You show Yourself
  ^{a}astute.
27 For You save an afflicted people,
  But haughty eyes You abase.
28 For You light my lamp;
  The LORD my God illumines my
  darkness.
29 For by You I can ^{b}run upon a troop;
  And by my God I can leap over a wall.

30 ¶ As for God, His way is blameless;
  The word of the LORD is tried;
  He is a shield to all who take refuge in
  Him.
31 For who is God, but the LORD?
  And who is a rock, except our God,
32 The God who girds me with strength
  And makes my way blameless?
33 He makes my feet like hinds' *feet*,
  And sets me upon my high places.
34 He trains my hands for battle,
  So that my arms can bend a bow of
  bronze.
35 You have also given me the shield of
  Your salvation,
  And Your right hand upholds me;
  And Your gentleness makes me great.
36 You enlarge my steps under me,
  And my feet have not slipped.

37 ¶ I pursued my enemies and overtook
  them,
  And I did not turn back until they were
  consumed.
38 I shattered them, so that they were not
  able to rise;
  They fell under my feet.
39 For You have girded me with strength
  for battle;
  You have subdued under me those who
  rose up against me.
40 You have also made my enemies turn
  their backs to me,
  And I ^{c}destroyed those who hated me.
41 They cried for help, but there was none
  to save,
  Even to the LORD, but He did not answer
  them.
42 Then I beat them fine as the dust before
  the wind;
  I emptied them out as the mire of the
  streets.

43 ¶ You have delivered me from the
  contentions of the people;
  You have placed me as head of the
  nations;
  A people whom I have not known
  serve me.
44 As soon as they hear, they obey me;

Foreigners ^{d}submit to me.
45 Foreigners fade away,
  And come trembling out of their
  fortresses.

46 ¶ The LORD lives, and blessed be my
  rock;
  And exalted be the God of my salvation,
47 The God who executes vengeance
  for me,
  And subdues peoples under me,
48 He delivers me from my enemies;
  Surely You lift me above those who rise
  up against me;
  You rescue me from the violent man.
49 Therefore I will give thanks to You
  among the nations, O LORD,
  And I will sing praises to Your name.

18:49 Going Public

*For the psalmists, praising God was more than
a personal matter between the believer and his
God. They praised God publicly—even in front
of unbelievers—often inviting their audience to
join in. Such public praise anticipated New
Testament evangelism, the spreading of good
news to the entire world. Paul quoted this verse
in Romans 15:9 to stress that God had always
meant his love to reach out from the Jews to
the rest of humanity.*

50 He gives great ^{e}deliverance to His king,
  And shows lovingkindness to His
  anointed,
  To David and his descendants forever.

Psalm 19

The Works and the Word of God.

For the choir director. A Psalm of David.

1 ¶ The heavens are telling of the glory of
  God;
  And their expanse is declaring the work
  of His hands.
2 Day to day pours forth speech,
  And night to night reveals knowledge.
3 There is no speech, nor are there words;
  Their voice is not heard.
4 Their ^{f}line has gone out through all the
  earth,
  And their utterances to the end of the
  world.
  In them He has placed a tent for the sun,
5 Which is as a bridegroom coming out of
  his chamber;
  It rejoices as a strong man to run his
  course.

---

^{a}Lit *twisted* ^{b}Or *crush a troop* ^{c}Or *silenced* ^{d}Lit *deceive me;* i.e. give feigned obedience ^{e}I.e. victories; lit
salvations ^{f}Another reading is *sound*

6 Its rising is from one end of the heavens,
And its circuit to the other end of
them;
And there is nothing hidden from
its heat.

7 ¶ The law of the LORD is ^aperfect,
restoring the soul;
The testimony of the LORD is sure,
making wise the simple.

19:7–14 The Names of God

After describing the skies as a reflection of God's glory in the first six verses, Psalm 19 switches gears. From the sun, moon, and stars it turns to consider the beauty of God's law. Reflecting that change, the poem in Hebrew uses a different, more personal name for God. The first six verses refer to God with a general name that anyone, of any religion, might use—just like our English word God. But from verse seven on, God is called "the LORD" (a translation of the Hebrew Yahweh)—the personal name God revealed to Moses from the burning bush (Exodus 3:15). The heavens declare the glory of God, but God's law reveals even more—his personal voice to his chosen people. He introduces himself to them by his first name, as it were.

8 The precepts of the LORD are right,
rejoicing the heart;
The commandment of the LORD is pure,
enlightening the eyes.
9 The fear of the LORD is clean, enduring
forever;
The judgments of the LORD are true; they
are righteous altogether.
10 They are more desirable than gold, yes,
than much fine gold;
Sweeter also than honey and the
drippings of the honeycomb.
11 Moreover, by them Your servant is
warned;
In keeping them there is great reward.
12 Who can discern *his* errors? Acquit me
of hidden *faults*.
13 Also keep back Your servant from
presumptuous *sins;*
Let them not rule over me;
Then I will be ^bblameless,
And I shall be acquitted of great
transgression.
14 Let the words of my mouth and the
meditation of my heart
Be acceptable in Your sight,
O LORD, my rock and my Redeemer.

Psalm 20

Prayer for Victory over Enemies.

For the choir director. A Psalm of David.

1 ¶ May the LORD answer you in the day
of trouble!
May the name of the God of Jacob set
you *securely* on high!
2 May He send you help from the
sanctuary
And support you from Zion!
3 May He remember all your meal
offerings
And find your burnt offering acceptable!
Selah.

4 ¶ May He grant you your heart's desire
And fulfill all your ^ccounsel!
5 We will sing for joy over your victory,
And in the name of our God we will set
up our banners.
May the LORD fulfill all your petitions.

6 ¶ Now I know that the LORD saves His
anointed;
He will answer him from His holy
heaven
With the saving strength of His right
hand.
7 Some *boast* in chariots and some in
horses,
But we will boast in the name of the
LORD, our God.
8 They have bowed down and fallen,
But we have risen and stood upright.
9 Save, O LORD;
May the King answer us in the day we
call.

Psalm 21

Praise for Deliverance.

For the choir director. A Psalm of David.

1 ¶ O LORD, in Your strength the king will
be glad,
And in Your ^dsalvation how greatly he
will rejoice!
2 You have given him his heart's desire,
And You have not withheld the request
of his lips. Selah.
3 For You meet him with the blessings of
good things;
You set a crown of fine gold on his head.
4 He asked life of You,
You gave it to him,
Length of days forever and ever.
5 His glory is great through Your
^dsalvation,
Splendor and majesty You place upon
him.
6 For You make him most blessed forever;

---

^a I.e. blameless   ^b Lit *complete*   ^c Or *purpose*   ^d Or *victory*

You make him joyful with gladness in
Your presence.

7 ¶ For the king trusts in the LORD,
And through the lovingkindness of the
Most High he will not be shaken.
8 Your hand will find out all your enemies;
Your right hand will find out those who
hate you.
9 You will make them as a fiery oven in
the time of your anger;
The LORD will swallow them up in His
wrath,
And fire will devour them.
10 Their ªoffspring You will destroy from
the earth,
And their ᵇdescendants from among the
sons of men.
11 Though they intended evil against You
And devised a plot,
They will not succeed.
12 For You will make them turn their back;
You will aim with Your bowstrings at
their faces.
13 Be exalted, O LORD, in Your strength;
We will sing and praise Your power.

Psalm 22

A Cry of Anguish and a Song of Praise.

For the choir director; upon ᶜAijeleth
Hashshahar. A Psalm of David.

1 ¶ My God, my God, why have You
forsaken me?
Far from my deliverance are the words of
my groaning.
2 O my God, I cry by day, but You do not
answer;
And by night, but I have no rest.
3 Yet You are holy,
O You who are enthroned upon the
praises of Israel.
4 In You our fathers trusted;
They trusted and You delivered them.
5 To You they cried out and were
delivered;
In You they trusted and were not
disappointed.

6 ¶ But I am a worm and not a man,
A reproach of men and despised by the
people.
7 All who see me sneer at me;
They ᵈseparate with the lip, they wag
the head, *saying,*
8 "ᵉCommit *yourself* to the LORD; let Him
deliver him;
Let Him rescue him, because He delights
in him."

9 ¶ Yet You are He who brought me forth
from the womb;
You made me trust *when* upon my
mother's breasts.
10 Upon You I was cast from birth;
You have been my God from my
mother's womb.

11 ¶ Be not far from me, for trouble is near;
For there is none to help.
12 Many bulls have surrounded me;
Strong *bulls* of Bashan have encircled me.
13 They open wide their mouth at me,
As a ravening and a roaring lion.
14 I am poured out like water,
And all my bones are out of joint;
My heart is like wax;
It is melted within me.
15 My strength is dried up like a potsherd,
And my tongue cleaves to my jaws;
And You lay me in the dust of death.
16 For dogs have surrounded me;
A band of evildoers has
encompassed me;
They pierced my hands and my feet.
17 I can count all my bones.
They look, they stare at me;
18 They divide my garments among them,
And for my clothing they cast lots.

19 ¶ But You, O LORD, be not far off;
O You my help, hasten to my assistance.
20 Deliver my soul from the sword,
My only *life* from the power of the dog.
21 Save me from the lion's mouth;
From the horns of the wild oxen You
answer me.

22 ¶ I will tell of Your name to my
brethren;
In the midst of the assembly I will
praise You.
23 You who fear the LORD, praise Him;
All you descendants of Jacob, glorify
Him,
And stand in awe of Him, all you
descendants of Israel.
24 For He has not despised nor abhorred
the affliction of the afflicted;
Nor has He hidden His face from him;
But when he cried to Him for help, He
heard.

25 ¶ From You *comes* my praise in the great
assembly;
I shall pay my vows before those who
fear Him.
26 The ᶠafflicted will eat and be satisfied;
Those who seek Him will praise the
LORD.
Let your heart live forever!

ª Lit *fruit*   ᵇ Lit *seed*   ᶜ Lit *the hind of the morning*   ᵈ I.e. make mouths at me   ᵉ Lit *Roll;* another reading is *He*
committed himself   ᶠ Or *poor*

27 All the ends of the earth will remember
    and turn to the LORD,
    And all the families of the nations will
    worship before You.
28 For the kingdom is the LORD'S
    And He rules over the nations.
29 All the prosperous of the earth will eat
    and worship,
    All those who go down to the dust will
    bow before Him,
    Even he who cannot keep his soul alive.
30 Posterity will serve Him;
    It will be told of the Lord to the *coming*
    generation.
31 They will come and will declare His
    righteousness

To a people who will be born, that He
    has performed *it*.

Psalm 23

The LORD, the Psalmist's Shepherd.

A Psalm of David.

1 ¶ The LORD is my shepherd,
    I shall not want.
2 He makes me lie down in green pastures;
    He leads me beside quiet waters.
3 He restores my soul;
    He guides me in the paths of
    righteousness
    For His name's sake.

The Song of the Cross
Even the best people sometimes suffer

> They divide my garments among them, and for my clothing they cast lots. 22:18

SUPERFICIALLY, THE OLD TESTAMENT CAN sometimes read like it's taken from old movies. The good guys are the Israelites, and they fight with the bad guys from nations around them. The Israelites have moments when they get off track, worshiping idols and acting like their "bad guy" neighbors. But when they turn back to God, they invariably win, and win big. The ending, in story after story, is happy. God *is* on their side.

Yet, in Psalm 22 and a few other places, the "good guy" story doesn't fit at all. This poem, credited to David, the great king and man "after God's own heart," tells of tremendous suffering with no relief from God. It sounds like a mob scene, a lynching. The "good guy's" enemies have him. They surround him, jeering, like a pack of dogs. He is helpless and exhausted. All he can do is cry to God.

The psalmist wavers back and forth, first crying out in misery, then taking stock of God's wonderful character, then describing his misery again. The whole poem is a prayer to God. Although this cry has gone up day and night (verse 2), God remains silent.

Whose Humiliations?

Then, at verse 22, the poem takes a dramatic turn, switching from grief to jubilation. Somehow, God has saved the sufferer, who, in great excitement, tells others about it. He sees more than his own good fortune: He foresees this deliverance spilling over into the whole world. He predicts the story of God's help told to future generations forever. God will be worshiped by the entire world.

A person might read Psalm 22 as an extravagantly poetic description of David's troubles. But Jesus and the writers of the New Testament saw something more in it. When Jesus was dying on the cross, he had this psalm on his lips (Matthew 27:46). Afterwards, when his disciples wanted to explain Jesus' life and sufferings, they turned to this psalm and others like it.

In them the disciples saw a pattern and a foreshadowing. The pattern is redemptive suffering. If good guys do not always win, if God seems actually to desert them—if David himself, the great leader and true man of God, knew these pains—then surely no one is exempt. And this suffering has a point. After it (and because of it) come victory and power, and the salvation of the world. This pattern helped Jesus' followers appreciate why Jesus, along with his followers, had to suffer.

A Fulfillment of Prophecy

Psalm 22 also helped the New Testament writers to see Jesus' life as a fulfillment of Old Testament prophecy. Jews had expected a Warrior-Messiah, a son of David who, like David, would lead his people to victory through battle. In Psalm 22 they saw that David had left another legacy: victory through suffering. The Messiah would lead his followers in suffering. Only Isaiah had put it more clearly, in his famous "servant" passages (Isaiah 42:1–9; 49:1–7; 50:4–9; 52:13–53:12). Psalm 22 stretches beyond the time of David; Jesus fits it perfectly.

Life Questions: Have you ever seen good come out of suffering for your friends or family?

4 ¶ Even though I walk through the
  ^avalley of the shadow of death,
I fear no ^bevil, for You are with me;
Your rod and Your staff, they
  comfort me.
5 You prepare a table before me in the
  presence of my enemies;
You have anointed my head with oil;
My cup overflows.
6 Surely goodness and lovingkindness will
  follow me all the days of my life,
And I will ^cdwell in the house of the
  LORD forever.

Psalm 24

The King of Glory Entering Zion.

A Psalm of David.

1 ¶ The earth is the LORD'S, and ^dall it
  contains,
The world, and those who dwell in it.
2 For He has founded it upon the seas
And established it upon the rivers.
3 Who may ascend into the hill of the
  LORD?
And who may stand in His holy place?
4 He who has clean hands and a pure
  heart,
Who has not lifted up his soul to
  falsehood
And has not sworn deceitfully.
5 He shall receive a blessing from the LORD
And righteousness from the God of his
  salvation.
6 This is the generation of those who seek
  Him,
Who seek Your face—*even* Jacob.   Selah.

7 ¶ Lift up your heads, O gates,
And be lifted up, O ^eancient doors,
That the King of glory may come in!
8 Who is the King of glory?
The LORD strong and mighty,
The LORD mighty in battle.
9 Lift up your heads, O gates,
And lift *them* up, O ^eancient doors,
That the King of glory may come in!
10 Who is this King of glory?
The LORD of hosts,
He is the King of glory.   Selah.

Psalm 25

Prayer for Protection, Guidance
and Pardon.

A Psalm of David.

1 ¶ To You, O LORD, I lift up my soul.
2 O my God, in You I trust,
Do not let me be ashamed;

Do not let my enemies exult over me.
3 Indeed, none of those who wait for You
  will be ashamed;
Those who deal treacherously without
  cause will be ashamed.

4 ¶ Make me know Your ways, O LORD;
Teach me Your paths.
5 Lead me in Your truth and teach me,
For You are the God of my salvation;
For You I wait all the day.
6 Remember, O LORD, Your compassion
  and Your lovingkindnesses,
For they have been ^ffrom of old.
7 Do not remember the sins of my youth
  or my transgressions;
According to Your lovingkindness
  remember me,
For Your goodness' sake, O LORD.

8 ¶ Good and upright is the LORD;
Therefore He instructs sinners in the
  way.
9 He leads the humble in justice,
And He teaches the humble His way.
10 All the paths of the LORD are
  lovingkindness and truth
To those who keep His covenant and His
  testimonies.
11 For Your name's sake, O LORD,
Pardon my iniquity, for it is great.

12 ¶ Who is the man who fears the LORD?
He will instruct him in the way he
  should choose.
13 His soul will abide in prosperity,
And his ^gdescendants will inherit the
  land.
14 The secret of the LORD is for those who
  fear Him,
And He will make them know His
  covenant.
15 My eyes are continually toward the LORD,
For He will pluck my feet out of the net.

16 ¶ Turn to me and be gracious to me,
For I am lonely and afflicted.
17 The troubles of my heart are enlarged;
Bring me out of my distresses.
18 Look upon my affliction and my
  ^htrouble,
And forgive all my sins.
19 Look upon my enemies, for they are
  many,
And they hate me with violent hatred.
20 Guard my soul and deliver me;
Do not let me be ashamed, for I take
  refuge in You.
21 Let integrity and uprightness
  preserve me,
For I wait for You.

---

^a Or *valley of deep darkness*   ^b Or *harm*   ^c Another reading is *return to*   ^d Lit *its fullness*   ^e Lit *everlasting*
^f Or *everlasting*   ^g Lit *seed*   ^h Lit *toil*

22 Redeem Israel, O God,
  Out of all his troubles.

Psalm 26

Protestation of Integrity and Prayer for Protection.

A Psalm of David.

1 ¶ *a*Vindicate me, O LORD, for I have
    walked in my integrity,
  And I have trusted in the LORD without
    wavering.
2 Examine me, O LORD, and try me;
  Test my *b*mind and my heart.
3 For Your lovingkindness is before my
    eyes,
  And I have walked in Your truth.
4 I do not sit with *c*deceitful men,
  Nor will I go with pretenders.
5 I hate the assembly of evildoers,
  And I will not sit with the wicked.
6 I shall wash my hands in innocence,
  And I will go about Your altar, O LORD,
7 That I may proclaim with the voice of
    thanksgiving
  And declare all Your wonders.

8 ¶ O LORD, I love the habitation of Your
    house
  And the place where Your glory dwells.
9 Do not take my soul away *along* with
    sinners,
  Nor my life with men of bloodshed,
10 In whose hands is a wicked scheme,
  And whose right hand is full of bribes.
11 But as for me, I shall walk in my
    integrity;
  Redeem me, and be gracious to me.
12 My foot stands on a level place;
  In the congregations I shall bless the
    LORD.

Psalm 27

A Psalm of Fearless Trust in God.

A Psalm of David.

1 ¶ The LORD is my light and my salvation;
    Whom shall I fear?
  The LORD is the defense of my life;
    Whom shall I dread?
2 When evildoers came upon me to devour
    my flesh,
  My adversaries and my enemies, they
    stumbled and fell.
3 Though a host encamp against me,
  My heart will not fear;
  Though war arise against me,
  In *spite of* this I shall be confident.

4 ¶ One thing I have asked from the LORD,
    that I shall seek:
  That I may dwell in the house of the
    LORD all the days of my life,
  To behold the *d*beauty of the LORD
  And to *e*meditate in His temple.

26:11 Self-Righteous?

*This claim to be blameless or righteous—
repeated many times in other psalms—should
not be stretched too far. Whenever the
psalmists examined themselves before God,
they acknowledged their deep need for
forgiveness (see 19:12; 32:1–5; 130:3; and
143:2).*

*Here, though, the issue is God's fairness.
Knowing little about life after death, the
psalmists expected that good people would do
better in this life than bad people. They were
deeply puzzled when they did not. Didn't God
control every event? In calling for justice, they
emphasized that they had been more faithful
to God than their enemies.*

*Compared to the people plotting murder and
betrayal against him, the psalmist was
blameless. In a wholehearted, sincere way he
had followed God. He was no hypocrite. He
responds like a person swearing in court about
his traffic accident: "My driving is blameless."
He doesn't mean he never makes a mistake. He
means only that he doesn't deserve
punishment.*

5 For in the day of trouble He will conceal
    me in His tabernacle;
  In the secret place of His tent He will
    hide me;
  He will lift me up on a rock.
6 And now my head will be lifted up above
    my enemies around me,
  And I will offer in His tent sacrifices with
    shouts of joy;
  I will sing, yes, I will sing praises to the
    LORD.

7 ¶ Hear, O LORD, when I cry with my
    voice,
  And be gracious to me and answer me.
8 *When You said,* "Seek My face," my
    heart said to You,
  "Your face, O LORD, I shall seek."
9 Do not hide Your face from me,
  Do not turn Your servant away in
    anger;
  You have been my help;
  Do not abandon me nor forsake me,
  O God of my salvation!

a Lit *Judge*   *b* Lit *kidneys,* figurative for inner man   *c* Or *worthless men;* lit *men of falsehood*   *d* Lit *delightfulness*
e Lit *inquire*

10 For my father and my mother have
         forsaken me,
    But the LORD will take me up.

11 ¶ Teach me Your way, O LORD,
    And lead me in a level path
    Because of my foes.
12 Do not deliver me over to the desire of
         my adversaries,
    For false witnesses have risen against me,
    And such as breathe out violence.
13 *I would have despaired* unless I had
         believed that I would see the
         goodness of the LORD
    In the land of the living.
14 Wait for the LORD;
    Be strong and let your heart take
         courage;
    Yes, wait for the LORD.

Psalm 28

A Prayer for Help,
and Praise for Its Answer.

A Psalm of David.

1 ¶ To You, O LORD, I call;
    My rock, do not be deaf to me,
    For if You are silent to me,
    I will become like those who go down to
         the pit.
2 Hear the voice of my supplications when
         I cry to You for help,
    When I lift up my hands toward ^aYour
         holy sanctuary.
3 Do not drag me away with the wicked
    And with those who work iniquity,
    Who speak peace with their neighbors,
    While evil is in their hearts.
4 Requite them according to their work
         and according to the evil of their
         practices;
    Requite them according to the deeds of
         their hands;
    Repay them their ^brecompense.
5 Because they do not regard the works of
         the LORD
    Nor the deeds of His hands,
    He will tear them down and not build
         them up.

6 ¶ Blessed be the LORD,
    Because He has heard the voice of my
         supplication.
7 The LORD is my strength and my shield;
    My heart trusts in Him, and I am helped;
    Therefore my heart exults,
    And with my song I shall thank Him.
8 The LORD is their strength,
    And He is a saving defense to His
         anointed.

9 Save Your people and bless Your
         inheritance;
    Be their shepherd also, and carry them
         forever.

Psalm 29

The Voice of the LORD in the Storm.

A Psalm of David.

1 ¶ Ascribe to the LORD, O sons of the
         mighty,
    Ascribe to the LORD glory and strength.
2 Ascribe to the LORD the glory due to His
         name;
    Worship the LORD in holy array.

3 ¶ The voice of the LORD is upon the
         waters;
    The God of glory thunders,
    The LORD is over many waters.
4 The voice of the LORD is powerful,
    The voice of the LORD is majestic.
5 The voice of the LORD breaks the cedars;
    Yes, the LORD breaks in pieces the cedars
         of Lebanon.
6 He makes Lebanon skip like a calf,
    And Sirion like a young wild ox.
7 The voice of the LORD hews out flames
         of fire.
8 The voice of the LORD shakes the
         wilderness;
    The LORD shakes the wilderness of
         Kadesh.
9 The voice of the LORD makes the deer to
         calve
    And strips the forests bare;
    And in His temple everything says,
         "Glory!"

10 ¶ The LORD sat *as King* at the flood;
    Yes, the LORD sits as King forever.
11 The LORD will give strength to His
         people;
    The LORD will bless His people with
         peace.

Psalm 30

Thanksgiving for Deliverance from Death.

A Psalm; a Song at the Dedication of the House.
A Psalm of David.

1 ¶ I will extol You, O LORD, for You have
         lifted me up,
    And have not let my enemies rejoice
         over me.
2 O LORD my God,
    I cried to You for help, and You
         healed me.
3 O LORD, You have brought up my soul
         from Sheol;

---

^a Lit *the innermost place of Your sanctuary*   ^b Or *dealings*

You have kept me alive, that I would not
go down to the pit.
4 Sing praise to the LORD, you His godly
ones,
And give thanks to His holy name.
5 For His anger is but for a moment,
His favor is for a lifetime;
Weeping may last for the night,
But a shout of joy *comes* in the morning.

30:5 One-night Guest

*The Bible never ignores the emotions of the
moment. Here, the psalmist acknowledges the
tough times that come with living as God's
child. But the Bible also insists on a long-range
perspective. Difficulties don't last; God's care
does. This psalm pictures "weeping" as a guest
who comes to stay for just a single night.*

6 ¶ Now as for me, I said in my prosperity,
"I will never be moved."
7 O LORD, by Your favor You have made
my mountain to stand strong;
You hid Your face, I was dismayed.
8 To You, O LORD, I called,
And to the Lord I made supplication:
9 "What profit is there in my blood, if I go
down to the pit?
Will the dust praise You? Will it declare
Your faithfulness?
10 ¶ "Hear, O LORD, and be gracious to me;
O LORD, be my helper."
11 You have turned for me my mourning
into dancing;
You have loosed my sackcloth and
girded me with gladness,
12 That *my* soul may sing praise to You and
not be silent.
O LORD my God, I will give thanks to
You forever.

Psalm 31

A Psalm of Complaint and of Praise.

For the choir director. A Psalm of David.

1 ¶ In You, O LORD, I have taken refuge;
Let me never be ashamed;
In Your righteousness deliver me.
2 Incline Your ear to me, rescue me
quickly;
Be to me a rock of strength,
A stronghold to save me.
3 For You are my rock and my fortress;
For Your name's sake You will lead me
and guide me.
4 You will pull me out of the net which
they have secretly laid for me,
For You are my strength.

5 Into Your hand I commit my spirit;
You have ransomed me, O LORD, God of
truth.
6 ¶ I hate those who regard vain idols,
But I trust in the LORD.
7 I will rejoice and be glad in Your
lovingkindness,
Because You have seen my affliction;
You have known the troubles of my
soul,
8 And You have not given me over into
the hand of the enemy;
You have set my feet in a large place.
9 ¶ Be gracious to me, O LORD, for I am in
distress;
My eye is wasted away from grief, my
soul and my body *also*.
10 For my life is spent with sorrow
And my years with sighing;
My strength has failed because of my
iniquity,
And my body has wasted away.
11 Because of all my adversaries, I have
become a reproach,
Especially to my neighbors,
And an object of dread to my
acquaintances;
Those who see me in the street flee
from me.
12 I am forgotten as a dead man, out of
mind;
I am like a broken vessel.
13 For I have heard the slander of many,
Terror is on every side;
While they took counsel together
against me,
They schemed to take away my life.
14 ¶ But as for me, I trust in You, O LORD,
I say, "You are my God."
15 My times are in Your hand;
Deliver me from the hand of my enemies
and from those who persecute me.
16 Make Your face to shine upon Your
servant;
Save me in Your lovingkindness.
17 Let me not be put to shame, O LORD, for
I call upon You;
Let the wicked be put to shame, let them
be silent in Sheol.
18 Let the lying lips be mute,
Which speak arrogantly against the
righteous
With pride and contempt.
19 ¶ How great is Your goodness,
Which You have stored up for those who
fear You,
Which You have wrought for those who
take refuge in You,
Before the sons of men!

20 You hide them in the secret place of
    Your presence from the conspiracies
    of man;
    You keep them secretly in a shelter from
    the strife of tongues.
21 Blessed be the LORD,
    For He has made marvelous His
    lovingkindness to me in a besieged
    city.
22 As for me, I said in my alarm,
    "I am cut off from before Your eyes";
    Nevertheless You heard the voice of my
    supplications
    When I cried to You.
23 ¶ O love the LORD, all you His godly
    ones!
    The LORD preserves the faithful
    And fully recompenses the proud
    doer.
24 Be strong and let your heart take
    courage,
    All you who hope in the LORD.

Psalm 32

Blessedness of Forgiveness and of Trust in God.

A Psalm of David. A [a]Maskil.

1 ¶ How blessed is he whose transgression
    is forgiven,
    Whose sin is covered!
2 How blessed is the man to whom the
    LORD does not impute iniquity,
    And in whose spirit there is no deceit!

32:2 The Benefits of Faith

Paul quoted this verse in Romans 4:6–8, while making his case that we do not earn status in God's eyes: God must credit righteousness on the basis of faith.

3 ¶ When I kept silent *about my sin*, my
    body wasted away
    Through my groaning all day long.
4 For day and night Your hand was heavy
    upon me;
    My vitality was drained away *as* with the
    fever heat of summer. Selah.
5 I acknowledged my sin to You,
    And my iniquity I did not hide;
    I said, "I will confess my transgressions
    to the LORD";
    And You forgave the guilt of my
    sin. Selah.

6 Therefore, let everyone who is godly pray
    to You in a time when You may be
    found;
    Surely in a flood of great waters they will
    not reach him.
7 You are my hiding place; You preserve
    me from trouble;
    You surround me with songs of
    deliverance. Selah.
8 ¶ I will instruct you and teach you in the
    way which you should go;
    I will counsel you with My eye upon
    you.
9 Do not be as the horse or as the mule
    which have no understanding,
    Whose trappings include bit and bridle
    to hold them in check,
    Otherwise they will not come near to
    you.
10 Many are the sorrows of the wicked,
    But he who trusts in the LORD,
    lovingkindness shall surround him.
11 Be glad in the LORD and rejoice, you
    righteous ones;
    And shout for joy, all you who are
    upright in heart.

Psalm 33

Praise to the Creator and Preserver.

1 ¶ Sing for joy in the LORD, O you
    righteous ones;
    Praise is becoming to the upright.
2 Give thanks to the LORD with the lyre;
    Sing praises to Him with a harp of ten
    strings.
3 Sing to Him a new song;
    Play skillfully with a shout of joy.
4 For the word of the LORD is upright,
    And all His work is *done* in faithfulness.
5 He loves righteousness and justice;
    The earth is full of the lovingkindness of
    the LORD.
6 ¶ By the word of the LORD the heavens
    were made,
    And by the breath of His mouth all their
    host.
7 He gathers the waters of the sea together
    as a heap;
    He lays up the deeps in storehouses.
8 Let all the earth fear the LORD;
    Let all the inhabitants of the world stand
    in awe of Him.
9 For He spoke, and it was done;
    He commanded, and it stood fast.
10 The LORD nullifies the counsel of the
    nations;

---

[a] Possibly *Contemplative*, or *Didactic*, or *Skillful Psalm*

He frustrates the plans of the peoples.
11 The counsel of the LORD stands forever,
The plans of His heart from generation
to generation.
12 Blessed is the nation whose God is the
LORD,
The people whom He has chosen for His
own inheritance.

13 ¶ The LORD looks from heaven;
He sees all the sons of men;
14 From His dwelling place He looks out
On all the inhabitants of the earth,
15 He who fashions the hearts of them all,
He who understands all their works.
16 The king is not saved by a mighty army;
A warrior is not delivered by great
strength.

17 A horse is a false hope for victory;
Nor does it deliver anyone by its great
strength.
18 ¶ Behold, the eye of the LORD is on those
who fear Him,
On those who hope for His
lovingkindness,
19 To deliver their soul from death
And to keep them alive in famine.
20 Our soul waits for the LORD;
He is our help and our shield.
21 For our heart rejoices in Him,
Because we trust in His holy name.
22 Let Your lovingkindness, O LORD,
be upon us,
According as we have hoped in
You.

Lyrics for the Living God
The psalms were meant to be sung—and shouted

WILLIAM BOOTH, BELIEVING THE 19TH-CENTURY English church had become too refined to reach the cities' poor, took the gospel into the streets. He organized his workers into a "salvation army," complete with uniforms and military rank.

Sing to Him a new song; play skillfully with a shout of joy.
33:3

With hecklers and drunks abounding, the "army" didn't always find preaching easy or safe. A local builder, Charles William Fry, offered himself and his three sons as bodyguards. As it happened all four played brass instruments, which they carried along to accompany singing.

Booth's rowdier supporters were soon dragging along concertinas, bells, hunting horns, banjos, tambourines, and drums to praise the Lord. Said one leader, "It sounds as if a brass band's gone out of its mind."

Salvation Army recruits did not stick to traditional hymns but invented their own words for rousing popular tunes. "Here's to Good Old Whiskey" became "Storm the Forts of Darkness." Booth had his doubts about this trend until one night, hearing a beautiful rendition of "Bless His Name, He Sets Me Free," he asked about the tune. "Why, Mr. Booth, that's 'Champagne Charlie Is My Name,'" the embarrassed singer replied.

"That settles it," Booth said. "Why *should* the devil have all the best tunes?" Soon 400 bands were crashing about England, playing hit tunes with Christian words.

The Best Music Available

David and his people would have liked that spirit. Many of the psalms were meant to be sung, and sung joyfully. Modern church formality seems far removed from their frequent command: "Sing for joy! Shout aloud!" Their instruments included cymbals, tambourines, trumpets, ram's horns, harps, and lyres. Sometimes dancing erupted. The world, in the psalmist's imagination, can't contain the delight God inspires. A *new* song must be sung. "Shout joyfully to the LORD, all the earth; break forth and sing for joy" (98:4).

First Chronicles 15:16 and 23:5 report that David appointed 4,000 professional musicians to provide their services to the temple. They offered the best music available, and the congregation joined in. Nobody knows exactly what it sounded like, but scholars doubt it was all soft and soothing. Musicians improvised. Most of the instruments used suggest rousing, rhythmic sound.

Every generation of Christians renews the discovery of this "new song," sometimes through the music of their forebears, sometimes in a form that shocks their solemn elders. The Salvation Army did, as did the Jesus Movement in the 60s and Christian rock music in the 80s and 90s. David would not have been surprised. He jolted his own wife with spontaneous dancing (see 1 Chronicles 15:29). When people know God, they come to life with a jubilant song on their lips.

Life Questions: When you sing to God, what kind of emotions do you hope to feel? What kind of music contributes to that?

Psalm 34

The LORD, a Provider and Deliverer.

A Psalm of David when he feigned madness before Abimelech, who drove him away and he departed.

1 ¶ I will bless the LORD at all times;
His praise shall continually be in my mouth.

2 My soul will make its boast in the LORD;
The humble will hear it and rejoice.

3 O magnify the LORD with me,
And let us exalt His name together.

4 ¶ I sought the LORD, and He answered me,
And delivered me from all my fears.

5 They looked to Him and were radiant,
And their faces will never be ashamed.

6 This poor man cried, and the LORD heard him
And saved him out of all his troubles.

7 The angel of the LORD encamps around those who fear Him,
And rescues them.

8 ¶ O taste and see that the LORD is good;
How blessed is the man who takes refuge in Him!

9 O fear the LORD, you His saints;
For to those who fear Him there is no want.

34:9 Is God Frightening?

"Fear of the LORD" is a phrase we find frequently in the Old Testament. Does it mean that we should be frightened of God? Apparently not. "Fear of the LORD" gradually became a standard phrase for a good relationship with God. A good relationship begins with a reverent sense that God is so powerful and righteous that we dare not take him lightly. But it goes on from awe to a sense of deep security, as this psalm fully demonstrates.

10 The young lions do lack and suffer hunger;
But they who seek the LORD shall not be in want of any good thing.

11 Come, you children, listen to me;
I will teach you the fear of the LORD.

12 Who is the man who desires life
And loves *length of* days that he may see good?

13 Keep your tongue from evil
And your lips from speaking deceit.

14 Depart from evil and do good;
Seek peace and pursue it.

15 ¶ The eyes of the LORD are toward the righteous
And His ears are *open* to their cry.

16 The face of the LORD is against evildoers,
To cut off the memory of them from the earth.

17 *The righteous* cry, and the LORD hears
And delivers them out of all their troubles.

18 The LORD is near to the brokenhearted
And saves those who are ᵃcrushed in spirit.

19 ¶ Many are the afflictions of the righteous,
But the LORD delivers him out of them all.

20 He keeps all his bones,
Not one of them is broken.

21 Evil shall slay the wicked,
And those who hate the righteous will be condemned.

22 The LORD redeems the soul of His servants,
And none of those who take refuge in Him will be condemned.

Psalm 35

Prayer for Rescue from Enemies.

A Psalm of David.

1 ¶ Contend, O LORD, with those who contend with me;
Fight against those who fight against me.

2 Take hold of ᵇbuckler and shield
And rise up for my help.

3 Draw also the spear and the battle-axe to meet those who pursue me;
Say to my soul, "I am your salvation."

4 Let those be ashamed and dishonored who seek my life;
Let those be turned back and humiliated who devise evil against me.

5 Let them be like chaff before the wind,
With the angel of the LORD driving *them* on.

6 Let their way be dark and slippery,
With the angel of the LORD pursuing them.

7 For without cause they hid their net for me;
Without cause they dug a pit for my soul.

8 Let destruction come upon him unawares,
And let the net which he hid catch himself;
Into that very destruction let him fall.

9 ¶ And my soul shall rejoice in the LORD;
It shall exult in His salvation.

ᵃ Or *contrite*   ᵇ I.e. small shield

10 All my bones will say, "LORD, who is
like You,
Who delivers the afflicted from him who
is too strong for him,
And the afflicted and the needy from
him who robs him?"

11 Malicious witnesses rise up;
They ask me of things that I do not
know.

12 They repay me evil for good,
To the bereavement of my soul.

13 But as for me, when they were sick, my
clothing was sackcloth;
I humbled my soul with fasting,
And my prayer kept returning to my
bosom.

14 I went about as though it were my friend
or brother;
I bowed down mourning, as one who
sorrows for a mother.

15 But at my ªstumbling they rejoiced and
gathered themselves together;
The smiters whom I did not know
gathered together against me,
They slandered me without ceasing.

16 Like godless jesters at a feast,
They gnashed at me with their teeth.

17 ¶ Lord, how long will You look on?
Rescue my soul from their ravages,
My only *life* from the lions.

18 I will give You thanks in the great
congregation;
I will praise You among a mighty throng.

19 Do not let those who are wrongfully my
enemies rejoice over me;
Nor let those who hate me without cause
wink maliciously.

20 For they do not speak peace,
But they devise deceitful words against
those who are quiet in the land.

21 They opened their mouth wide
against me;
They said, "Aha, aha, our eyes have
seen it!"

22 ¶ You have seen it, O LORD, do not keep
silent;
O Lord, do not be far from me.

23 Stir up Yourself, and awake to my right
And to my cause, my God and my Lord.

24 Judge me, O LORD my God, according to
Your righteousness,
And do not let them rejoice over me.

25 Do not let them say in their heart, "Aha,
our desire!"
Do not let them say, "We have
swallowed him up!"

26 Let those be ashamed and humiliated
altogether who rejoice at my
distress;

Let those be clothed with shame and
dishonor who magnify themselves
over me.

27 ¶ Let them shout for joy and rejoice, who
favor my vindication;
And let them say continually, "The LORD
be magnified,
Who delights in the prosperity of His
servant."

28 And my tongue shall declare Your
righteousness
And Your praise all day long.

Psalm 36

Wickedness of Men
and Lovingkindness of God.

For the choir director. *A Psalm* of David the
servant of the LORD.

1 ¶ Transgression speaks to the ungodly
within his heart;
There is no fear of God before his eyes.

2 For it flatters him in his *own*
eyes
Concerning the discovery of his iniquity
and the hatred *of it.*

3 The words of his mouth are wickedness
and deceit;
He has ceased to be wise *and* to do
good.

4 He plans wickedness upon his bed;
He sets himself on a path that is not
good;
He does not despise evil.

5 ¶ Your lovingkindness, O LORD, extends
to the heavens,
Your faithfulness *reaches* to the skies.

6 Your righteousness is like the mountains
of God;
Your judgments are *like* a great deep.
O LORD, You preserve man and beast.

7 How precious is Your lovingkindness,
O God!
And the children of men take refuge in
the shadow of Your wings.

8 They drink their fill of the abundance of
Your house;
And You give them to drink of the river
of Your delights.

9 For with You is the fountain of life;
In Your light we see light.

10 ¶ O continue Your lovingkindness to
those who know You,
And Your righteousness to the upright in
heart.

11 Let not the foot of pride come upon
me,

ª Or *limping*

And let not the hand of the wicked drive
    me away.
12 There the doers of iniquity have fallen;
    They have been thrust down and cannot
    rise.

36:9 Light Makes Light

*By itself, light is invisible; and yet everything is
invisible until light strikes it. So it is with God:
we can't see him, but "in his light" (under his
loving influence) we see and understand
his love in all that surrounds us. God's
overwhelming generosity stands in complete
contrast to the self-important plotting of
wicked human beings (verses 1–4).*

Psalm 37

Security of Those Who Trust in the LORD, and Insecurity of the Wicked.

A Psalm of David.

1 ¶ Do not fret because of evildoers,
    Be not envious toward wrongdoers.
2 For they will wither quickly like the grass
    And fade like the green herb.
3 Trust in the LORD and do good;
    Dwell in the land and *a*cultivate
    faithfulness.
4 Delight yourself in the LORD;
    And He will give you the desires of your
    heart.
5 Commit your way to the LORD,
    Trust also in Him, and He will do it.
6 He will bring forth your righteousness as
    the light
    And your judgment as the noonday.

7 ¶ *b*Rest in the LORD and wait *c*patiently
    for Him;
    Do not fret because of him who prospers
    in his way,
    Because of the man who carries out
    wicked schemes.
8 Cease from anger and forsake wrath;
    Do not fret; *it leads* only to evildoing.
9 For evildoers will be cut off,
    But those who wait for the LORD, they
    will inherit the land.
10 Yet a little while and the wicked man will
    be no more;
    And you will look carefully for his place
    and he will not be *there*.
11 But the humble will inherit the land
    And will delight themselves in abundant
    prosperity.

12 ¶ The wicked plots against the righteous
    And gnashes at him with his teeth.

13 The Lord laughs at him,
    For He sees his day is coming.
14 The wicked have drawn the sword and
    bent their bow
    To cast down the afflicted and the needy,
    To slay those who are upright in
    conduct.
15 Their sword will enter their own heart,
    And their bows will be broken.

16 ¶ Better is the little of the righteous
    Than the abundance of many wicked.
17 For the arms of the wicked will be
    broken,
    But the LORD sustains the righteous.
18 The LORD knows the days of the
    blameless,
    And their inheritance will be forever.
19 They will not be ashamed in the time of
    evil,
    And in the days of famine they will have
    abundance.
20 But the wicked will perish;
    And the enemies of the LORD will be like
    the *d*glory of the pastures,
    They vanish—like smoke they vanish
    away.
21 The wicked borrows and does not pay
    back,
    But the righteous is gracious and gives.
22 For those blessed by Him will inherit the
    land,
    But those cursed by Him will be cut off.

23 ¶ The steps of a man are established by
    the LORD,
    And He delights in his way.
24 When he falls, he will not be hurled
    headlong,
    Because the LORD is the One who holds
    his hand.
25 I have been young and now I am old,
    Yet I have not seen the righteous
    forsaken
    Or his descendants begging bread.

37:25 Never Abandoned

*Is life unfair? Psalm 37 ponders that
perplexing question. Its basic conclusion: The
success of wicked people won't last, while in the
long run people who do right will flourish. The
psalmist adds this observation, based on
experience: Through a lifetime of troubles and
anxieties, he has yet to see the righteous
abandoned by God and unable to provide the
basics of life for their children. Their generosity
doesn't bankrupt them.*

---

a Or *feed securely* or *feed on His faithfulness*   *b* Or *Be still*   *c* Or *longingly*   *d* I.e. flowers

26 All day long he is gracious and lends,
And his descendants are a blessing.
27 ¶ Depart from evil and do good,
So you will abide forever.
28 For the LORD loves justice
And does not forsake His godly ones;
They are preserved forever,
But the descendants of the wicked will be
cut off.
29 The righteous will inherit the land
And dwell in it forever.
30 The mouth of the righteous utters
wisdom,
And his tongue speaks justice.
31 The law of his God is in his heart;
His steps do not slip.
32 The wicked spies upon the righteous
And seeks to kill him.
33 The LORD will not leave him in his
hand
Or let him be condemned when he is
judged.
34 Wait for the LORD and keep His way,
And He will exalt you to inherit the
land;
When the wicked are cut off, you will
see it.
35 ¶ I have seen a wicked, violent man
Spreading himself like a luxuriant tree in
its native soil.
36 Then he passed away, and lo, he was no
more;
I sought for him, but he could not be
found.
37 Mark the blameless man, and behold the
upright;
For the man of peace will have a
posterity.
38 But transgressors will be altogether
destroyed;
The posterity of the wicked will be cut
off.
39 But the salvation of the righteous is from
the LORD;
He is their strength in time of trouble.
40 The LORD helps them and delivers them;
He delivers them from the wicked and
saves them,
Because they take refuge in Him.

Psalm 38

Prayer of a Suffering Penitent.

A Psalm of David, for a memorial.

1 ¶ O LORD, rebuke me not in Your
wrath,
And chasten me not in Your burning
anger.

2 For Your arrows have sunk deep
into me,
And Your hand has pressed down
on me.
3 There is no soundness in my flesh
because of Your indignation;
There is no health in my bones because
of my sin.
4 For my iniquities are gone over my
head;
As a heavy burden they weigh too much
for me.
5 My wounds grow foul *and* fester
Because of my folly.
6 I am bent over and greatly bowed down;
I go mourning all day long.
7 For my loins are filled with burning,
And there is no soundness in my flesh.
8 I am benumbed and badly crushed;
I groan because of the agitation of my
heart.
9 ¶ Lord, all my desire is before You;
And my sighing is not hidden from
You.
10 My heart throbs, my strength fails me;
And the light of my eyes, even that has
gone from me.
11 My loved ones and my friends stand
aloof from my plague;
And my kinsmen stand afar off.
12 Those who seek my life lay snares *for me;*
And those who seek to injure me have
threatened destruction,
And they devise treachery all day long.
13 ¶ But I, like a deaf man, do not hear;
And *I am* like a mute man who does not
open his mouth.
14 Yes, I am like a man who does not hear,
And in whose mouth are no arguments.
15 For I hope in You, O LORD;
You will answer, O Lord my God.
16 For I said, "May they not rejoice
over me,
Who, when my foot slips, would magnify
themselves against me."
17 For I am ready to fall,
And my ªsorrow is continually
before me.
18 For I confess my iniquity;
I am full of anxiety because of my sin.
19 But my enemies are vigorous *and*
ᵇstrong,
And many are those who hate me
wrongfully.
20 And those who repay evil for good,
They oppose me, because I follow what is
good.
21 Do not forsake me, O LORD;
O my God, do not be far from me!

ª Lit *pain*   ᵇ Or *numerous*

22 Make haste to help me,
   O Lord, my salvation!

Psalm 39

The Vanity of Life.

For the choir director, for Jeduthun.
A Psalm of David.

1 ¶ I said, "I will guard my ways
   That I may not sin with my tongue;
   I will guard my mouth as with a muzzle
   While the wicked are in my presence."
2 I was mute and silent,
   I *a*refrained *even* from good,
   And my *b*sorrow grew worse.
3 My heart was hot within me,
   While I was musing the fire burned;
   Then I spoke with my tongue:
4 "LORD, make me to know my end
   And what is the extent of my days;
   Let me know how transient I am.
5 "Behold, You have made my days *as*
   handbreadths,
   And my lifetime as nothing in Your
   sight;
   Surely every man at his best is a mere
   breath.   Selah.
6 "Surely every man walks about as *c*a
   phantom;
   Surely they make an uproar for nothing;
   He amasses *riches* and does not know
   who will gather them.

7 ¶ "And now, Lord, for what do I wait?
   My hope is in You.
8 "Deliver me from all my transgressions;
   Make me not the reproach of the foolish.
9 "I have become mute, I do not open my
   mouth,
   Because it is You who have done *it*.
10 "Remove Your plague from me;
   Because of the opposition of Your hand I
   am perishing.

11 "With reproofs You chasten a man for
   iniquity;
   You consume as a moth what is precious
   to him;
   Surely every man is a mere breath.   Selah.

12 ¶ "Hear my prayer, O LORD, and give ear
   to my cry;
   Do not be silent at my tears;
   For I am a stranger with You,
   A sojourner like all my fathers.
13 "Turn Your gaze away from me, that I
   may *d*smile *again*
   Before I depart and am no more."

Psalm 40

God Sustains His Servant.

For the choir director. A Psalm of David.

1 ¶ I waited *e*patiently for the LORD;
   And He inclined to me and heard my
   cry.
2 He brought me up out of the pit of
   destruction, out of the miry clay,
   And He set my feet upon a rock making
   my footsteps firm.
3 He put a new song in my mouth, a song
   of praise to our God;
   Many will see and fear
   And will trust in the LORD.

4 ¶ How blessed is the man who has made
   the LORD his trust,
   And has not turned to the proud, nor to
   those who lapse into falsehood.
5 Many, O LORD my God, are the wonders
   which You have done,
   And Your thoughts toward us;
   There is none to compare with You.
   If I would declare and speak of them,
   They would be too numerous to count.

6 ¶ Sacrifice and meal offering You have
   not desired;
   My ears You have *f*opened;
   Burnt offering and sin offering You have
   not required.

39:10 Wrestling with God

*Not all the psalms are happy. Some, such as
this one and Psalms 44 and 88, are intensely
sad. They try to make sense out of suffering,
and fail. They ask God for help and receive
none. The Bible's inclusion of such hopeless
cries eloquently testifies to God's acceptance of
human struggles. These psalms are not the
final word on suffering. They show, however,
that wrestling with God has value even when
we fail to find answers.*

40:6 A Better Sacrifice

*While the Old Testament law prescribed animal
and grain sacrifices to deal with the problem of
sin, Old Testament writers made clear that God
really wanted obedient lives, not ritual
performances. Hebrews 10:5–9 quotes these
verses (6–8) in explaining that Jesus' sacrifice
made all the animal sacrifices obsolete. Only
Jesus' sacrifice has the power to actually
forgive sins and change lives.*

a Lit *kept silence*   *b* Lit *pain*   *c* Lit *an image*   *d* Or *become cheerful*   *e* Or *intently*   *f* Lit *dug;* or possibly
pierced

7 Then I said, "Behold, I come;
In the scroll of the book it is written
of me.
8 I delight to do Your will, O my God;
Your Law is within my heart."

9 ¶ I have proclaimed glad tidings of
righteousness in the great
congregation;
Behold, I will not restrain my lips,
O Lord, You know.
10 I have not hidden Your righteousness
within my heart;
I have spoken of Your faithfulness and
Your salvation;
I have not concealed Your
lovingkindness and Your truth from
the great congregation.

11 ¶ You, O Lord, will not withhold Your
compassion from me;
Your lovingkindness and Your truth will
continually preserve me.
12 For evils beyond number have
surrounded me;
My iniquities have overtaken me, so that
I am not able to see;
They are more numerous than the hairs
of my head,
And my heart has failed me.

13 ¶ Be pleased, O Lord, to deliver me;
Make haste, O Lord, to help me.
14 Let those be ashamed and humiliated
together
Who seek my ªlife to destroy it;
Let those be turned back and dishonored
Who delight ᵇin my hurt.
15 Let those be appalled because of their
shame
Who say to me, "Aha, aha!"
16 Let all who seek You rejoice and be glad
in You;
Let those who love Your salvation say
continually,
"The Lord be magnified!"
17 Since I am afflicted and needy,
Let the Lord be mindful of me.
You are my help and my deliverer;
Do not delay, O my God.

Psalm 41

The Psalmist in Sickness Complains of Enemies and False Friends.

For the choir director. A Psalm of David.

1 ¶ How blessed is he who considers the
helpless;
The Lord will deliver him in a day of
trouble.

2 The Lord will protect him and keep him
alive,
And he shall be called blessed upon the
earth;

41:1 A Key Characteristic

The psalmist was severely ill. Enemies and rivals—and even a close friend, verse 9— whispered that he was dying. What made him so confident that God would heal him? He knew that God helps those who "consider the helpless." Because he had shown integrity in this, he confidently expected God to show mercy to him. Jesus reflected this value when he said, "Blessed are the merciful, for they shall receive mercy" (Matthew 5:7).

And do not give him over to the desire
of his enemies.
3 The Lord will sustain him upon his
sickbed;
In his illness, You ᶜrestore him to
health.

4 ¶ As for me, I said, "O Lord, be gracious
to me;
Heal my soul, for I have sinned
against You."
5 My enemies speak evil against me,
"When will he die, and his name perish?"
6 And when he comes to see *me*, he speaks
falsehood;
His heart gathers wickedness to itself;
When he goes outside, he tells it.
7 All who hate me whisper together
against me;
Against me they devise my hurt, *saying*,
8 "A wicked thing is poured out upon him,
That when he lies down, he will not rise
up again."
9 Even my close friend in whom I trusted,
Who ate my bread,
Has lifted up his heel against me.

10 ¶ But You, O Lord, be gracious to me
and raise me up,
That I may repay them.
11 By this I know that You are pleased
with me,
Because my enemy does not shout in
triumph over me.
12 As for me, You uphold me in my
integrity,
And You set me in Your presence
forever.

13 ¶ Blessed be the Lord, the God of Israel,
From everlasting to everlasting.
Amen and Amen.

ª Or *soul*   ᵇ Or *to injure me*   ᶜ Lit *turn all his bed*

BOOK 2

Psalm 42

Thirsting for God in Trouble and Exile.

For the choir director. A Maskil of the sons of Korah.

1 ¶ As the deer *a*pants for the water brooks,
So my soul pants for You, O God.
2 My soul thirsts for God, for the living God;
When shall I come and appear before God?
3 My tears have been my food day and night,
While *they* say to me all day long, "Where is your God?"
4 These things I remember and I pour out my soul within me.
For I used to go along with the throng *and* lead them in procession to the house of God,
With the voice of joy and thanksgiving, a multitude keeping festival.

5 ¶ Why are you in despair, O my soul?
And *why* have you become disturbed within me?
Hope in God, for I shall again praise Him
For the help of His presence.
6 O my God, my soul is in despair within me;
Therefore I remember You from the land of the Jordan
And the peaks of Hermon, from Mount Mizar.
7 Deep calls to deep at the sound of Your waterfalls;
All Your breakers and Your waves have rolled over me.
8 The LORD will command His lovingkindness in the daytime;
And His song will be with me in the night,
A prayer to the God of my life.

9 ¶ I will say to God my rock, "Why have You forgotten me?
Why do I go mourning because of the oppression of the enemy?"
10 As a shattering of my bones, my adversaries revile me,
While they say to me all day long, "Where is your God?"
11 Why are you in despair, O my soul?
And why have you become disturbed within me?
Hope in God, for I shall yet praise Him,

The help of my countenance and my God.

Psalm 43

Prayer for Deliverance.

1 ¶ Vindicate me, O God, and plead my case against an ungodly nation;
O deliver me from the deceitful and unjust man!
2 For You are the God of my strength; why have You rejected me?
Why do I go mourning because of the oppression of the enemy?

3 ¶ O send out Your light and Your truth, let them lead me;
Let them bring me to Your holy hill
And to Your dwelling places.
4 Then I will go to the altar of God,
To God my exceeding joy;
And upon the lyre I shall praise You, O God, my God.

5 ¶ Why are you in despair, O my soul?
And why are you disturbed within me?
Hope in God, for I shall again praise Him,
The help of my countenance and my God.

Psalm 44

Former Deliverances and Present Troubles.

For the choir director. A Maskil of the sons of Korah.

1 ¶ O God, we have heard with our ears,
Our fathers have told us
The work that You did in their days,
In the days of old.
2 You with Your own hand drove out the nations;
Then You planted them;
You afflicted the peoples,
Then You spread them abroad.
3 For by their own sword they did not possess the land,
And their own arm did not save them,
But Your right hand and Your arm and the light of Your presence,
For You favored them.

4 ¶ You are my King, O God;
Command victories for Jacob.
5 Through You we will push back our adversaries;
Through Your name we will trample down those who rise up against us.
6 For I will not trust in my bow,
Nor will my sword save me.
7 But You have saved us from our adversaries,

_{*a*} Lit *longs for*

And You have put to shame those who
hate us.
8 In God we have boasted all day long,
And we will give thanks to Your name
forever. Selah.

9 ¶ Yet You have rejected *us* and brought
us to dishonor,
And do not go out with our armies.
10 You cause us to turn back from the
adversary;
And those who hate us have taken spoil
for themselves.
11 You give us as sheep to be eaten
And have scattered us among the
nations.
12 You sell Your people cheaply,
And have not ªprofited by their sale.
13 You make us a reproach to our
neighbors,
A scoffing and a derision to those
around us.
14 You make us a byword among the
nations,
A laughingstock among the peoples.
15 All day long my dishonor is before me
And my humiliation has
overwhelmed me,
16 Because of the voice of him who
reproaches and reviles,
Because of the presence of the enemy
and the avenger.

17 ¶ All this has come upon us, but we have
not forgotten You,
And we have not dealt falsely with Your
covenant.
18 Our heart has not turned back,
And our steps have not deviated from
Your way,
19 Yet You have crushed us in a place of
jackals
And covered us with the shadow of
death.

20 ¶ If we had forgotten the name of our
God
Or extended our hands to a strange god,
21 Would not God find this out?
For He knows the secrets of the heart.
22 But for Your sake we are killed all day
long;
We are considered as sheep to be
slaughtered.
23 Arouse Yourself, why do You sleep,
O Lord?
Awake, do not reject us forever.
24 Why do You hide Your face
And forget our affliction and our
oppression?

25 For our soul has sunk down into the
dust;
Our body cleaves to the earth.
26 Rise up, be our help,
And redeem us for the sake of Your
lovingkindness.

44:22 No Happy Ending

*Not all the psalms have happy endings. This
one, while beginning with distant memories of
what God did in the past, ends with a poignant
plea for help. Prayers and faith in God have not
produced any results. Is God asleep?*

*Yet God works in bigger patterns than we
can see. The apostle Paul, considering the place
of suffering in a Christian's life, quoted this
verse to remind his readers that suffering was
nothing new for believers (Romans 8:35). He
asked, "Who will separate us from the love of
Christ?" His response: "No one! Nothing!" He
would have loved to go back in time and tell
the suffering psalmist about all the good things
in store for God's people.*

Psalm 45

A Song Celebrating the King's Marriage.

For the choir director; according to the
ᵇShoshannim. A Maskil of the sons of Korah.
A Song of Love.

1 ¶ My heart ᶜoverflows with a good
theme;
I address my verses to the King;
My tongue is the pen of a ready writer.
2 You are fairer than the sons of men;
Grace is poured upon Your lips;
Therefore God has blessed You forever.

3 ¶ Gird Your sword on *Your* thigh,
O Mighty One,
In Your splendor and Your majesty!
4 And in Your majesty ride on victoriously,
For the cause of truth and meekness *and*
righteousness;
Let Your right hand teach You awesome
things.
5 Your arrows are sharp;
The peoples fall under You;
Your arrows are in the heart of the
King's enemies.

6 ¶ Your throne, O God, is forever and
ever;
A scepter of uprightness is the scepter of
Your kingdom.
7 You have loved righteousness and hated
wickedness;

ª Or *set a high price on them*   ᵇ Or possibly *Lilies*   ᶜ Lit *is astir*

Therefore God, Your God, has
   anointed You
With the oil of joy above Your fellows.
8 All Your garments are *fragrant with*
      myrrh and aloes *and* cassia;
   Out of ivory palaces stringed instruments
      have made You glad.
9 Kings' daughters are among Your noble
      ladies;
   At Your right hand stands the queen in
      gold from Ophir.

10 ¶ Listen, O daughter, give attention and
      incline your ear:
   Forget your people and your father's
      house;
11 Then the King will desire your beauty.
   Because He is your Lord, bow down to
      Him.
12 The daughter of Tyre *will come* with a
      gift;

The rich among the people will seek your
   favor.
13 ¶ The King's daughter is all glorious
      within;
   Her clothing is interwoven with gold.
14 She will be led to the King in
      embroidered work;
   The virgins, her companions who follow
      her,
   Will be brought to You.
15 They will be led forth with gladness and
      rejoicing;
   They will enter into the King's palace.

16 ¶ In place of your fathers will be your
      sons;
   You shall make them princes in all the
      earth.
17 I will cause Your name to be
      remembered in all generations;

A Wedding Fit for a King
Why should this poem be found in a book of prayers?

> *Your throne, O God,*
> *is forever and ever.*
> *45:6*

IN THE MIDDLE OF A book of heartfelt prayers, a wedding poem suddenly appears. Does Psalm 45 belong here? Its "good theme" (verse 1) is not God's kindness, but the excellence of his majesty the king as he prepares to take a bride. While most of the psalms express an intimacy with God that could have been written yesterday, thrones, scepters, and royal robes make us think of an old Hollywood epic.

To understand why this psalm was included we need to know, first, that the king in Biblical times was more than just a symbol. He was the president and the commanding general and the chief justice of the Supreme Court, all rolled into one. An unjust or cowardly king could cost his people their lives. A clever, successful king, on the other hand, could assure them of prosperity.

When the Israelites wished the king well, therefore, they wished themselves well. Seeing their king decked out in finery was like looking at a picture of their own success. And when their king made a happy and fruitful marriage, it assured them of stable leadership for years to come. The king's welfare represented the welfare of God's people.

The Promise to David

David was the first good king Israel had known. God had told David that his "house" would endure forever (2 Samuel 7:16). This meant that Israel would endure, too. When David's people combined this promise with the other benefits God had promised to Abraham and Moses, they could foresee a great future for their small, poor, war-weary nation.

Yet David's descendants disappointed these hopes. Israel remained a small, hemmed-in nation. Gradually, Israelites began to expect another king who would live up to the Bible's praises and promises. They called him "the Anointed" (for kings and priests took office through an official anointing with oil, like our swearing in). When they read psalms that mentioned the king, they thought of this coming ruler.

As the years went by and Israel's kings failed miserably, Israel's longing grew stronger and stronger. People looked for "the consolation of Israel" (Luke 2:25). The word for "the Anointed" became *Messiah,* or (in Greek) *Christ.*

Only when "the Anointed" came—in Jesus—did the extravagant language of Psalm 45:6–7 (along with unusual descriptions in Psalms 2 and 110) make sense. These verses were quoted in Hebrews 1:8–9 to show that the king the Jews had long expected could be no ordinary man. The king turned out to *be* God—as verse 6 had suggested. The poem that seemed to be only about a king's marriage turned out, in the end, to be about God's marriage to humanity.

Life Questions: Are you more apt to picture God as a loving father or a majestic, regal monarch?

Therefore the peoples will give You
thanks forever and ever.

Psalm 46

God the Refuge of His People.

For the choir director. A Psalm of the sons
of Korah, [a]set to Alamoth. A Song.

1 ¶ God is our refuge and strength,
[b]A very present help in trouble.
2 Therefore we will not fear, though the
earth should change
And though the mountains slip into the
heart of the sea;
3 Though its waters roar and foam,
Though the mountains quake at its
swelling pride.   Selah.

4 ¶ There is a river whose streams make
glad the city of God,
The holy dwelling places of the Most
High.
5 God is in the midst of her, she will not
be moved;
God will help her when morning dawns.
6 The nations made an uproar, the
kingdoms tottered;
He raised His voice, the earth melted.
7 The LORD of hosts is with us;
The God of Jacob is our stronghold.
          Selah.

8 ¶ Come, behold the works of the LORD,
Who has wrought desolations in the
earth.
9 He makes wars to cease to the end of the
earth;
He breaks the bow and cuts the spear in
two;
He burns the chariots with fire.
10 "Cease striving and know that I am God;
I will be exalted among the nations, I will
be exalted in the earth."
11 The LORD of hosts is with us;
The God of Jacob is our stronghold.
          Selah.

Psalm 47

God the King of the Earth.

For the choir director. A Psalm of the sons
of Korah.

1 ¶ O clap your hands, all peoples;
Shout to God with the voice of joy.
2 For the LORD Most High is to be feared,
A great King over all the earth.
3 He subdues peoples under us
And nations under our feet.
4 He chooses our inheritance for us,
The glory of Jacob whom He
loves.   Selah.

5 ¶ God has ascended with a shout,
The LORD, with the sound of a trumpet.
6 Sing praises to God, sing praises;
Sing praises to our King, sing praises.
7 For God is the King of all the earth;
Sing praises with a skillful psalm.

47:7–9 Who Are God's People?

*While the Israelites often thought of themselves
as exclusively God's people, Psalms contains
frequent references to a day when "the nations"
—that is, all ethnic groups—will exultantly
praise God. In this psalm they not only join in,
they do so as "the people of the God of
Abraham"—that is, as insiders included in God's
covenant with the Israelites.*

8 God reigns over the nations,
God sits on His holy throne.
9 The princes of the people have assembled
themselves as the people of the God
of Abraham,
For the shields of the earth belong to
God;
He is highly exalted.

Psalm 48

The Beauty and Glory of Zion.

A Song; a Psalm of the sons of Korah.

1 ¶ Great is the LORD, and greatly to be
praised,
In the city of our God, His holy
mountain.
2 Beautiful in elevation, the joy of the
whole earth,
Is Mount Zion in the far north,
The city of the great King.
3 God, in her palaces,
Has made Himself known as a
stronghold.

4 ¶ For, lo, the kings assembled themselves,
They passed by together.
5 They saw it, then they were amazed;
They were terrified, they fled in alarm.
6 Panic seized them there,
Anguish, as of a woman in childbirth.
7 With the east wind
You break the ships of Tarshish.
8 As we have heard, so have we seen
In the city of the LORD of hosts, in the
city of our God;
God will establish her forever.   Selah.

9 ¶ We have thought on Your
lovingkindness, O God,
In the midst of Your temple.

---

[a] Possibly for soprano voices   [b] Or Abundantly available for help

10 As is Your name, O God,
So is Your praise to the ends of the
earth;
Your right hand is full of righteousness.
11 Let Mount Zion be glad,
Let the daughters of Judah rejoice
Because of Your judgments.
12 Walk about Zion and go around her;
Count her towers;
13 Consider her ramparts;
Go through her palaces,
That you may tell *it* to the next
generation.
14 For such is God,
Our God forever and ever;
He will guide us *a*until death.

Psalm 49

The Folly of Trusting in Riches.

For the choir director. A Psalm of the sons
of Korah.

1 ¶ Hear this, all peoples;
Give ear, all inhabitants of the world,
2 Both low and high,
Rich and poor together.
3 My mouth will speak wisdom,
And the meditation of my heart *will be*
understanding.
4 I will incline my ear to a proverb;
I will express my riddle on the harp.
5 ¶ Why should I fear in days of adversity,
When the iniquity of my foes
surrounds me,

49:5–20 Money Can't Buy Life

*How do you make sense of a world in which
bad people get rich and actually oppress good
people? This psalm ponders this riddle and
finds the answer on the other side of death.
Money can do many things, but it simply
cannot buy an escape from the grave. "No man
can by any means redeem his brother . . . for
the redemption of his soul is costly . . . that he
should live on eternally" (verses 7–9). But "God
will redeem my soul from the power of Sheol,"
says verse 15; "He will receive me."*

6 Even those who trust in their wealth
And boast in the abundance of their
riches?
7 No man can by any means redeem *his*
brother
Or give to God a ransom for him—
8 For the redemption of his soul is costly,
And he should cease *trying* forever—

9 That he should live on eternally,
That he should not *b*undergo decay.
10 ¶ For he sees *that even* wise men die;
The stupid and the senseless alike perish
And leave their wealth to others.
11 Their *c*inner thought is *that* their houses
are forever
And their dwelling places to all
generations;
They have called their lands after their
own names.
12 But man in *his* pomp will not endure;
He is like the beasts that perish.
13 ¶ This is the way of those who are
foolish,
And of those after them who approve
their words. Selah.
14 As sheep they are appointed for Sheol;
Death shall be their shepherd;
And the upright shall rule over them in
the morning,
And their form shall be for Sheol to
consume
So that they have no habitation.
15 But God will redeem my soul from the
power of Sheol,
For He will receive me. Selah.
16 ¶ Do not be afraid when a man becomes
rich,
When the *d*glory of his house is
increased;
17 For when he dies he will carry nothing
away;
His *d*glory will not descend after him.
18 Though while he lives he congratulates
himself—
And though *men* praise you when you
do well for yourself—
19 He shall go to the generation of his
fathers;
They will never see the light.
20 Man in *his* pomp, yet without
understanding,
Is like the beasts that perish.

Psalm 50

God the Judge of the Righteous
and the Wicked.

A Psalm of Asaph.

1 ¶ The Mighty One, God, the LORD, has
spoken,
And summoned the earth from the rising
of the sun to its setting.
2 Out of Zion, the perfection of beauty,
God has shone forth.
3 May our God come and not keep silence;

a Lit *upon;* some mss and the Gr read *forever*   *b* Or *see corruption* or *the pit*   *c* Some versions read *graves are their*
houses   *d* Or *wealth*

Fire devours before Him,
And it is very tempestuous around Him.
4 He summons the heavens above,
And the earth, to judge His people:
5 "Gather My godly ones to Me,
Those who have made a covenant with
Me by sacrifice."
6 And the heavens declare His
righteousness,
For God Himself is judge.   Selah.

7 ¶ "Hear, O My people, and I will speak;
O Israel, I will testify against you;
I am God, your God.
8 "I do not reprove you for your sacrifices,
And your burnt offerings are continually
before Me.
9 "I shall take no young bull out of your
house
Nor male goats out of your folds.

50:9–12 Does God Need Our Gifts?

People often try to bargain with God, thinking that by their good deeds they can get God to do what they want. Old Testament people sometimes viewed their animal sacrifices this way: not as an act of commitment and fellowship with God, but as a way to manipulate God into putting his stamp of approval on their plans. These majestic words from God scorn such a view. He is rich beyond their dreams; he has no need of their offerings. What matters to him is the attitude they take toward him.

10 "For every beast of the forest is Mine,
The cattle on a thousand hills.
11 "I know every bird of the mountains,
And everything that moves in the field is
ᵃMine.
12 "If I were hungry I would not tell you,
For the world is Mine, and all it
contains.
13 "Shall I eat the flesh of bulls
Or drink the blood of male goats?
14 "Offer to God a sacrifice of thanksgiving
And pay your vows to the Most High;
15 Call upon Me in the day of trouble;
I shall rescue you, and you will
honor Me."

16 ¶ But to the wicked God says,
"What right have you to tell of My
statutes
And to take My covenant in your
mouth?
17 "For you hate discipline,
And you cast My words behind you.

18 "When you see a thief, you are pleased
with him,
And you associate with adulterers.
19 "You let your mouth loose in evil
And your tongue frames deceit.
20 "You sit and speak against your brother;
You slander your own mother's son.
21 "These things you have done and I kept
silence;
You thought that I was just like you;
I will reprove you and state *the case* in
order before your eyes.

22 ¶ "Now consider this, you who forget
God,
Or I will tear *you* in pieces, and there
will be none to deliver.
23 "He who offers a sacrifice of thanksgiving
honors Me;
And to him who orders *his* way *aright*
I shall show the salvation of God."

Psalm 51

A Contrite Sinner's Prayer for Pardon.

For the choir director. A Psalm of David, when
Nathan the prophet came to him, after he had
gone in to Bathsheba.

1 ¶ Be gracious to me, O God, according
to Your lovingkindness;
According to the greatness of Your
compassion blot out my
transgressions.
2 Wash me thoroughly from my iniquity
And cleanse me from my sin.
3 For I know my transgressions,
And my sin is ever before me.
4 Against You, You only, I have sinned
And done what is evil in Your sight,
So that You ᵇare justified when You
speak
And blameless when You judge.

5 ¶ Behold, I was brought forth in iniquity,
And in sin my mother conceived me.
6 Behold, You desire truth in the
innermost being,
And in the hidden part You will make
me know wisdom.
7 Purify me with hyssop, and I shall be
clean;
Wash me, and I shall be whiter than
snow.
8 Make me to hear joy and gladness,
Let the bones which You have broken
rejoice.
9 Hide Your face from my sins
And blot out all my iniquities.

10 ¶ Create in me a clean heart, O God,
And renew a steadfast spirit within me.

ᵃOr *in My mind*; lit *with Me*   ᵇOr *may be in the right*

11 Do not cast me away from Your
   presence
   And do not take Your Holy Spirit
   from me.
12 Restore to me the joy of Your salvation
   And sustain me with a willing spirit.
13 *Then* I will teach transgressors Your
   ways,
   And sinners will ᵃbe converted to You.

14 ¶ Deliver me from bloodguiltiness,
   O God, the God of my salvation;
   Then my tongue will joyfully sing of
   Your righteousness.
15 O Lord, open my lips,
   That my mouth may declare Your praise.
16 For You do not delight in sacrifice,
   otherwise I would give it;
   You are not pleased with burnt offering.
17 The sacrifices of God are a broken spirit;
   A broken and a contrite heart, O God,
   You will not despise.

18 ¶ By Your favor do good to Zion;
   Build the walls of Jerusalem.

ᵃ Or *turn back*

19 Then You will delight in righteous
   sacrifices,
   In burnt offering and whole burnt
   offering;
   Then young bulls will be offered on Your
   altar.

Psalm 52

Futility of Boastful Wickedness.

For the choir director. A Maskil of David, when
Doeg the Edomite came and told Saul and said
to him, "David has come to the house
of Ahimelech."

1 ¶ Why do you boast in evil,
   O mighty man?
   The lovingkindness of God *endures* all
   day long.
2 Your tongue devises destruction,
   Like a sharp razor, O worker of deceit.
3 You love evil more than good,
   Falsehood more than speaking what is
   right.   Selah.
4 You love all words that devour,
   O deceitful tongue.

David Caught in the Act
Israel had a strange way to remember its heroes

> Against You, You
> only, I have sinned
> and done what is
> evil in Your sight.
> *51:4*

DAVID FOUND A PLACE IN the hearts of Israelites something like the one Abraham Lincoln found in the hearts of Americans. Both men led their nations through dark hours with courage, wisdom, and deep faith.

But there are essential differences in the way they are remembered. Suppose, for example, that Abraham Lincoln had been caught in the act of adultery. Would his private outpouring of grief before God have been included in America's July 4th celebration? Hardly: America tends to cover up the faults of its heroes, and even invent stories about their spotless honesty.

Yet, for David, no cover-up was attempted. Just the opposite: Psalm 51 publishes David's anguished reaction when he was caught in sin. The story behind the psalm is told in 2 Samuel 11 and 12—a sordid tale of adultery, intrigue, and murder. David, the greatest king in Israel's history, acted like the worst.

David apparently thought nothing of his crime until the prophet Nathan accused him to his face. Then, in tears, David confessed—and this poem was one result. It was recorded (along with the story of David's deeds) in the holy Scriptures. It may well have been used in worship services, as a guide for others' confession.

David's Greatest Legacy

All nations have heroes. Israel may have been alone in making heroic literature about its heroes' failings. In confessing his failures openly, David was certainly unique among all leaders of his day. He knew his place before God, and this humility made him an example for his people.

Ultimately Israel remembered David more for his devotion to God than for his military achievements. In centuries to come, Israel looked for a "son of David" to come and save them. They wanted a truly strong leader—one humble enough to know that God must lead the leaders.

Life Questions: When you fail, what is your response—to cover up your failure, or to publicize your confession?

5 ¶ But God will break you down forever;
 He will snatch you up and tear you away
  from *your* tent,
 And uproot you from the land of the
  living.   Selah.
6 The righteous will see and fear,
 And will laugh at him, *saying,*
7 "Behold, the man who would not make
  God his refuge,
 But trusted in the abundance of his
  riches
 And was strong in his *evil* desire."

8 ¶ But as for me, I am like a green olive
  tree in the house of God;
 I trust in the lovingkindness of God
  forever and ever.
9 I will give You thanks forever, because
  You have done *it,*
 And I will wait on Your name, for *it is*
  good, in the presence of Your godly
  ones.

Psalm 53

Folly and Wickedness of Men.

For the choir director; according to *a*Mahalath.
A Maskil of David.

1 ¶ The fool has said in his heart, "There is
  no God,"
 They are corrupt, and have committed
  abominable injustice;
 There is no one who does good.
2 God has looked down from heaven upon
  the sons of men
 To see if there is anyone who
  understands,
 Who seeks after God.
3 Every one of them has turned aside;
  together they have become corrupt;
 There is no one who does good, not
  even one.

53:3 Sound Familiar?

*Psalm 53 is nearly identical to Psalm 14.
Scholars think the book of Psalms bundled
together several different collections of hymns;
this duplication is one reason they believe so.*

4 ¶ Have the workers of wickedness no
  knowledge,
 Who eat up My people *as though* they
  ate bread
 And have not called upon God?
5 There they were in great fear *where* no
  fear had been;

For God scattered the bones of him who
  encamped against you;
 You put *them* to shame, because God
  had rejected them.
6 Oh, that the salvation of Israel would
  come out of Zion!
 When God restores His captive people,
 Let Jacob rejoice, let Israel be glad.

Psalm 54

Prayer for Defense against Enemies.

For the choir director; on stringed instruments.
A Maskil of David, when the Ziphites came and
said to Saul, "Is not David hiding
himself among us?"

1 ¶ Save me, O God, by Your name,
 And *b*vindicate me by Your power.
2 Hear my prayer, O God;
 Give ear to the words of my mouth.
3 For strangers have risen against me
 And violent men have sought my life;
 They have not set God before them.
                              Selah.

4 ¶ Behold, God is my helper;
 The Lord is the sustainer of my soul.
5 *c*He will recompense the evil to my foes;
 Destroy them in Your faithfulness.

6 ¶ Willingly I will sacrifice to You;
 I will give thanks to Your name, O LORD,
  for it is good.
7 For He has delivered me from all
  trouble,
 And my eye has looked *with satisfaction*
  upon my enemies.

Psalm 55

Prayer for the Destruction of the Treacherous.

For the choir director; on stringed instruments.
A Maskil of David.

1 ¶ Give ear to my prayer, O God;
 And do not hide Yourself from my
  supplication.
2 Give heed to me and answer me;
 I am restless in my complaint and *d*am
  surely distracted,
3 Because of the voice of the enemy,
 Because of the pressure of the wicked;
 For they bring down trouble upon me
 And in anger they bear a grudge
  against me.

4 ¶ My heart is in anguish within me,
 And the terrors of death have fallen
  upon me.
5 Fear and trembling come upon me,
 And horror has overwhelmed me.
6 I said, "Oh, that I had wings like a dove!

---

a I.e. sickness, a sad tone   *b* Lit *judge*   *c* Lit *The evil will return*   *d* Or *I must moan*

I would fly away and [a]be at rest.
7 "Behold, I would wander far away,
  I would lodge in the wilderness.   Selah.
8 "I would hasten to my place of refuge
  From the stormy wind *and* tempest."

9 ¶ Confuse, O Lord, divide their tongues,
  For I have seen violence and strife in the
    city.
10 Day and night they go around her upon
    her walls,
  And iniquity and mischief are in her
    midst.
11 Destruction is in her midst;
  Oppression and deceit do not depart
    from her streets.

12 ¶ For it is not an enemy who
    reproaches me,
  Then I could bear *it;*
  Nor is it one who hates me who has
    exalted himself against me,
  Then I could hide myself from him.
13 But it is you, a man my equal,
  My companion and my familiar friend;
14 We who had sweet [b]fellowship together
  Walked in the house of God in the
    throng.

55:14 Betrayed by a Friend

It is hard enough to deal with enemies, but far harder to face the fact of betrayal by a close friend. Feeling that he can no longer trust anyone, the psalmist turns to God for help. God, he knows, will never betray him.

15 Let death come deceitfully upon them;
  Let them go down alive to Sheol,
  For evil is in their dwelling, in their
    midst.

16 ¶ As for me, I shall call upon God,
  And the LORD will save me.
17 Evening and morning and at noon, I will
    complain and murmur,
  And He will hear my voice.
18 He will redeem my soul in peace from
    the battle *which is* against me,
  For they are many *who strive* with me.
19 God will hear and answer them—
  Even the one who sits enthroned from of
    old—   Selah.
  With whom there is no change,
  And who do not fear God.
20 He has put forth his hands against those
    who were at peace with him;
  He has [c]violated his covenant.

21 His speech was smoother than butter,
  But his heart was war;
  His words were softer than oil,
  Yet they were drawn swords.

22 ¶ Cast your burden upon the LORD and
    He will sustain you;
  He will never allow the righteous to be
    shaken.
23 But You, O God, will bring them down
    to the pit of destruction;
  Men of bloodshed and deceit will not live
    out half their days.
  But I will trust in You.

Psalm 56

Supplication for Deliverance and Grateful Trust in God.

For the choir director; according to Jonath elem rehokim. A Mikhtam of David, when the Philistines seized him in Gath.

1 ¶ Be gracious to me, O God, for man has
    trampled upon me;
  Fighting all day long he oppresses me.
2 My foes have trampled upon me all day
    long,
  For they are many who fight proudly
    against me.
3 When I am afraid,
  I will put my trust in You.
4 In God, whose word I praise,
  In God I have put my trust;
  I shall not be afraid.
  What can *mere* man do to me?
5 All day long they [d]distort my words;
  All their thoughts are against me for evil.
6 They [e]attack, they lurk,
  They watch my steps,
  As they have waited *to take* my life.
7 Because of wickedness, cast them forth,
  In anger put down the peoples, O God!

8 ¶ You have taken account of my
    wanderings;
  Put my tears in Your bottle.
  Are *they* not in Your book?
9 Then my enemies will turn back in the
    day when I call;
  This I know, [f]that God is for me.
10 In God, *whose* word I praise,
  In the LORD, *whose* word I praise,
11 In God I have put my [g]trust, I shall not
    be afraid.
  What can man do to me?
12 Your vows are *binding* upon me, O God;
  I will render thank offerings to You.
13 For You have delivered my soul from
    death,
  Indeed my feet from stumbling,

---

[a] Lit *settle down*   [b] Lit *counsel;* or *intimacy*   [c] Lit *profaned*   [d] Or *trouble my affairs*   [e] Or *stir up strife*   [f] Or
because   [g] Or *trust without fear*

So that I may walk before God
In the light of the living.

Psalm 57

Prayer for Rescue from Persecutors.

For the choir director; *set to* [a]Al-tashheth.
A Mikhtam of David, when he fled from Saul
in the cave.

1 ¶ Be gracious to me, O God, be gracious
to me,
For my soul takes refuge in You;
And in the shadow of Your wings I will
take refuge
Until destruction passes by.
2 I will cry to God Most High,
To God who accomplishes *all things*
for me.
3 He will send from heaven and save me;
He reproaches him who tramples upon
me.   Selah.
God will send forth His lovingkindness
and His truth.

4 ¶ My soul is among lions;
I must lie among those who breathe
forth fire,
Even the sons of men, whose teeth are
spears and arrows
And their tongue a sharp sword.
5 Be exalted above the heavens, O God;
Let Your glory *be* above all the earth.
6 They have [b]prepared a net for my steps;
My soul is bowed down;
They dug a pit before me;
They *themselves* have fallen into the
midst of it.   Selah.

7 ¶ My heart is steadfast, O God, my heart
is steadfast;
I will sing, yes, I will sing praises!
8 Awake, my glory!
Awake, harp and lyre!
I will awaken the dawn.
9 I will give thanks to You, O Lord, among
the peoples;
I will sing praises to You among the
nations.
10 For Your lovingkindness is great to the
heavens
And Your truth to the clouds.
11 Be exalted above the heavens, O God;
Let Your glory *be* above all the earth.

Psalm 58

Prayer for the Punishment of the Wicked.

For the choir director; *set to* Al-tashheth.
A Mikhtam of David.

1 ¶ Do you indeed speak righteousness,
O [c]gods?

Do you judge [d]uprightly, O sons
of men?
2 No, in heart you work unrighteousness;
On earth you weigh out the violence of
your hands.
3 The wicked are estranged from the
womb;
These who speak lies go astray from
birth.
4 They have venom like the venom of a
serpent;
Like a deaf cobra that stops up its
ear,
5 So that it does not hear the voice of
charmers,
Or a skillful caster of spells.

6 ¶ O God, shatter their teeth in their
mouth;
Break out the fangs of the young lions,
O LORD.
7 Let them flow away like water that runs
off;
When he aims his arrows, let them be as
headless shafts.
8 *Let them be* as a snail which melts away
as it goes along,
Like the miscarriages of a woman which
never see the sun.

58:8 Rough Words

*The psalmist's white-hot anger is never more
obvious than in these ardent words asking God
to punish wicked people. His demand for
retribution is a far cry from Jesus' command to
love your enemies; no Christian should make
this a model of prayer. We ought to remember,
though, that the psalmist is asking God for
justice—not planning how he will bring it about
himself. For more on this subject, see "What
About Curses?" page 680.*

9 Before your pots can feel *the fire of*
thorns
He will sweep them away with a
whirlwind, the green and the
burning alike.

10 ¶ The righteous will rejoice when he sees
the vengeance;
He will wash his feet in the blood of the
wicked.
11 And men will say, "Surely there is a
reward for the righteous;
Surely there is a God who judges on
earth!"

---

[a] Lit *Do Not Destroy*   [b] Or *spread*   [c] Or *mighty ones* or *judges*   [d] Or *uprightly the sons of men*

Psalm 59

Prayer for Deliverance from Enemies.

*For the choir director; set to Al-tashheth.
A Mikhtam of David, when Saul sent men and
they watched the house in order to kill him.*

1 ¶ Deliver me from my enemies, O my
   God;
   Set me *securely* on high away from those
      who rise up against me.
2 Deliver me from those who do iniquity
   And save me from men of bloodshed.
3 For behold, they have set an ambush for
      my life;
   Fierce men *a*launch an attack
      against me,
   Not for my transgression nor for my sin,
      O Lord,
4 For no guilt of *mine,* they run and set
      themselves against me.
   Arouse Yourself to help me, and see!
5 You, O Lord God of hosts, the God of
      Israel,
   Awake to punish all the nations;
   Do not be gracious to any *who are*
      treacherous in iniquity.   Selah.
6 They return at evening, they howl like a
      dog,
   And go around the city.
7 Behold, they belch forth with their
      mouth;
   Swords are in their lips,
   For, *they say,* "Who hears?"
8 But You, O Lord, laugh at them;
   You scoff at all the nations.

9 ¶ *Because of* *b*his strength I will watch
      for You,
   For God is my stronghold.
10 My God in His lovingkindness will
      meet me;
   God will let me look *triumphantly* upon
      my foes.
11 Do not slay them, or my people will
      forget;
   Scatter them by Your power, and bring
      them down,
   O Lord, our shield.
12 *On account of* the sin of their mouth *and*
      the words of their lips,
   Let them even be caught in their pride,
   And on account of curses and lies which
      they utter.
13 *c*Destroy *them* in wrath, *c*destroy *them*
      that they may be no more;
   That *men* may know that God rules in
      Jacob
   To the ends of the earth.   Selah.

14 They return at evening, they howl like a
      dog,
   And go around the city.
15 They wander about *d*for food
   And growl if they are not satisfied.

16 ¶ But as for me, I shall sing of Your
      strength;
   Yes, I shall joyfully sing of Your
      lovingkindness in the morning,
   For You have been my stronghold
   And a refuge in the day of my distress.
17 O my strength, I will sing praises to You;
   For God is my stronghold, the God who
      shows me lovingkindness.

Psalm 60

Lament over Defeat in Battle, and Prayer for Help.

*For the choir director; according to *e*Shushan
Eduth. A Mikhtam of David, to teach; when he
struggled with Aram-naharaim and with
Aram-zobah, and Joab returned, and smote twelve
thousand of Edom in the Valley of Salt.*

1 ¶ O God, You have rejected us. You have
      broken us;
   You have been angry; O, restore us.
2 You have made the land quake, You
      have split it open;
   Heal its breaches, for it totters.
3 You have made Your people experience
      hardship;
   You have given us wine to drink that
      makes us stagger.
4 You have given a banner to those who
      fear You,
   That it may be displayed because of the
      truth.   Selah.
5 That Your beloved may be delivered,
   Save with Your right hand, and
      answer us!

6 ¶ God has spoken in His *f*holiness:
   "I will exult, I will portion out Shechem
      and measure out the valley of
      Succoth.
7 "Gilead is Mine, and Manasseh is Mine;
   Ephraim also is the helmet of My head;
   Judah is My *g*scepter.
8 "Moab is My washbowl;
   Over Edom I shall throw My shoe;
   Shout loud, O Philistia, because of Me!"

9 ¶ Who will bring me into the besieged
      city?
   Who will lead me to Edom?
10 Have not You Yourself, O God,
      rejected us?
   And will You not go forth with our
      armies, O God?

---

a Or *stir up strife*   *b* Many mss and some ancient versions read *My strength*   *c* Lit *Bring to an end*   *d* Or *to devour*
e Lit *The lily of testimony*   *f* Or *sanctuary*   *g* Or *lawgiver*

11 O give us help against the adversary,
For deliverance by man is in vain.
12 Through God we shall do valiantly,
And it is He who will tread down our
adversaries.

Psalm 61

Confidence in God's Protection.

For the choir director; on a stringed instrument.
A Psalm of David.

1 ¶ Hear my cry, O God;
Give heed to my prayer.
2 From the end of the earth I call to You
when my heart is faint;
Lead me to the rock that is higher
than I.
3 For You have been a refuge for me,
A tower of strength against the enemy.
4 Let me dwell in Your tent forever;
Let me take refuge in the shelter of Your
wings. Selah.

5 ¶ For You have heard my vows, O God;
You have given *me* the inheritance of
those who fear Your name.
6 You will prolong the king's life;
His years will be as many generations.
7 He will abide before God forever;
Appoint lovingkindness and truth that
they may preserve him.
8 So I will sing praise to Your name
forever,
That I may pay my vows day by day.

Psalm 62

God Alone a Refuge from Treachery
and Oppression.

For the choir director; according to Jeduthun.
A Psalm of David.

1 ¶ My soul *waits* in silence for God only;
From Him is my salvation.
2 He only is my rock and my salvation,
My stronghold; I shall not be greatly
shaken.

3 ¶ How long will you assail a man,
That you may murder *him*, all of you,
Like a leaning wall, like a tottering fence?
4 They have counseled only to thrust him
down from his high position;
They delight in falsehood;
They bless with their mouth,
But inwardly they curse. Selah.

5 ¶ My soul, wait in silence for God only,
For my hope is from Him.
6 He only is my rock and my salvation,
My stronghold; I shall not be shaken.
7 On God my salvation and my glory *rest*;

The rock of my strength, my refuge is in
God.
8 Trust in Him at all times, O people;
Pour out your heart before Him;
God is a refuge for us. Selah.

9 ¶ Men of low degree are only vanity and
men of rank are a lie;

62:7 The Hideout

In the years when David was an outlaw from
King Saul, his hideouts included a "rock" in the
desert (1 Samuel 23:25–28), as well as a
"stronghold" (1 Samuel 22:4). As an
experienced fighter, David knew the value of
such defenses. He recognized, however, that he
owed his safety to God, his true rock and
fortress.

In the balances they go up;
They are together lighter than breath.
10 Do not trust in oppression
And do not vainly hope in robbery;
If riches increase, do not set *your* heart
upon them.

11 ¶ [a]Once God has spoken;
[b]Twice I have heard this:
That power belongs to God;
12 And lovingkindness is Yours, O Lord,
For You recompense a man according to
his work.

Psalm 63

The Thirsting Soul Satisfied in God.

A Psalm of David, when he was in the wilderness
of Judah.

1 ¶ O God, You are my God; I shall seek
You [c]earnestly;
My soul thirsts for You, my flesh yearns
for You,
In a dry and weary land where there is
no water.
2 Thus I have seen You in the sanctuary,
To see Your power and Your glory.
3 Because Your lovingkindness is better
than life,
My lips will praise You.
4 So I will bless You as long as I live;
I will lift up my hands in Your name.
5 My soul is satisfied as with [d]marrow
and fatness,
And my mouth offers praises with joyful
lips.

6 ¶ When I remember You on my bed,
I meditate on You in the night watches,
7 For You have been my help,

---

[a] Or *One thing* [b] Or *These two things I have heard* [c] Lit *early* [d] Lit *fat*

And in the shadow of Your wings I sing
for joy.
8 My soul clings to You;
Your right hand upholds me.

9 ¶ But those who seek my life to
destroy it,
Will go into the depths of the earth.
10 They will be delivered over to the power
of the sword;
They will be a prey for foxes.
11 But the king will rejoice in God;
Everyone who swears by Him will glory,
For the mouths of those who speak lies
will be stopped.

Psalm 64

Prayer for Deliverance from Secret Enemies.

For the choir director. A Psalm of David.

1 ¶ Hear my voice, O God, in my
ᵃcomplaint;
Preserve my life from dread of the
enemy.
2 Hide me from the secret counsel of
evildoers,
From the tumult of those who do
iniquity,
3 Who have sharpened their tongue like a
sword.
They aimed bitter speech as their arrow,
4 To shoot from concealment at the
blameless;
Suddenly they shoot at him, and do not
fear.
5 They hold fast to themselves an evil
purpose;
They talk of laying snares secretly;
They say, "Who can see them?"
6 They ᵇdevise injustices, saying,
"We are ready with a well-conceived
plot";
For the inward thought and the heart of
a man are ᶜdeep.

7 ¶ But God will shoot at them with an
arrow;
Suddenly they will be wounded.
8 So they will make him stumble;
Their own tongue is against them;
All who see them will shake the head.
9 Then all men will fear,
And they will declare the work of God,
And will consider what He has done.
10 The righteous man will be glad in the
LORD and will take refuge in Him;
And all the upright in heart will glory.

Psalm 65

God's Abundant Favor to Earth and Man.

For the choir director. A Psalm of David. A Song.

1 ¶ There will be silence before You, and
praise in Zion, O God,
And to You the vow will be performed.
2 O You who hear prayer,
To You all men come.
3 Iniquities prevail against me;
As for our transgressions, You forgive
them.
4 How blessed is the one whom You
choose and bring near to You
To dwell in Your courts.
We will be satisfied with the goodness of
Your house,
Your holy temple.

5 ¶ By awesome deeds You answer us in
righteousness, O God of our
salvation,
You who are the trust of all the ends of
the earth and of the farthest sea;
6 Who establishes the mountains by His
strength,
Being girded with might;
7 Who stills the roaring of the seas,
The roaring of their waves,
And the tumult of the peoples.
8 They who dwell in the ends of the earth
stand in awe of Your signs;
You make the dawn and the sunset shout
for joy.

65:8 God Reaches Out

God's Old Testament people primarily came from a specially chosen ethnic group. Some outsiders joined them in their faith (Ruth, for instance), but the Israelites didn't issue blanket invitations. Nevertheless, they recognized that God's love extended to people over the horizon. His care for the earth, so beautifully described here, called for a response everywhere, not just in Israel.

9 ¶ You visit the earth and cause it to
overflow;
You greatly enrich it;
The stream of God is full of water;
You prepare their grain, for thus You
prepare the earth.
10 You water its furrows abundantly,
You settle its ridges,
You soften it with showers,
You bless its growth.

ᵃ Or concern　　ᵇ Or search out　　ᶜ Or unsearchable

11 You have crowned the year with Your
　　bounty,
　　And Your paths drip *with* fatness.
12 The pastures of the wilderness drip,
　　And the hills gird themselves with
　　　rejoicing.
13 The meadows are clothed with flocks
　　And the valleys are covered with grain;
　　They shout for joy, yes, they sing.

Psalm 66

Praise for God's Mighty Deeds and for His Answer to Prayer.

For the choir director. A Song. A Psalm.

1 ¶ Shout joyfully to God, all the earth;
2 Sing the glory of His name;
　　Make His praise glorious.
3 Say to God, "How awesome are Your
　　works!
　　Because of the greatness of Your power
　　　Your enemies will give feigned
　　　obedience to You.
4 "All the earth will worship You,
　　And will sing praises to You;
　　They will sing praises to Your name."
　　　　　　　　　　　　　　　Selah.

5 ¶ Come and see the works of God,
　　Who is awesome in *His* deeds toward the
　　　sons of men.
6 He turned the sea into dry land;
　　They passed through the river on foot;
　　There let us rejoice in Him!
7 He rules by His might forever;
　　His eyes keep watch on the nations;
　　Let not the rebellious exalt themselves.
　　　　　　　　　　　　　　　Selah.

8 ¶ Bless our God, O peoples,
　　And sound His praise abroad,
9 Who keeps us in life
　　And does not allow our feet to slip.
10 For You have tried us, O God;
　　You have refined us as silver is refined.
11 You brought us into the net;
　　You laid an oppressive burden upon our
　　　loins.
12 You made men ride over our heads;
　　We went through fire and through water,
　　Yet You brought us out into *a place of*
　　　abundance.
13 I shall come into Your house with burnt
　　　offerings;
　　I shall pay You my vows,
14 Which my lips uttered
　　And my mouth spoke when I was in
　　　distress.
15 I shall offer to You burnt offerings of fat
　　　beasts,
　　With the smoke of rams;

I shall make *an offering of* bulls with
　　male goats.　　　　　　　　　Selah.

16 ¶ Come *and* hear, all who [a]fear God,
　　And I will tell of what He has done for
　　　my soul.
17 I cried to Him with my mouth,
　　And He was extolled with my tongue.
18 If I [b]regard wickedness in my heart,
　　The Lord will not hear;
19 But certainly God has heard;
　　He has given heed to the voice of my
　　　prayer.
20 Blessed be God,
　　Who has not turned away my prayer
　　Nor His lovingkindness from me.

Psalm 67

The Nations Exhorted to Praise God.

For the choir director; with stringed instruments.
A Psalm. A Song.

1 ¶ God be gracious to us and bless us,
　　And cause His face to shine upon us—
　　　　　　　　　　　　　　　Selah.
2 That Your way may be known on the
　　　earth,
　　Your salvation among all nations.
3 Let the peoples praise You, O God;
　　Let all the peoples praise You.
4 Let the nations be glad and sing for joy;
　　For You will judge the peoples with
　　　uprightness
　　And guide the nations on the earth.
　　　　　　　　　　　　　　　Selah.
5 Let the peoples praise You, O God;
　　Let all the peoples praise You.
6 The earth has yielded its produce;
　　God, our God, blesses us.
7 God blesses us,
　　[c]That all the ends of the earth may fear
　　　Him.

Psalm 68

The God of Sinai and of the Sanctuary.

For the choir director. A Psalm of David. A Song.

1 ¶ Let God arise, let His enemies be
　　　scattered,
　　And let those who hate Him flee before
　　　Him.
2 As smoke is driven away, *so drive them*
　　　away;
　　As wax melts before the fire,
　　So let the wicked perish before God.
3 But let the righteous be glad; let them
　　　exult before God;
　　Yes, let them rejoice with gladness.
4 Sing to God, sing praises to His name;

---

[a] Or *revere*　　[b] Or *had regarded*　　[c] Or *And let all...earth fear Him*

Lift up *a song* for Him who rides
    through the deserts,
Whose name is the LORD, and exult
    before Him.

5 ¶ A father of the fatherless and a judge
    [a]for the widows,
    Is God in His holy habitation.
6 God makes a home for the lonely;
    He leads out the prisoners into
      prosperity,
    Only the rebellious dwell in a parched
      land.

7 ¶ O God, when You went forth before
    Your people,
    When You marched through the
      wilderness,   Selah.
8 The earth quaked;
    The heavens also dropped *rain* at the
      presence of God;
    Sinai itself *quaked* at the presence of
      God, the God of Israel.
9 You shed abroad a plentiful rain, O God;
    You confirmed Your inheritance when it
      was parched.
10 Your creatures settled in it;
    You provided in Your goodness for the
      poor, O God.

11 ¶ The Lord gives the command;
    The women who proclaim the *good*
      tidings are a great host:
12 "Kings of armies flee, they flee,
    And she who remains at home will
      divide the spoil!"
13 [b]When you lie down among the
    [c]sheepfolds,
    You are like the wings of a dove covered
      with silver,
    And its pinions with glistening gold.
14 When the Almighty scattered the kings
    there,
    It was snowing in Zalmon.

15 ¶ A mountain of God is the mountain of
    Bashan;
    A mountain *of many* peaks is the
      mountain of Bashan.
16 Why do you look with envy,
    O mountains with *many* peaks,
    At the mountain which God has desired
      for His abode?
    Surely the LORD will dwell *there* forever.
17 The chariots of God are [d]myriads,
    thousands upon thousands;
    The Lord is among them *as at* Sinai, in
      holiness.
18 You have ascended on high, You have
    led captive *Your* captives;
    You have received gifts among men,

Even *among* the rebellious also, that the
    LORD God may dwell *there.*

19 ¶ Blessed be the Lord, who daily bears
    our burden,
    The God *who* is our salvation.   Selah.
20 God is to us a God of deliverances;
    And to GOD the Lord belong escapes
      from death.
21 Surely God will shatter the head of His
    enemies,
    The hairy crown of him who goes on in
      his guilty deeds.
22 The Lord said, "I will bring *them* back
    from Bashan.
    I will bring *them* back from the depths of
      the sea;
23 That your foot may shatter *them* in
    blood,
    The tongue of your dogs *may have* its
      portion from *your* enemies."

24 ¶ They have seen Your procession,
    O God,
    The procession of my God, my King,
      into the sanctuary.

68:24 The Way They Worshiped

Many of the psalms were sung in the temple, to worship God. Exactly how people worshiped, however, is difficult to know. This verse offers unmistakable clues to how this psalm was used—in a procession leading to the temple. It may have first been sung when David brought the ark—the sign of God's actual presence—into Jerusalem (2 Samuel 6; 1 Chronicles 15–16). Or it may have been used in one of the annual festivals that drew Israelites from all over to the capital.

25 The singers went on, the musicians after
    them,
    In the midst of the maidens beating
      tambourines.
26 Bless God in the congregations,
    Even the LORD, *you who are* of the
      fountain of Israel.
27 There is Benjamin, the youngest, ruling
    them,
    The princes of Judah *in* their throng,
    The princes of Zebulun, the princes of
      Naphtali.

28 ¶ Your God has commanded your
    strength;
    Show Yourself strong, O God, who have
      acted on our behalf.
29 Because of Your temple at Jerusalem
    Kings will bring gifts to You.

---

[a] Lit *of*   [b] Lit *If*   [c] Or *cooking stones* or *saddle bags*   [d] Lit *twice ten thousand*

30 Rebuke the beasts in the reeds,
The herd of bulls with the calves of the
peoples,
Trampling under foot the pieces of silver;
He has scattered the peoples who delight
in war.
31 Envoys will come out of Egypt;
Ethiopia will quickly stretch out her
hands to God.
32 ¶ Sing to God, O kingdoms of the earth,
Sing praises to the Lord,   Selah.
33 To Him who rides upon the highest
heavens, which are from ancient
times;
Behold, He speaks forth with His voice, a
mighty voice.
34 Ascribe strength to God;
His majesty is over Israel
And His strength is in the skies.
35 O God, *You are* awesome from Your
sanctuary.
The God of Israel Himself gives strength
and power to the people.
Blessed be God!

Psalm 69

A Cry of Distress and Imprecation on Adversaries.

For the choir director; according to *a*Shoshannim.
A Psalm of David.

1 ¶ Save me, O God,
For the waters have threatened my life.
2 I have sunk in deep mire, and there is no
foothold;
I have come into deep waters, and a
flood overflows me.
3 I am weary with my crying; my throat is
parched;
My eyes fail while I wait for my God.
4 Those who hate me without a cause are
more than the hairs of my head;
Those who would destroy me are
powerful, being wrongfully my
enemies;
What I did not steal, I then have to
restore.
5 ¶ O God, it is You who knows my folly,
And my wrongs are not hidden
from You.
6 May those who wait for You not be
ashamed through me, O Lord GOD
of hosts;
May those who seek You not be
dishonored through me, O God of
Israel,
7 Because for Your sake I have borne
reproach;
Dishonor has covered my face.

8 I have become estranged from my
brothers
And an alien to my mother's sons.
9 For zeal for Your house has
consumed me,
And the reproaches of those who
reproach You have fallen on me.

69:9 Foreshadowing Jesus

Psalm 69 was quoted repeatedly by New Testament writers, who identify Jesus as the righteous sufferer. "Zeal for Your house will consume me" was quoted in John 2:17, for instance, when Jesus drove out the money changers, and Romans 15:3 quoted the second half of that verse, referring to Jesus' self-sacrificial attitude.

Why did the New Testament writers see Jesus in this psalm? The psalm was attributed to David, the great king. Yet it is not David's greatness and majesty that are described here. Instead, the psalm is a cry of suffering from a righteous man, alienated even from his family because of his zeal for God. It is strange: Israel's greatest hero is portrayed as a helpless victim because of his faith in God. Yet Jesus filled this pattern completely. He did not, however, follow every part of the psalm: Instead of the curses this psalm directs toward enemies, Jesus prayed that God would forgive the men murdering him.

10 When I wept in my soul with fasting,
It became my reproach.
11 When I made sackcloth my clothing,
I became a byword to them.
12 Those who sit in the gate talk about me,
And I *am* the song of the drunkards.

13 ¶ But as for me, my prayer is to You,
O LORD, at an acceptable time;
O God, in the greatness of Your
lovingkindness,
Answer me with Your saving truth.
14 Deliver me from the mire and do not let
me sink;
May I be delivered from my foes and
from the deep waters.
15 May the flood of water not overflow me
Nor the deep swallow me up,
Nor the pit shut its mouth on me.

16 ¶ Answer me, O LORD, for Your
lovingkindness is good;
According to the greatness of Your
compassion, turn to me,
17 And do not hide Your face from Your
servant,
For I am in distress; answer me quickly.

18 Oh draw near to my soul *and* redeem it;
Ransom me because of my enemies!
19 You know my reproach and my shame
and my dishonor;
All my adversaries are *a*before You.

20 ¶ Reproach has broken my heart and I
am so sick.
And I looked for sympathy, but there
was none,
And for comforters, but I found none.
21 They also gave me *b*gall for my food
And for my thirst they gave me vinegar
to drink.

22 ¶ May their table before them become a
snare;
And when they are in peace, *may it
become* a trap.
23 May their eyes grow dim so that they
cannot see,
And make their loins shake continually.
24 Pour out Your indignation on them,
And may Your burning anger overtake
them.
25 May their camp be desolate;
May none dwell in their tents.
26 For they have persecuted him whom You
Yourself have smitten,
And they tell of the pain of those whom
You have wounded.
27 Add iniquity to their iniquity,
And may they not come into Your
righteousness.
28 May they be blotted out of the book of
life
And may they not be recorded with the
righteous.

29 ¶ But I am afflicted and in pain;
May Your salvation, O God, set me
securely on high.
30 I will praise the name of God with song
And magnify Him with thanksgiving.
31 And it will please the LORD better than
an ox
Or a young bull with horns and hoofs.
32 The humble have seen *it and* are glad;
You who seek God, let your heart revive.
33 For the LORD hears the needy
And does not despise His *who are*
prisoners.

34 ¶ Let heaven and earth praise Him,
The seas and everything that moves in
them.
35 For God will save Zion and build the
cities of Judah,
That they may dwell there and possess it.
36 The descendants of His servants will
inherit it,

And those who love His name will dwell
in it.

Psalm 70

Prayer for Help against Persecutors.

*For the choir director. A Psalm of David;
for a memorial.*

1 ¶ O God, *hasten* to deliver me;
O LORD, hasten to my help!
2 Let those be ashamed and humiliated
Who seek my life;
Let those be turned back and dishonored
Who delight in my hurt.
3 Let those be turned back because of their
shame
Who say, "Aha, aha!"

4 ¶ Let all who seek You rejoice and be
glad in You;
And let those who love Your salvation
say continually,
"Let God be magnified."
5 But I am afflicted and needy;
Hasten to me, O God!
You are my help and my deliverer;
O LORD, do not delay.

Psalm 71

Prayer of an Old Man for Deliverance.

1 ¶ In You, O LORD, I have taken refuge;
Let me never be ashamed.
2 In Your righteousness deliver me and
rescue me;
Incline Your ear to me and save me.
3 Be to me a rock of habitation to which I
may continually come;
You have given commandment to
save me,
For You are my rock and my fortress.
4 Rescue me, O my God, out of the hand
of the wicked,
Out of the grasp of the wrongdoer and
ruthless man,
5 For You are my hope;
O Lord GOD, *You are* my confidence
from my youth.
6 By You I have been sustained from *my*
birth;
You are He who took me from my
mother's womb;
My praise is continually of You.

7 ¶ I have become a marvel to many,
For You are my strong refuge.
8 My mouth is filled with Your praise
And with Your glory all day long.
9 Do not cast me off in the time of old
age;

a Or known *to You*   *b* Or *poison*

Do not forsake me when my strength
  fails.
10 For my enemies have spoken against me;
  And those who watch for my life have
    consulted together,
11 Saying, "God has forsaken him;
  Pursue and seize him, for there is no one
    to deliver."

12 ¶ O God, do not be far from me;
  O my God, hasten to my help!
13 Let those who are adversaries of my soul
    be ashamed *and* consumed;
  Let them be covered with reproach and
    dishonor, who seek to injure me.
14 But as for me, I will hope continually,
  And will praise You yet more and more.
15 My mouth shall tell of Your
    righteousness
  And of Your salvation all day long;
  For I do not know the sum *of them.*
16 I will come with the mighty deeds of the
    Lord GOD;
  I will make mention of Your
    righteousness, Yours alone.

17 ¶ O God, You have taught me from my
    youth,
  And I still declare Your wondrous deeds.
18 And even when *I am* old and gray,
  O God, do not forsake me,
  Until I declare Your strength to *this*
    generation,
  Your power to all who are to come.

71:18 A View from Old Age

Older people have a peculiar privilege: the
chance to see God's faithfulness over a lifetime.
Their troubles do not grow smaller as the years
go by (see verses 9–11), but their experiences
can strengthen confidence that God will deliver
as he always has (verses 20–21).

19 For Your righteousness, O God, *reaches*
    to the heavens,
  You who have done great things;
  O God, who is like You?
20 You who have shown ᵃme many
    troubles and distresses
  Will revive ᵃme again,
  And will bring ᵃme up again from the
    depths of the earth.
21 May You increase my greatness
  And turn *to* comfort me.

22 ¶ I will also praise You with a harp,
  Even Your truth, O my God;
  To You I will sing praises with the lyre,

O Holy One of Israel.
23 My lips will shout for joy when I sing
    praises to You;
  And my soul, which You have redeemed.
24 My tongue also will utter Your
    righteousness all day long;
  For they are ashamed, for they are
    humiliated who seek my hurt.

Psalm 72

The Reign of the Righteous King.

A Psalm of Solomon.

1 ¶ Give the king Your judgments, O God,
  And Your righteousness to the king's
    son.
2 May he judge Your people with
    righteousness
  And ᵇYour afflicted with justice.
3 Let the mountains bring peace to the
    people,
  And the hills, in righteousness.
4 May he vindicate the afflicted of the
    people,
  Save the children of the needy
  And crush the oppressor.

5 ¶ Let them fear You while the sun
    endures,
  And as long as the moon, throughout all
    generations.
6 May he come down like rain upon the
    mown grass,
  Like showers that water the earth.
7 In his days may the righteous flourish,
  And abundance of peace till the moon is
    no more.

8 ¶ May he also rule from sea to sea
  And from the River to the ends of the
    earth.
9 Let the nomads of the desert bow before
    him,
  And his enemies lick the dust.
10 Let the kings of Tarshish and of the
    islands bring presents;
  The kings of Sheba and Seba offer gifts.
11 And let all kings bow down before him,
  All nations serve him.

12 ¶ For he will deliver the needy when he
    cries for help,
  The afflicted also, and him who has no
    helper.
13 He will have compassion on the poor
    and needy,
  And the lives of the needy he will save.
14 He will rescue their life from oppression
    and violence,
  And their blood will be precious in his
    sight;

ᵃ Another reading is *us*   ᵇ Or *Your humble*

15 So may he live, and may the gold of
    Sheba be given to him;
    And let them pray for him continually;
    Let them bless him all day long.

16 ¶ May there be abundance of grain in the
    earth on top of the mountains;
    Its fruit will wave like *the cedars of*
    Lebanon;
    And may those from the city flourish like
    vegetation of the earth.

17 May his name endure forever;
    May his name increase as long as the sun
    shines;
    And let *men* bless themselves by him;
    Let all nations call him blessed.

18 ¶ Blessed be the LORD God, the God of
    Israel,
    Who alone works wonders.

19 And blessed be His glorious name
    forever;
    And may the whole earth be filled with
    His glory.
    Amen, and Amen.

20 ¶ The prayers of David the son of Jesse
    are ended.

BOOK 3

Psalm 73

The End of the Wicked Contrasted with That of the Righteous.

A Psalm of Asaph.

1 ¶ Surely God is good to Israel,
    To those who are pure in heart!

2 But as for me, my feet came close to
    stumbling,

73:1 The Five Books

Psalms was probably made into one big book from five separate collections. These are set off in our Bible as Book 1, Book 2, and so on, each book ending with a concluding line of praise. The contents sometimes overlap: Psalm 14 in Book 1 turns up again as Psalm 53 in Book 2. Part of Psalm 40 (Book 1) becomes Psalm 70 (Book 2), and parts of Psalms 57 and 60 make up Psalm 108 (Book 4). Other less noticeable differences stand out between the books. But perhaps the most eloquent proof that all these psalms were not originally collected together is found at the end of Psalm 72, "The prayers of David the son of Jesse are ended." Since 18 more "psalms of David" appear in Psalms, it seems very likely that Psalm 72:20 originally concluded a songbook. Later, this collection was incorporated into the book of Psalms.

    My steps had almost slipped.

3 For I was envious of the arrogant
    As I saw the prosperity of the wicked.

4 For there are no pains in their death,
    And their body is fat.

73:3–20 Short-Run Rewards

Some people are deeply disturbed when they see evil people living without a care. Does a bad life always make you unhappy? Not in the short run, according to this description. In fact, the life of the wicked sometimes looks enviable. Only in the light of eternity is godly living always more rewarding.

5 They are not in trouble *as other* men,
    Nor are they plagued like mankind.

6 Therefore pride is their necklace;
    The garment of violence covers them.

7 Their eye bulges from fatness;
    The imaginations of *their* heart run riot.

8 They mock and wickedly speak of
    oppression;
    They speak from on high.

9 They have set their mouth against the
    heavens,
    And their tongue parades through the
    earth.

10 ¶ Therefore his people return to this
    place,
    And waters of abundance are drunk by
    them.

11 They say, "How does God know?
    And is there knowledge with the Most
    High?"

12 Behold, these are the wicked;
    And always at ease, they have increased
    in wealth.

13 Surely in vain I have kept my heart pure
    And washed my hands in innocence;

14 For I have been stricken all day long
    And chastened every morning.

15 ¶ If I had said, "I will speak thus,"
    Behold, I would have betrayed the
    generation of Your children.

16 When I pondered to understand this,
    It was troublesome in my sight

17 Until I came into the sanctuary of God;
    Then I perceived their end.

18 Surely You set them in slippery places;
    You cast them down to destruction.

19 How they are destroyed in a moment!
    They are utterly swept away by sudden
    terrors!

20 Like a dream when one awakes,
    O Lord, when aroused, You will despise
    their form.

21 ¶ When my heart was embittered
And I was pierced within,
22 Then I was senseless and ignorant;
I was *like* a beast before You.
23 Nevertheless I am continually with You;
You have taken hold of my right hand.
24 With Your counsel You will guide me,
And afterward receive me to glory.

25 ¶ Whom have I in heaven *but You?*
And besides You, I desire nothing on
earth.
26 My flesh and my heart may fail,
But God is the strength of my heart and
my portion forever.
27 For, behold, those who are far from You
will perish;
You have destroyed all those who are
unfaithful to You.
28 But as for me, the nearness of God is my
good;
I have made the Lord GOD my refuge,
That I may tell of all Your works.

Psalm 74

An Appeal against the Devastation
of the Land by the Enemy.

A Maskil of Asaph.

1 ¶ O God, why have You rejected *us*
forever?
Why does Your anger smoke against the
sheep of Your pasture?
2 Remember Your congregation, which
You have purchased of old,
Which You have redeemed to be the
tribe of Your inheritance;
And this Mount Zion, where You have
dwelt.
3 Turn Your footsteps toward the perpetual
ruins;
The enemy has damaged everything
within the sanctuary.
4 Your adversaries have roared in the
midst of Your meeting place;
They have set up their own standards for
signs.
5 It seems as if one had lifted up
His axe in a forest of trees.
6 And now all its carved work
They smash with hatchet and hammers.
7 They have burned Your sanctuary to the
ground;
They have defiled the dwelling place of
Your name.
8 They said in their heart, "Let us
completely subdue them."
They have burned all the meeting places
of God in the land.
9 We do not see our signs;

There is no longer any prophet,
Nor is there any among us who knows
how long.
10 How long, O God, will the adversary
revile,
And the enemy spurn Your name
forever?
11 Why do You withdraw Your hand, even
Your right hand?
From within Your bosom, destroy *them!*

12 ¶ Yet God is my king from of old,
Who works deeds of deliverance in the
midst of the earth.
13 ª You divided the sea by Your strength;
You broke the heads of the sea monsters
in the waters.
14 You crushed the heads of Leviathan;
You gave him as food for the creatures
of the wilderness.
15 You broke open springs and torrents;
You dried up ever-flowing streams.
16 Yours is the day, Yours also is the night;
You have prepared the light and the sun.
17 You have established all the boundaries
of the earth;
You have made summer and winter.

18 ¶ Remember this, O LORD, that the
enemy has reviled,
And a foolish people has spurned Your
name.
19 Do not deliver the soul of Your
turtledove to the wild beast;
Do not forget the life of Your afflicted
forever.
20 Consider the covenant;
For the dark places of the land are full of
the habitations of violence.
21 Let not the oppressed return dishonored;
Let the afflicted and needy praise Your
name.

22 ¶ Arise, O God, *and* plead Your own
cause;
Remember how the foolish man
reproaches You all day long.
23 Do not forget the voice of Your
adversaries,
The uproar of those who rise against You
which ascends continually.

Psalm 75

God Abases the Proud, but Exalts
the Righteous.

For the choir director; *set to* Al-tashtheth. A Psalm
of Asaph, a Song.

1 ¶ We give thanks to You, O God, we
give thanks,
For Your name is near;

ª Or *You Yourself*

Men declare Your wondrous works.

2 "When I select an appointed time,
It is I who judge with equity.

3 "The earth and all who dwell in it
  ^amelt;
It is I who have firmly set its pillars.
                                    Selah.

4 "I said to the boastful, 'Do not boast,'
And to the wicked, 'Do not lift up the
  horn;

5 Do not lift up your horn on high,
Do not speak with insolent pride.' "

6 ¶ For not from the east, nor from the
  west,
Nor from the desert *comes* exaltation;

7 But God is the Judge;
He puts down one and exalts another.

8 For a cup is in the hand of the LORD,
  and the wine foams;
It is well mixed, and He pours out of
  this;
Surely all the wicked of the earth must
  drain *and* drink down its dregs.

9 ¶ But as for me, I will declare *it* forever;
I will sing praises to the God of Jacob.

10 And all the horns of the wicked He will
  cut off,
But the horns of the righteous will be
  lifted up.

Psalm 76

The Victorious Power of the God of Jacob.

For the choir director; on stringed instruments.
A Psalm of Asaph, a Song.

1 ¶ God is known in Judah;
His name is great in Israel.

2 His tabernacle is in Salem;
His dwelling place also is in Zion.

3 There He broke the flaming arrows,
The shield and the sword and the
  weapons of war.   Selah.

4 ¶ You are resplendent,
More majestic than the mountains of
  prey.

5 The stouthearted were plundered,
They sank into sleep;
And none of the warriors could use his
  hands.

6 At Your rebuke, O God of Jacob,
Both rider and horse were cast into a
  dead sleep.

7 You, even You, are to be feared;
And who may stand in Your presence
  when once You are angry?

8 ¶ You caused judgment to be heard from
  heaven;
The earth feared and was still

9 When God arose to judgment,
To save all the humble of the earth.
                                    Selah.

10 For the wrath of man shall praise You;
With a remnant of wrath You will gird
  Yourself.

11 ¶ Make vows to the LORD your God and
  fulfill *them;*
Let all who are around Him bring gifts
  to Him who is to be feared.

12 He will cut off the spirit of princes;
He is feared by the kings of the earth.

Psalm 77

Comfort in Trouble from Recalling God's
Mighty Deeds.

For the choir director; according to Jeduthun.
A Psalm of Asaph.

1 ¶ My voice *rises* to God, and I will cry
  aloud;
My voice *rises* to God, and He will
  hear me.

2 In the day of my trouble I sought the
  Lord;
In the night my hand was stretched out
  ^bwithout weariness;
My soul refused to be comforted.

3 *When* I remember God, then I am
  disturbed;
When I sigh, then my spirit grows faint.
                                    Selah.

77:3–12 Sleepless Nights

*Sleeplessness afflicts millions, and this psalm
shows it is nothing new. Anxiety tormented the
psalmist while he lay awake at night. What to
do? He deliberately turned his thoughts to the
past, remembering what God had done for him
and for his people.*

4 You have held my eyelids *open;*
I am so troubled that I cannot speak.

5 I have considered the days of old,
The years of long ago.

6 I will remember my song in the night;
I will meditate with my heart,
And my spirit ponders:

7 ¶ Will the Lord reject forever?
And will He never be favorable again?

8 Has His lovingkindness ceased forever?
Has *His* promise come to an end forever?

9 Has God forgotten to be gracious,
Or has He in anger withdrawn His
  compassion?   Selah.

^a Or *totter*   ^b Lit *and did not grow numb*

10 Then I said, "It is my grief,
   That the right hand of the Most High
      has changed."

11 ¶ I shall remember the deeds of the
      LORD;
   Surely I will remember Your wonders of
      old.

12 I will meditate on all Your work
   And muse on Your deeds.

13 Your way, O God, is holy;
   What god is great like our God?

14 You are the God who works wonders;
   You have made known Your strength
      among the peoples.

15 You have by Your power redeemed Your
      people,
   The sons of Jacob and Joseph.   Selah.

16 ¶ The waters saw You, O God;
   The waters saw You, they were in
      anguish;
   The deeps also trembled.

17 The clouds poured out water;
   The skies gave forth a sound;
   Your arrows flashed here and there.

18 The sound of Your thunder was in the
      whirlwind;
   The lightnings lit up the world;
   The earth trembled and shook.

19 Your way was in the sea
   And Your paths in the mighty waters,
   And Your footprints may not be
      known.

20 You led Your people like a flock
   By the hand of Moses and Aaron.

Remembering Back
The past can give you hope for the future

> I shall remember
> the deeds of the
> LORD. 77:11

MARRIED PEOPLE MAKE IT THEIR business to remember how love began. Anniversaries recall their wedding day, year after year. Wedding rings remind them of their commitment. Wedding photos capture the moment when "two become one." In remembering the beginning of their love, couples often find new hope for the future.

Forgetting, on the other hand, amounts to treason. If one person forgets the all-important anniversary, tears and anger may follow.

An Anniversary Day

The book of Psalms remembers too. When things get bad, these poems often refer to the past—particularly to the great events when, under Moses, the Israelite nation began. God freed the Israelites from Egyptian slavery, carried them through the Red Sea, gave them directions for living, and ushered them into the promised land. This miraculous beginning was as significant to Jews as the cross is to Christians.

The Israelites even had an "anniversary day"—known as Passover—to remember it. Every spring Passover reminded them of their escape from Egypt. It's no accident that Easter often falls on the same week. Both days celebrate liberation from slavery.

The memories weren't all positive. The Israelites could, in fact, be brutally frank about their early failings. Even as they remembered how persistently wonderful God had been, they also remembered how rebellious, complaining, and forgetful they had been. Yet they had one great, happy reason to celebrate: God had kept his promise to love them.

Hope in a Time of Despair

Psalm 77 is a "remembering" poem. It starts with deep despair. "Will the Lord reject forever? And will he never be favorable again?... Has God forgotten to be gracious, or has He in anger withdrawn His compassion?" (77:7,9). Imagine a wife asking such questions about her husband.

Then thoughts turn, deliberately, to the past. Remember the turmoil at the banks of the Red Sea? Could anything be worse? But in that turbulent water they had seen the Lord's power: God had led them through to safety. He would do the same again.

The historical psalms (77, 78, 105, 106) invite us, along with the Israelites, to relive history. Like married couples remembering back, we can recall God's work—his powerful victories recorded all through Scripture, his promises and proofs of love toward his people. And we can refer to God's history with us as individuals, too. Who cannot count some blessings, some undeserved favors? Through such remembering we are strengthened to face the future, and to recommit ourselves to trusting God's care.

Life Questions: If you were to refer to a single past event for encouragement, what would it be?

Psalm 78

God's Guidance of His People in Spite of Their Unfaithfulness.

A Maskil of Asaph.

1 ¶ Listen, O my people, to my instruction;
   Incline your ears to the words of my
      mouth.
2 I will open my mouth in a parable;
   I will utter dark sayings of old,

78:2 Speaking in Parables

Matthew saw this verse as foreshadowing Jesus' teaching style (Matthew 13:35). A "parable" or "proverb" (the Hebrew word is the same) simply compares one thing with another. This psalm compares the present to the past. By going over the great things God has done—and the great indifference God's people have often shown—the psalmist warns against making the same mistakes again.

3 Which we have heard and known,
   And our fathers have told us.
4 We will not conceal them from their
     children,
   But tell to the generation to come the
     praises of the LORD,
   And His strength and His wondrous
     works that He has done.

5 ¶ For He established a testimony in Jacob
   And appointed a law in Israel,
   Which He commanded our fathers
   That they should teach them to their
     children,
6 That the generation to come might
     know, *even* the children *yet* to be
     born,
   That they may arise and tell *them* to
     their children,
7 That they should put their confidence in
     God
   And not forget the works of God,
   But keep His commandments,
8 And not be like their fathers,
   A stubborn and rebellious generation,
   A generation that did not ªprepare its
     heart
   And whose spirit was not faithful to God.

9 ¶ The sons of Ephraim were archers
     equipped with bows,
   Yet they turned back in the day of battle.
10 They did not keep the covenant of God
   And refused to walk in His law;
11 They forgot His deeds
   And His miracles that He had shown
     them.
12 He wrought wonders before their fathers
   In the land of Egypt, in the field of Zoan.
13 He divided the sea and caused them to
     pass through,
   And He made the waters stand up like a
     heap.
14 Then He led them with the cloud by day
   And all the night with a light of fire.
15 He split the rocks in the wilderness
   And gave *them* abundant drink like the
     ocean depths.
16 He brought forth streams also from the
     rock
   And caused waters to run down like
     rivers.

17 ¶ Yet they still continued to sin against
     Him,
   To rebel against the Most High in the
     desert.
18 And in their heart they put God to the
     test
   By asking food according to their desire.
19 Then they spoke against God;
   They said, "Can God prepare a table in
     the wilderness?
20 "Behold, He struck the rock so that waters
     gushed out,
   And streams were overflowing;
   Can He give bread also?
   Will He provide meat for His people?"

21 ¶ Therefore the LORD heard and was full
     of wrath;
   And a fire was kindled against Jacob
   And anger also mounted against Israel,
22 Because they did not believe in God
   And did not trust in His salvation.
23 Yet He commanded the clouds above
   And opened the doors of heaven;
24 He rained down manna upon them
     to eat
   And gave them food from heaven.
25 Man did eat the bread of angels;
   He sent them food in abundance.
26 He caused the east wind to blow in the
     heavens
   And by His power He directed the south
     wind.
27 When He rained meat upon them like
     the dust,
   Even winged fowl like the sand of the
     seas,
28 Then He let *them* fall in the midst of
     their camp,
   Round about their dwellings.
29 So they ate and were well filled,
   And their desire He gave to them.
30 Before they had satisfied their desire,

ª Or *put right*

While their food was in their mouths,
31 The anger of God rose against them
    And killed some of their stoutest ones,
    And subdued the choice men of Israel.
32 In spite of all this they still sinned
    And did not believe in His wonderful
    works.
33 So He brought their days to an end in
    futility
    And their years in sudden terror.

34 ¶ When He killed them, then they sought
    Him,
    And returned and searched diligently for
    God;
35 And they remembered that God was
    their rock,
    And the Most High God their Redeemer.
36 But they deceived Him with their mouth
    And lied to Him with their tongue.
37 For their heart was not steadfast toward
    Him,
    Nor were they faithful in His covenant.
38 But He, being compassionate, forgave
    their iniquity and did not destroy
    them;
    And often He restrained His anger
    And did not arouse all His wrath.
39 Thus He remembered that they were but
    flesh,
    A wind that passes and does not return.

40 ¶ How often they rebelled against Him in
    the wilderness
    And grieved Him in the desert!
41 Again and again they *a*tempted God,
    And pained the Holy One of Israel.
42 They did not remember His power,
    The day when He redeemed them from
    the adversary,
43 When He performed His signs in Egypt
    And His marvels in the field of Zoan,
44 And turned their rivers to blood,
    And their streams, they could not drink.
45 He sent among them swarms of flies
    which devoured them,
    And frogs which destroyed them.
46 He gave also their crops to the
    grasshopper
    And the product of their labor to the
    locust.
47 He destroyed their vines with hailstones
    And their sycamore trees with frost.
48 He gave over their cattle also to the
    hailstones
    And their herds to bolts of lightning.
49 He sent upon them His burning anger,
    Fury and indignation and trouble,
    A band of destroying angels.
50 He leveled a path for His anger;
    He did not spare their soul from death,

But gave over their life to the plague,
51 And smote all the firstborn in Egypt,
    The first *issue* of their virility in the tents
    of Ham.
52 But He led forth His own people like
    sheep
    And guided them in the wilderness like a
    flock;
53 He led them safely, so that they did not
    fear;
    But the sea engulfed their enemies.

54 ¶ So He brought them to His holy land,
    To this hill country which His right hand
    had gained.
55 He also drove out the nations before
    them
    And apportioned them for an inheritance
    by measurement,
    And made the tribes of Israel dwell in
    their tents.
56 Yet they *b*tempted and rebelled against
    the Most High God
    And did not keep His testimonies,
57 But turned back and acted treacherously
    like their fathers;
    They turned aside like a treacherous bow.
58 For they provoked Him with their high
    places
    And aroused His jealousy with their
    graven images.
59 When God heard, He was filled with
    wrath
    And greatly abhorred Israel;
60 So that He abandoned the dwelling place
    at Shiloh,
    The tent which He had pitched among
    men,
61 And gave up His strength to captivity
    And His glory into the hand of the
    adversary.
62 He also delivered His people to the
    sword,
    And was filled with wrath at His
    inheritance.
63 Fire devoured His young men,
    And His virgins had no wedding songs.
64 His priests fell by the sword,
    And His widows could not weep.

65 ¶ Then the Lord awoke as *if from* sleep,
    Like a warrior overcome by wine.
66 He drove His adversaries backward;
    He put on them an everlasting reproach.
67 He also rejected the tent of Joseph,
    And did not choose the tribe of Ephraim,
68 But chose the tribe of Judah,
    Mount Zion which He loved.
69 And He built His sanctuary like the
    heights,

a Or *put God to the test* *b* Or *put to the test*

Like the earth which He has founded
    forever.
70 He also chose David His servant
    And took him from the sheepfolds;

78:64 The Bad Old Days

From the time they entered the promised land to the time when Saul was named their first king, Israelites had no central government. Instead they were governed by "judges," colorful volunteer leaders like Deborah, Gideon, and Samson. Israel had few nostalgic memories of those days. Psalm 78 portrays them as a time when Israel abandoned God— and God rejected Israel. These verses (59–64) draw from the events described in 1 Samuel 4.

71 From the care of the ewes with suckling
    lambs He brought him
    To shepherd Jacob His people,
    And Israel His inheritance.
72 So he shepherded them according to the
    integrity of his heart,
    And guided them with his skillful hands.

Psalm 79

A Lament over the Destruction
of Jerusalem, and Prayer for Help.

A Psalm of Asaph.

1 ¶ O God, the nations have invaded Your
    inheritance;
    They have defiled Your holy temple;
    They have laid Jerusalem in ruins.
2 They have given the dead bodies of Your
    servants for food to the birds of the
    heavens,
    The flesh of Your godly ones to the
    beasts of the earth.
3 They have poured out their blood like
    water round about Jerusalem;
    And there was no one to bury them.
4 We have become a reproach to our
    neighbors,
    A scoffing and derision to those
    around us.
5 How long, O LORD? Will You be angry
    forever?
    Will Your jealousy burn like fire?
6 Pour out Your wrath upon the nations
    which do not know You,
    And upon the kingdoms which do not
    call upon Your name.
7 For they have devoured Jacob
    And laid waste his habitation.

8 ¶ Do not remember the iniquities of *our*
    forefathers against us;

Let Your compassion come quickly to
    meet us,
    For we are brought very low.
9 Help us, O God of our salvation, for the
    glory of Your name;
    And deliver us and forgive our sins for
    Your name's sake.
10 Why should the nations say, "Where is
    their God?"
    Let there be known among the nations in
    our sight,
    Vengeance for the blood of Your
    servants which has been shed.
11 Let the groaning of the prisoner come
    before You;
    According to the greatness of Your
    power preserve those who are
    doomed to die.
12 And return to our neighbors sevenfold
    into their bosom
    The reproach with which they have
    reproached You, O Lord.
13 So we Your people and the sheep of
    Your pasture
    Will give thanks to You forever;
    To all generations we will tell of Your
    praise.

Psalm 80

God Implored to Rescue His People
from Their Calamities.

For the choir director; *set to* El Shoshannim;
Eduth. A Psalm of Asaph.

1 ¶ Oh, give ear, Shepherd of Israel,
    You who lead Joseph like a flock;
    You who are enthroned *above* the
    cherubim, shine forth!
2 Before Ephraim and Benjamin and
    Manasseh, stir up Your power
    And come to save us!
3 O God, restore us
    And cause Your face to shine *upon us,*
    and we will be saved.

4 ¶ O LORD God *of* hosts,
    How long will You be angry with the
    prayer of Your people?
5 You have fed them with the bread of
    tears,
    And You have made them to drink tears
    in large measure.
6 You make us ᵃan object of contention
    to our neighbors,
    And our enemies laugh among
    themselves.
7 O God *of* hosts, restore us
    And cause Your face to shine *upon us,*
    ᵇand we will be saved.

8 ¶ You removed a vine from Egypt;

ᵃLit *a strife to*   ᵇOr *that we may*

You drove out the nations and planted it.
9 You cleared *the ground* before it,
And it took deep root and filled the land.
10 The mountains were covered with its
shadow,
And the cedars of God with its boughs.
11 It was sending out its branches to the sea
And its shoots to the River.
12 Why have You broken down its hedges,
So that all who pass *that* way pick its
fruit?
13 A boar from the forest eats it away
And whatever moves in the field feeds
on it.

14 ¶ O God *of* hosts, turn again now, we
beseech You;
Look down from heaven and see, and
take care of this vine,

80:14 Grapevines

*The Old Testament often portrays God's people
as a vineyard. Jesus, too, used the image (see
Mark 12:1–9; John 15:1–5). Raising grapes
was as familiar to Israelites as playing baseball
is to Americans. Many sermon illustrations
have been made from both.*

15 Even the shoot which Your right hand
has planted,
And on the son whom You have
strengthened for Yourself.
16 It is burned with fire, it is cut down;
They perish at the rebuke of Your
countenance.
17 Let Your hand be upon the man of Your
right hand,
Upon the son of man whom You made
strong for Yourself.
18 Then we shall not turn back from You;
Revive us, and we will call upon Your
name.
19 O LORD God of hosts, restore us;
Cause Your face to shine *upon us,* and
we will be saved.

Psalm 81

God's Goodness and Israel's Waywardness.

*For the choir director; on the Gittith.
A Psalm of Asaph.*

1 ¶ Sing for joy to God our strength;
Shout joyfully to the God of Jacob.
2 Raise a song, strike the timbrel,
The sweet sounding lyre with the harp.
3 Blow the trumpet at the new moon,
At the full moon, on our feast day.
4 For it is a statute for Israel,
An ordinance of the God of Jacob.

5 He established it for a testimony in
Joseph
When he went throughout the land of
Egypt.
I heard a language that I did not know:

6 ¶ "I relieved his shoulder of the burden,
His hands were freed from the basket.
7 "You called in trouble and I rescued you;
I answered you in the hiding place of
thunder;
I proved you at the waters of Meribah.
Selah.
8 "Hear, O My people, and I will admonish
you;
O Israel, if you would listen to Me!
9 "Let there be no strange god among you;
Nor shall you worship any foreign god.
10 "I, the LORD, am your God,
Who brought you up from the land of
Egypt;
Open your mouth wide and I will fill it.

11 ¶ "But My people did not listen to My
voice,
And Israel did not obey Me.
12 "So I gave them over to the stubbornness
of their heart,
To walk in their own devices.
13 "Oh that My people would listen to Me,
That Israel would walk in My ways!
14 "I would quickly subdue their enemies
And turn My hand against their
adversaries.
15 "Those who hate the LORD would pretend
obedience to Him,
And their time *of punishment* would be
forever.
16 "But I would feed you with the finest of
the wheat,
And with honey from the rock I would
satisfy you."

Psalm 82

Unjust Judgments Rebuked.

A Psalm of Asaph.

1 ¶ God takes His stand in His own
congregation;
He judges in the midst of the rulers.
2 How long will you judge unjustly
And show partiality to the wicked? Selah.
3 Vindicate the weak and fatherless;
Do justice to the afflicted and destitute.
4 Rescue the weak and needy;
Deliver *them* out of the hand of the
wicked.

5 ¶ They do not know nor do they
understand;
They walk about in darkness;
All the foundations of the earth are
shaken.

6 I said, "You are gods,
    And all of you are sons of the Most
        High.
7 "Nevertheless you will die like men
    And fall like *any* one of the princes."

82:1 In the Midst of the Rulers

Human beings like to think of themselves as godlike—able to do whatever they like. Many commentators believe this psalm's snort of disdain is aimed at human judges and "powers that be" who set themselves up as little gods. What will become of their arrogance if they defy God? They will "die like men" (verse 7). The grave is a perfect answer to their pretensions.

When Jesus was accused of blasphemy for claiming to be God's Son, he referred his critics to this psalm (John 10:35). If Scripture could apply such lofty terminology to sinful human beings, was it not possible that a perfect man could be God's own Son?

8 Arise, O God, judge the earth!
    For it is You who possesses all the
        nations.

Psalm 83

God Implored to Confound His Enemies.

A Song, a Psalm of Asaph.

1 ¶ O God, do not remain quiet;
    Do not be silent and, O God, do not be
        still.
2 For behold, Your enemies make an
        uproar,
    And those who hate You have exalted
        themselves.
3 They make shrewd plans against Your
        people,
    And conspire together against Your
        treasured ones.
4 They have said, "Come, and let us wipe
        them out as a nation,
    That the name of Israel be remembered
        no more."
5 For they have conspired together with
        one mind;
    Against You they make a covenant:
6 The tents of Edom and the Ishmaelites,
    Moab and the Hagrites;
7 Gebal and Ammon and Amalek,
    Philistia with the inhabitants of Tyre;
8 Assyria also has joined with them;
    They have become a help to the children
        of Lot.   Selah.

9 ¶ Deal with them as with Midian,

As with Sisera *and* Jabin at the torrent of
    Kishon,
10 Who were destroyed at En-dor,
    Who became as dung for the ground.
11 Make their nobles like Oreb and Zeeb
    And all their princes like Zebah and
        Zalmunna,
12 Who said, "Let us possess for ourselves
    The pastures of God."

13 ¶ O my God, make them like the
        [a]whirling dust,
    Like chaff before the wind.
14 Like fire that burns the forest
    And like a flame that sets the mountains
        on fire,
15 So pursue them with Your tempest
    And terrify them with Your storm.
16 Fill their faces with dishonor,
    That they may seek Your name,
        O LORD.
17 Let them be ashamed and dismayed
        forever,
    And let them be humiliated and
        perish,
18 That they may know that You alone,
        whose name is the LORD,
    Are the Most High over all the earth.

Psalm 84

Longing for the Temple Worship.

*For the choir director; on the Gittith. A Psalm
of the sons of Korah.*

1 ¶ How lovely are Your dwelling places,
    O LORD of hosts!
2 My soul longed and even yearned for the
        courts of the LORD;
    My heart and my flesh sing for joy to the
        living God.
3 The bird also has found a house,
    And the swallow a nest for herself, where
        she may lay her young,
    Even Your altars, O LORD of hosts,
    My King and my God.
4 How blessed are those who dwell in Your
        house!
    They are ever praising You.   Selah.

5 ¶ How blessed is the man whose strength
        is in You,
    In whose heart are the highways *to*
        Zion!
6 Passing through the valley of [b]Baca
        they make it a spring;
    The early rain also covers it with
        blessings.
7 They go from strength to strength,
    Every one of them appears before God in
        Zion.

---

a Or *tumbleweed*   b Probably, *Weeping;* or *Balsam trees*

8 ¶ O LORD God of hosts, hear my prayer;
　Give ear, O God of Jacob!　　Selah.
9 Behold our shield, O God,
　And look upon the face of Your
　　anointed.
10 For a day in Your courts is better than a
　　thousand *outside*.
　I would rather stand at the threshold of
　　the house of my God
　Than dwell in the tents of wickedness.

84:10 Homecoming

"Home Sweet Home" probably adorns more plaques than any other motto. Home is a place where you can lay down your tired body and bruised ego in safety. Psalm 84 contains the same idea, but with a dramatic difference. Home is in God's house, a place that brings comfort right down into your bones. You'd rather spend one day near God, praising him, than a thousand days anywhere else.

11 For the LORD God is a sun and shield;
　The LORD gives grace and glory;
　No good thing does He withhold from
　　those who walk uprightly.
12 O LORD of hosts,
　How blessed is the man who trusts
　　in You!

Psalm 85

Prayer for God's Mercy upon the Nation.

For the choir director. A Psalm of the sons
of Korah.

1 ¶ O LORD, You showed favor to Your
　　land;
　You ªrestored the captivity of Jacob.
2 You forgave the iniquity of Your
　　people;
　You covered all their sin.　　Selah.
3 You withdrew all Your fury;
　You turned away from Your burning
　　anger.
4 ¶ Restore us, O God of our salvation,
　And cause Your indignation toward us to
　　cease.
5 Will You be angry with us forever?
　Will You prolong Your anger to all
　　generations?
6 Will You not Yourself revive us again,
　That Your people may rejoice in You?
7 Show us Your lovingkindness, O LORD,
　And grant us Your salvation.

8 ¶ I will hear what God the LORD will
　　say;

For He will speak peace to His people, to
　　His godly ones;
　But let them not turn back to folly.
9 Surely His salvation is near to those who
　　ᵇfear Him,
　That glory may dwell in our land.
10 Lovingkindness and truth have met
　　together;
　Righteousness and peace have kissed
　　each other.
11 Truth springs from the earth,
　And righteousness looks down from
　　heaven.
12 Indeed, the LORD will give what is good,
　And our land will yield its produce.
13 Righteousness will go before Him
　And will make His footsteps into a way.

Psalm 86

A Psalm of Supplication and Trust.

A Prayer of David.

1 ¶ Incline Your ear, O LORD, *and*
　　answer me;
　For I am afflicted and needy.
2 Preserve my soul, for I am a godly man;
　O You my God, save Your servant who
　　trusts in You.
3 Be gracious to me, O Lord,
　For to You I cry all day long.
4 Make glad the soul of Your servant,
　For to You, O Lord, I lift up my soul.
5 For You, Lord, are good, and ready to
　　forgive,
　And abundant in lovingkindness to all
　　who call upon You.
6 Give ear, O LORD, to my prayer;
　And give heed to the voice of my
　　supplications!
7 In the day of my trouble I shall call
　　upon You,
　For You will answer me.
8 There is no one like You among the
　　gods, O Lord,
　Nor are there any works like Yours.
9 All nations whom You have made shall
　　come and worship before You,
　　O Lord,
　And they shall glorify Your name.
10 For You are great and do wondrous
　　deeds;
　You alone are God.

11 ¶ Teach me Your way, O LORD;
　I will walk in Your truth;
　Unite my heart to fear Your name.
12 I will give thanks to You, O Lord my
　　God, with all my heart,
　And will glorify Your name forever.

ª Or *restore the fortunes*　　ᵇ Or *reverence*

13 For Your lovingkindness toward me is
   great,
   And You have delivered my soul from
   the depths of Sheol.

86:11 Heart Surgery

*David prays for an undivided heart, in order to
give all of it to God in his praise. "Heart" in the
Bible doesn't refer merely to emotions, but to
the whole person. David's prayer means, "Help
me aim myself in a single direction!"*

14 ¶ O God, arrogant men have risen up
   against me,
   And a band of violent men have sought
   my life,
   And they have not set You before them.
15 But You, O Lord, are a God merciful
   and gracious,
   Slow to anger and abundant in
   lovingkindness and truth.
16 Turn to me, and be gracious to me;
   Oh grant Your strength to Your servant,
   And save the son of Your handmaid.
17 Show me a sign for good,
   That those who hate me may see *it* and
   be ashamed,
   Because You, O Lord, have helped me
   and comforted me.

Psalm 87

The Privileges of Citizenship in Zion.

A Psalm of the sons of Korah. A Song.

1 ¶ His foundation is in the holy
   mountains.
2 The Lord loves the gates of Zion
   More than all the *other* dwelling places of
   Jacob.
3 Glorious things are spoken of you,
   O city of God.   Selah.
4 "I shall mention *a*Rahab and Babylon
   among those who know Me;
   Behold, Philistia and Tyre with Ethiopia:
   'This one was born there.'"
5 But of Zion it shall be said, "This one
   and that one were born in her";
   And the Most High Himself will establish
   her.
6 The Lord will count when He registers
   the peoples,
   "This one was born there."   Selah.
7 Then those who sing as well as those
   who play the flutes *shall say,*
   "All my springs *of joy* are in you."

Psalm 88

A Petition to Be Saved from Death.

A Song. A Psalm of the sons of Korah. For the
choir director; according to Mahalath Leannoth.
A Maskil of Heman the Ezrahite.

1 ¶ O Lord, the God of my salvation,
   I have cried out by day and in the night
   before You.

88:1 Bad Father, Good Kids

*Psalm 88 is the last of 12 psalms ascribed to
"the sons of Korah." Korah, a rebel against
Moses' leadership, died in his rebellion
(Numbers 16). His children were spared, and
many years later David chose their clan to
found a temple choir (1 Chronicles 6:31–37).
Apparently these psalms were part of a musical
collection they used.*

2 Let my prayer come before You;
   Incline Your ear to my cry!
3 For my soul has had enough troubles,
   And my life has drawn near to Sheol.
4 I am reckoned among those who go
   down to the pit;
   I have become like a man without
   strength,
5 Forsaken among the dead,
   Like the slain who lie in the grave,
   Whom You remember no more,
   And they are cut off from Your hand.
6 You have put me in the lowest pit,
   In dark places, in the depths.
7 Your wrath has rested upon me,
   And You have afflicted me with all Your
   waves.   Selah.
8 You have removed my acquaintances far
   from me;
   You have made me an *b*object of
   loathing to them;
   I am shut up and cannot go out.
9 My eye has wasted away because of
   affliction;
   I have called upon You every day,
   O Lord;
   I have spread out my hands to You.
10 ¶ Will You perform wonders for the
   dead?
   Will the departed spirits rise *and* praise
   You?   Selah.
11 Will Your lovingkindness be declared in
   the grave,
   Your faithfulness in Abaddon?
12 Will Your wonders be made known in
   the darkness?

a I.e. Egypt   *b* Lit *abomination to them*

And Your righteousness in the land of
forgetfulness?

13 ¶ But I, O LORD, have cried out to You
for help,
And in the morning my prayer comes
before You.

14 O LORD, why do You reject my soul?
Why do You hide Your face from me?

15 I was afflicted and about to die from my
youth on;
I suffer Your terrors; I am overcome.

16 Your burning anger has passed over me;
Your terrors have destroyed me.

17 They have surrounded me like water all
day long;
They have encompassed me altogether.

18 You have removed lover and friend far
from me;
My acquaintances are *in* darkness.

Psalm 89

The LORD's Covenant with David,
and Israel's Afflictions.

A Maskil of Ethan the Ezrahite.

1 ¶ I will sing of the lovingkindness of the
LORD forever;
To all generations I will make known
Your faithfulness with my mouth.

2 For I have said, "Lovingkindness will be
built up forever;
In the heavens You will establish Your
faithfulness."

3 "I have made a covenant with My chosen;
I have sworn to David My servant,

4 I will establish your seed forever
And build up your throne to all
generations." Selah.

5 ¶ The heavens will praise Your wonders,
O LORD;
Your faithfulness also in the assembly of
the holy ones.

6 For who in the skies is comparable to the
LORD?
Who among the sons of the mighty is
like the LORD,

7 A God greatly feared in the council of
the holy ones,
And awesome above all those who are
around Him?

8 O LORD God of hosts, who is like You,
O mighty LORD?
Your faithfulness also surrounds You.

9 You rule the swelling of the sea;
When its waves rise, You still them.

10 You Yourself crushed Rahab like one
who is slain;

You scattered Your enemies with Your
mighty arm.

11 ¶ The heavens are Yours, the earth also is
Yours;
The world and ᵃall it contains, You
have founded them.

12 The north and the south, You have
created them;
Tabor and Hermon shout for joy at Your
name.

13 You have a strong arm;
Your hand is mighty, Your right hand is
exalted.

14 Righteousness and justice are the
foundation of Your throne;
Lovingkindness and truth go before You.

15 How blessed are the people who know
the ᵇjoyful sound!
O LORD, they walk in the light of Your
countenance.

16 In Your name they rejoice all the day,
And by Your righteousness they are
exalted.

17 For You are the glory of their strength,
And by Your favor our horn is exalted.

18 For our shield belongs to the LORD,
ᶜAnd our king to the Holy One of
Israel.

19 ¶ Once You spoke in vision to Your
godly ones,
And said, "I have given help to one who
is mighty;
I have exalted one chosen from the
people.

20 "I have found David My servant;
With My holy oil I have anointed him,

21 With whom My hand will be established;
My arm also will strengthen him.

22 "The enemy will not ᵈdeceive him,
Nor the son of wickedness afflict him.

23 "But I shall crush his adversaries before
him,
And strike those who hate him.

24 "My faithfulness and My lovingkindness
will be with him,
And in My name his horn will be
exalted.

25 "I shall also set his hand on the sea
And his right hand on the rivers.

26 "He will cry to Me, 'You are my Father,
My God, and the rock of my salvation.'

27 "I also shall make him *My* firstborn,
The highest of the kings of the earth.

28 "My lovingkindness I will keep for him
forever,
And My covenant shall be confirmed to
him.

ᵃ Lit *its fullness* ᵇ Or *blast of the trumpet, shout of joy* ᶜ Or *Even to the Holy One of Israel our King* ᵈ Or *exact*
usury *from him*

29 "So I will establish his descendants forever
And his throne as the days of heaven.

30 ¶ "If his sons forsake My law
And do not walk in My judgments,

89:30–49 Shame Forever?

*God, as this psalm notes, had made
tremendous promises to David and to his
descendants (see 2 Samuel 7:4–17). But what
do you do when God's promises don't match
your experience? This psalm was probably
written after the Babylonians had deported the
young king Jehoiachin (see here and 2 Kings
24:8,15) and torn down Jerusalem (see verse
40 and 2 Kings 25:10). It gives no explanation
of how God's promises fit with this humiliation
and suffering. But it offers a model of how to
respond, taking the problem straight to God in
the frankest terms. Only when Jesus came
centuries later did Israel see God fulfill these
promises to honor and love a "son of David" as
his own Son (verses 26–29).*

---

31 If they ªviolate My statutes
And do not keep My commandments,
32 Then I will punish their transgression
with the rod
And their iniquity with stripes.
33 "But I will not break off My
lovingkindness from him,
Nor deal falsely in My faithfulness.
34 "My covenant I will not violate,
Nor will I alter the utterance of My lips.
35 "ᵇOnce I have sworn by My holiness;
I will not lie to David.
36 "His descendants shall endure forever
And his throne as the sun before Me.
37 "It shall be established forever like the
moon,
And the witness in the sky is faithful."
Selah.

38 ¶ But You have cast off and rejected,
You have been full of wrath against Your
anointed.
39 You have spurned the covenant of Your
servant;
You have profaned his crown in the dust.
40 You have broken down all his walls;
You have brought his strongholds to
ruin.
41 All who pass along the way plunder him;
He has become a reproach to his
neighbors.
42 You have exalted the right hand of his
adversaries;
You have made all his enemies rejoice.

43 You also turn back the edge of his sword
And have not made him stand in battle.
44 You have made his splendor to cease
And cast his throne to the ground.
45 You have shortened the days of his
youth;
You have covered him with shame. Selah.

46 ¶ How long, O LORD?
Will You hide Yourself forever?
Will Your wrath burn like fire?
47 Remember what my span of life is;
For what vanity You have created all the
sons of men!
48 What man can live and not see death?
Can he deliver his soul from the power
of Sheol? Selah.

49 ¶ Where are Your former
lovingkindnesses, O Lord,
Which You swore to David in Your
faithfulness?
50 Remember, O Lord, the reproach of
Your servants;
How I bear in my bosom *the reproach of*
all the many peoples,
51 With which Your enemies have
reproached, O LORD,
With which they have reproached the
footsteps of Your anointed.

52 ¶ Blessed be the LORD forever!
Amen and Amen.

BOOK 4

Psalm 90

God's Eternity and Man's Transitoriness.

A Prayer of Moses, the man of God.

1 ¶ Lord, You have been our ᶜdwelling
place in all generations.
2 Before the mountains were born
Or You gave birth to the earth and the
world,
Even from everlasting to everlasting, You
are God.

3 ¶ You turn man back into dust
And say, "Return, O children of men."
4 For a thousand years in Your sight
Are like yesterday when it passes by,
Or *as* a watch in the night.
5 You have swept them away like a flood,
they fall asleep;
In the morning they are like grass which
sprouts anew.
6 In the morning it flourishes and sprouts
anew;
Toward evening it fades and withers
away.

ª Lit *profane*   ᵇ Or *One thing*   ᶜ Or *hiding place*; some ancient mss read *place of refuge*

7 ¶ For we have been consumed by Your anger
And by Your wrath we have been dismayed.
8 You have placed our iniquities before You,
Our secret *sins* in the light of Your presence.
9 For all our days have declined in Your fury;
We have finished our years like a sigh.
10 As for the days of our life, they contain seventy years,
Or if due to strength, eighty years,
Yet their pride is *but* labor and sorrow;
For soon it is gone and we fly away.
11 Who understands the power of Your anger
And Your fury, according to the fear that is due You?
12 So teach us to number our days,
That we may present to You a heart of wisdom.
13 ¶ Do return, O LORD; how long *will it be?*
And be sorry for Your servants.
14 O satisfy us in the morning with Your lovingkindness,
That we may sing for joy and be glad all our days.
15 Make us glad according to the days You have afflicted us,
And the years we have seen [a]evil.
16 Let Your work appear to Your servants
And Your majesty to their children.
17 Let the favor of the Lord our God be upon us;
And [b]confirm for us the work of our hands;
Yes, [b]confirm the work of our hands.

Psalm 91

Security of the One Who Trusts in the LORD.

1 ¶ He who dwells in the shelter of the Most High
Will abide in the shadow of the Almighty.
2 I will say to the LORD, "My refuge and my fortress,
My God, in whom I trust!"
3 For it is He who delivers you from the snare of the trapper
And from the deadly pestilence.
4 He will cover you with His pinions,
And under His wings you may seek refuge;
His faithfulness is a shield and bulwark.

5 ¶ You will not be afraid of the terror by night,
Or of the arrow that flies by day;
6 Of the pestilence that stalks in darkness,
Or of the destruction that lays waste at noon.
7 A thousand may fall at your side
And ten thousand at your right hand,
But it shall not approach you.
8 You will only look on with your eyes
And see the recompense of the wicked.
9 For you have made the LORD, my refuge,
Even the Most High, your dwelling place.
10 No evil will befall you,
Nor will any plague come near your tent.
11 ¶ For He will give His angels charge concerning you,
To guard you in all your ways.
12 They will bear you up in their hands,
That you do not strike your foot against a stone.

91:12 Satan and the Bible

Satan knows Scripture. He quoted this promise to Jesus when tempting him to spiritual arrogance (see Matthew 4:6). Jesus recognized that Satan had twisted its meaning. The magnificent assurances in this psalm encourage us to rest in God, not test him.

13 You will tread upon the lion and cobra,
The young lion and the serpent you will trample down.
14 ¶ "Because he has loved Me, therefore I will deliver him;
I will set him *securely* on high, because he has known My name.
15 "He will call upon Me, and I will answer him;
I will be with him in trouble;
I will rescue him and honor him.
16 "With a long life I will satisfy him
And let him see My salvation."

Psalm 92

Praise for the LORD'S Goodness.

A Psalm, a Song for the Sabbath day.

1 ¶ It is good to give thanks to the LORD
And to sing praises to Your name,
O Most High;
2 To declare Your lovingkindness in the morning
And Your faithfulness by night,
3 With the ten-stringed lute and with the harp,

---

[a] Or *trouble*   [b] Or *give permanence to*

With resounding music upon the lyre.
4 For You, O Lord, have made me glad by
what You have done,
I will sing for joy at the works of Your
hands.

5 ¶ How great are Your works, O Lord!
Your thoughts are very deep.
6 A senseless man has no knowledge,
Nor does a stupid man understand this:
7 That when the wicked sprouted up like
grass
And all who did iniquity flourished,
It *was only* that they might be destroyed
forevermore.
8 But You, O Lord, are on high forever.
9 For, behold, Your enemies, O Lord,
For, behold, Your enemies will perish;
All who do iniquity will be scattered.

10 ¶ But You have exalted my horn like *that
of* the wild ox;
I have been anointed with fresh oil.
11 And my eye has looked *exultantly* upon
my foes,
My ears hear of the evildoers who rise up
against me.
12 The righteous man will flourish like the
palm tree,
He will grow like a cedar in Lebanon.
13 Planted in the house of the Lord,
They will flourish in the courts of our
God.
14 They will still yield fruit in old age;
They shall be ªfull of sap and very
green,
15 To declare that the Lord is upright;
He is my rock, and there is no
unrighteousness in Him.

Psalm 93

The Majesty of the Lord.

1 ¶ The Lord reigns, He is clothed with
majesty;
The Lord has clothed and girded
Himself with strength;
Indeed, the world is firmly established, it
will not be moved.
2 Your throne is established from of old;
You are from everlasting.

3 ¶ The floods have lifted up, O Lord,
The floods have lifted up their voice,
The floods lift up their pounding waves.
4 More than the sounds of many waters,
Than the mighty breakers of the sea,
The Lord on high is mighty.
5 Your testimonies are fully confirmed;
Holiness befits Your house,
O Lord, forevermore.

Psalm 94

The Lord Implored to Avenge His People.

1 ¶ O Lord, God of vengeance,
God of vengeance, shine forth!
2 Rise up, O Judge of the earth,
Render recompense to the proud.
3 How long shall the wicked, O Lord,
How long shall the wicked exult?
4 They pour forth *words,* they speak
arrogantly;
All who do wickedness vaunt themselves.
5 They crush Your people, O Lord,
And afflict Your heritage.
6 They slay the widow and the stranger
And murder the orphans.
7 They have said, "The Lord does not see,
Nor does the God of Jacob pay heed."

8 ¶ Pay heed, you senseless among the
people;
And when will you understand, stupid
ones?
9 He who planted the ear, does He not
hear?
He who formed the eye, does He
not see?
10 He who chastens the nations, will He not
rebuke,
Even He who teaches man knowledge?
11 The Lord knows the thoughts of man,
That they are a *mere* breath.

12 ¶ Blessed is the man whom You chasten,
O Lord,
And whom You teach out of Your law;
13 That You may grant him relief from the
days of adversity,
Until a pit is dug for the wicked.
14 For the Lord will not abandon His
people,
Nor will He forsake His inheritance.
15 For judgment will again be righteous,
And all the upright in heart will follow it.
16 Who will stand up for me against
evildoers?
Who will take his stand for me against
those who do wickedness?

17 ¶ If the Lord had not been my help,
My soul would soon have dwelt in *the
abode of* silence.
18 If I should say, "My foot has slipped,"
Your lovingkindness, O Lord, will hold
me up.
19 When my anxious thoughts multiply
within me,
Your consolations delight my soul.
20 Can a throne of destruction be allied
with You,
One which devises mischief by decree?

ª Lit *fat and*

21 They band themselves together against
the life of the righteous
And condemn the innocent to death.
22 But the LORD has been my stronghold,
And my God the rock of my refuge.
23 He has brought back their wickedness
upon them
And will destroy them in their evil;
The LORD our God will destroy them.

Psalm 95

Praise to the LORD, and Warning against Unbelief.

1 ¶ O come, let us sing for joy to the
LORD,
Let us shout joyfully to the rock of our
salvation.
2 Let us come before His presence with
thanksgiving,
Let us shout joyfully to Him with psalms.
3 For the LORD is a great God
And a great King above all gods,
4 In whose hand are the depths of the
earth,
The peaks of the mountains are His also.
5 The sea is His, for it was He who
made it,
And His hands formed the dry land.
6 ¶ Come, let us worship and bow down,
Let us kneel before the LORD our Maker.
7 For He is our God,
And we are the people of His pasture
and the sheep of His hand.
Today, if you would hear His voice,
8 Do not harden your hearts, as at
*a*Meribah,
As in the day of *b*Massah in the
wilderness,

95:8 Rebellion

*One of Israel's worst memories involved a place
known as Massah and Meribah. There, on their
way to the promised land, the Israelites ran out
of water (Exodus 17:1–7) and rebelled against
Moses and God. Because of their lack of faith,
God made them wander the wilderness for 40
years.*

*Now, hundreds of years later, Psalm 95
warns another generation of Israelites not to
repeat the mistake that had made their
forebears miss "His rest." In the New Testament,
Hebrews 4:1–13 argues that "His rest" means
not merely the promised land of Israel, but a
state of peaceful unity with God. The warning
still applies.*

9 "When your fathers tested Me,
They tried Me, though they had seen My
work.
10 "For forty years I loathed *that* generation,
And said they are a people who err in
their heart,
And they do not know My ways.
11 "Therefore I swore in My anger,
Truly they shall not enter into My rest."

Psalm 96

A Call to Worship the LORD the Righteous Judge.

1 ¶ Sing to the LORD a new song;
Sing to the LORD, all the earth.
2 Sing to the LORD, bless His name;
Proclaim good tidings of His salvation
from day to day.
3 Tell of His glory among the nations,
His wonderful deeds among all the
peoples.
4 For great is the LORD and greatly to be
praised;
He is to be feared above all gods.
5 For all the gods of the peoples are idols,
But the LORD made the heavens.
6 Splendor and majesty are before Him,
Strength and beauty are in His sanctuary.

7 ¶ *c*Ascribe to the LORD, O families of
the peoples,
*c*Ascribe to the LORD glory and
strength.
8 *c*Ascribe to the LORD the glory of His
name;
Bring an offering and come into His
courts.
9 Worship the LORD in *d*holy attire;
Tremble before Him, all the earth.
10 Say among the nations, "The LORD
reigns;
Indeed, the world is firmly established, it
will not be moved;
He will judge the peoples with *e*equity."

11 ¶ Let the heavens be glad, and let the
earth rejoice;
Let the sea roar, and all it contains;
12 Let the field exult, and all that is in it.
Then all the trees of the forest will sing
for joy
13 Before the LORD, for He is coming,
For He is coming to judge the earth.
He will judge the world in righteousness
And the peoples in His faithfulness.

Psalm 97

The LORD's Power and Dominion.

1 ¶ The LORD reigns, let the earth rejoice;

---

*a*Or *place of strife* *b*Or *temptation* *c*Lit *Give* *d*Or *the splendor of holiness* *e*Or *uprightness*

Let the many [a]islands be glad.
2 Clouds and thick darkness surround
 Him;
 Righteousness and justice are the
  foundation of His throne.
3 Fire goes before Him
 And burns up His adversaries round
  about.
4 His lightnings lit up the world;
 The earth saw and trembled.
5 The mountains melted like wax at the
  presence of the LORD,
 At the presence of the Lord of the whole
  earth.
6 The heavens declare His righteousness,
 And all the peoples have seen His glory.

7 ¶ Let all those be ashamed who serve
  graven images,
 Who boast themselves of idols;
 Worship Him, all you gods.
8 Zion heard *this* and was glad,
 And the daughters of Judah have rejoiced
 Because of Your judgments, O LORD.
9 For You are the LORD Most High over all
  the earth;
 You are exalted far above all gods.

10 ¶ Hate evil, you who love the LORD,
 Who preserves the souls of His godly
  ones;
 He delivers them from the hand of the
  wicked.
11 Light is sown *like seed* for the righteous
 And gladness for the upright in heart.
12 Be glad in the LORD, you righteous ones,
 And give thanks to His holy name.

Psalm 98

A Call to Praise the LORD for His Righteousness.

A Psalm.

1 ¶ O sing to the LORD a new song,
 For He has done wonderful things,
 His right hand and His holy arm have
  [b]gained the victory for Him.
2 The LORD has made known His
  salvation;
 He has revealed His righteousness in the
  sight of the nations.
3 He has remembered His lovingkindness
  and His faithfulness to the house of
  Israel;
 All the ends of the earth have seen the
  salvation of our God.

4 ¶ Shout joyfully to the LORD, all the
  earth;
 Break forth and sing for joy and sing
  praises.

5 Sing praises to the LORD with the lyre,
 With the lyre and the sound of melody.
6 With trumpets and the sound of the
  horn
 Shout joyfully before the King, the LORD.

7 ¶ Let the sea roar and all it contains,
 The world and those who dwell in it.
8 Let the rivers clap their hands,
 Let the mountains sing together for joy

98:8 Ecological Choir

Seas, rivers, and mountains crown this psalm with their praise. God's salvation doesn't just affect human beings. When rebellion against God finally ends, nature itself will celebrate. Romans 8:18–22 takes up this theme as part of the wonderful salvation God offers to all people.

9 Before the LORD, for He is coming to
  judge the earth;
 He will judge the world with
  righteousness
 And the peoples with equity.

Psalm 99

Praise to the LORD for His Fidelity to Israel.

1 ¶ The LORD reigns, let the peoples
  tremble;
 He is enthroned *above* the cherubim, let
  the earth shake!
2 The LORD is great in Zion,
 And He is exalted above all the peoples.
3 Let them praise Your great and awesome
  name;
 Holy is He.
4 The strength of the King loves [c]justice;
 You have established equity;
 You have executed [c]justice and
  righteousness in Jacob.
5 Exalt the LORD our God
 And worship at His footstool;
 Holy is He.

6 ¶ Moses and Aaron were among His
  priests,
 And Samuel was among those who called
  on His name;
 They called upon the LORD and He
  answered them.
7 He spoke to them in the pillar of cloud;
 They kept His testimonies
 And the statute that He gave them.
8 O LORD our God, You answered them;
 You were a forgiving God to them,

---

[a] Or *coastlands*   [b] Or *accomplished salvation*   [c] Or *judgment*

And *yet* an avenger of their *evil* deeds.
9 Exalt the LORD our God
    And worship at His holy hill,
    For holy is the LORD our God.

Psalm 100

All Men Exhorted to Praise God.

A Psalm for Thanksgiving.

1 ¶ Shout joyfully to the LORD, all the
    earth.
2 Serve the LORD with gladness;
    Come before Him with joyful singing.
3 Know that the LORD Himself is God;
    It is He who has made us, and *a*not we
        ourselves;
    We are His people and the sheep of His
        pasture.

4 ¶ Enter His gates with thanksgiving
    And His courts with praise.
    Give thanks to Him, bless His name.
5 For the LORD is good;
    His lovingkindness is everlasting
    And His faithfulness to all generations.

Psalm 101

The Psalmist's Profession of Uprightness.

A Psalm of David.

1 ¶ I will sing of lovingkindness and
    justice,
    To You, O LORD, I will sing praises.
2 I will give heed to the *b*blameless way.
    When will You come to me?
    I will walk within my house in the
        integrity of my heart.
3 I will set no worthless thing before my
    eyes;
    I hate the work of those who fall away;
    It shall not fasten its grip on me.
4 A perverse heart shall depart from me;
    I will know no evil.
5 Whoever secretly slanders his neighbor,
    him I will destroy;
    No one who has a haughty look and an
        arrogant heart will I endure.

6 ¶ My eyes shall be upon the faithful of
    the land, that they may dwell
        with me;
    He who walks in a *b*blameless way is the
        one who will minister to me.
7 He who practices deceit shall not dwell
    within my house;
    He who speaks falsehood shall not
        maintain his position before me.
8 Every morning I will *c*destroy all the
    wicked of the land,
    So as to cut off from the city of the
        LORD all those who do iniquity.

Psalm 102

Prayer of an Afflicted Man for Mercy on Himself and on Zion.

*A Prayer of the Afflicted when he is faint
and pours out his complaint before the LORD.*

1 ¶ Hear my prayer, O LORD!
    And let my cry for help come to You.

101:7 The Company You Keep

*Some friends build you up, others tear you
down. That's true for people in influential
positions as well. "Politics makes strange
bedfellows," they say, because a politician must
work with people from various political
factions, whether he or she admires them or
not. But here David, the head of state, pledges
to steer clear of all shady alliances. He wants a
clean administration, from the top down.*

2 Do not hide Your face from me in the
    day of my distress;
    Incline Your ear to me;
    In the day when I call answer me
        quickly.
3 For my days have been consumed in
    smoke,
    And my bones have been scorched like a
        hearth.
4 My heart has been smitten like grass and
    has withered away,
    Indeed, I forget to eat my bread.
5 Because of the loudness of my groaning
    My bones cling to my flesh.
6 I resemble a pelican of the wilderness;
    I have become like an owl of the waste
        places.
7 I lie awake,
    I have become like a lonely bird on a
        housetop.

8 ¶ My enemies have reproached me all
    day long;
    Those who deride me have used my
        name as a curse.
9 For I have eaten ashes like bread
    And mingled my drink with weeping
10 Because of Your indignation and Your
    wrath,
    For You have lifted me up and cast me
        away.
11 My days are like a lengthened shadow,
    And I wither away like grass.

12 ¶ But You, O LORD, abide forever,
    And Your name to all generations.
13 You will arise *and* have compassion on
    Zion;

---

a Some mss read *His we are*   *b* Or *way of integrity*   *c* Or *silence*

For it is time to be gracious to her,
For the appointed time has come.

14 Surely Your servants find pleasure in her
stones
And feel pity for her dust.
15 So the nations will fear the name of the
LORD
And all the kings of the earth Your
glory.
16 For the LORD has built up Zion;
He has appeared in His glory.
17 He has regarded the prayer of the
destitute
And has not despised their prayer.

18 ¶ This will be written for the generation
to come,
That a people yet to be created may
praise the LORD.
19 For He looked down from His holy
height;
From heaven the LORD gazed upon the
earth,
20 To hear the groaning of the prisoner,
To set free those who were doomed to
death,
21 That men may tell of the name of the
LORD in Zion
And His praise in Jerusalem,
22 When the peoples are gathered together,
And the kingdoms, to serve the LORD.

23 ¶ He has weakened my strength in the
way;
He has shortened my days.
24 I say, "O my God, do not take me away
in the midst of my days,
Your years are throughout all
generations.
25 "Of old You founded the earth,
And the heavens are the work of Your
hands.
26 "Even they will perish, but You endure;
And all of them will wear out like a
garment;
Like clothing You will change them and
they will be changed.
27 "But You are the same,
And Your years will not come to an end.

102:26 Outlasting the Universe

Is a diamond forever? Not according to the psalmist, who predicts that the universe, which God made, will wear out like old clothes. But God remains the same forever—and he will preserve his people, whom he is committed to far more than to his universe.

28 "The children of Your servants will
continue,
And their descendants will be established
before You."

Psalm 103

Praise for the LORD'S Mercies.

A Psalm of David.

1 ¶ Bless the LORD, O my soul,
And all that is within me, *bless* His holy
name.
2 Bless the LORD, O my soul,
And forget none of His benefits;
3 Who pardons all your iniquities,
Who heals all your diseases;
4 Who redeems your life from the pit,
Who crowns you with lovingkindness
and compassion;
5 Who satisfies your ᵃyears with good
things,
So that your youth is renewed like the
eagle.

6 ¶ The LORD performs righteous deeds
And judgments for all who are
oppressed.
7 He made known His ways to Moses,
His acts to the sons of Israel.
8 The LORD is compassionate and gracious,
Slow to anger and abounding in
lovingkindness.
9 He will not always strive *with us*,
Nor will He keep *His anger* forever.
10 He has not dealt with us according to
our sins,
Nor rewarded us according to our
iniquities.
11 For as high as the heavens are above the
earth,
So great is His lovingkindness toward
those who ᵇfear Him.
12 As far as the east is from the west,
So far has He removed our
transgressions from us.
13 Just as a father has compassion on *his*
children,
So the LORD has compassion on those
who fear Him.
14 For He Himself knows ᶜour frame;
He is mindful that we are *but* dust.

15 ¶ As for man, his days are like grass;
As a flower of the field, so he flourishes.
16 When the wind has passed over it, it is
no more,
And its place acknowledges it no longer.
17 But the lovingkindness of the LORD is
from everlasting to everlasting on
those who ᵇfear Him,

ᵃ Or *desire* ᵇ Or *revere* ᶜ I.e. what we are made of

And His righteousness to children's
children,
18 To those who keep His covenant
And remember His precepts to do them.

19 ¶ The LORD has established His throne in
the heavens,
And His *a*sovereignty rules over all.
20 Bless the LORD, you His angels,
Mighty in strength, who perform His
word,
Obeying the voice of His word!
21 Bless the LORD, all you His hosts,
You who serve Him, doing His will.
22 Bless the LORD, all you works of His,
In all places of His dominion;
Bless the LORD, O my soul!

a Or kingdom   *b* Lit The one who   *c* Or His angels, spirits

Psalm 104

The LORD's Care over All His Works.

1 ¶ Bless the LORD, O my soul!
O LORD my God, You are very great;
You are clothed with splendor and
majesty,
2 Covering Yourself with light as with a
cloak,
Stretching out heaven like a *tent* curtain.
3 *b*He lays the beams of His upper
chambers in the waters;
He makes the clouds His chariot;
He walks upon the wings of the wind;
4 He makes *c*the winds His messengers,
*d*Flaming fire His ministers.

d Or His ministers flames of fire

Ecology Plus
Creation sings God's praise

> *O LORD, how many are your works! In wisdom You have made them all.*
> *104:24*

IN 1962 BIOLOGIST RACHEL CARSON published *Silent Spring*, a book tracing the effects of pesticides—DDT in particular. Until then, DDT had been treated like a wonder chemical, sprayed almost at random to kill pests. Carson showed how it worked its way up the food chain, killing larger animals—like songbirds. If no birds were left to sing, we would have an ominously "silent spring."

Until then, *ecology* had been a word known only to specialists. But with Carson's book, ordinary people began to take an interest in what only biologists had known: the delicate balance of nature, in which each creature is intertwined with every other. The ecology movement had begun.

The Value in "Useless" Creatures

Ecology was new, but its ideas were old. You could have learned its basic principles from Psalm 104. It shows appreciation for every aspect of nature, even creatures like wild goats, lions, and the "leviathan," the crocodile or sea monster. The Israelites, as herders and farmers, had no romantic idealization of the outdoors. Nobody who herds sheep thinks of them as soft and fluffy pets. But to the poet who wrote Psalm 104, creatures that are of no "use" to anyone still have intrinsic worth—especially to God.

The author saw how the world fits together, everything in its proper sphere. At night wild animals hunt; at daybreak humans go out to work. The rain falls, nourishing crops for people and grass for cattle, but also watering the forest to provide a place for birds to nest.

Ecology Is God's Work

The intertwining of nature is not, for the psalmist, like a complex machine, dangerously sensitive. Things fit together because an intimate, personal God watches over his creation. Animals eat on schedule not just because their habitat contains adequate food, but because God gives them their food "at the proper time." Every breath of life depends on his will. So do the weather, the winds and clouds, the water supply, the very stability of the earth. The psalmist doesn't just marvel over the complexity and beauty of nature; in it he sees the work of God.

When modern people think of ecology, they are preoccupied with the fear of overcrowding and of poisoning the planet with landfills, oil spills, and toxic chemicals. The psalms show no such fear, for overcrowding and pollution were not major problems in that preindustrial civilization. Yet interestingly enough, this psalm ends with a wish that God would clean up the earth—cleanse it of sinners, who mar its perfection by their rejection of God's will. The beauty of the earth, made by God, calls out for purity—purity of the heart.

Life Questions: How does nature affect you? How do you affect it?

5 ¶ He established the earth upon its
    foundations,
So that it will not ªtotter forever and
    ever.
6 You covered it with the deep as with a
    garment;
The waters were standing above the
    mountains.
7 At Your rebuke they fled,
At the sound of Your thunder they
    hurried away.
8 The mountains rose; the valleys sank
    down
To the place which You established for
    them.
9 You set a boundary that they may not
    pass over,
So that they will not return to cover the
    earth.

10 ¶ He sends forth springs in the valleys;
They flow between the mountains;
11 They give drink to every beast of the
    field;
The wild donkeys quench their thirst.
12 Beside them the birds of the heavens
    dwell;
They lift up *their* voices among the
    branches.
13 He waters the mountains from His upper
    chambers;
The earth is satisfied with the fruit of His
    works.

14 ¶ He causes the grass to grow for the
    cattle,
And vegetation for the labor of man,
So that he may bring forth food from the
    earth,
15 And wine which makes man's heart glad,
So that he may make *his* face glisten with
    oil,
And food which sustains man's heart.
16 The trees of the LORD drink their fill,
The cedars of Lebanon which He
    planted,
17 Where the birds build their nests,
And the stork, whose home is the fir
    trees.
18 ¶ The high mountains are for the wild
    goats;
The cliffs are a refuge for the shephanim.
19 He made the moon for the seasons;
The sun knows the place of its setting.
20 You appoint darkness and it becomes
    night,
In which all the beasts of the forest prowl
    about.
21 The young lions roar after their prey
And seek their food from God.

22 *When* the sun rises they withdraw
And lie down in their dens.
23 Man goes forth to his work
And to his labor until evening.

24 ¶ O LORD, how many are Your works!
In wisdom You have made them all;
The earth is full of Your ᵇpossessions.
25 There is the sea, great and broad,
In which are swarms without number,
Animals both small and great.
26 There the ships move along,
And ᶜLeviathan, which You have
    formed to sport in it.

104:26 Just for Fun

What good is a leviathan (possibly a whale, but to the landlocked Israelites a frightening sea monster)? Why would God make such a creature? Simply "to frolic." God makes and delights in each creature for its own sake.

27 ¶ They all wait for You
To give them their food in ᵈdue season.
28 You give to them, they gather *it* up;
You open Your hand, they are satisfied
    with good.
29 You hide Your face, they are dismayed;
You take away their ᵉspirit, they expire
And return to their dust.
30 You send forth Your ᵉSpirit, they are
    created;
And You renew the face of the ground.

31 ¶ Let the glory of the LORD endure
    forever;
Let the LORD be glad in His works;
32 He looks at the earth, and it trembles;
He touches the mountains, and they
    smoke.
33 I will sing to the LORD as long as I live;
I will sing praise to my God while I have
    my being.
34 Let my meditation be pleasing to Him;
As for me, I shall be glad in the LORD.
35 Let sinners be consumed from the earth
And let the wicked be no more.
Bless the LORD, O my soul.
Praise the LORD!

Psalm 105

The LORD'S Wonderful Works in Behalf of Israel.

1 ¶ Oh give thanks to the LORD, call upon
    His name;
Make known His deeds among the
    peoples.

ª Or *move out of place*   ᵇ Or *creatures*   ᶜ Or *a sea monster*   ᵈ Lit *its appointed time*   ᵉ Or *breath*

2 Sing to Him, sing praises to Him;
    [a]Speak of all His wonders.
3 Glory in His holy name;
    Let the heart of those who seek the LORD
        be glad.
4 Seek the LORD and His strength;
    Seek His face continually.
5 Remember His wonders which He has
      done,
    His marvels and the judgments uttered
      by His mouth,
6 O seed of Abraham, His servant,
    O sons of Jacob, His chosen ones!
7 He is the LORD our God;
    His judgments are in all the earth.

8 ¶ He has remembered His covenant
      forever,
    The word which He commanded to a
      thousand generations,
9 *The covenant* which He made with
      Abraham,
    And His oath to Isaac.
10 Then He confirmed it to Jacob for a
      statute,
    To Israel as an everlasting covenant,
11 Saying, "To you I will give the land of
      Canaan
    As the portion of your inheritance,"
12 When they were only a few men in
      number,
    Very few, and strangers in it.
13 And they wandered about from nation to
      nation,
    From *one* kingdom to another people.
14 He permitted no man to oppress them,
    And He reproved kings for their sakes:
15 "Do not touch My anointed ones,
    And do My prophets no harm."

16 ¶ And He called for a famine upon the
      land;
    He broke the whole staff of bread.
17 He sent a man before them,
    Joseph, *who* was sold as a slave.
18 They afflicted his feet with fetters,
    He himself was laid in irons;
19 Until the time that his word came to
      pass,
    The word of the LORD tested him.
20 The king sent and released him,
    The ruler of peoples, and set him free.
21 He made him lord of his house
    And ruler over all his possessions,
22 To imprison his princes at will,
    That he might teach his elders wisdom.
23 Israel also came into Egypt;
    Thus Jacob sojourned in the land
      of Ham.
24 And He caused His people to be very
      fruitful,

    And made them stronger than their
      adversaries.

25 ¶ He turned their heart to hate His
      people,
    To deal craftily with His servants.
26 He sent Moses His servant,
    And Aaron, whom He had chosen.
27 They performed His wondrous acts
      among them,
    And miracles in the land of Ham.
28 He sent darkness and made *it* dark;
    And they did not rebel against His
      words.
29 He turned their waters into blood
    And caused their fish to die.
30 Their land swarmed with frogs
    Even in the chambers of their kings.
31 He spoke, and there came a swarm of
      flies
    And gnats in all their territory.
32 He gave them hail for rain,
    And flaming fire in their land.
33 He struck down their vines also and their
      fig trees,
    And shattered the trees of their territory.
34 He spoke, and locusts came,
    And young locusts, even without
      number,
35 And ate up all vegetation in their land,
    And ate up the fruit of their ground.
36 He also struck down all the firstborn in
      their land,
    The first fruits of all their vigor.

37 ¶ Then He brought them out with silver
      and gold,
    And among His tribes there was not one
      who stumbled.
38 Egypt was glad when they departed,
    For the dread of them had fallen upon
      them.
39 He spread a cloud for a [b]covering,
    And fire to illumine by night.
40 They asked, and He brought quail,
    And satisfied them with the bread of
      heaven.
41 He opened the rock and water flowed
      out;
    It ran in the dry places *like* a river.
42 For He remembered His holy word
    With Abraham His servant;
43 And He brought forth His people with
      joy,
    His chosen ones with a joyful shout.
44 He gave them also the lands of the
      nations,
    That they might take possession of *the*
      fruit of the peoples' labor,

[a] Or *Meditate on*   [b] Or *curtain*

45 So that they might keep His statutes
And observe His laws,
Praise the LORD!

Psalm 106

Israel's Rebelliousness and the LORD'S Deliverances.

1 ¶ Praise the LORD!
Oh give thanks to the LORD, for He is good;
For His lovingkindness is everlasting.
2 Who can speak of the mighty deeds of the LORD,
Or can show forth all His praise?
3 How blessed are those who keep justice,
Who practice righteousness at all times!

4 ¶ Remember me, O LORD, in *Your* favor toward Your people;
Visit me with Your salvation,
5 That I may see the prosperity of Your chosen ones,
That I may rejoice in the gladness of Your nation,
That I may glory with Your *a*inheritance.

6 ¶ We have sinned like our fathers,
We have committed iniquity, we have behaved wickedly.
7 Our fathers in Egypt did not understand Your wonders;
They did not remember Your abundant kindnesses,
But rebelled by the sea, at the *b*Red Sea.
8 Nevertheless He saved them for the sake of His name,
That He might make His power known.
9 Thus He rebuked the *b*Red Sea and it dried up,
And He led them through the deeps, as through the wilderness.
10 So He saved them from the hand of the one who hated *them,*
And redeemed them from the hand of the enemy.
11 The waters covered their adversaries;
Not one of them was left.
12 Then they believed His words;
They sang His praise.

13 ¶ They quickly forgot His works;
They did not wait for His counsel,
14 But craved intensely in the wilderness,
And tempted God in the desert.
15 So He gave them their request,
But sent a wasting disease among them.

16 ¶ When they became envious of Moses in the camp,
And of Aaron, the holy one of the LORD,

17 The earth opened and swallowed up Dathan,
And engulfed the company of Abiram.
18 And a fire blazed up in their company;
The flame consumed the wicked.

106:12 The Turning Point

When the Israelites praised God, their thoughts turned naturally back to the time when God (through Moses) freed them from slavery and gave them a country all their own. In it they saw God's pure graciousness. They had done nothing to win their freedom; God had done it all. Similarly, Christians look back to Jesus' death and resurrection, which freed them from sin's slavery.

19 ¶ They made a calf in Horeb
And worshiped a molten image.
20 Thus they exchanged their glory
For the image of an ox that eats grass.
21 They forgot God their Savior,
Who had done great things in Egypt,
22 Wonders in the land of Ham
And awesome things by the *b*Red Sea.
23 Therefore He said that He would destroy them,
Had not Moses His chosen one stood in the breach before Him,
To turn away His wrath from destroying *them.*
24 Then they despised the pleasant land;
They did not believe in His word,
25 But grumbled in their tents;
They did not listen to the voice of the LORD.
26 Therefore He swore to them
That He would cast them down in the wilderness,
27 And that He would cast their seed among the nations
And scatter them in the lands.

28 ¶ They joined themselves also to Baal-peor,
And ate sacrifices offered to the dead.
29 Thus they provoked *Him* to anger with their deeds,
And the plague broke out among them.
30 Then Phinehas stood up and interposed,
And so the plague was stayed.
31 And it was reckoned to him for righteousness,
To all generations forever.

a I.e. people   *b* Lit *Sea of Reeds*

32 ¶ They also provoked *Him* to wrath at
the waters of ᵃMeribah,
So that it went hard with Moses on their
account;
33 Because they were rebellious against His
Spirit,
He spoke rashly with his lips.

34 ¶ They did not destroy the peoples,
As the LORD commanded them,
35 But they mingled with the nations
And learned their practices,
36 And served their idols,
Which became a snare to them.
37 They even sacrificed their sons and their
daughters to the demons,
38 And shed innocent blood,
The blood of their sons and their
daughters,
Whom they sacrificed to the idols of
Canaan;
And the land was polluted with the blood.
39 Thus they became unclean in their
practices,
And played the harlot in their deeds.

40 ¶ Therefore the anger of the LORD was
kindled against His people
And He abhorred His inheritance.
41 Then He gave them into the hand of the
nations,
And those who hated them ruled over
them.
42 Their enemies also oppressed them,
And they were subdued under their
power.
43 Many times He would deliver them;
They, however, were rebellious in their
counsel,
And *so* sank down in their iniquity.

44 ¶ Nevertheless He looked upon their
distress
When He heard their cry;
45 And He remembered His covenant for
their sake,
And relented according to the greatness
of His lovingkindness.
46 He also made them *objects* of
compassion
In the presence of all their captors.

47 ¶ Save us, O LORD our God,
And gather us from among the nations,
To give thanks to Your holy name
And glory in Your praise.
48 Blessed be the LORD, the God of Israel,
From everlasting even to everlasting.
And let all the people say, "Amen."
Praise the LORD!

BOOK 5

Psalm 107

The LORD Delivers Men from Manifold Troubles.

1 ¶ Oh give thanks to the LORD, for He is
good,
For His lovingkindness is everlasting.
2 Let the redeemed of the LORD say *so*,
Whom He has redeemed from the hand
of the adversary
3 And gathered from the lands,
From the east and from the west,
From the north and from the south.

4 ¶ They wandered in the wilderness in a
desert region;
They did not find a way to an inhabited
city.
5 *They were* hungry and thirsty;
Their soul fainted within them.
6 Then they cried out to the LORD in their
trouble;
He delivered them out of their distresses.
7 He led them also by a straight way,
To go to an inhabited city.
8 Let them give thanks to the LORD for His
lovingkindness,
And for His wonders to the sons of men!
9 For He has satisfied the thirsty soul,
And the hungry soul He has filled with
what is good.

10 ¶ There were those who dwelt in
darkness and in the shadow of
death,
Prisoners in misery and chains,
11 Because they had rebelled against the
words of God
And spurned the counsel of the Most
High.
12 Therefore He humbled their heart with
labor;
They stumbled and there was none to help.
13 Then they cried out to the LORD in their
trouble;
He saved them out of their distresses.
14 He brought them out of darkness and
the shadow of death
And broke their bands apart.
15 Let them give thanks to the LORD for His
lovingkindness,
And for His wonders to the sons of men!
16 For He has shattered gates of bronze
And cut bars of iron asunder.

17 ¶ Fools, because of their rebellious way,
And because of their iniquities, were
afflicted.
18 Their soul abhorred all kinds of food,

ᵃ Lit *strife*

And they drew near to the gates of
   death.
19 Then they cried out to the LORD in their
   trouble;
He saved them out of their distresses.
20 He sent His word and healed them,
And delivered *them* from their
   *a*destructions.
21 Let them give thanks to the LORD for His
   lovingkindness,
And for His wonders to the sons of men!
22 Let them also offer sacrifices of
   thanksgiving,
And tell of His works with joyful singing.

23 ¶ Those who go down to the sea in
   ships,
Who do business on great waters;
24 They have seen the works of the LORD,
And His wonders in the deep.
25 For He spoke and raised up a stormy
   wind,
Which lifted up the waves of the sea.
26 They rose up to the heavens, they went
   down to the depths;
Their soul melted away in *their* misery.
27 They reeled and staggered like a drunken
   man,
And *b*were at their wits' end.

107:27 Worst Case

No problem is too great for God. This psalm imagines the worst calamities a Jew could think of: homelessness and starvation (verses 4–5), imprisonment (10–12), self-inflicted disease (17–18), and—the ultimate—imminent shipwreck (23–27). (Since Israel was landlocked, Jews had little experience with turbulent seas—and they dreaded them.) In all these cases, God was able to rescue those who called for his help.

28 Then they cried to the LORD in their
   trouble,
And He brought them out of their
   distresses.
29 He caused the storm to be still,
So that the waves of the sea were hushed.
30 Then they were glad because they were
   quiet,
So He guided them to their desired
   haven.
31 Let them give thanks to the LORD for His
   lovingkindness,
And for His wonders to the sons of men!
32 Let them extol Him also in the
   congregation of the people,
And praise Him at the seat of the elders.

33 ¶ He *c*changes rivers into a wilderness
And springs of water into a thirsty
   ground;
34 A fruitful land into a salt waste,
Because of the wickedness of those who
   dwell in it.
35 He changes a wilderness into a pool of
   water
And a dry land into springs of water;
36 And there He makes the hungry to dwell,
So that they may establish an inhabited
   city,
37 And sow fields and plant vineyards,
And gather a fruitful harvest.
38 Also He blesses them and they multiply
   greatly,
And He does not let their cattle decrease.

39 ¶ When they are diminished and bowed
   down
Through oppression, misery and sorrow,
40 He pours contempt upon princes
And makes them wander in a pathless
   waste.
41 But He sets the needy securely on high
   away from affliction,
And makes *his* families like a flock.
42 The upright see it and are glad;
But all unrighteousness shuts its mouth.
43 Who is wise? Let him give heed to these
   things,
And consider the lovingkindnesses of the
   LORD.

Psalm 108

God Praised and Supplicated to Give Victory.

A Song, a Psalm of David.

1 ¶ My heart is steadfast, O God;
I will sing, I will sing praises, even with
   my soul.
2 Awake, harp and lyre;
I will awaken the dawn!
3 I will give thanks to You, O LORD,
   among the peoples,
And I will sing praises to You among the
   nations.
4 For Your lovingkindness is great above
   the heavens,
And Your truth *reaches* to the skies.
5 Be exalted, O God, above the heavens,
And Your glory above all the earth.
6 That Your beloved may be delivered,
Save with Your right hand, and
   answer me!

7 ¶ God has spoken in His *d*holiness:
"I will exult, I will portion out Shechem
And measure out the valley of Succoth.
8 "Gilead is Mine, Manasseh is Mine;

---

a Or *pits*   *b* Lit *all their wisdom was swallowed up*   *c* Or *turns*   *d* Or *sanctuary*

Ephraim also is the helmet of My head;
Judah is My [a]scepter.
9 "Moab is My washbowl;
Over Edom I shall throw My shoe;
Over Philistia I will shout aloud."

10 ¶ Who will bring me into the besieged
city?
Who will lead me to Edom?
11 Have not You Yourself, O God,
rejected us?
And will You not go forth with our
armies, O God?
12 Oh give us help against the adversary,
For deliverance by man is in vain.
13 Through God we will do valiantly,
And it is He who shall tread down our
adversaries.

Psalm 109

Vengeance Invoked upon Adversaries.

For the choir director. A Psalm of David.

1 ¶ O God of my praise,
Do not be silent!
2 For they have opened the wicked and
deceitful mouth against me;
They have spoken against me with a
lying tongue.
3 They have also surrounded me with
words of hatred,
And fought against me without cause.
4 In return for my love they act as my
accusers;
But I am *in* prayer.
5 Thus they have repaid me evil for good
And hatred for my love.

6 ¶ Appoint a wicked man over him,
And let an accuser stand at his right
hand.
7 When he is judged, let him come forth
guilty,
And let his prayer become sin.
8 Let his days be few;
Let another take his office.
9 Let his children be fatherless
And his wife a widow.

109:8 The Judas Principle

*Peter applied this verse to Judas (Acts 1:20).
The New Testament writers saw David's life as
the pattern and foreshadowing of the Messiah,
David's son. The savage betrayal recorded in
this poem shows, as do many psalms, that
unexplained suffering comes to the most
devoted of God's people: first David, then Jesus.*

10 Let his children wander about and beg;
And let them seek *sustenance* far from
their ruined homes.
11 Let the creditor seize all that he has,
And let strangers plunder the product of
his labor.
12 Let there be none to extend
lovingkindness to him,
Nor any to be gracious to his fatherless
children.
13 Let his posterity be cut off;
In a following generation let their name
be blotted out.

14 ¶ Let the iniquity of his fathers be
remembered before the LORD,
And do not let the sin of his mother be
blotted out.
15 Let them be before the LORD continually,
That He may cut off their memory from
the earth;
16 Because he did not remember to show
lovingkindness,
But persecuted the afflicted and needy
man,
And the despondent in heart, to put
them to death.
17 He also loved cursing, so it came to him;
And he did not delight in blessing, so it
was far from him.
18 But he clothed himself with cursing as
with his garment,
And it entered into his body like water
And like oil into his bones.
19 Let it be to him as a garment with which
he covers himself,
And for a belt with which he constantly
girds himself.
20 Let this be the reward of my accusers
from the LORD,
And of those who speak evil against my
soul.

21 ¶ But You, O GOD, the Lord, deal *kindly*
with me for Your name's sake;
Because Your lovingkindness is good,
deliver me;
22 For I am afflicted and needy,
And my heart is wounded within me.
23 I am passing like a shadow when it
lengthens;
I am shaken off like the locust.
24 My knees are weak from fasting,
And my flesh has grown lean, without
fatness.
25 I also have become a reproach to them;
When they see me, they wag their head.
26 ¶ Help me, O LORD my God;
Save me according to Your
lovingkindness.

[a] Or *lawgiver*

27 And let them know that this is Your
hand;
You, LORD, have done it.
28 Let them curse, but You bless;
When they arise, they shall be ashamed,
But Your servant shall be glad.
29 Let my accusers be clothed with
dishonor,
And let them cover themselves with their
own shame as with a robe.

30 ¶ With my mouth I will give thanks
abundantly to the LORD;
And in the midst of many I will praise
Him.
31 For He stands at the right hand of the
needy,
To save him from those who judge his
soul.

Psalm 110

The LORD Gives Dominion to the King.

A Psalm of David.

1 ¶ The LORD says to my Lord:
"Sit at My right hand
Until I make Your enemies a footstool
for Your feet."

110:1 The Son of God

*Jesus quoted this verse in Mark 12:35–37 to
show that the Messiah would not be merely a
human military leader, as many Jews
expected. Here David refers to the coming King
(David's descendant) as "my Lord." If the
Messiah were strictly his human descendant,
David would not address him so respectfully.*

2 The LORD will stretch forth Your strong
scepter from Zion, *saying,*
"Rule in the midst of Your enemies."
3 Your people will volunteer freely in the
day of Your power;
In holy array, from the womb of the
dawn,
Your youth are to You *as* the dew.

4 ¶ The LORD has sworn and will not
change His mind,
"You are a priest forever
According to the order of Melchizedek."
5 The Lord is at Your right hand;
He will shatter kings in the day of His
wrath.
6 He will judge among the nations,
He will fill *them* with corpses,
He will shatter the chief men over a
broad country.

7 He will drink from the brook by the
wayside;
Therefore He will lift up *His* head.

Psalm 111

The LORD Praised for His Goodness.

1 ¶ Praise the LORD!
I will give thanks to the LORD with all *my*
heart,
In the company of the upright and in the
assembly.
2 Great are the works of the LORD;
They are studied by all who delight in
them.
3 Splendid and majestic is His work,
And His righteousness endures forever.
4 He has made His wonders to be
remembered;
The LORD is gracious and compassionate.
5 He has given food to those who ªfear
Him;
He will remember His covenant forever.
6 He has made known to His people the
power of His works,
In giving them the heritage of the
nations.

7 ¶ The works of His hands are truth and
justice;
All His precepts are sure.
8 They are upheld forever and ever;
They are performed in truth and
uprightness.
9 He has sent redemption to His people;
He has ordained His covenant forever;
Holy and awesome is His name.
10 The ᵇfear of the LORD is the beginning
of wisdom;
A good understanding have all those who
do *His commandments;*
His praise endures forever.

Psalm 112

Prosperity of the One Who Fears
the LORD.

1 ¶ Praise the LORD!
How blessed is the man who fears the
LORD,
Who greatly delights in His
commandments.
2 His ᶜdescendants will be mighty on
earth;
The generation of the upright will be
blessed.
3 Wealth and riches are in his house,
And his righteousness endures forever.
4 Light arises in the darkness for the
upright;

ª Or *revere*   ᵇ Or *reverence for*   ᶜ Lit *seed*

He is gracious and compassionate and
  righteous.
5 It is well with the man who is gracious
  and lends;
  He will maintain his cause in judgment.
6 For he will never be shaken;
  The righteous will be remembered
  forever.

7 ¶ He will not fear evil tidings;

His heart is steadfast, trusting in the
  LORD.
8 His heart is upheld, he will not fear,
  Until he looks *with satisfaction* on his
  adversaries.
9 He has given freely to the poor,
  His righteousness endures forever;
  His horn will be exalted in honor.

10 ¶ The wicked will see it and be vexed,

The Twelfth Man

He came "out of nowhere" to win great respect

> *"You are a priest forever, according to the order of Melchizedek."*
> 110:4

IN DALLAS, TEXAS, ON JANUARY 1, 1922, Texas A&M fought it out in the first bowl game ever played in the Southwest. Coach Dana Bible watched helplessly as, one by one, his running backs limped off the field with injuries. As the game neared half-time, he had only one reserve left.

What to do? He remembered a small, wiry back who had not made the traveling team. He had told Coach Bible, "I'll be in the stands if you need me." Bible sent a messenger to search for the young player, King Gill, and get him to suit up for the second half. The Texas A&M tradition of "the twelfth man" began.

Since then, a series of "twelfth men" have come from the student body to help Texas A&M teams. At some schools football players are a breed apart. But Texas A&M, with its "twelfth man" tradition, remembers that a football player may come "out of nowhere." Help doesn't always arrive in the proper uniform.

Mystery Man

The Bible has a kind of twelfth man, a shadowy figure who is mentioned only three times, yet has great importance. Melchizedek came "out of nowhere" in Genesis 14:18–20 as a priest whom Abraham honored. Melchizedek never reappeared. But Psalm 110 mentions him in referring to the Messiah, the conquering king whom Israelites expected. And in the New Testament, the book of Hebrews devotes more than a chapter to Melchizedek's significance. Why so? The answer has to do with Israel's longing for great leadership.

Much as the United States government recognizes three branches of government, Israel had three important kinds of leaders: prophets, priests, and kings. Prophets told the truth, revealing God's righteousness. Kings were to put righteousness into effect, as head of the government. Priests were to see that God met his people in worship: they represented God to the people, and the people to God. According to the God-given Israelite constitution, kings and priests always came from different tribes: a priest from the family of Levi and a king from the family of Judah. Ordinarily, a king could not be a priest.

Total Leadership

The Messiah, however, must be a total leader: a perfect king governing justly, a perfect prophet revealing God's truth, a perfect priest bringing God and people together. But how could he be all three, when priests and kings were supposed to come from different families? Wouldn't that violate God's law?

Psalm 110 suggests (and Hebrews 7 amplifies) the answer. Just as a football player need not necessarily come from the athletic dorm, so Melchizedek's example proves that a priest need not necessarily come from the proper family. Melchizedek was not an Israelite, let alone from the Levite family. He knew nothing about the temple or the Old Testament law, for these came after his time. Yet his spiritual power impressed Abraham. Melchizedek showed the kind of leadership Christ was to bring. He was both a priest and a king.

Psalm 110's brief praise provides a thread between the Old and New Testaments. It hints that the Messiah would be greater than David, while David's descendant. And by tracing the Messiah's roots to Melchizedek, it established his credibility as both priest and king.

Life Questions: What are the "proper channels" you expect to see spiritual leadership come from? Has God ever led you through someone outside those channels?

He will gnash his teeth and melt away;
The desire of the wicked will perish.

Psalm 113

The LORD Exalts the Humble.

1 ¶ Praise the LORD!
Praise, O servants of the LORD,
Praise the name of the LORD.

113:1 Psalms of the Last Supper

Psalms 113 to 118 were traditionally sung at the Passover meal—the first two before the meal, the last four after. These were probably the last songs Jesus sang with his disciples before his death (Mark 14:26).

2 Blessed be the name of the LORD
From this time forth and forever.
3 From the rising of the sun to its setting
The name of the LORD is to be praised.
4 The LORD is high above all nations;
His glory is above the heavens.

5 ¶ Who is like the LORD our God,
Who is enthroned on high,
6 Who humbles Himself to behold
The things that are in heaven and in the
earth?
7 He raises the poor from the dust
And lifts the needy from the ash heap,
8 To make *them* sit with princes,
With the princes of His people.
9 He makes the barren woman abide in the
house
As a joyful mother of children.
Praise the LORD!

Psalm 114

God's Deliverance of Israel from Egypt.

1 ¶ When Israel went forth from Egypt,
The house of Jacob from a people of
strange language,
2 Judah became His sanctuary,
Israel, His dominion.

3 ¶ The sea looked and fled;
The Jordan turned back.
4 The mountains skipped like rams,
The hills, like lambs.
5 What ails you, O sea, that you flee?
O Jordan, that you turn back?
6 O mountains, that you skip like rams?
O hills, like lambs?

7 ¶ Tremble, O earth, before the Lord,

Before the God of Jacob,
8 Who turned the rock into a pool of
water,
The flint into a fountain of water.

Psalm 115

Heathen Idols Contrasted with the LORD.

1 ¶ Not to us, O LORD, not to us,
But to Your name give glory
Because of Your lovingkindness, because
of Your truth.
2 Why should the nations say,
"Where, now, is their God?"
3 But our God is in the heavens;
He does whatever He pleases.
4 Their idols are silver and gold,
The work of man's hands.
5 They have mouths, but they cannot
speak;
They have eyes, but they cannot see;
6 They have ears, but they cannot hear;
They have noses, but they cannot smell;
7 They have hands, but they cannot feel;
They have feet, but they cannot walk;
They cannot make a sound with their
throat.
8 Those who make them will become like
them,
Everyone who trusts in them.

9 ¶ O Israel, trust in the LORD;
He is their help and their shield.
10 O house of Aaron, trust in the LORD;
He is their help and their shield.
11 You who [a]fear the LORD, trust in the
LORD;
He is their help and their shield.
12 The LORD has been mindful of us; He
will bless *us;*
He will bless the house of Israel;
He will bless the house of Aaron.
13 He will bless those who [a]fear the LORD,
The small together with the great.
14 May the LORD give you increase,
You and your children.
15 May you be blessed of the LORD,
Maker of heaven and earth.

16 ¶ The heavens are the heavens of the
LORD,
But the earth He has given to the sons of
men.
17 The dead do not praise the LORD,
Nor *do* any who go down into silence;
18 But as for us, we will bless the LORD
From this time forth and forever.
Praise the LORD!

[a] Or *revere*

Psalm 116

Thanksgiving for Deliverance from Death.

1 ¶ I love the LORD, because He hears
My voice *and* my supplications.
2 Because He has inclined His ear to me,
Therefore I shall call *upon Him* as long
as I live.
3 The cords of death encompassed me
And the terrors of Sheol came upon me;
I found distress and sorrow.
4 Then I called upon the name of the
LORD:
"O LORD, I beseech You, save my life!"

5 ¶ Gracious is the LORD, and righteous;
Yes, our God is compassionate.
6 The LORD preserves the simple;
I was brought low, and He saved me.
7 Return to your rest, O my soul,
For the LORD has dealt bountifully with
you.
8 For You have rescued my soul from
death,
My eyes from tears,
My feet from stumbling.
9 I shall walk before the LORD
In the land of the living.
10 I believed when I said,
"I am greatly afflicted."
11 I said in my alarm,
"All men are liars."

12 ¶ What shall I render to the LORD
For all His benefits toward me?
13 I shall lift up the cup of salvation
And call upon the name of the LORD.
14 I shall pay my vows to the LORD,
Oh *may it be* in the presence of all His
people.
15 Precious in the sight of the LORD
Is the death of His godly ones.

116:15 Precious Death

This verse, often read at funerals, in no way
implies that God enjoys the death of his people.
Instead, it means that he carefully watches
over their death, and that it matters deeply to
him. The whole psalm praises God for saving
from death. Psalm 72:14 uses a similar phrase
in a similar way: "their blood will be precious in
his sight."

16 O LORD, surely I am Your servant,
I am Your servant, the son of Your
handmaid,
You have loosed my bonds.

17 To You I shall offer a sacrifice of
thanksgiving,
And call upon the name of the LORD.
18 I shall pay my vows to the LORD,
Oh *may it be* in the presence of all His
people,
19 In the courts of the LORD's house,
In the midst of you, O Jerusalem.
Praise the LORD!

Psalm 117

A Psalm of Praise.

1 ¶ Praise the LORD, all nations;
Laud Him, all peoples!
2 For His lovingkindness [a]is great
toward us,
And the truth of the LORD is everlasting.
Praise the LORD!

Psalm 118

Thanksgiving for the LORD's Saving Goodness.

1 ¶ Give thanks to the LORD, for He is
good;
For His lovingkindness is everlasting.
2 Oh let Israel say,
"His lovingkindness is everlasting."
3 Oh let the house of Aaron say,
"His lovingkindness is everlasting."
4 Oh let those who [b]fear the LORD say,
"His lovingkindness is everlasting."

5 ¶ From *my* distress I called upon the
LORD;
The LORD answered me *and set me* in a
large place.
6 The LORD is for me; I will not fear;
What can man do to me?
7 The LORD is for me among those who
help me;
Therefore I will look *with satisfaction* on
those who hate me.
8 It is better to take refuge in the LORD
Than to trust in man.
9 It is better to take refuge in the LORD
Than to trust in princes.

10 ¶ All nations surrounded me;
In the name of the LORD I will surely cut
them off.
11 They surrounded me, yes, they
surrounded me;
In the name of the LORD I will surely cut
them off.
12 They surrounded me like bees;
They were extinguished as a fire of
thorns;
In the name of the LORD I will surely cut
them off.

---

[a] Lit *prevails over us*   [b] Or *revere*

13 You pushed me violently so that I was
falling,
But the LORD helped me.
14 The LORD is my strength and song,
And He has become my salvation.

15 ¶ The sound of joyful shouting and
salvation is in the tents of the
righteous;
The right hand of the LORD does
valiantly.
16 The right hand of the LORD is exalted;
The right hand of the LORD does
valiantly.
17 I will not die, but live,
And tell of the works of the LORD.
18 The LORD has disciplined me severely,
But He has not given me over to death.

19 ¶ Open to me the gates of righteousness;
I shall enter through them, I shall give
thanks to the LORD.
20 This is the gate of the LORD;
The righteous will enter through it.
21 I shall give thanks to You, for You have
answered me,
And You have become my salvation.

22 ¶ The stone which the builders rejected
Has become the chief corner *stone.*

118:22 Last-place Winner

*God has a habit of reversing people's status.
The poor and needy end up satisfied, while the
rich and arrogant lose their position. As Jesus
said, "many who are first will be last; and the
last, first" (Matthew 19:30). This psalm
expresses the concept with an image: A stone
builders considered unusable ends up holding
the whole building together. Jesus applied it to
himself, and it was quoted by Peter as a
prophecy fulfilled by Jesus' death and
resurrection (see Matthew 21:42; 1 Peter 2:7;
and Acts 4:11).*

23 This is *a*the LORD'S doing;
It is marvelous in our eyes.
24 This is the day which the LORD has
made;
Let us rejoice and be glad in it.
25 O LORD, do save, we beseech You;
O LORD, we beseech You, do send
prosperity!
26 Blessed is the one who comes in the
name of the LORD;
We have blessed you from the house of
the LORD.
27 The LORD is God, and He has given us
light;

Bind the festival sacrifice with cords to
the horns of the altar.
28 You are my God, and I give thanks
to You;
You are my God, I extol You.
29 Give thanks to the LORD, for He is good;
For His lovingkindness is everlasting.

Psalm 119

Meditations and Prayers Relating
to the Law of God.

א Aleph.

1 ¶ How blessed are those whose way is
*b*blameless,
Who walk in the law of the LORD.
2 How blessed are those who observe His
testimonies,
Who seek Him with all *their* heart.
3 They also do no unrighteousness;
They walk in His ways.
4 You have ordained Your precepts,
That we should keep *them* diligently.
5 Oh that my ways may be established
To keep Your statutes!
6 Then I shall not be ashamed
When I look upon all Your
commandments.
7 I shall give thanks to You with
uprightness of heart,
When I learn Your righteous judgments.
8 I shall keep Your statutes;
Do not forsake me utterly!

ב Beth.

9 ¶ How can a young man keep his way
pure?
By keeping *it* according to Your word.
10 With all my heart I have sought You;
Do not let me wander from Your
commandments.
11 Your word I have treasured in my heart,
That I may not sin against You.
12 Blessed are You, O LORD;
Teach me Your statutes.
13 With my lips I have told of
All the ordinances of Your mouth.
14 I have rejoiced in the way of Your
testimonies,
As much as in all riches.
15 I will meditate on Your precepts
And regard Your ways.
16 I shall delight in Your statutes;
I shall not forget Your word.

ג Gimel.

17 ¶ Deal bountifully with Your servant,
That I may live and keep Your word.
18 Open my eyes, that I may behold

a Lit *from the* LORD   *b* Lit *complete;* or *having integrity*

Wonderful things from Your law.
19 I am a stranger in the earth;
Do not hide Your commandments
from me.
20 My soul is crushed with longing
After Your ordinances at all times.
21 You rebuke the arrogant, the cursed,
Who wander from Your commandments.
22 Take away reproach and contempt
from me,
For I observe Your testimonies.
23 Even though princes sit *and* talk
against me,
Your servant meditates on Your statutes.
24 Your testimonies also are my delight;
They are my counselors.

ד   Daleth.

25 ¶ My soul cleaves to the dust;
Revive me according to Your word.
26 I have told of my ways, and You have
answered me;
Teach me Your statutes.
27 Make me understand the way of Your
precepts,
So I will meditate on Your wonders.
28 My soul weeps because of grief;
Strengthen me according to Your word.
29 Remove the false way from me,
And graciously grant me Your law.
30 I have chosen the faithful way;
I have placed Your ordinances *before me*.
31 I cling to Your testimonies;
O LORD, do not put me to shame!
32 I shall run the way of Your
commandments,
For You will enlarge my heart.

ה   He.

33 ¶ Teach me, O LORD, the way of Your
statutes,
And I shall observe it to the end.
34 Give me understanding, that I may
observe Your law
And keep it with all *my* heart.
35 Make me walk in the path of Your
commandments,
For I delight in it.
36 Incline my heart to Your testimonies
And not to *dishonest* gain.
37 Turn away my eyes from looking at
vanity,
And revive me in Your ways.
38 Establish Your word to Your servant,
As that which produces reverence
for You.
39 Turn away my reproach which I dread,
For Your ordinances are good.

40 Behold, I long for Your precepts;
Revive me through Your righteousness.

ו   Vav.

41 ¶ May Your lovingkindnesses also come
to me, O LORD,
Your salvation according to Your word;
42 So I will have an answer for him who
reproaches me,
For I trust in Your word.
43 And do not take the word of truth
utterly out of my mouth,
For I wait for Your ordinances.
44 So I will keep Your law continually,
Forever and ever.
45 And I will walk at liberty,
For I seek Your precepts.
46 I will also speak of Your testimonies
before kings
And shall not be ashamed.
47 I shall delight in Your commandments,
Which I love.
48 And I shall lift up my hands to Your
commandments,
Which I love;
And I will meditate on Your statutes.

ז   Zayin.

49 ¶ Remember the word to Your servant,
In which You have made me hope.
50 This is my comfort in my affliction,
That Your word has revived me.
51 The arrogant utterly deride me,
Yet I do not turn aside from Your law.
52 I have remembered Your ordinances
from *a*of old, O LORD,
And comfort myself.
53 Burning indignation has seized me
because of the wicked,
Who forsake Your law.
54 Your statutes are my songs
In the house of my pilgrimage.
55 O LORD, I remember Your name in the
night,
And keep Your law.

119:55 Lying in Bed

The psalms consider every aspect of life—even the thoughts that come while lying in bed at night. You can easily become obsessed with other people's wrongs against you. But you can also turn your thoughts to God and quiet your anxieties while strengthening your commitment. Other psalms that refer to such nighttime thoughts, good and bad, are these: 4:4; 6:6; 16:7; 17:3; 63:6; 77:2; 102:7; and 119:62,148.

a Or *everlasting*

56 This has become mine,
That I observe Your precepts.

ח Heth.

57 ¶ The LORD is my portion;
I have promised to keep Your words.
58 I sought Your favor with all *my* heart;
Be gracious to me according to Your
word.

59 I considered my ways
And turned my feet to Your testimonies.
60 I hastened and did not delay
To keep Your commandments.
61 The cords of the wicked have
encircled me,
But I have not forgotten Your law.
62 At midnight I shall rise to give thanks
to You

A Love Poem to God's Law
How could Scripture inspire such poetry?

FOR ALL THE HUNDREDS OF books written about William Shakespeare, he remains a mysterious figure. His "dark lady" prompts endless guesses. He wrote 26 passionate poems to her, yet we do not even know her name. Numerous books try to guess it, "proving" that one lady or another must have been the one.

> *And I shall lift up my hands to Your commandments, which I love.*
> *119:48*

One thing we do know: She had captivated Shakespeare. Seldom has love produced such writhing emotion as his sonnets express. Helplessly ravished by her unfashionable "black (brunette) beauty," Shakespeare longed to forget her, to escape her evil character. Yet he was uncontrollably drawn.

My thoughts and my discourse as madman's are . . .
For I have sworn thee fair, and thought thee bright,
Who art as black as hell, as dark as night.

But what an oddity to express such fevered emotion in sonnets! The sonnets require discipline: precisely 14 lines, an exact rhyming scheme, and iambic pentameter rhythm. How can a raging storm be reflected in such a small, still pond? Yet the evidence of the poems is unmistakable. The discipline gave wild emotion a backbone.

A Love Poem to the Law

Psalm 119 contains even greater oddities. As emotional as Shakespeare's sonnets, this poem also takes a very systematic form: the acrostic, where each line of each stanza begins with a letter from the Hebrew alphabet, *A* in the first stanza, *B* in the second, and so on, through all 22 letters of the Hebrew alphabet.

But the subject is the biggest surprise. Psalm 119 is a long, passionate love poem about God's law.

How do you fall in love with law? Most people admit that rules are necessary, and appreciate them grudgingly. But no one writes love poems to the federal drug abuse statutes.

The word translated "law" doesn't merely mean rules. It expresses the totality of God's written instructions. The poet sees life full of uncertainties, of enemies, of pain. But God has given a reliable guide for living—like pavement underfoot after you have been stuck in mud. Obeying God's law, to the psalmist, is no slavery—rather it is freedom. "I shall run the way of Your commandments, for you will enlarge my heart " (verse 32).

On the Edge of Death

Psalm 119 is not written from an ivory tower. The poet has apparently been near death (verse 87), and even as he writes, "the wicked wait for me to destroy me" (verse 95). But in this dangerous situation he has learned to hang on to God's wisdom. The lesson is so valuable he has become grateful for his sufferings: "It is good for me that I was afflicted, that I may learn Your statutes" (verse 71).

The psalmist simply does not see God's law as a dusty, rigid rulebook. He hears God's loving voice in it. "The earth is full of Your lovingkindness, O LORD; teach me Your statutes" (verse 64). "Your testimonies . . . are the joy of my heart" (verse 111).

God's laws channel God's love into the poet's life. They protect him from doing wrong and give him wisdom to understand his situation. They make new life flow into him. No wonder he writes with such thankfulness. In God's word he finds more than direction. He finds God himself.

Life Questions: Do you ever feel with the psalmist that life has become frighteningly out of control? How can God's law help you regain confidence?

Because of Your righteous ordinances.

63 I am a companion of all those who
    fear You,
    And of those who keep Your precepts.
64 The earth is full of Your lovingkindness,
    O LORD;
    Teach me Your statutes.

ט   Teth.

65 ¶ You have dealt well with Your servant,
    O LORD, according to Your word.
66 Teach me good discernment and
    knowledge,
    For I believe in Your commandments.
67 Before I was afflicted I went astray,
    But now I keep Your word.
68 You are good and do good;
    Teach me Your statutes.
69 The arrogant ᵃhave forged a lie
    against me;
    With all *my* heart I will observe Your
    precepts.
70 Their heart is covered with fat,
    But I delight in Your law.
71 It is good for me that I was afflicted,
    That I may learn Your statutes.
72 The law of Your mouth is better to me
    Than thousands of gold and silver *pieces.*

י   Yodh.

73 ¶ Your hands made me and
    ᵇfashioned me;
    Give me understanding, that I may learn
    Your commandments.
74 May those who fear You see me and be
    glad,
    Because I wait for Your word.
75 I know, O LORD, that Your judgments
    are righteous,
    And that in faithfulness You have
    afflicted me.
76 O may Your lovingkindness comfort me,
    According to Your word to Your servant.
77 May Your compassion come to me that I
    may live,
    For Your law is my delight.
78 May the arrogant be ashamed, for they
    subvert me with a lie;
    But I shall meditate on Your precepts.
79 May those who fear You turn to me,
    Even those who know Your testimonies.
80 May my heart be blameless in Your
    statutes,
    So that I will not be ashamed.

כ   Kaph.

81 ¶ My soul languishes for Your salvation;
    I wait for Your word.
82 My eyes fail *with longing* for Your word,

While I say, "When will You
    comfort me?"
83 Though I have become like a wineskin in
    the smoke,
    I do not forget Your statutes.
84 How many are the days of Your servant?
    When will You execute judgment on
    those who persecute me?
85 The arrogant have dug pits for me,
    Men who are not in accord with Your
    law.
86 All Your commandments are faithful;
    They have persecuted me with a lie;
    help me!
87 They almost destroyed me on earth,
    But as for me, I did not forsake Your
    precepts.
88 Revive me according to Your
    lovingkindness,
    So that I may keep the testimony of
    Your mouth.

ל   Lamedh.

89 ¶ Forever, O LORD,
    Your word ᶜis settled in heaven.
90 Your faithfulness *continues* throughout all
    generations;
    You established the earth, and it stands.
91 They stand this day according to Your
    ordinances,
    For all things are Your servants.
92 If Your law had not been my delight,
    Then I would have perished in my
    affliction.
93 I will never forget Your precepts,
    For by them You have revived me.
94 I am Yours, save me;
    For I have sought Your precepts.
95 The wicked wait for me to destroy me;
    I shall diligently consider Your
    testimonies.
96 I have seen a limit to all perfection;
    Your commandment is exceedingly
    broad.

119:96 Free At Last

People often wonder if following God's law will restrict them, but actual experience shows that God's law liberates—by freeing us from the destructive impact of sinful behavior, and by introducing us to the mind-expanding realm of God's wisdom. Like the author of Ecclesiastes, the psalmist had looked around and seen limits to everything. Only in following God's commands, he sees, can a person escape this frustrating sense of boundaries.

ᵃLit *besmear me with lies*   ᵇLit *established*   ᶜLit *stands firm*

מ Mem.

97 ¶ O how I love Your law!
It is my meditation all the day.
98 Your commandments make me wiser
than my enemies,
For they are ever mine.
99 I have more insight than all my teachers,
For Your testimonies are my meditation.
100 I understand more than the aged,
Because I have observed Your precepts.
101 I have restrained my feet from every evil
way,
That I may keep Your word.
102 I have not turned aside from Your
ordinances,
For You Yourself have taught me.
103 How sweet are Your words to my taste!
Yes, sweeter than honey to my mouth!
104 From Your precepts I get understanding;
Therefore I hate every false way.

נ Nun.

105 ¶ Your word is a lamp to my feet
And a light to my path.
106 I have sworn and I will confirm it,
That I will keep Your righteous
ordinances.
107 I am exceedingly afflicted;
Revive me, O LORD, according to Your
word.
108 O accept the freewill offerings of my
mouth, O LORD,
And teach me Your ordinances.
109 My life is continually ᵃin my hand,
Yet I do not forget Your law.
110 The wicked have laid a snare for me,
Yet I have not gone astray from Your
precepts.
111 I have inherited Your testimonies forever,
For they are the joy of my heart.
112 I have inclined my heart to perform
Your statutes
Forever, even to the end.

ס Samekh.

113 ¶ I hate those who are double-minded,
But I love Your law.
114 You are my hiding place and my shield;
I wait for Your word.
115 Depart from me, evildoers,
That I may observe the commandments
of my God.
116 Sustain me according to Your word, that
I may live;
And do not let me be ashamed of my
hope.
117 Uphold me that I may be safe,
That I may have regard for Your statutes
continually.

118 You have rejected all those who wander
from Your statutes,
For their deceitfulness is useless.
119 You have removed all the wicked of the
earth like dross;
Therefore I love Your testimonies.
120 My flesh trembles for fear of You,
And I am afraid of Your judgments.

ע Ayin.

121 ¶ I have done justice and righteousness;
Do not leave me to my oppressors.
122 Be surety for Your servant for good;
Do not let the arrogant oppress me.
123 My eyes fail with longing for Your
salvation
And for Your righteous word.
124 Deal with Your servant according to
Your lovingkindness
And teach me Your statutes.
125 I am Your servant; give me
understanding,
That I may know Your testimonies.
126 It is time for the LORD to act,
For they have broken Your law.
127 Therefore I love Your commandments
Above gold, yes, above fine gold.
128 Therefore I esteem right all Your precepts
concerning everything,
I hate every false way.

פ Pe.

129 ¶ Your testimonies are wonderful;
Therefore my soul observes them.
130 The unfolding of Your words gives light;
It gives understanding to the simple.
131 I opened my mouth wide and panted,
For I longed for Your commandments.
132 Turn to me and be gracious to me,
After Your manner with those who love
Your name.
133 Establish my footsteps in Your word,
And do not let any iniquity have
dominion over me.
134 Redeem me from the oppression of man,
That I may keep Your precepts.
135 Make Your face shine upon Your
servant,
And teach me Your statutes.
136 My eyes shed streams of water,
Because they do not keep Your law.

צ Tsadhe.

137 ¶ Righteous are You, O LORD,
And upright are Your judgments.
138 You have commanded Your testimonies
in righteousness
And exceeding faithfulness.
139 My zeal has consumed me,

ᵃ I.e. in danger

Because my adversaries have forgotten
  Your words.
140 Your word is very pure,
  Therefore Your servant loves it.
141 I am small and despised,
  Yet I do not forget Your precepts.
142 Your righteousness is an everlasting
    righteousness,
  And Your law is truth.
143 Trouble and anguish have come
    upon me,
  Yet Your commandments are my delight.
144 Your testimonies are righteous forever;
  Give me understanding that I may live.

ק Qoph.

145 ¶ I cried with all my heart; answer me,
    O LORD!
  I will observe Your statutes.
146 I cried to You; save me
  And I shall keep Your testimonies.
147 I rise before dawn and cry for help;
  I wait for Your words.
148 My eyes anticipate the night watches,
  That I may meditate on Your word.
149 Hear my voice according to Your
    lovingkindness;
  Revive me, O LORD, according to Your
    ordinances.
150 Those who follow after wickedness draw
    near;
  They are far from Your law.
151 You are near, O LORD,
  And all Your commandments are truth.

119:151 Near and Nearer

*The psalmist doesn't claim that God makes
problem people disappear. He merely points
out that while they are near, so is God. Big
problems gain a different perspective when we
remember the nearness of a bigger God.*

152 Of old I have known from Your
    testimonies
  That You have founded them forever.

ר Resh.

153 ¶ Look upon my affliction and
    rescue me,
  For I do not forget Your law.
154 Plead my cause and redeem me;
  Revive me according to Your word.
155 Salvation is far from the wicked,
  For they do not seek Your statutes.
156 Great are Your mercies, O LORD;
  Revive me according to Your ordinances.
157 Many are my persecutors and my
    adversaries,

Yet I do not turn aside from Your
    testimonies.
158 I behold the treacherous and loathe *them,*
  Because they do not keep Your word.
159 Consider how I love Your precepts;
  Revive me, O LORD, according to Your
    lovingkindness.
160 The sum of Your word is truth,
  And every one of Your righteous
    ordinances is everlasting.

ש Shin.

161 ¶ Princes persecute me without cause,
  But my heart stands in awe of Your
    words.
162 I rejoice at Your word,
  As one who finds great spoil.
163 I hate and despise falsehood,
  But I love Your law.
164 Seven times a day I praise You,
  Because of Your righteous ordinances.
165 Those who love Your law have great
    peace,
  And nothing causes them to stumble.
166 I hope for Your salvation, O LORD,
  And do Your commandments.
167 My soul keeps Your testimonies,
  And I love them exceedingly.
168 I keep Your precepts and Your
    testimonies,
  For all my ways are before You.

ת Tav.

169 ¶ Let my cry come before You, O LORD;
  Give me understanding according to
    Your word.
170 Let my supplication come before You;
  Deliver me according to Your word.
171 Let my lips utter praise,
  For You teach me Your statutes.
172 Let my tongue sing of Your word,
  For all Your commandments are
    righteousness.
173 Let Your hand be ready to help me,
  For I have chosen Your precepts.
174 I long for Your salvation, O LORD,
  And Your law is my delight.
175 Let my soul live that it may praise You,
  And let Your ordinances help me.
176 I have gone astray like a lost sheep; seek
    Your servant,
  For I do not forget Your
    commandments.

Psalm 120

Prayer for Deliverance
from the Treacherous.

A Song of Ascents.

1 ¶ In my trouble I cried to the LORD,
  And He answered me.

2 Deliver my soul, O LORD, from lying lips,
From a deceitful tongue.
3 What shall be given to you, and what
more shall be done to you,
You deceitful tongue?
4 Sharp arrows of the warrior,
With the *burning* coals of the broom
tree.

5 ¶ Woe is me, for I sojourn in Meshech,
For I dwell among the tents of Kedar!
6 Too long has my soul had its dwelling
With those who hate peace.
7 I am *for* peace, but when I speak,
They are for war.

Psalm 121

The LORD the Keeper of Israel.

A Song of Ascents.

1 ¶ I will lift up my eyes to the mountains;
From where shall my help come?
2 My help *comes* from the LORD,
Who made heaven and earth.
3 He will not allow your foot to slip;
He who keeps you will not slumber.
4 Behold, He who keeps Israel
Will neither slumber nor sleep.

5 ¶ The LORD is your keeper;
The LORD is your shade on your right
hand.
6 The sun will not smite you by day,
Nor the moon by night.
7 The LORD will *a*protect you from all
evil;
He will keep your soul.
8 The LORD will *a*guard your going out
and your coming in
From this time forth and forever.

Psalm 122

Prayer for the Peace of Jerusalem.

A Song of Ascents, of David.

1 ¶ I was glad when they said to me,
"Let us go to the house of the LORD."
2 Our feet are standing
Within your gates, O Jerusalem,
3 Jerusalem, that is built
As a city that is compact together;
4 To which the tribes go up, even the
tribes of the LORD—
An ordinance for Israel—
To give thanks to the name of the LORD.
5 For there thrones were set for judgment,
The thrones of the house of David.

6 ¶ Pray for the peace of Jerusalem:
"May they prosper who love you.
7 "May peace be within your walls,

And prosperity within your palaces."
8 For the sake of my brothers and my
friends,
I will now say, "May peace be within
you."
9 For the sake of the house of the LORD
our God,
I will seek your good.

Psalm 123

Prayer for the LORD'S Help.

A Song of Ascents.

1 ¶ To You I lift up my eyes,
O You who are enthroned in the
heavens!
2 Behold, as the eyes of servants *look* to
the hand of their master,
As the eyes of a maid to the hand of her
mistress,
So our eyes *look* to the LORD our God,
Until He is gracious to us.

3 ¶ Be gracious to us, O LORD, be gracious
to us,
For we are greatly filled with contempt.
4 Our soul is greatly filled
With the scoffing of those who are at
ease,
And with the contempt of the proud.

Psalm 124

Praise for Rescue from Enemies.

A Song of Ascents, of David.

1 ¶ "Had it not been the LORD who was on
our side,"
Let Israel now say,
2 "Had it not been the LORD who was on
our side
When men rose up against us,
3 Then they would have swallowed us alive,
When their anger was kindled against us;
4 Then the waters would have engulfed us,
The stream would have swept over our
soul;
5 Then the raging waters would have swept
over our soul."

6 ¶ Blessed be the LORD,
Who has not given us to be torn by their
teeth.
7 Our soul has escaped as a bird out of the
snare of the trapper;
The snare is broken and we have
escaped.
8 Our help is in the name of the LORD,
Who made heaven and earth.

a Or *keep*

Psalm 125

The LORD Surrounds His People.

A Song of Ascents.

1 ¶ Those who trust in the LORD
   Are as Mount Zion, which cannot be
      moved but abides forever.

124:7 Deeper and Deeper

Some trouble is quick—bang and it's over. If you get caught speeding, for instance, you pay your fine and that ends the whole affair. But with other trouble, trying to escape only gets you more deeply entangled. Spreading gossip, for instance, may lead you into all kinds of unexpected consequences as the gossip spreads. If you try to undo the damage, you only make it worse.

That's exactly the picture of "the snare of the trapper." The bird that caught its neck in the noose only tightened the snare's choke-hold by struggling. The bird could not get out by its own effort. But this time, says David, the snare has miraculously broken, and the bird has flown to safety. When you escape that way, there's only one person to thank: the Lord.

2 As the mountains surround Jerusalem,
   So the LORD surrounds His people
   From this time forth and forever.
3 For the scepter of wickedness shall not
      rest upon the land of the righteous,
   So that the righteous will not put forth
      their hands to do wrong.
4 ¶ Do good, O LORD, to those who are
      good
   And to those who are upright in their
      hearts.
5 But as for those who turn aside to their
      crooked ways,
   The LORD will lead them away with the
      doers of iniquity.
   Peace be upon Israel.

Psalm 126

Thanksgiving for Return from Captivity.

A Song of Ascents.

1 ¶ When the LORD brought back the
      captive ones of Zion,
   We were like those who dream.
2 Then our mouth was filled with laughter
   And our tongue with joyful shouting;
   Then they said among the nations,
   "The LORD has done great things for
      them."

3 The LORD has done great things for us;
   We are glad.
4 ¶ Restore our captivity, O LORD,
   As the streams in the South.
5 Those who sow in tears shall reap with
      joyful shouting.
6 He who goes to and fro weeping,
      carrying *his* bag of seed,
   Shall indeed come again with a shout of
      joy, bringing his sheaves *with him*.

Psalm 127

Prosperity Comes from the LORD.

A Song of Ascents, of Solomon.

1 ¶ Unless the LORD builds the house,
   They labor in vain who build it;
   Unless the LORD guards the city,
   The watchman keeps awake in vain.
2 It is vain for you to rise up early,
   To retire late,
   To eat the bread of painful labors;
   For He gives to His beloved *even in his*
      sleep.
3 ¶ Behold, children are a gift of the LORD,
   The fruit of the womb is a reward.
4 Like arrows in the hand of a warrior,
   So are the children of one's youth.
5 How blessed is the man whose quiver is
      full of them;
   They will not be ashamed
   When they speak with their enemies in
      the gate.

Psalm 128

Blessedness of the Fear of the LORD.

A Song of Ascents.

1 ¶ How blessed is everyone who fears the
      LORD,
   Who walks in His ways.
2 When you shall eat of the [a]fruit of your
      hands,
   You will be happy and it will be well
      with you.
3 Your wife shall be like a fruitful vine
   Within your house,
   Your children like olive plants
   Around your table.
4 Behold, for thus shall the man be blessed
   Who fears the LORD.
5 ¶ The LORD bless you from Zion,
   And may you see the prosperity of
      Jerusalem all the days of your life.
6 Indeed, may you see your children's
      children.
   Peace be upon Israel!

---

[a] Lit *labor*

Psalm 129

Prayer for the Overthrow of Zion's Enemies.

A Song of Ascents.

1 ¶ "Many times they have persecuted me
from my youth up,"
Let Israel now say,
2 "Many times they have persecuted me
from my youth up;
Yet they have not prevailed against me.
3 "The plowers plowed upon my back;
They lengthened their furrows."

129:3 The Right Words

You can't improve on the vivid images used in great poetry. If someone asks you, "What's it about?" you can only quote the poem. The psalms are full of such unforgettable language. "Plowers plowed upon my back; they lengthened their furrows" makes you grit your teeth with the sense of oppression. "Let them be like grass upon the housetops, which withers before it grows up" (verse 6) says it better than any alternate phrase like, "Let their successes amount to nothing."

4 The LORD is righteous;
He has cut in two the cords of the
wicked.
5 ¶ May all who hate Zion
Be put to shame and turned backward;
6 Let them be like grass upon the
housetops,
Which withers before it grows up;
7 With which the reaper does not fill his
hand,
Or the binder of sheaves his bosom;
8 Nor do those who pass by say,
"The blessing of the LORD be upon
you;
We bless you in the name of the LORD."

Psalm 130

Hope in the LORD's Forgiving Love.

A Song of Ascents.

1 ¶ Out of the depths I have cried to You,
O LORD.
2 Lord, hear my voice!
Let Your ears be attentive
To the voice of my supplications.
3 If You, LORD, should mark iniquities,
O Lord, who could stand?
4 But there is forgiveness with You,
That You may be feared.

5 ¶ I wait for the LORD, my soul does
wait,
And in His word do I hope.
6 My soul *waits* for the Lord
More than the watchmen for the
morning;
Indeed, more than the watchmen for the
morning.
7 O Israel, hope in the LORD;
For with the LORD there is
lovingkindness,
And with Him is abundant redemption.
8 And He will redeem Israel
From all his iniquities.

Psalm 131

Childlike Trust in the LORD.

A Song of Ascents, of David.

1 ¶ O LORD, my heart is not proud, nor
my eyes haughty;
Nor do I involve myself in great matters,
Or in things too difficult for me.
2 Surely I have composed and quieted my
soul;
Like a weaned child *rests* against his
mother,
My soul is like a weaned child
within me.

131:2 A Child with Its Mother

How trusting is a baby? Not very, some would say, for babies cry violently as soon as they feel the slightest hunger. It is the weaned child, a little older, who has learned to trust its mother, to fret less and simply ask for food instead of wailing. The profound simplicity of this patience is David's model for how he, and all Israel, should wait on the Lord. The apostle Paul comments similarly, "in any and every circumstance I have learned the secret of being filled . . . I can do all things through Him who strengthens me" (Philippians 4:12–13).

3 O Israel, hope in the LORD
From this time forth and forever.

Psalm 132

Prayer for the LORD's Blessing upon the Sanctuary.

A Song of Ascents.

1 ¶ Remember, O LORD, on David's behalf,
All his affliction;
2 How he swore to the LORD
And vowed to the Mighty One of Jacob,
3 "Surely I will not enter my house,
Nor lie on my bed;
4 I will not give sleep to my eyes

Or slumber to my eyelids,

5 Until I find a place for the LORD,
A dwelling place for the Mighty One of
Jacob."

6 ¶ Behold, we heard of it in Ephrathah,
We found it in the field of Jaar.
7 Let us go into His dwelling place;
Let us worship at His footstool.
8 Arise, O LORD, to Your resting place,
You and the ark of Your strength.
9 Let Your priests be clothed with
righteousness,
And let Your godly ones sing for joy.

10 ¶ For the sake of David Your servant,
Do not turn away the face of Your
anointed.
11 The LORD has sworn to David
A truth from which He will not turn
back:
"Of the fruit of your body I will set upon
your throne.

132:11–18 Promise to David

*God's covenant with David promised that he
and his descendants would always reign over
Israel. For Israel, this promise meant that God
would never let the nation disintegrate, that he
would always provide a leader. Over the
centuries, when Israel chafed under the
domination of other nations, Jews remembered
this promise and looked for a "Messiah" or
"anointed one" (a king) who would provide this
leadership. That is why the New Testament
often refers to Jesus as a "son of David."*

12 "If your sons will keep My covenant
And My testimony which I will teach
them,
Their sons also shall sit upon your
throne forever."

13 ¶ For the LORD has chosen Zion;
He has desired it for His habitation.
14 "This is My resting place forever;
Here I will dwell, for I have desired it.
15 "I will abundantly bless her provision;
I will satisfy her needy with bread.
16 "Her priests also I will clothe with
salvation,
And her godly ones will sing aloud for
joy.
17 "There I will cause the horn of David to
spring forth;
I have prepared a lamp for Mine
anointed.
18 "His enemies I will clothe with shame,
But upon himself his crown shall
shine."

Psalm 133

The Excellency of Brotherly Unity.

A Song of Ascents, of David.

1 ¶ Behold, how good and how pleasant
it is
For brothers to dwell together in unity!
2 It is like the precious oil upon the head,
Coming down upon the beard,
Even Aaron's beard,
Coming down upon the edge of his
robes.
3 It is like the dew of Hermon
Coming down upon the mountains of
Zion;
For there the LORD commanded the
blessing—life forever.

Psalm 134

Greetings of Night Watchers.

A Song of Ascents.

1 ¶ Behold, bless the LORD, all servants of
the LORD,
Who serve by night in the house of the
LORD!
2 Lift up your hands to the sanctuary
And bless the LORD.
3 May the LORD bless you from Zion,
He who made heaven and earth.

Psalm 135

Praise the LORD's Wonderful Works.
Vanity of Idols.

1 ¶ Praise the LORD!
Praise the name of the LORD;
Praise *Him,* O servants of the LORD,
2 You who stand in the house of the LORD,
In the courts of the house of our God!
3 Praise the LORD, for the LORD is good;
Sing praises to His name, for it is lovely.
4 For the LORD has chosen Jacob for
Himself,
Israel for His own possession.

5 ¶ For I know that the LORD is great
And that our Lord is above all gods.
6 Whatever the LORD pleases, He does,
In heaven and in earth, in the seas and
in all deeps.
7 He causes the vapors to ascend from the
ends of the earth;
Who makes lightnings for the rain,
Who brings forth the wind from His
treasuries.

8 ¶ He smote the firstborn of Egypt,
Both of man and beast.
9 He sent signs and wonders into your
midst, O Egypt,
Upon Pharaoh and all his servants.
10 He smote many nations

And slew mighty kings,
11 Sihon, king of the Amorites,
And Og, king of Bashan,
And all the kingdoms of Canaan;
12 And He gave their land as a heritage,
A heritage to Israel His people.
13 Your name, O LORD, is everlasting,
Your remembrance, O LORD, throughout
all generations.
14 For the LORD will judge His people
And will have compassion on His
servants.
15 The idols of the nations are *but* silver
and gold,
The work of man's hands.
16 They have mouths, but they do not
speak;
They have eyes, but they do not see;
17 They have ears, but they do not hear,
Nor is there any breath at all in their
mouths.
18 Those who make them will be like them,
Yes, everyone who trusts in them.

19 ¶ O house of Israel, bless the LORD;
O house of Aaron, bless the LORD;
20 O house of Levi, bless the LORD;
You who ªrevere the LORD, bless the
LORD.
21 Blessed be the LORD from Zion,
Who dwells in Jerusalem.
Praise the LORD!

Psalm 136

Thanks for the LORD's Goodness to Israel.

1 ¶ Give thanks to the LORD, for He is
good,
For His lovingkindness is everlasting.

136:1 Call and Response

*Scholars think most of the psalms were used in
temple worship, but they are unsure how they
were sung. This psalm seems like an example
of what is known in African-American music as
"call and response." A leader sings out a story,
and the congregation shouts back a rhythmic
refrain.*

2 Give thanks to the God of gods,
For His lovingkindness is everlasting.
3 Give thanks to the Lord of lords,
For His lovingkindness is everlasting.
4 To Him who alone does great wonders,
For His lovingkindness is everlasting;
5 To Him who made the heavens with
skill,
For His lovingkindness is everlasting;

6 To Him who spread out the earth above
the waters,
For His lovingkindness is everlasting;
7 To Him who made *the* great lights,
For His lovingkindness is everlasting:
8 The sun to rule by day,
For His lovingkindness is everlasting,
9 The moon and stars to rule by night,
For His lovingkindness is everlasting.

10 ¶ To Him who smote the Egyptians in
their firstborn,
For His lovingkindness is everlasting,
11 And brought Israel out from their
midst,
For His lovingkindness is everlasting,
12 With a strong hand and an outstretched
arm,
For His lovingkindness is everlasting.
13 To Him who divided the Red Sea
asunder,
For His lovingkindness is everlasting,
14 And made Israel pass through the midst
of it,
For His lovingkindness is everlasting;
15 But He overthrew Pharaoh and his army
in the Red Sea,
For His lovingkindness is everlasting.
16 To Him who led His people through the
wilderness,
For His lovingkindness is everlasting;
17 To Him who smote great kings,
For His lovingkindness is everlasting,
18 And slew mighty kings,
For His lovingkindness is everlasting:
19 Sihon, king of the Amorites,
For His lovingkindness is everlasting,
20 And Og, king of Bashan,
For His lovingkindness is everlasting,
21 And gave their land as a heritage,
For His lovingkindness is everlasting,
22 Even a heritage to Israel His servant,
For His lovingkindness is everlasting.

23 ¶ Who remembered us in our low estate,
For His lovingkindness is everlasting,
24 And has rescued us from our adversaries,
For His lovingkindness is everlasting;
25 Who gives food to all flesh,
For His lovingkindness is everlasting.
26 Give thanks to the God of heaven,
For His lovingkindness is everlasting.

Psalm 137

An Experience of the Captivity.

1 ¶ By the rivers of Babylon,
There we sat down and wept,
When we remembered Zion.
2 Upon the willows in the midst of it

ª Lit *fear*

We hung our harps.
3 For there our captors demanded of us
 songs,
And our tormentors mirth, *saying,*
"Sing us one of the songs of Zion."

4 ¶ How can we sing the LORD's song
 In a foreign land?
5 If I forget you, O Jerusalem,
 May my right hand forget *her skill.*
6 May my tongue cling to the roof of my
 mouth
If I do not remember you,
If I do not exalt Jerusalem
Above my chief joy.

7 ¶ Remember, O LORD, against the sons
 of Edom
The day of Jerusalem,
Who said, "Raze it, raze it
To its very foundation."
8 O daughter of Babylon, you devastated
 one,

How blessed will be the one who
 repays you
With the recompense with which you
 have repaid us.
9 How blessed will be the one who seizes
 and dashes your little ones
Against the rock.

Psalm 138

Thanksgiving for the LORD's Favor.

A Psalm of David.

1 ¶ I will give You thanks with all my
 heart;
I will sing praises to You before the
 gods.
2 I will bow down toward Your holy
 temple
And give thanks to Your name for Your
 lovingkindness and Your truth;
For You have magnified Your word
 according to all Your name.

What about Curses?
Bitter emotions expressed in sorrow

THE SO-CALLED "CURSING PSALMS" COME as a shock. Psalm 137 is the most famous example. In a gorgeous lament from exile, the poet crescendoes to wish that God would bless anyone who knocks a Babylonian baby's brains out.

To many people, this wish seems too bitter to belong in the Bible. Aren't Christians supposed to love their enemies and pray for those who persecute them (Matthew 5:44)? Even in the Old Testament, enemies were not to be treated unkindly (Exodus 23:4). How does this outburst fit into God's Word?

> *How blessed will be the one . . . who seizes and dashes your little ones against the rock. 137:8–9*

A Cry for Justice

To answer we must go to the courtroom, where more and more judges are allowing the victims of a crime to testify during sentencing. A mother who has lost her child to a murderer may spout wild and even vindictive emotions as she stands to demand the death sentence. Still the court needs to hear her. She alone knows fully what was lost. She alone feels the full outrage of the crime.

The cursing psalms voice such "victim testimony" to God, the judge. They always assume that the punishment they ask for is deserved. For example, Psalm 109 calls down curses on a man who "perse-cuted the afflicted and needy man, and the despondent in heart, to put them to death. He also loved the cursing, so it came to him" (109:16–17).

Psalm 137 was written out of similar anguish. As a nation, Babylon had callously murdered, earn-ing punishment. The Bible says that God hears the cries of the innocent. He promises to punish those who have hurt them.

With all his teaching on forgiving enemies, Jesus did not change this idea of justice. He taught that justice will be done by God after death. (See, for instance, Matthew 25:31–46.) But Old Testament Israelites had only vague ideas about life after death. For them, justice had to be done in this life, before their eyes. They asked for it in the cursing psalms.

Mercy for Your Enemies

What about mercy? Isn't our duty to forgive our enemies, and love them? How do the cursing psalms fit with that?

Three things must be said. First, while no mercy shows through in the cursing psalms, that doesn't mean the people who wrote them were wholly unmerciful. David, credited with some of the strongest cursing psalms, showed extraordinary mercy toward Saul, his vengeful enemy. The cursing psalms are

3 On the day I called, You answered me;
    You made me bold with strength in my
        soul.

4 ¶ All the kings of the earth will give
        thanks to You, O LORD,
    When they have heard the words of Your
        mouth.
5 And they will sing of the ways of the
        LORD,
    For great is the glory of the LORD.
6 For though the LORD is exalted,
    Yet He regards the lowly,
    But the haughty He knows from afar.

7 ¶ Though I walk in the midst of trouble,
        You will revive me;
    You will stretch forth Your hand against
        the wrath of my enemies,
    And Your right hand will save me.
8 The LORD will accomplish what
        concerns me;
    Your lovingkindness, O LORD, is
        everlasting;
    Do not forsake the works of Your hands.

Psalm 139

God's Omnipresence and Omniscience.

For the choir director. A Psalm of David.

1 ¶ O LORD, You have searched me and
        known *me*.
2 You know when I sit down and when I
        rise up;

You understand my thought from afar.
3 You scrutinize my path and my lying
        down,
    And are intimately acquainted with all
        my ways.
4 Even before there is a word on my
        tongue,
    Behold, O LORD, You know it all.
5 You have enclosed me behind and
        before,
    And laid Your hand upon me.
6 *Such* knowledge is too wonderful for me;
    It is *too* high, I cannot attain to it.

7 ¶ Where can I go from Your Spirit?
    Or where can I flee from Your presence?
8 If I ascend to heaven, You are there;
    If I make my bed in Sheol, behold, You
        are there.
9 If I take the wings of the dawn,
    If I dwell in the remotest part of the
        sea,
10 Even there Your hand will lead me,
    And Your right hand will lay hold of me.
11 If I say, "Surely the darkness will
        overwhelm me,
    And the light around me will be night,"
12 Even the darkness is not dark to You,
    And the night is as bright as the day.
    Darkness and light are alike *to You.*

13 ¶ For You formed my inward parts;
    You wove me in my mother's womb.

---

unbridled cries of agony. They honestly reflect the way people felt. Their authors' lives sometimes balanced this cry with compassion.

Second, the psalmists wrote before Jesus offered forgiveness to all by dying, as God's Son, in people's place. Even today many people find it difficult to accept Jesus' teaching on forgiving enemies, for it means forgiving rapists, child molesters, mass murderers. We can only forgive them because Jesus paid the price for their crimes. The psalmists lived before that payment.

Third, the cursing psalms prepared the way for forgiveness. You can only be genuinely merciful if you start with a full appreciation of guilt. The judge who carelessly lets a criminal off on a technicality is not showing mercy. Maybe he or she just lacks sympathy for the crime's victim. True mercy comes when victims themselves turn and forgive the people who hurt them, releasing them to liberty.

Jesus the Victim

The cursing psalms express the hideousness of violence and injustice. Unless you feel the depth of this, you cannot understand the depth of God's forgiveness, offered freely to anyone who pleads for mercy. God is not merely letting people off on a legal technicality. He hears the cry of their victims, and more: He shares it. In Jesus, God was the victim, beaten, cursed, killed.

The New Testament actually quoted two of the cursing psalms, referring to Judas's betrayal of Jesus. These psalms speak of bitter injustice, and Jesus suffered the ultimate injustice. But the final word comes from Jesus himself: "Father, forgive them, for they do not know what they are doing."

If we follow Jesus' example, we dare not mouth the cursing psalms when we think of our enemies. These psalms are not for us to borrow from, as are other psalms. Yet these cursing psalms remind us of the bitter suffering many experience, and reading them can impel us to fight for justice. More, they remind us to forgive. For God, hearing such cries from the victim, having suffered as they suffer, forgives. So can we.

Life Questions: What is the worst injustice you have ever experienced? Did you feel some of the anger expressed in the cursing psalms? Were you able to forgive?

14 I will give thanks to You, for ^aI am
  fearfully and wonderfully made;
Wonderful are Your works,
And my soul knows it very well.

139:13-16 Love Before Birth

Does life begin at conception, or at birth? This psalm doesn't directly answer that question, but it does make clear that God's loving involvement with our lives starts long before birth. Nothing can escape God's concern, according to this psalm—no person, no thought, no place, no time.

---

15 My frame was not hidden from You,
  When I was made in secret,
And skillfully wrought in the depths of
  the earth;
16 Your eyes have seen my unformed
  substance;
And in Your book were all written
The days that were ordained *for me,*
When as yet there was not one of them.

17 ¶ How precious also are Your thoughts
  to me, O God!
How vast is the sum of them!
18 If I should count them, they would
  outnumber the sand.
When I awake, I am still with You.

19 ¶ O that You would slay the wicked,
  O God;
Depart from me, therefore, men of
  bloodshed.
20 For they speak against You wickedly,
And Your enemies take *Your name* in
  vain.
21 Do I not hate those who hate You,
  O LORD?
And do I not loathe those who rise up
  against You?
22 I hate them with the utmost hatred;
They have become my enemies.

23 ¶ Search me, O God, and know my
  heart;
Try me and know my anxious thoughts;
24 And see if there be any hurtful way
  in me,
And lead me in the everlasting way.

Psalm 140

Prayer for Protection against the Wicked.

For the choir director. A Psalm of David.

1 ¶ Rescue me, O LORD, from evil men;
Preserve me from violent men

2 Who devise evil things in *their* hearts;
They continually stir up wars.
3 They sharpen their tongues as a
  serpent;
Poison of a viper is under their lips.
                                    Selah.

4 ¶ Keep me, O LORD, from the hands of
  the wicked;
Preserve me from violent men
Who have purposed to ^btrip up my
  feet.
5 The proud have hidden a trap for me,
  and cords;
They have spread a net by the wayside;
They have set snares for me.   Selah.

6 ¶ I said to the LORD, "You are my God;
Give ear, O LORD, to the voice of my
  supplications.
7 "O GOD the Lord, the strength of my
  salvation,
You have covered my head in the day of
  battle.
8 "Do not grant, O LORD, the desires of the
  wicked;
Do not promote his *evil* device, *that* they
  not be exalted.   Selah.

9 ¶ "As for the head of those who
  surround me,
May the mischief of their lips cover
  them.
10 "May burning coals fall upon them;
May they be cast into the fire,
Into deep pits from which they cannot
  rise.
11 "May a slanderer not be established in the
  earth;
May evil hunt the violent man
  ^cspeedily."

12 ¶ I know that the LORD will maintain the
  cause of the afflicted
And justice for the poor.

140:12 Justice for the Poor

In ancient societies (and in most of the world today) poor people lose all status. Nobody of influence will listen to them or take up their cause. In the Bible, though, God emphasizes his concern for the poor. He will see that they get just treatment. Naturally he expects his followers to do the same.

---

13 Surely the righteous will give thanks to
  Your name;
The upright will dwell in Your presence.

---

^a Some ancient versions read *You are fearfully wonderful*   ^b Lit *push violently*   ^c Lit *thrust upon thrust*

Psalm 141

An Evening Prayer for Sanctification and Protection.

A Psalm of David.

1 ¶ O LORD, I call upon You; hasten
  to me!
  Give ear to my voice when I call to You!
2 May my prayer be counted as incense
    before You;
  The lifting up of my hands as the
    evening offering.
3 Set a guard, O LORD, over my mouth;
  Keep watch over the door of my lips.
4 Do not incline my heart to any evil
    thing,
  To practice deeds of wickedness
  With men who do iniquity;
  And do not let me eat of their delicacies.

5 ¶ Let the righteous smite me in kindness
    and reprove me;
  It is oil upon the head;
  Do not let my head refuse it,
  For still my prayer is against their wicked
    deeds.
6 Their judges are thrown down by the
    sides of the rock,
  And they hear my words, for they are
    pleasant.
7 As when one plows and breaks open the
    earth,
  Our bones have been scattered at the
    mouth of Sheol.

8 ¶ For my eyes are toward You, O GOD,
    the Lord;
  In You I take refuge; do not leave me
    defenseless.
9 Keep me from the jaws of the trap which
    they have set for me,
  And from the snares of those who do
    iniquity.
10 Let the wicked fall into their own nets,
  While I pass by safely.

Psalm 142

Prayer for Help in Trouble.

*Maskil of David, when he was
in the cave. A Prayer.*

1 ¶ I cry aloud with my voice to the LORD;
  I make supplication with my voice to the
    LORD.
2 I pour out my complaint before Him;
  I declare my trouble before Him.
3 When my spirit was overwhelmed
    within me,
  You knew my path.
  In the way where I walk
  They have hidden a trap for me.

4 Look to the right and see;
  For there is no one who regards me;
  There is no escape for me;
  No one cares for my soul.

5 ¶ I cried out to You, O LORD;
  I said, "You are my refuge,
  My portion in the land of the living.
6 "Give heed to my cry,
  For I am brought very low;
  Deliver me from my persecutors,
  For they are too strong for me.
7 "Bring my soul out of prison,
  So that I may give thanks to Your name;
  The righteous will surround me,
  For You will deal bountifully with me."

Psalm 143

Prayer for Deliverance and Guidance.

A Psalm of David.

1 ¶ Hear my prayer, O LORD,
  Give ear to my supplications!
  Answer me in Your faithfulness, in Your
    righteousness!
2 And do not enter into judgment with
    Your servant,
  For in Your sight no man living is
    righteous.
3 For the enemy has persecuted my soul;
  He has crushed my life to the ground;
  He has made me dwell in dark places,
    like those who have long been dead.
4 Therefore my spirit is overwhelmed
    within me;
  My heart is ᵃappalled within me.

5 ¶ I remember the days of old;
  I meditate on all Your doings;
  I muse on the work of Your hands.
6 I stretch out my hands to You;
  My soul *longs* for You, as a parched
    land.   Selah.

7 ¶ Answer me quickly, O LORD, my spirit
    fails;
  Do not hide Your face from me,
  Or I will become like those who go down
    to the pit.
8 Let me hear Your lovingkindness in the
    morning;
  For I trust in You;
  Teach me the way in which I should
    walk;
  For to You I lift up my soul.
9 Deliver me, O LORD, from my enemies;
  I take refuge in You.

10 ¶ Teach me to do Your will,
  For You are my God;
  Let Your good Spirit lead me on level
    ground.

ᵃ Or desolate

11 For the sake of Your name, O LORD,
    revive me.
  In Your righteousness bring my soul out
    of trouble.
12 And in Your lovingkindness, cut off my
    enemies
  And destroy all those who afflict my
    soul,
  For I am Your servant.

Psalm 144

Prayer for Rescue and Prosperity.

A Psalm of David.

1 ¶ Blessed be the LORD, my rock,
  Who trains my hands for war,
  And my fingers for battle;
2 My lovingkindness and my fortress,
  My stronghold and my deliverer,
  My shield and He in whom I take refuge,
  Who subdues my people under me.
3 O LORD, what is man, that You take
    knowledge of him?
  Or the son of man, that You think
    of him?
4 Man is like a mere breath;
  His days are like a passing shadow.

5 ¶ Bow Your heavens, O LORD, and come
    down;
  Touch the mountains, that they may
    smoke.
6 Flash forth lightning and scatter them;
  Send out Your arrows and confuse them.
7 Stretch forth Your hand from on high;
  Rescue me and deliver me out of great
    waters,
  Out of the hand of aliens
8 Whose mouths speak deceit,
  And whose right hand is a right hand of
    falsehood.

9 ¶ I will sing a new song to You, O God;
  Upon a harp of ten strings I will sing
    praises to You,
10 Who gives salvation to kings,
  Who rescues David His servant from the
    evil sword.
11 Rescue me and deliver me out of the
    hand of aliens,
  Whose mouth speaks deceit
  And whose right hand is a right hand of
    falsehood.

12 ¶ Let our sons in their youth be as
    grown-up plants,
  And our daughters as corner pillars
    fashioned as for a palace;
13 Let our garners be full, furnishing every
    kind of produce,
  And our flocks bring forth thousands
    and ten thousands in our fields;
14 Let our cattle bear

Without mishap and without loss,
  Let there be no outcry in our streets!
15 How blessed are the people who are so
    situated;
  How blessed are the people whose God is
    the LORD!

Psalm 145

The LORD Extolled for His Goodness.

A Psalm of Praise, of David.

1 ¶ I will extol You, my God, O King,
  And I will bless Your name forever and
    ever.
2 Every day I will bless You,
  And I will praise Your name forever and
    ever.
3 Great is the LORD, and highly to be
    praised,
  And His greatness is unsearchable.
4 One generation shall praise Your works
    to another,
  And shall declare Your mighty acts.
5 On the glorious splendor of Your majesty
  And on Your wonderful works, I will
    meditate.
6 Men shall speak of the power of Your
    awesome acts,
  And I will tell of Your greatness.
7 They shall eagerly utter the memory of
    Your abundant goodness
  And will shout joyfully of Your
    righteousness.

8 ¶ The LORD is gracious and merciful;
  Slow to anger and great in
    lovingkindness.
9 The LORD is good to all,
  And His mercies are over all His works.
10 All Your works shall give thanks to You,
    O LORD,
  And Your godly ones shall bless You.
11 They shall speak of the glory of Your
    kingdom
  And talk of Your power;
12 To make known to the sons of men
    Your mighty acts
  And the glory of the majesty of Your
    kingdom.
13 Your kingdom is an everlasting kingdom,
  And Your dominion *endures* throughout
    all generations.

14 ¶ The LORD sustains all who fall
  And raises up all who are bowed down.
15 The eyes of all look to You,
  And You give them their food in due
    time.
16 You open Your hand
  And satisfy the desire of every living
    thing.

17 ¶ The LORD is righteous in all His ways

And kind in all His deeds.
18 The LORD is near to all who call upon
Him,
To all who call upon Him in truth.
19 He will fulfill the desire of those who fear
Him;
He will also hear their cry and will save
them.
20 The LORD keeps all who love Him,
But all the wicked He will destroy.
21 My mouth will speak the praise of the
LORD,
And all flesh will bless His holy name
forever and ever.

Psalm 146

The LORD an Abundant Helper.

1 ¶ Praise the LORD!
Praise the LORD, O my soul!
2 I will praise the LORD while I live;
I will sing praises to my God while I
have my being.
3 Do not trust in princes,
In mortal man, in whom there is no
salvation.
4 His spirit departs, he returns to the earth;
In that very day his thoughts perish.
5 How blessed is he whose help is the God
of Jacob,
Whose hope is in the LORD his God,
6 Who made heaven and earth,
The sea and all that is in them;
Who keeps faith forever;
7 Who executes justice for the oppressed;
Who gives food to the hungry.
The LORD sets the prisoners free.

8 ¶ The LORD opens the eyes of the blind;
The LORD raises up those who are bowed
down;
The LORD loves the righteous;
9 The LORD protects the strangers;
He supports the fatherless and the
widow,
But He thwarts the way of the wicked.
10 The LORD will reign forever,
Your God, O Zion, to all generations.
Praise the LORD!

Psalm 147

Praise for Jerusalem's Restoration and Prosperity.

1 ¶ Praise the LORD!
For it is good to sing praises to our God;
For ªit is pleasant and praise is
becoming.
2 The LORD builds up Jerusalem;
He gathers the outcasts of Israel.
3 He heals the brokenhearted

And binds up their ᵇwounds.
4 He counts the number of the stars;
He gives names to all of them.
5 Great is our Lord and abundant in
strength;
His understanding is infinite.
6 The LORD ᶜsupports the afflicted;
He brings down the wicked to the
ground.

7 ¶ Sing to the LORD with thanksgiving;
Sing praises to our God on the lyre,
8 Who covers the heavens with clouds,
Who provides rain for the earth,
Who makes grass to grow on the
mountains.
9 He gives to the beast its food,
And to the young ravens which cry.
10 He does not delight in the strength of the
horse;
He does not take pleasure in the legs of a
man.
11 The LORD favors those who fear Him,
Those who wait for His lovingkindness.

147:11 God's Great Concern

The Lord is a God of strength, as this song amply demonstrates. But power doesn't delight him (verse 10). More than anything he loves to be in a close relationship to people who respond to his love.

12 ¶ Praise the LORD, O Jerusalem!
Praise your God, O Zion!
13 For He has strengthened the bars of your
gates;
He has blessed your sons within you.
14 He makes peace in your borders;
He satisfies you with the finest of the
wheat.
15 He sends forth His command to the
earth;
His word runs very swiftly.
16 He gives snow like wool;
He scatters the frost like ashes.
17 He casts forth His ice as fragments;
Who can stand before His cold?
18 He sends forth His word and melts them;
He causes His wind to blow and the
waters to flow.
19 He declares His words to Jacob,
His statutes and His ordinances to Israel.
20 He has not dealt thus with any nation;
And as for His ordinances, they have not
known them.
Praise the LORD!

ª Or *He is gracious* ᵇ Lit *sorrows* ᶜ Or *relieves*

Psalm 148

The Whole Creation Invoked to Praise the LORD.

1 ¶ Praise the LORD!
Praise the LORD from the heavens;
Praise Him in the heights!
2 Praise Him, all His angels;
Praise Him, all His hosts!
3 Praise Him, sun and moon;
Praise Him, all stars of light!
4 Praise Him, highest heavens,
And the waters that are above the
heavens!
5 Let them praise the name of the LORD,
For He commanded and they were
created.
6 He has also established them forever and
ever;
He has made a decree which will not
pass away.

7 ¶ Praise the LORD from the earth,
Sea monsters and all deeps;
8 Fire and hail, snow and clouds;
Stormy wind, fulfilling His word;
9 Mountains and all hills;
Fruit trees and all cedars;
10 Beasts and all cattle;
Creeping things and winged fowl;
11 Kings of the earth and all peoples;
Princes and all judges of the earth;
12 Both young men and virgins;
Old men and children.

13 ¶ Let them praise the name of the LORD,
For His name alone is exalted;
His glory is above earth and heaven.
14 And He has lifted up a horn for His
people,
Praise for all His godly ones;
Even for the sons of Israel, a people near
to Him.
Praise the LORD!

Psalm 149

Israel Invoked to Praise the LORD.

1 ¶ Praise the LORD!
Sing to the LORD a new song,
And His praise in the congregation of the
godly ones.
2 Let Israel be glad in his Maker;
Let the sons of Zion rejoice in their King.
3 Let them praise His name with dancing;
Let them sing praises to Him with
timbrel and lyre.
4 For the LORD takes pleasure in His
people;
He will beautify the afflicted ones with
salvation.

5 ¶ Let the godly ones exult in glory;
Let them sing for joy on their beds.
6 Let the high praises of God be in their
mouth,
And a two-edged sword in their hand,
7 To execute vengeance on the nations
And punishment on the peoples,
8 To bind their kings with chains
And their nobles with fetters of iron,
9 To execute on them the judgment
written;
This is an honor for all His godly ones.
Praise the LORD!

Psalm 150

A Psalm of Praise.

1 ¶ Praise the LORD!
Praise God in His sanctuary;
Praise Him in His mighty expanse.
2 Praise Him for His mighty deeds;
Praise Him according to His excellent
greatness.

3 ¶ Praise Him with trumpet sound;
Praise Him with harp and lyre.
4 Praise Him with timbrel and dancing;
Praise Him with stringed instruments
and pipe.
5 Praise Him with loud cymbals;
Praise Him with resounding cymbals.
6 Let everything that has breath praise the
LORD.
Praise the LORD!

PROVERBS

Uncommon Sense
A most down-to-earth book

"SESAME STREET," THE EDUCATIONAL TV show, has changed a lot of people's ideas about education. It offers a kaleidoscopic mix of gentle fun that seems to have nothing to do with education at all. One episode may start with a band of puppet rock stars—the Beetles—singing an ode entitled "Letter B" (to a tune that sounds surprisingly like the Beatles' "Let It Be"). Then the picture cuts to Big Bird asking Oscar the Grouch to help him write a letter to his uncle—Uncle Bird, whose name just happens to start with the letter B. Five minutes later, a cartoon letter B is jumping in front of various letter combinations while a voice intones the words spelled out: "B-b-boy." "B-b-bathtub." "B-b-bicycle."

"Sesame Street" showed that teaching kids doesn't always mean forcing them to sit down and memorize lists. By watching Big Bird, Cookie Monster, and Oscar the Grouch, children painlessly learn the letter B as well as colors, shapes, and a lot more.

> *For if you cry for discernment, lift your voice for understanding; if you seek her as silver and search for her as for hidden treasures; then you will discern the fear of the LORD and discover the knowledge of God.*
> *2:3–5*

The book of Proverbs does for wisdom what "Sesame Street" does for the ABCs. Much of Proverbs reads like a collection of one-liners, moving quickly (and apparently illogically) from one subject to another. A proverb pleases the ear much as "Sesame Street" pleases the eye, using "shortness, sense and salt" to compress life into a handful of memorable words. But just as with the TV program, Proverbs has an overall objective behind its disorder. If you spend enough time in Proverbs, you will gain a subtle and practical understanding of life.

A Father's Guidance

Proverbs is probably the most down-to-earth book in the Bible. Its education prepares you for the street and the marketplace, not the schoolroom. (Proverbs 1:20–21 expresses this poetically.) The book offers the warm advice you get by growing up in a good family: practical guidance for successfully making your way in the world. It covers small questions as well as large: talking too much, visiting neighbors too often, being unbearably cheerful too early in the morning.

The first nine chapters, which explain the purpose of Proverbs's wisdom, are spoken from father to son. Fifteen times the fatherly voice says, "My son." Some of the advice seems particularly well suited to young people: warnings against joining gangs, for instance, or urgent cautions against sex outside marriage. But the central message of Proverbs applies to anyone, old or young: "Get wisdom at all costs." It is a plea to strain your mind and your ears searching for the wise way to live.

Virtue Is Not Its Only Reward

Anybody with a brain can find exceptions to Proverbs's generalities. For instance, Proverbs 28:19 proclaims that "he who tills his land will have plenty of food, but he who follows empty pursuits will have poverty in plenty." Yet farmers who work hard go hungry in a drought, and dreamers win $10 million in a lottery.

Proverbs simply tells how life works most of the time. You can worry about the exceptions after you have learned the rule. Try to live by the exceptions, and you court disaster.

The rule is that the godly, moral, hardworking, and wise will reap many rewards. Those who learn the practical and godly wisdom of Proverbs not only sleep better, they succeed and become able to help their family and friends. Fools and scoffers, though they appear successful, will eventually pay the cost of their lifestyle.

Much of Proverbs's practical advice makes no mention of God, and its concern for success may therefore seem quite secular. But if you take the book as a whole, it becomes obvious that the lifestyle Proverbs teaches depends on a healthy respect for God (1:7) affecting every aspect of life (3:5–7).

Proverbs frankly concedes that the wise path will not be chosen by many; it is easier to live carelessly and godlessly. But those who choose to live by Proverbs will get success and safety, and more: They will get to know God himself. "Then you will discern the fear of the Lord and discover the knowledge of God" (2:5).

How to Read Proverbs

People love to quote proverbs. Often they express truth about life in an elegant, witty kernel. You'll find more humor in Proverbs than anywhere else in the Bible.

Yet Proverbs may well be the most abused book in the Bible. People often quote the proverbs as though they were absolute promises from God or rigid rules for living. In fact, few of the proverbs should be read that way. And some proverbs, read alone, would give you a distorted point of view.

To understand Proverbs, you should not hunt through it for proverbs you like. You should study the whole book to get its overall point of view. This takes time, for Proverbs covers dozens of subjects in subtle detail.

Each of the more than 500 proverbs is a tough nut you have to crack before you get the inner meat. Read Proverbs slowly, but not for too long at one sitting.

Some people like to read a small number of proverbs each day in addition to their regular Bible readings. Others concentrate on memorizing proverbs, so they can run them through their heads as they go on about the day. Whatever technique you use, keep two things in mind: Think carefully about each proverb, and try to put each into the bigger context of the teachings of all of Proverbs. To help you see the total picture of Proverbs's teaching on some key subjects, ten Insights scattered thoughout Proverbs briefly introduce ten subjects and list relevant proverbs.

The book of Proverbs is divided into two main parts: an introduction in the first nine chapters and the proverbs themselves in the remaining 22 chapters. If you skip the introduction, you won't understand the point of Proverbs as a book. It introduces "Lady Wisdom," and explains what she can do for you.

3-TRACK READING PLAN

For an explanation and complete listing of the 3-track reading plan, turn to page 7.

TRACK 1: *Two-Week Courses on the Bible*
See page 7 for information on these courses.

TRACK 2: *An Overview of Proverbs in 3 Days*
☐ Day 1. Read the Introduction to Proverbs and chapter 4, which gives an introduction to the importance of wisdom and the style of life you need to pursue it.
☐ Day 2. Read chapter 10, which covers a fairly typical range of subject matter.
☐ Day 3. Read all the proverbs listed in "Verbal Dynamite," on page 703.
Now turn to page 9 for your next Track 2 reading project.

TRACK 3: *All of Proverbs in 31 Days*
After you have read through Proverbs, turn to pages 10–14 for your next Track 3 reading project.

☐1 ☐2 ☐3 ☐4 ☐5 ☐6 ☐7 ☐8
☐9 ☐10 ☐11 ☐12 ☐13 ☐14 ☐15 ☐16
☐17 ☐18 ☐19 ☐20 ☐21 ☐22 ☐23 ☐24
☐25 ☐26 ☐27 ☐28 ☐29 ☐30 ☐31

The Usefulness of Proverbs

1 The proverbs of Solomon the son of David,
king of Israel:

2 To know wisdom and instruction,
To discern the sayings of understanding,

3 To receive instruction in wise behavior,
Righteousness, justice and equity;

4 To give prudence to the naive,
To the youth knowledge and discretion,

5 A wise man will hear and increase in
learning,
And a man of understanding will acquire
wise counsel,

6 To understand a proverb and a figure,
The words of the wise and their riddles.

7 ¶ The fear of the LORD is the beginning
of knowledge;
Fools despise wisdom and instruction.

The Enticement of Sinners

8 ¶ Hear, my son, your father's instruction
And do not forsake your mother's
teaching;

9 Indeed, they are a graceful wreath to
your head
And ornaments about your neck.

10 My son, if sinners entice you,
Do not consent.

11 If they say, "Come with us,
Let us lie in wait for blood,
Let us ambush the innocent without
cause;

12 Let us swallow them alive like Sheol,
Even whole, as those who go down to
the pit;

13 We will find all *kinds* of precious wealth,
We will fill our houses with spoil;

14 Throw in your lot with us,
We shall all have one purse,"

15 My son, do not walk in the way with
them.
Keep your feet from their path,

16 For their feet run to evil
And they hasten to shed blood.

17 Indeed, it is useless to spread the
baited net
In the sight of any bird;

18 But they lie in wait for their own blood;
They ambush their own lives.

19 So are the ways of everyone who gains
by violence;
It takes away the life of its possessors.

Wisdom Warns

20 ¶ Wisdom shouts in the street,
She lifts her voice in the square;

21 At the head of the noisy *streets* she cries
out;

At the entrance of the gates in the city
she utters her sayings:

22 "How long, O naive ones, will you love
being simple-minded?
And scoffers delight themselves in
scoffing
And fools hate knowledge?

1:22 Three Problem People

Scoffers, fools, the naive: *Proverbs keeps using these words to define the "bad characters" we should stay away from. What kind of people are they? The "naive" are the least harmful group: they live without thinking and are too lazy to change. But they, like the others, will end up sorry. "Fools" have more smarts but have made a conscious decision to live by their own wits, independent of God and independent of advice. "Scoffers," worst of all, are rebels against God who make their prideful position known to everyone. They mock God, but God will mock them in the end (verse 26).*

23 "Turn to my reproof,
Behold, I will pour out my spirit on
you;
I will make my words known to you.

24 "Because I called and you refused,
I stretched out my hand and no one paid
attention;

25 And you neglected all my counsel
And did not want my reproof;

26 I will also laugh at your calamity;
I will mock when your dread comes,

27 When your dread comes like a storm
And your calamity comes like a
whirlwind,
When distress and anguish come upon
you.

28 "Then they will call on me, but I will not
answer;
They will seek me diligently but they will
not find me,

29 Because they hated knowledge
And did not choose the fear of the LORD.

30 "They would not accept my counsel,
They spurned all my reproof.

31 "So they shall eat of the fruit of their
own way
And be satiated with their own devices.

32 "For the waywardness of the naive will kill
them,
And the complacency of fools will
destroy them.

33 "But he who listens to me shall live
securely
And will be at ease from the dread of
evil."

The Pursuit of Wisdom Brings Security

2 My son, if you will receive my words
And treasure my commandments within
you,

2 Make your ear attentive to wisdom,
Incline your heart to understanding;
3 For if you cry for discernment,
Lift your voice for understanding;
4 If you seek her as silver
And search for her as for hidden
treasures;
5 Then you will discern the fear of the
LORD
And discover the knowledge of God.
6 For the LORD gives wisdom;
From His mouth *come* knowledge and
understanding.
7 He stores up sound wisdom for the
upright;
He is a shield to those who walk in
integrity,
8 Guarding the paths of justice,
And He preserves the way of His godly
ones.
9 Then you will discern righteousness and
justice
And equity *and* every good course.
10 For wisdom will enter your heart
And knowledge will be pleasant to your
soul;
11 Discretion will guard you,
Understanding will watch over you,
12 To deliver you from the way of evil,
From the man who speaks perverse
things;
13 From those who leave the paths of
uprightness
To walk in the ways of darkness;
14 Who delight in doing evil
And rejoice in the perversity of evil;
15 Whose paths are crooked,
And who are devious in their ways;
16 To deliver you from the strange woman,
From the adulteress who flatters with her
words;
17 That leaves the companion of her youth
And forgets the covenant of her God;
18 For her house sinks down to death
And her tracks *lead* to the dead;
19 None who go to her return again,
Nor do they reach the paths of life.
20 So you will walk in the way of good
men
And keep to the paths of the righteous.
21 For the upright will live in the land
And the blameless will remain in it;
22 But the wicked will be cut off from the
land
And the treacherous will be uprooted
from it.

The Rewards of Wisdom

3 My son, do not forget my teaching,
But let your heart keep my
commandments;

2 For length of days and years of life
And peace they will add to you.
3 Do not let kindness and truth leave you;
Bind them around your neck,
Write them on the tablet of your heart.
4 So you will find favor and good repute
In the sight of God and man.
5 Trust in the LORD with all your heart
And do not lean on your own
understanding.
6 In all your ways acknowledge Him,
And He will make your paths straight.

3:6 Walking with God

*In the original Hebrew, "in all your ways
acknowledge Him" is more literally "in all your
ways know him." This fundamental statement
of how to relate to God implies more than mere
reverence. Nodding in God's direction is not
enough: You must know him by living closely
with him, relating to him personally in every
aspect of your life.*

7 Do not be wise in your own eyes;
Fear the LORD and turn away from evil.
8 It will be healing to your body
And refreshment to your bones.
9 Honor the LORD from your wealth
And from the first of all your produce;
10 So your barns will be filled with plenty
And your vats will overflow with new
wine.
11 My son, do not reject the discipline of
the LORD
Or loathe His reproof,
12 For whom the LORD loves He reproves,
Even as a father *corrects* the son in
whom he delights.

13 ¶ How blessed is the man who finds
wisdom
And the man who gains understanding.
14 For her profit is better than the profit of
silver
And her gain better than fine gold.
15 She is more precious than jewels;
And nothing you desire compares with
her.
16 Long life is in her right hand;
In her left hand are riches and honor.
17 Her ways are pleasant ways
And all her paths are peace.
18 She is a tree of life to those who take
hold of her,
And happy are all who hold her fast.

19 The LORD by wisdom founded the earth,
By understanding He established the
heavens.
20 By His knowledge the deeps were
broken up
And the skies drip with dew.
21 My son, let them not vanish from your
sight;
Keep sound wisdom and discretion,
22 So they will be life to your soul
And adornment to your neck.
23 Then you will walk in your way securely
And your foot will not stumble.
24 When you lie down, you will not be
afraid;
When you lie down, your sleep will be
sweet.
25 Do not be afraid of sudden fear
Nor of the onslaught of the wicked when
it comes;
26 For the LORD will be your confidence
And will keep your foot from being
caught.

27 ¶ Do not withhold good from those to
whom it is due,
When it is in your power to do *it*.
28 Do not say to your neighbor, "Go, and
come back,
And tomorrow I will give *it*,"
When you have it with you.
29 Do not devise harm against your
neighbor,
While he lives securely beside you.
30 Do not contend with a man without
cause,
If he has done you no harm.
31 Do not envy a man of violence
And do not choose any of his ways.
32 For the devious are an abomination to
the LORD;
But He is intimate with the upright.
33 The curse of the LORD is on the house of
the wicked,
But He blesses the dwelling of the
righteous.
34 Though He scoffs at the scoffers,
Yet He gives grace to the afflicted.
35 The wise will inherit honor,
But fools display dishonor.

A Father's Instruction

4 Hear, O sons, the instruction of a father,
And give attention that you may gain
understanding,
2 For I give you sound teaching;
Do not abandon my instruction.
3 When I was a son to my father,
Tender and the only son in the sight of
my mother,
4 Then he taught me and said to me,
"Let your heart hold fast my words;

Keep my commandments and live;
5 Acquire wisdom! Acquire understanding!
Do not forget nor turn away from the
words of my mouth.
6 "Do not forsake her, and she will guard
you;
Love her, and she will watch over you.
7 "The beginning of wisdom *is*: Acquire
wisdom;
And with all your acquiring, get
understanding.

4:7 A Lifelong Quest

*A father's advice can easily degenerate into,
"Don't do this, don't do that." But the fatherly
advice of Proverbs isn't preoccupied with rules.
Instead, this father tries to help his son develop
a love for the best things in life—just as his
father did for him. This love for the best—and
most of all for wisdom—begins with listening to
your father's advice, but it goes beyond taking
instructions. The love of wisdom becomes a
lifelong quest that may make you wiser than
your father.*

8 "Prize her, and she will exalt you;
She will honor you if you embrace her.
9 "She will place on your head a garland of
grace;
She will present you with a crown of
beauty."

10 ¶ Hear, my son, and accept my sayings
And the years of your life will be many.
11 I have directed you in the way of
wisdom;
I have led you in upright paths.
12 When you walk, your steps will not be
impeded;
And if you run, you will not stumble.
13 Take hold of instruction; do not let go.
Guard her, for she is your life.
14 Do not enter the path of the wicked
And do not proceed in the way of evil
men.
15 Avoid it, do not pass by it;
Turn away from it and pass on.
16 For they cannot sleep unless they do evil;
And they are robbed of sleep unless they
make *someone* stumble.
17 For they eat the bread of wickedness
And drink the wine of violence.
18 But the path of the righteous is like the
light of dawn,
That shines brighter and brighter until
the full day.
19 The way of the wicked is like darkness;
They do not know over what they
stumble.

20 ¶ My son, give attention to my words;
   Incline your ear to my sayings.
21 Do not let them depart from your sight;
   Keep them in the midst of your heart.
22 For they are life to those who find them
   And health to all their body.
23 Watch over your heart with all diligence,
   For from it *flow* the springs of life.
24 Put away from you a deceitful mouth
   And put devious speech far from you.
25 Let your eyes look directly ahead
   And let your gaze be fixed straight in
   front of you.
26 Watch the path of your feet
   And all your ways will be established.
27 Do not turn to the right nor to the left;
   Turn your foot from evil.

Pitfalls of Immorality

5 My son, give attention to my wisdom,
   Incline your ear to my understanding;
2 That you may observe discretion
   And your lips may reserve knowledge.
3 For the lips of an adulteress drip honey
   And smoother than oil is her speech;
4 But in the end she is bitter as
   wormwood,
   Sharp as a two-edged sword.
5 Her feet go down to death,
   Her steps take hold of Sheol.
6 She does not ponder the path of life;
   Her ways are unstable, she does not
   know *it.*

7 ¶ Now then, *my* sons, listen to me
   And do not depart from the words of my
   mouth.
8 Keep your way far from her
   And do not go near the door of her
   house,
9 Or you will give your vigor to others
   And your years to the cruel one;
10 And strangers will be filled with your
   strength
   And your hard-earned goods *will go* to
   the house of an alien;
11 And you groan at your final end,
   When your flesh and your body are
   consumed;
12 And you say, "How I have hated
   instruction!
   And my heart spurned reproof!
13 "I have not listened to the voice of my
   teachers,
   Nor inclined my ear to my instructors!
14 "I was almost in utter ruin
   In the midst of the assembly and
   congregation."

15 ¶ Drink water from your own cistern
   And fresh water from your own well.
16 Should your springs be dispersed abroad,

Streams of water in the streets?
17 Let them be yours alone
   And not for strangers with you.
18 Let your fountain be blessed,
   And rejoice in the wife of your youth.
19 *As* a loving hind and a graceful doe,
   Let her breasts satisfy you at all times;
   Be exhilarated always with her love.
20 For why should you, my son, be
   exhilarated with an adulteress
   And embrace the bosom of a foreigner?
21 For the ways of a man are before the
   eyes of the LORD,
   And He watches all his paths.
22 His own iniquities will capture the
   wicked,
   And he will be held with the cords of his
   sin.
23 He will die for lack of instruction,
   And in the greatness of his folly he will
   go astray.

Parental Counsel

6 My son, if you have become surety for
   your neighbor,
   Have given a pledge for a stranger,

6:1–3 Danger in Debt

Proverbs warns against becoming "surety" for a neighbor—something like co-signing a loan for a friend who doesn't otherwise qualify. Proverbs supports generosity, but not open-ended charity in which the amount you must give and the timing are determined by circumstances beyond your control. Too often it leads to disaster. (See also 11:15; 17:18; 22:26–27.)

2 *If* you have been snared with the words
   of your mouth,
   Have been caught with the words of your
   mouth,
3 Do this then, my son, and deliver
   yourself;
   Since you have come into the hand of
   your neighbor,
   Go, humble yourself, and importune
   your neighbor.
4 Give no sleep to your eyes,
   Nor slumber to your eyelids;
5 Deliver yourself like a gazelle from *the
   hunter's* hand
   And like a bird from the hand of the
   fowler.

6 ¶ Go to the ant, O sluggard,
   Observe her ways and be wise,
7 Which, having no chief,
   Officer or ruler,

8 Prepares her food in the summer
And gathers her provision in the harvest.
9 How long will you lie down, O sluggard?
When will you arise from your sleep?
10 "A little sleep, a little slumber,
A little folding of the hands to rest"—
11 Your poverty will come in like a
vagabond
And your need like an armed man.

12 ¶ A worthless person, a wicked man,
Is the one who walks with a perverse
mouth,
13 Who winks with his eyes, who signals
with his feet,
Who points with his fingers;
14 Who *with* perversity in his heart
continually devises evil,
Who spreads strife.
15 Therefore his calamity will come
suddenly;
Instantly he will be broken and there will
be no healing.

16 ¶ There are six things which the LORD
hates,
Yes, seven which are an abomination to
Him:
17 Haughty eyes, a lying tongue,
And hands that shed innocent blood,
18 A heart that devises wicked plans,
Feet that run rapidly to evil,
19 A false witness *who* utters lies,
And one who spreads strife among
brothers.

20 ¶ My son, observe the commandment of
your father
And do not forsake the teaching of your
mother;
21 Bind them continually on your heart;
Tie them around your neck.
22 When you walk about, they will guide
you;
When you sleep, they will watch over
you;
And when you awake, they will talk to
you.
23 For the commandment is a lamp and the
teaching is light;
And reproofs for discipline are the way
of life
24 To keep you from the evil woman,
From the smooth tongue of the
adulteress.
25 Do not desire her beauty in your heart,
Nor let her capture you with her eyelids.
26 For on account of a harlot *one is reduced*
to a loaf of bread,
And an adulteress hunts for the precious
life.
27 Can a man take fire in his bosom
And his clothes not be burned?

28 Or can a man walk on hot coals
And his feet not be scorched?
29 So is the one who goes in to his
neighbor's wife;
Whoever touches her will not go
unpunished.
30 Men do not despise a thief if he steals
To satisfy himself when he is hungry;
31 But when he is found, he must repay
sevenfold;
He must give all the substance of his
house.
32 The one who commits adultery with a
woman is lacking sense;
He who would destroy himself does it.
33 Wounds and disgrace he will find,
And his reproach will not be blotted out.
34 For jealousy enrages a man,
And he will not spare in the day of
vengeance.
35 He will not accept any ransom,
Nor will he be satisfied though you give
many gifts.

The Wiles of the Harlot

7 My son, keep my words
And treasure my commandments within
you.
2 Keep my commandments and live,
And my teaching as the apple of your
eye.

7:2 The Apple of Your Eye

*The "apple of your eye" is an Old English
expression for the eye's center, or pupil. The
whole body is tuned to protect that pupil from
harm: eyelids reflexively snap shut at the
slightest hint of danger; tear ducts bathe your
eye with a cleansing liquid if any irritant
enters; nerve endings scream "danger" at the
slightest pain or pressure. Proverbs urges you
to take as much care of its teachings as you do
of your eye.*

3 Bind them on your fingers;
Write them on the tablet of your heart.
4 Say to wisdom, "You are my sister,"
And call understanding *your* intimate
friend;
5 That they may keep you from an
adulteress,
From the foreigner who flatters with her
words.

6 ¶ For at the window of my house
I looked out through my lattice,
7 And I saw among the naive,
And discerned among the youths
A young man lacking sense,

8 Passing through the street near her
corner;
And he takes the way to her house,
9 In the twilight, in the evening,
In the middle of the night and *in* the
darkness.
10 And behold, a woman *comes* to meet
him,
Dressed as a harlot and cunning of heart.
11 She is boisterous and rebellious,
Her feet do not remain at home;
12 *She is* now in the streets, now in the
squares,
And lurks by every corner.
13 So she seizes him and kisses him
And with a brazen face she says to him:
14 "I was due to offer peace offerings;
Today I have paid my vows.
15 "Therefore I have come out to meet you,
To seek your presence earnestly, and I
have found you.
16 "I have spread my couch with coverings,
With colored linens of Egypt.
17 "I have sprinkled my bed
With myrrh, aloes and cinnamon.
18 "Come, let us drink our fill of love until
morning;
Let us delight ourselves with caresses.
19 "For my husband is not at home,
He has gone on a long journey;
20 He has taken a bag of money with him,
At the full moon he will come home."
21 With her many persuasions she entices
him;
With her flattering lips she seduces him.
22 Suddenly he follows her
As an ox goes to the slaughter,
Or as *one in* fetters to the discipline of a
fool,
23 Until an arrow pierces through his liver;
As a bird hastens to the snare,
So he does not know that it *will cost him*
his life.

24 ¶ Now therefore, *my* sons, listen to me,
And pay attention to the words of my
mouth.
25 Do not let your heart turn aside to her
ways,
Do not stray into her paths.
26 For many are the victims she has cast
down,
And numerous are all her slain.
27 Her house is the way to Sheol,
Descending to the chambers of death.

The Commendation of Wisdom

8 Does not wisdom call,
And understanding lift up her voice?
2 On top of the heights beside the way,
Where the paths meet, she takes her
stand;

3 Beside the gates, at the opening to the
city,
At the entrance of the doors, she
cries out:
4 "To you, O men, I call,
And my voice is to the sons of men.
5 "O naive ones, understand prudence;
And, O fools, understand wisdom.
6 "Listen, for I will speak noble things;
And the opening of my lips *will reveal*
right things.
7 "For my mouth will utter truth;
And wickedness is an abomination to my
lips.
8 "All the utterances of my mouth are in
righteousness;
There is nothing crooked or perverted in
them.
9 "They are all straightforward to him who
understands,
And right to those who find knowledge.
10 "Take my instruction and not silver,
And knowledge rather than choicest gold.
11 "For wisdom is better than jewels;
And all desirable things cannot compare
with her.

12 ¶ "I, wisdom, dwell with prudence,
And I find knowledge *and* discretion.
13 "The fear of the LORD is to hate evil;
Pride and arrogance and the evil way
And the perverted mouth, I hate.

8:13 The Fear of the Lord

*The phrase "fear of the LORD" doesn't mean
fright or terror. It means "a good relationship
with God," based on reverence and respect for
him and his commands. Here, for instance, the
fear of the Lord means righteous living.*

14 "Counsel is mine and sound wisdom;
I am understanding, power is mine.
15 "By me kings reign,
And rulers decree justice.
16 "By me princes rule, and nobles,
All who judge rightly.
17 "I love those who love me;
And those who diligently seek me will
find me.
18 "Riches and honor are with me,
Enduring wealth and righteousness.
19 "My fruit is better than gold, even pure
gold,
And my yield *better* than choicest silver.
20 "I walk in the way of righteousness,
In the midst of the paths of justice,
21 To endow those who love me with
wealth,
That I may fill their treasuries.

22 ¶ "The LORD possessed me at the
  beginning of His way,
  Before His works of old.
23 "From everlasting I was established,
  From the beginning, from the earliest
  times of the earth.
24 "When there were no depths I was
  brought forth,
  When there were no springs abounding
  with water.
25 "Before the mountains were settled,
  Before the hills I was brought forth;
26 While He had not yet made the earth
  and the fields,
  Nor the first dust of the world.
27 "When He established the heavens, I was
  there,
  When He inscribed a circle on the face
  of the deep,
28 When He made firm the skies above,
  When the springs of the deep became
  fixed,
29 When He set for the sea its boundary
  So that the water would not transgress
  His command,
  When He marked out the foundations of
  the earth;
30 Then I was beside Him, *as* a master
  workman;
  And I was daily *His* delight,
  Rejoicing always before Him,
31 Rejoicing in the world, His earth,

And *having* my delight in the sons
  of men.

32 ¶ "Now therefore, O sons, listen to me,
  For blessed are they who keep my ways.
33 "Heed instruction and be wise,
  And do not neglect *it.*
34 "Blessed is the man who listens to me,
  Watching daily at my gates,
  Waiting at my doorposts.
35 "For he who finds me finds life
  And obtains favor from the LORD.
36 "But he who sins against me injures
  himself;
  All those who hate me love death."

Wisdom's Invitation

9 Wisdom has built her house,
  She has hewn out her seven pillars;
2 She has prepared her food, she has
  mixed her wine;
  She has also set her table;
3 She has sent out her maidens, she calls
  From the tops of the heights of the city:
4 "Whoever is naive, let him turn in here!"
  To him who lacks understanding she
  says,
5 "Come, eat of my food
  And drink of the wine I have mixed.
6 "Forsake *your* folly and live,
  And proceed in the way of
  understanding."

God and "How-to-Succeed"

Does Proverbs care more for success than for God?

> *The fear of the LORD is the beginning of wisdom. 9:10*

BOOKSTORES ARE FULL OF "HOW-TO" books, each promising to teach you how to make a success of yourself by just following a few simple rules. Is Proverbs an ancient "how-to" book? It seems, at first look, more interested in success and prosperity than in God. Many of the proverbs can be adopted by those who have no love for God.

But if you look at Proverbs as a book, rather than a collection of unrelated fragments, you will find that its "how-tos" of wise living can't be separated from God. While some proverbs observe the hard facts of life—that bribes are effective, for instance, or that money does buy friends of a kind—the book never for a moment endorses success techniques that involve immorality. More important, a deep sense of people's sin and their utter dependence on God pervades Proverbs. Wisdom, that fundamental tool for living, starts with the fear of God and leads to a knowledge of him.

The words *Lord* or *God* are actually mentioned nearly 100 times, so a complete study of God's place in Proverbs takes you through virtually the entire book.

Proverbs on God's relationship to wisdom: 1:7; 2:5–9; 8:22–31; 9:10; 22:17–19.
Proverbs on sin: 15:8; 16:6; 20:9; 24:11–12; 28:9,13.
Proverbs on trust in God: 3:5–12; 14:26–27; 16:20; 18:10; 19:21; 21:31; 29:25–26; 30:5–9.
Proverbs on God's blessing: 10:22,27,29; 15:16.
Other proverbs of particular interest: 11:1; 17:3; 19:3; 20:12; 21:3; 28:5.

Life Questions: What are your plans for success? Is God's will the basis of your plans, or is it an after-thought?

7 ¶ He who corrects a scoffer gets dishonor
for himself,
And he who reproves a wicked man *gets*
insults for himself.
8 Do not reprove a scoffer, or he will hate
you,
Reprove a wise man and he will love
you.
9 Give *instruction* to a wise man and he
will be still wiser,
Teach a righteous man and he will
increase *his* learning.
10 The fear of the LORD is the beginning of
wisdom,
And the knowledge of the Holy One is
understanding.
11 For by me your days will be multiplied,
And years of life will be added to you.
12 If you are wise, you are wise for yourself,
And if you scoff, you alone will bear it.

13 ¶ The woman of folly is boisterous,
She is naive and knows nothing.
14 She sits at the doorway of her house,
On a seat by the high places of the
city,
15 Calling to those who pass by,
Who are making their paths straight:
16 "Whoever is naive, let him turn in here,"
And to him who lacks understanding she
says,
17 "Stolen water is sweet;
And bread *eaten* in secret is pleasant."
18 But he does not know that the dead are
there,
That her guests are in the depths of
Sheol.

Contrast of the Righteous and the Wicked

10 The proverbs of Solomon.
A wise son makes a father glad,
But a foolish son is a grief to his mother.

10:1 Hebrew Poetry

"Parallelism" is a technical term for the form of Hebrew poetry that repeats a thought in slightly different ways. "Synonymous parallelism" is found in Proverbs 15:30, "Bright eyes gladden the heart; Good news puts fat on the bones." "Antithetical parallelism," in which a thought is followed by its opposite, is found in 14:30, "A tranquil heart is life to the body, but passion is rottenness to the bones."

In studying parallelism the trick is to compare each part with its pair in the other half of the proverb. For instance, in 14:30 "a tranquil heart" pairs with its opposite, "passion," and "rottenness to the bones" is the opposite of "is life to the body." Sometimes these comparisons bare subtle shades of meaning.

2 Ill-gotten gains do not profit,
But righteousness delivers from death.
3 The LORD will not allow the righteous to
hunger,
But He will reject the craving of the
wicked.
4 Poor is he who works with a negligent
hand,
But the hand of the diligent makes rich.
5 He who gathers in summer is a son who
acts wisely,

What Makes People Poor?
A clear-eyed view of wealth and poverty

POOR PEOPLE ARE LAZY," SAYS one person. Someone else claims the opposite: "They are poor because the rich control the system." People tend to oversimplify when they discuss wealth and poverty. Curiously, both sides may quote Proverbs to prove their point.

> *The rich man's wealth is his fortress, the ruin of the poor is their poverty.*
> 10:15

You have to read all of Proverbs to get its subtle view. It says people are poor for various reasons: because of laziness and drunkenness, but also because the rich oppress them. People get rich for various reasons too: because of hard work, because of the Lord's blessing, because they cheated.

Proverbs gives an evenhanded view of what money does for people. Wealth brings benefits, including eager friends, Proverbs says; but it also brings worries and troubles. Proverbs strongly urges the rich and powerful to be generous and fair to poor people. It remains remarkably clear-eyed about the tangled causes of poverty and about the dangers and benefits of wealth.

Proverbs on money: 10:4,15,22; 11:4,16,28; 13:8,18,22–23; 14:20,23,31; 15:16; 18:23; 19:1,4,17; 20:13; 21:5,17; 22:1–2,4,7,9,16,22–23; 23:5; 28:3,6,8,11,19,20,22,27; 29:7,14; 30:7–9.

Life Questions: Think of the richest and the poorest people you know. Have stereotypes about wealth and poverty affected your attitude toward them?

But he who sleeps in harvest is a son
who acts shamefully.
6 Blessings are on the head of the
righteous,
But the mouth of the wicked conceals
violence.
7 The memory of the righteous is blessed,
But the name of the wicked will rot.
8 The wise of heart will receive commands,
But a babbling fool will be ruined.
9 He who walks in integrity walks securely,
But he who perverts his ways will be
found out.
10 He who winks the eye causes trouble,
And a babbling fool will be ruined.
11 The mouth of the righteous is a fountain
of life,
But the mouth of the wicked conceals
violence.
12 Hatred stirs up strife,
But love covers all transgressions.

10:12 Love Is the Greatest

*If you think of love as restricted to the New
Testament, Proverbs will surprise you. Here
love is the all-purpose cure, covering all
wrongs. It is worth searching for. It should be
expressed openly.*

*Some of the proverbs on love are found in
the following passages: 3:3–4; 9:8; 10:12;
14:22; 15:17; 16:6; 17:9; 19:22; 20:6,28; 21:21;
27:5.*

13 On the lips of the discerning, wisdom is
found,
But a rod is for the back of him who
lacks understanding.
14 Wise men store up knowledge,
But with the mouth of the foolish, ruin is
at hand.
15 The rich man's wealth is his fortress,
The ruin of the poor is their poverty.
16 The wages of the righteous is life,
The income of the wicked, punishment.
17 He is *on* the path of life who heeds
instruction,
But he who ignores reproof goes astray.
18 He who conceals hatred *has* lying lips,
And he who spreads slander is a fool.
19 When there are many words,
transgression is unavoidable,
But he who restrains his lips is wise.
20 The tongue of the righteous is *as* choice
silver,
The heart of the wicked is *worth* little.
21 The lips of the righteous feed many,
But fools die for lack of understanding.
22 It is the blessing of the LORD that makes
rich,

And He adds no sorrow to it.
23 Doing wickedness is like sport to a fool,
And *so is* wisdom to a man of
understanding.
24 What the wicked fears will come upon
him,
But the desire of the righteous will be
granted.
25 When the whirlwind passes, the wicked is
no more,
But the righteous *has* an everlasting
foundation.
26 Like vinegar to the teeth and smoke to
the eyes,
So is the lazy one to those who send
him.
27 The fear of the LORD prolongs life,
But the years of the wicked will be
shortened.
28 The hope of the righteous is gladness,
But the expectation of the wicked
perishes.
29 The way of the LORD is a stronghold to
the upright,
But ruin to the workers of iniquity.
30 The righteous will never be shaken,
But the wicked will not dwell in the land.
31 The mouth of the righteous flows with
wisdom,
But the perverted tongue will be cut out.
32 The lips of the righteous bring forth what
is acceptable,
But the mouth of the wicked what is
perverted.

Contrast the Upright and the Wicked

11 A false balance is an abomination to the
LORD,
But a just weight is His delight.
2 When pride comes, then comes dishonor,
But with the humble is wisdom.
3 The integrity of the upright will guide
them,
But the crookedness of the treacherous
will destroy them.
4 Riches do not profit in the day of wrath,
But righteousness delivers from death.
5 The righteousness of the blameless will
smooth his way,
But the wicked will fall by his own
wickedness.
6 The righteousness of the upright will
deliver them,
But the treacherous will be caught by
their own greed.
7 When a wicked man dies, *his* expectation
will perish,
And the hope of strong men perishes.
8 The righteous is delivered from trouble,
But the wicked takes his place.

9 With *his* mouth the godless man destroys
his neighbor,
But through knowledge the righteous will
be delivered.
10 When it goes well with the righteous, the
city rejoices,
And when the wicked perish, there is
joyful shouting.
11 By the blessing of the upright a city is
exalted,
But by the mouth of the wicked it is torn
down.
12 He who despises his neighbor lacks
sense,
But a man of understanding keeps silent.
13 He who goes about as a talebearer
reveals secrets,
But he who is trustworthy conceals a
matter.
14 Where there is no guidance the people
fall,
But in abundance of counselors there is
victory.
15 He who is guarantor for a stranger will
surely suffer for it,
But he who hates being a guarantor is
secure.
16 A gracious woman attains honor,
And ruthless men attain riches.
17 The merciful man does himself good,
But the cruel man does himself harm.
18 The wicked earns deceptive wages,
But he who sows righteousness *gets* a
true reward.
19 He who is steadfast in righteousness *will
attain* to life,
And he who pursues evil *will bring about*
his own death.
20 The perverse in heart are an abomination
to the LORD,
But the blameless in *their* walk are His
delight.
21 Assuredly, the evil man will not go
unpunished,
But the descendants of the righteous will
be delivered.
22 *As* a ring of gold in a swine's snout
So is a beautiful woman who lacks
ᵃdiscretion.
23 The desire of the righteous is only good,

But the expectation of the wicked is
wrath.
24 There is one who scatters, and *yet*
increases all the more,
And there is one who withholds what is
justly due, *and yet it results* only in
want.
25 The generous man will be prosperous,
And he who waters will himself be
watered.
26 He who withholds grain, the people will
curse him,
But blessing will be on the head of him
who sells *it.*
27 He who diligently seeks good seeks favor,
But he who seeks evil, evil will come to
him.
28 He who trusts in his riches will fall,
But the righteous will flourish like the
green leaf.
29 He who troubles his own house will
inherit wind,
And the foolish will be servant to the
wisehearted.
30 The fruit of the righteous is a tree of life,
And he who is wise wins souls.
31 If the righteous will be rewarded in the
earth,
How much more the wicked and the
sinner!

Contrast the Upright and the Wicked

12 Whoever loves discipline loves knowledge,
But he who hates reproof is stupid.
2 A good man will obtain favor from the
LORD,
But He will condemn a man who devises
evil.
3 A man will not be established by
wickedness,
But the root of the righteous will not be
moved.
4 An excellent wife is the crown of her
husband,
But she who shames *him* is like
rottenness in his bones.
5 The thoughts of the righteous are just,
But the counsels of the wicked are
deceitful.
6 The words of the wicked lie in wait for
blood,
But the mouth of the upright will deliver
them.
7 The wicked are overthrown and are no
more,
But the house of the righteous will stand.
8 A man will be praised according to his
insight,
But one of perverse mind will be
despised.

11:22 Skin-deep Beauty

*Throughout Proverbs, character is what counts.
When not matched by inward beauty, good
looks seem ridiculous, as this saying
humorously suggests.*

ᵃ Lit *taste*

9 Better is he who is lightly esteemed and
    has a servant
Than he who honors himself and lacks
    bread.
10 A righteous man has regard for the life
    of his animal,
But *even* the compassion of the wicked is
    cruel.
11 He who tills his land will have plenty of
    bread,
But he who pursues worthless *things*
    lacks sense.
12 The wicked man desires the booty of evil
    men,
But the root of the righteous yields *fruit.*
13 An evil man is ensnared by the
    transgression of his lips,
But the righteous will escape from
    trouble.
14 A man will be satisfied with good by the
    fruit of his words,
And the deeds of a man's hands will
    return to him.
15 The way of a fool is right in his own
    eyes,
But a wise man is he who listens to
    counsel.
16 A fool's anger is known at once,
But a prudent man conceals dishonor.
17 He who speaks truth tells what is right,
But a false witness, deceit.

12:17 Deeper Meanings

*Some proverbs, disarmingly obvious at first
glance, offer deep truth when chewed on. For
instance, verse 17 seems to merely repeat the
obvious. But its underlying meaning is that a
person's character determines his or her
actions. You can reflect at length on what this
implies about why you do what you do.*

18 There is one who speaks rashly like the
    thrusts of a sword,
But the tongue of the wise brings healing.
19 Truthful lips will be established forever,
But a lying tongue is only for a moment.
20 Deceit is in the heart of those who devise
    evil,
But counselors of peace have joy.
21 No harm befalls the righteous,
But the wicked are filled with trouble.
22 Lying lips are an abomination to the
    LORD,
But those who deal faithfully are His
    delight.
23 A prudent man conceals knowledge,
But the heart of fools proclaims folly.

24 The hand of the diligent will rule,
But the slack *hand* will be put to forced
    labor.
25 Anxiety in a man's heart weighs it down,
But a good word makes it glad.
26 The righteous is a guide to his neighbor,
But the way of the wicked leads them
    astray.
27 A lazy man does not roast his prey,
But the precious possession of a man *is*
    diligence.
28 In the way of righteousness is life,
And in *its* pathway there is no death.

Contrast the Upright and the Wicked

13 A wise son *accepts his* father's discipline,
    But a scoffer does not listen to rebuke.
2 From the fruit of a man's mouth he
    enjoys good,
But the desire of the treacherous is
    violence.
3 The one who guards his mouth preserves
    his life;
The one who opens wide his lips comes
    to ruin.
4 The soul of the sluggard craves and *gets*
    nothing,
But the soul of the diligent is made fat.
5 A righteous man hates falsehood,
But a wicked man acts disgustingly and
    shamefully.
6 Righteousness guards the one whose way
    is blameless,
But wickedness subverts the sinner.
7 There is one who pretends to be rich,
    but has nothing;
Another pretends to be poor, but has
    great wealth.
8 The ransom of a man's life is his wealth,
But the poor hears no rebuke.
9 The light of the righteous ªrejoices,
But the lamp of the wicked goes out.
10 Through insolence comes nothing but
    strife,
But wisdom is with those who receive
    counsel.
11 Wealth *obtained* by fraud dwindles,
But the one who gathers by labor
    increases *it.*
12 Hope deferred makes the heart sick,
But desire fulfilled is a tree of life.
13 The one who despises the word will be in
    debt to it,
But the one who fears the commandment
    will be rewarded.
14 The teaching of the wise is a fountain of
    life,
To turn aside from the snares of death.
15 Good understanding produces favor,
But the way of the treacherous is hard.

ª I.e. shines brightly

16 Every prudent man acts with knowledge,
   But a fool displays folly.
17 A wicked messenger falls into adversity,
   But a faithful envoy *brings* healing.
18 Poverty and shame *will come* to him who
      neglects discipline,
   But he who regards reproof will be
      honored.
19 Desire realized is sweet to the soul,
   But it is an abomination to fools to turn
      away from evil.
20 He who walks with wise men will be
      wise,
   But the companion of fools will suffer
      harm.
21 Adversity pursues sinners,
   But the righteous will be rewarded with
      prosperity.
22 A good man leaves an inheritance to his
      children's children,
   And the wealth of the sinner is stored up
      for the righteous.
23 Abundant food *is in* the fallow ground of
      the poor,
   But it is swept away by injustice.
24 He who withholds his rod hates his son,
   But he who loves him disciplines him
      diligently.
25 The righteous has enough to satisfy his
      appetite,
   But the stomach of the wicked is in need.

Contrast the Upright and the Wicked

14 The wise woman builds her house,
   But the foolish tears it down with her
      own hands.

2 He who walks in his uprightness fears
      the LORD,
   But he who is devious in his ways
      despises Him.
3 In the mouth of the foolish is a rod for
      his back,
   But the lips of the wise will protect them.
4 Where no oxen are, the manger is clean,
   But much revenue *comes* by the strength
      of the ox.
5 A trustworthy witness will not lie,
   But a false witness utters lies.
6 A scoffer seeks wisdom and *finds* none,
   But knowledge is easy to one who has
      understanding.
7 Leave the presence of a fool,
   Or you will not discern words of
      knowledge.
8 The wisdom of the sensible is to
      understand his way,
   But the foolishness of fools is deceit.
9 Fools mock at sin,
   But among the upright there is good will.
10 The heart knows its own bitterness,
   And a stranger does not share its joy.
11 The house of the wicked will be
      destroyed,
   But the tent of the upright will flourish.
12 There is a way *which seems* right to a
      man,
   But its end is the way of death.
13 Even in laughter the heart may be in
      pain,
   And the end of joy may be grief.
14 The backslider in heart will have his fill
      of his own ways,
   But a good man will *be satisfied* with his.

The Supreme Gift of Wisdom
First, learn to listen

PROVERBS JUDGES EVERY THOUGHT OR action by one standard: "Is this wise?" The word *wisdom* brings up pictures of gray-haired old men muttering obscure philosophic maxims. But that is almost the opposite of what Proverbs means by the word. Wisdom is above all practical and down to earth. Young people as well as old can and should have it. Wisdom teaches you how to live. It combines understanding with discipline— the kind of discipline an athlete needs in training. It also adds a healthy dose of good common sense—except that common sense isn't, and never has been, common.

How do you become a wise person? You must first begin to listen. Wisdom is freely available to those who will stop talking and start paying attention—to God and his Word, to parents, to wise counselors. Anybody can become wise, Proverbs says. Wisdom is not reserved for a brainy elite. But becoming wise requires self-discipline to study and humbly seek wisdom at every opportunity.

Proverbs on becoming a wise person: 2:1–6; 9:1–10; 10:1,5,8,14,19,23; 11:2; 12:18; 13:10,20; 14:8; 15:7,31; 16:23; 17:24; 18:15; 19:11,20; 20:1; 21:11,20,30; 23:4; 29:3,8,11,15; 30:5–6.

> *He who walks with wise men will be wise, but the companion of fools will suffer harm.*
> 13:20

Life Questions: Think over the last two years of your life. To whom do you listen? Who has the greatest influence on you?

15 The naive believes everything,
But the sensible man considers his steps.
16 A wise man is cautious and turns away
from evil,
But a fool is arrogant and careless.

14:12 Be Careful

Proverbs offers common sense, but doesn't encourage simply trusting your own sense. Choices that seem perfectly right may end up destroying you. That is precisely why people need to cultivate wisdom: What looks good often isn't.

17 A quick-tempered man acts foolishly,
And a man of evil devices is hated.
18 The naive inherit foolishness,
But the sensible are crowned with
knowledge.
19 The evil will bow down before the good,
And the wicked at the gates of the
righteous.
20 The poor is hated even by his neighbor,
But those who love the rich are many.

14:20 Lucky Rich

Rich people have many friends, whereas the poor often get ignored. That's the way life is. But, according to the next proverb (verse 21), life isn't meant to be "the way it is." Verse 31 goes on to show God himself closely involved in the way we treat poor people.

a Or *reverence*

21 He who despises his neighbor sins,
But happy is he who is gracious to the
poor.
22 Will they not go astray who devise evil?
But kindness and truth *will be to* those
who devise good.
23 In all labor there is profit,
But mere talk *leads* only to poverty.
24 The crown of the wise is their riches,
But the folly of fools is foolishness.
25 A truthful witness saves lives,
But he who utters lies is treacherous.
26 In the *a*fear of the LORD there is strong
confidence,
And his children will have refuge.
27 The *a*fear of the LORD is a fountain of
life,
That one may avoid the snares of death.
28 In a multitude of people is a king's glory,
But in the dearth of people is a prince's
ruin.
29 He who is slow to anger has great
understanding,
But he who is quick-tempered exalts
folly.
30 A tranquil heart is life to the body,
But passion is rottenness to the bones.
31 He who oppresses the poor taunts his
Maker,
But he who is gracious to the needy
honors Him.
32 The wicked is thrust down by his
wrongdoing,
But the righteous has a refuge when he
dies.
33 Wisdom rests in the heart of one who
has understanding,

A Matter of Life and Death

More than mere survival

PROVERBS FREQUENTLY TALKS ABOUT LIFE and death. Wise living, it says, tends to make you live longer, while foolish living will push you into an early grave.

If you take this observation at face value, you'll have a problem: Plenty of people who live foolishly survive into old age. But the concept of life and death in Proverbs includes much more than physical survival. By life, Proverbs means "real living" full of peace and joy and wisdom. By death, it means spiritual as well as physical decay. A person who misses the way of wisdom may be as good as dead, even though he or she is still walking around.

Proverbs on "real living": 3:18,21–22; 4:23; 8:34–36; 10:11,16; 12:28; 13:12; 14:27,30; 15:4,27; 18:21; 19:23; 21:21; 28:16.
Proverbs on "real dying": 2:16–18; 5:3–6,22–23; 10:21; 14:12,32; 15:10; 19:16; 21:25; 27:20.

> There is a way which seems right to a man, but its end is the way of death.
> 14:12

Life Questions: Can you remember a specific experience that represents, for you, "real living"? How about "real dying"?

But in the hearts of fools it is made
    known.
34 Righteousness exalts a nation,
    But sin is a disgrace to *any* people.
35 The king's favor is toward a servant who
        acts wisely,
    But his anger is toward him who acts
        shamefully.

Contrast the Upright and the Wicked

15 A gentle answer turns away wrath,
    But a harsh word stirs up anger.
2 The tongue of the wise makes knowledge
        acceptable,
    But the mouth of fools spouts folly.
3 The eyes of the LORD are in every place,
    Watching the evil and the good.
4 A soothing tongue is a tree of life,
    But perversion in it crushes the spirit.
5 A fool rejects his father's discipline,
    But he who regards reproof is sensible.
6 Great wealth is *in* the house of the
        righteous,
    But trouble is in the income of the
        wicked.
7 The lips of the wise spread knowledge,
    But the hearts of fools are not so.
8 The sacrifice of the wicked is an
        abomination to the LORD,
    But the prayer of the upright is His
        delight.
9 The way of the wicked is an abomination
        to the LORD,
    But He loves one who pursues
        righteousness.
10 Grievous punishment is for him who
        forsakes the way;
    He who hates reproof will die.
11 Sheol and Abaddon *lie open* before the
        LORD,
    How much more the hearts of men!
12 A scoffer does not love one who reproves
        him,
    He will not go to the wise.
13 A joyful heart makes a cheerful face,
    But when the heart is sad, the spirit is
        broken.
14 The mind of the intelligent seeks
        knowledge,
    But the mouth of fools feeds on folly.
15 All the days of the afflicted are bad,
    But a cheerful heart *has* a continual feast.
16 Better is a little with the fear of the LORD
    Than great treasure and turmoil with it.
17 Better is a dish of vegetables where
        love is
    Than a fattened ox *served* with hatred.
18 A hot-tempered man stirs up strife,
    But the slow to anger calms a dispute.
19 The way of the lazy is as a hedge of
        thorns,

But the path of the upright is a highway.
20 A wise son makes a father glad,
    But a foolish man despises his mother.
21 Folly is joy to him who lacks sense,
    But a man of understanding walks
        straight.
22 Without consultation, plans are
        frustrated,
    But with many counselors they succeed.
23 A man has joy in an apt answer,
    And how delightful is a timely word!
24 The path of life *leads* upward for the
        wise
    That he may keep away from Sheol
        below.
25 The LORD will tear down the house of
        the proud,
    But He will establish the boundary of the
        widow.

15:25 Poor and Helpless

*In Old Testament society the most helpless
person was the widow. With no one to protect
her, she could only watch as her late husband's
land was grabbed by bullying neighbors. But a
widow was never completely helpless. The Lord
was on her side. In the final analysis her
condition was more secure than that of her
proud, rich neighbor.*

26 Evil plans are an abomination to the
        LORD,
    But pleasant words are pure.
27 He who profits illicitly troubles his own
        house,
    But he who hates bribes will live.
28 The heart of the righteous ponders how
        to answer,
    But the mouth of the wicked pours out
        evil things.
29 The LORD is far from the wicked,
    But He hears the prayer of the righteous.
30 Bright eyes gladden the heart;
    Good news puts fat on the bones.
31 He whose ear listens to the life-giving
        reproof
    Will dwell among the wise.
32 He who neglects discipline despises
        himself,
    But he who listens to reproof acquires
        understanding.
33 The fear of the LORD is the instruction
        for wisdom,
    And before honor *comes* humility.

Contrast the Upright and the Wicked

16 The plans of the heart belong to man,
    But the answer of the tongue is from the
        LORD.

2 All the ways of a man are clean in his
  own sight,
  But the LORD weighs the motives.
3 Commit your works to the LORD
  And your plans will be established.
4 The LORD has made everything for its
  own purpose,
  Even the wicked for the day of evil.
5 Everyone who is proud in heart is an
  abomination to the LORD;
  Assuredly, he will not be unpunished.
6 By lovingkindness and truth iniquity is
  atoned for,
  And by the fear of the LORD one keeps
  away from evil.
7 When a man's ways are pleasing to the
  LORD,
  He makes even his enemies to be at
  peace with him.
8 Better is a little with righteousness
  Than great income with injustice.
9 The mind of man plans his way,
  But the LORD directs his steps.
10 A divine decision is in the lips of the
  king;
  His mouth should not err in judgment.
11 A just balance and scales belong to the
  LORD;
  All the weights of the bag are His
  concern.
12 It is an abomination for kings to commit
  wicked acts,
  For a throne is established on
  righteousness.
13 Righteous lips are the delight of kings,
  And he who speaks right is loved.

14 The fury of a king is *like* messengers of
  death,
  But a wise man will appease it.
15 In the light of a king's face is life,
  And his favor is like a cloud with the
  spring rain.
16 How much better it is to get wisdom
  than gold!
  And to get understanding is to be chosen
  above silver.
17 The highway of the upright is to depart
  from evil;
  He who watches his way preserves his
  life.
18 Pride *goes* before destruction,
  And a haughty spirit before stumbling.
19 It is better to be humble in spirit with
  the lowly
  Than to divide the spoil with the proud.
20 He who gives attention to the word will
  find good,
  And blessed is he who trusts in the
  LORD.
21 The wise in heart will be called
  understanding,
  And sweetness of speech increases
  persuasiveness.
22 Understanding is a fountain of life to one
  who has it,
  But the discipline of fools is folly.
23 The heart of the wise instructs his mouth
  And adds persuasiveness to his lips.
24 Pleasant words are a honeycomb,
  Sweet to the soul and healing to the
  bones.
25 There is a way *which seems* right to a
  man,

Verbal Dynamite

Even truthful words can damage other people

WHAT COULD BE WRONG WITH just talking, as long as you
don't actually lie? Proverbs sees plenty of danger. Words are dynamite;
they can destroy people. They should be carefully weighed before they are
spoken. Even truthful words can damage. Yet they can also save a friend
from going wrong. Proverbs speaks strongly about both the danger of gossip
and the good done when someone justly rebukes his or her friend.

> *A perverse man spreads strife, and a slanderer separates intimate friends.*
> 16:28

"Death and life are in the power of the tongue," Proverbs 18:21 says, "and those who love it will
eat its fruit." Proverbs teaches the skill of speaking so as to give life.

Proverbs on the importance of words: 10:11,20; 12:14; 15:4; 17:10; 18:21; 25:11.
Proverbs on the wrong way to speak: 6:16–19; 11:9,12–13; 12:18; 13:3; 16:27–28; 18:8,13; 26:23–28;
29:5.
Proverbs on the right way to speak: 10:14,21,32; 12:25; 15:1,23,28; 16:13,23–24; 17:27–28; 25:12,15;
27:5–6; 28:23.
Proverbs on the dangers of words: 10:19; 14:23.

Life Questions: Have you said anything recently that you wish you could take back? What are the most
life-giving words you've spoken lately?

But its end is the way of death.

26 A worker's appetite works for him,
For his hunger urges him *on.*

27 A worthless man digs up evil,
While his words are like scorching fire.

28 A perverse man spreads strife,
And a slanderer separates intimate friends.

29 A man of violence entices his neighbor
And leads him in a way that is not good.

30 He who winks his eyes *does so* to devise perverse things;
He who compresses his lips brings evil to pass.

31 A gray head is a crown of glory;
It is found in the way of righteousness.

32 He who is slow to anger is better than the mighty,
And he who rules his spirit, than he who captures a city.

33 The lot is cast into the lap,
But its every decision is from the LORD.

Contrast the Upright and the Wicked

17 Better is a dry morsel and quietness with it
Than a house full of feasting with strife.

2 A servant who acts wisely will rule over a son who acts shamefully,
And will share in the inheritance among brothers.

3 The refining pot is for silver and the furnace for gold,
But the LORD tests hearts.

4 An evildoer listens to wicked lips;
A liar pays attention to a destructive tongue.

5 He who mocks the poor taunts his Maker;
He who rejoices at calamity will not go unpunished.

6 Grandchildren are the crown of old men,
And the glory of sons is their fathers.

7 Excellent speech is not fitting for a fool,
Much less are lying lips to a prince.

8 A bribe is a charm in the sight of its owner;
Wherever he turns, he prospers.

9 He who conceals a transgression seeks love,

17:8 Bribery Works Wonders!

Proverbs is utterly realistic about the hard facts of life. One is that bribery works. A complete education ought to include that fact! But does that make bribery right? No—just a few verses later (verse 23), Proverbs condemns bribery.

But he who repeats a matter separates intimate friends.

10 A rebuke goes deeper into one who has understanding
Than a hundred blows into a fool.

11 A rebellious man seeks only evil,
So a cruel messenger will be sent against him.

12 Let a man meet a bear robbed of her cubs,
Rather than a fool in his folly.

13 He who returns evil for good,
Evil will not depart from his house.

14 The beginning of strife is *like* letting out water,
So abandon the quarrel before it breaks out.

15 He who justifies the wicked and he who condemns the righteous,
Both of them alike are an abomination to the LORD.

16 Why is there a price in the hand of a fool to buy wisdom,
When he has no sense?

17 A friend loves at all times,
And a brother is born for adversity.

17:17 How to Be a Good Friend

The Old Testament puts great emphasis on close family relationships. Surprisingly, Proverbs rates a good friend even higher, for he or she "sticks closer than a brother" (18:24). Fair-weather friends are common (14:20), and the wrong kind of companions will bring you trouble. But a true friend loves you at all times, even when things are bad.

Some key proverbs on being a good friend and neighbor can be found in the following passages: 3:27–28; 11:12; 12:26; 17:9,17; 18:24; 22:24–25; 25:20; 26:18–19; 27:6,9–10,14,17; 28:23; 29:5.

18 A man lacking in sense pledges
And becomes guarantor in the presence of his neighbor.

19 He who loves transgression loves strife;
He who raises his door seeks destruction.

20 He who has a crooked mind finds no good,
And he who is perverted in his language falls into evil.

21 He who sires a fool *does so* to his sorrow,
And the father of a fool has no joy.

22 A joyful heart is good medicine,
But a broken spirit dries up the bones.

23 A wicked man receives a bribe from the bosom
To pervert the ways of justice.

24 Wisdom is in the presence of the one
  who has understanding,
  But the eyes of a fool are on the ends of
  the earth.
25 A foolish son is a grief to his father
  And bitterness to her who bore him.
26 It is also not good to fine the righteous,
  Nor to strike the noble for *their*
  uprightness.
27 He who restrains his words has
  knowledge,
  And he who has a cool spirit is a man of
  understanding.
28 Even a fool, when he keeps silent, is
  considered wise;
  When he closes his lips, he is *considered*
  prudent.

Contrast the Upright and the Wicked

18 He who separates himself seeks *his own*
  desire,
  He quarrels against all sound wisdom.
2 A fool does not delight in understanding,
  But only in revealing his own mind.
3 When a wicked man comes, contempt
  also comes,
  And with dishonor *comes* scorn.
4 The words of a man's mouth are deep
  waters;
  The fountain of wisdom is a bubbling
  brook.
5 To show partiality to the wicked is not
  good,
  Nor to thrust aside the righteous in
  judgment.
6 A fool's lips bring strife,
  And his mouth calls for blows.
7 A fool's mouth is his ruin,
  And his lips are the snare of his soul.
8 The words of a whisperer are like dainty
  morsels,
  And they go down into the innermost
  parts of the body.
9 He also who is slack in his work
  Is brother to him who destroys.
10 The name of the LORD is a strong tower;
  The righteous runs into it and is safe.
11 A rich man's wealth is his strong city,
  And like a high wall in his own
  imagination.
12 Before destruction the heart of man is
  haughty,
  But humility *goes* before honor.
13 He who gives an answer before he hears,
  It is folly and shame to him.
14 The spirit of a man can endure his
  sickness,
  But *as for* a broken spirit who can
  bear it?
15 The mind of the prudent acquires
  knowledge,

And the ear of the wise seeks knowledge.
16 A man's gift makes room for him
  And brings him before great men.
17 The first to plead his case *seems* right,
  Until another comes and examines him.
18 The *cast* lot puts an end to strife
  And decides between the mighty ones.
19 A brother offended *is harder to be won*
  than a strong city,
  And contentions are like the bars of a
  citadel.
20 With the fruit of a man's mouth his
  stomach will be satisfied;
  He will be satisfied *with* the product of
  his lips.
21 Death and life are in the power of the
  tongue,
  And those who love it will eat its fruit.
22 He who finds a wife finds a good thing
  And obtains favor from the LORD.
23 The poor man utters supplications,
  But the rich man answers roughly.
24 A man of *too many* friends *comes* to
  ruin,
  But there is a friend who sticks closer
  than a brother.

On Life and Conduct

19 Better is a poor man who walks in his
  integrity
  Than he who is perverse in speech and is
  a fool.
2 Also it is not good for a person to be
  without knowledge,
  And he who hurries his footsteps errs.
3 The foolishness of man ruins his way,
  And his heart rages against the LORD.
4 Wealth adds many friends,
  But a poor man is separated from his
  friend.
5 A false witness will not go unpunished,
  And he who tells lies will not escape.
6 Many will seek the favor of a generous
  man,
  And every man is a friend to him who
  gives gifts.
7 All the brothers of a poor man hate him;
  How much more do his friends
  abandon him!
  He pursues *them with* words, *but they*
  are gone.
8 He who gets wisdom loves his own soul;
  He who keeps understanding will find
  good.
9 A false witness will not go unpunished,
  And he who tells lies will perish.
10 Luxury is not fitting for a fool;
  Much less for a slave to rule over
  princes.
11 A man's discretion makes him slow to
  anger,

And it is his glory to overlook a transgression.
12 The king's wrath is like the roaring of a lion,
But his favor is like dew on the grass.
13 A foolish son is destruction to his father,
And the contentions of a wife are a constant dripping.
14 House and wealth are an inheritance from fathers,
But a prudent wife is from the LORD.
15 Laziness casts into a deep sleep,
And an idle man will suffer hunger.
16 He who keeps the commandment keeps his soul,
But he who is careless of conduct will die.
17 One who is gracious to a poor man lends to the LORD,
And He will repay him for his good deed.
18 Discipline your son while there is hope,
And do not desire his death.
19 *A man of* great anger will bear the penalty,
For if you rescue *him,* you will only have to do it again.
20 Listen to counsel and accept discipline,
That you may be wise the rest of your days.
21 Many plans are in a man's heart,
But the counsel of the LORD will stand.
22 What is desirable in a man is his ªkindness,
And *it is* better to be a poor man than a liar.
23 The fear of the LORD *leads* to life,
So that one may sleep satisfied, untouched by evil.
24 The sluggard buries his hand in the dish,
But will not even bring it back to his mouth.
25 Strike a scoffer and the naive may become shrewd,
But reprove one who has understanding and he will gain knowledge.
26 He who assaults *his* father *and* drives *his* mother away
Is a shameful and disgraceful son.
27 Cease listening, my son, to discipline,
And you will stray from the words of knowledge.
28 A rascally witness makes a mockery of justice,
And the mouth of the wicked spreads iniquity.
29 Judgments are prepared for scoffers,
And blows for the back of fools.

ª Or *loyalty*

On Life and Conduct

20 Wine is a mocker, strong drink a brawler,
And whoever is intoxicated by it is not wise.
2 The terror of a king is like the growling of a lion;
He who provokes him to anger forfeits his own life.
3 Keeping away from strife is an honor for a man,
But any fool will quarrel.
4 The sluggard does not plow after the autumn,
So he begs during the harvest and has nothing.
5 A plan in the heart of a man is *like* deep water,
But a man of understanding draws it out.
6 Many a man proclaims his own loyalty,
But who can find a trustworthy man?
7 A righteous man who walks in his integrity—
How blessed are his sons after him.
8 A king who sits on the throne of justice
Disperses all evil with his eyes.
9 Who can say, "I have cleansed my heart,
I am pure from my sin"?
10 Differing weights and differing measures,
Both of them are abominable to the LORD.
11 It is by his deeds that a lad distinguishes himself
If his conduct is pure and right.
12 The hearing ear and the seeing eye,
The LORD has made both of them.
13 Do not love sleep, or you will become poor;
Open your eyes, *and* you will be satisfied with food.
14 "Bad, bad," says the buyer,
But when he goes his way, then he boasts.
15 There is gold, and an abundance of jewels;
But the lips of knowledge are a more precious thing.
16 Take his garment when he becomes surety for a stranger;
And for foreigners, hold him in pledge.
17 Bread obtained by falsehood is sweet to a man,
But afterward his mouth will be filled with gravel.
18 Prepare plans by consultation,
And make war by wise guidance.
19 He who goes about as a slanderer reveals secrets,
Therefore do not associate with a gossip.

20 He who curses his father or his mother,
His lamp will go out in time of darkness.
21 An inheritance gained hurriedly at the
beginning
Will not be blessed in the end.
22 Do not say, "I will repay evil";
Wait for the LORD, and He will save you.
23 Differing weights are an abomination to
the LORD,
And a false scale is not good.
24 Man's steps are *ordained* by the LORD,
How then can man understand his way?
25 It is a trap for a man to say rashly, "It is
holy!"
And after the vows to make inquiry.
26 A wise king winnows the wicked,
And drives the *threshing* wheel over
them.
27 The spirit of man is the lamp of the
LORD,
Searching all the innermost parts of his
being.
28 Loyalty and truth preserve the king,
And he upholds his throne by
righteousness.
29 The glory of young men is their strength,
And the honor of old men is their gray
hair.
30 Stripes that wound scour away evil,
And strokes *reach* the innermost parts.

On Life and Conduct

21 The king's heart is *like* channels of water
in the hand of the LORD;
He turns it wherever He wishes.
2 Every man's way is right in his own eyes,
But the LORD weighs the hearts.
3 To do righteousness and justice
Is desired by the LORD more than
sacrifice.
4 Haughty eyes and a proud heart,
The lamp of the wicked, is sin.
5 The plans of the diligent *lead* surely to
advantage,
But everyone who is hasty *comes* surely
to poverty.
6 The acquisition of treasures by a lying
tongue
Is a fleeting vapor, the pursuit of death.
7 The violence of the wicked will drag
them away,
Because they refuse to act with justice.
8 The way of a guilty man is crooked,
But as for the pure, his conduct is
upright.
9 It is better to live in a corner of a roof
Than in a house shared with a
contentious woman.
10 The soul of the wicked desires evil;
His neighbor finds no favor in his eyes.
11 When the scoffer is punished, the naive
becomes wise;
But when the wise is instructed, he
receives knowledge.
12 The righteous one considers the house of
the wicked,
Turning the wicked to ruin.
13 He who shuts his ear to the cry of the
poor
Will also cry himself and not be
answered.
14 A gift in secret subdues anger,

Whom Should You Marry?

A good partner can make or break your life

> It is better to live in a corner of a roof than in a house shared with a contentious woman.
> 21:9

IN ANCIENT TIMES WOMEN WERE often viewed as men's property, good for bearing children and not much more. Proverbs, addressed to young men approaching the age of marriage, takes a different view. It holds up marriage as a crucial choice, to be made with great care.

A good wife (or husband, we can assume) will make or break her partner's life. Her duties lay the foundation for her family's welfare (14:1; 31:10–31). She shares with her husband the most significant task of teaching their children the way of wisdom (1:8–9; 6:20). Therefore, her character matters far more than her physical beauty.

Not that Proverbs ignores the physical side of love. It urges marriage partners to rejoice in their love, to be captivated by it (5:18–19). It warns young people against sexual sin precisely because this wastes sexuality on unsatisfying, unloving relationships. Sex ought to be saved for the long-lasting, productive joy of marriage.

Proverbs on sexual sin: 2:16–19; 5:1–23; 6:20–35; 7:6–27; 23:26–28.
Proverbs on marriage: 5:15–19; 12:4; 14:1; 18:22; 19:13–14; 21:9,19; 27:15–16; 31:10–31.

Life Questions: What do you look for in a mate? How does your list compare with Proverbs's rating of attributes such as physical attractiveness?

And a bribe in the bosom, strong wrath.
15 The exercise of justice is joy for the
righteous,
But is terror to the workers of iniquity.

21:11 Learning the Easy Way

*"The naive"—those who live without thinking—
are rarely persuaded to change, because they
don't listen. One lesson may get through to
them, though: seeing a troublemaker—the
"scoffer"—get punished. Wise people learn in a
much less painful way. When told something,
they pay attention.*

16 A man who wanders from the way of
understanding
Will rest in the assembly of the dead.
17 He who loves pleasure *will become* a
poor man;
He who loves wine and oil will not
become rich.
18 The wicked is a ransom for the
righteous,
And the treacherous is in the place of the
upright.
19 It is better to live in a desert land
Than with a contentious and vexing
woman.
20 There is precious treasure and oil in the
dwelling of the wise,
But a foolish man swallows it up.
21 He who pursues righteousness and
loyalty
Finds life, righteousness and honor.
22 A wise man scales the city of the mighty

And brings down the stronghold in
which they trust.
23 He who guards his mouth and his
tongue,
Guards his soul from troubles.
24 "Proud," "Haughty," "Scoffer," are his
names,
Who acts with insolent pride.
25 The desire of the sluggard puts him to
death,
For his hands refuse to work;
26 All day long he is craving,
While the righteous gives and does not
hold back.
27 The sacrifice of the wicked is an
abomination,
How much more when he brings it with
evil intent!
28 A false witness will perish,
But the man who listens *to the truth* will
speak forever.
29 A wicked man displays a bold face,
But as for the upright, he makes his way
sure.
30 There is no wisdom and no
understanding
And no counsel against the LORD.
31 The horse is prepared for the day of
battle,
But victory belongs to the LORD.

On Life and Conduct

22 A *good* name is to be more desired than
great wealth,
Favor is better than silver and gold.
2 The rich and the poor have a common
bond,
The LORD is the maker of them all.

How to Raise Children
Family members should be allies, not adversaries

"SPARE THE ROD AND SPOIL the child" may be the most
famous of the Bible's proverbs. Proverbs calls punishment a form of love
and says that parents who won't discipline their children are in danger of
ruining them (29:15). But that much-quoted maxim is only a small part of
what Proverbs has to offer on the subject of bringing up children.

The overwhelming emphasis of Proverbs is on verbal encouragement and
teaching. The whole book is framed as a father's words to his son, teaching him
those "facts of life" that have nothing to do with biology. Again and again he pleads, "Listen, my son."
Mother has equally important words (1:8; 6:20). The parent-child conversation is a warm one, and
Proverbs 17:6 bears out what the whole book implies: Parents and children are not meant to be adversaries, but allies in life who are proud of each other.

> Train up a child in
> the way he should
> go, even when he is
> old he will not
> depart from it.
> 22:6

Proverbs on parent-child relationships: 3:11–12; 10:1,5; 13:1,24; 14:26; 15:20; 17:6,21; 19:18,26–27;
20:20; 22:6,15; 23:13–16,22–25; 27:11; 29:15,17; 31:28.

Life Questions: In your upbringing, which had the most effect: punishment and discipline, or verbal
instruction and encouragement?

3 The prudent sees the evil and hides
himself,
But the naive go on, and are punished
for it.
4 The reward of humility *and* the fear of
the LORD
Are riches, honor and life.
5 Thorns *and* snares are in the way of the
perverse;
He who guards himself will be far from
them.
6 Train up a child in the way he
should go,
Even when he is old he will not depart
from it.

22:6 Good Parenting

*An individual proverb shouldn't be read as
either an invariable rule or a binding promise
from God. Proverbs 10:4 generalizes truthfully,
"the hand of the diligent makes rich," but you
would not have to look too far to find an
exception to the rule. Verse 6, a famous
proverb, reinforces the importance of early
training in forming a person's lifelong
character. But you can find individuals who,
though well brought up, choose to reject their
training. Proverbs studies life the way it
normally works. The general rule is this: Good
parents raise good children.*

7 The rich rules over the poor,
And the borrower *becomes* the lender's
slave.
8 He who sows iniquity will reap vanity,
And the rod of his fury will perish.
9 He who is generous will be blessed,
For he gives some of his food to the
poor.
10 Drive out the scoffer, and contention will
go out,
Even strife and dishonor will cease.
11 He who loves purity of heart
And whose speech is gracious, the king is
his friend.
12 The eyes of the LORD preserve
knowledge,
But He overthrows the words of the
treacherous man.
13 The sluggard says, "There is a lion
outside;
I will be killed in the streets!"
14 The mouth of an adulteress is a deep pit;
He who is cursed of the LORD will fall
into it.
15 Foolishness is bound up in the heart of a
child;
The rod of discipline will remove it far
from him.

16 He who oppresses the poor to make
more for himself
Or who gives to the rich, *will* only *come*
to poverty.

17 ¶ Incline your ear and hear the words of
the wise,
And apply your mind to my knowledge;
18 For it will be pleasant if you keep them
within you,
That they may be ready on your lips.
19 So that your trust may be in the LORD,
I have taught you today, even you.
20 Have I not written to you excellent
things
Of counsels and knowledge,
21 To make you know the certainty of the
words of truth
That you may correctly answer him who
sent you?

22 ¶ Do not rob the poor because he is
poor,
Or crush the afflicted at the gate;
23 For the LORD will plead their case
And take the life of those who rob them.

24 ¶ Do not associate with a man *given* to
anger;
Or go with a hot-tempered man,
25 Or you will learn his ways
And find a snare for yourself.

26 ¶ Do not be among those who give
pledges,
Among those who become guarantors for
debts.
27 If you have nothing with which to pay,
Why should he take your bed from
under you?

28 ¶ Do not move the ancient boundary
Which your fathers have set.

29 ¶ Do you see a man skilled in his work?
He will stand before kings;
He will not stand before obscure men.

On Life and Conduct

23 When you sit down to dine with a ruler,
Consider carefully what is before you,
2 And put a knife to your throat
If you are a man of *great* appetite.
3 Do not desire his delicacies,
For it is deceptive food.

4 ¶ Do not weary yourself to gain wealth,
Cease from your consideration *of it.*
5 When you set your eyes on it, it is gone.
For *wealth* certainly makes itself wings
Like an eagle that flies *toward* the
heavens.

6 ¶ Do not eat the bread of a selfish man,
Or desire his delicacies;

7 For as he thinks within himself, so he is.
He says to you, "Eat and drink!"
But his heart is not with you.

8 You will vomit up the morsel you have
eaten,
And waste your compliments.

9 ¶ Do not speak in the hearing of a fool,
For he will despise the wisdom of your
words.

10 ¶ Do not move the ancient boundary
Or go into the fields of the fatherless,

11 For their Redeemer is strong;
He will plead their case against you.

12 Apply your heart to discipline
And your ears to words of knowledge.

13 ¶ Do not hold back discipline from the
child,
Although you strike him with the rod, he
will not die.

14 You shall strike him with the rod
And rescue his soul from Sheol.

15 ¶ My son, if your heart is wise,
My own heart also will be glad;

16 And my inmost being will rejoice
When your lips speak what is right.

17 ¶ Do not let your heart envy sinners,
But *live* in the fear of the LORD always.

18 Surely there is a future,
And your hope will not be cut off.

19 Listen, my son, and be wise,
And direct your heart in the way.

20 Do not be with heavy drinkers of wine,
Or with gluttonous eaters of meat;

21 For the heavy drinker and the glutton
will come to poverty,
And drowsiness will clothe *one* with rags.

22 ¶ Listen to your father who begot you,
And do not despise your mother when
she is old.

23 Buy truth, and do not sell *it*,
Get wisdom and instruction and
understanding.

24 ¶ The father of the righteous will greatly
rejoice,
And he who sires a wise son will be glad
in him.

25 Let your father and your mother be glad,
And let her rejoice who gave birth
to you.

26 ¶ Give me your heart, my son,
And let your eyes delight in my ways.

27 For a harlot is a deep pit
And an adulterous woman is a narrow
well.

28 Surely she lurks as a robber,
And increases the faithless among men.

29 ¶ Who has woe? Who has sorrow?
Who has contentions? Who has
complaining?
Who has wounds without cause?
Who has redness of eyes?

30 Those who linger long over wine,
Those who go to taste mixed wine.

31 Do not look on the wine when it is red,
When it sparkles in the cup,
When it goes down smoothly;

32 At the last it bites like a serpent
And stings like a viper.

33 Your eyes will see strange things
And your mind will utter perverse things.

34 And you will be like one who lies down
in the middle of the sea,
Or like one who lies down on the top of
a *a*mast.

35 "They struck me, *but* I did not become ill;
They beat me, *but* I did not know *it*.
When shall I awake?
I will seek another drink."

23:35 The Dangers of Wine

*Wine was common in biblical times, but its
dangers were recognized. Proverbs contains
some of the Bible's strongest warnings against
overindulgence: 20:1; 21:17; 23:20–21, 30–35;
31:4–7.*

Precepts and Warnings

24 Do not be envious of evil men,
Nor desire to be with them;

2 For their minds devise violence,
And their lips talk of trouble.

3 ¶ By wisdom a house is built,
And by understanding it is established;

4 And by knowledge the rooms are filled
With all precious and pleasant riches.

5 ¶ A wise man is strong,
And a man of knowledge increases
power.

6 For by wise guidance you will wage war,
And in abundance of counselors there is
victory.

7 ¶ Wisdom is *too* exalted for a fool,
He does not open his mouth in the gate.

8 ¶ One who plans to do evil,
Men will call a schemer.

9 The devising of folly is sin,
And the scoffer is an abomination
to men.

10 ¶ If you are slack in the day of distress,
Your strength is limited.

a Or *lookout*

11 ¶ Deliver those who are being taken away
  to death,
And those who are staggering to
  slaughter, Oh hold *them* back.
12 If you say, "See, we did not know this,"
Does He not consider *it* who weighs the
  hearts?
And does He not know *it* who keeps
  your soul?
And will He not render to man
  according to his work?

13 ¶ My son, eat honey, for it is good,
Yes, the honey from the comb is sweet to
  your taste;
14 Know *that* wisdom is thus for your soul;
If you find *it*, then there will be a future,
And your hope will not be cut off.

15 ¶ Do not lie in wait, O wicked man,
  against the dwelling of the righteous;
Do not destroy his resting place;
16 For a righteous man falls seven times,
  and rises again,
But the wicked stumble in *time of*
  calamity.

17 ¶ Do not rejoice when your enemy falls,
And do not let your heart be glad when
  he stumbles;
18 Or the LORD will see *it* and be displeased,
And turn His anger away from him.

19 ¶ Do not fret because of evildoers
Or be envious of the wicked;
20 For there will be no future for the evil
  man;
The lamp of the wicked will be put out.

21 ¶ My son, fear the LORD and the king;

Do not associate with those who are
  given to change,
22 For their calamity will rise suddenly,
And who knows the ruin *that comes*
  from both of them?

23 ¶ These also are sayings of the wise.
To show partiality in judgment is not
  good.
24 He who says to the wicked, "You are
  righteous,"
Peoples will curse him, nations will abhor
  him;
25 But to those who rebuke the *wicked* will
  be delight,
And a good blessing will come upon
  them.
26 He kisses the lips
Who gives a right answer.

27 ¶ Prepare your work outside
And make it ready for yourself in the
  field;
Afterwards, then, build your house.

28 ¶ Do not be a witness against your
  neighbor without cause,
And do not deceive with your lips.
29 Do not say, "Thus I shall do to him as
  he has done to me;
I will render to the man according to his
  work."

30 ¶ I passed by the field of the sluggard
And by the vineyard of the man lacking
  sense,
31 And behold, it was completely overgrown
  with thistles;
Its surface was covered with nettles,
And its stone wall was broken down.

The Problem with Laziness
Becoming a sluggard requires little effort

THE "SLUGGARD" IS LAZIER THAN a pig on vacation. His only exercise is turning on his bed; Proverbs says he is *hinged* to it. Any farfetched excuse—"there is a lion in the road!"—will keep him from going to work. Proverbs laughs at the sluggard a little, but uses him to teach serious lessons. You can be like him very easily, for it doesn't require much: "A little sleep, a little slumber, a little folding of the hands to rest." Putting things off, making excuses, sleeping in—who doesn't sometimes fall victim to these tendencies?

> *"A little sleep, a little slumber, a little folding of the hands to rest,"* then *your poverty will come as a robber.* 24:33

The result of such a life? Poverty, frustration, broken relationships. The sluggard still wants the luxuries hard work earns, but he never gets them. "The desire of the sluggard puts him to death" (21:25).

Proverbs on laziness: 6:6–11; 10:4,26; 12:24,27; 13:4; 15:19; 19:15,24; 20:4; 21:25; 22:13; 24:30–34; 26:13–16.

Life Questions: What attributes of a sluggard do you recognize in yourself? Do you think of these as serious?

32 When I saw, I reflected upon it;
I looked, *and* received instruction.
33 "A little sleep, a little slumber,
A little folding of the hands to rest,"
34 Then your poverty will come *as* a robber
And your want like an armed man.

Similitudes, Instructions

25 These also are proverbs of Solomon which the men of Hezekiah, king of Judah, transcribed.

25:1 Good Government

Proverbs lists three kings in its credits: Solomon (1:1; 10:1), Hezekiah (25:1), and Lemuel (31:1). So, naturally, it shows concern for what makes good government. The qualities needed in a king still apply to governmental heads today. Proverbs doesn't mention political philosophy or administrative efficiency. Justice and fairness matter most.
Proverbs on good government include the following: 14:35; 16:10,12–13; 20:26; 22:11; 25:4–5; 29:4,14; 31:3–5.

2 ¶ It is the glory of God to conceal a matter,
But the glory of kings is to search out a matter.
3 *As* the heavens for height and the earth for depth,
So the heart of kings is unsearchable.
4 Take away the dross from the silver,
And there comes out a vessel for the smith;
5 Take away the wicked before the king,
And his throne will be established in righteousness.
6 Do not claim honor in the presence of the king,
And do not stand in the place of great men;
7 For it is better that it be said to you,
"Come up here,"
Than for you to be placed lower in the presence of the prince,
Whom your eyes have seen.
8 ¶ Do not go out hastily to argue *your case;*
Otherwise, what will you do in the end,
When your neighbor humiliates you?
9 Argue your case with your neighbor,
And do not reveal the secret of another,
10 Or he who hears *it* will reproach you,
And the evil report about you will not pass away.
11 ¶ *Like* apples of gold in settings of silver
Is a word spoken in right circumstances.

12 *Like* an earring of gold and an ornament of fine gold
Is a wise reprover to a listening ear.
13 Like the cold of snow in the time of harvest
Is a faithful messenger to those who send him,
For he refreshes the soul of his masters.
14 *Like* clouds and wind without rain
Is a man who boasts of his gifts falsely.
15 By forbearance a ruler may be persuaded,
And a soft tongue breaks the bone.
16 Have you found honey? Eat *only* what you need,
That you not have it in excess and vomit it.
17 Let your foot rarely be in your neighbor's house,
Or he will become weary of you and hate you.
18 *Like* a club and a sword and a sharp arrow
Is a man who bears false witness against his neighbor.
19 *Like* a bad tooth and an unsteady foot
Is confidence in a faithless man in time of trouble.
20 *Like* one who takes off a garment on a cold day, *or like* vinegar on soda,
Is he who sings songs to a troubled heart.
21 If your enemy is hungry, give him food to eat;
And if he is thirsty, give him water to drink;
22 For you will heap burning coals on his head,
And the LORD will reward you.
23 The north wind brings forth rain,
And a backbiting tongue, an angry countenance.
24 It is better to live in a corner of the roof
Than in a house shared with a contentious woman.
25 *Like* cold water to a weary soul,
So is good news from a distant land.
26 *Like* a trampled spring and a polluted well
Is a righteous man who gives way before the wicked.
27 It is not good to eat much honey,
Nor is it glory to search out one's own glory.
28 *Like* a city that is broken into *and* without walls
Is a man who has no control over his spirit.

Similitudes, Instructions

26 Like snow in summer and like rain in harvest,

So honor is not fitting for a fool.
2 Like a sparrow in *its* flitting, like a
swallow in *its* flying,
So a curse without cause does not alight.
3 A whip is for the horse, a bridle for the
donkey,
And a rod for the back of fools.
4 Do not answer a fool according to his
folly,
Or you will also be like him.
5 Answer a fool as his folly *deserves,*
That he not be wise in his own eyes.
6 He cuts off *his own* feet *and* drinks
violence
Who sends a message by the hand of a
fool.
7 *Like* the legs *which* are useless to the
lame,
So is a proverb in the mouth of fools.
8 Like one who binds a stone in a sling,
So is he who gives honor to a fool.
9 *Like* a thorn *which* falls into the hand of
a drunkard,
So is a proverb in the mouth of fools.
10 *Like* an archer who wounds everyone,
So is he who hires a fool or who hires
those who pass by.
11 Like a dog that returns to its vomit
Is a fool who repeats his folly.
12 Do you see a man wise in his own eyes?
There is more hope for a fool than for
him.
13 The sluggard says, "There is a lion in the
road!
A lion is in the open square!"
14 *As* the door turns on its hinges,
So *does* the sluggard on his bed.
15 The sluggard buries his hand in the
dish;

He is weary of bringing it to his mouth
again.
16 The sluggard is wiser in his own eyes
Than seven men who can give a discreet
answer.

26:13 The Excuses of a Lazy Man

*At first glance some proverbs, like this one,
appear incomplete and pointless. But this
proverb cleverly pinpoints a lazy man's habit of
seeing dangerous obstacles to every plan and
making incredible excuses. He will not go
anywhere (on a road) or even get out of his
house (into the streets) because his imagination
conjures up all the things that could go wrong.*

17 *Like* one who takes a dog by the ears
Is he who passes by *and* meddles with
strife not belonging to him.
18 Like a madman who throws
Firebrands, arrows and death,
19 So is the man who deceives his neighbor,
And says, "Was I not joking?"
20 For lack of wood the fire goes out,
And where there is no whisperer,
contention quiets down.
21 *Like* charcoal to hot embers and wood to
fire,
So is a contentious man to kindle strife.
22 The words of a whisperer are like dainty
morsels,
And they go down into the innermost
parts of the body.
23 *Like* an earthen vessel overlaid with silver
dross
Are burning lips and a wicked heart.
24 He who hates disguises *it* with his lips,

The Making of a Fool
Even a genius can be one

> *Like a dog that returns to its vomit is a fool who repeats his folly. 26:11*

FOOLS, IN MODERN ENGLISH, ARE people who lack brains.
But the word has a different meaning in the Bible. Fools may have high
IQs. People may admire their reputation for success. Yet a wise person
views them as a disaster.
One of the Bible's worst insults is "You fool!" People become fools by ignoring the wisdom God
offers them, preferring to follow the crowd or their own conceited opinions. They may think themselves very clever, but their cleverness will land them in trouble.
Proverbs aims its sharpest warnings, not against acting immorally, but against becoming a fool. If
you develop such a character, no set of rules can keep you out of trouble. A wise person ought to
learn to recognize a fool from far away, and stay out of his or her path.
Poignant proverbs on foolishness: 1:7; 10:8; 12:15–16,23; 14:8–9,16,24; 15:14; 17:10,12,16; 18:2,6;
20:3; 26:3,11; 27:22; 28:26; 29:11.

Life Questions: Do you know anyone whom Proverbs would call a fool? If so, how should you relate to
him or her?

But he lays up deceit in his heart.
25 When he speaks graciously, do not
     believe him,
   For there are seven abominations in his
     heart.
26 *Though his* hatred covers itself with guile,
   His wickedness will be revealed before
     the assembly.
27 He who digs a pit will fall into it,
   And he who rolls a stone, it will come
     back on him.
28 A lying tongue hates those it crushes,
   And a flattering mouth works ruin.

Warnings and Instructions

27 Do not boast about tomorrow,
   For you do not know what a day may
     bring forth.
2 Let another praise you, and not your
     own mouth;
   A stranger, and not your own lips.
3 A stone is heavy and the sand weighty,
   But the provocation of a fool is heavier
     than both of them.
4 Wrath is fierce and anger is a flood,
   But who can stand before jealousy?
5 Better is open rebuke
   Than love that is concealed.
6 Faithful are the wounds of a friend,
   But deceitful are the kisses of an enemy.
7 A sated man loathes honey,
   But to a famished man any bitter thing is
     sweet.
8 Like a bird that wanders from her nest,
   So is a man who wanders from his
     home.
9 Oil and perfume make the heart glad,
   So a man's counsel is sweet to his friend.
10 Do not forsake your own friend or your
     father's friend,
   And do not go to your brother's house
     in the day of your calamity;
   Better is a neighbor who is near than a
     brother far away.
11 Be wise, my son, and make my heart
     glad,
   That I may reply to him who
     reproaches me.
12 A prudent man sees evil *and* hides
     himself,
   The naive proceed *and* pay the penalty.
13 Take his garment when he becomes
     surety for a stranger;
   And for an adulterous woman hold him
     in pledge.
14 He who blesses his friend with a loud
     voice early in the morning,
   It will be reckoned a curse to him.
15 A constant dripping on a day of steady
     rain
   And a contentious woman are alike;

16 He who would restrain her restrains the
     wind,
   And grasps oil with his right hand.
17 Iron sharpens iron,
   So one man sharpens another.
18 He who tends the fig tree will eat its
     fruit,
   And he who cares for his master will be
     honored.
19 As in water face *reflects* face,
   So the heart of man *reflects* man.
20 Sheol and Abaddon are never satisfied,
   Nor are the eyes of man ever satisfied.
21 The crucible is for silver and the furnace
     for gold,
   And each *is tested* by the praise accorded
     him.
22 Though you pound a fool in a mortar
     with a pestle along with crushed
     grain,
   Yet his foolishness will not depart
     from him.

23 ¶ Know well the condition of your flocks,
   And pay attention to your herds;
24 For riches are not forever,
   Nor does a crown *endure* to all
     generations.
25 *When* the grass disappears, the new
     growth is seen,
   And the herbs of the mountains are
     gathered in,
26 The lambs *will be* for your clothing,
   And the goats *will bring* the price of a
     field,
27 And *there will be* goats' milk enough for
     your food,
   For the food of your household,
   And sustenance for your maidens.

Warnings and Instructions

28 The wicked flee when no one is pursuing,
   But the righteous are bold as a lion.
2 By the transgression of a land many are
     its princes,
   But by a man of understanding *and*
     knowledge, so it endures.
3 A poor man who oppresses the lowly
   Is *like* a driving rain which leaves no
     food.
4 Those who forsake the law praise the
     wicked,
   But those who keep the law strive with
     them.
5 Evil men do not understand justice,
   But those who seek the LORD understand
     all things.
6 Better is the poor who walks in his
     integrity
   Than he who is crooked though he be
     rich.

7 He who keeps the law is a discerning
son,
But he who is a companion of gluttons
humiliates his father.
8 He who increases his wealth by interest
and usury
Gathers it for him who is gracious to the
poor.
9 He who turns away his ear from listening
to the law,
Even his prayer is an abomination.
10 He who leads the upright astray in an
evil way
Will himself fall into his own pit,
But the blameless will inherit good.
11 The rich man is wise in his own eyes,
But the poor who has understanding sees
through him.
12 When the righteous triumph, there is
great glory,
But when the wicked rise, men hide
themselves.
13 He who conceals his transgressions will
not prosper,
But he who confesses and forsakes *them*
will find compassion.
14 How blessed is the man who fears
always,
But he who hardens his heart will fall
into calamity.
15 *Like* a roaring lion and a rushing bear
Is a wicked ruler over a poor people.
16 A leader who is a great oppressor lacks
understanding,
But he who hates unjust gain will
prolong *his* days.
17 A man who is laden with the guilt of
human blood
Will be a fugitive until death; let no one
support him.
18 He who walks blamelessly will be
delivered,

But he who is crooked will fall all at
once.
19 He who tills his land will have plenty of
food,
But he who follows empty *pursuits* will
have poverty in plenty.
20 A faithful man will abound with
blessings,
But he who makes haste to be rich will
not go unpunished.
21 To show partiality is not good,
Because for a piece of bread a man will
transgress.
22 A man with an evil eye hastens after
wealth
And does not know that want will come
upon him.
23 He who rebukes a man will afterward
find *more* favor
Than he who flatters with the tongue.
24 He who robs his father or his mother
And says, "It is not a transgression,"
Is the companion of a man who destroys.
25 An arrogant man stirs up strife,
But he who trusts in the LORD will
prosper.
26 He who trusts in his own heart is a fool,
But he who walks wisely will be
delivered.
27 He who gives to the poor will never
want,
But he who shuts his eyes will have many
curses.
28 When the wicked rise, men hide
themselves;
But when they perish, the righteous
increase.

Warnings and Instructions

29 A man who hardens *his* neck after much
reproof
Will suddenly be broken beyond remedy.

Five Dangerous Responses
Inner attitudes can destroy you

> *A fool always loses his temper, but a wise man holds it back. 29:11*

ANGER WILL DESTROY YOU BEFORE it destroys anyone else.
Control your temper! Read Proverbs 14:17; 14:29; 15:18; 19:19; 22:24–25;
29:11; 29:22.

Pride will lead to your downfall. Humility is far more rewarding. See Proverbs 3:34; 11:2; 13:10;
16:5,18–19; 18:12; 21:4.

Jealousy grows like a cancer. Read Proverbs 14:30; 23:17; 24:1; 27:4.

Fear of people is unnecessary if you trust God. See Proverbs 3:25–26; 29:25.

Conceit is ugly. A conceited person forgets God's place in his or her life. Read Proverbs 16:2; 25:27;
26:12; 27:2; 28:11,13.

Life Questions: Which of these responses tempts you most? Why?

2 When the righteous increase, the people
   rejoice,
  But when a wicked man rules, people
   groan.
3 A man who loves wisdom makes his
   father glad,
  But he who keeps company with harlots
   wastes *his* wealth.
4 The king gives stability to the land by
   justice,
  But a man who takes bribes
   overthrows it.
5 A man who flatters his neighbor
  Is spreading a net for his steps.

29:5 Dangerous Flattery

"Flattery can get you anywhere," some say. But flattery—the art of making someone feel good by stretching the truth—can be downright harmful. It can leave a trusting friend unprepared for troubles ahead. Instead of flattering, we should warn a friend where he or she is headed (see 28:23).

6 By transgression an evil man is ensnared,
  But the righteous sings and rejoices.
7 The righteous is concerned for the rights
   of the poor,
  The wicked does not understand *such*
   concern.
8 Scorners set a city aflame,
  But wise men turn away anger.
9 When a wise man has a controversy with
   a foolish man,
  The foolish man either rages or laughs,
   and there is no rest.
10 Men of bloodshed hate the blameless,
  But the upright are concerned for his life.
11 A fool always loses his temper,
  But a wise man holds it back.
12 If a ruler pays attention to falsehood,
  All his ministers *become* wicked.
13 The poor man and the oppressor have
   this in common:
  The LORD gives light to the eyes of both.
14 If a king judges the poor with truth,
  His throne will be established forever.
15 The rod and reproof give wisdom,
  But a child who gets his own way brings
   shame to his mother.
16 When the wicked increase, transgression
   increases;
  But the righteous will see their fall.
17 Correct your son, and he will give you
   comfort;
  He will also delight your soul.
18 Where there is no vision, the people are
   unrestrained,
  But happy is he who keeps the law.

19 A slave will not be instructed by words
   alone;
  For though he understands, there will be
   no response.
20 Do you see a man who is hasty in his
   words?
  There is more hope for a fool than for
   him.
21 He who pampers his slave from
   childhood
  Will in the end find him to be a son.
22 An angry man stirs up strife,
  And a hot-tempered man abounds in
   transgression.
23 A man's pride will bring him low,
  But a humble spirit will obtain honor.
24 He who is a partner with a thief hates his
   own life;
  He hears the oath but tells nothing.
25 The fear of man brings a snare,
  But he who trusts in the LORD will be
   exalted.
26 Many seek the ruler's favor,
  But justice for man *comes* from the
   LORD.
27 An unjust man is abominable to the
   righteous,
  And he who is upright in the way is
   abominable to the wicked.

The Words of Agur

30 The words of Agur the son of Jakeh, the
   oracle.
  ¶ The man declares to Ithiel, to Ithiel and Ucal:
2 Surely I am more stupid than any man,
  And I do not have the understanding of
   a man.
3 Neither have I learned wisdom,
  Nor do I have the knowledge of the
   Holy One.
4 Who has ascended into heaven and
   descended?
  Who has gathered the wind in His fists?
  Who has wrapped the waters in His
   garment?
  Who has established all the ends of the
   earth?
  What is His name or His son's name?
  Surely you know!

5 ¶ Every word of God is tested;
  He is a shield to those who take refuge
   in Him.
6 Do not add to His words
  Or He will reprove you, and you will be
   proved a liar.
7 ¶ Two things I asked of You,
  Do not refuse me before I die:
8 Keep deception and lies far from me,
  Give me neither poverty nor riches;

Feed me with the food that is my
portion,
9 That I not be full and deny *You* and say,
"Who is the LORD?"
Or that I not be in want and steal,
And profane the name of my God.

10 ¶ Do not slander a slave to his master,
Or he will curse you and you will be
found guilty.

11 ¶ There is a *a*kind of *man* who curses
his father
And does not bless his mother.
12 There is a kind who is pure in his own
eyes,
Yet is not washed from his filthiness.
13 There is a kind—oh how lofty are his
eyes!
And his eyelids are raised *in arrogance.*
14 There is a kind of *man* whose teeth are
like swords
And his jaw teeth *like* knives,
To devour the afflicted from the earth
And the needy from among men.

15 ¶ The leech has two daughters,
"Give," "Give."
There are three things that will not be
satisfied,
Four that will not say, "Enough":
16 Sheol, and the barren womb,
Earth that is never satisfied with water,
And fire that never says, "Enough."
17 The eye that mocks a father
And scorns a mother,
The ravens of the valley will pick it out,
And the young eagles will eat it.

18 ¶ There are three things which are too
wonderful for me,
Four which I do not understand:
19 The way of an eagle in the sky,
The way of a serpent on a rock,
The way of a ship in the middle of the
sea,
And the way of a man with a maid.
20 This is the way of an adulterous woman:
She eats and wipes her mouth,
And says, "I have done no wrong."

21 ¶ Under three things the earth quakes,
And under four, it cannot bear up:
22 Under a slave when he becomes king,
And a fool when he is satisfied with
food,
23 Under an unloved woman when she gets
a husband,
And a maidservant when she supplants
her mistress.

24 ¶ Four things are small on the earth,
But they are exceedingly wise:

25 The ants are not a strong people,
But they prepare their food in the
summer;
26 The shephanim are not mighty people,
Yet they make their houses in the rocks;
27 The locusts have no king,
Yet all of them go out in ranks;
28 The lizard you may grasp with the hands,
Yet it is in kings' palaces.

29 ¶ There are three things which are stately
in *their* march,
Even four which are stately when they
walk:
30 The lion *which* is mighty among beasts
And does not retreat before any,
31 The strutting rooster, the male goat also,
And a king *when his* army is with him.

32 ¶ If you have been foolish in exalting
yourself
Or if you have plotted *evil, put your*
hand on your mouth.
33 For the churning of milk produces
butter,
And pressing the nose brings forth
blood;
So the churning of anger produces strife.

The Words of Lemuel

31 The words of King Lemuel, the oracle which
his mother taught him:
2 ¶ What, O my son?
And what, O son of my womb?
And what, O son of my vows?
3 Do not give your strength to women,
Or your ways to that which destroys
kings.
4 It is not for kings, O Lemuel,
It is not for kings to drink wine,
Or for rulers to desire strong drink,
5 For they will drink and forget what is
decreed,
And pervert the rights of all the afflicted.
6 Give strong drink to him who is
perishing,
And wine to him whose life is bitter.
7 Let him drink and forget his poverty
And remember his trouble no more.
8 Open your mouth for the mute,
For the rights of all the unfortunate.
9 Open your mouth, judge righteously,
And defend the rights of the afflicted and
needy.

Description of a Worthy Woman

10 ¶ An excellent wife, who can find?
For her worth is far above jewels.
11 The heart of her husband trusts in her,
And he will have no lack of gain.
12 She does him good and not evil

a Or *generation*

All the days of her life.
13 She looks for wool and flax
And works with her hands in delight.
14 She is like merchant ships;
She brings her food from afar.

31:8 For the Voiceless

The German pastor Dietrich Bonhoeffer frequently quoted this verse in the years before World War II. He was urging his fellow Christians to speak up for Hitler's victims, particularly Jews who had been stripped of their civil rights.

15 She rises also while it is still night
And gives food to her household
And portions to her maidens.
16 She considers a field and buys it;
From her earnings she plants a vineyard.
17 She girds herself with strength
And makes her arms strong.
18 She senses that her gain is good;
Her lamp does not go out at night.
19 She stretches out her hands to the distaff,
And her hands grasp the spindle.
20 She extends her hand to the poor,
And she stretches out her hands to the
needy.

21 She is not afraid of the snow for her
household,
For all her household are clothed with
scarlet.
22 She makes coverings for herself;
Her clothing is fine linen and purple.
23 Her husband is known in the gates,
When he sits among the elders of the
land.
24 She makes linen garments and sells *them,*
And supplies belts to the tradesmen.
25 Strength and dignity are her clothing,
And she smiles at the future.
26 She opens her mouth in wisdom,
And the teaching of kindness is on her
tongue.
27 She looks well to the ways of her
household,
And does not eat the bread of idleness.
28 Her children rise up and bless her;
Her husband *also,* and he praises her,
saying:
29 "Many daughters have done nobly,
But you excel them all."
30 Charm is deceitful and beauty is vain,
But a woman who fears the LORD, she
shall be praised.
31 Give her the product of her hands,
And let her works praise her in the
gates.

ECCLESIASTES

When Life Seems Senseless
A book for our time

I
N THIS WORLD THERE ARE only two tragedies," said Irish writer Oscar Wilde. "One is not getting what one wants, and the other is getting it." This paradoxical proverb has often proved true. Consider a larger-than-life character from the 20th century, a man named Howard Hughes.

> *"Vanity of vanities,"*
> *says the Preacher,*
> *"Vanity of vanities!*
> *All is vanity." 1:2*

World's Richest Man

At age 45 Hughes was one of the most glamorous men in America. He courted actresses, piloted exotic test aircraft, and worked on top-secret CIA contracts. He owned a string of hotels around the world, and even an airline—TWA—to carry him on global jaunts.

Twenty years later, at 65, Howard Hughes still had plenty of money—$2.3 billion, to be exact. But the world's richest man had become one of its most pathetic. He lived in small, dark rooms atop his hotels, without sun and without joy. He was unkempt: A scraggly beard had grown waist-length, his hair fell well down his back, and his fingernails were two inches long. His once-powerful 6'4" frame had shrunk to about 100 pounds.

This famous man spent most of his time watching movies over and over, with the same movie showing as many as 150 times. He lay naked in bed, deathly afraid of germs. Life held no meaning for him. Finally, emaciated and hooked on drugs, he died at age 67, for lack of a medical device his own company had helped to develop.

A King's Charmed Life

Howard Hughes is an extreme example of a syndrome that can afflict the rich and famous. His attitude toward life closely followed the thoughts of another successful man, a great king who ruled Israel long ago. This book, Ecclesiastes, records what happened to that man who had everything.

The author of Ecclesiastes had tasted just about everything life has to offer. Wealth? No one could exceed him in luxurious lifestyle (2:4–9). Wisdom? His was world-renowned (1:13–18). Fame? He was king, the most famous man of his time (1:12). Systematically, he sampled all of life's powers and pleasures, yet all ultimately disappointed him. All proved meaningless.

What is the point of life? he asked. You work hard, and someone else gets all the credit. You struggle to be good, and evil people take advantage of you. You accumulate money, and it just goes to spoiled heirs. You seek pleasure, and it turns sour on you. And everyone—rich or poor, good or evil—meets the same end. We all die. There is only one word to describe this life: meaningless!

Life Under the Sun

Ecclesiastes strikes a responsive chord in our age. Its words show up in folk songs and at presidential inaugurations. No generation has seen such progress, and yet such despair. What is the purpose of life anyway? Is there any ultimate meaning? "Is that all there is?" asked one songwriter after listing life's pleasures.

A key phrase in this book, "under the sun," describes the world lived on one level, apart from God and without any belief in the afterlife. If you live on that level, you may well conclude that life is meaningless.

Ecclesiastes gives some words of hope, including the final summary: "Fear God and keep his commandments, because this applies to every person" (12:13). That's the positive message, the "lesson" of

Ecclesiastes. But such positive words are almost overwhelmed by the author's powerful negative example. You could summarize his whole life in Jesus' one statement, "For what will it profit a man if he gains the whole world and forfeits his soul?" (Matthew 16:26).

How to Read Ecclesiastes

Ecclesiastes attracts extreme reactions. For several hundred years, Jewish scholars fiercely debated whether the book should even be included in the Old Testament. Yet American novelist Thomas Wolfe said of it, "Ecclesiastes is the greatest single piece of writing I have ever known, and the wisdom expressed in it the most lasting and profound."

Because of the book's unique nature, it is important to keep certain principles in mind while reading it. Consider Ecclesiastes as a whole. The Teacher was exploring various philosophies of life. During his search, he tried different approaches, including hedonism, the unrestrained pursuit of pleasure. The book honestly records the author's search without endorsing it.

At times the author concludes with despairing statements that directly contradict other parts of the Bible (for example, the recurring phrase, "All is vanity"). Read such individual statements in their context. Just as the book of Job contains arguments that God directly refuted later, so Ecclesiastes contains many isolated statements that contradict its final conclusion.

Ecclesiastes performs two very valuable functions. First, it should stimulate compassion for those who are trapped in despair and live in a meaningless world, alone, without God. The author brilliantly captures the futility and meaninglessness of that world, expressing a philosophy of life widespread in our times.

But the book includes more than despair. It also blends in proverbs about how life should be lived, pungent observations that can be easily overlooked. Look for these nuggets of wisdom, especially toward the end of the book. (You may also find it helpful to balance out Ecclesiastes with the more confident advice of Proverbs.)

By asking questions, the author of Ecclesiastes helped prepare for the answers God ultimately provided. The Teacher concluded, "All is vanity" under the sun, but when Jesus Christ came, he promised life "abundantly" (John 10:10).

3-TRACK READING PLAN

For an explanation and complete listing of the 3-track reading plan, turn to page 7.

TRACK 1: *Two-Week Courses on the Bible*
See page 7 for information on these courses.

TRACK 2: *An Overview of Ecclesiastes in 1 Day*
☐ Day 1. Read the Introduction to Ecclesiastes and then chapter 3, perhaps the most enduring portion of the book's poetry. Folksinger Pete Seeger used the first part verbatim in a famous song, and former United States president John F. Kennedy had these words read at his inauguration.

Now turn to page 9 for your next Track 2 reading project.

TRACK 3: *All of Ecclesiastes in 12 Days*
After you have read through Ecclesiastes, turn to pages 10–14 for your next Track 3 reading project.
☐1 ☐2 ☐3 ☐4 ☐5 ☐6 ☐7 ☐8
☐9 ☐10 ☐11 ☐12

The Futility of All Endeavor

1 The words of the Preacher, the son of David, king in Jerusalem.

2 "*a*Vanity of vanities," says the Preacher,
"*a*Vanity of vanities! All is vanity."

3 ¶ What advantage does man have in all
his work
Which he does under the sun?
4 A generation goes and a generation
comes,
But the earth remains forever.
5 Also, the sun rises and the sun sets;
And hastening to its place it rises there
again.
6 Blowing toward the south,
Then turning toward the north,
The wind continues swirling along;
And on its circular courses the wind
returns.
7 All the rivers flow into the sea,
Yet the sea is not full.
To the place where the rivers flow,
There they flow again.
8 All things are wearisome;
Man is not able to tell *it.*
The eye is not satisfied with seeing,
Nor is the ear filled with hearing.
9 That which has been is that which
will be,
And that which has been done is that
which will be done.
So there is nothing new under the sun.
10 Is there anything of which one might say,
"See this, it is new"?
Already it has existed for ages
Which were before us.
11 There is no remembrance of earlier
things;
And also of the later things which will
occur,
There will be for them no remembrance
Among those who will come later *still.*

The Futility of Wisdom

12 ¶ I, the Preacher, have been king over Israel in Jerusalem.
13 And I set my mind to seek and explore by wisdom concerning all that has been done under heaven. *It* is a grievous task *which* God has given to the sons of men to be afflicted with.
14 I have seen all the works which have been done under the sun, and behold, all is vanity and striving after wind.
15 What is crooked cannot be straightened and what is lacking cannot be counted.
16 ¶ I said to myself, "Behold, I have magnified and increased wisdom more than all who were over Jerusalem before me; and my mind has observed a wealth of wisdom and knowledge."

17 And I set my mind to know wisdom and to know madness and folly; I realized that this also is striving after wind.
18 Because in much wisdom there is much grief, and increasing knowledge *results in* increasing pain.

The Futility of Pleasure and Possessions

2 I said to myself, "Come now, I will test you with pleasure. So enjoy yourself." And behold, it too was futility.

2:1 Outside the Palace

The first two chapters of Ecclesiastes tell of "the Preacher's" own experience of despair and meaninglessness. The life described in this autobiographical section resembles that of King Solomon. In the rest of the book, the Preacher examines the world around him to see if others have found answers to life "under the sun." To his disappointment, he finds the same pattern repeated over and over.

2 I said of laughter, "It is madness," and of pleasure, "What does it accomplish?"
3 I explored with my mind *how* to stimulate my body with wine while my mind was guiding *me* wisely, and how to take hold of folly, until I could see what good there is for the sons of men to do under heaven the few years of their lives.
4 I enlarged my works: I built houses for myself, I planted vineyards for myself;
5 I made gardens and parks for myself and I planted in them all kinds of fruit trees;
6 I made ponds of water for myself from which to irrigate a forest of growing trees.
7 I bought male and female slaves and I had homeborn slaves. Also I possessed flocks and herds larger than all who preceded me in Jerusalem.
8 Also, I collected for myself silver and gold and the treasure of kings and provinces. I provided for myself male and female singers and the pleasures of men—many concubines.
9 ¶ Then I became great and increased more than all who preceded me in Jerusalem. My wisdom also stood by me.
10 All that my eyes desired I did not refuse them. I did not withhold my heart from any pleasure, for my heart was pleased because of all my labor and this was my reward for all my labor.
11 Thus I considered all my activities which my hands had done and the labor which I had exerted, and behold all was *b*vanity and striving after wind and there was no profit under the sun.

---

a Or *Futility of futilities*   *b* Or *futility,* and so throughout the ch

Wisdom Excels Folly

12 ¶ So I turned to consider wisdom, madness and folly; for what *will* the man *do* who will come after the king *except* what has already been done?

13 And I saw that wisdom excels folly as light excels darkness.

14 The wise man's eyes are in his head, but the fool walks in darkness. And yet I know that one fate befalls them both.

15 Then I said to myself, "As is the fate of the fool, it will also befall me. Why then have I been extremely wise?" So I said to myself, "This too is vanity."

16 For there is no lasting remembrance of the wise man *as* with the fool, inasmuch as *in* the coming days all will be forgotten. And how the wise man and the fool alike die!

17 So I hated life, for the work which had been done under the sun was grievous to me; because everything is futility and striving after wind.

The Futility of Labor

18 ¶ Thus I hated all the fruit of my labor for which I had labored under the sun, for I must leave it to the man who will come after me.

19 And who knows whether he will be a wise man or a fool? Yet he will have control over all the fruit of my labor for which I have labored by acting wisely under the sun. This too is vanity.

20 Therefore I completely despaired of all the fruit of my labor for which I had labored under the sun.

21 When there is a man who has labored with wisdom, knowledge and skill, then he gives his legacy to one who has not labored with them. This too is vanity and a great evil.

22 For what does a man get in all his labor and in his striving with which he labors under the sun?

23 Because all his days his task is painful and grievous; even at night his mind does not rest. This too is vanity.

24 ¶ There is nothing better for a man *than* to eat and drink and tell himself that his labor is good. This also I have seen that it is from the hand of God.

25 For who can eat and who can have enjoyment without Him?

26 For to a person who is good in His sight He has given wisdom and knowledge and joy, while to the sinner He has given the task of gathering and collecting so that he may give to one who is good in God's sight. This too is vanity and striving after wind.

A Time for Everything

3 There is an appointed time for everything. And there is a time for every event under heaven—

2 A time to give birth and a time to die;

A time to plant and a time to uproot what is planted.

3 A time to kill and a time to heal;
A time to tear down and a time to build up.

4 A time to weep and a time to laugh;
A time to mourn and a time to dance.

3:4 Change or No Change?

At first the Preacher complained that nothing ever changes (1:10–14). Now in this passage—made famous by a popular song in the 1960s—he indicates that life is full of changes. The French proverb, "The more things change, the more they stay the same," expresses this same paradox. For someone in despair who can see no meaning in life, everything that happens seems like an endless, repetitive cycle of futility.

5 A time to throw stones and a time to gather stones;
A time to embrace and a time to shun embracing.

6 A time to search and a time to give up as lost;
A time to keep and a time to throw away.

7 A time to tear apart and a time to sew together;
A time to be silent and a time to speak.

8 A time to love and a time to hate;
A time for war and a time for peace.

9 ¶ What profit is there to the worker from that in which he toils?

10 I have seen the task which God has given the sons of men with which to occupy themselves.

God Set Eternity in the Heart of Man

11 He has made everything *a*appropriate in its time. He has also set eternity in their heart, yet so that man will not find out the work which God has done from the beginning even to the end.

12 ¶ I know that there is nothing better for them than to rejoice and to do good in one's lifetime;

13 moreover, that every man who eats and drinks sees good in all his labor—it is the gift of God.

14 I know that everything God does will remain forever; there is nothing to add to it and there is nothing to take from it, for God has *so* worked that men should fear Him.

15 That which is has been already and that which will be has already been, for God seeks what has passed by.

16 ¶ Furthermore, I have seen under the sun *that* in the place of justice there is wickedness and

a Lit *beautiful*

in the place of righteousness there is wickedness.

17 I said to myself, "God will judge both the righteous man and the wicked man," for a time for every matter and for every deed is there.

18 I said to myself concerning the sons of men, "God has surely tested them in order for them to see that they are but beasts."

19 For the fate of the sons of men and the fate of beasts is the same. As one dies so dies the other; indeed, they all have the same breath and there is no advantage for man over beast, for all is vanity.

20 All go to the same place. All came from the dust and all return to the dust.

3:20 Is There an Afterlife?

Old Testament writers said very little about the afterlife. Not until Jesus' coming did God reveal details about heaven and hell. In this passage, the author wonders aloud whether death will be the end of everything. Yet he also adds some intriguing hints about the future. God "has also set eternity in their heart," he declares (verse 11). He also refers to a time of future judgment (verse 17).

21 Who knows that the breath of man ascends upward and the breath of the beast descends downward to the earth?

22 I have seen that nothing is better than that man should be happy in his activities, for that is his lot. For who will bring him to see what will occur after him?

The Evils of Oppression

4 Then I looked again at all the acts of oppression which were being done under the sun. And behold *I saw* the tears of the oppressed and *that* they had no one to comfort *them;* and on the side of their oppressors was power, but they had no one to comfort *them.*

2 So I congratulated the dead who are already dead more than the living who are still living.

3 But better *off* than both of them is the one who has never existed, who has never seen the evil activity that is done under the sun.

4 ¶ I have seen that every labor and every skill which is done is *the result of* rivalry between a man and his neighbor. This too is vanity and striving after wind.

5 The fool folds his hands and consumes his own flesh.

6 One hand full of rest is better than two fists full of labor and striving after wind.

7 ¶ Then I looked again at vanity under the sun.

8 There was a certain man without a dependent, having neither a son nor a brother, yet there was no end to all his labor. Indeed, his eyes were not satisfied with riches *and he never asked,* "And

for whom am I laboring and depriving myself of pleasure?" This too is vanity and it is a grievous task.

9 ¶ Two are better than one because they have a good return for their labor.

10 For if either of them falls, the one will lift up his companion. But woe to the one who falls when there is not another to lift him up.

11 Furthermore, if two lie down together they keep warm, but how can one be warm *alone?*

12 And if one can overpower him who is alone, two can resist him. A cord of three *strands* is not quickly torn apart.

13 ¶ A poor yet wise lad is better than an old and foolish king who no longer knows *how* to receive instruction.

14 For he has come out of prison to become king, even though he was born poor in his kingdom.

15 I have seen all the living under the sun throng to the side of the second lad who replaces him.

16 There is no end to all the people, to all who were before them, and even the ones who will come later will not be happy with him, for this too is vanity and striving after wind.

Your Attitude Toward God

5 Guard your steps as you go to the house of God and draw near to listen rather than to offer the sacrifice of fools; for they do not know they are doing evil.

2 Do not be hasty in word or impulsive in thought to bring up a matter in the presence of God. For God is in heaven and you are on the earth; therefore let your words be few.

3 For the dream comes through much effort and the voice of a fool through many words.

4 ¶ When you make a vow to God, do not be late in paying it; for *He takes* no delight in fools. Pay what you vow!

5 It is better that you should not vow than that you should vow and not pay.

6 Do not let your speech cause you to sin and do not say in the presence of the messenger *of God* that it was a mistake. Why should God be angry on account of your voice and destroy the work of your hands?

7 For in many dreams and in many words there is emptiness. Rather, fear God.

8 ¶ If you see oppression of the poor and denial of justice and righteousness in the province, do not be shocked at the sight; for one official watches over another official, and there are higher officials over them.

9 After all, a king who cultivates the field is an advantage to the land.

The Folly of Riches

10 ¶ He who loves money will not be satisfied

with money, nor he who loves abundance *with its* income. This too is vanity.

11 When good things increase, those who consume them increase. So what is the advantage to their owners except to look on?

5:10 Never Enough

Someone asked John D. Rockefeller, the richest man of his time, how much money is enough. He replied with a perfect definition of greed: "Just a little bit more." A real estate tycoon said something similar: "I don't want all the land in the world, just whatever touches mine."

12 The sleep of the working man is pleasant, whether he eats little or much; but the full stomach of the rich man does not allow him to sleep.

13 ¶ There is a grievous evil *which* I have seen under the sun: riches being hoarded by their owner to his hurt.

14 When those riches were lost through a bad investment and he had fathered a son, then there was nothing to support him.

15 As he had come naked from his mother's womb, so will he return as he came. He will take nothing from the fruit of his labor that he can carry in his hand.

16 This also is a grievous evil—exactly as a man is born, thus will he die. So what is the advantage to him who toils for the wind?

17 Throughout his life *he* also eats in darkness with great vexation, sickness and anger.

18 ¶ Here is what I have seen to be good and fitting: to eat, to drink and enjoy oneself in all one's labor in which he toils under the sun *during* the few years of his life which God has given him; for this is his reward.

5:18 Good for Something

As he tasted various attractions in life—work, food, drink, success—the Preacher decided that all are "vanity." None gave ultimate satisfaction. But in passages like this one, he admits that such good things are gifts from God and have a temporary value. Some possessions are better than none, wisdom is better than ignorance, life is better than death.

19 Furthermore, as for every man to whom God has given riches and wealth, He has also empowered him to eat from them and to receive his reward and rejoice in his labor; this is the gift of God.

20 For he will not often consider the years of his life, because God keeps him occupied with the gladness of his heart.

The Futility of Life

6 There is an evil which I have seen under the sun and it is prevalent among men—

2 a man to whom God has given riches and wealth and honor so that his soul lacks nothing of all that he desires; yet God has not empowered him to eat from them, for a foreigner enjoys them. This is vanity and a severe affliction.

3 If a man fathers a hundred *children* and lives many years, however many they be, but his soul is not satisfied with good things and he does not even have a *proper* burial, *then* I say, "Better the miscarriage than he,

4 for it comes in futility and goes into obscurity; and its name is covered in obscurity.

5 "It never sees the sun and it never knows *anything;* it is better off than he.

6 "Even if the *other* man lives a thousand years twice and does not enjoy good things—do not all go to one place?"

7 ¶ All a man's labor is for his mouth and yet the appetite is not satisfied.

8 For what advantage does the wise man have over the fool? What *advantage* does the poor man have, knowing *how* to walk before the living?

9 What the eyes see is better than what the soul desires. This too is futility and a striving after wind.

10 ¶ Whatever exists has already been named, and it is known what man is; for he cannot dispute with him who is stronger than he is.

11 For there are many words which increase futility. What *then* is the advantage to a man?

12 For who knows what is good for a man during *his* lifetime, *during* the few years of his futile life? He will spend them like a shadow. For who can tell a man what will be after him under the sun?

Wisdom and Folly Contrasted

7 A good name is better than a good
    ointment,
And the day of *one's* death is better than
    the day of one's birth.
2 It is better to go to a house of mourning
    Than to go to a house of feasting,
Because that is the end of every man,
    And the living takes *it* to heart.
3 Sorrow is better than laughter,
    For when a face is sad a heart may be
    happy.
4 The mind of the wise is in the house of
    mourning,
While the mind of fools is in the house
    of pleasure.
5 It is better to listen to the rebuke of a
    wise man
Than for one to listen to the song of
    fools.
6 For as the crackling of thorn bushes
    under a pot,

So is the laughter of the fool;
And this too is futility.
7 For oppression makes a wise man mad,
And a bribe corrupts the heart.
8 The end of a matter is better than its
beginning;
Patience of spirit is better than
haughtiness of spirit.
9 Do not be eager in your heart to be
angry,
For anger resides in the bosom of fools.
10 Do not say, "Why is it that the former
days were better than these?"
For it is not from wisdom that you ask
about this.
11 Wisdom along with an inheritance is
good
And an advantage to those who see the
sun.
12 For wisdom is protection *just as* money
is protection,
But the advantage of knowledge is that
wisdom preserves the lives of its
possessors.
13 Consider the work of God,
For who is able to straighten what He
has bent?
14 In the day of prosperity be happy,
But in the day of adversity consider—
God has made the one as well as the
other
So that man will not discover anything
that will be after him.
15 ¶ I have seen everything during my lifetime
of futility; there is a righteous man who perishes in
his righteousness and there is a wicked man who
prolongs *his life* in his wickedness.

7:15 Companion Book

*Passages in Ecclesiastes sound eerily like the
book of Job. Both books are "philosophical,"
asking the hardest questions about life. Both
authors battled despair, but for opposite
reasons: Job was overwhelmed by tragedy and
pain while the Preacher was jaded by luxury
and success. No matter what their status in life,
everyone has to face the same basic issues: Is
there a God? Is life unfair? Does it have
meaning?*

16 Do not be excessively righteous and do not
be overly wise. Why should you ruin yourself?
17 Do not be excessively wicked and do not be
a fool. Why should you die before your time?
18 It is good that you grasp one thing and also
not let go of the other; for the one who fears God
comes forth with both of them.
19 ¶ Wisdom strengthens a wise man more
than ten rulers who are in a city.

20 Indeed, there is not a righteous man on
earth who *continually* does good and who never
sins.
21 Also, do not take seriously all words which
are spoken, so that you will not hear your servant
cursing you.
22 For you also have realized that you likewise
have many times cursed others.
23 ¶ I tested all this with wisdom, *and* I said, "I
will be wise," but it was far from me.
24 What has been is remote and exceedingly
mysterious. Who can discover it?
25 I directed my mind to know, to investigate
and to seek wisdom and an explanation, and to
know the evil of folly and the foolishness of madness.
26 And I discovered more bitter than death the
woman whose heart is snares and nets, whose
hands are chains. One who is pleasing to God will
escape from her, but the sinner will be captured by
her.
27 ¶ "Behold, I have discovered this," says the
Preacher, "*adding* one thing to another to find an
explanation,
28 which I am still seeking but have not found.
I have found one man among a thousand, but I
have not found a woman among all these.
29 "Behold, I have found only this, that God
made men upright, but they have sought out
many devices."

Obey Rulers

8 Who is like the wise man and who knows the
interpretation of a matter? A man's wisdom
illumines him and causes his stern face to beam.
2 ¶ I say, "Keep the command of the king
because of the oath before God.
3 "Do not be in a hurry to leave him. Do not
join in an evil matter, for he will do whatever he
pleases."
4 Since the word of the king is authoritative,
who will say to him, "What are you doing?"
5 ¶ He who keeps a *royal* command experiences no trouble, for a wise heart knows the proper time and procedure.
6 For there is a proper time and procedure for
every delight, though a man's trouble is heavy
upon him.
7 If no one knows what will happen, who can
tell him when it will happen?
8 No man has authority to restrain the wind
with the wind, or authority over the day of death;
and there is no discharge in the time of war, and
evil will not deliver those who practice it.
9 All this I have seen and applied my mind to
every deed that has been done under the sun
wherein a man has exercised authority over *another* man to his hurt.
10 ¶ So then, I have seen the wicked buried,
those who used to go in and out from the holy

place, and they are *soon* forgotten in the city where they did thus. This too is futility.

11 Because the sentence against an evil deed is not executed quickly, therefore the hearts of the sons of men among them are given fully to do evil.

12 Although a sinner does evil a hundred *times* and may lengthen his *life*, still I know that it will be well for those who fear God, who fear Him openly.

13 But it will not be well for the evil man and he will not lengthen his days like a shadow, because he does not fear God.

14 ¶ There is futility which is done on the earth, that is, there are righteous men to whom it happens according to the deeds of the wicked. On the other hand, there are evil men to whom it happens according to the deeds of the righteous. I say that this too is futility.

15 So I commended pleasure, for there is nothing good for a man under the sun except to eat and to drink and to be merry, and this will stand by him in his toils *throughout* the days of his life which God has given him under the sun.

16 ¶ When I gave my heart to know wisdom and to see the task which has been done on the earth (even though one should never sleep day or night),

17 and I saw every work of God, *I concluded* that man cannot discover the work which has been done under the sun. Even though man should seek laboriously, he will not discover; and though the wise man should say, "I know," he cannot discover.

8:17 God's Fault?

Despite their similarities, Job and Ecclesiastes reveal important differences. As this verse shows, the Preacher never really expected to solve life's riddles; his attitude of resignation contrasts with Job's combativeness. Also, in his anguish, Job sometimes questioned the character of God himself, demanding a personal explanation. At no time did the Preacher blame God for the unfairness and meaninglessness he saw around him. "God made men upright," he concludes, "but they have sought out many devices" (7:29).

Men Are in the Hand of God

9 For I have taken all this to my heart and explain it that righteous men, wise men, and their deeds are in the hand of God. Man does not know whether *it will be* love or hatred; anything awaits him.

2 ¶ It is the same for all. There is one fate for the righteous and for the wicked; for the good, for the clean and for the unclean; for the man who offers a sacrifice and for the one who does not sacrifice. As the good man is, so is the sinner; as

the swearer is, so is the one who is afraid to swear.

3 This is an evil in all that is done under the sun, that there is one fate for all men. Furthermore, the hearts of the sons of men are full of evil and insanity is in their hearts throughout their lives. Afterwards they *go* to the dead.

4 For whoever is joined with all the living, there is hope; surely a live dog is better than a dead lion.

5 For the living know they will die; but the dead do not know anything, nor have they any longer a reward, for their memory is forgotten.

6 Indeed their love, their hate and their zeal have already perished, and they will no longer have a share in all that is done under the sun.

7 ¶ Go *then,* eat your bread in happiness and drink your wine with a cheerful heart; for God has already approved your works.

8 Let your clothes be white all the time, and let not oil be lacking on your head.

9 Enjoy life with the woman whom you love all the days of your fleeting life which He has given to you under the sun; for this is your reward in life and in your toil in which you have labored under the sun.

Whatever Your Hand Finds to Do

10 ¶ Whatever your hand finds to do, do *it* with *all* your might; for there is no activity or planning or knowledge or wisdom in Sheol where you are going.

11 ¶ I again saw under the sun that the race is not to the swift and the battle is not to the warriors, and neither is bread to the wise nor wealth to the discerning nor favor to men of ability; for time and chance overtake them all.

9:11 Life Is Unfair

Chapters 8 and 9 eloquently voice the unfairness of life. People don't get what they deserve, claims the Preacher. Good people suffer while wicked people prosper. Everything seems determined only by time and chance. The Preacher's doubts about the afterlife (see 3:20) affected all his thinking, because he saw the utter unfairness of life around him. In contrast, New Testament authors, with a solid belief in the afterlife, showed confidence that God would ultimately judge all people with fairness.

12 Moreover, man does not know his time: like fish caught in a treacherous net and birds trapped in a snare, so the sons of men are ensnared at an evil time when it suddenly falls on them.

13 ¶ Also this I came to see as wisdom under the sun, and it impressed me.

14 There was a small city with few men in it

and a great king came to it, surrounded it and constructed large siegeworks against it.

15 But there was found in it a poor wise man and he delivered the city by his wisdom. Yet no one remembered that poor man.

16 So I said, "Wisdom is better than strength." But the wisdom of the poor man is despised and his words are not heeded.

17 The words of the wise heard in quietness are *better* than the shouting of a ruler among fools.

18 Wisdom is better than weapons of war, but one sinner destroys much good.

A Little Foolishness

10 Dead flies make a perfumer's oil stink, so a little foolishness is weightier than wisdom *and* honor.

2 A wise man's heart *directs him* toward the right, but the foolish man's heart *directs him* toward the left.

3 Even when the fool walks along the road, his sense is lacking and he demonstrates to everyone *that* he is a fool.

4 If the ruler's temper rises against you, do not abandon your position, because composure allays great offenses.

5 ¶ There is an evil I have seen under the sun, like an error which goes forth from the ruler—

6 folly is set in many exalted places while rich men sit in humble places.

7 I have seen slaves *riding* on horses and princes walking like slaves on the land.

8 ¶ He who digs a pit may fall into it, and a serpent may bite him who breaks through a wall.

9 He who quarries stones may be hurt by them, and he who splits logs may be endangered by them.

10 If the axe is dull and he does not sharpen *its* edge, then he must exert more strength. Wisdom has the advantage of giving success.

11 If the serpent bites before being charmed, there is no profit for the charmer.

12 Words from the mouth of a wise man are gracious, while the lips of a fool consume him;

13 the beginning of his talking is folly and the end of it is wicked madness.

14 Yet the fool multiplies words. No man knows what will happen, and who can tell him what will come after him?

15 The toil of a fool *so* wearies him that he does not *even* know how to go to a city.

16 Woe to you, O land, whose king is a lad and whose princes feast in the morning.

17 Blessed are you, O land, whose king is of nobility and whose princes eat at the appropriate time—for strength and not for drunkenness.

18 Through indolence the rafters sag, and through slackness the house leaks.

19 *Men* prepare a meal for enjoyment, and wine makes life merry, and money is the answer to everything.

20 Furthermore, in your bedchamber do not curse a king, and in your sleeping rooms do not curse a rich man, for a bird of the heavens will carry the sound and the winged creature will make the matter known.

Cast Your Bread on the Waters

11 Cast your bread on the surface of the waters, for you will find it after many days.

2 Divide your portion to seven, or even to eight, for you do not know what misfortune may occur on the earth.

3 If the clouds are full, they pour out rain upon the earth; and whether a tree falls toward the south or toward the north, wherever the tree falls, there it lies.

4 He who watches the wind will not sow and he who looks at the clouds will not reap.

5 Just as you do not know the path of the wind and how bones *are formed* in the womb of the pregnant woman, so you do not know the activity of God who makes all things.

11:5 Beyond Understanding

Even the Preacher, a man who possessed brilliant powers of wisdom and observation, had to conclude some things are beyond understanding. Failing in his attempt to "figure out" life, he fell back on simple advice: Fear God and obey him, no matter how things seem to you. In essence, he concluded in favor of a life of faith. For him, an old man, much of life had already passed; in eloquent poetry he describes the decay that was already at work in his body (12:1–7). Thus he stressed, "Remember also your Creator in the days of your youth" (12:1).

6 ¶ Sow your seed in the morning and do not be idle in the evening, for you do not know whether morning or evening sowing will succeed, or whether both of them alike will be good.

7 ¶ The light is pleasant, and *it is* good for the eyes to see the sun.

8 Indeed, if a man should live many years, let him rejoice in them all, and let him remember the days of darkness, for they will be many. Everything that is to come *will be* futility.

9 ¶ Rejoice, young man, during your childhood, and let your heart be pleasant during the days of young manhood. And follow the impulses of your heart and the desires of your eyes. Yet know that God will bring you to judgment for all these things.

10 So, remove grief and anger from your heart and put away pain from your body, because childhood and the prime of life are fleeting.

Remember God in Your Youth

12 Remember also your Creator in the days of your youth, before the evil days come and the years draw near when you will say, "I have no delight in them";

2 before the sun and the light, the moon and the stars are darkened, and clouds return after the rain;

3 in the day that the watchmen of the house tremble, and mighty men stoop, the grinding ones stand idle because they are few, and those who look through windows grow dim;

4 and the doors on the street are shut as the sound of the grinding mill is low, and one will arise at the sound of the bird, and all the daughters of song will sing softly.

5 Furthermore, men are afraid of a high place and of terrors on the road; the almond tree blossoms, the grasshopper drags himself along, and the caperberry is ineffective. For man goes to his eternal home while mourners go about in the street.

6 *Remember Him* before the silver cord is broken and the golden bowl is crushed, the pitcher by the well is shattered and the wheel at the cistern is crushed;

7 then the dust will return to the earth as it was, and the spirit will return to God who gave it.

8 "Vanity of vanities," says the Preacher, "all is vanity!"

Purpose of the Preacher

9 ¶ In addition to being a wise man, the Preacher also taught the people knowledge; and he pondered, searched out and arranged many proverbs.

10 The Preacher sought to find delightful words and to write words of truth correctly.

11 ¶ The words of wise men are like goads, and masters of *these* collections are like well-driven nails; they are given by one Shepherd.

12 But beyond this, my son, be warned: the writing of many books is endless, and excessive devotion *to books* is wearying to the body.

13 ¶ The conclusion, when all has been heard, *is:* fear God and keep His commandments, because this *applies to* every person.

14 For God will bring every act to judgment, everything which is hidden, whether it is good or evil.

12:13 The Gamble

Having tried everything life has to offer, the Preacher circles back to this uncomplicated formula for making sense of our time on earth. Although Ecclesiastes displays little of the confidence of the book of Proverbs preceding it, both arrive at exactly the same conclusion (see Proverbs 1:7).

The 17th-century mathematician and philosopher Blaise Pascal, who similarly struggled with issues of meaninglessness, concluded that faith sometimes resembles a wager. He told his friends, "If I believe in God and life after death and you do not, and if there is no God, we both lose when we die. However, if there is a God, you still lose and I gain everything."

SONG OF SOLOMON

An Intoxicating Love

A poem about love the way it's meant to be

> Many waters cannot quench love, nor will rivers overflow it.
> 8:7

SNAP THE RADIO ON, ZIP to any station, and what are you likely to hear? Love songs. Songs of new love, songs of disappointed love, songs of grateful love, songs of crazy love. Times change, but through history the flow of love songs is a constant.

Plenty of people are shocked to find an explicit love song in the Bible—complete with erotic lyrics. But Song of Solomon is exactly that. It shows no embarrassment about lovers enjoying each other's bodies, and talking about it. Consequently, intermittent attempts have been made to rule Song of Solomon out of the Bible or to make it for "Adults Only." In 16th-century Spain, for instance, professor Fray Luis de Leon was dragged out of his classroom and imprisoned for four years. His crime? He translated Song of Solomon into Spanish.

Allegorical Interpretation

More often, Song of Solomon has been read as though it had nothing to do with lovers at all. Many have interpreted it as an allegory of love between God and his people. Some of these interpretations identify every poetic detail with some corresponding facet of our relationship to God. For instance, the bride's hair may be interpreted as non-Jewish nations who come to Christ. The famous 12th-century monk Saint Bernard of Clairvaux, using this allegorical approach, wrote 86 sermons on the first two chapters of Song of Solomon.

Nowadays, few follow that kind of interpretation. Most scholars believe that the poem was intended to celebrate love between a newly married couple. God values love between a man and a woman. That's why he placed this song in his holy Bible. It may have been sung first at a wedding.

Naked and Unashamed

These lovers love to look at each other. They love to tell each other what they feel. They revel in the sensuous: the beauty of nature, the scent of perfumes and spices. They are openly erotic.

Their intoxication with love sounds quite up-to-date, not so different from what you hear on the radio. Yet Song of Solomon conveys a very different atmosphere from most modern love songs. The explicit lyrics never become even slightly dirty. This love comes from the Garden of Eden, when both man and woman were naked and unashamed. It is tender, filled with delight, natural. You sense no shame or guilt; you feel that God is with the two as they love.

The lovers act as equals. Both woman and man take the initiative in praising each other. They don't flirt or play games: they say what they mean.

Yet they show caution and dignity in their love. While at the peak of joy, the lovers repeatedly warn others not to stir up love prematurely (2:7; 3:5; 8:4). They recognize the dangerously explosive side of love. "For love is as strong as death, jealousy is as severe as Sheol; its flashes are flashes of fire" (8:6).

How to Read Song of Solomon

Since love songs are always popular, many people approach Song of Solomon with great expectations. However, readers often find the book different from what they had expected.

Two main problems may hinder today's reader. One is the poetic imagery. No modern lover would say, "Your hair is like a flock of goats" (4:1), or, "Your nose is like the tower of Lebanon" (7:4). While some images in Song of Solomon appeal—"And his banner over me is love" (2:4) or "For love is as strong as death" (8:6)—the majority of the book's metaphors sound strange to our ears.

Most of the comparisons aren't visual, but emotional. For instance, when the lover tells his beloved that "your two breasts are like two fawns" (4:5), he isn't saying that her breasts look like deer. He is saying that they bring out the same tender feelings baby deer do. When you read strange-sounding metaphors in Song of Solomon, don't ask, "What did these things (pomegranates, myrrh, a flock of sheep) look like?" but ask, "What did the lovers *feel* when they thought of them?"

A second problem: Song of Solomon is hard to follow. One part doesn't seem connected to the next. Think of it as a series of snapshots of a couple in love—snapshots not necessarily in order. Put together in one photo album, they show the profound feelings of newly married lovers.

Though Song of Solomon is primarily about love on the human level, many Christians and Jews have read it as a book about God's love. This was probably not the author's original intent, but it is a legitimate and inspiring way to look at the book. After all, God made human love, and other parts of the Bible suggest its similarity to God's love. (See Hosea 1–3 and Ephesians 5:22–33.) Song of Solomon never makes this connection, but it does present a love so rich, so full, so unashamed that it's natural to think of God and his love for us.

3-TRACK READING PLAN

For an explanation and complete listing of the 3-track reading plan, turn to page 7.

TRACK 1: **Two-Week Courses on the Bible**
See page 7 for information on these courses.

TRACK 2: **An Overview of Song of Solomon in 1 Day**
☐ Day 1. Read the Introduction to Song of Solomon and chapter 2, a beautiful love poem.

Now turn to page 9 for your next Track 2 reading project.

TRACK 3: **All of Song of Solomon in 8 Days**
After you have read through Song of Solomon, turn to pages 10–14 for your next Track 3 reading project.

☐1   ☐2   ☐3   ☐4   ☐5   ☐6   ☐7   ☐8

The Young Shulammite Bride and Jerusalem's Daughters

1 The ªSong of Songs, which is Solomon's.

2 ¶ ᵇMay he kiss me with the kisses of his mouth!
For your love is better than wine.
3 "Your oils have a pleasing fragrance,
Your name is *like* purified oil;
Therefore the maidens love you.
4 "Draw me after you *and* let us run *together!*
The king has brought me into his chambers."

¶ ꞌWe will rejoice in you and be glad;
We will extol your love more than wine.
Rightly do they love you."

5 ¶ ᵇI am black but lovely,
O daughters of Jerusalem,
Like the tents of Kedar,
Like the curtains of Solomon.
6 "Do not stare at me because I am swarthy,
For the sun has burned me.
My mother's sons were angry with me;
They made me caretaker of the vineyards,
But I have not taken care of my own vineyard.
7 "Tell me, O you whom my soul loves,
Where do you pasture *your flock,*
Where do you make *it* lie down at noon?
For why should I be like one who veils herself
Beside the flocks of your companions?"

ª Or *Best of the Songs*   ᵇ BRIDE   ꞌ CHORUS

Solomon, the Lover, Speaks

8 ¶ "*a*If you yourself do not know,
Most beautiful among women,
Go forth on the trail of the flock

1:6 Tan Lines

Modern Americans, who lavish millions of dollars on tanning lotions and tanning salons, consider a suntan desirable, despite its health risks. Not so in Victorian times—or in Solomon's time. Soft white skin marked a more refined person who had not been required to work outdoors.

And pasture your young goats
By the tents of the shepherds.

9 ¶ "To me, my darling, you are like
My mare among the chariots of Pharaoh.
10 "Your cheeks are lovely with ornaments,
Your neck with strings of beads."

11 ¶ "*b*We will make for you ornaments of
gold
With beads of silver."

12 ¶ "*c*While the king was at his table,
My perfume gave forth its fragrance.
13 "My beloved is to me a pouch of myrrh
Which lies all night between my breasts.
14 "My beloved is to me a cluster of henna
blossoms
In the vineyards of Engedi."

15 ¶ "*a*How beautiful you are, my darling,
How beautiful you are!
Your eyes are *like* doves."

16 ¶ "*c*How handsome you are, my
beloved,
And so pleasant!
Indeed, our couch is luxuriant!
17 "The beams of our houses are cedars,
Our rafters, cypresses.

The Bride's Admiration

2 "*c*I am the rose of Sharon,
The lily of the valleys."

2 ¶ "*a*Like a lily among the thorns,
So is my darling among the maidens."

3 ¶ "*c*Like an apple tree among the trees
of the forest,
So is my beloved among the young men.
In his shade I took great delight and sat
down,
And his fruit was sweet to my taste.
4 "He has brought me to *his* banquet hall,
And his banner over me is love.

5 "Sustain me with raisin cakes,
Refresh me with apples,
Because I am lovesick.
6 "Let his left hand be under my head
And his right hand embrace me."

2:4 His Banner over Me

A "banner" was a large military flag that held a fighting unit together in battle. In the noise and dust of the fight, soldiers needed a visible sign to keep them oriented. For these lovers, a public and visible declaration of love forms a "banner," keeping them together.

---

7 ¶ "*a*I adjure you, O daughters of
Jerusalem,
By the gazelles or by the hinds of the
field,
That you do not arouse or awaken *my*
love
Until she pleases."

8 ¶ "*c*Listen! My beloved!
Behold, he is coming,
Climbing on the mountains,
Leaping on the hills!
9 "My beloved is like a gazelle or a young
stag.
Behold, he is standing behind our wall,
He is looking through the windows,
He is peering through the lattice.

10 ¶ "My beloved responded and said
to me,
'Arise, my darling, my beautiful one,
And come along.
11 'For behold, the winter is past,
The rain is over *and* gone.
12 'The flowers have *already* appeared in the
land;
The time has arrived for pruning *the
vines*,
And the voice of the turtledove has been
heard in our land.
13 'The fig tree has ripened its figs,
And the vines in blossom have given
forth *their* fragrance.
Arise, my darling, my beautiful one,
And come along!' "

14 ¶ "O my dove, in the clefts of the rock,
In the secret place of the steep pathway,
Let me see your form,
Let me hear your voice;
For your voice is sweet,
And your form is lovely."

15 ¶ "Catch the foxes for us,

---

a BRIDEGROOM   *b* CHORUS   *c* BRIDE

The little foxes that are ruining the
vineyards,
While our vineyards are in blossom."

16 ¶ "My beloved is mine, and I am his;
He pastures *his flock* among the lilies.
17 "Until the cool of the day when the
shadows flee away,
Turn, my beloved, and be like a gazelle
Or a young stag on the mountains of
Bether."

The Bride's Troubled Dream

3 "*a*On my bed night after night I
sought him
Whom my soul loves;
I sought him but did not find him.
2 'I must arise now and go about the city;
In the streets and in the squares
I must seek him whom my soul loves.'
I sought him but did not find him.
3 "The watchmen who make the rounds in
the city found me,
And I said, 'Have you seen him whom
my soul loves?'
4 "Scarcely had I left them
When I found him whom my soul loves;
I held on to him and would not let
him go
Until I had brought him to my mother's
house,
And into the room of her who
conceived me."

5 ¶ "*b*I adjure you, O daughters of
Jerusalem,
By the gazelles or by the hinds of the
field,
That you will not arouse or awaken *my*
love
Until she pleases."

3:5 Let Love Sleep

*If love is so wonderful, as this poem beautifully
sings, shouldn't people pursue it recklessly? Yet
the beloved warns them not to. Three times she
urges others not to force love, but to let it
develop at its own rate. Love should wait for its
proper time.*

Solomon's Wedding Day

6 ¶ "*c*What is this coming up from the
wilderness
Like columns of smoke,
Perfumed with myrrh and frankincense,
With all scented powders of the
merchant?

7 "Behold, it is the *traveling* couch of
Solomon;
Sixty mighty men around it,
Of the mighty men of Israel.
8 "All of them are wielders of the sword,
Expert in war;
Each man has his sword at his side,
Guarding against the terrors of the night.
9 "King Solomon has made for himself a
sedan chair
From the timber of Lebanon.
10 "He made its posts of silver,
Its back of gold
And its seat of purple fabric,
With its interior lovingly fitted out
By the daughters of Jerusalem.
11 "Go forth, O daughters of Zion,
And gaze on King Solomon with the
crown
With which his mother has crowned him
On the day of his wedding,
And on the day of his gladness of heart."

Solomon's Love Expressed

4 "*b*How beautiful you are, my darling,
How beautiful you are!
Your eyes are *like* doves behind your
veil;
Your hair is like a flock of goats
That have descended from Mount Gilead.
2 "Your teeth are like a flock of *newly* shorn
ewes
Which have come up from *their* washing,
All of which bear twins,
And not one among them has lost her
young.
3 "Your lips are like a scarlet thread,
And your mouth is lovely.
Your temples are like a slice of a
pomegranate
Behind your veil.
4 "Your neck is like the tower of David,
Built with rows of stones
On which are hung a thousand shields,
All the round shields of the mighty men.
5 "Your two breasts are like two fawns,
Twins of a gazelle
Which feed among the lilies.
6 "Until the cool of the day
When the shadows flee away,
I will go my way to the mountain of
myrrh
And to the hill of frankincense.

7 ¶ "You are altogether beautiful, my
darling,
And there is no blemish in you.
8 "*Come* with me from Lebanon, *my* bride,
May you come with me from Lebanon.

*a*BRIDE   *b*BRIDEGROOM   *c*CHORUS

Journey down from the summit of
Amana,
From the summit of Senir and Hermon,
From the dens of lions,
From the mountains of leopards.
9 "You have made my heart beat faster, my
sister, *my* bride;
You have made my heart beat faster with
a single *glance* of your eyes,
With a single strand of your necklace.
10 "How beautiful is your love, my sister, *my*
bride!
How much better is your love than wine,
And the fragrance of your oils
Than all *kinds* of spices!
11 "Your lips, *my* bride, drip honey;
Honey and milk are under your tongue,
And the fragrance of your garments is
like the fragrance of Lebanon.
12 "A garden locked is my sister, *my* bride,
A rock garden locked, a spring sealed up.
13 "Your shoots are an orchard of
pomegranates
With choice fruits, henna with nard
plants,
14 Nard and saffron, calamus and
cinnamon,
With all the trees of frankincense,
Myrrh and aloes, along with all the finest
spices.
15 "*You are* a garden spring,
A well of fresh water,
And streams *flowing* from Lebanon."

16 ¶ "*a*Awake, O north *wind,*
And come, *wind of* the south;
Make my garden breathe out *fragrance,*
Let its spices be wafted abroad.
May my beloved come into his garden
And eat its choice fruits!"

The Torment of Separation

5 "*b*I have come into my garden, my sister,
my bride;
I have gathered my myrrh along with my
balsam.
I have eaten my honeycomb and my
honey;
I have drunk my wine and my milk.
Eat, friends;
Drink and imbibe deeply, O lovers."

2 ¶ "*a*I was asleep but my heart was
awake.
A voice! My beloved was knocking:
'Open to me, my sister, my darling,
My dove, my perfect one!
For my head is drenched with dew,
My locks with the damp of the night.'
3 "I have taken off my dress,
How can I put it on *again?*

I have washed my feet,
How can I dirty them *again?*
4 "My beloved extended his hand through
the opening,
And my feelings were aroused for him.

5:2–8 A Nightmare

*This short passage and the first five verses of
chapter 3 are strange and troubling interludes.
Many scholars think they are dream
sequences, nightmares showing that the
beauty of love also brings an increased
vulnerability to pain and fear. Here, the
beloved is slow to get out of bed to welcome
her lover. As a result, he is gone when she
reaches the door.*

5 "I arose to open to my beloved;
And my hands dripped with myrrh,
And my fingers with liquid myrrh,
On the handles of the bolt.
6 "I opened to my beloved,
But my beloved had turned away *and*
had gone!
My heart went out *to him* as he spoke.
I searched for him but I did not find
him;
I called him but he did not answer me.
7 "The watchmen who make the rounds in
the city found me,
They struck me *and* wounded me;
The guardsmen of the walls took away
my shawl from me.
8 "I adjure you, O daughters of Jerusalem,
If you find my beloved,
As to what you will tell him:
For I am lovesick."

9 ¶ "*c*What kind of beloved is your
beloved,
O most beautiful among women?
What kind of beloved is your beloved,
That thus you adjure us?"

Admiration by the Bride

10 ¶ "*a*My beloved is dazzling and ruddy,
Outstanding among ten thousand.
11 "His head is *like* gold, pure gold;
His locks are *like* clusters of dates
And black as a raven.
12 "His eyes are like doves
Beside streams of water,
Bathed in milk,
And reposed in *their* setting.
13 "His cheeks are like a bed of balsam,
Banks of sweet-scented herbs;
His lips are lilies
Dripping with liquid myrrh.

a BRIDE   *b* BRIDEGROOM   *c* CHORUS

14 "His hands are rods of gold
  Set with beryl;
  His abdomen is carved ivory
  Inlaid with sapphires.
15 "His legs are pillars of alabaster
  Set on pedestals of pure gold;
  His appearance is like Lebanon
  Choice as the cedars.
16 "His mouth is *full of* sweetness.
  And he is wholly desirable.
  This is my beloved and this is my friend,
  O daughters of Jerusalem."

Mutual Delight in Each Other

6 "*a*Where has your beloved gone,
  O most beautiful among women?
  Where has your beloved turned,
  That we may seek him with you?"

2 ¶ "*b*My beloved has gone down to his
    garden,
  To the beds of balsam,
  To pasture *his flock* in the gardens
  And gather lilies.
3 "I am my beloved's and my beloved is
    mine,
  He who pastures *his flock* among the
    lilies."

4 ¶ "*c*You are as beautiful as Tirzah, my
    darling,
  As lovely as Jerusalem,
  As awesome as an army with banners.
5 "Turn your eyes away from me,
  For they have confused me;
  Your hair is like a flock of goats
  That have descended from Gilead.
6 "Your teeth are like a flock of ewes
  Which have come up from *their* washing,
  All of which bear twins,
  And not one among them has lost her
    young.
7 "Your temples are like a slice of a
    pomegranate
  Behind your veil.
8 "There are sixty queens and eighty
    concubines,
  And maidens without number;
9 *But* my dove, my perfect one, is unique:
  She is her mother's only *daughter;*
  She is the pure *child* of the one who bore
    her.
  The maidens saw her and called her
    blessed,
  The queens and the concubines *also*, and
    they praised her, *saying*,

10 ¶ 'Who is this that grows like the dawn,
  As beautiful as the full moon,
  As pure as the sun,
  As awesome as an army with banners?'

11 "I went down to the orchard of nut trees
  To see the blossoms of the valley,
  To see whether the vine had budded
  Or the pomegranates had bloomed.
12 "Before I was aware, my soul set me
  Over the chariots of my noble people."

13 ¶ "*a*Come back, come back,
  O Shulammite;
  Come back, come back, that we may
    gaze at you!"

¶ "*c*Why should you gaze at the
    Shulammite,
  As at the dance of the two companies?

Admiration by the Bridegroom

7 "How beautiful are your feet in sandals,
  O prince's daughter!
  The curves of your hips are like jewels,
  The work of the hands of an artist.
2 "Your navel is *like* a round goblet
  Which never lacks mixed wine;
  Your belly is like a heap of wheat
  Fenced about with lilies.
3 "Your two breasts are like two fawns,
  Twins of a gazelle.
4 "Your neck is like a tower of ivory,
  Your eyes *like* the pools in Heshbon
  By the gate of Bath-rabbim;
  Your nose is like the tower of Lebanon,
  Which faces toward Damascus.
5 "Your head crowns you like Carmel,
  And the flowing locks of your head are
    like purple threads;
  The king is captivated by *your* tresses.
6 "How beautiful and how delightful you
    are,
  My love, with *all* your charms!
7 "Your stature is like a palm tree,
  And your breasts are *like its* clusters.
8 "I said, 'I will climb the palm tree,
  I will take hold of its fruit stalks.'
  Oh, may your breasts be like clusters of
    the vine,
  And the fragrance of your breath like
    apples,
9 And your mouth like the best wine!"

¶ "*b*It goes *down* smoothly for my
    beloved,
  Flowing gently *through* the lips of those
    who fall asleep.

The Union of Love

10 ¶ "I am my beloved's,
  And his desire is for me.
11 "Come, my beloved, let us go out into the
    country,
  Let us spend the night in the villages.
12 "Let us rise early *and go* to the vineyards;

Let us see whether the vine has budded
And its blossoms have opened,
And whether the pomegranates have
bloomed.
There I will give you my love.
13 "The mandrakes have given forth
fragrance;
And over our doors are all choice *fruits,*
Both new and old,
Which I have saved up for you, my
beloved.

The Lovers Speak

8 "Oh that you were like a brother to me
Who nursed at my mother's breasts.
If I found you outdoors, I would kiss
you;
No one would despise me, either.

8:1 A Brotherly Kiss

*In oriental culture, even a married couple could
not express their love publicly. Only a brother
and sister could openly kiss. The beloved is
wishing she had the right to show their love to
the world.*

---

2 "I would lead you *and* bring you
Into the house of my mother, who used
to instruct me;
I would give you spiced wine to drink
from the juice of my pomegranates.
3 "Let his left hand be under my head
And his right hand embrace me."

4 ¶ "*a*I want you to swear, O daughters of
Jerusalem,
Do not arouse or awaken *my* love
Until she pleases."

5 ¶ "*b*Who is this coming up from the
wilderness
Leaning on her beloved?"

¶ "*c*Beneath the apple tree I awakened
you;
There your mother was in labor with
you,
There she was in labor *and* gave you
birth.
6 "Put me like a *d* seal over your heart,
Like a seal on your arm.
For love is as strong as death,

Jealousy is as severe as Sheol;
Its flashes are flashes of fire,
The *very* flame of the LORD.
7 "Many waters cannot quench love,
Nor will rivers overflow it;
If a man were to give all the riches of his
house for love,
It would be utterly despised."

8:6 Love and Death

*Death sweeps everything away. It yields to no
one, and once you are in its power you cannot
escape. So with love: It takes control of your
life, and like a gigantic fire, it cannot be doused.
Love must be treated with the greatest caution
and respect.*

---

8 ¶ "*b*We have a little sister,
And she has no breasts;
What shall we do for our sister
On the day when she is spoken for?
9 "If she is a wall,
We will build on her a battlement of
silver;
But if she is a door,
We will barricade her with planks of
cedar."

10 ¶ "*c*I was a wall, and my breasts were
like towers;
Then I became in his eyes as one who
finds peace.
11 "Solomon had a vineyard at Baal-hamon;
He entrusted the vineyard to caretakers.
Each one was to bring a thousand *shekels*
of silver for its fruit.
12 "My very own vineyard is at my disposal;
The thousand *shekels* are for you,
Solomon,
And two hundred are for those who take
care of its fruit."

13 ¶ "*a*O you who sit in the gardens,
My companions are listening for your
voice—
Let me hear it!"

14 ¶ "*c*Hurry, my beloved,
And be like a gazelle or a young stag
On the mountains of spices."

---

a BRIDEGROOM   *b* CHORUS   *c* BRIDE   *d* Or *signe*

ISAIAH

Prophet, Poet, and Politician
His nation at a crossroads, Isaiah rose to meet the challenge

T HE PROPHET ISAIAH WAS A giant of Jewish history. He was the Shakespeare of Hebrew literature, and the New Testament quotes him more than all the other prophets combined. No other biblical author can match his rich vocabulary and use of imagery.

And yet Isaiah spent his days not in an ivory tower, but in the corridors of power. He served as adviser to the kings of Judah and helped set the course of his nation.

> *Thus He looked for justice, but behold, bloodshed; for righteousness, but behold, a cry of distress. 5:7*

Days of Crisis

Isaiah lived at a crucial time, midway between the founding of the kingdom under Saul and David and its eventual destruction. A civil war had split the Israelites into North (Israel) and South (Judah), and Isaiah lived in the more pious Southern Kingdom.

When Isaiah began his work, the nation seemed strong and wealthy. But Isaiah saw signs of grave danger. People were using their power to harass the poor. Men went around drunk; women cared more about their clothes than about their neighbors' hunger. People gave lip service to God and kept up the outward appearance of religion but did little more.

Outside dangers loomed even larger. The armies of neighboring Israel were rattling swords and spears at the border. On all sides, monster empires were growing, especially Egypt and Assyria. Judah was caught in a pincers. Should the nation choose one of the empires as an ally?

Harsh Words from an Uncompromising Prophet

The nation of Judah, said Isaiah, stood at a crossroads: It could either regain its footing or begin a dangerous slide downward. The prophet did not temper his message for the sake of popular opinion. He had harsh and unyielding words about what changes must take place.

Although he moved in royal circles, Isaiah was hardly a yes-man in politics. Sometimes he stood alone against a tide of optimism. His very name meant "The LORD saves," and he warned kings that relying on military power or wealth or any force other than God would lead to disaster.

Isaiah outlasted four kings, but he finally offended one beyond repair. King Manasseh (notorious for practicing infant sacrifice) found Isaiah's strong words too much to bear. Tradition records that he had Isaiah killed by fastening him between two planks of wood and sawing his body in half.

Manasseh has long since disappeared into obscurity. But Isaiah, through this book, endures as one of the great authors of all time. Sometimes the pen *is* mightier than the sword.

How to Read Isaiah

I n the eighth century B.C., about the time Homer was writing *The Iliad* and *The Odyssey*, Isaiah wrote the book that bears his name. It is arguably the most eloquent book in the Old Testament, and you will likely recognize many verses and phrases.

Isaiah is full of profound insights into the nature of God and his plan for the earth. Due to its length and its peculiar organization, however, the book may seem hard to grasp.

Remember that Isaiah consists of a collection of many messages on various topics, pulled together into groupings. To understand Isaiah, it helps to think of "road markers" that set off the major groupings. Here is a summary of them:

Isaiah 1–12: Isaiah's call and messages of warning to Judah during the prosperous days of the kingdom. (These came mostly in the reigns of Jotham and Ahaz: see "A Lineup of Rulers," pages 1417–1425.)

Isaiah 13–23: Isaiah's messages to all the nations around Judah—including enemies and close allies.

Isaiah 24–35: A view of the earth's future (24–27) and specific messages to the people of Judah as they faced Assyria's imminent invasion.

Isaiah 36–39: An interlude telling of great crises faced by King Hezekiah. The focus of the book moves from Assyria to Babylon.

Isaiah 40–48: Prophecies addressed to a very different situation, 200 years into the future. Now Babylon, not Assyria, is the great enemy.

Isaiah 49–55: A word of hope about final deliverance through the "suffering servant."

Isaiah 56–66: General warnings to Judah, and a view of the future.

PEOPLE YOU'LL MEET IN ISAIAH

ISAIAH (p. 736)
CYRUS (p. 781)

3-TRACK READING PLAN

For an explanation and complete listing of the 3-track reading plan, turn to page 7.

TRACK 1: *Two-Week Courses on the Bible*
The Track 1 reading program on the Old Testament includes one chapter from Isaiah. See page 8 for a complete listing of this course.

TRACK 2: *An Overview of Isaiah in 6 Days*
☐ Day 1. Read the Introduction to Isaiah and also chapter 6. This chapter describes Isaiah's dramatic call.
☐ Day 2. Read chapter 25, a song of praise.
☐ Day 3. Read chapter 40, a great description of God and his power over the whole earth.
☐ Day 4. Read chapter 52, which gives detailed descriptions of God's ultimate plan.
☐ Day 5. Read chapter 53, a remarkable prophecy quoted at least ten times in the New Testament.
☐ Day 6. Read chapter 55, a word of great comfort from God.

Now turn to page 9 for your next Track 2 reading project.

TRACK 3: *All of Isaiah in 63 Days*
After you have read through Isaiah, turn to pages 10–14 for your next Track 3 reading project.

☐1	☐2	☐3	☐4–5	☐6	☐7	☐8	☐9
☐10	☐11	☐12	☐13	☐14	☐15	☐16	☐17
☐18	☐19–20	☐21	☐22	☐23	☐24	☐25	☐26
☐27	☐28	☐29	☐30	☐31	☐32	☐33	☐34
☐35	☐36	☐37	☐38–39	☐40	☐41	☐42	☐43
☐44	☐45	☐46	☐47	☐48	☐49	☐50	☐51
☐52	☐53	☐54	☐55	☐56	☐57	☐58	☐59
☐60	☐61	☐62	☐63	☐64	☐65	☐66	

Rebellion of God's People

1 The vision of Isaiah the son of Amoz concerning Judah and Jerusalem, which he saw during the reigns of Uzziah, Jotham, Ahaz *and* Hezekiah, kings of Judah.

2 Listen, O heavens, and hear, O earth;
    For the LORD speaks,
    "Sons I have reared and brought up,
    But they have revolted against Me.
3 "An ox knows its owner,
    And a donkey its master's manger,
    But Israel does not know,
    My people do not understand."

4 ¶ Alas, sinful nation,
    People weighed down with iniquity,
    Offspring of evildoers,
    Sons who act corruptly!
    They have abandoned the LORD,
    They have despised the Holy One of
        Israel,
    They have turned away from Him.

5 ¶ Where will you be stricken again,
    As you continue in *your* rebellion?
    The whole head is sick
    And the whole heart is faint.
6 From the sole of the foot even to the
        head
    There is nothing sound in it,
    Only bruises, welts and raw wounds,
    Not pressed out or bandaged,
    Nor softened with oil.

7 ¶ Your land is desolate,
    Your cities are burned with fire,
    Your fields—strangers are devouring
        them in your presence;
    It is desolation, as overthrown by
        strangers.
8 The daughter of Zion is left like a shelter
        in a vineyard,
    Like a watchman's hut in a cucumber
        field, like a besieged city.
9 Unless the LORD of hosts
    Had left us a few survivors,
    We would be like Sodom,
    We would be like Gomorrah.

God Has Had Enough

10 ¶ Hear the word of the LORD,
    You rulers of Sodom;
    Give ear to the instruction of our God,
    You people of Gomorrah.
11 "What are your multiplied sacrifices
        to Me?"
    Says the LORD.
    "I have had enough of burnt offerings of
        rams
    And the fat of fed cattle;
    And I take no pleasure in the blood of
        bulls, lambs or goats.

12 "When you come to appear before Me,
    Who requires of you this trampling of
        My courts?
13 "Bring your worthless offerings no longer,
    Incense is an abomination to Me.
    New moon and sabbath, the calling of
        assemblies—
    I cannot endure iniquity and the solemn
        assembly.
14 "I hate your new moon *festivals* and your
        appointed feasts,
    They have become a burden to Me;
    I am weary of bearing *them*.

1:14 The New Sodom

Is God finished with Israel? He denounces them as "Sodom and Gomorrah" (verse 10), judging their worship worthless, and their prayers an insult. But just when his tirade reaches its peak, God invites the Israelites to "come . . . reason" with him. Sins "as scarlet" shall be "as white as snow" (verse 18). God judges his people not to destroy them, but to bring them to repentance, forgiveness, and redemption.

15 "So when you spread out your hands *in*
        prayer,
    I will hide My eyes from you;
    Yes, even though you multiply prayers,
    I will not listen.
    Your hands are covered with blood.

16 ¶ "Wash yourselves, make yourselves
        clean;
    Remove the evil of your deeds from My
        sight.
    Cease to do evil,
17 Learn to do good;
    Seek justice,
    Reprove the ruthless,
    Defend the orphan,
    Plead for the widow.

"Let Us Reason"

18 ¶ "Come now, and let us reason
        together,"
    Says the LORD,
    "Though your sins are as scarlet,
    They will be as white as snow;
    Though they are red like crimson,
    They will be like wool.
19 "If you consent and obey,
    You will eat the best of the land;
20 "But if you refuse and rebel,
    You will be devoured by the sword."
    Truly, the mouth of the LORD has
        spoken.

Zion Corrupted, to be Redeemed

21 ¶ How the faithful city has become a
harlot,
She *who* was full of justice!
Righteousness once lodged in her,
But now murderers.
22 Your silver has become dross,
Your drink diluted with water.
23 Your rulers are rebels
And companions of thieves;
Everyone loves a bribe
And chases after rewards.
They do not defend the orphan,
Nor does the widow's plea come before
them.

1:23 Justice, Not Religion

*Isaiah 1 paints a striking picture of conditions
in Judah. Descriptions of luxury indicate the
nation was prospering economically. There
was no shortage of offerings, prayers, and
religious celebrations (verses 11–17). But Isaiah
condemned Judah for not putting religion into
practice by defending weak people, such as
widows and the fatherless. The country's
prosperity had come at the poor's expense.*

24 ¶ Therefore the Lord GOD of hosts,
The Mighty One of Israel, declares,
"Ah, I will be relieved of My adversaries
And avenge Myself on My foes.
25 "I will also turn My hand against you,
And will smelt away your dross as
with lye
And will remove all your alloy.
26 "Then I will restore your judges as at the
first,
And your counselors as at the beginning;
After that you will be called the city of
righteousness,
A faithful city."

27 ¶ Zion will be redeemed with justice
And her repentant ones with
righteousness.
28 But transgressors and sinners will be
crushed together,
And those who forsake the LORD will
come to an end.
29 Surely you will be ashamed of the oaks
which you have desired,
And you will be embarrassed at the
gardens which you have chosen.
30 For you will be like an oak whose leaf
fades away
Or as a garden that has no water.
31 The strong man will become tinder,
His work also a spark.

Thus they shall both burn together
And there will be none to quench *them*.

God's Universal Reign

2 The word which Isaiah the son of Amoz saw
concerning Judah and Jerusalem.
2 ¶ Now it will come about that
In the last days
The mountain of the house of the LORD
Will be established as the chief of the
mountains,
And will be raised above the hills;
And all the nations will stream to it.
3 And many peoples will come and say,
"Come, let us go up to the mountain of
the LORD,
To the house of the God of Jacob;
That He may teach us concerning His
ways
And that we may walk in His paths."
For the law will go forth from Zion
And the word of the LORD from
Jerusalem.
4 And He will judge between the nations,
And will render decisions for many
peoples;
And they will hammer their swords into
plowshares and their spears into
pruning hooks.
Nation will not lift up sword against
nation,
And never again will they learn war.

5 ¶ Come, house of Jacob, and let us walk
in the light of the LORD.
6 For You have abandoned Your people,
the house of Jacob,
Because they are filled *with influences*
from the east,
And *they are* soothsayers like the
Philistines,
And they strike *bargains* with the
children of foreigners.
7 Their land has also been filled with silver
and gold
And there is no end to their treasures;
Their land has also been filled with
horses
And there is no end to their chariots.
8 Their land has also been filled with idols;
They worship the work of their hands,
That which their fingers have made.
9 So the *common* man has been humbled
And the man *of importance* has been
abased,
But do not forgive them.
10 Enter the rock and hide in the dust
From the terror of the LORD and from
the splendor of His majesty.
11 The proud look of man will be abased
And the loftiness of man will be
humbled,

And the LORD alone will be exalted in
that day.

A Day of Reckoning Coming

12 ¶ For the LORD of hosts will have a day
of reckoning
Against everyone who is proud and lofty
And against everyone who is lifted up,
That he may be abased.
13 And *it will be* against all the cedars of
Lebanon that are lofty and lifted up,
Against all the oaks of Bashan,
14 Against all the lofty mountains,
Against all the hills that are lifted up,
15 Against every high tower,
Against every fortified wall,
16 Against all the ships of Tarshish
And against all the beautiful craft.
17 The pride of man will be humbled
And the loftiness of men will be abased;
And the LORD alone will be exalted in
that day,
18 But the idols will completely vanish.
19 *Men* will go into caves of the rocks
And into holes of the ground
Before the terror of the LORD
And the splendor of His majesty,
When He arises to make the earth
tremble.
20 In that day men will cast away to the
moles and the bats
Their idols of silver and their idols of
gold,
Which they made for themselves to
worship,
21 In order to go into the caverns of the
rocks and the clefts of the cliffs
Before the terror of the LORD and the
splendor of His majesty,
When He arises to make the earth
tremble.
22 Stop regarding man, whose breath *of life*
is in his nostrils;
For why should he be esteemed?

God Will Remove the Leaders

3 For behold, the Lord GOD of hosts is
going to remove from Jerusalem and
Judah
Both supply and support, the whole
supply of bread
And the whole supply of water;
2 The mighty man and the warrior,
The judge and the prophet,
The diviner and the elder,
3 The captain of fifty and the honorable
man,
The counselor and the expert artisan,
And the skillful enchanter.
4 And I will make mere lads their princes,

And capricious children will rule over
them,
5 And the people will be oppressed,
Each one by another, and each one by
his neighbor;
The youth will storm against the elder
And the inferior against the honorable.
6 When a man lays hold of his brother in
his father's house, *saying,*
"You have a cloak, you shall be our ruler,
And these ruins will be under your
charge,"

3:6 Total Anarchy

*Isaiah foresees a time of judgment on Judah,
when total anarchy will prevail. Leaders will be
chosen at random, and the nation's supply of
young men will be decimated by war (verse
25). The vivid passage on the proud women of
Zion (3:16–4:1) shows why this book is
admired for its writing style.*

7 He will protest on that day, saying,
"I will not be *your* healer,
For in my house there is neither bread
nor cloak;
You should not appoint me ruler of the
people."
8 For Jerusalem has stumbled and Judah
has fallen,
Because their speech and their actions are
against the LORD,
To rebel against His glorious presence.
9 The expression of their faces bears
witness against them,
And they display their sin like Sodom;
They do not *even* conceal *it.*
Woe to them!
For they have brought evil on themselves.
10 Say to the righteous that *it will go* well
with them,
For they will eat the fruit of their actions.
11 Woe to the wicked! *It will go* badly
with him,
For what he deserves will be done to
him.
12 O My people! Their oppressors are
children,
And women rule over them.
O My people! Those who guide you lead
you astray
And confuse the direction of your paths.

God Will Judge

13 ¶ The LORD arises to contend,
And stands to judge the people.
14 The LORD enters into judgment with the
elders and princes of His people,

"It is you who have devoured the
vineyard;
The plunder of the poor is in your
houses.
15 "What do you mean by crushing My
people
And grinding the face of the poor?"
Declares the Lord GOD of hosts.

Judah's Women Denounced

16 ¶ Moreover, the LORD said, "Because the
daughters of Zion are proud
And walk with heads held high and
seductive eyes,
And go along with mincing steps
And tinkle the bangles on their feet,
17 Therefore the Lord will afflict the scalp of
the daughters of Zion with scabs,
And the LORD will make their foreheads
bare."
18 In that day the Lord will take away the beauty of *their* anklets, headbands, crescent ornaments,
19 dangling earrings, bracelets, veils,
20 headdresses, ankle chains, sashes, perfume
boxes, amulets,
21 finger rings, nose rings,
22 festal robes, outer tunics, cloaks, money
purses,
23 hand mirrors, undergarments, turbans and
veils.
24 Now it will come about that instead of
sweet perfume there will be
putrefaction;
Instead of a belt, a rope;
Instead of well-set hair, a plucked-out
scalp;
Instead of fine clothes, a donning of
sackcloth;
And branding instead of beauty.
25 Your men will fall by the sword
And your mighty ones in battle.
26 And her gates will lament and mourn,
And deserted she will sit on the ground.

A Remnant Prepared

4 For seven women will take hold of one man in
that day, saying, "We will eat our own bread
and wear our own clothes, only let us be called by
your name; take away our reproach!"
2 ¶ In that day the Branch of the LORD will be
beautiful and glorious, and the fruit of the earth
will be the pride and the adornment of the survivors of Israel.
3 It will come about that he who is left in Zion
and remains in Jerusalem will be called holy—everyone who is recorded for life in Jerusalem.
4 When the Lord has washed away the filth of
the daughters of Zion and purged the bloodshed
of Jerusalem from her midst, by the spirit of judgment and the spirit of burning,
5 then the LORD will create over the whole

area of Mount Zion and over her assemblies a
cloud by day, even smoke, and the brightness of a
flaming fire by night; for over all the glory will be
a canopy.
6 There will be a shelter to *give* shade from the
heat by day, and refuge and protection from the
storm and the rain.

Parable of the Vineyard

5 Let me sing now for my well-beloved
A song of my beloved concerning His
vineyard.
My well-beloved had a vineyard on a
fertile hill.
2 He dug it all around, removed its stones,
And planted it with the choicest vine.
And He built a tower in the middle of it
And also hewed out a wine vat in it;
Then He expected *it* to produce *good*
grapes,
But it produced *only* worthless ones.

3 ¶ "And now, O inhabitants of Jerusalem
and men of Judah,
Judge between Me and My vineyard.
4 "What more was there to do for My
vineyard that I have not done in it?
Why, when I expected *it* to produce *good*
grapes did it produce worthless
ones?

5:4 What Can God Do?

*The "Parable of the Vineyard" beautifully
summarizes God's message to Judah. Although
he had done everything possible to care for the
nation, his "vineyard"–the house of Israel–had
produced only wild grapes. What else could he
do but allow it to grow wild and uncultivated?
Jesus used a related analogy in some of his
parables (Matthew 20:1–16; 21:33–46; Mark
12:1–12; Luke 13:6–9; 20:9–19).*

5 "So now let Me tell you what I am going
to do to My vineyard:
I will remove its hedge and it will be
consumed;
I will break down its wall and it will
become trampled ground.
6 "I will lay it waste;
It will not be pruned or hoed,
But briars and thorns will come up.
I will also charge the clouds to rain no
rain on it."

7 ¶ For the vineyard of the LORD of hosts
is the house of Israel
And the men of Judah His delightful
plant.
Thus He looked for justice, but behold,
bloodshed;

For righteousness, but behold, a cry of
distress.

Woes for the Wicked

8 ¶ Woe to those who add house to house
   and join field to field,
   Until there is no more room,
   So that you have to live alone in the
      midst of the land!
9 In my ears the LORD of hosts *has sworn,*
   "Surely, many houses shall become
      desolate,
   Even great and fine ones, without
      occupants.
10 "For ten acres of vineyard will yield *only*
   one ᵃbath *of wine,*
   And a homer of seed will yield *but* an
   ᵇephah of grain."
11 Woe to those who rise early in the
   morning that they may pursue
      strong drink,
   Who stay up late in the evening that
      wine may inflame them!
12 Their banquets are *accompanied* by lyre
   and harp, by tambourine and flute,
   and by wine;
   But they do not pay attention to the
      deeds of the LORD,
   Nor do they consider the work of His
      hands.

13 ¶ Therefore My people go into exile for
   their lack of knowledge;
   And their honorable men are famished,
   And their multitude is parched with
      thirst.
14 Therefore Sheol has enlarged its throat
   and opened its mouth without
      measure;
   And Jerusalem's splendor, her multitude,
   her din *of revelry* and the jubilant
   within her, descend *into it.*
15 So the *common* man will be humbled
   and the man of *importance* abased,
   The eyes of the proud also will be
      abased.
16 But the LORD of hosts will be exalted in
      judgment,
   And the holy God will show Himself
   holy in righteousness.
17 Then the lambs will graze as in their
      pasture,
   And strangers will eat in the waste places
      of the wealthy.

18 ¶ Woe to those who drag iniquity with
   the cords of falsehood,
   And sin as if with cart ropes;
19 Who say, "Let Him make speed, let Him
   hasten His work, that we may see *it;*

And let the purpose of the Holy One of
   Israel draw near
And come to pass, that we may
   know *it!*"
20 Woe to those who call evil good, and
      good evil;
   Who substitute darkness for light and
   light for darkness;
   Who substitute bitter for sweet and sweet
   for bitter!
21 Woe to those who are wise in their own
      eyes
   And clever in their own sight!
22 Woe to those who are heroes in drinking
      wine
   And valiant men in mixing strong drink,
23 Who justify the wicked for a bribe,
   And take away the rights of the ones
      who are in the right!

24 ¶ Therefore, as a tongue of fire consumes
      stubble
   And dry grass collapses into the flame,
   So their root will become like rot and
      their blossom blow away as dust;
   For they have rejected the law of the
   LORD of hosts
   And despised the word of the Holy One
   of Israel.
25 On this account the anger of the LORD
   has burned against His people,
   And He has stretched out His hand
      against them and struck them down.
   And the mountains quaked, and their
   corpses lay like refuse in the middle
   of the streets.
   For all this His anger is not spent,
   But His hand is still stretched out.

26 ¶ He will also lift up a standard to the
   distant nation,
   And will whistle for it from the ends of
   the earth;
   And behold, it will come with speed
      swiftly.
27 No one in it is weary or stumbles,
   None slumbers or sleeps;
   Nor is the belt at its waist undone,
   Nor its sandal strap broken.
28 Its arrows are sharp and all its bows are
      bent;
   The hoofs of its horses seem like flint
   and its *chariot* wheels like a
      whirlwind.
29 Its roaring is like a lioness, and it roars
   like young lions;
   It growls as it seizes the prey
   And carries *it* off with no one to
      deliver *it.*
30 And it will growl over it in that day like
   the roaring of the sea.

ᵃ I.e. Approx 10 1/2 gal.   ᵇ I.e. Approx one bu

If one looks to the land, behold, there is
    darkness *and* distress;
Even the light is darkened by its clouds.

Isaiah's Vision

6 In the year of King Uzziah's death I saw the
Lord sitting on a throne, lofty and exalted,
with the train of His robe filling the temple.
2 Seraphim stood above Him, each having six
wings: with two he covered his face, and with two
he covered his feet, and with two he flew.

6:2 A Message from God

*Isaiah experienced a dramatic call from God to
become a prophet. The message was
personally delivered by seraphim, a term that
appears only here and means "something
burning and dazzling." Evidently, seraphim
were angels who acted as spokesmen for God.*

3 And one called out to another and said,
    "Holy, Holy, Holy, is the LORD of hosts,
    The whole earth is full of His glory."
4 And the foundations of the thresholds trembled at the voice of him who called out, while the
temple was filling with smoke.
5 Then I said,
    "Woe is me, for I am ruined!
    Because I am a man of unclean lips,
    And I live among a people of unclean
        lips;
    For my eyes have seen the King, the
        LORD of hosts."
6 ¶ Then one of the seraphim flew to me with
a burning coal in his hand, which he had taken
from the altar with tongs.
7 He touched my mouth *with it* and said, "Behold, this has touched your lips; and your iniquity
is taken away and your sin is forgiven."

Isaiah's Commission

8 Then I heard the voice of the Lord, saying,
"Whom shall I send, and who will go for Us?"
Then I said, "Here am I. Send me!"
9 He said, "Go, and tell this people:
    'Keep on listening, but do not perceive;
    Keep on looking, but do not understand.'
10 "Render the hearts of this people
        insensitive,
    Their ears dull,
    And their eyes dim,
    Otherwise they might see with their eyes,
    Hear with their ears,
    Understand with their hearts,
    And return and be healed."
11 Then I said, "Lord, how long?" And He
answered,
    "Until cities are devastated *and* without
        inhabitant,

Houses are without people
    And the land is utterly desolate,
12 "The LORD has removed men far away,
    And the forsaken places are many in the
        midst of the land.
13 "Yet there will be a tenth portion in it,
    And it will again be *subject* to burning,
    Like a terebinth or an oak
    Whose stump remains when it is felled.
The holy seed is its stump."

War against Jerusalem

7 Now it came about in the days of Ahaz, the
son of Jotham, the son of Uzziah, king of Judah, that Rezin the king of Aram and Pekah the
son of Remaliah, king of Israel, went up to Jerusalem to *wage* war against it, but could not conquer it.
2 When it was reported to the house of David,
saying, "The Arameans have camped in Ephraim," his heart and the hearts of his people shook
as the trees of the forest shake with the wind.
3 ¶ Then the LORD said to Isaiah, "Go out
now to meet Ahaz, you and your son Shear-
jashub, at the end of the conduit of the upper
pool, on the highway to the fuller's field,
4 and say to him, 'Take care and be calm,
have no fear and do not be fainthearted because of
these two stubs of smoldering firebrands, on account of the fierce anger of Rezin and Aram and
the son of Remaliah.
5 'Because Aram, *with* Ephraim and the son of
Remaliah, has planned evil against you, saying,
6 "Let us go up against Judah and terrorize it,
and make for ourselves a breach in its walls and
set up the son of Tabeel as king in the midst of it,"
7 thus says the Lord GOD: "It shall not stand
nor shall it come to pass.
8 "For the head of Aram is Damascus and the
head of Damascus is Rezin (now within another
65 years Ephraim will be shattered, *so that it is* no
longer a people),
9 and the head of Ephraim is Samaria and the
head of Samaria is the son of Remaliah. If you will
not believe, you surely shall not last." ' "

The Child Immanuel

10 ¶ Then the LORD spoke again to Ahaz, saying,
11 "Ask a sign for yourself from the LORD your
God; make *it* deep as Sheol or high as heaven."
12 But Ahaz said, "I will not ask, nor will I test
the LORD!"
13 Then he said, "Listen now, O house of David! Is it too slight a thing for you to try the
patience of men, that you will try the patience of
my God as well?
14 "Therefore the Lord Himself will give you a

sign: Behold, a virgin will be with child and bear a son, and she will call His name *a*Immanuel.

15 "He will eat curds and honey at the time He knows *enough* to refuse evil and choose good.

7:14 A Famous Sign

Like so many prophecies, this one probably had two meanings: one for Isaiah's time and another much later. Isaiah urged King Ahaz to seek a sign from God about Judah's safety from its neighbors. Ahaz, notoriously stubborn and ungodly, refused.

Isaiah told of the sign anyway: A young boy would be born, and before he grew out of childhood Judah's feared enemies would be destroyed. Only 12 years after this prediction, the Northern Kingdom of Israel fell. The New Testament sees a further meaning in this prophecy, applying it to the birth of Jesus Christ (Matthew 1:23).

16 "For before the boy will know *enough* to refuse evil and choose good, the land whose two kings you dread will be forsaken.

Trials to Come for Judah

17 "The LORD will bring on you, on your people, and on your father's house such days as have never come since the day that Ephraim separated from Judah, the king of Assyria."

18 ¶ In that day the LORD will whistle for the fly that is in the remotest part of the rivers of Egypt and for the bee that is in the land of Assyria.

19 They will all come and settle on the steep ravines, on the ledges of the cliffs, on all the thorn bushes and on all the watering places.

20 ¶ In that day the Lord will shave with a razor, hired from regions beyond the Euphrates (*that is*, with the king of Assyria), the head and the hair of the legs; and it will also remove the beard.

21 ¶ Now in that day a man may keep alive a heifer and a pair of sheep;

22 and because of the abundance of the milk produced he will eat curds, for everyone that is left within the land will eat curds and honey.

23 ¶ And it will come about in that day, that every place where there used to be a thousand vines, *valued* at a thousand *shekels* of silver, will become briars and thorns.

24 *People* will come there with bows and arrows because all the land will be briars and thorns.

25 As for all the hills which used to be cultivated with the hoe, you will not go there for fear of briars and thorns; but they will become a place for pasturing oxen and for sheep to trample.

Damascus and Samaria Fall

8 Then the LORD said to me, "Take for yourself a large tablet and write on it in ordinary letters: Swift is the booty, speedy is the prey.

2 "And I will take to Myself faithful witnesses for testimony, Uriah the priest and Zechariah the son of Jeberechiah."

3 So I approached the prophetess, and she conceived and gave birth to a son. Then the LORD said to me, "Name him *b*Maher-shalal-hash-baz;

4 for before the boy knows how to cry out 'My father' or 'My mother,' the wealth of Damascus and the spoil of Samaria will be carried away before the king of Assyria."

5 ¶ Again the LORD spoke to me further, saying,

6 "Inasmuch as these people have rejected
   the gently flowing waters of Shiloah
And rejoice in Rezin and the son of
   Remaliah;

7 "Now therefore, behold, the Lord is about
   to bring on them the strong and
   abundant waters of the Euphrates,
Even the king of Assyria and all his
   glory;
And it will rise up over all its channels
   and go over all its banks.

8 "Then it will sweep on into Judah, it will
   overflow and pass through,
It will reach even to the neck;
And the spread of its wings will fill the
   breadth of your land, O Immanuel.

A Believing Remnant

9 ¶ "Be broken, O peoples, and be
   shattered;
And give ear, all remote places of the
   earth.
Gird yourselves, yet be shattered;
Gird yourselves, yet be shattered.

10 "Devise a plan, but it will be thwarted;
State a proposal, but it will not stand,
For God is with us."

11 ¶ For thus the LORD spoke to me with mighty power and instructed me not to walk in the way of this people, saying,

12 "You are not to say, '*It is* a conspiracy!'
In regard to all that this people call a
   conspiracy,
And you are not to fear what they fear
   or be in dread of *it.*

13 "It is the LORD of hosts whom you should
   regard as holy.
And He shall be your fear,
And He shall be your dread.

14 "Then He shall become a sanctuary;
But to both the houses of Israel, a stone
   to strike and a rock to stumble over,

---

a I.e. God is with us   *b* I.e. swift is the booty, speedy is the prey

And a snare and a trap for the
    inhabitants of Jerusalem.
15 "Many will stumble over them,
    Then they will fall and be broken;
    They will even be snared and caught."
16 ¶ Bind up the testimony, seal the law among my disciples.

17 And I will wait for the LORD who is hiding His face from the house of Jacob; I will even look eagerly for Him.

18 Behold, I and the children whom the LORD has given me are for signs and wonders in Israel from the LORD of hosts, who dwells on Mount Zion.

19 ¶ When they say to you, "Consult the mediums and the spiritists who whisper and mutter," should not a people consult their God? *Should they consult* the dead on behalf of the living?

20 To the law and to the testimony! If they do not speak according to this word, it is because they have no dawn.

8:20 Whom to Believe?

King Ahaz and his people sought guidance from every source but the right one. They consulted mediums, spiritists, even the dead. Isaiah suggests ironically that they try God. "To the law and to the testimony!" he says—that is, to the Scriptures, which give God's commandments and the testimony of what great things he has done.

21 They will pass through the land hardpressed and famished, and it will turn out that when they are hungry, they will be enraged and curse their king and their God as they face upward.

22 Then they will look to the earth, and behold, distress and darkness, the gloom of anguish; and *they will be* driven away into darkness.

Birth and Reign of the Prince of Peace

9 But there will be no *more* gloom for her who was in anguish; in earlier times He treated the land of Zebulun and the land of Naphtali with contempt, but later on He shall make *it* glorious, by the way of the sea, on the other side of Jordan, Galilee of the Gentiles.

2 The people who walk in darkness
    Will see a great light;
    Those who live in a dark land,
    The light will shine on them.
3 You shall multiply the nation,
    You shall increase their gladness;
    They will be glad in Your presence
    As with the gladness of harvest,
    As men rejoice when they divide the
      spoil.

4 For You shall break the yoke of their
    burden and the staff on their
    shoulders,
    The rod of their oppressor, as at the
    battle of Midian.
5 For every boot of the booted warrior in
    the *battle* tumult,
    And cloak rolled in blood, will be for
    burning, fuel for the fire.
6 For a child will be born to us, a son will
    be given to us;
    And the government will rest on His
    shoulders;
    And His name will be called Wonderful
    Counselor, Mighty God,
    Eternal Father, Prince of Peace.

9:6 A Child Is Born

Isaiah includes many direct predictions of the coming Messiah, including this passage, which established that the Messiah will come from Galilee (verse 1). The lands Isaiah mentions as "treated . . . with contempt" in verse 1 are the very regions devastated by Assyria's armies (2 Kings 15:29). Thus Isaiah offers a word of distant hope for those parts of his nation most affected by war.

7 There will be no end to the increase of
    His government or of peace,
    On the throne of David and over his
    kingdom,
    To establish it and to uphold it with
    justice and righteousness
    From then on and forevermore.
    The zeal of the LORD of hosts will
    accomplish this.

God's Anger with Israel's Arrogance

8 ¶ The Lord sends a message against
    Jacob,
    And it falls on Israel.
9 And all the people know *it*,
    That is, Ephraim and the inhabitants of
    Samaria,
    Asserting in pride and in arrogance of
    heart:
10 "The bricks have fallen down,
    But we will rebuild with smooth stones;
    The sycamores have been cut down,
    But we will replace *them* with cedars."
11 Therefore the LORD raises against them
    adversaries from Rezin
    And spurs their enemies on,
12 The Arameans on the east and the
    Philistines on the west;
    And they devour Israel with gaping jaws.

In *spite of* all this, His anger does not
turn away
And His hand is still stretched out.

13 ¶ Yet the people do not turn back to
Him who struck them,
Nor do they seek the LORD of hosts.
14 So the LORD cuts off head and tail from
Israel,
Both palm branch and bulrush in a single
day.
15 The head is the elder and honorable
man,
And the prophet who teaches falsehood
is the tail.
16 For those who guide this people are
leading *them* astray;
And those who are guided by them are
brought to confusion.
17 Therefore the Lord does not take
pleasure in their young men,
Nor does He have pity on their orphans
or their widows;
For every one of them is godless and an
evildoer,
And every mouth is speaking foolishness.
In *spite of* all this, His anger does not
turn away
And His hand is still stretched out.

18 ¶ For wickedness burns like a fire;
It consumes briars and thorns;
It even sets the thickets of the forest
aflame
And they roll upward in a column of
smoke.
19 By the fury of the LORD of hosts the land
is burned up,
And the people are like fuel for the fire;
No man spares his brother.
20 They slice off *what is* on the right hand
but *still* are hungry,
And they eat *what is* on the left hand but
they are not satisfied;
Each of them eats the flesh of his own
arm.
21 Manasseh *devours* Ephraim, and Ephraim
Manasseh,
And together they are against Judah.
In *spite of* all this, His anger does not
turn away
And His hand is still stretched out.

Assyria Is God's Instrument

10 Woe to those who enact evil statutes
And to those who constantly record
unjust decisions,
2 So as to deprive the needy of justice
And rob the poor of My people of *their*
rights,
So that widows may be their spoil
And that they may plunder the orphans.

3 Now what will you do in the day of
punishment,
And in the devastation which will come
from afar?
To whom will you flee for help?
And where will you leave your wealth?
4 Nothing *remains* but to crouch among
the captives
Or fall among the slain.
In *spite of* all this, His anger does not
turn away
And His hand is still stretched out.

5 ¶ Woe to Assyria, the rod of My anger
And the staff in whose hands is My
indignation,
6 I send it against a godless nation
And commission it against the people of
My fury
To capture booty and to seize plunder,
And to trample them down like mud in
the streets.
7 Yet it does not so intend,
Nor does it plan so in its heart,
But rather it is its purpose to destroy
And to cut off many nations.

10:7 God's Hand in History

*In this comment, God reveals how he works
through history in hidden, indirect ways. The
pagan empire Assyria had no idea it was being
used by the true God—it dealt with Jerusalem
just as it dealt with any nation and its idols
(verse 11). Nevertheless, Assyria would serve
God's purpose, and would one day be punished
for its own pride and greed (verse 12).*

8 For it says, "Are not my princes all
kings?
9 "Is not Calno like Carchemish,
Or Hamath like Arpad,
Or Samaria like Damascus?
10 "As my hand has reached to the
kingdoms of the idols,
Whose graven images *were* greater than
those of Jerusalem and Samaria,
11 Shall I not do to Jerusalem and her
images
Just as I have done to Samaria and her
idols?"

12 ¶ So it will be that when the Lord has completed all His work on Mount Zion and on Jerusalem, *He will say,* "I will punish the fruit of the
arrogant heart of the king of Assyria and the
pomp of his haughtiness."
13 For he has said,
"By the power of my hand and by my
wisdom I did *this,*
For I have understanding;

And I removed the boundaries of the
    peoples
And plundered their treasures,
And like a mighty man I brought down
    their inhabitants,

14 And my hand reached to the riches of
    the peoples like a nest,
And as one gathers abandoned eggs, I
    gathered all the earth;
And there was not one that flapped its
    wing or opened *its* beak or chirped."

15 ¶ Is the axe to boast itself over the one
    who chops with it?
Is the saw to exalt itself over the one
    who wields it?
That would be like a club wielding those
    who lift it,
Or like a rod lifting *him who* is not
    wood.

16 Therefore the Lord, the GOD of hosts,
    will send a wasting disease among
    his stout warriors;
And under his glory a fire will be kindled
    like a burning flame.

17 And the light of Israel will become a fire
    and his Holy One a flame,
And it will burn and devour his thorns
    and his briars in a single day.

18 And He will destroy the glory of his
    forest and of his fruitful garden,
    both soul and body,
And it will be as when a sick man wastes
    away.

19 And the rest of the trees of his forest will
    be so small in number
That a child could write them down.

A Remnant Will Return

20 ¶ Now in that day the remnant of Israel, and
those of the house of Jacob who have escaped, will
never again rely on the one who struck them, but
will truly rely on the LORD, the Holy One of Israel.

21 A remnant will return, the remnant of
    Jacob, to the mighty God.

22 For though your people, O Israel, may be
    like the sand of the sea,
Only a remnant within them will return;
A destruction is determined, overflowing
    with righteousness.

23 For a complete destruction, one that is decreed, the Lord GOD of hosts will execute in the
midst of the whole land.

24 ¶ Therefore thus says the Lord GOD of
hosts, "O My people who dwell in Zion, do not
fear the Assyrian who strikes you with the rod and
lifts up his staff against you, the way Egypt *did*.

25 "For in a very little while My indignation
against you will be spent and My anger *will be
directed* to their destruction."

26 The LORD of hosts will arouse a scourge
against him like the slaughter of Midian at the
rock of Oreb; and His staff will be over the sea and
He will lift it up the way *He did* in Egypt.

27 So it will be in that day, that his burden will
be removed from your shoulders and his yoke
from your neck, and the yoke will be broken because of fatness.

28 ¶ He has come against Aiath,
    He has passed through Migron;
    At Michmash he deposited his baggage.

29 They have gone through the pass, *saying*,
    "Geba will be our lodging place."
    Ramah is terrified, and Gibeah of Saul
      has fled away.

30 Cry aloud with your voice, O daughter of
    Gallim!
    Pay attention, Laishah *and* wretched
      Anathoth!

31 Madmenah has fled.
    The inhabitants of Gebim have sought
      refuge.

32 Yet today he will halt at Nob;
    He shakes his fist at the mountain of the
      daughter of Zion, the hill of
      Jerusalem.

33 ¶ Behold, the Lord, the GOD of hosts,
    will lop off the boughs with a
      terrible crash;
Those also who are tall in stature will be
    cut down
And those who are lofty will be abased.

34 He will cut down the thickets of the
    forest with an iron *axe*,
And Lebanon will fall by the
    Mighty One.

Righteous Reign of the Branch

11 Then a shoot will spring from the stem of
    Jesse,
And a branch from his roots will bear
    fruit.

11:1–16 The Good Old Days

*To express his message of hope to the Israelite
people, Isaiah appealed to their fondest
memories. This chapter borrows images from
three of the greatest events from the past: the
prosperous dynasty of David when Israel was
united (verse 1); the Garden of Eden (verses
6–9); and the miracles of the exodus from
Egypt (verse 15). Whatever the state of "the
good old days," the future time of peace will
exceed it.*

2 The Spirit of the LORD will rest on Him,
    The spirit of wisdom and understanding,
    The spirit of counsel and strength,
    The spirit of knowledge and the fear of
      the LORD.

3 And He will delight in the fear of the
LORD,
And He will not judge by what His eyes
see,
Nor make a decision by what His ears
hear;
4 But with righteousness He will judge the
poor,
And decide with fairness for the afflicted
of the earth;
And He will strike the earth with the rod
of His mouth,
And with the breath of His lips He will
slay the wicked.
5 Also righteousness will be the belt about
His loins,
And faithfulness the belt about His waist.

6 ¶ And the wolf will dwell with the lamb,
And the leopard will lie down with the
young goat,
And the calf and the young lion *and
the fatling together;
And a little boy will lead them.
7 Also the cow and the bear will graze,
Their young will lie down together,
And the lion will eat straw like the ox.
8 The nursing child will play by the hole of
the cobra,
And the weaned child will put his hand
on the viper's den.
9 They will not hurt or destroy in all My
holy mountain,
For the earth will be full of the
knowledge of the LORD
As the waters cover the sea.

10 ¶ Then in that day
The nations will resort to the root of
Jesse,
Who will stand as a signal for the
peoples;
And His resting place will be glorious.

The Restored Remnant

11 ¶ Then it will happen on that day that
the Lord
Will again recover the second time with
His hand
The remnant of His people, who will
remain,
From Assyria, Egypt, Pathros, Cush,
Elam, Shinar, Hamath,
And from the islands of the sea.
12 And He will lift up a standard for the
nations
And assemble the banished ones of
Israel,
And will gather the dispersed of Judah
From the four corners of the earth.
13 Then the jealousy of Ephraim will depart,

And those who harass Judah will be cut
off;
Ephraim will not be jealous of Judah,
And Judah will not harass Ephraim.
14 They will swoop down on the slopes of
the Philistines on the west;
Together they will plunder the sons of
the east;
They will possess Edom and Moab,
And the sons of Ammon will be subject
to them.
15 And the LORD will utterly destroy
The tongue of the Sea of Egypt;
And He will wave His hand over the
River
With His scorching wind;
And He will strike it into seven streams
And make *men* walk over dry-shod.
16 And there will be a highway from Assyria
For the remnant of His people who will
be left,
Just as there was for Israel
In the day that they came up out of the
land of Egypt.

Thanksgiving Expressed

12 Then you will say on that day,
"I will give thanks to You, O LORD;
For although You were angry with me,
Your anger is turned away,
And You comfort me.
2 "Behold, God is my salvation,
I will trust and not be afraid;
For the LORD GOD is my strength and
song,
And He has become my salvation."
3 Therefore you will joyously draw water
From the springs of salvation.
4 And in that day you will say,
"Give thanks to the LORD, call on His
name.
Make known His deeds among the
peoples;
Make *them* remember that His name is
exalted."
5 Praise the LORD in song, for He has done
excellent things;
Let this be known throughout the earth.
6 Cry aloud and shout for joy,
O inhabitant of Zion,
For great in your midst is the Holy One
of Israel.

Prophecies about Babylon

13 The oracle concerning Babylon which Isaiah
the son of Amoz saw.
2 Lift up a standard on the *b*bare hill,
Raise your voice to them,
Wave the hand that they may enter the
doors of the nobles.

a Some versions read *will feed together*   *b* Or *wind-swept mountain*

3 I have commanded My consecrated ones,
I have even called My mighty warriors,
My proudly exulting ones,
To *execute* My anger.

4 A sound of tumult on the mountains,
Like that of many people!
A sound of the uproar of kingdoms,
Of nations gathered together!
The LORD of hosts is mustering the army
for battle.
5 They are coming from a far country,
From the farthest horizons,
The LORD and His instruments of
indignation,
To destroy the whole land.

Judgment on the Day of the LORD

6 Wail, for the day of the LORD is near!
It will come as destruction from the
Almighty.
7 Therefore all hands will fall limp,
And every man's heart will melt.
8 They will be terrified,
Pains and anguish will take hold of *them;*
They will writhe like a woman in labor,
They will look at one another in
astonishment,
Their faces aflame.
9 Behold, the day of the LORD is coming,
Cruel, with fury and burning anger,
To make the land a desolation;
And He will exterminate its sinners
from it.
10 For the stars of heaven and their
constellations
Will not flash forth their light;
The sun will be dark when it rises
And the moon will not shed its light.
11 Thus I will punish the world for its evil
And the wicked for their iniquity;
I will also put an end to the arrogance of
the proud
And abase the haughtiness of the
ruthless.
12 I will make mortal man scarcer than
pure gold
And mankind than the gold of Ophir.

13 Therefore I will make the heavens
tremble,
And the earth will be shaken from its
place
At the fury of the LORD of hosts
In the day of His burning anger.
14 And it will be that like a hunted gazelle,
Or like sheep with none to gather *them,*
They will each turn to his own people,
And each one flee to his own land.
15 Anyone who is found will be thrust
through,
And anyone who is captured will fall by
the sword.
16 Their little ones also will be dashed to
pieces
Before their eyes;
Their houses will be plundered
And their wives ravished.

Babylon Will Fall to the Medes

17 ¶ Behold, I am going to stir up the
Medes against them,
Who will not value silver or take pleasure
in gold.
18 And *their* bows will mow down the
young men,
They will not even have compassion on
the fruit of the womb,
Nor will their eye pity children.
19 And Babylon, the beauty of kingdoms,
the glory of the Chaldeans' pride,
Will be as when God overthrew Sodom
and Gomorrah.
20 It will never be inhabited or lived in
from generation to generation;
Nor will the Arab pitch *his* tent there,
Nor will shepherds make *their flocks* lie
down there.
21 But desert creatures will lie down there,
And their houses will be full of owls;
Ostriches also will live there, and shaggy
goats will frolic there.
22 Hyenas will howl in their fortified towers
And jackals in their luxurious palaces.
Her *fateful* time also will soon come
And her days will not be prolonged.

Israel's Taunt

14 When the LORD will have compassion on
Jacob and again choose Israel, and settle
them in their own land, then strangers will join
them and attach themselves to the house of
Jacob.
2 The peoples will take them along and bring
them to their place, and the house of Israel will
possess them as an inheritance in the land of the
LORD as male servants and female servants; and
they will take their captors captive and will rule
over their oppressors.

3 ¶ And it will be in the day when the LORD gives you rest from your pain and turmoil and harsh service in which you have been enslaved,

4 that you will take up this taunt against the king of Babylon, and say,

"How the oppressor has ceased,
And how fury has ceased!

5 "The LORD has broken the staff of the wicked,
The scepter of rulers

6 Which used to strike the peoples in fury with unceasing strokes,
Which subdued the nations in anger with unrestrained persecution.

7 "The whole earth is at rest *and* is quiet;
They break forth into shouts of joy.

8 "Even the cypress trees rejoice over you,
and the cedars of Lebanon, *saying,*
'Since you were laid low, no *tree* cutter comes up against us.'

Faith in God or the Military?

Where does a weak nation turn for help?

IN 1944, WILD CHEERING GREETED the Russian tanks that rolled into Poland. The Russians were freeing Poland from the Nazis, and grateful Poles showered the liberating soldiers with fresh flowers.

But 45 years later, Russian troops had worn out their welcome, and the Polish government asked them to leave. The Polish experience offers living proof of a painful lesson of history: Military help from great powers usually comes with strings attached.

> *"This is the plan devised against the whole earth; and this is the hand that is stretched out against all the nations."* 14:26

A Small Nation Seeks Help

What can a small nation do when facing a military giant? Judah found itself in that predicament early in Isaiah's career. When two neighboring nations invaded, the tiny kingdom suffered heavy losses. King Ahaz and the people of Judah were shaken, "as the trees of the forest shake with the wind" (7:2). Panicked, Ahaz sought Isaiah's advice.

Isaiah had received a "call" to ministry as dramatic as any recorded in the Bible (chapter 6). King Ahaz knew that Isaiah would deliver a message straight from God, no matter how unpopular. Still, Ahaz was hardly prepared for what Isaiah said: Stay calm, don't worry, simply trust God.

The attacking kings were mere "stubs of smoldering firebrands," Isaiah declared (7:4). Whatever happens, don't seek help from an empire like Assyria; if you do, you will invite in the very army that will one day destroy you.

The Long Slide Begins

But Ahaz, reeling from the invasion, wanted quick relief. Ignoring Isaiah's warnings, he negotiated a treaty with mighty Assyria, using as a bribe the treasury of the temple in Jerusalem.

In the short term, Ahaz's decision brought results. No army of that day could match the Assyrian war machine, and all Judah's enemies fell to the onslaught. Israel, to the north, was wiped off the map. At last Judah had peace. But at what cost?

Perhaps as part of the treaty with Assyria, Ahaz began corrupting Judah's religion. He first closed the doors of the temple to worship, and later replaced the sacred altar to God with a foreign one. He officially adopted Assyria's state religion, going so far as to make a human sacrifice of his sons in a fire. In every way King Ahaz became a puppet king, under the thumb of Assyria. Foreign armies stayed in Judah. Indeed, Assyria's help had come with strings attached.

Messages for Then and Now

The prophet Isaiah was furious. He had grown up in a boom time in Judah, under a good king. Suddenly he saw his country become a mere pawn of Assyria, trading away even its great religious heritage.

Chapters 7–19 record his passionate words, not only against Judah, but against her neighbors also. He told of a reckoning day, when each nation would be punished for its sin and rebellion. The immediate future looked very bleak, and Isaiah minced no words in describing it.

But Isaiah did not stop there. He went on to project far into the future, in familiar words that still stir up hope and longing. This section begins with a question from a king about where to turn for help. It ends with a grand sweep of all of history.

Life Questions: What do you think Isaiah would say if he were writing today about such superpower countries as the United States and Russia?

9 "Sheol from beneath is excited over you
　　to meet you when you come;
　It arouses for you the spirits of the dead,
　　all the leaders of the earth;
　It raises all the kings of the nations from
　　their thrones.
10 "They will all respond and say to you,
　'Even you have been made weak as we,
　You have become like us.
11 'Your pomp *and* the music of your harps
　Have been brought down to Sheol;
　Maggots are spread out *as your bed*
　　beneath you
　And worms are your covering.'
12 "How you have fallen from heaven,
　O star of the morning, son of the dawn!
　You have been cut down to the earth,
　You who have weakened the nations!

14:12 Fall of the Morning Star

*A name used of Satan—"Lucifer," or "star of the
morning,"—comes from this verse. The word
Lucifer refers to Venus, one of the brightest
objects in the sky. Yet, when the sun rises, the
light of even the brightest morning star is
totally eclipsed.*

*In context, Isaiah was describing the cruelly
oppressive king of Babylon, who swelled with
pride but would be brought down to defeat.
However, Isaiah may be hinting at a force
behind the human king: Satan himself. Isaiah's
metaphor of the faded morning star aptly
describes the eclipse of the haughty king of
Babylon—and of Satan.*

13 "But you said in your heart,
　'I will ascend to heaven;
　I will raise my throne above the stars of
　　God,
　And I will sit on the mount of assembly
　In the recesses of the north.
14 'I will ascend above the heights of the
　　clouds;
　I will make myself like the Most High.'
15 "Nevertheless you will be thrust down to
　　Sheol,
　To the recesses of the pit.
16 "Those who see you will gaze at you,
　They will ponder over you, *saying,*
　'Is this the man who made the earth
　　tremble,
　Who shook kingdoms,
17 Who made the world like a wilderness
　And overthrew its cities,
　Who did not allow his prisoners to *go*
　　home?'
18 "All the kings of the nations lie in glory,
　Each in his own tomb.
19 "But you have been cast out of your tomb

Like a rejected branch,
　Clothed with the slain who are pierced
　　with a sword,
　Who go down to the stones of the pit
　Like a trampled corpse.
20 "You will not be united with them in
　　burial,
　Because you have ruined your country,
　You have slain your people.
　May the offspring of evildoers not be
　　mentioned forever.
21 "Prepare for his sons a place of slaughter
　Because of the iniquity of their fathers.
　They must not arise and take possession
　　of the earth
　And fill the face of the world with cities."

22 "I will rise up against them," declares the
LORD of hosts, "and will cut off from Babylon
name and survivors, offspring and posterity," declares the LORD.

23 "I will also make it a possession for the
hedgehog and swamps of water, and I will sweep
it with the broom of destruction," declares the
LORD of hosts.

Judgment on Assyria

24 The LORD of hosts has sworn saying, "Surely, just as I have intended so it has happened, and
just as I have planned so it will stand,

25 to break Assyria in My land, and I will trample him on My mountains. Then his yoke will
be removed from them and his burden removed
from their shoulder.

26 "This is the plan devised against the whole
earth; and this is the hand that is stretched out
against all the nations.

27 "For the LORD of hosts has planned, and who
can frustrate *it?* And as for His stretched-out
hand, who can turn it back?"

28 ¶ In the year that King Ahaz died this oracle
came:

Judgment on Philistia

29 "Do not rejoice, O Philistia, all of you,
　Because the rod that struck you is
　　broken;
　For from the serpent's root a viper will
　　come out,
　And its fruit will be a flying serpent.
30 "Those who are most helpless will eat,
　And the needy will lie down in security;
　I will destroy your root with famine,
　And it will kill off your survivors.
31 "Wail, O gate; cry, O city;
　Melt away, O Philistia, all of you;
　For smoke comes from the north,
　And there is no straggler in his ranks.
32 "How then will one answer the
　　messengers of the nation?
　That the LORD has founded Zion,

And the afflicted of His people will seek
refuge in it."

Judgment on Moab

15 The oracle concerning Moab.
Surely in a night Ar of Moab is
devastated *and* ruined;
Surely in a night Kir of Moab is
devastated *and* ruined.
2 They have gone up to the temple and *to*
Dibon, *even* to the high places to
weep.
Moab wails over Nebo and Medeba;
Everyone's head is bald *and* every beard
is cut off.
3 In their streets they have girded
themselves with sackcloth;
On their housetops and in their squares
Everyone is wailing, dissolved in tears.
4 Heshbon and Elealeh also cry out,
Their voice is heard all the way to Jahaz;
Therefore the armed men of Moab cry
aloud;
His soul trembles within him.
5 My heart cries out for Moab;
His fugitives are as far as Zoar *and*
Eglath-shelishiyah,
For they go up the ascent of Luhith
weeping;
Surely on the road to Horonaim they
raise a cry of distress over *their* ruin.
6 For the waters of Nimrim are desolate.
Surely the grass is withered, the tender
grass died out,
There is no green thing.
7 Therefore the abundance *which* they have
acquired and stored up
They carry off over the brook of Arabim.
8 For the cry of distress has gone around
the territory of Moab,
Its wail *goes* as far as Eglaim and its
wailing even to Beer-elim.
9 For the waters of Dimon are full of
blood;
Surely I will bring added *woes* upon
Dimon,
A lion upon the fugitives of Moab and
upon the remnant of the land.

Prophecy of Moab's Devastation

16 Send the *tribute* lamb to the ruler of the
land,
From Sela by way of the wilderness to
the mountain of the daughter of
Zion.
2 Then, like fleeing birds *or* scattered
nestlings,
The daughters of Moab will be at the
fords of the Arnon.
3 "Give *us* advice, make a decision;

Cast your shadow like night at high
noon;
Hide the outcasts, do not betray the
fugitive.
4 "Let the outcasts of Moab stay with you;
Be a hiding place to them from the
destroyer."
For the extortioner has come to an end,
destruction has ceased,
Oppressors have completely *disappeared*
from the land.
5 A throne will even be established in
lovingkindness,
And a judge will sit on it in faithfulness
in the tent of David;
Moreover, he will seek justice
And be prompt in righteousness.

6 ¶ We have heard of the pride of Moab,
an excessive pride;
Even of his arrogance, pride, and fury;
His idle boasts are false.
7 Therefore Moab will wail; everyone of
Moab will wail.
You will moan for the raisin cakes of
Kir-hareseth
As those who are utterly stricken.
8 For the fields of Heshbon have withered,
the vines of Sibmah *as well*;
The lords of the nations have trampled
down its choice clusters
Which reached as far as Jazer *and*
wandered to the deserts;
Its tendrils spread themselves out *and*
passed over the sea.
9 Therefore I will weep bitterly for Jazer,
for the vine of Sibmah;
I will drench you with my tears,
O Heshbon and Elealeh;
For the shouting over your summer
fruits and your harvest has fallen
away.

16:9 A Prophet's Pain

*Although Isaiah often delivered bad news to
the nations around him, he never took pleasure
in it. Remarkably, he often deeply identified
with the pain of other, non-Israelite nations
such as Moab (see 15:5). Chapters 15–16 were
likely used as sources for Jeremiah 48.
(Jeremiah was another prophet who suffered
greatly.)*

10 Gladness and joy are taken away from
the fruitful field;
In the vineyards also there will be no
cries of joy or jubilant shouting,
No treader treads out wine in the
presses,

For I have made the shouting to cease.
11 Therefore my heart intones like a harp
    for Moab
    And my inward feelings for Kir-hareseth.
12 So it will come about when Moab
    presents himself,
    When he wearies himself upon *his* high
    place
    And comes to his sanctuary to pray,
    That he will not prevail.
13 ¶ This is the word which the LORD spoke
earlier concerning Moab.
14 But now the LORD speaks, saying, "Within
three years, as a hired man would count them, the
glory of Moab will be degraded along with all *his*
great population, and *his* remnant will be very
small *and* impotent."

Prophecy about Damascus

17 The oracle concerning Damascus.
    "Behold, Damascus is about to be
    removed from being a city
    And will become a fallen ruin.
2 "The cities of Aroer are forsaken;
    They will be for flocks to lie down in,
    And there will be no one to frighten
    them.
3 "The fortified city will disappear from
    Ephraim,
    And sovereignty from Damascus
    And the remnant of Aram;
    They will be like the glory of the sons of
    Israel,"
    Declares the LORD of hosts.

4 ¶ Now in that day the glory of Jacob will
    fade,
    And the fatness of his flesh will become
    lean.
5 It will be even like the reaper gathering
    the standing grain,
    As his arm harvests the ears,
    Or it will be like one gleaning ears of
    grain
    In the valley of Rephaim.
6 Yet gleanings will be left in it like the
    shaking of an olive tree,
    Two *or* three olives on the topmost
    bough,
    Four *or* five on the branches of a fruitful
    tree,
    Declares the LORD, the God of Israel.
7 In that day man will have regard for his
    Maker
    And his eyes will look to the Holy One
    of Israel.
8 He will not have regard for the altars, the
    work of his hands,
    Nor will he look to that which his fingers
    have made,

    Even the *a*Asherim and incense stands.
9 In that day their strong cities will be like
    forsaken places in the forest,
    Or like branches which they abandoned
    before the sons of Israel;
    And the land will be a desolation.
10 For you have forgotten the God of your
    salvation
    And have not remembered the rock of
    your refuge.
    Therefore you plant delightful plants
    And set them with vine slips of a
    strange *god.*
11 In the day that you plant *it* you carefully
    fence *it* in,
    And in the morning you bring your seed
    to blossom;
    But the harvest will *be* a heap
    In a day of sickliness and incurable pain.

12 ¶ Alas, the uproar of many peoples
    Who roar like the roaring of the seas,
    And the rumbling of nations
    Who rush on like the rumbling of
    mighty waters!
13 The nations rumble on like the rumbling
    of many waters,
    But He will rebuke them and they will
    flee far away,
    And be chased like chaff in the
    mountains before the wind,
    Or like whirling dust before a gale.
14 At evening time, behold, *there is* terror!
    Before morning they are no more.
    Such *will be* the portion of those who
    plunder us
    And the lot of those who pillage us.

Message to Ethiopia

18 Alas, oh land of whirring wings
    Which lies beyond the rivers of *b*Cush,
2 Which sends envoys by the sea,
    Even in papyrus vessels on the surface of
    the waters.
    Go, swift messengers, to a nation tall and
    smooth,
    To a people feared far and wide,
    A powerful and oppressive nation
    Whose land the rivers divide.
3 All you inhabitants of the world and
    dwellers on earth,
    As soon as a standard is raised on the
    mountains, you will see *it,*
    And as soon as the trumpet is blown,
    you will hear *it.*
4 For thus the LORD has told me,
    "I will look from My dwelling place
    quietly
    Like dazzling heat in the sunshine,

---

a I.e. wooden symbols of a female deity   *b* Or *Ethiopia*

Like a cloud of dew in the heat of
harvest."
5 For before the harvest, as soon as the
bud blossoms

18:2 Foreign Policy

Isaiah never balked at direct political involvement. He consistently lobbied against alliances with any foreign powers. Here, he warned against the "envoys by the sea" coming from Cush, a region near Ethiopia or Sudan. Judah's king was often tempted to make alliances with Ethiopia or Egypt, but according to Isaiah, both nations would meet disaster.

And the flower becomes a ripening
grape,
Then He will cut off the sprigs with
pruning knives
And remove *and* cut away the spreading
branches.
6 They will be left together for mountain
birds of prey,
And for the beasts of the earth;
And the birds of prey will spend the
summer *feeding* on them,
And all the beasts of the earth will spend
harvest time on them.
7 At that time a gift of homage will be
brought to the LORD of hosts
From a people tall and smooth,
Even from a people feared far and wide,
A powerful and oppressive nation,
Whose land the rivers divide—
To the place of the name of the LORD of
hosts, *even* Mount Zion.

Message to Egypt

19 The oracle concerning Egypt.
Behold, the LORD is riding on a swift
cloud and is about to come to
Egypt;
The idols of Egypt will tremble at His
presence,
And the heart of the Egyptians will melt
within them.
2 "So I will incite Egyptians against
Egyptians;
And they will each fight against his
brother and each against his
neighbor,
City against city *and* kingdom against
kingdom.
3 "Then the spirit of the Egyptians will be
demoralized within them;
And I will confound their strategy,
So that they will resort to idols and
ghosts of the dead
And to mediums and spiritists.

4 "Moreover, I will deliver the Egyptians
into the hand of a cruel master,
And a mighty king will rule over them,"
declares the Lord GOD of hosts.
5 ¶ The waters from the sea will dry up,
And the river will be parched and dry.
6 The canals will emit a stench,
The streams of Egypt will thin out and
dry up;
The reeds and rushes will rot away.
7 The bulrushes by the Nile, by the edge of
the Nile
And all the sown fields by the Nile
Will become dry, be driven away, and be
no more.
8 And the fishermen will lament,
And all those who cast a line into the
Nile will mourn,
And those who spread nets on the waters
will pine away.
9 Moreover, the manufacturers of linen
made from combed flax
And the weavers of white cloth will be
utterly dejected.
10 And the pillars *of Egypt* will be crushed;
All the hired laborers will be grieved in
soul.
11 ¶ The princes of Zoan are mere fools;
The advice of Pharaoh's wisest advisers
has become stupid.
How can you *men* say to Pharaoh,
"I am a son of the wise, a son of ancient
kings"?
12 Well then, where are your wise men?
Please let them tell you,
And let them understand what the LORD
of hosts
Has purposed against Egypt.
13 The princes of Zoan have acted foolishly,
The princes of Memphis are deluded;
Those who are the cornerstone of her
tribes
Have led Egypt astray.
14 The LORD has mixed within her a spirit
of distortion;
They have led Egypt astray in all that it
does,
As a drunken man staggers in his vomit.
15 There will be no work for Egypt
Which *its* head or tail, *its* palm branch or
bulrush, may do.
16 ¶ In that day the Egyptians will become like
women, and they will tremble and be in dread
because of the waving of the hand of the LORD of
hosts, which He is going to wave over them.
17 The land of Judah will become a terror to
Egypt; everyone to whom it is mentioned will be
in dread of it, because of the purpose of the LORD
of hosts which He is purposing against them.
18 ¶ In that day five cities in the land of Egypt

will be speaking the language of Canaan and swearing *allegiance* to the LORD of hosts; one will be called the City of [a]Destruction.

19 ¶ In that day there will be an altar to the LORD in the midst of the land of Egypt, and a pillar to the LORD near its border.

20 It will become a sign and a witness to the LORD of hosts in the land of Egypt; for they will cry to the LORD because of oppressors, and He will send them a Savior and a Champion, and He will deliver them.

21 Thus the LORD will make Himself known to Egypt, and the Egyptians will know the LORD in that day. They will even worship with sacrifice and offering, and will make a vow to the LORD and perform it.

22 The LORD will strike Egypt, striking but healing; so they will return to the LORD, and He will respond to them and will heal them.

23 ¶ In that day there will be a highway from Egypt to Assyria, and the Assyrians will come into Egypt and the Egyptians into Assyria, and the Egyptians will worship with the Assyrians.

24 ¶ In that day Israel will be the third *party* with Egypt and Assyria, a blessing in the midst of the earth,

25 whom the LORD of hosts has blessed, saying, "Blessed is Egypt My people, and Assyria the work of My hands, and Israel My inheritance."

Prophecy about Egypt and Ethiopia

20 In the year that the commander came to Ashdod, when Sargon the king of Assyria sent him and he fought against Ashdod and captured it,

2 at that time the LORD spoke through Isaiah the son of Amoz, saying, "Go and loosen the sackcloth from your hips and take your shoes off your feet." And he did so, going naked and barefoot.

20:2 A Dramatic Object Lesson

Isaiah was an educated and urbane prophet, at home in the corridors of power. His reputation must have made this object lesson very shocking: For three years he walked around stripped and barefoot, in the guise of a slave, to protest a planned alliance with Egypt and Cush. He had originally opposed an alliance with Assyria. Now he opposed a treaty with other nations as well.

3 And the LORD said, "Even as My servant Isaiah has gone naked and barefoot three years as a sign and token against Egypt and Cush,

4 so the king of Assyria will lead away the captives of Egypt and the exiles of Cush, young and old, naked and barefoot with buttocks uncovered, to the shame of Egypt.

5 "Then they will be dismayed and ashamed because of Cush their hope and Egypt their boast.

6 "So the inhabitants of this coastland will say in that day, 'Behold, such is our hope, where we fled for help to be delivered from the king of Assyria; and we, how shall we escape?'"

God Commands That Babylon Be Taken

21 The oracle concerning the [b]wilderness of the sea.

As windstorms in the Negev sweep on,
It comes from the wilderness, from a
   terrifying land.
2 A harsh vision has been shown to me;
The treacherous one *still* deals
   treacherously, and the destroyer *still*
   destroys.
Go up, Elam, lay siege, Media;
I have made an end of all the groaning
   she has caused.
3 For this reason my loins are full of
   anguish;
Pains have seized me like the pains of a
   woman in labor.
I am so bewildered I cannot hear, so
   terrified I cannot see.
4 My mind reels, horror overwhelms me;
The twilight I longed for has been turned
   for me into trembling.
5 They set the table, they [c]spread out the
   cloth, they eat, they drink;
"Rise up, captains, oil the shields,"
6 For thus the Lord says to me,
"Go, station the lookout, let him report
   what he sees.
7 "When he sees riders, horsemen in pairs,
A train of donkeys, a train of camels,
Let him pay close attention, very close
   attention."
8 Then the lookout called,
"O Lord, I stand continually by day on
   the watchtower,
And I am stationed every night at my
   guard post.
9 "Now behold, here comes a troop of
   riders, horsemen in pairs."
And one said, "Fallen, fallen is Babylon;
And all the images of her gods are
   shattered on the ground."
10 O my threshed *people,* and my afflicted
   of the threshing floor!
What I have heard from the LORD of
   hosts,
The God of Israel, I make known to you.

Oracles about Edom and Arabia

11 ¶ The oracle concerning Edom.

---

[a] Some ancient mss and versions read *the Sun*   [b] Or *sandy wastes, sea country*   [c] Or *spread out the rugs* or possibly *they arranged the seating*

One keeps calling to me from Seir,
"Watchman, *how far gone is the night?
Watchman, *how far gone is the night?"
12 The watchman says,
"Morning comes but also night.
If you would inquire, inquire;
Come back again."

13 ¶ The oracle about Arabia.
In the thickets of Arabia you must spend
the night,
O caravans of Dedanites.
14 Bring water for the thirsty,
O inhabitants of the land of Tema,
Meet the fugitive with bread.
15 For they have fled from the swords,
From the drawn sword, and from the
bent bow
And from the press of battle.

a Lit *what is the time of the night?*

16 ¶ For thus the Lord said to me, "In a year,
as a hired man would count it, all the splendor of
Kedar will terminate;
17 and the remainder of the number of bowmen, the mighty men of the sons of Kedar, will be
few; for the LORD God of Israel has spoken."

The Valley of Vision

22 The oracle concerning the valley of vision.
What is the matter with you now, that
you have all gone up to the
housetops?
2 You who were full of noise,
You boisterous town, you exultant city;
Your slain were not slain with the sword,
Nor did they die in battle.
3 All your rulers have fled together,
And have been captured without the
bow;

Catastrophes Through God's Eyes
An endless cycle of war and death—what did it mean?

THERE IS ONE EASY WAY to picture the Middle East of Isaiah's
day: Simply follow today's newspaper headlines and project backward in
time. Then, as now, one nation would invade its neighbor, leveling cities
and devastating the land and its people. The prophet Isaiah longed for an
end to the cycle, much as modern-day residents of Lebanon or Israel do
today.
Isaiah looked at the world with a kind of split vision. Around him he saw
spiritual decay and the dreary cycle of war and death. Yet God had given him a
clear vision of what his nation could one day become: a pure people, faithful to
God, living in peace where "war no more."

*For this reason my
loins are full of
anguish; pains have
seized me like the
pains of a woman
in labor. I am so
bewildered I cannot
hear, so terrified I
cannot see.
21:3*

A Kingdom for a Purpose

With God's view of the future shining brightly before him, Isaiah went about reinterpreting history.
Others in Judah looked upon military invasions as terrible catastrophes. In contrast, Isaiah—though he
felt anguish over the events—saw glimpses of a higher purpose.
Isaiah said that Judah had to endure pain and suffering in order to be purified. He counseled
against making political alliances to forestall the punishment. God's people had to go through the fire,
and from the trials a *remnant*—a small remaining number of persons—would emerge that God could
then use to accomplish his work. Isaiah went so far as to name his own son "a remnant shall return" as
a walking object lesson of his message to Judah.
Why had the Jews been called by God in the first place? They were to be a "light to the nations,"
Isaiah said, a nation used by God to bring his truth to other nations. And out of the land of Judah God
would raise up a great Prince who would rule over all the earth.

Who Is in Charge?

In short, God had not discarded his people, no matter how bleak things looked. The Israelites
would ultimately become a missionary nation, pointing others to God.
Above all messages, Isaiah stressed this one: God is in charge of history. To Judah—surrounded by
enemies, staggering from invasion, weary of bloodshed—God seemed far away and distant. Isaiah
assured them that the great powers of earth were mere tools in God's hands; he would use them and
fling them aside.

Life Questions: Isaiah described people who felt afraid and abandoned by God. Have you ever felt like
that? How does Isaiah's message offer hope for us today?

All of you who were found were taken
  captive together,
Though they had fled far away.
4 Therefore I say, "Turn your eyes away
    from me,
Let me weep bitterly,
Do not try to comfort me concerning the
  destruction of the daughter of my
  people."
5 For the Lord GOD of hosts has a day of
    panic, subjugation and confusion
In the valley of vision,
A breaking down of walls
And a crying to the mountain.
6 Elam took up the quiver
With the chariots, infantry *and*
  horsemen;
And Kir uncovered the shield.
7 Then your choicest valleys were full of
    chariots,
And the horsemen took up fixed
  positions at the gate.
8 And He removed the defense of Judah.
In that day you depended on the
  weapons of the house of the forest,
9 And you saw that the breaches
In the *wall* of the city of David were
  many;
And you collected the waters of the lower
  pool.
10 Then you counted the houses of
     Jerusalem
And tore down houses to fortify the
  wall.
11 And you made a reservoir between the
     two walls
For the waters of the old pool.
But you did not depend on Him who
  made it,
Nor did you take into consideration Him
  who planned it long ago.

12 ¶ Therefore in that day the Lord GOD of
     hosts called *you* to weeping, to
     wailing,

22:12 Smiles Instead of Tears

*This chapter may refer to Jerusalem's
deliverance recorded in Isaiah 36–37. Isaiah
was distressed because, although great
devastation was prophesied, Jerusalem was
celebrating, not mourning. People had
reinforced walls and built water reservoirs to
prepare for war, but had not turned to God for
help (verse 11). Israelites at that time had a
certain cockiness about the city of Jerusalem,
believing that God would never allow it to fall
into enemy hands.*

To shaving the head and to wearing
  sackcloth.
13 Instead, there is gaiety and gladness,
Killing of cattle and slaughtering of
  sheep,
Eating of meat and drinking of wine:
"Let us eat and drink, for tomorrow we
  may die."
14 But the LORD of hosts revealed Himself
     to me,
"Surely this iniquity shall not be
  forgiven you
Until you die," says the Lord GOD of
  hosts.

15 ¶ Thus says the Lord GOD of hosts,
"Come, go to this steward,
To Shebna, who is in charge of the *royal*
  household,
16 'What right do you have here,
And whom do you have here,
That you have hewn a tomb for yourself
  here,
You who hew a tomb on the height,
You who carve a resting place for
  yourself in the rock?
17 'Behold, the LORD is about to hurl you
     headlong, O man.
And He is about to grasp you firmly
18 *And* roll you tightly like a ball,
To be cast into a vast country;
There you will die
And there your splendid chariots will be,
You shame of your master's house.'
19 "I will depose you from your office,
And I will pull you down from your
  station.
20 "Then it will come about in that day,
That I will summon My servant Eliakim
  the son of Hilkiah,
21 And I will clothe him with your tunic
And tie your sash securely about him.
I will entrust him with your authority,
And he will become a father to the
  inhabitants of Jerusalem and to the
  house of Judah.
22 "Then I will set the key of the house of
     David on his shoulder,
When he opens no one will shut,
When he shuts no one will open.
23 "I will drive him *like* a peg in a firm
     place,
And he will become a throne of glory to
  his father's house.
24 "So they will hang on him all the glory of his
father's house, offspring and issue, all the least of
vessels, from bowls to all the jars.
25 "In that day," declares the LORD of hosts,
"the peg driven in a firm place will give way; it will
even break off and fall, and the load hanging on it
will be cut off, for the LORD has spoken."

The Fall of Tyre

23 The oracle concerning Tyre.
Wail, O ships of Tarshish,
For *Tyre* is destroyed, without house *or*
harbor;
It is reported to them from the land of
Cyprus.

23:1 The Decline of Tyre

*In Isaiah's day the city of Tyre was a major
power, dominating the sea trade in the eastern
Mediterranean. Her many colonies included the
island of Cyprus, and her merchants traveled
as far as the Indian Ocean and the English
Channel. But not long after this prophecy
Assyria conquered the city, and Tyre's king fled
to Cyprus.*

2 Be silent, you inhabitants of the
coastland,
You merchants of Sidon;
Your messengers crossed the sea
3 And *were* on many waters.
The grain of the Nile, the harvest of the
River was her revenue;
And she was the market of nations.
4 Be ashamed, O Sidon;
For the sea speaks, the stronghold of the
sea, saying,
"I have neither travailed nor given birth,
I have neither brought up young men
nor reared virgins."
5 When the report *reaches* Egypt,
They will be in anguish at the report of
Tyre.
6 Pass over to Tarshish;
Wail, O inhabitants of the coastland.
7 Is this your jubilant *city*,
Whose origin is from antiquity,
Whose feet used to carry her to colonize
distant places?
8 ¶ Who has planned this against Tyre, the
bestower of crowns,
Whose merchants were princes, whose
traders were the honored of the
earth?
9 The LORD of hosts has planned it, to
defile the pride of all beauty,
To despise all the honored of the earth.
10 Overflow your land like the Nile,
O daughter of Tarshish,
There is no more restraint.
11 He has stretched His hand out over the
sea,
He has made the kingdoms tremble;
The LORD has given a command
concerning Canaan to demolish its
strongholds.

12 ¶ He has said, "You shall exult no more,
O crushed virgin daughter of Sidon.
Arise, pass over to Cyprus; even there
you will find no rest."
13 ¶ Behold, the land of the Chaldeans—this is
the people *which* was not; Assyria appointed it for
desert creatures—they erected their siege towers,
they stripped its palaces, they made it a ruin.
14 Wail, O ships of Tarshish,
For your stronghold is destroyed.
15 Now in that day Tyre will be forgotten for
seventy years like the days of one king. At the end
of seventy years it will happen to Tyre as *in* the
song of the harlot:
16 Take *your* harp, walk about the city,
O forgotten harlot;
Pluck the strings skillfully, sing many
songs,
That you may be remembered.
17 It will come about at the end of seventy
years that the LORD will visit Tyre. Then she will
go back to her harlot's wages and will play the
harlot with all the kingdoms on the face of the
earth.
18 Her gain and her harlot's wages will be set
apart to the LORD; it will not be stored up or
hoarded, but her gain will become sufficient food
and choice attire for those who dwell in the presence of the LORD.

Judgment on the Earth

24 Behold, the LORD lays the earth waste,
devastates it, distorts its surface and scatters
its inhabitants.
2 And the people will be like the priest, the
servant like his master, the maid like her mistress,
the buyer like the seller, the lender like the borrower, the creditor like the debtor.
3 The earth will be completely laid waste and
completely despoiled, for the LORD has spoken
this word.
4 The earth mourns *and* withers, the world
fades *and* withers, the exalted of the people of the
earth fade away.
5 The earth is also polluted by its inhabitants,
for they transgressed laws, violated statutes, broke
the everlasting covenant.
6 Therefore, a curse devours the earth, and
those who live in it are held guilty. Therefore, the
inhabitants of the earth are burned, and few men
are left.
7 ¶ The new wine mourns,
The vine decays,
All the merry-hearted sigh.
8 The gaiety of tambourines ceases,
The noise of revelers stops,
The gaiety of the harp ceases.
9 They do not drink wine with song;
Strong drink is bitter to those who
drink it.

10 The city of chaos is broken down;
　Every house is shut up so that none may
　　enter.
11 There is an outcry in the streets
　　concerning the wine;
　All joy turns to gloom.
　The gaiety of the earth is banished.
12 Desolation is left in the city
　And the gate is battered to ruins.
13 For thus it will be in the midst of the
　　earth among the peoples,
　As the shaking of an olive tree,
　As the gleanings when the grape harvest
　　is over.
14 They raise their voices, they shout for
　　joy;
　They cry out from the west concerning
　　the majesty of the Lord.
15 Therefore glorify the Lord in the east,
　The name of the Lord, the God of
　　Israel,
　In the coastlands of the sea.
16 From the ends of the earth we hear
　　songs, "Glory to the
　　Righteous One,"
　But I say, "Woe to me! Woe to me! Alas
　　for me!
　The treacherous deal treacherously,
　And the treacherous deal very
　　treacherously."
17 Terror and pit and snare
　Confront you, O inhabitant of the earth.
18 Then it will be that he who flees the
　　report of disaster will fall into the
　　pit,
　And he who climbs out of the pit will be
　　caught in the snare;
　For the windows above are opened, and
　　the foundations of the earth shake.
19 The earth is broken asunder,
　The earth is split through,
　The earth is shaken violently.
20 The earth reels to and fro like a
　　drunkard
　And it totters like a shack,
　For its transgression is heavy upon it,
　And it will fall, never to rise again.
21 So it will happen in that day,
　That the Lord will punish the host of
　　heaven on high,
　And the kings of the earth on earth.
22 They will be gathered together
　Like prisoners in the dungeon,
　And will be confined in prison;
　And after many days they will be
　　punished.
23 Then the moon will be abashed and the
　　sun ashamed,
　For the Lord of hosts will reign on
　　Mount Zion and in Jerusalem,
　And His glory will be before His elders.

Song of Praise for God's Favor

25 O Lord, You are my God;
　I will exalt You, I will give thanks to
　　Your name;
　For You have worked wonders,
　Plans *formed* long ago, with perfect
　　faithfulness.
2 For You have made a city into a heap,
　A fortified city into a ruin;
　A palace of strangers is a city no more,
　It will never be rebuilt.
3 Therefore a strong people will
　　glorify You;
　Cities of ruthless nations will revere You.
4 For You have been a defense for the
　　helpless,
　A defense for the needy in his distress,
　A refuge from the storm, a shade from
　　the heat;
　For the breath of the ruthless
　Is like a *rain* storm *against* a wall.
5 Like heat in drought, You subdue the
　　uproar of aliens;
　Like heat by the shadow of a cloud, the
　　song of the ruthless is silenced.

6 ¶ The Lord of hosts will prepare a lavish
　　banquet for all peoples on this
　　mountain;
　A banquet of aged wine, choice pieces
　　with marrow,
　And refined, aged wine.

25:6 A Promise of Eternal Life

The Old Testament includes only a few hints about resurrection and the afterlife, and this is one of the strongest. Isaiah follows a devastating chapter on God's judgment of the whole earth (chapter 24) with a bright promise of a future life. Then, death and pain will be abolished (see verses 7–8 and 26:19), and God will reign with perfect justice.

7 And on this mountain He will swallow
　　up the covering which is over all
　　peoples,
　Even the veil which is stretched over all
　　nations.
8 He will swallow up death for all time,
　And the Lord God will wipe tears away
　　from all faces,
　And He will remove the reproach of His
　　people from all the earth;
　For the Lord has spoken.
9 And it will be said in that day,
　"Behold, this is our God for whom we
　　have waited that He might save us.
　This is the Lord for whom we have
　　waited;

Let us rejoice and be glad in His
salvation."

10 For the hand of the LORD will rest on
this mountain,
And Moab will be trodden down in his
place
As straw is trodden down in the water of
a manure pile.

11 And he will spread out his hands in the
middle of it
As a swimmer spreads out *his hands* to
swim,
But *the Lord* will lay low his pride
together with the trickery of his
hands.

12 The unassailable fortifications of your
walls He will bring down,
Lay low *and* cast to the ground, even to
the dust.

Song of Trust in God's Protection

26 In that day this song will be sung in the
land of Judah:
"We have a strong city;
He sets up walls and ramparts for
security.

2 "Open the gates, that the righteous nation
may enter,
The one that remains faithful.

3 "The steadfast of mind You will keep in
perfect peace,
Because he trusts in You.

26:3 Perfect Peace

*Isaiah, who lived in a time of tremendous
turmoil, predicted more of the same. Godly
people would suffer along with everybody else,
he said. How should believers cope? Isaiah
urged them to focus on a reality greater than
their current troubles: to keep their minds
steady on God, who never loses control over
events.*

4 "Trust in the LORD forever,
For in GOD the LORD, *we have* an
everlasting Rock.

5 "For He has brought low those who dwell
on high, the unassailable city;
He lays it low, He lays it low to the
ground, He casts it to the dust.

6 "The foot will trample it,
The feet of the afflicted, the steps of the
helpless."

7 ¶ The way of the righteous is smooth;
O Upright One, make the path of the
righteous level.

8 Indeed, *while following* the way of Your
judgments, O LORD,
We have waited for You eagerly;
Your name, even Your memory, is the
desire of *our* souls.

9 At night my soul longs for You,
Indeed, my spirit within me seeks You
diligently;
For when the earth experiences Your
judgments
The inhabitants of the world learn
righteousness.

10 *Though* the wicked is shown favor,
He does not learn righteousness;
He deals unjustly in the land of
uprightness,
And does not perceive the majesty of the
LORD.

11 ¶ O LORD, Your hand is lifted up *yet*
they do not see it.
They see *Your* zeal for the people and
are put to shame;
Indeed, fire will devour Your enemies.

12 LORD, You will establish peace for us,
Since You have also performed for us all
our works.

13 O LORD our God, other masters besides
You have ruled us;
But through You alone we confess Your
name.

14 The dead will not live, the departed
spirits will not rise;
Therefore You have punished and
destroyed them,
And You have wiped out all
remembrance of them.

15 You have increased the nation, O LORD,
You have increased the nation, You are
glorified;
You have extended all the borders of the
land.

16 O LORD, they sought You in distress;
They could only whisper a prayer,
Your chastening was upon them.

17 As the pregnant woman approaches *the
time* to give birth,
She writhes *and* cries out in her labor
pains,
Thus were we before You, O LORD.

18 We were pregnant, we writhed *in labor*,
We gave birth, as it seems, *only* to wind.
We could not accomplish deliverance for
the earth,
Nor were inhabitants of the world born.

19 Your dead will live;
Their corpses will rise.
You who lie in the dust, awake and
shout for joy,
For your dew *is as* the dew of the dawn,
And the earth will give birth to the
departed spirits.

20 ¶ Come, my people, enter into your
     rooms
And close your doors behind you;
Hide for a little while
Until indignation runs *its* course.
21 For behold, the LORD is about to come
     out from His place
To punish the inhabitants of the earth
     for their iniquity;
And the earth will reveal her bloodshed
And will no longer cover her slain.

The Deliverance of Israel

27 In that day the LORD will punish
     Leviathan the fleeing serpent,
With His fierce and great and mighty
     sword,
Even Leviathan the twisted serpent;
And He will kill the dragon who *lives* in
     the sea.

27:1 A Prophecy for the World

*Most of Isaiah 1–39 concerns specific nations
in the prophet's own time. But chapters 24 to
27 form a unit that seems to sum up all world
history. Those chapters contain some of
Isaiah's strongest imagery.*

2 ¶ In that day,
"A vineyard of wine, sing of it!
3 "I, the LORD, am its keeper;
I water it every moment.
So that no one will damage it,
I guard it night and day.
4 "I have no wrath.
Should someone give Me briars *and*
     thorns in battle,
Then I would step on them, I would
     burn them completely.
5 "Or let him rely on My protection,
Let him make peace with Me,
Let him make peace with Me."
6 In the days to come Jacob will take root,
Israel will blossom and sprout,
And they will fill the whole world with
     fruit.

7 ¶ Like the striking of Him who has
     struck them, has He struck them?
Or like the slaughter of His slain, have
     they been slain?
8 You contended with them by banishing
     them, by driving them away.
With His fierce wind He has expelled
     them on the day of the east wind.
9 Therefore through this Jacob's iniquity
     will be forgiven;
And this will be the full price of the
     pardoning of his sin:

When he makes all the altar stones like
     pulverized chalk stones;
When Asherim and incense altars will not
     stand.
10 For the fortified city is isolated,
A homestead forlorn and forsaken like
     the desert;
There the calf will graze,
And there it will lie down and feed on its
     branches.
11 When its limbs are dry, they are broken
     off;
Women come *and* make a fire with
     them,
For they are not a people of discernment,
Therefore their Maker will not have
     compassion on them.
And their Creator will not be gracious to
     them.
12 ¶ In that day the LORD will start *His* threshing from the flowing stream of the Euphrates to
the brook of Egypt, and you will be gathered up
one by one, O sons of Israel.
13 It will come about also in that day that a
great trumpet will be blown, and those who were
perishing in the land of Assyria and who were
scattered in the land of Egypt will come and worship the LORD in the holy mountain at Jerusalem.

Ephraim's Captivity Predicted

28 Woe to the proud crown of the
     drunkards of Ephraim,
And to the fading flower of its glorious
     beauty,
Which is at the head of the fertile valley
Of those who are overcome with wine!
2 Behold, the Lord has a strong and
     mighty *agent;*
As a storm of hail, a tempest of
     destruction,
Like a storm of mighty overflowing
     waters,
He has cast *it* down to the earth with *His*
     hand.
3 The proud crown of the drunkards of
     Ephraim is trodden under foot.
4 And the fading flower of its glorious
     beauty,
Which is at the head of the fertile valley,
Will be like the first-ripe fig prior to
     summer,
Which one sees,
And as soon as it is in his hand,
He swallows it.
5 In that day the LORD of hosts will
     become a beautiful crown
And a glorious diadem to the remnant of
     His people;
6 A spirit of justice for him who sits in
     judgment,

A strength to those who repel the
    onslaught at the gate.
7 And these also reel with wine and stagger
    from strong drink:
The priest and the prophet reel with
    strong drink,
They are confused by wine, they stagger
    from strong drink;
They reel while having visions,
They totter *when rendering* judgment.
8 For all the tables are full of filthy vomit,
    without a *single clean* place.

9 ¶ "To whom would He teach knowledge,
And to whom would He interpret the
    message?
Those *just* weaned from milk?
Those *just* taken from the breast?
10 "For *He says,*
    'Order on order, order on order,
    Line on line, line on line,
    A little here, a little there.' "
11 Indeed, He will speak to this people
    Through stammering lips and a foreign
    tongue,
12 He who said to them, "Here is rest, give
    rest to the weary,"
And, "Here is repose," but they would
    not listen.
13 So the word of the LORD to them will be,
    "Order on order, order on order,
    Line on line, line on line,
    A little here, a little there,"
That they may go and stumble backward,
    be broken, snared and taken captive.

Judah Is Warned

14 Therefore, hear the word of the LORD,
    O scoffers,
Who rule this people who are in
    Jerusalem,
15 Because you have said, "We have made a
    covenant with death,
And with Sheol we have made a pact.
The overwhelming scourge will not reach
    us when it passes by,
For we have made falsehood our refuge
    and we have concealed ourselves
    with deception."
16 Therefore thus says the Lord GOD,
    "Behold, I am laying in Zion a stone, a
    tested stone,
A costly cornerstone *for* the foundation,
    firmly placed.
He who believes *in it* will not be
    disturbed.
17 "I will make justice the measuring line
And righteousness the level;
Then hail will sweep away the refuge of
    lies
And the waters will overflow the secret
    place.

18 "Your covenant with death will be
    canceled,
And your pact with Sheol will not stand;
When the overwhelming scourge passes
    through,
Then you become its trampling *place.*
19 "As often as it passes through, it will seize
    you;
For morning after morning it will pass
    through, *anytime* during the day or
    night,
And it will be sheer terror to understand
    what it means."
20 The bed is too short on which to stretch
    out,
And the blanket is too small to wrap
    oneself in.
21 For the LORD will rise up as *at* Mount
    Perazim,
He will be stirred up as in the valley of
    Gibeon,
To do His task, His unusual task,
And to work His work, His extraordinary
    work.
22 And now do not carry on as scoffers,
Or your fetters will be made stronger;
For I have heard from the Lord GOD of
    hosts
Of decisive destruction on all the earth.

23 ¶ Give ear and hear my voice,
Listen and hear my words.
24 Does the farmer plow continually to
    plant seed?
Does he *continually* turn and harrow the
    ground?

28:24 Like a Wise Farmer

Drawing an analogy from farming, Isaiah shows that God varies his treatment of nations, depending on conditions. Just as different crops—grain, barley, dill, cummin—require different farming techniques, so each nation requires individual treatment. Those who readily repent need only light punishment, while stubborn nations need further discipline.

25 Does he not level its surface
And sow dill and scatter cummin
And plant wheat in rows,
Barley in its place and rye within its
    area?
26 For his God instructs and teaches him
    properly.
27 For dill is not threshed with a threshing
    sledge,
Nor is the cartwheel driven over
    cummin;

But dill is beaten out with a rod, and
  cummin with a club.
28 *Grain for* bread is crushed,
Indeed, he does not continue to thresh it
  forever.
Because the wheel of *his* cart and his
  horses *eventually* damage *it,*
He does not thresh it longer.
29 This also comes from the LORD of hosts,
Who has made *His* counsel wonderful
  and *His* wisdom great.

Jerusalem Is Warned

29 Woe, O Ariel, Ariel the city *where* David
  once camped!
Add year to year, observe *your* feasts on
  schedule.
2 I will bring distress to Ariel,
And she will be *a city of* lamenting and
  mourning;
And she will be like an Ariel to me.
3 I will camp against you encircling *you,*
And I will set siegeworks against you,
And I will raise up battle towers against
  you.
4 Then you will be brought low;
From the earth you will speak,
And from the dust *where* you are
  prostrate
Your words *will* come.
Your voice will also be like that of a
  spirit from the ground,
And your speech will whisper from the
  dust.
5 ¶ But the multitude of your enemies will
  become like fine dust,
And the multitude of the ruthless ones
  like the chaff which blows away;
And it will happen instantly, suddenly.
6 From the LORD of hosts you will be
  punished with thunder and
  earthquake and loud noise,
With whirlwind and tempest and the
  flame of a consuming fire.
7 And the multitude of all the nations who
  wage war against Ariel,
Even all who wage war against her and
  her stronghold, and who distress
  her,
Will be like a dream, a vision of the
  night.
8 It will be as when a hungry man
  dreams—
And behold, he is eating;
But when he awakens, his hunger is not
  satisfied,
Or as when a thirsty man dreams—
And behold, he is drinking,
But when he awakens, behold, he is faint
And his thirst is not quenched.

Thus the multitude of all the nations
  will be
Who wage war against Mount Zion.

9 ¶ Be delayed and wait,
Blind yourselves and be blind;
They become drunk, but not with wine,
They stagger, but not with strong drink.
10 For the LORD has poured over you a
  spirit of deep sleep,
He has shut your eyes, the prophets;
And He has covered your heads, the
  seers.

11 The entire vision will be to you like the
words of a sealed book, which when they give it to
the one who is literate, saying, "Please read this,"
he will say, "I cannot, for it is sealed."

12 Then the book will be given to the one who
is illiterate, saying, "Please read this." And he will
say, "I cannot read."

13 ¶ Then the Lord said,
"Because this people draw near with their
  words
And honor Me with their lip service,
But they remove their hearts far
  from Me,
And their reverence for Me consists of
  tradition learned *by rote,*

29:13 Hypocrites

*Again and again, Isaiah blasts the Israelites for
a superficial faith—all words and no heart.
Hundreds of years later, Jesus quoted this
verse, saying that it applied precisely to people
of his day (Mark 7:6–7).*

14 Therefore behold, I will once again deal
  marvelously with this people,
  wondrously marvelous;
And the wisdom of their wise men will
  perish,
And the discernment of their discerning
  men will be concealed."

15 ¶ Woe to those who deeply hide their
  plans from the LORD,
And whose deeds are *done* in a dark
  place,
And they say, "Who sees us?" or "Who
  knows us?"
16 You turn *things* around!
Shall the potter be considered as equal
  with the clay,
That what is made would say to its
  maker, "He did not make me";
Or what is formed say to him who
  formed it, "He has no
  understanding"?

Blessing after Discipline

17 ¶ Is it not yet just a little while
  Before Lebanon will be turned into a
    fertile field,
  And the fertile field will be considered as
    a forest?
18 On that day the deaf will hear words of a
    book,
  And out of *their* gloom and darkness the
    eyes of the blind will see.
19 The afflicted also will increase their
    gladness in the LORD,
  And the needy of mankind will rejoice in
    the Holy One of Israel.
20 For the ruthless will come to an end and
    the scorner will be finished,
  Indeed all who are intent on doing evil
    will be cut off;
21 Who cause a person to be indicted by a
    word,
  And ensnare him who adjudicates at the
    gate,
  And defraud the one in the right with
    meaningless arguments.
22 ¶ Therefore thus says the LORD, who re-
deemed Abraham, concerning the house of Jacob:
  "Jacob shall not now be ashamed, nor
    shall his face now turn pale;
23 But when he sees his children, the work
    of My hands, in his midst,
  They will sanctify My name;
  Indeed, they will sanctify the Holy One
    of Jacob
  And will stand in awe of the God of
    Israel.
24 "Those who err in mind will know the
    truth,
  And those who criticize will accept
    instruction.

Judah Warned against Egyptian Alliance

30 "Woe to the rebellious children," declares
    the LORD,
  "Who execute a plan, but not Mine,
  And make an alliance, but not of My
    Spirit,
  In order to add sin to sin;
2 Who proceed down to Egypt
  Without consulting Me,
  To take refuge in the safety of Pharaoh
  And to seek shelter in the shadow of
    Egypt!
3 "Therefore the safety of Pharaoh will be
    your shame
  And the shelter in the shadow of Egypt,
    your humiliation.
4 "For their princes are at Zoan
  And their ambassadors arrive at Hanes.
5 "Everyone will be ashamed because of a
    people who cannot profit them,

Who are not for help or profit, but for
  shame and also for reproach."

6 ¶ The oracle concerning the beasts of the
Negev.
  Through a land of distress and anguish,
  From where *come* lioness and lion, viper
    and flying serpent,
  They carry their riches on the backs of
    young donkeys
  And their treasures on camels' humps,
  To a people who cannot profit *them;*

30:1 Isaiah in His Prime

*Isaiah delivered the messages of chapters
28–35 at the peak of his ministry, under
Hezekiah. He unleashed six great "woes," or
warnings: (1) to drunken, scoffing politicians,
28:1; (2) to those who carry on the form of
religion, without true faith, 29:1; (3) to those
who hide their plans from God (possibly
referring to secret political intrigues), 29:15; (4)
to the pro-Egyptian party lobbying for a
political alliance, 30:1; (5) to those who trust in
military power (horses and chariots) instead of
God, 31:1; and (6) to the Assyrian destroyer,
33:1. Seemingly invincible at the time, the
Assyrian empire would face a judgment day.*

7 Even Egypt, whose help is vain and
    empty.
  Therefore, I have called her
  "Rahab who has been exterminated."
8 Now go, write it on a tablet before them
  And inscribe it on a scroll,
  That it may serve in the time to come
  As a witness forever.
9 For this is a rebellious people, false sons,
  Sons who refuse to listen
  To the instruction of the LORD;
10 Who say to the seers, "You must not see
    visions";
  And to the prophets, "You must not
    prophesy to us what is right,
  Speak to us pleasant words,
  Prophesy illusions.
11 "Get out of the way, turn aside from the
    path,
  Let us hear no more about the Holy One
    of Israel."
12 Therefore thus says the Holy One of Israel,
  "Since you have rejected this word
  And have put your trust in oppression
    and guile, and have relied on them,
13 Therefore this iniquity will be to you
  Like a breach about to fall,
  A bulge in a high wall,
  Whose collapse comes suddenly in an
    instant,

14 Whose collapse is like the smashing of a
potter's jar,
So ruthlessly shattered
That a sherd will not be found among its
pieces
To take fire from a hearth
Or to scoop water from a cistern."
15 For thus the Lord GOD, the Holy One of
Israel, has said,
"In repentance and rest you will be saved,
In quietness and trust is your strength."
But you were not willing,
16 And you said, "No, for we will flee on
horses,"
Therefore you shall flee!
"And we will ride on swift *horses*,"
Therefore those who pursue you shall be
swift.
17 One thousand *will flee* at the threat of
one *man*;
You will flee at the threat of five,
Until you are left as a flag on a
mountain top
And as a signal on a hill.

God Is Gracious and Just

18 ¶ Therefore the LORD longs to be
gracious to you,
And therefore He waits on high to have
compassion on you.
For the LORD is a God of justice;
How blessed are all those who long for
Him.
19 ¶ O people in Zion, inhabitant in Jerusalem, you will weep no longer. He will surely be
gracious to you at the sound of your cry; when He
hears it, He will answer you.
20 Although the Lord has given you bread of
privation and water of oppression, *He,* your
Teacher will no longer hide Himself, but your eyes
will behold your Teacher.
21 Your ears will hear a word behind you,
"This is the way, walk in it," whenever you turn to
the right or to the left.
22 And you will defile your graven images
overlaid with silver, and your molten images plated with gold. You will scatter them as an impure
thing, *and* say to them, "Be gone!"
23 ¶ Then He will give *you* rain for the seed
which you will sow in the ground, and bread *from*
the yield of the ground, and it will be rich and
plenteous; on that day your livestock will graze in
a roomy pasture.
24 Also the oxen and the donkeys which work
the ground will eat salted fodder, which has been
winnowed with shovel and fork.
25 On every lofty mountain and on every high
hill there will be streams running with water on
the day of the great slaughter, when the towers fall.
26 The light of the moon will be as the light of

the sun, and the light of the sun will be seven times
brighter, like the light of seven days, on the day the
LORD binds up the fracture of His people and
heals the bruise He has inflicted.
27 ¶ Behold, the name of the LORD comes
from a remote place;
Burning is His anger and dense is *His*
smoke;
His lips are filled with indignation
And His tongue is like a consuming fire;

30:27 An End to Punishment

*Isaiah minces no words in his fierce
descriptions of the punishment awaiting Judah.
But as this chapter shows, the punishment will
reach an end, and then God will turn on the
surrounding evil nations. The fire of judgment
will culminate in Topheth (verse 33), a valley
near Jerusalem where human sacrifices were
offered to the god Molech (referred to here as
"the king").*

28 His breath is like an overflowing torrent,
Which reaches to the neck,
To shake the nations back and forth in a
sieve,
And to *put* in the jaws of the peoples the
bridle which leads to ruin.
29 You will have songs as in the night when
you keep the festival,
And gladness of heart as when one
marches to *the sound of* the flute,
To go to the mountain of the LORD, to
the Rock of Israel.
30 And the LORD will cause His voice of
authority to be heard,
And the descending of His arm to be
seen in fierce anger,
And *in* the flame of a consuming fire
In cloudburst, downpour and hailstones.
31 For at the voice of the LORD Assyria will
be terrified,
When He strikes with the rod.
32 And every blow of the rod of
punishment,
Which the LORD will lay on him,
Will be with *the music of* tambourines
and lyres;
And in battles, brandishing weapons, He
will fight them.
33 For *a*Topheth has long been ready,
Indeed, it has been prepared for the king.
He has made it deep and large,
A pyre of fire with plenty of wood;
The breath of the LORD, like a torrent of
brimstone, sets it afire.

a I.e. the place of human sacrifice to Molech

Help Not in Egypt but in God

31 Woe to those who go down to Egypt for
help
And rely on horses,
And trust in chariots because they are
many
And in horsemen because they are very
strong,
But they do not look to the Holy One of
Israel, nor seek the LORD!
2 Yet He also is wise and will bring
disaster
And does not retract His words,

But will arise against the house of
evildoers
And against the help of the workers of
iniquity.
3 Now the Egyptians are men and not
God,
And their horses are flesh and not spirit;
So the LORD will stretch out His hand,
And he who helps will stumble
And he who is helped will fall,
And all of them will come to an end
together.

4 ¶ For thus says the LORD to me,

A Time of Crisis
Defeat seemed certain to everyone but Isaiah

AFTER TWO DISMAL DECADES UNDER King Ahaz, Judah
finally saw a ray of hope when Hezekiah ascended the throne. Second
Kings summarizes his reign this way: "There was none like him among
all the kings of Judah, nor among those who were before him" (2 Kings 18:5).
Isaiah reached the peak of his ministry under King Hezekiah, who often sought his advice. The
king needed Isaiah's help; he had inherited a kingdom in mortal danger from Assyria.

> *And the Assyrian will fall by a sword not of man.* 31:8

Protesting a Foolish Rebellion

How could Judah break free from Assyrian domination? Like other kings before him, Hezekiah
thought of joining with other countries. Both Egypt and a rising Babylon seemed eager to court Judah
as an ally.
Isaiah, however, said no. He urged Hezekiah to trust only in God. To dramatize his point, the court
prophet did a shocking thing: he stalked around stripped and barefoot for three years as a protest
against the pro-Egypt lobby (20:1–6). This protest forms the background for some of the strongest
speeches in Isaiah's book (chapters 18–20; 30–31).
Isaiah's protest failed, however. Not even Hezekiah could resist the temptation to oppose Assyria.
First, he shored up the defenses of Jerusalem and built up the city's water supplies. Then he formed an
alliance of small kingdoms and led an outright rebellion against Assyria.

Revenge of an Empire

Assyria lowered the boom. Its armies smashed into Judah, leveling 46 walled cities and carrying
away 200,150 captives. The Assyrian king demanded huge sums of money from Hezekiah, whom he
mockingly described as "a bird in a cage."
Hezekiah, cowering under siege in Jerusalem, once more turned to Isaiah for advice. Should he
surrender? Assyrian soldiers were already pressing in around the walls, hurling insults at the demoralized citizens inside.
Isaiah avoided an "I told you so" attitude. Against all odds, he again recommended prayer and
reliance on the power of God. Have faith, he said; don't surrender, don't fear. Assyria will return home,
wounded (37:5–7).
Isaiah's deep courage and optimism raised the morale of all Jerusalem. And in a spectacular way
(37:36; also 2 Kings 19), God took care of the Assyrian army.

An Authentic Hero

Chapters 18–35 contain Isaiah's messages from this period, including many of the very words that
stirred a desperate nation to faith. Without his inspiring example, Jerusalem might have surrendered.
Many of the prophets of Israel and Judah were loners, voices "crying in the desert." Isaiah was an
exception. He had the king's ear at a critical moment in Judah's history. Because of his effectiveness,
Isaiah went down in history as a great statesman and hero.

Life Questions: In your life, what experience has called for the most courage and faith? How did you
respond at the time?

"As the lion or the young lion growls over
his prey,
Against which a band of shepherds is
called out,
And he will not be terrified at their voice
nor disturbed at their noise,
So will the LORD of hosts come down to
wage war on Mount Zion and on its
hill."
5 Like flying birds so the LORD of hosts
will protect Jerusalem.
He will protect and deliver *it;*
He will pass over and rescue *it.*
6 ¶ Return to Him from whom you have
deeply defected, O sons of Israel.
7 For in that day every man will cast away his
silver idols and his gold idols, which your sinful
hands have made for you as a sin.
8 And the Assyrian will fall by a sword not
of man,
And a sword not of man will devour
him.
So he will not escape the sword,
And his young men will become forced
laborers.
9 "His rock will pass away because of panic,
And his princes will be terrified at the
standard,"
Declares the LORD, whose fire is in Zion
and whose furnace is in Jerusalem.

The Glorious Future

32 Behold, a king will reign righteously
And princes will rule justly.

32:1–20 Shifting Stance in Time

*Isaiah's writings often shift confusingly,
describing the present surroundings and then
moving on to predict the future. At times Isaiah
even projects himself into the future, writing in
the past tense about events that have not yet
happened. Note the shifting time sequence in
this chapter.*

2 Each will be like a refuge from the wind
And a shelter from the storm,
Like streams of water in a dry country,
Like the shade of a huge rock in a
parched land.
3 Then the eyes of those who see will not
be blinded,
And the ears of those who hear will
listen.
4 The mind of the hasty will discern the
truth,
And the tongue of the stammerers will
hasten to speak clearly.
5 No longer will the fool be called noble,
Or the rogue be spoken of *as* generous.

6 For a fool speaks nonsense,
And his heart inclines toward
wickedness:
To practice ungodliness and to speak
error against the LORD,
To keep the hungry person unsatisfied
And to withhold drink from the thirsty.
7 As for a rogue, his weapons are evil;
He devises wicked schemes
To destroy *the* afflicted with slander,
Even though *the* needy one speaks what
is right.
8 But the noble man devises noble plans;
And by noble plans he stands.
9 ¶ Rise up, you women who are at ease,
And hear my voice;
Give ear to my word,
You complacent daughters.
10 Within a year and *a few* days
You will be troubled, O complacent
daughters;
For the vintage is ended,
And the *fruit* gathering will not come.
11 Tremble, you *women* who are at ease;
Be troubled, you complacent *daughters;*
Strip, undress and put *sackcloth* on *your*
waist,
12 Beat your breasts for the pleasant fields,
for the fruitful vine,
13 For the land of my people *in which*
thorns *and* briars shall come up;
Yea, for all the joyful houses *and for* the
jubilant city.
14 Because the palace has been abandoned,
the populated city forsaken.
Hill and watch-tower have become caves
forever,
A delight for wild donkeys, a pasture for
flocks;
15 Until the Spirit is poured out upon us
from on high,
And the wilderness becomes a fertile
field,
And the fertile field is considered as a
forest.
16 Then justice will dwell in the wilderness
And righteousness will abide in the fertile
field.
17 And the work of righteousness will be
peace,
And the service of righteousness,
quietness and confidence forever.
18 Then my people will live in a peaceful
habitation,
And in secure dwellings and in
undisturbed resting places;
19 And it will hail when the forest comes
down,
And the city will be utterly laid low.
20 How blessed will you be, you who sow
beside all waters,

Who let out freely the ox and the
    donkey.

The Judgment of God

33 Woe to you, O destroyer,
    While you were not destroyed;
And he who is treacherous, while *others*
    did not deal treacherously with him.
As soon as you finish destroying, you
    will be destroyed;
As soon as you cease to deal
    treacherously, *others* will deal
    treacherously with you.
2 O LORD, be gracious to us; we have
    waited for You.
Be their strength every morning,
Our salvation also in the time of distress.
3 At the sound of the tumult peoples flee;
At the lifting up of Yourself nations
    disperse.
4 Your spoil is gathered *as* the caterpillar
    gathers;
As locusts rushing about men rush about
    on it.
5 The LORD is exalted, for He dwells on
    high;
He has filled Zion with justice and
    righteousness.
6 And He will be the stability of your
    times,
A wealth of salvation, wisdom and
    knowledge;
The fear of the LORD is his treasure.
7 Behold, their brave men cry in the
    streets,
The ambassadors of peace weep bitterly.
8 The highways are desolate, the traveler
    has ceased,
He has broken the covenant, he has
    despised the cities,
He has no regard for man.
9 The land mourns *and* pines away,
Lebanon is shamed *and* withers;
Sharon is like a desert plain,
And Bashan and Carmel lose *their*
    foliage.
10 "Now I will arise," says the LORD,
"Now I will be exalted, now I will be
    lifted up.
11 "You have conceived chaff, you will give
    birth to stubble;
My breath will consume you like a fire.
12 "The peoples will be burned to lime,
Like cut thorns which are burned in the
    fire.
13 ¶ "You who are far away, hear what I
    have done;
And you who are near, acknowledge My
    might."
14 Sinners in Zion are terrified;
Trembling has seized the godless.

"Who among us can live with the
    consuming fire?
Who among us can live with continual
    burning?"
15 He who walks righteously and speaks
    with sincerity,
He who rejects unjust gain
And shakes his hands so that they hold
    no bribe;
He who stops his ears from hearing
    about bloodshed
And shuts his eyes from looking upon
    evil;
16 He will dwell on the heights,
His refuge will be the impregnable rock;
His bread will be given *him*,
His water will be sure.
17 ¶ Your eyes will see the King in His
    beauty;
They will behold a far-distant land.
18 Your heart will meditate on terror:
"Where is he who counts?
Where is he who weighs?
Where is he who counts the towers?"
19 You will no longer see a fierce people,
A people of unintelligible speech which
    no one comprehends,
Of a stammering tongue which no one
    understands.
20 Look upon Zion, the city of our
    appointed feasts;
Your eyes will see Jerusalem, an
    undisturbed habitation,
A tent which will not be folded;
Its stakes will never be pulled up,
Nor any of its cords be torn apart.
21 But there the majestic *One*, the LORD,
    will be for us
A place of rivers *and* wide canals
On which no boat with oars will go,
And on which no mighty ship will
    pass—
22 For the LORD is our judge,
The LORD is our lawgiver,
The LORD is our king;
He will save us—
23 Your tackle hangs slack;
It cannot hold the base of its mast firmly,
Nor spread out the sail.
Then the prey of an abundant spoil will
    be divided;
The lame will take the plunder.
24 And no resident will say, "I am sick";
The people who dwell there will be
    forgiven *their* iniquity.

God's Wrath against Nations

34 Draw near, O nations, to hear; and listen,
    O peoples!

Let the earth and all it contains hear, and
the world and all that springs
from it.
2 For the LORD's indignation is against all
the nations,

34:1 Isaiah the Historian

*Isaiah's book includes many references to
nations and leaders of his day. Perhaps more
than any other prophet, Isaiah had a deep
sense of history. In fact, he wrote an account of
the life of King Uzziah and a record of the
rulers of Israel and Judah (see 2 Chronicles
26:22; 32:32). Although neither of these books
has survived, the one that bears his name
gives a blow-by-blow analysis of all the
nations of his time.*

And *His* wrath against all their armies;
He has utterly destroyed them,
He has given them over to slaughter.
3 So their slain will be thrown out,
And their corpses will give off their
stench,
And the mountains will be drenched with
their blood.
4 And all the host of heaven will wear
away,
And the sky will be rolled up like a
scroll;
All their hosts will also wither away
As a leaf withers from the vine,
Or as *one* withers from the fig tree.
5 For My sword is satiated in heaven,
Behold it shall descend for judgment
upon Edom
And upon the people whom I have
devoted to destruction.
6 The sword of the LORD is filled with
blood,
It is sated with fat, with the blood of
lambs and goats,
With the fat of the kidneys of rams.
For the LORD has a sacrifice in Bozrah
And a great slaughter in the land of
Edom.
7 Wild oxen will also fall with them
And young bulls with strong ones;
Thus their land will be soaked with
blood,
And their dust become greasy with fat.
8 For the LORD has a day of vengeance,
A year of recompense for the cause of
Zion.
9 Its streams will be turned into pitch,
And its loose earth into brimstone,
And its land will become burning pitch.
10 It will not be quenched night or day;
Its smoke will go up forever.

From generation to generation it will be
desolate;
None will pass through it forever and
ever.
11 But pelican and hedgehog will possess it,
And owl and raven will dwell in it;
And He will stretch over it the line of
desolation
And the plumb line of emptiness.
12 Its nobles—there is no one there
Whom they may proclaim king—
And all its princes will be nothing.
13 Thorns will come up in its fortified
towers,
Nettles and thistles in its fortified cities;
It will also be a haunt of jackals
And an abode of ostriches.
14 The desert creatures will meet with the
wolves,
The hairy goat also will cry to its kind;
Yes, the night monster will settle there
And will find herself a resting place.
15 The tree snake will make its nest and lay
eggs there,
And it will hatch and gather *them* under
its protection.
Yes, the hawks will be gathered there,
Every one with its kind.

16 ¶ Seek from the book of the LORD, and read:
Not one of these will be missing;
None will lack its mate.
For His mouth has commanded,
And His Spirit has gathered them.
17 He has cast the lot for them,
And His hand has divided it to them by
line.
They shall possess it forever;
From generation to generation they will
dwell in it.

Zion's Happy Future

35 The wilderness and the desert will be
glad,
And the Arabah will rejoice and blossom;
Like the crocus
2 It will blossom profusely
And rejoice with rejoicing and shout of
joy.
The glory of Lebanon will be given to it,
The majesty of Carmel and Sharon.
They will see the glory of the LORD,
The majesty of our God.
3 Encourage the exhausted, and strengthen
the feeble.
4 Say to those with anxious heart,
"Take courage, fear not.
Behold, your God will come *with*
vengeance;
The recompense of God will come,
But He will save you."
5 Then the eyes of the blind will be opened

And the ears of the deaf will be
  unstopped.
6 Then the lame will leap like a deer,
  And the tongue of the mute will shout
    for joy.
  For waters will break forth in the
    wilderness
  And streams in the Arabah.
7 The scorched land will become a pool
  And the thirsty ground springs of water;
  In the haunt of jackals, its resting place,
  Grass *becomes* reeds and rushes.
8 A highway will be there, a roadway,
  And it will be called the Highway of
    Holiness.
  The unclean will not travel on it,
  But it *will* be for him who walks *that*
    way,
  And fools will not wander *on it.*
9 No lion will be there,
  Nor will any vicious beast go up on it;
  These will not be found there.
  But the redeemed will walk *there,*
10 And the ransomed of the LORD will
    return
  And come with joyful shouting to Zion,
  With everlasting joy upon their heads.
  They will find gladness and joy,
  And sorrow and sighing will flee away.

Sennacherib Invades Judah

36 Now in the fourteenth year of King Hezekiah, Sennacherib king of Assyria came up against all the fortified cities of Judah and seized them.

36:1 Bridge Chapters

After a beautiful poem describing the renewed world God will make, Isaiah plunges into a historical account of Judah's troubles with the superpower Assyria. These next four historical chapters (which closely follow 2 Kings 18:13–20:19) form a bridge between problems with Assyria (chapters 1–35) and those with Babylon (chapters 40–66). They record some of the greatest crises in Isaiah's and King Hezekiah's lives, beginning with Assyria's final assault on Jerusalem and ending with Hezekiah's biggest blunder. That blunder led to Isaiah's prediction that Babylon would someday destroy Judah.

2 And the king of Assyria sent Rabshakeh from Lachish to Jerusalem to King Hezekiah with a large army. And he stood by the conduit of the upper pool on the highway of the fuller's field.

3 Then Eliakim the son of Hilkiah, who was over the household, and Shebna the scribe, and Joah the son of Asaph, the recorder, came out to him.

4 ¶ Then Rabshakeh said to them, "Say now to Hezekiah, 'Thus says the great king, the king of Assyria, "What is this confidence that you have?

5 "I say, 'Your counsel and strength for the war are only empty words.' Now on whom do you rely, that you have rebelled against me?

6 "Behold, you rely on the staff of this crushed reed, *even* on Egypt, on which if a man leans, it will go into his hand and pierce it. So is Pharaoh king of Egypt to all who rely on him.

7 "But if you say to me, 'We trust in the LORD our God,' is it not He whose high places and whose altars Hezekiah has taken away and has said to Judah and to Jerusalem, 'You shall worship before this altar'?

8 "Now therefore, come make a bargain with my master the king of Assyria, and I will give you two thousand horses, if you are able on your part to set riders on them.

9 "How then can you repulse one official of the least of my master's servants and rely on Egypt for chariots and for horsemen?

10 "Have I now come up without the LORD's approval against this land to destroy it? The LORD said to me, 'Go up against this land and destroy it.' " " "

11 ¶ Then Eliakim and Shebna and Joah said to Rabshakeh, "Speak now to your servants in Aramaic, for we understand *it;* and do not speak with us in Judean in the hearing of the people who are on the wall."

36:11 Fear in the City

The Assyrian commander showed great skill in demoralizing the besieged residents of Jerusalem. King Hezekiah's own officials were terrified (36:22–37:4). Only Isaiah stood firm in believing that God could save the city. Earlier (see 22:15–25), God had expressed through Isaiah utter contempt for these very officials of Hezekiah.

12 But Rabshakeh said, "Has my master sent me only to your master and to you to speak these words, *and* not to the men who sit on the wall, *doomed* to eat their own dung and drink their own urine with you?"

13 ¶ Then Rabshakeh stood and cried with a loud voice in Judean and said, "Hear the words of the great king, the king of Assyria.

14 "Thus says the king, 'Do not let Hezekiah deceive you, for he will not be able to deliver you;

15 nor let Hezekiah make you trust in the LORD, saying, "The LORD will surely deliver us, this city will not be given into the hand of the king of Assyria."

16 'Do not listen to Hezekiah,' for thus says the

king of Assyria, 'Make your peace with me and come out to me, and eat each of his vine and each of his fig tree and drink each of the waters of his own cistern,

17 until I come and take you away to a land like your own land, a land of grain and new wine, a land of bread and vineyards.

18 'Beware that Hezekiah does not mislead you, saying, "The LORD will deliver us." Has any one of the gods of the nations delivered his land from the hand of the king of Assyria?

19 'Where are the gods of Hamath and Arpad? Where are the gods of Sepharvaim? And when have they delivered Samaria from my hand?

20 'Who among all the gods of these lands have delivered their land from my hand, that the LORD would deliver Jerusalem from my hand?' "

21 ¶ But they were silent and answered him not a word; for the king's commandment was, "Do not answer him."

22 Then Eliakim the son of Hilkiah, who was over the household, and Shebna the scribe and Joah the son of Asaph, the recorder, came to Hezekiah with their clothes torn and told him the words of Rabshakeh.

Hezekiah Seeks Isaiah's Help

37 And when King Hezekiah heard it, he tore his clothes, covered himself with sackcloth and entered the house of the LORD.

2 Then he sent Eliakim who was over the household with Shebna the scribe and the elders of the priests, covered with sackcloth, to Isaiah the prophet, the son of Amoz.

3 They said to him, "Thus says Hezekiah, 'This day is a day of distress, rebuke and rejection; for children have come to birth, and there is no strength to deliver.

4 'Perhaps the LORD your God will hear the words of Rabshakeh, whom his master the king of Assyria has sent to reproach the living God, and will rebuke the words which the LORD your God has heard. Therefore, offer a prayer for the remnant that is left.' "

5 ¶ So the servants of King Hezekiah came to Isaiah.

6 Isaiah said to them, "Thus you shall say to your master, 'Thus says the LORD, "Do not be afraid because of the words that you have heard, with which the servants of the king of Assyria have blasphemed Me.

7 "Behold, I will put a spirit in him so that he will hear a rumor and return to his own land. And I will make him fall by the sword in his own land." ' "

8 ¶ Then Rabshakeh returned and found the king of Assyria fighting against Libnah, for he had heard that the king had left Lachish.

9 When he heard them say concerning Tirhakah king of Cush, "He has come out to fight

against you," and when he heard it he sent messengers to Hezekiah, saying,

10 "Thus you shall say to Hezekiah king of Judah, 'Do not let your God in whom you trust deceive you, saying, "Jerusalem will not be given into the hand of the king of Assyria."

11 'Behold, you have heard what the kings of Assyria have done to all the lands, destroying them completely. So will you be spared?

12 'Did the gods of those nations which my fathers have destroyed deliver them, even Gozan and Haran and Rezeph and the sons of Eden who were in Telassar?

13 'Where is the king of Hamath, the king of Arpad, the king of the city of Sepharvaim, and of Hena and Ivvah?' "

Hezekiah's Prayer in the Temple

14 ¶ Then Hezekiah took the letter from the hand of the messengers and read it, and he went up to the house of the LORD and spread it out before the LORD.

15 Hezekiah prayed to the LORD saying,

16 "O LORD of hosts, the God of Israel, who is enthroned above the cherubim, You are the God, You alone, of all the kingdoms of the earth. You have made heaven and earth.

17 "Incline Your ear, O LORD, and hear; open Your eyes, O LORD, and see; and listen to all the words of Sennacherib, who sent them to reproach the living God.

18 "Truly, O LORD, the kings of Assyria have devastated all the countries and their lands,

19 and have cast their gods into the fire, for they were not gods but the work of men's hands, wood and stone. So they have destroyed them.

20 "Now, O LORD our God, deliver us from his hand that all the kingdoms of the earth may know that You alone, LORD, are God."

God Answers through Isaiah

21 ¶ Then Isaiah the son of Amoz sent word to Hezekiah, saying, "Thus says the LORD, the God of Israel, 'Because you have prayed to Me about Sennacherib king of Assyria,

22 this is the word that the LORD has spoken against him:

"She has despised you and mocked you,
The virgin daughter of Zion;
She has shaken her head behind you,
The daughter of Jerusalem!
23 "Whom have you reproached and
blasphemed?
And against whom have you raised your
voice
And haughtily lifted up your eyes?
Against the Holy One of Israel!
24 "Through your servants you have
reproached the Lord,

And you have said, 'With my many
chariots I came up to the heights of
the mountains,
To the remotest parts of Lebanon;
And I cut down its tall cedars *and* its
choice cypresses.
And I will go to its highest peak, its
thickest forest.
25 'I dug *wells* and drank waters,
And with the sole of my feet I dried up
All the rivers of Egypt.'
26 "Have you not heard?
Long ago I did it,
From ancient times I planned it.
Now I have brought it to pass,
That you should turn fortified cities into
ruinous heaps.
27 "Therefore their inhabitants were short of
strength,
They were dismayed and put to shame;
They were *as* the vegetation of the field
and *as* the green herb,
As grass on the housetops is scorched
before it is grown up.
28 "But I know your sitting down
And your going out and your coming in
And your raging against Me.
29 "Because of your raging against Me
And because your arrogance has come
up to My ears,
Therefore I will put My hook in your
nose
And My bridle in your lips,
And I will turn you back by the way
which you came.

30 ¶ "Then this shall be the sign for you: you
will eat this year what grows of itself, in the second
year what springs from the same, and in the third
year sow, reap, plant vineyards and eat their fruit.
31 "The surviving remnant of the house of Judah will again take root downward and bear fruit
upward.
32 "For out of Jerusalem will go forth a remnant
and out of Mount Zion survivors. The zeal of the
LORD of hosts will perform this." '
33 ¶ "Therefore, thus says the LORD concerning the king of Assyria, 'He will not come to this
city or shoot an arrow there; and he will not come
before it with a shield, or throw up a siege ramp
against it.
34 'By the way that he came, by the same he will
return, and he will not come to this city,' declares
the LORD.
35 'For I will defend this city to save it for My
own sake and for My servant David's sake.' "

Assyrians Destroyed

36 ¶ Then the angel of the LORD went out and
struck 185,000 in the camp of the Assyrians; and
when men arose early in the morning, behold, all
of these were dead.

37 So Sennacherib king of Assyria departed
and returned *home* and lived at Nineveh.
38 It came about as he was worshiping in the
house of Nisroch his god, that Adrammelech and
Sharezer his sons killed him with the sword; and
they escaped into the land of Ararat. And Esarhaddon his son became king in his place.

Hezekiah Healed

38 In those days Hezekiah became mortally ill.
And Isaiah the prophet the son of Amoz
came to him and said to him, "Thus says the
LORD, 'Set your house in order, for you shall die
and not live.' "

38:1 Fifteen More Years

*When the doctor solemnly pronounces a
disease terminal, who doesn't crave a second
chance? After Isaiah announced to Hezekiah
that his disease would be fatal, Hezekiah did
not give up. He wept bitterly and asked God to
remember his devotion. In response, God sent
Isaiah back with an amazing message: He had
granted Hezekiah fifteen additional years.
Here, as so often in the Bible, God changes
events because of prayer.*

2 Then Hezekiah turned his face to the wall
and prayed to the LORD,
3 and said, "Remember now, O LORD, I beseech You, how I have walked before You in truth
and with a whole heart, and have done what is
good in Your sight." And Hezekiah wept bitterly.
4 ¶ Then the word of the LORD came to Isaiah, saying,
5 "Go and say to Hezekiah, 'Thus says the
LORD, the God of your father David, "I have heard
your prayer, I have seen your tears; behold, I will
add fifteen years to your life.
6 "I will deliver you and this city from the hand
of the king of Assyria; and I will defend this city." '
7 ¶ "This shall be the sign to you from the
LORD, that the LORD will do this thing that He has
spoken:
8 "Behold, I will cause the shadow on the stairway, which has gone down with the sun on the
stairway of Ahaz, to go back ten steps." So the
sun's *shadow* went back ten steps on the stairway
on which it had gone down.
9 ¶ A writing of Hezekiah king of Judah after
his illness and recovery:
10 I said, "In the middle of my life
I am to enter the gates of Sheol;
I am to be deprived of the rest of my
years."
11 I said, "I will not see the LORD,
The LORD in the land of the living;
I will look on man no more among the
inhabitants of the world.

12 "Like a shepherd's tent my dwelling is
    pulled up and removed from me;
As a weaver I rolled up my life.
He cuts me off from the loom;
From day until night You make an end
    of me.
13 "I composed *my soul* until morning.
Like a lion—so He breaks all my bones,
From day until night You make an end
    of me.
14 "Like a swallow, *like* a crane, so I twitter;
I moan like a dove;
My eyes look wistfully to the heights;
O Lord, I am oppressed, be my security.

15 ¶ "What shall I say?
For He has spoken to me, and He
    Himself has done it;
I will wander about all my years because
    of the bitterness of my soul.
16 "O Lord, by *these* things *men* live,
And in all these is the life of my spirit;
O restore me to health and let me live!
17 "Lo, for *my own* welfare I had great
    bitterness;
It is You who has kept my soul from the
    pit of nothingness,
For You have cast all my sins behind
    Your back.
18 "For Sheol cannot thank You,
Death cannot praise You;
Those who go down to the pit cannot
    hope for Your faithfulness.
19 "It is the living who give thanks to You,
    as I do today;
A father tells his sons about Your
    faithfulness.
20 "The LORD will surely save me;
So we will play my songs on stringed
    instruments
All *the* days of our life at the house of
    the LORD."

21 ¶ Now Isaiah had said, "Let them take a cake of figs and apply it to the boil, that he may recover." 22 Then Hezekiah had said, "What is the sign that I shall go up to the house of the LORD?"

Hezekiah Shows His Treasures

39 At that time Merodach-baladan son of Baladan, king of Babylon, sent letters and a present to Hezekiah, for he heard that he had been sick and had recovered. 2 Hezekiah was pleased, and showed them *all* his treasure house, the silver and the gold and the spices and the precious oil and his whole armory and all that was found in his treasuries. There was nothing in his house nor in all his dominion that Hezekiah did not show them. 3 Then Isaiah the prophet came to King Hezekiah and said to him, "What did these men say, and from where have they come to you?" And

Hezekiah said, "They have come to me from a far country, from Babylon." 4 He said, "What have they seen in your house?" So Hezekiah answered, "They have seen all that is in my house; there is nothing among my treasuries that I have not shown them."

5 ¶ Then Isaiah said to Hezekiah, "Hear the word of the LORD of hosts, 6 'Behold, the days are coming when all that is in your house and all that your fathers have laid up in store to this day will be carried to Babylon; nothing will be left,' says the LORD. 7 'And *some* of your sons who will issue from you, whom you will beget, will be taken away, and they will become officials in the palace of the king of Babylon.' "

8 Then Hezekiah said to Isaiah, "The word of the LORD which you have spoken is good." For he thought, "For there will be peace and truth in my days."

The Greatness of God

40 "Comfort, O comfort My people," says your God.
2 "Speak kindly to Jerusalem;
And call out to her, that her warfare has
    ended,
That her iniquity has been removed,
That she has received of the LORD's hand
Double for all her sins."

3 ¶ A voice is calling,
"Clear the way for the LORD in the
    wilderness;
Make smooth in the desert a highway for
    our God.

40:3 Voice in the Wilderness

Beginning here, Isaiah's emphasis shifts away from judgment and toward comfort. The comfort will ultimately come through God's glorious arrival, which God's people should prepare for by building a "highway" for God to travel on. In the New Testament, John the Baptist identified himself as the "voice" calling for this preparation (John 1:23). The "earthmoving" he demanded was repentance from sin, a preparation for Jesus' arrival.

4 "Let every valley be lifted up,
And every mountain and hill be made
    low;
And let the rough ground become a
    plain,
And the rugged terrain a broad valley;
5 Then the glory of the LORD will be
    revealed,
And all flesh will see *it* together;
For the mouth of the LORD has spoken."

A New Song

A dramatic change in tone: comfort and hope for the worst of times

YOU CAN SENSE THE CHANGE in the very first words of chapter 40. "Comfort, O comfort My people," says your God. "Speak kindly to Jerusalem; and call out to her, that her warfare has ended." Soft, reassuring words replace the harsh warnings of Isaiah's earlier chapters.

During much of Isaiah's life, Judah was confident and strong. But the prophecies beginning in chapter 40 project forward to a radically different scene. The land of Judah has been devastated, and the Jews have been taken captive. Jerusalem lies in ruins. Some 200 years separate what is described in the first part of Isaiah from the latter part. (Many scholars believe these later prophecies were given by another prophet.)

> *Yet those who wait for the LORD will gain new strength; they will mount up with wings like eagles, they will run and not get tired, they will walk and not become weary. 40:31*

What Happened in the Meantime

To understand the rest of the book of Isaiah, you need to understand what happened in those 200 years. The confident nation Isaiah once knew slid further and further downward. At the same time a new empire, Babylon, gained strength. This new enemy invaded Judah.

The armies of Babylon did something no army had accomplished since King David's time: they conquered Jerusalem itself. Siege engines breached the walls. Judah's king was led out of Jerusalem, blinded. Their homes destroyed, most of the city's inhabitants followed their king in chains. The dark period of Babylonian captivity began.

Prophets of this period, and those who prophesied in advance about the coming catastrophes, faced huge questions. Was God abandoning his "eternal" throne of David? How could he watch in silence as his own nation—his own temple—was ripped to shreds by pagan armies?

Three Great Hopes

Reflecting the change in circumstances, Isaiah 40–66 shifts into a new key. Gone are the bleak predictions of judgment on the Jews. Instead, a majestic message of hope and joy and light breaks in, beginning with the opening words of comfort. The prophet sets out to reestablish faith in God.

What happened to Judah, Isaiah teaches, was not God's defeat. God had in mind a new thing, a plan far more grand than anything seen before.

The author of Isaiah expresses the plan as a series of wonderful reasons for hope. First, he says, will come deliverance from the Babylonian captivity. A new star, a ruler named Cyrus, will arise in the east and set the Jews free. He will allow them to return to Jerusalem to begin the long task of rebuilding a city and a nation. Chapters 40–48 detail God's confident predictions about Cyrus and the relief he would give captive Jews.

Indeed, just such a ruler did ascend to the throne in ancient Persia (present-day Iran). Cyrus smashed Babylon's armies in one decisive battle. As recorded in Ezra 1:1–4, he granted the Jews permission to return to their city and rebuild.

In words that have become very familiar, the book of Isaiah tells of two further hopes for the future. A mysterious figure called "the servant" appears in chapter 49. That servant, through his suffering, would provide a way to rescue the entire world. Finally, in conclusion, the prophet turns to a faraway time, when God will usher in peace for all in a new heaven and new earth. "The Holy One of Israel" (one of Isaiah's favorite names for God) will rule as the God of the whole earth.

Surviving Tough Times

Isaiah 40–66 had immense practical value for the people who first heard it. The Jews, facing a series of great crises, needed the prophet's message of hope: Forgiveness was on the way; the Jews, though scattered, would one day be gathered "one by one."

Further, Isaiah teaches that no matter how difficult the circumstances, God can use them for our benefit. Again and again in the Israelites' history, good times led to decadence. In contrast, times of suffering tested and refined the true people of God. Ultimately, suffering would lead to the salvation of all the world.

Life Questions: Try to put yourself in the circumstances of the Jews back then. Would you have found the prophet's words comforting?

6 A voice says, "Call out."
   Then he answered, "What shall I call
      out?"
   All flesh is grass, and all its loveliness is
      like the flower of the field.
7 The grass withers, the flower fades,
   When the breath of the LORD blows
      upon it;
   Surely the people are grass.
8 The grass withers, the flower fades,
   But the word of our God stands forever.

9 ¶ Get yourself up on a high mountain,
   O Zion, bearer of good news,
   Lift up your voice mightily,
   O Jerusalem, bearer of good news;
   Lift it up, do not fear.
   Say to the cities of Judah,
   "Here is your God!"
10 Behold, the Lord GOD will come with
      might,
   With His arm ruling for Him.
   Behold, His reward is with Him
   And His recompense before Him.
11 Like a shepherd He will tend His flock,
   In His arm He will gather the lambs
   And carry them in His bosom;
   He will gently lead the nursing ewes.

12 ¶ Who has measured the waters in the
      hollow of His hand,
   And marked off the heavens by the span,
   And calculated the dust of the earth by
      the measure,
   And weighed the mountains in a balance
   And the hills in a pair of scales?
13 Who has directed the Spirit of the LORD,
   Or as His counselor has informed Him?
14 With whom did He consult and who
      gave Him understanding?
   And who taught Him in the path of
      justice and taught Him knowledge
   And informed Him of the way of
      understanding?
15 Behold, the nations are like a drop from
      a bucket,
   And are regarded as a speck of dust on
      the scales;
   Behold, He lifts up the islands like fine
      dust.
16 Even Lebanon is not enough to burn,
   Nor its beasts enough for a burnt
      offering.
17 All the nations are as nothing before
      Him,
   They are regarded by Him as less than
      nothing and meaningless.

18 ¶ To whom then will you liken God?
   Or what likeness will you compare with
      Him?

19 As for the idol, a craftsman casts it,
   A goldsmith plates it with gold,
   And a silversmith fashions chains of
      silver.
20 He who is too impoverished for such an
      offering
   Selects a tree that does not rot;
   He seeks out for himself a skillful
      craftsman
   To prepare an idol that will not totter.

21 ¶ Do you not know? Have you not
      heard?
   Has it not been declared to you from the
      beginning?
   Have you not understood from the
      foundations of the earth?
22 It is He who ᵃsits above the ᵇcircle of
      the earth,
   And its inhabitants are like grasshoppers,
   Who stretches out the heavens like a
      curtain
   And spreads them out like a tent to
      dwell in.
23 He it is who reduces rulers to nothing,
   Who makes the judges of the earth
      meaningless.
24 ᶜScarcely have they been planted,
   ᶜScarcely have they been sown,
   ᶜScarcely has their stock taken root in
      the earth,
   But He merely blows on them, and they
      wither,
   And the storm carries them away like
      stubble.
25 "To whom then will you liken Me
   That I would be his equal?" says the
      Holy One.
26 Lift up your eyes on high
   And see who has created these stars,
   The One who leads forth their host by
      number,
   He calls them all by name;
   Because of the greatness of His might
      and the strength of His power,
   Not one of them is missing.

27 ¶ Why do you say, O Jacob, and assert,
      O Israel,
   "My way is hidden from the LORD,
   And the justice due me escapes the
      notice of my God"?
28 Do you not know? Have you not heard?
   The Everlasting God, the LORD, the
      Creator of the ends of the earth
   Does not become weary or tired.
   His understanding is inscrutable.
29 He gives strength to the weary,
   And to him who lacks might He
      increases power.
30 Though youths grow weary and tired,

ᵃ Or is enthroned   ᵇ Or vault   ᶜ Or Not even

And vigorous young men stumble badly,
31 Yet those who wait for the LORD
Will gain new strength;
They will mount up *with* wings like
eagles,
They will run and not get tired,
They will walk and not become weary.

Israel Encouraged

41 "Coastlands, listen to Me in silence,
And let the peoples gain new strength;
Let them come forward, then let them
speak;
Let us come together for judgment.
2 "Who has aroused one from the east
Whom He calls in righteousness to His
feet?
He delivers up nations before him
And subdues kings.
He makes them like dust with his sword,
As the wind-driven chaff with his bow.
3 "He pursues them, passing on in safety,
By a way he had not been traversing with
his feet.
4 "Who has performed and accomplished *it,*
Calling forth the generations from the
beginning?
'I, the LORD, am the first, and with the
last. I am He.' "

41:4 How to Understand God

Chapters 40–46 echo the majestic chapters at
the end of Job. God shows himself as master of
the universe. Before him, nations are like a
drop from a bucket (40:15) and people are like
grasshoppers (40:22). He taunts all other so-
called "gods": such idols are carved of the same
tree used to cook supper! (44:12–20). The true
God, the God of the Israelites, is the One who
created the universe (45:12,18), who called
Abraham (41:8), who rescued the Israelites
from slavery in Egypt. For the dispirited Jewish
survivors of Babylon's invasion, this exalted
view of God was a reminder that God had
neither vanished nor rejected them.

5 ¶ The coastlands have seen and are
afraid;
The ends of the earth tremble;
They have drawn near and have come.
6 Each one helps his neighbor
And says to his brother, "Be strong!"
7 So the craftsman encourages the smelter,
And he who smooths *metal* with the
hammer *encourages* him who beats
the anvil,
Saying of the soldering, "It is good";
And he fastens it with nails,
So that it will not totter.

8 "But you, Israel, My servant,
Jacob whom I have chosen,
Descendant of Abraham My friend,
9 You whom I have taken from the ends of
the earth,
And called from its remotest parts
And said to you, 'You are My servant,
I have chosen you and not rejected you.
10 'Do not fear, for I am with you;
Do not anxiously look about you, for I
am your God.
I will strengthen you, surely I will help
you,
Surely I will uphold you with My
righteous right hand.'
11 "Behold, all those who are angered at you
will be shamed and dishonored;
Those who contend with you will be as
nothing and will perish.
12 "You will seek those who quarrel with
you, but will not find them,
Those who war with you will be as
nothing and non-existent.
13 "For I am the LORD your God, who
upholds your right hand,
Who says to you, 'Do not fear, I will
help you.'
14 "Do not fear, you worm Jacob, you men
of Israel;
I will help you," declares the LORD, "and
your Redeemer is the Holy One of
Israel.
15 "Behold, I have made you a new, sharp
threshing sledge with double edges;
You will thresh the mountains and
pulverize *them,*
And will make the hills like chaff.
16 "You will winnow them, and the wind will
carry them away,
And the storm will scatter them;
But you will rejoice in the LORD,
You will glory in the Holy One of Israel.

17 ¶ "The afflicted and needy are seeking
water, but there is none,
And their tongue is parched with thirst;
I, the LORD, will answer them Myself,
As the God of Israel I will not forsake
them.
18 "I will open rivers on the bare heights
And springs in the midst of the valleys;
I will make the wilderness a pool of
water
And the dry land fountains of water.
19 "I will put the cedar in the wilderness,
The acacia and the myrtle and the olive
tree;
I will place the juniper in the desert
Together with the box tree and the
cypress,
20 That they may see and recognize,
And consider and gain insight as well,

That the hand of the LORD has done this,
And the Holy One of Israel has
created it.

21 ¶ "Present your case," the LORD says.
"Bring forward your strong *arguments*,"
The King of Jacob says.
22 Let them bring forth and declare to us
what is going to take place;
As for the former *events*, declare what
they *were*,
That we may consider them and know
their outcome.
Or announce to us what is coming;
23 Declare the things that are going to come
afterward,
That we may know that you are gods;
Indeed, do good or evil, that we may
anxiously look about us and fear
together.
24 Behold, you are of no account,
And your work amounts to nothing;
He who chooses you is an abomination.

25 ¶ "I have aroused one from the north,
and he has come;
From the rising of the sun he will call on
My name;
And he will come upon rulers as *upon*
mortar,
Even as the potter treads clay."
26 Who has declared *this* from the
beginning, that we might know?
Or from former times, that we may say,
"*He is* right!"?
Surely there was no one who declared,
Surely there was no one who proclaimed,
Surely there was no one who heard your
words.
27 "Formerly *I said* to Zion, 'Behold, here
they are.'
And to Jerusalem, 'I will give a
messenger of good news.'
28 "But when I look, there is no one,
And there is no counselor among them
Who, if I ask, can give an answer.
29 "Behold, all of them are ᵃfalse;
Their works are worthless,
Their molten images are wind and
emptiness.

God's Promise Concerning His Servant

42 "Behold, My Servant, whom I uphold;
My chosen one *in whom* My soul
delights.
I have put My Spirit upon Him;
He will bring forth justice to the nations.
2 "He will not cry out or raise *His voice*,
Nor make His voice heard in the street.
3 "A bruised reed He will not break

ᵃ Another reading is *nothing*

And a dimly burning wick He will not
extinguish;
He will faithfully bring forth justice.

42:1 The Solution

*Having described shocking injustice, Isaiah
now gives the solution: God's servant, who in a
quiet, gentle, steady way will bring justice not
only to Israel but to "the nations"—that is, the
entire earth. Matthew 12:18–21, quoting this
passage, identifies the servant as Jesus.*

4 "He will not be disheartened or crushed
Until He has established justice in the
earth;
And the coastlands will wait expectantly
for His law."

5 ¶ Thus says God the LORD,
Who created the heavens and stretched
them out,
Who spread out the earth and its
offspring,
Who gives breath to the people on it
And spirit to those who walk in it,
6 "I am the LORD, I have called you in
righteousness,
I will also hold you by the hand and
watch over you,
And I will appoint you as a covenant to
the people,
As a light to the nations,
7 To open blind eyes,
To bring out prisoners from the dungeon
And those who dwell in darkness from
the prison.
8 "I am the LORD, that is My name;
I will not give My glory to another,
Nor My praise to graven images.
9 "Behold, the former things have come to
pass,
Now I declare new things;
Before they spring forth I proclaim *them*
to you."

10 ¶ Sing to the LORD a new song,
Sing His praise from the end of the
earth!
You who go down to the sea, and all that
is in it.
You islands, and those who dwell on
them.
11 Let the wilderness and its cities lift up
their voices,
The settlements where Kedar inhabits.
Let the inhabitants of Sela sing aloud,
Let them shout for joy from the tops of
the mountains.

12 Let them give glory to the LORD
And declare His praise in the coastlands.
13 The LORD will go forth like a warrior,
He will arouse *His* zeal like a man of
war.
He will utter a shout, yes, He will raise a
war cry.
He will prevail against His enemies.

The Blindness of the People

14 ¶ "I have kept silent for a long time,
I have kept still and restrained Myself.
Now like a woman in labor I will groan,
I will both gasp and pant.

42:14 Does God Care?

After telling of his power, God goes on to describe the depth of his feelings for his people. He uses tender and sometimes shocking language, especially in this comparison of his pain to that of childbirth.

15 "I will lay waste the mountains and hills
And wither all their vegetation;
I will make the rivers into coastlands
And dry up the ponds.
16 "I will lead the blind by a way they do
not know,
In paths they do not know I will guide
them.
I will make darkness into light before
them
And rugged places into plains.
These are the things I will do,
And I will not leave them undone."
17 They will be turned back *and* be utterly
put to shame,
Who trust in idols,
Who say to molten images,
"You are our gods."

18 ¶ Hear, you deaf!
And look, you blind, that you may see.
19 Who is blind but My servant,
Or so deaf as My messenger whom I
send?
Who is so blind as he that is at peace
with Me,
Or so blind as the servant of the LORD?
20 You have seen many things, but you do
not observe *them;*
Your ears are open, but none hears.
21 The LORD was pleased for His
righteousness' sake
To make the law great and glorious.
22 But this is a people plundered and
despoiled;
All of them are trapped in caves,
Or are hidden away in prisons;

They have become a prey with none to
deliver *them,*
And a spoil, with none to say, "Give
them back!"

23 ¶ Who among you will give ear to this?
Who will give heed and listen hereafter?
24 Who gave Jacob up for spoil, and Israel
to plunderers?
Was it not the LORD, against whom we
have sinned,
And in whose ways they were not willing
to walk,
And whose law they did not obey?
25 So He poured out on him the heat of
His anger
And the fierceness of battle;
And it set him aflame all around,
Yet he did not recognize *it;*
And it burned him, but he paid no
attention.

Israel Redeemed

43 But now, thus says the LORD, your
Creator, O Jacob,
And He who formed you, O Israel,
"Do not fear, for I have redeemed you;
I have called you by name; you are
Mine!
2 "When you pass through the waters,
I will be with you;
And through the rivers, they will not
overflow you.
When you walk through the fire, you will
not be scorched,
Nor will the flame burn you.
3 "For I am the LORD your God,
The Holy One of Israel, your Savior;
I have given Egypt as your ransom,
Cush and Seba in your place.

43:3 Ransom for the Captives

God speaks of providing the nations of Egypt, Cush, and Seba as a ransom or reward for allowing the Jews to return to their land. Historically, Cyrus of Persia permitted the Jews to resettle in the sixth century B.C. Shortly after that, Persia conquered the territories mentioned here.

4 "Since you are precious in My sight,
Since you are honored and I love you,
I will give *other* men in your place and
other peoples in exchange for your
life.
5 "Do not fear, for I am with you;
I will bring your offspring from the east,

And gather you from the west.

6 "I will say to the north, 'Give *them* up!'
And to the south, 'Do not hold *them*
back.'
Bring My sons from afar
And My daughters from the ends of the
earth,

7 Everyone who is called by My name,
And whom I have created for My glory,
Whom I have formed, even whom I have
made."

Israel Is God's Witness

8 ¶ Bring out the people who are blind,
even though they have eyes,
And the deaf, even though they have
ears.

9 All the nations have gathered together
So that the peoples may be assembled.
Who among them can declare this
And proclaim to us the former things?
Let them present their witnesses that they
may be justified,
Or let them hear and say, "It is true."

10 "You are My witnesses," declares the
LORD,
"And My servant whom I have chosen,
So that you may know and believe Me
And understand that I am He.
Before Me there was no God formed,
And there will be none after Me.

43:10 Courtroom Drama

*Isaiah pictures a courtlike drama, in which the
world assembles to decide who is really God. As
each would-be god calls witnesses in turn, the
God of Israel calls his people to witness for him.
They had heard God's prediction that he would
bring back his people, scattered all over the
Middle East, to reestablish their nation. As his
witnesses, they need only testify that he has
done what he promised.*

11 "I, even I, am the LORD,
And there is no savior besides Me.

12 "It is I who have declared and saved and
proclaimed,
And there was no strange *god* among
you;
So you are My witnesses," declares the
LORD,
"And I am God.

13 "Even from eternity I am He,
And there is none who can deliver out of
My hand;
I act and who can reverse It?"

Babylon to Be Destroyed

14 ¶ Thus says the LORD your Redeemer, the
Holy One of Israel,
"For your sake I have sent to Babylon,
And will bring them all down as
fugitives,
[a]Even the Chaldeans, into the ships in
which they rejoice.

15 "I am the LORD, your Holy One,
The Creator of Israel, your King."

16 Thus says the LORD,
Who makes a way through the sea
And a path through the mighty waters,

17 Who brings forth the chariot and the
horse,
The army and the mighty man
(They will lie down together *and* not rise
again;
They have been quenched *and*
extinguished like a wick):

18 "Do not call to mind the former things,
Or ponder things of the past.

19 "Behold, I will do something new,
Now it will spring forth;
Will you not be aware of it?
I will even make a roadway in the
wilderness,
Rivers in the desert.

20 "The beasts of the field will glorify Me,
The jackals and the ostriches,
Because I have given waters in the
wilderness
And rivers in the desert,
To give drink to My chosen people.

21 "The people whom I formed for Myself
Will declare My praise.

The Shortcomings of Israel

22 ¶ "Yet you have not called on Me,
O Jacob;
But you have become weary of Me,
O Israel.

23 "You have not brought to Me the sheep
of your burnt offerings,
Nor have you honored Me with your
sacrifices.
I have not burdened you with offerings,
Nor wearied you with incense.

24 "You have bought Me not sweet cane with
money,
Nor have you filled Me with the fat of
your sacrifices;
Rather you have burdened Me with your
sins,
You have wearied Me with your
iniquities.

25 ¶ "I, even I, am the one who wipes out
your transgressions for My own
sake,

[a] Another reading is *As for the Chaldeans, their rejoicing* is turned *into lamentations*

And I will not remember your sins.
26 "Put Me in remembrance, let us argue our
case together;
State your *cause,* that you may be proved
right.
27 "Your first forefather sinned,
And your spokesmen have transgressed
against Me.
28 "So I will pollute the princes of the
sanctuary,
And I will consign Jacob to the ban and
Israel to revilement.

The Blessings of Israel

44 "But now listen, O Jacob, My servant,
And Israel, whom I have chosen:
2 Thus says the LORD who made you
And formed you from the womb, who
will help you,
'Do not fear, O Jacob My servant;
And you Jeshurun whom I have chosen.
3 'For I will pour out water on the thirsty
land
And streams on the dry ground;
I will pour out My Spirit on your
offspring
And My blessing on your descendants;
4 And they will spring up among the grass
Like poplars by streams of water.'
5 "This one will say, 'I am the LORD's';
And that one will call on the name of
Jacob;
And another will write *on* his hand,
'Belonging to the LORD,'
And will name Israel's name with honor.

6 ¶ "Thus says the LORD, the King of Israel
and his Redeemer, the LORD of hosts:
'I am the first and I am the last,
And there is no God besides Me.
7 'Who is like Me? Let him proclaim and
declare it;
Yes, let him recount it to Me in order,
From the time that I established the
ancient nation.
And let them declare to them the things
that are coming
And the events that are going to take
place.
8 'Do not tremble and do not be afraid;
Have I not long since announced *it* to
you and declared *it?*
And you are My witnesses.
Is there any God besides Me,
Or is there any *other* Rock?
I know of none.' "

The Folly of Idolatry

9 ¶ Those who fashion a graven image are all
of them futile, and their precious things are of no
profit; even their own witnesses fail to see or
know, so that they will be put to shame.

10 Who has fashioned a god or cast an idol to
no profit?
11 Behold, all his companions will be put to
shame, for the craftsmen are mere
men. Let them all assemble themselves, let them
stand up, let them tremble, let them together be
put to shame.
12 ¶ The man shapes iron into a cutting tool
and does his work over the coals, fashioning it
with hammers and working it with his strong arm.
He also gets hungry and his strength fails; he
drinks no water and becomes weary.
13 *Another* shapes wood, he extends a measuring line; he outlines it with red chalk. He works it
with planes and outlines it with a compass, and
makes it like the form of a man, like the beauty of
man, so that it may sit in a house.
14 Surely he cuts cedars for himself, and takes
a cypress or an oak and raises *it* for himself among
the trees of the forest. He plants a fir, and the rain
makes it grow.
15 Then it becomes *something* for a man to
burn, so he takes one of them and warms himself;
he also makes a fire to bake bread. He also makes
a god and worships it; he makes it a graven image
and falls down before it.
16 Half of it he burns in the fire; over *this* half
he eats meat as he roasts a roast and is satisfied.
He also warms himself and says, "Aha! I am
warm, I have seen the fire."
17 But the rest of it he makes into a god, his
graven image. He falls down before it and worships; he also prays to it and says, "Deliver me, for
you are my god."
18 ¶ They do not know, nor do they understand, for He has smeared over their eyes so that
they cannot see and their hearts so that they cannot comprehend.
19 No one recalls, nor is there knowledge or
understanding to say, "I have burned half of it in
the fire and also have baked bread over its coals.
I roast meat and eat *it.* Then I make the rest of it
into an abomination, I fall down before a block of
wood!"
20 He feeds on ashes; a deceived heart has
turned him aside. And he cannot deliver himself,
nor say, "Is there not a lie in my right hand?"

God Forgives and Redeems

21 ¶ "Remember these things, O Jacob,
And Israel, for you are My servant;
I have formed you, you are My servant,
O Israel, you will not be forgotten
by Me.
22 "I have wiped out your transgressions like
a thick cloud
And your sins like a heavy mist.
Return to Me, for I have redeemed you."
23 Shout for joy, O heavens, for the LORD
has done *it!*

Shout joyfully, you lower parts of the
earth;
Break forth into a shout of joy, you
mountains,
O forest, and every tree in it;
For the LORD has redeemed Jacob
And in Israel He shows forth His glory.

24 ¶ Thus says the LORD, your Redeemer, and
the one who formed you from the womb,
"I, the LORD, am the maker of all things,
Stretching out the heavens by Myself
And spreading out the earth all alone,
25 Causing the omens of boasters to fail,
Making fools out of diviners,
Causing wise men to draw back
And turning their knowledge into
foolishness,
26 Confirming the word of His servant
And performing the purpose of His
messengers.
It is I who says of Jerusalem, 'She shall
be inhabited!'
And of the cities of Judah, 'They shall be
built.'
And I will raise up her ruins *again.*
27 "*It is I* who says to the depth of the sea,
'Be dried up!'
And I will make your rivers dry.
28 "*It is I* who says of Cyrus, '*He is* My
shepherd!
And he will perform all My desire.'
And he declares of Jerusalem, 'She will
be built,'
And of the temple, 'Your foundation will
be laid.' "

God Uses Cyrus

45 Thus says the LORD to Cyrus His anointed,
Whom I have taken by the right hand,
To subdue nations before him
And to loose the loins of kings;
To open doors before him so that gates
will not be shut:
2 "I will go before you and make the rough
places smooth;
I will shatter the doors of bronze and cut
through their iron bars.
3 "I will give you the treasures of darkness
And hidden wealth of secret places,
So that you may know that it is I,
The LORD, the God of Israel, who calls
you by your name.
4 "For the sake of Jacob My servant,
And Israel My chosen *one,*
I have also called you by your name;
I have given you a title of honor
Though you have not known Me.
5 "I am the LORD, and there is no other;
Besides Me there is no God.
I will gird you, though you have not
known Me;
6 That men may know from the rising to
the setting of the sun
That there is no one besides Me.
I am the LORD, and there is no other,
7 The One forming light and creating
darkness,
Causing well-being and creating calamity;
I am the LORD who does all these.

God's Supreme Power

8 ¶ "Drip down, O heavens, from above,

CYRUS *Good Shepherd?*

GOD REFERRED TO HIM AS "My shepherd," delegated to him the rebuilding of Jerusalem and the temple (44:28), summoned him by name and bestowed on him "a title of honor" (45:4). Who was this ruler so favored by God? Surprisingly, Cyrus was not one of God's faithful followers at all. He was a foreigner, the emperor and founder of the great Persian Empire. A political and military genius, Cyrus had melded the Medes and the Persians into a unified nation and used his power to overthrow the cruel Babylonians.

Cyrus introduced a genuinely fresh idea onto the world stage: tolerance. Rather than smashing small countries, killing or deporting their people and destroying their religion and identity, Cyrus began a policy of encouraging ethnic minorities. He let them return to their homelands and helped them reestablish their places of worship.

The Jews benefited greatly from this policy (as the book of Ezra recounts in detail). Cyrus allowed the captive Jews to return to Jerusalem and rebuild their temple. Some 42,360 made the long trek home. Amazingly, Cyrus restored to the Jews the temple vessels stolen by the Babylonians and even contributed financially to the Jewish cause.

From the story of Cyrus, Isaiah draws the strong lesson that God has complete control over human history. He can use anybody to accomplish his work, even a great emperor who does not acknowledge him. All people of the earth belong to God, whether they know it or not.

Life Questions: Do you think God is using powerful leaders today to accomplish his will? How?

And let the clouds pour down
righteousness;
Let the earth open up and salvation bear
fruit,
And righteousness spring up with it.
I, the LORD, have created it.

9 ¶ "Woe to the one who quarrels with his
Maker—
An earthenware vessel among the vessels
of earth!
Will the clay say to the potter, 'What are
you doing?'
Or the thing you are making say, 'He has
no hands'?

45:9 Quarrels with God

*Quarreling with your Maker goes far beyond
the spirited dialogue that Moses, Job, and
Jeremiah engaged in. Isaiah is describing an
insolent assault on God's competence. Not only
is it wrong, it is ridiculous—as ridiculous as a
pot complaining about the shape the potter
gives it. In Romans 9:20, Paul applies this
analogy to complaints that God had treated the
Jews unfairly.*

10 "Woe to him who says to a father, 'What
are you begetting?'
Or to a woman, 'To what are you giving
birth?' "

11 ¶ Thus says the LORD, the Holy One of Israel, and his Maker:
"Ask Me about the things to come
concerning My sons,
And you shall commit to Me the work of
My hands.
12 "It is I who made the earth, and created
man upon it.
I stretched out the heavens with My
hands
And I ordained all their host.
13 "I have aroused him in righteousness
And I will make all his ways smooth;
He will build My city and will let My
exiles go free,
Without any payment or reward," says
the LORD of hosts.

14 ¶ Thus says the LORD,
"The products of Egypt and the
merchandise of Cush
And the Sabeans, men of stature,
Will come over to you and will be yours;
They will walk behind you, they will
come over in chains
And will bow down to you;
They will make supplication to you:

'Surely, God is with you, and there is
none else,
No other God.' "
15 Truly, You are a God who hides Himself,
O God of Israel, Savior!
16 They will be put to shame and even
humiliated, all of them;
The manufacturers of idols will go away
together in humiliation.
17 Israel has been saved by the LORD
With an everlasting salvation;
You will not be put to shame or
humiliated
To all eternity.

18 ¶ For thus says the LORD, who created the
heavens (He is the God who formed the earth and
made it, He established it and did not create it a
waste place, but formed it to be inhabited),
"I am the LORD, and there is none else.
19 "I have not spoken in secret,
In some dark land;
I did not say to the offspring of Jacob,
'Seek Me in a waste place';
I, the LORD, speak righteousness,
Declaring things that are upright.

20 ¶ "Gather yourselves and come;
Draw near together, you fugitives of the
nations;
They have no knowledge,
Who carry about their wooden idol
And pray to a god who cannot save.
21 "Declare and set forth your case;
Indeed, let them consult together.
Who has announced this from of old?
Who has long since declared it?
Is it not I, the LORD?
And there is no other God besides
Me,
A righteous God and a Savior;
There is none except Me.

45:21 Foretelling the Future

*Isaiah contains many predictions of future
events. These chapters tell of Cyrus's rise from
the east. Elsewhere, the prophet gives specific
predictions about the coming Messiah and
about events near the end of time. God uses
these predictions as proof of his power and
knowledge, challenging the pagan gods to
foretell anything (41:23).*

22 "Turn to Me and be saved, all the ends of
the earth;
For I am God, and there is no other.
23 "I have sworn by Myself,

The word has gone forth from My
mouth in righteousness
And will not turn back,
That to Me every knee will bow, every
tongue will swear *allegiance*.
24 "They will say of Me, 'Only in the LORD
are righteousness and strength.'
Men will come to Him,
And all who were angry at Him will be
put to shame.
25 "In the LORD all the offspring of Israel
Will be justified and will glory."

Babylon's Idols and the True God

46 Bel has bowed down, Nebo stoops over;
Their images are *consigned* to the beasts
and the cattle.
The things that you carry are
burdensome,
A load for the weary *beast*.
2 They stooped over, they have bowed
down together;
They could not rescue the burden,
But have themselves gone into captivity.

3 ¶ "Listen to Me, O house of Jacob,
And all the remnant of the house of
Israel,
You who have been borne by Me from
birth
And have been carried from the womb;
4 Even to *your* old age I will be the same,
And even to *your* graying years I will
bear *you!*
I have done *it,* and I will carry *you;*
And I will bear *you* and I will
deliver *you.*

46:4 I Carried You

*Is religion a burden? For idol worshipers,
certainly, in the most literal sense: Their
helpless gods had to be carried around on carts
(verse 1). In contrast, God carries his people,
and has done so from the time of their
conception and birth. He won't stop; he will
sustain and rescue them in their old age.*

5 ¶ "To whom would you liken Me
And make Me equal and compare Me,
That we would be alike?
6 "Those who lavish gold from the purse
And weigh silver on the scale
Hire a goldsmith, and he makes it *into* a
god;
They bow down, indeed they worship it.
7 "They lift it upon the shoulder *and*
carry it;
They set it in its place and it stands
there.

It does not move from its place.
Though one may cry to it, it cannot
answer;
It cannot deliver him from his distress.

8 ¶ "Remember this, and be assured;
Recall it to mind, you transgressors.
9 "Remember the former things long past,
For I am God, and there is no other;
I am God, and there is no one like Me,
10 Declaring the end from the beginning,
And from ancient times things which
have not been done,
Saying, 'My purpose will be established,
And I will accomplish all My good
pleasure';
11 Calling a bird of prey from the east,
The man of My purpose from a far
country.
Truly I have spoken; truly I will bring it
to pass.
I have planned *it, surely* I will do it.

12 ¶ "Listen to Me, you stubborn-minded,
Who are far from righteousness.
13 "I bring near My righteousness, it is not
far off;
And My salvation will not delay.
And I will grant salvation in Zion,
And My glory for Israel.

Lament for Babylon

47 "Come down and sit in the dust,
O virgin daughter of Babylon;
Sit on the ground without a throne,
O daughter of the Chaldeans!
For you shall no longer be called tender
and delicate.
2 "Take the millstones and grind meal.
Remove your veil, strip off the skirt,
Uncover the leg, cross the rivers.
3 "Your nakedness will be uncovered,
Your shame also will be exposed;
I will take vengeance and will not spare a
man."
4 Our Redeemer, the LORD of hosts is His
name,
The Holy One of Israel.
5 "Sit silently, and go into darkness,
O daughter of the Chaldeans,
For you will no longer be called
The queen of kingdoms.
6 "I was angry with My people,
I profaned My heritage
And gave them into your hand.
You did not show mercy to them,
On the aged you made your yoke very
heavy.
7 "Yet you said, 'I will be a queen forever.'
These things you did not consider
Nor remember the outcome of them.

8 ¶ "Now, then, hear this, you sensual one,

Who dwells securely,
Who says in your heart,
'I am, and there is no one besides me.
I will not sit as a widow,
Nor know loss of children.'

47:7 An Evil Queen

Over the centuries, Babylon became a byword for evil among the Jews, for she was the nation that had destroyed Jerusalem and its temple. Psalm 137, composed by captive Jews in Babylon, expresses their anguish. But in this chapter God predicts that the great queen will become a prostitute, surprised by a sudden catastrophe. The same theme is echoed in the book of Revelation, which applies the symbolism of "Babylon the great" to another evil empire (Revelation 18).

9 "But these two things will come on you
    suddenly in one day:
Loss of children and widowhood.
They will come on you in full measure
In spite of your many sorceries,
In spite of the great power of your spells.
10 "You felt secure in your wickedness and
    said,
'No one sees me,'
Your wisdom and your knowledge, they
    have deluded you;
For you have said in your heart,
'I am, and there is no one besides me.'
11 "But evil will come on you
Which you will not know how to charm
    away;
And disaster will fall on you
For which you cannot atone;
And destruction about which you do not
    know
Will come on you suddenly.

12 ¶ "Stand *fast* now in your spells
And in your many sorceries
With which you have labored from your
    youth;
Perhaps you will be able to profit,
Perhaps you may cause trembling.
13 "You are wearied with your many
    counsels;
Let now the astrologers,
Those who prophesy by the stars,
Those who predict by the new moons,
Stand up and save you from what will
    come upon you.
14 "Behold, they have become like stubble,
Fire burns them;
They cannot deliver themselves from the
    power of the flame;
There will be no coal to warm by
Nor a fire to sit before!

15 "So have those become to you with whom
    you have labored,
Who have trafficked with you from your
    youth;
Each has wandered in his own way;
There is none to save you.

Israel's Obstinacy

48 "Hear this, O house of Jacob, who are
    named Israel
And who came forth from the loins of
    Judah,
Who swear by the name of the LORD
And invoke the God of Israel,
But not in truth nor in righteousness.
2 "For they call themselves after the holy
    city
And lean on the God of Israel;
The LORD of hosts is His name.
3 "I declared the former things long ago
And they went forth from My mouth,
    and I proclaimed them.
Suddenly I acted, and they came to pass.
4 "Because I know that you are obstinate,
And your neck is an iron sinew
And your forehead bronze,
5 Therefore I declared *them* to you long
    ago,
Before they took place I proclaimed *them*
    to you,
So that you would not say, 'My idol has
    done them,
And my graven image and my molten
    image have commanded them.'
6 "You have heard; look at all this.
And you, will you not declare it?
I proclaim to you new things from this
    time,
Even hidden things which you have not
    known.
7 "They are created now and not long ago;
And before today you have not heard
    them,
So that you will not say, 'Behold, I knew
    them.'
8 "You have not heard, you have not
    known.
Even from long ago your ear has not
    been open,
Because I knew that you would deal very
    treacherously;
And you have been called a rebel from
    birth.
9 "For the sake of My name I delay My
    wrath,
And *for* My praise I restrain *it* for you,
In order not to cut you off.
10 "Behold, I have refined you, but not as
    silver;
I have tested you in the furnace of
    affliction.

11 "For My own sake, for My own sake, I
will act;
For how can *My name* be profaned?
And My glory I will not give to another.

Deliverance Promised

12 ¶ "Listen to Me, O Jacob, even Israel
whom I called;
I am He, I am the first, I am also the
last.
13 "Surely My hand founded the earth,
And My right hand spread out the
heavens;
When I call to them, they stand together.
14 "Assemble, all of you, and listen!
Who among them has declared these
things?
The LORD loves him; he will carry out
His good pleasure on Babylon,
And His arm *will be against* the
Chaldeans.
15 "I, even I, have spoken; indeed I have
called him,
I have brought him, and He will make
his ways successful.
16 "Come near to Me, listen to this:
From the first I have not spoken in
secret,
From the time it took place, I was there.
And now the Lord GOD has sent Me,
and His Spirit."

17 ¶ Thus says the LORD, your Redeemer, the
Holy One of Israel,
"I am the LORD your God, who teaches
you to profit,
Who leads you in the way you
should go.
18 "If only you had paid attention to My
commandments!
Then your well-being would have been
like a river,
And your righteousness like the waves of
the sea.
19 "Your descendants would have been like
the sand,
And your offspring like its grains;
Their name would never be cut off or
destroyed from My presence."

20 ¶ Go forth from Babylon! Flee from the
Chaldeans!
Declare with the sound of joyful
shouting, proclaim this,
Send it out to the end of the earth;
Say, "The LORD has redeemed His
servant Jacob."
21 They did not thirst when He led them
through the deserts.
He made the water flow out of the rock
for them;

He split the rock and the water gushed
forth.
22 "There is no peace for the wicked," says
the LORD.

Salvation Reaches to the End of the Earth

49 Listen to Me, O islands,
And pay attention, you peoples from
afar.
The LORD called Me from the womb;
From the body of My mother He
named Me.
2 He has made My mouth like a sharp
sword,
In the shadow of His hand He has
concealed Me;
And He has also made Me a select
arrow,
He has hidden Me in His quiver.
3 He has said to Me, "You are My Servant,
Israel,
In Whom I will show My glory."
4 But I said, "I have toiled in vain,
I have spent My strength for nothing and
vanity;
Yet surely the justice *due* to Me is with
the LORD,
And My reward with My God."

5 ¶ And now says the LORD, who formed
Me from the womb to be His
Servant,
To bring Jacob back to Him, so that
Israel might be gathered to Him
(For I am honored in the sight of the
LORD,
And My God is My strength),
6 He says, "It is too small a thing that You
should be My Servant
To raise up the tribes of Jacob and to
restore the preserved ones of Israel;
I will also make You a light of the
nations
So that My salvation may reach to the
end of the earth."

49:6 Israel's Final Destiny

*The book of Isaiah spells out Israel's ultimate
destiny: to be a light of the nations and to bring
salvation to the ends of the earth. Isaiah is
not introducing a brand-new thought—God
had made clear his intentions in the original
covenant (Genesis 22:18). But, along the way,
Israel and Judah's desire for political greatness
had obscured their original calling.*

7 Thus says the LORD, the Redeemer of
Israel *and* its Holy One,
To the despised One,

To the One abhorred by the nation,
To the Servant of rulers,
"Kings will see and arise,
Princes will also bow down,
Because of the LORD who is faithful, the
 Holy One of Israel who has
 chosen You."

8 ¶ Thus says the LORD,
"In a favorable time I have answered You,
And in a day of salvation I have
 helped You;
And I will keep You and give You for a
 covenant of the people,
To restore the land, to make *them* inherit
 the desolate heritages;
9 Saying to those who are bound, 'Go
 forth,'
To those who are in darkness, 'Show
 yourselves.'
Along the roads they will feed,
And their pasture *will be* on all bare
 heights.
10 "They will not hunger or thirst,
Nor will the scorching heat or sun strike
 them down;
For He who has compassion on them
 will lead them
And will guide them to springs of water.
11 "I will make all My mountains a road,
And My highways will be raised up.
12 "Behold, these will come from afar;
And lo, these *will come* from the north
 and from the west,
And these from the land of Sinim."
13 Shout for joy, O heavens! And rejoice,
 O earth!
Break forth into joyful shouting,
 O mountains!
For the LORD has comforted His people
And will have compassion on His
 afflicted.

Promise to Zion

14 ¶ But Zion said, "The LORD has
 forsaken me,
And the Lord has forgotten me."
15 "Can a woman forget her nursing child
And have no compassion on the son of
 her womb?
Even these may forget, but I will not
 forget you.
16 "Behold, I have inscribed you on the
 palms *of My hands;*
Your walls are continually before Me.
17 "Your builders hurry;
Your destroyers and devastators
Will depart from you.
18 "Lift up your eyes and look around;
All of them gather together, they come to
 you.
As I live," declares the LORD,

"You will surely put on all of them as
 jewels and bind them on as a bride.
19 "For your waste and desolate places and
 your destroyed land—
Surely now you will be too cramped for
 the inhabitants,
And those who swallowed you will be far
 away.
20 "The children of whom you were bereaved
 will yet say in your ears,
'The place is too cramped for me;
Make room for me that I may live *here.*'
21 "Then you will say in your heart,
'Who has begotten these for me,
Since I have been bereaved of my
 children
And am barren, an exile and a wanderer?
And who has reared these?
Behold, I was left alone;
From where did these come?' "

22 ¶ Thus says the Lord GOD,
"Behold, I will lift up My hand to the
 nations
And set up My standard to the peoples;
And they will bring your sons in *their*
 bosom,
And your daughters will be carried on
 their shoulders.
23 "Kings will be your guardians,
And their princesses your nurses.
They will bow down to you with their
 faces to the earth
And lick the dust of your feet;
And *you* will know that I am the LORD;
Those who hopefully wait for Me will not
 be put to shame.

24 ¶ "Can the prey be taken from the
 mighty man,
Or the captives of a tyrant be rescued?"
25 Surely, thus says the LORD,
"Even the captives of the mighty man will
 be taken away,
And the prey of the tyrant will be
 rescued;
For I will contend with the one who
 contends with you,
And I will save your sons.
26 "I will feed your oppressors with their
 own flesh,
And they will become drunk with their
 own blood as with sweet wine;
And all flesh will know that I, the LORD,
 am your Savior
And your Redeemer, the Mighty One of
 Jacob."

God Helps His Servant

50 Thus says the LORD,
"Where is the certificate of divorce

By which I have sent your mother
    away?
Or to whom of My creditors did I
    sell you?
Behold, you were sold for your iniquities,
And for your transgressions your mother
    was sent away.
2 "Why was there no man when I came?
When I called, *why* was there none to
    answer?
Is My hand so short that it cannot
    ransom?
Or have I no power to deliver?
Behold, I dry up the sea with My rebuke,
I make the rivers a wilderness;
Their fish stink for lack of water
And die of thirst.
3 "I clothe the heavens with blackness
And make sackcloth their covering."

4 ¶ The Lord GOD has given Me the
    tongue of disciples,
That I may know how to sustain the
    weary one with a word.
He awakens *Me* morning by morning,
He awakens My ear to listen as a
    disciple.
5 The Lord GOD has opened My ear;
And I was not disobedient
Nor did I turn back.
6 I gave My back to those who strike *Me*,
And My cheeks to those who pluck out
    the beard;
I did not cover My face from humiliation
    and spitting.
7 For the Lord GOD helps Me,
Therefore, I am not disgraced;
Therefore, I have set My face like flint,
And I know that I will not be ashamed.
8 He who vindicates Me is near;
Who will contend with Me?
Let us stand up to each other;
Who has a case against Me?
Let him draw near to Me.
9 Behold, the Lord GOD helps Me;
Who is he who condemns Me?
Behold, they will all wear out like a
    garment;
The moth will eat them.
10 Who is among you that fears the LORD,
That obeys the voice of His servant,
That walks in darkness and has no light?
Let him trust in the name of the LORD
    and rely on his God.
11 Behold, all you who kindle a fire,
Who encircle yourselves with firebrands,
Walk in the light of your fire
And among the brands you have set
    ablaze.
This you will have from My hand:
You will lie down in torment.

Israel Exhorted

51 "Listen to me, you who pursue
    righteousness,
Who seek the LORD:
Look to the rock from which you were
    hewn
And to the quarry from which you were
    dug.
2 "Look to Abraham your father
And to Sarah who gave birth to you in
    pain;
When *he was but* one I called him,
Then I blessed him and multiplied him."
3 Indeed, the LORD will comfort Zion;
He will comfort all her waste places.
And her wilderness He will make like
    Eden,
And her desert like the garden of the
    LORD;
Joy and gladness will be found in her,
Thanksgiving and sound of a melody.

4 ¶ "Pay attention to Me, O My people,
And give ear to Me, O My nation;
For a law will go forth from Me,
And I will set My justice for a light of
    the peoples.
5 "My righteousness is near, My salvation
    has gone forth,
And My arms will judge the peoples;
The coastlands will wait for Me,
And for My arm they will wait
    expectantly.
6 "Lift up your eyes to the sky,
Then look to the earth beneath;
For the sky will vanish like smoke,
And the earth will wear out like a
    garment
And its inhabitants will die in like
    manner;
But My salvation will be forever,
And My righteousness will not wane.
7 "Listen to Me, you who know
    righteousness,
A people in whose heart is My law;
Do not fear the reproach of man,
Nor be dismayed at their revilings.
8 "For the moth will eat them like a
    garment,
And the grub will eat them like wool.
But My righteousness will be forever,
And My salvation to all generations."

9 ¶ Awake, awake, put on strength, O arm
    of the LORD;
Awake as in the days of old, the
    generations of long ago.
Was it not You who cut Rahab in pieces,
Who pierced the dragon?
10 Was it not You who dried up the sea,
The waters of the great deep;

Who made the depths of the sea a
pathway
For the redeemed to cross over?

51:9 Rahab the Monster

*The Rahab in Isaiah (here and in 30:7) should
not be confused with the Rahab who helped
Joshua's spies in Jericho (Joshua 2). Rather, the
word refers to a sea-monster that appears in
much Middle Eastern mythology. Because the
mythological monster lived in the Nile River
region, Rahab can stand for the nation of
Egypt, as it does here.*

11 So the ransomed of the LORD will return
And come with joyful shouting to Zion,
And everlasting joy *will be* on their
heads.
They will obtain gladness and joy,
And sorrow and sighing will flee away.

12 ¶ "I, even I, am He who comforts you.
Who are you that you are afraid of man
who dies
And of the son of man who is made like
grass,

13 That you have forgotten the LORD your
Maker,
Who stretched out the heavens
And laid the foundations of the earth,
That you fear continually all day long
because of the fury of the oppressor,
As he makes ready to destroy?
But where is the fury of the oppressor?

14 "The exile will soon be set free, and will not
die in the dungeon, nor will his bread be lacking.

15 "For I am the LORD your God, who stirs up
the sea and its waves roar (the LORD of hosts is His
name).

16 "I have put My words in your mouth and
have covered you with the shadow of My hand, to
establish the heavens, to found the earth, and to
say to Zion, 'You are My people.' "

17 ¶ Rouse yourself! Rouse yourself! Arise,
O Jerusalem,
You who have drunk from the LORD's
hand the cup of His anger;
The chalice of reeling you have drained
to the dregs.

18 There is none to guide her among all the
sons she has borne,
Nor is there one to take her by the hand
among all the sons she has reared.

19 These two things have befallen you;
Who will mourn for you?
The devastation and destruction, famine
and sword;
How shall I comfort you?

20 Your sons have fainted,
They lie *helpless* at the head of every
street,
Like an antelope in a net,
Full of the wrath of the LORD,
The rebuke of your God.

21 ¶ Therefore, please hear this, you
afflicted,
Who are drunk, but not with wine:

22 Thus says your Lord, the LORD, even
your God
Who contends for His people,
"Behold, I have taken out of your hand
the cup of reeling,
The chalice of My anger;
You will never drink it again.

23 "I will put it into the hand of your
tormentors,
Who have said to you, 'Lie down that we
may walk over *you*.'
You have even made your back like the
ground
And like the street for those who walk
over *it*."

Cheer for Prostrate Zion

52 Awake, awake,
Clothe yourself in your strength, O Zion;
Clothe yourself in your beautiful
garments,
O Jerusalem, the holy city;
For the uncircumcised and the unclean
Will no longer come into you.

2 Shake yourself from the dust, rise up,
O captive Jerusalem;
Loose yourself from the chains around
your neck,
O captive daughter of Zion.

3 ¶ For thus says the LORD, "You were sold
for nothing and you will be redeemed without
money."

4 For thus says the Lord GOD, "My people
went down at the first into Egypt to reside there;
then the Assyrian oppressed them without cause.

5 "Now therefore, what do I have here," declares the LORD, "seeing that My people have been
taken away without cause?" *Again* the LORD declares, "Those who rule over them howl, and My
name is continually blasphemed all day long.

6 "Therefore My people shall know My name;
therefore in that day I am the one who is speaking,
'Here I am.' "

7 ¶ How lovely on the mountains
Are the feet of him who brings good
news,
Who announces peace
And brings good news of happiness,
Who announces salvation,
And says to Zion, "Your God reigns!"

8 Listen! Your watchmen lift up *their*
voices,
They shout joyfully together;

For they will see with their own eyes
When the LORD restores Zion.
9 Break forth, shout joyfully together,
You waste places of Jerusalem;

52:7 Lovely Feet

Isaiah portrays the joy of carrying good news to those desperately hoping for it—perhaps a city waiting for news of a battle in which all their young men were at risk. But Isaiah's news is not of war; it is of God's people returning from exile, with the Lord himself leading the way. In Romans 10:15, Paul applied this joyful cheer to the messengers who, like himself, bore the good news of Jesus Christ.

For the LORD has comforted His people,
He has redeemed Jerusalem.
10 The LORD has bared His holy arm
In the sight of all the nations,
That all the ends of the earth may see
The salvation of our God.

11 ¶ Depart, depart, go out from there,
Touch nothing unclean;
Go out of the midst of her, purify
yourselves,
You who carry the vessels of the LORD.
12 But you will not go out in haste,
Nor will you go as fugitives;
For the LORD will go before you,
And the God of Israel *will be* your rear
guard.

The Exalted Servant

13 ¶ Behold, My servant will prosper,
He will be high and lifted up and greatly
exalted.
14 Just as many were astonished at you, *My
people,*
So His appearance was marred more
than any man
And His form more than the sons of
men.
15 Thus He will sprinkle many nations,
Kings will shut their mouths on account
of Him;
For what had not been told them they
will see,
And what they had not heard they will
understand.

The Suffering Servant

53 Who has believed our message?
And to whom has the arm of the LORD
been revealed?
2 For He grew up before Him like a tender
shoot,

And like a root out of parched ground;
He has no *stately* form or majesty
That we should look upon Him,
Nor appearance that we should [a]be
attracted to Him.

3 He was despised and forsaken of men,
A man of sorrows and acquainted with
grief;
And like one from whom men hide their
face
He was despised, and we did not esteem
Him.

4 ¶ Surely our [b]griefs He Himself bore,
And our sorrows He carried;
Yet we ourselves esteemed Him stricken,
Smitten of God, and afflicted.
5 But He was [c]pierced through for our
transgressions,
He was crushed for our iniquities;
The chastening for our well-being *fell*
upon Him,
And by His scourging we are healed.

53:5 Healing Wounds

Throughout the New Testament, the Suffering Servant described here is understood to be Jesus. This astounding verse claims that his wounds heal us. Peter explained it this way: when Jesus died on the cross, his suffering and death "healed" us of our sins, enabling us to live for righteousness (1 Peter 2:24).

6 All of us like sheep have gone astray,
Each of us has turned to his own way;
But the LORD has caused the iniquity of
us all
To fall on Him.
7 ¶ He was oppressed and He was afflicted,
Yet He did not open His mouth;
Like a lamb that is led to slaughter,
And like a sheep that is silent before its
shearers,
So He did not open His mouth.
8 By oppression and judgment He was
taken away;
And as for His generation, who
considered
That He was cut off out of the land of
the living
For the transgression of my people, to
whom the stroke *was due?*
9 His grave was assigned with wicked men,
Yet He was with a rich man in His
death,
Because He had done no violence,
Nor was there any deceit in His mouth.

[a] Lit *desire*   [b] Or *sickness*   [c] Or *wounded*

10 ¶ But the LORD was pleased
   To crush Him, putting *Him* to grief;
   If He would render Himself *as* a guilt
      offering,
   He will see *His* offspring,
   He will prolong *His* days,
   And the good pleasure of the LORD will
      prosper in His hand.
11 As a result of the anguish of His soul,
   He will see *it and* be satisfied;
   By His knowledge the Righteous One,

My Servant, will justify the many,
   As He will bear their iniquities.
12 Therefore, I will allot Him a portion with
      the great,
   And He will divide the booty with the
      strong;
   Because He poured out Himself to death,
   And was numbered with the
      transgressors;
   Yet He Himself bore the sin of many,
   And interceded for the transgressors.

The Suffering Servant
A great victory looked at first like defeat

> *He was despised and forsaken of men, a man of sorrows and acquainted with grief. 53:3*

CHAPTERS 49–55 OF ISAIAH TELL of a "suffering servant" who will come from Israel to bring light to all nations. Who is this suffering servant?

Jewish scholars puzzled over these passages for centuries. Many considered them the most significant part of the entire Old Testament, and yet they could not agree on exactly what the prophet meant. (Four passages especially are called the "servant songs": 42:1–9; 49:1–13; 50:4–9; 52:13–53:12.)

A Nation or a Person?

Sometimes the verses speak about the nation of Israel as a whole: "You are My Servant, Israel, in Whom I will show My glory" (49:3). But in other places the servant seems to refer to a specific individual, a great leader who suffers terribly.

Isaiah presents the servant as the deliverer of all humankind. And yet it portrays him more as a tragic figure than as a hero: "He has no stately form or majesty that. . . . we should be attracted to Him . . . . He was oppressed and He was afflicted, yet He did not open His mouth; like a lamb that is led to slaughter" (53:2,7).

Some Jewish scholars guessed the prophet was describing himself or another prophet, such as Jeremiah. Still others focused their hopes on a Messiah to come. They expected a king from very humble origins, whose power would depend not on swords, but on the spirits of people committed to him.

An Answer from the New Testament

The idea of the suffering servant did not really catch on among the Jewish nation. They longed for a victorious Messiah, not a suffering one. The image of the suffering servant went underground, as it were, lying dormant for centuries.

Then, in a very dramatic scene early in his ministry, Jesus quoted from one of the servant passages in Isaiah (Luke 4:18–19). "And He closed the book, gave it back to the attendant and sat down; and the eyes of all in the synagogue were fixed on Him. And He began to say to them, 'Today this Scripture has been fulfilled in your hearing' " (Luke 4:20–21).

Following his example, the New Testament writers named Jesus as the servant, at least ten times. In one instance, Philip corrected an Ethiopian official who had wondered if the suffering servant referred to an ancient prophet (Acts 8:26–35).

The Final Sacrifice

Isaiah 49–55 includes vivid scenes of the servant's sufferings, predictions that found their fulfillment in Jesus' death on the cross. Written like an eyewitness account, they were actually composed centuries before Christ's death.

According to Isaiah, the servant died for a very specific purpose: "He was pierced through for our transgressions" (53:5). Through his wounds, the suffering servant won a great victory. His death made possible a future when all that is wrong on earth will be set right. Significantly, the book of Isaiah does not end with the suffering servant image. It goes on to describe a wonderful life in a new heaven and new earth made possible by the servant's death.

Life Questions: If you had been a Jew in Jesus' day, would you have been disappointed in the Messiah? Why did Jesus choose to come as a suffering servant rather than, say, a triumphant army general?

The Fertility of Zion

54 "Shout for joy, O barren one, you who
have borne no *child*;
Break forth into joyful shouting and cry
aloud, you who have not travailed;
For the sons of the desolate one *will be*
more numerous
Than the sons of the married woman,"
says the LORD.
2 "Enlarge the place of your tent;
Stretch out the curtains of your
dwellings, spare not;
Lengthen your cords
And strengthen your pegs.
3 "For you will spread abroad to the right
and to the left.
And your descendants will possess
nations
And will resettle the desolate cities.

4 ¶ "Fear not, for you will not be put to
shame;
And do not feel humiliated, for you will
not be disgraced;
But you will forget the shame of your
youth,
And the reproach of your widowhood
you will remember no more.
5 "For your husband is your Maker,
Whose name is the LORD of hosts;
And your Redeemer is the Holy One of
Israel,
Who is called the God of all the earth.
6 "For the LORD has called you,
Like a wife forsaken and grieved in spirit,
Even like a wife of *one's* youth when she
is rejected,"
Says your God.

54:6 Jerusalem's Future

*The book of Isaiah insists that God will not
permanently divorce the nation of Israel. It
foretells a time when the ruined capital city will
be rebuilt and achieve a greatness it has never
known. Yet the description in these chapters
goes far beyond what has ever been realized in
Jerusalem. It merges into a vision of the future,
when sin and sorrow will be no more and
people will live in final peace with God.*

7 "For a brief moment I forsook you,
But with great compassion I will gather
you.
8 "In an outburst of anger
I hid My face from you for a moment,
But with everlasting lovingkindness I will
have compassion on you,"
Says the LORD your Redeemer.

9 ¶ "For this is like the days of Noah
to Me,
When I swore that the waters of Noah
Would not flood the earth again;
So I have sworn that I will not be angry
with you
Nor will I rebuke you.
10 "For the mountains may be removed and
the hills may shake,
But My lovingkindness will not be
removed from you,
And My covenant of peace will not be
shaken,"
Says the LORD who has compassion
on you.

11 ¶ "O afflicted one, storm-tossed, *and* not
comforted,
Behold, I will set your stones in
antimony,
And your foundations I will lay in
sapphires.
12 "Moreover, I will make your battlements
of rubies,
And your gates of crystal,
And your entire wall of precious stones.
13 "All your sons will be taught of the LORD;
And the well-being of your sons will be
great.
14 "In righteousness you will be established;
You will be far from oppression, for you
will not fear;
And from terror, for it will not come
near you.
15 "If anyone fiercely assails *you* it will not
be from Me.
Whoever assails you will fall because of
you.
16 "Behold, I Myself have created the smith
who blows the fire of coals
And brings out a weapon for its work;
And I have created the destroyer to ruin.
17 "No weapon that is formed against you
will prosper;
And every tongue that accuses you in
judgment you will condemn.
This is the heritage of the servants of the
LORD,
And their vindication is from Me,"
declares the LORD.

The Free Offer of Mercy

55 "Ho! Every one who thirsts, come to the
waters;
And you who have no money come, buy
and eat.
Come, buy wine and milk
Without money and without cost.
2 "Why do you spend money for what is
not bread,
And your wages for what does not
satisfy?

Listen carefully to Me, and eat what is
good,
And delight yourself in abundance.

55:1 Who Can Be Saved?

*God, through Isaiah, issues an open invitation
to "every one . . . who thirsts." Anyone can eat
and drink this meal, free of charge. The only
requirement is that they come. In verse 6 Isaiah
urges everyone to take this opportunity for
forgiveness while it is so freely available.*

3 "Incline your ear and come to Me.
Listen, that you may live;
And I will make an everlasting covenant
with you,
According to the faithful mercies shown
to David.
4 "Behold, I have made him a witness to the
peoples,
A leader and commander for the peoples.
5 "Behold, you will call a nation you do not
know,
And a nation which knows you not will
run to you,
Because of the LORD your God, even the
Holy One of Israel;
For He has glorified you."

6 ¶ Seek the LORD while He may be found;
Call upon Him while He is near.
7 Let the wicked forsake his way
And the unrighteous man his thoughts;
And let him return to the LORD,
And He will have compassion on him,
And to our God,
For He will abundantly pardon.
8 "For My thoughts are not your thoughts,
Nor are your ways My ways," declares
the LORD.
9 "For *as* the heavens are higher than the
earth,
So are My ways higher than your ways
And My thoughts than your thoughts.
10 "For as the rain and the snow come down
from heaven,
And do not return there without
watering the earth
And making it bear and sprout,
And furnishing seed to the sower and
bread to the eater;
11 So will My word be which goes forth
from My mouth;
It will not return to Me empty,
Without accomplishing what I desire,
And without succeeding *in the matter* for
which I sent it.
12 "For you will go out with joy
And be led forth with peace;

The mountains and the hills will break
forth into shouts of joy before you,
And all the trees of the field will clap
their hands.
13 "Instead of the thorn bush the cypress will
come up,
And instead of the nettle the myrtle will
come up,
And it will be a memorial to the LORD,
For an everlasting sign which will not be
cut off."

Rewards for Obedience to God

56 Thus says the LORD,
"Preserve justice and do righteousness,
For My salvation is about to come
And My righteousness to be revealed.
2 "How blessed is the man who does this,
And the son of man who takes hold
of it;
Who keeps from profaning the sabbath,
And keeps his hand from doing any
evil."
3 Let not the foreigner who has joined
himself to the LORD say,
"The LORD will surely separate me from
His people."
Nor let the eunuch say, "Behold, I am a
dry tree."
4 For thus says the LORD,
"To the eunuchs who keep My sabbaths,
And choose what pleases Me,
And hold fast My covenant;
5 To them I will give in My house and
within My walls a memorial,
And a name better than that of sons and
daughters;
I will give them an everlasting name
which will not be cut off.

6 ¶ "Also the foreigners who join
themselves to the LORD,
To minister to Him, and to love the
name of the LORD,
To be His servants, every one who keeps
from profaning the sabbath
And holds fast My covenant;
7 Even those I will bring to My holy
mountain
And make them joyful in My house of
prayer.
Their burnt offerings and their sacrifices
will be acceptable on My altar;
For My house will be called a house of
prayer for all the peoples."
8 The Lord GOD, who gathers the
dispersed of Israel, declares,
"Yet *others* I will gather to them, to those
already gathered."

9 ¶ All you beasts of the field,
All you beasts in the forest,

Come to eat.
10 His watchmen are blind,
All of them know nothing.
All of them are mute dogs unable to
bark,

56:7 House of Prayer

*Traditionally, foreigners and eunuchs were
excluded from worshiping God (see Exodus
12:43; Deuteronomy 23:1,3,7–8). But now God
promises to welcome all those once excluded.
The New Testament church welcomed
foreigners and eunuchs into God's family; in
contrast, the temple in Jerusalem never made
non-Jews welcome. Jesus complained that
rather than creating a "house of prayer for all
the nations," merchants had turned it into a
"robbers' den" (Mark 11:17).*

Dreamers lying down, who love to
slumber;
11 And the dogs are greedy, they are not
satisfied.
And they are shepherds who have no
understanding;
They have all turned to their own way,
Each one to his unjust gain, to the last
one.

56:10–11 Doglike Prophets

*This passage gives one of the most scathing
denunciations of Israel's corrupt spiritual
leaders in the entire Bible.*

12 "Come," they say, "let us get wine, and let
us drink heavily of strong drink;
And tomorrow will be like today, only
more so."

Evil Leaders Rebuked

57 The righteous man perishes, and no man
takes it to heart;
And devout men are taken away, while
no one understands.
For the righteous man is taken away
from evil,
2 He enters into peace;
They rest in their beds,
Each one who walked in his upright way.
3 "But come here, you sons of a sorceress,
Offspring of an adulterer and a
prostitute.
4 "Against whom do you jest?
Against whom do you open wide your
mouth
And stick out your tongue?

Are you not children of rebellion,
Offspring of deceit,
5 Who inflame yourselves among the oaks,
Under every luxuriant tree,
Who slaughter the children in the
ravines,
Under the clefts of the crags?
6 "Among the smooth stones of the ravine
Is your portion, they are your lot;
Even to them you have poured out a
drink offering,
You have made a grain offering.
Shall I relent concerning these things?
7 "Upon a high and lofty mountain
You have made your bed.
You also went up there to offer sacrifice.
8 "Behind the door and the doorpost
You have set up your sign;
Indeed, far removed from Me, you have
uncovered yourself,
And have gone up and made your bed
wide.
And you have made an agreement for
yourself with them,
You have loved their bed,
You have looked on their manhood.
9 "You have journeyed to the king with oil
And increased your perfumes;
You have sent your envoys a great
distance
And made them go down to Sheol.
10 "You were tired out by the length of your
road,
Yet you did not say, 'It is hopeless.'
You found renewed strength,
Therefore you did not faint.

11 ¶ "Of whom were you worried and
fearful
When you lied, and did not
remember Me
Nor give Me a thought?
Was I not silent even for a long time
So you do not fear Me?
12 "I will declare your righteousness and
your deeds,
But they will not profit you.
13 "When you cry out, let your collection of
idols deliver you.
But the wind will carry all of them up,
And a breath will take them away.
But he who takes refuge in Me will
inherit the land
And will possess My holy mountain."

14 ¶ And it will be said,
"Build up, build up, prepare the way,
Remove every obstacle out of the way of
My people."
15 For thus says the high and exalted One
Who lives forever, whose name is Holy,
"I dwell on a high and holy place,

And *also* with the contrite and lowly of
spirit
In order to revive the spirit of the lowly
And to revive the heart of the contrite.
16 "For I will not contend forever,
Nor will I always be angry;
For the spirit would grow faint
before Me,
And the breath *of those whom* I have
made.
17 "Because of the iniquity of his unjust gain
I was angry and struck him;
I hid *My face* and was angry,
And he went on turning away, in the
way of his heart.
18 "I have seen his ways, but I will heal him;
I will lead him and restore comfort to
him and to his mourners,
19 Creating the praise of the lips.
Peace, peace to him who is far and to
him who is near,"
Says the LORD, "and I will heal him."
20 But the wicked are like the tossing sea,
For it cannot be quiet,
And its waters toss up refuse and mud.
21 "There is no peace," says my God, "for
the wicked."

Observances of Fasts

58 "Cry loudly, do not hold back;
Raise your voice like a trumpet,
And declare to My people their
transgression
And to the house of Jacob their sins.
2 "Yet they seek Me day by day and delight
to know My ways,
As a nation that has done righteousness
And has not forsaken the ordinance of
their God.
They ask Me *for* just decisions,
They delight in the nearness of God.
3 'Why have we fasted and You do not see?
Why have we humbled ourselves and
You do not notice?'
Behold, on the day of your fast you find
your desire,
And drive hard all your workers.
4 "Behold, you fast for contention and strife
and to strike with a wicked fist.
You do not fast like *you do* today to
make your voice heard on high.
5 "Is it a fast like this which I choose, a day
for a man to humble himself?
Is it for bowing one's head like a reed
And for spreading out sackcloth and
ashes as a bed?
Will you call this a fast, even an
acceptable day to the LORD?
6 "Is this not the fast which I choose,
To loosen the bonds of wickedness,
To undo the bands of the yoke,

And to let the oppressed go free
And break every yoke?
7 "Is it not to divide your bread with the
hungry

58:6 Religion at Its Best

*The book of Isaiah begins in chapter 1 by
exposing false religion that had the right form
and ritual, but no true sincerity. This chapter
gives the other side: the spiritual work God
prefers. The book of James includes a similar
perspective (1:27).*

And bring the homeless poor into the
house;
When you see the naked, to cover him;
And not to hide yourself from your own
flesh?
8 "Then your light will break out like the
dawn,
And your recovery will speedily spring
forth;
And your righteousness will go before
you;
The glory of the LORD will be your rear
guard.
9 "Then you will call, and the LORD will
answer;
You will cry, and He will say, 'Here
I am.'
If you remove the yoke from your midst,
The pointing of the finger and speaking
wickedness,
10 And if you give yourself to the hungry
And satisfy the desire of the afflicted,
Then your light will rise in darkness
And your gloom *will become* like midday.
11 "And the LORD will continually guide you,
And satisfy your desire in scorched
places,
And give strength to your bones;
And you will be like a watered garden,
And like a spring of water whose waters
do not fail.
12 "Those from among you will rebuild the
ancient ruins;
You will raise up the age-old
foundations;
And you will be called the repairer of the
breach,
The restorer of the streets in which to
dwell.

Keeping the Sabbath

13 ¶ "If because of the sabbath, you turn
your foot
From doing your *own* pleasure on My
holy day,

And call the sabbath a delight, the holy
   day of the Lord honorable,
And honor it, desisting from your *own*
   ways,
From seeking your *own* pleasure
And speaking *your own* word,
14 Then you will take delight in the Lord,
   And I will make you ride on the heights
      of the earth;
   And I will feed you *with* the heritage of
      Jacob your father,
For the mouth of the Lord has spoken."

Separation from God

59 Behold, the Lord's hand is not so short
    That it cannot save;
   Nor is His ear so dull
   That it cannot hear.
2 But your iniquities have made a
    separation between you and your
    God,
   And your sins have hidden *His* face from
    you so that He does not hear.
3 For your hands are defiled with blood
   And your fingers with iniquity;
   Your lips have spoken falsehood,
   Your tongue mutters wickedness.
4 No one sues righteously and no one
    pleads honestly.
   They trust in confusion and speak lies;
   They conceive mischief and bring forth
    iniquity.
5 They hatch adders' eggs and weave the
    spider's web;
   He who eats of their eggs dies,
   And *from* that which is crushed a snake
    breaks forth.
6 Their webs will not become clothing,
   Nor will they cover themselves with their
    works;
   Their works are works of iniquity,
   And an act of violence is in their hands.
7 Their feet run to evil,
   And they hasten to shed innocent blood;
   Their thoughts are thoughts of iniquity,
   Devastation and destruction are in their
    highways.
8 They do not know the way of peace,
   And there is no justice in their tracks;
   They have made their paths crooked,
   Whoever treads on them does not know
    peace.

A Confession of Wickedness

9 ¶ Therefore justice is far from us,
   And righteousness does not overtake us;
   We hope for light, but behold, darkness,
   For brightness, but we walk in gloom.
10 We grope along the wall like blind men,
   We grope like those who have no eyes;
   We stumble at midday as in the twilight,

Among those who are vigorous *we are*
   like dead men.
11 All of us growl like bears,
   And moan sadly like doves;
   We hope for justice, but there is none,
   For salvation, *but* it is far from us.
12 For our transgressions are multiplied
    before You,
   And our sins testify against us;
   For our transgressions are with us,
   And we know our iniquities:
13 Transgressing and denying the Lord,
   And turning away from our God,
   Speaking oppression and revolt,
   Conceiving *in* and uttering from the
    heart lying words.
14 Justice is turned back,
   And righteousness stands far away;
   For truth has stumbled in the street,
   And uprightness cannot enter.
15 Yes, truth is lacking;
   And he who turns aside from evil makes
    himself a prey.

   ¶ Now the Lord saw,
And it was displeasing in His sight that
   there was no justice.
16 And He saw that there was no man,
   And was astonished that there was no
    one to intercede;
   Then His own arm brought salvation to
    Him,
   And His righteousness upheld Him.
17 He put on righteousness like a
    breastplate,
   And a helmet of salvation on His head;
   And He put on garments of vengeance
    for clothing
   And wrapped Himself with zeal as a
    mantle.
18 According to *their* deeds, so He will
    repay,
   Wrath to His adversaries, recompense to
    His enemies;
   To the coastlands He will make
    recompense.
19 So they will fear the name of the Lord
    from the west
   And His glory from the rising of the sun,
   For He will come like a rushing stream
   Which the wind of the Lord drives.
20 "A Redeemer will come to Zion,
   And to those who turn from
    transgression in Jacob," declares the
    Lord.
21 ¶ "As for Me, this is My covenant with
them," says the Lord: "My Spirit which is upon
you, and My words which I have put in your
mouth shall not depart from your mouth, nor
from the mouth of your offspring, nor from
the mouth of your offspring's offspring," says the
Lord, "from now and forever."

A Glorified Zion

60 "Arise, shine; for your light has come,
And the glory of the LORD has risen
upon you.

2 "For behold, darkness will cover the earth
And deep darkness the peoples;
But the LORD will rise upon you
And His glory will appear upon you.

3 "Nations will come to your light,
And kings to the brightness of your
rising.

4 ¶ "Lift up your eyes round about and
see;
They all gather together, they come to
you.
Your sons will come from afar,
And your daughters will be carried in the
arms.

5 "Then you will see and be radiant,
And your heart will thrill and rejoice;
Because the abundance of the sea will be
turned to you,
The wealth of the nations will come to
you.

6 "A multitude of camels will cover you,
The young camels of Midian and Ephah;
All those from Sheba will come;
They will bring gold and frankincense,
And will bear good news of the praises
of the LORD.

7 "All the flocks of Kedar will be gathered
together to you,
The rams of Nebaioth will minister to
you;
They will go up with acceptance on My
altar,
And I shall glorify My glorious house.

8 "Who are these who fly like a cloud
And like the doves to their lattices?

9 "Surely the coastlands will wait for Me;
And the ships of Tarshish *will come* first,
To bring your sons from afar,
Their silver and their gold with them,
For the name of the LORD your God,
And for the Holy One of Israel because
He has glorified you.

10 ¶ "Foreigners will build up your walls,
And their kings will minister to you;
For in My wrath I struck you,
And in My favor I have had compassion
on you.

11 "Your gates will be open continually;
They will not be closed day or night,
So that *men* may bring to you the wealth
of the nations,
With their kings led in procession.

12 "For the nation and the kingdom which
will not serve you will perish,
And the nations will be utterly ruined.

13 "The glory of Lebanon will come to you,

The juniper, the box tree and the cypress
together,
To beautify the place of My sanctuary;
And I shall make the place of My feet
glorious.

14 "The sons of those who afflicted you will
come bowing to you,
And all those who despised you will bow
themselves at the soles of your feet;
And they will call you the city of the
LORD,
The Zion of the Holy One of Israel.

15 ¶ "Whereas you have been forsaken and
hated
With no one passing through,
I will make you an everlasting pride,
A joy from generation to generation.

16 "You will also suck the milk of nations
And suck the breast of kings;
Then you will know that I, the LORD, am
your Savior
And your Redeemer, the Mighty One of
Jacob.

17 "Instead of bronze I will bring gold,
And instead of iron I will bring silver,
And instead of wood, bronze,
And instead of stones, iron.
And I will make peace your
administrators
And righteousness your overseers.

18 "Violence will not be heard again in your
land,
Nor devastation or destruction within
your borders;
But you will call your walls salvation, and
your gates praise.

19 "No longer will you have the sun for light
by day,
Nor for brightness will the moon give
you light;
But you will have the LORD for an
everlasting light,
And your God for your glory.

20 "Your sun will no longer set,
Nor will your moon wane;
For you will have the LORD for an
everlasting light,
And the days of your mourning will be
over.

21 "Then all your people *will be* righteous;
They will possess the land forever,
The branch of My planting,
The work of My hands,
That I may be glorified.

22 "The smallest one will become a clan,
And the least one a mighty nation.
I, the LORD, will hasten it in its time."

Exaltation of the Afflicted

61 The Spirit of the Lord GOD is upon me,
Because the LORD has anointed me

To bring good news to the afflicted;
He has sent me to bind up the
brokenhearted,
To proclaim liberty to captives
And freedom to prisoners;

61:1 Jesus Began Here

**When Jesus was ready to announce himself
and his mission, he began with a dramatic
quotation of this passage (Luke 4:18–19).
Notably, he stopped in mid-sentence, before he
reached the phrase "the day of vengeance of
our God." Jesus taught that this day of
vengeance would indeed take place, but at the
time of his second coming, not his first.**

2 To proclaim the favorable year of the
LORD
And the day of vengeance of our God;
To comfort all who mourn,
3 To grant those who mourn *in* Zion,
Giving them a garland instead of ashes,
The oil of gladness instead of mourning,
The mantle of praise instead of a spirit of
fainting.
So they will be called oaks of
righteousness,
The planting of the LORD, that He may
be glorified.
4 ¶ Then they will rebuild the ancient
ruins,
They will raise up the former
devastations;
And they will repair the ruined cities,
The desolations of many generations.
5 Strangers will stand and pasture your
flocks,
And foreigners will be your farmers and
your vinedressers.
6 But you will be called the priests of the
LORD;
You will be spoken of *as* ministers of our
God.
You will eat the wealth of nations,
And in their riches you will boast.
7 Instead of your shame *you will have a*
double *portion,*
And *instead of* humiliation they will
shout for joy over their portion.
Therefore they will possess a double
portion in their land,
Everlasting joy will be theirs.
8 For I, the LORD, love justice,
I hate robbery in the burnt offering;
And I will faithfully give them their
recompense
And make an everlasting covenant with
them.

9 Then their offspring will be known
among the nations,
And their descendants in the midst of
the peoples.
All who see them will recognize them
Because they are the offspring *whom* the
LORD has blessed.

10 ¶ I will rejoice greatly in the LORD,
My soul will exult in my God;
For He has clothed me with garments of
salvation,
He has wrapped me with a robe of
righteousness,
As a bridegroom decks himself with a
garland,
And as a bride adorns herself with her
jewels.
11 For as the earth brings forth its sprouts,
And as a garden causes the things sown
in it to spring up,
So the Lord GOD will cause righteousness
and praise
To spring up before all the nations.

Zion's Glory and New Name

62 For Zion's sake I will not keep silent,
And for Jerusalem's sake I will not keep
quiet,
Until her righteousness goes forth like
brightness,
And her salvation like a torch that is
burning.
2 The nations will see your righteousness,
And all kings your glory;
And you will be called by a new name
Which the mouth of the LORD will
designate.
3 You will also be a crown of beauty in the
hand of the LORD,
And a royal diadem in the hand of your
God.
4 It will no longer be said to you,
"Forsaken,"
Nor to your land will it any longer be
said, "Desolate";
But you will be called, "My delight is
in her,"
And your land, "Married";
For the LORD delights in you,
And *to Him* your land will be married.
5 For *as* a young man marries a virgin,
So your sons will marry you;
And *as* the bridegroom rejoices over the
bride,
So your God will rejoice over you.
6 ¶ On your walls, O Jerusalem, I have
appointed watchmen;
All day and all night they will never keep
silent.

You who remind the LORD, take no rest
 for yourselves;
7 And give Him no rest until He
 establishes
And makes Jerusalem a praise in the
 earth.

8 The LORD has sworn by His right hand
 and by His strong arm,
"I will never again give your grain *as* food
 for your enemies;
Nor will foreigners drink your new wine
 for which you have labored."

9 But those who garner it will eat it and
 praise the LORD;
And those who gather it will drink it in
 the courts of My sanctuary.

10 ¶ Go through, go through the gates,
Clear the way for the people;
Build up, build up the highway,
Remove the stones, lift up a standard
 over the peoples.

11 Behold, the LORD has proclaimed to the
 end of the earth,
Say to the daughter of Zion, "Lo, your
 salvation comes;
Behold His reward is with Him, and His
 recompense before Him."

12 And they will call them, "The holy
 people,
The redeemed of the LORD";
And you will be called, "Sought out, a
 city not forsaken."

God's Vengeance on the Nations

63 Who is this who comes from Edom,
 With garments of glowing colors from
 Bozrah,
This One who is majestic in His apparel,
Marching in the greatness of His
 strength?
"It is I who speak in righteousness,
 mighty to save."

2 Why is Your apparel red,

A Glimpse of Things to Come

When all our best dreams will come true

EVERYBODY WANTS A GLIMPSE INTO the future, and the last part of Isaiah gives just that. It tells what will happen at the end of our age on earth. The account is not easy to decipher, however, because the prophet shifts back and forth between his own time and the final events on earth.

"For behold, I create new heavens and a new earth; and the former things will not be remembered or come to mind."
65:17

A Missionary Book

To the original audience of Israelites, Isaiah makes one thing clear: God would not permanently divorce Israel. "For a brief moment I forsook you," says God, "but with great compassion I will gather you " (54:7). There is a future for his chosen people.

Isaiah declares that Israel's future involves other nations. Foreigners will flock to Jerusalem: "My house will be called a house of prayer for all the peoples" (56:7). Word about God will go out to nations nearby and far away, and to distant islands that have never heard of him (66:18–21).

Thus the last part of Isaiah, addressed to a people facing deep despair, opens the door for the Jews to become a gift to all people. This prophecy saw fulfillment in Jesus, who recruited disciples to take his message to everyone. Through his life and death, the suffering servant indeed introduced the gospel to the entire world.

What Isaiah Says to Us

The book of Isaiah goes on to describe a new beginning, a time of final triumph and peace. In that day, there will be no need for tears. Wild animals will tamely lie down together. The sun and moon will fade, overwhelmed by the brightness of God's glory.

In chapters 60 and 65, the prophet describes the future with such eloquence that New Testament books like Revelation could not improve on the language; they merely quoted Isaiah. Even today some of these phrases—"hammer their swords into plowshares," for example—surface in popular language, expressing our deepest longings for peace.

We dream of a time of peace, without pain or fear or disease or death. Isaiah assures us that one day those dreams will come true.

Life Questions: What would you most like to see changed about your world? Does Isaiah speak to that change?

And Your garments like the one who
treads in the wine press?
3 "I have trodden the wine trough alone,
And from the peoples there was no man
with Me.
I also trod them in My anger
And trampled them in My wrath;
And their lifeblood is sprinkled on My
garments,
And I stained all My raiment.
4 "For the day of vengeance was in My
heart,
And My year of redemption has come.
5 "I looked, and there was no one to help,
And I was astonished and there was no
one to uphold;
So My own arm brought salvation to
Me,
And My wrath upheld Me.
6 "I trod down the peoples in My anger
And made them drunk in My wrath,
And I poured out their lifeblood on the
earth."

God's Ancient Mercies Recalled

7 ¶ I shall make mention of the
lovingkindnesses of the LORD, the
praises of the LORD,
According to all that the LORD has
granted us,
And the great goodness toward the house
of Israel,
Which He has granted them according to
His compassion
And according to the abundance of His
lovingkindnesses.
8 For He said, "Surely, they are My people,
Sons who will not deal falsely."
So He became their Savior.
9 In all their affliction He was afflicted,
And the angel of His presence saved
them;
In His love and in His mercy He
redeemed them,
And He lifted them and carried them all
the days of old.
10 But they rebelled
And grieved His Holy Spirit;
Therefore He turned Himself to become
their enemy,
He fought against them.
11 Then His people remembered the days of
old, of Moses.
Where is He who brought them up out
of the sea with the shepherds of His
flock?
Where is He who put His Holy Spirit in
the midst of them,
12 Who caused His glorious arm to go at
the right hand of Moses,

Who divided the waters before them to
make for Himself an everlasting
name,
13 Who led them through the depths?
Like the horse in the wilderness, they did
not stumble;

63:9–17 A Lesson from History

*The Babylonian captivity brought a grave crisis
to the Israelites. To them, God's own integrity
was at stake. They had a treaty, or covenant,
with him. Had he abandoned them? In this
chapter, the prophet reviews all the good
things God has done for the Israelites and says
that, even in the worst times, "in all their
affliction He was afflicted." If God had been
with them in the past, then he would be with
them in the future. Then he turns to God
directly and makes an impassioned appeal for
help: "Oh, that You would rend the heavens and
come down" (64:1).*

14 As the cattle which go down into the
valley,
The Spirit of the LORD gave them rest.
So You led Your people,
To make for Yourself a glorious name.

"You Are Our Father"

15 ¶ Look down from heaven and see from
Your holy and glorious habitation;
Where are Your zeal and Your mighty
deeds?
The stirrings of Your heart and Your
compassion are restrained
toward me.
16 For You are our Father, though Abraham
does not know us
And Israel does not recognize us.
You, O LORD, are our Father,
Our Redeemer from of old is Your
name.
17 Why, O LORD, do You cause us to stray
from Your ways
And harden our heart from fearing You?
Return for the sake of Your servants, the
tribes of Your heritage.
18 Your holy people possessed Your
sanctuary for a little while,
Our adversaries have trodden *it* down.
19 We have become *like* those over whom
You have never ruled,
Like those who were not called by Your
name.

Prayer for Mercy and Help

64 Oh, that You would rend the heavens
and come down,

That the mountains might quake at Your
presence—
2 As fire kindles the brushwood, *as* fire
causes water to boil—
To make Your name known to Your
adversaries,
That the nations may tremble at Your
presence!
3 When You did awesome things which we
did not expect,
You came down, the mountains quaked
at Your presence.
4 For from days of old they have not heard
or perceived by ear,
Nor has the eye seen a God besides You,
Who acts in behalf of the one who waits
for Him.
5 You meet him who rejoices in doing
righteousness,
Who remembers You in Your ways.
Behold, You were angry, for we sinned,
We continued in them a long time;
And shall we be saved?
6 For all of us have become like one who
is unclean,
And all our righteous deeds are like a
filthy garment;
And all of us wither like a leaf,
And our iniquities, like the wind, take us
away.
7 There is no one who calls on Your name,
Who arouses himself to take hold
of You;
For You have hidden Your face from us
And have delivered us into the power of
our iniquities.

8 ¶ But now, O LORD, You are our Father,
We are the clay, and You our potter;
And all of us are the work of Your hand.
9 Do not be angry beyond measure,
O LORD,
Nor remember iniquity forever;
Behold, look now, all of us are Your
people.
10 Your holy cities have become a
wilderness,
Zion has become a wilderness,
Jerusalem a desolation.
11 Our holy and beautiful house,
Where our fathers praised You,
Has been burned *by* fire;
And all our precious things have become
a ruin.
12 Will You restrain Yourself at these
things, O LORD?
Will You keep silent and afflict us
beyond measure?

A Rebellious People

65 "I permitted Myself to be sought by those
who did not ask *for Me;*

I permitted Myself to be found by those
who did not seek Me.
I said, 'Here am I, here am I,'
To a nation which did not call on My
name.
2 "I have spread out My hands all day long
to a rebellious people,
Who walk *in* the way which is not good,
following their own thoughts,
3 A people who continually provoke Me to
My face,
Offering sacrifices in gardens and
burning incense on bricks;

65:3 Provoking God

*In this speech, God is directly attacking the
most repulsive practices of Judah, notably its
idolatry. "Gardens" refers to the gardens that
usually surrounded pagan shrines. Verse 4
mentions the superstitious practice of sitting in
cemeteries to seek help from the dead. And the
"swine's flesh" was eaten in a sacrificial meal
for a pagan god—faithful Jews did not eat pork.*

4 Who sit among graves and spend the
night in secret places;
Who eat swine's flesh,
And the broth of unclean meat is *in* their
pots.
5 "Who say, 'Keep to yourself, do not come
near me,
For I am holier than you!'
These are smoke in My nostrils,
A fire that burns all the day.
6 "Behold, it is written before Me,
I will not keep silent, but I will repay;
I will even repay into their bosom,
7 Both their own iniquities and the
iniquities of their fathers together,"
says the LORD.
"Because they have burned incense on the
mountains
And scorned Me on the hills,
Therefore I will measure their former
work into their bosom."

8 ¶ Thus says the LORD,
"As the new wine is found in the cluster,
And one says, 'Do not destroy it, for
there is benefit in it,'
So I will act on behalf of My servants
In order not to destroy all of them.
9 "I will bring forth offspring from Jacob,
And an heir of My mountains from
Judah;
Even My chosen ones shall inherit it,
And My servants will dwell there.
10 "Sharon will be a pasture land for flocks,

And the valley of Achor a resting place
for herds,
For My people who seek Me.
11 "But you who forsake the LORD,
Who forget My holy mountain,
Who set a table for Fortune,
And who fill *cups* with mixed wine for
Destiny,
12 I will destine you for the sword,
And all of you will bow down to the
slaughter.
Because I called, but you did not answer;
I spoke, but you did not hear.
And you did evil in My sight
And chose that in which I did not
delight."

13 ¶ Therefore, thus says the Lord GOD,
"Behold, My servants will eat, but you will
be hungry.
Behold, My servants will drink, but you
will be thirsty.
Behold, My servants will rejoice, but you
will be put to shame.
14 "Behold, My servants will shout joyfully
with a glad heart,
But you will cry out with a heavy heart,
And you will wail with a broken spirit.
15 "You will leave your name for a curse to
My chosen ones,
And the Lord GOD will slay you.
But My servants will be called by another
name.
16 "Because he who is blessed in the earth
Will be blessed by the God of truth;
And he who swears in the earth
Will swear by the God of truth;
Because the former troubles are
forgotten,
And because they are hidden from My
sight!

New Heavens and a New Earth

17 ¶ "For behold, I create new heavens and
a new earth;
And the former things will not be
remembered or come to mind.

65:17 New Earth

Human beings have always longed for a utopia. Isaiah repeatedly promises just that, here and in chapters 11 and 35. He has in mind a whole new earth, in which people will build and farm, work and raise children—but without frustration. The violence and sadness that mark our earth will vanish. The key to that new era will be an intimate relationship with God. "Before they call I will answer; and while they are still speaking, I will hear" (verse 24).

18 "But be glad and rejoice forever in what I
create;
For behold, I create Jerusalem *for*
rejoicing
And her people *for* gladness.
19 "I will also rejoice in Jerusalem and be
glad in My people;
And there will no longer be heard in her
The voice of weeping and the sound of
crying.
20 "No longer will there be in it an infant
who lives but a few days,
Or an old man who does not live out his
days;
For the youth will die at the age of one
hundred
And the one who does not reach the age
of one hundred
Will be *thought* accursed.
21 "They will build houses and inhabit *them;*
They will also plant vineyards and eat
their fruit.
22 "They will not build and another inhabit,
They will not plant and another eat;
For as the lifetime of a tree, *so will be* the
days of My people,
And My chosen ones will wear out the
work of their hands.
23 "They will not labor in vain,
Or bear *children* for calamity;
For they are the offspring of those
blessed by the LORD,
And their descendants with them.
24 "It will also come to pass that before they
call, I will answer; and while they are still speaking,
I will hear.
25 "The wolf and the lamb will graze together,
and the lion will eat straw like the ox; and dust will
be the serpent's food. They will do no evil or harm
in all My holy mountain," says the LORD.

Heaven Is God's Throne

66 Thus says the LORD,
"Heaven is My throne and the earth is
My footstool.
Where then is a house you could build
for Me?
And where is a place that I may rest?
2 "For My hand made all these things,
Thus all these things came into being,"
declares the LORD.
"But to this one I will look,
To him who is humble and contrite of
spirit, and who trembles at My
word.

Hypocrisy Rebuked

3 ¶ "*But* he who kills an ox is *like* one who
slays a man;
He who sacrifices a lamb is *like* the one
who breaks a dog's neck;

He who offers a grain offering *is like one
who offers* swine's blood;
He who burns incense is *like* the one
who blesses an idol.
As they have chosen their *own* ways,
And their soul delights in their
abominations,
4 So I will choose their punishments
And will bring on them what they dread.
Because I called, but no one answered;
I spoke, but they did not listen.
And they did evil in My sight
And chose that in which I did not
delight."
5 Hear the word of the LORD, you who
tremble at His word:
"Your brothers who hate you, who
exclude you for My name's sake,
Have said, 'Let the LORD be glorified,
that we may see your joy.'
But they will be put to shame.
6 "A voice of uproar from the city, a voice
from the temple,
The voice of the LORD who is rendering
recompense to His enemies.

7 ¶ "Before she travailed, she brought
forth;
Before her pain came, she gave birth to a
boy.
8 "Who has heard such a thing? Who has
seen such things?
Can a land be born in one day?
Can a nation be brought forth all at
once?
As soon as Zion travailed, she also
brought forth her sons.

66:9 Pain with a Purpose

*Nowhere does the book of Isaiah minimize the
pain Israel went through; the prophet shared
the nation's agony. But God makes clear that
the pain was not arbitrary and purposeless.
Like childbirth, this pain will lead to something
happy and good. "As one whom his mother
comforts, so I will comfort you" (verse 13). In
one last word of triumph, God reaffirms that
the suffering of the Israelites will one day lead
to a great missionary outreach among all
humanity (verses 19,23).*

9 "Shall I bring to the point of birth and
not give delivery?" says the LORD.
"Or shall I who gives delivery shut *the
womb?*" says your God.

Joy in Jerusalem's Future

10 "Be joyful with Jerusalem and rejoice for
her, all you who love her;

Be exceedingly glad with her, all you who
mourn over her,
11 That you may nurse and be satisfied with
her comforting breasts,
That you may suck and be delighted with
her bountiful bosom."
12 For thus says the LORD, "Behold, I
extend peace to her like a river,
And the glory of the nations like an
overflowing stream;
And you will be nursed, you will be
carried on the hip and fondled on
the knees.
13 "As one whom his mother comforts, so I
will comfort you;
And you will be comforted in Jerusalem."
14 Then you will see *this,* and your heart
will be glad,
And your bones will flourish like the new
grass;
And the hand of the LORD will be made
known to His servants,
But He will be indignant toward His
enemies.
15 For behold, the LORD will come in fire
And His chariots like the whirlwind,
To render His anger with fury,
And His rebuke with flames of fire.
16 For the LORD will execute judgment by
fire
And by His sword on all flesh,
And those slain by the LORD will be
many.
17 "Those who sanctify and purify themselves
to go to the gardens,
Following one in the center,
Who eat swine's flesh, detestable things
and mice,
Will come to an end altogether," declares
the LORD.

18 ¶ "For I know their works and their
thoughts; the time is coming to gather all nations
and tongues. And they shall come and see My
glory.
19 "I will set a sign among them and will send
survivors from them to the nations: Tarshish, Put,
Lud, Meshech, Rosh, Tubal and Javan, to the distant coastlands that have neither heard My fame
nor seen My glory. And they will declare My glory
among the nations.
20 "Then they shall bring all your brethren from
all the nations as a grain offering to the LORD, on
horses, in chariots, in litters, on mules and on
camels, to My holy mountain Jerusalem," says
the LORD, "just as the sons of Israel bring their
grain offering in a clean vessel to the house of the
LORD.
21 "I will also take some of them for priests *and*
for Levites," says the LORD.

22 "For just as the new heavens and the new
    earth
    Which I make will endure before Me,"
        declares the LORD,
    "So your offspring and your name will
        endure.
23 "And it shall be from new moon to new
    moon
    And from sabbath to sabbath,

All mankind will come to bow down
    before Me," says the LORD.
24 "Then they will go forth and look
    On the corpses of the men
    Who have transgressed against Me.
    For their worm will not die
    And their fire will not be quenched;
    And they will be an abhorrence to all
        mankind."

JEREMIAH

God's Reluctant Messenger
Jeremiah felt frightened and insecure—but he burned with a message

> *"Do not be afraid of them, for I am with you to deliver you,"* declares the LORD.
> *1:8*

JEREMIAH LIVED ONE OF THE most dramatic lives in the Bible, and that is saying something. But he never learned to like his role. Through all the excitement he remained reluctant, insecure, and often unhappy.

God chose him to be "over the nations and over the kingdoms, to pluck up and to break down, to destroy and to overthrow, to build and to plant" (1:10). To accomplish that, Jeremiah had only one resource—his mouth. How did he respond to such an awesome challenge? "Then I said, 'Alas, Lord GOD! Behold, I do not know how to speak, because I am a youth'" (1:6). He didn't stride forward; he barely hung on. He wanted out of the job.

His only encouragement was God's promise: "I have made you today as a fortified city and as a pillar of iron and as walls of bronze against the whole land" (1:18). For 40 years Jeremiah gave top officials a warning they hated to hear and refused to heed. Several times they arrested and imprisoned him; they nearly killed him.

His message? With God's approval, the savage Babylonians would sweep down into Judah. Clever alliances with other powers like Egypt would not help, said Jeremiah. Neither would Judah's halfhearted religion. Judah's only hope lay in renewing an alliance with the living God.

A Disturbing Glimpse of Jeremiah's Mind

The book of Jeremiah stands out not for beautiful poetry or great ideas. Its power comes from its disturbing glimpse of Jeremiah's mind. Jeremiah talked like a man who has awakened from a nightmare, convinced that the nightmare is coming true. His words were sledgehammer blows designed to crack the hardest, most indifferent skull. Though he wished to keep quiet, he found that God's word "in my heart. . . . becomes like a burning fire shut up in my bones" (20:9).

No prophet exposed his feelings more than Jeremiah. His relationship with God was streaked with quarrels, reproaches, and outbursts. He told God he wished he were dead (20:14–18). He accused God of being unreliable (15:18). But God offered no sympathy. Rather, he promised more of the same, reminding Jeremiah of his promise to stand by him (12:5–6; 15:19–20). Their relationship, doubts and all, forms one of the best examples in the Bible of what it means to follow God in spite of everything.

Reason to Fear

Jeremiah frankly feared death. He wearied of ridicule. He hated standing alone against the crowd. He told God how he felt. Yet he obeyed God, and in the end his message proved true. He stands as a far greater man than the kings in their luxurious palaces who imprisoned him and burned his writings.

He spoke a gloomy message in a gloomy time, and as a result his words are not always pleasant to read. He reminds us, in an era of artificial cheer and television smiles, that God's message is not always comforting and encouraging. People who disregard God will have reason to fear. For a world that defies him, he plans judgment. And no one, not even his chosen messengers, will escape suffering. God's presence will make them strong enough to face it.

How to Read Jeremiah

Suppose you find, in an old trunk, a thick packet of letters written by your great uncle. You soon realize they are all out of order. One he wrote from the trenches of France during World War I. The next also refers to a war, but from the references to British prime minister Winston Churchill you soon recognize it as World War II, over 20 years later.

Those letters might contain the whole of your uncle's life, but to get his story straight, you'd have to read the whole packet. A reader of Jeremiah finds a very similar situation. The book is an anthology of prophecies given at different times. They jump forward and backward in history, and if you imagine that the book is in chronological order, you will become very confused. Fortunately, it is not hard to reconstruct the order of the main events of Jeremiah's life.

Jeremiah spoke to a nation about to be destroyed by war. Three hundred years before him, the Israelites had split into two countries, Israel in the North and Judah in the South. About 100 years before Jeremiah, Assyria had conquered the Northern Kingdom. This disaster was "World War I" in Old Testament history.

Now, during Jeremiah's life, World War II threatened. Another fierce kingdom, Babylon, assembled troops against the remaining Southern Kingdom. Would God save his chosen people? Jeremiah loudly insisted for more than 20 years that God would punish Judah just as he had Israel, by letting Babylon take them into captivity. He lived to see his predictions come true.

Many passages in Jeremiah refer to the five kings he knew. When you see their names, use them as a reference point in figuring out the order of events:

> Josiah (17 years)
> Jehoahaz (3 months)
> Jehoiakim (12 years)
> Jehoiachin (3 months)
> Zedekiah (11 years)

Second Kings 23–25 or 2 Chronicles 34–36 gives an overall historical summary of their reigns. You can read a brief synopsis in "A Lineup of Rulers," pages 1417–1425. The better you grasp the historical situation Jeremiah lived in, the more insight you will have into his words.

To capture the full emotion of Jeremiah, you may want to read the first few chapters out loud.

PEOPLE YOU'LL MEET IN JEREMIAH

JEREMIAH *(p. 804)*

3-TRACK READING PLAN

For an explanation and complete listing of the 3-track reading plan, turn to page 7.

TRACK 1: *Two-Week Courses on the Bible*
See page 7 for information on these courses.

TRACK 2: *An Overview of Jeremiah in 4 Days*
☐ Day 1. Read the Introduction to Jeremiah and chapter 2, for God's passionate indictment of his people.
☐ Day 2. Read chapter 15, part of an emotional dialogue between Jeremiah and God.
☐ Day 3. Read chapter 31, God's promise of restoration and a new covenant.
☐ Day 4. Read chapter 38, for Jeremiah's dramatic skirmishes with death in the last days of Jerusalem.

Now turn to page 9 for your next Track 2 reading project.

TRACK 3: *All of Jeremiah in 51 Days*
After you have read through Jeremiah, turn to pages 10–14 for your next Track 3 reading project.

☐1	☐2	☐3	☐4	☐5	☐6	☐7	☐8
☐9	☐10	☐11	☐12	☐13	☐14	☐15	☐16
☐17	☐18	☐19	☐20	☐21	☐22	☐23	☐24
☐25	☐26	☐27	☐28	☐29	☐30	☐31	☐32
☐33	☐34	☐35	☐36	☐37	☐38	☐39	☐40
☐41	☐42	☐43	☐44–45	☐46	☐47	☐48	☐49
☐50	☐51	☐52					

Jeremiah's Call and Commission

1 The words of Jeremiah the son of Hilkiah, of the priests who were in Anathoth in the land of Benjamin,

2 to whom the word of the LORD came in the days of Josiah the son of Amon, king of Judah, in the thirteenth year of his reign.

3 It came also in the days of Jehoiakim the son of Josiah, king of Judah, until the end of the eleventh year of Zedekiah the son of Josiah, king of Judah, until the exile of Jerusalem in the fifth month.

4 ¶ Now the word of the LORD came to me saying,

5 "Before I formed you in the womb I knew you,
And before you were born I consecrated you;
I have appointed you a prophet to the nations."

6 Then I said, "Alas, Lord GOD!
Behold, I do not know how to speak,
Because I am a youth."

7 But the LORD said to me,
"Do not say, 'I am a youth,'
Because everywhere I send you, you shall go,
And all that I command you, you shall speak.

8 "Do not be afraid of them,
For I am with you to deliver you,"
declares the LORD.

9 Then the LORD stretched out His hand and touched my mouth, and the LORD said to me,
"Behold, I have put My words in your mouth.

10 "See, I have appointed you this day over the nations and over the kingdoms,
To pluck up and to break down,
To destroy and to overthrow,
To build and to plant."

The Almond Rod and Boiling Pot

11 ¶ The word of the LORD came to me saying, "What do you see, Jeremiah?" And I said, "I see a rod of an almond tree."

12 Then the LORD said to me, "You have seen well, for I am watching over My word to perform it."

13 ¶ The word of the LORD came to me a second time saying, "What do you see?" And I said, "I see a boiling pot, facing away from the north."

14 Then the LORD said to me, "Out of the north the evil will break forth on all the inhabitants of the land.

15 "For, behold, I am calling all the families of the kingdoms of the north," declares the LORD; "and they will come and they will set each one his throne at the entrance of the gates of Jerusalem, and against all its walls round about and against all the cities of Judah.

16 "I will pronounce My judgments on them concerning all their wickedness, whereby they have forsaken Me and have offered sacrifices to other gods, and worshiped the works of their own hands.

17 "Now, gird up your loins and arise, and speak to them all which I command you. Do not be dismayed before them, or I will dismay you before them.

18 "Now behold, I have made you today as a fortified city and as a pillar of iron and as walls of bronze against the whole land, to the kings of Judah, to its princes, to its priests and to the people of the land.

1:18 Too Young?

Like Moses before him, Jeremiah responded reluctantly to God's call. "I am a youth," he protested, feeling too inexperienced to carry such responsibility (verse 6). But God contradicted him. Age and experience did not matter; God's presence did (verse 8). In the face of powerful opposition, God would make Jeremiah as strong as iron.

19 "They will fight against you, but they will not overcome you, for I am with you to deliver you," declares the LORD.

Judah's Apostasy

2 Now the word of the LORD came to me saying,
2 "Go and proclaim in the ears of Jerusalem, saying, 'Thus says the LORD,
'I remember concerning you the devotion of your youth,
The love of your betrothals,
Your following after Me in the wilderness,
Through a land not sown.

3 "Israel was holy to the LORD,
The first of His harvest.
All who ate of it became guilty;
Evil came upon them," declares the LORD.' "

4 ¶ Hear the word of the LORD, O house of Jacob, and all the families of the house of Israel.

5 Thus says the LORD,
"What injustice did your fathers find in Me,
That they went far from Me
And walked after emptiness and became empty?

6 "They did not say, 'Where is the LORD
Who brought us up out of the land of Egypt,
Who led us through the wilderness,
Through a land of deserts and of pits,
Through a land of drought and of deep darkness,

Through a land that no one crossed
And where no man dwelt?'
7 "I brought you into the fruitful land
To eat its fruit and its good things.
But you came and defiled My land,
And My inheritance you made an
abomination.
8 "The priests did not say, 'Where is the
LORD?'
And those who handle the law did not
know Me;
The rulers also transgressed against Me,
And the prophets prophesied by Baal
And walked after things that did not
profit.
9 ¶ "Therefore I will yet contend with
you," declares the LORD,
"And with your sons' sons I will contend.
10 "For cross to the coastlands of Kittim and
see,
And send to Kedar and observe closely
And see if there has been such a thing as
this!
11 "Has a nation changed gods
When they were not gods?
But My people have changed their glory
For that which does not profit.
12 "Be appalled, O heavens, at this,
And shudder, be very desolate," declares
the LORD.
13 "For My people have committed two evils:
They have forsaken Me,
The fountain of living waters,
To hew for themselves cisterns,
Broken cisterns
That can hold no water.

2:13 An Astounding Trade

*Jeremiah piles image on top of image,
searching for a way to express the astounding
fact that Israelites had traded the living God for
the idols of their neighbors. Here he compares
the deed to exchanging a spring of living water
for a leaky cistern. In verse 20 he graphically
compares idolatry to sexual promiscuity. In an
interesting twist, Jesus offered "living water" to
a sexually promiscuous Samaritan woman in
John 4:10.*

14 ¶ "Is Israel a slave? Or is he a homeborn
servant?
Why has he become a prey?
15 "The young lions have roared at him,
They have roared loudly.
And they have made his land a waste;
His cities have been destroyed, without
inhabitant.

16 "Also the men of Memphis and
Tahpanhes
Have shaved the crown of your head.
17 "Have you not done this to yourself
By your forsaking the LORD your God
When He led you in the way?
18 "But now what are you doing on the road
to Egypt,
To drink the waters of the Nile?
Or what are you doing on the road to
Assyria,
To drink the waters of the Euphrates?
19 "Your own wickedness will correct you,
And your apostasies will reprove you;
Know therefore and see that it is evil and
bitter
For you to forsake the LORD your God,
And the dread of Me is not in you,"
declares the Lord GOD of hosts.

20 ¶ "For long ago I broke your yoke
And tore off your bonds;
But you said, 'I will not serve!'
For on every high hill
And under every green tree
You have lain down as a harlot.
21 "Yet I planted you a choice vine,
A completely faithful seed.
How then have you turned yourself
before Me
Into the degenerate shoots of a foreign
vine?
22 "Although you wash yourself with lye
And use much soap,
The stain of your iniquity is before Me,"
declares the Lord GOD.
23 "How can you say, 'I am not defiled,
I have not gone after the Baals'?
Look at your way in the valley!
Know what you have done!
You are a swift young camel entangling
her ways,
24 A wild donkey accustomed to the
wilderness,
That sniffs the wind in her passion.
In the time of her heat who can turn her
away?
All who seek her will not become weary;
In her month they will find her.
25 "Keep your feet from being unshod
And your throat from thirst;
But you said, 'It is hopeless!
No! For I have loved strangers,
And after them I will walk.'
26 ¶ "As the thief is shamed when he is
discovered,
So the house of Israel is shamed;
They, their kings, their princes
And their priests and their prophets,
27 Who say to a tree, 'You are my father,'
And to a stone, 'You gave me birth.'

For they have turned *their* back to Me,
And not *their* face;
But in the time of their trouble they will
say,
'Arise and save us.'
28 "But where are your gods
Which you made for yourself?
Let them arise, if they can save you
In the time of your trouble;
For *according to* the number of your
cities
Are your gods, O Judah.

29 ¶ "Why do you contend with Me?
You have all transgressed against Me,"
declares the LORD.
30 "In vain I have struck your sons;
They accepted no chastening.
Your sword has devoured your prophets
Like a destroying lion.
31 "O generation, heed the word of the
LORD.
Have I been a wilderness to Israel,
Or a land of thick darkness?
Why do My people say, 'We *are free to*
roam;
We will no longer come to You'?
32 "Can a virgin forget her ornaments,
Or a bride her attire?
Yet My people have forgotten Me
Days without number.
33 "How well you prepare your way
To seek love!
Therefore even the wicked women
You have taught your ways.
34 "Also on your skirts is found
The lifeblood of the innocent poor;
You did not find them breaking in.
But in spite of all these things,
35 Yet you said, 'I am innocent;
Surely His anger is turned away
from me.'
Behold, I will enter into judgment
with you
Because you say, 'I have not sinned.'
36 "Why do you go around so much
Changing your way?
Also, you will be put to shame by Egypt
As you were put to shame by Assyria.
37 "From this *place* also you will go out
With your hands on your head;
For the LORD has rejected those in whom
you trust,
And you will not prosper with them."

The Polluted Land

3 God says, "If a husband divorces his wife
And she goes from him
And belongs to another man,
Will he still return to her?
Will not that land be completely
polluted?

But you are a harlot *with* many lovers;
Yet you turn to Me," declares the LORD.
2 "Lift up your eyes to the bare heights and
see;
Where have you not been violated?
By the roads you have sat for them
Like an Arab in the desert,
And you have polluted a land
With your harlotry and with your
wickedness.

3:2 Ritual Sex

Today, the news that a minister or priest has committed adultery sends shock waves through the community. But Israel's neighbors in ancient times actually incorporated adultery into their religious rites. Pagans worshiped their gods through cultic prostitution, believing sex would put them in tune with divine power. This ritual sex went on at religious shrines located on the "high places" (hilltops). When Israel joined in their neighbors' worship, God properly called it adultery—both physical and spiritual. Israel was going out with every god in town.

3 "Therefore the showers have been
withheld,
And there has been no spring rain.
Yet you had a harlot's forehead;
You refused to be ashamed.
4 "Have you not just now called to Me,
'My Father, You are the friend of my
youth?
5 'Will He be angry forever?
Will He be indignant to the end?'
Behold, you have spoken
And have done evil things,
And you have had your way."

Faithless Israel

6 ¶ Then the LORD said to me in the days of Josiah the king, "Have you seen what faithless Israel did? She went up on every high hill and under every green tree, and she was a harlot there. 7 "I thought, 'After she has done all these things she will return to Me'; but she did not return, and her treacherous sister Judah saw it. 8 "And I saw that for all the adulteries of faithless Israel, I had sent her away and given her a writ of divorce, yet her treacherous sister Judah did not fear; but she went and was a harlot also. 9 "Because of the lightness of her harlotry, she polluted the land and committed adultery with stones and trees. 10 "Yet in spite of all this her treacherous sister Judah did not return to Me with all her heart, but rather in deception," declares the LORD.

God Invites Repentance

11 ¶ And the LORD said to me, "Faithless Israel has proved herself more righteous than treacherous Judah.

3:10 A Superficial Change

King Josiah, one of the few good kings in Judah's history, led a massive religious reform (see 2 Kings 22 and 23). While Josiah was unquestionably sincere, Jeremiah saw that the nation's return to God wasn't. Jeremiah's accusation was borne out after King Josiah's death: Judah returned quickly to her former ways.

12 "Go and proclaim these words toward the north and say,
'Return, faithless Israel,' declares the
LORD;
'I will not look upon you in anger.
For I am gracious,' declares the LORD;
'I will not be angry forever.
13 'Only acknowledge your iniquity,
That you have transgressed against the
LORD your God
And have scattered your favors to the
strangers under every green tree,
And you have not obeyed My voice,'
declares the LORD.
14 'Return, O faithless sons,' declares the
LORD;
'For I am a master to you,

A Lover's Quarrel
The violent emotions of a scorned lover

THE CALL COMES LATE, AFTER midnight, to a police officer who grimaces and shakes his head. Then, siren screaming, he races toward the house. Neighbors heard a woman's cries. Someone saw a man threatening her with a knife. As the police officer pulls up to the house, he hears her high-pitched shrieks. She is begging for mercy—from her husband.

> *"But you are a harlot with many lovers; yet you turn to Me," declares the LORD. 3:1*

Such cases are called "domestic disturbances." They happen nearly every night, and particularly on weekends. The police usually dislike getting called in. Both husband and wife can turn on the person who is "interfering."

Lovers' quarrels may seem silly to outsiders, but they are deadly serious to those involved. Some turn violent, even murderous. The most precious, desired gift anyone can offer has been abused. Love has been betrayed. Lovers react to that with violent emotions.

Words that Tear His Heart

It is a lovers' quarrel that Jeremiah exposes in chapters 2 and 3, and the emotions are violent and helpless. Again and again God makes his charge against Judah. Of all the nations, he had picked her; he had tenderly offered his protection and care. But she keeps sleeping with other men. He warns her again and again, but she ignores him. She saw how he divorced her sister Israel. Doesn't she know he will do the same to her?

God's words bleed pain. He accuses as though he cannot help himself, although his words tear his own heart. First, he is tender, full of memories: "I remember . . . the love of your betrothals, your following after Me in the wilderness" (2:2). But then you "tore off your bonds; but you said, 'I will not serve!' For on every high hill and under every green tree you have lain down as a harlot" (2:20). In disgust God compares Judah to a donkey in heat, who "sniffs the wind in her passion. . . . All who seek her will not become weary" (2:24). But the comparison hurts him more than her. His love, not hers, is scorned.

Married to a Whore

The prophet Hosea was the first to draw the picture of God married to a prostitute. Jeremiah amplifies it. The comparison cries out both the passionate love God feels for his people and the terrible, wounded pain he feels at their betrayal. Jeremiah's imagery is violent and dark, but underneath it, something wonderful shines out: the tender and personal love of God for his people.

The "adultery" Jeremiah wrote about focuses on the worship of idols. Most modern people find it hard to understand why Israelites felt any impulse to kneel before wooden or metal statues, or why their doing so made God furious. But when Jeremiah refers to it as adultery, God's hatred of idolatry becomes understandable. God meant his people to have only one true love in their lives—God himself. God the lover will not take second place; he refuses to share his bride.

Life Questions: Have you ever fought with God? What issues were you fighting about?

And I will take you one from a city and
two from a family,
And I will bring you to Zion.'

15 ¶ "Then I will give you shepherds after My own heart, who will feed you on knowledge and understanding.

16 "It shall be in those days when you are multiplied and increased in the land," declares the LORD, "they will no longer say, 'The ark of the covenant of the LORD.' And it will not come to mind, nor will they remember it, nor will they miss *it*, nor will it be made again.

17 "At that time they will call Jerusalem 'The Throne of the LORD,' and all the nations will be gathered to it, to Jerusalem, for the name of the LORD; nor will they walk anymore after the stubbornness of their evil heart.

18 "In those days the house of Judah will walk with the house of Israel, and they will come together from the land of the north to the land that I gave your fathers as an inheritance.

19 ¶ "Then I said,
'How I would set you among My sons
And give you a pleasant land,
The most beautiful inheritance of the
nations!'
And I said, 'You shall call Me, My
Father,
And not turn away from following Me.'

20 "Surely, as a woman treacherously departs
from her lover,
So you have dealt treacherously with Me,
O house of Israel," declares the LORD.

21 ¶ A voice is heard on the bare heights,
The weeping *and* the supplications of the
sons of Israel;
Because they have perverted their way,
They have forgotten the LORD their God.

22 "Return, O faithless sons,
I will heal your faithlessness."
"Behold, we come to You;
For You are the LORD our God.

23 "Surely, the hills are a deception,
A tumult *on* the mountains.
Surely in the LORD our God
Is the salvation of Israel.

24 ¶ "But the shameful thing has consumed the labor of our fathers since our youth, their flocks and their herds, their sons and their daughters.

25 "Let us lie down in our shame, and let our humiliation cover us; for we have sinned against the LORD our God, we and our fathers, from our youth even to this day. And we have not obeyed the voice of the LORD our God."

Judah Threatened with Invasion

4 "If you will return, O Israel," declares the
LORD,
"Then you should return to Me.

And if you will put away your detested
things from My presence,
And will not waver,

2 And you will swear, 'As the LORD lives,'
In truth, in justice and in righteousness;
Then the nations will bless themselves in
Him,
And in Him they will glory."

3 ¶ For thus says the LORD to the men of Judah and to Jerusalem,
"Break up your fallow ground,
And do not sow among thorns.

4 "Circumcise yourselves to the LORD
And remove the foreskins of your heart,
Men of Judah and inhabitants of
Jerusalem,
Or else My wrath will go forth like fire
And burn with none to quench it,
Because of the evil of your deeds."

4:4 Circumcised Hearts

All male Jewish babies underwent circumcision, a sign of their "set-apartness" as God's chosen people. Often, though, circumcision became just a ritual, not reflecting any real difference in the way people lived. Jeremiah used a startling metaphor—"remove the foreskins of your heart"—to remind the Israelites that membership in God's family should make a difference inside, not just on the surface. The apostle Paul wrote that Christ brings about this inner circumcision (Colossians 2:11).

5 ¶ Declare in Judah and proclaim in
Jerusalem, and say,
"Blow the trumpet in the land;
Cry aloud and say,
'Assemble yourselves, and let us go
Into the fortified cities.'

6 "Lift up a standard toward Zion!
Seek refuge, do not stand *still*,
For I am bringing evil from the north,
And great destruction.

7 "A lion has gone up from his thicket,
And a destroyer of nations has set out;
He has gone out from his place
To make your land a waste.
Your cities will be ruins
Without inhabitant.

8 "For this, put on sackcloth,
Lament and wail;
For the fierce anger of the LORD
Has not turned back from us."

9 "It shall come about in that day," declares the LORD, "that the heart of the king and the heart of the princes will fail; and the priests will be appalled and the prophets will be astounded."

10 ¶ Then I said, "Ah, Lord GOD! Surely You have utterly deceived this people and Jerusalem,

saying, 'You will have peace'; whereas a sword touches the throat."

11 ¶ In that time it will be said to this people and to Jerusalem, "A scorching wind from the bare heights in the wilderness in the direction of the daughter of My people—not to winnow and not to cleanse,

12 a wind too strong for this—will come at My command; now I will also pronounce judgments against them.

13 "Behold, he goes up like clouds,
And his chariots like the whirlwind;
His horses are swifter than eagles.
Woe to us, for we are ruined!"

14 ¶ Wash your heart from evil,
O Jerusalem,
That you may be saved.
How long will your wicked thoughts
Lodge within you?

15 For a voice declares from Dan,
And proclaims wickedness from Mount Ephraim.

16 "Report it to the nations, now!
Proclaim over Jerusalem,
'Besiegers come from a far country,
And lift their voices against the cities of Judah.

17 'Like watchmen of a field they are against her round about,
Because she has rebelled against Me,'
declares the LORD.

18 "Your ways and your deeds
Have brought these things to you.
This is your evil. How bitter!
How it has touched your heart!"

Lament over Judah's Devastation

19 ¶ My soul, my soul! I am in anguish! Oh, my heart!
My heart is pounding in me;
I cannot be silent,
Because you have heard, O my soul,
The sound of the trumpet,
The alarm of war.

20 Disaster on disaster is proclaimed,
For the whole land is devastated;
Suddenly my tents are devastated,
My curtains in an instant.

21 How long must I see the standard
And hear the sound of the trumpet?

22 "For My people are foolish,
They know Me not;
They are stupid children
And have no understanding.
They are shrewd to do evil,
But to do good they do not know."

23 ¶ I looked on the earth, and behold, it was formless and void;
And to the heavens, and they had no light.

24 I looked on the mountains, and behold, they were quaking,
And all the hills moved to and fro.

4:23 Return to the Void

Jeremiah used words from Genesis 1:2 to describe the effect of the Israelites' sin. It was as though the Israelites were carrying the earth back to the chaos before creation, destroying all the beauty and order God had made.

25 I looked, and behold, there was no man,
And all the birds of the heavens had fled.

26 I looked, and behold, the fruitful land was a wilderness,
And all its cities were pulled down
Before the LORD, before His fierce anger.

27 ¶ For thus says the LORD,
"The whole land shall be a desolation,
Yet I will not execute a complete destruction.

28 "For this the earth shall mourn
And the heavens above be dark,
Because I have spoken, I have purposed,
And I will not change My mind, nor will I turn from it."

29 At the sound of the horseman and bowman every city flees;
They go into the thickets and climb among the rocks;
Every city is forsaken,
And no man dwells in them.

30 And you, O desolate one, what will you do?
Although you dress in scarlet,
Although you decorate *yourself with* ornaments of gold,
Although you enlarge your eyes with paint,
In vain you make yourself beautiful.
Your lovers despise you;
They seek your life.

31 For I heard a cry as of a woman in labor,
The anguish as of one giving birth to her first child,
The cry of the daughter of Zion gasping for breath,
Stretching out her hands, *saying*,
"Ah, woe is me, for I faint before murderers."

Jerusalem's Godlessness

5 "Roam to and fro through the streets of Jerusalem,
And look now and take note.
And seek in her open squares,
If you can find a man,

If there is one who does justice, who
   seeks truth,
Then I will pardon her.

5:1 Search for an Honest Person

*In Genesis 18:22–33, Abraham tried to
convince God not to destroy Sodom and
Gomorrah if as many as ten righteous people
could be found. God agreed, but evidently the
ten did not exist. Here, God offers to forgive
Jerusalem if a single honest person can be
found. God's people had sunk to Sodom's level
(23:14).*

2 "And although they say, 'As the LORD
   lives,'
Surely they swear falsely."
3 O LORD, do not Your eyes *look* for truth?
You have smitten them,
But they did not weaken;
You have consumed them,
But they refused to take correction.
They have made their faces harder than
   rock;
They have refused to repent.

4 ¶ Then I said, "They are only the poor,
They are foolish;
For they do not know the way of the
   LORD
Or the ordinance of their God.
5 "I will go to the great
And will speak to them,
For they know the way of the LORD
And the ordinance of their God."
But they too, with one accord, have
   broken the yoke
And burst the bonds.
6 Therefore a lion from the forest will slay
   them,
A wolf of the deserts will destroy them,
A leopard is watching their cities.
Everyone who goes out of them will be
   torn in pieces,
Because their transgressions are many,
Their apostasies are numerous.

7 ¶ "Why should I pardon you?
Your sons have forsaken Me
And sworn by those who are not gods.
When I had fed them to the full,
They committed adultery
And trooped to the harlot's house.
8 "They were well-fed lusty horses,
Each one neighing after his neighbor's
   wife.
9 "Shall I not punish these *people*," declares
   the LORD,

"And on a nation such as this
Shall I not avenge Myself?

10 ¶ "Go up through her vine rows and
   destroy,
But do not execute a complete
   destruction;
Strip away her branches,
For they are not the LORD's.
11 "For the house of Israel and the house of
   Judah
Have dealt very treacherously with Me,"
   declares the LORD.
12 They have lied about the LORD
And said, "^aNot He;
Misfortune will not come on us,
And we will not see sword or famine.

5:12 Don't Worry, Be Happy

*Nobody likes bad news, and if you can find a
way to shrug it off, you probably will. So the
people of Judah treated Jeremiah's gloomy
prophecies as so much hot air. To protect their
comfortable lifestyles, they pictured a God who
was uninvolved, either unable or unwilling to
interfere.*

13 "The prophets are *as* wind,
And the word is not in them.
Thus it will be done to them!"

Judgment Proclaimed

14 ¶ Therefore, thus says the LORD, the God
   of hosts,
"Because you have spoken this word,
Behold, I am making My words in your
   mouth fire
And this people wood, and it will
   consume them.
15 "Behold, I am bringing a nation against
   you from afar, O house of Israel,"
   declares the LORD.
"It is an enduring nation,
It is an ancient nation,
A nation whose language you do not
   know,
Nor can you understand what they say.
16 "Their quiver is like an open grave,
All of them are mighty men.
17 "They will devour your harvest and your
   food;
They will devour your sons and your
   daughters;
They will devour your flocks and your
   herds;
They will devour your vines and your fig
   trees;

---

^a Lit *He is not*

They will demolish with the sword your
    fortified cities in which you trust.
18 ¶ "Yet even in those days," declares the
LORD, "I will not make you a complete destruction.
19 "It shall come about when they say, 'Why has
the LORD our God done all these things to us?'
then you shall say to them, 'As you have forsaken
Me and served foreign gods in your land, so you
will serve strangers in a land that is not yours.'
20 ¶ "Declare this in the house of Jacob
    And proclaim it in Judah, saying,
21 'Now hear this, O foolish and senseless
    people,
    Who have eyes but do not see;
    Who have ears but do not hear.
22 'Do you not fear Me?' declares the LORD.
    'Do you not tremble in My presence?
    For I have placed the sand as a boundary
      for the sea,
    An eternal decree, so it cannot cross
      over it.
    Though the waves toss, yet they cannot
      prevail;
    Though they roar, yet they cannot cross
      over it.
23 'But this people has a stubborn and
      rebellious heart;
    They have turned aside and departed.
24 'They do not say in their heart,
    "Let us now fear the LORD our God,
    Who gives rain in its season,
    Both the autumn rain and the spring
      rain,
    Who keeps for us
    The appointed weeks of the harvest."
25 'Your iniquities have turned these away,
    And your sins have withheld good from
      you.
26 'For wicked men are found among My
      people,
    They watch like fowlers lying in wait;
    They set a trap,
    They catch men.
27 'Like a cage full of birds,
    So their houses are full of deceit;
    Therefore they have become great and
      rich.
28 'They are fat, they are sleek,
    They also *a*excel in deeds of wickedness;
    They do not plead the cause,
    The cause of the orphan, that they may
      prosper;
    And they do not defend the rights of the
      poor.
29 'Shall I not punish these *people?*' declares
      the LORD,
    'On a nation such as this
    Shall I not avenge Myself?'

30 ¶ "An appalling and horrible thing
    Has happened in the land:
31 The prophets prophesy falsely,
    And the priests rule on their *own*
      authority;
    And My people love it so!
    But what will you do at the end of it?

Destruction of Jerusalem Impending

6 "Flee for safety, O sons of Benjamin,
    From the midst of Jerusalem!
    Now blow a trumpet in Tekoa
    And raise a signal over *b*Beth-haccerem;
    For evil looks down from the north,
    And a great destruction.
2 "The comely and dainty one, the daughter
      of Zion, I will cut off.
3 "Shepherds and their flocks will come to
      her,
    They will pitch *their* tents around her,
    They will pasture each in his place.
4 "Prepare war against her;
    Arise, and let us attack at noon.
    Woe to us, for the day declines,
    For the shadows of the evening lengthen!
5 "Arise, and let us attack by night
    And destroy her palaces!"
6 For thus says the LORD of hosts,
    "Cut down her trees
    And cast up a siege against Jerusalem.
    This is the city to be punished,
    In whose midst there is only oppression.
7 "As a well keeps its waters fresh,
    So she keeps fresh her wickedness.
    Violence and destruction are heard in
      her;
    Sickness and wounds are ever before Me.
8 "Be warned, O Jerusalem,
    Or I shall be alienated from you,
    And make you a desolation,
    A land not inhabited."

9 ¶ Thus says the LORD of hosts,
    "They will thoroughly glean as the vine
      the remnant of Israel;
    Pass your hand again like a grape
      gatherer
    Over the branches."
10 To whom shall I speak and give warning
    That they may hear?
    Behold, their ears are closed
    And they cannot listen.
    Behold, the word of the LORD has
      become a reproach to them;
    They have no delight in it.
11 But I am full of the wrath of the LORD;
    I am weary with holding *it* in.
    "Pour *it* out on the children in the street
    And on the gathering of young men
      together;

a Lit *pass over,* or, *overlook deeds*   *b* I.e. house of the vineyard

For both husband and wife shall be
taken,
The aged and the very old.
12 "Their houses shall be turned over to
others,
Their fields and their wives together;
For I will stretch out My hand
Against the inhabitants of the land,"
declares the LORD.
13 "For from the least of them even to the
greatest of them,
Everyone is greedy for gain,
And from the prophet even to the priest
Everyone deals falsely.
14 "They have healed the brokenness of My
people superficially,
Saying, 'Peace, peace,'
But there is no peace.

6:14 Greedy Doctors

A good doctor sometimes has to convey bad tidings, delivering a diagnosis of cancer, for example. But in Judah the spiritual "doctors" (prophets and priests) only gave out good news. They covered up serious wounds with a Band-Aid.

15 "Were they ashamed because of the
abomination they have done?
They were not even ashamed at all;
They did not even know how to blush.
Therefore they shall fall among those
who fall;
At the time that I punish them,
They shall be cast down," says the LORD.

16 ¶ Thus says the LORD,
"Stand by the ways and see and ask for
the ancient paths,
Where the good way is, and walk in it;
And you will find rest for your souls.
But they said, 'We will not walk *in it.*'
17 "And I set watchmen over you, *saying,*
'Listen to the sound of the trumpet!'
But they said, 'We will not listen.'
18 "Therefore hear, O nations,
And know, O congregation, what is
among them.
19 "Hear, O earth: behold, I am bringing
disaster on this people,
The fruit of their plans,
Because they have not listened to My
words,
And as for My law, they have rejected it
also.
20 "For what purpose does frankincense
come to Me from Sheba
And the sweet cane from a distant land?
Your burnt offerings are not acceptable

And your sacrifices are not pleasing
to Me."
21 Therefore, thus says the LORD,
"Behold, I am laying stumbling blocks
before this people.
And they will stumble against them,
Fathers and sons together;
Neighbor and friend will perish."

The Enemy from the North

22 ¶ Thus says the LORD,
"Behold, a people is coming from the
north land,
And a great nation will be aroused from
the remote parts of the earth.
23 "They seize bow and spear;
They are cruel and have no mercy;
Their voice roars like the sea,
And they ride on horses,
Arrayed as a man for the battle
Against you, O daughter of Zion!"
24 We have heard the report of it;
Our hands are limp.
Anguish has seized us,
Pain as of a woman in childbirth.
25 Do not go out into the field
And do not walk on the road,
For the enemy has a sword,
Terror is on every side.
26 O daughter of my people, put on
sackcloth
And roll in ashes;
Mourn as for an only son,
A lamentation most bitter.
For suddenly the destroyer
Will come upon us.

27 ¶ "I have made you an assayer *and* a
tester among My people,
That you may know and assay their
way."
28 All of them are stubbornly rebellious,
Going about as a talebearer.
They are bronze and iron;
They, all of them, are corrupt.
29 The bellows blow fiercely,
The lead is consumed by the fire;
In vain the refining goes on,
But the wicked are not separated.
30 They call them rejected silver,
Because the LORD has rejected them.

Message at the Temple Gate

7 The word that came to Jeremiah from the
LORD, saying,
2 "Stand in the gate of the LORD's house and
proclaim there this word and say, 'Hear the word
of the LORD, all you of Judah, who enter by these
gates to worship the LORD!'"
3 Thus says the LORD of hosts, the God of
Israel, "Amend your ways and your deeds, and I
will let you dwell in this place.

4 "Do not trust in deceptive words, saying, 'This is the temple of the LORD, the temple of the LORD, the temple of the LORD.'

5 "For if you truly amend your ways and your deeds, if you truly practice justice between a man and his neighbor,

6 if you do not oppress the alien, the orphan, or the widow, and do not shed innocent blood in this place, nor walk after other gods to your own ruin,

7 then I will let you dwell in this place, in the land that I gave to your fathers forever and ever.

8 ¶ "Behold, you are trusting in deceptive words to no avail.

9 "Will you steal, murder, and commit adultery and swear falsely, and offer sacrifices to Baal and walk after other gods that you have not known,

10 then come and stand before Me in this house, which is called by My name, and say, 'We are delivered!'—that you may do all these abominations?

11 "Has this house, which is called by My name, become a den of robbers in your sight? Behold, I, even I, have seen it," declares the LORD.

7:11 A Den of Robbers

Israelites of Jeremiah's time felt they were safe from invasion as long as they had the temple. After all, they thought, God would not let his home be destroyed (verse 4). But the Lord, through Jeremiah, said that the temple had become "a den of robbers" and would be demolished. In Jeremiah's lifetime this prediction came true. Jesus quoted the reference to a den of robbers when driving out money changers from the rebuilt temple (Mark 11:17).

12 ¶ "But go now to My place which was in Shiloh, where I made My name dwell at the first, and see what I did to it because of the wickedness of My people Israel.

13 "And now, because you have done all these things," declares the LORD, "and I spoke to you, rising up early and speaking, but you did not hear, and I called you but you did not answer,

14 therefore, I will do to the house which is called by My name, in which you trust, and to the place which I gave you and your fathers, as I did to Shiloh.

15 "I will cast you out of My sight, as I have cast out all your brothers, all the offspring of Ephraim.

16 ¶ "As for you, do not pray for this people, and do not lift up cry or prayer for them, and do not intercede with Me; for I do not hear you.

17 "Do you not see what they are doing in the cities of Judah and in the streets of Jerusalem?

18 "The children gather wood, and the fathers kindle the fire, and the women knead dough to make cakes for the queen of heaven; and *they* pour out drink offerings to other gods in order to spite Me.

19 "Do they spite Me?" declares the LORD. "Is it not themselves *they spite*, to their own shame?"

20 Therefore thus says the Lord GOD, "Behold, My anger and My wrath will be poured out on this place, on man and on beast and on the trees of the field and on the fruit of the ground; and it will burn and not be quenched."

21 ¶ Thus says the LORD of hosts, the God of Israel, "Add your burnt offerings to your sacrifices and eat flesh.

22 "For I did not speak to your fathers, or command them in the day that I brought them out of the land of Egypt, concerning burnt offerings and sacrifices.

23 "But this is what I commanded them, saying, 'Obey My voice, and I will be your God, and you will be My people; and you will walk in all the way which I command you, that it may be well with you.'

24 "Yet they did not obey or incline their ear, but walked in *their own* counsels *and* in the stubbornness of their evil heart, and went backward and not forward.

25 "Since the day that your fathers came out of the land of Egypt until this day, I have sent you all My servants the prophets, daily rising early and sending *them.*

26 "Yet they did not listen to Me or incline their ear, but stiffened their neck; they did more evil than their fathers.

27 ¶ "You shall speak all these words to them, but they will not listen to you; and you shall call to them, but they will not answer you.

28 "You shall say to them, 'This is the nation that did not obey the voice of the LORD their God or accept correction; truth has perished and has been cut off from their mouth.

29 'Cut off your hair and cast *it* away,
And take up a lamentation on the bare heights;
For the LORD has rejected and forsaken
The generation of His wrath.'

30 "For the sons of Judah have done that which is evil in My sight," declares the LORD, "they have set their detestable things in the house which is called by My name, to defile it.

31 "They have built the high places of Topheth, which is in the valley of the son of Hinnom, to burn their sons and their daughters in the fire, which I did not command, and it did not come into My mind.

32 ¶ "Therefore, behold, days are coming," declares the LORD, "when it will no longer be called Topheth, or the valley of the son of Hinnom, but the valley of the Slaughter; for they will bury in Topheth because there is no *other* place.

33 "The dead bodies of this people will be food

for the birds of the sky and for the beasts of the earth; and no one will frighten *them away.*

34 "Then I will make to cease from the cities of Judah and from the streets of Jerusalem the voice of joy and the voice of gladness, the voice of the bridegroom and the voice of the bride; for the land will become a ruin.

The Sin and Treachery of Judah

8 "At that time," declares the LORD, "they will bring out the bones of the kings of Judah and the bones of its princes, and the bones of the priests and the bones of the prophets, and the bones of the inhabitants of Jerusalem from their graves.

2 "They will spread them out to the sun, the moon and to all the host of heaven, which they have loved and which they have served, and which they have gone after and which they have sought, and which they have worshiped. They will not be gathered or buried; they will be as dung on the face of the ground.

3 "And death will be chosen rather than life by all the remnant that remains of this evil family, that remains in all the places to which I have driven them," declares the LORD of hosts.

4 "You shall say to them, 'Thus says the LORD,

"Do *men* fall and not get up again?
Does one turn away and not repent?

5 "Why then has this people, Jerusalem,
Turned away in continual apostasy?
They hold fast to deceit,
They refuse to return.

6 "I have listened and heard,
They have spoken what is not right;
No man repented of his wickedness,
Saying, 'What have I done?'
Everyone turned to his course,
Like a horse charging into the battle.

7 "Even the stork in the sky
Knows her seasons;
And the turtledove and the swift and the thrush
Observe the time of their migration;
But My people do not know
The ordinance of the LORD.

8 ¶ "How can you say, 'We are wise,
And the law of the LORD is with us'?
But behold, the lying pen of the scribes
Has made *it* into a lie.

9 "The wise men are put to shame,
They are dismayed and caught;
Behold, they have rejected the word of the LORD,
And what kind of wisdom do they have?

10 "Therefore I will give their wives to others,
Their fields to new owners;
Because from the least even to the greatest
Everyone is greedy for gain;

From the prophet even to the priest
Everyone practices deceit.

11 "They heal the brokenness of the daughter of My people superficially,
Saying, 'Peace, peace,'
But there is no peace.

12 "Were they ashamed because of the abomination they had done?
They certainly were not ashamed,
And they did not know how to blush;
Therefore they shall fall among those who fall;
At the time of their punishment they shall be brought down,"
Says the LORD.

13 ¶ "I will surely snatch them away," declares the LORD;
"There will be no grapes on the vine
And no figs on the fig tree,
And the leaf will wither;
And what I have given them will pass away." ' "

14 Why are we sitting still?
Assemble yourselves, and let us go into the fortified cities
And let us perish there,
Because the LORD our God has doomed us
And given us poisoned water to drink,
For we have sinned against the LORD.

15 *We* waited for peace, but no good *came;*
For a time of healing, but behold, terror!

16 From Dan is heard the snorting of his horses;
At the sound of the neighing of his stallions
The whole land quakes;
For they come and devour the land and its fullness,
The city and its inhabitants.

17 "For behold, I am sending serpents against you,
Adders, for which there is no charm,
And they will bite you," declares the LORD.

18 ¶ My sorrow is beyond healing,
My heart is faint *within me!*

19 Behold, listen! The cry of the daughter of my people from a distant land:
"Is the LORD not in Zion? Is her King not within her?"
"Why have they provoked Me with their graven images, with foreign idols?"

20 "Harvest is past, summer is ended,
And we are not saved."

21 For the brokenness of the daughter of my people I am broken;
I mourn, dismay has taken hold of me.

22 Is there no balm in Gilead?
Is there no physician there?

Why then has not the health of the
daughter of my people been
restored?

A Lament over Zion

9 Oh that my head were waters
And my eyes a fountain of tears,
That I might weep day and night
For the slain of the daughter of my
people!

9:1 A Fountain of Tears

*Jeremiah never stood aside like a stern
moralist, enjoying others' well-deserved
sufferings. He felt the bitterness of the
judgment he announced. "For the brokenness
of the daughter of my people I am broken; I
mourn, dismay has taken hold of me" (8:21).
In the end, Jeremiah swallowed the bitter
medicine of exile like the others.*

*Jeremiah reminds us of another "man of
sorrows." Like Jesus, Jeremiah wept over
Jerusalem. Like Jesus, he was rejected by his
own hometown (11:18–23). Jeremiah even
compared himself to a lamb led to the
slaughter (11:19), language that would later be
applied to Jesus' sacrifice for our sins.*

2 Oh that I had in the desert
A wayfarers' lodging place;
That I might leave my people
And go from them!
For all of them are adulterers,
An assembly of treacherous men.
3 "They bend their tongue *like* their bow;
Lies and not truth prevail in the land;
For they proceed from evil to evil,
And they do not know Me," declares the
LORD.
4 "Let everyone be on guard against his
neighbor,
And do not trust any brother;
Because every brother deals craftily,
And every neighbor goes about as a
slanderer.
5 "Everyone deceives his neighbor
And does not speak the truth,
They have taught their tongue to speak
lies;
They weary themselves committing
iniquity.
6 "Your dwelling is in the midst of deceit;
Through deceit they refuse to know Me,"
declares the LORD.

7 ¶ Therefore thus says the LORD of hosts,
"Behold, I will refine them and assay
them;
For what *else* can I do, because of the
daughter of My people?

8 "Their tongue is a deadly arrow;
It speaks deceit;
With his mouth one speaks peace to his
neighbor,
But inwardly he sets an ambush for him.
9 "Shall I not punish them for these
things?" declares the LORD.
"On a nation such as this
Shall I not avenge Myself?

10 ¶ "For the mountains I will take up a
weeping and wailing,
And for the pastures of the wilderness a
dirge,
Because they are laid waste so that no
one passes through,
And the lowing of the cattle is not heard;
Both the birds of the sky and the beasts
have fled; they are gone.
11 "I will make Jerusalem a heap of ruins,
A haunt of jackals;
And I will make the cities of Judah a
desolation, without inhabitant."

12 ¶ Who is the wise man that may understand
this? And *who is* he to whom the mouth of the
LORD has spoken, that he may declare it? Why is
the land ruined, laid waste like a desert, so that no
one passes through?

13 The LORD said, "Because they have forsaken
My law which I set before them, and have not
obeyed My voice nor walked according to it,
14 but have walked after the stubbornness of
their heart and after the Baals, as their fathers
taught them,"
15 therefore thus says the LORD of hosts, the
God of Israel, "behold, I will feed them, this people, with wormwood and give them poisoned water to drink.
16 "I will scatter them among the nations,
whom neither they nor their fathers have known;
and I will send the sword after them until I have
annihilated them."

17 ¶ Thus says the LORD of hosts,
"Consider and call for the mourning
women, that they may come;
And send for the wailing women, that
they may come!
18 "Let them make haste and take up a
wailing for us,
That our eyes may shed tears
And our eyelids flow with water.
19 "For a voice of wailing is heard from
Zion,
'How are we ruined!
We are put to great shame,
For we have left the land,
Because they have cast down our
dwellings.' "
20 Now hear the word of the LORD, O you
women,
And let your ear receive the word of His
mouth;

Teach your daughters wailing,
And everyone her neighbor a dirge.
21 For death has come up through our
windows;
It has entered our palaces
To cut off the children from the streets,
The young men from the town squares.
22 Speak, "Thus says the LORD,
'The corpses of men will fall like dung on
the open field,
And like the sheaf after the reaper,
But no one will gather *them.*'"
23 ¶ Thus says the LORD, "Let not a wise man boast of his wisdom, and let not the mighty man boast of his might, let not a rich man boast of his riches;
24 but let him who boasts boast of this, that he understands and knows Me, that I am the LORD who exercises lovingkindness, justice and righteousness on earth; for I delight in these things," declares the LORD.

9:24 Bragging on God

In dire circumstances like those Jeremiah predicts, what has value? Wisdom? Strength? Money? In the midst of a devastating invasion, these will get you nothing. Only one thing will count: a living, confident relationship with God. If you have that, it's worth boasting about. Paul quoted this verse in writing to the Corinthians (1 Corinthians 1:31); he said God seems to prefer to work through weak and poor people, those who have little else to brag about.

25 ¶ "Behold, the days are coming," declares the LORD, "that I will punish all who are circumcised and yet uncircumcised—
26 Egypt and Judah, and Edom and the sons of Ammon, and Moab and all those inhabiting the desert who clip the hair on their temples; for all the nations are uncircumcised, and all the house of Israel are uncircumcised of heart."

A Satire on Idolatry

10 Hear the word which the LORD speaks to you, O house of Israel.
2 Thus says the LORD,
"Do not learn the way of the nations,
And do not be terrified by the signs of
the heavens
Although the nations are terrified by
them;
3 For the customs of the peoples are
delusion;
Because it is wood cut from the forest,
The work of the hands of a craftsman
with a cutting tool.
4 "They decorate *it* with silver and with
gold;

They fasten it with nails and with
hammers
So that it will not totter.
5 "Like a scarecrow in a cucumber field are
they,
And they cannot speak;
They must be carried,
Because they cannot walk!
Do not fear them,
For they can do no harm,
Nor can they do any good."
6 ¶ There is none like You, O LORD;
You are great, and great is Your name in
might.
7 Who would not fear You, O King of the
nations?
Indeed it is Your due!
For among all the wise men of the
nations
And in all their kingdoms,
There is none like You.
8 But they are altogether stupid and foolish
In their discipline of delusion—their idol
is wood!
9 Beaten silver is brought from Tarshish,
And gold from Uphaz,
The work of a craftsman and of the
hands of a goldsmith;
Violet and purple are their clothing;
They are all the work of skilled men.
10 But the LORD is the true God;
He is the living God and the everlasting
King.
At His wrath the earth quakes,
And the nations cannot endure His
indignation.
11 ¶ Thus you shall say to them, "The gods that did not make the heavens and the earth will perish from the earth and from under the heavens."
12 ¶ *It is* He who made the earth by His
power,
Who established the world by His
wisdom;
And by His understanding He has
stretched out the heavens.
13 When He utters His voice, *there is* a
tumult of waters in the heavens,
And He causes the clouds to ascend from
the end of the earth;
He makes lightning for the rain,
And brings out the wind from His
storehouses.
14 Every man is stupid, devoid of
knowledge;
Every goldsmith is put to shame by his
idols;
For his molten images are deceitful,
And there is no breath in them.
15 They are worthless, a work of mockery;

In the time of their punishment they will
perish.
16 The portion of Jacob is not like these;
For the Maker of all is He,
And Israel is the tribe of His inheritance;
The LORD of hosts is His name.

17 ¶ Pick up your bundle from the ground,
You who dwell under siege!
18 For thus says the LORD,
"Behold, I am slinging out the inhabitants
of the land
At this time,
And will cause them distress,
That they may be found."

19 ¶ Woe is me, because of my injury!
My wound is incurable.
But I said, "Truly this is a sickness,
And I must bear it."
20 My tent is destroyed,
And all my ropes are broken;
My sons have gone from me and are no
more.
There is no one to stretch out my tent
again
Or to set up my curtains.
21 For the shepherds have become stupid
And have not sought the LORD;
Therefore they have not prospered,
And all their flock is scattered.
22 The sound of a report! Behold, it
comes—
A great commotion out of the land of
the north—
To make the cities of Judah
A desolation, a haunt of jackals.

23 ¶ I know, O LORD, that a man's way is
not in himself,
Nor is it in a man who walks to direct
his steps.
24 Correct me, O LORD, but with justice;
Not with Your anger, or You will bring
me to nothing.
25 Pour out Your wrath on the nations that
do not know You
And on the families that do not call Your
name;
For they have devoured Jacob;
They have devoured him and
consumed him
And have laid waste his habitation.

The Broken Covenant

11 The word which came to Jeremiah from the
LORD, saying,
2 "Hear the words of this covenant, and speak
to the men of Judah and to the inhabitants of
Jerusalem;
3 and say to them, 'Thus says the LORD, the
God of Israel, "Cursed is the man who does not
heed the words of this covenant

4 which I commanded your forefathers in the
day that I brought them out of the land of Egypt,
from the iron furnace, saying, 'Listen to My voice,
and do according to all which I command you; so
you shall be My people, and I will be your God,'
5 in order to confirm the oath which I swore
to your forefathers, to give them a land flowing
with milk and honey, as *it is* this day." ' " Then I
said, "Amen, O LORD."

6 ¶ And the LORD said to me, "Proclaim all
these words in the cities of Judah and in the streets
of Jerusalem, saying, 'Hear the words of this covenant and do them.
7 'For I solemnly warned your fathers in the
day that I brought them up from the land of
Egypt, even to this day, warning persistently, saying, "Listen to My voice."
8 'Yet they did not obey or incline their ear,
but walked, each one, in the stubbornness of his
evil heart; therefore I brought on them all the
words of this covenant, which I commanded *them*
to do, but they did not.' "

11:8 Day of Reckoning

*If you sign a note to buy a house, you have to
follow through. Miss too many payments, and
the bank will evict you. So it was with Israel.
Hundreds of years before Jeremiah's time, God
had made a "covenant" with them—a treaty
binding him to be their God, in exchange for
their obedience (see "The Covenant," page 106).
This was formally ratified, along with a series
of "blessings" and "curses"—good consequences
for obedience, bad consequences for
disobedience—as recorded in Deuteronomy 28.
Now, God announces, because the covenant
has been broken, severe punishment must
follow.*

9 ¶ Then the LORD said to me, "A conspiracy
has been found among the men of Judah and
among the inhabitants of Jerusalem.
10 "They have turned back to the iniquities of
their ancestors who refused to hear My words, and
they have gone after other gods to serve them; the
house of Israel and the house of Judah have broken My covenant which I made with their fathers."
11 Therefore thus says the LORD, "Behold I am
bringing disaster on them which they will not be
able to escape; though they will cry to Me, yet I
will not listen to them.
12 "Then the cities of Judah and the inhabitants
of Jerusalem will go and cry to the gods to whom
they burn incense, but they surely will not save
them in the time of their disaster.
13 "For your gods are as many as your cities,
O Judah; and as many as the streets of Jerusalem

are the altars you have set up to the shameful thing, altars to burn incense to Baal.

14 ¶ "Therefore do not pray for this people, nor lift up a cry or prayer for them; for I will not listen when they call to Me because of their disaster.

15 "What right has My beloved in My house
When she has done many vile deeds?
Can the sacrificial flesh take away from
you your disaster,
So *that* you can rejoice?"
16 The LORD called your name,
"A green olive tree, beautiful in fruit and
form";
With the noise of a great tumult
He has kindled fire on it,
And its branches are worthless.

17 The LORD of hosts, who planted you, has pronounced evil against you because of the evil of the house of Israel and of the house of Judah, which they have done to provoke Me by offering up sacrifices to Baal.

Plots against Jeremiah

18 ¶ Moreover, the LORD made it known to
me and I knew it;
Then You showed me their deeds.
19 But I was like a gentle lamb led to the
slaughter;
And I did not know that they had
devised plots against me, *saying*,
"Let us destroy the tree with its fruit,
And let us cut him off from the land of
the living,
That his name be remembered no more."
20 But, O LORD of hosts, who judges
righteously,
Who tries the feelings and the heart,
Let me see Your vengeance on them,
For to You have I committed my cause.

21 ¶ Therefore thus says the LORD concerning the men of Anathoth, who seek your life, saying, "Do not prophesy in the name of the LORD, so that you will not die at our hand";
22 therefore, thus says the LORD of hosts, "Behold, I am about to punish them! The young men will die by the sword, their sons and daughters will die by famine;
23 and a remnant will not be left to them, for I will bring disaster on the men of Anathoth—the year of their punishment."

11:23 Hometown Enemies

Jeremiah's life was endangered several times because of his message. On this occasion, men from his hometown were plotting against him. Though Jeremiah was completely unprepared for their attack, God protected him. Other prophets, however, had been killed (2:30).

Jeremiah's Prayer

12 Righteous are You, O LORD, that I would
plead *my* case with You;
Indeed I would discuss matters of justice
with You:
Why has the way of the wicked
prospered?
Why are all those who deal in treachery
at ease?
2 You have planted them, they have also
taken root;
They grow, they have even produced
fruit.
You are near to their lips
But far from their mind.
3 But You know me, O LORD;
You see me;
And You examine my heart's *attitude*
toward You.
Drag them off like sheep for the
slaughter
And set them apart for a day of carnage!
4 How long is the land to mourn
And the vegetation of the countryside to
wither?
For the wickedness of those who dwell
in it,
Animals and birds have been snatched
away,
Because *men* have said, "He will not see
our latter ending."

5 ¶ "If you have run with footmen and
they have tired you out,
Then how can you compete with horses?
If you fall down in a land of peace,
How will you do in the thicket of the
Jordan?
6 "For even your brothers and the
household of your father,
Even they have dealt treacherously with
you,
Even they have cried aloud after you.
Do not believe them, although they may
say nice things to you."

God's Answer

7 ¶ "I have forsaken My house,
I have abandoned My inheritance;
I have given the beloved of My soul
Into the hand of her enemies.
8 "My inheritance has become to Me
Like a lion in the forest;
She has roared against Me;
Therefore I have come to hate her.
9 "Is My inheritance like a speckled bird of
prey to Me?
Are the birds of prey against her on
every side?
Go, gather all the beasts of the field,
Bring them to devour!

10 "Many shepherds have ruined My
vineyard,
They have trampled down My field;
They have made My pleasant field
A desolate wilderness.
11 "It has been made a desolation,
Desolate, it mourns before Me;
The whole land has been made desolate,
Because no man lays it to heart.
12 "On all the bare heights in the wilderness
Destroyers have come,
For a sword of the LORD is devouring
From one end of the land even to the
other;
There is no peace for anyone.
13 "They have sown wheat and have reaped
thorns,
They have strained themselves to no
profit.
But be ashamed of your harvest
Because of the fierce anger of the LORD."

14 ¶ Thus says the LORD concerning all My
wicked neighbors who strike at the inheritance
with which I have endowed My people Israel, "Behold I am about to uproot them from their land
and will uproot the house of Judah from among
them.

15 "And it will come about that after I have
uprooted them, I will again have compassion on
them; and I will bring them back, each one to his
inheritance and each one to his land.

16 "Then if they will really learn the ways of My
people, to swear by My name, 'As the LORD lives,'
even as they taught My people to swear by Baal,
they will be built up in the midst of My people.

12:16 Hope for the Gentiles

*Through most of the Old Testament, Israel's
Gentile neighbors seem to have no part in
God's plan. Here, though, God clearly promises
them his salvation.*

17 "But if they will not listen, then I will uproot
that nation, uproot and destroy it," declares the
LORD.

The Ruined Waistband

13 Thus the LORD said to me, "Go and buy
yourself a linen waistband and put it around
your waist, but do not put it in water."

2 So I bought the waistband in accordance
with the word of the LORD and put it around my
waist.

3 Then the word of the LORD came to me a
second time, saying,

4 "Take the waistband that you have bought,
which is around your waist, and arise, go to the
Euphrates and hide it there in a crevice of the
rock."

5 So I went and hid it by the Euphrates, as the
LORD had commanded me.

6 After many days the LORD said to me,
"Arise, go to the Euphrates and take from there
the waistband which I commanded you to hide
there."

7 Then I went to the Euphrates and dug, and
I took the waistband from the place where I had
hidden it; and lo, the waistband was ruined, it was
totally worthless.

8 ¶ Then the word of the LORD came to me,
saying,

9 "Thus says the LORD, 'Just so will I destroy
the pride of Judah and the great pride of Jerusalem.

10 'This wicked people, who refuse to listen to
My words, who walk in the stubbornness of their
hearts and have gone after other gods to serve
them and to bow down to them, let them be just
like this waistband which is totally worthless.

11 'For as the waistband clings to the waist of a
man, so I made the whole household of Israel and
the whole household of Judah cling to Me,' declares the LORD, 'that they might be for Me a
people, for renown, for praise and for glory; but
they did not listen.'

Captivity Threatened

12 ¶ "Therefore you are to speak this word to
them, 'Thus says the LORD, the God of Israel, "Every jug is to be filled with wine."' And when they
say to you, 'Do we not very well know that every
jug is to be filled with wine?'

13 then say to them, 'Thus says the LORD, "Behold I am about to fill all the inhabitants of this
land—the kings that sit for David on his throne,
the priests, the prophets and all the inhabitants of
Jerusalem—with drunkenness!

14 "I will dash them against each other, both the
fathers and the sons together," declares the LORD.
"I will not show pity nor be sorry nor have compassion so as not to destroy them."'"

15 ¶ Listen and give heed, do not be
haughty,
For the LORD has spoken.
16 Give glory to the LORD your God,
Before He brings darkness
And before your feet stumble
On the dusky mountains,
And while you are hoping for light
He makes it into deep darkness,
And turns *it* into gloom.
17 But if you will not listen to it,
My soul will sob in secret for *such* pride;
And my eyes will bitterly weep
And flow down with tears,
Because the flock of the LORD has been
taken captive.
18 Say to the king and the queen mother,
"Take a lowly seat,
For your beautiful crown

Has come down from your head."

19 The cities of the Negev have been
   locked up,
   And there is no one to open *them;*
   All Judah has been carried into exile,
   Wholly carried into exile.

20 ¶ "Lift up your eyes and see
   Those coming from the north.
   Where is the flock that was given you,
   Your beautiful sheep?

21 "What will you say when He appoints
   over you—
   And you yourself had taught them—
   Former companions to be head
   over you?
   Will not pangs take hold of you
   Like a woman in childbirth?

22 "If you say in your heart,
   'Why have these things happened to me?'
   Because of the magnitude of your
   iniquity
   Your skirts have been removed
   And your heels have been exposed.

23 "Can the Ethiopian change his skin
   Or the leopard his spots?
   Then you also can do good
   Who are accustomed to doing evil.

24 "Therefore I will scatter them like drifting
   straw
   To the desert wind.

25 "This is your lot, the portion measured
   to you
   From Me," declares the LORD,
   "Because you have forgotten Me
   And trusted in falsehood.

26 "So I Myself have also stripped your skirts
   off over your face,
   That your shame may be seen.

27 "As for your adulteries and your *lustful*
   neighings,
   The lewdness of your prostitution
   On the hills in the field,
   I have seen your abominations.
   Woe to you, O Jerusalem!
   How long will you remain unclean?"

Drought and a Prayer for Mercy

14 That which came as the word of the LORD to
   Jeremiah in regard to the drought:

2 "Judah mourns
   And her gates languish;
   They sit on the ground in mourning,
   And the cry of Jerusalem has ascended.

3 "Their nobles have sent their servants for
   water;
   They have come to the cisterns and
   found no water.
   They have returned with their vessels
   empty;
   They have been put to shame and
   humiliated,
   And they cover their heads.

4 "Because the ground is cracked,
   For there has been no rain on the land;
   The farmers have been put to shame,
   They have covered their heads.

5 "For even the doe in the field has given
   birth only to abandon *her young,*
   Because there is no grass.

6 "The wild donkeys stand on the bare
   heights;
   They pant for air like jackals,
   Their eyes fail
   For there is no vegetation.

7 "Although our iniquities testify against us,
   O LORD, act for Your name's sake!
   Truly our apostasies have been many,
   We have sinned against You.

8 "O Hope of Israel,
   Its Savior in time of distress,
   Why are You like a stranger in the land
   Or like a traveler who has pitched his
   tent for the night?

9 "Why are You like a man dismayed,
   Like a mighty man who cannot save?
   Yet You are in our midst, O LORD,
   And we are called by Your name;
   Do not forsake us!"

10 ¶ Thus says the LORD to this people, "Even
so they have loved to wander; they have not kept
their feet in check. Therefore the LORD does not
accept them; now He will remember their iniquity
and call their sins to account."

11 So the LORD said to me, "Do not pray for
the welfare of this people.

14:11 God's Patience Exhausted

*God gave Jeremiah these dreaded instructions,
repeated nowhere else in the Bible: "Do not
pray for this people . . . for I will not listen"
(11:14). He repeated that message twice (7:16;
14:11). He told Jeremiah, "Even though Moses
and Samuel were to stand before Me, My heart
would not be with this people; send them away
from My presence!" (15:1).*

12 "When they fast, I am not going to listen to
their cry; and when they offer burnt offering and
grain offering, I am not going to accept them.
Rather I am going to make an end of them by the
sword, famine and pestilence."

False Prophets

13 ¶ But, "Ah, Lord GOD!" I said, "Look, the
prophets are telling them, 'You will not see the
sword nor will you have famine, but I will give you
lasting peace in this place.' "

14 Then the LORD said to me, "The prophets
are prophesying falsehood in My name. I have
neither sent them nor commanded them nor spo-

ken to them; they are prophesying to you a false vision, divination, futility and the deception of their own minds.

15 "Therefore thus says the LORD concerning the prophets who are prophesying in My name, although it was not I who sent them—yet they keep saying, 'There will be no sword or famine in this land'—by sword and famine those prophets shall meet their end!

16 "The people also to whom they are prophesying will be thrown out into the streets of Jerusalem because of the famine and the sword; and there will be no one to bury them—*neither* them, *nor* their wives, nor their sons, nor their daughters—for I will pour out their *own* wickedness on them.

17 "You will say this word to them,
'Let my eyes flow down with tears night
    and day,
And let them not cease;
For the virgin daughter of my people has
    been crushed with a mighty blow,
With a sorely infected wound.
18 'If I go out to the country,
Behold, those slain with the sword!
Or if I enter the city,
Behold, diseases of famine!
For both prophet and priest
Have gone roving about in the land that
    they do not know.' "

19 ¶ Have You completely rejected Judah?
Or have You loathed Zion?
Why have You stricken us so that we are
    beyond healing?
We waited for peace, but nothing good
    came;
And for a time of healing, but behold,
    terror!
20 We know our wickedness, O LORD,
The iniquity of our fathers, for we have
    sinned against You.
21 Do not despise *us*, for Your own name's
    sake;
Do not disgrace the throne of Your
    glory;
Remember *and* do not annul Your
    covenant with us.
22 Are there any among the idols of the
    nations who give rain?
Or can the heavens grant showers?
Is it not You, O LORD our God?
Therefore we hope in You,
For You are the one who has done all
    these things.

Judgment Must Come

15 Then the LORD said to me, "Even though Moses and Samuel were to stand before Me, My heart would not be with this people; send them away from My presence and let them go!

2 "And it shall be that when they say to you,

'Where should we go?' then you are to tell them, 'Thus says the LORD:

"Those *destined* for death, to death;
And those *destined* for the sword, to the
    sword;
And those *destined* for famine, to famine;
And those *destined* for captivity, to
    captivity." '

3 "I will appoint over them four kinds *of doom*," declares the LORD: "the sword to slay, the dogs to drag off, and the birds of the sky and the beasts of the earth to devour and destroy.

4 "I will make them an object of horror among all the kingdoms of the earth because of Manasseh, the son of Hezekiah, the king of Judah, for what he did in Jerusalem.

5 ¶ "Indeed, who will have pity on you,
    O Jerusalem,
Or who will mourn for you,
Or who will turn aside to ask about your
    welfare?
6 "You who have forsaken Me," declares the
    LORD,
"You keep going backward.
So I will stretch out My hand against you
    and destroy you;
I am tired of relenting!
7 "I will winnow them with a winnowing
    fork
At the gates of the land;
I will bereave *them* of children, I will
    destroy My people;
They did not repent of their ways.
8 "Their widows will be more numerous
    before Me
Than the sand of the seas;
I will bring against them, against the
    mother of a young man,
A destroyer at noonday;
I will suddenly bring down on her
    Anguish and dismay.
9 "She who bore seven *sons* pines away;
Her breathing is labored.
Her sun has set while it was yet day;
She has been shamed and humiliated.
So I will give over their survivors to the
    sword
Before their enemies," declares the LORD.

10 ¶ Woe to me, my mother, that you have
    borne me
As a man of strife and a man of
    contention to all the land!
I have not lent, nor have men lent
    money to me,
Yet everyone curses me.
11 The LORD said, "Surely I will set you free
    for *purposes of* good;
Surely I will cause the enemy to make
    supplication to you
In a time of disaster and a time of
    distress.

12 ¶ "Can anyone smash iron,
Iron from the north, or bronze?
13 "Your wealth and your treasures
I will give for booty without cost,
Even for all your sins
And within all your borders.
14 "Then I will cause your enemies to
bring *it*
Into a land you do not know;
For a fire has been kindled in My anger,
It will burn upon you."

Jeremiah's Prayer and God's Answer

15 ¶ You who know, O LORD,
Remember me, take notice of me,
And take vengeance for me on my
persecutors.
Do not, in view of Your patience, take
me away;
Know that for Your sake I endure
reproach.
16 Your words were found and I ate them,
And Your words became for me a joy
and the delight of my heart;
For I have been called by Your name,
O LORD God of hosts.
17 I did not sit in the circle of merrymakers,
Nor did I exult.
Because of Your hand *upon me* I sat
alone,
For You filled me with indignation.
18 Why has my pain been perpetual
And my wound incurable, refusing to be
healed?
Will You indeed be to me like a
deceptive *stream*
With water that is unreliable?

19 ¶ Therefore, thus says the LORD,
"If you return, then I will restore you—
Before Me you will stand;
And if you extract the precious from the
worthless,
You will become My spokesman.
They for their part may turn to you,
But as for you, you must not turn to
them.
20 "Then I will make you to this people
A fortified wall of bronze;
And though they fight against you,
They will not prevail over you;
For I am with you to save you
And deliver you," declares the LORD.
21 "So I will deliver you from the hand of
the wicked,
And I will redeem you from the grasp of
the violent."

Distresses Foretold

16 The word of the LORD also came to me saying,

2 "You shall not take a wife for yourself nor have sons or daughters in this place."

3 For thus says the LORD concerning the sons and daughters born in this place, and concerning their mothers who bear them, and their fathers who beget them in this land:

4 "They will die of deadly diseases, they will not be lamented or buried; they will be as dung on the surface of the ground and come to an end by sword and famine, and their carcasses will become food for the birds of the sky and for the beasts of the earth."

5 ¶ For thus says the LORD, "Do not enter a house of mourning, or go to lament or to console them; for I have withdrawn My peace from this people," declares the LORD, "*My* lovingkindness and compassion.

6 "Both great men and small will die in this land; they will not be buried, they will not be lamented, nor will anyone gash himself or shave his head for them.

7 "Men will not break *bread* in mourning for them, to comfort anyone for the dead, nor give them a cup of consolation to drink for anyone's father or mother.

8 "Moreover you shall not go into a house of feasting to sit with them to eat and drink."

16:8 No Social Life

Jeremiah was a man swallowed up in his work. He had no family and little social life, because God told him never to marry and not to attend weddings, funerals, or any other ceremonial feasts (verses 1–9). God's message through him was so negative that a tale of woe or complaint came to be known as a "jeremiad." Other prophets kept predicting peace (14:13), but Jeremiah couldn't say what people wanted to hear. He told the truth, and the truth was bleak. Nevertheless, Jeremiah experienced the joy and delight of receiving God's word, and bearing God's name (15:16).

9 For thus says the LORD of hosts, the God of Israel: "Behold, I am going to eliminate from this place, before your eyes and in your time, the voice of rejoicing and the voice of gladness, the voice of the groom and the voice of the bride.

10 ¶ "Now when you tell this people all these words, they will say to you, 'For what reason has the LORD declared all this great calamity against us? And what is our iniquity, or what is our sin which we have committed against the LORD our God?'

11 "Then you are to say to them, '*It is* because your forefathers have forsaken Me,' declares the LORD, 'and have followed other gods and served them and bowed down to them; but Me they have forsaken and have not kept My law.

12 'You too have done evil, *even* more than your forefathers; for behold, you are each one walking according to the stubbornness of his own evil heart, without listening to Me.

13 'So I will hurl you out of this land into the land which you have not known, neither you nor your fathers; and there you will serve other gods day and night, for I will grant you no favor.'

God Will Restore Them

14 ¶ "Therefore behold, days are coming," declares the LORD, "when it will no longer be said, 'As the LORD lives, who brought up the sons of Israel out of the land of Egypt,'

15 but, 'As the LORD lives, who brought up the sons of Israel from the land of the north and from all the countries where He had banished them.' For I will restore them to their own land which I gave to their fathers.

16 ¶ "Behold, I am going to send for many fishermen," declares the LORD, "and they will fish for them; and afterwards I will send for many hunters, and they will hunt them from every mountain and every hill and from the clefts of the rocks.

17 "For My eyes are on all their ways; they are not hidden from My face, nor is their iniquity concealed from My eyes.

18 "I will first doubly repay their iniquity and their sin, because they have polluted My land; they have filled My inheritance with the carcasses of their detestable idols and with their abominations."

19 ¶ O LORD, my strength and my
    stronghold,
  And my refuge in the day of distress,
  To You the nations will come
  From the ends of the earth and say,
  "Our fathers have inherited nothing but
    falsehood,
  Futility and things of no profit."
20 Can man make gods for himself?
  Yet they are not gods!

21 ¶ "Therefore behold, I am going to make
    them know—
  This time I will make them know
  My power and My might;
  And they shall know that My name is the
    LORD."

The Deceitful Heart

17 The sin of Judah is written down with an iron stylus;
  With a diamond point it is engraved
    upon the tablet of their heart
  And on the horns of their altars,
2 As they remember their children,
  So they *remember* their altars and their
    Asherim
  By green trees on the high hills.
3 O mountain of Mine in the countryside,

  I will give over your wealth and all your
    treasures for booty,
  Your high places for sin throughout your
    borders.
4 And you will, even of yourself, let go of
    your inheritance
  That I gave you;
  And I will make you serve your enemies
  In the land which you do not know;
  For you have kindled a fire in My anger
  Which will burn forever.

5 ¶ Thus says the LORD,
  "Cursed is the man who trusts in
    mankind
  And makes flesh his strength,
  And whose heart turns away from the
    LORD.
6 "For he will be like a bush in the desert
  And will not see when prosperity comes,
  But will live in stony wastes in the
    wilderness,
  A land of salt without inhabitant.

17:6 Whom to Trust?

Buy two identical plants in a nursery. Plant one in a desert, and one by a river. For a few days they'll look alike, but what happens after a few weeks? That's the image Jeremiah uses. The person who trusts in human beings will end up like a shriveled bush (verse 6), while the person who trusts God will be like a tree that has its roots sunk deep beside a stream (verse 8).

7 "Blessed is the man who trusts in the
    LORD
  And whose trust is the LORD.
8 "For he will be like a tree planted by the
    water,
  That extends its roots by a stream
  And will not fear when the heat comes;
  But its leaves will be green,
  And it will not be anxious in a year of
    drought
  Nor cease to yield fruit.

9 ¶ "The heart is more deceitful than all
    else
  And is desperately sick;
  Who can understand it?
10 "I, the LORD, search the heart,
  I test the mind,
  Even to give to each man according to
    his ways,
  According to the results of his deeds.
11 "As a partridge that hatches eggs which it
    has not laid,
  So is he who makes a fortune, but
    unjustly;

In the midst of his days it will forsake
    him,
And in the end he will be a fool."

12 ¶ A glorious throne on high from the
    beginning
Is the place of our sanctuary.
13 O LORD, the hope of Israel,
All who forsake You will be put to
    shame.
Those who turn away on earth will be
    written down,
Because they have forsaken the fountain
    of living water, even the LORD.
14 Heal me, O LORD, and I will be healed;
Save me and I will be saved,
For You are my praise.
15 Look, they keep saying to me,
"Where is the word of the LORD?
Let it come now!"
16 But as for me, I have not hurried away
    from *being* a shepherd after You,
Nor have I longed for the woeful day;
You Yourself know that the utterance of
    my lips
Was in Your presence.
17 Do not be a terror to me;
You are my refuge in the day of disaster.
18 Let those who persecute me be put to
    shame, but as for me, let me not be
    put to shame;
Let them be dismayed, but let me not be
    dismayed.
Bring on them a day of disaster,
And crush them with twofold
    destruction!

The Sabbath Must Be Kept

19 ¶ Thus the LORD said to me, "Go and stand
in the public gate, through which the kings of
Judah come in and go out, as well as in all the
gates of Jerusalem;
20 and say to them, 'Listen to the word of the
LORD, kings of Judah, and all Judah and all inhabitants of Jerusalem who come in through these
gates:
21 'Thus says the LORD, "Take heed for yourselves, and do not carry any load on the sabbath
day or bring anything in through the gates of Jerusalem.
22 "You shall not bring a load out of your
houses on the sabbath day nor do any work, but
keep the sabbath day holy, as I commanded your
forefathers.
23 "Yet they did not listen or incline their ears,
but stiffened their necks in order not to listen or
take correction.
24 ¶ "But it will come about, if you listen attentively to Me," declares the LORD, "to bring no load
in through the gates of this city on the sabbath

day, but to keep the sabbath day holy by doing no
work on it,
25 then there will come in through the gates of
this city kings and princes sitting on the throne of
David, riding in chariots and on horses, they and
their princes, the men of Judah and the inhabitants of Jerusalem, and this city will be inhabited
forever.
26 "They will come in from the cities of Judah
and from the environs of Jerusalem, from the land
of Benjamin, from the lowland, from the hill
country and from the Negev, bringing burnt offerings, sacrifices, grain offerings and incense, and
bringing sacrifices of thanksgiving to the house of
the LORD.
27 "But if you do not listen to Me to keep the
sabbath day holy by not carrying a load and coming in through the gates of Jerusalem on the sabbath day, then I will kindle a fire in its gates and
it will devour the palaces of Jerusalem and not be
quenched." ' "

The Potter and the Clay

18 The word which came to Jeremiah from the
    LORD saying,
2 "Arise and go down to the potter's house,
and there I will announce My words to you."
3 Then I went down to the potter's house, and
there he was, making something on the wheel.
4 But the vessel that he was making of clay
was spoiled in the hand of the potter; so he
remade it into another vessel, as it pleased the
potter to make.
5 ¶ Then the word of the LORD came to me
saying,
6 "Can I not, O house of Israel, deal with you
as this potter *does?*" declares the LORD. "Behold,
like the clay in the potter's hand, so are you in My
hand, O house of Israel.

18:6 The Potter and the Clay

*God is in control—a message vividly portrayed
to Jeremiah as he watched a potter start over
on a pot that did not take the shape he wanted
it to take. Israelites had gradually come to
think that God, because he had chosen them as
his people, was obliged to protect them. But
their unnatural behavior toward him had
brought God to the point of "starting over." In
Romans 9:21, Paul returned to this metaphor to
answer people who were claiming God was
unjust.*

7 "At one moment I might speak concerning a
nation or concerning a kingdom to uproot, to pull
down, or to destroy *it;*
8 if that nation against which I have spoken

turns from its evil, I will ^arelent concerning the calamity I planned to bring on it.

9 "Or at another moment I might speak concerning a nation or concerning a kingdom to build up or to plant *it;*

10 if it does evil in My sight by not obeying My voice, then I will ^bthink better of the good with which I had promised to bless it.

11 "So now then, speak to the men of Judah and against the inhabitants of Jerusalem saying, 'Thus says the LORD, "Behold, I am fashioning calamity against you and devising a plan against you. Oh turn back, each of you from his evil way, and reform your ways and your deeds." '

12 "But they will say, 'It's hopeless! For we are going to follow our own plans, and each of us will act according to the stubbornness of his evil heart.'

13 ¶ "Therefore thus says the LORD,
'Ask now among the nations,
Who ever heard the like of this?
The virgin of Israel
Has done a most appalling thing.

14 'Does the snow of Lebanon forsake the rock of the open country?
Or is the cold flowing water *from* a foreign *land* ever snatched away?

15 'For My people have forgotten Me,
They burn incense to worthless gods
And they have stumbled from their ways,
From the ancient paths,
To walk in bypaths,
Not on a highway,

16 To make their land a desolation,
An object of perpetual hissing;
Everyone who passes by it will be astonished
And shake his head.

17 'Like an east wind I will scatter them
Before the enemy;
I will show them My back and not *My* face
In the day of their calamity.' "

18 ¶ Then they said, "Come and let us devise plans against Jeremiah. Surely the law is not going to be lost to the priest, nor counsel to the sage, nor the *divine* word to the prophet! Come on and let us strike at him with *our* tongue, and let us give no heed to any of his words."

19 ¶ Do give heed to me, O LORD,
And listen to what my opponents are saying!

20 Should good be repaid with evil?
For they have dug a pit for me.
Remember how I stood before You
To speak good on their behalf,
So as to turn away Your wrath from them.

21 Therefore, give their children over to famine

And deliver them up to the power of the sword;
And let their wives become childless and widowed.
Let their men also be smitten to death,
Their young men struck down by the sword in battle.

22 May an outcry be heard from their houses,
When You suddenly bring raiders upon them;
For they have dug a pit to capture me
And hidden snares for my feet.

23 Yet You, O LORD, know
All their deadly designs against me;
Do not forgive their iniquity
Or blot out their sin from Your sight.
But may they be overthrown before You;
Deal with them in the time of Your anger!

The Broken Jar

19 Thus says the LORD, "Go and buy a potter's earthenware jar, and *take* some of the elders of the people and some of the senior priests.

2 "Then go out to the valley of Ben-hinnom, which is by the entrance of the potsherd gate, and proclaim there the words that I tell you,

3 and say, 'Hear the word of the LORD, O kings of Judah and inhabitants of Jerusalem: thus says the LORD of hosts, the God of Israel, "Behold I am about to bring a calamity upon this place, at which the ears of everyone that hears of it will tingle.

4 "Because they have forsaken Me and have made this an alien place and have burned sacrifices in it to other gods, that neither they nor their forefathers nor the kings of Judah had *ever* known, and *because* they have filled this place with the blood of the innocent

5 and have built the high places of Baal to burn their sons in the fire as burnt offerings to Baal, a thing which I never commanded or spoke of, nor did it *ever* enter My mind;

6 therefore, behold, days are coming," declares the LORD, "when this place will no longer be called Topheth or the valley of Ben-hinnom, but rather the valley of Slaughter.

7 "I will make void the counsel of Judah and Jerusalem in this place, and I will cause them to fall by the sword before their enemies and by the hand of those who seek their life; and I will give over their carcasses as food for the birds of the sky and the beasts of the earth.

8 "I will also make this city a desolation and an *object of* hissing; everyone who passes by it will be astonished and hiss because of all its disasters.

9 "I will make them eat the flesh of their sons and the flesh of their daughters, and they will eat one another's flesh in the siege and in the distress

^a Lit *repent of*   ^b Lit *repent*

with which their enemies and those who seek their life will distress them." '

10 ¶ "Then you are to break the jar in the sight of the men who accompany you

11 and say to them, 'Thus says the LORD of hosts, "Just so will I break this people and this city, even as one breaks a potter's vessel, which cannot

again be repaired; and they will bury in Topheth because there is no *other* place for burial.

12 "This is how I will treat this place and its inhabitants," declares the LORD, "so as to make this city like Topheth.

13 "The houses of Jerusalem and the houses of the kings of Judah will be defiled like the place

Idolatry
It still flourishes, even without statues

> "They have forsaken Me and have made this an alien place . . . to other gods." 19:4

SUPPOSE YOU FOUND A FRIEND carving a small statue out of a piece of wood. "What are you going to do with that?" you ask. "I'm going to worship it," he says. "I've got a nice spot in my bedroom where I can kneel down and ask it for things."

Or imagine people on a suburban street pooling their wedding rings and other jewelry to make a statue they can put in the park. They plan to kill animals and leave the meat out in front of the statue.

To moderns, idolatry is as weird as cannibalism; we're not tempted to try it. But since a great part of the Old Testament is concerned with idolatry, we need to get some idea of what people saw in it—and why God condemned it.

Mixing Religions

In Jeremiah's day, practically everybody practiced idolatry. Israelites had a hard time seeing that a few statues interfered with their relationship with the one true God. They worshiped the God of Abraham, but mixed in the gods of countries surrounding them. They had idols right in the Jerusalem temple (7:30). They could go to worship God right after burning incense to Baal (7:9–10).

They had built shrines on top of many hills—the "high places"—and under the tallest trees so that worship could be carried out conveniently, without a trip to Jerusalem. They ignored the prophets' warnings that God hated this "mixed" religion.

Judah's neighbors believed in many gods, each having its sphere of influence. The Jews themselves had begun to wonder: Why should their God be so different? Why should he want to knock out all competition? If idols were a fraud, mere carvings (10:4), why should God worry about them?

The Evils Idols Stood For

Idols were far from innocent, however. They stood for vile, angry gods who could hurt you unless you bartered for peace. The highest sacrifice? Slaughter your own son. The Israelites had adopted this practice (19:5).

According to these idol-worshiping religions, success came through the fertile power of nature and the gods. You could tune in to such power by having sex with temple prostitutes, either male or female. The Israelites also borrowed this (2 Kings 23:7). These ideas disgusted the God of Israel. By mixing such practices with their devotion to him, God's people were becoming confused about his true character. (For more on idolatry, see "Why All the Fuss about Idols?" page 417.)

Idolatry Today

The New Testament broadens the definition of idolatry so that it applies to us, even though we worship no statues. Paul said that greed is idolatry (Ephesians 5:5; Colossians 3:5). The things people get greedy for—money, sex, power, even food—can function as little gods. When we feel depressed, we turn to them for comfort. When we're happy, we give them the credit. We gradually become their slaves. But this is exactly the place for God in our lives, and God alone. If something else takes his place, we are as guilty of idolatry as the people Jeremiah spoke to. God cannot share us. He is either the only God, or he is not God at all.

Jealousy is an ugly emotion, but in some situations it is the only appropriate response. A father is jealous of his children; he will fight never to give them up to another family. A husband is jealous of his wife; he will not share her most intimate love with anyone else. So God feels about his people. They belong to him, and to him alone.

Life Questions: Where do you turn when you're troubled? Do money, success, popularity, or other factors serve as substitutes for God?

Topheth, because of all the houses on whose rooftops they burned sacrifices to all the heavenly host and poured out drink offerings to other gods." ' "

14 ¶ Then Jeremiah came from Topheth, where the LORD had sent him to prophesy; and he stood in the court of the LORD's house and said to all the people:

15 "Thus says the LORD of hosts, the God of Israel, 'Behold, I am about to bring on this city and all its towns the entire calamity that I have declared against it, because they have stiffened their necks so as not to heed My words.' "

Pashhur Persecutes Jeremiah

20 When Pashhur the priest, the son of Immer, who was chief officer in the house of the LORD, heard Jeremiah prophesying these things,

2 Pashhur had Jeremiah the prophet beaten and put him in the stocks that were at the upper Benjamin Gate, which was by the house of the LORD.

3 On the next day, when Pashhur released Jeremiah from the stocks, Jeremiah said to him, "Pashhur is not the name the LORD has called you, but rather *a*Magor-missabib.

4 "For thus says the LORD, 'Behold, I am going to make you a terror to yourself and to all your friends; and while your eyes look on, they will fall by the sword of their enemies. So I will give over all Judah to the hand of the king of Babylon, and he will carry them away as exiles to Babylon and will slay them with the sword.

5 'I will also give over all the wealth of this city, all its produce and all its costly things; even all the treasures of the kings of Judah I will give over to the hand of their enemies, and they will plunder them, take them away and bring them to Babylon.

6 'And you, Pashhur, and all who live in your house will go into captivity; and you will enter Babylon, and there you will die and there you will be buried, you and all your friends to whom you have falsely prophesied.' "

Jeremiah's Complaint

7 ¶ O LORD, You have deceived me and I
    was deceived;
You have overcome me and prevailed.
I have become a laughingstock all day
    long;
Everyone mocks me.
8 For each time I speak, I cry aloud;
I proclaim violence and destruction,
Because for me the word of the LORD has
    resulted
In reproach and derision all day long.
9 But if I say, "I will not remember Him
Or speak anymore in His name,"
Then in my heart it becomes like a
    burning fire

Shut up in my bones;
And I am weary of holding *it* in,
And I cannot endure *it*.

20:9 Fire in His Bones

When Jeremiah spoke to God, he often complained angrily about the role God had given him. Here he claimed that God had "overcome" him into carrying a message that people ridiculed (verse 7). Jeremiah cursed his own birth, wishing he had been stillborn (verses 14–18). Just how did God "overcome" Jeremiah? God's message was like fire in his bones, so powerful that he could not resist telling it. The "force" God used on Jeremiah was the power of truth.

10 For I have heard the whispering of many,
    "Terror on every side!
    Denounce *him*; yes, let us
        denounce him!"
    All my trusted friends,
    Watching for my fall, say:
    "Perhaps he will be deceived, so that we
        may prevail against him
    And take our revenge on him."
11 But the LORD is with me like a dread
        champion;
    Therefore my persecutors will stumble
        and not prevail.
    They will be utterly ashamed, because
        they have failed,
    With an everlasting disgrace that will not
        be forgotten.
12 Yet, O LORD of hosts, You who test the
        righteous,
    Who see the mind and the heart;
    Let me see Your vengeance on them;
    For to You I have set forth my cause.
13 Sing to the LORD, praise the LORD!
    For He has delivered the soul of the
        needy one
    From the hand of evildoers.

14 ¶ Cursed be the day when I was born;
    Let the day not be blessed when my
        mother bore me!
15 Cursed be the man who brought the
        news
    To my father, saying,
    "A baby boy has been born to you!"
    And made him very happy.
16 But let that man be like the cities
    Which the LORD overthrew without
        *b*relenting,
    And let him hear an outcry in the
        morning
    And a shout of alarm at noon;

---

a I.e. terror on every side   *b* Lit *being sorry*

17 Because he did not kill me before birth,
So that my mother would have been my
grave,
And her womb ever pregnant.
18 Why did I ever come forth from the
womb
To look on trouble and sorrow,
So that my days have been spent in
shame?

Jeremiah's Message for Zedekiah

21 The word which came to Jeremiah from the
LORD when King Zedekiah sent to him
Pashhur the son of Malchijah, and Zephaniah the
priest, the son of Maaseiah, saying,
2 "Please inquire of the LORD on our behalf,
for Nebuchadnezzar king of Babylon is warring
against us; perhaps the LORD will deal with us
according to all His wonderful acts, so that *the
enemy* will withdraw from us."
3 ¶ Then Jeremiah said to them, "You shall
say to Zedekiah as follows:
4 'Thus says the LORD God of Israel, "Behold,
I am about to turn back the weapons of war which
are in your hands, with which you are warring
against the king of Babylon and the Chaldeans
who are besieging you outside the wall; and I will
gather them into the center of this city.
5 "I Myself will war against you with an outstretched hand and a mighty arm, even in anger
and wrath and great indignation.
6 "I will also strike down the inhabitants of this
city, both man and beast; they will die of a great
pestilence.
7 "Then afterwards," declares the LORD, "I will
give over Zedekiah king of Judah and his servants
and the people, even those who survive in this city
from the pestilence, the sword and the famine,
into the hand of Nebuchadnezzar king of Babylon,
and into the hand of their foes and into the hand
of those who seek their lives; and he will strike
them down with the edge of the sword. He will not
spare them nor have pity nor compassion." '
8 ¶ "You shall also say to this people, 'Thus

21:7 God's Answer: No

*Prayer changes things, but the results depend
on who's asking and what their motives are.
Faced with a crisis, King Zedekiah asked
Jeremiah to pray to God on his behalf. He
hoped for a miracle, but the answer Jeremiah
received was anything but good news. Not only
would God not help, he would fight against
Zedekiah and his people. Why was God's
response so negative? Because nobody had
paid attention to his warnings. Judah wanted
to be rescued—not to alter its behavior.*

---

says the LORD, "Behold, I set before you the way
of life and the way of death.
9 "He who dwells in this city will die by the
sword and by famine and by pestilence; but he
who goes out and falls away to the Chaldeans who
are besieging you will live, and he will have his
own life as booty.
10 "For I have set My face against this city for
harm and not for good," declares the LORD. "It
will be given into the hand of the king of Babylon
and he will burn it with fire." '"
11 ¶ "Then *say* to the household of the king of
Judah, 'Hear the word of the LORD,
12 O house of David, thus says the LORD:
"Administer justice every morning;
And deliver the *person* who has been
robbed from the power of *his*
oppressor,
That My wrath may not go forth like
fire
And burn with none to extinguish *it*,
Because of the evil of their deeds.
13 ¶ "Behold, I am against you, O valley
dweller,
O rocky plain," declares the LORD,
"You men who say, 'Who will come down
against us?
Or who will enter into our habitations?'
14 "But I will punish you according to the
results of your deeds," declares the
LORD,
"And I will kindle a fire in its forest
That it may devour all its environs." ' "

Warning of Jerusalem's Fall

22 Thus says the LORD, "Go down to the house
of the king of Judah, and there speak this
word
2 and say, 'Hear the word of the LORD,
O king of Judah, who sits on David's throne, you
and your servants and your people who enter
these gates.
3 'Thus says the LORD, "Do justice and righteousness, and deliver the one who has been
robbed from the power of *his* oppressor. Also do
not mistreat *or* do violence to the stranger, the
orphan, or the widow; and do not shed innocent
blood in this place.
4 "For if you men will indeed perform this
thing, then kings will enter the gates of this house,
sitting in David's place on his throne, riding in
chariots and on horses, *even the king* himself and
his servants and his people.
5 "But if you will not obey these words, I swear
by Myself," declares the LORD, "that this house
will become a desolation." ' "
6 For thus says the LORD concerning the
house of the king of Judah:
"You are *like* Gilead to Me,
Like the summit of Lebanon;

Yet most assuredly I will make you like a
wilderness,
Like cities which are not inhabited.
7 "For I will set apart destroyers against
you,
Each with his weapons;
And they will cut down your choicest
cedars
And throw *them* on the fire.

8 ¶ "Many nations will pass by this city; and
they will say to one another, 'Why has the LORD
done thus to this great city?'

9 "Then they will answer, 'Because they forsook the covenant of the LORD their God and
bowed down to other gods and served them.' "

10 ¶ Do not weep for the dead or mourn
for him,
But weep continually for the one who
goes away;
For he will never return
Or see his native land.

11 ¶ For thus says the LORD in regard to Shallum the son of Josiah, king of Judah, who became
king in the place of Josiah his father, who went
forth from this place, "He will never return there;
12 but in the place where they led him captive,
there he will die and not see this land again.

Messages about the Kings

13 ¶ "Woe to him who builds his house
without righteousness
And his upper rooms without justice,
Who uses his neighbor's services
without pay
And does not give him his wages,
14 Who says, 'I will build myself a roomy
house
With spacious upper rooms,
And cut out its windows,
Paneling *it* with cedar and painting *it*
bright red.'
15 "Do you become a king because you are
competing in cedar?
Did not your father eat and drink
And do justice and righteousness?
Then it was well with him.
16 "He pled the cause of the afflicted and
needy;
Then it was well.
Is not that what it means to know Me?"
Declares the LORD.
17 "But your eyes and your heart
Are *intent* only upon your own dishonest
gain,
And on shedding innocent blood
And on practicing oppression and
extortion."

18 ¶ Therefore thus says the LORD in regard to
Jehoiakim the son of Josiah, king of Judah,

"They will not lament for him:
'Alas, my brother!' or, 'Alas, sister!'
They will not lament for him:
'Alas for the master!' or, 'Alas for his
splendor!'
19 "He will be buried with a donkey's burial,
Dragged off and thrown out beyond the
gates of Jerusalem.
20 "Go up to Lebanon and cry out,
And lift up your voice in Bashan;
Cry out also from Abarim,
For all your lovers have been crushed.
21 "I spoke to you in your prosperity;
But you said, 'I will not listen!'
This has been your practice from your
youth,
That you have not obeyed My voice.
22 "The wind will sweep away all your
shepherds,
And your lovers will go into captivity;
Then you will surely be ashamed and
humiliated
Because of all your wickedness.
23 "You who dwell in Lebanon,
Nested in the cedars,
How you will groan when pangs come
upon you,
Pain like a woman in childbirth!

24 ¶ "As I live," declares the LORD, "even
though *a*Coniah the son of Jehoiakim king of
Judah were a signet *ring* on My right hand, yet I
would pull you off;
25 and I will give you over into the hand of
those who are seeking your life, yes, into the hand
of those whom you dread, even into the hand of
Nebuchadnezzar king of Babylon and into the
hand of the Chaldeans.
26 "I will hurl you and your mother who bore
you into another country where you were not
born, and there you will die.
27 "But as for the land to which they desire to
return, they will not return to it.
28 "Is this man Coniah a despised,
shattered jar?
Or is he an undesirable vessel?
Why have he and his descendants been
hurled out
And cast into a land that they had not
known?
29 "O land, land, land,
Hear the word of the LORD!
30 "Thus says the LORD,
'Write this man down childless,
A man who will not prosper in his
days;
For no man of his descendants will
prosper
Sitting on the throne of David
Or ruling again in Judah.' "

a I.e. Jehoiachin

The Coming Messiah: the Righteous Branch

23 "Woe to the shepherds who are destroying and scattering the sheep of My pasture!" declares the LORD.

2 Therefore thus says the LORD God of Israel concerning the shepherds who are tending My people: "You have scattered My flock and driven them away, and have not attended to them; behold, I am about to attend to you for the evil of your deeds," declares the LORD.

3 "Then I Myself will gather the remnant of My flock out of all the countries where I have driven them and bring them back to their pasture, and they will be fruitful and multiply.

4 "I will also raise up shepherds over them and they will tend them; and they will not be afraid any longer, nor be terrified, nor will any be missing," declares the LORD.

5 ¶ "Behold, *the* days are coming," declares the LORD,
"When I will raise up for David a
      righteous Branch;
And He will reign as king and act wisely
And do justice and righteousness in the
      land.
6 "In His days Judah will be saved,
And Israel will dwell securely;
And this is His name by which He will
      be called,
'The LORD our righteousness.'

23:6 The Messianic Promise

Long before, God had promised David that his descendants would always rule Israel. But the kings who followed David had been more like wolves than shepherds of God's people. Jeremiah predicted that the kings of his day would either be killed or carried into captivity—which in fact occurred. He also predicted that a good king would replace them—the Messiah.

7 ¶ "Therefore behold, *the* days are coming," declares the LORD, "when they will no longer say, 'As the LORD lives, who brought up the sons of Israel from the land of Egypt,'

8 but, 'As the LORD lives, who brought up and led back the descendants of the household of Israel from *the* north land and from all the countries where I had driven them.' Then they will live on their own soil."

False Prophets Denounced

9 ¶ As for the prophets:
My heart is broken within me,
All my bones tremble;
I have become like a drunken man,
Even like a man overcome with wine,
Because of the LORD
And because of His holy words.
10 For the land is full of adulterers;
For the land mourns because of the
      curse.
The pastures of the wilderness have
      dried up.
Their course also is evil
And their might is not right.
11 "For both prophet and priest are polluted;
Even in My house I have found their
      wickedness," declares the LORD.
12 "Therefore their way will be like slippery
      paths to them,
They will be driven away into the gloom
      and fall down in it;
For I will bring calamity upon them,
The year of their punishment," declares
      the LORD.
13 ¶ "Moreover, among the prophets of
      Samaria I saw an offensive thing:
They prophesied by Baal and led My
      people Israel astray.
14 "Also among the prophets of Jerusalem I
      have seen a horrible thing:
The committing of adultery and walking
      in falsehood;
And they strengthen the hands of
      evildoers,
So that no one has turned back from his
      wickedness.
All of them have become to Me like
      Sodom,
And her inhabitants like Gomorrah.
15 "Therefore thus says the LORD of hosts concerning the prophets,
'Behold, I am going to feed them
      wormwood
And make them drink poisonous water,
For from the prophets of Jerusalem
Pollution has gone forth into all the
      land.' "

16 ¶ Thus says the LORD of hosts,
"Do not listen to the words of the
      prophets who are prophesying to
      you.
They are leading you into futility;
They speak a vision of their own
      imagination,
Not from the mouth of the LORD.
17 "They keep saying to those who
      despise Me,
'The LORD has said, "You will have
      peace" ';
And as for everyone who walks in the
      stubbornness of his own heart,
They say, 'Calamity will not come
      upon you.'
18 "But who has stood in the council of the
      LORD,

That he should see and hear His word?
Who has given heed to His word and
listened?
19 "Behold, the storm of the LORD has gone
forth in wrath,
Even a whirling tempest;
It will swirl down on the head of the
wicked.
20 "The anger of the LORD will not turn back
Until He has performed and carried out
the purposes of His heart;
In the last days you will clearly
understand it.
21 "I did not send *these* prophets,
But they ran.
I did not speak to them,
But they prophesied.
22 "But if they had stood in My council,
Then they would have announced My
words to My people,
And would have turned them back from
their evil way
And from the evil of their deeds.

23 ¶ "Am I a God who is near," declares the
LORD,
"And not a God far off?
24 "Can a man hide himself in hiding places
So I do not see him?" declares the LORD.
"Do I not fill the heavens and the earth?"
declares the LORD.
25 ¶ "I have heard what the prophets have said
who prophesy falsely in My name, saying, 'I had
a dream, I had a dream!'

23:25 Questionable Dreams

For the casual observer, it must have been difficult to tell real prophets from false prophets in Jeremiah's day. Jeremiah was outnumbered by optimists who claimed God gave them dreams and messages. In reality, their dreams had nothing to do with God's word, and anyone who compared their message with Scripture could have seen the difference. They predicted peace when God had promised severe punishment for his people's sins.

26 "How long? Is there *anything* in the hearts of
the prophets who prophesy falsehood, even *these*
prophets of the deception of their own heart,
27 who intend to make My people forget My
name by their dreams which they relate to one
another, just as their fathers forgot My name because of Baal?
28 "The prophet who has a dream may relate *his*
dream, but let him who has My word speak My
word in truth. What does straw have *in common*
with grain?" declares the LORD.

29 "Is not My word like fire?" declares the
LORD, "and like a hammer which shatters a rock?
30 "Therefore behold, I am against the prophets," declares the LORD, "who steal My words from
each other.
31 "Behold, I am against the prophets," declares
the LORD, "who use their tongues and declare,
'*The Lord* declares.'
32 "Behold, I am against those who have prophesied false dreams," declares the LORD, "and related them and led My people astray by their false-
hoods and reckless boasting; yet I did not send
them or command them, nor do they furnish this
people the slightest benefit," declares the LORD.
33 ¶ "Now when this people or the prophet or
a priest asks you saying, 'What is the ᵃoracle of
the LORD?' then you shall say to them, 'What oracle?' The LORD declares, 'I will abandon you.'
34 "Then as for the prophet or the priest or the
people who say, 'The oracle of the LORD,' I will
bring punishment upon that man and his household.
35 "Thus will each of you say to his neighbor
and to his brother, 'What has the LORD answered?'
or, 'What has the LORD spoken?'
36 "For you will no longer remember the oracle
of the LORD, because every man's own word will
become the oracle, and you have perverted the
words of the living God, the LORD of hosts, our
God.
37 "Thus you will say to *that* prophet, 'What has
the LORD answered you?' and, 'What has the LORD
spoken?'
38 "For if you say, 'The oracle of the LORD!'
surely thus says the LORD, 'Because you said this
word, "The oracle of the LORD!" I have also sent
to you, saying, "You shall not say, 'The oracle of
the LORD!'"'
39 "Therefore behold, I will surely forget you
and cast you away from My presence, along with
the city which I gave you and your fathers.
40 "I will put an everlasting reproach on you
and an everlasting humiliation which will not be
forgotten."

Baskets of Figs and the Returnees

24 After Nebuchadnezzar king of Babylon had
carried away captive Jeconiah the son of
Jehoiakim, king of Judah, and the officials of Judah with the craftsmen and smiths from Jerusalem
and had brought them to Babylon, the LORD
showed me: behold, two baskets of figs set before
the temple of the LORD!
2 One basket had very good figs, like first-ripe
figs, and the other basket had very bad figs which
could not be eaten due to rottenness.
3 Then the LORD said to me, "What do you
see, Jeremiah?" And I said, "Figs, the good figs,
very good; and the bad *figs*, very bad, which cannot be eaten due to rottenness."

ᵃ Or *burden,* and so throughout the ch

4 ¶ Then the word of the LORD came to me, saying,

5 "Thus says the LORD God of Israel, 'Like these good figs, so I will regard as good the captives of Judah, whom I have sent out of this place *into* the land of the Chaldeans.

6 'For I will set My eyes on them for good, and I will bring them again to this land; and I will build them up and not overthrow them, and I will plant them and not pluck them up.

7 'I will give them a heart to know Me, for I am the LORD; and they will be My people, and I will be their God, for they will return to Me with their whole heart.

8 ¶ 'But like the bad figs which cannot be eaten due to rottenness—indeed, thus says the LORD—so I will abandon Zedekiah king of Judah and his officials, and the remnant of Jerusalem who remain in this land and the ones who dwell in the land of Egypt.

9 'I will make them a terror *and an* evil for all the kingdoms of the earth, as a reproach and a proverb, a taunt and a curse in all places where I will scatter them.

10 'I will send the sword, the famine and the pestilence upon them until they are destroyed from the land which I gave to them and their forefathers.' "

Prophecy of the Captivity

25 The word that came to Jeremiah concerning all the people of Judah, in the fourth year of Jehoiakim the son of Josiah, king of Judah (that was the first year of Nebuchadnezzar king of Babylon),

2 which Jeremiah the prophet spoke to all the people of Judah and to all the inhabitants of Jerusalem, saying,

3 "From the thirteenth year of Josiah the son of Amon, king of Judah, even to this day, these twenty-three years the word of the LORD has come to me, and I have spoken to you again and again, but you have not listened.

4 "And the LORD has sent to you all His servants the prophets again and again, but you have not listened nor inclined your ear to hear,

5 saying, 'Turn now everyone from his evil way and from the evil of your deeds, and dwell on the land which the LORD has given to you and your forefathers forever and ever;

6 and do not go after other gods to serve them and to worship them, and do not provoke Me to anger with the work of your hands, and I will do you no harm.'

7 "Yet you have not listened to Me," declares the LORD, "in order that you might provoke Me to anger with the work of your hands to your own harm.

8 ¶ "Therefore thus says the LORD of hosts, 'Because you have not obeyed My words,

9 behold, I will send and take all the families

of the north,' declares the LORD, 'and *I will send* to Nebuchadnezzar king of Babylon, My servant, and will bring them against this land and against its inhabitants and against all these nations round about; and I will utterly destroy them and make them a horror and a hissing, and an everlasting desolation.

10 'Moreover, I will take from them the voice of joy and the voice of gladness, the voice of the bridegroom and the voice of the bride, the sound of the millstones and the light of the lamp.

11 'This whole land will be a desolation and a horror, and these nations will serve the king of Babylon seventy years.

25:11–12 Gone, But Not Forever

Seventy years of captivity, God predicted. This probably represents a rounded-off number; the precise length of the captivity can be calculated in different ways, since several waves of captives were taken away and several waves of exiles returned. The number 70 has a deeper significance, though: It says that the punishment, though long and severe (at least two generations would die far from home), will not last forever. Unlike other nations taken into captivity, Israel will return. God's judgment is limited, but his mercy is forever.

Babylon Will Be Judged

12 ¶ 'Then it will be when seventy years are completed I will punish the king of Babylon and that nation,' declares the LORD, 'for their iniquity, and the land of the Chaldeans; and I will make it an everlasting desolation.

13 'I will bring upon that land all My words which I have pronounced against it, all that is written in this book which Jeremiah has prophesied against all the nations.

14 '(For many nations and great kings will make slaves of them, even them; and I will recompense them according to their deeds and according to the work of their hands.)' "

15 ¶ For thus the LORD, the God of Israel, says to me, "Take this cup of the wine of wrath from My hand and cause all the nations to whom I send you to drink it.

16 "They will drink and stagger and go mad because of the sword that I will send among them."

17 ¶ Then I took the cup from the LORD's hand and made all the nations to whom the LORD sent me drink it:

18 Jerusalem and the cities of Judah and its kings *and* its princes, to make them a ruin, a horror, a hissing and a curse, as it is this day;

19 Pharaoh king of Egypt, his servants, his princes and all his people;

20 and all the foreign people, all the kings of

the land of Uz, all the kings of the land of the Philistines (even Ashkelon, Gaza, Ekron and the remnant of Ashdod);

21 Edom, Moab and the sons of Ammon;

22 and all the kings of Tyre, all the kings of Sidon and the kings of the coastlands which are beyond the sea;

23 and Dedan, Tema, Buz and all who cut the corners *of their hair;*

24 and all the kings of Arabia and all the kings of the foreign people who dwell in the desert;

25 and all the kings of Zimri, all the kings of Elam and all the kings of Media;

26 and all the kings of the north, near and far, one with another; and all the kingdoms of the earth which are upon the face of the ground, and the king of Sheshach shall drink after them.

27 ¶ "You shall say to them, 'Thus says the LORD of hosts, the God of Israel, "Drink, be drunk, vomit, fall and rise no more because of the sword which I will send among you." '

28 "And it will be, if they refuse to take the cup from your hand to drink, then you will say to them, 'Thus says the LORD of hosts: "You shall surely drink!

29 "For behold, I am beginning to work calamity in *this* city which is called by My name, and shall you be completely free from punishment? You will not be free from punishment; for I am summoning a sword against all the inhabitants of the earth," declares the LORD of hosts.'

30 ¶ "Therefore you shall prophesy against them all these words, and you shall say to them, 'The LORD will roar from on high
And utter His voice from His holy habitation;
He will roar mightily against His fold.
He will shout like those who tread *the grapes,*
Against all the inhabitants of the earth.

31 'A clamor has come to the end of the earth,
Because the LORD has a controversy with the nations.
He is entering into judgment with all flesh;
As for the wicked, He has given them to the sword,' declares the LORD."

32 ¶ Thus says the LORD of hosts,
"Behold, evil is going forth
From nation to nation,
And a great storm is being stirred up
From the remotest parts of the earth.

33 ¶ "Those slain by the LORD on that day will be from one end of the earth to the other. They will not be lamented, gathered or buried; they will be like dung on the face of the ground.

34 "Wail, you shepherds, and cry;
And wallow *in ashes,* you masters of the flock;

For the days of your slaughter and your dispersions have come,
And you will fall like a choice vessel.

35 "Flight will perish from the shepherds,
And escape from the masters of the flock.

36 "*Hear* the sound of the cry of the shepherds,
And the wailing of the masters of the flock!
For the LORD is destroying their pasture,

37 "And the peaceful folds are made silent
Because of the fierce anger of the LORD.

38 "He has left His hiding place like the lion;
For their land has become a horror
Because of the fierceness of the oppressing *sword*
And because of His fierce anger."

Cities of Judah Warned

26 In the beginning of the reign of Jehoiakim the son of Josiah, king of Judah, this word came from the LORD, saying,

2 "Thus says the LORD, 'Stand in the court of the LORD's house, and speak to all the cities of Judah who have come to worship *in* the LORD's house all the words that I have commanded you to speak to them. Do not omit a word!

3 'Perhaps they will listen and everyone will turn from his evil way, that I may repent of the calamity which I am planning to do to them because of the evil of their deeds.'

4 "And you will say to them, 'Thus says the LORD, "If you will not listen to Me, to walk in My law which I have set before you,

5 to listen to the words of My servants the prophets, whom I have been sending to you again and again, but you have not listened;

6 then I will make this house like Shiloh, and this city I will make a curse to all the nations of the earth." ' "

A Plot to Murder Jeremiah

7 ¶ The priests and the prophets and all the people heard Jeremiah speaking these words in the house of the LORD.

8 When Jeremiah finished speaking all that the LORD had commanded *him* to speak to all the people, the priests and the prophets and all the people seized him, saying, "You must die!

9 "Why have you prophesied in the name of the LORD saying, 'This house will be like Shiloh and this city will be desolate, without inhabitant'?" And all the people gathered about Jeremiah in the house of the LORD.

10 ¶ When the officials of Judah heard these things, they came up from the king's house to the house of the LORD and sat in the entrance of the New Gate of the LORD's *house.*

11 Then the priests and the prophets spoke to the officials and to all the people, saying, "A death

sentence for this man! For he has prophesied against this city as you have heard in your hearing."

12 ¶ Then Jeremiah spoke to all the officials and to all the people, saying, "The LORD sent me to prophesy against this house and against this city all the words that you have heard.

13 "Now therefore amend your ways and your deeds and obey the voice of the LORD your God; and the LORD will change His mind about the misfortune which He has pronounced against you.

14 "But as for me, behold, I am in your hands; do with me as is good and right in your sight.

15 "Only know for certain that if you put me to death, you will bring innocent blood on yourselves, and on this city and on its inhabitants; for truly the LORD has sent me to you to speak all these words in your hearing."

Jeremiah Is Spared

16 ¶ Then the officials and all the people said to the priests and to the prophets, "No death sentence for this man! For he has spoken to us in the name of the LORD our God."

17 Then some of the elders of the land rose up and spoke to all the assembly of the people, saying,

18 "Micah of Moresheth prophesied in the days of Hezekiah king of Judah; and he spoke to all the people of Judah, saying, 'Thus the LORD of hosts has said,

"Zion will be plowed *as* a field,
And Jerusalem will become ruins,
And the mountain of the house as the
high places of a forest." '

19 "Did Hezekiah king of Judah and all Judah put him to death? Did he not fear the LORD and entreat the favor of the LORD, and the LORD changed His mind about the misfortune which He had pronounced against them? But we are committing a great evil against ourselves."

26:19 Scripture Saves a Life

Jeremiah's scorn for the temple was considered sacrilege and might have cost him his life. (Another prophet, Uriah, was assassinated for the same message—see verses 20–23.) But some of the elders remembered the treatment given Micah years before. Hezekiah—a good king—had listened to Micah. Based on this precedent, Jeremiah was allowed to live.

20 ¶ Indeed, there was also a man who prophesied in the name of the LORD, Uriah the son of Shemaiah from Kiriath-jearim; and he prophesied against this city and against this land words similar to all those of Jeremiah.

21 When King Jehoiakim and all his mighty men and all the officials heard his words, then the king sought to put him to death; but Uriah heard *it*, and he was afraid and fled and went to Egypt.

22 Then King Jehoiakim sent men to Egypt: Elnathan the son of Achbor and *certain* men with him *went* into Egypt.

23 And they brought Uriah from Egypt and led him to King Jehoiakim, who slew him with a sword and cast his dead body into the burial place of the common people.

24 ¶ But the hand of Ahikam the son of Shaphan was with Jeremiah, so that he was not given into the hands of the people to put him to death.

The Nations to Submit to Nebuchadnezzar

27 In the beginning of the reign of Zedekiah the son of Josiah, king of Judah, this word came to Jeremiah from the LORD, saying—

2 thus says the LORD to me—"Make for yourself bonds and yokes and put them on your neck,

3 and send word to the king of Edom, to the king of Moab, to the king of the sons of Ammon, to the king of Tyre and to the king of Sidon by the messengers who come to Jerusalem to Zedekiah king of Judah.

4 "Command them *to go* to their masters, saying, 'Thus says the LORD of hosts, the God of Israel, thus you shall say to your masters,

5 "I have made the earth, the men and the beasts which are on the face of the earth by My great power and by My outstretched arm, and I will give it to the one who is pleasing in My sight.

6 "Now I have given all these lands into the hand of Nebuchadnezzar king of Babylon, My servant, and I have given him also the wild animals of the field to serve him.

7 "All the nations shall serve him and his son and his grandson until the time of his own land comes; then many nations and great kings will make him their servant.

8 ¶ "It will be, *that* the nation or the kingdom which will not serve him, Nebuchadnezzar king of Babylon, and which will not put its neck under the yoke of the king of Babylon, I will punish that nation with the sword, with famine and with pestilence," declares the LORD, "until I have destroyed it by his hand.

9 "But as for you, do not listen to your prophets, your diviners, your dreamers, your soothsayers or your sorcerers who speak to you, saying, 'You will not serve the king of Babylon.'

10 "For they prophesy a lie to you in order to remove you far from your land; and I will drive you out and you will perish.

11 "But the nation which will bring its neck under the yoke of the king of Babylon and serve him, I will let remain on its land," declares the LORD, "and they will till it and dwell in it." ' "

12 ¶ I spoke words like all these to Zedekiah king of Judah, saying, "Bring your necks under

the yoke of the king of Babylon and serve him and his people, and live!

13 "Why will you die, you and your people, by the sword, famine and pestilence, as the LORD has spoken to that nation which will not serve the king of Babylon?

14 "So do not listen to the words of the prophets who speak to you, saying, 'You will not serve the king of Babylon,' for they prophesy a lie to you;

15 for I have not sent them," declares the LORD, "but they prophesy falsely in My name, in order that I may drive you out and that you may perish, you and the prophets who prophesy to you."

16 ¶ *Then* I spoke to the priests and to all this people, saying, "Thus says the LORD: Do not listen to the words of your prophets who prophesy to you, saying, 'Behold, the vessels of the LORD's house will now shortly be brought again from Babylon'; for they are prophesying a lie to you.

17 "Do not listen to them; serve the king of Babylon, and live! Why should this city become a ruin?

18 "But if they are prophets, and if the word of the LORD is with them, let them now entreat the LORD of hosts that the vessels which are left in the house of the LORD, in the house of the king of Judah and in Jerusalem may not go to Babylon.

19 "For thus says the LORD of hosts concerning the pillars, concerning the sea, concerning the stands and concerning the rest of the vessels that are left in this city,

20 which Nebuchadnezzar king of Babylon did not take when he carried into exile Jeconiah the son of Jehoiakim, king of Judah, from Jerusalem to Babylon, and all the nobles of Judah and Jerusalem.

21 "Yes, thus says the LORD of hosts, the God of Israel, concerning the vessels that are left in the house of the LORD and in the house of the king of Judah and in Jerusalem,

22 'They will be carried to Babylon and they will be there until the day I visit them,' declares the LORD. 'Then I will bring them back and restore them to this place.' "

Hananiah's False Prophecy

28 Now in the same year, in the beginning of the reign of Zedekiah king of Judah, in the fourth year, in the fifth month, Hananiah the son of Azzur, the prophet, who was from Gibeon, spoke to me in the house of the LORD in the presence of the priests and all the people, saying,

2 "Thus says the LORD of hosts, the God of Israel, 'I have broken the yoke of the king of Babylon.

3 'Within two years I am going to bring back to this place all the vessels of the LORD's house, which Nebuchadnezzar king of Babylon took away from this place and carried to Babylon.

4 'I am also going to bring back to this place Jeconiah the son of Jehoiakim, king of Judah, and all the exiles of Judah who went to Babylon,' declares the LORD, 'for I will break the yoke of the king of Babylon.' "

5 ¶ Then the prophet Jeremiah spoke to the prophet Hananiah in the presence of the priests and in the presence of all the people who were standing in the house of the LORD,

6 and the prophet Jeremiah said, "Amen! May the LORD do so; may the LORD confirm your words which you have prophesied to bring back the vessels of the LORD's house and all the exiles, from Babylon to this place.

7 "Yet hear now this word which I am about to speak in your hearing and in the hearing of all the people!

8 "The prophets who were before me and before you from ancient times prophesied against many lands and against great kingdoms, of war and of calamity and of pestilence.

9 "The prophet who prophesies of peace, when the word of the prophet comes to pass, then that prophet will be known *as* one whom the LORD has truly sent."

10 ¶ Then Hananiah the prophet took the yoke from the neck of Jeremiah the prophet and broke it.

11 Hananiah spoke in the presence of all the people, saying, "Thus says the LORD, 'Even so will I break within two full years the yoke of Nebuchadnezzar king of Babylon from the neck of all the nations.' " Then the prophet Jeremiah went his way.

12 ¶ The word of the LORD came to Jeremiah after Hananiah the prophet had broken the yoke from off the neck of the prophet Jeremiah, saying,

13 "Go and speak to Hananiah, saying, 'Thus says the LORD, "You have broken the yokes of wood, but you have made instead of them yokes of iron."

14 'For thus says the LORD of hosts, the God of Israel, "I have put a yoke of iron on the neck of all these nations, that they may serve Nebuchadnezzar king of Babylon; and they will serve him. And I have also given him the beasts of the field." ' "

15 Then Jeremiah the prophet said to Hana-

27:12 Counseling Surrender

By the time Zedekiah took office, Israel had twice surrendered to Babylon. Two groups of Israelites had already been exiled, including in their number King Jehoiachin. The desire for independence did not die easily, however. Zedekiah, who had been put into office as a puppet king, soon began scheming for revolution. Jeremiah persistently counseled submission to Babylon—unpopular advice that nearly cost him his life when he was accused of treason.

niah the prophet, "Listen now, Hananiah, the LORD has not sent you, and you have made this people trust in a lie.

16 "Therefore thus says the LORD, 'Behold, I am about to remove you from the face of the earth. This year you are going to die, because you have counseled rebellion against the LORD.' "

17 ¶ So Hananiah the prophet died in the same year in the seventh month.

Message to the Exiles

29 Now these are the words of the letter which Jeremiah the prophet sent from Jerusalem to the rest of the elders of the exile, the priests, the prophets and all the people whom Nebuchadnezzar had taken into exile from Jerusalem to Babylon.

2 (This was after King Jeconiah and the queen mother, the court officials, the princes of Judah and Jerusalem, the craftsmen and the smiths had departed from Jerusalem.)

3 *The letter was sent* by the hand of Elasah the son of Shaphan, and Gemariah the son of Hilkiah, whom Zedekiah king of Judah sent to Babylon to Nebuchadnezzar king of Babylon, saying,

4 "Thus says the LORD of hosts, the God of Israel, to all the exiles whom I have sent into exile from Jerusalem to Babylon,

5 'Build houses and live *in them;* and plant gardens and eat their produce.

29:5 Writing to Ezekiel

During the last years of Jeremiah's work, a sizable community of exiles were already living in Babylon. Among them were Daniel, a young man who would rise to tremendous power in court, and the prophet Ezekiel. Ezekiel was preaching at the same time as Jeremiah, and their messages are similar in many ways. Since neither one mentions the other, however, we can't be sure whether they were acquainted.

6 'Take wives and become the fathers of sons and daughters, and take wives for your sons and give your daughters to husbands, that they may bear sons and daughters; and multiply there and do not decrease.

7 'Seek the welfare of the city where I have sent you into exile, and pray to the LORD on its behalf; for in its welfare you will have welfare.'

8 "For thus says the LORD of hosts, the God of Israel, 'Do not let your prophets who are in your midst and your diviners deceive you, and do not listen to the dreams which they dream.

9 'For they prophesy falsely to you in My name; I have not sent them,' declares the LORD.

10 ¶ "For thus says the LORD, 'When seventy years have been completed for Babylon, I will visit you and fulfill My good word to you, to bring you back to this place.

11 'For I know the plans that I have for you,' declares the LORD, 'plans for welfare and not for calamity to give you a future and a hope.

12 'Then you will call upon Me and come and pray to Me, and I will listen to you.

13 'You will seek Me and find *Me* when you search for Me with all your heart.

14 'I will be found by you,' declares the LORD, 'and I will restore your fortunes and will gather you from all the nations and from all the places where I have driven you,' declares the LORD, 'and I will bring you back to the place from where I sent you into exile.'

15 ¶ "Because you have said, 'The LORD has raised up prophets for us in Babylon'—

16 for thus says the LORD concerning the king who sits on the throne of David, and concerning all the people who dwell in this city, your brothers who did not go with you into exile—

17 thus says the LORD of hosts, 'Behold, I am sending upon them the sword, famine and pestilence, and I will make them like split-open figs that cannot be eaten due to rottenness.

18 'I will pursue them with the sword, with famine and with pestilence; and I will make them a terror to all the kingdoms of the earth, to be a curse and a horror and a hissing, and a reproach among all the nations where I have driven them,

19 because they have not listened to My words,' declares the LORD, 'which I sent to them again and again by My servants the prophets; but you did not listen,' declares the LORD.

20 "You, therefore, hear the word of the LORD, all you exiles, whom I have sent away from Jerusalem to Babylon.

21 ¶ "Thus says the LORD of hosts, the God of Israel, concerning Ahab the son of Kolaiah and concerning Zedekiah the son of Maaseiah, who are prophesying to you falsely in My name, 'Behold, I will deliver them into the hand of Nebuchadnezzar king of Babylon, and he will slay them before your eyes.

22 'Because of them a curse will be used by all the exiles from Judah who are in Babylon, saying, "May the LORD make you like Zedekiah and like Ahab, whom the king of Babylon roasted in the fire,

23 because they have acted foolishly in Israel, and have committed adultery with their neighbors' wives and have spoken words in My name falsely, which I did not command them; and I am He who knows and am a witness," declares the LORD.'

24 ¶ To Shemaiah the Nehelamite you shall speak, saying,

25 "Thus says the LORD of hosts, the God of Israel, 'Because you have sent letters in your own name to all the people who are in Jerusalem, and

to Zephaniah the son of Maaseiah, the priest, and to all the priests, saying,

26 "The LORD has made you priest instead of Jehoiada the priest, to be the overseer in the house of the LORD over every madman who prophesies, to put him in the stocks and in the iron collar,

27 now then, why have you not rebuked Jeremiah of Anathoth who prophesies to you?

28 "For he has sent to us in Babylon, saying, 'The exile will be long; build houses and live in them and plant gardens and eat their produce.' " ' "

29 ¶ Zephaniah the priest read this letter to Jeremiah the prophet.

30 Then came the word of the LORD to Jeremiah, saying,

31 "Send to all the exiles, saying, 'Thus says the LORD concerning Shemaiah the Nehelamite, "Because Shemaiah has prophesied to you, although I did not send him, and he has made you trust in a lie,"

32 therefore thus says the LORD, "Behold, I am about to punish Shemaiah the Nehelamite and his descendants; he will not have anyone living among this people, and he will not see the good that I am about to do to My people," declares the LORD, "because he has preached rebellion against the LORD." ' "

Deliverance from Captivity Promised

30 The word which came to Jeremiah from the LORD, saying,

2 "Thus says the LORD, the God of Israel, 'Write all the words which I have spoken to you in a book.

3 'For behold, days are coming,' declares the LORD, 'when I will restore the fortunes of My people Israel and Judah.' The LORD says, 'I will also bring them back to the land that I gave to their forefathers and they shall possess it.' "

4 ¶ Now these are the words which the LORD spoke concerning Israel and concerning Judah:

5 ¶ "For thus says the LORD,
'I have heard a sound of terror,
Of dread, and there is no peace.

6 'Ask now, and see
If a male can give birth.
Why do I see every man
With his hands on his loins, as a woman in childbirth?
And why have all faces turned pale?

7 'Alas! for that day is great,
There is none like it;
And it is the time of Jacob's distress,
But he will be saved from it.

8 ¶ 'It shall come about on that day,' declares the LORD of hosts, 'that I will break his yoke from off their neck and will tear off their bonds; and strangers will no longer make them their slaves.

9 'But they shall serve the LORD their God and David their king, whom I will raise up for them.

10 'Fear not, O Jacob My servant,' declares the LORD,
'And do not be dismayed, O Israel;
For behold, I will save you from afar
And your offspring from the land of their captivity.
And Jacob will return and will be quiet and at ease,
And no one will make him afraid.

11 'For I am with you,' declares the LORD,
'to save you;
For I will destroy completely all the nations where I have scattered you,
Only I will not destroy you completely.
But I will chasten you justly
And will by no means leave you unpunished.'

30:11 Free Again

Though Jeremiah mainly spoke of God's judgment, he also offered hope beyond judgment. Someday, Israel would be free again. The prophecy of this verse has been fulfilled: not one of the powerful cultures surrounding Israel has endured, but the Jews have survived with their language, customs, and religion intact.

12 ¶ "For thus says the LORD,
'Your wound is incurable
And your injury is serious.

13 'There is no one to plead your cause;
No healing for your sore,
No recovery for you.

14 'All your lovers have forgotten you,
They do not seek you;
For I have wounded you with the wound of an enemy,
With the punishment of a cruel one,
Because your iniquity is great
And your sins are numerous.

15 'Why do you cry out over your injury?
Your pain is incurable.
Because your iniquity is great
And your sins are numerous,
I have done these things to you.

16 'Therefore all who devour you will be devoured;
And all your adversaries, every one of them, will go into captivity;
And those who plunder you will be for plunder,
And all who prey upon you I will give for prey.

17 'For I will restore you to health
And I will heal you of your wounds,'
declares the LORD,

The People Who Refuse to Die

Their powerful neighbors have disappeared—but the Jews live on

IF YOU GET LOST IN Brooklyn, New York, and wander into the section called Williamsburg, prepare to do a double take. Boys playing baseball look odd: long, uncut curls of hair trail from above their ears down to their chests. Men in black, with long, untrimmed beards, coach from the sidelines. All the women you see wear wigs because they've shaved their heads completely. Is this a new cult from California? The latest punk fashion from London?

You've stumbled into a community of Hasidic Jews. They live, not by the latest fad, but by ancient rules based on Old Testament laws. They follow complicated dietary regulations. They keep one set of bowls for meat, and another for dairy products. Young men devote long hours of study to the Hebrew Old Testament. Though they are Americans living in New York, their cultural compass points to Mount Sinai, where God gave Moses the Law.

> "'I will save you from afar and your offspring from the land of their captivity. And Jacob will return and will be quiet and at ease, and no one will make him afraid.'"
> 30:10

Jews Outlived Their Enemies

The Jewish people have survived, astonishingly. Who in Jeremiah's time could have predicted their persistence, when they were hemmed in and threatened with total destruction? The Babylonians conquered and carried them into exile. But where are the Babylonians today? They have vanished. Desert sand covers their capital.

The story of the Jews is a long chronicle of discrimination, exile, punishment, and slaughter. Against no other people have such destructive measures been taken. Yet they have survived, and thrived. Their language endures. Their book, the Old Testament, is part of the great best seller of all time. They have rebuilt their nation.

Even more remarkably, this durability was predicted in writing 2,500 years ago. God promised in the clearest terms that he would never reject his people.

The New Covenant

Jeremiah, known for his stinging denunciations and repeated predictions of savage destruction, also brought word of God's eternal faithfulness and of a new covenant replacing the old, broken one. The new covenant would improve generously on the old one, Jeremiah said. God would no longer simply list rules for his people to obey. He would plant those rules in their hearts, so they would want to obey (31:33). Each individual would know the Lord personally. God would offer forgiveness for sins.

Jeremiah promised more than that. He said a new king from David's line would come to rule. He would be called "The LORD our righteousness" (23:5–8). Israel would return from exile to their land. They would farm there again. They would rebuild Jerusalem and again worship God there. Jeremiah wrote these rosy words in the face of Israel's worst catastrophe.

Jeremiah didn't just deliver these messages. He acted them out. He made what was either one of the stupidest financial investments of all time, or a remarkable act of faith. He bought property from a relative at the height of the Babylonian siege (chapter 32). God had promised Jeremiah that someday the property would be worth money again to his family. He believed and invested in that distant prospect. He bet on the survival of Israel.

The Fulfillment of Prophecy

Christians agree that the new king Jeremiah predicted was Jesus. They agree that Jesus brought the new covenant, which puts the law into people's hearts and enables them to know God. But on the restoration of Israel Christians hold different opinions. Some feel that the modern nation of Israel is, at least partly, the reincarnated nation Jeremiah wrote about. Others feel that the New Testament teaches that Christians of all races form Jeremiah's "new nation" of God's people, and that the promises apply allegorically to them.

All agree, though, that what Jesus set out to do is not yet finished. Someday he will destroy the forces of evil and fully establish his new kingdom.

Life Questions: Jeremiah bought a field as a sign of his faith in the future of Israel. By what "investments" can you demonstrate practical faith in God's kingdom?

'Because they have called you an outcast,
saying:
"It is Zion; no one cares for her." '

Restoration of Jacob

18 ¶ "Thus says the LORD,
'Behold, I will restore the fortunes of the
tents of Jacob
And have compassion on his dwelling
places;
And the city will be rebuilt on its ruin,
And the palace will stand on its rightful
place.
19 'From them will proceed thanksgiving
And the voice of those who celebrate;
And I will multiply them and they will
not be diminished;
I will also honor them and they will not
be insignificant.
20 'Their children also will be as formerly,
And their congregation shall be
established before Me;
And I will punish all their oppressors.
21 'Their leader shall be one of them,
And their ruler shall come forth from
their midst;
And I will bring him near and he shall
approach Me;
For who would dare to risk his life to
approach Me?' declares the LORD.
22 'You shall be My people,
And I will be your God.' "

23 ¶ Behold, the tempest of the LORD!
Wrath has gone forth,
A sweeping tempest;
It will burst on the head of the wicked.
24 The fierce anger of the LORD will not
turn back
Until He has performed and until He has
accomplished
The intent of His heart;
In the latter days you will understand
this.

Israel's Mourning Turned to Joy

31 "At that time," declares the LORD, "I will be
the God of all the families of Israel, and they
shall be My people."
2 ¶ Thus says the LORD,
"The people who survived the sword
Found grace in the wilderness—
Israel, when it went to find its rest."
3 The LORD appeared to him from afar,
saying,
"I have loved you with an everlasting love;
Therefore I have drawn you with
lovingkindness.
4 "Again I will build you and you will be
rebuilt,
O virgin of Israel!

Again you will take up your tambourines,
And go forth to the dances of the
merrymakers.
5 "Again you will plant vineyards
On the hills of Samaria;
The planters will plant
And will enjoy *them.*
6 "For there will be a day when watchmen
On the hills of Ephraim call out,
'Arise, and let us go up *to* Zion,
To the LORD our God.' "

7 ¶ For thus says the LORD,
"Sing aloud with gladness for Jacob,
And shout among the chief of the
nations;
Proclaim, give praise and say,
'O LORD, save Your people,
The remnant of Israel.'
8 "Behold, I am bringing them from the
north country,
And I will gather them from the remote
parts of the earth,
Among them the blind and the lame,
The woman with child and she who is in
labor with child, together;
A great company, they will return here.
9 "With weeping they will come,
And by supplication I will lead them;
I will make them walk by streams of
waters,
On a straight path in which they will not
stumble;
For I am a father to Israel,
And Ephraim is My firstborn."

10 ¶ Hear the word of the LORD, O nations,
And declare in the coastlands afar off,
And say, "He who scattered Israel will
gather him
And keep him as a shepherd keeps his
flock."
11 For the LORD has ransomed Jacob
And redeemed him from the hand of
him who was stronger than he.
12 "They will come and shout for joy on the
height of Zion,
And they will be radiant over the bounty
of the LORD—
Over the grain and the new wine and the
oil,
And over the young of the flock and the
herd;
And their life will be like a watered
garden,
And they will never languish again.
13 "Then the virgin will rejoice in the dance,
And the young men and the old,
together,
For I will turn their mourning into joy
And will comfort them and give them
joy for their sorrow.

14 "I will fill the soul of the priests with
    abundance,
And My people will be satisfied with My
    goodness," declares the LORD.

15 ¶ Thus says the LORD,
"A voice is heard in Ramah,
Lamentation *and* bitter weeping.
Rachel is weeping for her children;
She refuses to be comforted for her
    children,
Because they are no more."

31:15 Pain in Redemption

*The Babylonians used Ramah, a town north of
Jerusalem, as a collection point for the captives
they were about to exile. Rachel, the "mother of
Israel," was buried near there, and she is
portrayed as weeping over the exiles. But the
Lord's voice answers hers, offering hope for
their return. Matthew related this verse to King
Herod's slaughter of all baby boys in the
vicinity of Bethlehem (Matthew 2:18). In
deepest grief, God is not absent: He is planning
redemption.*

---

16 Thus says the LORD,
"Restrain your voice from weeping
And your eyes from tears;
For your work will be rewarded,"
    declares the LORD.
"And they will return from the land of the
    enemy.
17 "There is hope for your future," declares
    the LORD,
"And *your* children will return to their
    own territory.
18 "I have surely heard Ephraim grieving,
'You have chastised me, and I was
    chastised,
Like an untrained calf;
Bring me back that I may be restored,
For You are the LORD my God.
19 'For after I turned back, I repented;
And after I was instructed, I smote on
    my thigh;
I was ashamed and also humiliated
Because I bore the reproach of my
    youth.'
20 "Is Ephraim My dear son?
Is he a delightful child?
Indeed, as often as I have spoken against
    him,
I certainly *still* remember him;
Therefore My heart yearns for him;
I will surely have mercy on him,"
    declares the LORD.
21 ¶ "Set up for yourself roadmarks,
Place for yourself guideposts;

Direct your mind to the highway,
The way by which you went.
Return, O virgin of Israel,
Return to these your cities.
22 "How long will you go here and there,
O faithless daughter?
For the LORD has created a new thing in
    the earth—
A woman will encompass a man."

23 ¶ Thus says the LORD of hosts, the God of
Israel, "Once again they will speak this word in the
land of Judah and in its cities when I restore their
fortunes,
'The LORD bless you, O abode of
    righteousness,
O holy hill!'
24 "Judah and all its cities will dwell together in
it, the farmer and they who go about with flocks.
25 "For I satisfy the weary ones and refresh everyone who languishes."
26 At this I awoke and looked, and my sleep
was pleasant to me.

A New Covenant

27 ¶ "Behold, days are coming," declares the
LORD, "when I will sow the house of Israel and the
house of Judah with the seed of man and with the
seed of beast.
28 "As I have watched over them to pluck up, to
break down, to overthrow, to destroy and to bring
disaster, so I will watch over them to build and to
plant," declares the LORD.
29 "In those days they will not say again,
'The fathers have eaten sour grapes,
And the children's teeth are set on edge.'
30 "But everyone will die for his own iniquity;
each man who eats the sour grapes, his teeth will
be set on edge.
31 ¶ "Behold, days are coming," declares the
LORD, "when I will make a new covenant with the
house of Israel and with the house of Judah,
32 not like the covenant which I made with
their fathers in the day I took them by the hand to
bring them out of the land of Egypt, My covenant
which they broke, although I was a husband to
them," declares the LORD.
33 "But this is the covenant which I will make
with the house of Israel after those days," declares
the LORD, "I will put My law within them and on
their heart I will write it; and I will be their God,
and they shall be My people.
34 "They will not teach again, each man his
neighbor and each man his brother, saying, 'Know
the LORD,' for they will all know Me, from the least
of them to the greatest of them," declares the
LORD, "for I will forgive their iniquity, and their
sin I will remember no more."
35 ¶ Thus says the LORD,
Who gives the sun for light by day
And the fixed order of the moon and the
    stars for light by night,

Who stirs up the sea so that its waves
    roar;
  The LORD of hosts is His name:
36 "If this fixed order departs
    From before Me," declares the LORD,
  "Then the offspring of Israel also will
    cease
    From being a nation before Me forever."

31:33–34 Law in Their Hearts

*The book of Hebrews quotes this passage
(Hebrews 8:8–12) in explaining why Christians
no longer live by Old Testament regulations.
The written law was useful, and God-given. But
as the history of Israel proved, it didn't have the
power to transform people's inner attitudes.
Something more was needed. God would have
to change his people from the inside out,
putting his law into their hearts through his
Holy Spirit.*

37 Thus says the LORD,
  "If the heavens above can be measured
    And the foundations of the earth
      searched out below,
  Then I will also cast off all the offspring
    of Israel
  For all that they have done," declares the
    LORD.
38 ¶ "Behold, days are coming," declares the
LORD, "when the city will be rebuilt for the LORD
from the Tower of Hananel to the Corner Gate.
39 "The measuring line will go out farther
straight ahead to the hill Gareb; then it will turn to
Goah.
40 "And the whole valley of the dead bodies and
of the ashes, and all the fields as far as the brook
Kidron, to the corner of the Horse Gate toward
the east, shall be holy to the LORD; it will not be
plucked up or overthrown anymore forever."

Jeremiah Imprisoned

32 The word that came to Jeremiah from the
LORD in the tenth year of Zedekiah king of
Judah, which was the eighteenth year of Nebuchadnezzar.
2 Now at that time the army of the king of
Babylon was besieging Jerusalem, and Jeremiah
the prophet was shut up in the court of the guard,
which *was in* the house of the king of Judah,
3 because Zedekiah king of Judah had shut
him up, saying, "Why do you prophesy, saying,
'Thus says the LORD, "Behold, I am about to give
this city into the hand of the king of Babylon, and
he will take it;
4 and Zedekiah king of Judah will not escape
out of the hand of the Chaldeans, but he will surely be given into the hand of the king of Babylon,

and he will speak with him face to face and see
him eye to eye;
5 and he will take Zedekiah to Babylon, and
he will be there until I visit him," declares the
LORD. "If you fight against the Chaldeans, you will
not succeed" "?"
6 ¶ And Jeremiah said, "The word of the
LORD came to me, saying,
7 'Behold, Hanamel the son of Shallum your
uncle is coming to you, saying, "Buy for yourself
my field which is at Anathoth, for you have the
right of redemption to buy *it*." '

32:7 Bargain Hunting

*Jerusalem, under siege from the most powerful
army in the world, hardly looked like a prime
market for real estate. God told
Jeremiah to buy up family property that was
presently occupied by Babylonians. Though
worthless in the short run, it would grow
valuable when Jeremiah's heirs returned from
exile. Through his outrageous investment,
Jeremiah put his money where his mouth was.
He showed practical faith that God would bring
his people back.*

8 "Then Hanamel my uncle's son came to me
in the court of the guard according to the word of
the LORD and said to me, 'Buy my field, please,
that is at Anathoth, which is in the land of Benjamin; for you have the right of possession and the
redemption is yours; buy *it* for yourself.' Then I
knew that this was the word of the LORD.
9 ¶ "I bought the field which was at Anathoth
from Hanamel my uncle's son, and I weighed out
the silver for him, seventeen shekels of silver.
10 "I signed and sealed the deed, and called in
witnesses, and weighed out the silver on the scales.
11 "Then I took the deeds of purchase, both the
sealed *copy containing* the terms and conditions
and the open *copy;*
12 and I gave the deed of purchase to Baruch
the son of Neriah, the son of Mahseiah, in the
sight of Hanamel my uncle's *son* and in the sight
of the witnesses who signed the deed of purchase,
before all the Jews who were sitting in the court of
the guard.
13 "And I commanded Baruch in their presence, saying,
14 'Thus says the LORD of hosts, the God of
Israel, "Take these deeds, this sealed deed of purchase and this open deed, and put them in an
earthenware jar, that they may last a long time."
15 'For thus says the LORD of hosts, the God of
Israel, "Houses and fields and vineyards will again
be bought in this land." '

Jeremiah Prays and God Explains

16 ¶ "After I had given the deed of purchase to

Baruch the son of Neriah, then I prayed to the LORD, saying,

17 'Ah Lord GOD! Behold, You have made the heavens and the earth by Your great power and by Your outstretched arm! Nothing is too difficult for You,

18 who shows lovingkindness to thousands, but repays the iniquity of fathers into the bosom of their children after them, O great and mighty God. The LORD of hosts is His name;

19 great in counsel and mighty in deed, whose eyes are open to all the ways of the sons of men, giving to everyone according to his ways and according to the fruit of his deeds;

20 who has set signs and wonders in the land of Egypt, *and* even to this day both in Israel and among mankind; and You have made a name for Yourself, as at this day.

21 'You brought Your people Israel out of the land of Egypt with signs and with wonders, and with a strong hand and with an outstretched arm and with great terror;

22 and gave them this land, which You swore to their forefathers to give them, a land flowing with milk and honey.

23 'They came in and took possession of it, but they did not obey Your voice or walk in Your law; they have done nothing of all that You commanded them to do; therefore You have made all this calamity come upon them.

24 'Behold, the siege ramps have reached the city to take it; and the city is given into the hand of the Chaldeans who fight against it, because of the sword, the famine and the pestilence; and what You have spoken has come to pass; and behold, You see *it.*

25 'You have said to me, O Lord GOD, "Buy for yourself the field with money and call in witnesses"—although the city is given into the hand of the Chaldeans.' "

26 ¶ Then the word of the LORD came to Jeremiah, saying,

27 "Behold, I am the LORD, the God of all flesh; is anything too difficult for Me?"

28 Therefore thus says the LORD, "Behold, I am about to give this city into the hand of the Chaldeans and into the hand of Nebuchadnezzar king of Babylon, and he will take it.

29 "The Chaldeans who are fighting against this city will enter and set this city on fire and burn it, with the houses where *people* have offered incense to Baal on their roofs and poured out drink offerings to other gods to provoke Me to anger.

30 "Indeed the sons of Israel and the sons of Judah have been doing only evil in My sight from their youth; for the sons of Israel have been only provoking Me to anger by the work of their hands," declares the LORD.

31 "Indeed this city has been to Me *a provocation of* My anger and My wrath from the day that they built it, even to this day, so that it should be removed from before My face,

32 because of all the evil of the sons of Israel and the sons of Judah which they have done to provoke Me to anger—they, their kings, their leaders, their priests, their prophets, the men of Judah and the inhabitants of Jerusalem.

33 "They have turned *their* back to Me and not *their* face; though *I* taught them, teaching again and again, they would not listen and receive instruction.

34 "But they put their detestable things in the house which is called by My name, to defile it.

35 "They built the high places of Baal that are in the valley of Ben-hinnom to cause their sons and their daughters to pass through *the fire* to Molech, which I had not commanded them nor had it entered My mind that they should do this abomination, to cause Judah to sin.

36 ¶ "Now therefore thus says the LORD God of Israel concerning this city of which you say, 'It is given into the hand of the king of Babylon by sword, by famine and by pestilence.'

37 "Behold, I will gather them out of all the lands to which I have driven them in My anger, in My wrath and in great indignation; and I will bring them back to this place and make them dwell in safety.

38 "They shall be My people, and I will be their God;

39 and I will give them one heart and one way, that they may fear Me always, for their own good and for *the good of* their children after them.

40 "I will make an everlasting covenant with them that I will not turn away from them, to do them good; and I will put the fear of Me in their hearts so that they will not turn away from Me.

32:40 A New Covenant

The foundation of Israel was its covenant with God. It bound both sides together on the basis of clear-cut expectations (see "The Covenant," page 106). Israel had never really lived up to the covenant, however. Here (and in 31:31–34) God promised a new covenant, far better than the old one. It would change the people's thinking. Paul amplified the contrast in 2 Corinthians 2:12–3:18. The new covenant came in Christ.

41 "I will rejoice over them to do them good and will faithfully plant them in this land with all My heart and with all My soul.

42 "For thus says the LORD, 'Just as I brought all this great disaster on this people, so I am going to bring on them all the good that I am promising them.

43 'Fields will be bought in this land of which you say, "It is a desolation, without man or beast; it is given into the hand of the Chaldeans."

44 'Men will buy fields for money, sign and seal deeds, and call in witnesses in the land of Benjamin, in the environs of Jerusalem, in the cities of Judah, in the cities of the hill country, in the cities of the lowland and in the cities of the *a*Negev; for I will restore their fortunes,' declares the LORD."

Restoration Promised

33 Then the word of the LORD came to Jeremiah the second time, while he was still confined in the court of the guard, saying,

2 "Thus says the LORD who made *the earth,* the LORD who formed it to establish it, the LORD is His name,

3 'Call to Me and I will answer you, and I will tell you great and mighty things, which you do not know.'

4 "For thus says the LORD God of Israel concerning the houses of this city, and concerning the houses of the kings of Judah which are broken down *to make a defense* against the siege ramps and against the sword,

5 'While *they* are coming to fight with the Chaldeans and to fill them with the corpses of men whom I have slain in My anger and in My wrath, and I have hidden My face from this city because of all their wickedness:

6 'Behold, I will bring to it health and healing, and I will heal them; and I will reveal to them an abundance of peace and truth.

7 'I will restore the fortunes of Judah and the fortunes of Israel and will rebuild them as they were at first.

8 'I will cleanse them from all their iniquity by which they have sinned against Me, and I will pardon all their iniquities by which they have sinned against Me and by which they have transgressed against Me.

9 '*b*It will be to Me a name of joy, praise and glory before all the nations of the earth which will hear of all the good that I do for them, and they will fear and tremble because of all the good and all the peace that I make for it.'

10 ¶ "Thus says the LORD, 'Yet again there will be heard in this place, of which you say, "It is a waste, without man and without beast," *that is,* in the cities of Judah and in the streets of Jerusalem that are desolate, without man and without inhabitant and without beast,

11 the voice of joy and the voice of gladness, the voice of the bridegroom and the voice of the bride, the voice of those who say,

"Give thanks to the LORD of hosts,
For the LORD is good,
For His lovingkindness is everlasting";
and of those who bring a thank offering into the house of the LORD. For I will restore the fortunes of the land as they were at first,' says the LORD.

12 ¶ "Thus says the LORD of hosts, 'There will again be in this place which is waste, without man

or beast, and in all its cities, a habitation of shepherds who rest their flocks.

13 'In the cities of the hill country, in the cities of the lowland, in the cities of the Negev, in the land of Benjamin, in the environs of Jerusalem and in the cities of Judah, the flocks will again pass under the hands of the one who numbers them,' says the LORD.

The Davidic Kingdom

14 ¶ 'Behold, days are coming,' declares the LORD, 'when I will fulfill the good word which I have spoken concerning the house of Israel and the house of Judah.

15 'In those days and at that time I will cause a righteous Branch of David to spring forth; and He shall execute justice and righteousness on the earth.

16 'In those days Judah will be saved and Jerusalem will dwell in safety; and this is *the name* by which she will be called: the LORD is our righteousness.'

17 "For thus says the LORD, 'David shall never lack a man to sit on the throne of the house of Israel;

18 and the Levitical priests shall never lack a man before Me to offer burnt offerings, to burn grain offerings and to prepare sacrifices continually.'"

33:18 Unchanged Promises

Jerusalem lay in rubble, and survivors must surely have wondered whether God's covenants had been irrevocably broken. In this message through Jeremiah, God says that his promises still stand. Israel will always have an heir of David to provide leadership, and priests to lead in worship. The New Testament, and particularly the book of Hebrews, teaches that these promises are fulfilled forever in Jesus, who is both priest and king.

19 ¶ The word of the LORD came to Jeremiah, saying,

20 "Thus says the LORD, 'If you can break My covenant for the day and My covenant for the night, so that day and night will not be at their appointed time,

21 then My covenant may also be broken with David My servant so that he will not have a son to reign on his throne, and with the Levitical priests, My ministers.

22 'As the host of heaven cannot be counted and the sand of the sea cannot be measured, so I will multiply the descendants of David My servant and the Levites who minister to Me.'"

---

a I.e. South country *b* I.e. This city

23 ¶ And the word of the LORD came to Jeremiah, saying,

24 "Have you not observed what this people have spoken, saying, 'The two families which the LORD chose, He has rejected them'? Thus they despise My people, no longer are they as a nation in their sight.

25 "Thus says the LORD, 'If My covenant *for* day and night *stand* not, *and* the fixed patterns of heaven and earth I have not established,

26 then I would reject the descendants of Jacob and David My servant, not taking from his descendants rulers over the descendants of Abraham, Isaac and Jacob. But I will restore their fortunes and will have mercy on them.' "

A Prophecy against Zedekiah

34 The word which came to Jeremiah from the LORD, when Nebuchadnezzar king of Babylon and all his army, with all the kingdoms of the earth that were under his dominion and all the peoples, were fighting against Jerusalem and against all its cities, saying,

2 "Thus says the LORD God of Israel, 'Go and speak to Zedekiah king of Judah and say to him: "Thus says the LORD, 'Behold, I am giving this city into the hand of the king of Babylon, and he will burn it with fire.

3 'You will not escape from his hand, for you will surely be captured and delivered into his hand; and you will see the king of Babylon eye to eye, and he will speak with you face to face, and you will go to Babylon.' " '

4 "Yet hear the word of the LORD, O Zedekiah king of Judah! Thus says the LORD concerning you, 'You will not die by the sword.

5 'You will die in peace; and as *spices* were burned for your fathers, the former kings who were before you, so they will burn *spices* for you; and they will lament for you, "Alas, lord!" ' For I have spoken the word," declares the LORD.

6 ¶ Then Jeremiah the prophet spoke all these words to Zedekiah king of Judah in Jerusalem

7 when the army of the king of Babylon was fighting against Jerusalem and against all the remaining cities of Judah, *that is,* Lachish and Azekah, for they *alone* remained as fortified cities among the cities of Judah.

8 ¶ The word which came to Jeremiah from the LORD after King Zedekiah had made a covenant with all the people who were in Jerusalem to proclaim release to them:

9 that each man should set free his male servant and each man his female servant, a Hebrew man or a Hebrew woman; so that no one should keep them, a Jew his brother, in bondage.

10 And all the officials and all the people obeyed who had entered into the covenant that each man should set free his male servant and

each man his female servant, so that no one should keep them any longer in bondage; they obeyed, and set *them* free.

11 But afterward they turned around and took back the male servants and the female servants whom they had set free, and brought them into subjection for male servants and for female servants.

12 ¶ Then the word of the LORD came to Jeremiah from the LORD, saying,

13 "Thus says the LORD God of Israel, 'I made a covenant with your forefathers in the day that I brought them out of the land of Egypt, from the house of bondage, saying,

14 "At the end of seven years each of you shall set free his Hebrew brother who has been sold to you and has served you six years, you shall send him out free from you; but your forefathers did not obey Me or incline their ear to Me.

15 "Although recently you *had* turned and done what is right in My sight, each man proclaiming release to his neighbor, and you had made a covenant before Me in the house which is called by My name.

16 "Yet you turned and profaned My name, and each man took back his male servant and each man his female servant whom you had set free according to their desire, and you brought them into subjection to be your male servants and female servants." '

17 ¶ "Therefore thus says the LORD, 'You have not obeyed Me in proclaiming release each man to his brother and each man to his neighbor. Behold, I am proclaiming a release to you,' declares the LORD, 'to the sword, to the pestilence and to the famine; and I will make you a terror to all the kingdoms of the earth.

18 'I will give the men who have transgressed My covenant, who have not fulfilled the words of the covenant which they made before Me, *when* they cut the calf in two and passed between its parts—

19 the officials of Judah and the officials of Jerusalem, the court officers and the priests and all the people of the land who passed between the parts of the calf—

20 I will give them into the hand of their enemies and into the hand of those who seek their life. And their dead bodies will be food for the birds of the sky and the beasts of the earth.

21 'Zedekiah king of Judah and his officials I will give into the hand of their enemies and into the hand of those who seek their life, and into the hand of the army of the king of Babylon which has gone away from you.

22 'Behold, I am going to command,' declares the LORD, 'and I will bring them back to this city; and they will fight against it and take it and burn

it with fire; and I will make the cities of Judah a desolation without inhabitant.'"

The Rechabites' Obedience

35 The word which came to Jeremiah from the LORD in the days of Jehoiakim the son of Josiah, king of Judah, saying,

2 "Go to the house of the Rechabites and speak to them, and bring them into the house of the LORD, into one of the chambers, and give them wine to drink."

3 Then I took Jaazaniah the son of Jeremiah, son of Habazziniah, and his brothers and all his sons and the whole house of the Rechabites,

4 and I brought them into the house of the LORD, into the chamber of the sons of Hanan the son of Igdaliah, the man of God, which was near the chamber of the officials, which was above the chamber of Maaseiah the son of Shallum, the doorkeeper.

5 Then I set before the men of the house of the Rechabites pitchers full of wine and cups; and I said to them, "Drink wine!"

6 But they said, "We will not drink wine, for Jonadab the son of Rechab, our father, commanded us, saying, 'You shall not drink wine, you or your sons, forever.

7 'You shall not build a house, and you shall not sow seed and you shall not plant a vineyard or own one; but in tents you shall dwell all your days, that you may live many days in the land where you sojourn.'

8 "We have obeyed the voice of Jonadab the son of Rechab, our father, in all that he commanded us, not to drink wine all our days, we, our wives, our sons or our daughters,

9 nor to build ourselves houses to dwell in; and we do not have vineyard or field or seed.

10 "We have only dwelt in tents, and have obeyed and have done according to all that Jonadab our father commanded us.

11 "But when Nebuchadnezzar king of Babylon came up against the land, we said, 'Come and let us go to Jerusalem before the army of the Chaldeans and before the army of the Arameans.' So we have dwelt in Jerusalem."

Living Parables
Jeremiah's bizarre protests

OCCASIONALLY THE EVENING NEWS BRINGS us word of someone's bizarre protest. Anti-military demonstrators pour pigs' blood on a sidewalk. Monks set themselves on fire. Environmental activists chain themselves to trees to protest logging. Marchers block the entrance to a nuclear power station. Such protests leave many people feeling uneasy. We can't easily imagine a serious political figure, or a respectable pastor, acting that way.

> "'You have not inclined your ear or listened to Me.'"
> 35:15

But Jeremiah's life was full of such protests, at the express command of God. He made an ox yoke and wore it everywhere until the false prophet Hananiah took it off and broke it in the temple one day. (Jeremiah prophesied Hananiah's death, and within two months he was gone.) Jeremiah's point? He wanted to emphasize the yoke of captivity the king of Babylon would put on Judah's shoulders. The story is in chapters 27–28.

On another occasion (chapter 35) Jeremiah invited a group of well-known nondrinkers into a room in the temple and offered them wine. They refused, and that made another sermon. If they could remember their vows not to drink, then why couldn't the people of Judah and Jerusalem remember the words of the living God?

Nothing Was Too Undignified

Jeremiah bought a beautiful linen sash and buried it in a hole until it was ruined (chapter 13). He invited the rulers of Jerusalem on a trip outside the city, and in the midst of a sermon about God's anger smashed a pot to smithereens (chapter 19). And in his most famous "enacted parable," Jeremiah bought a farm while the Babylonian army was knocking at Jerusalem's door (chapter 32). He might as well have been a Jew buying property within a German concentration camp during World War II, for all the hope he had of using it. But his action demonstrated bold hope. Someday his family would farm there again.

Why such weird activity? It says less about Jeremiah than it does about the God who gave the orders. God would not let go of his people until he had done all in his power to turn them around. Nothing was too undignified; no carnival ploy was too corny. So long as he had the slightest hope of breaking through to them, he would keep shouting.

Life Questions: How does God get through to you? Does he use dramatic means like Jeremiah's or quieter methods?

Judah Rebuked

12 ¶ Then the word of the LORD came to Jeremiah, saying,

13 "Thus says the LORD of hosts, the God of Israel, 'Go and say to the men of Judah and the inhabitants of Jerusalem, "Will you not receive instruction by listening to My words?" declares the LORD.

14 "The words of Jonadab the son of Rechab, which he commanded his sons not to drink wine, are observed. So they do not drink *wine* to this day, for they have obeyed their father's command. But I have spoken to you again and again; yet you have not listened to Me.

35:14 Teetotalers

The Rechabites had a family tradition of not drinking, and nothing Jeremiah said or did could budge them from it. He made their tenacity the basis of a sermon. If family traditions are carried on for generations, why not God's traditions?

15 "Also I have sent to you all My servants the prophets, sending *them* again and again, saying: 'Turn now every man from his evil way and amend your deeds, and do not go after other gods to worship them. Then you will dwell in the land which I have given to you and to your forefathers; but you have not inclined your ear or listened to Me.

16 'Indeed, the sons of Jonadab the son of Rechab have observed the command of their father which he commanded them, but this people has not listened to Me.' " '

17 "Therefore thus says the LORD, the God of hosts, the God of Israel, 'Behold, I am bringing on Judah and on all the inhabitants of Jerusalem all the disaster that I have pronounced against them; because I spoke to them but they did not listen, and I have called them but they did not answer.' "

18 ¶ Then Jeremiah said to the house of the Rechabites, "Thus says the LORD of hosts, the God of Israel, 'Because you have obeyed the command of Jonadab your father, kept all his commands and done according to all that he commanded you;

19 therefore thus says the LORD of hosts, the God of Israel, "Jonadab the son of Rechab shall not lack a man to stand before Me always." ' "

Jeremiah's Scroll Read in the Temple

36 In the fourth year of Jehoiakim the son of Josiah, king of Judah, this word came to Jeremiah from the LORD, saying,

2 "Take a scroll and write on it all the words which I have spoken to you concerning Israel and concerning Judah, and concerning all the nations,

from the day I *first* spoke to you, from the days of Josiah, even to this day.

3 "Perhaps the house of Judah will hear all the calamity which I plan to bring on them, in order that every man will turn from his evil way; then I will forgive their iniquity and their sin."

4 ¶ Then Jeremiah called Baruch the son of Neriah, and Baruch wrote on a scroll at the dictation of Jeremiah all the words of the LORD which He had spoken to him.

5 Jeremiah commanded Baruch, saying, "I am restricted; I cannot go into the house of the LORD.

6 "So you go and read from the scroll which you have written at my dictation the words of the LORD to the people in the LORD's house on a fast day. And also you shall read them to all *the people of* Judah who come from their cities.

7 "Perhaps their supplication will come before the LORD, and everyone will turn from his evil way, for great is the anger and the wrath that the LORD has pronounced against this people."

8 Baruch the son of Neriah did according to all that Jeremiah the prophet commanded him, reading from the book the words of the LORD in the LORD's house.

9 ¶ Now in the fifth year of Jehoiakim the son of Josiah, king of Judah, in the ninth month, all the people in Jerusalem and all the people who came from the cities of Judah to Jerusalem proclaimed a fast before the LORD.

10 Then Baruch read from the book the words of Jeremiah in the house of the LORD in the chamber of Gemariah the son of Shaphan the scribe, in the upper court, at the entry of the New Gate of the LORD's house, to all the people.

11 ¶ Now when Micaiah the son of Gemariah, the son of Shaphan, had heard all the words of the LORD from the book,

12 he went down to the king's house, into the scribe's chamber. And behold, all the officials were sitting there—Elishama the scribe, and Delaiah the son of Shemaiah, and Elnathan the son of Achbor, and Gemariah the son of Shaphan, and Zedekiah the son of Hananiah, and all the *other* officials.

13 Micaiah declared to them all the words that he had heard when Baruch read from the book to the people.

14 Then all the officials sent Jehudi the son of Nethaniah, the son of Shelemiah, the son of Cushi, to Baruch, saying, "Take in your hand the scroll from which you have read to the people and come." So Baruch the son of Neriah took the scroll in his hand and went to them.

15 They said to him, "Sit down, please, and read it to us." So Baruch read it to them.

16 When they had heard all the words, they turned in fear one to another and said to Baruch, "We will surely report all these words to the king."

17 And they asked Baruch, saying, "Tell us,

please, how did you write all these words? *Was it at his dictation?*"

18 Then Baruch said to them, "He dictated all these words to me, and I wrote them with ink on the book."

19 Then the officials said to Baruch, "Go, hide yourself, you and Jeremiah, and do not let anyone know where you are."

The Scroll Is Burned

20 ¶ So they went to the king in the court, but they had deposited the scroll in the chamber of Elishama the scribe, and they reported all the words to the king.

21 Then the king sent Jehudi to get the scroll, and he took it out of the chamber of Elishama the scribe. And Jehudi read it to the king as well as to all the officials who stood beside the king.

22 Now the king was sitting in the winter house in the ninth month, with *a* fire burning in the brazier before him.

23 When Jehudi had read three or four columns, *the king* cut it with a scribe's knife and threw *it* into the fire that was in the brazier, until all the scroll was consumed in the fire that was in the brazier.

24 Yet the king and all his servants who heard all these words were not afraid, nor did they rend their garments.

25 Even though Elnathan and Delaiah and Gemariah pleaded with the king not to burn the scroll, he would not listen to them.

26 And the king commanded Jerahmeel the king's son, Seraiah the son of Azriel, and Shelemiah the son of Abdeel to seize Baruch the scribe and Jeremiah the prophet, but the LORD hid them.

The Scroll Is Replaced

27 ¶ Then the word of the LORD came to Jeremiah after the king had burned the scroll and the words which Baruch had written at the dictation of Jeremiah, saying,

28 "Take again another scroll and write on it all the former words that were on the first scroll which Jehoiakim the king of Judah burned.

29 "And concerning Jehoiakim king of Judah you shall say, 'Thus says the LORD, "You have burned this scroll, saying, 'Why have you written on it that the king of Babylon will certainly come and destroy this land, and will make man and beast to cease from it?'"

30 'Therefore thus says the LORD concerning Jehoiakim king of Judah, "He shall have no one to sit on the throne of David, and his dead body shall be cast out to the heat of the day and the frost of the night.

31 "I will also punish him and his descendants and his servants for their iniquity, and I will bring on them and the inhabitants of Jerusalem and the men of Judah all the calamity that I have declared to them—but they did not listen."'"

32 ¶ Then Jeremiah took another scroll and gave it to Baruch the son of Neriah, the scribe, and he wrote on it at the dictation of Jeremiah all the words of the book which Jehoiakim king of Judah had burned in the fire; and many similar words were added to them.

Jeremiah Warns against Trust in Pharaoh

37 Now Zedekiah the son of Josiah whom Nebuchadnezzar king of Babylon had made king in the land of Judah, reigned as king in place of Coniah the son of Jehoiakim.

2 But neither he nor his servants nor the people of the land listened to the words of the LORD which He spoke through Jeremiah the prophet.

3 ¶ Yet King Zedekiah sent Jehucal the son of Shelemiah, and Zephaniah the son of Maaseiah, the priest, to Jeremiah the prophet, saying, "Please pray to the LORD our God on our behalf."

4 Now Jeremiah was *still* coming in and going out among the people, for they had not *yet* put him in the prison.

5 Meanwhile, Pharaoh's army had set out from Egypt; and when the Chaldeans who had been besieging Jerusalem heard the report about them, they lifted the *siege* from Jerusalem.

37:5 The Siege Lifted

Israel was a small nation, hemmed in by bigger powers such as Egypt and Babylon. Israelite kings often attempted to keep their independence by playing off the big powers against each other. King Zedekiah tried to get Egypt to intervene against Babylon, and during this brief period it seemed he had succeeded. Because the Egyptian army marched out, Nebuchadnezzar lifted his siege of Jerusalem. Jeremiah, who had warned that this foreign policy must ultimately fail, was arrested for treason.

6 ¶ Then the word of the LORD came to Jeremiah the prophet, saying,

7 "Thus says the LORD God of Israel, 'Thus you are to say to the king of Judah, who sent you to Me to inquire of Me: "Behold, Pharaoh's army which has come out for your assistance is going to return to its own land of Egypt.

8 "The Chaldeans will also return and fight against this city, and they will capture it and burn it with fire."'

9 "Thus says the LORD, 'Do not deceive yourselves, saying, "The Chaldeans will surely go away from us," for they will not go.

10 'For even if you had defeated the entire army of Chaldeans who were fighting against you, and there were *only* wounded men left among them, each man in his tent, they would rise up and burn this city with fire.'"

Jeremiah Imprisoned

11 ¶ Now it happened when the army of the Chaldeans had lifted *the siege* from Jerusalem because of Pharaoh's army,

12 that Jeremiah went out from Jerusalem to go to the land of Benjamin in order to take possession of *some* property there among the people.

13 While he was at the Gate of Benjamin, a captain of the guard whose name was Irijah, the son of Shelemiah the son of Hananiah was there; and he arrested Jeremiah the prophet, saying, "You are going over to the Chaldeans!"

14 But Jeremiah said, "A lie! I am not going over to the Chaldeans"; yet he would not listen to him. So Irijah arrested Jeremiah and brought him to the officials.

15 Then the officials were angry at Jeremiah and beat him, and they put him in jail in the house of Jonathan the scribe, which they had made into the prison.

16 For Jeremiah had come into the dungeon, that is, the vaulted cell; and Jeremiah stayed there many days.

17 ¶ Now King Zedekiah sent and took him *out;* and in his palace the king secretly asked him and said, "Is there a word from the LORD?" And Jeremiah said, "There is!" Then he said, "You will be given into the hand of the king of Babylon!"

18 Moreover Jeremiah said to King Zedekiah, "*In* what *way* have I sinned against you, or against your servants, or against this people, that you have put me in prison?

19 "Where then are your prophets who prophesied to you, saying, 'The king of Babylon will not come against you or against this land'?

20 "But now, please listen, O my lord the king; please let my petition come before you and do not make me return to the house of Jonathan the scribe, that I may not die there."

21 Then King Zedekiah gave commandment, and they committed Jeremiah to the court of the guardhouse and gave him a loaf of bread daily from the bakers' street, until all the bread in the city was gone. So Jeremiah remained in the court of the guardhouse.

Jeremiah Thrown into the Cistern

38 Now Shephatiah the son of Mattan, and Gedaliah the son of Pashhur, and Jucal the son of Shelemiah, and Pashhur the son of Malchijah heard the words that Jeremiah was speaking to all the people, saying,

2 "Thus says the LORD, 'He who stays in this city will die by the sword and by famine and by pestilence, but he who goes out to the Chaldeans will live and have his *own* life as booty and stay alive.'

3 "Thus says the LORD, 'This city will certainly be given into the hand of the army of the king of Babylon and he will capture it.' "

4 Then the officials said to the king, "Now let this man be put to death, inasmuch as he is discouraging the men of war who are left in this city and all the people, by speaking such words to them; for this man is not seeking the well-being of this people but rather their harm."

5 So King Zedekiah said, "Behold, he is in your hands; for the king can *do* nothing against you."

6 Then they took Jeremiah and cast him into the cistern *of* Malchijah the king's son, which was in the court of the guardhouse; and they let Jeremiah down with ropes. Now in the cistern there was no water but only mud, and Jeremiah sank into the mud.

7 But Ebed-melech the Ethiopian, a eunuch, while he was in the king's palace, heard that they had put Jeremiah into the cistern. Now the king was sitting in the Gate of Benjamin;

8 and Ebed-melech went out from the king's palace and spoke to the king, saying,

9 "My lord the king, these men have acted wickedly in all that they have done to Jeremiah the prophet whom they have cast into the cistern; and he will die right where he is because of the famine, for there is no more bread in the city."

38:9 Close to Death

Jeremiah was arrested during the long, final siege of Jerusalem—a time when food became so short some Israelites resorted to cannibalism. Imprisoned at the bottom of an empty cistern, the prophet could easily have starved to death. Interestingly, only a foreigner cared enough to go to the king and convince him to let Jeremiah out. For this, Ebed-melech received a special message from God (39:15–18).

10 Then the king commanded Ebed-melech the Ethiopian, saying, "Take thirty men from here under your authority and bring up Jeremiah the prophet from the cistern before he dies."

11 So Ebed-melech took the men under his authority and went into the king's palace to *a place* beneath the storeroom and took from there worn-out clothes and worn-out rags and let them down by ropes into the cistern to Jeremiah.

12 Then Ebed-melech the Ethiopian said to Jeremiah, "Now put these worn-out clothes and rags under your armpits under the ropes"; and Jeremiah did so.

13 So they pulled Jeremiah up with the ropes and lifted him out of the cistern, and Jeremiah stayed in the court of the guardhouse.

14 ¶ Then King Zedekiah sent and had Jeremiah the prophet brought to him at the third entrance that is in the house of the LORD; and the king said to Jeremiah, "I am going to ask you something; do not hide anything from me."

15 Then Jeremiah said to Zedekiah, "If I tell you, will you not certainly put me to death? Besides, if I give you advice, you will not listen to me."

16 But King Zedekiah swore to Jeremiah in secret saying, "As the LORD lives, who made this life for us, surely I will not put you to death nor will I give you over to the hand of these men who are seeking your life."

Interview with Zedekiah

17 ¶ Then Jeremiah said to Zedekiah, "Thus says the LORD God of hosts, the God of Israel, 'If you will indeed go out to the officers of the king of Babylon, then you will live, this city will not be burned with fire, and you and your household will survive.

18 'But if you will not go out to the officers of the king of Babylon, then this city will be given over to the hand of the Chaldeans; and they will burn it with fire, and you yourself will not escape from their hand.' "

19 Then King Zedekiah said to Jeremiah, "I dread the Jews who have gone over to the Chaldeans, for they may give me over into their hand and they will abuse me."

20 But Jeremiah said, "They will not give you over. Please obey the LORD in what I am saying to you, that it may go well with you and you may live.

21 "But if you keep refusing to go out, this is the word which the LORD has shown me:

22 'Then behold, all of the women who have been left in the palace of the king of Judah are going to be brought out to the officers of the king of Babylon; and those women will say,

"Your close friends
Have misled and overpowered you;
While your feet were sunk in the mire,
They turned back."

23 'They will also bring out all your wives and your sons to the Chaldeans, and you yourself will not escape from their hand, but will be seized by the hand of the king of Babylon, and this city will be burned with fire.' "

24 ¶ Then Zedekiah said to Jeremiah, "Let no man know about these words and you will not die.

25 "But if the officials hear that I have talked with you and come to you and say to you, 'Tell us now what you said to the king and what the king said to you; do not hide it from us and we will not put you to death,'

26 then you are to say to them, 'I was presenting my petition before the king, not to make me return to the house of Jonathan to die there.' "

27 Then all the officials came to Jeremiah and questioned him. So he reported to them in accordance with all these words which the king had commanded; and they ceased speaking with him, since the conversation had not been overheard.

28 So Jeremiah stayed in the court of the guardhouse until the day that Jerusalem was captured.

Jerusalem Captured

39 Now when Jerusalem was captured in the ninth year of Zedekiah king of Judah, in the tenth month, Nebuchadnezzar king of Babylon and all his army came to Jerusalem and laid siege to it;

2 in the eleventh year of Zedekiah, in the fourth month, in the ninth *day* of the month, the city *wall* was breached.

3 Then all the officials of the king of Babylon came in and sat down at the Middle Gate: Nergal-sar-ezer, Samgar-nebu, Sar-sekim the Rab-saris, Nergal-sar-ezer *the* Rab-mag, and all the rest of the officials of the king of Babylon.

4 When Zedekiah the king of Judah and all the men of war saw them, they fled and went out of the city at night by way of the king's garden through the gate between the two walls; and he went out toward the a Arabah.

5 But the army of the Chaldeans pursued them and overtook Zedekiah in the plains of Jericho; and they seized him and brought him up to Nebuchadnezzar king of Babylon at Riblah in the land of Hamath, and he passed sentence on him.

6 Then the king of Babylon slew the sons of Zedekiah before his eyes at Riblah; the king of Babylon also slew all the nobles of Judah.

7 He then blinded Zedekiah's eyes and bound him in fetters of bronze to bring him to Babylon.

8 The Chaldeans also burned with fire the king's palace and the houses of the people, and they broke down the walls of Jerusalem.

9 As for the rest of the people who were left in the city, the deserters who had gone over to him and the rest of the people who remained, Nebuzaradan the captain of the bodyguard carried *them* into exile in Babylon.

10 But some of the poorest people who had nothing, Nebuzaradan the captain of the bodyguard left behind in the land of Judah, and gave them vineyards and fields at that time.

Jeremiah Spared

11 ¶ Now Nebuchadnezzar king of Babylon gave orders about Jeremiah through Nebuzaradan the captain of the bodyguard, saying,

12 "Take him and look after him, and do nothing harmful to him, but rather deal with him just as he tells you."

13 So Nebuzaradan the captain of the bodyguard sent *word*, along with Nebushazban the Rab-saris, and Nergal-sar-ezer the Rab-mag, and all the leading officers of the king of Babylon;

14 they even sent and took Jeremiah out of the court of the guardhouse and entrusted him to Gedaliah, the son of Ahikam, the son of Shaphan,

---

a I.e. Jordan valley

to take him home. So he stayed among the people.

15 ¶ Now the word of the LORD had come to Jeremiah while he was confined in the court of the guardhouse, saying,

16 "Go and speak to Ebed-melech the Ethiopian, saying, 'Thus says the LORD of hosts, the God of Israel, "Behold, I am about to bring My words on this city for disaster and not for prosperity; and they will take place before you on that day.

17 "But I will deliver you on that day," declares the LORD, "and you will not be given into the hand of the men whom you dread.

18 "For I will certainly rescue you, and you will not fall by the sword; but you will have your *own* life as booty, because you have trusted in Me," declares the LORD.' "

Jeremiah Remains in Judah

40 The word which came to Jeremiah from the LORD after Nebuzaradan captain of the bodyguard had released him from Ramah, when he had taken him bound in chains among all the exiles of Jerusalem and Judah who were being exiled to Babylon.

2 Now the captain of the bodyguard had taken Jeremiah and said to him, "The LORD your God promised this calamity against this place;

3 and the LORD has brought *it* on and done just as He promised. Because you *people* sinned against the LORD and did not listen to His voice, therefore this thing has happened to you.

4 "But now, behold, I am freeing you today from the chains which are on your hands. If you would prefer to come with me to Babylon, come *along*, and I will look after you; but if you would prefer not to come with me to Babylon, never mind. Look, the whole land is before you; go wherever it seems good and right for you to go."

5 As Jeremiah was still not going back, *he said*, "Go on back then to Gedaliah the son of Ahikam, the son of Shaphan, whom the king of Babylon has appointed over the cities of Judah, and stay with him among the people; or else go anywhere it seems right for you to go." So the captain of the bodyguard gave him a ration and a gift and let him go.

6 Then Jeremiah went to Mizpah to Gedaliah the son of Ahikam and stayed with him among the people who were left in the land.

7 ¶ Now all the commanders of the forces that were in the field, they and their men, heard that the king of Babylon had appointed Gedaliah the son of Ahikam over the land and that he had put him in charge of the men, women and children, those of the poorest of the land who had not been exiled to Babylon.

8 So they came to Gedaliah at Mizpah, along with Ishmael the son of Nethaniah, and Johanan and Jonathan the sons of Kareah, and Seraiah the son of Tanhumeth, and the sons of Ephai the Netophathite, and Jezaniah the son of the Maacathite, *both* they and their men.

9 Then Gedaliah the son of Ahikam, the son of Shaphan, swore to them and to their men, saying, "Do not be afraid of serving the Chaldeans; stay in the land and serve the king of Babylon, that it may go well with you.

10 "Now as for me, behold, I am going to stay at Mizpah to stand *for you* before the Chaldeans who come to us; but as for you, gather in wine and summer fruit and oil and put *them* in your *storage* vessels, and live in your cities that you have taken over."

11 Likewise, also all the Jews who were in Moab and among the sons of Ammon and in Edom and who were in all the *other* countries, heard that the king of Babylon had left a remnant for Judah, and that he had appointed over them Gedaliah the son of Ahikam, the son of Shaphan.

12 Then all the Jews returned from all the places to which they had been driven away and came to the land of Judah, to Gedaliah at Mizpah, and gathered in wine and summer fruit in great abundance.

13 ¶ Now Johanan the son of Kareah and all the commanders of the forces that were in the field came to Gedaliah at Mizpah

14 and said to him, "Are you well aware that Baalis the king of the sons of Ammon has sent Ishmael the son of Nethaniah to take your life?" But Gedaliah the son of Ahikam did not believe them.

15 Then Johanan the son of Kareah spoke secretly to Gedaliah in Mizpah, saying, "Let me go and kill Ishmael the son of Nethaniah, and not a man will know! Why should he take your life, so that all the Jews who are gathered to you would be

scattered and the remnant of Judah would perish?"

16 But Gedaliah the son of Ahikam said to Johanan the son of Kareah, "Do not do this thing, for you are telling a lie about Ishmael."

Gedaliah Is Murdered

41 In the seventh month Ishmael the son of Nethaniah, the son of Elishama, of the royal family and *one* of the chief officers of the king, along with ten men, came to Mizpah to Gedaliah the son of Ahikam. While they were eating bread together there in Mizpah,

2 Ishmael the son of Nethaniah and the ten men who were with him arose and struck down Gedaliah the son of Ahikam, the son of Shaphan, with the sword and put to death the one whom the king of Babylon had appointed over the land.

3 Ishmael also struck down all the Jews who were with him, *that is* with Gedaliah at Mizpah, and the Chaldeans who were found there, the men of war.

4 ¶ Now it happened on the next day after the killing of Gedaliah, when no one knew about *it,*

5 that eighty men came from Shechem, from Shiloh, and from Samaria with their beards shaved off and their clothes torn and their bodies gashed, having grain offerings and incense in their hands to bring to the house of the LORD.

6 Then Ishmael the son of Nethaniah went out from Mizpah to meet them, weeping as he went; and as he met them, he said to them, "Come to Gedaliah the son of Ahikam!"

7 Yet it turned out that as soon as they came inside the city, Ishmael the son of Nethaniah and the men that were with him slaughtered them *and cast them* into the cistern.

8 But ten men who were found among them said to Ishmael, "Do not put us to death; for we have stores of wheat, barley, oil and honey hidden in the field." So he refrained and did not put them to death along with their companions.

9 ¶ Now as for the cistern where Ishmael had cast all the corpses of the men whom he had struck down because of Gedaliah, it was the one that King Asa had made on account of Baasha, king of Israel; Ishmael the son of Nethaniah filled it with the slain.

10 Then Ishmael took captive all the remnant of the people who were in Mizpah, the king's daughters and all the people who were left in Mizpah, whom Nebuzaradan the captain of the bodyguard had put under the charge of Gedaliah the son of Ahikam; thus Ishmael the son of Nethaniah took them captive and proceeded to cross over to the sons of Ammon.

Johanan Rescues the People

11 ¶ But Johanan the son of Kareah and all the commanders of the forces that were with him heard of all the evil that Ishmael the son of Nethaniah had done.

12 So they took all the men and went to fight with Ishmael the son of Nethaniah and they found him by the great pool that is in Gibeon.

13 Now as soon as all the people who were with Ishmael saw Johanan the son of Kareah and the commanders of the forces that were with him, they were glad.

14 So all the people whom Ishmael had taken captive from Mizpah turned around and came back, and went to Johanan the son of Kareah.

15 But Ishmael the son of Nethaniah escaped from Johanan with eight men and went to the sons of Ammon.

16 Then Johanan the son of Kareah and all the commanders of the forces that were with him took from Mizpah all the remnant of the people whom he had recovered from Ishmael the son of Nethaniah, after he had struck down Gedaliah the son of Ahikam, *that is,* the men who were soldiers, *the* women, *the* children, and *the* eunuchs, whom he had brought back from Gibeon.

17 And they went and stayed in Geruth Chimham, which is beside Bethlehem, in order to proceed into Egypt

18 because of the Chaldeans; for they were afraid of them, since Ishmael the son of Nethaniah had struck down Gedaliah the son of Ahikam, whom the king of Babylon had appointed over the land.

Warning against Going to Egypt

42 Then all the commanders of the forces, Johanan the son of Kareah, Jezaniah the son of Hoshaiah, and all the people both small and great approached

2 and said to Jeremiah the prophet, "Please let our petition come before you, and pray for us to the LORD your God, *that is* for all this remnant; because we are left *but* a few out of many, as your own eyes *now* see us,

3 that the LORD your God may tell us the way in which we should walk and the thing that we should do."

4 Then Jeremiah the prophet said to them, "I have heard *you.* Behold, I am going to pray to the LORD your God in accordance with your words; and I will tell you the whole message which the LORD will answer you. I will not keep back a word from you."

5 Then they said to Jeremiah, "May the LORD be a true and faithful witness against us if we do not act in accordance with the whole message with which the LORD your God will send you to us.

6 "Whether *it* is pleasant or unpleasant, we will listen to the voice of the LORD our God to whom we are sending you, so that it may go well with us when we listen to the voice of the LORD our God."

7 ¶ Now at the end of ten days the word of the LORD came to Jeremiah.

8 Then he called for Johanan the son of Kareah and all the commanders of the forces that were with him, and for all the people both small and great,

9 and said to them, "Thus says the LORD the God of Israel, to whom you sent me to present your petition before Him:

10 'If you will indeed stay in this land, then I will build you up and not tear you down, and I will plant you and not uproot you; for I will relent concerning the calamity that I have inflicted on you.

11 'Do not be afraid of the king of Babylon, whom you are *now* fearing; do not be afraid of him,' declares the LORD, 'for I am with you to save you and deliver you from his hand.

12 'I will also show you compassion, so that he will have compassion on you and restore you to your own soil.

13 'But if you are going to say, "We will not stay in this land," so as not to listen to the voice of the LORD your God,

14 saying, "No, but we will go to the land of Egypt, where we will not see war or hear the sound of a trumpet or hunger for bread, and we will stay there";

15 then in that case listen to the word of the LORD, O remnant of Judah. Thus says the LORD of hosts, the God of Israel, "If you really set your mind to enter Egypt and go in to reside there,

16 then the sword, which you are afraid of, will overtake you there in the land of Egypt; and the famine, about which you are anxious, will follow closely after you there *in* Egypt, and you will die there.

17 "So all the men who set their mind to go to Egypt to reside there will die by the sword, by famine and by pestilence; and they will have no survivors or refugees from the calamity that I am going to bring on them."'"

18 ¶ For thus says the LORD of hosts, the God of Israel, "As My anger and wrath have been poured out on the inhabitants of Jerusalem, so My wrath will be poured out on you when you enter Egypt. And you will become a curse, an object of horror, an imprecation and a reproach; and you will see this place no more."

19 The LORD has spoken to you, O remnant of Judah, "Do not go into Egypt!" You should clearly understand that today I have testified against you.

20 For you have *only* deceived yourselves; for it is you who sent me to the LORD your God, saying, "Pray for us to the LORD our God; and whatever the LORD our God says, tell us so, and we will do it."

21 So I have told you today, but you have not obeyed the LORD your God, even in whatever He has sent me to *tell* you.

22 Therefore you should now clearly understand that you will die by the sword, by famine and by pestilence, in the place where you wish to go to reside.

In Egypt Jeremiah Warns of Judgment

43 But as soon as Jeremiah, whom the LORD their God had sent, had finished telling all the people all the words of the LORD their God—that is, all these words—

2 Azariah the son of Hoshaiah, and Johanan the son of Kareah, and all the arrogant men said to Jeremiah, "You are telling a lie! The LORD our God has not sent you to say, 'You are not to enter Egypt to reside there';

3 but Baruch the son of Neriah is inciting you against us to give us over into the hand of the Chaldeans, so they will put us to death or exile us to Babylon."

43:3 Closed Minds

Jeremiah was kidnapped by the few Israelites remaining in Jerusalem. Fearful that the Babylonians would blame them for the governor's murder, they took Jeremiah with them as they headed for Egypt. They stopped near Bethlehem to ask Jeremiah if they were doing the right thing. When he told them God wanted them to go back, they called him a liar. Jeremiah was disbelieved from the beginning to the end of his ministry, even by those who had seen some of his predictions come true.

4 So Johanan the son of Kareah and all the commanders of the forces, and all the people, did not obey the voice of the LORD to stay in the land of Judah.

5 But Johanan the son of Kareah and all the commanders of the forces took the entire remnant of Judah who had returned from all the nations to which they had been driven away, in order to reside in the land of Judah—

6 the men, the women, the children, the king's daughters and every person that Nebuzaradan the captain of the bodyguard had left with Gedaliah the son of Ahikam and grandson of Shaphan, together with Jeremiah the prophet and Baruch the son of Neriah—

7 and they entered the land of Egypt (for they did not obey the voice of the LORD) and went in as far as Tahpanhes.

8 ¶ Then the word of the LORD came to Jeremiah in Tahpanhes, saying,

9 "Take *some* large stones in your hands and hide them in the mortar in the brick *terrace* which is at the entrance of Pharaoh's palace in Tahpanhes, in the sight of some *of the* Jews;

10 and say to them, 'Thus says the LORD of hosts, the God of Israel, "Behold, I am going to send and get Nebuchadnezzar the king of Babylon, My servant, and I am going to set his throne

right over these stones that I have hidden; and he will spread his canopy over them.

11 "He will also come and strike the land of Egypt; those who are *meant* for death *will be given over* to death, and those for captivity to captivity, and those for the sword to the sword.

12 "And I shall set fire to the temples of the gods of Egypt, and he will burn them and take them captive. So he will wrap himself with the land of Egypt as a shepherd wraps himself with his garment, and he will depart from there safely.

13 "He will also shatter the obelisks of Heliopolis, which is in the land of Egypt; and the temples of the gods of Egypt he will burn with fire." ' "

Conquest of Egypt Predicted

44 The word that came to Jeremiah for all the Jews living in the land of Egypt, those who were living in Migdol, Tahpanhes, Memphis, and the land of Pathros, saying,

2 "Thus says the LORD of hosts, the God of Israel, 'You yourselves have seen all the calamity that I have brought on Jerusalem and all the cities of Judah; and behold, this day they are in ruins and no one lives in them,

3 because of their wickedness which they committed so as to provoke Me to anger by continuing to burn sacrifices *and* to serve other gods whom they had not known, *neither* they, you, nor your fathers.

4 'Yet I sent you all My servants the prophets, again and again, saying, "Oh, do not do this abominable thing which I hate."

5 'But they did not listen or incline their ears to turn from their wickedness, so as not to burn sacrifices to other gods.

6 'Therefore My wrath and My anger were poured out and burned in the cities of Judah and in the streets of Jerusalem, so they have become a ruin and a desolation as it is this day.

7 'Now then thus says the LORD God of hosts, the God of Israel, "Why are you doing great harm to yourselves, so as to cut off from you man and woman, child and infant, from among Judah, leaving yourselves without remnant,

8 provoking Me to anger with the works of your hands, burning sacrifices to other gods in the land of Egypt, where you are entering to reside, so that you might be cut off and become a curse and a reproach among all the nations of the earth?

9 "Have you forgotten the wickedness of your fathers, the wickedness of the kings of Judah, and the wickedness of their wives, your own wickedness, and the wickedness of your wives, which they committed in the land of Judah and in the streets of Jerusalem?

10 "But they have not become contrite even to this day, nor have they feared nor walked in My law or My statutes, which I have set before you and before your fathers." '

11 ¶ "Therefore thus says the LORD of hosts, the God of Israel, 'Behold, I am going to set My face against you for woe, even to cut off all Judah.

12 'And I will take away the remnant of Judah who have set their mind on entering the land of Egypt to reside there, and they will all meet their end in the land of Egypt; they will fall by the sword *and* meet their end by famine. Both small and great will die by the sword and famine; and they will become a curse, an object of horror, an imprecation and a reproach.

13 'And I will punish those who live in the land of Egypt, as I have punished Jerusalem, with the sword, with famine and with pestilence.

14 'So there will be no refugees or survivors for the remnant of Judah who have entered the land of Egypt to reside there and then to return to the land of Judah, to which they are longing to return and live; for none will return except *a few* refugees.' "

15 ¶ Then all the men who were aware that their wives were burning sacrifices to other gods, along with all the women who were standing by, *as* a large assembly, including all the people who were living in Pathros in the land of Egypt, responded to Jeremiah, saying,

16 "As for the message that you have spoken to us in the name of the LORD, we are not going to listen to you!

17 "But rather we will certainly carry out every word that has proceeded from our mouths, by burning sacrifices to the queen of heaven and pouring out drink offerings to her, just as we ourselves, our forefathers, our kings and our princes did in the cities of Judah and in the streets of Jerusalem; for *then* we had plenty of food and were well off and saw no misfortune.

18 "But since we stopped burning sacrifices to the queen of heaven and pouring out drink offerings to her, we have lacked everything and have met our end by the sword and by famine."

44:18 Queen of Heaven

"Queen of heaven" was a title for Ishtar, a Babylonian goddess of fertility. Israelites— women especially—had worshiped her for a very long time, until the revival sparked by King Josiah put a stop to the practice (2 Kings 22). Now, about 35 years after Josiah's campaign, Israelites blamed their downfall on his reform. Jeremiah tried to set the record straight: It was persistence in pagan worship that had led to their destruction.

19 "And," *said the women,* "when we were burning sacrifices to the queen of heaven and were pouring out drink offerings to her, was it without our husbands that we made for her *sacrificial* cakes in her image and poured out drink offerings to her?"

Calamity for the Jews

20 ¶ Then Jeremiah said to all the people, to the men and women—even to all the people who were giving him *such* an answer—saying,

21 "As for the smoking sacrifices that you burned in the cities of Judah and in the streets of Jerusalem, you and your forefathers, your kings and your princes, and the people of the land, did not the LORD remember them and did not *all this* come into His mind?

22 "So the LORD was no longer able to endure *it*, because of the evil of your deeds, because of the abominations which you have committed; thus your land has become a ruin, an object of horror and a curse, without an inhabitant, as *it is* this day.

23 "Because you have burned sacrifices and have sinned against the LORD and not obeyed the voice of the LORD or walked in His law, His statutes or His testimonies, therefore this calamity has befallen you, as *it has* this day."

24 ¶ Then Jeremiah said to all the people, including all the women, "Hear the word of the LORD, all Judah who are in the land of Egypt,

25 thus says the LORD of hosts, the God of Israel, as follows: 'As for you and your wives, you have spoken with your mouths and fulfilled *it* with your hands, saying, "We will certainly perform our vows that we have vowed, to burn sacrifices to the queen of heaven and pour out drink offerings to her." Go ahead and confirm your vows, and certainly perform your vows!'

26 "Nevertheless hear the word of the LORD, all Judah who are living in the land of Egypt, 'Behold, I have sworn by My great name,' says the LORD, 'never shall My name be invoked again by the mouth of any man of Judah in all the land of Egypt, saying, "As the Lord GOD lives."

27 'Behold, I am watching over them for harm and not for good, and all the men of Judah who are in the land of Egypt will meet their end by the sword and by famine until they are completely gone.

28 'Those who escape the sword will return out of the land of Egypt to the land of Judah few in number. Then all the remnant of Judah who have gone to the land of Egypt to reside there will know whose word will stand, Mine or theirs.

29 'This will be the sign to you,' declares the LORD, 'that I am going to punish you in this place, so that you may know that My words will surely stand against you for harm.'

30 "Thus says the LORD, 'Behold, I am going to give over Pharaoh Hophra king of Egypt to the hand of his enemies, to the hand of those who seek his life, just as I gave over Zedekiah king of Judah to the hand of Nebuchadnezzar king of Babylon, *who was* his enemy and was seeking his life.'"

Message to Baruch

45 *This is* the message which Jeremiah the prophet spoke to Baruch the son of Neriah, when he had written down these words in a book at Jeremiah's dictation, in the fourth year of Jehoiakim the son of Josiah, king of Judah, saying:

2 "Thus says the LORD the God of Israel to you, O Baruch:

3 'You said, "Ah, woe is me! For the LORD has added sorrow to my pain; I am weary with my groaning and have found no rest." '

4 "Thus you are to say to him, 'Thus says the LORD, "Behold, what I have built I am about to tear down, and what I have planted I am about to uproot, that is, the whole land."

5 'But you, are you seeking great things for yourself? Do not seek *them;* for behold, I am going to bring disaster on all flesh,' declares the LORD, 'but I will give your life to you as booty in all the places where you may go.' "

Defeat of Pharaoh Foretold

46 That which came as the word of the LORD to Jeremiah the prophet concerning the nations.

2 ¶ To Egypt, concerning the army of Pharaoh Neco king of Egypt, which was by the Euphrates River at Carchemish, which Nebuchadnezzar king of Babylon defeated in the fourth year of Jehoiakim the son of Josiah, king of Judah:

3 "Line up the shield and buckler,
And draw near for the battle!
4 "Harness the horses,
And mount the steeds,
And take your stand with helmets *on!*
Polish the spears,
Put on the scale-armor!
5 "Why have I seen *it?*
They are terrified,
They are drawing back,
And their mighty men are defeated
And have taken refuge in flight,
Without facing back;
Terror is on every side!"
Declares the LORD.
6 Let not the swift man flee,
Nor the mighty man escape;
In the north beside the river Euphrates
They have stumbled and fallen.
7 Who is this that rises like the Nile,
Like the rivers whose waters surge about?
8 Egypt rises like the Nile,
Even like the rivers whose waters surge
about;
And He has said, "I will rise and cover
that land;
I will surely destroy the city and its
inhabitants."
9 Go up, you horses, and drive madly, you
chariots,
That the mighty men may march
forward:

Ethiopia and Put, that handle the shield,
And the Lydians, that handle *and* bend
the bow.

10 For that day belongs to the Lord GOD of
hosts,
A day of vengeance, so as to avenge
Himself on His foes;
And the sword will devour and be
satiated
And drink its fill of their blood;
For there will be a slaughter for the Lord
GOD of hosts,
In the land of the north by the river
Euphrates.

11 Go up to Gilead and obtain balm,
O virgin daughter of Egypt!
In vain have you multiplied remedies;
There is no healing for you.

12 The nations have heard of your shame,
And the earth is full of your cry *of
distress;*
For one warrior has stumbled over
another,
And both of them have fallen down
together.

13 ¶ *This is* the message which the LORD spoke
to Jeremiah the prophet about the coming of Neb-

uchadnezzar king of Babylon to smite the land of
Egypt:

14 "Declare in Egypt and proclaim in
Migdol,
Proclaim also in Memphis and
Tahpanhes;
Say, 'Take your stand and get yourself
ready,
For the sword has devoured those
around you.'

15 "Why have your mighty ones become
prostrate?
They do not stand because the LORD has
thrust them down.

16 "They have repeatedly stumbled;
Indeed, they have fallen one against
another.
Then they said, 'Get up! And let us go
back
To our own people and our native
land
Away from the sword of the oppressor.'

17 "They cried there, 'Pharaoh king of Egypt
is but a big noise;
He has let the appointed time pass by!'

18 "As I live," declares the King
Whose name is the LORD of hosts,

World at War
While nations battle, God is in control

> The sword will devour and be satiated and drink its fill of their blood.
> 46:10

FLIP ON THE TV NEWS. Scenes from around the world flash across the screen. In the Middle East, a bomb explodes and a building collapses. Bodies lie in the gutter. Women howl with anguish over their dead.

Seconds later you are in Africa. Revolutionaries, rifles brandished over their heads, march through captured streets. The camera zeroes in on the crumpled body of their former president.

The scene shifts to a Central American capital. Sirens scream around a burning restaurant while stretcher-bearers carry out the moaning victims of a drug-lord attack. Next, in Africa again, starving children grimace at you, too far gone to beg for food. Then you see snatches of violence in United States ghettoes, scenes of ethnic unrest in Europe, and political protests in Tibet and India. The world is whirling out of control. Your mind cannot take it in; one disaster muddles with another.

God Is in Control

In chapters 46 to 50, Jeremiah gives a similar portrait of the world. We flash by imagination from one country to the next. We smell the rotting bodies; we hear the exultant cries of conquerors. Jeremiah shows, in vivid color, a world as frightening as ours.

But there is a difference. TV news leaves viewers with a dizzy feeling that chaos reigns. But Jeremiah's vision shows, paradoxically, that God is in control. Through these disasters God punishes those who have opposed his will. As Israel's neighbors are destroyed, exiled Jews are freed to return to their land. History is not just "one thing after another." God gives it a sense of direction.

Jeremiah delivered his longest and most biting message to Babylon, Judah's conqueror. Their sheer arrogance, their assumption that they could do whatever they liked, drew God's fury. To a lesser degree, other countries followed the same pattern. God did not judge them by his law, because they never knew it. He judged them for their pride. They ought to have shown humility before God.

Life Questions: Can you discern any pattern or purpose to the violence in the world today?

"Surely one shall come *who looms up* like
    Tabor among the mountains,
Or like Carmel by the sea.
19 "Make your baggage ready for exile,
    O daughter dwelling in Egypt,
For Memphis will become a desolation;
    It will even be burned down *and* bereft
        of inhabitants.
20 "Egypt is a pretty heifer,
    But a horsefly is coming from the
        north—it is coming!
21 "Also her mercenaries in her midst
    Are like fattened calves,
For even they too have turned back *and*
    have fled away together;
They did not stand *their ground.*
For the day of their calamity has come
    upon them,
The time of their punishment.
22 "Its sound moves along like a serpent;
    For they move on like an army
And come to her as woodcutters with
    axes.
23 "They have cut down her forest," declares
    the LORD;
"Surely it will no *more* be found,
    Even though they are *now* more
        numerous than locusts
And are without number.
24 "The daughter of Egypt has been put to
    shame,
Given over to the power of the people of
    the north."

25 ¶ The LORD of hosts, the God of Israel, says,
"Behold, I am going to punish Amon of Thebes,
and Pharaoh, and Egypt along with her gods and
her kings, even Pharaoh and those who trust in
him.
26 "I shall give them over to the power of those
who are seeking their lives, even into the hand of
Nebuchadnezzar king of Babylon and into the
hand of his officers. Afterwards, however, it will be
inhabited as in the days of old," declares the LORD.
27 ¶ "But as for you, O Jacob My servant,
    do not fear,
Nor be dismayed, O Israel!
For, see, I am going to save you from
    afar,
And your descendants from the land of
    their captivity;
And Jacob will return and be
    undisturbed
And secure, with no one making *him*
    tremble.
28 "O Jacob My servant, do not fear,"
    declares the LORD,
"For I am with you.
For I will make a full end of all the
    nations
Where I have driven you,

Yet I will not make a full end of you;
But I will correct you properly
And by no means leave you
    unpunished."

Prophecy against Philistia

47 That which came as the word of the LORD
    to Jeremiah the prophet concerning the
Philistines, before Pharaoh conquered Gaza.
2 Thus says the LORD:
"Behold, waters are going to rise from the
    north
And become an overflowing torrent,
And overflow the land and all its fullness,
The city and those who live in it;
And the men will cry out,
And every inhabitant of the land will
    wail.
3 "Because of the noise of the galloping
    hoofs of his stallions,
The tumult of his chariots, *and* the
    rumbling of his wheels,
The fathers have not turned back for
    their children,
Because of the limpness of *their* hands,
4 On account of the day that is coming
    To destroy all the Philistines,
To cut off from Tyre and Sidon
    Every ally that is left;
For the LORD is going to destroy the
    Philistines,
The remnant of the coastland of Caphtor.
5 "Baldness has come upon Gaza;
    Ashkelon has been ruined.
O remnant of their valley,
    How long will you gash yourself?
6 "Ah, sword of the LORD,
    How long will you not be quiet?
Withdraw into your sheath;
    Be at rest and stay still.
7 "How can it be quiet,
    When the LORD has given it an order?
Against Ashkelon and against the
    seacoast—
There He has assigned it.' "

Prophecy against Moab

48 Concerning Moab. Thus says the LORD of
    hosts, the God of Israel,
"Woe to Nebo, for it has been destroyed;
    Kiriathaim has been put to shame, it has
        been captured;
The lofty stronghold has been put to
    shame and shattered.
2 "There is praise for Moab no longer;
    In Heshbon they have devised calamity
        against her:
'Come and let us cut her off from *being* a
    nation!'

You too, *Madmen, will be silenced;
The sword will follow after you.
3 "The sound of an outcry from Horonaim,
'Devastation and great destruction!'
4 "Moab is broken,
Her little ones have sounded out a cry *of
distress.*
5 "For by the ascent of Luhith
They will ascend with continual weeping;
For at the descent of Horonaim
They have heard the anguished cry of
destruction.
6 "Flee, save your lives,
That you may be like a juniper in the
wilderness.
7 "For because of your trust in your own
achievements and treasures,
Even you yourself will be captured;
And Chemosh will go off into exile
Together with his priests and his princes.

48:7 An Exiled God

*The gods of the Middle East tended to occupy a
certain territory—thus each city had its own
god. Chemosh, the chief god of Moab, was
worshiped through child sacrifice (2 Kings
3:27). Here Jeremiah predicts that not only
would the Moabites go into exile—their god
would too. These gods were powerless before
the God of Israel.*

8 "A destroyer will come to every city,
So that no city will escape;
The valley also will be ruined
And the plateau will be destroyed,
As the LORD has said.
9 "Give wings to Moab,
For she will flee away;
And her cities will become a desolation,
Without inhabitants in them.
10 "Cursed be the one who does the LORD'S
work negligently,
And cursed be the one who restrains his
sword from blood.

11 ¶ "Moab has been at ease since his
youth;
He has also been undisturbed, *like wine*
on its dregs,
And he has not been emptied from vessel
to vessel,
Nor has he gone into exile.
Therefore he retains his flavor,
And his aroma has not changed.
12 "Therefore behold, the days are coming," declares the LORD, "when I will send to him those
who tip *vessels,* and they will tip him over, and
they will empty his vessels and shatter his jars.

13 "And Moab will be ashamed of Chemosh, as
the house of Israel was ashamed of Bethel, their
confidence.
14 "How can you say, 'We are mighty
warriors,
And men valiant for battle'?
15 "Moab has been destroyed and men have
gone up to his cities;
His choicest young men have also gone
down to the slaughter,"
Declares the King, whose name is the
LORD of hosts.
16 "The disaster of Moab will soon come,
And his calamity has swiftly hastened.
17 "Mourn for him, all you who *live* around
him,
Even all of you who know his name;
Say, 'How has the mighty scepter been
broken,
A staff of splendor!'
18 "Come down from your glory
And sit on the parched ground,
O daughter dwelling in Dibon,
For the destroyer of Moab has come up
against you,
He has ruined your strongholds.
19 "Stand by the road and keep watch,
O inhabitant of Aroer;
Ask him who flees and her who escapes
And say, 'What has happened?'
20 "Moab has been put to shame, for it has
been shattered.
Wail and cry out;
Declare by the Arnon
That Moab has been destroyed.
21 ¶ "Judgment has also come upon the plain,
upon Holon, Jahzah and against Mephaath,
22 against Dibon, Nebo and Beth-diblathaim,
23 against Kiriathaim, Beth-gamul and Beth-
meon,
24 against Kerioth, Bozrah and all the cities of
the land of Moab, far and near.
25 "The horn of Moab has been cut off and his
arm broken," declares the LORD.
26 "Make him drunk, for he has become arrogant toward the LORD; so Moab will wallow in his
vomit, and he also will become a laughingstock.
27 "Now was not Israel a laughingstock to you?
Or was he caught among thieves? For each time
you speak about him you shake *your head in
scorn.*
28 "Leave the cities and dwell among the
crags,
O inhabitants of Moab,
And be like a dove that nests
Beyond the mouth of the chasm.
29 "We have heard of the pride of Moab—
he *is* very proud—
Of his haughtiness, his pride, his
arrogance and his self-exaltation.

I.e. a city of Moab

30 "I know his fury," declares the LORD,
  "But it is futile;
  His idle boasts have accomplished
    nothing.
31 "Therefore I will wail for Moab,
  Even for all Moab will I cry out;
  I will moan for the men of Kir-heres.
32 "More than the weeping for Jazer
  I will weep for you, O vine of Sibmah!
  Your tendrils stretched across the sea,
  They reached to the sea of Jazer;
  Upon your summer fruits and your
    grape harvest
  The destroyer has fallen.
33 "So gladness and joy are taken away
  From the fruitful field, even from the
    land of Moab.
  And I have made the wine to cease from
    the wine presses;
  No one will tread *them* with shouting,
  The shouting will not be shouts *of joy*.
34 "From the outcry at Heshbon even to Elealeh, even to Jahaz they have raised their voice,
from Zoar even to Horonaim *and to* Eglath-
shelishiyah; for even the waters of Nimrim will
become desolate.
35 "I will make an end of Moab," declares the
LORD, "the one who offers *sacrifice* on the high
place and the one who burns incense to his gods.
36 ¶ "Therefore My heart wails for Moab like
flutes; My heart also wails like flutes for the men
of Kir-heres. Therefore they have lost the abundance it produced.
37 "For every head is bald and every beard cut
short; there are gashes on all the hands and sackcloth on the loins.
38 "On all the housetops of Moab and in its
streets there is lamentation everywhere; for I have
broken Moab like an undesirable vessel," declares
the LORD.
39 "How shattered it is! *How* they have wailed!
How Moab has turned his back—he is ashamed!
So Moab will become a laughingstock and an object of terror to all around him."
40 ¶ For thus says the LORD:
  "Behold, one will fly swiftly like an eagle
  And spread out his wings against Moab.
41 "Kerioth has been captured
  And the strongholds have been seized,
  So the hearts of the mighty men of Moab
    in that day
  Will be like the heart of a woman in
    labor.
42 "Moab will be destroyed from *being* a
    people
  Because he has become arrogant toward
    the LORD.
43 "Terror, pit and snare are *coming* upon
    you,
  O inhabitant of Moab," declares the
    LORD.

44 "The one who flees from the terror
  Will fall into the pit,
  And the one who climbs up out of
    the pit

48:43 Well-turned Phrase

Some of Jeremiah's language eludes translation, especially when, as here, he chooses Hebrew words for the sake of sound. "Terror, pit, snare" are translations of "pahad, pahat, pah." Isaiah (or some poet before him) had already minted the phrase, generations before Jeremiah (see Isaiah 24:17).

  Will be caught in the snare;
  For I shall bring upon her, *even* upon
    Moab,
  The year of their punishment," declares
    the LORD.

45 ¶ "In the shadow of Heshbon
  The fugitives stand without strength;
  For a fire has gone forth from Heshbon
  And a flame from the midst of Sihon,
  And it has devoured the forehead of
    Moab
  And the scalps of the riotous revelers.
46 "Woe to you, Moab!
  The people of Chemosh have perished;
  For your sons have been taken away
    captive
  And your daughters into captivity.
47 "Yet I will restore the fortunes of Moab
  In the latter days," declares the LORD.
¶ Thus far the judgment on Moab.

Prophecy against Ammon

49 Concerning the sons of Ammon. Thus
says the LORD:
  "Does Israel have no sons?
  Or has he no heirs?
  Why then has Malcam taken possession
    of Gad
  And his people settled in its cities?
2 "Therefore behold, the days are coming,"
    declares the LORD,
  "That I will cause a trumpet blast of war
    to be heard
  Against Rabbah of the sons of Ammon;
  And it will become a desolate heap,
  And her towns will be set on fire.
  Then Israel will take possession of his
    possessors,"
  Says the LORD.
3 "Wail, O Heshbon, for Ai has been
    destroyed!
  Cry out, O daughters of Rabbah,
  Gird yourselves with sackcloth and
    lament,

And rush back and forth inside the walls;
For Malcam will go into exile
Together with his priests and his princes.
4 "How boastful you are about the valleys!
Your valley is flowing *away,*
O backsliding daughter
Who trusts in her treasures, *saying,*
'Who will come against me?'
5 "Behold, I am going to bring terror
upon you,"
Declares the Lord GOD of hosts,
"From all *directions* around you;
And each of you will be driven out
headlong,
With no one to gather the fugitives
together.
6 "But afterward I will restore
The fortunes of the sons of Ammon,"
Declares the LORD.

Prophecy against Edom

7 ¶ Concerning Edom.
Thus says the LORD of hosts,
"Is there no longer any wisdom in
Teman?
Has good counsel been lost to the
prudent?
Has their wisdom decayed?
8 "Flee away, turn back, dwell in the depths,
O inhabitants of Dedan,
For I will bring the disaster of Esau
upon him
At the time I punish him.
9 "If grape gatherers came to you,
Would they not leave gleanings?
If thieves *came* by night,
They would destroy *only* until they had
enough.
10 "But I have stripped Esau bare,
I have uncovered his hiding places
So that he will not be able to conceal
himself;
His offspring has been destroyed along
with his relatives
And his neighbors, and he is no more.
11 "Leave your orphans behind, I will keep
them alive;
And let your widows trust in Me."
12 ¶ For thus says the LORD, "Behold, those
who were not sentenced to drink the cup will certainly drink *it,* and are you the one who will be
completely acquitted? You will not be acquitted,
but you will certainly drink *it.*
13 "For I have sworn by Myself," declares the
LORD, "that Bozrah will become an object of horror, a reproach, a ruin and a curse; and all its cities
will become perpetual ruins."
14 ¶ I have heard a message from the LORD,
And an envoy is sent among the nations,
saying,

"Gather yourselves together and come
against her,
And rise up for battle!"
15 "For behold, I have made you small
among the nations,
Despised among men.
16 "As for the terror of you,
The arrogance of your heart has deceived
you,
O you who live in the clefts of the rock,
Who occupy the height of the hill.
Though you make your nest as high as
an eagle's,
I will bring you down from there,"
declares the LORD.
17 ¶ "Edom will become an object of horror;
everyone who passes by it will be horrified and
will hiss at all its wounds.
18 "Like the overthrow of Sodom and Gomorrah with its neighbors," says the LORD, "no one
will live there, nor will a son of man reside in it.
19 "Behold, one will come up like a lion from
the thickets of the Jordan against a perennially
watered pasture; for in an instant I will make him
run away from it, and whoever is chosen I shall
appoint over it. For who is like Me, and who will
summon Me *into court?* And who then is the
shepherd who can stand against Me?"
20 ¶ Therefore hear the plan of the LORD which
He has planned against Edom, and His purposes
which He has purposed against the inhabitants of
Teman: surely they will drag them off, *even* the
little ones of the flock; surely He will make their
pasture desolate because of them.
21 The earth has quaked at the noise of their
downfall. There is an outcry! The noise of it has
been heard at the Red Sea.
22 Behold, He will mount up and swoop like
an eagle and spread out His wings against Bozrah;
and the hearts of the mighty men of Edom in that
day will be like the heart of a woman in labor.

Prophecy against Damascus

23 ¶ Concerning Damascus.
"Hamath and Arpad are put to shame,
For they have heard bad news;
They are disheartened.
There is anxiety by the sea,
It cannot be calmed.
24 "Damascus has become helpless;
She has turned away to flee,
And panic has gripped her;
Distress and pangs have taken hold
of her
Like a woman in childbirth.
25 "How the city of praise has not been
deserted,
The town of My joy!
26 "Therefore, her young men will fall in her
streets,

And all the men of war will be silenced
in that day," declares the LORD of
hosts.
27 "I will set fire to the wall of Damascus,
And it will devour the fortified towers of
Ben-hadad."

Prophecy against Kedar and Hazor

28 ¶ Concerning Kedar and the kingdoms of
Hazor, which Nebuchadnezzar king of Babylon
defeated. Thus says the LORD,
"Arise, go up to Kedar
And devastate the men of the east.
29 "They will take away their tents and their
flocks;
They will carry off for themselves
Their tent curtains, all their goods and
their camels,
And they will call out to one another,
'Terror on every side!'
30 "Run away, flee! Dwell in the depths,
O inhabitants of Hazor," declares the
LORD;
"For Nebuchadnezzar king of Babylon has
formed a plan against you
And devised a scheme against you.
31 "Arise, go up against a nation which is at
ease,
Which lives securely," declares the LORD.
"It has no gates or bars;
They dwell alone.
32 "Their camels will become plunder,
And their many cattle for booty,
And I will scatter to all the winds those
who cut the corners of their hair;
And I will bring their disaster from every
side," declares the LORD.
33 "Hazor will become a haunt of jackals,
A desolation forever;
No one will live there,
Nor will a son of man reside in it."

Prophecy against Elam

34 ¶ That which came as the word of the LORD
to Jeremiah the prophet concerning Elam, at the
beginning of the reign of Zedekiah king of Judah,
saying:
35 ¶ "Thus says the LORD of hosts,
'Behold, I am going to break the bow of
Elam,
The finest of their might.
36 'I will bring upon Elam the four winds
From the four ends of heaven,
And will scatter them to all these winds;
And there will be no nation
To which the outcasts of Elam will
not go.
37 'So I will shatter Elam before their
enemies
And before those who seek their lives;

And I will bring calamity upon them,
Even My fierce anger,' declares the LORD,
'And I will send out the sword after them
Until I have consumed them.
38 'Then I will set My throne in Elam
And destroy out of it king and princes,'
Declares the LORD.
39 'But it will come about in the last days
That I will restore the fortunes of
Elam,' "
Declares the LORD.

Prophecy against Babylon

50 The word which the LORD spoke concerning Babylon, the land of the Chaldeans,
through Jeremiah the prophet:
2 "Declare and proclaim among the nations.
Proclaim it and lift up a standard.
Do not conceal it but say,
'Babylon has been captured,
Bel has been put to shame, Marduk has
been shattered;
Her images have been put to shame, her
idols have been shattered.'
3 "For a nation has come up against her out of
the north; it will make her land an object of horror, and there will be no inhabitant in it. Both man
and beast have wandered off, they have gone
away!

50:1–3 None Escape

*Chapters 46–50 record a virtual catalog of
Israel's enemies. Jeremiah begins with Egypt,
goes on to Israel's immediate (small)
neighbors, and ends with archenemy Babylon.
No nation is exempt from God's justice.*

4 ¶ "In those days and at that time," declares
the LORD, "the sons of Israel will come, both they
and the sons of Judah as well; they will go along
weeping as they go, and it will be the LORD their
God they will seek.
5 "They will ask for the way to Zion, turning
their faces in its direction; they will come that they
may join themselves to the LORD in an everlasting
covenant that will not be forgotten.
6 ¶ "My people have become lost sheep;
Their shepherds have led them astray.
They have made them turn aside on the
mountains;
They have gone along from mountain to
hill
And have forgotten their resting place.
7 "All who came upon them have devoured
them;
And their adversaries have said, 'We are
not guilty,

Inasmuch as they have sinned against the
LORD *who is* the habitation of
righteousness,
Even the LORD, the hope of their fathers.'

8 ¶ "Wander away from the midst of
Babylon
And go forth from the land of the
Chaldeans;
Be also like male goats at the head of the
flock.
9 "For behold, I am going to arouse and
bring up against Babylon
A horde of great nations from the land
of the north,
And they will draw up *their* battle lines
against her;
From there she will be taken captive.
Their arrows will be like an expert
warrior
Who does not return empty-handed.
10 "Chaldea will become plunder;
All who plunder her will have enough,"
declares the LORD.

11 ¶ "Because you are glad, because you are
jubilant,
O you who pillage My heritage,
Because you skip about like a threshing
heifer
And neigh like stallions,
12 Your mother will be greatly ashamed,
She who gave you birth will be
humiliated.
Behold, *she will be* the least of the
nations,
A wilderness, a parched land and a
desert.
13 "Because of the indignation of the LORD
she will not be inhabited,
But she will be completely desolate;
Everyone who passes by Babylon will be
horrified
And will hiss because of all her wounds.
14 "Draw up your battle lines against
Babylon on every side,
All you who bend the bow;
Shoot at her, do not be sparing with *your*
arrows,
For she has sinned against the LORD.
15 "Raise your battle cry against her on every
side!
She has given herself up, her pillars have
fallen,
Her walls have been torn down.
For this is the vengeance of the LORD:
Take vengeance on her;
As she has done *to others, so* do to her.
16 "Cut off the sower from Babylon
And the one who wields the sickle at the
time of harvest;

From before the sword of the oppressor
They will each turn back to his own
people
And they will each flee to his own land.
17 ¶ "Israel is a scattered flock, the lions have
driven *them* away. The first one *who* devoured
him was the king of Assyria, and this last one *who*
has broken his bones is Nebuchadnezzar king of
Babylon.
18 "Therefore thus says the LORD of hosts, the
God of Israel: 'Behold, I am going to punish the
king of Babylon and his land, just as I punished
the king of Assyria.
19 'And I will bring Israel back to his pasture
and he will graze on Carmel and Bashan, and his
desire will be satisfied in the hill country of Ephraim and Gilead.
20 'In those days and at that time,' declares the
LORD, 'search will be made for the iniquity of Israel, but there will be none; and for the sins of
Judah, but they will not be found; for I will pardon
those whom I leave as a remnant.'

50:20 An End to Guilt

*For 50 chapters the book of Jeremiah hammers
away at Israel's guilt. Because of it, punishment
was bound to come. Yet the forgiveness to
come from God will be as absolute as the guilt:
A search for Israel's sins will not uncover a
single one.*

21 ¶ "Against the land of [a]Merathaim, go
up against it,
And against the inhabitants of [b]Pekod.
Slay and utterly destroy them," declares
the LORD,
"And do according to all that I have
commanded you.
22 "The noise of battle is in the land,
And great destruction.
23 "How the hammer of the whole earth
Has been cut off and broken!
How Babylon has become
An object of horror among the nations!
24 "I set a snare for you and you were also
caught, O Babylon,
While you yourself were not aware;
You have been found and also seized
Because you have engaged in conflict
with the LORD."
25 The LORD has opened His armory
And has brought forth the weapons of
His indignation,
For it is a work of the Lord GOD of hosts
In the land of the Chaldeans.
26 Come to her from the farthest border;
Open up her barns,

Pile her up like heaps
And utterly destroy her,
Let nothing be left to her.
27 Put all her young bulls to the sword;
Let them go down to the slaughter!
Woe be upon them, for their day has
come,
The time of their punishment.

28 ¶ There is a sound of fugitives and
refugees from the land of Babylon,
To declare in Zion the vengeance of the
LORD our God,
Vengeance for His temple.

29 ¶ "Summon [a]many against Babylon,
All those who bend the bow:
Encamp against her on every side,
Let there be no escape.
Repay her according to her work;
According to all that she has done, so do
to her;
For she has become arrogant against the
LORD,
Against the Holy One of Israel.
30 "Therefore her young men will fall in her
streets,
And all her men of war will be silenced
in that day," declares the LORD.
31 "Behold, I am against you,
O arrogant one,"
Declares the Lord GOD of hosts,
"For your day has come,
The time when I will punish you.
32 "The arrogant one will stumble and fall
With no one to raise him up;
And I will set fire to his cities
And it will devour all his environs."

33 ¶ Thus says the LORD of hosts,
"The sons of Israel are oppressed,
And the sons of Judah as well;
And all who took them captive have held
them fast,
They have refused to let them go.
34 "Their Redeemer is strong, the LORD of
hosts is His name;
He will vigorously plead their case
So that He may bring rest to the earth,
But turmoil to the inhabitants of
Babylon.
35 "A sword against the Chaldeans," declares
the LORD,
"And against the inhabitants of Babylon
And against her officials and her
wise men!
36 "A sword against the oracle priests, and
they will become fools!
A sword against her mighty men, and
they will be shattered!

37 "A sword against their horses and against
their chariots
And against all the foreigners who are in
the midst of her,
And they will become women!
A sword against her treasures, and they
will be plundered!
38 "A drought on her waters, and they will
be dried up!
For it is a land of idols,
And they are mad over fearsome idols.

39 ¶ "Therefore the desert creatures will live
there along with the jackals;
The ostriches also will live in it,
And it will never again be inhabited
Or dwelt in from generation to
generation.
40 "As when God overthrew Sodom
And Gomorrah with its neighbors,"
declares the LORD,
"No man will live there,
Nor will any son of man reside in it.

41 ¶ "Behold, a people is coming from the
north,
And a great nation and many kings
Will be aroused from the remote parts of
the earth.
42 "They seize their bow and javelin;
They are cruel and have no mercy.
Their voice roars like the sea;
And they ride on horses,
Marshalled like a man for the battle
Against you, O daughter of Babylon.
43 "The king of Babylon has heard the report
about them,
And his hands hang limp;
Distress has gripped him,
Agony like a woman in childbirth.

44 ¶ "Behold, one will come up like a lion from
the thicket of the Jordan to a perennially watered
pasture; for in an instant I will make them run
away from it, and whoever is chosen I will appoint
over it. For who is like Me, and who will summon
Me into court? And who then is the shepherd who
can stand before Me?"
45 Therefore hear the plan of the LORD which
He has planned against Babylon, and His purposes which He has purposed against the land of
the Chaldeans: surely they will drag them off, even
the little ones of the flock; surely He will make
their pasture desolate because of them.
46 At the shout, "Babylon has been seized!" the
earth is shaken, and an outcry is heard among the
nations.

Babylon Judged for Sins against Israel

51 Thus says the LORD:
"Behold, I am going to arouse against
Babylon

[a] Another reading is archers

And against the inhabitants of
[a]Leb-kamai
The spirit of a destroyer.

2 "I will dispatch foreigners to Babylon that
they may winnow her
And may devastate her land;
For on every side they will be opposed
to her
In the day of *her* calamity.

3 "Let not him who bends his bow bend *it*,
Nor let him rise up in his scale-armor;
So do not spare her young men;
Devote all her army to destruction.

4 "They will fall down slain in the land of
the Chaldeans,
And pierced through in their streets."

5 ¶ For neither Israel nor Judah has been
forsaken
By his God, the LORD of hosts,
Although their land is full of guilt
Before the Holy One of Israel.

6 Flee from the midst of Babylon,
And each of you save his life!
Do not be destroyed in her punishment,
For this is the LORD'S time of vengeance;
He is going to render recompense to her.

7 Babylon has been a golden cup in the
hand of the LORD,
Intoxicating all the earth.
The nations have drunk of her wine;
Therefore the nations are going mad.

8 Suddenly Babylon has fallen and been
broken;
Wail over her!
Bring balm for her pain;
Perhaps she may be healed.

9 We applied healing to Babylon, but she
was not healed;
Forsake her and let us each go to his
own country,
For her judgment has reached to heaven
And towers up to the very skies.

10 The LORD has brought about our
vindication;
Come and let us recount in Zion
The work of the LORD our God!

11 ¶ Sharpen the arrows, fill the quivers!
The LORD has aroused the spirit of the
kings of the Medes,
Because His purpose is against Babylon
to destroy it;
For it is the vengeance of the LORD,
vengeance for His temple.

12 Lift up a signal against the walls of
Babylon;
Post a strong guard,
Station sentries,
Place men in ambush!

For the LORD has both purposed and
performed
What He spoke concerning the
inhabitants of Babylon.

13 O you who dwell by many waters,
Abundant in treasures,
Your end has come,
The measure of your end.

51:13 Waters of Babylon

Water has always been precious in the Middle East, and Babylon's mighty Euphrates River, complemented by a magnificent system of irrigation canals, was a major source of wealth and security in times of drought. The modern-day nations of Iraq, Iran, and Turkey still argue—and sometimes fight—over this resource.

14 The LORD of hosts has sworn by Himself:
"Surely I will fill you with a population
like locusts,
And they will cry out with shouts of
victory over you."

15 ¶ *It is* He who made the earth by His
power,
Who established the world by His
wisdom,
And by His understanding He stretched
out the heavens.

16 When He utters His voice, *there is* a
tumult of waters in the heavens,
And He causes the clouds to ascend from
the end of the earth;
He makes lightning for the rain
And brings forth the wind from His
storehouses.

17 All mankind is stupid, devoid of
knowledge;
Every goldsmith is put to shame by his
idols,
For his molten images are deceitful,
And there is no breath in them.

18 They are worthless, a work of mockery;
In the time of their punishment they will
perish.

19 The portion of Jacob is not like these;
For the Maker of all is He,
And of the tribe of His inheritance;
The LORD of hosts is His name.

20 *He says,* "You are My war-club, *My*
weapon of war;
And with you I shatter nations,
And with you I destroy kingdoms.

21 "With you I shatter the horse and his
rider,

[a] Cryptic name for Chaldea; or *the heart of those who rise up against Me*

And with you I shatter the chariot and
    its rider,
22 And with you I shatter man and woman,
    And with you I shatter old man and
        youth,
    And with you I shatter young man and
        virgin,
23 And with you I shatter the shepherd and
        his flock,
    And with you I shatter the farmer and
        his team,
    And with you I shatter governors and
        prefects.
24 ¶ "But I will repay Babylon and all the inhabitants of Chaldea for all their evil that they
have done in Zion before your eyes," declares the
LORD.
25 "Behold, I am against you, O destroying
        mountain,
    Who destroys the whole earth," declares
        the LORD,
  "And I will stretch out My hand against
        you,
    And roll you down from the crags,
    And I will make you a burnt out
        mountain.
26 "They will not take from you *even* a stone
        for a corner
    Nor a stone for foundations,
    But you will be desolate forever,"
        declares the LORD.

27 ¶ Lift up a signal in the land,
    Blow a trumpet among the nations!
    Consecrate the nations against her,
    Summon against her the kingdoms of
        Ararat, Minni and Ashkenaz;
    Appoint a marshal against her,
    Bring up the horses like bristly locusts.
28 Consecrate the nations against her,
    The kings of the Medes,
    Their governors and all their prefects,
    And every land of their dominion.
29 So the land quakes and writhes,
    For the purposes of the LORD against
        Babylon stand,
    To make the land of Babylon
    A desolation without inhabitants.
30 The mighty men of Babylon have ceased
        fighting,
    They stay in the strongholds;
    Their strength is exhausted,
    They are becoming *like* women;
    Their dwelling places are set on fire,
    The bars of her *gates* are broken.
31 One courier runs to meet another,
    And one messenger to meet another,
    To tell the king of Babylon
    That his city has been captured from end
        to end;

32 The fords also have been seized,
    And they have burned the marshes with
        fire,
    And the men of war are terrified.

33 ¶ For thus says the LORD of hosts, the God
of Israel:
  "The daughter of Babylon is like a
        threshing floor
    At the time it is stamped firm;
    Yet in a little while the time of harvest
        will come for her."

34 ¶ "Nebuchadnezzar king of Babylon has
        devoured me *and* crushed me,
    He has set me down *like* an empty vessel;
    He has swallowed me like a monster,
    He has filled his stomach with my
        delicacies;
    He has washed me away.
35 "May the violence *done* to me and to my
        flesh be upon Babylon,"
    The inhabitant of Zion will say;
    And, "May my blood be upon the
        inhabitants of Chaldea,"
    Jerusalem will say.
36 Therefore thus says the LORD,
  "Behold, I am going to plead your case
    And exact full vengeance for you;
    And I will dry up her sea
    And make her fountain dry.
37 "Babylon will become a heap *of ruins*, a
        haunt of jackals,
    An object of horror and hissing, without
        inhabitants.
38 "They will roar together like young lions,
    They will growl like lions' cubs.
39 "When they become heated up, I will
        serve *them* their banquet
    And make them drunk, that they may
        become jubilant
    And may sleep a perpetual sleep
    And not wake up," declares the LORD.
40 "I will bring them down like lambs to the
        slaughter,
    Like rams together with male goats.

41 ¶ "How *a*Sheshak has been captured,
    And the praise of the whole earth been
        seized!
    How Babylon has become an object of
        horror among the nations!
42 "The sea has come up over Babylon;
    She has been engulfed with its
        tumultuous waves.
43 "Her cities have become an object of
        horror,
    A parched land and a desert,
    A land in which no man lives
    And through which no son of man
        passes.

a Cryptic name for Babylon

44 "I will punish Bel in Babylon,
And I will make what he has swallowed
come out of his mouth;
And the nations will no longer stream to
him.
Even the wall of Babylon has fallen
down!

45 ¶ "Come forth from her midst, My
people,
And each of you save yourselves
From the fierce anger of the LORD.

46 "Now so that your heart does not grow
faint,
And you are not afraid at the report that
will be heard in the land—
For the report will come one year,
And after that another report in another
year,
And violence *will be* in the land
With ruler against ruler—

47 Therefore behold, days are coming
When I will punish the idols of Babylon;
And her whole land will be put to shame
And all her slain will fall in her midst.

48 "Then heaven and earth and all that is in
them
Will shout for joy over Babylon,
For the destroyers will come to her from
the north,"
Declares the LORD.

49 ¶ Indeed Babylon is to fall *for* the slain of
Israel,
As also for Babylon the slain of all the
earth have fallen.

50 You who have escaped the sword,
Depart! Do not stay!
Remember the LORD from afar,
And let Jerusalem come to your mind.

51 We are ashamed because we have heard
reproach;
Disgrace has covered our faces,
For aliens have entered
The holy places of the LORD'S house.

52 ¶ "Therefore behold, the days are
coming," declares the LORD,
"When I will punish her idols,
And the mortally wounded will groan
throughout her land.

53 "Though Babylon should ascend to the
heavens,
And though she should fortify her lofty
stronghold,
From Me destroyers will come to her,"
declares the LORD.

54 ¶ The sound of an outcry from Babylon,
And of great destruction from the land
of the Chaldeans!

55 For the LORD is going to destroy
Babylon,

And He will make *her* loud noise vanish
from her.
And their waves will roar like many
waters;
The tumult of their voices sounds forth.

51:53 Apocalyptic Arrogance

The arrogance of Babylon—her sense of absolute, untouchable power—became an emblem of the forces God will ultimately destroy. Jeremiah probably was thinking only of Babylon's towering ziggurat (or temple) and double wall defenses. But Babylon's attempt to "ascend to the heavens" suggested an image of a nation trying to compete with God. Revelation 18—written long after Jeremiah's Babylon had been destroyed—described the fall of another proud and wealthy "Babylon" at the end of the age.

56 For the destroyer is coming against her,
against Babylon,
And her mighty men will be captured,
Their bows are shattered;
For the LORD is a God of recompense,
He will fully repay.

57 "I will make her princes and her wise men
drunk,
Her governors, her prefects and her
mighty men,
That they may sleep a perpetual sleep
and not wake up,"
Declares the King, whose name is the
LORD of hosts.

58 Thus says the LORD of hosts,
"The broad wall of Babylon will be
completely razed
And her high gates will be set on fire;
So the peoples will toil for nothing,
And the nations become exhausted *only*
for fire."

59 ¶ The message which Jeremiah the prophet
commanded Seraiah the son of Neriah, the grandson of Mahseiah, when he went with Zedekiah the
king of Judah to Babylon in the fourth year of his
reign. (Now Seraiah was quartermaster.)

60 So Jeremiah wrote in a single scroll all the
calamity which would come upon Babylon, *that is,*
all these words which have been written concerning Babylon.

61 Then Jeremiah said to Seraiah, "As soon as
you come to Babylon, then see that you read all
these words aloud,

62 and say, 'You, O LORD, have promised concerning this place to cut it off, so that there will be
nothing dwelling in it, whether man or beast, but
it will be a perpetual desolation.'

63 "And as soon as you finish reading this scroll,

you will tie a stone to it and throw it into the middle of the Euphrates,

64 and say, 'Just so shall Babylon sink down and not rise again because of the calamity that I am going to bring upon her; and they will become exhausted.' " Thus far are the words of Jeremiah.

The Fall of Jerusalem

52 Zedekiah was twenty-one years old when he became king, and he reigned eleven years in Jerusalem; and his mother's name was Hamutal the daughter of Jeremiah of Libnah.

2 He did evil in the sight of the LORD like all that Jehoiakim had done.

3 For through the anger of the LORD *this* came about in Jerusalem and Judah until He cast them out from His presence. And Zedekiah rebelled against the king of Babylon.

4 Now it came about in the ninth year of his reign, on the tenth *day* of the tenth month, that Nebuchadnezzar king of Babylon came, he and all his army, against Jerusalem, camped against it and built a siege wall all around it.

5 So the city was under siege until the eleventh year of King Zedekiah.

6 On the ninth *day* of the fourth month the famine was so severe in the city that there was no food for the people of the land.

7 Then the city was broken into, and all the men of war fled and went forth from the city at night by way of the gate between the two walls which *was* by the king's garden, though the Chaldeans were all around the city. And they went by way of the Arabah.

8 But the army of the Chaldeans pursued the king and overtook Zedekiah in the plains of Jericho, and all his army was scattered from him.

9 Then they captured the king and brought him up to the king of Babylon at Riblah in the land of Hamath, and he passed sentence on him.

10 The king of Babylon slaughtered the sons of Zedekiah before his eyes, and he also slaughtered all the princes of Judah in Riblah.

11 Then he blinded the eyes of Zedekiah; and the king of Babylon bound him with bronze fetters and brought him to Babylon and put him in prison until the day of his death.

12 ¶ Now on the tenth *day* of the fifth month, which was the nineteenth year of King Nebuchadnezzar, king of Babylon, Nebuzaradan the captain of the bodyguard, who was in the service of the king of Babylon, came to Jerusalem.

13 He burned the house of the LORD, the king's house and all the houses of Jerusalem; even every large house he burned with fire.

14 So all the army of the Chaldeans who *were* with the captain of the guard broke down all the walls around Jerusalem.

15 Then Nebuzaradan the captain of the guard carried away into exile some of the poorest of the people, the rest of the people who were left in the city, the deserters who had deserted to the king of Babylon and the rest of the artisans.

16 But Nebuzaradan the captain of the guard left some of the poorest of the land to be vine-dressers and plowmen.

52:13 Total Destruction

A small but subtle change telegraphs a huge turnabout. Verse 4 gives the date in terms of (Israelite) King Zedekiah's reign; verse 12 gives it in terms of (Babylonian) King Nebuchadnezzar. From this point on in history, Israel survived only on the periphery of other nations' empires. Instead of reckoning years in terms of their own leaders' time in office, Israel would base their calendar on the empires that ruled them.

17 ¶ Now the bronze pillars which belonged to the house of the LORD and the stands and the bronze sea, which were in the house of the LORD, the Chaldeans broke in pieces and carried all their bronze to Babylon.

18 They also took away the pots, the shovels, the snuffers, the basins, the pans and all the bronze vessels which were used in *temple* service.

19 The captain of the guard also took away the bowls, the firepans, the basins, the pots, the lampstands, the pans and the drink offering bowls, what was fine gold and what was fine silver.

20 The two pillars, the one sea, and the twelve bronze bulls that were under the sea, *and* the stands, which King Solomon had made for the house of the LORD—the bronze of all these vessels was beyond weight.

21 As for the pillars, the height of each pillar *was* eighteen cubits, and it *was* twelve cubits in circumference and four fingers in thickness, *and* hollow.

22 Now a capital of bronze was on it; and the height of each capital was five cubits, with network and pomegranates upon the capital all around, all of bronze. And the second pillar was like these, including pomegranates.

23 There were ninety-six exposed pomegranates; all the pomegranates *numbered* a hundred on the network all around.

24 ¶ Then the captain of the guard took Seraiah the chief priest and Zephaniah the second priest, with the three officers of the temple.

25 He also took from the city one official who was overseer of the men of war, and seven of the king's advisers who were found in the city, and the scribe of the commander of the army who mustered the people of the land, and sixty men of the people of the land who were found in the midst of the city.

26 Nebuzaradan the captain of the guard took

them and brought them to the king of Babylon at Riblah.

27 Then the king of Babylon struck them down and put them to death at Riblah in the land of Hamath. So Judah was led away into exile from its land.

28 ¶ These are the people whom Nebuchadnezzar carried away into exile: in the seventh year 3,023 Jews;

29 in the eighteenth year of Nebuchadnezzar 832 persons from Jerusalem;

30 in the twenty-third year of Nebuchadnezzar, Nebuzaradan the captain of the guard carried into exile 745 Jewish people; there were 4,600 persons in all.

31 ¶ Now it came about in the thirty-seventh year of the exile of Jehoiachin king of Judah, in the twelfth month, on the twenty-fifth of the month, that Evil-merodach king of Babylon, in the *first* year of his reign, showed favor to Jehoiachin king of Judah and brought him out of prison.

32 Then he spoke kindly to him and set his throne above the thrones of the kings who *were* with him in Babylon.

33 So Jehoiachin changed his prison clothes, and had his meals in the king's presence regularly all the days of his life.

34 For his allowance, a regular allowance was given him by the king of Babylon, a daily portion all the days of his life until the day of his death.

LAMENTATIONS

A City in Ruins
There was nothing left to do but weep

"Is it nothing to all you who pass this way?" 1:12

EVERY YEAR THE WORLD PAUSES to remember one awful day in Hiroshima, Japan, when the power of the atom came out of the sky. Opinions vary over whether an atom bomb was necessary to end World War II. Necessary or not, however, Hiroshima was a horrible tragedy. Though the survivors have gone on with their lives, they cannot forget. Nor can the rest of the world. Hiroshima's shadow stretches through to our time.

Five Poems of Grief

Lamentations offers five poems written from a state of dazed grief worthy of Hiroshima. A whole city has been destroyed. Brothers, sisters, children, friends are all gone. Men the town admired wander the body-littered streets, their skins shriveled and their faces barely recognizable. Starvation has even compelled women to cook their own children (4:10).

And so the author mourns. He carefully reviews everything he has seen and felt, his pain darkening every line. He writes the first four poems in an acrostic style, following the Hebrew alphabet, one letter for each stanza. Perhaps this system helps him to pursue the subject thoroughly and not to break down in spasms of emotion. When he thinks of the starving children, he nearly does (2:11).

God Caused the Carnage

The author of Lamentations—tradition ascribes it to Jeremiah—evidently had seen the siege and destruction of Jerusalem in 586 B.C., when the Babylonian army burned and destroyed all the principal buildings and carried most of the surviving inhabitants into exile. Lamentations conducts a kind of postmortem on the death of Jerusalem, examining the body in clinical detail.

Like a doctor, Lamentations' author seeks to know the cause of death. He has no final doubt: Though the Babylonians did the work, ultimately God was responsible. But could God willingly create such misery? The author seems stunned that God has actually destroyed his own people, though he admits they richly deserved the punishment. "The Lord has become like an enemy," he cries in astonishment (2:5). "Even when I cry out and call for help, he shuts out my prayer" (3:8). "He has turned aside my ways and torn me to pieces; He has made me desolate" (3:11). "He has broken my teeth with gravel" (3:16).

But, though astonished and grief-stricken, the author never doubts God's justice. Jerusalem's destruction came as a result of sin (1:5). This fact prompts quiet hope, based on the character of God. "For if He causes grief, then He will have compassion according to His abundant lovingkindness. For He does not afflict willingly or grieve the sons of men" (3:32–33). When sin is eliminated, the Lord acts quickly to forgive and heal.

Looking for Recovery

Though the grief of Lamentations is as deep and heavy as any ever written, hope lies at the bottom. The author does not say "Cheer up!" to himself or anyone else. He mourns passionately and fully. But in mourning he looks to recovery. Lamentations ends with a prayer to God, asking him to restore his people, "unless You have utterly rejected us and are exceedingly angry with us"(5:22). Behind that "unless" lies confidence. God can never be angry without limits.

The author of Lamentations doesn't soften his words to God for fear of offending him. He expresses the full and dreadful horror of what he has seen, and he gives God full responsibility. But, remembering that the Lord is a loving God, he counts on God to heal Israel's wounds. This time of mourning will be followed by another time, a time to dance.

How to Read Lamentations

Lamentations is poetry, one poem per chapter. Its main purpose is not to describe events, nor to teach lessons, though it does both. Its intent is to express grief, to pour out before God the horror and bitterness of what has happened to Jerusalem. These five poems can help you to understand what it meant for Jews to see Jerusalem destroyed. They can also help you learn to deal appropriately with grief, your own or others'. Read them expressively, preferably out loud, so that you catch the deep emotion. Note that the author does not rush to express his hope in God, but fully grieves for the tragedy he was involved in.

Lamentations is not difficult to understand, though some of the poetical allusions may become clearer if you use a Bible dictionary or a commentary. For a summary of the destruction that inspired Lamentations, read 2 Kings 25.

3-TRACK READING PLAN

For an explanation and complete listing of the 3-track reading plan, turn to page 7.

TRACK 1: Two-Week Courses on the Bible

See page 7 for information on these courses.

TRACK 2: An Overview of Lamentations in 1 Day
☐ Day 1. Read the Introduction to Lamentations and chapter 3, which contains both bitter grief and quiet hope.

Now turn to page 9 for your next Track 2 reading project.

TRACK 3: All of Lamentations in 5 Days

After you have read through Lamentations, turn to pages 10–14 for your next Track 3 reading project.

☐1   ☐2   ☐3   ☐4   ☐5

The Sorrows of Zion

1 How lonely sits the city
That was full of people!
She has become like a widow
Who was *once* great among the nations!
She who was a princess among the
provinces
Has become a forced laborer!
2 She weeps bitterly in the night
And her tears are on her cheeks;
She has none to comfort her
Among all her lovers.
All her friends have dealt treacherously
with her;
They have become her enemies.
3 Judah has gone into exile under affliction
And under harsh servitude;
She dwells among the nations,
But she has found no rest;
All her pursuers have overtaken her
In the midst of distress.
4 The roads of Zion are in mourning
Because no one comes to the appointed
feasts.
All her gates are desolate;
Her priests are groaning,
Her virgins are afflicted,

And she herself is bitter.
5 Her adversaries have become her
masters,
Her enemies prosper;

1:4–5 Structured Passion

Middle Easterners often commemorated catastrophes in poetry and song, as a kind of dirge in memory of the event. (See Psalm 137 for another example.) Lamentations, a response to the destruction of Jerusalem, contains as much passion as any book in the Bible. Yet, remarkably, the author has poured his passion into a highly structured form of poetry. Note that each chapter contains exactly 22 verses, or "stanzas," except for chapter 3, which has 66 verses (3 times 22). There were 22 letters in the Hebrew alphabet, and all but one of these poems follow an acrostic form, with each stanza beginning with a different letter of the alphabet.

For the LORD has caused her grief
Because of the multitude of her
transgressions;

Her little ones have gone away
As captives before the adversary.
6 All her majesty
Has departed from the daughter of Zion;
Her princes have become like deer
That have found no pasture;
And they have fled without strength
Before the pursuer.
7 In the days of her affliction and
homelessness
Jerusalem remembers all her precious
things
That were from the days of old,
When her people fell into the hand of
the adversary
And no one helped her.
The adversaries saw her,
They mocked at her ruin.
8 Jerusalem sinned greatly,
Therefore she has become an unclean
thing.
All who honored her despise her
Because they have seen her nakedness;
Even she herself groans and turns away.
9 Her uncleanness was in her skirts;
She did not consider her future.
Therefore she has fallen astonishingly;
She has no comforter.
"See, O LORD, my affliction,
For the enemy has magnified himself!"
10 The adversary has stretched out his hand
Over all her precious things,
For she has seen the nations enter her
sanctuary,
The ones whom You commanded
That they should not enter into Your
congregation.

1:10 The Temple Destroyed

*Non-Jews were barred from the holy places of
the temple. But when the Babylonians
conquered Jerusalem, they not only entered the
temple; they looted and burned it. This shook
devout Jews deeply; more than anything else it
showed that God had given them up. Even
today Orthodox Jews observe the anniversary
of the temple's destruction by reading the book
of Lamentations aloud, and pilgrims daily
recite its prayers at the Wailing Wall in
Jerusalem.*

11 All her people groan seeking bread;
They have given their precious things for
food
To restore their lives themselves.
"See, O LORD, and look,
For I am despised."
12 "Is it nothing to all you who pass
this way?

Look and see if there is any pain like my
pain
Which was severely dealt out to me,
Which the LORD inflicted on the day of
His fierce anger.
13 "From on high He sent fire into my
bones,
And it prevailed *over them.*
He has spread a net for my feet;
He has turned me back;
He has made me desolate,
Faint all day long.
14 "The yoke of my transgressions is bound;
By His hand they are knit together.
They have come upon my neck;
He has made my strength fail.
The Lord has given me into the hands
Of *those against whom* I am not able to
stand.
15 "The Lord has rejected all my strong men
In my midst;
He has called an appointed time
against me
To crush my young men;
The Lord has trodden *as in* a wine press
The virgin daughter of Judah.
16 "For these things I weep;
My eyes run down with water;
Because far from me is a comforter,
One who restores my soul.
My children are desolate
Because the enemy has prevailed."
17 Zion stretches out her hands;
There is no one to comfort her;
The LORD has commanded concerning
Jacob
That the ones round about him should
be his adversaries;
Jerusalem has become an unclean thing
among them.
18 "The LORD is righteous;
For I have rebelled against His
command;
Hear now, all peoples,
And behold my pain;
My virgins and my young men
Have gone into captivity.
19 "I called to my lovers, *but they*
deceived me;
My priests and my elders perished in the
city
While they sought food to restore their
strength themselves.
20 "See, O LORD, for I am in distress;
My spirit is greatly troubled;
My heart is overturned within me,
For I have been very rebellious.
In the street the sword slays;
In the house it is like death.
21 "They have heard that I groan;
There is no one to comfort me;

All my enemies have heard of my
    calamity;
They are glad that You have done *it*.
Oh, that You would bring the day which
    You have proclaimed,
That they may become like me.
22 "Let all their wickedness come before You;
    And deal with them as You have dealt
      with me
For all my transgressions;
For my groans are many and my heart is
    faint."

God's Anger over Israel

2 How the Lord has covered the daughter
    of Zion
With a cloud in His anger!
He has cast from heaven to earth
The glory of Israel,
And has not remembered His footstool
In the day of His anger.
2 The Lord has swallowed up; He has not
    spared
All the habitations of Jacob.
In His wrath He has thrown down
The strongholds of the daughter of
    Judah;
He has brought *them* down to the
    ground;
He has profaned the kingdom and its
    princes.
3 In fierce anger He has cut off
All the strength of Israel;
He has drawn back His right hand
From before the enemy.
And He has burned in Jacob like a
    flaming fire
Consuming round about.
4 He has bent His bow like an enemy;
He has set His right hand like an
    adversary
And slain all that were pleasant to the
    eye;
In the tent of the daughter of Zion
He has poured out His wrath like fire.
5 The Lord has become like an enemy.
He has swallowed up Israel;
He has swallowed up all its palaces,
He has destroyed its strongholds
And multiplied in the daughter of Judah
Mourning and moaning.
6 And He has violently treated His
    tabernacle like a garden *booth;*
He has destroyed His appointed meeting
    place.
The LORD has caused to be forgotten
The appointed feast and sabbath in Zion,
And He has despised king and priest
In the indignation of His anger.
7 The Lord has rejected His altar,
He has abandoned His sanctuary;

He has delivered into the hand of the
    enemy
The walls of her palaces.
They have made a noise in the house of
    the LORD
As in the day of an appointed feast.
8 The LORD determined to destroy
The wall of the daughter of Zion.
He has stretched out a line,
He has not restrained His hand from
    destroying,
And He has caused rampart and wall to
    lament;
They have languished together.
9 Her gates have sunk into the ground,
He has destroyed and broken her bars.
Her king and her princes are among the
    nations;
The law is no more.
Also, her prophets find
No vision from the LORD.
10 The elders of the daughter of Zion
Sit on the ground, they are silent.
They have thrown dust on their heads;
They have girded themselves with
    sackcloth.
The virgins of Jerusalem
Have bowed their heads to the ground.
11 My eyes fail because of tears,
My spirit is greatly troubled;
My heart is poured out on the earth
Because of the destruction of the
    daughter of my people,
When little ones and infants faint
In the streets of the city.
12 They say to their mothers,
    "Where is grain and wine?"
As they faint like a wounded man
In the streets of the city,
As their life is poured out
On their mothers' bosom.

2:12 Pity the Children

*Everyone suffered in the destruction of
Jerusalem, rich and poor, young and old, male
and female. Lamentations grieves for them all,
but especially for the children, who were dying
of hunger. During the long siege, hunger grew
so fierce that mothers ate their own children
(2:20; 4:10). Compassion for children had
disappeared (4:3–4).*

13 How shall I admonish you?
To what shall I compare you,
O daughter of Jerusalem?
To what shall I liken you as I comfort
    you,
O virgin daughter of Zion?
For your ruin is as vast as the sea;

Who can heal you?

14 Your prophets have seen for you
False and foolish *visions;*
And they have not exposed your iniquity
So as to restore you from captivity,
But they have seen for you false and
misleading oracles.

15 All who pass along the way
Clap their hands *in derision* at you;
They hiss and shake their heads
At the daughter of Jerusalem,
"Is this the city of which they said,
'The perfection of beauty,
A joy to all the earth'?"

16 All your enemies
Have opened their mouths wide against
you;
They hiss and gnash *their* teeth.
They say, "We have swallowed *her* up!
Surely this is the day for which we
waited;
We have reached *it,* we have seen *it.*"

17 The LORD has done what He purposed;
He has accomplished His word
Which He commanded from days of old.
He has thrown down without sparing,
And He has caused the enemy to rejoice
over you;
He has exalted the might of your
adversaries.

18 Their heart cried out to the Lord,
"O wall of the daughter of Zion,
Let *your* tears run down like a river day
and night;
Give yourself no relief,
Let your eyes have no rest.

19 "Arise, cry aloud in the night
At the beginning of the night watches;
Pour out your heart like water
Before the presence of the Lord;
Lift up your hands to Him
For the life of your little ones
Who are faint because of hunger
At the head of every street."

20 See, O LORD, and look!
With whom have You dealt thus?
Should women eat their offspring,
The little ones who were born healthy?
Should priest and prophet be slain
In the sanctuary of the Lord?

21 On the ground in the streets
Lie young and old;
My virgins and my young men
Have fallen by the sword.
You have slain *them* in the day of Your
anger,
You have slaughtered, not sparing.

22 You called as in the day of an appointed
feast
My terrors on every side;

And there was no one who escaped or
survived
In the day of the LORD'S anger.
Those whom I bore and reared,
My enemy annihilated them.

Jeremiah Shares Israel's Affliction

3 I am the man who has seen affliction
Because of the rod of His wrath.

3:1 Autobiography of Pain

Ancient traditions say that Jeremiah wrote the book of Lamentations, and if so, this chapter records that doleful prophet's autobiography of pain. He was persecuted by enemies, thrown in a well, dragged captive, and jailed. Jeremiah knew, of course, that the people who did those things were God's enemies too, and he had delivered strong pronouncements against them. Yet to a person in pain—like Job, like Jeremiah—it often feels as if God himself has turned his back.

2 He has driven me and made me walk
In darkness and not in light.

3 Surely against me He has turned His
hand
Repeatedly all the day.

4 He has caused my flesh and my skin to
waste away,
He has broken my bones.

5 He has besieged and encompassed me
with bitterness and hardship.

6 In dark places He has made me dwell,
Like those who have long been dead.

7 He has walled me in so that I cannot go
out;
He has made my chain heavy.

8 Even when I cry out and call for help,
He shuts out my prayer.

9 He has blocked my ways with hewn
stone;
He has made my paths crooked.

10 He is to me like a bear lying in wait,
Like a lion in secret places.

11 He has turned aside my ways and torn
me to pieces;
He has made me desolate.

12 He bent His bow
And set me as a target for the arrow.

13 He made the arrows of His quiver
To enter into my inward parts.

14 I have become a laughingstock to all my
people,
Their *mocking* song all the day.

15 He has filled me with bitterness,
He has made me drunk with wormwood.

16 He has broken my teeth with gravel;
He has made me cower in the dust.

17 My soul has been rejected from peace;
   I have forgotten happiness.
18 So I say, "My strength has perished,
   And so has my hope from the LORD."

Hope of Relief in God's Mercy

19 ¶ Remember my affliction and my
      wandering, the wormwood and
      bitterness.
20 Surely my soul remembers
   And is bowed down within me.
21 This I recall to my mind,
   Therefore I have hope.
22 The LORD's lovingkindnesses indeed
      never cease,
   For His compassions never fail.
23 They are new every morning;
   Great is Your faithfulness.
24 "The LORD is my portion," says my soul,
   "Therefore I have hope in Him."
25 The LORD is good to those who wait for
      Him,
   To the person who seeks Him.
26 It is good that he waits silently
   For the salvation of the LORD.
27 It is good for a man that he should bear
   The yoke in his youth.
28 Let him sit alone and be silent
   Since He has laid it on him.
29 Let him put his mouth in the dust,
   Perhaps there is hope.
30 Let him give his cheek to the smiter,
   Let him be filled with reproach.
31 For the Lord will not reject forever,
32 For if He causes grief,
   Then He will have compassion
   According to His abundant
      lovingkindness.
33 For He does not afflict willingly
   Or grieve the sons of men.

3:33 Hope for the Grieving

*Lamentations bares the full horror of suffering,
yet offers hope based on the character of God.
He has let some survive (verse 22), and he is
not a God to be angry with them forever. Their
duty is to accept fully their grief, and quietly
meditate on its meaning while waiting for the
Lord.*

34 To crush under His feet
   All the prisoners of the land,
35 To deprive a man of justice
   In the presence of the Most High,
36 To defraud a man in his lawsuit—
   Of these things the Lord does not
      approve.
37 Who is there who speaks and it comes to
   pass,

Unless the Lord has commanded it?
38 Is it not from the mouth of the Most
      High
   That both good and ill go forth?
39 ¶ Why should any living mortal, or any
      man,
   Offer complaint in view of his sins?
40 Let us examine and probe our ways,
   And let us return to the LORD.
41 We lift up our heart and hands
   Toward God in heaven;
42 We have transgressed and rebelled,
   You have not pardoned.
43 You have covered Yourself with anger
   And pursued us;
   You have slain and have not spared.
44 You have covered Yourself with a cloud
   So that no prayer can pass through.
45 You have made us mere offscouring and
      refuse
   In the midst of the peoples.
46 All our enemies have opened their
      mouths against us.
47 Panic and pitfall have befallen us,
   Devastation and destruction;
48 My eyes run down with streams of water
   Because of the destruction of the
      daughter of my people.
49 My eyes pour down unceasingly,
   Without stopping,
50 Until the LORD looks down
   And sees from heaven.
51 My eyes bring pain to my soul
   Because of all the daughters of my city.
52 My enemies without cause
   Hunted me down like a bird;
53 They have silenced me in the pit
   And have placed a stone on me.
54 Waters flowed over my head;
   I said, "I am cut off!"
55 I called on Your name, O LORD,
   Out of the lowest pit.
56 You have heard my voice,
   "Do not hide Your ear from my prayer for
      relief,
   From my cry for help."
57 You drew near when I called on You;
   You said, "Do not fear!"
58 O Lord, You have pleaded my soul's
      cause;
   You have redeemed my life.
59 O LORD, You have seen my oppression;
   Judge my case.
60 You have seen all their vengeance,
   All their schemes against me.
61 You have heard their reproach, O LORD,
   All their schemes against me.
62 The lips of my assailants and their
      whispering
   Are against me all day long.
63 Look on their sitting and their rising;

I am their mocking song.

64 You will recompense them, O LORD,
According to the work of their hands.

65 You will give them hardness of heart,
Your curse will be on them.

66 You will pursue them in anger and
destroy them
From under the heavens of the LORD!

Distress of the Siege Described

4 How dark the gold has become,
How the pure gold has changed!
The sacred stones are poured out
At the corner of every street.

2 The precious sons of Zion,
Weighed against fine gold,
How they are regarded as earthen jars,
The work of a potter's hands!

3 Even jackals offer the breast,
They nurse their young;
But the daughter of my people has
become cruel
Like ostriches in the wilderness.

4 The tongue of the infant cleaves
To the roof of its mouth because of
thirst;
The little ones ask for bread,
But no one breaks *it* for them.

4:4 Starving to Death

Horrible scenes of starvation, like those shown in documentaries of African famines in recent times, were seen in the streets of Jerusalem during the Babylonian invasion. Foreign armies encircled the city for two years, cutting off all sources of food. The residents of this once-proud city resorted to eating their own children (verse 10) just to stay alive.

5 Those who ate delicacies
Are desolate in the streets;
Those reared in purple
Embrace ash pits.

6 For the iniquity of the daughter of my
people
Is greater than the sin of Sodom,
Which was overthrown as in a moment,
And no hands were turned toward her.

7 Her consecrated ones were purer than
snow,
They were whiter than milk;
They were more ruddy *in* body than
corals,
Their polishing *was like* lapis lazuli.

8 Their appearance is blacker than soot,
They are not recognized in the streets;
Their skin is shriveled on their bones,
It is withered, it has become like wood.

9 Better are those slain with the sword

Than those slain with hunger;
For they pine away, being stricken
For lack of the fruits of the field.

10 The hands of compassionate women
Boiled their own children;
They became food for them
Because of the destruction of the
daughter of my people.

11 The LORD has accomplished His wrath,
He has poured out His fierce anger;
And He has kindled a fire in Zion
Which has consumed its foundations.

12 The kings of the earth did not believe,
Nor *did* any of the inhabitants of the
world,
That the adversary and the enemy
Could enter the gates of Jerusalem.

13 Because of the sins of her prophets
And the iniquities of her priests,
Who have shed in her midst
The blood of the righteous;

14 They wandered, blind, in the streets;
They were defiled with blood
So that no one could touch their
garments.

15 "Depart! Unclean!" they cried of
themselves.
"Depart, depart, do not touch!"
So they fled and wandered;
Men among the nations said,
"They shall not continue to dwell
with us."

16 The presence of the LORD has scattered
them,
He will not continue to regard them;
They did not honor the priests,
They did not favor the elders.

17 Yet our eyes failed,
Looking for help was useless;
In our watching we have watched
For a nation that could not save.

4:17 False Hope

In the last decades before Jerusalem was conquered, Judah's kings frequently tried to play Egypt, another superpower, against Babylon. Right to the end they expected Egypt's armies to rescue them. But as Jeremiah had warned, Egypt proved to be an unreliable ally (Jeremiah 2:36–37; 37:5–8).

18 They hunted our steps
So that we could not walk in our streets;
Our end drew near,
Our days were finished
For our end had come.

19 Our pursuers were swifter
Than the eagles of the sky;
They chased us on the mountains,

They waited in ambush for us in the wilderness.

20 The breath of our nostrils, the LORD'S anointed,
Was captured in their pits,
Of whom we had said, "Under his shadow
We shall live among the nations."

21 Rejoice and be glad, O daughter of Edom,
Who dwells in the land of Uz;
But the cup will come around to you as well,
You will become drunk and make yourself naked.

22 *The punishment* of your iniquity has been completed, O daughter of Zion;
He will exile you no longer.
But He will punish your iniquity,
O daughter of Edom;
He will expose your sins!

A Prayer for Mercy

5 Remember, O LORD, what has befallen us;
Look, and see our reproach!

2 Our inheritance has been turned over to strangers,
Our houses to aliens.

3 We have become orphans without a father,
Our mothers are like widows.

4 We have to pay for our drinking water,
Our wood comes *to us* at a price.

5 Our pursuers are at our necks;
We are worn out, there is no rest for us.

6 We have submitted to Egypt *and* Assyria to get enough bread.

7 Our fathers sinned, *and* are no more;

It is we who have borne their iniquities.

8 Slaves rule over us;
There is no one to deliver us from their hand.

9 We get our bread at the risk of our lives
Because of the sword in the wilderness.

10 Our skin has become as hot as an oven,
Because of the burning heat of famine.

11 They ravished the women in Zion,
The virgins in the cities of Judah.

12 Princes were hung by their hands;
Elders were not respected.

13 Young men worked at the grinding mill,
And youths stumbled under *loads* of wood.

14 Elders are gone from the gate,
Young men from their music.

15 The joy of our hearts has ceased;
Our dancing has been turned into mourning.

16 The crown has fallen from our head;
Woe to us, for we have sinned!

17 Because of this our heart is faint,
Because of these things our eyes are dim;

18 Because of Mount Zion which lies desolate,
Foxes prowl in it.

19 ¶ You, O LORD, rule forever;
Your throne is from generation to generation.

20 Why do You forget us forever?
Why do You forsake us so long?

21 Restore us to You, O LORD, that we may be restored;
Renew our days as of old,

22 Unless You have utterly rejected us
And are exceedingly angry with us.

EZEKIEL

Seeing the Unseen God
God showed himself to Ezekiel in unearthly radiance

E ZEKIEL BEGINS WITH A DESCRIPTION so unearthly that some have suggested the prophet saw a UFO. Indeed, there are similarities: glowing lights, quick movements, inhuman figures shrouded with fire. But at least one critical difference sets Ezekiel's story apart. UFOs typically appear in remote places and then mysteriously zoom off, never to be heard from again. The majestic being Ezekiel described was not rushing off to disappear. He wanted to be known—by everyone.

For Ezekiel was quite sure that he had seen and heard the God of the Bible. While few have been privileged to see him as Ezekiel did, this God had been speaking plainly for generations. His words were on record.

> *As the appearance of the rainbow in the clouds on a rainy day. . . . such was the appearance of the likeness of the glory of the LORD. And when I saw it, I fell on my face.* 1:28

Before such splendor Ezekiel felt utterly weak and inadequate, just as Isaiah had during a similar vision (Isaiah 6). He fell on his face, repeatedly. But God raised Ezekiel to his feet and gave him a message to deliver.

A Stunning Portrait of God

In describing his call by God, Ezekiel groped for words. He portrayed a God of stunning grandeur, above and beyond our world. Yet this supernatural God was inescapably near and real. He demanded complete obedience. Surprisingly, he appeared to Ezekiel in Babylon—the last place an Israelite expected to see him. This God could not be locked in by national or geographical boxes. He ruled the earth.

Ezekiel repeated this classic message over 60 times: "You will know that I am the LORD." God said it when promising the destruction of Jerusalem in the first 24 chapters. He said it when predicting the downfall of Israel's neighbors in chapters 25 through 32. And, after Jerusalem had fallen, God said it when promising a great future in the last 16 chapters. God did not want to remain vague or far off. He wanted his people to know him. More, Ezekiel's God wanted to live with his people. He wanted to make his home in the center of their city.

A Strange Book

Ezekiel has a reputation for strangeness, partly because of the unearthly visions with which his book begins and ends, and partly because Ezekiel acted out God's messages through some bizarre behavior. (For instance, for months at a time he lay in public on his side, bound by ropes, facing a clay model of Jerusalem.) Strange? When a car is speeding down a road unaware of a bridge washout, you may take strange measures to get the driver's attention. You may scream and gesture so wildly people think you are insane. So it was with Ezekiel. His message came in the most vivid form possible, meant to force people to pay attention.

Ezekiel lived in perhaps the most tragic period of his people's existence. They had been tempting fate for generations, ignoring God's messengers (prophets like Micah, Amos, Isaiah) who warned that if they didn't listen to God, they would be destroyed. Finally, Babylonian armies swept through Judah, deporting large groups of citizens.

Ezekiel had gone into exile in one of the first groups, as had Daniel. Ezekiel became God's messenger as a captive in Babylon. His voice blended in stereo with Jeremiah's, still in Jerusalem. Both prophets warned their people (who kept plotting ways to break free of Babylon) that the captives were going to be in Babylon for a long time. They predicted that Babylon's oppression would grow heavier: Jerusalem and the temple would be destroyed. Since Judah had ignored God's repeated warnings, God would use another means to get their attention: suffering.

A New Jerusalem

Yet even while punishing them, God's aim remained the same: to make himself known. God had warned Ezekiel that the Israelites were unlikely to listen (3:7), even from captivity. They preferred idols to the living God. Yet Ezekiel's messages and dramas and visions continued to come, year after year. It's as though God were saying through him, "Some way, some day, I will get through to them. If the message doesn't reach their hearts one way, I'll try another."

Ezekiel ends with hope. The final chapters show a new Jerusalem rising from the ruins of the old. The renewed city would never die, for it would be built on an unshifting reality: "They will know that I am the Lord." The burning vision of God that Ezekiel had seen would become accessible to all. God would make himself at home there forever. Ezekiel's last verse says it all: "And the name of the city from that day shall be: The Lord is there."

How to Read Ezekiel

The special difficulty in reading Ezekiel is the dizzying variety of forms he used to get his message across. The book is like a multimedia package—a mix of visions, messages, dramas, poems. But three remarkable visions of God bracket the package, beginning, middle, and end (1:1—3:15; 8:1—6 and 11:16—25; 40:1—4 and 43:1—9). And throughout, one line is repeated: "You will know that I am the Lord." All God's messages are meant to shock his people into restoring a living relationship with him.

As you read Ezekiel, note down when each prophecy was made and its dominant image—Jerusalem as a prostitute, as a spreading grapevine, as a shaved head, etc. (For insight into why Ezekiel sometimes acted out his message in bizarre fashion, read "Living Parables," page 847.) Don't skip ahead too fast as you read—take time to think about the message in each section. Remember that the book of Ezekiel compresses messages God gave over 22 years. Try to imagine the impact of each message on the people who first heard or saw it.

Most of what Ezekiel said in Babylonia concerned a dramatic military situation hundreds of miles away in Jerusalem. His message changed from doom to hope in chapter 33; the turning point came with news of Jerusalem's fall. You can get to know the historical situation by reading 2 Kings 23:36—25:12. "A Lineup of Rulers," page 1417—1425, can help you place Ezekiel in Israel's history.

A fascinating though difficult study is the design of the renewed temple, which Ezekiel described in chapters 40—43. A commentary on Ezekiel or a Bible dictionary (under "Ezekiel" or "temple") can help immensely in understanding these visions.

PEOPLE YOU'LL MEET IN EZEKIEL

EZEKIEL (p. 882)

3-TRACK READING PLAN

For an explanation and complete listing of the 3-track reading plan, turn to page 7.

TRACK 1: **Two-Week Courses on the Bible**
See page 7 for information on these courses.

TRACK 2: **An Overview of Ezekiel in 4 Days**
☐ Day 1. Read the Introduction to Ezekiel and chapter 1, the majestic vision of a living God who appeared to Ezekiel.
☐ Day 2. Read chapters 2—3, which tell how God called Ezekiel to deliver a difficult message.
☐ Day 3. Read chapter 4, one of the most dramatic of the "enacted parables" Ezekiel performed.
☐ Day 4. Read chapter 37, a message of hope and resurrection for a defeated people.

Now turn to page 9 for your next Track 2 reading project.

TRACK 3: **All of Ezekiel in 47 Days**
After you have read through Ezekiel, turn to pages 10–14 for your next Track 3
reading project.

☐1	☐2–3	☐4	☐5	☐6	☐7	☐8	☐9
☐10	☐11	☐12	☐13	☐14	☐15	☐16	☐17
☐18	☐19	☐20	☐21	☐22	☐23	☐24	☐25
☐26	☐27	☐28	☐29	☐30	☐31	☐32	☐33
☐34	☐35	☐36	☐37	☐38	☐39	☐40	☐41
☐42	☐43	☐44	☐45	☐46	☐47	☐48	

The Vision of Four Figures

1 Now it came about in the thirtieth year, on the fifth *day* of the fourth month, while I was by the river Chebar among the exiles, the heavens were opened and I saw visions of God.

2 (On the fifth of the month in the fifth year of King Jehoiachin's exile,

3 the word of the LORD came expressly to Ezekiel the priest, son of Buzi, in the land of the Chaldeans by the river Chebar; and there the hand of the LORD came upon him.)

1:3 Foreign Appearance

Most ancient religions worshiped tribal gods, whose rule extended only within the tribal territory. As an exile, Ezekiel may have wondered whether the God of Israel would still speak so far from home. But it was in Babylon that God appeared. The terrifying vision in a windstorm revealed a God who ruled over the entire world, awesome, magnificent, exalted, far more powerful than the Babylonian armies.

4 ¶ As I looked, behold, a storm wind was coming from the north, a great cloud with fire flashing forth continually and a bright light around it, and in its midst something like glowing metal in the midst of the fire.

5 Within it there were figures resembling four living beings. And this was their appearance: they had human form.

6 Each of them had four faces and four wings.

7 Their legs were straight and their feet were like a calf's hoof, and they gleamed like burnished bronze.

8 Under their wings on their four sides *were* human hands. As for the faces and wings of the four of them,

9 their wings touched one another; *their faces* did not turn when they moved, each went straight forward.

10 As for the form of their faces, *each* had the face of a man; all four had the face of a lion on the right and the face of a bull on the left, and all four had the face of an eagle.

11 Such were their faces. Their wings were spread out above; each had two touching another *being,* and two covering their bodies.

12 And each went straight forward; wherever the spirit was about to go, they would go, without turning as they went.

13 In the midst of the living beings there was something that looked like burning coals of fire, like torches darting back and forth among the living beings. The fire was bright, and lightning was flashing from the fire.

14 And the living beings ran to and fro like bolts of lightning.

15 ¶ Now as I looked at the living beings, behold, there was one wheel on the earth beside the living beings, for *each of* the four of them.

16 The appearance of the wheels and their workmanship *was* like sparkling beryl, and all four of them had the same form, their appearance and workmanship *being* as if one wheel were within another.

17 Whenever they moved, they moved in any of their four directions without turning as they moved.

18 As for their rims they were lofty and awesome, and the rims of all four of them were full of eyes round about.

19 Whenever the living beings moved, the wheels moved with them. And whenever the living beings rose from the earth, the wheels rose *also.*

20 Wherever the spirit was about to go, they would go in that direction. And the wheels rose close beside them; for the spirit of the living beings *was* in the wheels.

21 Whenever those went, these went; and whenever those stood still, these stood still. And whenever those rose from the earth, the wheels rose close beside them; for the spirit of the living beings *was* in the wheels.

Vision of Divine Glory

22 ¶ Now over the heads of the living beings *there was* something like an expanse, like the awesome gleam of crystal, spread out over their heads.

23 Under the expanse their wings *were* stretched out straight, one toward the other; each one also had two wings covering its body on the one side and on the other.

24 I also heard the sound of their wings like the sound of abundant waters as they went, like the voice of the Almighty, a sound of tumult like the sound of an army camp; whenever they stood still, they dropped their wings.

25 And there came a voice from above the expanse that was over their heads; whenever they stood still, they dropped their wings.

26 ¶ Now above the expanse that was over their heads there was something resembling a throne, like lapis lazuli in appearance; and on that which resembled a throne, high up, *was* a figure with the appearance of a man.

27 Then I noticed from the appearance of His loins and upward something like glowing metal that looked like fire all around within it, and from the appearance of His loins and downward I saw something like fire; and *there was* a radiance around Him.

28 As the appearance of the rainbow in the clouds on a rainy day, so *was* the appearance of the surrounding radiance. Such *was* the appearance of the likeness of the glory of the LORD. And when I saw *it*, I fell on my face and heard a voice speaking.

The Prophet's Call

2 Then He said to me, "Son of man, stand on your feet that I may speak with you!"

2 As He spoke to me the Spirit entered me and set me on my feet; and I heard *Him* speaking to me.

3 Then He said to me, "Son of man, I am sending you to the sons of Israel, to a rebellious people who have rebelled against Me; they and their fathers have transgressed against Me to this very day.

4 "I am sending you to them who are stubborn and obstinate children, and you shall say to them, 'Thus says the Lord GOD.'

5 "As for them, whether they listen or not—for they are a rebellious house—they will know that a prophet has been among them.

6 "And you, son of man, neither fear them nor fear their words, though thistles and thorns are with you and you sit on scorpions; neither fear their words nor be dismayed at their presence, for they are a rebellious house.

7 "But you shall speak My words to them whether they listen or not, for they are rebellious.

8 ¶ "Now you, son of man, listen to what I am speaking to you; do not be rebellious like that rebellious house. Open your mouth and eat what I am giving you."

9 Then I looked, and behold, a hand was extended to me; and lo, a scroll *was* in it.

10 When He spread it out before me, it was written on the front and back, and written on it were lamentations, mourning and woe.

Ezekiel's Commission

3 Then He said to me, "Son of man, eat what you find; eat this scroll, and go, speak to the house of Israel."

2 So I opened my mouth, and He fed me this scroll.

3 He said to me, "Son of man, feed your stomach and fill your body with this scroll which I am giving you." Then I ate it, and it was sweet as honey in my mouth.

3:3 Eat the Scroll

The scroll with words of woe looked inedible, but tasted sweet as honey to Ezekiel. Most of God's prophets gave bitter messages of warning, but God's word sustained and strengthened them as they served him. (See also Jeremiah's experience, in Jeremiah 15:16.) Similarly, the book of Revelation tells of a scroll being eaten (Revelation 10:9–11). Many of Ezekiel's images are paralleled in that book.

4 ¶ Then He said to me, "Son of man, go to the house of Israel and speak with My words to them.

5 "For you are not being sent to a people of unintelligible speech or difficult language, *but* to the house of Israel,

6 nor to many peoples of unintelligible speech or difficult language, whose words you cannot understand. But I have sent you to them who should listen to you;

7 yet the house of Israel will not be willing to listen to you, since they are not willing to listen to Me. Surely the whole house of Israel is stubborn and obstinate.

8 "Behold, I have made your face as hard as their faces and your forehead as hard as their foreheads.

9 "Like emery harder than flint I have made your forehead. Do not be afraid of them or be dismayed before them, though they are a rebellious house."

10 Moreover, He said to me, "Son of man, take into your heart all My words which I will speak to you and listen closely.

11 "Go to the exiles, to the sons of your people, and speak to them and tell them, whether they listen or not, 'Thus says the Lord GOD.' "

12 ¶ Then the Spirit lifted me up, and I heard a great rumbling sound behind me, "Blessed be the glory of the LORD in His place."

13 And I *heard* the sound of the wings of the living beings touching one another and the sound of the wheels beside them, even a great rumbling sound.

14 So the Spirit lifted me up and took me away; and I went embittered in the rage of my spirit, and the hand of the LORD was strong on me.

15 Then I came to the exiles who lived beside the river Chebar at Tel-abib, and I sat there seven days where they were living, causing consternation among them.

16 ¶ At the end of seven days the word of the LORD came to me, saying,

17 "Son of man, I have appointed you a watchman to the house of Israel; whenever you hear a word from My mouth, warn them from Me.

18 "When I say to the wicked, 'You will surely die,' and you do not warn him or speak out to warn the wicked from his wicked way that he may live, that wicked man shall die in his iniquity, but his blood I will require at your hand.

19 "Yet if you have warned the wicked and he does not turn from his wickedness or from his wicked way, he shall die in his iniquity; but you have delivered yourself.

20 "Again, when a righteous man turns away from his righteousness and commits iniquity, and I place an obstacle before him, he will die; since you have not warned him, he shall die in his sin, and his righteous deeds which he has done shall not be remembered; but his blood I will require at your hand.

21 "However, if you have warned the righteous man that the righteous should not sin and he does not sin, he shall surely live because he took warning; and you have delivered yourself."

22 ¶ The hand of the LORD was on me there, and He said to me, "Get up, go out to the plain, and there I will speak to you."

23 So I got up and went out to the plain; and behold, the glory of the LORD was standing there, like the glory which I saw by the river Chebar, and I fell on my face.

24 The Spirit then entered me and made me stand on my feet, and He spoke with me and said to me, "Go, shut yourself up in your house.

25 "As for you, son of man, they will put ropes on you and bind you with them so that you cannot go out among them.

26 "Moreover, I will make your tongue stick to the roof of your mouth so that you will be mute and cannot be a man who rebukes them, for they are a rebellious house.

27 "But when I speak to you, I will open your mouth and you will say to them, 'Thus says the Lord GOD.' He who hears, let him hear; and he who refuses, let him refuse; for they are a rebellious house.

Siege of Jerusalem Predicted

4 "Now you son of man, get yourself a brick, place it before you and inscribe a city on it, Jerusalem.

2 "Then lay siege against it, build a siege wall, raise up a ramp, pitch camps and place battering rams against it all around.

3 "Then get yourself an iron plate and set it up as an iron wall between you and the city, and set your face toward it so that it is under siege, and besiege it. This is a sign to the house of Israel.

4 ¶ "As for you, lie down on your left side and lay the iniquity of the house of Israel on it; you shall bear their iniquity for the number of days that you lie on it.

5 "For I have assigned you a number of days

EZEKIEL *Radical Priest*

SOME GREAT HISTORICAL FIGURES ARE known only by their accomplishments. The artists who created the great European cathedrals, for example—in most cases we do not even know their names. They fashioned beautiful monuments to God, not to themselves.

In some ways Ezekiel fits this pattern. He created a major book of the Bible and acted as God's messenger in some hinge moments of history. We know what he did, yet we know next to nothing about *him*: his personality, his background, his family life. Ezekiel recounted his calling as a prophet in detail and mentioned his work as a priest, but otherwise his book includes only a few shreds of personal information (such as the fact that he was married). His work swallowed up his life.

Ezekiel's story begins with King Nebuchadnezzar taking him captive from Jerusalem to Babylon—the site of present-day Iraq. No doubt the foreign setting made him feel lonely and homesick. He was a priest far from God's temple, as fruitless a combination as a basketball coach without a gym. What could Ezekiel do?

Complicating Ezekiel's life, God told him to deliver a very unpopular message—that God would continue to punish his people because they had not repented from their sin. Moreover, God instructed Ezekiel to dramatize that message in bizarre ways. At various times he ate a book, shaved his head, cooked with cow manure, and lay outdoors beside a model of Jerusalem. Looking back, some of Ezekiel's "object lessons" seem downright weird.

For one short period, when his predictions came true, Ezekiel enjoyed popularity and acceptance (33:30–32). More often, though, he needed God's prodding and encouragement: "Neither fear them nor fear their words, though thistles and thorns are with you and you sit on scorpions" (2:6). God had vital work for him to do. For Ezekiel, that made for a worthy life, regardless of the cost.

Life Questions: If you were to die today, what "monument" would you leave behind?

corresponding to the years of their iniquity, three hundred and ninety days; thus you shall bear the iniquity of the house of Israel.

6 "When you have completed these, you shall lie down a second time, *but* on your right side and bear the iniquity of the house of Judah; I have assigned it to you for forty days, a day for each year.

7 "Then you shall set your face toward the siege of Jerusalem with your arm bared and prophesy against it.

8 "Now behold, I will put ropes on you so that you cannot turn from one side to the other until you have completed the days of your siege.

Defiled Bread

9 ¶ "But as for you, take wheat, barley, beans, lentils, millet and spelt, put them in one vessel and make them into bread for yourself; you shall eat it according to the number of the days that you lie on your side, three hundred and ninety days.

10 "Your food which you eat *shall be* twenty shekels a day by weight; you shall eat it from time to time.

11 "The water you drink shall be the sixth part of a hin by measure; you shall drink it from time to time.

12 "You shall eat it as a barley cake, having baked *it* in their sight over human dung."

13 Then the LORD said, "Thus will the sons of Israel eat their bread unclean among the nations where I will banish them."

14 But I said, "Ah, Lord GOD! Behold, I have never been defiled; for from my youth until now I have never eaten what died of itself or was torn by beasts, nor has any unclean meat ever entered my mouth."

15 Then He said to me, "See, I will give you cow's dung in place of human dung over which you will prepare your bread."

16 Moreover, He said to me, "Son of man, behold, I am going to break the staff of bread in Jerusalem, and they will eat bread by weight and with anxiety, and drink water by measure and in horror,

17 because bread and water will be scarce; and they will be appalled with one another and waste away in their iniquity.

Jerusalem's Desolation Foretold

5 "As for you, son of man, take a sharp sword; take and use it *as* a barber's razor on your head and beard. Then take scales for weighing and divide the hair.

2 "One third you shall burn in the fire at the center of the city, when the days of the siege are completed. Then you shall take one third and strike *it* with the sword all around the city, and one third you shall scatter to the wind; and I will unsheathe a sword behind them.

3 "Take also a few in number from them and bind them in the edges of your *robes*.

4 "Take again some of them and throw them into the fire and burn them in the fire; from it a fire will spread to all the house of Israel.

5 ¶ "Thus says the Lord GOD, 'This is Jerusalem; I have set her at the center of the nations, with lands around her.

5:5 Navel of the Universe

Maps dating from the Middle Ages often showed Jerusalem and Israel as the center of a flat world. The practice probably stemmed from several verses like this one, referring to Jerusalem as "the center of the nations." Geography was not what God had in mind, however. Jerusalem was at the center of his love. A lover might say something similar: "You're the center of my universe."

6 'But she has rebelled against My ordinances more wickedly than the nations and against My statutes more than the lands which surround her; for they have rejected My ordinances and have not walked in My statutes.'

7 "Therefore, thus says the Lord GOD, 'Because you have more turmoil than the nations which surround you *and* have not walked in My statutes, nor observed My ordinances, nor observed the ordinances of the nations which surround you,'

8 therefore, thus says the Lord GOD, 'Behold, I, even I, am against you, and I will execute judgments among you in the sight of the nations.

9 'And because of all your abominations, I will do among you what I have not done, and the like of which I will never do again.

10 'Therefore, fathers will eat *their* sons among you, and sons will eat their fathers; for I will execute judgments on you and scatter all your remnant to every wind.

11 'So as I live,' declares the Lord GOD, 'surely, because you have defiled My sanctuary with all your detestable idols and with all your abominations, therefore I will also withdraw, and My eye will have no pity and I will not spare.

12 'One third of you will die by plague or be consumed by famine among you, one third will fall by the sword around you, and one third I will scatter to every wind, and I will unsheathe a sword behind them.

13 ¶ 'Thus My anger will be spent and I will satisfy My wrath on them, and I will be appeased; then they will know that I, the LORD, have spoken in My zeal when I have spent My wrath upon them.

14 'Moreover, I will make you a desolation and a reproach among the nations which surround you, in the sight of all who pass by.

15 'So it will be a reproach, a reviling, a warning

and an object of horror to the nations who surround you when I execute judgments against you in anger, wrath and raging rebukes. I, the LORD, have spoken.

16 'When I send against them the deadly arrows of famine which were for the destruction of those whom I will send to destroy you, then I will also intensify the famine upon you and break the staff of bread.

17 'Moreover, I will send on you famine and wild beasts, and they will bereave you of children; plague and bloodshed also will pass through you, and I will bring the sword on you. I, the LORD, have spoken.' "

Idolatrous Worship Denounced

6 And the word of the LORD came to me saying, 2 "Son of man, set your face toward the mountains of Israel, and prophesy against them

3 and say, 'Mountains of Israel, listen to the word of the Lord GOD! Thus says the Lord GOD to the mountains, the hills, the ravines and the valleys: "Behold, I Myself am going to bring a sword on you, and I will destroy your high places.

4 "So your altars will become desolate and your incense altars will be smashed; and I will make your slain fall in front of your idols.

5 "I will also lay the dead bodies of the sons of Israel in front of their idols; and I will scatter your bones around your altars.

6 "In all your dwellings, cities will become waste and the high places will be desolate, that your altars may become waste and desolate, your idols may be broken and brought to an end, your incense altars may be cut down, and your works may be blotted out.

7 "The slain will fall among you, and you will know that I am the LORD.

8 ¶ "However, I will leave a remnant, for you will have those who escaped the sword among the nations when you are scattered among the countries.

9 "Then those of you who escape will remember Me among the nations to which they will be carried captive, how I have been hurt by their adulterous hearts which turned away from Me, and by their eyes which played the harlot after their idols; and they will loathe themselves in their own sight for the evils which they have committed, for all their abominations.

10 "Then they will know that I am the LORD; I have not said in vain that I would inflict this disaster on them." '

11 ¶ "Thus says the Lord GOD, 'Clap your hand, stamp your foot and say, "Alas, because of all the evil abominations of the house of Israel, which will fall by sword, famine and plague!

12 "He who is far off will die by the plague, and he who is near will fall by the sword, and he who remains and is besieged will die by the famine. Thus will I spend My wrath on them.

13 "Then you will know that I am the LORD, when their slain are among their idols around their altars, on every high hill, on all the tops of the mountains, under every green tree and under

6:9 A Dim View of Idolatry

Ezekiel said little about exploitation and injustice. He concentrated on Israel's rejection of a relationship with the living God; they preferred idols instead. The Hebrew word translated "idols" here is used 38 times in Ezekiel, nine in the rest of the Old Testament. Some scholars believe the word is derived from "pellet of dung," indicating Ezekiel's scorn.

every leafy oak—the places where they offered soothing aroma to all their idols.

14 "So throughout all their habitations I will stretch out My hand against them and make the land more desolate and waste than the wilderness toward Diblah; thus they will know that I am the LORD." ' "

Punishment for Wickedness Foretold

7 Moreover, the word of the LORD came to me saying,

2 "And you, son of man, thus says the Lord GOD to the land of Israel, 'An end! The end is coming on the four corners of the land.

3 'Now the end is upon you, and I will send My anger against you; I will judge you according to your ways and bring all your abominations upon you.

4 'For My eye will have no pity on you, nor will I spare you, but I will bring your ways upon you, and your abominations will be among you; then you will know that I am the LORD!'

5 ¶ "Thus says the Lord GOD, 'A disaster, unique disaster, behold it is coming!

6 'An end is coming; the end has come! It has awakened against you; behold, it has come!

7 'Your doom has come to you, O inhabitant of the land. The time has come, the day is near—tumult rather than joyful shouting on the mountains.

8 'Now I will shortly pour out My wrath on you and spend My anger against you; judge you according to your ways and bring on you all your abominations.

9 'My eye will show no pity nor will I spare. I will repay you according to your ways, while your abominations are in your midst; then you will know that I, the LORD, do the smiting.

10 ¶ 'Behold, the day! Behold, it is coming! Your doom has gone forth; the rod has budded, arrogance has blossomed.

11 'Violence has grown into a rod of wickedness. None of them shall remain, none of their

people, none of their wealth, nor anything eminent among them.

12 'The time has come, the day has arrived. Let not the buyer rejoice nor the seller mourn; for wrath is against all their multitude.

13 'Indeed, the seller will not regain what he sold as long as they *both* live; for the vision regarding all their multitude will not be averted, nor will any of them maintain his life by his iniquity.

14 ¶ 'They have blown the trumpet and made everything ready, but no one is going to the battle, for My wrath is against all their multitude.

15 'The sword is outside and the plague and the famine are within. He who is in the field will die by the sword; famine and the plague will also consume those in the city.

16 'Even when their survivors escape, they will be on the mountains like doves of the valleys, all of them mourning, each over his own iniquity.

17 'All hands will hang limp and all knees will become *like* water.

18 'They will gird themselves with sackcloth and shuddering will overwhelm them; and shame *will be* on all faces and baldness on all their heads.

19 'They will fling their silver into the streets and their gold will become an abhorrent thing; their silver and their gold will not be able to deliver them in the day of the wrath of the LORD. They cannot satisfy their appetite nor can they fill their stomachs, for their iniquity has become an occasion of stumbling.

The Temple Profaned

20 'They transformed the beauty of His ornaments into pride, and they made the images of their abominations *and* their detestable things with it; therefore I will make it an abhorrent thing to them.

21 'I will give it into the hands of the foreigners as plunder and to the wicked of the earth as spoil, and they will profane it.

22 'I will also turn My face from them, and they will profane My secret place; then robbers will enter and profane it.

23 ¶ 'Make the chain, for the land is full of bloody crimes and the city is full of violence.

24 'Therefore, I will bring the worst of the nations, and they will possess their houses. I will also make the pride of the strong ones cease, and their holy places will be profaned.

25 'When anguish comes, they will seek peace, but there will be none.

26 'Disaster will come upon disaster and rumor will be *added* to rumor; then they will seek a vision from a prophet, but the law will be lost from the priest and counsel from the elders.

27 'The king will mourn, the prince will be clothed with horror, and the hands of the people of the land will tremble. According to their conduct I will deal with them, and by their judgments I will judge them. And they will know that I am the LORD.' "

Vision of Abominations in Jerusalem

8 It came about in the sixth year, on the fifth *day* of the sixth month, as I was sitting in my house with the elders of Judah sitting before me, that the hand of the Lord GOD fell on me there.

2 Then I looked, and behold, a likeness as the appearance of a man; from His loins and downward *there was* the appearance of fire, and from His loins and upward the appearance of brightness, like the appearance of glowing metal.

3 He stretched out the form of a hand and caught me by a lock of my head; and the Spirit lifted me up between earth and heaven and brought me in the visions of God to Jerusalem, to the entrance of the north gate of the inner *court*, where the seat of the idol of jealousy, which provokes to jealousy, was *located*.

4 And behold, the glory of the God of Israel *was* there, like the appearance which I saw in the plain.

5 ¶ Then He said to me, "Son of man, raise your eyes now toward the north." So I raised my eyes toward the north, and behold, to the north of the altar gate *was* this idol of jealousy at the entrance.

6 And He said to me, "Son of man, do you see what they are doing, the great abominations which the house of Israel are committing here, so that I would be far from My sanctuary? But yet you will see still greater abominations."

8:6 Detestable Things

Ezekiel, a priest, had a special concern about the abuses going on in the temple. Here, in a vision, he sees painful details of these practices, notably idol worship (verses 5,10) and sun worship (verse 16). The leaders of Israel had lost faith in their God, and were desperately trying alternatives. Here and elsewhere Ezekiel accuses leaders by name; his original audience would have known them well.

7 ¶ Then He brought me to the entrance of the court, and when I looked, behold, a hole in the wall.

8 He said to me, "Son of man, now dig through the wall." So I dug through the wall, and behold, an entrance.

9 And He said to me, "Go in and see the wicked abominations that they are committing here."

10 So I entered and looked, and behold, every form of creeping things and beasts *and* detestable things, with all the idols of the house of Israel, were carved on the wall all around.

11 Standing in front of them were seventy el-

ders of the house of Israel, with Jaazaniah the son of Shaphan standing among them, each man with his censer in his hand and the fragrance of the cloud of incense rising.

12 Then He said to me, "Son of man, do you see what the elders of the house of Israel are committing in the dark, each man in the room of his carved images? For they say, 'The LORD does not see us; the LORD has forsaken the land.' "

13 And He said to me, "Yet you will see still greater abominations which they are committing."

14 ¶ Then He brought me to the entrance of the gate of the LORD'S house which was toward the north; and behold, women were sitting there weeping for Tammuz.

15 He said to me, "Do you see this, son of man? Yet you will see still greater abominations than these."

16 ¶ Then He brought me into the inner court of the LORD'S house. And behold, at the entrance to the temple of the LORD, between the porch and the altar, were about twenty-five men with their backs to the temple of the LORD and their faces toward the east; and they were prostrating themselves eastward toward the sun.

17 He said to me, "Do you see this, son of man? Is it too light a thing for the house of Judah to commit the abominations which they have committed here, that they have filled the land with violence and provoked Me repeatedly? For behold, they are putting the twig to their nose.

18 "Therefore, I indeed will deal in wrath. My eye will have no pity nor will I spare; and though they cry in My ears with a loud voice, yet I will not listen to them."

The Vision of Slaughter

9 Then He cried out in my hearing with a loud voice saying, "Draw near, O executioners of the city, each with his destroying weapon in his hand."

2 Behold, six men came from the direction of the upper gate which faces north, each with his shattering weapon in his hand; and among them was a certain man clothed in linen with a writing case at his loins. And they went in and stood beside the bronze altar.

3 ¶ Then the glory of the God of Israel went up from the cherub on which it had been, to the threshold of the temple. And He called to the man clothed in linen at whose loins was the writing case.

4 The LORD said to him, "Go through the midst of the city, even through the midst of Jerusalem, and put a mark on the foreheads of the men who sigh and groan over all the abominations which are being committed in its midst."

5 But to the others He said in my hearing, "Go through the city after him and strike; do not let your eye have pity and do not spare.

6 "Utterly slay old men, young men, maidens, little children, and women, but do not touch any man on whom is the mark; and you shall start from My sanctuary." So they started with the elders who were before the temple.

9:4 The Saving Mark

The man in linen marked those to be saved with a taw, the final letter in the Hebrew alphabet, written in the oldest script as "x"— a cross, as Christians have noted.

7 And He said to them, "Defile the temple and fill the courts with the slain. Go out!" Thus they went out and struck down the people in the city.

8 As they were striking the people and I alone was left, I fell on my face and cried out saying, "Alas, Lord GOD! Are You destroying the whole remnant of Israel by pouring out Your wrath on Jerusalem?"

9 ¶ Then He said to me, "The iniquity of the house of Israel and Judah is very, very great, and the land is filled with blood and the city is full of perversion; for they say, 'The LORD has forsaken the land, and the LORD does not see!'

10 "But as for Me, My eye will have no pity nor will I spare, but I will bring their conduct upon their heads."

11 ¶ Then behold, the man clothed in linen at whose loins was the writing case reported, saying, "I have done just as You have commanded me."

Vision of God's Glory Departing from the Temple

10 Then I looked, and behold, in the expanse that was over the heads of the cherubim something like a sapphire stone, in appearance resembling a throne, appeared above them.

2 And He spoke to the man clothed in linen and said, "Enter between the whirling wheels under the cherubim and fill your hands with coals of fire from between the cherubim and scatter them over the city." And he entered in my sight.

3 ¶ Now the cherubim were standing on the right side of the temple when the man entered, and the cloud filled the inner court.

4 Then the glory of the LORD went up from the cherub to the threshold of the temple, and the temple was filled with the cloud and the court was filled with the brightness of the glory of the LORD.

5 Moreover, the sound of the wings of the cherubim was heard as far as the outer court, like the voice of God Almighty when He speaks.

6 ¶ It came about when He commanded the man clothed in linen, saying, "Take fire from between the whirling wheels, from between the cherubim," he entered and stood beside a wheel.

7 Then the cherub stretched out his hand from between the cherubim to the fire which was

between the cherubim, took *some* and put *it* into the hands of the one clothed in linen, who took *it* and went out.

8 The cherubim appeared to have the form of a man's hand under their wings.

9 ¶ Then I looked, and behold, four wheels beside the cherubim, one wheel beside each cherub; and the appearance of the wheels *was* like the gleam of a Tarshish stone.

10 As for their appearance, all four of them had the same likeness, as if one wheel were within another wheel.

11 When they moved, they went in *any of* their four directions without turning as they went; but they followed in the direction which they faced, without turning as they went.

12 Their whole body, their backs, their hands, their wings and the wheels were full of eyes all around, the wheels belonging to all four of them.

13 The wheels were called in my hearing, the whirling wheels.

14 And each one had four faces. The first face *was* the face of a cherub, the second face *was* the face of a man, the third the face of a lion, and the fourth the face of an eagle.

15 ¶ Then the cherubim rose up. They are the living beings that I saw by the river Chebar.

16 Now when the cherubim moved, the wheels would go beside them; also when the cherubim lifted up their wings to rise from the ground, the wheels would not turn from beside them.

17 When the cherubim stood still, the wheels would stand still; and when they rose up, the wheels would rise with them, for the spirit of the living beings *was* in them.

18 ¶ Then the glory of the LORD departed from the threshold of the temple and stood over the cherubim.

10:18 Good-bye, God

What would it mean if the President of the United States grew so disgusted with the government that he moved out of the White House—and vanished? It would mean spectacular news, and trouble for the nation. Ezekiel's vision indicates even bigger problems for the Israelites. God—the same powerful God who appeared to Ezekiel in Babylon (chapter 1) —leaves the temple. Sick of his people's corruption, he simply moves out.

19 When the cherubim departed, they lifted their wings and rose up from the earth in my sight with the wheels beside them; and they stood still at the entrance of the east gate of the LORD's house, and the glory of the God of Israel hovered over them.

20 ¶ These are the living beings that I saw beneath the God of Israel by the river Chebar; so I knew that they *were* cherubim.

21 Each one had four faces and each one four wings, and beneath their wings *was* the form of human hands.

22 As for the likeness of their faces, they were the same faces whose appearance I had seen by the river Chebar. Each one went straight ahead.

Evil Rulers to Be Judged

11 Moreover, the Spirit lifted me up and brought me to the east gate of the LORD's house which faced eastward. And behold, *there were* twenty-five men at the entrance of the gate, and among them I saw Jaazaniah son of Azzur and Pelatiah son of Benaiah, leaders of the people.

2 He said to me, "Son of man, these are the men who devise iniquity and give evil advice in this city,

3 who say, 'Is not *the time* near to build houses? This *city* is the pot and we are the flesh.'

4 "Therefore, prophesy against them, son of man, prophesy!"

5 ¶ Then the Spirit of the LORD fell upon me, and He said to me, "Say, 'Thus says the LORD, "So you think, house of Israel, for I know your thoughts.

6 "You have multiplied your slain in this city, filling its streets with them."

7 'Therefore, thus says the Lord GOD, "Your slain whom you have laid in the midst of the city are the flesh and this *city* is the pot; but I will bring you out of it.

8 "You have feared a sword; so I will bring a sword upon you," the Lord GOD declares.

9 "And I will bring you out of the midst of the city and deliver you into the hands of strangers and execute judgments against you.

10 "You will fall by the sword. I will judge you to the border of Israel; so you shall know that I am the LORD.

11 "This *city* will not be a pot for you, nor will you be flesh in the midst of it, *but* I will judge you to the border of Israel.

12 "Thus you will know that I am the LORD; for you have not walked in My statutes nor have you executed My ordinances, but have acted according to the ordinances of the nations around you." ' "

13 ¶ Now it came about as I prophesied, that Pelatiah son of Benaiah died. Then I fell on my face and cried out with a loud voice and said, "Alas, Lord GOD! Will You bring the remnant of Israel to a complete end?"

Promise of Restoration

14 ¶ Then the word of the LORD came to me, saying,

15 "Son of man, your brothers, your relatives, your fellow exiles and the whole house of Israel, all of them, *are those* to whom the inhabitants of

Jerusalem have said, 'Go far from the LORD; this land has been given us as a possession.'

16 "Therefore say, 'Thus says the Lord GOD, "Though I had removed them far away among the nations and though I had scattered them among the countries, yet I was a sanctuary for them a little while in the countries where they had gone." '

17 "Therefore say, 'Thus says the Lord GOD, "I will gather you from the peoples and assemble you out of the countries among which you have been scattered, and I will give you the land of Israel." '

18 "When they come there, they will remove all its detestable things and all its abominations from it.

19 "And I will give them one heart, and put a new spirit within them. And I will take the heart of stone out of their flesh and give them a heart of flesh,

20 that they may walk in My statutes and keep My ordinances and do them. Then they will be My people, and I shall be their God.

21 "But as for those whose hearts go after their detestable things and abominations, I will bring their conduct down on their heads," declares the Lord GOD.

22 ¶ Then the cherubim lifted up their wings with the wheels beside them, and the glory of the God of Israel hovered over them.

23 The glory of the LORD went up from the midst of the city and stood over the mountain which is east of the city.

24 And the Spirit lifted me up and brought me in a vision by the Spirit of God to the exiles in Chaldea. So the vision that I had seen left me.

25 Then I told the exiles all the things that the LORD had shown me.

Ezekiel Prepares for Exile

12 Then the word of the LORD came to me, saying,

2 "Son of man, you live in the midst of the rebellious house, who have eyes to see but do not see, ears to hear but do not hear; for they are a rebellious house.

3 "Therefore, son of man, prepare for yourself baggage for exile and go into exile by day in their sight; even go into exile from your place to another place in their sight. Perhaps they will understand though they are a rebellious house.

4 "Bring your baggage out by day in their sight, as baggage for exile. Then you will go out at evening in their sight, as those going into exile.

5 "Dig a hole through the wall in their sight and go out through it.

6 "Load the baggage on your shoulder in their sight and carry it out in the dark. You shall cover your face so that you cannot see the land, for I have set you as a sign to the house of Israel."

7 ¶ I did so, as I had been commanded. By day I brought out my baggage like the baggage of an exile. Then in the evening I dug through the wall with my hands; I went out in the dark and carried the baggage on my shoulder in their sight.

8 ¶ In the morning the word of the LORD came to me, saying,

9 "Son of man, has not the house of Israel, the rebellious house, said to you, 'What are you doing?'

10 "Say to them, 'Thus says the Lord GOD, "This burden concerns the prince in Jerusalem as well as all the house of Israel who are in it." '

11 "Say, 'I am a sign to you. As I have done, so it will be done to them; they will go into exile, into captivity.'

12 "The prince who is among them will load his baggage on his shoulder in the dark and go out. They will dig a hole through the wall to bring it out. He will cover his face so that he can not see the land with his eyes.

12:12 Out Through the Hole

Ezekiel's prediction of Jerusalem's leader leaving through a hole in the wall was literally fulfilled. You can read about it in 2 Kings 25:4–7 or Jeremiah 39:4–7.

13 "I will also spread My net over him, and he will be caught in My snare. And I will bring him to Babylon in the land of the Chaldeans; yet he will not see it, though he will die there.

14 "I will scatter to every wind all who are around him, his helpers and all his troops; and I will draw out a sword after them.

15 "So they will know that I am the LORD when I scatter them among the nations and spread them among the countries.

16 "But I will spare a few of them from the sword, the famine and the pestilence that they may tell all their abominations among the nations where they go, and may know that I am the LORD."

17 ¶ Moreover, the word of the LORD came to me saying,

18 "Son of man, eat your bread with trembling and drink your water with quivering and anxiety.

19 "Then say to the people of the land, 'Thus says the Lord GOD concerning the inhabitants of Jerusalem in the land of Israel, "They will eat their bread with anxiety and drink their water with horror, because their land will be stripped of its fullness on account of the violence of all who live in it.

20 "The inhabited cities will be laid waste and the land will be a desolation. So you will know that I am the LORD." ' "

21 ¶ Then the word of the LORD came to me, saying,

22 "Son of man, what is this proverb you people have concerning the land of Israel, saying, 'The days are long and every vision fails'?

23 "Therefore say to them, 'Thus says the Lord GOD, "I will make this proverb cease so that they will no longer use it as a proverb in Israel." But tell them, "The days draw near as well as the fulfillment of every vision.

24 "For there will no longer be any false vision or flattering divination within the house of Israel.

25 "For I the LORD will speak, and whatever word I speak will be performed. It will no longer be delayed, for in your days, O rebellious house, I will speak the word and perform it," declares the Lord GOD.' "

26 ¶ Furthermore, the word of the LORD came to me, saying,

27 "Son of man, behold, the house of Israel is saying, 'The vision that he sees is for many years *from now*, and he prophesies of times far off.'

28 "Therefore say to them, 'Thus says the Lord GOD, "None of My words will be delayed any longer. Whatever word I speak will be performed," ' " declares the Lord GOD.

False Prophets Condemned

13 Then the word of the LORD came to me saying,

2 "Son of man, prophesy against the prophets of Israel who prophesy, and say to those who prophesy from their own inspiration, 'Listen to the word of the LORD!

3 'Thus says the Lord GOD, "Woe to the foolish prophets who are following their own spirit and have seen nothing.

4 "O Israel, your prophets have been like foxes among ruins.

5 "You have not gone up into the breaches, nor did you build the wall around the house of Israel to stand in the battle on the day of the LORD.

6 "They see falsehood and lying divination who are saying, 'The LORD declares,' when the LORD has not sent them; yet they hope for the fulfillment of *their* word.

7 "Did you not see a false vision and speak a lying divination when you said, 'The LORD declares,' but it is not I who have spoken?" ' "

8 ¶ Therefore, thus says the Lord GOD, "Because you have spoken falsehood and seen a lie, therefore behold, I am against you," declares the Lord GOD.

9 "So My hand will be against the prophets who see false visions and utter lying divinations. They will have no place in the council of My people, nor will they be written down in the register of the house of Israel, nor will they enter the land of Israel, that you may know that I am the Lord GOD.

10 "It is definitely because they have misled My people by saying, 'Peace!' when there is no peace. And when anyone builds a wall, behold, they plaster it over with whitewash;

11 *so* tell those who plaster *it* over with whitewash, that it will fall. A flooding rain will come, and you, O hailstones, will fall; and a violent wind will break out.

12 "Behold, when the wall has fallen, will you not be asked, 'Where is the plaster with which you plastered *it?*' "

13:10–16 Whitewash

The Hebrew word translated "whitewash" means "to plaster over." The picture is of a poorly constructed wall that is carefully plastered so it looks well built. False prophets, wanting everyone to be happy, spoke cheerfully about the future. But they were only covering up the surface of fundamental problems. A storm, God warns, will strip off their coat of whitewash, and the flawed wall will collapse. In contrast, real prophets were unafraid of exposing the truth, however bad, for only then could problems be remedied.
Ezekiel 13:6–9 asserts that the false prophets thought up messages, then attributed them to God. Ezekiel, on the other hand, was repeatedly seized by a supernatural power. See, for examples, Ezekiel 8:1–5; 10:1–2; 24:1–2; and 33:21–22.

13 Therefore, thus says the Lord GOD, "I will make a violent wind break out in My wrath. There will also be in My anger a flooding rain and hailstones to consume *it* in wrath.

14 "So I will tear down the wall which you plastered over with whitewash and bring it down to the ground, so that its foundation is laid bare; and when it falls, you will be consumed in its midst. And you will know that I am the LORD.

15 "Thus I will spend My wrath on the wall and on those who have plastered it over with whitewash; and I will say to you, 'The wall is gone and its plasterers are gone,

16 *along with* the prophets of Israel who prophesy to Jerusalem, and who see visions of peace for her when there is no peace,' declares the Lord GOD.

17 ¶ "Now you, son of man, set your face against the daughters of your people who are prophesying from their own inspiration. Prophesy against them

18 and say, 'Thus says the Lord GOD, "Woe to the women who sew *magic* bands on all wrists and make veils for the heads of *persons* of every stature to hunt down lives! Will you hunt down the lives of My people, but preserve the lives *of others* for yourselves?

19 "For handfuls of barley and fragments of bread, you have profaned Me to My people to put to death some who should not die and to keep others alive who should not live, by your lying to My people who listen to lies." ' "

20 ¶ Therefore, thus says the Lord GOD, "Be-

hold, I am against your *magic* bands by which you hunt lives there as birds and I will tear them from your arms; and I will let them go, even those lives whom you hunt as birds.

21 "I will also tear off your veils and deliver My people from your hands, and they will no longer be in your hands to be hunted; and you will know that I am the LORD.

22 "Because you disheartened the righteous with falsehood when I did not cause him grief, but have encouraged the wicked not to turn from his wicked way *and* preserve his life,

23 therefore, you women will no longer see false visions or practice divination, and I will deliver My people out of your hand. Thus you will know that I am the LORD."

Idolatrous Elders Condemned

14 Then some elders of Israel came to me and sat down before me.

2 And the word of the LORD came to me, saying,

3 "Son of man, these men have set up their idols in their hearts and have put right before their faces the stumbling block of their iniquity. Should I be consulted by them at all?

4 "Therefore speak to them and tell them, 'Thus says the Lord GOD, "Any man of the house of Israel who sets up his idols in his heart, puts right before his face the stumbling block of his iniquity, and *then* comes to the prophet, I the LORD will be brought to give him an answer in the matter in view of the multitude of his idols,

5 in order to lay hold of the hearts of the house of Israel who are estranged from Me through all their idols." '

6 ¶ "Therefore say to the house of Israel, 'Thus says the Lord GOD, "Repent and turn away from your idols and turn your faces away from all your abominations.

7 "For anyone of the house of Israel or of the immigrants who stay in Israel who separates himself from Me, sets up his idols in his heart, puts right before his face the stumbling block of his iniquity, and *then* comes to the prophet to inquire of Me for himself, I the LORD will be brought to answer him in My own person.

8 "I will set My face against that man and make him a sign and a proverb, and I will cut him off from among My people. So you will know that I am the LORD.

9 ¶ "But if the prophet is prevailed upon to speak a word, it is I, the LORD, who have prevailed upon that prophet, and I will stretch out My hand against him and destroy him from among My people Israel.

10 "They will bear *the punishment of* their iniquity; as the iniquity of the inquirer is, so the iniquity of the prophet will be,

11 in order that the house of Israel may no longer stray from Me and no longer defile themselves with all their transgressions. Thus they will be My people, and I shall be their God," ' declares the Lord GOD."

The City Will Not Be Spared

12 ¶ Then the word of the LORD came to me saying,

13 "Son of man, if a country sins against Me by committing unfaithfulness, and I stretch out My hand against it, destroy its supply of bread, send famine against it and cut off from it both man and beast,

14 even *though* these three men, Noah, Daniel and Job were in its midst, by their *own* righteousness they could *only* deliver themselves," declares the Lord GOD.

15 "If I were to cause wild beasts to pass through the land and they depopulated it, and it became desolate so that no one would pass through it because of the beasts,

16 *though* these three men were in its midst, as I live," declares the Lord GOD, "they could not deliver either *their* sons or *their* daughters. They alone would be delivered, but the country would be desolate.

17 "Or *if* I should bring a sword on that country and say, 'Let the sword pass through the country and cut off man and beast from it,'

18 even *though* these three men were in its midst, as I live," declares the Lord GOD, "they could not deliver either *their* sons or *their* daughters, but they alone would be delivered.

19 "Or *if* I should send a plague against that country and pour out My wrath in blood on it to cut off man and beast from it,

20 even *though* Noah, Daniel and Job were in its midst, as I live," declares the Lord GOD, "they could not deliver either *their* son or *their* daughter. They would deliver only themselves by their righteousness."

21 ¶ For thus says the Lord GOD, "How much more when I send My four severe judgments against Jerusalem: sword, famine, wild beasts and plague to cut off man and beast from it!

22 "Yet, behold, survivors will be left in it who will be brought out, *both* sons and daughters. Behold, they are going to come forth to you and you will see their conduct and actions; then you will be comforted for the calamity which I have brought against Jerusalem for everything which I have brought upon it.

23 "Then they will comfort you when you see their conduct and actions, for you will know that I have not done in vain whatever I did to it," declares the Lord GOD.

Jerusalem like a Useless Vine

15 Then the word of the LORD came to me, saying,

2 "Son of man, how is the wood of the vine

better than any wood of a branch which is among the trees of the forest?

3 "Can wood be taken from it to make anything, or can *men* take a peg from it on which to hang any vessel?

4 "If it has been put into the fire for fuel, *and* the fire has consumed both of its ends and its middle part has been charred, is it *then* useful for anything?

5 "Behold, while it is intact, it is not made into anything. How much less, when the fire has consumed it and it is charred, can it still be made into anything!

6 "Therefore, thus says the Lord GOD, 'As the wood of the vine among the trees of the forest, which I have given to the fire for fuel, so have I given up the inhabitants of Jerusalem;

7 and I set My face against them. *Though* they have come out of the fire, yet the fire will consume them. Then you will know that I am the LORD, when I set My face against them.

8 'Thus I will make the land desolate, because they have acted unfaithfully,'" declares the Lord GOD.

God's Grace to Unfaithful Jerusalem

16 Then the word of the LORD came to me, saying,

2 "Son of man, make known to Jerusalem her abominations

3 and say, 'Thus says the Lord GOD to Jerusalem, "Your origin and your birth are from the land of the Canaanite, your father was an Amorite and your mother a Hittite.

4 "As for your birth, on the day you were born your navel cord was not cut, nor were you washed with water for cleansing; you were not rubbed with salt or even wrapped in cloths.

5 "No eye looked with pity on you to do any of these things for you, to have compassion on you. Rather you were thrown out into the open field, for you were abhorred on the day you were born.

6 ¶ "When I passed by you and saw you squirming in your blood, I said to you *while you were* in your blood, 'Live!' Yes, I said to you *while you were* in your blood, 'Live!'

7 "I made you numerous like plants of the field. Then you grew up, became tall and reached the age for fine ornaments; *your* breasts were formed and your hair had grown. Yet you were naked and bare.

8 ¶ "Then I passed by you and saw you, and behold, you were at the time for love; so I spread My skirt over you and covered your nakedness. I also swore to you and entered into a covenant with you so that you became Mine," declares the Lord GOD.

9 "Then I bathed you with water, washed off your blood from you and anointed you with oil.

10 "I also clothed you with embroidered cloth and put sandals of porpoise skin on your feet; and

I wrapped you with fine linen and covered you with silk.

11 "I adorned you with ornaments, put bracelets on your hands and a necklace around your neck.

12 "I also put a ring in your nostril, earrings in your ears and a beautiful crown on your head.

13 "Thus you were adorned with gold and silver, and your dress was of fine linen, silk and embroidered cloth. You ate fine flour, honey and oil; so you were exceedingly beautiful and advanced to royalty.

14 "Then your fame went forth among the nations on account of your beauty, for it was perfect because of My splendor which I bestowed on you," declares the Lord GOD.

15 ¶ "But you trusted in your beauty and played the harlot because of your fame, and you poured out your harlotries on every passer-by who might be *willing*.

16 "You took some of your clothes, made for yourself high places of various colors and played the harlot on them, which should never come about nor happen.

17 "You also took your beautiful jewels *made* of My gold and of My silver, which I had given you, and made for yourself male images that you might play the harlot with them.

18 "Then you took your embroidered cloth and covered them, and offered My oil and My incense before them.

19 "Also My bread which I gave you, fine flour, oil and honey with which I fed you, you would offer before them for a soothing aroma; so it happened," declares the Lord GOD.

20 "Moreover, you took your sons and daughters whom you had borne to Me and sacrificed them to idols to be devoured. Were your harlotries so small a matter?

21 "You slaughtered My children and offered them up to idols by causing them to pass through *the* fire.

22 "Besides all your abominations and harlotries you did not remember the days of your youth, when you were naked and bare and squirming in your blood.

23 ¶ "Then it came about after all your wickedness ('Woe, woe to you!' declares the Lord GOD),

24 that you built yourself a shrine and made yourself a high place in every square.

25 "You built yourself a high place at the top of every street and made your beauty abominable, and you spread your legs to every passer-by to multiply your harlotry.

26 "You also played the harlot with the Egyptians, your lustful neighbors, and multiplied your harlotry to make Me angry.

27 "Behold now, I have stretched out My hand against you and diminished your rations. And I delivered you up to the desire of those who hate

you, the daughters of the Philistines, who are ashamed of your lewd conduct.

28 "Moreover, you played the harlot with the Assyrians because you were not satisfied; you

16:26 Worse than a Whore

In this graphic allegory, Ezekiel compares Jerusalem to an abandoned baby whom God rescues and raises with great tenderness. (Female children, often unwanted, were sometimes left to die.) Yet she rebels, preferring life on the wild side. She becomes a prostitute, then sinks even lower. Rather than being paid for her services, she actually pays for sex (verse 34). Ezekiel is depicting Israel's eagerness to adopt the religious practices of her neighbors.

played the harlot with them and still were not satisfied.

29 "You also multiplied your harlotry with the land of merchants, Chaldea, yet even with this you were not satisfied." ' "

30 ¶ "How languishing is your heart," declares the Lord GOD, "while you do all these things, the actions of a bold-faced harlot.

31 "When you built your shrine at the beginning of every street and made your high place in every square, in disdaining money, you were not like a harlot.

32 "You adulteress wife, who takes strangers instead of her husband!

33 "Men give gifts to all harlots, but you give your gifts to all your lovers to bribe them to come to you from every direction for your harlotries.

34 "Thus you are different from those women in your harlotries, in that no one plays the harlot as you do, because you give money and no money is given you; thus you are different."

35 ¶ Therefore, O harlot, hear the word of the LORD.

36 Thus says the Lord GOD, "Because your lewdness was poured out and your nakedness uncovered through your harlotries with your lovers and with all your detestable idols, and because of the blood of your sons which you gave to idols,

37 therefore, behold, I will gather all your lovers with whom you took pleasure, even all those whom you loved *and* all those whom you hated. So I will gather them against you from every direction and expose your nakedness to them that they may see all your nakedness.

38 "Thus I will judge you like women who commit adultery or shed blood are judged; and I will bring on you the blood of wrath and jealousy.

39 "I will also give you into the hands of your lovers, and they will tear down your shrines, demolish your high places, strip you of your cloth-

ing, take away your jewels, and will leave you naked and bare.

40 "They will incite a crowd against you and they will stone you and cut you to pieces with their swords.

41 "They will burn your houses with fire and execute judgments on you in the sight of many women. Then I will stop you from playing the harlot, and you will also no longer pay your lovers.

42 "So I will calm My fury against you and My jealousy will depart from you, and I will be pacified and angry no more.

43 "Because you have not remembered the days of your youth but have enraged Me by all these things, behold, I in turn will bring your conduct down on your own head," declares the Lord GOD, "so that you will not commit this lewdness on top of all your *other* abominations.

44 ¶ "Behold, everyone who quotes proverbs will quote *this* proverb concerning you, saying, 'Like mother, like daughter.'

45 "You are the daughter of your mother, who loathed her husband and children. You are also the sister of your sisters, who loathed their husbands and children. Your mother was a Hittite and your father an Amorite.

46 "Now your older sister is Samaria, who lives north of you with her daughters; and your younger sister, who lives south of you, is Sodom with her daughters.

47 "Yet you have not merely walked in their ways or done according to their abominations; but, as if that were too little, you acted more corruptly in all your conduct than they.

48 "As I live," declares the Lord GOD, "Sodom, your sister and her daughters have not done as you and your daughters have done.

49 "Behold, this was the guilt of your sister Sodom: she and her daughters had arrogance, abundant food and careless ease, but she did not help the poor and needy.

16:49 The Sin of Sodom

Why had God destroyed Sodom and Gomorrah? The Genesis 19 account suggests sexual perversion and violence as the cause. Ezekiel here adds an interesting aspect: arrogant, uncaring wealth. The attempt at homosexual gang rape, chronicled in Genesis, was only part of a bigger problem.

50 "Thus they were haughty and committed abominations before Me. Therefore I removed them when I saw *it*.

51 "Furthermore, Samaria did not commit half of your sins, for you have multiplied your abominations more than they. Thus you have made your sisters appear righteous by all your abominations which you have committed.

52 "Also bear your disgrace in that you have made judgment favorable for your sisters. Because of your sins in which you acted more abominably than they, they are more in the right than you. Yes, be also ashamed and bear your disgrace, in that you made your sisters appear righteous.

53 ¶ "Nevertheless, I will restore their captivity, the captivity of Sodom and her daughters, the captivity of Samaria and her daughters, and along with them your own captivity,

54 in order that you may bear your humiliation and feel ashamed for all that you have done when you become a consolation to them.

55 "Your sisters, Sodom with her daughters and Samaria with her daughters, will return to their former state, and you with your daughters will *also* return to your former state.

56 "As *the name of* your sister Sodom was not heard from your lips in your day of pride,

57 before your wickedness was uncovered, so now you have become the reproach of the daughters of Edom and of all who are around her, of the daughters of the Philistines—those surrounding *you* who despise you.

58 "You have borne *the penalty of* your lewdness and abominations," the LORD declares.

59 For thus says the Lord GOD, "I will also do with you as you have done, you who have despised the oath by breaking the covenant.

The Covenant Remembered

60 ¶ "Nevertheless, I will remember My covenant with you in the days of your youth, and I will establish an everlasting covenant with you.

61 "Then you will remember your ways and be ashamed when you receive your sisters, *both* your older and your younger; and I will give them to you as daughters, but not because of your covenant.

62 "Thus I will establish My covenant with you, and you shall know that I am the LORD,

63 so that you may remember and be ashamed and never open your mouth anymore because of your humiliation, when I have forgiven you for all that you have done," the Lord GOD declares.

Parable of Two Eagles and a Vine

17 Now the word of the LORD came to me saying,

2 "Son of man, propound a riddle and speak a parable to the house of Israel,

3 saying, 'Thus says the Lord GOD, "A great eagle with great wings, long pinions and a full plumage of many colors came to Lebanon and took away the top of the cedar.

4 "He plucked off the topmost of its young twigs and brought it to a land of merchants; he set it in a city of traders.

5 "He also took some of the seed of the land and planted it in fertile soil. He placed *it* beside abundant waters; he set it *like* a willow.

6 "Then it sprouted and became a low, spreading vine with its branches turned toward him, but its roots remained under it. So it became a vine and yielded shoots and sent out branches.

7 ¶ "But there was another great eagle with great wings and much plumage; and behold, this vine bent its roots toward him and sent out its branches toward him from the beds where it was planted, that he might water it.

8 "It was planted in good soil beside abundant waters, that it might yield branches and bear fruit *and* become a splendid vine." '

9 "Say, 'Thus says the Lord GOD, "Will it thrive? Will he not pull up its roots and cut off its fruit, so that it withers—so that all its sprouting leaves wither? And neither by great strength nor by many people can it be raised from its roots *again*.

10 "Behold, though it is planted, will it thrive? Will it not completely wither as soon as the east wind strikes it—wither on the beds where it grew?" ' "

Zedekiah's Rebellion

11 ¶ Moreover, the word of the LORD came to me, saying,

12 "Say now to the rebellious house, 'Do you not know what these things *mean?*' Say, 'Behold, the king of Babylon came to Jerusalem, took its king and princes and brought them to him in Babylon.

13 'He took one of the royal family and made a covenant with him, putting him under oath. He also took away the mighty of the land,

14 that the kingdom might be in subjection, not exalting itself, *but* keeping his covenant that it might continue.

15 'But he rebelled against him by sending his envoys to Egypt that they might give him horses and many troops. Will he succeed? Will he who does such things escape? Can he indeed break the covenant and escape?

16 'As I live,' declares the Lord GOD, 'Surely in the country of the king who put him on the throne, whose oath he despised and whose covenant he broke, in Babylon he shall die.

17 'Pharaoh with *his* mighty army and great company will not help him in the war, when they cast up ramps and build siege walls to cut off many lives.

18 'Now he despised the oath by breaking the covenant, and behold, he pledged his allegiance, yet did all these things; he shall not escape.' "

19 Therefore, thus says the Lord GOD, "As I live, surely My oath which he despised and My covenant which he broke, I will inflict on his head.

20 "I will spread My net over him, and he will be caught in My snare. Then I will bring him to Babylon and enter into judgment with him there *regarding* the unfaithful act which he has committed against Me.

21 "All the choice men in all his troops will fall by the sword, and the survivors will be scattered to every wind; and you will know that I, the LORD, have spoken."

22 ¶ Thus says the Lord GOD, "I will also take *a sprig* from the lofty top of the cedar and set *it* out; I will pluck from the topmost of its young twigs a tender one and I will plant *it* on a high and lofty mountain.

23 "On the high mountain of Israel I will plant it, that it may bring forth boughs and bear fruit and become a stately cedar. And birds of every kind will nest under it; they will nest in the shade of its branches.

24 "All the trees of the field will know that I am the LORD; I bring down the high tree, exalt the low tree, dry up the green tree and make the dry tree flourish. I am the LORD; I have spoken, and I will perform *it.*"

God Deals Justly with Individuals

18 Then the word of the LORD came to me, saying,

2 "What do you mean by using this proverb concerning the land of Israel, saying,

'The fathers eat the sour grapes,
But the children's teeth are set on edge'?

18:2 Jeremiah and Ezekiel

This proverb, which suggests the way children pay for their parents' sins, was also quoted by Jeremiah (Jeremiah 31:29). While Ezekiel did his work in Babylon, Jeremiah carried out a parallel work in Jerusalem. Neither mentions the other, but their messages carry many similarities. Note particularly Jeremiah 1:14–19; 3:6–13; 6:27–30; 8:10–11; 15:1–2; 16:5–8; 23:16–40; 24; 29; 31:27–34; 39—all passages that have close parallels in Ezekiel.

3 "As I live," declares the Lord GOD, "you are surely not going to use this proverb in Israel anymore.

4 "Behold, all souls are Mine; the soul of the father as well as the soul of the son is Mine. The soul who sins will die.

5 ¶ "But if a man is righteous and practices justice and righteousness,

6 and does not eat at the mountain *shrines* or lift up his eyes to the idols of the house of Israel, or defile his neighbor's wife or approach a woman during her menstrual period—

7 if a man does not oppress anyone, but restores to the debtor his pledge, does not commit robbery, *but* gives his bread to the hungry and covers the naked with clothing,

8 if he does not lend *money* on interest or take increase, *if* he keeps his hand from iniquity *and* executes true justice between man and man,

9 *if* he walks in My statutes and My ordinances so as to deal faithfully—he is righteous *and* will surely live," declares the Lord GOD.

10 ¶ "Then he may have a violent son who sheds blood and who does any of these things to a brother

11 (though he himself did not do any of these things), that is, he even eats at the mountain *shrines,* and defiles his neighbor's wife,

12 oppresses the poor and needy, commits robbery, does not restore a pledge, but lifts up his eyes to the idols *and* commits abomination,

13 he lends *money* on interest and takes increase; will he live? He will not live! He has committed all these abominations, he will surely be put to death; his blood will be on his own head.

14 ¶ "Now behold, he has a son who has observed all his father's sins which he committed, and observing does not do likewise.

15 "He does not eat at the mountain *shrines* or lift up his eyes to the idols of the house of Israel, or defile his neighbor's wife,

16 or oppress anyone, or retain a pledge, or commit robbery, *but* he gives his bread to the hungry and covers the naked with clothing,

17 he keeps his hand from the poor, does not take interest or increase, *but* executes My ordinances, and walks in My statutes; he will not die for his father's iniquity, he will surely live.

18 "As for his father, because he practiced extortion, robbed *his* brother and did what was not good among his people, behold, he will die for his iniquity.

19 ¶ "Yet you say, 'Why should the son not bear the punishment for the father's iniquity?' When the son has practiced justice and righteousness and has observed all My statutes and done them, he shall surely live.

20 "The person who sins will die. The son will not bear the punishment for the father's iniquity, nor will the father bear the punishment for the son's iniquity; the righteousness of the righteous will be upon himself, and the wickedness of the wicked will be upon himself.

21 ¶ "But if the wicked man turns from all his sins which he has committed and observes all My statutes and practices justice and righteousness, he shall surely live; he shall not die.

22 "All his transgressions which he has committed will not be remembered against him; because of his righteousness which he has practiced, he will live.

23 "Do I have any pleasure in the death of the wicked," declares the Lord GOD, "rather than that he should turn from his ways and live?

24 ¶ "But when a righteous man turns away from his righteousness, commits iniquity and does according to all the abominations that a wicked man does, will he live? All his righteous deeds which he has done will not be remembered for his

treachery which he has committed and his sin which he has committed; for them he will die.

25 "Yet you say, 'The way of the Lord is not right.' Hear now, O house of Israel! Is My way not right? Is it not your ways that are not right?

26 "When a righteous man turns away from his righteousness, commits iniquity and dies because of it, for his iniquity which he has committed he will die.

27 "Again, when a wicked man turns away from his wickedness which he has committed and practices justice and righteousness, he will save his life.

28 "Because he considered and turned away from all his transgressions which he had committed, he shall surely live; he shall not die.

29 "But the house of Israel says, 'The way of the Lord is not right.' Are My ways not right, O house of Israel? Is it not your ways that are not right?

30 ¶ "Therefore I will judge you, O house of Israel, each according to his conduct," declares the Lord GOD. "Repent and turn away from all your transgressions, so that iniquity may not become a stumbling block to you.

31 "Cast away from you all your transgressions which you have committed and make yourselves a new heart and a new spirit! For why will you die, O house of Israel?

32 "For I have no pleasure in the death of anyone who dies," declares the Lord GOD. "Therefore, repent and live."

Lament for the Princes of Israel

19 "As for you, take up a lamentation for the princes of Israel

2 and say,

'What was your mother?
    A lioness among lions!
She lay down among young lions,
    She reared her cubs.
3 'When she brought up one of her cubs,
    He became a lion,
And he learned to tear *his* prey;
    He devoured men.
4 'Then nations heard about him;
    He was captured in their pit,
And they brought him with hooks
    To the land of Egypt.
5 'When she saw, as she waited,

That her hope was lost,
    She took another of her cubs
And made him a young lion.
6 'And he walked about among the lions;
    He became a young lion,
He learned to tear *his* prey;
    He devoured men.
7 'He destroyed their fortified towers
    And laid waste their cities;
And the land and its fullness were
        appalled
    Because of the sound of his roaring.
8 'Then nations set against him
    On every side from *their* provinces,
And they spread their net over him;
    He was captured in their pit.
9 'They put him in a cage with hooks
    And brought him to the king of Babylon;
They brought him in hunting nets
So that his voice would be heard no
        more
    On the mountains of Israel.
10 'Your mother was like a vine in your
        vineyard,
    Planted by the waters;
It was fruitful and full of branches
    Because of abundant waters.
11 'And it had strong branches *fit* for
        scepters of rulers,
    And its height was raised above the
        clouds
So that it was seen in its height with the
        mass of its branches.
12 'But it was plucked up in fury;
    It was cast down to the ground;
And the east wind dried up its fruit.
    Its strong branch was torn off
So that it withered;
    The fire consumed it.
13 'And now it is planted in the wilderness,
    In a dry and thirsty land.
14 'And fire has gone out from *its* branch;
    It has consumed its shoots *and* fruit,
So that there is not in it a strong branch,
    A scepter to rule.' "

This is a lamentation, and has become a lamentation.

God's Dealings with Israel Rehearsed

20 Now in the seventh year, in the fifth *month,* on the tenth of the month, certain of the elders of Israel came to inquire of the LORD, and sat before me.

2 And the word of the LORD came to me saying,

3 "Son of man, speak to the elders of Israel and say to them, 'Thus says the Lord GOD, "Do you come to inquire of Me? As I live," declares the Lord GOD, "I will not be inquired of by you." '

4 "Will you judge them, will you judge them,

son of man? Make them know the abominations of their fathers;

5 and say to them, 'Thus says the Lord GOD, "On the day when I chose Israel and swore to the

20:3 Don't Ask God

Does God always want people to pray? According to this passage, time sometimes runs out on prayer. When elders came to Ezekiel to ask God for direction, God said: Don't bother. What is the use, when he has told them over and over what the problem is? He has nothing more to say.

descendants of the house of Jacob and made Myself known to them in the land of Egypt, when I swore to them, saying, I am the LORD your God,

6 on that day I swore to them, to bring them out from the land of Egypt into a land that I had selected for them, flowing with milk and honey, which is the glory of all lands.

7 "I said to them, 'Cast away, each of you, the detestable things of his eyes, and do not defile yourselves with the idols of Egypt; I am the LORD your God.'

8 "But they rebelled against Me and were not willing to listen to Me; they did not cast away the detestable things of their eyes, nor did they forsake the idols of Egypt.

¶ Then I resolved to pour out My wrath on them, to accomplish My anger against them in the midst of the land of Egypt.

9 "But I acted for the sake of My name, that it should not be profaned in the sight of the nations among whom they *lived,* in whose sight I made Myself known to them by bringing them out of the land of Egypt.

10 "So I took them out of the land of Egypt and brought them into the wilderness.

11 "I gave them My statutes and informed them of My ordinances, by which, if a man observes them, he will live.

12 "Also I gave them My sabbaths to be a sign between Me and them, that they might know that I am the LORD who sanctifies them.

13 "But the house of Israel rebelled against Me in the wilderness. They did not walk in My statutes and they rejected My ordinances, by which, if a man observes them, he will live; and My sabbaths they greatly profaned. Then I resolved to pour out My wrath on them in the wilderness, to annihilate them.

14 "But I acted for the sake of My name, that it should not be profaned in the sight of the nations, before whose sight I had brought them out.

15 "Also I swore to them in the wilderness that I would not bring them into the land which I had

given them, flowing with milk and honey, which is the glory of all lands,

16 because they rejected My ordinances, and as for My statutes, they did not walk in them; they even profaned My sabbaths, for their heart continually went after their idols.

17 "Yet My eye spared them rather than destroying them, and I did not cause their annihilation in the wilderness.

18 ¶ "I said to their children in the wilderness, 'Do not walk in the statutes of your fathers or keep their ordinances or defile yourselves with their idols.

19 'I am the LORD your God; walk in My statutes and keep My ordinances and observe them.

20 'Sanctify My sabbaths; and they shall be a sign between Me and you, that you may know that I am the LORD your God.'

21 "But the children rebelled against Me; they did not walk in My statutes, nor were they careful to observe My ordinances, by which, *if* a man observes them, he will live; they profaned My sabbaths. So I resolved to pour out My wrath on them, to accomplish My anger against them in the wilderness.

22 "But I withdrew My hand and acted for the sake of My name, that it should not be profaned in the sight of the nations in whose sight I had brought them out.

23 "Also I swore to them in the wilderness that I would scatter them among the nations and disperse them among the lands,

24 because they had not observed My ordinances, but had rejected My statutes and had profaned My sabbaths, and their eyes were on the idols of their fathers.

25 "I also gave them statutes that were not good and ordinances by which they could not live;

26 and I pronounced them unclean because of their gifts, in that they caused all their firstborn to pass through *the fire* so that I might make them desolate, in order that they might know that I am the LORD." '

27 ¶ "Therefore, son of man, speak to the house of Israel and say to them, 'Thus says the Lord GOD, "Yet in this your fathers have blasphemed Me by acting treacherously against Me.

28 "When I had brought them into the land which I swore to give to them, then they saw every high hill and every leafy tree, and they offered there their sacrifices and there they presented the provocation of their offering. There also they made their soothing aroma and there they poured out their drink offerings.

29 "Then I said to them, 'What is the high place to which you go?' So its name is called *a*Bamah to this day." '

30 "Therefore, say to the house of Israel, 'Thus says the Lord GOD, "Will you defile yourselves

a Or High Place

after the manner of your fathers and play the harlot after their detestable things?

31 "When you offer your gifts, when you cause your sons to pass through the fire, you are defiling yourselves with all your idols to this day. And shall I be inquired of by you, O house of Israel? As I live," declares the Lord GOD, "I will not be inquired of by you.

32 "What comes into your mind will not come about, when you say: 'We will be like the nations, like the tribes of the lands, serving wood and stone.'

20:32 Like Everybody Else

"Everybody does it!" children sometimes whine to their parents. Good parents aren't swayed, however. They want their children to live up to their own potential, not mimic everybody else.

Like those children, Israelites grew tired of their calling. They wanted to relax and live like other nations. But God swears he will never let it happen. He will remain strict, even putting them through another desert experience to purify them, but he absolutely refuses to let them conform.

God Will Restore Israel to Her Land

33 ¶ "As I live," declares the Lord GOD, "surely with a mighty hand and with an outstretched arm and with wrath poured out, I shall be king over you.

34 "I will bring you out from the peoples and gather you from the lands where you are scattered, with a mighty hand and with an outstretched arm and with wrath poured out;

35 and I will bring you into the wilderness of the peoples, and there I will enter into judgment with you face to face.

36 "As I entered into judgment with your fathers in the wilderness of the land of Egypt, so I will enter into judgment with you," declares the Lord GOD.

37 "I will make you pass under the rod, and I will bring you into the bond of the covenant;

38 and I will purge from you the rebels and those who transgress against Me; I will bring them out of the land where they sojourn, but they will not enter the land of Israel. Thus you will know that I am the LORD.

39 ¶ "As for you, O house of Israel," thus says the Lord GOD, "Go, serve everyone his idols; but later you will surely listen to Me, and My holy name you will profane no longer with your gifts and with your idols.

40 "For on My holy mountain, on the high mountain of Israel," declares the Lord GOD, "there the whole house of Israel, all of them, will serve Me in the land; there I will accept them and there

I will seek your contributions and the choicest of your gifts, with all your holy things.

41 "As a soothing aroma I will accept you when I bring you out from the peoples and gather you from the lands where you are scattered; and I will prove Myself holy among you in the sight of the nations.

42 "And you will know that I am the LORD, when I bring you into the land of Israel, into the land which I swore to give to your forefathers.

43 "There you will remember your ways and all your deeds with which you have defiled yourselves; and you will loathe yourselves in your own sight for all the evil things that you have done.

44 "Then you will know that I am the LORD when I have dealt with you for My name's sake, not according to your evil ways or according to your corrupt deeds, O house of Israel," declares the Lord GOD.' "

45 ¶ Now the word of the LORD came to me, saying,

46 "Son of man, set your face toward Teman, and speak out against the south and prophesy against the forest land of the Negev,

47 and say to the forest of the Negev, 'Hear the word of the LORD: thus says the Lord GOD, "Behold, I am about to kindle a fire in you, and it will consume every green tree in you, as well as every dry tree; the blazing flame will not be quenched and the whole surface from south to north will be burned by it.

48 "All flesh will see that I, the LORD, have kindled it; it shall not be quenched." ' "

49 Then I said, "Ah Lord GOD! They are saying of me, 'Is he not *just* speaking parables?' "

Parable of the Sword of the LORD

21 And the word of the LORD came to me saying,

2 "Son of man, set your face toward Jerusalem, and speak against the sanctuaries and prophesy against the land of Israel;

3 and say to the land of Israel, 'Thus says the LORD, "Behold, I am against you; and I will draw My sword out of its sheath and cut off from you the righteous and the wicked.

4 "Because I will cut off from you the righteous and the wicked, therefore My sword will go forth from its sheath against all flesh from south *to* north.

5 "Thus all flesh will know that I, the LORD, have drawn My sword out of its sheath. It will not return *to its sheath* again." '

6 "As for you, son of man, groan with breaking heart and bitter grief, groan in their sight.

7 "And when they say to you, 'Why do you groan?' you shall say, 'Because of the news that is coming; and every heart will melt, all hands will be feeble, every spirit will faint and all knees will be weak as water. Behold, it comes and it will happen,' declares the Lord GOD."

8 ¶ Again the word of the LORD came to me, saying,

9 "Son of man, prophesy and say, 'Thus says the LORD.' Say,

'A sword, a sword sharpened
And also polished!

10 'Sharpened to make a slaughter,
Polished to flash like lightning!'

Or shall we rejoice, the rod of My son despising every tree?

11 "It is given to be polished, that it may be handled; the sword is sharpened and polished, to give it into the hand of the slayer.

12 "Cry out and wail, son of man; for it is against My people, it is against all the officials of Israel. They are delivered over to the sword with My people, therefore strike *your* thigh.

13 "For *there is* a testing; and what if even the rod which despises will be no more?" declares the Lord GOD.

14 ¶ "You therefore, son of man, prophesy and clap *your* hands together; and let the sword be doubled the third time, the sword for the slain. It is the sword for the great one slain, which surrounds them,

15 that *their* hearts may melt, and many fall at all their gates. I have given the glittering sword. Ah! It is made *for striking* like lightning, it is wrapped up *in readiness* for slaughter.

16 "Show yourself sharp, go to the right; set yourself; go to the left, wherever your edge is appointed.

17 "I will also clap My hands together, and I will appease My wrath; I, the LORD, have spoken."

The Instrument of God's Judgment

18 ¶ The word of the LORD came to me saying,

19 "As for you, son of man, make two ways for the sword of the king of Babylon to come; both of them will go out of one land. And make a signpost; make it at the head of the way to the city.

20 "You shall mark a way for the sword to come to Rabbah of the sons of Ammon, and to Judah into fortified Jerusalem.

21 "For the king of Babylon stands at the parting of the way, at the head of the two ways, to use divination; he shakes the arrows, he consults the household idols, he looks at the liver.

22 "Into his right hand came the divination, 'Jerusalem,' to set battering rams, to open the mouth for slaughter, to lift up the voice with a battle cry, to set battering rams against the gates, to cast up ramps, to build a siege wall.

23 "And it will be to them like a false divination in their eyes; they have *sworn* solemn oaths. But he brings iniquity to remembrance, that they may be seized.

24 ¶ "Therefore, thus says the Lord GOD, 'Because you have made your iniquity to be remembered, in that your transgressions are uncovered, so that in all your deeds your sins appear—because you have come to remembrance, you will be seized with the hand.

25 'And you, O slain, wicked one, the prince of Israel, whose day has come, in the time of the punishment of the end,'

21:21 Liver-Gazing

This verse shows how an ancient Babylonian king might seek direction from his gods. Divination with arrows apparently meant marking arrows with various alternatives, putting them in a quiver, and drawing one out. Consulting idols would mean praying to them, perhaps hoping for a dream or an omen. The livers of animals, like tea leaves today, were often studied in ancient times; their shape or color was supposed to tell the future.

26 thus says the Lord GOD, 'Remove the turban and take off the crown; this *will* no longer *be* the same. Exalt that which is low and abase that which is high.

27 'A ruin, a ruin, a ruin, I will make it. This also will be no more until He comes whose right it is, and I will give it *to Him.*'

28 ¶ "And you, son of man, prophesy and say, 'Thus says the Lord GOD concerning the sons of Ammon and concerning their reproach,' and say: 'A sword, a sword is drawn, polished for the slaughter, to cause it to consume, that it may be like lightning—

29 while they see for you false visions, while they divine lies for you—to place you on the necks of the wicked who are slain, whose day has come, in the time of the punishment of the end.

30 'Return *it* to its sheath. In the place where you were created, in the land of your origin, I will judge you.

31 'I will pour out My indignation on you; I will blow on you with the fire of My wrath, and I will give you into the hand of brutal men, skilled in destruction.

32 'You will be fuel for the fire; your blood will be in the midst of the land. You will not be remembered, for I, the LORD, have spoken.' "

The Sins of Israel

22 Then the word of the LORD came to me, saying,

2 "And you, son of man, will you judge, will you judge the bloody city? Then cause her to know all her abominations.

3 "You shall say, 'Thus says the Lord GOD, "A city shedding blood in her midst, so that her time will come, and that makes idols, contrary to her *interest*, for defilement!

4 "You have become guilty by the blood which you have shed, and defiled by your idols which you have made. Thus you have brought your day

near and have come to your years; therefore I have made you a reproach to the nations and a mocking to all the lands.

5 "Those who are near and those who are far from you will mock you, you of ill repute, full of turmoil.

6 ¶ "Behold, the rulers of Israel, each according to his power, have been in you for the purpose of shedding blood.

7 "They have treated father and mother lightly within you. The alien they have oppressed in your midst; the fatherless and the widow they have wronged in you.

8 "You have despised My holy things and profaned My sabbaths.

9 "Slanderous men have been in you for the purpose of shedding blood, and in you they have eaten at the mountain *shrines*. In your midst they have committed acts of lewdness.

10 "In you they have uncovered *their* fathers' nakedness; in you they have humbled her who was unclean in her menstrual impurity.

11 "One has committed abomination with his neighbor's wife and another has lewdly defiled his daughter-in-law. And another in you has humbled his sister, his father's daughter.

12 "In you they have taken bribes to shed blood; you have taken interest and profits, and you have injured your neighbors for gain by oppression, and you have forgotten Me," declares the Lord GOD.

13 ¶ "Behold, then, I smite My hand at your dishonest gain which you have acquired and at the bloodshed which is among you.

14 "Can your heart endure, or can your hands be strong in the days that I will deal with you? I, the LORD, have spoken and will act.

15 "I will scatter you among the nations and I will disperse you through the lands, and I will consume your uncleanness from you.

16 "You will profane yourself in the sight of the nations, and you will know that I am the LORD." ' "

17 ¶ And the word of the LORD came to me, saying,

18 "Son of man, the house of Israel has become dross to Me; all of them are bronze and tin and iron and lead in the furnace; they are the dross of silver.

19 "Therefore, thus says the Lord GOD, 'Because all of you have become dross, therefore, behold, I am going to gather you into the midst of Jerusalem.

20 'As they gather silver and bronze and iron and lead and tin into the furnace to blow fire on it in order to melt *it*, so I will gather *you* in My anger and in My wrath and I will lay you *there* and melt you.

21 'I will gather you and blow on you with the fire of My wrath, and you will be melted in the midst of it.

22 'As silver is melted in the furnace, so you will be melted in the midst of it; and you will know that I, the LORD, have poured out My wrath on you.' "

23 ¶ And the word of the LORD came to me, saying,

24 "Son of man, say to her, 'You are a land that is not cleansed or rained on in the day of indignation.'

25 "There is a conspiracy of her prophets in her midst like a roaring lion tearing the prey. They have devoured lives; they have taken treasure and precious things; they have made many widows in the midst of her.

26 "Her priests have done violence to My law and have profaned My holy things; they have made no distinction between the holy and the profane, and they have not taught the difference between the unclean and the clean; and they hide their eyes from My sabbaths, and I am profaned among them.

27 "Her princes within her are like wolves tearing the prey, by shedding blood *and* destroying lives in order to get dishonest gain.

28 "Her prophets have smeared whitewash for them, seeing false visions and divining lies for them, saying, 'Thus says the Lord GOD,' when the LORD has not spoken.

29 "The people of the land have practiced oppression and committed robbery, and they have wronged the poor and needy and have oppressed the sojourner without justice.

30 "I searched for a man among them who would build up the wall and stand in the gap before Me for the land, so that I would not destroy it; but I found no one.

31 "Thus I have poured out My indignation on them; I have consumed them with the fire of My wrath; their way I have brought upon their heads," declares the Lord GOD.

Oholah and Oholibah's Sin and Its Consequences

23 The word of the LORD came to me again, saying,

2 "Son of man, there were two women, the daughters of one mother;

3 and they played the harlot in Egypt. They played the harlot in their youth; there their breasts were pressed and there their virgin bosom was handled.

4 "Their names were Oholah the elder and Oholibah her sister. And they became Mine, and they bore sons and daughters. And *as for* their names, Samaria is Oholah and Jerusalem is Oholibah.

5 ¶ "Oholah played the harlot while she was Mine; and she lusted after her lovers, after the Assyrians, *her* neighbors,

6 who were clothed in purple, governors and

officials, all of them desirable young men, horsemen riding on horses.

7 "She bestowed her harlotries on them, all of whom *were* the choicest men of Assyria; and with all whom she lusted after, with all their idols she defiled herself.

8 "She did not forsake her harlotries from *the time in* Egypt; for in her youth men had lain with her, and they handled her virgin bosom and poured out their lust on her.

9 "Therefore, I gave her into the hand of her lovers, into the hand of the Assyrians, after whom she lusted.

10 "They uncovered her nakedness; they took her sons and her daughters, but they slew her with the sword. Thus she became a byword among women, and they executed judgments on her.

11 ¶ "Now her sister Oholibah saw *this,* yet she was more corrupt in her lust than she, and her harlotries were more than the harlotries of her sister.

12 "She lusted after the Assyrians, governors and officials, the ones near, magnificently dressed,

13 "I saw that she had defiled herself; they both took the same way.

14 "So she increased her harlotries. And she saw men portrayed on the wall, images of the Chaldeans portrayed with vermilion,

15 girded with belts on their loins, with flowing turbans on their heads, all of them looking like officers, like the Babylonians *in* Chaldea, the land of their birth.

16 "When she saw them she lusted after them and sent messengers to them in Chaldea.

17 "The Babylonians came to her to the bed of love and defiled her with their harlotry. And when she had been defiled by them, she became disgusted with them.

18 "She uncovered her harlotries and uncovered her nakedness; then I became disgusted with her, as I had become disgusted with her sister.

19 "Yet she multiplied her harlotries, remembering the days of her youth, when she played the harlot in the land of Egypt.

The Runaways
A story meant to make you sick

> "Will they now commit adultery with her when she is thus?'" 23:43

THIS STORY, WHICH USES SEXUALLY explicit language, turns you off, not on. It tells of two sisters who choose promiscuous sex. Once they are involved, nothing satisfies them. They go from one man to the next. God calls them prostitutes, but they don't do it for the money. They do it because they like to live perversely.

Finally, in grief and frustration, God turns them over to their chosen lovers, who treat them like trash. God seems to take angry satisfaction in this. Love makes him angry—angry enough to weep.

An Allegory of Love

Ezekiel doesn't pretend that these two sisters are real people. From the beginning he identifies them with the capitals of the two halves of Israel—Samaria in the North, which the Assyrians had wiped out over 100 years before, and Jerusalem in the South. Samaria was properly rewarded for her prostitution, Ezekiel says, and Jerusalem will be too. The story of the two sisters is, in a sense, one more graphic way of saying that God has been patient with Jerusalem long enough. (A similar story is told in Ezekiel 16.)

A Drastic Dose of Reality

God had promised the Israelites everything their hearts desired if they would stick by him. But they were always cozying up to other nations whose prosperity and power they envied. In those days, a little nation like Israel couldn't just sign a friendship pact with a big power. Political alliances meant accepting the big power's religion and worshiping its gods alongside your own. God warned Israel against this repeatedly, but they ignored the warning. Therefore, Ezekiel says, they will get their wish. They will experience firsthand the care and concern of their Babylonian "lovers."

God responds like a father who has finally given up trying to regulate his daughter's bad habits. He tells her, "Get out! Find out for yourself what life is like on the street!" God says, "You will drink your sister's cup, which is deep and wide. You will be laughed at and held in derision; it contains much. . . . You will drink it and drain it. Then you will gnaw its fragments and tear your breasts " (23:32–34). He says it in anger, but also in hope that such bitter grief will awaken Israel to the disastrous choices she made in rejecting God's care.

Life Questions: Have you ever loved someone who didn't love you back? What emotions did you feel?

20 "She lusted after their paramours, whose flesh is *like* the flesh of donkeys and whose issue is *like* the issue of horses.

21 "Thus you longed for the lewdness of your youth, when the Egyptians handled your bosom because of the breasts of your youth.

22 ¶ "Therefore, O Oholibah, thus says the Lord GOD, 'Behold I will arouse your lovers against you, from whom you were alienated, and I will bring them against you from every side:

23 the Babylonians and all the Chaldeans, Pekod and Shoa and Koa, *and* all the Assyrians with them; desirable young men, governors and officials all of them, officers and men of renown, all of them riding on horses.

24 'They will come against you with weapons, chariots and wagons, and with a company of peoples. They will set themselves against you on every side with buckler and shield and helmet; and I will commit the judgment to them, and they will judge you according to their customs.

25 'I will set My jealousy against you, that they may deal with you in wrath. They will remove your nose and your ears; and your survivors will fall by the sword. They will take your sons and your daughters; and your survivors will be consumed by the fire.

26 'They will also strip you of your clothes and take away your beautiful jewels.

27 'Thus I will make your lewdness and your harlotry *brought* from the land of Egypt to cease from you, so that you will not lift up your eyes to them or remember Egypt anymore.'

28 "For thus says the Lord GOD, 'Behold, I will give you into the hand of those whom you hate, into the hand of those from whom you were alienated.

29 'They will deal with you in hatred, take all your property, and leave you naked and bare. And the nakedness of your harlotries will be uncovered, both your lewdness and your harlotries.

30 'These things will be done to you because you have played the harlot with the nations, because you have defiled yourself with their idols.

31 'You have walked in the way of your sister; therefore I will give her cup into your hand.'

32 "Thus says the Lord GOD,

'You will drink your sister's cup,
Which is deep and wide.
You will be laughed at and held in
    derision;
It contains much.

33 'You will be filled with drunkenness and
    sorrow,
The cup of horror and desolation,
The cup of your sister Samaria.

34 'You will drink it and drain it.
Then you will gnaw its fragments
And tear your breasts;

for I have spoken,' declares the Lord GOD.

35 "Therefore, thus says the Lord GOD, 'Because

you have forgotten Me and cast Me behind your back, bear now the *punishment* of your lewdness and your harlotries.' "

36 ¶ Moreover, the LORD said to me, "Son of man, will you judge Oholah and Oholibah? Then declare to them their abominations.

37 "For they have committed adultery, and blood is on their hands. Thus they have committed adultery with their idols and even caused their sons, whom they bore to Me, to pass through *the fire* to them as food.

38 "Again, they have done this to Me: they have defiled My sanctuary on the same day and have profaned My sabbaths.

39 "For when they had slaughtered their children for their idols, they entered My sanctuary on the same day to profane it; and lo, thus they did within My house.

40 ¶ "Furthermore, they have even sent for men who come from afar, to whom a messenger was sent; and lo, they came—for whom you bathed, painted your eyes and decorated yourselves with ornaments;

41 and you sat on a splendid couch with a table arranged before it on which you had set My incense and My oil.

42 "The sound of a carefree multitude was with her; and drunkards were brought from the wilderness with men of the common sort. And they put bracelets on the hands of the women and beautiful crowns on their heads.

43 ¶ "Then I said concerning her who was worn out by adulteries, 'Will they now commit adultery with her when she is *thus?*'

44 "But they went in to her as they would go in to a harlot. Thus they went in to Oholah and to Oholibah, the lewd women.

45 "But they, righteous men, will judge them with the judgment of adulteresses and with the judgment of women who shed blood, because they are adulteresses and blood is on their hands.

46 ¶ "For thus says the Lord GOD, 'Bring up a company against them and give them over to terror and plunder.

47 'The company will stone them with stones and cut them down with their swords; they will slay their sons and their daughters and burn their houses with fire.

48 'Thus I will make lewdness cease from the land, that all women may be admonished and not commit lewdness as you have done.

49 'Your lewdness will be requited upon you, and you will bear the penalty of *worshiping* your idols; thus you will know that I am the Lord GOD.' "

Parable of the Boiling Pot

24 And the word of the LORD came to me in the ninth year, in the tenth month, on the tenth of the month, saying,

2 "Son of man, write the name of the day, this

very day. The king of Babylon has laid siege to Jerusalem this very day.

3 "Speak a parable to the rebellious house and say to them, 'Thus says the Lord GOD,

"Put on the pot, put *it* on and also pour
water in it;

24:2 Prophet's Proof

With Ezekiel living in Babylon, news from Israel took months to reach him. By recording the date when God told him the final siege of Jerusalem had begun, Ezekiel would have evidence that he was genuinely a prophet of God.

---

4 Put in it the pieces,
　　Every good piece, the thigh and the
　　　　shoulder;
　　Fill *it* with choice bones.
5 "Take the choicest of the flock,
　　And also pile wood under the pot.
　　Make it boil vigorously.
　　Also seethe its bones in it."

6 ¶ 'Therefore, thus says the Lord GOD,
　　"Woe to the bloody city,
　　To the pot in which there is rust
　　And whose rust has not gone out of it!
　　Take out of it piece after piece,
　　Without making a choice.
7 "For her blood is in her midst;
　　She placed it on the bare rock;
　　She did not pour it on the ground
　　To cover it with dust.
8 "That it may cause wrath to come up to
　　　　take vengeance,
　　I have put her blood on the bare rock,
　　That it may not be covered."
9 'Therefore, thus says the Lord GOD,
　　"Woe to the bloody city!
　　I also will make the pile great.
10 "Heap on the wood, kindle the fire,
　　Boil the flesh well
　　And mix in the spices,
　　And let the bones be burned.
11 "Then set it empty on its coals
　　So that it may be hot
　　And its bronze may glow
　　And its filthiness may be melted in it,
　　Its rust consumed.
12 "She has wearied *Me* with toil,
　　Yet her great rust has not gone from her;
　　Let her rust *be* in the fire!
13 "In your filthiness is lewdness.
　　Because I *would* have cleansed you,
　　Yet you are not clean,
　　You will not be cleansed from your
　　　　filthiness again
　　Until I have spent My wrath on you.

14 "I, the LORD, have spoken; it is coming and I will act. I will not relent, and I will not pity and I will not be sorry; according to your ways and according to your deeds I will judge you," declares the Lord GOD.' "

Death of Ezekiel's Wife Is a Sign

15 ¶ And the word of the LORD came to me saying,

16 "Son of man, behold, I am about to take from you the desire of your eyes with a blow; but you shall not mourn and you shall not weep, and your tears shall not come.

17 "Groan silently; make no mourning for the dead. Bind on your turban and put your shoes on your feet, and do not cover *your* mustache and do not eat the bread of men."

18 So I spoke to the people in the morning, and in the evening my wife died. And in the morning I did as I was commanded.

19 The people said to me, "Will you not tell us what these things that you are doing mean for us?"

20 Then I said to them, "The word of the LORD came to me saying,

21 'Speak to the house of Israel, "Thus says the Lord GOD, 'Behold, I am about to profane My sanctuary, the pride of your power, the desire of your eyes and the delight of your soul; and your sons and your daughters whom you have left behind will fall by the sword.

22 'You will do as I have done; you will not cover *your* mustache and you will not eat the bread of men.

23 'Your turbans will be on your heads and your shoes on your feet. You will not mourn and you will not weep, but you will rot away in your iniquities and you will groan to one another.

24 'Thus Ezekiel will be a sign to you; according to all that he has done you will do; when it comes, then you will know that I am the Lord GOD.' "

25 ¶ 'As for you, son of man, will *it* not be on the day when I take from them their stronghold, the joy of their pride, the desire of their eyes and their heart's delight, their sons and their daughters,

26 that on that day he who escapes will come to you with information for *your* ears?

27 'On that day your mouth will be opened to him who escaped, and you will speak and be mute no longer. Thus you will be a sign to them, and they will know that I am the LORD.' "

Judgment on Gentile Nations—Ammon

25 And the word of the LORD came to me saying,

2 "Son of man, set your face toward the sons of Ammon and prophesy against them,

3 and say to the sons of Ammon, 'Hear the word of the Lord GOD! Thus says the Lord GOD,

"Because you said, 'Aha!' against My sanctuary when it was profaned, and against the land of Israel when it was made desolate, and against the house of Judah when they went into exile,

4 therefore, behold, I am going to give you to the sons of the east for a possession, and they will set their encampments among you and make their dwellings among you; they will eat your fruit and drink your milk.

5 "I will make Rabbah a pasture for camels and the sons of Ammon a resting place for flocks. Thus you will know that I am the LORD."

6 'For thus says the Lord GOD, "Because you have clapped your hands and stamped your feet and rejoiced with all the scorn of your soul against the land of Israel,

7 therefore, behold, I have stretched out My hand against you and I will give you for spoil to the nations. And I will cut you off from the peoples and make you perish from the lands; I will

Just What They Deserved
God will judge every nation in the world

WORLD WAR II ENDED IN Europe with the surrender of the German army. People danced in the streets.

But the victorious allies could not simply pack and go home. They had captured thousands of Nazis. Among them were some of the most brutal murderers the world has ever known— monsters, really, who had enriched themselves with the gold and jewelry of the millions of Jews they had exterminated.

> "'I will execute great vengeance on them with wrathful rebukes; and they will know that I am the LORD.'" 25:17

A question came up: Under what law could the Nazis be tried? American, British, or French law didn't apply in Germany. Faced with this dilemma, the Allies invented something new: the Nuremberg trials for war crimes. Judgments were based on a belief in a higher law—an international code of right and wrong that applies to every person, regardless of country. Under this unwritten law many Nazi leaders were condemned to death.

Nations on Trial

Ezekiel introduces a similar concept of justice, beginning in chapter 25. In the first 24 chapters he had spoken harsh words to the Israelites, who had repeatedly broken the law God had given them. But now Ezekiel's vision expands to nations who never had that law. Ezekiel marches through Ammon, Moab, Edom, Philistia—four nations that, on the small scale of Palestinian geography, could be seen with the naked eye from Jerusalem.

Each nation has its moment in court, and each is condemned for its inhumane malice against Israel. (The sentences Ezekiel gave were soon carried out historically. The nations listed vanished from the face of the earth, victims of the same violence they had used against Israel.)

Ezekiel goes on to Tyre, 100 miles up the coast. Tyre's soul was profit; its merchants controlled trade for the whole Mediterranean. Because of their wealth and success, they considered themselves virtual gods (28:2,6). They had callously rejoiced in Jerusalem's downfall, seeing it as a chance for increased trade (26:2). For such unfeeling arrogance, God would sentence them. Nebuchadnezzar began this punishment in Ezekiel's era, and centuries later Alexander the Great finished it off by razing the city. Tyre became, as Ezekiel had predicted, "a bare rock, and . . . a place for the spreading of fishnets" (26:14).

A Comic Condemnation

Pausing briefly to give a judgment against Sidon, Ezekiel travels on to Egypt. His words might have seemed comic. Who does he think he is, passing judgment on one of the great powers of his day? Ezekiel, a captive from a two-bit country about to be overrun, sounds rather like a refugee from Haiti shaking his fist at the United States. Yet Ezekiel confidently asserts that Egypt can start mourning now. As it happened, Egypt, a great power for many centuries, lost its dominance and has never regained it (29:15).

Perhaps, in taking up these nations' fates, Ezekiel intended to build suspense for the climactic tragedy of Jerusalem's fall. But certainly this trial of the nations demonstrated that Jerusalem had not been singled out for justice. Every nation would be judged by the standard of right and wrong that they knew. If God was harder on Judah, it was only because Judah knew so much more about God and his expectations.

Life Questions: Do you believe in universal standards of right and wrong? What "code of conduct" applies to everybody, regardless of their upbringing?

destroy you. Thus you will know that I am the LORD."

Moab

8 ¶ Thus says the Lord GOD, "Because Moab and Seir say, 'Behold, the house of Judah is like all the nations,'

9 therefore, behold, I am going to deprive the flank of Moab of *its* cities, of its cities which are on its frontiers, the glory of the land, Beth-jeshimoth, Baal-meon and Kiriathaim,

10 and I will give it for a possession along with the sons of Ammon to the sons of the east, so that the sons of Ammon will not be remembered among the nations.

11 "Thus I will execute judgments on Moab, and they will know that I am the LORD."

Edom

12 ¶ 'Thus says the Lord GOD, "Because Edom has acted against the house of Judah by taking vengeance, and has incurred grievous guilt, and avenged themselves upon them,"

13 therefore thus says the Lord GOD, "I will also stretch out My hand against Edom and cut off man and beast from it. And I will lay it waste; from Teman even to Dedan they will fall by the sword.

14 "I will lay My vengeance on Edom by the hand of My people Israel. Therefore, they will act in Edom according to My anger and according to My wrath; thus they will know My vengeance," declares the Lord GOD.

Philistia

15 ¶ 'Thus says the Lord GOD, "Because the Philistines have acted in revenge and have taken vengeance with scorn of soul to destroy with everlasting enmity,"

16 therefore thus says the Lord GOD, "Behold, I will stretch out My hand against the Philistines, even cut off the Cherethites and destroy the remnant of the seacoast.

17 "I will execute great vengeance on them with wrathful rebukes; and they will know that I am the LORD when I lay My vengeance on them." ' "

Judgment on Tyre

26 Now in the eleventh year, on the first of the month, the word of the LORD came to me saying,

2 "Son of man, because Tyre has said concerning Jerusalem, 'Aha, the gateway of the peoples is broken; it has opened to me. I shall be filled, *now that* she is laid waste,'

3 therefore thus says the Lord GOD, 'Behold, I am against you, O Tyre, and I will bring up many nations against you, as the sea brings up its waves.

4 'They will destroy the walls of Tyre and break down her towers; and I will scrape her debris from her and make her a bare rock.

5 'She will be a place for the spreading of nets in the midst of the sea, for I have spoken,' declares the Lord GOD, 'and she will become spoil for the nations.

6 'Also her daughters who are on the mainland will be slain by the sword, and they will know that I am the LORD.' "

7 ¶ For thus says the Lord GOD, "Behold, I will bring upon Tyre from the north Nebuchadnezzar king of Babylon, king of kings, with horses, chariots, cavalry and a great army.

8 "He will slay your daughters on the mainland with the sword; and he will make siege walls against you, cast up a ramp against you and raise up a large shield against you.

9 "The blow of his battering rams he will direct against your walls, and with his axes he will break down your towers.

10 "Because of the multitude of his horses, the dust *raised by* them will cover you; your walls will shake at the noise of cavalry and wagons and chariots when he enters your gates as men enter a city that is breached.

11 "With the hoofs of his horses he will trample all your streets. He will slay your people with the sword; and your strong pillars will come down to the ground.

12 "Also they will make a spoil of your riches and a prey of your merchandise, break down your walls and destroy your pleasant houses, and throw your stones and your timbers and your debris into the water.

13 "So I will silence the sound of your songs, and the sound of your harps will be heard no more.

14 "I will make you a bare rock; you will be a place for the spreading of nets. You will be built no more, for I the LORD have spoken," declares the Lord GOD.

26:14 Alexander the Great

Tyre, a city on the Mediterranean coast, included two rocky offshore islands. Nebuchadnezzar captured the mainland city in 572 B.C., just 12 years after the fall of Jerusalem. But the islands were not taken until Alexander the Great destroyed them two centuries later. True to this prophecy, the city has never been rebuilt.

15 ¶ Thus says the Lord GOD to Tyre, "Shall not the coastlands shake at the sound of your fall when the wounded groan, when the slaughter occurs in your midst?

16 "Then all the princes of the sea will go down from their thrones, remove their robes and strip off their embroidered garments. They will clothe

themselves with trembling; they will sit on the ground, tremble every moment and be appalled at you.

17 "They will take up a lamentation over you and say to you,

'How you have perished, O inhabited one,
From the seas, O renowned city,
Which was mighty on the sea,
She and her inhabitants,
Who imposed her terror
On all her inhabitants!

18 'Now the coastlands will tremble
On the day of your fall;
Yes, the coastlands which are by the sea
Will be terrified at your passing.' "

19 ¶ For thus says the Lord GOD, "When I make you a desolate city, like the cities which are not inhabited, when I bring up the deep over you and the great waters cover you,

20 then I will bring you down with those who go down to the pit, to the people of old, and I will make you dwell in the lower parts of the earth, like the ancient waste places, with those who go down to the pit, so that you will not be inhabited; but I will set glory in the land of the living.

21 "I will bring terrors on you and you will be no more; though you will be sought, you will never be found again," declares the Lord GOD.

Lament over Tyre

27 Moreover, the word of the LORD came to me saying,

2 "And you, son of man, take up a lamentation over Tyre;

3 and say to Tyre, who dwells at the entrance to the sea, merchant of the peoples to many coastlands, 'Thus says the Lord GOD,

"O Tyre, you have said, 'I am perfect in beauty.'

4 "Your borders are in the heart of the seas;
Your builders have perfected your beauty.

5 "They have made all *your* planks of fir trees from Senir;
They have taken a cedar from Lebanon to make a mast for you.

6 "Of oaks from Bashan they have made your oars;
With ivory they have inlaid your deck of boxwood from the coastlands of Cyprus.

7 "Your sail was of fine embroidered linen from Egypt
So that it became your distinguishing mark;
Your awning was blue and purple from the coastlands of Elishah.

8 "The inhabitants of Sidon and Arvad were your rowers;

Your wise men, O Tyre, were aboard;
they were your pilots.

9 "The elders of Gebal and her wise men were with you repairing your seams;
All the ships of the sea and their sailors were with you in order to deal in your merchandise.

10 ¶ "Persia and Lud and Put were in your army, your men of war. They hung shield and helmet in you; they set forth your splendor.

11 "The sons of Arvad and your army were on your walls, *all* around, and the Gammadim were in your towers. They hung their shields on your walls *all* around; they perfected your beauty.

12 ¶ "Tarshish was your customer because of the abundance of all *kinds* of wealth; with silver, iron, tin and lead they paid for your wares.

13 "Javan, Tubal and Meshech, they were your traders; with the lives of men and vessels of bronze they paid for your merchandise.

14 "Those from Beth-togarmah gave horses and war horses and mules for your wares.

15 "The sons of Dedan were your traders. Many coastlands were your market; ivory tusks and ebony they brought as your payment.

16 "Aram was your customer because of the abundance of your goods; they paid for your wares with emeralds, purple, embroidered work, fine linen, coral and rubies.

17 "Judah and the land of Israel, they were your traders; with the wheat of Minnith, cakes, honey, oil and balm they paid for your merchandise.

18 "Damascus was your customer because of the abundance of your goods, because of the abundance of all *kinds* of wealth, because of the wine of Helbon and white wool.

19 "Vedan and Javan paid for your wares from Uzal; wrought iron, cassia and sweet cane were among your merchandise.

20 "Dedan traded with you in saddlecloths for riding.

21 "Arabia and all the princes of Kedar, they were your customers for lambs, rams and goats; for these they were your customers.

22 "The traders of Sheba and Raamah, they traded with you; they paid for your wares with the best of all *kinds* of spices, and with all *kinds* of precious stones and gold.

23 "Haran, Canneh, Eden, the traders of Sheba, Asshur *and* Chilmad traded with you.

24 "They traded with you in choice garments, in clothes of blue and embroidered work, and in carpets of many colors *and* tightly wound cords, *which were* among your merchandise.

25 "The ships of Tarshish were the carriers for your merchandise.

And you were filled and were very glorious
In the heart of the seas.

26 ¶ "Your rowers have brought you
Into great waters;

The east wind has broken you
In the heart of the seas.
27 "Your wealth, your wares, your
    merchandise,
Your sailors and your pilots,
Your repairers of seams, your dealers in
    merchandise
And all your men of war who are in you,
With all your company that is in your
    midst,
Will fall into the heart of the seas
On the day of your overthrow.
28 "At the sound of the cry of your pilots
The pasture lands will shake.
29 "All who handle the oar,
The sailors *and* all the pilots of the sea
Will come down from their ships;
They will stand on the land,
30 And they will make their voice heard
    over you
And will cry bitterly.
They will cast dust on their heads,
They will wallow in ashes.
31 "Also they will make themselves bald
    for you
And gird themselves with sackcloth;
And they will weep for you in bitterness
    of soul
With bitter mourning.
32 "Moreover, in their wailing they will take
    up a lamentation for you
And lament over you:
'Who is like Tyre,
Like her who is silent in the midst of
    the sea?
33 'When your wares went out from the
    seas,
You satisfied many peoples;
With the abundance of your wealth and
    your merchandise
You enriched the kings of earth.
34 'Now that you are broken by the seas
In the depths of the waters,
Your merchandise and all your company
Have fallen in the midst of you.
35 'All the inhabitants of the coastlands
Are appalled at you,
And their kings are horribly afraid;
They are troubled in countenance.
36 'The merchants among the peoples hiss at
    you;
You have become terrified
And you will cease to be forever.' " ' "

Tyre's King Overthrown

28 The word of the LORD came again to me,
saying,
2 "Son of man, say to the leader of Tyre, 'Thus
says the Lord GOD,
    "Because your heart is lifted up
    And you have said, 'I am a god,

I sit in the seat of gods
In the heart of the seas';
Yet you are a man and not God,
Although you make your heart like the
    heart of God—
3 Behold, you are wiser than Daniel;
There is no secret that is a match for
    you.

28:3 Different Daniel

*This Daniel, also mentioned in 14:14, is
probably not the prophet Daniel, but an earlier
patriarch revered for his wisdom. The prophet
Daniel, Ezekiel's fellow exile in Babylon, would
not likely have gained such renown so soon.
Also, his name is spelled slightly differently in
Hebrew.*

4 "By your wisdom and understanding
You have acquired riches for yourself
And have acquired gold and silver for
    your treasuries.
5 "By your great wisdom, by your trade
You have increased your riches
And your heart is lifted up because of
    your riches—
6 Therefore thus says the Lord GOD,
'Because you have made your heart
Like the heart of God,
7 Therefore, behold, I will bring strangers
    upon you,
The most ruthless of the nations.
And they will draw their swords
Against the beauty of your wisdom
And defile your splendor.
8 'They will bring you down to the pit,
And you will die the death of those who
    are slain
In the heart of the seas.
9 'Will you still say, "I am a god,"
In the presence of your slayer,
Though you are a man and not God,
In the hands of those who wound you?
10 'You will die the death of the
    uncircumcised
By the hand of strangers,
For I have spoken!' declares the
    Lord GOD!' ' "

11 ¶ Again the word of the LORD came to me
saying,
12 "Son of man, take up a lamentation over
the king of Tyre and say to him, 'Thus says the
Lord GOD,
    "You had the seal of perfection,
    Full of wisdom and perfect in beauty.
13 "You were in Eden, the garden of God;
Every precious stone was your covering:
The ruby, the topaz and the diamond;
The beryl, the onyx and the jasper;

The lapis lazuli, the turquoise and the
emerald;
And the gold, the workmanship of your
settings and sockets,
Was in you.
On the day that you were created
They were prepared.
14 "You were the anointed cherub who
covers,
And I placed you *there.*
You were on the holy mountain of God;
You walked in the midst of the stones of
fire.
15 "You were blameless in your ways
From the day you were created
Until unrighteousness was found in you.
16 "By the abundance of your trade
You were internally filled with violence,
And you sinned;
Therefore I have cast you as profane
From the mountain of God.
And I have destroyed you, O covering
cherub,
From the midst of the stones of fire.
17 "Your heart was lifted up because of your
beauty;
You corrupted your wisdom by reason of
your splendor.
I cast you to the ground;
I put you before kings,
That they may see you.
18 "By the multitude of your iniquities,
In the unrighteousness of your trade
You profaned your sanctuaries.
Therefore I have brought fire from the
midst of you;
It has consumed you,
And I have turned you to ashes on the
earth
In the eyes of all who see you.
19 "All who know you among the peoples
Are appalled at you;
You have become terrified
And you will cease to be forever." ' "

Judgment of Sidon

20 ¶ And the word of the LORD came to me
saying,
21 "Son of man, set your face toward Sidon,
prophesy against her
22 and say, 'Thus says the Lord GOD,
"Behold, I am against you, O Sidon,
And I will be glorified in your midst.
Then they will know that I am the LORD
when I execute judgments in her,
And I will manifest My holiness in her.
23 "For I will send pestilence to her
And blood to her streets,
And the wounded will fall in her midst
By the sword upon her on every side;
Then they will know that I am the LORD.

24 "And there will be no more for the house of
Israel a prickling brier or a painful thorn from any
round about them who scorned them; then they
will know that I am the Lord GOD."

Israel Regathered

25 ¶ 'Thus says the Lord GOD, "When I gather
the house of Israel from the peoples among whom
they are scattered, and will manifest My holiness
in them in the sight of the nations, then they will
live in their land which I gave to My servant Jacob.
26 "They will live in it securely; and they will
build houses, plant vineyards and live securely
when I execute judgments upon all who scorn
them round about them. Then they will know that
I am the LORD their God." ' "

Judgment of Egypt

29 In the tenth year, in the tenth *month,* on the
twelfth of the month, the word of the LORD
came to me saying,
2 "Son of man, set your face against Pharaoh
king of Egypt and prophesy against him and
against all Egypt.
3 "Speak and say, 'Thus says the Lord GOD,
"Behold, I am against you, Pharaoh king
of Egypt,
The great monster that lies in the midst
of his rivers,
That has said, 'My Nile is mine, and I
myself have made *it.*'
4 "I will put hooks in your jaws
And make the fish of your rivers cling to
your scales.
And I will bring you up out of the midst
of your rivers,
And all the fish of your rivers will cling
to your scales.
5 "I will abandon you to the wilderness, you
and all the fish of your rivers;
You will fall on the open field; you will
not be brought together or gathered.
I have given you for food to the beasts of
the earth and to the birds of the sky.
6 "Then all the inhabitants of Egypt will
know that I am the LORD,
Because they have been *only* a staff *made*
of reed to the house of Israel.
7 "When they took hold of you with the
hand,
You broke and tore all their hands;
And when they leaned on you,
You broke and made all their loins
quake."
8 ¶ 'Therefore thus says the Lord GOD, "Behold, I will bring upon you a sword and I will cut
off from you man and beast.
9 "The land of Egypt will become a desolation
and waste. Then they will know that I am the
LORD.

¶ Because you said, 'The Nile is mine, and I have made *it*,'

10 therefore, behold, I am against you and against your rivers, and I will make the land of

Egypt an utter waste and desolation, from Migdol *to* Syene and even to the border of Ethiopia.

11 "A man's foot will not pass through it, and the foot of a beast will not pass through it, and it will not be inhabited for forty years.

12 "So I will make the land of Egypt a desolation in the midst of desolated lands. And her cities, in the midst of cities that are laid waste, will be desolate forty years; and I will scatter the Egyptians among the nations and disperse them among the lands."

13 ¶ 'For thus says the Lord GOD, "At the end of forty years I will gather the Egyptians from the peoples among whom they were scattered.

14 "I will turn the fortunes of Egypt and make them return to the land of Pathros, to the land of their origin, and there they will be a lowly kingdom.

15 "It will be the lowest of the kingdoms, and it will never again lift itself up above the nations. And I will make them so small that they will not rule over the nations.

16 "And it will never again be the confidence of the house of Israel, bringing to mind the iniquity of their having turned to Egypt. Then they will know that I am the Lord GOD." ' "

17 ¶ Now in the twenty-seventh year, in the first *month*, on the first of the month, the word of the LORD came to me saying,

18 "Son of man, Nebuchadnezzar king of Babylon made his army labor hard against Tyre; every head was made bald and every shoulder was rubbed bare. But he and his army had no wages from Tyre for the labor that he had performed against it."

19 Therefore thus says the Lord GOD, "Behold, I will give the land of Egypt to Nebuchadnezzar king of Babylon. And he will carry off her wealth and capture her spoil and seize her plunder; and it will be wages for his army.

20 "I have given him the land of Egypt *for* his labor which he performed, because they acted for Me," declares the Lord GOD.

21 ¶ "On that day I will make a horn sprout for the house of Israel, and I will open your mouth in their midst. Then they will know that I am the LORD."

Lament over Egypt

30 The word of the LORD came again to me saying,

2 "Son of man, prophesy and say, 'Thus says the Lord GOD,

"Wail, 'Alas for the day!'

3 "For the day is near,
Even the day of the LORD is near;
It will be a day of clouds,
A time *of doom* for the nations.

4 "A sword will come upon Egypt,
And anguish will be in Ethiopia;
When the slain fall in Egypt,
They take away her wealth,
And her foundations are torn down.

5 "Ethiopia, Put, Lud, all Arabia, Libya and the people of the land that is in league will fall with them by the sword."

6 ¶ 'Thus says the LORD,
"Indeed, those who support Egypt will fall
And the pride of her power will come down;
From Migdol *to* Syene
They will fall within her by the sword,"
Declares the Lord GOD.

7 "They will be desolate
In the midst of the desolated lands;
And her cities will be
In the midst of the devastated cities.

8 "And they will know that I am the LORD,
When I set a fire in Egypt
And all her helpers are broken.

9 "On that day messengers will go forth from Me in ships to frighten secure Ethiopia; and anguish will be on them as on the day of Egypt; for behold, it comes!"

10 ¶ 'Thus says the Lord GOD,
"I will also make the hordes of Egypt cease
By the hand of Nebuchadnezzar king of Babylon.

11 "He and his people with him,
The most ruthless of the nations,
Will be brought in to destroy the land;
And they will draw their swords against Egypt
And fill the land with the slain.

12 "Moreover, I will make the Nile canals dry
 And sell the land into the hands of evil
  men.
 And I will make the land desolate
 And all that is in it,
 By the hand of strangers; I the LORD
  have spoken."

13 ¶ 'Thus says the Lord GOD,
 "I will also destroy the idols
 And make the images cease from
  Memphis.
 And there will no longer be a prince in
  the land of Egypt;
 And I will put fear in the land of Egypt.
14 "I will make Pathros desolate,
 Set a fire in Zoan
 And execute judgments on ᵃThebes.
15 "I will pour out My wrath on ᵇSin,
 The stronghold of Egypt;
 I will also cut off the hordes of Thebes.
16 "I will set a fire in Egypt;
 Sin will writhe in anguish,
 Thebes will be breached
 And ᶜMemphis *will have* distresses
  daily.
17 "The young men of ᵈOn and of
  Pi-beseth
 Will fall by the sword,
 And the women will go into captivity.
18 "In Tehaphnehes the day will be dark
 When I break there the yoke bars of
  Egypt.
 Then the pride of her power will cease in
  her;
 A cloud will cover her,
 And her daughters will go into captivity.
19 "Thus I will execute judgments on Egypt,
 And they will know that I am the
  LORD."' "

Victory for Babylon

20 ¶ In the eleventh year, in the first *month,* on
the seventh of the month, the word of the LORD
came to me saying,
21 "Son of man, I have broken the arm of Pharaoh king of Egypt; and, behold, it has not been
bound up for healing or wrapped with a bandage,
that it may be strong to hold the sword.
22 "Therefore thus says the Lord GOD, 'Behold,
I am against Pharaoh king of Egypt and will break
his arms, both the strong and the broken; and I
will make the sword fall from his hand.
23 'I will scatter the Egyptians among the nations and disperse them among the lands.
24 'For I will strengthen the arms of the king of
Babylon and put My sword in his hand; and I will
break the arms of Pharaoh, so that he will groan
before him with the groanings of a wounded man.
25 'Thus I will strengthen the arms of the king

of Babylon, but the arms of Pharaoh will fall. Then
they will know that I am the LORD, when I put My
sword into the hand of the king of Babylon and he
stretches it out against the land of Egypt.
26 'When I scatter the Egyptians among the nations and disperse them among the lands, then
they will know that I am the LORD.' "

Pharaoh Warned of Assyria's Fate

31 In the eleventh year, in the third *month,* on
 the first of the month, the word of the LORD
came to me saying,
2 "Son of man, say to Pharaoh king of Egypt
and to his hordes,
 'Whom are you like in your greatness?
3 'Behold, Assyria *was* a cedar in Lebanon
 With beautiful branches and forest shade,
 And very high,
 And its top was among the clouds.
4 'The waters made it grow, the deep made
  it high.
 With its rivers it continually extended all
  around its planting place,
 And sent out its channels to all the trees
  of the field.
5 'Therefore its height was loftier than all
  the trees of the field
 And its boughs became many and its
  branches long
 Because of many waters as it spread
  them out.
6 'All the birds of the heavens nested in its
  boughs,
 And under its branches all the beasts of
  the field gave birth,
 And all great nations lived under its
  shade.
7 'So it was beautiful in its greatness, in the
  length of its branches;
 For its roots extended to many waters.
8 'The cedars in God's garden could not
  match it;
 The cypresses could not compare with its
  boughs,
 And the plane trees could not match its
  branches.
 No tree in God's garden could compare
  with it in its beauty.
9 'I made it beautiful with the multitude of
  its branches,
 And all the trees of Eden, which were in
  the garden of God, were jealous
  of it.

10 ¶ 'Therefore thus says the Lord GOD, "Because it is high in stature and has set its top among
the clouds, and its heart is haughty in its loftiness,
11 therefore I will give it into the hand of a
despot of the nations; he will thoroughly deal with
it. According to its wickedness I have driven it
away.

ᵃ Or *No*   ᵇ Or *Pelusium*   ᶜ Or *Noph*   ᵈ Or *Aven*

12 "Alien tyrants of the nations have cut it down and left it; on the mountains and in all the valleys its branches have fallen and its boughs have been broken in all the ravines of the land. And all the peoples of the earth have gone down from its shade and left it.

13 "On its ruin all the birds of the heavens will dwell, and all the beasts of the field will be on its *fallen* branches

14 so that all the trees by the waters may not be exalted in their stature, nor set their top among the clouds, nor their well-watered mighty ones stand *erect* in their height. For they have all been given over to death, to the earth beneath, among the sons of men, with those who go down to the pit."

15 ¶ 'Thus says the Lord GOD, "On the day when it went down to Sheol I caused lamentations; I closed the deep over it and held back its rivers. And *its* many waters were stopped up, and I made Lebanon mourn for it, and all the trees of the field wilted away on account of it.

16 "I made the nations quake at the sound of its fall when I made it go down to Sheol with those who go down to the pit; and all the well-watered trees of Eden, the choicest and best of Lebanon, were comforted in the earth beneath.

17 "They also went down with it to Sheol to those who were slain by the sword; and those who were its strength lived under its shade among the nations.

18 ¶ "To which among the trees of Eden are you thus equal in glory and greatness? Yet you will be brought down with the trees of Eden to the earth beneath; you will lie in the midst of the uncircumcised, with those who were slain by the sword. So is Pharaoh and all his hordes!"' declares the Lord GOD."

Lament over Pharaoh and Egypt

32 In the twelfth year, in the twelfth *month,* on the first of the month, the word of the LORD came to me saying,

2 "Son of man, take up a lamentation over Pharaoh king of Egypt and say to him,

'You compared yourself to a young lion
    of the nations,
Yet you are like the monster in the seas;
And you burst forth in your rivers
And muddied the waters with your feet
And fouled their rivers.' "

3 ¶ Thus says the Lord GOD,
"Now I will spread My net over you
With a company of many peoples,
And they shall lift you up in My net.
4 "I will leave you on the land;
I will cast you on the open field.
And I will cause all the birds of the
    heavens to dwell on you,
And I will satisfy the beasts of the whole
    earth with you.

5 "I will lay your flesh on the mountains
And fill the valleys with your refuse.
6 "I will also make the land drink the
    discharge of your blood
As far as the mountains,
And the ravines will be full of you.
7 "And when *I* extinguish you,
I will cover the heavens and darken their
    stars;
I will cover the sun with a cloud
And the moon will not give its light.
8 "All the shining lights in the heavens
I will darken over you
And will set darkness on your land,"
Declares the Lord GOD.

9 "I will also trouble the hearts of many peoples when I bring your destruction among the nations, into lands which you have not known.

10 "I will make many peoples appalled at you, and their kings will be horribly afraid of you when I brandish My sword before them; and they will tremble every moment, every man for his own life, on the day of your fall."

11 ¶ For thus says the Lord GOD, "The sword of the king of Babylon will come upon you.

12 "By the swords of the mighty ones I will cause your hordes to fall; all of them are tyrants of the nations,
And they will devastate the pride of
    Egypt,
And all its hordes will be destroyed.
13 "I will also destroy all its cattle from
    beside many waters;
And the foot of man will not muddy
    them anymore
And the hoofs of beasts will not muddy
    them.
14 "Then I will make their waters settle
And will cause their rivers to run
    like oil,"
Declares the Lord GOD.
15 "When I make the land of Egypt a
    desolation,
And the land is destitute of that which
    filled it,
When I smite all those who live in it,
Then they shall know that I am the
    LORD.

16 "This is a lamentation and they shall chant it. The daughters of the nations shall chant it. Over Egypt and over all her hordes they shall chant it," declares the Lord GOD.

17 ¶ In the twelfth year, on the fifteenth of the month, the word of the LORD came to me saying,

18 "Son of man, wail for the hordes of Egypt and bring it down, her and the daughters of the powerful nations, to the nether world, with those who go down to the pit;

19 'Whom do you surpass in beauty?
Go down and make your bed with the
    uncircumcised.'

20 "They shall fall in the midst of those who are slain by the sword. She is given over to the sword; they have drawn her and all her hordes away.

21 "The strong among the mighty ones shall speak of him *and* his helpers from the midst of Sheol, 'They have gone down, they lie still, the uncircumcised, slain by the sword.'

32:21 The Afterlife

Though eternal life shines through a few Old Testament passages (see "Life after Death," page 603), life after death was extremely vague in most of the Old Testament. The grave was represented by a place called "Sheol." The fate of the nations described here as "from the midst of Sheol" gives a vivid, eerie sense of death.

22 ¶ "Assyria is there and all her company; her graves are round about her. All of them are slain, fallen by the sword,

23 whose graves are set in the remotest parts of the pit and her company is round about her grave. All of them are slain, fallen by the sword, who spread terror in the land of the living.

24 ¶ "Elam is there and all her hordes around her grave; all of them slain, fallen by the sword, who went down uncircumcised to the lower parts of the earth, who instilled their terror in the land of the living and bore their disgrace with those who went down to the pit.

25 "They have made a bed for her among the slain with all her hordes. Her graves are around it, they are all uncircumcised, slain by the sword (although their terror was instilled in the land of the living), and they bore their disgrace with those who go down to the pit; they were put in the midst of the slain.

26 ¶ "Meshech, Tubal and all their hordes are there; their graves surround them. All of them were slain by the sword uncircumcised, though they instilled their terror in the land of the living.

27 "Nor do they lie beside the fallen heroes of the uncircumcised, who went down to Sheol with their weapons of war and whose swords were laid under their heads; but the punishment for their iniquity rested on their bones, though the terror of *these* heroes *was once* in the land of the living.

28 "But in the midst of the uncircumcised you will be broken and lie with those slain by the sword.

29 ¶ "There also is Edom, its kings and all its princes, who for *all* their might are laid with those slain by the sword; they will lie with the uncircumcised and with those who go down to the pit.

30 ¶ "There also are the chiefs of the north, all of them, and all the Sidonians, who in spite of the terror resulting from their might, in shame went down with the slain. So they lay down uncircum-

cised with those slain by the sword and bore their disgrace with those who go down to the pit.

31 ¶ "These Pharaoh will see, and he will be comforted for all his hordes slain by the sword, *even* Pharaoh and all his army," declares the Lord GOD.

32 "Though I instilled a terror of him in the land of the living, yet he will be made to lie down among *the* uncircumcised *along* with those slain by the sword, *even* Pharaoh and all his hordes," declares the Lord GOD.

The Watchman's Duty

33 And the word of the LORD came to me, saying,

2 "Son of man, speak to the sons of your people and say to them, 'If I bring a sword upon a land, and the people of the land take one man from among them and make him their watchman,

3 and he sees the sword coming upon the land and blows on the trumpet and warns the people,

4 then he who hears the sound of the trumpet and does not take warning, and a sword comes and takes him away, his blood will be on his *own* head.

5 'He heard the sound of the trumpet but did not take warning; his blood will be on himself. But had he taken warning, he would have delivered his life.

6 'But if the watchman sees the sword coming and does not blow the trumpet and the people are not warned, and a sword comes and takes a person from them, he is taken away in his iniquity; but his blood I will require from the watchman's hand.'

7 ¶ "Now as for you, son of man, I have appointed you a watchman for the house of Israel; so you will hear a message from My mouth and give them warning from Me.

33:7 Watch Out

You don't hire a watchman to fight off robbers single-handed; he is responsible for sounding the alarm. God assigns Ezekiel the watchman's role, here and earlier (3:18). It's tragic when someone dies for his or her sins, but when he or she dies without being warned, that is inexcusable—for the watchman was assigned to offer a chance to repent.

8 "When I say to the wicked, 'O wicked man, you will surely die,' and you do not speak to warn the wicked from his way, that wicked man shall die in his iniquity, but his blood I will require from your hand.

9 "But if you on your part warn a wicked man to turn from his way and he does not turn from his way, he will die in his iniquity, but you have delivered your life.

10 ¶ "Now as for you, son of man, say to the house of Israel, 'Thus you have spoken, saying, "Surely our transgressions and our sins are upon us, and we are rotting away in them; how then can we survive?"'

11 "Say to them, 'As I live!' declares the Lord GOD, 'I take no pleasure in the death of the wicked, but rather that the wicked turn from his way and live. Turn back, turn back from your evil ways! Why then will you die, O house of Israel?'

12 "And you, son of man, say to your fellow citizens, 'The righteousness of a righteous man will not deliver him in the day of his transgression, and as for the wickedness of the wicked, he will not stumble because of it in the day when he turns from his wickedness; whereas a righteous man will not be able to live by his righteousness on the day when he commits sin.'

13 "When I say to the righteous he will surely live, and he *so* trusts in his righteousness that he commits iniquity, none of his righteous deeds will be remembered; but in that same iniquity of his which he has committed he will die.

14 "But when I say to the wicked, 'You will surely die,' and he turns from his sin and practices justice and righteousness,

15 *if a* wicked man restores a pledge, pays back what he has taken by robbery, walks by the stat-

The Turning Point
From here forward, Ezekiel offers good news

TO THEIR CHILDREN PARENTS CAN seem frighteningly inconsistent. One minute a father is gripping his son's wrist, shouting about something. The next moment, punishment over, he is talking about going camping together next summer. How can he change so drastically? Why so angry one minute and so loving the next?

The sudden change makes sense only if you grasp that most parents hate the role of disciplinarian. They punish in order to correct something they see as harmful. Afterwards, they put punishment behind them as quickly as possible, because they dream of better times in the future.

> In the twelfth year of our exile . . . the refugees from Jerusalem came to me, saying, "The city has been taken." 33:21

A Happier Life for Ezekiel

Ezekiel portrays just such a drastic change between God and Israel. Until chapter 33 he had offered mostly anger and threats. Suddenly, in verse 21, the news of Jerusalem's fall reached Ezekiel. The punishment, long threatened, had come. From this point on, Ezekiel's message from God became dominated by dreams of the future—happy dreams. Ezekiel's life became happier too. After seven years of virtual silence (3:26–27—he spoke only what God told him to), he opened his mouth freely again.

God, speaking through Ezekiel, began to paint the future with the same vivid colors he had used to promise punishment. He spoke of Israel as a flock of sheep and himself as their loving shepherd (chapter 34). He previewed the mountains of Israel as they will look under his full blessing (chapter 36)—very different from the prediction given those same mountains in chapter 6.

God showed Ezekiel a valley of dry bones rising up and taking life (chapter 37), a vision that has inspired musicians and preachers ever since. He forecast a fantastic battle with evil forces from the north, Gog and Magog, in which God's people would triumph magnificently (chapters 38–39). Then, in his final vision, God showed Ezekiel the nation of Israel restored, with its boundaries extended far into hostile territory, its temple rebuilt in new splendor (chapters 40–48). The Lord would come back to his home, to live with his people.

The Temple's Significance

The temple, to Israel, was a sign of God's love. By taking up a home there, he committed himself to be with them permanently—not to come and go but to be available at any and all times to his people. When he left the temple (10:18) and let it be razed by the Babylonians (2 Kings 25:9), he communicated clearly that Israel had forfeited any right to his care.

So Ezekiel's vision of a rebuilt temple, with God's glory filling it, was a promise of new hope. The temple has never been rebuilt according to the precise description Ezekiel gave (chapters 40–43), and many scholars understand his portrayal as symbolic. But the central beauty of the temple is this: "The LORD is there." The glorious, astonishing God whom Ezekiel first saw in the Babylonian desert will make his home in the center of the land. He will not always be angry. He has great plans for the happiness of his people.

Life Questions: In your relationship with God, are you more concerned with past failures? Or with hopes for the future?

utes which ensure life without committing iniquity, he shall surely live; he shall not die.

16 "None of his sins that he has committed will be remembered against him. He has practiced justice and righteousness; he shall surely live.

17 ¶ "Yet your fellow citizens say, 'The way of the Lord is not right,' when it is their own way that is not right.

18 "When the righteous turns from his righteousness and commits iniquity, then he shall die in it.

19 "But when the wicked turns from his wickedness and practices justice and righteousness, he will live by them.

20 "Yet you say, 'The way of the Lord is not right.' O house of Israel, I will judge each of you according to his ways."

Word of Jerusalem's Capture

21 ¶ Now in the twelfth year of our exile, on the fifth of the tenth month, the refugees from Jerusalem came to me, saying, "The city has been taken."

22 Now the hand of the LORD had been upon me in the evening, before the refugees came. And He opened my mouth at the time they came to me in the morning; so my mouth was opened and I was no longer speechless.

33:22 End of the Silence

For nearly eight years, since the beginning of his ministry, Ezekiel had been silent except when giving God's words. Now, an exile arrived in Babylon with bad news from Jerusalem: The temple had been burned, the city destroyed. Ezekiel's long silence ended, by God's permission. His message of doom ended too, for his prediction of punishment had come true. From this point on, Ezekiel's prophecies take up a more hopeful theme, of rebuilding a broken people.

23 ¶ Then the word of the LORD came to me saying,

24 "Son of man, they who live in these waste places in the land of Israel are saying, 'Abraham was only one, yet he possessed the land; so to us who are many the land has been given as a possession.'

25 "Therefore say to them, 'Thus says the Lord GOD, "You eat meat with the blood in it, lift up your eyes to your idols as you shed blood. Should you then possess the land?

26 "You rely on your sword, you commit abominations and each of you defiles his neighbor's wife. Should you then possess the land?" '

27 "Thus you shall say to them, 'Thus says the Lord GOD, "As I live, surely those who are in the waste places will fall by the sword, and whoever is in the open field I will give to the beasts to be devoured, and those who are in the strongholds and in the caves will die of pestilence.

28 "I will make the land a desolation and a waste, and the pride of her power will cease; and the mountains of Israel will be desolate so that no one will pass through.

29 "Then they will know that I am the LORD, when I make the land a desolation and a waste because of all their abominations which they have committed." '

30 ¶ "But as for you, son of man, your fellow citizens who talk about you by the walls and in the doorways of the houses, speak to one another, each to his brother, saying, 'Come now and hear what the message is which comes forth from the LORD.'

31 "They come to you as people come, and sit before you as My people and hear your words, but they do not do them, for they do the lustful desires expressed by their mouth, and their heart goes after their gain.

32 "Behold, you are to them like a sensual song by one who has a beautiful voice and plays well on an instrument; for they hear your words but they do not practice them.

33:32 Prophetic Entertainment

Ezekiel's popularity soared after Jerusalem's fall, for his warnings had all come true. Even so, his audience listened just for entertainment, as they would to music. God reminds Ezekiel that the true purpose of prophecy is to change people's lives, not to draw a crowd.

33 "So when it comes to pass—as surely it will—then they will know that a prophet has been in their midst."

Prophecy against the Shepherds of Israel

34 Then the word of the LORD came to me saying,

2 "Son of man, prophesy against the shepherds of Israel. Prophesy and say to those shepherds, 'Thus says the Lord GOD, "Woe, shepherds of Israel who have been feeding themselves! Should not the shepherds feed the flock?

3 "You eat the fat and clothe yourselves with the wool, you slaughter the fat sheep without feeding the flock.

4 "Those who are sickly you have not strengthened, the diseased you have not healed, the broken you have not bound up, the scattered you have not brought back, nor have you sought for the lost; but with force and with severity you have dominated them.

5 "They were scattered for lack of a shepherd, and they became food for every beast of the field and were scattered.

6 "My flock wandered through all the mountains and on every high hill; My flock was scattered over all the surface of the earth, and there was no one to search or seek *for them*." ' "

7 ¶ Therefore, you shepherds, hear the word of the LORD:

8 "As I live," declares the Lord GOD, "surely because My flock has become a prey, My flock has even become food for all the beasts of the field for lack of a shepherd, and My shepherds did not search for My flock, but *rather* the shepherds fed themselves and did not feed My flock;

9 therefore, you shepherds, hear the word of the LORD:

10 'Thus says the Lord GOD, "Behold, I am against the shepherds, and I will demand My sheep from them and make them cease from feeding sheep. So the shepherds will not feed themselves anymore, but I will deliver My flock from their mouth, so that they will not be food for them." ' "

The Restoration of Israel

11 ¶ For thus says the Lord GOD, "Behold, I Myself will search for My sheep and seek them out.

12 "As a shepherd cares for his herd in the day when he is among his scattered sheep, so I will care for My sheep and will deliver them from all the places to which they were scattered on a cloudy and gloomy day.

13 "I will bring them out from the peoples and gather them from the countries and bring them to their own land; and I will feed them on the mountains of Israel, by the streams, and in all the inhabited places of the land.

The Sad Truth

Ezekiel became popular overnight—but the praise was empty

GOD WARNED EZEKIEL IT WOULD be a terrible job. Nobody would listen to his message. He would find his own people "stubborn and obstinate" (3:7). And how would God help him? "I have made your face as hard as their faces" (3:8).

As a result Ezekiel lived a lonely life. Those few who believed his prophecies expected nothing to happen in their lifetime (12:27). People thought of Ezekiel as someone just telling stories (20:49). They couldn't believe that God would let Jerusalem fall, as Ezekiel was stubbornly predicting.

> "They come to you as people come, and sit before you as My people and hear your words, but they do not do them." 33:31

Then, after years of prophecy, news came that Babylon had conquered Jerusalem (33:21). Suddenly Ezekiel was popular. People talked about him, flocked to hear his words, expressed devotion. But they listened to Ezekiel without changing their hearts. He was "to them like a sensual song by one who has a beautiful voice" (33:32). The people heard his words but did not put them into practice.

A Dreadful Message

In some ways Ezekiel could sympathize with the people's negative attitude. He did not like his message either; sometimes it horrified him. Twice, seeing God's judgment, he fell facedown in horror, crying out (9:8; 11:13). When God told him to cook food over human excrement, a symbol of defilement, he was too shocked to agree (4:14). When his wife, "the desire of his eyes," died, he was not even allowed to weep (24:15–24).

Ezekiel had to subordinate ordinary human emotions to the unpleasant task God had given him: to tell the truth, the whole truth, and nothing but the truth, and to tell it in a way that the Israelites could not ignore. "'As I live!' declares the Lord GOD, 'I take no pleasure in the death of the wicked, but rather that the wicked turn from his way and live. Turn back, turn back from your evil ways! Why then will you die, O house of Israel?' " (33:11).

Phony Optimism

The false prophets, by contrast, tended to be optimists. They overlooked their nation's corruption and predicted that everything would work out. Chapter 13 records Ezekiel's words against them. "Woe to the foolish prophets who are following their own spirit and have seen nothing," he said (13:3). They would "whitewash" a bad situation with claims that God could never let Jerusalem be destroyed (13:10–16).

In the end Ezekiel got to deliver genuine good news: the promise of restored life. He saw a vision that still lives in song: scattered, bleached bones coming to life (37:1–14). In another vision, he saw God return to live in Jerusalem (43:1–5). Ezekiel didn't live to see these hopeful predictions fulfilled. But you can be sure he enjoyed making them far more than he enjoyed his predictions of disaster.

Life Questions: Is there any place today for "bad news" of the kind Ezekiel proclaimed?

14 "I will feed them in a good pasture, and their grazing ground will be on the mountain heights of Israel. There they will lie down on good grazing ground and feed in rich pasture on the mountains of Israel.

34:11–16 The Good Shepherd

Ezekiel, who used strong imagery throughout his writing, developed the image of God as a shepherd with more detail than any other author in the Bible. To people who herded sheep for a living, the simile had tremendous impact.

The same comparison is used repeatedly throughout the Bible. One much-loved passage is Psalm 23, which begins, "The Lord is my shepherd." Jesus called himself "the good shepherd" (John 10:11–16) and had compassion on crowds because they were like "sheep without a shepherd" (Mark 6:34). The image of God as a shepherd begins with Jacob (Genesis 48:15) and ends with Revelation 7:17.

15 "I will feed My flock and I will lead them to rest," declares the Lord GOD.

16 "I will seek the lost, bring back the scattered, bind up the broken and strengthen the sick; but the fat and the strong I will destroy. I will feed them with judgment.

17 ¶ "As for you, My flock, thus says the Lord GOD, 'Behold, I will judge between one sheep and another, between the rams and the male goats.

18 'Is it too slight a thing for you that you should feed in the good pasture, that you must tread down with your feet the rest of your pastures? Or that you should drink of the clear waters, that you must foul the rest with your feet?

19 'As for My flock, they must eat what you tread down with your feet and drink what you foul with your feet!' "

20 ¶ Therefore, thus says the Lord GOD to them, "Behold, I, even I, will judge between the fat sheep and the lean sheep.

21 "Because you push with side and with shoulder, and thrust at all the weak with your horns until you have scattered them abroad,

22 therefore, I will deliver My flock, and they will no longer be a prey; and I will judge between one sheep and another.

23 ¶ "Then I will set over them one shepherd, My servant David, and he will feed them; he will feed them himself and be their shepherd.

24 "And I, the LORD, will be their God, and My servant David will be prince among them; I the LORD have spoken.

25 ¶ "I will make a covenant of peace with them and eliminate harmful beasts from the land so that they may live securely in the wilderness and sleep in the woods.

26 "I will make them and the places around My hill a blessing. And I will cause showers to come down in their season; they will be showers of blessing.

27 "Also the tree of the field will yield its fruit and the earth will yield its increase, and they will be secure on their land. Then they will know that I am the LORD, when I have broken the bars of their yoke and have delivered them from the hand of those who enslaved them.

28 "They will no longer be a prey to the nations, and the beasts of the earth will not devour them; but they will live securely, and no one will make *them* afraid.

29 "I will establish for them a renowned planting place, and they will not again be victims of famine in the land, and they will not endure the insults of the nations anymore.

30 "Then they will know that I, the LORD their God, am with them, and that they, the house of Israel, are My people," declares the Lord GOD.

31 "As for you, My sheep, the sheep of My pasture, you are men, and I am your God," declares the Lord GOD.

Prophecy against Mount Seir

35 Moreover, the word of the LORD came to me saying,

2 "Son of man, set your face against Mount Seir, and prophesy against it

3 and say to it, 'Thus says the Lord GOD,
"Behold, I am against you, Mount Seir,
And I will stretch out My hand
against you
And make you a desolation and a waste.

4 "I will lay waste your cities
And you will become a desolation.
Then you will know that I am the LORD.

5 "Because you have had everlasting enmity and have delivered the sons of Israel to the power of the sword at the time of their calamity, at the time of the punishment of the end,

35:5 Bad Blood

Ill will between two clans dated from the beginning, when Jacob cheated his brother Esau out of the family inheritance. Over the centuries Esau's descendants became the nation of Edom, and Jacob's became Israel. Bad feelings persisted. To Israelites, however, this incident was the ultimate offense: When Babylon burned down Jerusalem, the Edomites looted the city and egged on the Babylonians.

6 therefore as I live," declares the Lord GOD, "I will give you over to bloodshed, and bloodshed will pursue you; since you have not hated bloodshed, therefore bloodshed will pursue you.

7 "I will make Mount Seir a waste and a deso-

lation and I will cut off from it the one who passes through and returns.

8 "I will fill its mountains with its slain; on your hills and in your valleys and in all your ravines those slain by the sword will fall.

9 "I will make you an everlasting desolation and your cities will not be inhabited. Then you will know that I am the LORD.

10 ¶ "Because you have said, 'These two nations and these two lands will be mine, and we will possess them,' although the LORD was there,

11 therefore as I live," declares the Lord GOD, "I will deal *with you* according to your anger and according to your envy which you showed because of your hatred against them; so I will make Myself known among them when I judge you.

12 "Then you will know that I, the LORD, have heard all your revilings which you have spoken against the mountains of Israel saying, 'They are laid desolate; they are given to us for food.'

13 "And you have spoken arrogantly against Me and have multiplied your words against Me; I have heard *it*."

14 'Thus says the Lord GOD, "As all the earth rejoices, I will make you a desolation.

15 "As you rejoiced over the inheritance of the house of Israel because it was desolate, so I will do to you. You will be a desolation, O Mount Seir, and all Edom, all of it. Then they will know that I am the LORD." '

The Mountains of Israel to Be Blessed

36 "And you, son of man, prophesy to the mountains of Israel and say, 'O mountains of Israel, hear the word of the LORD.

2 'Thus says the Lord GOD, "Because the enemy has spoken against you, 'Aha!' and, 'The everlasting heights have become our possession,'

3 therefore prophesy and say, 'Thus says the Lord GOD, "For good reason they have made you desolate and crushed you from every side, that you would become a possession of the rest of the nations and you have been taken up in the talk and the whispering of the people." ' "

4 'Therefore, O mountains of Israel, hear the word of the Lord GOD. Thus says the Lord GOD to the mountains and to the hills, to the ravines and to the valleys, to the desolate wastes and to the forsaken cities which have become a prey and a derision to the rest of the nations which are round about,

5 therefore thus says the Lord GOD, "Surely in the fire of My jealousy I have spoken against the rest of the nations, and against all Edom, who appropriated My land for themselves as a possession with wholehearted joy *and* with scorn of soul, to drive it out for a prey."

6 'Therefore prophesy concerning the land of Israel and say to the mountains and to the hills, to the ravines and to the valleys, "Thus says the Lord GOD, 'Behold, I have spoken in My jealousy and

in My wrath because you have endured the insults of the nations.'

7 "Therefore thus says the Lord GOD, 'I have sworn that surely the nations which are around you will themselves endure their insults.

8 'But you, O mountains of Israel, you will put forth your branches and bear your fruit for My people Israel; for they will soon come.

9 'For, behold, I am for you, and I will turn to you, and you will be cultivated and sown.

10 'I will multiply men on you, all the house of Israel, all of it; and the cities will be inhabited and the waste places will be rebuilt.

11 'I will multiply on you man and beast; and they will increase and be fruitful; and I will cause you to be inhabited as you were formerly and will treat you better than at the first. Thus you will know that I am the LORD.

12 'Yes, I will cause men—My people Israel—to walk on you and possess you, so that you will become their inheritance and never again bereave them of children.'

13 ¶ "Thus says the Lord GOD, 'Because they say to you, "You are a devourer of men and have bereaved your nation of children,"

14 therefore you will no longer devour men and no longer bereave your nation of children,' declares the Lord GOD.

15 "I will not let you hear insults from the nations anymore, nor will you bear disgrace from the peoples any longer, nor will you cause your nation to stumble any longer," declares the Lord GOD.' "

16 ¶ Then the word of the LORD came to me saying,

17 "Son of man, when the house of Israel was living in their own land, they defiled it by their ways and their deeds; their way before Me was like the uncleanness of a woman in her impurity.

18 "Therefore I poured out My wrath on them for the blood which they had shed on the land, because they had defiled it with their idols.

19 "Also I scattered them among the nations and they were dispersed throughout the lands. According to their ways and their deeds I judged them.

20 "When they came to the nations where they went, they profaned My holy name, because it was said of them, 'These are the people of the LORD; yet they have come out of His land.'

21 "But I had concern for My holy name, which the house of Israel had profaned among the nations where they went.

Israel to Be Renewed for His Name's Sake

22 ¶ "Therefore say to the house of Israel, 'Thus says the Lord GOD, "It is not for your sake, O house of Israel, that I am about to act, but for My holy name, which you have profaned among the nations where you went.

23 "I will vindicate the holiness of My great

name which has been profaned among the nations, which you have profaned in their midst. Then the nations will know that I am the LORD," declares the Lord GOD, "when I prove Myself holy among you in their sight.

24 "For I will take you from the nations, gather you from all the lands and bring you into your own land.

25 "Then I will sprinkle clean water on you, and you will be clean; I will cleanse you from all your filthiness and from all your idols.

26 "Moreover, I will give you a new heart and put a new spirit within you; and I will remove the heart of stone from your flesh and give you a heart of flesh.

27 "I will put My Spirit within you and cause you to walk in My statutes, and you will be careful to observe My ordinances.

36:27 A New Spirit

Like Jeremiah, Ezekiel realized that Israel needed more than a fresh start. To avoid making the same mistakes all over again, they needed new motivation and orientation. God must work radical surgery on them, to implant a new heart and a new spirit. Jesus' followers believed that this began when the Holy Spirit came at Pentecost (Acts 2:17–21).

28 "You will live in the land that I gave to your forefathers; so you will be My people, and I will be your God.

29 "Moreover, I will save you from all your uncleanness; and I will call for the grain and multiply it, and I will not bring a famine on you.

30 "I will multiply the fruit of the tree and the produce of the field, so that you will not receive again the disgrace of famine among the nations.

31 "Then you will remember your evil ways and your deeds that were not good, and you will loathe yourselves in your own sight for your iniquities and your abominations.

32 "I am not doing *this* for your sake," declares the Lord GOD, "let it be known to you. Be ashamed and confounded for your ways, O house of Israel!"

33 ¶ 'Thus says the Lord GOD, "On the day that I cleanse you from all your iniquities, I will cause the cities to be inhabited, and the waste places will be rebuilt.

34 "The desolate land will be cultivated instead of being a desolation in the sight of everyone who passes by.

35 "They will say, 'This desolate land has become like the garden of Eden; and the waste, desolate and ruined cities are fortified *and* inhabited.'

36 "Then the nations that are left round about

you will know that I, the LORD, have rebuilt the ruined places *and* planted that which was desolate; I, the LORD, have spoken and will do it."

37 ¶ 'Thus says the Lord GOD, "This also I will let the house of Israel ask Me to do for them: I will increase their men like a flock.

38 "Like the flock for sacrifices, like the flock at Jerusalem during her appointed feasts, so will the waste cities be filled with flocks of men. Then they will know that I am the LORD." ' "

Vision of the Valley of Dry Bones

37 The hand of the LORD was upon me, and He brought me out by the Spirit of the LORD and set me down in the middle of the valley; and it was full of bones.

2 He caused me to pass among them round about, and behold, *there were* very many on the surface of the valley; and lo, *they were* very dry.

3 He said to me, "Son of man, can these bones live?" And I answered, "O Lord GOD, You know."

4 Again He said to me, "Prophesy over these bones and say to them, 'O dry bones, hear the word of the LORD.'

5 "Thus says the Lord GOD to these bones, 'Behold, I will cause *a*breath to enter you that you may come to life.

6 'I will put sinews on you, make flesh grow back on you, cover you with skin and put breath in you that you may come alive; and you will know that I am the LORD.' "

7 ¶ So I prophesied as I was commanded; and as I prophesied, there was a noise, and behold, a rattling; and the bones came together, bone to its bone.

8 And I looked, and behold, sinews were on them, and flesh grew and skin covered them; but there was no breath in them.

9 Then He said to me, "Prophesy to the breath, prophesy, son of man, and say to the breath, 'Thus says the Lord GOD, "Come from the four winds, O breath, and breathe on these slain, that they come to life." ' "

10 So I prophesied as He commanded me, and the breath came into them, and they came to life and stood on their feet, an exceedingly great army.

The Vision Explained

11 ¶ Then He said to me, "Son of man, these bones are the whole house of Israel; behold, they say, 'Our bones are dried up and our hope has perished. We are completely cut off.'

12 "Therefore prophesy and say to them, 'Thus says the Lord GOD, "Behold, I will open your graves and cause you to come up out of your graves, My people; and I will bring you into the land of Israel.

13 "Then you will know that I am the LORD, when I have opened your graves and caused you to come up out of your graves, My people.

---

a Or *spirit*, and so throughout the ch

14 "I will put My ^aSpirit within you and you will come to life, and I will place you on your own land. Then you will know that I, the LORD, have spoken and done it," declares the LORD.'"

37:9 Dry Bones

This marvelous vision, celebrated in a famous song, begins with a collection of bones littering a valley floor. Before Ezekiel's eyes, the bones come together, assembling into skeletons and growing flesh and skin. The bodies stay dead, however, until in a dramatic moment God puts breath into them. The Hebrew for "breath" also means Spirit, and the vision would have reminded any Jew of Genesis 2:7, where God breathed life into the first man.

God is reminding Ezekiel that it would take a miracle to bring the remnants of Israel back together from the many locations where they were scattered. But to be truly alive, Israel will need a greater miracle: a new Spirit, breathed by God. Only a new creation can resurrect Israel or anyone else.

Reunion of Judah and Israel

15 ¶ The word of the LORD came again to me saying,

16 "And you, son of man, take for yourself one stick and write on it, 'For Judah and for the sons of Israel, his companions'; then take another stick and write on it, 'For Joseph, the stick of Ephraim and all the house of Israel, his companions.'

17 "Then join them for yourself one to another into one stick, that they may become one in your hand.

18 "When the sons of your people speak to you saying, 'Will you not declare to us what you mean by these?'

19 say to them, 'Thus says the Lord GOD, "Behold, I will take the stick of Joseph, which is in the hand of Ephraim, and the tribes of Israel, his companions; and I will put them with it, with the stick of Judah, and make them one stick, and they will be one in My hand."'

20 "The sticks on which you write will be in your hand before their eyes.

21 "Say to them, 'Thus says the Lord GOD, "Behold, I will take the sons of Israel from among the nations where they have gone, and I will gather them from every side and bring them into their own land;

22 and I will make them one nation in the land, on the mountains of Israel; and one king will be king for all of them; and they will no longer be two nations and no longer be divided into two kingdoms.

23 "They will no longer defile themselves with their idols, or with their detestable things, or with any of their transgressions; but I will deliver them from all their ^bdwelling places in which they have sinned, and will cleanse them. And they will be My people, and I will be their God.

37:22 North and South Reunited

Israel longed to be reunited. The Jews had been split into two nations (sometimes at war) since the days of Solomon, over 300 years before. Yet, like East and West Germany, now united again, and North and South Korea today, they had not forgotten their common origin. God promised to reunite the two—even though one had been in exile, scattered among other nations, for over 100 years.

The Davidic Kingdom

24 ¶ "My servant David will be king over them, and they will all have one shepherd; and they will walk in My ordinances and keep My statutes and observe them.

25 "They will live on the land that I gave to Jacob My servant, in which your fathers lived; and they will live on it, they, and their sons and their sons' sons, forever; and David My servant will be their prince forever.

26 "I will make a covenant of peace with them; it will be an everlasting covenant with them. And I will place them and multiply them, and will set My sanctuary in their midst forever.

27 "My dwelling place also will be with them; and I will be their God, and they will be My people.

28 "And the nations will know that I am the LORD who sanctifies Israel, when My sanctuary is in their midst forever."'"

Prophecy about Gog and Future Invasion of Israel

38 And the word of the LORD came to me saying,

2 "Son of man, set your face toward Gog of the land of Magog, the prince of Rosh, Meshech and Tubal, and prophesy against him

3 and say, 'Thus says the Lord GOD, "Behold, I am against you, O Gog, prince of Rosh, Meshech and Tubal.

4 "I will turn you about and put hooks into your jaws, and I will bring you out, and all your army, horses and horsemen, all of them splendidly attired, a great company *with* buckler and shield, all of them wielding swords;

5 Persia, Ethiopia and Put with them, all of them *with* shield and helmet;

6 Gomer with all its troops; Beth-togarmah

---

^a Or *breath*   ^b Another reading is *backslidings*

from the remote parts of the north with all its troops—many peoples with you.

7 ¶ "Be prepared, and prepare yourself, you and all your companies that are assembled about you, and be a guard for them.

8 "After many days you will be summoned; in the latter years you will come into the land that is restored from the sword, *whose inhabitants* have been gathered from many nations to the mountains of Israel which had been a continual waste; but its people were brought out from the nations, and they are living securely, all of them.

9 "You will go up, you will come like a storm; you will be like a cloud covering the land, you and all your troops, and many peoples with you."

10 ¶ 'Thus says the Lord GOD, "It will come about on that day, that thoughts will come into your mind and you will devise an evil plan,

11 and you will say, 'I will go up against the land of ªunwalled villages. I will go against those who are at rest, that live securely, all of them living without walls and having no bars or gates,

12 to capture spoil and to seize plunder, to turn your hand against the waste places which are *now* inhabited, and against the people who are gathered from the nations, who have acquired cattle and goods, who live at the center of the world.'

13 "Sheba and Dedan and the merchants of Tarshish with all its villages will say to you, 'Have you come to capture spoil? Have you assembled your company to seize plunder, to carry away silver and gold, to take away cattle and goods, to capture great spoil?' " '

14 ¶ "Therefore prophesy, son of man, and say to Gog, 'Thus says the Lord GOD, "On that day when My people Israel are living securely, will you not know *it*?

15 "You will come from your place out of the remote parts of the north, you and many peoples with you, all of them riding on horses, a great assembly and a mighty army;

16 and you will come up against My people Israel like a cloud to cover the land. It shall come about in the last days that I will bring you against My land, so that the nations may know Me when I am sanctified through you before their eyes, O Gog."

17 ¶ 'Thus says the Lord GOD, "Are you the one of whom I spoke in former days through My servants the prophets of Israel, who prophesied in those days for *many* years that I would bring you against them?

18 "It will come about on that day, when Gog comes against the land of Israel," declares the Lord GOD, "that My fury will mount up in My anger.

19 "In My zeal and in My blazing wrath I declare *that* on that day there will surely be a great earthquake in the land of Israel.

20 "The fish of the sea, the birds of the heavens, the beasts of the field, all the creeping things that creep on the earth, and all the men who are on the face of the earth will shake at My presence; the mountains also will be thrown down, the steep pathways will collapse and every wall will fall to the ground.

21 "I will call for a sword against him on all My mountains," declares the Lord GOD. "Every man's sword will be against his brother.

22 "With pestilence and with blood I will enter into judgment with him; and I will rain on him and on his troops, and on the many peoples who are with him, a torrential rain, with hailstones, fire and brimstone.

23 "I will magnify Myself, sanctify Myself, and make Myself known in the sight of many nations; and they will know that I am the LORD." '

Prophecy against Gog—Invaders Destroyed

39 "And you, son of man, prophesy against Gog and say, 'Thus says the Lord GOD, "Behold, I am against you, O Gog, prince of Rosh, Meshech and Tubal;

39:1 Gog and Magog

Who are Gog and Magog? Bible interpreters disagree. At the very least, they represent an evil empire that attacks Israel from the north. More than ordinary enemies, they are a personification of evil—the evil that has fought God's people from the very beginning. These chapters show God delivering his people by destroying Gog. The two names, Gog and Magog, reappear in Revelation 20:8, participating in the final battle with evil.

2 and I will turn you around, drive you on, take you up from the remotest parts of the north and bring you against the mountains of Israel.

3 "I will strike your bow from your left hand and dash down your arrows from your right hand.

4 "You will fall on the mountains of Israel, you and all your troops and the peoples who are with you; I will give you as food to every kind of predatory bird and beast of the field.

5 "You will fall on the open field; for it is I who have spoken," declares the Lord GOD.

6 "And I will send fire upon Magog and those who inhabit the coastlands in safety; and they will know that I am the LORD.

7 ¶ "My holy name I will make known in the midst of My people Israel; and I will not let My holy name be profaned anymore. And the nations will know that I am the LORD, the Holy One in Israel.

8 "Behold, it is coming and it shall be done,"

ª Or *open country*

declares the Lord GOD. "That is the day of which I have spoken.

9 ¶ "Then those who inhabit the cities of Israel will go out and make fires with the weapons and burn *them*, both shields and bucklers, bows and arrows, war clubs and spears, and for seven years they will make fires of them.

10 "They will not take wood from the field or gather firewood from the forests, for they will make fires with the weapons; and they will take the spoil of those who despoiled them and seize the plunder of those who plundered them," declares the Lord GOD.

11 ¶ "On that day I will give Gog a burial ground there in Israel, the valley of those who pass by east of the sea, and it will block off those who would pass by. So they will bury Gog there with all his horde, and they will call *it* the valley of Hamon-gog.

12 "For seven months the house of Israel will be burying them in order to cleanse the land.

13 "Even all the people of the land will bury *them;* and it will be to their renown *on* the day that I glorify Myself," declares the Lord GOD.

14 "They will set apart men who will constantly pass through the land, burying those who were passing through, even those left on the surface of the ground, in order to cleanse it. At the end of seven months they will make a search.

15 "As those who pass through the land pass through and anyone sees a man's bone, then he will set up a marker by it until the buriers have buried it in the valley of Hamon-gog.

16 "And even *the* name of *the* city will be Hamonah. So they will cleanse the land." '

17 ¶ "As for you, son of man, thus says the Lord GOD, 'Speak to every kind of bird and to every beast of the field, "Assemble and come, gather from every side to My sacrifice which I am going to sacrifice for you, as a great sacrifice on the mountains of Israel, that you may eat flesh and drink blood.

18 "You will eat the flesh of mighty men and drink the blood of the princes of the earth, as *though they were* rams, lambs, goats and bulls, all of them fatlings of Bashan.

19 "So you will eat fat until you are glutted, and drink blood until you are drunk, from My sacrifice which I have sacrificed for you.

20 "You will be glutted at My table with horses and charioteers, with mighty men and all the men of war," declares the Lord GOD.

21 ¶ "And I will set My glory among the nations; and all the nations will see My judgment which I have executed and My hand which I have laid on them.

22 "And the house of Israel will know that I am the LORD their God from that day onward.

23 "The nations will know that the house of Israel went into exile for their iniquity because they acted treacherously against Me, and I hid My face from them; so I gave them into the hand of their adversaries, and all of them fell by the sword.

24 "According to their uncleanness and according to their transgressions I dealt with them, and I hid My face from them." ' "

Israel Restored

25 ¶ Therefore thus says the Lord GOD, "Now I will restore the fortunes of Jacob and have mercy on the whole house of Israel; and I will be jealous for My holy name.

26 "They will [a]forget their disgrace and all their treachery which they [b]perpetrated against Me, when they live securely on their *own* land with no one to make *them* afraid.

27 "When I bring them back from the peoples and gather them from the lands of their enemies, then I shall be sanctified through them in the sight of the many nations.

28 "Then they will know that I am the LORD their God because I made them go into exile among the nations, and then gathered them *again* to their own land; and I will leave none of them there any longer.

29 "I will not hide My face from them any longer, for I will have poured out My Spirit on the house of Israel," declares the Lord GOD.

Vision of the Man with a Measuring Rod

40 In the twenty-fifth year of our exile, at the beginning of the year, on the tenth of the month, in the fourteenth year after the city was taken, on that same day the hand of the LORD was upon me and He brought me there.

2 In the visions of God He brought me into the land of Israel and set me on a very high mountain, and on it to the south *there was* a structure like a city.

3 So He brought me there; and behold, there was a man whose appearance was like the appearance of bronze, with a line of flax and a measuring rod in his hand; and he was standing in the gateway.

4 The man said to me, "Son of man, see with your eyes, hear with your ears, and give attention to all that I am going to show you; for you have been brought here in order to show *it* to you. Declare to the house of Israel all that you see."

Measurements Relating to the Temple

5 ¶ And behold, there was a wall on the outside of the temple all around, and in the man's hand was a measuring rod of six cubits, *each of which was* a cubit and a handbreadth. So he measured the thickness of the wall, one rod; and the height, one rod.

6 Then he went to the gate which faced east, went up its steps and measured the threshold of

---

a Another reading is *bear*   *b* Lit *did treacherously* the gate, one rod in width; and the other threshold *was* one rod in width.

7 The guardroom *was* one rod long and one rod wide; and *there were* five cubits between the

40:5 Taking Measurements

When Moses and Solomon supervised the building of God's dwelling place, they placed great emphasis on exact specifications for its construction. Ezekiel does the same, even though the temple he measured with such care was never constructed. Some scholars see the details as symbolic, emphasizing how important renewed worship in the temple would be. The symmetry and beauty of the new temple witness to the perfection of God's plan for his people.

guardrooms. And the threshold of the gate by the porch of the gate facing inward *was* one rod.

8 Then he measured the porch of the gate facing inward, one rod.

9 He measured the porch of the gate, eight cubits; and its side pillars, two cubits. And the porch of the gate was faced inward.

10 The guardrooms of the gate toward the east *numbered* three on each side; the three of them had the same measurement. The side pillars also had the same measurement on each side.

11 And he measured the width of the gateway, ten cubits, and the length of the gate, thirteen cubits.

12 *There was* a barrier *wall* one cubit *wide* in front of the guardrooms on each side; and the guardrooms *were* six cubits *square* on each side.

13 He measured the gate from the roof of the one guardroom to the roof of the other, a width of twenty-five cubits from *one* door to *the* door opposite.

14 He made the side pillars sixty cubits *high;* the gate *extended* round about to the side pillar of the courtyard.

15 *From* the front of the entrance gate to the front of the inner porch of the gate *was* fifty cubits.

16 *There were* shuttered windows *looking* toward the guardrooms, and toward their side pillars within the gate all around, and likewise for the porches. And *there were* windows all around inside; and on *each* side pillar *were* palm tree ornaments.

17 ¶ Then he brought me into the outer court, and behold, *there were* chambers and a pavement made for the court all around; thirty chambers faced the pavement.

18 The pavement (*that is,* the lower pavement) *was* by the side of the gates, corresponding to the length of the gates.

19 Then he measured the width from the front of the lower gate to the front of the exterior of the inner court, a hundred cubits on the east and on the north.

20 ¶ *As for* the gate of the outer court which faced the north, he measured its length and its width.

21 It had three guardrooms on each side; and its side pillars and its porches had the same measurement as the first gate. Its length *was* fifty cubits and the width twenty-five cubits.

22 Its windows and its porches and its palm tree ornaments *had* the same measurements as the gate which faced toward the east; and it was reached by seven steps, and its porch *was* in front of them.

23 The inner court had a gate opposite the gate on the north as well as *the gate* on the east; and he measured a hundred cubits from gate to gate.

24 ¶ Then he led me toward the south, and behold, there was a gate toward the south; and he measured its side pillars and its porches according to those same measurements.

25 The gate and its porches had windows all around like those other windows; the length *was* fifty cubits and the width twenty-five cubits.

26 *There were* seven steps going up to it, and its porches *were* in front of them; and it had palm tree ornaments on its side pillars, one on each side.

27 The inner court had a gate toward the south; and he measured from gate to gate toward the south, a hundred cubits.

28 ¶ Then he brought me to the inner court by the south gate; and he measured the south gate according to those same measurements.

29 Its guardrooms also, its side pillars and its porches *were* according to those same measurements. And the gate and its porches had windows all around; it *was* fifty cubits long and twenty-five cubits wide.

30 *There were* porches all around, twenty-five cubits long and five cubits wide.

31 Its porches *were* toward the outer court; and palm tree ornaments *were* on its side pillars, and its stairway *had* eight steps.

32 ¶ He brought me into the inner court toward the east. And he measured the gate according to those same measurements.

33 Its guardrooms also, its side pillars and its porches *were* according to those same measurements. And the gate and its porches had windows all around; it *was* fifty cubits long and twenty-five cubits wide.

34 Its porches *were* toward the outer court; and palm tree ornaments *were* on its side pillars, on each side, and its stairway *had* eight steps.

35 ¶ Then he brought me to the north gate; and he measured *it* according to those same measurements,

36 *with* its guardrooms, its side pillars and its porches. And the gate had windows all around;

the length *was* fifty cubits and the width twenty-five cubits.

37 Its side pillars *were* toward the outer court; and palm tree ornaments *were* on its side pillars on each side, and its stairway had eight steps.

38 ¶ A chamber with its doorway was by the side pillars at the gates; there they rinse the burnt offering.

39 In the porch of the gate *were* two tables on each side, on which to slaughter the burnt offering, the sin offering and the guilt offering.

40 On the outer side, as one went up to the gateway toward the north, *were* two tables; and on the other side of the porch of the gate *were* two tables.

41 Four tables *were* on each side next to the gate; *or*, eight tables on which they slaughter *sacrifices.*

42 For the burnt offering *there were* four tables of hewn stone, a cubit and a half long, a cubit and a half wide and one cubit high, on which they lay the instruments with which they slaughter the burnt offering and the sacrifice.

43 The double hooks, one handbreadth in length, were installed in the house all around; and on the tables *was* the flesh of the offering.

44 ¶ From the outside to the inner gate were chambers for the singers in the inner court, *one of* which was at the side of the north gate, with its front toward the south, and one at the side of the south gate facing toward the north.

45 He said to me, "This is the chamber which faces toward the south, *intended* for the priests who keep charge of the temple;

46 but the chamber which faces toward the north is for the priests who keep charge of the altar. These are the sons of Zadok, who from the sons of Levi come near to the LORD to minister to Him."

47 He measured the court, a *perfect* square, a hundred cubits long and a hundred cubits wide; and the altar was in front of the temple.

48 ¶ Then he brought me to the porch of the temple and measured *each* side pillar of the porch, five cubits on each side; and the width of the gate was three cubits on each side.

49 The length of the porch *was* twenty cubits and the width eleven cubits; and at the stairway by which it was ascended *were* columns belonging to the side pillars, one on each side.

The Inner Temple

41 Then he brought me to the nave and measured the side pillars; six cubits wide on each side *was* the width of the side pillar.

2 The width of the entrance *was* ten cubits and the sides of the entrance *were* five cubits on each side. And he measured the length of the nave, forty cubits, and the width, twenty cubits.

3 Then he went inside and measured each side pillar of the doorway, two cubits, and the doorway, six cubits *high;* and the width of the doorway, seven cubits.

4 He measured its length, twenty cubits, and the width, twenty cubits, before the nave; and he said to me, "This is the most holy *place.*"

41:2 Seeing the New Temple

You'll find it easier to visualize Ezekiel's temple if you look at a sketch from a Bible dictionary. (Look under "Temple" or "Ezekiel.") Ezekiel's description reveals fascinating insights. For instance, the number of steps up toward the Holy Place grows greater at each stage, so that a worshiper mounts increasingly higher. But the doorways grow narrower (40:48; 41:2–3)— suggesting that the nearer to God's presence one climbs, the narrower the path he or she must follow.

5 ¶ Then he measured the wall of the temple, six cubits; and the width of the side chambers, four cubits, all around about the house on every side.

6 The side chambers were in three stories, one above another, and thirty in each story; and the side chambers extended to the wall which *stood* on their inward side all around, that they might be fastened, and not be fastened into the wall of the temple *itself.*

7 The side chambers surrounding the temple were wider at each successive story. Because the structure surrounding the temple went upward by stages on all sides of the temple, therefore the width of the temple *increased* as it went higher; and thus one went up from the lowest *story* to the highest by way of the second *story.*

8 I saw also that the house had a raised platform all around; the foundations of the side chambers were a full rod of six long cubits *in height.*

9 The thickness of the outer wall of the side chambers *was* five cubits. But the free space between the side chambers belonging to the temple

10 and the *outer* chambers *was* twenty cubits in width all around the temple on every side.

11 The doorways of the side chambers toward the free space *consisted of* one doorway toward the north and another doorway toward the south; and the width of the free space *was* five cubits all around.

12 ¶ The building that *was* in front of the separate area at the side toward the west *was* seventy cubits wide; and the wall of the building *was* five cubits thick all around, and its length *was* ninety cubits.

13 ¶ Then he measured the temple, a hundred cubits long; the separate area with the building and its walls *were* also a hundred cubits long.

14 Also the width of the front of the temple

and *that of* the separate areas along the east *side* totaled a hundred cubits.

15 ¶ He measured the length of the building along the front of the separate area behind it, with a gallery on each side, a hundred cubits; *he* also *measured* the inner nave and the porches of the court.

16 The thresholds, the latticed windows and the galleries round about their three stories, opposite the threshold, were paneled with wood all around, and *from* the ground to the windows (but the windows were covered),

17 over the entrance, and to the inner house, and on the outside, and on all the wall all around inside and outside, by measurement.

18 It was carved with cherubim and palm trees; and a palm tree was between cherub and cherub, and every cherub had two faces,

19 a man's face toward the palm tree on one side and a young lion's face toward the palm tree on the other side; they were carved on all the house all around.

20 From the ground to above the entrance cherubim and palm trees were carved, as well as *on* the wall of the nave.

21 ¶ The doorposts of the nave were square; as for the front of the sanctuary, the appearance of one doorpost was like that of the other.

22 The altar *was* of wood, three cubits high and its length two cubits; its corners, its base and its sides *were* of wood. And he said to me, "This is the table that is before the LORD."

23 The nave and the sanctuary each had a double door.

24 Each of the doors had two leaves, two swinging leaves; two *leaves* for one door and two leaves for the other.

25 Also there were carved on them, on the doors of the nave, cherubim and palm trees like those carved on the walls; and *there was* a threshold of wood on the front of the porch outside.

26 *There were* latticed windows and palm trees on one side and on the other, on the sides of the porch; thus *were* the side chambers of the house and the thresholds.

Chambers of the Temple

42 Then he brought me out into the outer court, the way toward the north; and he brought me to the chamber which *was* opposite the separate area and opposite the building toward the north.

2 Along the length, *which was* a hundred cubits, *was* the north door; the width *was* fifty cubits.

3 Opposite the twenty *cubits* which belonged to the inner court, and opposite the pavement which belonged to the outer court, *was* gallery corresponding to gallery in three stories.

4 Before the chambers *was* an inner walk ten cubits wide, a way of one *hundred* cubits; and their openings *were* on the north.

5 Now the upper chambers *were* smaller because the galleries took more *space* away from them than from the lower and middle ones in the building.

6 For they *were* in three stories and had no pillars like the pillars of the courts; therefore *the upper chambers* were set back from the ground upward, more than the lower and middle ones.

7 As for the outer wall by the side of the chambers, toward the outer court facing the chambers, its length *was* fifty cubits.

8 For the length of the chambers which *were* in the outer court *was* fifty cubits; and behold, *the length of those* facing the temple *was* a hundred cubits.

9 Below these chambers *was* the entrance on the east side, as one enters them from the outer court.

10 ¶ In the thickness of the wall of the court toward the east, facing the separate area and facing the building, *there were* chambers.

11 The way in front of them *was* like the appearance of the chambers which *were* on the north, according to their length so was their width, and all their exits *were* both according to their arrangements and openings.

12 Corresponding to the openings of the chambers which were toward the south was an opening at the head of the way, the way in front of the wall toward the east, as one enters them.

13 ¶ Then he said to me, "The north chambers *and* the south chambers, which are opposite the separate area, they are the holy chambers where the priests who are near to the LORD shall eat the most holy things. There they shall lay the most holy things, the grain offering, the sin offering and the guilt offering; for the place is holy.

14 "When the priests enter, then they shall not go out into the outer court from the sanctuary without laying there their garments in which they minister, for they are holy. They shall put on other garments; then they shall approach that which is for the people."

15 ¶ Now when he had finished measuring the inner house, he brought me out by the way of the gate which faced toward the east and measured it all around.

16 He measured on the east side with the measuring reed five hundred reeds by the measuring reed.

17 He measured on the north side five hundred reeds by the measuring reed.

18 On the south side he measured five hundred reeds with the measuring reed.

19 He turned to the west side *and* measured five hundred reeds with the measuring reed.

20 He measured it on the four sides; it had a wall all around, the length five hundred and the width five hundred, to divide between the holy and the profane.

Vision of the Glory of God Filling the Temple

43 Then he led me to the gate, the gate facing toward the east;

2 and behold, the glory of the God of Israel was coming from the way of the east. And His voice was like the sound of many waters; and the earth shone with His glory.

3 And *it was* like the appearance of the vision which I saw, like the vision which I saw when He came to destroy the city. And the visions *were* like the vision which I saw by the river Chebar; and I fell on my face.

4 And the glory of the LORD came into the house by the way of the gate facing toward the east.

43:4–9 The Glory Returns

Nineteen years had passed since Ezekiel saw the glory of the Lord leave the temple (11:22–23). That temple was now dust and ashes and broken stones: The conquering Babylonians had burnt and destroyed it. The new temple Ezekiel saw in this vision symbolized that God would again live with his renewed people.

5 And the Spirit lifted me up and brought me into the inner court; and behold, the glory of the LORD filled the house.

6 ¶ Then I heard one speaking to me from the house, while a man was standing beside me.

7 He said to me, "Son of man, *this is* the place of My throne and the place of the soles of My feet, where I will dwell among the sons of Israel forever. And the house of Israel will not again defile My holy name, neither they nor their kings, by their harlotry and by the *a*corpses of their kings *b*when they die,

8 by setting their threshold by My threshold and their door post beside My door post, with *only* the wall between Me and them. And they have defiled My holy name by their abominations which they have committed. So I have consumed them in My anger.

9 "Now let them put away their harlotry and the *a*corpses of their kings far from Me; and I will dwell among them forever.

10 ¶ "As for you, son of man, describe the temple to the house of Israel, that they may be ashamed of their iniquities; and let them measure the plan.

11 "If they are ashamed of all that they have done, make known to them the design of the house, its structure, its exits, its entrances, all its designs, all its statutes, and all its laws. And write

it in their sight, so that they may observe its whole design and all its statutes and do them.

12 "This is the law of the house: its entire area on the top of the mountain all around *shall be* most holy. Behold, this is the law of the house.

The Altar of Sacrifice

13 ¶ "And these are the measurements of the altar by cubits (the cubit being a cubit and a handbreadth): the base *shall be* a cubit and the width a cubit, and its border on its edge round about one span; and this *shall be* the *height* of the base of the altar.

14 "From the base on the ground to the lower ledge *shall be* two cubits and the width one cubit; and from the smaller ledge to the larger ledge *shall be* four cubits and the width one cubit.

15 "The altar hearth *shall be* four cubits; and from the altar hearth shall extend upwards four horns.

16 "Now the altar hearth *shall be* twelve *cubits* long by twelve wide, square in its four sides.

17 "The ledge *shall be* fourteen *cubits* long by fourteen wide in its four sides, the border around it *shall be* half a cubit and its base *shall be* a cubit round about; and its steps shall face the east."

The Offerings

18 ¶ And He said to me, "Son of man, thus says the Lord GOD, 'These are the statutes for the altar on the day it is built, to offer burnt offerings on it and to sprinkle blood on it.

19 'You shall give to the Levitical priests who are from the offspring of Zadok, who draw near to Me to minister to Me,' declares the Lord GOD, 'a young bull for a sin offering.

20 'You shall take some of its blood and put it on its four horns and on the four corners of the ledge and on the border round about; thus you shall cleanse it and make atonement for it.

21 'You shall also take the bull for the sin offering, and it *shall be* burned in the appointed place of the house, outside the sanctuary.

22 ¶ 'On the second day you shall offer a male goat without blemish for a sin offering, and they shall cleanse the altar as they cleansed *it* with the bull.

23 'When you have finished cleansing *it,* you shall present a young bull without blemish and a ram without blemish from the flock.

24 'You shall present them before the LORD, and the priests shall throw salt on them, and they shall offer them up as a burnt offering to the LORD.

25 'For seven days you shall prepare daily a goat for a sin offering; also a young bull and a ram from the flock, without blemish, shall be prepared.

26 'For seven days they shall make atonement for the altar and purify it; so shall they consecrate it.

27 'When they have completed the days, it shall

---

a Or *monuments* as in Ugaritic   *b* Or *in their high places* be that on the eighth day and onward, the priests shall offer your burnt offerings on the altar, and your peace offerings; and I will accept you,' declares the Lord GOD."

Gate for the Prince

44 Then He brought me back by the way of the outer gate of the sanctuary, which faces the east; and it was shut.

2 The LORD said to me, "This gate shall be shut; it shall not be opened, and no one shall enter by it, for the LORD God of Israel has entered by it; therefore it shall be shut.

3 "As for the prince, he shall sit in it as prince to eat bread before the LORD; he shall enter by way of the porch of the gate and shall go out by the same way."

4 ¶ Then He brought me by way of the north gate to the front of the house; and I looked, and behold, the glory of the LORD filled the house of the LORD, and I fell on my face.

5 The LORD said to me, "Son of man, mark well, see with your eyes and hear with your ears all that I say to you concerning all the statutes of the house of the LORD and concerning all its laws; and mark well the entrance of the house, with all exits of the sanctuary.

6 "You shall say to the rebellious ones, to the house of Israel, 'Thus says the Lord GOD, "Enough of all your abominations, O house of Israel,

7 when you brought in foreigners, uncircumcised in heart and uncircumcised in flesh, to be in My sanctuary to profane it, *even* My house, when you offered My food, the fat and the blood; for they made My covenant void—*this* in addition to all your abominations.

8 "And you have not kept charge of My holy things yourselves, but you have set *foreigners* to keep charge of My sanctuary."

9 ¶ 'Thus says the Lord GOD, "No foreigner uncircumcised in heart and uncircumcised in flesh, of all the foreigners who are among the sons of Israel, shall enter My sanctuary.

10 "But the Levites who went far from Me when Israel went astray, who went astray from Me after their idols, shall bear the punishment for their iniquity.

11 "Yet they shall be ministers in My sanctuary, having oversight at the gates of the house and ministering in the house; they shall slaughter the burnt offering and the sacrifice for the people, and they shall stand before them to minister to them.

12 "Because they ministered to them before their idols and became a stumbling block of iniquity to the house of Israel, therefore I have sworn against them," declares the Lord GOD, "that they shall bear *the punishment for* their iniquity.

13 "And they shall not come near to Me to serve as a priest to Me, nor come near to any of My holy

things, to the things that are most holy; but they will bear their shame and their abominations which they have committed.

14 "Yet I will appoint them to keep charge of the house, of all its service and of all that shall be done in it.

Ordinances for the Levites

15 ¶ "But the Levitical priests, the sons of Zadok, who kept charge of My sanctuary when the sons of Israel went astray from Me, shall come near to Me to minister to Me; and they shall stand before Me to offer Me the fat and the blood," declares the Lord GOD.

16 "They shall enter My sanctuary; they shall come near to My table to minister to Me and keep My charge.

17 "It shall be that when they enter at the gates of the inner court, they shall be clothed with linen garments; and wool shall not be on them while they are ministering in the gates of the inner court and in the house.

18 "Linen turbans shall be on their heads and linen undergarments shall be on their loins; they shall not gird themselves with *anything which makes them* sweat.

19 "When they go out into the outer court, into the outer court to the people, they shall put off their garments in which they have been ministering and lay them in the holy chambers; then they shall put on other garments so that they will not transmit holiness to the people with their garments.

20 "Also they shall not shave their heads, yet they shall not let their locks grow long; they shall only trim *the hair of* their heads.

21 "Nor shall any of the priests drink wine when they enter the inner court.

22 "And they shall not marry a widow or a divorced woman but shall take virgins from the offspring of the house of Israel, or a widow who is the widow of a priest.

23 "Moreover, they shall teach My people *the difference* between the holy and the profane, and cause them to discern between the unclean and the clean.

24 "In a dispute they shall take their stand to judge; they shall judge it according to My ordinances. They shall also keep My laws and My statutes in all My appointed feasts and sanctify My sabbaths.

25 "They shall not go to a dead person to defile *themselves;* however, for father, for mother, for son, for daughter, for brother, or for a sister who has not had a husband, they may defile themselves.

26 "After he is cleansed, seven days shall *a*elapse for him.

27 "On the day that he goes into the sanctuary, into the inner court to minister in the sanctuary,

---

a Lit *be counted*

he shall offer his sin offering," declares the Lord GOD.

28 ¶ "And it shall be with regard to an inheritance for them, *that* I am their inheritance; and you shall give them no possession in Israel—I am their possession.

29 "They shall eat the grain offering, the sin offering and the guilt offering; and every devoted thing in Israel shall be theirs.

30 "The first of all the first fruits of every kind and every contribution of every kind, from all your contributions, shall be for the priests; you shall also give to the priest the first of your dough to cause a blessing to rest on your house.

31 "The priests shall not eat any bird or beast that has died a natural death or has been torn to pieces.

The LORD'S Portion of the Land

45 "And when you divide by lot the land for inheritance, you shall offer an allotment to the LORD, a holy portion of the land; the length shall be the length of 25,000 *cubits,* and the width shall be 20,000. It shall be holy within all its boundary round about.

2 "Out of this there shall be for the holy place a square round about five hundred by five hundred *cubits,* and fifty cubits for its open space round about.

3 "From this area you shall measure a length of 25,000 *cubits* and a width of 10,000 *cubits;* and in it shall be the sanctuary, the most holy place.

4 "It shall be the holy portion of the land; it shall be for the priests, the ministers of the sanctuary, who come near to minister to the LORD, and it shall be a place for their houses and a holy place for the sanctuary.

5 "An area 25,000 *cubits* in length and 10,000 in width shall be for the Levites, the ministers of the house, *and* for their possession cities to dwell in.

6 ¶ "You shall give the city possession of *an area* 5,000 *cubits* wide and 25,000 *cubits* long, alongside the ªallotment of the holy portion; it shall be for the whole house of Israel.

Portion for the Prince

7 ¶ "The prince shall have *land* on either side of the holy ªallotment and the property of the city, adjacent to the holy ªallotment and the property of the city, on the west side toward the west and on the east side toward the east, and in length comparable to one of the portions, from the west border to the east border.

8 "This shall be his land for a possession in Israel; so My princes shall no longer oppress My people, but they shall give *the rest of* the land to the house of Israel according to their tribes."

9 ¶ 'Thus says the Lord GOD, "Enough, you princes of Israel; put away violence and destruc-

tion, and practice justice and righteousness. Stop your expropriations from My people," declares the Lord GOD.

10 ¶ "You shall have just balances, a just ephah and a just bath.

45:10 Honest Weight

The Bible, always practical, doesn't bother to define honesty in philosophic terms. It merely says, "Don't cheat on your measures." Such cheating was a common problem in Judah (see, for instance, Micah 6:10–12). Archaeologists have found many weights once used in Hebrew marketplaces, but very few have weighed exactly the weight inscribed on them.

11 "The ephah and the bath shall be the same quantity, so that the bath will contain a tenth of a homer and the ephah a tenth of a homer; their standard shall be according to the homer.

12 "The shekel shall be twenty gerahs; twenty shekels, twenty-five shekels, *and* fifteen shekels shall be your maneh.

13 ¶ "This is the offering that you shall offer: a sixth of an ephah from a homer of wheat; a sixth of an ephah from a homer of barley;

14 and the prescribed portion of oil (*namely,* the bath of oil), a tenth of a bath from *each* kor (*which is* ten baths *or* a homer, for ten baths are a homer);

15 and one sheep from *each* flock of two hundred from the watering places of Israel—for a grain offering, for a burnt offering and for peace offerings, to make atonement for them," declares the Lord GOD.

16 "All the people of the land shall give to this offering for the prince in Israel.

17 "It shall be the prince's part *to provide* the burnt offerings, the grain offerings and the drink offerings, at the feasts, on the new moons and on the sabbaths, at all the appointed feasts of the house of Israel; he shall provide the sin offering, the grain offering, the burnt offering and the peace offerings, to make atonement for the house of Israel."

18 ¶ 'Thus says the Lord GOD, "In the first *month,* on the first of the month, you shall take a young bull without blemish and cleanse the sanctuary.

19 "The priest shall take some of the blood from the sin offering and put *it* on the door posts of the house, on the four corners of the ledge of the altar and on the posts of the gate of the inner court.

20 "Thus you shall do on the seventh *day* of the month for everyone who goes astray or is naive; so you shall make atonement for the house.

21 ¶ "In the first *month,* on the fourteenth day

of the month, you shall have the Passover, a feast of seven days; unleavened bread shall be eaten.

22 "On that day the prince shall provide for himself and all the people of the land a bull for a sin offering.

23 "*During* the seven days of the feast he shall provide as a burnt offering to the LORD seven bulls and seven rams without blemish on every day of the seven days, and a male goat daily for a sin offering.

24 "He shall provide as a grain offering an ephah with a bull, an ephah with a ram and a hin of oil with an ephah.

25 "In the seventh *month,* on the fifteenth day of the month, at the feast, he shall provide like this, seven days for the sin offering, the burnt offering, the grain offering and the oil."

The Prince's Offerings

46 'Thus says the Lord GOD, "The gate of the inner court facing east shall be shut the six working days; but it shall be opened on the sabbath day and opened on the day of the new moon.

2 "The prince shall enter by way of the porch of the gate from outside and stand by the post of the gate. Then the priests shall provide his burnt offering and his peace offerings, and he shall worship at the threshold of the gate and then go out; but the gate shall not be shut until the evening.

3 "The people of the land shall also worship at the doorway of that gate before the LORD on the sabbaths and on the new moons.

4 "The burnt offering which the prince shall offer to the LORD on the sabbath day shall be six lambs without blemish and a ram without blemish;

5 and the grain offering shall be an ephah with the ram, and the grain offering with the lambs as much as he is able to give, and a hin of oil with an ephah.

6 "On the day of the new moon *he shall offer* a young bull without blemish, also six lambs and a ram, *which* shall be without blemish.

7 "And he shall provide a grain offering, an ephah with the bull and an ephah with the ram, and with the lambs as much as he is able, and a hin of oil with an ephah.

8 "When the prince enters, he shall go in by way of the porch of the gate and go out by the same way.

9 "But when the people of the land come before the LORD at the appointed feasts, he who enters by way of the north gate to worship shall go out by way of the south gate. And he who enters by way of the south gate shall go out by way of the north gate. No one shall return by way of the gate by which he entered but shall go straight out.

10 "When they go in, the prince shall go in among them; and when they go out, he shall go out.

11 ¶ "At the festivals and the appointed feasts the grain offering shall be an ephah with a bull and an ephah with a ram, and with the lambs as much as one is able to give, and a hin of oil with an ephah.

12 "When the prince provides a freewill offering, a burnt offering, or peace offerings *as* a freewill offering to the LORD, the gate facing east shall be opened for him. And he shall provide his burnt offering and his peace offerings as he does on the sabbath day. Then he shall go out, and the gate shall be shut after he goes out.

13 ¶ "And you shall provide a lamb a year old without blemish for a burnt offering to the LORD daily; morning by morning you shall provide it.

14 "Also you shall provide a grain offering with it morning by morning, a sixth of an ephah and a third of a hin of oil to moisten the fine flour, a grain offering to the LORD continually by a perpetual ordinance.

15 "Thus they shall provide the lamb, the grain offering and the oil, morning by morning, for a continual burnt offering."

16 ¶ 'Thus says the Lord GOD, "If the prince gives a gift *out of* his inheritance to any of his sons, it shall belong to his sons; it is their possession by inheritance.

17 "But if he gives a gift from his inheritance to one of his servants, it shall be his until the year of liberty; then it shall return to the prince. His inheritance *shall be* only his sons'; it shall belong to them.

18 "The prince shall not take from the people's inheritance, thrusting them out of their possession; he shall give his sons inheritance from his own possession so that My people will not be scattered, anyone from his possession." ' "

The Boiling Places

19 ¶ Then he brought me through the entrance, which *was* at the side of the gate, into the holy chambers for the priests, which faced north; and behold, there *was* a place at the extreme rear toward the west.

20 He said to me, "This is the place where the priests shall boil the guilt offering and the sin offering *and* where they shall bake the grain offering, in order that they may not bring *them* out into the outer court to transmit holiness to the people."

21 ¶ Then he brought me out into the outer court and led me across to the four corners of the court; and behold, in every corner of the court *there was* a *small* court.

22 In the four corners of the court *there were* enclosed courts, forty *cubits* long and thirty wide; these four in the corners *were* the same size.

23 *There was* a row *of masonry* round about in them, around the four of them, and boiling places were made under the rows round about.

24 Then he said to me, "These are the boiling places where the ministers of the house shall boil the sacrifices of the people."

Water from the Temple

47 Then he brought me back to the door of the house; and behold, water was flowing from under the threshold of the house toward the east, for the house faced east. And the water was flowing down from under, from the right side of the house, from south of the altar.

2 He brought me out by way of the north gate and led me around on the outside to the outer gate by way of *the gate* that faces east. And behold, water was trickling from the south side.

3 ¶ When the man went out toward the east with a line in his hand, he measured a thousand cubits, and he led me through the water, water *reaching* the ankles.

4 Again he measured a thousand and led me through the water, water *reaching* the knees. Again he measured a thousand and led me through *the water*, water *reaching* the loins.

5 Again he measured a thousand; *and it was* a river that I could not ford, for the water had risen, *enough* water to swim in, a river that could not be forded.

6 He said to me, "Son of man, have you seen *this?*" Then he brought me back to the bank of the river.

7 Now when I had returned, behold, on the bank of the river there *were* very many trees on the one side and on the other.

8 Then he said to me, "These waters go out toward the eastern region and go down into the Arabah; then they go toward the sea, being made to flow into the sea, and the waters *of the sea* become fresh.

9 "It will come about that every living creature which swarms in every place where the river goes, will live. And there will be very many fish, for these waters go there and *the others* become fresh; so everything will live where the river goes.

10 "And it will come about that fishermen will stand beside it; from Engedi to Eneglaim there will be a place for the spreading of nets. Their fish will be according to their kinds, like the fish of the Great Sea, very many.

11 "But its swamps and marshes will not become fresh; they will be left for salt.

12 "By the river on its bank, on one side and on the other, will grow all *kinds of* trees for food. Their leaves will not wither and their fruit will not fail. They will bear every month because their water flows from the sanctuary, and their fruit will be for food and their leaves for healing."

Boundaries and Division of the Land

13 ¶ Thus says the Lord GOD, "This *shall be* the boundary by which you shall divide the land for an inheritance among the twelve tribes of Israel; Joseph *shall have* two portions.

14 "You shall divide it for an inheritance, each one equally with the other; for I swore to give it to your forefathers, and this land shall fall to you as an inheritance.

15 ¶ "This *shall be* the boundary of the land: on the north side, from the Great Sea *by* the way of Hethlon, to the entrance of Zedad;

47:12 River from the Temple

This river, flowing from the temple, had miraculous properties: it reversed the deadly saltiness of the Dead Sea and produced healing fruit on its banks. The early Christians used similar symbolism; in John's vision of a new Jerusalem (Revelation 22), he saw a river of life flowing from the throne of God.

16 Hamath, Berothah, Sibraim, which is between the border of Damascus and the border of Hamath; Hazer-hatticon, which is by the border of Hauran.

17 "The boundary shall extend from the sea *to* Hazar-enan *at* the border of Damascus, and on the north toward the north is the border of Hamath. This is the north side.

18 ¶ "The east side, from between Hauran, Damascus, Gilead and the land of Israel, *shall be* the Jordan; from the *north* border to the eastern sea you shall measure. This is the east side.

19 ¶ "The south side toward the south *shall extend* from Tamar as far as the waters of Meribath-kadesh, to the brook *of Egypt and* to the Great Sea. This is the south side toward the south.

20 ¶ "The west side *shall be* the Great Sea, from the *south* border to a point opposite Lebo-hamath. This is the west side.

21 ¶ "So you shall divide this land among yourselves according to the tribes of Israel.

22 "You shall divide it by lot for an inheritance among yourselves and among the aliens who stay in your midst, who bring forth sons in your midst. And they shall be to you as the native-born among the sons of Israel; they shall be allotted an inheritance with you among the tribes of Israel.

23 "And in the tribe with which the alien stays, there you shall give *him* his inheritance," declares the Lord GOD.

Division of the Land

48 "Now these are the names of the tribes: from the northern extremity, beside the way of Hethlon to Lebo-hamath, *as far as* Hazar-enan *at* the border of Damascus, toward the north beside Hamath, running from east to west, Dan, one *portion*.

2 "Beside the border of Dan, from the east side to the west side, Asher, one *portion*.

3 "Beside the border of Asher, from the east side to the west side, Naphtali, one *portion*.

4 "Beside the border of Naphtali, from the east side to the west side, Manasseh, one *portion*.

5 "Beside the border of Manasseh, from the east side to the west side, Ephraim, one *portion*.

6 "Beside the border of Ephraim, from the east side to the west side, Reuben, one *portion*.

7 "Beside the border of Reuben, from the east side to the west side, Judah, one *portion*.

8 ¶ "And beside the border of Judah, from the east side to the west side, shall be the *a*allotment which you shall set apart, 25,000 *cubits* in width, and in length like one of the portions, from the east side to the west side; and the sanctuary shall be in the middle of it.

9 "The allotment that you shall set apart to the LORD *shall be* 25,000 *cubits* in length and 10,000 in width.

Portion for the Priests

10 "The holy allotment shall be for these, *namely* for the priests, toward the north 25,000 *cubits in length*, toward the west 10,000 in width, toward the east 10,000 in width, and toward the south 25,000 in length; and the sanctuary of the LORD shall be in its midst.

11 "*It shall be* for the priests who are sanctified of the sons of Zadok, who have kept My charge, who did not go astray when the sons of Israel went astray as the Levites went astray.

12 "It shall be an allotment to them from the allotment of the land, a most holy place, by the border of the Levites.

13 "Alongside the border of the priests the Levites *shall have* 25,000 *cubits* in length and 10,000 in width. The whole length *shall be* 25,000 *cubits* and the width 10,000.

14 "Moreover, they shall not sell or exchange any of it, or alienate this choice *portion* of land; for it is holy to the LORD.

15 ¶ "The remainder, 5,000 *cubits* in width and 25,000 in length, shall be for common use for the city, for dwellings and for open spaces; and the city shall be in its midst.

16 "These *shall be* its measurements: the north side 4,500 *cubits*, the south side 4,500 *cubits*, the east side 4,500 *cubits*, and the west side 4,500 *cubits*.

17 "The city shall have open spaces: on the north 250 *cubits*, on the south 250 *cubits*, on the east 250 *cubits*, and on the west 250 *cubits*.

18 "The remainder of the length alongside the holy allotment shall be 10,000 *cubits* toward the east and 10,000 toward the west; and it shall be alongside the holy allotment. And its produce shall be food for the workers of the city.

19 "The workers of the city, out of all the tribes of Israel, shall cultivate it.

20 "The whole allotment *shall be* 25,000 by 25,000 *cubits;* you shall set apart the holy allotment, a square, with the property of the city.

Portion for the Prince

21 ¶ "The remainder *shall be* for the prince, on the one side and on the other of the holy allotment and of the property of the city; in front of the 25,000 *cubits* of the allotment toward the east border and westward in front of the 25,000 toward the west border, alongside the portions, *it shall be* for the prince. And the holy allotment and the sanctuary of the house shall be in the middle of it.

22 "Exclusive of the property of the Levites and the property of the city, *which* are in the middle of that which belongs to the prince, *everything* between the border of Judah and the border of Benjamin shall be for the prince.

Portion for Other Tribes

23 ¶ "As for the rest of the tribes: from the east side to the west side, Benjamin, one *portion*.

24 "Beside the border of Benjamin, from the east side to the west side, Simeon, one *portion*.

25 "Beside the border of Simeon, from the east side to the west side, Issachar, one *portion*.

26 "Beside the border of Issachar, from the east side to the west side, Zebulun, one *portion*.

27 "Beside the border of Zebulun, from the east side to the west side, Gad, one *portion*.

28 "And beside the border of Gad, at the south side toward the south, the border shall be from Tamar to the waters of Meribath-kadesh, to the brook *of Egypt,* to the Great Sea.

29 "This is the land which you shall divide by lot to the tribes of Israel for an inheritance, and these are their *several* portions," declares the Lord GOD.

The City Gates

30 ¶ "These are the exits of the city: on the north side, 4,500 *cubits* by measurement,

48:30 Gates to the City

These twelve gates, named after the twelve tribes of Israel, are also described in the new Jerusalem (Revelation 21:12). Other details of Ezekiel's vision are echoed in Revelation 21–22: for example, the view from a high mountain (Ezekiel 40:2), the angel guide (40:3), and the healing river (47:12). The most important similarity is reflected in the name of Ezekiel's city: "The LORD is there" (48:35). As Revelation expresses it, "Behold, the tabernacle of God is among men, and He will dwell among them . . . and God Himself will be among them" (Revelation 21:3).

31 shall be the gates of the city, named for the tribes of Israel, three gates toward the north: the gate of Reuben, one; the gate of Judah, one; the gate of Levi, one.

a Or *contribution,* and so throughout the ch

32 "On the east side, 4,500 *cubits,* shall be three gates: the gate of Joseph, one; the gate of Benjamin, one; the gate of Dan, one.

33 "On the south side, 4,500 *cubits* by measurement, shall be three gates: the gate of Simeon, one; the gate of Issachar, one; the gate of Zebulun, one.

34 "On the west side, 4,500 *cubits, shall be* three gates: the gate of Gad, one; the gate of Asher, one; the gate of Naphtali, one.

35 "*The city shall be* 18,000 *cubits* round about; and the name of the city from *that* day *shall be,* 'The LORD is there.'"

DANIEL

"Kidnapped"
Even as prime minister, Daniel remained a lonely outsider

A S A YOUNG MAN, DANIEL could have anticipated an outstanding future in Jerusalem. He came from a prominent family, and he had a first-rate mind (1:4). But, when the Babylonian army dragged him captive to a faraway country, they didn't ask about his plans and dreams.

True, the Babylonians recognized Daniel's potential and put him into a top civil service training program. But even the study material was distasteful to a Jew: It covered sorcery, magic, and a pagan, multigod religion. After graduation Daniel was put to work for the Babylonian king, who continued to war against Daniel's people for nearly 20 more years.

Anyone far from home feels lonely. But Daniel was one of those whose lives get lost in the shuffle of history—refugees, captives. He was destined to spend his life as an alien in Babylon. We have no record that he ever married or had family members nearby.

> But Daniel made up his mind that he would not defile himself with the king's choice food or with the wine which he drank; so he sought permission from the commander of the officials that he might not defile himself. 1:8

Great Personal Courage

Through his ability and God's blessing he rose to the post of prime minister of Babylon. Yet he remained an outsider. The higher he rose, the more prominent a target he became. Babylonians resented his foreign background and his political success. Their plots put him under pressure to compromise his faith, to fit in, to bend his principles. His life was often at risk.

Daniel's career near the top lasted at least 66 years, so that by the time he was thrown into the lions' den (chapter 6), he must have been in his 80s. Throughout these years he labored with great effectiveness for Babylon. He was respectful and diligent, even though working for pagan kings. Yet he never compromised his faith. He would not bend, even when threatened with death. The Bible gives no better model of how to live with and serve those who don't share or respect your beliefs.

The Shape of the Future

Near the end of Daniel's life God gave him a series of visions, described in chapters 7–12. In graphic images God showed Daniel the pattern of future history. Daniel's people would duplicate his own experience, but on a world stage.

The Jews, Daniel's visions showed, would be caught in a political storm, battered about by a series of world empires. Daniel foresaw nations raging in battle against each other. He foresaw God's people thrown in between these nations, suffering through no fault of their own. They would be helpless until God himself rescued them from their troubles. Daniel foresaw, in the end, all people falling down to worship "one like a Son of Man" (7:13). This was the title Jesus applied to himself when he came, nearly six centuries after Daniel, to bring the good news of salvation for all people.

Spreading the Word

Daniel's people had thought of God in terms of their own small community, their own capital city and the temple there. Not only were the Jews God's chosen people, but (they tended to think) they held exclusive rights to him.

But God had never intended his blessings to stop with the Jews. He had the world in mind. At the time he called Abraham, he had promised that through Abraham's offspring he would bless the whole earth (Genesis 12:3).

The Jews had found it difficult enough to keep their own faith, let alone spread it to others. Only while captives in Babylon, unwillingly dragged far from home, did they begin to convince others that their God deserved honor. The proclamations Nebuchadnezzar and Darius made because of Daniel (4:2–3; 6:26–27) honored God more than anything a king of Judah had done in years.

How to Read Daniel

Daniel breaks into two parts, each quite different from the other. The first six chapters tell the "famous" Daniel stories—including the stories of three men thrown into a fiery furnace and Daniel in the lions' den. Any of these chapters would make a script for a thriller. As you read them, reflect on the principles Daniel lived by, far from home and in dangerous circumstances. Ask yourself what Daniel can teach you about faithfulness to God in similarly "alien" circumstances.

Most people find chapters 7–12 far more difficult: They record Daniel's visions about the future of world history. Such symbolism was a familiar mode of expression in the ancient world, but it reads very strangely now—almost like science fiction. Look for broad impressions of how God's people can live, caught in the jaws of brutal world politics. Let the visual symbols engage your emotions and imagination.

If you seek a more detailed understanding of these visions, a commentary on Daniel will be a great help. In some passages, background information on ancient world history is essential. A good commentary can offer this, along with an interpretation of difficult symbols.

You can place Daniel's message in the context of Israelite history by looking at "A Lineup of Rulers," pages 1417–1425.

PEOPLE YOU'LL MEET IN DANIEL

DANIEL *(p. 931)*
NEBUCHADNEZZAR *(p. 937)*

3-TRACK READING PLAN

For an explanation and complete listing of the 3-track reading plan, turn to page 7.

TRACK 1: *Two-Week Courses on the Bible*
The Track 1 reading program on the Old Testament includes one chapter from Daniel. See page 8 for a complete listing of this course.

TRACK 2: *An Overview of Daniel in 4 Days*
☐ Day 1. Read the Introduction to Daniel and chapter 1, which describes Daniel's courage in rejecting compromise. He set a lifelong pattern.
☐ Day 2. Read chapter 3, the famous story of three men thrown into a fiery furnace.
☐ Day 3. Read chapter 5, the "handwriting on the wall" that announced the destruction of a great empire.
☐ Day 4. Read chapter 6, Daniel in the lions' den.
Now turn to page 9 for your next Track 2 reading project.

TRACK 3: *All of Daniel in 12 Days*
After you have read through Daniel, turn to pages 10–14 for your next Track 3 reading project.

☐1 ☐2 ☐3 ☐4 ☐5 ☐6 ☐7 ☐8
☐9 ☐10 ☐11 ☐12

The Choice Young Men

1 In the third year of the reign of Jehoiakim king of Judah, Nebuchadnezzar king of Babylon came to Jerusalem and besieged it.

2 The Lord gave Jehoiakim king of Judah into his hand, along with some of the vessels of the house of God; and he brought them to the land of Shinar, to the house of his ᵃgod, and he brought the vessels into the treasury of his ᵃgod.

3 ¶ Then the king ordered Ashpenaz, the chief of his ᵇofficials, to bring in some of the sons of Israel, including some of the royal family and of the nobles,

4 youths in whom was no defect, who were good-looking, showing intelligence in every *branch of* wisdom, endowed with understanding and discerning knowledge, and who had ability for serving in the king's court; and *he ordered him* to teach them the ᶜliterature and language of the Chaldeans.

5 The king appointed for them a daily ration from the king's choice food and from the wine which he drank, and *appointed* that they should be educated three years, at the end of which they were to enter the king's personal service.

6 Now among them from the sons of Judah were Daniel, Hananiah, Mishael and Azariah.

7 Then the commander of the officials assigned *new* names to them; and to Daniel he assigned *the name* Belteshazzar, to Hananiah Shadrach, to Mishael Meshach and to Azariah Abed-nego.

Daniel's Resolve

8 ¶ But Daniel made up his mind that he would not defile himself with the king's choice food or with the wine which he drank; so he sought *permission* from the commander of the officials that he might not defile himself.

9 Now God granted Daniel favor and compassion in the sight of the commander of the officials,

10 and the commander of the officials said to Daniel, "I am afraid of my lord the king, who has appointed your food and your drink; for why should he see your faces looking more haggard than the youths who are your own age? Then you would make me forfeit my head to the king."

11 But Daniel said to the overseer whom the commander of the officials had appointed over Daniel, Hananiah, Mishael and Azariah,

12 "Please test your servants for ten days, and let us be given some vegetables to eat and water to drink.

13 "Then let our appearance be observed in your presence and the appearance of the youths who are eating the king's choice food; and deal with your servants according to what you see."

14 ¶ So he listened to them in this matter and tested them for ten days.

15 At the end of ten days their appearance seemed better and they were fatter than all the youths who had been eating the king's choice food.

16 So the overseer continued to withhold their choice food and the wine they were to drink, and kept giving them vegetables.

17 ¶ As for these four youths, God gave them knowledge and intelligence in every *branch of* literature and wisdom; Daniel even understood all *kinds of* visions and dreams.

18 ¶ Then at the end of the days which the king had specified for presenting them, the commander of the officials presented them before Nebuchadnezzar.

19 The king talked with them, and out of them all not one was found like Daniel, Hananiah, Mishael and Azariah; so they entered the king's personal service.

20 As for every matter of wisdom and understanding about which the king consulted them, he found them ten times better than all the magicians *and* conjurers who *were* in all his realm.

21 And Daniel continued until the first year of Cyrus the king.

The King's Forgotten Dream

2 Now in the second year of the reign of Nebuchadnezzar, Nebuchadnezzar had dreams; and his spirit was troubled and his sleep left him.

2 Then the king gave orders to call in the ᵈmagicians, the conjurers, the sorcerers and the ᵉChaldeans to tell the king his dreams. So they came in and stood before the king.

3 The king said to them, "I had a dream and my spirit is anxious to understand the dream."

4 ¶ Then the Chaldeans spoke to the king in Aramaic: "O king, live forever! Tell the dream to your servants, and we will declare the interpretation."

5 The king replied to the Chaldeans, "The command from me is firm: if you do not make

2:4 A Change in Language

The astrologers spoke in Aramaic, the most common language of the Middle East during this period. From this point through chapter 7, Daniel was written in Aramaic, instead of Hebrew. Only the book of Ezra is similarly split into two languages. Some theorize that these chapters would have been of general interest throughout the Middle East and so were put in a language everyone could understand.

ᵃOr *gods* ᵇOr *eunuchs*, and so throughout the ch ᶜOr *writing* ᵈOr *soothsayer priests* ᵉOr *master*
astrologers, and so throughout the ch

known to me the dream and its interpretation, you will be torn limb from limb and your houses will be made a rubbish heap.

6 "But if you declare the dream and its interpretation, you will receive from me gifts and a reward and great honor; therefore declare to me the dream and its interpretation."

7 They answered a second time and said, "Let the king tell the dream to his servants, and we will declare the interpretation."

8 The king replied, "I know for certain that you are bargaining for time, inasmuch as you have seen that the command from me is firm,

9 that if you do not make the dream known to me, there is only one decree for you. For you have agreed together to speak lying and corrupt words before me until the situation is changed; therefore tell me the dream, that I may know that you can declare to me its interpretation."

10 The Chaldeans answered the king and said, "There is not a man on earth who could declare the matter for the king, inasmuch as no great king or ruler has *ever* asked anything like this of any magician, conjurer or Chaldean.

11 "Moreover, the thing which the king demands is difficult, and there is no one else who could declare it to the king except gods, whose dwelling place is not with *mortal* flesh."

12 ¶ Because of this the king became indignant and very furious and gave orders to destroy all the wise men of Babylon.

13 So the decree went forth that the wise men should be slain; and they looked for Daniel and his friends to kill *them*.

14 ¶ Then Daniel replied with discretion and discernment to Arioch, the captain of the king's bodyguard, who had gone forth to slay the wise men of Babylon;

15 he said to Arioch, the king's commander, "For what reason is the decree from the king *so* urgent?" Then Arioch informed Daniel about the matter.

16 So Daniel went in and requested of the king that he would give him time, in order that he might declare the interpretation to the king.

17 ¶ Then Daniel went to his house and informed his friends, Hananiah, Mishael and Azariah, about the matter,

18 so that they might request compassion from the God of heaven concerning this mystery, so that Daniel and his friends would not be destroyed with the rest of the wise men of Babylon.

The Secret Is Revealed to Daniel

19 Then the mystery was revealed to Daniel in a night vision. Then Daniel blessed the God of heaven;

20 Daniel said,
"Let the name of God be blessed forever
      and ever,
For wisdom and power belong to Him.

21 "It is He who changes the times and the
      epochs;
He removes kings and establishes kings;
He gives wisdom to wise men
And knowledge to men of understanding.

22 "It is He who reveals the profound and
      hidden things;
He knows what is in the darkness,
And the light dwells with Him.
23 "To You, O God of my fathers, I give
      thanks and praise,
For You have given me wisdom and
      power;
Even now You have made known to me
      what we requested of You,
For You have made known to us the
      king's matter."

24 ¶ Therefore, Daniel went in to Arioch, whom the king had appointed to destroy the wise men of Babylon; he went and spoke to him as follows: "Do not destroy the wise men of Babylon! Take me into the king's presence, and I will declare the interpretation to the king."

25 ¶ Then Arioch hurriedly brought Daniel into the king's presence and spoke to him as follows: "I have found a man among the exiles from Judah who can make the interpretation known to the king!"

26 The king said to Daniel, whose name was Belteshazzar, "Are you able to make known to me the dream which I have seen and its interpretation?"

27 Daniel answered before the king and said, "As for the mystery about which the king has inquired, neither wise men, conjurers, magicians *nor* diviners are able to declare *it* to the king.

28 "However, there is a God in heaven who reveals mysteries, and He has made known to King Nebuchadnezzar what will take place in the latter days. This was your dream and the visions in your mind *while* on your bed.

29 "As for you, O king, *while* on your bed your thoughts turned to what would take place in the future; and He who reveals mysteries has made known to you what will take place.

30 "But as for me, this mystery has not been

revealed to me for any wisdom residing in me more than in any other living man, but for the purpose of making the interpretation known to the king, and that you may understand the thoughts of your mind.

The King's Dream

31 ¶ "You, O king, were looking and behold, there was a single great statue; that statue, which was large and of extraordinary splendor, was standing in front of you, and its appearance was awesome.

32 "The head of that statue was made of fine gold, its breast and its arms of silver, its belly and its thighs of bronze,

33 its legs of iron, its feet partly of iron and partly of clay.

34 "You continued looking until a stone was cut out without hands, and it struck the statue on its feet of iron and clay and crushed them.

35 "Then the iron, the clay, the bronze, the silver and the gold were crushed all at the same time and became like chaff from the summer threshing floors; and the wind carried them away so that not a trace of them was found. But the stone that struck the statue became a great mountain and filled the whole earth.

The Interpretation—Babylon the First Kingdom

36 ¶ "This was the dream; now we will tell its interpretation before the king.

37 "You, O king, are the king of kings, to whom the God of heaven has given the kingdom, the power, the strength and the glory;

38 and wherever the sons of men dwell, or the beasts of the field, or the birds of the sky, He has given them into your hand and has caused you to rule over them all. You are the head of gold.

Medo-Persia and Greece

39 "After you there will arise another kingdom inferior to you, then another third kingdom of bronze, which will rule over all the earth.

Rome

40 "Then there will be a fourth kingdom as strong as iron; inasmuch as iron crushes and shatters all things, so, like iron that breaks in pieces, it will crush and break all these in pieces.

41 "In that you saw the feet and toes, partly of potter's clay and partly of iron, it will be a divided kingdom; but it will have in it the toughness of iron, inasmuch as you saw the iron mixed with common clay.

42 "As the toes of the feet were partly of iron and partly of pottery, so some of the kingdom will be strong and part of it will be brittle.

43 "And in that you saw the iron mixed with common clay, they will combine with one another in the seed of men; but they will not adhere to one another, even as iron does not combine with pottery.

The Divine Kingdom

44 "In the days of those kings the God of heaven will set up a kingdom which will never be destroyed, and that kingdom will not be left for another people; it will crush and put an end to all these kingdoms, but it will itself endure forever.

45 "Inasmuch as you saw that a stone was cut out of the mountain without hands and that it crushed the iron, the bronze, the clay, the silver and the gold, the great God has made known to the king what will take place in the future; so the dream is true and its interpretation is trustworthy."

Daniel Promoted

46 ¶ Then King Nebuchadnezzar fell on his face and did homage to Daniel, and gave orders to present to him an offering and fragrant incense.

47 The king answered Daniel and said, "Surely your God is a God of gods and a Lord of kings and a revealer of mysteries, since you have been able to reveal this mystery."

48 Then the king promoted Daniel and gave him many great gifts, and he made him ruler over the whole province of Babylon and chief prefect over all the wise men of Babylon.

2:48 A Nation of Dreamers

The Babylonians highly valued dream interpretation, for they believed the gods spoke to them through dreams. "If a man cannot remember the dream he saw, his personal god is angry with him," says one Babylonian proverb. That proverb helps explain Nebuchadnezzar's panic over forgetting his dream—and his lavish reward to Daniel for recalling and interpreting it.

49 And Daniel made request of the king, and he appointed Shadrach, Meshach and Abed-nego over the administration of the province of Babylon, while Daniel was at the king's court.

The King's Golden Image

3 Nebuchadnezzar the king made an image of gold, the height of which was sixty cubits and its width six cubits; he set it up on the plain of Dura in the province of Babylon.

2 Then Nebuchadnezzar the king sent word to assemble the satraps, the prefects and the governors, the counselors, the treasurers, the judges, the magistrates and all the rulers of the provinces to come to the dedication of the image that Nebuchadnezzar the king had set up.

3 Then the satraps, the prefects and the governors, the counselors, the treasurers, the judges, the

magistrates and all the rulers of the provinces were assembled for the dedication of the image that Nebuchadnezzar the king had set up; and they stood before the image that Nebuchadnezzar had set up.

4 Then the herald loudly proclaimed: "To you the command is given, O peoples, nations and *men of every* language,

5 that at the moment you hear the sound of the horn, flute, lyre, trigon, psaltery, bagpipe and all kinds of music, you are to fall down and worship the golden image that Nebuchadnezzar the king has set up.

6 "But whoever does not fall down and worship shall immediately be cast into the midst of a furnace of blazing fire."

7 Therefore at that time, when all the peoples heard the sound of the horn, flute, lyre, trigon, psaltery, bagpipe and all kinds of music, all the peoples, nations and *men of every* language fell down *and* worshiped the golden image that Nebuchadnezzar the king had set up.

Worship of the Image Refused

8 ¶ For this reason at that time certain Chaldeans came forward and brought charges against the Jews.

9 They responded and said to Nebuchadnezzar the king: "O king, live forever!

10 "You, O king, have made a decree that every man who hears the sound of the horn, flute, lyre, trigon, psaltery, and bagpipe and all kinds of music, is to fall down and worship the golden image.

11 "But whoever does not fall down and worship shall be cast into the midst of a furnace of blazing fire.

12 "There are certain Jews whom you have appointed over the administration of the province of Babylon, *namely* Shadrach, Meshach and Abednego. These men, O king, have disregarded you; they do not serve your gods or worship the golden image which you have set up."

13 ¶ Then Nebuchadnezzar in rage and anger gave orders to bring Shadrach, Meshach and Abed-nego; then these men were brought before the king.

14 Nebuchadnezzar responded and said to them, "Is it true, Shadrach, Meshach and Abednego, that you do not serve my gods or worship the golden image that I have set up?

15 "Now if you are ready, at the moment you hear the sound of the horn, flute, lyre, trigon, psaltery and bagpipe and all kinds of music, to fall down and worship the image that I have made, *very well.* But if you do not worship, you will immediately be cast into the midst of a furnace of blazing fire; and what god is there who can deliver you out of my hands?"

16 ¶ Shadrach, Meshach and Abed-nego replied to the king, "O Nebuchadnezzar, we do not need to give you an answer concerning this matter.

17 "If it be *so,* our God whom we serve is able to deliver us from the furnace of blazing fire; and He will deliver us out of your hand, O king.

18 "But *even* if *He does* not, let it be known to you, O king, that we are not going to serve your gods or worship the golden image that you have set up."

3:18 Whether Rescued or Not

Daniel's three friends illustrated perfectly the quality of faith that is later commended in Hebrews 11. When allegiance to God led them to commit an act of civil disobedience, they were willing to face the consequences whether or not God rescued them. Daniel himself faced a severe test of faith, with a similarly happy ending (see chapter 6). Along with Elijah and Elisha, he was one of the few Old Testament prophets whose ministry was marked by miracles.

Daniel's Friends Protected

19 ¶ Then Nebuchadnezzar was filled with wrath, and his facial expression was altered toward Shadrach, Meshach and Abed-nego. He answered by giving orders to heat the furnace seven times more than it was usually heated.

20 He commanded certain valiant warriors who *were* in his army to tie up Shadrach, Meshach and Abed-nego in order to cast *them* into the furnace of blazing fire.

21 Then these men were tied up in their trousers, their coats, their caps and their *other* clothes, and were cast into the midst of the furnace of blazing fire.

22 For this reason, because the king's command *was* urgent and the furnace had been made extremely hot, the flame of the fire slew those men who carried up Shadrach, Meshach and Abed-nego.

23 But these three men, Shadrach, Meshach and Abed-nego, fell into the midst of the furnace of blazing fire *still* tied up.

24 ¶ Then Nebuchadnezzar the king was astounded and stood up in haste; he said to his high officials, "Was it not three men we cast bound into the midst of the fire?" They replied to the king, "Certainly, O king."

25 He said, "Look! I see four men loosed *and* walking *about* in the midst of the fire without harm, and the appearance of the fourth is like a son of *the* gods!"

26 Then Nebuchadnezzar came near to the door of the furnace of blazing fire; he responded and said, "Shadrach, Meshach and Abed-nego, come out, you servants of the Most High God, and

come here!" Then Shadrach, Meshach and Abed-nego came out of the midst of the fire.

27 The satraps, the prefects, the governors and the king's high officials gathered around *and* saw in regard to these men that the fire had no effect on the bodies of these men nor was the hair of their head singed, nor were their trousers damaged, nor had the smell of fire *even* come upon them.

28 ¶ Nebuchadnezzar responded and said, "Blessed be the God of Shadrach, Meshach and Abed-nego, who has sent His angel and delivered His servants who put their trust in Him, violating the king's command, and yielded up their bodies so as not to serve or worship any god except their own God.

29 "Therefore I make a decree that any people, nation or tongue that speaks anything offensive against the God of Shadrach, Meshach and Abed-nego shall be torn limb from limb and their houses reduced to a rubbish heap, inasmuch as there is no other god who is able to deliver in this way."

30 Then the king caused Shadrach, Meshach and Abed-nego to prosper in the province of Babylon.

The King Acknowledges God

4 Nebuchadnezzar the king to all the peoples, nations, and *men of every* language that live in all the earth: "May your peace abound!

2 "It has seemed good to me to declare the signs and wonders which the Most High God has done for me.

a Or possibly *the Spirit of the holy God,* and so throughout the ch

3 "How great are His signs
And how mighty are His wonders!
His kingdom is an everlasting kingdom
And His dominion is from generation to
generation.

The Vision of a Great Tree

4 ¶ "I, Nebuchadnezzar, was at ease in my house and flourishing in my palace.

5 "I saw a dream and it made me fearful; and *these* fantasies as I lay on my bed and the visions in my mind kept alarming me.

6 "So I gave orders to bring into my presence all the wise men of Babylon, that they might make known to me the interpretation of the dream.

7 "Then the magicians, the conjurers, the Chaldeans and the diviners came in and I related the dream to them, but they could not make its interpretation known to me.

8 "But finally Daniel came in before me, whose name is Belteshazzar according to the name of my god, and in whom is ªa spirit of the holy gods; and I related the dream to him, *saying,*

9 'O Belteshazzar, chief of the magicians, since I know that a spirit of the holy gods is in you and no mystery baffles you, tell *me* the visions of my dream which I have seen, along with its interpretation.

10 ¶ 'Now *these were* the visions in my mind as I lay on my bed: I was looking, and behold, *there was* a tree in the midst of the earth and its height *was* great.

11 'The tree grew large and became strong
And its height reached to the sky,

NEBUCHADNEZZAR *Power and Pride*

NEBUCHADNEZZAR, THE WORLD'S MOST POWERFUL man, had reason to be proud. He captained the mighty Babylonian army (based in what is now Iraq) on its march through the Middle East, annihilating all opposition and demanding tribute. No one could withstand him.

The kingdom of Judah, vastly reduced by previous wars, was just one small country among many that sent money and captives to try to appease this tyrant. Ultimately Nebuchadnezzar destroyed Jerusalem and its temple and dragged its remaining citizens into exile. Jews still look back on that time as one of the darkest periods of Jewish history.

On the home front, Nebuchadnezzar went on a lavish building campaign. He decorated the sacred Procession Way with 120 lions flanking its length of nearly a mile. He adorned the Ishtar Gate with enameled brickwork depicting 575 dragons and bulls. He built spectacular palaces and temples and also the "Hanging Gardens of Babylon," one of the Seven Wonders of the Ancient World.

The book of Daniel, however, shows Nebuchadnezzar in a different light: as a vulnerable man who needed to recognize the King of kings. Some of the hapless Jews whom Nebuchadnezzar carried into exile became his trusted officials. Through them, and through a humiliating (but God-given) bout of insanity, Nebuchadnezzar came to terms with his pride. He learned his lesson while living out in the fields like a wild animal, eating grass.

In the end, the mighty Nebuchadnezzar himself wrote of Daniel's God: "He is able to humble those who walk in pride" (4:37).

Life Questions: Do the most powerful people you know recognize God's "higher power"? What could you do to help them see it?

And it *was* visible to the end of the
whole earth.

12 'Its foliage *was* beautiful and its fruit
abundant,

4:8 The Name of a God

*Names were extremely important in Biblical
times, for they conveyed something of a
person's identity. Thus God sometimes gave a
person a new name to indicate a changed life.
However, the name the Babylonians presented
to Daniel, Belteshazzar, was no gift from God. It
was taken from "Bel," a title for the Babylonian
god Marduk. Daniel was surrounded by an
alien culture and could not avoid every aspect
of it.*

And in it *was* food for all.
The beasts of the field found shade
under it,
And the birds of the sky dwelt in its
branches,
And all living creatures fed themselves
from it.

13 ¶ 'I was looking in the visions in my mind
as I lay on my bed, and behold, an *angelic* watcher, a holy one, descended from heaven.

14 'He shouted out and spoke as follows:
"Chop down the tree and cut off its
branches,
Strip off its foliage and scatter its fruit;
Let the beasts flee from under it
And the birds from its branches.

15 "Yet leave the stump with its roots in the
ground,
But with a band of iron and bronze
around it
In the new grass of the field;
And let him be drenched with the dew of
heaven,
And let him share with the beasts in the
grass of the earth.

16 "Let his mind be changed from *that of*
a man
And let a beast's mind be given to him,
And let seven periods of time pass over
him.

17 "This sentence is by the decree of the
angelic watchers
And the decision is a command of the
holy ones,
In order that the living may know
That the Most High is ruler over the
realm of mankind,
And bestows it on whom He wishes
And sets over it the lowliest of men."

18 'This is the dream *which* I, King Nebuchadnezzar, have seen. Now you, Belteshazzar, tell *me*
its interpretation, inasmuch as none of the wise

men of my kingdom is able to make known to me
the interpretation; but you are able, for a spirit of
the holy gods is in you.'

Daniel Interprets the Vision

19 ¶ "Then Daniel, whose name is Belteshazzar, was appalled for a while as his thoughts
alarmed him. The king responded and said, 'Belteshazzar, do not let the dream or its interpretation alarm you.' Belteshazzar replied, 'My lord, *if
only* the dream applied to those who hate you and
its interpretation to your adversaries!

20 'The tree that you saw, which became large
and grew strong, whose height reached to the sky
and was visible to all the earth

21 and whose foliage *was* beautiful and its fruit
abundant, and in which *was* food for all, under
which the beasts of the field dwelt and in whose
branches the birds of the sky lodged—

22 it is you, O king; for you have become great
and grown strong, and your majesty has become
great and reached to the sky and your dominion
to the end of the earth.

23 'In that the king saw an *angelic* watcher, a
holy one, descending from heaven and saying,
"Chop down the tree and destroy it; yet leave the
stump with its roots in the ground, but with a
band of iron and bronze *around it* in the new grass
of the field, and let him be drenched with the dew
of heaven, and let him share with the beasts of the
field until seven periods of time pass over him,"

24 this is the interpretation, O king, and this is
the decree of the Most High, which has come
upon my lord the king:

25 that you be driven away from mankind and
your dwelling place be with the beasts of the field,
and you be given grass to eat like cattle and be
drenched with the dew of heaven; and seven periods of time will pass over you, until you recognize
that the Most High is ruler over the realm of mankind and bestows it on whomever He wishes.

26 'And in that it was commanded to leave the
stump with the roots of the tree, your kingdom
will be assured to you after you recognize that *it is*
Heaven *that* rules.

27 'Therefore, O king, may my advice be pleasing to you: break away now from your sins by
doing righteousness and from your iniquities
by showing mercy to *the* poor, in case there may
be a prolonging of your prosperity.'

The Vision Fulfilled

28 ¶ "All *this* happened to Nebuchadnezzar the
king.

29 "Twelve months later he was walking on the
roof of the royal palace of Babylon.

30 "The king reflected and said, 'Is this not Babylon the great, which I myself have built as a royal
residence by the might of my power and for the
glory of my majesty?'

31 "While the word *was* in the king's mouth, a

voice came from heaven, *saying,* 'King Nebuchadnezzar, to you it is declared: sovereignty has been removed from you,

32 and you will be driven away from mankind, and your dwelling place *will be* with the beasts of the field. You will be given grass to eat like cattle, and seven periods of time will pass over you until you recognize that the Most High is ruler over the realm of mankind and bestows it on whomever He wishes.'

33 "Immediately the word concerning Nebuchadnezzar was fulfilled; and he was driven away from mankind and began eating grass like cattle, and his body was drenched with the dew of heaven until his hair had grown like eagles' *feathers* and his nails like birds' *claws.*

34 ¶ "But at the end of that period, I, Nebuchadnezzar, raised my eyes toward heaven and my reason returned to me, and I blessed the Most High and praised and honored Him who lives forever;

For His dominion is an everlasting dominion,
And His kingdom *endures* from generation to generation.

35 "All the inhabitants of the earth are accounted as nothing,
But He does according to His will in the host of heaven
And *among* the inhabitants of earth;
And no one can ward off His hand
Or say to Him, 'What have You done?'

36 "At that time my reason returned to me. And my majesty and splendor were restored to me for the glory of my kingdom, and my counselors and my nobles began seeking me out; so I was reestablished in my sovereignty, and surpassing greatness was added to me.

37 "Now I, Nebuchadnezzar, praise, exalt and honor the King of heaven, for all His works are true and His ways just, and He is able to humble those who walk in pride."

Belshazzar's Feast

5 Belshazzar the king held a great feast for a thousand of his nobles, and he was drinking wine in the presence of the thousand.

2 When Belshazzar tasted the wine, he gave orders to bring the gold and silver vessels which

5:1 The Throne Room

Modern archaeological excavation has found, in the Babylonian palace, a large room (about 150 feet by 50 feet—one quarter the size of a football field) that has become known as the Throne Room. One wall had a design of blue enameled bricks, but the other three were covered in white plaster (see verse 5).

Nebuchadnezzar his father had taken out of the temple which *was* in Jerusalem, so that the king and his nobles, his wives and his concubines might drink from them.

3 Then they brought the gold vessels that had been taken out of the temple, the house of God which *was* in Jerusalem; and the king and his nobles, his wives and his concubines drank from them.

4 They drank the wine and praised the gods of gold and silver, of bronze, iron, wood and stone.

5 ¶ Suddenly the fingers of a man's hand emerged and began writing opposite the lampstand on the plaster of the wall of the king's palace, and the king saw the back of the hand that did the writing.

6 Then the king's face grew pale and his thoughts alarmed him, and his hip joints went slack and his knees began knocking together.

7 The king called aloud to bring in the conjurers, the Chaldeans and the diviners. The king spoke and said to the wise men of Babylon, "Any man who can read this inscription and explain its interpretation to me shall be clothed with purple and *have* a necklace of gold around his neck, and have authority as third *ruler* in the kingdom."

8 Then all the king's wise men came in, but they could not read the inscription or make known its interpretation to the king.

9 Then King Belshazzar was greatly alarmed, his face grew *even* paler, and his nobles were perplexed.

10 ¶ The queen entered the banquet hall because of the words of the king and his nobles; the queen spoke and said, "O king, live forever! Do not let your thoughts alarm you or your face be pale.

11 "There is a man in your kingdom in whom is a spirit of the holy gods; and in the days of your father, illumination, insight and wisdom like the wisdom of the gods were found in him. And King Nebuchadnezzar, your father, your father the king, appointed him chief of the magicians, conjurers, Chaldeans *and* diviners.

12 "*This was* because an extraordinary spirit, knowledge and insight, interpretation of dreams, explanation of enigmas and solving of difficult problems were found in this Daniel, whom the king named Belteshazzar. Let Daniel now be summoned and he will declare the interpretation."

Daniel Interprets Handwriting on the Wall

13 ¶ Then Daniel was brought in before the king. The king spoke and said to Daniel, "Are you that Daniel who is one of the exiles from Judah, whom my father the king brought from Judah?

14 "Now I have heard about you that a spirit of the gods is in you, and that illumination, insight and extraordinary wisdom have been found in you.

15 "Just now the wise men *and* the conjurers

were brought in before me that they might read this inscription and make its interpretation known to me, but they could not declare the interpretation of the message.

16 "But I personally have heard about you, that you are able to give interpretations and solve difficult problems. Now if you are able to read the inscription and make its interpretation known to me, you will be clothed with purple and *wear a* necklace of gold around your neck, and you will have authority as the third *ruler* in the kingdom."

17 ¶ Then Daniel answered and said before the king, "Keep your gifts for yourself or give your rewards to someone else; however, I will read the inscription to the king and make the interpretation known to him.

18 "O king, the Most High God granted sovereignty, grandeur, glory and majesty to Nebuchadnezzar your father.

19 "Because of the grandeur which He bestowed on him, all the peoples, nations and *men of every* language feared and trembled before him; whomever he wished he killed and whomever he wished he spared alive; and whomever he wished he elevated and whomever he wished he humbled.

20 "But when his heart was lifted up and his spirit became so proud that he behaved arrogantly, he was deposed from his royal throne and *his* glory was taken away from him.

21 "He was also driven away from mankind, and his heart was made like *that of* beasts, and his dwelling place *was* with the wild donkeys. He was given grass to eat like cattle, and his body was drenched with the dew of heaven until he recognized that the Most High God is ruler over the realm of mankind and *that* He sets over it whomever He wishes.

22 "Yet you, his son, Belshazzar, have not humbled your heart, even though you knew all this,

23 but you have exalted yourself against the Lord of heaven; and they have brought the vessels of His house before you, and you and your nobles, your wives and your concubines have been drinking wine from them; and you have praised the gods of silver and gold, of bronze, iron, wood and stone, which do not see, hear or understand. But the God in whose hand are your life-breath and your ways, you have not glorified.

24 "Then the hand was sent from Him and this inscription was written out.

25 ¶ "Now this is the inscription that was written out: 'MENĒ, MENĒ, TEKEL, UPHARSIN.'

26 "This is the interpretation of the message: 'MENĒ'—God has numbered your kingdom and put an end to it.

27 " 'TEKĒL'—you have been weighed on the scales and found deficient.

28 " 'PERĒS'—your kingdom has been divided and given over to the Medes and Persians."

29 ¶ Then Belshazzar gave orders, and they clothed Daniel with purple and *put* a necklace of gold around his neck, and issued a proclamation concerning him that he *now* had authority as the third *ruler* in the kingdom.

30 ¶ That same night Belshazzar the Chaldean king was slain.

5:30 Sneak Attack

Two empires, the Medes and the Persians, joined forces to overthrow Babylon, the dominant power of the day. Invading armies diverted the river Euphrates to another channel, then marched along the dry riverbed underneath the city walls. The site of ancient Babylon lies about fifty miles from modern-day Baghdad, Iraq.

31 So Darius the Mede received the kingdom at about the age of sixty-two.

Daniel Serves Darius

6 It seemed good to Darius to appoint 120 satraps over the kingdom, that they would be in charge of the whole kingdom,

2 and over them three commissioners (of whom Daniel was one), that these satraps might be accountable to them, and that the king might not suffer loss.

3 Then this Daniel began distinguishing himself among the commissioners and satraps because he possessed an extraordinary spirit, and the king planned to appoint him over the entire kingdom.

4 Then the commissioners and satraps began trying to find a ground of accusation against Daniel in regard to government affairs; but they could find no ground of accusation or *evidence of* corruption, inasmuch as he was faithful, and no negligence or corruption was *to be* found in him.

5 Then these men said, "We will not find any ground of accusation against this Daniel unless we find *it* against him with regard to the law of his God."

6 ¶ Then these commissioners and satraps came by agreement to the king and spoke to him as follows: "King Darius, live forever!

7 "All the commissioners of the kingdom, the prefects and the satraps, the high officials and the governors have consulted together that the king should establish a statute and enforce an injunction that anyone who makes a petition to any god or man besides you, O king, for thirty days, shall be cast into the lions' den.

8 "Now, O king, establish the injunction and sign the document so that it may not be changed, according to the law of the Medes and Persians, which may not be revoked."

9 Therefore King Darius signed the document, that is, the injunction.

10 ¶ Now when Daniel knew that the docu-

ment was signed, he entered his house (now in his roof chamber he had windows open toward Jerusalem); and he continued kneeling on his knees three times a day, praying and giving thanks before his God, as he had been doing previously.

6:10–11 A Jewish Orientation

Daniel had lost much of his Jewish heritage— even his name had been changed to a Babylonian one (1:7). Certainly he could not worship God in the way God's law commanded, through sacrifices at the temple in Jerusalem. He did, however, point himself toward the promised land three times a day in prayer. Not even the threat of death could make him vary this practice. By this time Daniel had been in Babylon over 60 years; he was probably in his 80s.

11 Then these men came by agreement and found Daniel making petition and supplication before his God.

12 Then they approached and spoke before the king about the king's injunction, "Did you not sign an injunction that any man who makes a petition to any god or man besides you, O king, for thirty days, is to be cast into the lions' den?" The king replied, "The statement is true, according to the law of the Medes and Persians, which may not be revoked."

13 Then they answered and spoke before the king, "Daniel, who is one of the exiles from Judah, pays no attention to you, O king, or to the injunction which you signed, but keeps making his petition three times a day."

14 ¶ Then, as soon as the king heard this statement, he was deeply distressed and set *his* mind on delivering Daniel; and even until sunset he kept exerting himself to rescue him.

15 Then these men came by agreement to the king and said to the king, "Recognize, O king, that it is a law of the Medes and Persians that no injunction or statute which the king establishes may be changed."

Daniel in the Lions' Den

16 ¶ Then the king gave orders, and Daniel was brought in and cast into the lions' den. The king spoke and said to Daniel, "Your God whom you constantly serve will Himself deliver you."

17 A stone was brought and laid over the mouth of the den; and the king sealed it with his own signet ring and with the signet rings of his nobles, so that nothing would be changed in regard to Daniel.

18 Then the king went off to his palace and spent the night fasting, and no entertainment was brought before him; and his sleep fled from him.

19 ¶ Then the king arose at dawn, at the break of day, and went in haste to the lions' den.

20 When he had come near the den to Daniel, he cried out with a troubled voice. The king spoke and said to Daniel, "Daniel, servant of the living God, has your God, whom you constantly serve, been able to deliver you from the lions?"

21 Then Daniel spoke to the king, "O king, live forever!

22 "My God sent His angel and shut the lions' mouths and they have not harmed me, inasmuch as I was found innocent before Him; and also toward you, O king, I have committed no crime."

23 Then the king was very pleased and gave orders for Daniel to be taken up out of the den. So Daniel was taken up out of the den and no injury whatever was found on him, because he had trusted in his God.

24 The king then gave orders, and they brought those men who had maliciously accused Daniel, and they cast them, their children and their wives into the lions' den; and they had not reached the bottom of the den before the lions overpowered them and crushed all their bones.

25 ¶ Then Darius the king wrote to all the peoples, nations and *men of every* language who were living in all the land: "May your peace abound!

26 "I make a decree that in all the dominion of my kingdom men are to fear and tremble before the God of Daniel;

For He is the living God and enduring forever,
And His kingdom is one which will not be destroyed,
And His dominion *will be* forever.

27 "He delivers and rescues and performs signs and wonders
In heaven and on earth,
Who has *also* delivered Daniel from the power of the lions."

28 ¶ So this Daniel enjoyed success in the reign of Darius and in the reign of Cyrus the Persian.

Vision of the Four Beasts

7 In the first year of Belshazzar king of Babylon Daniel saw a dream and visions in his mind *as he lay* on his bed; then he wrote the dream down *and* related the *following* summary of it.

2 Daniel said, "I was looking in my vision by night, and behold, the four winds of heaven were stirring up the great sea.

3 "And four great beasts were coming up from the sea, different from one another.

4 "The first *was* like a lion and had *the* wings of an eagle. I kept looking until its wings were plucked, and it was lifted up from the ground and made to stand on two feet like a man; a human mind also was given to it.

5 "And behold, another beast, a second one, resembling a bear. And it was raised up on one side, and three ribs *were* in its mouth between its

teeth; and thus they said to it, 'Arise, devour much meat!'

6 "After this I kept looking, and behold, another one, like a leopard, which had on its back four wings of a bird; the beast also had four heads, and dominion was given to it.

7 "After this I kept looking in the night visions, and behold, a fourth beast, dreadful and terrifying and extremely strong; and it had large iron teeth. It devoured and crushed and trampled down the remainder with its feet; and it was different from all the beasts that were before it, and it had ten horns.

8 "While I was contemplating the horns, behold, another horn, a little one, came up among them, and three of the first horns were pulled out by the roots before it; and behold, this horn possessed eyes like the eyes of a man and a mouth uttering great *boasts*.

The Ancient of Days Reigns

9 ¶ "I kept looking
Until thrones were set up,
And the Ancient of Days took *His* seat;
His vesture *was* like white snow
And the hair of His head like pure wool.
His throne *was* ablaze with flames,
Its wheels *were* a burning fire.

10 "A river of fire was flowing
And coming out from before Him;
Thousands upon thousands were
attending Him,
And myriads upon myriads were
standing before Him;
The court sat,
And the books were opened.

11 "Then I kept looking because of the sound of the boastful words which the horn was speaking; I kept looking until the beast was slain, and its body was destroyed and given to the burning fire.

12 "As for the rest of the beasts, their dominion was taken away, but an extension of life was granted to them for an appointed period of time.

The Son of Man Presented

13 ¶ "I kept looking in the night visions,
And behold, with the clouds of heaven
One like a Son of Man was coming,
And He came up to the Ancient of Days
And was presented before Him.

14 "And to Him was given dominion,
Glory and a kingdom,
That all the peoples, nations and *men of
every* language
Might serve Him.
His dominion is an everlasting dominion

Symbols of Power
The bigger the tyrant, the more statues litter the landscape

IT'S NO SURPRISE THAT NEBUCHADNEZZAR erected a gold image for people to worship (chapter 3). Kings and rulers love to display statues or gigantic photos as symbols of their power. The bigger the tyrants, the more of their statues litter the landscape.

It seems reasonable, then, that Daniel's visions depict political realms through statues and symbolic animals. But since each of the visions uses a different set of symbols, you can easily lose track of what the symbols stand for. This chart may help you coordinate Daniel's view of four great empires—and the almighty God who overwhelms their power in the end:

"I kept looking in the night visions, and behold, a fourth beast, … terrifying and extremely strong; and it had large iron teeth. It devoured and crushed and trampled down the remainder with its feet." 7:7

	Babylon	Medo-Persia	Greece	Rome	Kingdom of God
Chapter 2	gold	silver	bronze	iron	supernatural rock
Chapter 7	lion	bear	leopard	beast with horns	Ancient of Days, Son of Man
Chapter 8	–	ram	goat		
Chapter 11	–	–	king of North		

Life Questions: What images "litter the landscape" in our time? Are they symbols of power? If so, how does that power affect you?

Which will not pass away;
And His kingdom is one
Which will not be destroyed.

The Vision Interpreted

15 ¶ "As for me, Daniel, my spirit was distressed within me, and the visions in my mind kept alarming me.

7:13–14 A Son of Man

God's power is given to one "like a Son of Man" rather than to those like beasts. The contrast suggests God's kingdom has power that is humane, not savage or bestial. Jesus adopted this term for himself.

16 "I approached one of those who were standing by and began asking him the exact meaning of all this. So he told me and made known to me the interpretation of these things:

17 'These great beasts, which are four *in number*, are four kings *who* will arise from the earth.

18 'But the saints of the Highest One will receive the kingdom and possess the kingdom forever, for all ages to come.'

19 ¶ "Then I desired to know the exact meaning of the fourth beast, which was different from all the others, exceedingly dreadful, with its teeth of iron and its claws of bronze, *and which* devoured, crushed and trampled down the remainder with its feet,

20 and *the meaning* of the ten horns that *were* on its head and the other *horn* which came up, and before which three *of them* fell, namely, that horn which had eyes and a mouth uttering great *boasts* and which was larger in appearance than its associates.

21 "I kept looking, and that horn was waging war with the saints and overpowering them

22 until the Ancient of Days came and judgment was passed in favor of the saints of the Highest One, and the time arrived when the saints took possession of the kingdom.

23 ¶ "Thus he said: 'The fourth beast will be a fourth kingdom on the earth, which will be different from all the *other* kingdoms and will devour the whole earth and tread it down and crush it.

24 'As for the ten horns, out of this kingdom ten kings will arise; and another will arise after them, and he will be different from the previous ones and will subdue three kings.

25 'He will speak out against the Most High and wear down the saints of the Highest One, and he will intend to make alterations in times and in law; and they will be given into his hand for a time, times, and half a time.

26 'But the court will sit *for judgment,* and his

dominion will be taken away, annihilated and destroyed forever.

27 'Then the sovereignty, the dominion and the greatness of *all* the kingdoms under the whole heaven will be given to the people of the saints of the Highest One; His kingdom *will be* an everlasting kingdom, and all the dominions will serve and obey Him.'

28 ¶ "At this point the revelation ended. As for me, Daniel, my thoughts were greatly alarming me and my face grew pale, but I kept the matter to myself."

Vision of the Ram and Goat

8 In the third year of the reign of Belshazzar the king a vision appeared to me, Daniel, subsequent to the one which appeared to me previously.

2 I looked in the vision, and while I was looking I was in the citadel of Susa, which is in the province of Elam; and I looked in the vision and I myself was beside the Ulai Canal.

3 Then I lifted my eyes and looked, and behold, a ram which had two horns was standing in front of the canal. Now the two horns *were* long, but one *was* longer than the other, with the longer one coming up last.

4 I saw the ram butting westward, northward, and southward, and no *other* beasts could stand before him nor was there anyone to rescue from his power, but he did as he pleased and magnified *himself.*

5 ¶ While I was observing, behold, a male goat was coming from the west over the surface of the whole earth without touching the ground; and the goat *had* a conspicuous horn between his eyes.

6 He came up to the ram that had the two horns, which I had seen standing in front of the canal, and rushed at him in his mighty wrath.

7 I saw him come beside the ram, and he was enraged at him; and he struck the ram and shattered his two horns, and the ram had no strength to withstand him. So he hurled him to the ground and trampled on him, and there was none to rescue the ram from his power.

8 Then the male goat magnified *himself* exceedingly. But as soon as he was mighty, the large horn was broken; and in its place there came up four conspicuous *horns* toward the four winds of heaven.

The Little Horn

9 ¶ Out of one of them came forth a rather small horn which grew exceedingly great toward the south, toward the east, and toward the *a*Beautiful *Land.*

10 It grew up to the host of heaven and caused some of the host and some of the stars to fall to the earth, and it trampled them down.

11 It even magnified *itself* to be equal with the

---

a I.e. Palestine

Commander of the host; and it removed the regular sacrifice from Him, and the place of His sanctuary was thrown down.

12 And on account of transgression the host will be given over to the horn along with the regular sacrifice; and it will fling truth to the ground and perform its will and prosper.

13 Then I heard a holy one speaking, and another holy one said to that particular one who was speaking, "How long will the vision about the regular sacrifice apply, while the transgression causes horror, so as to allow both the holy place and the host to be trampled?"

14 He said to me, "For 2,300 evenings and mornings; then the holy place will be properly restored."

Interpretation of the Vision

15 ¶ When I, Daniel, had seen the vision, I sought to understand it; and behold, standing before me was one who looked like a man.

16 And I heard the voice of a man between the banks of Ulai, and he called out and said, "Gabriel, give this man an understanding of the vision."

17 So he came near to where I was standing, and when he came I was frightened and fell on my face; but he said to me, "Son of man, understand that the vision pertains to the time of the end."

18 ¶ Now while he was talking with me, I sank into a deep sleep with my face to the ground; but he touched me and made me stand upright.

19 He said, "Behold, I am going to let you know what will occur at the final period of the indignation, for it pertains to the appointed time of the end.

The Ram's Identity

20 "The ram which you saw with the two horns represents the kings of Media and Persia.

The Goat

21 "The shaggy goat represents the kingdom of Greece, and the large horn that is between his eyes is the first king.

22 "The broken horn and the four horns that arose in its place represent four kingdoms which will arise from his nation, although not with his power.

23 "In the latter period of their rule,
When the transgressors have run their course,
A king will arise,
Insolent and skilled in intrigue.

24 "His power will be mighty, but not by his own power,
And he will destroy to an extraordinary degree
And prosper and perform his will;
He will destroy mighty men and the holy people.

25 "And through his shrewdness

He will cause deceit to succeed by his influence;
And he will magnify himself in his heart,
And he will destroy many while they are at ease.
He will even oppose the Prince of princes,
But he will be broken without human agency.

26 "The vision of the evenings and mornings
Which has been told is true;
But keep the vision secret,
For it pertains to many days in the future."

8:26 Long Delay

Twice (here and 12:4) the angel tells Daniel to seal up the vision because it concerns the distant future. Pointedly, in Revelation, the last book of the Bible, an angel tells John, "Do not seal up the words of the prophecy of this book, for the time is near" (Revelation 22:10). Daniel and Revelation, written hundreds of years apart, arrive at the same conclusion: No matter how bad things look, God is in control of history and will one day reclaim the earth.

27 ¶ Then I, Daniel, was exhausted and sick for days. Then I got up again and carried on the king's business; but I was astounded at the vision, and there was none to explain it.

Daniel's Prayer for His People

9 In the first year of Darius the son of Ahasuerus, of Median descent, who was made king over the kingdom of the Chaldeans—

2 in the first year of his reign, I, Daniel, observed in the books the number of the years which was revealed as the word of the LORD to Jeremiah the prophet for the completion of the desolations of Jerusalem, namely, seventy years.

9:2 Favored by God and Kings

This chapter gives a rare glimpse of one prophet, Daniel, being comforted by the words of another, Jeremiah. Daniel's response shows that, despite his government service to two enemy empires (Babylon and Persia), loyalty to his homeland never faltered. The remarkable prayer that follows expresses well his intimate relationship with God.

3 So I gave my attention to the Lord God to seek Him by prayer and supplications, with fasting, sackcloth and ashes.

4 I prayed to the LORD my God and confessed

and said, "Alas, O Lord, the great and awesome God, who keeps His covenant and lovingkindness for those who love Him and keep His commandments,

5 we have sinned, committed iniquity, acted wickedly and rebelled, even turning aside from Your commandments and ordinances.

6 "Moreover, we have not listened to Your servants the prophets, who spoke in Your name to our kings, our princes, our fathers and all the people of the land.

7 ¶ "Righteousness belongs to You, O Lord, but to us open shame, as it is this day—to the men of Judah, the inhabitants of Jerusalem and all Israel, those who are nearby and those who are far away in all the countries to which You have driven them, because of their unfaithful deeds which they have committed against You.

8 "Open shame belongs to us, O Lord, to our kings, our princes and our fathers, because we have sinned against You.

9 "To the Lord our God *belong* compassion and forgiveness, for we have rebelled against Him;

10 nor have we obeyed the voice of the LORD our God, to walk in His teachings which He set before us through His servants the prophets.

11 "Indeed all Israel has transgressed Your law and turned aside, not obeying Your voice; so the curse has been poured out on us, along with the oath which is written in the law of Moses the servant of God, for we have sinned against Him.

12 "Thus He has confirmed His words which He had spoken against us and against our rulers who ruled us, to bring on us great calamity; for under the whole heaven there has not been done *anything* like what was done to Jerusalem.

13 "As it is written in the law of Moses, all this calamity has come on us; yet we have not sought the favor of the LORD our God by turning from our iniquity and giving attention to Your truth.

14 "Therefore the LORD has kept the calamity in store and brought it on us; for the LORD our God is righteous with respect to all His deeds which He has done, but we have not obeyed His voice.

15 ¶ "And now, O Lord our God, who have brought Your people out of the land of Egypt with a mighty hand and have made a name for Yourself, as it is this day—we have sinned, we have been wicked.

16 "O Lord, in accordance with all Your righteous acts, let now Your anger and Your wrath turn away from Your city Jerusalem, Your holy mountain; for because of our sins and the iniquities of our fathers, Jerusalem and Your people *have become* a reproach to all those around us.

17 "So now, our God, listen to the prayer of Your servant and to his supplications, and for Your sake, O Lord, let Your face shine on Your desolate sanctuary.

18 "O my God, incline Your ear and hear! Open Your eyes and see our desolations and the city which is called by Your name; for we are not presenting our supplications before You on account of any merits of our own, but on account of Your great compassion.

19 "O Lord, hear! O Lord, forgive! O Lord, listen and take action! For Your own sake, O my God, do not delay, because Your city and Your people are called by Your name."

Gabriel Brings an Answer

20 ¶ Now while I was speaking and praying, and confessing my sin and the sin of my people Israel, and presenting my supplication before the LORD my God in behalf of the holy mountain of my God,

21 while I was still speaking in prayer, then the man Gabriel, whom I had seen in the vision previously, came to me in *my* extreme weariness about the time of the evening offering.

22 He gave *me* instruction and talked with me and said, "O Daniel, I have now come forth to give you insight with understanding.

23 "At the beginning of your supplications the command was issued, and I have come to tell *you*, for you are highly esteemed; so give heed to the message and gain understanding of the vision.

Seventy Weeks and the Messiah

24 ¶ "Seventy weeks have been decreed for your people and your holy city, to finish the transgression, to make an end of sin, to make atonement for iniquity, to bring in everlasting righteousness, to seal up vision and prophecy and to anoint the most holy *place.*

25 "So you are to know and discern *that* from the issuing of a decree to restore and rebuild Jerusalem until Messiah the Prince *there will be* seven weeks and sixty-two weeks; it will be built again, with plaza and moat, even in times of distress.

26 "Then after the sixty-two weeks the Messiah will be cut off and have nothing, and the people of the prince who is to come will destroy the city and the sanctuary. And its end *will come* with a flood; even to the end there will be war; desolations are determined.

27 "And he will make a firm covenant with the many for one week, but in the middle of the week he will put a stop to sacrifice and grain offering; and on the wing of abominations *will come* one who makes desolate, even until a complete destruction, one that is decreed, is poured out on the one who makes desolate."

Daniel Is Terrified by a Vision

10 In the third year of Cyrus king of Persia a message was revealed to Daniel, who was named Belteshazzar; and the message was true and *one of* great conflict, but he understood the message and had an understanding of the vision.

2 ¶ In those days, I, Daniel, had been mourning for three entire weeks.

3 I did not eat any tasty food, nor did meat or wine enter my mouth, nor did I use any ointment at all until the entire three weeks were completed.

4 On the twenty-fourth day of the first month, while I was by the bank of the great river, that is, the Tigris,

5 I lifted my eyes and looked, and behold, there was a certain man dressed in linen, whose waist was girded with *a belt of* pure gold of Uphaz.

6 His body also *was* like beryl, his face had the appearance of lightning, his eyes were like flaming torches, his arms and feet like the gleam of polished bronze, and the sound of his words like the sound of a tumult.

7 Now I, Daniel, alone saw the vision, while the men who were with me did not see the vision; nevertheless, a great dread fell on them, and they ran away to hide themselves.

8 So I was left alone and saw this great vision; yet no strength was left in me, for my natural color turned to a deathly pallor, and I retained no strength.

9 But I heard the sound of his words; and as soon as I heard the sound of his words, I fell into a deep sleep on my face, with my face to the ground.

Daniel Comforted

10 ¶ Then behold, a hand touched me and set me trembling on my hands and knees.

11 He said to me, "O Daniel, man of high esteem, understand the words that I am about to tell you and stand upright, for I have now been sent to you." And when he had spoken this word to me, I stood up trembling.

12 Then he said to me, "Do not be afraid, Daniel, for from the first day that you set your heart on understanding *this* and on humbling yourself before your God, your words were heard, and I have come in response to your words.

13 "But the prince of the kingdom of Persia was withstanding me for twenty-one days; then behold, Michael, one of the chief princes, came to help me, for I had been left there with the kings of Persia.

14 "Now I have come to give you an understanding of what will happen to your people in the latter days, for the vision pertains to the days yet *future*."

15 ¶ When he had spoken to me according to these words, I turned my face toward the ground and became speechless.

16 And behold, one who resembled a human being was touching my lips; then I opened my mouth and spoke and said to him who was standing before me, "O my lord, as a result of the vision anguish has come upon me, and I have retained no strength.

17 "For how can such a servant of my lord talk with such as my lord? As for me, there remains just now no strength in me, nor has any breath been left in me."

18 ¶ Then *this* one with human appearance touched me again and strengthened me.

19 He said, "O man of high esteem, do not be afraid. Peace be with you; take courage and be courageous!" Now as soon as he spoke to me, I received strength and said, "May my lord speak, for you have strengthened me."

20 Then he said, "Do you understand why I came to you? But I shall now return to fight against the prince of Persia; so I am going forth, and behold, the prince of Greece is about to come.

10:20 Slow to Answer Prayer

These comments come from what seems to be an angelic messenger. They hint at heavenly warfare human beings know little about. When prayers go unanswered for long periods, more may be involved than we ever dream.

21 "However, I will tell you what is inscribed in the writing of truth. Yet there is no one who stands firmly with me against these *forces* except Michael your prince.

Conflicts to Come

11 "In the first year of Darius the Mede, I arose to be an encouragement and a protection for him.

2 "And now I will tell you the truth. Behold, three more kings are going to arise in Persia. Then a fourth will gain far more riches than all *of them;* as soon as he becomes strong through his riches, he will arouse the whole *empire* against the realm of Greece.

3 "And a mighty king will arise, and he will rule with great authority and do as he pleases.

4 "But as soon as he has arisen, his kingdom will be broken up and parceled out toward the four points of the compass, though not to his *own* descendants, nor according to his authority which he wielded, for his sovereignty will be uprooted and *given* to others besides them.

5 ¶ "Then the king of the South will grow strong, along with *one* of his princes who will gain ascendancy over him and obtain dominion; his domain *will be* a great dominion *indeed.*

6 "After some years they will form an alliance, and the daughter of the king of the South will come to the king of the North to carry out a peaceful arrangement. But she will not retain her position of power, nor will he remain with his power, but she will be given up, along with those who brought her in and the one who sired her as well as he who supported her in *those* times.

7 "But one of the descendants of her line will arise in his place, and he will come against *their*

army and enter the fortress of the king of the North, and he will deal with them and display *great* strength.

8 "Also their gods with their metal images *and* their precious vessels of silver and gold he will take into captivity to Egypt, and he on his part will refrain from *attacking* the king of the North for *some* years.

9 "Then the latter will enter the realm of the king of the South, but will return to his *own* land.

10 ¶ "His sons will mobilize and assemble a multitude of great forces; and one of them will keep on coming and overflow and pass through, that he may again wage war up to his *very* fortress.

11 "The king of the South will be enraged and go forth and fight with the king of the North. Then the latter will raise a great multitude, but *that* multitude will be given into the hand of the *former*.

12 "When the multitude is carried away, his heart will be lifted up, and he will cause tens of thousands to fall; yet he will not prevail.

13 "For the king of the North will again raise a greater multitude than the former, and after an interval of some years he will press on with a great army and much equipment.

14 ¶ "Now in those times many will rise up against the king of the South; the violent ones

In the Hands of Tyrants
Daniel's visions portray history as one bestial empire after another

> "Then the king will do as he pleases, and he will exalt and magnify himself above every god and will speak monstrous things against the God of gods." 11:36

JOSEF STALIN, HEAD OF THE Soviet Union from 1924 to 1953, murdered millions. His supporters knew that the slightest slip would lead them to the executioner. Of 1,966 delegates to one Party Congress, Stalin had 1,108—all Stalin supporters—arrested and killed. Of the 139 Central Committee members, 98 were shot.

In spite of this, the nation virtually worshiped Stalin. He had made himself a god. Every public park displayed his statue. Every newspaper published lavish tributes daily. For one of his birthdays, an entire museum in Moscow was stripped so it could be filled with his birthday presents. He was called Father of the Peoples, the Greatest Genius in History, the Shining Sun of Humanity, the Life-giving Force of Socialism.

He was not the first, nor the last, of his kind. Increasingly, it seems, totalitarian leaders promise everything—and demand everything. They brutally dispose of anyone who opposes them. Hitler, Stalin, Idi Amin, Chairman Mao, the Ayatollah Khomeini, Saddam Hussein . . . the list grows longer.

A Single, Cruel King

Daniel's visions predicted such tyrants. History, in these visions, is one terrible empire after another. Each is stronger but more bestial than the last.

The focus narrows (in 8:23–25 and 11:21–45) to a single, cruel king. Most scholars agree the description matches Antiochus IV of Syria. An obscure tyrant who ruled a century and a half before Jesus, he was the Jews' worst enemy in history, until Hitler.

Antiochus, never totally victorious against archenemy Egypt, took out his frustrations on little Jerusalem. He determined to make that city Greek rather than Jewish by rooting out its religion. He sold the high priest's position to an opportunist and transformed the temple into an altar for the Greek god Zeus. This desecration sparked one of history's earliest guerrilla wars, the Maccabean revolt that began in 168 B.C. Antiochus conquered Jerusalem twice, slaughtering thousands. He outlawed Judaism and proclaimed himself to be God incarnate.

The End of the Tyrant

And yet, for all his power and terror, Antiochus died raving from insanity, and his mark on history has virtually disappeared. Ironically, the religion he sought to destroy has endured and touched the whole world. This is just what you could expect from reading Daniel. Terrible rulers rise up one after another, but they disappear just as quickly. We can expect political terror. But we can count on God.

The New Testament suggests that Antiochus's brutal pattern will culminate someday in the antichrist, an arrogant leader who will dominate the world and persecute God's people as never before. Many scholars believe that the last part of Daniel's final vision refers to this character. Yet despite the antichrist's power, he too will fall in the end. God's justice will rule the earth. Those who believe in such an outcome have reason to be as brave as Daniel.

Life Questions: How does Daniel's view of history affect your perspective on world politics? How should a Christian regard the human "powers-that-be"?

among your people will also lift themselves up in order to fulfill the vision, but they will fall down.

15 "Then the king of the North will come, cast up a siege ramp and capture a well-fortified city; and the forces of the South will not stand *their ground,* not even their choicest troops, for there will be no strength to make a stand.

16 "But he who comes against him will do as he pleases, and no one will *be able to* withstand him; he will also stay *for a time* in the Beautiful Land, with destruction in his hand.

17 "He will set his face to come with the power of his whole kingdom, bringing with him a proposal of peace which he will put into effect; he will also give him the daughter of women to ruin it. But she will not take a stand *for him* or be on his side.

18 "Then he will turn his face to the coastlands and capture many. But a commander will put a stop to his scorn against him; moreover, he will repay him for his scorn.

19 "So he will turn his face toward the fortresses of his own land, but he will stumble and fall and be found no more.

20 ¶ "Then in his place one will arise who will send an oppressor through the [a]Jewel of *his* kingdom; yet within a few days he will be shattered, though not in anger nor in battle.

21 "In his place a despicable person will arise, on whom the honor of kingship has not been conferred, but he will come in a time of tranquility and seize the kingdom by intrigue.

22 "The overflowing forces will be flooded away before him and shattered, and also the prince of the covenant.

23 "After an alliance is made with him he will practice deception, and he will go up and gain power with a small *force of* people.

24 "In a time of tranquility he will enter the richest *parts* of the realm, and he will accomplish what his fathers never did, nor his ancestors; he will distribute plunder, booty and possessions among them, and he will devise his schemes against strongholds, but *only* for a time.

25 "He will stir up his strength and courage against the king of the South with a large army; so the king of the South will mobilize an extremely large and mighty army for war; but he will not stand, for schemes will be devised against him.

26 "Those who eat his choice food will destroy him, and his army will overflow, but many will fall down slain.

27 "As for both kings, their hearts will be *intent* on evil, and they will speak lies *to each other* at the same table; but it will not succeed, for the end is still *to come* at the appointed time.

28 "Then he will return to his land with much plunder; but his heart will be *set* against the holy covenant, and he will take action and *then* return to his *own* land.

[a] Lit *adornment;* i.e. probably Jerusalem and its temple

29 ¶ "At the appointed time he will return and come into the South, but this last time it will not turn out the way it did before.

30 "For ships of Kittim will come against him; therefore he will be disheartened and will return and become enraged at the holy covenant and take action; so he will come back and show regard for those who forsake the holy covenant.

31 "Forces from him will arise, desecrate the sanctuary fortress, and do away with the regular sacrifice. And they will set up the abomination of desolation.

32 "By smooth *words* he will turn to godlessness those who act wickedly toward the covenant, but the people who know their God will display strength and take action.

33 "Those who have insight among the people will give understanding to the many; yet they will fall by sword and by flame, by captivity and by plunder for *many* days.

34 "Now when they fall they will be granted a little help, and many will join with them in hypocrisy.

35 "Some of those who have insight will fall, in order to refine, purge and make them pure until the end time; because *it is* still *to come* at the appointed time.

36 ¶ "Then the king will do as he pleases, and he will exalt and magnify himself above every god and will speak monstrous things against the God of gods; and he will prosper until the indignation is finished, for that which is decreed will be done.

37 "He will show no regard for the gods of his fathers or for the desire of women, nor will he show regard for any *other* god; for he will magnify himself above *them* all.

11:37 Exalted above the Gods

The tyrant Antiochus IV, whom most commentators believe is described here, minted many coins showing his portrait. The early coins were merely stamped, "King Antiochus." But, as he grew more obsessed with his own importance, he added features to his portrait that made him look like the Greek gods Apollo or Zeus, and to his given name he appended the title "Epiphanes"—"God Manifest." Such behavior earned him the nickname "Antiochus Epimanes"—"crazy Antiochus."

38 "But instead he will honor a god of fortresses, a god whom his fathers did not know; he will honor *him* with gold, silver, costly stones and treasures.

39 "He will take action against the strongest of fortresses with *the help of* a foreign god; he will give great honor to those who acknowledge *him*

and will cause them to rule over the many, and will parcel out land for a price.

40 ¶ "At the end time the king of the South will collide with him, and the king of the North will storm against him with chariots, with horsemen and with many ships; and he will enter countries, overflow *them* and pass through.

41 "He will also enter the Beautiful Land, and many *countries* will fall; but these will be rescued out of his hand: Edom, Moab and the foremost of the sons of Ammon.

42 "Then he will stretch out his hand against *other* countries, and the land of Egypt will not escape.

43 "But he will gain control over the hidden treasures of gold and silver and over all the precious things of Egypt; and Libyans and Ethiopians *will follow* at his heels.

44 "But rumors from the East and from the North will disturb him, and he will go forth with great wrath to destroy and annihilate many.

45 "He will pitch the tents of his royal pavilion between the seas and the beautiful Holy Mountain; yet he will come to his end, and no one will help him.

The Time of the End

12 "Now at that time Michael, the great prince who stands *guard* over the sons of your people, will arise. And there will be a time of distress such as never occurred since there was a nation until that time; and at that time your people, everyone who is found written in the book, will be rescued.

2 "Many of those who sleep in the dust of the ground will awake, these to everlasting life, but the others to disgrace *and* everlasting contempt.

3 "Those who have insight will shine brightly like the brightness of the expanse of heaven, and those who lead the many to righteousness, like the stars forever and ever.

4 "But as for you, Daniel, conceal these words and seal up the book until the end of time; many

will go back and forth, and knowledge will increase."

5 ¶ Then I, Daniel, looked and behold, two others were standing, one on this bank of the river and the other on that bank of the river.

12:2 Resurrection

While eternal life is usually portrayed cloudily in the Old Testament, this verse clearly predicts that we will live forever.

6 And one said to the man dressed in linen, who was above the waters of the river, "How long *will it be* until the end of *these* wonders?"

7 I heard the man dressed in linen, who was above the waters of the river, as he raised his right hand and his left toward heaven, and swore by Him who lives forever that it would be for a time, times, and half *a time;* and as soon as they finish shattering the power of the holy people, all these *events* will be completed.

8 As for me, I heard but could not understand; so I said, "My lord, what *will be* the outcome of these *events?*"

9 He said, "Go *your way,* Daniel, for *these* words are concealed and sealed up until the end time.

10 "Many will be purged, purified and refined, but the wicked will act wickedly; and none of the wicked will understand, but those who have insight will understand.

11 "From the time that the regular sacrifice is abolished and the abomination of desolation is set up, *there will be* 1,290 days.

12 "How blessed is he who keeps waiting and attains to the 1,335 days!

13 "But as for you, go *your way* to the end; then you will enter into rest and rise *again* for your allotted portion at the end of the age."

HOSEA

Tearing God's Heart
Why would he love such a woman?

HOSEA BEGINS WITH A LOVE story—a painful, personal love story, the prophet's very own. Hosea had married a woman who acted like a prostitute. Yet the more she went out on him, the more Hosea loved her. He gave her everything a good wife deserved: his love, his home, his name, his reputation. She responded by sleeping around with other men. He warned her, he pleaded with her, he punished her. She humiliated him until he wanted to cry, yet still he clung to her.

Why did Hosea begin with his personal life? Because God had expressly told him to relate it to another, more tragic love story: the painful love of God for his people. God could have simply declared, "Israel is like a wife to me—an adulterous wife." Instead, he used Hosea to act out the treachery in real life—and to show in living color God's fury, his jealousy, and above all else, his love for his people.

> *"I will punish her for the days of the Baals when she used to offer sacrifices to them and adorn herself with her earrings and jewelry, and follow her lovers, so that she forgot Me," declares the LORD. 2:13*

Winding Down to a Bitter End

Virtually every chapter of Hosea talks about the "prostitution" or "adultery" and 'harlotry' of God's people (1:2; 2:2,4; 3:1; 4:2,10–15,18; 5:3–4; 6:10; 7:4; 8:9; 9:1). Underlying some hard words is a remarkably tender revelation: God doesn't want to be only "master" to his people. He wants to be a husband, giving all of himself in intimate love.

Hosea spoke and acted these messages to the northern part of God's divided country—Israel or "Ephraim," as Hosea sometimes called it. King Jeroboam II's reign was a time of prosperity; the prophet Amos blasted the rich for their greedy injustices toward the poor. But soon after Jeroboam's death the national fabric began to unravel. In just over 20 years six kings took the throne—four of them by murdering the previous king. Hosea probably lived to see the massive Assyrian armies storm the capital and deport all the Israelite citizens to other lands. God's "wife" was carried off, just as he had warned.

God Is a Lover

When most people must have been preoccupied with politics and military matters, Hosea kept his message aimed at idol worship, which he referred to as adultery. He saw that as the root of Israel's problems.

Israel tended to mix religions freely—to think that everybody's religion had a little truth in it, and the more religion you got, the better off you would be. Many prophets attacked Israel's idol worship. Hosea shows that God's concern about idolatry is no fussy, religious matter. It is terribly personal. God, the lover, will not share his bride with anyone else.

God's anger and jealousy, expressed so often throughout the Old Testament, reflect his powerful love. Sin does not merely break God's law, it breaks his heart. He punishes to get his lover's attention. Yet even when she turns her back on him, he sticks with her. He is willing to suffer, in the hope that someday she will change. Hosea shows that God longs not to punish, but to love.

How to Read Hosea

Hosea is one of the most emotional books in the Bible, an outpouring of suffering love from God's heart. This shows in the writing, which jumps impulsively from one thought to the next. Read a chapter dramatically aloud, and you will get this sense. It is almost like listening in on a husband-and-wife fight.

The book divides into two parts. In the first three chapters, the prophet Hosea briefly describes his marriage to an adulterous woman and makes the connection to Israel's unfaithfulness to God. From chapter 4 onward this dramatic, personal beginning is not mentioned again. But it has set the stage. God's deep love, his disappointment and anger, and his determination to persevere with his unfaithful wife pour out in a series of vivid speeches.

For a historical perspective on Hosea's times, read from 2 Kings 14:23 to 17:41, noting that some sections describe Judah, the southern nation, while the rest relate to the deteriorating Israel Hosea knew. This history is summarized in "A Lineup of Rulers," pages 1417–1425. The prophet Amos spoke to the North at about the same time as Hosea, but from a noticeably different point of view. Amos concentrated on law and justice, with special concern for the poor, while Hosea concentrated on the broken relationship with God that led to this injustice. Together, these two prophets provide a three-dimensional view of Israel's problems.

Because Hosea is so emotional, he doesn't stop to explain a large number of images or biblical references. A Bible dictionary will help you understand the names and places you aren't familiar with.

3-TRACK READING PLAN

For an explanation and complete listing of the 3-track reading plan, turn to page 7.

TRACK 1: *Two-Week Courses on the Bible*
See page 7 for information on these courses.

TRACK 2: *An Overview of Hosea in 2 Days*
☐ Day 1. Read the Introduction to Hosea and chapters 2 and 3, which compare Hosea's marriage to Israel's relationship with God.
☐ Day 2. Read chapter 11, which shows God's powerful, competing emotions as he thinks of Israel.

Now turn to page 9 for your next Track 2 reading project.

TRACK 3: *All of Hosea in 10 Days*
After you have read through Hosea, turn to pages 10–14 for your next Track 3 reading project.

☐1   ☐2–3   ☐4   ☐5   ☐6–7   ☐8   ☐9   ☐10
☐11–12 ☐13–14

Hosea's Wife and Children

1 The word of the LORD which came to Hosea the son of Beeri, during the days of Uzziah, Jotham, Ahaz *and* Hezekiah, kings of Judah, and during the days of Jeroboam the son of Joash, king of Israel.

2 ¶ When the LORD first spoke through Hosea, the LORD said to Hosea, "Go, take to yourself a wife of harlotry and *have* children of harlotry; for the land commits flagrant harlotry, forsaking the LORD."

3 So he went and took Gomer the daughter of Diblaim, and she conceived and bore him a son.

4 And the LORD said to him, "Name him Jezreel; for yet a little while, and I will punish the house of Jehu for the bloodshed of Jezreel, and I will put an end to the kingdom of the house of Israel.

5 "On that day I will break the bow of Israel in the valley of Jezreel."

6 ¶ Then she conceived again and gave birth to a daughter. And the LORD said to him, "Name her *a*Lo-ruhamah, for I will no longer have compassion on the house of Israel, that I would ever forgive them.

7 "But I will have compassion on the house of Judah and deliver them by the LORD their God, and will not deliver them by bow, sword, battle, horses or horsemen."

8 ¶ When she had weaned Lo-ruhamah, she conceived and gave birth to a son.

9 And the LORD said, "Name him *b*Lo-ammi, for you are not My people and I am not your God."

10 ¶ Yet the number of the sons of Israel
Will be like the sand of the sea,
Which cannot be measured or
    numbered;
And in the place
Where it is said to them,
"You are not My people,"
It will be said to them,

---

a I.e. she has not obtained compassion   *b* I.e. not my people

"*You are* the sons of the living God."
11 And the sons of Judah and the sons of
  Israel will be gathered together,
  And they will appoint for themselves one
    leader,

1:4 Children's Strange Names

*At God's direction, Hosea named his three
children in a way that symbolized God's anger.
Their names show God's increasing judgment
against Israel's adultery: first comes
punishment, then a loss of love, finally total
divorce. The first name, Jezreel, refers to a
historical incident from 2 Kings 9–10. Jezreel
was the place where King Jehu slaughtered a
wicked king and all his associates (2 Kings
10:11). Hosea lived to see his prediction of
punishment on Jehu's house fulfilled, when the
last king in Jehu's line was murdered (2 Kings
15:8–12).*

*Punishment, however, was not the last word.
Jezreel has a double meaning—both to
"scatter" and to "sow." In verse 11 and in verses
22–23 of chapter 2, Jezreel takes on the
hopeful sense of planting new life. Hosea's
other two children's names are similarly turned
from curses to blessings. God's anger leads to
new life.*

And they will go up from the land,
For great will be the day of Jezreel.

Israel's Unfaithfulness Condemned

2 Say to your brothers, "[a]Ammi," and to your
  sisters, "[b]Ruhamah."
2 "Contend with your mother, contend,
  For she is not my wife, and I am not her
    husband;
  And let her put away her harlotry from
    her face
  And her adultery from between her
    breasts,
3 Or I will strip her naked
  And expose her as on the day when she
    was born.
  I will also make her like a wilderness,
  Make her like desert land
  And slay her with thirst.
4 "Also, I will have no compassion on her
    children,
  Because they are children of harlotry.
5 "For their mother has played the harlot;
  She who conceived them has acted
    shamefully.
  For she said, 'I will go after my lovers,
  Who give *me* my bread and my water,
  My wool and my flax, my oil and my
    drink.'

6 "Therefore, behold, I will hedge up her
    way with thorns,
  And I will build a wall against her so
    that she cannot find her paths.
7 "She will pursue her lovers, but she will
    not overtake them;
  And she will seek them, but will not find
    them.
  Then she will say, 'I will go back to my
    first husband,
  For it was better for me then than now!'
8 ¶ "For she does not know that it was I
    who gave her the grain, the new
    wine and the oil,
  And lavished on her silver and gold,
  Which they used for Baal.
9 "Therefore, I will take back My grain at
    harvest time
  And My new wine in its season.
  I will also take away My wool and My
    flax
  Given to cover her nakedness.
10 "And then I will uncover her lewdness
    In the sight of her lovers,
  And no one will rescue her out of My
    hand.
11 "I will also put an end to all her gaiety,
  Her feasts, her new moons, her sabbaths
  And all her festal assemblies.
12 "I will destroy her vines and fig trees,
  Of which she said, 'These are my wages
  Which my lovers have given me.'
  And I will make them a forest,
  And the beasts of the field will devour
    them.
13 "I will punish her for the days of the
    Baals
  When she used to offer sacrifices to them
  And adorn herself with her earrings and
    jewelry,
  And follow her lovers, so that she forgot
    Me," declares the LORD.

Restoration of Israel

14 ¶ "Therefore, behold, I will allure her,
  Bring her into the wilderness
  And speak kindly to her.
15 "Then I will give her her vineyards from
    there,
  And the valley of Achor as a door of
    hope.
  And she will sing there as in the days of
    her youth,
  As in the day when she came up from
    the land of Egypt.
16 "It will come about in that day," declares
    the LORD,
  "That you will call Me [c]Ishi
  And will no longer call Me [d]Baali.

---

[a] I.e. my people   [b] I.e. she has obtained compassion   [c] I.e. my husband   [d] I.e. my master, or my Baal

17 "For I will remove the names of the Baals
    from her mouth,
So that they will be mentioned by their
    names no more.
18 "In that day I will also make a covenant
    for them
With the beasts of the field,
The birds of the sky
And the creeping things of the ground.
And I will abolish the bow, the sword
    and war from the land,
And will make them lie down in safety.
19 "I will betroth you to Me forever;
Yes, I will betroth you to Me in
    righteousness and in justice,
In lovingkindness and in compassion,
20 And I will betroth you to Me in
    faithfulness.
Then you will know the LORD.

21 ¶ "It will come about in that day that I
    will respond," declares the LORD.
"I will respond to the heavens, and they
    will respond to the earth,
22 And the earth will respond to the grain,
    to the new wine and to the oil,
And they will respond to *a*Jezreel.
23 "I will sow her for Myself in the land.
I will also have compassion on her who
    had not obtained compassion,
And I will say to those who were not My
    people,
'You are My people!'
And they will say, '*You are* my God!' "

Hosea's Second Symbolic Marriage

3 Then the LORD said to me, "Go again, love a
woman *who* is loved by *her* husband, yet an
adulteress, even as the LORD loves the sons of
Israel, though they turn to other gods and love
raisin cakes."

3:1 Parable of Love

*No other prophet lived out an object lesson
with quite the same emotional force as Hosea
did. Gomer had sunk so low as to sell herself
into slavery, but Hosea purchased her back and
reclaimed her as his wife. That remarkable
deed, certainly the subject of his countrymen's
gossip, symbolized God's undying love for his
people. Though they had dragged his name in
the mud, still he welcomed them back.*

2 So I bought her for myself for fifteen *shekels*
of silver and a homer and a half of barley.
3 Then I said to her, "You shall stay with me
for many days. You shall not play the harlot, nor

---

shall you have a man; so I will also be toward
you."
4 For the sons of Israel will remain for many
days without king or prince, without sacrifice or
sacred pillar and without ephod or household
idols.
5 Afterward the sons of Israel will return and
seek the LORD their God and David their king; and
they will come trembling to the LORD and to His
goodness in the last days.

God's Controversy with Israel

4 Listen to the word of the LORD, O sons of
    Israel,
For the LORD has a case against the
    inhabitants of the land,
Because there is no faithfulness or
    kindness
Or knowledge of God in the land.
2 *There is* swearing, deception, murder,
    stealing and adultery.
They employ violence, so that bloodshed
    follows bloodshed.
3 Therefore the land mourns,
And everyone who lives in it languishes
Along with the beasts of the field and the
    birds of the sky,
And also the fish of the sea disappear.

4 ¶ Yet let no one find fault, and let none
    offer reproof;
For your people are like those who
    contend with the priest.
5 So you will stumble by day,
And the prophet also will stumble with
    you by night;
And I will destroy your mother.
6 My people are destroyed for lack of
    knowledge.
Because you have rejected knowledge,
I also will reject you from being My
    priest.
Since you have forgotten the law of your
    God,
I also will forget your children.

7 ¶ The more they multiplied, the more
    they sinned against Me;
I will change their glory into shame.
8 They feed on the sin of My people
And direct their desire toward their
    iniquity.
9 And it will be, like people, like priest;
So I will punish them for their ways
And repay them for their deeds.
10 They will eat, but not have enough;
They will play the harlot, but not
    increase,
Because they have stopped giving heed to
    the LORD.

a I.e. God sows

11 ¶ Harlotry, wine and new wine take away
   the understanding.
12 My people consult their wooden idol,
   and their *diviner's* wand informs
   them;

4:7 Poor Trade

*Early in its history, the Northern Kingdom of
Israel began appointing its own priests from
ineligible tribes (1 Kings 12:31). These priests
led the people in the worship of golden calves—
idols—instead of in the worship of the God of
Abraham and Moses. This verse has an echo in
Romans 1:23, where Paul blasts pagans who
exchange the glory of immortal God for mere
statues of birds, animals, and reptiles.*

For a spirit of harlotry has led *them*
   astray,
And they have played the harlot,
   departing from their God.
13 They offer sacrifices on the tops of the
   mountains
And burn incense on the hills,
Under oak, poplar and terebinth,
Because their shade is pleasant.
Therefore your daughters play the harlot
And your brides commit adultery.

4:13 Real Prostitution

*In each of the first nine chapters of his book,
Hosea describes Israel's sin as prostitution or
adultery. This is primarily symbolism meant to
emphasize God's deep, personal love for Israel
and his pain when the Israelites desert him to
go after other gods.*

*But prostitution has a literal meaning also.
The religions Israel pursued taught that human
sexuality was tied to agricultural fertility. To
encourage good crops, believers in these
religions practiced their human fertility. This
meant organized prostitution, done as part of
their worship experience.*

14 I will not punish your daughters when
   they play the harlot
Or your brides when they commit
   adultery,
For *the men* themselves go apart with
   harlots
And offer sacrifices with temple
   prostitutes;
So the people without understanding are
   ruined.
15 ¶ Though you, Israel, play the harlot,
Do not let Judah become guilty;

Also do not go to Gilgal,
Or go up to Beth-aven
And take the oath:
"As the LORD lives!"
16 Since Israel is stubborn
Like a stubborn heifer,
Can the LORD now pasture them
Like a lamb in a large field?
17 Ephraim is joined to idols;
Let him alone.
18 Their liquor gone,
They play the harlot continually;
Their rulers dearly love shame.
19 The wind wraps them in its wings,
And they will be ashamed because of
   their sacrifices.

The People's Apostasy Rebuked

5 Hear this, O priests!
   Give heed, O house of Israel!
   Listen, O house of the king!
   For the judgment applies to you,
   For you have been a snare at Mizpah
   And a net spread out on Tabor.
2 The revolters have gone deep in
   depravity,
   But I will chastise all of them.
3 I know Ephraim, and Israel is not hidden
   from Me;
   For now, O Ephraim, you have played
      the harlot,
   Israel has defiled itself.
4 Their deeds will not allow them
   To return to their God.
   For a spirit of harlotry is within them,
   And they do not know the LORD.
5 Moreover, the pride of Israel testifies
   against him,
   And Israel and Ephraim stumble in their
      iniquity;
   Judah also has stumbled with them.
6 They will go with their flocks and herds
   To seek the LORD, but they will not
      find *Him*;
   He has withdrawn from them.
7 They have dealt treacherously against the
   LORD,
   For they have borne illegitimate children.
   Now the new moon will devour them
      with their land.

8 ¶ Blow the horn in Gibeah,
   The trumpet in Ramah.
   Sound an alarm at Beth-aven:
   "Behind you, Benjamin!"
9 Ephraim will become a desolation in the
   day of rebuke;
   Among the tribes of Israel I declare what
      is sure.
10 The princes of Judah have become like
   those who move a boundary;

On them I will pour out My wrath like
water.
11 Ephraim is oppressed, crushed in
judgment,
Because he was determined to follow
man's command.
12 Therefore I am like a moth to Ephraim
And like rottenness to the house of
Judah.
13 When Ephraim saw his sickness,
And Judah his wound,
Then Ephraim went to Assyria
And sent to King Jareb.
But he is unable to heal you,
Or to cure you of your wound.
14 For I *will be* like a lion to Ephraim
And like a young lion to the house of
Judah.
I, even I, will tear to pieces and go away,
I will carry away, and there will be none
to deliver.
15 I will go away *and* return to My place
Until they acknowledge their guilt and
seek My face;
In their affliction they will earnestly
seek Me.

The Response to God's Rebuke

6 "Come, let us return to the LORD.
For He has torn *us,* but He will heal us;
He has wounded *us,* but He will
bandage us.
2 "He will revive us after two days;
He will raise us up on the third day,
That we may live before Him.
3 "So let us know, let us press on to know
the LORD.
His going forth is as certain as the dawn;
And He will come to us like the rain,
Like the spring rain watering the earth."

4 ¶ What shall I do with you, O Ephraim?
What shall I do with you, O Judah?
For your loyalty is like a morning cloud
And like the dew which goes away early.
5 Therefore I have hewn *them* in pieces by
the prophets;
I have slain them by the words of My
mouth;
And the judgments on you are *like* the
light that goes forth.
6 For I delight in loyalty rather than
sacrifice,
And in the knowledge of God rather
than burnt offerings.
7 But like Adam they have transgressed the
covenant;
There they have dealt treacherously
against Me.
8 Gilead is a city of wrongdoers,
Tracked with bloody *footprints.*
9 And as raiders wait for a man,

So a band of priests murder on the way
to Shechem;
Surely they have committed crime.
10 In the house of Israel I have seen a
horrible thing;
Ephraim's harlotry is there, Israel has
defiled itself.
11 Also, O Judah, there is a harvest
appointed for you,
When I restore the fortunes of My
people.

Ephraim's Iniquity

7 When I would heal Israel,
The iniquity of Ephraim is uncovered,
And the evil deeds of Samaria,
For they deal falsely;
The thief enters in,
Bandits raid outside,
2 And they do not consider in their hearts
That I remember all their wickedness.
Now their deeds are all around them;
They are before My face.
3 With their wickedness they make the
king glad,
And the princes with their lies.
4 They are all adulterers,
Like an oven heated by the baker
Who ceases to stir up *the fire*
From the kneading of the dough until it
is leavened.

7:4 Smoldering Passion

*In parts of the Middle East, ovens are made of
clay and shaped like a large cone or beehive.
The baker builds a fire inside and tends it until
the clay gets very hot. Then, fire and wood ash
can be pulled out and the fresh dough placed
inside. It rises due to the heat contained inside
the oven, which stays hot long after the fire has
been removed. Such was Israel's lust for other
gods: It kept on smoldering, like a self-fueling
oven (verse 6).*

5 On the day of our king, the princes
became sick with the heat of wine;
He stretched out his hand with scoffers,
6 For their hearts are like an oven
As they approach their plotting;
Their anger smolders all night,
In the morning it burns like a flaming
fire.
7 All of them are hot like an oven,
And they consume their rulers;
All their kings have fallen.
None of them calls on Me.

8 ¶ Ephraim mixes himself with the
nations;

Ephraim has become a cake not turned.
9 Strangers devour his strength,
Yet he does not know *it*;
Gray hairs also are sprinkled on him,
Yet he does not know *it*.
10 Though the pride of Israel testifies
against him,
Yet they have not returned to the LORD
their God,
Nor have they sought Him, for all this.
11 So Ephraim has become like a silly dove,
without sense;
They call to Egypt, they go to Assyria.
12 When they go, I will spread My net over
them;
I will bring them down like the birds of
the sky.
I will chastise them in accordance with
the proclamation to their assembly.
13 Woe to them, for they have strayed
from Me!
Destruction is theirs, for they have
rebelled against Me!
I would redeem them, but they speak lies
against Me.
14 And they do not cry to Me from their
heart
When they wail on their beds;
For the sake of grain and new wine they
assemble themselves,
They turn away from Me.
15 Although I trained *and* strengthened
their arms,
Yet they devise evil against Me.
16 They turn, *but* not upward,
They are like a deceitful bow;
Their princes will fall by the sword
Because of the insolence of their tongue.
This *will be* their derision in the land of
Egypt.

Israel Reaps the Whirlwind

8 *Put* the trumpet to your lips!
Like an eagle *the enemy comes* against the
house of the LORD,
Because they have transgressed My
covenant
And rebelled against My law.
2 They cry out to Me,
"My God, we of Israel know You!"
3 Israel has rejected the good;
The enemy will pursue him.
4 They have set up kings, but not by Me;
They have appointed princes, but I did
not know *it*.
With their silver and gold they have
made idols for themselves,
That they might be cut off.
5 He has rejected your calf, O Samaria,
saying,
"My anger burns against them!"

How long will they be incapable of
innocence?
6 For from Israel is even this!
A craftsman made it, so it is not God;
Surely the calf of Samaria will be broken
to pieces.
7 For they sow the wind
And they reap the whirlwind.
The standing grain has no heads;
It yields no grain.
Should it yield, strangers would swallow
it up.

8 ¶ Israel is swallowed up;
They are now among the nations
Like a vessel in which no one delights.
9 For they have gone up to Assyria,
Like a wild donkey all alone;
Ephraim has hired lovers.
10 Even though they hire *allies* among the
nations,
Now I will gather them up;
And they will begin to diminish
Because of the burden of the king of
princes.
11 ¶ Since Ephraim has multiplied altars for
sin,
They have become altars of sinning for
him.

8:11 How to Be Religious Without Pleasing God

The Israelites didn't think they were rejecting God. In fact, they became increasingly pious. (See 6:1–3; 8:2,11,13; and 10:1 for their expressions of faith.) But they wanted to worship on their terms, not God's. While their sacrifices to God increased, they kept on worshiping idols as well.

12 Though I wrote for him ten thousand
precepts of My law,
They are regarded as a strange thing.
13 As for My sacrificial gifts,
They sacrifice the flesh and eat *it,*
But the LORD has taken no delight in
them.
Now He will remember their iniquity,
And punish *them* for their sins;
They will return to Egypt.
14 For Israel has forgotten his Maker and
built palaces;
And Judah has multiplied fortified cities,
But I will send a fire on its cities that it
may consume its palatial dwellings.

Ephraim Punished

9 Do not rejoice, O Israel, with exultation
like the nations!

For you have played the harlot, forsaking
your God.
You have loved *harlots'* earnings on
every threshing floor.
2 Threshing floor and wine press will not
feed them,
And the new wine will fail them.
3 They will not remain in the LORD's land,
But Ephraim will return to Egypt,
And in Assyria they will eat unclean *food.*
4 They will not pour out drink offerings of
wine to the LORD,
Their sacrifices will not please Him.
Their bread will be like mourners' bread;
All who eat of it will be defiled,
For their bread will be for themselves
alone;
It will not enter the house of the LORD.
5 What will you do on the day of the
appointed festival
And on the day of the feast of the LORD?
6 For behold, they will go because of
destruction;
Egypt will gather them up, Memphis will
bury them.
Weeds will take over their treasures of
silver;
Thorns *will be* in their tents.

7 ¶ The days of punishment have come,
The days of retribution have come;
Let Israel know *this!*
The prophet is a fool,
The inspired man is demented,
Because of the grossness of your iniquity,
And *because* your hostility is *so* great.
8 Ephraim *was* a watchman with my God,
a prophet;
Yet the snare of a bird catcher is in all
his ways,
And there is *only* hostility in the house of
his God.
9 They have gone deep in depravity
As in the days of Gibeah;
He will remember their iniquity,
He will punish their sins.

10 ¶ I found Israel like grapes in the
wilderness;
I saw your forefathers as the earliest fruit
on the fig tree in its first *season.*
But they came to Baal-peor and devoted
themselves to [a]shame,
And they became as detestable as that
which they loved.
11 As for Ephraim, their glory will fly away
like a bird—
No birth, no pregnancy and no
conception!
12 Though they bring up their children,

[a] I.e. Baal

Yet I will bereave them until not a man
is left.
Yes, woe to them indeed when I depart
from them!

9:9 Two Instances of Evil

*The "days of Gibeah" evidently refers to the
vicious murder of a woman, told in Judges
19–21. This horrifying incident was a version
of Sodom and Gomorrah right in Israel.
Another incident (verse 10), equally bad in its
own way, occurred at Baal of Peor (see
Numbers 25:1–3). Israelite men en route to the
promised land slept with Moabite women and
worshiped their gods. From both these
incidents, Hosea proves that sin is nothing new
to Israel.*

13 Ephraim, as I have seen,
Is planted in a pleasant meadow like
Tyre;
But Ephraim will bring out his children
for slaughter.
14 Give them, O LORD—what will You give?
Give them a miscarrying womb and dry
breasts.

15 ¶ All their evil is at Gilgal;
Indeed, I came to hate them there!
Because of the wickedness of their deeds
I will drive them out of My house!
I will love them no more;
All their princes are rebels.
16 Ephraim is stricken, their root is
dried up,
They will bear no fruit.
Even though they bear children,
I will slay the precious ones of their
womb.
17 My God will cast them away
Because they have not listened to Him;
And they will be wanderers among the
nations.

Retribution for Israel's Sin

10 Israel is a luxuriant vine;
He produces fruit for himself.
The more his fruit,
The more altars he made;
The richer his land,
The better he made the *sacred* pillars.
2 Their heart is faithless;
Now they must bear their guilt.
The LORD will break down their altars
And destroy their *sacred* pillars.

3 ¶ Surely now they will say, "We have no
king,

For we do not revere the LORD.
As for the king, what can he do for us?"

4 They speak *mere* words,
With worthless oaths they make
covenants;
And judgment sprouts like poisonous
weeds in the furrows of the field.

5 The inhabitants of Samaria will fear
For the calf of Beth-aven.
Indeed, its people will mourn for it,
And its idolatrous priests will cry out
over it,
Over its glory, since it has departed
from it.

10:5 The New Golden Calf

Beth-aven ("house of wickedness") is a sarcastic reference to Bethel ("house of God"), which is mentioned more times in the Bible than any other city except Jerusalem. When Israel split into North and South, the northern king, Jeroboam I, made Bethel the chief religious sanctuary, to replace Jerusalem. There he put up a golden calf for people to worship (1 Kings 12:26–30). Mixing worship of the one true God with the idol worship of Baal was, according to Hosea, the root of Israel's trouble.

6 The thing itself will be carried to Assyria
As tribute to King Jareb;
Ephraim will be seized with shame
And Israel will be ashamed of its own
counsel.

7 Samaria will be cut off *with* her king
Like a stick on the surface of the water.

8 Also the high places of Aven, the sin of
Israel, will be destroyed;
Thorn and thistle will grow on their
altars;
Then they will say to the mountains,
"Cover us!" And to the hills, "Fall on us!"

9 From the days of Gibeah you have
sinned, O Israel;
There they stand!
Will not the battle against the sons of
iniquity overtake them in Gibeah?

10 When it is My desire, I will chastise
them;
And the peoples will be gathered against
them
When they are bound for their double
guilt.

11 ¶ Ephraim is a trained heifer that loves to
thresh,
But I will come over her fair neck *with a
yoke*;
I will harness Ephraim,

Judah will plow, Jacob will harrow for
himself.

12 Sow with a view to righteousness,
Reap in accordance with kindness;
Break up your fallow ground,
For it is time to seek the LORD
Until He comes to rain righteousness on
you.

13 You have plowed wickedness, you have
reaped injustice,
You have eaten the fruit of lies.
Because you have trusted in your way, in
your numerous warriors,

14 Therefore a tumult will arise among your
people,
And all your fortresses will be destroyed,
As Shalman destroyed Beth-arbel on the
day of battle,
When mothers were dashed in pieces
with *their* children.

15 Thus it will be done to you at Bethel
because of your great wickedness.
At dawn the king of Israel will be
completely cut off.

God Yearns over His People

11 When Israel *was* a youth I loved him,
And out of Egypt I called My son.

11:1 Rebel Son

God has already illustrated his unquenchable love for Israel through the real-life parable of Hosea and his unfaithful wife. Now he introduces yet another picture: a rebellious son. According to the laws of Deuteronomy, a rebel son could be sentenced to death by stoning (Deuteronomy 21:18–21). But God cannot make himself carry out that sentence (verses 8–9). He gives his people one more chance.

2 The more they called them,
The more they went from them;
They kept sacrificing to the Baals
And burning incense to idols.

3 Yet it is I who taught Ephraim to walk,
I took them in My arms;
But they did not know that I healed
them.

4 I led them with cords of a man, with
bonds of love,
And I became to them as one who lifts
the yoke from their jaws;
And I bent down *and* fed them.

5 ¶ They will not return to the land of
Egypt;
But Assyria—he will be their king
Because they refused to return *to Me.*

6 The sword will whirl against their cities,

And will demolish their gate bars
And consume *them* because of their
counsels.
7 So My people are bent on turning
from Me.
Though they call them to *the One* on
high,
None at all exalts *Him.*

8 ¶ How can I give you up, O Ephraim?
How can I surrender you, O Israel?
How can I make you like Admah?
How can I treat you like Zeboiim?
My heart is turned over within Me,
All My compassions are kindled.
9 I will not execute My fierce anger;
I will not destroy Ephraim again.
For I am God and not man, the Holy
One in your midst,
And I will not come in wrath.
10 They will walk after the LORD,
He will roar like a lion;
Indeed He will roar
And *His* sons will come trembling from
the west.
11 They will come trembling like birds from
Egypt
And like doves from the land of Assyria;
And I will settle them in their houses,
declares the LORD.

12 ¶ Ephraim surrounds Me with lies
And the house of Israel with deceit;
Judah is also unruly against God,
Even against the Holy One who is
faithful.

Ephraim Reminded

12 Ephraim feeds on wind,
And pursues the east wind continually;
He multiplies lies and violence.
Moreover, he makes a covenant with
Assyria,
And oil is carried to Egypt.
2 The LORD also has a dispute with Judah,
And will punish Jacob according to his
ways;
He will repay him according to his deeds.
3 In the womb he took his brother by the
heel,
And in his maturity he contended with
God.
4 Yes, he wrestled with the angel and
prevailed;
He wept and sought His favor.
He found Him at Bethel
And there He spoke with us,
5 Even the LORD, the God of hosts,
The LORD is His name.
6 Therefore, return to your God,
Observe kindness and justice,
And wait for your God continually.

7 A merchant, in whose hands are false
balances,
He loves to oppress.
8 And Ephraim said, "Surely I have
become rich,

12:2–5 Jacob, a Man and a Country

"Israel" was a nation named after a man—a man also known as Jacob, whose story is told principally in Genesis 25–35. He was greedy and grasping, and he went into exile for it. Yet he had another side: an eagerness to meet God and be blessed by him, culminating in his nighttime "wrestling with God" (Genesis 32). Though Jacob went into exile, as would Israel, he came back with God's blessing on his future. So, Hosea suggests, could the nation that carried his name.

I have found wealth for myself;
In all my labors they will find in me
No iniquity, which *would be* sin."
9 But I *have been* the LORD your God since
the land of Egypt;
I will make you live in tents again,
As in the days of the appointed festival.
10 I have also spoken to the prophets,
And I gave numerous visions,
And through the prophets I gave
parables.
11 Is there iniquity *in* Gilead?
Surely they are worthless.
In Gilgal they sacrifice bulls,
Yes, their altars are like the stone heaps
Beside the furrows of the field.

12 ¶ Now Jacob fled to the land of Aram,
And Israel worked for a wife,
And for a wife he kept *sheep.*
13 But by a prophet the LORD brought Israel
from Egypt,
And by a prophet he was kept.
14 Ephraim has provoked to bitter anger;
So his Lord will leave his bloodguilt
on him
And bring back his reproach to him.

Ephraim's Idolatry

13 When Ephraim spoke, *there was*
trembling.
He exalted himself in Israel,
But through Baal he did wrong and died.
2 And now they sin more and more,
And make for themselves molten images,
Idols skillfully made from their silver,
All of them the work of craftsmen.
They say of them, "Let the men who
sacrifice kiss the calves!"
3 Therefore they will be like the morning
cloud

And like dew which soon disappears,
Like chaff which is blown away from the
    threshing floor
And like smoke from a chimney.

13:3 As Reliable as the Wind

*The fruitlessness of Israel's deeds is beautifully
expressed in the metaphor of wind: They feed
on it, they pursue it all day (12:1), they sow it,
and they reap the whirlwind (8:7). Their love is
like the morning cloud, or dew (6:4), and their
lives will be as lasting as the early dew or as
chaff or as smoke from a chimney (13:3).*

4 ¶ Yet I *have been* the LORD your God
    Since the land of Egypt;
    And you were not to know any god
        except Me,
    For there is no savior besides Me.
5 I cared for you in the wilderness,
    In the land of drought.
6 As *they had* their pasture, they became
        satisfied,
    And being satisfied, their heart became
        proud;
    Therefore they forgot Me.
7 So I will be like a lion to them;
    Like a leopard I will lie in wait by the
        wayside.
8 I will encounter them like a bear robbed
        of her cubs,
    And I will tear open their chests;
    There I will also devour them like a
        lioness,
    As a wild beast would tear them.

9 ¶ *It is* your destruction, O Israel,
    That *you are* against Me, against your
        help.
10 Where now is your king
    That he may save you in all your cities,
    And your judges of whom you requested,
    "Give me a king and princes"?
11 I gave you a king in My anger
    And took him away in My wrath.

12 ¶ The iniquity of Ephraim is bound up;
    His sin is stored up.
13 The pains of childbirth come upon him;
    He is not a wise son,
    For it is not the time that he should
        delay at the opening of the womb.
14 Shall I ransom them from the power of
        Sheol?
    Shall I redeem them from death?
    O Death, where are your thorns?
    O Sheol, where is your sting?
    Compassion will be hidden from My
        sight.

15 ¶ Though he flourishes among the reeds,
    An east wind will come,
    The wind of the LORD coming up from
        the wilderness;
    And his fountain will become dry
    And his spring will be dried up;
    It will plunder *his* treasury of every
        precious article.
16 Samaria will be held guilty,
    For she has rebelled against her God.
    They will fall by the sword,
    Their little ones will be dashed in pieces,
    And their pregnant women will be ripped
        open.

Israel's Future Blessing

14 Return, O Israel, to the LORD your God,
    For you have stumbled because of your
        iniquity.
2 Take words with you and return to the
        LORD.
    Say to Him, "Take away all iniquity
    And receive *us* graciously,
    That we may present the fruit of our lips.
3 "Assyria will not save us,
    We will not ride on horses;
    Nor will we say again, 'Our god,'
    To the work of our hands;
    For in You the orphan finds mercy."

4 ¶ I will heal their apostasy,
    I will love them freely,
    For My anger has turned away from
        them.
5 I will be like the dew to Israel;
    He will blossom like the lily,
    And he will take root like *the cedars of*
        Lebanon.

14:5 New Hope

*In its conclusion the book of Hosea, so full of
torment, dissolves into a series of serene
images of what Israel can become. God
compares the nation to a lily (beauty), a cedar
(strength), an olive tree (value), a fragrant tree
(delight), grain (abundance), a grapevine
(fruitfulness). Thus a book dominated by
images of unfaithfulness—an adulterous wife, a
rebellious son—ends with the firm promise of
restoration.*

6 His shoots will sprout,
    And his beauty will be like the olive tree
    And his fragrance like *the cedars of*
        Lebanon.
7 Those who live in his shadow
    Will again raise grain,
    And they will blossom like the vine.

His renown *will be* like the wine of
Lebanon.

8 ¶ O Ephraim, what more have I to do
with idols?
It is I who answer and look after you.
I am like a luxuriant cypress;
From Me comes your fruit.

9 ¶ Whoever is wise, let him understand
these things;
Whoever is discerning, let him know
them.
For the ways of the LORD are right,
And the righteous will walk in them,
But transgressors will stumble in
them.

JOEL

The Meaning of a Natural Disaster
What's behind a devastating locust plague?

> Before them the earth quakes, the heavens tremble, the sun and the moon grow dark and the stars lose their brightness. 2:10

HEIR NUMBER WAS ASTOUNDING; THE whole face of the mountain was black with them. On they came like a living deluge. We dug trenches, and kindled fires, and beat and burned to death 'heaps upon heaps'; but the effort was utterly useless. Wave after wave rolled up the mountainside and poured over rocks, walls, ditches and hedges—those behind covering up and bridging over the masses already killed. It was perfectly appalling to watch this animated river as it flowed up the road and ascended the hill above my house. For four days they continued to pass on toward the east . . . .'

Eyewitness W. M. Thomson is describing a locust plague. Descriptions of the aftermath sound just as awful. When locusts have passed, the terrain looks as though it has been swept by a scorching fire.

Why Have I Lived?

Many awestruck observers have written accounts of locust swarms, but none more graphically than the prophet Joel. In striking, polished imagery he described the devastation. His people faced starvation. Joel drew a verbal portrait of grief and fear.

Natural disasters provoke questions. Why did God allow this disaster to happen? Why have I lived and others died? Is there a lesson here? For Joel, a plague of locusts led to deep insights into God's universal plan.

Joel had no doubt that God was behind the plague. In fact, he pictured God leading the locusts like an army into battle (2:11). They represented "the day of the LORD," a judgment on Israel. Unlike many of the other prophets, Joel did not devote time to an analysis of Israel's failings. He concentrated, instead, on a cure.

Joel urged the priests to call a nationwide day of prayer and fasting to lead the people back to God. Then God would roll back the damage done by the locusts, and more: "You will have plenty to eat and be satisfied and praise the name of the LORD your God, who has dealt wondrously with you" (2:26). They would emerge from the experience with new, durable confidence in God's love. So it has often proved for God's people: A disaster has pressed them to a deeper relationship with him.

God's Bigger Plans

Though the locust plague was by far the worst Joel had ever heard of (1:2–3), no historical record of this particular invasion has endured, other than the one Joel left us. The truth is, even the worst natural disasters fade from memory. Joel wanted the disaster to turn people's attention toward something more lasting—toward an eternal God.

Joel wanted God's people to believe that God controlled the locusts, and, even more important, that God shaped the entire course of history to his plan. As terribly as the locusts had destroyed, and as wonderfully as God had rolled back their destruction, these events only foreshadowed far more terrible and wonderful things. Joel saw that God's Spirit would transform his people into those who love him constantly, not just when a disaster catches their attention. After a time of terrible judgment, God would create a renewed, secure city for his people, in which he himself would live.

How to Read Joel

Joel breaks naturally into two parts. Up to 2:28, it talks about a locust invasion and the response of God's people to such a natural disaster. From that verse on, however, Joel's view rises above the local situation and deals with the far-off future.

Joel rarely refers to unfamiliar people, places, or events, so you can read it fairly easily without using any outside reference like a Bible dictionary. The challenge is to connect his understanding of a natural disaster—a locust plague—with his vision of the future.

The Bible often refers to "the day of the LORD" as the time when God will completely take charge of our world. But Joel seems to see "the day of the LORD" partly revealed in the disasters of his day. As you read, try to see the similarities Joel draws between the locust invasion and the final consummation of history. Ask yourself: How do I respond to disaster? How would Joel want me to respond?

3-TRACK READING PLAN

For an explanation and complete listing of the 3-track reading plan, turn to page 7.

TRACK 1: *Two-Week Courses on the Bible*
See page 7 for information on these courses.

TRACK 2: *An Overview of Joel in 1 Day*
☐ Day 1. Read the Introduction to Joel and chapter 2, which describes the locust plague and its effect on the people's relationship with God.

Now turn to page 9 for your next Track 2 reading project.

TRACK 3: *All of Joel in 3 Days*
After you have read through Joel, turn to pages 10–14 for your next Track 3 reading project.
☐1   ☐2   ☐3

The Devastation of Locusts

1 The word of the LORD that came to Joel, the son of Pethuel:

2 Hear this, O elders,
And listen, all inhabitants of the land.
Has *anything like* this happened in your days
Or in your fathers' days?
3 Tell your sons about it,
And *let* your sons *tell* their sons,
And their sons the next generation.

4 ¶ What the gnawing locust has left, the swarming locust has eaten;
And what the swarming locust has left, the creeping locust has eaten;
And what the creeping locust has left, the stripping locust has eaten.
5 Awake, drunkards, and weep;
And wail, all you wine drinkers,
On account of the sweet wine
That is cut off from your mouth.
6 For a nation has invaded my land,
Mighty and without number;
Its teeth are the teeth of a lion,
And it has the fangs of a lioness.
7 It has made my vine a waste
And my fig tree splinters.

It has stripped them bare and cast *them* away;
Their branches have become white.

8 ¶ Wail like a virgin girded with sackcloth
For the bridegroom of her youth.

1:4 Doomsday

Nowadays we tend to think of doomsday in terms of nuclear holocaust. But until recent times the most powerful weapons in the world belonged to nature. Earthquakes, floods, and plagues of illness caused far more destruction than arrows, spears, and swords. Natural disasters were frightening and unpredictable: A plague of locusts, for example, could wipe out an entire food supply overnight.

9 The grain offering and the drink offering are cut off
From the house of the LORD.
The priests mourn,
The ministers of the LORD.
10 The field is ruined,
The land mourns;

For the grain is ruined,
The new wine dries up,
Fresh oil fails.
11 Be ashamed, O farmers,
Wail, O vinedressers,
For the wheat and the barley;
Because the harvest of the field is
destroyed.
12 The vine dries up
And the fig tree fails;
The pomegranate, the palm also, and the
apple tree,
All the trees of the field dry up.
Indeed, rejoicing dries up
From the sons of men.

13 ¶ Gird yourselves *with sackcloth*
And lament, O priests;
Wail, O ministers of the altar!
Come, spend the night in sackcloth
O ministers of my God,
For the grain offering and the drink
offering
Are withheld from the house of your
God.

Starvation and Drought

14 Consecrate a fast,
Proclaim a solemn assembly;
Gather the elders
And all the inhabitants of the land
To the house of the LORD your God,
And cry out to the LORD.
15 Alas for the day!
For the day of the LORD is near,
And it will come as destruction from the
Almighty.
16 Has not food been cut off before our
eyes,
Gladness and joy from the house of our
God?
17 The seeds shrivel under their clods;
The storehouses are desolate,
The barns are torn down,
For the grain is dried up.
18 How the beasts groan!
The herds of cattle wander aimlessly
Because there is no pasture for them;
Even the flocks of sheep suffer.

1:18 Total Devastation

No wine for the drunkards, no husbands for young brides, no crops for the farmers, no offerings for the priests—the disaster was affecting every part of society. Cattle groaned, cattle wandered in starvation. People had nowhere to turn but God, concluded Joel. So why didn't they?

19 To You, O LORD, I cry;
For fire has devoured the pastures of the
wilderness
And the flame has burned up all the
trees of the field.
20 Even the beasts of the field pant for You;
For the water brooks are dried up
And fire has devoured the pastures of the
wilderness.

The Terrible Visitation

2 Blow a trumpet in Zion,
And sound an alarm on My holy
mountain!
Let all the inhabitants of the land
tremble,
For the day of the LORD is coming;
Surely it is near,
2 A day of darkness and gloom,
A day of clouds and thick darkness.
As the dawn is spread over the
mountains,
So there is a great and mighty people;
There has never been *anything* like it,
Nor will there be again after it
To the years of many generations.
3 A fire consumes before them
And behind them a flame burns.
The land is like the garden of Eden
before them
But a desolate wilderness behind them,
And nothing at all escapes them.
4 Their appearance is like the appearance
of horses;
And like war horses, so they run.
5 With a noise as of chariots
They leap on the tops of the mountains,
Like the crackling of a flame of fire
consuming the stubble,
Like a mighty people arranged for
battle.
6 Before them the people are in anguish;
All faces turn pale.
7 They run like mighty men,
They climb the wall like soldiers;
And they each march in line,
Nor do they deviate from their paths.
8 They do not crowd each other,
They march everyone in his path;
When they burst through the defenses,
They do not break ranks.
9 They rush on the city,
They run on the wall;
They climb into the houses,
They enter through the windows like a
thief.
10 Before them the earth quakes,
The heavens tremble,
The sun and the moon grow dark
And the stars lose their brightness.

11 The LORD utters His voice before His
army;
Surely His camp is very great,
For strong is he who carries out His
word.
The day of the LORD is indeed great and
very awesome,
And who can endure it?
12 "Yet even now," declares the LORD,
"Return to Me with all your heart,
And with fasting, weeping and mourning;
13 And rend your heart and not your
garments."
Now return to the LORD your God,
For He is gracious and compassionate,
Slow to anger, abounding in
lovingkindness
And relenting of evil.

2:13 Torn Hearts

*In the Old Testament, men and women tore
their robes as a sign of sorrow and mourning.
(Some Middle Easterners do so still.) Jacob,
Moses, Joshua, Elijah, David, and Job all tore
their clothes as an expression of grief or
anguish. In Joel's day, however, God looked for
change on the inside, not just another outward
show of remorse. He sought broken hearts, not
torn garments.*

14 Who knows whether He will *not* turn
and relent
And leave a blessing behind Him,
Even a grain offering and a drink
offering
For the LORD your God?
15 Blow a trumpet in Zion,
Consecrate a fast, proclaim a solemn
assembly,
16 Gather the people, sanctify the
congregation,
Assemble the elders,
Gather the children and the nursing
infants.
Let the bridegroom come out of his
room
And the bride out of her *bridal* chamber.
17 Let the priests, the LORD's ministers,
Weep between the porch and the altar,
And let them say, "Spare Your people,
O LORD,
And do not make Your inheritance a
reproach,
A byword among the nations.
Why should they among the peoples
say,
'Where is their God?' "

Deliverance Promised

18 ¶ Then the LORD will be zealous for His
land
And will have pity on His people.
19 The LORD will answer and say to His
people,
"Behold, I am going to send you grain,
new wine and oil,
And you will be satisfied *in full* with
them;
And I will never again make you a
reproach among the nations.
20 "But I will remove the northern *army* far
from you,
And I will drive it into a parched and
desolate land,
And its vanguard into the eastern sea,
And its rear guard into the western sea.
And its stench will arise and its foul
smell will come up,
For it has done great things."

21 ¶ Do not fear, O land, rejoice and be
glad,
For the LORD has done great things.
22 Do not fear, beasts of the field,
For the pastures of the wilderness have
turned green,
For the tree has borne its fruit,
The fig tree and the vine have yielded in
full.
23 So rejoice, O sons of Zion,
And be glad in the LORD your God;
For He has given you *a*the early rain for
your vindication.
And He has poured down for you the
rain,
The *b*early and *c*latter rain as before.
24 The threshing floors will be full of grain,
And the vats will overflow with the new
wine and oil.
25 "Then I will make up to you for the years
That the swarming locust has eaten,
The creeping locust, the stripping locust
and the gnawing locust,
My great army which I sent among you.
26 "You will have plenty to eat and be
satisfied
And praise the name of the LORD your
God,
Who has dealt wondrously with you;
Then My people will never be put to
shame.
27 "Thus you will know that I am in the
midst of Israel,
And that I am the LORD your God,
And there is no other;
And My people will never be put to
shame.

---

a I.e. autumn; or possibly *the teacher for righteousness*   *b* I.e. autumn   *c* I.e. spring

The Promise of the Spirit

28 ¶ "It will come about after this
   That I will pour out My Spirit on all
      mankind;
   And your sons and daughters will
      prophesy,
   Your old men will dream dreams,
   Your young men will see visions.
29 "Even on the male and female servants
   I will pour out My Spirit in those days.

2:29 The Spirit Poured Out

This prophecy was quoted by Peter on the day of Pentecost (Acts 2:17–21). He said it had been fulfilled when the Holy Spirit came on Jesus' disciples. Paul also quoted verse 32 in Romans 10:12–13, making the point that God would respond to Jews and non-Jews without distinction.

The Day of the LORD

30 "I will display wonders in the sky and on
      the earth,
   Blood, fire and columns of smoke.
31 "The sun will be turned into darkness
   And the moon into blood
   Before the great and awesome day of the
      LORD comes.
32 "And it will come about that whoever calls
      on the name of the LORD
   Will be delivered;
   For on Mount Zion and in Jerusalem
   There will be those who escape,
   As the LORD has said,
   Even among the survivors whom the
      LORD calls.

The Nations Will Be Judged

3 "For behold, in those days and at that
      time,
   When I restore the fortunes of Judah and
      Jerusalem,
2 I will gather all the nations
   And bring them down to the valley of
      Jehoshaphat.
   Then I will enter into judgment with
      them there
   On behalf of My people and My
      inheritance, Israel,
   Whom they have scattered among the
      nations;
   And they have divided up My land.
3 "They have also cast lots for My people,
   Traded a boy for a harlot
   And sold a girl for wine that they may
      drink.
4 "Moreover, what are you to Me, O Tyre, Si-
don and all the regions of Philistia? Are you ren-

dering Me a recompense? But if you do recompense Me, swiftly and speedily I will return your
recompense on your head.
5 "Since you have taken My silver and My
gold, brought My precious treasures to your temples,

3:3 Gambling Prizes

The Babylonians who invaded Judah fulfilled this prophecy literally: They seized captives as part of the spoils of war, divided them up by casting lots, then traded them for prostitutes and wine. In this section, God promises vengeance on such war crimes.

6 and sold the sons of Judah and Jerusalem to
the Greeks in order to remove them far from their
territory,
7 behold, I am going to arouse them from the
place where you have sold them, and return your
recompense on your head.
8 "Also I will sell your sons and your daughters
into the hand of the sons of Judah, and they will
sell them to the Sabeans, to a distant nation," for
the LORD has spoken.
9 ¶ Proclaim this among the nations:
   Prepare a war; rouse the mighty men!
   Let all the soldiers draw near, let them
      come up!
10 Beat your plowshares into swords
   And your pruning hooks into spears;
   Let the weak say, "I am a mighty man."
11 Hasten and come, all you surrounding
      nations,
   And gather yourselves there.
   Bring down, O LORD, Your mighty ones.
12 Let the nations be aroused
   And come up to the valley of
      Jehoshaphat,
   For there I will sit to judge
   All the surrounding nations.
13 Put in the sickle, for the harvest is ripe.
   Come, tread, for the wine press is full;
   The vats overflow, for their wickedness is
      great.
14 Multitudes, multitudes in the valley of
      decision!
   For the day of the LORD is near in the
      valley of decision.
15 The sun and moon grow dark
   And the stars lose their brightness.
16 The LORD roars from Zion
   And utters His voice from Jerusalem,
   And the heavens and the earth tremble.
   But the LORD is a refuge for His people
   And a stronghold to the sons of Israel.
17 Then you will know that I am the LORD
      your God,
   Dwelling in Zion, My holy mountain.

So Jerusalem will be holy,
And strangers will pass through it no
more.

Judah Will Be Blessed

18 ¶ And in that day
The mountains will drip with sweet
wine,
And the hills will flow with milk,
And all the brooks of Judah will flow
with water;
And a spring will go out from the house
of the LORD

To water the valley of Shittim.
19 Egypt will become a waste,
And Edom will become a desolate
wilderness,
Because of the violence done to the sons
of Judah,
In whose land they have shed innocent
blood.
20 But Judah will be inhabited forever
And Jerusalem for all generations.
21 And I will avenge their blood which I
have not avenged,
For the LORD dwells in Zion.

AMOS

Justice!

A simple farmer takes on a materialistic nation

> "But let justice roll down like waters and righteousness like an ever-flowing stream." 5:24

BUSINESS HAD NEVER BEEN BETTER. For the first time in generations, Israel faced no military threat. Since they controlled the crucial trade routes, merchants piled up big profits. Luxuries became readily available—new stone houses, ivory-inlaid furniture, top-grade meat and fine wine, the best body lotions.

Amid such peace and prosperity, one lone voice scraped like fingernails on a blackboard. Amos spoke bluntly with a farmer's vocabulary, calling the city socialites "cows" (4:1). A mere shepherd—among the poorest of all professions—he treated luxury with scorn. Worst of all, Amos was a foreigner from the South—from Tekoa, a small town in Judah. Since Israel had split from the South about 170 years before, Israelite leaders did not take kindly to criticism from a southerner.

But to Amos, social acceptance didn't matter. He was no professional prophet, making his living talking smoothly about God (7:14). God had called him to leave his job and carry a message. God had said go, and Amos had obeyed.

God's View of "Religion"

The people Amos addressed had plenty of "religion." They went regularly to shrines for worship. They looked forward to "the day of the LORD," when God would fulfill all their expectations for their country. But Amos brought unexpected bad news from God: "I hate, I reject your festivals" (5:21). God didn't want sacrifice or singing. He demanded justice.

Amos listed all Israel's neighbors, announcing God's judgment for their crimes against humanity. Israelites liked this kind of talk; they felt superior to all these nations. But having caught the Israelites' attention, Amos circled dramatically home. God would judge Israel too. The people, their beautiful homes, their sacred altars—all would be destroyed.

The Character of God

More than any other book in the Bible, Amos concentrates on injustice. Israel had plenty of other faults he might have blasted. Their religious system, for instance, centered on two calf-idols. But Amos wasted little breath on that. He focused on the facts that met his eyes and ears in every marketplace: oppression of the poor, dishonest business, bribery in court, privilege bought with money.

The wealthy Israelites were getting their luxuries at the expense of the poor. They congratulated themselves on their devotion to God with no sense that they had cut the heart out of their relationship to him. They wanted God to fit conveniently into life as an additive. God showed himself through Amos as lordly, absolute, inescapable. He must be master over all of life, including business affairs.

How to Read Amos

Perhaps because he was a farmer, Amos used a plain writing style, filled with strong country language. The organization of his book is clear too: chapters 1–2 line up the Middle Eastern nations for trial, chapters 3–6 give a series of messages from God (usually beginning with "Hear this word"), and the last three chapters convey God's judgment through five graphic visions.

Throughout, Amos sticks close to his main concern: cruelty and inhumanity between people. The injustices Amos condemns often sound familiar today. As you read, ask yourself, "What would Amos say about me and about my people?"

It is a good idea to read Amos and Hosea together, for they give two views of the same situation. A visitor from the South, Amos was shocked by the injustices he saw in every marketplace. Hosea emphasized the inner dimension, an abused relationship to a loving God.

Amos predicted that Israel would be punished, and his prediction proved right. After King Jeroboam, the government deteriorated. Five kings took the throne in the next 13 years; four were assassinated. In 30 years Israel was permanently dismantled by Assyrian armies. For historical background, read 2 Kings 14:23–17:41, noting that the kings of both Israel and Judah are interspersed. For a briefer account, read the summaries of their reigns in "A Lineup of Rulers," pages 1417–1425.

3-TRACK READING PLAN

For an explanation and complete listing of the 3-track reading plan, turn to page 7.

TRACK 1: *Two-Week Courses on the Bible*
The Track 1 reading program on the Old Testament includes one chapter from Amos. See page 8 for a complete listing of this course.

TRACK 2: *An Overview of Amos in 1 Day*
☐ Day 1. Read the Introduction to Amos and chapter 4, which sums up God's majestic anger against his people.

Now turn to page 9 for your next Track 2 reading project.

TRACK 3: *All of Amos in 9 Days*
After you have read through Amos, turn to pages 10–14 for your next Track 3 reading project.

☐1　　☐2　　☐3　　☐4　　☐5　　☐6　　☐7　　☐8
☐9

Judgment on Neighbor Nations

1 The words of Amos, who was among the sheepherders from Tekoa, which he envisioned in visions concerning Israel in the days of Uzziah king of Judah, and in the days of Jeroboam son of Joash, king of Israel, two years before the earthquake.

2 He said,
"The LORD roars from Zion
And from Jerusalem He utters His
　voice;
And the shepherds' pasture grounds
　mourn,
And the summit of Carmel dries up."

3 ¶ Thus says the LORD,
"For three transgressions of Damascus
　and for four
I will not revoke its *punishment,*
Because they threshed Gilead with
　implements of sharp iron.
4 "So I will send fire upon the house of
　Hazael
And it will consume the citadels of
　Ben-hadad.
5 "I will also break the *gate* bar of
　Damascus,

And cut off the inhabitant from the
　valley of Aven,
And him who holds the scepter, from
　Beth-eden;
So the people of Aram will go exiled
　to Kir,"
Says the LORD.

6 ¶ Thus says the LORD,
"For three transgressions of Gaza and for
　four
I will not revoke its *punishment,*
Because they deported an entire
　population
To deliver *it* up to Edom.
7 "So I will send fire upon the wall of Gaza
And it will consume her citadels.
8 "I will also cut off the inhabitant from
　Ashdod,
And him who holds the scepter, from
　Ashkelon;
I will even unleash My power upon
　Ekron,
And the remnant of the Philistines will
　perish,"
Says the Lord GOD.

9 ¶ Thus says the LORD,

"For three transgressions of Tyre and for
four
I will not revoke its *punishment,*
Because they delivered up an entire
population to Edom
And did not remember *the* covenant of
brotherhood.

1:9 Atrocities

Amos began with thundering pronouncements against the enemies of Israel and Judah. His local audience must have cheered as he called down judgment on the blatant misdeeds of their neighbors: selling slaves, breaking treaties, ripping open pregnant women, desecrating the dead. But then Amos turned his attention to his own countrymen (2:4–16). God held his people to a far higher standard of morality. Israelites failed by breaking God's law; their neighbors were judged guilty of "crimes against humanity," for breaking laws of common decency.

10 "So I will send fire upon the wall of Tyre
And it will consume her citadels."

11 ¶ Thus says the LORD,
"For three transgressions of Edom and for
four
I will not revoke its *punishment,*
Because he pursued his brother with the
sword,
While he stifled his compassion;
His anger also tore continually,
And he maintained his fury forever.
12 "So I will send fire upon Teman
And it will consume the citadels of
Bozrah."

13 ¶ Thus says the LORD,
"For three transgressions of the sons of
Ammon and for four
I will not revoke its *punishment,*
Because they ripped open the pregnant
women of Gilead
In order to enlarge their borders.
14 "So I will kindle a fire on the wall of
Rabbah
And it will consume her citadels
Amid war cries on the day of battle,
And a storm on the day of tempest.
15 "Their king will go into exile,
He and his princes together," says the
LORD.

Judgment on Judah and Israel

2 Thus says the LORD,
"For three transgressions of Moab and
for four
I will not revoke its *punishment,*

Because he burned the bones of the king
of Edom to lime.
2 "So I will send fire upon Moab
And it will consume the citadels of
Kerioth;
And Moab will die amid tumult,
With war cries and the sound of a
trumpet.
3 "I will also cut off the judge from her
midst
And slay all her princes with him," says
the LORD.

4 ¶ Thus says the LORD,
"For three transgressions of Judah and for
four
I will not revoke its *punishment,*
Because they rejected the law of the LORD
And have not kept His statutes;
Their lies also have led them astray,
Those after which their fathers walked.
5 "So I will send fire upon Judah
And it will consume the citadels of
Jerusalem."

6 ¶ Thus says the LORD,
"For three transgressions of Israel and for
four
I will not revoke its *punishment,*
Because they sell the righteous for money
And the needy for a pair of sandals.
7 "These who pant after the *very* dust of the
earth on the head of the helpless
Also turn aside the way of the humble;
And a man and his father resort to the
same girl
In order to profane My holy name.
8 "On garments taken as pledges they
stretch out beside every altar,
And in the house of their God they drink
the wine of those who have been
fined.

2:8 Ruthless Bill Collectors

Bankers making loans usually want collateral to back up the promise to repay. In Amos's day poor people resorted to pledging the very clothes on their backs as collateral. Bill collectors who took a debtor's garments flagrantly violated God's law (Exodus 22:25–27). Worse, they were using the clothes as bedding when they went to their shrines to worship God.

9 ¶ "Yet it was I who destroyed the
Amorite before them,
Though his height *was* like the height of
cedars
And he *was* strong as the oaks;

I even destroyed his fruit above and his
root below.
10 "It was I who brought you up from the
land of Egypt,
And I led you in the wilderness forty
years
That you might take possession of the
land of the Amorite.
11 "Then I raised up some of your sons to
be prophets
And some of your young men to be
Nazirites.
Is this not so, O sons of Israel?" declares
the LORD.
12 "But you made the Nazirites drink wine,
And you commanded the prophets
saying, 'You shall not prophesy!'
13 "Behold, I am weighted down
beneath you
As a wagon is weighted down when filled
with sheaves.
14 "Flight will perish from the swift,
And the stalwart will not strengthen his
power,
Nor the mighty man save his life.
15 "He who grasps the bow will not stand *his
ground,*
The swift of foot will not escape,
Nor will he who rides the horse save his
life.
16 "Even the bravest among the warriors will
flee naked in that day," declares the
LORD.

All the Tribes Are Guilty

3 Hear this word which the LORD has spoken
against you, sons of Israel, against the entire
family which He brought up from the land of
Egypt:
2 "You only have I chosen among all the
families of the earth;
Therefore I will punish you for all your
iniquities."
3 Do two men walk together unless they
have made an appointment?
4 Does a lion roar in the forest when he
has no prey?
Does a young lion growl from his den
unless he has captured *something?*
5 Does a bird fall into a trap on the
ground when there is no bait in it?
Does a trap spring up from the earth
when it captures nothing at all?
6 If a trumpet is blown in a city will not
the people tremble?
If a calamity occurs in a city has not the
LORD done it?
7 Surely the Lord GOD does nothing
Unless He reveals His secret counsel
To His servants the prophets.
8 A lion has roared! Who will not fear?

The Lord GOD has spoken! Who can but
prophesy?
9 ¶ Proclaim on the citadels in Ashdod and
on the citadels in the land of Egypt and say, "Assemble yourselves on the mountains of Samaria
and see *the* great tumults within her and *the* op-
pressions in her midst.
10 "But they do not know how to do what is
right," declares the LORD, "these who hoard up
violence and devastation in their citadels."
11 ¶ Therefore, thus says the Lord GOD,
"An enemy, even one surrounding the
land,
Will pull down your strength from you
And your citadels will be looted."
12 Thus says the LORD,
"Just as the shepherd snatches from the
lion's mouth a couple of legs or a
piece of an ear,
So will the sons of Israel dwelling in
Samaria be snatched away—
With *the* corner of a bed and *the* cover
of a couch!
13 "Hear and testify against the house of
Jacob,"
Declares the Lord GOD, the God of hosts.
14 "For on the day that I punish Israel's
transgressions,
I will also punish the altars of Bethel;
The horns of the altar will be cut off
And they will fall to the ground.
15 "I will also smite the winter house
together with the summer house;
The houses of ivory will also perish
And the great houses will come to
an end,"
Declares the LORD.

"Yet You Have Not Returned to Me"

4 Hear this word, you cows of Bashan who
are on the mountain of Samaria,
Who oppress the poor, who crush the
needy,
Who say to your husbands, "Bring now,
that we may drink!"
2 The Lord GOD has sworn by His
holiness,

4:1 Prize Cows

*With searing scornfulness, Amos paints a
picture of women living in sheer luxury. These
"cows" thought only of their pleasure, not of
the oppressed poor who made their life of
luxury possible. Amos paints their punishment
just as vividly. The brutal Assyrian armies, who
later captured Israel and took its people into
exile, left monuments portraying their captives
being dragged off with hooks in their mouths.*

"Behold, the days are coming upon you
 When they will take you away with meat
  hooks,
 And the last of you with fish hooks.
3 "You will go out *through* breaches *in the
  walls,*
 Each one straight before her,
 And you will be cast to Harmon,"
  declares the LORD.

4 ¶ "Enter Bethel and transgress;
 In Gilgal multiply transgression!
 Bring your sacrifices every morning,
 Your tithes every three days.
5 "Offer a thank offering also from that
  which is leavened,
 And proclaim freewill offerings, make
  them known.
 For so you love *to do,* you sons of
  Israel,"
 Declares the Lord GOD.

6 ¶ "But I gave you also cleanness of teeth
  in all your cities
 And lack of bread in all your places,
 Yet you have not returned to Me,"
  declares the LORD.
7 "Furthermore, I withheld the rain
  from you
 While *there were* still three months until
  harvest.
 Then I would send rain on one city
 And on another city I would not send
  rain;
 One part would be rained on,
 While the part not rained on would
  dry up.
8 "So two or three cities would stagger to
  another city to drink water,
 But would not be satisfied;
 Yet you have not returned to Me,"
  declares the LORD.
9 "I smote you with scorching *wind* and
  mildew;
 And the caterpillar was devouring
 Your many gardens and vineyards, fig
  trees and olive trees;
 Yet you have not returned to Me,"
  declares the LORD.
10 "I sent a plague among you after the
  manner of Egypt;
 I slew your young men by the sword
  along with your captured horses,
 And I made the stench of your camp rise
  up in your nostrils;
 Yet you have not returned to Me,"
  declares the LORD.
11 "I overthrew you, as God overthrew
  Sodom and Gomorrah,
 And you were like a firebrand snatched
  from a blaze;

Yet you have not returned to Me,"
 declares the LORD.
12 "Therefore thus I will do to you, O Israel;
 Because I will do this to you,
 Prepare to meet your God, O Israel."

4:12 Before It's Too Late

This is the most famous verse in Amos, thanks to graffiti artists who write "Prepare to meet thy God!" in unlikely places. Amos has just reviewed a series of natural disasters—famine, drought, blight, plagues, war—any of which should have been enough to turn the nation to God. But Israel did not respond, and now Amos is holding out one last chance for repentance.

13 For behold, He who forms mountains
  and creates the wind
 And declares to man what are His
  thoughts,
 He who makes dawn into darkness
 And treads on the high places of the
  earth,
 The LORD God of hosts is His name.

"Seek Me that You May Live"

5 Hear this word which I take up for you as
  a dirge, O house of Israel:
2 She has fallen, she will not rise again—
  The virgin Israel.
 She *lies* neglected on her land;
 There is none to raise her up.
3 For thus says the Lord GOD,
 "The city which goes forth a thousand
  strong
 Will have a hundred left,
 And the one which goes forth a hundred
  strong
 Will have ten left to the house of Israel."

4 ¶ For thus says the LORD to the house of
Israel,
 "Seek Me that you may live.
5 "But do not resort to Bethel
 And do not come to Gilgal,
 Nor cross over to Beersheba;
 For Gilgal will certainly go into captivity
 And Bethel will come to trouble.
6 "Seek the LORD that you may live,
 Or He will break forth like a fire,
  O house of Joseph,
 And it will consume with none to
  quench *it* for Bethel,
7 *For* those who turn justice into
  wormwood
 And cast righteousness down to the
  earth."

8 ¶ He who made the Pleiades and Orion

And changes deep darkness into
morning,
Who also darkens day *into* night,
Who calls for the waters of the sea
And pours them out on the surface of
the earth,
The LORD is His name.
9 It is He who flashes forth *with*
destruction upon the strong,
So that destruction comes upon the
fortress.
10 ¶ They hate him who reproves in the
gate,
And they abhor him who speaks *with*
integrity.
11 Therefore because you impose heavy rent
on the poor
And exact a tribute of grain from them,
Though you have built houses of
well-hewn stone,
Yet you will not live in them;
You have planted pleasant vineyards, yet
you will not drink their wine.
12 For I know your transgressions are many
and your sins are great,
You who distress the righteous *and*
accept bribes
And turn aside the poor in the gate.
13 Therefore at such a time the prudent
person keeps silent, for it is an evil
time.
14 ¶ Seek good and not evil, that you may
live;
And thus may the LORD God of hosts be
with you,
Just as you have said!
15 Hate evil, love good,
And establish justice in the gate!
Perhaps the LORD God of hosts
May be gracious to the remnant of
Joseph.
16 ¶ Therefore thus says the LORD God of
hosts, the Lord,
"There is wailing in all the plazas,
And in all the streets they say, 'Alas!
Alas!'
They also call the farmer to mourning
And professional mourners to
lamentation.
17 "And in all the vineyards *there is* wailing,
Because I will pass through the midst of
you," says the LORD.
18 ¶ Alas, you who are longing for the day
of the LORD,
For what purpose *will* the day of the
LORD *be* to you?
It *will be* darkness and not light;
19 As when a man flees from a lion
And a bear meets him,

Or goes home, leans his hand against the
wall
And a snake bites him.
20 *Will* not the day of the LORD *be* darkness
instead of light,
Even gloom with no brightness in it?

5:20 The Day of the Lord

In Amos's day as today, some religious people looked forward to "the day of the LORD," when God will intervene personally in history and save his people. Israelites, assuming that "God is on our side," thought it would be a great day for them. But Amos contradicted their expectations. In a few words he depicted "the day of the LORD" as a nightmare.

---

21 ¶ "I hate, I reject your festivals,
Nor do I delight in your solemn
assemblies.
22 "Even though you offer up to Me burnt
offerings and your grain offerings,
I will not accept *them;*
And I will not *even* look at the peace
offerings of your fatlings.
23 "Take away from Me the noise of your
songs;
I will not even listen to the sound of
your harps.
24 "But let justice roll down like waters
And righteousness like an ever-flowing
stream.
25 ¶ "Did you present Me with sacrifices and
grain offerings in the wilderness for forty years,
O house of Israel?
26 "You also carried along Sikkuth your king
and Kiyyun, your images, the star of your gods
which you made for yourselves.
27 "Therefore, I will make you go into exile beyond Damascus," says the LORD, whose name is
the God of hosts.

"Those at Ease in Zion"

6 Woe to those who are at ease in Zion
And to those who *feel* secure in the
mountain of Samaria,
The distinguished men of the foremost of
nations,
To whom the house of Israel comes.
2 Go over to Calneh and look,
And go from there to Hamath the great,
Then go down to Gath of the Philistines.
Are they better than these kingdoms,
Or is their territory greater than yours?
3 Do you put off the day of calamity,
And would you bring near the seat of
violence?
4 ¶ Those who recline on beds of ivory

And sprawl on their couches,
And eat lambs from the flock
And calves from the midst of the stall,
5 Who improvise to the sound of the harp,
And like David have composed songs for
themselves,

6:1 Soft and Fat

Amos is at his sarcastic best in this message to "the distinguished men of the foremost of nations." Consistently, Israel proved much better at handling hardship than success. In prosperous times like Amos's they grew addicted to luxury and power, forgetting all about God. Hundreds of years before, Moses had warned against this very syndrome (Deuteronomy 8:10–20).

6 Who drink wine from sacrificial bowls
While they anoint themselves with the
finest of oils,
Yet they have not grieved over the ruin
of Joseph.
7 Therefore, they will now go into exile at
the head of the exiles,
And the sprawlers' banqueting will pass
away.

8 ¶ The Lord GOD has sworn by Himself,
the LORD God of hosts has declared:
"I loathe the arrogance of Jacob,
And detest his citadels;
Therefore I will deliver up *the* city and
all it contains."

9 And it will be, if ten men are left in one house, they will die.
10 Then one's uncle, or his undertaker, will lift him up to carry out *his* bones from the house, and he will say to the one who is in the innermost part of the house, "Is anyone else with you?" And that one will say, "No one." Then he will answer, "Keep quiet. For the name of the LORD is not to be mentioned."
11 For behold, the LORD is going to command that the great house be smashed to pieces and the small house to fragments.

12 ¶ Do horses run on rocks?
Or does one plow them with oxen?
Yet you have turned justice into poison
And the fruit of righteousness into
ᵃwormwood,
13 You who rejoice in ᵇLodebar,
And say, "Have we not by our *own*
strength taken ᶜKarnaim for
ourselves?"
14 "For behold, I am going to raise up a
nation against you,

O house of Israel," declares the LORD
God of hosts,
"And they will afflict you from the
entrance of Hamath
To the brook of the Arabah."

Warning Through Visions

7 Thus the Lord GOD showed me, and behold, He was forming a locust-swarm when the spring crop began to sprout. And behold, the spring crop *was* after the king's mowing.
2 And it came about, when it had finished eating the vegetation of the land, that I said,
"Lord GOD, please pardon!
How can Jacob stand,
For he is small?"
3 The LORD changed His mind about this.
"It shall not be," said the LORD.
4 ¶ Thus the Lord GOD showed me, and behold, the Lord GOD was calling to contend *with them* by fire, and it consumed the great deep and began to consume the farm land.
5 Then I said,
"Lord GOD, please stop!
How can Jacob stand, for he is small?"
6 The LORD changed His mind about this.
"This too shall not be," said the
Lord GOD.
7 ¶ Thus He showed me, and behold, the Lord was standing by a vertical wall with a plumb line in His hand.
8 The LORD said to me, "What do you see, Amos?" And I said, "A plumb line." Then the Lord said,
"Behold I am about to put a plumb line
In the midst of My people Israel.
I will spare them no longer.

7:8 A Plumb Line

A plumb line is a weight on the end of a string; builders use it to make certain that their walls stand straight. A wall may look right, but if it doesn't match a plumb line, it is out of kilter. Similarly God will use a plumb line to judge whether Israel is "straight" by his standards.

9 "The high places of Isaac will be desolated
And the sanctuaries of Israel laid waste.
Then I will rise up against the house of
Jeroboam with the sword."

Amos Accused, Answers

10 ¶ Then Amaziah, the priest of Bethel, sent word to Jeroboam king of Israel, saying, "Amos has conspired against you in the midst of the house of Israel; the land is unable to endure all his words.

ᵃ I.e. bitterness   ᵇ Lit *a thing of nothing*   ᶜ Lit *a pair of horns*

11 "For thus Amos says, 'Jeroboam will die by the sword and Israel will certainly go from its land into exile.' "

12 Then Amaziah said to Amos, "Go, you seer, flee away to the land of Judah and there eat bread and there do your prophesying!

13 "But no longer prophesy at Bethel, for it is a sanctuary of the king and a royal residence."

14 ¶ Then Amos replied to Amaziah, "I am not a prophet, nor am I the son of a prophet; for I am a herdsman and a grower of sycamore figs.

15 "But the LORD took me from following the flock and the LORD said to me, 'Go prophesy to My people Israel.'

16 "Now hear the word of the LORD: you are saying, 'You shall not prophesy against Israel nor shall you speak against the house of Isaac.'

17 "Therefore, thus says the LORD, 'Your wife will become a harlot in the city, your sons and your daughters will fall by the sword, your land will be parceled up by a *measuring* line and you yourself will die upon unclean soil. Moreover, Israel will certainly go from its land into exile.' "

Basket of Fruit and Israel's Captivity

8 Thus the Lord GOD showed me, and behold, there was a basket of summer fruit.

2 He said, "What do you see, Amos?" And I said, "A basket of summer fruit." Then the LORD said to me, "The end has come for My people Israel. I will spare them no longer.

3 "The songs of the palace will turn to wailing in that day," declares the Lord GOD. "Many *will be* the corpses; in every place they will cast them forth in silence."

4 ¶ Hear this, you who trample the needy, to do away with the humble of the land,

5 saying,
"When will the new moon be over,
So that we may sell grain,
And the sabbath, that we may open the
wheat *market,*
To make the bushel smaller and the
shekel bigger,
And to cheat with dishonest scales,

6 So as to buy the helpless for money
And the needy for a pair of sandals,
And *that* we may sell the refuse of the
wheat?"

7 ¶ The LORD has sworn by the pride of
Jacob,
"Indeed, I will never forget any of their
deeds.

8 "Because of this will not the land quake
And everyone who dwells in it mourn?
Indeed, all of it will rise up like the Nile,
And it will be tossed about
And subside like the Nile of Egypt.

9 "It will come about in that day," declares
the Lord GOD,

"That I will make the sun go down at
noon
And make the earth dark in broad
daylight.

10 "Then I will turn your festivals into
mourning
And all your songs into lamentation;
And I will bring sackcloth on everyone's
loins
And baldness on every head.
And I will make it like *a time of*
mourning for an only son,
And the end of it will be like a
bitter day.

11 ¶ "Behold, days are coming," declares the
Lord GOD,
"When I will send a famine on the land,
Not a famine for bread or a thirst for
water,
But rather for hearing the words of the
LORD.

8:11 Worst of All Famines

In this chapter, God describes devastations that will fall upon Israel if they do not repent. One judgment, however stands out above all others: The nation will experience the silence of God, a famine of the words of the Lord. A few more prophets succeeded Amos, but after Malachi no prophet appeared in Israel for four centuries, until John the Baptist came to announce Jesus.

12 "People will stagger from sea to sea
And from the north even to the east;
They will go to and fro to seek the word
of the LORD,
But they will not find *it.*

13 "In that day the beautiful virgins
And the young men will faint from
thirst.

14 "*As for* those who swear by the guilt of
Samaria,
Who say, 'As your god lives, O Dan,'
And, 'As the way of Beersheba lives,'
They will fall and not rise again."

God's Judgment Unavoidable

9 I saw the Lord standing beside the altar, and
He said,
"Smite the capitals so that the thresholds
will shake,
And break them on the heads of
them all!
Then I will slay the rest of them with the
sword;
They will not have a fugitive who will
flee,

Or a refugee who will escape.
2 "Though they dig into Sheol,
From there will My hand take them;
And though they ascend to heaven,
From there will I bring them down.
3 "Though they hide on the summit of Carmel,
I will search them out and take them from there;
And though they conceal themselves from My sight on the floor of the sea,
From there I will command the serpent and it will bite them.
4 "And though they go into captivity before their enemies,
From there I will command the sword that it slay them,
And I will set My eyes against them for evil and not for good."

9:4 An Inescapable God

The beautiful verses of Psalm 139:7–12 describe God's inescapable presence as a comfort. Here, in similar poetry, Amos gives the opposite side of that truth. Those whom God opposes can find no refuge. They may hide on top of Mount Carmel, or even at the very bottom of the sea, but God's eye will follow them.

5 ¶ The Lord GOD of hosts,
The One who touches the land so that it melts,
And all those who dwell in it mourn,
And all of it rises up like the Nile
And subsides like the Nile of Egypt;
6 The One who builds His upper chambers in the heavens
And has founded His vaulted dome over the earth,
He who calls for the waters of the sea
And pours them out on the face of the earth,
The LORD is His name.

7 ¶ "Are you not as the sons of Ethiopia to Me,
O sons of Israel?" declares the LORD.

"Have I not brought up Israel from the land of Egypt,
And the Philistines from Caphtor and the Arameans from Kir?
8 "Behold, the eyes of the Lord GOD are on the sinful kingdom,
And I will destroy it from the face of the earth;
Nevertheless, I will not totally destroy the house of Jacob,"
Declares the LORD.
9 "For behold, I am commanding,
And I will shake the house of Israel among all nations
As *grain* is shaken in a sieve,
But not a kernel will fall to the ground.
10 "All the sinners of My people will die by the sword,
Those who say, 'The calamity will not overtake or confront us.'

The Restoration of Israel

11 ¶ "In that day I will raise up the fallen booth of David,
And wall up its breaches;
I will also raise up its ruins
And rebuild it as in the days of old;
12 That they may possess the remnant of Edom
And all the nations who are called by My name,"
Declares the LORD who does this.

13 ¶ "Behold, days are coming," declares the LORD,
"When the plowman will overtake the reaper
And the treader of grapes him who sows seed;
When the mountains will drip sweet wine
And all the hills will be dissolved.
14 "Also I will restore the captivity of My people Israel,
And they will rebuild the ruined cities and live *in them;*
They will also plant vineyards and drink their wine,
And make gardens and eat their fruit.
15 "I will also plant them on their land,
And they will not again be rooted out from their land
Which I have given them,"
Says the LORD your God.

OBADIAH

Poetic Justice
Obadiah gave the final word on a blood feud

> "As you have done, it will be done to you." 15

THE FEUD BEGAN WITH TWIN brothers, Jacob and Esau. Esau, the older by minutes, would have inherited family leadership, but in a moment of hunger he traded it for a meal (Genesis 25:19–34). Jacob went on to become the founding father of the nation of Israel. Esau, a born hunter, moved southeast to desolate mountain country. He founded the nation of Edom.

Their descendants continued the quarrel. Over hundreds of years the two nations battled repeatedly but inconclusively. The Edomites' capital, Sela, sat on a high plateau above a sheer cliff; the only access was by a deep ravine. From that well-protected enclave, the Edomites raided Israel.

Though the Israelites had been commanded, "You shall not detest an Edomite, for he is your brother" (Deuteronomy 23:7), they grew to regard the Edomites as cruel and heartless. Repeatedly the prophets predicted Edom's punishment by God. The final straw came when Babylon dismembered Jerusalem and took its citizens into exile. The Edomites egged on the conquering army, preyed on fleeing Israelites, and helped plunder Jerusalem. Psalm 137, one of the saddest passages in the Bible, records the Israelite bitterness over this. As Esau had cared more for a meal than for the family name, so his descendants cared more for the profit they could get from plunder than for the compassion they owed a brother.

Fair Return for Cruelty

Obadiah predicts poetic justice for proud Edom: their treachery toward Judah (verses 11–12) repaid with treachery from their own allies (7), their robbery (13) repaid with robbery (5–6), their violence (10) with violence (9), their love of destruction (12–14) repaid with utter destruction (10,18). Obadiah predicts that downtrodden Israel will rise again, while Edom will disappear from the face of the earth.

This prediction came precisely true. Edom was destroyed, not by Israel but by a series of foreign invaders. The last remnant of Edomites were destroyed in the Roman siege of Jerusalem in A.D. 70. Ironically, the nation that had tormented Jews in Jerusalem later died defending that city.

Why does this blood feud earn a place in Scripture? It demonstrates God's ongoing protection of his people from their enemies. It also shows that God's standards extend beyond his chosen people. Every nation will be judged, like Edom, by their own standard: "As you have done, it will be done to you" (15).

How to Read Obadiah

The shortest book in the Old Testament, Obadiah can easily be read and understood in one sitting. Many readers, however, have a hard time seeing the importance of this ongoing border feud between blood relatives.

A Bible dictionary can summarize the centuries of violence. Look under "Edom." Perhaps, though, you can only fully appreciate Israel's feelings by reflecting on your own when a close relative treats you cruelly. A family betrayal is uniquely offensive to God and humanity. Obadiah reminds us that justice will be done.

3-TRACK READING PLAN

For an explanation and complete listing of the 3-track reading plan, turn to page 7.

TRACK 1: **_Two-Week Courses on the Bible_**
See page 7 for information on these courses.

TRACK 2: **_An Overview of Obadiah in 1 Day_**
☐ Day 1. Read the Introduction to Obadiah and all of Obadiah.
Now turn to page 9 for your next Track 2 reading project.

TRACK 3: **_All of Obadiah in 1 Day_**
After you have read through Obadiah, turn to pages 10–14 for your next Track 3 reading project.
☐ Obadiah

Edom Will Be Humbled

1 The vision of Obadiah.
¶ Thus says the Lord GOD concerning Edom—
We have heard a report from the LORD,
And an envoy has been sent among the nations *saying,*
"Arise and let us go against her for battle"—
2 "Behold, I will make you small among the nations;
You are greatly despised.
3 "The arrogance of your heart has deceived you,
You who live in the clefts of the rock,
In the loftiness of your dwelling place,
Who say in your heart,
'Who will bring me down to earth?'
4 "Though you build high like the eagle,
Though you set your nest among the stars,
From there I will bring you down,"
declares the LORD.
5 "If thieves came to you,
If robbers by night—
O how you will be ruined!—
Would they not steal *only* until they had enough?
If grape gatherers came to you,
Would they not leave *some* gleanings?
6 "O how Esau will be ransacked,
And his hidden treasures searched out!
7 "All the men allied with you
Will send you forth to the border,
And the men at peace with you
Will deceive you and overpower you.
They who eat your bread
Will set an ambush for you.
(There is no understanding in him.)
8 "Will I not on that day," declares the LORD,
"Destroy wise men from Edom

And understanding from the mountain of Esau?
9 "Then your mighty men will be dismayed, O Teman,
So that everyone may be cut off from the mountain of Esau by slaughter.
10 ¶ "Because of violence to your brother Jacob,
You will be covered *with* shame,
And you will be cut off forever.
11 "On the day that you stood aloof,
On the day that strangers carried off his wealth,
And foreigners entered his gate
And cast lots for Jerusalem—
You too were as one of them.
12 "Do not gloat over your brother's day,
The day of his misfortune.
And do not rejoice over the sons of Judah
In the day of their destruction;
Yes, do not boast
In the day of *their* distress.
13 "Do not enter the gate of My people
In the day of their disaster.
Yes, you, do not gloat over their calamity
In the day of their disaster.
And do not loot their wealth
In the day of their disaster.
14 "Do not stand at the fork of the road
To cut down their fugitives;
And do not imprison their survivors
In the day of their distress.

The Day of the LORD and the Future

15 ¶ "For the day of the LORD draws near on all the nations.
As you have done, it will be done to you.
Your dealings will return on your own head.
16 "Because just as you drank on My holy mountain,

All the nations will drink continually.
They will drink and swallow
And become as if they had never existed.
17 "But on Mount Zion there will be those
who escape,
And it will be holy.
And the house of Jacob will possess their
possessions.
18 "Then the house of Jacob will be a fire
And the house of Joseph a flame;
But the house of Esau *will be* as
stubble.
And they will set them on fire and
consume them,
So that there will be no survivor of the
house of Esau,"
For the LORD has spoken.

19 Then *those of* the ᵃNegev will possess
the mountain of Esau,
And *those of* the ᵇShephelah the
Philistine *plain;*
Also, possess the territory of Ephraim
and the territory of Samaria,
And Benjamin *will possess* Gilead.
20 And the exiles of this host of the sons of
Israel,
Who are *among* the Canaanites as far as
Zarephath,
And the exiles of Jerusalem who are in
Sepharad
Will possess the cities of the Negev.
21 The deliverers will ascend Mount Zion
To judge the mountain of Esau,
And the kingdom will be the LORD'S.

ᵃ I.e. South country   ᵇ I.e. the foothills

JONAH

Good News for the Enemy?
Jonah balked at loving the cruel Assyrians

JESUS TOLD HIS FOLLOWERS, "LOVE your enemies and pray for those who persecute you" (Matthew 5:44). While everyone talks admiringly about that command, loving your enemies is no easy thing. Many people doubt whether it is even right. Should we forgive the Nazis? Should we make a point to be kind to the Ku Klux Klan? Should we have compassion on dictators like Saddam Hussein?

> "Should I not have compassion on Nineveh, the great city in which there are more than 120,000 persons?" 4:11

The book of Jonah tells the story of a man whom God instructed to love his enemies in Nineveh. True to life, the prophet Jonah did just the opposite of what God commanded. He refused to go to the people he hated. Instead, he tried to run away from the Lord.

Nineveh was a large, important city in Assyria, situated on the river Tigris. It posed a grave military threat to tiny Israel. God sent Jonah there, and he responded without hesitation: In Joppa he caught a boat going in the opposite direction. Obviously, Jonah didn't want to warn Nineveh's citizens they were about to be destroyed. He suspected they would repent and God would forgive them.

Why Jonah Didn't Want to Go

We can't be sure why Jonah hated Assyria, but another short Old Testament book, Nahum, gives a clue. This book, also completely dedicated to Nineveh, describes a ruthless, bloodthirsty people. The Assyrians themselves left monuments to their cruelty—long, boastful inscriptions describing their torture and slaughter of people who opposed them.

Israelites had reasons to hate and fear Nineveh. But God *loved* Nineveh. He wanted to save the city, not destroy it. He knew Nineveh was ripe for change. When Jonah finally preached there, the entire city believed his message and repented. Though cruel and hardened, Nineveh was ready to believe God. Israel had never responded to a prophet like these Assyrians did.

An Attitude Like God's

Since God repeatedly warned the Israelites not to intermarry with people of other religions, and even ordered them to drive other nations out of the promised land, some readers conclude that the Old Testament is racially narrow-minded. They say the New Testament gives the first indication that God cares for non-Jewish people.

The book of Jonah contradicts that view. It shows, instead, that God wanted to use Israelites like Jonah as agents of his concern. They would preach doom but always with the hope that the warning would lead to repentance.

Jonah needed to develop an attitude like God's toward his enemies. Insistently, God led Jonah to this understanding of his own mind and heart. The book of Jonah is a story of a miraculous change in Nineveh, but even more a story of miraculous change in Jonah.

How to Read Jonah

Like Esther and Ruth, Jonah is a delightful short narrative by a master writer. Its spiritual implications are powerful and obvious. You can easily read it at one sitting.

As you read Jonah, notice the changes that the city of Nineveh goes through. Try also to trace the changes that occur in Jonah, and observe how God pushes him to make these changes. Then ask yourself: What did this book say to its original Jewish readers? What does it say to me?

You may also be interested in following Nineveh's entire history. Though the Ninevites repented in Jonah's time, they later returned to old patterns. Later prophets (Nahum and Zephaniah) predicted Nineveh's downfall for endless cruelty (Nahum 3:19), and in 612 B.C. that city was destroyed, never to be inhabited again. A Bible dictionary can summarize Nineveh's long history as a world power; look under "Assyria." To place Jonah in Israelite history, see "A Lineup of Rulers," pages 1417–1425.

Is Jonah a "fish story"? Interpreters differ over whether it should be read as a parable (not necessarily factual) or as historical fact. At least one reliable account exists of a man swallowed by a sperm whale and later found, alive, in the whale's stomach. Jonah's historical basis cannot be dismissed simply because of the "great fish."

More to the point, Jesus compared himself to Jonah, and the people of his time to the Ninevites (Matthew 12:39–41; Luke 11:29–32). He predicted that "the men of Nineveh will stand up with this generation at the judgment, and will condemn it because they repented at the preaching of Jonah; and behold, something greater than Jonah is here." It is hard to see how fictional characters could stand up at an event Jesus evidently believed would be historical.

3-TRACK READING PLAN

For an explanation and complete listing of the 3-track reading plan, turn to page 7.

TRACK 1: *Two-Week Courses on the Bible*
See page 7 for information on these courses.

TRACK 2: *An Overview of Jonah in 1 Day*
☐ Day 1. Read the Introduction to Jonah and chapters 3 and 4. These two short chapters tell the less familiar part of the story: How Jonah got to Nineveh and became more bitter than before.

Now turn to page 9 for your next Track 2 reading project.

TRACK 3: *All of Jonah in 2 Days*
After you have read through Jonah, turn to pages 10–14 for your next Track 3 reading project.
☐1–2   ☐3–4

Jonah's Disobedience

1 The word of the LORD came to Jonah the son of Amittai saying,

2 "Arise, go to Nineveh the great city and cry against it, for their wickedness has come up before Me."

3 But Jonah rose up to flee to Tarshish from the presence of the LORD. So he went down to Joppa, found a ship which was going to Tarshish, paid the fare and went down into it to go with them to Tarshish from the presence of the LORD.

4 ¶ The LORD hurled a great wind on the sea and there was a great storm on the sea so that the ship was about to break up.

5 Then the sailors became afraid and every man cried to his god, and they threw the cargo which was in the ship into the sea to lighten *it* for them. But Jonah had gone below into the hold of the ship, lain down and fallen sound asleep.

6 So the captain approached him and said, "How is it that you are sleeping? Get up, call on your god. Perhaps *your* god will be concerned about us so that we will not perish."

7 ¶ Each man said to his mate, "Come, let us cast lots so we may learn on whose account this calamity *has* struck us." So they cast lots and the lot fell on Jonah.

8 Then they said to him, "Tell us, now! On whose account *has* this calamity *struck* us? What is your occupation? And where do you come from? What is your country? From what people are you?"

9 He said to them, "I am a Hebrew, and I fear the LORD God of heaven who made the sea and the dry land."

10 ¶ Then the men became extremely frightened and they said to him, "How could you do this?" For the men knew that he was fleeing from the presence of the LORD, because he had told them.

11 So they said to him, "What should we do to you that the sea may become calm for us?"—for the sea was becoming increasingly stormy.

12 He said to them, "Pick me up and throw me into the sea. Then the sea will become calm for you, for I know that on account of me this great storm *has come* upon you."

13 However, the men rowed *desperately* to return to land but they could not, for the sea was becoming *even* stormier against them.

14 Then they called on the LORD and said, "We earnestly pray, O LORD, do not let us perish on account of this man's life and do not put innocent blood on us; for You, O LORD, have done as You have pleased."

15 ¶ So they picked up Jonah, threw him into the sea, and the sea stopped its raging.

16 Then the men feared the LORD greatly, and they offered a sacrifice to the LORD and made vows.

17 ¶ And the LORD appointed a great fish to swallow Jonah, and Jonah was in the stomach of the fish three days and three nights.

Jonah's Prayer

2 Then Jonah prayed to the LORD his God from the stomach of the fish,

2 and he said,
"I called out of my distress to the LORD,
And He answered me.
I cried for help from the depth of Sheol;
You heard my voice.
3 "For You had cast me into the deep,
Into the heart of the seas,
And the current engulfed me.
All Your breakers and billows passed
over me.
4 "So I said, 'I have been expelled from
Your sight.
Nevertheless I will look again toward
Your holy temple.'
5 "Water encompassed me to the point of
death.
The great deep engulfed me,
Weeds were wrapped around my head.
6 "I descended to the roots of the
mountains.
The earth with its bars *was* around me
forever,
But You have brought up my life from
the pit, O LORD my God.
7 "While I was fainting away,
I remembered the LORD,
And my prayer came to You,
Into Your holy temple.
8 "Those who regard vain idols
Forsake their faithfulness,
9 But I will sacrifice to You
With the voice of thanksgiving.
That which I have vowed I will pay.
Salvation is from the LORD."

10 ¶ Then the LORD commanded the fish, and it vomited Jonah up onto the dry land.

a Lit *a great city to God*

Nineveh Repents

3 Now the word of the LORD came to Jonah the second time, saying,

2 "Arise, go to Nineveh the great city and proclaim to it the proclamation which I am going to tell you."

3 So Jonah arose and went to Nineveh according to the word of the LORD. Now Nineveh was *a*an exceedingly great city, a three days' walk.

3:3 How Big a City?

Archaeologists who have dug up Nineveh report that at its peak its walls were 7¾ miles in circumference. Since it would not take three days to go around a city of that size, most probably the "three days" refers to the administrative district of which Nineveh was the capital. This comprised four cities with a circumference of about 60 miles. Another possibility: Perhaps it took Jonah three days to go to every neighborhood, marketplace, and city gate with his message.

4 Then Jonah began to go through the city one day's walk; and he cried out and said, "Yet forty days and Nineveh will be overthrown."

5 ¶ Then the people of Nineveh believed in God; and they called a fast and put on sackcloth from the greatest to the least of them.

6 When the word reached the king of Nineveh, he arose from his throne, laid aside his robe from him, covered *himself* with sackcloth and sat on the ashes.

7 He issued a proclamation and it said, "In Nineveh by the decree of the king and his nobles: Do not let man, beast, herd, or flock taste a thing. Do not let them eat or drink water.

8 "But both man and beast must be covered with sackcloth; and let men call on God earnestly that each may turn from his wicked way and from the violence which is in his hands.

9 "Who knows, God may turn and relent and withdraw His burning anger so that we will not perish."

10 ¶ When God saw their deeds, that they turned from their wicked way, then God relented concerning the calamity which He had declared He would bring upon them. And He did not do *it*.

Jonah's Displeasure Rebuked

4 But it greatly displeased Jonah and he became angry.

2 He prayed to the LORD and said, "Please LORD, was not this what I said while I was still in my *own* country? Therefore in order to forestall

this I fled to Tarshish, for I knew that You are a gracious and compassionate God, slow to anger and abundant in lovingkindness, and one who relents concerning calamity.

3 "Therefore now, O LORD, please take my life from me, for death is better to me than life."

4:2 Too Merciful a God?

The poet Robert Frost said, "After Jonah, you could never trust God not to be merciful again." The balky prophet discloses why he ran away from God in the first place: He was afraid God would forgive his archenemies. In fact, God did just that, after Nineveh repented with an eagerness that the Jews themselves often lacked (see Matthew 12:41). Pointedly, the book of Jonah ends with a question. Can anyone put limits on God's mercy and forgiveness?

4 The LORD said, "Do you have good reason to be angry?"

5 ¶ Then Jonah went out from the city and sat east of it. There he made a shelter for himself and sat under it in the shade until he could see what would happen in the city.

6 So the LORD God appointed a plant and it grew up over Jonah to be a shade over his head to deliver him from his discomfort. And Jonah was extremely happy about the plant.

7 But God appointed a worm when dawn came the next day and it attacked the plant and it withered.

8 When the sun came up God appointed a scorching east wind, and the sun beat down on Jonah's head so that he became faint and begged with *all* his soul to die, saying, "Death is better to me than life."

9 ¶ Then God said to Jonah, "Do you have good reason to be angry about the plant?" And he said, "I have good reason to be angry, even to death."

10 Then the LORD said, "You had compassion on the plant for which you did not work and *which* you did not cause to grow, which came up overnight and perished overnight.

11 "Should I not have compassion on Nineveh, the great city in which there are more than 120,000 persons who do not know *the difference* between their right and left hand, as well as many animals?"

MICAH

Light in a Dark Time
Evil and violence were creeping south toward Jerusalem

> *And what does the LORD require of you but to do justice, to love kindness, and to walk humbly with your God? 6:8*

COUNTRY BOYS OFTEN LOSE PERSPECTIVE in the big city. They gawk at the tall buildings, the fancy clothes, and the showy symbols of power. Micah was a country boy from Moresheth, a small village in the no-man's-land southwest of Jerusalem. While his contemporary, Isaiah, moved in and out of the king's palace, Micah shows no sign of traveling in such circles.

Yet this country boy kept his sense of perspective. The blood and violence of his day did not overwhelm him, nor was he intimidated by powerful and wealthy people. He spoke like a person who had seen the world through God's eyes.

Micah lived in one of the darkest times in Israel's history, a time of brutal warfare. The country had long been split into North and South. Micah saw war break out between these sides, with 120,000 deaths on the southern side alone (2 Chronicles 28:6). Then Assyria, the brutal chief power of the day, smashed the Northern Kingdom after a three-year siege of its capital, Samaria. Only a miracle kept those same Assyrian armies out of Jerusalem (2 Chronicles 32). But for how long would the South remain free?

The Sin of the South

Micah had no doubt how to interpret these chaotic events. God had punished the northern nation of Israel for sins summarized in 2 Kings 17:16–17: idolatry, Baal worship, child sacrifice, magic and sorcery. Now these same activities were creeping south into Judah—so much so that Micah referred in disgust to Jerusalem as a "high place," the traditional setting for pagan idol worship (1:5). The same judgment the North had suffered would come to Judah if people continued to disobey God.

Other historical accounts give more details of the South's sins. They describe how King Ahaz set up a foreign altar in God's temple, altering the temple construction "because of the king of Assyria" (2 Kings 16:18). He gave his own children in human sacrifice and shut the Lord's temple, substituting altars on every street corner (2 Chronicles 28:3,24–25). Along with this religious corruption came every other kind of sin: dishonesty (Micah 6:10–11), bribery (3:11), injustice (2:2), and distrust that destroyed families (7:5–6).

Beyond the Darkness

Yet Micah saw light ahead. He perceived a majestic God over all events, who punished his people only to purify and restore them. Along with making some of the Bible's frankest predictions of destruction, Micah gave some of the clearest predictions of the Messiah, the leader who would come to save Israel. Micah's perspective encompassed not only the events of his time but events far into the future, when the nations "will hammer their swords into plowshares" (4:3).

Micah looked straight at the darkness of his time and at the darkness yet to come. But his perspective—God's perspective—enabled him to see beyond darkness. "Do not rejoice over me, O my enemy. Though I fall I will rise; though I dwell in darkness, the LORD is a light for me" (7:8).

How to Read Micah

Micah had the big view of history, and thus he covered a lot of ground. His book, only seven chapters, is loaded with pronouncements on the events of several thousand years. Because so much is jammed into so short a space, reading Micah can be confusing. A fragment may deal with the Messiah, for instance, and without warning the next few verses shift to the battle against Assyria.

To grasp Micah's message, think of his book as a collection of short speeches. One speech doesn't necessarily lead into the next. Instead of reading quickly from start to finish, pause after each short section to see whether you understand what it says. Try to understand who is speaking. Sometimes God speaks, sometimes Micah, sometimes the rebellious people.

In general, Micah follows this outline: chapters 1–3 indict both Northern and Southern Kingdoms, with their leaders; chapters 4 and 5 turn to the wonderful future God is planning; the last two chapters give the trial, punishment, and hope of the guilty nations.

It's very helpful to understand Micah's historical situation. Micah 1:1 names the kings of Judah he worked under. You can read about these kings, and their northern counterparts, in 2 Kings 15:27–20:21 and 2 Chronicles 27–32. For a brief summary, see "A Lineup of Rulers," pages 1417–1425.

3-TRACK READING PLAN

For an explanation and complete listing of the 3-track reading plan, turn to page 7.

TRACK 1: *Two-Week Courses on the Bible*
See page 7 for information on these courses.

TRACK 2: *An Overview of Micah in 1 Day*
☐ Day 1. Read the Introduction to Micah and chapter 6, which includes one of the most succinct statements in the Old Testament of what God wants our lives to be.

Now turn to page 9 for your next Track 2 reading project.

TRACK 3: *All of Micah in 7 Days*
After you have read through Micah, turn to pages 10–14 for your next Track 3 reading project.
☐1　　☐2　　☐3　　☐4　　☐5　　☐6　　☐7

Destruction in Israel and Judah

1 The word of the LORD which came *to* Micah of Moresheth in the days of Jotham, Ahaz *and* Hezekiah, kings of Judah, which he saw concerning Samaria and Jerusalem.

2 Hear, O peoples, all of you;
　Listen, O earth and all it contains,
　And let the Lord GOD be a witness
　　against you,
　The Lord from His holy temple.

3 For behold, the LORD is coming forth
　　from His place.
　He will come down and tread on the
　　high places of the earth.

4 The mountains will melt under Him
　And the valleys will be split,
　Like wax before the fire,
　Like water poured down a steep
　　place.

5 All this is for the rebellion of Jacob
　And for the sins of the house of Israel.
　What is the rebellion of Jacob?
　Is it not Samaria?
　What is the high place of Judah?
　Is it not Jerusalem?

6 For I will make Samaria a heap of ruins
　　in the open country,
　Planting places for a vineyard.
　I will pour her stones down into the
　　valley
　And will lay bare her foundations.

7 All of her idols will be smashed,
　All of her earnings will be burned with
　　fire
　And all of her images I will make
　　desolate,
　For she collected *them* from a harlot's
　　earnings,
　And to the earnings of a harlot they will
　　return.

8 ¶ Because of this I must lament and wail,
　I must go barefoot and naked;
　I must make a lament like the jackals
　And a mourning like the ostriches.

9 For her wound is incurable,
　For it has come to Judah;
　It has reached the gate of my people,
　Even to Jerusalem.

10 Tell it not in Gath,
　Weep not at all.

At ^aBeth-le-aphrah roll yourself in the
dust.

11 Go on your way, inhabitant of ^bShaphir,
in shameful nakedness.

1:10 A Passion for Punning

Puns stump even the best translators. In verses 10–15 Micah plays on the names of a series of Israelite towns—probably marking the path Assyrian invaders followed. The puns were not meant to be funny. They extracted grief from the place-names of the invasion.

The inhabitant of ^cZaanan does not
escape.
The lamentation of ^dBethezel: "He will
take from you its support."

12 For the inhabitant of ^eMaroth
Becomes weak waiting for good,
Because a calamity has come down from
the LORD
To the gate of Jerusalem.

13 Harness the chariot to the team of
horses,
O inhabitant of Lachish—
She was the beginning of sin
To the daughter of Zion—
Because in you were found
The rebellious acts of Israel.

14 Therefore you will give parting gifts
On behalf of Moresheth-gath;
The houses of Achzib *will* become a
deception
To the kings of Israel.

15 Moreover, I will bring on you
The one who takes possession,
O inhabitant of ^fMareshah.
The glory of Israel will enter Adullam.

16 Make yourself bald and cut off your hair,
Because of the children of your delight;
Extend your baldness like the eagle,
For they will go from you into exile.

Woe to Oppressors

2 Woe to those who scheme iniquity,
Who work out evil on their beds!
When morning comes, they do it,
For it is in the power of their hands.

2 They covet fields and then seize *them*,
And houses, and take *them* away.
They rob a man and his house,
A man and his inheritance.

3 Therefore thus says the LORD,
"Behold, I am planning against this family
a calamity

From which you cannot remove your
necks;
And you will not walk haughtily,
For it will be an evil time.

4 "On that day they will take up against you
a taunt
And utter a bitter lamentation *and* say,
'We are completely destroyed!
He exchanges the portion of my people;
How He removes it from me!
To the apostate He apportions our
fields.'

5 "Therefore you will have no one
stretching a measuring line
For you by lot in the assembly of the
LORD.

6 ¶ 'Do not speak out,' *so* they speak out.
But if they do not speak out concerning
these things,
Reproaches will not be turned back.

7 "Is it being said, O house of Jacob:
'Is the Spirit of the LORD impatient?
Are these His doings?'
Do not My words do good
To the one walking uprightly?

8 "Recently My people have arisen as an
enemy—
You strip the robe off the garment
From unsuspecting passers-by,
From those returned from war.

9 "The women of My people you evict,
Each *one* from her pleasant house.
From her children you take My splendor
forever.

10 "Arise and go,
For this is no place of rest
Because of the uncleanness that brings on
destruction,
A painful destruction.

11 "If a man walking after wind and
falsehood
Had told lies *and said,*
'I will speak out to you concerning wine
and liquor,'
He would be spokesman to this people.

2:11 Plenty of Beer

Modern politicians avoid the phrase like poison: "tax hike." They love to proclaim "a new day in America," and hate to bring bad news. Prophets in Micah's time were just the same. They insisted that Micah stop predicting bad news (2:6; 3:5) and join their peace bandwagon. In fact, says Micah sarcastically, the ideal prophet for feel-good Israel would predict plenty of wine and liquor.

---

^a I.e. house of dust   ^b I.e. pleasantness   ^c I.e. going out
possession   ^d I.e. house of removal   ^e I.e. bitterness   ^f I.e.

12 ¶ "I will surely assemble all of you,
        Jacob,
    I will surely gather the remnant of Israel.
    I will put them together like sheep in the
        fold;
    Like a flock in the midst of its pasture
    They will be noisy with men.
13 "The breaker goes up before them;
    They break out, pass through the gate
        and go out by it.
    So their king goes on before them,
    And the LORD at their head."

Rulers Denounced

3 And I said,
    "Hear now, heads of Jacob
    And rulers of the house of Israel.
    Is it not for you to know justice?
2 "You who hate good and love evil,
    Who tear off their skin from them
    And their flesh from their bones,
3 Who eat the flesh of my people,
    Strip off their skin from them,
    Break their bones
    And chop *them* up as for the pot
    And as meat in a kettle."
4 Then they will cry out to the LORD,
    But He will not answer them.
    Instead, He will hide His face from them
        at that time
    Because they have practiced evil deeds.

5 ¶ Thus says the LORD concerning the
prophets
    Who lead my people astray;
    When they have *something* to bite with
        their teeth,
    They cry, "Peace,"
    But against him who puts nothing in
        their mouths
    They declare holy war.
6 Therefore *it will be* night for you—
        without vision,
    And darkness for you—without
        divination.
    The sun will go down on the prophets,
    And the day will become dark over
        them.
7 The seers will be ashamed
    And the diviners will be embarrassed.
    Indeed, they will all cover *their* mouths
    Because there is no answer from God.
8 On the other hand I am filled with
        power—
    With the Spirit of the LORD—
    And with justice and courage
    To make known to Jacob his rebellious
        act,
    Even to Israel his sin.
9 Now hear this, heads of the house of
        Jacob
    And rulers of the house of Israel,

Who abhor justice
    And twist everything that is straight,
10 Who build Zion with bloodshed
    And Jerusalem with violent injustice.
11 Her leaders pronounce judgment for a
        bribe,
    Her priests instruct for a price
    And her prophets divine for money.
    Yet they lean on the LORD saying,
    "Is not the LORD in our midst?
    Calamity will not come upon us."
12 Therefore, on account of you
    Zion will be plowed as a field,
    Jerusalem will become a heap of ruins,
    And the mountain of the temple *will
        become* high places of a forest.

3:12 Life-saving Prophecy

*One hundred years after this clear prophecy of
its destruction, Jerusalem still stood. By that
time Jeremiah was making similar predictions,
which led to his arrest for treason. Some of the
city leaders, however, quoted Micah's "ancient"
prophecy, pointing out that since Micah had
not been put to death, neither should Jeremiah
be (Jeremiah 26:18–19). Their memory
probably saved Jeremiah's life.*
    *Within another 20 years, both Micah's and
Jeremiah's predictions came true and
Jerusalem was reduced to rubble.*

Peaceful Latter Days

4 And it will come about in the last days
    That the mountain of the house of the
        LORD
    Will be established as the chief of the
        mountains.
    It will be raised above the hills,
    And the peoples will stream to it.
2 Many nations will come and say,
    "Come and let us go up to the mountain
        of the LORD
    And to the house of the God of Jacob,
    That He may teach us about His ways
    And that we may walk in His paths."
    For from Zion will go forth the law,
    Even the word of the LORD from
        Jerusalem.
3 And He will judge between many peoples
    And render decisions for mighty, distant
        nations.
    Then they will hammer their swords into
        plowshares
    And their spears into pruning hooks;
    Nation will not lift up sword against
        nation,
    And never again will they train for war.
4 Each of them will sit under his vine
    And under his fig tree,

With no one to make *them* afraid,
For the mouth of the LORD of hosts has
spoken.

4:3 Parallel with Isaiah

Micah 4:1–3, which describes the wonderful
future in store for the world, has an almost
exact parallel in Isaiah 2:2–4. Isaiah must have
quoted Micah, or vice versa, or perhaps both
quoted a third unknown prophet. Both
prophets spoke in Jerusalem at about the same
time.

5 Though all the peoples walk
Each in the name of his god,
As for us, we will walk
In the name of the LORD our God
forever and ever.

6 ¶ "In that day," declares the LORD,
"I will assemble the lame
And gather the outcasts,
Even those whom I have afflicted.
7 "I will make the lame a remnant
And the outcasts a strong nation,
And the LORD will reign over them in
Mount Zion
From now on and forever.
8 "As for you, tower of the flock,
Hill of the daughter of Zion,
To you it will come—
Even the former dominion will come,
The kingdom of the daughter of
Jerusalem.
9 ¶ "Now, why do you cry out loudly?
Is there no king among you,
Or has your counselor perished,
That agony has gripped you like a
woman in childbirth?
10 "Writhe and labor to give birth,
Daughter of Zion,
Like a woman in childbirth;
For now you will go out of the city,
Dwell in the field,
And go to Babylon.
There you will be rescued;
There the LORD will redeem you
From the hand of your enemies.
11 "And now many nations have been
assembled against you
Who say, 'Let her be polluted,
And let our eyes gloat over Zion.'
12 "But they do not know the thoughts of
the LORD,
And they do not understand His
purpose;
For He has gathered them like sheaves to
the threshing floor.
13 "Arise and thresh, daughter of Zion,

For your horn I will make iron
And your hoofs I will make bronze,
That you may pulverize many peoples,
That you may devote to the LORD their
unjust gain
And their wealth to the Lord of all the
earth.

Birth of the King in Bethlehem

5 "Now muster yourselves in troops,
daughter of troops;
They have laid siege against us;
With a rod they will smite the judge of
Israel on the cheek.
2 "But as for you, Bethlehem Ephrathah,
Too little to be among the clans of Judah,
From you One will go forth for Me to be
ruler in Israel.
His goings forth are from long ago,
From the days of eternity."

5:2 Messiah's Birthplace

When the Magi came looking for a newborn
"king of the Jews," King Herod asked the
Biblical scholars where to search. They referred
him to this passage (see Matthew 2:6), which
predicted that the Messiah would come from
the small town of Bethlehem. Micah also
describes Christ as a shepherd who will not
merely bring peace, but be Israel's peace.

3 Therefore He will give them *up* until the
time
When she who is in labor has borne a
child.
Then the remainder of His brethren
Will return to the sons of Israel.
4 And He will arise and shepherd *His flock*
In the strength of the LORD,
In the majesty of the name of the LORD
His God.
And they will remain,
Because at that time He will be great
To the ends of the earth.
5 This One will be *our* peace.

¶ When the Assyrian invades our land,
When he tramples on our citadels,
Then we will raise against him
Seven shepherds and eight leaders of
men.
6 They will shepherd the land of Assyria
with the sword,
The land of Nimrod at its entrances;
And He will deliver *us* from the Assyrian
When he attacks our land
And when he tramples our territory.

7 ¶ Then the remnant of Jacob
Will be among many peoples

Like dew from the LORD,
Like showers on vegetation
Which do not wait for man
Or delay for the sons of men.
8 The remnant of Jacob
   Will be among the nations,
   Among many peoples
   Like a lion among the beasts of the
      forest,
   Like a young lion among flocks of sheep,
   Which, if he passes through,
   Tramples down and tears,
   And there is none to rescue.
9 Your hand will be lifted up against your
      adversaries,
   And all your enemies will be cut off.

10 ¶ "It will be in that day," declares the
      LORD,
   "That I will cut off your horses from
      among you
   And destroy your chariots.
11 "I will also cut off the cities of your land
   And tear down all your fortifications.
12 "I will cut off sorceries from your hand,
   And you will have fortune-tellers no
      more.
13 "I will cut off your carved images
   And your *sacred* pillars from among
      you,
   So that you will no longer bow down
   To the work of your hands.
14 "I will root out your Asherim from
      among you
   And destroy your cities.

15 "And I will execute vengeance in anger
      and wrath
   On the nations which have not obeyed."

God's Indictment of His People

6 Hear now what the LORD is saying,
   "Arise, plead your case before the
      mountains,
   And let the hills hear your voice.
2 "Listen, you mountains, to the indictment
      of the LORD,
   And you enduring foundations of the
      earth,
   Because the LORD has a case against His
      people;
   Even with Israel He will dispute.
3 "My people, what have I done to you,
   And how have I wearied you?
      Answer Me.
4 "Indeed, I brought you up from the land
      of Egypt
   And ransomed you from the house of
      slavery,
   And I sent before you Moses, Aaron and
      Miriam.
5 "My people, remember now
   What Balak king of Moab counseled
   And what Balaam son of Beor answered
      him,
   And from Shittim to Gilgal,
   So that you might know the righteous
      acts of the LORD."

What God Requires of Man

6 ¶ With what shall I come to the LORD

Seeing in Two Dimensions
Little distinction between next week and the next thousand years

WHEN YOU SEE A MOUNTAIN range from a distance, it's very difficult to tell which peak is highest. A smaller mountain may loom largest simply because it is closer to you than a higher peak.

Micah, and many of the other Old Testament prophets, saw the future like that. They made little distinction between events coming next week and events that would come a thousand years later. They seemed to see the future with limited "depth perception."

> *They will hammer their swords into plowshares and their spears into pruning hooks.*
> 4:3

In the space of one verse, for instance, Micah shifts from a prediction (3:12) that Jerusalem will become a heap of ruins—a prophecy fulfilled about 100 years later—to a prophecy (4:1) that the same mountain will be lifted up as "chief of the mountains"—something that has yet to be fulfilled today. In 5:2 comes a prediction that Matthew 2:6 records as fulfilled by Jesus' birth in Bethlehem 700 years later.

In Micah, the thousands of years between these fulfillments are unclear. They all seem to be about the same distance into the future. Almost certainly, Micah himself saw them unclearly. First Peter 1:10–11 comments that "the prophets ... made careful searches and inquiries, seeking to know what person or time the Spirit of Christ within them was indicating as He predicted the sufferings of Christ and the glories to follow."

Life Questions: What emotions do you feel knowing that some prophecies have not yet been fulfilled?

And bow myself before the God on high?
Shall I come to Him with burnt offerings,
With yearling calves?

6:5 Names with Meaning

Speaking to people who knew their own history well, Micah needed only to mention names like Balaam and Balak to recall God's goodness and humankind's disobedience. Numbers 22–24 tells the story of Balaam, in which Balak tried to get Balaam to curse Israel. Balaam gave this famous reply: "How shall I curse whom God has not cursed?" (Numbers 23:8). The trip from Shittim to Gilgal apparently refers to Israel's miraculous crossing of the Jordan River (Joshua 3:1; 4:19–20), the final stage in their journey from slavery in Egypt to freedom in the promised land. These events, which had occurred about 500 years before, were as real to the Israelites as yesterday.

Verse 16 offers a different kind of memory: "The statutes of Omri and all the works of the house of Ahab." Omri and his son Ahab were two of the most notoriously wicked kings in Israelite history (1 Kings 16:21–33). Ahab went so far as to marry Jezebel, a Phoenician princess, and set up a temple for her god, Baal, in the new capital of Samaria. He sponsored her massacre of genuine prophets.

7 Does the LORD take delight in thousands
   of rams,
   In ten thousand rivers of oil?
   Shall I present my firstborn *for* my
   rebellious acts,
   The fruit of my body for the sin of my
   soul?
8 He has told you, O man, what is good;
   And what does the LORD require of
   you
   But to do justice, to love kindness,
   And to walk humbly with your God?

9 ¶ The voice of the LORD will call to the
   city—

6:8 What God Wants

Micah's most famous pronouncement summarizes the qualities that matter to God. Jesus spoke in similar terms to the Pharisees about their religious hypocrisy: They gave a tenth of even their spices to God, yet they neglected justice, mercy, and faithfulness (Matthew 23:23).

And it is sound wisdom to fear Your
   name:
   "Hear, O tribe. Who has appointed its
   time?
10 "Is there yet a man in the wicked house,
   Along with treasures of wickedness
   And a short measure *that is* cursed?
11 "Can I justify wicked scales
   And a bag of deceptive weights?
12 "For the rich men of *the* city are full of
   violence,
   Her residents speak lies,
   And their tongue is deceitful in their
   mouth.
13 "So also I will make *you* sick, striking you
   down,
   Desolating *you* because of your sins.
14 "You will eat, but you will not be
   satisfied,
   And your [a]vileness will be in your
   midst.
   You will *try to* remove *for safekeeping,*
   But you will not preserve *anything,*
   And what you do preserve I will give to
   the sword.
15 "You will sow but you will not reap.
   You will tread the olive but will not
   anoint yourself with oil;
   And the grapes, but you will not drink
   wine.
16 "The statutes of Omri
   And all the works of the house of Ahab
   are observed;
   And in their devices you walk.
   Therefore I will give you up for
   destruction
   And your inhabitants for derision,
   And you will bear the reproach of My
   people."

The Prophet Acknowledges

7 Woe is me! For I am
   Like the fruit pickers, like the grape
   gatherers.
   There is not a cluster of grapes to eat,
   Or a first-ripe fig *which* I crave.
2 The godly person has perished from the
   land,
   And there is no upright *person* among
   men.
   All of them lie in wait for bloodshed;
   Each of them hunts the other with a net.
3 Concerning evil, both hands do it well.
   The prince asks, also the judge, for a
   bribe,
   And a great man speaks the desire of his
   soul;
   So they weave it together.
4 The best of them is like a briar,
   The most upright like a thorn hedge.

[a] Or possibly *garbage* or *excreta*

The day when you post your watchmen,
Your punishment will come.
Then their confusion will occur.
5 Do not trust in a neighbor;
Do not have confidence in a friend.
From her who lies in your bosom
Guard your lips.
6 For son treats father contemptuously,
Daughter rises up against her mother,
Daughter-in-law against her
mother-in-law;
A man's enemies are the men of his own
household.

God Is the Source of Salvation and Light

7 ¶ But as for me, I will watch expectantly
for the LORD;
I will wait for the God of my salvation.
My God will hear me.
8 Do not rejoice over me, O my enemy.
Though I fall I will rise;
Though I dwell in darkness, the LORD is
a light for me.
9 ¶ I will bear the indignation of the LORD
Because I have sinned against Him,
Until He pleads my case and executes
justice for me.
He will bring me out to the light,
And I will see His righteousness.
10 Then my enemy will see,
And shame will cover her who said
to me,
"Where is the LORD your God?"
My eyes will look on her;
At that time she will be trampled down
Like mire of the streets.
11 *It will be* a day for building your walls.
On that day will your boundary be
extended.
12 It *will be* a day when they will come
to you
From Assyria and the cities of Egypt,
From Egypt even to the Euphrates,
Even from sea to sea and mountain to
mountain.
13 And the earth will become desolate
because of her inhabitants,
On account of the fruit of their deeds.

14 ¶ Shepherd Your people with Your
scepter,
The flock of Your possession
Which dwells by itself in the woodland,
In the midst of a fruitful field.
Let them feed in Bashan and Gilead
As in the days of old.
15 "As in the days when you came out from
the land of Egypt,
I will show you miracles."
16 Nations will see and be ashamed
Of all their might.
They will put *their* hand on *their* mouth,
Their ears will be deaf.
17 They will lick the dust like a serpent,
Like reptiles of the earth.
They will come trembling out of their
fortresses;
To the LORD our God they will come in
dread
And they will be afraid before You.
18 Who is a God like You, who pardons
iniquity
And passes over the rebellious act of the
remnant of His possession?
He does not retain His anger forever,
Because He delights in unchanging love.

7:18 Nobody Like God

Theologians use big words to describe God's unique qualities: transcendence, omnipotence, omnipresence. Micah marveled even more over this: God's forgiveness. Unlike the angry gods of other nations, Israel's God delighted to show mercy.

19 He will again have compassion on us;
He will tread our iniquities under foot.
Yes, You will cast all their sins
Into the depths of the sea.
20 You will give truth to Jacob
And unchanging love to Abraham,
Which You swore to our forefathers
From the days of old.

NAHUM

God's Answer to Injustice

A power above the powers

Who can stand before His indignation? Who can endure the burning of His anger? 1:6

I S LIFE FAIR? IT RARELY seems so, especially in international politics. The most vicious dictators thrive, and raw power is the key ingredient in a successful foreign policy. Weak people get trampled.

As a citizen of Judah, the prophet Nahum felt the force of such injustice. His message from God concerned the greatest city of the time, Nineveh. This city, the capital of Assyria, represented raw, brutal power—"evil passed continually," as Nahum put it (3:19). Though Nineveh was hundreds of miles northeast of Judah, Assyrian power dominated the Middle East. In contrast, Judah was a small, fragile state barely clinging to independence.

Nahum's Nerve

Judah's sister nation to the north, Israel, had already been defeated by Assyria and carried into exile. Only God's miraculous intervention had saved Judah on that occasion. And now, in Nahum's time, the Assyrians had returned. They dragged off Manasseh, the king, with a hook in his nose (2 Chronicles 33:11). Judah was forced to pay tribute as a vassal state.

Few people can stare into the face of such raw power and come away unimpressed. Nahum did so only because he had seen a far greater power—the power of a God whose wrath could shatter rocks. If God was angry, how could Nineveh stand? Nahum's absolute confidence in God is underlined throughout this book.

It took nerve to stand up and predict the downfall of the most powerful nation in the world. Yet, in this book, Nahum sounds unintimidated, almost lordly. He spoke with confidence because he knew God's character: "The LORD will by no means leave the guilty unpunished" (1:3).

Decline and Fall of Nineveh

Within a few years, Nahum's predictions came true. Nineveh did fall, never to rise again. The greatest city in the world became a pile of rubble overgrown with grass. Both Alexander the Great and Napoleon camped near it but had no idea a city had ever been there. The site became known as "the mound of many sheep."

The name *Nahum* means "comfort." Though Nahum describes God's anger, his message offers comfort to those who live with injustice and evil. "The LORD is good," said Nahum, "a stronghold in the day of trouble, and He knows those who take refuge in Him. But with an overflowing flood . . . [He] will pursue His enemies into darkness" (1:7–8). Nineveh is gone, but Nahum's testimony lives on, reminding us that though God's justice may seem slow, nothing can ultimately escape it.

How to Read Nahum

N ahum stands out from the other short prophetic books in two ways. He addressed a foreign city—Nineveh—instead of his own home nation, and he used unusually vivid language.

You can read more background on Judah and its relationship to Nineveh in the following historical accounts: 2 Kings 17–19 and 2 Chronicles 32–33:13. The background will help you understand why God was so angry at Nineveh.

As you read Nahum, pay special attention to the vivid imagery. Some of the best examples are the following:

Descriptions of warfare: 2:3–7; 3:1–3
Nineveh like a pool with its water draining out: 2:8
Nineveh like a lions' den, full of bones: 2:11–12
Nineveh like a prostitute shamed in the streets: 3:5–6
Nineveh's fortresses like fig trees, with fruit shaken into the mouth of their attacker: 3:12
Nineveh's numerous citizens like grasshoppers: prolific, voracious, and quickly disappearing: 3:15–17

3-TRACK READING PLAN

For an explanation and complete listing of the 3-track reading plan, turn to page 7.

TRACK 1:   *Two-Week Courses on the Bible*
See page 8 for information on these courses.

TRACK 2:   *An Overview of Nahum in 1 Day*
☐ Day 1. Read the Introduction to Nahum and chapter 1, which portrays God's anger against Nineveh's injustice.

Now turn to page 9 for your next Track 2 reading project.

TRACK 3:   *All of Nahum in 3 Days*
After you have read through Nahum, turn to pages 10–14 for your next Track 3 reading project.

☐1   ☐2   ☐3

God Is Awesome

1 The ᵃoracle of Nineveh. The book of the vision of Nahum the Elkoshite.

2 ¶ A jealous and avenging God is the
    LORD;
    The LORD is avenging and wrathful.
    The LORD takes vengeance on His
        adversaries,
    And He reserves wrath for His enemies.
3 The LORD is slow to anger and great in
        power,
    And the LORD will by no means leave *the
        guilty* unpunished.
    In whirlwind and storm is His way,
    And clouds are the dust beneath His feet.
4 He rebukes the sea and makes it dry;
    He dries up all the rivers.
    Bashan and Carmel wither;
    The blossoms of Lebanon wither.
5 Mountains quake because of Him
    And the hills dissolve;
    Indeed the earth is upheaved by His
        presence,
    The world and all the inhabitants in it.
6 Who can stand before His indignation?
    Who can endure the burning of His
        anger?
    His wrath is poured out like fire
    And the rocks are broken up by Him.
7 The LORD is good,

A stronghold in the day of trouble,
And He knows those who take refuge in
    Him.

1:3 God Is Slow to Anger

God's anger against Nineveh had not appeared overnight. Assyria had been the dominant world power for at least 300 years. Once before, Jonah had carried a message of condemnation to its chief city, Nineveh. As was always true with God's prophets, Jonah's condemnation sounded absolute. Actually, it included an escape clause. In Jeremiah 18:7–10, God spelled it out: "At one moment I might speak concerning a nation or concerning a kingdom to uproot, to pull down, or to destroy it; if that nation against which I have spoken turns from its evil, I will relent." Hearing Jonah, the Ninevites had repented, and God had spared their city.

The repentance had not lasted, however. By Nineveh's time, Nineveh had returned to her evil ways. God's anger, while slow to develop, was sure.

8 But with an overflowing flood
    He will make a complete end of its site,
    And will pursue His enemies into
        darkness.

ᵃ Or *burden*

9 ¶ Whatever you devise against the
LORD,
He will make a complete end of it.
Distress will not rise up twice.
10 Like tangled thorns,
And like those who are drunken with
their drink,
They are consumed
As stubble completely withered.
11 From you has gone forth
One who plotted evil against the LORD,
A wicked counselor.
12 Thus says the LORD,
"Though they are at full *strength* and
likewise many,
Even so, they will be cut off and pass
away.
Though I have afflicted you,
I will afflict you no longer.
13 "So now, I will break his yoke bar from
upon you,
And I will tear off your shackles."

14 ¶ The LORD has issued a command
concerning you:
"Your name will no longer be
perpetuated.
I will cut off idol and image
From the house of your gods.
I will prepare your grave,
For you are contemptible."

15 ¶ Behold, on the mountains the feet of
him who brings good news,
Who announces peace!
Celebrate your feasts, O Judah;
Pay your vows.
For never again will the wicked one pass
through you;
He is cut off completely.

The Overthrow of Nineveh

2 The one who scatters has come up against
you.
Man the fortress, watch the road;
Strengthen your back, summon all *your*
strength.
2 For the LORD will restore the splendor of
Jacob
Like the splendor of Israel,
Even though devastators have devastated
them
And destroyed their vine branches.

3 ¶ The shields of his mighty men are
colored red,
The warriors are dressed in scarlet,
The chariots are *enveloped* in flashing
steel
When he is prepared *to march,*
And the cypress *spears* are brandished.

4 The chariots race madly in the streets,
They rush wildly in the squares,
Their appearance is like torches,
They dash to and fro like lightning
flashes.
5 He remembers his nobles;
They stumble in their march,
They hurry to her wall,
And the mantelet is set up.

2:5 Battle Tactics

*To most people, mighty Nineveh seemed
impregnable. A thick protective wall eight miles
long encircled the city, and just to reach the
wall attackers had to cross a moat 150 feet
wide. Behind those fortifications waited the
Assyrian troops, renowned for their cruelty.
One Assyrian king boasted of erecting a
pyramid of chopped-off heads in front of an
enemy's city. Even so, Nahum predicted
Nineveh's complete downfall.*

6 The gates of the rivers are opened
And the palace is dissolved.
7 It is fixed:
She is stripped, she is carried away,
And her handmaids are moaning like the
sound of doves,
Beating on their breasts.

8 ¶ Though Nineveh *was* like a pool of
water throughout her days,
Now they are fleeing;
"Stop, stop,"
But no one turns back.
9 Plunder the silver!
Plunder the gold!
For there is no limit to the treasure—
Wealth from every kind of desirable
object.
10 She is emptied! Yes, she is desolate and
waste!
Hearts are melting and knees knocking!
Also anguish is in the whole body
And all their faces are grown pale!
11 Where is the den of the lions
And the feeding place of the young lions,
Where the lion, lioness and lion's cub
prowled,
With nothing to disturb *them?*
12 The lion tore enough for his cubs,
Killed *enough* for his lionesses,
And filled his lairs with prey
And his dens with torn flesh.
13 ¶ "Behold, I am against you," declares the
LORD of hosts. "I will burn up her chariots in
smoke, a sword will devour your young lions; I
will cut off your prey from the land, and no longer
will the voice of your messengers be heard."

Nineveh's Complete Ruin

3 Woe to the bloody city, completely full of
lies *and* pillage;
Her prey never departs.
2 The noise of the whip,
The noise of the rattling of the wheel,
Galloping horses
And bounding chariots!
3 Horsemen charging,
Swords flashing, spears gleaming,
Many slain, a mass of corpses,
And countless dead bodies—
They stumble over the dead bodies!
4 *All* because of the many harlotries of the
harlot,
The charming one, the mistress of
sorceries,
Who sells nations by her harlotries
And families by her sorceries.
5 "Behold, I am against you," declares the
LORD of hosts;
"And I will lift up your skirts over your
face,
And show to the nations your nakedness
And to the kingdoms your disgrace.
6 "I will throw filth on you
And make you vile,
And set you up as a spectacle.
7 "And it will come about that all who
see you
Will shrink from you and say,
'Nineveh is devastated!
Who will grieve for her?'
Where will I seek comforters for you?"

8 ¶ Are you better than [a]No-amon,
Which was situated by the waters of the
Nile,
With water surrounding her,
Whose rampart *was* the sea,
Whose wall *consisted* of the sea?
9 Ethiopia was *her* might,
And Egypt too, without limits.

3:8 Another Powerful City

*In approximately 663 B.C. Assyria overwhelmed
No-amon, the ancient, wealthy capital of Upper
Egypt. This victory seemed to symbolize
Assyria's absolute power. To Nahum, however,
the battle told a different tale. If No-amon was
vulnerable, so was proud Nineveh. About 50
years after capturing No-amon, Nineveh fell to
the Babylonians. The mention of No-amon's
downfall enables us to date Nahum's message
within that 50-year period.*

Put and Lubim were among her helpers.
10 Yet she became an exile,
She went into captivity;
Also her small children were dashed to
pieces
At the head of every street;
They cast lots for her honorable men,
And all her great men were bound with
fetters.
11 You too will become drunk,
You will be hidden.
You too will search for a refuge from the
enemy.
12 All your fortifications are fig trees with
ripe fruit—
When shaken, they fall into the eater's
mouth.
13 Behold, your people are women in your
midst!
The gates of your land are opened wide
to your enemies;
Fire consumes your gate bars.
14 Draw for yourself water for the siege!
Strengthen your fortifications!
Go into the clay and tread the mortar!
Take hold of the brick mold!
15 There fire will consume you,
The sword will cut you down;
It will consume you as the locust *does*.

¶ Multiply yourself like the creeping
locust,
Multiply yourself like the swarming
locust.
16 You have increased your traders more
than the stars of heaven—
The creeping locust strips and flies away.
17 Your guardsmen are like the swarming
locust.
Your marshals are like hordes of
grasshoppers
Settling in the stone walls on a cold
day.
The sun rises and they flee,
And the place where they are is not
known.
18 Your shepherds are sleeping, O king of
Assyria;
Your nobles are lying down.
Your people are scattered on the
mountains
And there is no one to regather *them*.
19 There is no relief for your breakdown,
Your wound is incurable.
All who hear about you
Will clap *their* hands over you,
For on whom has not your evil passed
continually?

---

[a] I.e. the city of Amon: Thebes

HABAKKUK

The Problem of Evil

Habakkuk's question: "Why is God silent while the wicked succeed?"

> *"The righteous will live by his faith."*
> 2:4

THE BOOK OF HABAKKUK BEGINS with a complaint. The prophet saw injustice, violence, and evil in his own country, yet God remained silent and invisible. Why didn't God intervene? Why did he give no answer when Habakkuk called out for help? Habakkuk took these questions directly to God, in prayer.

God answered him, but hardly in the way Habakkuk had anticipated. God said he was sending the Babylonians to punish Judah. God's words described a ruthless, savage army that would tear Israel apart.

So Habakkuk complained again. Could this be justice—punishing Judah through an even more evil nation? Deeply perplexed, Habakkuk waited to see what answer God would give to his second complaint.

How long he had to wait, we do not know. But God did reply, and his answer is perhaps the best explanation we have of God's attitude toward evil. It satisfied Habakkuk, so that his book, which begins with a complaint, ends with one of the most beautiful songs in the Bible.

Two Certainties to Live By

God pointed out two certainties to Habakkuk. First, the violent, proud Babylonians would be paid back with the very weapons they had used on others. Just as they destroyed nations, they would be destroyed. "Is it not indeed from the LORD of hosts that . . . nations grow weary for nothing?" (2:13). Evil may dominate the earth, but it always wears itself out.

The second certainty was God's character. He may be silent for a time, but not forever. "The earth will be filled with the knowledge of the glory of the LORD, as the waters cover the sea" (2:14). In chapter 3, Habakkuk "saw" this powerful glory, and his heart pounded. It changed his attitude from complaining to joy.

Because the future belongs to God, a believer can cling to the truth embodied in 2:4: "The righteous will live by his faith." Habakkuk beautifully expressed this attitude of faith in the last three verses of his book: No matter how hard life might become, he would rejoice and find strength in the Lord.

Living by Faith

Did Habakkuk explain why God allows evil? Not precisely. He did affirm that God has not lost control. Evil is moving toward its own logical end of self-destruction, and God's glory will someday fill the earth. Habakkuk offers no proof of this, merely the record of God's communication to him. A believer can find hope and joy through faith in God, regardless of circumstances. Habakkuk's capsule of faith was quoted at three crucial points in the New Testament: Romans 1:17; Galatians 3:11; and Hebrews 10:38.

Though Habakkuk probably did not live to see it, the Babylonians were destroyed. Today they are merely a memory. Yet we, like Habakkuk, must still wait in faith to see the earth "filled with the knowledge of the glory of the LORD."

How to Read Habakkuk

Other prophets carried messages from God to humankind; Habakkuk addressed God alone. He pondered deep riddles of life while wrestling with two terrible realities: the degeneration of his own nation and the certainty that it was about to be overrun by another, worse nation. How can a just God allow, even use, such evil? To fully delve into

Habakkuk's questions, you may want to read the book of Job and Psalm 73, which explore related issues.

The first two chapters of Habakkuk tell of two questions and two answers. As you read, try to imagine the emotional changes Habakkuk experienced as he talked with God. Then read the joyful psalm of chapter 3 (set to music, either by Habakkuk or someone else) and ask yourself: Where did this joyful confidence come from?

3-TRACK READING PLAN

For an explanation and complete listing of the 3-track reading plan, turn to page 7.

TRACK 1: **Two-Week Courses on the Bible**
See page 8 for information on these courses.

TRACK 2: **An Overview of Habakkuk in 1 Day**
☐ Day 1. Read the Introduction to Habakkuk and chapter 1, which gives you a flavor of the dialogue between God and the prophet.
Now turn to page 9 for your next Track 2 reading project.

TRACK 3: **All of Habakkuk in 3 Days**
After you have read through Habakkuk, turn to pages 10–14 for your next Track 3 reading project.
☐1   ☐2   ☐3

Chaldeans Used to Punish Judah

1 The ᵃoracle which Habakkuk the prophet saw.

2 ¶ How long, O LORD, will I call for help,
And You will not hear?
I cry out to You, "Violence!"
Yet You do not save.

3 Why do You make me see iniquity,
And cause *me* to look on wickedness?
Yes, destruction and violence are before me;
Strife exists and contention arises.

4 Therefore the law is ignored
And justice is never upheld.
For the wicked surround the righteous;
Therefore justice comes out perverted.

5 ¶ "Look among the nations! Observe!
Be astonished! Wonder!
Because *I am* doing something in your days—
You would not believe if you were told.

6 "For behold, I am raising up the Chaldeans,
That fierce and impetuous people
Who march throughout the earth
To seize dwelling places which are not theirs.

7 "They are dreaded and feared;
Their justice and authority originate with themselves.

8 "Their horses are swifter than leopards

And keener than wolves in the evening.
Their horsemen come galloping,
Their horsemen come from afar;
They fly like an eagle swooping *down* to devour.

1:5 Unbelievable!

To Habakkuk and his fellow Israelites, it seemed unbelievable. How could God hand his own people over to the cruel and arrogant Babylonians? But incredible reversals can happen to people who think they have an automatic entitlement with God. Hundreds of years later the apostle Paul quoted this verse to a synagogue congregation (Acts 13:41), urging them not to let complacency keep them from accepting Jesus.

9 "All of them come for violence.
Their horde of faces *moves* forward.
They collect captives like sand.

10 "They mock at kings
And rulers are a laughing matter to them.
They laugh at every fortress
And heap up rubble to capture it.

11 "Then they will sweep through *like* the wind and pass on.
But they will be held guilty,
They whose strength is their god."

ᵃ Or burden

12 ¶ Are You not from everlasting,
O Lord, my God, my Holy One?
We will not die.
You, O Lord, have appointed them to
judge;

1:11 Worshiping the Military

The Babylonians had their own gods, but Habakkuk claimed that they really worshiped their "net," that is, their military might (verse 16). God described them as "guilty, they whose strength is their god" (verse 11).

And You, O Rock, have established them
to correct.
13 *Your* eyes are too pure to approve evil,
And You can not look on wickedness
with favor.
Why do You look with favor
On those who deal treacherously?
Why are You silent when the wicked
swallow up
Those more righteous than they?
14 *Why* have You made men like the fish of
the sea,
Like creeping things without a ruler over
them?
15 *The Chaldeans* bring all of them up with
a hook,
Drag them away with their net,
And gather them together in their fishing
net.
Therefore they rejoice and are glad.
16 Therefore they offer a sacrifice to
their net
And burn incense to their fishing net;
Because through these things their catch
is large,
And their food is plentiful.
17 Will they therefore empty their net
And continually slay nations without
sparing?

God Answers the Prophet

2 I will stand on my guard post
And station myself on the rampart;
And I will keep watch to see what He
will speak to me,
And how I may reply when I am
reproved.
2 Then the Lord answered me and said,
"Record the vision
And inscribe *it* on tablets,
That the one who reads it may run.
3 "For the vision is yet for the appointed
time;
It hastens toward the goal and it will not
fail.
Though it tarries, wait for it;

For it will certainly come, it will not
delay.
4 ¶ "Behold, as for the proud one,
His soul is not right within him;
But the righteous will live by his faith.

2:4 Righteous by Faith

Has any brief slogan made a bigger impact than this one? For Habakkuk, "the righteous will live by his faith" meant that righteous people must patiently trust God in a difficult time. The New Testament quoted Habakkuk in a wider context (Romans 1:17; Galatians 3:11; Hebrews 10:38–39), saying not only that believers must live by faith, but that they are saved by grace through faith. When Martin Luther read that quote in Romans, it changed his life, and "righteousness by faith" became a rallying cry of the Protestant Reformation.

---

5 "Furthermore, wine betrays the haughty
man,
So that he does not stay at home.
He enlarges his appetite like Sheol,
And he is like death, never satisfied.
He also gathers to himself all nations
And collects to himself all peoples.

6 ¶ "Will not all of these take up a
taunt-song against him,
Even mockery *and* insinuations
against him
And say, 'Woe to him who increases
what is not his—
For how long—
And makes himself rich with loans?'
7 "Will not your creditors rise up suddenly,
And those who collect from you awaken?
Indeed, you will become plunder for
them.
8 "Because you have looted many nations,
All the remainder of the peoples will
loot you—
Because of human bloodshed and
violence done to the land,
To the town and all its inhabitants.

9 ¶ "Woe to him who gets evil gain for his
house
To put his nest on high,
To be delivered from the hand of
calamity!
10 "You have devised a shameful thing for
your house
By cutting off many peoples;
So you are sinning against yourself.
11 "Surely the stone will cry out from the
wall,
And the rafter will answer it from the
framework.

12 ¶ "Woe to him who builds a city with
bloodshed
And founds a town with violence!
13 "Is it not indeed from the LORD of hosts
That peoples toil for fire,
And nations grow weary for nothing?
14 "For the earth will be filled
With the knowledge of the glory of the
LORD,
As the waters cover the sea.

15 ¶ "Woe to you who make your neighbors
drink,
Who mix in your venom even to make
them drunk
So as to look on their nakedness!
16 "You will be filled with disgrace rather
than honor.
Now you yourself drink and expose your
own nakedness.
The cup in the LORD'S right hand will
come around to you,
And utter disgrace *will come* upon your
glory.
17 "For the violence done to Lebanon will
overwhelm you,
And the devastation of *its* beasts by
which you terrified them,
Because of human bloodshed and
violence done to the land,
To the town and all its inhabitants.

18 ¶ "What profit is the idol when its maker
has carved it,
Or an image, a teacher of falsehood?
For *its* maker trusts in his *own*
handiwork
When he fashions speechless idols.
19 "Woe to him who says to a *piece of* wood,
'Awake!'
To a mute stone, 'Arise!'
And that is *your* teacher?
Behold, it is overlaid with gold and silver,
And there is no breath at all inside it.
20 "But the LORD is in His holy temple.
Let all the earth be silent before Him."

God's Deliverance of His People

3 A prayer of Habakkuk the prophet, according
to [a]Shigionoth.
2 ¶ LORD, I have heard the report about
You *and* I fear.
O LORD, revive Your work in the midst
of the years,
In the midst of the years make it known;
In wrath remember mercy.

3 ¶ God comes from Teman,
And the Holy One from Mount
Paran.   Selah.
His splendor covers the heavens,

And the earth is full of His praise.
4 *His* radiance is like the sunlight;
He has rays *flashing* from His hand,
And there is the hiding of His power.
5 Before Him goes pestilence,
And plague comes after Him.
6 He stood and surveyed the earth;
He looked and startled the nations.
Yes, the perpetual mountains were
shattered,
The ancient hills collapsed.
His ways are everlasting.
7 I saw the tents of Cushan under distress,
The tent curtains of the land of Midian
were trembling.

8 ¶ Did the LORD rage against the rivers,
Or *was* Your anger against the rivers,
Or *was* Your wrath against the sea,
That You rode on Your horses,
On Your chariots of salvation?
9 Your bow was made bare,
The rods of chastisement were sworn.
                                    Selah.
You cleaved the earth with rivers.
10 The mountains saw You *and* quaked;
The downpour of waters swept by.
The deep uttered forth its voice,
It lifted high its hands.
11 Sun *and* moon stood in their places;
They went away at the light of Your
arrows,
At the radiance of Your gleaming spear.
12 In indignation You marched through the
earth;
In anger You trampled the nations.
13 You went forth for the salvation of Your
people,
For the salvation of Your anointed.
You struck the head of the house of the
evil
To lay him open from thigh to neck.
                                    Selah.

14 You pierced with his own spears
The head of his throngs.
They stormed in to scatter us;

---

[a] I.e. a highly emotional poetic form

Their exultation *was* like those
Who devour the oppressed in secret.
15 You trampled on the sea with Your
horses,
On the surge of many waters.

16 ¶ I heard and my inward parts trembled,
At the sound my lips quivered.
Decay enters my bones,
And in my place I tremble.
Because I must wait quietly for the day
of distress,
For the people to arise *who* will
invade us.
17 Though the fig tree should not blossom

And there be no fruit on the vines,
Though the yield of the olive should fail
And the fields produce no food,
Though the flock should be cut off from
the fold
And there be no cattle in the stalls,
18 Yet I will exult in the LORD,
I will rejoice in the God of my salvation.
19 The Lord GOD is my strength,
And He has made my feet like hinds'
feet,
And makes me walk on my high places.

For the choir director, on my stringed instruments.

ZEPHANIAH

Beyond Darkness
A worldwide catastrophe and a shining light

> "The LORD . . . will be quiet in His love, He will rejoice over you with shouts of joy."
> 3:17

ZEPHANIAH WROTE NOT LONG AFTER Manasseh had ended his 50-year reign in Judah. One of the worst kings on record, Manasseh had made idol worship and child sacrifice common practice. He had built altars for star worshipers in God's temple and had encouraged male prostitution as part of the religious ritual. He had also "shed very much innocent blood until he had filled Jerusalem from one end to another" (2 Kings 21:16). His son Amon carried on in the same way during his short reign.

Then came King Josiah, who took the throne at the age of eight, after his father's assassination. The Bible says there was never a king like Josiah (2 Kings 23:25). He led a reform, destroying all the pagan idols and restoring the temple. He organized the first Passover celebration in generations.

Zephaniah, who was probably related to the king through his great-great-grandfather King Hezekiah, apparently spoke just before the big changes. The nation's future hung in the balance, and Zephaniah's words may well have helped tip it toward renewal of faith in God.

From Gloom to Exultation

Zephaniah's book begins in deep gloom. Like other prophets, he condemned the sins of his nation and predicted judgment from God. But he went one big step further. He talked repeatedly about "the day of the LORD" and saw that it would be a supernatural event sweeping clean the whole planet. Zephaniah offered no hope that it could be avoided. The Lord had warned and pleaded, but to no avail (3:6–7). Zephaniah saw hope for a minority only. A faithful, humble remnant could be sheltered from disaster if they would seek God.

Beyond the judgment fires Zephaniah saw something remarkably bright. He predicted that a purified remnant of God's people, truthful and humble, would trust in God. He foresaw a remade world learning to worship God.

Therefore this short book, which starts with such gloom, ends with an ecstatic song of joy: an anticipation of the kingdom to come after the judgment. God's blessing will flow freely as every nation worships him. Zephaniah's words may have been influential in encouraging Josiah's reforms, but his vision extended far beyond. The New Testament speaks often, like Zephaniah, of the worldwide judgment and a renewed world to come.

How to Read Zephaniah

Zephaniah will seem more interesting if you grasp the historical situation in which he wrote. For the decadence that led to King Josiah's reforms, read 2 Kings 21. Josiah's history is told in chapters 22 and 23. Second Chronicles 33–35 tells the same story with slightly different details. You can find a brief summary of these reigns in "A Lineup of Rulers," pages 1417–1425.

Zephaniah is easily understood. It has a clear and symmetrical structure, opening (after a brief introduction) with a warning of judgment for Judah and its capital of Jerusalem, then extending the judgment to Judah's neighbors, and closing in chapter 3 with good news about Jerusalem.

3-TRACK READING PLAN

For an explanation and complete listing of the 3-track reading plan, turn to page 7.

TRACK 1: **Two-Week Courses on the Bible**
See page 7 for information on these courses.

TRACK 2: **An Overview of Zephaniah in 1 Day**
☐ Day 1: Read the Introduction to Zephaniah and chapter 3, with its hopeful portrait of Jerusalem after the judgment.

Now turn to page 9 for your next Track 2 reading project.

TRACK 3: **All of Zephaniah in 3 Days**
After you have read through Zephaniah, turn to pages 10–14 for your next Track 3 reading project.

☐1　　☐2　　☐3

Day of Judgment on Judah

1 The word of the LORD which came to Zephaniah son of Cushi, son of Gedaliah, son of Amariah, son of Hezekiah, in the days of Josiah son of Amon, king of Judah:

2 ¶ "I will completely remove all *things*
From the face of the earth," declares the LORD.

1:1 Royal Blood

Prophets had to be hand-picked by God. Education or family background didn't qualify them for the job. Zephaniah, however, came from an impressive family. His great-great-grandfather was King Hezekiah. Despite his royal blood, Zephaniah was blunt and uncompromising; he took no white-glove approach to prophecy.

3 "I will remove man and beast;
I will remove the birds of the sky
And the fish of the sea,
And the ruins along with the wicked;
And I will cut off man from the face of
the earth," declares the LORD.
4 "So I will stretch out My hand against
Judah
And against all the inhabitants of
Jerusalem.
And I will cut off the remnant of Baal
from this place,
And the names of the idolatrous priests
along with the priests.
5 "And those who bow down on the
housetops to the host of heaven,
And those who bow down *and* swear to
the LORD and *yet* swear by Milcom,

6 And those who have turned back from
following the LORD,
And those who have not sought the
LORD or inquired of Him."

7 ¶ Be silent before the Lord GOD!
For the day of the LORD is near,
For the LORD has prepared a sacrifice,
He has consecrated His guests.
8 "Then it will come about on the day of
the LORD'S sacrifice
That I will punish the princes, the king's
sons
And all who clothe themselves with
foreign garments.
9 "And I will punish on that day all who
leap on the *temple* threshold,
Who fill the house of their lord with
violence and deceit.
10 "On that day," declares the LORD,
"There will be the sound of a cry from
the Fish Gate,
A wail from the ᵃSecond Quarter,
And a loud crash from the hills.
11 "Wail, O inhabitants of the ᵃMortar,
For all the people of Canaan will be
silenced;
All who weigh out silver will be cut
off.
12 "It will come about at that time
That I will search Jerusalem with lamps,
And I will punish the men
Who are stagnant in spirit,
Who say in their hearts,
'The LORD will not do good or evil!'
13 "Moreover, their wealth will become
plunder
And their houses desolate;
Yes, they will build houses but not
inhabit *them*,

ᵃ I.e. a district of Jerusalem

And plant vineyards but not drink their
    wine."

14 ¶ Near is the great day of the LORD,
    Near and coming very quickly;

1:12 Practical Atheism

*The people of Judah did terrible things, such as
worshiping Milcom (verse 5), the Ammonite
god who sometimes required child sacrifice.
Zephaniah singled out another sin, however,
that was just as damaging: complacency. They
weren't formal atheists, but they acted like it.*

Listen, the day of the LORD!
    In it the warrior cries out bitterly.
15 A day of wrath is that day,
    A day of trouble and distress,
    A day of destruction and desolation,
    A day of darkness and gloom,
    A day of clouds and thick darkness,
16 A day of trumpet and battle cry
    Against the fortified cities
    And the high corner towers.
17 I will bring distress on men
    So that they will walk like the blind,
    Because they have sinned against the
      LORD;
    And their blood will be poured out like
      dust
    And their flesh like dung.
18 Neither their silver nor their gold
    Will be able to deliver them
    On the day of the LORD's wrath;
    And all the earth will be devoured
    In the fire of His jealousy,
    For He will make a complete end,
    Indeed a terrifying one,
    Of all the inhabitants of the earth.

Judgments on Judah's Enemies

2 Gather yourselves together, yes, gather,
    O nation without shame,
2 Before the decree takes effect—
    The day passes like the chaff—
    Before the burning anger of the LORD
      comes upon you,
    Before the day of the LORD's anger
      comes upon you.
3 Seek the LORD,
    All you humble of the earth
    Who have carried out His ordinances;
    Seek righteousness, seek humility.
    Perhaps you will be hidden
    In the day of the LORD's anger.

4 ¶ For Gaza will be abandoned
    And Ashkelon a desolation;

Ashdod will be driven out at noon
    And Ekron will be uprooted.
5 Woe to the inhabitants of the seacoast,
    The nation of the *a*Cherethites!
    The word of the LORD is against you,
    O Canaan, land of the Philistines;
    And I will destroy you
    So that there will be no inhabitant.
6 So the seacoast will be pastures,
    With caves for shepherds and folds for
      flocks.
7 And the coast will be
    For the remnant of the house of Judah,
    They will pasture on it.
    In the houses of Ashkelon they will lie
      down at evening;
    For the LORD their God will care for
      them
    And restore their fortune.

8 ¶ "I have heard the taunting of Moab
    And the revilings of the sons of Ammon,
    With which they have taunted My people
    And become arrogant against their
      territory.
9 "Therefore, as I live," declares the LORD of
      hosts,
    The God of Israel,
    "Surely Moab will be like Sodom
    And the sons of Ammon like
      Gomorrah—
    A place possessed by nettles and salt pits,
    And a perpetual desolation.
    The remnant of My people will plunder
      them
    And the remainder of My nation will
      inherit them."
10 This they will have in return for their pride,
because they have taunted and become arrogant
against the people of the LORD of hosts.
11 The LORD will be terrifying to them, for He
will starve all the gods of the earth; and all the
coastlands of the nations will bow down to Him,
everyone from his *own* place.

12 ¶ "You also, O Ethiopians, will be slain
      by My sword."
13 And He will stretch out His hand against
      the north
    And destroy Assyria,
    And He will make Nineveh a desolation,
    Parched like the wilderness.
14 Flocks will lie down in her midst,
    All beasts which range in herds;
    Both the pelican and the hedgehog
    Will lodge in the tops of her pillars;
    Birds will sing in the window,
    Desolation *will be* on the threshold;
    For He has laid bare the cedar work.
15 This is the exultant city
    Which dwells securely,

---

a I.e. a segment of the Philistines with roots in Crete

Who says in her heart,
"I am, and there is no one besides me."
How she has become a desolation,
A resting place for beasts!
Everyone who passes by her will hiss
And wave his hand *in contempt*.

Woe to Jerusalem and the Nations

3 Woe to her who is rebellious and defiled,
The tyrannical city!

2 She heeded no voice,
She accepted no instruction.
She did not trust in the LORD,
She did not draw near to her God.

3 Her princes within her are roaring lions,
Her judges are wolves at evening;
They leave nothing for the morning.

4 Her prophets are reckless, treacherous
men;
Her priests have profaned the sanctuary.
They have done violence to the law.

5 The LORD is righteous within her;
He will do no injustice.
Every morning He brings His justice to
light;
He does not fail.
But the unjust knows no shame.

6 "I have cut off nations;
Their corner towers are in ruins.
I have made their streets desolate,
With no one passing by;
Their cities are laid waste,
Without a man, without an inhabitant.

7 "I said, 'Surely you will revere Me,
Accept instruction.'
So her dwelling will not be cut off
According to all that I have appointed
concerning her.
But they were eager to corrupt all their
deeds.

8 ¶ "Therefore wait for Me," declares the
LORD,
"For the day when I rise up as a witness.
Indeed, My decision is to gather nations,
To assemble kingdoms,
To pour out on them My indignation,
All My burning anger;
For all the earth will be devoured
By the fire of My zeal.

9 "For then I will give to the peoples
purified lips,
That all of them may call on the name of
the LORD,
To serve Him shoulder to shoulder.

10 "From beyond the rivers of Ethiopia
My worshipers, My dispersed ones,
Will bring My offerings.

11 "In that day you will feel no shame
Because of all your deeds

By which you have rebelled against
Me;
For then I will remove from your
midst
Your proud, exulting ones,
And you will never again be haughty
On My holy mountain.

A Remnant of Israel

12 "But I will leave among you
A humble and lowly people,
And they will take refuge in the name of
the LORD.

3:12 Meek Will Inherit

As on Wall Street, as in the streets of many cities, "survival of the fittest" might have been Jerusalem's motto. Its officials were like wolves, devouring everything in sight (verse 3). Could only the ruthless survive? Zephaniah said no. In fact, he claimed, only the meek and the humble, those who trust God and simply tell the truth, would live in security. Jesus said something similar: "Blessed are the gentle, for they shall inherit the earth" (Matthew 5:5).

---

13 "The remnant of Israel will do no wrong
And tell no lies,
Nor will a deceitful tongue
Be found in their mouths;
For they will feed and lie down
With no one to make them tremble."

14 ¶ Shout for joy, O daughter of Zion!
Shout *in triumph*, O Israel!
Rejoice and exult with all *your* heart,
O daughter of Jerusalem!

15 The LORD has taken away *His* judgments
against you,
He has cleared away your enemies.
The King of Israel, the LORD, is in your
midst;
You will fear disaster no more.

16 In that day it will be said to Jerusalem:
"Do not be afraid, O Zion;
Do not let your hands fall limp.

17 "The LORD your God is in your midst,
A victorious warrior.
He will exult over you with joy,
He will be quiet in His love,
He will rejoice over you with shouts of
joy.

18 "I will gather those who grieve about the
appointed feasts—
They came from you, O Zion;
The reproach *of exile* is a burden on
them.

19 "Behold, I am going to deal at that time
    With all your oppressors,
    I will save the lame
    And gather the outcast,
    And I will turn their shame into praise
        and renown
    In all the earth.
20 "At that time I will bring you in,
    Even at the time when I gather you
        together;
    Indeed, I will give you renown and
        praise
    Among all the peoples of the earth,
    When I restore your fortunes before your
        eyes,"
    Says the LORD.

HAGGAI

The Prophet Who Got Results
For once, God's people listened

S
OMETIMES, AT CRUCIAL MOMENTS, A single voice can stir a directionless mass of people to action. Prime minister Winston Churchill's inspiring oratory may have saved Britain in World War II. American clergyman and civil rights leader Martin Luther King's sermons and speeches captured America's conscience in the 1950s and 60s.

All the remnant of the people obeyed the voice of the LORD their God and the words of Haggai the prophet, as the LORD their God had sent him. 1:12

Haggai's words, similarly, rang clear in a time of confusion. The Jews had come back from their exile in Babylon nearly 20 years before. But they seemed to have forgotten the point of returning. After one false start on the temple, the returned exiles had devoted their energy to building their own houses. The ruins of Solomon's temple stood as a nagging reminder that they had neglected God.

Now Haggai urged these pioneers to "consider your ways." He did not rage like Jeremiah or build eloquent poems like Isaiah. He put it simply and logically. They had worked hard, but what had it earned them? Their crops were unsuccessful. Their money disappeared as soon as they earned it. Why? Haggai asked. Because they had mistaken their priorities. They needed to put God first. They needed to rebuild his temple.

A Response from the Heart

People responded to Haggai immediately. Prophets before him, such as Amos, Isaiah, and Jeremiah, had spoken for decades without seeing such a heartfelt reaction. Haggai's messages span a mere four months, but he accomplished everything he set out to do. In four years the temple was complete.

What made the temple so important? After all, the proper sacrifices and rituals could be carried out on a makeshift altar. But God's reputation was at stake. He could not be properly honored so long as the house he called home lay in ruins. The temple symbolized God's presence, and Israel's priorities.

Would rebuilding the temple change Israel's financial situation? Haggai's first words promised nothing. He simply said, "Consider your ways," and pointed out that Israel's lack of prosperity was God's doing. They had worked hard, but God had withheld the rain their crops needed. A month later (2:1–9) Haggai said that God had glorious plans for Israel, plans that would shake the whole earth. But he referred to God's presence with them, not to good crops.

Only on the last day accounted for in this brief book did Haggai get back to the subject of harvests. He said that God wanted his people to "consider" again—this time to the dramatic difference they would see in their harvests now that they had put God first. "From this day on I will bless you," God said through Haggai (2:18–19).

How to Read Haggai

O
ne of the shortest books in the Bible, Haggai can easily be read at one sitting. Haggai's words came at a critical time in the life of the nation of Israel. They mark one of the few times in all history when God spoke and his people quickly and unquestioningly obeyed. For the historical background, read Ezra 1–6. Haggai's crucial message is mentioned in Ezra 5:1–2. "A Lineup of Rulers," pages 1417–1425, can help you place Haggai in Israelite history.

There is a progression to God's warnings and his promises through Haggai. Study each of Haggai's messages, and note what *encouragement*, what *warning*, and what *hope* God offered Israel. How did God motivate them to obey him?

3-TRACK READING PLAN

For an explanation and complete listing of the 3-track reading plan, turn to page 7.

TRACK 1: **Two-Week Courses on the Bible**
See page 7 for information on these courses.

TRACK 2: **An Overview of Haggai in 1 Day**
☐ Day 1. Read the Introduction to Haggai and chapter 1, which tells how Haggai's message changed Israel's direction.
Now turn to page 9 for your next Track 2 reading project.

TRACK 3: **All of Haggai in 2 Days**
After you have read through Haggai, turn to pages 10–14 for your next Track 3 reading project.
☐1   ☐2

Haggai Begins Temple Building

1 In the second year of Darius the king, on the first day of the sixth month, the word of the LORD came by the prophet Haggai to Zerubbabel the son of Shealtiel, governor of Judah, and to Joshua the son of Jehozadak, the high priest, saying,

2 Thus says the LORD of hosts, 'This people says, "The time has not come, *even* the time for the house of the LORD to be rebuilt." ' "

1:2–13 Change of Tone

For two decades the Israelites had ignored God's strong desire for them to rebuild the temple. When they finally responded and got to work, however, God's sternness melted immediately. "I am with you," he told them. And though the new temple going up seemed a sad imitation of Solomon's masterpiece, God still spoke with gentleness and kindness (2:2–5). Haggai, one of the last prophets, indicates God's eagerness to respond with mercy.

3 Then the word of the LORD came by Haggai the prophet, saying,

4 "Is it time for you yourselves to dwell in your paneled houses while this house *lies* desolate?"

5 Now therefore, thus says the LORD of hosts, "Consider your ways!

6 "You have sown much, but harvest little; *you* eat, but *there is* not *enough* to be satisfied; *you* drink, but *there is* not *enough* to become drunk; *you* put on clothing, but no one is warm *enough*; and he who earns, earns wages *to put* into a purse with holes."

7 ¶ Thus says the LORD of hosts, "Consider your ways!

8 "Go up to the mountains, bring wood and rebuild the temple, that I may be pleased with it and be glorified," says the LORD.

9 "*You* look for much, but behold, *it comes* to little; when you bring *it* home, I blow it *away*. Why?" declares the LORD of hosts, "Because of My house which *lies* desolate, while each of you runs to his own house.

10 "Therefore, because of you the sky has withheld its dew and the earth has withheld its produce.

11 "I called for a drought on the land, on the mountains, on the grain, on the new wine, on the oil, on what the ground produces, on men, on cattle, and on all the labor of your hands."

12 ¶ Then Zerubbabel the son of Shealtiel, and Joshua the son of Jehozadak, the high priest, with all the remnant of the people, obeyed the voice of the LORD their God and the words of Haggai the prophet, as the LORD their God had sent him. And the people showed reverence for the LORD.

13 Then Haggai, the messenger of the LORD, spoke by the commission of the LORD to the people saying, " 'I am with you,' declares the LORD."

14 So the LORD stirred up the spirit of Zerubbabel the son of Shealtiel, governor of Judah, and the spirit of Joshua the son of Jehozadak, the high priest, and the spirit of all the remnant of the people; and they came and worked on the house of the LORD of hosts, their God,

15 on the twenty-fourth day of the sixth month in the second year of Darius the king.

The Builders Encouraged

2 On the twenty-first of the seventh month, the word of the LORD came by Haggai the prophet saying,

2 "Speak now to Zerubbabel the son of Shealtiel, governor of Judah, and to Joshua the son of Jehozadak, the high priest, and to the remnant of the people saying,

3 'Who is left among you who saw this temple in its former glory? And how do you see it now?

Does it not seem to you like nothing in comparison?

4 'But now take courage, Zerubbabel,' declares the LORD, 'take courage also, Joshua son of Jehozadak, the high priest, and all you people of the land take courage,' declares the LORD, 'and work; for I am with you,' declares the LORD of hosts.

5 'As for the promise which I made you when you came out of Egypt, My Spirit is abiding in your midst; do not fear!'

6 "For thus says the LORD of hosts, 'Once more in a little while, I am going to shake the heavens and the earth, the sea also and the dry land.

7 'I will shake all the nations; and they will come with the wealth of all nations, and I will fill this house with glory,' says the LORD of hosts.

8 'The silver is Mine and the gold is Mine,' declares the LORD of hosts.

9 'The latter glory of this house will be greater than the former,' says the LORD of hosts, 'and in this place I will give peace,' declares the LORD of hosts."

10 ¶ On the twenty-fourth of the ninth *month,* in the second year of Darius, the word of the LORD came to Haggai the prophet, saying,

11 "Thus says the LORD of hosts, 'Ask now the priests *for* a ruling:

12 'If a man carries holy meat in the fold of his garment, and touches bread with this fold, or cooked food, wine, oil, or any *other* food, will it become holy?' " And the priests answered, "No."

2:12 One-way Contamination

"One bad apple spoils the barrel," the saying goes; but one good apple doesn't clean up the rotten ones. In a similar vein, Haggai asked, "Which is contagious, good or evil?" In the Old Testament law, he found that consecrated meat—set aside to be used in sacrificial worship—did not "spread" its holiness. But a person who became "unclean" did spread his or her defilement. Under the Old Testament law, evil spread, but goodness did not. The Israelites' failure to rebuild the temple had defiled everything they touched—even their good deeds.

13 Then Haggai said, "If one who is unclean from a corpse touches any of these, will *the latter* become unclean?" And the priests answered, "It will become unclean."

14 Then Haggai said, " 'So is this people. And so is this nation before Me,' declares the LORD,

'and so is every work of their hands; and what they offer there is unclean.

15 'But now, do consider from this day onward: before one stone was placed on another in the temple of the LORD,

16 from that time *when* one came to a *grain* heap of twenty *measures,* there would be only ten; and *when* one came to the wine vat to draw fifty measures, there would be *only* twenty.

17 'I smote you *and* every work of your hands with blasting wind, mildew and hail; yet you *did* not *come back* to Me,' declares the LORD.

18 'Do consider from this day onward, from the twenty-fourth day of the ninth *month;* from the day when the temple of the LORD was founded, consider:

19 'Is the seed still in the barn? Even including the vine, the fig tree, the pomegranate and the olive tree, it has not borne *fruit.* Yet from this day on I will bless *you.'* "

20 ¶ Then the word of the LORD came a second time to Haggai on the twenty-fourth *day* of the month, saying,

21 "Speak to Zerubbabel governor of Judah, saying, 'I am going to shake the heavens and the earth.

22 'I will overthrow the thrones of kingdoms and destroy the power of the kingdoms of the nations; and I will overthrow the chariots and their riders, and the horses and their riders will go down, everyone by the sword of another.'

23 'On that day,' declares the LORD of hosts, 'I will take you, Zerubbabel, son of Shealtiel, My servant,' declares the LORD, 'and I will make you like a signet *ring,* for I have chosen you,' " declares the LORD of hosts.

2:23 The Imprint of the Master

Some 78 years before, Coniah (King Jehoiachin) had been captured and taken to Babylon. God had rejected him: "Even though Coniah . . . were a signet ring on My right hand, yet I would pull you off" (Jeremiah 22:24).

But now his grandson Zerubbabel had come back to Jerusalem, chosen again as the Lord's "signet ring." Such a ring was used in place of a signature, to impress the king's seal on important documents. God had accepted men from the royal line of David as his chosen leaders again. The complete fulfillment of this prophecy would have to wait for Zerubbabel's descendant Jesus, a son of David who fully printed God's image on humanity.

ZECHARIAH

Starting Over
How could they rebuild with broken pieces?

> "Therefore thus says the LORD, 'I will return to Jerusalem with compassion; My house will be built in it.' "
>
> 1:16

WHEN THE JEWS REVIEWED THEIR history, it looked like a long slide downhill. Consistently, they had responded to God's love by grumbling against him, by disobeying his law, by worshiping idols. Finally, after centuries of warning, punishment had come. Jerusalem was flattened. The survivors marched off in chains toward the other end of the world.

They had not merely lost a battle. They had lost, seemingly, their place in God's heart and their future as his special people.

But hope for a new start came in exile. When Persian emperor Cyrus took power, he offered Jews a chance to return to their land and rebuild their temple. Some jumped at the chance. They took the long journey to a homeland most of them had never seen (you can read about the trip in the first chapters of Ezra). They wanted not merely to rebuild; they hoped somehow to escape the downward, anti-God trend that had plagued their nation from its beginnings.

Hope Begins to Fade

They found a disheartening scene. Their once-beautiful city was a ghost town. Everything of value had been destroyed. Fertile fields were overgrown. The region was almost empty of people.

The small band of returned exiles built an altar on the grounds of the ruined temple. But soon they grew discouraged about actual rebuilding. They had enough trouble finding shelter and scratching out a living from the land. When their non-Jewish neighbors fought against rebuilding the temple, the former exiles gave up. Their hopes of a glorious "new beginning" began to fade.

The temple stayed in a state of disrepair for nearly 20 years, until the prophets Haggai and Zechariah stirred up renewed interest. These prophets saw that as long as the temple lay in ruins, Israel's distinctive character as a people of God was ruined, too. At their urging, the Jews organized to build again.

The book of Zechariah is a record from that critical period of rebuilding. Its first recorded message dates from approximately two months after the temple foundation was laid. The temple was completed four years later, at least partly due to Zechariah's encouraging words.

Needed: A Change of Heart

Zechariah wasn't mainly interested in a building, however. More important was the relationship with God that the temple symbolized. In his first recorded words Zechariah warned his people not to be like their ancestors. What good had a temple done them? A really new beginning required a change of heart. " 'Return to Me,' declares the LORD of hosts, 'that I may return to you' "(1:3).

The last half of Zechariah widens its view to the whole world. The small refugee community of Jews, Zechariah says, holds the world's future. Their new beginning would become the hope of the world.

How to Read Zechariah

Most people find Zechariah difficult to understand. Throughout the book you will find references to people and events that are hard to interpret. A commentary can be a great help, clarifying the meaning of these details. For historical background on Zechariah's times, read Ezra 1–6. Zechariah is mentioned by name in Ezra 5:1.

The book of Zechariah breaks into three parts. The first six chapters offer eight symbolic visions, which were meant to encourage the builders of the temple. They are not too difficult to understand if you take them one at a time and don't rush through them. Their main emphasis: God is at work again. He plans to live with his people in Jerusalem. He will protect them from their enemies, cleanse them from their sins, banish evil. He is making a new beginning for them.

Chapters 7–8 address the quality of life God wants his renewed people to enjoy. These words contain many encouraging promises to Israel.

The last six chapters are packed with puzzling references to the struggles Israel must endure in becoming what God wants. You will find predictions of terrible suffering and absolute victory. These chapters, as complex as they are, helped the Gospel writers understand Jesus' suffering, death, and resurrection. The writers quoted these chapters as they wrote of Jesus' final days. The book of Revelation, telling of the final goal of history, also drew on Zechariah's predictions.

3-TRACK READING PLAN

For an explanation and complete listing of the 3-track reading plan, turn to page 7.

TRACK 1: *Two-Week Courses on the Bible*
See page 7 for information on these courses.

TRACK 2: *An Overview of Zechariah in 1 Day*
☐ Day 1. Read the Introduction to Zechariah and chapter 8, which describes the future God has in mind for his people.

Now turn to page 9 for your next Track 2 reading project.

TRACK 3: *All of Zechariah in 11 Days*
After you have read through Zechariah, turn to pages 10–14 for your next Track 3 reading project.

☐1   ☐2–3   ☐4–5   ☐6   ☐7   ☐8   ☐9   ☐10
☐11   ☐12–13 ☐14

A Call to Repentance

1 In the eighth month of the second year of Darius, the word of the LORD came to Zechariah the prophet, the son of Berechiah, the son of Iddo saying,

2 "The LORD was very angry with your fathers.

3 "Therefore say to them, 'Thus says the LORD of hosts, "Return to Me," declares the LORD of hosts, "that I may return to you," says the LORD of hosts.

4 "Do not be like your fathers, to whom the former prophets proclaimed, saying, 'Thus says the LORD of hosts, "Return now from your evil ways and from your evil deeds."' But they did not listen or give heed to Me," declares the LORD.

5 "Your fathers, where are they? And the prophets, do they live forever?

6 "But did not My words and My statutes, which I commanded My servants the prophets, overtake your fathers? Then they repented and said, 'As the LORD of hosts purposed to do to us in accordance with our ways and our deeds, so He has dealt with us.'" ' "

Patrol of the Earth

7 ¶ On the twenty-fourth day of the eleventh month, which is the month Shebat, in the second year of Darius, the word of the LORD came to Zechariah the prophet, the son of Berechiah, the son of Iddo, as follows:

8 I saw at night, and behold, a man was riding on a red horse, and he was standing among the myrtle trees which were in the ravine, with red, sorrel and white horses behind him.

9 Then I said, "My lord, what are these?" And the angel who was speaking with me said to me, "I will show you what these are."

10 And the man who was standing among the myrtle trees answered and said, "These are those whom the LORD has sent to patrol the earth."

11 So they answered the angel of the LORD who was standing among the myrtle trees and said, "We have patrolled the earth, and behold, all the earth is peaceful and quiet."

12 ¶ Then the angel of the LORD said, "O LORD of hosts, how long will You have no compassion for Jerusalem and the cities of Judah, with which You have been indignant these seventy years?"

13 The LORD answered the angel who was

speaking with me with gracious words, comforting words.

14 So the angel who was speaking with me said to me, "Proclaim, saying, 'Thus says the LORD of hosts, "I am exceedingly jealous for Jerusalem and Zion.

15 "But I am very angry with the nations who are at ease; for while I was only a little angry, they furthered the disaster."

16 'Therefore thus says the LORD, "I will return to Jerusalem with compassion; My house will be built in it," declares the LORD of hosts, "and a measuring line will be stretched over Jerusalem."'

17 "Again, proclaim, saying, 'Thus says the LORD of hosts, "My cities will again overflow with prosperity, and the LORD will again comfort Zion and again choose Jerusalem."'"

18 ¶ Then I lifted up my eyes and looked, and behold, *there were* four horns.

1:18 Brute Power

In an agricultural society that does its plowing with oxen, nothing is stronger than a bull. Probably because of this, horns are frequently used as symbols of power in the Old Testament. In our day we might say "bulldozer."

19 So I said to the angel who was speaking with me, "What are these?" And he answered me, "These are the horns which have scattered Judah, Israel and Jerusalem."

20 Then the LORD showed me four craftsmen.

21 I said, "What are these coming to do?" And he said, "These are the horns which have scattered Judah so that no man lifts up his head; but these *craftsmen* have come to terrify them, to throw down the horns of the nations who have lifted up *their* horns against the land of Judah in order to scatter it."

God's Favor to Zion

2 Then I lifted up my eyes and looked, and behold, *there was* a man with a measuring line in his hand.

2 So I said, "Where are you going?" And he said to me, "To measure Jerusalem, to see how wide it is and how long it is."

3 And behold, the angel who was speaking with me was going out, and another angel was coming out to meet him,

4 and said to him, "Run, speak to that young man, saying, 'Jerusalem will be inhabited without walls because of the multitude of men and cattle within it.

5 'For I,' declares the LORD, 'will be a wall of fire around her, and I will be the glory in her midst.'"

6 ¶ "Ho there! Flee from the land of the north," declares the LORD, "for I have dispersed

you as the four winds of the heavens," declares the LORD.

7 "Ho, Zion! Escape, you who are living with the daughter of Babylon."

8 For thus says the LORD of hosts, "After glory He has sent me against the nations which plunder you, for he who touches you, touches the apple of His eye.

9 "For behold, I will wave My hand over them so that they will be plunder for their slaves. Then you will know that the LORD of hosts has sent Me.

10 "Sing for joy and be glad, O daughter of Zion; for behold I am coming and I will dwell in your midst," declares the LORD.

11 "Many nations will join themselves to the LORD in that day and will become My people. Then I will dwell in your midst, and you will know that the LORD of hosts has sent Me to you.

12 "The LORD will possess Judah as His portion in the holy land, and will again choose Jerusalem.

13 ¶ "Be silent, all flesh, before the LORD; for He is aroused from His holy habitation."

Joshua, the High Priest

3 Then he showed me Joshua the high priest standing before the angel of the LORD, and Satan standing at his right hand to accuse him.

3:1–4 Bad News, Good News

References to the high priest Joshua also appear throughout Haggai. Whereas Zechariah uses him as a symbol of the rebellious nation, Haggai tells of Joshua's later transformation and obedience to God. Although Haggai and Zechariah cover the same time period, they show radically different styles. Haggai emphasizes the positive and gives a very straightforward message; Zechariah warns of danger and conveys his message in visions and symbols.

2 The LORD said to Satan, "The LORD rebuke you, Satan! Indeed, the LORD who has chosen Jerusalem rebuke you! Is this not a brand plucked from the fire?"

3 Now Joshua was clothed with filthy garments and standing before the angel.

4 He spoke and said to those who were standing before him, saying, "Remove the filthy garments from him." Again he said to him, "See, I have taken your iniquity away from you and will clothe you with festal robes."

5 Then I said, "Let them put a clean turban on his head." So they put a clean turban on his head and clothed him with garments, while the angel of the LORD was standing by.

6 ¶ And the angel of the LORD admonished Joshua, saying,

7 "Thus says the LORD of hosts, 'If you will

walk in My ways and if you will perform My service, then you will also govern My house and also have charge of My courts, and I will grant you free access among these who are standing *here.*

The Branch

8 'Now listen, Joshua the high priest, you and your friends who are sitting in front of you—indeed they are men who are a symbol, for behold, I am going to bring in My servant the Branch.

9 'For behold, the stone that I have set before Joshua; on one stone are seven eyes. Behold, I will engrave an inscription on it,' declares the LORD of hosts, 'and I will remove the iniquity of that land in one day.

10 'In that day,' declares the LORD of hosts, 'every one of you will invite his neighbor to *sit* under *his* vine and under *his* fig tree.' "

The Golden Lampstand and Olive Trees

4 Then the angel who was speaking with me returned and roused me, as a man who is awakened from his sleep.

2 He said to me, "What do you see?" And I said, "I see, and behold, a lampstand all of gold with its bowl on the top of it, and its seven lamps on it with seven spouts belonging to each of the lamps which are on the top of it;

3 also two olive trees by it, one on the right side of the bowl and the other on its left side."

4 Then I said to the angel who was speaking with me saying, "What are these, my lord?"

5 So the angel who was speaking with me answered and said to me, "Do you not know what these are?" And I said, "No, my lord."

6 Then he said to me, "This is the word of the LORD to Zerubbabel saying, 'Not by might nor by power, but by My Spirit,' says the LORD of hosts.

7 'What are you, O great mountain? Before Zerubbabel *you will become* a plain; and he will bring forth the top stone with shouts of "Grace, grace to it!" ' "

8 ¶ Also the word of the LORD came to me, saying,

9 "The hands of Zerubbabel have laid the foundation of this house, and his hands will finish *it.* Then you will know that the LORD of hosts has sent me to you.

10 "For who has despised the day of small things? But these seven will be glad when they see the plumb line in the hand of Zerubbabel—*these are* the eyes of the LORD which range to and fro throughout the earth."

11 ¶ Then I said to him, "What are these two olive trees on the right of the lampstand and on its left?"

12 And I answered the second time and said to him, "What are the two olive branches which are beside the two golden pipes, which empty the golden *oil* from themselves?"

13 So he answered me, saying, "Do you not know what these are?" And I said, "No, my lord."

14 Then he said, "These are the two anointed ones who are standing by the Lord of the whole earth."

The Flying Scroll

5 Then I lifted up my eyes again and looked, and behold, *there was* a flying scroll.

5:1 A Message for Everyone

The flying scroll probably symbolizes God's law, which condemns sin. It is unrolled and flying like a banner for all to read—not rolled up for only priests to read.

2 And he said to me, "What do you see?" And I answered, "I see a flying scroll; its length is twenty cubits and its width ten cubits."

3 Then he said to me, "This is the curse that is going forth over the face of the whole land; surely everyone who steals will be purged away according to the writing on one side, and everyone who swears will be purged away according to the writing on the other side.

4 "I will make it go forth," declares the LORD of hosts, "and it will enter the house of the thief and the house of the one who swears falsely by My name; and it will spend the night within that house and consume it with its timber and stones."

5 ¶ Then the angel who was speaking with me went out and said to me, "Lift up now your eyes and see what this is going forth."

6 I said, "What is it?" And he said, "This is the ephah going forth." Again he said, "This is their appearance in all the land

7 (and behold, a lead cover was lifted up); and this is a woman sitting inside the ephah."

8 Then he said, "This is Wickedness!" And he threw her down into the middle of the ephah and cast the lead weight on its opening.

9 Then I lifted up my eyes and looked, and there two women were coming out with the wind in their wings; and they had wings like the wings of a stork, and they lifted up the ephah between the earth and the heavens.

10 I said to the angel who was speaking with me, "Where are they taking the ephah?"

11 Then he said to me, "To build a temple for her in the land of Shinar; and when it is prepared, she will be set there on her own pedestal."

The Four Chariots

6 Now I lifted up my eyes again and looked, and behold, four chariots were coming forth from between the two mountains; and the mountains *were* bronze mountains.

2 With the first chariot *were* red horses, with the second chariot black horses,

3 with the third chariot white horses, and with the fourth chariot strong dappled horses.

4 Then I spoke and said to the angel who was speaking with me, "What are these, my lord?"

5 The angel replied to me, "These are the four spirits of heaven, going forth after standing before the Lord of all the earth,

6 with one of which the black horses are going forth to the north country; and the white ones go forth after them, while the dappled ones go forth to the south country.

7 "When the strong ones went out, they were eager to go to patrol the earth." And He said, "Go, patrol the earth." So they patrolled the earth.

8 Then He cried out to me and spoke to me saying, "See, those who are going to the land of the north have appeased My wrath in the land of the north."

9 ¶ The word of the LORD also came to me, saying,

10 "Take an offering from the exiles, from Heldai, Tobijah and Jedaiah; and you go the same day and enter the house of Josiah the son of Zephaniah, where they have arrived from Babylon.

The Symbolic Crowns

11 "Take silver and gold, make an ornate crown and set it on the head of Joshua the son of Jehozadak, the high priest.

12 "Then say to him, 'Thus says the LORD of hosts, "Behold, a man whose name is Branch, for He will branch out from where He is; and He will build the temple of the LORD.

13 "Yes, it is He who will build the temple of the LORD, and He who will bear the honor and sit and rule on His throne. Thus, He will be a priest on His throne, and the counsel of peace will be between the two offices." '

14 "Now the crown will become a reminder in the temple of the LORD to Helem, Tobijah, Jedaiah and Hen the son of Zephaniah.

15 "Those who are far off will come and build the temple of the LORD." Then you will know that the LORD of hosts has sent me to you. And it will take place if you completely obey the LORD your God.

Hearts like Flint

7 In the fourth year of King Darius, the word of the LORD came to Zechariah on the fourth day of the ninth month, which is Chislev.

2 Now the town of Bethel had sent Sharezer and Regemmelech and their men to seek the favor of the LORD,

3 speaking to the priests who belong to the house of the LORD of hosts, and to the prophets, saying, "Shall I weep in the fifth month and abstain, as I have done these many years?"

4 Then the word of the LORD of hosts came to me, saying,

5 "Say to all the people of the land and to the priests, 'When you fasted and mourned in the fifth and seventh months these seventy years, was it actually for Me that you fasted?

6 'When you eat and drink, do you not eat for yourselves and do you not drink for yourselves?

7:3 Repent for How Long?

While in exile, Jews had fasted and mourned on certain days in memory of the siege and overthrow of Jerusalem. Now that they had returned to Jerusalem they wanted to know: Should we keep fasting? Zechariah's answer came in 8:19: Fasting should now be replaced with feasting. But Zechariah warned that all religious ceremonies, however proper, were meaningless unless people's lives were controlled by God.

7 'Are not these the words which the LORD proclaimed by the former prophets, when Jerusalem was inhabited and prosperous along with its cities around it, and the Negev and the foothills were inhabited?' "

8 ¶ Then the word of the LORD came to Zechariah saying,

9 "Thus has the LORD of hosts said, 'Dispense true justice and practice kindness and compassion each to his brother;

10 and do not oppress the widow or the orphan, the stranger or the poor; and do not devise evil in your hearts against one another.'

11 "But they refused to pay attention and turned a stubborn shoulder and stopped their ears from hearing.

12 "They made their hearts like flint so that they could not hear the law and the words which the LORD of hosts had sent by His Spirit through the former prophets; therefore great wrath came from the LORD of hosts.

13 "And just as He called and they would not listen, so they called and I would not listen," says the LORD of hosts;

14 "but I scattered them with a storm wind among all the nations whom they have not known. Thus the land is desolated behind them so that no one went back and forth, for they made the pleasant land desolate."

The Coming Peace and Prosperity of Zion

8 Then the word of the LORD of hosts came, saying,

2 "Thus says the LORD of hosts, 'I am exceedingly jealous for Zion, yes, with great wrath I am jealous for her.'

3 "Thus says the LORD, 'I will return to Zion and will dwell in the midst of Jerusalem. Then Jerusalem will be called the City of Truth, and the mountain of the LORD of hosts will be called the Holy Mountain.'

4 "Thus says the LORD of hosts, 'Old men and old women will again sit in the ^astreets of Jerusalem, each man with his staff in his hand because of age.

8:4 Safe Streets

To refugees inhabiting a city overrun by conquerors, the promise of streets safe for senior citizens and playful children seemed almost too much to ask. But God assured them Jerusalem would once again become stable and secure. "Will it also be too difficult in My sight?" he asks, with a touch of irony (verse 6).

5 'And the ^astreets of the city will be filled with boys and girls playing in its ^astreets.'

6 "Thus says the LORD of hosts, 'If it is too difficult in the sight of the remnant of this people in those days, will it also be too difficult in My sight?' declares the LORD of hosts.

7 "Thus says the LORD of hosts, 'Behold, I am going to save My people from the land of the east and from the land of the west;

8 and I will bring them *back* and they will live in the midst of Jerusalem; and they shall be My people, and I will be their God in truth and righteousness.'

9 ¶ "Thus says the LORD of hosts, 'Let your hands be strong, you who are listening in these days to these words from the mouth of the prophets, *those* who *spoke* in the day that the foundation of the house of the LORD of hosts was laid, to the end that the temple might be built.

10 'For before those days there was no wage for man or any wage for animal; and for him who went out or came in there was no peace because of his enemies, and I set all men one against another.

11 'But now I will not treat the remnant of this people as in the former days,' declares the LORD of hosts.

12 'For *there will be* peace for the seed: the vine will yield its fruit, the land will yield its produce and the heavens will give their dew; and I will cause the remnant of this people to inherit all these *things*.

13 'It will come about that just as you were a curse among the nations, O house of Judah and house of Israel, so I will save you that you may become a blessing. Do not fear; let your hands be strong.'

14 ¶ "For thus says the LORD of hosts, 'Just as I purposed to do harm to you when your fathers provoked Me to wrath,' says the LORD of hosts, 'and I have not relented,

15 so I have again purposed in these days to do good to Jerusalem and to the house of Judah. Do not fear!

16 'These are the things which you should do: speak the truth to one another; judge with truth and judgment for peace in your ^bgates.

17 'Also let none of you devise evil in your heart against another, and do not love perjury; for all these are what I hate,' declares the LORD."

18 ¶ Then the word of the LORD of hosts came to me, saying,

19 "Thus says the LORD of hosts, 'The fast of the fourth, the fast of the fifth, the fast of the seventh and the fast of the tenth *months* will become joy, gladness, and cheerful feasts for the house of Judah; so love truth and peace.'

20 ¶ "Thus says the LORD of hosts, '*It will* yet *be* that peoples will come, even the inhabitants of many cities.

21 'The inhabitants of one will go to another, saying, "Let us go at once to entreat the favor of the LORD, and to seek the LORD of hosts; I will also go."

22 'So many peoples and mighty nations will come to seek the LORD of hosts in Jerusalem and to entreat the favor of the LORD.'

23 "Thus says the LORD of hosts, 'In those days ten men from all the nations will grasp the garment of a Jew, saying, "Let us go with you, for we have heard that God is with you." ' "

Prophecies against Neighboring Nations

9 The burden of the word of the LORD is against the land of Hadrach, with Damascus as its resting place (for the eyes of men, especially of all the tribes of Israel, are toward the LORD),

2 And Hamath also, which borders on it;
   Tyre and Sidon, though they are very
      wise.
3 For Tyre built herself a fortress
   And piled up silver like dust,
   And gold like the mire of the streets.
4 Behold, the Lord will dispossess her
   And cast her wealth into the sea;
   And she will be consumed with fire.
5 Ashkelon will see *it* and be afraid.
   Gaza too will writhe in great pain;
   Also Ekron, for her expectation has been
      confounded.
   Moreover, the king will perish from
      Gaza,
   And Ashkelon will not be inhabited.
6 And a mongrel race will dwell in
      Ashdod,
   And I will cut off the pride of the
      Philistines.
7 And I will remove their blood from their
      mouth
   And their detestable things from between
      their teeth.

^a Or *squares*   ^b I.e. the place where court was held

Then they also will be a remnant for our God,
And be like a clan in Judah,
And Ekron like a Jebusite.

8 But I will camp around My house
  because of an army,
Because of him who passes by and
  returns;
And no oppressor will pass over them
  anymore,
For now I have seen with My eyes.

9 Rejoice greatly, O daughter of Zion!
Shout *in triumph*, O daughter of
  Jerusalem!
Behold, your king is coming to you;
He is just and endowed with salvation,
Humble, and mounted on a donkey,
Even on a colt, the foal of a donkey.

10 I will cut off the chariot from Ephraim
And the horse from Jerusalem;
And the bow of war will be cut off.
And He will speak peace to the nations;
And His dominion will be from sea to
  sea,
And from the *a*River to the ends of the
  earth.

a I.e. Euphrates

Deliverance of Judah and Ephraim

11 ¶ As for you also, because of the blood
  of *My* covenant with you,
I have set your prisoners free from the
  waterless pit.

9:9 Donkey of Peace

The Gospel writers refer back to this verse in connection with Jesus' triumphal entry into Jerusalem (Matthew 21:5; John 12:15). More warlike leaders normally rode on stallions, but Zechariah pointedly notes that the coming king will ban chariots and horses (verse 10). Jesus scrupulously followed the pattern of a king described here—often disappointing his followers, who sought a more militaristic leader.

12 Return to the stronghold, O prisoners
  who have the hope;
This very day I am declaring that I will
  restore double to you.

13 For I will bend Judah as My bow,

New King, New Kingdom
The paradox of leadership that triumphs through suffering

THE BOOK OF ZECHARIAH TAKES a radical turn at chapter 9. A series of messages from God, expressed in fragmented images, tells the future of the world—and the role of God's people in it.

These chapters are difficult to understand, even in our day. The ultimate future is clearly good, however: Instead of remaining a small, subject nation, God's people will shake the world. The nations will worship at Jerusalem. "The LORD will be king over all the earth" (14:9).

> Your king is coming to you; He is just and endowed with salvation, humble, and mounted on a donkey. 9:9

How could it be? Even for the Israelites this dream sounded farfetched. In Zechariah's day they needed clearance from the far-off Persian government just to rebuild their temple. Persia was the center of their world. Jerusalem hardly mattered. How could Israel become a great nation?

A Rejected Leader

These chapters of Zechariah show Israel's greatness emerging through struggle and suffering. No one who reads these words could have a glib idea that God makes things easy. Evil and misery virtually triumph before God's final intervention.

The key to Israel's future is a coming leader—a very unusual leader. People naturally expected the Messiah to be a triumphant warrior, especially since many Old Testament prophecies spoke of him that way. But this king would come on a donkey instead of a war-horse (9:9). Zechariah speaks of a shepherd—a term for "leader"—who would be rejected by the nation (11:4–17). It describes a nation in mourning for the one "whom they have pierced" (12:10).

All these predictions of a coming leader were quoted in the New Testament as applying to Jesus: a king without an army, whose crown was made of thorns. In all the Old Testament, only Isaiah (especially in chapter 53) captures so fully the paradox of Jesus' life: gentle leadership that triumphs through suffering.

Life Questions: Who is the "greatest" person you've known up close? Did some kind of suffering contribute to his or her greatness?

I will fill the bow with Ephraim.
And I will stir up your sons, O Zion,
    against your sons, O Greece;
And I will make you like a warrior's
    sword.
14 Then the LORD will appear over them,
And His arrow will go forth like
    lightning;
And the Lord GOD will blow the
    trumpet,
And will march in the storm winds of
    the south.
15 The LORD of hosts will defend them.
And they will devour and trample on the
    sling stones;
And they will drink *and* be boisterous as
    with wine;
And they will be filled like a *sacrificial*
    basin,
Drenched like the corners of the altar.
16 And the LORD their God will save them
    in that day
As the flock of His people;
For *they are as* the stones of a crown,
Sparkling in His land.
17 For what comeliness and beauty *will be*
    theirs!
Grain will make the young men flourish,
    and new wine the virgins.

God Will Bless Judah and Ephraim

10 Ask rain from the LORD at the time of the
    spring rain—
The LORD who makes the storm clouds;
And He will give them showers of rain,
    vegetation in the field to *each* man.
2 For the teraphim speak iniquity,
And the diviners see lying visions
And tell false dreams;
They comfort in vain.
Therefore *the people* wander like sheep,
They are afflicted, because there is no
    shepherd.
3 "My anger is kindled against the
    shepherds,
And I will punish the male goats;
For the LORD of hosts has visited His
    flock, the house of Judah,
And will make them like His majestic
    horse in battle.
4 "From them will come the cornerstone,
From them the tent peg,
From them the bow of battle,
From them every ruler, *all* of them
    together.
5 "They will be as mighty men,
Treading down *the enemy* in the mire of
    the streets in battle;
And they will fight, for the LORD *will be*
    with them;

And the riders on horses will be put to
    shame.
6 "I will strengthen the house of Judah,
And I will save the house of Joseph,
And I will bring them back,
Because I have had compassion on them;
And they will be as though I had not
    rejected them,
For I am the LORD their God and I will
    answer them.
7 "Ephraim will be like a mighty man,
And their heart will be glad as if *from*
    wine;
Indeed, their children will see *it* and be
    glad,
Their heart will rejoice in the LORD.
8 "I will whistle for them to gather them
    together,
For I have redeemed them;
And they will be as numerous as they
    were before.
9 "When I scatter them among the peoples,
They will remember Me in far countries,
And they with their children will live and
    come back.
10 "I will bring them back from the land of
    Egypt
And gather them from Assyria;
And I will bring them into the land of
    Gilead and Lebanon
Until no *room* can be found for them.
11 "And they will pass through the sea *of*
    distress
And He will strike the waves in the sea,
So that all the depths of the Nile will
    dry up;
And the pride of Assyria will be brought
    down
And the scepter of Egypt will depart.
12 "And I will strengthen them in the LORD,
And in His name they will walk,"
    declares the LORD.

The Doomed Flock

11 Open your doors, O Lebanon,
    That a fire may feed on your cedars.
2 Wail, O cypress, for the cedar has fallen,
Because the glorious *trees* have been
    destroyed;
Wail, O oaks of Bashan,
For the impenetrable forest has come
    down.
3 There is a sound of the shepherds' wail,
For their glory is ruined;
There is a sound of the young lions'
    roar,
For the pride of the Jordan is ruined.

4 ¶ Thus says the LORD my God, "Pasture the
flock *doomed* to slaughter.
5 "Those who buy them slay them and go unpunished, and *each of* those who sell them says,

'Blessed be the LORD, for I have become rich!' And their own shepherds have no pity on them.

6 "For I will no longer have pity on the inhabitants of the land," declares the LORD; "but behold, I will cause the men to fall, each into another's power and into the power of his king; and they will strike the land, and I will not deliver *them* from their power."

7 ¶ So I pastured the flock *doomed* to slaughter, hence the afflicted of the flock. And I took for myself two staffs: the one I called Favor and the other I called Union; so I pastured the flock.

11:7 Who Are the Shepherds?

The prophets' messages often had a double meaning: one for the people who first heard them, and another, deeper meaning for future times. In this passage, Zechariah plays the role of the good shepherd who is rejected, an image that Jesus later applied to himself. Similarly, the Jews in Zechariah's day had many "foolish shepherd" leaders, but this description (verses 15–17) may also foreshadow the New Testament's "antichrist."

8 Then I annihilated the three shepherds in one month, for my soul was impatient with them, and their soul also was weary of me.

9 Then I said, "I will not pasture you. What is to die, let it die, and what is to be annihilated, let it be annihilated; and let those who are left eat one another's flesh."

10 I took my staff Favor and cut it in pieces, to break my covenant which I had made with all the peoples.

11 So it was broken on that day, and ᵃthus the afflicted of the flock who were watching me realized that it was the word of the LORD.

12 I said to them, "If it is good in your sight, give *me* my wages; but if not, never mind!" So they weighed out thirty *shekels* of silver as my wages.

13 Then the LORD said to me, "Throw it to the potter, *that* magnificent price at which I was valued by them." So I took the thirty *shekels* of silver and threw them to the potter in the house of the LORD.

14 Then I cut in pieces my second staff Union, to break the brotherhood between Judah and Israel.

15 ¶ The LORD said to me, "Take again for yourself the equipment of a foolish shepherd.

16 "For behold, I am going to raise up a shepherd in the land who will not care for the perishing, seek the scattered, heal the broken, or sustain the one standing, but will devour the flesh of the fat *sheep* and tear off their hoofs.

17 "Woe to the worthless shepherd

Who leaves the flock!
A sword will be on his arm
And on his right eye!
His arm will be totally withered
And his right eye will be blind."

Jerusalem to Be Attacked

12 The ᵇburden of the word of the LORD concerning Israel.

¶ *Thus* declares the LORD who stretches out the heavens, lays the foundation of the earth, and forms the spirit of man within him,

2 "Behold, I am going to make Jerusalem a cup that causes reeling to all the peoples around; and when the siege is against Jerusalem, it will also be against Judah.

3 "It will come about in that day that I will make Jerusalem a heavy stone for all the peoples; all who lift it will be severely injured. And all the nations of the earth will be gathered against it.

4 "In that day," declares the LORD, "I will strike every horse with bewilderment and his rider with madness. But I will watch over the house of Judah, while I strike every horse of the peoples with blindness.

5 "Then the clans of Judah will say in their hearts, 'A strong support for us are the inhabitants of Jerusalem through the LORD of hosts, their God.'

6 ¶ "In that day I will make the clans of Judah like a firepot among pieces of wood and a flaming torch among sheaves, so they will consume on the right hand and on the left all the surrounding peoples, while the inhabitants of Jerusalem again dwell on their own sites in Jerusalem.

7 "The LORD also will save the tents of Judah first, so that the glory of the house of David and the glory of the inhabitants of Jerusalem will not be magnified above Judah.

8 "In that day the LORD will defend the inhabitants of Jerusalem, and the one who is feeble among them in that day will be like David, and the house of David *will be* like God, like the angel of the LORD before them.

9 "And in that day I will set about to destroy all the nations that come against Jerusalem.

10 ¶ "I will pour out on the house of David and on the inhabitants of Jerusalem, the Spirit of grace and of supplication, so that they will look on Me whom they have pierced; and they will mourn for Him, as one mourns for an only son, and they will weep bitterly over Him like the bitter weeping over a firstborn.

11 "In that day there will be great mourning in Jerusalem, like the mourning of Hadadrimmon in the plain of Megiddo.

12 "The land will mourn, every family by itself; the family of the house of David by itself and their wives by themselves; the family of the house of Nathan by itself and their wives by themselves;

ᵃ Another reading is *the sheep dealers who*   ᵇ Or *oracle*

13 the family of the house of Levi by itself and their wives by themselves; the family of the Shime-ites by itself and their wives by themselves;

14 all the families that remain, every family by itself and their wives by themselves.

False Prophets Ashamed

13 "In that day a fountain will be opened for the house of David and for the inhabitants of Jerusalem, for sin and for impurity.

2 ¶ "It will come about in that day," declares the LORD of hosts, "that I will cut off the names of the idols from the land, and they will no longer be remembered; and I will also remove the prophets and the unclean spirit from the land.

3 "And if anyone still prophesies, then his fa-ther and mother who gave birth to him will say to him, 'You shall not live, for you have spoken false-ly in the name of the LORD'; and his father and mother who gave birth to him will pierce him through when he prophesies.

4 "Also it will come about in that day that the prophets will each be ashamed of his vision when he prophesies, and they will not put on a hairy robe in order to deceive;

5 but he will say, 'I am not a prophet; I am a tiller of the ground, for a man sold me as a slave in my youth.'

6 "And one will say to him, 'What are these wounds between your arms?' Then he will say, 'Those with which I was wounded in the house of my friends.'

7 ¶ "Awake, O sword, against My
Shepherd,
And against the man, My Associate,"
Declares the LORD of hosts.
"Strike the Shepherd that the sheep may
be scattered;
And I will turn My hand against the little
ones.

13:7 A Prophecy of Jesus

Jesus applied this verse to himself just before he died (Matthew 26:31). Some commentators believe that his words about the shepherd who "lays down His life for the sheep" (John 10:11) also drew on this passage. Zechariah's prophecies were on the minds of the Gospel writers: 9:9 is quoted in Matthew 21:5; 12:10 in John 19:37; and 11:12–13 in Matthew 27:9.

8 "It will come about in all the land,"
Declares the LORD,
"That two parts in it will be cut off and
perish;
But the third will be left in it.

9 "And I will bring the third part through
the fire,
Refine them as silver is refined,

And test them as gold is tested.
They will call on My name,
And I will answer them;
I will say, 'They are My people,'
And they will say, 'The LORD is my
God.'"

God Will Battle Jerusalem's Foes

14 Behold, a day is coming for the LORD when the spoil taken from you will be divided among you.

2 For I will gather all the nations against Jeru-salem to battle, and the city will be captured, the houses plundered, the women ravished and half of the city exiled, but the rest of the people will not be cut off from the city.

3 Then the LORD will go forth and fight against those nations, as when He fights on a day of battle.

4 In that day His feet will stand on the Mount of Olives, which is in front of Jerusalem on the east; and the Mount of Olives will be split in its middle from east to west by a very large valley, so that half of the mountain will move toward the north and the other half toward the south.

5 You will flee by the valley of My mountains, for the valley of the mountains will reach to Azel; yes, you will flee just as you fled before the earth-quake in the days of Uzziah king of Judah. Then the LORD, my God, will come, *and* all the holy ones with Him!

6 ¶ In that day there will be no light; the lumi-naries will dwindle.

7 For it will be a unique day which is known to the LORD, neither day nor night, but it will come about that at evening time there will be light.

8 ¶ And in that day living waters will flow out of Jerusalem, half of them toward the eastern sea and the other half toward the western sea; it will be in summer as well as in winter.

God Will Be King over All

9 ¶ And the LORD will be king over all the

14:9 Catastrophes to Come?

Biblical scholars disagree on how to understand the images in this chapter. To some, the catastrophes portrayed—a mountain splitting in two, a day without light or cold, people rotting on their feet (verses 4,6,12)—take on added significance in an era of nuclear weapons and a possible greenhouse effect. Others interpret these images in more symbolic ways. Regardless, Zechariah makes clear that the end result of the earth's turmoil will be good news for all followers of God.

earth; in that day the LORD will be *the only* one, and His name *the only* one.

10 ¶ All the land will be changed into a plain from Geba to Rimmon south of Jerusalem; but Jerusalem will rise and remain on its site from Benjamin's Gate as far as the place of the First Gate to the Corner Gate, and from the Tower of Hananel to the king's wine presses.

11 People will live in it, and there will no longer be a curse, for Jerusalem will dwell in security.

12 ¶ Now this will be the plague with which the LORD will strike all the peoples who have gone to war against Jerusalem; their flesh will rot while they stand on their feet, and their eyes will rot in their sockets, and their tongue will rot in their mouth.

13 It will come about in that day that a great panic from the LORD will fall on them; and they will seize one another's hand, and the hand of one will be lifted against the hand of another.

14 Judah also will fight at Jerusalem; and the wealth of all the surrounding nations will be gathered, gold and silver and garments in great abundance.

15 So also like this plague will be the plague on the horse, the mule, the camel, the donkey and all the cattle that will be in those camps.

16 ¶ Then it will come about that any who are left of all the nations that went against Jerusalem will go up from year to year to worship the King, the LORD of hosts, and to celebrate the Feast of Booths.

17 And it will be that whichever of the families of the earth does not go up to Jerusalem to wor-

ship the King, the LORD of hosts, there will be no rain on them.

18 If the family of Egypt does not go up or enter, then no *rain will fall* on them; it will be the

14:21 No More Separation

The priests and the temple had always been separate and more holy than the rest of Israel. "HOLY TO THE LORD" had been inscribed on the priests' turbans (Exodus 28:36) as a symbol of this. But, Zechariah predicted, in the future such words would decorate even horses. Ordinary kitchen pots would become as sacred as the holy sacramental vessels. There would no longer be a distinction between the sacred and secular, for everything would be sacred.

plague with which the LORD smites the nations who do not go up to celebrate the Feast of Booths.

19 This will be the punishment of Egypt, and the punishment of all the nations who do not go up to celebrate the Feast of Booths.

20 ¶ In that day there will *be inscribed* on the bells of the horses, "HOLY TO THE LORD." And the cooking pots in the LORD's house will be like the bowls before the altar.

21 Every cooking pot in Jerusalem and in Judah will be holy to the LORD of hosts; and all who sacrifice will come and take of them and boil in them. And there will no longer be a Canaanite in the house of the LORD of hosts in that day.

MALACHI

When Faith Grows Weary
Malachi spoke to people "going through the motions"

S UCCESS HAS DANGERS OF ITS own. When you reach the top, you may tend to slack off. Spiritual life can gradually deteriorate too.

Malachi, in this short book, tried to awaken Israel from slackness in relating to God. Years before, they had optimistically returned to Jerusalem after a long exile. Their faith had grown deeper through difficulties. Despite fierce opposition they had rebuilt the temple, the symbol of their hope in God. They had expected God to supernaturally fill it with his glory and make their nation the center of the world.

> *"A son honors his father, and a servant his master . . . And if I am a master, where is My respect?"* 1:6

By Malachi's time Israel's hope had faded. In fact, life seemed to have passed the Israelites by. They could not see that God loved them (1:2), and they felt that serving God brought no reward (2:17; 3:14).

No Big Sinners

The people of Jerusalem had become lukewarm. Their complaints showed it, and so did their actions. They were not "big" sinners like the people before the exile, who had practiced child sacrifice and brought idols into the temple. Malachi's people had kept their religion, but they had lost contact with the God whom the religion was all about.

While Malachi mentioned the same injustices and evils earlier prophets had blasted (3:5), he concentrated most of his energy on problems that may seem petty in comparison: mixed marriages, divorce, and apathetic worship (shown in their second-rate offerings). Through Malachi's eyes, we see the Israelites going through the motions of their faith, doing the bare minimum.

How do you heat up a lukewarm faith? Malachi used several tactics. He began with God's love. To his audience, it was not apparent. But if they would compare their situation with neighboring Edom's, they would see that God had been caring for them all along.

Curing a Careless Attitude

Malachi then challenged the Jews to take obedience seriously. They were bringing injured or sick animals to God for offerings. "Why not offer it to your governor!" Malachi said. "Would he be pleased with you?" (1:8). Malachi urged them to bring the perfect animals God's law demands and his honor requires. Malachi further demanded that they stop marrying women of other religions, a practice that inevitably introduced religious compromise. They must also put an end to divorce. And finally, they must bring a full tenth—the "tithe"—of their income to God at the temple. Their skimping amounted to robbery—robbery from God.

Malachi didn't demand these changes just because they were in the rulebook. They were actions meant to symbolize an inner attitude. The people must practice their faith seriously. "Test Me now in this," says the LORD of hosts, "if I will not open for you the windows of heaven and pour out for you a blessing until it overflows" (3:10).

The Last Voice

Malachi's was the last Old Testament voice. It reverberated through 400 or more years of biblical silence. During those years at least some of Malachi's message took hold. Led by the Pharisees, Jews became increasingly devoted to keeping the Old Testament law. Unfortunately, many of them lost Malachi's main point. They forgot that the law was not an end in itself. It was a means by which to give God the honor he deserves.

How to Read Malachi

God's voice dominates Malachi, the voice of a loving father pleading with his children. The people's response is given in the form of seven questions or complaints. The result is a kind of dialogue—almost an argument—which lets you see into the personal attitudes of God and the people he is speaking to.

As in most arguments, a variety of issues are raised, but they are all rooted in a few basic attitudes. As you read through Malachi, try to see what attitudes lay behind the questions, complaints, and problems of God's people. Also note what attitudes lay behind God's words and promises to them.

You can place Malachi's message in the context of Israelite history by looking up 'A Lineup of Rulers,' pages 1417–1425.

3-TRACK READING PLAN

For an explanation and complete listing of the 3-track reading plan, turn to page 7.

TRACK 1: *Two-Week Courses on the Bible*
See page 7 for information on these courses.

TRACK 2: *An Overview of Malachi in 1 Day*
☐ Day 1. Read the Introduction to Malachi and chapter 3, which lays out some of God's promises and expectations for his people.

Now turn to page 9 for your next Track 2 reading project.

TRACK 3: *All of Malachi in 3 Days*
After you have read through Malachi, turn to pages 10–14 for your next Track 3 reading project.

☐1   ☐2   ☐3–4

God's Love for Jacob

1 The oracle of the word of the LORD to Israel through Malachi.

2 ¶ "I have loved you," says the LORD. But you say, "How have You loved us?" "*Was* not Esau Jacob's brother?" declares the LORD. "Yet I have loved Jacob;

1:2 Spurned

Lovers remember when they first fell for someone. They also remember how that person responded, especially if their love met rejection.

In Malachi, God starts the conversation: "I have loved you." Then he traces all of Israel's sins back to their underlying contempt for that love. They have not honored him as a father (verse 6) or worshiped him as the great King he is (verse 11). Instead, they have shown contempt, bringing second-rate offerings (verse 8), saying, "how tiresome it is!" and sniffing contemptuously at his table (verse 13).

3 but I have hated Esau, and I have made his mountains a desolation and *appointed* his inheritance for the jackals of the wilderness."

4 Though Edom says, "We have been beaten down, but we will return and build up the ruins"; thus says the LORD of hosts, "They may build, but I will tear down; and *men* will call them the wicked territory, and the people toward whom the LORD is indignant forever."

5 Your eyes will see this and you will say, "The LORD be magnified beyond the border of Israel!"

Sin of the Priests

6 ¶ " 'A son honors *his* father, and a servant his master. Then if I am a father, where is My honor? And if I am a master, where is My respect?' says the LORD of hosts to you, O priests who despise My name. But you say, 'How have we despised Your name?'

7 "*You* are presenting defiled food upon My altar. But you say, 'How have we defiled You?' In that you say, 'The table of the LORD is to be despised.'

8 "But when you present the blind for sacrifice, is it not evil? And when you present the lame and sick, is it not evil? Why not offer it to your governor? Would he be pleased with you? Or would he receive you kindly?" says the LORD of hosts.

9 "But now will you not entreat God's favor, that He may be gracious to us? With such an

offering on your part, will He receive any of you kindly?" says the LORD of hosts.

10 "Oh that there were one among you who would shut the gates, that you might not uselessly kindle *fire on* My altar! I am not pleased with you," says the LORD of hosts, "nor will I accept an offering from you.

11 "For from the rising of the sun even to its setting, My name *will be* great among the nations, and in every place incense is going to be offered to My name, and a grain offering *that is* pure; for My name *will be* great among the nations," says the LORD of hosts.

12 "But you are profaning it, in that you say, 'The table of the Lord is defiled, and as for its fruit, its food is to be despised.'

13 "You also say, 'My, how tiresome it is!' And you disdainfully sniff at it," says the LORD of hosts, "and you bring what was taken by robbery and *what is* lame or sick; so you bring the offering! Should I receive that from your hand?" says the LORD.

14 "But cursed be the swindler who has a male in his flock and vows it, but sacrifices a blemished animal to the Lord, for I am a great King," says the LORD of hosts, "and My name is feared among the nations."

Priests to Be Disciplined

2 "And now this commandment is for you, O priests.

2 "If you do not listen, and if you do not take it to heart to give honor to My name," says the LORD of hosts, "then I will send the curse upon you and I will curse your blessings; and indeed, I have cursed them *already*, because you are not taking *it* to heart.

3 "Behold, I am going to rebuke your offspring, and I will spread refuse on your faces, the refuse of your feasts; and you will be taken away with it.

4 "Then you will know that I have sent this commandment to you, that My covenant may continue with Levi," says the LORD of hosts.

5 "My covenant with him was *one of* life and peace, and I gave them to him *as an object of* reverence; so he revered Me and stood in awe of My name.

6 "True instruction was in his mouth and unrighteousness was not found on his lips; he walked with Me in peace and uprightness, and he turned many back from iniquity.

7 "For the lips of a priest should preserve knowledge, and men should seek instruction from his mouth; for he is the messenger of the LORD of hosts.

8 "But as for you, you have turned aside from the way; you have caused many to stumble by the instruction; you have corrupted the covenant of Levi," says the LORD of hosts.

9 "So I also have made you despised and abased before all the people, just as you are not keeping My ways but are showing partiality in the instruction.

Sin in the Family

10 ¶ "Do we not all have one father? Has not one God created us? Why do we deal treacherously each against his brother so as to profane the covenant of our fathers?

11 "Judah has dealt treacherously, and an abomination has been committed in Israel and in Jerusalem; for Judah has profaned the sanctuary of the LORD which He loves and has married the daughter of a foreign god.

12 "*As* for the man who does this, may the LORD cut off from the tents of Jacob *everyone* who awakes and answers, or who presents an offering to the LORD of hosts.

13 ¶ "This is another thing you do: you cover the altar of the LORD with tears, with weeping and with groaning, because He no longer regards the offering or accepts *it with* favor from your hand.

14 "Yet you say, 'For what reason?' Because the LORD has been a witness between you and the wife of your youth, against whom you have dealt treacherously, though she is your companion and your wife by covenant.

15 "But not one has done *so* who has a remnant of the Spirit. And what did *that* one *do* while he was seeking a godly offspring? Take heed then to your spirit, and let no one deal treacherously against the wife of your youth.

16 "For I hate divorce," says the LORD, the God of Israel, "and him who covers his garment with wrong," says the LORD of hosts. "So take heed to your spirit, that you do not deal treacherously."

2:16 I Hate Divorce

Divorce was legal in Israel (see Deuteronomy 24:1–4), so perhaps people made no connection between their troubles and the divorce statistics. Malachi straightens them out. God hates divorce, legal or not. The marriage covenant between a man and woman should be kept faithfully. Jesus said much the same thing in Matthew 19:1–9.

17 ¶ You have wearied the LORD with your words. Yet you say, "How have we wearied *Him*?" In that you say, "Everyone who does evil is good in the sight of the LORD, and He delights in them," or, "Where is the God of justice?"

The Purifier

3 "Behold, I am going to send My messenger, and he will clear the way before Me. And the Lord, whom you seek, will suddenly come to His temple; and the messenger of the covenant, in whom you delight, behold, He is coming," says the LORD of hosts.

2 "But who can endure the day of His coming? And who can stand when He appears? For He is like a refiner's fire and like fullers' soap.

2:17 Why Serve God?

Here and in 3:14 people harshly complained they could see no point in serving God, when you got no special reward. In responding, God did not try to convince them that the righteous were, in fact, better off. He told them that he keeps a "book of remembrance" (3:16), on which he records those who fear him, and that sometime in the future he will come as judge, destroying the wicked and preserving those who fear him. The value of serving him will be obvious someday, even if it is not today.

3 "He will sit as a smelter and purifier of silver, and He will purify the sons of Levi and refine them like gold and silver, so that they may present to the LORD offerings in righteousness.

4 "Then the offering of Judah and Jerusalem will be pleasing to the LORD as in the days of old and as in former years.

5 ¶ "Then I will draw near to you for judgment; and I will be a swift witness against the sorcerers and against the adulterers and against those who swear falsely, and against those who oppress the wage earner in his wages, the widow and the orphan, and those who turn aside the alien and do not fear Me," says the LORD of hosts.

6 "For I, the LORD, do not change; therefore you, O sons of Jacob, are not consumed.

7 ¶ "From the days of your fathers you have turned aside from My statutes and have not kept *them.* Return to Me, and I will return to you," says the LORD of hosts. "But you say, 'How shall we return?'

You Have Robbed God

8 ¶ "Will a man *a*rob God? Yet you are robbing Me! But you say, 'How have we robbed You?' In tithes and offerings.

9 "You are cursed with a curse, for you are *b*robbing Me, the whole nation *of you!*

10 "Bring the whole tithe into the storehouse, so that there may be food in My house, and test Me now in this," says the LORD of hosts, "if I will not open for you the windows of heaven and pour out for you a blessing until *c*it overflows.

11 "Then I will rebuke the devourer for you, so that it will not destroy the fruits of the ground; nor

will your vine in the field cast *its grapes,*" says the LORD of hosts.

12 "All the nations will call you blessed, for you shall be a delightful land," says the LORD of hosts.

13 ¶ "Your words have been arrogant against Me," says the LORD. "Yet you say, 'What have we spoken against You?'

3:10 Testing the Tithe

Like a salesman offering a free sample, God urges the Israelites to test him out. If they bring their tithes to the temple, they will see how God blesses them, opening the "windows of heaven" to pour out an abundance. The "tithe" was at least a tenth of their income, used to feed the priests, pay temple expenses, and help the poor.

14 "You have said, 'It is vain to serve God; and what profit is it that we have kept His charge, and that we have walked in mourning before the LORD of hosts?

15 'So now we call the arrogant blessed; not only are the doers of wickedness built up but they also test God and escape.' "

The Book of Remembrance

16 ¶ Then those who *d*feared the LORD spoke to one another, and the LORD gave attention and heard *it,* and a book of remembrance was written before Him for those who *d*fear the LORD and who esteem His name.

17 "They will be Mine," says the LORD of hosts, "on the day that I prepare *My* own possession, and I will spare them as a man spares his own son who serves him."

18 So you will again distinguish between the righteous and the wicked, between one who serves God and one who does not serve Him.

Final Admonition

4 "For behold, the day is coming, burning like a furnace; and all the arrogant and every evildoer will be chaff; and the day that is coming will set them ablaze," says the LORD of hosts, "so that it will leave them neither root nor branch."

2 "But for you who *d*fear My name, the sun of righteousness will rise with healing in its wings; and you will go forth and skip about like calves from the stall.

3 "You will tread down the wicked, for they will be ashes under the soles of your feet on the day which I am preparing," says the LORD of hosts.

4 ¶ "Remember the law of Moses My servant,

---

a Or *defraud*   *b* Or *defrauding*   *c* Or *there is not* room *enough*   *d* Or *revere(d) even the* statutes and ordinances which I commanded him in Horeb for all Israel.

5 ¶ "Behold, I am going to send you Elijah the prophet before the coming of the great and terrible day of the LORD.

6 "He will restore the hearts of the fathers to *their* children and the hearts of the children to their fathers, so that I will not come and smite the land with a curse."

4:5 The Second Elijah

The prophet Elijah, Malachi predicted, would precede the Lord. This prophecy was carefully noted in the New Testament. Jesus identified John the Baptist as the one predicted (Matthew 11:14; 17:9–13).

Outline of Old Testament History

This outline emphasizes broad historical periods rather than specific events. Dates, which often depend on scholarly interpretation, are approximate.

ADAM AND EVE

ABRAHAM

ISAAC

JACOB

JOSEPH

MOSES

JOSHUA

THE JUDGES

PATRIARCHAL AGE

CONQUEST OF CANAAN

UNITED

EXODUS

SOJOURN IN EGYPT

GENESIS

EXODUS TO JUDGES

2000 B.C.

1500 B.C.

ISRAEL

SAMUEL
SAUL
DAVID
SOLOMON

EXILE TO
ASSYRIA

DIVIDED KINGDOM

PERIOD OF
THE JUDGES

KINGDOM

EXILES RETURN   JESUS

JUDAH

EXILE TO BABYLON

1 AND 2 SAMUEL
1 CHRONICLES

1 AND 2 KINGS
2 CHRONICLES
AND MOST PROPHETS

EZEKIEL
DANIEL

EZRA
NEHEMIAH
ESTHER

1000 B.C.

500 B.C.

0 A.D.

THE
NEW
TESTAMENT

MATTHEW

A Bridge from Old to New
Why start with a list of names?

> *"She will bear a Son; and you shall call His name Jesus, for He will save His people from their sins."*
> **1:21**

OR FOUR HUNDRED YEARS, NOTHING new was added to the Bible. The prophets fell silent. During this time, Middle Eastern empires rose and fell, and the tiny nation of Israel suffered under the domination of greater powers like Greece and Rome.

And then something momentous happened. A baby was born—a baby unlike any who had ever come before. By introducing this baby who grew into the man Jesus, the book of Matthew opens a whole new section of the Bible—the New Testament.

Matthew makes his intentions clear from the very first sentence: He connects Jesus' arrival with the Old Testament story line. Jesus was a Jew, he says, the son of Abraham. And also a king, the son of David. Matthew then sets out to prove an audacious claim: This Jesus, from the humble town of Nazareth, is the very "Messiah," the deliverer promised back in the Old Testament. (*Christ* is a Greek translation of the word *Messiah*.)

Jesus' Family Tree

People all over the world, especially Jews, had been eagerly awaiting the Messiah. His coming would change the entire history of the world, they believed. Could this carpenter's son be the long-expected king? To answer that question, Matthew starts with a genealogy.

Genealogies—long lists of names—rarely prove interesting to anyone but the people directly involved. To those people, however, the lists are anything but boring.

Listen to one modern author describe what it was like to hear an ancient genealogy: "There is an expression, 'the peak experience,' a moment which emotionally can never again be equaled in your life. I had mine, that first day in the village of Juffure, in black west Africa . . . Goose bumps came out on me the size of marbles." With those words, Alex Haley, author of *Roots*, recalls the day he first heard, from the lips of an aged storyteller, the account of young Kunta Kinte being taken captive by slave traders in 1752.

The Importance of Roots

Haley's ancestors in Tennessee and Virginia had descended directly from a native African captured in a tiny village in Gambia. The day he listened to the gentle African elder recite, "And so-and-so took as a wife so-and-so, and begat so-and-so," the final link in Haley's family chain snapped into place. *Roots* tells the story of this connection.

In a similar way, the book of Matthew doesn't begin with Jesus' birth, but reaches back further to establish his roots. If indeed Jesus is the Messiah, his ancestors must match up to that claim. As any student of history knows, kings don't merely declare themselves; they must belong to a royal line. Matthew traces Jesus' lineage to the father of the Jewish race, Abraham—who first received the promise of the Messiah—then to the great Jewish king David.

Links to the Old Testament

After recording Jesus' bloodline, Matthew narrates the story of Jesus' life on earth. He relies heavily on the Old Testament, quoting it more frequently than does any other New Testament author. (Note such phrases as "So was fulfilled what was spoken through the prophets.")

The first book in the New Testament, then, stands as the Gospel that pulls things together, the link between the old and the new. Matthew starts with Jesus' roots, but he also contrasts Jesus with the traditional Jewish picture of the Messiah. Jesus, a king, ended thousands of years of eager waiting. But he came to establish a wholly new kind of kingdom—a kingdom different from what anyone expected.

How to Read Matthew

Anybody who has looked over an Internal Revenue Service (IRS) form knows what tax collectors like: neat, orderly rows of figures, with all expenses and income classified by type and source. Fittingly, the Gospel attributed to former tax collector Matthew reflects systematic, ledger-sheet thinking. He doesn't tell Jesus' story chronologically; he groups facts topically.

Matthew collects Jesus' sayings in five main places. First comes the famous Sermon on the Mount in chapters 5–7. Chapter 10 records Jesus' instructions to his disciples about their mission; chapter 13, a series of parables on the kingdom; chapter 18, Christ's words on the church as a community; and chapters 23–25, Jesus' thoughts on religious hypocrisy and his predictions of the future. Sandwiched in among these five great discourses you'll find connected scenes of Jesus in action.

The skillful blending of Jesus' action and teaching has helped earn this Gospel an esteemed place in literature. Artists are often drawn to it as a capsule summary of Jesus' ministry: witness J.S. Bach's greatest choral work, *Saint Matthew's Passion,* the joyous play *Godspell,* and Italian film maker Pasolini's film *The Gospel according to Saint Matthew.* The French skeptic Renan praised Matthew as "the most important book of Christendom—the most important book that has ever been written."

Two approaches will help in a detailed study of Matthew. First, consider how it differs from the other three Gospels; this will give you some idea of Matthew's distinctive purpose. Then, you will find it enlightening to look up many of Matthew's references to the Old Testament.

Many passages in the Gospels are parallel, dealing with the same event. Nearly identical passages are noted at the section heading with "pp," while similar passages are noted with "Ref."

PEOPLE YOU'LL MEET IN MATTHEW

JOSEPH *(p. 1035)*
JOHN THE BAPTIST *(p. 1045)*
THE HERODS *(p. 1050)*

3-TRACK READING PLAN

For an explanation and complete listing of the 3-track reading plan, turn to page 7.

TRACK 1: **Two-Week Courses on the Bible**
The Track 1 reading program on the Life and Teachings of Jesus includes four chapters from Matthew. See page 7 for a complete listing of this course.

TRACK 2: **An Overview of Matthew in 7 Days**
☐ Day 1. Read the Introduction to Matthew. Then turn to Matthew 5 and begin the Sermon on the Mount.
☐ Day 2. Read chapter 6, a continuation of Jesus' longest single speech, perhaps the most familiar passage in the entire Bible.
☐ Day 3. Matthew 13 records some of Jesus' parables—concise stories with a powerful meaning behind them. Read these parables about the "kingdom of heaven," referring to "What Should a Leader Look Like?" page 1048, for help in understanding.
☐ Day 4. As a former tax collector, Matthew was especially sensitive to what Jesus had to say about money. Read his comments on this and other topics in chapter 19.
☐ Day 5. The last three chapters of Matthew give a complete, factual account of Jesus' death. Read chapter 26, the story of the arrest and trial.
☐ Day 6. Continue the crucifixion story with chapter 27.
☐ Day 7. Read chapter 28, which tells of Jesus' resurrection.

Now turn to page 9 for your next Track 2 reading project.

TRACK 3: **All of Matthew in 28 Days**
After you have read through Matthew a chapter a day, turn to pages 10–14 for your next Track 3 reading project.

☐1 ☐2 ☐3 ☐4 ☐5 ☐6 ☐7 ☐8
☐9 ☐10 ☐11 ☐12 ☐13 ☐14 ☐15 ☐16
☐17 ☐18 ☐19 ☐20 ☐21 ☐22 ☐23 ☐24
☐25 ☐26 ☐27 ☐28

The Genealogy of Jesus the Messiah

1:1–17pp — Luke 3:23–38
1:3–6pp — Ruth 4:18–22
1:7–11pp — 1 Chr 3:10–17

1 The record of the genealogy of Jesus the Messiah, the son of David, the son of Abraham:

2 ¶ Abraham was the father of Isaac, Isaac the father of Jacob, and Jacob the father of ᵃJudah and his brothers.

3 Judah was the father of Perez and Zerah by Tamar, Perez was the father of Hezron, and Hezron the father of Ram.

4 Ram was the father of Amminadab, Amminadab the father of Nahshon, and Nahshon the father of Salmon.

5 Salmon was the father of Boaz by Rahab, Boaz was the father of Obed by Ruth, and Obed the father of Jesse.

6 Jesse was the father of David the king.

¶ David was the father of Solomon by ᵇBathsheba who had been the wife of Uriah.

1:6 Shady Ancestors

Matthew's list differs from many Jewish genealogies by including women, and a surprising selection of women at that. Tamar, a Gentile, tricked and seduced her father-in-law, then bore illegitimate twins (Genesis 38); Rahab, another Gentile, once worked as a prostitute (Joshua 2; 6); Ruth also grew up as a pagan Gentile (Ruth 1–4); and Uriah's wife Bathsheba committed adultery with King David (2 Samuel 11–12). Many of the men listed had unsavory pasts as well; taken together, these ancestors of Jesus vividly demonstrate God's ability to work with all sorts of people.

7 Solomon was the father of Rehoboam, Rehoboam the father of Abijah, and Abijah the father of Asa.

8 Asa was the father of Jehoshaphat, Jehoshaphat the father of Joram, and Joram the father of Uzziah.

9 Uzziah was the father of Jotham, Jotham the father of Ahaz, and Ahaz the father of Hezekiah.

10 Hezekiah was the father of Manasseh, Manasseh the father of Amon, and Amon the father of Josiah.

11 Josiah became the father of Jeconiah and his brothers, at the time of the deportation to Babylon.

12 ¶ After the deportation to Babylon: Jeconiah became the father of Shealtiel, and Shealtiel the father of Zerubbabel.

13 Zerubbabel was the father of Abihud, Abihud the father of Eliakim, and Eliakim the father of Azor.

14 Azor was the father of Zadok, Zadok the father of Achim, and Achim the father of Eliud.

15 Eliud was the father of Eleazar, Eleazar the father of Matthan, and Matthan the father of Jacob.

16 Jacob was the father of Joseph the husband of Mary, by whom Jesus was born, who is called the Messiah.

17 ¶ So all the generations from Abraham to David are fourteen generations; from David to the deportation to Babylon, fourteen generations; and from the deportation to Babylon to the Messiah, fourteen generations.

Conception and Birth of Jesus

18 ¶ Now the birth of Jesus Christ was as follows: when His mother Mary had been betrothed to Joseph, before they came together she was found to be with child by the Holy Spirit.

19 And Joseph her husband, being a righteous man and not wanting to disgrace her, planned ᶜto send her away secretly.

20 But when he had considered this, behold, an angel of the Lord appeared to him in a dream, saying, "Joseph, son of David, do not be afraid to take Mary as your wife; for the Child who has been ᵈconceived in her is of the Holy Spirit.

21 "She will bear a Son; and you shall call His name Jesus, for He will save His people from their sins."

22 Now all this took place to fulfill what was spoken by the Lord through the prophet:

23 "BEHOLD, THE VIRGIN SHALL BE WITH CHILD AND SHALL BEAR A SON, AND THEY SHALL CALL HIS

ᵃ Gr *Judas*; names of people in the Old Testament are given in their Old Testament form   ᵇ Lit *her of Uriah*   ᶜ Or *to divorce her*   ᵈ Lit *begotten*

NAME IMMANUEL," which translated means, "GOD WITH US."

24 And Joseph awoke from his sleep and did as the angel of the Lord commanded him, and took *Mary* as his wife,

1:18–20 More Than Engaged

Jewish custom in Joseph and Mary's day recognized a state called "betrothal" that fell somewhere between our modern commitments of engagement and marriage. A betrothal was more binding than an engagement: It could only be broken with an act of divorce. And if a betrothed woman became pregnant, she was regarded as an adulteress.

25 [a]but kept her a virgin until she gave birth to a Son; and he called His name Jesus.

The Visit of the Magi

2 Now after Jesus was born in Bethlehem of Judea in the days of Herod the king, [b]magi from the east arrived in Jerusalem, saying,

2 "Where is He who has been born King of the Jews? For we saw His star in the east and have come to worship Him."

3 When Herod the king heard *this*, he was troubled, and all Jerusalem with him.

4 Gathering together all the chief priests and scribes of the people, he inquired of them where the Messiah was to be born.

5 They said to him, "In Bethlehem of Judea; for this is what has been written by the prophet:

6 'AND YOU, BETHLEHEM, LAND OF JUDAH,
ARE BY NO MEANS LEAST AMONG THE
  LEADERS OF JUDAH;
FOR OUT OF YOU SHALL COME FORTH A
  RULER
WHO WILL SHEPHERD MY PEOPLE
  ISRAEL.' "

7 ¶ Then Herod secretly called the magi and determined from them the exact time the star appeared.

8 And he sent them to Bethlehem and said, "Go and search carefully for the Child; and when you have found *Him*, report to me, so that I too may come and worship Him."

9 After hearing the king, they went their way; and the star, which they had seen in the east, went on before them until it came and stood over *the place* where the Child was.

10 When they saw the star, they rejoiced exceedingly with great joy.

11 After coming into the house they saw the Child with Mary His mother; and they fell to the ground and worshiped Him. Then, opening their treasures, they presented to Him gifts of gold, frankincense, and myrrh.

2:11 The Wise Men

Of the four Gospels, Matthew alone tells of the visit of the Magi, or Wise Men. This incident shows that people from other parts of the world, not just from Israel, were anticipating the Messiah. The Magi's visit underscores that Jesus came for all people, not just the Jews. The last words of this Gospel spell out that mission very clearly.

12 And having been warned *by God* in a dream not to return to Herod, the magi left for their own country by another way.

The Flight to Egypt

13 ¶ Now when they had gone, behold, an angel of the Lord *appeared to Joseph in a dream and said, "Get up! Take the Child and His mother and flee to Egypt, and remain there until I tell you; for Herod is going to search for the Child to destroy Him."

14 ¶ So Joseph got up and took the Child and His mother while it was still night, and left for Egypt.

15 He remained there until the death of Herod. *This was* to fulfill what had been spoken by the Lord through the prophet: "OUT OF EGYPT I CALLED MY SON."

Herod Slaughters Babies

16 ¶ Then when Herod saw that he had been tricked by the magi, he became very enraged, and sent and slew all the male children who were in Bethlehem and all its vicinity, from two years old and under, according to the time which he had determined from the magi.

17 Then what had been spoken through Jeremiah the prophet was fulfilled:

18 "A VOICE WAS HEARD IN RAMAH,
WEEPING AND GREAT MOURNING,
RACHEL WEEPING FOR HER CHILDREN;
AND SHE REFUSED TO BE COMFORTED,
BECAUSE THEY WERE NO MORE."

19 ¶ But when Herod died, behold, an angel of the Lord *appeared in a dream to Joseph in Egypt, and said,

20 "Get up, take the Child and His mother, and go into the land of Israel; for those who sought the Child's life are dead."

21 So Joseph got up, took the Child and His mother, and came into the land of Israel.

---

[a] Lit *and was not knowing her*   [b] A caste of wise men specializing in astronomy, astrology, and natural science

22 But when he heard that Archelaus was reigning over Judea in place of his father Herod, he was afraid to go there. Then after being warned *by God* in a dream, he left for the regions of Galilee,

23 and came and lived in a city called Nazareth. *This was* to fulfill what was spoken through the prophets: "He shall be called a Nazarene."

The Preaching of John the Baptist

3:1–12pp — Mark 1:3–8; Luke 3:2–17

3 Now in those days John the Baptist *came, preaching in the wilderness of Judea, saying,

2 "Repent, for the kingdom of heaven is at hand."

3 For this is the one referred to by Isaiah the prophet when he said,

"THE VOICE OF ONE CRYING IN THE
WILDERNESS,
'MAKE READY THE WAY OF THE LORD,
MAKE HIS PATHS STRAIGHT!' "

4 Now John himself had a garment of camel's hair and a leather belt around his waist; and his food was locusts and wild honey.

5 Then Jerusalem was going out to him, and all Judea and all the district around the Jordan;

6 and they were being baptized by him in the Jordan River, as they confessed their sins.

7 ¶ But when he saw many of the Pharisees and Sadducees coming for baptism, he said to them, "You brood of vipers, who warned you to flee from the wrath to come?

8 "Therefore bear fruit in keeping with repentance;

9 and do not suppose that you can say to yourselves, 'We have Abraham for our father'; for I say to you that from these stones God is able to raise up children to Abraham.

10 "The axe is already laid at the root of the trees; therefore every tree that does not bear good fruit is cut down and thrown into the fire.

11 ¶ "As for me, I baptize you [a]with water for repentance, but He who is coming after me is mightier than I, and I am not fit to remove His sandals; He will baptize you with the Holy Spirit and fire.

12 "His winnowing fork is in His hand, and He will thoroughly clear His threshing floor; and He will gather His wheat into the barn, but He will burn up the chaff with unquenchable fire."

The Baptism of Jesus

3:13–17pp — Mark 1:9–11; Luke 3:21,22; John 1:31–34

13 ¶ Then Jesus *arrived from Galilee at the Jordan *coming* to John, to be baptized by him.

14 But John tried to prevent Him, saying, "I have need to be baptized by You, and do You come to me?"

15 But Jesus answering said to him, "Permit *it* at this time; for in this way it is fitting for us to fulfill all righteousness." Then he *permitted Him.

16 After being baptized, Jesus came up immediately from the water; and behold, the heavens were opened, and he saw the Spirit of God descending as a dove *and* lighting on Him,

17 and behold, a voice out of the heavens said, "This is [b]My beloved Son, in whom I am well-pleased."

[a] The Gr here can be translated *in, with* or *by*   [b] Or *My Son, the Beloved*

JOSEPH *Stepfather*

STEPPARENTS TAKE ON ONE OF the hardest tasks in life—raising a child who isn't biologically theirs. When Joseph first learned that his fiancée Mary was bearing someone else's child, he must have felt deep heartache. By law, he had the right to accuse Mary of adultery and have her executed. Then an angel brought instructions in a dream: Joseph was to stay with Mary, for her child was from God.

Three times Joseph received angelic messages in dreams, and each time they called for moves he had not planned and could hardly wish. First he was called to care for a wife he had never slept with and a child who was not his. Then he was ordered to flee as a refugee to far-off Egypt. Finally an angel told him to return home, where skeptical neighbors probably remembered that Mary had been pregnant before her marriage.

We know one thing about Joseph: He obeyed, following the angel's orders in each difficult case. A dutiful stepfather, he treated his son as his own, raising him according to the Jewish law. As a carpenter, he taught Jesus to hammer and saw. As a righteous man, he modeled for him an obedient life.

We last hear of Joseph when Jesus was 12. After that, the Bible only mentions Jesus' mother, Mary, and Jesus' brothers. (Joseph probably died before Jesus began his ministry. From the cross, Jesus committed the care of his mother to one of his disciples [John 19:25–27].) Through his faithfulness as a stepfather, however, Joseph made a lasting contribution to the world.

Life Questions: Has God asked you to do any thankless tasks? What were they, and how did they turn out?

The Temptation of Jesus

4:1–11pp — Mark 1:12,13; Luke 4:1–13

4 Then Jesus was led up by the Spirit into the wilderness to be tempted by the devil.

2 And after He had fasted forty days and forty nights, He ªbecame hungry.

3 And the tempter came and said to Him, "If You are the Son of God, command that these stones become bread."

4 But He answered and said, "It is written, 'MAN SHALL NOT LIVE ON BREAD ALONE, BUT ON EVERY WORD THAT PROCEEDS OUT OF THE MOUTH OF GOD.'"

5 ¶ Then the devil *took Him into the holy city and had Him stand on the pinnacle of the temple,

6 and *said to Him, "If You are the Son of God, throw Yourself down; for it is written,

'HE WILL COMMAND HIS ANGELS
    CONCERNING YOU';

and

'ON *their* HANDS THEY WILL BEAR YOU UP,
SO THAT YOU WILL NOT STRIKE YOUR
    FOOT AGAINST A STONE.'"

7 Jesus said to him, "On the other hand, it is written, 'YOU SHALL NOT PUT THE LORD YOUR GOD TO THE TEST.'"

8 ¶ Again, the devil *took Him to a very high mountain and *showed Him all the kingdoms of the world and their glory;

9 and he said to Him, "All these things I will give You, if You fall down and worship me."

10 Then Jesus *said to him, "Go, Satan! For it is written, 'YOU SHALL WORSHIP THE LORD YOUR GOD, AND SERVE HIM ONLY.'"

11 Then the devil *left Him; and behold, angels came and *began* to minister to Him.

Jesus Begins His Ministry

12 ¶ Now when Jesus heard that John had been taken into custody, He withdrew into Galilee;

13 and leaving Nazareth, He came and settled in Capernaum, which is by the sea, in the region of Zebulun and Naphtali.

14 *This was* to fulfill what was spoken through Isaiah the prophet:

15 "THE LAND OF ZEBULUN AND THE LAND OF
        NAPHTALI,
    BY THE WAY OF THE SEA, BEYOND THE
        JORDAN, GALILEE OF THE
        ᵇGENTILES—

16 "THE PEOPLE WHO WERE SITTING IN
        DARKNESS SAW A GREAT LIGHT,
    AND THOSE WHO WERE SITTING IN THE
        LAND AND SHADOW OF DEATH,
    UPON THEM A LIGHT DAWNED."

17 ¶ From that time Jesus began to preach and say, "Repent, for the kingdom of heaven is at hand."

The First Disciples

4:18–22pp — Mark 1:16–20; Luke 5:2–11; John 1:35–42

18 ¶ Now as Jesus was walking by the Sea of Galilee, He saw two brothers, Simon who was called Peter, and Andrew his brother, casting a net into the sea; for they were fishermen.

19 And He *said to them, "Follow Me, and I will make you fishers of men."

4:17 Words for Jewish Readers

Matthew wrote for a primarily Jewish audience. Starting with his opening chapter, he affirms that Jesus is the Messiah, backing up that claim by constant reference to the Old Testament. Often Matthew leaves Jewish phrases and customs unexplained, assuming that his readers are familiar with them. And, where other Gospel writers say, "kingdom of God," he uses the phrase "kingdom of heaven," out of respect for Jews, who never wrote out the word God.

20 Immediately they left their nets and followed Him.

21 Going on from there He saw two other brothers, James the *son* of Zebedee, and John his brother, in the boat with Zebedee their father, mending their nets; and He called them.

22 Immediately they left the boat and their father, and followed Him.

Ministry in Galilee

23 ¶ Jesus was going throughout all Galilee, teaching in their synagogues and proclaiming the gospel of the kingdom, and healing every kind of disease and every kind of sickness among the people.

24 ¶ The news about Him spread throughout all Syria; and they brought to Him all who were ill, those suffering with various diseases and pains, demoniacs, epileptics, paralytics; and He healed them.

25 Large crowds followed Him from Galilee and *the* Decapolis and Jerusalem and Judea and *from* beyond the Jordan.

The Sermon on the Mount
The Beatitudes

5:3–12pp — Luke 6:20–23

5 When Jesus saw the crowds, He went up on the mountain; and after He sat down, His disciples came to Him.

2 He opened His mouth and *began* to teach them, saying,

ª Lit *later became*; or *afterward became*   ᵇ Lit *nations*, usually non-Jewish

3 ¶ "Blessed are the poor in spirit, for theirs is the kingdom of heaven.

4 ¶ "Blessed are those who mourn, for they shall be comforted.

5 ¶ "Blessed are the *a*gentle, for they shall inherit the earth.

6 ¶ "Blessed are those who hunger and thirst for righteousness, for they shall be satisfied.

7 ¶ "Blessed are the merciful, for they shall receive mercy.

8 ¶ "Blessed are the pure in heart, for they shall see God.

9 ¶ "Blessed are the peacemakers, for they shall be called sons of God.

10 ¶ "Blessed are those who have been persecuted for the sake of righteousness, for theirs is the kingdom of heaven.

11 ¶ "Blessed are you when *people* insult you and persecute you, and falsely say all kinds of evil against you because of Me.

12 "Rejoice and be glad, for your reward in heaven is great; for in the same way they persecuted the prophets who were before you.

Disciples and the World

13 ¶ "You are the salt of the earth; but if the salt has become tasteless, how can it be made salty *again*? It is no longer good for anything, except to be thrown out and trampled under foot by men.

14 ¶ "You are the light of the world. A city set on a hill cannot be hidden;

15 nor does *anyone* light a lamp and put it under a basket, but on the lampstand, and it gives light to all who are in the house.

16 "Let your light shine before men in such a way that they may see your good works, and glorify your Father who is in heaven.

17 ¶ "Do not think that I came to abolish the Law or the Prophets; I did not come to abolish but to fulfill.

18 "For truly I say to you, until heaven and earth pass away, not the smallest letter or stroke shall pass from the Law until all is accomplished.

19 "Whoever then annuls one of the least of these commandments, and teaches others *to do* the same, shall be called least in the kingdom of

heaven; but whoever keeps and teaches *them,* he shall be called great in the kingdom of heaven.

20 ¶ "For I say to you that unless your righteousness surpasses *that* of the scribes and Pharisees, you will not enter the kingdom of heaven.

Personal Relationships

5:25,26pp — Luke 12:58,59

21 ¶ "You have heard that the ancients were told, 'YOU SHALL NOT COMMIT MURDER' and 'Whoever commits murder shall be *b*liable to the court.'

22 "But I say to you that everyone who is angry with his brother shall be guilty before the court; and whoever says to his brother, '*c*You good-for-nothing,' shall be guilty before *d*the supreme court; and whoever says, 'You fool,' shall be guilty *enough to go* into the *e*fiery hell.

23 "Therefore if you are presenting your offering at the altar, and there remember that your brother has something against you,

24 leave your offering there before the altar and go; first be reconciled to your brother, and then come and present your offering.

25 "Make friends quickly with your opponent at law while you are with him on the way, so that your opponent may not hand you over to the judge, and the judge to the officer, and you be thrown into prison.

26 "Truly I say to you, you will not come out of there until you have paid up the last *f*cent.

27 ¶ "You have heard that it was said, 'YOU SHALL NOT COMMIT ADULTERY';

28 but I say to you that everyone who looks at a woman with lust for her has already committed adultery with her in his heart.

29 "If your right eye makes you stumble, tear it out and throw it from you; for it is better for you to lose one of the parts of your body, than for your whole body to be thrown into hell.

30 "If your right hand makes you stumble, cut it off and throw it from you; for it is better for you to lose one of the parts of your body, than for your whole body to go into hell.

31 ¶ "It was said, 'WHOEVER SENDS HIS WIFE AWAY, LET HIM GIVE HER A CERTIFICATE OF DIVORCE';

32 but I say to you that everyone who divorces his wife, except for *the* reason of unchastity, makes her commit adultery; and whoever marries a divorced woman commits adultery.

33 ¶ "Again, you have heard that the ancients were told, 'YOU SHALL NOT MAKE FALSE VOWS, BUT SHALL FULFILL YOUR VOWS TO THE LORD.'

34 "But I say to you, make no oath at all, either by heaven, for it is the throne of God,

35 or by the earth, for it is the footstool of His feet, or by Jerusalem, for it is THE CITY OF THE GREAT KING.

5:17 Jesus and Moses' Law

In this statement, Jesus clarifies his relationship to the Law of Moses. The next verses get more specific, contrasting Jesus' teaching with many common interpretations of that Law. "You have heard that it was said . . . ," he begins, and then concludes, "But I say to you . . ." Jesus revealed the true intent of the Old Testament law, rather than its legalistic interpretations.

---

a Or humble, meek   *b* Or guilty before   *c* Or empty-head; Gr Raka (Raca) fr Aram reqa   *d* Lit the Sanhedrin
e Lit Gehenna of fire   *f* Lit quadrans (equaling two mites); i.e. 1/64 of a daily wage

36 "Nor shall you make an oath by your head, for you cannot make one hair white or black.

37 "But let your statement be, 'Yes, yes' or 'No, no'; anything beyond these is of evil.

38 ¶ "You have heard that it was said, 'AN EYE FOR AN EYE, AND A TOOTH FOR A TOOTH.'

39 "But I say to you, do not resist an evil person; but whoever slaps you on your right cheek, turn the other to him also.

40 "If anyone wants to sue you and take your ªshirt, let him have your ᵇcoat also.

41 "Whoever forces you to go one mile, go with him two.

42 "Give to him who asks of you, and do not turn away from him who wants to borrow from you.

43 ¶ "You have heard that it was said, 'YOU SHALL LOVE YOUR NEIGHBOR and hate your enemy.'

44 "But I say to you, love your enemies and pray for those who persecute you,

5:44 Praying for Persecutors

Jesus got a chance to live out these words when, nailed to a cross, he prayed for his persecutors (Luke 23:34). The example of Stephen, the first Christian martyr (Acts 7:60), shows that some followers also put Jesus' command into practice—a fact that surely impressed one persecutor named Saul.

45 so that you may be sons of your Father who is in heaven; for He causes His sun to rise on *the* evil and *the* good, and sends rain on *the* righteous and *the* unrighteous.

46 "For if you love those who love you, what reward do you have? Do not even the tax collectors do the same?

47 "If you greet only your brothers, what more are you doing *than others*? Do not even the Gentiles do the same?

48 "Therefore you are to be perfect, as your heavenly Father is perfect.

Giving to the Poor and Prayer

6:9–13pp — Luke 11:2–4

6 "Beware of practicing your righteousness before men to be noticed by them; otherwise you have no reward with your Father who is in heaven.

2 ¶ "So when you give to the poor, do not sound a trumpet before you, as the hypocrites do in the synagogues and in the streets, so that they may be honored by men. Truly I say to you, they have their reward in full.

3 "But when you give to the poor, do not let your left hand know what your right hand is doing,

4 so that your giving will be in secret; and your Father who sees *what is done* in secret will reward you.

5 ¶ "When you pray, you are not to be like the hypocrites; for they love to stand and pray in the synagogues and on the street corners so that they may be seen by men. Truly I say to you, they have their reward in full.

6 "But you, when you pray, go into your inner room, close your door and pray to your Father who is in secret, and your Father who sees *what is done* in secret will reward you.

7 ¶ "And when you are praying, do not use meaningless repetition as the Gentiles do, for they suppose that they will be heard for their many words.

8 "So do not be like them; for your Father knows what you need before you ask Him.

9 ¶ "Pray, then, in this way:
'Our Father who is in heaven,
Hallowed be Your name.

10 'Your kingdom come.
Your will be done,
On earth as it is in heaven.

11 'Give us this day our daily bread.

12 'And forgive us our debts, as we also have forgiven our debtors.

13 'And do not lead us into temptation, but deliver us from evil. [For Yours is the kingdom and the power and the glory forever. Amen.]'

14 "For if you forgive others for their transgressions, your heavenly Father will also forgive you.

15 "But if you do not forgive others, then your Father will not forgive your transgressions.

Fasting
The True Treasure
Wealth (Mammon)

6:22,23pp — Luke 11:34–36

16 ¶ "Whenever you fast, do not put on a gloomy face as the hypocrites *do*, for they neglect their appearance so that they will be noticed by men when they are fasting. Truly I say to you, they have their reward in full.

17 "But you, when you fast, anoint your head and wash your face

18 so that your fasting will not be noticed by men, but by your Father who is in secret; and your Father who sees *what is done* in secret will reward you.

19 ¶ "Do not store up for yourselves treasures on earth, where moth and rust destroy, and where thieves break in and steal.

20 "But store up for yourselves treasures in heaven, where neither moth nor rust destroys, and where thieves do not break in or steal;

21 for where your treasure is, there your heart will be also.

ª Lit *tunic*; i.e. a garment worn next to the body   ᵇ Lit *cloak*; i.e. an outer garment

22 ¶ "The eye is the lamp of the body; so then if your eye is clear, your whole body will be full of light.

23 "But if your eye is bad, your whole body will be full of darkness. If then the light that is in you is darkness, how great is the darkness!

24 ¶ "No one can serve two masters; for either he will hate the one and love the other, or he will be devoted to one and despise the other. You cannot serve God and ªwealth.

The Cure for Anxiety

6:25-33pp — Luke 12:22-31

25 ¶ "For this reason I say to you, do not be worried about your life, as to what you will eat or what you will drink; nor for your body, as to what you will put on. Is not life more than food, and the body more than clothing?

26 "Look at the birds of the air, that they do not sow, nor reap nor gather into barns, and yet your heavenly Father feeds them. Are you not worth much more than they?

27 "And who of you by being worried can add a single hour to his life?

28 "And why are you worried about clothing? Observe how the lilies of the field grow; they do not toil nor do they spin,

29 yet I say to you that not even Solomon in all his glory clothed himself like one of these.

30 "But if God so clothes the grass of the field, which is alive today and tomorrow is thrown into the furnace, will He not much more clothe you? You of little faith!

31 "Do not worry then, saying, 'What will we eat?' or 'What will we drink?' or 'What will we wear for clothing?'

32 "For the Gentiles eagerly seek all these things;

ª mamona, Gr for Ara mammon; i.e. wealth, etc, personified as an object of worship

---

Letting the Inside Match the Outside

Is everyone a hypocrite?

ALMOST ALL OF US LIVE two lives: what people see outside and what is really going on inside. In school we learn what outward signs of attention will please the teacher. At a job we learn to "put up a good front" whenever the boss happens to stroll by. As if putting on masks, we style our hair, choose our clothes, and use body language to impress those around us. Over time, we learn to excel at hiding truly serious problems.

> "Your Father, who sees what is done in secret will reward you." 6:4

People tend to judge by outward appearances and so can easily be fooled. Acquaintances are often shocked when a mass-murderer is arrested. "He seemed like such a nice man!" they insist. The outside appearance did not match the inside reality.

A Blast at Hypocrites

Chapters 5–7 announce that the time has come for us to change not just the outside, but also the inside. In Jesus' day, religious people tried to impress each other with showy outward behavior. They wore gaunt and hungry looks during a brief fast, prayed grandiosely if people were watching, and went so far as to wear Bible verses strapped to their foreheads and left arms.

In his famous Sermon on the Mount, Jesus blasts the hypocrisy behind such seemingly harmless practices. God is not fooled by appearances. We cannot fake behavior to impress him. He knows that inside the best of us lurk dark thoughts of hatred, pride, and lust—internal problems only he can deal with. Jesus goes on to present a truly radical way of life, free of pretense.

Familiar Yet Startling Words

These three chapters, among the most analyzed in the entire Bible, present a fresh view of the world. You will likely recognize many familiar sections, including the Golden Rule and the Lord's Prayer.

In one sense, Jesus says, the truths presented here are not new: they fulfill, rather than abolish the Old Testament law. In another sense the way of life described is more radical than anything before or since. Jesus' words turn many normal assumptions upside down. With statements like, "Blessed are the poor in spirit ... those who mourn ... the gentle ... the peacemakers ... those who have been persecuted," Jesus attacks those who strive to build a good image by appearing powerful, successful, and assertive.

Perhaps most radical of all, The Sermon on the Mount introduces the possibility of living solely for God and not for appearances. At last we can bring our inner and outer lives together.

Life Questions: Do other people see what you're really like inside? How do your friends try to impress each other?

for your heavenly Father knows that you need all these things.

33 "But seek first His kingdom and His righteousness, and all these things will be added to you.

34 ¶ "So do not worry about tomorrow; for tomorrow will care for itself. Each day has enough trouble of its own.

Judging Others

7:3–5pp — Luke 6:41,42

7 "Do not judge so that you will not be judged. 2 "For in the way you judge, you will be judged; and by your standard of measure, it will be measured to you.

3 "Why do you look at the speck that is in your brother's eye, but do not notice the log that is in your own eye?

4 "Or how can you say to your brother, 'Let me take the speck out of your eye,' and behold, the log is in your own eye?

5 "You hypocrite, first take the log out of your own eye, and then you will see clearly to take the speck out of your brother's eye.

6 ¶ "Do not give what is holy to dogs, and do not throw your pearls before swine, or they will trample them under their feet, and turn and tear you to pieces.

Prayer and the Golden Rule

7:7–11pp — Luke 11:9–13

7 ¶ "Ask, and it will be given to you; seek, and you will find; knock, and it will be opened to you.

8 "For everyone who asks receives, and he who seeks finds, and to him who knocks it will be opened.

9 "Or what man is there among you who, when his son asks for a loaf, will give him a stone?

10 "Or if he asks for a fish, he will not give him a snake, will he?

11 "If you then, being evil, know how to give good gifts to your children, how much more will your Father who is in heaven give what is good to those who ask Him!

12 ¶ "In everything, therefore, treat people the same way you want them to treat you, for this is the Law and the Prophets.

The Narrow and Wide Gates

13 ¶ "Enter through the narrow gate; for the

gate is wide and the way is broad that leads to destruction, and there are many who enter through it.

14 "For the gate is small and the way is narrow that leads to life, and there are few who find it.

A Tree and Its Fruit

15 ¶ "Beware of the false prophets, who come to you in sheep's clothing, but inwardly are ravenous wolves.

16 "You will know them by their fruits. Grapes are not gathered from thorn *bushes* nor figs from thistles, are they?

17 "So every good tree bears good fruit, but the bad tree bears bad fruit.

18 "A good tree cannot produce bad fruit, nor can a bad tree produce good fruit.

19 "Every tree that does not bear good fruit is cut down and thrown into the fire.

20 "So then, you will know them by their fruits.

21 ¶ "Not everyone who says to Me, 'Lord, Lord,' will enter the kingdom of heaven, but he who does the will of My Father who is in heaven *will enter.*

22 "Many will say to Me on that day, 'Lord, Lord, did we not prophesy in Your name, and in Your name cast out demons, and in Your name perform many miracles?'

23 "And then I will declare to them, 'I never knew you; DEPART FROM ME, YOU WHO PRACTICE LAWLESSNESS.'

The Two Foundations

7:24–27pp — Luke 6:47–49

24 ¶ "Therefore everyone who hears these words of Mine and acts on them, may be compared to a wise man who built his house on the rock.

25 "And the rain fell, and the floods came, and the winds blew and slammed against that house; and *yet* it did not fall, for it had been founded on the rock.

26 "Everyone who hears these words of Mine and does not act on them, will be like a foolish man who built his house on the sand.

27 "The rain fell, and the floods came, and the winds blew and slammed against that house; and it fell—and great was its fall."

28 ¶ When Jesus had finished these words, the crowds were amazed at His teaching;

29 for He was teaching them as *one* having authority, and not as their scribes.

Jesus Cleanses a Leper
The Centurion's Faith

8:2–4pp — Mark 1:40–44; Luke 5:12–14
8:5–13pp — Luke 7:1–10

8 When Jesus came down from the mountain, large crowds followed Him.

2 And a leper came to Him and bowed down

7:12 Golden Rule

Other religions (Judaism, Hinduism, Buddhism, Confucianism) had some form of this saying, but most were stated negatively: "Don't treat people the same way you wouldn't want them to treat you." Jesus' version is far more open-ended and challenging.

before Him, and said, "Lord, if You are willing, You can make me clean."

3 Jesus stretched out His hand and touched him, saying, "I am willing; be cleansed." And immediately his leprosy was cleansed.

4 And Jesus *said to him, "See that you tell no one; but go, show yourself to the priest and present the offering that Moses commanded, as a testimony to them."

5 ¶ And when Jesus entered Capernaum, a centurion came to Him, imploring Him,

6 and saying, "Lord, my servant is lying paralyzed at home, fearfully tormented."

7 Jesus *said to him, "I will come and heal him."

8 But the centurion said, "Lord, I am not worthy for You to come under my roof, but just say the word, and my servant will be healed.

9 "For I also am a man under authority, with soldiers under me; and I say to this one, 'Go!' and he goes, and to another, 'Come!' and he comes, and to my slave, 'Do this!' and he does it."

10 Now when Jesus heard this, He marveled and said to those who were following, "Truly I say to you, I have not found such great faith with anyone in Israel.

11 "I say to you that many will come from east and west, and *a*recline at the table with Abraham, Isaac and Jacob in the kingdom of heaven;

12 but the sons of the kingdom will be cast out into the outer darkness; in that place there will be weeping and gnashing of teeth."

13 And Jesus said to the centurion, "Go; it shall be done for you as you have believed." And the servant was healed that very moment.

Peter's Mother-in-law and Many Others Healed

8:14-16pp — Mark 1:29-34; Luke 4:38-41

14 ¶ When Jesus came into Peter's home, He saw his mother-in-law lying sick in bed with a fever.

8:14 Actions Follow Words

Typically, Matthew blends together Jesus' words and actions. Chapters 5–7 contain Jesus' longest recorded speech, the Sermon on the Mount–a speech that greatly impressed the audience. The next few chapters mention ten miracles performed by Jesus, which further established his authority. Those who benefited–a despised leprosy victim, a Roman officer, a housewife, two violent demoniacs, a quadriplegic, a synagogue ruler–demonstrate the "wideness in God's mercy" Jesus had just described.

15 He touched her hand, and the fever left her; and she got up and waited on Him.

16 When evening came, they brought to Him many who were demon-possessed; and He cast out the spirits with a word, and healed all who were ill.

17 This was to fulfill what was spoken through Isaiah the prophet: "HE HIMSELF TOOK OUR INFIRMITIES AND CARRIED AWAY OUR DISEASES."

Discipleship Tested

8:19-22pp — Luke 9:57-60
8:23-27pp — Mark 4:36-41; Luke 8:22-25
8:23-27Ref — Matt 14:22-33

18 ¶ Now when Jesus saw a crowd around Him, He gave orders to depart to the other side of the sea.

19 Then a scribe came and said to Him, "Teacher, I will follow You wherever You go."

20 Jesus *said to him, "The foxes have holes and the birds of the air have nests, but the Son of Man has nowhere to lay His head."

21 Another of the disciples said to Him, "Lord, permit me first to go and bury my father."

22 But Jesus *said to him, "Follow Me, and allow the dead to bury their own dead."

23 ¶ When He got into the boat, His disciples followed Him.

24 And behold, there arose a great storm on the sea, so that the boat was being covered with the waves; but Jesus Himself was asleep.

25 And they came to Him and woke Him, saying, "Save us, Lord; we are perishing!"

26 He *said to them, "Why are you afraid, you men of little faith?" Then He got up and rebuked the winds and the sea, and it became perfectly calm.

27 The men were amazed, and said, "What kind of a man is this, that even the winds and the sea obey Him?"

Jesus Casts Out Demons

8:28-34pp — Mark 5:1-17; Luke 8:26-37

28 ¶ When He came to the other side into the country of the Gadarenes, two men who were demon-possessed met Him as they were coming out of the tombs. They were so extremely violent that no one could pass by that way.

29 And they cried out, saying, "What business do we have with each other, Son of God? Have You come here to torment us before the time?"

30 Now there was a herd of many swine feeding at a distance from them.

31 The demons began to entreat Him, saying, "If You are going to cast us out, send us into the herd of swine."

32 And He said to them, "Go!" And they came out and went into the swine, and the whole herd

a Or dine

rushed down the steep bank into the sea and perished in the waters.

33 The herdsmen ran away, and went to the city and reported everything, including what had happened to the demoniacs.

34 And behold, the whole city came out to meet Jesus; and when they saw Him, they implored Him to leave their region.

A Paralytic Healed

9:2–8pp — Mark 2:3–12; Luke 5:18–26

9 Getting into a boat, Jesus crossed over *the sea* and came to His own city.

2 ¶ And they brought to Him a paralytic lying on a bed. Seeing their faith, Jesus said to the paralytic, "Take courage, son; your sins are forgiven."

3 And some of the scribes said to themselves, "This *fellow* blasphemes."

4 And Jesus knowing their thoughts said, "Why are you thinking evil in your hearts?

5 "Which is easier, to say, 'Your sins are forgiven,' or to say, 'Get up, and walk'?

6 "But so that you may know that the Son of Man has authority on earth to forgive sins"—then He *said to the paralytic, "Get up, pick up your bed and go home."

7 And he got up and went home.

8 But when the crowds saw *this*, they were awestruck, and glorified God, who had given such authority to men.

Matthew Called

9:9–13pp — Mark 2:14–17; Luke 5:27–32

9 ¶ As Jesus went on from there, He saw a man called Matthew, sitting in the tax collector's booth; and He *said to him, "Follow Me!" And he got up and followed Him.

10 ¶ Then it happened that as Jesus was reclining *at the table* in the house, behold, many tax collectors and sinners came and were dining with Jesus and His disciples.

11 When the Pharisees saw *this*, they said to His disciples, "Why is your Teacher eating with the tax collectors and sinners?"

12 But when Jesus heard *this*, He said, "*It is* not those who are healthy who need a physician, but those who are sick.

13 "But go and learn what this means: 'I DESIRE COMPASSION, ᵃAND NOT SACRIFICE,' for I did not come to call the righteous, but sinners."

The Question about Fasting

9:14–17pp — Mark 2:18–22; Luke 5:33–39

14 ¶ Then the disciples of John *came to Him, asking, "Why do we and the Pharisees fast, but Your disciples do not fast?"

15 And Jesus said to them, "The attendants of the bridegroom cannot mourn as long as the bridegroom is with them, can they? But the days will come when the bridegroom is taken away from them, and then they will fast.

16 "But no one puts a patch of unshrunk cloth on an old garment; for the patch pulls away from the garment, and a worse tear results.

17 "Nor do *people* put new wine into old wineskins; otherwise the wineskins burst, and the wine pours out and the wineskins are ruined; but they put new wine into fresh wineskins, and both are preserved."

Miracles of Healing

9:18–26pp — Mark 5:22–43; Luke 8:41–56

18 ¶ While He was saying these things to them, a *synagogue* official came and bowed down before Him, and said, "My daughter has just died; but come and lay Your hand on her, and she will live."

19 Jesus got up and *began* to follow him, and *so did* His disciples.

20 ¶ And a woman who had been suffering from a hemorrhage for twelve years, came up behind Him and touched the fringe of His cloak;

21 for she was saying to herself, "If I only touch His garment, I will get well."

22 But Jesus turning and seeing her said, "Daughter, take courage; your faith has made you well." At once the woman was made well.

23 ¶ When Jesus came into the official's house, and saw the flute-players and the crowd in noisy disorder,

24 He said, "Leave; for the girl has not died, but is asleep." And they *began* laughing at Him.

25 But when the crowd had been sent out, He entered and took her by the hand, and the girl got up.

26 This news spread throughout all that land.

27 ¶ As Jesus went on from there, two blind men followed Him, crying out, "Have mercy on us, Son of David!"

9:9 Unpopular Profession

Tax collectors like Matthew were even less popular in Jesus' day than now. Many Jews viewed them as traitors serving the hated Roman empire. To make things worse, they worked on a commission basis, allowing them to set their own rates, which often led to extortion.

In this poignant scene, the Gospel tells how Jesus first called Matthew and then came to his house to mingle freely with "tax collectors and 'sinners'." By following Jesus, Matthew turned his back on a lucrative government job. He was gradually transformed into a loyal disciple who applied his orderly mind to organize this account of Jesus' life.

ᵃ I.e. more than

28 When He entered the house, the blind men came up to Him, and Jesus *said to them, "Do you believe that I am able to do this?" They *said to Him, "Yes, Lord."

29 Then He touched their eyes, saying, "It shall be done to you according to your faith."

30 And their eyes were opened. And Jesus sternly warned them: "See that no one knows *about this!*"

31 But they went out and spread the news about Him throughout all that land.

32 ¶ As they were going out, a mute, demon-possessed man was brought to Him.

33 After the demon was cast out, the mute man spoke; and the crowds were amazed, *and were* saying, "Nothing like this has ever been seen in Israel."

34 But the Pharisees were saying, "He casts out the demons by the ruler of the demons."

35 ¶ Jesus was going through all the cities and villages, teaching in their synagogues and proclaiming the gospel of the kingdom, and healing every kind of disease and every kind of sickness.

36 ¶ Seeing the people, He felt compassion for them, because they were distressed and dispirited like sheep without a shepherd.

37 Then He *said to His disciples, "The harvest is plentiful, but the workers are few.

38 "Therefore beseech the Lord of the harvest to send out workers into His harvest."

The Twelve Disciples
Instructions for Service

10:2–4pp — Mark 3:16–19; Luke 6:14–16; Acts 1:13
10:9–15pp — Mark 6:8–11; Luke 9:3–5; 10:4–12

10 Jesus summoned His twelve disciples and gave them authority over unclean spirits, to cast them out, and to heal every kind of disease and every kind of sickness.

2 ¶ Now the names of the twelve apostles are these: The first, Simon, who is called Peter, and Andrew his brother; and James the son of Zebedee, and John his brother;

3 Philip and Bartholomew; Thomas and Matthew the tax collector; James the son of Alphaeus, and Thaddaeus;

4 Simon the Zealot, and Judas Iscariot, the one who betrayed Him.

5 ¶ These twelve Jesus sent out after instructing them: "Do not go in *the* way of *the* Gentiles, and do not enter *any* city of the Samaritans;

6 but rather go to the lost sheep of the house of Israel.

7 "And as you go, preach, saying, 'The kingdom of heaven is at hand.'

8 "Heal *the* sick, raise *the* dead, cleanse *the* lepers, cast out demons. Freely you received, freely give.

9 "Do not acquire gold, or silver, or copper for your money belts,

10 or a bag for *your* journey, or even two coats, or sandals, or a staff; for the worker is worthy of his support.

11 "And whatever city or village you enter, inquire who is worthy in it, and stay at his house until you leave *that city.*

12 "As you enter the house, give it your greeting.

13 "If the house is worthy, give it your *blessing of* peace. But if it is not worthy, take back your *blessing of* peace.

14 "Whoever does not receive you, nor heed your words, as you go out of that house or that city, shake the dust off your feet.

15 "Truly I say to you, it will be more tolerable for *the* land of Sodom and Gomorrah in the day of judgment than for that city.

A Hard Road before Them

10:19–22pp — Mark 13:11–13; Luke 21:12–17

16 ¶ "Behold, I send you out as sheep in the midst of wolves; so be shrewd as serpents and innocent as doves.

17 "But beware of men, for they will hand you over to *the* courts and scourge you in their synagogues;

18 and you will even be brought before governors and kings for My sake, as a testimony to them and to the Gentiles.

19 "But when they hand you over, do not worry about how or what you are to say; for it will be given you in that hour what you are to say.

20 "For it is not you who speak, but *it is* the Spirit of your Father who speaks in you.

21 ¶ "Brother will betray brother to death, and a father *his* child; and children will rise up against parents and cause them to be put to death.

22 "You will be hated by all because of My name, but it is the one who has endured to the end who will be saved.

23 ¶ "But whenever they persecute you in one city, flee to the next; for truly I say to you, you will not finish *going through* the cities of Israel until the Son of Man comes.

The Meaning of Discipleship

10:26–33pp — Luke 12:2–9
10:34,35pp — Luke 12:51–53

24 ¶ "A disciple is not above his teacher, nor a slave above his master.

25 "It is enough for the disciple that he become like his teacher, and the slave like his master. If they have called the head of the house Beelzebul, how much more *will they malign* the members of his household!

26 ¶ "Therefore do not fear them, for there is nothing concealed that will not be revealed, or hidden that will not be known.

27 "What I tell you in the darkness, speak in the light; and what you hear *whispered* in *your* ear, proclaim upon the housetops.

28 "Do not fear those who kill the body but are

unable to kill the soul; but rather fear Him who is able to destroy both soul and body in hell.

29 "Are not two sparrows sold for a [a]cent? And *yet* not one of them will fall to the ground apart from your Father.

30 "But the very hairs of your head are all numbered.

31 "So do not fear; you are more valuable than many sparrows.

32 ¶ "Therefore everyone who confesses Me before men, I will also confess him before My Father who is in heaven.

33 "But whoever denies Me before men, I will also deny him before My Father who is in heaven.

34 ¶ "Do not think that I came to bring peace on the earth; I did not come to bring peace, but a sword.

35 "For I came to SET A MAN AGAINST HIS FATHER, AND A DAUGHTER AGAINST HER MOTHER, AND A DAUGHTER-IN-LAW AGAINST HER MOTHER-IN-LAW;

36 and a MAN'S ENEMIES WILL BE THE MEMBERS OF HIS HOUSEHOLD.

37 ¶ "He who loves father or mother more than Me is not worthy of Me; and he who loves son or daughter more than Me is not worthy of Me.

38 "And he who does not take his cross and follow after Me is not worthy of Me.

39 "He who has found his life will lose it, and he who has lost his life for My sake will find it.

The Reward of Service

40 ¶ "He who receives you receives Me, and he who receives Me receives Him who sent Me.

41 "He who receives a prophet in *the* name of a prophet shall receive a prophet's reward; and he who receives a righteous man in the name of a righteous man shall receive a righteous man's reward.

42 "And whoever in the name of a disciple gives to one of these little ones even a cup of cold water to drink, truly I say to you, he shall not lose his reward."

John's Questions

11:2-19pp — Luke 7:18-35

11 When Jesus had finished giving instructions to His twelve disciples, He departed from there to teach and preach in their cities.

2 ¶ Now when John, while imprisoned, heard of the works of Christ, he sent *word* by his disciples

3 and said to Him, "Are You the Expected One, or shall we look for someone else?"

4 Jesus answered and said to them, "Go and report to John what you hear and see:

5 *the* BLIND RECEIVE SIGHT and *the* lame walk, *the* lepers are cleansed and *the* deaf hear, *the* dead

are raised up, and *the* POOR HAVE THE GOSPEL PREACHED TO THEM.

6 "And blessed is he who does not take offense at Me."

11:2 The One to Come?

John's question here may reflect confusion over the Messiah's role. If, like many Jews, John was expecting a political Messiah who would overthrow the Romans, his imprisonment may have caused him to wonder why Jesus wasn't taking action. Jesus responded by clarifying the kind of kingdom he came to establish: a kingdom that brought healing, liberation, and good news—but not necessarily political power.

Jesus' Tribute to John

7 ¶ As these men were going *away*, Jesus began to speak to the crowds about John, "What did you go out into the wilderness to see? A reed shaken by the wind?

8 "But what did you go out to see? A man dressed in soft *clothing*? Those who wear soft *clothing* are in kings' palaces!

9 "But what did you go out to see? A prophet? Yes, I tell you, and one who is more than a prophet.

10 "This is the one about whom it is written,

'BEHOLD, I SEND MY MESSENGER AHEAD OF YOU,
WHO WILL PREPARE YOUR WAY BEFORE YOU.'

11 "Truly I say to you, among those born of women there has not arisen *anyone* greater than John the Baptist! Yet the one who is least in the kingdom of heaven is greater than he.

12 "From the days of John the Baptist until now the kingdom of heaven suffers violence, and violent men take it by force.

13 "For all the prophets and the Law prophesied until John.

14 "And if you are willing to accept *it*, John himself is Elijah who was to come.

15 "He who has ears to hear, let him hear.

16 ¶ "But to what shall I compare this generation? It is like children sitting in the market places, who call out to the other *children*,

17 and say, 'We played the flute for you, and you did not dance; we sang a dirge, and you did not mourn.'

18 "For John came neither eating nor drinking, and they say, 'He has a demon!'

19 "The Son of Man came eating and drinking, and they say, 'Behold, a gluttonous man and a drunkard, a friend of tax collectors and sinners!' Yet wisdom is vindicated by her deeds."

---

[a] Gr *assarion*, the smallest copper coin

The Unrepenting Cities

11:21–23pp — Luke 10:13–15

20 ¶ Then He began to denounce the cities in which most of His miracles were done, because they did not repent.

11:20 Miracles Aren't Enough

Surprisingly, seeing supernatural miracles didn't lead people to repent and follow Jesus' teaching. Throughout his ministry, Jesus showed annoyance with crowds who flocked to see a popular leader do something supernatural. He wanted from them not applause, but commitment. Gradually, he relied more and more on parables, which, in private, he would explain to his disciples (see 13:11–17).

21 "Woe to you, Chorazin! Woe to you, Bethsaida! For if the miracles had occurred in Tyre and Sidon which occurred in you, they would have repented long ago in sackcloth and ashes.

22 "Nevertheless I say to you, it will be more tolerable for Tyre and Sidon in *the* day of judgment than for you.

23 "And you, Capernaum, will not be exalted to heaven, will you? You will descend to Hades; for if the miracles had occurred in Sodom which occurred in you, it would have remained to this day.

24 "Nevertheless I say to you that it will be more tolerable for the land of Sodom in *the* day of judgment, than for you."

Come to Me

11:25–27pp — Luke 10:21,22

25 ¶ At that time Jesus said, "I praise You, Father, Lord of heaven and earth, that You have hidden these things from *the* wise and intelligent and have revealed them to infants.

26 "Yes, Father, for this way was well-pleasing in Your sight.

27 "All things have been handed over to Me by My Father; and no one knows the Son except the Father; nor does anyone know the Father except the Son, and anyone to whom the Son wills to reveal *Him*.

28 ¶ "Come to Me, all who are weary and heavy-laden, and I will give you rest.

29 "Take My yoke upon you and learn from Me, for I am gentle and humble in heart, and YOU WILL FIND REST FOR YOUR SOULS.

30 "For My yoke is easy and My burden is light."

Sabbath Questions

12:1–8pp — Mark 2:23–28; Luke 6:1–5

12 At that time Jesus went through the grainfields on the Sabbath, and His disciples became hungry and began to pick the heads *of grain* and eat.

2 But when the Pharisees saw *this*, they said to

JOHN THE BAPTIST *Something New*

FASHION STARTS WITH A SINGLE purpose: to turn people's heads. At first the new look is a shock. Many say, "Wow"; some say, "Ugh!" Whether it's short skirts or long nose rings or earrings, paisleys or pastels, the new must stand out to gain attention.

John the Baptist was something new, and he certainly stood out from his surroundings. Though he could have been a priest like his father, he exchanged those linen robes for a garment of coarse camel's hair. He took to the wilderness, scavenging grasshoppers and wild honey rather than settling in Jerusalem where he could have savored a portion of the offerings people presented to God.

John's unusual style helped direct attention to his burning message: The Messiah was about to arrive, and people must change their ways. Crowds flocked to hear John, and he baptized them in the Jordan River as a sign of their repentance, thus earning himself the nickname "the Baptist."

No less an authority than Jesus said that John was as great as any man who had ever lived (11:11). In the same breath Jesus added that the lowest-ranking person in the kingdom of God, now drawing near, was even greater than John. Although John represented the best of the old order, the new order of God's kingdom would outshine his greatness by far.

John had no difficulty accepting this comparison. When he saw Jesus he recognized "the Lamb of God who takes away the sin of the world" (John 1:29). He considered himself unworthy even to untie Jesus' sandals. John the Baptist did not intend to attract attention to himself; rather, he pointed to Jesus.

When Herod Antipas arrested and executed John (14:1–12), most of John's disciples followed Jesus. It took a long time, however, for some who lived in far-off parts of the world to get the full message about Jesus (see Acts 18:24–26, 19:1–7). They, too, quickly adopted the Christian way. Despite John's great influence, it was a mark of his success that he left no distinctive "church" of his own. His followers were ready for Jesus.

Life Questions: How can your lifestyle help prepare people for Jesus?

Him, "Look, Your disciples do what is not lawful to do on a Sabbath."

3 But He said to them, "Have you not read what David did when he became hungry, he and his companions,

4 how he entered the house of God, and they ate the consecrated bread, which was not lawful for him to eat nor for those with him, but for the priests alone?

5 "Or have you not read in the Law, that on the Sabbath the priests in the temple break the Sabbath and are innocent?

6 "But I say to you that something greater than the temple is here.

7 "But if you had known what this means, 'I DESIRE COMPASSION, AND NOT A SACRIFICE,' you would not have condemned the innocent.

Lord of the Sabbath

12:9–14pp — Mark 3:1–6; Luke 6:6–11

8 "For the Son of Man is Lord of the Sabbath."

9 ¶ Departing from there, He went into their synagogue.

10 And a man *was there* whose hand was withered. And they questioned Jesus, asking, "Is it lawful to heal on the Sabbath?"—so that they might accuse Him.

11 And He said to them, "What man is there among you who has a sheep, and if it falls into a pit on the Sabbath, will he not take hold of it and lift it out?

12 "How much more valuable then is a man than a sheep! So then, it is lawful to do good on the Sabbath."

12:12 Pharisees Take Offense

Chapter 12 gives insight into why the Pharisees were offended by Jesus. First, his disciples picked grain on the Sabbath (verses 1–7), something forbidden by the Pharisees. A provocative healing on the Sabbath followed. Jesus accused the Pharisees of caring more for the letter of the law than the spirit, so much so that they showed more concern for animal life than human.

13 Then He *said to the man, "Stretch out your hand!" He stretched it out, and it was restored to normal, like the other.

14 But the Pharisees went out and conspired against Him, *as to* how they might destroy Him.

15 ¶ But Jesus, aware of *this*, withdrew from there. Many followed Him, and He healed them all,

16 and warned them not to tell who He was.

17 *This was* to fulfill what was spoken through Isaiah the prophet:

18 "BEHOLD, MY SERVANT WHOM I HAVE CHOSEN;

MY BELOVED IN WHOM MY SOUL is WELL-PLEASED;
I WILL PUT MY SPIRIT UPON HIM,
AND HE SHALL PROCLAIM JUSTICE TO THE GENTILES;

19 "HE WILL NOT QUARREL, NOR CRY OUT;
NOR WILL ANYONE HEAR HIS VOICE IN THE STREETS.

20 "A BATTERED REED HE WILL NOT BREAK OFF,
AND A SMOLDERING WICK HE WILL NOT PUT OUT,
UNTIL HE LEADS JUSTICE TO VICTORY.

21 "AND IN HIS NAME THE GENTILES WILL HOPE."

The Pharisees Rebuked

12:25–29pp — Mark 3:23–27; Luke 11:17–22

22 ¶ Then a demon-possessed man *who was* blind and mute was brought to Jesus, and He healed him, so that the mute man spoke and saw.

23 All the crowds were amazed, and were saying, "This man cannot be the Son of David, can he?"

24 But when the Pharisees heard *this*, they said, "This man casts out demons only by Beelzebul the ruler of the demons."

25 ¶ And knowing their thoughts Jesus said to them, "Any kingdom divided against itself is laid waste; and any city or house divided against itself will not stand.

26 "If Satan casts out Satan, he is divided against himself; how then will his kingdom stand?

27 "If I by Beelzebul cast out demons, by whom do your sons cast *them* out? For this reason they will be your judges.

28 "But if I cast out demons by the Spirit of God, then the kingdom of God has come upon you.

29 "Or how can anyone enter the strong man's house and carry off his property, unless he first binds the strong *man*? And then he will plunder his house.

The Unpardonable Sin

30 "He who is not with Me is against Me; and he who does not gather with Me scatters.

31 ¶ "Therefore I say to you, any sin and blasphemy shall be forgiven people, but blasphemy against the Spirit shall not be forgiven.

32 "Whoever speaks a word against the Son of Man, it shall be forgiven him; but whoever speaks against the Holy Spirit, it shall not be forgiven him, either in this age or in the *age* to come.

Words Reveal Character

33 ¶ "Either make the tree good and its fruit good, or make the tree bad and its fruit bad; for the tree is known by its fruit.

34 "You brood of vipers, how can you, being

evil, speak what is good? For the mouth speaks out of that which fills the heart.

35 "The good man brings out of *his* good treasure what is good; and the evil man brings out of *his* evil treasure what is evil.

36 "But I tell you that every careless word that people speak, they shall give an accounting for it in the day of judgment.

37 "For by your words you will be justified, and by your words you will be condemned."

The Desire for Signs

12:39–42pp — Luke 11:29–32
12:43–45pp — Luke 11:24–26

38 ¶ Then some of the scribes and Pharisees said to Him, "Teacher, we want to see a sign from You."

39 But He answered and said to them, "An evil and adulterous generation craves for a sign; and *yet* no sign will be given to it but the sign of Jonah the prophet;

40 for just as JONAH WAS THREE DAYS AND THREE NIGHTS IN THE BELLY OF THE SEA MONSTER, so will the Son of Man be three days and three nights in the heart of the earth.

41 "The men of Nineveh will stand up with this generation at the judgment, and will condemn it because they repented at the preaching of Jonah; and behold, something greater than Jonah is here.

42 "*The* Queen of *the* South will rise up with this generation at the judgment and will condemn it, because she came from the ends of the earth to hear the wisdom of Solomon; and behold, something greater than Solomon is here.

43 ¶ "Now when the unclean spirit goes out of a man, it passes through waterless places seeking rest, and does not find *it*.

44 "Then it says, 'I will return to my house from which I came'; and when it comes, it finds *it* unoccupied, swept, and put in order.

45 "Then it goes and takes along with it seven other spirits more wicked than itself, and they go in and live there; and the last state of that man becomes worse than the first. That is the way it will also be with this evil generation."

Changed Relationships

12:46–50pp — Mark 3:31–35; Luke 8:19–21

46 ¶ While He was still speaking to the crowds, behold, His mother and brothers were standing outside, seeking to speak to Him.

47 Someone said to Him, "Behold, Your mother and Your brothers are standing outside seeking to speak to You."

48 But Jesus answered the one who was telling Him and said, "Who is My mother and who are My brothers?"

49 And stretching out His hand toward His disciples, He said, "Behold My mother and My brothers!

50 "For whoever does the will of My Father who is in heaven, he is My brother and sister and mother."

Jesus Teaches in Parables

13:1–15pp — Mark 4:1–12; Luke 8:4–10
13:16,17pp — Luke 10:23,24
13:18–23pp — Mark 4:13–20; Luke 8:11–15

13 That day Jesus went out of the house and was sitting by the sea.

2 And large crowds gathered to Him, so He got into a boat and sat down, and the whole crowd was standing on the beach.

3 ¶ And He spoke many things to them in parables, saying, "Behold, the sower went out to sow;

4 and as he sowed, some *seeds* fell beside the road, and the birds came and ate them up.

5 "Others fell on the rocky places, where they did not have much soil; and immediately they sprang up, because they had no depth of soil.

6 "But when the sun had risen, they were scorched; and because they had no root, they withered away.

7 "Others fell among the thorns, and the thorns came up and choked them out.

8 "And others fell on the good soil and *yielded a crop, some a hundredfold, some sixty, and some thirty.

9 "He who has ears, let him hear."

An Explanation

10 ¶ And the disciples came and said to Him, "Why do You speak to them in parables?"

13:10 Stories to Remember

An illiterate society (like much of Palestine in Jesus' day) passes down wisdom in the form of proverbs and stories. Everybody likes a story, and stories are easier to remember than concepts or logical outlines. Jesus spoke in terms that would hold the interest of a society of farmers and fishermen, and about 30 of his masterful parables—stories with a point—have survived in the Gospels.

11 Jesus answered them, "To you it has been granted to know the mysteries of the kingdom of heaven, but to them it has not been granted.

12 "For whoever has, to him *more* shall be given, and he will have an abundance; but whoever does not have, even what he has shall be taken away from him.

13 "Therefore I speak to them in parables; because while seeing they do not see, and while hearing they do not hear, nor do they understand.

14 "In their case the prophecy of Isaiah is being fulfilled, which says,
'YOU WILL KEEP ON HEARING, BUT WILL NOT UNDERSTAND;

YOU WILL KEEP ON SEEING, BUT WILL NOT
  PERCEIVE;
15 FOR THE HEART OF THIS PEOPLE HAS
  BECOME DULL,
WITH THEIR EARS THEY SCARCELY HEAR,
AND THEY HAVE CLOSED THEIR EYES,
OTHERWISE THEY WOULD SEE WITH THEIR
  EYES,
HEAR WITH THEIR EARS,

AND UNDERSTAND WITH THEIR HEART AND
  RETURN,
AND I WOULD HEAL THEM.'
16 "But blessed are your eyes, because they see;
and your ears, because they hear.
17 "For truly I say to you that many prophets
and righteous men desired to see what you see,
and did not see *it*, and to hear what you hear, and
did not hear *it*.

What Should a Leader Look Like?
Not everyone wanted Jesus' kind of kingdom

> "Where did this man get this wisdom and these miraculous powers? Is not this the carpenter's son?"
> 13:54–55

IMPORTANT LEADERS, SUCH AS PRESIDENTS and prime ministers, work hard to convey an impression of confidence and power. A leader, they assume, should look like a leader, and many of them hire an "image specialist" to learn how. Wherever they go, press agents, bodyguards, loyal assistants, and throngs of eager admirers follow in their wake.

Matthew depicts Jesus as a true leader—a king, in fact—but one who broke stereotypes. Jesus had undeniable power. He could quiet an angry storm and even walk on the surface of a lake. Yet he used that power compassionately, for the sake of others: to feed the hungry and heal the sick. He wasn't concerned about a powerful image.

A New Kind of Kingdom

First-century Jews, who hated the Roman empire, would have rallied eagerly around a militant Jewish king. They rebelled often until a vengeful Roman general flattened Jerusalem in A.D. 70. The kingdom Jesus presented, however, didn't meet their expectations.

At the beginning of his ministry, Jesus turned down a tempting offer of glory and territory (4:8–11), and he consistently bucked the pressures of the crowd. Although he was the most powerful leader ever, he spent his time telling stories, not raising an army. As a true Messiah, he sought not to satisfy people's false image of him, but to please God.

In chapter 13, Matthew collects several of the stories Jesus told to describe his "kingdom of heaven"—a phrase used 32 times in Matthew. Although Jesus never concisely defined the phrase, he gave many clues about the nature of his kingdom. The kingdom is so important, he said, that belonging to it is worth selling everything a person owns.

Jesus said his kingdom doesn't have geographical boundaries. Unlike, say, Greece or China or Spain, it can't be charted on a map. Its followers live right among their enemies, not separated from them by a moat or a wall. Yet Jesus predicted that his kingdom would show remarkable growth even in an evil environment bent on its destruction.

The Disciples Fail to Understand

The "kingdom of heaven" consists of the rule of God in the world. It's made up of people of all races and from all nations who loyally follow God's will on earth. Jesus stressed that this new kingdom was a major advance in God's plan: its least member, he said, is even greater than John the Baptist (11:11).

The disciples, accustomed to more traditional images of power and leadership, couldn't quite grasp Jesus' concept of the kingdom. They kept asking him to explain his parables even as they jockeyed vainly for status.

As the days passed, the disciples became convinced that Jesus was "the Christ, the Son of the living God." Peter won warm praise for that assertion (16:17). But he received Jesus' strongest rebuke in the next scene when he recoiled from the idea that his leader might soon suffer and die.

The paradoxes of Jesus' style of leadership deepened as he neared Jerusalem, the capital city. He allowed one moment of public triumph, on the day we call Palm Sunday. Yet, even then he rode not a chariot or a stallion, but a donkey colt. And a few days later he left his followers an enduring emblem: not a royal banner or a scepter, but an executioner's cross.

Life Questions: Could Jesus run for political office in the United States? What kind of leader do people want today?

The Sower Explained

18 ¶ "Hear then the parable of the sower.

19 "When anyone hears the word of the kingdom and does not understand it, the evil *one* comes and snatches away what has been sown in his heart. This is the one on whom seed was sown beside the road.

20 "The one on whom seed was sown on the rocky places, this is the man who hears the word and immediately receives it with joy;

21 yet he has no *firm* root in himself, but is *only* temporary, and when affliction or persecution arises because of the word, immediately he falls away.

22 "And the one on whom seed was sown among the thorns, this is the man who hears the word, and the worry of the world and the deceitfulness of wealth choke the word, and it becomes unfruitful.

23 "And the one on whom seed was sown on the good soil, this is the man who hears the word and understands it; who indeed bears fruit and brings forth, some a hundredfold, some sixty, and some thirty."

Tares among Wheat

24 ¶ Jesus presented another parable to them, saying, "The kingdom of heaven may be compared to a man who sowed good seed in his field.

25 "But while his men were sleeping, his enemy came and sowed *a*tares among the wheat, and went away.

26 "But when the wheat sprouted and bore grain, then the tares became evident also.

27 "The slaves of the landowner came and said to him, 'Sir, did you not sow good seed in your field? How then does it have tares?'

28 "And he said to them, 'An enemy has done this!' The slaves *said to him, 'Do you want us, then, to go and gather them up?'

29 "But he *said, 'No; for while you are gathering up the tares, you may uproot the wheat with them.

30 'Allow both to grow together until the harvest; and in the time of the harvest I will say to the reapers, "First gather up the tares and bind them in bundles to burn them up; but gather the wheat into my barn."'"

The Mustard Seed

13:31,32pp — Mark 4:30–32
13:31–33pp — Luke 13:18–21

31 ¶ He presented another parable to them, saying, "The kingdom of heaven is like a mustard seed, which a man took and sowed in his field;

32 and this is smaller than all *other* seeds, but when it is full grown, it is larger than the garden plants and becomes a tree, so that THE BIRDS OF THE AIR come and NEST IN ITS BRANCHES."

a Or *darnel*, a weed resembling wheat

The Leaven

33 ¶ He spoke another parable to them, "The kingdom of heaven is like leaven, which a woman took and hid in three pecks of flour until it was all leavened."

34 ¶ All these things Jesus spoke to the crowds in parables, and He did not speak to them without a parable.

35 *This was* to fulfill what was spoken through the prophet:

"I WILL OPEN MY MOUTH IN PARABLES;
I WILL UTTER THINGS HIDDEN SINCE THE
   FOUNDATION OF THE WORLD."

The Tares Explained

36 ¶ Then He left the crowds and went into the house. And His disciples came to Him and said, "Explain to us the parable of the tares of the field."

37 And He said, "The one who sows the good seed is the Son of Man,

38 and the field is the world; and *as for* the good seed, these are the sons of the kingdom; and the tares are the sons of the evil *one;*

39 and the enemy who sowed them is the devil, and the harvest is the end of the age; and the reapers are angels.

40 "So just as the tares are gathered up and burned with fire, so shall it be at the end of the age.

41 "The Son of Man will send forth His angels, and they will gather out of His kingdom all stumbling blocks, and those who commit lawlessness,

42 and will throw them into the furnace of fire; in that place there will be weeping and gnashing of teeth.

43 "Then THE RIGHTEOUS WILL SHINE FORTH AS THE SUN in the kingdom of their Father. He who has ears, let him hear.

Hidden Treasure

44 ¶ "The kingdom of heaven is like a treasure hidden in the field, which a man found and hid *again*; and from joy over it he goes and sells all that he has and buys that field.

A Costly Pearl

45 ¶ "Again, the kingdom of heaven is like a merchant seeking fine pearls,

46 and upon finding one pearl of great value, he went and sold all that he had and bought it.

A Dragnet

47 ¶ "Again, the kingdom of heaven is like a dragnet cast into the sea, and gathering fish of every kind;

48 and when it was filled, they drew it up on the beach; and they sat down and gathered the good *fish* into containers, but the bad they threw away.

49 "So it will be at the end of the age; the angels

will come forth and take out the wicked from among the righteous,

50 and will throw them into the furnace of fire; in that place there will be weeping and gnashing of teeth.

51 ¶ "Have you understood all these things?" They *said to Him, "Yes."

52 And Jesus said to them, "Therefore every scribe who has become a disciple of the kingdom of heaven is like a head of a household, who brings out of his treasure things new and old."

Jesus Revisits Nazareth

13:54-58pp — Mark 6:1-6

53 ¶ When Jesus had finished these parables, He departed from there.

54 He came to His hometown and *began* teaching them in their synagogue, so that they were astonished, and said, "Where *did* this man *get* this wisdom and *these* miraculous powers?

55 "Is not this the carpenter's son? Is not His mother called Mary, and His brothers, James and Joseph and Simon and Judas?

56 "And His sisters, are they not all with us? Where then *did* this man *get* all these things?"

57 And they took offense at Him. But Jesus said to them, "A prophet is not without honor

except in his hometown and in his *own* household."

13:57 No Respect at Home

Jesus had opened his ministry at home in a synagogue, an occasion marked by a near-riot. When he returned later, he aroused great curiosity but little belief. The townsfolk couldn't fathom that one who'd been raised in their midst by a carpenter was now teaching like a rabbi and performing miracles. Jesus declined to display his supernatural power for them, and quietly withdrew.

58 And He did not do many miracles there because of their unbelief.

John the Baptist Beheaded

14:1-12pp — Mark 6:14-29

14 At that time Herod the tetrarch heard the news about Jesus,

2 and said to his servants, "This is John the Baptist; he has risen from the dead, and that is why miraculous powers are at work in him."

THE HERODS *Lower Authority*

THE HEROD FAMILY WEAVES ITS way through the background of the New Testament, like minor supporting characters in a play. Oddly enough, in their own minds—and in the minds of most people then—they were major players.

Like the Kennedys in modern America, or the many royal families in European history, the Herods were a family dynasty. They ruled on behalf of the Romans with nearly absolute power. Such power did not impress the early Christians, however. They worshiped a higher authority, one whom the Herods were too spiritually dense to recognize.

Three different rulers go by the name of Herod in the New Testament. (A fourth, Agrippa, descended from the same family [see Agrippa, page 1215].) All three clashed with Jesus or his followers.

Herod the Great reigned as king when Jesus was born. He met the Magi, pointed them toward Bethlehem and then, when they disappeared without identifying the baby king, had all the infants in the area slaughtered (Matthew 2). Other historical sources suggest that such behavior was all too typical of this Herod—he even had his own sons murdered when he thought they threatened his power.

Herod the tetrarch, also known as Herod Antipas, was among Herod the Great's sons who survived the violence. At his father's death, he took command over Jesus' home area of Galilee. When John the Baptist offended Herod and his mistress by criticizing their morals, Herod imprisoned John and later had him beheaded. Jesus himself fell into this Herod's hands during his trial. Herod had heard of Jesus and hoped to see him do a miracle; when Jesus wouldn't cooperate, Herod ridiculed him and sent him back to Pilate (Luke 23:6-12).

Herod Agrippa I, grandson of Herod the Great, continued the pattern into the next generation. He ruled Jerusalem when the church first began growing there. He clamped down on the early Christians, executing James and arresting a number of others, including Peter. When Peter "escaped" with God's help, Herod had the guards executed (Acts 12). Acts tells us that Herod Agrippa died a sudden death, because he "did not give God the glory" when a crowd of admirers hailed him as divine (Acts 12:23).

As modern people we tend to focus on the Herods' brutal behavior, but most rulers behaved brutally in those days. Even more importantly, in the Bible's eyes, the Herods failed to recognize the real power on earth—that belonging to God.

Life Questions: What dangers do Christians in the modern world face from the "lower authority" of politicians and rulers?

3 ¶ For when Herod had John arrested, he bound him and put him in prison because of Herodias, the wife of his brother Philip.

4 For John had been saying to him, "It is not lawful for you to have her."

5 Although Herod wanted to put him to death, he feared the crowd, because they regarded John as a prophet.

14:5 A Wife's Revenge

John the Baptist offended King Herod with his blunt accusations, but Mark 6 points out that most of the venom came from Herod's wife (whom the king had stolen from his brother Philip). Herod had mixed feelings about John. He liked to listen to the prophet and had a respectful fear of him and his stern message. After falling into a trap set by his wife and stepdaughter, however, he succumbed to peer pressure and ordered John's execution.

6 ¶ But when Herod's birthday came, the daughter of Herodias danced before *them* and pleased Herod,

7 so *much* that he promised with an oath to give her whatever she asked.

8 Having been prompted by her mother, she *said, "Give me here on a platter the head of John the Baptist."

9 Although he was grieved, the king commanded *it* to be given because of his oaths, and because of his dinner guests.

10 He sent and had John beheaded in the prison.

11 And his head was brought on a platter and given to the girl, and she brought it to her mother.

12 His disciples came and took away the body and buried it; and they went and reported to Jesus.

Five Thousand Fed

14:13–21pp — Mark 6:32–44; Luke 9:10–17; John 6:1–13
14:13–21Ref — Matt 15:32–38

13 ¶ Now when Jesus heard *about John,* He withdrew from there in a boat to a secluded place by Himself; and when the people heard *of this,* they followed Him on foot from the cities.

14 When He went ashore, He saw a large crowd, and felt compassion for them and healed their sick.

15 ¶ When it was evening, the disciples came to Him and said, "This place is desolate and the hour is already late; so send the crowds away, that they may go into the villages and buy food for themselves."

16 But Jesus said to them, "They do not need to go away; you give them *something* to eat!"

17 They *said to Him, "We have here only five loaves and two fish."

18 And He said, "Bring them here to Me."

19 Ordering the people to sit down on the grass, He took the five loaves and the two fish, and looking up toward heaven, He blessed *the food,* and breaking the loaves He gave them to the disciples, and the disciples *gave them* to the crowds,

20 and they all ate and were satisfied. They picked up what was left over of the broken pieces, twelve full baskets.

21 There were about five thousand men who ate, besides women and children.

Jesus Walks on the Water

14:22–33pp — Mark 6:45–51; John 6:16–21
14:34–36pp — Mark 6:53–56

22 ¶ Immediately He made the disciples get into the boat and go ahead of Him to the other side, while He sent the crowds away.

23 After He had sent the crowds away, He went up on the mountain by Himself to pray; and when it was evening, He was there alone.

24 But the boat was already *a long distance from the land, battered by the waves; for the wind was contrary.

25 And in the *bfourth watch of the night He came to them, walking on the sea.

26 When the disciples saw Him walking on the sea, they were terrified, and said, "It is a ghost!" And they cried out in fear.

27 But immediately Jesus spoke to them, saying, "Take courage, it is I; do not be afraid."

28 ¶ Peter said to Him, "Lord, if it is You, command me to come to You on the water."

29 And He said, "Come!" And Peter got out of the boat, and walked on the water and came toward Jesus.

30 But seeing the wind, he became frightened, and beginning to sink, he cried out, "Lord, save me!"

31 Immediately Jesus stretched out His hand and took hold of him, and *said to him, "You of little faith, why did you doubt?"

32 When they got into the boat, the wind stopped.

33 And those who were in the boat worshiped Him, saying, "You are certainly God's Son!"

34 ¶ When they had crossed over, they came to land at Gennesaret.

35 And when the men of that place recognized Him, they sent *word* into all that surrounding district and brought to Him all who were sick;

36 and they implored Him that they might just touch the fringe of His cloak; and as many as touched *it* were cured.

---

a Lit *many stadia from*; a stadion was about 600 feet or about 182 meters   *b* I.e. 3–6 a.m.

Tradition and Commandment

15:1–20pp — Mark 7:1–23

15 Then some Pharisees and scribes *came to Jesus from Jerusalem and said,

2 "Why do Your disciples break the tradition of the elders? For they do not wash their hands when they eat bread."

15:1 Attacking Legalism

The Pharisees and teachers of the law considered their own strict traditions as binding as Old Testament law. In this passage, Jesus points out glaring inconsistencies in those traditions.

3 And He answered and said to them, "Why do you yourselves transgress the commandment of God for the sake of your tradition?

4 "For God said, 'HONOR YOUR FATHER AND MOTHER,' and, 'HE WHO SPEAKS EVIL OF FATHER OR MOTHER IS TO BE PUT TO DEATH.'

5 "But you say, 'Whoever says to *his* father or mother, "Whatever I have that would help you has been given *to God*,"

6 he is not to honor his father or his mother*ᵃ*.' And *by this* you invalidated the word of God for the sake of your tradition.

7 "You hypocrites, rightly did Isaiah prophesy of you:

8 'THIS PEOPLE HONORS ME WITH THEIR LIPS,
   BUT THEIR HEART IS FAR AWAY FROM ME.

9 'BUT IN VAIN DO THEY WORSHIP ME,
   TEACHING AS DOCTRINES THE PRECEPTS OF MEN.' "

10 ¶ After Jesus called the crowd to Him, He said to them, "Hear and understand.

11 "*It is* not what enters into the mouth *that* defiles the man, but what proceeds out of the mouth, this defiles the man."

12 ¶ Then the disciples *came and *said to Him, "Do You know that the Pharisees were offended when they heard this statement?"

13 But He answered and said, "Every plant which My heavenly Father did not plant shall be uprooted.

14 "Let them alone; they are blind guides *ᵇ*of the blind. And if a blind man guides a blind man, both will fall into a pit."

The Heart of Man

15 ¶ Peter said to Him, "Explain the parable to us."

16 Jesus said, "Are you still lacking in understanding also?

17 "Do you not understand that everything that goes into the mouth passes into the stomach, and is eliminated?

18 "But the things that proceed out of the mouth come from the heart, and those defile the man.

19 "For out of the heart come evil thoughts, murders, adulteries, fornications, thefts, false witness, slanders.

20 "These are the things which defile the man; but to eat with unwashed hands does not defile the man."

The Syrophoenician Woman

15:21–28pp — Mark 7:24–30

21 ¶ Jesus went away from there, and withdrew into the district of Tyre and Sidon.

22 And a Canaanite woman from that region came out and *began* to cry out, saying, "Have mercy on me, Lord, Son of David; my daughter is cruelly demon-possessed."

23 But He did not answer her a word. And His disciples came and implored Him, saying, "Send her away, because she keeps shouting at us."

24 But He answered and said, "I was sent only to the lost sheep of the house of Israel."

25 But she came and *began* to bow down before Him, saying, "Lord, help me!"

26 And He answered and said, "It is not good to take the children's bread and throw it to the dogs."

27 But she said, "Yes, Lord; but even the dogs feed on the crumbs which fall from their masters' table."

28 Then Jesus said to her, "O woman, your faith is great; it shall be done for you as you wish." And her daughter was healed at once.

Healing Crowds

15:29–31pp — Mark 7:31–37

29 ¶ Departing from there, Jesus went along by the Sea of Galilee, and having gone up on the mountain, He was sitting there.

30 And large crowds came to Him, bringing

15:29–39 Two Feedings

In back-to-back chapters, Matthew reports on two incidents that can be easily confused. The feeding of the 5,000 (chapter 14) came at the height of Jesus' popularity and made a huge impression: all four Gospels report on it. Only Matthew and Mark, however, record this separate miracle performed for a slightly smaller crowd. In Mark's account (Mark 8:1–10), Jesus seems amazed that his disciples, having seen the first miracle, doubt his ability to supply a crowd's needs this second time.

ᵃ I.e. by supporting them with it   *ᵇ* Later mss add *of the blind* with them *those who were* lame, crippled, blind, mute, and many others, and they laid them down at His feet; and He healed them.

31 So the crowd marveled as they saw the mute speaking, the crippled restored, and the lame walking, and the blind seeing; and they glorified the God of Israel.

Four Thousand Fed

15:32–39pp — Mark 8:1–10
15:32–39Ref — Matt 14:13–21

32 ¶ And Jesus called His disciples to Him, and said, "I feel compassion for the people, because they have remained with Me now three days and have nothing to eat; and I do not want to send them away hungry, for they might faint on the way."

33 The disciples *said to Him, "Where would we get so many loaves in *this* desolate place to satisfy such a large crowd?"

34 And Jesus *said to them, "How many loaves do you have?" And they said, "Seven, and a few small fish."

35 And He directed the people to sit down on the ground;

36 and He took the seven loaves and the fish; and giving thanks, He broke them and started giving them to the disciples, and the disciples *gave them* to the people.

37 And they all ate and were satisfied, and they picked up what was left over of the broken pieces, seven large baskets full.

38 And those who ate were four thousand men, besides women and children.

39 ¶ And sending away the crowds, Jesus got into the boat and came to the region of Magadan.

Pharisees Test Jesus

16:1–12pp — Mark 8:11–21

16 The Pharisees and Sadducees came up, and testing Jesus, they asked Him to show them a sign from heaven.

2 But He replied to them, "When it is evening, you say, '*It will be* fair weather, for the sky is red.'

3 "And in the morning, '*There will be* a storm today, for the sky is red and threatening.' Do you know how to discern the appearance of the sky, but cannot *discern* the signs of the times?

4 "An evil and adulterous generation seeks after a sign; and a sign will not be given it, except the sign of Jonah." And He left them and went away.

5 ¶ And the disciples came to the other side *of the sea*, but they had forgotten to bring *any* bread.

6 And Jesus said to them, "Watch out and beware of the leaven of the Pharisees and Sadducees."

7 They began to discuss *this* among themselves, saying, "*He said that* because we did not bring *any* bread."

8 But Jesus, aware of this, said, "You men of little faith, why do you discuss among yourselves that you have no bread?

9 "Do you not yet understand or remember the five loaves of the five thousand, and how many baskets *full* you picked up?

10 "Or the seven loaves of the four thousand, and how many large baskets *full* you picked up?

11 "How is it that you do not understand that I did not speak to you concerning bread? But beware of the leaven of the Pharisees and Sadducees."

12 Then they understood that He did not say to beware of the leaven of bread, but of the teaching of the Pharisees and Sadducees.

Peter's Confession of Christ

16:13–16pp — Mark 8:27–29; Luke 9:18–20

13 ¶ Now when Jesus came into the district of Caesarea Philippi, He was asking His disciples, "Who do people say that the Son of Man is?"

16:13 Peter's Highs and Lows

The disciple Peter earned a reputation for impulsiveness, and this chapter shows him at his very best and very worst. He won highest praise for discerning Jesus' true identity, but in the very next paragraph he made one of his biggest blunders. He wanted Jesus to avoid pain, not understanding that the pain of the cross would bring salvation to the whole world.

14 And they said, "Some *say* John the Baptist; and others, Elijah; but still others, Jeremiah, or one of the prophets."

15 He *said to them, "But who do you say that I am?"

16 Simon Peter answered, "You are the Christ, the Son of the living God."

17 And Jesus said to him, "Blessed are you, Simon Barjona, because flesh and blood did not reveal *this* to you, but My Father who is in heaven.

18 "I also say to you that you are Peter, and upon this rock I will build My church; and the gates of Hades will not overpower it.

19 "I will give you the keys of the kingdom of heaven; and whatever you bind on earth shall have been bound in heaven, and whatever you loose on earth shall have been loosed in heaven."

20 Then He warned the disciples that they should tell no one that He was the Christ.

Jesus Foretells His Death

16:21–28pp — Mark 8:31–9:1; Luke 9:22–27

21 ¶ From that time Jesus began to show His disciples that He must go to Jerusalem, and suffer many things from the elders and chief priests and scribes, and be killed, and be raised up on the third day.

22 Peter took Him aside and began to rebuke Him, saying, "God forbid *it*, Lord! This shall never happen to You."

23 But He turned and said to Peter, "Get behind Me, Satan! You are a stumbling block to Me; for you are not setting your mind on God's interests, but man's."

Discipleship Is Costly

24 ¶ Then Jesus said to His disciples, "If anyone wishes to come after Me, he must deny himself, and take up his cross and follow Me.

25 "For whoever wishes to save his life will lose it; but whoever loses his life for My sake will find it.

26 "For what will it profit a man if he gains the whole world and forfeits his soul? Or what will a man give in exchange for his soul?

27 "For the Son of Man is going to come in the glory of His Father with His angels, and WILL THEN REPAY EVERY MAN ACCORDING TO HIS DEEDS.

28 ¶ "Truly I say to you, there are some of those who are standing here who will not taste death until they see the Son of Man coming in His kingdom."

The Transfiguration

17:1–8pp — Luke 9:28–36
17:1–13pp — Mark 9:2–13

17 Six days later Jesus *took with Him Peter and James and John his brother, and *led them up on a high mountain by themselves.

2 And He was transfigured before them; and His face shone like the sun, and His garments became as white as light.

3 And behold, Moses and Elijah appeared to them, talking with Him.

4 Peter said to Jesus, "Lord, it is good for us to be here; if You wish, I will make three tabernacles here, one for You, and one for Moses, and one for Elijah."

5 While he was still speaking, a bright cloud overshadowed them, and behold, a voice out of the cloud said, "This is My beloved Son, with whom I am well-pleased; listen to Him!"

6 When the disciples heard *this*, they fell face down to the ground and were terrified.

17:5 Unforgettable Moment

Three of Jesus' disciples had the opportunity to observe this dramatic scene of God's approving of his Son Jesus. Moses, the first great lawgiver, and Elijah, the first great prophet, appeared with Jesus, and God spoke from heaven. The apostle Peter described the impact of this experience in 2 Peter 1:16–18.

7 And Jesus came to *them* and touched them and said, "Get up, and do not be afraid."

8 And lifting up their eyes, they saw no one except Jesus Himself alone.

9 ¶ As they were coming down from the mountain, Jesus commanded them, saying, "Tell the vision to no one until the Son of Man has risen from the dead."

10 And His disciples asked Him, "Why then do the scribes say that Elijah must come first?"

11 And He answered and said, "Elijah is coming and will restore all things;

12 but I say to you that Elijah already came, and they did not recognize him, but did to him whatever they wished. So also the Son of Man is going to suffer at their hands."

13 Then the disciples understood that He had spoken to them about John the Baptist.

The Demoniac

17:14–19pp — Mark 9:14–28; Luke 9:37–42

14 ¶ When they came to the crowd, a man came up to Jesus, falling on his knees before Him and saying,

15 "Lord, have mercy on my son, for he is a lunatic and is very ill; for he often falls into the fire and often into the water.

16 "I brought him to Your disciples, and they could not cure him."

17 And Jesus answered and said, "You unbelieving and perverted generation, how long shall I be with you? How long shall I put up with you? Bring him here to Me."

18 And Jesus rebuked him, and the demon came out of him, and the boy was cured at once.

19 ¶ Then the disciples came to Jesus privately and said, "Why could we not drive it out?"

20 And He *said to them, "Because of the littleness of your faith; for truly I say to you, if you have faith the size of a mustard seed, you will say to this mountain, 'Move from here to there,' and it will move; and nothing will be impossible to you.

21 ["*a*But this kind does not go out except by prayer and fasting."]

22 ¶ And while they were gathering together in Galilee, Jesus said to them, "The Son of Man is going to be delivered into the hands of men;

23 and they will kill Him, and He will be raised on the third day." And they were deeply grieved.

The Tribute Money

24 ¶ When they came to Capernaum, those who collected the *b*two-drachma *tax* came to Peter and said, "Does your teacher not pay the *b*two-drachma *tax*?"

25 He *said, "Yes." And when he came into the house, Jesus spoke to him first, saying, "What do you think, Simon? From whom do the kings of the

---

a Early mss do not contain this v   *b* Equivalent to two denarii or two days' wages, paid as a temple tax earth collect customs or poll-tax, from their sons or from strangers?"

26 When Peter said, "From strangers," Jesus said to him, "Then the sons are exempt.

27 "However, so that we do not offend them, go to the sea and throw in a hook, and take the first fish that comes up; and when you open its mouth, you will find *a shekel. Take that and give it to them for you and Me."

Rank in the Kingdom

18:1–5pp — Mark 9:33–37; Luke 9:46–48

18 At that time the disciples came to Jesus and said, "Who then is greatest in the kingdom of heaven?"

2 And He called a child to Himself and set him before them,

3 and said, "Truly I say to you, unless you are converted and become like children, you will not enter the kingdom of heaven.

4 "Whoever then humbles himself as this child, he is the greatest in the kingdom of heaven.

5 "And whoever receives one such child in My name receives Me;

6 but whoever causes one of these little ones who believe in Me to stumble, it would be better for him to have a heavy millstone hung around his neck, and to be drowned in the depth of the sea.

Stumbling Blocks

7 ¶ "Woe to the world because of *its* stumbling blocks! For it is inevitable that stumbling blocks come; but woe to that man through whom the stumbling block comes!

8 ¶ "If your hand or your foot causes you to stumble, cut it off and throw it from you; it is better for you to enter life crippled or lame, than to have two hands or two feet and be cast into the eternal fire.

9 "If your eye causes you to stumble, pluck it out and throw it from you. It is better for you to enter life with one eye, than to have two eyes and be cast into the fiery hell.

10 ¶ "See that you do not despise one of these little ones, for I say to you that their angels in heaven continually see the face of My Father who is in heaven.

11 ["*b*For the Son of Man has come to save that which was lost.]

Ninety-nine Plus One

18:12–14pp — Luke 15:4–7

12 ¶ "What do you think? If any man has a hundred sheep, and one of them has gone astray, does he not leave the ninety-nine on the mountains and go and search for the one that is straying?

13 "If it turns out that he finds it, truly I say to

you, he rejoices over it more than over the ninety-nine which have not gone astray.

14 "So it is not *the* will of your Father who is in heaven that one of these little ones perish.

Discipline and Prayer

15 ¶ "If your brother sins*c*, go and show him his fault in private; if he listens to you, you have won your brother.

16 "But if he does not listen *to you,* take one or two more with you, so that BY THE MOUTH OF TWO OR THREE WITNESSES EVERY FACT MAY BE CONFIRMED.

17 "If he refuses to listen to them, tell it to the church; and if he refuses to listen even to the church, let him be to you as a Gentile and a tax collector.

18 "Truly I say to you, whatever you bind on earth shall have been bound in heaven; and whatever you loose on earth shall have been loosed in heaven.

19 ¶ "Again I say to you, that if two of you agree on earth about anything that they may ask, it shall be done for them by My Father who is in heaven.

20 "For where two or three have gathered together in My name, I am there in their midst."

Forgiveness

21 ¶ Then Peter came and said to Him, "Lord, how often shall my brother sin against me and I forgive him? Up to seven times?"

22 Jesus *said to him, "I do not say to you, up to seven times, but up to seventy times seven.

23 ¶ "For this reason the kingdom of heaven may be compared to a king who wished to settle accounts with his slaves.

18:23 Matthew and Money

Just as Luke, a doctor, gives more descriptive accounts of physical healings, Matthew, a former tax collector, highlights stories about money. This story in chapter 18, as well as others in chapters 20 and 25, appears only in Matthew's Gospel. Significantly, the former tax collector records Jesus' strongest words on treatment of the poor and needy.

24 "When he had begun to settle *them,* one who owed him *d*ten thousand talents was brought to him.

25 "But since he did not have *the means* to repay, his lord commanded him to be sold, along with his wife and children and all that he had, and repayment to be made.

26 "So the slave fell *to the ground* and prostrated

---

a Lit *standard coin,* which was a shekel   *b* Early mss do not contain this v   *c* Late mss add *against you*   *d* A talent
was worth more than fifteen years' wages of a laborer

himself before him, saying, 'Have patience with me and I will repay you everything.'

27 "And the lord of that slave felt compassion and released him and forgave him the debt.

28 "But that slave went out and found one of his fellow slaves who owed him a hundred *a*denarii; and he seized him and *began* to choke *him,* saying, 'Pay back what you owe.'

29 "So his fellow slave fell *to the ground* and *began* to plead with him, saying, 'Have patience with me and I will repay you.'

30 "But he was unwilling and went and threw him in prison until he should pay back what was owed.

31 "So when his fellow slaves saw what had happened, they were deeply grieved and came and reported to their lord all that had happened.

32 "Then summoning him, his lord *said to him, 'You wicked slave, I forgave you all that debt because you pleaded with me.

33 'Should you not also have had mercy on your fellow slave, in the same way that I had mercy on you?'

34 "And his lord, moved with anger, handed him over to the torturers until he should repay all that was owed him.

35 "My heavenly Father will also do the same to you, if each of you does not forgive his brother from your heart."

Concerning Divorce

19:1–9pp — Mark 10:1–12

19 When Jesus had finished these words, He departed from Galilee and came into the region of Judea beyond the Jordan;

2 and large crowds followed Him, and He healed them there.

3 ¶ *Some* Pharisees came to Jesus, testing Him and asking, "Is it lawful *for a man* to divorce his wife for any reason at all?"

4 And He answered and said, "Have you not read that He who created *them* from the beginning MADE THEM MALE AND FEMALE,

5 and said, 'FOR THIS REASON A MAN SHALL LEAVE HIS FATHER AND MOTHER AND BE JOINED TO HIS WIFE, AND THE TWO SHALL BECOME ONE FLESH'?

6 "So they are no longer two, but one flesh. What therefore God has joined together, let no man separate."

7 They *said to Him, "Why then did Moses command to GIVE HER A CERTIFICATE OF DIVORCE AND SEND *her* AWAY?"

8 He *said to them, "Because of your hardness of heart Moses permitted you to divorce your wives; but from the beginning it has not been this way.

9 "And I say to you, whoever divorces his wife, except for immorality, and marries another woman commits adultery ."

---

a The denarius was a day's wages

10 ¶ The disciples *said to Him, "If the relationship of the man with his wife is like this, it is better not to marry."

11 But He said to them, "Not all men *can* accept this statement, but *only* those to whom it has been given.

19:9 No-Fault Divorce?

In Jesus' day Pharisees debated how to interpret Old Testament rules concerning divorce. As usual, they tried to pull Jesus into the dispute. A famous rabbi named Hillel taught that a man could divorce his wife if she did anything at all to displease him, such as burning his food. A stricter school headed by Shammai limited grounds for divorce to marital infidelity. Jesus clearly sided with Shammai but pointed much deeper, beyond the technicalities of divorce to God's original design for marriage.

12 "For there are eunuchs who were born that way from their mother's womb; and there are eunuchs who were made eunuchs by men; and there are *also* eunuchs who made themselves eunuchs for the sake of the kingdom of heaven. He who is able to accept *this,* let him accept *it.*"

Jesus Blesses Little Children

19:13–15pp — Mark 10:13–16; Luke 18:15–17

13 ¶ Then *some* children were brought to Him so that He might lay His hands on them and pray; and the disciples rebuked them.

14 But Jesus said, "Let the children alone, and do not hinder them from coming to Me; for the kingdom of heaven belongs to such as these."

15 After laying His hands on them, He departed from there.

The Rich Young Ruler

19:16–29pp — Mark 10:17–30; Luke 18:18–30

16 ¶ And someone came to Him and said, "Teacher, what good thing shall I do that I may obtain eternal life?"

17 And He said to him, "Why are you asking Me about what is good? There is *only* One who is good; but if you wish to enter into life, keep the commandments."

18 *Then* he *said to Him, "Which ones?" And Jesus said, "YOU SHALL NOT COMMIT MURDER; YOU SHALL NOT COMMIT ADULTERY; YOU SHALL NOT STEAL; YOU SHALL NOT BEAR FALSE WITNESS;

19 HONOR YOUR FATHER AND MOTHER; and YOU SHALL LOVE YOUR NEIGHBOR AS YOURSELF."

20 The young man *said to Him, "All these things I have kept; what am I still lacking?"

21 Jesus said to him, "If you wish to be com-

plete, go *and* sell your possessions and give to *the* poor, and you will have treasure in heaven; and come, follow Me."

22 But when the young man heard this statement, he went away grieving; for he was one who owned much property.

23 ¶ And Jesus said to His disciples, "Truly I say to you, it is hard for a rich man to enter the kingdom of heaven.

24 "Again I say to you, it is easier for a camel to go through the eye of a needle, than for a rich man to enter the kingdom of God."

25 When the disciples heard *this*, they were very astonished and said, "Then who can be saved?"

26 And looking at *them* Jesus said to them, "With people this is impossible, but with God all things are possible."

The Disciples' Reward

27 ¶ Then Peter said to Him, "Behold, we have left everything and followed You; what then will there be for us?"

28 And Jesus said to them, "Truly I say to you, that you who have followed Me, in the regeneration when the Son of Man will sit on His glorious throne, you also shall sit upon twelve thrones, judging the twelve tribes of Israel.

29 "And everyone who has left houses or brothers or sisters or father or mother *a*or children or farms for My name's sake, will receive many times as much, and will inherit eternal life.

30 "But many *who are* first will be last; and *the* last, first.

Laborers in the Vineyard

20 "For the kingdom of heaven is like a landowner who went out early in the morning to hire laborers for his vineyard.

20:1 Unfair Pay

Jesus' story makes little economic sense, which was his point exactly. He is giving a parable about grace, and you can't calculate the grace of God like you can a day's wages. We receive it as a gift from God, not as something we work hard to earn. The person who comes to God at the end of life—like the robber on the cross— enjoys the same ultimate benefits as someone who follows God from early childhood.
Jealousy of another's "unfair" rewards can take the joy from your own.

---

2 "When he had agreed with the laborers for a *b*denarius for the day, he sent them into his vineyard.

3 "And he went out about the *c*third hour and saw others standing idle in the market place;

4 and to those he said, 'You also go into the vineyard, and whatever is right I will give you.' And *so* they went.

5 "Again he went out about the *d*sixth and the ninth hour, and did the same thing.

6 "And about the *e*eleventh *hour* he went out and found others standing *around*; and he *said to them, 'Why have you been standing here idle all day long?'

7 "They *said to him, 'Because no one hired us.' He *said to them, 'You go into the vineyard too.'

8 ¶ "When evening came, the owner of the vineyard *said to his foreman, 'Call the laborers and pay them their wages, beginning with the last *group* to the first.'

9 "When those *hired* about the eleventh hour came, each one received a *b*denarius.

10 "When those *hired* first came, they thought that they would receive more; but each of them also received a denarius.

11 "When they received it, they grumbled at the landowner,

12 saying, 'These last men have worked *only* one hour, and you have made them equal to us who have borne the burden and the scorching heat of the day.'

13 "But he answered and said to one of them, 'Friend, I am doing you no wrong; did you not agree with me for a denarius?

14 'Take what is yours and go, but I wish to give to this last man the same as to you.

15 'Is it not lawful for me to do what I wish with what is my own? Or is your eye envious because I am generous?'

16 "So the last shall be first, and the first, last."

Death, Resurrection Foretold

20:17–19pp — Mark 10:32–34; Luke 18:31–33

17 ¶ As Jesus was about to go up to Jerusalem, He took the twelve *disciples* aside by themselves, and on the way He said to them,

18 "Behold, we are going up to Jerusalem; and the Son of Man will be delivered to the chief priests and scribes, and they will condemn Him to death,

19 and will hand Him over to the Gentiles to mock and scourge and crucify *Him*, and on the third day He will be raised up."

Preferment Asked

20:20–28pp — Mark 10:35–45

20 ¶ Then the mother of the sons of Zebedee came to Jesus with her sons, bowing down and making a request of Him.

21 And He said to her, "What do you wish?"

---

a One early ms adds *or wife*   *b* The denarius was a day's wages   *c* I.e. 9 a.m.   *d* I.e. noon and 3 p.m.
e I.e. 5 p.m.

She *said to Him, "Command that in Your kingdom these two sons of mine may sit one on Your right and one on Your left."

22 But Jesus answered, "You do not know what you are asking. Are you able to drink the cup that I am about to drink?" They *said to Him, "We are able."

23 He *said to them, "My cup you shall drink; but to sit on My right and on *My* left, this is not Mine to give, but it is for those for whom it has been prepared by My Father."

24 ¶ And hearing *this*, the ten became indignant with the two brothers.

25 But Jesus called them to Himself and said, "You know that the rulers of the Gentiles lord it over them, and *their* great men exercise authority over them.

26 "It is not this way among you, but whoever wishes to become great among you shall be your servant,

27 and whoever wishes to be first among you shall be your slave;

28 just as the Son of Man did not come to be served, but to serve, and to give His life a ransom for many."

Sight for the Blind

20:29–34pp — Mark 10:46–52; Luke 18:35–43

29 ¶ As they were leaving Jericho, a large crowd followed Him.

30 And two blind men sitting by the road, hearing that Jesus was passing by, cried out, "Lord, have mercy on us, Son of David!"

31 The crowd sternly told them to be quiet, but they cried out all the more, "Lord, Son of David, have mercy on us!"

32 And Jesus stopped and called them, and said, "What do you want Me to do for you?"

33 They *said to Him, "Lord, *we want* our eyes to be opened."

34 Moved with compassion, Jesus touched their eyes; and immediately they regained their sight and followed Him.

The Triumphal Entry

21:1–9pp — Mark 11:1–10; Luke 19:29–38
21:4–9pp — John 12:12–15

21 When they had approached Jerusalem and had come to Bethphage, at the Mount of Olives, then Jesus sent two disciples,

2 saying to them, "Go into the village opposite you, and immediately you will find a donkey tied *there* and a colt with her; untie them and bring them to Me.

3 "If anyone says anything to you, you shall say, 'The Lord has need of them,' and immediately he will send them."

4 This took place to fulfill what was spoken through the prophet:

5 "SAY TO THE DAUGHTER OF ZION,
  'BEHOLD YOUR KING IS COMING TO YOU,

  GENTLE, AND MOUNTED ON A DONKEY,
  EVEN ON A COLT, THE FOAL OF A BEAST OF
    BURDEN.' "

6 The disciples went and did just as Jesus had instructed them,

7 and brought the donkey and the colt, and laid their coats on them; and He sat on the coats.

8 Most of the crowd spread their coats in the road, and others were cutting branches from the trees and spreading them in the road.

9 The crowds going ahead of Him, and those who followed, were shouting,
  "Hosanna to the Son of David;
  BLESSED IS HE WHO COMES IN THE NAME
    OF THE LORD;
  Hosanna in the highest!"

10 When He had entered Jerusalem, all the city was stirred, saying, "Who is this?"

11 And the crowds were saying, "This is the prophet Jesus, from Nazareth in Galilee."

Cleansing the Temple

21:12–16pp — Mark 11:15–18; Luke 19:45–47

12 ¶ And Jesus entered the temple and drove out all those who were buying and selling in the temple, and overturned the tables of the money changers and the seats of those who were selling doves.

21:12 Drastic Action

In Jesus' day, activities at the temple, supposedly the center for worship of God, had taken on a commercial cast. Merchants sold sacrificial animals to pilgrims and foreigners at inflated prices. The system was designed more for profit than for true worship. Jesus responded first by aggressively turning out these "robbers," and then by turning his attention to the people with real needs, the blind and the lame.

13 And He *said to them, "It is written, 'MY HOUSE SHALL BE CALLED A HOUSE OF PRAYER'; but you are making it a ROBBERS' DEN."

14 ¶ And *the* blind and *the* lame came to Him in the temple, and He healed them.

15 But when the chief priests and the scribes saw the wonderful things that He had done, and the children who were shouting in the temple, "Hosanna to the Son of David," they became indignant

16 and said to Him, "Do You hear what these *children* are saying?" And Jesus *said to them, "Yes; have you never read, 'OUT OF THE MOUTH OF INFANTS AND NURSING BABIES YOU HAVE PREPARED PRAISE FOR YOURSELF'?"

17 And He left them and went out of the city to Bethany, and spent the night there.

The Barren Fig Tree

21:18–22pp — Mark 11:12–14,20–24

18 ¶ Now in the morning, when He was returning to the city, He became hungry.

19 Seeing a lone fig tree by the road, He came to it and found nothing on it except leaves only; and He *said to it, "No longer shall there ever be *any* fruit from you." And at once the fig tree withered.

20 ¶ Seeing *this*, the disciples were amazed and asked, "How did the fig tree wither *all* at once?"

21 And Jesus answered and said to them, "Tru-ly I say to you, if you have faith and do not doubt, you will not only do what was done to the fig tree, but even if you say to this mountain, 'Be taken up and cast into the sea,' it will happen.

22 "And all things you ask in prayer, believing, you will receive."

Authority Challenged

21:23–27pp — Mark 11:27–33; Luke 20:1–8

23 ¶ When He entered the temple, the chief priests and the elders of the people came to Him while He was teaching, and said, "By what author-

---

Out to Get Jesus

Jesus confronts his enemies

THE MERE BIRTH OF JESUS had threatened King Herod so much that he had ordered a bloody slaughter of boy babies. The pattern of opposition continued. Early on, Jesus openly predicted his own death.

Beginning in chapter 19, Matthew explains some of the escalating tensions between Jesus and the groups who resisted him. Enemies followed him from town to town, setting traps. Even so, Jesus neither tempered his words nor tried to hide. Instead, he used the occasions of conflict to warn his disciples and the watching crowds against those enemies, whose fury only increased.

Chapter 22 shows Jesus confronting three different groups of enemies on the same day: two religious sects, the Pharisees and the Sadducees, as well as the political Herodians. Jesus easily avoided their carefully devised verbal traps. In fact, he succeeded so brilliantly that Matthew concludes, "nor did anyone dare from that day on to ask Him another question" (22:46).

When the chief priests and the Pharisees heard His parables, they understood that He was speaking about them. When they sought to seize Him, they feared the people, because they considered Him to be a prophet.
21:45–46

What Did Jesus Have Against the Pharisees?

Students of history have often puzzled over why Jesus lashed out so strongly at one Jewish sect, the Pharisees—a group the New Testament mentions 100 times. At first glance, they seem like people Jesus should have liked. They were the most religious people of the day. More than any other group, they strove to follow the letter of the Old Testament law. Their very name, meaning "separatists," hinted at their desire to rise above normal behavior.

Pharisees were legalists. Besides unduly focusing on minute details of the law, they embellished it with their own strict traditions. For example, a person could ride a donkey without breaking the Sabbath rules, but if he carried a switch to speed up the animal, he would be guilty of laying a burden on it.

A Pharisee could give to a beggar on the Sabbath only if the beggar stuck his hand inside the home of the Pharisee so that the Pharisee needn't reach outside. A woman couldn't look in the mirror on the Sabbath—she might see a gray hair and be tempted to pull it out.

Matthew 23 records Jesus' eloquent verdict on the Pharisees. He chastised them for being proud and cliquish and petty, and for refusing to admit their wrongs. External, showy forms of legalism, he said, tend to divert attention away from a person's inner attitude toward God and other people.

Are There Pharisees Now?

As he entered into the last weeks of his life on earth, Jesus polarized people. He boldly contrasted his own teaching with that of his opponents. In addition, he warned his followers about what to expect after his death. Opposition from enemies like the Pharisees wouldn't fade away when he departed. Rather, it would crescendo until the day of final judgment.

Jesus singled out the Pharisees as an example of legalism carried to an extreme. But he wasn't talking merely against an ancient Jewish sect. His words describe persistent tendencies of human beings, then and now. The errors he mentioned have characterized the church throughout its history. Christians still battle against pride and intolerance and a religion based on deeds.

Life Questions: Jesus describes characteristics of Pharisees in the first century. But what about our own time? What Pharisee-like qualities exist in your church? In you?

ity are You doing these things, and who gave You this authority?"

24 Jesus said to them, "I will also ask you one thing, which if you tell Me, I will also tell you by what authority I do these things.

25 "The baptism of John was from what *source*, from heaven or from men?" And they *began* reasoning among themselves, saying, "If we say, 'From heaven,' He will say to us, 'Then why did you not believe him?'

26 "But if we say, 'From men,' we fear the people; for they all regard John as a prophet."

27 And answering Jesus, they said, "We do not know." He also said to them, "Neither will I tell you by what authority I do these things.

Parable of Two Sons

28 ¶ "But what do you think? A man had two sons, and he came to the first and said, 'Son, go work today in the vineyard.'

29 "And he answered, 'I will not'; but afterward he regretted it and went.

30 "The man came to the second and said the same thing; and he answered, 'I *will*, sir'; but he did not go.

31 "Which of the two did the will of his father?" They *said, "The first." Jesus *said to them, "Truly I say to you that the tax collectors and prostitutes will get into the kingdom of God before you.

32 "For John came to you in the way of righteousness and you did not believe him; but the tax collectors and prostitutes did believe him; and you, seeing *this*, did not even feel remorse afterward so as to believe him.

Parable of the Landowner

21:33–46pp — Mark 12:1–12; Luke 20:9–19

33 ¶ "Listen to another parable. There was a landowner who PLANTED A VINEYARD AND PUT A WALL AROUND IT AND DUG A WINE PRESS IN IT, AND BUILT A TOWER, and rented it out to vine-growers and went on a journey.

34 "When the harvest time approached, he sent his slaves to the vine-growers to receive his produce.

35 "The vine-growers took his slaves and beat one, and killed another, and stoned a third.

36 "Again he sent another group of slaves larger than the first; and they did the same thing to them.

37 "But afterward he sent his son to them, saying, 'They will respect my son.'

38 "But when the vine-growers saw the son, they said among themselves, 'This is the heir; come, let us kill him and seize his inheritance.'

39 "They took him, and threw him out of the vineyard and killed him.

40 "Therefore when the owner of the vineyard comes, what will he do to those vine-growers?"

41 They *said to Him, "He will bring those wretches to a wretched end, and will rent out the vineyard to other vine-growers who will pay him the proceeds at the *proper* seasons."

42 ¶ Jesus *said to them, "Did you never read in the Scriptures,

'THE STONE WHICH THE BUILDERS REJECTED,
THIS BECAME THE CHIEF CORNER *stone*;
THIS CAME ABOUT FROM THE LORD,
AND IT IS MARVELOUS IN OUR EYES'?

43 "Therefore I say to you, the kingdom of God will be taken away from you and given to a people, producing the fruit of it.

44 "And he who falls on this stone will be broken to pieces; but on whomever it falls, it will scatter him like dust."

45 ¶ When the chief priests and the Pharisees heard His parables, they understood that He was speaking about them.

46 When they sought to seize Him, they feared the people, because they considered Him to be a prophet.

Parable of the Marriage Feast

22:2–14Ref — Luke 14:16–24

22 Jesus spoke to them again in parables, saying,

2 "The kingdom of heaven may be compared to a king who gave a wedding feast for his son.

3 "And he sent out his slaves to call those who had been invited to the wedding feast, and they were unwilling to come.

4 "Again he sent out other slaves saying, 'Tell those who have been invited, "Behold, I have prepared my dinner; my oxen and my fattened livestock are *all* butchered and everything is ready; come to the wedding feast." '

5 "But they paid no attention and went their way, one to his own farm, another to his business,

6 and the rest seized his slaves and mistreated them and killed them.

7 "But the king was enraged, and he sent his armies and destroyed those murderers and set their city on fire.

8 "Then he *said to his slaves, 'The wedding is ready, but those who were invited were not worthy.

9 'Go therefore to the main highways, and as many as you find *there*, invite to the wedding feast.'

10 "Those slaves went out into the streets and gathered together all they found, both evil and good; and the wedding hall was filled with dinner guests.

11 ¶ "But when the king came in to look over the dinner guests, he saw a man there who was not dressed in wedding clothes,

12 and he *said to him, 'Friend, how did you come in here without wedding clothes?' And the man was speechless.

13 "Then the king said to the servants, 'Bind him hand and foot, and throw him into the outer

darkness; in that place there will be weeping and gnashing of teeth.'

14 "For many are called, but few *are* chosen."

Tribute to Caesar

22:15–22pp — Mark 12:13–17; Luke 20:20–26

15 ¶ Then the Pharisees went and plotted together how they might trap Him in what He said.

16 And they *sent their disciples to Him, along with the Herodians, saying, "Teacher, we know that You are truthful and teach the way of God in truth, and defer to no one; for You are not partial to any.

17 "Tell us then, what do You think? Is it lawful to give a poll-tax to Caesar, or not?"

22:17 A Double Bind

The Pharisees, allied with a party following King Herod, posed a question designed to trap Jesus regardless of his answer. If Jesus said, Pay the taxes, he would lose the support of the independence-minded Jews; if he said, Don't pay, he could be turned in to Rome for breaking the law.

18 But Jesus perceived their malice, and said, "Why are you testing Me, you hypocrites?

19 "Show Me the coin *used* for the poll-tax." And they brought Him a denarius.

20 And He *said to them, "Whose likeness and inscription is this?"

21 They *said to Him, "Caesar's." Then He *said to them, "Then render to Caesar the things that are Caesar's; and to God the things that are God's."

22 And hearing *this*, they were amazed, and leaving Him, they went away.

Jesus Answers the Sadducees

22:23–33pp — Mark 12:18–27; Luke 20:27–40
22:34–40pp — Mark 12:28–31
22:41–46pp — Mark 12:35–37; Luke 20:41–44

23 ¶ On that day *some* Sadducees (who say there is no resurrection) came to Jesus and questioned Him,

24 asking, "Teacher, Moses said, 'IF A MAN DIES HAVING NO CHILDREN, HIS BROTHER AS NEXT OF KIN SHALL MARRY HIS WIFE, AND RAISE UP CHILDREN FOR HIS BROTHER.'

25 "Now there were seven brothers with us; and the first married and died, and having no children left his wife to his brother;

26 so also the second, and the third, down to the seventh.

27 "Last of all, the woman died.

28 "In the resurrection, therefore, whose wife of the seven will she be? For they all had *married* her."

29 ¶ But Jesus answered and said to them, "You are mistaken, not understanding the Scriptures nor the power of God.

30 "For in the resurrection they neither marry nor are given in marriage, but are like angels in heaven.

31 "But regarding the resurrection of the dead, have you not read what was spoken to you by God:

32 'I AM THE GOD OF ABRAHAM, AND THE GOD OF ISAAC, AND THE GOD OF JACOB'? He is not the God of the dead but of the living."

33 When the crowds heard *this*, they were astonished at His teaching.

34 ¶ But when the Pharisees heard that Jesus had silenced the Sadducees, they gathered themselves together.

35 One of them, *a* lawyer, asked Him *a question*, testing Him,

36 "Teacher, which is the great commandment in the Law?"

37 And He said to him, " 'YOU SHALL LOVE THE LORD YOUR GOD WITH ALL YOUR HEART, AND WITH ALL YOUR SOUL, AND WITH ALL YOUR MIND.'

38 "This is the great and foremost commandment.

39 "The second is like it, 'YOU SHALL LOVE YOUR NEIGHBOR AS YOURSELF.'

40 "On these two commandments depend the whole Law and the Prophets."

41 ¶ Now while the Pharisees were gathered together, Jesus asked them a question:

42 "What do you think about the Christ, whose son is He?" They *said to Him, "*The son* of David."

43 He *said to them, "Then how does David in the Spirit call Him 'Lord,' saying,

44 'THE LORD SAID TO MY LORD,
"SIT AT MY RIGHT HAND,
UNTIL I PUT YOUR ENEMIES BENEATH YOUR FEET" '?

45 "If David then calls Him 'Lord,' how is He his son?"

46 No one was able to answer Him a word, nor did anyone dare from that day on to ask Him another question.

Pharisaism Exposed

23:1–7pp — Mark 12:38,39; Luke 20:45,46

23 Then Jesus spoke to the crowds and to His disciples,

2 saying: "The scribes and the Pharisees have seated themselves in the chair of Moses;

3 therefore all that they tell you, do and observe, but do not do according to their deeds; for they say *things* and do not do *them*.

---

a I.e. an expert in the Mosaic Law

4 "They tie up heavy burdens and lay them on men's shoulders, but they themselves are unwilling to move them with *so much as* a finger.

5 "But they do all their deeds to be noticed by men; for they broaden their *a*phylacteries and lengthen the tassels *of their garments.*

6 "They love the place of honor at banquets and the chief seats in the synagogues,

7 and respectful greetings in the market places, and being called Rabbi by men.

8 "But do not be called Rabbi; for One is your Teacher, and you are all brothers.

9 "Do not call *anyone* on earth your father; for One is your Father, He who is in heaven.

10 "Do not be called leaders; for One is your Leader, *that is,* Christ.

11 "But the greatest among you shall be your servant.

12 "Whoever exalts himself shall be humbled; and whoever humbles himself shall be exalted.

Eight Woes

13 ¶ "But woe to you, scribes and Pharisees, hypocrites, because you shut off the kingdom of heaven from people; for you do not enter in yourselves, nor do you allow those who are entering to go in.

14 ["*b*Woe to you, scribes and Pharisees, hypocrites, because you devour widows' houses, and for a pretense you make long prayers; therefore you will receive greater condemnation.]

15 ¶ "Woe to you, scribes and Pharisees, hypocrites, because you travel around on sea and land to make one proselyte; and when he becomes one, you make him twice as much a son of hell as yourselves.

16 ¶ "Woe to you, blind guides, who say, 'Whoever swears by the temple, *that* is nothing; but whoever swears by the gold of the temple is obligated.'

17 "You fools and blind men! Which is more important, the gold or the temple that sanctified the gold?

18 "And, 'Whoever swears by the altar, *that* is nothing, but whoever swears by the offering on it, he is obligated.'

19 "You blind men, which is more important, the offering, or the altar that sanctifies the offering?

20 "Therefore, whoever swears by the altar, swears *both* by the altar and by everything on it.

21 "And whoever swears by the temple, swears *both* by the temple and by Him who dwells within it.

22 "And whoever swears by heaven, swears *both* by the throne of God and by Him who sits upon it.

23 ¶ "Woe to you, scribes and Pharisees, hypocrites! For you tithe the mint and dill and cummin,

and have neglected the weightier provisions of the law: justice and mercy and faithfulness; but these are the things you should have done without neglecting the others.

24 "You blind guides, who strain out a gnat and swallow a camel!

23:24–28 Straining at Gnats

The Pharisees, who literally strained water through a cloth to filter out unclean gnats, could hardly miss the point of Jesus' biting humor. Jesus was not attacking them for being strict per se, but rather for fixating on trivial matters while ignoring more important issues: justice, mercy, faithfulness. He blasted their smug, hypocritical sense of superiority.

25 ¶ "Woe to you, scribes and Pharisees, hypocrites! For you clean the outside of the cup and of the dish, but inside they are full of robbery and self-indulgence.

26 "You blind Pharisee, first clean the inside of the cup and of the dish, so that the outside of it may become clean also.

27 ¶ "Woe to you, scribes and Pharisees, hypocrites! For you are like whitewashed tombs which on the outside appear beautiful, but inside they are full of dead men's bones and all uncleanness.

28 "So you, too, outwardly appear righteous to men, but inwardly you are full of hypocrisy and lawlessness.

29 ¶ "Woe to you, scribes and Pharisees, hypocrites! For you build the tombs of the prophets and adorn the monuments of the righteous,

30 and say, 'If we had been *living* in the days of our fathers, we would not have been partners with them in *shedding* the blood of the prophets.'

31 "So you testify against yourselves, that you are sons of those who murdered the prophets.

32 "Fill up, then, the measure *of the guilt* of your fathers.

33 "You serpents, you brood of vipers, how will you escape the sentence of hell?

34 ¶ "Therefore, behold, I am sending you prophets and wise men and scribes; some of them you will kill and crucify, and some of them you will scourge in your synagogues, and persecute from city to city,

35 so that upon you may fall *the guilt of* all the righteous blood shed on earth, from the blood of righteous Abel to the blood of Zechariah, the son of Berechiah, whom you murdered between the temple and the altar.

36 "Truly I say to you, all these things will come upon this generation.

---

a I.e. small cases containing Scripture texts worn on the left arm and forehead for religious purposes   *b* This v not found in early mss

Lament over Jerusalem

23:37–39pp — Luke 13:34,35

37 ¶ "Jerusalem, Jerusalem, who kills the prophets and stones those who are sent to her! How often I wanted to gather your children together, the way a hen gathers her chicks under her wings, and you were unwilling.

38 "Behold, your house is being left to you desolate!

39 "For I say to you, from now on you will not see Me until you say, 'BLESSED IS HE WHO COMES IN THE NAME OF THE LORD!' "

Signs of Christ's Return

24:1–51pp — Mark 13:1–37; Luke 21:5–36

24 Jesus came out from the temple and was going away when His disciples came up to point out the temple buildings to Him.

2 And He said to them, "Do you not see all these things? Truly I say to you, not one stone here will be left upon another, which will not be torn down."

24:2 Stones Overturned

Jesus' prediction came true four decades after his death, in A.D. 70, when the Roman army crushed a Jewish rebellion in Jerusalem. Soldiers knocked down the massive stones of the temple in search of the melted gold that had run down between the stones as the temple burned. The largest stones weighed over 400 tons, but General Titus's soldiers leveled them all.

3 ¶ As He was sitting on the Mount of Olives, the disciples came to Him privately, saying, "Tell us, when will these things happen, and what *will be* the sign of Your coming, and of the end of the age?"

4 ¶ And Jesus answered and said to them, "See to it that no one misleads you.

5 "For many will come in My name, saying, 'I am the Christ,' and will mislead many.

6 "You will be hearing of wars and rumors of wars. See that you are not frightened, for *those things* must take place, but *that* is not yet the end.

7 "For nation will rise against nation, and kingdom against kingdom, and in various places there will be famines and earthquakes.

8 "But all these things are *merely* the beginning of birth pangs.

9 ¶ "Then they will deliver you to tribulation, and will kill you, and you will be hated by all nations because of My name.

10 "At that time many will fall away and will betray one another and hate one another.

11 "Many false prophets will arise and will mislead many.

12 "Because lawlessness is increased, most people's love will grow cold.

13 "But the one who endures to the end, he will be saved.

14 "This gospel of the kingdom shall be preached in the whole world as a testimony to all the nations, and then the end will come.

Perilous Times

15 ¶ "Therefore when you see the ABOMINATION OF DESOLATION which was spoken of through Daniel the prophet, standing in the holy place (let the reader understand),

16 then those who are in Judea must flee to the mountains.

17 "Whoever is on the housetop must not go down to get the things out that are in his house.

18 "Whoever is in the field must not turn back to get his cloak.

19 "But woe to those who are pregnant and to those who are nursing babies in those days!

20 "But pray that your flight will not be in the winter, or on a Sabbath.

21 "For then there will be a great tribulation, such as has not occurred since the beginning of the world until now, nor ever will.

22 "Unless those days had been cut short, no life would have been saved; but for the sake of the elect those days will be cut short.

23 "Then if anyone says to you, 'Behold, here is the Christ,' or 'There *He is,*' do not believe *him*.

24 "For false Christs and false prophets will arise and will show great signs and wonders, so as to mislead, if possible, even the elect.

25 "Behold, I have told you in advance.

26 "So if they say to you, 'Behold, He is in the wilderness,' do not go out, *or,* 'Behold, He is in the inner rooms,' do not believe *them*.

27 "For just as the lightning comes from the east and flashes even to the west, so will the coming of the Son of Man be.

28 "Wherever the corpse is, there the vultures will gather.

The Glorious Return

29 ¶ "But immediately after the tribulation of those days THE SUN WILL BE DARKENED, AND THE MOON WILL NOT GIVE ITS LIGHT, AND THE STARS WILL FALL from the sky, and the powers of the heavens will be shaken.

30 "And then the sign of the Son of Man will appear in the sky, and then all the tribes of the earth will mourn, and they will see the SON OF MAN COMING ON THE CLOUDS OF THE SKY with power and great glory.

31 "And He will send forth His angels with A GREAT TRUMPET and THEY WILL GATHER TOGETHER His elect from the four winds, from one end of the sky to the other.

Parable of the Fig Tree

24:37–39pp — Luke 17:26,27

32 ¶ "Now learn the parable from the fig tree: when its branch has already become tender and puts forth its leaves, you know that summer is near;

33 so, you too, when you see all these things, recognize that He is near, *right* at the door.

34 "Truly I say to you, this generation will not pass away until all these things take place.

35 "Heaven and earth will pass away, but My words will not pass away.

36 ¶ "But of that day and hour no one knows, not even the angels of heaven, nor the Son, but the Father alone.

24:36 When Will Jesus Return?

Matthew 24 records one of Jesus' longest statements about the future. Jesus gives direct clues to events that will precede his second coming. But, notably, almost half the chapter consists of warnings that no one can predict the precise time of his coming.

37 "For the coming of the Son of Man will be just like the days of Noah.

38 "For as in those days before the flood they were eating and drinking, marrying and giving in marriage, until the day that Noah entered the ark,

39 and they did not understand until the flood came and took them all away; so will the coming of the Son of Man be.

40 "Then there will be two men in the field; one will be taken and one will be left.

41 "Two women *will be* grinding at the mill; one will be taken and one will be left.

Be Ready for His Coming

24:45–51pp — Luke 12:42–46

42 ¶ "Therefore be on the alert, for you do not know which day your Lord is coming.

43 "But be sure of this, that if the head of the house had known at what time of the night the thief was coming, he would have been on the alert and would not have allowed his house to be broken into.

44 "For this reason you also must be ready; for the Son of Man is coming at an hour when you do not think *He will.*

45 ¶ "Who then is the faithful and sensible slave whom his master put in charge of his household to give them their food at the proper time?

46 "Blessed is that slave whom his master finds so doing when he comes.

47 "Truly I say to you that he will put him in charge of all his possessions.

48 "But if that evil slave says in his heart, 'My master is not coming for a long time,'

49 and begins to beat his fellow slaves and eat and drink with drunkards;

50 the master of that slave will come on a day when he does not expect *him* and at an hour which he does not know,

51 and will cut him in pieces and assign him a place with the hypocrites; in that place there will be weeping and gnashing of teeth.

Parable of Ten Virgins

25 "Then the kingdom of heaven will be comparable to ten virgins, who took their lamps and went out to meet the bridegroom.

2 "Five of them were foolish, and five were prudent.

3 "For when the foolish took their lamps, they took no oil with them,

4 but the prudent took oil in flasks along with their lamps.

5 "Now while the bridegroom was delaying, they all got drowsy and *began* to sleep.

6 "But at midnight there was a shout, 'Behold, the bridegroom! Come out to meet *him.*'

7 "Then all those virgins rose and trimmed their lamps.

8 "The foolish said to the prudent, 'Give us some of your oil, for our lamps are going out.'

9 "But the prudent answered, 'No, there will not be enough for us and you *too*; go instead to the dealers and buy *some* for yourselves.'

10 "And while they were going away to make the purchase, the bridegroom came, and those who were ready went in with him to the wedding feast; and the door was shut.

11 "Later the other virgins also came, saying, 'Lord, lord, open up for us.'

12 "But he answered, 'Truly I say to you, I do not know you.'

13 "Be on the alert then, for you do not know the day nor the hour.

Parable of the Talents

25:14–30Ref — Luke 19:12–27

14 ¶ "For *it is* just like a man *about* to go on a journey, who called his own slaves and entrusted his possessions to them.

15 "To one he gave five talents, to another, two, and to another, one, each according to his own ability; and he went on his journey.

16 "Immediately the one who had received the five talents went and traded with them, and gained five more talents.

17 "In the same manner the one who *had received* the two *talents* gained two more.

18 "But he who received the one *talent* went away, and dug *a hole* in the ground and hid his master's money.

19 ¶ "Now after a long time the master of those slaves *came and *settled accounts with them.

20 "The one who had received the five talents came up and brought five more talents, saying,

'Master, you entrusted five talents to me. See, I have gained five more talents.'

21 "His master said to him, 'Well done, good and faithful slave. You were faithful with a few

25:15–30 Original Talent

Today when we speak of a "talented" musician or athlete, we are actually harking back to this parable. A talent in Jesus' time was a valuable sum of money worth about two years' wages. Because of this parable, the word acquired a different meaning. Each person in the kingdom of heaven is given a certain number of gifts and opportunities ("talents") to serve God. We can either waste those opportunities or invest them in a way that furthers the kingdom.

things, I will put you in charge of many things; enter into the joy of your master.'

22 ¶ "Also the one who *had received* the two talents came up and said, 'Master, you entrusted two talents to me. See, I have gained two more talents.'

23 "His master said to him, 'Well done, good and faithful slave. You were faithful with a few things, I will put you in charge of many things; enter into the joy of your master.'

24 ¶ "And the one also who had received the one talent came up and said, 'Master, I knew you to be a hard man, reaping where you did not sow and gathering where you scattered no *seed*.

25 'And I was afraid, and went away and hid your talent in the ground. See, you have what is yours.'

26 ¶ "But his master answered and said to him, 'You wicked, lazy slave, you knew that I reap where I did not sow and gather where I scattered no *seed*.

27 'Then you ought to have put my money in the bank, and on my arrival I would have received my *money* back with interest.

28 'Therefore take away the talent from him, and give it to the one who has the ten talents.'

29 ¶ "For to everyone who has, *more* shall be given, and he will have an abundance; but from the one who does not have, even what he does have shall be taken away.

30 "Throw out the worthless slave into the outer darkness; in that place there will be weeping and gnashing of teeth.

The Judgment

31 ¶ "But when the Son of Man comes in His glory, and all the angels with Him, then He will sit on His glorious throne.

32 "All the nations will be gathered before Him; and He will separate them from one another, as the shepherd separates the sheep from the goats;

33 and He will put the sheep on His right, and the goats on the left.

34 ¶ "Then the King will say to those on His right, 'Come, you who are blessed of My Father, inherit the kingdom prepared for you from the foundation of the world.

35 'For I was hungry, and you gave Me *something* to eat; I was thirsty, and you gave Me *something* to drink; I was a stranger, and you invited Me in;

36 naked, and you clothed Me; I was sick, and you visited Me; I was in prison, and you came to Me.'

37 "Then the righteous will answer Him, 'Lord, when did we see You hungry, and feed You, or thirsty, and give You *something* to drink?

38 'And when did we see You a stranger, and invite You in, or naked, and clothe You?

39 'When did we see You sick, or in prison, and come to You?'

40 "The King will answer and say to them, 'Truly I say to you, to the extent that you did it to one of these brothers of Mine, *even* the least *of them,* you did it to Me.'

41 ¶ "Then He will also say to those on His left, 'Depart from Me, accursed ones, into the eternal fire which has been prepared for the devil and his angels;

42 for I was hungry, and you gave Me *nothing* to eat; I was thirsty, and you gave Me nothing to drink;

43 I was a stranger, and you did not invite Me in; naked, and you did not clothe Me; sick, and in prison, and you did not visit Me.'

44 "Then they themselves also will answer, 'Lord, when did we see You hungry, or thirsty, or a stranger, or naked, or sick, or in prison, and did not take care of You?'

45 "Then He will answer them, 'Truly I say to you, to the extent that you did not do it to one of the least of these, you did not do it to Me.'

46 "These will go away into eternal punishment, but the righteous into eternal life."

The Plot to Kill Jesus

26:2–5pp — Mark 14:1,2; Luke 22:1,2

26 When Jesus had finished all these words, He said to His disciples,

2 "You know that after two days the Passover is coming, and the Son of Man is *to be* handed over for crucifixion."

3 ¶ Then the chief priests and the elders of the people were gathered together in the court of the high priest, named Caiaphas;

4 and they plotted together to seize Jesus by stealth and kill Him.

5 But they were saying, "Not during the festival, otherwise a riot might occur among the people."

The Precious Ointment

26:6–13pp — Mark 14:3–9
26:6–13Ref — Luke 7:37,38; John 12:1–8

6 ¶ Now when Jesus was in Bethany, at the home of Simon the leper,

26:4 "Some Sly Way"

The religious leaders failed in their plan to dispose of Jesus quietly. He was killed during a national holiday while Jerusalem swarmed with pilgrims. Yet his death sparked no riots, and in the end even his devoted followers abandoned him. The chief priests and elders might have congratulated themselves on a successful mission—except for what happened on Easter Sunday.

7 a woman came to Him with an alabaster vial of very costly perfume, and she poured it on His head as He reclined *at the table.*

8 But the disciples were indignant when they saw *this,* and said, "Why this waste?

9 "For this *perfume* might have been sold for a high price and *the money* given to the poor."

10 But Jesus, aware of this, said to them, "Why do you bother the woman? For she has done a good deed to Me.

11 "For you always have the poor with you; but you do not always have Me.

12 "For when she poured this perfume on My body, she did it to prepare Me for burial.

13 "Truly I say to you, wherever this gospel is preached in the whole world, what this woman has done will also be spoken of in memory of her."

Judas's Bargain

26:14–16pp — Mark 14:10,11; Luke 22:3–6
26:17–19pp — Mark 14:12–16; Luke 22:7–13

14 ¶ Then one of the twelve, named Judas Iscariot, went to the chief priests

15 and said, "What are you willing to give me to betray Him to you?" And they weighed out thirty pieces of silver to him.

16 From then on he *began* looking for a good opportunity to betray Jesus.

17 ¶ Now on the first *day* of Unleavened Bread the disciples came to Jesus and asked, "Where do You want us to prepare for You to eat the Passover?"

18 And He said, "Go into the city to a certain man, and say to him, 'The Teacher says, "My time is near; I *am* to keep the Passover at your house with My disciples." ' "

19 The disciples did as Jesus had directed them; and they prepared the Passover.

The Last Passover

26:20–24pp — Mark 14:17–21

20 ¶ Now when evening came, Jesus was reclining *at the table* with the twelve disciples.

21 As they were eating, He said, "Truly I say to you that one of you will betray Me."

22 Being deeply grieved, they each one began to say to Him, "Surely not I, Lord?"

23 And He answered, "He who dipped his hand with Me in the bowl is the one who will betray Me.

24 "The Son of Man *is to* go, just as it is written of Him; but woe to that man by whom the Son of Man is betrayed! It would have been good for that man if he had not been born."

25 And Judas, who was betraying Him, said, "Surely it is not I, Rabbi?" Jesus *said to him, "You have said *it* yourself."

The Lord's Supper Instituted

26:26–29pp — Mark 14:22–25; Luke 22:17–20;
1 Cor 11:23–25
26:31–35pp — Mark 14:27–31; Luke 22:31–34

26 ¶ While they were eating, Jesus took *some* bread, and after a blessing, He broke *it* and gave *it* to the disciples, and said, "Take, eat; this is My body."

27 And when He had taken a cup and given thanks, He gave *it* to them, saying, "Drink from it, all of you;

28 for this is My blood of the covenant, which is poured out for many for forgiveness of sins.

29 "But I say to you, I will not drink of this fruit of the vine from now on until that day when I drink it new with you in My Father's kingdom."

30 ¶ After singing a hymn, they went out to the Mount of Olives.

31 ¶ Then Jesus *said to them, "You will all fall away because of Me this night, for it is written, 'I WILL STRIKE DOWN THE SHEPHERD, AND THE SHEEP OF THE FLOCK SHALL BE SCATTERED.'

32 "But after I have been raised, I will go ahead of you to Galilee."

33 But Peter said to Him, "*Even* though all may fall away because of You, I will never fall away."

34 Jesus said to him, "Truly I say to you that this *very* night, before a rooster crows, you will deny Me three times."

35 Peter *said to Him, "Even if I have to die with You, I will not deny You." All the disciples said the same thing too.

The Garden of Gethsemane

26:36–46pp — Mark 14:32–42; Luke 22:40–46

36 ¶ Then Jesus *came with them to a place called Gethsemane, and *said to His disciples, "Sit here while I go over there and pray."

37 And He took with Him Peter and the two sons of Zebedee, and began to be grieved and distressed.

38 Then He *said to them, "My soul is deeply

grieved, to the point of death; remain here and keep watch with Me."

39 ¶ And He went a little beyond *them,* and fell on His face and prayed, saying, "My Father, if it is possible, let this cup pass from Me; yet not as I will, but as You will."

40 And He *came to the disciples and *found them sleeping, and *said to Peter, "So, you *men* could not keep watch with Me for one hour?

41 "Keep watching and praying that you may not enter into temptation; the spirit is willing, but the flesh is weak."

42 ¶ He went away again a second time and prayed, saying, "My Father, if this cannot pass away unless I drink it, Your will be done."

43 Again He came and found them sleeping, for their eyes were heavy.

44 And He left them again, and went away and prayed a third time, saying the same thing once more.

45 Then He *came to the disciples and *said to them, "Are you still sleeping and resting? Behold, the hour is at hand and the Son of Man is being betrayed into the hands of sinners.

46 "Get up, let us be going; behold, the one who betrays Me is at hand!"

Jesus' Betrayal and Arrest

26:47–56pp — Mark 14:43–50; Luke 22:47–53

47 ¶ While He was still speaking, behold, Judas, one of the twelve, came up accompanied by a large crowd with swords and clubs, *who came* from the chief priests and elders of the people.

26:47 A Name Disgraced

Judas (like Jesus) was a common name for Jewish men in those days; it is the Greek form of Judah. He came from a region called Judea, whereas all the other disciples came from Galilee. Yet he gained enough trust to be named the disciples' treasurer. The Bible gives few details on Judas's motive for betraying Jesus. He may have become disillusioned when Jesus didn't fulfill his expectations of a powerful king and Messiah.

48 Now he who was betraying Him gave them a sign, saying, "Whomever I kiss, He is the one; seize Him."

49 Immediately Judas went to Jesus and said, "Hail, Rabbi!" and kissed Him.

50 And Jesus said to him, "Friend, *do* what you have come for." Then they came and laid hands on Jesus and seized Him.

51 ¶ And behold, one of those who were with Jesus reached and drew out his sword, and struck the slave of the high priest and cut off his ear.

52 Then Jesus *said to him, "Put your sword back into its place; for all those who take up the sword shall perish by the sword.

53 "Or do you think that I cannot appeal to My Father, and He will at once put at My disposal more than twelve *a*legions of angels?

54 "How then will the Scriptures be fulfilled, *which say* that it must happen this way?"

55 ¶ At that time Jesus said to the crowds, "Have you come out with swords and clubs to arrest Me as *you would* against a robber? Every day I used to sit in the temple teaching and you did not seize Me.

56 "But all this has taken place to fulfill the Scriptures of the prophets." Then all the disciples left Him and fled.

Jesus before Caiaphas

26:57–68pp — Mark 14:53–65; John 18:12,13,19–24

57 ¶ Those who had seized Jesus led Him away to Caiaphas, the high priest, where the scribes and the elders were gathered together.

58 But Peter was following Him at a distance as far as the courtyard of the high priest, and entered in, and sat down with the officers to see the outcome.

59 ¶ Now the chief priests and the whole Council kept trying to obtain false testimony against Jesus, so that they might put Him to death.

60 They did not find *any,* even though many false witnesses came forward. But later on two came forward,

61 and said, "This man stated, 'I am able to destroy the temple of God and to rebuild it in three days.' "

62 The high priest stood up and said to Him, "Do You not answer? What is it that these men are testifying against You?"

63 But Jesus kept silent. And the high priest said to Him, "I adjure You by the living God, that You tell us whether You are the Christ, the Son of God."

64 Jesus *said to him, "You have said it *yourself;* nevertheless I tell you, hereafter you will see THE SON OF MAN SITTING AT THE RIGHT HAND OF POWER, and COMING ON THE CLOUDS OF HEAVEN."

65 ¶ Then the high priest tore his robes and said, "He has blasphemed! What further need do we have of witnesses? Behold, you have now heard the blasphemy;

66 what do you think?" They answered, "He deserves death!"

67 ¶ Then they spat in His face and beat Him with their fists; and others slapped Him,

68 and said, "Prophesy to us, You Christ; who is the one who hit You?"

Peter's Denials

26:69–75pp — Mark 14:66–72; Luke 22:55–62; John 18:16–18,25–27

69 ¶ Now Peter was sitting outside in the

---

a A legion equaled 6,000 troops

courtyard, and a servant-girl came to him and said, "You too were with Jesus the Galilean."

70 But he denied it before them all, saying, "I do not know what you are talking about."

71 When he had gone out to the gateway, another *servant-girl* saw him and *said to those who were there, "This man was with Jesus of Nazareth."

72 And again he denied *it* with an oath, "I do not know the man."

73 A little later the bystanders came up and said to Peter, "Surely you too are *one* of them; for even the way you talk gives you away."

26:73 Telltale Accent

Revolutionaries and troublemakers in Palestine usually operated in the rugged countryside. In Jerusalem, a city abuzz with rumors, Peter's Galilean accent made him suspect, for it marked him as a non-local. Jesus, also from Galilee, had already been arrested.

74 Then he began to curse and swear, "I do not know the man!" And immediately a rooster crowed.

75 And Peter remembered the word which Jesus had said, "Before a rooster crows, you will deny Me three times." And he went out and wept bitterly.

Judas's Remorse

27 Now when morning came, all the chief priests and the elders of the people conferred together against Jesus to put Him to death;

2 and they bound Him, and led Him away and delivered Him to Pilate the governor.

3 ¶ Then when Judas, who had betrayed Him, saw that He had been condemned, he felt remorse and returned the thirty pieces of silver to the chief priests and elders,

4 saying, "I have sinned by betraying innocent blood." But they said, "What is that to us? See *to that* yourself."

5 And he threw the pieces of silver into the temple sanctuary and departed; and he went away and hanged himself.

6 The chief priests took the pieces of silver and said, "It is not lawful to put them into the temple treasury, since it is the price of blood."

7 And they conferred together and with the money bought the Potter's Field as a burial place for strangers.

8 For this reason that field has been called the Field of Blood to this day.

9 Then that which was spoken through Jere-

The Killing of a King
Arrest, trial, and execution

IN SPARE, UNADORNED LANGUAGE THE last three chapters of Matthew draw together the deep ironies of Jesus' life. From the first sentence, Matthew has stressed that Jesus is the Messiah, a true king. This Gospel is sometimes called the "royal" Gospel because it refers so many times to kingship.

But at the end of his life, the man whom wise men had crossed a continent to worship was sold, like a slave, for thirty pieces of silver. Jesus got a royal robe and crown at last—but as a cruel, mocking joke. Blood from the wounds on his back clotted on the robe, and the crown of thorns streaked his face with more blood.

A short time before, he had blistered the religious leaders with accusations. But when they put him on the stand and accused him, his strong voice stayed mostly silent.

> Pilate said to them, "Then what shall I do with Jesus who is called Christ?" They all said, "Crucify Him!" 27:22

Jesus' Self-Defense

Jesus' enemies asked him two chief questions: "Are You the King of the Jews?" and "Are you the Messiah?" He answered with a simple "It is as you say" (27:11), confirming the major themes woven throughout Matthew's book. Finally he was executed, with his "crime"—being a king—posted above his sagging body.

Jesus was indeed a king, but not the kind of king people expected. Even his disciples, who had known Jesus intimately for three years, slipped away in doubt.

The story, however, doesn't end with the death scene in chapter 27. Good Friday would never have been called "good" without the miracle described next. The king came back! And the writer who opened his book by tracing Jesus' Jewish roots ends it with Jesus' stirring call to take the good news to all nations.

Life Questions: The people who crucified Jesus—what did they hate in him? Is it the same today?

miah the prophet was fulfilled: "AND THEY TOOK THE THIRTY PIECES OF SILVER, THE PRICE OF THE ONE WHOSE PRICE HAD BEEN SET by the sons of Israel;

10 AND THEY GAVE THEM FOR THE POTTER'S FIELD, AS THE LORD DIRECTED ME."

Jesus before Pilate

27:11-26pp — Mark 15:2-15; Luke 23:2,3,18-25; John 18:29-19:16

11 ¶ Now Jesus stood before the governor, and the governor questioned Him, saying, "Are You the King of the Jews?" And Jesus said to him, "*It is as* you say."

12 And while He was being accused by the chief priests and elders, He did not answer.

13 Then Pilate *said to Him, "Do You not hear how many things they testify against You?"

14 And He did not answer him with regard to even a *single* charge, so the governor was quite amazed.

15 ¶ Now at *the* feast the governor was accustomed to release for the people *any* one prisoner whom they wanted.

16 At that time they were holding a notorious prisoner, called Barabbas.

17 So when the people gathered together, Pilate said to them, "Whom do you want me to release for you? Barabbas, or Jesus who is called Christ?"

18 For he knew that because of envy they had handed Him over.

19 ¶ While he was sitting on the judgment seat, his wife sent him a *message*, saying, "Have nothing to do with that righteous Man; for last night I suffered greatly in a dream because of Him."

20 But the chief priests and the elders persuaded the crowds to ask for Barabbas and to put Jesus to death.

21 But the governor said to them, "Which of the two do you want me to release for you?" And they said, "Barabbas."

22 Pilate *said to them, "Then what shall I do with Jesus who is called Christ?" They all *said, "Crucify Him!"

23 And he said, "Why, what evil has He done?" But they kept shouting all the more, saying, "Crucify Him!"

24 ¶ When Pilate saw that he was accomplishing nothing, but rather that a riot was starting, he took water and washed his hands in front of the crowd, saying, "I am innocent of this Man's blood; see *to that* yourselves."

25 And all the people said, "His blood shall be on us and on our children!"

26 Then he released Barabbas for them; but after having Jesus scourged, he handed Him over to be crucified.

Jesus Is Mocked

27:27-31pp — Mark 15:16-20

27 ¶ Then the soldiers of the governor took Jesus into the Praetorium and gathered the whole *Roman* cohort around Him.

28 They stripped Him and put a scarlet robe on Him.

29 And after twisting together a crown of thorns, they put it on His head, and a reed in His right hand; and they knelt down before Him and mocked Him, saying, "Hail, King of the Jews!"

30 They spat on Him, and took the reed and *began* to beat Him on the head.

31 After they had mocked Him, they took the *scarlet* robe off Him and put His *own* garments back on Him, and led Him away to crucify Him.

32 ¶ As they were coming out, they found a man of Cyrene named Simon, whom they pressed into service to bear His cross.

The Crucifixion

27:33-44pp — Mark 15:22-32; Luke 23:33-43; John 19:17-24
27:45-56pp — Mark 15:33-41; Luke 23:44-49; John 19:29-30

33 ¶ And when they came to a place called Golgotha, which means Place of a Skull,

34 they gave Him wine to drink mixed with gall; and after tasting *it*, He was unwilling to drink.

35 ¶ And when they had crucified Him, they divided up His garments among themselves by casting lots.

36 And sitting down, they *began* to keep watch over Him there.

37 And above His head they put up the charge against Him which read, "THIS IS JESUS THE KING OF THE JEWS."

38 ¶ At that time two robbers *were crucified with Him, one on the right and one on the left.

39 And those passing by were hurling abuse at Him, wagging their heads

40 and saying, "You who *are going to* destroy the temple and rebuild it in three days, save Yourself! If You are the Son of God, come down from the cross."

41 In the same way the chief priests also, along with the scribes and elders, were mocking *Him* and saying,

42 "He saved others; He cannot save Himself. He is the King of Israel; let Him now come down from the cross, and we will believe in Him.

43 "HE TRUSTS IN GOD; LET GOD RESCUE *Him* now, IF HE DELIGHTS IN HIM; for He said, 'I am the Son of God.' "

44 The robbers who had been crucified with Him were also insulting Him with the same words.

45 ¶ Now from the *a*sixth hour darkness fell upon all the land until the *b*ninth hour.

46 About the ninth hour Jesus cried out with a

---

a I.e. noon　　*b* I.e. 3 p.m.

loud voice, saying, "ELI, ELI, LAMA SABACHTHANI?" that is, "MY GOD, MY GOD, WHY HAVE YOU FORSAKEN ME?"

47 And some of those who were standing there, when they heard it, *began* saying, "This man is calling for Elijah."

48 Immediately one of them ran, and taking a sponge, he filled it with sour wine and put it on a reed, and gave Him a drink.

49 But the rest *of them* said, "Let us see whether Elijah will come to save Him."*a*

50 And Jesus cried out again with a loud voice, and yielded up His spirit.

51 And behold, the veil of the temple was torn in two from top to bottom; and the earth shook and the rocks were split.

27:51 A Curtain Is Torn

At Jesus' death, the massive, thick curtain in the temple in Jerusalem ripped in two. This curtain sealed off the holy of holies. No one except the high priest was allowed into the presence of God in that holy of holies. And the high priest was permitted in only once a year, on a special day. The author of Hebrews looked on the miraculously torn curtain as symbolic: it signified the immediate access to God made possible by Jesus' death (Hebrews 10:19–20).

52 The tombs were opened, and many bodies of the saints who had fallen asleep were raised;

53 and coming out of the tombs after His resurrection they entered the holy city and appeared to many.

54 Now the centurion, and those who were with him keeping guard over Jesus, when they saw the earthquake and the things that were happening, became very frightened and said, "Truly this was the Son of God!"

55 ¶ Many women were there looking on from a distance, who had followed Jesus from Galilee while ministering to Him.

56 Among them was Mary Magdalene, and Mary the mother of James and Joseph, and the mother of the sons of Zebedee.

Jesus Is Buried

27:57–61pp — Mark 15:42–47; Luke 23:50–56; John 19:38–42

57 ¶ When it was evening, there came a rich man from Arimathea, named Joseph, who himself had also become a disciple of Jesus.

58 This man went to Pilate and asked for the body of Jesus. Then Pilate ordered it to be given *to him.*

59 And Joseph took the body and wrapped it in a clean linen cloth,

60 and laid it in his own new tomb, which he had hewn out in the rock; and he rolled a large stone against the entrance of the tomb and went away.

61 And Mary Magdalene was there, and the other Mary, sitting opposite the grave.

62 ¶ Now on the next day, the day after the preparation, the chief priests and the Pharisees gathered together with Pilate,

63 and said, "Sir, we remember that when He was still alive that deceiver said, 'After three days I *am* to rise again.'

64 "Therefore, give orders for the grave to be made secure until the third day, otherwise His disciples may come and steal Him away and say to the people, 'He has risen from the dead,' and the last deception will be worse than the first."

65 Pilate said to them, "You have a guard; go, make it *as* secure as you know how."

66 And they went and made the grave secure, and along with the guard they set a seal on the stone.

Jesus Is Risen!

28:1–8pp — Mark 16:1–8; Luke 24:1–10; John 20:1–8

28 Now after the Sabbath, as it began to dawn toward the first *day* of the week, Mary Magdalene and the other Mary came to look at the grave.

2 And behold, a severe earthquake had occurred, for an angel of the Lord descended from heaven and came and rolled away the stone and sat upon it.

3 And his appearance was like lightning, and his clothing as white as snow.

4 The guards shook for fear of him and became like dead men.

28:4 Coverup

Throughout Jesus' extraordinary life, people found all sorts of reasons to doubt him, even in the face of unexplainable events. These guards, for instance, were virtual eyewitnesses of the greatest miracle of all time, Jesus' resurrection. Yet a few hours later they made a deal with the chief priests to cover up the story (verses 11–15). Then, as now, people who choose not to believe can always find a rationale.

5 The angel said to the women, "Do not be afraid; for I know that you are looking for Jesus who has been crucified.

6 "He is not here, for He has risen, just as He said. Come, see the place where He was lying.

7 "Go quickly and tell His disciples that He has risen from the dead; and behold, He is going

---

a Some early mss read *And another took a spear and pierced His side, and there came out water and blood* (cf John 19:34) ahead of you into Galilee, there you will see Him; behold, I have told you."

8 ¶ And they left the tomb quickly with fear and great joy and ran to report it to His disciples.

9 And behold, Jesus met them and greeted them. And they came up and took hold of His feet and worshiped Him.

10 Then Jesus *said to them, "Do not be afraid; go and take word to My brethren to leave for Galilee, and there they will see Me."

11 ¶ Now while they were on their way, some of the guard came into the city and reported to the chief priests all that had happened.

12 And when they had assembled with the elders and consulted together, they gave a large sum of money to the soldiers,

13 and said, "You are to say, 'His disciples came by night and stole Him away while we were asleep.'

14 "And if this should come to the governor's ears, we will win him over and keep you out of trouble."

15 And they took the money and did as they had been instructed; and this story was widely spread among the Jews, *and is* to this day.

The Great Commission

16 ¶ But the eleven disciples proceeded to Galilee, to the mountain which Jesus had designated.

17 When they saw Him, they worshiped *Him*; but some were doubtful.

18 And Jesus came up and spoke to them, saying, "All authority has been given to Me in heaven and on earth.

19 "Go therefore and make disciples of all the nations, baptizing them in the name of the Father and the Son and the Holy Spirit,

20 teaching them to observe all that I commanded you; and lo, I am with you always, even to the end of the age."

MARK

The Fast-paced Gospel
Mark reads like the script for an action movie

> *Immediately the news about Him spread everywhere into all the surrounding district of Galilee. 1:28*

BRIEF INTRODUCTORY CREDITS FLASH ON the screen. Then the camera pans across an expanse of bleached sand, inhabited mostly by scorpions, lizards, and tarantulas. At last, through the shimmering heat, a lone figure appears: an eccentric wearing camel's hair and crying something in the thin desert air. So begins Mark.

It helps to imagine the book of Mark as a concisely edited documentary film. Unlike the other Gospels, this one has little tolerance for dialogue and personal reflection. The author is writing to a restless, impatient audience—people more like moviegoers than readers.

Mark deftly controls camera angles, alternately panning across large crowds and zooming in on individual people. He leaves no doubt about the main character. After the opening shot of John the Baptist, he moves Jesus to center stage and the camera follows him everywhere.

An Emphasis on Action

Those who look for an outline in Mark come away baffled: all the spliced-together scenes defy structure. One author observed that Mark shows Jesus "scattering miracles like rice at a wedding." Matthew and Luke each give four chapters of historical warm-up before recording a miracle by Jesus; Mark covers three miracles and a group event in the first chapter alone.

In contrast to all its action scenes, the book includes only a sampling of Jesus' parables. It focuses on events, not speeches or editorial comments. Mark shows gymnasium-size crowds pressing around Jesus so tightly that he launches a boat to escape them. Wherever he goes, the crowds follow, buzzing about his remarkable life. "Is he the Holy One of God?" "Is he mad?" "Isn't this the carpenter's boy?"

A Breathless Pace

By dispensing with all but bare-bones action, Mark manages to achieve more drama than perhaps any other Biblical writer. Action guarantees an attentive audience, and Mark jams sequences together breathlessly. *At once* the Spirit sends Jesus into the desert; *at once* the disciples respond to Jesus' call to follow him; Jesus' touch *immediately* heals a man with leprosy—42 times this book uses the Greek hurry-up adverb translated several different ways into English.

Characters rush from place to place, jostle among crowds, are astonished at mighty works. Mark is a Gospel of exclamation points, full of words like *amazed, astonished, terrified*. A phenomenon is loose on the earth, and the author is determined to capture its impact for future generations.

How to Read Mark

About 90 percent of Mark's content appears in the other three Gospels, but the book makes an ideal starting place for someone who knows little about Jesus. Its style—simple sentences, without complicated transitions or long speeches—makes understanding easier. In fact, Mark was probably written as a missionary book to people who knew next to nothing about the new Christian faith.

Except where he cites Jesus' own quotations, Mark quotes the Old Testament directly in only one place (1:2–3). In addition, Mark doesn't refer to the Old Testament Law, a striking difference from the other Gospels. Such facts indicate his book was written to a non-Jewish audience, probably the Romans.

You'll need no special instructions on reading Mark. This book's breezy style makes it as understandable as a newspaper. Because it loosely follows the chronology of Jesus' life, Mark offers an excellent introduction to the life of Jesus. As you read, stop and ponder the events Mark records. Why did the author select these facts? What meaning did they have for the people in Jesus' day? What about for you?

Many passages in the Gospels are parallel, dealing with the same event. Nearly identical passages are noted at the section heading with "pp," while similar passages are noted with "Ref."

PEOPLE YOU'LL MEET IN MARK

JAMES *(p. 1089)*

3-TRACK READING PLAN

For an explanation and complete listing of the 3-track reading plan, turn to page 7.

TRACK 1: *Two-Week Courses on the Bible*
The Track 1 reading program on the Life and Teachings of Jesus includes two chapters from Mark. See page 7 for a complete listing of this course.

TRACK 2: *An Overview of Mark in 15 Days*
Reading Mark will give you a quick summary of Jesus' acts on this earth. For this reason, plan to spend two weeks reading all 16 chapters of Mark.

☐ Day 1. Read the Introduction to Mark, then chapter 1.
☐ Day 2. Read chapter 2's record of scenes from Jesus' life during a period of popular acclaim.
☐ Day 3. Read chapter 3, which shows Jesus calling his 12 disciples.
☐ Day 4. Read the brief parables and the account of the calming of a storm in chapter 4.
☐ Day 5. Mark 5 tells of three miracles of healing; note the different crowd reaction to each one.
☐ Day 6. Read chapter 6, which includes several famous miracles and also the story of John the Baptist's beheading.
☐ Day 7. Read chapter 7, which shows the Pharisees' opposition to Jesus beginning to mount.
☐ Day 8. As you read chapter 8, notice, on the one hand, Jesus' increasing popularity and, on the other, the growing tension that will eventually culminate in his death.
☐ Day 9. Read the account of Jesus' transfiguration and the other events recorded in chapter 9.
☐ Day 10. Mark 10 records Jesus' teaching on divorce, humility, and wealth.
☐ Day 11. Read chapter 11's account of Jesus' entry into Jerusalem for the last week of his life.
☐ Day 12. Read chapter 12, which includes Jesus' teaching on a variety of topics.
☐ Day 13. Read chapter 13 for Jesus' predictions of the end of the world.
☐ Day 14. Mark 14 records the events leading up to Jesus' arrest, as well as his trial before a Jewish court.
☐ Day 15. Read chapters 15 and 16, which report the last events in Jesus' life on earth.

Now turn to page 9 for your next Track 2 reading project.

TRACK 3: *All of Mark in 15 Days*
After you have read through Mark, turn to pages 10–14 for your next Track 3 reading project.

☐1 ☐2 ☐3 ☐4 ☐5 ☐6 ☐7 ☐8
☐9 ☐10 ☐11 ☐12 ☐13 ☐14 ☐15–16

Preaching of John the Baptist

1:2–8pp — Matt 3:1–11; Luke 3:2–16

1 The beginning of the gospel of Jesus Christ, the Son of God.

2 ¶ As it is written in Isaiah the prophet:
"BEHOLD, I SEND MY MESSENGER AHEAD
OF YOU,
WHO WILL PREPARE YOUR WAY;

3 THE VOICE OF ONE CRYING IN THE
WILDERNESS,
'MAKE READY THE WAY OF THE LORD,
MAKE HIS PATHS STRAIGHT.' "

4 John the Baptist appeared in the wilderness *a*preaching a baptism of repentance for the forgiveness of sins.

5 And all the country of Judea was going out to him, and all the people of Jerusalem; and they were being baptized by him in the Jordan River, confessing their sins.

6 John was clothed with camel's hair and *wore* a leather belt around his waist, and his diet was locusts and wild honey.

7 And he was preaching, and saying, "After me One is coming who is mightier than I, and I am not fit to stoop down and untie the thong of His sandals.

8 "I baptized you *b*with water; but He will baptize you *b*with the Holy Spirit."

The Baptism of Jesus

1:9–11pp — Matt 3:13–17; Luke 3:21,22
1:12,13pp — Matt 4:1–11; Luke 4:1–13

9 ¶ In those days Jesus came from Nazareth in Galilee and was baptized by John in the Jordan.

10 Immediately coming up out of the water, He saw the heavens opening, and the Spirit like a dove descending upon Him;

11 and a voice came out of the heavens: "You are My beloved Son, in You I am well-pleased."

12 ¶ Immediately the Spirit *impelled Him *to* go out into the wilderness.

13 And He was in the wilderness forty days being tempted by Satan; and He was with the wild beasts, and the angels were ministering to Him.

Jesus Preaches in Galilee

1:16–20pp — Matt 4:18–22; Luke 5:2–11; John 1:35–42
1:21–28pp — Luke 4:31–37

14 ¶ Now after John had been taken into custody, Jesus came into Galilee, preaching the gospel of God,

15 and saying, "The time is fulfilled, and the kingdom of God is at hand; repent and believe in the gospel."

16 ¶ As He was going along by the Sea of Galilee, He saw Simon and Andrew, the brother of Simon, casting a net in the sea; for they were fishermen.

17 And Jesus said to them, "Follow Me, and I will make you become fishers of men."

18 Immediately they left their nets and followed Him.

1:14 Into the Countryside

Possibly, Jesus withdrew to Galilee in order to escape the political turmoil spawned by John's arrest. He went on to spend almost two-thirds of his working life in this rather remote northern region, the lushest and most picturesque portion of Palestine. Except for festival times when he traveled to Jerusalem, Jesus showed a marked preference for rural and small-town areas.

19 Going on a little farther, He saw James the son of Zebedee, and John his brother, who were also in the boat mending the nets.

20 Immediately He called them; and they left their father Zebedee in the boat with the hired servants, and went away to follow Him.

21 ¶ They *went into Capernaum; and immediately on the Sabbath He entered the synagogue and *began* to teach.

22 They were amazed at His teaching; for He was teaching them as *one* having authority, and not as the scribes.

23 Just then there was a man in their synagogue with an unclean spirit; and he cried out,

24 saying, "What business do we have with each other, Jesus *c*of Nazareth? Have You come to destroy us? I know who You are—the Holy One of God!"

25 And Jesus rebuked him, saying, "Be quiet, and come out of him!"

26 Throwing him into convulsions, the unclean spirit cried out with a loud voice and came out of him.

27 They were all amazed, so that they debated among themselves, saying, "What is this? A new teaching with authority! He commands even the unclean spirits, and they obey Him."

28 Immediately the news about Him spread everywhere into all the surrounding district of Galilee.

Crowds Healed

1:29–31pp — Matt 8:14,15; Luke 4:38,39
1:32–34pp — Matt 8:16,17; Luke 4:40,41
1:35–38pp — Luke 4:42,43
1:40–44pp — Matt 8:2–4; Luke 5:12–14

29 ¶ And immediately after they came out of the synagogue, they came into the house of Simon and Andrew, with James and John.

30 Now Simon's mother-in-law was lying sick

---

a Or *proclaiming*   *b* The Gr here can be translated *in, with* or *by*   *c* Lit *the Nazarene* with a fever; and immediately they *spoke to Jesus about her.

31 And He came to her and raised her up, taking her by the hand, and the fever left her, and she ªwaited on them.

32 ¶ When evening came, after the sun had set, they *began* bringing to Him all who were ill and those who were demon-possessed.

33 And the whole city had gathered at the door.

34 And He healed many who were ill with various diseases, and cast out many demons; and He was not permitting the demons to speak, because they knew who He was.

35 ¶ In the early morning, while it was still dark, Jesus got up, left *the house*, and went away to a secluded place, and was praying there.

36 Simon and his companions searched for Him;

37 they found Him, and *said to Him, "Everyone is looking for You."

38 He *said to them, "Let us go somewhere else to the towns nearby, so that I may preach there also; for that is what I came for."

39 And He went into their synagogues throughout all Galilee, preaching and casting out the demons.

40 ¶ And a leper *came to Jesus, beseeching Him and falling on his knees before Him, and saying, "If You are willing, You can make me clean."

41 Moved with compassion, Jesus stretched out His hand and touched him, and *said to him, "I am willing; be cleansed."

42 Immediately the leprosy left him and he was cleansed.

43 And He sternly warned him and immediately sent him away,

44 and He *said to him, "See that you say nothing to anyone; but go, show yourself to the priest and offer for your cleansing what Moses commanded, as a testimony to them."

45 But he went out and began to proclaim it freely and to spread the news around, to such an extent that Jesus could no longer publicly enter a city, but ᵇstayed out in unpopulated areas; and they were coming to Him from everywhere.

The Paralytic Healed

2:3–12pp — Matt 9:2–8; Luke 5:18–26

2 When He had come back to Capernaum several days afterward, it was heard that He was at home.

2 And many were gathered together, so that there was no longer room, not even near the door; and He was speaking the word to them.

3 And they *came, bringing to Him a paralytic, carried by four men.

4 Being unable to get to Him because of the crowd, they removed the roof above Him; and when they had dug an opening, they let down the pallet on which the paralytic was lying.

2:4 Barriers to the Disabled

One disabled person has pointed out this story's relevance to the modern controversy over accessibility. "Any disabled person can supply lots of stories like this one—entering a church through the sacristy (or, worse, having to be carried up the front steps like a child), coming into a lecture hall by means of a freight elevator and then through the kitchen or utility room before being able to join the 'normal' people who come in the front door." The paralytic's friends found a rather drastic solution to the problem, and Jesus, impressed, honored their (plural) faith.

---

5 And Jesus seeing their faith *said to the paralytic, "ᶜSon, your sins are forgiven."

6 But some of the scribes were sitting there and reasoning in their hearts,

7 "Why does this man speak that way? He is blaspheming; who can forgive sins but God alone?"

8 Immediately Jesus, aware in His spirit that they were reasoning that way within themselves, *said to them, "Why are you reasoning about these things in your hearts?

9 "Which is easier, to say to the paralytic, 'Your sins are forgiven'; or to say, 'Get up, and pick up your pallet and walk'?

10 "But so that you may know that the Son of Man has authority on earth to forgive sins"—He *said to the paralytic,

11 "I say to you, get up, pick up your pallet and go home."

12 And he got up and immediately picked up the pallet and went out in the sight of everyone, so that they were all amazed and were glorifying God, saying, "We have never seen anything like this."

13 ¶ And He went out again by the seashore; and all the people were coming to Him, and He was teaching them.

Levi (Matthew) Called

2:14–17pp — Matt 9:9–13; Luke 5:27–32
2:18–22pp — Matt 9:14–17; Luke 5:33–38

14 As He passed by, He saw Levi the *son* of Alphaeus sitting in the tax booth, and He *said to him, "Follow Me!" And he got up and followed Him.

15 ¶ And it *happened that He was reclining *at the table* in his house, and many tax collectors and sinners were dining with Jesus and His disciples;

ª Or *served*   ᵇ Lit *was*   ᶜ Lit *child*

for there were many of them, and they were following Him.

16 When the scribes of the Pharisees saw that He was eating with the sinners and tax collectors, they said to His disciples, "Why is He eating and drinking with tax collectors and sinners?"

17 And hearing *this*, Jesus *said to them, "*It is* not those who are healthy who need a physician, but those who are sick; I did not come to call the righteous, but sinners."

18 ¶ John's disciples and the Pharisees were fasting; and they *came and *said to Him, "Why do John's disciples and the disciples of the Pharisees fast, but Your disciples do not fast?"

19 And Jesus said to them, "While the bridegroom is with them, the attendants of the bridegroom cannot fast, can they? So long as they have the bridegroom with them, they cannot fast.

20 "But the days will come when the bridegroom is taken away from them, and then they will fast in that day.

21 ¶ "No one sews a patch of unshrunk cloth on an old garment; otherwise the patch pulls away from it, the new from the old, and a worse tear results.

22 "No one puts new wine into old wineskins; otherwise the wine will burst the skins, and the wine is lost and the skins *as well*; but *one puts* new wine into fresh wineskins."

Question of the Sabbath

2:23–28pp — Matt 12:1–8; Luke 6:1–5

23 ¶ And it happened that He was passing through the grainfields on the Sabbath, and His disciples began to make their way along while picking the heads *of grain*.

24 The Pharisees were saying to Him, "Look, why are they doing what is not lawful on the Sabbath?"

25 And He *said to them, "Have you never read what David did when he was in need and he and his companions became hungry;

26 how he entered the house of God in the time of Abiathar *the* high priest, and ate the consecrated bread, which is not lawful for *anyone* to eat except the priests, and he also gave it to those who were with him?"

27 Jesus said to them, "The Sabbath was made for man, and not man for the Sabbath.

28 "So the Son of Man is Lord even of the Sabbath."

Jesus Heals on the Sabbath

3:1–6pp — Matt 12:9–14; Luke 6:6–11
3:7–12pp — Matt 12:15,16; Luke 6:17–19

3 He entered again into a synagogue; and a man was there whose hand was withered.

2 They were watching Him *to see* if He would

heal him on the Sabbath, so that they might accuse Him.

3 He *said to the man with the withered hand, "Get up and come forward!"

4 And He *said to them, "Is it lawful to do good or to do harm on the Sabbath, to save a life or to kill?" But they kept silent.

5 After looking around at them with anger, grieved at their hardness of heart, He *said to the man, "Stretch out your hand." And he stretched it out, and his hand was restored.

6 The Pharisees went out and immediately *began* conspiring with the Herodians against Him, *as to* how they might destroy Him.

7 ¶ Jesus withdrew to the sea with His disciples; and a great multitude from Galilee followed; and *also* from Judea,

8 and from Jerusalem, and from Idumea, and beyond the Jordan, and the vicinity of Tyre and Sidon, a great number of people heard of all that He was doing and came to Him.

9 And He told His disciples that a boat should stand ready for Him because of the crowd, so that they would not crowd Him;

10 for He had healed many, with the result that all those who had afflictions pressed around Him in order to touch Him.

11 Whenever the unclean spirits saw Him, they would fall down before Him and shout, "You are the Son of God!"

12 And He earnestly warned them not to tell who He was.

The Twelve Are Chosen

3:16–19pp — Matt 10:2–4; Luke 6:14–16; Acts 1:13
3:23–27pp — Matt 12:25–29; Luke 11:17–22
3:31–35pp — Matt 12:46–50; Luke 8:19–21

13 ¶ And He *went up on the mountain and * summoned those whom He Himself wanted, and they came to Him.

14 And He appointed twelve, so that they would be with Him and that He *could* send them out to preach,

15 and to have authority to cast out the demons.

16 And He appointed the twelve: Simon (to whom He gave the name Peter),

17 and James, the *son* of Zebedee, and John the brother of James (to them He gave the name Boanerges, which means, "Sons of Thunder");

18 and Andrew, and Philip, and Bartholomew, and Matthew, and Thomas, and James the son of Alphaeus, and Thaddaeus, and Simon the Zealot;

19 and Judas Iscariot, who betrayed Him.

20 ¶ And He *came *home, and the crowd *gathered again, to such an extent that they could not even eat a meal.

21 When His own *people heard *of this*, they went out to take custody of Him; for they were saying, "He has lost His senses."

---

a Lit *into a house*   *b* Or *kinsmen*

22 The scribes who came down from Jerusalem were saying, "He is possessed by Beelzebul," and "He casts out the demons by the ruler of the demons."

23 And He called them to Himself and began speaking to them in parables, "How can Satan cast out Satan?

24 "If a kingdom is divided against itself, that kingdom cannot stand.

25 "If a house is divided against itself, that house will not be able to stand.

26 "If Satan has risen up against himself and is divided, he cannot stand, but he is finished!

27 "But no one can enter the strong man's

Why Come to Earth?
The only way God could get through

AMERICAN RADIO BROADCASTER PAUL HARVEY once told a modern parable about a religious skeptic who worked as a farmer. One raw winter night the man heard an irregular thumping sound against the kitchen storm door. He went to a window and watched as tiny, shivering sparrows, attracted to the evident warmth inside, beat in vain against the glass.

Touched, the farmer bundled up and trudged through fresh snow to open the barn door for the struggling birds. He turned on the lights and tossed some hay in a corner. But the sparrows, which had scattered in all directions when he emerged from the house, hid in the darkness, afraid.

The man tried various tactics to get them into the barn. He laid down a trail of saltine cracker crumbs to direct them. He tried circling behind the birds to drive them toward the barn. Nothing worked. He, a huge, alien creature, had terrified them; the birds couldn't comprehend that he actually desired to help.

The farmer withdrew to his house and watched the doomed sparrows through a window. As he stared, a thought hit him like lightning from a clear blue sky: *If only I could become a bird—one of them—just for a moment. Then I wouldn't frighten them so. I could show them the way to warmth and safety.*

At the same moment, another thought dawned on him. He had grasped the reason Jesus was born.

> They became very much afraid and said to one another, "Who then is this, that even the wind and the sea obey Him?" 4:41

When God Came to Earth

A man becoming a bird is nothing compared to God becoming a man. The concept of a sovereign eternal being who created the universe confining himself to a human body was—and is—too much for some people to believe. But how else could God truly communicate with us?

We don't know what God looked like as a man; no Gospel writer described the physical appearance of Jesus. But, in other ways, Mark painted a full picture of his humanity. Jesus, who claimed to be God, didn't have a supernatural "glow" about him. His own neighbors and family marveled that he seemed so, well, normal.

Mark does not diminish Jesus. He shows the power of a man who healed the blind with a simple touch (8:25), and the authority of a teacher so captivating that people sat three days straight, with empty stomachs, just to hear him (8:2). Even after Jesus hushed them, people wouldn't stop talking about his miracles.

But Mark also reveals the full range of Jesus' emotions: a surge of compassion for a person with leprosy (1:41), a deep sigh in response to nagging Pharisees (8:12), a look of anger and distress at cold-hearted legalists (3:5), and then an awful cry on the cross, "My God, My God, why have You forsaken me?" (15:34). Jesus was sometimes witty, and he sometimes cried. He got tired: Five times, Mark records, he sought a quiet place for rest away from the crowds.

Like No One Else

Jesus was like no other person who ever lived. Twelve men left their jobs and families at a single command to follow him. Yet Jesus was also fully "one of us." He needed food and friends. He got lonely and tired. He showed anger and disappointment. Because Jesus experienced all we experience as human beings, he can understand us completely, and share in our joys and sorrows.

Mark portrays both sides of Jesus—the divine and the human. The disciples needed to see both dimensions to give their lives to him.

Life Questions: Suppose that Jesus had never come, that God had merely sent an elaborate love note. What difference would that make?

house and plunder his property unless he first binds the strong man, and then he will plunder his house.

28 ¶ "Truly I say to you, all sins shall be forgiven the sons of men, and whatever blasphemies they utter;

29 but whoever blasphemes against the Holy Spirit never has forgiveness, but is guilty of an eternal sin"—

30 because they were saying, "He has an unclean spirit."

3:30 Out of His Mind?

Jesus provoked a strong reaction in just about everyone. In this instance, Jesus' own family members questioned his sanity, and teachers of the law wondered about demon-possession. He aroused the fiercest opposition among his own neighbors and among the religious "professionals" of his day. But, as Mark shows, throngs of other people were amazed by his authoritative teaching and his miraculous powers. Personal contact with Jesus left virtually no one unmoved.

31 ¶ Then His mother and His brothers *arrived, and standing outside they sent *word* to Him and called Him.

32 A crowd was sitting around Him, and they *said to Him, "Behold, Your mother and Your brothers are outside looking for You."

33 Answering them, He *said, "Who are My mother and My brothers?"

34 Looking about at those who were sitting around Him, He *said, "Behold My mother and My brothers!

35 "For whoever does the will of God, he is My brother and sister and mother."

Parable of the Sower and Soils

4:1–12pp — Matt 13:1–15; Luke 8:4–10

4 He began to teach again by the sea. And such a very large crowd gathered to Him that He got into a boat in the sea and sat down; and the whole crowd was by the sea on the land.

2 And He was teaching them many things in parables, and was saying to them in His teaching,

3 "Listen *to this*! Behold, the sower went out to sow;

4 as he was sowing, some *seed* fell beside the road, and the birds came and ate it up.

5 "Other *seed* fell on the rocky *ground* where it did not have much soil; and immediately it sprang up because it had no depth of soil.

6 "And after the sun had risen, it was scorched; and because it had no root, it withered away.

7 "Other *seed* fell among the thorns, and the

thorns came up and choked it, and it yielded no crop.

8 "Other *seeds* fell into the good soil, and as they grew up and increased, they yielded a crop and produced thirty, sixty, and a hundredfold."

9 And He was saying, "He who has ears to hear, let him hear."

10 ¶ As soon as He was alone, His followers, along with the twelve, *began* asking Him *about* the parables.

11 And He was saying to them, "To you has been given the mystery of the kingdom of God, but those who are outside get everything in parables,

12 so that WHILE SEEING, THEY MAY SEE AND NOT PERCEIVE, AND WHILE HEARING, THEY MAY HEAR AND NOT UNDERSTAND, OTHERWISE THEY MIGHT RETURN AND BE FORGIVEN."

Explanation

4:13–20pp — Matt 13:18–23; Luke 8:11–15

13 ¶ And He *said to them, "Do you not understand this parable? How will you understand all the parables?

14 "The sower sows the word.

15 "These are the ones who are beside the road where the word is sown; and when they hear, immediately Satan comes and takes away the word which has been sown in them.

16 "In a similar way these are the ones on whom seed was sown on the rocky *places,* who, when they hear the word, immediately receive it with joy;

17 and they have no *firm* root in themselves, but are *only* temporary; then, when affliction or persecution arises because of the word, immediately they fall away.

18 "And others are the ones on whom seed was sown among the thorns; these are the ones who have heard the word,

19 but the worries of the ªworld, and the deceitfulness of riches, and the desires for other things enter in and choke the word, and it becomes unfruitful.

20 "And those are the ones on whom seed was sown on the good soil; and they hear the word and accept it and bear fruit, thirty, sixty, and a hundredfold."

21 ¶ And He was saying to them, "A lamp is not brought to be put under a basket, is it, or under a bed? Is it not *brought* to be put on the lampstand?

22 "For nothing is hidden, except to be revealed; nor has *anything* been secret, but that it would come to light.

23 "If anyone has ears to hear, let him hear."

24 And He was saying to them, "Take care what you listen to. By your standard of measure it will be measured to you; and more will be given you besides.

ª Or *age*

25 "For whoever has, to him *more* shall be given; and whoever does not have, even what he has shall be taken away from him."

Parable of the Seed

26 ¶ And He was saying, "The kingdom of God is like a man who casts seed upon the soil;

27 and he goes to bed at night and gets up by day, and the seed sprouts and grows—how, he himself does not know.

28 "The soil produces crops by itself; first the blade, then the head, then the mature grain in the head.

29 "But when the crop permits, he immediately puts in the sickle, because the harvest has come."

Parable of the Mustard Seed

4:30-32pp — Matt 13:31,32; Luke 13:18,19

30 ¶ And He said, "How shall we *a*picture the kingdom of God, or by what parable shall we present it?

4:30 Scarce Parables

Unlike Matthew and Luke, Mark devotes little space to parables, the unique form of teaching Jesus often relied on. Yet Mark includes as many miracles as does any Gospel. Clearly, this book emphasizes action over words.

31 "*It is* like a mustard seed, which, when sown upon the soil, though it is smaller than all the seeds that are upon the soil,

32 yet when it is sown, it grows up and becomes larger than all the garden plants and forms large branches; so that THE BIRDS OF THE *b*AIR can NEST UNDER ITS SHADE."

33 ¶ With many such parables He was speaking the word to them, so far as they were able to hear it;

34 and He did not speak to them without a parable; but He was explaining everything privately to His own disciples.

Jesus Stills the Sea

4:35-41pp — Matt 8:18,23-27; Luke 8:22-25

35 ¶ On that day, when evening came, He *said to them, "Let us go over to the other side."

36 Leaving the crowd, they *took Him along with them in the boat, just as He was; and other boats were with Him.

37 And there *arose a fierce gale of wind, and the waves were breaking over the boat so much that the boat was already filling up.

38 Jesus Himself was in the stern, asleep on the cushion; and they *woke Him and *said to Him, "Teacher, do You not care that we are perishing?"

39 And He got up and rebuked the wind and said to the sea, "Hush, be still." And the wind died down and it became perfectly calm.

40 And He said to them, "Why are you afraid? Do you still have no faith?"

41 They became very much afraid and said to one another, "Who then is this, that even the wind and the sea obey Him?"

The Gerasene Demoniac

5:1-17pp — Matt 8:28-34; Luke 8:26-37
5:18-20pp — Luke 8:38,39

5 They came to the other side of the sea, into the country of the Gerasenes.

2 When He got out of the boat, immediately a man from the tombs with an unclean spirit met Him,

3 and he had his dwelling among the tombs. And no one was able to bind him anymore, even with a chain;

4 because he had often been bound with shackles and chains, and the chains had been torn apart by him and the shackles broken in pieces, and no one was strong enough to subdue him.

5 Constantly, night and day, he was screaming among the tombs and in the mountains, and gashing himself with stones.

6 Seeing Jesus from a distance, he ran up and bowed down before Him;

7 and shouting with a loud voice, he *said, "What business do we have with each other, Jesus, Son of the Most High God? I implore You by God, do not torment me!"

8 For He had been saying to him, "Come out of the man, you unclean spirit!"

9 And He was asking him, "What is your name?" And he *said to Him, "My name is Legion; for we are many."

10 And he *began* to implore Him earnestly not to send them out of the country.

11 Now there was a large herd of swine feeding nearby on the mountain.

12 *The demons* implored Him, saying, "Send us into the swine so that we may enter them."

13 Jesus gave them permission. And coming out, the unclean spirits entered the swine; and the herd rushed down the steep bank into the sea, about two thousand *of them*; and they were drowned in the sea.

14 ¶ Their herdsmen ran away and reported it in the city and in the country. And *the people* came to see what it was that had happened.

15 They *came to Jesus and *observed the man who had been demon-possessed sitting down, clothed and in his right mind, the very man who had had the "legion"; and they became frightened.

16 Those who had seen it described to them how it had happened to the demon-possessed man, and *all* about the swine.

a Lit *compare*   *b* Or *sky*

17 And they began to implore Him to leave their region.

18 As He was getting into the boat, the man who had been demon-possessed was imploring Him that he might accompany Him.

19 And He did not let him, but He *said to him, "Go home to your people and report to them ªwhat great things the Lord has done for you, and how He had mercy on you."

20 And he went away and began to proclaim in Decapolis what great things Jesus had done for him; and everyone was amazed.

Miracles and Healing
5:22–43pp — Matt 9:18–26; Luke 8:41–56

21 ¶ When Jesus had crossed over again in the boat to the other side, a large crowd gathered around Him; and so He stayed by the seashore.

22 One of the synagogue officials named Jairus *came up, and on seeing Him, *fell at His feet

23 and *implored Him earnestly, saying, "My little daughter is at the point of death; please come and lay Your hands on her, so that she will get well and live."

24 And He went off with him; and a large crowd was following Him and pressing in on Him.

25 ¶ A woman who had had a hemorrhage for twelve years,

26 and had endured much at the hands of many physicians, and had spent all that she had and was not helped at all, but rather had grown worse—

27 after hearing about Jesus, she came up in the crowd behind Him and touched His cloak.

28 For she thought, "If I just touch His garments, I will get well."

29 Immediately the flow of her blood was dried up; and she felt in her body that she was healed of her affliction.

30 Immediately Jesus, perceiving in Himself that the power proceeding from Him had gone forth, turned around in the crowd and said, "Who touched My garments?"

31 And His disciples said to Him, "You see the crowd pressing in on You, and You say, 'Who touched Me?'"

32 And He looked around to see the woman who had done this.

33 But the woman fearing and trembling, aware of what had happened to her, came and fell down before Him and told Him the whole truth.

34 And He said to her, "Daughter, your faith has made you well; go in peace and be healed of your affliction."

35 ¶ While He was still speaking, they *came from the house of the synagogue official, saying, "Your daughter has died; why trouble the Teacher anymore?"

36 But Jesus, overhearing what was being spo-

ken, *said to the synagogue official, "Do not be afraid any longer, only believe."

37 And He allowed no one to accompany Him, except Peter and James and John the brother of James.

38 They *came to the house of the synagogue official; and He *saw a commotion, and people loudly weeping and wailing.

39 And entering in, He *said to them, "Why make a commotion and weep? The child has not died, but is asleep."

40 They began laughing at Him. But putting them all out, He *took along the child's father and mother and His own companions, and *entered the room where the child was.

41 Taking the child by the hand, He *said to her, "Talitha kum!" (which translated means, "Little girl, I say to you, get up!").

42 Immediately the girl got up and began to walk, for she was twelve years old. And immediately they were completely astounded.

43 And He gave them strict orders that no one should know about this, and He said that something should be given her to eat.

5:43 Don't Tell

Seven times in Mark, Jesus asked people who had seen a miracle not to tell anyone. He was protecting himself from the crush of crowds that flocked to him when word of his miracles spread—as it usually did, despite his orders—and from the opposition forces who were already tailing him. Jesus recognized early on that the kind of excitement generated by miracles did not automatically convert into the life-changing faith he sought to arouse.

Teaching at Nazareth
6:1–6pp — Matt 13:54–58

6 Jesus went out from there and *came into His hometown; and His disciples *followed Him.

2 When the Sabbath came, He began to teach in the synagogue; and the many listeners were astonished, saying, "Where did this man get these things, and what is this wisdom given to Him, and such miracles as these performed by His hands?

3 "Is not this the carpenter, the son of Mary, and brother of James and Joses and Judas and Simon? Are not His sisters here with us?" And they took offense at Him.

4 Jesus said to them, "A prophet is not without honor except in his hometown and among his own relatives and in his own household."

5 And He could do no miracle there except that He laid His hands on a few sick people and healed them.

ª Or everything that

6 And He wondered at their unbelief.

¶ And He was going around the villages teaching.

The Twelve Sent Out

6:7–11pp — Matt 10:1,9–14; Luke 9:1,3–5

7 ¶ And He *summoned the twelve and began to send them out in pairs, and gave them authority over the unclean spirits;

8 and He instructed them that they should take nothing for *their* journey, except a mere staff—no bread, no bag, no money in their belt—

9 but to wear sandals; and *He added*, "Do not put on two *a*tunics."

10 And He said to them, "Wherever you enter a house, stay there until you leave town.

11 "Any place that does not receive you or listen to you, as you go out from there, shake the dust off the soles of your feet for a testimony against them."

12 They went out and preached that *men* should repent.

a Or *inner garments*

13 And they were casting out many demons and were anointing with oil many sick people and healing them.

John's Fate Recalled

6:14–29pp — Matt 14:1–12
6:14–16pp — Luke 9:7–9
6:32–44pp — Matt 14:13–21; Luke 9:10–17; John 6:5–13
6:32–44Ref — Mark 8:2–9

14 ¶ And King Herod heard *of it,* for His name had become well known; and *people* were saying, "John the Baptist has risen from the dead, and that is why these miraculous powers are at work in Him."

15 But others were saying, "He is Elijah." And others were saying, "*He is* a prophet, like one of the prophets *of old.*"

16 But when Herod heard *of it,* he kept saying, "John, whom I beheaded, has risen!"

17 ¶ For Herod himself had sent and had John

Eyewitness Reports
Where did Mark get his facts?

WHEN PEOPLE TRANSLATE THE BIBLE into a new language, they have a lot of explaining to do. How do you convey Christianity to someone who has never heard of Abraham or Moses or the apostles Peter and Paul? Where do you start?

More often than not, translators begin with the book of Mark. Its simple sentences and brief, action-filled scenes allow for easier translation. It reads like a newspaper. And the book seems written for a foreign culture (perhaps the Romans) in the first place: Common Jewish customs are explained in parentheses.

> He allowed no one to accompany Him, except Peter and James and John the brother of James.
> 5:37

The Peter Connection

Perhaps the most compelling feature of Mark to an unfamiliar reader, though, is its vividness. It has the feel of an eyewitness account. Those who study such things have concluded that Mark probably got his facts from Peter, one of Jesus' intimate disciples. Peter, or someone like him, provided believable, close-up details.

Jesus spent his time in the desert "with the wild beasts" (1:13). When he went to pray, he got up "in the early morning, while it was still dark" (1:35)—a memorable detail to Jesus' disciples, sometimes known for their untimely sleeping habits. In the midst of a furious squall Jesus lay in a boat "asleep on the cushion" (4:38).

Whoever told Mark about the scene on the Mount of Transfiguration described Jesus' clothes as "radiant and exceedingly white, as no launderer on earth can whiten them" (9:3). And only Mark tells us that Peter sat with the guards during Jesus' trial, warming himself by the fire.

Why Details Matter

You can say these details don't matter, and it's true that Matthew and Luke recounted the same events without them. But as any good writer knows, details like these make a story come alive. Vivid images that stuck in the eyewitness's memory will likely stick with the reader as well.

For example, Mark could have matter-of-factly told of people being healed, but it just didn't happen that way. A blind man, "throwing aside his cloak ... jumped up and came to Jesus" (10:50). And after the paralytic stood up, "they were all amazed and were glorifying God, saying, 'We have never seen anything like this!' " (2:12).

Life Questions: As you read Mark, what "eyewitness details" stand out to you?

arrested and bound in prison on account of Herodias, the wife of his brother Philip, because he had married her.

18 For John had been saying to Herod, "It is not lawful for you to have your brother's wife."

19 Herodias had a grudge against him and wanted to put him to death and could not *do so;*

20 for Herod was afraid of John, knowing that he was a righteous and holy man, and he kept him safe. And when he heard him, he was very perplexed; but he used to enjoy listening to him.

21 A strategic day came when Herod on his birthday gave a banquet for his lords and military commanders and the leading men of Galilee;

22 and when the daughter of Herodias herself came in and danced, she pleased Herod and his dinner guests; and the king said to the girl, "Ask me for whatever you want and I will give it to you."

23 And he swore to her, "Whatever you ask of me, I will give it to you; up to half of my kingdom."

24 And she went out and said to her mother, "What shall I ask for?" And she said, "The head of John the Baptist."

25 Immediately she came in a hurry to the king and asked, saying, "I want you to give me at once the head of John the Baptist on a platter."

26 And although the king was very sorry, *yet* because of his oaths and because of his dinner guests, he was unwilling to refuse her.

27 Immediately the king sent an executioner and commanded *him* to bring *back* his head. And he went and had him beheaded in the prison,

28 and brought his head on a platter, and gave it to the girl; and the girl gave it to her mother.

29 When his disciples heard *about this,* they came and took away his body and laid it in a tomb.

6:29 New Recruits

Jesus got some of his original disciples from John the Baptist (see John 1:35,40), and after John's execution even more of them joined up with Jesus. But as Acts 19:1–5 makes clear, some of John's disciples never got the word about Jesus. Two decades after John's death, Paul stumbled across a group of loyal followers in Ephesus, hundreds of miles away.

30 ¶ The apostles *gathered together with Jesus; and they reported to Him all that they had done and taught.

31 And He *said to them, "Come away by yourselves to a secluded place and rest a while." (For there were many *people* coming and going, and they did not even have time to eat.)

a The denarius was equivalent to one day's wage

32 They went away in the boat to a secluded place by themselves.

Five Thousand Fed

33 *The people* saw them going, and many recognized *them* and ran there together on foot from all the cities, and got there ahead of them.

6:31 The Need to Get Away

Mark graphically shows the press of the crowds around Jesus. Wherever he went, people followed, bringing him the sick to heal and challenging him with questions. In five separate places (3:7–9; 6:31; 6:45; 7:24; 9:30) Mark records that Jesus took his disciples aside to some quiet place to escape the crush of the crowd.

34 When Jesus went ashore, He saw a large crowd, and He felt compassion for them because they were like sheep without a shepherd; and He began to teach them many things.

35 When it was already quite late, His disciples came to Him and said, "This place is desolate and it is already quite late;

36 send them away so that they may go into the surrounding countryside and villages and buy themselves something to eat."

37 But He answered them, "You give them *something* to eat!" And they *said to Him, "Shall we go and spend two hundred *a*denarii on bread and give them *something* to eat?"

38 And He *said to them, "How many loaves do you have? Go look!" And when they found out, they *said, "Five, and two fish."

39 And He commanded them all to sit down by groups on the green grass.

40 They sat down in groups of hundreds and of fifties.

41 And He took the five loaves and the two fish, and looking up toward heaven, He blessed the food and broke the loaves and He kept giving *them* to the disciples to set before them; and He divided up the two fish among them all.

42 They all ate and were satisfied,

43 and they picked up twelve full baskets of the broken pieces, and also of the fish.

44 There were five thousand men who ate the loaves.

Jesus Walks on the Water

6:45–51pp — Matt 14:22–32; John 6:15–21
6:53–56pp — Matt 14:34–36

45 ¶ Immediately Jesus made His disciples get into the boat and go ahead of *Him* to the other side to Bethsaida, while He Himself was sending the crowd away.

46 After bidding them farewell, He left for the mountain to pray.

47 ¶ When it was evening, the boat was in the middle of the sea, and He was alone on the land.

48 Seeing them straining at the oars, for the wind was against them, at about the fourth watch of the night He *came to them, walking on the sea; and He intended to pass by them.

49 But when they saw Him walking on the sea, they supposed that it was a ghost, and cried out;

50 for they all saw Him and were terrified. But immediately He spoke with them and *said to them, "Take courage; it is I, do not be afraid."

51 Then He got into the boat with them, and the wind stopped; and they were utterly astonished,

52 for they had not gained any insight from the *incident of* the loaves, but their heart was hardened.

Healing at Gennesaret

53 ¶ When they had crossed over they came to land at Gennesaret, and moored to the shore.

54 When they got out of the boat, immediately *the people* recognized Him,

55 and ran about that whole country and began to carry here and there on their pallets those who were sick, to the place they heard He was.

56 Wherever He entered villages, or cities, or countryside, they were laying the sick in the market places, and imploring Him that they might just touch the fringe of His cloak; and as many as touched it were being cured.

Followers of Tradition

7:1–23pp — Matt 15:1–20

7 The Pharisees and some of the scribes gathered around Him when they had come from Jerusalem,

2 and had seen that some of His disciples were eating their bread with impure hands, that is, unwashed.

3 (For the Pharisees and all the Jews do not eat unless they carefully wash their hands, *thus* observing the traditions of the elders;

7:3 Explaining Jewish Customs

The parenthetical remark in verses 3–4 explains a common Jewish custom of ceremonial hand-washing. Such remarks as these indicate Mark was writing to a non-Jewish audience who needed background explanations.

4 and *when they come* from the market place, they do not eat unless they cleanse themselves; and there are many other things which they have received in order to observe, such as the washing of cups and pitchers and copper pots.)

5 The Pharisees and the scribes *asked Him, "Why do Your disciples not walk according to the tradition of the elders, but eat their bread with impure hands?"

6 And He said to them, "Rightly did Isaiah prophesy of you hypocrites, as it is written:

'THIS PEOPLE HONORS ME WITH THEIR LIPS,
BUT THEIR HEART IS FAR AWAY FROM ME.

7 'BUT IN VAIN DO THEY WORSHIP ME,
TEACHING AS DOCTRINES THE PRECEPTS OF MEN.'

8 "Neglecting the commandment of God, you hold to the tradition of men."

9 ¶ He was also saying to them, "You are experts at setting aside the commandment of God in order to keep your tradition.

10 "For Moses said, 'HONOR YOUR FATHER AND YOUR MOTHER'; and, 'HE WHO SPEAKS EVIL OF FATHER OR MOTHER, IS TO BE PUT TO DEATH';

11 but you say, 'If a man says to *his* father or *his* mother, whatever I have that would help you is Corban (that is to say, *a*given *to God*),'

12 you no longer permit him to do anything for *his* father or *his* mother;

13 *thus* invalidating the word of God by your tradition which you have handed down; and you do many things such as that."

The Heart of Man

14 ¶ After He called the crowd to Him again, He *began* saying to them, "Listen to Me, all of you, and understand:

15 there is nothing outside the man which can defile him if it goes into him; but the things which proceed out of the man are what defile the man.

16 ["*b*If anyone has ears to hear, let him hear."]

17 ¶ When he had left the crowd *and* entered the house, His disciples questioned Him about the parable.

18 And He *said to them, "Are you so lacking in understanding also? Do you not understand that whatever goes into the man from outside cannot defile him,

19 because it does not go into his heart, but into his stomach, and is eliminated?" (*Thus He* declared all foods clean.)

20 And He was saying, "That which proceeds out of the man, that is what defiles the man.

21 "For from within, out of the heart of men, proceed the evil thoughts, fornications, thefts, murders, adulteries,

22 deeds of coveting *and* wickedness, *as well as* deceit, sensuality, envy, slander, pride *and* foolishness.

23 "All these evil things proceed from within and defile the man."

---

a Or *a gift,* i.e. *an offering*   *b* Early mss do not contain this verse

The Syrophoenician Woman

7:24–30pp — Matt 15:21–28
7:31–37pp — Matt 15:29–31

24 ¶ Jesus got up and went away from there to the region of Tyre[a]. And when He had entered a house, He wanted no one to know *of it*; yet He could not escape notice.

25 But after hearing of Him, a woman whose little daughter had an unclean spirit immediately came and fell at His feet.

26 Now the woman was a [b]Gentile, of the Syrophoenician race. And she kept asking Him to cast the demon out of her daughter.

27 And He was saying to her, "Let the children be satisfied first, for it is not good to take the children's bread and throw it to the dogs."

28 But she answered and *said to Him, "Yes, Lord, *but* even the dogs under the table feed on the children's crumbs."

29 And He said to her, "Because of this answer go; the demon has gone out of your daughter."

30 And going back to her home, she found the child lying on the bed, the demon having left.

31 ¶ Again He went out from the region of Tyre, and came through Sidon to the Sea of Galilee, within the region of Decapolis.

32 They *brought to Him one who was deaf and spoke with difficulty, and they *implored Him to lay His hand on him.

33 Jesus took him aside from the crowd, by himself, and put His fingers into his ears, and after spitting, He touched his tongue *with the saliva;*

34 and looking up to heaven with a deep sigh, He *said to him, "Ephphatha!" that is, "Be opened!"

35 And his ears were opened, and the impediment of his tongue was removed, and he *began* speaking plainly.

36 And He gave them orders not to tell anyone; but the more He ordered them, the more widely they continued to proclaim it.

37 They were utterly astonished, saying, "He has done all things well; He makes even the deaf to hear and the mute to speak."

Four Thousand Fed

8:1–9pp — Matt 15:32–39
8:1–9Ref — Mark 6:32–44
8:11–21pp — Matt 16:1–12

8 In those days, when there was again a large crowd and they had nothing to eat, Jesus called His disciples and *said to them,

2 "I feel compassion for the people because they have remained with Me now three days and have nothing to eat.

3 "If I send them away hungry to their homes, they will faint on the way; and some of them have come from a great distance."

4 And His disciples answered Him, "Where will anyone be able *to find enough* bread here in *this* desolate place to satisfy these people?"

5 And He was asking them, "How many loaves do you have?" And they said, "Seven."

6 And He *directed the people to sit down on the ground; and taking the seven loaves, He gave thanks and broke them, and started giving them to His disciples to serve to them, and they served them to the people.

7 They also had a few small fish; and after He had blessed them, He ordered these to be served as well.

8 And they ate and were satisfied; and they picked up seven large baskets full of what was left over of the broken pieces.

8:8 Lost in Translation

Often details get lost when a book is translated from one language to another. For example, the Greek word for the "baskets" used in the feeding of the 5,000 (6:43) is used for small, lunchbox-size baskets. In the feeding of the 4,000, leftovers filled seven large baskets; the same word describes the basket the apostle Paul would hide in to escape from Damascus (Acts 9:25).

9 About four thousand were *there*; and He sent them away.

10 And immediately He entered the boat with His disciples and came to the district of Dalmanutha.

11 ¶ The Pharisees came out and began to argue with Him, seeking from Him a sign from heaven, to test Him.

12 Sighing deeply in His spirit, He *said, "Why does this generation seek for a sign? Truly I say to you, no sign will be given to this generation."

13 Leaving them, He again embarked and went away to the other side.

14 ¶ And they had forgotten to take bread, and did not have more than one loaf in the boat with them.

15 And He was giving orders to them, saying, "Watch out! Beware of the leaven of the Pharisees and the leaven of Herod."

16 They *began* to discuss with one another the fact that they had no bread.

17 And Jesus, aware of this, *said to them, "Why do you discuss *the fact* that you have no bread? Do you not yet see or understand? Do you have a hardened heart?

18 "HAVING EYES, DO YOU NOT SEE? AND HAVING EARS, DO YOU NOT HEAR? And do you not remember,

19 when I broke the five loaves for the five

---

[a] Two early mss add *and Sidon*   [b] Lit *Greek*

thousand, how many baskets full of broken pieces you picked up?" They *said to Him, "Twelve."

20 "When *I broke* the seven for the four thousand, how many large baskets full of broken pieces did you pick up?" And they *said to Him, "Seven."

21 And He was saying to them, "Do you not yet understand?"

22 ¶ And they *came to Bethsaida. And they *brought a blind man to Jesus and *implored Him to touch him.

23 Taking the blind man by the hand, He brought him out of the village; and after spitting on his eyes and laying His hands on him, He asked him, "Do you see anything?"

24 And he looked up and said, "I see men, for I see *them* like trees, walking around."

25 Then again He laid His hands on his eyes; and he looked intently and was restored, and *began* to see everything clearly.

26 And He sent him to his home, saying, "Do not even enter the village."

Peter's Confession of Christ

8:27–29pp — Matt 16:13–16; Luke 9:18–20
8:31 — 9:1pp — Matt 16:21–28; Luke 9:22–27

27 ¶ Jesus went out, along with His disciples, to the villages of Caesarea Philippi; and on the way He questioned His disciples, saying to them, "Who do people say that I am?"

28 They told Him, saying, "John the Baptist; and others *say* Elijah; but others, one of the prophets."

29 And He *continued* by questioning them, "But who do you say that I am?" Peter *answered and *said to Him, "You are the Christ."

8:29 Peter Learns Humility

Most scholars believe that Mark got his eyewitness details from the disciple Peter. If so, the book reveals something about how Peter changed. Mark tells of three separate instances when Jesus rebuked Peter (see, for example, verse 33), but omits several compliments paid him. For example, compare this passage to a parallel account in Matthew 16:13–20, where Jesus commended Peter highly. Evidently, brash Peter learned a few lessons about humility along the way.

30 And He warned them to tell no one about Him.

31 ¶ And He began to teach them that the Son of Man must suffer many things and be rejected by the elders and the chief priests and the scribes, and be killed, and after three days rise again.

32 And He was stating the matter plainly. And

Peter took Him aside and began to rebuke Him.

33 But turning around and seeing His disciples, He rebuked Peter and *said, "Get behind Me, Satan; for you are not setting your mind on *a*God's interests, but man's."

34 ¶ And He summoned the crowd with His disciples, and said to them, "If anyone wishes to come after Me, he must deny himself, and take up his cross and follow Me.

35 "For whoever wishes to save his life will lose it, but whoever loses his life for My sake and the gospel's will save it.

36 "For what does it profit a man to gain the whole world, and forfeit his soul?

37 "For what will a man give in exchange for his soul?

38 "For whoever is ashamed of Me and My words in this adulterous and sinful generation, the Son of Man will also be ashamed of him when He comes in the glory of His Father with the holy angels."

The Transfiguration

9:2–8pp — Luke 9:28–36
9:2–13pp — Matt 17:1–13

9 And Jesus was saying to them, "Truly I say to you, there are some of those who are standing here who will not taste death until they see the kingdom of God after it has come with power."

2 ¶ Six days later, Jesus *took with Him Peter and James and John, and *brought them up on a high mountain by themselves. And He was transfigured before them;

3 and His garments became radiant and exceedingly white, as no launderer on earth can whiten them.

4 Elijah appeared to them along with Moses; and they were talking with Jesus.

5 Peter *said to Jesus, "Rabbi, it is good for us to be here; let us make three tabernacles, one for You, and one for Moses, and one for Elijah."

6 For he did not know what to answer; for they became terrified.

7 Then a cloud formed, overshadowing them, and a voice came out of the cloud, "This is My beloved Son, listen to Him!"

8 All at once they looked around and saw no one with them anymore, except Jesus alone.

9 ¶ As they were coming down from the mountain, He gave them orders not to relate to anyone what they had seen, until the Son of Man rose from the dead.

10 They seized upon that statement, discussing with one another what rising from the dead meant.

11 They asked Him, saying, "*Why is it* that the scribes say that Elijah must come first?"

12 And He said to them, "Elijah does first come and restore all things. And *yet* how is it

a Lit *the things of God*

written of the Son of Man that He will suffer many things and be treated with contempt?

13 "But I say to you that Elijah has indeed come, and they did to him whatever they wished, just as it is written of him."

All Things Possible

9:14–28,30–32pp — Matt 17:14–19,22,23; Luke 9:37–45

14 ¶ When they came *back* to the disciples, they saw a large crowd around them, and *some* scribes arguing with them.

15 Immediately, when the entire crowd saw Him, they were amazed and *began* running up to greet Him.

16 And He asked them, "What are you discussing with them?"

17 And one of the crowd answered Him, "Teacher, I brought You my son, possessed with a spirit which makes him mute;

18 and whenever it seizes him, it slams him *to* the ground and he foams *at the mouth*, and grinds his teeth and stiffens out. I told Your disciples to cast it out, and they could not *do it.*"

19 And He *answered them and *said, "O unbelieving generation, how long shall I be with you? How long shall I put up with you? Bring him to Me!"

20 They brought the boy to Him. When he saw Him, immediately the spirit threw him into a convulsion, and falling to the ground, he *began* rolling around and foaming *at the mouth*.

21 And He asked his father, "How long has this been happening to him?" And he said, "From childhood.

22 "It has often thrown him both into the fire and into the water to destroy him. But if You can do anything, take pity on us and help us!"

23 And Jesus said to him, " 'If You can?' All things are possible to him who believes."

24 Immediately the boy's father cried out and said, "I do believe; help my unbelief."

Training the 12 Disciples
A most unpromising group of recruits

A SKILLED DRAMATIST, MARK DESCRIBES THE crowd reactions to Jesus all through his account. He shows people astonished, confused, and upset by Jesus' actions. Always, twelve people, the disciples, linger in the background, working out the logistics of Jesus' ministry.

> *"Having eyes, do you not see? And having ears, do you not hear?"* 8:18

At first, the disciples did not distinguish themselves—to put it mildly. Their most obvious trait was denseness: "Are you so lacking in understanding also?" Jesus asked (7:18), and again, "How long shall I put up with you?" (9:19).

Dense Disciples

About halfway through the book of Mark (chapter 8), the focus shifts away from the crowds and onto the disciples. In spite of their erratic performance, Jesus devoted much of his time to them. Outsiders still gathered to watch and listen, but Jesus concentrated on training the Twelve, preparing them to carry on his work after his departure.

How did the disciples handle the increased attention? If anything, they proved even more inept. When Jesus referred to his coming death, they either missed the point or foolishly protested his plans. Sometimes they squabbled about who deserved the most favored position. They obviously didn't understand the dazzling events going on around them. In short, the disciples amply demonstrated the mixture of good and bad present in all of us.

Near the end of Mark, as events conspired toward Jesus' death, the disciples grew more anxious and assertive. Jesus singled out two followers in particular, John and Peter, for his strongest reprimands. Ultimately, despite vigorous pronouncements of loyalty, each one of the Twelve sneaked quietly and ashamedly away from Jesus in his moment of deepest need.

A Decisive Change

One event, however, dramatically altered them. Something passed through their lives like a flame: Jesus' resurrection from death. After that, Jesus' patient hours of training seemed to bear fruit at last.

The disciples' change in behavior is astonishing. Of the proofs for the resurrection of Jesus, one of the most compelling is simply to compare these cowering disciples as portrayed in a Gospel like Mark with the bold, confident figures in the book of Acts. There, in a remarkable irony, we see the incredible advance of the early church being led by the two disciples with the thickest heads of all: Peter and John.

Life Questions: Sometimes we think of the disciples as saints or heroes, but Mark shows their weak spots. What weak spots keep you from following Jesus as you might?

25 When Jesus saw that a crowd was rapidly gathering, He rebuked the unclean spirit, saying to it, "You deaf and mute spirit, I command you, come out of him and do not enter him again."

26 After crying out and throwing him into terrible convulsions, it came out; and *the boy* became so much like a corpse that most *of them* said, "He is dead!"

27 But Jesus took him by the hand and raised him; and he got up.

28 When He came into *the* house, His disciples *began* questioning Him privately, "Why could we not drive it out?"

29 And He said to them, "This kind cannot come out by anything but prayer."

Death and Resurrection Foretold
9:33-37pp — Matt 18:1-5; Luke 9:46-48

30 ¶ From there they went out and *began* to go through Galilee, and He did not want anyone to know *about it.*

31 For He was teaching His disciples and telling them, "The Son of Man is to be *a*delivered into the hands of men, and they will kill Him; and when He has been killed, He will rise three days later."

9:31 Baffling Thoughts

At the height of his popularity, as throngs of people were following him, Jesus began to talk about his suffering and death. Such talk baffled his disciples, whose image of a Messiah included no such dark notions. (When reality finally hit, they would all desert him and flee 14:50.) Although Jesus made a point of mentioning his resurrection whenever he talked about his death, the disciples grasped neither concept—until he had died and then come back.

32 But they did not understand *this* statement, and they were afraid to ask Him.

33 ¶ They came to Capernaum; and when He was in the house, He *began* to question them, "What were you discussing on the way?"

34 But they kept silent, for on the way they had discussed with one another which *of them was* the greatest.

35 Sitting down, He called the twelve and *said to them, "If anyone wants to be first, he shall be last of all and servant of all."

36 Taking a child, He set him before them, and taking him in His arms, He said to them,

37 "Whoever receives one child like this in My name receives Me; and whoever receives Me does not receive Me, but Him who sent Me."

Dire Warnings
9:38-40pp — Luke 9:49,50

38 ¶ John said to Him, "Teacher, we saw someone casting out demons in Your name, and we tried to prevent him because he was not following us."

39 But Jesus said, "Do not hinder him, for there is no one who will perform a miracle in My name, and be able soon afterward to speak evil of Me.

40 "For he who is not against us is *b*for us.

41 "For whoever gives you a cup of water to drink because of your name as *followers* of Christ, truly I say to you, he will not lose his reward.

42 ¶ "Whoever causes one of these little ones who believe to stumble, it would be better for him if, with a heavy millstone hung around his neck, he had been cast into the sea.

43 "If your hand causes you to stumble, cut it off; it is better for you to enter life crippled, than, having your two hands, to go into hell, into the unquenchable fire,

44 [*c*where THEIR WORM DOES NOT DIE, AND THE FIRE IS NOT QUENCHED.]

45 "If your foot causes you to stumble, cut it off; it is better for you to enter life lame, than, having your two feet, to be cast into hell,

46 [*d*where THEIR WORM DOES NOT DIE, AND THE FIRE IS NOT QUENCHED.]

47 "If your eye causes you to stumble, throw it out; it is better for you to enter the kingdom of God with one eye, than, having two eyes, to be cast into hell,

48 where THEIR WORM DOES NOT DIE, AND THE FIRE IS NOT QUENCHED.

49 ¶ "For everyone will be salted with fire.

50 "Salt is good; but if the salt becomes unsalty, with what will you make it salty *again*? Have salt in yourselves, and be at peace with one another."

Jesus' Teaching about Divorce
10:1-12pp — Matt 19:1-9

10 Getting up, He *went from there to the region of Judea and beyond the Jordan; crowds *gathered around Him again, and, according to His custom, He once more *began* to teach them.

2 ¶ *Some* Pharisees came up to Jesus, testing Him, and *began* to question Him whether it was lawful for a man to divorce a wife.

3 And He answered and said to them, "What did Moses command you?"

4 They said, "Moses permitted *a man* TO WRITE A CERTIFICATE OF DIVORCE AND SEND *her* AWAY."

5 But Jesus said to them, "Because of your hardness of heart he wrote you this commandment.

---

a Or *betrayed*   *b* Or *on our side*   *c* Vv 44 and 46, which are identical to v 48, are not found in the early mss
d See v 44 note

6 "But from the beginning of creation, *God*
MADE THEM MALE AND FEMALE.

7 "FOR THIS REASON A MAN SHALL LEAVE HIS FA-
THER AND MOTHER,[a]

10:2–12 Teaching on Divorce

*The Pharisees tested Jesus with questions
about common practices of divorce and
remarriage. Jesus responded by pointing back
to the origin of marriage at creation. His
disciples were surprised by his strict views on
divorce, and questioned him further in private.
For other passages on this topic, see Matthew
19:1–12 and 1 Corinthians 7:1–16.*

8 AND THE TWO SHALL BECOME ONE FLESH; so
they are no longer two, but one flesh.

9 "What therefore God has joined together, let
no man separate."

10 ¶ In the house the disciples *began* questioning Him about this again.

11 And He *said to them, "Whoever divorces
his wife and marries another woman commits
adultery against her;

12 and if she herself divorces her husband and
marries another man, she is committing adultery."

Jesus Blesses Little Children

10:13–16pp — Matt 19:13–15; Luke 18:15–17

13 ¶ And they were bringing children to Him
so that He might touch them; but the disciples
rebuked them.

14 But when Jesus saw this, He was indignant
and said to them, "Permit the children to come to
Me; do not hinder them; for the kingdom of God
belongs to such as these.

15 "Truly I say to you, whoever does not receive
the kingdom of God like a child will not enter it
at all."

16 And He took them in His arms and *began*
blessing them, laying His hands on them.

The Rich Young Ruler

10:17–31pp — Matt 19:16–30; Luke 18:18–30

17 ¶ As He was setting out on a journey, a man
ran up to Him and knelt before Him, and asked
Him, "Good Teacher, what shall I do to inherit
eternal life?"

18 And Jesus said to him, "Why do you call Me
good? No one is good except God alone.

19 "You know the commandments, 'DO NOT
MURDER, DO NOT COMMIT ADULTERY, DO NOT
STEAL, DO NOT BEAR FALSE WITNESS, Do not de-
fraud, HONOR YOUR FATHER AND MOTHER.' "

20 And he said to Him, "Teacher, I have kept
all these things from my youth up."

21 Looking at him, Jesus felt a love for him and
said to him, "One thing you lack: go and sell all
you possess and give to the poor, and you will
have treasure in heaven; and come, follow Me."

22 But at these words he was saddened, and he
went away grieving, for he was one who owned
much property.

23 ¶ And Jesus, looking around, *said to His
disciples, "How hard it will be for those who are
wealthy to enter the kingdom of God!"

24 The disciples were amazed at His words.
But Jesus *answered again and *said to them,
"Children, how hard it is to enter the kingdom of
God!

25 "It is easier for a camel to go through the eye
of a needle than for a rich man to enter the kingdom of God."

26 They were even more astonished and said to
Him, "Then who can be saved?"

10:26 The Wealth Barrier

*Religious teachers of that time saw wealth as a
positive sign of God's approval, which explains
the disciples' bewilderment. Jesus contradicted
such ideas by teaching that wealth can actually
be a barrier keeping people out of the kingdom
of God.*

27 Looking at them, Jesus *said, "With people
it is impossible, but not with God; for all things are
possible with God."

28 ¶ Peter began to say to Him, "Behold, we
have left everything and followed You."

29 Jesus said, "Truly I say to you, there is no
one who has left house or brothers or sisters or
mother or father or children or farms, for My sake
and for the gospel's sake,

30 but that he will receive a hundred times as
much now in the present age, houses and brothers
and sisters and mothers and children and farms,
along with persecutions; and in the age to come,
eternal life.

31 "But many *who are* first will be last, and the
last, first."

Jesus' Sufferings Foretold

10:32–34pp — Matt 20:17–19; Luke 18:31–33
10:35–45pp — Matt 20:20–28

32 ¶ They were on the road going up to Jerusalem, and Jesus was walking on ahead of them; and
they were amazed, and those who followed were
fearful. And again He took the twelve aside and
began to tell them what was going to happen to
Him,

33 *saying,* "Behold, we are going up to Jerusalem, and the Son of Man will be [b]delivered to the
chief priests and the scribes; and they will con-

---

[a] Many late mss add *and shall cling to his wife*   [b] Or *betrayed*

your Father who is in heaven forgive your transgressions."]

Jesus' Authority Questioned

11:27–33pp — Matt 21:23–27; Luke 20:1–8

27 ¶ They *came again to Jerusalem. And as He was walking in the temple, the chief priests and the scribes and the elders *came to Him,

28 and *began* saying to Him, "By what authority are You doing these things, or who gave You this authority to do these things?"

29 And Jesus said to them, "I will ask you one question, and you answer Me, and *then* I will tell you by what authority I do these things.

30 "Was the baptism of John from heaven, or from men? Answer Me."

31 They *began* reasoning among themselves, saying, "If we say, 'From heaven,' He will say, 'Then why did you not believe him?'

32 "But shall we say, 'From men'?"—they were afraid of the people, for everyone considered John to have been a real prophet.

33 Answering Jesus, they *said, "We do not know." And Jesus *said to them, "Nor will I tell you by what authority I do these things."

Parable of the Vine-growers

12:1–12pp — Matt 21:33–46; Luke 20:9–19

12 And He began to speak to them in parables: "A man PLANTED A VINEYARD AND PUT A WALL AROUND IT, AND DUG A VAT UNDER THE WINE PRESS AND BUILT A TOWER, and rented it out to ᵃvine-growers and went on a journey.

2 "At the *harvest* time he sent a slave to the vine-growers, in order to receive *some* of the produce of the vineyard from the vine-growers.

3 "They took him, and beat him and sent him away empty-handed.

4 "Again he sent them another slave, and they wounded him in the head, and treated him shamefully.

5 "And he sent another, and that one they killed; and *so with* many others, beating some and killing others.

6 "He had one more *to send,* a beloved son; he sent him last *of all* to them, saying, 'They will respect my son.'

7 "But those vine-growers said to one another, 'This is the heir; come, let us kill him, and the inheritance will be ours!'

8 "They took him, and killed him and threw him out of the vineyard.

9 "What will the owner of the vineyard do? He will come and destroy the vine-growers, and will give the vineyard to others.

10 "Have you not even read this Scripture:
'THE STONE WHICH THE BUILDERS REJECTED,
THIS BECAME THE CHIEF CORNER *stone*;

11 THIS CAME ABOUT FROM THE LORD,
AND IT IS MARVELOUS IN OUR EYES'?"

12 ¶ And they were seeking to seize Him, and *yet* they feared the people, for they understood that He spoke the parable against them. And *so* they left Him and went away.

Jesus Answers the Pharisees, Sadducees and Scribes

12:13–17pp — Matt 22:15–22; Luke 20:20–26
12:18–27pp — Matt 22:23–33; Luke 20:27–38
12:28–34pp — Matt 22:34–40
12:35–37pp — Matt 22:41–46; Luke 20:41–44
12:38–40pp — Matt 23:1–7; Luke 20:45–47

13 ¶ Then they *sent some of the Pharisees and Herodians to Him in order to trap Him in a statement.

12:13 Opposition Heats Up

While in Jerusalem, Jesus was surrounded by hostile groups. Mark 12 records a series of attempts to bait him: by the Pharisees and Sadducees, by the political Herodians, and by the teachers of the law. Each group challenged Jesus with a situation designed to trap him and anger the crowd.

14 They *came and *said to Him, "Teacher, we know that You are truthful and defer to no one; for You are not partial to any, but teach the way of God in truth. Is it lawful to pay a poll-tax to Caesar, or not?

15 "Shall we pay or shall we not pay?" But He, knowing their hypocrisy, said to them, "Why are you testing Me? Bring Me a ᵇdenarius to look at."

16 They brought *one.* And He *said to them, "Whose likeness and inscription is this?" And they said to Him, "Caesar's."

17 And Jesus said to them, "Render to Caesar the things that are Caesar's, and to God the things that are God's." And they were amazed at Him.

18 ¶ *Some* Sadducees (who say that there is no resurrection) *came to Jesus, and *began* questioning Him, saying,

19 "Teacher, Moses wrote for us that IF A MAN'S BROTHER DIES and leaves behind a wife AND LEAVES NO CHILD, HIS BROTHER SHOULD MARRY THE WIFE AND RAISE UP CHILDREN TO HIS BROTHER.

20 "There were seven brothers; and the first took a wife, and died leaving no children.

21 "The second one married her, and died leaving behind no children; and the third likewise;

22 and *so* all seven left no children. Last of all the woman died also.

23 "In the resurrection, ᶜwhen they rise again,

ᵃ Or *tenant farmers,* also vv 2, 7, 9   ᵇ The denarius was a day's wages   ᶜ Early mss do not contain *when they rise again* which one's wife will she be? For all seven had married her."

24 Jesus said to them, "Is this not the reason you are mistaken, that you do not understand the Scriptures or the power of God?

25 "For when they rise from the dead, they neither marry nor are given in marriage, but are like angels in heaven.

26 "But regarding the fact that the dead rise again, have you not read in the book of Moses, in the *passage* about *the burning* bush, how God spoke to him, saying, 'I AM THE GOD OF ABRAHAM, AND THE GOD OF ISAAC, and the God of Jacob'?

27 "He is not the God of the dead, but of the living; you are greatly mistaken."

28 ¶ One of the scribes came and heard them arguing, and recognizing that He had answered them well, asked Him, "What commandment is the foremost of all?"

29 Jesus answered, "The foremost is, 'HEAR, O ISRAEL! THE LORD OUR GOD IS ONE LORD;

30 AND YOU SHALL LOVE THE LORD YOUR GOD WITH ALL YOUR HEART, AND WITH ALL YOUR SOUL, AND WITH ALL YOUR MIND, AND WITH ALL YOUR STRENGTH.'

31 "The second is this, 'YOU SHALL LOVE YOUR NEIGHBOR AS YOURSELF.' There is no other commandment greater than these."

32 The scribe said to Him, "Right, Teacher; You have truly stated that HE IS ONE, AND THERE IS NO ONE ELSE BESIDES HIM;

33 AND TO LOVE HIM WITH ALL THE HEART AND WITH ALL THE UNDERSTANDING AND WITH ALL THE STRENGTH, AND TO LOVE ONE'S NEIGHBOR AS HIMSELF, is much more than all burnt offerings and sacrifices."

34 When Jesus saw that he had answered intelligently, He said to him, "You are not far from the kingdom of God." After that, no one would venture to ask Him any more questions.

35 ¶ And Jesus *began* to say, as He taught in the temple, "How *is it that* the scribes say that the Christ is the son of David?

36 "David himself said in the Holy Spirit,
'THE LORD SAID TO MY LORD,
"SIT AT MY RIGHT HAND,
UNTIL I PUT YOUR ENEMIES BENEATH
YOUR FEET." '

37 "David himself calls Him 'Lord'; so in what sense is He his son?" And the large crowd enjoyed listening to Him.

38 ¶ In His teaching He was saying: "Beware of the scribes who like to walk around in long robes, and *like* respectful greetings in the market places,

39 and chief seats in the synagogues and places of honor at banquets,

40 who devour widows' houses, and for appearance's sake offer long prayers; these will receive greater condemnation."

The Widow's Mite

12:41–44pp — Luke 21:1–4

41 ¶ And He sat down opposite the treasury, and *began* observing how the people were putting money into the treasury; and many rich people were putting in large sums.

42 A poor widow came and put in two small copper coins, which amount to a cent.

12:42 Exploiting Widows

The simple act of faithfulness by an impoverished widow made a stark contrast to others' pompous public displays. Some teachers "devour widows' houses," Jesus had said (verse 40). Teachers of the law lived off the gifts of supporters, and, then as now, the gullible poor made a tempting target.

43 Calling His disciples to Him, He said to them, "Truly I say to you, this poor widow put in more than all the contributors to the treasury;

44 for they all put in out of their surplus, but she, out of her poverty, put in all she owned, all she had to live on."

Things to Come

13:1–37pp — Matt 24:1–51; Luke 21:5–36

13 As He was going out of the temple, one of His disciples *said to Him, "Teacher, behold [a]what wonderful stones and what wonderful buildings!"

2 And Jesus said to him, "Do you see these great buildings? Not one stone will be left upon another which will not be torn down."

3 ¶ As He was sitting on the Mount of Olives opposite the temple, Peter and James and John and Andrew were questioning Him privately,

4 "Tell us, when will these things be, and what *will be* the sign when all these things are going to be fulfilled?"

5 And Jesus began to say to them, "See to it that no one misleads you.

6 "Many will come in My name, saying, 'I am *He!*' and will mislead many.

7 "When you hear of wars and rumors of wars, do not be frightened; *those things* must take place; but *that is* not yet the end.

8 "For nation will rise up against nation, and kingdom against kingdom; there will be earthquakes in various places; there will *also* be famines. These things are *merely* the beginning of birth pangs.

9 ¶ "But be on your guard; for they will deliver you to *the* courts, and you will be flogged in *the* synagogues, and you will stand before governors and kings for My sake, as a testimony to them.

[a] Lit *how great*

10 "The gospel must first be preached to all the nations.

11 "When they arrest you and hand you over, do not worry beforehand about what you are to

13:10 To All Nations

Preaching the gospel to all nations was probably a new thought to the disciples, who still thought in terms of a Messiah for the Jews. But some of them would spend the remainder of their lives making this prophecy come true.

say, but say whatever is given you in that hour; for it is not you who speak, but *it is* the Holy Spirit.

12 "Brother will betray brother to death, and a father *his* child; and children will rise up against parents and have them put to death.

13 "You will be hated by all because of My name, but the one who endures to the end, he will be saved.

14 ¶ "But when you see the ABOMINATION OF DESOLATION standing where it should not be (let the reader understand), then those who are in Judea must flee to the mountains.

15 "The one who is on the housetop must not go down, or go in to get anything out of his house;

16 and the one who is in the field must not turn back to get his coat.

17 "But woe to those who are pregnant and to those who are nursing babies in those days!

18 "But pray that it may not happen in the winter.

19 "For those days will be a *time of* tribulation such as has not occurred since the beginning of the creation which God created until now, and never will.

20 "Unless the Lord had shortened *those* days, no life would have been saved; but for the sake of the elect, whom He chose, He shortened the days.

21 "And then if anyone says to you, 'Behold, here is the Christ'; or, 'Behold, *He is* there'; do not believe *him;*

22 for false Christs and false prophets will arise, and will show signs and wonders, in order to lead astray, if possible, the elect.

23 "But take heed; behold, I have told you everything in advance.

The Return of Christ

24 ¶ "But in those days, after that tribulation, THE SUN WILL BE DARKENED AND THE MOON WILL NOT GIVE ITS LIGHT,

25 AND THE STARS WILL BE FALLING from heaven, and the powers that are in the heavens will be shaken.

26 "Then they will see THE SON OF MAN COMING IN CLOUDS with great power and glory.

27 "And then He will send forth the angels, and will gather together His elect from the four winds, from the farthest end of the earth to the farthest end of heaven.

28 ¶ "Now learn the parable from the fig tree: when its branch has already become tender and puts forth its leaves, you know that summer is near.

29 "Even so, you too, when you see these things happening, recognize that He is near, *right* at the door.

30 "Truly I say to you, this [a]generation will not pass away until all these things take place.

31 "Heaven and earth will pass away, but My words will not pass away.

32 "But of that day or hour no one knows, not even the angels in heaven, nor the Son, but the Father *alone.*

33 ¶ "Take heed, keep on the alert; for you do not know when the *appointed* time will come.

34 *"It is* like a man away on a journey, *who* upon leaving his house and putting his slaves in charge, *assigning* to each one his task, also commanded the doorkeeper to stay on the alert.

35 "Therefore, be on the alert—for you do not know when the master of the house is coming, whether in the evening, at midnight, or when the rooster crows, or in the morning—

36 in case he should come suddenly and find you asleep.

37 "What I say to you I say to all, 'Be on the alert!' "

Death Plot and Anointing

14:1–11pp — Matt 26:2–16
14:1,2,10,11pp — Luke 22:1–6
14:3–8Ref — John 12:1–8

14 Now the Passover and Unleavened Bread were two days away; and the chief priests and the scribes were seeking how to seize Him by stealth and kill *Him;*

14:1 Festival Time in Jerusalem

The Passover, celebrating the Jews' deliverance from Egypt, was one of the high points of the Jewish calendar. All males older than age 12 went to Jerusalem for the holiday. Thus the city was filled with hundreds of thousands of pilgrims at the time of Jesus' death.

2 for they were saying, "Not during the festival, otherwise there might be a riot of the people."

3 ¶ While He was in Bethany at the home of Simon the leper, and reclining *at the table,* there came a woman with an alabaster vial of very costly perfume of pure nard; *and* she broke the vial and poured it over His head.

[a] Or *race*

4 But some were indignantly *remarking* to one another, "Why has this perfume been wasted? 5 "For this perfume might have been sold for over three hundred ªdenarii, and *the money* given to the poor." And they were scolding her.

6 But Jesus said, "Let her alone; why do you bother her? She has done a good deed to Me.

7 "For you always have the poor with you, and whenever you wish you can do good to them; but you do not always have Me.

8 "She has done what she could; she has anointed My body beforehand for the burial.

9 "Truly I say to you, wherever the gospel is preached in the whole world, what this woman has done will also be spoken of in memory of her."

10 ¶ Then Judas Iscariot, who was one of the twelve, went off to the chief priests in order to betray Him to them.

11 They were glad when they heard *this*, and promised to give him money. And he *began* seeking how to betray Him at an opportune time.

The Last Passover

14:12–26pp — Matt 26:17–30; Luke 22:7–23

12 ¶ On the first day of Unleavened Bread, when the Passover *lamb* was being sacrificed, His disciples *said to Him, "Where do You want us to go and prepare for You to eat the Passover?"

13 And He *sent two of His disciples and *said to them, "Go into the city, and a man will meet you carrying a pitcher of water; follow him;

14 and wherever he enters, say to the owner of the house, 'The Teacher says, "Where is My guest room in which I may eat the Passover with My disciples?" '

15 "And he himself will show you a large upper room furnished *and* ready; prepare for us there."

16 The disciples went out and came to the city, and found *it* just as He had told them; and they prepared the Passover.

17 ¶ When it was evening He *came with the twelve.

18 As they were reclining *at the table* and eating, Jesus said, "Truly I say to you that one of you will betray Me—one who is eating with Me."

19 They began to be grieved and to say to Him one by one, "Surely not I?"

20 And He said to them, "*It is* one of the twelve, one who dips with Me in the bowl.

21 "For the Son of Man *is to* go just as it is written of Him; but woe to that man by whom the Son of Man is betrayed! *It would have been* good for that man if he had not been born."

The Lord's Supper

14:22–25pp — 1 Cor 11:23–25
14:27–31pp — Matt 26:31–35

22 ¶ While they were eating, He took *some* bread, and after a blessing He broke *it*, and gave it to them, and said, "Take *it*; this is My body."

23 And when He had taken a cup *and* given thanks, He gave *it* to them, and they all drank from it.

14:22–26 Original Lord's Supper

Virtually all Christian churches celebrate the practice of Communion (Mass, Eucharist, or Lord's Supper) in some form. Matthew, Mark, and Luke each record the original Passover meal when Jesus instituted the practice.

24 And He said to them, "This is My blood of the covenant, which is poured out for many.

25 "Truly I say to you, I will never again drink of the fruit of the vine until that day when I drink it new in the kingdom of God."

26 ¶ After singing a hymn, they went out to the Mount of Olives.

27 ¶ And Jesus *said to them, "You will all fall away, because it is written, 'I WILL STRIKE DOWN THE SHEPHERD, AND THE SHEEP SHALL BE SCATTERED.'

28 "But after I have been raised, I will go ahead of you to Galilee."

29 But Peter said to Him, "*Even* though all may fall away, yet I will not."

30 And Jesus *said to him, "Truly I say to you, that this very night, before a rooster crows twice, you yourself will deny Me three times."

31 But *Peter* kept saying insistently, "*Even* if I have to die with You, I will not deny You!" And they all were saying the same thing also.

Jesus in Gethsemane

14:32–42pp — Matt 26:36–46; Luke 22:40–46

32 ¶ They *came to a place named Gethsemane; and He *said to His disciples, "Sit here until I have prayed."

14:32 Seeking Privacy

Where to pray? The temple was crowded, and synagogues were reserved for public meetings. In order to find some privacy, Jesus would often rise early in the morning or spend all night in prayer. Luke reports that this garden was one of Jesus' favorite places (Luke 22:39).

33 And He *took with Him Peter and James and John, and began to be very distressed and troubled.

34 And He *said to them, "My soul is deeply grieved to the point of death; remain here and keep watch."

ª The denarius was equivalent to a day's wages

35 And He went a little beyond *them,* and fell to the ground and *began* to pray that if it were possible, the hour might pass Him by.

36 And He was saying, "Abba! Father! All things are possible for You; remove this cup from Me; yet not what I will, but what You will."

37 And He *came and *found them sleeping, and *said to Peter, "Simon, are you asleep? Could you not keep watch for one hour?

38 "Keep watching and praying that you may not come into temptation; the spirit is willing, but the flesh is weak."

39 Again He went away and prayed, saying the same words.

40 And again He came and found them sleeping, for their eyes were very heavy; and they did not know what to answer Him.

41 And He *came the third time, and *said to them, "Are you still sleeping and resting? It is enough; the hour has come; behold, the Son of Man is being betrayed into the hands of sinners.

42 "Get up, let us be going; behold, the one who betrays Me is at hand!"

Betrayal and Arrest

14:43–50pp — Matt 26:47–56; Luke 22:47–50; John 18:3–11

43 ¶ Immediately while He was still speaking, Judas, one of the twelve, *came up accompanied by a crowd with swords and clubs, *who were* from the chief priests and the scribes and the elders.

44 Now he who was betraying Him had given them a signal, saying, "Whomever I kiss, He is the one; seize Him and lead Him away under guard."

45 After coming, Judas immediately went to Him, saying, "Rabbi!" and kissed Him.

46 They laid hands on Him and seized Him.

47 But one of those who stood by drew his sword, and struck the slave of the high priest and cut off his ear.

48 And Jesus said to them, "Have you come out with swords and clubs to arrest Me, as *you would* against a robber?

49 "Every day I was with you in the temple teaching, and you did not seize Me; but *this has taken place* to fulfill the Scriptures."

50 And they all left Him and fled.

51 ¶ A young man was following Him, wearing *nothing but* a linen sheet over *his* naked *body*; and they *seized him.

14:51 The Anonymous Author?

Many scholars believe the young man in this verse was none other than Mark himself, author of this Gospel. Often, in ancient days, an author wouldn't use his name, but would plant a clue such as this (see John 21:24).

52 But he pulled free of the linen sheet and escaped naked.

Jesus before His Accusers

14:53–65pp — Matt 26:57–68; John 18:12,13,19–24
14:61–63pp — Luke 22:67–71

53 ¶ They led Jesus away to the high priest; and all the chief priests and the elders and the scribes *gathered together.

54 Peter had followed Him at a distance, right into the courtyard of the high priest; and he was sitting with the officers and warming himself at the fire.

55 Now the chief priests and the whole [a]Council kept trying to obtain testimony against Jesus to put Him to death, and they were not finding any.

56 For many were giving false testimony against Him, but their testimony was not consistent.

57 Some stood up and *began* to give false testimony against Him, saying,

58 "We heard Him say, 'I will destroy this temple made with hands, and in three days I will build another made without hands.' "

59 Not even in this respect was their testimony consistent.

60 The high priest stood up *and came* forward and questioned Jesus, saying, "Do You not answer? What is it that these men are testifying against You?"

61 But He kept silent and did not answer. Again the high priest was questioning Him, and saying to Him, "Are You the Christ, the Son of the Blessed *One?*"

62 And Jesus said, "I am; and you shall see THE SON OF MAN SITTING AT THE RIGHT HAND OF POWER, and COMING WITH THE CLOUDS OF HEAVEN."

63 Tearing his clothes, the high priest *said, "What further need do we have of witnesses?

64 "You have heard the blasphemy; how does it seem to you?" And they all condemned Him to be deserving of death.

65 Some began to spit at Him, and to blindfold Him, and to beat Him with their fists, and to say to Him, "Prophesy!" And the officers received Him with slaps *in the face.*

Peter's Denials

14:66–72pp — Matt 26:69–75; Luke 22:56–62; John 18:16–18,25–27

66 ¶ As Peter was below in the courtyard, one of the servant-girls of the high priest *came,

67 and seeing Peter warming himself, she looked at him and *said, "You also were with Jesus the Nazarene."

68 But he denied *it,* saying, "I neither know nor understand what you are talking about."

a Or *Sanhedrin*

And he went out onto the porch, and a rooster crowed.[a]

69 The servant-girl saw him, and began once more to say to the bystanders, "This is one of them!"

70 But again he denied it. And after a little while the bystanders were again saying to Peter, "Surely you are one of them, for you are a Galilean too."

71 But he began to curse and swear, "I do not know this man you are talking about!"

---

[a] Later mss add and a rooster crowed

72 Immediately a rooster crowed a second time. And Peter remembered how Jesus had made the remark to him, "Before a rooster crows twice, you will deny Me three times." And he began to weep.

Jesus before Pilate

15:2–15pp — Matt 27:11–26; Luke 23:2,3,18–25; John 18:29–19:16

15 Early in the morning the chief priests with the elders and scribes and the whole

The Day of Execution
The disciples were totally unprepared

EVENTS IN JESUS' LIFE—THE BIRTH in a manger, the death on a cross—can become so familiar that we miss the point. They're too close to us. In thinking about them, it sometimes helps to let the mind wander and search out whole new images.

A Bible study group was asked to suggest word images that might apply to Jesus. Common ones surfaced first: a shepherd, a lamb, a door. Then out of nowhere came a wildly different metaphor: "fireworks in reverse." Everyone turned, puzzled, to the middle-aged woman who had spoken.

"Think about it," she said. "Fireworks explode with brilliant, dazzling colors and loud noises ... yet they start out in an ordinary-looking paper package. When God became a man, the opposite happened. The Creator of everything in the universe confined himself to an unimpressive human package."

> When the centurion, who was standing right in front of Him, saw the way He breathed His last, he said, "Truly this man was the Son of God!" 15:39

When the Impossible Happened

No event in the life of Jesus fits the woman's metaphor better than his execution in Jerusalem. The idea was inconceivable, even to Jesus' closest followers. The Son of God die? How could this be?

Could the Creator of all things succumb to his creation? Disciples who had slogged through every other confrontation by his side now forsook him. It made no sense for Jesus, the Messiah, to die.

Not until later would other thoughts click into place: memories of Old Testament customs that hauntingly pointed to a cross, prophecies of a Messiah who was King but also a Suffering Servant (see Isaiah 53). To die was, after all, the central reason Jesus came to earth; he had insisted on that from the beginning.

The Most Important Week

Jesus' last week so impressed the disciples that the four chroniclers of his life, including Mark, devoted one-third of their space to that final week in Jerusalem. By the time they wrote it down, of course, they could see his death in a new light: as a mournful prelude to the greatest miracle of all, his resurrection.

Even so, nothing could erase the impact of those fear-filled, final days. When the eerie darkness had lifted and Jesus had breathed his last, the disciples had learned something profound about God, and about love.

Dorothy Sayers put it this way: "Whatever game He is playing with His creation, He has kept His own rules and played fair. He can exact nothing from man that He has not exacted from Himself. He has Himself gone through the whole of human experience, from the trivial irritations of family life and the cramping restriction of hard work and lack of money to the worst horrors of pain and humiliation, defeat, despair, and death. When He was a man, He played the man. He was born in poverty and died in disgrace and thought it well worthwhile" (from Christian Letters to a Post-Christian World).

At no other point in history did the fireworks appear so powerless as the day Jesus died. They had not yet been lit.

Life Questions: Put yourself in the disciples' place. How would you have responded to news of Jesus' death? Would you have believed in him still?

aCouncil, immediately held a consultation; and binding Jesus, they led Him away and delivered Him to Pilate.

2 Pilate questioned Him, "Are You the King

15:1 Appeal for a Death Penalty

Roman law granted the Jews many freedoms, including the right to their Jewish court system, a council called the Sanhedrin. However, the Sanhedrin had no authority to order the death penalty. Seeking that sentence, Jesus' opponents sent him to Pilate, the Roman governor.

of the Jews?" And He *answered him, "It is *as* you say."

3 The chief priests *began* to accuse Him harshly.

4 Then Pilate questioned Him again, saying, "Do You not answer? See how many charges they bring against You!"

5 But Jesus made no further answer; so Pilate was amazed.

6 ¶ Now at *the* feast he used to release for them *any* one prisoner whom they requested.

7 The man named Barabbas had been imprisoned with the insurrectionists who had committed murder in the insurrection.

8 The crowd went up and began asking him *to do* as he had been accustomed to do for them.

9 Pilate answered them, saying, "Do you want me to release for you the King of the Jews?"

10 For he was aware that the chief priests had handed Him over because of envy.

11 But the chief priests stirred up the crowd *to ask* him to release Barabbas for them instead.

12 Answering again, Pilate said to them, "Then what shall I do with Him whom you call the King of the Jews?"

13 They shouted back, "Crucify Him!"

14 But Pilate said to them, "Why, what evil has He done?" But they shouted all the more, "Crucify Him!"

15 Wishing to satisfy the crowd, Pilate released Barabbas for them, and after having Jesus scourged, he handed Him over to be crucified.

Jesus Is Mocked

15:16–20pp — Matt 27:27–31

16 ¶ The soldiers took Him away into the palace (that is, the Praetorium), and they *called together the whole Roman bcohort.

17 They *dressed Him up in purple, and after twisting a crown of thorns, they put it on Him;

18 and they began to acclaim Him, "Hail, King of the Jews!"

19 They kept beating His head with a creed, and spitting on Him, and kneeling and bowing before Him.

20 After they had mocked Him, they took the purple robe off Him and put His *own* garments on Him. And they *led Him out to crucify Him.

21 ¶ They *pressed into service a passer-by coming from the country, Simon of Cyrene (the father of Alexander and Rufus), to bear His cross.

The Crucifixion

15:22–32pp — Matt 27:33–44; Luke 23:33–43; John 19:17–24
15:33–41pp — Matt 27:45–56; Luke 23:44–49; John 19:29,30

22 ¶ Then they *brought Him to the place Golgotha, which is translated, Place of a Skull.

23 They tried to give Him wine mixed with myrrh; but He did not take it.

24 And they *crucified Him, and *divided up His garments among themselves, casting lots for them *to decide* what each man should take.

25 It was the dthird hour when they crucified Him.

15:25 Death Without Dignity

Romans reserved their cruelest form of execution—crucifixion—for slaves and the worst criminals. Skeletons of crucifixion victims show that thick nails were pounded through the wrist and heel bones. Death (from asphyxiation) usually took many hours or even several days.

26 The inscription of the charge against Him read, "THE KING OF THE JEWS."

27 ¶ They *crucified two robbers with Him, one on His right and one on His left.

28 [eAnd the Scripture was fulfilled which says, "And He was numbered with transgressors."]

29 Those passing by were hurling abuse at Him, wagging their heads, and saying, "Ha! You who *are going to* destroy the temple and rebuild it in three days,

30 save Yourself, and come down from the cross!"

31 In the same way the chief priests also, along with the scribes, were mocking *Him* among themselves and saying, "He saved others; He cannot save Himself.

32 "Let *this* Christ, the King of Israel, now come down from the cross, so that we may see and believe!" Those who were crucified with Him were also insulting Him.

---

a Or *Sanhedrin*   b Or *battalion*   c Or *staff* (made of a reed)   d I.e. 9 a.m.   e Early mss do not contain this v

33 ¶ When the [a]sixth hour came, darkness fell over the whole land until the [b]ninth hour.

34 At the ninth hour Jesus cried out with a loud voice, "ELOI, ELOI, LAMA SABACHTHANI?" which is translated, "MY GOD, MY GOD, WHY HAVE YOU FORSAKEN ME?"

35 When some of the bystanders heard it, they *began* saying, "Behold, He is calling for Elijah."

36 Someone ran and filled a sponge with sour wine, put it on a reed, and gave Him a drink, saying, "Let us see whether Elijah will come to take Him down."

37 And Jesus uttered a loud cry, and breathed His last.

38 And the veil of the temple was torn in two from top to bottom.

39 When the centurion, who was standing right in front of Him, saw the way He breathed His last, he said, "Truly this man was the Son of God!"

40 ¶ There were also *some* women looking on from a distance, among whom *were* Mary Magdalene, and Mary the mother of James the Less and Joses, and Salome.

41 When He was in Galilee, they used to follow Him and minister to Him; and *there were* many other women who came up with Him to Jerusalem.

Jesus Is Buried

15:42–47pp — Matt 27:57–61; Luke 23:50–56; John 19:38–42

42 ¶ When evening had already come, because it was the preparation day, that is, the day before the Sabbath,

43 Joseph of Arimathea came, a prominent member of the Council, who himself was waiting for the kingdom of God; and he gathered up courage and went in before Pilate, and asked for the body of Jesus.

44 Pilate wondered if He was dead by this time, and summoning the centurion, he questioned him as to whether He was already dead.

45 And ascertaining this from the centurion, he granted the body to Joseph.

46 Joseph bought a linen cloth, took Him down, wrapped Him in the linen cloth and laid Him in a tomb which had been hewn out in the rock; and he rolled a stone against the entrance of the tomb.

47 Mary Magdalene and Mary the *mother* of Joses were looking on *to see* where He was laid.

The Resurrection

16:1–8pp — Matt 28:1–8; Luke 24:1–10

16 When the Sabbath was over, Mary Magdalene, and Mary the *mother* of James, and Salome, bought spices, so that they might come and anoint Him.

2 Very early on the first day of the week, they *came to the tomb when the sun had risen.

3 They were saying to one another, "Who will roll away the stone for us from the entrance of the tomb?"

16:1 A Late Anointing

Jewish rules forbade handling dead bodies during the Sabbath. Because Jesus died during the Sabbath celebration, his friends and relatives couldn't properly embalm and prepare his body. They returned to the tomb later for this purpose, only to find the greatest surprise of their lives.

4 Looking up, they *saw that the stone had been rolled away, although it was extremely large.

5 Entering the tomb, they saw a young man sitting at the right, wearing a white robe; and they were amazed.

6 And he *said to them, "Do not be amazed; you are looking for Jesus the Nazarene, who has been crucified. He has risen; He is not here; behold, *here is* the place where they laid Him.

7 "But go, tell His disciples and Peter, 'He is going ahead of you to Galilee; there you will see Him, just as He told you.' "

16:7 . . . and Peter

The messenger who informed the women about Jesus' resurrection pointedly asked them to tell "His disciples and Peter," singling out the disciple who had vehemently denied Jesus. John 21 records a further, moving scene in which Jesus specifically reinstated Peter.

8 They went out and fled from the tomb, for trembling and astonishment had gripped them; and they said nothing to anyone, for they were afraid.

9 ¶ [[c]Now after He had risen early on the first day of the week, He first appeared to Mary Magdalene, from whom He had cast out seven demons.

10 She went and reported to those who had been with Him, while they were mourning and weeping.

11 When they heard that He was alive and had been seen by her, they refused to believe it.

12 ¶ After that, He appeared in a different form to two of them while they were walking along on their way to the country.

13 They went away and reported it to the others, but they did not believe them either.

The Disciples Commissioned

14 ¶ Afterward He appeared to the eleven themselves as they were reclining *at the table*; and He reproached them for their unbelief and hardness of heart, because they had not believed those who had seen Him after He had risen.

15 And He said to them, "Go into all the world and preach the gospel to all creation.

16 "He who has believed and has been baptized shall be saved; but he who has disbelieved shall be condemned.

17 "These signs will accompany those who have believed: in My name they will cast out demons, they will speak with new tongues;

18 they will pick up serpents, and if they drink any deadly *poison*, it will not hurt them; they will lay hands on the sick, and they will recover."

19 ¶ So then, when the Lord Jesus had spoken to them, He was received up into heaven and sat down at the right hand of God.

20 And they went out and preached everywhere, while the Lord worked with them, and confirmed the word by the signs that followed.]

¶ [*a*And they promptly reported all these instructions to Peter and his companions. And after that, Jesus Himself sent out through them from east to west the sacred and imperishable proclamation of eternal salvation.]

---

a A few late mss and versions contain this paragraph, usually after v 8; a few have it at the end of ch

LUKE

Like a Joy-filled Musical
Something was brewing on planet Earth

> *But the angel said to them, "Do not be afraid; for behold, I bring you good news of great joy which will be for all the people." 2:10*

ALTHOUGH LUKE COVERS THE SAME basic territory as Matthew and Mark, he gives away his own slant in the very first chapters. Matthew begins with a formal family genealogy; Mark opens with a bleached desert scene. In contrast, Luke describes a hearty celebration.

The way Luke tells it, events surrounding Jesus' birth resembled a joy-filled musical. Characters crowded into the scene: a white-haired great-uncle, an astonished virgin, a tottery old prophetess. They all smiled broadly and, as likely as not, burst into song.

Once Mary had recovered from the shock of seeing an angel, she let loose with a beautiful hymn. The old priest Zacharias broke nine months of muteness with a rousing poem, and even the unborn John the Baptist kicked for joy inside his mother's womb (1:44). When Jesus finally made an entrance, in an inconspicuous stable, the sky filled with singing angels. Clearly, something was brewing on planet Earth.

History Split in Two

You get the feeling when you read his account that Luke wanted to capture in words the spirit of "great joy" that the angel predicted (2:10). Among dreary, defeated villagers in a remote corner of the Roman empire, something climactically good was bursting out.

The author tells us (1:1–4) that he researched many accounts of Jesus' life. Intimate details in these first two chapters show he relied heavily on eyewitnesses, for no other Gospel writer picked up so many facts. Careful attention to detail and an undergirding tone of joy characterize Luke's book.

Jesus' birth literally split history into two parts; we memorialize the event whenever we write a date. The book of Luke takes us back to the world before there was an A.D. or B.C., when Jesus' life was just beginning.

Even now, approximately 2,000 years later, the commemoration of Jesus' birth still gives cause for joy. We eat better during the Christmas season, buy gifts for others, donate to charity, and sing more often. Our feelings of celebration are gentle aftershocks, reminders of the remarkable moment when God became a man and lived on earth.

How to Read Luke

Luke probably did not know Jesus personally. But as a dedicated convert in the early church, he accompanied the apostle Paul on missionary trips. In three of his letters, Paul refers to Luke with great affection.

As he mentions in his introduction, Luke eventually saw the need to draw up a carefully researched account of the life of Christ. Many accounts of varying quality existed then, but Luke set out to interview eyewitnesses and compose a thoughtful summary. His book shows thoroughness and detail. It starts before Jesus' birth, and ends with his ascension into heaven.

You should find Luke a very appealing book to read. Luke was a gifted writer, and the stories he recorded have won their place among the classics of literature: the Good Samaritan, the Prodigal Son, the Rich Man and Lazarus. If Mark is a Gospel of action, Luke is a Gospel of relationships. It contains very good character descriptions.

Look for the many different ethnic, religious, economic, and social groups in Luke. Think of the diverse groups in a country like the United States today. How do you think each of them would respond to Jesus in the flesh?

Note especially two large sections of Luke that present material found nowhere else: chapters 1–2 and chapters 10–19.

Many passages in the Gospels are parallel, dealing with the same event. Nearly identical passages are noted at the section heading with "pp," while similar passages are noted with "Ref."

PEOPLE YOU'LL MEET IN LUKE

ELIZABETH AND ZACHARIAS *(p. 1102)*
MARY, MOTHER OF JESUS *(p. 1104)*
MARTHA AND MARY OF BETHANY *(p. 1120)*

3-TRACK READING PLAN

For an explanation and complete listing of the 3-track reading plan, turn to page 7.

TRACK 1:　***Two-Week Courses on the Bible***
The Track 1 reading program on the Life and Teachings of Jesus includes four chapters from Luke. See page 7 for a complete listing of this course.

TRACK 2:　***An Overview of Luke in 8 Days***
Over the next eight days, read from the material that's found in no other Gospel but Luke's.

　☐ Day 1. Read the Introduction to Luke and then Luke's account in chapter 1 of the events preceding Jesus' birth.
　☐ Day 2. Read the familiar Christmas passage, chapter 2.
　☐ Day 3. Read chapter 10, which includes the parable of the Good Samaritan.
　☐ Day 4. Read chapter 12, in which Jesus draws a strong contrast between those who trust him, no matter how poor, and haughty rich people.
　☐ Day 5. Read the famous parables, or short stories, that Jesus tells in chapter 15.
　☐ Day 6. Read chapter 16's two familiar stories: the shrewd manager and the rich man and Lazarus.
　☐ Day 7. Read chapter 18.
　☐ Day 8. How did Jesus' disciples react to his resurrection? Read a good description in chapter 24.

Now turn to page 9 for your next Track 2 reading project.

TRACK 3:　***All of Luke in 24 Days***
After you have read through Luke, turn to pages 10–14 for your next Track 3 reading project.

☐1　　☐2　　☐3　　☐4　　☐5　　☐6　　☐7　　☐8
☐9　　☐10　☐11　☐12　☐13　☐14　☐15　☐16
☐17　☐18　☐19　☐20　☐21　☐22　☐23　☐24

Introduction

1:1–4Ref — Acts 1:1

1 Inasmuch as many have undertaken to compile an account of the things accomplished among us,

2 just as they were handed down to us by those who from the beginning were eyewitnesses and servants of the [a]word,

3 it seemed fitting for me as well, having in-vestigated everything carefully from the beginning, to write *it* out for you in consecutive order, most excellent Theophilus;

4 so that you may know the exact truth about the things you have been taught.

Birth of John the Baptist Foretold

5 ¶ In the days of Herod, king of Judea, there was a priest named Zacharias, of the division of

[a] I.e. gospel

^aAbijah; and he had a wife ^bfrom the daughters of Aaron, and her name was Elizabeth.

6 They were both righteous in the sight of God, walking blamelessly in all the commandments and requirements of the Lord.

1:3 Luke the Historian

A historian looks for original sources of information—people who were personally involved in the events being described. Luke doesn't claim to be an eyewitness himself, but he had carefully interviewed many who were. As the apostle Paul's traveling companion, Luke must have met many such sources. The Gospel of Luke is the first of a two-part work; the book of Acts continues the story.

7 But they had no child, because Elizabeth was barren, and they were both advanced in years.

8 ¶ Now it happened *that* while he was performing his priestly service before God in the *appointed* order of his division,

9 according to the custom of the priestly office, he was chosen by lot to enter the temple of the Lord and burn incense.

10 And the whole multitude of the people were in prayer outside at the hour of the incense offering.

11 And an angel of the Lord appeared to him, standing to the right of the altar of incense.

12 Zacharias was troubled when he saw *the angel,* and fear gripped him.

13 But the angel said to him, "Do not be afraid, Zacharias, for your petition has been heard, and your wife Elizabeth will bear you a son, and you will give him the name John.

14 "You will have joy and gladness, and many will rejoice at his birth.

15 "For he will be great in the sight of the Lord; and he will drink no wine or liquor, and he will be filled with the Holy Spirit while yet in his mother's womb.

16 "And he will turn many of the sons of Israel back to the Lord their God.

17 "It is he who will go *as a forerunner* before Him in the spirit and power of Elijah, TO TURN THE HEARTS OF THE FATHERS BACK TO THE CHILDREN, and the disobedient to the attitude of the righteous, so as to make ready a people prepared for the Lord."

18 ¶ Zacharias said to the angel, "How will I know this *for certain*? For I am an old man and my wife is advanced in years."

19 The angel answered and said to him, "I am Gabriel, who stands in the presence of God, and I have been sent to speak to you and to bring you this good news.

20 "And behold, you shall be silent and unable to speak until the day when these things take place, because you did not believe my words, which will be fulfilled in their proper time."

21 ¶ The people were waiting for Zacharias, and were wondering at his delay in the temple.

^a Gr *Abia*   ^b I.e. of priestly descent

ELIZABETH AND ZACHARIAS *End of an Era*

"THE END OF AN ERA," people say when a retiring coach hands over his clipboard to a young assistant. Similarly, when a new president, a new pastor or a new principal moves in, one era ends and another begins. As fresh faces take over, new ways surely follow.

Elizabeth and Zacharias were among the very first to sense the change that came with Jesus. Devout believers from priestly families, they represented the best of the old order. They had devoted many years to serving God under the Old Testament law. Yet a cloud of sadness hung over their lives, for they were growing old and the greatest blessing they could imagine had been denied them. Childless, they knew their line would die out when they passed away.

Then the new era abruptly broke in. One day as Zacharias was performing his duties in the temple, an angel brought some astounding news: He would have a son! Zacharias, long past the age of parenthood, asked for proof and got perhaps more than he bargained for (1:20).

A short while later a relative of Elizabeth's named Mary brought even greater news. The Messiah, the Savior the Jews had been longing for, was on the way! Not only had God answered Elizabeth's and Zacharias's personal prayers, their nation's long waiting would soon come to an end as well.

Soon the old priest Zacharias and his elderly wife Elizabeth were bringing up the young and vigorous John the Baptist, a true original who would prepare the way for Jesus. With unusual foresight, the old couple greeted the new era with joy. In it they saw not the loss of their old order, but the fulfillment of their dreams.

Life Questions: Think of a time in your life when an "old era" ended and something quite new began: a move, a marriage, a new job or perhaps an experience with God. What made the change difficult? What made it joyful? How was God involved?

22 But when he came out, he was unable to speak to them; and they realized that he had seen a vision in the temple; and he kept making signs to them, and remained mute.

23 When the days of his priestly service were ended, he went back home.

24 ¶ After these days Elizabeth his wife became pregnant, and she kept herself in seclusion for five months, saying,

25 "This is the way the Lord has dealt with me in the days when He looked *with favor* upon *me,* to take away my disgrace among men."

Jesus' Birth Foretold

26 ¶ Now in the sixth month the angel Gabriel was sent from God to a city in Galilee called Nazareth,

27 to a virgin engaged to a man whose name was Joseph, of the descendants of David; and the virgin's name was Mary.

28 And coming in, he said to her, "Greetings, favored one! The Lord *is* with you."

29 But she was very perplexed at *this* statement, and kept pondering what kind of salutation this was.

30 The angel said to her, "Do not be afraid, Mary; for you have found favor with God.

31 "And behold, you will conceive in your womb and bear a son, and you shall name Him Jesus.

32 "He will be great and will be called the Son of the Most High; and the Lord God will give Him the throne of His father David;

33 and He will reign over the house of Jacob forever, and His kingdom will have no end."

34 Mary said to the angel, "How can this be, since I am a virgin?"

35 The angel answered and said to her, "The Holy Spirit will come upon you, and the power of the Most High will overshadow you; and for that reason the holy Child shall be called the Son of God.

36 "And behold, even your relative Elizabeth has also conceived a son in her old age; and she who was called barren is now in her sixth month.

37 "For nothing will be impossible with God."

38 And Mary said, "Behold, the *a*bondslave of the Lord; may it be done to me according to your word." And the angel departed from her.

Mary Visits Elizabeth

39 ¶ Now at this time Mary arose and went in a hurry to the hill country, to a city of Judah,

40 and entered the house of Zacharias and greeted Elizabeth.

41 When Elizabeth heard Mary's greeting, the baby leaped in her womb; and Elizabeth was filled with the Holy Spirit.

42 And she cried out with a loud voice and

said, "Blessed *are* you among women, and blessed *is* the fruit of your womb!

43 "And how has it *happened* to me, that the mother of my Lord would come to me?

44 "For behold, when the sound of your greeting reached my ears, the baby leaped in my womb for joy.

45 "And blessed *is* she who believed that there would be a fulfillment of what had been spoken to her by the Lord."

The Magnificat

1:46–53pp — 1 Sam 2:1–10

46 ¶ And Mary said:
"My soul exalts the Lord,
47 And my spirit has rejoiced in God my Savior.
48 "For He has had regard for the humble state of His bondslave;
For behold, from this time on all generations will count me blessed.
49 "For the Mighty One has done great things for me;
And holy is His name.
50 "AND HIS MERCY IS UPON GENERATION AFTER GENERATION
TOWARD THOSE WHO FEAR HIM.
51 "He has done mighty deeds with His arm;
He has scattered *those who were* proud in the thoughts of their heart.
52 "He has brought down rulers from *their* thrones,
And has exalted those who were humble.
53 "HE HAS FILLED THE HUNGRY WITH GOOD THINGS;
And sent away the rich empty-handed.
54 "He has given help to Israel His servant,
In remembrance of His mercy,
55 As He spoke to our fathers,
To Abraham and his descendants forever."

56 ¶ And Mary stayed with her about three months, and *then* returned to her home.

John Is Born

57 ¶ Now the time had come for Elizabeth to give birth, and she gave birth to a son.

58 Her neighbors and her relatives heard that the Lord had displayed His great mercy toward her; and they were rejoicing with her.

59 ¶ And it happened that on the eighth day they came to circumcise the child, and they were going to call him Zacharias, after his father.

60 But his mother answered and said, "No indeed; but he shall be called John."

61 And they said to her, "There is no one among your relatives who is called by that name."

62 And they made signs to his father, as to what he wanted him called.

a I.e. female slave

63 And he asked for a tablet and wrote as follows, "His name is John." And they were all astonished.

64 And at once his mouth was opened and his tongue *loosed*, and he *began* to speak in praise of God.

65 Fear came on all those living around them; and all these matters were being talked about in all the hill country of Judea.

66 All who heard them kept them in mind, saying, "What then will this child *turn out to* be?" For the hand of the Lord was certainly with him.

Zacharias's Prophecy

67 ¶ And his father Zacharias was filled with the Holy Spirit, and prophesied, saying:

68 "Blessed *be* the Lord God of Israel,
     For He has visited us and accomplished
          redemption for His people,

69 And has raised up a horn of salvation
          for us
     In the house of David His servant—

70 As He spoke by the mouth of His holy
          prophets from of old—

71 Salvation FROM OUR ENEMIES,
     And FROM THE HAND OF ALL WHO
          HATE US;

72 To show mercy toward our fathers,
     And to remember His holy covenant,

73 The oath which He swore to Abraham
          our father,

74 To grant us that we, being rescued from
          the hand of our enemies,
     Might serve Him without fear,

75 In holiness and righteousness before Him
          all our days.

76 "And you, child, will be called the prophet
          of the Most High;

---

a I.e. the Roman empire   *b* Gr *Kyrenios*

For you will go on BEFORE THE LORD TO
     PREPARE HIS WAYS;

77 To give to His people *the* knowledge of
          salvation
     By the forgiveness of their sins,

78 Because of the tender mercy of our God,
     With which the Sunrise from on high
          will visit us,

79 TO SHINE UPON THOSE WHO SIT IN
          DARKNESS AND THE SHADOW OF
          DEATH,
     To guide our feet into the way of peace."

80 ¶ And the child continued to grow and to become strong in spirit, and he lived in the deserts until the day of his public appearance to Israel.

Jesus' Birth in Bethlehem

2 Now in those days a decree went out from Caesar Augustus, that a census be taken of all *a*the inhabited earth.

2 This was the first census taken while *b*Quirinius was governor of Syria.

2:1 Dating by Emperors

Among Biblical writers, only Luke dated the events he wrote about by referring to Roman emperors. He had determined (1:1–4) to write a thorough, factual account of Jesus' life, which included setting the events in historical context. Because of the Roman census mentioned here, Mary had to travel from her hometown in a very advanced state of pregnancy. As a result, the Messiah was born in Bethlehem, fulfilling an ancient prophecy.

MARY, MOTHER OF JESUS *Saying Yes to God*

MARY RECEIVED THE GREATEST HONOR God can pay: He chose her to mother his son. Probably a teenager at the time, Mary had done nothing to deserve such favor. Yet her simple response spoke deeply of her humble faith. "Behold, the bondslave of the Lord; may it be done to me according to your word" (Luke 1:38). Without hesitation, Mary said yes to God's plan to take over her life.

Saying yes to God usually involves sacrifice. It did for Mary, who endured the doubts of her fiancé and the scorn of neighbors who saw her pregnant before marriage. Saying yes meant bearing the pain of childbirth. It meant fleeing to far-off Egypt to protect her baby from Herod's soldiers. It meant raising a child she did not completely understand. (Once during his ministry she came to take charge of Jesus, thinking him out of his mind [Mark 3:21].) Most of all, it meant watching her son die on the cross.

Our last glimpse of Mary, though, shows her among the disciples after the resurrection, praying for the Holy Spirit Jesus had promised (Acts 1:14). Mary had begun her relationship with Jesus by holding his tiny form in her arms. In the end she realized she must let Jesus hold her. He was not only her child, he was her Lord. To that, too, Mary said yes.

Life Questions: To what is God asking you to say yes? What sacrifice may be involved?

3 And everyone was on his way to register for the census, each to his own city.

4 Joseph also went up from Galilee, from the city of Nazareth, to Judea, to the city of David which is called Bethlehem, because he was of the house and family of David,

5 in order to register along with Mary, who was engaged to him, and was with child.

6 While they were there, the days were completed for her to give birth.

7 And she gave birth to her firstborn son; and she wrapped Him in cloths, and laid Him in a manger, because there was no room for them in the inn.

8 ¶ In the same region there were *some* shepherds staying out in the fields and keeping watch over their flock by night.

9 And an angel of the Lord suddenly stood before them, and the glory of the Lord shone around them; and they were terribly frightened.

10 But the angel said to them, "Do not be afraid; for behold, I bring you good news of great joy which will be for all the people;

11 for today in the city of David there has been born for you a Savior, who is *a*Christ the Lord.

12 "This *will be* a sign for you: you will find a baby wrapped in cloths and lying in a manger."

13 And suddenly there appeared with the angel a multitude of the heavenly host praising God and saying,

14 "Glory to God in the highest,
And on earth peace among men *b*with
whom He is pleased."

15 ¶ When the angels had gone away from them into heaven, the shepherds *began* saying to one another, "Let us go straight to Bethlehem then, and see this thing that has happened which the Lord has made known to us."

16 So they came in a hurry and found their way to Mary and Joseph, and the baby as He lay in the manger.

17 When they had seen this, they made known the statement which had been told them about this Child.

18 And all who heard it wondered at the things which were told them by the shepherds.

19 But Mary treasured all these things, pondering them in her heart.

20 The shepherds went back, glorifying and praising God for all that they had heard and seen, just as had been told them.

Jesus Presented at the Temple

21 ¶ And when eight days had passed, before His circumcision, His name was *then* called Jesus, the name given by the angel before He was conceived in the womb.

22 ¶ And when the days for their purification according to the law of Moses were completed, they brought Him up to Jerusalem to present Him to the Lord

23 (as it is written in the Law of the Lord, "EVERY *firstborn* MALE THAT OPENS THE WOMB SHALL BE CALLED HOLY TO THE LORD"),

24 and to offer a sacrifice according to what was said in the Law of the Lord, "A PAIR OF TURTLEDOVES OR TWO YOUNG PIGEONS."

25 ¶ And there was a man in Jerusalem whose name was Simeon; and this man was righteous and devout, looking for the consolation of Israel; and the Holy Spirit was upon him.

26 And it had been revealed to him by the Holy Spirit that he would not see death before he had seen the Lord's Christ.

27 And he came in the Spirit into the temple; and when the parents brought in the child Jesus, to carry out for Him the custom of the Law,

28 then he took Him into his arms, and blessed God, and said,

29 "Now Lord, You are releasing Your
bond-servant to depart in peace,
According to Your word;

30 For my eyes have seen Your salvation,

31 Which You have prepared in the
presence of all peoples,

32 A LIGHT OF REVELATION TO THE GENTILES,
And the glory of Your people Israel."

33 ¶ And His father and mother were amazed at the things which were being said about Him.

34 And Simeon blessed them and said to Mary His mother, "Behold, this *Child* is appointed for the fall and rise of many in Israel, and for a sign to be opposed—

35 and a sword will pierce even your own soul—to the end that thoughts from many hearts may be revealed."

36 ¶ And there was a prophetess, Anna the daughter of Phanuel, of the tribe of Asher. She was advanced in years and had lived with *her* husband seven years after her marriage,

37 and then as a widow to the age of eighty-

2:16 Cast of Characters

If a public relations firm planned the introduction of God's Son on earth, whom would they invite? Certainly not the group Luke introduces. No Roman emperor or Greek philosopher attended. Instead, Luke tells of an obscure priest and his wife, a carpenter and his young fiancée, a group of shepherds, and two elderly people. Jesus never had much to do with the high and mighty, except during his trial and execution. He would change the world through the lives of ordinary people.

a I.e. Messiah   *b* Lit *of good pleasure*; or *of good will* four. She never left the temple, serving night and day with fastings and prayers.

38 At that very moment she came up and *began* giving thanks to God, and continued to speak of Him to all those who were looking for the redemption of Jerusalem.

Return to Nazareth

39 ¶ When they had performed everything according to the Law of the Lord, they returned to Galilee, to their own city of Nazareth.

40 The Child continued to grow and become strong, increasing in wisdom; and the grace of God was upon Him.

Visit to Jerusalem

41 ¶ Now His parents went to Jerusalem every year at the Feast of the Passover.

2:41 Jesus' Childhood

Most Christmas pageants rely heavily on Luke because of his thoroughness in reporting the facts of Jesus' birth. And only Luke recorded the brief glimpses of Jesus' early years given in this chapter. For this reason, many scholars believe Luke must have interviewed Mary, mother of Jesus, during his investigations into Jesus' life.

42 And when He became twelve, they went up *there* according to the custom of the Feast;

43 and as they were returning, after spending the full number of days, the boy Jesus stayed behind in Jerusalem. But His parents were unaware of it,

44 but supposed Him to be in the caravan, and went a day's journey; and they *began* looking for Him among their relatives and acquaintances.

45 When they did not find Him, they returned to Jerusalem looking for Him.

46 Then, after three days they found Him in the temple, sitting in the midst of the teachers, both listening to them and asking them questions.

47 And all who heard Him were amazed at His understanding and His answers.

48 When they saw Him, they were astonished; and His mother said to Him, "Son, why have You treated us this way? Behold, Your father and I have been anxiously looking for You."

49 And He said to them, "Why is it that you were looking for Me? Did you not know that I had to be in My Father's *house?*"

50 But they did not understand the statement which He had made to them.

51 And He went down with them and came to Nazareth, and He continued in subjection to them; and His mother treasured all *these* things in her heart.

52 ¶ And Jesus kept increasing in wisdom and stature, and in favor with God and men.

John the Baptist Preaches

3:2–10pp — Matt 3:1–10; Mark 1:3–5
3:16,17pp — Matt 3:11,12; Mark 1:7,8

3 Now in the fifteenth year of the reign of Tiberius Caesar, when Pontius Pilate was governor of Judea, and Herod was tetrarch of Galilee, and his brother Philip was tetrarch of the region of Ituraea and Trachonitis, and Lysanias was tetrarch of Abilene,

2 in the high priesthood of Annas and Caiaphas, the word of God came to John, the son of Zacharias, in the wilderness.

3 And he came into all the district around the Jordan, preaching a baptism of repentance for the forgiveness of sins;

4 as it is written in the book of the words of Isaiah the prophet,

"THE VOICE OF ONE CRYING IN THE
    WILDERNESS,
'MAKE READY THE WAY OF THE LORD,
MAKE HIS PATHS STRAIGHT.

5 'EVERY RAVINE WILL BE FILLED,
AND EVERY MOUNTAIN AND HILL WILL BE
    BROUGHT LOW;
THE CROOKED WILL BECOME STRAIGHT,
AND THE ROUGH ROADS SMOOTH;

6 AND ALL FLESH WILL SEE THE SALVATION
    OF GOD.' "

7 ¶ So he *began* saying to the crowds who were going out to be baptized by him, "You brood of vipers, who warned you to flee from the wrath to come?

8 "Therefore bear fruits in keeping with repentance, and do not begin to say to yourselves, 'We have Abraham for our father,' for I say to you that from these stones God is able to raise up children to Abraham.

9 "Indeed the axe is already laid at the root of the trees; so every tree that does not bear good fruit is cut down and thrown into the fire."

10 ¶ And the crowds were questioning him, saying, "Then what shall we do?"

11 And he would answer and say to them, "The man who has two tunics is to share with him who has none; and he who has food is to do likewise."

12 And *some* tax collectors also came to be baptized, and they said to him, "Teacher, what shall we do?"

13 And he said to them, "Collect no more than what you have been ordered to."

14 *Some* soldiers were questioning him, saying, "And *what about* us, what shall we do?" And he said to them, "Do not take money from anyone by force, or accuse *anyone* falsely, and be content with your wages."

15 ¶ Now while the people were in a state of expectation and all were wondering in their hearts about John, as to whether he was the Christ,

16 John answered and said to them all, "As for me, I baptize you with water; but One is coming

who is mightier than I, and I am not fit to untie the thong of His sandals; He will baptize you with the Holy Spirit and fire.

17 "His winnowing fork is in His hand to thoroughly clear His threshing floor, and to gather the wheat into His barn; but He will burn up the chaff with unquenchable fire."

18 ¶ So with many other exhortations he preached the gospel to the people.

19 But when Herod the tetrarch was reprimanded by him because of Herodias, his brother's wife, and because of all the wicked things which Herod had done,

20 Herod also added this to them all: he locked John up in prison.

Jesus Is Baptized

3:21,22pp — Matt 3:13–17; Mark 1:9–11
3:23–38pp — Matt 1:1–17

21 ¶ Now when all the people were baptized, Jesus was also baptized, and while He was praying, heaven was opened,

22 and the Holy Spirit descended upon Him in bodily form like a dove, and a voice came out of heaven, "You are My beloved Son, in You I am well-pleased."

Genealogy of Jesus

23 ¶ When He began His ministry, Jesus Himself was about thirty years of age, being, as was supposed, the son of Joseph, the son of Eli,

24 the son of Matthat, the son of Levi, the son of Melchi, the son of Jannai, the son of Joseph,

25 the son of Mattathias, the son of Amos, the son of Nahum, the son of Hesli, the son of Naggai,

26 the son of Maath, the son of Mattathias, the son of Semein, the son of Josech, the son of Joda,

27 the son of Joanan, the son of Rhesa, the son of Zerubbabel, the son of Shealtiel, the son of Neri,

28 the son of Melchi, the son of Addi, the son of Cosam, the son of Elmadam, the son of Er,

29 the son of Joshua, the son of Eliezer, the son of Jorim, the son of Matthat, the son of Levi,

30 the son of Simeon, the son of Judah, the son of Joseph, the son of Jonam, the son of Eliakim,

31 the son of Melea, the son of Menna, the son of Mattatha, the son of Nathan, the son of David,

32 the son of Jesse, the son of Obed, the son of Boaz, the son of Salmon, the son of Nahshon,

33 the son of Amminadab, the son of Admin, the son of Ram, the son of Hezron, the son of Perez, the son of Judah,

34 the son of Jacob, the son of Isaac, the son of Abraham, the son of Terah, the son of Nahor,

35 the son of Serug, the son of Reu, the son of Peleg, the son of Heber, the son of Shelah,

36 the son of Cainan, the son of Arphaxad, the son of Shem, the son of Noah, the son of Lamech,

37 the son of Methuselah, the son of Enoch, the son of Jared, the son of Mahalaleel, the son of Cainan,

38 the son of Enosh, the son of Seth, the son of Adam, the son of God.

The Temptation of Jesus

4:1–13pp — Matt 4:1–11; Mark 1:12,13

4 Jesus, full of the Holy Spirit, returned from the Jordan and was led around by the Spirit in the wilderness

3:38 A Gospel for the Gentiles

Matthew's Gospel traced Jesus' roots back to Abraham, father of the Jewish race. But Luke, probably the only Gentile writer of the New Testament, emphasized that Jesus' good news was for all people, not just the Jews. In keeping with that purpose, he carried Jesus' lineage all the way back to the first man, Adam.

2 for forty days, being tempted by the devil. And He ate nothing during those days, and when they had ended, He became hungry.

3 And the devil said to Him, "If You are the Son of God, tell this stone to become bread."

4 And Jesus answered him, "It is written, 'MAN SHALL NOT LIVE ON BREAD ALONE.' "

5 ¶ And he led Him up and showed Him all the kingdoms of the world in a moment of time.

6 And the devil said to Him, "I will give You all this domain and its glory; for it has been handed over to me, and I give it to whomever I wish.

7 "Therefore if You worship before me, it shall all be Yours."

8 Jesus answered him, "It is written, 'YOU SHALL WORSHIP THE LORD YOUR GOD AND SERVE HIM ONLY.' "

9 ¶ And he led Him to Jerusalem and had Him stand on the pinnacle of the temple, and said to Him, "If You are the Son of God, throw Yourself down from here;

10 for it is written,

'HE WILL COMMAND HIS ANGELS
    CONCERNING YOU TO GUARD YOU,'

11 and,

'ON *their* HANDS THEY WILL BEAR YOU UP,
SO THAT YOU WILL NOT STRIKE YOUR
    FOOT AGAINST A STONE.' "

12 And Jesus answered and said to him, "It is said, 'YOU SHALL NOT PUT THE LORD YOUR GOD TO THE TEST.' "

13 ¶ When the devil had finished every temptation, he left Him until an opportune time.

Jesus' Public Ministry

4:31–37pp — Mark 1:21–28

14 ¶ And Jesus returned to Galilee in the power of the Spirit, and news about Him spread through all the surrounding district.

15 And He *began* teaching in their synagogues and was praised by all.

16 ¶ And He came to Nazareth, where He had been brought up; and as was His custom, He entered the synagogue on the Sabbath, and stood up to read.

17 And the book of the prophet Isaiah was handed to Him. And He opened the book and found the place where it was written,

18 "THE SPIRIT OF THE LORD IS UPON ME,
    BECAUSE HE ANOINTED ME TO PREACH THE
        GOSPEL TO THE POOR.
    HE HAS SENT ME TO PROCLAIM RELEASE TO
        THE CAPTIVES,
    AND RECOVERY OF SIGHT TO THE BLIND,
    TO SET FREE THOSE WHO ARE OPPRESSED,

19 TO PROCLAIM THE FAVORABLE YEAR OF THE
        LORD."

20 And He closed the book, gave it back to the attendant and sat down; and the eyes of all in the synagogue were fixed on Him.

21 And He began to say to them, "Today this Scripture has been fulfilled in your hearing."

22 And all were speaking well of Him, and wondering at the gracious words which were falling from His lips; and they were saying, "Is this not Joseph's son?"

23 And He said to them, "No doubt you will quote this proverb to Me, 'Physician, heal yourself! Whatever we heard was done at Capernaum, do here in your hometown as well.' "

24 And He said, "Truly I say to you, no prophet is welcome in his hometown.

25 "But I say to you in truth, there were many widows in Israel in the days of Elijah, when the sky was shut up for three years and six months, when a great famine came over all the land;

26 and yet Elijah was sent to none of them, but only to Zarephath, *in the land* of Sidon, to a woman who was a widow.

27 "And there were many lepers in Israel in the time of Elisha the prophet; and none of them was cleansed, but only Naaman the Syrian."

4:27 Hard Words for the Jews

Luke's book stresses the universal appeal of the gospel. In both of these Old Testament stories (the Zarephath widow and Naaman), God sent a prophet to perform a miracle for foreigners (non-Jews). Such an emphasis scandalized the Jews, who saw themselves as God's uniquely chosen people. Jesus' words proved so inflammatory that a mob attempted to kill him. As far as is known, Jesus never returned to his home territory of Nazareth.

28 And all *the people* in the synagogue were filled with rage as they heard these things;

29 and they got up and drove Him out of the city, and led Him to the brow of the hill on which their city had been built, in order to throw Him down the cliff.

30 But passing through their midst, He went His way.

31 ¶ And He came down to Capernaum, a city of Galilee, and He was teaching them on the Sabbath;

32 and they were amazed at His teaching, for His message was with authority.

33 In the synagogue there was a man possessed by the spirit of an unclean demon, and he cried out with a loud voice,

34 "Let us alone! What business do we have with each other, Jesus of Nazareth? Have You come to destroy us? I know who You are—the Holy One of God!"

35 But Jesus rebuked him, saying, "Be quiet and come out of him!" And when the demon had thrown him down in the midst *of the people*, he came out of him without doing him any harm.

36 And amazement came upon them all, and they *began* talking with one another saying, "What is this message? For with authority and power He commands the unclean spirits and they come out."

37 And the report about Him was spreading into every locality in the surrounding district.

Many Are Healed

4:38–41pp — Matt 8:14–17
4:38–43pp — Mark 1:29–38

38 ¶ Then He got up and *left* the synagogue, and entered Simon's home. Now Simon's mother-in-law was suffering from a high fever, and they asked Him to help her.

39 And standing over her, He rebuked the fever, and it left her; and she immediately got up and waited on them.

40 ¶ While the sun was setting, all those who had any *who were* sick with various diseases brought them to Him; and laying His hands on each one of them, He was healing them.

41 Demons also were coming out of many, shouting, "You are the Son of God!" But rebuking them, He would not allow them to speak, because they knew Him to be the Christ.

42 ¶ When day came, Jesus left and went to a secluded place; and the crowds were searching for Him, and came to Him and tried to keep Him from going away from them.

43 But He said to them, "I must preach the kingdom of God to the other cities also, for I was sent for this purpose."

44 ¶ So He kept on preaching in the synagogues of [a]Judea.

[a] I.e. the country of the Jews (including Galilee)

The First Disciples

5:1–11pp — Matt 4:18–22; Mark 1:16–20; John 1:40–42

5 Now it happened that while the crowd was pressing around Him and listening to the word of God, He was standing by the lake of Gennesaret;

2 and He saw two boats lying at the edge of the lake; but the fishermen had gotten out of them and were washing their nets.

3 And He got into one of the boats, which was Simon's, and asked him to put out a little way from the land. And He sat down and *began* teaching the people from the boat.

4 When He had finished speaking, He said to Simon, "Put out into the deep water and let down your nets for a catch."

5 Simon answered and said, "Master, we worked hard all night and caught nothing, but I will do as You say *and* let down the nets.

6 When they had done this, they enclosed a great quantity of fish, and their nets *began* to break;

7 so they signaled to their partners in the other boat for them to come and help them. And they came and filled both of the boats, so that they began to sink.

8 But when Simon Peter saw *that*, he fell down at Jesus' feet, saying, "Go away from me Lord, for I am a sinful man, O Lord!"

9 For amazement had seized him and all his

A Physician Looks at the Poor
The surprising emphasis of an upper-class writer

A GREAT DOCTOR ONCE COMPARED HIS professional duties to working at the complaint desk of a large department store. "All through medical school I studied the body's wonderful engineering. A healthy body is perfect—absolutely beautiful to observe. But in practice I spend my time treating people whose bodies don't work right. I hear only complaints. After a while, it's easy to lose perspective."

> "It is not those who are well who need a physician, but those who are sick." 5:31

Luke, a physician, knew firsthand about sick and suffering people; he, too, heard their daily complaints. Yet somehow he never became callous. In fact, his Gospel focuses on Jesus' ministry to society's "complaint desk": the poor, the sick, and the neglected.

Jesus Announces His Mission

In Luke, even Mary's opening song strikes a chord for the poor and hungry (1:46–55). Using his favorite title for Jesus ("Son of Man") 25 times, Luke reveals him as a true servant of all humanity.

Luke 4 shows Jesus boldly declaring why he came to earth. He had just resisted temptations of wealth and power, and returned from the desert to his hometown. There Jesus, a local village boy, announced his unique mission from God: to preach good news to the poor, to free prisoners, heal the blind, and release the oppressed (4:18–19).

With little editorial comment, Luke follows Jesus from town to town. Jesus avoided such fashionable places as the resort town of Tiberias. He stayed near the farming communities and fishing villages clustered around the Sea of Galilee, serving the needs of humble people.

Reaction to Jesus varied. Naturally, the sick clamored for his attention, begging for healing. Even a few powerful people believed in him, including a respected Roman centurion and a synagogue ruler. But the religious leaders constantly challenged his actions, and his own neighbors angrily chased him out of town.

An Unlikely Friend of the Poor

Luke skillfully brings his characters to life in vignettes. Learned and sophisticated, he uses the finest Greek of any Gospel writer; but, ironically, he focuses mainly on the poor and the outcast. Women, largely ignored by ancient historians, play a large role: Luke introduces 13 women mentioned in no other Gospel. He also shows a delight and appreciation for children.

It may seem strange that Luke, by education and profession a member of the upper class, emerged as a champion of the poor and the oppressed. Evidently Jesus' message had affected him deeply. As Jesus said, "It is not those who are well who need a physician, but those who are sick. I have not come to call the righteous but sinners to repentance" (5:31–32).

Life Questions: As Luke tells it, Jesus threatened the rich and powerful, but appealed to the poor and outcast. If Jesus came today, how would those two groups in our society respond to him?

companions because of the catch of fish which they had taken;

10 and so also *were* James and John, sons of Zebedee, who were partners with Simon. And Jesus said to Simon, "Do not fear, from now on you will be catching men."

11 When they had brought their boats to land, they left everything and followed Him.

The Leper and the Paralytic

5:12–14pp — Matt 8:2–4; Mark 1:40–44
5:18–26pp — Matt 9:2–8; Mark 2:3–12

12 ¶ While He was in one of the cities, behold, *there was* a man covered with leprosy; and when he saw Jesus, he fell on his face and implored Him, saying, "Lord, if You are willing, You can make me clean."

13 And He stretched out His hand and touched him, saying, "I am willing; be cleansed." And immediately the leprosy left him.

14 And He ordered him to tell no one, "But go and show yourself to the priest and make an offering for your cleansing, just as Moses commanded, as a testimony to them."

15 But the news about Him was spreading even farther, and large crowds were gathering to hear *Him* and to be healed of their sicknesses.

16 But Jesus Himself would *often* slip away to the wilderness and pray.

17 ¶ One day He was teaching; and there were *some* Pharisees and teachers of the law sitting *there,* who had come from every village of Galilee and Judea and *from* Jerusalem; and the power of the Lord was *present* for Him to perform healing.

18 And *some* men *were* carrying on a bed a man who was paralyzed; and they were trying to bring him in and to set him down in front of Him.

19 But not finding any *way* to bring him in because of the crowd, they went up on the roof and let him down through the tiles with his stretcher, into the middle *of the crowd*, in front of Jesus.

20 Seeing their faith, He said, "Friend, your sins are forgiven you."

5:20 Group Faith

The paralytic's friends showed remarkable determination to get him to Jesus. Luke writes that their faith—the man's and his friends'—moved Jesus to forgive and to heal. Jesus recognized that a helpless man needed help to come to him. Often an individual comes to Christ only with the persistent encouragement of friends and family.

21 The scribes and the Pharisees began to reason, saying, "Who is this *man* who speaks blasphemies? Who can forgive sins, but God alone?"

22 But Jesus, aware of their reasonings, an-

swered and said to them, "Why are you reasoning in your hearts?

23 "Which is easier, to say, 'Your sins have been forgiven you,' or to say, 'Get up and walk'?

24 "But, so that you may know that the Son of Man has authority on earth to forgive sins,"—He said to the paralytic—"I say to you, get up, and pick up your stretcher and go home."

25 Immediately he got up before them, and picked up what he had been lying on, and went home glorifying God.

26 They were all struck with astonishment and *began* glorifying God; and they were filled with fear, saying, "We have seen remarkable things today."

Call of Levi (Matthew)

5:27–32pp — Matt 9:9–13; Mark 2:14–17
5:33–39pp — Matt 9:14–17; Mark 2:18–22

27 ¶ After that He went out and noticed a tax collector named Levi sitting in the tax booth, and He said to him, "Follow Me."

28 And he left everything behind, and got up and *began* to follow Him.

29 ¶ And Levi gave a big reception for Him in his house; and there was a great crowd of tax collectors and other *people* who were reclining *at the table* with them.

30 The Pharisees and their scribes *began* grumbling at His disciples, saying, "Why do you eat and drink with the tax collectors and sinners?"

31 And Jesus answered and said to them, "*It is* not those who are well who need a physician, but those who are sick.

32 "I have not come to call the righteous but sinners to repentance."

33 ¶ And they said to Him, "The disciples of John often fast and offer prayers, the *disciples* of the Pharisees also do the same, but Yours eat and drink."

34 And Jesus said to them, "You cannot make the attendants of the bridegroom fast while the bridegroom is with them, can you?

35 "But *the* days will come; and when the bridegroom is taken away from them, then they will fast in those days."

36 And He was also telling them a parable: "No one tears a piece of cloth from a new garment and puts it on an old garment; otherwise he will both tear the new, and the piece from the new will not match the old.

37 "And no one puts new wine into old wineskins; otherwise the new wine will burst the skins and it will be spilled out, and the skins will be ruined.

38 "But new wine must be put into fresh wineskins.

39 "And no one, after drinking old *wine* wishes for new; for he says, 'The old is good *enough.*' "

Jesus Is Lord of the Sabbath

6:1–11pp — Matt 12:1–14; Mark 2:23–3:6

6 Now it happened that He was passing through *some* grainfields on a Sabbath; and His disciples were picking the heads of grain, rubbing them in their hands, and eating *the grain*.

2 But some of the Pharisees said, "Why do you do what is not lawful on the Sabbath?"

3 And Jesus answering them said, "Have you not even read what David did when he was hungry, he and those who were with him,

4 how he entered the house of God, and took and ate the ªconsecrated bread which is not lawful for any to eat except the priests alone, and gave it to his companions?"

5 And He was saying to them, "The Son of Man is Lord of the Sabbath."

6 ¶ On another Sabbath He entered the synagogue and was teaching; and there was a man there whose right hand was withered.

7 The scribes and the Pharisees were watching Him closely *to see* if He healed on the Sabbath, so that they might find *reason* to accuse Him.

8 But He knew what they were thinking, and He said to the man with the withered hand, "Get up and come forward!" And he got up and came forward.

9 And Jesus said to them, "I ask you, is it lawful to do good or to do harm on the Sabbath, to save a life or to destroy it?"

6:9 Rules Without Love

Luke's vignettes on Jesus and the Sabbath (see also 13:10–17) demonstrate the legalism Jesus opposed. Jews of his day observed very strict rules governing what could be done on the Sabbath. Religious leaders became furious at Jesus for "breaking" the traditions. His crime? Healing people on the Sabbath. Jesus refused to let traditions interfere with compassion for needy people.

10 After looking around at them all, He said to him, "Stretch out your hand!" And he did *so*; and his hand was restored.

11 But they themselves were filled with rage, and discussed together what they might do to Jesus.

Choosing the Twelve

6:13–16pp — Matt 10:2–4; Mark 3:16–19; Acts 1:13

12 ¶ It was at this time that He went off to the mountain to pray, and He spent the whole night in prayer to God.

13 And when day came, He called His disciples to Him and chose twelve of them, whom He also named as apostles:

14 Simon, whom He also named Peter, and Andrew his brother; and James and John; and Philip and Bartholomew;

15 and Matthew and Thomas; James *the son* of Alphaeus, and Simon who was called the Zealot;

16 Judas *the son* of James, and Judas Iscariot, who became a traitor.

17 ¶ Jesus came down with them and stood on a level place; and *there was* a large crowd of His disciples, and a great throng of people from all Judea and Jerusalem and the coastal region of Tyre and Sidon,

18 who had come to hear Him and to be healed of their diseases; and those who were troubled with unclean spirits were being cured.

19 And all the people were trying to touch Him, for power was coming from Him and healing *them* all.

The Beatitudes

6:20–23pp — Matt 5:3–12
6:29,30pp — Matt 5:39–42
6:37–42pp — Matt 7:1–5
6:43,44pp — Matt 7:16,18,20

20 ¶ And turning His gaze toward His disciples, He *began* to say, "Blessed *are* you *who are* poor, for yours is the kingdom of God.

21 "Blessed *are* you who hunger now, for you shall be satisfied. Blessed *are* you who weep now, for you shall laugh.

22 "Blessed are you when men hate you, and ostracize you, and insult you, and scorn your name as evil, for the sake of the Son of Man.

23 "Be glad in that day and leap *for joy*, for behold, your reward is great in heaven. For in the same way their fathers used to treat the prophets.

24 "But woe to you who are rich, for you are receiving your comfort in full.

25 "Woe to you who are well-fed now, for you shall be hungry. Woe *to you* who laugh now, for you shall mourn and weep.

26 "Woe *to you* when all men speak well of you, for their fathers used to treat the false prophets in the same way.

27 ¶ "But I say to you who hear, love your enemies, do good to those who hate you,

28 bless those who curse you, pray for those who mistreat you.

29 "Whoever hits you on the cheek, offer him the other also; and whoever takes away your coat, do not withhold your shirt from him either.

30 "Give to everyone who asks of you, and whoever takes away what is yours, do not demand it back.

31 "Treat others the same way you want them to treat you.

32 "If you love those who love you, what credit is *that* to you? For even sinners love those who love them.

ª Or *showbread*; lit *loaves of presentation*

33 "If you do good to those who do good to you, what credit is *that* to you? For even sinners do the same.

34 "If you lend to those from whom you expect to receive, what credit is *that* to you? Even sinners lend to sinners in order to receive back the same *amount.*

35 "But love your enemies, and do good, and lend, expecting nothing in return; and your reward will be great, and you will be sons of the Most High; for He Himself is kind to ungrateful and evil *men.*

36 "Be merciful, just as your Father is merciful.

37 ¶ "Do not judge, and you will not be judged; and do not condemn, and you will not be condemned; pardon, and you will be pardoned.

38 "Give, and it will be given to you. They will pour into your lap a good measure—pressed down, shaken together, *and* running over. For by your standard of measure it will be measured to you in return."

39 ¶ And He also spoke a parable to them: "A blind man cannot guide a blind man, can he? Will they not both fall into a pit?

40 "A pupil is not above his teacher; but everyone, after he has been fully trained, will be like his teacher.

41 "Why do you look at the speck that is in your brother's eye, but do not notice the log that is in your own eye?

42 "Or how can you say to your brother, 'Brother, let me take out the speck that is in your eye,' when you yourself do not see the log that is in your own eye? You hypocrite, first take the log out of your own eye, and then you will see clearly to take out the speck that is in your brother's eye.

43 "For there is no good tree which produces bad fruit, nor, on the other hand, a bad tree which produces good fruit.

44 "For each tree is known by its own fruit. For men do not gather figs from thorns, nor do they pick grapes from a briar bush.

45 "The good man out of the good treasure of his heart brings forth what is good; and the evil *man* out of the evil *treasure* brings forth what is evil; for his mouth speaks from that which fills his heart.

Builders and Foundations

6:47–49pp — Matt 7:24–27

46 ¶ "Why do you call Me, 'Lord, Lord,' and do not do what I say?

47 "Everyone who comes to Me and hears My words and acts on them, I will show you whom he is like:

48 he is like a man building a house, who dug deep and laid a foundation on the rock; and when a flood occurred, the torrent burst against that house and could not shake it, because it had been well built.

49 "But the one who has heard and has not acted *accordingly,* is like a man who built a house on the ground without any foundation; and the torrent burst against it and immediately it collapsed, and the ruin of that house was great."

Jesus Heals a Centurion's Servant

7:1–10pp — Matt 8:5–13
7:11–16Ref — 1 Kin 17:17–24; 2 Kin 4:32–37;
Mark 5:21–24,35–43; John 11:1–44

7 When He had completed all His discourse in the hearing of the people, He went to Capernaum.

2 ¶ And a centurion's slave, who was highly regarded by him, was sick and about to die.

3 When he heard about Jesus, he sent some Jewish elders asking Him to come and save the life of his slave.

4 When they came to Jesus, they earnestly implored Him, saying, "He is worthy for You to grant this to him;

5 for he loves our nation and it was he who built us our synagogue."

6 Now Jesus *started* on His way with them; and when He was not far from the house, the centurion sent friends, saying to Him, "Lord, do not trouble Yourself further, for I am not worthy for You to come under my roof;

7 for this reason I did not even consider myself worthy to come to You, but *just* say the word, and my servant will be healed.

8 "For I also am a man placed under authority, with soldiers under me; and I say to this one, 'Go!' and he goes, and to another, 'Come!' and he comes, and to my slave, 'Do this!' and he does it."

9 Now when Jesus heard this, He marveled at him, and turned and said to the crowd that was following Him, "I say to you, not even in Israel have I found such great faith."

10 When those who had been sent returned to the house, they found the slave in good health.

11 ¶ Soon afterwards He went to a city called Nain; and His disciples were going along with Him, accompanied by a large crowd.

12 Now as He approached the gate of the city, a dead man was being carried out, the only son of his mother, and she was a widow; and a sizeable crowd from the city was with her.

13 When the Lord saw her, He felt compassion for her, and said to her, "Do not weep."

14 And He came up and touched the coffin; and the bearers came to a halt. And He said, "Young man, I say to you, arise!"

15 The dead man sat up and began to speak. And *Jesus* gave him back to his mother.

16 Fear gripped them all, and they *began* glorifying God, saying, "A great prophet has arisen among us!" and, "God has visited His people!"

17 This report concerning Him went out all over Judea and in all the surrounding district.

A Deputation from John

7:18–35pp — Matt 11:2–19
7:37–39Ref — Matt 26:6–13; Mark 14:3–9;
John 12:1–8

18 ¶ The disciples of John reported to him about all these things.

19 Summoning two of his disciples, John sent them to the Lord, saying, "Are You the Expected One, or do we look for someone else?"

7:19 Even John Questioned

The crowds Jesus attracted wavered between enthusiastic support and outright rejection of him. Evidently, some of the controversy even affected John the Baptist, who had baptized Jesus and pronounced him the Son of God (see John 1:34). John, then in prison, sent his disciples to confirm whether Jesus was the true Messiah. Jesus reassured him with a direct reference to the prophecies of Isaiah 61 (see also Luke 4:18–21).

20 When the men came to Him, they said, "John the Baptist has sent us to You, to ask, 'Are You the Expected One, or do we look for someone else?'"

21 At that very time He cured many *people* of diseases and afflictions and evil spirits; and He gave sight to many *who were* blind.

22 And He answered and said to them, "Go and report to John what you have seen and heard: *the* BLIND RECEIVE SIGHT, *the* lame walk, *the* lepers are cleansed, and *the* deaf hear, *the* dead are raised up, *the* POOR HAVE THE GOSPEL PREACHED TO THEM.

23 "Blessed is he who does not take offense at Me."

24 ¶ When the messengers of John had left, He began to speak to the crowds about John, "What did you go out into the wilderness to see? A reed shaken by the wind?

25 "But what did you go out to see? A man dressed in soft clothing? Those who are splendidly clothed and live in luxury are *found* in royal palaces!

26 "But what did you go out to see? A prophet? Yes, I say to you, and one who is more than a prophet.

27 "This is the one about whom it is written,
'BEHOLD, I SEND MY MESSENGER AHEAD OF
    YOU,
WHO WILL PREPARE YOUR WAY BEFORE
    YOU.'

28 "I say to you, among those born of women there is no one greater than John; yet he who is least in the kingdom of God is greater than he."

29 When all the people and the tax collectors heard *this*, they acknowledged God's justice, having been baptized with the baptism of John.

30 But the Pharisees and the [a]lawyers rejected God's purpose for themselves, not having been baptized by John.

31 ¶ "To what then shall I compare the men of this generation, and what are they like?

32 "They are like children who sit in the market place and call to one another, and they say, 'We played the flute for you, and you did not dance; we sang a dirge, and you did not weep.'

33 "For John the Baptist has come eating no bread and drinking no wine, and you say, 'He has a demon!'

34 "The Son of Man has come eating and drinking, and you say, 'Behold, a gluttonous man and a drunkard, a friend of tax collectors and sinners!'

35 "Yet wisdom is vindicated by all her children."

36 ¶ Now one of the Pharisees was requesting Him to dine with him, and He entered the Pharisee's house and reclined *at the table*.

37 And there was a woman in the city who was a sinner; and when she learned that He was reclining *at the table* in the Pharisee's house, she brought an alabaster vial of perfume,

38 and standing behind *Him* at His feet, weeping, she began to wet His feet with her tears, and kept wiping them with the hair of her head, and kissing His feet and anointing them with the perfume.

39 Now when the Pharisee who had invited Him saw this, he said to himself, "If this man were a prophet He would know who and what sort of person this woman is who is touching Him, that she is a sinner."

Parable of Two Debtors

7:41,42Ref — Matt 18:23–34

40 And Jesus answered him, "Simon, I have something to say to you." And he replied, "Say it, Teacher."

41 "A moneylender had two debtors: one owed five hundred [b]denarii, and the other fifty.

42 "When they were unable to repay, he graciously forgave them both. So which of them will love him more?"

43 Simon answered and said, "I suppose the one whom he forgave more." And He said to him, "You have judged correctly."

44 Turning toward the woman, He said to Simon, "Do you see this woman? I entered your house; you gave Me no water for My feet, but she has wet My feet with her tears and wiped them with her hair.

45 "You gave Me no kiss; but she, since the time I came in, has not ceased to kiss My feet.

46 "You did not anoint My head with oil, but she anointed My feet with perfume.

47 "For this reason I say to you, her sins, which

---

[a] I.e. experts in the Mosaic Law   [b] The denarius was equivalent to a day's wages

are many, have been forgiven, for she loved much; but he who is forgiven little, loves little."

48 Then He said to her, "Your sins have been forgiven."

49 Those who were reclining *at the table* with Him began to say to themselves, "Who is this *man* who even forgives sins?"

50 And He said to the woman, "Your faith has saved you; go in peace."

Ministering Women

8 Soon afterwards, He *began* going around from one city and village to another, proclaiming and preaching the kingdom of God. The twelve were with Him,

2 and *also* some women who had been healed of evil spirits and sicknesses: Mary who was called Magdalene, from whom seven demons had gone out,

3 and Joanna the wife of Chuza, Herod's steward, and Susanna, and many others who were contributing to their support out of their private means.

8:3 Jesus' Support

In the Middle East of that day, teachers traveled from town to town, accepting the gifts of appreciative listeners. Luke points out that certain women who had been healed by Jesus helped provide for him. In all, Luke introduces 13 women who do not appear in the other Gospels.

Parable of the Sower

8:4–15pp — Matt 13:2–23; Mark 4:1–20

4 ¶ When a large crowd was coming together, and those from the various cities were journeying to Him, He spoke by way of a parable:

5 "The sower went out to sow his seed; and as he sowed, some fell beside the road, and it was trampled under foot and the birds of the air ate it up.

6 "Other *seed* fell on rocky *soil,* and as soon as it grew up, it withered away, because it had no moisture.

7 "Other *seed* fell among the thorns; and the thorns grew up with it and choked it out.

8 "Other *seed* fell into the good soil, and grew up, and produced a crop a hundred times as great." As He said these things, He would call out, "He who has ears to hear, let him hear."

9 ¶ His disciples *began* questioning Him as to what this parable meant.

10 And He said, "To you it has been granted to know the mysteries of the kingdom of God, but to the rest *it is* in parables, so that SEEING THEY MAY NOT SEE, AND HEARING THEY MAY NOT UNDERSTAND.

11 ¶ "Now the parable is this: the seed is the word of God.

12 "Those beside the road are those who have heard; then the devil comes and takes away the word from their heart, so that they will not believe and be saved.

13 "Those on the rocky *soil are* those who, when they hear, receive the word with joy; and these have no *firm* root; they believe for a while, and in time of temptation fall away.

14 "The *seed* which fell among the thorns, these are the ones who have heard, and as they go on their way they are choked with worries and riches and pleasures of *this* life, and bring no fruit to maturity.

15 "But the *seed* in the good soil, these are the ones who have heard the word in an honest and good heart, and hold it fast, and bear fruit with perseverance.

Parable of the Lamp

8:19–21pp — Matt 12:46–50; Mark 3:31–35

16 ¶ "Now no one after lighting a lamp covers it over with a container, or puts it under a bed; but he puts it on a lampstand, so that those who come in may see the light.

17 "For nothing is hidden that will not become evident, nor *anything* secret that will not be known and come to light.

18 "So take care how you listen; for whoever has, to him *more* shall be given; and whoever does not have, even what he thinks he has shall be taken away from him."

19 ¶ And His mother and brothers came to Him, and they were unable to get to Him because of the crowd.

20 And it was reported to Him, "Your mother and Your brothers are standing outside, wishing to see You."

21 But He answered and said to them, "My mother and My brothers are these who hear the word of God and do it."

Jesus Stills the Sea

8:22–25pp — Matt 8:23–27; Mark 4:36–41
8:22–25Ref — Mark 6:47–52; John 6:16–21

22 ¶ Now on one of *those* days Jesus and His disciples got into a boat, and He said to them, "Let us go over to the other side of the lake." So they launched out.

23 But as they were sailing along He fell asleep; and a fierce gale of wind descended on the lake, and they *began* to be swamped and to be in danger.

24 They came to Jesus and woke Him up, saying, "Master, Master, we are perishing!" And He got up and rebuked the wind and the surging waves, and they stopped, and it became calm.

25 And He said to them, "Where is your faith?" They were fearful and amazed, saying to one an-

other, "Who then is this, that He commands even the winds and the water, and they obey Him?"

The Demoniac Cured

8:26–37pp — Matt 8:28–34
8:26–39pp — Mark 5:1–20

26 ¶ Then they sailed to the country of the Gerasenes, which is opposite Galilee.

27 And when He came out onto the land, He was met by a man from the city who was possessed with demons; and who had not put on any clothing for a long time, and was not living in a house, but in the tombs.

8:27 Homeless

Much as some mentally troubled people live under bridges today, this disturbed man had fled society to live in the tombs. Cemeteries in the ancient world were located far from town, because people feared the spirits of the dead. The man was violent and uncontrollable, and he greeted Jesus with bizarre behavior. Jesus, rather than avoiding him, went straight to the heart of his problem.

28 Seeing Jesus, he cried out and fell before Him, and said in a loud voice, "What business do we have with each other, Jesus, Son of the Most High God? I beg You, do not torment me."

29 For He had commanded the unclean spirit to come out of the man. For it had seized him many times; and he was bound with chains and shackles and kept under guard, and *yet* he would break his bonds and be driven by the demon into the desert.

30 And Jesus asked him, "What is your name?" And he said, "Legion"; for many demons had entered him.

31 They were imploring Him not to command them to go away into the abyss.

32 ¶ Now there was a herd of many swine feeding there on the mountain; and *the demons* implored Him to permit them to enter the swine. And He gave them permission.

33 And the demons came out of the man and entered the swine; and the herd rushed down the steep bank into the lake and was drowned.

34 ¶ When the herdsmen saw what had happened, they ran away and reported it in the city and *out* in the country.

35 *The people* went out to see what had happened; and they came to Jesus, and found the man from whom the demons had gone out, sitting down at the feet of Jesus, clothed and in his right mind; and they became frightened.

36 Those who had seen it reported to them how the man who was demon-possessed had been made well.

37 And all the people of the country of the Gerasenes and the surrounding district asked Him to leave them, for they were gripped with great fear; and He got into a boat and returned.

38 But the man from whom the demons had gone out was begging Him that he might accompany Him; but He sent him away, saying,

39 "Return to your house and describe what great things God has done for you." So he went away, proclaiming throughout the whole city what great things Jesus had done for him.

Miracles of Healing

8:40–56pp — Matt 9:18–26; Mark 5:22–43

40 ¶ And as Jesus returned, the people welcomed Him, for they had all been waiting for Him.

41 And there came a man named Jairus, and he was an official of the synagogue; and he fell at Jesus' feet, and *began* to implore Him to come to his house;

42 for he had an only daughter, about twelve years old, and she was dying. But as He went, the crowds were pressing against Him.

43 ¶ And a woman who had a hemorrhage for twelve years, and could not be healed by anyone,

44 came up behind Him and touched the fringe of His cloak, and immediately her hemorrhage stopped.

45 And Jesus said, "Who is the one who touched Me?" And while they were all denying it, Peter said, "Master, the people are crowding and pressing in on You."

46 But Jesus said, "Someone did touch Me, for I was aware that power had gone out of Me."

47 When the woman saw that she had not escaped notice, she came trembling and fell down before Him, and declared in the presence of all the people the reason why she had touched Him, and how she had been immediately healed.

48 And He said to her, "Daughter, your faith has made you well; go in peace."

49 ¶ While He was still speaking, someone *came from *the house of* the synagogue official, saying, "Your daughter has died; do not trouble the Teacher anymore."

50 But when Jesus heard *this,* He answered him, "Do not be afraid *any longer;* only believe, and she will be made well."

51 When He came to the house, He did not allow anyone to enter with Him, except Peter and John and James, and the girl's father and mother.

52 Now they were all weeping and lamenting for her; but He said, "Stop weeping, for she has not died, but is asleep."

53 And they *began* laughing at Him, knowing that she had died.

54 He, however, took her by the hand and called, saying, "Child, arise!"

55 And her spirit returned, and she got up immediately; and He gave orders for *something* to be given her to eat.

56 Her parents were amazed; but He instructed them to tell no one what had happened.

Ministry of the Twelve

9:3–5pp — Matt 10:9–15; Mark 6:8–11
9:7–9pp — Matt 14:1,2; Mark 6:14–16
9:10–17pp — Matt 14:13–21; Mark 6:32–44; John 6:5–13

9 And He called the twelve together, and gave them power and authority over all the demons and to heal diseases.

2 And He sent them out to proclaim the kingdom of God and to perform healing.

3 And He said to them, "Take nothing for *your* journey, neither a staff, nor a bag, nor bread, nor money; and do not *even* have two tunics apiece.

4 "Whatever house you enter, stay there until you leave that city.

5 "And as for those who do not receive you, as you go out from that city, shake the dust off your feet as a testimony against them."

6 Departing, they *began* going throughout the villages, preaching the gospel and healing everywhere.

7 ¶ Now Herod the tetrarch heard of all that was happening; and he was greatly perplexed, because it was said by some that John had risen from the dead,

8 and by some that Elijah had appeared, and by others that one of the prophets of old had risen again.

9 Herod said, "I myself had John beheaded; but who is this man about whom I hear such things?" And he kept trying to see Him.

10 ¶ When the apostles returned, they gave an account to Him of all that they had done. Taking them with Him, He withdrew by Himself to a city called Bethsaida.

11 But the crowds were aware of this and followed Him; and welcoming them, He *began* speaking to them about the kingdom of God and curing those who had need of healing.

Five Thousand Fed

9:13–17Ref — 2 Kin 4:42–44
9:18–20pp — Matt 16:13–16; Mark 8:27–29
9:22–27pp — Matt 16:21–28; Mark 8:31–9:1

12 ¶ Now the day was ending, and the twelve came and said to Him, "Send the crowd away, that they may go into the surrounding villages and countryside and find lodging and get something to eat; for here we are in a desolate place."

13 But He said to them, "You give them *something* to eat!" And they said, "We have no more than five loaves and two fish, unless perhaps we go and buy food for all these people."

14 (For there were about five thousand men.) And He said to His disciples, "Have them sit down *to eat* in groups of about fifty each."

15 They did so, and had them all sit down.

16 Then He took the five loaves and the two fish, and looking up to heaven, He blessed them, and broke *them,* and kept giving *them* to the disciples to set before the people.

17 And they all ate and were satisfied; and the broken pieces which they had left over were picked up, twelve baskets *full.*

18 ¶ And it happened that while He was praying alone, the disciples were with Him, and He questioned them, saying, "Who do the people say that I am?"

19 They answered and said, "John the Baptist, and others *say* Elijah; but others, that one of the prophets of old has risen again."

20 And He said to them, "But who do you say that I am?" And Peter answered and said, "The Christ of God."

21 But He warned them and instructed *them* not to tell this to anyone,

22 saying, "The Son of Man must suffer many things and be rejected by the elders and chief priests and scribes, and be killed and be raised up on the third day."

23 ¶ And He was saying to *them* all, "If anyone wishes to come after Me, he must deny himself, and take up his cross daily and follow Me.

24 "For whoever wishes to save his life will lose it, but whoever loses his life for My sake, he is the one who will save it.

25 "For what is a man profited if he gains the whole world, and loses or forfeits himself?

26 "For whoever is ashamed of Me and My words, the Son of Man will be ashamed of him when He comes in His glory, and *the glory* of the Father and of the holy angels.

27 "But I say to you truthfully, there are some of those standing here who will not taste death until they see the kingdom of God."

The Transfiguration

9:28–36pp — Matt 17:1–8; Mark 9:2–8
9:37–42,43–45pp — Matt 17:14–18,22,23; Mark 9:14–27,30–32

28 ¶ Some eight days after these sayings, He took along Peter and John and James, and went up on the mountain to pray.

29 And while He was praying, the appearance of His face became different, and His clothing *became* white *and* gleaming.

30 And behold, two men were talking with Him; and they were Moses and Elijah,

31 who, appearing in glory, were speaking of His departure which He was about to accomplish at Jerusalem.

32 Now Peter and his companions had been overcome with sleep; but when they were fully awake, they saw His glory and the two men standing with Him.

33 And as these were leaving Him, Peter said to Jesus, "Master, it is good for us to be here; let us make three tabernacles: one for You, and one for

Moses, and one for Elijah"—not realizing what he was saying.

34 While he was saying this, a cloud formed and *began* to overshadow them; and they were afraid as they entered the cloud.

9:28–33 Seeing the Kingdom

Jesus predicted that some of his disciples would "see the kingdom of God" (verse 27) before tasting death. Eight days later, three of them witnessed Jesus gleaming like a flash of lightning and talking with the long-dead Moses and Elijah (verses 29–30). Many scholars think the Transfiguration fulfilled Jesus' "seeing the kingdom" prediction. Apart from this moment, Jesus looked like any other man during his years on earth. He had none of the brilliant glory associated with God in the Old Testament (see Exodus 40:34).

35 Then a voice came out of the cloud, saying, "This is My Son, *My* Chosen One; listen to Him!"

36 And when the voice had spoken, Jesus was found alone. And they kept silent, and reported to no one in those days any of the things which they had seen.

37 ¶ On the next day, when they came down from the mountain, a large crowd met Him.

38 And a man from the crowd shouted, saying, "Teacher, I beg You to look at my son, for he is my only *boy*,

39 and a spirit seizes him, and he suddenly screams, and it throws him into a convulsion with foaming *at the mouth*; and only with difficulty does it leave him, mauling him *as it leaves*.

40 "I begged Your disciples to cast it out, and they could not."

41 And Jesus answered and said, "You unbelieving and perverted generation, how long shall I be with you and put up with you? Bring your son here."

42 While he was still approaching, the demon slammed him *to the ground* and threw him into a convulsion. But Jesus rebuked the unclean spirit, and healed the boy and gave him back to his father.

43 And they were all amazed at the greatness of God.

¶ But while everyone was marveling at all that He was doing, He said to His disciples,

44 "Let these words sink into your ears; for the Son of Man is going to be delivered into the hands of men."

45 But they did not understand this statement, and it was concealed from them so that they would not perceive it; and they were afraid to ask Him about this statement.

The Test of Greatness

9:46–48pp — Matt 18:1–5
9:46–50pp — Mark 9:33–40

46 ¶ An argument started among them as to which of them might be the greatest.

47 But Jesus, knowing what they were thinking in their heart, took a child and stood him by His side,

48 and said to them, "Whoever receives this child in My name receives Me, and whoever receives Me receives Him who sent Me; for the one who is least among all of you, this is the one who is great."

49 ¶ John answered and said, "Master, we saw someone casting out demons in Your name; and we tried to prevent him because he does not follow along with us."

50 But Jesus said to him, "Do not hinder *him*; for he who is not against you is for you."

51 ¶ When the days were approaching for His ascension, He was determined to go to Jerusalem;

52 and He sent messengers on ahead of Him, and they went and entered a village of the Samaritans to make arrangements for Him.

53 But they did not receive Him, because He was traveling toward Jerusalem.

54 When His disciples James and John saw *this*, they said, "Lord, do You want us to command fire to come down from heaven and consume them?"

55 But He turned and rebuked them, [and said, "You do not know what kind of spirit you are of;

56 for the Son of Man did not come to destroy men's lives, but to save them."] And they went on to another village.

Exacting Discipleship

9:57–60pp — Matt 8:19–22

57 ¶ As they were going along the road, someone said to Him, "I will follow You wherever You go."

58 And Jesus said to him, "The foxes have holes and the birds of the air *have* nests, but the Son of Man has nowhere to lay His head."

59 And He said to another, "Follow Me." But he said, "Lord, permit me first to go and bury my father."

60 But He said to him, "Allow the dead to bury their own dead; but as for you, go and proclaim everywhere the kingdom of God."

61 Another also said, "I will follow You, Lord; but first permit me to say good-bye to those at home."

62 But Jesus said to him, "No one, after putting

his hand to the plow and looking back, is fit for the kingdom of God."

9:59 Burying His Father

The man's request to "permit me first to go and bury my father" didn't necessarily mean that the man's father had just died. Possibly the expression was a figure of speech, a way of saying, "Let me wait until my father has died." Jesus instead stressed the urgency of his mission.

The Power of a Name
Jesus' time on earth was running out

CHRISTIANS SPEAK "IN THE NAME of Jesus." But that familiar phrase may have lost meaning for some of us. Consider:

College sophomore Tom Bowers took a summer job as an intern on the governor of Michigan's staff. He spent the first few weeks cranking out memos, returning mundane phone calls, and straightening files. But one day a harried manager asked Tom to write a public statement on the state's new law enforcement program. Tom composed a brief announcement and took it to the governor.

The next day, as he rounded the corner of a newsstand, his eyes snapped wide open. Headlined across the front page of the *Detroit News* was the announcement he had composed. It dawned on him that, all over the city, people would be reading his very own words as the governor's.

Throughout that summer, Tom discovered the power of the governor's name. If he sent a letter to a mayor under his own signature, it would likely be filed under "Ignore." Who was Tom Bowers, sophomore summer intern? If, however, the governor put his name at the bottom, the letter got instant attention anywhere in the state. That summer Tom worked "in the name of the governor"—he represented the governor.

Jesus' Crash Training Course

It is one thing to represent the governor of Michigan; it is quite another to represent God and use his name. Yet Jesus had exactly that plan in mind for his followers. He hand-selected simple folk like James and Andrew to bear his name and represent him to the world. In the same way that a governor or president delegates authority to people acting on his behalf, Jesus gave his followers his own authority and power.

Jesus' time on earth was running out. Luke 9:51 records that he "was determined to go to Jerusalem," on his way to die. Only a few weeks remained for him to train those people who would be left behind to carry his name: "Christians." Jesus used the time as a crash training course for his followers.

Chapters 9–19 contain many of Jesus' events and sayings found nowhere else in the Bible. First he sent out the Twelve, then 72 others, to announce his message to all who would listen. These chapters convey Jesus' last detailed instructions to his loyal followers.

Final Instructions

Everything about Jesus' life increased in intensity along the treacherous road to Jerusalem. As he taught his small group of disciples, gawking crowds shoved in from all sides, sometimes even trampling each other. From those crowds, Pharisees tossed out loaded questions, seeking to trap Jesus.

Jesus did not soften his words in the face of danger. Instead, he emphasized the severe cost of following him. Frequently he talked about prayer, the church's life-giving connection to the Father.

Later, the apostle Paul would say that we, the church, actually form Christ's body in the world. By coming to earth and then leaving, Jesus ushered in a completely new chapter in history. And, as he prepared for departure, he called on his people—the disciples and us—to represent him. In every sense, we bear his name.

Life Questions: What does it mean to pray "in Jesus' name"? How can your life have the power and authority of Jesus behind it?

The Seventy Sent Out
10:4–12pp — Luke 9:3–5
10:13–15,21,22pp — Matt 11:21–23,25–27

10 Now after this the Lord appointed seventy others, and sent them in pairs ahead of Him to every city and place where He Himself was going to come.

2 And He was saying to them, "The harvest is plentiful, but the laborers are few; therefore beseech the Lord of the harvest to send out laborers into His harvest.

3 "Go; behold, I send you out as lambs in the midst of wolves.

"The one who listens to you listens to Me, and the one who rejects you rejects Me." 10:16

4 "Carry no money belt, no bag, no shoes; and greet no one on the way.

5 "Whatever house you enter, first say, 'Peace *be* to this house.'

6 "If a man of peace is there, your peace will rest on him; but if not, it will return to you.

7 "Stay in that house, eating and drinking what they give you; for the laborer is worthy of his wages. Do not keep moving from house to house.

8 "Whatever city you enter and they receive you, eat what is set before you;

9 and heal those in it who are sick, and say to them, 'The kingdom of God has come near to you.'

10 "But whatever city you enter and they do not receive you, go out into its streets and say,

11 'Even the dust of your city which clings to our feet we wipe off *in protest* against you; yet be sure of this, that the kingdom of God has come near.'

12 "I say to you, it will be more tolerable in that day for Sodom than for that city.

13 ¶ "Woe to you, Chorazin! Woe to you, Bethsaida! For if the miracles had been performed in Tyre and Sidon which occurred in you, they would have repented long ago, sitting in sackcloth and ashes.

14 "But it will be more tolerable for Tyre and Sidon in the judgment than for you.

15 "And you, Capernaum, will not be exalted to heaven, will you? You will be brought down to Hades!

16 ¶ "The one who listens to you listens to Me, and the one who rejects you rejects Me; and he who rejects Me rejects the One who sent Me."

The Happy Results

10:23,24pp — Matt 13:16,17
10:25-28pp — Matt 22:34-40; Mark 12:28-31

17 ¶ The seventy returned with joy, saying, "Lord, even the demons are subject to us in Your name."

18 And He said to them, "I was watching Satan fall from heaven like lightning.

19 "Behold, I have given you authority to tread on serpents and scorpions, and over all the power of the enemy, and nothing will injure you.

20 "Nevertheless do not rejoice in this, that the spirits are subject to you, but rejoice that your names are recorded in heaven."

21 ¶ At that very time He rejoiced greatly in the Holy Spirit, and said, "I praise You, O Father, Lord of heaven and earth, that You have hidden these things from *the* wise and intelligent and have revealed them to infants. Yes, Father, for this way was well-pleasing in Your sight.

22 "All things have been handed over to Me by My Father, and no one knows who the Son is except the Father, and who the Father is except the

Son, and anyone to whom the Son wills to reveal *Him*."

23 ¶ Turning to the disciples, He said privately, "Blessed *are* the eyes which see the things you see,

10:20 Taste of Power

Power can go to your head, especially if you've never had any. The disciples—mainly farmers and fishermen—were overwhelmed to discover their spiritual authority. Jesus urged them to keep it in perspective. Their salvation, he said— their names written in heaven—mattered more than their power. The Bible often speaks of God's people having their names recorded in a heavenly book (Daniel 12:1; Revelation 3:5).

24 for I say to you, that many prophets and kings wished to see the things which you see, and did not see *them*, and to hear the things which you hear, and did not hear *them*."

25 ¶ And a lawyer stood up and put Him to the test, saying, "Teacher, what shall I do to inherit eternal life?"

26 And He said to him, "What is written in the Law? How does it read to you?"

27 And he answered, "YOU SHALL LOVE THE LORD YOUR GOD WITH ALL YOUR HEART, AND WITH ALL YOUR SOUL, AND WITH ALL YOUR STRENGTH, AND WITH ALL YOUR MIND; AND YOUR NEIGHBOR AS YOURSELF."

28 And He said to him, "You have answered correctly; DO THIS AND YOU WILL LIVE."

29 But wishing to justify himself, he said to Jesus, "And who is my neighbor?"

The Good Samaritan

30 Jesus replied and said, "A man was going down from Jerusalem to Jericho, and fell among robbers, and they stripped him and beat him, and went away leaving him half dead.

31 "And by chance a priest was going down on that road, and when he saw him, he passed by on the other side.

10:31 Which One Showed Love?

The priest saw the robbery victim in a half-dead state. According to Old Testament law, a priest who touched a dead body made himself ceremonially impure (Leviticus 21:1-4). The priest and religious Levite decided not to get involved. Jesus' audience might have been expecting the third character to be a Jewish layperson. But Jesus added a twist by making the one who showed love a Samaritan—a racial minority despised in Israel. In this way, Jesus contrasted mere religious beliefs with true love.

32 "Likewise a Levite also, when he came to the place and saw him, passed by on the other side.

33 "But a Samaritan, who was on a journey, came upon him; and when he saw him, he felt compassion,

34 and came to him and bandaged up his wounds, pouring oil and wine on *them*; and he put him on his own beast, and brought him to an inn and took care of him.

35 "On the next day he took out two [a]denarii and gave them to the innkeeper and said, 'Take care of him; and whatever more you spend, when I return I will repay you.'

36 "Which of these three do you think proved to be a neighbor to the man who fell into the robbers' *hands?*"

37 And he said, "The one who showed mercy toward him." Then Jesus said to him, "Go and do the same."

Martha and Mary

38 ¶ Now as they were traveling along, He entered a village; and a woman named Martha welcomed Him into her home.

39 She had a sister called Mary, who was seated at the Lord's feet, listening to His word.

40 But Martha was distracted with all her preparations; and she came up *to Him* and said, "Lord, do You not care that my sister has left me to do all the serving alone? Then tell her to help me."

41 But the Lord answered and said to her, "Martha, Martha, you are worried and bothered about so many things;

42 but *only* one thing is necessary, for Mary has chosen the good part, which shall not be taken away from her."

Instruction about Prayer

11:2–4pp — Matt 6:9–13
11:9–13pp — Matt 7:7–11

11 It happened that while Jesus was praying in a certain place, after He had finished, one of His disciples said to Him, "Lord, teach us to pray just as John also taught his disciples."

2 And He said to them, "When you pray, say:
'[b]Father, hallowed be Your name.
Your kingdom come.
3 'Give us each day our daily bread.
4 'And forgive us our sins,
For we ourselves also forgive everyone
who is indebted to us.
And lead us not into temptation.'"

5 ¶ Then He said to them, "Suppose one of you has a friend, and goes to him at midnight and says to him, 'Friend, lend me three loaves;

6 for a friend of mine has come to me from a journey, and I have nothing to set before him';

7 and from inside he answers and says, 'Do not bother me; the door has already been shut and my children and I are in bed; I cannot get up and give you *anything*.'

8 "I tell you, even though he will not get up and give him *anything* because he is his friend, yet because of his persistence he will get up and give him as much as he needs.

9 ¶ "So I say to you, ask, and it will be given to you; seek, and you will find; knock, and it will be opened to you.

10 "For everyone who asks, receives; and he who seeks, finds; and to him who knocks, it will be opened.

11 "Now suppose one of you fathers is asked by his son for a fish; he will not give him a snake instead of a fish, will he?

---

[a] The denarius was equivalent to a day's wages   [b] Later mss add phrases from Matt 6:9-13 to make the two passages closely similar

MARTHA AND MARY OF BETHANY *Doer and Seeker*

MARY AND MARTHA BOTH HAD a close relationship with Jesus, who loved them deeply. He visited the sisters' home three times that we know of, and probably many more. They lived with their brother Lazarus in Bethany, a village just outside Jerusalem. Like many sisters, Mary and Martha had quite different personalities, and we can see the difference clearly in how they related to Jesus.

Mary could drop everything and listen to Jesus. When he called, she answered instantly. She showed her love for him in extravagant ways, once lavishing a huge amount of expensive perfume on his feet (John 12:3). For Mary, everything stopped when Jesus was present.

Mary's ways sometimes annoyed her sister Martha, who showed more obsessive concern about getting things done. "Duty first" was Martha's motto. She served Jesus by preparing meals and doing the work of hosting.

Which way was better? Martha preferred her own hard-working style, and she asked Jesus to set Mary straight. Jesus gently disagreed. Mary, who simply sat at his feet and listened, did the one really necessary thing in life, he said, and he would not reprove her (10:41).

Life Questions: Are you more like Mary or like Martha? Why do you think Jesus preferred Mary's way?

12 "Or *if* he is asked for an egg, he will not give him a scorpion, will he?

13 "If you then, being evil, know how to give good gifts to your children, how much more will *your* heavenly Father give the Holy Spirit to those who ask Him?"

Pharisees' Blasphemy

11:14,15,17–22,24–26pp — Matt 12:22,24–29,43–45
11:17–22pp — Mark 3:23–27

14 ¶ And He was casting out a demon, and it was mute; when the demon had gone out, the mute man spoke; and the crowds were amazed.

15 But some of them said, "He casts out demons by Beelzebul, the ruler of the demons."

16 Others, to test *Him,* were demanding of Him a sign from heaven.

17 But He knew their thoughts and said to them, "Any kingdom divided against itself is laid waste; and a house *divided* against itself falls.

11:17 Jesus or Lincoln?

Abraham Lincoln is often credited with saying, "A house divided against itself cannot stand." Actually, Lincoln quoted Jesus, who was refuting a frivolous accusation that his power came from Satan (Beelzebul). Jesus suggested that if Satan used his power against his own cause, Satan's kingdom would soon fall. Lincoln applied this principle to the not-so-United States just before the Civil War: A nation divided over such a fundamental issue as slavery could not endure.

18 "If Satan also is divided against himself, how will his kingdom stand? For you say that I cast out demons by Beelzebul.

19 "And if I by Beelzebul cast out demons, by whom do your sons cast them out? So they will be your judges.

20 "But if I cast out demons by the finger of God, then the kingdom of God has come upon you.

21 "When a strong *man,* fully armed, guards his own house, his possessions are undisturbed.

22 "But when someone stronger than he attacks him and overpowers him, he takes away from him all his armor on which he had relied and distributes his plunder.

23 "He who is not with Me is against Me; and he who does not gather with Me, scatters.

24 ¶ "When the unclean spirit goes out of a man, it passes through waterless places seeking rest, and not finding any, it says, 'I will return to my house from which I came.'

25 "And when it comes, it finds it swept and put in order.

26 "Then it goes and takes *along* seven other spirits more evil than itself, and they go in and live there; and the last state of that man becomes worse than the first."

27 ¶ While Jesus was saying these things, one of the women in the crowd raised her voice and said to Him, "Blessed is the womb that bore You and the breasts at which You nursed."

28 But He said, "On the contrary, blessed are those who hear the word of God and observe it."

The Sign of Jonah

11:29–32pp — Matt 12:39–42
11:34,35pp — Matt 6:22,23

29 ¶ As the crowds were increasing, He began to say, "This generation is a wicked generation; it seeks for a sign, and *yet* no sign will be given to it but the sign of Jonah.

11:29 Sensation-Seekers

Jesus had no tolerance for people who begged for miraculous signs. Here and elsewhere he declared that no amount of proof would convince those who stubbornly refused to believe in him. In contrast, certain Old Testament Gentiles believed even though they had far less evidence.

30 "For just as Jonah became a sign to the Ninevites, so will the Son of Man be to this generation.

31 "The Queen of the South will rise up with the men of this generation at the judgment and condemn them, because she came from the ends of the earth to hear the wisdom of Solomon; and behold, something greater than Solomon is here.

32 "The men of Nineveh will stand up with this generation at the judgment and condemn it, because they repented at the preaching of Jonah; and behold, something greater than Jonah is here.

33 ¶ "No one, after lighting a lamp, puts it away in a cellar nor under a basket, but on the lampstand, so that those who enter may see the light.

34 "The eye is the lamp of your body; when your eye is clear, your whole body also is full of light; but when it is bad, your body also is full of darkness.

35 "Then watch out that the light in you is not darkness.

36 "If therefore your whole body is full of light, with no dark part in it, it will be wholly illumined, as when the lamp illumines you with its rays."

Woes upon the Pharisees

37 ¶ Now when He had spoken, a Pharisee *asked Him to have lunch with him; and He went in, and reclined *at the table.*

38 When the Pharisee saw it, he was surprised that He had not first ceremonially washed before the meal.

39 But the Lord said to him, "Now you Phari-

sees clean the outside of the cup and of the platter; but inside of you, you are full of robbery and wickedness.

40 "You foolish ones, did not He who made the outside make the inside also?

41 "But give that which is within as charity, and then all things are clean for you.

42 ¶ "But woe to you Pharisees! For you pay tithe of mint and rue and *every kind of* garden herb, and *yet* disregard justice and the love of God; but these are the things you should have done without neglecting the others.

43 "Woe to you Pharisees! For you love the chief seats in the synagogues and the respectful greetings in the market places.

44 "Woe to you! For you are like concealed tombs, and the people who walk over *them* are unaware *of it.*"

45 ¶ One of the ᵃlawyers *said to Him in reply, "Teacher, when You say this, You insult us too."

46 But He said, "Woe to you lawyers as well! For you weigh men down with burdens hard to bear, while you yourselves will not even touch the burdens with one of your fingers.

47 "Woe to you! For you build the tombs of the prophets, and *it was* your fathers *who* killed them.

48 "So you are witnesses and approve the deeds of your fathers; because it was they who killed them, and you build *their tombs.*

49 "For this reason also the wisdom of God said, 'I will send to them prophets and apostles, and *some* of them they will kill and *some* they will persecute,

50 so that the blood of all the prophets, shed since the foundation of the world, may be charged against this generation,

51 from the blood of Abel to the blood of Zechariah, who was killed between the altar and the house *of God*; yes, I tell you, it shall be charged against this generation.'

52 "Woe to you lawyers! For you have taken away the key of knowledge; you yourselves did not enter, and you hindered those who were entering."

53 ¶ When He left there, the scribes and the Pharisees began to be very hostile and to question Him closely on many subjects,

54 plotting against Him to catch *Him* in something He might say.

God Knows and Cares

12:2-9pp — Matt 10:26-33

12 Under these circumstances, after so many thousands of people had gathered together that they were stepping on one another, He began saying to His disciples first *of all*, "Beware of the leaven of the Pharisees, which is hypocrisy.

2 "But there is nothing covered up that will not

be revealed, and hidden that will not be known.

3 "Accordingly, whatever you have said in the dark will be heard in the light, and what you have whispered in the inner rooms will be proclaimed upon the housetops.

4 ¶ "I say to you, My friends, do not be afraid of those who kill the body and after that have no more that they can do.

5 "But I will warn you whom to fear: fear the One who, after He has killed, has authority to cast into hell; yes, I tell you, fear Him!

6 "Are not five sparrows sold for two cents? Yet not one of them is forgotten before God.

7 "Indeed, the very hairs of your head are all numbered. Do not fear; you are more valuable than many sparrows.

8 ¶ "And I say to you, everyone who confesses Me before men, the Son of Man will confess him also before the angels of God;

9 but he who denies Me before men will be denied before the angels of God.

10 "And everyone who speaks a word against the Son of Man, it will be forgiven him; but he who blasphemes against the Holy Spirit, it will not be forgiven him.

11 "When they bring you before the synagogues and the rulers and the authorities, do not worry about how or what you are to speak in your defense, or what you are to say;

12 for the Holy Spirit will teach you in that very hour what you ought to say."

Covetousness Denounced

12:22-31pp — Matt 6:25-33

13 ¶ Someone in the crowd said to Him, "Teacher, tell my brother to divide the *family* inheritance with me."

14 But He said to him, "Man, who appointed Me a judge or arbitrator over you?"

15 Then He said to them, "Beware, and be on your guard against every form of greed; for not *even* when one has an abundance does his life consist of his possessions."

12:15 When Money Is Useless

Jesus refused to get involved in a family dispute about money. In this statement, he neatly summarized his usual approach to money. He did not condemn the possession of it. But he did warn against putting faith in money to secure the future. The rich man's money did him absolutely no good the night of his death. To emphasize his point, Jesus referred back to King Solomon, the richest man in the Old Testament (verse 27). The lesson: Trust in God and his kingdom, and free yourself of worry about money and possessions.

ᵃ I.e. experts in the Mosaic Law

16 And He told them a parable, saying, "The land of a rich man was very productive.

17 "And he began reasoning to himself, saying, 'What shall I do, since I have no place to store my crops?'

18 "Then he said, 'This is what I will do: I will tear down my barns and build larger ones, and there I will store all my grain and my goods.

19 'And I will say to my soul, "Soul, you have many goods laid up for many years *to come*; take your ease, eat, drink *and* be merry." '

20 "But God said to him, 'You fool! This *very* night your soul is required of you; and *now* who will own what you have prepared?'

21 "So is the man who stores up treasure for himself, and is not rich toward God."

22 ¶ And He said to His disciples, "For this reason I say to you, do not worry about *your* life, *as to* what you will eat; nor for your body, *as to* what you will put on.

23 "For life is more than food, and the body more than clothing.

24 "Consider the ravens, for they neither sow nor reap; they have no storeroom nor barn, and *yet* God feeds them; how much more valuable you are than the birds!

25 "And which of you by worrying can add a single *a*hour to his *b*life's span?

26 "If then you cannot do even a very little thing, why do you worry about other matters?

27 "Consider the lilies, how they grow: they neither toil nor spin; but I tell you, not even Solomon in all his glory clothed himself like one of these.

28 "But if God so clothes the grass in the field, which is *alive* today and tomorrow is thrown into the furnace, how much more *will He clothe* you? You men of little faith!

29 "And do not seek what you will eat and what you will drink, and do not keep worrying.

30 "For all these things the nations of the world eagerly seek; but your Father knows that you need these things.

31 "But seek His kingdom, and these things will be added to you.

32 "Do not be afraid, little flock, for your Father has chosen gladly to give you the kingdom.

33 ¶ "Sell your possessions and give to charity; make yourselves money belts which do not wear out, an unfailing treasure in heaven, where no thief comes near nor moth destroys.

34 "For where your treasure is, there your heart will be also.

Be in Readiness

12:35,36pp — Matt 25:1-13; Mark 13:33-37
12:39,40,42-46pp — Matt 24:43-51

35 ¶ "Be dressed in readiness, and *keep* your lamps lit.

36 "Be like men who are waiting for their master when he returns from the wedding feast, so that they may immediately open *the door* to him when he comes and knocks.

37 "Blessed are those slaves whom the master will find on the alert when he comes; truly I say to you, that he will gird himself *to serve*, and have them recline *at the table*, and will come up and wait on them.

38 "Whether he comes in the *c*second watch, or even in the *d*third, and finds *them* so, blessed are those *slaves*.

39 ¶ "But be sure of this, that if the head of the house had known at what hour the thief was coming, he would not have allowed his house to be broken into.

40 "You too, be ready; for the Son of Man is coming at an hour that you do not expect."

41 ¶ Peter said, "Lord, are You addressing this parable to us, or to everyone *else* as well?"

42 And the Lord said, "Who then is the faithful and sensible steward, whom his master will put in charge of his servants, to give them their rations at the proper time?

43 "Blessed is that slave whom his master finds so doing when he comes.

44 "Truly I say to you that he will put him in charge of all his possessions.

45 "But if that slave says in his heart, 'My master will be a long time in coming,' and begins to beat the slaves, *both* men and women, and to eat and drink and get drunk;

46 the master of that slave will come on a day when he does not expect *him* and at an hour he does not know, and will cut him in pieces, and assign him a place with the unbelievers.

47 "And that slave who knew his master's will and did not get ready or act in accord with his will, will receive many lashes,

48 but the one who did not know *it*, and committed deeds worthy of a flogging, will receive but few. From everyone who has been given much, much will be required; and to whom they entrusted much, of him they will ask all the more.

Christ Divides Men

12:51-53pp — Matt 10:34-36

49 ¶ "I have come to cast fire upon the earth; and how I wish it were already kindled!

50 "But I have a baptism to undergo, and how distressed I am until it is accomplished!

51 "Do you suppose that I came to grant peace on earth? I tell you, no, but rather division;

52 for from now on five *members* in one household will be divided, three against two and two against three.

53 "They will be divided, father against son and son against father, mother against daughter and daughter against mother, mother in-law against

---

a Lit *cubit* (approx 18 in.)   *b* Or *height*   *c* I.e. 9 p.m. to midnight   *d* I.e. midnight to 3 a.m.

daughter-in-law and daughter-in-law against mother-in-law."

54 ¶ And He was also saying to the crowds, "When you see a cloud rising in the west, immediately you say, 'A shower is coming,' and so it turns out.

55 "And when *you see* a south wind blowing, you say, 'It will be a hot day,' and it turns out *that way.*

56 "You hypocrites! You know how to analyze the appearance of the earth and the sky, but why do you not analyze this present time?

57 ¶ "And why do you not even on your own initiative judge what is right?

58 "For while you are going with your opponent to appear before the magistrate, on *your* way *there* make an effort to settle with him, so that he may not drag you before the judge, and the judge turn you over to the officer, and the officer throw you into prison.

59 "I say to you, you will not get out of there until you have paid the very last cent."

Call to Repent

13 Now on the same occasion there were some present who reported to Him about the Galileans whose blood Pilate had mixed with their sacrifices.

2 And Jesus said to them, "Do you suppose that these Galileans were *greater* sinners than all *other* Galileans because they suffered this *fate?*

3 "I tell you, no, but unless you repent, you will all likewise perish.

4 "Or do you suppose that those eighteen on whom the tower in Siloam fell and killed them were *worse* culprits than all the men who live in Jerusalem?

5 "I tell you, no, but unless you repent, you will all likewise perish."

6 ¶ And He *began* telling this parable: "A man had a fig tree which had been planted in his vineyard; and he came looking for fruit on it and did not find any.

7 "And he said to the vineyard-keeper, 'Behold, for three years I have come looking for fruit on this fig tree without finding any. Cut it down! Why does it even use up the ground?'

8 "And he answered and said to him, 'Let it alone, sir, for this year too, until I dig around it and put in fertilizer;

9 and if it bears fruit next year, *fine;* but if not, cut it down.' "

Healing on the Sabbath

10 ¶ And He was teaching in one of the synagogues on the Sabbath.

11 And there was a woman who for eighteen years had had a sickness caused by a spirit; and she was bent double, and could not straighten up at all.

12 When Jesus saw her, He called her over and

said to her, "Woman, you are freed from your sickness."

13 And He laid His hands on her; and immediately she was made erect again and *began* glorifying God.

14 But the synagogue official, indignant because Jesus had healed on the Sabbath, *began* saying to the crowd in response, "There are six days in which work should be done; so come during them and get healed, and not on the Sabbath day."

15 But the Lord answered him and said, "You hypocrites, does not each of you on the Sabbath untie his ox or his donkey from the stall and lead him away to water *him?*

16 "And this woman, a daughter of Abraham as she is, whom Satan has bound for eighteen long years, should she not have been released from this bond on the Sabbath day?"

17 As He said this, all His opponents were being humiliated; and the entire crowd was rejoicing over all the glorious things being done by Him.

Parables of Mustard Seed and Leaven

13:18,19pp — Mark 4:30–32
13:18–21pp — Matt 13:31–33

18 ¶ So He was saying, "What is the kingdom of God like, and to what shall I compare it?

19 "It is like a mustard seed, which a man took and threw into his own garden; and it grew and became a tree, and THE BIRDS OF THE AIR NESTED IN ITS BRANCHES."

20 ¶ And again He said, "To what shall I compare the kingdom of God?

21 "It is like leaven, which a woman took and hid in three pecks of flour until it was all leavened."

Teaching in the Villages

13:34,35pp — Matt 23:37–39
13:34,35Ref — Luke 19:41

22 ¶ And He was passing through from one city and village to another, teaching, and proceeding on His way to Jerusalem.

23 And someone said to Him, "Lord, are there *just* a few who are being saved?" And He said to them,

24 "Strive to enter through the narrow door; for many, I tell you, will seek to enter and will not be able.

25 "Once the head of the house gets up and shuts the door, and you begin to stand outside and knock on the door, saying, 'Lord, open up to us!' then He will answer and say to you, 'I do not know where you are from.'

26 "Then you will begin to say, 'We ate and drank in Your presence, and You taught in our streets';

27 and He will say, 'I tell you, I do not know where you are from; DEPART FROM ME, ALL YOU EVILDOERS.'

28 "In that place there will be weeping and

gnashing of teeth when you see Abraham and Isaac and Jacob and all the prophets in the kingdom of God, but yourselves being thrown out.

29 "And they will come from east and west and from north and south, and will recline *at the table* in the kingdom of God.

30 "And behold, *some* are last who will be first and *some* are first who will be last."

31 ¶ Just at that time some Pharisees approached, saying to Him, "Go away, leave here, for Herod wants to kill You."

32 And He said to them, "Go and tell that fox, 'Behold, I cast out demons and perform cures today and tomorrow, and the third *day* I reach My goal.'

13:32 Who Had Real Power?

Jesus was executed by powerful political authorities, among them the Roman official Herod. But this statement, spoken before his arrest, reveals who had the real power. Jesus dismissed Herod as "that fox," a Jewish expression for a worthless or insignificant person. Jesus' death on a cross came as no surprise to him; in fact, here Jesus calls it his "goal."

33 "Nevertheless I must journey on today and tomorrow and the next *day*; for it cannot be that a prophet would perish outside of Jerusalem.

34 "O Jerusalem, Jerusalem, *the city* that kills the prophets and stones those sent to her! How often I wanted to gather your children together, just as a hen *gathers* her brood under her wings, and you would not *have it!*

35 "Behold, your house is left to you *desolate*; and I say to you, you will not see Me until *the time* comes when you say, 'BLESSED IS HE WHO COMES IN THE NAME OF THE LORD!' "

Jesus Heals on the Sabbath

14:8–10Ref — Prov 25:6,7

14 It happened that when He went into the house of one of the leaders of the Pharisees on *the* Sabbath to eat bread, they were watching Him closely.

2 And there in front of Him was a man suffering from dropsy.

3 And Jesus answered and spoke to the lawyers and Pharisees, saying, "Is it lawful to heal on the Sabbath, or not?"

4 But they kept silent. And He took hold of him and healed him, and sent him away.

5 And He said to them, "Which one of you will have a son or an ox fall into a well, and will not immediately pull him out on a Sabbath day?"

6 And they could make no reply to this.

Parable of the Guests

14:16–24Ref — Matt 22:2-14

7 ¶ And He *began* speaking a parable to the invited guests when He noticed how they had been picking out the places of honor *at the table*, saying to them,

8 "When you are invited by someone to a wedding feast, do not take the place of honor, for someone more distinguished than you may have been invited by him,

9 and he who invited you both will come and say to you, 'Give *your* place to this man,' and then in disgrace you proceed to occupy the last place.

10 "But when you are invited, go and recline at the last place, so that when the one who has invited you comes, he may say to you, 'Friend, move up higher'; then you will have honor in the sight of all who are at the table with you.

11 "For everyone who exalts himself will be humbled, and he who humbles himself will be exalted."

12 ¶ And He also went on to say to the one who had invited Him, "When you give a luncheon or a dinner, do not invite your friends or your brothers or your relatives or rich neighbors, otherwise they may also invite you in return and *that* will be your repayment.

13 "But when you give a reception, invite *the* poor, *the* crippled, *the* lame, *the* blind,

14 and you will be blessed, since they do not have *the means* to repay you; for you will be repaid at the resurrection of the righteous."

15 ¶ When one of those who were reclining *at the table* with Him heard this, he said to Him, "Blessed is everyone who will eat bread in the kingdom of God!"

Parable of the Dinner

16 But He said to him, "A man was giving a big dinner, and he invited many;

17 and at the dinner hour he sent his slave to say to those who had been invited, 'Come; for everything is ready now.'

18 "But they all alike began to make excuses. The first one said to him, 'I have bought a piece of land and I need to go out and look at it; please consider me excused.'

19 "Another one said, 'I have bought five yoke of oxen, and I am going to try them out; please consider me excused.'

20 "Another one said, 'I have married a wife, and for that reason I cannot come.'

21 "And the slave came *back* and reported this to his master. Then the head of the household became angry and said to his slave, 'Go out at once into the streets and lanes of the city and bring in here the poor and crippled and blind and lame.'

22 "And the slave said, 'Master, what you commanded has been done, and still there is room.'

23 "And the master said to the slave, 'Go out

into the highways and along the hedges, and compel *them* to come in, so that my house may be filled.

24 'For I tell you, none of those men who were invited shall taste of my dinner.' "

Discipleship Tested

25 ¶ Now large crowds were going along with Him; and He turned and said to them,

26 "If anyone comes to Me, and does not [a]hate his own father and mother and wife and children and brothers and sisters, yes, and even his own life, he cannot be My disciple.

27 "Whoever does not carry his own cross and come after Me cannot be My disciple.

28 "For which one of you, when he wants to build a tower, does not first sit down and calculate the cost to see if he has enough to complete it?

29 "Otherwise, when he has laid a foundation and is not able to finish, all who observe it begin to ridicule him,

30 saying, 'This man began to build and was not able to finish.'

31 "Or what king, when he sets out to meet another king in battle, will not first sit down and consider whether he is strong enough with ten thousand *men* to encounter the one coming against him with twenty thousand?

32 "Or else, while the other is still far away, he sends a delegation and asks for terms of peace.

33 "So then, none of you can be My disciple who does not give up all his own possessions.

34 ¶ "Therefore, salt is good; but if even salt has become tasteless, with what will it be seasoned?

35 "It is useless either for the soil or for the manure pile; it is thrown out. He who has ears to hear, let him hear."

The Lost Sheep

15:4–7pp — Matt 18:12–14

15 Now all the tax collectors and the sinners were coming near Him to listen to Him.

2 Both the Pharisees and the scribes *began* to grumble, saying, "This man receives sinners and eats with them."

3 ¶ So He told them this parable, saying,

4 "What man among you, if he has a hundred sheep and has lost one of them, does not leave the ninety-nine in the open pasture and go after the one which is lost until he finds it?

5 "When he has found it, he lays it on his shoulders, rejoicing.

6 "And when he comes home, he calls together his friends and his neighbors, saying to them, 'Rejoice with me, for I have found my sheep which was lost!'

7 "I tell you that in the same way, there will be *more* joy in heaven over one sinner who repents

[a] I.e. by comparison of his love for Me

than over ninety-nine righteous persons who need no repentance.

The Lost Coin

8 ¶ "Or what woman, if she has ten silver coins and loses one coin, does not light a lamp and sweep the house and search carefully until she finds it?

9 "When she has found it, she calls together her friends and neighbors, saying, 'Rejoice with me, for I have found the coin which I had lost!'

10 "In the same way, I tell you, there is joy in the presence of the angels of God over one sinner who repents."

The Prodigal Son

11 ¶ And He said, "A man had two sons.

12 "The younger of them said to his father, 'Father, give me the share of the estate that falls to me.' So he divided his wealth between them.

13 "And not many days later, the younger son gathered everything together and went on a journey into a distant country, and there he squandered his estate with loose living.

14 "Now when he had spent everything, a severe famine occurred in that country, and he began to be impoverished.

15 "So he went and hired himself out to one of the citizens of that country, and he sent him into his fields to feed swine.

16 "And he would have gladly filled his stomach with the pods that the swine were eating, and no one was giving *anything* to him.

17 "But when he came to his senses, he said, 'How many of my father's hired men have more than enough bread, but I am dying here with hunger!

18 'I will get up and go to my father, and will say to him, "Father, I have sinned against heaven, and in your sight;

19 I am no longer worthy to be called your son; make me as one of your hired men."'

20 "So he got up and came to his father. But while he was still a long way off, his father saw him

and felt compassion *for him*, and ran and embraced him and kissed him.

21 "And the son said to him, 'Father, I have sinned against heaven and in your sight; I am no longer worthy to be called your son.'

22 "But the father said to his slaves, 'Quickly bring out the best robe and put it on him, and put a ring on his hand and sandals on his feet;

23 and bring the fattened calf, kill it, and let us eat and celebrate;

24 for this son of mine was dead and has come to life again; he was lost and has been found.' And they began to celebrate.

25 ¶ "Now his older son was in the field, and when he came and approached the house, he heard music and dancing.

26 "And he summoned one of the servants and *began* inquiring what these things could be.

27 "And he said to him, 'Your brother has come, and your father has killed the fattened calf because he has received him back safe and sound.'

28 "But he became angry and was not willing to go in; and his father came out and *began* pleading with him.

15:28 Two Lost Brothers?

The parable of the Lost Son actually tells of two sons, one irresponsible, the other hardworking. One wastes his life and comes home humbled; the other proudly refuses to celebrate his brother's homecoming. The story ends with one son in a joyful family celebration, and his brother outside, bitterly unwilling to forgive. Which son is really lost?

29 "But he answered and said to his father, 'Look! For so many years I have been serving you and I have never neglected a command of yours; and *yet* you have never given me a young goat, so that I might celebrate with my friends;

30 but when this son of yours came, who has devoured your wealth with prostitutes, you killed the fattened calf for him.'

31 "And he said to him, 'Son, you have always been with me, and all that is mine is yours.

32 'But we had to celebrate and rejoice, for this brother of yours was dead and *has begun* to live, and *was* lost and has been found.'"

The Unrighteous Steward

16 Now He was also saying to the disciples, "There was a rich man who had a manager, and this *manager* was reported to him as squandering his possessions.

2 "And he called him and said to him, 'What is this I hear about you? Give an accounting of your management, for you can no longer be manager.'

3 "The manager said to himself, 'What shall I do, since my master is taking the management away from me? I am not strong enough to dig; I am ashamed to beg.

4 'I know what I shall do, so that when I am removed from the management people will welcome me into their homes.'

5 "And he summoned each one of his master's debtors, and he *began* saying to the first, 'How much do you owe my master?'

6 "And he said, 'A hundred measures of oil.' And he said to him, 'Take your bill, and sit down quickly and write fifty.'

7 "Then he said to another, 'And how much do you owe?' And he said, 'A hundred measures of wheat.' He *said to him, 'Take your bill, and write eighty.'

8 "And his master praised the unrighteous manager because he had acted shrewdly; for the sons of this age are more shrewd in relation to their own kind than the sons of light.

9 "And I say to you, make friends for yourselves by means of the ᵃwealth of unrighteousness, so that when it fails, they will receive you into the eternal dwellings.

10 ¶ "He who is faithful in a very little thing is faithful also in much; and he who is unrighteous in a very little thing is unrighteous also in much.

11 "Therefore if you have not been faithful in the *use of* unrighteous wealth, who will entrust the true *riches* to you?

12 "And if you have not been faithful in *the use of* that which is another's, who will give you that which is your own?

13 "No servant can serve two masters; for either he will hate the one and love the other, or else he will be devoted to one and despise the other. You cannot serve God and wealth."

14 ¶ Now the Pharisees, who were lovers of money, were listening to all these things and were scoffing at Him.

15 And He said to them, "You are those who justify yourselves in the sight of men, but God knows your hearts; for that which is highly esteemed among men is detestable in the sight of God.

16 ¶ "The Law and the Prophets *were proclaimed* until John; since that time the gospel of the kingdom of God has been preached, and everyone is forcing his way into it.

17 "But it is easier for heaven and earth to pass away than for one stroke of a letter of the Law to fail.

18 ¶ "Everyone who divorces his wife and marries another commits adultery, and he who marries one who is divorced from a husband commits adultery.

ᵃ Gr *mammon*, fr Aram *mamona*, signifying riches, wealth, etc, personified as an object of worship

The Rich Man and Lazarus

19 ¶ "Now there was a rich man, and he habitually dressed in purple and fine linen, joyously living in splendor every day.

20 "And a poor man named Lazarus was laid at his gate, covered with sores,

21 and longing to be fed with the *crumbs* which were falling from the rich man's table; besides, even the dogs were coming and licking his sores.

22 "Now the poor man died and was carried away by the angels to Abraham's bosom; and the rich man also died and was buried.

23 "In Hades he lifted up his eyes, being in torment, and *saw Abraham far away and Lazarus in his bosom.

24 "And he cried out and said, 'Father Abraham, have mercy on me, and send Lazarus so that he may dip the tip of his finger in water and cool off my tongue, for I am in agony in this flame.'

25 "But Abraham said, 'Child, remember that during your life you received your good things, and likewise Lazarus bad things; but now he is being comforted here, and you are in agony.

26 'And besides all this, between us and you there is a great chasm fixed, so that those who wish to come over from here to you will not be able, and *that* none may cross over from there to us.'

27 "And he said, 'Then I beg you, father, that you send him to my father's house—

28 for I have five brothers—in order that he may warn them, so that they will not also come to this place of torment.'

29 "But Abraham *said, 'They have Moses and the Prophets; let them hear them.'

30 "But he said, 'No, father Abraham, but if someone goes to them from the dead, they will repent!'

31 "But he said to him, 'If they do not listen to Moses and the Prophets, they will not be persuaded even if someone rises from the dead.' "

16:31 Stubbornly Unconvinced

With the concluding statement in this famous story of Lazarus, Jesus made a poignant prophecy, although his listeners at the time probably missed the point. Many of them, especially the Pharisees, refused to believe him even after he rose from the dead.

Instructions

17 He said to His disciples, "It is inevitable that stumbling blocks come, but woe to him through whom they come!

2 "It would be better for him if a millstone were hung around his neck and he were thrown

into the sea, than that he would cause one of these little ones to stumble.

3 "Be on your guard! If your brother sins, rebuke him; and if he repents, forgive him.

4 "And if he sins against you seven times a day, and returns to you seven times, saying, 'I repent,' forgive him."

5 ¶ The apostles said to the Lord, "Increase our faith!"

6 And the Lord said, "If you had faith like a mustard seed, you would say to this mulberry tree, 'Be uprooted and be planted in the sea'; and it would obey you.

7 ¶ "Which of you, having a slave plowing or tending sheep, will say to him when he has come in from the field, 'Come immediately and sit down to eat'?

8 "But will he not say to him, 'Prepare something for me to eat, and *properly* clothe yourself and serve me while I eat and drink; and afterward you may eat and drink'?

9 "He does not thank the slave because he did the things which were commanded, does he?

10 "So you too, when you do all the things which are commanded you, say, 'We are unworthy slaves; we have done *only* that which we ought to have done.' "

Ten Lepers Cleansed

17:26,27pp — Matt 24:37–39

11 ¶ While He was on the way to Jerusalem, He was passing between Samaria and Galilee.

12 As He entered a village, ten leprous men who stood at a distance met Him;

13 and they raised their voices, saying, "Jesus, Master, have mercy on us!"

14 When He saw them, He said to them, "Go and show yourselves to the priests." And as they were going, they were cleansed.

15 Now one of them, when he saw that he had been healed, turned back, glorifying God with a loud voice,

16 and he fell on his face at His feet, giving thanks to Him. And he was a Samaritan.

17 Then Jesus answered and said, "Were there not ten cleansed? But the nine—where are they?

18 "Was no one found who returned to give glory to God, except this foreigner?"

19 And He said to him, "Stand up and go; your faith ªhas made you well."

20 ¶ Now having been questioned by the Pharisees as to when the kingdom of God was coming, He answered them and said, "The kingdom of God is not coming with signs to be observed;

21 nor will they say, 'Look, here *it is!*' or, 'There *it is!*' For behold, the kingdom of God is in your midst."

ª Lit *has saved you*

Second Coming Foretold

22 ¶ And He said to the disciples, "The days will come when you will long to see one of the days of the Son of Man, and you will not see it.

23 "They will say to you, 'Look there! Look here!' Do not go away, and do not run after *them*.

24 "For just like the lightning, when it flashes out of one part of the sky, shines to the other part of the sky, so will the Son of Man be in His day.

25 "But first He must suffer many things and be rejected by this generation.

26 "And just as it happened in the days of Noah, so it will be also in the days of the Son of Man:

27 they were eating, they were drinking, they were marrying, they were being given in marriage, until the day that Noah entered the ark, and the flood came and destroyed them all.

28 "It was the same as happened in the days of Lot: they were eating, they were drinking, they were buying, they were selling, they were planting, they were building;

29 but on the day that Lot went out from Sodom it rained fire and brimstone from heaven and destroyed them all.

30 "It will be just the same on the day that the Son of Man is revealed.

31 "On that day, the one who is on the housetop and whose goods are in the house must not go down to take them out; and likewise the one who is in the field must not turn back.

32 "Remember Lot's wife.

33 "Whoever seeks to keep his life will lose it, and whoever loses *his life* will preserve it.

34 "I tell you, on that night there will be two in one bed; one will be taken and the other will be left.

35 "There will be two women grinding at the same place; one will be taken and the other will be left.

36 ["*a*Two men will be in the field; one will be taken and the other will be left."]

37 And answering they *said to Him, "Where, Lord?" And He said to them, "Where the body *is*, there also the vultures will be gathered."

Parables on Prayer

18 Now He was telling them a parable to show that at all times they ought to pray and not to lose heart,

2 saying, "In a certain city there was a judge who did not fear God and did not respect man.

3 "There was a widow in that city, and she kept coming to him, saying, 'Give me legal protection from my opponent.'

4 "For a while he was unwilling; but afterward he said to himself, 'Even though I do not fear God nor respect man,

5 yet because this widow bothers me, I will give her legal protection, otherwise by continually coming she will wear me out.' "

6 And the Lord said, "Hear what the unrighteous judge *said;

7 now, will not God bring about justice for His elect who cry to Him day and night, and will He delay long over them?

8 "I tell you that He will bring about justice for them quickly. However, when the Son of Man comes, will He find faith on the earth?"

The Pharisee and the Publican

18:15–17pp — Matt 19:13–15; Mark 10:13–16

9 ¶ And He also told this parable to some people who trusted in themselves that they were righteous, and viewed others with contempt:

18:9 Luke and the Underdog

Luke's concern for the humble comes through clearly in the stories he selected, especially in chapters 18 and 19. The parable of the Pharisee and the tax collector, for example, draws a sharp contrast between the proud and the humble. Stories that follow also feature the humble: little children, a blind beggar, another tax collector.

10 "Two men went up into the temple to pray, one a Pharisee and the other a tax collector.

11 "The Pharisee stood and was praying this to himself: 'God, I thank You that I am not like other people: swindlers, unjust, adulterers, or even like this tax collector.

12 'I fast twice a week; I pay tithes of all that I get.'

13 "But the tax collector, standing some distance away, was even unwilling to lift up his eyes to heaven, but was beating his breast, saying, 'God, be merciful to me, the sinner!'

14 "I tell you, this man went to his house justified rather than the other; for everyone who exalts himself will be humbled, but he who humbles himself will be exalted."

15 ¶ And they were bringing even their babies to Him so that He would touch them, but when the disciples saw it, they *began* rebuking them.

16 But Jesus called for them, saying, "Permit the children to come to Me, and do not hinder them, for the kingdom of God belongs to such as these.

17 "Truly I say to you, whoever does not receive the kingdom of God like a child will not enter it *at all.*"

a Early mss do not contain this v

The Rich Young Ruler

18:18–30pp — Matt 19:16–29; Mark 10:17–30
18:31–33pp — Matt 20:17–19; Mark 10:32–34

18 ¶ A ruler questioned Him, saying, "Good Teacher, what shall I do to inherit eternal life?"

19 And Jesus said to him, "Why do you call Me good? No one is good except God alone.

20 "You know the commandments, 'DO NOT COMMIT ADULTERY, DO NOT MURDER, DO NOT STEAL, DO NOT BEAR FALSE WITNESS, HONOR YOUR FATHER AND MOTHER.' "

21 And he said, "All these things I have kept from *my* youth."

22 When Jesus heard *this*, He said to him, "One thing you still lack; sell all that you possess and distribute it to the poor, and you shall have treasure in heaven; and come, follow Me."

23 But when he had heard these things, he became very sad, for he was extremely rich.

24 And Jesus looked at him and said, "How hard it is for those who are wealthy to enter the kingdom of God!

25 "For it is easier for a camel to go through the eye of a needle than for a rich man to enter the kingdom of God."

26 They who heard it said, "Then who can be saved?"

27 But He said, "The things that are impossible with people are possible with God."

28 ¶ Peter said, "Behold, we have left our own *homes* and followed You."

29 And He said to them, "Truly I say to you, there is no one who has left house or wife or brothers or parents or children, for the sake of the kingdom of God,

30 who will not receive many times as much at this time and in the age to come, eternal life."

31 ¶ Then He took the twelve aside and said to them, "Behold, we are going up to Jerusalem, and all things which are written through the prophets about the Son of Man will be accomplished.

32 "For He will be handed over to the Gentiles, and will be mocked and mistreated and spit upon,

33 and after they have scourged Him, they will kill Him; and the third day He will rise again."

34 But the disciples understood none of these things, and *the meaning of* this statement was hidden from them, and they did not comprehend the things that were said.

Bartimaeus Receives Sight

18:35–43pp — Matt 20:29–34; Mark 10:46–52

35 ¶ As Jesus was approaching Jericho, a blind man was sitting by the road begging.

36 Now hearing a crowd going by, he *began* to inquire what this was.

37 They told him that Jesus of Nazareth was passing by.

38 And he called out, saying, "Jesus, Son of David, have mercy on me!"

39 Those who led the way were sternly telling him to be quiet; but he kept crying out all the more, "Son of David, have mercy on me!"

40 And Jesus stopped and commanded that he be brought to Him; and when he came near, He questioned him,

41 "What do you want Me to do for you?" And he said, "Lord, *I want* to regain my sight!"

42 And Jesus said to him, "Receive your sight; your faith has made you well."

43 Immediately he regained his sight and *began* following Him, glorifying God; and when all the people saw it, they gave praise to God.

Zaccheus Converted

19 He entered Jericho and was passing through.

2 And there was a man called by the name of Zaccheus; he was a chief tax collector and he was rich.

3 Zaccheus was trying to see who Jesus was, and was unable because of the crowd, for he was small in stature.

4 So he ran on ahead and climbed up into a sycamore tree in order to see Him, for He was about to pass through that way.

5 When Jesus came to the place, He looked up and said to him, "Zaccheus, hurry and come down, for today I must stay at your house."

6 And he hurried and came down and received Him gladly.

7 When they saw it, they all *began* to grumble, saying, "He has gone to be the guest of a man who is a sinner."

8 Zaccheus stopped and said to the Lord, "Behold, Lord, half of my possessions I will give to the poor, and if I have defrauded anyone of anything, I will give back four times as much."

9 And Jesus said to him, "Today salvation has come to this house, because he, too, is a son of Abraham.

10 "For the Son of Man has come to seek and to save that which was lost."

Parable of Money Usage

19:12–27Ref — Matt 25:14–30

11 ¶ While they were listening to these things,

19:10 Seek and Save

A Jew who had sided with the hated Roman oppressors, Zaccheus still had enough religious sensitivity to be curious about Jesus. Seeing his interest, Jesus took the initiative. He stopped the procession and called out to Zaccheus, inviting himself to a meal at Zaccheus's home. Though befriending this tax collector upset the crowd, Jesus proclaimed it as typical of his ministry: to seek and to save the lost.

Jesus went on to tell a parable, because He was near Jerusalem, and they supposed that the kingdom of God was going to appear immediately.

12 So He said, "A nobleman went to a distant country to receive a kingdom for himself, and *then* return.

13 "And he called ten of his slaves, and gave them ten *a*minas and said to them, 'Do business *with this* until I come *back*.'

14 "But his citizens hated him and sent a delega-tion after him, saying, 'We do not want this man to reign over us.'

15 "When he returned, after receiving the kingdom, he ordered that these slaves, to whom he had given the money, be called to him so that he might know what business they had done.

16 "The first appeared, saying, 'Master, your mina has made ten minas more.'

17 "And he said to him, 'Well done, good slave, because you have been faithful in a very little

a A mina is equal to about 100 days' wages

Handling Tough Questions
Why so many stories?

SUFFERING STRIKES LIKE AN EARTHQUAKE, without warning, causing sudden devastation. Twenty-nine teenagers die when a school bus plunges off a bridge. A hurricane smashes into Mexico. An epidemic of cholera breaks out in South America.

Psychological tremors follow, often in the form of questions. "Why did God let this happen? Did we do something wrong? Why does God permit such suffering?"

In Jesus' day, rumors buzzed about two catastrophes: Pontius Pilate's slaughter of Galileans and the collapse of a tower (13:1–4). Naturally, people around Jesus questioned him about these events, but his answers puzzled them. He refused to be drawn into a discussion of the age-old problem of pain. He merely dismissed the common opinion that tragedies happen to people who deserve them and deflected the issue back to the questioners as a general warning (13:4–5; see also "What Job Teaches about Suffering," page 588).

> The chief priests and the scribes and the leading men among the people were trying to destroy Him, and they could not find anything that they might do, for all the people were hanging on to every word He said. 19:47–48

The Heart of the Question

Jesus' response to the questions on suffering illustrate how he dealt with difficult issues. Religious leaders and philosophical types were constantly trying to stop him with an arsenal of tough questions. Usually their tactics backfired as Jesus expertly turned their questions back on them.

Conscious of the listening crowds, Jesus avoided long arguments, instead emphasizing the need for people to change behavior. His answers cut to the heart of the question, and to the hearts of his listeners.

When teaching, Jesus often relied on a parable—a compact short story with a moral. Speaking in parables allowed him to continue training his disciples "privately," despite the throngs of onlookers (8:10). He could explain the meaning to the disciples later on when they were alone together. Parables also helped preserve his message: Years later, as people reflected on what Jesus taught, his parables came to mind in vivid detail.

Simple Stories with a Profound Point

Luke, a master storyteller, collected 18 parables that appear nowhere else, and he also retold some of the most familiar. While Matthew emphasizes parables of the kingdom, Luke adds those that focus on people: the good Samaritan, a persistent widow, the lost son. His parables speak to heavy subjects, but in an unexpectedly disarming way.

Jesus' style of handling tough questions contrasts sharply with Paul's. The apostle Paul wrapped concepts in theological words and gave formal explanations. In careful prose he patiently probed such complex words as *forgiveness* and *justification*.

Jesus, speaking to a restless crowd of thousands, communicated the same message in three progressive stories—The Lost Sheep, The Lost Coin, and The Prodigal Son (15:1–32). Scottish Christians like to call that last story "The Wonderful Father." It expresses the heart of Jesus' message about as well as any ten-volume theological work.

Life Questions: What one question would you most like to ask Jesus in person? Given how he handled tough questions in Luke, can you imagine how he might respond to yours?

thing, you are to be in authority over ten cities.'

18 "The second came, saying, 'Your mina, master, has made five minas.'

19 "And he said to him also, 'And you are to be over five cities.'

20 "Another came, saying, 'Master, here is your mina, which I kept put away in a handkerchief;

21 for I was afraid of you, because you are an exacting man; you take up what you did not lay down and reap what you did not sow.'

22 "He *said to him, 'By your own words I will judge you, you worthless slave. Did you know that I am an exacting man, taking up what I did not lay down and reaping what I did not sow?

23 'Then why did you not put my money in the bank, and having come, I would have collected it with interest?'

24 "Then he said to the bystanders, 'Take the mina away from him and give it to the one who has the ten minas.'

25 "And they said to him, 'Master, he has ten minas *already.*'

26 "I tell you that to everyone who has, more shall be given, but from the one who does not have, even what he does have shall be taken away.

27 "But these enemies of mine, who did not want me to reign over them, bring them here and slay them in my presence."

Triumphal Entry

19:29–38pp — Matt 21:1–9; Mark 11:1–10
19:35–38pp — John 12:12–15

28 ¶ After He had said these things, He was going on ahead, going up to Jerusalem.

29 ¶ When He approached Bethphage and Bethany, near the mount that is called Olivet, He sent two of the disciples,

30 saying, "Go into the village ahead of *you;* there, as you enter, you will find a colt tied on which no one yet has ever sat; untie it and bring it *here.*

31 "If anyone asks you, 'Why are you untying it?' you shall say, 'The Lord has need of it.' "

32 So those who were sent went away and found it just as He had told them.

33 As they were untying the colt, its owners said to them, "Why are you untying the colt?"

34 They said, "The Lord has need of it."

35 They brought it to Jesus, and they threw their coats on the colt and put Jesus *on it.*

36 As He was going, they were spreading their coats on the road.

37 As soon as He was approaching, near the descent of the Mount of Olives, the whole crowd of the disciples began to praise God joyfully with a loud voice for all the miracles which they had seen,

38 shouting:

"BLESSED IS THE KING WHO COMES IN THE
NAME OF THE LORD;

Peace in heaven and glory in the
highest!"

39 Some of the Pharisees in the crowd said to Him, "Teacher, rebuke Your disciples."

40 But Jesus answered, "I tell you, if these become silent, the stones will cry out!"

41 ¶ When He approached *Jerusalem*, He saw the city and wept over it,

42 saying, "If you had known in this day, even you, the things which make for peace! But now they have been hidden from your eyes.

43 "For the days will come upon you when your enemies will throw up a barricade against you, and surround you and hem you in on every side,

44 and they will level you to the ground and your children within you, and they will not leave in you one stone upon another, because you did not recognize the time of your visitation."

19:44 Wailing Wall

Jesus' tearful prediction of total destruction was fulfilled in A.D. 70, when the Romans crushed a Jewish revolt by razing the city. In modern Jerusalem, the Wailing Wall is one of the few places where some of the original stonework of Jerusalem can still be seen.

Traders Driven from the Temple

19:45,46pp — Matt 21:12–16; Mark 11:15–18; John 2:13–16

45 ¶ Jesus entered the temple and began to drive out those who were selling,

46 saying to them, "It is written, 'AND MY HOUSE SHALL BE A HOUSE OF PRAYER,' but you have made it a ROBBERS' DEN."

47 ¶ And He was teaching daily in the temple; but the chief priests and the scribes and the leading men among the people were trying to destroy Him,

48 and they could not find anything that they might do, for all the people were hanging on to every word He said.

Jesus' Authority Questioned

20:1–8pp — Matt 21:23–27; Mark 11:27–33

20 On one of the days while He was teaching the people in the temple and preaching the gospel, the chief priests and the scribes with the elders confronted *Him,*

2 and they spoke, saying to Him, "Tell us by what authority You are doing these things, or who is the one who gave You this authority?"

3 Jesus answered and said to them, "I will also ask you a question, and you tell Me:

4 "Was the baptism of John from heaven or from men?"

5 They reasoned among themselves, saying,

"If we say, 'From heaven,' He will say, 'Why did you not believe him?'

6 "But if we say, 'From men,' all the people will stone us to death, for they are convinced that John was a prophet."

7 So they answered that they did not know where *it came* from.

8 And Jesus said to them, "Nor will I tell you by what authority I do these things."

Parable of the Vine-growers

20:9–19pp — Matt 21:33–46; Mark 12:1–12

9 ¶ And He began to tell the people this parable: "A man planted a vineyard and rented it out to vine-growers, and went on a journey for a long time.

10 "At the *harvest* time he sent a slave to the vine-growers, so that they would give him *some* of the produce of the vineyard; but the vine-growers beat him and sent him away empty-handed.

11 "And he proceeded to send another slave; and they beat him also and treated him shamefully and sent him away empty-handed.

12 "And he proceeded to send a third; and this one also they wounded and cast out.

13 "The owner of the vineyard said, 'What shall I do? I will send my beloved son; perhaps they will respect him.'

14 "But when the vine-growers saw him, they reasoned with one another, saying, 'This is the heir; let us kill him so that the inheritance will be ours.'

15 "So they threw him out of the vineyard and killed him. What, then, will the owner of the vineyard do to them?

16 "He will come and destroy these vine-growers and will give the vineyard to others." When they heard it, they said, "May it never be!"

17 But Jesus looked at them and said, "What then is this that is written:

'THE STONE WHICH THE BUILDERS REJECTED,
THIS BECAME THE CHIEF CORNER *stone*'?

18 "Everyone who falls on that stone will be broken to pieces; but on whomever it falls, it will scatter him like dust."

Tribute to Caesar

20:20–26pp — Matt 22:15–22; Mark 12:13–17

19 ¶ The scribes and the chief priests tried to lay hands on Him that very hour, and they feared the people; for they understood that He spoke this parable against them.

20 So they watched Him, and sent spies who pretended to be righteous, in order that they might catch Him in some statement, so that they *could* deliver Him to the rule and the authority of the governor.

21 They questioned Him, saying, "Teacher, we know that You speak and teach correctly, and You

are not partial to any, but teach the way of God in truth.

22 "Is it lawful for us to pay taxes to Caesar, or not?"

23 But He detected their trickery and said to them,

24 "Show Me a *a*denarius. Whose likeness and inscription does it have?" They said, "Caesar's."

25 And He said to them, "Then render to Caesar the things that are Caesar's, and to God the things that are God's."

26 And they were unable to catch Him in a saying in the presence of the people; and being amazed at His answer, they became silent.

Is There a Resurrection?

20:27–40pp — Matt 22:23–33; Mark 12:18–27
20:41–47pp — Matt 22:41–23:7; Mark 12:35–40

27 ¶ Now there came to Him some of the Sadducees (who say that there is no resurrection),

28 and they questioned Him, saying, "Teacher, Moses wrote for us that IF A MAN'S BROTHER DIES, having a wife, AND HE IS CHILDLESS, HIS BROTHER SHOULD MARRY THE WIFE AND RAISE UP CHILDREN TO HIS BROTHER.

29 "Now there were seven brothers; and the first took a wife and died childless;

30 and the second

31 and the third married her; and in the same way all seven died, leaving no children.

32 "Finally the woman died also.

33 "In the resurrection therefore, which one's wife will she be? For all seven had married her."

34 ¶ Jesus said to them, "The sons of this age marry and are given in marriage,

35 but those who are considered worthy to attain to that age and the resurrection from the dead, neither marry nor are given in marriage;

36 for they cannot even die anymore, because they are like angels, and are sons of God, being sons of the resurrection.

37 "But that the dead are raised, even Moses showed, in the *passage about the burning* bush, where he calls the Lord THE GOD OF ABRAHAM, AND THE GOD OF ISAAC, AND THE GOD OF JACOB.

38 "Now He is not the God of the dead but of the living; for all live to Him."

39 Some of the scribes answered and said, "Teacher, You have spoken well."

40 For they did not have courage to question Him any longer about anything.

41 ¶ Then He said to them, "How *is it that* they say *b*the Christ is David's son?

42 "For David himself says in the book of Psalms,

'THE LORD SAID TO MY LORD,
"SIT AT MY RIGHT HAND,

43 UNTIL I MAKE YOUR ENEMIES A FOOTSTOOL FOR YOUR FEET." '

---

a The denarius was a day's wages　　*b* I.e. the Messiah

44 "Therefore David calls Him 'Lord,' and how is He his son?"

45 ¶ And while all the people were listening, He said to the disciples,

20:41–44 Jesus Asks a Question

In the midst of many questions thrown at him, Jesus offers one back. The passage, quoting Psalm 110:1, is difficult to understand, but Jesus may have been trying to clear up a misunderstanding about the Messiah. Nationalistic Jews of that day were expecting a Messiah, or a "Son of David," out of the same mold as the great Jewish king who defeated Israel's enemies. But Jesus shows that David himself acknowledged the Messiah to come as "Lord," or One far greater than a mere earthly king.

46 "Beware of the scribes, who like to walk around in long robes, and love respectful greetings in the market places, and chief seats in the synagogues and places of honor at banquets,

47 who devour widows' houses, and for appearance's sake offer long prayers. These will receive greater condemnation."

The Widow's Gift

21:1–4pp — Mark 12:41–44
21:5–36pp — Matt 24; Mark 13
21:12–17pp — Matt 10:17–22

21 And He looked up and saw the rich putting their gifts into the treasury.

2 And He saw a poor widow putting in two small copper coins.

3 And He said, "Truly I say to you, this poor widow put in more than all *of them;*

4 for they all out of their surplus put into the offering; but she out of her poverty put in all that she had to live on."

5 ¶ And while some were talking about the temple, that it was adorned with beautiful stones and votive gifts, He said,

6 "*As for* these things which you are looking at, the days will come in which there will not be left one stone upon another which will not be torn down."

7 ¶ They questioned Him, saying, "Teacher, when therefore will these things happen? And what *will be* the sign when these things are about to take place?"

8 And He said, "See to it that you are not misled; for many will come in My name, saying, 'I am *He*,' and, 'The time is near.' Do not go after them.

9 "When you hear of wars and disturbances, do not be terrified; for these things must take place first, but the end *does* not *follow* immediately."

Things to Come

10 ¶ Then He continued by saying to them, "Nation will rise against nation and kingdom against kingdom,

11 and there will be great earthquakes, and in various places plagues and famines; and there will be terrors and great signs from heaven.

12 ¶ "But before all these things, they will lay their hands on you and will persecute you, delivering you to the synagogues and prisons, bringing you before kings and governors for My name's sake.

13 "It will lead to an opportunity for your testimony.

14 "So make up your minds not to prepare beforehand to defend yourselves;

15 for I will give you utterance and wisdom which none of your opponents will be able to resist or refute.

16 "But you will be betrayed even by parents and brothers and relatives and friends, and they will put *some* of you to death,

17 and you will be hated by all because of My name.

18 "Yet not a hair of your head will perish.

19 "By your endurance you will gain your lives.

20 ¶ "But when you see Jerusalem surrounded by armies, then recognize that her desolation is near.

21 "Then those who are in Judea must flee to the mountains, and those who are in the midst of the city must leave, and those who are in the country must not enter the city;

22 because these are days of vengeance, so that all things which are written will be fulfilled.

23 "Woe to those who are pregnant and to those who are nursing babies in those days; for there will be great distress upon the land and wrath to this people;

24 and they will fall by the edge of the sword, and will be led captive into all the nations; and Jerusalem will be trampled under foot by the Gentiles until the times of the Gentiles are fulfilled.

The Return of Christ

25 ¶ "There will be signs in sun and moon and stars, and on the earth dismay among nations, in perplexity at the roaring of the sea and the waves,

26 men fainting from fear and the expectation of the things which are coming upon the world; for the powers of the heavens will be shaken.

27 "Then they will see THE SON OF MAN COMING IN A CLOUD with power and great glory.

28 "But when these things begin to take place, straighten up and lift up your heads, because your redemption is drawing near."

29 ¶ Then He told them a parable: "Behold the fig tree and all the trees;

30 as soon as they put forth *leaves,* you see it and know for yourselves that summer is now near.

31 "So you also, when you see these things hap-

pening, recognize that the kingdom of God is near.

32 "Truly I say to you, this generation will not pass away until all things take place.

33 "Heaven and earth will pass away, but My words will not pass away.

34 ¶ "Be on guard, so that your hearts will not be weighted down with dissipation and drunkenness and the worries of life, and that day will not come on you suddenly like a trap;

35 for it will come upon all those who dwell on the face of all the earth.

36 "But keep on the alert at all times, praying that you may have strength to escape all these things that are about to take place, and to stand before the Son of Man."

37 ¶ Now during the day He was teaching in the temple, but at evening He would go out and spend the night on the mount that is called Olivet.

38 And all the people would get up early in the morning *to come* to Him in the temple to listen to Him.

Preparing the Passover

22:1,2pp — Matt 26:2–5; Mark 14:1,2,10,11
22:7–13pp — Matt 26:17–19; Mark 14:12–16

22 Now the Feast of Unleavened Bread, which is called the Passover, was approaching.

2 The chief priests and the scribes were seeking how they might put Him to death; for they were afraid of the people.

3 ¶ And Satan entered into Judas who was called Iscariot, belonging to the number of the twelve.

4 And he went away and discussed with the chief priests and officers how he might betray Him to them.

5 They were glad and agreed to give him money.

6 So he consented, and *began* seeking a good opportunity to betray Him to them apart from the crowd.

7 ¶ Then came the *first* day of Unleavened Bread on which the Passover *lamb* had to be sacrificed.

8 And Jesus sent Peter and John, saying, "Go and prepare the Passover for us, so that we may eat it."

9 They said to Him, "Where do You want us to prepare it?"

10 And He said to them, "When you have entered the city, a man will meet you carrying a pitcher of water; follow him into the house that he enters.

11 "And you shall say to the owner of the house, 'The Teacher says to you, "Where is the guest room in which I may eat the Passover with My disciples?" '

12 "And he will show you a large, furnished upper room; prepare it there."

13 And they left and found *everything* just as

He had told them; and they prepared the Passover.

The Lord's Supper

22:17–20pp — Matt 26:26–29; Mark 14:22–25;
1 Cor 11:23–25
22:21–23pp — Matt 26:21–24; Mark 14:18–21;
John 13:21–30
22:25–27pp — Matt 20:25–28; Mark 10:42–45
22:33,34pp — Matt 26:33–35; Mark 14:29–31;
John 13:37,38

14 ¶ When the hour had come, He reclined *at the table,* and the apostles with Him.

15 And He said to them, "I have earnestly desired to eat this Passover with you before I suffer;

16 for I say to you, I shall never again eat it until it is fulfilled in the kingdom of God."

17 And when He had taken a cup *and* given thanks, He said, "Take this and share it among yourselves;

18 for I say to you, I will not drink of the fruit of the vine from now on until the kingdom of God comes."

19 And when He had taken *some* bread *and* given thanks, He broke it and gave it to them, saying, "This is My body which is given for you; do this in remembrance of Me."

20 And in the same way *He took* the cup after they had eaten, saying, "This cup which is poured out for you is the new covenant in My blood.

21 "But behold, the hand of the one betraying Me is with Mine on the table.

22 "For indeed, the Son of Man is going as it has been determined; but woe to that man by whom He is betrayed!"

23 And they began to discuss among themselves which one of them it might be who was going to do this thing.

Who Is Greatest

24 ¶ And there arose also a dispute among them *as to* which one of them was regarded to be greatest.

22:24 Status-conscious Disciples

Even at the emotional Last Supper scene described here, the disciples fell into their habit of worrying about rank and status. Not until after Jesus had died and returned did they understand the true nature of the kingdom he was setting into motion. It is a kingdom primarily of spiritual, not political, power. And in it, the greatest is the one who serves others.

25 And He said to them, "The kings of the Gentiles lord it over them; and those who have authority over them are called 'Benefactors.'

26 "But *it is* not this way with you, but the one who is the greatest among you must become like the youngest, and the leader like the servant.

27 "For who is greater, the one who reclines *at the table* or the one who serves? Is it not the one who reclines *at the table*? But I am among you as the one who serves.

28 ¶ "You are those who have stood by Me in My trials;

29 and just as My Father has granted Me a kingdom, I grant you

30 that you may eat and drink at My table in My kingdom, and you will sit on thrones judging the twelve tribes of Israel.

31 ¶ "Simon, Simon, behold, Satan has demanded *permission* to sift you like wheat;

32 but I have prayed for you, that your faith may not fail; and you, when once you have turned again, strengthen your brothers."

33 But he said to Him, "Lord, with You I am ready to go both to prison and to death!"

34 And He said, "I say to you, Peter, the rooster will not crow today until you have denied three times that you know Me."

35 ¶ And He said to them, "When I sent you out without money belt and bag and sandals, you did not lack anything, did you?" They said, "*No,* nothing."

36 And He said to them, "But now, whoever has a money belt is to take it along, likewise also a bag, and whoever has no sword is to sell his coat and buy one.

37 "For I tell you that this which is written must be fulfilled in Me, 'AND HE WAS NUMBERED WITH TRANSGRESSORS'; for that which refers to Me has *its* fulfillment."

38 They said, "Lord, look, here are two swords." And He said to them, "It is enough."

The Garden of Gethsemane

22:40–46pp — Matt 26:36–46; Mark 14:32–42

39 ¶ And He came out and proceeded as was His custom to the Mount of Olives; and the disciples also followed Him.

40 When He arrived at the place, He said to them, "Pray that you may not enter into temptation."

41 And He withdrew from them about a stone's throw, and He knelt down and *began* to pray,

42 saying, "Father, if You are willing, remove this cup from Me; yet not My will, but Yours be done."

43 Now an angel from heaven appeared to Him, strengthening Him.

44 And being in agony He was praying very fervently; and His sweat became like drops of blood, falling down upon the ground.

45 When He rose from prayer, He came to the disciples and found them sleeping from sorrow,

46 and said to them, "Why are you sleeping? Get up and pray that you may not enter into temptation."

Jesus Betrayed by Judas

22:47–53pp — Matt 26:47–56; Mark 14:43–50; John 18:3–11

47 ¶ While He was still speaking, behold, a crowd *came,* and the one called Judas, one of the twelve, was preceding them; and he approached Jesus to kiss Him.

48 But Jesus said to him, "Judas, are you betraying the Son of Man with a kiss?"

49 When those who were around Him saw what was going to happen, they said, "Lord, shall we strike with the sword?"

50 And one of them struck the slave of the high priest and cut off his right ear.

51 But Jesus answered and said, "Stop! No more of this." And He touched his ear and healed him.

52 Then Jesus said to the chief priests and officers of the temple and elders who had come against Him, "Have you come out with swords and clubs as you would against a robber?

53 "While I was with you daily in the temple, you did not lay hands on Me; but this hour and the power of darkness are yours."

Jesus' Arrest

22:55–62pp — Matt 26:69–75; Mark 14:66–72; John 18:16–18,25–27
22:63–65pp — Matt 26:67,68; Mark 14:65; John 18:22,23

54 ¶ Having arrested Him, they led Him *away* and brought Him to the house of the high priest; but Peter was following at a distance.

55 After they had kindled a fire in the middle of the courtyard and had sat down together, Peter was sitting among them.

56 And a servant-girl, seeing him as he sat in the firelight and looking intently at him, said, "This man was with Him too."

57 But he denied *it,* saying, "Woman, I do not know Him."

58 A little later, another saw him and said, "You are *one* of them too!" But Peter said, "Man, I am not!"

59 After about an hour had passed, another

22:58 Deserted by His Friends

Peter showed courage by following Jesus, rather than going into hiding. Perhaps trying to gain information, he even went into the high priest's courtyard. But there he was recognized, partly because of his Galilean accent (see Matthew 26:73). After denying that he knew Jesus, Peter remembered with pain his boast that he would be willing to die with Jesus (verse 33). Jesus had accurately predicted even Peter would desert him.

man *began* to insist, saying, "Certainly this man also was with Him, for he is a Galilean too."

60 But Peter said, "Man, I do not know what you are talking about." Immediately, while he was still speaking, a rooster crowed.

61 The Lord turned and looked at Peter. And Peter remembered the word of the Lord, how He had told him, "Before a rooster crows today, you will deny Me three times."

62 And he went out and wept bitterly.

63 ¶ Now the men who were holding Jesus in custody were mocking Him and beating Him,

64 and they blindfolded Him and were asking Him, saying, "Prophesy, who is the one who hit You?"

65 And they were saying many other things against Him, blaspheming.

Jesus before the Sanhedrin

22:67–71pp — Matt 26:63–66; Mark 14:61–63;
John 18:19–21

66 ¶ When it was day, the [a]Council of elders of the people assembled, both chief priests and scribes, and they led Him away to their council *chamber,* saying,

67 "If You are the Christ, tell us." But He said to them, "If I tell you, you will not believe;

68 and if I ask a question, you will not answer.

69 "But from now on THE SON OF MAN WILL BE SEATED AT THE RIGHT HAND of the power OF GOD."

70 And they all said, "Are You the Son of God, then?" And He said to them, "Yes, I am."

71 Then they said, "What further need do we have of testimony? For we have heard it ourselves from His own mouth."

Jesus before Pilate

23:2,3pp — Matt 27:11–14; Mark 15:2–5;
John 18:29–37

23 Then the whole body of them got up and brought Him before Pilate.

2 And they began to accuse Him, saying, "We found this man misleading our nation and forbidding to pay taxes to Caesar, and saying that He Himself is Christ, a King."

3 So Pilate asked Him, saying, "Are You the King of the Jews?" And He answered him and said, "*It is as* you say."

4 Then Pilate said to the chief priests and the crowds, "I find no guilt in this man."

5 But they kept on insisting, saying, "He stirs up the people, teaching all over Judea, starting from Galilee even as far as this place."

6 ¶ When Pilate heard it, he asked whether the man was a Galilean.

7 And when he learned that He belonged to Herod's jurisdiction, he sent Him to Herod, who himself also was in Jerusalem at that time.

Jesus before Herod

8 ¶ Now Herod was very glad when he saw Jesus; for he had wanted to see Him for a long time, because he had been hearing about Him and was hoping to see some sign performed by Him.

9 And he questioned Him at some length; but He answered him nothing.

10 And the chief priests and the scribes were standing there, accusing Him vehemently.

11 And Herod with his soldiers, after treating Him with contempt and mocking Him, dressed Him in a gorgeous robe and sent Him back to Pilate.

12 Now Herod and Pilate became friends with one another that very day; for before they had been enemies with each other.

Pilate Seeks Jesus' Release

23:18–25pp — Matt 27:15–26; Mark 15:6–15;
John 18:39–19:16

13 ¶ Pilate summoned the chief priests and the rulers and the people,

14 and said to them, "You brought this man to me as one who incites the people to rebellion, and behold, having examined Him before you, I have found no guilt in this man regarding the charges which you make against Him.

15 "No, nor has Herod, for he sent Him back to us; and behold, nothing deserving death has been done by Him.

16 "Therefore I will punish Him and release Him."

17 [[b]Now he was obliged to release to them at the feast one prisoner.]

18 ¶ But they cried out all together, saying, "Away with this man, and release for us Barabbas!"

19 (He was one who had been thrown into prison for an insurrection made in the city, and for murder.)

20 Pilate, wanting to release Jesus, addressed them again,

21 but they kept on calling out, saying, "Crucify, crucify Him!"

22 And he said to them the third time, "Why, what evil has this man done? I have found in Him no guilt *demanding* death; therefore I will punish Him and release Him."

23 But they were insistent, with loud voices asking that He be crucified. And their voices *began* to prevail.

24 And Pilate pronounced sentence that their demand be granted.

25 And he released the man they were asking for who had been thrown into prison for insurrec-

---

[a] Or *Sanhedrin*   [b] Early mss do not contain this v

tion and murder, but he delivered Jesus to their will.

Simon Bears the Cross

26 ¶ When they led Him away, they seized a man, Simon of Cyrene, coming in from the country, and placed on him the cross to carry behind Jesus.

27 ¶ And following Him was a large crowd of the people, and of women who were mourning and lamenting Him.

28 But Jesus turning to them said, "Daughters of Jerusalem, stop weeping for Me, but weep for yourselves and for your children.

29 "For behold, the days are coming when they will say, 'Blessed are the barren, and the wombs that never bore, and the breasts that never nursed.'

30 "Then they will begin TO SAY TO THE MOUNTAINS, 'FALL ON US,' AND TO THE HILLS, 'COVER US.'

31 "For if they do these things when the tree is green, what will happen when it is dry?"

32 ¶ Two others also, who were criminals, were being led away to be put to death with Him.

Final Glimpses of Jesus
The most important week in history

EVERYTHING ABOUT JESUS SEEMED TO come together during his last few days on earth, and surely those days offer a key to understanding him. As if on a roller coaster, people's reactions to him plunged from heady exhilaration to murderous rejection overnight.

Those last days included one scene of triumph, a grand entry into Jerusalem. Pilgrims were filling the streets in holiday celebration. In a gallant gesture for Jesus, they laid their coats before him, and they roared their approval as he approached. But against that tumultuous background, Jesus sat weeping, painfully aware that their praise was hollow.

Even as Jesus' popularity with the masses was soaring, spies joined the ranks of onlookers, assailing him with questions and verbal traps. Jesus knew he wasn't safe anywhere, even in an intimate gathering with his disciples. During his and his disciples' last meal together, one of the Twelve rose and left the room to bargain for Jesus' life.

> But they were insistent, with loud voices asking that He be crucified. And their voices began to prevail. 23:23

The Darkest Day and the Brightest

At Jesus' arrest, the religious and political power brokers had a look at him at last. They had heard many intriguing rumors, and hoped he would perform for them like a magician (23:8). Jesus declined. He had never sought their kind of power, and would not then, even with his life at stake.

Outside, the crowd that previously had shouted, "Blessed is the king!" took up a very different chant: "Crucify him!" Jesus' life was doomed. The one who had come to save the world was about to be destroyed by it.

In two back-to-back closing chapters Luke records the darkest day in history . . . and the brightest. No one was more surprised than Jesus' disciples to hear reports that the man they had seen die on Friday was walking around on Sunday. It seemed like hysterical nonsense at first—until he did appear, and they could deny it no longer.

Ordinary People, an Extraordinary Discovery

Luke adds one scene that captures the terrible confusion of those final days. Two of Jesus' disciples were walking away from Jerusalem, downhearted. Their dream was over; all the mounting hopes of the last few years had died with Jesus on the cross.

A strange man appeared beside the two forlorn disciples. Bizarrely, he seemed the only man alive who hadn't heard about the incredible week in Jerusalem. He talked with them, tracing the whole story of the gospel, beginning with Moses and the prophets.

The stranger intrigued them, and they asked him to stay longer. At mealtime the last link snapped into place. It was Jesus! No one else. Without a doubt, he was alive.

Ordinary people, with more than a touch of cowardice, had followed Jesus, listened to him, and watched him die (from a distance, to keep themselves safe). But seeing Jesus alive changed all that. Luke's story began with joy, and it ends that way: "And they, after worshiping Him, returned to Jerusalem with great joy" (24:52). Before long they were out telling the world about it.

Life Questions: Suppose you had been in the room to hear the first news of Jesus' resurrection. Would you have believed it? What makes you believe it now?

The Crucifixion

23:33–43pp — Matt 27:33–44; Mark 15:22–32; John 19:17–24
23:44–49pp — Matt 27:45–56; Mark 15:33–41; John 19:29,30

33 ¶ When they came to the place called The Skull, there they crucified Him and the criminals, one on the right and the other on the left.

23:25 Who Should Try Jesus?

The Gospels record a "pass-the-buck" sequence in Jesus' encounter with Roman justice. The Jewish court, or Sanhedrin, judged Jesus guilty of blasphemy, but it had no authority to carry out a death sentence. Therefore, the religious leaders took Jesus to Pilate, the Roman governor of Judea. Along the way, they changed the religious charge against Jesus to a political one, which alone would call for Roman punishment.

Pilate showed cowardice. First, he deferred the case to Herod, who had jurisdiction over Jesus' home region. Herod taunted and mocked Jesus, and then sent him back. Three times Pilate tried to get the Jewish leaders to release Jesus, but finally he yielded to the demands for capital punishment.

34 But Jesus was saying, "Father, forgive them; for they do not know what they are doing." And they cast lots, dividing up His garments among themselves.

35 And the people stood by, looking on. And even the rulers were sneering at Him, saying, "He saved others; let Him save Himself if this is the Christ of God, His Chosen One."

36 The soldiers also mocked Him, coming up to Him, offering Him sour wine,

37 and saying, "If You are the King of the Jews, save Yourself!"

38 Now there was also an inscription above Him, "THIS IS THE KING OF THE JEWS."

39 ¶ One of the criminals who were hanged *there* was hurling abuse at Him, saying, "Are You not the Christ? Save Yourself and us!"

40 But the other answered, and rebuking him said, "Do you not even fear God, since you are under the same sentence of condemnation?

41 "And we indeed *are suffering* justly, for we are receiving what we deserve for our deeds; but this man has done nothing wrong."

42 And he was saying, "Jesus, remember me when You come in Your kingdom!"

43 And He said to him, "Truly I say to you, today you shall be with Me in Paradise."

44 ¶ It was now about *a*the sixth hour, and darkness fell over the whole land until *b*the ninth hour,

45 because the sun was obscured; and the veil of the temple was torn in two.

46 And Jesus, crying out with a loud voice, said, "Father, INTO YOUR HANDS I COMMIT MY SPIRIT." Having said this, He breathed His last.

47 Now when the centurion saw what had happened, he *began* praising God, saying, "Certainly this man was innocent."

48 And all the crowds who came together for this spectacle, when they observed what had happened, *began* to return, beating their breasts.

49 And all His acquaintances and the women who accompanied Him from Galilee were standing at a distance, seeing these things.

Jesus Is Buried

23:50–56pp — Matt 27:57–61; Mark 15:42–47; John 19:38–42

50 ¶ And a man named Joseph, who was a member of the Council, a good and righteous man

51 (he had not consented to their plan and action), *a man* from Arimathea, a city of the Jews, who was waiting for the kingdom of God;

52 this man went to Pilate and asked for the body of Jesus.

53 And he took it down and wrapped it in a linen cloth, and laid Him in a tomb cut into the rock, where no one had ever lain.

54 It was the preparation day, and the Sabbath was about to begin.

55 Now the women who had come with Him out of Galilee followed, and saw the tomb and how His body was laid.

56 Then they returned and prepared spices and perfumes.

¶ And on the Sabbath they rested according to the commandment.

The Resurrection

24:1–10pp — Matt 28:1–8; Mark 16:1–8; John 20:1–8

24 But on the first day of the week, at early dawn, they came to the tomb bringing the spices which they had prepared.

2 And they found the stone rolled away from the tomb,

3 but when they entered, they did not find the body of the Lord Jesus.

4 While they were perplexed about this, behold, two men suddenly stood near them in dazzling clothing;

5 and as *the women* were terrified and bowed their faces to the ground, *the men* said to them, "Why do you seek the living One among the dead?

6 "He is not here, but He has risen. Remember how He spoke to you while He was still in Galilee,

7 saying that the Son of Man must be delivered into the hands of sinful men, and be crucified, and the third day rise again."

---

a I.e. noon   *b* I.e. 3 p.m.

8 And they remembered His words,

9 and returned from the tomb and reported all these things to the eleven and to all the rest.

10 Now they were Mary Magdalene and Joanna and Mary the *mother* of James; also the other women with them were telling these things to the apostles.

11 But these words appeared to them as nonsense, and they would not believe them.

12 But Peter got up and ran to the tomb; stooping and looking in, he *saw the linen wrappings only; and he went away to his home, marveling at what had happened.

The Road to Emmaus

13 ¶ And behold, two of them were going that very day to a village named Emmaus, which was ªabout seven miles from Jerusalem.

14 And they were talking with each other about all these things which had taken place.

15 While they were talking and discussing, Jesus Himself approached and *began* traveling with them.

16 But their eyes were prevented from recognizing Him.

17 And He said to them, "What are these words that you are exchanging with one another as you are walking?" And they stood still, looking sad.

18 One *of them*, named Cleopas, answered and said to Him, "Are You the only one visiting Jerusalem and unaware of the things which have happened here in these days?"

19 And He said to them, "What things?" And they said to Him, "The things about Jesus the Nazarene, who was a prophet mighty in deed and word in the sight of God and all the people,

20 and how the chief priests and our rulers delivered Him to the sentence of death, and crucified Him.

21 "But we were hoping that it was He who was going to redeem Israel. Indeed, besides all this, it is the third day since these things happened.

22 "But also some women among us amazed us. When they were at the tomb early in the morning,

23 and did not find His body, they came, saying that they had also seen a vision of angels who said that He was alive.

24 "Some of those who were with us went to the tomb and found it just exactly as the women also had said; but Him they did not see."

25 And He said to them, "O foolish men and slow of heart to believe in all that the prophets have spoken!

26 "Was it not necessary for the Christ to suffer these things and to enter into His glory?"

27 Then beginning with Moses and with all the prophets, He explained to them the things concerning Himself in all the Scriptures.

28 ¶ And they approached the village where they were going, and He acted as though He were going farther.

29 But they urged Him, saying, "Stay with us, for it is *getting* toward evening, and the day is now nearly over." So He went in to stay with them.

24:27 Old Testament 101

When the disciples first began to tell about Jesus' resurrection, they quoted Old Testament Scriptures and explained how Jesus fulfilled their predictions. (See, for example, Peter's sermons in Acts 2 and 3.) They were probably following what Jesus had taught on the road to Emmaus. Jesus went through the entire Old Testament, explaining how his life crowned centuries of God's work.

30 When He had reclined *at the table* with them, He took the bread and blessed *it*, and breaking *it*, He *began* giving *it* to them.

31 Then their eyes were opened and they recognized Him; and He vanished from their sight.

32 They said to one another, "Were not our hearts burning within us while He was speaking to us on the road, while He was explaining the Scriptures to us?"

33 And they got up that very hour and returned to Jerusalem, and found gathered together the eleven and those who were with them,

34 saying, "The Lord has really risen and has appeared to Simon."

35 They *began* to relate their experiences on the road and how He was recognized by them in the breaking of the bread.

Other Appearances

36 ¶ While they were telling these things, He Himself stood in their midst and *said to them, "Peace be to you."

37 But they were startled and frightened and thought that they were seeing a spirit.

38 And He said to them, "Why are you troubled, and why do doubts arise in your hearts?

39 "See My hands and My feet, that it is I Myself; touch Me and see, for a spirit does not have flesh and bones as you see that I have."

40 And when He had said this, He showed them His hands and His feet.

41 While they still could not believe *it* because of their joy and amazement, He said to them, "Have you anything here to eat?"

42 They gave Him a piece of a broiled fish;

43 and He took it and ate *it* before them.

44 ¶ Now He said to them, "These are My words which I spoke to you while I was still with you, that all things which are written about Me in

---

ª Lit *60 stadia*; one stadion was about 600 ft

the Law of Moses and the Prophets and the Psalms must be fulfilled."

45 Then He opened their minds to understand the Scriptures,

46 and He said to them, "Thus it is written, that the Christ would suffer and rise again from the dead the third day,

47 and that repentance for forgiveness of sins would be proclaimed in His name to all the nations, beginning from Jerusalem.

48 "You are witnesses of these things.

49 "And behold, I am sending forth the promise of My Father upon you; but you are to stay in the city until you are clothed with power from on high."

The Ascension

50 ¶ And He led them out as far as Bethany, and He lifted up His hands and blessed them.

51 While He was blessing them, He parted from them and was carried up into heaven.

52 And they, after worshiping Him, returned to Jerusalem with great joy,

53 and were continually in the temple praising God.

JOHN

God Breaks the Silence
He spoke in the only way we could truly understand

> *The Word became flesh, and dwelt among us. 1:14*

UNLESS A PERSON COMMUNICATES TO you, in speech or gestures or even facial expressions, you can't get to know him or her. What goes on behind the mask of skin will always remain a mystery.

God, too, was a mystery until he broke his silence. He spoke once, and all creation sprang to life—quasars, oceans, whales, giraffes, orchids, and beetles. He spoke again, says John, and this time the Word took the form of a man, Jesus Christ. John's book tells the story of that Word who became flesh.

Different from Other Gospels

It's clear from the first few paragraphs that John broke sharply from the style of Matthew, Mark, and Luke. The other Gospel writers focused on events, following Jesus through the bustling marketplaces and villages.

Unlike them, John assumed readers knew the basic facts about Jesus. Instead of focusing on facts, he mulled over the profound meaning of what Jesus had said and done. The book of John reads as if it were written under a great, shady tree by an author who had lots of time for reflection.

In his first sentence, John highlights Christ's nature. There are no Christmas scenes here: no stables, shepherds, or wise men. John tells nothing of Jesus' birth and youth. He introduces him as the adult Son of God. After an eloquent prologue, the book shows John the Baptist humbly pointing to Jesus, "the thong of whose sandal I am not worthy to untie" (1:27).

Jesus Sent with a Mission

John selected vignettes from no more than 20 days in Jesus' life, and arranged them so that they present a Messiah who knows "where I came from and where I am going" (8:14). Jesus was not simply a "man who fell to earth," but God's Son, sent to do the work of the Father. His repeated references to the One "who sent me" give a cadence to the book.

According to John, Christ participated in the original creation act. But later he was sent to earth as the Word, the sum of all that God wanted to say. God spoke in the only way we could truly understand: by becoming one of us.

How to Read John

New Christians often turn to the book of John because it spells out so clearly the basics of the faith. Jesus proves who he is, diagnoses humanity's problems, and bluntly describes what is necessary for conversion. You will likely recognize familiar verses and phrases in this remarkable book (such as Jesus' "I am" sayings).

John selected seven "signs" or miracles (five of which aren't reported elsewhere) and built a story around them. As you read John, note how the author weaves together his story and its meaning.

It's best to read John in units. Don't just read a paragraph or a chapter. Follow the bold-face sectional headings and read a complete section, both the action and the commentary on it. John does not primarily relate events; he interprets those events.

Look carefully for the audiences Jesus addresses. Is he talking to his disciples? To his opponents? To the large crowds? He treats each audience differently.

Many passages in the Gospels are parallel, dealing with the same event. Nearly identical passages are noted at the section heading with "pp," while similar passages are noted with "Ref."

PEOPLE YOU'LL MEET IN JOHN

NICODEMUS *(p. 1146)*
ANDREW *(p. 1151)*
JUDAS *(p. 1153)*
ANNAS AND CAIAPHAS *(p. 1161)*

THOMAS *(p. 1165)*
PONTIUS PILATE *(p. 1171)*
MARY MAGDALENE *(p. 1173)*
JOHN *(p. 1174)*

3-TRACK READING PLAN

For an explanation and complete listing of the 3-track reading plan, turn to page 7.

TRACK 1:   *Two-Week Courses on the Bible*
The Track 1 reading program on the Life and Teachings of Jesus includes four chapters from John. See page 7 for a complete listing of this course.

TRACK 2:   *An Overview of John in 8 Days*
☐ Day 1. Read the Introduction to John and then turn to John 3, which contains perhaps the best-known verse in the entire Bible (verse 16). Read Jesus' conversation with Nicodemus.
☐ Day 2. John 5 and 6 contain Jesus' blunt teaching about who he was and why he came to earth. Read chapter 6, noting how John weaves together a miracle, the crowd's reaction to it, then Jesus' comments on it.
☐ Day 3. Read chapter 10, another familiar passage.
☐ Day 4. The next four readings are taken from John's report of the Last Supper. Begin with chapter 14.
☐ Day 5. Read chapter 15, where Jesus explains the image of a vine and its branches.
☐ Day 6. Read chapter 16, noting especially what Jesus says about the Holy Spirit. John contains more teaching about the Holy Spirit than any other Gospel.
☐ Day 7. Read chapter 17, a farewell prayer Jesus prayed for his disciples.
☐ Day 8. Read John's account of Jesus' resurrection, chapter 20.

Now turn to page 9 for your next Track 2 reading project.

TRACK 3:   *All of John in 21 Days*
After you have read through John, turn to pages 10–14 for your next Track 3 reading project.

☐1   ☐2   ☐3   ☐4   ☐5   ☐6   ☐7   ☐8
☐9   ☐10   ☐11   ☐12   ☐13   ☐14   ☐15   ☐16
☐17   ☐18   ☐19   ☐20   ☐21

The Deity of Jesus Christ

1 In the beginning was the Word, and the Word was with God, and the Word was God.

2 He was in the beginning with God.

3 All things came into being through Him, and apart from Him nothing came into being that has come into being.

4 In Him was life, and the life was the Light of men.

5 The Light shines in the darkness, and the darkness did not *a*comprehend it.

The Witness John

6 ¶ There *b*came a man sent from God, whose name was John.

7 He came as a witness, to testify about the Light, so that all might believe through him.

8 He was not the Light, but *he came* to testify about the Light.

9 ¶ There was the true Light *c*which, coming into the world, enlightens every man.

10 He was in the world, and the world was made through Him, and the world did not know Him.

---

a Or *overpower*   *b* Or *came into being*   *c* Or *which enlightens every person coming into the world*

11 He came to His [a]own, and those who were His own did not receive Him.

12 But as many as received Him, to them He gave the right to become children of God, *even* to those who believe in His name,

13 who were born, not of blood nor of the will of the flesh nor of the will of man, but of God.

The Word Made Flesh

14 ¶ And the Word became flesh, and dwelt among us, and we saw His glory, glory as of the only begotten from the Father, full of grace and truth.

1:14 Jesus the Word

John used language with special meaning for both Greek and Jewish readers. In Greek philosophy, "word" (logos) was a key term, often referring to the power of reason undergirding all creation. For Jews, too, "word" had great significance, for God spoke his word to create the world and to transform his people. Yet John's meaning passed beyond the Greek and Jewish ideas. An eight-year-old girl expressed it well. When asked why Jesus was called the Word, she said, "Because Jesus is all God wanted to say to us."

15 John *testified about Him and cried out, saying, "This was He of whom I said, 'He who comes after me has a higher rank than I, for He existed before me.'"

16 For of His fullness we have all received, and grace upon grace.

17 For the Law was given through Moses; grace and truth were realized through Jesus Christ.

18 No one has seen God at any time; the only begotten God who is in the bosom of the Father, He has explained *Him*.

The Testimony of John

19 ¶ This is the testimony of John, when the Jews sent to him priests and Levites from Jerusalem to ask him, "Who are you?"

20 And he confessed and did not deny, but confessed, "I am not the Christ."

21 They asked him, "What then? Are you Elijah?" And he *said, "I am not." "Are you the Prophet?" And he answered, "No."

22 Then they said to him, "Who are you, so that we may give an answer to those who sent us? What do you say about yourself?"

23 He said, "I am A VOICE OF ONE CRYING IN THE WILDERNESS, 'MAKE STRAIGHT THE WAY OF THE LORD,'" as Isaiah the prophet said."

24 ¶ Now they had been sent from the Pharisees.

25 They asked him, and said to him, "Why then are you baptizing, if you are not the Christ, nor Elijah, nor the Prophet?"

26 John answered them saying, "I baptize [b]in water, *but* among you stands One whom you do not know.

27 "*It is* He who comes after me, the thong of whose sandal I am not worthy to untie."

28 These things took place in Bethany beyond the Jordan, where John was baptizing.

29 ¶ The next day he *saw Jesus coming to him and *said, "Behold, the Lamb of God who takes away the sin of the world!

30 "This is He on behalf of whom I said, 'After me comes a Man who has a higher rank than I, for He existed before me.'

31 "I did not recognize Him, but so that He might be manifested to Israel, I came baptizing [b]in water."

32 John testified saying, "I have seen the Spirit descending as a dove out of heaven, and He remained upon Him.

33 "I did not recognize Him, but He who sent me to baptize [b]in water said to me, 'He upon whom you see the Spirit descending and remaining upon Him, this is the One who baptizes in the Holy Spirit.'

34 "I myself have seen, and have testified that this is the Son of God."

Jesus' Public Ministry, First Converts

1:40–42pp — Matt 4:18–22; Mark 1:16–20; Luke 5:2–11

35 ¶ Again the next day John was standing with two of his disciples,

36 and he looked at Jesus as He walked, and *said, "Behold, the Lamb of God!"

37 The two disciples heard him speak, and they followed Jesus.

38 And Jesus turned and saw them following, and *said to them, "What do you seek?" They said to Him, "Rabbi (which translated means Teacher), where are You staying?"

39 He *said to them, "Come, and you will see." So they came and saw where He was staying; and they stayed with Him that day, for it was about the [c]tenth hour.

40 One of the two who heard John *speak* and followed Him, was Andrew, Simon Peter's brother.

41 He *found first his own brother Simon and *said to him, "We have found the Messiah" (which translated means Christ).

42 He brought him to Jesus. Jesus looked at him and said, "You are Simon the son of John; you shall be called Cephas" (which is translated Peter).

[a] Or *own things, possessions, domain*   [b] The Gr here can be translated *in, with* or *by*   [c] Perhaps 10 a.m. (Roman time)

43 ¶ The next day He purposed to go into Galilee, and He *found Philip. And Jesus *said to him, "Follow Me."

44 Now Philip was from Bethsaida, of the city of Andrew and Peter.

1:39 Gradual Disciples

Other Gospels show the disciples dropping their nets and following Jesus instantly. John describes a more gradual process. When two of John the Baptist's disciples grew curious, Jesus invited them to come and spend a day with him. Soon, they were ready to tell others what they had seen and heard.

45 Philip *found Nathanael and *said to him, "We have found Him of whom Moses in the Law and *also* the Prophets wrote—Jesus of Nazareth, the son of Joseph."

46 Nathanael said to him, "Can any good thing come out of Nazareth?" Philip *said to him, "Come and see."

47 Jesus saw Nathanael coming to Him, and *said of him, "Behold, an Israelite indeed, in whom there is no deceit!"

48 Nathanael *said to Him, "How do You know me?" Jesus answered and said to him, "Before Philip called you, when you were under the fig tree, I saw you."

49 Nathanael answered Him, "Rabbi, You are the Son of God; You are the King of Israel."

50 Jesus answered and said to him, "Because I said to you that I saw you under the fig tree, do you believe? You will see greater things than these."

51 And He *said to him, "Truly, truly, I say to you, you will see the heavens opened and the angels of God ascending and descending on the Son of Man."

Miracle at Cana

2 On the third day there was a wedding in Cana of Galilee, and the mother of Jesus was there;

2 and both Jesus and His disciples were invited to the wedding.

3 When the wine ran out, the mother of Jesus *said to Him, "They have no wine."

4 And Jesus *said to her, "Woman, what does that have to do with us? My hour has not yet come."

5 His mother *said to the servants, "Whatever He says to you, do it."

6 Now there were six stone waterpots set there for the Jewish custom of purification, containing twenty or thirty gallons each.

7 Jesus *said to them, "Fill the waterpots with water." So they filled them up to the brim.

8 And He *said to them, "Draw *some* out now and take it to the ªheadwaiter." So they took it *to him.*

9 When the headwaiter tasted the water which had become wine, and did not know where it came from (but the servants who had drawn the water knew), the headwaiter *called the bridegroom,

10 and *said to him, "Every man serves the good wine first, and when *the people* have drunk freely, *then he serves* the poorer *wine; but* you have kept the good wine until now."

2:6 Eyewitness Details

Numerous specific details show that an eyewitness wrote the book of John. Here, the author describes stone waterpots; elsewhere, he records the exact number of fish caught (21:11).

11 This beginning of *His* signs Jesus did in Cana of Galilee, and manifested His glory, and His disciples believed in Him.

12 ¶ After this He went down to Capernaum, He and His mother and *His* brothers and His disciples; and they stayed there a few days.

First Passover—Cleansing the Temple

2:14–16pp — Matt 21:12,13; Mark 11:15–17; Luke 19:45,46

13 ¶ The Passover of the Jews was near, and Jesus went up to Jerusalem.

14 And He found in the temple those who were selling oxen and sheep and doves, and the money changers seated *at their tables.*

15 And He made a scourge of cords, and drove *them* all out of the temple, with the sheep and the oxen; and He poured out the coins of the money changers and overturned their tables;

16 and to those who were selling the doves He said, "Take these things away; stop making My Father's house a place of business."

17 His disciples remembered that it was written, "Zeal for Your house will consume Me."

18 The Jews then said to Him, "What sign do You show us as your authority for doing these things?"

19 Jesus answered them, "Destroy this temple, and in three days I will raise it up."

20 The Jews then said, "It took forty-six years to build this temple, and will You raise it up in three days?"

21 But He was speaking of the temple of His body.

ª Or steward

22 So when He was raised from the dead, His disciples remembered that He said this; and they believed the Scripture and the word which Jesus had spoken.

23 ¶ Now when He was in Jerusalem at the Passover, during the feast, many believed in His name, observing His signs which He was doing.

24 But Jesus, on His part, was not entrusting Himself to them, for He knew all men,

25 and because He did not need anyone to testify concerning man, for He Himself knew what was in man.

The New Birth

3 Now there was a man of the Pharisees, named Nicodemus, a ruler of the Jews;

2 this man came to Jesus by night and said to Him, "Rabbi, we know that You have come from God *as* a teacher; for no one can do these signs that You do unless God is with him."

3 Jesus answered and said to him, "Truly, truly, I say to you, unless one is born again he cannot see the kingdom of God."

4 ¶ Nicodemus *said to Him, "How can a man be born when he is old? He cannot enter a second time into his mother's womb and be born, can he?"

5 Jesus answered, "Truly, truly, I say to you, unless one is born of water and the Spirit he cannot enter into the kingdom of God.

6 "That which is born of the flesh is flesh, and that which is born of the Spirit is spirit.

7 "Do not be amazed that I said to you, 'You must be born again.'

8 "The wind blows where it wishes and you

hear the sound of it, but do not know where it comes from and where it is going; so is everyone who is born of the Spirit."

9 ¶ Nicodemus said to Him, "How can these things be?"

10 Jesus answered and said to him, "Are you the teacher of Israel and do not understand these things?

11 "Truly, truly, I say to you, we speak of what we know and testify of what we have seen, and you do not accept our testimony.

12 "If I told you earthly things and you do not believe, how will you believe if I tell you heavenly things?

13 "No one has ascended into heaven, but He who descended from heaven: the Son of Man.

14 "As Moses lifted up the serpent in the wilderness, even so must the Son of Man be lifted up;

15 so that whoever [a]believes will in Him have eternal life.

16 ¶ "For God so loved the world, that He gave His only begotten Son, that whoever believes in Him shall not perish, but have eternal life.

17 "For God did not send the Son into the world

3:16 The Gospel in a Nutshell

This verse has probably been memorized more than any other in the Bible. In a few words it tells the story of salvation: God's love for the world, God's gift of his Son, and the opportunity for anyone who believes to be saved.

[a] Or believes in Him will have eternal life

NICODEMUS *A Reputation at Stake*

MOST OF JESUS' DISCIPLES WERE ordinary people with no status to worry about losing. A fisherman or tax collector would not forfeit much standing if he followed an unorthodox teacher. In contrast, Nicodemus had quite a reputation at stake. As a member of the Jewish Sanhedrin, he held an important ruling post. As a Pharisee, he was committed to a certain set of beliefs. And as a prominent religious teacher, he was a respected interpreter of God's law.

No doubt that is why Nicodemus first asked Jesus to meet him at night. As time went on, however, Nicodemus grew more bold. When the Sanhedrin discussed Jesus, he spoke out against their willingness to condemn the man without talking to him. For that, Nicodemus received scalding criticism (7:50–52).

After Jesus' death, Nicodemus let his sentiments become more public. Along with Joseph of Arimathea, he took Jesus' body from Calvary and prepared it for burial.

The Bible tells us no more about Nicodemus, so we can't be sure whether he ever openly confessed faith in Jesus. It seems likely, however, that John mentions these incidents because Nicodemus was willing to talk about what he had seen and heard and believed. How else would John have learned the intimate details of Nicodemus's actions? This Gospel gives reason to hope that Nicodemus sacrificed his reputation—and gained a new birth—in the end.

Life Questions: Are there questions about God you feel you cannot ask in public? What are they, and who could you ask in private?

to judge the world, but that the world might be saved through Him.

18 "He who believes in Him is not judged; he who does not believe has been judged already, because he has not believed in the name of the only begotten Son of God.

19 "This is the judgment, that the Light has come into the world, and men loved the darkness rather than the Light, for their deeds were evil.

20 "For everyone who does evil hates the Light, and does not come to the Light for fear that his deeds will be exposed.

21 "But he who practices the truth comes to the Light, so that his deeds may be manifested as having been wrought in God."

John's Last Testimony

22 ¶ After these things Jesus and His disciples came into the land of Judea, and there He was spending time with them and baptizing.

23 John also was baptizing in Aenon near Salim, because there was much water there; and *people* were coming and were being baptized—

24 for John had not yet been thrown into prison.

25 ¶ Therefore there arose a discussion on the part of John's disciples with a Jew about purification.

26 And they came to John and said to him, "Rabbi, He who was with you beyond the Jordan, to whom you have testified, behold, He is baptizing and all are coming to Him."

27 John answered and said, "A man can receive nothing unless it has been given him from heaven.

28 "You yourselves are my witnesses that I said, 'I am not the Christ,' but, 'I have been sent ahead of Him.'

29 "He who has the bride is the bridegroom; but the friend of the bridegroom, who stands and hears him, rejoices greatly because of the bridegroom's voice. So this joy of mine has been made full.

30 "He must increase, but I must decrease."

31 ¶ "He who comes from above is above all, he who is of the earth is from the earth and speaks of the earth. He who comes from heaven is above all.

32 "What He has seen and heard, of that He testifies; and no one receives His testimony.

33 "He who has received His testimony has set his seal to *this*, that God is true.

34 "For He whom God has sent speaks the words of God; for He gives the Spirit without measure.

35 "The Father loves the Son and has given all things into His hand.

36 "He who believes in the Son has eternal life; but he who does not obey the Son will not see life, but the wrath of God abides on him."

Jesus Goes to Galilee

4 Therefore when the Lord knew that the Pharisees had heard that Jesus was making and baptizing more disciples than John

2 (although Jesus Himself was not baptizing, but His disciples were),

3 He left Judea and went away again into Galilee.

4 And He had to pass through Samaria.

5 So He *came to a city of Samaria called Sychar, near the parcel of ground that Jacob gave to his son Joseph;

6 and Jacob's well was there. So Jesus, being wearied from His journey, was sitting thus by the well. It was about *a*the sixth hour.

The Woman of Samaria

7 ¶ There *came a woman of Samaria to draw water. Jesus *said to her, "Give Me a drink."

8 For His disciples had gone away into the city to buy food.

9 Therefore the Samaritan woman *said to Him, "How is it that You, being a Jew, ask me for a drink since I am a Samaritan woman?" (For Jews have no dealings with Samaritans.)

4:9 Bridging Differences

When one church brands another a cult, it usually creates long-standing bitterness. The Samaritans and the Jews felt that way about each other. Samaritan religion closely resembled Judaism, but on key issues its followers had gone their own way. They accepted only the first five books of the Old Testament, and insisted that Mount Gerizim, not Jerusalem, was the proper place to worship God. Though Jews and Samaritans usually avoided each other, Jesus reached across these barriers.

10 Jesus answered and said to her, "If you knew the gift of God, and who it is who says to you, 'Give Me a drink,' you would have asked Him, and He would have given you living water."

11 She *said to Him, "Sir, You have nothing to draw with and the well is deep; where then do You get that living water?

12 "You are not greater than our father Jacob, are You, who gave us the well, and drank of it himself and his sons and his cattle?"

13 Jesus answered and said to her, "Everyone who drinks of this water will thirst again;

14 but whoever drinks of the water that I will give him shall never thirst; but the water that I will give him will become in him a well of water springing up to eternal life."

15 ¶ The woman *said to Him, "Sir, give me

---

a Perhaps 6 p.m. Roman time or noon Jewish time

this water, so I will not be thirsty nor come all the way here to draw."

16 He *said to her, "Go, call your husband and come here."

17 The woman answered and said, "I have no husband." Jesus *said to her, "You have correctly said, 'I have no husband';

18 for you have had five husbands, and the one whom you now have is not your husband; this you have said truly."

19 The woman *said to Him, "Sir, I perceive that You are a prophet.

20 "Our fathers worshiped in this mountain, and you *people* say that in Jerusalem is the place where men ought to worship."

21 Jesus *said to her, "Woman, believe Me, an hour is coming when neither in this mountain nor in Jerusalem will you worship the Father.

22 "You worship what you do not know; we worship what we know, for salvation is from the Jews.

23 "But an hour is coming, and now is, when the true worshipers will worship the Father in spirit and truth; for such people the Father seeks to be His worshipers.

24 "God is spirit, and those who worship Him must worship in spirit and truth."

25 The woman *said to Him, "I know that Messiah is coming (He who is called Christ); when that One comes, He will declare all things to us."

26 Jesus *said to her, "I who speak to you am He."

27 ¶ At this point His disciples came, and they were amazed that He had been speaking with a woman, yet no one said, "What do You seek?" or, "Why do You speak with her?"

Conversations with Jesus
How did Jesus talk to ordinary people?

WATER. WHERE IT'S PLENTIFUL, WE tend to take it for granted, like air. We linger in the shower, hose down a dusty driveway, let a sprinkler spurt for hours to keep the lawn green.

Not so in the desert, where even plants hoard water with bristly defenses. There, water takes on a mythical aura. Taunting visions of pools and streams dance in the heat waves. A craving for water crowds out all other thoughts, and one spoonful, on a parched tongue, is worth gold.

To a woman in a dry land who spent part of each day hauling clay jugs to and from a well, water was the most powerful symbol imaginable. Little wonder that when Jesus offered "living water" that would never run dry (4:10,14), the Samaritan woman paid attention.

> The woman said, "I know that Messiah is coming (He who is called Christ); when that One comes, He will declare all things to us." Jesus said to her, "I who speak to you am He." 4:25-26

Profoundly Simple Words

A simple word or phrase with a profound meaning: that is the style of Jesus' teaching as presented in John. No Biblical author used simpler, more commonplace words: *water, world, light, life, birth, love, truth.* Yet John used them with such depth that hundreds of authors since have tried to plumb their meaning.

Reading John is like sitting in a canoe in the middle of a deep, pristine lake. The clarity of the water reveals everything under the surface—you think. Yet, as you gaze deeper, you can never see the bottom. Something always remains hidden.

Those who look for a neat scheme of organization in John usually fail. John's Gospel omits many of the events recorded in Mark, most of the long public speeches of Matthew, and all of the parables of Luke. Its teaching emerges mainly through Jesus' intimate encounters with diverse people.

Listening in on Private Conversations

Jesus uttered some of his most memorable sayings in the midst of very ordinary conversations. The book of John rarely shows him speaking to large crowds. Instead, we see Jesus meeting secretly with a nervous religious leader (3:1–21), or talking with a promiscuous woman (4:5–26) beside a well. Both visitors carried away simple-yet-profound images (a second birth, living water), and today we recall those words as among the most familiar in all the Bible.

John paints close-ups of individuals who responded to Jesus on earth. Some followed him courageously, others remained skeptical, and still others reacted with hostility. Often, John reports, people simply did not understand, despite Jesus' use of visual images. In short, response to the Son of God on earth nearly 2,000 years ago bears a striking resemblance to the world's response to him now.

Life Questions: Imagine yourself in a private conversation with Jesus, much like the Samaritan woman's. What would you want to talk about?

28 So the woman left her waterpot, and went into the city and *said to the men,

29 "Come, see a man who told me all the things that I *have* done; this is not the Christ, is it?"

30 They went out of the city, and were coming to Him.

31 ¶ Meanwhile the disciples were urging Him, saying, "Rabbi, eat."

32 But He said to them, "I have food to eat that you do not know about."

33 So the disciples were saying to one another, "No one brought Him *anything* to eat, did he?"

34 Jesus *said to them, "My food is to do the will of Him who sent Me and to accomplish His work.

35 "Do you not say, 'There are yet four months, and *then* comes the harvest'? Behold, I say to you, lift up your eyes and look on the fields, that they are white for harvest.

36 "Already he who reaps is receiving wages and is gathering fruit for life eternal; so that he who sows and he who reaps may rejoice together.

37 "For in this *case* the saying is true, 'One sows and another reaps.'

38 "I sent you to reap that for which you have not labored; others have labored and you have entered into their labor."

The Samaritans

39 ¶ From that city many of the Samaritans believed in Him because of the word of the woman who testified, "He told me all the things that I *have* done."

40 So when the Samaritans came to Jesus, they were asking Him to stay with them; and He stayed there two days.

41 Many more believed because of His word;

42 and they were saying to the woman, "It is no longer because of what you said that we believe, for we have heard for ourselves and know that this One is indeed the Savior of the world."

43 ¶ After the two days He went forth from there into Galilee.

44 For Jesus Himself testified that a prophet has no honor in his own country.

45 So when He came to Galilee, the Galileans received Him, having seen all the things that He did in Jerusalem at the feast; for they themselves also went to the feast.

Healing a Nobleman's Son

46 ¶ Therefore He came again to Cana of Galilee where He had made the water wine. And there was a royal official whose son was sick at Capernaum.

47 When he heard that Jesus had come out of Judea into Galilee, he went to Him and was imploring *Him* to come down and heal his son; for he was at the point of death.

48 So Jesus said to him, "Unless you *people* see signs and wonders, you *simply* will not believe."

49 The royal official *said to Him, "Sir, come down before my child dies."

50 Jesus *said to him, "Go; your son lives." The man believed the word that Jesus spoke to him and started off.

4:50 A Long-distance Miracle

This miracle has certain similarities to another performed at the request of a Roman centurion (Luke 7:2–10; Matthew 8:5–13). Of Jesus' two dozen recorded miracles of healing, only these occurred over a distance.

51 As he was now going down, *his* slaves met him, saying that his son was living.

52 So he inquired of them the hour when he began to get better. Then they said to him, "Yesterday at the *a*seventh hour the fever left him."

53 So the father knew that *it was* at that hour in which Jesus said to him, "Your son lives"; and he himself believed and his whole household.

54 This is again a second sign that Jesus performed when He had come out of Judea into Galilee.

The Healing at Bethesda

5 After these things there was a feast of the Jews, and Jesus went up to Jerusalem.

2 ¶ Now there is in Jerusalem by the sheep *gate* a pool, which is called in Hebrew Bethesda, having five porticoes.

3 In these lay a multitude of those who were sick, blind, lame, and withered, [*b*waiting for the moving of the waters;

4 for an angel of the Lord went down at certain seasons into the pool and stirred up the water; whoever then first, after the stirring up of the water, stepped in was made well from whatever disease with which he was afflicted.]

5 A man was there who had been ill for thirty-eight years.

6 When Jesus saw him lying *there*, and knew that he had already been a long time *in that condition*, He *said to him, "Do you wish to get well?"

7 The sick man answered Him, "Sir, I have no man to put me into the pool when the water is stirred up, but while I am coming, another steps down before me."

8 Jesus *said to him, "Get up, pick up your pallet and walk."

9 Immediately the man became well, and picked up his pallet and *began* to walk.

¶ Now it was the Sabbath on that day.

10 So the Jews were saying to the man who was

cured, "It is the Sabbath, and it is not permissible for you to carry your pallet."

11 But he answered them, "He who made me well was the one who said to me, 'Pick up your pallet and walk.'"

12 They asked him, "Who is the man who said to you, 'Pick up *your pallet* and walk'?"

13 But the man who was healed did not know who it was, for Jesus had slipped away while there was a crowd in *that* place.

14 Afterward Jesus *found him in the temple and said to him, "Behold, you have become well; do not sin anymore, so that nothing worse happens to you."

15 The man went away, and told the Jews that it was Jesus who had made him well.

16 For this reason the Jews were persecuting Jesus, because He was doing these things on the Sabbath.

17 But He answered them, "My Father is working until now, and I Myself am working."

Jesus' Equality with God

18 For this reason therefore the Jews were seeking all the more to kill Him, because He not only was breaking the Sabbath, but also was calling God His own Father, making Himself equal with God.

19 ¶ Therefore Jesus answered and was saying to them, "Truly, truly, I say to you, the Son can do nothing of Himself, unless *it is* something He sees the Father doing; for whatever the Father does, these things the Son also does in like manner.

20 "For the Father loves the Son, and shows Him all things that He Himself is doing; and *the Father* will show Him greater works than these, so that you will marvel.

21 "For just as the Father raises the dead and gives them life, even so the Son also gives life to whom He wishes.

22 "For not even the Father judges anyone, but He has given all judgment to the Son,

23 so that all will honor the Son even as they honor the Father. He who does not honor the Son does not honor the Father who sent Him.

24 ¶ "Truly, truly, I say to you, he who hears My word, and believes Him who sent Me, has eternal life, and does not come into judgment, but has passed out of death into life.

Two Resurrections

25 "Truly, truly, I say to you, an hour is coming and now is, when the dead will hear the voice of the Son of God, and those who hear will live.

26 "For just as the Father has life in Himself, even so He gave to the Son also to have life in Himself;

27 and He gave Him authority to execute judgment, because He is *the* Son of Man.

28 "Do not marvel at this; for an hour is com-

ing, in which all who are in the tombs will hear His voice,

29 and will come forth; those who did the good *deeds* to a resurrection of life, those who committed the evil *deeds* to a resurrection of judgment.

30 ¶ "I can do nothing on My own initiative. As I hear, I judge; and My judgment is just, because I do not seek My own will, but the will of Him who sent Me.

31 ¶ "If I *alone* testify about Myself, My testimony is not true.

32 "There is another who testifies of Me, and I know that the testimony which He gives about Me is true.

Witness of John

33 "You have sent to John, and he has testified to the truth.

34 "But the testimony which I receive is not from man, but I say these things so that you may be saved.

35 "He was the lamp that was burning and was shining and you were willing to rejoice for a while in his light.

Witness of Works

36 "But the testimony which I have is greater than *the testimony of* John; for the works which the Father has given Me to accomplish—the very works that I do—testify about Me, that the Father has sent Me.

Witness of the Father

37 "And the Father who sent Me, He has testified of Me. You have neither heard His voice at any time nor seen His form.

38 "You do not have His word abiding in you, for you do not believe Him whom He sent.

Witness of the Scripture

39 "*a*You search the Scriptures because you think that in them you have eternal life; it is these that testify about Me;

40 and you are unwilling to come to Me so that you may have life.

41 "I do not receive glory from men;

42 but I know you, that you do not have the love of God in yourselves.

43 "I have come in My Father's name, and you do not receive Me; if another comes in his own name, you will receive him.

44 "How can you believe, when you receive glory from one another and you do not seek the glory that is from the *one and* only God?

45 "Do not think that I will accuse you before the Father; the one who accuses you is Moses, in whom you have set your hope.

46 "For if you believed Moses, you would believe Me, for he wrote about Me.

---

a Or (a command) *Search the Scriptures!*

47 "But if you do not believe his writings, how will you believe My words?"

Five Thousand Fed

6:1–13pp — Matt 14:13–21; Mark 6:32–44; Luke 9:10–17

6 After these things Jesus went away to the other side of the Sea of Galilee (or Tiberias).

2 A large crowd followed Him, because they saw the signs which He was performing on those who were sick.

3 Then Jesus went up on the mountain, and there He sat down with His disciples.

4 Now the Passover, the feast of the Jews, was near.

5 Therefore Jesus, lifting up His eyes and seeing that a large crowd was coming to Him, *said to Philip, "Where are we to buy bread, so that these may eat?"

6 This He was saying to test him, for He Himself knew what He was intending to do.

7 Philip answered Him, "Two hundred *a*denarii worth of bread is not sufficient for them, for everyone to receive a little."

8 One of His disciples, Andrew, Simon Peter's brother, *said to Him,

9 "There is a lad here who has five barley loaves and two fish, but what are these for so many people?"

10 Jesus said, "Have the people sit down." Now there was much grass in the place. So the men sat down, in number about five thousand.

11 Jesus then took the loaves, and having given thanks, He distributed to those who were seated; likewise also of the fish as much as they wanted.

12 When they were filled, He *said to His disciples, "Gather up the leftover fragments so that nothing will be lost."

13 So they gathered them up, and filled twelve baskets with fragments from the five barley loaves which were left over by those who had eaten.

14 Therefore when the people saw the sign

a The denarius was equivalent to a day's wages

which He had performed, they said, "This is truly the Prophet who is to come into the world."

Jesus Walks on the Water

6:16–21pp — Matt 14:22–33; Mark 6:47–51

15 ¶ So Jesus, perceiving that they were intending to come and take Him by force to make Him king, withdrew again to the mountain by Himself alone.

6:9 Better Bread

The feeding of the five thousand is the only miracle (except Jesus' resurrection) that all four Gospels record. It shows Jesus meeting the most basic human need, using barley loaves, the least expensive kind of bread. Many Jews believed that the Messiah would renew the miraculous manna that their ancestors had eaten under Moses. Jesus pointed to a better, life-changing meal—himself. As the bread of life (verse 35), he would nourish his people far better than any miraculous meal.

16 ¶ Now when evening came, His disciples went down to the sea,

17 and after getting into a boat, they *started to* cross the sea to Capernaum. It had already become dark, and Jesus had not yet come to them.

18 The sea *began* to be stirred up because a strong wind was blowing.

19 Then, when they had rowed about three or four miles, they *saw Jesus walking on the sea and drawing near to the boat; and they were frightened.

20 But He *said to them, "It is I; do not be afraid."

21 So they were willing to receive Him into the boat, and immediately the boat was at the land to which they were going.

22 ¶ The next day the crowd that stood on the

ANDREW *Out of the Spotlight*

ANDREW OPERATED MOSTLY BEHIND THE scenes. As Simon Peter's brother and one of Jesus' first followers, he got involved in many important happenings. Yet all of Andrew's appearances in the Gospels show him directing attention to someone else, not himself.

His greatest recorded achievement was making an introduction. When Andrew heard John the Baptist commend Jesus as "the Lamb of God," he dropped everything to follow Jesus. (He was one of the first to recognize Jesus as the "Messiah.") Then, after spending the day with Jesus, he went to fetch Peter, his brother and fishing partner. Andrew introduced the two, and the rest is history (see 1:35–42).

The Gospels show two other occasions on which Andrew served as a facilitator: He drew Jesus' attention to a boy carrying a lunch (6:8–9) and helped introduce Jesus to some Greek visitors (12:20). Both incidents led to impressive miracles.

Life Questions: How can a behind-the-scenes person today have a role in introducing others to Jesus?

other side of the sea saw that there was no other small boat there, except one, and that Jesus had not entered with His disciples into the boat, but *that* His disciples had gone away alone.

23 There came other small boats from Tiberias near to the place where they ate the bread after the Lord had given thanks.

24 So when the crowd saw that Jesus was not there, nor His disciples, they themselves got into the small boats, and came to Capernaum seeking Jesus.

25 When they found Him on the other side of the sea, they said to Him, "Rabbi, when did You get here?"

Words to the People

26 ¶ Jesus answered them and said, "Truly, truly, I say to you, you seek Me, not because you saw signs, but because you ate of the loaves and were filled.

27 "Do not work for the food which perishes, but for the food which endures to eternal life, which the Son of Man will give to you, for on Him the Father, God, has set His seal."

28 Therefore they said to Him, "What shall we do, so that we may work the works of God?"

29 Jesus answered and said to them, "This is the work of God, that you believe in Him whom He has sent."

30 So they said to Him, "What then do You do for a sign, so that we may see, and believe You? What work do You perform?

31 "Our fathers ate the manna in the wilderness; as it is written, 'HE GAVE THEM BREAD OUT OF HEAVEN TO EAT.' "

32 Jesus then said to them, "Truly, truly, I say to you, it is not Moses who has given you the bread out of heaven, but it is My Father who gives you the true bread out of heaven.

33 "For the bread of God is *a*that which comes down out of heaven, and gives life to the world."

34 Then they said to Him, "Lord, always give us this bread."

35 ¶ Jesus said to them, "I am the bread of life; he who comes to Me will not hunger, and he who believes in Me will never thirst.

36 "But I said to you that you have seen Me, and yet do not believe.

37 "All that the Father gives Me will come to Me, and the one who comes to Me I will certainly not cast out.

38 "For I have come down from heaven, not to do My own will, but the will of Him who sent Me.

39 "This is the will of Him who sent Me, that of all that He has given Me I lose nothing, but raise it up on the last day.

40 "For this is the will of My Father, that everyone who beholds the Son and believes in Him will have eternal life, and I Myself will raise him up on the last day."

Words to the Jews

41 ¶ Therefore the Jews were grumbling about Him, because He said, "I am the bread that came down out of heaven."

42 They were saying, "Is not this Jesus, the son of Joseph, whose father and mother we know? How does He now say, 'I have come down out of heaven'?"

43 Jesus answered and said to them, "Do not grumble among yourselves.

44 "No one can come to Me unless the Father who sent Me draws him; and I will raise him up on the last day.

45 "It is written in the prophets, 'AND THEY SHALL ALL BE TAUGHT OF GOD.' Everyone who has heard and learned from the Father, comes to Me.

46 "Not that anyone has seen the Father, except the One who is from God; He has seen the Father.

47 "Truly, truly, I say to you, he who believes has eternal life.

48 "I am the bread of life.

49 "Your fathers ate the manna in the wilderness, and they died.

50 "This is the bread which comes down out of heaven, so that one may eat of it and not die.

51 "I am the living bread that came down out of heaven; if anyone eats of this bread, he will live forever; and the bread also which I will give for the life of the world is My flesh."

52 ¶ Then the Jews *began* to argue with one another, saying, "How can this man give us *His* flesh to eat?"

53 So Jesus said to them, "Truly, truly, I say to you, unless you eat the flesh of the Son of Man and drink His blood, you have no life in yourselves.

54 "He who eats My flesh and drinks My blood has eternal life, and I will raise him up on the last day.

55 "For My flesh is true food, and My blood is true drink.

56 "He who eats My flesh and drinks My blood abides in Me, and I in him.

57 "As the living Father sent Me, and I live because of the Father, so he who eats Me, he also will live because of Me.

58 "This is the bread which came down out of heaven; not as the fathers ate and died; he who eats this bread will live forever."

Words to the Disciples

59 These things He said in the synagogue as He taught in Capernaum.

60 ¶ Therefore many of His disciples, when they heard *this* said, "This is a difficult statement; who can listen to it?"

61 But Jesus, conscious that His disciples grumbled at this, said to them, "Does this cause you to stumble?

a Or *He who comes*

62 *"What* then if you see the Son of Man ascending to where He was before?

63 "It is the Spirit who gives life; the flesh profits nothing; the words that I have spoken to you are spirit and are life.

6:60 Too Hard to Swallow

Chapter 6 shows the full cycle of people's response to Jesus. At first, excited by his miracle of feeding the 5,000, people tried to make him king. But Jesus escaped. The next day he rebuked them for having an interest only in physical concerns, not in spiritual truth (verse 26). He used the miracle of the feeding to give an important lesson on the bread of life, using words that were later applied to the Lord's Supper, or the Eucharist. These words, however, so disappointed the sensation-seeking crowd that many turned away from him.

64 "But there are some of you who do not believe." For Jesus knew from the beginning who they were who did not believe, and who it was that would betray Him.

65 And He was saying, "For this reason I have said to you, that no one can come to Me unless it has been granted him from the Father."

Peter's Confession of Faith

66 ¶ As a result of this many of His disciples withdrew and were not walking with Him anymore.

67 So Jesus said to the twelve, "You do not want to go away also, do you?"

68 Simon Peter answered Him, "Lord, to whom shall we go? You have words of eternal life.

69 "We have believed and have come to know that You are the Holy One of God."

70 Jesus answered them, "Did I Myself not choose you, the twelve, and *yet* one of you is a devil?"

71 Now He meant Judas *the son* of Simon Iscariot, for he, one of the twelve, was going to betray Him.

Jesus Teaches at the Feast

7 After these things Jesus was walking in Galilee, for He was unwilling to walk in Judea because the Jews were seeking to kill Him.

2 Now the feast of the Jews, the Feast of Booths, was near.

3 Therefore His brothers said to Him, "Leave here and go into Judea, so that Your disciples also may see Your works which You are doing.

4 "For no one does anything in secret when he himself seeks to be *known* publicly. If You do these things, show Yourself to the world."

5 For not even His brothers were believing in Him.

6 So Jesus *said to them, "My time is not yet here, but your time is always opportune.

7 "The world cannot hate you, but it hates Me because I testify of it, that its deeds are evil.

JUDAS *Devil Man*

HUMAN BEINGS ARE BOTH "THE scum and glory of the universe," said Blaise Pascal. The Bible, too, paints a realistic picture of people as definite mixtures of good and bad. Apart from Jesus, no one is so good as to be flawless, but rarely is anyone portrayed as all bad.

Judas Iscariot is a major exception. No doubt he had some good qualities, or else why would Jesus have picked him as a disciple? Yet these good qualities were swallowed up by characteristics the Bible clearly labels satanic. In fact, Jesus himself described Judas as a devil (6:70).

How does a human being fall so low? From the evidence of the New Testament, it seems that Judas let greed get the better of him. While handling the cash as the disciples' treasurer, he began to take money for himself (12:6).

Possibly, too, Judas became frustrated over Jesus' unwillingness to be crowned king and lead a revolt against the Romans. Although other disciples struggled with that same issue, only Judas left himself so open to evil that Satan took control. Both John and Luke say that Satan entered into Judas (Luke 22:3; John 13:27). In a final, terrible act, he betrayed his Master, identifying him with a kiss in a crowd on a dark night.

Afterward, Judas felt shame and remorse. But so did the other disciples, who had also abandoned and denied Jesus. Judas should have gone to Jesus for forgiveness—after all, Jesus mercifully forgave Peter's brazen denial. Instead Judas went to the wrong people, attempting to undo his betrayal by meeting with the very ones who had financed it.

Rebuffed by his co-conspirators, Judas killed himself (Matthew 27:5). He went down in history as perhaps the most famous of all of Jesus' disciples—famous as an object lesson of what can happen, even among Jesus' followers, if they let evil have its way.

Life Questions: In Judas's life, one sin led to other, bigger ones. Have you ever seen this process in action? Where and how? What steps can you take to counteract this process?

8 "Go up to the feast yourselves; I do not go up to this feast because My time has not yet fully come."

9 Having said these things to them, He stayed in Galilee.

10 ¶ But when His brothers had gone up to the feast, then He Himself also went up, not publicly, but as if, in secret.

11 So the Jews were seeking Him at the feast and were saying, "Where is He?"

12 There was much grumbling among the crowds concerning Him; some were saying, "He is a good man"; others were saying, "No, on the contrary, He leads the people astray."

7:12 Public Opinion

At one time a musician who wanted a national reputation had to play at New York's Carnegie Hall, the nation's cultural center. Similarly, Jesus' brothers wanted him to appear in Jerusalem, Israel's political and religious center. But Jesus had less faith than they in public opinion, and John shows why. The crowds that came to Jerusalem were curious but skeptical. Some thought Jesus a good man, some considered him a con artist. They were amazed at his knowledge of Scripture, but attributed his ideas to demon-possession (verse 20). They couldn't agree whether he was the Messiah (verse 43).

13 Yet no one was speaking openly of Him for fear of the Jews.

14 ¶ But when it was now the midst of the feast Jesus went up into the temple, and *began to* teach.

15 The Jews then were astonished, saying, "How has this man become learned, having never been educated?"

16 So Jesus answered them and said, "My teaching is not Mine, but His who sent Me.

17 "If anyone is willing to do His will, he will know of the teaching, whether it is of God or *whether* I speak from Myself.

18 "He who speaks from himself seeks his own glory; but He who is seeking the glory of the One who sent Him, He is true, and there is no unrighteousness in Him.

19 ¶ "Did not Moses give you the Law, and *yet* none of you carries out the Law? Why do you seek to kill Me?"

20 The crowd answered, "You have a demon! Who seeks to kill You?"

21 Jesus answered them, "I did one deed, and you all marvel.

22 "For this reason Moses has given you circumcision (not because it is from Moses, but from the fathers), and on *the* Sabbath you circumcise a man.

23 "If a man receives circumcision on *the* Sab-

bath so that the Law of Moses will not be broken, are you angry with Me because I made an entire man well on *the* Sabbath?

24 "Do not judge according to appearance, but judge with righteous judgment."

25 ¶ So some of the people of Jerusalem were saying, "Is this not the man whom they are seeking to kill?

26 "Look, He is speaking publicly, and they are saying nothing to Him. The rulers do not really know that this is the Christ, do they?

27 "However, we know where this man is from; but whenever the Christ may come, no one knows where He is from."

28 Then Jesus cried out in the temple, teaching and saying, "You both know Me and know where I am from; and I have not come of Myself, but He who sent Me is true, whom you do not know.

29 "I know Him, because I am from Him, and He sent Me."

30 So they were seeking to seize Him; and no man laid his hand on Him, because His hour had not yet come.

31 But many of the crowd believed in Him; and they were saying, "When the Christ comes, He will not perform more signs than those which this man has, will He?"

32 ¶ The Pharisees heard the crowd muttering these things about Him, and the chief priests and the Pharisees sent officers to seize Him.

33 Therefore Jesus said, "For a little while longer I am with you, then I go to Him who sent Me.

34 "You will seek Me, and will not find Me; and where I am, you cannot come."

35 The Jews then said to one another, "Where does this man intend to go that we will not find Him? He is not intending to go to the Dispersion among the Greeks, and teach the Greeks, is He?

36 "What is this statement that He said, 'You will seek Me, and will not find Me; and where I am, you cannot come'?"

37 ¶ Now on the last day, the great *day* of the feast, Jesus stood and cried out, saying, "If anyone is thirsty, let him come to Me and drink.

38 "He who believes in Me, as the Scripture said, 'From his innermost being will flow rivers of living water.'"

39 But this He spoke of the Spirit, whom those who believed in Him were to receive; for the Spirit was not yet *given*, because Jesus was not yet glorified.

Division of People over Jesus

40 ¶ *Some* of the people therefore, when they heard these words, were saying, "This certainly is the Prophet."

41 Others were saying, "This is the Christ." Still others were saying, "Surely the Christ is not going to come from Galilee, is He?

42 "Has not the Scripture said that the Christ

comes from the descendants of David, and from Bethlehem, the village where David was?"

43 So a division occurred in the crowd because of Him.

44 Some of them wanted to seize Him, but no one laid hands on Him.

45 ¶ The officers then came to the chief priests and Pharisees, and they said to them, "Why did you not bring Him?"

46 The officers answered, "Never has a man spoken the way this man speaks."

47 The Pharisees then answered them, "You have not also been led astray, have you?

48 "No one of the rulers or Pharisees has believed in Him, has he?

49 "But this crowd which does not know the Law is accursed."

50 Nicodemus (he who came to Him before, being one of them) *said to them,

51 "Our Law does not judge a man unless it first hears from him and knows what he is doing, does it?"

52 They answered him, "You are not also from Galilee, are you? Search, and see that no prophet arises out of Galilee."

53 [*Everyone went to his home.

The Adulterous Woman

8 But Jesus went to the Mount of Olives.
2 Early in the morning He came again into the temple, and all the people were coming to Him; and He sat down and *began* to teach them.

3 The scribes and the Pharisees *brought a woman caught in adultery, and having set her in the center *of the court*,

4 they *said to Him, "Teacher, this woman has been caught in adultery, in the very act.

5 "Now in the Law Moses commanded us to stone such women; what then do You say?"

6 They were saying this, testing Him, so that they might have grounds for accusing Him. But Jesus stooped down and with His finger wrote on the ground.

7 But when they persisted in asking Him, He straightened up, and said to them, "He who is

8:6 Belong in the Bible?

Because most ancient manuscripts don't include this story about the woman caught in adultery, many scholars question whether it was added later or perhaps originally fell at a different place in the Gospel. According to the story, the Pharisees weren't following Moses' law, which required the woman's partner in crime to appear also. Interestingly, verse 6 records the only scene of Jesus writing.

without sin among you, let him *be the* first to throw a stone at her."

8 Again He stooped down and wrote on the ground.

9 When they heard it, they *began* to go out one by one, beginning with the older ones, and He was left alone, and the woman, where she was, in the center *of the court*.

10 Straightening up, Jesus said to her, "Woman, where are they? Did no one condemn you?"

11 She said, "No one, Lord." And Jesus said, "I do not condemn you, either. Go. From now on sin no more."]

Jesus Is the Light of the World

12 ¶ Then Jesus again spoke to them, saying, "I am the Light of the world; he who follows Me will not walk in the darkness, but will have the Light of life."

13 So the Pharisees said to Him, "You are testifying about Yourself; Your testimony is not true."

14 Jesus answered and said to them, "Even if I testify about Myself, My testimony is true, for I know where I came from and where I am going; but you do not know where I come from or where I am going.

15 "You judge according to the flesh; I am not judging anyone.

16 "But even if I do judge, My judgment is true; for I am not alone *in it,* but I and the Father who sent Me.

17 "Even in your law it has been written that the testimony of two men is true.

18 "I am He who testifies about Myself, and the Father who sent Me testifies about Me."

19 So they were saying to Him, "Where is Your Father?" Jesus answered, "You know neither Me nor My Father; if you knew Me, you would know My Father also."

20 These words He spoke in the treasury, as He taught in the temple; and no one seized Him, because His hour had not yet come.

21 ¶ Then He said again to them, "I go away, and you will seek Me, and will die in your sin; where I am going, you cannot come."

22 So the Jews were saying, "Surely He will not kill Himself, will He, since He says, 'Where I am going, you cannot come'?"

23 And He was saying to them, "You are from below, I am from above; you are of this world, I am not of this world.

24 "Therefore I said to you that you will die in your sins; for unless you believe that I am *He*, you will die in your sins."

25 So they were saying to Him, "Who are You?" Jesus said to them, "What have I been saying to you *from* the beginning?

26 "I have many things to speak and to judge concerning you, but He who sent Me is true; and

---

a Later mss add the story of the adulterous woman, numbering it as John 7:53-8:11

the things which I heard from Him, these I speak to the world."

27 They did not realize that He had been speaking to them about the Father.

28 So Jesus said, "When you lift up the Son of Man, then you will know that I am *He,* and I do nothing on My own initiative, but I speak these things as the Father taught Me.

29 "And He who sent Me is with Me; He has not left Me alone, for I always do the things that are pleasing to Him."

30 As He spoke these things, many came to believe in Him.

The Truth Will Make You Free

31 ¶ So Jesus was saying to those Jews who had believed Him, "If you continue in My word, *then* you are truly disciples of Mine;

32 and you will know the truth, and the truth will make you free."

33 They answered Him, "We are Abraham's descendants and have never yet been enslaved to anyone; how is it that You say, 'You will become free'?"

34 ¶ Jesus answered them, "Truly, truly, I say to you, everyone who commits sin is the slave of sin.

35 "The slave does not remain in the house forever; the son does remain forever.

36 "So if the Son makes you free, you will be free indeed.

37 "I know that you are Abraham's descendants; yet you seek to kill Me, because My word has no place in you.

38 "I speak the things which I have seen with *My* Father; therefore you also do the things which you heard from *your* father."

39 ¶ They answered and said to Him, "Abraham is our father." Jesus *said to them, "If you are Abraham's children, do the deeds of Abraham.

40 "But as it is, you are seeking to kill Me, a man who has told you the truth, which I heard from God; this Abraham did not do.

41 "You are doing the deeds of your father." They said to Him, "We were not born of fornication; we have one Father: God."

42 Jesus said to them, "If God were your Father, you would love Me, for I proceeded forth and have come from God, for I have not even come on My own initiative, but He sent Me.

43 "Why do you not understand what I am saying? *It is* because you cannot hear My word.

44 "You are of *your* father the devil, and you want to do the desires of your father. He was a murderer from the beginning, and does not stand in the truth because there is no truth in him. Whenever he speaks a lie, he speaks from his own *nature,* for he is a liar and the father of lies.

45 "But because I speak the truth, you do not believe Me.

46 "Which one of you convicts Me of sin? If I speak truth, why do you not believe Me?

47 "He who is of God hears the words of God; for this reason you do not hear *them,* because you are not of God."

48 ¶ The Jews answered and said to Him, "Do we not say rightly that You are a Samaritan and have a demon?"

49 Jesus answered, "I do not have a demon; but I honor My Father, and you dishonor Me.

50 "But I do not seek My glory; there is One who seeks and judges.

51 "Truly, truly, I say to you, if anyone keeps My word he will never see death."

52 The Jews said to Him, "Now we know that You have a demon. Abraham died, and the prophets *also*; and You say, 'If anyone keeps My word, he will never taste of death.'

53 "Surely You are not greater than our father Abraham, who died? The prophets died too; whom do You make Yourself out *to be*?"

54 Jesus answered, "If I glorify Myself, My glory is nothing; it is My Father who glorifies Me, of whom you say, 'He is our God';

55 and you have not come to know Him, but I know Him; and if I say that I do not know Him, I will be a liar like you, but I do know Him and keep His word.

56 "Your father Abraham rejoiced to see My day, and he saw *it* and was glad."

57 So the Jews said to Him, "You are not yet fifty years old, and have You seen Abraham?"

58 Jesus said to them, "Truly, truly, I say to you, before Abraham was born, I am."

59 Therefore they picked up stones to throw at Him, but Jesus hid Himself and went out of the temple.

Healing the Man Born Blind

9 As He passed by, He saw a man blind from birth.

2 And His disciples asked Him, "Rabbi, who sinned, this man or his parents, that he would be born blind?"

9:2 Suffering and Sin

In this story, Jesus corrects a commonly held notion that suffering comes because of sin. The healed man became a loyal spokesman for Jesus. His testimony, however, failed to convince the Pharisees, who also rejected Jesus' teaching about why the man had been born blind (verse 34). In typical style, John wove together the incident with Jesus' comments on a different kind of blindness.

3 Jesus answered, "*It was* neither *that* this man sinned, nor his parents; but *it was* so that the works of God might be displayed in him.

4 "We must work the works of Him who sent Me as long as it is day; night is coming when no one can work.

5 "While I am in the world, I am the Light of the world."

6 When He had said this, He spat on the ground, and made clay of the spittle, and applied the clay to his eyes,

7 and said to him, "Go, wash in the pool of Siloam" (which is translated, Sent). So he went away and washed, and came *back* seeing.

8 Therefore the neighbors, and those who previously saw him as a beggar, were saying, "Is not this the one who used to sit and beg?"

9 Others were saying, "This is he," *still* others were saying, "No, but he is like him." He kept saying, "I am the one."

10 So they were saying to him, "How then were your eyes opened?"

11 He answered, "The man who is called Jesus made clay, and anointed my eyes, and said to me, 'Go to Siloam and wash'; so I went away and washed, and I received sight."

12 They said to him, "Where is He?" He *said, "I do not know."

Controversy over the Man

13 ¶ They *brought to the Pharisees the man who was formerly blind.

14 Now it was a Sabbath on the day when Jesus made the clay and opened his eyes.

15 Then the Pharisees also were asking him again how he received his sight. And he said to them, "He applied clay to my eyes, and I washed, and I see."

16 Therefore some of the Pharisees were saying, "This man is not from God, because He does not keep the Sabbath." But others were saying, "How can a man who is a sinner perform such signs?" And there was a division among them.

17 So they *said to the blind man again, "What do you say about Him, since He opened your eyes?" And he said, "He is a prophet."

18 ¶ The Jews then did not believe *it* of him, that he had been blind and had received sight, until they called the parents of the very one who had received his sight,

19 and questioned them, saying, "Is this your son, who you say was born blind? Then how does he now see?"

20 His parents answered them and said, "We know that this is our son, and that he was born blind;

21 but how he now sees, we do not know; or who opened his eyes, we do not know. Ask him; he is of age, he will speak for himself."

22 His parents said this because they were afraid of the Jews; for the Jews had already agreed that if anyone confessed Him to be Christ, he was to be put out of the synagogue.

23 For this reason his parents said, "He is of age; ask him."

24 ¶ So a second time they called the man who had been blind, and said to him, "Give glory to God; we know that this man is a sinner."

25 He then answered, "Whether He is a sinner, I do not know; one thing I do know, that though I was blind, now I see."

26 So they said to him, "What did He do to you? How did He open your eyes?"

27 He answered them, "I told you already and you did not listen; why do you want to hear *it* again? You do not want to become His disciples too, do you?"

28 They reviled him and said, "You are His disciple, but we are disciples of Moses.

29 "We know that God has spoken to Moses, but as for this man, we do not know where He is from."

30 The man answered and said to them, "Well, here is an amazing thing, that you do not know where He is from, and *yet* He opened my eyes.

31 "We know that God does not hear sinners; but if anyone is God-fearing and does His will, He hears him.

32 "Since the beginning of time it has never been heard that anyone opened the eyes of a person born blind.

33 "If this man were not from God, He could do nothing."

34 They answered him, "You were born entirely in sins, and are you teaching us?" So they put him out.

Jesus Affirms His Deity

35 ¶ Jesus heard that they had put him out, and finding him, He said, "Do you believe in the Son of Man?"

36 He answered, "Who is He, Lord, that I may believe in Him?"

37 Jesus said to him, "You have both seen Him, and He is the one who is talking with you."

38 And he said, "Lord, I believe." And he worshiped Him.

39 And Jesus said, "For judgment I came into this world, so that those who do not see may see, and that those who see may become blind."

40 Those of the Pharisees who were with Him heard these things and said to Him, "We are not blind too, are we?"

41 Jesus said to them, "If you were blind, you would have no sin; but since you say, 'We see,' your sin remains.

Parable of the Good Shepherd

10 "Truly, truly, I say to you, he who does not enter by the door into the fold of the sheep, but climbs up some other way, he is a thief and a robber.

2 "But he who enters by the door is a shepherd of the sheep.

3 "To him the doorkeeper opens, and the sheep hear his voice, and he calls his own sheep by name and leads them out.

4 "When he puts forth all his own, he goes ahead of them, and the sheep follow him because they know his voice.

5 "A stranger they simply will not follow, but will flee from him, because they do not know the voice of strangers."

6 This figure of speech Jesus spoke to them, but they did not understand what those things were which He had been saying to them.

7 ¶ So Jesus said to them again, "Truly, truly, I say to you, I am the door of the sheep.

8 "All who came before Me are thieves and robbers, but the sheep did not hear them.

9 "I am the door; if anyone enters through Me, he will be saved, and will go in and out and find pasture.

10 "The thief comes only to steal and kill and

A Modern Shepherd
What a "good shepherd" would look like today

SOME OF THE BIBLE'S RURAL illustrations simply do not transfer easily into modern life. What is a "good shepherd" like? What did Jesus mean by the term?

A small drama that took place on the slopes of Washington's Mount Rainier may shed light on the meaning of the "good shepherd." One Memorial Day weekend a Christian dentist named James Reddick was teaching his 12-year-old daughter and 11-year-old son the joy of mountain hiking. A sudden storm came up, battering them with hurricane-force winds and thick, wet sheets of snow. A blinding "whiteout" made it impossible to see or move on the steep slopes.

"I came that they may have life, and have it abundantly."
10:10

Willing to Die

Reddick laboriously dug an oblong trench with an aluminum mess kit, then tucked his children into sleeping bags away from the entrance. He covered the opening with a tarp, but it kept blowing away, exposing the trench to the swirling snow outside. Reddick found he had to lie directly across the opening, using his own weight to hold down the edges of the tarp. His body protected his son and daughter from the howling wind.

Two days passed before searchers finally noticed the corner of a backpack protruding from deep snow. They rushed to the site, hoping the snow-covered mound would contain the three missing hikers. Inside, they found Sharon and David Reddick, very much alive. But the stiff body of their father lay against one wall of the snow cave. He had "taken the cold spot," in one searcher's words, by using his own back as the outer wall.

An image something like that must have filled the minds of Jesus' listeners as he described a good shepherd who "lays down his life" for his sheep (10:11). Nothing—not ravaging cold, thieves, or wolves—would come between the good shepherd and his sheep. He would die for their protection.

Popularity, for a While

As Jesus headed toward final tragedy in Jerusalem, the theme of death, *his* death, kept surfacing in his parables and direct statements. Ironically, his followers were growing in numbers. His popularity had reached a peak with the feeding of 5,000 people on a handful of morsels, a miracle mentioned by all four Gospel writers.

The ground swell of support to make Jesus king deeply impressed his followers; Jesus, however, escaped into the hills (6:15). He would not be a king on the crowd's terms. He continued on his lonely mission, stirring up controversy and hatred by healing people on the Sabbath and by proclaiming himself equal with God.

Ignoring an Impressive Miracle

Many Jews came over to Jesus after one of his most impressive signs: bringing Lazarus back to life. But, simultaneously, religious leaders concluded callously that it was best for one man (Jesus) to die rather than upset the whole nation (11:50). Four separate times they tried to seize him.

Jesus came to offer "life"—one of those one-syllable words, swollen with meaning, that John threaded through his narrative. Lazarus received that life in an astonishingly literal way, providing yet another sign of Jesus' ultimate power. Jesus, though, made preparations to give up his own life, making the ultimate sacrifice of the good shepherd.

Life Questions: What have you sacrificed for the sake of another person?

destroy; I came that they may have life, and have *it* abundantly.

11 ¶ "I am the good shepherd; the good shepherd lays down His life for the sheep.

10:4 Good Shepherd

Unlike modern-day shepherds, who use dogs to drive their flocks, Palestinian shepherds walked ahead, calling the sheep to follow. Only a familiar voice would make them come. In the Old Testament, God was called the "Shepherd of Israel" (Psalm 80:1), and God's appointed leaders were often referred to as shepherds. In claiming to be the good shepherd, Jesus was asserting his leadership over a flock he was willing to die for.

12 "He who is a hired hand, and not a shepherd, who is not the owner of the sheep, sees the wolf coming, and leaves the sheep and flees, and the wolf snatches them and scatters *them*.

13 *"He flees* because he is a hired hand and is not concerned about the sheep.

14 "I am the good shepherd, and I know My own and My own know Me,

15 even as the Father knows Me and I know the Father; and I lay down My life for the sheep.

16 "I have other sheep, which are not of this fold; I must bring them also, and they will hear My voice; and they will become one flock *with* one shepherd.

17 "For this reason the Father loves Me, because I lay down My life so that I may take it again.

18 "No one has taken it away from Me, but I lay it down on My own initiative. I have authority to lay it down, and I have authority to take it up again. This commandment I received from My Father."

19 ¶ A division occurred again among the Jews because of these words.

20 Many of them were saying, "He has a demon and is insane. Why do you listen to Him?"

21 Others were saying, "These are not the sayings of one demon-possessed. A demon cannot open the eyes of the blind, can he?"

Jesus Asserts His Deity

22 ¶ At that time the Feast of the Dedication took place at Jerusalem;

23 it was winter, and Jesus was walking in the temple in the portico of Solomon.

24 The Jews then gathered around Him, and were saying to Him, "How long will You keep us in suspense? If You are the Christ, tell us plainly."

25 Jesus answered them, "I told you, and you do not believe; the works that I do in My Father's name, these testify of Me.

26 "But you do not believe because you are not of My sheep.

27 "My sheep hear My voice, and I know them, and they follow Me;

28 and I give eternal life to them, and they will never perish; and no one will snatch them out of My hand.

29 "ᵃMy Father, who has given *them* to Me, is greater than all; and no one is able to snatch *them* out of the Father's hand.

30 "I and the Father are one."

31 ¶ The Jews picked up stones again to stone Him.

32 Jesus answered them, "I showed you many good works from the Father; for which of them are you stoning Me?"

33 The Jews answered Him, "For a good work we do not stone You, but for blasphemy; and because You, being a man, make Yourself out *to be* God."

34 Jesus answered them, "Has it not been written in your Law, 'I SAID, YOU ARE GODS'?

35 "If he called them gods, to whom the word of God came (and the Scripture cannot be broken),

36 do you say of Him, whom the Father sanctified and sent into the world, 'You are blaspheming,' because I said, 'I am the Son of God'?

37 "If I do not do the works of My Father, do not believe Me;

38 but if I do them, though you do not believe Me, believe the works, so that you may know and understand that the Father is in Me, and I in the Father."

39 Therefore they were seeking again to seize Him, and He eluded their grasp.

40 ¶ And He went away again beyond the Jordan to the place where John was first baptizing, and He was staying there.

41 Many came to Him and were saying, "While John performed no sign, yet everything John said about this man was true."

42 Many believed in Him there.

The Death and Resurrection of Lazarus

11 Now a certain man was sick, Lazarus of Bethany, the village of Mary and her sister Martha.

2 It was the Mary who anointed the Lord with ointment, and wiped His feet with her hair, whose brother Lazarus was sick.

3 So the sisters sent *word* to Him, saying, "Lord, behold, he whom You love is sick."

4 But when Jesus heard *this*, He said, "This sickness is not to end in death, but for the glory of God, so that the Son of God may be glorified by it."

5 Now Jesus loved Martha and her sister and Lazarus.

6 So when He heard that he was sick, He then stayed two days *longer* in the place where He was.

ᵃ One early ms reads *What My Father has given Me is greater than all*

7 Then after this He *said to the disciples, "Let us go to Judea again."

8 The disciples *said to Him, "Rabbi, the Jews were just now seeking to stone You, and are You going there again?"

9 Jesus answered, "Are there not twelve hours in the day? If anyone walks in the day, he does not stumble, because he sees the light of this world.

10 "But if anyone walks in the night, he stumbles, because the light is not in him."

11 This He said, and after that He *said to them, "Our friend Lazarus has fallen asleep; but I go, so that I may awaken him out of sleep."

12 The disciples then said to Him, "Lord, if he has fallen asleep, he will recover."

13 Now Jesus had spoken of his death, but they thought that He was speaking of literal sleep.

14 So Jesus then said to them plainly, "Lazarus is dead,

15 and I am glad for your sakes that I was not there, so that you may believe; but let us go to him."

16 Therefore Thomas, who is called Didymus, said to *his* fellow disciples, "Let us also go, so that we may die with Him."

17 ¶ So when Jesus came, He found that he had already been in the tomb four days.

18 Now Bethany was near Jerusalem, about two miles off;

19 and many of the Jews had come to Martha and Mary, to console them concerning *their* brother.

20 Martha therefore, when she heard that Jesus was coming, went to meet Him, but Mary stayed at the house.

21 Martha then said to Jesus, "Lord, if You had been here, my brother would not have died."

11:21 If Only . . .

Mary and Martha had very different personalities, but the same response to pain. Both sisters, meeting Jesus, said the same thing: "If You had been here, my brother would not have died" (verses 21,32). They had asked Jesus to come, and for reasons they could not understand, he had delayed. The healing they longed for had not occurred. Jesus gave the sisters no explanation of his timing, but showed he had a reason: to demonstrate his power over death.

22 "Even now I know that whatever You ask of God, God will give You."

23 Jesus *said to her, "Your brother will rise again."

24 Martha *said to Him, "I know that he will rise again in the resurrection on the last day."

25 Jesus said to her, "I am the resurrection and the life; he who believes in Me will live even if he dies,

26 and everyone who lives and believes in Me will never die. Do you believe this?"

27 She *said to Him, "Yes, Lord; I have believed that You are the Christ, the Son of God, *even* He who comes into the world."

28 ¶ When she had said this, she went away and called Mary her sister, saying secretly, "The Teacher is here and is calling for you."

29 And when she heard it, she *got up quickly and was coming to Him.

30 ¶ Now Jesus had not yet come into the village, but was still in the place where Martha met Him.

31 Then the Jews who were with her in the house, and consoling her, when they saw that Mary got up quickly and went out, they followed her, supposing that she was going to the tomb to weep there.

32 Therefore, when Mary came where Jesus was, she saw Him, and fell at His feet, saying to Him, "Lord, if You had been here, my brother would not have died."

33 When Jesus therefore saw her weeping, and the Jews who came with her *also* weeping, He was deeply moved in spirit and was troubled,

34 and said, "Where have you laid him?" They *said to Him, "Lord, come and see."

35 Jesus wept.

36 So the Jews were saying, "See how He loved him!"

37 But some of them said, "Could not this man, who opened the eyes of the blind man, have kept this man also from dying?"

38 ¶ So Jesus, again being deeply moved within, *came to the tomb. Now it was a cave, and a stone was lying against it.

39 Jesus *said, "Remove the stone." Martha, the sister of the deceased, *said to Him, "Lord, by this time there will be a stench, for he has been *dead* four days."

40 Jesus *said to her, "Did I not say to you that if you believe, you will see the glory of God?"

41 So they removed the stone. Then Jesus raised His eyes, and said, "Father, I thank You that You have heard Me.

42 "I knew that You always hear Me; but because of the people standing around I said it, so that they may believe that You sent Me."

43 When He had said these things, He cried out with a loud voice, "Lazarus, come forth."

44 The man who had died came forth, bound hand and foot with wrappings, and his face was wrapped around with a cloth. Jesus *said to them, "Unbind him, and let him go."

45 ¶ Therefore many of the Jews who came to Mary, and saw what He had done, believed in Him.

46 But some of them went to the Pharisees and told them the things which Jesus had done.

Conspiracy to Kill Jesus

47 ¶ Therefore the chief priests and the Pharisees convened a council, and were saying, "What are we doing? For this man is performing many signs.

48 "If we let Him *go on* like this, all men will believe in Him, and the Romans will come and take away both our place and our nation."

49 But one of them, Caiaphas, who was high priest that year, said to them, "You know nothing at all,

50 nor do you take into account that it is expedient for you that one man die for the people, and that the whole nation not perish."

51 Now he did not say this on his own initiative, but being high priest that year, he prophesied that Jesus was going to die for the nation,

52 and not for the nation only, but in order that He might also gather together into one the children of God who are scattered abroad.

53 So from that day on they planned together to kill Him.

54 ¶ Therefore Jesus no longer continued to walk publicly among the Jews, but went away from there to the country near the wilderness, into a city called Ephraim; and there He stayed with the disciples.

55 ¶ Now the Passover of the Jews was near, and many went up to Jerusalem out of the country before the Passover to purify themselves.

56 So they were seeking for Jesus, and were saying to one another as they stood in the temple, "What do you think; that He will not come to the feast at all?"

57 Now the chief priests and the Pharisees had given orders that if anyone knew where He was, he was to report it, so that they might seize Him.

Mary Anoints Jesus

12:1–8Ref — Matt 26:6–13; Mark 14:3–9; Luke 7:37–39

12 Jesus, therefore, six days before the Passover, came to Bethany where Lazarus was, whom Jesus had raised from the dead.

11:53 Climax of the Drama

John wrote his book with a great sense of drama. The first six chapters reveal the identity of Jesus. The next six chapters (7–12) show the increasingly divided opinions about Jesus. On the one hand, his disciples were won over, and Jesus gained a loyal following among the people. On the other hand, his enemies rejected all the evidence about him. Their opposition culminated in this plot, which finally brought about Jesus' death.

2 So they made Him a supper there, and Martha was serving; but Lazarus was one of those reclining *at the table* with Him.

3 Mary then took a pound of very costly perfume of pure nard, and anointed the feet of Jesus and wiped His feet with her hair; and the house was filled with the fragrance of the perfume.

4 But Judas Iscariot, one of His disciples, who was intending to betray Him, *said,

ANNAS AND CAIAPHAS *Collaborators*

THE ANCIENT ROMANS KNEW HOW the Jews valued their faith, which is why they insisted on appointing Israel's high priest. Much like the Soviet Communists and German Nazis in our own time, first-century Romans sought to keep the religious dimension of life under their control.

Annas and Caiaphas fit the Romans' plans perfectly. Caiaphas held office during Jesus' ministry, but Annas, his father-in-law and a former high priest, retained so much influence that he was sometimes called by the title. Both were Sadducees, an aristocratic group who had a very this-worldly understanding of Judaism. Sadducees bent over backward to cooperate with whatever group held political power, and as a result they prospered.

When Jesus started making waves in Israel, Annas and Caiaphas viewed him as a political threat. As John explains it, they feared Jesus would attract so many followers that the Romans would grow alarmed and step in. In classic "Don't rock the boat" thinking, Caiaphas concluded it was better to do away with Jesus than jeopardize the future of Israel. Jesus' miracles, his teachings and his character made no difference to Caiaphas. Political survival mattered above all (11:45–53).

With that in mind, religious leaders secretly kidnapped Jesus, put him on trial, and brought him to the Romans for execution. They later persecuted the church that sprang up after Jesus' resurrection.

The nation of Israel did survive, though not for long. In A.D. 70 the Romans wiped Israel out of existence, in the process destroying the temple where the high priest officiated. Not until 1948 would the Jews again control Jerusalem.

Life Questions: Is it possible to be so concerned with keeping the peace that you end up opposing what God is doing? What examples can you think of today?

5 "Why was this perfume not sold for [a]three hundred denarii and given to poor *people*?"

6 Now he said this, not because he was concerned about the poor, but because he was a thief, and as he had the money box, he used to pilfer what was put into it.

7 Therefore Jesus said, "Let her alone, so that she may keep [b]it for the day of My burial.

8 "For you always have the poor with you, but you do not always have Me."

9 ¶ The large crowd of the Jews then learned that He was there; and they came, not for Jesus' sake only, but that they might also see Lazarus, whom He raised from the dead.

10 But the chief priests planned to put Lazarus to death also;

11 because on account of him many of the Jews were going away and were believing in Jesus.

Jesus Enters Jerusalem

12:12–15pp — Matt 21:4–9; Mark 11:7–10;
Luke 19:35–38

12 ¶ On the next day the large crowd who had come to the feast, when they heard that Jesus was coming to Jerusalem,

13 took the branches of the palm trees and went out to meet Him, and *began* to shout, "Hosanna! BLESSED IS HE WHO COMES IN THE NAME OF THE LORD, even the King of Israel."

14 Jesus, finding a young donkey, sat on it; as it is written,

15 "FEAR NOT, DAUGHTER OF ZION; BEHOLD, YOUR KING IS COMING, SEATED ON A DONKEY'S COLT."

16 These things His disciples did not understand at the first; but when Jesus was glorified, then they remembered that these things were written of Him, and that they had done these things to Him.

17 So the people, who were with Him when He called Lazarus out of the tomb and raised him from the dead, continued to testify *about Him.*

18 For this reason also the people went and met Him, because they heard that He had performed this sign.

19 So the Pharisees said to one another, "You see that you are not doing any good; look, the world has gone after Him."

Greeks Seek Jesus

20 ¶ Now there were some Greeks among those who were going up to worship at the feast;

21 these then came to Philip, who was from Bethsaida of Galilee, and *began to* ask him, saying, "Sir, we wish to see Jesus."

22 Philip *came and *told Andrew; Andrew and Philip *came and *told Jesus.

23 And Jesus *answered them, saying, "The hour has come for the Son of Man to be glorified.

24 "Truly, truly, I say to you, unless a grain of wheat falls into the earth and dies, it remains alone; but if it dies, it bears much fruit.

25 "He who loves his life loses it, and he who hates his life in this world will keep it to life eternal.

26 "If anyone serves Me, he must follow Me; and where I am, there My servant will be also; if anyone serves Me, the Father will honor him.

Jesus Foretells His Death

27 ¶ "Now My soul has become troubled; and what shall I say, 'Father, save Me from this hour'? But for this purpose I came to this hour.

28 "Father, glorify Your name." Then a voice came out of heaven: "I have both glorified it, and will glorify it again."

29 So the crowd *of people* who stood by and heard it were saying that it had thundered; others were saying, "An angel has spoken to Him."

30 Jesus answered and said, "This voice has not come for My sake, but for your sakes.

31 "Now judgment is upon this world; now the ruler of this world will be cast out.

32 "And I, if I am lifted up from the earth, will draw all men to Myself."

33 But He was saying this to indicate the kind of death by which He was to die.

34 The crowd then answered Him, "We have heard out of the Law that the Christ is to remain forever; and how can You say, 'The Son of Man must be lifted up'? Who is this Son of Man?"

35 So Jesus said to them, "For a little while longer the Light is among you. Walk while you have the Light, so that darkness will not overtake you; he who walks in the darkness does not know where he goes.

36 "While you have the Light, believe in the Light, so that you may become sons of Light."

¶ These things Jesus spoke, and He went away and hid Himself from them.

37 But though He had performed so many signs before them, *yet* they were not believing in Him.

38 *This was* to fulfill the word of Isaiah the prophet which he spoke: "LORD, WHO HAS BELIEVED OUR REPORT? AND TO WHOM HAS THE ARM OF THE LORD BEEN REVEALED?"

39 For this reason they could not believe, for Isaiah said again,

40 "HE HAS BLINDED THEIR EYES AND HE HARDENED THEIR HEART, SO THAT THEY WOULD NOT SEE WITH THEIR EYES AND PERCEIVE WITH THEIR HEART, AND BE CONVERTED AND I HEAL THEM."

41 These things Isaiah said because he saw His glory, and he spoke of Him.

42 Nevertheless many even of the rulers believed in Him, but because of the Pharisees they were not confessing *Him,* for fear that they would be put out of the synagogue;

---

[a] Equivalent to 11 months' wages   [b] I.e. the custom of preparing the body for burial

43 for they loved the approval of men rather than the approval of God.

44 ¶ And Jesus cried out and said, "He who believes in Me, does not believe in Me but in Him who sent Me.

45 "He who sees Me sees the One who sent Me.

46 "I have come *as* Light into the world, so that everyone who believes in Me will not remain in darkness.

47 "If anyone hears My sayings and does not keep them, I do not judge him; for I did not come to judge the world, but to save the world.

48 "He who rejects Me and does not receive My sayings, has one who judges him; the word I spoke is what will judge him at the last day.

49 "For I did not speak on My own initiative, but the Father Himself who sent Me has given Me a commandment *as to* what to say and what to speak.

50 "I know that His commandment is eternal life; therefore the things I speak, I speak just as the Father has told Me."

The Lord's Supper

13 Now before the Feast of the Passover, Jesus knowing that His hour had come that He would depart out of this world to the Father, having loved His own who were in the world, He loved them to the end.

2 During supper, the devil having already put into the heart of Judas Iscariot, *the son* of Simon, to betray Him,

3 *Jesus,* knowing that the Father had given all things into His hands, and that He had come forth from God and was going back to God,

4 *got up from supper, and *laid aside His garments; and taking a towel, He girded Himself.

13:4 The Role of a Servant

Before beginning an intimate meal with his disciples, Jesus gave them a lesson about humility. Normally, slaves performed the act of washing the feet of dinner guests. Here Jesus, the guest of honor, dressed himself like a slave, with a towel around his waist, and insisted on washing the feet of his disciples. Paul comments on Jesus' servanthood in Philippians 2:5–11.

Jesus Washes the Disciples' Feet

5 Then He *poured water into the basin, and began to wash the disciples' feet and to wipe them with the towel with which He was girded.

6 So He *came to Simon Peter. He *said to Him, "Lord, do You wash my feet?"

7 Jesus answered and said to him, "What I do you do not realize now, but you will understand hereafter."

8 Peter *said to Him, "Never shall You wash my feet!" Jesus answered him, "If I do not wash you, you have no part with Me."

9 Simon Peter *said to Him, "Lord, *then wash* not only my feet, but also my hands and my head."

10 Jesus *said to him, "He who has bathed needs only to wash his feet, but is completely clean; and you are clean, but not all *of you.*"

11 For He knew the one who was betraying Him; for this reason He said, "Not all of you are clean."

12 ¶ So when He had washed their feet, and taken His garments and reclined *at the table* again, He said to them, "Do you know what I have done to you?

13 "You call Me Teacher and Lord; and you are right, for *so* I am.

14 "If I then, the Lord and the Teacher, washed your feet, you also ought to wash one another's feet.

15 "For I gave you an example that you also should do as I did to you.

16 "Truly, truly, I say to you, a slave is not greater than his master, nor *is* one who is sent greater than the one who sent him.

17 "If you know these things, you are blessed if you do them.

18 "I do not speak of all of you. I know the ones I have chosen; but *it is* that the Scripture may be fulfilled, 'HE WHO EATS MY BREAD HAS LIFTED UP HIS HEEL AGAINST ME.'

19 "From now on I am telling you before *it* comes to pass, so that when it does occur, you may believe that I am *He.*

20 "Truly, truly, I say to you, he who receives whomever I send receives Me; and he who receives Me receives Him who sent Me."

Jesus Predicts His Betrayal

13:37,38pp — Matt 26:33–35; Mark 14:29–31; Luke 22:33,34

21 ¶ When Jesus had said this, He became troubled in spirit, and testified and said, "Truly, truly, I say to you, that one of you will betray Me."

22 The disciples *began* looking at one another, at a loss *to know* of which one He was speaking.

23 There was reclining on Jesus' bosom one of His disciples, whom Jesus loved.

24 So Simon Peter *gestured to him, and *said to him, "Tell *us* who it is of whom He is speaking."

25 He, leaning back thus on Jesus' bosom, *said to Him, "Lord, who is it?"

26 Jesus then *answered, "That is the one for whom I shall dip the morsel and give it to him." So when He had dipped the morsel, He *took and *gave it to Judas, *the son* of Simon Iscariot.

27 After the morsel, Satan then entered into him. Therefore Jesus *said to him, "What you do, do quickly."

28 Now no one of those reclining *at the table* knew for what purpose He had said this to him.

29 For some were supposing, because Judas had the money box, that Jesus was saying to him, "Buy the things we have need of for the feast"; or else, that he should give something to the poor.

30 So after receiving the morsel he went out immediately; and it was night.

31 ¶ Therefore when he had gone out, Jesus *said, "Now is the Son of Man glorified, and God is glorified in Him;

32 if God is glorified in Him, God will also glorify Him in Himself, and will glorify Him immediately.

33 "Little children, I am with you a little while longer. You will seek Me; and as I said to the Jews, now I also say to you, 'Where I am going, you cannot come.'

34 "A new commandment I give to you, that you love one another, even as I have loved you, that you also love one another.

35 "By this all men will know that you are My disciples, if you have love for one another."

36 ¶ Simon Peter *said to Him, "Lord, where are You going?" Jesus answered, "Where I go, you cannot follow Me now; but you will follow later."

37 Peter *said to Him, "Lord, why can I not follow You right now? I will lay down my life for You."

38 Jesus *answered, "Will you lay down your

John's Reason for Writing
Handpicked incidents that prove a point

PRESIDENT ABRAHAM LINCOLN ATTRACTS BIOGRAPHERS like candy attracts ants; books about his life would easily fill a large room. Some explore his religious beliefs, some his military strategy, some his eloquence, and others his character. Imagine, though, a biography written about only one aspect of the man: Lincoln the lawyer.

> "Believe Me that I am in the Father and the Father is in Me; otherwise believe because of the works themselves." 14:11

Stories from the childhood of Abe—his reading by light filtered through chinks in the wall or his traipsing across town to return a customer's change—would likely never make it into such a book. Yet the precise wording of the Emancipation Proclamation might merit an entire chapter. Long chapters would dwell on an obscure period in Springfield, Illinois, when Lincoln practiced law. But his political campaigns would get scarce mention.

Such an incomplete biography would serve one purpose: to establish Lincoln's ability in law. All other details would fade into the background.

Everything for a Purpose

Like such a biographer, John wrote his book about Jesus for a similarly limited purpose, which he states very clearly: "But these have been written so that you may believe that Jesus is the Christ, the Son of God; and that believing you may have life in His name" (20:31). The book is not so much a biography as an argument. Its author has handpicked incidents to demonstrate that Jesus is unlike any man who has ever lived; he is the Son of God.

This purpose shows up, for example, in how John treats Jesus' miracles. Although Matthew, Mark, and Luke all record miracles, John goes one step further and calls them "signs." A sign points to something. In John, supernatural acts are one more proof of Jesus' unique nature. Jesus refused to perform miracles as magic to dazzle the crowds but used them instead as object lessons to teach about himself. After feeding 5,000 people from one sack lunch, Jesus described himself as the bread of life (6:1–59). Just before restoring sight to a blind man, he called himself the Light of the world (9:1–7). Nothing "just happens" in John; everything underscores the author's overall theme.

Merely a Great Man?

Because Jesus is so clear in describing his own nature, a statement like "I'm ready to accept Jesus as a great moral teacher, but I don't accept his claim to be God" doesn't hold up. As C.S. Lewis has said, "That is the one thing we must not say. A man who was merely a man and said the sort of things Jesus said would not be a great moral teacher. He would either be a lunatic—on a level with the man who says he is a poached egg—or else he would be the Devil of Hell. You must make your choice. Either this man was, and is, the Son of God: or else a madman or something worse."

According to John, not everyone believed Jesus was divine: "Whom do You make Yourself out to be?" some indignantly demanded (8:53). Doubters had him killed for making such an audacious claim. But it is hardly possible to read John without being convinced that Jesus himself claimed to be God.

Life Questions: Despite what C.S. Lewis says, many people do think of Jesus as "merely a great man." How do they rationalize it?

life for Me? Truly, truly, I say to you, a rooster will not crow until you deny Me three times.

Jesus Comforts His Disciples

14 "Do not let your heart be troubled; [a]believe in God, believe also in Me.

2 "In My Father's house are many dwelling places; if it were not so, I would have told you; for I go to prepare a place for you.

3 "If I go and prepare a place for you, I will come again and receive you to Myself, that where I am, *there* you may be also.

4 "And you know the way where I am going."

5 Thomas *said to Him, "Lord, we do not know where You are going, how do we know the way?"

6 Jesus *said to him, "I am the way, and the truth, and the life; no one comes to the Father but through Me.

Oneness with the Father

7 "If you had known Me, you would have known My Father also; from now on you know Him, and have seen Him."

8 ¶ Philip *said to Him, "Lord, show us the Father, and it is enough for us."

9 Jesus *said to him, "Have I been so long with you, and *yet* you have not come to know Me, Philip? He who has seen Me has seen the Father; how *can* you say, 'Show us the Father'?

10 "Do you not believe that I am in the Father, and the Father is in Me? The words that I say to you I do not speak on My own initiative, but the Father abiding in Me does His works.

11 "Believe Me that I am in the Father and the Father is in Me; otherwise believe because of the works themselves.

12 "Truly, truly, I say to you, he who believes in Me, the works that I do, he will do also; and greater *works* than these he will do; because I go to the Father.

13 "Whatever you ask in My name, that will I do, so that the Father may be glorified in the Son.

14 "If you ask Me anything in My name, I will do *it*.

15 ¶ "If you love Me, you will keep My commandments.

Role of the Spirit

16 "I will ask the Father, and He will give you another Helper, that He may be with you forever;

17 *that is* the Spirit of truth, whom the world cannot receive, because it does not see Him or know Him, *but* you know Him because He abides with you and will be in you.

18 ¶ "I will not leave you as orphans; I will come to you.

19 "After a little while the world will no longer see Me, but you *will* see Me; because I live, you will live also.

20 "In that day you will know that I am in My Father, and you in Me, and I in you.

21 "He who has My commandments and keeps them is the one who loves Me; and he who loves Me will be loved by My Father, and I will love him and will disclose Myself to him."

22 Judas (not Iscariot) *said to Him, "Lord, what then has happened that You are going to disclose Yourself to us and not to the world?"

23 Jesus answered and said to him, "If anyone loves Me, he will keep My word; and My Father will love him, and We will come to him and make Our abode with him.

24 "He who does not love Me does not keep My

---

[a] Or *you believe in God*

THOMAS *Honest Questions*

BETWEEN STUBBORN SKEPTICISM AND HONEST questioning there is a huge gap, and the disciple named Thomas illustrates the difference. Popularly known as "Doubting Thomas," this disciple stands out for his practical honesty, not for his unbelief.

When Jesus' friend Lazarus died, Thomas frankly showed his anxiety over the danger in going into Judea, along with his intense loyalty to Jesus: "Let us also go [to Lazarus's grave], so that we may die with Him" (11:16). At Jesus' last meal with his disciples, he expressed the confusion that was surely on all the disciples' minds (14:5). Thomas never pretended. If he didn't understand something, he said so; if he felt discouraged, he acted like it.

Thomas got his reputation as a doubter primarily because of his reaction when told of Jesus' resurrection. He simply insisted, "I need to see it for myself." The implications of a risen Jesus were too great, he believed, to take someone else's word for it. Jesus honored this honest doubt, and when he visited Thomas in person to offer proof, Thomas responded with the ultimate statement of faith: "My Lord and my God" (20:28). He was, in fact, the only disciple who specifically addressed Jesus as God.

Thomas's questions led to faith because he expressed them sincerely and looked for answers. The last mention of him in the Bible shows Thomas not questioning but praying, waiting with the other disciples for the Holy Spirit to come (Acts 1:12–14).

Life Questions: What honest questions do you need to bring before God?

words; and the word which you hear is not Mine, but the Father's who sent Me.

25 ¶ "These things I have spoken to you while abiding with you.

26 "But the Helper, the Holy Spirit, whom the Father will send in My name, He will teach you all things, and bring to your remembrance all that I said to you.

27 "Peace I leave with you; My peace I give to you; not as the world gives do I give to you. Do not let your heart be troubled, nor let it be fearful.

28 "You heard that I said to you, 'I go away, and I will come to you.' If you loved Me, you would have rejoiced because I go to the Father, for the Father is greater than I.

29 "Now I have told you before it happens, so that when it happens, you may believe.

30 "I will not speak much more with you, for the ruler of the world is coming, and he has nothing in Me;

31 but so that the world may know that I love the Father, I do exactly as the Father commanded Me. Get up, let us go from here.

Jesus Is the Vine—Followers Are Branches

15 "I am the true vine, and My Father is the vinedresser.

15:1 Jesus as the Vine

Old Testament prophets referred to the Israelites as God's "vine," or "vineyard." But as Jesus often pointed out, the Jews had failed to bear fruit. Here he claims the image for himself, "I am the true vine."

John frequently records Jesus' use of the words I am: "I am the bread of life," "I am the way and the truth and the life." The phrase stood out sharply to Jewish leaders, because God had been known as the great I AM to the Jews (Exodus 3:14). Jewish unbelievers, recognizing that Jesus was claiming to be God, reacted with shock and outrage.

2 "Every branch in Me that does not bear fruit, He takes away; and every *branch* that bears fruit, He ªprunes it so that it may bear more fruit.

3 "You are already clean because of the word which I have spoken to you.

4 "Abide in Me, and I in you. As the branch cannot bear fruit of itself unless it abides in the vine, so neither *can* you unless you abide in Me.

5 "I am the vine, you are the branches; he who abides in Me and I in him, he bears much fruit, for apart from Me you can do nothing.

6 "If anyone does not abide in Me, he is thrown away as a branch and dries up; and they gather them, and cast them into the fire and they are burned.

7 "If you abide in Me, and My words abide in you, ask whatever you wish, and it will be done for you.

8 "My Father is glorified by this, that you bear much fruit, and *so* prove to be My disciples.

9 "Just as the Father has loved Me, I have also loved you; abide in My love.

10 "If you keep My commandments, you will abide in My love; just as I have kept My Father's commandments and abide in His love.

11 "These things I have spoken to you so that My joy may be in you, and *that* your joy may be made full.

Disciples' Relation to Each Other

12 ¶ "This is My commandment, that you love one another, just as I have loved you.

13 "Greater love has no one than this, that one lay down his life for his friends.

14 "You are My friends if you do what I command you.

15 "No longer do I call you slaves, for the slave does not know what his master is doing; but I have called you friends, for all things that I have heard from My Father I have made known to you.

16 "You did not choose Me but I chose you, and appointed you that you would go and bear fruit, and *that* your fruit would remain, so that whatever you ask of the Father in My name He may give to you.

17 "This I command you, that you love one another.

Disciples' Relation to the World

18 ¶ "If the world hates you, you know that it has hated Me before *it hated* you.

19 "If you were of the world, the world would love its own; but because you are not of the world, but I chose you out of the world, because of this the world hates you.

20 "Remember the word that I said to you, 'A slave is not greater than his master.' If they persecuted Me, they will also persecute you; if they kept My word, they will keep yours also.

21 "But all these things they will do to you for My name's sake, because they do not know the One who sent Me.

22 "If I had not come and spoken to them, they would not have sin, but now they have no excuse for their sin.

23 "He who hates Me hates My Father also.

24 "If I had not done among them the works which no one else did, they would not have sin; but now they have both seen and hated Me and My Father as well.

25 "But *they have done this* to fulfill the word that is written in their Law, 'THEY HATED ME WITHOUT A CAUSE.'

ª Lit *cleans*; used to describe pruning

26 ¶ "When the Helper comes, whom I will send to you from the Father, *that is* the Spirit of truth who proceeds from the Father, He will testify about Me,

27 and you *will* testify also, because you have been with Me from the beginning.

Jesus' Warning

16 "These things I have spoken to you so that you may be kept from stumbling.

2 "They will make you outcasts from the synagogue, but an hour is coming for everyone who kills you to think that he is offering service to God.

3 "These things they will do because they have not known the Father or Me.

4 "But these things I have spoken to you, so that when their hour comes, you may remember that I told you of them. These things I did not say to you at the beginning, because I was with you.

The Holy Spirit Promised

5 ¶ "But now I am going to Him who sent Me; and none of you asks Me, 'Where are You going?'

6 "But because I have said these things to you, sorrow has filled your heart.

7 "But I tell you the truth, it is to your advantage that I go away; for if I do not go away, the Helper will not come to you; but if I go, I will send Him to you.

8 "And He, when He comes, will convict the world concerning sin and righteousness and judgment;

9 concerning sin, because they do not believe in Me;

10 and concerning righteousness, because I go to the Father and you no longer see Me;

11 and concerning judgment, because the ruler of this world has been judged.

The Last Meal Together
The longest, most emotional night of Jesus' life

> "You will grieve, but your grief will be turned into joy."
> 16:20

JOHN DEVOTED ONE-THIRD OF HIS book to the last 24-hour period Jesus spent on earth. Five chapters (13–17) describe one of the scenes from that period, and nothing like these chapters exists elsewhere in the Bible. In their slow-motion, realistic detail, they provide an intimate memoir of Jesus' most anguished evening.

Leonardo da Vinci immortalized the setting in his famous painting *The Last Supper,* with the participants arranged on one side of the table as if posing for the artist. But John gives few physical details; instead, he focuses on a whirlpool of emotional currents.

John holds a light to the disciples' faces, and you can almost see the awareness flickering in their eyes. All that Jesus had told them was slowly settling in. As for Jesus, "Having loved His own who were in the world, He loved them to the end" (13:1).

Jesus Prepares to Leave

Never before had Jesus been so direct with them. Around the table he avoided parables and painstakingly answered the disciples' redundant questions. Never was he more "theological." He alone fully recognized the significance of this last evening before his death. The world was about to undergo a convulsive trauma, and the 11 fearful men with him were his hope for that world.

"It is to your advantage that I go away," Jesus said (16:7), but the disciples were too busy discussing the meaning of "go away" to comprehend the good that would follow.

Nevertheless, Jesus kept explaining until at last the disciples showed signs of understanding. God's Son had entered the world to reside in one body. He was leaving earth to return to the Father. But the Spirit would come and reside in many bodies. Jesus seemed aware that much of what they nodded their heads at now would not sink in until later.

Pain before Joy

Jesus concluded his words with a ringing declaration, "Take courage; I have overcome the world" (16:33). How hollow this statement would seem the next evening, when his pale, abused body hung on an executioner's cross. The disciples' emotions—and faith—would rise and plummet in one unforgettable day. Jesus predicted this, too, likening the pain to the spasms of childbirth before great joy breaks through (16:21–22).

In his longest recorded prayer, Jesus summed up his feelings and his plans for the tight circle of friends gathered around him. He prayed, too, for the others who would follow them, stretching in an unbroken chain throughout history. And then he led the little band to his appointment with death.

Life Questions: Have you ever been around someone facing death? How did he or she act? What does Jesus' response to impending death reveal about why he came to earth?

12 ¶ "I have many more things to say to you, but you cannot bear *them* now.

13 "But when He, the Spirit of truth, comes, He will guide you into all the truth; for He will not speak on His own initiative, but whatever He hears, He will speak; and He will disclose to you what is to come.

14 "He will glorify Me, for He will take of Mine and will disclose *it* to you.

15 "All things that the Father has are Mine; therefore I said that He takes of Mine and will disclose *it* to you.

Jesus' Death and Resurrection Foretold

16 ¶ "A little while, and you will no longer see Me; and again a little while, and you will see Me."

17 *Some* of His disciples then said to one another, "What is this thing He is telling us, 'A little while, and you will not see Me; and again a little while, and you will see Me'; and, 'because I go to the Father'?"

18 So they were saying, "What is this that He says, 'A little while'? We do not know what He is talking about."

19 Jesus knew that they wished to question Him, and He said to them, "Are you deliberating together about this, that I said, 'A little while, and you will not see Me, and again a little while, and you will see Me'?

20 "Truly, truly, I say to you, that you will weep and lament, but the world will rejoice; you will grieve, but your grief will be turned into joy.

16:20 Filled with Grief

Good-byes are always sad, and for the disciples this farewell speech was especially so. They had staked their lives on Jesus, and without him they could see no future. Jesus, however, promised that he was leaving for their own good. He would send the Holy Spirit to guide them into "all the truth" (verse 13). In fact, as Acts shows, only after Jesus' departure did these confused disciples fully grasp the meaning of his death and resurrection and begin to proclaim it joyfully to everyone around them.

21 "Whenever a woman is in labor she has pain, because her hour has come; but when she gives birth to the child, she no longer remembers the anguish because of the joy that a child has been born into the world.

22 "Therefore you too have grief now; but I will see you again, and your heart will rejoice, and no one *will* take your joy away from you.

Prayer Promises

23 "In that day you will not question Me about anything. Truly, truly, I say to you, if you ask the Father for anything in My name, He will give it to you.

24 "Until now you have asked for nothing in My name; ask and you will receive, so that your joy may be made full.

25 ¶ "These things I have spoken to you in figurative language; an hour is coming when I will no longer speak to you in figurative language, but will tell you plainly of the Father.

26 "In that day you will ask in My name, and I do not say to you that I will request of the Father on your behalf;

27 for the Father Himself loves you, because you have loved Me and have believed that I came forth from the Father.

28 "I came forth from the Father and have come into the world; I am leaving the world again and going to the Father."

29 ¶ His disciples *said, "Lo, now You are speaking plainly and are not using a figure of speech.

30 "Now we know that You know all things, and have no need for anyone to question You; by this we believe that You came from God."

31 Jesus answered them, "Do you now believe?

32 "Behold, an hour is coming, and has *already* come, for you to be scattered, each to his own *home,* and to leave Me alone; and *yet* I am not alone, because the Father is with Me.

33 "These things I have spoken to you, so that in Me you may have peace. In the world you have tribulation, but take courage; I have overcome the world."

The High Priestly Prayer

17 Jesus spoke these things; and lifting up His eyes to heaven, He said, "Father, the hour has come; glorify Your Son, that the Son may glorify You,

2 even as You gave Him authority over all flesh, that to all whom You have given Him, He may give eternal life.

3 "This is eternal life, that they may know You, the only true God, and Jesus Christ whom You have sent.

4 "I glorified You on the earth, having accomplished the work which You have given Me to do.

5 "Now, Father, glorify Me together with Yourself, with the glory which I had with You before the world was.

6 ¶ "I have manifested Your name to the men whom You gave Me out of the world; they were Yours and You gave them to Me, and they have kept Your word.

7 "Now they have come to know that everything You have given Me is from You;

8 for the words which You gave Me I have given to them; and they received *them* and truly

understood that I came forth from You, and they believed that You sent Me.

9 "I ask on their behalf; I do not ask on behalf of the world, but of those whom You have given Me; for they are Yours;

10 and all things that are Mine are Yours, and Yours are Mine; and I have been glorified in them.

11 "I am no longer in the world; and *yet* they themselves are in the world, and I come to You. Holy Father, keep them in Your name, *the name* which You have given Me, that they may be one even as We *are.*

12 "While I was with them, I was keeping them in Your name which You have given Me; and I guarded them and not one of them perished but the son of perdition, so that the Scripture would be fulfilled.

The Disciples in the World

13 "But now I come to You; and these things I speak in the world so that they may have My joy made full in themselves.

14 "I have given them Your word; and the world has hated them, because they are not of the world, even as I am not of the world.

15 "I do not ask You to take them out of the world, but to keep them from the evil *one.*

16 "They are not of the world, even as I am not of the world.

17 "Sanctify them in the truth; Your word is truth.

18 "As You sent Me into the world, I also have sent them into the world.

19 "For their sakes I sanctify Myself, that they themselves also may be sanctified in truth.

20 ¶ "I do not ask on behalf of these alone, but for those also who believe in Me through their word;

21 that they may all be one; even as You, Father, *are* in Me and I in You, that they also may be in Us, so that the world may believe that You sent Me.

17:21 Jesus' Longest Prayer

The famous prayer recorded here concludes a kind of commissioning or graduation. In it, Jesus turns over his mission to the disciples and, by extension, to all believers who would follow.

Their Future Glory

22 "The glory which You have given Me I have given to them, that they may be one, just as We are one;

23 I in them and You in Me, that they may be perfected in unity, so that the world may know that You sent Me, and loved them, even as You have loved Me.

24 "Father, I desire that they also, whom You have given Me, be with Me where I am, so that they may see My glory which You have given Me, for You loved Me before the foundation of the world.

25 ¶ "O righteous Father, although the world has not known You, yet I have known You; and these have known that You sent Me;

26 and I have made Your name known to them, and will make it known, so that the love with which You loved Me may be in them, and I in them."

Judas Betrays Jesus

18:3–11pp — Matt 26:47–56; Mark 14:43–50; Luke 22:47–53

18 When Jesus had spoken these words, He went forth with His disciples over the ravine of the Kidron, where there was a garden, in which He entered with His disciples.

2 Now Judas also, who was betraying Him, knew the place, for Jesus had often met there with His disciples.

3 Judas then, having received the *Roman* cohort and officers from the chief priests and the Pharisees, *came there with lanterns and torches and weapons.

4 So Jesus, knowing all the things that were coming upon Him, went forth and *said to them, "Whom do you seek?"

5 They answered Him, "Jesus the Nazarene." He *said to them, "I am *He.*" And Judas also, who was betraying Him, was standing with them.

6 So when He said to them, "I am *He,*" they drew back and fell to the ground.

7 Therefore He again asked them, "Whom do you seek?" And they said, "Jesus the Nazarene."

8 Jesus answered, "I told you that I am *He;* so if you seek Me, let these go their way,"

9 to fulfill the word which He spoke, "Of those whom You have given Me I lost not one."

10 Simon Peter then, having a sword, drew it and struck the high priest's slave, and cut off his right ear; and the slave's name was Malchus.

11 So Jesus said to Peter, "Put the sword into the sheath; the cup which the Father has given Me, shall I not drink it?"

Jesus before the Priests

18:12,13pp — Matt 26:57
18:16–18pp — Matt 26:69,70; Mark 14:66–68; Luke 22:55–57
18:19–24pp — Matt 26:59–68; Mark 14:55–65; Luke 22:63–71

12 ¶ So the *Roman* cohort and the commander and the officers of the Jews, arrested Jesus and bound Him,

13 and led Him to Annas first; for he was father-in-law of Caiaphas, who was high priest that year.

14 Now Caiaphas was the one who had advised

the Jews that it was expedient for one man to die on behalf of the people.

15 ¶ Simon Peter was following Jesus, and *so was* another disciple. Now that disciple was known to the high priest, and entered with Jesus into the court of the high priest,

16 but Peter was standing at the door outside. So the other disciple, who was known to the high priest, went out and spoke to the doorkeeper, and brought Peter in.

17 Then the slave-girl who kept the door *said to Peter, "You are not also *one* of this man's disciples, are you?" He *said, "I am not."

18 Now the slaves and the officers were standing *there*, having made a charcoal fire, for it was cold and they were warming themselves; and Peter was also with them, standing and warming himself.

19 ¶ The high priest then questioned Jesus about His disciples, and about His teaching.

20 Jesus answered him, "I have spoken openly to the world; I always taught in synagogues and in the temple, where all the Jews come together; and I spoke nothing in secret.

21 "Why do you question Me? Question those who have heard what I spoke to them; they know what I said."

22 When He had said this, one of the officers standing nearby struck Jesus, saying, "Is that the way You answer the high priest?"

23 Jesus answered him, "If I have spoken wrongly, testify of the wrong; but if rightly, why do you strike Me?"

24 So Annas sent Him bound to Caiaphas the high priest.

Peter's Denial of Jesus

18:25–27pp — Matt 26:71–75; Mark 14:69–72; Luke 22:58–62

25 ¶ Now Simon Peter was standing and warming himself. So they said to him, "You are not also *one* of His disciples, are you?" He denied *it*, and said, "I am not."

26 One of the slaves of the high priest, being a relative of the one whose ear Peter cut off, *said, "Did I not see you in the garden with Him?"

27 Peter then denied *it* again, and immediately a rooster crowed.

Jesus before Pilate

18:29–40pp — Matt 27:11–18,20–23; Mark 15:2–15; Luke 23:2,3,18–25

28 ¶ Then they *led Jesus from Caiaphas into the ᵃPraetorium, and it was early; and they themselves did not enter into the Praetorium so that they would not be defiled, but might eat the Passover.

29 Therefore Pilate went out to them and *said,

"What accusation do you bring against this Man?"

30 They answered and said to him, "If this Man were not an evildoer, we would not have delivered Him to you."

31 So Pilate said to them, "Take Him yourselves, and judge Him according to your law." The Jews said to him, "We are not permitted to put anyone to death,"

32 to fulfill the word of Jesus which He spoke, signifying by what kind of death He was about to die.

33 ¶ Therefore Pilate entered again into the Praetorium, and summoned Jesus and said to Him, "Are You the King of the Jews?"

34 Jesus answered, "Are you saying this on your own initiative, or did others tell you about Me?"

35 Pilate answered, "I am not a Jew, am I? Your own nation and the chief priests delivered You to me; what have You done?"

36 Jesus answered, "My kingdom is not of this world. If My kingdom were of this world, then My servants would be fighting so that I would not be handed over to the Jews; but as it is, My kingdom is not ᵇof this realm."

37 Therefore Pilate said to Him, "So You are a king?" Jesus answered, "You say *correctly* that I am a king. For this I have been born, and for this I have come into the world, to testify to the truth. Everyone who is of the truth hears My voice."

38 Pilate *said to Him, "What is truth?"

¶ And when he had said this, he went out again to the Jews and *said to them, "I find no guilt in Him.

39 "But you have a custom that I release someone for you at the Passover; do you wish then that I release for you the King of the Jews?"

40 So they cried out again, saying, "Not this Man, but Barabbas." Now Barabbas was a robber.

The Crown of Thorns

19:1–16pp — Matt 27:27–31; Mark 15:16–20

19 Pilate then took Jesus and scourged Him.

2 And the soldiers twisted together a crown of thorns and put it on His head, and put a purple robe on Him;

3 and they *began* to come up to Him and say, "Hail, King of the Jews!" and to give Him slaps *in the face*.

4 Pilate came out again and *said to them, "Behold, I am bringing Him out to you so that you may know that I find no guilt in Him."

5 Jesus then came out, wearing the crown of thorns and the purple robe. *Pilate* *said to them, "Behold, the Man!"

6 So when the chief priests and the officers saw Him, they cried out saying, "Crucify, crucify!"

ᵃ I.e. governor's official residence　　ᵇ Lit *from here*

Pilate *said to them, "Take Him yourselves and crucify Him, for I find no guilt in Him."

7 The Jews answered him, "We have a law, and by that law He ought to die because He made Himself out *to be* the Son of God."

8 ¶ Therefore when Pilate heard this statement, he was *even* more afraid;

9 and he entered into the *a*Praetorium again and *said to Jesus, "Where are You from?" But Jesus gave him no answer.

10 So Pilate *said to Him, "You do not speak to me? Do You not know that I have authority to release You, and I have authority to crucify You?"

11 Jesus answered, "You would have no authority over Me, unless it had been given you from above; for this reason he who delivered Me to you has *the* greater sin."

12 As a result of this Pilate made efforts to release Him, but the Jews cried out saying, "If you release this Man, you are no friend of Caesar; everyone who makes himself out *to be* a king opposes Caesar."

13 ¶ Therefore when Pilate heard these words, he brought Jesus out, and sat down on the judgment seat at a place called The Pavement, but in Hebrew, Gabbatha.

14 Now it was the day of preparation for the Passover; it was about the *b*sixth hour. And he *said to the Jews, "Behold, your King!"

15 So they cried out, "Away with *Him,* away with *Him,* crucify Him!" Pilate *said to them,

"Shall I crucify your King?" The chief priests answered, "We have no king but Caesar."

The Crucifixion

19:17–24pp — Matt 27:33–44; Mark 15:22–32;
Luke 23:33–43
19:29,30pp — Matt 27:48,50; Mark 15:36,37;
Luke 23:36

16 So he then handed Him over to them to be crucified.

17 ¶ They took Jesus, therefore, and He went out, bearing His own cross, to the place called the Place of a Skull, which is called in Hebrew, Golgotha.

18 There they crucified Him, and with Him two other men, one on either side, and Jesus in between.

19 Pilate also wrote an inscription and put it on the cross. It was written, "JESUS THE NAZARENE, THE KING OF THE JEWS."

20 Therefore many of the Jews read this inscription, for the place where Jesus was crucified was near the city; and it was written in Hebrew, Latin *and* in Greek.

21 So the chief priests of the Jews were saying to Pilate, "Do not write, 'The King of the Jews'; but that He said, 'I am King of the Jews.' "

22 Pilate answered, "What I have written I have written."

23 ¶ Then the soldiers, when they had crucified Jesus, took His outer garments and made four parts, a part to every soldier and *also* the *c*tunic;

---

a I.e. governor's official residence   *b* Perhaps 6 a.m.   *c* Gr *khiton,* the garment worn next to the skin

---

PONTIUS PILATE *Governor Cynic*

WHENEVER LOCAL RULERS FAILED TO keep the colonies in line, Rome appointed its own strongmen, called "procurators" or "governors." Pilate served as Roman procurator of Judea, a regional ruler for the most powerful empire in the history of the planet up to that time. Yet, as Pilate discovered, having absolute power does not guarantee peace. The Jews hated Roman rule, and religious and nationalist emotions constantly flared up in Judea.

According to the first-century historian Josephus, Pilate marched Roman soldiers into Jerusalem, learning too late that Jews would die to keep Rome's military emblems out. (They considered images of the emperor blasphemous.) When Pilate set out to build an aqueduct for Jerusalem, he caused a bloody riot by appropriating temple offerings to pay the bill. Pilate's soldiers brutally put down many such disturbances.

When Pilate met Jesus, he mainly saw one more source of trouble. Pilate tried to pass the buck (to Herod). He even offered to set the prisoner free. But in the end Pilate was willing to sacrifice Jesus if that would buy order. Pilate's most famous words were a cynical question, "What is truth?" (18:38). The answer was standing right in front of him, but Pilate didn't really want to know.

Pilate must have considered Jesus' execution a success (it didn't start any riots), but his balancing act was upturned just a few years later. Some Samaritans—the mixed-race group whom Jews despised—heard a crazy report that Moses had buried treasures on Mt. Gerizim. A crowd gathered to climb the mountain. Pilate, thinking these pilgrims might be dangerous, sent in troops. Soon he had a massacre on his hands. For his overreaction he was relieved from command and sent back to Rome to stand trial.

Life Questions: Are there situations in your life where you would buy peace at any cost? What happens to the truth when you do so?

now the tunic was seamless, woven in one piece.

24 So they said to one another, "Let us not tear it, but cast lots for it, *to decide* whose it shall be"; *this was* to fulfill the Scripture: "THEY DIVIDED MY OUTER GARMENTS AMONG THEM, AND FOR MY CLOTHING THEY CAST LOTS."

25 Therefore the soldiers did these things.

¶ But standing by the cross of Jesus were His mother, and His mother's sister, Mary the *wife* of Clopas, and Mary Magdalene.

26 When Jesus then saw His mother, and the disciple whom He loved standing nearby, He *said to His mother, "Woman, behold, your son!"

27 Then He *said to the disciple, "Behold, your mother!" From that hour the disciple took her into his own *household*.

28 ¶ After this, Jesus, knowing that all things had already been accomplished, to fulfill the Scripture, *said, "I am thirsty."

29 A jar full of sour wine was standing there; so they put a sponge full of the sour wine upon *a branch of* hyssop and brought it up to His mouth.

30 Therefore when Jesus had received the sour wine, He said, "It is finished!" And He bowed His head and gave up His spirit.

Care of the Body of Jesus

19:38–42pp — Matt 27:57–61; Mark 15:42–47; Luke 23:50–56

31 ¶ Then the Jews, because it was the day of preparation, so that the bodies would not remain on the cross on the Sabbath (for that Sabbath was a high day), asked Pilate that their legs might be broken, and *that* they might be taken away.

19:31 Speeding up Death

Soldiers broke the bones of crucified men to speed up their dying, so the bodies could be removed before the holy day that followed. Jesus had already died, so his bones were left intact. This fulfilled Old Testament promises that the Messiah's bones would not be broken and that his side would be pierced with a spear (Exodus 12:46; Zechariah 12:10).

32 So the soldiers came, and broke the legs of the first man and of the other who was crucified with Him;

33 but coming to Jesus, when they saw that He was already dead, they did not break His legs.

34 But one of the soldiers pierced His side with a spear, and immediately blood and water came out.

35 And he who has seen has testified, and his testimony is true; and he knows that he is telling the truth, so that you also may believe.

36 For these things came to pass to fulfill the Scripture, "NOT A BONE OF HIM SHALL BE BROKEN."

37 And again another Scripture says, "THEY SHALL LOOK ON HIM WHOM THEY PIERCED."

38 ¶ After these things Joseph of Arimathea, being a disciple of Jesus, but a secret *one* for fear of the Jews, asked Pilate that he might take away the body of Jesus; and Pilate granted permission. So he came and took away His body.

39 Nicodemus, who had first come to Him by night, also came, bringing a mixture of myrrh and aloes, about a hundred pounds *weight*.

40 So they took the body of Jesus and bound it in linen wrappings with the spices, as is the burial custom of the Jews.

41 Now in the place where He was crucified there was a garden, and in the garden a new tomb in which no one had yet been laid.

42 Therefore because of the Jewish day of preparation, since the tomb was nearby, they laid Jesus there.

The Empty Tomb

20:1–8pp — Matt 28:1–8; Mark 16:1–8; Luke 24:1–10

20 Now on the first *day* of the week Mary Magdalene *came early to the tomb, while it *was still dark, and *saw the stone *already* taken away from the tomb.

2 So she *ran and *came to Simon Peter and to the other disciple whom Jesus loved, and *said to them, "They have taken away the Lord out of the tomb, and we do not know where they have laid Him."

3 So Peter and the other disciple went forth, and they were going to the tomb.

4 The two were running together; and the other disciple ran ahead faster than Peter and came to the tomb first;

5 and stooping and looking in, he *saw the linen wrappings lying *there*; but he did not go in.

6 And so Simon Peter also *came, following him, and entered the tomb; and he *saw the linen wrappings lying *there*,

7 and the face-cloth which had been on His head, not lying with the linen wrappings, but rolled up in a place by itself.

8 So the other disciple who had first come to the tomb then also entered, and he saw and believed.

9 For as yet they did not understand the Scripture, that He must rise again from the dead.

10 So the disciples went away again to their own homes.

11 ¶ But Mary was standing outside the tomb weeping; and so, as she wept, she stooped and looked into the tomb;

12 and she *saw two angels in white sitting, one at the head and one at the feet, where the body of Jesus had been lying.

13 And they *said to her, "Woman, why are you weeping?" She *said to them, "Because they have taken away my Lord, and I do not know where they have laid Him."

14 When she had said this, she turned around and *saw Jesus standing *there,* and did not know that it was Jesus.

15 Jesus *said to her, "Woman, why are you weeping? Whom are you seeking?" Supposing Him to be the gardener, she *said to Him, "Sir, if you have carried Him away, tell me where you have laid Him, and I will take Him away."

16 Jesus *said to her, "Mary!" She turned and *said to Him in Hebrew, "Rabboni!" (which means, Teacher).

17 Jesus *said to her, "Stop clinging to Me, for I have not yet ascended to the Father; but go to My brethren and say to them, 'I ascend to My Father and your Father, and My God and your God.'"

18 Mary Magdalene *came, announcing to the disciples, "I have seen the Lord," and *that* He had said these things to her.

Jesus among His Disciples

19 ¶ So when it was evening on that day, the first *day* of the week, and when the doors were shut where the disciples were, for fear of the Jews, Jesus came and stood in their midst and *said to them, "Peace *be* with you."

20 And when He had said this, He showed them both His hands and His side. The disciples then rejoiced when they saw the Lord.

21 So Jesus said to them again, "Peace *be* with you; as the Father has sent Me, I also send you."

22 And when He had said this, He breathed on them and *said to them, "Receive the Holy Spirit.

23 "If you forgive the sins of any, *their sins* have been forgiven them; if you retain the *sins* of any, they have been retained."

24 ¶ But Thomas, one of the twelve, called Didymus, was not with them when Jesus came.

25 So the other disciples were saying to him, "We have seen the Lord!" But he said to them,

"Unless I see in His hands the imprint of the nails, and put my finger into the place of the nails, and put my hand into His side, I will not believe."

26 ¶ After eight days His disciples were again

20:25 Doubting Thomas

The skeptical Thomas is sometimes singled out, as though he had unusual doubts. In reality, none of the disciples believed in Jesus' resurrection until they saw him for themselves. Thomas had been absent, though, when Jesus first appeared to the others. He stayed skeptical until Jesus appeared again, and summoned Thomas to touch him. Seeing was believing for all the disciples, but Jesus specially commended those who believed without such firsthand evidence.

inside, and Thomas with them. Jesus *came, the doors having been shut, and stood in their midst and said, "Peace *be* with you."

27 Then He *said to Thomas, "Reach here with your finger, and see My hands; and reach here your hand and put it into My side; and do not be unbelieving, but believing."

28 Thomas answered and said to Him, "My Lord and my God!"

29 Jesus *said to him, "Because you have seen Me, have you believed? Blessed *are* they who did not see, and *yet* believed."

Why This Gospel Was Written

30 ¶ Therefore many other signs Jesus also performed in the presence of the disciples, which are not written in this book;

31 but these have been written so that you may

MARY MAGDALENE *First to See*

MARY MAGDALENE HAS BECOME FAMOUS. *Jesus Christ Superstar* and other plays and movies have portrayed her as a sensuous woman, sometimes as a reformed prostitute. In reality, the Bible gives no indication of anything tawdry about her. All we know is that she came from Magdala, a city on the Sea of Galilee, and that Jesus drove seven demons from her. Having been healed by him, she dedicated her life to Jesus.

The Gospels, which focus on Jesus' twelve disciples, also mention that a good-sized crowd of women left their homes and families to follow Jesus (Matthew 27:55–56). Mary Magdalene heads the list of the women who helped finance his ministry.

When Jesus was crucified in Jerusalem, far from his home in Galilee, Mary Magdalene stayed near him. She carefully observed where he was buried and faithfully went there at the earliest opportunity to care for his body. As a result, she was the very first person to see Jesus risen from the dead and the first to spread the word (20:18).

Women in that time were usually given second place, if any place at all. Jewish courts did not even accept their testimony. At the great miracle of Jesus' resurrection, however, Mary Magdalene had the honor of being the first witness on the scene.

Life Questions: Have you been able to witness God's work? Where and how?

believe that Jesus is the Christ, the Son of God; and that believing you may have life in His name.

Jesus Appears at the Sea of Galilee

21 After these things Jesus manifested Himself again to the disciples at the Sea of Tiberias, and He manifested *Himself* in this way.

2 Simon Peter, and Thomas called Didymus, and Nathanael of Cana in Galilee, and the *sons* of Zebedee, and two others of His disciples were together.

3 Simon Peter *said to them, "I am going fishing." They *said to him, "We will also come with you." They went out and got into the boat; and that night they caught nothing.

4 ¶ But when the day was now breaking, Jesus stood on the beach; yet the disciples did not know that it was Jesus.

5 So Jesus *said to them, "Children, you do not have any fish, do you?" They answered Him, "No."

6 And He said to them, "Cast the net on the right-hand side of the boat and you will find *a catch.*" So they cast, and then they were not able to haul it in because of the great number of fish.

7 Therefore that disciple whom Jesus loved *said to Peter, "It is the Lord." So when Simon Peter heard that it was the Lord, he put his outer garment on (for he was stripped *for work*), and threw himself into the sea.

8 But the other disciples came in the little boat, for they were not far from the land, but about one hundred yards away, dragging the net *full* of fish.

9 ¶ So when they got out on the land, they *saw a charcoal fire *already* laid and fish placed on it, and bread.

10 Jesus *said to them, "Bring some of the fish which you have now caught."

11 Simon Peter went up and drew the net to land, full of large fish, a hundred and fifty-three; and although there were so many, the net was not torn.

Jesus Provides

12 Jesus *said to them, "Come *and* have breakfast." None of the disciples ventured to question Him, "Who are You?" knowing that it was the Lord.

13 Jesus *came and *took the bread and *gave *it* to them, and the fish likewise.

14 This is now the third time that Jesus was manifested to the disciples, after He was raised from the dead.

The Love Motivation

15 ¶ So when they had finished breakfast, Jesus *said to Simon Peter, "Simon, *son* of John, do you love Me more than these?" He *said to Him, "Yes, Lord; You know that I love You." He *said to him, "Tend My lambs."

16 He *said to him again a second time, "Si-

A Change of Heart and Mind
Whatever happened to the "Son of Thunder"?

THE DISCIPLE JOHN HAD BEEN favored to share private moments with Jesus. As part of an inner circle of three, he saw Jesus transfigured, watched him bring Jairus's daughter back to life, and waited for him in the Garden of Gethsemane.

After Jesus was arrested, John witnessed the sequence of his trials. He was the only disciple mentioned as being near the cross at Jesus' death and one of the very first to learn of Christ's resurrection. Somehow, this process changed John.

This is the disciple who is testifying to these things and wrote these things, and we know that his testimony is true. 21:24

From Thunder to Love

John wore an amusing nickname, "Son of Thunder" (Mark 3:17), and several incidents in the Gospels hint that this name reflected his stormy personality. John jealously resented competition from rival miracle workers (Mark 9:38), and he insisted on the best seat in the kingdom of heaven for himself. Once, he wanted to call fire down from heaven to destroy a hostile town (Luke 9:54).

Somewhere in his life, the thunderclouds broke apart. Eventually he got a new nickname: "the apostle of love." John's books—this Gospel and the letters John wrote later—are marked by a recurring emphasis on love.

Naturally, John's spiritual pilgrimage influenced his written record of Jesus' life. His changed personality may provide a clue to his unique style of telling Jesus' story through a handful of poignant episodes. Perhaps these few scenes are the memories of Jesus that finally convinced John himself that Jesus was, indeed, the Son of God.

Life Questions: Getting to know Jesus changes a person. How have you been changed?

mon, *son* of John, do you love Me?" He *said to Him, "Yes, Lord; You know that I love You." He *said to him, "Shepherd My sheep."

17 He *said to him the third time, "Simon, *son* of John, do you love Me?" Peter was grieved because He said to him the third time, "Do you love Me?" And he said to Him, "Lord, You know all things; You know that I love You." Jesus *said to him, "Tend My sheep.

Our Times Are in His Hand

18 "Truly, truly, I say to you, when you were younger, you used to gird yourself and walk wher-

---

21:15 Do You Love Me?

John ends his book with a moving scene in which Jesus spoke to Peter and "the disciple whom Jesus loved," presumably John himself. Jesus asked Peter the same question three times, a painful reminder of Peter's three denials of him. But this reinstatement helped embolden Peter to become one of the early church's most fearless spokesmen.

---

ever you wished; but when you grow old, you will stretch out your hands and someone else will gird you, and bring you where you do not wish to *go*."

19 Now this He said, signifying by what kind of death he would glorify God. And when He had spoken this, He *said to him, "Follow Me!"

20 ¶ Peter, turning around, *saw the disciple whom Jesus loved following *them*; the one who also had leaned back on His bosom at the supper and said, "Lord, who is the one who betrays You?"

21 So Peter seeing him *said to Jesus, "Lord, and what about this man?"

22 Jesus *said to him, "If I want him to remain until I come, what *is that* to you? You follow Me!"

23 Therefore this saying went out among the brethren that that disciple would not die; yet Jesus did not say to him that he would not die, but *only*, "If I want him to remain until I come, what *is that* to you?"

24 ¶ This is the disciple who is testifying to these things and wrote these things, and we know that his testimony is true.

25 ¶ And there are also many other things which Jesus did, which if they *were written in detail, I suppose that even the world itself *would not contain the books that *would be written.

ACTS

The Linking Book
Imagine a Bible without the book of Acts

> "You will receive power when the Holy Spirit has come upon you; and you shall be My witnesses." 1:8

THE NEW TESTAMENT DIVIDES NEATLY into two nearly equal sections. The first consists of four Gospels that tell about Jesus' life on earth. The second section, beginning with Romans, concerns churches that sprang up after Jesus left. In between stands the book of Acts.

The best way to appreciate Acts is to imagine a Bible without it. You have just read the life of Jesus, underscored by four different authors, and you turn to Romans: "Paul, a bond-servant of Christ Jesus . . . to all who are beloved of God in Rome, called as saints." Rome? How did the story get there from Jerusalem?

Next you'd find two books, also from Paul (who's he?), addressed to "the church of God which is at Corinth." Another book follows, written to the church in Galatia, then one to Ephesus, and so on with more letters to other exotic locales. Obviously, something is missing. Without Acts, the New Testament leaps from an orderly history of one man, Jesus, to a collection of unexplained personal correspondence.

A Plan Revealed by Jesus

With Acts, everything fits into place. This book gives a transition from the life of Christ to the new church. It introduces Paul and explains how a minority religion crossed the sea to Rome, the capital of the empire. A reader of Acts visits key cities sprinkled around the Mediterranean, meets the principal leaders of the new movement, and gets a strong scent of the problems that will occupy Paul's letters.

Luke, a physician, had written the third Gospel as an account of "all that Jesus began to do and teach" (Acts 1:1). The book of Acts resumes the story, hinting that this history, too, will show Jesus at work, but in a quite different form. "I will build My church," Jesus had promised (Matthew 16:18), and Acts graphically shows how that process began.

Jesus himself had laid out the plot in his last recorded words on earth: "You shall be My witnesses both in Jerusalem, and in all Judea and Samaria, and even to the remotest part of the earth" (1:8). Acts faithfully follows that outline: The first seven chapters show the church in Jerusalem, the next five focus on Judea and Samaria, and the rest of the book follows the spread of the gospel to the outposts of Roman civilization.

Boisterous Beginnings

The book opens in Jerusalem, during the Pentecost holiday. Over a million pilgrims were milling about the city when suddenly a group of 120 believers came alive. Jesus' followers hit the streets with a bold new style, and 3,000 joined up on the first day alone. Starting with that boisterous scene, Luke spins a historical adventure tale.

Due to Luke's writing skill, Acts reads like a novel, skipping from one exhilarating scene to the next. Wherever the apostles went, action swirled, riots erupted, and a small church took root. In an era when new religions were a dime a dozen, the Christian faith became a worldwide phenomenon. Acts tells how.

How to Read Acts

Acts reads like well-written history. It follows a logical plan, includes fascinating details, and focuses on the most dramatic events. In that sense, it is self-explanatory.

3 And there appeared to them tongues as of fire distributing themselves, and they rested on each one of them.

4 And they were all filled with the Holy Spirit and began to speak with other tongues, as the Spirit was giving them utterance.

5 ¶ Now there were Jews living in Jerusalem, devout men from every nation under heaven.

6 And when this sound occurred, the crowd came together, and were bewildered because each one of them was hearing them speak in his own language.

7 They were amazed and astonished, saying, "Why, are not all these who are speaking Galileans?

8 "And how is it that we each hear *them* in our own language to which we were born?

9 "Parthians and Medes and Elamites, and residents of Mesopotamia, Judea and Cappadocia, Pontus and Asia,

10 Phrygia and Pamphylia, Egypt and the districts of Libya around Cyrene, and visitors from Rome, both Jews and *a*proselytes,

11 Cretans and Arabs—we hear them in our *own* tongues speaking of the mighty deeds of God."

12 And they all continued in amazement and great perplexity, saying to one another, "What does this mean?"

13 But others were mocking and saying, "They are full of sweet wine."

Peter's Sermon

14 ¶ But Peter, taking his stand with the eleven, raised his voice and declared to them: "Men of Judea and all you who live in Jerusalem, let this be known to you and give heed to my words.

15 "For these men are not drunk, as you suppose, for it is *only* the *b*third hour of the day;

16 but this is what was spoken of through the prophet Joel:

17 'AND IT SHALL BE IN THE LAST DAYS,' God says,
'THAT I WILL POUR FORTH OF MY SPIRIT ON ALL MANKIND;
AND YOUR SONS AND YOUR DAUGHTERS SHALL PROPHESY,
AND YOUR YOUNG MEN SHALL SEE VISIONS,
AND YOUR OLD MEN SHALL DREAM DREAMS;

18 EVEN ON MY BONDSLAVES, BOTH MEN AND WOMEN,
I WILL IN THOSE DAYS POUR FORTH OF MY SPIRIT
And they shall prophesy.

19 'AND I WILL GRANT WONDERS IN THE SKY ABOVE
AND SIGNS ON THE EARTH BELOW,
BLOOD, AND FIRE, AND VAPOR OF SMOKE.

20 'THE SUN WILL BE TURNED INTO DARKNESS

AND THE MOON INTO BLOOD,
BEFORE THE GREAT AND GLORIOUS DAY OF THE LORD SHALL COME.

21 'AND IT SHALL BE THAT EVERYONE WHO CALLS ON THE NAME OF THE LORD WILL BE SAVED.'

22 ¶ "Men of Israel, listen to these words: Jesus the Nazarene, a man attested to you by God with miracles and wonders and signs which God performed through Him in your midst, just as you yourselves know—

23 this *Man*, delivered over by the predetermined plan and foreknowledge of God, you nailed to a cross by the hands of godless men and put *Him* to death.

24 "But God raised Him up again, putting an end to the agony of death, since it was impossible for Him to be held in its power.

25 "For David says of Him,
'I SAW THE LORD ALWAYS IN MY PRESENCE;
FOR HE IS AT MY RIGHT HAND, SO THAT I WILL NOT BE SHAKEN.

26 'THEREFORE MY HEART WAS GLAD AND MY TONGUE EXULTED;
MOREOVER MY FLESH ALSO WILL LIVE IN HOPE;

27 BECAUSE YOU WILL NOT ABANDON MY SOUL TO HADES,
NOR ALLOW YOUR HOLY ONE TO UNDERGO DECAY.

28 'YOU HAVE MADE KNOWN TO ME THE WAYS OF LIFE;
YOU WILL MAKE ME FULL OF GLADNESS WITH YOUR PRESENCE.'

29 ¶ "Brethren, I may confidently say to you regarding the patriarch David that he both died and was buried, and his tomb is with us to this day.

30 "And so, because he was a prophet and knew that GOD HAD SWORN TO HIM WITH AN OATH TO SEAT *one* OF HIS DESCENDANTS ON HIS THRONE,

31 he looked ahead and spoke of the resurrection of *c*the Christ, that HE WAS NEITHER ABANDONED TO HADES, NOR DID His flesh SUFFER DECAY.

32 "This Jesus God raised up again, to which we are all witnesses.

33 "Therefore having been exalted to the right hand of God, and having received from the Father the promise of the Holy Spirit, He has poured forth this which you both see and hear.

34 "For it was not David who ascended into heaven, but he himself says:
'THE LORD SAID TO MY LORD,
"SIT AT MY RIGHT HAND,

35 UNTIL I MAKE YOUR ENEMIES A FOOTSTOOL FOR YOUR FEET."'

36 "Therefore let all the house of Israel know for certain that God has made Him both Lord and Christ—this Jesus whom you crucified."

---

a I.e. Gentile converts to Judaism   *b* I.e. 9 a.m.   *c* I.e. the Messiah

The Ingathering

37 ¶ Now when they heard *this*, they were pierced to the heart, and said to Peter and the rest of the apostles, "Brethren, what shall we do?"

38 Peter *said* to them, "Repent, and each of you be baptized in the name of Jesus Christ for the forgiveness of your sins; and you will receive the gift of the Holy Spirit.

39 "For the promise is for you and your children and for all who are far off, as many as the Lord our God will call to Himself."

40 And with many other words he solemnly testified and kept on exhorting them, saying, "Be saved from this perverse generation!"

41 So then, those who had received his word were baptized; and that day there were added about three thousand *a*souls.

42 They were continually devoting themselves to the apostles' teaching and to fellowship, to the breaking of bread and to prayer.

2:42 Infant Church

Acts records a series of stages through which the Christian church became a separate movement. At this point, the followers of Jesus were still keeping the pattern of traditional Jewish worship: prayers in the temple at 9 A.M., 3 P.M., and sunset (3:1). Yet this paragraph shows them also developing a new form of "house churches" based on communal sharing and fellowship.

43 ¶ Everyone kept feeling a sense of awe; and many wonders and signs were taking place through the apostles.

44 And all those who had believed *b*were together and had all things in common;

45 and they *began* selling their property and possessions and were sharing them with all, as anyone might have need.

46 Day by day continuing with one mind in the temple, and breaking bread from house to house, they were taking their meals together with gladness and sincerity of heart,

47 praising God and having favor with all the people. And the Lord was adding to their number day by day those who were being saved.

Healing the Lame Beggar

3 Now Peter and John were going up to the temple at the *c*ninth *hour,* the hour of prayer.

2 And a man who had been lame from his mother's womb was being carried along, whom they used to set down every day at the gate of the temple which is called Beautiful, in order to beg *d*alms of those who were entering the temple.

3 When he saw Peter and John about to go into the temple, he *began* asking to receive alms.

4 But Peter, along with John, fixed his gaze on him and said, "Look at us!"

5 And he *began* to give them his attention, expecting to receive something from them.

6 But Peter said, "I do not possess silver and gold, but what I do have I give to you: In the name of Jesus Christ the Nazarene—walk!"

7 And seizing him by the right hand, he raised him up; and immediately his feet and his ankles were strengthened.

8 With a leap he stood upright and *began* to walk; and he entered the temple with them, walking and leaping and praising God.

9 And all the people saw him walking and praising God;

10 and they were taking note of him as being the one who used to sit at the Beautiful Gate of the temple to *beg* alms, and they were filled with wonder and amazement at what had happened to him.

Peter's Second Sermon

11 ¶ While he was clinging to Peter and John, all the people ran together to them at the so-called portico of Solomon, full of amazement.

12 But when Peter saw *this,* he replied to the people, "Men of Israel, why are you amazed at this, or why do you gaze at us, as if by our own power or piety we had made him walk?

3:12 Knowing the Audience

Peter's speeches in chapters 2 and 3 offer excellent examples of adapting the gospel message to a particular audience. Preaching to Jews gathered in Jerusalem to celebrate Pentecost, he relied heavily on quotations from the Old Testament. Although his main intent was to tell them about Jesus, he referred to Joel, David, Abraham, Isaac, Jacob, Moses, and Samuel. His words proved so effective that 3,000 people were converted the first day. Jewish leaders soon arrested Peter and John.

13 "The God of Abraham, Isaac and Jacob, the God of our fathers, has glorified His servant Jesus, *the one* whom you delivered and disowned in the presence of Pilate, when he had decided to release Him.

14 "But you disowned the Holy and Righteous One and asked for a murderer to be granted to you,

15 but put to death the Prince of life, *the one* whom God raised from the dead, *a fact* to which we are witnesses.

16 "And on the basis of faith in His name, *it is* the name of Jesus which has strengthened this man whom you see and know; and the faith which

---

a I.e. persons   *b* One early ms does not contain *were* and *and*   *c* I.e. 3 p.m.   *d* Or *a gift of charity comes* through Him has given him this perfect health in the presence of you all.

17 ¶ "And now, brethren, I know that you acted in ignorance, just as your rulers did also.

18 "But the things which God announced beforehand by the mouth of all the prophets, that His Christ would suffer, He has thus fulfilled.

19 "Therefore repent and return, so that your sins may be wiped away, in order that times of refreshing may come from the presence of the Lord;

20 and that He may send Jesus, the Christ appointed for you,

21 whom heaven must receive until *the* period of restoration of all things about which God spoke by the mouth of His holy prophets from ancient time.

22 "Moses said, 'THE LORD GOD WILL RAISE UP FOR YOU A PROPHET LIKE ME FROM YOUR BRETHREN; TO HIM YOU SHALL GIVE HEED to everything He says to you.

23 'And it will be that every soul that does not heed that prophet shall be utterly destroyed from among the people.'

24 "And likewise, all the prophets who have spoken, from Samuel and *his* successors onward, also announced these days.

25 "It is you who are the sons of the prophets

More than a Ghost
The best proof that Jesus is alive

"HE LOOKS AS IF HE'S seen a ghost!" What image comes to mind when you hear that? A face drained of blood, a trembling jaw, pasty skin and thin lips, a look of terror.

Seeing a ghost doesn't make a person stronger and more confident. The witness is usually reluctant to talk about the experience. Self-doubt attacks in waves: *Was it real? Maybe I was hallucinating . . . it was so dark and eerie.*

> "But put to death the Prince of life, the one whom God raised from the dead, a fact to which we are witnesses." 3:15

A Convincing Change

When Jesus showed up after his death, his disciples went through a did-we-see-a-ghost? phase, complete with terror, disbelief, and wild rumors. But it didn't last long. In 40 days Jesus made enough undeniable appearances to convince each of his disciples—even skeptical Thomas—that he had indeed overthrown death.

As Acts shows, the disciples began acting the opposite of people who think they've seen a ghost. Rather, they acted like people who had just witnessed the most astounding event in all history. They couldn't wait to tell the world about it.

Exuberance, not fear, lit up the disciples' faces. In the streets of Jerusalem and in the temple, to anyone who would listen, they cried out the news that couldn't be true, but was. "Jesus is alive! The man who died has come back—he's the Messiah we've been waiting for!"

If you're ever tempted to doubt Jesus' resurrection, take a sober look at his changed followers in Acts. Consider Peter, for instance. He had cowered in the shadows at the trial scene, trying to look inconspicuous. Out of fear of arrest, he had even cursed and denied knowing Jesus. Could this be the same man, standing before the most distinguished religious leaders in the land, blasting them as murderers (chapter 3)? Something ignited Peter that would not easily be snuffed out.

Response to a New Message

When Jesus was on earth he mostly preached "the kingdom," sometimes even warning his followers not to mention he was the Messiah. In Acts, the word is out. Jesus is the theme of every speech, whether delivered in the temple square or in the luxurious setting of a royal palace, to working-class pagans or cultured Greek philosophers. Reports of his resurrection resound throughout Acts.

To those who heard, the message sounded like the first note of music to people born deaf. Five thousand men believed (4:4), as did many priests (6:7) and many thousands of Jews (21:20). The scanty band of followers Jesus had left behind was soon organizing and electing officers to handle the needs of a growing church.

Acts follows the core of leaders from place to place, as a remarkable drama unfolds. A few men, mostly unlearned, were setting into motion a worldwide outreach that would ultimately reshape civilization. A revolution was underway, but not one with weapons. This one was powered by the work of God in simple men who had seen a miracle. As Peter said, "We cannot stop speaking about what we have seen and heard" (4:20).

Life Questions: The disciples led mass conversions to Christ. What made them such effective spokesmen?

and of the covenant which God made with your fathers, saying to Abraham, 'AND IN YOUR SEED ALL THE FAMILIES OF THE EARTH SHALL BE BLESSED.' 26 "For you first, God raised up His Servant and sent Him to bless you by turning every one *of you* from your wicked ways."

Peter and John Arrested

4 As they were speaking to the people, the priests and the captain of the temple *guard* and the Sadducees came up to them,

4:1 Alarmed Sadducees

The coalition arrayed against the disciples resembled the group that had arrested Jesus in Gethsemane. The priests were working hand in hand with Roman rulers, who allowed them to maintain a police force (or "temple guard") to keep order in the temple. Reports of Jesus' resurrection from the dead especially alarmed the Sadducees, a party of priests who denied there would ever be a resurrection from the dead (see also 5:17 and 23:6–8).

2 being greatly disturbed because they were teaching the people and proclaiming in Jesus the resurrection from the dead.

3 And they laid hands on them and put them in jail until the next day, for it was already evening.

4 But many of those who had heard the message believed; and the number of the men came to be about five thousand.

5 ¶ On the next day, their rulers and elders and scribes were gathered together in Jerusalem;

6 and Annas the high priest *was there,* and Caiaphas and John and Alexander, and all who were of high-priestly descent.

7 When they had placed them in the center, they *began to* inquire, "By what power, or in what name, have you done this?"

8 Then Peter, filled with the Holy Spirit, said to them, "Rulers and elders of the people,

9 if we are on trial today for a benefit done to a sick man, as to how this man has been made well,

10 let it be known to all of you and to all the people of Israel, that by the name of Jesus Christ the Nazarene, whom you crucified, whom God raised from the dead—by this *name* this man stands here before you in good health.

11 "He is the STONE WHICH WAS REJECTED by you, THE BUILDERS, *but* WHICH BECAME THE CHIEF CORNER *stone.*

12 "And there is salvation in no one else; for there is no other name under heaven that has been given among men by which we must be saved."

Threat and Release

13 ¶ Now as they observed the confidence of Peter and John and understood that they were uneducated and untrained men, they were amazed, and *began* to recognize them as having been with Jesus.

14 And seeing the man who had been healed standing with them, they had nothing to say in reply.

15 But when they had ordered them to leave the Council, they *began* to confer with one another,

16 saying, "What shall we do with these men? For the fact that a noteworthy miracle has taken place through them is apparent to all who live in Jerusalem, and we cannot deny it.

17 "But so that it will not spread any further among the people, let us warn them to speak no longer to any man in this name."

18 And when they had summoned them, they commanded them not to speak or teach at all in the name of Jesus.

19 But Peter and John answered and said to them, "Whether it is right in the sight of God to give heed to you rather than to God, you be the judge;

20 for we cannot stop speaking about what we have seen and heard."

21 When they had threatened them further, they let them go (finding no basis on which to punish them) on account of the people, because they were all glorifying God for what had happened;

22 for the man was more than forty years old on whom this miracle of healing had been performed.

23 ¶ When they had been released, they went to their own *companions* and reported all that the chief priests and the elders had said to them.

24 And when they heard *this,* they lifted their voices to God with one accord and said, "O Lord, it is You who MADE THE HEAVEN AND THE EARTH AND THE SEA, AND ALL THAT IS IN THEM,

25 who by the Holy Spirit, *through* the mouth of our father David Your servant, said,

'WHY DID THE *a*GENTILES RAGE,
AND THE PEOPLES DEVISE FUTILE THINGS?

26 'THE KINGS OF THE EARTH TOOK THEIR STAND,
AND THE RULERS WERE GATHERED TOGETHER
AGAINST THE LORD AND AGAINST HIS CHRIST.'

27 "For truly in this city there were gathered together against Your holy servant Jesus, whom You anointed, both Herod and Pontius Pilate, along with the Gentiles and the peoples of Israel,

28 to do whatever Your hand and Your purpose predestined to occur.

a Or *nations*

29 "And now, Lord, take note of their threats, and grant that Your bond-servants may speak Your word with all confidence,

30 while You extend Your hand to heal, and signs and wonders take place through the name of Your holy servant Jesus."

31 And when they had prayed, the place where they had gathered together was shaken, and they were all filled with the Holy Spirit and *began* to speak the word of God with boldness.

Sharing among Believers

32 ¶ And the congregation of those who believed were of one heart and soul; and not one *of them* claimed that anything belonging to him was his own, but all things were common property to them.

33 And with great power the apostles were giving testimony to the resurrection of the Lord Jesus, and abundant grace was upon them all.

34 For there was not a needy person among them, for all who were owners of land or houses

would sell them and bring the proceeds of the sales

35 and lay them at the apostles' feet, and they would be distributed to each as any had need.

36 ¶ Now Joseph, a Levite of Cyprian birth, who was also called Barnabas by the apostles (which translated means Son of Encouragement),

37 and who owned a tract of land, sold it and brought the money and laid it at the apostles' feet.

Fate of Ananias and Sapphira

5 But a man named Ananias, with his wife Sapphira, sold a piece of property,

2 and kept back *some* of the price for himself, with his wife's full knowledge, and bringing a portion of it, he laid it at the apostles' feet.

3 But Peter said, "Ananias, why has Satan filled your heart to lie to the Holy Spirit and to keep back *some* of the price of the land?

4 "While it remained *unsold*, did it not remain your own? And after it was sold, was it not under your control? Why is it that you have conceived

The Secret to the Early Church
The real power at work in Acts

AUTHOR J.B. PHILLIPS, AFTER SPENDING 14 years translating the New Testament, sat back and reflected on his most lasting impressions. He kept returning to the book of Acts and its portrait of an infant church. "The sick are not merely prayed about," said Phillips, "they are healed, often suddenly and dramatically. . . . Human nature is changed. The fresh air of Heaven blows gustily through these pages.

"The early church lived dangerously, but never before has such a handful of people exerted such widespread influence. . . . To put it shortly, the lasting excitement which follows the reading of the book is this: *the thing works!*"

> *"I say to you, stay away from these men and let them alone, for if this plan or action is of men, it will be overthrown; but if it is of God, you will not be able to overthrow them; or else you may even be found fighting against God."*
> 5:38–39

Who Was behind the Success?

Why did it work? Acts points decisively to the power of God, through his Holy Spirit. Luke carefully notes that every major decision of the young church was made under the Spirit's guidance. Indeed, some have suggested Acts should really be titled *Acts of the Holy Spirit* because of his dominant role. Luke mentions the Holy Spirit 57 times in Acts.

The disciples waited on the Spirit in Jerusalem before beginning to preach (2:4). According to Luke, the Holy Spirit fell on each new group of believers: on Jews (4:31), then on Samaritans (8:17), then on Gentiles (10:44), and finally on John the Baptist's disciples (19:6).

For Their Good

As the church grew, the disciples gradually began to understand what Jesus had meant when he said, "It is to your advantage that I go away; for if I do not go away, the Helper will not come to you; but if I go, I will send Him to you" (John 16:7). Although Jesus himself departed, God became present in each one of them, making his activity in the world more widespread than ever before.

The Spirit personally directed each major advance of the church. He sent Philip into the desert to meet an Ethiopian (8:29), set apart missionaries in Antioch (13:2), guided the first big church council (15:1–28), and helped plan Paul's itinerary (13:4; 16:6). As presented in Acts, the Spirit was no vague mist but a living person who spoke, guided in decisions, and fueled the church with the energy of faith.

Life Questions: How is the Holy Spirit active in your life?

this deed in your heart? You have not lied to men but to God."

5 And as he heard these words, Ananias fell down and breathed his last; and great fear came over all who heard of it.

5:4 Deadly Deceit

As Peter makes clear, Ananias and Sapphira were punished not for holding back money but for lying about it. They were misrepresenting themselves spiritually, trying to appear especially pious and generous. At the very beginning of the church (the word first appears in Acts in 5:11), God set a stern standard of absolute honesty and integrity.

6 The young men got up and covered him up, and after carrying him out, they buried him.

7 ¶ Now there elapsed an interval of about three hours, and his wife came in, not knowing what had happened.

8 And Peter responded to her, "Tell me whether you sold the land for such and such a price?" And she said, "Yes, that was the price."

9 Then Peter *said* to her, "Why is it that you have agreed together to put the Spirit of the Lord to the test? Behold, the feet of those who have buried your husband are at the door, and they will carry you out *as well*."

10 And immediately she fell at his feet and breathed her last, and the young men came in and found her dead, and they carried her out and buried her beside her husband.

11 And great fear came over the whole church, and over all who heard of these things.

12 ¶ At the hands of the apostles many signs and wonders were taking place among the people; and they were all with one accord in Solomon's portico.

13 But none of the rest dared to associate with them; however, the people held them in high esteem.

14 And all the more believers in the Lord, multitudes of men and women, were constantly added to *their number*,

15 to such an extent that they even carried the sick out into the streets and laid them on cots and pallets, so that when Peter came by at least his shadow might fall on any one of them.

16 Also the people from the cities in the vicinity of Jerusalem were coming together, bringing people who were sick *a*or afflicted with unclean spirits, and they were all being healed.

Imprisonment and Release

17 ¶ But the high priest rose up, along with all his associates (that is the sect of the Sadducees), and they were filled with jealousy.

18 They laid hands on the apostles and put them in a public jail.

19 But during the night an angel of the Lord opened the gates of the prison, and taking them out he said,

20 "Go, stand and speak to the people in the temple the whole message of this Life."

21 Upon hearing *this*, they entered into the temple about daybreak and *began* to teach.

¶ Now when the high priest and his associates came, they called the Council together, even all the Senate of the sons of Israel, and sent *orders* to the prison house for them to be brought.

22 But the officers who came did not find them in the prison; and they returned and reported back,

23 saying, "We found the prison house locked quite securely and the guards standing at the doors; but when we had opened up, we found no one inside."

24 Now when the captain of the temple *guard* and the chief priests heard these words, they were greatly perplexed about them as to what would come of this.

25 But someone came and reported to them, "The men whom you put in prison are standing in the temple and teaching the people!"

26 Then the captain went along with the officers and *proceeded* to bring them *back* without violence (for they were afraid of the people, that they might be stoned).

27 ¶ When they had brought them, they stood them before the Council. The high priest questioned them,

28 saying, "We gave you strict orders not to continue teaching in this name, and yet, you have filled Jerusalem with your teaching and intend to bring this man's blood upon us."

29 But Peter and the apostles answered, "We must obey God rather than men.

30 "The God of our fathers raised up Jesus, whom you had put to death by hanging Him on a cross.

31 "He is the one whom God exalted to His right hand as a Prince and a Savior, to grant repentance to Israel, and forgiveness of sins.

32 "And we are witnesses *b*of these things; and *so is* the Holy Spirit, whom God has given to those who obey Him."

Gamaliel's Counsel

33 ¶ But when they heard this, they were cut to the quick and intended to kill them.

34 But a Pharisee named Gamaliel, a teacher of the Law, respected by all the people, stood up in the Council and gave orders to put the men outside for a short time.

a Lit *and*   *b* One early ms adds *in Him*

35 And he said to them, "Men of Israel, take care what you propose to do with these men.

36 "For some time ago Theudas rose up, claiming to be somebody, and a group of about four

5:34 Ancient Terrorism

Terrorist acts have had a long history in the Middle East, as Gamaliel's speech shows. During the years surrounding Jesus' life, several revolutionaries had led armed uprisings, two of whom Gamaliel refers to here. Several decades later, the apostle Paul was mistaken for an Egyptian who had staged a terrorist revolt in the desert (21:38).

Gamaliel, who urged a cautious approach on the issue, was a revered and wise rabbi in his day. He followed the progressive branch of Judaism that originated with the rabbi Hillel, and Saul (who became the apostle Paul) was one of his pupils (22:3).

hundred men joined up with him. But he was killed, and all who followed him were dispersed and came to nothing.

37 "After this man, Judas of Galilee rose up in the days of the census and drew away *some* people after him; he too perished, and all those who followed him were scattered.

38 "So in the present case, I say to you, stay away from these men and let them alone, for if this plan or action is of men, it will be overthrown;

39 but if it is of God, you will not be able to overthrow them; or else you may even be found fighting against God."

40 ¶ They took his advice; and after calling the apostles in, they flogged them and ordered them not to speak in the name of Jesus, and *then* released them.

41 So they went on their way from the presence of the Council, rejoicing that they had been considered worthy to suffer shame for *His* name.

42 And every day, in the temple and from house to house, they kept right on teaching and preaching Jesus *as* the Christ.

Choosing of the Seven

6 Now at this time while the disciples were increasing *in number*, a complaint arose on the part of the *a*Hellenistic *Jews* against the *native* Hebrews, because their widows were being overlooked in the daily serving *of food*.

2 So the twelve summoned the congregation of the disciples and said, "It is not desirable for us to neglect the word of God in order to serve tables.

3 "Therefore, brethren, select from among you

seven men of good reputation, full of the Spirit and of wisdom, whom we may put in charge of this task.

4 "But we will devote ourselves to prayer and to the ministry of the word."

5 The statement found approval with the whole congregation; and they chose Stephen, a man full of faith and of the Holy Spirit, and Philip, Prochorus, Nicanor, Timon, Parmenas and Nicolas, a *b*proselyte from Antioch.

6:5 A Cure for Discrimination

Early on, the church ran into complaints from a neglected minority, the Grecian Jews, or Hellenists. This branch of Jews retained many Greek customs and chose to speak Greek rather than Hebrew. The disciples' response in creating a new church office shows considerable diplomacy. The names of the seven appointees indicate they were all Grecian Jews. In other words, the disciples entrusted the minority with full authority to solve their own problems. The first Christian martyr, Stephen, came out of that group of seven.

6 And these they brought before the apostles; and after praying, they laid their hands on them.

7 ¶ The word of God kept on spreading; and the number of the disciples continued to increase greatly in Jerusalem, and a great many of the priests were becoming obedient to the faith.

8 ¶ And Stephen, full of grace and power, was performing great wonders and signs among the people.

9 But some men from what was called the Synagogue of the Freedmen, *including* both Cyrenians and Alexandrians, and some from Cilicia and Asia, rose up and argued with Stephen.

10 But they were unable to cope with the wisdom and the Spirit with which he was speaking.

11 Then they secretly induced men to say, "We have heard him speak blasphemous words against Moses and *against* God."

12 And they stirred up the people, the elders and the scribes, and they came up to him and dragged him away and brought him before the Council.

13 They put forward false witnesses who said, "This man incessantly speaks against this holy place and the Law;

14 for we have heard him say that this Nazarene, Jesus, will destroy this place and alter the customs which Moses handed down to us."

15 And fixing their gaze on him, all who were sitting in the Council saw his face like the face of an angel.

a Jews who adopted the Gr language and much of Gr culture through acculturation   *b* I.e. a Gentile convert to Judaism

Stephen's Defense

7 The high priest said, "Are these things so?" 2 ¶ And he said, "Hear me, brethren and fathers! The God of glory appeared to our father Abraham when he was in Mesopotamia, before he lived in Haran,

3 and said to him, 'LEAVE YOUR COUNTRY AND YOUR RELATIVES, AND COME INTO THE LAND THAT I WILL SHOW YOU.'

4 "Then he left the land of the Chaldeans and settled in Haran. From there, after his father died, God had him move to this country in which you are now living.

5 "But He gave him no inheritance in it, not even a foot of ground, and yet, even when he had no child, He promised that HE WOULD GIVE IT TO HIM AS A POSSESSION, AND TO HIS DESCENDANTS AFTER HIM.

6 "But God spoke to this effect, that his DESCENDANTS WOULD BE ALIENS IN A FOREIGN LAND, AND THAT THEY WOULD BE ENSLAVED AND MISTREATED FOR FOUR HUNDRED YEARS.

7 " 'AND WHATEVER NATION TO WHICH THEY WILL BE IN BONDAGE I MYSELF WILL JUDGE,' said God, 'AND AFTER THAT THEY WILL COME OUT AND *a*SERVE ME IN THIS PLACE.'

8 "And He gave him the covenant of circumcision; and so *Abraham* became the father of Isaac, and circumcised him on the eighth day; and Isaac *became the father of* Jacob, and Jacob *of* the twelve patriarchs.

a Or *worship*

9 ¶ "The patriarchs became jealous of Joseph and sold him into Egypt. *Yet* God was with him,

10 and rescued him from all his afflictions, and granted him favor and wisdom in the sight of Pharaoh, king of Egypt, and he made him governor over Egypt and all his household.

11 ¶ "Now a famine came over all Egypt and Canaan, and great affliction *with it,* and our fathers could find no food.

12 "But when Jacob heard that there was grain in Egypt, he sent our fathers *there* the first time.

13 "On the second *visit* Joseph made himself known to his brothers, and Joseph's family was disclosed to Pharaoh.

14 "Then Joseph sent *word* and invited Jacob his father and all his relatives to come to him, seventy-five persons *in all.*

15 "And Jacob went down to Egypt and *there* he and our fathers died.

16 "*From there* they were removed to Shechem and laid in the tomb which Abraham had purchased for a sum of money from the sons of Hamor in Shechem.

17 ¶ "But as the time of the promise was approaching which God had assured to Abraham, the people increased and multiplied in Egypt,

18 until THERE AROSE ANOTHER KING OVER EGYPT WHO KNEW NOTHING ABOUT JOSEPH.

19 "It was he who took shrewd advantage of our race and mistreated our fathers so that they would expose their infants and they would not survive.

STEPHEN *Dying to Live*

THOUSANDS OF CHRISTIANS HAVE DIED for their faith over the centuries. Even today Christians are persecuted in countries like Algeria, Iran, Sudan and China. Stephen was the first martyr, setting the standard for all Christians who have come under fire for their faith.

While on trial, Stephen spoke so courageously and clearly that members of the sophisticated Sanhedrin lost all control. They gnashed their teeth, covered their ears and, yelling at the top of their voices, rushed at Stephen in their fury. Then, in a mob action, they stoned him to death.

Stephen had begun his public service for Christ when the apostles chose him, with six others, to make sure that Greek-speaking widows got their fair share of food. As it turned out, he did far more than administrate charity. God gave him the power to do miracles and to speak convincingly to other Greek-speaking Jews.

Stephen angered the religious establishment for some of the same reasons Jesus did. The Jews claimed that he had dishonored their revered temple and the Old Testament Law. There was a shred of truth in the charges. For Stephen, God's grace was greater than any building or any rule book.

At his trial, Stephen presented his case loud and clear. He recast the history of Israel as the story of God saving his people *in spite of* their stubborn resistance. Had anything changed? The very people who most honored the temple and the Law—weren't these the same ones who "betrayed and murdered" Jesus?

Like Jesus, Stephen was tried and executed because he upset the establishment. Like Jesus, he died breathing forgiveness, not condemnation. Even while dying, he prayed for those who stoned him. Stephen's final prayer was answered spectacularly, for a man named Saul stood among the persecutors. As Augustine said, "If Stephen had not prayed, the church would not have had Paul."

Life Questions: How would you react if you were put on trial and asked to justify your faith in Christ? What would you say?

20 "It was at this time that Moses was born; and he was lovely in the sight of God, and he was nurtured three months in his father's home.

21 "And after he had been set outside, Pharaoh's daughter took him away and nurtured him as her own son.

22 "Moses was educated in all the learning of the Egyptians, and he was a man of power in words and deeds.

23 "But when he was approaching the age of forty, it entered his mind to visit his brethren, the sons of Israel.

24 "And when he saw one *of them* being treated unjustly, he defended him and took vengeance for the oppressed by striking down the Egyptian.

25 "And he supposed that his brethren understood that God was granting them deliverance through him, but they did not understand.

26 "On the following day he appeared to them as they were fighting together, and he tried to reconcile them in peace, saying, 'Men, you are brethren, why do you injure one another?'

27 "But the one who was injuring his neighbor pushed him away, saying, 'WHO MADE YOU A RULER AND JUDGE OVER US?

28 'YOU DO NOT MEAN TO KILL ME AS YOU KILLED THE EGYPTIAN YESTERDAY, DO YOU?'

29 "At this remark, MOSES FLED AND BECAME AN ALIEN IN THE LAND OF MIDIAN, where he became the father of two sons.

30 ¶ "After forty years had passed, AN ANGEL APPEARED TO HIM IN THE WILDERNESS OF MOUNT Sinai, IN THE FLAME OF A BURNING THORN BUSH.

31 "When Moses saw it, he marveled at the sight; and as he approached to look *more* closely, there came the voice of the Lord:

32 'I AM THE GOD OF YOUR FATHERS, THE GOD OF ABRAHAM AND ISAAC AND JACOB.' Moses shook with fear and would not venture to look.

33 "BUT THE LORD SAID TO HIM, 'TAKE OFF THE SANDALS FROM YOUR FEET, FOR THE PLACE ON WHICH YOU ARE STANDING IS HOLY GROUND.

34 'I HAVE CERTAINLY SEEN THE OPPRESSION OF MY PEOPLE IN EGYPT AND HAVE HEARD THEIR GROANS, AND I HAVE COME DOWN TO RESCUE THEM; COME NOW, AND I WILL SEND YOU TO EGYPT.'

35 ¶ "This Moses whom they disowned, saying, 'WHO MADE YOU A RULER AND A JUDGE?' is the one whom God sent *to be* both a ruler and a deliverer with the help of the angel who appeared to him in the thorn bush.

36 "This man led them out, performing wonders and signs in the land of Egypt and in the Red Sea and in the wilderness for forty years.

37 "This is the Moses who said to the sons of Israel, 'GOD WILL RAISE UP FOR YOU A PROPHET LIKE ME FROM YOUR BRETHREN.'

38 "This is the one who was in the congregation in the wilderness together with the angel who was speaking to him on Mount Sinai, and *who was*

with our fathers; and he received living oracles to pass on to you.

39 "Our fathers were unwilling to be obedient to him, but repudiated him and in their hearts turned back to Egypt,

7:35 Provocative Words

The early part of Stephen's speech must have pleased his Jewish audience. He was, in effect, giving a capsule view of history from the Jewish point of view, featuring such famous ancestors as Abraham, Joseph, Moses, and David. But then Stephen turned the tables, directly attacking the Jewish establishment.

He compared their treatment of Jesus with earlier Jewish rejection of God's messengers. He also called into question Jewish temple worship, claiming that "the Most High does not dwell in houses made by human hands" (verse 48). He ended the speech by calling them traitors and murderers. Stephen's death and the resulting persecution in Jerusalem scattered the disciples, helping to fulfill what Jesus had predicted just before leaving the earth (1:8).

40 SAYING TO AARON, 'MAKE FOR US GODS WHO WILL GO BEFORE US; FOR THIS MOSES WHO LED US OUT OF THE LAND OF EGYPT—WE DO NOT KNOW WHAT HAPPENED TO HIM.'

41 "At that time they made a calf and brought a sacrifice to the idol, and were rejoicing in the works of their hands.

42 "But God turned away and delivered them up to serve the host of heaven; as it is written in the book of the prophets, 'IT WAS NOT TO ME THAT YOU OFFERED VICTIMS AND SACRIFICES FORTY YEARS IN THE WILDERNESS, WAS IT, O HOUSE OF ISRAEL?

43 'YOU ALSO TOOK ALONG THE TABERNACLE OF MOLOCH AND THE STAR OF THE GOD ROMPHA, THE IMAGES WHICH YOU MADE TO WORSHIP. I ALSO WILL REMOVE YOU BEYOND BABYLON.'

44 ¶ "Our fathers had the tabernacle of testimony in the wilderness, just as He who spoke to Moses directed *him* to make it according to the pattern which he had seen.

45 "And having received it in their turn, our fathers brought it in with Joshua upon dispossessing the nations whom God drove out before our fathers, until the time of David.

46 "*David* found favor in God's sight, and asked that he might find a dwelling place for the ªGod of Jacob.

47 "But it was Solomon who built a house for Him.

48 "However, the Most High does not dwell in *houses* made by *human* hands; as the prophet says:

49 'HEAVEN IS MY THRONE,

ª The earliest mss read *house* instead of *God*; the Septuagint reads *God*

AND EARTH IS THE FOOTSTOOL OF MY
   FEET;
WHAT KIND OF HOUSE WILL YOU BUILD
   FOR ME?' says the Lord,
'OR WHAT PLACE IS THERE FOR MY REPOSE?
50 'WAS IT NOT MY HAND WHICH MADE ALL
   THESE THINGS?'

51 ¶ "You men who are stiff-necked and un-circumcised in heart and ears are always resisting the Holy Spirit; you are doing just as your fathers did.

52 "Which one of the prophets did your fathers not persecute? They killed those who had previously announced the coming of the Righteous One, whose betrayers and murderers you have now become;

53 you who received the law as ordained by angels, and *yet* did not keep it."

Stephen Put to Death

54 ¶ Now when they heard this, they were cut to the quick, and they *began* gnashing their teeth at him.

55 But being full of the Holy Spirit, he gazed intently into heaven and saw the glory of God, and Jesus standing at the right hand of God;

56 and he said, "Behold, I see the heavens opened up and the Son of Man standing at the right hand of God."

57 But they cried out with a loud voice, and covered their ears and rushed at him with one impulse.

58 When they had driven him out of the city, they *began* stoning *him*; and the witnesses laid aside their robes at the feet of a young man named Saul.

59 They went on stoning Stephen as he called on *the Lord* and said, "Lord Jesus, receive my spirit!"

60 Then falling on his knees, he cried out with a loud voice, "Lord, do not hold this sin against them!" Having said this, he fell asleep.

Saul Persecutes the Church

8 Saul was in hearty agreement with putting him to death.

¶ And on that day a great persecution began against the church in Jerusalem, and they were all scattered throughout the regions of Judea and Samaria, except the apostles.

2 *Some* devout men buried Stephen, and made loud lamentation over him.

3 But Saul *began* ravaging the church, entering house after house, and dragging off men and women, he would put them in prison.

Philip in Samaria

4 ¶ Therefore, those who had been scattered went about preaching the word.

5 Philip went down to the city of Samaria and *began* proclaiming Christ to them.

6 The crowds with one accord were giving attention to what was said by Philip, as they heard and saw the signs which he was performing.

7 For *in the case of* many who had unclean

8:5 Crossing Racial Barriers

Philip's visit to Samaria was quite remarkable in its day. Jewish people had little to do with the Samaritans, whom they looked down on for racial and religious reasons. Later, Philip met with an Ethiopian official on a mission that crossed racial barriers. The modern Christian church in Ethiopia claims an uninterrupted descent from the conversion described in chapter 8.

spirits, they were coming out *of them* shouting with a loud voice; and many who had been paralyzed and lame were healed.

8 So there was much rejoicing in that city.

9 ¶ Now there was a man named Simon, who formerly was practicing magic in the city and astonishing the people of Samaria, claiming to be someone great;

10 and they all, from smallest to greatest, were giving attention to him, saying, "This man is what is called the Great Power of God."

11 And they were giving him attention because he had for a long time astonished them with his magic arts.

12 But when they believed Philip preaching the good news about the kingdom of God and the name of Jesus Christ, they were being baptized, men and women alike.

13 Even Simon himself believed; and after being baptized, he continued on with Philip, and as he observed signs and great miracles taking place, he was constantly amazed.

14 ¶ Now when the apostles in Jerusalem heard that Samaria had received the word of God, they sent them Peter and John,

15 who came down and prayed for them that they might receive the Holy Spirit.

16 For He had not yet fallen upon any of them; they had simply been baptized in the name of the Lord Jesus.

17 Then they *began* laying their hands on them, and they were receiving the Holy Spirit.

18 Now when Simon saw that the Spirit was bestowed through the laying on of the apostles' hands, he offered them money,

19 saying, "Give this authority to me as well, so that everyone on whom I lay my hands may receive the Holy Spirit."

20 But Peter said to him, "May your silver perish with you, because you thought you could obtain the gift of God with money!

21 "You have no part or portion in this matter, for your heart is not right before God.

22 "Therefore repent of this wickedness of yours, and pray the Lord that, if possible, the intention of your heart may be forgiven you.

23 "For I see that you are in the gall of bitterness and in the bondage of iniquity."

24 But Simon answered and said, "Pray to the Lord for me yourselves, so that nothing of what you have said may come upon me."

An Ethiopian Receives Christ

25 ¶ So, when they had solemnly testified and spoken the word of the Lord, they started back to Jerusalem, and were preaching the gospel to many villages of the Samaritans.

26 ¶ But an angel of the Lord spoke to Philip saying, "Get up and go south to the road that descends from Jerusalem to Gaza." (This is a desert *road*.)

27 So he got up and went; and there was an Ethiopian eunuch, a court official of Candace, queen of the Ethiopians, who was in charge of all her treasure; and he had come to Jerusalem to worship,

28 and he was returning and sitting in his chariot, and was reading the prophet Isaiah.

8:20 Gospel Greed

The tendency to exploit spiritual power for material profit did not originate with the television age. Simon, a local magician, saw the gospel as a way to increase his own fame. The disciples had no more tolerance for his attitude than they had for the lies of Ananias and Sapphira (Acts 5).

The Danger in Being a Christian

It began as a Jewish sect; fierce persecution only helped it spread

IN SOME COUNTRIES, A PERSON who becomes a Christian forfeits a good education and job. And in a few countries, a person who converts risks his or her life. One church historian estimates more Christians have been martyred in this century than in all preceding centuries put together.

Yet, strangely, more often than not, intense persecution of Christians leads to a spurt of growth in the church. An ancient saying expresses this phenomenon, "The blood of martyrs is the seed of the church."

> *On that day a great persecution began against the church in Jerusalem, and they were all scattered throughout the regions of Judea and Samaria, except the apostles. 8:1*

The First Big Advance

For a while, the new faith enjoyed popular favor. But very soon it involved grave risk. In the book of Acts, the persecution that produced the first Christian martyr, Stephen, ironically brought about the advance of Christianity outside its Jewish base. Forced out of stormy Jerusalem, the scattering Jewish Christians turned to other races and ethnic groups. Philip preached first to the despised Samaritans, and then crossed racial barriers by helping to convert an official from Ethiopia.

Acts documents a dramatic change in the faith. What had been viewed as an offshoot of the Jewish religion, a "sect of the Nazarenes," began to encompass people from other religions, races, and cultures. Before long, the center of church activity moved from Jerusalem to the city of Antioch. There, people coined the word *Christian*, indicating how separate the new faith had become. Never again would it be considered "just a Jewish thing."

Breaking the Jewish Mold

As Luke tells it, the transition to other ethnic groups required some adjustments. Jewish disciples balked at letting go of their centuries-old traditions and allowing the church to be flooded with non-Jews.

Peter, one of the most loyal Jews, explained his dilemma this way, "Who was I that I could stand in God's way?" (11:17). A direct, unmistakable vision from God (10:9–23) overcame Peter's resistance to accepting non-Jews, and later a decisive church council settled on a policy toward them (15:1–21).

As the pages of Acts turn, whole provinces and cultures open up to the gospel. The faith that had been guarded by a small knot of intimates, all Jews who knew Jesus personally, broke out into a rough world of soldiers, sorcerers, merchants, and antagonists from other religions. This process was not without its bloody and frightening moments.

Life Questions: If severe persecution came to the church in your region today, what would happen to your faith?

29 Then the Spirit said to Philip, "Go up and join this chariot."

30 Philip ran up and heard him reading Isaiah the prophet, and said, "Do you understand what you are reading?"

31 And he said, "Well, how could I, unless someone guides me?" And he invited Philip to come up and sit with him.

32 Now the passage of Scripture which he was reading was this:

"HE WAS LED AS A SHEEP TO SLAUGHTER;
AND AS A LAMB BEFORE ITS SHEARER IS
    SILENT,
SO HE DOES NOT OPEN HIS MOUTH.

33 "IN HUMILIATION HIS JUDGMENT WAS
    TAKEN AWAY;
WHO WILL RELATE HIS GENERATION?
FOR HIS LIFE IS REMOVED FROM THE
    EARTH."

34 The eunuch answered Philip and said, "Please *tell me*, of whom does the prophet say this? Of himself or of someone else?"

35 Then Philip opened his mouth, and beginning from this Scripture he preached Jesus to him.

36 As they went along the road they came to some water; and the eunuch *said, "Look! Water! What prevents me from being baptized?"

37 [a And Philip said, "If you believe with all your heart, you may." And he answered and said, "I believe that Jesus Christ is the Son of God."]

38 And he ordered the chariot to stop; and they both went down into the water, Philip as well as the eunuch, and he baptized him.

39 When they came up out of the water, the Spirit of the Lord snatched Philip away; and the eunuch no longer saw him, but went on his way rejoicing.

40 But Philip found himself at Azotus, and as he passed through he kept preaching the gospel to all the cities until he came to Caesarea.

The Conversion of Saul

9 Now Saul, still breathing threats and murder against the disciples of the Lord, went to the high priest,

2 and asked for letters from him to the synagogues at Damascus, so that if he found any belonging to the Way, both men and women, he might bring them bound to Jerusalem.

3 As he was traveling, it happened that he was approaching Damascus, and suddenly a light from heaven flashed around him;

4 and he fell to the ground and heard a voice saying to him, "Saul, Saul, why are you persecuting Me?"

5 And he said, "Who are You, Lord?" And He *said*, "I am Jesus whom you are persecuting,

a Early mss do not contain this v

PHILIP *Breakthrough Man*

RELIGION EASILY GETS ASSOCIATED WITH ethnic groups. Arabs are stereotypically Muslim, Indians are Hindu, Japanese are Shinto or Buddhist. Initially, that same pattern held true for early Christians as well. All the original disciples were Jews, and although Jesus had told them to spread the good news to all ethnic groups they found such a prospect hard to imagine.

Philip (not to be confused with the apostle Philip, one of Jesus' original Twelve) was one of the very first to put the Great Commission into practice. He was a pioneer in carrying Jesus' love across racial lines.

Philip originally came to prominence as one of seven men named by the early church to care for poor widows (6:1–7). Greek-speaking Jews had complained about being overlooked, and the apostles wanted someone to take on the problems of providing food and care for these and other individuals. By appointing Philip and six of his colleagues (all Greek-speaking themselves, to judge from their Greek names), the apostles showed their concern for Christians who were not traditional Hebrews.

Still, no one thought of inviting Samaritans—people who had some Jewish blood but were disdained by Jews as heretics and half-breeds—into the fellowship. Then Philip, pushed out of Jerusalem by persecution, began preaching to Samaritans, with amazing results. For the first time, non-Jews joined in following Jesus.

And Philip was just beginning. Next he brought the word about Jesus to a traveling Ethiopian official. Thus Philip was responsible for the first African Christian (8:26–40), and legend has it that the strong North African church of the first few centuries could be traced back to this convert.

Years later the apostle Paul visited Philip, staying with him on his way to Jerusalem (21:7–16). Acts mentions that Philip "the evangelist" had four daughters who prophesied. Since women rarely had a public role in those days, this may indicate that Philip was involved in one more breakthrough—this time involving his own family.

Life Questions: Think of some barriers that you would like to see the gospel "break through." What kind of men or women of God will be needed for that to happen? Are you one of those individuals?

6 but get up and enter the city, and it will be told you what you must do."

7 The men who traveled with him stood speechless, hearing the voice but seeing no one.

9:2 Naming the New Religion

In the early days of the church, its believers were given a variety of labels. Here, they are called members of "the Way"; elsewhere, "the brethren" (9:30), "all those who had believed" (2:44), and "sect of the Nazarenes" (24:5). Luke reports (11:26) that in the city of Antioch they were first called "Christians," a name that stuck. Roman writers often used the word Christian in a derisive sense, reflecting the hostility that greeted the first believers.

8 Saul got up from the ground, and though his eyes were open, he could see nothing; and leading him by the hand, they brought him into Damascus.

9 And he was three days without sight, and neither ate nor drank.

10 ¶ Now there was a disciple at Damascus named Ananias; and the Lord said to him in a vision, "Ananias." And he said, "Here I am, Lord."

11 And the Lord *said* to him, "Get up and go to the street called Straight, and inquire at the house of Judas for a man from Tarsus named Saul, for he is praying,

12 and he has seen *a*in a vision a man named Ananias come in and lay his hands on him, so that he might regain his sight."

13 But Ananias answered, "Lord, I have heard from many about this man, how much harm he did to Your saints at Jerusalem;

14 and here he has authority from the chief priests to bind all who call on Your name."

15 But the Lord said to him, "Go, for he is a chosen *b*instrument of Mine, to bear My name before the Gentiles and kings and the sons of Israel;

16 for I will show him how much he must suffer for My name's sake."

17 So Ananias departed and entered the house, and after laying his hands on him said, "Brother Saul, the Lord Jesus, who appeared to you on the road by which you were coming, has sent me so that you may regain your sight and be filled with the Holy Spirit."

18 And immediately there fell from his eyes something like scales, and he regained his sight, and he got up and was baptized;

19 and he took food and was strengthened.

Saul Begins to Preach Christ

¶ Now for several days he was with the disciples who were at Damascus,

20 and immediately he *began* to proclaim Jesus in the synagogues, saying, "He is the Son of God."

21 All those hearing him continued to be amazed, and were saying, "Is this not he who in Jerusalem destroyed those who called on this name, and *who* had come here for the purpose of bringing them bound before the chief priests?"

9:21 Altered Mission

Damascus, said to be the oldest continually occupied city in the world, is now capital of present-day Syria. Saul undertook the 150-mile journey from Jerusalem in order to persecute Christians there, but on the "Damascus Road" he had an encounter that changed his life forever. In the end, Paul had to flee the Jewish zealots he had originally come to aid.

Although Luke does not mention it, sometime during this period Paul withdrew to Arabia, where he had an extended time to think through his new faith and mission (Galatians 1:17).

22 But Saul kept increasing in strength and confounding the Jews who lived at Damascus by proving that this *Jesus* is the Christ.

23 ¶ When many days had elapsed, the Jews plotted together to do away with him,

24 but their plot became known to Saul. They were also watching the gates day and night so that they might put him to death;

25 but his disciples took him by night and let him down through *an opening in* the wall, lowering him in a large basket.

26 ¶ When he came to Jerusalem, he was trying to associate with the disciples; but they were all afraid of him, not believing that he was a disciple.

27 But Barnabas took hold of him and brought him to the apostles and described to them how he had seen the Lord on the road, and that He had talked to him, and how at Damascus he had spoken out boldly in the name of Jesus.

28 And he was with them, moving about freely in Jerusalem, speaking out boldly in the name of the Lord.

29 And he was talking and arguing with the Hellenistic *Jews*; but they were attempting to put him to death.

30 But when the brethren learned *of it*, they brought him down to Caesarea and sent him away to Tarsus.

31 ¶ So the church throughout all Judea and Galilee and Samaria enjoyed peace, being built up; and going on in the fear of the Lord and in the

---

a A few early mss do not contain *in a vision*   *b* Or *vessel* comfort of the Holy Spirit, it continued to increase.

Peter's Ministry

32 ¶ Now as Peter was traveling through all *those regions,* he came down also to the saints who lived at Lydda.

33 There he found a man named Aeneas, who had been bedridden eight years, for he was paralyzed.

34 Peter said to him, "Aeneas, Jesus Christ heals you; get up and make your bed." Immediately he got up.

35 And all who lived at Lydda and Sharon saw him, and they turned to the Lord.

36 ¶ Now in Joppa there was a disciple named Tabitha (which translated *in Greek* is called Dorcas); this woman was abounding with deeds of kindness and charity which she continually did.

37 And it happened at that time that she fell sick and died; and when they had washed her body, they laid it in an upper room.

38 Since Lydda was near Joppa, the disciples, having heard that Peter was there, sent two men to him, imploring him, "Do not delay in coming to us."

39 So Peter arose and went with them. When he arrived, they brought him into the upper room; and all the widows stood beside him, weeping and showing all the *a*tunics and garments that Dorcas used to make while she was with them.

40 But Peter sent them all out and knelt down and prayed, and turning to the body, he said, "Tabitha, arise." And she opened her eyes, and when she saw Peter, she sat up.

41 And he gave her his hand and raised her up; and calling the saints and widows, he presented her alive.

42 It became known all over Joppa, and many believed in the Lord.

43 And Peter stayed many days in Joppa with a tanner *named* Simon.

Cornelius's Vision

10 Now *there was* a man at Caesarea named Cornelius, a centurion of what was called the Italian *b*cohort,

2 a devout man and one who feared God with all his household, and gave many *c*alms to the Jewish people and prayed to God continually.

3 About the *d*ninth hour of the day he clearly saw in a vision an angel of God who had *just* come in and said to him, "Cornelius!"

4 And fixing his gaze on him and being much alarmed, he said, "What is it, Lord?" And he said to him, "Your prayers and *e*alms have ascended as a memorial before God.

5 "Now dispatch *some* men to Joppa and send for a man *named* Simon, who is also called Peter;

6 he is staying with a tanner *named* Simon, whose house is by the sea."

7 When the angel who was speaking to him had left, he summoned two of his servants and a devout soldier of those who were his personal attendants,

8 and after he had explained everything to them, he sent them to Joppa.

9 ¶ On the next day, as they were on their way and approaching the city, Peter went up on the housetop about the *f*sixth hour to pray.

10:9 A Shift from Peter to Paul

The first part of Acts, especially chapters 9–12, concentrates on the life of Peter. He represented the conservative Jewish contingent, and Acts reports that God gave him direct revelation to understand his plan of outreach to the Gentiles. But a man named Saul had been converted, and beginning with chapter 13, Acts follows his story almost exclusively.

10 But he became hungry and was desiring to eat; but while they were making preparations, he fell into a trance;

11 and he *saw the sky opened up, and an *g*object like a great sheet coming down, lowered by four corners to the ground,

12 and there were in it all *kinds of* four-footed animals and *h*crawling creatures of the earth and birds of the air.

13 A voice came to him, "Get up, Peter, kill and eat!"

14 But Peter said, "By no means, Lord, for I have never eaten anything unholy and unclean."

15 Again a voice *came* to him a second time, "What God has cleansed, no *longer* consider unholy."

16 This happened three times, and immediately the object was taken up into the sky.

17 ¶ Now while Peter was greatly perplexed in mind as to what the vision which he had seen might be, behold, the men who had been sent by Cornelius, having asked directions for Simon's house, appeared at the gate;

18 and calling out, they were asking whether Simon, who was also called Peter, was staying there.

19 While Peter was reflecting on the vision, the Spirit said to him, "Behold, three men are looking for you.

20 "But get up, go downstairs and accompany them without misgivings, for I have sent them Myself."

21 Peter went down to the men and said,

---

a Or *inner garments*   *b* Or *battalion*   *c* Or *gifts of charity*   *d* I.e. 3 p.m.   *e* Or *deeds of charity*   *f* I.e. noon
g Or *vessel*   *h* Or *reptiles*

Recruiting from the Opposition

A former bounty hunter breaks through to the Gentiles

WITH A TOUCH OF THEATRICS, the Indianapolis judge shook his head very slowly back and forth as his clerk read off John Erwin's offenses from a red record book. He had skipped school too many times to count. He had stolen petty items, like flashlight batteries, only to discard them. He had stolen bicycles, ridden them to the junkyard, and destroyed them.

Most recently, twelve-year-old John had joined a gang of young toughs and threatened his foster parents with a .22 rifle. The judge leaned forward and announced, "Young man, I don't know how any one boy can be as mean as they say you are. But I'm convinced you'll never change. I'm going to send you to a Manual Labor Institute for correction, and I predict you'll spend most of your life in institutions."

> *All those hearing him continued to be amazed, and were saying, "Is this not he who in Jerusalem destroyed those who called on this name?"*
> 9:21

Voluntary Life Imprisonment

Three decades later the judge's prophecy has been partially fulfilled: In all, John Erwin has spent over 25 years in a large, notorious institution—Chicago's Cook County jail. But not as an inmate. The judge was mostly wrong: John did change. Remarkably.

During a stint in the army, Erwin met a family who adopted him, determined to show him the same love they had shown their own children. The defenses he had built up in a childhood of violence and sexual abuse slowly melted. He experienced God's love and forgiveness, and he became a new person.

As a free man determined to help set others free, he founded and led the PACE Institute, one of America's most successful prison rehabilitation programs. Then he went on to join the staff of Charles Colson's Prison Fellowship.

When asked why he has been so effective in the failure-littered field of prison work, Erwin replies, "Maybe it's because I've been behind bars, like these prisoners. Most of them came from miserable homes also, and were abused by their parents. I understand what makes life so hard for them—and my story gives them hope. I don't give up on people. If God can change me, he can change them too."

A Complete Turnaround

Converts like John Erwin often make the best crusaders. Former alcoholics can convince others of drinking's dangers. Exiles from Communist countries, such as Alexander Solzhenitsyn, often become the most vehement anti-Communists. And when the book of Acts introduces the most effective Christian missionary of all time, he turns out to be a former bounty hunter of Christians.

How did a Jewish sect become the largest Gentile religion? How did an Asian faith become associated with European civilization? The answers trace back to the remarkable career of Paul, apostle to the Gentiles.

Paul (formerly called Saul) made his first appearance in Acts (8:1), assisting at the brutal stoning of Stephen. Later, he led a gang of persecutors on a violent campaign against Christian believers. But then came a miraculous turnabout on the road to Damascus (9:1–19).

A Courageous Career

Acts is constructed like a drama that delays introducing the hero until the stage is finally set. Beginning in chapter 13, the spotlight in Acts moves from Peter to Paul and follows him throughout the rest of the book. Other Christians, knowing Paul's old reputation, were initially skeptical about his conversion. But he soon proved to be as fiery and intense in preaching Christ as he had been in working against him.

Paul spearheaded the campaign to grant Gentiles full acceptance without subjecting them to Jewish law. He had himself been liberated from bondage to confining laws, and he insisted on a life based on God's free forgiveness, not legalism.

During his journeys, Paul wrote half the New Testament books, and in them he laid the groundwork for much of Christian theology. All the while he carried on a courageous career despite jailings, beatings and riots. He was perhaps the most thoroughly converted man who ever lived.

Life Questions: Has your life changed quickly and dramatically, as Paul's did, or slowly and gradually?

"Behold, I am the one you are looking for; what is the reason for which you have come?"

22 They said, "Cornelius, a centurion, a righteous and God-fearing man well spoken of by the entire nation of the Jews, was *divinely* directed by a holy angel to send for you *to come* to his house and hear a message from you."

23 So he invited them in and gave them lodging.

Peter at Caesarea

¶ And on the next day he got up and went away with them, and some of the brethren from Joppa accompanied him.

24 On the following day he entered Caesarea. Now Cornelius was waiting for them and had called together his relatives and close friends.

25 When Peter entered, Cornelius met him, and fell at his feet and worshiped *him.*

26 But Peter raised him up, saying, "Stand up; I too am *just* a man."

27 As he talked with him, he entered and *found many people assembled.

28 And he said to them, "You yourselves know how unlawful it is for a man who is a Jew to associate with a foreigner or to visit him; and *yet* God has shown me that I should not call any man unholy or unclean.

29 "That is why I came without even raising any objection when I was sent for. So I ask for what reason you have sent for me."

30 ¶ Cornelius said, "Four days ago to this

a I.e. 3 to 4 p.m.

hour, I was praying in my house during the *a*ninth hour; and behold, a man stood before me in shining garments,

31 and he *said, 'Cornelius, your prayer has been heard and your alms have been remembered before God.

32 'Therefore send to Joppa and invite Simon, who is also called Peter, to come to you; he is staying at the house of Simon *the* tanner by the sea.'

33 "So I sent for you immediately, and you have been kind enough to come. Now then, we are all here present before God to hear all that you have been commanded by the Lord."

Gentiles Hear Good News

34 ¶ Opening his mouth, Peter said:

¶ "I most certainly understand *now* that God is not one to show partiality,

35 but in every nation the man who fears Him and does what is right is welcome to Him.

36 "The word which He sent to the sons of Israel, preaching peace through Jesus Christ (He is Lord of all)—

37 you yourselves know the thing which took place throughout all Judea, starting from Galilee, after the baptism which John proclaimed.

38 "*You know of* Jesus of Nazareth, how God anointed Him with the Holy Spirit and with power, and *how* He went about doing good and healing all who were oppressed by the devil, for God was with Him.

CORNELIUS *Least Likely Convert*

WHO WOULD YOU NOMINATE AS "least likely to become a Christian?" A fundamentalist Muslim from Iran? A drug dealer? A hardened, hate-filled criminal? Most of us have a stereotype of who is—and is not—a candidate for Christianity.

To Jesus' first disciples, Cornelius certainly fit the "least likely" description. He was a Roman, which meant that he represented the absolute opposite of Jewish culture and religion. A good Jew could never even enter the home of a Roman, let alone share a meal with him.

Furthermore, Cornelius held the position of centurion, an officer in the brutal occupying army that all good Jews resented and despised. A Jewish fisherman like Simon Peter would never have expected such a man to become a Christian. And Cornelius never would have, had not God used supernatural means to bring Cornelius and Peter together. (The vision Peter received helps explain why Christians today eat such foods as pork and shrimp rather than following Jewish dietary laws.)

While Cornelius the Roman soldier made an unlikely candidate for conversion, Cornelius the *man* was far more ready than most. Acts tells us he gave generously to the poor, prayed often and actively sought God. In short, he had a sterling character. When an angel told him where to seek help, Cornelius responded immediately. Not only did he send for Peter, but he had enough faith to assemble friends and relatives in his home in expectation of Peter's arrival.

Peter, who probably had never stepped inside a non-Jewish house before, was stunned when he heard Cornelius's story. He quickly grasped the point: "I most certainly understand now that God is not one to show partiality, but in every nation the man who fears Him and does what is right is welcome to Him" (10:34,35).

Life Questions: Who in your circle do you feel is "least likely" to become a Christian? Do you really know what goes on underneath the surface, or are you making assumptions?

39 "We are witnesses of all the things He did both in the land of the Jews and in Jerusalem. They also put Him to death by hanging Him on a cross.

40 "God raised Him up on the third day and granted that He become visible,

41 not to all the people, but to witnesses who were chosen beforehand by God, *that is,* to us who ate and drank with Him after He arose from the dead.

42 "And He ordered us to preach to the people, and solemnly to testify that this is the One who has been appointed by God as Judge of the living and the dead.

43 "Of Him all the prophets bear witness that through His name everyone who believes in Him receives forgiveness of sins."

44 ¶ While Peter was still speaking these words, the Holy Spirit fell upon all those who were listening to the message.

45 All the circumcised believers who came with Peter were amazed, because the gift of the Holy Spirit had been poured out on the Gentiles also.

46 For they were hearing them speaking with tongues and exalting God. Then Peter answered,

47 "Surely no one can refuse the water for these to be baptized who have received the Holy Spirit just as we *did,* can he?"

48 And he ordered them to be baptized in the name of Jesus Christ. Then they asked him to stay on for a few days.

Peter Reports at Jerusalem

11 Now the apostles and the brethren who were throughout Judea heard that the Gentiles also had received the word of God.

11:1 Earthshaking Change

Nearly 2,000 years later, the decision to accept Gentiles into the church on equal footing with Jews may seem minor, but at the time it was a hotly debated issue of enormous consequence. Antioch, the first church with a large number of Gentile members, sparked a major controversy with the Jewish-dominated church in Jerusalem (see Acts 15). The third largest city in the Roman empire, Antioch was a crossroads between the Mediterranean and the eastern world, and from here the first missionaries went out to other nations and cultures.

2 And when Peter came up to Jerusalem, those who were circumcised took issue with him,

3 saying, "You went to uncircumcised men and ate with them."

4 But Peter began *speaking* and *proceeded* to explain to them in orderly sequence, saying,

5 "I was in the city of Joppa praying; and in a trance I saw a vision, an object coming down like a great sheet lowered by four corners from the sky; and it came right down to me,

6 and when I had fixed my gaze on it and was observing it I saw the four-footed animals of the earth and the wild beasts and the *a*crawling creatures and the birds of the air.

7 "I also heard a voice saying to me, 'Get up, Peter; kill and eat.'

8 "But I said, 'By no means, Lord, for nothing unholy or unclean has ever entered my mouth.'

9 "But a voice from heaven answered a second time, 'What God has cleansed, no longer consider unholy.'

10 "This happened three times, and everything was drawn back up into the sky.

11 "And behold, at that moment three men appeared at the house in which we were *staying,* having been sent to me from Caesarea.

12 "The Spirit told me to go with them without misgivings. These six brethren also went with me and we entered the man's house.

13 "And he reported to us how he had seen the angel standing in his house, and saying, 'Send to Joppa and have Simon, who is also called Peter, brought here;

14 and he will speak words to you by which you will be saved, you and all your household.'

15 "And as I began to speak, the Holy Spirit fell upon them just as *He did* upon us at the beginning.

16 "And I remembered the word of the Lord, how He used to say, 'John baptized with water, but you will be baptized with the Holy Spirit.'

17 "Therefore if God gave to them the same gift as *He gave* to us also after believing in the Lord Jesus Christ, who was I that I could stand in God's way?"

18 When they heard this, they quieted down and glorified God, saying, "Well then, God has granted to the Gentiles also the repentance *that leads* to life."

The Church at Antioch

19 ¶ So then those who were scattered because of the persecution that occurred in connection with Stephen made their way to Phoenicia and Cyprus and Antioch, speaking the word to no one except to Jews alone.

20 But there were some of them, men of Cyprus and Cyrene, who came to Antioch and *began* speaking to the *b*Greeks also, preaching the Lord Jesus.

21 And the hand of the Lord was with them, and a large number who believed turned to the Lord.

22 The news about them reached the ears of the church at Jerusalem, and they sent Barnabas off to Antioch.

---

a Or reptiles   *b* Lit *Hellenists*; people who lived by Greek customs and culture

23 Then when he arrived and witnessed the grace of God, he rejoiced and *began* to encourage them all with resolute heart to remain *true* to the Lord;

24 for he was a good man, and full of the Holy Spirit and of faith. And considerable numbers were brought to the Lord.

25 And he left for Tarsus to look for Saul;

26 and when he had found him, he brought him to Antioch. And for an entire year they met with the church and taught considerable numbers; and the disciples were first called Christians in Antioch.

27 ¶ Now at this time some prophets came down from Jerusalem to Antioch.

28 One of them named Agabus stood up and *began* to indicate by the Spirit that there would certainly be a great famine all over the world. And this took place in the *reign* of Claudius.

11:28 In the Reign of . . .

The historian Luke is the only New Testament author who dates his books by referring to Roman emperors. He refers to Claudius three times in Acts; the events in Luke's Gospel occur during the reigns of Tiberius and Augustus.

29 And in the proportion that any of the disciples had means, each of them determined to send *a contribution* for the relief of the brethren living in Judea.

30 And this they did, sending it in charge of Barnabas and Saul to the elders.

Peter's Arrest and Deliverance

12 Now about that time Herod the king laid hands on some who belonged to the church in order to mistreat them.

2 And he had James the brother of John put to death with a sword.

3 When he saw that it pleased the Jews, he proceeded to arrest Peter also. Now it was during the days of Unleavened Bread.

4 When he had seized him, he put him in prison, delivering him to four squads of soldiers to guard him, intending after the Passover to bring him out before the people.

5 So Peter was kept in the prison, but prayer for him was being made fervently by the church to God.

6 ¶ On the very night when Herod was about to bring him forward, Peter was sleeping between two soldiers, bound with two chains, and guards in front of the door were watching over the prison.

7 And behold, an angel of the Lord suddenly appeared and a light shone in the cell; and he struck Peter's side and woke him up, saying, "Get up quickly." And his chains fell off his hands.

8 And the angel said to him, "Gird yourself and put on your sandals." And he did so. And he *said to him, "Wrap your cloak around you and follow me."

9 And he went out and continued to follow, and he did not know that what was being done by the angel was real, but thought he was seeing a vision.

10 When they had passed the first and second guard, they came to the iron gate that leads into the city, which opened for them by itself; and they went out and went along one street, and immediately the angel departed from him.

11 When Peter came to himself, he said, "Now I know for sure that the Lord has sent forth His angel and rescued me from the hand of Herod and from all that the Jewish people were expecting."

12 And when he realized *this*, he went to the house of Mary, the mother of John who was also called Mark, where many were gathered together and were praying.

13 When he knocked at the door of the gate, a servant-girl named Rhoda came to answer.

14 When she recognized Peter's voice, because of her joy she did not open the gate, but ran in and announced that Peter was standing in front of the gate.

15 They said to her, "You are out of your mind!" But she kept insisting that it was so. They kept saying, "It is his angel."

16 But Peter continued knocking; and when they had opened *the door*, they saw him and were amazed.

17 But motioning to them with his hand to be silent, he described to them how the Lord had led him out of the prison. And he said, "Report these things to James and the brethren." Then he left and went to another place.

18 ¶ Now when day came, there was no small disturbance among the soldiers *as to* what could have become of Peter.

19 When Herod had searched for him and had not found him, he examined the guards and ordered that they be led away *to execution*. Then he went down from Judea to Caesarea and was spending time there.

12:19 Guards Without Allies

The soldiers who had unsuccessfully guarded Jesus' tomb were protected by a conspiracy hatched by the Jewish establishment (Matthew 28:12–15). This passage sheds light on their eagerness to agree to a cover-up plan: Rome dealt harshly with guards who did not perform their duty. In contrast, the guards who had been on duty when Peter "escaped" (he was set free by an angel) had no one to plead for them. Herod ordered their execution.

Death of Herod

20 ¶ Now he was very angry with the people of Tyre and Sidon; and with one accord they came to him, and having won over Blastus the king's chamberlain, they were asking for peace, because their country was fed by the king's country.

21 On an appointed day Herod, having put on his royal apparel, took his seat on the rostrum and *began* delivering an address to them.

22 The people kept crying out, "The voice of a god and not of a man!"

23 And immediately an angel of the Lord struck him because he did not give God the glory, and he was eaten by worms and died.

24 ¶ But the word of the Lord continued to grow and to be multiplied.

25 ¶ And Barnabas and Saul returned from Jerusalem when they had fulfilled their mission, taking along with *them* John, who was also called Mark.

First Missionary Journey

13 Now there were at Antioch, in the church that was *there*, prophets and teachers: Barnabas, and Simeon who was called Niger, and Lucius of Cyrene, and Manaen who had been brought up with Herod the tetrarch, and Saul.

2 While they were ministering to the Lord and fasting, the Holy Spirit said, "Set apart for Me Barnabas and Saul for the work to which I have called them."

3 Then, when they had fasted and prayed and laid their hands on them, they sent them away.

4 ¶ So, being sent out by the Holy Spirit, they went down to Seleucia and from there they sailed to Cyprus.

5 When they reached Salamis, they *began* to proclaim the word of God in the synagogues of the Jews; and they also had John as their helper.

6 When they had gone through the whole island as far as Paphos, they found a magician, a Jewish false prophet whose name was Bar-Jesus,

7 who was with the proconsul, Sergius Paulus, a man of intelligence. This man summoned Barnabas and Saul and sought to hear the word of God.

8 But Elymas the magician (for so his name is translated) was opposing them, seeking to turn the proconsul away from the faith.

9 But Saul, who was also *known as* Paul, filled with the Holy Spirit, fixed his gaze on him,

10 and said, "You who are full of all deceit and fraud, you son of the devil, you enemy of all righteousness, will you not cease to make crooked the straight ways of the Lord?

11 "Now, behold, the hand of the Lord is upon you, and you will be blind and not see the sun for a time." And immediately a mist and a darkness fell upon him, and he went about seeking those who would lead him by the hand.

12 Then the proconsul believed when he saw what had happened, being amazed at the teaching of the Lord.

13 ¶ Now Paul and his companions put out to sea from Paphos and came to Perga in Pamphylia; but John left them and returned to Jerusalem.

14 But going on from Perga, they arrived at Pisidian Antioch, and on the Sabbath day they went into the synagogue and sat down.

15 After the reading of the Law and the Prophets the synagogue officials sent to them, saying, "Brethren, if you have any word of exhortation for the people, say it."

16 Paul stood up, and motioning with his hand said,

BARNABAS *The Encourager*

THOUGH HIS REAL NAME WAS Joseph, he became known as "Barnabas," an apt nickname meaning "Son of Encouragement." Barnabas had a knack for recognizing and encouraging others' potential. His most notable beneficiary? None other than the apostle Paul.

Even after his dramatic conversion, Paul frightened Jewish Christians—so much so that when he reached Jerusalem they all kept their distance. Wasn't this the fire-breather who had hurt so many believers? But Barnabas took his life in his hands and went to see Paul. Convinced that his conversion was genuine, Barnabas led Paul to the apostles and introduced them (9:26–27).

Later, when the first Gentile church sprang to life in Antioch, Barnabas encouraged these new Christians and then thought of a role for Paul (11:25–26). Barnabas helped Paul find his real calling: to nurture churches that crossed Jewish-Gentile lines. (Paul would eventually become known as the "Apostle to the Gentiles.") Soon God would hand-pick the two of them to leave Antioch on the first missionary journey (13:1–3).

Ironically, Barnabas's encouraging outlook put him at odds with Paul. On that first trip they took along Barnabas's young cousin John Mark, who quit in mid-journey. When they were planning a second trip, Barnabas wanted to give Mark another chance, but Paul refused. Consequently they split and went their separate ways (15:36–40). Barnabas proved right on this point, for Mark proved trustworthy and Paul ultimately came to depend on him (2 Timothy 4:11).

Life Questions: Whom do you encourage, and how do you do it? Who encourages you?

¶ "Men of Israel, and you who fear God, listen:

17 "The God of this people Israel chose our fathers and made the people great during their stay in the land of Egypt, and with an uplifted arm He led them out from it.

13:15 Visiting Speaker

Synagogue rulers customarily invited a visiting rabbi to address the congregation, and in this case the apostle Paul responded by delivering his longest-recorded sermon. The rulers got more than they bargained for: The next week virtually the whole city turned out to hear him, resulting in a near-riot (verses 44–45).

18 "For a period of about forty years He put up with them in the wilderness.

19 "When He had destroyed seven nations in the land of Canaan, He distributed their land as an inheritance—*all of which took* about four hundred and fifty years.

20 "After these things He gave *them* judges until Samuel the prophet.

21 "Then they asked for a king, and God gave them Saul the son of Kish, a man of the tribe of Benjamin, for forty years.

22 "After He had removed him, He raised up David to be their king, concerning whom He also testified and said, 'I HAVE FOUND DAVID the son of Jesse, A MAN AFTER MY HEART, who will do all My will.'

23 "From the descendants of this man, according to promise, God has brought to Israel a Savior, Jesus,

24 after John had proclaimed before His coming a baptism of repentance to all the people of Israel.

25 "And while John was completing his course, he kept saying, 'What do you suppose that I am? I am not *He*. But behold, one is coming after me the sandals of whose feet I am not worthy to untie.'

26 ¶ "Brethren, sons of Abraham's family, and those among you who fear God, to us the message of this salvation has been sent.

27 "For those who live in Jerusalem, and their rulers, recognizing neither Him nor the utterances of the prophets which are read every Sabbath, fulfilled *these* by condemning Him.

28 "And though they found no ground for *putting Him to* death, they asked Pilate that He be executed.

29 "When they had carried out all that was written concerning Him, they took Him down from the cross and laid Him in a tomb.

30 "But God raised Him from the dead;

31 and for many days He appeared to those who came up with Him from Galilee to Jerusalem,

the very ones who are now His witnesses to the people.

32 "And we preach to you the good news of the promise made to the fathers,

33 that God has fulfilled this *promise* to our children in that He raised up Jesus, as it is also written in the second Psalm, 'YOU ARE MY SON; TODAY I HAVE BEGOTTEN YOU.'

34 "*As for the fact* that He raised Him up from the dead, no longer to return to decay, He has spoken in this way: 'I WILL GIVE YOU THE HOLY *and* SURE *blessings* OF DAVID.'

35 "Therefore He also says in another *Psalm*, 'YOU WILL NOT ALLOW YOUR HOLY ONE TO UNDERGO DECAY.'

36 "For David, after he had served the purpose of God in his own generation, fell asleep, and was laid among his fathers and underwent decay;

37 but He whom God raised did not undergo decay.

38 "Therefore let it be known to you, brethren, that through Him forgiveness of sins is proclaimed to you,

39 and through Him everyone who believes is freed from all things, from which you could not be freed through the Law of Moses.

40 "Therefore take heed, so that the thing spoken of in the Prophets may not come upon *you*:

41 'BEHOLD, YOU SCOFFERS, AND MARVEL, AND
　　PERISH;
　FOR I AM ACCOMPLISHING A WORK IN
　　YOUR DAYS,
　A WORK WHICH YOU WILL NEVER BELIEVE,
　　THOUGH SOMEONE SHOULD DESCRIBE
　　IT TO YOU.' "

42 ¶ As Paul and Barnabas were going out, the people kept begging that these things might be spoken to them the next Sabbath.

43 Now when *the meeting of* the synagogue had broken up, many of the Jews and of the God-fearing proselytes followed Paul and Barnabas, who, speaking to them, were urging them to continue in the grace of God.

Paul Turns to the Gentiles

44 ¶ The next Sabbath nearly the whole city assembled to hear the word of the Lord.

45 But when the Jews saw the crowds, they were filled with jealousy and *began* contradicting the things spoken by Paul, and were blaspheming.

46 Paul and Barnabas spoke out boldly and said, "It was necessary that the word of God be spoken to you first; since you repudiate it and judge yourselves unworthy of eternal life, behold, we are turning to the Gentiles.

47 "For so the Lord has commanded us,
'I HAVE PLACED YOU AS A LIGHT FOR THE
　　GENTILES,
THAT YOU MAY BRING SALVATION TO THE
　　END OF THE EARTH.' "

48 ¶ When the Gentiles heard this, they *began*

rejoicing and glorifying the word of the Lord; and as many as had been appointed to eternal life believed.

49 And the word of the Lord was being spread through the whole region.

50 But the Jews incited the devout women of prominence and the leading men of the city, and instigated a persecution against Paul and Barnabas, and drove them out of their district.

51 But they shook off the dust of their feet *in protest* against them and went to Iconium.

52 And the disciples were continually filled with joy and with the Holy Spirit.

Acceptance and Opposition

14 In Iconium they entered the synagogue of the Jews together, and spoke in such a manner that a large number of people believed, both of Jews and of Greeks.

2 But the Jews who disbelieved stirred up the minds of the Gentiles and embittered them against the brethren.

3 Therefore they spent a long time *there* speaking boldly *with reliance* upon the Lord, who was testifying to the word of His grace, granting that signs and wonders be done by their hands.

4 But the people of the city were divided; and some sided with the Jews, and some with the apostles.

5 And when an attempt was made by both the Gentiles and the Jews with their rulers, to mistreat and to stone them,

6 they became aware of it and fled to the cities of Lycaonia, Lystra and Derbe, and the surrounding region;

7 and there they continued to preach the gospel.

8 ¶ At Lystra a man was sitting who had no strength in his feet, lame from his mother's womb, who had never walked.

9 This man was listening to Paul as he spoke, who, when he had fixed his gaze on him and had seen that he had faith to be made well,

10 said with a loud voice, "Stand upright on your feet." And he leaped up and *began* to walk.

11 When the crowds saw what Paul had done,

they raised their voice, saying in the Lycaonian language, "The gods have become like men and have come down to us."

12 And they *began* calling Barnabas, Zeus, and Paul, Hermes, because he was the chief speaker.

13 The priest of Zeus, whose *temple* was just outside the city, brought oxen and garlands to the gates, and wanted to offer sacrifice with the crowds.

14 But when the apostles Barnabas and Paul heard of it, they tore their robes and rushed out into the crowd, crying out

15 and saying, "Men, why are you doing these things? We are also men of the same nature as you, and preach the gospel to you that you should turn from these *a*vain things to a living God, WHO MADE THE HEAVEN AND THE EARTH AND THE SEA AND ALL THAT IS IN THEM.

16 "In the generations gone by He permitted all the nations to go their own ways;

17 and yet He did not leave Himself without witness, in that He did good and gave you rains from heaven and fruitful seasons, satisfying your hearts with food and gladness."

18 *Even* saying these things, with difficulty they restrained the crowds from offering sacrifice to them.

19 ¶ But Jews came from Antioch and Iconium, and having won over the crowds, they stoned Paul and dragged him out of the city, supposing him to be dead.

20 But while the disciples stood around him, he got up and entered the city. The next day he went away with Barnabas to Derbe.

21 After they had preached the gospel to that city and had made many disciples, they returned to Lystra and to Iconium and to Antioch,

22 strengthening the souls of the disciples, encouraging them to continue in the faith, and *saying,* "Through many tribulations we must enter the kingdom of God."

23 When they had appointed elders for them in every church, having prayed with fasting, they commended them to the Lord in whom they had believed.

24 ¶ They passed through Pisidia and came into Pamphylia.

25 When they had spoken the word in Perga, they went down to Attalia.

26 From there they sailed to Antioch, from which they had been commended to the grace of God for the work that they had accomplished.

27 When they had arrived and gathered the church together, they *began* to report all things that God had done with them and how He had opened a door of faith to the Gentiles.

28 And they spent a long time with the disciples.

a I.e. idols

The Council at Jerusalem

15 Some men came down from Judea and *began* teaching the brethren, "Unless you are circumcised according to the custom of Moses, you cannot be saved."

2 And when Paul and Barnabas had great dissension and debate with them, *the brethren* determined that Paul and Barnabas and some others of them should go up to Jerusalem to the apostles and elders concerning this issue.

3 Therefore, being sent on their way by the church, they were passing through both Phoenicia and Samaria, describing in detail the conversion of the Gentiles, and were bringing great joy to all the brethren.

4 When they arrived at Jerusalem, they were received by the church and the apostles and the elders, and they reported all that God had done with them.

5 But some of the sect of the Pharisees who had believed stood up, saying, "It is necessary to circumcise them and to direct them to observe the Law of Moses."

6 ¶ The apostles and the elders came together to look into this matter.

7 After there had been much debate, Peter stood up and said to them, "Brethren, you know that in the early days God made a choice among you, that by my mouth the Gentiles would hear the word of the gospel and believe.

15:7 The First Church Council

Chapter 15 gives a fascinating glimpse into Jewish/Gentile politics in the early church, recounting a debate between such leaders as Peter, Paul, and James. "Brethren, you know that in the early days," Peter began his speech—about ten years had passed since his startling experience with Gentiles recorded in Acts 10. By now Gentiles probably outnumbered Jewish believers worldwide.

The leaders agreed on a compromise position that removed some of the barriers between the two groups. They issued a formal position paper, reproduced here, in which Jewish Christians asked the Gentiles to honor four of their practices, two moral issues and two cultural. The two on food relate to a "kosher" method of food preparation designed to keep people from ingesting any animal blood.

8 "And God, who knows the heart, testified to them giving them the Holy Spirit, just as He also did to us;

9 and He made no distinction between us and them, cleansing their hearts by faith.

10 "Now therefore why do you put God to the test by placing upon the neck of the disciples a yoke which neither our fathers nor we have been able to bear?

11 "But we believe that we are saved through the grace of the Lord Jesus, in the same way as they also are."

12 ¶ All the people kept silent, and they were listening to Barnabas and Paul as they were relating what signs and wonders God had done through them among the Gentiles.

James's Judgment

13 After they had stopped speaking, James answered, saying, "Brethren, listen to me.

14 "Simeon has related how God first concerned Himself about taking from among the Gentiles a people for His name.

15 "With this the words of the Prophets agree, just as it is written,

16 'AFTER THESE THINGS I will return,
AND I WILL REBUILD THE TABERNACLE OF
DAVID WHICH HAS FALLEN,
AND I WILL REBUILD ITS RUINS,
AND I WILL RESTORE IT,

17 SO THAT THE REST OF MANKIND MAY SEEK
THE LORD,
AND ALL THE GENTILES WHO ARE CALLED
BY MY NAME,'

18 SAYS THE LORD, WHO MAKES THESE
THINGS KNOWN FROM LONG AGO.

19 "Therefore it is my judgment that we do not trouble those who are turning to God from among the Gentiles,

20 but that we write to them that they abstain from things contaminated by idols and from fornication and from what is strangled and from blood.

21 "For Moses from ancient generations has in every city those who preach him, since he is read in the synagogues every Sabbath."

22 ¶ Then it seemed good to the apostles and the elders, with the whole church, to choose men from among them to send to Antioch with Paul and Barnabas—Judas called Barsabbas, and Silas, leading men among the brethren,

23 and they sent this letter by them,

"The apostles and the brethren who are elders, to the brethren in Antioch and Syria and Cilicia who are from the Gentiles, greetings.

24 "Since we have heard that some of our number to whom we gave no instruction have disturbed you with *their* words, unsettling your souls,

25 it seemed good to us, having become of one mind, to select men to send to you with our beloved Barnabas and Paul,

26 men who have risked their lives for the name of our Lord Jesus Christ.

27 "Therefore we have sent Judas and Silas, who themselves will also report the same things by word *of mouth*.

28 "For it seemed good to the Holy Spirit and to us to lay upon you no greater burden than these essentials:

29 that you abstain from things sacrificed to idols and from blood and from things strangled and from fornication; if you keep yourselves free from such things, you will do well. Farewell."

30 ¶ So when they were sent away, they went down to Antioch; and having gathered the congregation together, they delivered the letter.

31 When they had read it, they rejoiced because of its encouragement.

32 Judas and Silas, also being prophets themselves, encouraged and strengthened the brethren with a lengthy message.

33 After they had spent time *there*, they were sent away from the brethren in peace to those who had sent them out.

34 [*But it seemed good to Silas to remain there.]

35 But Paul and Barnabas stayed in Antioch, teaching and preaching with many others also, the word of the Lord.

Second Missionary Journey

36 ¶ After some days Paul said to Barnabas, "Let us return and visit the brethren in every city in which we proclaimed the word of the Lord, *and see* how they are."

37 Barnabas wanted to take John, called Mark, along with them also.

38 But Paul kept insisting that they should not

a Early mss do not contain this v

take him along who had deserted them in Pamphylia and had not gone with them to the work.

39 And there occurred such a sharp disagreement that they separated from one another, and Barnabas took Mark with him and sailed away to Cyprus.

40 But Paul chose Silas and left, being committed by the brethren to the grace of the Lord.

41 And he was traveling through Syria and Cilicia, strengthening the churches.

The Macedonian Vision

16 Paul came also to Derbe and to Lystra. And a disciple was there, named Timothy, the son of a Jewish woman who was a believer, but his father was a Greek,

2 and he was well spoken of by the brethren who were in Lystra and Iconium.

3 Paul wanted this man to go with him; and he took him and circumcised him because of the Jews who were in those parts, for they all knew that his father was a Greek.

4 Now while they were passing through the cities, they were delivering the decrees which had been decided upon by the apostles and elders who were in Jerusalem, for them to observe.

5 So the churches were being strengthened in the faith, and were increasing in number daily.

6 ¶ They passed through the Phrygian and Galatian region, having been forbidden by the Holy Spirit to speak the word in Asia;

7 and after they came to Mysia, they were

MARK (JOHN MARK) *Slow Starter*

FOR MORE THAN 75 YEARS, England has chosen an All-England soccer team for players under the age of 15. Selections each year represent the very best young players, England's future. Yet a long-term study of these players unearthed a disturbing fact. Of more than 1,200 young players, only 29 went on to play for the All-England adult team. In other words, only two percent of the best remained the best as adults.

It's risky to size someone up too early. Why? Because people change. That was the case with John Mark. As a young man living in Jerusalem, he had a ringside seat for the coming of Christ and the early days of the church. His mother Mary, apparently a widow, opened her home to the early Christians. His cousin Barnabas served as one of the early deacons. Surely Mark would become an outstanding Christian leader!

Paul and Barnabas certainly must have thought so when they took Mark along on their first missionary journey. But the young man failed, deserting them in the middle of the trip. Terribly disappointed, Paul refused to allow Mark on the next journey. This refusal led to a rift with Barnabas (15:39).

Although Paul may have sized up the young man as hopeless, he later changed his opinion. Mark eventually became a valued assistant to Paul, and three of the apostle's letters mention him with gratitude.

Another apostle, Peter, refers warmly to Mark as "my son" (1 Peter 5:13). Tradition has it that Mark accompanied Peter to Rome, where Peter helped him write the Gospel account that bears Mark's name.

Life Questions: If someone were to evaluate you now, as against five years ago, would you show improvement?

trying to go into Bithynia, and the Spirit of Jesus did not permit them;

8 and passing by Mysia, they came down to Troas.

9 A vision appeared to Paul in the night: a man of Macedonia was standing and appealing to him, and saying, "Come over to Macedonia and help us."

10 When he had seen the vision, immediately we sought to go into Macedonia, concluding that God had called us to preach the gospel to them.

16:10 Firsthand Report

In Acts 16, 21, and 28, Luke uses "we" in writing, for he accompanied the apostle Paul on some of his trips. His close association with Paul meant he had immediate access to the central character in Acts 13–28.

11 ¶ So putting out to sea from Troas, we ran a straight course to Samothrace, and on the day following to Neapolis;

12 and from there to Philippi, which is a leading city of the district of Macedonia, a *Roman* colony; and we were staying in this city for some days.

13 And on the Sabbath day we went outside the gate to a riverside, where we were supposing that there would be a place of prayer; and we sat down and began speaking to the women who had assembled.

First Convert in Europe

14 A woman named Lydia, from the city of Thyatira, a seller of purple fabrics, a worshiper of God, was listening; and the Lord opened her heart to respond to the things spoken by Paul.

15 And when she and her household had been baptized, she urged us, saying, "If you have judged me to be faithful to the Lord, come into my house and stay." And she prevailed upon us.

16 ¶ It happened that as we were going to the place of prayer, a slave-girl having a spirit of divination met us, who was bringing her masters much profit by fortune-telling.

17 Following after Paul and us, she kept crying out, saying, "These men are bond-servants of the Most High God, who are proclaiming to you the way of salvation."

18 She continued doing this for many days. But Paul was greatly annoyed, and turned and said to the spirit, "I command you in the name of Jesus Christ to come out of her!" And it came out at that very moment.

19 ¶ But when her masters saw that their hope of profit was gone, they seized Paul and Silas and dragged them into the market place before the authorities,

20 and when they had brought them to the chief magistrates, they said, "These men are throwing our city into confusion, being Jews,

21 and are proclaiming customs which it is not lawful for us to accept or to observe, being Romans."

Paul and Silas Imprisoned

22 The crowd rose up together against them, and the chief magistrates tore their robes off them and proceeded to order *them* to be beaten with rods.

23 When they had struck them with many blows, they threw them into prison, commanding the jailer to guard them securely;

24 and he, having received such a command, threw them into the inner prison and fastened their feet in the stocks.

25 ¶ But about midnight Paul and Silas were praying and singing hymns of praise to God, and the prisoners were listening to them;

26 and suddenly there came a great earthquake, so that the foundations of the prison house were shaken; and immediately all the doors were opened and everyone's chains were unfastened.

27 When the jailer awoke and saw the prison doors opened, he drew his sword and was about to kill himself, supposing that the prisoners had escaped.

28 But Paul cried out with a loud voice, saying, "Do not harm yourself, for we are all here!"

29 And he called for lights and rushed in, and trembling with fear he fell down before Paul and Silas,

30 and after he brought them out, he said, "Sirs, what must I do to be saved?"

The Jailer Converted

31 They said, "Believe in the Lord Jesus, and you will be saved, you and your household."

32 And they spoke the word of the Lord to him together with all who were in his house.

33 And he took them that *very* hour of the night and washed their wounds, and immediately he was baptized, he and all his *household*.

34 And he brought them into his house and set food before them, and rejoiced greatly, having believed in God with his whole household.

35 ¶ Now when day came, the chief magistrates sent their policemen, saying, "Release those men."

36 And the jailer reported these words to Paul, *saying*, "The chief magistrates have sent to release you. Therefore come out now and go in peace."

37 But Paul said to them, "They have beaten us in public without trial, men who are Romans, and have thrown us into prison; and now are they sending us away secretly? No indeed! But let them come themselves and bring us out."

38 The policemen reported these words to the chief magistrates. They were afraid when they heard that they were Romans,

39 and they came and appealed to them, and

when they had brought them out, they kept begging them to leave the city.

40 They went out of the prison and entered *the house of* Lydia, and when they saw the brethren, they encouraged them and departed.

Paul at Thessalonica

17 Now when they had traveled through Amphipolis and Apollonia, they came to Thessalonica, where there was a synagogue of the Jews.

2 And according to Paul's custom, he went to them, and for three Sabbaths reasoned with them from the Scriptures,

3 explaining and giving evidence that the Christ had to suffer and rise again from the dead, and *saying*, "This Jesus whom I am proclaiming to you is the Christ."

4 And some of them were persuaded and joined Paul and Silas, along with a large number of the God-fearing Greeks and a number of the leading women.

5 But the Jews, becoming jealous and taking along some wicked men from the market place, formed a mob and set the city in an uproar; and attacking the house of Jason, they were seeking to bring them out to the people.

6 When they did not find them, they *began* dragging Jason and some brethren before the city authorities, shouting, "These men who have upset *a*the world have come here also;

7 and Jason has welcomed them, and they all act contrary to the decrees of Caesar, saying that there is another king, Jesus."

8 They stirred up the crowd and the city authorities who heard these things.

a Lit *the inhabited earth*

9 And when they had received a pledge from Jason and the others, they released them.

Paul at Berea

10 ¶ The brethren immediately sent Paul and Silas away by night to Berea, and when they arrived, they went into the synagogue of the Jews.

11 Now these were more noble-minded than those in Thessalonica, for they received the word with great eagerness, examining the Scriptures daily *to see* whether these things were so.

12 Therefore many of them believed, along with a number of prominent Greek women and men.

13 But when the Jews of Thessalonica found out that the word of God had been proclaimed by Paul in Berea also, they came there as well, agitating and stirring up the crowds.

14 Then immediately the brethren sent Paul out to go as far as the sea; and Silas and Timothy remained there.

15 Now those who escorted Paul brought him as far as Athens; and receiving a command for Silas and Timothy to come to him as soon as possible, they left.

Paul at Athens

16 ¶ Now while Paul was waiting for them at Athens, his spirit was being provoked within him as he was observing the city full of idols.

17 So he was reasoning in the synagogue with the Jews and the God-fearing *Gentiles*, and in the market place every day with those who happened to be present.

18 And also some of the Epicurean and Stoic philosophers were conversing with him. Some

SILAS *Singing in Prison*

THE NEW CHURCH EXPLODED OUTWARD, persecution pounded inward and change hung everywhere in the air. Boredom never troubled the early Christians—especially the small band who, with the apostle Paul, boldly carried the good news into uncharted territory.

Silas was one of that elite, brave group. A leader in the Jerusalem church, he journeyed to Antioch with an official church message. Something about that city's multicultural church apparently got under his skin, because he volunteered to accompany the apostle Paul on a lengthy missionary trip. Any trip with the fearless Paul guaranteed excitement.

Even today, in some parts of the world, missionary work can be risky business. In those early days of the church, Paul and Silas found trouble ready at hand. In Philippi, the authorities beat up the two missionaries and threw them in jail. While they were singing hymns at midnight behind bars, an earthquake freed them, yet the two stayed around to lead the jailer to faith in Christ. At the next stop, Thessalonica, the pair inadvertently started a riot. Narrowly escaping injury, they went on to Berea, where more trouble ensued.

Such excitement came with the job. The message about Jesus proved challenging and sometimes offensive to those who heard. Silas dedicated his life to spreading the word. Besides preaching the good news, he evidently helped in the writing of 1 and 2 Thessalonians and 1 Peter (1 Thessalonians 1:1; 2 Thessalonians 1:1; 1 Peter 5:12)

Life Questions: Can you imagine serving God as exciting? What would make it so for you?

were saying, "What would this idle babbler wish to say?" Others, "He seems to be a proclaimer of strange deities,"—because he was preaching Jesus and the resurrection.

17:16 Flexible Approach

In places like Thessalonica and Berea, Paul went first to the synagogues, where he tried to convince fellow Jews that Jesus Christ was the Messiah promised in the Old Testament. In Athens he initially took that same approach, but few Athenians had the Old Testament background to understand his argument. Paul soon began comparing his God to the many gods they worshiped. The ancients used to say, "It is easier to find a god than a man in Athens."

19 And they took him and brought him to the Areopagus, saying, "May we know what this new teaching is which you are proclaiming?

20 "For you are bringing some strange things to our ears; so we want to know what these things mean."

21 (Now all the Athenians and the strangers visiting there used to spend their time in nothing other than telling or hearing something new.)

Sermon on Mars Hill

22 ¶ So Paul stood in the midst of the Areopagus and said, "Men of Athens, I observe that you are very religious in all respects.

23 "For while I was passing through and examining the objects of your worship, I also found an altar with this inscription, 'TO AN UNKNOWN GOD.' Therefore what you worship in ignorance, this I proclaim to you.

24 "The God who made the world and all things in it, since He is Lord of heaven and earth, does not dwell in temples made with hands;

25 nor is He served by human hands, as though He needed anything, since He Himself gives to all *people* life and breath and all things;

26 and He made from one *man* every nation of mankind to live on all the face of the earth, having determined *their* appointed times and the boundaries of their habitation,

27 that they would seek God, if perhaps they might grope for Him and find Him, though He is not far from each one of us;

28 for in Him we live and move and exist, as even some of your own poets have said, 'For we also are His children.'

29 "Being then the children of God, we ought not to think that the Divine Nature is like gold or silver or stone, an image formed by the art and thought of man.

30 "Therefore having overlooked the times of

ignorance, God is now declaring to men that all *people* everywhere should repent,

31 because He has fixed a day in which He will judge the world in righteousness through a Man whom He has appointed, having furnished proof to all men by raising Him from the dead."

32 ¶ Now when they heard of the resurrection of the dead, some *began* to sneer, but others said, "We shall hear you again concerning this."

17:32 A Tough Audience

Paul gave a remarkable speech to a gathering of philosophers and thinkers in the sophisticated university city of Athens. It appears he met with little success, and the results may have troubled him greatly. Acts 18:5 hints at a shift in his approach. Some scholars believe that the first four chapters of 1 Corinthians, reflecting on this period of time, may describe the strong impact of his experience in Athens.

33 So Paul went out of their midst.

34 But some men joined him and believed, among whom also were Dionysius the Areopagite and a woman named Damaris and others with them.

Paul at Corinth

18 After these things he left Athens and went to Corinth.

2 And he found a Jew named Aquila, a native of Pontus, having recently come from Italy with his wife Priscilla, because Claudius had commanded all the Jews to leave Rome. He came to them,

3 and because he was of the same trade, he stayed with them and they were working, for by trade they were tent-makers.

4 And he was reasoning in the synagogue every Sabbath and trying to persuade Jews and Greeks.

5 ¶ But when Silas and Timothy came down from Macedonia, Paul *began* devoting himself completely to the word, solemnly testifying to the Jews that Jesus was the Christ.

6 But when they resisted and blasphemed, he shook out his garments and said to them, "Your blood *be* on your own heads! I am clean. From now on I will go to the Gentiles."

7 Then he left there and went to the house of a man named Titius Justus, a worshiper of God, whose house was next to the synagogue.

8 Crispus, the leader of the synagogue, believed in the Lord with all his household, and many of the Corinthians when they heard were believing and being baptized.

9 And the Lord said to Paul in the night by a vision, "Do not be afraid *any longer*, but go on speaking and do not be silent;

10 for I am with you, and no man will attack you in order to harm you, for I have many people in this city."

11 And he settled *there* a year and six months, teaching the word of God among them.

12 ¶ But while Gallio was proconsul of Achaia, the Jews with one accord rose up against Paul and brought him before the judgment seat,

13 saying, "This man persuades men to worship God contrary to the law."

14 But when Paul was about to open his mouth, Gallio said to the Jews, "If it were a matter of wrong or of vicious crime, O Jews, it would be reasonable for me to put up with you;

15 but if there are questions about words and names and your own law, look after it yourselves; I am unwilling to be a judge of these matters."

16 And he drove them away from the judgment seat.

17 And they all took hold of Sosthenes, the leader of the synagogue, and *began* beating him in front of the judgment seat. But Gallio was not concerned about any of these things.

18 ¶ Paul, having remained many days longer, took leave of the brethren and put out to sea for Syria, and with him were Priscilla and Aquila. In Cenchrea he had his hair cut, for he was keeping a vow.

19 They came to Ephesus, and he left them there. Now he himself entered the synagogue and reasoned with the Jews.

On the Road with the Apostle Paul

Paul, both Jewish and Roman, took the gospel into the melting pot

THE BOOK OF ACTS FOLLOWS Paul on three distinct missionary journeys along the northeastern shores of the Mediterranean Sea. Normally in the ancient world, travel posed great hazards, with pirates, barbarian armies, and hostile border guards clogging up the roads. But by Paul's lifetime, Rome had established absolute mastery over a vast territory. Empire-wide peace, the famous *Pax Romana*—a condition that existed only twice in 700 years—prevailed.

Roman engineers had crisscrossed the empire with a network of roads (built so well that many still survive), and as a Roman citizen Paul had a passport to any destination. Language, too, was unified. The Greek tongue, as well as the Greek style of thinking, crossed ethnic barriers.

> But when they resisted and blasphemed, he shook out his garments and said to them, "Your blood be on your own heads! I am clean. From now on I will go to the Gentiles." 18:6

Paul's Strategy

In his missionary ventures, Paul focused primarily on chief trade towns, capital cities, and Roman colonies. Like modern cities today, these comprised a melting pot of diverse cultures. From these places, the gospel message would be carried across the globe.

Usually, Paul began with a visit to a local synagogue, establishing contact with fellow Jews. If they rejected his message, as often happened, he quickly turned to a non-Jewish audience.

When a promising church was established, Paul stayed on—sometimes as long as three years—to teach and to direct its spiritual growth. His letters glow with affection for the friends he developed in this way. (Acts 20 gives a glimpse of the intimacy he shared with one such group.) On his second and third journeys Paul revisited many of the churches he had founded.

Unusual Qualifications, Impressive Results

Paul's background uniquely qualified him for his adventures. A Pharisee who had studied with the famous teacher Gamaliel, he fully understood the Jewish mind. Roman citizenship gave him the status and respect he needed to gain official recognition and to survive threatening legal scrapes.

Paul's mastery of languages helped him also. He used Aramaic to relate to the early church leaders in Jerusalem, and fluency in Greek made possible a speech before philosophers in Athens.

Sometimes Paul was used by God to work miracles. In one tragicomic episode, a sleepy listener succumbed to Paul's all-night sermon and fell out of a third-story window (20:7–12); Paul raised him from the dead.

By the end of his eventful life, Paul had left a ring of burgeoning churches around the eastern Mediterranean. To make sure his work would go on, he trained such leaders as Silas, Titus, Timothy, and the man who recorded much of what we know about Paul's life—Luke himself.

Life Questions: Why did God choose Paul to lead the early church? What special qualifications do you have that God could use?

20 When they asked him to stay for a longer time, he did not consent,

21 but taking leave of them and saying, "I will return to you again if God wills," he set sail from Ephesus.

18:15 A Secular View

Like many Roman officials, Gallio showed little interest in religious matters. However, his decision not to hear charges against Paul had far-reaching consequences. Gallio was an important ruler—brother of the philosopher Seneca and in line for a high office in Rome. By treating Christianity as a part of Judaism he was granting it a form of official protection, for Judaism had already been formally recognized as a religion.

Ironically, when Gallio eventually returned to Rome, he was killed on the orders of Nero—one of the first emperors to begin persecuting Christians.

22 ¶ When he had landed at Caesarea, he went up and greeted the church, and went down to Antioch.

Third Missionary Journey

23 And having spent some time *there*, he left and passed successively through the Galatian region and Phrygia, strengthening all the disciples.

24 ¶ Now a Jew named Apollos, an Alexandrian by birth, an eloquent man, came to Ephesus; and he was mighty in the Scriptures.

25 This man had been instructed in the way of the Lord; and being fervent in spirit, he was speaking and teaching accurately the things concerning Jesus, being acquainted only with the baptism of John;

26 and he began to speak out boldly in the synagogue. But when Priscilla and Aquila heard him, they took him aside and explained to him the way of God more accurately.

27 And when he wanted to go across to Achaia, the brethren encouraged him and wrote to the disciples to welcome him; and when he had arrived, he greatly helped those who had believed through grace,

28 for he powerfully refuted the Jews in public, demonstrating by the Scriptures that Jesus was the Christ.

Paul at Ephesus

19 It happened that while Apollos was at Corinth, Paul passed through the upper country and came to Ephesus, and found some disciples.

2 He said to them, "Did you receive the Holy Spirit when you believed?" And they *said* to him, "No, we have not even heard whether there is a Holy Spirit."

3 And he said, "Into what then were you baptized?" And they said, "Into John's baptism."

4 Paul said, "John baptized with the baptism of repentance, telling the people to believe in Him who was coming after him, that is, in Jesus."

5 When they heard this, they were baptized in the name of the Lord Jesus.

6 And when Paul had laid his hands upon them, the Holy Spirit came on them, and they *began* speaking with tongues and prophesying.

7 There were in all about twelve men.

PRISCILLA AND AQUILA *Power Couple*

MOST LEADERS IN THE NEW Testament were married, but Priscilla and Aquila stand out for making their impact together as a married couple. The Bible never mentions one without the other. Together they worked as tentmakers (18:3), as a couple they sponsored churches in their home (1 Corinthians 16:19; Romans 16:3–5), and in tandem they quietly straightened out a powerful evangelist's doctrine (18:26). More often than not, Priscilla's name comes first—which certainly leaves an impression that in the eyes of their friends she was at least her husband's equal.

Priscilla and Aquila rank among the apostle Paul's closest friends. They first met when Paul arrived alone and weary in the sophisticated, immoral city of Corinth. Priscilla and Aquila were recent arrivals as well—refugees, in fact. Along with all Jews, they had been evicted from Rome by the emperor Claudius. Paul stayed with them and—since he, too, had been trained as a tentmaker—worked alongside them. No doubt the three talked long and thoughtfully as they worked together making tents.

Later Priscilla and Aquila accompanied Paul to the port city of Ephesus, where they became leaders in that new and dynamic church. Churches often met in homes then, just as they do today in places such as Communist China. Under such circumstances the hospitality of hosts like Priscilla and Aquila was crucial to the believers' fellowship.

Since Paul was constantly on the go, he had to rely on letters and occasional visits to sustain his friendship with Priscilla and Aquila. At some point they risked their lives for him (Romans 16:4). When he sent greetings in public letters, this couple headed the list (Romans 16:3; 2 Timothy 4:19).

Life Questions: Think of a married couple you know who have a ministry together. What attitudes toward each other do they show?

8 ¶ And he entered the synagogue and continued speaking out boldly for three months, reasoning and persuading *them* about the kingdom of God.

9 But when some were becoming hardened and disobedient, speaking evil of the Way before the people, he withdrew from them and took away the disciples, reasoning daily in the school of Tyrannus.

19:9 Sports and Education

Greek lecture halls or gymnasiums, such as this one at Tyrannus, often were built as training rooms for Olympic athletes and later converted to educational purposes. (The word "gymnasium" comes from a Greek word that means, literally, "to train in the nude.") Modern Americans use this ancient word for athletic facilities; Europeans, especially Germans, use it in referring to college-prep schools.

10 This took place for two years, so that all who lived in Asia heard the word of the Lord, both Jews and Greeks.

Miracles at Ephesus

11 ¶ God was performing extraordinary miracles by the hands of Paul,

12 so that handkerchiefs or aprons were even carried from his body to the sick, and the diseases left them and the evil spirits went out.

13 But also some of the Jewish exorcists, who went from place to place, attempted to name over those who had the evil spirits the name of the Lord Jesus, saying, "I adjure you by Jesus whom Paul preaches."

14 Seven sons of one Sceva, a Jewish chief priest, were doing this.

15 And the evil spirit answered and said to them, "I recognize Jesus, and I know about Paul, but who are you?"

16 And the man, in whom was the evil spirit, leaped on them and subdued all of them and overpowered them, so that they fled out of that house naked and wounded.

17 This became known to all, both Jews and Greeks, who lived in Ephesus; and fear fell upon them all and the name of the Lord Jesus was being magnified.

18 Many also of those who had believed kept coming, confessing and disclosing their practices.

19 And many of those who practiced magic brought their books together and *began* burning them in the sight of everyone; and they counted up the price of them and found it fifty thousand pieces of silver.

20 So the word of the Lord was growing mightily and prevailing.

21 ¶ Now after these things were finished, Paul purposed in the spirit to go to Jerusalem after he had passed through Macedonia and Achaia, saying, "After I have been there, I must also see Rome."

22 And having sent into Macedonia two of those who ministered to him, Timothy and Erastus, he himself stayed in Asia for a while.

23 ¶ About that time there occurred no small disturbance concerning the Way.

24 For a man named Demetrius, a silversmith, who made silver shrines of Artemis, was bringing no little business to the craftsmen;

19:24 Commercialized Religion

Ephesus was devoted to idolatry and to profit, and Paul's message threatened both. The citizens took great pride in their temple, one of the seven wonders of the ancient world, and were outraged at anyone who might interfere with their profitable businesses dependent on religious pilgrims. The story presents a clear case of mob psychology. Paul started a riot, but he also founded one of his strongest churches, a community that later inspired the book of Ephesians.

25 these he gathered together with the workmen of similar *trades*, and said, "Men, you know that our prosperity depends upon this business.

26 "You see and hear that not only in Ephesus, but in almost all of Asia, this Paul has persuaded and turned away a considerable number of people, saying that gods made with hands are no gods *at all*.

27 "Not only is there danger that this trade of ours fall into disrepute, but also that the temple of the great goddess Artemis be regarded as worthless and that she whom all of Asia and the world worship will even be dethroned from her magnificence."

28 ¶ When they heard *this* and were filled with rage, they *began* crying out, saying, "Great is Artemis of the Ephesians!"

29 The city was filled with the confusion, and they rushed with one accord into the theater, dragging along Gaius and Aristarchus, Paul's traveling companions from Macedonia.

30 And when Paul wanted to go into the assembly, the disciples would not let him.

31 Also some of the *a*Asiarchs who were friends of his sent to him and repeatedly urged him not to venture into the theater.

32 So then, some were shouting one thing and

---

a I.e. political or religious officials of the province of Asia some another, for the assembly was in confusion and the majority did not know for what reason they had come together.

33 Some of the crowd concluded *it was* Alexander, since the Jews had put him forward; and having motioned with his hand, Alexander was intending to make a defense to the assembly.

34 But when they recognized that he was a Jew, a *single* outcry arose from them all as they shouted for about two hours, "Great is Artemis of the Ephesians!"

35 After quieting the crowd, the town clerk *said, "Men of Ephesus, what man is there after all who does not know that the city of the Ephesians is guardian of the temple of the great Artemis and of the *image* which fell down from heaven?

36 "So, since these are undeniable facts, you ought to keep calm and to do nothing rash.

37 "For you have brought these men *here* who are neither robbers of temples nor blasphemers of our goddess.

38 "So then, if Demetrius and the craftsmen who are with him have a complaint against any man, the courts are in session and proconsuls are *available*; let them bring charges against one another.

39 "But if you want anything beyond this, it shall be settled in the lawful assembly.

40 "For indeed we are in danger of being accused of a riot in connection with today's events, since there is no *real* cause *for it*, and in this connection we will be unable to account for this disorderly gathering."

41 After saying this he dismissed the assembly.

Paul in Macedonia and Greece

20 After the uproar had ceased, Paul sent for the disciples, and when he had exhorted

---

Paul's Legal Battles
470 Roman soldiers protected him from a lynch mob

THE DRUMBEAT STARTS WITH THE last verse in chapter 20: "grieving especially over the word which he had spoken, that they would not see his face again." After this, wherever he went, Paul's friends begged him not to go to Jerusalem. One of them bound his own hands and feet with Paul's belt, publicly role-playing what was in store for Paul (21:10–11).

But Paul had survived shipwrecks, a stoning, beatings, and long nights in jail, and fear had never stopped him. Besides, he knew that God wanted him to take his word to Rome, and no disaster in Jerusalem could prevent that.

A Dangerous Revolutionary?

Thus, against all advice Paul went to Jerusalem. His reputation as a Christian missionary had spread, to such an extent that it took a brigade of 470 Roman soldiers to protect him from a Jewish lynch mob.

Luke details the process of Roman justice so thoroughly that some have speculated he wrote Acts as a legal brief for Paul's defense. Was Paul a violent terrorist intent on inciting revolt? Luke meticulously records that, no, Paul had no political ambitions and consistently worked within Roman law.

Most of the time, Roman law found Paul innocent. An official in Corinth dismissed charges against him (18:15), as did the town clerk at Ephesus (19:35–41). In Judea Governor Festus and King Agrippa both concluded Paul might have been freed outright had he not appealed to Caesar (26:32).

The Beginning of the End

Paul's last days of freedom summarize his turbulent life. His friends' fears regarding Jerusalem proved well-founded. A murderous mob there assailed him with trumped-up charges, and he had to be rescued bodily by soldiers.

In typical brazen style, Paul asked to address the unruly crowd, using the chance to confront them with his life's testimony. The crowd listened until he got to the part about a mission to the Gentiles; then it erupted.

In his speech (22:3–21), Paul referred back to the day he stood on the sidelines cheering as Stephen, the first Christian martyr, was killed. That violent scene was forever etched in Paul's mind as a reminder of his former life. But another memory was even more powerful: the blinding light on the road to Damascus. Ever after that event in Damascus, Paul seemed determined to stun the human race as he had been stunned on that desert road. No matter how many nights in jail it cost him.

Life Questions: Acts 20 shows Paul's closeness to other Christians. What produced such intense feelings? What could increase your closeness with others?

> "And now, behold, bound in spirit, I am on my way to Jerusalem, not knowing what will happen to me there, except that the Holy Spirit solemnly testifies to me in every city, saying that bonds and afflictions await me."
> 20:22–23

them and taken his leave of them, he left to go to Macedonia.

2 When he had gone through those districts and had given them much exhortation, he came to Greece.

3 And *there* he spent three months, and when a plot was formed against him by the Jews as he was about to set sail for Syria, he decided to return through Macedonia.

4 And he was accompanied by Sopater of Berea, *the son* of Pyrrhus, and by Aristarchus and Secundus of the Thessalonians, and Gaius of Derbe, and Timothy, and Tychicus and Trophimus of Asia.

20:4 No Cheating

In the days before electronic banking, money had to be carried in person. Thus Paul's plan to transfer the famine relief funds collected in Greece and Asia to the churches in Judea (see 24:17) posed some problems. Eager to avoid suspicion, Paul invited representatives from the donating churches to accompany him. That way he could assure everyone the money was used as promised, and not for personal gain. Second Corinthians 8 gives more details about this offering.

5 But these had gone on ahead and were waiting for us at Troas.

6 We sailed from Philippi after the days of Unleavened Bread, and came to them at Troas within five days; and there we stayed seven days.

7 ¶ On the first day of the week, when we were gathered together to break bread, Paul *began* talking to them, intending to leave the next day, and he prolonged his message until midnight.

8 There were many lamps in the upper room where we were gathered together.

9 And there was a young man named Eutychus sitting on the window sill, sinking into a deep sleep; and as Paul kept on talking, he was overcome by sleep and fell down from the third floor and was picked up dead.

10 But Paul went down and fell upon him, and after embracing him, he said, "Do not be troubled, for his life is in him."

11 When he had gone *back* up and had broken the bread and eaten, he talked with them a long while until daybreak, and then left.

12 They took away the boy alive, and were greatly comforted.

Troas to Miletus

13 ¶ But we, going ahead to the ship, set sail for Assos, intending from there to take Paul on board; for so he had arranged it, intending himself to go by land.

14 And when he met us at Assos, we took him on board and came to Mitylene.

15 Sailing from there, we arrived the following day opposite Chios; and the next day we crossed over to Samos; and the day following we came to Miletus.

16 For Paul had decided to sail past Ephesus so that he would not have to spend time in Asia; for he was hurrying to be in Jerusalem, if possible, on the day of Pentecost.

Farewell to Ephesus

17 ¶ From Miletus he sent to Ephesus and called to him the elders of the church.

18 And when they had come to him, he said to them,

¶ "You yourselves know, from the first day that I set foot in Asia, how I was with you the whole time,

19 serving the Lord with all humility and with tears and with trials which came upon me through the plots of the Jews;

20 how I did not shrink from declaring to you anything that was profitable, and teaching you publicly and from house to house,

21 solemnly testifying to both Jews and Greeks of repentance toward God and faith in our Lord Jesus Christ.

22 "And now, behold, bound in spirit, I am on my way to Jerusalem, not knowing what will happen to me there,

23 except that the Holy Spirit solemnly testifies to me in every city, saying that bonds and afflictions await me.

24 "But I do not consider my life of any account as dear to myself, so that I may finish my course and the ministry which I received from the Lord Jesus, to testify solemnly of the gospel of the grace of God.

25 ¶ "And now, behold, I know that all of you, among whom I went about preaching the kingdom, will no longer see my face.

26 "Therefore, I testify to you this day that I am innocent of the blood of all men.

27 "For I did not shrink from declaring to you the whole purpose of God.

28 "Be on guard for yourselves and for all the flock, among which the Holy Spirit has made you overseers, to shepherd the church of God which He purchased with His own blood.

29 "I know that after my departure savage wolves will come in among you, not sparing the flock;

30 and from among your own selves men will arise, speaking perverse things, to draw away the disciples after them.

31 "Therefore be on the alert, remembering that night and day for a period of three years I did not cease to admonish each one with tears.

32 "And now I commend you to God and to the word of His grace, which is able to build *you* up

and to give *you* the inheritance among all those who are sanctified.

33 "I have coveted no one's silver or gold or clothes.

34 "You yourselves know that these hands ministered to my *own* needs and to the men who were with me.

35 "In everything I showed you that by working hard in this manner you must help the weak and remember the words of the Lord Jesus, that He Himself said, 'It is more blessed to give than to receive.' "

20:35 Emotional Farewell

Paul had worked in Ephesus longer than any other city. Before leaving on his fateful trip to Jerusalem, he called the elders to Miletus for a final farewell (verse 17). In his speech, he quotes a saying from Jesus—the only New Testament quotation from Jesus not found in the Gospels.

36 ¶ When he had said these things, he knelt down and prayed with them all.

37 And they *began* to weep aloud and embraced Paul, and repeatedly kissed him,

38 grieving especially over the word which he had spoken, that they would not see his face again. And they were accompanying him to the ship.

Paul Sails from Miletus

21 When we had parted from them and had set sail, we ran a straight course to Cos and the next day to Rhodes and from there to Patara;

2 and having found a ship crossing over to Phoenicia, we went aboard and set sail.

3 When we came in sight of Cyprus, leaving it on the left, we kept sailing to Syria and landed at Tyre; for there the ship was to unload its cargo.

4 After looking up the disciples, we stayed there seven days; and they kept telling Paul through the Spirit not to set foot in Jerusalem.

5 When our days there were ended, we left and started on our journey, while they all, with wives and children, escorted us until *we were* out of the city. After kneeling down on the beach and praying, we said farewell to one another.

6 Then we went on board the ship, and they returned home again.

7 ¶ When we had finished the voyage from Tyre, we arrived at Ptolemais, and after greeting the brethren, we stayed with them for a day.

8 On the next day we left and came to Caesarea, and entering the house of Philip the evangelist, who was one of the seven, we stayed with him.

9 Now this man had four virgin daughters who were prophetesses.

10 As we were staying there for some days, a prophet named Agabus came down from Judea.

11 And coming to us, he took Paul's belt and bound his own feet and hands, and said, "This is what the Holy Spirit says: 'In this way the Jews at Jerusalem will bind the man who owns this belt and deliver him into the hands of the Gentiles.' "

12 When we had heard this, we as well as the local residents *began* begging him not to go up to Jerusalem.

13 Then Paul answered, "What are you doing, weeping and breaking my heart? For I am ready not only to be bound, but even to die at Jerusalem for the name of the Lord Jesus."

14 And since he would not be persuaded, we fell silent, remarking, "The will of the Lord be done!"

Paul at Jerusalem

15 ¶ After these days we got ready and started on our way up to Jerusalem.

16 *Some* of the disciples from Caesarea also came with us, taking us to Mnason of Cyprus, a disciple of long standing with whom we were to lodge.

17 ¶ After we arrived in Jerusalem, the brethren received us gladly.

18 And the following day Paul went in with us to James, and all the elders were present.

19 After he had greeted them, he *began* to relate one by one the things which God had done among the Gentiles through his ministry.

20 And when they heard it they *began* glorifying God; and they said to him, "You see, brother, how many thousands there are among the Jews of those who have believed, and they are all zealous for the Law;

21 and they have been told about you, that you are teaching all the Jews who are among the Gentiles to forsake Moses, telling them not to circumcise their children nor to walk according to the customs.

22 "What, then, is *to be done*? They will certainly hear that you have come.

23 "Therefore do this that we tell you. We have four men who are under a vow;

24 take them and purify yourself along with them, and pay their expenses so that they may shave their heads; and all will know that there is nothing to the things which they have been told about you, but that you yourself also walk orderly, keeping the Law.

25 "But concerning the Gentiles who have believed, we wrote, having decided that they should abstain from meat sacrificed to idols and from blood and from what is strangled and from fornication."

26 Then Paul took the men, and the next day, purifying himself along with them, went into the temple giving notice of the completion of the days of purification, until the sacrifice was offered for each one of them.

Paul Seized in the Temple

27 ¶ When the seven days were almost over, the Jews from Asia, upon seeing him in the temple, *began* to stir up all the crowd and laid hands on him,

28 crying out, "Men of Israel, come to our aid! This is the man who preaches to all men everywhere against our people and the Law and this place; and besides he has even brought Greeks into the temple and has defiled this holy place."

21:28 A Trumped-up Charge

Ironically, the arrest that led to Paul's final imprisonment came about because of a misunderstanding. He was actually trying to reassure the Jerusalem church of his loyalty by agreeing to take Jewish vows. But a rumor spread that Paul had illegally taken an "unclean" Gentile into a forbidden part of the temple, and a mob scene ensued. The remainder of Acts reports on various stages of Paul's legal appeals.

29 For they had previously seen Trophimus the Ephesian in the city with him, and they supposed that Paul had brought him into the temple.

30 Then all the city was provoked, and the people rushed together, and taking hold of Paul they dragged him out of the temple, and immediately the doors were shut.

31 While they were seeking to kill him, a report came up to the *a*commander of the *Roman* cohort that all Jerusalem was in confusion.

32 At once he took along *some* soldiers and centurions and ran down to them; and when they saw the commander and the soldiers, they stopped beating Paul.

33 Then the commander came up and took hold of him, and ordered him to be bound with two chains; and he *began* asking who he was and what he had done.

34 But among the crowd some were shouting one thing *and* some another, and when he could not find out the facts because of the uproar, he ordered him to be brought into the barracks.

35 When he got to the stairs, he was carried by the soldiers because of the violence of the mob;

36 for the multitude of the people kept following them, shouting, "Away with him!"

37 ¶ As Paul was about to be brought into the barracks, he said to the commander, "May I say something to you?" And he *said, "Do you know Greek?

38 "Then you are not the Egyptian who some time ago stirred up a revolt and led the four thousand men of the Assassins out into the wilderness?"

39 But Paul said, "I am a Jew of Tarsus in Cilicia, a citizen of no insignificant city; and I beg you, allow me to speak to the people."

40 When he had given him permission, Paul, standing on the stairs, motioned to the people with his hand; and when there was a great hush, he spoke to them in the Hebrew dialect, saying,

Paul's Defense before the Jews

22 "Brethren and fathers, hear my defense which I now *offer* to you."

2 ¶ And when they heard that he was addressing them in the Hebrew dialect, they became even more quiet; and he *said,

3 ¶ "I am a Jew, born in Tarsus of Cilicia, but brought up in this city, educated under Gamaliel, strictly according to the law of our fathers, being zealous for God just as you all are today.

4 "I persecuted this Way to the death, binding and putting both men and women into prisons,

5 as also the high priest and all the Council of the elders can testify. From them I also received letters to the brethren, and started off for Damascus in order to bring even those who were there to Jerusalem as prisoners to be punished.

6 ¶ "But it happened that as I was on my way, approaching Damascus about noontime, a very bright light suddenly flashed from heaven all around me,

22:6 Three Versions

Paul's change from persecutor to Christian missionary makes for one of the most dramatic conversion stories in the New Testament. Acts gives three versions: Luke's historical report in chapter 9; Paul's self-defense here before a Jewish mob; and his formal testimony before Agrippa (chapter 26), a descendant of the ruler who tried to kill the infant Jesus in Bethlehem. Each version adds new details custom-tailored to the specific audience.

7 and I fell to the ground and heard a voice saying to me, 'Saul, Saul, why are you persecuting Me?'

8 "And I answered, 'Who are You, Lord?' And He said to me, 'I am Jesus the Nazarene, whom you are persecuting.'

9 "And those who were with me saw the light, to be sure, but did not understand the voice of the One who was speaking to me.

10 "And I said, 'What shall I do, Lord?' And the Lord said to me, 'Get up and go on into Damascus, and there you will be told of all that has been appointed for you to do.'

11 "But since I could not see because of the brightness of that light, I was led by the hand by

---

a I.e. chiliarch, in command of one thousand troops

those who were with me and came into Damascus.

12 ¶ "A certain Ananias, a man who was devout by the standard of the Law, *and* well spoken of by all the Jews who lived there,

13 came to me, and standing near said to me, 'Brother Saul, receive your sight!' And at that very time I looked up at him.

14 "And he said, 'The God of our fathers has appointed you to know His will and to see the Righteous One and to hear an utterance from His mouth.

15 'For you will be a witness for Him to all men of what you have seen and heard.

16 'Now why do you delay? Get up and be baptized, and wash away your sins, calling on His name.'

17 ¶ "It happened when I returned to Jerusalem and was praying in the temple, that I fell into a trance,

18 and I saw Him saying to me, 'Make haste, and get out of Jerusalem quickly, because they will not accept your testimony about Me.'

19 "And I said, 'Lord, they themselves understand that in one synagogue after another I used to imprison and beat those who believed in You.

20 'And when the blood of Your witness Stephen was being shed, I also was standing by approving, and watching out for the coats of those who were slaying him.'

21 "And He said to me, 'Go! For I will send you far away to the Gentiles.' "

22 ¶ They listened to him up to this statement, and *then* they raised their voices and said, "Away with such a fellow from the earth, for he should not be allowed to live!"

23 And as they were crying out and throwing off their cloaks and tossing dust into the air,

24 the [a]commander ordered him to be brought into the barracks, stating that he should be examined by scourging so that he might find out the reason why they were shouting against him that way.

25 But when they stretched him out with thongs, Paul said to the centurion who was standing by, "Is it lawful for you to scourge a man who is a Roman and uncondemned?"

26 When the centurion heard *this*, he went to the commander and told him, saying, "What are you about to do? For this man is a Roman."

27 The commander came and said to him, "Tell me, are you a Roman?" And he said, "Yes."

28 The commander answered, "I acquired this citizenship with a large sum of money." And Paul said, "But I was actually born *a citizen*."

29 Therefore those who were about to examine him immediately let go of him; and the commander also was afraid when he found out that he was a Roman, and because he had put him in chains.

30 ¶ But on the next day, wishing to know for certain why he had been accused by the Jews, he released him and ordered the chief priests and all the Council to assemble, and brought Paul down and set him before them.

Paul before the Council

23 Paul, looking intently at the Council, said, "Brethren, I have lived my life with a perfectly good conscience before God up to this day."

2 The high priest Ananias commanded those standing beside him to strike him on the mouth.

3 Then Paul said to him, "God is going to strike you, you whitewashed wall! Do you sit to try me according to the Law, and in violation of the Law order me to be struck?"

4 But the bystanders said, "Do you revile God's high priest?"

5 And Paul said, "I was not aware, brethren, that he was high priest; for it is written, 'YOU SHALL NOT SPEAK EVIL OF A RULER OF YOUR PEOPLE.' "

6 ¶ But perceiving that one group were Sadducees and the other Pharisees, Paul *began* crying out in the Council, "Brethren, I am a Pharisee, a son of Pharisees; I am on trial for the hope and resurrection of the dead!"

23:6 Paul under Attack

Under pressure, Paul proved to be a formidable opponent. In this scene, he spoke back to a priest who struck him on the mouth. Using great skill, Paul divided his accusers by exploiting the differences between two Jewish sects, the Pharisees and Sadducees (see note on 4:1). Paul managed to arouse such intense opposition that a group of 40 conspirators vowed not to eat or drink until they had killed him.

7 As he said this, there occurred a dissension between the Pharisees and Sadducees, and the assembly was divided.

8 For the Sadducees say that there is no resurrection, nor an angel, nor a spirit, but the Pharisees acknowledge them all.

9 And there occurred a great uproar; and some of the scribes of the Pharisaic party stood up and *began* to argue heatedly, saying, "We find nothing wrong with this man; suppose a spirit or an angel has spoken to him?"

10 And as a great dissension was developing, the [a]commander was afraid Paul would be torn to pieces by them and ordered the troops to go down and take him away from them by force, and bring him into the barracks.

11 ¶ But on the night *immediately* following, the Lord stood at his side and said, "Take courage;

---

[a] I.e. chiliarch, in command of one thousand troops

for as you have solemnly witnessed to My cause at Jerusalem, so you must witness at Rome also."

A Conspiracy to Kill Paul

12 ¶ When it was day, the Jews formed a conspiracy and bound themselves under an oath, saying that they would neither eat nor drink until they had killed Paul.

13 There were more than forty who formed this plot.

14 They came to the chief priests and the elders and said, "We have bound ourselves under a solemn oath to taste nothing until we have killed Paul.

15 "Now therefore, you and the Council notify the commander to bring him down to you, as though you were going to determine his case by a more thorough investigation; and we for our part are ready to slay him before he comes near *the place.*"

16 ¶ But the son of Paul's sister heard of their ambush, and he came and entered the barracks and told Paul.

23:16 Paul's Family

This mention of Paul's nephew is the only reference to Paul's family. Born a Roman citizen in Tarsus (22:28), Paul likely came from a rather prominent family. Only a minority of people in the Roman empire held citizenship, especially in occupied lands. Citizenship could be purchased at a great price or awarded by Roman authorities, but Paul specifies his came through inheritance.

17 Paul called one of the centurions to him and said, "Lead this young man to the commander, for he has something to report to him."

18 So he took him and led him to the commander and *said, "Paul the prisoner called me to him and asked me to lead this young man to you since he has something to tell you."

19 The commander took him by the hand and stepping aside, *began* to inquire of him privately, "What is it that you have to report to me?"

20 And he said, "The Jews have agreed to ask you to bring Paul down tomorrow to the Council, as though they were going to inquire somewhat more thoroughly about him.

21 "So do not listen to them, for more than forty of them are lying in wait for him who have bound themselves under a curse not to eat or drink until they slay him; and now they are ready and waiting for the promise from you."

22 So the commander let the young man go, instructing him, "Tell no one that you have notified me of these things."

Paul Moved to Caesarea

23 And he called to him two of the centurions and said, "Get two hundred soldiers ready by ᵃthe third hour of the night to proceed to Caesarea, with seventy horsemen and two hundred spearmen."

24 *They were* also to provide mounts to put Paul on and bring him safely to Felix the governor.

25 And he wrote a letter having this form:

26 ¶ "Claudius Lysias, to the most excellent governor Felix, greetings.

27 ¶ "When this man was arrested by the Jews and was about to be slain by them, I came up to them with the troops and rescued him, having learned that he was a Roman.

28 "And wanting to ascertain the charge for which they were accusing him, I brought him down to their Council;

29 and I found him to be accused over questions about their Law, but under no accusation deserving death or imprisonment.

30 ¶ "When I was informed that there would be a plot against the man, I sent him to you at once, also instructing his accusers to bring charges against him before you."

31 ¶ So the soldiers, in accordance with their orders, took Paul and brought him by night to Antipatris.

32 But the next day, leaving the horsemen to go on with him, they returned to the barracks.

33 When these had come to Caesarea and delivered the letter to the governor, they also presented Paul to him.

34 When he had read it, he asked from what province he was, and when he learned that he was from Cilicia,

35 he said, "I will give you a hearing after your accusers arrive also," giving orders for him to be kept in Herod's ᵇPraetorium.

Paul before Felix

24 After five days the high priest Ananias came down with some elders, with an attorney *named* Tertullus, and they brought charges to the governor against Paul.

2 After *Paul* had been summoned, Tertullus began to accuse him, saying *to the governor,*

¶ "Since we have through you attained much peace, and since by your providence reforms are being carried out for this nation,

3 we acknowledge *this* in every way and everywhere, most excellent Felix, with all thankfulness.

4 "But, that I may not weary you any further, I beg you to grant us, by your kindness, a brief hearing.

5 "For we have found this man a real pest and a fellow who stirs up dissension among all the Jews

---

ᵃ I.e. 9 p.m.   ᵇ I.e. governor's official residence

throughout [a]the world, and a ringleader of the sect of the Nazarenes.

6 "And he even tried to desecrate the temple; and then we arrested him. [[b]We wanted to judge him according to our own Law.

7 "But Lysias the commander came along, and with much violence took him out of our hands,

8 ordering his accusers to come before you.] By examining him yourself concerning all these matters you will be able to ascertain the things of which we accuse him."

9 The Jews also joined in the attack, asserting that these things were so.

10 ¶ When the governor had nodded for him to speak, Paul responded:

¶ "Knowing that for many years you have been a judge to this nation, I cheerfully make my defense,

11 since you can take note of the fact that no more than twelve days ago I went up to Jerusalem to worship.

12 "Neither in the temple, nor in the synagogues, nor in the city *itself* did they find me carrying on a discussion with anyone or causing a riot.

13 "Nor can they prove to you *the charges* of which they now accuse me.

14 "But this I admit to you, that according to the Way which they call a sect I do serve the God of our fathers, believing everything that is in accordance with the Law and that is written in the Prophets;

15 having a hope in God, which these men cherish themselves, that there shall certainly be a resurrection of both the righteous and the wicked.

16 "In view of this, I also do my best to maintain always a blameless conscience *both* before God and before men.

17 "Now after several years I came to bring [c]alms to my nation and to present offerings;

18 in which they found me *occupied* in the temple, having been purified, without *any* crowd or uproar. But *there were* some Jews from Asia—

19 who ought to have been present before you and to make accusation, if they should have anything against me.

20 "Or else let these men themselves tell what misdeed they found when I stood before the Council,

21 other than for this one statement which I shouted out while standing among them, 'For the resurrection of the dead I am on trial before you today.' "

22 ¶ But Felix, having a more exact knowledge about the Way, put them off, saying, "When Lysias the [d]commander comes down, I will decide your case."

23 Then he gave orders to the centurion for him to be kept in custody and *yet* have *some* free-

dom, and not to prevent any of his friends from ministering to him.

24 ¶ But some days later Felix arrived with Drusilla, his wife who was a Jewess, and sent for Paul and heard him *speak* about faith in Christ Jesus.

25 But as he was discussing righteousness, self-control and the judgment to come, Felix became frightened and said, "Go away for the present, and when I find time I will summon you."

26 At the same time too, he was hoping that money would be given him by Paul; therefore he also used to send for him quite often and converse with him.

27 But after two years had passed, Felix was succeeded by Porcius Festus, and wishing to do the Jews a favor, Felix left Paul imprisoned.

24:27 Left in Chains

Felix was unpopular with the Jews of Palestine. The brief report in Acts shows him to be shrewd and even corrupt (verse 26). Recalled by Rome because of his troubles with the Jews, Felix left Paul in chains for a period of two years. When the new Roman ruler arrived, the controversy over Paul hadn't died down. Jewish leaders immediately confronted Festus with their charges against Paul.

Paul before Festus

25 Festus then, having arrived in the province, three days later went up to Jerusalem from Caesarea.

2 And the chief priests and the leading men of the Jews brought charges against Paul, and they were urging him,

3 requesting a concession against Paul, that he might have him brought to Jerusalem (*at the same time,* setting an ambush to kill him on the way).

4 Festus then answered that Paul was being kept in custody at Caesarea and that he himself was about to leave shortly.

5 "Therefore," he *said, "let the influential men among you go there with me, and if there is anything wrong about the man, let them prosecute him."

6 ¶ After he had spent not more than eight or ten days among them, he went down to Caesarea, and on the next day he took his seat on the tribunal and ordered Paul to be brought.

7 After Paul arrived, the Jews who had come down from Jerusalem stood around him, bringing many and serious charges against him which they could not prove,

8 while Paul said in his own defense, "I have

---

[a] Lit *the inhabited earth* [b] The early mss do not contain the remainder of v 6, v 7, nor the first part of v 8 [c] Or *gifts to charity* [d] I.e. chiliarch, in command of one thousand troops

committed no offense either against the Law of the Jews or against the temple or against Caesar."

9 But Festus, wishing to do the Jews a favor, answered Paul and said, "Are you willing to go up to Jerusalem and stand trial before me on these charges?"

10 But Paul said, "I am standing before Caesar's tribunal, where I ought to be tried. I have done no wrong to the Jews, as you also very well know.

11 "If, then, I am a wrongdoer and have committed anything worthy of death, I do not refuse to die; but if none of those things is true of which these men accuse me, no one can hand me over to them. I appeal to Caesar."

12 Then when Festus had conferred with his council, he answered, "You have appealed to Caesar, to Caesar you shall go."

13 ¶ Now when several days had elapsed, King Agrippa and Bernice arrived at Caesarea and paid their respects to Festus.

14 While they were spending many days there, Festus laid Paul's case before the king, saying, "There is a man who was left as a prisoner by Felix;

15 and when I was at Jerusalem, the chief priests and the elders of the Jews brought charges against him, asking for a sentence of condemnation against him.

16 "I answered them that it is not the custom of the Romans to hand over any man before the accused meets his accusers face to face and has an opportunity to make his defense against the charges.

a Lit the Augustus's (in this case Nero)

17 "So after they had assembled here, I did not delay, but on the next day took my seat on the tribunal and ordered the man to be brought before me.

18 "When the accusers stood up, they began bringing charges against him not of such crimes as I was expecting,

25:13 Two Rulers

In Jesus' day Rome ruled Palestine through local rulers (the Herods) and their overseer Pilate, a governor who reported directly to Rome. Now, around A.D. 59 or 60, their counterparts were the Roman governor Festus and the last of the Herods, Agrippa II. Festus, a responsible leader, dealt with Paul's case promptly, whereas his predecessor Felix had stalled for two years, leaving Paul in prison. Festus used the visit of Herod Agrippa to schedule this special inquiry into Paul's case.

19 but they simply had some points of disagreement with him about their own religion and about a dead man, Jesus, whom Paul asserted to be alive.

20 "Being at a loss how to investigate such matters, I asked whether he was willing to go to Jerusalem and there stand trial on these matters.

21 "But when Paul appealed to be held in custody for athe Emperor's decision, I ordered him to be kept in custody until I send him to Caesar."

AGRIPPA *Roman Heart*

MEMBERS OF THE HEROD FAMILY were native to Palestine, but their loyalties lay elsewhere—in Rome, where their bread was buttered. The Herods play a leading role in New Testament history, but mostly a negative one.

Agrippa, known to historians as Herod Agrippa II, was the last of a series of Herods who ruled Palestine on Rome's behalf. His great uncle had beheaded John the Baptist and presided over one of Jesus' trials; that man's father had ordered the massacre of babies after Jesus' birth. Now, Agrippa had to pass judgment on the apostle Paul, fiery missionary of the new cause.

Educated in Rome, Agrippa came to power at the age of 17 when his father died. Apparently Agrippa picked up some loose morals in Rome as well; his sister Bernice, who accompanied him to hear Paul's trial, was also his mistress. She tried marriage a number of times, and was mistress to other powerful men, but always she returned to her brother. Their incest fueled Roman gossip.

Nonetheless Paul assumed that Agrippa had some background knowledge of the gospel. As overseer of the Jewish temple, he knew about the increasing number of Jesus-followers and their claims that the prophets' predictions of a Messiah had been fulfilled. Agrippa, however, brushed off Paul's appeal. He was not about to get into a Biblical discussion in front of a Roman governor.

As far as we know, Agrippa stayed loyal to Rome until the end. When Jerusalem revolted against Nero in the year 66, Agrippa backed Rome completely. He was involved in Rome's complete destruction of Jerusalem and its temple in A.D. 70. His death marked the end of the Herods.

Life Questions: Agrippa put his loyalty to Rome above God's claims. Do you feel any conflict between competing loyalties? Where and why?

22 Then Agrippa *said* to Festus, "I also would like to hear the man myself." "Tomorrow," he *said, "you shall hear him."

Paul before Agrippa

23 ¶ So, on the next day when Agrippa came together with Bernice amid great pomp, and entered the auditorium *a*accompanied by the commanders and the prominent men of the city, at the command of Festus, Paul was brought in.

24 Festus *said, "King Agrippa, and all you gentlemen here present with us, you see this man about whom all the people of the Jews appealed to me, both at Jerusalem and here, loudly declaring that he ought not to live any longer.

25 "But I found that he had committed nothing worthy of death; and since he himself appealed to the Emperor, I decided to send him.

26 "Yet I have nothing definite about him to write to my lord. Therefore I have brought him before you *all* and especially before you, King Agrippa, so that after the investigation has taken place, I may have something to write.

27 "For it seems absurd to me in sending a prisoner, not to indicate also the charges against him."

Paul's Defense before Agrippa

26 Agrippa said to Paul, "You are permitted to speak for yourself." Then Paul stretched out his hand and *proceeded* to make his defense:

2 ¶ "In regard to all the things of which I am accused by the Jews, I consider myself fortunate, King Agrippa, that I am about to make my defense before you today;

3 especially because you are an expert in all customs and questions among *the* Jews; therefore I beg you to listen to me patiently.

4 ¶ "So then, all Jews know my manner of life from my youth up, which from the beginning was spent among my *own* nation and at Jerusalem;

5 since they have known about me for a long time, if they are willing to testify, that I lived *as* a Pharisee according to the strictest sect of our religion.

6 "And now I am standing trial for the hope of the promise made by God to our fathers;

7 *the promise* to which our twelve tribes hope to attain, as they earnestly serve *God* night and day. And for this hope, O King, I am being accused by Jews.

8 "Why is it considered incredible among you *people* if God does raise the dead?

9 ¶ "So then, I thought to myself that I had to do many things hostile to the name of Jesus of Nazareth.

10 "And this is just what I did in Jerusalem; not only did I lock up many of the saints in prisons, having received authority from the chief priests, but also when they were being put to death I cast my vote against them.

11 "And as I punished them often in all the synagogues, I tried to force them to blaspheme; and being furiously enraged at them, I kept pursuing them even to foreign cities.

12 ¶ "While so engaged as I was journeying to Damascus with the authority and commission of the chief priests,

13 at midday, O King, I saw on the way a light from heaven, brighter than the sun, shining all around me and those who were journeying with me.

14 "And when we had all fallen to the ground, I heard a voice saying to me in the Hebrew dialect, 'Saul, Saul, why are you persecuting Me? It is hard for you to kick against the goads.'

26:14 Kicking the Oxgoads

The proverb comes from a sharp "goad" farmers used to control their oxen hitched to a plow. It means something like, "You are only hurting yourself."

15 "And I said, 'Who are You, Lord?' And the Lord said, 'I am Jesus whom you are persecuting.

16 'But get up and stand on your feet; for this purpose I have appeared to you, to appoint you a minister and a witness not only to the things which you have seen, but also to the things in which I will appear to you;

17 rescuing you from the *Jewish* people and from the Gentiles, to whom I am sending you,

18 to open their eyes so that they may turn from darkness to light and from the dominion of Satan to God, that they may receive forgiveness of sins and an inheritance among those who have been sanctified by faith in Me.'

19 ¶ "So, King Agrippa, I did not prove disobedient to the heavenly vision,

20 but *kept* declaring both to those of Damascus first, and *also* at Jerusalem and *then* throughout all the region of Judea, and *even* to the Gentiles, that they should repent and turn to God, performing deeds appropriate to repentance.

21 "For this reason *some* Jews seized me in the temple and tried to put me to death.

22 "So, having obtained help from God, I stand to this day testifying both to small and great, stating nothing but what the Prophets and Moses said was going to take place;

23 that the Christ was to suffer, *and* that by reason of *His* resurrection from the dead He would be the first to proclaim light both to the *Jewish* people and to the Gentiles."

24 ¶ While *Paul* was saying this in his defense, Festus *said in a loud voice, "Paul, you are out of

---

a Lit *and with*

your mind! *Your* great learning is driving you mad."

25 But Paul *said, "I am not out of my mind, most excellent Festus, but I utter words of sober truth.

26 "For the king knows about these matters, and I speak to him also with confidence, since I am persuaded that none of these things escape his notice; for this has not been done in a corner.

27 "King Agrippa, do you believe the Prophets? I know that you do."

28 Agrippa *replied* to Paul, "In a short time you will persuade me to become a Christian."

29 And Paul *said*, "I would wish to God, that whether in a short or long time, not only you, but also all who hear me this day, might become such as I am, except for these chains."

30 ¶ The king stood up and the governor and Bernice, and those who were sitting with them,

31 and when they had gone aside, they *began* talking to one another, saying, "This man is not doing anything worthy of death or imprisonment."

32 And Agrippa said to Festus, "This man might have been set free if he had not appealed to Caesar."

a Or *battalion*

Paul Is Sent to Rome

27 When it was decided that we would sail for Italy, they proceeded to deliver Paul and some other prisoners to a centurion of the Augustan *a*cohort named Julius.

2 And embarking in an Adramyttian ship, which was about to sail to the regions along the coast of Asia, we put out to sea accompanied by Aristarchus, a Macedonian of Thessalonica.

3 The next day we put in at Sidon; and Julius treated Paul with consideration and allowed him to go to his friends and receive care.

4 From there we put out to sea and sailed under the shelter of Cyprus because the winds were contrary.

5 When we had sailed through the sea along the coast of Cilicia and Pamphylia, we landed at Myra in Lycia.

6 There the centurion found an Alexandrian ship sailing for Italy, and he put us aboard it.

7 When we had sailed slowly for a good many days, and with difficulty had arrived off Cnidus, since the wind did not permit us *to go* farther, we sailed under the shelter of Crete, off Salmone;

8 and with difficulty sailing past it we came to

Rome at Last
Paul finally made it to the capital—in chains

ACTS RECORDS 18 SPEECHES IN all, the last three of which were delivered before a very select audience. Roman officials, intrigued by the most talked-about prisoner in their corner of the empire, brought Paul out and asked him to perform, like a trained bear. As a result of their inquisition, he got his long-awaited trip to Rome.

It is hard for us today to realize how completely the city of Rome then dominated the world. "All roads lead to Rome" was more than a figure of speech. Like a center of gravity, the city attracted all the roads and commerce, all the leaders and thinkers and fortune-seekers of the empire. Political and military power fanned out from Rome. It was the indisputable capital of the world. If Christianity was to gain a foothold anywhere, it had to be in Rome.

A Missionary in Chains

Ironically, Paul, the greatest spokesman for the Christian faith, arrived in Rome as a prisoner. He was exhausted, having just survived a harrowing shipwreck. In Rome, Paul got hours of quiet solitude to work on fond letters to the churches he had left behind.

In one sense, Acts ends anticlimactically, for Luke leaves Paul's life dangling. Most scholars believe Paul was released from this imprisonment and expanded his ministry into new frontiers. Luke records nothing of this period, and nothing about the trial of Paul or his eventual fate. He ends with a single memory, frozen in time: Paul, confined to his house, welcoming and preaching to all who come.

Paul could no longer choose his audience; they had to seek him. But boldly, in the heart of mighty Rome, he talked of a new kingdom and a new king. Christianity had made the journey, and the transition, from Jerusalem to Rome.

He was explaining to them by solemnly testifying about the kingdom of God and trying to persuade them concerning Jesus, from both the Law of Moses and from the Prophets, from morning until evening.
28:23

Life Questions: Is it better for Christianity to be popular or unpopular?

a place called Fair Havens, near which was the city of Lasea.

9 ¶ When considerable time had passed and the voyage was now dangerous, since even the [a]fast was already over, Paul began to admonish them,

10 and said to them, "Men, I perceive that the voyage will certainly be with damage and great loss, not only of the cargo and the ship, but also of our lives."

11 But the centurion was more persuaded by the pilot and the captain of the ship than by what was being said by Paul.

12 Because the harbor was not suitable for wintering, the majority reached a decision to put out to sea from there, if somehow they could reach Phoenix, a harbor of Crete, facing southwest and northwest, and spend the winter there.

13 ¶ When a moderate south wind came up, supposing that they had attained their purpose, they weighed anchor and began sailing along Crete, close inshore.

27:13–41 Sailing Log

Luke was no sailor, but he portrays an authentically detailed account of the trip and storm. For example, sailors can sense they are "approaching some land" (verse 27) long before they see it, both by an acutely developed sense of smell and also by the sound of breaking waves, which carries far out to sea. In the eastern Mediterranean, autumn winds blow from the west, which made westward sailing difficult for ships of that day.

Shipwreck

14 But before very long there rushed down from the land a violent wind, called [b]Euraquilo;

15 and when the ship was caught in it and could not face the wind, we gave way to it and let ourselves be driven along.

16 Running under the shelter of a small island called Clauda, we were scarcely able to get the ship's boat under control.

17 After they had hoisted it up, they used supporting cables in undergirding the ship; and fearing that they might run aground on the shallows of Syrtis, they let down the sea anchor and in this way let themselves be driven along.

18 The next day as we were being violently storm-tossed, they began to jettison the cargo;

19 and on the third day they threw the ship's tackle overboard with their own hands.

20 Since neither sun nor stars appeared for many days, and no small storm was assailing us,

from then on all hope of our being saved was gradually abandoned.

21 ¶ When they had gone a long time without food, then Paul stood up in their midst and said, "Men, you ought to have followed my advice and not to have set sail from Crete and incurred this damage and loss.

22 "Yet now I urge you to keep up your courage, for there will be no loss of life among you, but only of the ship.

23 "For this very night an angel of the God to whom I belong and whom I serve stood before me,

24 saying, 'Do not be afraid, Paul; you must stand before Caesar; and behold, God has granted you all those who are sailing with you.'

25 "Therefore, keep up your courage, men, for I believe God that it will turn out exactly as I have been told.

26 "But we must run aground on a certain island."

27 ¶ But when the fourteenth night came, as we were being driven about in the Adriatic Sea, about midnight the sailors began to surmise that they were approaching some land.

28 They took soundings and found it to be twenty fathoms; and a little farther on they took another sounding and found it to be fifteen fathoms.

29 Fearing that we might run aground somewhere on the rocks, they cast four anchors from the stern and wished for daybreak.

30 But as the sailors were trying to escape from the ship and had let down the ship's boat into the sea, on the pretense of intending to lay out anchors from the bow,

31 Paul said to the centurion and to the soldiers, "Unless these men remain in the ship, you yourselves cannot be saved."

32 Then the soldiers cut away the ropes of the ship's boat and let it fall away.

33 ¶ Until the day was about to dawn, Paul was encouraging them all to take some food, saying, "Today is the fourteenth day that you have been constantly watching and going without eating, having taken nothing.

34 "Therefore I encourage you to take some food, for this is for your preservation, for not a hair from the head of any of you will perish."

35 Having said this, he took bread and gave thanks to God in the presence of all, and he broke it and began to eat.

36 All of them were encouraged and they themselves also took food.

37 All of us in the ship were two hundred and seventy-six persons.

38 When they had eaten enough, they began to lighten the ship by throwing out the wheat into the sea.

---

[a] I.e. Day of Atonement in September or October, which was a dangerous time of year for navigation   [b] I.e. a northeaster

39 ¶ When day came, they could not recognize the land; but they did observe a bay with a beach, and they resolved to drive the ship onto it if they could.

40 And casting off the anchors, they left them in the sea while at the same time they were loosening the ropes of the rudders; and hoisting the foresail to the wind, they were heading for the beach.

41 But striking a reef where two seas met, they ran the vessel aground; and the prow stuck fast and remained immovable, but the stern *began* to be broken up by the force *of the waves.*

42 The soldiers' plan was to kill the prisoners, so that none *of them* would swim away and escape;

43 but the centurion, wanting to bring Paul safely through, kept them from their intention, and commanded that those who could swim should jump overboard first and get to land,

44 and the rest *should follow,* some on planks, and others on various things from the ship. And so it happened that they all were brought safely to land.

Safe at Malta

28 When they had been brought safely through, then we found out that the island was called Malta.

2 The natives showed us extraordinary kindness; for because of the rain that had set in and because of the cold, they kindled a fire and received us all.

3 But when Paul had gathered a bundle of sticks and laid them on the fire, a viper came out because of the heat and fastened itself on his hand.

4 When the natives saw the creature hanging from his hand, they *began* saying to one another, "Undoubtedly this man is a murderer, and though he has been saved from the sea, justice has not allowed him to live."

5 However he shook the creature off into the fire and suffered no harm.

6 But they were expecting that he was about to swell up or suddenly fall down dead. But after they had waited a long time and had seen nothing unusual happen to him, they changed their minds and *began* to say that he was a god.

7 ¶ Now in the neighborhood of that place were lands belonging to the leading man of the island, named Publius, who welcomed us and entertained us courteously three days.

8 And it happened that the father of Publius was lying *in bed* afflicted with *recurrent* fever and dysentery; and Paul went in *to see* him and after he had prayed, he laid his hands on him and healed him.

9 After this had happened, the rest of the people on the island who had diseases were coming to him and getting cured.

10 They also honored us with many marks of respect; and when we were setting sail, they supplied *us* with all we needed.

Paul Arrives at Rome

11 ¶ At the end of three months we set sail on an Alexandrian ship which had wintered in the island, and which had the Twin Brothers for its figurehead.

12 After we put in at Syracuse, we stayed there for three days.

13 From there we sailed around and arrived at Rhegium, and a day later a south wind sprang up, and on the second day we came to Puteoli.

14 There we found *some* brethren, and were invited to stay with them for seven days; and thus we came to Rome.

15 And the brethren, when they heard about us, came from there as far as the Market of Appius and Three Inns to meet us; and when Paul saw them, he thanked God and took courage.

16 ¶ When we entered Rome, Paul was allowed to stay by himself, with the soldier who was guarding him.

28:16 Time on His Hands

Luke reports that controversy about the Christian "sect" had preceded Paul to Rome (verse 22). The apostle put his time of house arrest to good use, evangelizing all who came to see him and writing to the churches he had founded along the way. Such New Testament books as Philippians, Colossians, Ephesians, and Philemon came out of this period of protective custody, which may have lasted four years.

17 ¶ After three days Paul called together those who were the leading men of the Jews, and when they came together, he *began* saying to them, "Brethren, though I had done nothing against our people or the customs of our fathers, yet I was delivered as a prisoner from Jerusalem into the hands of the Romans.

18 "And when they had examined me, they were willing to release me because there was no ground for putting me to death.

19 "But when the Jews objected, I was forced to appeal to Caesar, not that I had any accusation against my nation.

20 "For this reason, therefore, I requested to see you and to speak with you, for I am wearing this chain for the sake of the hope of Israel."

21 They said to him, "We have neither received letters from Judea concerning you, nor have any of the brethren come here and reported or spoken anything bad about you.

22 "But we desire to hear from you what your views are; for concerning this sect, it is known to us that it is spoken against everywhere."

23 ¶ When they had set a day for Paul, they came to him at his lodging in large numbers; and he was explaining to them by solemnly testifying about the kingdom of God and trying to persuade them concerning Jesus, from both the Law of Moses and from the Prophets, from morning until evening.

24 Some were being persuaded by the things spoken, but others would not believe.

25 And when they did not agree with one another, they *began* leaving after Paul had spoken one *parting* word, "The Holy Spirit rightly spoke through Isaiah the prophet to your fathers,

26 saying,

'GO TO THIS PEOPLE AND SAY,
"YOU WILL KEEP ON HEARING, BUT WILL
    NOT UNDERSTAND;
AND YOU WILL KEEP ON SEEING, BUT WILL
    NOT PERCEIVE;

27 FOR THE HEART OF THIS PEOPLE HAS
    BECOME DULL,
AND WITH THEIR EARS THEY SCARCELY
    HEAR,
AND THEY HAVE CLOSED THEIR EYES;
OTHERWISE THEY MIGHT SEE WITH THEIR
    EYES,
AND HEAR WITH THEIR EARS,
AND UNDERSTAND WITH THEIR HEART AND
    RETURN,
AND I WOULD HEAL THEM." '

28 "Therefore let it be known to you that this salvation of God has been sent to the Gentiles; they will also listen."

29 [ªWhen he had spoken these words, the Jews departed, having a great dispute among themselves.]

30 ¶ And he stayed two full years in his own rented quarters and was welcoming all who came to him,

31 preaching the kingdom of God and teaching concerning the Lord Jesus Christ with all openness, unhindered.

ª Early mss do not contain this v

ROMANS

A Most Demanding Audience

If you were stranded on a deserted island, what book would you want along?

> *I thank my God through Jesus Christ for you all because your faith is being proclaimed throughout the whole world.* 1:8

IMAGINE YOURSELF IN A COLLEGE speech course. Your assignment: a brief speech on "the meaning of life." Over late-night cups of coffee, you outline the Christian faith and what it means to you. You devote a lot of time to this assignment—after all, this speech may be the only clear expression of faith your classmates will ever hear.

But what if you were asked to write up the speech for your local paper? Instead of a few dozen listeners, you would have thousands of readers. Undoubtedly, you would devote even more time and care to preparation.

Letter to the Center of the World

Let your imagination run even further. How would you react if you were asked to adapt this same speech for a front-page story in the *New York Times*? This newspaper has sophisticated, demanding readers. In writing for them, you would meticulously pore over every word, polishing phrases and making sure your thoughts were complete and well-expressed.

You can see a similar process at work in the apostle Paul's various letters. Some of his letters were, like a college speech, addressed to a small cluster of people he knew by name. Often they consisted of warm, personal words of advice or even fatherly scolding.

But, *Romans* . . . the very title of this book conjures up images of the powerful empire that ruled the western world. To people of Paul's day, Rome was the center of the world in every way: law, culture, power, and learning. A letter to this sophisticated audience had to be impressive indeed.

In Romans, Paul brilliantly set down the whole scope of Christian doctrine, which, at that time, was still being passed along orally from town to town. Paul wanted to convince those demanding readers that Christ held the answers to all of life's important questions.

One-Volume Summary

Literary types are often asked questions like this: "What one book would you most want along if you were stranded on a deserted island?" (Victorian author G.K. Chesterton gave a classic reply: *"Thomas's Guide to Practical Shipbuilding"!*) If asked the same question about a single book of the Bible, many Christians would choose Romans. Compact enough to fit on one spread of a modern newspaper, Romans yet manages to encompass all essentials of the Christian faith.

Despite its thoroughness, however, Romans does not read like a dry book of theology. Great revivals in church history have been spawned by a study of this book. Augustine, Martin Luther, and John Wesley all trace their spiritual renewals to a reading of Romans. It gives the apostle Paul's final answer to questions about the "meaning of life."

How to Read Romans

Romans is a book to savor, slowly and carefully. Paul is developing an argument, and his logic unfolds thought by thought from the very first chapter. You may recognize many well-known verses in Romans; note these in their context as a part of Paul's overall presentation.

Romans divides into a clear outline. Chapters 1–3 introduce the book and give the need for the good news of the gospel. The end of chapter 3, called the "central theological passage in the Bible," compresses the core message in a brief paragraph. Chapters 4 and 5 expand on that message.

Romans 6–8 discuss the working out of the gospel in a Christian's life. Paul then pauses for three chapters (9–11) to link his argument to the Old Testament history of the Jews. From there, he proceeds to give practical advice on specific problems (12–16).

It will require time and concentration to grasp fully the teachings of Romans; few people would claim to have "mastered" this book. But it has no equal as a concise, reasonable statement of the Christian faith.

PEOPLE YOU'LL MEET IN ROMANS

PAUL *(p. 1224)*

3-TRACK READING PLAN

For an explanation and complete listing of the 3-track reading plan, turn to page 7.

TRACK 1: *Two-Week Courses on the Bible*
The Track 1 reading program on the Life and Teachings of Paul includes three chapters from Romans. See page 7 for a complete listing of this course.

TRACK 2: *An Overview of Romans in 4 Days*
☐ Day 1. Read the Introduction to Romans and then read chapter 3 as a summary of the whole book. Take your time as you read the end, verses 21–31.
☐ Day 2. Read of Paul's struggles against sin in chapter 7.
☐ Day 3. Paul concludes this great section on the Christian life with the triumphant message of chapter 8.
☐ Day 4. Paul gets practical toward the end of the book. Read his direct instructions on how to live in chapter 12.

Now turn to page 9 for your next Track 2 reading project.

TRACK 3: *All of Romans in 14 Days*
After you have read through Romans, turn to pages 10–14 for your next Track 3 reading project.
☐1   ☐2   ☐3   ☐4   ☐5   ☐6   ☐7   ☐8
☐9   ☐10   ☐11   ☐12–13 ☐14   ☐15–16

The Gospel Exalted

1 Paul, a bond-servant of Christ Jesus, called *as* an apostle, set apart for the gospel of God,

2 which He promised beforehand through His prophets in the holy Scriptures,

3 concerning His Son, who was born of a descendant of David according to the flesh,

4 who was declared the Son of God with power [a]by the resurrection from the dead, according to the Spirit of holiness, Jesus Christ our Lord,

5 through whom we have received grace and apostleship to bring about *the* obedience of faith among all the Gentiles for His name's sake,

6 among whom you also are the called of Jesus Christ;

7 ¶ to all who are beloved of God in Rome, called *as* saints: Grace to you and peace from God our Father and the Lord Jesus Christ.

8 ¶ First, I thank my God through Jesus Christ for you all, because your faith is being proclaimed throughout the whole world.

9 For God, whom I serve in my spirit in the *preaching of the* gospel of His Son, is my witness *as to* how unceasingly I make mention of you,

10 always in my prayers making request, if perhaps now at last by the will of God I may succeed in coming to you.

11 For I long to see you so that I may impart some spiritual gift to you, that you may be established;

12 that is, that I may be encouraged together with you *while* among you, each of us by the other's faith, both yours and mine.

[a] Or *as a result of*

13 I do not want you to be unaware, brethren, that often I have planned to come to you (and have been prevented so far) so that I may obtain some fruit among you also, even as among the rest of the Gentiles.

14 I am *a*under obligation both to Greeks and to barbarians, both to the wise and to the foolish.

15 So, for my part, I am eager to preach the gospel to you also who are in Rome.

16 ¶ For I am not ashamed of the gospel, for it is the power of God for salvation to everyone who believes, to the Jew first and also to the Greek.

17 For in it *the* righteousness of God is revealed from faith to faith; as it is written, "BUT THE RIGHTEOUS *man* SHALL LIVE BY FAITH."

1:17 Luther's Gateway

Verses 16–17, a capsule summary of Paul's message to the Romans, changed Martin Luther forever. After he finally understood the phrase "righteousness of God," Luther said, "I felt myself to be reborn and to have gone through open doors into paradise. The whole of Scripture took on a new meaning . . . . This passage of Paul became to me a gateway to heaven."

Unbelief and Its Consequences

18 ¶ For the wrath of God is revealed from heaven against all ungodliness and unrighteousness of men who suppress the truth in unrighteousness,

19 because that which is known about God is evident within them; for God made it evident to them.

20 For since the creation of the world His invisible attributes, His eternal power and divine nature, have been clearly seen, being understood through what has been made, so that they are without excuse.

21 For even though they knew God, they did not *b*honor Him as God or give thanks, but they

1:20 No Excuses

From Adam and Eve onward, people have tended to blame others, not themselves, for what goes wrong. Romans 1–3 sets forth an important principle that has been widely recognized by recovery groups such as Alcoholics Anonymous: Unless you first accept responsibility for wrong behavior and stop blaming others, you'll never get well.

became futile in their speculations, and their foolish heart was darkened.

22 Professing to be wise, they became fools,

23 and exchanged the glory of the incorruptible God for an image in the form of corruptible man and of birds and four-footed animals and *c*crawling creatures.

24 ¶ Therefore God gave them over in the lusts of their hearts to impurity, so that their bodies would be dishonored among them.

25 For they exchanged the truth of God for a lie, and worshiped and served the creature rather than the Creator, who is blessed forever. Amen.

26 ¶ For this reason God gave them over to degrading passions; for their women exchanged the natural function for that which is unnatural,

27 and in the same way also the men abandoned the natural function of the woman and burned in their desire toward one another, men with men committing indecent acts and receiving in their own persons the due penalty of their error.

28 ¶ And just as they did not see fit to acknowledge God any longer, God gave them over to a depraved mind, to do those things which are not proper,

29 being filled with all unrighteousness, wickedness, greed, evil; full of envy, murder, strife, deceit, malice; *they are* gossips,

30 slanderers, haters of God, insolent, arrogant, boastful, inventors of evil, disobedient to parents,

31 without understanding, untrustworthy, unloving, unmerciful;

32 and although they know the ordinance of God, that those who practice such things are worthy of death, they not only do the same, but also give hearty approval to those who practice them.

The Impartiality of God

2 Therefore you have no excuse, everyone of you who passes judgment, for in that which you judge another, you condemn yourself; for you who judge practice the same things.

2:1 Unsettling Proverbs

"It takes one to know one." "The pot calls the kettle black." Or, as the Spanish say, "The donkey calls the pig 'long ears.'" All these proverbs echo Paul's point: We often criticize in others the very thing we ourselves say or do.

2 And we know that the judgment of God rightly falls upon those who practice such things.

3 But do you suppose this, O man, when you pass judgment on those who practice such things and do the same *yourself,* that you will escape the judgment of God?

---

a Lit *debtor*   *b* Lit *glorify*   *c* Or *reptiles*

4 Or do you think lightly of the riches of His kindness and tolerance and patience, not knowing that the kindness of God leads you to repentance? 5 But because of your stubbornness and unrepentant heart you are storing up wrath for yourself in the day of wrath and revelation of the righteous judgment of God, 6 who WILL RENDER TO EACH PERSON ACCORDING TO HIS DEEDS: 7 to those who by perseverance in doing good seek for glory and honor and immortality, eternal life; 8 but to those who are selfishly ambitious and do not obey the truth, but obey unrighteousness, wrath and indignation. 9 *There will be* tribulation and distress for every soul of man who does evil, of the Jew first and also of the Greek, 10 but glory and honor and peace to everyone who does good, to the Jew first and also to the Greek. 11 For there is no partiality with God.

12 ¶ For all who have sinned without the Law will also perish without the Law, and all who have sinned under the Law will be judged by the Law;

13 for *it is* not the hearers of the Law *who* are just before God, but the doers of the Law will be justified. 14 For when Gentiles who do not have the Law do instinctively the things of the Law, these, not having the Law, are a law to themselves, 15 in that they show the work of the Law written in their hearts, their conscience bearing witness and their thoughts alternately accusing or else defending them, 16 on the day when, according to my gospel, God will judge the secrets of men through Christ Jesus.

The Jew Is Condemned by the Law

17 ¶ But if you bear the name "Jew" and rely upon the Law and boast in God, 18 and know *His* will and approve the things that are essential, being instructed out of the Law, 19 and are confident that you yourself are a guide to the blind, a light to those who are in darkness, 20 a corrector of the foolish, a teacher of the immature, having in the Law the embodiment of knowledge and of the truth,

PAUL *Turnaround*

THOUGH PAUL BEGAN HIS CAREER as a fanatical enemy of Christianity, he became its greatest leader. After Jesus, he is unquestionably the most important person in the New Testament. Paul was not just an activist committed to the cause, and not just a theologian thinking deep thoughts about God. He was *both*—and his passionate, committed life still serves as a model.

Unlike the twelve apostles, Paul started out with status and education. He was born a Roman citizen, a rare and precious privilege for any Jew. Paul's fluent Greek writings show him to be a man of the world, well versed in secular literature.

Fundamentally, though, Paul saw himself as a devout Jew. He had studied theology in Jerusalem under the famous rabbi Gamaliel. He joined the campaign to arrest, imprison and even execute Christians because he believed they were blaspheming God by worshiping a man, and he was determined to stamp out such heresy.

Jesus' searing appearance on the road to Damascus turned Paul's life upside down (Acts 9:1–19). In one of the most dramatic conversions ever, Paul became the very thing he had so hated—a Christian. Paul later wrote to the Philippian believers, "For to me, to live is Christ" (Philippians 1:21). Nobody could doubt it. A passionate focus on Jesus shines through every line he wrote and was the reason for every mile he traveled. He remains what every Christian means by "Christ-centered."

Some years passed, though, before Paul found his role. He discovered it in Antioch, an important Roman city in modern-day Turkey, where the first sizable congregation of non-Jewish Christians sprang up. From then on Paul was every inch a missionary, taking the Good News about Jesus to the whole world. He traveled almost incessantly, moving from city to city around the Mediterranean Sea, preaching to both Jews and Gentiles.

Paul's life was marked with excitement: a shipwreck, a snakebite, beatings, narrow escapes. He started many churches, and thirteen letters of the New Testament have his name on them—all of them addressing problems in those first churches.

Though Paul never stopped thinking of himself as a devout Jew, he spent much of his life explaining that Jews and Gentiles were equally loved by God. Many people talk about racial reconciliation. Paul was one of the first to fight for it. He struggled hard against those who wanted Gentiles to submit to the whole Jewish law. Non-Jewish Christians, he was determined, should be considered first-class citizens of the kingdom of God. Faith in Jesus was all that God required.

Life Questions: To what role does God call you? How does your pursuit of that compare with the apostle Paul's?

21 you, therefore, who teach another, do you not teach yourself? You who preach that one shall not steal, do you steal?

22 You who say that one should not commit adultery, do you commit adultery? You who abhor idols, do you rob temples?

23 You who boast in the Law, through your breaking the Law, do you dishonor God?

24 For "THE NAME OF GOD IS BLASPHEMED AMONG THE GENTILES BECAUSE OF YOU," just as it is written.

25 ¶ For indeed circumcision is of value if you practice the Law; but if you are a transgressor of the Law, your circumcision has become uncircumcision.

26 So if the uncircumcised man keeps the requirements of the Law, will not his uncircumcision be regarded as circumcision?

27 And he who is physically uncircumcised, if he keeps the Law, will he not judge you who though having the letter *of the Law* and circumcision are a transgressor of the Law?

28 For he is not a Jew who is one outwardly, nor is circumcision that which is outward in the flesh.

29 But he is a Jew who is one inwardly; and circumcision is that which is of the heart, by the Spirit, not by the letter; and his praise is not from men, but from God.

All the World Guilty

3 Then what advantage has the Jew? Or what is the benefit of circumcision?

2 Great in every respect. First of all, that they were entrusted with the oracles of God.

3 What then? If some did not believe, their unbelief will not nullify the faithfulness of God, will it?

4 May it never be! Rather, let God be found true, though every man *be found* a liar, as it is written,

"THAT YOU MAY BE JUSTIFIED IN YOUR WORDS,
AND PREVAIL WHEN YOU ARE JUDGED."

5 But if our unrighteousness demonstrates the righteousness of God, what shall we say? The God who inflicts wrath is not unrighteous, is He? (I am speaking in human terms.)

6 May it never be! For otherwise, how will God judge the world?

7 But if through my lie the truth of God abounded to His glory, why am I also still being judged as a sinner?

8 And why not *say* (as we are slanderously reported and as some claim that we say), "Let us do evil that good may come"? Their condemnation is just.

9 ¶ What then? Are we better than they? Not at all; for we have already charged that both Jews and Greeks are all under sin;

10 as it is written,

"THERE IS NONE RIGHTEOUS, NOT EVEN ONE;
11 THERE IS NONE WHO UNDERSTANDS,
THERE IS NONE WHO SEEKS FOR GOD;
12 ALL HAVE TURNED ASIDE, TOGETHER THEY HAVE BECOME USELESS;

3:10–18 Need for a Cure

If a doctor suddenly appeared on a television news program announcing, in an excited voice, a cure for the Paraguayan flu, who would notice? For his discovery to impress us so deeply that we would seek vaccination, he would first need to prove the terrible danger of the unknown virus.

Paul's message in Romans is the great news about God's amazing grace: A complete cure is available to all. But people won't seek a cure until they know they are ill. Thus, Romans begins with one of the darkest descriptions in the Bible. Paul concludes, "There is none righteous, not even one." The entire world is doomed to spiritual death unless a cure can be found.

THERE IS NONE WHO DOES GOOD,
THERE IS NOT EVEN ONE."
13 "THEIR THROAT IS AN OPEN GRAVE,
WITH THEIR TONGUES THEY KEEP DECEIVING,"
"THE POISON OF ASPS IS UNDER THEIR LIPS";
14 "WHOSE MOUTH IS FULL OF CURSING AND BITTERNESS";
15 "THEIR FEET ARE SWIFT TO SHED BLOOD,
16 DESTRUCTION AND MISERY ARE IN THEIR PATHS,
17 AND THE PATH OF PEACE THEY HAVE NOT KNOWN."
18 "THERE IS NO FEAR OF GOD BEFORE THEIR EYES."

19 ¶ Now we know that whatever the Law says, it speaks to those who are under the Law, so that every mouth may be closed and all the world may become accountable to God;

20 because by the works of the Law no flesh will be justified in His sight; for through the Law *comes* the knowledge of sin.

Justification by Faith

21 ¶ But now apart from the Law *the* righteousness of God has been manifested, being witnessed by the Law and the Prophets,

22 even *the* righteousness of God through faith in Jesus Christ for all those who believe; for there is no distinction;

23 for all have sinned and fall short of the glory of God,

24 being justified as a gift by His grace through the redemption which is in Christ Jesus;

25 whom God displayed publicly as a propitia-

tion in His blood through faith. *This was* to demonstrate His righteousness, because in the forbearance of God He passed over the sins previously committed;

26 for the demonstration, *I say*, of His righteousness at the present time, so that He would be just and the justifier of the one who has faith in Jesus.

27 ¶ Where then is boasting? It is excluded. By what kind of law? Of works? No, but by a law of faith.

28 For we maintain that a man is justified by faith apart from works of the Law.

29 Or is God *the God* of Jews only? Is He not *the God* of Gentiles also? Yes, of Gentiles also,

30 since indeed God who will justify the circumcised by faith and the uncircumcised through faith is one.

31 ¶ Do we then nullify the Law through faith? May it never be! On the contrary, we establish the Law.

Justification by Faith Evidenced in Old Testament

4 What then shall we say that Abraham, our forefather according to the flesh, has found?

2 For if Abraham was justified by works, he has something to boast about, but not before God.

3 For what does the Scripture say? "ABRAHAM BELIEVED GOD, AND IT WAS CREDITED TO HIM AS RIGHTEOUSNESS."

4 Now to the one who works, his wage is not credited as a favor, but as what is due.

5 But to the one who does not work, but believes in Him who justifies the ungodly, his faith is credited as righteousness,

6 just as David also speaks of the blessing on the man to whom God credits righteousness apart from works:

7 "BLESSED ARE THOSE WHOSE LAWLESS DEEDS
    HAVE BEEN FORGIVEN,
AND WHOSE SINS HAVE BEEN COVERED.

8 "BLESSED IS THE MAN WHOSE SIN THE LORD
    WILL NOT TAKE INTO ACCOUNT."

9 ¶ Is this blessing then on the circumcised, or on the uncircumcised also? For we say, "FAITH WAS CREDITED TO ABRAHAM AS RIGHTEOUSNESS."

10 How then was it credited? While he was circumcised, or uncircumcised? Not while circumcised, but while uncircumcised;

11 and he received the sign of circumcision, a seal of the righteousness of the faith which he had while uncircumcised, so that he might be the father of all who believe without being circumcised, that righteousness might be credited to them,

12 and the father of circumcision to those who not only are of the circumcision, but who also follow in the steps of the faith of our father Abraham which he had while uncircumcised.

13 ¶ For the promise to Abraham or to his descendants that he would be heir of the world was not through the Law, but through the righteousness of faith.

14 For if those who are of the Law are heirs, faith is made void and the promise is nullified;

4:13 How to Please God

Paul goes to great lengths in chapter 4 to make a theological point. He traces the Jewish heritage back to Abraham, who lived hundreds of years before Moses and the Old Testament law. Abraham, says Paul, pleased God exactly as we do: through faith. The Old Testament law was never meant to bridge the gap between God and people. Only Jesus Christ could do that. Paul stresses that the law was given not to bring about redemption, but to point up the need for it (5:20).

15 for the Law brings about wrath, but where there is no law, there also is no violation.

16 ¶ For this reason *it is* by faith, in order that *it may be* in accordance with grace, so that the promise will be guaranteed to all the descendants, not only to those who are of the Law, but also to those who are of the faith of Abraham, who is the father of us all,

17 (as it is written, "A FATHER OF MANY NATIONS HAVE I MADE YOU") in the presence of Him whom he believed, *even* God, who gives life to the dead and calls into being that which does not exist.

18 In hope against hope he believed, so that he might become a father of many nations according to that which had been spoken, "SO SHALL YOUR DESCENDANTS BE."

19 Without becoming weak in faith he contemplated his own body, now as good as dead since he was about a hundred years old, and the deadness of Sarah's womb;

20 yet, with respect to the promise of God, he did not waver in unbelief but grew strong in faith, giving glory to God,

21 and being fully assured that what God had promised, He was able also to perform.

22 Therefore IT WAS ALSO CREDITED TO HIM AS RIGHTEOUSNESS.

23 Now not for his sake only was it written that it was credited to him,

24 but for our sake also, to whom it will be credited, as those who believe in Him who raised Jesus our Lord from the dead,

25 *He* who was delivered over because of our transgressions, and was raised because of our justification.

Results of Justification

5 Therefore, having been justified by faith, we have peace with God through our Lord Jesus Christ,

A Modern Peace Child

God spans the gulf

> For one will hardly die for a righteous man; though perhaps for the good man someone would dare even to die. But God demonstrates His own love toward us, in that while we were yet sinners, Christ died for us.
> 5:7–8

DON RICHARDSON SPENT SEVERAL FRUSTRATING years among the Sawi tribe in New Guinea. He had come from America as an anthropologist/missionary, hoping to bring the Christian message to a nearly stone-age tribe. But his message kept colliding with the tribe's unusual beliefs.

Christian values of love and forgiveness had no appeal to the Sawi, for they held up deceit as the highest virtue. They saw no reason to change their patterns of cruelty and cannibalism. In fact, when Richardson told them the story of Jesus, only one incident sparked their interest: the story of Judas's betrayal! To the Sawi, Judas was a genuine hero; he had shrewdly penetrated the trusted inner circle of disciples before turning against Jesus.

A Mysterious Ceremony

Every time Richardson tried to share Christ with the Sawi, the attempt miscarried. Finally, after watching the fourteenth bloody battle fought outside his home, Richardson reached the end of his patience. How could he ever break through to such violent people? He decided to leave New Guinea, despite the Sawi's pleas that he stay.

Just before Richardson left, the Sawi and their deadly enemies, the Haenam tribe, staged an elaborate ceremony in front of his home. It was their final effort to convince the missionary to stay.

The entire village gathered to watch the event. All were silent except the Sawi chief's wife. She screamed loudly as the chief seized their six-month-old baby from her arms and held him high in the air. The chief then carried his son to the enemy chief and gave him to his enemies. A member of the tribe explained to Richardson that the Haenam tribe would rename the baby and rear him as one of its own.

Breakthrough

Richardson knew that no Sawi could be fully trusted, since any action might be part of an elaborate deception. But that memorable day he learned of the one great exception: the peace child. A chief's giving his own son to his enemies—that profound, painful act would overcome all suspicion. By mutual agreement, as long as the peace child lived, no wars could be fought between the two tribes.

Something clicked in Don Richardson's mind as he watched the spectacle. At last he had found an analogy—a parallel story—built into the Sawi's culture that could convey the message of a forgiving God. He gathered members of the tribe around him and, with a pounding heart and dry throat, told them of God's peace child. God had sent his own Son, Jesus, to live among enemies, to make peace with humankind.

A Key Passage

Perhaps Paul felt that same pounding heart and dry throat as he presented in 11 concise verses, Romans 3:21–31, the meaning of God's offering of his peace child Jesus. The first part of Romans spelled out the vast gulf between God and people. Now Paul describes how God spanned this gulf. Some have called this section "the central theological passage in the Bible."

After stating the facts, Paul backs them up with historical proofs in chapters 4 and 5. American politicians often defend their positions by appealing to founding fathers, men like George Washington and Abraham Lincoln. Similarly, Paul keeps his Jewish audience in mind. He supports his concepts by citing Abraham, Moses, and even Adam.

Christ's death, says Paul, was not a new idea, an addition to the Old Testament law. Rather, it was the completion of the law, what the Old Testament implied and foreshadowed. Like the Sawi, the Jewish culture had its own "redemptive analogies"; and they all found true fulfillment in Jesus Christ.

Life Questions: Have you ever felt far from God? Does Romans 3–5 say anything that might help during those times?

2 through whom also we have obtained our introduction by faith into this grace in which we stand; and we exult in hope of the glory of God.

3 And not only this, but we also exult in

5:1 What It's There For

In Romans, Paul constructs a step-by-step argument much like a legal brief, as shown by his frequent use of the legalese word "therefore" (20 times in all). Step one: No one is righteous and we all need help (3:20); Step two: God has provided that help in the form of his Son, making peace with us (5:11); Step three: Therefore God no longer condemns those who are in Christ (8:1).

our tribulations, knowing that tribulation brings about perseverance;

4 and perseverance, proven character; and proven character, hope;

5 and hope does not disappoint, because the love of God has been poured out within our hearts through the Holy Spirit who was given to us.

6 ¶ For while we were still helpless, at the right time Christ died for the ungodly.

7 For one will hardly die for a righteous man; though perhaps for the good man someone would dare even to die.

8 But God demonstrates His own love toward us, in that while we were yet sinners, Christ died for us.

9 Much more then, having now been justified by His blood, we shall be saved from the wrath *of God* through Him.

10 For if while we were enemies we were reconciled to God through the death of His Son, much more, having been reconciled, we shall be saved by His life.

11 And not only this, but we also exult in God through our Lord Jesus Christ, through whom we have now received the reconciliation.

12 ¶ Therefore, just as through one man sin entered into the world, and death through sin, and so death spread to all men, because all sinned—

13 for until the Law sin was in the world, but sin is not imputed when there is no law.

14 Nevertheless death reigned from Adam until Moses, even over those who had not sinned in the likeness of the offense of Adam, who is a ªtype of Him who was to come.

15 ¶ But the free gift is not like the transgression. For if by the transgression of the one the many died, much more did the grace of God and the gift by the grace of the one Man, Jesus Christ, abound to the many.

16 The gift is not like *that which came* through the one who sinned; for on the one hand the judg-

ment *arose* from one *transgression* resulting in condemnation, but on the other hand the free gift *arose* from many transgressions resulting in justification.

17 For if by the transgression of the one, death reigned through the one, much more those who receive the abundance of grace and of the gift of righteousness will reign in life through the One, Jesus Christ.

18 ¶ So then as through one transgression there resulted condemnation to all men, even so through one act of righteousness there resulted justification of life to all men.

19 For as through the one man's disobedience the many were made sinners, even so through the obedience of the One the many will be made righteous.

20 The Law came in so that the transgression would increase; but where sin increased, grace abounded all the more,

21 so that, as sin reigned in death, even so grace would reign through righteousness to eternal life through Jesus Christ our Lord.

Believers Are Dead to Sin, Alive to God

6 What shall we say then? Are we to continue in sin so that grace may increase?

6:1 More Sin, More Forgiveness?

Paul often uses this writing technique: He pauses in the middle of an argument to answer objections or questions that may be occurring to the reader. Some people have actually reached the conclusion that horrifies Paul in this passage. The Russian monk Rasputin, for example, concluded, "I'll sin more to earn more forgiveness." He lived a bizarre life of immorality.

2 May it never be! How shall we who died to sin still live in it?

3 Or do you not know that all of us who have been baptized into Christ Jesus have been baptized into His death?

4 Therefore we have been buried with Him through baptism into death, so that as Christ was raised from the dead through the glory of the Father, so we too might walk in newness of life.

5 For if we have become united with *Him* in the likeness of His death, certainly we shall also be *in the likeness* of His resurrection,

6 knowing this, that our old self was crucified with *Him,* in order that our body of sin might be done away with, so that we would no longer be slaves to sin;

7 for he who has died is freed from sin.

ª Or *foreshadowing*

8 ¶ Now if we have died with Christ, we believe that we shall also live with Him,

9 knowing that Christ, having been raised from the dead, is never to die again; death no longer is master over Him.

10 For the death that He died, He died to sin once for all; but the life that He lives, He lives to God.

11 Even so consider yourselves to be dead to sin, but alive to God in Christ Jesus.

12 ¶ Therefore do not let sin reign in your mortal body so that you obey its lusts,

13 and do not go on presenting the members of your body to sin *as* instruments of unrighteousness; but present yourselves to God as those alive from the dead, and your members *as* instruments of righteousness to God.

14 For sin shall not be master over you, for you are not under law but under grace.

15 ¶ What then? Shall we sin because we are not under law but under grace? May it never be!

16 Do you not know that when you present yourselves to someone *as* slaves for obedience, you are slaves of the one whom you obey, either of sin resulting in death, or of obedience resulting in righteousness?

17 But thanks be to God that though you were slaves of sin, you became obedient from the heart to that form of teaching to which you were committed,

18 and having been freed from sin, you became slaves of righteousness.

19 I am speaking in human terms because of the weakness of your flesh. For just as you presented your members as slaves to impurity and to lawlessness, resulting in *further* lawlessness, so now present your members as slaves to righteousness, resulting in sanctification.

20 ¶ For when you were slaves of sin, you were free in regard to righteousness.

21 Therefore what benefit were you then deriving from the things of which you are now ashamed? For the outcome of those things is death.

22 But now having been freed from sin and enslaved to God, you derive your benefit, resulting in sanctification, and the outcome, eternal life.

23 For the wages of sin is death, but the free gift of God is eternal life in Christ Jesus our Lord.

Believers United to Christ

7 Or do you not know, brethren (for I am speaking to those who know the law), that the law has jurisdiction over a person as long as he lives?

2 For the married woman is bound by law to her husband while he is living; but if her husband dies, she is released from the law concerning the husband.

3 So then, if while her husband is living she is joined to another man, she shall be called an adulteress; but if her husband dies, she is free from the law, so that she is not an adulteress though she is joined to another man.

4 ¶ Therefore, my brethren, you also were made to die to the Law through the body of Christ, so that you might be joined to another, to Him who was raised from the dead, in order that we might bear fruit for God.

5 For while we were in the flesh, the sinful passions, which were *aroused* by the Law, were at work in the members of our body to bear fruit for death.

6 But now we have been released from the Law, having died to that by which we were bound, so that we serve in newness of the [a]Spirit and not in oldness of the letter.

7 ¶ What shall we say then? Is the Law sin? May it never be! On the contrary, I would not have come to know sin except through the Law; for I would not have known about coveting if the Law had not said, "YOU SHALL NOT COVET."

7:7 Hidden Dangers

A strict disciplinarian like Paul had little trouble keeping most of the Ten Commandments. Outward actions such as swearing, murder, adultery, stealing, and lying could be measured and controlled. But the internal, invisible sin of coveting proved far more bedeviling. As Jesus made clear in the Sermon on the Mount, invisible sins like coveting, lust, and anger can have the same toxic effects as the more outward manifestations of stealing, adultery, and murder.

8 But sin, taking opportunity through the commandment, produced in me coveting of every kind; for apart from the Law sin *is* dead.

9 I was once alive apart from the Law; but when the commandment came, sin became alive and I died;

10 and this commandment, which was to result in life, proved to result in death for me;

11 for sin, taking an opportunity through the commandment, deceived me and through it killed me.

12 So then, the Law is holy, and the commandment is holy and righteous and good.

13 ¶ Therefore did that which is good become *a cause of* death for me? May it never be! Rather it was sin, in order that it might be shown to be sin by effecting my death through that which is good, so that through the commandment sin would become utterly sinful.

The Conflict of Two Natures

14 ¶ For we know that the Law is spiritual, but I am of flesh, sold into bondage to sin.

15 For what I am doing, I do not understand; for I am not practicing what I *would* like to *do*, but I am doing the very thing I hate.

16 But if I do the very thing I do not want *to do*, I agree with the Law, *confessing* that the Law is good.

17 So now, no longer am I the one doing it, but sin which dwells in me.

18 For I know that nothing good dwells in me, that is, in my flesh; for the willing is present in me, but the doing of the good *is* not.

19 For the good that I want, I do not do, but I practice the very evil that I do not want.

20 But if I am doing the very thing I do not want, I am no longer the one doing it, but sin which dwells in me.

21 ¶ I find then the principle that evil is present in me, the one who wants to do good.

22 For I joyfully concur with the law of God in the inner man,

23 but I see a different law in the members of my body, waging war against the law of my mind and making me a prisoner of the law of sin which is in my members.

24 Wretched man that I am! Who will set me free from the body of this death?

25 Thanks be to God through Jesus Christ our Lord! So then, on the one hand I myself with my mind am serving the law of God, but on the other, with my flesh the law of sin.

Deliverance from Bondage

8 Therefore there is now no condemnation for those who are in Christ Jesus.

2 For the law of the Spirit of life in Christ Jesus has set you free from the law of sin and of death.

3 For what the Law could not do, weak as it was through the flesh, God *did*: sending His own

Inner Struggles
A battle, and a victory

THE FIRST PART OF ROMANS paints a grand picture of God's grace and forgiveness, so grand that Paul opens himself up to some tricky questions. "I think I like what I'm hearing," a devious person may exclaim as he or she finishes the first part of Romans. "The more I sin, the more opportunity God has to forgive me, right? Then I can live any way I want!"

> *I find then the principle that evil is present in me, the one who wants to do good.*
> *7:21*

In chapter 6, Paul reacts to the "Now I have an excuse to sin" line of thinking with shock and outrage. And then he turns to practical issues in the Christian life. Why is it that sin is so hard to overcome? Does God forgive every sin, no matter how bad? What really happens when we become Christians? Do we change or don't we?

Illustrations from Life

When Paul was trying to be a good person (by keeping all the law) in his own strength, he was ultimately defeated by the sin problem. Although his intentions were good, he was attempting to win the battle over sin by his own plan and ability. There is only one solution to that kind of struggle. Paul concludes at the end, "Wretched man that I am! Who will set me free from the body of this death? Thanks be to God through Jesus Christ our Lord!" (7:24–25a).

The very best proof of the Christian faith is a believer with a changed life. Paul calls Christians to "consider yourselves to be dead to sin, but alive to God in Christ Jesus" (6:11), and he wrote as if this were really possible!

A Final Answer

Then, like a gust of fresh air, chapter 8 follows with one of the most hopeful passages in the Bible. The Holy Spirit is its theme, and Paul defines the Spirit's role in our lives. The Spirit works alongside us as we relate to God, even praying for us when we don't know what to ask (8:26). Mainly, the Spirit teaches us the benefits of being a child of God.

Conflict won't disappear completely yet, says Paul, for we are part of a "groaning," imperfect creation (8:18–25). But with God working for us, we can be *more than* conquerors, and one day God will make all of creation perfect again. That promise should assure us that nothing can separate us from God's love (8:38–39).

Life Questions: Which person do you identify with—the one who is struggling to please God on personal strength alone, or the one who is trusting in Christ for victory over sin?

Son in the likeness of sinful flesh and *as an offering for sin*, He condemned sin in the flesh,

4 so that the requirement of the Law might be fulfilled in us, who do not walk according to the flesh but according to the Spirit.

5 For those who are according to the flesh set their minds on the things of the flesh, but those who are according to the Spirit, the things of the Spirit.

6 For the mind set on the flesh is death, but the mind set on the Spirit is life and peace,

7 because the mind set on the flesh is hostile toward God; for it does not subject itself to the law of God, for it is not even able *to do so*,

8 and those who are in the flesh cannot please God.

9 ¶ However, you are not in the flesh but in the Spirit, if indeed the Spirit of God dwells in you. But if anyone does not have the Spirit of Christ, he does not belong to Him.

10 If Christ is in you, though the body is dead because of sin, yet the spirit is alive because of righteousness.

11 But if the Spirit of Him who raised Jesus from the dead dwells in you, He who raised Christ Jesus from the dead will also give life to your mortal bodies *a*through His Spirit who dwells in you.

12 ¶ So then, brethren, we are under obligation, not to the flesh, to live according to the flesh—

13 for if you are living according to the flesh, you must die; but if by the Spirit you are putting to death the deeds of the body, you will live.

14 For all who are being led by the Spirit of God, these are sons of God.

15 For you have not received a spirit of slavery leading to fear again, but you have received a spirit of adoption as sons by which we cry out, "Abba! Father!"

16 The Spirit Himself testifies with our spirit that we are children of God,

17 and if children, heirs also, heirs of God and fellow heirs with Christ, if indeed we suffer with *Him* so that we may also be glorified with *Him*.

18 ¶ For I consider that the sufferings of this present time are not worthy to be compared with the glory that is to be revealed to us.

19 For the anxious longing of the creation waits eagerly for the revealing of the sons of God.

20 For the creation was subjected to futility, not willingly, but because of Him who subjected it, *b*in hope

21 that the creation itself also will be set free from its slavery to corruption into the freedom of the glory of the children of God.

22 For we know that the whole creation groans and suffers the pains of childbirth together until now.

23 And not only this, but also we ourselves, having the first fruits of the Spirit, even we ourselves groan within ourselves, waiting eagerly for *our* adoption as sons, the redemption of our body.

24 For in hope we have been saved, but hope

8:18 Worth the Struggle

Paul never minimizes suffering; after all, his own life included beatings, imprisonment, shipwrecks, assassination attempts, and chronic illness. But he insists with absolute conviction that future rewards will outweigh all present sufferings.

Olympic athletes endure years of eight-hour practice sessions and much discipline and pain for the goal of winning a gold medal. Similarly, the Christian's life on earth may involve many difficulties (verses 22–23), but the end result will make them seem worthwhile.

that is seen is not hope; for who hopes for what he *already* sees?

25 But if we hope for what we do not see, with perseverance we wait eagerly for it.

Our Victory in Christ

26 ¶ In the same way the Spirit also helps our weakness; for we do not know how to pray as we should, but the Spirit Himself intercedes for *us* with groanings too deep for words;

27 and He who searches the hearts knows what the mind of the Spirit is, because He intercedes for the saints according to *the will of* God.

28 ¶ And we know that *c*God causes all things to work together for good to those who love God, to those who are called according to *His* purpose.

8:28 Only Good Things?

This famous verse is often misquoted or stretched to mean more than it says. It should be read along with the next two paragraphs. Paul doesn't promise that only good, or pleasurable, things will come to the Christian. What he does say is that even the difficult experiences described in verses 35–39 can be used in God's overall plan for good. And nothing can separate us from the love of God.

29 For those whom He foreknew, He also predestined *to become* conformed to the image of His Son, so that He would be the firstborn among many brethren;

30 and these whom He predestined, He also called; and these whom He called, He also justi-

---

a One early ms reads *because of*   *b* Or *in hope; because the creation*   *c* One early ms reads *all things work together for good* fied; and these whom He justified, He also glorified.

31 ¶ What then shall we say to these things? If God *is* for us, who *is* against us?

32 He who did not spare His own Son, but delivered Him over for us all, how will He not also with Him freely give us all things?

33 Who will bring a charge against God's elect? God is the one who justifies;

34 who is the one who condemns? Christ Jesus is He who died, yes, rather who was [a]raised, who is at the right hand of God, who also intercedes for us.

35 Who will separate us from the love of [b]Christ? Will tribulation, or distress, or persecution, or famine, or nakedness, or peril, or sword?

36 Just as it is written,

"FOR YOUR SAKE WE ARE BEING PUT TO
    DEATH ALL DAY LONG;
WE WERE CONSIDERED AS SHEEP TO BE
    SLAUGHTERED."

37 But in all these things we overwhelmingly conquer through Him who loved us.

38 For I am convinced that neither death, nor life, nor angels, nor principalities, nor things present, nor things to come, nor powers,

39 nor height, nor depth, nor any other created thing, will be able to separate us from the love of God, which is in Christ Jesus our Lord.

Solicitude for Israel

9 I am telling the truth in Christ, I am not lying, my conscience testifies with me in the Holy Spirit,

2 that I have great sorrow and unceasing grief in my heart.

3 For I could wish that I myself were accursed, *separated* from Christ for the sake of my brethren, my kinsmen according to the flesh,

4 who are Israelites, to whom belongs the adoption as sons, and the glory and the covenants and the giving of the Law and the *temple* service and the promises,

5 whose are the fathers, and from whom is the Christ according to the flesh, who is over all, God blessed forever. Amen.

6 ¶ But *it is* not as though the word of God has failed. For they are not all Israel who are *descended* from Israel;

7 nor are they all children because they are Abraham's descendants, but: "THROUGH ISAAC YOUR DESCENDANTS WILL BE NAMED."

8 That is, it is not the children of the flesh who are children of God, but the children of the promise are regarded as descendants.

9 For this is the word of promise: "AT THIS TIME I WILL COME, AND SARAH SHALL HAVE A SON."

10 And not only this, but there was Rebekah

[a] One early ms reads *raised from the dead*   [b] Two early mss read *God*

A Crushing Blow to Paul
Does God break his promises?

> *I have great sorrow and unceasing grief in my heart.* **9:2**

DOES ANYTHING BRING MORE PAIN to a new Christian than family rejection? A teenager converts to Christianity. Her parents overreact, assuming their daughter has fallen for some weird cult. They slap away all her attempts to present the appealing facts of the gospel. What is good news for her is seen as bad news by the family.

Some new Christians can melt down the walls of suspicion and hostility. But others are treated like diseased persons by other family members and forced to live in a state of emotional quarantine.

Anyone who has lived through such an experience can understand the agonizing dilemma Paul faced. Members of his own race, the Jews, were rejecting the gospel he had committed his life to.

Can God Be Trusted?

Rejection by the Jews was a crushing blow to Paul, and he interrupted his letter to the Romans to consider the dilemma. These three chapters (9–11) contain some of his strongest words ever, including an offer to forfeit his own relationship with Christ for the sake of his race (9:3).

The issues discussed here apply to non-Jews as well, for they raise basic questions about God. Had he given up on the Jewish people, ignoring the promises he made to them in Old Testament times? If so, couldn't he also break promises made to us today?

For Paul, a Jew who called himself an apostle to the Gentiles, no other issue was so important to resolve. He couldn't rest until he linked the brilliant theology set forth in Romans to God's past, present, and future activity among the Jews.

Life Questions: Romans 9–11 explains how God worked with people disappointed in him: the Jews. Have you ever been deeply disappointed in God? What does Paul say that might help answer your questions?

also, when she had conceived *twins* by one man, our father Isaac;

11 for though *the twins* were not yet born and had not done anything good or bad, so that God's purpose according to *His* choice would stand, not because of works but because of Him who calls,

12 it was said to her, "THE OLDER WILL SERVE THE YOUNGER."

13 Just as it is written, "JACOB I LOVED, BUT ESAU I HATED."

14 ¶ What shall we say then? There is no injustice with God, is there? May it never be!

15 For He says to Moses, "I WILL HAVE MERCY ON WHOM I HAVE MERCY, AND I WILL HAVE COMPASSION ON WHOM I HAVE COMPASSION."

16 So then it *does* not *depend* on the man who wills or the man who runs, but on God who has mercy.

17 For the Scripture says to Pharaoh, "FOR THIS VERY PURPOSE I RAISED YOU UP, TO DEMONSTRATE MY POWER IN YOU, AND THAT MY NAME MIGHT BE PROCLAIMED THROUGHOUT THE WHOLE EARTH."

18 So then He has mercy on whom He desires, and He hardens whom He desires.

19 ¶ You will say to me then, "Why does He still find fault? For who resists His will?"

9:19 Questions, Anyone?

Frequently Paul interrupts his writing with a question or series of questions. In doing so, he is imitating the style he learned from rabbis in his earlier training. The story is told of one student who asked, "Why do you rabbis so often put your teaching in the form of a question?" The reply: "So what's wrong with a question?"

20 On the contrary, who are you, O man, who answers back to God? The thing molded will not say to the molder, "Why did you make me like this," will it?

21 Or does not the potter have a right over the clay, to make from the same lump one vessel for honorable use and another for common use?

22 What if God, although willing to demonstrate His wrath and to make His power known, endured with much patience vessels of wrath prepared for destruction?

23 And *He did so* to make known the riches of His glory upon vessels of mercy, which He prepared beforehand for glory,

24 *even* us, whom He also called, not from among Jews only, but also from among Gentiles.

25 As He says also in Hosea,
"I WILL CALL THOSE WHO WERE NOT MY
    PEOPLE, 'MY PEOPLE,'
AND HER WHO WAS NOT BELOVED,
    'BELOVED.' "

26 "AND IT SHALL BE THAT IN THE PLACE
    WHERE IT WAS SAID TO THEM, 'YOU
    ARE NOT MY PEOPLE,'
THERE THEY SHALL BE CALLED SONS OF THE
    LIVING GOD."

27 ¶ Isaiah cries out concerning Israel, "THOUGH THE NUMBER OF THE SONS OF ISRAEL BE LIKE THE SAND OF THE SEA, IT IS THE REMNANT THAT WILL BE SAVED;

28 FOR THE LORD WILL EXECUTE HIS WORD ON THE EARTH, THOROUGHLY AND QUICKLY."

29 And just as Isaiah foretold,
"UNLESS THE LORD OF SABAOTH HAD LEFT
    TO US A POSTERITY,
WE WOULD HAVE BECOME LIKE SODOM,
    AND WOULD HAVE RESEMBLED
    GOMORRAH."

30 ¶ What shall we say then? That Gentiles, who did not pursue righteousness, attained righteousness, even the righteousness which is by faith;

31 but Israel, pursuing a law of righteousness, did not arrive at *that* law.

32 Why? Because *they did* not *pursue it* by faith, but as though *it were* by works. They stumbled over the stumbling stone,

33 just as it is written,
"BEHOLD, I LAY IN ZION A STONE OF
    STUMBLING AND A ROCK OF OFFENSE,
AND HE WHO BELIEVES IN HIM WILL NOT
    BE DISAPPOINTED."

The Word of Faith Brings Salvation

10 Brethren, my heart's desire and my prayer to God for them is for *their* salvation.

2 For I testify about them that they have a zeal for God, but not in accordance with knowledge.

3 For not knowing about God's righteousness and seeking to establish their own, they did not subject themselves to the righteousness of God.

4 For Christ is the end of the law for righteousness to everyone who believes.

5 ¶ For Moses writes that the man who practices the righteousness which is based on law shall live by that righteousness.

6 But the righteousness based on faith speaks as follows: "DO NOT SAY IN YOUR HEART, 'WHO WILL ASCEND INTO HEAVEN?' (that is, to bring Christ down),

7 or 'WHO WILL DESCEND INTO THE ABYSS?' (that is, to bring Christ up from the dead)."

8 But what does it say? "THE WORD IS NEAR YOU, in your mouth and in your heart"—that is, the word of faith which we are preaching,

9 that if you confess with your mouth Jesus *as* Lord, and believe in your heart that God raised Him from the dead, you will be saved;

10 for with the heart a person believes, resulting in righteousness, and with the mouth he confesses, resulting in salvation.

11 For the Scripture says, "WHOEVER BELIEVES IN HIM WILL NOT BE DISAPPOINTED."

12 For there is no distinction between Jew and Greek; for the same *Lord* is Lord of all, abounding in riches for all who call on Him;

13 for "WHOEVER WILL CALL ON THE NAME OF THE LORD WILL BE SAVED."

14 ¶ How then will they call on Him in whom they have not believed? How will they believe in Him whom they have not heard? And how will they hear without a preacher?

15 How will they preach unless they are sent? Just as it is written, "HOW BEAUTIFUL ARE THE FEET OF THOSE WHO BRING GOOD NEWS OF GOOD THINGS!"

16 ¶ However, they did not all heed the good news; for Isaiah says, "LORD, WHO HAS BELIEVED OUR REPORT?"

17 So faith *comes* from hearing, and hearing by the word of Christ.

18 ¶ But I say, surely they have never heard, have they? Indeed they have;

"THEIR VOICE HAS GONE OUT INTO ALL THE
EARTH,
AND THEIR WORDS TO THE ENDS OF THE
WORLD."

19 But I say, surely Israel did not know, did they? First Moses says,

"I WILL MAKE YOU JEALOUS BY THAT WHICH
IS NOT A NATION,
BY A NATION WITHOUT UNDERSTANDING
WILL I ANGER YOU."

20 And Isaiah is very bold and says,

"I WAS FOUND BY THOSE WHO DID NOT
SEEK ME,
I BECAME MANIFEST TO THOSE WHO DID
NOT ASK FOR ME."

21 But as for Israel He says, "ALL THE DAY LONG I HAVE STRETCHED OUT MY HANDS TO A DISOBEDI-ENT AND OBSTINATE PEOPLE."

Israel Is Not Cast Away

11 I say then, God has not rejected His people, has He? May it never be! For I too am an Israelite, a descendant of Abraham, of the tribe of Benjamin.

2 God has not rejected His people whom He foreknew. Or do you not know what the Scripture says in *the passage about* Elijah, how he pleads with God against Israel?

3 "Lord, THEY HAVE KILLED YOUR PROPHETS, THEY HAVE TORN DOWN YOUR ALTARS, AND I ALONE AM LEFT, AND THEY ARE SEEKING MY LIFE."

4 But what is the divine response to him? "I HAVE KEPT for Myself SEVEN THOUSAND MEN WHO HAVE NOT BOWED THE KNEE TO BAAL."

5 In the same way then, there has also come to be at the present time a remnant according to *God's* gracious choice.

6 But if it is by grace, it is no longer on the basis of works, otherwise grace is no longer grace.

7 ¶ What then? What Israel is seeking, it has not obtained, but those who were chosen obtained it, and the rest were hardened;

8 just as it is written,

"GOD GAVE THEM A SPIRIT OF STUPOR,
EYES TO SEE NOT AND EARS TO HEAR NOT,
DOWN TO THIS VERY DAY."

9 And David says,

"LET THEIR TABLE BECOME A SNARE AND A
TRAP,
AND A STUMBLING BLOCK AND A
RETRIBUTION TO THEM.

10 "LET THEIR EYES BE DARKENED TO SEE NOT,
AND BEND THEIR BACKS FOREVER."

11 ¶ I say then, they did not stumble so as to fall, did they? May it never be! But by their trans-gression salvation *has come* to the Gentiles, to make them jealous.

11:11 The Future of the Jews

In chapters 9 and 10, Paul painfully admits that, on the whole, the Jews did not believe in Christ. Despite all the advantages of Old Testament history, they "stumbled over the 'stumbling stone' " (9:32). In chapter 11, Paul goes back over that history and asks whether it was futile. Will the Jews come to believe in Christ some day? Did their tragic experience produce any advantage for the rest of the world? This chapter clearly shows God's eternal love for his chosen people. Paul concludes with a poetic outburst, celebrating God's mysterious ways of working on earth.

12 Now if their transgression is riches for the world and their failure is riches for the Gentiles, how much more will their fulfillment be!

13 But I am speaking to you who are Gentiles. Inasmuch then as I am an apostle of Gentiles, I magnify my ministry,

14 if somehow I might move to jealousy my fellow countrymen and save some of them.

15 For if their rejection is the reconciliation of the world, what will *their* acceptance be but life from the dead?

16 If the first piece *of dough* is holy, the lump is also; and if the root is holy, the branches are too.

17 ¶ But if some of the branches were broken off, and you, being a wild olive, were grafted in among them and became partaker with them of the rich root of the olive tree,

18 do not be arrogant toward the branches; but if you are arrogant, *remember that* it is not you who supports the root, but the root *supports* you.

19 You will say then, "Branches were broken off so that I might be grafted in."

20 Quite right, they were broken off for their unbelief, but you stand by your faith. Do not be conceited, but fear;

21 for if God did not spare the natural branches, He will not spare you, either.

22 Behold then the kindness and severity of God; to those who fell, severity, but to you, God's kindness, if you continue in His kindness; otherwise you also will be cut off.

23 And they also, if they do not continue in their unbelief, will be grafted in, for God is able to graft them in again.

24 For if you were cut off from what is by nature a wild olive tree, and were grafted contrary to nature into a cultivated olive tree, how much more will these who are the natural *branches* be grafted into their own olive tree?

11:17 Unnatural Botany

Botanists and orchard growers commonly use grafting to improve their stock of flowers and fruit. Usually they graft a weaker, cultivated branch onto a wild but sturdy root stock. Paul admits that "contrary to nature" God has grafted the wild branches (Gentiles) onto the cultivated roots (Jews)—a reverse technique sometimes used to reinvigorate an olive tree.

25 ¶ For I do not want you, brethren, to be uninformed of this mystery—so that you will not be wise in your own estimation—that a partial hardening has happened to Israel until the fullness of the Gentiles has come in;

26 and so all Israel will be saved; just as it is written,

"THE DELIVERER WILL COME FROM ZION,
HE WILL REMOVE UNGODLINESS FROM
JACOB."

27 "THIS IS MY COVENANT WITH THEM,
WHEN I TAKE AWAY THEIR SINS."

28 From the standpoint of the gospel they are enemies for your sake, but from the standpoint of *God's* choice they are beloved for the sake of the fathers;

29 for the gifts and the calling of God are irrevocable.

30 For just as you once were disobedient to God, but now have been shown mercy because of their disobedience,

31 so these also now have been disobedient, that because of the mercy shown to you they also may now be shown mercy.

32 For God has shut up all in disobedience so that He may show mercy to all.

33 ¶ Oh, the depth of the riches both of the wisdom and knowledge of God! How unsearchable are His judgments and unfathomable His ways!

34 For WHO HAS KNOWN THE MIND OF THE LORD, OR WHO BECAME HIS COUNSELOR?

35 Or WHO HAS FIRST GIVEN TO HIM THAT IT MIGHT BE PAID BACK TO HIM AGAIN?

36 For from Him and through Him and to Him are all things. To Him *be* the glory forever. Amen.

Dedicated Service

12 Therefore I urge you, brethren, by the mercies of God, to present your bodies a living and holy sacrifice, acceptable to God, *which is* your spiritual service of worship.

2 And do not be conformed to this world, but be transformed by the renewing of your mind, so that you may prove what the will of God is, that which is good and acceptable and perfect.

3 ¶ For through the grace given to me I say to everyone among you not to think more highly of himself than he ought to think; but to think so as to have sound judgment, as God has allotted to each a measure of faith.

4 For just as we have many members in one body and all the members do not have the same function,

5 so we, who are many, are one body in Christ, and individually members one of another.

6 Since we have gifts that differ according to the grace given to us, *each of us is to exercise them accordingly*: if prophecy, according to the proportion of his faith;

7 if service, in his serving; or he who teaches, in his teaching;

8 or he who exhorts, in his exhortation; he who gives, with *a*liberality; he who leads, with diligence; he who shows mercy, with cheerfulness.

9 ¶ *Let* love *be* without hypocrisy. Abhor what is evil; cling to what is good.

10 *Be* devoted to one another in brotherly love; give preference to one another in honor;

11 not lagging behind in diligence, fervent in spirit, serving the Lord;

12 rejoicing in hope, persevering in tribulation, devoted to prayer,

13 contributing to the needs of the saints, practicing hospitality.

14 ¶ Bless those who persecute *b*you; bless and do not curse.

15 Rejoice with those who rejoice, and weep with those who weep.

16 Be of the same mind toward one another; do not be haughty in mind, but associate with the lowly. Do not be wise in your own estimation.

17 Never pay back evil for evil to anyone. Respect what is right in the sight of all men.

18 If possible, so far as it depends on you, be at peace with all men.

19 Never take your own revenge, beloved, but leave room for the wrath *of God,* for it is written, "VENGEANCE IS MINE, I WILL REPAY," says the Lord.

20 "BUT IF YOUR ENEMY IS HUNGRY, FEED HIM,

a Or *simplicity*   *b* Two early mss do not contain *you*

AND IF HE IS THIRSTY, GIVE HIM A DRINK; FOR IN SO DOING YOU WILL HEAP BURNING COALS ON HIS HEAD."

21 Do not be overcome by evil, but overcome evil with good.

Be Subject to Government

13 Every person is to be in subjection to the governing authorities. For there is no authority except from God, and those which exist are established by God.

13:1 Christians and the Empire

For most of his ministry, Paul benefited from the legal protection of the Roman empire. The first generation of Christians received the same freedom of worship and legal protection as did the Jews. But soon emperors such as Nero vengefully turned on Christians, torturing and murdering thousands of them, probably including Paul himself. History shows that most of them followed Paul's difficult advice in this passage, refusing to revolt against the government no matter how hostile it became.

2 Therefore whoever resists authority has opposed the ordinance of God; and they who have opposed will receive condemnation upon themselves.

3 For rulers are not a cause of fear for good behavior, but for evil. Do you want to have no fear of authority? Do what is good and you will have praise from the same;

4 for it is a minister of God to you for good. But if you do what is evil, be afraid; for it does not bear the sword for nothing; for it is a minister of God, an avenger who brings wrath on the one who practices evil.

5 Therefore it is necessary to be in subjection, not only because of wrath, but also for conscience' sake.

6 For because of this you also pay taxes, for *rulers* are servants of God, devoting themselves to this very thing.

7 Render to all what is due them: tax to whom tax *is due*; custom to whom custom; fear to whom fear; honor to whom honor.

8 ¶ Owe nothing to anyone except to love one another; for he who loves his neighbor has fulfilled *the* law.

9 For this, "YOU SHALL NOT COMMIT ADULTERY, YOU SHALL NOT MURDER, YOU SHALL NOT STEAL, YOU SHALL NOT COVET," and if there is any other commandment, it is summed up in this saying, "YOU SHALL LOVE YOUR NEIGHBOR AS YOURSELF."

10 Love does no wrong to a neighbor; therefore love is the fulfillment of *the* law.

11 ¶ *Do* this, knowing the time, that it is already the hour for you to awaken from sleep; for

Down-To-Earth Problems

When Christians disagree about what's right and wrong

> Abhor what is evil; cling to what is good. 12:9

TOO OFTEN THEOLOGY IS VIEWED as stuff for hermits and marooned shipwreck victims. When there's nothing else to do, *then* is the time to ask abstract questions about God.

Such a notion would surely have exasperated the apostle Paul. To him, theology *was* worthless unless it made a difference in how people lived. Therefore, he concluded the most concise theological book in the Bible with a down-to-earth discussion of contemporary problems.

Revolutionaries and Weaker Brothers

The issue of politics surfaces in Romans (13:1–7). How should a Christian relate to government? In Paul's day, when Christians were living under Nero's tyrannical regime, that question was hotly debated, as it still is in our revolution-oriented era.

Christians in Rome were also disagreeing on what was proper behavior for a Christian (14:1–15:4). One person was sure another was sinning; but that "offender" was convinced his accuser was hopelessly narrow-minded. Who was right? The specific issues change with each culture, but Paul's guidelines on the proper attitudes apply to all.

Paul did not live as an intellectual recluse. He applied his theology to life, practicing what he preached. In fact, the lofty book of Romans was written while he was out raising money for famine victims in Jerusalem (15:25–27).

Life Questions: Christians in Paul's day hotly debated such issues as eating meat, celebrating holidays, and drinking wine. What issues do Christians debate today? What attitude should we have toward Christians we differ with?

now [a]salvation is nearer to us than when we believed.

12 The night is almost gone, and the day is near. Therefore let us lay aside the deeds of darkness and put on the armor of light.

13 Let us behave properly as in the day, not in carousing and drunkenness, not in sexual promiscuity and sensuality, not in strife and jealousy.

14 But put on the Lord Jesus Christ, and make no provision for the flesh in regard to *its* lusts.

Principles of Conscience

14 Now accept the one who is weak in faith, *but* not for *the purpose of* passing judgment on his opinions.

2 One person has faith that he may eat all things, but he who is weak eats vegetables *only*.

14:2 Weak or Strong?

According to Paul, a weaker brother is a new believer who needs many rules and regulations. Christians in Paul's day debated such issues as vegetarianism, eating meat sacrificed to idols, and celebrating pagan festival days. Paul's advice to both weak and strong Christians of his day applies to people in all cultures who debate questionable issues. Elsewhere, Paul speaks to legalists: "strong" Christians who nevertheless insist on many rules and regulations (see Colossians 2:16–23).

3 The one who eats is not to regard with contempt the one who does not eat, and the one who does not eat is not to judge the one who eats, for God has accepted him.

4 Who are you to judge the servant of another? To his own master he stands or falls; and he will stand, for the Lord is able to make him stand.

5 ¶ One person regards one day above another, another regards every day *alike*. Each person must be fully convinced in his own mind.

6 He who observes the day, observes it for the Lord, and he who eats, does so for the Lord, for he gives thanks to God; and he who eats not, for the Lord he does not eat, and gives thanks to God.

7 For not one of us lives for himself, and not one dies for himself;

8 for if we live, we live for the Lord, or if we die, we die for the Lord; therefore whether we live or die, we are the Lord's.

9 For to this end Christ died and lived again, that He might be Lord both of the dead and of the living.

10 ¶ But you, why do you judge your brother? Or you again, why do you regard your brother with contempt? For we will all stand before the judgment seat of God.

11 For it is written,

"AS I LIVE, SAYS THE LORD, EVERY KNEE
    SHALL BOW TO ME,
AND EVERY TONGUE SHALL GIVE PRAISE
    TO GOD."

12 So then each one of us will give an account of himself to God.

13 ¶ Therefore let us not judge one another anymore, but rather determine this—not to put an obstacle or a stumbling block in a brother's way.

14 I know and am convinced in the Lord Jesus that nothing is unclean in itself; but to him who thinks anything to be unclean, to him it is unclean.

15 For if because of food your brother is hurt, you are no longer walking according to love. Do not destroy with your food him for whom Christ died.

16 Therefore do not let what is for you a good thing be spoken of as evil;

17 for the kingdom of God is not eating and drinking, but righteousness and peace and joy in the Holy Spirit.

18 For he who in this *way* serves Christ is acceptable to God and approved by men.

19 So then [b]we pursue the things which make for peace and the building up of one another.

20 Do not tear down the work of God for the sake of food. All things indeed are clean, but they are evil for the man who eats and gives offense.

21 It is good not to eat meat or to drink wine, or *to do anything* by which your brother stumbles.

22 The faith which you have, have as your own conviction before God. Happy is he who does not condemn himself in what he approves.

23 But he who doubts is condemned if he eats, because *his eating is* not from faith; and whatever is not from faith is sin.

Self-denial on Behalf of Others

15 Now we who are strong ought to bear the weaknesses of those without strength and not *just* please ourselves.

2 Each of us is to please his neighbor for his good, to his edification.

3 For even Christ did not please Himself; but as it is written, "THE REPROACHES OF THOSE WHO REPROACHED YOU FELL ON ME."

4 For whatever was written in earlier times was written for our instruction, so that through perseverance and the encouragement of the Scriptures we might have hope.

5 Now may the God who gives perseverance and encouragement grant you to be of the same mind with one another according to Christ Jesus,

6 so that with one accord you may with one voice glorify the God and Father of our Lord Jesus Christ.

7 ¶ Therefore, accept one another, just as Christ also accepted us to the glory of God.

---

[a] Or *our salvation is nearer than when*   [b] Later mss read *let us pursue*

8 For I say that Christ has become a servant to the circumcision on behalf of the truth of God to confirm the promises *given* to the fathers,

9 and for the Gentiles to glorify God for His mercy; as it is written,

"THEREFORE I WILL GIVE PRAISE TO YOU
AMONG THE GENTILES,
AND I WILL SING TO YOUR NAME."

10 Again he says,

"REJOICE, O GENTILES, WITH HIS PEOPLE."

11 And again,

"PRAISE THE LORD ALL YOU GENTILES,
AND LET ALL THE PEOPLES PRAISE HIM."

12 Again Isaiah says,

"THERE SHALL COME THE ROOT OF JESSE,
AND HE WHO ARISES TO RULE OVER THE
GENTILES,
IN HIM SHALL THE GENTILES HOPE."

13 Now may the God of hope fill you with all joy and peace in believing, so that you will abound in hope by the power of the Holy Spirit.

14 ¶ And concerning you, my brethren, I myself also am convinced that you yourselves are full of goodness, filled with all knowledge and able also to admonish one another.

15 But I have written very boldly to you on some points so as to remind you again, because of the grace that was given me from God,

16 to be a minister of Christ Jesus to the Gentiles, ministering as a priest the gospel of God, so that *my* offering of the Gentiles may become acceptable, sanctified by the Holy Spirit.

17 Therefore in Christ Jesus I have found reason for boasting in things pertaining to God.

18 For I will not presume to speak of anything except what Christ has accomplished through me, resulting in the obedience of the Gentiles by word and deed,

19 in the power of signs and wonders, in the power of the Spirit; so that from Jerusalem and round about as far as Illyricum I have fully preached the gospel of Christ.

20 And thus I aspired to preach the gospel, not where Christ was *already* named, so that I would not build on another man's foundation;

21 but as it is written,

"THEY WHO HAD NO NEWS OF HIM
SHALL SEE,
AND THEY WHO HAVE NOT HEARD SHALL
UNDERSTAND."

22 ¶ For this reason I have often been prevented from coming to you;

23 but now, with no further place for me in these regions, and since I have had for many years a longing to come to you

24 whenever I go to Spain—for I hope to see you in passing, and to be helped on my way there by you, when I have first enjoyed your company for a while—

25 but now, I am going to Jerusalem serving the saints.

26 For Macedonia and Achaia have been pleased to make a contribution for the poor among the saints in Jerusalem.

27 Yes, they were pleased *to do so*, and they are

15:26 Paul the Fund-raiser

Paul wrote Romans while traveling to raise funds for famine relief. Another letter (2 Corinthians 8) gives more details on this mercy mission on behalf of the Jews in Jerusalem. Paul's actions set an example of unity for a church composed of both Jews and Gentiles—unity sorely needed by groups racked by the divisions described in chapter 14.

indebted to them. For if the Gentiles have shared in their spiritual things, they are indebted to minister to them also in material things.

28 Therefore, when I have finished this, and have put my seal on this fruit of theirs, I will go on by way of you to Spain.

29 I know that when I come to you, I will come in the fullness of the blessing of Christ.

30 ¶ Now I urge you, brethren, by our Lord Jesus Christ and by the love of the Spirit, to strive together with me in your prayers to God for me,

31 that I may be rescued from those who are disobedient in Judea, and *that* my service for Jerusalem may prove acceptable to the saints;

32 so that I may come to you in joy by the will of God and find *refreshing* rest in your company.

33 Now the God of peace be with you all. Amen.

Greetings and Love Expressed

16 I commend to you our sister Phoebe, who is a servant of the church which is at Cenchrea;

2 that you receive her in the Lord in a manner worthy of the saints, and that you help her in whatever matter she may have need of you; for she herself has also been a helper of many, and of myself as well.

3 ¶ Greet Prisca and Aquila, my fellow workers in Christ Jesus,

4 who for my life risked their own necks, to whom not only do I give thanks, but also all the churches of the Gentiles;

5 also *greet* the church that is in their house. Greet Epaenetus, my beloved, who is the first convert to Christ from Asia.

6 Greet Mary, who has worked hard for you.

7 Greet Andronicus and Junias, my kinsmen and my fellow prisoners, who are outstanding among the apostles, who also were in Christ before me.

8 Greet Ampliatus, my beloved in the Lord.

9 Greet Urbanus, our fellow worker in Christ, and Stachys my beloved.

10 Greet Apelles, the approved in Christ. Greet those who are of the *household* of Aristobulus.

11 Greet Herodion, my kinsman. Greet those of the *household* of Narcissus, who are in the Lord.

12 Greet Tryphaena and Tryphosa, workers in the Lord. Greet Persis the beloved, who has worked hard in the Lord.

13 Greet Rufus, a choice man in the Lord, also his mother and mine.

14 Greet Asyncritus, Phlegon, Hermes, Patrobas, Hermas and the brethren with them.

15 Greet Philologus and Julia, Nereus and his sister, and Olympas, and all the saints who are with them.

16 Greet one another with a holy kiss. All the churches of Christ greet you.

17 ¶ Now I urge you, brethren, keep your eye on those who cause dissensions and hindrances contrary to the teaching which you learned, and turn away from them.

18 For such men are slaves, not of our Lord Christ but of their own appetites; and by their smooth and flattering speech they deceive the hearts of the unsuspecting.

19 For the report of your obedience has reached to all; therefore I am rejoicing over you, but I want you to be wise in what is good and innocent in what is evil.

20 The God of peace will soon crush Satan under your feet.

¶ The grace of our Lord Jesus be with you.

21 ¶ Timothy my fellow worker greets you, and *so do* Lucius and Jason and Sosipater, my kinsmen.

22 ¶ I, Tertius, who write this letter, greet you in the Lord.

23 ¶ Gaius, host to me and to the whole church, greets you. Erastus, the city treasurer greets you, and Quartus, the brother.

24 [*a*The grace of our Lord Jesus Christ be with you all. Amen.]

16:23 Paul's Friends

This chapter contains a fascinating list of Paul's friends and co-workers, many of whom would be unknown apart from their mention here. Although Paul himself had not yet visited Rome, a Christian community had taken root in the imperial capital. The list includes prominent women in the church (Phoebe, Prisca, Junias, Tryphaena, Tryphosa, Persis), common slave names (Ampliatus, Urbanus, Stachys, Apelles), and possible royalty (the household of Aristobulus—probably the grandson of Herod the Great).

Paul was writing from Corinth, where his friends included the city's director of public works. At Corinth archaeologists have dug up a block of stone that may refer to this man: It bears the Latin inscription "Erastus, commissioner of public works, bore the expense of this pavement."

25 ¶ Now to Him who is able to establish you according to my gospel and the preaching of Jesus Christ, according to the revelation of the mystery which has been kept secret for long ages past,

26 but now is manifested, and by the Scriptures of the prophets, according to the commandment of the eternal God, has been made known to all the nations, *leading* to obedience of faith;

27 to the only wise God, through Jesus Christ, be the glory forever. Amen.

a Early mss do not contain this v

1 CORINTHIANS

The Last Place to Start a Church
No one expected much from crazy Corinth

EVERY LARGE CITY HAS ONE pocket where prostitutes, strippers, gamblers, and drug dealers hang out. Tourists stroll by to gawk at the sights. In New York, it's Times Square; in San Francisco, the North Beach district; in New Orleans, Bourbon Street; and in Las Vegas, it's virtually anywhere.

In the ancient world, the whole city of Corinth was known for that kind of lifestyle. Romans made the Corinthians the butt of dirty jokes, and playwrights consistently portrayed them as drunken brawlers. The Greek verb "to Corinthianize" meant to live shamelessly and immorally.

A Wide-Open City

Everyone knew what the Corinthians worshiped: money and the kinky things it could buy. Money flowed freely, for Corinth straddled one of the Roman empire's most vital trade routes. When a ship wrecked nearby, salvage companies housed the hapless sailors at inflated prices while they scrambled to auction off the ship's cargo. The city was a sprawling open-air market, filled with slaves, Orientals, Jews, Greeks, Egyptians, sailors, athletes, gamblers, and charioteers.

Yet Corinth was no blue-collar town. It had a population of 700,000, second only to Rome's, and as the capital of a large province, the city hosted a parade of Roman diplomats and dignitaries. Its clever citizens showcased new "Corinthian" architecture and prided themselves on having a cosmopolitan outlook.

For their religious ideal, the fun-loving Corinthians adopted Venus, the goddess of love. A temple built in her honor employed more than 1,000 prostitutes.

Paul Takes on the Corinthians

Due to all these influences, Corinth loomed as the one city "least likely to convert" to the Christian faith. What crazy cults and new religions did spring up there quickly gave in to the prevailing good-time atmosphere.

The mighty Paul, reeling from one of his most difficult missionary assignments in Athens, came to Corinth "in weakness and in fear and in much trembling" (2:3). He knew its strategic importance: If the gospel could take root there, it could transplant anywhere—and probably would, considering Corinth's crossroads location.

Paul worked in Corinth for 18 months. To everyone's surprise , the church he founded became one of the largest in the first century. But several years later he heard reports that the church, true to its city's heritage, had broken out in a series of spiritual ills. The distressing news prompted the letter known as 1 Corinthians.

The tone of this letter differs drastically from the one that precedes it. If Romans was stylistically carved in stone, 1 Corinthians was dashed off in tears and anger. One of Paul's longest letters, it covers the greatest variety of topics, partly because the Corinthians added bizarre new twists to ethical issues. In it, Paul gives practical advice on a series of church problems as well as a fascinating glimpse into the personal lives of early Christians.

> For consider your calling, brethren, that there were not many wise according to the flesh, not many mighty, not many noble; but God has chosen the foolish things of the world to shame the wise, and God has chosen the weak things of the world to shame the things which are strong.
> 1:26–27

How to Read 1 Corinthians

To fully appreciate Paul's letters, keep in mind that they are personal correspondence. We are actually reading someone else's mail.

In 1 Corinthians a riled-up apostle gives direct, forthright advice to a troubled local church. Paul saw alarming trends at work, and he used his full literary powers to set its members on the right course. He tried sarcasm, emotional pleas, autobiography, poetry, and lengthy arguments.

First, you will encounter the problems that had been reported to Paul: divisions in the church, a case of incest, court cases, the abuse of Christian freedom, chaos in the worship services. Paul lunges into these problems early in the book. Then, beginning with chapter 7, he takes up some other problems the Corinthians had written him about: marriage and the single life, pagan festivals, behavior of women, spiritual gifts, and the resurrection of the dead.

This first letter to the Corinthians presents a foundation for practical Christian ethics. Use the boldface sectional headings throughout the book to locate those issues that especially trouble you. Not all the problems discussed will apply directly to modern situations. But the general principles underlying Paul's advice do apply. As you read, look for those principles behind Paul's arguments.

PEOPLE YOU'LL MEET IN 1 CORINTHIANS

APOLLOS *(p. 1245)*

3-TRACK READING PLAN

For an explanation and complete listing of the 3-track reading plan, turn to page 7.

TRACK 1: *Two-Week Courses on the Bible*
The Track 1 reading program on the Life and Teachings of Paul includes two chapters from 1 Corinthians. See page 7 for a complete listing of this course.

TRACK 2: *An Overview of 1 Corinthians in 2 Days*
The emotional tone of 1 Corinthians makes for exciting reading throughout, but two chapters especially can't be missed.
☐ Day 1. Read the Introduction to 1 Corinthians, then chapter 13. Paul is at the top of his literary form as he defines love in one of the most famous passages in all of literature.
☐ Day 2. Read chapter 15, a crucial passage on life after death and resurrection from the dead.

Now turn to page 9 for your next Track 2 reading project.

TRACK 3: *All of 1 Corinthians in 14 Days*
After you have read through 1 Corinthians, turn to pages 10–14 for your next Track 3 reading project.

☐1   ☐2   ☐3   ☐4–5   ☐6   ☐7   ☐8–9   ☐10
☐11   ☐12   ☐13   ☐14   ☐15   ☐16

Appeal to Unity

1 Paul, called *as* an apostle of Jesus Christ by the will of God, and Sosthenes our brother,

2 ¶ To the church of God which is at Corinth, to those who have been sanctified in Christ Jesus, saints by calling, with all who in every place call on the name of our Lord Jesus Christ, their *Lord* and ours:

3 ¶ Grace to you and peace from God our Father and the Lord Jesus Christ.

4 ¶ I thank [a]my God always concerning you for the grace of God which was given you in Christ Jesus,

5 that in everything you were enriched in Him, in all speech and all knowledge,

6 even as the testimony concerning Christ was confirmed in you,

7 so that you are not lacking in any gift, awaiting eagerly the revelation of our Lord Jesus Christ,

8 who will also confirm you to the end, blameless in the day of our Lord Jesus Christ.

9 God is faithful, through whom you were called into fellowship with His Son, Jesus Christ our Lord.

10 ¶ Now I exhort you, brethren, by the name of our Lord Jesus Christ, that you all agree and that there be no divisions among you, but that you be made complete in the same mind and in the same judgment.

11 For I have been informed concerning you, my brethren, by Chloe's *people*, that there are quarrels among you.

12 Now I mean this, that each one of you is saying, "I am of Paul," and "I of Apollos," and "I of Cephas," and "I of Christ."

13 Has Christ been divided? Paul was not crucified for you, was he? Or were you baptized in the name of Paul?

14 [b]I thank God that I baptized none of you except Crispus and Gaius,

15 so that no one would say you were baptized in my name.

16 Now I did baptize also the household of Stephanas; beyond that, I do not know whether I baptized any other.

17 For Christ did not send me to baptize, but to preach the gospel, not in cleverness of speech, so that the cross of Christ would not be made void.

The Wisdom of God

18 ¶ For the word of the cross is foolishness to those who are perishing, but to us who are being saved it is the power of God.

19 For it is written,
"I WILL DESTROY THE WISDOM OF THE WISE,
AND THE CLEVERNESS OF THE CLEVER I
WILL SET ASIDE."

20 Where is the wise man? Where is the scribe? Where is the debater of this age? Has not God made foolish the wisdom of the world?

21 For since in the wisdom of God the world through its wisdom did not *come to* know God, God was well-pleased through the foolishness of the message preached to save those who believe.

22 For indeed Jews ask for signs and Greeks search for wisdom;

23 but we preach [c]Christ crucified, to Jews a stumbling block and to Gentiles foolishness,

24 but to those who are the called, both Jews and Greeks, Christ the power of God and the wisdom of God.

25 Because the foolishness of God is wiser than men, and the weakness of God is stronger than men.

26 ¶ For consider your calling, brethren, that there were not many wise according to the flesh, not many mighty, not many noble;

27 but God has chosen the foolish things of the world to shame the wise, and God has chosen the weak things of the world to shame the things which are strong,

28 and the base things of the world and the despised God has chosen, the things that are not, so that He may nullify the things that are,

29 so that no man may boast before God.

30 But by His doing you are in Christ Jesus, who became to us wisdom from God, and righteousness and sanctification, and redemption,

31 so that, just as it is written, "LET HIM WHO BOASTS, BOAST IN THE LORD."

Paul's Reliance upon the Spirit

2 And when I came to you, brethren, I did not come with superiority of speech or of wisdom, proclaiming to you the [d]testimony of God.

2 For I determined to know nothing among you except Jesus Christ, and Him crucified.

3 I was with you in weakness and in fear and in much trembling,

4 and my message and my preaching were not

2:3 Paul at a Crossroads

This brief paragraph hints at a grave personal crisis in the apostle Paul's ministry, and Acts 16–18 gives important background. In three cities Paul saw a promising beginning crushed by fanatical Jews. Then in Athens he met little success in communicating to the intelligentsia. Many scholars believe that he reached Corinth shaken and discouraged and that he resolved to make Christ the sole subject of his teaching and preaching while there.

---

[a] Two early mss do not contain *my*   [b] Two early mss read *I give thanks that*   [c] I.e. Messiah   [d] One early ms reads *mystery*

in persuasive words of wisdom, but in demonstration of the Spirit and of power,

5 so that your faith would not rest on the wisdom of men, but on the power of God.

6 ¶ Yet we do speak wisdom among those who are mature; a wisdom, however, not of this age nor of the rulers of this age, who are passing away;

7 but we speak God's wisdom in a mystery, the hidden *wisdom* which God predestined before the ages to our glory;

8 *the wisdom* which none of the rulers of this age has understood; for if they had understood it they would not have crucified the Lord of glory;

9 but just as it is written,
"THINGS WHICH EYE HAS NOT SEEN AND EAR
    HAS NOT HEARD,
AND *which* HAVE NOT ENTERED THE HEART
    OF MAN,
ALL THAT GOD HAS PREPARED FOR THOSE
    WHO LOVE HIM."

10 *a*For to us God revealed *them* through the Spirit; for the Spirit searches all things, even the depths of God.

11 For who among men knows the *thoughts* of a man except the spirit of the man which is in him? Even so the *thoughts* of God no one knows except the Spirit of God.

12 Now we have received, not the spirit of the world, but the Spirit who is from God, so that we may know the things freely given to us by God,

13 which things we also speak, not in words taught by human wisdom, but in those taught by the Spirit, combining spiritual *thoughts* with spiritual *words*.

14 ¶ But a natural man does not accept the things of the Spirit of God, for they are foolishness to him; and he cannot understand them, because they are spiritually appraised.

15 But he who is spiritual appraises all things, yet he himself is appraised by no one.

16 For WHO HAS KNOWN THE MIND OF THE LORD, THAT HE WILL INSTRUCT HIM? But we have the mind of Christ.

Foundations for Living

3 And I, brethren, could not speak to you as to spiritual men, but as to men of flesh, as to infants in Christ.

2 I gave you milk to drink, not solid food; for you were not yet able *to receive it.* Indeed, even now you are not yet able,

3 for you are still fleshly. For since there is jealousy and strife among you, are you not fleshly, and are you not walking like mere men?

4 For when one says, "I am of Paul," and another, "I am of Apollos," are you not *mere* men?

5 ¶ What then is Apollos? And what is Paul?

Servants through whom you believed, even as the Lord gave *opportunity* to each one.

6 I planted, Apollos watered, but God was causing the growth.

3:5–9 Personality Cults

In this chapter, Paul expands on a theme first introduced in 1:12. Converts were lining up behind various church leaders: Peter, who had walked and talked with Christ on earth; Apollos, with his sophisticated, cultivated style; Paul, the famous missionary; and Christ himself. Paul had no tolerance for that kind of hero worship. He stressed vigorously that the Corinthians belonged only to God, not to any human worker.

7 So then neither the one who plants nor the one who waters is anything, but God who causes the growth.

8 Now he who plants and he who waters are one; but each will receive his own reward according to his own labor.

9 For we are God's fellow workers; you are God's field, God's building.

10 ¶ According to the grace of God which was given to me, like a wise master builder I laid a foundation, and another is building on it. But each man must be careful how he builds on it.

11 For no man can lay a foundation other than the one which is laid, which is Jesus Christ.

12 Now if any man builds on the foundation with gold, silver, precious stones, wood, hay, straw,

13 each man's work will become evident; for the day will show it because it is *to be* revealed with fire, and the fire itself will test the quality of each man's work.

14 If any man's work which he has built on it remains, he will receive a reward.

15 If any man's work is burned up, he will suffer loss; but he himself will be saved, yet so as through fire.

16 ¶ Do you not know that you are a temple of God and *that* the Spirit of God dwells in you?

17 If any man destroys the temple of God, God will destroy him, for the temple of God is holy, and that is what you are.

18 ¶ Let no man deceive himself. If any man among you thinks that he is wise in this age, he must become foolish, so that he may become wise.

19 For the wisdom of this world is foolishness before God. For it is written, "*He is* THE ONE WHO CATCHES THE WISE IN THEIR CRAFTINESS";

20 and again, "THE LORD KNOWS THE REASONINGS of the wise, THAT THEY ARE USELESS."

---

a One early ms reads But

21 So then let no one boast in men. For all things belong to you,

22 whether Paul or Apollos or Cephas or the world or life or death or things present or things to come; all things belong to you,

23 and you belong to Christ; and Christ belongs to God.

Servants of Christ

4 Let a man regard us in this manner, as servants of Christ and stewards of the mysteries of God.

2 In this case, moreover, it is required of stewards that one be found trustworthy.

3 But to me it is a very small thing that I may be examined by you, or by *any* human court; in fact, I do not even examine myself.

4 For I am conscious of nothing against myself, yet I am not by this acquitted; but the one who examines me is the Lord.

5 Therefore do not go on passing judgment before *a*the time, *but wait* until the Lord comes who will both bring to light the things hidden in

a I.e. the appointed time of judgment

the darkness and disclose the motives of *men's* hearts; and then each man's praise will come to him from God.

6 ¶ Now these things, brethren, I have figuratively applied to myself and Apollos for your sakes, so that in us you may learn not to exceed what is written, so that no one of you will become arrogant in behalf of one against the other.

7 For who regards you as superior? What do you have that you did not receive? And if you did receive it, why do you boast as if you had not received it?

8 ¶ You are already filled, you have already become rich, you have become kings without us; and indeed, *I* wish that you had become kings so that we also might reign with you.

9 For, I think, God has exhibited us apostles last of all, as men condemned to death; because we have become a spectacle to the world, both to angels and to men.

10 We are fools for Christ's sake, but you are prudent in Christ; we are weak, but you are

---

Like an Angry Letter from Home
A well-deserved scolding from a grieving "parent"

IMAGINE A COLLEGE FRESHMAN, STANDING in a corridor amid a swirl of chattering students. In two minutes the next class will begin. But, for her, time has stopped. She has just opened a tearstained, 12-page letter from her parents.

> I do not write these things to shame you, but to admonish you as my beloved children.
> 4:14

The tone of the letter takes her by surprise. Her parents are normally reserved, not given to emotional outbursts. Their letters are warm and friendly. Not this time. Somehow they have heard about her recent behavior on campus, and they are very hurt. In a torrent of words, they pour out their feelings for her and their equally deep disappointment.

First Corinthians reflects the same tone: it is an intimate, well-deserved scolding from a grieved parent. "I do not write these things to shame you," says Paul, "but to admonish you as my beloved children" (4:14).

Paul's Shifting Moods

No other letter in the New Testament reveals such a wide range of Paul's emotions. At his own financial expense, he had invested 18 risk-filled months in Corinth. But afterwards his rebellious "children" had launched personal attacks against him. Paul reacted like any parent first informed of his child's shocking behavior. His moods in 1 Corinthians bounce from anger to shame, from sorrow to indignation.

Chapter 3, for example, begins with a stern lecture to "infants in Christ." This leads to biting sarcasm (4:8), which melts into the tender pleas of a spiritual father. Six times in chapter 6 Paul asks, "Do you not know . . . ?" Finally, in chapter 7, he gets to the practical questions that had prompted his letter in the first place.

The apostle Paul was a superbly educated logician who could skillfully weave together history and philosophy. But he also brooded over his missionary churches like a parent. He asked the Corinthians pointedly, "Shall I come to you with a rod, or with love and a spirit of gentleness?" (4:21). In this letter, we see a little of both.

Life Questions: How do you react when someone—a parent, teacher, boss, pastor—tries to straighten you out?

strong; you are distinguished, but we are without honor.

11 To this present hour we are both hungry and thirsty, and are poorly clothed, and are roughly treated, and are homeless;

4:8–13 A Hint of Trials to Come

Paul's intense feelings come to the surface in this paragraph, as sharply worded as any in the New Testament. He alludes (verse 9) to the Roman practice of parading the gladiators condemned to death—a poignant reference in light of the martyr's fate that awaited him and other apostles.

12 and we toil, working with our own hands; when we are reviled, we bless; when we are persecuted, we endure;

13 when we are slandered, we try to conciliate; we have become as the scum of the world, the dregs of all things, *even* until now.

14 ¶ I do not write these things to shame you, but to admonish you as my beloved children.

15 For if you were to have countless tutors in Christ, yet *you would* not *have* many fathers, for in Christ Jesus I became your father through the gospel.

16 Therefore I exhort you, be imitators of me.

17 For this reason I have sent to you Timothy, who is my beloved and faithful child in the Lord, and he will remind you of my ways which are in Christ, just as I teach everywhere in every church.

18 Now some have become arrogant, as though I were not coming to you.

19 But I will come to you soon, if the Lord

a Two early mss do not contain *Jesus*

wills, and I shall find out, not the words of those who are arrogant but their power.

20 For the kingdom of God does not consist in words but in power.

21 What do you desire? Shall I come to you with a rod, or with love and a spirit of gentleness?

Immorality Rebuked

5 It is actually reported that there is immorality among you, and immorality of such a kind as does not exist even among the Gentiles, that someone has his father's wife.

2 You have become arrogant and have not mourned instead, so that the one who had done this deed would be removed from your midst.

3 ¶ For I, on my part, though absent in body but present in spirit, have already judged him who has so committed this, as though I were present.

4 In the name of our Lord Jesus, when you are assembled, and I with you in spirit, with the power of our Lord Jesus,

5 *I have decided* to deliver such a one to Satan for the destruction of his flesh, so that his spirit may be saved in the day of the Lord *a*Jesus.

5:5 Handed Over to Satan

The strong phrase used in this verse has a Biblical parallel in 1 Timothy 1:20. To Paul, expelling someone from the church and Christian privileges meant pushing them out into the world ruled by Satan. In both references, however, Paul stresses that the action was designed to teach the offender a lesson.

APOLLOS *Brimming with Confidence*

APOLLOS CAME ON THE SCENE at Ephesus like a whirlwind (Acts 18:24–26). He knew the Scriptures inside out and went immediately to the Jewish synagogue to present Jesus as their long-awaited Messiah. Apollos had a few things to learn (Priscilla and Aquila found it necessary to update his information privately), but he was fearless in telling what he knew.

Brimming with confidence, Apollos hailed from one of the largest, most cultured cities in the world. Alexandria in Egypt boasted a centuries-old university and library, and had a thriving, scholarly Jewish sector. It was in Alexandria that the Old Testament had been translated into Greek.

Apollos later traveled to Corinth, where he became an extremely effective leader in the church. Indeed, he made such an impact that a "pro-Apollos" faction gathered around him, threatening to split the church in two. The apostle Paul had to warn the Corinthians to stay together, rather than taking sides.

When Paul wrote this letter, Apollos apparently was with him (16:12). Paul urged Apollos to return to Corinth, but he declined. Divisions in the church were no doubt as troubling to Apollos as they were to Paul.

Life Questions: How can charismatic leaders avoid attracting attention to themselves rather than their message?

6 ¶ Your boasting is not good. Do you not know that a little leaven leavens the whole lump *of dough*?

7 Clean out the old leaven so that you may be a new lump, just as you are *in fact* unleavened. For Christ our Passover also has been sacrificed.

8 Therefore let us celebrate the feast, not with old leaven, nor with the leaven of malice and wickedness, but with the unleavened bread of sincerity and truth.

9 ¶ I wrote you in my letter not to associate with immoral people;

10 I *did* not at all *mean* with the immoral people of this world, or with the covetous and swindlers, or with idolaters, for then you would have to go out of the world.

11 But actually, I wrote to you not to associate with any so-called brother if he is an immoral person, or covetous, or an idolater, or a reviler, or a drunkard, or a swindler—not even to eat with such a one.

12 For what have I to do with judging outsiders? Do you not judge those who are within *the church*?

13 But those who are outside, God judges. REMOVE THE WICKED MAN FROM AMONG YOURSELVES.

Lawsuits Discouraged

6 Does any one of you, when he has a case against his neighbor, dare to go to law before the unrighteous and not before the saints?

2 Or do you not know that the saints will judge the world? If the world is judged by you, are you not competent *to constitute* the smallest law courts?

3 Do you not know that we will judge angels? How much more matters of this life?

4 So if you have law courts dealing with matters of this life, do you appoint them as judges who are of no account in the church?

5 I say *this* to your shame. *Is it* so, *that* there is not among you one wise man who will be able to decide between his brethren,

6 but brother goes to law with brother, and that before unbelievers?

7 ¶ Actually, then, it is already a defeat for you, that you have lawsuits with one another. Why not rather be wronged? Why not rather be defrauded?

8 On the contrary, you yourselves wrong and defraud. *You do* this even to *your* brethren.

9 ¶ Or do you not know that the unrighteous will not inherit the kingdom of God? Do not be deceived; neither fornicators, nor idolaters, nor adulterers, nor [a]effeminate, nor homosexuals,

10 nor thieves, nor *the* covetous, nor drunkards, nor revilers, nor swindlers, will inherit the kingdom of God.

11 Such were some of you; but you were washed, but you were sanctified, but you were justified in the name of the Lord Jesus Christ and in the Spirit of our God.

The Body Is the Lord's

12 ¶ All things are lawful for me, but not all things are profitable. All things are lawful for me, but I will not be mastered by anything.

6:12 Corinthian Slogans

The phrases given here in quotes ("All things are lawful for me"; "Food is for the stomach and the stomach is for food") appear to be slogans the Corinthians had used in justifying their loose behavior. Paul doesn't refute their ideas outright, but rather points to the ultimate effect of their excesses.

13 Food is for the stomach and the stomach is for food, but God will do away with both of them. Yet the body is not for immorality, but for the Lord, and the Lord is for the body.

14 Now God has not only raised the Lord, but will also raise us up through His power.

15 Do you not know that your bodies are members of Christ? Shall I then take away the members of Christ and make them members of a prostitute? May it never be!

16 Or do you not know that the one who joins himself to a prostitute is one body *with her*? For He says, "THE TWO SHALL BECOME ONE FLESH."

17 But the one who joins himself to the Lord is one spirit *with Him*.

18 Flee immorality. Every *other* sin that a man commits is outside the body, but the immoral man sins against his own body.

19 Or do you not know that your body is a temple of the Holy Spirit who is in you, whom you have from God, and that you are not your own?

20 For you have been bought with a price: therefore glorify God in your body.

Teaching on Marriage

7 Now concerning the things about which you wrote, it is good for a man not to touch a woman.

2 But because of immoralities, each man is to have his own wife, and each woman is to have her own husband.

3 The husband must fulfill his duty to his wife, and likewise also the wife to her husband.

4 The wife does not have authority over her own body, but the husband *does*; and likewise also the husband does not have authority over his own body, but the wife *does*.

5 Stop depriving one another, except by agreement for a time, so that you may devote

---

[a] I.e. effeminate by perversion

yourselves to prayer, and come together again so that Satan will not tempt you because of your lack of self-control.

6 But this I say by way of concession, not of command.

7 ᵃYet I wish that all men were even as I myself am. However, each man has his own gift from God, one in this manner, and another in that.

8 ¶ But I say to the unmarried and to widows that it is good for them if they remain even as I.

9 But if they do not have self-control, let them marry; for it is better to marry than to burn *with passion.*

10 ¶ But to the married I give instructions, not I, but the Lord, that the wife should not leave her husband

11 (but if she does leave, she must remain unmarried, or else be reconciled to her husband), and that the husband should not divorce his wife.

12 ¶ But to the rest I say, not the Lord, that if any brother has a wife who is an unbeliever, and she consents to live with him, he must not divorce her.

13 And a woman who has an unbelieving husband, and he consents to live with her, she must not send her husband away.

14 For the unbelieving husband is sanctified through his wife, and the unbelieving wife is sanctified through her believing husband; for otherwise your children are unclean, but now they are holy.

15 Yet if the unbelieving one leaves, let him leave; the brother or the sister is not under bondage in such *cases,* but God has called ᵇus to peace.

16 For how do you know, O wife, whether you will save your husband? Or how do you know, O husband, whether you will save your wife?

17 ¶ Only, as the Lord has assigned to each one, as God has called each, in this manner let him walk. And so I direct in all the churches.

18 Was any man called *when he was already* circumcised? He is not to become uncircumcised. Has anyone been called in uncircumcision? He is not to be circumcised.

19 Circumcision is nothing, and uncircumcision is nothing, but *what matters is* the keeping of the commandments of God.

20 Each man must remain in that condition in which he was called.

21 ¶ Were you called while a slave? Do not worry about it; but if you are able also to become free, rather do that.

22 For he who was called in the Lord while a slave, is the Lord's freedman; likewise he who was called while free, is Christ's slave.

23 You were bought with a price; do not become slaves of men.

24 Brethren, each one is to remain with God in that *condition* in which he was called.

25 ¶ Now concerning virgins I have no command of the Lord, but I give an opinion as one who by the mercy of the Lord is trustworthy.

26 I think then that this is good in view of the

7:25 Paul's Personal Opinions

In discussing the thorny issue of singleness and marriage, Paul carefully distinguishes what is his personal opinion and what is a clear revelation from God. He explains in verse 29 why he reached these conclusions.

present distress, that it is good for a man to remain as he is.

27 Are you bound to a wife? Do not seek to be released. Are you released from a wife? Do not seek a wife.

28 But if you marry, you have not sinned; and if a virgin marries, she has not sinned. Yet such will have trouble in this life, and I am trying to spare you.

29 But this I say, brethren, the time has been shortened, so that from now on those who have wives should be as though they had none;

30 and those who weep, as though they did not weep; and those who rejoice, as though they did not rejoice; and those who buy, as though they did not possess;

31 and those who use the world, as though they did not make full use of it; for the form of this world is passing away.

32 ¶ But I want you to be free from concern. One who is unmarried is concerned about the things of the Lord, how he may please the Lord;

33 but one who is married is concerned about the things of the world, how he may please his wife,

34 and *his interests* are divided. The woman who is unmarried, and the virgin, is concerned about the things of the Lord, that she may be holy both in body and spirit; but one who is married is concerned about the things of the world, how she may please her husband.

35 This I say for your own benefit; not to put a restraint upon you, but to promote what is appropriate and *to secure* undistracted devotion to the Lord.

36 ¶ But if any man thinks that he is acting unbecomingly toward his virgin *daughter,* if she is past her youth, and if it must be so, let him do what he wishes, he does not sin; let her marry.

37 But he who stands firm in his heart, being under no constraint, but has authority over his own will, and has decided this in his own heart, to keep his own virgin *daughter,* he will do well.

38 So then both he who gives his own virgin

ᵃ One early ms reads *For*   ᵇ One early ms reads *you*

daughter in marriage does well, and he who does not give her in marriage will do better.

39 ¶ A wife is bound as long as her husband lives; but if her husband is dead, she is free to be married to whom she wishes, only in the Lord.

40 But in my opinion she is happier if she remains as she is; and I think that I also have the Spirit of God.

Take Care with Your Liberty

8 Now concerning things sacrificed to idols, we know that we all have knowledge. Knowledge makes arrogant, but love edifies.

2 If anyone supposes that he knows anything, he has not yet known as he ought to know;

3 but if anyone loves God, he is known by Him.

4 ¶ Therefore concerning the eating of things sacrificed to idols, we know that *a*there is no such thing as an idol in the world, and that there is no God but one.

5 For even if there are so-called gods whether in heaven or on earth, as indeed there are many gods and many lords,

6 yet for us there is *but* one God, the Father, from whom are all things and we *exist* for Him; and one Lord, Jesus Christ, by whom are all things, and we *exist* through Him.

7 ¶ However not all men have this knowledge;

but some, being accustomed to the idol until now, eat *food* as if it were sacrificed to an idol; and their conscience being weak is defiled.

8 But food will not commend us to God; we are neither the worse if we do not eat, nor the better if we do eat.

9 But take care that this liberty of yours does not somehow become a stumbling block to the weak.

10 For if someone sees you, who have knowledge, dining in an idol's temple, will not his conscience, if he is weak, be strengthened to eat things sacrificed to idols?

11 For through your knowledge he who is weak is ruined, the brother for whose sake Christ died.

12 And so, by sinning against the brethren and wounding their conscience when it is weak, you sin against Christ.

13 Therefore, if food causes my brother to stumble, I will never eat meat again, so that I will not cause my brother to stumble.

Paul's Use of Liberty

9 Am I not free? Am I not an apostle? Have I not seen Jesus our Lord? Are you not my work in the Lord?

2 If to others I am not an apostle, at least I am

---

a Lit *nothing is an idol in the world*; i.e. an idol has no real existence

When Everything Goes Wrong
A church of former idolaters, adulterers, thieves, and drunkards

> *Now concerning the things about which you wrote. . . 7:1*

"IF ANYTHING CAN GO WRONG, it will." This tongue-in-cheek principle, known as Murphy's Law, is cited by economists, sports team owners, and big-city mayors. Human nature somehow guarantees that nothing turns out quite the way it's supposed to. And the church at Corinth provides a darkly shining example of Murphy's Law.

To be sure, Corinthian Christians started out with the odds stacked against them. Imagine a church composed of converted idolaters, adulterers, male prostitutes, thieves, drunkards, and swindlers (6:9–11). The church made up of people from such backgrounds soon encountered a thicket of problems. Paul faced a huge challenge: For one thing, he had to convince these people of the immorality of sexual activities that had been a part of everyday worship under their old religion.

Local and Universal Issues

First Corinthians is Paul's careful response to that thicket of problems, some of which had been posed to him as questions in a letter (7:1). Many of his answers relate directly to Corinth's local situation. In that culture, as in Muslim countries today, whether or not to wear a veil was a major issue for women (11:3–10). Eating meat sacrificed to pagan idols also disturbed some new Christians (10:18–33).

But other problems discussed here turn up in every culture: divisions in the church, lawsuits, immorality, the single life, the extent of Christian freedoms, differing views of worship and the place of tongue-speaking and other spiritual gifts. Not every breakdown in Corinth will recur in churches today, but Paul's principles apply to our own unpredictable experiences with Murphy's Law.

Life Questions: Think of the most "Corinthian" television show you know. Then imagine: If the lead characters became Christians, what problems would they encounter?

to you; for you are the seal of my apostleship in the Lord.

3 ¶ My defense to those who examine me is this:

4 Do we not have a right to eat and drink?

5 Do we not have a right to take along a believing wife, even as the rest of the apostles and the brothers of the Lord and Cephas?

6 Or do only Barnabas and I not have a right to refrain from working?

7 Who at any time serves as a soldier at his own expense? Who plants a vineyard and does not eat the fruit of it? Or who tends a flock and does not use the milk of the flock?

8 ¶ I am not speaking these things according to human judgment, am I? Or does not the Law also say these things?

9 For it is written in the Law of Moses, "YOU SHALL NOT MUZZLE THE OX WHILE HE IS THRESHING." God is not concerned about oxen, is He?

10 Or is He speaking altogether for our sake? Yes, for our sake it was written, because the plowman ought to plow in hope, and the thresher *to thresh* in hope of sharing *the crops.*

11 If we sowed spiritual things in you, is it too much if we reap material things from you?

12 If others share the right over you, do we not more? Nevertheless, we did not use this right, but we endure all things so that we will cause no hindrance to the gospel of Christ.

13 Do you not know that those who perform sacred services eat the *food* of the temple, *and* those who attend regularly to the altar have their share from the altar?

14 So also the Lord directed those who proclaim the gospel to get their living from the gospel.

15 ¶ But I have used none of these things. And I am not writing these things so that it will be done so in my case; for it would be better for me to die than have any man make my boast an empty one.

16 For if I preach the gospel, I have nothing to boast of, for I am under compulsion; for woe is me if I do not preach the gospel.

17 For if I do this voluntarily, I have a reward; but if against my will, I have a stewardship entrusted to me.

18 What then is my reward? That, when I preach the gospel, I may offer the gospel without charge, so as not to make full use of my right in the gospel.

19 ¶ For though I am free from all *men,* I have made myself a slave to all, so that I may win more.

20 To the Jews I became as a Jew, so that I might win Jews; to those who are under the Law, as under the Law though not being myself under the Law, so that I might win those who are under the Law;

21 to those who are without law, as without law, though not being without the law of God but under the law of Christ, so that I might win those who are without law.

22 To the weak I became weak, that I might win the weak; I have become all things to all men, so that I may by all means save some.

23 I do all things for the sake of the gospel, so that I may become a fellow partaker of it.

9:22 A Positive and a Negative

After discussing the specific questions that had surfaced in the church at Corinth, Paul gives two examples from life. The first, a positive one, points to the actions of the apostles. Although they had certain "rights" and freedoms, they didn't insist on them. Rather, they adapted to the practices of people around them to win them over. In contrast, the ancient Israelites (chapter 10) had consistently given in to their own weaknesses. Paul urges the Corinthians to follow his example, not that of the Israelites (11:1).

24 ¶ Do you not know that those who run in a race all run, but *only* one receives the prize? Run in such a way that you may win.

25 Everyone who competes in the games exercises self-control in all things. They then *do it* to receive a perishable wreath, but we an imperishable.

26 Therefore I run in such a way, as not without aim; I box in such a way, as not beating the air;

27 but I discipline my body and make it my slave, so that, after I have preached to others, I myself will not be disqualified.

Avoid Israel's Mistakes

10 For I do not want you to be unaware, brethren, that our fathers were all under the cloud and all passed through the sea;

2 and all were baptized into Moses in the cloud and in the sea;

3 and all ate the same spiritual food;

4 and all drank the same spiritual drink, for they were drinking from a spiritual rock which followed them; and the rock was Christ.

5 Nevertheless, with most of them God was not well-pleased; for they were laid low in the wilderness.

6 ¶ Now these things happened as examples for us, so that we would not crave evil things as they also craved.

7 Do not be idolaters, as some of them were; as it is written, "THE PEOPLE SAT DOWN TO EAT AND DRINK, AND STOOD UP TO PLAY."

8 Nor let us act immorally, as some of them did, and twenty-three thousand fell in one day.

9 Nor let us try the Lord, as some of them did, and were destroyed by the serpents.

10 Nor grumble, as some of them did, and were destroyed by the destroyer.

11 Now these things happened to them as an example, and they were written for our instruction, upon whom the ends of the ages have come.

12 Therefore let him who thinks he stands take heed that he does not fall.

13 No temptation has overtaken you but such as is common to man; and God is faithful, who will not allow you to be tempted beyond what you are able, but with the temptation will provide the way of escape also, so that you will be able to endure it.

14 ¶ Therefore, my beloved, flee from idolatry.

15 I speak as to wise men; you judge what I say.

16 Is not the cup of blessing which we bless a sharing in the blood of Christ? Is not the bread which we break a sharing in the body of Christ?

17 Since there is one bread, we who are many are one body; for we all partake of the one bread.

18 Look at the nation Israel; are not those who eat the sacrifices sharers in the altar?

19 What do I mean then? That a thing sacrificed to idols is anything, or that an idol is anything?

20 No, but I say that the things which the Gentiles sacrifice, they sacrifice to demons and not to God; and I do not want you to become sharers in demons.

21 You cannot drink the cup of the Lord and the cup of demons; you cannot partake of the table of the Lord and the table of demons.

22 Or do we provoke the Lord to jealousy? We are not stronger than He, are we?

23 ¶ All things are lawful, but not all things are profitable. All things are lawful, but not all things edify.

24 Let no one seek his own good, but that of his neighbor.

25 Eat anything that is sold in the meat market without asking questions for conscience' sake;

26 FOR THE EARTH IS THE LORD'S, AND ALL IT CONTAINS.

27 If one of the unbelievers invites you and you want to go, eat anything that is set before you without asking questions for conscience' sake.

28 But if anyone says to you, "This is meat sacrificed to idols," do not eat it, for the sake of the one who informed you, and for conscience' sake;

29 I mean not your own conscience, but the other man's; for why is my freedom judged by another's conscience?

30 If I partake with thankfulness, why am I slandered concerning that for which I give thanks?

31 ¶ Whether, then, you eat or drink or whatever you do, do all to the glory of God.

32 Give no offense either to Jews or to Greeks or to the church of God;

33 just as I also please all men in all things, not seeking my own profit but the profit of the many, so that they may be saved.

Christian Order

11 Be imitators of me, just as I also am of Christ.

2 ¶ Now I praise you because you remember me in everything and hold firmly to the traditions, just as I delivered them to you.

3 But I want you to understand that Christ is the head of every man, and the man is the head of a woman, and God is the head of Christ.

4 Every man who has something on his head while praying or prophesying disgraces his head.

5 But every woman who has her head uncovered while praying or prophesying disgraces her head, for she is one and the same as the woman whose head is shaved.

11:5 Women in Corinth

In the Middle East, a woman who appeared in public barefaced, without a veil, showed loose morals. Some Muslim countries today still retain that custom. Paul's advice applied directly to the cultural situation in Corinth, where unruly women were disrupting the worship services.

6 For if a woman does not cover her head, let her also have her hair cut off; but if it is disgraceful for a woman to have her hair cut off or her head shaved, let her cover her head.

7 For a man ought not to have his head covered, since he is the image and glory of God; but the woman is the glory of man.

8 For man does not originate from woman, but woman from man;

9 for indeed man was not created for the woman's sake, but woman for the man's sake.

10 Therefore the woman ought to have a symbol of authority on her head, because of the angels.

11 However, in the Lord, neither is woman independent of man, nor is man independent of woman.

12 For as the woman originates from the man, so also the man has his birth through the woman; and all things originate from God.

13 Judge for yourselves: is it proper for a woman to pray to God with her head uncovered?

14 Does not even nature itself teach you that if a man has long hair, it is a dishonor to him,

15 but if a woman has long hair, it is a glory to her? For her hair is given to her for a covering.

16 But if one is inclined to be contentious, we have no other practice, nor have the churches of God.

17 ¶ But in giving this instruction, I do not praise you, because you come together not for the better but for the worse.

18 For, in the first place, when you come together as a church, I hear that divisions exist among you; and in part I believe it.

19 For there must also be factions among you, so that those who are approved may become evident among you.

20 Therefore when you meet together, it is not to eat the Lord's Supper,

21 for in your eating each one takes his own supper first; and one is hungry and another is drunk.

22 What! Do you not have houses in which to eat and drink? Or do you despise the church of God and shame those who have nothing? What shall I say to you? Shall I praise you? In this I will not praise you.

The Lord's Supper

23 ¶ For I received from the Lord that which I also delivered to you, that the Lord Jesus in the night in which He was betrayed took bread;

24 and when He had given thanks, He broke it and said, "This is My body, which is for you; do this in remembrance of Me."

25 In the same way He *took* the cup also after supper, saying, "This cup is the new covenant in My blood; do this, as often as you drink *it*, in remembrance of Me."

26 For as often as you eat this bread and drink the cup, you proclaim the Lord's death until He comes.

27 ¶ Therefore whoever eats the bread or drinks the cup of the Lord in an unworthy manner, shall be guilty of the body and the blood of the Lord.

28 But a man must examine himself, and in so doing he is to eat of the bread and drink of the cup.

29 For he who eats and drinks, eats and drinks judgment to himself if he does not judge the body rightly.

30 For this reason many among you are weak and sick, and a number sleep.

31 But if we judged ourselves rightly, we would not be judged.

32 But when we are judged, we are disciplined by the Lord so that we will not be condemned along with the world.

33 ¶ So then, my brethren, when you come together to eat, wait for one another.

34 If anyone is hungry, let him eat at home, so that you will not come together for judgment. The remaining matters I will arrange when I come.

The Use of Spiritual Gifts

12 Now concerning spiritual *gifts,* brethren, I do not want you to be unaware.

2 You know that when you were pagans, *you were* led astray to the mute idols, however you were led.

3 Therefore I make known to you that no one speaking by the Spirit of God says, "Jesus is accursed"; and no one can say, "Jesus is Lord," except by the Holy Spirit.

4 ¶ Now there are varieties of gifts, but the same Spirit.

5 And there are varieties of ministries, and the same Lord.

6 There are varieties of effects, but the same God who works all things in all *persons.*

7 But to each one is given the manifestation of the Spirit for the common good.

8 For to one is given the word of wisdom through the Spirit, and to another the word of knowledge according to the same Spirit;

9 to another faith by the same Spirit, and to another gifts of healing by the one Spirit,

10 and to another the effecting of miracles, and to another prophecy, and to another the distinguishing of spirits, to another *various* kinds of tongues, and to another the interpretation of tongues.

11 But one and the same Spirit works all these things, distributing to each one individually just as He wills.

12 ¶ For even as the body is one and *yet* has many members, and all the members of the body, though they are many, are one body, so also is Christ.

13 For by one Spirit we were all baptized into one body, whether Jews or Greeks, whether slaves or free, and we were all made to drink of one Spirit.

14 ¶ For the body is not one member, but many.

15 If the foot says, "Because I am not a hand, I am not *a part* of the body," it is not for this reason any the less *a part* of the body.

16 And if the ear says, "Because I am not an eye, I am not *a part* of the body," it is not for this reason any the less *a part* of the body.

17 If the whole body were an eye, where would the hearing be? If the whole were hearing, where would the sense of smell be?

18 But now God has placed the members, each one of them, in the body, just as He desired.

19 If they were all one member, where would the body be?

20 But now there are many members, but one body.

21 And the eye cannot say to the hand, "I have no need of you"; or again the head to the feet, "I have no need of you."

22 On the contrary, it is much truer that the members of the body which seem to be weaker are necessary;

23 and those *members* of the body which we deem less honorable, on these we bestow more abundant honor, and our less presentable members become much more presentable,

24 whereas our more presentable members have no need *of it.* But God has *so* composed the body, giving more abundant honor to that *member* which lacked,

25 so that there may be no division in the

body, but *that* the members may have the same care for one another.

26 And if one member suffers, all the members suffer with it; if *one* member is honored, all the members rejoice with it.

27 ¶ Now you are Christ's body, and individually members of it.

28 And God has appointed in the church, first apostles, second prophets, third teachers, then miracles, then gifts of healings, helps, administrations, *various* kinds of tongues.

29 All are not apostles, are they? All are not prophets, are they? All are not teachers, are they? All are not *workers of* miracles, are they?

30 All do not have gifts of healings, do they? All do not speak with tongues, do they? All do not interpret, do they?

31 But earnestly desire the greater gifts.

¶ And I show you a still more excellent way.

a Early mss read *that I may boast*

The Excellence of Love

13 If I speak with the tongues of men and of angels, but do not have love, I have become a noisy gong or a clanging cymbal.

2 If I have *the gift of* prophecy, and know all mysteries and all knowledge; and if I have all faith, so as to remove mountains, but do not have love, I am nothing.

3 And if I give all my possessions to feed *the poor,* and if I surrender my body *a*to be burned, but do not have love, it profits me nothing.

4 ¶ Love is patient, love is kind *and* is not jealous; love does not brag *and* is not arrogant,

5 does not act unbecomingly; it does not seek its own, is not provoked, does not take into account a wrong *suffered,*

6 does not rejoice in unrighteousness, but rejoices with the truth;

Lessons from the Human Body
The body needs an eye, and the eye needs a body

CAN YOU GET ALONG IN life without eyes? Of course, but you must make adjustments. You must rely more on other senses and depend on friends, or perhaps a seeing-eye dog, for extra help. Regardless of what adjustments you make, however, your body will remain incomplete without eyes. You will miss out on color and design and all the visual delights this world offers.

An eyeless body can cope, but a bodyless eye is unimaginable. The most beautiful eyes in the world, when detached from a body, are lifeless and worthless. Eyes need a body that will bring them blood and receive their nerve impulses.

> For even as the body is one and yet has many members, and all the members of the body, though they are many, are one body, so also is Christ. 12:12

Many Parts, All Working Together

In chapter 12 Paul gives a clever anatomy lesson, with a purpose. By comparing members of the church of Christ to parts of a human body, he neatly explains two complementary truths the Corinthians had failed to comprehend. Any part of a body, he says—such as an eye or a foot—makes a valuable contribution to the whole body. Whenever a single member is missing, the entire body suffers.

And, he continues, no member can survive if isolated from the rest. Alone, an eye is useless. All parts must cooperate to form a single, unified body.

Paul relied on body images to explain both the diversity and unity of God's followers. The body analogy fit so well that he referred to it two dozen times in his various letters. It became his favorite way of portraying the church.

An Emphasis on Unity

A church as diverse as Corinth knew about the differences among various members, so Paul's letter to them stressed the unity part of the analogy. How can diverse people work together in a spiritual body? He answered that question with the famous lyrical description of love in chapter 13. After that eloquent statement, he went on to discuss the Corinthians' various spiritual gifts.

Chapters 12–14 address issues that troubled the patchwork Corinthian church and that still disturb the church today. The solution, in our time as well as Paul's, is for each person to respect other members of the body and to take direction from Jesus Christ, the head.

Life Questions: Of Paul's list of spiritual gifts, which are prominent in your church? Are any overlooked? How do you fit in?

7 bears all things, believes all things, hopes all things, endures all things.

8 ¶ Love never fails; but if *there are gifts of* prophecy, they will be done away; if *there are* tongues, they will cease; if *there is* knowledge, it will be done away.

9 For we know in part and we prophesy in part;

10 but when the perfect comes, the partial will be done away.

11 When I was a child, I used to speak like a child, think like a child, reason like a child; when I became a man, I did away with childish things.

12 For now we see in a mirror dimly, but then face to face; now I know in part, but then I will know fully just as I also have been fully known.

13 But now faith, hope, love, abide these three; but the greatest of these is love.

Prophecy a Superior Gift

14 Pursue love, yet desire earnestly spiritual *gifts*, but especially that you may prophesy.

2 For one who speaks in a tongue does not speak to men but to God; for no one understands, but in *his* spirit he speaks mysteries.

14:2 Speaking in Tongues

1 Corinthians 12–14 gives the New Testament's most complete teaching on supernatural gifts such as healing and speaking in tongues. Paul stresses two concerns: (1) "Sensational" gifts must not be given higher rank than they deserve (chapter 13 stresses the superiority of simple love). (2) These gifts should contribute to orderly and proper worship, not confusion. The Corinthians seemed to take everything to excess—whether practicing immorality, celebrating the Lord's Supper, or exercising spiritual gifts.

3 But one who prophesies speaks to men for edification and exhortation and consolation.

4 One who speaks in a tongue edifies himself; but one who prophesies edifies the church.

5 Now I wish that you all spoke in tongues, but *even* more that you would prophesy; and greater is one who prophesies than one who speaks in tongues, unless he interprets, so that the church may receive edifying.

6 ¶ But now, brethren, if I come to you speaking in tongues, what will I profit you unless I speak to you either by way of revelation or of knowledge or of prophecy or of teaching?

7 Yet *even* lifeless things, either flute or harp, in producing a sound, if they do not produce a distinction in the tones, how will it be known what is played on the flute or on the harp?

8 For if the bugle produces an indistinct sound, who will prepare himself for battle?

9 So also you, unless you utter by the tongue speech that is clear, how will it be known what is spoken? For you will be speaking into the air.

10 There are, perhaps, a great many kinds of languages in the world, and no *kind* is without meaning.

11 If then I do not know the meaning of the language, I will be to the one who speaks a barbarian, and the one who speaks will be a barbarian to me.

12 So also you, since you are zealous of spiritual *gifts*, seek to abound for the edification of the church.

13 ¶ Therefore let one who speaks in a tongue pray that he may interpret.

14 For if I pray in a tongue, my spirit prays, but my mind is unfruitful.

15 What is *the outcome* then? I will pray with the spirit and I will pray with the mind also; I will sing with the spirit and I will sing with the mind also.

16 Otherwise if you bless in the spirit *only*, how will the one who fills the place of the ungifted say the "Amen" at your giving of thanks, since he does not know what you are saying?

17 For you are giving thanks well enough, but the other person is not edified.

18 I thank God, I speak in tongues more than you all;

19 however, in the church I desire to speak five words with my mind so that I may instruct others also, rather than ten thousand words in a tongue.

Instruction for the Church

20 ¶ Brethren, do not be children in your thinking; yet in evil be infants, but in your thinking be mature.

21 In the Law it is written, "BY MEN OF STRANGE TONGUES AND BY THE LIPS OF STRANGERS I WILL SPEAK TO THIS PEOPLE, AND EVEN SO THEY WILL NOT LISTEN TO ME," says the Lord.

22 So then tongues are for a sign, not to those who believe but to unbelievers; but prophecy *is for a sign*, not to unbelievers but to those who believe.

23 Therefore if the whole church assembles together and all speak in tongues, and ungifted men or unbelievers enter, will they not say that you are mad?

24 But if all prophesy, and an unbeliever or an ungifted man enters, he is convicted by all, he is called to account by all;

25 the secrets of his heart are disclosed; and so he will fall on his face and worship God, declaring that God is certainly among you.

26 ¶ What is *the outcome* then, brethren? When you assemble, each one has a psalm, has a teaching, has a revelation, has a tongue, has an interpretation. Let all things be done for edification.

27 If anyone speaks in a tongue, *it should be* by

two or at the most three, and *each* in turn, and one must interpret;

28 but if there is no interpreter, he must keep silent in the church; and let him speak to himself and to God.

29 Let two or three prophets speak, and let the others pass judgment.

30 But if a revelation is made to another who is seated, the first one must keep silent.

31 For you can all prophesy one by one, so that all may learn and all may be exhorted;

32 and the spirits of prophets are subject to prophets;

33 for God is not *a God* of confusion but of peace, as in all the churches of the saints.

34 ¶ The women are to keep silent in the churches; for they are not permitted to speak, but are to subject themselves, just as the Law also says.

35 If they desire to learn anything, let them ask their own husbands at home; for it is improper for a woman to speak in church.

36 Was it from you that the word of God *first* went forth? Or has it come to you only?

37 ¶ If anyone thinks he is a prophet or spiritual, let him recognize that the things which I write to you are the Lord's commandment.

38 But if anyone does not recognize *this*, he *a*is not recognized.

39 ¶ Therefore, my brethren, desire earnestly to prophesy, and do not forbid to speak in tongues.

a Two early mss read *is not to be recognized*

40 But all things must be done properly and in an orderly manner.

The Fact of Christ's Resurrection

15 Now I make known to you, brethren, the gospel which I preached to you, which also you received, in which also you stand,

2 by which also you are saved, if you hold fast the word which I preached to you, unless you believed in vain.

3 ¶ For I delivered to you as of first importance what I also received, that Christ died for our sins according to the Scriptures,

4 and that He was buried, and that He was raised on the third day according to the Scriptures,

5 and that He appeared to Cephas, then to the twelve.

6 After that He appeared to more than five hundred brethren at one time, most of whom remain until now, but some have fallen asleep;

7 then He appeared to James, then to all the apostles;

8 and last of all, as to one untimely born, He appeared to me also.

9 For I am the least of the apostles, and not fit to be called an apostle, because I persecuted the church of God.

10 But by the grace of God I am what I am, and His grace toward me did not prove vain; but I

The Worst Danger of All
Why believe in life after death?

MOST OF THE PROBLEMS RAISED by the church at Corinth concerned personal behavior. After tackling each of those problems, Paul turned to one last question, a matter of doctrine. Some people in the church were challenging the Christian belief in an afterlife. Death, they said, is the end.

Many people have questioned the afterlife. In Jesus' day, a Jewish sect called Sadducees denied the resurrection from the dead. Doubters persist today (among them: many Black Muslims, Buddhists, and Marxists and most atheists). But Paul saw the matter of life after death as the most explosive issue in the Corinthian church.

> But if there is no resurrection of the dead, not even Christ has been raised; and if Christ has not been raised, then our preaching is vain, your faith also is vain.
> 15:13-14

Pitiable Christians

If there's no future life, he thundered, the entire Christian message would be a lie. He, Paul, would have no reason to continue as a minister; Christ's death would have merely wasted blood; and Christians would be the most pitiable of all people.

Chapter 15 weaves together the threads of Christian belief about death. It shows how death is finally conquered and becomes, not an end, but a beginning. Cheered by such a triumphant note, the apostle Paul sums up his counsel to the Corinthians with a ringing challenge to "be steadfast."

Life Questions: Which of Paul's arguments in chapter 15 do you find most convincing? How does belief in an afterlife affect you?

labored even more than all of them, yet not I, but the grace of God with me.

11 Whether then *it was* I or they, so we preach and so you believed.

15:8 Basic Christianity

Paul stresses the basics every Christian must believe: that Christ died for our sins, that he was buried (really dead), and that he rose again. Listing some of the many people who saw Jesus after his resurrection, Paul includes himself last of all. He is referring to his encounter with Christ on the road to Damascus (see Acts 9).

12 ¶ Now if Christ is preached, that He has been raised from the dead, how do some among you say that there is no resurrection of the dead?

13 But if there is no resurrection of the dead, not even Christ has been raised;

14 and if Christ has not been raised, then our preaching is vain, your faith also is vain.

15 Moreover we are even found *to be* false witnesses of God, because we testified against God that He raised [a]Christ, whom He did not raise, if in fact the dead are not raised.

16 For if the dead are not raised, not even Christ has been raised;

17 and if Christ has not been raised, your faith is worthless; you are still in your sins.

18 Then those also who have fallen asleep in Christ have perished.

19 If we have hoped in Christ in this life only, we are of all men most to be pitied.

The Order of Resurrection

20 ¶ But now Christ has been raised from the dead, the first fruits of those who are asleep.

21 For since by a man *came* death, by a man also *came* the resurrection of the dead.

22 For as in Adam all die, so also in Christ all will be made alive.

23 But each in his own order: Christ the first fruits, after that those who are Christ's at His coming,

24 then *comes* the end, when He hands over the kingdom to the God and Father, when He has abolished all rule and all authority and power.

25 For He must reign until He has put all His enemies under His feet.

26 The last enemy that will be abolished is death.

27 For HE HAS PUT ALL THINGS IN SUBJECTION UNDER HIS FEET. But when He says, "All things are put in subjection," it is evident that He is excepted who put all things in subjection to Him.

28 When all things are subjected to Him, then the Son Himself also will be subjected to the One who subjected all things to Him, so that God may be all in all.

29 ¶ Otherwise, what will those do who are baptized for the dead? If the dead are not raised at all, why then are they baptized for them?

30 Why are we also in danger every hour?

31 I affirm, brethren, by the boasting in you which I have in Christ Jesus our Lord, I die daily.

32 If from human motives I fought with wild beasts at Ephesus, what does it profit me? If the dead are not raised, LET US EAT AND DRINK, FOR TOMORROW WE DIE.

33 Do not be deceived: "Bad company corrupts good morals."

34 Become sober-minded as you ought, and stop sinning; for some have no knowledge of God. I speak *this* to your shame.

35 ¶ But someone will say, "How are the dead raised? And with what kind of body do they come?"

36 You fool! That which you sow does not come to life unless it dies;

37 and that which you sow, you do not sow the body which is to be, but a bare grain, perhaps of wheat or of something else.

38 But God gives it a body just as He wished, and to each of the seeds a body of its own.

39 All flesh is not the same flesh, but there is one *flesh* of men, and another flesh of beasts, and another flesh of birds, and another of fish.

40 There are also heavenly bodies and earthly bodies, but the glory of the heavenly is one, and the *glory* of the earthly is another.

41 There is one glory of the sun, and another glory of the moon, and another glory of the stars; for star differs from star in glory.

42 ¶ So also is the resurrection of the dead. It is sown a perishable *body*, it is raised an imperishable *body*;

43 it is sown in dishonor, it is raised in glory; it is sown in weakness, it is raised in power;

44 it is sown a natural body, it is raised a spiritual body. If there is a natural body, there is also a spiritual *body*.

45 So also it is written, "The first MAN, Adam, BECAME A LIVING SOUL." The last Adam *became* a life-giving spirit.

46 However, the spiritual is not first, but the natural; then the spiritual.

47 The first man is from the earth, earthy; the second man is from heaven.

48 As is the earthy, so also are those who are earthy; and as is the heavenly, so also are those who are heavenly.

49 Just as we have borne the image of the earthy, [b]we will also bear the image of the heavenly.

[a] I.e. the Messiah   [b] Two early mss read *let us also*

The Mystery of Resurrection

50 ¶ Now I say this, brethren, that flesh and blood cannot inherit the kingdom of God; nor does the perishable inherit the imperishable.

51 Behold, I tell you a mystery; we will not all sleep, but we will all be changed,

52 in a moment, in the twinkling of an eye, at the last trumpet; for the trumpet will sound, and the dead will be raised imperishable, and we will be changed.

53 For this perishable must put on the imperishable, and this mortal must put on immortality.

54 But when this perishable will have put on the imperishable, and this mortal will have put on immortality, then will come about the saying that is written, "DEATH IS SWALLOWED UP in victory.

55 "O DEATH, WHERE IS YOUR VICTORY? O DEATH, WHERE IS YOUR STING?"

56 The sting of death is sin, and the power of sin is the law;

57 but thanks be to God, who gives us the victory through our Lord Jesus Christ.

58 ¶ Therefore, my beloved brethren, be steadfast, immovable, always abounding in the work of the Lord, knowing that your toil is not *in* vain in the Lord.

Instructions and Greetings

16 Now concerning the collection for the saints, as I directed the churches of Galatia, so do you also.

16:1 Remembering the Poor

Paul's deep concern for the poor in Jerusalem comes up often in the New Testament. He mentions taking a collection here, as well as in Romans and 2 Corinthians. He knew that widespread concern for the mother church in Jerusalem would do much to further unity between Jewish and Gentile Christians.

2 On the first day of every week each one of you is to put aside and save, as he may prosper, so that no collections be made when I come.

3 When I arrive, whomever you may approve, I will send them with letters to carry your gift to Jerusalem;

4 and if it is fitting for me to go also, they will go with me.

5 ¶ But I will come to you after I go through Macedonia, for I am going through Macedonia;

6 and perhaps I will stay with you, or even spend the winter, so that you may send me on my way wherever I may go.

7 For I do not wish to see you now *just* in passing; for I hope to remain with you for some time, if the Lord permits.

8 But I will remain in Ephesus until Pentecost;

9 for a wide door for effective *service* has opened to me, and there are many adversaries.

10 ¶ Now if Timothy comes, see that he is with you without cause to be afraid, for he is doing the Lord's work, as I also am.

11 So let no one despise him. But send him on his way in peace, so that he may come to me; for I expect him with the brethren.

12 ¶ But concerning Apollos our brother, I encouraged him greatly to come to you with the brethren; and it was not at all *his* desire to come now, but he will come when he has opportunity.

13 ¶ Be on the alert, stand firm in the faith, act like men, be strong.

14 Let all that you do be done in love.

15 ¶ Now I urge you, brethren (you know the household of Stephanas, that they were the first fruits of Achaia, and that they have devoted themselves for ministry to the saints),

16 that you also be in subjection to such men and to everyone who helps in the work and labors.

17 I rejoice over the coming of Stephanas and Fortunatus and Achaicus, because they have supplied what was lacking on your part.

18 For they have refreshed my spirit and yours. Therefore acknowledge such men.

19 ¶ The churches of Asia greet you. Aquila and Prisca greet you heartily in the Lord, with the church that is in their house.

20 All the brethren greet you. Greet one another with a holy kiss.

21 ¶ The greeting is in my own hand—Paul.

22 If anyone does not love the Lord, he is to be accursed. Maranatha.

23 The grace of the Lord Jesus be with you.

24 My love be with you all in Christ Jesus. Amen.

2 CORINTHIANS

A Book of Joy and Sadness
Why isn't Paul celebrating his victory?

ATHLETES SOMETIMES HAVE A STRANGE reaction to a great victory. Some call it "morning-after sickness." An Olympic gymnast who has trained for 15 years wakes up the day after her gold medal performance feeling oddly depressed. Paradoxically, the sweet taste of victory can take on a bitter edge.

An even more pungent feeling may hit those who prevail in personal disputes. The man who wins a crucial court case is stabbed by sympathy for those he defeated. The politician who waves jubilantly to a cheering crowd on primary night winces inwardly at the bruises she suffered—and inflicted—during the campaign. The husband who insisted on a divorce leaves the final settlement feeling sad and burdened.

> Indeed, we had the sentence of death within ourselves so that we would not trust in ourselves, but in God who raises the dead.
> 1:9

Lingering Pain

Something like that bittersweet state must have plagued the apostle Paul when he wrote 2 Corinthians. He had just won a great victory in convincing the Corinthians to come over to his side. His spirit had surged upon hearing Titus's news of their wave of support for him (7:6–16). His previous letter, a personal risk, had paid off. Reflecting Paul's triumph, this letter spontaneously breaks out in jubilant praise and thanksgiving.

And yet, in no other letter does Paul so openly admit his frustrations. Immediately after a spare greeting he mentions hardships so severe that "we despaired even of life" (1:8). Numerous references crop up regarding the tense relations he and the Corinthians have had. Paul wonders aloud if he has been too hard on them; he acknowledges his own lingering pain.

A Diary for Two Audiences

Second Corinthians, full of allusions and personal references, reads more like a diary than a public document. If 1 Corinthians analyzes the problems of the Corinthian church, this sequel reveals the problems Paul himself experienced.

He doesn't gloat over his victory in getting the Corinthians' support. Rather, he makes himself vulnerable and opens a window into his inner self. He summarizes his state as "afflicted in every way, but not crushed; perplexed, but not despairing; persecuted, but not forsaken; struck down, but not destroyed" (4:8–9).

Although random selections from 2 Corinthians demonstrate the author's seesawing moods, the book as a whole reveals a tenacious man on the rebound. Paul expresses relief that the Corinthians' problems are being resolved, even as he points out new danger signs in the church. Always he keeps in mind a dual readership: the majority who support him, for whom he has warm, loving words, and the minority of dissenters who pose a grave threat to church unity.

How to Read 2 Corinthians

Of all Paul's letters, 2 Corinthians reads most like a personal letter and least like a public document. He wrote it when an intense struggle with the Corinthian church was coming to a head. As a result, it reveals much about Paul's troubled state. He half-apologized for speaking so freely, for appearing to be boasting, and for spending time on "foolishness."

Read 2 Corinthians like you would read any personal letter. Try to visualize the mood of the apostle Paul as he was writing, and look between the lines for clues that would help explain his relationship with the church at Corinth. What were his enemies accusing him of? Watch especially for Paul's spirited reply to criticism, especially in the last four chapters. He tells about certain events in his life that are recorded nowhere else.

You will likely notice that Paul is tying up loose ends in this letter: for example, he is preparing for a third visit to Corinth and asking them to get a collection ready. Yet amid these practical matters he pauses to write profound words on such topics as suffering, giving, and personal ministry.

3-TRACK READING PLAN

For an explanation and complete listing of the 3-track reading plan, turn to page 7.

TRACK 1: *Two-Week Courses on the Bible*
See page 7 for information on these courses.

TRACK 2: *An Overview of 2 Corinthians in 2 Days*
☐ Day 1. Read the Introduction to 2 Corinthians, then chapter 4. It helps explain how Paul kept going despite all his hardships.
☐ Day 2. Read chapter 12, which includes a brief description of Paul's "out-of-the-body" experience and his mysterious "thorn in the flesh."

Now turn to page 9 for your next Track 2 reading project.

TRACK 3: *All of 2 Corinthians in 10 Days*
After you have read through 2 Corinthians, turn to pages 10–14 for your next Track 3 reading project.

☐1　　☐2–3　☐4　　☐5　　☐6　　☐7　　☐8–9　☐10
☐11　　☐12–13

Introduction

1 Paul, an apostle of Christ Jesus by the will of God, and Timothy *our* brother,

¶ To the church of God which is at Corinth with all the saints who are throughout Achaia:

2 ¶ Grace to you and peace from God our Father and the Lord Jesus Christ.

3 ¶ Blessed *be* the God and Father of our Lord Jesus Christ, the Father of mercies and God of all comfort,

4 who comforts us in all our affliction so that we will be able to comfort those who are in any affliction with the comfort with which we ourselves are comforted by God.

5 For just as the sufferings of Christ are ours in abundance, so also our comfort is abundant through Christ.

6 But if we are afflicted, it is for your comfort and salvation; or if we are comforted, it is for your comfort, which is effective in the patient enduring of the same sufferings which we also suffer;

7 and our hope for you is firmly grounded, knowing that as you are sharers of our sufferings, so also you are *sharers* of our comfort.

8 ¶ For we do not want you to be unaware, brethren, of our affliction which came *to us* in Asia, that we were burdened excessively, beyond our strength, so that we despaired even of life;

9 indeed, we had the sentence of death within

ourselves so that we would not trust in ourselves, but in God who raises the dead;

10 who delivered us from so great a *peril of death*, and will deliver *us*, He on whom we have set our hope. And He will yet deliver us,

1:8 On the Rebound

Paul does not tell what specific hardships he had faced in Asia; they were probably known to the original audience. But four separate places in this letter (chapters 4,6,11,12) he spells out an accumulation of hardships that plagued his ministry. Such life-threatening trials had recently driven him into a deep state of despair. He survived, though, and was now using his newfound vitality to comfort and reassure concerned friends in Corinth.

11 you also joining in helping us through your prayers, so that thanks may be given by many persons on our behalf for the favor bestowed on us through *the prayers of* many.

Paul's Integrity

12 ¶ For our proud confidence is this: the testimony of our conscience, that in holiness and godly sincerity, not in fleshly wisdom but in the grace

of God, we have conducted ourselves in the world, and especially toward you.

13 For we write nothing else to you than what you read and understand, and I hope you will understand until the end;

14 just as you also partially did understand us, that we are your reason to be proud as you also are ours, in the day of our Lord Jesus.

15 ¶ In this confidence I intended at first to come to you, so that you might twice receive a blessing;

16 that is, to pass your way into Macedonia, and again from Macedonia to come to you, and by you to be helped on my journey to Judea.

17 Therefore, I was not vacillating when I intended to do this, was I? Or what I purpose, do I purpose according to the flesh, so that with me there will be yes, yes and no, no *at the same time*?

18 But as God is faithful, our word to you is not yes and no.

19 For the Son of God, Christ Jesus, who was preached among you by us—by me and Silvanus and Timothy—was not yes and no, but is yes in Him.

20 For as many as are the promises of God, in Him they are yes; therefore also through Him is our Amen to the glory of God through us.

21 Now He who establishes us with you in Christ and anointed us is God,

22 who also sealed us and gave *us* the Spirit in our hearts as a pledge.

23 ¶ But I call God as witness to my soul, that to spare you I did not come again to Corinth.

24 Not that we lord it over your faith, but are workers with you for your joy; for in your faith you are standing firm.

Reaffirm Your Love

2 But I determined this for my own sake, that I would not come to you in sorrow again.

A Mysterious Visit
Paul's break with the Corinthians

THOSE WHO TRY TO PIECE together Paul's life story from fragments in the two Corinthian letters and the book of Acts usually come away puzzled. Paul, addressing friends who knew that history intimately, saw no need to review every stage of their relationship. Yet for us, reading centuries later, some chronology would help explain his allusions and his emotional state.

> But I determined this for my own sake, that I would not come to you in sorrow again.
> 2:1

Many scholars believe two events occurred to which Paul refers only in passing: the "come to you in sorrow" and the letter written "out of much affliction."

A Change in Plans

In the first two chapters Paul explains a change of plans whereby he decided not to visit Corinth because he didn't want to come in "sorrow again" (2:1). What visit was he referring to?

During his first visit to Corinth, spanning 18 months, the church took shape (Acts 18:11). Paul probably would not have described that time as a time of "sorrow," for his relationship with them at that time was basically positive. Evidently he made a second visit to Corinth, not recorded in Acts, that included a painful confrontation.

Paul planned a third visit to Corinth, but postponed it because he didn't want to stir up the conflict. Later, he wondered about rescheduling that third visit (12:14; 13:1).

The Longed-for Reconciliation

Second Corinthians also mentions a letter written out of much affliction and with many tears (2:4; 7:8). This letter, coming after Paul's unsettling second visit, contained such strong wording that he feared the Corinthians' response. He fleetingly regretted having written the letter. Had it ruptured their relationship? While he preached in the seaport town of Troas, Paul anxiously awaited some report of their reaction, through Titus.

One can imagine Paul rushing to the dock as ships from Macedonia came to unload, fervently scanning the vessels for some sign of Titus. Finally, unable to find peace of mind, he left his ministry in Troas to seek out Titus in Macedonia.

News from Titus at last calmed Paul. The Corinthians had indeed repented (7:7–9) and now wanted to restore ties with him. Feeling encouraged, Paul contemplated a third visit as he wrote 2 Corinthians. He used the letter to rebuild his relationship with them and to spell out his reasons for coming.

Life Questions: Have you ever experienced a tear in a relationship like the one described here? How have you found healing?

2 For if I cause you sorrow, who then makes me glad but the one whom I made sorrowful?

3 This is the very thing I wrote you, so that when I came, I would not have sorrow from those who ought to make me rejoice; having confidence in you all that my joy would be *the joy* of you all.

4 For out of much affliction and anguish of heart I wrote to you with many tears; not so that you would be made sorrowful, but that you might know the love which I have especially for you.

5 ¶ But if any has caused sorrow, he has caused sorrow not to me, but in some degree—in order not to say too much—to all of you.

6 Sufficient for such a one is this punishment which *was inflicted* by the majority,

7 so that on the contrary you should rather forgive and comfort *him*, otherwise such a one might be overwhelmed by excessive sorrow.

8 Wherefore I urge you to reaffirm *your* love for him.

9 For to this end also I wrote, so that I might put you to the test, whether you are obedient in all things.

10 But one whom you forgive anything, I *forgive* also; for indeed what I have forgiven, if I have forgiven anything, I *did it* for your sakes in the presence of Christ,

11 so that no advantage would be taken of us by Satan, for we are not ignorant of his schemes.

12 ¶ Now when I came to Troas for the gospel of Christ and when a door was opened for me in the Lord,

13 I had no rest for my spirit, not finding Titus my brother; but taking my leave of them, I went on to Macedonia.

14 ¶ But thanks be to God, who always leads us in triumph in Christ, and manifests through us the sweet aroma of the knowledge of Him in every place.

2:14 Victory Party

On their return from battle, Roman generals were honored with a triumphal procession, much like the ticker-tape parades given modern heroes. As the victorious army paraded their loot and conquered captives, the streets would be filled with fragrance from burning incense and the smells of the victory feast being prepared.

15 For we are a fragrance of Christ to God among those who are being saved and among those who are perishing;

16 to the one an aroma from death to death, to the other an aroma from life to life. And who is adequate for these things?

17 For we are not like many, *a*peddling the

a Or *corrupting*

---

word of God, but as from sincerity, but as from God, we speak in Christ in the sight of God.

Ministers of a New Covenant

3 Are we beginning to commend ourselves again? Or do we need, as some, letters of commendation to you or from you?

2 You are our letter, written in our hearts, known and read by all men;

3:2 A Human Letter

Chapters 3–5 form one of the Bible's great passages on professional ministry: what is involved in representing Christ on earth. Responding to attacks, Paul defends his "style" of ministry. He discusses the ultimate goal of ministry and the grace of God in using mere "earthen vessels" (4:7) to accomplish his work. But the final proof of effectiveness, he says, is people's lives. In this way, the Corinthians themselves are his best letter of recommendation, for he brought them the gospel in the first place.

3 being manifested that you are a letter of Christ, cared for by us, written not with ink but with the Spirit of the living God, not on tablets of stone but on tablets of human hearts.

4 ¶ Such confidence we have through Christ toward God.

5 Not that we are adequate in ourselves to consider anything as *coming* from ourselves, but our adequacy is from God,

6 who also made us adequate *as* servants of a new covenant, not of the letter but of the Spirit; for the letter kills, but the Spirit gives life.

7 ¶ But if the ministry of death, in letters engraved on stones, came with glory, so that the sons of Israel could not look intently at the face of Moses because of the glory of his face, fading *as* it was,

8 how will the ministry of the Spirit fail to be even more with glory?

9 For if the ministry of condemnation has glory, much more does the ministry of righteousness abound in glory.

10 For indeed what had glory, in this case has no glory because of the glory that surpasses *it*.

11 For if that which fades away *was* with glory, much more that which remains *is* in glory.

12 ¶ Therefore having such a hope, we use great boldness in *our* speech,

13 and *are* not like Moses, *who* used to put a veil over his face so that the sons of Israel would not look intently at the end of what was fading away.

14 But their minds were hardened; for until

this very day at the reading of the old covenant the same veil remains unlifted, because it is removed in Christ.

15 But to this day whenever Moses is read, a veil lies over their heart;

16 but whenever a person turns to the Lord, the veil is taken away.

17 Now the Lord is the Spirit, and where the Spirit of the Lord is, *there* is liberty.

18 But we all, with unveiled face, beholding as in a mirror the glory of the Lord, are being transformed into the same image from glory to glory, just as from the Lord, the Spirit.

Paul's Apostolic Ministry

4 Therefore, since we have this ministry, as we received mercy, we do not lose heart,

2 but we have renounced the things hidden because of shame, not walking in craftiness or adulterating the word of God, but by the manifestation of truth commending ourselves to every man's conscience in the sight of God.

3 And even if our gospel is veiled, it is veiled to those who are perishing,

4 in whose case the god of this world has blinded the minds of the unbelieving so that they might not see the light of the gospel of the glory of Christ, who is the image of God.

5 For we do not preach ourselves but Christ Jesus as Lord, and ourselves as your bond-servants for Jesus' sake.

6 For God, who said, "Light shall shine out of darkness," is the One who has shone in our hearts to give the Light of the knowledge of the glory of God in the face of Christ.

7 ¶ But we have this treasure in earthen vessels, so that the surpassing greatness of the power will be of God and not from ourselves;

8 *we are* afflicted in every way, but not crushed; perplexed, but not despairing;

9 persecuted, but not forsaken; struck down, but not destroyed;

10 always carrying about in the body the dying of Jesus, so that the life of Jesus also may be manifested in our body.

11 For we who live are constantly being delivered over to death for Jesus' sake, so that the life of Jesus also may be manifested in our mortal flesh.

12 So death works in us, but life in you.

13 ¶ But having the same spirit of faith, according to what is written, "I BELIEVED, THEREFORE I SPOKE," we also believe, therefore we also speak,

14 knowing that He who raised the Lord Jesus will raise us also with Jesus and will present us with you.

15 For all things *are* for your sakes, so that the grace which is spreading to more and more people may cause the giving of thanks to abound to the glory of God.

16 ¶ Therefore we do not lose heart, but though our outer man is decaying, yet our inner man is being renewed day by day.

17 For momentary, light affliction is producing for us an eternal weight of glory far beyond all comparison,

18 while we look not at the things which are seen, but at the things which are not seen; for the things which are seen are temporal, but the things which are not seen are eternal.

The Temporal and Eternal

5 For we know that if the earthly tent which is our house is torn down, we have a building from God, a house not made with hands, eternal in the heavens.

4:7 A Picture of Weakness

Where would you keep expensive jewelry? You would want a safe, secure place. You wouldn't stash valuables in, say, a tattered cardboard box. Yet this image comes close to the one Paul used to describe his ministry: "earthen vessels." In his day these vessels were about as common—and as safe—as cardboard boxes are today.

The treasure Paul refers to is the incredible message of the gospel: God's good news of forgiveness and the promise of life forever. Yet, amazingly, God chose to enclose that treasure in people who are like "earthen vessels." Earthen vessels are ordinary and highly breakable, and Paul tells us he is both. An immortal God chooses mere humans as his personal representatives. "And who is adequate for these things?" Paul asks (2:16). He determines to draw attention to the treasure inside him, not to himself.

5:1 The Body as a Tent

Paul often refers to his frail and abused body in this letter. But in this passage he looks past life on earth to a future life when, he says, we will have new bodies "not made with hands." The contrast between tent and house shows the temporary nature of a body in this life compared to what is to come.

2 For indeed in this *house* we groan, longing to be clothed with our dwelling from heaven,

3 inasmuch as we, having put it on, will not be found naked.

4 For indeed while we are in this tent, we groan, being burdened, because we do not want to be unclothed but to be clothed, so that what is mortal will be swallowed up by life.

5 Now He who prepared us for this very purpose is God, who gave to us the Spirit as a pledge.

6 ¶ Therefore, being always of good courage,

and knowing that while we are at home in the body we are absent from the Lord—

7 for we walk by faith, not by sight—

8 we are of good courage, I say, and prefer rather to be absent from the body and to be at home with the Lord.

9 Therefore we also have as our ambition, whether at home or absent, to be pleasing to Him.

10 For we must all appear before the judgment seat of Christ, so that each one may be recompensed for his deeds in the body, according to what he has done, whether good or bad.

11 ¶ Therefore, knowing the fear of the Lord, we persuade men, but we are made manifest to God; and I hope that we are made manifest also in your consciences.

12 We are not again commending ourselves to you but *are* giving you an occasion to be proud of us, so that you will have *an answer* for those who take pride in appearance and not in heart.

13 For if we are beside ourselves, it is for God; if we are of sound mind, it is for you.

14 For the love of Christ controls us, having concluded this, that one died for all, therefore all died;

15 and He died for all, so that they who live might no longer live for themselves, but for Him who died and rose again on their behalf.

16 ¶ Therefore from now on we recognize no one according to the flesh; even though we have known Christ according to the flesh, yet now we know *Him in this way* no longer.

17 Therefore if anyone is in Christ, *he is* a new creature; the old things passed away; behold, new things have come.

18 Now all *these* things are from God, who reconciled us to Himself through Christ and gave us the ministry of reconciliation,

19 namely, that God was in Christ reconciling the world to Himself, not counting their trespasses against them, and He has committed to us the word of reconciliation.

20 ¶ Therefore, we are ambassadors for Christ, as though God were making an appeal through us; we beg you on behalf of Christ, be reconciled to God.

21 He made Him who knew no sin *to be* sin on our behalf, so that we might become the righteousness of God in Him.

Their Ministry Commended

6 And working together *with Him,* we also urge you not to receive the grace of God in vain—

2 for He says,

"AT THE ACCEPTABLE TIME I LISTENED
    TO YOU,
AND ON THE DAY OF SALVATION I HELPED
    YOU."

Behold, now is "THE ACCEPTABLE TIME," behold, now is "THE DAY OF SALVATION"—

3 giving no cause for offense in anything, so that the ministry will not be discredited,

4 but in everything commending ourselves as servants of God, in much endurance, in afflictions, in hardships, in distresses,

5 in beatings, in imprisonments, in tumults, in labors, in sleeplessness, in hunger,

6 in purity, in knowledge, in patience, in kindness, in the Holy Spirit, in genuine love,

7 in the word of truth, in the power of God; by the weapons of righteousness for the right hand and the left,

8 by glory and dishonor, by evil report and good report; *regarded* as deceivers and yet true;

9 as unknown yet well-known, as dying yet behold, we live; as punished yet not put to death,

10 as sorrowful yet always rejoicing, as poor yet making many rich, as having nothing yet possessing all things.

11 ¶ Our mouth has spoken freely to you, O Corinthians, our heart is opened wide.

12 You are not restrained by us, but you are restrained in your own affections.

13 Now in a like exchange—I speak as to children—open wide *to us* also.

14 ¶ Do not be bound together with unbelievers; for what partnership have righteousness and lawlessness, or what fellowship has light with darkness?

6:14 Unequal Yokes

A yoke is a curved wooden bar that fits across the necks of two animals used to pull a plow or wagon. Yoke together a short, speedy calf with a tall, sluggish ox, and you're asking for trouble. Paul probably had in mind the false teachers who so often bedeviled the Corinthians, but his wise principle applies to many other alliances between believers and unbelievers.

15 Or what harmony has Christ with Belial, or what has a believer in common with an unbeliever?

16 Or what agreement has the temple of God with idols? For we are the temple of the living God; just as God said,

"I WILL DWELL IN THEM AND WALK AMONG
    THEM;
AND I WILL BE THEIR GOD, AND THEY
    SHALL BE MY PEOPLE.

17 "Therefore, COME OUT FROM THEIR MIDST
    AND BE SEPARATE," says the Lord.
"AND DO NOT TOUCH WHAT IS UNCLEAN;
    And I will welcome you.

18 "And I will be a father to you,
    And you shall be sons and daughters
      to Me,"
Says the Lord Almighty.

Paul Reveals His Heart

7 Therefore, having these promises, beloved, let us cleanse ourselves from all defilement of flesh and spirit, perfecting holiness in the fear of God.

2 ¶ Make room for us *in your hearts*; we wronged no one, we corrupted no one, we took advantage of no one.

3 I do not speak to condemn you, for I have said before that you are in our hearts to die together and to live together.

4 Great is my confidence in you; great is my boasting on your behalf. I am filled with comfort; I am overflowing with joy in all our affliction.

5 ¶ For even when we came into Macedonia our flesh had no rest, but we were afflicted on every side: conflicts without, fears within.

6 But God, who comforts the depressed, comforted us by the coming of Titus;

7 and not only by his coming, but also by the comfort with which he was comforted in you, as he reported to us your longing, your mourning, your zeal for me; so that I rejoiced even more.

8 For though I caused you sorrow by my letter, I do not regret it; though I did regret it—*for* I see that that letter caused you sorrow, though only for a while—

9 I now rejoice, not that you were made sorrowful, but that you were made sorrowful to *the point of* repentance; for you were made sorrowful according to *the will of* God, so that you might not suffer loss in anything through us.

10 For the sorrow that is according to *the will of* God produces a repentance without regret, *leading* to salvation, but the sorrow of the world produces death.

11 For behold what earnestness this very thing, this godly sorrow, has produced in you: what vindication of yourselves, what indignation, what fear, what longing, what zeal, what avenging of wrong! In everything you demonstrated yourselves to be innocent in the matter.

12 So although I wrote to you, *it was* not for the sake of the offender nor for the sake of the one offended, but that your earnestness on our behalf

7:11 What Suffering Produces

When he wrote about suffering, Paul concentrated not merely on the pain itself, but on what qualities it produced in those who had faith. In this case, he cites the emotional suffering the Corinthians had experienced because of his letter. Although the suffering was unpleasant, it produced something of great value: an abrupt change in their attitudes.

might be made known to you in the sight of God.

13 For this reason we have been comforted.

¶ And besides our comfort, we rejoiced even much more for the joy of Titus, because his spirit has been refreshed by you all.

14 For if in anything I have boasted to him about you, I was not put to shame; but as we spoke all things to you in truth, so also our boasting before Titus proved to be *the* truth.

15 His affection abounds all the more toward you, as he remembers the obedience of you all, how you received him with fear and trembling.

16 I rejoice that in everything I have confidence in you.

Great Generosity

8 Now, brethren, we *wish to* make known to you the grace of God which has been given in the churches of Macedonia,

2 that in a great ordeal of affliction their abundance of joy and their deep poverty overflowed in the wealth of their liberality.

3 For I testify that according to their ability, and beyond their ability, *they gave* of their own accord,

4 begging us with much urging for the favor of participation in the support of the saints,

5 and *this*, not as we had expected, but they first gave themselves to the Lord and to us by the will of God.

6 So we urged Titus that as he had previously made a beginning, so he would also complete in you this gracious work as well.

7 ¶ But just as you abound in everything, in faith and utterance and knowledge and in all earnestness and in the [a]love we inspired in you, *see* that you abound in this gracious work also.

8 I am not speaking *this* as a command, but as proving through the earnestness of others the sincerity of your love also.

9 For you know the grace of our Lord Jesus Christ, that though He was rich, yet for your sake He became poor, so that you through His poverty might become rich.

10 I give *my* opinion in this matter, for this is to your advantage, who were the first to begin a year ago not only to do *this*, but also to desire *to do it*.

11 But now finish doing it also, so that just as *there was* the readiness to desire it, so *there may be* also the completion of it by your ability.

12 For if the readiness is present, it is acceptable according to what *a person* has, not according to what he does not have.

13 For *this* is not for the ease of others *and* for your affliction, but by way of equality—

14 at this present time your abundance *being a* supply for their need, so that their abundance also may become *a supply* for your need, that there may be equality;

---

[a] Lit *love from us in you*; one early ms reads *your love for us*

15 as it is written, "HE WHO *gathered* MUCH DID NOT HAVE TOO MUCH, AND HE WHO *gathered* LITTLE HAD NO LACK."

16 ¶ But thanks be to God who puts the same earnestness on your behalf in the heart of Titus.

17 For he not only accepted our appeal, but being himself very earnest, he has gone to you of his own accord.

18 We have sent along with him the brother whose fame in *the things of* the gospel *has spread* through all the churches;

19 and not only *this*, but he has also been appointed by the churches to travel with us in this gracious work, which is being administered by us for the glory of the Lord Himself, and *to show* our readiness,

20 taking precaution so that no one will discredit us in our administration of this generous gift;

21 for we have regard for what is honorable, not only in the sight of the Lord, but also in the sight of men.

22 We have sent with them our brother, whom we have often tested and found diligent in many things, but now even more diligent because of *his* great confidence in you.

23 As for Titus, *he is* my partner and fellow worker among you; as for our brethren, *they are* messengers of the churches, a glory to Christ.

24 Therefore openly before the churches, show them the proof of your love and of our reason for boasting about you.

God Gives Most

9 For it is superfluous for me to write to you about this ministry to the saints;

2 for I know your readiness, of which I boast about you to the Macedonians, *namely,* that Achaia has been prepared since last year, and your zeal has stirred up most of them.

3 But I have sent the brethren, in order that our boasting about you may not be made empty in this case, so that, as I was saying, you may be prepared;

4 otherwise if any Macedonians come with me and find you unprepared, we—not to speak of you—will be put to shame by this confidence.

5 So I thought it necessary to urge the brethren that they would go on ahead to you and arrange beforehand your previously promised bountiful gift, so that the same would be ready as a bountiful gift and not affected by covetousness.

6 ¶ Now this *I say,* he who sows sparingly will also reap sparingly, and he who sows bountifully will also reap bountifully.

7 Each one *must do* just as he has purposed in his heart, not grudgingly or under compulsion, for God loves a cheerful giver.

8 And God is able to make all grace abound to you, so that always having all sufficiency in

Don't Forget the Poor
A fund-raising letter from Paul himself

EVERY DAY IN MILLIONS OF mailboxes across the United States, letters with special "non-profit" postage stamps appear, stuffed among catalogs, magazines, and flyers from retail stores. Fund-raising through the mail is big business for Jews, Catholics, Protestants and a passel of charitable organizations.

> Each one must do just as he has purposed in his heart, not grudgingly or under compulsion, for God loves a cheerful giver. 9:7

The apostle Paul assuredly never engineered a million-piece charity appeal—the empire's postal service and the cost of papyrus made such an idea unthinkable. But 2 Corinthians does present a direct appeal for funds (chapters 8–9). Jewish Christians near Jerusalem were reportedly on the edge of starvation. Paul seized on the crisis as a perfect chance for Gentile Christians to reach out in compassion and demonstrate their spiritual unity with Jewish Christians.

Practicing What He Preached

In these two chapters, Paul outlines a philosophy of Christian giving, holding up Jesus Christ as a model. He explains the goal of such giving and the proper attitude of the givers. He even applies a little pressure by citing examples of Christians less well-heeled than the Corinthians (8:1–6; 9:1–5).

This brief passage on giving shows Paul's holistic concerns. While still recuperating from personal trauma, he had agreed to head up a major fund-raising drive on behalf of the needy in Jerusalem. Later, working on that very project, he paused to write the profoundly theological book of Romans (Romans 15:25–26). His scholarship didn't dampen a zeal for practical Christian love; his concern for souls didn't crowd out concern for their hungry bodies.

Life Questions: Compare Paul's appeal for funds with those you see in the mail and in the media. Is there a different emphasis?

everything, you may have an abundance for every good deed;

9 as it is written,

"HE SCATTERED ABROAD, HE GAVE TO THE POOR,

HIS RIGHTEOUSNESS ENDURES FOREVER."

9:6 Bonuses of Giving

In taking his collection for poor people, Paul mainly appealed to the Christian responsibility to help those in need. But in this passage he details generosity's side effects. Giving actually enriches and benefits the giver, he says. Also, a gift can serve as an act of worship to God and can inspire other people's faith and thanksgiving.

10 Now He who supplies seed to the sower and bread for food will supply and multiply your seed for sowing and increase the harvest of your righteousness;

11 you will be enriched in everything for all liberality, which through us is producing thanksgiving to God.

12 For the ministry of this service is not only fully supplying the needs of the saints, but is also overflowing through many thanksgivings to God.

13 Because of the proof given by this ministry, they will glorify God for *your* obedience to your confession of the gospel of Christ and for the liberality of your contribution to them and to all,

14 while they also, by prayer on your behalf, yearn for you because of the surpassing grace of God in you.

15 Thanks be to God for His indescribable gift!

Paul Describes Himself

10 Now I, Paul, myself urge you by the meekness and gentleness of Christ—I who am meek when face to face with you, but bold toward you when absent!

2 I ask that when I am present I *need* not be bold with the confidence with which I propose to be courageous against some, who regard us as if we walked according to the flesh.

3 For though we walk in the flesh, we do not war according to the flesh,

Paul Has Had Enough
Answering his critics

> Again I say, let no one think me foolish. 11:16

VERSE 1 OF CHAPTER 10 introduces a dramatic shift in tone. The first nine chapters mainly show Paul's relief at seeing encouraging signs in Corinth. But these last four chapters make clear that hostility was still raging. In fact, some have guessed this section was taken from the painful letter Paul referred to earlier (2:4). Here at the end of 2 Corinthians, Paul boldly confronts his critics.

Who were his antagonists? A picture of them emerges if you compile all the accusations Paul answers throughout the letter. Basically, they were carping troublemakers. In their eyes, Paul could do nothing right.

Paul's enemies in Corinth had blasted him for not visiting them as promised; yet when he did visit they gossiped, "his personal presence is unimpressive and his speech contemptible" (10:10). They had criticized him for not taking a salary and then hinted he was misusing funds (8:20; 11:7–9). To these "most eminent apostles" (11:5), Paul somehow appeared simultaneously unimpressive and yet crafty; overly strict and yet worldly. Some even hinted he was out of his mind (5:13).

A Ringing Self-Defense

You can almost sense Paul declaring "I've had it!" and then rolling up his sleeves to refute the charges. He insists that the future of the Corinthian church, not just his own reputation, is at stake. What does he feel? Something like the burning jealousy of a father who watches his virgin daughter being seduced away from her true lover (11:2–3).

These four remarkable chapters show Paul's passionate nature. Frustrated by having to defend himself, he almost stammers in print. He is determined to convince the Corinthians that he is motivated by a desire to serve God, not by any schemes of profit or power. Along the way, he lists an amazing catalog of his physical sufferings and reveals intimate details of his spiritual life, including one incident still shrouded in mystery (12:1–6).

Judge for yourself, Paul seems to say, to the Corinthians and to all of us. Look at my life and decide, Whose fool am I?

Life Questions: Have you ever been wrongly accused of something? How did you react to your accusers?

4 for the weapons of our warfare are not of the flesh, but divinely powerful for the destruction of fortresses.

5 *We are* destroying speculations and every lofty thing raised up against the knowledge of God, and *we are* taking every thought captive to the obedience of Christ,

6 and we are ready to punish all disobedience, whenever your obedience is complete.

7 ¶ You are looking at things as they are outwardly. If anyone is confident in himself that he is Christ's, let him consider this again within himself, that just as he is Christ's, so also are we.

10:7–18 Style or Substance?

Paul had an image problem, and his enemies were taking advantage of it by ridiculing his unimpressive personal style. Though a powerful, direct, and engaging speaker, Paul was spurned by those who preferred a more golden-tongued style, with lots of rhetorical flourish (verse 10). Such orators may have attracted applause and money, but Paul was looking for results in the form of changed lives, not profit or fame.

In the next two chapters, Paul reviews his qualifications, but he also ironically "boasts" of his weaknesses. Judge a messenger by the substance of the gospel he or she preaches, Paul seems to say—not by fancy words or a flashy style.

8 For even if I boast somewhat further about our authority, which the Lord gave for building you up and not for destroying you, I will not be put to shame,

9 for I do not wish to seem as if I would terrify you by my letters.

10 For they say, "His letters are weighty and strong, but his personal presence is unimpressive and his speech contemptible."

11 Let such a person consider this, that what we are in word by letters when absent, such persons *we are* also in deed when present.

12 ¶ For we are not bold to class or compare ourselves with some of those who commend themselves; but when they measure themselves by themselves and compare themselves with themselves, they are without understanding.

13 But we will not boast beyond *our* measure, but within the measure of the sphere which God apportioned to us as a measure, to reach even as far as you.

14 For we are not overextending ourselves, as if we did not reach to you, for we were the first to come even as far as you in the gospel of Christ;

15 not boasting beyond *our* measure, *that is,* in other men's labors, but with the hope that as your faith grows, we will be, within our sphere, enlarged even more by you,

16 so as to preach the gospel even to the regions beyond you, *and* not to boast in what has been accomplished in the sphere of another.

17 But HE WHO BOASTS IS TO BOAST IN THE LORD.

18 For it is not he who commends himself that is approved, but he whom the Lord commends.

Paul Defends His Apostleship

11 I wish that you would bear with me in a little foolishness; but indeed you are bearing with me.

2 For I am jealous for you with a godly jealousy; for I betrothed you to one husband, so that to Christ I might present you *as* a pure virgin.

3 But I am afraid that, as the serpent deceived Eve by his craftiness, your minds will be led astray from the simplicity and purity *of devotion* to Christ.

4 For if one comes and preaches another Jesus whom we have not preached, or you receive a different spirit which you have not received, or a different gospel which you have not accepted, you bear *this* beautifully.

5 For I consider myself not in the least inferior to the most eminent apostles.

6 But even if I am unskilled in speech, yet I am not *so* in knowledge; in fact, in every way we have made *this* evident to you in all things.

7 ¶ Or did I commit a sin in humbling myself so that you might be exalted, because I preached the gospel of God to you without charge?

8 I robbed other churches by taking wages *from them* to serve you;

9 and when I was present with you and was in need, I was not a burden to anyone; for when the brethren came from Macedonia they fully supplied my need, and in everything I kept myself from being a burden to you, and will continue to do so.

10 As the truth of Christ is in me, this boasting of mine will not be stopped in the regions of Achaia.

11 Why? Because I do not love you? God knows I *do!*

12 ¶ But what I am doing I will continue to do, so that I may cut off opportunity from those who desire an opportunity to be regarded just as we are in the matter about which they are boasting.

13 For such men are false apostles, deceitful workers, disguising themselves as apostles of Christ.

14 No wonder, for even Satan disguises himself as an angel of light.

15 Therefore it is not surprising if his servants also disguise themselves as servants of righteousness, whose end will be according to their deeds.

16 ¶ Again I say, let no one think me foolish; but if *you do,* receive me even as foolish, so that I also may boast a little.

17 What I am saying, I am not saying as the Lord would, but as in foolishness, in this confidence of boasting.

18 Since many boast according to the flesh, I will boast also.

19 For you, being *so* wise, tolerate the foolish gladly.

20 For you tolerate it if anyone enslaves you, anyone devours you, anyone takes advantage of you, anyone exalts himself, anyone hits you in the face.

21 To *my* shame I *must* say that we have been weak *by comparison*.

¶ But in whatever respect anyone *else* is bold—I speak in foolishness—I am just as bold myself.

22 Are they Hebrews? So am I. Are they Israelites? So am I. Are they descendants of Abraham? So am I.

23 Are they servants of Christ?—I speak as if insane—I more so; in far more labors, in far more imprisonments, beaten times without number, often in danger of death.

24 Five times I received from the Jews thirty-nine *lashes.*

11:24 Paul's Many Trials

Acts records many of the apostle Paul's adventures and trials, but this passage shows that other disasters occurred as well. "Thirty-nine lashes" was the maximum punishment allowed under Jewish law—five times Paul had been judged and sentenced by the Jews for his activities as a Christian. In addition, he was often imprisoned under Roman law and sometimes beaten with rods (an illegal punishment for a Roman citizen such as Paul).

25 Three times I was beaten with rods, once I was stoned, three times I was shipwrecked, a night and a day I have spent in the deep.

26 *I have been* on frequent journeys, in dangers from rivers, dangers from robbers, dangers from *my* countrymen, dangers from the Gentiles, dangers in the city, dangers in the wilderness, dangers on the sea, dangers among false brethren;

27 *I have been* in labor and hardship, through many sleepless nights, in hunger and thirst, often without food, in cold and exposure.

28 Apart from *such* external things, there is the daily pressure on me *of* concern for all the churches.

29 Who is weak without my being weak? Who is led into sin without my intense concern?

30 ¶ If I have to boast, I will boast of what pertains to my weakness.

31 The God and Father of the Lord Jesus, He who is blessed forever, knows that I am not lying.

32 In Damascus the ethnarch under Aretas the king was guarding the city of the Damascenes in order to seize me,

33 and I was let down in a basket through a window in the wall, and *so* escaped his hands.

Paul's Vision

12 Boasting is necessary, though it is not profitable; but I will go on to visions and revelations of the Lord.

2 I know a man in Christ who fourteen years ago—whether in the body I do not know, or out of the body I do not know, God knows—such a man was caught up to the third heaven.

3 And I know how such a man—whether in the body or apart from the body I do not know, God knows—

4 was caught up into Paradise and heard inexpressible words, which a man is not permitted to speak.

5 On behalf of such a man I will boast; but on my own behalf I will not boast, except in regard to *my* weaknesses.

6 For if I do wish to boast I will not be foolish, for I will be speaking the truth; but I refrain *from this*, so that no one will credit me with more than he sees *in* me or hears from me.

A Thorn in the Flesh

7 Because of the surpassing greatness of the revelations, for this reason, to keep me from exalting myself, there was given me a thorn in the flesh, a messenger of Satan to torment me—to keep me from exalting myself!

12:7 The Thorn in Paul's Flesh

Bible scholars don't agree on the precise nature of Paul's "thorn." Some suggest a physical ailment, such as an eye disease, malaria, or epilepsy. Others interpret it as a spiritual temptation, or a sequence of failures in his ministry. The Bible gives no clear evidence on the precise nature of this affliction. Regardless, Paul stresses that God permitted the thorn to continue, despite his prayers for relief, to teach him an important lesson about grace and dependence. This conclusion echoes Paul's thoughts on the Corinthians' suffering in chapter 7.

8 Concerning this I implored the Lord three times that it might leave me.

9 And He has said to me, "My grace is sufficient for you, for power is perfected in weakness." Most gladly, therefore, I will rather boast about my weaknesses, so that the power of Christ may dwell in me.

10 Therefore I am well content with weaknesses, with insults, with distresses, with persecu-

tions, with difficulties, for Christ's sake; for when I am weak, then I am strong.

11 ¶ I have become foolish; you yourselves compelled me. Actually I should have been commended by you, for in no respect was I inferior to the most eminent apostles, even though I am a nobody.

12 The signs of a true apostle were performed among you with all perseverance, by signs and wonders and miracles.

13 For in what respect were you treated as inferior to the rest of the churches, except that I myself did not become a burden to you? Forgive me this wrong!

14 ¶ Here for this third time I am ready to come to you, and I will not be a burden to you; for I do not seek what is yours, but you; for children are not responsible to save up for *their* parents, but parents for *their* children.

15 I will most gladly spend and be expended for your souls. If I love you more, am I to be loved less?

16 But be that as it may, I did not burden you myself; nevertheless, crafty fellow that I am, I took you in by deceit.

17 *Certainly* I have not taken advantage of you through any of those whom I have sent to you, have I?

18 I urged Titus *to go,* and I sent the brother with him. Titus did not take any advantage of you, did he? Did we not conduct ourselves in the same spirit *and walk* in the same steps?

19 ¶ All this time you have been thinking that we are defending ourselves to you. *Actually,* it is in the sight of God that we have been speaking in Christ; and all for your upbuilding, beloved.

20 For I am afraid that perhaps when I come I may find you to be not what I wish and may be found by you to be not what you wish; that perhaps *there will be* strife, jealousy, angry tempers, disputes, slanders, gossip, arrogance, disturbances;

21 I am afraid that when I come again my God may humiliate me before you, and I may mourn over many of those who have sinned in the past and not repented of the impurity, immorality and sensuality which they have practiced.

Examine Yourselves

13 This is the third time I am coming to you. EVERY FACT IS TO BE CONFIRMED BY THE TESTIMONY OF TWO OR THREE WITNESSES.

2 I have previously said when present the second time, and though now absent I say in advance to those who have sinned in the past and to all the rest *as well,* that if I come again I will not spare *anyone,*

3 since you are seeking for proof of the Christ who speaks in me, and who is not weak toward you, but mighty in you.

4 For indeed He was crucified because of weakness, yet He lives because of the power of God. For we also are weak *a*in Him, yet we will live with Him because of the power of God *directed* toward you.

5 ¶ Test yourselves *to see* if you are in the faith; examine yourselves! Or do you not recognize this about yourselves, that Jesus Christ is in you—unless indeed you fail the test?

6 But I trust that you will realize that we ourselves do not fail the test.

7 Now we pray to God that you do no wrong; not that we ourselves may appear approved, but that you may do what is right, even though we may appear unapproved.

8 For we can do nothing against the truth, but *only* for the truth.

9 For we rejoice when we ourselves are weak but you are strong; this we also pray for, that you be made complete.

10 For this reason I am writing these things while absent, so that when present I *need* not use severity, in accordance with the authority which the Lord gave me for building up and not for tearing down.

11 ¶ Finally, brethren, rejoice, be made complete, be comforted, be like-minded, live in peace; and the God of love and peace will be with you.

12 Greet one another with a holy kiss.

13 All the saints greet you.

14 ¶ The grace of the Lord Jesus Christ, and the love of God, and the fellowship of the Holy Spirit, be with you all.

---

a One early ms reads *with Him*

GALATIANS

No Second-Class Christians
A protest against treason

P AUL IS ANGRY. YOU CAN almost see his face: flushed red, with lines of tension working in his jaw. Typically, he greets his readers briefly and then launches into warm praise of them. But in this letter shock and dismay replace the usual warmth. A crisis threatens the Galatians, and Paul opens with a withering blast against the people responsible.

> But even if we, or an angel from heaven, should preach to you a gospel contrary to what we have preached to you, he is to be accursed! 1:8

What's the Problem?

Yet, when you read a few chapters, you may wonder why the apostle is so upset. Galatia seems innocent of the kinkiness of Corinth; Paul describes no incest or idolatry here. Instead, he brings up common, everyday Jewish affairs such as the observance of festival days and the practice of ancient traditions, especially circumcision. Where is the big crisis?

Paul could foresee the outcome of the Galatians' thinking: By unduly stressing their Jewish heritage, the Galatians would soon devalue what Christ had done. They would start trusting in their own human effort (their keeping of "the Law") to gain acceptance by God (3:1–5).

If the Galatians continued their policies, the bedrock of the gospel would crumble. Faith in Christ would become just one of many steps in salvation, not the only one. The gospel itself would be perverted (1:6–9).

A Dangerous Class Structure

Paul saw other ominous dangers ahead for the fledgling Christian church. As a Jewish Roman citizen who spoke Greek, he knew well the innate human tendency to look down on people. Roman citizens snubbed non-Romans; Greeks looked down their noses at Romans; and Jews, with their exalted history and highly developed religion, felt superior to other cultures.

The Galatians' insistence on strict Jewish rules would inevitably bring side effects. Subtle distinctions between Christians would inevitably creep in: *Faith in Christ is fine, but a circumcised person who keeps the Jewish law . . . that's far better*. Already, such thoughts had infected two esteemed apostles, Peter and Barnabas. Circumcised Christians were snubbing uncircumcised ones as second-class citizens.

The letter to the Galatians, then, is protesting against treason. It lashes out against subtle dangers that can ultimately pervert the gospel and divide the church. Paul insists that Jesus Christ came to tear down walls between people, not to build them up. In him there is neither Jew nor Greek, slave nor free, male nor female (3:28). Faith in him, not anyone's set of laws (2:16), opens the door to acceptance by God.

How to Read Galatians

G alatians reads like a dramatic court trial. On one side of the courtroom stand Paul's accusers. Persuasive and powerful, these "Judaizers" have followed Paul from town to town, spreading rumors and contradicting his version of the Christian faith.

On the other side sits the jury, the Galatian Christians. They have enjoyed warm friendship with Paul in the past, but some of the charges against him are serious. Did he invent parts of the gospel he preached to them? Has God really given him a special insight? Is it true that his message of "freedom" will lead to a weak, immoral church? Should they turn their backs on their Jewish heritage?

Paul, acting in his own self-defense, paces the courtroom. He uses a variety of debating styles: tight logic, historical reviews, and personal outrage. His integrity, and ultimately Jesus Christ's integrity, is at stake.

In topical content, Galatians covers much the same ground as Romans. But in style, it crackles with a fighting spirit. As you read it, try to visualize that courtroom scene, and judge for yourself Paul's effectiveness as a defendant.

3-TRACK READING PLAN

For an explanation and complete listing of the 3-track reading plan, turn to page 7.

TRACK 1: *Two-Week Courses on the Bible*
The Track 1 reading program on the Life and Teachings of Paul includes one chapter from Galatians. See page 7 for a complete listing of this course.

TRACK 2: *An Overview of Galatians in 1 Day*
☐ Day 1. Read the Introduction to Galatians, then chapter 3. You'll have to concentrate to follow all the arguments. But this chapter gives an essential interpretation of the Old Testament. Study it as a sample of Paul's defense in Galatians.

Now turn to page 9 for your next Track 2 reading project.

TRACK 3: *All of Galatians in 5 Days*
After you have read through Galatians, turn to pages 10–14 for your next Track 3 reading project.
☐1   ☐2   ☐3   ☐4   ☐5–6

Introduction

1 Paul, an apostle (not *sent* from men nor through the agency of man, but through Jesus Christ and God the Father, who raised Him from the dead),

2 and all the brethren who are with me,
¶ To the churches of Galatia:

3 ¶ Grace to you and peace from God our Father and the Lord Jesus Christ,

4 who gave Himself for our sins so that He might rescue us from this present evil age, according to the will of our God and Father,

5 to whom *be* the glory forevermore. Amen.

Perversion of the Gospel

6 ¶ I am amazed that you are so quickly deserting Him who called you by the grace of Christ, for a different gospel;

7 which is *really* not another; only there are some who are disturbing you and want to distort the gospel of Christ.

8 But even if we, or an angel from heaven, should preach to you a gospel contrary to what we have preached to you, he is to be accursed!

9 As we have said before, so I say again now, if any man is preaching to you a gospel contrary to what you received, he is to be accursed!

10 ¶ For am I now seeking the favor of men, or of God? Or am I striving to please men? If I were still trying to please men, I would not be a bond-servant of Christ.

Paul Defends His Ministry

11 ¶ For I would have you know, brethren, that the gospel which was preached by me is not according to man.

12 For I neither received it from man, nor was I taught it, but *I received it* through a revelation of Jesus Christ.

13 ¶ For you have heard of my former manner of life in Judaism, how I used to persecute the church of God beyond measure and tried to destroy it;

14 and I was advancing in Judaism beyond many of my contemporaries among my countrymen, being more extremely zealous for my ancestral traditions.

15 But when God, who had set me apart *even* from my mother's womb and called me through His grace, was pleased

16 to reveal His Son in me so that I might preach Him among the Gentiles, I did not immediately consult with flesh and blood,

17 nor did I go up to Jerusalem to those who were apostles before me; but I went away to Arabia, and returned once more to Damascus.

18 ¶ Then three years later I went up to Jerusalem to become acquainted with Cephas, and stayed with him fifteen days.

19 But I did not see any other of the apostles except James, the Lord's brother.

20 (Now in what I am writing to you, I assure you before God that I am not lying.)

21 Then I went into the regions of Syria and Cilicia.

22 I was *still* unknown by sight to the churches of Judea which were in Christ;

23 but only, they kept hearing, "He who once persecuted us is now preaching the faith which he once tried to destroy."

24 And they were glorifying God because of me.

The Council at Jerusalem

2 Then after an interval of fourteen years I went up again to Jerusalem with Barnabas, taking Titus along also.

2 It was because of a revelation that I went up; and I submitted to them the gospel which I preach among the Gentiles, but *I did so* in private to those who were of reputation, for fear that I might be running, or had run, in vain.

3 But not even Titus, who was with me, though he was a Greek, was compelled to be circumcised.

4 But *it was* because of the false brethren secretly brought in, who had sneaked in to spy out our liberty which we have in Christ Jesus, in order to bring us into bondage.

5 But we did not yield in subjection to them for even an hour, so that the truth of the gospel would remain with you.

6 But from those who were of high reputation (what they were makes no difference to me; God shows no partiality)—well, those who were of reputation contributed nothing to me.

7 But on the contrary, seeing that I had been entrusted with the gospel to the uncircumcised, just as Peter *had been* to the circumcised

8 (for He who effectually worked for Peter in *his* apostleship to the circumcised effectually worked for me also to the Gentiles),

9 and recognizing the grace that had been given to me, James and Cephas and John, who were reputed to be pillars, gave to me and Barnabas the right hand of fellowship, so that we *might go* to the Gentiles and they to the circumcised.

10 *They* only *asked* us to remember the poor—the very thing I also was eager to do.

Peter (Cephas) Opposed by Paul

11 ¶ But when Cephas came to Antioch, I opposed him to his face, because he stood condemned.

12 For prior to the coming of certain men from James, he used to eat with the Gentiles; but when they came, he *began* to withdraw and hold himself aloof, fearing the party of the circumcision.

13 The rest of the Jews joined him in hypocrisy, with the result that even Barnabas was carried away by their hypocrisy.

14 But when I saw that they were not straightforward about the truth of the gospel, I said to Cephas in the presence of all, "If you, being a Jew, live like the Gentiles and not like the Jews, how *is it that* you compel the Gentiles to live like Jews?

15 ¶ "We *are* Jews by nature and not sinners from among the Gentiles;

2:11 Forcing a Confrontation

Galatians 2 gives a fascinating behind-the-scenes account of how the Jewish/Gentile question was splitting the early church. Peter and James, sympathetic to Jewish Christians, acted hypocritically in their treatment of Gentiles until Paul confronted them publicly. Acts 15 gives a more detailed account of the official disagreements and how they were finally resolved.

16 nevertheless knowing that a man is not justified by the works of the Law but through faith in Christ Jesus, even we have believed in Christ Jesus, so that we may be justified by faith in Christ and not by the works of the Law; since by the works of the Law no flesh will be justified.

17 "But if, while seeking to be justified in Christ, we ourselves have also been found sinners, is Christ then a minister of sin? May it never be!

18 "For if I rebuild what I have *once* destroyed, I prove myself to be a transgressor.

19 "For through the Law I died to the Law, so that I might live to God.

20 "I have been crucified with Christ; and it is no longer I who live, but Christ lives in me; and the *life* which I now live in the flesh I live by faith in the Son of God, who loved me and gave Himself up for me.

21 "I do not nullify the grace of God, for if righteousness *comes* through the Law, then Christ died needlessly."

Faith Brings Righteousness

3 You foolish Galatians, who has bewitched you, before whose eyes Jesus Christ was publicly portrayed *as* crucified?

2 This is the only thing I want to find out from you: did you receive the Spirit by the works of the Law, or by hearing with faith?

3 Are you so foolish? Having begun by the Spirit, are you now being perfected by the flesh?

4 Did you suffer so many things in vain—if indeed it was in vain?

5 So then, does He who provides you with the Spirit and works miracles among you, do it by the works of the Law, or by hearing with faith?

6 ¶ Even so Abraham BELIEVED GOD, AND IT WAS RECKONED TO HIM AS RIGHTEOUSNESS.

7 Therefore, be sure that it is those who are of faith who are sons of Abraham.

8 The Scripture, foreseeing that God would justify the Gentiles by faith, preached the gospel beforehand to Abraham, *saying*, "ALL THE NATIONS WILL BE BLESSED IN YOU."

9 So then those who are of faith are blessed with Abraham, the believer.

10 ¶ For as many as are of the works of the Law are under a curse; for it is written, "CURSED IS EVERYONE WHO DOES NOT ABIDE BY ALL THINGS WRITTEN IN THE BOOK OF THE LAW, TO PERFORM THEM."

11 Now that no one is justified by the Law before God is evident; for, "THE RIGHTEOUS MAN SHALL LIVE BY FAITH."

12 However, the Law is not of faith; on the contrary, "HE WHO PRACTICES THEM SHALL LIVE BY THEM."

13 Christ redeemed us from the curse of the Law, having become a curse for us—for it is written, "CURSED IS EVERYONE WHO HANGS ON A TREE"—

14 in order that in Christ Jesus the blessing of Abraham might come to the Gentiles, so that we would receive the promise of the Spirit through faith.

Intent of the Law

15 ¶ Brethren, I speak in terms of human relations: even though it is *only* a man's covenant, yet when it has been ratified, no one sets it aside or adds conditions to it.

16 Now the promises were spoken to Abraham and to his seed. He does not say, "And to seeds," as *referring* to many, but *rather* to one, "And to your seed," that is, Christ.

17 What I am saying is this: the Law, which came four hundred and thirty years later, does not invalidate a covenant previously ratified by God, so as to nullify the promise.

3:17 The 430-Year Gap

In chapter 3, Paul uses clever arguments to put the entire Old Testament law in a new perspective. The law was never intended to make possible a way to God, he says (verses 11,21). Rather, the law was given to "lead us to Christ" (verse 24) by convincing us of the impossibility of gaining God's acceptance on our own. To prove his point, Paul mentions a 430-year gap between Abraham and Moses. God gave his promises to Abraham, who lived long before Moses ever received the law; therefore, Abraham couldn't possibly have depended on the law. God's promise reached final fulfillment in Jesus, whom Paul calls Abraham's "seed" (verse 16).

18 For if the inheritance is based on law, it is no longer based on a promise; but God has granted it to Abraham by means of a promise.

Legalism
Can we do anything to make God love us more?

BEFORE HIS CONVERSION, PAUL WAS one of the best legalists who ever lived. A loyal Jew, he tortured Christians who stepped outside Jewish tradition to follow Christ. If a person could reach God by obeying the law, then he, the strict Pharisee, would have done it.

But in Galatians, he blasts the idea that God's love is conditioned by how many rules we obey. Legalism is like a cage: It can only condemn people and lock them behind bars. As Paul points out, no one has kept all of God's laws perfectly, and all who try ultimately fail (3:10–11).

But now that you have come to know God, or rather to be known by God, how is it that you turn back again to the weak and worthless elemental things? 4:9

No Strings Attached

Chapters 3–4 draw sharp contrasts: a prisoner and a free man, a sheltered child and an adult. Don't act like a slave or a child, Paul says. Act like a privileged son, an heir to a great fortune!

Galatians has been called the "Magna Carta of Christian liberty." "It was for freedom that Christ set us free," Paul declares (5:1). Galatians teaches that there is nothing we can do to make God love us more—or love us less. We don't have to "earn" God's love by slavishly following rules.

Martin Luther said Galatians was "my own little epistle. I have betrothed myself to it; it is my Katie von Bora [Luther's wife]." This slim book proclaims that God has given his love freely, with no strings attached. We should never get over the awesome implications of that truth, Galatians says. Evidently, Paul didn't.

Life Questions: The early Christians went in two directions. Some, like the people in Galatia, became obsessed with legalism. Others took their Christian freedom too far: They refused to follow anyone's rules. Which is the greater danger in your circle?

19 ¶ Why the Law then? It was added because of transgressions, having been ordained through angels by the agency of a mediator, until the seed would come to whom the promise had been made.

20 Now a mediator is not for one *party only*; whereas God is *only* one.

21 Is the Law then contrary to the promises of God? May it never be! For if a law had been given which was able to impart life, then righteousness would indeed have been based on law.

22 But the Scripture has shut up everyone under sin, so that the promise by faith in Jesus Christ might be given to those who believe.

23 ¶ But before faith came, we were kept in custody under the law, being shut up to the faith which was later to be revealed.

24 Therefore the Law has become our tutor *to lead us* to Christ, so that we may be justified by faith.

25 But now that faith has come, we are no longer under a tutor.

26 For you are all sons of God through faith in Christ Jesus.

27 For all of you who were baptized into Christ have clothed yourselves with Christ.

28 There is neither Jew nor Greek, there is neither slave nor free man, there is neither male nor female; for you are all one in Christ Jesus.

29 And if you belong to Christ, then you are Abraham's descendants, heirs according to promise.

Sonship in Christ

4 Now I say, as long as the heir is a child, he does not differ at all from a slave although he is owner of everything,

2 but he is under guardians and managers until the date set by the father.

3 So also we, while we were children, were held in bondage under the elemental things of the world.

4 But when the fullness of the time came, God sent forth His Son, born of a woman, born under the Law,

5 so that He might redeem those who were under the Law, that we might receive the adoption as sons.

6 Because you are sons, God has sent forth the Spirit of His Son into our hearts, crying, "Abba! Father!"

7 Therefore you are no longer a slave, but a son; and if a son, then an heir through God.

8 ¶ However at that time, when you did not know God, you were slaves to those which by nature are no gods.

9 But now that you have come to know God, or rather to be known by God, how is it that you turn back again to the weak and worthless elemental things, to which you desire to be enslaved all over again?

10 You observe days and months and seasons and years.

11 I fear for you, that perhaps I have labored over you in vain.

12 ¶ I beg of you, brethren, become as I *am*, for I also *have become* as you *are*. You have done me no wrong;

13 but you know that it was because of a bodily illness that I preached the gospel to you the first time;

14 and that which was a trial to you in my bodily condition you did not despise or loathe, but you received me as an angel of God, as Christ Jesus *Himself*.

15 Where then is that sense of blessing you had? For I bear you witness that, if possible, you would have plucked out your eyes and given them to me.

16 So have I become your enemy by telling you the truth?

4:16 Paul's Anguish

Paul's letter wavers between abstract reasoning and intensely emotional pleading. As this paragraph shows, Paul had once enjoyed intimate closeness with the people of Galatia. He feels anguish and personal rejection because they now seem to be turning their backs on the faith he had carefully taught them. He is in the pains of childbirth, he says, waiting anxiously for them to grow out of their false ideas (verse 19).

17 They eagerly seek you, not commendably, but they wish to shut you out so that you will seek them.

18 But it is good always to be eagerly sought in a commendable manner, and not only when I am present with you.

19 My children, with whom I am again in labor until Christ is formed in you—

20 but I could wish to be present with you now and to change my tone, for I am perplexed about you.

Bond and Free

21 ¶ Tell me, you who want to be under law, do you not listen to the law?

22 For it is written that Abraham had two sons, one by the bondwoman and one by the free woman.

23 But the son by the bondwoman was born according to the flesh, and the son by the free woman through the promise.

24 This is allegorically speaking, for these

women are two covenants: one *proceeding* from Mount Sinai bearing children who are to be slaves; she is Hagar.

25 Now this Hagar is Mount Sinai in Arabia and corresponds to the present Jerusalem, for she is in slavery with her children.

26 But the Jerusalem above is free; she is our mother.

27 For it is written,

"REJOICE, BARREN WOMAN WHO DOES NOT
BEAR;
BREAK FORTH AND SHOUT, YOU WHO ARE
NOT IN LABOR;
FOR MORE NUMEROUS ARE THE CHILDREN
OF THE DESOLATE
THAN OF THE ONE WHO HAS A HUSBAND."

28 And you brethren, like Isaac, are children of promise.

29 But as at that time he who was born according to the flesh persecuted him *who was born* according to the Spirit, so it is now also.

30 But what does the Scripture say?

"CAST OUT THE BONDWOMAN AND HER SON,
FOR THE SON OF THE BONDWOMAN SHALL
NOT BE AN HEIR WITH THE SON OF THE
FREE WOMAN."

31 So then, brethren, we are not children of a bondwoman, but of the free woman.

Walk by the Spirit

5 It was for freedom that Christ set us free; therefore keep standing firm and do not be subject again to a yoke of slavery.

2 ¶ Behold I, Paul, say to you that if you receive circumcision, Christ will be of no benefit to you.

3 And I testify again to every man who receives circumcision, that he is under obligation to keep the whole Law.

4 You have been severed from Christ, you who are seeking to be justified by law; you have fallen from grace.

5 For we through the Spirit, by faith, are waiting for the hope of righteousness.

6 For in Christ Jesus neither circumcision nor uncircumcision means anything, but faith working through love.

7 ¶ You were running well; who hindered you from obeying the truth?

8 This persuasion *did* not *come* from Him who calls you.

9 A little leaven leavens the whole lump *of dough.*

10 I have confidence in you in the Lord that you will adopt no other view; but the one who is disturbing you will bear his judgment, whoever he is.

Paul Fights Back
When freedom gets dangerous

OVER THE YEARS PAUL CAUGHT on to his opponents' crafty ways of undermining him. Galatians provides a textbook case of his response to critics.

First, Paul answered their personal attacks. Some had questioned his right to be called an apostle. In chapters 1 and 2, Paul insists that he received the gospel directly from God. In addition, he has met every criterion of an apostle.

> *For in Christ Jesus neither circumcision nor uncircumcision means anything, but faith working through love. 5:6*

Chapters 3 and 4 deal with Paul's ideas. Had he strayed too far from Old Testament law and customs? Some hinted that Paul was preaching an incomplete gospel. He answered those objections with a carefully reasoned look at the Old Testament, focusing on Abraham, the father of the Jewish race.

What to Do with Freedom

Then Paul turned to more practical matters. Stressing freedom, not rules, left him open to criticism. Did his strong emphasis on freedom lead to loose morals? To answer this question, he ended Galatians, a letter devoted to Christian liberty, with a warning.

"Why did Christ set us free?" Paul asks. To make possible a life of orgies, drunkenness, and witchcraft? Obviously no. Christ freed us from worrying about whether we are "doing enough" to please God and from uselessly following external forms. But we should use that freedom to serve one another in love and to live a Spirit-filled life.

His arguments and emotions exhausted, Paul concludes, "For neither is circumcision anything, nor uncircumcision, but a new creation" (6:15). A released prisoner, a freed slave, the bountiful fruit of a living tree—all the images in Galatians convey *life*, an abundant life in the Spirit of God, readily available to every Christian.

Life Questions: Read over the qualities of life in the Spirit listed in 5:22–23. Do these characterize your life?

11 But I, brethren, if I still preach circumcision, why am I still persecuted? Then the stumbling block of the cross has been abolished.

12 I wish that those who are troubling you would even mutilate themselves.

13 ¶ For you were called to freedom, brethren; only *do* not *turn* your freedom into an opportunity for the flesh, but through love serve one another.

14 For the whole Law is fulfilled in one word, in the *statement*, "YOU SHALL LOVE YOUR NEIGHBOR AS YOURSELF."

15 But if you bite and devour one another, take care that you are not consumed by one another.

16 ¶ But I say, walk by the Spirit, and you will not carry out the desire of the flesh.

17 For the flesh sets its desire against the Spirit, and the Spirit against the flesh; for these are in opposition to one another, so that you may not do the things that you please.

18 But if you are led by the Spirit, you are not under the Law.

19 Now the deeds of the flesh are evident, which are: immorality, impurity, sensuality,

20 idolatry, sorcery, enmities, strife, jealousy, outbursts of anger, disputes, dissensions, factions,

21 envying, drunkenness, carousing, and things like these, of which I forewarn you, just as I have forewarned you, that those who practice such things will not inherit the kingdom of God.

22 But the fruit of the Spirit is love, joy, peace, patience, kindness, goodness, faithfulness,

23 gentleness, self-control; against such things there is no law.

24 Now those who belong to Christ Jesus have crucified the flesh with its passions and desires.

25 ¶ If we live by the Spirit, let us also walk by the Spirit.

26 Let us not become boastful, challenging one another, envying one another.

Bear One Another's Burdens

6 Brethren, even if anyone is caught in any trespass, you who are spiritual, restore such a one in a spirit of gentleness; *each one* looking to yourself, so that you too will not be tempted.

2 Bear one another's burdens, and thereby fulfill the law of Christ.

3 For if anyone thinks he is something when he is nothing, he deceives himself.

4 But each one must examine his own work, and then he will have *reason for* boasting in regard to himself alone, and not in regard to another.

5 For each one will bear his own load.

6 ¶ The one who is taught the word is to share all good things with the one who teaches *him.*

7 Do not be deceived, God is not mocked; for whatever a man sows, this he will also reap.

8 For the one who sows to his own flesh will from the flesh reap corruption, but the one who sows to the Spirit will from the Spirit reap eternal life.

9 Let us not lose heart in doing good, for in due time we will reap if we do not grow weary.

6:2 Mixing Gentleness with Harshness

Galatians contains some of Paul's harshest language, for he sensed a danger that could destroy the church's faith. But the book also includes some of Paul's most familiar and comforting words. Chapter 6 describes a spirit of tolerance and forgiveness toward those who fail. It also offers encouragement for people who grow tired of doing good when it appears justice is not working out.

10 So then, while we have opportunity, let us do good to all people, and especially to those who are of the household of the faith.

11 ¶ See with what large letters I am writing to you with my own hand.

12 Those who desire to make a good showing in the flesh try to compel you to be circumcised, simply so that they will not be persecuted for the cross of Christ.

13 For those who *a*are circumcised do not even keep the Law themselves, but they desire to have you circumcised so that they may boast in your flesh.

14 But may it never be that I would boast, except in the cross of our Lord Jesus Christ, through which the world has been crucified to me, and I to the world.

15 For neither is circumcision anything, nor uncircumcision, but a new creation.

16 And those who will walk by this rule, peace and mercy *be* upon them, and upon the Israel of God.

17 ¶ From now on let no one cause trouble for me, for I bear on my body the brand-marks of Jesus.

18 ¶ The grace of our Lord Jesus Christ be with your spirit, brethren. Amen.

a Two early mss read *have been*

EPHESIANS

For the Discouraged
Good news for those who feel abandoned and unloved

I MAGINE YOURSELF A CHILD, ABANDONED on the streets of New York. Your immigrant parents died on the ship on the way to America. You have no money and no relatives. You can't speak English. And you are left to fend for yourself.

You are no longer strangers and aliens, but you are fellow citizens with the saints, and are of God's household.
2:19

As many as 30,000 orphans found themselves in exactly that predicament in 1850. They slept in alleys, huddling for warmth in boxes or metal drums. To survive, the boys mostly stole, caught rats to eat, or rummaged in garbage cans. Girls sometimes worked as "panel thieves" for prostitutes, slipping their tiny hands through camouflaged openings in the walls to lift a watch or wallet from a preoccupied customer.

Immigrants were flooding New York City then, and no one had the time or money to look after the orphans—no one, that is, except Charles Loring Brace, a 26-year-old minister. Horrified by their plight, he organized a unique solution, the Orphan Train. The idea was simple: Pack hundreds of orphans on a train heading west and announce to towns along the way that anyone could claim a new son or daughter when the Orphan Train chugged through.

Adopted into a New Life

By the time the last Orphan Train steamed west in 1929, 100,000 children had found new homes and new lives. Two orphans from such trains became governors, one served as a United States congressman, and still another was a U.S. Supreme Court justice.

The Orphan Train provides a vivid parable of the message of Ephesians. To capture Paul's enthusiasm in this book, imagine one more stage in your life as a street urchin in New York.

You have learned to survive and fight off starvation. But one day, someone takes you and puts you on a smoke-belching train jammed with hundreds of other foreign-speaking youngsters. Three days later you are selected by a kindly middle-aged couple in Michigan who introduce themselves as Mr. and Mrs. Henry Ford. You are driven (in an automobile!) to the largest house you have ever seen, and they quietly explain that you are now part of their family. Everything they have is yours to use and enjoy. At long last, by some miracle, you have a family and a home—and what a home!

Welcome to the Family

Paul conveys a feeling something like that in Ephesians, a rich book that expands the message of Jesus' parable of the Lost Son (Luke 15). A big "Welcome Home!" banner is stretched across the lawn, confetti swirls in the air, balloons lunge skyward, and a band plays. Christians have been adopted directly into the family of God. This is a good news book, to put it mildly.

If you feel discouraged or wonder if God really cares or question whether the Christian life is worth the effort, read Ephesians. You will no longer feel like an orphan. Paul describes the "riches of Christ" available to all and points to us, God's adopted children, as his sparkling "Exhibit A" in all the universe (3:10).

Ephesians contains staggering thoughts. Paul wants his readers to grasp "the breadth and length and height and depth" of the love of Christ (3:18). He cranks up the volume to express that love, and not one low, mournful note sneaks in.

How to Read Ephesians

In many ways, Ephesians is Paul's "summing-up" book. The same subjects appear in greater detail in books like Romans, 1 Corinthians and 1 Thessalonians. But in Ephesians, Paul gives an overall view of the grand scheme of the gospel. Only now, Paul says, has God's hidden plan for all of history come to light.

Because it compresses such large thoughts into such a short space, Ephesians deserves very careful study. Read the first three chapters slowly, digesting one paragraph at a time. Such study will prove rewarding: Ephesians gives exuberant good news about the nature of the universe and God's plan for believers.

Like other letters from Paul, Ephesians divides fairly neatly between doctrine (chapters 1–3) and practical advice (4–6). The last half details how our lives should change as a result of the great things described in the first part.

3-TRACK READING PLAN

For an explanation and complete listing of the 3-track reading plan, turn to page 7.

TRACK 1: *Two-Week Courses on the Bible*
The Track 1 reading program on the Life and Teachings of Paul includes one chapter from Ephesians. See page 7 for a complete listing of this course.

TRACK 2: *An Overview of Ephesians in 2 Days*
☐ Day 1. Read the Introduction to Ephesians, then chapter 2.
☐ Day 2. Read chapter 3. You may also want to look at the famous "armor" passage (6:10–18).
Now turn to page 9 for your next Track 2 reading project.

TRACK 3: *All of Ephesians in 6 Days*
After you have read through Ephesians, turn to pages 10–14 for your next Track 3 reading project.
☐1   ☐2   ☐3   ☐4   ☐5   ☐6

The Blessings of Redemption

1 Paul, an apostle of Christ Jesus by the will of God,

¶ To the saints who are ᵃat Ephesus and *who are* faithful in Christ Jesus:

2 Grace to you and peace from God our Father and the Lord Jesus Christ.

3 ¶ Blessed *be* the God and Father of our Lord Jesus Christ, who has blessed us with every spiritual blessing in the heavenly *places* in Christ,

4 just as He chose us in Him before the foundation of the world, that we would be holy and blameless before ᵇHim. In love

5 He predestined us to adoption as sons through Jesus Christ to Himself, according to the kind intention of His will,

6 to the praise of the glory of His grace, which He freely bestowed on us in the Beloved.

7 In Him we have redemption through His blood, the forgiveness of our trespasses, according to the riches of His grace

8 which He lavished on us. In all wisdom and insight

9 He made known to us the mystery of His will, according to His kind intention which He purposed in Him

10 with a view to an administration suitable to the fullness of the times, *that is*, the summing up of all things in Christ, things in the heavens and things on the earth. In Him

11 also we have obtained an inheritance, having been predestined according to His purpose who works all things after the counsel of His will,

12 to the end that we who were the first to hope in ᶜChrist would be to the praise of His glory.

13 In Him, you also, after listening to the message of truth, the gospel of your salvation—having also believed, you were sealed in Him with the Holy Spirit of promise,

14 who is given as a pledge of our inheritance, with a view to the redemption of *God's own* possession, to the praise of His glory.

15 ¶ For this reason I too, having heard of the

ᵃ Three early mss do not contain *at Ephesus*   ᵇ Or *Him, in love*   ᶜ I.e. the Messiah faith in the Lord Jesus which *exists* among you and [a]your love for all the saints,

16 do not cease giving thanks for you, while making mention *of you* in my prayers;

1:13 Branded

Cattle ranchers brand their cattle, loggers carve a symbol on a tree, dignitaries seal their important papers with wax—all these are marks of ownership. According to Paul, the Holy Spirit is God's proof of ownership for Christians. More, he is a "pledge" guaranteeing a great inheritance.

17 that the God of our Lord Jesus Christ, the Father of glory, may give to you a spirit of wisdom and of revelation in the knowledge of Him.

18 *I pray that* the eyes of your heart may be enlightened, so that you will know what is the hope of His calling, what are the riches of the glory of His inheritance in the saints,

19 and what is the surpassing greatness of His power toward us who believe. *These are* in accordance with the working of the strength of His might

20 which He brought about in Christ, when He raised Him from the dead and seated Him at His right hand in the heavenly *places*,

21 far above all rule and authority and power and dominion, and every name that is named, not only in this age but also in the one to come.

1:19 Proven Power

Throughout the Old Testament, God cites the liberation of slaves from Egypt as evidence of his power (over the most powerful nation of the time). "I am the God who brought you out of Egypt," he says. The New Testament holds up an even greater proof: God's ability to give life to the dead. That same life-giving power is available to the individual believer, Paul proclaims.

22 And He put all things in subjection under His feet, and gave Him as head over all things to the church,

23 which is His body, the fullness of Him who fills all in all.

Made Alive in Christ

2 And you were dead in your trespasses and sins,

2 in which you formerly walked according to the course of this world, according to the prince of the power of the air, of the spirit that is now working in the sons of disobedience.

3 Among them we too all formerly lived in the lusts of our flesh, indulging the desires of the flesh and of the mind, and were by nature children of wrath, even as the rest.

4 But God, being rich in mercy, because of His great love with which He loved us,

5 even when we were dead in our transgressions, made us alive together [b]with Christ (by grace you have been saved),

6 and raised us up with Him, and seated us with Him in the heavenly *places* in Christ Jesus,

7 so that in the ages to come He might show the surpassing riches of His grace in kindness toward us in Christ Jesus.

8 For by grace you have been saved through faith; and that not of yourselves, *it is* the gift of God;

2:8 Given, Not Earned

As a converted legalist, Paul insisted on one fact of the gospel: Eternal life comes not by any ritual of rule-keeping (which he calls "works"), but by the grace of God. Yet in this paragraph he notes that God intends for us for "good works." Paul makes a clear distinction: Good works do nothing to help us obtain God's favor, but they follow naturally as we experience the love of Christ.

9 not as a result of works, so that no one may boast.

10 For we are His workmanship, created in Christ Jesus for good works, which God prepared beforehand so that we would walk in them.

11 ¶ Therefore remember that formerly you, the Gentiles in the flesh, who are called "Uncircumcision" by the so-called "Circumcision," *which is* performed in the flesh by human hands—

12 *remember* that you were at that time separate from Christ, excluded from the commonwealth of Israel, and strangers to the covenants of promise, having no hope and without God in the world.

13 But now in Christ Jesus you who formerly were far off have been brought near by the blood of Christ.

14 For He Himself is our peace, who made both *groups into* one and broke down the barrier of the dividing wall,

15 by abolishing in His flesh the enmity, *which is* the Law of commandments *contained* in ordinances, so that in Himself He might make the two into one new man, *thus* establishing peace,

16 and might reconcile them both in one body

---

[a] Three early mss do not contain *your love*   [b] Two early mss read *in Christ*

to God through the cross, by it having put to death the enmity.

17 AND HE CAME AND PREACHED PEACE TO YOU WHO WERE FAR AWAY, AND PEACE TO THOSE WHO WERE NEAR;

2:14 Destroying the Barriers

A Jewish missionary to the Gentiles, Paul wrote and talked constantly about tearing down the barriers between Jews and Gentiles. Jews kept themselves separate from Gentiles by many cultural and religious barriers. Perhaps the most vivid symbol of separation was an actual wall in the temple. Non-Jews could never enter the temple courts beyond that wall, and a further wall separated Jewish men from Jewish women. Here Paul describes how Christ utterly destroyed the "barrier of the dividing wall." (See also Galatians 3:28.)

18 for through Him we both have our access in one Spirit to the Father.

19 So then you are no longer strangers and aliens, but you are fellow citizens with the saints, and are of God's household,

20 having been built on the foundation of the apostles and prophets, Christ Jesus Himself being the corner *stone*,

21 in whom the whole building, being fitted together, is growing into a holy temple in the Lord,

22 in whom you also are being built together into a dwelling of God in the Spirit.

Paul's Stewardship

3 For this reason I, Paul, the prisoner of Christ Jesus for the sake of you Gentiles—

2 if indeed you have heard of the stewardship of God's grace which was given to me for you;

3 that by revelation there was made known to me the mystery, as I wrote before in brief.

4 By referring to this, when you read you can understand my insight into the mystery of Christ,

5 which in other generations was not made known to the sons of men, as it has now been revealed to His holy apostles and prophets in the Spirit;

6 *to be specific*, that the Gentiles are fellow heirs and fellow members of the body, and fellow partakers of the promise in Christ Jesus through the gospel,

7 of which I was made a minister, according to the gift of God's grace which was given to me according to the working of His power.

8 To me, the very least of all saints, this grace was given, to preach to the Gentiles the unfathomable riches of Christ,

9 and to bring to light what is the administration of the mystery which for ages has been hidden in God who created all things;

10 so that the manifold wisdom of God might now be made known through the church to the rulers and the authorities in the heavenly *places*.

11 *This was* in accordance with the eternal purpose which He carried out in Christ Jesus our Lord,

12 in whom we have boldness and confident access through faith in Him.

13 Therefore I ask you not to lose heart at my tribulations on your behalf, for they are your glory.

14 ¶ For this reason I bow my knees before the Father,

15 from whom every family in heaven and on earth derives its name,

16 that He would grant you, according to the riches of His glory, to be strengthened with power through His Spirit in the inner man,

3:16 Reading Between Lines

Paul's prayers often give some of the best insights into the local situation. This prayer (verses 14–21) and the one in chapter 1 (verses 15–23) indicate the church at Ephesus was well-grounded. In Ephesians Paul does not dwell on any urgent problems; instead, he tries to raise the sights of young Christians who have not fully grasped the extent of God's love and grace.

17 so that Christ may dwell in your hearts through faith; *and* that you, being rooted and grounded in love,

18 may be able to comprehend with all the saints what is the breadth and length and height and depth,

19 and to know the love of Christ which surpasses knowledge, that you may be filled up to all the fullness of God.

20 ¶ Now to Him who is able to do far more abundantly beyond all that we ask or think, according to the power that works within us,

21 to Him *be* the glory in the church and in Christ Jesus to all generations forever and ever. Amen.

Unity of the Spirit

4 Therefore I, the prisoner of the Lord, implore you to walk in a manner worthy of the calling with which you have been called,

2 with all humility and gentleness, with patience, showing tolerance for one another in love,

3 being diligent to preserve the unity of the Spirit in the bond of peace.

4 *There is* one body and one Spirit, just as also you were called in one hope of your calling;

5 one Lord, one faith, one baptism,

6 one God and Father of all who is over all and through all and in all.

7 ¶ But to each one of us grace was given according to the measure of Christ's gift.

8 Therefore it says,

"WHEN HE ASCENDED ON HIGH,
HE LED CAPTIVE A HOST OF CAPTIVES,
AND HE GAVE GIFTS TO MEN."

9 (Now this *expression,* "He ascended," what does it mean except that He also had descended into the lower parts of the earth?

10 He who descended is Himself also He who ascended far above all the heavens, so that He might fill all things.)

11 And He gave some *as* apostles, and some *as* prophets, and some *as* evangelists, and some *as* pastors and teachers,

12 for the equipping of the saints for the work of service, to the building up of the body of Christ;

13 until we all attain to the unity of the faith, and of the knowledge of the Son of God, to a mature man, to the measure of the stature which belongs to the fullness of Christ.

14 As a result, we are no longer to be children, tossed here and there by waves and carried about by every wind of doctrine, by the trickery of men, by craftiness in deceitful scheming;

15 but speaking the truth in love, we are to grow up in all *aspects* into Him who is the head, *even* Christ,

16 from whom the whole body, being fitted and held together by what every joint supplies, according to the proper working of each individual part, causes the growth of the body for the building up of itself in love.

The Christian's Walk

17 ¶ So this I say, and affirm together with the Lord, that you walk no longer just as the Gentiles also walk, in the futility of their mind,

18 being darkened in their understanding, excluded from the life of God because of the igno-

Letters from Prison
Time at last to tackle the grandest question of all

TO STIMULATE CREATIVITY, MANY AUTHORS seek out a scenic setting. Yet some of the world's most famous literature originated in, of all places, a prison cell. John Bunyan wrote his *Pilgrim's Progress* there. Russian novelist Alexander Solzhenitsyn's vast output had its conception behind barbed wire, as did his compatriot Dostoevski's.

Parts of the Bible were written in prison as well. Ephesians represents one of Paul's "prison letters" (along with Philippians, Colossians, and Philemon).

> *For which I am an ambassador in chains; that in proclaiming [the gospel] I may speak boldly, as I ought to speak. 6:20*

Time on His Hands

Prison offers authors one precious commodity: time to think and reflect. When Paul wrote his prison letters, he was no longer journeying from town to town, stamping out fires set by his enemies. Settled into passably comfortable surroundings (probably confined to a house), he could slip off his sandals and devote attention to lofty concepts.

Unlike Paul's other letters, Ephesians does not address any urgent problems. With a sigh of relief, the apostle turned to the grandest question of all: "What is God's overall purpose for this world?" Paul answers the question this way: "the summing up of all things in Christ, things in the heavens and things on the earth" (1:10).

A Positive Approach

The apostle Paul often borrowed from the language of athletics to press home a crucial point, and Ephesians ends with a well-composed pep talk. In keeping with this letter's uplifting style, Paul does not scold or warn; rather, he begins, "I . . . implore you to walk in a manner worthy of the calling with which you have been called" (4:1).

Already Paul has taught that Christ lives in each Christian—we are his body. Now he exhorts his readers to think through what it means to represent Christ in the world. When people look at Christians, do they see the qualities of Christ on display?

The last half of Ephesians spells out practical steps toward Christian maturity. Paul blends each new thought into his overall theme, urging us to love *as Christ loved,* to forgive *as Christ forgave,* to submit *as you would to Christ* (5:2; 4:32; 5:21).

Ironically, it took a stint in prison to free up Paul for this endeavor. The book of Ephesians can hardly introduce a new thought without bursting into a song or a prayer. It is no wonder the English poet Samuel Taylor Coleridge called the book "the divinest composition of man."

Life Questions: Suppose you were put in prison. What kind of letters would you write?

rance that is in them, because of the hardness of their heart;

19 and they, having become callous, have given themselves over to sensuality for the practice of every kind of impurity with greediness.

4:19 Loss of Sensitivity

Medical conditions that destroy nerves—leprosy, spinal cord injury, diabetes—are among the most difficult to treat. Without a sense of touch or pain, the patient can get a bedsore by lying in the same position too long, or a footsore by wearing too-tight shoes. The body no longer warns of danger. According to Paul, people can also develop a kind of moral insensitivity, silencing their consciences and hardening their hearts. That condition can prove fatal.

20 But you did not learn Christ in this way,

21 if indeed you have heard Him and have been taught in Him, just as truth is in Jesus,

22 that, in reference to your former manner of life, you lay aside the old self, which is being corrupted in accordance with the lusts of deceit,

23 and that you be renewed in the spirit of your mind,

24 and put on the new self, which in *the likeness of* God has been created in righteousness and holiness of the truth.

25 ¶ Therefore, laying aside falsehood, SPEAK TRUTH EACH ONE *of you* WITH HIS NEIGHBOR, for we are members of one another.

26 BE ANGRY, AND *yet* DO NOT SIN; do not let the sun go down on your anger,

27 and do not give the devil an opportunity.

28 He who steals must steal no longer; but rather he must labor, performing with his own hands what is good, so that he will have *something* to share with one who has need.

29 Let no unwholesome word proceed from your mouth, but only such *a word* as is good for edification according to the need *of the moment*, so that it will give grace to those who hear.

30 Do not grieve the Holy Spirit of God, by whom you were sealed for the day of redemption.

31 Let all bitterness and wrath and anger and clamor and slander be put away from you, along with all malice.

32 Be kind to one another, tender-hearted, forgiving each other, just as God in Christ also has forgiven [a]you.

Be Imitators of God

5 Therefore be imitators of God, as beloved children;

2 and walk in love, just as Christ also loved

[b]you and gave Himself up for us, an offering and a sacrifice to God as a fragrant aroma.

3 ¶ But immorality or any impurity or greed must not even be named among you, as is proper among saints;

4 and *there must be no* filthiness and silly talk, or coarse jesting, which are not fitting, but rather giving of thanks.

5 For this you know with certainty, that no immoral or impure person or covetous man, who is an idolater, has an inheritance in the kingdom of Christ and God.

6 ¶ Let no one deceive you with empty words, for because of these things the wrath of God comes upon the sons of disobedience.

7 Therefore do not be partakers with them;

8 for you were formerly darkness, but now you are Light in the Lord; walk as children of Light

9 (for the fruit of the Light *consists* in all goodness and righteousness and truth),

10 trying to learn what is pleasing to the Lord.

11 Do not participate in the unfruitful deeds of darkness, but instead even expose them;

12 for it is disgraceful even to speak of the things which are done by them in secret.

13 But all things become visible when they are exposed by the light, for everything that becomes visible is light.

14 For this reason it says,
    "Awake, sleeper,
        And arise from the dead,
        And Christ will shine on you."

15 ¶ Therefore be careful how you walk, not as unwise men but as wise,

16 making the most of your time, because the days are evil.

17 So then do not be foolish, but understand what the will of the Lord is.

18 And do not get drunk with wine, for that is dissipation, but be filled with the Spirit,

19 speaking to one another in psalms and hymns and spiritual songs, singing and making melody with your heart to the Lord;

20 always giving thanks for all things in the name of our Lord Jesus Christ to God, even the Father;

21 and be subject to one another in the fear of Christ.

Marriage Like Christ and the Church

22 ¶ Wives, *be subject* to your own husbands, as to the Lord.

23 For the husband is the head of the wife, as Christ also is the head of the church, He Himself *being* the Savior of the body.

24 But as the church is subject to Christ, so also the wives *ought to be* to their husbands in everything.

25 ¶ Husbands, love your wives, just as Christ also loved the church and gave Himself up for her,

---

[a] Two early mss read *us*   [b] One early ms reads *us*

26 so that He might sanctify her, having cleansed her by the washing of water with the word,

27 that He might present to Himself the church

5:21 The Key to Submission

Many readers have struggled with the advice Paul gives in the next few paragraphs. This simple sentence sets the tone for all that follows: We are to submit to others because of our reverence for Christ. In other words, in any human relationship—husband and wife, child and parent, slave and master—a third party is involved, Christ himself. Paul urges us to conduct those relationships in light of Christ's own spirit.

in all her glory, having no spot or wrinkle or any such thing; but that she would be holy and blameless.

28 So husbands ought also to love their own wives as their own bodies. He who loves his own wife loves himself;

29 for no one ever hated his own flesh, but nourishes and cherishes it, just as Christ also *does* the church,

30 because we are members of His body.

31 FOR THIS REASON A MAN SHALL LEAVE HIS FATHER AND MOTHER AND SHALL BE JOINED TO HIS WIFE, AND THE TWO SHALL BECOME ONE FLESH.

32 This mystery is great; but I am speaking with reference to Christ and the church.

33 Nevertheless, each individual among you also is to love his own wife even as himself, and the wife must *see to it* that she respects her husband.

Family Relationships

6 Children, obey your parents in the Lord, for this is right.

2 HONOR YOUR FATHER AND MOTHER (which is the first commandment with a promise),

3 SO THAT IT MAY BE WELL WITH YOU, AND THAT YOU MAY LIVE LONG ON THE EARTH.

4 ¶ Fathers, do not provoke your children to anger, but bring them up in the discipline and instruction of the Lord.

5 ¶ Slaves, be obedient to those who are your masters according to the flesh, with fear and trembling, in the sincerity of your heart, as to Christ;

6 not by way of eyeservice, as men-pleasers, but as slaves of Christ, doing the will of God from the heart.

7 With good will render service, as to the Lord, and not to men,

8 knowing that whatever good thing each one does, this he will receive back from the Lord, whether slave or free.

9 ¶ And masters, do the same things to them, and give up threatening, knowing that both their Master and yours is in heaven, and there is no partiality with Him.

The Armor of God

10 ¶ Finally, be strong in the Lord and in the strength of His might.

11 Put on the full armor of God, so that you will be able to stand firm against the schemes of the devil.

6:11 The Armor of God

Ephesians concludes with a concise analogy, perhaps inspired by a glimpse of a Roman soldier, outfitted in armor, patrolling the grounds of Paul's prison. Paul viewed the Christian life as a kind of warfare, and he wanted his readers to prepare for combat with a dangerous opponent. Bible scholars often note two details: (1) Only the "sword of the Spirit" is an offensive weapon; all the rest were used for defense. (2) No armor protects the back and rear; Paul made no provision for running away from a spiritual battle.

12 For our struggle is not against flesh and blood, but against the rulers, against the powers, against the world forces of this darkness, against the spiritual *forces* of wickedness in the heavenly *places*.

13 Therefore, take up the full armor of God, so that you will be able to resist in the evil day, and having done everything, to stand firm.

14 Stand firm therefore, HAVING GIRDED YOUR LOINS WITH TRUTH, and HAVING PUT ON THE BREASTPLATE OF RIGHTEOUSNESS,

15 and having shod YOUR FEET WITH THE PREPARATION OF THE GOSPEL OF PEACE;

16 in addition to all, taking up the shield of faith with which you will be able to extinguish all the flaming arrows of the evil *one.*

17 And take THE HELMET OF SALVATION, and the sword of the Spirit, which is the word of God.

18 ¶ With all prayer and petition pray at all times in the Spirit, and with this in view, be on the alert with all perseverance and petition for all the saints,

19 and *pray* on my behalf, that utterance may be given to me in the opening of my mouth, to make known with boldness the mystery of the gospel,

20 for which I am an ambassador in chains; that *a*in *proclaiming* it I may speak boldly, as I ought to speak.

21 ¶ But that you also may know about my circumstances, how I am doing, Tychicus, the be-

a Two early mss read *I may speak it boldly*

loved brother and faithful minister in the Lord, will make everything known to you.

22 I have sent him to you for this very purpose, so that you may know about us, and that he may comfort your hearts.

23 ¶ Peace be to the brethren, and love with faith, from God the Father and the Lord Jesus Christ.

24 Grace be with all those who love our Lord Jesus Christ with incorruptible *love*.

PHILIPPIANS

Cheerful Sounds from a Jail Cell
Joy when it's least expected

> Finally, my brethren, rejoice in the Lord.
> 3:1

JOY. THE WORD HAS A quick, poignant ring to it. Yet it, like other words, has been drained of meaning over the years, even tapped as a name for a dishwashing detergent. Nowadays *joy* is used most commonly for a sensation like *thrill*.

We think of joy as something you save up for months to experience and then splurge on in a moment of exhilaration: a trip to Disney World, a free-fall dive, a heart-stopping ride on the world's meanest roller coaster, a hot-air balloon trip. Paul had a different understanding of the word, as this letter reveals.

When You Feel Like Despairing

Philippians uses the word *joy* or *rejoice* every few paragraphs, but the joy it describes doesn't vanish after your heart starts beating normally again. Rejoice, says Paul, when someone selfishly tries to steal the limelight from you. And when you meet persecution for your faith. And when you are facing death.

In fact, the most joyous book in the Bible comes from the pen of an author chained to a Roman guard. Many scholars believe Paul wrote Philippians in Rome just about the time Nero began tossing Christians to ravenous lions and burning them as torches to illuminate his banquets. How could a rational man devote a letter to the topic of joy while his survival was in serious jeopardy? In such an environment, how could joy possibly thrive?

Turning Evil into Good

Paul hints at an answer in a burst of eloquence in chapter 2 (verses 5–11). This pithy, metrical paragraph may have been a hymn familiar to the early church. In it, Paul discusses Christ's perspective in coming to earth.

During the Christmas season we celebrate the grand night God visited earth as a baby. But to the rest of the universe the event looked like an astounding humiliation. God, the Creator of all, took on the unimpressive body of a human being to endure a confining life and grisly death on planet Earth.

Paul points to this death to show that God can take even the darkest moment in history and turn it into good. The cross, and Jesus' not staying dead, proves that nothing is powerful enough to stamp out a reason for joy—joy "in the Lord," as Paul says.

Victory in Jail

Thus even the normally depressing state of imprisonment didn't bother Paul. As he wrote Philippians, he must have recalled his first visit to Philippi. Then, a most unusual jailbreak occurred: The jail broke, but the prisoners didn't (Acts 16:22–28).

Even when Paul stayed in jail for long periods, God used the experience to advance the gospel. As he wrote Philippians, conversions were occurring among the Roman palace soldiers, forced by guard duty to overhear Paul's daily ministry.

Paul summarized his life philosophy in a famous "to be or not to be" soliloquy, concluding that "to live is Christ and to die is gain" (1:21). God is even stronger than death, and that makes a Christian's joy indestructible.

How to Read Philippians

Philippians is simple and straightforward. It's not a formal treatise, but a warm letter to friends. Read it like you would read any personal letter. From the clues Paul gives, try to imagine the relationship between him and the Philippians. What did he like about them? Why were they so important to him?

The Introduction refers to the common use of the words *joy* and *rejoice*. Check out each of these, noticing how Paul can find joy in any circumstances. Use Philippians like a devotional book, first reflecting on what it says, then applying it to your own life.

3-TRACK READING PLAN

For an explanation and complete listing of the 3-track reading plan, turn to page 7.

TRACK 1: *Two-Week Courses on the Bible*
The Track 1 reading program on the Life and Teachings of Paul includes one chapter from Philippians. See page 7 for a complete listing of this course.

TRACK 2: *An Overview of Philippians in 1 Day*
☐ Day 1. Read the Introduction to Philippians, then chapter 2, noticing especially the central passage set off in poetic form (verses 5–11).
Now turn to page 9 for your next Track 2 reading project.

TRACK 3: *All of Philippians in 4 Days*
After you have read through Philippians, turn to pages 10–14 for your next Track 3 reading project.
☐1   ☐2   ☐3   ☐4

Thanksgiving

1 Paul and Timothy, bond-servants of Christ Jesus,

¶ To all the saints in Christ Jesus who are in Philippi, including the overseers and deacons:

2 Grace to you and peace from God our Father and the Lord Jesus Christ.

3 ¶ I thank my God in all my remembrance of you,

4 always offering prayer with joy in my every prayer for you all,

5 in view of your participation in the gospel from the first day until now.

6 For I am confident of this very thing, that He who began a good work in you will perfect it until the day of Christ Jesus.

7 For it is only right for me to feel this way about you all, because I have you in my heart, since both in my imprisonment and in the defense and confirmation of the gospel, you all are partakers of grace with me.

8 For God is my witness, how I long for you all with the affection of Christ Jesus.

9 And this I pray, that your love may abound still more and more in real knowledge and all discernment,

10 so that you may approve the things that are excellent, in order to be sincere and blameless until the day of Christ;

11 having been filled with the fruit of righteousness which *comes* through Jesus Christ, to the glory and praise of God.

The Gospel Is Preached

12 ¶ Now I want you to know, brethren, that my circumstances have turned out for the greater progress of the gospel,

1:7 Paul's Partners

Strong-minded though he was, Paul never worked alone. The warmth in this book comes partly from his confidence that the Philippian Christians were his partners (verse 5), sharing in God's grace. He counted on their prayers (verse 19). At the end of this letter, Paul returns to this theme of partnership, rejoicing in the Philippians' love and thoughtfulness (4:10–19).

13 so that my imprisonment in *the cause of* Christ has become well known throughout the whole ᵃpraetorian guard and to everyone else,

14 and that most of the brethren, trusting in the Lord because of my imprisonment, have far

ᵃ Or *governor's palace*

more courage to speak the word of God without fear.

15 Some, to be sure, are preaching Christ even from envy and strife, but some also from good will;

16 the latter *do it* out of love, knowing that I am appointed for the defense of the gospel;

17 the former proclaim Christ out of selfish ambition rather than from pure motives, thinking to cause me distress in my imprisonment.

18 What then? Only that in every way, whether in pretense or in truth, Christ is proclaimed; and in this I rejoice.

¶ Yes, and I will rejoice,

19 for I know that this will turn out for my deliverance through your prayers and the provision of the Spirit of Jesus Christ,

20 according to my earnest expectation and hope, that I will not be put to shame in anything, but *that* with all boldness, Christ will even now, as always, be exalted in my body, whether by life or by death.

To Live Is Christ

21 For to me, to live is Christ and to die is gain.

22 But if *I am* to live *on* in the flesh, this *will mean* fruitful labor for me; and I do not know which to choose.

23 But I am hard-pressed from both *directions*, having the desire to depart and be with Christ, for *that* is very much better;

24 yet to remain on in the flesh is more necessary for your sake.

25 Convinced of this, I know that I will remain and continue with you all for your progress and joy in the faith,

26 so that your proud confidence in me may abound in Christ Jesus through my coming to you again.

27 ¶ Only conduct yourselves in a manner worthy of the gospel of Christ, so that whether I come and see you or remain absent, I will hear of you that you are standing firm in one spirit, with one mind striving together for the faith of the gospel;

28 in no way alarmed by *your* opponents—which is a sign of destruction for them, but of salvation for you, and that *too*, from God.

29 For to you it has been granted for Christ's sake, not only to believe in Him, but also to suffer for His sake,

30 experiencing the same conflict which you saw in me, and now hear *to be* in me.

Be Like Christ

2 Therefore if there is any encouragement in Christ, if there is any consolation of love, if there is any fellowship of the Spirit, if any affection and compassion,

2 make my joy complete by being of the same mind, maintaining the same love, united in spirit, intent on one purpose.

3 Do nothing from selfishness or empty conceit, but with humility of mind regard one another as more important than yourselves;

4 do not *merely* look out for your own personal interests, but also for the interests of others.

5 Have this attitude in yourselves which was also in Christ Jesus,

6 who, although He existed in the form of God, did not regard equality with God a thing to be grasped,

7 but [a]emptied Himself, taking the form of a bond-servant, *and* being made in the likeness of men.

8 Being found in appearance as a man, He humbled Himself by becoming obedient to the point of death, even death on a cross.

9 For this reason also, God highly exalted Him, and bestowed on Him the name which is above every name,

10 so that at the name of Jesus EVERY KNEE WILL BOW, of those who are in heaven and on earth and under the earth,

11 and that every tongue will confess that Jesus Christ is Lord, to the glory of God the Father.

12 ¶ So then, my beloved, just as you have always obeyed, not as in my presence only, but now much more in my absence, work out your salvation with fear and trembling;

2:12–13 Working with God

Philippians, a practical book, presents theology simply and without elaboration. These verses describe both the human and divine element in our faith: We "work out" our salvation, and yet God "works" in us to accomplish it. Philippians 3:16 expresses a similar paradox: Paul urges that we keep "living by that same standard to which we have attained."

13 for it is God who is at work in you, both to will and to work for *His* good pleasure.

14 ¶ Do all things without grumbling or disputing;

15 so that you will prove yourselves to be blameless and innocent, children of God above reproach in the midst of a crooked and perverse generation, among whom you appear as lights in the world,

16 holding fast the word of life, so that in the day of Christ I will have reason to glory because I did not run in vain nor toil in vain.

17 But even if I am being poured out as a drink offering upon the sacrifice and service of your faith, I rejoice and share my joy with you all.

[a] I.e. laid aside His privileges

18 You too, *I urge you*, rejoice in the same way and share your joy with me.

Timothy and Epaphroditus

19 ¶ But I hope in the Lord Jesus to send Timothy to you shortly, so that I also may be encouraged when I learn of your condition.

20 For I have no one *else* of kindred spirit who will genuinely be concerned for your welfare.

21 For they all seek after their own interests, not those of Christ Jesus.

22 But you know of his proven worth, that he served with me in the furtherance of the gospel like a child *serving* his father.

23 Therefore I hope to send him immediately, as soon as I see how things *go* with me;

24 and I trust in the Lord that I myself also will be coming shortly.

25 But I thought it necessary to send to you Epaphroditus, my brother and fellow worker and fellow soldier, who is also your messenger and minister to my need;

26 because he was longing *a* for you all and

a One early ms reads *to see you all*

was distressed because you had heard that he was sick.

27 For indeed he was sick to the point of death, but God had mercy on him, and not on him only

2:25 A Helper for Paul

The paragraph on Epaphroditus reveals the warm feelings between Paul and the church at Philippi. If Paul was imprisoned at Rome, as many scholars believe, then Epaphroditus traveled more than 700 miles to be with him. He fell sick while visiting Paul and was now returning to Philippi, probably carrying this letter to hand-deliver.

but also on me, so that I would not have sorrow upon sorrow.

28 Therefore I have sent him all the more eagerly so that when you see him again you may rejoice and I may be less concerned *about you.*

Paul's Favorite Church
When others failed, these friends didn't

> I thank my God in all my remembrance of you. 1:3

THE CHRISTIAN CHURCH HASN'T HAD a perfect record throughout history. If you take a random sample of adjectives people use to describe the church, the list will likely include such labels as *racist, judgmental, narrow, divided, pompous.*

The church of Jesus Christ has fallen far short of the ideals he entrusted to it—so far short that we may sometimes forget what the church is supposed to look like. Problems existed from the beginning: Paul's letters to Galatia, Corinth, and Colossae flame with indignation against defects in the early church.

Occasionally, however, a church came along that worked, against all odds. Philippi was one of those rare congregations.

Loyal Friends

From its birth, the church in Philippi had two strikes against it. Its first recorded converts were an Asiatic Jewish merchant, a Greek slave girl employed as a sideshow fortune-teller, and a gruff Roman jailer (Acts 16). Yet more than a decade later, when Paul wrote the church, he could hardly find words warm enough to express his pride and affection.

Paul turned down money gifts from other churches, out of fear that his enemies might twist the facts and accuse him of being a crook. But he trusted the Philippians. At least four separate times they sacrificed to meet his needs. And they also sent Epaphroditus on an arduous journey to care for Paul in prison.

Paul wrote Philippians, in fact, mainly as a thank-you for all that his friends had done. Its bright, happy tone reflects the fondness he felt for his favorite church.

Nevertheless, Paul couldn't resist an opportunity to give some fatherly advice. In a fireside-chat tone, he warned of encroaching dangers: divisions, a strain of perfectionism, and inroads by those who wished to turn Christians back to the Jewish faith. Always, though, he returned to his underlying theme of joy, an emotion that seemed to come easily when Paul remembered the Philippians.

Life Questions: What does Paul single out for praise in the Philippian church? How are those qualities present in your church?

29 Receive him then in the Lord with all joy, and hold men like him in high regard;

30 because he came close to death for the work of Christ, risking his life to complete what was deficient in your service to me.

The Goal of Life

3 Finally, my brethren, rejoice in the Lord. To write the same things *again* is no trouble to me, and it is a safeguard for you.

2 ¶ Beware of the dogs, beware of the evil workers, beware of the false circumcision;

3 for we are the *true* circumcision, who worship in the Spirit of God and glory in Christ Jesus and put no confidence in the flesh,

4 although I myself might have confidence even in the flesh. If anyone else has a mind to put confidence in the flesh, I far more:

5 circumcised the eighth day, of the nation of Israel, of the tribe of Benjamin, a Hebrew of Hebrews; as to the Law, a Pharisee;

6 as to zeal, a persecutor of the church; as to the righteousness which is in the Law, found blameless.

7 ¶ But whatever things were gain to me, those things I have counted as loss for the sake of Christ.

8 More than that, I count all things to be loss in view of the surpassing value of knowing Christ Jesus my Lord, for whom I have suffered the loss of all things, and count them but rubbish so that I may gain Christ,

9 and may be found in Him, not having a righteousness of my own derived from *the* Law, but that which is through faith in Christ, the righteousness which *comes* from God on the basis of faith,

10 that I may know Him and the power of His resurrection and the fellowship of His sufferings, being conformed to His death;

11 in order that I may attain to the resurrection from the dead.

12 ¶ Not that I have already obtained *it* or have already become perfect, but I press on so that I may lay hold of that for which also I was laid hold of by Christ Jesus.

13 Brethren, I do not regard myself as having laid hold of *it* yet; but one thing *I do*: forgetting what *lies* behind and reaching forward to what *lies* ahead,

14 I press on toward the goal for the prize of the upward call of God in Christ Jesus.

15 Let us therefore, as many as are perfect, have this attitude; and if in anything you have a different attitude, God will reveal that also to you;

16 however, let us keep living by that same *standard* to which we have attained.

17 ¶ Brethren, join in following my example, and observe those who walk according to the pattern you have in us.

18 For many walk, of whom I often told you, and now tell you even weeping, *that they are* enemies of the cross of Christ,

19 whose end is destruction, whose god is *their* appetite, and *whose* glory is in their shame, who set their minds on earthly things.

20 For our citizenship is in heaven, from which also we eagerly wait for a Savior, the Lord Jesus Christ;

21 who will transform the body of our humble state into conformity with the body of His glory, by the exertion of the power that He has even to subject all things to Himself.

Think of Excellence

4 Therefore, my beloved brethren whom I long *to see*, my joy and crown, in this way stand firm in the Lord, my beloved.

2 ¶ I urge Euodia and I urge Syntyche to live in harmony in the Lord.

4:2 Women in the Church

Although these two women were stirring up trouble in Philippi, women played a positive role in that church. In fact, Paul's first convert in Europe was Lydia, a businesswoman. Paul met with her and a group of women by a river, and later stayed in her house (see Acts 16).

3 Indeed, true companion, I ask you also to help these women who have shared my struggle in *the cause of* the gospel, together with Clement also and the rest of my fellow workers, whose names are in the book of life.

4 ¶ Rejoice in the Lord always; again I will say, rejoice!

5 Let your gentle *spirit* be known to all men. The Lord is near.

6 Be anxious for nothing, but in everything by prayer and supplication with thanksgiving let your requests be made known to God.

7 And the peace of God, which surpasses all comprehension, will guard your hearts and your minds in Christ Jesus.

8 ¶ Finally, brethren, whatever is true, whatever is honorable, whatever is right, whatever is pure, whatever is lovely, whatever is of good repute, if there is any excellence and if anything worthy of praise, dwell on these things.

9 The things you have learned and received and heard and seen in me, practice these things, and the God of peace will be with you.

God's Provisions

10 ¶ But I rejoiced in the Lord greatly, that now at last you have revived your concern for me; indeed, you were concerned *before*, but you lacked opportunity.

11 Not that I speak from want, for I have learned to be content in whatever circumstances I am.

12 I know how to get along with humble means, and I also know how to live in prosperity; in any and every circumstance I have learned the secret of being filled and going hungry, both of having abundance and suffering need.

13 I can do all things through Him who strengthens me.

14 Nevertheless, you have done well to share *with me* in my affliction.

4:13 Paul's Secret

Shipwrecked, beaten, imprisoned, Paul had seen the down side of life. He had also known prosperity. Both, he suggests, offer temptations. But Paul had discovered a secret for contentment in all situations: his deeply personal sense of living in Christ. In this he found strength to handle anything.

15 ¶ You yourselves also know, Philippians, that at the first preaching of the gospel, after I left Macedonia, no church shared with me in the matter of giving and receiving but you alone;

16 for even in Thessalonica you sent *a gift* more than once for my needs.

17 Not that I seek the gift itself, but I seek for the profit which increases to your account.

18 But I have received everything in full and have an abundance; I am amply supplied, having received from Epaphroditus what you have sent, a fragrant aroma, an acceptable sacrifice, well-pleasing to God.

19 And my God will supply all your needs according to His riches in glory in Christ Jesus.

20 Now to our God and Father *be* the glory forever and ever. Amen.

21 ¶ Greet every saint in Christ Jesus. The brethren who are with me greet you.

22 All the saints greet you, especially those of Caesar's household.

23 ¶ The grace of the Lord Jesus Christ be with your spirit.

COLOSSIANS

Battling the Cults
For everything worthwhile, there exists a counterfeit

> *See to it that no one takes you captive through philosophy and empty deception. 2:8*

YOU SEE THEM IN STRANGE outfits on street corners, chanting phrases with too many vowels and punctuating the chants with a noisy tambourine. Or in airports, thrusting books or flowers into your face. Or in California, all over California. You think of them as crazy cults, populated by misfits. Then one day you hear about a friend of yours.

She seemed normal until suddenly, without warning, she snapped. Her parents searched desperately, even hiring private detectives to help get her back. They found her surrounded by allies, with a new name, a new hairstyle, and, so it seemed, a new brain. She stared at them with clear eyes and told them they were missing out on the most wonderful experience of life. She had joined a cult.

A Breeding Ground

Cults come in all varieties, some recent spin-offs from the New Age movement, others sporting exotic names like Hare Krishna or the Church of Scientology. They demand much from their members: a lifetime of discipline and absolute loyalty. And they also promise much in return: the pathway to a secret, hidden knowledge available only to those who follow them.

The first-century town of Colossae was a perfect breeding ground for cults. Situated on a major trade route from the East, Colossae entertained a steady stream of Oriental traders with mysterious religious ideas. Even Jews in that area worshiped angels and river spirits.

Early Christian converts soon confronted new variations of the gospel. Then, as now, many cults didn't reject Jesus Christ outright; they merely worked him into a more elaborate scheme. Christ and simple forms of worship, they taught, were fine for beginners, but for the "deep things of God," well, some further steps would be required.

The Best Defense

Paul doesn't give a complete glossary of the "philosophy and empty deception" the Colossians were sorting through. From his arguments, we can gather that the philosophy must have included strains of Jewish legalism mixed in with angel worship, Greek philosophy, and strict self-denial.

The best defense is a good offense. Rather than attacking each peculiar belief point by point, Paul countered with a positive theology. The principles he outlines in this book can be used today to judge new cults.

"Christ is enough," Paul declares. He is God, the fullness of God, the One who made the world, the reason that everything exists. All the mystery and treasure and wisdom you could ask for are found in the person of Jesus Christ; there is no need to look elsewhere.

Approach God Directly

Because Jesus bridged the chasm between God and us, we don't have to approach God indirectly, through a ladder of angels or other gods. We have no need to prove our worth through superior behavior. We can come to God directly and boldly because of Christ.

As for Jewish practices, they were mere shadows, made obsolete by Christ's coming. Why not concentrate on the actual image that God sent to earth?

Before Christ, Paul grants, a mystery was kept hidden for many centuries (1:26). But with Christ, everything broke out into the open. The fullness of God lived, died, and came back from death in broad daylight. Why settle for counterfeits?

How to Read Colossians

Although this letter was written to counter specific problems in the church at Colossae, it includes some of Paul's most eloquent writing about Jesus Christ. Chapter 1 contains a soaring paragraph (1:15–20) that may have been used as a hymn by the early church. Note in this book how Paul concludes all his arguments by referring to Christ.

Chapters 2 and 3 deal with dangerous tendencies in Colossae. Paul argues against a "mystery" religion by firmly asserting that Christ is the complete expression of the mystery of God. As you read these two chapters, try to imagine what kind of behavior at Colossae troubled Paul.

3-TRACK READING PLAN

For an explanation and complete listing of the 3-track reading plan, turn to page 7.

TRACK 1: *Two-Week Courses on the Bible*
See page 7 for information on these courses.

TRACK 2: *An Overview of Colossians in 1 Day*
☐ Day 1. Read the Introduction to Colossians, then chapter 1, noting especially Paul's prayer, which precedes the hymnlike paragraph (verses 15–20).

Now turn to page 9 for your next Track 2 reading project.

TRACK 3: *All of Colossians in 4 Days*
After you have read through Colossians, turn to pages 10–14 for your next Track 3 reading project.
☐1   ☐2   ☐3   ☐4

Thankfulness for Spiritual Attainments

1 Paul, an apostle of Jesus Christ by the will of God, and Timothy our brother,

2 ¶ To the saints and faithful brethren in Christ *who are* at Colossae: Grace to you and peace from God our Father.

3 ¶ We give thanks to God, the Father of our Lord Jesus Christ, praying always for you,

4 since we heard of your faith in Christ Jesus and the love which you have for all the saints;

5 because of the hope laid up for you in heaven, of which you previously heard in the word of truth, the gospel

6 which has come to you, just as in all the world also it is constantly bearing fruit and increasing, even as *it has been doing* in you also since the day you heard *of it* and understood the grace of God in truth;

7 just as you learned *it* from Epaphras, our beloved fellow bond-servant, who is a faithful servant of Christ on our behalf,

8 and he also informed us of your love in the Spirit.

9 ¶ For this reason also, since the day we heard *of it*, we have not ceased to pray for you and to ask that you may be filled with the knowledge of His will in all spiritual wisdom and understanding,

10 so that you will walk in a manner worthy of the Lord, to please *Him* in all respects, bearing fruit in every good work and increasing in the knowledge of God;

11 strengthened with all power, according to His glorious might, for the attaining of all steadfastness and patience; joyously

12 giving thanks to the Father, who has qualified us to share in the inheritance of the saints in Light.

The Incomparable Christ

13 For He rescued us from the domain of darkness, and transferred us to the kingdom of His beloved Son,

14 in whom we have redemption, the forgiveness of sins.

15 ¶ He is the image of the invisible God, the firstborn of all creation.

16 For by Him all things were created, *both* in the heavens and on earth, visible and invisible, whether thrones or dominions or rulers or authorities—all things have been created through Him and for Him.

17 He is before all things, and in Him all things hold together.

18 He is also head of the body, the church; and He is the beginning, the firstborn from the dead, so that He Himself will come to have first place in everything.

19 For it was the *Father's* good pleasure for all the fullness to dwell in Him,

20 and through Him to reconcile all things to Himself, having made peace through the blood of His cross; through Him, *I say*, whether things on earth or things in heaven.

21 ¶ And although you were formerly alienated and hostile in mind, *engaged* in evil deeds,

1:21 Getting Practical

Although Paul's letters often launch out into theological deep water, they always lead back to practical issues: What difference does theology make to daily life? The preceding paragraph (verses 15–20) contains a compressed summary of the absolute supremacy of Christ. Now Paul turns to the practical: Christ's supreme power does not distance us from but rather brings us closer to God. He alone has the ability to span the vast gap between God and humanity.

22 yet He has now reconciled you in His fleshly body through death, in order to present you before Him holy and blameless and beyond reproach—

23 if indeed you continue in the faith firmly established and steadfast, and not moved away from the hope of the gospel that you have heard, which was proclaimed in all creation under heaven, and of which I, Paul, was made a minister.

24 ¶ Now I rejoice in my sufferings for your sake, and in my flesh I do my share on behalf of His body, which is the church, in filling up what is lacking in Christ's afflictions.

25 Of *this church* I was made a minister according to the stewardship from God bestowed on me for your benefit, so that I might fully carry out the *preaching of* the word of God,

26 *that is,* the mystery which has been hidden from the *past* ages and generations, but has now been manifested to His saints,

27 to whom God willed to make known what is the riches of the glory of this mystery among the Gentiles, which is Christ in you, the hope of glory.

28 We proclaim Him, admonishing every man and teaching every man with all wisdom, so that we may present every man complete in Christ.

29 For this purpose also I labor, striving according to His power, which mightily works within me.

You Are Built Up in Christ

2 For I want you to know how great a struggle I have on your behalf and for those who are at Laodicea, and for all those who have not personally seen my face,

2 that their hearts may be encouraged, having been knit together in love, and *attaining* to all the wealth that comes from the full assurance of understanding, *resulting* in a true knowledge of God's mystery, *that is,* Christ *Himself,*

3 in whom are hidden all the treasures of wisdom and knowledge.

4 I say this so that no one will delude you with persuasive argument.

5 For even though I am absent in body, nevertheless I am with you in spirit, rejoicing to see your good discipline and the stability of your faith in Christ.

6 ¶ Therefore as you have received Christ Jesus the Lord, *so* walk in Him,

7 having been firmly rooted *and now* being built up in Him and established [a]in your faith, just as you were instructed, *and* overflowing with gratitude.

8 ¶ See to it that no one takes you captive through philosophy and empty deception, according to the tradition of men, according to the elementary principles of the world, rather than according to Christ.

9 For in Him all the fullness of Deity dwells in bodily form,

10 and in Him you have been made complete, and He is the head over all rule and authority;

11 and in Him you were also circumcised with a circumcision made without hands, in the removal of the body of the flesh by the circumcision of Christ;

12 having been buried with Him in baptism, in which you were also raised up with Him through faith in the working of God, who raised Him from the dead.

13 When you were dead in your transgressions and the uncircumcision of your flesh, He made you alive together with Him, having forgiven us all our transgressions,

14 having canceled out the certificate of debt consisting of decrees against us, which was hostile to us; and He has taken it out of the way, having nailed it to the cross.

15 When He had disarmed the rulers and authorities, He made a public display of them, having triumphed over them through Him.

16 ¶ Therefore no one is to act as your judge in regard to food or drink or in respect to a festival or a new moon or a Sabbath day—

17 things which are a *mere* shadow of what is to come; but the substance belongs to Christ.

18 Let no one keep defrauding you of your prize by delighting in self-abasement and the worship of the angels, taking his stand on *visions* he has seen, inflated without cause by his fleshly mind,

19 and not holding fast to the head, from whom the entire body, being supplied and held together by the joints and ligaments, grows with a growth which is from God.

20 ¶ If you have died with Christ to the ele-

[a] Or *by*

mentary principles of the world, why, as if you were living in the world, do you submit yourself to decrees, such as,

21 "Do not handle, do not taste, do not touch!"

2:16 The Search for Wholeness

Legalism in Paul's day concerned such issues as diet, festival days, and religious ceremony. In these two paragraphs, Paul tells why such rules that appear "spiritual" can actually lead a person away from God. Then, in chapter 3, he details what holy living should look like.

In his letter, Paul portrays the Christian life very optimistically. The Christians in Colosse were searching to be "made complete" in the same way modern people work to become "holistic" or "self-actualized." After first affirming that Jesus contains all the fullness of God, Paul asserts that true fullness is found only in Christ (verse 10).

---

22 (which all *refer to* things destined to perish with use)—in accordance with the commandments and teachings of men?

23 These are matters which have, to be sure, the appearance of wisdom in self-made religion and self-abasement and severe treatment of the body, *but are* of no value against fleshly indulgence.

Put On the New Self

3 Therefore if you have been raised up with Christ, keep seeking the things above, where Christ is, seated at the right hand of God.

3:1 Familiar Words

If Colossians strikes you as vaguely familiar, don't be surprised. Paul's letters tend to follow a pattern: a greeting, a prayer, some doctrine, and a practical application of how we should live. Colossians sounds especially familiar because many of its verses have close parallels in Ephesians. In fact, of Ephesians's 155 verses, 78 appear in some form in Colossians.

---

2 Set your mind on the things above, not on the things that are on earth.

3 For you have died and your life is hidden with Christ in God.

4 When Christ, who is our life, is revealed, then you also will be revealed with Him in glory.

5 ¶ Therefore consider the members of your earthly body as dead to immorality, impurity, passion, evil desire, and greed, which amounts to idolatry.

6 For it is because of these things that the wrath of God will come *a*upon the sons of disobedience,

7 and in them you also once walked, when you were living in them.

8 But now you also, put them all aside: anger, wrath, malice, slander, *and* abusive speech from your mouth.

9 Do not lie to one another, since you laid aside the old self with its *evil* practices,

10 and have put on the new self who is being renewed to a true knowledge according to the image of the One who created him—

11 *a renewal* in which there is no *distinction* between Greek and Jew, circumcised and uncircumcised, barbarian, Scythian, slave and freeman, but Christ is all, and in all.

3:11 The Original Barbarians

The word "barbarians" meant those who did not speak Greek. To civilized people of that day, their languages sounded like a stammering repetition of the same syllables—barbarbarbar—hence the word barbarian. Scythians were likewise considered uncivilized and brutish. By mentioning such people, Paul was underscoring the all-encompassing breadth of God's grace.

---

12 ¶ So, as those who have been chosen of God, holy and beloved, put on a heart of compassion, kindness, humility, gentleness and patience;

13 bearing with one another, and forgiving each other, whoever has a complaint against anyone; just as the Lord forgave you, so also should you.

14 Beyond all these things *put on* love, which is the perfect bond of unity.

15 Let the peace of Christ rule in your hearts, to which indeed you were called in one body; and be thankful.

16 Let the word of *b*Christ richly dwell within you, with all wisdom teaching and admonishing one another with psalms *and* hymns *and* spiritual songs, singing with thankfulness in your hearts to God.

17 Whatever you do in word or deed, *do* all in the name of the Lord Jesus, giving thanks through Him to God the Father.

Family Relations

18 ¶ Wives, be subject to your husbands, as is fitting in the Lord.

19 Husbands, love your wives and do not be embittered against them.

20 Children, be obedient to your parents in all things, for this is well-pleasing to the Lord.

---

a Two early mss do not contain *upon the sons of disobedience*   *b* One early ms reads *the Lord*

21 Fathers, do not exasperate your children, so that they will not lose heart.

22 ¶ Slaves, in all things obey those who are your masters on earth, not with external service, as those who *merely* please men, but with sincerity of heart, fearing the Lord.

23 Whatever you do, do your work heartily, as for the Lord rather than for men,

24 knowing that from the Lord you will receive the reward of the inheritance. It is the Lord Christ whom you serve.

25 For he who does wrong will receive the consequences of the wrong which he has done, and that without partiality.

Fellow Workers

4 Masters, grant to your slaves justice and fairness, knowing that you too have a Master in heaven.

2 ¶ Devote yourselves to prayer, keeping alert in it with *an attitude of* thanksgiving;

3 praying at the same time for us as well, that God will open up to us a door for the word, so that we may speak forth the mystery of Christ, for which I have also been imprisoned;

4 that I may make it clear in the way I ought to speak.

5 ¶ Conduct yourselves with wisdom toward outsiders, making the most of the opportunity.

6 Let your speech always be with grace, *as though* seasoned with salt, so that you will know how you should respond to each person.

7 ¶ As to all my affairs, Tychicus, *our* beloved brother and faithful servant and fellow bondservant in the Lord, will bring you information.

8 *For* I have sent him to you for this very purpose, that you may know about our circumstances and that he may encourage your hearts;

9 and with him Onesimus, *our* faithful and beloved brother, who is one of your *number*. They will inform you about the whole situation here.

10 ¶ Aristarchus, my fellow prisoner, sends you his greetings; and *also* Barnabas's cousin Mark (about whom you received instructions; if he comes to you, welcome him);

11 and *also* Jesus who is called Justus; these are the only fellow workers for the kingdom of God who are from the circumcision, and they have proved to be an encouragement to me.

12 Epaphras, who is one of your number, a bondslave of Jesus Christ, sends you his greetings, always laboring earnestly for you in his prayers, that you may stand perfect and fully assured in all the will of God.

13 For I testify for him that he has a deep concern for you and for those who are in Laodicea and Hierapolis.

14 Luke, the beloved physician, sends you his greetings, and *also* Demas.

15 Greet the brethren who are in Laodicea and also [a]Nympha and the church that is in her house.

16 When this letter is read among you, have it also read in the church of the Laodiceans; and

4:12 Prominent Names

Characteristically, Paul ended his letters with personal messages. Epaphras, who is mentioned twice in Colossians (1:7; 4:12), served with Paul and may have founded the church there. The short book of Philemon (verse 23) mentions him as a fellow prisoner with Paul. The main characters in that book, Philemon and his slave Onesimus, also came from Colossae, and Paul refers to a hoped-for visit to Colossae in his letter to Philemon (verse 22).

you, for your part read my letter *that is coming* from Laodicea.

17 Say to Archippus, "Take heed to the ministry which you have received in the Lord, that you may fulfill it."

18 ¶ I, Paul, write this greeting with my own hand. Remember my imprisonment. Grace be with you.

1 THESSALONIANS

What Made Paul Successful?

The apostle fusses over the city that once chased him away

A MODERN-DAY EVANGELIST LAMENTED, "WHENEVER THE apostle Paul visited a city, the residents started a riot; when I visit one, they serve tea." The church in Thessalonica, like many of Paul's churches, was born amid violent upheaval. An angry mob took offense at Paul's work and chased him out of town, accusing him of having "upset the world" (Acts 17:6).

Generally, people do not start riots without a good reason, and in Paul's case they had one. Almost everywhere he visited, an enthusiastic church came to life, provoking the jealousy of the Jewish and Roman establishments.

> *For what thanks can we render to God for you in return for all the joy with which we rejoice before our God on your account. 3:9*

A Concerned Parent

This letter, 1 Thessalonians, gives important clues into what made Paul so effective at founding churches. Accepted as one of the earliest of Paul's letters, it probably dates from A.D. 50 or 51 and provides a firsthand account of Paul's relationship with a missionary church barely 20 years after Jesus' departure.

Someone once asked John and Charles Wesley's mother which of her ten surviving children she loved the most. She replied, "The one who is sick until he's well, and the one who's away from home until he's back." If someone had asked Paul which church concerned him most, he probably would have answered, "The one with the most problems until it's healthy, the one I've been separated from longest until I return."

When Paul lived with the Thessalonians, he was gentle and loving, "as a nursing mother tenderly cares for her own children" (2:7). Later, absent from them, he wrote as if he had only them on his mind all day. In 1 Thessalonians, he praised their strengths, fussed over reports of their weaknesses, and continually thanked God for their spiritual progress.

Questioning Paul's Motives

Some people in the church had questioned Paul's motives, so he opened the letter with a careful review of his work among them. In those days free-lance teachers of religion and philosophy sought a profit; Paul reminded the Thessalonians that he had worked night and day to avoid becoming a financial burden. He also painstakingly explained his unavoidable absence from them.

First Thessalonians stands out from the four books that precede it because, unlike them, this letter doesn't major in theology. Rather, it reveals the gratitude, disappointment, and joy of a beloved missionary who can't stop thinking about the church he left behind. Surely one reason for Paul's success centers on his churches' having made as big an impression on Paul as he made on them.

How to Read 1 Thessalonians

This book provides a touching glimpse of Paul as a pastor. Paul visited Thessalonica at a troubled time in his ministry, while enemies were tailing him from town to town (see Acts 16–17). After he left, the church continued to meet hostility.

First Thessalonians is our earliest record of the life of a Christian community. Paul wrote this letter after receiving a mostly positive report (from Timothy) on the Thessalonians' spiritual health. He rejoiced at the good news, but also showed concern over the church's problems.

As you read 1 Thessalonians, notice the issues that Paul addresses: Christians were raising questions about Jesus' return to earth and were disagreeing on matters of morality. But mainly, look for signs of Paul's relationship to the church at Thessalonica.

3-TRACK READING PLAN

For an explanation and complete listing of the 3-track reading plan, turn to page 7.

TRACK 1: *Two-Week Courses on the Bible*
See page 7 for information on these courses.

TRACK 2: *An Overview of 1 Thessalonians in 1 Day*
☐ Day 1. Read the Introduction to 1 Thessalonians, then chapters 3 and 4. The chapters are very short, so you can easily read two together.
Now turn to page 9 for your next Track 2 reading project.

TRACK 3: *All of 1 Thessalonians in 3 Days*
After you have read through 1 Thessalonians, turn to pages 10–14 for your next Track 3 reading project.
☐1–2   ☐3–4   ☐5

Thanksgiving for These Believers

1 Paul and Silvanus and Timothy,
¶ To the church of the Thessalonians in God the Father and the Lord Jesus Christ: Grace to you and peace.

2 ¶ We give thanks to God always for all of you, making mention *of you* in our prayers;

3 constantly bearing in mind your work of faith and labor of love and steadfastness of hope in our Lord Jesus Christ in the presence of our God and Father,

4 knowing, brethren beloved by God, *His* choice of you;

5 for our gospel did not come to you in word only, but also in power and in the Holy Spirit and with full conviction; just as you know what kind of men we proved to be among you for your sake.

6 You also became imitators of us and of the Lord, having received the word in much tribulation with the joy of the Holy Spirit,

7 so that you became an example to all the believers in Macedonia and in Achaia.

8 For the word of the Lord has sounded forth from you, not only in Macedonia and Achaia, but also in every place your faith toward God has gone forth, so that we have no need to say anything.

9 For they themselves report about us what kind of a reception we had with you, and how you turned to God from idols to serve a living and true God,

10 and to wait for His Son from heaven, whom He raised from the dead, *that is* Jesus, who rescues us from the wrath to come.

Paul's Ministry

2 For you yourselves know, brethren, that our coming to you was not in vain,

2 but after we had already suffered and been mistreated in Philippi, as you know, we had the boldness in our God to speak to you the gospel of God amid much opposition.

3 For our exhortation does not *come* from error or impurity or by way of deceit;

4 but just as we have been approved by God to be entrusted with the gospel, so we speak, not as pleasing men, but God who examines our hearts.

5 For we never came with flattering speech, as you know, nor with a pretext for greed—God is witness—

6 nor did we seek glory from men, either from you or from others, even though as apostles of Christ we might have asserted our authority.

7 But we proved to be ᵃgentle among you, as a nursing *mother* tenderly cares for her own children.

8 Having so fond an affection for you, we were well-pleased to impart to you not only the gospel of God but also our own lives, because you had become very dear to us.

9 ¶ For you recall, brethren, our labor and hardship, *how* working night and day so as not to be a burden to any of you, we proclaimed to you the gospel of God.

10 You are witnesses, and *so is* God, how devoutly and uprightly and blamelessly we behaved toward you believers;

11 just as you know how we *were* exhorting

ᵃ Three early mss read *babes*

and encouraging and imploring each one of you as a father *would* his own children,

12 so that you would walk in a manner worthy of the God who calls you into His own kingdom and glory.

2:9 Working for a Living

Paul supported his own ministry with a trade (tentmaking) rather than take funds from others. He did this to avoid suspicion that he was profiting financially from his spiritual work. With the Thessalonians, his hard work gave another advantage: It set a good example for those who were quitting their jobs in anticipation of Christ's return to earth.

13 ¶ For this reason we also constantly thank God that when you received the word of God which you heard from us, you accepted *it* not *as* the word of men, but *for* what it really is, the word of God, which also performs its work in you who believe.

14 For you, brethren, became imitators of the churches of God in Christ Jesus that are in Judea, for you also endured the same sufferings at the hands of your own countrymen, even as they *did* from the Jews,

15 who both killed the Lord Jesus and the prophets, and drove us out. They are not pleasing to God, but hostile to all men,

16 hindering us from speaking to the Gentiles so that they may be saved; with the result that they always fill up the measure of their sins. But wrath has come upon them *a*to the utmost.

17 ¶ But we, brethren, having been taken away from you for a short while—in person, not in spirit—were all the more eager with great desire to see your face.

18 For we wanted to come to you—I, Paul, more than once—and *yet* Satan hindered us.

19 For who is our hope or joy or crown of exultation? Is it not even you, in the presence of our Lord Jesus at His coming?

20 For you are our glory and joy.

Encouragement of Timothy's Visit

3 Therefore when we could endure *it* no longer, we thought it best to be left behind at Athens alone,

2 and we sent Timothy, our brother and God's fellow worker in the gospel of Christ, to strengthen and encourage you as to your faith,

3 so that no one would be disturbed by these afflictions; for you yourselves know that we have been destined for this.

4 For indeed when we were with you, we *kept*

telling you in advance that we were going to suffer affliction; and so it came to pass, as you know.

5 For this reason, when I could endure *it* no longer, I also sent to find out about your faith, for fear that the tempter might have tempted you, and our labor would be in vain.

6 ¶ But now that Timothy has come to us from you, and has brought us good news of your faith and love, and that you always think kindly of us, longing to see us just as we also long to see you,

7 for this reason, brethren, in all our distress and affliction we were comforted about you through your faith;

8 for now we *really* live, if you stand firm in the Lord.

9 For what thanks can we render to God for you in return for all the joy with which we rejoice before our God on your account,

10 as we night and day keep praying most earnestly that we may see your face, and may complete what is lacking in your faith?

3:4 Paul Defends His Actions

First Thessalonians indicates some people had questioned Paul's true motives regarding their church. Throughout his ministry, Paul endured constant criticism and personal attacks. Here he replies by reviewing his history with the church. This section (2:17–3:10) details Paul's foiled attempts at a personal visit and then his sending Timothy as a messenger.

11 ¶ Now may our God and Father Himself and Jesus our Lord direct our way to you;

12 and may the Lord cause you to increase and abound in love for one another, and for all people, just as we also *do* for you;

13 so that He may establish your hearts without blame in holiness before our God and Father at the coming of our Lord Jesus with all His saints.

Sanctification and Love

4 Finally then, brethren, we request and exhort you in the Lord Jesus, that as you received from us *instruction* as to how you ought to walk and please God (just as you actually do *b*walk), that you excel still more.

2 For you know what commandments we gave you *c*by *the authority of* the Lord Jesus.

3 For this is the will of God, your sanctification; *that is,* that you abstain from sexual immorality;

4 that each of you know how to possess his own *d*vessel in sanctification and honor,

5 not in lustful passion, like the Gentiles who do not know God;

6 *and* that no man transgress and defraud his

---

a Or *forever* or *altogether*; lit *to the end*   *b* Or *conduct yourselves*   *c* Lit *through the Lord*   *d* I.e. body; or wife brother in the matter because the Lord is *the* avenger in all these things, just as we also told you before and solemnly warned *you.*

7 For God has not called us for the purpose of impurity, but in sanctification.

8 So, he who rejects *this* is not rejecting man but the God who gives His Holy Spirit to you.

9 ¶ Now as to the love of the brethren, you have no need for *anyone* to write to you, for you yourselves are taught by God to love one another;

10 for indeed you do practice it toward all the brethren who are in all Macedonia. But we urge you, brethren, to excel still more,

11 and to make it your ambition to lead a quiet life and attend to your own business and work with your hands, just as we commanded you,

12 so that you will behave properly toward outsiders and not be in any need.

Those Who Died in Christ

13 ¶ But we do not want you to be uninformed, brethren, about those who are asleep, so that you will not grieve as do the rest who have no hope.

4:13 The Sleep of Death

The Bible sometimes uses the word asleep to describe people who have died. In this context, Paul was answering a question the Thessalonians had asked. What of people who died before Christ's second coming—would they be left behind? Paul assures them that all people in Christ would have an afterlife with him—not just those still alive when he returned.

Preparing for the End
Obsessed with Jesus' second coming

YOU SEE THEM OCCASIONALLY ON the street corners of modern cities: strange-looking people with hand-lettered wooden signs draped over their bodies. "Jesus is coming again!" they proclaim. "Prepare to meet thy doom!" Similar messages are scrawled on rocks or on highway overpasses. And every few years a new prophet comes along suggesting a new, revised date for Jesus' return.

> *Now as to the times and the epochs, brethren, you have no need of anything to be written to you.*
> *5:1*

Archaeologists have yet to unearth Thessalonican graffiti, but this letter makes clear that 19 centuries ago people were already awaiting Jesus' promised return to earth. In fact, they were worried. What about people who died before Jesus returned? they wondered. Would they somehow miss out on life after death? Paul gives a direct and encouraging answer.

A Mixture of Fear and Hope

The Thessalonians had good reason to concern themselves with the future: They lived in constant danger of persecution by the authorities. On any night a knock on the door or the scrape of footsteps outside could mean imprisonment or death. Understandably, the young church looked to Jesus' second coming with longing and hope.

Paul assured them that hope in the future was well-founded, whether or not they lived to see Jesus' return. But he warned against an undue fixation on the future. He urged the Thessalonians to get back to work, indicating that some enthusiasts had quit their jobs to prepare for Jesus' return. Lead a quiet life and attend to your own business, Paul advised (4:11).

Waiting for Jesus' Return

The Thessalonians were merely the first in a long line of Christians obsessed with future events. Whole generations since have been caught up in frenzied speculations on the exact time and place of the second coming, only to watch their predictions misfire. Paul shrugs off such speculation (5:1–2). He presents the right way and the wrong way to prepare for Jesus' return.

Paul does not show undue alarm. The mild tone of his rebukes indicates his confidence in the Thessalonians. He asks that they follow God "still more ," as in fact they are already doing (4:1,10; 5:11).

History records that the first readers of this letter responded well. Despite lurking problems (4:3–12), the church in Thessalonica continued to show vigor and health for many years. Christians there stayed so faithful throughout persecutions that their city became known as "The City of Orthodoxy."

Life Questions: How should Jesus' second coming affect us and how can we prepare for it? What extremes does Paul warn against?

14 For if we believe that Jesus died and rose again, even so God will bring with Him those who have fallen asleep in Jesus.

15 For this we say to you by the word of the Lord, that we who are alive and remain until the coming of the Lord, will not precede those who have fallen asleep.

16 For the Lord Himself will descend from heaven with a shout, with the voice of *the* archangel and with the trumpet of God, and the dead in Christ will rise first.

17 Then we who are alive and remain will be caught up together with them in the clouds to meet the Lord in the air, and so we shall always be with the Lord.

18 Therefore comfort one another with these words.

The Day of the Lord

5 Now as to the times and the epochs, brethren, you have no need of anything to be written to you.

2 For you yourselves know full well that the day of the Lord will come just like a thief in the night.

3 While they are saying, "Peace and safety!" then destruction will come upon them suddenly like labor pains upon a woman with child, and they will not escape.

4 But you, brethren, are not in darkness, that the day would overtake you like a thief;

5 for you are all sons of light and sons of day. We are not of night nor of darkness;

6 so then let us not sleep as others do, but let us be alert and ^asober.

7 For those who sleep do their sleeping at night, and those who get drunk get drunk at night.

8 But since we are of *the* day, let us be ^asober, having put on the breastplate of faith and love, and as a helmet, the hope of salvation.

9 For God has not destined us for wrath, but

for obtaining salvation through our Lord Jesus Christ,

10 who died for us, so that whether we are awake or asleep, we will live together with Him.

11 Therefore encourage one another and build up one another, just as you also are doing.

Christian Conduct

12 ¶ But we request of you, brethren, that you appreciate those who diligently labor among you, and have charge over you in the Lord and give you instruction,

13 and that you esteem them very highly in love because of their work. Live in peace with one another.

14 We urge you, brethren, admonish the unruly, encourage the fainthearted, help the weak, be patient with everyone.

15 See that no one repays another with evil for evil, but always seek after that which is good for one another and for all people.

16 Rejoice always;

17 pray without ceasing;

18 in everything give thanks; for this is God's will for you in Christ Jesus.

19 Do not quench the Spirit;

20 do not despise prophetic ^butterances.

21 But examine everything *carefully*; hold fast to that which is good;

22 abstain from every ^cform of evil.

23 ¶ Now may the God of peace Himself sanctify you entirely; and may your spirit and soul and body be preserved complete, without blame at the coming of our Lord Jesus Christ.

24 Faithful is He who calls you, and He also will bring it to pass.

25 ¶ Brethren, pray for us^d.

26 ¶ Greet all the brethren with a holy kiss.

27 I adjure you by the Lord to have this letter read to all the brethren.

28 ¶ The grace of our Lord Jesus Christ be with you.

---

^a Or *self-controlled*   ^b Or *gifts*   ^c Or *appearance*   ^d Two early mss add *also*

2 THESSALONIANS

A Patient Who Didn't Follow Orders

When good advice goes ignored

HIS LIGHT HUMOR AND CASUAL manner are gone now. When he was setting the bone, the doctor joked about the benefits of your wearing your arm in a sling every day: instant sympathy from your friends, an opportunity for wild stories on how you got hurt, an easy alibi to avoid heavy work.

> But as for you, brethren, do not grow weary of doing good. 3:13

But now, three weeks later, lines of concern crease his forehead as he studies the X-rays and notes the slow progress of healing. "I told you to take it easy! Are you giving that arm any rest at all? You can't expect new bone to grow overnight, you know."

When you describe the throbbing pain of the last few days, he grimaces, shakes his head, and scribbles something on a prescription pad. "You shouldn't be feeling pain at this stage," he grumbles. "If you had followed my advice from the beginning you wouldn't need these pills." He then repeats all the instructions he gave you on the first visit, using stronger, less friendly words.

Same Advice, Sterner Words

The book of 2 Thessalonians resembles such a follow-up visit to a family doctor. If you list the topics Paul covers, you will find an uncanny similarity to the subjects of his first letter: Jesus' second coming, spiritual growth, idleness among certain nonworkers. However, a sterner, more formal approach replaces the warm tenderness of the first letter.

Obviously, the Thessalonians failed to listen well the first time. Paul wrote this second letter just a few months later, summarizing his message this way: "So then, brethren, stand firm and hold to the traditions which you were taught, whether by word of mouth or by letter" (2:15). Instead of coaxing, Paul now commands.

Squelching a Rumor

One topic, Jesus' return, dominates 2 Thessalonians more than any other. Church members were stirred up by a false report, allegedly from Paul, claiming the last days had already arrived (2:2). Paul denies the report and outlines several events that must occur before the day of the Lord arrives.

Here, as elsewhere, the Bible does not focus on the last days in an abstract, theoretical way. Rather, it draws a practical application to how we should live. Paul cautions his readers to be patient and steady. He asks them to trust that Jesus' return will finally bring justice to the earth, urges them to live worthily for that day, and commands them not to tolerate idleness—a prescription for health that has equal potency today.

How to Read 2 Thessalonians

Second Thessalonians has many parallels to its companion letter. The Christians in Thessalonica were still struggling with major problems, and each of the three chapters of this book concerns one of them.

Chapter 1 gives encouragement to Christians who were undergoing persecution for their faith. Chapter 2 attacks head-on the false teaching about the day of the Lord. Rumors about the day of the Lord had caused great excitement and speculation, leading to the practical errors Paul addresses in chapter 3.

Paul's specific words about what must happen before the day of the Lord make this letter a key part of New Testament prophecy. The prophecy passages aren't self-explanatory, and may require a Bible reference book for understanding.

Although 2 Thessalonians is Paul's shortest letter to a church, it contains four of his prayers. Note especially his concern for the Thessalonians as expressed in the prayers.

3-TRACK READING PLAN

For an explanation and complete listing of the 3-track reading plan, turn to page 7.

TRACK 1: *Two-Week Courses on the Bible*
See page 7 for information on these courses.

TRACK 2: *An Overview of 2 Thessalonians in 1 Day*
☐ Day 1. Read the Introduction to 2 Thessalonians, then chapter 2, the key chapter predicting what events will precede Jesus' return.

Now turn to page 9 for your next Track 2 reading project.

TRACK 3: *All of 2 Thessalonians in 2 Days*
After you have read through 2 Thessalonians, turn to pages 10–14 for your next Track 3 reading project.

☐1–2   ☐3

Thanksgiving for Faith and Perseverance

1 Paul and Silvanus and Timothy,
¶ To the church of the Thessalonians in God our Father and the Lord Jesus Christ:
2 Grace to you and peace from God the Father and the Lord Jesus Christ.
3 ¶ We ought always to give thanks to God for you, brethren, as is *only* fitting, because your faith is greatly enlarged, and the love of each one of you toward one another grows *ever* greater;
4 therefore, we ourselves speak proudly of you among the churches of God for your perseverance and faith in the midst of all your persecutions and afflictions which you endure.
5 *This is* a plain indication of God's righteous judgment so that you will be considered worthy of the kingdom of God, for which indeed you are suffering.
6 For after all it is *only* just for God to repay with affliction those who afflict you,
7 and to give relief to you who are afflicted and to us as well when the Lord Jesus will be

revealed from heaven with His mighty angels in flaming fire,
8 dealing out retribution to those who do not know God and to those who do not obey the gospel of our Lord Jesus.
9 These will pay the penalty of eternal destruction, away from the presence of the Lord and from the glory of His power,
10 when He comes to be glorified in His saints on that day, and to be marveled at among all who have believed—for our testimony to you was believed.
11 To this end also we pray for you always, that our God will count you worthy of your calling, and fulfill every desire for goodness and the work of faith with power,
12 so that the name of our Lord Jesus will be glorified in you, and you in Him, according to the grace of our God and *the* Lord Jesus Christ.

Man of Lawlessness

2 Now we request you, brethren, with regard to the coming of our Lord Jesus Christ and our gathering together to Him,
2 that you not be quickly shaken from your composure or be disturbed either by a spirit or a message or a letter as if from us, to the effect that the day of the Lord has come.
3 Let no one in any way deceive you, for *it will not come* unless the ᵃapostasy comes first, and the man of lawlessness is revealed, the son of destruction,
4 who opposes and exalts himself above every

1:6 Is Life Unfair?

This question bothers nearly everyone who gets persecuted or who sees someone profit from wrongdoing. Paul's answer would likely be, "Yes, but only temporarily." He had the firm conviction that one day God would indeed turn the tables on the unfairness of life.

ᵃ Or *falling away* from the faith

so-called god or object of worship, so that he takes his seat in the temple of God, displaying himself as being God.

5 Do you not remember that while I was still with you, I was telling you these things?

6 And you know what restrains him now, so that in his time he will be revealed.

7 For the mystery of lawlessness is already at work; only he who now restrains *will do so* until he is taken out of the way.

2:7 Exactly What Will Happen?

Nearly every age has come up with a different interpretation of this passage. No one is certain about the "mystery of lawlessness" or "he who now restrains." A British writer, Tom Davies, quite sincerely, proposes television as the lawless one, since it has made violence so popular. This passage is obscure because Paul refers to further information he had taught the Thessalonians in person. (Even another New Testament author admitted that Paul's letters contain "some things hard to understand" [2 Peter 3:16].)

8 Then that lawless one will be revealed whom the Lord will slay with the breath of His mouth and bring to an end by the appearance of His coming;

9 *that is,* the one whose coming is in accord with the activity of Satan, with all power and signs and false wonders,

10 and with all the deception of wickedness for those who perish, because they did not receive the love of the truth so as to be saved.

11 For this reason God will send upon them a deluding influence so that they will believe what is false,

12 in order that they all may be judged who did not believe the truth, but took pleasure in wickedness.

13 ¶ But we should always give thanks to God for you, brethren beloved by the Lord, because God has chosen you *a*from the beginning for salvation through sanctification by the Spirit and faith in the truth.

14 It was for this He called you through our gospel, that you may gain the glory of our Lord Jesus Christ.

15 So then, brethren, stand firm and hold to the traditions which you were taught, whether by word *of mouth* or by letter from us.

16 ¶ Now may our Lord Jesus Christ Himself and God our Father, who has loved us and given us eternal comfort and good hope by grace,

17 comfort and strengthen your hearts in every good work and word.

Exhortation

3 Finally, brethren, pray for us that the word of the Lord will spread rapidly and be glorified, just as *it did* also with you;

2 and that we will be rescued from perverse and evil men; for not all have faith.

3 But the Lord is faithful, and He will strengthen and protect you from the evil *one.*

4 We have confidence in the Lord concerning you, that you are doing and will *continue to* do what we command.

5 May the Lord direct your hearts into the love of God and into the steadfastness of Christ.

6 ¶ Now we command you, brethren, in the name of our Lord Jesus Christ, that you keep away from every brother who leads an unruly life and not according to the tradition which you received from us.

7 For you yourselves know how you ought to follow our example, because we did not act in an undisciplined manner among you,

8 nor did we eat anyone's bread without paying for it, but with labor and hardship we *kept* working night and day so that we would not be a burden to any of you;

9 not because we do not have the right *to this,* but in order to offer ourselves as a model for you, so that you would follow our example.

10 For even when we were with you, we used to give you this order: if anyone is not willing to work, then he is not to eat, either.

3:10 No Work, No Eat

Paul's first letter to the Thessalonians had affirmed that Jesus could return at any time, unexpectedly. Evidently, this anticipation had prompted some to quit their jobs and do nothing but wait for the second coming. (Dozens of times religious sects have followed the same pattern in the United States by heading for remote areas to await Christ's return.) To correct the imbalance, in this second letter Paul stresses that certain events must happen before Christ's return. He also strongly warns against idleness.

11 For we hear that some among you are leading an undisciplined life, doing no work at all, but acting like busybodies.

12 Now such persons we command and exhort in the Lord Jesus Christ to work in quiet fashion and eat their own bread.

13 But as for you, brethren, do not grow weary of doing good.

a One early ms reads *first fruits*

14 ¶ If anyone does not obey our instruction in this letter, take special note of that person and do not associate with him, so that he will be put to shame.

15 *Yet* do not regard him as an enemy, but admonish him as a brother.

16 ¶ Now may the Lord of peace Himself continually grant you peace in every circumstance. The Lord be with you all!

17 ¶ I, Paul, write this greeting with my own hand, and this is a distinguishing mark in every letter; this is the way I write.

18 The grace of our Lord Jesus Christ be with you all.

1 TIMOTHY

The Hardest Job
Timothy steps into a hornet's nest

> *Let no one look down on your youthfulness, but . . . show yourself an example of those who believe.*
> **4:12**

WHO HAS THE MOST DIFFICULT job? A brain surgeon? A trapeze artist who risks death with every leap? A nuclear engineer? Or perhaps an air traffic controller, who determines the safety of thousands of passengers. A number of professions might be nominated as the most difficult of all.

But if the apostle Paul were alive today, to that question he would very likely reply, "Without doubt—a pastor's job is hardest." In contrast to professionals who specialize, a pastor must call upon wide-ranging skills. In a given week a pastor may act as a psychologist, priest, social worker, hospital chaplain, administrator, personnel supervisor, philosopher, and communicator.

Paul was acutely aware of the vital nature of such a job. Churches sprouted up wherever he visited, but whether they survived or failed depended largely on what kind of local leadership developed.

Final Words to a Young Friend

To assure that his work would continue, Paul turned more and more to a few loyal friends, especially Timothy and Titus. He wrote them explicit instructions in the three letters that follow, known collectively as "The Pastoral Letters."

Paul wrote 1 Timothy near the end of his life. Rugged years of ministry had passed, years marked by stonings, beatings, jailings, and riots. Paul knew that his age, his enemies, or the increasingly brutal Roman empire would soon catch up with him.

Timothy, a young man, ranked high in Paul's esteem. Converted during Paul's first missionary journey, he had over the years gained the apostle's complete trust. When a volcano of discontent rumbled in some distant church like Corinth or Thessalonica, Paul quickly dispatched Timothy to try and prevent an eruption.

"I have no one else of kindred spirit," Paul once wrote of Timothy. "He served with me in the furtherance of the gospel like a child serving his father" (Philippians 2:20,22). Through a swarm of controversies, into prison, on the road—wherever Paul went—Timothy loyally followed. Six of Paul's letters begin with the news that Timothy is at his side.

Timothy Becomes a Pastor

Timothy took on, at Paul's request, that difficult job of heading a local church. The congregation at Ephesus, loose and informal, needed order and a more defined structure. To muddle the scene further, certain members of the church had embraced false doctrines. In this letter, Paul advises his understudy on such matters as worship procedures, the control of unruly women, leadership standards, and policies regarding widows, slaves, and rich people.

Although this book addresses a historical situation from the first century, many problems in the early church—underpaid staff members, a generation gap, an integrity shortage, abuse of social aid, love of money—persist today. A pastor's job description hasn't changed much, or grown any easier, over the centuries.

How to Read 1 Timothy

Despite a weak stomach and timid disposition, Timothy had proved his mettle to Paul in many ways, and Paul wrote this letter to challenge him to a difficult task.

Paul doesn't give many details on the false doctrines Timothy had to combat. These letters, however, include vague hints about super-spiritual living, Jewish genealogies, myths, and fables. Look for the problems Paul alludes to and ask yourself whether they have any modern equivalents.

In his instructions, Paul counseled Timothy to combat heresy not by being forceful and argumentative, but by living an exemplary life and by bringing order to the church. Paul's challenge to live a model life applies directly to us; it remains a powerful prescription for the Christian life.

PEOPLE YOU'LL MEET IN 1 TIMOTHY

TIMOTHY *(p. 1304)*

3-TRACK READING PLAN

For an explanation and complete listing of the 3-track reading plan, turn to page 7.

TRACK 1: *Two-Week Courses on the Bible*
See page 7 for information on these courses.

TRACK 2: *An Overview of 1 Timothy in 1 Day*
☐ Day 1. Read the Introduction to 1 Timothy, then chapter 1, which serves as a good introduction to Paul's "Pastoral Letters."
Now turn to page 9 for your next Track 2 reading project.

TRACK 3: *All of 1 Timothy in 4 Days*
After you have read through 1 Timothy, turn to pages 10–14 for your next Track 3 reading project.
☐ 1–2   ☐ 3–4   ☐ 5   ☐ 6

Misleadings in Doctrine and Living

1 Paul, an apostle of Christ Jesus according to the commandment of God our Savior, and of Christ Jesus, *who is* our hope,

2 ¶ To Timothy, *my* true child in *the* faith: Grace, mercy *and* peace from God the Father and Christ Jesus our Lord.

3 ¶ As I urged you upon my departure for Macedonia, remain on at Ephesus so that you may instruct certain men not to teach strange doctrines,

4 nor to pay attention to myths and endless genealogies, which give rise to mere speculation rather than *furthering* the administration of God which is by faith.

5 But the goal of our instruction is love from a pure heart and a good conscience and a sincere faith.

6 For some men, straying from these things, have turned aside to fruitless discussion,

7 wanting to be teachers of the Law, even though they do not understand either what they are saying or the matters about which they make confident assertions.

8 ¶ But we know that the Law is good, if one uses it lawfully,

9 realizing the fact that law is not made for a

1:3 Strategic Place

The city of Ephesus crops up throughout the New Testament, which indicates its strategic importance as gateway to Asia. Paul's first visit there resulted in a major riot (Acts 19). He nevertheless stayed on three years, instructing believers and establishing a powerful church. As this letter was written, Paul's trusted associate Timothy was serving as pastor in Ephesus. Revelation 2 indicates that Timothy had mixed success in combating the problems identified in this letter.

righteous person, but for those who are lawless and rebellious, for the ungodly and sinners, for the unholy and profane, for those who kill their fathers or mothers, for murderers

10 and immoral men and homosexuals and kidnappers and liars and perjurers, and whatever else is contrary to sound teaching,

11 according to the glorious gospel of the blessed God, with which I have been entrusted.

12 ¶ I thank Christ Jesus our Lord, who has strengthened me, because He considered me faithful, putting me into service,

13 even though I was formerly a blasphemer and a persecutor and a violent aggressor. Yet I was shown mercy because I acted ignorantly in unbelief;

14 and the grace of our Lord was more than abundant, with the faith and love which are *found* in Christ Jesus.

15 It is a trustworthy statement, deserving full acceptance, that Christ Jesus came into the world to save sinners, among whom I am foremost *of all.*

16 Yet for this reason I found mercy, so that in me as the foremost, Jesus Christ might demonstrate His perfect patience as an example for those who would believe in Him for eternal life.

17 Now to the King eternal, immortal, invisible, the only God, *be* honor and glory forever and ever. Amen.

18 ¶ This command I entrust to you, Timothy, *my* son, in accordance with the prophecies previously made concerning you, that by them you fight the good fight,

1:18 Timothy's Calling

In three separate places in his letters to Timothy, Paul refers to his associate's special calling to the ministry. This passage alludes to prophecies made about him. 1 Timothy 4:14 mentions a special ceremony when the church elders laid hands on him. And in 2 Timothy (1:6) Paul specifies that he, too, had been part of such a ceremony. Timothy came from a Christian household; both his grandmother and mother were believers (2 Timothy 1:5).

19 keeping faith and a good conscience, which some have rejected and suffered shipwreck in regard to their faith.

20 Among these are Hymenaeus and Alexander, whom I have handed over to Satan, so that they will be taught not to blaspheme.

A Call to Prayer

2 First of all, then, I urge that entreaties *and* prayers, petitions *and* thanksgivings, be made on behalf of all men,

2 for kings and all who are in authority, so that we may lead a tranquil and quiet life in all godliness and dignity.

3 This is good and acceptable in the sight of God our Savior,

3:1 Time to Get Organized

Chapters 2 and 3 give detailed instructions concerning worship and church organization. When Paul wrote this letter, near the end of his life, churches such as Ephesus had been established for many years. The time had come for a more formal organization and for instructions governing appropriate and inappropriate behavior in church.

4 who desires all men to be saved and to come to the knowledge of the truth.

5 For there is one God, *and* one mediator also between God and men, *the* man Christ Jesus,

6 who gave Himself as a ransom for all, the testimony *given* at the proper time.

7 For this I was appointed a preacher and an apostle (I am telling the truth, I am not lying) as a teacher of the Gentiles in faith and truth.

8 ¶ Therefore I want the men in every place to pray, lifting up holy hands, without wrath and dissension.

Women Instructed

9 Likewise, *I want* women to adorn themselves with proper clothing, modestly and discreetly, not with braided hair and gold or pearls or costly garments,

10 but rather by means of good works, as is proper for women making a claim to godliness.

11 A woman must quietly receive instruction with entire submissiveness.

12 But I do not allow a woman to teach or exercise authority over a man, but to remain quiet.

13 For it was Adam who was first created, *and* then Eve.

14 And *it was* not Adam *who* was deceived, but the woman being deceived, fell into transgression.

15 But *women* will be preserved through the bearing of children if they continue in faith and love and sanctity with self-restraint.

Overseers and Deacons

3 It is a trustworthy statement: if any man aspires to the office of overseer, it is a fine work he desires *to do.*

2 An overseer, then, must be above reproach, the husband of one wife, temperate, prudent, respectable, hospitable, able to teach,

3 not addicted to wine or pugnacious, but gentle, peaceable, free from the love of money.

4 *He must be* one who manages his own

household well, keeping his children under control with all dignity

5 (but if a man does not know how to manage his own household, how will he take care of the church of God?),

6 *and* not a new convert, so that he will not become conceited and fall into the condemnation incurred by the devil.

7 And he must have a good reputation with those outside *the church,* so that he will not fall into reproach and the snare of the devil.

8 ¶ Deacons likewise *must be* men of dignity, not double-tongued, or addicted to much wine or fond of sordid gain,

9 *but* holding to the mystery of the faith with a clear conscience.

10 These men must also first be tested; then let them serve as deacons if they are beyond reproach.

3:10 Too Young for the Job?

Few people succeed in athletics or professional careers without practice, time, and effort. Paul looked for some of those same qualities in choosing experienced leaders for churches. Ironically, however, Timothy himself was only in his thirties. His upbringing had prepared him early for spiritual leadership, and in his case Paul urged boldness and confidence (4:12).

11 Women *must* likewise *be* dignified, not malicious gossips, but temperate, faithful in all things.

12 Deacons must be husbands of *only* one wife, *and* good managers of *their* children and their own households.

13 For those who have served well as deacons obtain for themselves a high standing and great confidence in the faith that is in Christ Jesus.

14 ¶ I am writing these things to you, hoping to come to you before long;

15 but in case I am delayed, *I write* so that you will know how one ought to conduct himself in the household of God, which is the church of the living God, the pillar and support of the truth.

16 By common confession, great is the mystery of godliness:

He who was revealed in the flesh,
Was vindicated in the Spirit,
Seen by angels,
Proclaimed among the nations,
Believed on in the world,
Taken up in glory.

Apostasy

4 But the Spirit explicitly says that in later times some will fall away from the faith, paying attention to deceitful spirits and doctrines of demons,

2 by means of the hypocrisy of liars seared in their own conscience as with a branding iron,

3 *men* who forbid marriage *and advocate* abstaining from foods which God has created to be gratefully shared in by those who believe and know the truth.

4 For everything created by God is good, and nothing is to be rejected if it is received with gratitude;

5 for it is sanctified by means of the word of God and prayer.

A Good Minister's Discipline

6 ¶ In pointing out these things to the brethren, you will be a good servant of Christ Jesus, *constantly* nourished on the words of the faith and of the sound doctrine which you have been following.

7 But have nothing to do with worldly fables fit only for old women. On the other hand, discipline yourself for the purpose of godliness;

8 for bodily discipline is only of little profit, but godliness is profitable for all things, since it holds promise for the present life and *also* for the *life* to come.

9 It is a trustworthy statement deserving full acceptance.

10 For it is for this we labor and strive, because we have fixed our hope on the living God, who is the Savior of all men, especially of believers.

11 ¶ Prescribe and teach these things.

12 Let no one look down on your youthfulness, but *rather* in speech, conduct, love, faith *and* purity, show yourself an example of those who believe.

13 Until I come, give attention to the *public* reading *of Scripture,* to exhortation and teaching.

14 Do not neglect the spiritual gift within you, which was bestowed on you through prophetic utterance with the laying on of hands by the presbytery.

15 Take pains with these things; be *absorbed* in them, so that your progress will be evident to all.

16 Pay close attention to yourself and to your teaching; persevere in these things, for as you do this you will ensure salvation both for yourself and for those who hear you.

Honor Widows

5 Do not sharply rebuke an older man, but *rather* appeal to *him* as a father, *to* the younger men as brothers,

2 the older women as mothers, *and* the younger women as sisters, in all purity.

3 ¶ Honor widows who are widows indeed;

4 but if any widow has children or grandchildren, they must first learn to practice piety in regard to their own family and to make some return to their parents; for this is acceptable in the sight of God.

5 Now she who is a widow indeed and who has been left alone, has fixed her hope on God and

continues in entreaties and prayers night and day.

6 But she who gives herself to wanton pleasure is dead even while she lives.

7 Prescribe these things as well, so that they may be above reproach.

8 But if anyone does not provide for his own, and especially for those of his household, he has denied the faith and is worse than an unbeliever.

9 ¶ A widow is to be put on the list only if she is not less than sixty years old, *having been* the wife of one man,

10 having a reputation for good works; *and* if she has brought up children, if she has shown hospitality to strangers, if she has washed the saints' feet, if she has assisted those in distress, *and* if she has devoted herself to every good work.

Athlete in Training
Overcoming personal disabilities

> *Discipline yourself for the purpose of godliness; for bodily discipline is only of little profit, but godliness is profitable for all things, since it holds promise for the present life and also for the life to come.*
> *4:7–8*

BRAD LAUWERS WAS IN THE locker room, showering after a grueling football workout, when he first noticed the lump. He bent down and rubbed his ankle gently, cupping his hand around the swelling. He felt no pain or stiffness. *Probably just some fluid,* he thought. *It will disappear in a few days.*

But the swelling didn't disappear, and a month later Brad lay in a hospital bed awaiting amputation of his left leg. The lump turned out to be a malignant tumor that was sending runners out in several directions in Brad's foot. The next day a surgeon removed Brad's leg just inches below the knee.

Of all the adjustments to his new life—including "one-legged" jokes, the awkward reactions of friends, and learning to walk on an artificial leg—Brad most feared the loss of athletics, his main love in life. He had been a standout on his high school basketball and football teams in Alaska, a sports-crazy state. His doctor, also an amputee (from a war injury), tried to be encouraging: "Remember, Brad, there's *nothing* you cannot do."

Against All Odds

Four months later, Brad visited the campus of UCLA for a prosthetic leg fitting. Even before fully learning to walk on his artificial leg, he sought out a basketball backboard and began tossing up reverse lay-ups. The designers had warned him against subjecting the leg to the jarring stops and turns of basketball and had vetoed football outright, suggesting he take up swimming or water-skiing instead. But Brad never gave up his dream of returning to his two favorite sports.

As he trained, his artificial limb rubbed his leg stump raw and covered it with blisters. Undaunted, he ran until the blisters hardened into calluses. Then he began working on jumps and pivots.

Incredibly, in August, less than one year after the amputation, Brad played his first game as a one-legged quarterback for Dimond High School. Some thought his appearance was a mere sentimental gesture. They were wrong: Brad ended the year leading the state in passing! He completed 58 percent of his passes and racked up 662 yards in seven games as a part-time quarterback on the state championship squad. After football season, he started on Dimond's basketball team. From there, he went on to major in physical education at Washington State University.

When asked about his exploits, Brad shrugs and mentions two factors in his extraordinary achievement: gritty determination and long hours of often painful training.

A Lesson from Athletics

Paul uses the analogy of physical training in his letter to Timothy, urging him to train himself for godliness the same way disciplined athletes train for competition. Brad Lauwers had to overcome physical barriers; Timothy faced personality barriers. Several times Paul refers to Timothy's reserved, timid disposition, which probably contributed to his chronic stomach trouble.

Given his shyness and his half-Jewish, half-Gentile ancestry, Timothy did not seem the ideal choice for a heresy fighter in a turbulent church. But Paul was convinced he could do the job. He encouraged Timothy with such motivational phrases as "I charge you" and "I urge you." He also reminded Timothy of his ordination, a commitment he had made long before.

Harassed Christians need a model, an example of how they should live, perhaps even more than they need words of wisdom. In 1 Timothy, Paul urges his loyal friend to become that model by accepting the discipline and hard work required.

Life Questions: Do you have any personality traits that make Christian service seem difficult? What specific "training instructions" did Paul give Timothy that might also apply to you?

11 But refuse *to put* younger widows *on the list*, for when they feel sensual desires in disregard of Christ, they want to get married,

12 *thus* incurring condemnation, because they have set aside their previous pledge.

5:9 Welfare Mentality

Chapter 5 gives fascinating insight into early church problems that have parallels in today's social programs. Evidently, some members of the Ephesus congregation had been taking advantage of others' charity. Young widows were using the church's resources when they should have been looking for other means of support. Paul outlines a form of "enrollment" to establish who was truly needy.

13 At the same time they also learn *to be* idle, as they go around from house to house; and not merely idle, but also gossips and busybodies, talking about things not proper *to mention*.

14 Therefore, I want younger *widows* to get married, bear children, keep house, *and* give the enemy no occasion for reproach;

15 for some have already turned aside to follow Satan.

16 If any woman who is a believer has *dependent* widows, she must assist them and the church must not be burdened, so that it may assist those who are widows indeed.

Concerning Elders

17 ¶ The elders who rule well are to be considered worthy of double honor, especially those who work hard at preaching and teaching.

18 For the Scripture says, "YOU SHALL NOT MUZZLE THE OX WHILE HE IS THRESHING," and "The laborer is worthy of his wages."

19 Do not receive an accusation against an elder except on the basis of two or three witnesses.

20 Those who continue in sin, rebuke in the presence of all, so that the rest also will be fearful *of sinning*.

21 I solemnly charge you in the presence of God and of Christ Jesus and of *His* chosen angels, to maintain these *principles* without bias, doing nothing in a *spirit of* partiality.

22 Do not lay hands upon anyone *too* hastily and thereby share *responsibility for* the sins of others; keep yourself free from sin.

23 ¶ No longer drink water *exclusively,* but use a little wine for the sake of your stomach and your frequent ailments.

24 ¶ The sins of some men are quite evident, going before them to judgment; for others, their *sins* follow after.

25 Likewise also, deeds that are good are quite evident, and those which are otherwise cannot be concealed.

Instructions to Those Who Minister

6 All who are under the yoke as slaves are to regard their own masters as worthy of all honor so that the name of God and *our* doctrine will not be spoken against.

2 Those who have believers as their masters must not be disrespectful to them because they are brethren, but must serve them all the more, because those who partake of the benefit are believers and beloved. Teach and preach these *principles.*

3 ¶ If anyone advocates a different doctrine and does not agree with sound words, those of our Lord Jesus Christ, and with the doctrine conforming to godliness,

4 he is conceited *and* understands nothing; but he has a morbid interest in controversial questions and disputes about words, out of which arise envy, strife, abusive language, evil suspicions,

5 and constant friction between men of depraved mind and deprived of the truth, who suppose that godliness is a means of gain.

6 But godliness *actually* is a means of great gain when accompanied by contentment.

7 For we have brought nothing into the world, so we cannot take anything out of it either.

6:7 Two Familiar Quotes

Paul's parting advice to Timothy includes two sayings that have become familiar quotations. Verse 7 is usually quoted accurately. But verse 10, also familiar, is often misquoted as "money is the root of all evil." An established church had already developed a professional class of Christian workers, and Paul warned against the motive of profit-seeking.

8 If we have food and covering, with these we shall be content.

9 But those who want to get rich fall into temptation and a snare and many foolish and harmful desires which plunge men into ruin and destruction.

10 For the love of money is a root of all sorts of evil, and some by longing for it have wandered away from the faith and pierced themselves with many griefs.

11 ¶ But flee from these things, you man of God, and pursue righteousness, godliness, faith, love, perseverance *and* gentleness.

12 Fight the good fight of faith; take hold of the eternal life to which you were called, and you made the good confession in the presence of many witnesses.

13 I charge you in the presence of God, who gives life to all things, and of Christ Jesus,

who testified the good confession before Pontius Pilate,

14 that you keep the commandment without stain or reproach until the appearing of our Lord Jesus Christ,

15 which He will bring about at the proper time—He who is the blessed and only Sovereign, the King of kings and Lord of lords,

16 who alone possesses immortality and dwells in unapproachable light, whom no man has seen or can see. To Him *be* honor and eternal dominion! Amen.

17 ¶ Instruct those who are rich in this present world not to be conceited or to fix their hope on the uncertainty of riches, but on God, who richly supplies us with all things to enjoy.

18 *Instruct them* to do good, to be rich in good works, to be generous and ready to share,

19 storing up for themselves the treasure of a good foundation for the future, so that they may take hold of that which is life indeed.

20 ¶ O Timothy, guard what has been entrusted to you, avoiding worldly *and* empty chatter *and* the opposing arguments of what is falsely called "knowledge"—

21 which some have professed and thus gone astray from the faith.

¶ Grace be with you.

2 TIMOTHY

Passing the Torch
The apostle Paul's last known words

> The things which you have heard from me in the presence of many witnesses, entrust these to faithful men who will be able to teach others also. **2:2**

E VERY FOUR YEARS THE WORLD watches an ancient ritual unfold: the passing of the Olympic torch. The spectacular pageantry of the opening ceremonies cannot begin until the final carrier of the torch arrives in the stadium. The torch symbolically links the modern Olympic Games to their 2,700-year history.

"Passing the torch" has become a familiar phrase, used when the president of a corporation such as General Motors introduces his successor to the public, or when an esteemed orchestra conductor hands over his baton, or a great sports figure tutors her replacement. Often the retiring person delivers an emotional farewell speech. He or she has finished the work; the time has come to pass the torch to another.

Choosing Timothy

As the weary apostle Paul neared certain death, with imprisonment preventing him from traveling, he, too, began to think of a successor. It was time to pass the torch, and he decided on the young man Timothy.

At first glance, shy Timothy hardly seemed an adequate replacement, but Paul had few options. "All who are in Asia turned away from me," he lamented (1:15). This letter, 2 Timothy, reveals his deep reliance on Timothy's loyal friendship. Life was closing in on the apostle, and he felt a somber sense of abandonment.

At times in this letter, Paul lectures Timothy like a master sergeant, calling on him to stand firm, overcome shame, and hold to the faith. Elsewhere, his tone softens into the fond affirmation of a grateful father. Throughout, the bonds of deep friendship are evident: from Paul recalling Timothy's family heritage (1:5) to his urging Timothy to bring him a heavy coat before winter (4:13,21).

An Emotional Moment

Paul's moods alternate between sadness and confidence, nostalgia and grave concern. As he wrote this letter, he contemplated the disquieting months ahead and the prospect of young, divided churches left without his guidance. In these, his last known written words, he sought to prepare Timothy for the inevitable day when the message of God would depend on him and other reliable workers (2:2).

Despite his circumstances, Paul's farewell message from behind bars is gracious, even triumphant. The spreading of the gospel is far too big a task to be limited to any one man. "I suffer... even to imprisonment as a criminal," Paul declares, "but the word of God is not imprisoned" (2:9).

How to Read 2 Timothy

S econd Timothy has proved encouraging to Christian workers throughout history. Paul, facing death, did not wallow in self-pity, but instead used this last communication to inspire and challenge his associate Timothy.

This letter reveals much about Paul's emotional state and physical circumstances. As you read it, look for glimpses into Paul's loneliness and suffering. The apostle tells where he turned for strength when he faced personal trials.

In addition, 2 Timothy gives much valuable counsel to those of us who, like Timothy, have inherited the task of representing Christ on earth. Paul stresses the importance of relying on Scripture and of living a life of discipline. As you read this letter, put yourself in Timothy's place; imagine receiving one last personal letter from your great mentor. What final words of advice does he give?

3-TRACK READING PLAN

For an explanation and complete listing of the 3-track reading plan, turn to page 7.

TRACK 1: **Two-Week Courses on the Bible**
See page 7 for information on these courses.

TRACK 2: **An Overview of 2 Timothy in 1 Day**
☐ Day 1. Read the Introduction to 2 Timothy and then chapter 2, which contains a summary of Paul's challenge to Timothy.
Now turn to page 9 for your next Track 2 reading project.

TRACK 3: **All of 2 Timothy in 4 Days**
After you have read through 2 Timothy, turn to pages 10–14 for your next Track 3 reading project.
☐1   ☐2   ☐3   ☐4

Timothy Charged to Guard His Trust

1 Paul, an apostle of Christ Jesus by the will of God, according to the promise of life in Christ Jesus,

2 ¶ To Timothy, my beloved son: Grace, mercy *and* peace from God the Father and Christ Jesus our Lord.

3 ¶ I thank God, whom I serve with a clear conscience the way my forefathers did, as I constantly remember you in my prayers night and day,

4 longing to see you, even as I recall your tears, so that I may be filled with joy.

5 For I am mindful of the sincere faith within you, which first dwelt in your grandmother Lois and your mother Eunice, and I am sure that *it is* in you as well.

6 For this reason I remind you to kindle afresh the gift of God which is in you through the laying on of my hands.

7 For God has not given us a spirit of timidity, but of power and love and discipline.

8 ¶ Therefore do not be ashamed of the testimony of our Lord or of me His prisoner, but join with *me* in suffering for the gospel according to the power of God,

9 who has saved us and called us with a holy calling, not according to our works, but according to His own purpose and grace which was granted us in Christ Jesus from all eternity,

10 but now has been revealed by the appearing of our Savior Christ Jesus, who abolished death and brought life and immortality to light through the gospel,

11 for which I was appointed a preacher and an apostle and a teacher.

12 For this reason I also suffer these things, but I am not ashamed; for I know whom I have believed and I am convinced that He is able to guard what I have entrusted to Him until that day.

13 Retain the standard of sound words which you have heard from me, in the faith and love which are in Christ Jesus.

14 Guard, through the Holy Spirit who dwells in us, the treasure which has been entrusted to *you.*

15 ¶ You are aware of the fact that all who are in Asia turned away from me, among whom are Phygelus and Hermogenes.

16 The Lord grant mercy to the house of Onesiphorus, for he often refreshed me and was not ashamed of my chains;

17 but when he was in Rome, he eagerly searched for me and found me—

18 the Lord grant to him to find mercy from the Lord on that day—and you know very well what services he rendered at Ephesus.

Be Strong

2 You therefore, my son, be strong in the grace that is in Christ Jesus.

2 The things which you have heard from me in the presence of many witnesses, entrust these to faithful men who will be able to teach others also.

3 Suffer hardship with *me,* as a good soldier of Christ Jesus.

4 No soldier in active service entangles himself in the affairs of everyday life, so that he may please the one who enlisted him as a soldier.

5 Also if anyone competes as an athlete, he does not win the prize unless he competes according to the rules.

6 The hard-working farmer ought to be the first to receive his share of the crops.

2:4 Soldier, Athlete, Farmer

Writing to a friend who knew him well, Paul saw no need to expand on the three analogies in this paragraph; he simply mentions them and tells Timothy to reflect on them. Paul was fully conscious of the threats and dangers facing his own life, and he wanted Timothy to train himself in preparation for any hardships that he might have to face.

7 Consider what I say, for the Lord will give you understanding in everything.

8 ¶ Remember Jesus Christ, risen from the dead, descendant of David, according to my gospel,

9 for which I suffer hardship even to imprisonment as a criminal; but the word of God is not imprisoned.

10 For this reason I endure all things for the sake of those who are chosen, so that they also may obtain the salvation which is in Christ Jesus *and* with *it* eternal glory.

11 It is a trustworthy statement:
　For if we died with Him, we will also live
　　with Him;

12 If we endure, we will also reign with
　　Him;
　If we deny Him, He also will deny us;

13 If we are faithless, He remains faithful,
　　for He cannot deny Himself.

An Unashamed Workman

14 ¶ Remind *them* of these things, and solemnly charge *them* in the presence of God not to wrangle about words, which is useless *and leads* to the ruin of the hearers.

15 Be diligent to present yourself approved to God as a workman who does not need to be ashamed, accurately handling the word of truth.

16 But avoid worldly *and* empty chatter, for it will lead to further ungodliness,

17 and their talk will spread like *a*gangrene. Among them are Hymenaeus and Philetus,

18 *men* who have gone astray from the truth saying that the resurrection has already taken place, and they upset the faith of some.

19 Nevertheless, the firm foundation of God stands, having this seal, "The Lord knows those who are His," and, "Everyone who names the name of the Lord is to abstain from wickedness."

20 ¶ Now in a large house there are not only gold and silver vessels, but also vessels of wood and of earthenware, and some to honor and some to dishonor.

21 Therefore, if anyone cleanses himself from these *things*, he will be a vessel for honor, sanctified, useful to the Master, prepared for every good work.

22 Now flee from youthful lusts and pursue righteousness, faith, love *and* peace, with those who call on the Lord from a pure heart.

23 But refuse foolish and ignorant speculations, knowing that they produce quarrels.

24 The Lord's bond-servant must not be quarrelsome, but be kind to all, able to teach, patient when wronged,

25 with gentleness correcting those who are in opposition, if perhaps God may grant them repentance leading to the knowledge of the truth,

26 and they may come to their senses *and escape* from the snare of the devil, having been held captive by him to do his will.

"Difficult Times Will Come"

3 But realize this, that in the last days difficult times will come.

2 For men will be lovers of self, lovers of money, boastful, arrogant, revilers, disobedient to parents, ungrateful, unholy,

3 unloving, irreconcilable, malicious gossips, without self-control, brutal, haters of good,

4 treacherous, reckless, conceited, lovers of pleasure rather than lovers of God,

5 holding to a form of godliness, although they have denied its power; Avoid such men as these.

6 For among them are those who enter into households and captivate weak women weighed down with sins, led on by various impulses,

7 always learning and never able to come to the knowledge of the truth.

8 Just as Jannes and Jambres opposed Moses, so these *men* also oppose the truth, men of depraved mind, rejected in regard to the faith.

3:8 Who Were Jannes and Jambres?

These names, not mentioned in the Old Testament, were handed down in Jewish tradition as the names of the Egyptian magicians who opposed Moses during the ten plagues against Egypt (Exodus 7:11; 9:11).

9 But they will not make further progress; for their folly will be obvious to all, just as Jannes's and Jambres's folly was also.

10 ¶ Now you followed my teaching, conduct, purpose, faith, patience, love, perseverance,

11 persecutions, *and* sufferings, such as hap-

a Or cancer

pened to me at Antioch, at Iconium *and* at Lystra; what persecutions I endured, and out of them all the Lord rescued me!

12 Indeed, all who desire to live godly in Christ Jesus will be persecuted.

13 But evil men and impostors will proceed *from bad* to worse, deceiving and being deceived.

14 You, however, continue in the things you have learned and become convinced of, knowing from whom you have learned *them,*

15 and that from childhood you have known the sacred writings which are able to give you the wisdom that leads to salvation through faith which is in Christ Jesus.

16 All Scripture is inspired by God and profitable for teaching, for reproof, for correction, for training in righteousness;

17 so that the man of God may be adequate, equipped for every good work.

"Preach the Word"

4 I solemnly charge *you* in the presence of God and of Christ Jesus, who is to judge the living and the dead, and by His appearing and His kingdom:

2 preach the word; be ready in season *and* out of season; reprove, rebuke, exhort, with great patience and instruction.

3 For the time will come when they will not

3:16 Scripture Is God-breathed

This important verse gives the origin of the term inspiration, *which literally means "God-breathed." Although the Bible doesn't spell out the mechanics of how God inspired the writers, it makes clear the ultimate source was God himself.*

endure sound doctrine; but *wanting* to have their ears tickled, they will accumulate for themselves teachers in accordance to their own desires,

4 and will turn away their ears from the truth and will turn aside to myths.

5 But you, be sober in all things, endure hardship, do the work of an evangelist, fulfill your ministry.

6 ¶ For I am already being poured out as a

A Letter from Death Row
Paul sees the end

OCCASIONALLY, WRITINGS SURFACE FROM DEATH row, the earnest scratchings of prisoners who know each word may be their last. Whole books, for example, were discovered amid the ruins of Nazi death camps. Understandably, these writings don't usually dwell on abstract, philosophical themes. They chronicle the day-to-day reality of the struggle to survive.

I am already being poured out as a drink offering, and the time of my departure has come.
4:6

Quite naturally, Paul did not devote much space to doctrine in his death row letter. He stuck to personal advice on vital issues such as courage and personal integrity.

Paul's Grim Future

Although Paul does not elaborate on his present circumstances in 2 Timothy, he mentions that at his first trial not a single witness came forward to defend him (4:16). Through supernatural strength he successfully defended himself, but his prospects in a new trial appeared grim (4:6).

Paul's arrest probably occurred in the wave of anti-Christian persecutions begun by Nero in A.D. 64. That crazed emperor tortured Christians by crucifying them, by wrapping them in animal skins and turning his hunting dogs loose on them, and by burning them alive, as human torches, to illuminate the games in his garden. Is it any wonder that Paul, imprisoned in that era, exhorted Timothy on the need for boldness and the likelihood of suffering for Christ?

The Coming Conflict

Toward the end of his life, Paul viewed the future as a growing struggle. Immorality and false teaching would "spread like gangrene" (2:17); he urged Christians to counteract those forces with personal purity. The battle between good and evil would only intensify, he said.

After making some predictions about "the last days," Paul composed a formal charge to Timothy—a last will and testament to his spiritual son (4:1–8). He concluded, "I have fought the good fight, I have finished the course, I have kept the faith" (4:7). Tradition teaches that Paul was killed by Rome for his faith. But because of his life and the legacy he passed on, the world would never be the same.

Life Questions: If you drafted a spiritual "last will and testament" for your friends, what would you say?

drink offering, and the time of my departure has come.

7 I have fought the good fight, I have finished the course, I have kept the faith;

8 in the future there is laid up for me the crown of righteousness, which the Lord, the righteous Judge, will award to me on that day; and not only to me, but also to all who have loved His appearing.

Personal Concerns

9 ¶ Make every effort to come to me soon;

10 for Demas, having loved this present world, has deserted me and gone to Thessalonica; Crescens *has gone* to Galatia, Titus to Dalmatia.

11 Only Luke is with me. Pick up Mark and bring him with you, for he is useful to me for service.

12 But Tychicus I have sent to Ephesus.

13 When you come bring the cloak which I left at Troas with Carpus, and the books, especially the parchments.

14 Alexander the coppersmith did me much harm; the Lord will repay him according to his deeds.

15 Be on guard against him yourself, for he vigorously opposed our teaching.

16 ¶ At my first defense no one supported me, but all deserted me; may it not be counted against them.

17 But the Lord stood with me and strengthened me, so that through me the proclamation might be fully accomplished, and that all the Gentiles might hear; and I was rescued out of the lion's mouth.

4:17 Second Imprisonment in Rome

Acts 28 describes a period when Paul was held under house arrest in Rome, but the conditions hinted at in this letter are quite different. Paul wrote 2 Timothy much later, after the Roman empire had turned against Christians, and the tone of this letter (verses 6–9) implies that he had little hope of freedom. His request for a cloak and parchments (verse 13) indicates he was arrested suddenly, without warning.

18 The Lord will rescue me from every evil deed, and will bring me safely to His heavenly kingdom; to Him *be* the glory forever and ever. Amen.

19 ¶ Greet Prisca and Aquila, and the household of Onesiphorus.

20 Erastus remained at Corinth, but Trophimus I left sick at Miletus.

21 Make every effort to come before winter. Eubulus greets you, also Pudens and Linus and Claudia and all the brethren.

22 ¶ The Lord be with your spirit. Grace be with you.

TITUS

Diverse People, Diverse Problems
An island of liars, brutes, and gluttons

> These things speak and exhort and reprove. 2:15

MODERN PEOPLE READING ABOUT THE past can blur people together into a uniform, faceless crowd of strangers. It's hard to visualize individual people you read about.

Actually, the people Paul addressed were as diverse as those you might meet on the streets of Los Angeles or New York City today. Consider Crete, an island populated by five fiercely independent ethnic groups. Its main knowledge of the outside world came through pirates and coarse sailors. Add to that mix a large community of straight-laced Jews, and you can see why the Cretan church was born amid conflict.

Titus the Troubleshooter

When problems erupted in this stormy congregation, Paul dispatched Titus, his trusted associate of 15 years. The book of Galatians (2:1–5) introduced Titus as proof that a non-Jew could become a fully acceptable Christian.

When Titus's name occurs in the New Testament, he is usually seen serving as Paul's troubleshooter, the one called on to deal with local crises. Twice he was sent on a diplomatic mission to the rowdy church at Corinth. This letter indicates he faced an equally challenging task on Crete. Paul wrote the book of Titus as a set of personal instructions on how to handle a difficult assignment.

Because he was writing to people who knew the local circumstances well, Paul rarely bothered to give background for us years-later "over-the-shoulder" readers. But we can gain insights into the conditions by reading between the lines. For example, when Paul tells Titus to search for a leader "not quick-tempered, not addicted to wine, not pugnacious, not fond of sordid gain" (1:7), that description implies something about the average Cretan. One of the island's own poets described Cretans as "always liars, evil beasts, lazy gluttons" (1:12), and the Greeks had even coined a special verb for lying: "to Cretize."

Practical Theology

Titus 2 lists some of the diverse groups in the church: older men, older women, younger women, young men, slaves. Each presented a set of problems that needed attention, and Paul gave Titus specific counsel on each group. Although he was mainly emphasizing the need for good living, Paul also dropped in a few concise restatements of the gospel message. His theology was never distantly theoretical; he applied it to real-life human problems.

Taken as a group, the three pastoral letters (1 and 2 Timothy plus Titus) show Paul, an old man now, learning to rely more and more on capable assistants to carry on his work. The Cretans needed a hard-hitting, practical reminder of "sound doctrine" based on a God "who cannot lie" (1:2). The instructions in Titus give the man for whom the book was named—and us—the needed jolt.

How to Read Titus

Like 1 and 2 Timothy, Titus was written to an individual, not a church. This letter has similarities to 1 Timothy, but is less personal and more official. The book of Acts doesn't mention Titus, but 14 references to him in Paul's letters indicate that he was one of Paul's most trusted helpers.

In some letters, such as Galatians, Paul fought valiantly against legalism. But the church on Crete, full of immature Christians, needed basic lessons in morality, and Paul spelled them out for Titus. Using a very straightforward style, he told his associate what he would prescribe in such circumstances.

Because it is written in such a direct style—almost like a training manual—Titus needs little explanation. Paul's meaning comes through clearly. Note particularly how Paul adapts his overall principles to specific groups in chapter 2. And give careful study to the "nuggets" of theology in these passages: 1:1–4, 2:11–14, and 3:4–7.

PEOPLE YOU'LL MEET IN TITUS

TITUS *(p. 1316)*

3-TRACK READING PLAN

For an explanation and complete listing of the 3-track reading plan, turn to page 7.

TRACK 1: *Two-Week Courses on the Bible*
See page 7 for information on these courses.

TRACK 2: *An Overview of Titus in 1 Day*
☐ Day 1. Read the Introduction to Titus, then chapter 2, which contains Paul's practical advice for the diverse groups in the Cretan church.

Now turn to page 9 for your next Track 2 reading project.

TRACK 3: *All of Titus in 2 Days*
After you have read through Titus, turn to pages 10–14 for your next Track 3 reading project.
☐1   ☐2–3

Salutation

1 Paul, a bond-servant of God and an apostle of Jesus Christ, for the faith of those chosen of God and the knowledge of the truth which is according to godliness,

2 in the hope of eternal life, which God, who cannot lie, promised long ages ago,

1:2 No Lies

Right away Paul characterizes God as the One who does not lie. God's truthfulness made a sharp contrast to the Cretans themselves (verse 12) as well as to many gods of that era. The Romans exalted their emperors, worshiping them as divine despite the flaws and weaknesses that everyone knew about. Paul contrasts the message about Jesus as the eternal "word" of truth.

3 but at the proper time manifested, *even* His word, in the proclamation with which I was entrusted according to the commandment of God our Savior,

4 ¶ To Titus, my true child in a common faith: Grace and peace from God the Father and Christ Jesus our Savior.

Qualifications of Elders

5 ¶ For this reason I left you in Crete, that you would set in order what remains and appoint elders in every city as I directed you,

6 *namely,* if any man is above reproach, the husband of one wife, having children who believe, not accused of dissipation or rebellion.

7 For the overseer must be above reproach as God's steward, not self-willed, not quick-tempered, not addicted to wine, not pugnacious, not fond of sordid gain,

8 but hospitable, loving what is good, sensible, just, devout, self-controlled,

9 holding fast the faithful word which is in accordance with the teaching, so that he will be able both to exhort in sound doctrine and to refute those who contradict.

10 ¶ For there are many rebellious men, empty talkers and deceivers, especially those of the circumcision,

11 who must be silenced because they are up-

setting whole families, teaching things they should not *teach* for the sake of sordid gain.

12 One of themselves, a prophet of their own, said, "Cretans are always liars, evil beasts, lazy gluttons."

13 This testimony is true. For this reason reprove them severely so that they may be sound in the faith,

14 not paying attention to Jewish myths and commandments of men who turn away from the truth.

15 To the pure, all things are pure; but to those who are defiled and unbelieving, nothing is pure, but both their mind and their conscience are defiled.

16 They profess to know God, but by *their* deeds they deny *Him*, being detestable and disobedient and worthless for any good deed.

Duties of the Older and Younger

2 But as for you, speak the things which are fitting for sound doctrine.

2 Older men are to be temperate, dignified, sensible, sound in faith, in love, in perseverance.

3 ¶ Older women likewise are to be reverent in their behavior, not malicious gossips nor enslaved to much wine, teaching what is good,

4 so that they may encourage the young women to love their husbands, to love their children,

5 *to be* sensible, pure, workers at home, kind, being subject to their own husbands, so that the word of God will not be dishonored.

6 ¶ Likewise urge the young men to be sensible;

7 in all things show yourself to be an example of good deeds, *with* purity in doctrine, dignified,

8 sound *in* speech which is beyond reproach, so that the opponent will be put to shame, having nothing bad to say about us.

9 ¶ *Urge* bondslaves to be subject to their own masters in everything, to be well-pleasing, not argumentative,

10 not pilfering, but showing all good faith so that they will adorn the doctrine of God our Savior in every respect.

11 ¶ For the grace of God has appeared, bringing salvation to all men,

12 instructing us to deny ungodliness and worldly desires and to live sensibly, righteously and godly in the present age,

13 looking for the blessed hope and the appearing of the glory of our great God and Savior, Christ Jesus,

14 who gave Himself for us to redeem us from every lawless deed, and to purify for Himself a people for His own possession, zealous for good deeds.

15 ¶ These things speak and exhort and reprove with all authority. Let no one disregard you.

Godly Living

3 Remind them to be subject to rulers, to authorities, to be obedient, to be ready for every good deed,

2:15 Foolish Questions

In addition to the problems hinted at in chapter 2, the Cretan church struggled with issues its Jewish members introduced. These trends toward myths and "foolish controversies and genealogies and strife and disputes about the Law" (3:9) resemble the heresies Paul had warned against in the book of Colossians. Titus had to be prepared to deal with problems both of doctrine and of righteous living.

2 to malign no one, to be peaceable, gentle, showing every consideration for all men.

3 For we also once were foolish ourselves, disobedient, deceived, enslaved to various lusts and pleasures, spending our life in malice and envy, hateful, hating one another.

4 But when the kindness of God our Savior and *His* love for mankind appeared,

5 He saved us, not on the basis of deeds which we have done in righteousness, but according to His mercy, by the washing of regeneration and renewing by the Holy Spirit,

6 whom He poured out upon us richly through Jesus Christ our Savior,

7 so that being justified by His grace we would be made heirs according to *the* hope of eternal life.

3:5 Nuggets of Theology

Despite its practical, instructive tone, Titus contains three outstanding passages of Paul's theology. They appear in 1:1–4, 2:11–14, and 3:4–7. This last passage balances off Paul's stress on clean living in Titus. Verse 5 makes clear that "deeds . . . done in righteousness" do not earn us acceptance by God. Rather, they are a natural response from people who have experienced God's forgiveness and love.

8 This is a trustworthy statement; and concerning these things I want you to speak confidently, so that those who have believed God will be careful to engage in good deeds. These things are good and profitable for men.

9 But avoid foolish controversies and genealogies and strife and disputes about the Law, for they are unprofitable and worthless.

10 Reject a factious man after a first and second warning,

11 knowing that such a man is perverted and is sinning, being self-condemned.

Personal Concerns

12 ¶ When I send Artemas or Tychicus to you, make every effort to come to me at Nicopolis, for I have decided to spend the winter there.

13 Diligently help Zenas the lawyer and Apollos on their way so that nothing is lacking for them.

14 Our people must also learn to engage in good deeds to meet pressing needs, so that they will not be unfruitful.

15 ¶ All who are with me greet you. Greet those who love us in *the* faith.

¶ Grace be with you all.

3:12 Mail Carriers

In Roman times, the most reliable postal system was to give a letter to a trusted friend. Paul used Tychicus to carry letters both to Ephesus and to Colosse. Tychicus also accompanied Paul on his trip to distribute gifts to the poor of Jerusalem (Acts 20:4).

PHILEMON

Letter to a Slave Owner
A slave's life hangs in the balance

O NESIMUS WAS A RUNAWAY SLAVE, a hunted fugitive whose life was in constant danger. He had two options. He could spend his days hiding in the dark, grimy alleys of a Roman city, dodging soldiers and bounty hunters. Or, he could do the unthinkable and return to his master.

The laws of the empire were harsh. If Onesimus did return, his master Philemon had the legal power to sentence him to immediate execution. If Philemon mercifully decided to let him live, Onesimus would have the letter F (for *Fugitivus*) seared on his forehead with a branding iron, marking him for life.

> Though I have enough confidence in Christ to order you to do what is proper, yet for love's sake I rather appeal to you. 8–9

Paul Defends a Runaway

His conversion to Christ through Paul's ministry greatly complicated the decision of the runaway slave. Onesimus knew he couldn't keep running all his life. He had wronged his legal owner, and, painful as it seemed, he needed to make amends.

The apostle Paul, sympathetic to the slave's cause, agreed to use his full influence on Philemon. Onesimus's life hung in the balance. This 468-word letter to the slave owner masterfully brings together Paul's skills of persuasion and diplomacy.

Every phrase in Philemon is crafted to produce the best possible effect. Paul appeals to Philemon's friendship, his status as a Christian leader, his sense of love and compassion. He doesn't outright order Philemon to consent, yet he applies blatant pressure, reminding Philemon that "you owe to me even your own self as well" (verse 19). Addressing the letter to Philemon's church (verse 2) increases the pressure, as does Paul's promise of a personal visit (verse 22).

Christianity and Slavery

Slavery existed for 1,800 years after this letter was written, and it took the full moral force of Christianity to ban it from the globe. But the tiny book of Philemon shows that the faith had a profound impact on slavery long before abolition.

Christ can revolutionize any social relationship. Onesimus, a runaway, decided to turn himself in. In Philemon, Paul asks for a second miracle. He pleads with the owner to "accept him as you would me" (verse 17). Such an attitude, in that culture, was social dynamite.

How to Read Philemon

O bviously, Paul had a close relationship with both the slave Onesimus and his owner Philemon. Some scholars believe that Onesimus first heard about Christ when he shared a jail cell with the apostle (see verses 9–10). As you read Philemon, look for clues into Paul's relationship with each person.

Philemon gives us a model of Christian diplomacy. As you read it, think of awkward social situations you know about: two estranged friends or a parent-child conflict, for example. Notice the kind of persuasion used by Paul, and try to apply it to your own circumstances.

3-TRACK READING PLAN

For an explanation and complete listing of the 3-track reading plan, turn to page 7.

TRACK 1: **Two-Week Courses on the Bible**
See page 7 for information on these courses.

TRACK 2: **Philemon in 1 Day**
☐ Day 1. Just one chapter long, Philemon will take only a few minutes to read.
Now turn to page 9 for your next Track 2 reading project.

TRACK 3: **All of Philemon in 1 Day**
After you have read through Philemon, turn to pages 10–14 for your next Track 3 reading project.
☐Philemon

Salutation

1 Paul, a prisoner of Christ Jesus, and Timothy our brother,

¶ To Philemon our beloved *brother* and fellow worker,

2 and to Apphia our sister, and to Archippus our fellow soldier, and to the church in your house:

3 Grace to you and peace from God our Father and the Lord Jesus Christ.

Philemon's Love and Faith

4 ¶ I thank my God always, making mention of you in my prayers,

5 because I hear of your love and of the faith which you have toward the Lord Jesus and toward all the saints;

6 *and I pray* that the fellowship of your faith may become effective *a*through the knowledge of every good thing which is in you for Christ's sake.

7 For I have come to have much joy and comfort in your love, because the hearts of the saints have been refreshed through you, brother.

8 ¶ Therefore, though I have enough confidence in Christ to order you *to do* what is proper,

9 yet for love's sake I rather appeal *to you*— since I am such a person as Paul, the aged, and now also a prisoner of Christ Jesus—

Plea for Onesimus, a Free Man

10 I appeal to you for my child *b*Onesimus, whom I have begotten in my imprisonment,

11 who formerly was useless to you, but now is useful both to you and to me.

12 I have sent him back to you in person, that is, *sending* my very heart,

13 whom I wished to keep with me, so that on your behalf he might minister to me in my imprisonment for the gospel;

14 but without your consent I did not want to do anything, so that your goodness would not be, in effect, by compulsion but of your own free will.

15 For perhaps he was for this reason separated *from you* for a while, that you would have him back forever,

16 no longer as a slave, but more than a slave, a beloved brother, especially to me, but how much more to you, both in the flesh and in the Lord.

11 No Longer Useless

Onesimus *in Greek means "useful," and Paul playfully makes a pun from the name. A runaway slave was useless; a converted former slave can prove very useful—provided Philemon receives him in the right spirit. Accept him back, urges Paul, "no longer as a slave, but . . . a beloved brother" (verse 16).*

17 ¶ If then you regard me a partner, accept him as *you would* me.

18 But if he has wronged you in any way or owes you anything, charge that to my account;

19 I, Paul, am writing this with my own hand, I will repay it (not to mention to you that you owe to me even your own self as well).

20 Yes, brother, let me benefit from you in the Lord; refresh my heart in Christ.

a Or *in*   *b* I.e. useful

21 ¶ Having confidence in your obedience, I write to you, since I know that you will do even more than what I say.

22 ¶ At the same time also prepare me a lodging, for I hope that through your prayers I will be given to you.

23 ¶ Epaphras, my fellow prisoner in Christ Jesus, greets you,

24 *as do* Mark, Aristarchus, Demas, Luke, my fellow workers.

25 ¶ The grace of the Lord Jesus Christ be with your spirit.[a]

HEBREWS

Time to Decide
Does it matter what you believe as long as you're sincere?

> How will we escape if we neglect so great a salvation?
> 2:3

YOU CAN GO THROUGH MUCH of life deliberately avoiding hard decisions. But sometimes you have no choice; the situation forces you to make a decision. Consider an example from the sport of rock-climbing.

Sooner or later, every rock-climber faces a dreaded section of slick granite that offers no ledges or cracks to grasp. When you come to such a wall, you can abandon the climb. Or, you can risk a move like "the pendulum."

The Pendulum

The pendulum works the way it sounds: as high above you as you can reach, you fasten a loop with a metal nut and slide the rope through the loop. Then you climb down a few feet, dangle on the end of the rope, and try to swing across the sheer section. It takes nerve. You must lean out against the rope into empty space and, with a well-timed push, vault across the face of the cliff. If your lunge toward a safer spot fails, you swing helplessly back and try again.

After your entire party has swung the pendulum, you pull the rope all the way through the loop. From then on, there's no turning back. You have crossed a section of cliff that requires a rope to swing on and a loop to attach it to. The loop is now out of your reach, and the rope coiled at your feet. There is only one way to go: up.

Worth the Risk?

The author of Hebrews wrote to people who faced just such a climactic, can't-turn-back decision. It involved not a rock climb, but their entire future. Should they stick with the familiar routine of the Jewish religion? After all, it enjoyed Rome's official protection and had traditions going back thousands of years. Or should they take a risk and join the growing body of people who called themselves Christians? Those readers needed some compelling reasons to choose Christianity. At that time new converts were being thrown out of Jewish temples, tossed into jail, and even tortured. Was faith in Christ worth the risk?

The tug of the old and the fear of the new kept many interested people, especially Jews, teetering on the edge of Christianity. And the book of Hebrews seems designed to push such people toward a decisive commitment, in one direction or the other. Point by point, the author shows how Christ improved on the Jewish way. Hebrews is a no-holds-barred argument on why Christianity is *better* (a key word in Hebrews) than Judaism. The new faith is worth any risk.

Drawing on the Old Testament

For the sake of Jewish readers, the author painstakingly cites Old Testament passages, more than 80 times in all. He develops the case for Christ like a lawyer, but with the charged emotions befitting the life-and-death issues involved.

Although Hebrews mainly focuses on the Jewish religion, comparing it to Christianity, the book also speaks to our time. Today people ask, "Are religions all that different? Isn't the most important thing to be sincere?" Hebrews insists there are decisive reasons to choose Christ. The author urges his readers to leap forward to a new experience with God through Jesus.

How to Read Hebrews

Who wrote Hebrews? Did the author have a particular group of readers in mind? Scholars have debated these questions for centuries without reaching agreement. The truth is, no one knows for certain either the author or the intended audience of Hebrews.

Nevertheless, the book does give some information about its first readers. They had heard the gospel through contemporaries of Jesus (2:3), and their conversion had brought on physical persecution (10:32–34). One fact leaps out: Their spiritual state greatly distressed the unidentified author. Five times in the book of Hebrews he interrupts a careful line of reasoning to fire off a warning (2:1; 3:7; 5:11; 10:26; 12:25).

Hebrews is actually a commentary on the Old Testament. It examines many Jewish customs and shows how Jesus brought about a "better covenant" to replace many of those laws. (*Covenant* means the same thing as *Testament:* a firm agreement between God and humanity.) Therefore, to fully appreciate Hebrews, you should have some familiarity with such books as Exodus, Leviticus, and Numbers.

To follow the logic in Hebrews, note each use of the word *better* and *superior*. The author compares Jesus Christ to the angels, to Moses, to the priests Aaron and Melchizedek, and to Abraham.

3-TRACK READING PLAN

For an explanation and complete listing of the 3-track reading plan, turn to page 7.

TRACK 1: **Two-Week Courses on the Bible**
See page 7 for information on these courses.

TRACK 2: **An Overview of Hebrews in 3 Days**
☐ Day 1. Read the Introduction to Hebrews, then chapter 2. There you will learn about God's decision to send his Son to earth and why it was so important that Jesus come as a fully human being, not as some kind of alien.
☐ Day 2. Hebrews 11 lists many Old Testament heroes, with a capsule description of how each one demonstrated faith. Read this famous chapter.
☐ Day 3. Read Hebrews 12, which combines a pep talk with a brief summary of the entire book.

Now turn to page 9 for your next Track 2 reading project.

TRACK 3: **All of Hebrews in 11 Days**
After you have read through Hebrews, turn to pages 10–14 for your next Track 3 reading project.

☐1　　☐2　　☐3–4　☐5–6　☐7　　☐8　　☐9　　☐10
☐11　 ☐12　 ☐13

God's Final Word in His Son

1 God, after He spoke long ago to the fathers in the prophets in many portions and in many ways,

2 in these last days has spoken to us in His Son, whom He appointed heir of all things, through whom also He made the world.

3 And He is the radiance of His glory and the exact representation of His nature, and upholds all things by the word of His power. When He had made purification of sins, He sat down at the right hand of the Majesty on high,

4 having become as much better than the an-gels, as He has inherited a more excellent name than they.

5 ¶ For to which of the angels did He ever say,
"YOU ARE MY SON,
TODAY I HAVE BEGOTTEN YOU"?
And again,
"I WILL BE A FATHER TO HIM
AND HE SHALL BE A SON TO ME"?

6 And when He again brings the firstborn into the world, He says,
"AND LET ALL THE ANGELS OF GOD
WORSHIP HIM."

7 And of the angels He says,

"WHO MAKES HIS ANGELS WINDS,
AND HIS MINISTERS A FLAME OF FIRE."
8 But of the Son He says,
"YOUR THRONE, O GOD, IS FOREVER AND
EVER,
AND THE RIGHTEOUS SCEPTER IS THE
SCEPTER OF [a]HIS KINGDOM.
9 "YOU HAVE LOVED RIGHTEOUSNESS AND
HATED LAWLESSNESS;
THEREFORE GOD, YOUR GOD, HAS
ANOINTED YOU
WITH THE OIL OF GLADNESS ABOVE YOUR
COMPANIONS."
10 And,
"YOU, LORD, IN THE BEGINNING LAID THE
FOUNDATION OF THE EARTH,
AND THE HEAVENS ARE THE WORKS OF
YOUR HANDS;

1:10 Not by Chance

Quotations from the Old Testament fill the book of Hebrews from the second paragraph onwards. The author is making the point that God's plan, unfolding from the beginning of time, has now culminated in the visit of the Son to earth.

11 THEY WILL PERISH, BUT YOU REMAIN;
AND THEY ALL WILL BECOME OLD LIKE A
GARMENT,
12 AND LIKE A MANTLE YOU WILL ROLL
THEM UP;
LIKE A GARMENT THEY WILL ALSO BE
CHANGED.
BUT YOU ARE THE SAME,
AND YOUR YEARS WILL NOT COME TO
AN END."
13 But to which of the angels has He ever said,
"SIT AT MY RIGHT HAND,
UNTIL I MAKE YOUR ENEMIES
A FOOTSTOOL FOR YOUR FEET"?
14 Are they not all ministering spirits, sent out to render service for the sake of those who will inherit salvation?

Give Heed

2 For this reason we must pay much closer attention to what we have heard, so that we do not drift away *from it.*
2 For if the word spoken through angels proved unalterable, and every transgression and disobedience received a just penalty,
3 how will we escape if we neglect so great a salvation? After it was at the first spoken through the Lord, it was confirmed to us by those who heard,

4 God also testifying with them, both by signs and wonders and by various miracles and by gifts of the Holy Spirit according to His own will.

Earth Subject to Man

5 ¶ For He did not subject to angels the world to come, concerning which we are speaking.

1:14 Respect for Angels

In earlier times, people freely accepted the existence of angels and accorded them honor and respect. Jewish people retold stories of how angels had assisted Abraham, Moses, Elijah, Balaam, and Daniel. (In fact, several New Testament letters warn Jewish Christians against the common practice of worshiping angels.) To prove its argument about Christ being superior, Hebrews must show that angels served his purposes, not vice versa.

6 But one has testified somewhere, saying,
"WHAT IS MAN, THAT YOU REMEMBER HIM?
OR THE SON OF MAN, THAT YOU ARE
CONCERNED ABOUT HIM?
7 "YOU HAVE MADE HIM FOR A LITTLE WHILE
LOWER THAN THE ANGELS;
YOU HAVE CROWNED HIM WITH GLORY
AND HONOR,
[b]AND HAVE APPOINTED HIM OVER THE
WORKS OF YOUR HANDS;
8 YOU HAVE PUT ALL THINGS IN SUBJECTION
UNDER HIS FEET."
For in subjecting all things to him, He left nothing that is not subject to him. But now we do not yet see all things subjected to him.

Jesus Briefly Humbled

9 But we do see Him who was made for a little while lower than the angels, *namely,* Jesus, because of the suffering of death crowned with glory and honor, so that by the grace of God He might taste death for everyone.
10 ¶ For it was fitting for Him, for whom are all things, and through whom are all things, in bringing many sons to glory, to perfect the author of their salvation through sufferings.
11 For both He who sanctifies and those who are sanctified are all from one *Father*; for which reason He is not ashamed to call them brethren,
12 saying,
"I WILL PROCLAIM YOUR NAME TO MY
BRETHREN,
IN THE MIDST OF THE CONGREGATION I
WILL SING YOUR PRAISE."

---

[a] Late mss read *Your*   [b] Two early mss do not contain *And...hands*

13 And again,
"I WILL PUT MY TRUST IN HIM."
And again,
"BEHOLD, I AND THE CHILDREN WHOM GOD
HAS GIVEN ME."

14 ¶ Therefore, since the children share in flesh and blood, He Himself likewise also partook of the same, that through death He might render powerless him who had the power of death, that is, the devil,

15 and might free those who through fear of death were subject to slavery all their lives.

16 For assuredly He does not give help to angels, but He gives help to the descendant of Abraham.

17 Therefore, He had to be made like His brethren in all things, so that He might become a merciful and faithful high priest in things pertaining to God, to make propitiation for the sins of the people.

18 For since He Himself was tempted in that which He has suffered, He is able to come to the aid of those who are tempted.

Jesus Our High Priest

3 Therefore, holy brethren, partakers of a heavenly calling, consider Jesus, the Apostle and High Priest of our confession;

2:17 Like Us in Every Way

Hebrews goes further than any other New Testament book in explaining Jesus' human nature. Why was it so important that Jesus share our humanity? Hebrews stresses three reasons: (1) so that, in dying, he could free us from the power of death (verses 14–15); (2) so that, by becoming the final sacrifice for sin, he could reconcile us to God (5:8–9); and (3) so that, in experiencing temptation, he can better help us with our own temptations (verse 18).

2 He was faithful to Him who appointed Him, as Moses also was in all His house.

3 For He has been counted worthy of more

Is Christ Better?
The uniqueness of Jesus

IN TIME, A WORK OF art by a great artist gains enormous value because of its creator's reputation. Even a musty notebook full of scratchings, if found to be Leonardo da Vinci's, would suddenly be worth millions of dollars. Similarly, every house designed by American architect Frank Lloyd Wright retains high value simply because of his name.

To dramatize his argument that Christ is superior to any religious system, the author of Hebrews uses an analogy: Which has greater honor, the builder of a house or the house itself? Obviously, the builder has more honor; the house is just one expression of his genius.

For He [Jesus] has been counted worthy of more glory than Moses, by just so much as the builder of the house has more honor than the house. 3:3

In a Category by Himself

Likewise, Hebrews says, Christ has more honor than anyone else on earth. As Creator of the universe, he actually designed and made all people (1:2). That puts him in a different category of greatness, far above Moses, Aaron, and other Jewish heroes.

"Therefore," Hebrews urges, "consider Jesus" (3:1). He deserves all respect and allegiance. By becoming human, Jesus learned firsthand the temptations and sufferings that people undergo, so that he can now represent us sympathetically to God (4:14–15). The author goes on to prove that Jesus fulfilled all the Old Testament requirements. He was the one priest who could permanently bring together God and the human race (7:23–27). And, as God, he had the power through his death to remove the final barrier of sin between God and humankind (9:11–15).

Free Access to God

Over time, the author argues, God chose various ways to reveal himself: creation, the prophets, and the Old Testament Scriptures. But the final, complete self-expression culminated in his Son. Jesus is the one worthy of honor.

Because of Jesus, we no longer have to approach God through a priest, as the Israelites did. Christ's work makes God available to all who have faith in him. And God no longer dwells in an elaborately designed temple; we have become his house (3:6), his work of art.

Life Questions: People sometimes say about Jesus, "I don't believe he was God, but he was a very fine man—like Gandhi or Buddha." What arguments does the author of Hebrews use to contradict this?

glory than Moses, by just so much as the builder of the house has more honor than the house.

4 For every house is built by someone, but the builder of all things is God.

5 Now Moses was faithful in all His house as a servant, for a testimony of those things which were to be spoken later;

6 but Christ *was faithful* as a Son over His house—whose house we are, if we hold fast our confidence and the boast of our hope firm until the end.

7 ¶ Therefore, just as the Holy Spirit says,
"TODAY IF YOU HEAR HIS VOICE,
8 DO NOT HARDEN YOUR HEARTS AS WHEN
  THEY PROVOKED ME,
  AS IN THE DAY OF TRIAL IN THE
  WILDERNESS,
9 WHERE YOUR FATHERS TRIED *Me* BY
  TESTING *Me*,
  AND SAW MY WORKS FOR FORTY YEARS.
10 "THEREFORE I WAS ANGRY WITH THIS
  GENERATION,
  AND SAID, 'THEY ALWAYS GO ASTRAY IN
  THEIR HEART,
  AND THEY DID NOT KNOW MY WAYS';
11 AS I SWORE IN MY WRATH,
  'THEY SHALL NOT ENTER MY REST.' "

The Peril of Unbelief

12 Take care, brethren, that there not be in any one of you an evil, unbelieving heart that falls away from the living God.

13 But encourage one another day after day, as long as it is *still* called "Today," so that none of you will be hardened by the deceitfulness of sin.

14 For we have become partakers of Christ, if we hold fast the beginning of our assurance firm until the end,

15 while it is said,
"TODAY IF YOU HEAR HIS VOICE,
  DO NOT HARDEN YOUR HEARTS, AS WHEN
  THEY PROVOKED ME."

16 For who provoked *Him* when they had heard? Indeed, did not all those who came out of Egypt *led* by Moses?

17 And with whom was He angry for forty years? Was it not with those who sinned, whose bodies fell in the wilderness?

18 And to whom did He swear that they would not enter His rest, but to those who were disobedient?

19 *So* we see that they were not able to enter because of unbelief.

The Believer's Rest

4 Therefore, let us fear if, while a promise remains of entering His rest, any one of you may seem to have come short of it.

2 For indeed we have had good news preached to us, just as they also; but the word they heard did not profit them, because it was not united by faith in those who heard.

3 For we who have believed enter that rest, just as He has said,
"AS I SWORE IN MY WRATH,
  THEY SHALL NOT ENTER MY REST,"
although His works were finished from the foundation of the world.

4 For He has said somewhere concerning the seventh *day*: "AND GOD RESTED ON THE SEVENTH DAY FROM ALL HIS WORKS";

5 and again in this *passage*, "THEY SHALL NOT ENTER MY REST."

6 Therefore, since it remains for some to enter it, and those who formerly had good news preached to them failed to enter because of disobedience,

7 He again fixes a certain day, "Today," saying through David after so long a time just as has been said before,
"TODAY IF YOU HEAR HIS VOICE,
  DO NOT HARDEN YOUR HEARTS."

8 For if Joshua had given them rest, He would not have spoken of another day after that.

9 So there remains a Sabbath rest for the people of God.

10 For the one who has entered His rest has himself also rested from his works, as God did from His.

11 Therefore let us be diligent to enter that rest, so that no one will fall, through *following* the same example of disobedience.

12 For the word of God is living and active and sharper than any two-edged sword, and piercing as far as the division of soul and spirit, of both joints and marrow, and able to judge the thoughts and intentions of the heart.

13 And there is no creature hidden from His sight, but all things are open and laid bare to the eyes of Him with whom we have to do.

4:13 Mind Reader

Advances in technology—MRI tests, x-ray machines, CAT scans—make it possible for doctors to peer inside the human body and judge what goes on there. But no one has yet devised a machine that can peer inside the brain to detect thoughts and attitudes. God has such ability; why try to hide?

14 ¶ Therefore, since we have a great high priest who has passed through the heavens, Jesus the Son of God, let us hold fast our confession.

15 For we do not have a high priest who cannot sympathize with our weaknesses, but One who has been tempted in all things as *we are, yet* without sin.

16 Therefore let us draw near with confidence

to the throne of grace, so that we may receive mercy and find grace to help in time of need.

The Perfect High Priest

5 For every high priest taken from among men is appointed on behalf of men in things pertaining to God, in order to offer both gifts and sacrifices for sins;

2 he can deal gently with the ignorant and misguided, since he himself also is beset with weakness;

3 and because of it he is obligated to offer *sacrifices* for sins, as for the people, so also for himself.

4 And no one takes the honor to himself, but *receives it* when he is called by God, even as Aaron was.

5 ¶ So also Christ did not glorify Himself so as to become a high priest, but He who said to Him,

"YOU ARE MY SON,
TODAY I HAVE BEGOTTEN YOU";

6 just as He says also in another *passage*,
"YOU ARE A PRIEST FOREVER
ACCORDING TO THE ORDER OF
MELCHIZEDEK."

7 In the days of His flesh, He offered up both prayers and supplications with loud crying and tears to the One able to save Him from death, and He was heard because of His piety.

8 Although He was a Son, He learned obedience from the things which He suffered.

9 And having been made perfect, He became to all those who obey Him the source of eternal salvation,

10 being designated by God as a high priest according to the order of Melchizedek.

11 ¶ Concerning [a]him we have much to say, and *it is* hard to explain, since you have become dull of hearing.

12 For though by this time you ought to be teachers, you have need again for someone to teach you the elementary principles of the oracles of God, and you have come to need milk and not solid food.

13 For everyone who partakes *only* of milk is not accustomed to the word of righteousness, for he is an infant.

14 But solid food is for the mature, who because of practice have their senses trained to discern good and evil.

The Peril of Falling Away

6 Therefore leaving the elementary teaching about the Christ, let us press on to maturity, not laying again a foundation of repentance from dead works and of faith toward God,

2 of instruction about washings and laying on of hands, and the resurrection of the dead and eternal judgment.

[a] Lit *whom* or *which*

3 And this we will do, if God permits.

4 For in the case of those who have once been enlightened and have tasted of the heavenly gift and have been made partakers of the Holy Spirit,

6:4 Can a Believer Fall Away?

This passage has caused interpreters great difficulty. People who don't believe in "eternal security" think the passage refers to Christians who fall away from the faith. Others, such as John Calvin, insist that the author of Hebrews must be referring to people who never fully became Christians, because other verses seem to teach the eternal security of those in Christ (see John 5:24; 6:37; Romans 8:1; Hebrews 8:12). Regardless, the author is writing about a hypothetical situation. He is not describing what happened, but only what could happen: If such a falling away ever did occur, it would be impossible to rescue such people again. A somewhat similar argument appears at the end of chapter 10.

5 and have tasted the good word of God and the powers of the age to come,

6 and *then* have fallen away, it is impossible to renew them again to repentance, since they again crucify to themselves the Son of God and put Him to open shame.

7 For ground that drinks the rain which often falls on it and brings forth vegetation useful to those for whose sake it is also tilled, receives a blessing from God;

8 but if it yields thorns and thistles, it is worthless and close to being cursed, and it ends up being burned.

Better Things for You

9 ¶ But, beloved, we are convinced of better things concerning you, and things that accompany salvation, though we are speaking in this way.

10 For God is not unjust so as to forget your work and the love which you have shown toward His name, in having ministered and in still ministering to the saints.

11 And we desire that each one of you show the same diligence so as to realize the full assurance of hope until the end,

12 so that you will not be sluggish, but imitators of those who through faith and patience inherit the promises.

13 ¶ For when God made the promise to Abraham, since He could swear by no one greater, He swore by Himself,

14 saying, "I WILL SURELY BLESS YOU AND I WILL SURELY MULTIPLY YOU."

15 And so, having patiently waited, he obtained the promise.

16 For men swear by one greater *than themselves*, and with them an oath *given* as confirmation is an end of every dispute.

17 In the same way God, desiring even more to show to the heirs of the promise the unchangeableness of His purpose, interposed with an oath,

18 so that by two unchangeable things in which it is impossible for God to lie, we who have taken refuge would have strong encouragement to take hold of the hope set before us.

19 This hope we have as an anchor of the soul, a *hope* both sure and steadfast and one which enters within the veil,

20 where Jesus has entered as a forerunner for us, having become a high priest forever according to the order of Melchizedek.

Melchizedek's Priesthood Like Christ's

7 For this Melchizedek, king of Salem, priest of the Most High God, who met Abraham as he was returning from the slaughter of the kings and blessed him,

7:1 Who Is Melchizedek?

This mysterious person appears in only two places in the Old Testament: Genesis 14 and Psalm 110. Although a Gentile, Melchizedek worshiped the true God. In addition to being a priest, he was also a king. The Jews would never have permitted such dual office-holding.) Hebrews demonstrates that the priesthood of Melchizedek was superior to that of Aaron; but both of them were exceeded by the great high priest, Jesus himself. Because he is both priest and king, Jesus is "in the order of" Melchizedek. (See "The Twelfth Man," page 666, for more details.)

2 to whom also Abraham apportioned a tenth part of all *the spoils*, was first of all, by the translation *of his name*, king of righteousness, and then also king of Salem, which is king of peace.

3 Without father, without mother, without genealogy, having neither beginning of days nor end of life, but made like the Son of God, he remains a priest perpetually.

4 ¶ Now observe how great this man was to whom Abraham, the patriarch, gave a tenth of the choicest spoils.

5 And those indeed of the sons of Levi who receive the priest's office have commandment in the Law to collect a tenth from the people, that is, from their brethren, although these are descended from Abraham.

6 But the one whose genealogy is not traced from them collected a tenth from Abraham and blessed the one who had the promises.

7 But without any dispute the lesser is blessed by the greater.

8 In this case mortal men receive tithes, but in that case one *receives them*, of whom it is witnessed that he lives on.

9 And, so to speak, through Abraham even Levi, who received tithes, paid tithes,

10 for he was still in the loins of his father when Melchizedek met him.

11 ¶ Now if perfection was through the Levitical priesthood (for on the basis of it the people received the Law), what further need *was there* for another priest to arise according to the order of Melchizedek, and not be designated according to the order of Aaron?

12 For when the priesthood is changed, of necessity there takes place a change of law also.

13 For the one concerning whom these things are spoken belongs to another tribe, from which no one has officiated at the altar.

14 For it is evident that our Lord was descended from Judah, a tribe with reference to which Moses spoke nothing concerning priests.

15 And this is clearer still, if another priest arises according to the likeness of Melchizedek,

16 who has become *such* not on the basis of a law of physical requirement, but according to the power of an indestructible life.

17 For it is attested *of Him*,

"YOU ARE A PRIEST FOREVER
ACCORDING TO THE ORDER OF
MELCHIZEDEK."

18 For, on the one hand, there is a setting aside of a former commandment because of its weakness and uselessness

19 (for the Law made nothing perfect), and on the other hand there is a bringing in of a better hope, through which we draw near to God.

7:19 Drawing Near

The original Jewish readers of Hebrews were still following the "old covenant" law, and this book was written to show them how things had changed to their benefit. In Old Testament times only the high priest could "draw near" to God, and that only once a year when he entered the curtained-off holy place. As Hebrews points out, Jesus entered that inner room on our behalf (6:20). When he died, the curtain ripped in two; now any of us can draw near without fear.

20 And inasmuch as *it was* not without an oath

21 (for they indeed became priests without an oath, but He with an oath through the One who said to Him,

"THE LORD HAS SWORN
AND WILL NOT CHANGE HIS MIND,
'YOU ARE A PRIEST FOREVER'");

22 so much the more also Jesus has become the guarantee of a better covenant.

23 ¶ The *former* priests, on the one hand, existed in greater numbers because they were prevented by death from continuing,

24 but Jesus, on the other hand, because He continues forever, holds His priesthood permanently.

25 Therefore He is able also to save forever those who draw near to God through Him, since He always lives to make intercession for them.

26 ¶ For it was fitting for us to have such a high priest, holy, innocent, undefiled, separated from sinners and exalted above the heavens;

27 who does not need daily, like those high priests, to offer up sacrifices, first for His own sins and then for the *sins* of the people, because this He did once for all when He offered up Himself.

28 For the Law appoints men as high priests who are weak, but the word of the oath, which came after the Law, *appoints* a Son, made perfect forever.

A Better Ministry

8 Now the main point in what has been said *is this*: we have such a high priest, who has taken His seat at the right hand of the throne of the Majesty in the heavens,

2 a minister in the sanctuary and in the true tabernacle, which the Lord pitched, not man.

New Light on the Old Testament
The advantages of living now

> For if that first covenant had been faultless, there would have been no occasion sought for a second. 8:7

TO UNDERSTAND THE DIFFERENCE BETWEEN an original and a copy, consider trying to photograph the largest animal, a whale. Roy Chapman Andrews describes it:

"Once in Alaska we raised a humpback's spout and ran up close before the animal submerged. Ten minutes later, without warning, the floor of the ocean seemed to rise and a mountainous black body, dripping with foam, heaved upward, almost over our heads. It paused an instant, then fell sidewise to be swallowed up by a vortex of green water. With the camera ready in my hands I stared at the thing. The whale had dropped back scarcely twenty feet away; if it had fallen the other way, the vessel would have been crushed beneath its forty tons."

How can you adequately communicate the impact of something that immense? Photographers have recorded humpback whales bursting from the water, or "lobtailing" (standing on their heads and waving their mighty flukes high in the air). But no photograph can capture the sheer bigness of such an animal. A baby blue whale gains a ton of weight a month. An adult blue whale's heart weighs 1,000 pounds. How can any two-dimensional photograph convey such gargantuan size?

Comparing the Copy to the Original

Even the best photograph is just a copy, a representation of its subject's reality. No 8x10 rectangle can contain a whale. No photo sequence of the Grand Canyon is as grand as the canyon itself. The photograph preserves a mere two-dimensional copy of reality.

Hebrews uses that word *copy* to describe the images and rituals of the Old Testament: Passover feasts, sacrifices, and other priestly duties. They were mere shadows, expressing the reality to come in Jesus Christ. No ceremony alone, however elaborate, can adequately express the experience of God himself, any more than a photograph of a whale or a mountain can adequately represent a whale or a mountain.

According to Hebrews, the Old Testament rituals were a copy, but Christ is the original. The author pulls up time-hallowed images from the Jewish tradition—sacrifices, laws, blood, the tabernacle, the priest, the Day of Atonement—and explains how Christ revealed once and for all the meaning these images only hinted at. The incomplete, shadowy copy contrasts with the perfect, genuine reality.

Which Is Better?

As always, Hebrews stresses the advantages of living now, rather than in the Old Testament ("the first covenant"). Because of Christ, sacrifices are no longer necessary (10:11–12), and God's laws are now written in our minds and on our hearts, not in a formal code (8:10). "It is finished," Christ cried out from the cross (John 19:30); the author of Hebrews describes how.

Copies have some value. A photograph of a whale, for example, conveys much to those who will never encounter one. But, as the author of Hebrews asks, who would prefer a copy to the real thing?

Life Questions: What practical help does Hebrews give on how to read the Old Testament? Of what value are the Old Testament laws and religious rituals?

3 For every high priest is appointed to offer both gifts and sacrifices; so it is necessary that this *high priest* also have something to offer.

4 Now if He were on earth, He would not be a priest at all, since there are those who offer the gifts according to the Law;

5 who serve a copy and shadow of the heavenly things, just as Moses was warned *by God* when he was about to erect the tabernacle; for, "SEE," He says, "THAT YOU MAKE all things ACCORDING TO THE PATTERN WHICH WAS SHOWN YOU ON THE MOUNTAIN."

6 But now He has obtained a more excellent ministry, by as much as He is also the mediator of a better covenant, which has been enacted on better promises.

A New Covenant

7 For if that first *covenant* had been faultless, there would have been no occasion sought for a second.

8 For finding fault with them, He says,
"BEHOLD, DAYS ARE COMING, SAYS THE
LORD,
WHEN I WILL EFFECT A NEW COVENANT
WITH THE HOUSE OF ISRAEL AND WITH THE
HOUSE OF JUDAH;
9 NOT LIKE THE COVENANT WHICH I MADE
WITH THEIR FATHERS
ON THE DAY WHEN I TOOK THEM BY THE
HAND
TO LEAD THEM OUT OF THE LAND OF
EGYPT;
FOR THEY DID NOT CONTINUE IN MY
COVENANT,
AND I DID NOT CARE FOR THEM, SAYS THE
LORD.
10 "FOR THIS IS THE COVENANT THAT I WILL
MAKE WITH THE HOUSE OF ISRAEL
AFTER THOSE DAYS, SAYS THE LORD:
I WILL PUT MY LAWS INTO THEIR MINDS,
AND I WILL WRITE THEM ON THEIR
HEARTS.
AND I WILL BE THEIR GOD,
AND THEY SHALL BE MY PEOPLE.
11 "AND THEY SHALL NOT TEACH EVERYONE HIS
FELLOW CITIZEN,
AND EVERYONE HIS BROTHER, SAYING,
'KNOW THE LORD,'
FOR ALL WILL KNOW ME,
FROM THE LEAST TO THE GREATEST OF
THEM.
12 "FOR I WILL BE MERCIFUL TO THEIR
INIQUITIES,
AND I WILL REMEMBER THEIR SINS NO
MORE."

13 When He said, "A new *covenant*," He has made the first obsolete. But whatever is becoming obsolete and growing old is ready to disappear.

The Old and the New

9 Now even the first *covenant* had regulations of divine worship and the earthly sanctuary.

2 For there was a tabernacle prepared, the outer one, in which *were* the lampstand and the table and the sacred bread; this is called the holy place.

3 Behind the second veil there was a tabernacle which is called the Holy of Holies,

4 having a golden altar of incense and the ark of the covenant covered on all sides with gold, in which was a golden jar holding the manna, and Aaron's rod which budded, and the tables of the covenant;

5 and above it *were* the cherubim of glory overshadowing the mercy seat; but of these things we cannot now speak in detail.

6 ¶ Now when these things have been so prepared, the priests are continually entering the outer tabernacle performing the divine worship,

7 but into the second, only the high priest *enters* once a year, not without *taking* blood, which he offers for himself and for the sins of the people committed in ignorance.

8 The Holy Spirit *is* signifying this, that the way into the holy place has not yet been disclosed while the outer tabernacle is still standing,

9 which *is* a symbol for the present time. Accordingly both gifts and sacrifices are offered which cannot make the worshiper perfect in conscience,

10 since they *relate* only to food and drink and various washings, regulations for the body imposed until a time of reformation.

11 ¶ But when Christ appeared *as* a high priest of the good things *a*to come, *He entered* through the greater and more perfect tabernacle, not made with hands, that is to say, not of this creation;

9:11 More Perfect

Descriptions of the tabernacle and offerings take up much of Exodus, Leviticus, Numbers, and Deuteronomy, leading some scholars to judge it the largest single subject covered in the Bible. Yet Hebrews, concerned to prove the superiority of a new covenant, devotes a mere 10 verses to the tabernacle (verses 1–10). The great high priest, Christ himself, has made the old system obsolete.

12 and not through the blood of goats and calves, but through His own blood, He entered the holy place once for all, having obtained eternal redemption.

13 For if the blood of goats and bulls and the ashes of a heifer sprinkling those who have been defiled sanctify for the cleansing of the flesh,

a Two early mss read *that have come*

14 how much more will the blood of Christ, who through the eternal Spirit offered Himself without blemish to God, cleanse your conscience from dead works to serve the living God?

15 ¶ For this reason He is the mediator of a new covenant, so that, since a death has taken place for the redemption of the transgressions that were *committed* under the first covenant, those who have been called may receive the promise of the eternal inheritance.

16 For where a covenant is, there must of necessity be the death of the one who made it.

17 For a covenant is valid *only* when men are dead, [a]for it is never in force while the one who made it lives.

18 Therefore even the first *covenant* was not inaugurated without blood.

19 For when every commandment had been spoken by Moses to all the people according to the Law, he took the blood of the calves and the goats, with water and scarlet wool and hyssop, and sprinkled both the book itself and all the people,

20 saying, "THIS IS THE BLOOD OF THE COVENANT WHICH GOD COMMANDED YOU."

21 And in the same way he sprinkled both the tabernacle and all the vessels of the ministry with the blood.

22 And according to the Law, *one may* almost *say,* all things are cleansed with blood, and without shedding of blood there is no forgiveness.

23 ¶ Therefore it was necessary for the copies of the things in the heavens to be cleansed with these, but the heavenly things themselves with better sacrifices than these.

24 For Christ did not enter a holy place made with hands, a *mere* copy of the true one, but into heaven itself, now to appear in the presence of God for us;

25 nor was it that He would offer Himself often, as the high priest enters the holy place year by year with blood that is not his own.

26 Otherwise, He would have needed to suffer often since the foundation of the world; but now once at the consummation of the ages He has been manifested to put away sin by the sacrifice of Himself.

27 And inasmuch as it is appointed for men to die once and after this *comes* judgment,

28 so Christ also, having been offered once to bear the sins of many, will appear a second time for salvation without *reference to* sin, to those who eagerly await Him.

One Sacrifice of Christ Is Sufficient

10 For the Law, since it has *only* a shadow of the good things to come *and* not the very form of things, [b]can never, by the same sacrifices which they offer continually year by year, make perfect those who draw near.

2 Otherwise, would they not have ceased to be offered, because the worshipers, having once been cleansed, would no longer have had consciousness of sins?

3 But in those *sacrifices* there is a reminder of sins year by year.

9:26 A Once-for-all Sacrifice

Jewish readers of Hebrews were very familiar with the religious rituals described in this chapter (see Leviticus 9 and 16 for the original instructions). Step by step, the author shows how Christ's new covenant improves on the old one. Instead of many sacrifices, he made only one, himself, thus gaining free and complete forgiveness for us. The chapter uses an analogy to explain why Christ's death was necessary (verse 17). It compares God's grace to a will. Wealth is only passed down when a death occurs; Christ's death freed the inheritance for us.

4 For it is impossible for the blood of bulls and goats to take away sins.

5 Therefore, when He comes into the world, He says,
"SACRIFICE AND OFFERING YOU HAVE NOT
    DESIRED,
  BUT A BODY YOU HAVE PREPARED FOR ME;
6 IN WHOLE BURNT OFFERINGS AND *sacrifices*
    FOR SIN YOU HAVE TAKEN NO
    PLEASURE.
7 "THEN I SAID, 'BEHOLD, I HAVE COME
  (IN THE SCROLL OF THE BOOK IT IS WRITTEN
    OF ME)
  TO DO YOUR WILL, O GOD.' "

8 After saying above, "SACRIFICES AND OFFERINGS AND WHOLE BURNT OFFERINGS AND *sacrifices* FOR SIN YOU HAVE NOT DESIRED, NOR HAVE YOU TAKEN PLEASURE *in them*" (which are offered according to the Law),

9 then He said, "BEHOLD, I HAVE COME TO DO YOUR WILL." He takes away the first in order to establish the second.

10 By this will we have been sanctified through the offering of the body of Jesus Christ once for all.

11 ¶ Every priest stands daily ministering and offering time after time the same sacrifices, which can never take away sins;

12 but He, having offered one sacrifice for sins for all time, SAT DOWN AT THE RIGHT HAND OF GOD,

13 waiting from that time onward UNTIL HIS ENEMIES BE MADE A FOOTSTOOL FOR HIS FEET.

14 For by one offering He has perfected for all time those who are sanctified.

15 And the Holy Spirit also testifies to us; for after saying,

---

[a] Two early mss read *for is it then...lives?* [b] Two early mss read *they can*

16 "THIS IS THE COVENANT THAT I WILL MAKE
   WITH THEM
AFTER THOSE DAYS, SAYS THE LORD:
I WILL PUT MY LAWS UPON THEIR HEART,
AND ON THEIR MIND I WILL WRITE THEM,"

He then says,

17 "AND THEIR SINS AND THEIR LAWLESS DEEDS
I WILL REMEMBER NO MORE."

18 Now where there is forgiveness of these things, there is no longer *any* offering for sin.

A New and Living Way

19 ¶ Therefore, brethren, since we have confidence to enter the holy place by the blood of Jesus,

20 by a new and living way which He inaugurated for us through the veil, that is, His flesh,

10:12 Why Christ Sat Down

Hebrews makes special mention that Christ "sat down" after finishing his priestly duties. Jewish priests never sat down; the tabernacle and the temple did not have seats. They did their work standing up as a symbol that it was never finished. Having finished the work of a priest once for all, Christ "sat down."

21 and since *we have* a great priest over the house of God,

22 let us draw near with a sincere heart in full assurance of faith, having our hearts sprinkled *clean* from an evil conscience and our bodies washed with pure water.

23 Let us hold fast the confession of our hope without wavering, for He who promised is faithful;

24 and let us consider how to stimulate one another to love and good deeds,

25 not forsaking our own assembling together, as is the habit of some, but encouraging *one another*; and all the more as you see the day drawing near.

Christ or Judgment

26 ¶ For if we go on sinning willfully after receiving the knowledge of the truth, there no longer remains a sacrifice for sins,

27 but a terrifying expectation of judgment and THE FURY OF A FIRE WHICH WILL CONSUME THE ADVERSARIES.

28 Anyone who has set aside the Law of Moses dies without mercy on *the testimony of* two or three witnesses.

29 How much severer punishment do you think he will deserve who has trampled under foot the Son of God, and has regarded as unclean the blood of the covenant by which he was sanctified, and has insulted the Spirit of grace?

30 For we know Him who said, "VENGEANCE IS MINE, I WILL REPAY." And again, "THE LORD WILL JUDGE HIS PEOPLE."

31 It is a terrifying thing to fall into the hands of the living God.

32 ¶ But remember the former days, when, after being enlightened, you endured a great conflict of sufferings,

33 partly by being made a public spectacle through reproaches and tribulations, and partly by becoming sharers with those who were so treated.

34 For you showed sympathy to the prisoners and accepted joyfully the seizure of your property, knowing that you have for yourselves a better possession and a lasting one.

35 Therefore, do not throw away your confidence, which has a great reward.

36 For you have need of endurance, so that when you have done the will of God, you may receive what was promised.

37 FOR YET IN A VERY LITTLE WHILE,
   HE WHO IS COMING WILL COME, AND WILL
      NOT DELAY.
38 BUT MY RIGHTEOUS ONE SHALL LIVE BY
      FAITH;
   AND IF HE SHRINKS BACK, MY SOUL HAS NO
      PLEASURE IN HIM.

39 But we are not of those who shrink back to destruction, but of those who have faith to the preserving of the soul.

The Triumphs of Faith

11 Now faith is the assurance of *things* hoped for, the conviction of things not seen.

2 For by it the men of old gained approval.

3 ¶ By faith we understand that the worlds were prepared by the word of God, so that what is seen was not made out of things which are visible.

4 By faith Abel offered to God a better sacrifice than Cain, through which he obtained the testimony that he was righteous, God testifying about his gifts, and through faith, though he is dead, he still speaks.

5 By faith Enoch was taken up so that he would not see death; AND HE WAS NOT FOUND BECAUSE GOD TOOK HIM UP; for he obtained the witness that before his being taken up he was pleasing to God.

6 And without faith it is impossible to please *Him*, for he who comes to God must believe that He is and *that* He is a rewarder of those who seek Him.

7 By faith Noah, being warned *by God* about things not yet seen, in reverence prepared an ark for the salvation of his household, by which he condemned the world, and became an heir of the righteousness which is according to faith.

8 ¶ By faith Abraham, when he was called, obeyed by going out to a place which he was to receive for an inheritance; and he went out, not knowing where he was going.

9 By faith he lived as an alien in the land of promise, as in a foreign *land*, dwelling in tents

with Isaac and Jacob, fellow heirs of the same promise;

10 for he was looking for the city which has foundations, whose architect and builder is God.

11 By faith even Sarah herself received ability to conceive, even beyond the proper time of life, since she considered Him faithful who had promised.

12 Therefore there was born even of one man, and him as good as dead at that, *as many descendants* AS THE STARS OF HEAVEN IN NUMBER, AND INNUMERABLE AS THE SAND WHICH IS BY THE SEASHORE.

13 ¶ All these died in faith, without receiving the promises, but having seen them and having welcomed them from a distance, and having confessed that they were strangers and exiles on the earth.

14 For those who say such things make it clear that they are seeking a country of their own.

15 And indeed if they had been thinking of that *country* from which they went out, they would have had opportunity to return.

16 But as it is, they desire a better *country*, that is, a heavenly one. Therefore God is not ashamed to be called their God; for He has prepared a city for them.

11:16 Not Ashamed

The list of God's favorites in Hebrews 11 includes blemished characters such as Samson and Rahab, triumphant winners such as David and Barak, and then a whole list of anonymous "failures" who faced torture and persecution. Yet at some point all of these displayed the kind of faith that pleases God.

17 ¶ By faith Abraham, when he was tested, offered up Isaac, and he who had received the promises was offering up his only begotten *son;*

18 *it was he* to whom it was said, "IN ISAAC YOUR DESCENDANTS SHALL BE CALLED."

19 He considered that God is able to raise peo-

What Is True Faith?

Not even giants of faith get exactly what they want

WHAT IS FAITH? AND HOW can you be sure you've got it? Some Christians think of faith as an almost magical force: If you muster up enough of it, you'll get rich, stay healthy, and live a contented life, they say. Yet how does one "muster up" faith? What are signs of true faith?

The author of Hebrews launches into a detailed description of faith, complete with references to several dozen biographical models. (Some have dubbed Hebrews 11 the "Faith Hall of Fame.") "Without faith," Hebrews says bluntly, "it is impossible to please Him [God]" (11:6).

> And all these, having gained approval through their faith, did not receive what was promised.
> 11:39

Not What You'd Expect

But the picture of faith emerging from these chapters contains some surprises. The author uses words and phrases like "endurance," "endure," "lose heart." In many instances, the heroes cited did not receive the promise they hoped for; some ended up flogged and destitute, hiding out in goatskins (11:36–38). Many died horrible deaths.

Faith, concludes the author, most resembles a difficult race. The runner has his or her eyes on the winner's prize, and, despite nagging temptations to slacken the pace, refuses to let up until he or she crosses the finish line. "Lay aside every encumbrance," Hebrews coaches (12:1). "Strengthen the hands that are weak and the knees that are feeble" (12:12).

Is It Worth the Struggle?

Why do people punish their bodies to run a grueling marathon race? Most runners name two reasons: the sense of personal reward they get and the physical benefits of the exercise. The same two rewards apply in the spiritual realm: Great prizes await those who persevere, and the very process of living by faith builds strong character. In this race, no one loses. If you finish, you get the reward.

Here, as elsewhere, Hebrews holds up Jesus, who endured great suffering for our sakes (12:2–3), as the ultimate example. The faith described in Hebrews is not sugarcoated; God does not guarantee a life of luxury and ease. It is tough faith: a constant commitment to hang on and believe God against all odds, no matter what.

Life Questions: Hebrews 11 mentions some people who prospered and some who suffered, yet all had faith. Taking Into account what this passage says, try to come up with your own definition of faith.

ple even from the dead, from which he also received him back as a type.

20 By faith Isaac blessed Jacob and Esau, even regarding things to come.

21 By faith Jacob, as he was dying, blessed each of the sons of Joseph, and worshiped, *leaning* on the top of his staff.

22 By faith Joseph, when he was dying, made mention of the exodus of the sons of Israel, and gave orders concerning his bones.

23 ¶ By faith Moses, when he was born, was hidden for three months by his parents, because they saw he was a beautiful child; and they were not afraid of the king's edict.

24 By faith Moses, when he had grown up, refused to be called the son of Pharaoh's daughter,

25 choosing rather to endure ill-treatment with the people of God than to enjoy the passing pleasures of sin,

26 considering the reproach of Christ greater riches than the treasures of Egypt; for he was looking to the reward.

27 By faith he left Egypt, not fearing the wrath of the king; for he endured, as seeing Him who is unseen.

28 By faith he kept the Passover and the sprinkling of the blood, so that he who destroyed the firstborn would not touch them.

29 By faith they passed through the Red Sea as though *they were passing* through dry land; and the Egyptians, when they attempted it, were drowned.

30 ¶ By faith the walls of Jericho fell down after they had been encircled for seven days.

31 By faith Rahab the harlot did not perish along with those who were disobedient, after she had welcomed the spies in peace.

32 ¶ And what more shall I say? For time will fail me if I tell of Gideon, Barak, Samson, Jephthah, of David and Samuel and the prophets,

33 who by faith conquered kingdoms, performed *acts of* righteousness, obtained promises, shut the mouths of lions,

34 quenched the power of fire, escaped the edge of the sword, from weakness were made strong, became mighty in war, put foreign armies to flight.

35 Women received *back* their dead by resurrection; and others were tortured, not accepting their release, so that they might obtain a better resurrection;

36 and others experienced mockings and scourgings, yes, also chains and imprisonment.

37 They were stoned, they were sawn in two, [a]they were tempted, they were put to death with the sword; they went about in sheepskins, in goatskins, being destitute, afflicted, ill-treated

38 (*men* of whom the world was not worthy), wandering in deserts and mountains and caves and holes in the ground.

39 ¶ And all these, having gained approval through their faith, did not receive what was promised,

40 because God had provided something better for us, so that apart from us they would not be made perfect.

Jesus, the Example

12 Therefore, since we have so great a cloud of witnesses surrounding us, let us also lay aside every encumbrance and the sin which so easily entangles us, and let us run with endurance the race that is set before us,

12:1 Pep Talk

Chapter 12 makes clear why Hebrews 11 devoted such attention to martyrs from the past. The early Christians who first read this book were facing persecution, and their faith was bending under the pressure. Think of the "great cloud of witnesses" who have gone before, Hebrews urges, and fix your eyes on Jesus, who volunteered to die on your behalf. With its imagery borrowed from athletics, this portion of Hebrews sounds like a coach's halftime speech delivered to competitors in danger of giving up.

2 fixing our eyes on Jesus, the author and perfecter of faith, who for the joy set before Him endured the cross, despising the shame, and has sat down at the right hand of the throne of God.

3 ¶ For consider Him who has endured such hostility by sinners against Himself, so that you will not grow weary and lose heart.

A Father's Discipline

4 You have not yet resisted to the point of shedding blood in your striving against sin;

5 and you have forgotten the exhortation which is addressed to you as sons,

"MY SON, DO NOT REGARD LIGHTLY THE
　　DISCIPLINE OF THE LORD,
　NOR FAINT WHEN YOU ARE REPROVED
　　BY HIM;
6 FOR THOSE WHOM THE LORD LOVES HE
　　DISCIPLINES,
　AND HE SCOURGES EVERY SON WHOM HE
　　RECEIVES."

7 It is for discipline that you endure; God deals with you as with sons; for what son is there whom *his* father does not discipline?

8 But if you are without discipline, of which all have become partakers, then you are illegitimate children and not sons.

9 Furthermore, we had earthly fathers to discipline us, and we respected them; shall we not

---

[a] One early ms does not contain *they were tempted*

much rather be subject to the Father of spirits, and live?

10 For they disciplined us for a short time as seemed best to them, but He *disciplines us* for *our* good, so that we may share His holiness.

11 All discipline for the moment seems not to be joyful, but sorrowful; yet to those who have been trained by it, afterwards it yields the peaceful fruit of righteousness.

12 ¶ Therefore, strengthen the hands that are weak and the knees that are feeble,

13 and make straight paths for your feet, so that *the limb* which is lame may not be put out of joint, but rather be healed.

14 ¶ Pursue peace with all men, and the sanctification without which no one will see the Lord.

15 See to it that no one comes short of the grace of God; that no root of bitterness springing up causes trouble, and by it many be defiled;

16 that *there be* no immoral or godless person like Esau, who sold his own birthright for a *single* meal.

17 For you know that even afterwards, when he desired to inherit the blessing, he was rejected, for he found no place for repentance, though he sought for it with tears.

Contrast of Sinai and Zion

18 ¶ For you have not come to *a mountain* that can be touched and to a blazing fire, and to darkness and gloom and whirlwind,

12:18 A Vivid Contrast

The author of Hebrews has been arguing that Christ's new covenant is far better than the old one between God and the Jews. This one section (verses 18–28) uses powerful images to summarize the great difference between encountering God in the way Moses did in the Old Testament and encountering him through Jesus. It also predicts that even greater things are in store: a new kingdom and new creation.

19 and to the blast of a trumpet and the sound of words which *sound was such that* those who heard begged that no further word be spoken to them.

20 For they could not bear the command, "IF EVEN A BEAST TOUCHES THE MOUNTAIN, IT WILL BE STONED."

21 And so terrible was the sight, *that* Moses said, "I AM FULL OF FEAR and trembling."

22 But you have come to Mount Zion and to the city of the living God, the heavenly Jerusalem, and to myriads of angels,

23 to the general assembly and church of the firstborn who are enrolled in heaven, and to God, the Judge of all, and to the spirits of *the* righteous made perfect,

24 and to Jesus, the mediator of a new covenant, and to the sprinkled blood, which speaks better than *the blood* of Abel.

The Unshaken Kingdom

25 ¶ See to it that you do not refuse Him who is speaking. For if those did not escape when they refused him who warned *them* on earth, much less *will* we *escape* who turn away from Him who *warns* from heaven.

26 And His voice shook the earth then, but now He has promised, saying, "YET ONCE MORE I WILL SHAKE NOT ONLY THE EARTH, BUT ALSO THE HEAVEN."

27 This *expression,* "Yet once more," denotes the removing of those things which can be shaken, as of created things, so that those things which cannot be shaken may remain.

28 Therefore, since we receive a kingdom which cannot be shaken, let us show gratitude, by which we may offer to God an acceptable service with reverence and awe;

29 for our God is a consuming fire.

The Changeless Christ

13 Let love of the brethren continue.

2 Do not neglect to show hospitality to strangers, for by this some have entertained angels without knowing it.

3 Remember the prisoners, as though in prison with them, *and* those who are ill-treated, since you yourselves also are in the body.

4 Marriage *is to be held* in honor among all, and the *marriage* bed *is to be* undefiled; for fornicators and adulterers God will judge.

5 *Make sure that* your character is free from the love of money, being content with what you have; for He Himself has said, "I WILL NEVER DESERT YOU, NOR WILL I EVER FORSAKE YOU,"

6 so that we confidently say,

"THE LORD IS MY HELPER, I WILL NOT BE
    AFRAID.
WHAT WILL MAN DO TO ME?"

7 ¶ Remember those who led you, who spoke the word of God to you; and considering the result of their conduct, imitate their faith.

8 Jesus Christ *is* the same yesterday and today and forever.

9 Do not be carried away by varied and strange teachings; for it is good for the heart to be strengthened by grace, not by foods, through which those who were so occupied were not benefited.

10 We have an altar from which those who serve the tabernacle have no right to eat.

11 For the bodies of those animals whose blood is brought into the holy place by the high priest *as an offering* for sin, are burned outside the camp.

12 Therefore Jesus also, that He might sanctify

the people through His own blood, suffered outside the gate.

13 So, let us go out to Him outside the camp, bearing His reproach.

14 For here we do not have a lasting city, but we are seeking *the city* which is to come.

God-pleasing Sacrifices

15 Through Him then, let us continually offer up a sacrifice of praise to God, that is, the fruit of lips that give thanks to His name.

13:15 Sacrifice of Praise

In form, Hebrews is more theological than practical. But in the last chapter the author adds a list of specific commands and suggestions. Even here, however, he makes one last reference to sacrifice. Now, we have only a "sacrifice of praise" to offer, because Christ accomplished all that was needed.

16 And do not neglect doing good and sharing, for with such sacrifices God is pleased.

17 ¶ Obey your leaders and submit *to them*, for they keep watch over your souls as those who will give an account. Let them do this with joy and not with grief, for this would be unprofitable for you.

18 ¶ Pray for us, for we are sure that we have a good conscience, desiring to conduct ourselves honorably in all things.

19 And I urge *you* all the more to do this, so that I may be restored to you the sooner.

Benediction

20 ¶ Now the God of peace, who brought up from the dead the great Shepherd of the sheep through the blood of the eternal covenant, *even* Jesus our Lord,

21 equip you in every good thing to do His will, working in us that which is pleasing in His sight, through Jesus Christ, to whom *be* the glory forever and ever. Amen.

22 ¶ But I urge you, brethren, bear with this word of exhortation, for I have written to you briefly.

23 Take notice that our brother Timothy has been released, with whom, if he comes soon, I will see you.

24 Greet all of your leaders and all the saints. Those from Italy greet you.

25 ¶ Grace be with you all.

JAMES

Words Are Not Enough
You can believe all the right things, yet still be dead wrong

> *But prove yourselves doers of the word, and not merely hearers who delude themselves. 1:22*

WHERE THERE IS LIFE, THERE is motion. Some antelopes, as well as the cheetah, can sprint faster than some cars on the highway. Bighorn sheep, charging one another headfirst, collide with such force that the sound echoes like a gunshot through mountain ranges. Canada geese, fanned out across the sky in an orderly V, battle winds for 1,000 miles, nonstop, before dropping back to earth.

Sometimes we keep relics of life: an elkhead hanging above a fireplace, a fragile, perfect seashell, an exotic butterfly mounted on a pin. But these are mere mementos: life has gone from them, and with it motion.

A Sure Sign of Life

Authors of the Bible often look to nature for analogies to express spiritual truth. And the book of James, controversial because of its emphasis on "good works," is perhaps best understood through the analogy of motion. In the spiritual realm also, where there's life there will be motion.

When a person becomes a Christian, new life begins, and inevitably that life must express itself through "spiritual motion," or good deeds. In James's words, "What use is it . . . if someone says he has faith but he has no works?" (2:14).

Movement does not cause life, but it does invariably follow life. It's a sure sign that life is present. Similarly, genuine faith in Christ should always result in actions that demonstrate faith.

Does James Contradict Paul?

James is not writing about how to become a Christian, but rather how to act like one. Having all the correct beliefs about God will hardly suffice: Even demons believe in God. Real, life-giving faith should produce motion, and James minces no words in describing the specific spiritual actions expected of Christians.

Christian thinkers, notably Martin Luther, have struggled to reconcile the message of James with that of Paul, who so firmly warned against slavish legalism. But Paul never belittled holy living. When he wrote to carousers, such as in his letters to the Corinthians, he railed against immorality as strongly as James.

Evidently, James's readers were not even flirting with legalism. They lived at the other extreme, ignoring those laws God had clearly revealed. James had a simple remedy: "Prove yourselves doers of the word and not merely hearers" (1:22).

Straight to the Point

Unlike the apostle Paul, James was no urbane man of letters. He was a simple, homespun preacher, perturbed at people who were not living right. His letter covers a wide range of topics, applying the Christian faith to specific problems and commanding readers to live out their beliefs.

Be humble! James orders. *Submit to God! Stop sinning!* James is as forthright as an Old Testament prophet; it's hard to miss his point.

Modern readers of James face the same dilemma as the first recipients of this unsettling letter. His words are easy enough to understand, but are we doing what he says? What kind of motion characterizes our spiritual lives? As Luther himself said, "You are saved by faith alone, but if faith is alone it is not faith."

How to Read James

Few New Testament writers achieve the clarity or the "punch" of James. He doesn't spend time expanding subpoints or worrying about literary structure. As a result, the book of James reads like a collection of pithy proverbs. (It's sometimes called the "Proverbs of the New Testament.") In your study, it may help to group the material by subject; James tends to return to themes repeatedly.

As leader of the headquarters church in Jerusalem, James knew how to speak with authority. You don't have to look for hidden meanings in this book. James tells you clearly how you should act, in 54 direct commands. Note that many of these have parallels to Jesus' Sermon on the Mount. As you read, keep in mind the diverse audience he was addressing, which included the rich and the poor. Note his "asides" to specific groups.

3-TRACK READING PLAN

For an explanation and complete listing of the 3-track reading plan, turn to page 7.

TRACK 1:   *Two-Week Courses on the Bible*
See page 7 for information on these courses.

TRACK 2:   *An Overview of James in 1 Day*
☐ Day 1. Read the Introduction to James, then chapter 1, on how the Christian should respond to tough times, or "trials."
Now turn to page 9 for your next Track 2 reading project.

TRACK 3:   *All of James in 4 Days*
After you have read through James, turn to pages 10–14 for your next Track 3 reading project.
☐1   ☐2   ☐3–4   ☐5

Testing Your Faith

1 James, a bond-servant of God and of the Lord Jesus Christ,

¶ To the twelve tribes who are dispersed abroad: Greetings.

2 ¶ Consider it all joy, my brethren, when you encounter various trials,

3 knowing that the testing of your faith produces endurance.

1:3 Productive Pain

James's call for joy in the face of trials may seem shocking or even insensitive at first. A close reading, though, makes clear that James finds joy in the results of the trials, not in the trials themselves. Even difficult times can produce good qualities, such as perseverance. This positive, or "redemptive," approach to suffering surfaces throughout the New Testament (see Romans 5:1–5; 1 Peter 1:3–9).

4 And let endurance have *its* perfect result, so that you may be perfect and complete, lacking in nothing.

5 ¶ But if any of you lacks wisdom, let him ask of God, who gives to all generously and without reproach, and it will be given to him.

6 But he must ask in faith without any doubting, for the one who doubts is like the surf of the sea, driven and tossed by the wind.

7 For that man ought not to expect that he will receive anything from the Lord,

8 *being* a double-minded man, unstable in all his ways.

9 ¶ But the brother of humble circumstances is to glory in his high position;

10 and the rich man *is to glory* in his humiliation, because like flowering grass he will pass away.

11 For the sun rises with a scorching wind and withers the grass; and its flower falls off and the beauty of its appearance is destroyed; so too the rich man in the midst of his pursuits will fade away.

12 ¶ Blessed is a man who perseveres under trial; for once he has been approved, he will receive the crown of life which *the Lord* has promised to those who love Him.

13 Let no one say when he is tempted, "I am being tempted by God"; for God cannot be tempted by evil, and He Himself does not tempt anyone.

14 But each one is tempted when he is carried away and enticed by his own lust.

15 Then when lust has conceived, it gives birth to sin; and when sin is accomplished, it brings forth death.

16 Do not be deceived, my beloved brethren.

17 Every good thing given and every perfect gift is from above, coming down from the Father of lights, with whom there is no variation or shifting shadow.

18 In the exercise of His will He brought us forth by the word of truth, so that we would be a kind of first fruits among His creatures.

19 ¶ *a This* you know, my beloved brethren. But everyone must be quick to hear, slow to speak *and* slow to anger;

20 for the anger of man does not achieve the righteousness of God.

21 Therefore, putting aside all filthiness and *all* that remains of wickedness, in humility receive the word implanted, which is able to save your souls.

22 But prove yourselves doers of the word, and not merely hearers who delude themselves.

23 For if anyone is a hearer of the word and not a doer, he is like a man who looks at his natural face in a mirror;

24 for *once* he has looked at himself and gone away, he has immediately forgotten what kind of person he was.

25 But one who looks intently at the perfect law, the *law* of liberty, and abides by it, not having become a forgetful hearer but an effectual doer, this man will be blessed in what he does.

26 ¶ If anyone thinks himself to be religious, and yet does not bridle his tongue but deceives his *own* heart, this man's religion is worthless.

27 Pure and undefiled religion in the sight of *our* God and Father is this: to visit orphans and widows in their distress, *and* to keep oneself unstained by the world.

The Sin of Partiality

2 My brethren, do not hold your faith in our glorious Lord Jesus Christ with *an attitude of* personal favoritism.

2:1 Play No Favorites

James 1 tells Christians to act out their faith. James 2 gives a very pointed example of church members deferring to the wealthy and powerful. This direct application, hitting close to home, characterizes James. He leaves no room for ambiguity.

2 For if a man comes into your assembly with a gold ring and dressed in fine clothes, and there also comes in a poor man in dirty clothes,

3 and you pay special attention to the one who is wearing the fine clothes, and say, "You sit here in a good place," and you say to the poor man, "You stand over there, or sit down by my footstool,"

4 have you not made distinctions among yourselves, and become judges with evil motives?

5 Listen, my beloved brethren: did not God choose the poor of this world *to be* rich in faith and heirs of the kingdom which He promised to those who love Him?

6 But you have dishonored the poor man. Is it not the rich who oppress you and personally drag you into court?

7 Do they not blaspheme the fair name by which you have been called?

8 ¶ If, however, you are fulfilling the royal law according to the Scripture, "YOU SHALL LOVE YOUR NEIGHBOR AS YOURSELF," you are doing well.

9 But if you show partiality, you are committing sin *and* are convicted by the law as transgressors.

10 For whoever keeps the whole law and yet stumbles in one *point,* he has become guilty of all.

11 For He who said, "DO NOT COMMIT ADULTERY," also said, "DO NOT COMMIT MURDER." Now if you do not commit adultery, but do commit murder, you have become a transgressor of the law.

12 So speak and so act as those who are to be judged by *the* law of liberty.

13 For judgment *will be* merciless to one who has shown no mercy; mercy triumphs over judgment.

Faith and Works

14 ¶ What use is it, my brethren, if someone says he has faith but he has no works? Can that faith save him?

15 If a brother or sister is without clothing and in need of daily food,

16 and one of you says to them, "Go in peace, be warmed and be filled," and yet you do not give them what is necessary for *their* body, what use is that?

17 Even so faith, if it has no works, is dead, *being* by itself.

18 ¶ But someone may *well* say, "You have faith and I have works; show me your faith without the works, and I will show you my faith by my works."

19 You believe that *b* God is one. You do well; the demons also believe, and shudder.

20 But are you willing to recognize, you foolish fellow, that faith without works is useless?

21 Was not Abraham our father justified by works when he offered up Isaac his son on the altar?

22 You see that faith was working with his works, and as a result of the works, faith was perfected;

23 and the Scripture was fulfilled which says,

a Or *Know* this   *b* One early ms reads *there is one God*

"AND ABRAHAM BELIEVED GOD, AND IT WAS RECKONED TO HIM AS RIGHTEOUSNESS," and he was called the friend of God.

24 You see that a man is justified by works and not by faith alone.

25 In the same way, was not Rahab the harlot also justified by works when she received the messengers and sent them out by another way?

26 For just as the body without the spirit is dead, so also faith without works is dead.

The Tongue Is a Fire

3 Let not many of you become teachers, my brethren, knowing that as such we will incur a stricter judgment.

2 For we all stumble in many ways. If anyone does not stumble in what he says, he is a perfect man, able to bridle the whole body as well.

3 Now if we put the bits into the horses' mouths so that they will obey us, we direct their entire body as well.

3:3 Colorful Language

Vivid, homey pictures from nature give a visual character to James's words, almost as if each thought were a photograph. He refers to sea froth, wilted flowers, a forest fire, a horse's bit, the morning mist, a hungry moth, the farmer's spring rains, a giant ship, and a saltwater spring. Paul, a more educated writer, alluded to culture and athletics and human relationships. But James felt most comfortable borrowing simple images from nature.

4 Look at the ships also, though they are so great and are driven by strong winds, are still directed by a very small rudder wherever the inclination of the pilot desires.

5 So also the tongue is a small part of the body, and yet it boasts of great things.

¶ See how great a forest is set aflame by such a small fire!

6 And the tongue is a fire, the very world of iniquity; the tongue is set among our members as that which defiles the entire body, and sets on fire the course of our life, and is set on fire by hell.

7 For every species of beasts and birds, of reptiles and creatures of the sea, is tamed and has been tamed by the human race.

8 But no one can tame the tongue; it is a restless evil and full of deadly poison.

9 With it we bless our Lord and Father, and with it we curse men, who have been made in the likeness of God;

10 from the same mouth come both blessing and cursing. My brethren, these things ought not to be this way.

11 Does a fountain send out from the same opening both fresh and bitter water?

12 Can a fig tree, my brethren, produce olives, or a vine produce figs? Nor can salt water produce fresh.

Wisdom from Above

13 ¶ Who among you is wise and understanding? Let him show by his good behavior his deeds in the gentleness of wisdom.

14 But if you have bitter jealousy and selfish ambition in your heart, do not be arrogant and so lie against the truth.

15 This wisdom is not that which comes down from above, but is earthly, natural, demonic.

16 For where jealousy and selfish ambition exist, there is disorder and every evil thing.

17 But the wisdom from above is first pure, then peaceable, gentle, reasonable, full of mercy and good fruits, unwavering, without hypocrisy.

18 And the seed whose fruit is righteousness is sown in peace by those who make peace.

Things to Avoid

4 What is the source of quarrels and conflicts among you? Is not the source your pleasures that wage war in your members?

4:1 The Need for Self-Control

If you had to distill the message of James into one word, it might be self-control. Chapters 4 and 5, which contain some of James's most striking imagery, show how simple greed and desire can corrode the church and destroy unity. And, indeed, many of the Jewish Christians he was writing to soon experienced an abrupt turn of fortune. They lost their wealth and suffered severe persecution.

2 You lust and do not have; so you commit murder. You are envious and cannot obtain; so you fight and quarrel. You do not have because you do not ask.

3 You ask and do not receive, because you ask with wrong motives, so that you may spend it on your pleasures.

4 You adulteresses, do you not know that friendship with the world is hostility toward God? Therefore whoever wishes to be a friend of the world makes himself an enemy of God.

5 Or do you think that the Scripture speaks to no purpose: "*a*He jealously desires the Spirit which He has made to dwell in us"?

6 But He gives a greater grace. Therefore it says, "GOD IS OPPOSED TO THE PROUD, BUT GIVES GRACE TO THE HUMBLE."

---

a Or The spirit which He has made to dwell in us lusts with envy

7 Submit therefore to God. Resist the devil and he will flee from you.

8 Draw near to God and He will draw near to you. Cleanse your hands, you sinners; and purify your hearts, you double-minded.

9 Be miserable and mourn and weep; let your laughter be turned into mourning and your joy to gloom.

10 Humble yourselves in the presence of the Lord, and He will exalt you.

11 ¶ Do not speak against one another, brethren. He who speaks against a brother or judges his brother, speaks against the law and judges the law; but if you judge the law, you are not a doer of the law but a judge *of it.*

12 There is *only* one Lawgiver and Judge, the One who is able to save and to destroy; but who are you who judge your neighbor?

13 ¶ Come now, you who say, "Today or tomorrow we will go to such and such a city, and spend a year there and engage in business and make a profit."

14 Yet you do not know what your life will be like tomorrow. You are *just* a vapor that appears for a little while and then vanishes away.

15 Instead, *you ought* to say, "If the Lord wills, we will live and also do this or that."

16 But as it is, you boast in your arrogance; all such boasting is evil.

17 Therefore, to one who knows *the* right thing to do and does not do it, to him it is sin.

Misuse of Riches

5 Come now, you rich, weep and howl for your miseries which are coming upon you.

2 Your riches have rotted and your garments have become moth-eaten.

3 Your gold and your silver have rusted; and their rust will be a witness against you and will consume your flesh like fire. It is in the last days that you have stored up your treasure!

4 Behold, the pay of the laborers who mowed your fields, *and* which has been withheld by you, cries out *against you*; and the outcry of those who did the harvesting has reached the ears of the Lord of Sabaoth.

5 You have lived luxuriously on the earth and led a life of wanton pleasure; you have fattened your hearts in a day of slaughter.

6 You have condemned and put to death the righteous *man*; he does not resist you.

Conflicts of Rich and Poor
A different kind of class struggle

OUR SOCIETY TENDS TO DIVIDE the rich and the poor. The two groups have little daily contact, and you would have a very hard time communicating a unified message to both the very rich and the very poor.

> "God is opposed to the proud, but gives grace to the humble." 4:6

Yet it seems James's original readers included both those groups. In one paragraph James addresses the haughty, privileged people of wealth, and in the next paragraph he turns to poor people undergoing severe trials. (Note the shift between 5:1 and 5:7.)

The two groups had different problems. The wealthy were selfish. They showed insensitivity and snobbishness to the poor. For their part, the poor responded with envy and grumbling. They blamed God for their poverty.

Who Is Double-minded?

James gave advice on the specific problems of each group, but he also implied they have much in common. For both rich and poor the most important struggle is not outside—the conditions we live in—but rather inside. All of us experience the inner conflict of being pulled by powerful, contrary forces. Will we move toward Christ and the life he taught, or in the opposite direction? Will we trust God or reject him?

James coined a new word to describe this inner conflict: he called it being "double-minded" (4:8). For rich and poor, this conflict may express itself in different ways, as James went on to explain. But double-mindedness is a tug-of-war between divided loyalties. The essential struggle to obey God is no different for either group.

As he discussed the rich and the poor, James relied on many of the actual phrases Jesus had used, especially in the Sermon on the Mount. (This is quite understandable if the author was James the brother of Jesus, as many scholars believe.) He applied what Jesus taught in a fresh, new way, calling on all of us—rich and poor—to be single-minded in our commitment to follow that way.

Life Questions: James 2 warns against favoritism based on social class. Does such favoritism happen among Christians today? Is there any difference between the way rich and poor people think about following Jesus?

Exhortation

7 ¶ Therefore be patient, brethren, until the coming of the Lord. The farmer waits for the precious produce of the soil, being patient about it, until it gets the early and late rains.

8 You too be patient; strengthen your hearts, for the coming of the Lord is near.

9 Do not complain, brethren, against one another, so that you yourselves may not be judged; behold, the Judge is standing right at the door.

10 As an example, brethren, of suffering and patience, take the prophets who spoke in the name of the Lord.

11 We count those blessed who endured. You have heard of the endurance of Job and have seen the outcome of the Lord's dealings, that the Lord is full of compassion and is merciful.

12 ¶ But above all, my brethren, do not swear, either by heaven or by earth or with any other oath; but your yes is to be yes, and your no, no, so that you may not fall under judgment.

13 ¶ Is anyone among you suffering? Then he must pray. Is anyone cheerful? He is to sing praises.

14 Is anyone among you sick? Then he must call for the elders of the church and they are to pray over him, anointing him with oil in the name of the Lord;

15 and the prayer offered in faith will [a]restore the one who is sick, and the Lord will raise him up, and if he has committed sins, they will be forgiven him.

16 Therefore, confess your sins to one another, and pray for one another so that you may be healed. The effective prayer of a righteous man can accomplish much.

17 Elijah was a man with a nature like ours, and he prayed earnestly that it would not rain, and it did not rain on the earth for three years and six months.

18 Then he prayed again, and the sky poured rain and the earth produced its fruit.

19 ¶ My brethren, if any among you strays from the truth and one turns him back,

20 let him know that he who turns a sinner from the error of his way will save his soul from death and will cover a multitude of sins.

5:10 Waiting It Out

In this section, James expands on the idea (1:2–4) that God can use suffering for our benefit. He realistically concedes that rejoicing in the face of trials may not come right away. To develop such an attitude will take patience and perseverance. James mentions two sources of support for someone trying to cope with suffering: (1) the past example of people like the prophets and Job; (2) the church's ministry of healing and prayer.

[a] Or save

1 PETER

A Word to the Suffering
What to do when trouble comes

A DISTANT, SWIRLING CLOUD OF DUST signaled the approach of Turkish death squads. But who could escape? The villages of Armenia sat exposed and defenseless on a rocky plain. Doomed Christians clung together on the floors of their homes, praying, singing, and shivering with fear.

This scene was repeated often during World War I, and it usually ended in a massacre. The Turkish assault against Armenian Christians was one of history's worst religion-inspired bloodbaths: Over one million people died. But, sadly, the Armenian tragedy was but one of many attacks against 20th-century Christians.

> Beloved, do not be surprised at the fiery ordeal among you . . . as though some strange thing were happening to you. 4:12

More people have died for their religious faith in the 20th-century than in all the rest of history combined. Thousands of Christians died in East Africa, first in the Mau Mau uprising and then during Ugandan dictator Idi Amin's reign of terror. Millions more suffered under Soviet and Chinese governments. And the oppression goes on: Even today some countries imprison and torture converts to Christianity. This fact alone makes the book of 1 Peter starkly relevant for modern readers.

How to Respond to Persecution

What advice would you give Christians about to undergo persecution? The apostle Peter took up that challenge just as ominous rumblings from Rome were striking fear in every Christian community. Half-crazed Nero had seized on believers as scapegoats for the ills of his empire.

Should the persecuted Christians flee or resist? Should they tone down their outward signs of faith? Give up? Peter's readers, their lives in danger, needed clear advice on suffering.

They also wanted explanations of the meaning of suffering. Why does God allow it? Can good result? Does God care? In short, they were asking the questions that occur to any Christian who goes through great trial.

According to Peter, suffering should not catch a Christian off guard. We are strangers in a hostile world, and where Christians thrive, storm clouds may gather. Suffering is an expected part of a life of sincere faith.

Peter's Own Experience

On the subject of suffering, Peter makes an ideal counselor for readers then and now. He had been flogged and imprisoned for his own faith, once even expecting execution (Acts 12). Also, Peter had personally watched Jesus endure suffering, and in this letter he points to him as an example of how to respond.

Peter encourages his readers to "keep your behavior excellent among the Gentiles, so that in the thing in which they slander you as evildoers, they may because of your good deeds . . . glorify God" (2:12). Suffering can refine believers and give us an opportunity to prove our faith, the result thus working out for our benefit.

This book emphasizes a further point also: Suffering is temporary, to be endured only for "a little while" (1:6; 5:10). Those who suffer with Christ will also glory with him in a life forever free of pain. Skeptics have criticized the church for stressing a future life rather than working to improve this one. "You promise pie in the sky by and by," they taunt. But to Peter's readers—wary of enemies on the prowl, unsure of surviving another day—that message was as tangible and nourishing as food.

According to 1 Peter, our hope that suffering will one day cease is not a mirage but a "living hope" (1:3) in the One who has conquered death.

How to Read 1 Peter

At first Christianity enjoyed official toleration by the Roman empire, but gradually the government turned against it. Rome resented the Christians' talk about another kingdom and their objections to idolatry and decadence.

Although 1 Peter was originally written to people in severe danger, its lessons apply to all of us, for we all experience pain of some kind. Why don't things work out the way we want? Is God trying to tell us something? Peter gives authoritative answers. As you read, try to apply what he says to your own situation.

Peter's writing style reveals his simple fisherman background: He uses pithy peasant expressions and awkwardly shifts back and forth between doctrine and advice. Chapter 2 (verses 18–25) shows an excellent example. Peter gives a deep insight into what it meant for Christ to suffer on our behalf, but he includes it in a practical section on slaves and governments. Thus, he blends doctrine (what to believe) with practice (how to behave).

More a preacher than a writer, Peter structured his book like a rambling sermon. Look for the 34 direct commands included. Peter's reliance on common figures of speech—a cornerstone, a lamb, a shepherd—makes the book very quotable.

But Peter was not simply giving homespun advice; he was well-grounded in the teachings of Jesus and the prophets. Proportionately, he quotes from the Old Testament more than any other New Testament author.

PEOPLE YOU'LL MEET IN 1 PETER

PETER *(p. 1348)*

3-TRACK READING PLAN

For an explanation and complete listing of the 3-track reading plan, turn to page 7.

TRACK 1: *Two-Week Courses on the Bible*
See page 7 for information on these courses.

TRACK 2: *An Overview of 1 Peter in 1 Day*
☐ Day 1. Read the Introduction to 1 Peter, then chapter 1 for a capsule summary of the letter's style and message.
Now turn to page 9 for your next Track 2 reading project.

TRACK 3: *All of 1 Peter in 4 Days*
After you have read through 1 Peter, turn to pages 10–14 for your next Track 3 reading project.
☐1   ☐2   ☐3   ☐4–5

A Living Hope, and a Sure Salvation

1 Peter, an apostle of Jesus Christ,
¶ To those who reside as aliens, scattered throughout Pontus, Galatia, Cappadocia, Asia, and Bithynia, who are chosen

2 according to the foreknowledge of God the Father, by the sanctifying work of the Spirit, to obey Jesus Christ and be sprinkled with His blood: May grace and peace be yours in the fullest measure.

3 ¶ Blessed be the God and Father of our Lord Jesus Christ, who according to His great mercy has caused us to be born again to a living hope through the resurrection of Jesus Christ from the dead,

4 to *obtain* an inheritance *which is* imperishable and undefiled and will not fade away, reserved in heaven for you,

5 who are protected by the power of God through faith for a salvation ready to be revealed in the last time.

6 In this you greatly rejoice, even though now for a little while, if necessary, you have been distressed by various trials,

7 so that the proof of your faith, *being* more precious than gold which is perishable, even though tested by fire, may be found to result in

praise and glory and honor at the revelation of Jesus Christ;

8 and though you have not seen Him, you love Him, and though you do not see Him now,

1:7 Refiner's Fire

A prospector who discovers gold-bearing rock sends it to an assayer for evaluation. Testing by fire will melt off most impurities, and the true gold will emerge purified. Suffering acts in much the same way, says Peter: It exposes and refines true faith. In addition, faith in the midst of such trials will earn future rewards.

but believe in Him, you greatly rejoice with joy inexpressible and full of glory,

9 obtaining as the outcome of your faith the salvation of [a]your souls.

10 ¶ As to this salvation, the prophets who prophesied of the grace that *would come* to you made careful searches and inquiries,

11 seeking to know what person or time the Spirit of Christ within them was indicating as He predicted the sufferings of Christ and the glories to follow.

12 It was revealed to them that they were not serving themselves, but you, in these things which now have been announced to you through those who preached the gospel to you by the Holy Spirit sent from heaven—things into which angels long to look.

13 ¶ Therefore, prepare your minds for action, keep sober *in spirit,* fix your hope completely on the grace to be brought to you at the revelation of Jesus Christ.

14 As obedient children, do not be conformed to the former lusts *which were yours* in your ignorance,

15 but like the Holy One who called you, be holy yourselves also in all *your* behavior;

16 because it is written, "YOU SHALL BE HOLY, FOR I AM HOLY."

17 ¶ If you address as Father the One who impartially judges according to each one's work, conduct yourselves in fear during the time of your stay *on earth;*

18 knowing that you were not redeemed with perishable things like silver or gold from your futile way of life inherited from your forefathers,

19 but with precious blood, as of a lamb unblemished and spotless, *the blood* of Christ.

20 For He was foreknown before the foundation of the world, but has appeared in these last times for the sake of you

21 who through Him are believers in God, who raised Him from the dead and gave Him glory, so that your faith and hope are in God.

22 ¶ Since you have in obedience to the truth purified your souls for a sincere love of the brethren, fervently love one another from [b]the heart,

23 for you have been born again not of seed which is perishable but imperishable, *that is,* through the living and enduring word of God.

24 For,
"ALL FLESH IS LIKE GRASS,
AND ALL ITS GLORY LIKE THE FLOWER OF
    GRASS.
THE GRASS WITHERS,
AND THE FLOWER FALLS OFF,
25 BUT THE WORD OF THE LORD ENDURES
    FOREVER."
And this is the word which was preached to you.

As Newborn Babes

2 Therefore, putting aside all malice and all deceit and hypocrisy and envy and all slander,

2 like newborn babies, long for the pure milk of the word, so that by it you may grow in respect to salvation,

3 if you have tasted the kindness of the Lord.

As Living Stones

4 ¶ And coming to Him as to a living stone which has been rejected by men, but is choice and precious in the sight of God,

2:4 A Play on Words

In verses 4–9, Peter constructs a detailed metaphor out of a very common object: a stone. He refers to Christ as a stone rejected by builders, the kind of useless rock someone trips over. Yet this stone, Jesus, becomes the cornerstone of a new building composed of Christians ("living stones"). This metaphor has much in common with Paul's references to the "body of Christ," but Peter (nicknamed the "rock") uses architectural rather than biological terms.

5 you also, as living stones, are being built up as a spiritual house for a holy priesthood, to offer up spiritual sacrifices acceptable to God through Jesus Christ.

6 For *this* is contained in Scripture:
"BEHOLD, I LAY IN ZION A CHOICE STONE, A
    PRECIOUS CORNER *stone,*
AND HE WHO BELIEVES IN HIM WILL NOT
    BE DISAPPOINTED."

7 This precious value, then, is for you who believe; but for those who disbelieve,
"THE STONE WHICH THE BUILDERS
    REJECTED,
THIS BECAME THE VERY CORNER *stone,*"
8 and,

[a] One early ms does not contain *your*   [b] Two early mss read *a clean heart*

"A STONE OF STUMBLING AND A ROCK OF OFFENSE"; for they stumble because they are disobedient to the word, and to this *doom* they were also appointed.

9 ¶ But you are A CHOSEN RACE, A royal PRIESTHOOD, A HOLY NATION, A PEOPLE FOR *God's* OWN POSSESSION, so that you may proclaim the excellencies of Him who has called you out of darkness into His marvelous light;

10 for you once were NOT A PEOPLE, but now you are THE PEOPLE OF GOD; you had NOT RECEIVED MERCY, but now you have RECEIVED MERCY.

11 ¶ Beloved, I urge you as aliens and strangers to abstain from fleshly lusts which wage war against the soul.

2:11 Endangered Strangers

At first Christians had enjoyed the official protection of the Roman empire. Under Nero (A.D. 54–68) all that changed, and the apostles Peter and Paul were probably martyred during Nero's regime. Peter addressed this letter to "those who reside as aliens" (1:1), an indication that Christians were now viewed as a separate, persecuted minority without legal rights.

12 Keep your behavior excellent among the Gentiles, so that in the thing in which they slander you as evildoers, they may because of your good deeds, as they observe *them*, glorify God in the day of ªvisitation.

Honor Authority

13 ¶ Submit yourselves for the Lord's sake to every human institution, whether to a king as the one in authority,

14 or to governors as sent by him for the punishment of evildoers and the praise of those who do right.

15 For such is the will of God that by doing right you may silence the ignorance of foolish men.

16 *Act* as free men, and do not use your freedom as a covering for evil, but *use it* as bondslaves of God.

17 Honor all people, love the brotherhood, fear God, honor the king.

18 ¶ Servants, be submissive to your masters with all respect, not only to those who are good and gentle, but also to those who are unreasonable.

19 For this *finds* favor, if for the sake of conscience toward God a person bears up under sorrows when suffering unjustly.

20 For what credit is there if, when you sin and are harshly treated, you endure it with patience? But if when you do what is right and suffer *for it* you patiently endure it, this *finds* favor with God.

Christ Is Our Example

21 For you have been called for this purpose, since Christ also suffered for you, leaving you an example for you to follow in His steps,

22 WHO COMMITTED NO SIN, NOR WAS ANY DECEIT FOUND IN HIS MOUTH;

23 and while being reviled, He did not revile in return; while suffering, He uttered no threats, but kept entrusting *Himself* to Him who judges righteously;

24 and He Himself bore our sins in His body on the cross, so that we might die to sin and live to righteousness; for by His wounds you were healed.

25 For you were continually straying like sheep, but now you have returned to the Shepherd and Guardian of your souls.

Godly Living

3 In the same way, you wives, be submissive to your own husbands so that even if any *of them* are disobedient to the word, they may be won without a word by the behavior of their wives,

2 as they observe your chaste and respectful behavior.

3 Your adornment must not be *merely* external—braiding the hair, and wearing gold jewelry, or putting on dresses;

4 but *let it be* the hidden person of the heart, with the imperishable quality of a gentle and quiet spirit, which is precious in the sight of God.

5 For in this way in former times the holy women also, who hoped in God, used to adorn themselves, being submissive to their own husbands;

6 just as Sarah obeyed Abraham, calling him lord, and you have become her children if you do what is right without being frightened by any fear.

7 ¶ You husbands in the same way, live with *your wives* in an understanding way, as with someone weaker, since she is a woman; and show her honor as a fellow heir of the grace of life, so that your prayers will not be hindered.

8 ¶ To sum up, all of you be harmonious, sympathetic, brotherly, kindhearted, and humble in spirit;

9 not returning evil for evil or insult for insult, but giving a blessing instead; for you were called for the very purpose that you might inherit a blessing.

10 For,
"THE ONE WHO DESIRES LIFE, TO LOVE AND
    SEE GOOD DAYS,
MUST KEEP HIS TONGUE FROM EVIL AND HIS
    LIPS FROM SPEAKING DECEIT.

ª I.e. Christ's coming again in judgment

11 "HE MUST TURN AWAY FROM EVIL AND DO
        GOOD;
    HE MUST SEEK PEACE AND PURSUE IT.
12 "FOR THE EYES OF THE LORD ARE TOWARD
        THE RIGHTEOUS,
    AND HIS EARS ATTEND TO THEIR PRAYER,
    BUT THE FACE OF THE LORD IS AGAINST
        THOSE WHO DO EVIL."

13 ¶ Who is there to harm you if you prove zealous for what is good?

14 But even if you should suffer for the sake of righteousness, you are blessed. AND DO NOT FEAR THEIR INTIMIDATION, AND DO NOT BE TROUBLED,

15 but ªsanctify Christ as Lord in your hearts,

ª I.e. set apart

always *being* ready to make a defense to everyone who asks you to give an account for the hope that is in you, yet with gentleness and reverence;

16 and keep a good conscience so that in the thing in which you are slandered, those who revile your good behavior in Christ will be put to shame.

17 For it is better, if God should will it so, that you suffer for doing what is right rather than for doing what is wrong.

18 For Christ also died for sins once for all, *the* just for *the* unjust, so that He might bring us to God, having been put to death in the flesh, but made alive in the spirit;

A Man Named "The Rock"
Peter slowly learned how to live up to his nickname

YOU CAN'T MISS PETER IN the four Gospels. He stands out like a bumpkin, pushing to the head of the line and coming out with loud, outrageous assertions. Every list of the disciples names him first, and Peter is often seen elbowing his way to center stage.

He was likable enough, with a big heart and unlimited enthusiasm. He just had too many rough edges. He swung like a pendulum, bold and courageous at one moment, yet cowardly when it really counted.

> Therefore humble yourselves under the mighty hand of God, that He may exalt you at the proper time. 5:6

Signs of Mellowing

But by the time Peter sat down to write this letter, late in his life, a lot had changed. You can sense the change in the very words he chooses: words like *humble* and *submit*. This book contains nothing of the brash, aggressive style evident in the Gospels. He is heeding Jesus' last command to him: "Tend my sheep" (John 21:17). Gruff Peter has become a tender shepherd.

To get the full impact of Peter's transformation, you must read about him in the Gospels (especially in Mark), and then turn directly to this letter. Blustery, loudmouthed Peter now counsels wives to have "the imperishable quality of a gentle and quiet spirit" (3:4) and husbands to treat their wives with consideration and respect (3:7). The man who sliced off an ear in Jesus' defense (John 18:10) now advises submission to every government authority (2:13). Peter once vigorously protested Jesus' prediction of death (Mark 8:32); now he solemnly commends Christ's suffering as an ideal (2:21–24).

It's easy to believe Peter is describing himself when he writes such statements as "for you once were not a people, but now you are the people of God" (2:10) and "For you were continually straying like sheep, but now you have returned to the Shepherd and Guardian of your souls" (2:25). Over time the shifting sand of Peter's personality solidified into granite.

Never Too Late

Peter finally earned the nickname that Jesus gave him long before: the "rock" (Matthew 16:18). And when he instructs his readers to stand fast in the true grace of God (5:12), you get the feeling Peter has learned through hard experience the lessons he is now passing on to others.

If Paul is the apostle of faith, Peter is the apostle of hope. God does not give up on people, as Peter's life amply demonstrates. We have reason to hope, whatever our circumstances—even when facing suffering or death.

Tradition reports that Peter was crucified head downward on a Roman cross; he thought himself unworthy to die right side up like Jesus. Peter died still believing his promise of a happy ending: "the God of all grace, who called you to His eternal glory in Christ, will Himself perfect, confirm, strengthen and establish you" (5:10). He wrote like a man who knew.

Life Questions: If Jesus were to give you a nickname, what would it be? Has your personality undergone major changes? What still needs work?

19 in which also He went and made proclamation to the spirits *now* in prison,

20 who once were disobedient, when the patience of God kept waiting in the days of Noah, during the construction of the ark, in which a few, that is, eight persons, were brought safely through *the* water.

3:19 The Spirits in Prison

At least 18 major theories have been proposed to explain Peter's meaning in verses 18–22. Primarily, scholars differ over what the phrase "spirits now in prison" refers to. Were "the spirits" people in some intermediate state of death, or the fallen angels alluded to in Genesis 6:1–4? No one knows for sure. Peter uses the obscure reference to make a point about the ultimate good that came from the suffering Jesus endured.

21 Corresponding to that, baptism now saves you—not the removal of dirt from the flesh, but an appeal to God for a good conscience—through the resurrection of Jesus Christ,

22 who is at the right hand of God, having gone into heaven, after angels and authorities and powers had been subjected to Him.

Keep Fervent in Your Love

4 Therefore, since Christ has [a]suffered in the flesh, arm yourselves also with the same purpose, because he who has suffered in the flesh has ceased from sin,

2 so as to live the rest of the time in the flesh no longer for the lusts of men, but for the will of God.

3 For the time already past is sufficient *for you* to have carried out the desire of the Gentiles, having pursued a course of sensuality, lusts, drunkenness, carousing, drinking parties and abominable idolatries.

4 In *all* this, they are surprised that you do not run with *them* into the same excesses of dissipation, and they malign *you*;

5 but they will give account to Him who is ready to judge the living and the dead.

6 For the gospel has for this purpose been preached even to those who are dead, that though they are judged in the flesh as men, they may live in the spirit according to *the will of* God.

7 ¶ The end of all things is near; therefore, be of sound judgment and sober *spirit* for the purpose of prayer.

8 Above all, keep fervent in your love for one another, because love covers a multitude of sins.

9 Be hospitable to one another without complaint.

10 As each one has received a *special* gift, employ it in serving one another as good stewards of the manifold grace of God.

11 Whoever speaks, *is to do so* as one who is speaking the utterances of God; whoever serves *is to do so* as one who is serving by the strength which God supplies; so that in all things God may be glorified through Jesus Christ, to whom belongs the glory and dominion forever and ever. Amen.

Share the Sufferings of Christ

12 ¶ Beloved, do not be surprised at the fiery ordeal among you, which comes upon you for your testing, as though some strange thing were happening to you;

13 but to the degree that you share the sufferings of Christ, keep on rejoicing, so that also at the revelation of His glory you may rejoice with exultation.

4:13 Radical Shift

This one verse, above all others, shows how much Peter had changed. He received Jesus' strongest rebuke (Mark 8:33) for objecting to the suggestion that Jesus would suffer. But now he presents suffering for Christ as a privilege, a way to participate in Christ's glory.

14 If you are reviled for the name of Christ, you are blessed, because the Spirit of glory and of God rests on you.

15 Make sure that none of you suffers as a murderer, or thief, or evildoer, or a troublesome meddler;

16 but if *anyone suffers* as a Christian, he is not to be ashamed, but is to glorify God in this name.

17 For *it is* time for judgment to begin with the household of God; and if *it begins* with us first, what *will be* the outcome for those who do not obey the gospel of God?

18 AND IF IT IS WITH DIFFICULTY THAT THE RIGHTEOUS IS SAVED, WHAT WILL BECOME OF THE GODLESS MAN AND THE SINNER?

19 Therefore, those also who suffer according to the will of God shall entrust their souls to a faithful Creator in doing what is right.

Serve God Willingly

5 Therefore, I exhort the elders among you, as *your* fellow elder and witness of the sufferings of Christ, and a partaker also of the glory that is to be revealed,

2 shepherd the flock of God among you, exercising oversight not under compulsion, but volun-

[a] I.e. suffered death

tarily, according to *the will of* God; and not for sordid gain, but with eagerness;

3 nor yet as lording it over those allotted to your charge, but proving to be examples to the flock.

4 And when the Chief Shepherd appears, you will receive the unfading crown of glory.

5 You younger men, likewise, be subject to *your* elders; and all of you, clothe yourselves with humility toward one another, for GOD IS OPPOSED TO THE PROUD, BUT GIVES GRACE TO THE HUMBLE.

6 ¶ Therefore humble yourselves under the mighty hand of God, that He may exalt you at the proper time,

7 casting all your anxiety on Him, because He cares for you.

8 Be of sober *spirit*, be on the alert. Your adversary, the devil, prowls around like a roaring lion, seeking someone to devour.

9 But resist him, firm in *your* faith, knowing that the same experiences of suffering are being accomplished by your brethren who are in the world.

10 After you have suffered for a little while, the God of all grace, who called you to His eternal glory in Christ, will Himself perfect, confirm, strengthen *and* establish you.

11 To Him *be* dominion forever and ever. Amen.

12 ¶ Through Silvanus, our faithful brother (for so I regard *him*), I have written to you briefly, exhorting and testifying that this is the true grace of God. Stand firm in it!

13 She who is in Babylon, chosen together with you, sends you greetings, and *so does* my son, Mark.

14 Greet one another with a kiss of love.

¶ Peace be to you all who are in Christ.

2 PETER

A Threat from Within
The worst dangers aren't always well marked

> This is now, beloved, the second letter I am writing to you in which I am stirring up your sincere mind by way of reminder.
> 3:1

FIRST-CENTURY APOSTLES MUST HAVE FELT like pioneers in a mosquito-infested swamp. A pest attacked them. *Slap!* They'd kill it, and instantly another would land. Wherever they went new dangers swarmed up.

One group denied Jesus was God; then another declared him God but not fully man. The apostles denounced legalism, only to encounter free-swingers who assumed "anything goes." Members of one church quit work and huddled together to await Jesus' return; those of another gave up on his returning at all.

Second Peter was written in response to a young church's jumpy tendencies. Whereas 1 Peter centered on fearsome dangers from outside, this letter speaks to dangers from within. False teachers were stirring up dissent, questioning basic doctrines, and leading Christians into immorality.

Warning Signs

In its advice to the various squabbling groups, 2 Peter calls for a return to the true gospel. "I will always be ready to remind you of these things," the author says (1:12) and proceeds to go over some basic facts of how Christians should believe and behave. The book doesn't introduce many new insights; rather, it erects a giant warning sign against common pitfalls that endanger the church.

A key word, *knowledge*, echoes throughout this letter: 2 Peter refreshes readers' memories regarding the proper knowledge that makes possible "everything pertaining to life and godliness" (1:3). The author carefully grounds his knowledge in Old Testament prophets and eyewitness accounts of Jesus' life, not in "cleverly devised tales" (1:16). And he urges his readers to resist dangers by living blamelessly.

The answer to false knowledge, the author bluntly insists, is true knowledge; the answer to immoral living is moral living. As he prepares to die (1:14), the author of 2 Peter gets in one last appeal for truth.

How to Read 2 Peter

Although 1 and 2 Peter claim the same author, they have large differences in style and approach. Second Peter is unrefined in writing style, more shrill and less gentle than the first letter. (Many scholars question whether the apostle Peter actually wrote the whole letter, but the letter does claim his authorship and shows some signs of his influence.)

Perhaps the difference in audiences explains the two approaches. The Bible views suffering—persecution from outside—as a purifying influence that often results in an even stronger church. Thus 1 Peter has an encouraging and devotional tone. But the real danger to a church comes from the inside, from immoral behavior and false teaching. Second Peter, in strong words, addresses those "inside" dangers.

As you read it, try to put yourself in the place of the original audience. What dangers does the author warn against? Are there parallels today? Chapters 1 and 3 can be universally applied. Chapter 2 concerns itself more directly with the particular false teachers plaguing the first-century church.

In tone and actual content, 2 Peter resembles the tiny book of Jude. Both deal with the same problems and propose the same solutions.

When reading 2 Peter, look for the key word *knowledge*, and related words like *remind/ reminder* and *remember*. The author appeals to true knowledge that can correct many of the young church's errors.

3-TRACK READING PLAN

For an explanation and complete listing of the 3-track reading plan, turn to page 7.

TRACK 1: *Two-Week Courses on the Bible*
See page 7 for information on these courses.

TRACK 2: *An Overview of 2 Peter in 1 Day*
☐ Day 1. Read the Introduction to 2 Peter, then chapter 1.
Now turn to page 9 for your next Track 2 reading project.

TRACK 3: *All of 2 Peter in 3 Days*
After you have read through 2 Peter, turn to pages 10–14 for your next Track 3 reading project.
☐1   ☐2   ☐3

Growth in Christian Virtue

1 Simon Peter, a bond-servant and apostle of Jesus Christ,

¶ To those who have received a faith of the same kind as ours, by the righteousness of our God and Savior, Jesus Christ:

2 Grace and peace be multiplied to you in the knowledge of God and of Jesus our Lord;

3 seeing that His divine power has granted to us everything pertaining to life and godliness, through the true knowledge of Him who called us by His own glory and excellence.

4 For by these He has granted to us His precious and magnificent promises, so that by them you may become partakers of *the* divine nature, having escaped the corruption that is in the world by lust.

5 Now for this very reason also, applying all diligence, in your faith supply moral excellence, and in *your* moral excellence, knowledge,

6 and in *your* knowledge, self-control, and in *your* self-control, perseverance, and in *your* perseverance, godliness,

7 and in *your* godliness, brotherly kindness, and in *your* brotherly kindness, love.

8 For if these *qualities* are yours and are increasing, they render you neither useless nor unfruitful in the true knowledge of our Lord Jesus Christ.

9 For he who lacks these *qualities* is blind *or* short-sighted, having forgotten *his* purification from his former sins.

10 Therefore, brethren, be all the more diligent to make certain about His calling and choosing you; for as long as you practice these things, you will never stumble;

11 for in this way the entrance into the eternal kingdom of our Lord and Savior Jesus Christ will be abundantly supplied to you.

12 ¶ Therefore, I will always be ready to remind you of these things, even though you *already* know *them*, and have been established in the truth which is present with *you*.

13 I consider it right, as long as I am in this *earthly* dwelling, to stir you up by way of reminder,

14 knowing that the laying aside of my *earthly* dwelling is imminent, as also our Lord Jesus Christ has made clear to me.

1:14 Approaching Death

The person writing these words was nearing death, a fact that may partially explain the book's forceful tone. An eyewitness (verse 16) of Jesus on earth was watching a young church stray from Christ's clear teaching. This letter may offer the last chance to oppose the deterioration.

15 And I will also be diligent that at any time after my departure you will be able to call these things to mind.

Eyewitnesses

16 ¶ For we did not follow cleverly devised tales when we made known to you the power and coming of our Lord Jesus Christ, but we were eyewitnesses of His majesty.

17 For when He received honor and glory from God the Father, such an utterance as this was made to Him by the Majestic Glory, "This is My beloved Son with whom I am well-pleased"—

18 and we ourselves heard this utterance made

from heaven when we were with Him on the holy mountain.

19 ¶ So we have the prophetic word *made* more sure, to which you do well to pay attention as to a lamp shining in a dark place, until the day dawns and the morning star arises in your hearts.

20 But know this first of all, that no prophecy of Scripture is *a matter* of one's own interpretation,

21 for no prophecy was ever made by an act of human will, but men moved by the Holy Spirit spoke from God.

The Rise of False Prophets

2 But false prophets also arose among the people, just as there will also be false teachers among you, who will secretly introduce destructive heresies, even denying the Master who bought them, bringing swift destruction upon themselves.

2 Many will follow their sensuality, and because of them the way of the truth will be maligned;

3 and in *their* greed they will exploit you with false words; their judgment from long ago is not idle, and their destruction is not asleep.

4 ¶ For if God did not spare angels when they sinned, but cast them into hell and committed them to pits of darkness, reserved for judgment;

5 and did not spare the ancient world, but preserved Noah, a preacher of righteousness, with seven others, when He brought a flood upon the world of the ungodly;

2:5 Three Worlds

Second Peter refers to three great ages of the earth. The first, the ancient world, was destroyed by the flood in Noah's day. The present time, in which we are now living, will be destroyed by fire (3:10). But the author points with hope to an age that has not yet come: a new heaven and a new earth (3:13).

6 and *if* He condemned the cities of Sodom and Gomorrah to destruction by reducing *them* to ashes, having made them an example to those who would live ungodly *lives* thereafter;

7 and *if* He rescued righteous Lot, oppressed by the sensual conduct of unprincipled men

8 (for by what he saw and heard *that* righteous man, while living among them, felt *his* righteous soul tormented day after day by *their* lawless deeds),

9 *then* the Lord knows how to rescue the godly from temptation, and to keep the unrighteous under punishment for the day of judgment,

10 and especially those who indulge the flesh in *its* corrupt desires and despise authority.

¶ Daring, self-willed, they do not tremble when they revile angelic majesties,

11 whereas angels who are greater in might and power do not bring a reviling judgment against them before the Lord.

12 But these, like unreasoning animals, born as creatures of instinct to be captured and killed, reviling where they have no knowledge, will in the destruction of those creatures also be destroyed,

13 suffering wrong as the wages of doing wrong. They count it a pleasure to revel in the daytime. They are stains and blemishes, reveling in their *a*deceptions, as they carouse with you,

14 having eyes full of adultery that never cease from sin, enticing unstable souls, having a heart trained in greed, accursed children;

15 forsaking the right way, they have gone astray, having followed the way of Balaam, the *son* of Beor, who loved the wages of unrighteousness;

16 but he received a rebuke for his own transgression, *for* a mute donkey, speaking with a voice of a man, restrained the madness of the prophet.

17 ¶ These are springs without water and mists driven by a storm, for whom the black darkness has been reserved.

18 For speaking out arrogant *words* of vanity they entice by fleshly desires, by sensuality, those who barely escape from the ones who live in error,

19 promising them freedom while they themselves are slaves of corruption; for by what a man is overcome, by this he is enslaved.

20 For if, after they have escaped the defilements of the world by the knowledge of the Lord and Savior Jesus Christ, they are again entangled in them and are overcome, the last state has become worse for them than the first.

21 For it would be better for them not to have known the way of righteousness, than having known it, to turn away from the holy commandment handed on to them.

22 It has happened to them according to the true proverb, "A DOG RETURNS TO ITS OWN VOMIT," and, "A sow, after washing, *returns* to wallowing in the mire."

Purpose of This Letter

3 This is now, beloved, the second letter I am writing to you in which I am stirring up your sincere mind by way of reminder,

2 that you should remember the words spoken beforehand by the holy prophets and the commandment of the Lord and Savior *spoken* by your apostles.

The Coming Day of the Lord

3 Know this first of all, that in the last days mockers will come with *their* mocking, following after their own lusts,

4 and saying, "Where is the promise of His

---

a One early ms reads *love feasts*

coming? For *ever* since the fathers fell asleep, all continues just as it was from the beginning of creation."

5 For when they maintain this, it escapes their notice that by the word of God *the* heavens existed long ago and *the* earth was formed out of water and by water,

6 through which the world at that time was destroyed, being flooded with water.

7 But by His word the present heavens and earth are being reserved for fire, kept for the day of judgment and destruction of ungodly men.

8 ¶ But do not let this one *fact* escape your notice, beloved, that with the Lord one day is like a thousand years, and a thousand years like one day.

9 The Lord is not slow about His promise, as some count slowness, but is patient toward you, not wishing for any to perish but for all to come to repentance.

A New Heaven and Earth

10 But the day of the Lord will come like a thief, in which the heavens will pass away with a roar and the elements will be destroyed with intense heat, and the earth and its works will be [a]burned up.

3:10 The Fate of the Earth

The time of global destruction described here was a common theme in letters to the early churches. Talk of a coming judgment and the overthrow of the existing world threatened and alarmed Rome, the chief power in the existing world then. Such doomsday prophecies aroused Roman hostility against Christians.

11 ¶ Since all these things are to be destroyed in this way, what sort of people ought you to be in holy conduct and godliness,

12 looking for and hastening the coming of the day of God, because of which the heavens will be destroyed by burning, and the elements will melt with intense heat!

13 But according to His promise we are looking for new heavens and a new earth, in which righteousness dwells.

14 ¶ Therefore, beloved, since you look for these things, be diligent to be found by Him in peace, spotless and blameless,

15 and regard the patience of our Lord *as* salvation; just as also our beloved brother Paul, according to the wisdom given him, wrote to you,

3:15 A Fellow Author

This comment is one of the rare instances in which a New Testament author refers directly to another New Testament book. Evidently, 2 Peter was written late enough that a group of Paul's letters already existed. Scholars use clues like this one to date books of the Bible.

16 as also in all *his* letters, speaking in them of these things, in which are some things hard to understand, which the untaught and unstable distort, as *they do* also the rest of the Scriptures, to their own destruction.

17 You therefore, beloved, knowing this beforehand, be on your guard so that you are not carried away by the error of unprincipled men and fall from your own steadfastness,

18 but grow in the grace and knowledge of our Lord and Savior Jesus Christ. To Him *be* the glory, both now and to the day of eternity. Amen.

---

[a] Two early mss read *discovered*

1 JOHN

Words That Get Polluted
A problem with the new generation

> Let us not love with word or with tongue, but in deed and truth. 3:18

OVER TIME, COMMON PHRASES CAN be stripped of meaning and applied to something else entirely. Take "born again," for example. First coined by Jesus, this phrase was resurrected in the sixties during the Jesus Movement. Soon it was snatched up as an advertising slogan to describe such things as a used car and even a comeback football player.

Christianity has been around so long that people borrow its words for quite different meanings. *Jesus*, the center of our faith, is also a common curse word.

Same Words, Different Meanings

This tendency to pollute language is not new. Even at the close of the first century, words were being twisted and drained of their original meanings. When the apostle John wrote his letters, the Christian faith was perhaps 50 or 60 years old. A generation had grown up in Christian homes, and a distinct subculture was already developing.

Some people were using familiar phrases such as "knowing God," "walk in the light," and "born of God," but with new, distorted meanings. The apostle responded with fire. He knew that a confused, subtle distortion of truth is harder to resist than an outright denial.

In this book, John chooses key words (*light, sin, Christ, love, faith,* etc.), "disinfects" them, and then restores their original meanings. He points back to the truths behind the words. Repeatedly, he begins with the phrase "If we say . . . " and proceeds to show what actions must result if we claim to live in the true light and to know God.

A Step Further

John wrote his Gospel account of Jesus' life in order to bring readers to a belief in Christ (John 20:31). He directed this letter to people who were already Christians, outlining how that faith should affect a person's life. God is light, he says; so walk in the light. He is spirit; so worship him in the proper spirit. He is love; so demonstrate that love to others.

At times John shows the tender concern of a pastor, calling his readers "my little children" (2:1) and urging them to "love one another" (3:11). But in other places his stern language hints at why he once wore the nickname "Son of Thunder."

John was probably the last surviving apostle when he wrote this book. He lived almost to the end of the first century. But he was not too old to fight vigorously against whatever might corrupt the faith that had inspired him for so many years.

How to Read 1 John

First John is constructed like a piece of music. Its author states a few simple themes—light, truth, life, love—then builds variations on them. Relying on simple words and a rhythmic style, John writes in universal terms that apply to any time period.

Yet the book is understood far better if you know something about the environment in which John was writing. Therefore, begin your reading with "Who Were the Gnostics?" on page 1359.

As you read John, note the pattern. He defines a word, such as *light*, discusses its opposite, *darkness*, and then describes what a life in the light should look like. In every case, he shows God as the source of power in the Christian life.

3-TRACK READING PLAN

For an explanation and complete listing of the 3-track reading plan, turn to page 7.

TRACK 1: **Two-Week Courses on the Bible**
See page 7 for information on these courses.

TRACK 2: **An Overview of 1 John in 1 Day**
☐ Day 1. Read the Introduction to 1 John, then chapter 3, a great summary of the love of God and how it should affect our lives.
Now turn to page 9 for your next Track 2 reading project.

TRACK 3: **All of 1 John in 4 Days**
After you have read through 1 John, turn to pages 10–14 for your next Track 3 reading project.
☐1–2   ☐3   ☐4   ☐5

Introduction
The Incarnate Word

1 What was from the beginning, what we have heard, what we have seen with our eyes, what we have looked at and touched with our hands, concerning the Word of Life—

2 and the life was manifested, and we have seen and testify and proclaim to you the eternal life, which was with the Father and was manifested to us—

3 what we have seen and heard we proclaim to you also, so that you too may have fellowship with us; and indeed our fellowship is with the Father, and with His Son Jesus Christ.

1:3–4 Eyewitness

In contrast to most New Testament letters, this one does not identify its author. Certain hints and distinctive patterns of style, though, make it very likely that the apostle John wrote it in advanced age. Simply compare the first paragraph of this letter with the first few paragraphs of the Gospel of John to see the similarities. The author also emphasizes that he was a close eyewitness of Jesus' life, a fact consistent with the "disciple whom Jesus loved."

4 These things we write, so that our joy may be made complete.

God Is Light

5 ¶ This is the message we have heard from Him and announce to you, that God is Light, and in Him there is no darkness at all.

6 If we say that we have fellowship with Him and *yet* walk in the darkness, we lie and do not practice the truth;

7 but if we walk in the Light as He Himself is in the Light, we have fellowship with one another, and the blood of Jesus His Son cleanses us from all sin.

8 If we say that we have no sin, we are deceiving ourselves and the truth is not in us.

9 If we confess our sins, He is faithful and righteous to forgive us our sins and to cleanse us from all unrighteousness.

10 If we say that we have not sinned, we make Him a liar and His word is not in us.

Christ Is Our Advocate

2 My little children, I am writing these things to you so that you may not sin. And if anyone sins, we have an ⁿAdvocate with the Father, Jesus Christ the righteous;

2 and He Himself is the propitiation for our sins; and not for ours only, but also for *those of* the whole world.

3 ¶ By this we know that we have come to know Him, if we keep His commandments.

4 The one who says, "I have come to know Him," and does not keep His commandments, is a liar, and the truth is not in him;

5 but whoever keeps His word, in him the love of God has truly been perfected. By this we know that we are in Him:

6 the one who says he abides in Him ought himself to walk in the same manner as He walked.

7 ¶ Beloved, I am not writing a new com-

ⁿ Gr *Paracletos*, one called alongside to help; or *Intercessor* mandment to you, but an old commandment which you have had from the beginning; the old commandment is the word which you have heard.

8 On the other hand, I am writing a new commandment to you, which is true in Him and in you, because the darkness is passing away and the true Light is already shining.

9 The one who says he is in the Light and *yet* hates his brother is in the darkness until now.

10 The one who loves his brother abides in the Light and there is no cause for stumbling in him.

11 But the one who hates his brother is in the darkness and walks in the darkness, and does not know where he is going because the darkness has blinded his eyes.

12 ¶ I am writing to you, little children, because your sins have been forgiven you for His name's sake.

2:12 A Friendly Interruption

John begins his book with a stern warning against false ideas. But this lyrical section interrupts the flow with a warm greeting to true believers in the church. Many commentators believe that John intended the three categories (little children, young men, fathers) to represent three different stages in his readers' spiritual lives.

13 I am writing to you, fathers, because you know Him who has been from the beginning. I am writing to you, young men, because you have overcome the evil one. I have written to you, children, because you know the Father.

14 I have written to you, fathers, because you know Him who has been from the beginning. I have written to you, young men, because you are strong, and the word of God abides in you, and you have overcome the evil one.

Do Not Love the World

15 ¶ Do not love the world nor the things in the world. If anyone loves the world, the love of the Father is not in him.

16 For all that is in the world, the lust of the flesh and the lust of the eyes and the boastful pride of life, is not from the Father, but is from the world.

17 The world is passing away, and *also* its lusts; but the one who does the will of God lives forever.

18 ¶ Children, it is the last hour; and just as you heard that antichrist is coming, even now many antichrists have appeared; from this we know that it is the last hour.

19 They went out from us, but they were not *really* of us; for if they had been of us, they would have remained with us; but *they went out,* so that it would be shown that they all are not of us.

20 But you have an anointing from the Holy One, and you all know.

21 I have not written to you because you do not know the truth, but because you do know it, and because no lie is of the truth.

22 Who is the liar but the one who denies that Jesus is the Christ? This is the antichrist, the one who denies the Father and the Son.

2:22 Tough Love

John had two nicknames. "The apostle of love" uses the word love *35 times in this brief letter alone. But the letter also hints why he earned his original nickname, "Son of Thunder" (Mark 3:17). As one of Jesus' disciples, John had wanted to call fire down from heaven on unresponsive villages (Luke 9:54). Jesus rebuked such a notion, and John mellowed considerably over the years. Still, he reserves some choice words for enemies of the gospel: He brands them antichrists (2:18), liars (2:22), and children of the devil (3:10).*

23 Whoever denies the Son does not have the Father; the one who confesses the Son has the Father also.

24 As for you, let that abide in you which you heard from the beginning. If what you heard from the beginning abides in you, you also will abide in the Son and in the Father.

The Promise Is Eternal Life

25 This is the promise which He Himself made to us: eternal life.

26 ¶ These things I have written to you concerning those who are trying to deceive you.

27 As for you, the anointing which you received from Him abides in you, and you have no need for anyone to teach you; but as His anointing teaches you about all things, and is true and is not a lie, and just as it has taught you, you abide in Him.

28 ¶ Now, little children, abide in Him, so that when He appears, we may have confidence and not shrink away from Him in shame at His coming.

29 If you know that He is righteous, you know that everyone also who practices righteousness is born of Him.

Children of God Love One Another

3 See how great a love the Father has bestowed on us, that we would be called children of God; and *such* we are. For this reason the world does not know us, because it did not know Him.

2 Beloved, now we are children of God, and it has not appeared as yet what we will be. We know that when He appears, we will be like Him, because we will see Him just as He is.

3 And everyone who has this hope *fixed* on Him purifies himself, just as He is pure.

4 ¶ Everyone who practices sin also practices lawlessness; and sin is lawlessness.

5 You know that He appeared in order to take away sins; and in Him there is no sin.

6 No one who abides in Him sins; no one who sins has seen Him or knows Him.

7 Little children, make sure no one deceives you; the one who practices righteousness is righteous, just as He is righteous;

8 the one who practices sin is of the devil; for the devil has sinned from the beginning. The Son of God appeared for this purpose, to destroy the works of the devil.

9 No one who is born of God practices sin, because His seed abides in him; and he cannot sin, because he is born of God.

10 By this the children of God and the children of the devil are obvious: anyone who does not practice righteousness is not of God, nor the one who does not love his brother.

11 ¶ For this is the message which you have heard from the beginning, that we should love one another;

3:11 Love Versus Hate

Very often John defines words in relation to their opposites: light versus darkness, truth versus falsehood, life versus death. In this paragraph, he begins with a command to "love one another," then goes on to illustrate the life of hate before coming back to define love. Many of 1 John's themes are developed in this "circular" method.

12 not as Cain, *who* was of the evil one and slew his brother. And for what reason did he slay him? Because his deeds were evil, and his brother's were righteous.

13 ¶ Do not be surprised, brethren, if the world hates you.

14 We know that we have passed out of death into life, because we love the brethren. He who does not love abides in death.

15 Everyone who hates his brother is a murderer; and you know that no murderer has eternal life abiding in him.

16 We know love by this, that He laid down His life for us; and we ought to lay down our lives for the brethren.

17 But whoever has the world's goods, and sees his brother in need and closes his heart against him, how does the love of God abide in him?

18 Little children, let us not love with word or with tongue, but in deed and truth.

19 We will know by this that we are of the truth, and will assure our heart before Him

20 in whatever our heart condemns us; for God is greater than our heart and knows all things.

21 Beloved, if our heart does not condemn us, we have confidence before God;

22 and whatever we ask we receive from Him, because we keep His commandments and do the things that are pleasing in His sight.

23 ¶ This is His commandment, that we believe in the name of His Son Jesus Christ, and love one another, just as He commanded us.

24 The one who keeps His commandments abides in Him, and He in him. We know by this that He abides in us, by the Spirit whom He has given us.

Testing the Spirits

4 Beloved, do not believe every spirit, but test the spirits to see whether they are from God, because many false prophets have gone out into the world.

2 By this you know the Spirit of God: every spirit that confesses that Jesus Christ has come in the flesh is from God;

3 and every spirit that does not confess Jesus is not from God; this is the *spirit* of the antichrist, of which you have heard that it is coming, and now it is already in the world.

4 You are from God, little children, and have overcome them; because greater is He who is in you than he who is in the world.

5 They are from the world; therefore they speak *as* from the world, and the world listens to them.

6 We are from God; he who knows God listens to us; he who is not from God does not listen to us. By this we know the spirit of truth and the spirit of error.

God Is Love

7 ¶ Beloved, let us love one another, for love is from God; and everyone who loves is born of God and knows God.

8 The one who does not love does not know God, for God is love.

9 By this the love of God was manifested in us, that God has sent His only begotten Son into the world so that we might live through Him.

10 In this is love, not that we loved God, but that He loved us and sent His Son *to be* the propitiation for our sins.

11 Beloved, if God so loved us, we also ought to love one another.

12 No one has seen God at any time; if we love one another, God abides in us, and His love is perfected in us.

13 By this we know that we abide in Him and He in us, because He has given us of His Spirit.

14 We have seen and testify that the Father has sent the Son *to be* the Savior of the world.

15 ¶ Whoever confesses that Jesus is the Son of God, God abides in him, and he in God.

16 We have come to know and have believed the love which God has for us. God is love, and the one who abides in love abides in God, and God abides in him.

17 By this, love is perfected with us, so that we may have confidence in the day of judgment; because as He is, so also are we in this world.

18 There is no fear in love; but perfect love casts out fear, because fear involves punishment, and the one who fears is not perfected in love.

19 We love, because He first loved us.

20 If someone says, "I love God," and hates his brother, he is a liar; for the one who does not love his brother whom he has seen, cannot love God whom he has not seen.

21 And this commandment we have from Him, that the one who loves God should love his brother also.

Overcoming the World

5 Whoever believes that Jesus is the [a]Christ is born of God, and whoever loves the Father loves the *child* born of Him.

2 By this we know that we love the children of God, when we love God and observe His commandments.

3 For this is the love of God, that we keep His commandments; and His commandments are not burdensome.

4 For whatever is born of God overcomes the world; and this is the victory that has overcome the world—our faith.

[a] I.e. Messiah

Who Were the Gnostics?
A dangerous cult that proved fatally attractive

AS CHRISTIANITY SPREAD ACROSS THE Mediterranean, it came into contact with other religions. Greeks and Romans tried to absorb the faith into their own philosophies, just as some Jews had initially.

Intellectual centers of the Mediterranean raised questions about Jesus: Who was he? If he was God, how could he die? And a popular new cult called Gnosticism (from the Greek word for knowledge, *gnosis*) gained ground in an attempt to explain these things. The cult thrived, especially among the intellectual elite.

> By this you know the Spirit of God: every spirit that confesses that Jesus Christ has come in the flesh is from God. 4:2

Could God Have a Body?

Gnostics balked at the Christian concept of God's becoming human. Because they believed a physical body was intrinsically evil, they denied that a pure God could take on a body. Some dealt with the problem by claiming that Jesus was never a real human being, but a phantom, a temporary appearance of God who only looked human. Others proposed that God had "descended" on Jesus at his baptism, but left him before his death.

The apostle John debated in person with Gnostics of his day, and he had Gnostic thinking in mind when he wrote this letter. The very first sentence expressly states that the author has seen, heard, and touched Jesus—implying he could not have been a phantom, or pure spirit. Throughout the letter, and especially in 4:2–3, the author lambastes those who deny that Jesus came in the flesh.

Live As You Please

To Gnostics, all matter was evil. Only the spirit was pure, and Gnostics sought to rise to a higher, more spiritual plane. This teaching often produced a side effect: People who strove to rise above matter didn't care about personal ethics. Their pure spirits could not be tainted by "earthly" sin. Thus, they could act any way they wanted.

Aging John roared out against the twin dangers of Gnosticism: immoral living and doubts that Christ became a man. Beliefs must be judged by the actions they produce, and John stresses the theme of brotherly love. He primarily refutes errors by presenting a wholesome picture of the Christian life as it is supposed to be lived.

True fellowship is not a secret initiation into a New Age-type elite, but a relationship with the Father through Christ. And that also entails responsibilities to others in God's family.

Life Questions: Gnosticism showed itself in several ways: the belief that matter was evil, a desire for "super-spirituality," a tendency toward loose morals. How can we counter those same trends among Christians today?

5 ¶ Who is the one who overcomes the world, but he who believes that Jesus is the Son of God?

6 This is the One who came by water and blood, Jesus Christ; not with the water only, but with the water and with the blood. It is the Spirit who testifies, because the Spirit is the truth.

7 For there are three that testify:

8 ªthe Spirit and the water and the blood; and the three are in agreement.

9 If we receive the testimony of men, the testimony of God is greater; for the testimony of God is this, that He has testified concerning His Son.

10 The one who believes in the Son of God has the testimony in himself; the one who does not believe God has made Him a liar, because he has not believed in the testimony that God has given concerning His Son.

11 And the testimony is this, that God has given us eternal life, and this life is in His Son.

12 He who has the Son has the life; he who does not have the Son of God does not have the life.

This Is Written That You May Know

13 ¶ These things I have written to you who believe in the name of the Son of God, so that you may know that you have eternal life.

14 This is the confidence which we have before Him, that, if we ask anything according to His will, He hears us.

15 And if we know that He hears us *in* whatever we ask, we know that we have the requests which we have asked from Him.

16 ¶ If anyone sees his brother committing a sin not *leading* to death, he shall ask and *God* will for him give life to those who commit sin not *leading* to death. There is a sin *leading* to death; I do not say that he should make request for this.

5:8 Water, Blood, and Spirit

The apostle John relied heavily on symbolic language in his Gospel account of Jesus' life. Here, too, he uses symbols in giving proofs of Jesus. Water may refer to Jesus' baptism, blood to his death on the cross, and the Spirit to the Holy Spirit who descended on Jesus. John refers to these three as a "testimony" from God about his Son.

17 All unrighteousness is sin, and there is a sin not *leading* to death.

18 ¶ We know that no one who is born of God sins; but He who was born of God keeps him, and the evil one does not touch him.

19 We know that we are of God, and that the whole world lies in *the power of* the evil one.

20 And we know that the Son of God has come, and has given us understanding so that we may know Him who is true; and we are in Him who is true, in His Son Jesus Christ. This is the true God and eternal life.

21 ¶ Little children, guard yourselves from idols.

ª A few late mss add *...in heaven, the Father, the Word, and the Holy Spirit, and these three are one. And there are three that testify on earth, the Spirit*

2 JOHN

Undesirable Guests
When a "Welcome" sign is inappropriate

R OMAN ROADS MADE FIRST-CENTURY TRAVEL safer and easier than ever before, but Holiday Inns were still centuries away. Therefore, when teachers of the Christian faith traveled the empire, they relied on local Christians for food and lodging.

> Watch yourselves, that you do not lose what we have accomplished. 8

Before long, false teachers (such as Gnostics) also hit the circuit, joined by religious racketeers attracted primarily to the free food and lodging. The two letters, 2 John and 3 John, the shortest books in the entire Bible, concern themselves with the mounting problems of hospitality for the "circuit-rider" teachers.

Show Discretion, But Also Love

Heresies had already sprung up in many local churches, and 2 John urges true Christians to use discretion in testing a visitor's message and motive. The author cautions against entertaining visitors who do not teach the truth about Christ.

True to his nickname, the apostle of love repeats his motto, "Love one another," even in this letter of warning. The ancient writer Jerome (A.D. 374–419) tells of the frail apostle John, in extreme old age, being carried into his congregation mumbling only, "Love one another." When asked why he talked of nothing else, John replied, "Because it is the Lord's command, and if this only is done, it is enough."

How to Read 2 and 3 John

T hese two books are best read together, since each gives one side of a problem facing a young church. Try to imagine the setting back then, when Christianity was still new and many teachers came along claiming special insights. Do you see any parallels among Christians today? Look for the specific advice John gave in those circumstances.

3-TRACK READING PLAN

For an explanation and complete listing of the 3-track reading plan, turn to page 7.

TRACK 1: *Two-Week Courses on the Bible*
See page 7 for information on these courses.

TRACK 2: *Read 2 and 3 John Together in 1 Day*
☐ Day 1. These books are only one short chapter each, so you can easily read the two together.
Now turn to page 9 for your next Track 2 reading project.

TRACK 3: *All of 2 and 3 John in 1 Day*
Read both books in one day. After you have finished, turn to pages 10–14 for your next Track 3 reading project.
☐ 2 John, 3 John

Walk According to His Commandments

1 The elder to the chosen lady and her children, whom I love in truth; and not only I, but also all who know the truth,

2 for the sake of the truth which abides in us and will be with us forever:

3 Grace, mercy *and* peace will be with us, from God the Father and from Jesus Christ, the Son of the Father, in truth and love.

4 ¶ I was very glad to find *some* of your children walking in truth, just as we have received commandment *to do* from the Father.

5 Now I ask you, lady, not as though *I were* writing to you a new commandment, but the one which we have had from the beginning, that we love one another.

6 And this is love, that we walk according to His commandments. This is the commandment, just as you have heard from the beginning, that you should walk in it.

7 ¶ For many deceivers have gone out into the world, those who do not acknowledge Jesus Christ *as* coming in the flesh. This is the deceiver and the antichrist.

8 Watch yourselves, that you do not lose what we have accomplished, but that you may receive a full reward.

9 Anyone who goes too far and does not abide in the teaching of Christ, does not have God; the one who abides in the teaching, he has both the Father and the Son.

7 Pesky Deceivers

This paragraph shows that the enemies warned about in 1 John were still roaming about, stirring up trouble in the churches. The description of their beliefs—"who do not acknowledge Jesus Christ as coming in the flesh"—brings to mind the teaching of the Gnostics (see "Who Were the Gnostics?" page 1359), one of the main targets of that first letter.

10 If anyone comes to you and does not bring this teaching, do not receive him into *your* house, and do not give him a greeting;

11 for the one who gives him a greeting participates in his evil deeds.

12 ¶ Though I have many things to write to you, I do not want to *do so* with paper and ink; but I hope to come to you and speak face to face, so that your joy may be made full.

13 ¶ The children of your chosen sister greet you.

3 JOHN

Guidelines for Hospitality
The same questions crop up in every age, in every place

T AKEN TOGETHER, THIS LETTER AND its companion give a balanced view of proper Christian hospitality. Second John warned against entertaining false teachers. But 3 John praises a man named Gaius for warmly welcoming genuine Christian teachers. His actions had been opposed by Diotrephes, a cantankerous church dictator, who was also gossiping against John.

In a very condensed form, John's two letters deal with heresy and church splits, two problems that have plagued the church in every age, in every place. To defend against those dangers, John urges love and discernment. Believers must know whom to accept and support, and whom to resist.

> *I have no greater joy than this, to hear of my children walking in the truth. 4*

How to Read 3 John

See How to Read 2 and 3 John, page 1361.

You Walk in the Truth

1 The elder to the beloved Gaius, whom I love in truth.

2 ¶ Beloved, I pray that in all respects you may prosper and be in good health, just as your soul prospers.

3 For I was very glad when brethren came and testified to your truth, *that is,* how you are walking in truth.

4 I have no greater joy than this, to hear of my children walking in the truth.

4 No Greater Joy

Scholars estimate that the apostle John was between 80 and 90 years old when he wrote the letters bearing his name. He identifies himself as "the elder" (which may also refer to his office in a local church) and writes fondly of "my children." The letters carry the tone of an old man dispensing his last words of advice and taking grandfatherly pride in the progress of his spiritual heirs.

5 ¶ Beloved, you are acting faithfully in whatever you accomplish for the brethren, and especially *when they are* strangers;

6 and they have testified to your love before the church. You will do well to send them on their way in a manner worthy of God.

7 For they went out for the sake of the Name, accepting nothing from the Gentiles.

8 Therefore we ought to support such men, so that we may be fellow workers with the truth.

9 ¶ I wrote something to the church; but Diotrephes, who loves to be first among them, does not accept what we say.

10 For this reason, if I come, I will call attention to his deeds which he does, unjustly accusing us with wicked words; and not satisfied with this, he himself does not receive the brethren, either, and he forbids those who desire *to do so* and puts *them* out of the church.

11 ¶ Beloved, do not imitate what is evil, but what is good. The one who does good is of God; the one who does evil has not seen God.

12 Demetrius has received a *good* testimony from everyone, and from the truth itself; and we add our testimony, and you know that our testimony is true.

13 ¶ I had many things to write to you, but I am not willing to write *them* to you with pen and ink;

14 but I hope to see you shortly, and we will speak face to face.

15 ¶ Peace *be* to you. The friends greet you. Greet the friends by name.

JUDE

Watch Out!
Sounding an alarm

I
F YOU SIGN UP FOR a driver's training course, you'll begin with several hours of classroom lectures on "Rules of the Road." The instructor will drill you on the shapes and colors of warning signs—signs that announce danger on the highways.

> I felt the necessity to write to you appealing that you contend earnestly for the faith. 3

Driving seems all very academic, until you slide behind the wheel. There, a missed stop sign won't just lower a test score; it could cost you your life. Your instructor, rather than calmly correcting you, will shout, "Look out!"

Jude writes in the style of a teacher who is watching a freight train bear down on his student driver. Bells ring out, crossing gates go down, red lights flash. He admits this kind of letter isn't his preference; he intended a more high-minded treatise on salvation (verse 3). But the church was facing mortal dangers, and so Jude dashed off a vehement warning.

Who Were the Troublemakers?

Jude doesn't elaborate on what the troublemakers (verse 4) were teaching—perhaps he didn't want to honor their ideas by discussing them. Their behavior, however, is fair game: He fires away at their hypocrisy, divisiveness, and loose morals. He calls them spies and urges believers to fight for the true faith. At his poetic best, he borrows vivid images from nature to describe these people (12–13).

Short and vigorous, the book of Jude brings to mind a message from one of the fiery Old Testament prophets. Yet Jude holds out hope for his readers. Sincere believers can keep themselves in God's love, and some wavering souls can still be snatched "out of the fire" (21–23). (Even when battling heretics, Jude does not hint at persecuting the offenders—no burnings at the stake here.)

Jude closes with a familiar and joy-filled doxology, the one part of his letter still quoted widely in modern churches.

How to Read Jude

I
n tone, Jude reads a lot like James and 2 Peter: It is simple, hard-hitting, and stern. In fact, it seems to copy entire sections of 2 Peter.

You can read through Jude in a few minutes, to get the force of his argument. But to truly appreciate his letter, you should reflect on (and look up) his various Old Testament references. Jude supports his arguments with extensive illustrations from history, and he even quotes from two Jewish books not accepted as part of the Bible, *The Assumption of Moses* (verse 9) and the book of *Enoch* (verse 14).

All these citations support Jude's main thrust, which he summarizes eloquently in the last few paragraphs.

3-TRACK READING PLAN

For an explanation and complete listing of the 3-track reading plan, turn to page 7.

TRACK 1:   *Two-Week Courses on the Bible*
See page 7 for information on these courses.

TRACK 2:   *Read Jude in 1 Day*
☐ Day 1. Just one chapter long, Jude will take only a few minutes to read.
Now turn to page 9 for your next Track 2 reading project.

TRACK 3:   *All of Jude in 1 Day*
After you have read Jude, turn to pages 10–14 for your next Track 3 reading project.
☐Jude

The Warnings of History to the Ungodly

1 Jude, a bond-servant of Jesus Christ, and brother of James,

¶ To those who are the called, beloved in God the Father, and kept for Jesus Christ:

2 May mercy and peace and love be multiplied to you.

3 ¶ Beloved, while I was making every effort to write you about our common salvation, I felt the necessity to write to you appealing that you contend earnestly for the faith which was once for all handed down to the saints.

4 For certain persons have crept in unnoticed, those who were long beforehand marked out for this condemnation, ungodly persons who turn the grace of our God into licentiousness and deny our only Master and Lord, Jesus Christ.

5 ¶ Now I desire to remind you, though you know all things once for all, that ᵃthe Lord, after saving a people out of the land of Egypt, subsequently destroyed those who did not believe.

6 And angels who did not keep their own domain, but abandoned their proper abode, He has kept in eternal bonds under darkness for the judgment of the great day,

7 just as Sodom and Gomorrah and the cities around them, since they in the same way as these indulged in gross immorality and went after strange flesh, are exhibited as an example in undergoing the punishment of eternal fire.

8 ¶ Yet in the same way these men, also by dreaming, defile the flesh, and reject authority, and revile angelic majesties.

9 But Michael the archangel, when he disputed with the devil and argued about the body of Moses, did not dare pronounce against him a railing judgment, but said, "The Lord rebuke you!"

10 But these men revile the things which they do not understand; and the things which they know by instinct, like unreasoning animals, by these things they are destroyed.

11 Woe to them! For they have gone the way of Cain, and for pay they have rushed headlong into the error of Balaam, and perished in the rebellion of Korah.

12 These are the men who are hidden reefs in your love feasts when they feast with you without fear, caring for themselves; clouds without water, carried along by winds; autumn trees without fruit, doubly dead, uprooted;

13 wild waves of the sea, casting up their own shame like foam; wandering stars, for whom the black darkness has been reserved forever.

11 Bad Models

Jude mentions three Old Testament characters as powerful illustrations of qualities to avoid: the selfishness of Cain, the greed of Balaam, the rebelliousness of Korah. (Their stories can be found in Genesis 4, Numbers 22, and Numbers 16.) After filling his letter with such negative examples, however, Jude concludes triumphantly that God "is able to keep you from stumbling" (verse 24).

14 ¶ *It was* also about these men *that* Enoch, *in* the seventh *generation* from Adam, prophesied, saying, "Behold, the Lord came with many thousands of His holy ones,

15 to execute judgment upon all, and to convict all the ungodly of all their ungodly deeds which they have done in an ungodly way, and of all the harsh things which ungodly sinners have spoken against Him."

16 These are grumblers, finding fault, following after their *own* lusts; they speak arrogantly, flattering people for the sake of *gaining an* advantage.

Keep Yourselves in the Love of God

17 ¶ But you, beloved, ought to remember the words that were spoken beforehand by the apostles of our Lord Jesus Christ,

18 that they were saying to you, "In the last time there will be mockers, following after their own ungodly lusts."

19 These are the ones who cause divisions, worldly-minded, devoid of the Spirit.

ᵃ Two early mss read *Jesus*

20 But you, beloved, building yourselves up on your most holy faith, praying in the Holy Spirit,

21 keep yourselves in the love of God, waiting anxiously for the mercy of our Lord Jesus Christ to eternal life.

22 And have mercy on some, who are doubting;

23 save others, snatching them out of the fire; and on some have mercy with fear, hating even the garment polluted by the flesh.

24 ¶ Now to Him who is able to keep you from stumbling, and to make you stand in the presence of His glory blameless with great joy,

25 to the only God our Savior, through Jesus Christ our Lord, be glory, majesty, dominion and authority, before all time and now and forever. Amen.

REVELATION

A Book Full of Mysteries
Why Revelation is hard to understand

THE ROMAN EMPIRE HAD ITS own version of Alcatraz: a rocky island called Patmos. Prisoners banished to that hard-labor colony usually wasted away and died. In that desolate setting a man named John had a series of visions he wrote down as Revelation, the strangest book in the New Testament.

John probably wrote this book about 60 years after Jesus left the earth. Questions were troubling the church. Was Jesus coming back as he had promised? Where did he go? To do what? Why didn't he return immediately? Revelation addresses those issues.

> Blessed is he who reads and those who hear the words of the prophecy, and heed the things which are written in it; for the time is near. 1:3

Writing in Code

No other New Testament book resembles Revelation in style. Yet during its time similar Jewish "apocalyptic" books (books that symbolically picture the ultimate destruction of evil and the triumph of good) flourished. Authors, writing to persecuted Christians anxious about their future, predicted what would take place. Often, they used coded language to protect themselves; for example, they substituted a word like *Babylon* when criticizing Rome, just in case their writings fell into the wrong hands.

The codes in Revelation are effective—so effective that few people today agree on exactly what they mean. Some people think many of the predictions in Revelation have not yet been fulfilled; perhaps John was writing about events that will come to pass in our own generation, they say. A best-selling book, Hal Lindsey's *The Late Great Planet Earth,* interprets Revelation that way.

Others explain Revelation in terms of the first century, concluding that many of the events prophesied in code took place during the Roman empire. Still others find clues to John's meaning spread out over 2,000 years of church history, or surmise that he employed symbols merely to describe an idealized battle of good and evil.

Two Dangers

Because of all the conflicting theories about Revelation, readers are tempted to respond in one of two ways. Some judge the book so perplexingly weird that they can find no reason to read it at all. How can anyone be sure of its meaning?

Others fall prey to the opposite danger. They pore over Revelation and conclude they have discovered the secret explanation of each obscure detail. To the latter group, it may be humbling to learn that every generation since the first century has come up with different interpretations of the prophecies.

Why Read Revelation?

Why read this strange book? John gives a good clue in the first phrase, which introduces this book as "the Revelation of Jesus Christ." Revelation gives a unique picture of Jesus Christ, and the New Testament would be incomplete without it. The Gospels describe Jesus' life on earth from four different viewpoints. The letters discuss the deep significance of the resurrected Christ and what he accomplished. But Revelation shows Jesus Christ from a new perspective: as the mighty ruler of the cosmic forces of good. When John saw him in this exalted state, he fell at Jesus' feet as though dead (1:17).

Although Revelation does not remove the mystery surrounding Jesus' return and the end of the world, it does throw light on those events. It cannot be reduced to a mere timetable of events; it speaks lasting truths to every generation of readers. Revelation tells of Christ's future triumph over all the evil in the universe. This crucial message of final hope was needed by its original readers in the first century and is still needed by us today.

How to Read Revelation

Revelation is probably the most intimidating book in the Bible. It packs in so many symbols and obscure details that most readers find themselves plagued by the sensation that they are missing something.

All new forms of writing seem intimidating at first: for example, consider your very first science fiction book, filled with weird names and unearthly creatures, and governed by its own rules of writing. Science fiction seems very strange until you learn the techniques used by virtually all science fiction writers. Once you understand the form, it makes more sense. The same applies to Revelation. It will likely seem strange at first, because it uses techniques of symbolism and visions not commonly used elsewhere in the New Testament.

It is best to read Revelation one vision at a time, rather than all at once. The seven main visions give a view of similar events from different angles.

1. The church on earth (1–3)
2. The Lamb and the seven seals (4–7)
3. Seven angels with trumpets (8–11)
4. The church persecuted by Satan and the beast (12–14)
5. The seven bowls of God's wrath (15–16)
6. Judgment of Babylon (17–19:10).
7. Final judgment and final victory (19:11 to end).

Try to read completely through a vision, following the boldface sectional headings marked in the Bible text.

As you read, look behind the visual symbols for the meaning they point to. Ask yourself, What does this tell me about Christ, about God, about the real meaning of history? Don't try to analyze details at first; just follow the main flow of thought.

Keep in mind also the condition of the persecuted Christians who first received this book. They needed not a precise calendar of future events, but rather a word of encouragement and hope. They needed faith that, no matter how things looked, God was in charge of history and good would ultimately triumph. Revelation provides this hope, for them and for us.

Finally, a good Bible dictionary or commentary will clear up much of the confusion about Revelation.

3-TRACK READING PLAN

For an explanation and complete listing of the 3-track reading plan, turn to page 7.

TRACK 1: *Two-Week Courses on the Bible*
See page 7 for information on these courses.

TRACK 2: *An Overview of Revelation in 3 Days*
☐ Day 1. Read the Introduction to Revelation, then chapter 1, to see how John introduces this book.
☐ Day 2. Read chapter 12 as a sample of the writing contained in this book of visions.
☐ Day 3. Read chapter 21 for a glimpse of the final end of the universe.
Now turn to page 9 for your next Track 2 reading project.

TRACK 3: *All of Revelation in 19 Days*
After you have read through Revelation, turn to pages 10–14 for your next Track 3 reading project.

☐1 ☐2 ☐3 ☐4–5 ☐6 ☐7 ☐8 ☐9
☐10–11 ☐12 ☐13 ☐14 ☐15–16 ☐17 ☐18 ☐19
☐20 ☐21 ☐22

The Revelation of Jesus Christ

1 The Revelation of Jesus Christ, which God gave Him to show to His bond-servants, the things which must soon take place; and He sent and communicated *it* by His angel to His bond-servant John,

2 who testified to the word of God and to the testimony of Jesus Christ, *even* to all that he saw.

3 Blessed is he who reads and those who hear the words of the prophecy, and heed the things which are written in it; for the time is near.

Message to the Seven Churches

4 ¶ John to the seven churches that are in Asia: Grace to you and peace, from Him who is and who was and who is to come, and from the seven Spirits who are before His throne,

5 and from Jesus Christ, the faithful witness, the firstborn of the dead, and the ruler of the kings of the earth. To Him who loves us and released us from our sins by His blood—

6 and He has made us *to be* a kingdom, priests to His God and Father—to Him *be* the glory and the dominion forever and ever. Amen.

7 BEHOLD, HE IS COMING WITH THE CLOUDS, and every eye will see Him, even those who pierced Him; and all the tribes of the earth will mourn over Him. So it is to be. Amen.

8 ¶ "I am the Alpha and the Omega," says the Lord God, "who is and who was and who is to come, the Almighty."

The Patmos Vision

9 ¶ I, John, your brother and fellow partaker in the tribulation and kingdom and perseverance *which are* in Jesus, was on the island called Patmos because of the word of God and the testimony of Jesus.

10 I was ᵃin the Spirit on the Lord's day, and I heard behind me a loud voice like *the sound* of a trumpet,

11 saying, "Write in a book what you see, and send *it* to the seven churches: to Ephesus and to Smyrna and to Pergamum and to Thyatira and to Sardis and to Philadelphia and to Laodicea."

12 ¶ Then I turned to see the voice that was speaking with me. And having turned I saw seven golden lampstands;

13 and in the middle of the lampstands *I saw* one like ᵇa son of man, clothed in a robe reaching to the feet, and girded across His chest with a golden sash.

14 His head and His hair were white like white wool, like snow; and His eyes were like a flame of fire.

15 His feet *were* like burnished bronze, when it has been made to glow in a furnace, and His voice *was* like the sound of many waters.

16 In His right hand He held seven stars, and out of His mouth came a sharp two-edged sword; and His face was like the sun shining in its strength.

17 ¶ When I saw Him, I fell at His feet like a

1:13 Familiar Title

Revelation's original readers would have recognized this description immediately, for Jesus used the title "son of man" about 90 times in the Gospels. The phrase first appears in Daniel 7:13, introducing the Messiah who would rule all history.

dead man. And He placed His right hand on me, saying, "Do not be afraid; I am the first and the last,

18 and the living One; and I was dead, and behold, I am alive forevermore, and I have the keys of death and of Hades.

19 "Therefore write the things which you have seen, and the things which are, and the things which will take place after these things.

20 "As for the mystery of the seven stars which you saw in My right hand, and the seven golden lampstands: the seven stars are the angels of the seven churches, and the seven lampstands are the seven churches.

Message to Ephesus

2 "To the angel of the church in Ephesus write: ¶ The One who holds the seven stars in His right hand, the One who walks among the seven golden lampstands, says this:

2 ¶ 'I know your deeds and your toil and perseverance, and that you cannot tolerate evil men, and you put to the test those who call themselves apostles, and they are not, and you found them *to be* false;

3 and you have perseverance and have endured for My name's sake, and have not grown weary.

4 'But I have *this* against you, that you have left your first love.

5 'Therefore remember from where you have fallen, and repent and do the deeds you did at first; or else I am coming to you and will remove your lampstand out of its place—unless you repent.

6 'Yet this you do have, that you hate the deeds of the Nicolaitans, which I also hate.

7 'He who has an ear, let him hear what the Spirit says to the churches. To him who overcomes, I will grant to eat of the tree of life which is in the Paradise of God.'

ᵃ Or *in spirit*   ᵇ Or *the Son of Man*

Message to Smyrna

8 ¶ "And to the angel of the church in Smyrna write:

¶ The first and the last, who was dead, and has come to life, says this:

9 ¶ 'I know your tribulation and your poverty (but you are rich), and the blasphemy by those who say they are Jews and are not, but are a synagogue of Satan.

10 'Do not fear what you are about to suffer. Behold, the devil is about to cast some of you into prison, so that you will be tested, and you will have tribulation for ten days. Be faithful until death, and I will give you the crown of life.

11 'He who has an ear, let him hear what the Spirit says to the churches. He who overcomes will not be hurt by the second death.'

Message to Pergamum

12 ¶ "And to the angel of the church in Pergamum write:

¶ The One who has the sharp two-edged sword says this:

13 ¶ 'I know where you dwell, where Satan's throne is; and you hold fast My name, and did not deny My faith even in the days of Antipas, My witness, My faithful one, who was killed among you, where Satan dwells.

2:13 Satan's Throne

When John wrote Revelation, the first century was drawing to a close. Now clearly separate from Judaism, the Christian church had lost its semi-official protection, and Roman emperors such as Nero had directed bloody persecutions. Antipas, mentioned here, was the first martyr of western Asia. The city of Pergamum served as headquarters for several pagan cults, and the practice of emperor worship spread from here throughout the region—possibly the meaning behind the phrase "where Satan dwells."

14 'But I have a few things against you, because you have there some who hold the teaching of Balaam, who kept teaching Balak to put a stumbling block before the sons of Israel, to eat things sacrificed to idols and to commit *acts of* immorality.

15 'So you also have some who in the same way hold the teaching of the Nicolaitans.

16 'Therefore repent; or else I am coming to you quickly, and I will make war against them with the sword of My mouth.

17 'He who has an ear, let him hear what the Spirit says to the churches. To him who overcomes, to him I will give *some* of the hidden man-

na, and I will give him a white stone, and a new name written on the stone which no one knows but he who receives it.'

Message to Thyatira

18 ¶ "And to the angel of the church in Thyatira write:

¶ The Son of God, who has eyes like a flame of fire, and His feet are like burnished bronze, says this:

19 ¶ 'I know your deeds, and your love and faith and service and perseverance, and that your deeds of late are greater than at first.

20 'But I have *this* against you, that you tolerate the woman Jezebel, who calls herself a prophetess, and she teaches and leads My bond-servants astray so that they commit *acts of* immorality and eat things sacrificed to idols.

21 'I gave her time to repent, and she does not want to repent of her immorality.

22 'Behold, I will throw her on a bed *of sickness*, and those who commit adultery with her into great tribulation, unless they repent of [a]her deeds.

23 'And I will kill her children with pestilence, and all the churches will know that I am He who searches the minds and hearts; and I will give to each one of you according to your deeds.

24 'But I say to you, the rest who are in Thyatira, who do not hold this teaching, who have not known the deep things of Satan, as they call them—I place no other burden on you.

25 'Nevertheless what you have, hold fast until I come.

26 'He who overcomes, and he who keeps My deeds until the end, TO HIM I WILL GIVE AUTHORITY OVER THE NATIONS;

27 AND HE SHALL RULE THEM WITH A ROD OF IRON, AS THE VESSELS OF THE POTTER ARE BROKEN TO PIECES, as I also have received *authority* from My Father;

28 and I will give him the morning star.

29 'He who has an ear, let him hear what the Spirit says to the churches.'

Message to Sardis

3 "To the angel of the church in Sardis write:

¶ He who has the seven Spirits of God and the seven stars, says this: 'I know your deeds, that you have a name that you are alive, but you are dead.

2 'Wake up, and strengthen the things that remain, which were about to die; for I have not found your deeds completed in the sight of My God.

3 'So remember what you have received and heard; and keep *it*, and repent. Therefore if you do not wake up, I will come like a thief, and you will not know at what hour I will come to you.

4 'But you have a few people in Sardis who

---

[a] One early ms reads *their*

have not soiled their garments; and they will walk with Me in white, for they are worthy.

5 'He who overcomes will thus be clothed in white garments; and I will not erase his name from

3:1 Cities on a Mail Route

The cities mentioned in chapters 2 and 3 were actual cities in the ancient world where a church existed. John listed them in the order in which a messenger on the road would have found them, starting with the chief city of Ephesus and then circling back clockwise. The cities lie in what is now part of modern Turkey. Religious wars took their toll: None of the churches in these cities survived.

the book of life, and I will confess his name before My Father and before His angels.

6 'He who has an ear, let him hear what the Spirit says to the churches.'

Message to Philadelphia

7 ¶ "And to the angel of the church in Philadelphia write:

¶ He who is holy, who is true, who has the key of David, who opens and no one will shut, and who shuts and no one opens, says this:

8 ¶ 'I know your ᵃdeeds. Behold, I have put before you an open door which no one can shut, because you have a little power, and have kept My word, and have not denied My name.

9 'Behold, I will cause *those* of the synagogue of Satan, who say that they are Jews and are not, but lie—I will make them come and bow down at your feet, and *make them* know that I have loved you.

10 'Because you have kept the word of My perseverance, I also will keep you from the hour of testing, that *hour* which is about to come upon the whole world, to test those who dwell on the earth.

11 'I am coming quickly; hold fast what you have, so that no one will take your crown.

12 'He who overcomes, I will make him a pillar in the temple of My God, and he will not go out from it anymore; and I will write on him the name of My God, and the name of the city of My God, the new Jerusalem, which comes down out of heaven from My God, and My new name.

13 'He who has an ear, let him hear what the Spirit says to the churches.'

Message to Laodicea

14 ¶ "To the angel of the church in Laodicea write:

¶ The Amen, the faithful and true Witness, the ᵇBeginning of the creation of God, says this:

15 ¶ 'I know your deeds, that you are neither cold nor hot; I wish that you were cold or hot.

16 'So because you are lukewarm, and neither hot nor cold, I will spit you out of My mouth.

17 'Because you say, "I am rich, and have become wealthy, and have need of nothing," and you do not know that you are wretched and miserable and poor and blind and naked,

18 I advise you to buy from Me gold refined by fire so that you may become rich, and white garments so that you may clothe yourself, and *that* the shame of your nakedness will not be revealed; and eye salve to anoint your eyes so that you may see.

19 'Those whom I love, I reprove and discipline; therefore be zealous and repent.

20 'Behold, I stand at the door and knock; if anyone hears My voice and opens the door, I will come in to him and will dine with him, and he with Me.

21 'He who overcomes, I will grant to him to sit down with Me on My throne, as I also overcame and sat down with My Father on His throne.

22 'He who has an ear, let him hear what the Spirit says to the churches.' "

Scene in Heaven

4 After these things I looked, and behold, a door *standing* open in heaven, and the first voice which I had heard, like *the sound* of a trumpet speaking with me, said, "Come up here, and I will show you what must take place after these things."

2 Immediately I was ᶜin the Spirit; and behold, a throne was standing in heaven, and One sitting on the throne.

3 And He who was sitting *was* like a jasper stone and a sardius in appearance; and *there was* a rainbow around the throne, like an emerald in appearance.

4 Around the throne *were* twenty-four thrones; and upon the thrones *I* saw twenty-four elders sitting, clothed in white garments, and golden crowns on their heads.

The Throne and Worship of the Creator

5 Out from the throne come flashes of lightning and sounds and peals of thunder. And *there were* seven lamps of fire burning before the throne, which are the seven Spirits of God;

6 and before the throne *there was something* like a sea of glass, like crystal; and in the center and around the throne, four living creatures full of eyes in front and behind.

7 The first creature *was* like a lion, and the second creature like a calf, and the third creature had a face like that of a man, and the fourth creature *was* like a flying eagle.

8 And the four living creatures, each one of them having six wings, are full of eyes around and within; and day and night they do not cease to say,

---

ᵃ Or *deeds (behold...shut), that you have*   ᵇ I.e. Origin or Source   ᶜ Or *in spirit*

"HOLY, HOLY, HOLY *is* THE LORD GOD, THE ALMIGHTY, WHO WAS AND WHO IS AND WHO IS TO COME."

9 And when the living creatures give glory

4:7 Strange Creatures

The Old Testament prophet Ezekiel had a somewhat similar vision (Ezekiel 1:9–10). In his version, however, each individual creature had four faces: human, lion, bull, and eagle. These symbols held special meaning for people of that day, much as the American eagle or British lion does today. For more information see "A Startling Image of Jesus," below.

---

and honor and thanks to Him who sits on the throne, to Him who lives forever and ever,

10 the twenty-four elders will fall down before Him who sits on the throne, and will worship Him

who lives forever and ever, and will cast their crowns before the throne, saying,

11 "Worthy are You, our Lord and our God, to receive glory and honor and power; for You created all things, and because of Your will they existed, and were created."

The Book with Seven Seals

5 I saw in the right hand of Him who sat on the throne a book written inside and on the back, sealed up with seven seals.

2 And I saw a strong angel proclaiming with a loud voice, "Who is worthy to open the book and to break its seals?"

3 And no one in heaven or on the earth or under the earth was able to open the book or to look into it.

4 Then I *began* to weep greatly because no one was found worthy to open the book or to look into it;

5 and one of the elders *said to me, "Stop weeping; behold, the Lion that is from the tribe of

---

A Startling Image of Jesus

A helpless lamb—the mightiest of all creatures

IMAGES OF JESUS ABOUND IN Revelation, and one way to study the book is to follow a single image through the entire book. After his luminous appearance in the first chapter, Jesus is presented as a king, a child, a warrior on a horse, the Lord of the whole earth, the husband of a bride. Of all the images, however, none is so startling and unlikely as the one in John's second vision. Yet it takes hold and appears repeatedly throughout the book.

> Then I began to weep greatly because no one was found worthy to open the book or to look into it. 5:4

To set the stage for this vision, the book of Revelation uses more visual drama than a science fiction movie. Lightning flashes, the sky growls, and awesome creatures encircle a lofty throne. Four of the creatures (4:6) seem to symbolize the most impressive examples of all creation, for a common saying in those days went,

> *The mightiest among the birds is the eagle.*
> *The mightiest among the domestic animals is the bull.*
> *The mightiest among the wild beasts is the lion.*
> *And the mightiest of all is man.*

Only One Worthy

A question resounds in the heavens, "Who is worthy to open the book and to break its seals?" (5:2). In other words, who is worthy to introduce the next phase of history? No one can answer, much to John's dismay. Not one of the four impressive creatures qualifies.

But suddenly John sees another creature, a "Lamb standing, as if slain" (5:6). The image contains a great paradox. None of the majestic angels or elders or living creatures has the right to break the seals. Only a Lamb does—a helpless, slaughtered Lamb.

John records a song of celebration ("Worthy are You to take the book and to break its seals; for You were slain, and purchased for God with Your blood men from every tribe and tongue and people and nation" [5:9]), a song later set to earthly music in Handel's *Messiah*. And elsewhere in Revelation true believers are identified as being recorded in the "Lamb's book of life" (21:27).

This powerful image resurfaces often in Revelation, a book of warfare between good and evil. Christ the King is also the Lamb, the one who died for us. His death on the cross, seemingly a great defeat, actually ushered in a decisive victory, for him and for us. Good was not destroyed; it triumphed.

Life Questions: What meaning does the image of Jesus as a slain Lamb have for you? What are your favorite "pictures" or images of Jesus?

Judah, the Root of David, has overcome so as to open the book and its seven seals."

6 ¶ And I saw ᵃbetween the throne (with the four living creatures) and the elders a Lamb standing, as if slain, having seven horns and seven eyes, which are the seven Spirits of God, sent out into all the earth.

5:1 Seals and Scrolls

Certain words and phrases used in Revelation had a clearer meaning to ancient readers familiar with the objects. For example, important documents were sent written on a papyrus scroll sealed with several wax seals. Only the proper person, in the presence of witnesses, could open the document. Thus in this vision, only the "worthy" creature is able to break the seal.

7 And He came and took the book out of the right hand of Him who sat on the throne.

8 When He had taken the book, the four living creatures and the twenty-four elders fell down before the Lamb, each one holding a harp and golden bowls full of incense, which are the prayers of the saints.

9 And they *sang a new song, saying,

"Worthy are You to take the book and to break its seals; for You were slain, and purchased for God with Your blood *men* from every tribe and tongue and people and nation.

10 "You have made them *to be* a kingdom and priests to our God; and they will reign upon the earth."

Angels Exalt the Lamb

11 ¶ Then I looked, and I heard the voice of many angels around the throne and the living creatures and the elders; and the number of them was myriads of myriads, and thousands of thousands,

12 saying with a loud voice,

"Worthy is the Lamb that was slain to receive power and riches and wisdom and might and honor and glory and blessing."

13 And every created thing which is in heaven and on the earth and under the earth and on the sea, and all things in them, I heard saying,

"To Him who sits on the throne, and to the Lamb, *be* blessing and honor and glory and dominion forever and ever."

14 And the four living creatures kept saying, "Amen." And the elders fell down and worshiped.

The Book Opened
The First Seal—The False Christ

6 Then I saw when the Lamb broke one of the seven seals, and I heard one of the four living creatures saying as with a voice of thunder, "Come."

2 I looked, and behold, a white horse, and he who sat on it had a bow; and a crown was given to him, and he went out conquering and to conquer.

The Second Seal—War

3 ¶ When He broke the second seal, I heard the second living creature saying, "Come."

4 And another, a red horse, went out; and to him who sat on it, it was granted to take peace from the earth, and that *men* would slay one another; and a great sword was given to him.

The Third Seal—Famine

5 ¶ When He broke the third seal, I heard the third living creature saying, "Come." I looked, and behold, a black horse; and he who sat on it had a pair of scales in his hand.

6 And I heard *something* like a voice in the center of the four living creatures saying, "A ᵇquart of wheat for a ᶜdenarius, and three quarts of barley for a denarius; and do not damage the oil and the wine."

The Fourth Seal—Death

7 ¶ When the Lamb broke the fourth seal, I heard the voice of the fourth living creature saying, "Come."

8 I looked, and behold, an ashen horse; and he who sat on it had the name Death; and Hades was following with him. Authority was given to them over a fourth of the earth, to kill with sword and with famine and with pestilence and by the wild beasts of the earth.

The Fifth Seal—Martyrs

9 ¶ When the Lamb broke the fifth seal, I saw underneath the altar the souls of those who had been slain because of the word of God, and because of the testimony which they had maintained;

10 and they cried out with a loud voice, saying, "How long, O Lord, holy and true, will You refrain from judging and avenging our blood on those who dwell on the earth?"

11 And there was given to each of them a white robe; and they were told that they should rest for a little while longer, until *the number of* their fellow servants and their brethren who were to be killed even as they had been, would be completed also.

ᵃ Lit *in the middle of the throne and of the four living creatures, and in the middle of the elders*   ᵇ Gr *choenix*; i.e. a dry measure almost equal to a qt   ᶜThe denarius was equivalent to a day's wages

The Sixth Seal—Terror

12 ¶ I looked when He broke the sixth seal, and there was a great earthquake; and the sun became black as sackcloth *made* of hair, and the whole moon became like blood;

13 and the stars of the sky fell to the earth, as a fig tree casts its unripe figs when shaken by a great wind.

14 The sky was split apart like a scroll when it is rolled up, and every mountain and island were moved out of their places.

15 Then the kings of the earth and the great men and the [a]commanders and the rich and the strong and every slave and free man hid themselves in the caves and among the rocks of the mountains;

16 and they *said to the mountains and to the rocks, "Fall on us and hide us from the presence of Him who sits on the throne, and from the wrath of the Lamb;

17 for the great day of their wrath has come, and who is able to stand?"

An Interlude

7 After this I saw four angels standing at the four corners of the earth, holding back the four winds of the earth, so that no wind would blow on the earth or on the sea or on any tree.

7:1 Significant Numbers

Numbers had a great symbolic significance in the Bible, and especially to the writer of Revelation. This concept is foreign to most modern readers; a rough parallel might be the "unlucky" significance some attach to the number 13. The most obviously symbolic numbers in Revelation are 4, 7, 12, and their multiples.

The number 4 seems to stand for the created universe (four points of the compass, four winds of the earth), and thus the four living creatures (4:6) represent all creation. In the Bible, the number 7 denotes perfection or completion, probably because the Genesis creation account covers seven days. The 12 tribes of Israel in the Old Testament and 12 apostles in the New Testament indicate that the number 12 stands for the church, or God's redeemed people from both covenants.

A number multiplied by 10s, such as 144,000 (12x12x10x10x10), suggests an indefinite but very large figure. Therefore, 144,000 may stand for the entire church throughout history.

2 And I saw another angel ascending from the rising of the sun, having the seal of the living God; and he cried out with a loud voice to the four angels to whom it was granted to harm the earth and the sea,

3 saying, "Do not harm the earth or the sea or the trees until we have sealed the bond-servants of our God on their foreheads."

A Remnant of Israel—144,000

4 ¶ And I heard the number of those who were sealed, one hundred and forty-four thousand sealed from every tribe of the sons of Israel:

5 from the tribe of Judah, twelve thousand *were* sealed, from the tribe of Reuben twelve thousand, from the tribe of Gad twelve thousand,

6 from the tribe of Asher twelve thousand, from the tribe of Naphtali twelve thousand, from the tribe of Manasseh twelve thousand,

7 from the tribe of Simeon twelve thousand, from the tribe of Levi twelve thousand, from the tribe of Issachar twelve thousand,

8 from the tribe of Zebulun twelve thousand, from the tribe of Joseph twelve thousand, from the tribe of Benjamin, twelve thousand *were* sealed.

A Multitude from the Tribulation

9 ¶ After these things I looked, and behold, a great multitude which no one could count, from every nation and *all* tribes and peoples and tongues, standing before the throne and before the Lamb, clothed in white robes, and palm branches *were* in their hands;

10 and they cry out with a loud voice, saying,

¶ "Salvation to our God who sits on the throne, and to the Lamb."

11 And all the angels were standing around the throne and *around* the elders and the four living creatures; and they fell on their faces before the throne and worshiped God,

12 saying,

¶ "Amen, blessing and glory and wisdom and thanksgiving and honor and power and might, *be* to our God forever and ever. Amen."

13 ¶ Then one of the elders answered, saying to me, "These who are clothed in the white robes, who are they, and where have they come from?"

14 I said to him, "My lord, you know." And he said to me, "These are the ones who come out of the great tribulation, and they have washed their robes and made them white in the blood of the Lamb.

15 "For this reason, they are before the throne of God; and they serve Him day and night in His temple; and He who sits on the throne will spread His tabernacle over them.

16 "They will hunger no longer, nor thirst anymore; nor will the sun beat down on them, nor any heat;

17 for the Lamb in the center of the throne will

---

[a] I.e. chiliarchs, in command of one thousand troops

be their shepherd, and will guide them to springs of the water of life; and God will wipe every tear from their eyes."

The Seventh Seal—the Trumpets

8 When the Lamb broke the seventh seal, there was silence in heaven for about half an hour.

7:14 The Great Tribulation

Bible interpreters have proposed many theories to explain "the great tribulation," a time of intense persecution for Christians. Some believe it will occur in the future, around the time of Christ's return. (For more detail, see "Forty-two Months of Trials," page 1380.) Others believe John was referring to persecutions against the church occurring in his own day. Regardless, John stresses the overarching promise that the time of tribulation does not last forever. One day the faithful will no longer hunger or thirst and will never again have reason to cry (verses 16–17).

2 And I saw the seven angels who stand before God, and seven trumpets were given to them.

3 ¶ Another angel came and stood at the altar, holding a golden censer; and much incense was given to him, so that he might add it to the prayers of all the saints on the golden altar which was before the throne.

4 And the smoke of the incense, with the prayers of the saints, went up before God out of the angel's hand.

5 Then the angel took the censer and filled it with the fire of the altar, and threw it to the earth; and there followed peals of thunder and sounds and flashes of lightning and an earthquake.

8:1 Dramatic Structure

Revelation unfolds with a sense of ever-increasing drama, hinged on the symbolic number 7. Here, heaven itself pauses in silence before the opening of the seventh seal. Chapter 11 includes a long pause before the seventh trumpet sounds its judgment. Finally, in chapter 16 the seventh bowl introduces the greatest calamity of all, the battle of Armageddon.

6 ¶ And the seven angels who had the seven trumpets prepared themselves to sound them.

7 ¶ The first sounded, and there came hail and fire, mixed with blood, and they were thrown to the earth; and a third of the earth was burned up, and a third of the trees were burned up, and all the green grass was burned up.

8 ¶ The second angel sounded, and *something* like a great mountain burning with fire was thrown into the sea; and a third of the sea became blood,

9 and a third of the creatures which were in the sea and had life, died; and a third of the ships were destroyed.

10 ¶ The third angel sounded, and a great star fell from heaven, burning like a torch, and it fell on a third of the rivers and on the springs of waters.

11 The name of the star is called Wormwood; and a third of the waters became wormwood, and many men died from the waters, because they were made bitter.

12 ¶ The fourth angel sounded, and a third of the sun and a third of the moon and a third of the stars were struck, so that a third of them would be darkened and the day would not shine for a third of it, and the night in the same way.

13 ¶ Then I looked, and I heard an eagle flying in midheaven, saying with a loud voice, "Woe, woe, woe to those who dwell on the earth, because of the remaining blasts of the trumpet of the three angels who are about to sound!"

The Fifth Trumpet—the Bottomless Pit

9 Then the fifth angel sounded, and I saw a star from heaven which had fallen to the earth; and the key of the bottomless pit was given to him.

2 He opened the bottomless pit, and smoke went up out of the pit, like the smoke of a great furnace; and the sun and the air were darkened by the smoke of the pit.

3 Then out of the smoke came locusts upon the earth, and power was given them, as the scorpions of the earth have power.

4 They were told not to hurt the grass of the earth, nor any green thing, nor any tree, but only the men who do not have the seal of God on their foreheads.

5 And they were not permitted to kill anyone, but to torment for five months; and their torment was like the torment of a scorpion when it stings a man.

6 And in those days men will seek death and will not find it; they will long to die, and death flees from them.

7 ¶ The appearance of the locusts was like horses prepared for battle; and on their heads appeared to be crowns like gold, and their faces were like the faces of men.

8 They had hair like the hair of women, and their teeth were like *the teeth* of lions.

9 They had breastplates like breastplates of iron; and the sound of their wings was like the sound of chariots, of many horses rushing to battle.

10 They have tails like scorpions, and stings; and in their tails is their power to hurt men for five months.

11 They have as king over them, the angel of the abyss; his name in Hebrew is *a*Abaddon, and in the Greek he has the name Apollyon.

12 ¶ The first woe is past; behold, two woes are still coming after these things.

a I.e. destruction   *b* Two early mss do not contain *four*

The Sixth Trumpet—Army from the East

13 ¶ Then the sixth angel sounded, and I heard a voice from the *b*four horns of the golden altar which is before God,

14 one saying to the sixth angel who had the

Revelation's Use of Symbols
Why are there so many theories explaining Revelation?

"THERE NEVER HAS BEEN A book provoking more delirium, foolishness, and irrational movements, without any relationship to Jesus Christ," concluded Jacques Ellul, author of a commentary on Revelation. Readers tend to fixate wildly on details, mainly because John relied so heavily on symbols to express his meaning in this book.

Creatures covered with eyes and sprouting horns, eagles wheeling in the sky, molten mountains hurtling into the ocean—such rich imagery excites frenzied attempts to explain every word. John interprets some symbols for us—"The seven stars are the angels of the seven churches" (1:20)—and hints broadly at the meaning of others, such as the four horsemen in chapter 6. But many questions remain unanswered. For example, do the major visions describe consecutive periods of history, or do they foretell the same events from different angles?

> The appearance of the locusts was like horses prepared for battle; and on their heads appeared to be crowns like gold, and their faces were like the faces of men. 9:7

Look at the Broad Picture

Artists find that symbols communicate with special power. When Spanish artist Pablo Picasso painted his massive *Guernica*, he attempted to express what had happened in war-ravaged Spain on April 28, 1937. He created a work of art, not a photographic record. The painting does communicate the tragedy at Guernica, but artfully, symbolically.

In a similar way, John poetically renders human events so strange and climactic as to be otherwise inexpressible. If he had wanted to, God could have revealed a precise timetable of future events, but instead Jesus warned specifically against such speculation about the future. In keeping with that approach, Revelation does not so much outline future events as hint at the cosmic significance that goes on *behind* history.

Readers new to Revelation should start by viewing scenes as a whole, looking for an overall meaning. The visions are like Jesus' parables: Each has a main thrust, and some of the details may serve merely to dramatize or add literary fullness to the scene. No one can find the precise meaning behind every detail in John's visions. Those who seek to explain each symbol too quickly may easily miss the meaning of the symbol as well as the grand emotional sweep of the book.

Searching for a System

Revelation will always attract scholars who search for the meaning behind each symbol. It is no easy undertaking: Over 300 allusions to the Old Testament and an elaborate system of symbolic numbers must be factored into any explanation. History has proved thousands of explainers wrong. People from every generation—especially in the hectic days around A.D. 1000 and in the 14th and 19th centuries, as well as in contemporary times dominated by Middle East tensions—have insisted the end of the world was just around the corner.

Today, some believe that Revelation's symbols—statues that talk, fire coming from heaven, totalitarian economic control, massive changes in the earth and sea—come hauntingly close to 20th-century phenomena. The wholesale devastation of earth prophesied in the middle chapters seems eerily up-to-date.

Yet, calamities merely provide a backdrop to John's main thrust: Followers of Christ will be made safe at last. "God will wipe every tear from their eyes," he says (7:17). Much of Revelation remains shrouded in mystery, but the final results shine out clearly.

Life Questions: Two potential dangers in reading Revelation (see Introduction) are avoiding it entirely or getting obsessed with its details. Which danger are you most familiar with? Why do we need the message of Revelation today?

trumpet, "Release the four angels who are bound at the great river Euphrates."

15 And the four angels, who had been prepared for the hour and day and month and year,

9:12 Judgments for a Purpose

Revelation records a number of severe judgments, in chapters 6, 9, and 16. It carefully mentions the purpose of these judgments: to convince humankind that its rebellion is futile and encourage it to repent (9:20). In this way, the judgments are similar to the 10 plagues against Egypt. Like the 10 plagues, these judgments do not ultimately work. The failure of people to repent makes necessary the final judgment against the source of all evil.

were released, so that they would kill a third of mankind.

16 The number of the armies of the horsemen was two hundred million; I heard the number of them.

17 And this is how I saw in the vision the horses and those who sat on them: *the riders* had breastplates *the color* of fire and of hyacinth and of brimstone; and the heads of the horses are like the heads of lions; and out of their mouths proceed fire and smoke and brimstone.

18 A third of mankind was killed by these three plagues, by the fire and the smoke and the brimstone which proceeded out of their mouths.

19 For the power of the horses is in their mouths and in their tails; for their tails are like serpents and have heads, and with them they do harm.

20 ¶ The rest of mankind, who were not killed by these plagues, did not repent of the works of their hands, so as not to worship demons, and the idols of gold and of silver and of brass and of stone and of wood, which can neither see nor hear nor walk;

21 and they did not repent of their murders nor of their sorceries nor of their immorality nor of their thefts.

The Angel and the Little Book

10 I saw another strong angel coming down out of heaven, clothed with a cloud; and the rainbow was upon his head, and his face was like the sun, and his feet like pillars of fire;

2 and he had in his hand a little book which was open. He placed his right foot on the sea and his left on the land;

3 and he cried out with a loud voice, as when a lion roars; and when he had cried out, the seven peals of thunder uttered their voices.

4 When the seven peals of thunder had spoken, I was about to write; and I heard a voice from heaven saying, "Seal up the things which the seven

peals of thunder have spoken and do not write them."

5 Then the angel whom I saw standing on the sea and on the land lifted up his right hand to heaven,

6 and swore by Him who lives forever and ever, WHO CREATED HEAVEN AND THE THINGS IN IT, AND THE EARTH AND THE THINGS IN IT, AND THE SEA AND THE THINGS IN IT, that there will be delay no longer,

7 but in the days of the voice of the seventh angel, when he is about to sound, then the mystery of God is finished, as He preached to His servants the prophets.

8 ¶ Then the voice which I heard from heaven, *I heard* again speaking with me, and saying, "Go, take the book which is open in the hand of the angel who stands on the sea and on the land."

9 So I went to the angel, telling him to give me the little book. And he *said to me, "Take it and eat it; it will make your stomach bitter, but in your mouth it will be sweet as honey."

10 I took the little book out of the angel's hand and ate it, and in my mouth it was sweet as honey; and when I had eaten it, my stomach was made bitter.

11 And they *said to me, "You must prophesy again concerning many peoples and nations and tongues and kings."

The Two Witnesses

11 Then there was given me a measuring rod like a staff; and someone said, "Get up and measure the temple of God and the altar, and those who worship in it.

11:1 Old Testament Echoes

A full understanding of Revelation requires detailed study of such Old Testament prophets as Ezekiel and Daniel. John frequently borrows images from those books. For example, the passage here on the temple of God parallels Ezekiel 40. Similarly, many passages referring to kings and political empires are reminiscent of Daniel's visions.

2 "Leave out the court which is outside the temple and do not measure it, for it has been given to the nations; and they will tread under foot the holy city for forty-two months.

3 "And I will grant *authority* to my two witnesses, and they will prophesy for twelve hundred and sixty days, clothed in sackcloth."

4 These are the two olive trees and the two lampstands that stand before the Lord of the earth.

5 And if anyone wants to harm them, fire flows out of their mouth and devours their ene-

mies; so if anyone wants to harm them, he must be killed in this way.

6 These have the power to shut up the sky, so that rain will not fall during the days of their prophesying; and they have power over the waters to turn them into blood, and to strike the earth with every plague, as often as they desire.

7 ¶ When they have finished their testimony, the beast that comes up out of the abyss will make war with them, and overcome them and kill them.

8 And their dead bodies *will lie* in the street of the great city which [a]mystically is called Sodom and Egypt, where also their Lord was crucified.

9 Those from the peoples and tribes and tongues and nations *will* look at their dead [b]bodies for three and a half days, and will not permit their dead bodies to be laid in a tomb.

10 And those who dwell on the earth *will* rejoice over them and celebrate; and they will send gifts to one another, because these two prophets tormented those who dwell on the earth.

11 ¶ But after the three and a half days, the breath of life from God came into them, and they stood on their feet; and great fear fell upon those who were watching them.

12 And they heard a loud voice from heaven saying to them, "Come up here." Then they went up into heaven in the cloud, and their enemies watched them.

13 And in that hour there was a great earthquake, and a tenth of the city fell; seven thousand people were killed in the earthquake, and the rest were terrified and gave glory to the God of heaven.

14 ¶ The second woe is past; behold, the third woe is coming quickly.

The Seventh Trumpet—Christ's Reign Foreseen

15 ¶ Then the seventh angel sounded; and there were loud voices in heaven, saying,

¶ "The kingdom of the world has become *the kingdom* of our Lord and of His [c]Christ; and He will reign forever and ever."

16 And the twenty-four elders, who sit on their thrones before God, fell on their faces and worshiped God,

17 saying,

¶ "We give You thanks, O Lord God, the Almighty, who are and who were, because You have taken Your great power and have begun to reign.

18 "And the nations were enraged, and Your wrath came, and the time *came* for the dead to be judged, and *the time* to reward Your bondservants the prophets and the saints and those who fear Your name, the small and the great, and to destroy those who destroy the earth."

19 ¶ And the temple of God which is in heaven was opened; and the ark of His covenant appeared in His temple, and there were flashes of lightning

and sounds and peals of thunder and an earthquake and a great hailstorm.

The Woman, Israel

12 A great sign appeared in heaven: a woman clothed with the sun, and the moon under her feet, and on her head a crown of twelve stars;

2 and she was with child; and she *cried out, being in labor and in pain to give birth.

The Red Dragon, Satan

3 Then another sign appeared in heaven: and behold, a great red dragon having seven heads and ten horns, and on his heads *were* seven diadems.

4 And his tail *swept away a third of the stars of heaven and threw them to the earth. And the dragon stood before the woman who was about to give birth, so that when she gave birth he might devour her child.

The Male Child, Christ

5 And she gave birth to a son, a male *child*, who is to rule all the nations with a rod of iron; and her child was caught up to God and to His throne.

6 Then the woman fled into the wilderness where she *had a place prepared by God, so that there she would be nourished for one thousand two hundred and sixty days.

The Angel, Michael

7 ¶ And there was war in heaven, Michael and his angels waging war with the dragon. The dragon and his angels waged war,

8 and they were not strong enough, and there was no longer a place found for them in heaven.

9 And the great dragon was thrown down, the serpent of old who is called the devil and Satan, who deceives the whole world; he was thrown down to the earth, and his angels were thrown down with him.

10 Then I heard a loud voice in heaven, saying,

¶ "Now the salvation, and the power, and the kingdom of our God and the authority of His Christ have come, for the accuser of our brethren has been thrown down, he who accuses them before our God day and night.

11 "And they overcame him because of the blood of the Lamb and because of the word of their testimony, and they did not love their life even when faced with death.

12 "For this reason, rejoice, O heavens and you who dwell in them. Woe to the earth and the sea, because the devil has come down to you, having great wrath, knowing that he has *only* a short time."

13 ¶ And when the dragon saw that he was thrown down to the earth, he persecuted the woman who gave birth to the male *child*.

14 But the two wings of the great eagle were

---

[a] Lit *spiritually*   [b] Lit *body*   [c] I.e. Messiah

given to the woman, so that she could fly into the wilderness to her place, where she *was nourished for a time and times and half a time, from the presence of the serpent.

15 And the serpent poured water like a river out of his mouth after the woman, so that he might cause her to be swept away with the flood.

16 But the earth helped the woman, and the earth opened its mouth and drank up the river which the dragon poured out of his mouth.

17 So the dragon was enraged with the woman, and went off to make war with the rest of her children, who keep the commandments of God and hold to the testimony of Jesus.

The Beast from the Sea

13 And the dragon stood on the sand of the seashore.

¶ Then I saw a beast coming up out of the sea, having ten horns and seven heads, and on his horns *were* ten diadems, and on his heads *were* blasphemous names.

2 And the beast which I saw was like a leopard, and his feet were like *those* of a bear, and his mouth like the mouth of a lion. And the dragon gave him his power and his throne and great authority.

3 *I saw* one of his heads as if it had been slain, and his fatal wound was healed. And the whole earth was amazed *and followed* after the beast;

4 they worshiped the dragon because he gave his authority to the beast; and they worshiped the beast, saying, "Who is like the beast, and who is able to wage war with him?"

5 There was given to him a mouth speaking arrogant words and blasphemies, and authority to act for forty-two months was given to him.

6 And he opened his mouth in blasphemies

A Look Behind the Scenes
Christmas from heaven's perspective

CHRISTMAS DAY. WE CELEBRATE IT with a sudden splurge of money and gifts and an attempt to rediscover the joy of the first Christmas. Manger displays in town squares recreate the scene in Bethlehem on that day long ago.

As many interpret it, chapter 12 describes Christmas day also, but its point of view differs radically from that of the Gospels. Revelation does not tell of shepherds, a crazed king bent on infanticide, and a stable; rather, it pictures a murderous dragon leading a ferocious struggle in heaven. His attack when Christ was born launches a series of bloody rebellions against the forces of good.

> The dragon stood before the woman who was about to give birth, so that when she gave birth he might devour her child. 12:4

Two Histories at Once

The view of Christ's birth in Revelation 12 gives a glimpse into the pattern of the entire book. John is fusing things seen with things normally not seen. In daily life, two parallel histories occur simultaneously: one on earth and one in heaven. Revelation, however, views them together. It parts the curtain, allowing a quick look behind the scenes at the cosmic impact of what happens on earth.

Every inch of this planet is claimed by God and counterclaimed by Satan. We normally experience only the visible, everyday effects of this struggle. We feel it, for example, when we make a choice between what we know is wrong and what is right. But, as we are living out our lives on earth, the supernatural universe is simultaneously at war. Revelation draws the contrasts sharply: good versus evil, the Lamb versus the dragon, Jerusalem versus Babylon, the bride versus the prostitute.

Is God in Control of History?

Sometimes the "war in heaven" can break out into actual violence on earth, as it did when Jesus came. Revelation was originally written to people who were facing extreme persecution from the Roman empire. Revelation establishes that a war is being waged on this planet between good and evil, a war that reflects a larger struggle in the whole universe. But, no matter how it looks, God is in firm control of history. To first-century Christians, Rome was the arch-villain, and allusions to that empire crop up in these chapters. John asserts that Jesus Christ, and not an emperor, determines the flow of history.

Events are marching onward to a definite climax; history has meaning. Ultimately, even the despots of history will end up fulfilling the plan mapped out for them by God. Pontius Pilate and his Roman soldiers demonstrated that truth starkly. They thought they were getting rid of Jesus by crucifying him. Instead, they made possible the salvation of the world.

Life Questions: As Revelation tells it, events that appear tragic can work great good. Have you ever experienced that in your life?

against God, to blaspheme His name and His tabernacle, *that is*, those who dwell in heaven.

7 ¶ It was also given to him to make war with the saints and to overcome them, and authority

---

13:5 Forty-two Months of Trials

This mysterious number has prompted much speculation. Literally it means "a time, times and half a time" (see 12:14), that is, one year plus two years plus half a year, or three and a half years. It occurs several places in Revelation. Could it simply be half the perfect number 7, thus representing the age of the new covenant (the time between the first and second coming of Christ)? Or does it refer to literal months: a brief but intense three-and-one-half year period of great persecution against the church? If so, did these 42 months already take place during the Roman persecutions of Christians? Or are they still in the future?

Those who believe the 42 months are in the future frequently speak of the period as "the great tribulation" and call the beast the antichrist, a name used elsewhere in the Bible. Several schools of thought have developed around the tribulation. Pre-tribulationists believe that Jesus will come to remove the church from earth just before the great tribulation. Post-tribulationists believe the church will go through a time of trials before Jesus returns. Mid-tribulationists believe the church will be taken away during the tribulation.

---

over every tribe and people and tongue and nation was given to him.

8 All who dwell on the earth will worship him, *everyone* whose name has not been [a]written from the foundation of the world in the book of life of the Lamb who has been slain.

9 If anyone has an ear, let him hear.

10 If anyone [b]*is destined* for captivity, to captivity he goes; if anyone kills with the sword, with the sword he must be killed. Here is the perseverance and the faith of the saints.

The Beast from the Earth

11 ¶ Then I saw another beast coming up out of the earth; and he had two horns like a lamb and he spoke as a dragon.

12 He exercises all the authority of the first beast in his presence. And he makes the earth and those who dwell in it to worship the first beast, whose fatal wound was healed.

13 He performs great signs, so that he even

makes fire come down out of heaven to the earth in the presence of men.

14 And he deceives those who dwell on the earth because of the signs which it was given him to perform in the presence of the beast, telling those who dwell on the earth to make an image to the beast who *had the wound of the sword and has come to life.

15 And it was given to him to give breath to the image of the beast, so that the image of the beast would even [c]speak and cause as many as do not worship the image of the beast to be killed.

16 And he causes all, the small and the great, and the rich and the poor, and the free men and the slaves, to be given a mark on their right hand or on their forehead,

17 and *he provides* that no one will be able to buy or to sell, except the one who has the mark, *either* the name of the beast or the number of his name.

18 Here is wisdom. Let him who has understanding calculate the number of the beast, for the number is that of a man; and his number is [d]six hundred and sixty-six.

The Lamb and the 144,000 on Mount Zion

14 Then I looked, and behold, the Lamb *was* standing on Mount Zion, and with Him one hundred and forty-four thousand, having His name and the name of His Father written on their foreheads.

14:1 Good News with Bad

According to Revelation, human history will end not with a whimper but with a series of loud bangs. And yet John frequently reminds his readers that the spasms of violence will lead to a time of eternal peace, with God ruling over a restored heaven and earth. The peaceful scene of a heavenly choir in this chapter is sandwiched between two accounts of tribulation and judgment. John drops in such scenes like orchestral interludes in the midst of a tumultuous opera: They reassure us of a future in which all creation performs together in harmony.

---

2 And I heard a voice from heaven, like the sound of many waters and like the sound of loud thunder, and the voice which I heard *was* like *the sound* of harpists playing on their harps.

3 And they *sang a new song before the throne and before the four living creatures and the elders; and no one could learn the song except the one hundred and forty-four thousand who had been purchased from the earth.

4 These are the ones who have not been de-

---

[a] Or *written in the book...slain from the foundation of the world and he will cause*   [d] One early ms reads 616

[b] Or leads *into captivity*   [c] One early ms reads *speak,*

filed with women, for they [a]have kept themselves chaste. These *are* the ones who follow the Lamb wherever He goes. These have been purchased from among men as first fruits to God and to the Lamb.

5 And no lie was found in their mouth; they are blameless.

Vision of the Angel with the Gospel

6 ¶ And I saw another angel flying in midheaven, having an eternal gospel to preach to those who live on the earth, and to every nation and tribe and tongue and people;

7 and he said with a loud voice, "Fear God, and give Him glory, because the hour of His judgment has come; worship Him who made the heaven and the earth and sea and springs of waters."

8 ¶ And another angel, a second one, followed, saying, "Fallen, fallen is Babylon the great, she who has made all the nations drink of the wine of the passion of her immorality."

Doom for Worshipers of the Beast

9 ¶ Then another angel, a third one, followed them, saying with a loud voice, "If anyone worships the beast and his image, and receives a mark on his forehead or on his hand,

10 he also will drink of the wine of the wrath of God, which is mixed in full strength in the cup of His anger; and he will be tormented with fire and brimstone in the presence of the holy angels and in the presence of the Lamb.

11 "And the smoke of their torment goes up forever and ever; they have no rest day and night, those who worship the beast and his image, and whoever receives the mark of his name."

12 Here is the perseverance of the saints who keep the commandments of God and their faith in Jesus.

13 ¶ And I heard a voice from heaven, saying, "Write, 'Blessed are the dead who die in the Lord from now on!' " "Yes," says the Spirit, "so that they may rest from their labors, for their deeds follow with them."

The Reapers

14 ¶ Then I looked, and behold, a white cloud, and sitting on the cloud *was* one like [b]a son of man, having a golden crown on His head and a sharp sickle in His hand.

15 And another angel came out of the temple, crying out with a loud voice to Him who sat on the cloud, "Put in your sickle and reap, for the hour to reap has come, because the harvest of the earth is ripe."

16 Then He who sat on the cloud swung His sickle over the earth, and the earth was reaped.

17 ¶ And another angel came out of the temple which is in heaven, and he also had a sharp sickle.

18 Then another angel, the one who has power over fire, came out from the altar; and he called with a loud voice to him who had the sharp sickle, saying, "Put in your sharp sickle and gather the clusters from the vine of the earth, because her grapes are ripe."

19 So the angel swung his sickle to the earth and gathered *the clusters from* the vine of the earth, and threw them into the great wine press of the wrath of God.

20 And the wine press was trodden outside the city, and blood came out from the wine press, up to the horses' bridles, for a distance of [c]two hundred miles.

A Scene of Heaven

15 Then I saw another sign in heaven, great and marvelous, seven angels who had seven plagues, *which are* the last, because in them the wrath of God is finished.

2 ¶ And I saw something like a sea of glass mixed with fire, and those who had been victorious over the beast and his image and the number of his name, standing on the sea of glass, holding harps of God.

3 And they *sang the song of Moses, the bond-servant of God, and the song of the Lamb, saying,

¶ "Great and marvelous are Your works,
O Lord God, the Almighty;
Righteous and true are Your ways,
King of the [d]nations!
4 "Who will not fear, O Lord, and glorify
Your name?
For You alone are holy;
For ALL THE NATIONS WILL COME AND
WORSHIP BEFORE YOU,
FOR YOUR RIGHTEOUS ACTS HAVE BEEN
REVEALED."

5 ¶ After these things I looked, and the temple of the tabernacle of testimony in heaven was opened,

6 and the seven angels who had the seven plagues came out of the temple, clothed in [e]linen, clean *and* bright, and girded around their chests with golden sashes.

7 Then one of the four living creatures gave to the seven angels seven golden bowls full of the wrath of God, who lives forever and ever.

8 And the temple was filled with smoke from the glory of God and from His power; and no one was able to enter the temple until the seven plagues of the seven angels were finished.

Six Bowls of Wrath

16 Then I heard a loud voice from the temple, saying to the seven angels, "Go and pour out on the earth the seven bowls of the wrath of God."

---

[a] Lit *are chaste men*   [b] Or *the Son of Man*   [c] Lit *sixteen hundred stadia*; a stadion was approx 600 ft   [d] Two early mss read *ages*   [e] One early ms reads *stone*

2 ¶ So the first *angel* went and poured out his bowl on the earth; and it became a loathsome and malignant sore on the people who had the mark of the beast and who worshiped his image.

3 ¶ The second *angel* poured out his bowl into the sea, and it became blood like *that* of a dead man; and every living ªthing in the sea died.

4 ¶ Then the third *angel* poured out his bowl into the rivers and the springs of waters; and they became blood.

5 And I heard the angel of the waters saying, "Righteous are You, who are and who were, O Holy One, because You judged these things;

6 for they poured out the blood of saints and prophets, and You have given them blood to drink. They deserve it."

7 And I heard the altar saying, "Yes, O Lord God, the Almighty, true and righteous are Your judgments."

8 ¶ The fourth *angel* poured out his bowl upon the sun, and it was given to it to scorch men with fire.

9 Men were scorched with fierce heat; and they blasphemed the name of God who has the power over these plagues, and they did not repent so as to give Him glory.

10 ¶ Then the fifth *angel* poured out his bowl on the throne of the beast, and his kingdom became darkened; and they gnawed their tongues because of pain,

11 and they blasphemed the God of heaven because of their pains and their sores; and they did not repent of their deeds.

12 ¶ The sixth *angel* poured out his bowl on the great river, the Euphrates; and its water was dried up, so that the way would be prepared for the kings from the east.

Armageddon

13 And I saw *coming* out of the mouth of the dragon and out of the mouth of the beast and out of the mouth of the false prophet, three unclean spirits like frogs;

14 for they are spirits of demons, performing signs, which go out to the kings of the whole world, to gather them together for the war of the great day of God, the Almighty.

15 ("Behold, I am coming like a thief. Blessed is the one who stays awake and keeps his clothes, so that he will not walk about naked and men will not see his shame.")

16 And they gathered them together to the place which in Hebrew is called ᵇHar-Magedon.

Seventh Bowl of Wrath

17 ¶ Then the seventh *angel* poured out his bowl upon the air, and a loud voice came out of the temple from the throne, saying, "It is done."

18 And there were flashes of lightning and sounds and peals of thunder; and there was a great earthquake, such as there had not been since man came to be upon the earth, so great an earthquake *was it, and* so mighty.

19 The great city was split into three parts, and the cities of the nations fell. Babylon the great was remembered before God, to give her the cup of the wine of His fierce wrath.

16:16 The Battle of Armageddon

Armageddon has been the site of many military struggles in Israel's history. Some historians estimate more wars have been fought here than any other location in the world. It is an appropriate setting (or symbol) for the final struggle between good and evil.

20 And every island fled away, and the mountains were not found.

21 And huge hailstones, about ᶜone hundred pounds each, *came down from heaven upon men; and men blasphemed God because of the plague of the hail, because its plague *was extremely severe.

The Doom of Babylon

17 Then one of the seven angels who had the seven bowls came and spoke with me, saying, "Come here, I will show you the judgment of the great harlot who sits on many waters,

2 with whom the kings of the earth committed *acts of* immorality, and those who dwell on the earth were made drunk with the wine of her immorality."

3 And he carried me away ᵈin the Spirit into a wilderness; and I saw a woman sitting on a scarlet beast, full of blasphemous names, having seven heads and ten horns.

4 The woman was clothed in purple and scarlet, and adorned with gold and precious stones and pearls, having in her hand a gold cup full of abominations and of the unclean things of her immorality,

5 and on her forehead a name *was* written, a mystery, "BABYLON THE GREAT, THE MOTHER OF HARLOTS AND OF THE ABOMINATIONS OF THE EARTH."

6 And I saw the woman drunk with the blood of the saints, and with the blood of the witnesses of Jesus. When I saw her, I wondered greatly.

7 And the angel said to me, "Why do you wonder? I will tell you the mystery of the woman and of the beast that carries her, which has the seven heads and the ten horns.

8 ¶ "The beast that you saw was, and is not, and is about to come up out of the abyss and ᵉgo

---

ª Lit *soul*   ᵇ Two early mss read *Armagedon*   ᶜ Lit *the weight of a talent*   ᵈ Or *in spirit*   ᵉ One early ms reads *is going* to destruction. And those who dwell on the earth, whose name has not been written in the book of life from the foundation of the world, will wonder when they see the beast, that he was and is not and will come.

9 "Here is the mind which has wisdom. The seven heads are seven mountains on which the woman sits,

10 and they are seven kings; five have fallen, one is, the other has not yet come; and when he comes, he must remain a little while.

11 "The beast which was and is not, is himself also an eighth and is *one* of the seven, and he goes to destruction.

12 "The ten horns which you saw are ten kings who have not yet received a kingdom, but they receive authority as kings with the beast for one hour.

13 "These have one purpose, and they give their power and authority to the beast.

Victory for the Lamb

14 "These will wage war against the Lamb, and the Lamb will overcome them, because He is Lord of lords and King of kings, and those who are with Him *are the* called and chosen and faithful."

15 ¶ And he *said to me, "The waters which you saw where the harlot sits, are peoples and multitudes and nations and tongues.

16 "And the ten horns which you saw, and the beast, these will hate the harlot and will make her desolate and naked, and will eat her flesh and will burn her up with fire.

17 "For God has put it in their hearts to execute His purpose by having a common purpose, and by giving their kingdom to the beast, until the words of God will be fulfilled.

18 "The woman whom you saw is the great city, which reigns over the kings of the earth."

Babylon Is Fallen

18 After these things I saw another angel coming down from heaven, having great authority, and the earth was illumined with his glory.

2 And he cried out with a mighty voice, saying, "Fallen, fallen is Babylon the great! She has become a dwelling place of demons and a prison of every unclean spirit, and a prison of every unclean and hateful bird.

3 "For all the nations *a*have drunk of the wine of the passion of her immorality, and the kings of the earth have committed *acts of* immorality with her, and the merchants of the earth have become rich by the wealth of her sensuality."

4 ¶ I heard another voice from heaven, saying, "Come out of her, my people, so that you will not participate in her sins and receive of her plagues;

5 for her sins have piled up as high as heaven, and God has remembered her iniquities.

6 "Pay her back even as she has paid, and give back *to her* double according to her deeds; in the cup which she has mixed, mix twice as much for her.

18:2 What Is Babylon?

Many people believe Babylon was a coded substitute for Rome, the city set on seven hills (17:9). Revelation was almost surely written to Christians undergoing great persecution from harsh Roman emperors. Scholars who see Babylon as Rome sometimes try to identify the kings mentioned here as specific Roman rulers.

However, not all interpreters agree. Some suggest that Babylon stands for Jerusalem, and others believe we cannot clearly identify Babylon. Rather, they say, it can represent all powerful world systems that kill faithful Christians and seduce people away from God. Regardless, chapter 18 reveals that the great enemy, Babylon, will disappear forever (verse 21).

---

7 "To the degree that she glorified herself and lived sensuously, to the same degree give her torment and mourning; for she says in her heart, 'I SIT *as* A QUEEN AND I AM NOT A WIDOW, and will never see mourning.'

8 "For this reason in one day her plagues will come, pestilence and mourning and famine, and she will be burned up with fire; for the Lord God who judges her is strong.

Lament for Babylon

9 ¶ "And the kings of the earth, who committed *acts of* immorality and lived sensuously with her, will weep and lament over her when they see the smoke of her burning,

10 standing at a distance because of the fear of her torment, saying, 'Woe, woe, the great city, Babylon, the strong city! For in one hour your judgment has come.'

11 ¶ "And the merchants of the earth weep and mourn over her, because no one buys their cargoes any more—

12 cargoes of gold and silver and precious stones and pearls and fine linen and purple and silk and scarlet, and every *kind of* citron wood and every article of ivory and every article *made* from very costly wood and bronze and iron and marble,

13 and cinnamon and spice and incense and perfume and frankincense and wine and olive oil and fine flour and wheat and cattle and sheep, and *cargoes* of horses and chariots and slaves and human lives.

14 "The fruit you long for has gone from you, and all things that were luxurious and splendid

---

a Two early ancient mss read *have fallen by*

have passed away from you and *men* will no longer find them.

15 "The merchants of these things, who became rich from her, will stand at a distance because of the fear of her torment, weeping and mourning,

16 saying, 'Woe, woe, the great city, she who was clothed in fine linen and purple and scarlet, and adorned with gold and precious stones and pearls;

17 for in one hour such great wealth has been laid waste!' And every shipmaster and every passenger and sailor, and as many as make their living by the sea, stood at a distance,

18 and were crying out as they saw the smoke of her burning, saying, 'What *city* is like the great city?'

19 "And they threw dust on their heads and were crying out, weeping and mourning, saying, 'Woe, woe, the great city, in which all who had ships at sea became rich by her wealth, for in one hour she has been laid waste!'

20 "Rejoice over her, O heaven, and you saints and apostles and prophets, because God has pronounced judgment for you against her."

21 ¶ Then a strong angel took up a stone like a great millstone and threw it into the sea, saying, "So will Babylon, the great city, be thrown down with violence, and will not be found any longer.

18:21 Newspaper Prophecy

The fact that Baghdad, Iraq, sits just 50 miles from the historical site of Babylon led some commentators to predict that the Gulf War of 1991 would escalate into the battle of Armageddon. Instead, the "mother of all battles" on the ground lasted just 100 hours.

Revelation has defied many such prognosticators. A man who claimed to have cracked the Biblical code wrote the best-selling book 88 Reasons Why the Rapture Will Be in 1988. And not long before that a well-known television evangelist predicted the Soviet Union would invade Israel in 1982. Revelation contains a code intriguing enough to hold the interest of every generation, but obscure enough to have kept the best scholars guessing for almost 2,000 years. That may have been John's intent: to have each new wave of readers grapple with its meaning in their own historical context.

22 "And the sound of harpists and musicians and flute-players and trumpeters will not be heard in you any longer; and no craftsman of any craft will be found in you any longer; and the sound of a mill will not be heard in you any longer;

23 and the light of a lamp will not shine in you any longer; and the voice of the bridegroom and bride will not be heard in you any longer; for your merchants were the great men of the earth, because all the nations were deceived by your sorcery.

24 "And in her was found the blood of prophets and of saints and of all who have been slain on the earth."

The Fourfold Hallelujah

19 After these things I heard something like a loud voice of a great multitude in heaven, saying,

¶ "Hallelujah! Salvation and glory and power belong to our God;

2 BECAUSE HIS JUDGMENTS ARE TRUE AND RIGHTEOUS; for He has judged the great harlot who was corrupting the earth with her immorality, and HE HAS AVENGED THE BLOOD OF HIS BOND-SERVANTS ON HER."

3 And a second time they said, "Hallelujah! HER SMOKE RISES UP FOREVER AND EVER."

4 And the twenty-four elders and the four living creatures fell down and worshiped God who sits on the throne saying, "Amen. Hallelujah!"

5 And a voice came from the throne, saying,

¶ "Give praise to our God, all you His bond-servants, you who fear Him, the small and the great."

6 Then I heard *something* like the voice of a great multitude and like the sound of many waters and like the sound of mighty peals of thunder, saying,

¶ "Hallelujah! For the Lord our God, the Almighty, reigns.

Marriage of the Lamb

7 "Let us rejoice and be glad and give the glory to Him, for the marriage of the Lamb has come and His bride has made herself ready."

8 It was given to her to clothe herself in fine linen, bright *and* clean; for the fine linen is the righteous acts of the saints.

9 ¶ Then he *said to me, "Write, 'Blessed are those who are invited to the marriage supper of the Lamb.'" And he *said to me, "These are true words of God."

10 Then I fell at his feet to worship him. But he *said to me, "Do not do that; I am a fellow servant of yours and your brethren who hold the testimony of Jesus; worship God. For the testimony of Jesus is the spirit of prophecy."

The Coming of Christ

11 ¶ And I saw heaven opened, and behold, a white horse, and He who sat on it *is* called Faithful and True, and in righteousness He judges and wages war.

12 His eyes *are* a flame of fire, and on His head *are* many diadems; and He has a name written *on* Him which no one knows except Himself.

13 *He is* clothed with a robe dipped in blood, and His name is called The Word of God.

14 And the armies which are in heaven, clothed

in fine linen, white *and* clean, were following Him on white horses.

15 From His mouth comes a sharp sword, so that with it He may strike down the nations, and He will rule them with a rod of iron; and He treads the wine press of the fierce wrath of God, the Almighty.

16 And on His robe and on His thigh He has a name written, "KING OF KINGS, AND LORD OF LORDS."

17 ¶ Then I saw an angel standing in the sun, and he cried out with a loud voice, saying to all the birds which fly in midheaven, "Come, assemble for the great supper of God,

18 so that you may eat the flesh of kings and the flesh of [a]commanders and the flesh of mighty men and the flesh of horses and of those who sit on them and the flesh of all men, both free men and slaves, and small and great."

19 ¶ And I saw the beast and the kings of the earth and their armies assembled to make war against Him who sat on the horse and against His army.

Doom of the Beast and False Prophet

20 And the beast was seized, and with him the false prophet who performed the signs in his presence, by which he deceived those who had received the mark of the beast and those who wor-

[a] I.e. chiliarchs, in command of one thousand troops

shiped his image; these two were thrown alive into the lake of fire which burns with brimstone.

21 And the rest were killed with the sword which came from the mouth of Him who sat on the horse, and all the birds were filled with their flesh.

Satan Bound

20 Then I saw an angel coming down from heaven, holding the key of the abyss and a great chain in his hand.

2 And he laid hold of the dragon, the serpent of old, who is the devil and Satan, and bound him for a thousand years;

3 and he threw him into the abyss, and shut *it* and sealed *it* over him, so that he would not deceive the nations any longer, until the thousand years were completed; after these things he must be released for a short time.

4 ¶ Then I saw thrones, and they sat on them, and judgment was given to them. And I *saw* the souls of those who had been beheaded because of their testimony of Jesus and because of the word of God, and those who had not worshiped the beast or his image, and had not received the mark on their forehead and on their hand; and they came to life and reigned with Christ for a thousand years.

5 The rest of the dead did not come to life

A Happy Ending after All
The last word is the best news of all

> Then I saw a new heaven and a new earth. 21:1

WE SENSE IT AT RARE moments. The first real day of spring, when the air is heavy with the scent of blooms and new life sprouts everywhere. Or even in winter, when an unexpected snowstorm clothes a gray, dingy city in pure white. Or when we watch a baby animal at play in the zoo. Or remember the first sudden twinge of romantic love.

This world may be full of pollution, war, crime, and hate. But inside us, all of us, linger remnants that remind us of what the world could be like—of what we could be like. The Old Testament prophets dreamed of "that day" when creation would be made new. And those sensations, following a dismal monotone of predicted catastrophes, burst out of the last few chapters of Revelation. That perfect world is not merely a dream; it will come true.

A New World at Last

There will be no more tears then, nor pain. Wild animals will frolic, not kill. Once again creation will work the way God intended. Peace will reign not only between God and individuals, but between him and all creation. The kingdom comes out into the open. The City of God flings wide its gates.

Revelation ends on a note of great triumph. Somehow, out of all the bad news augured here, good news emerges—spectacular Good News. To those who believe, Revelation becomes a book not of fear, but of hope. God will prevail. All will be made new.

The Bible began, back in Genesis, with a tragic defeat when humanity, made in the image of God, rebelled. It ends with a reunion—a marriage, Revelation calls it. There is a happy ending after all.

Life Questions: If you could design a perfect world, what would it look like?

until the thousand years were completed. This is the first resurrection.

6 Blessed and holy is the one who has a part in the first resurrection; over these the second

---

20:3 The Millennium

Christians interpret the thousand-year reign referred to here in a variety of ways:

1. Postmillennialism believes that the church itself will, through its expanding influence, bring about a time of peace and prosperity in preparation for the return of Christ. This view was far more popular in the 19th century, when people were optimistic about progress and the future.

2. Premillennialism believes that Christ will return to earth and reign here in person, ushering in a period of great peace. During this period, Satan will be bound up, but will lead a final revolt at the end of the thousand years.

3. Amillennialism interprets this passage much less literally. Some amillennialists hold that the millennium has already been going on, but the reign of Christ is taking place in heaven, not on earth. Others believe the church is establishing the kingdom of Christ now, between Jesus' first and second coming.

Because so little information is given on the millennium, no one can be completely sure. The "thousand year" period itself may be symbolic, standing for a very long period of time. Regardless, all positions agree that ultimately this world will end with Jesus' establishment of an eternal kingdom.

---

death has no power, but they will be priests of God and of Christ and will reign with Him for a thousand years.

Satan Freed, Doomed

7 ¶ When the thousand years are completed, Satan will be released from his prison,

8 and will come out to deceive the nations which are in the four corners of the earth, Gog and Magog, to gather them together for the war; the number of them is like the sand of the seashore.

9 And they came up on the broad plain of the earth and surrounded the camp of the saints and the beloved city, and fire came down from heaven and devoured them.

10 And the devil who deceived them was thrown into the lake of fire and brimstone, where the beast and the false prophet are also; and they will be tormented day and night forever and ever.

Judgment at the Throne of God

11 ¶ Then I saw a great white throne and Him who sat upon it, from whose presence earth and

heaven fled away, and no place was found for them.

12 And I saw the dead, the great and the small, standing before the throne, and books were opened; and another book was opened, which is *the book* of life; and the dead were judged from the things which were written in the books, according to their deeds.

13 And the sea gave up the dead which were in it, and death and Hades gave up the dead which were in them; and they were judged, every one *of them* according to their deeds.

14 Then death and Hades were thrown into the lake of fire. This is the second death, the lake of fire.

15 And if anyone's name was not found written in the book of life, he was thrown into the lake of fire.

The New Heaven and Earth

21 Then I saw a new heaven and a new earth; for the first heaven and the first earth passed away, and there is no longer *any* sea.

2 And I saw the holy city, new Jerusalem, coming down out of heaven from God, made ready as a bride adorned for her husband.

3 And I heard a loud voice from the throne, saying, "Behold, the tabernacle of God is among men, and He will dwell among them, and they shall be His people, and God Himself will be among them,[a]

4 and He will wipe away every tear from their eyes; and there will no longer be *any* death; there will no longer be *any* mourning, or crying, or pain; the first things have passed away."

5 ¶ And He who sits on the throne said, "Behold, I am making all things new." And He *said, "Write, for these words are faithful and true."

6 Then He said to me, "It is done. I am the Alpha and the Omega, the beginning and the end. I will give to the one who thirsts from the spring of the water of life without cost.

7 "He who overcomes will inherit these things, and I will be his God and he will be My son.

8 "But for the cowardly and unbelieving and abominable and murderers and immoral persons and sorcerers and idolaters and all liars, their part *will be* in the lake that burns with fire and brimstone, which is the second death."

9 ¶ Then one of the seven angels who had the seven bowls full of the seven last plagues came and spoke with me, saying, "Come here, I will show you the bride, the wife of the Lamb."

The New Jerusalem

10 And he carried me away [b]in the Spirit to a great and high mountain, and showed me the holy city, Jerusalem, coming down out of heaven from God,

11 having the glory of God. Her brilliance was

---

[a] One early ms reads, and be *their God*   [b] Or *in spirit*

like a very costly stone, as a stone of crystal-clear jasper.

12 It had a great and high wall, with twelve gates, and at the gates twelve angels; and names *were* written on them, which are *the names* of the twelve tribes of the sons of Israel.

13 *There were* three gates on the east and three gates on the north and three gates on the south and three gates on the west.

14 And the wall of the city had twelve foundation stones, and on them *were* the twelve names of the twelve apostles of the Lamb.

15 ¶ The one who spoke with me had a gold measuring rod to measure the city, and its gates and its wall.

16 The city is laid out as a square, and its length is as great as the width; and he measured the city with the rod, [a]fifteen hundred miles; its length and width and height are equal.

17 And he measured its wall, [b]seventy-two yards, *according to* human measurements, which are *also* angelic *measurements.*

18 The material of the wall was jasper; and the city was pure gold, like clear glass.

19 The foundation stones of the city wall were adorned with every kind of precious stone. The first foundation stone was jasper; the second, sapphire; the third, chalcedony; the fourth, emerald;

20 the fifth, sardonyx; the sixth, sardius; the seventh, chrysolite; the eighth, beryl; the ninth, topaz; the tenth, chrysoprase; the eleventh, jacinth; the twelfth, amethyst.

21 And the twelve gates were twelve pearls; each one of the gates was a single pearl. And the street of the city was pure gold, like transparent glass.

22 ¶ I saw no temple in it, for the Lord God the Almighty and the Lamb are its temple.

23 And the city has no need of the sun or of the moon to shine on it, for the glory of God has illumined it, and its lamp *is* the Lamb.

24 The nations will walk by its light, and the kings of the earth will bring their glory into it.

25 In the daytime (for there will be no night there) its gates will never be closed;

26 and they will bring the glory and the honor of the nations into it;

27 and nothing unclean, and no one who practices abomination and lying, shall ever come into it, but only those whose names are written in the Lamb's book of life.

The River and the Tree of Life

22 Then he showed me a river of the water of life, clear as crystal, coming from the throne of God and of [c]the Lamb,

2 in the middle of its street. On either side of the river was the tree of life, bearing twelve [d]kinds *of* fruit, yielding its fruit every month; and the leaves of the tree were for the healing of the nations.

3 There will no longer be any curse; and the throne of God and of the Lamb will be in it, and His bond-servants will serve Him;

22:1 Eden Regained

The last two chapters of Revelation contain numerous parallels to the description of the Garden of Eden in the first three chapters of Genesis. Revelation describes a new creation that excludes all the things that spoiled Eden. There will be no night and no death. Satan will disappear forever, and nothing impure will enter the new city. People will walk with God again, just as they did in Eden. There will be no crying or pain. Once again humankind will rule over creation, this time with open access to the tree of life. Everything put wrong by human rebellion in Eden will be set right. In Eden, Adam and Eve were driven from the garden; in the new earth, they will see God's face.

4 they will see His face, and His name *will be* on their foreheads.

5 And there will no longer be *any* night; and they will not have need of the light of a lamp nor the light of the sun, because the Lord God will illumine them; and they will reign forever and ever.

6 ¶ And he said to me, "These words are faithful and true"; and the Lord, the God of the spirits of the prophets, sent His angel to show to His bond-servants the things which must soon take place.

7 ¶ "And behold, I am coming quickly. Blessed is he who heeds the words of the prophecy of this book."

8 ¶ I, John, am the one who heard and saw these things. And when I heard and saw, I fell down to worship at the feet of the angel who showed me these things.

9 But he *said to me, "Do not do that. I am a fellow servant of yours and of your brethren the prophets and of those who heed the words of this book. Worship God."

The Final Message

10 ¶ And he *said to me, "Do not seal up the words of the prophecy of this book, for the time is near.

11 "Let the one who does wrong, still do wrong; and the one who is filthy, still be filthy; and let the one who is righteous, still practice righteousness; and the one who is holy, still keep himself holy."

12 ¶ "Behold, I am coming quickly, and My

---

[a] Lit *twelve thousand stadia*; a stadion was approx 600 ft middle *of its street, and on either side of the river, was*   [b] Lit *one hundred forty-four cubits*   [c] Or *the Lamb. In the*   [d] Or *crops of fruit*

reward *is* with Me, to render to every man according to what he has done.

13 "I am the Alpha and the Omega, the first and the last, the beginning and the end."

14 ¶ Blessed are those who wash their robes, so that they may have the right to the tree of life, and may enter by the gates into the city.

15 Outside are the dogs and the sorcerers and the immoral persons and the murderers and the idolaters, and everyone who loves and practices lying.

16 ¶ "I, Jesus, have sent My angel to testify to you these things for the churches. I am the root and the descendant of David, the bright morning star."

17 ¶ The Spirit and the bride say, "Come." And let the one who hears say, "Come." And let the one who is thirsty come; let the one who wishes take the water of life without cost.

18 ¶ I testify to everyone who hears the words of the prophecy of this book: if anyone adds to them, God will add to him the plagues which are written in this book;

19 and if anyone takes away from the words of the book of this prophecy, God will take away his part from the tree of life and from the holy city, which are written in this book.

20 ¶ He who testifies to these things says, "Yes, I am coming quickly." Amen. Come, Lord Jesus.

21 ¶ The grace of the Lord Jesus be with *a*all. Amen.

---

a One early ms reads *the saints*

ACKNOWLEDGMENTS

ABOUT THE N.A.S.B

PRINCIPLES OF TRANSLATION

WHERE TO FIND IT

Acknowledgments

Philip Yancey, General Editor of *The Student Bible,* came up with the original concept while serving as Editor of *Campus Life* magazine. He has authored more than thirteen books, including *Where Is God When It Hurts?, Disappointment with God, The Jesus I Never Knew,* and *What's So Amazing About Grace?*

Tim Stafford wrote many of the notes for *The Student Bible,* especially in the Old Testament portions. His books include *That's Not What I Meant, Sexual Chaos,* and *Knowing the Face of God.*

Not long after its publication in 1986, *The Student Bible* became the best-selling edition of the Bible in the United States, and since then it has attracted over three million readers. Many of these readers wrote to say that the combination of scholarship and simplicity opened up the Bible for them in a new way. Partly in response to those letters, *The Student Bible* has undergone substantial revisions.

In 1992 a new edition updated existing material and added many new features, including 400 new Highlights and a greatly expanded Subject Guide. This edition also included a "parallel passages" feature under many boldface sectional headings in Matthew, Mark, Luke and John, sending you to other places where the same event or teaching is recorded. Note also the Glossary of Nonbiblical People and Places beginning on page 1405, where you will find a brief description of names used in Introductions, Insights and Highlights. Hunter and Edith Norwood and Chase and Harriet Stafford did much of the research and initial writing of the added Highlights, and Connie Van Dyke prepared additional material for the Subject Guide.

In the ten-year (1996) edition, *The Student Bible* has undergone further revision. Tim Stafford wrote the profiles of "100 People You Should Know." Sharon Wright redesigned the entire Bible, creatively combining new graphic elements and typefaces. And many changes were made to the "Where to Find It" section in the back, making it a more useful and convenient reference resource.

Any Bible publishing project relies on many people, and the following are a few of those who helped with *The Student Bible:*

Nathan Young designed the original *Student Bible* and was invaluably cheerful, flexible and skilled.

Dirk Buursma, Michael Vander Klipp, Doris Rikkers and Sandra Vander Zicht, editors at Zondervan, helped refine both words and design. In addition, they watched over the many complicated details of typesetting and production.

Virginia Vagt, through her research and common sense, turned the original concept for *The Student Bible* in new directions.

Scott Bolinder and Harold Myra helped greatly in improving, encouraging, and aiding the work.

Dr. Kenneth Kantzer made careful suggestions about questions of scholarship and theology.

Lenora Rand, Connie Van Dyke and Verlyn Verbrugge did much of the painstaking work for the Subject Guide.

In the process of developing *The Student Bible,* many helpful people and organizations contributed their insights, especially these: Association of Christian Schools International, Billy Graham Evangelistic Association, Campus Crusade for Christ, Dr. Jim Engel, Focus on the Family, Fuller Theological Seminary, the International Bible Society, InterVarsity Christian Fellowship, Josh McDowell, National Network of Youth Ministries, the Navigators, Search Institute, Student Venture, Chuck Swindoll, Dr. Mel White, Young Life, Youth for Christ and Youth Specialties.

About the N.A.S.B.

In the history of English Bible translations, the King James Version is the most prestigious. This time-honored version of 1611, itself a revision of the Bishops' Bible of 1568, became the basis for the English Revised Version appearing in 1881 (New Testament) and 1885 (Old Testament). The American counterpart of this last work was published in 1901 as the American Standard Version. The ASV, a product of both British and American scholarship, has been highly regarded for its scholarship and accuracy. Recognizing the values of the American Standard Version, The Lockman Foundation felt an urgency to preserve these and other lasting values of the ASV by incorporating recent discoveries of Hebrew and Greek textual sources and by rendering it into more current English. Therefore, in 1959 a new translation project was launched, based on the time-honored principles of translation of the ASV and KJV. The result is the New American Standard Bible.

Translation work for the NASB was begun in 1959. In the preparation of this work numerous other translations have been consulted along with the linguistic tools and literature of biblical scholarship. Decisions about English renderings were made by consensus of a team composed of educators and pastors. Subsequently, review and evaluation by other Hebrew and Greek scholars outside the Editorial Board were sought and carefully considered.

The Editorial Board has continued to function since publication of the complete Bible in 1971. This edition of the NASB represents revisions and refinements recommended over the last several years as well as thorough research based on modern English usage.

Scriptural Promise

"The grass withers, the flower fades, but the word of our God stands forever."

Isaiah 40:8

The New American Standard Bible has been produced with the conviction that the words of Scripture as originally penned in the Hebrew, Aramaic, and Greek were inspired by God. Since they are the eternal Word of God, the Holy Scriptures speak with fresh power to each generation, to give wisdom that leads to salvation, that men may serve Christ to the glory of God.

The Fourfold Aim
of
The Lockman Foundation

1. These publications shall be true to the original Hebrew, Aramaic, and Greek.

2. They shall be grammatically correct.

3. They shall be understandable.

4. They shall give the Lord Jesus Christ His proper place, the place which the Word gives Him; therefore, no work will ever be personalized.

Principles of Translation

MODERN ENGLISH USAGE: The attempt has been made to render the grammar and terminology in contemporary English. When it was felt that the word-for-word literalness was unacceptable to the modern reader, a change was made in the direction of a more current English idiom. In the instances where this has been done, the more literal rendering has been indicated in the notes. There are a few exceptions to this procedure. In particular, frequently "And" is not translated at the beginning of sentences because of differences in style between ancient and modern writing. Punctuation is a relatively modern invention, and ancient writers often linked most of their sentences with "and" or other connectives. Also, the Hebrew idiom "answered and said" is sometimes reduced to "answered" or "said" as demanded by the context. For current English the idiom "it came about that" has not been translated in the New Testament except when a major transition is needed.

ALTERNATIVE READINGS: In addition to the more literal renderings, notations have been made to include alternate translations, reading of variant manuscripts and explanatory equivalents of the text. Only such notations have been used as have been felt justified in assisting the reader's comprehension of the terms used by the original author.

HEBREW TEXT: In the present translation the latest edition of Rudolf Kittel's *BIBLIA HEBRAICA* has been employed together with the most recent light from lexicography, cognate languages, and the Dead Sea Scrolls.

HEBREW TENSES: Consecution of tenses in Hebrew remains a puzzling factor in translation. The translators have been guided by the requirements of a literal translation, the sequence of tenses, and the immediate and broad contexts.

THE PROPER NAME OF GOD IN THE OLD TESTAMENT: In the Scriptures, the name of God is most significant and understandably so. It is inconceivable to think of spiritual matters without a proper designation for the Supreme Deity. Thus the most common name for the Deity is God, a translation of the original *Elohim.* One of the titles for God is Lord, a translation of *Adonai.* There is yet another name which is particularly assigned to God as His special or proper name, that is, the four letters YHWH (Exodus 3:14 and Isaiah 42:8). This name has not been pronounced by the Jews because of reverence for the great sacredness of the divine name. Therefore, it has been consistently translated LORD. The only exception to this translation of YHWH is when it occurs in immediate proximity to the word *Lord*, that is, *Adonai.* In that case it is regularly translated GOD in order to avoid confusion.

It is known that for many years YHWH has been transliterated as Yahweh, however no complete certainty attaches to this pronunciation.

GREEK TEXT: Consideration was given to the latest available manuscripts with a view to determining the best Greek text. In most instances the 26th edition of Eberhard Nestle's *NOVUM TESTAMENTUM GRAECE* was followed.

GREEK TENSES: A careful distinction has been made in the treatment of the Greek aorist tense (usually translated as the English past, "He did") and the Greek imperfect tense (normally rendered either as English past progressive, "He was doing"; or, if inceptive, as "He began to do" or "He started to do"; or else if customary past, as "He used to do"). "Began" is italicized if it renders an imperfect tense, in order to distinguish it from the Greek verb for "begin." In some contexts the difference between the Greek imperfect and the English past is conveyed better by the choice of vocabulary or by other words in the context, and in such cases the Greek imperfect may be rendered as a simple past tense (e.g. "had an illness for many years" would be preferable to "was having an illness for many years" and would be understood in the same way).

On the other hand, not all aorists have been rendered as English pasts ("He did"), for some of them are clearly to be rendered as English perfects ("He has done"), or even as past perfects ("He had done"), judging from the context in which they occur. Such aorists have been rendered as perfects or past perfects in this translation.

As for the distinction between aorist and present imperatives, the translators have usually rendered these imperatives in the customary manner, rather than attempting any such fine distinction as "Begin to do!" (for the aorist imperative), or, "Continually do!" (for the present imperative).

As for sequence of tenses, the translators took care to follow English rules rather than Greek in translating Greek presents, imperfects and aorists. Thus, where English says, "We knew that he was doing," Greek puts it, "We knew that he does"; similarly, "We knew that he had done" is the Greek, "We knew that he did." Likewise, the English, "When he had come, they met him," is represented in Greek by, "When he came, they met him." In all cases a consistent transfer has been made from the Greek tense in the subordinate clause to the appropriate tense in English.

In the rendering of negative questions introduced by the particle *mē* (which always expects the answer "No") the wording has been altered from a mere, "Will he not do this?" to a more accurate, "He will not do this, will he?"

THE LOCKMAN FOUNDATION

WHERE
TO FIND IT

100 People
YOU SHOULD KNOW

Glossary
OF NONBIBLICAL PEOPLE AND PLACES

This glossary lists the names and gives brief descriptions of most of the nonbiblical people and places cited in Introductions, Insights, and Highlights. We have made every effort to be accurate and comprehensive, while acknowledging the limitations of such a list.

Alcatraz an island in the San Francisco Bay, former site of a famous U.S. prison (reference can be found on page 1367).

Idi Amin (1925–) at one time the cruel dictator of the East African nation of Uganda, known for his persecution of Christians (references can be found on pages 947 and 1344).

Roy Chapman Andrews (1884–1960) U.S. naturalist and explorer, best known for books on his central Asiatic field trips (reference can be found on page 1330).

Armenia a region and ancient kingdom in southwestern Asia, now divided between Russia, Turkey and Iran (reference can be found on page 1344).

Augustine (354–430) bishop of Hippo in Roman Africa who was in his day the dominant personality of the Western church (reference can be found on page 1221).

Joseph Bayly American author, educator, and longtime columnist for *Eternity* magazine, known for books such as *The View From a Hearse* and *Psalms of My Life* (reference can be found on page 567).

Bernard of Clairvaux (1090–1153) the abbot of Clairvaux in France, a mystic and reformer known as a writer of sermons and treatises (reference can be found on page 729).

William Booth (1829–1912) founder of the Salvation Army, deeply committed to evangelistic and social justice activities (reference can be found on page 614).

Dietrich Bonhoeffer (1906–1945) German theologian who resisted the Nazi regime and was executed for treason; known for such books as *The Cost of Discipleship* (reference can be found on page 718).

Charles Loring Brace (1826–1890) U.S. reformer and pioneer social welfare worker, founder and director of the Children's Aid Society of New York City (reference can be found on page 1276).

Buddha (563–483 B.C.) Indian philosopher, founder of Buddhism (reference can be found on page 1326).

Frederick Buechner (1926–) ordained Presbyterian minister, called by the *New York Times* the leading clergyman/writer in the U.S., the widely read author of many novels and works of nonfiction (reference can be found on page 590).

John Bunyan (1628–1688) English Puritan minister, considered to be the greatest literary genius to come out of the Puritan movement (reference can be found on page 1280).

John Calvin (1509–1564) French-born Genevan theologian and reformer, a leader in the Protestant Reformation of the 16th century (reference can be found on page 1328).

Rachel Carson (1907–1964) U.S. scientist and writer, a pioneer in the environmentalist movement, especially in her warnings about the effects of pesticides on the environment (reference can be found on page 658).

Chartres a city in northwestern France, site of the great cathedral of Notre Dame (reference can be found on page 124).

G.K. Chesterton (1874–1936) English journalist and author, outstanding as critic, polemicist, and rhetorical poet (reference can be found on page 1221).

Winston Churchill (1874–1965) British statesman and orator, the great national leader during World War II (references can be found on pages 804 and 1006).

Samuel Taylor Coleridge (1772–1834) English poet, lecturer, journalist, and critic of literature, theology, philosophy, and society (reference can be found on page 1280).

Charles Colson U.S. government official during Richard Nixon's presidency, convicted for his role in the Watergate scandal; now active as an evangelical Christian author and the founder and leader of a prison ministry (reference can be found on page 1193).

Leonardo da Vinci (1452–1519) Florentine artist and scientist, known for such works as *The Last Supper* and the *Mona Lisa* (references can be found on pages 1167 and 1326).

Fedor Mikhailovich Dostoevski (1821–1881) Russian novelist of international reputation, generally acknowledged as one of the profoundest creative artists of the 19th century, known for such works as *The Brothers Karamazov* (reference can be found on page 1280).

Albert Einstein (1879–1955) German-born physicist, who emigrated to the United States; creator of the theory of relativity (reference can be found on page 590).

Jacques Ellul (1912–1994) French historian and sociologist known for works such as *The Meaning of the City* and *The Technological Society* (reference can be found on page 1376).

Henry Ford (1863–1947) U.S. industrialist known as the creator of modern mass production, most notably in the assembly-line method of automobile production (reference can be found on page 1276).

Robert Frost (1874–1963) American poet who used symbols from common life to express the values of rural New England, four-time winner of the Pulitzer Prize (reference can be found on page 993).

Mohandas Karamchand Gandhi (1869–1948) architect of India's freedom through a nonviolent revolution (references can be found on pages 84 and 1326).

Grand Canyon an immense gorge cut by the Colorado River into the high plateaus of the northern part of Arizona (reference can be found on page 1330).

Alex Haley (1923–1992) African-American author best known for his book *Roots*, the basis of a made-for-television mini-series (reference can be found on page 1031).

Georg Friedrich Handel (1685–1759) German-born composer who spent the majority of his life in England; the greatest English composer of the late baroque era, known best for his oratorio *The Messiah* (reference can be found on page 1372).

Hare Krishna a religious sect of Hindu character, founded by an Indian holy man; its followers are characterized by rhythmic chanting of the "Hare Krsna" (reference can be found on page 1290).

Paul Harvey (1918–) an American radio newscaster known for his unique intonation and special interest stories (reference can be found on page 1077).

Herodotus (5th century B.C.) Greek author of a history of the Persian Wars (references can be found on pages 442, 549, 552).

Hindus adherents of Hinduism, a religious system whose precepts govern a vast range of human activity outside the scope of most modern religions; the Republic of India is home to more than 95 percent of all Hindus (reference can be found on page 437).

Hiroshima a seaport city in southwestern Japan, the first city on which the U.S. air force dropped an atomic bomb in 1945 (reference can be found on page 870).

Adolf Hitler (1889–1945) Austrian-born politician, leader of the Nazi party, who became dictator of Germany in 1933 and led the nation into World War II (references can be found on pages 86, 416, 548, 947).

Homer Greek epic poet, regarded as the author of many narrative poems, and according to later tradition, author of the *Iliad* and *Odyssey* (reference can be found on page 736).

Howard Hughes (1905–1976) an eccentric American businessman who amassed a fortune but died a miserable recluse (reference can be found on page 719).

Samuel Huntington (1731–1796) signer of the Declaration of Independence, president of the continental congress (1779-81) and governor of Connecticut (reference can be found on page 325).

Saddam Hussein (1937–) the cruel president of Iraq, who led his nation into the Persian Gulf War (1991) as a result of Iraq's invasion of Kuwait (references can be found on pages 86, 947, 980).

Kali Hindu goddess, usually represented as black with bloody hands, eyes, teeth, and tongue, whose worship appears to be an extension of the widespread mother-goddess cult (reference can be found on page 437).

John F. Kennedy (1917–1963) 35th president of the U.S., the youngest man and first Roman Catholic to be elected to that office; fourth U.S. president in history to die by an assassin's bullet (reference can be found on page 498).

Ruholla Mussavi Khomeini (1900–1989) one-time religious leader of Iran, served as the leader of the Shi'ite Muslims, who comprise about 90 percent of Iran's population (reference can be found on page 947).

Derek Kidner former warden of Tyndale House, Cambridge, and author of numerous Old Testament commentaries and expositions (reference can be found on page 57).

Martin Luther King (1929–1968) U.S. African-American clergyman who received the 1964 Nobel Peace Prize for his leadership in the nonviolent struggle for racial equality in the U.S. (reference can be found on page 1006).

Ku Klux Klan a secret, masked organization that, after the American Civil War, became the chief instrument of the white underground resistance movement in the south against northerners and African-Americans (reference can be found on page 980).

Ann Landers (1918–) born Esther Pauline Friedman, she is best known as "Ann Landers," syndicated advice-column writer for newspapers around the U.S. (reference can be found on page 68).

C.S. Lewis (1898–1963) Irish-born author who achieved worldwide fame for books on Christian apologetics and other subjects; known for books such as *The Screwtape Letters, Mere Christianity*, and *The Chronicles of Narnia* (reference can be found on page 1164).

Abraham Lincoln (1809–1865) 16th president of the U.S., led the nation during the Civil War; the issuer of the Emancipation Proclamation, which directly or indirectly led to freedom for hundreds of thousands of slaves (references can be found on pages 84, 627, 1121, 1164, 1327).

Martin Luther (1483–1546) German religious leader who began the Protestant Reformation (references can be found on pages 998, 1221, 1223, 1272, 1338).

Douglas MacArthur (1880–1964) American general who gained fame for his military leadership in World War II (reference can be found on page 354).

Mao Tse Tung (1893–1976) Chinese revolutionist and statesman, Communist Party leader and founder of the Chinese communist state (reference can be found on page 947).

Mau Mau a nativistic cult among the Kikuya tribe in Kenya responsible for a 1950 rebellion directed against the presence of Europeans in Kenya and their ownership of land (reference can be found on page 1344).

Michelangelo (1475–1564) a native Italian, he is considered to be the greatest painter of the Renaissance and the most famous of all sculptors since the time of the Greeks, best known for his statue of "David" and his four-year painting project in the Sistine Chapel in Rome (reference can be found on page 23).

Bill Miner (1847–1913) notorious outlaw who terrorized stagecoach runs in the western U.S. (reference can be found on page 242).

Nazis followers of the National Socialist party in Germany, a party headed by Adolf Hitler, who took control of the country in 1933 (reference can be found on page 980).

John Newton (1725–1807) one of the leaders of the Evangelical revival in England, a former seafarer who after his conversion to Christianity wrote hymns (most notably *Amazing Grace*) and devotional letters (reference can be found on page 560).

Blaise Pascal (1623–1662) French mathematician and philosopher, author of a comprehensive treatise on Christian apologetics (reference can be found on page 728).

Louis Pasteur (1822–1895) French chemist and microbiologist who developed a vaccine for rabies and the method of heat pasteurization for liquid foods and beverages (reference can be found on page 142).

J.B. Phillips British pastor who devoted much of his life to writing a fresh translation of the New Testament, publishing the entire New Testament in 1958 and revising it in 1972 (reference can be found on page 1183).

Pablo Picasso (1881–1973) Spanish painter, sculptor, and engraver, the most influential independent artist of the 20th century (reference can be found on page 1376).

Grigori Efimovich Rasputin (1872–1916) Russian peasant and mystic notorious for his phenomenal sexual appetite and his impact as the voice of the peasantry (reference can be found on page 1228).

John D. Rockefeller (1874–1960) American oil magnate and philanthropist (reference can be found on page 724).

Franklin Delano Roosevelt (1882–1945) the U.S.'s 32nd president and only president to be reelected three times, he served during the New Deal era and World War II (reference can be found on page 210).

Dorothy Sayers (1893–1957) noted English writer of mystery novels, featuring the sleuth Lord Peter Wimsey (reference can be found on page 1096).

Scientology, Church of a quasi-scientific and religious discipline founded by American Ron Hubbard, it formally became the Church of Scientology in 1955 (reference can be found on page 1290).

Ignaz Philipp Semmelweis (1818–1865) Hungarian physician who had a dramatic influence on the development of knowledge and control of infection, notably through his work in the control of puerperal (childbirth) fever (reference can be found on page 142).

William Shakespeare (1564–1616) Elizabethan Englishman generally acknowledged as not only England's, but the world's, greatest poet and playwright (references can be found on pages 671 and 736).

Sistine Chapel the pope's private chapel, built under commission from Sixtus IV; Julius II commissioned Michelangelo to paint its ceiling (reference can be found on page 23).

Aleksandr Solzhenitsyn (1918–) noted Russian author known for such works as *One Day in the Life of Ivan Denisovich* and *The Gulag Archipelago* (references can be found on pages 568, 1193, 1280).

Josef Stalin (1879–1953) leader of the Communist party of the Soviet Union, generalissimo and dictator of the USSR and one of the most powerful, complex, and controversial figures in world history (reference can be found on page 784).

J.R.R. Tolkien (1892–1973) English author best known for his imaginative works such as *Lord of the Rings* (reference can be found on page 408).

Harry Truman (1884–1972) 33rd president of the U.S., serving from 1945-1953 (reference can be found on page 354).

Abigail Van Buren (1918–) born Pauline Esther Friedman, she is best known for her work as writer of the advice column "Dear Abby" for U.S. newspapers (reference can be found on page 68).

Katie von Bora (1499–1552) a former nun, she married Protestant Reformer Martin Luther in 1525 (reference can be found on page 1272).

Lech Walesa champion of the working class in Poland who rallied the nation to independence from Russian influence (reference can be found on page 84).

George Washington (1732–1799) commander in chief, statesman, and first president of the U.S. (references can be found on pages 84, 325, 341, 481, 1227).

Charles Wesley (1707–1788) English clergyman, poet, and hymnwriter who, together with his brother John, started the Methodist movement in the Church of England (reference can be found on page 1295).

John Wesley (1703–1791) English clergyman and founder of Methodism (references can be found on pages 1221 and 1295).

Oscar Wilde (1854–1900) Irish poet and dramatist, author of such works as *The Importance of Being Earnest* and *The Picture of Dorian Gray* (reference can be found on page 719).

Thomas Wolfe (1900–1938) American novelist, known for such works as *Look Homeward, Angel* (reference can be found on page 720).

Frank Lloyd Wright (1867–1959) U.S. architect who became world famous as creator and expounder of "organic architecture," designing buildings that harmonize with users and the environment (reference can be found on page 1326).

Well-known Biblical Events

OVERVIEW OF BIBLICAL EVENTS

(in approximate order of occurrence)

Creation: *Genesis 1–2*

The first sin, or fall: *Genesis 3*

Cain kills Abel: *Genesis 4*

Noah and the ark: *Genesis 6–9*

Sodom and Gomorrah: *Genesis 18–19*

Abraham sacrifices Isaac: *Genesis 22*

Jacob's ladder: *Genesis 28:10–22*

Joseph and the coat of many colors: *Genesis 37*

Moses' birth: *Exodus 2*

Moses and the burning bush: *Exodus 3*

Plagues on Egypt: *Exodus 7–11*

The exodus: *Exodus 12–13*

The Ten Commandments: *Exodus 20*

The battle of Jericho: *Joshua 6*

Gideon and the fleece: *Judges 6–7*

Samson and Delilah: *Judges 13–16*

God calls young Samuel: *1 Samuel 1–3*

David and Goliath: *1 Samuel 17*

David and Bathsheba: *2 Samuel 11*

Elijah versus the priests of Baal: *1 Kings 18*

The miracles of Elisha: *2 Kings 4–5*

Ezekiel and the dry bones: *Ezekiel 37*

Daniel in the lions' den: *Daniel 6*

Jonah and the fish: *Jonah 1*

Hosea and his adulterous wife: *Hosea 1–3*

Jesus' birth: *Luke 1–2*

Jesus' baptism: *Mark 1:9–11*

Temptation of Jesus: *Luke 4:1–13*

Jesus clears the temple: *John 2:12–25*

The transfiguration of Jesus: *Matthew 17:1–13*

Jesus raises Lazarus from the dead: *John 11:1–46*

Jesus' triumphal entry into Jerusalem: *Mark 11:1–11*

Jesus and the widow's offering: *Mark 12:41–44*

The Last Supper: *Luke 22:7–38*

Jesus washes his disciples' feet: *John 13:1–17*

Jesus at Gethsemane: *Matthew 26:36–56*

Judas betrays Jesus: *Luke 22:1–53*

Peter denies Christ: *Luke 22:54–62*

Jesus' crucifixion: *Matthew 26:57–27:66*

Jesus' resurrection and ascension: *Luke 24*

Holy Spirit at Pentecost: *Acts 2*

Stephen martyred: *Acts 6–7*

Paul's conversion: *Acts 9:1–31*

Peter's escape from prison: *Acts 12:1–19*

Paul and Silas in prison: *Acts 16:16–40*

MINISTRY OF JESUS
(in Biblical order)

Jesus baptized: *Matthew 3:13–17; Mark 1:9–11; Luke 3:21–22; John 1:29–34*

Jesus tempted by Satan: *Matthew 4:1–11; Mark 1:12–13; Luke 4:1–13*

Jesus' first miracle: *John 2:1–11*

Jesus and Nicodemus: *John 3:1–21*

Jesus talks to a Samaritan woman: *John 4:5–42*

Jesus heals an official's son: *John 4:46–54*

People of Nazareth try to kill Jesus: *Luke 4:16–30*

Jesus calls four fishermen: *Matthew 4:18–22; Mark 1:16–20; Luke 5:1–11*

Jesus heals Peter's mother–in–law: *Matthew 8:14–15; Mark 1:29–31; Luke 4:38–39*

Jesus begins preaching in Galilee: *Matthew 4:23–25; Mark 1:35–39; Luke 4:42–44*

Matthew decides to follow Jesus: *Matthew 9:9–13; Mark 2:13–17; Luke 5:27–32*

Jesus chooses twelve disciples: *Matthew 10:2–4; Mark 3:13–19; Luke 6:12–15*

Jesus preaches the Sermon on the Mount: *Matthew 5:1–7:29; Luke 6:20–49*

A sinful woman anoints Jesus: *Luke 7:36–50*

Jesus travels again through Galilee: *Luke 8:1–3*

Jesus tells kingdom parables: *Matthew 13:1–52; Mark 4:1–34; Luke 8:4–18*

Jesus quiets the storm: *Matthew 8:23–27; Mark 4:35–41; Luke 8:22–25*

Jairus's daughter raised to life: *Matthew 9:18–26; Mark 5:21–23; Luke 8:40–56*

Jesus sends out the twelve: *Matthew 9:35–11:1; Mark 6:6–13; Luke 9:1–6*

John the Baptist killed by Herod: *Matthew 14:1–12; Mark 6:14–29; Luke 9:7–9*

Jesus feeds the 5,000: *Matthew 14:13–21; Mark 6:30–44; Luke 9:10–17; John 6:1–14*

Jesus walks on water: *Matthew 14:22–32; Mark 6:47–52; John 6:16–21*

Jesus feeds the 4,000: *Matthew 15:32–39; Mark 8:1–10*

Peter confesses Jesus as the Son of God: *Matthew 16:13–20; Mark 8:27–30; Luke 9:18–21*

Jesus predicts his death: *Matthew 16:21–26; Mark 8:31–37; Luke 9:22–25*

Jesus is transfigured: *Matthew 17:1–13; Mark 9:2–13; Luke 9:28–36*

Jesus pays his temple taxes: *Matthew 17:24–27*

Jesus attends the Feast of Tabernacles: *John 7:10–52*

Jesus heals a man born blind: *John 9:1–41*

Jesus visits Mary and Martha: *Luke 10:38–42*

Jesus raises Lazarus from the dead: *John 11:1–44*

Jesus begins his last trip to Jerusalem: *Luke 17:11*

Jesus blesses the little children: *Matthew 19:13–15; Mark 10:13–16; Luke 18:15–17*

Jesus talks to the rich young man: *Matthew 19:16–30; Mark 10:17–31; Luke 18:18–30*

Jesus again predicts his death: *Matthew 20:17–19; Mark 10:32–34; Luke 18:31–34*

Jesus heals blind Bartimaeus: *Matthew 20:29–34; Mark 10:46–52; Luke 18:35–43*

Jesus talks to Zaccheus: *Luke 19:1–10*

Jesus visits Mary and Martha again: *John 12:1–11*

MIRACLES OF JESUS

(in Biblical order)

HEALING OF INDIVIDUALS

Man with leprosy: *Matthew 8:1–4; Mark 1:40–44; Luke 5:12–14*

Roman centurion's servant: *Matthew 8:5–13; Luke 7:1–10*

Peter's mother-in-law: *Matthew 8:14–15; Mark 1:30–31; Luke 4:38–39*

Two demon-possessed men from Gadara: *Matthew 8:28–34; Mark 5:1–15; Luke 8:27–39*

Paralyzed man: *Matthew 9:2–7; Mark 2:3–12; Luke 5:18–26*

Woman with bleeding: *Matthew 9:20–22; Mark 5:25–34; Luke 8:43–48*

Two blind men: *Matthew 9:27–31*

Mute, demon-possessed man: *Matthew 9:32–33*

Man with a shriveled hand: *Matthew 12:10–13; Mark 3:1–5; Luke 6:6–11*

Blind, mute and demon-possessed man: *Matthew 12:22–23; Luke 11:14*

Canaanite woman's daughter: *Matthew 15:21–28; Mark 7:24–30*

Boy with epilepsy: *Matthew 17:14–21; Mark 9:17–29; Luke 9:38–43*

Two blind men (including Bartimaeus): *Matthew 20:29–34; Mark 10:46–52; Luke 18:35–43*

Demon-possessed man in synagogue: *Mark 1:21–28; Luke 4:31–37*

Blind man at Bethsaida: *Mark 8:22–26*

Crippled woman: *Luke 13:10–17*

Man with dropsy: *Luke 14:1–4*

Ten men with leprosy: *Luke 17:11–19*

The high priest's servant: *Luke 22:50–51*

Official's son at Capernaum: *John 4:46–54*

Sick man at the pool of Bethesda: *John 5:1–15*

Man born blind: *John 9:1–41*

CONTROL OF NATURE

Calming the storm: *Matthew 8:23–27; Mark 4:37–41; Luke 8:22–25*

Feeding of 5,000: *Matthew 14:1–21; Mark 6:30–44; Luke 9:10–17; John 6:1–14*

Walking on water: *Matthew 14:22–32; Mark 6:47–52; John 6:16–21*

Feeding of 4,000: *Matthew 15:32–39; Mark 8:1–9*

Fish with coin: *Matthew 17:24–27*

Fig tree withers: *Matthew 21:18–22; Mark 11:12–14, 20–25*

Huge catch of fish: *Luke 5:4–11; John 21:1–11*

Water into wine: *John 2:1–11*

RAISING THE DEAD

Jairus's daughter: *Matthew 9:18–26; Mark 5:21–43; Luke 8:40–56*

Widow at Nain's son: *Luke 7:11–17*

Lazarus: *John 11:1–44*

PARABLES OF JESUS

(in alphabetical order)

Canceled debts: *Luke 7:41–43*

Cost of discipleship: *Luke 14:28–33*

Faithful servant: *Matthew 24:45–51; Luke 12:42–48*

Fig tree: *Matthew 24:32–35; Mark 13:28–31; Luke 21:29–33*

Good Samaritan: *Luke 10:30–37*

The great dinner: *Luke 14:16–24*

Growing seed: *Mark 4:26–29*

Hidden treasure and pearl: *Matthew 13:44–46*

Honor at a banquet: *Luke 14:7–14*

Laborers in the vineyard: *Matthew 20:1–16*

Light of the world: *Matthew 5:14–16; Mark 4:21–22; Luke 8:16; 11:33–36*

Lost coin: *Luke 15:8–10*

Lost sheep: *Matthew 18:12–14; Luke 15:4–7*

Mustard seed: *Matthew 13:31–32; Mark 4:30–32; Luke 13:18–19*

New cloth on an old garment: *Matthew 9:16; Mark 2:21; Luke 5:36*

New wine in old wineskins: *Matthew 9:17; Mark 2:22; Luke 5:37–39*

Net: *Matthew 13:47–50*

Obedient servants: *Luke 17:7–10*

Owner of a house: *Matthew 13:52*

Persistent friend: *Luke 11:5–8*

Persistent widow: *Luke 18:2–8*

Pharisee and the tax collector: *Luke 18:10–14*

Prodigal (lost) son: *Luke 15:11–32*

Rich fool: *Luke 12:16–21*

Rich man and Lazarus: *Luke 16:19–31*

Sheep and goats: *Matthew 25:31–46*

Shrewd manager: *Luke 16:1–8*

Sower: *Matthew 13:1–8, 18–23; Mark 4:3–8, 14–20; Luke 8:5–8, 11–15*

Talents: *Matthew 25:14–30*

Tenants: *Matthew 21:33–34; Mark 12:1–11; Luke 20:9–18*

Ten minas: *Luke 19:12–27*

Ten bridesmaids: *Matthew 25:1–13*

Two sons: *Matthew 21:28–32*

Unforgiving servant: *Matthew 18:23–35*

Unfruitful fig tree: *Luke 13:6–9*

Watchful slaves: *Mark 13:34–37; Luke 12:35–40*

Wedding banquet: *Matthew 22:2–14*

Weeds: *Matthew 13:24–30, 36–43*

Wise and foolish builders: *Matthew 7:24–27; Luke 6:47–49*

Yeast: *Matthew 13:33; Luke 13:20–21*

TEACHINGS OF JESUS

(in alphabetical order)

Beatitudes: *Matthew 5:1–12*

Bread of life: *John 6:25–59*

Born again: *John 3:1–21*

Discipleship: *Luke 14:25–35*

Give to Caesar: *Mark 12:13–17*

Good shepherd: *John 10:1–21*

Golden Rule: *Luke 6:31*

Greatest commandment: *Matthew 22:34–40*

Living water: *John 4:1–26*

Lord's prayer: *Matthew 6:5–15*

Sending out the Twelve: *Matthew 10*

Sermon on the Mount: *Matthew 5–7*

Vine and branches: *John 15:1–17*

The way and the truth and the life: *John 14:5–14*

Wealth: *Matthew 19:16–30*

Worry: *Luke 12:22–34*

JESUS' LAST WEEK

(in Biblical order)

The triumphal entry: *Matthew 21:1–11; Mark 11:1–11; Luke 19:29–44; John 12:12–19*

Jesus curses the fig tree: *Matthew 21:18–22; Mark 11:12–14*

Jesus clears the temple: *Matthew 21:12–13; Mark 11:15–18; Luke 19:45–48*

Jesus' authority questioned: *Matthew 21:23–27; Mark 11:27–33; Luke 20:1–8*

Jesus teaches in the temple: *Matthew 21:28–23:39; Mark 12:1–44; Luke 20:9–21:4*

Jesus' feet anointed: *Matthew 26:6–13; Mark 14:3–9; John 12:2–11*

The plot against Jesus: *Matthew 26:14–16; Mark 14:10–11; Luke 22:3–6*

The Last Supper: *Matthew 26:17–29; Mark 14:12–25; Luke 22:7–38; John 13:1–38*

Jesus comforts his disciples: *John 14:1–16:33*

Jesus' high priestly prayer: *John 17:1–26*

Gethsemane: *Matthew 26:36–46; Mark 14:32–42; Luke 22:40–46*

Jesus' arrest and trial: *Matthew 26:47–27:26; Mark 14:43–15:15; Luke 22:47–23:25; John 18:2–19:16*

Jesus' crucifixion and death: *Matthew 27:27–56; Mark 15:16–41; Luke 23:26–49; John 19:17–37*

Jesus' burial: *Matthew 27:57–66; Mark 15:42–47; Luke 23:50–56; John 19:38–42*

JESUS' RESURRECTION APPEARANCES
(in Biblical order)

The empty tomb : *Matthew 28:1–8; Mark 16:1–8; Luke 24:1–12; John 20:1–10*

To Mary Magdalene in the garden: *Mark 16:9–11; John 20:11–18*

To other women: *Matthew 28:9–10*

To two people going to Emmaus: *Mark 16:12–13; Luke 24:13–32*

To Peter: *Luke 24:34; 1 Corinthians 15:5*

To the ten disciples in the upper room: *Luke 24:36–43; John 20:19–25*

To the eleven disciples in the upper room: *Mark 16:14; John 20:26–31; 1 Corinthians 15:5*

To seven disciples fishing: *John 21:1–14*

To the eleven disciples on a mountain: *Matthew 28:16–20; Mark 16:15–18*

To more than 500 people: *1 Corinthians 15:6*

To James: *1 Corinthians 15:7*

To his disciples at his ascension: *Luke 24:36–51; Acts 1:3–9; 1 Corinthians 15:7*

To Paul: *Acts 9:1–19; 22:3–16; 26:9–18; 1 Corinthians 9:1*

Some Notable Psalms

A plea for help in time of trouble: *5, 17, 25, 31, 61*

A prayer when near despair: *39, 42, 43, 55, 73, 77, 86, 88, 102, 130*

A prayer for forgiveness and help: *6, 32, 38, 51, 143*

Rest in God's goodness: *4, 11, 23, 27, 63, 67, 91, 115, 121, 125, 139*

Israel's cry of anguish at God's anger: *44, 74, 80, 85*

Praise with shouts and singing: *33, 47, 66, 81, 95, 96, 98, 149, 150*

Praise for God's personal blessings: *18, 30, 34, 40, 92, 103, 107, 113, 116, 118, 146*

Praise for God's blessings to Israel: *68, 77, 100, 108, 124, 126, 129*

Praise for God's awesome majesty: *8, 24, 29, 46, 50, 90, 93, 114, 145*

Praise for God's law: *19, 119*

Songs of war and vindication: *35, 58, 76, 79, 83, 109, 137*

The history of God and the people of Israel: *78, 105, 106*

Nature: *19, 65, 104, 147, 148*

The Messiah: *2, 16, 22, 45, 69, 89, 110, 132*

Jerusalem and the temple: *48, 84, 87, 122*

The fates of the wicked and the righteous: *1, 15, 37, 49*

A Lineup of Rulers

The two-part book of Kings can be confusing. First, there's one nation to keep track of, then two, then one again. In all, 39 rulers are profiled. Little wonder it takes a Biblical scholar to keep all the details straight.

The following list of 38 kings and one queen should help clarify the history of Israel in the North and Judah in the South. As you come across the name of a ruler in one of the history books or in a book of the prophets, simply refer to the capsule description below for a brief summary of life during the time of that ruler or prophet.

In all, the kingdoms of Israel and Judah were united for 120 years and divided for just over 200 years. Then Israel disappeared and Judah lasted alone another 135 years. After that, no independent Jewish nation existed until the 20th century.

The timeline on the bottom of pages 1419–1425 places the major prophets in the appropriate time period, along with the rulers of their era. Prophets whose names appear in darker gray boxes spoke to Israel; those listed against a lighter gray background spoke to Judah. (Dating of some rulers is inexact because of overlapping reigns.)

UNITED KINGDOM

SAUL
DAVID
SOLOMON

These first three kings of Israel each ruled approximately 40 years, and so for 120 years, Israel was one nation. The books of Samuel and Chronicles, along with 1 Kings, describe their reigns in great detail. Later, Jews would look back on this time as the Golden Age of Israel.

DIVIDED KINGDOM

ISRAEL

JEROBOAM I   22 Years

He was handpicked by God to lead a reform, but this first king of the Northern Kingdom proved to be one of Israel's worst. For years afterward, evil kings were described as "walking in the ways of Jeroboam." It was he who firmly established the split-off nation of Israel, uniting 10 rebel tribes. To prevent his people from worshiping in Jerusalem (now enemy territory), he built a new capital city and set up the notorious "high places" as alternative worship sites. The high places and calf worship plagued Israel throughout its entire history. First Kings records that God decided to abandon Israel during the reign of Jeroboam, the Northern Kingdom's very first ruler. (1 Kings 11:26–15:25; 2 Chronicles 10:2–13:20)

JUDAH

REHOBOAM   17 Years

Judah's first king had a checkered career. Sometimes he obeyed God and listened to the prophets; sometimes he did not. At first, the Jewish religion gained strength when all priests and Levites came over to Judah. But, before long, idolatry found its way into Judah as well as into Israel, and Judah suffered humiliating punishment from the armies of Egypt. Thus Judah's first king set an unfortunate pattern for his successors. (1 Kings 11:43–14:31; 2 Chronicles 10–12)

ABIJAH   3 Years

War with Israel in the North dragged on throughout Abijah's three-year reign. The two splinter nations were still adjusting to each other's independence. Abijah offered no improvement on his father Rehoboam's immoral ways. (1 Kings 15:1-8; 2 Chronicles 13:1–14:1)

ISRAEL

JEROBOAM I (CONTINUED)

NADAB 2 Years

Jeroboam's son followed the errors of his father in every way, and his reign merits only eight verses. Israel's first dynasty ended abruptly when Nadab fell victim to a murder plot launched by Baasha. (1 Kings 15:25-32)

BAASHA 24 Years

After gaining the throne in a violent manner, Baasha lasted 24 years. He showed no inclination to reverse the evil practice begun by Jeroboam. The prophet Jehu predicted his death. (1Kings 15:33—16:7; 2 Chronicles 16)

ELAH 2 years

The Bible records only one incident from Elah's reign: His chariot commander staged a military coup while Elah was off getting drunk. Elah was killed, along with all other descendants of his father, Baasha. Israel's second dynasty, therefore, only lasted 26 years, and another family took the throne. (1 Kings 16:8-14)

ZIMRI 7 Days

Evidently, mutinous chariot commander Zimri acted without his army's support. The army revolted against him, and his "reign" ended seven days after it had begun, in a suicidal fire set in his palace. (1Kings 16:15-20)

JUDAH

ASA 41 Years

Asa and his son Jehoshaphat were the only kings mentioned in 1 Kings who did "what was right in the sight of the Lord." Second Chronicles gives a much fuller account of Asa's 41 years. He began religious reforms that turned into a kind of wildfire revival. He drove heathen cults out of the land—even removing his own grandmother as queen mother because of her idolatry. Asa also welcomed to Judah many refugees from Israel. Late in his reign he backslid and got bogged down in foreign wars, making an alliance with neighboring Aram to hold Israel at bay. (1 Kings 15:9-24; 2 Chronicles 14—16)

ISRAEL

OMRI   12 Years
Secular historians rate Omri as one of Israel's most powerful and capable political rulers. In fact, Assyrian records call Israel "the land of Omri." He outlasted a rival to the throne, expanded Israel's lands, and founded the city of Samaria, which would remain Israel's capital for 150 years. But he gets scant mention in the Bible; it dismisses him for sinning more "than all who were before him." (1 Kings 16:21-28)

AHAB   22 Years
In a competition for all-time worst king of Israel, Ahab would win hands down. He married the notorious Jezebel, a pagan priestess who promptly installed Baal worship as Israel's official religion. First Kings departs from its usually brief style to give a detailed treatment of Ahab's life and the great spiritual crisis then. During that time, Elijah appeared on the scene to represent the true God against Queen Jezebel's religion. God gave Ahab plenty of opportunities to reform. Ahab humbled himself at least once, postponing disaster, but a nasty incident over Naboth's vineyard sealed his fate. Politically, Ahab forged a successful alliance with Israel's neighbor, Judah, and the divided kingdoms lived at peace for the first time since Jeroboam. Ultimately, however, his evil practices would spread into Judah. (1 Kings 16:29—22:40; 2 Chronicles 18)

AHAZIAH   2 years
Like his father, Ahab, and mother, Jezebel, Ahaziah continued to worship Baal and to fight against Elijah. He was no match. His reign lasted only part of two years, and the descriptions of him reveal a weak, vengeful ruler. (1 Kings 22:40—2 Kings 1:18)

JORAM   12 Years

JUDAH

ASA (CONTINUED)

JEHOSHAPHAT   25 Years
Judah enjoyed the rare blessing of two good kings back to back. Jehoshaphat continued the spirit of Asa's rule, and found ways to further it. He sent out princes to teach from the Book of the Law in the cities of Judah and established courts of justice throughout the country. With a large army and well-fortified cities, he attained a level of peace and prosperity rare in Judah's history. His one serious mistake was in linking himself to Israel's wicked king Ahab through marriage and military alliance. (1 Kings 22:41-50; 2 Chronicles 17—20)

885 B.C.		AHAB	AHAZIAH	JORAM	850 B.C.
PROPHETS		ELIJAH			
ASA		JEHOSHAPHAT			

ISRAEL

JORAM (CONTINUED)

Although an improvement over his father and mother (Ahab and Jezebel), Joram ultimately failed to do right. He modified some of the worship of Baal, and at times had a respectful relationship with the prophet Elisha. But Joram lived in treacherous times. The nation of Aram was attacking from the east, and God had set in motion an internal plot, led by Jehu, against Ahab's heirs. Finally Joram fell victim to Jehu's arrow, ending the evil dynasty founded by Omri. (2 Kings 3:1–9:26)

JEHU   28 years

Not to be confused with the prophet of the same name, this Jehu was a fast-driving, impetuous military man. He began a holy mission to purge Ahab's influence out of Israel and Judah, but considerably overstepped his bounds. He killed Joram, had Jezebel thrown from a window, and slew 70 princes, piling their heads in two heaps by a gate. Then he slew all the priests and prophets of Baal and tricked the worshipers of Baal into a trap that led to a mass slaughter. Unfortunately, Jehu's zeal for violence did not translate into zeal for justice. His actions tore Israel apart for generations, and he did little to attend to the nation's spiritual health. Israel also began to lose political strength. (2 Kings 9–10)

JUDAH

JEHORAM   8 Years

After 60 good years under Asa and Jehoshaphat, Judah experienced a terrible regression under Jehoram. He began by killing his brothers and then marrying Athaliah, daughter of Israel's Ahab and Jezebel. She promptly led him into Baal worship. Elijah, who mostly prophesied to Israel, sent Judah's king Jehoram a letter predicting the severe bowel disease that would lead to his death. Second Chronicles reports that "he departed with no one's regret." (2 Kings 8:16-24; 2 Chronicles 21)

AHAZIAH   1 Year

In effect Ahaziah served as a mere puppet representative of the notorious queen Athaliah, daughter of Ahab and Jezebel. He fell victim to the bloody purge of Jehu. (2 Kings 8:25-29; 2 Chronicles 22:1-9)

ATHALIAH   7 Years

Queen Athaliah first corrupted her husband Jehoram and dominated her son Ahaziah. Then, after Ahaziah's death, she killed off her infant grandchildren to remove rivals to the throne. She ruled Judah for seven years, leading the kingdom into a dark time of Baal worship and evil. Providentially, however, one heir escaped her reach. The young Joash, hidden away by a relative, emerged at the age of seven. This led to a popular revolt against Athaliah. Athaliah, the only woman to rule either of the two kingdoms, was the last of Ahab's family to die. She had come within one baby of wiping out King David's royal line. (2 Kings 11; 2 Chronicles 22:10–23:21)

JOASH   40 Years

JEHU

ELISHA

JEHORAM   AHAZIAH   ATHALIAH   JOASH

ISRAEL

JEHU (CONTINUED)

JEHOAHAZ   17 Years

After all his father Jehu had done to exterminate Baal worship, Jehoahaz immediately reinstated it. He ruled 17 years, marked by a series of embarrassing military defeats at the hands of neighboring Aram. He did turn to God in desperation at least once, and Israel got some reprieve. (2 Kings 13:1-9)

JEHOASH   16 Years

Although Jehoash did not break the evil pattern of Israel's kings, he showed some bright spots. He honored the prophet Elisha, and God allowed him to recover much of the territory that Aram had taken from Israel. (Note that Judah also had a king named Joash, the shortened version of Jehoash.) (2 Kings 13:10–14:16)

JEROBOAM II   41 Years

It seems that God gave Israel one last chance under King Jeroboam II. This king ruled a strong and prosperous nation. The Bible gives scant mention of his reign, but it lasted 41 years, during which Israel recovered nearly all its former territory. The prophet Jonah lived then, possibly assisting the king in his frontier defense against Assyria. In addition, Amos and Hosea were active, railing against the terrible social and religious corruption of those affluent times. In a remarkable turn of events, Israel survived as a nation for only a few decades after this stable period. (2 Kings 14:23-29)

ZECHARIAH   6 Months
SHALLUM   1 Month

After Jeroboam II, the nation splintered into rival factions. The first king (Zechariah) ruled for six months, the second (Shallum) only one month. Both died violently. (2 Kings 15:8-16)

JUDAH

JOASH (CONTINUED)

He swept into power at the crest of a revolt against his wicked grandmother Athaliah. And as long as Joash followed the advice of Jehoiada the priest, he did well. Most notably, he organized massive projects to repair the temple. After Jehoiada died, however, Joash allowed idolatry to prosper once more. He strayed so far from the ideals of his youth that he ordered the prophet Zechariah to be stoned—the same Zechariah whose father, Jehoiada, had saved his life. Punishment came swiftly, at the hands of a plundering army. Finally, Joash's own servants turned against him and avenged Zechariah's murder. (2 Kings 12; 2 Chronicles 24)

AMAZIAH   29 Years

Second Kings concludes that Amaziah "did right in the sight of the LORD, but not like David his father." Yet the author mostly comments on Amaziah's failures. He began his rule by executing those who had killed his father. Then he ignored a prophet's advice and attacked Edom, bringing back idols from there. Flush with military success, he launched a foolhardy campaign against Israel. The trouncing that resulted discredited his leadership, and he spent his last 12 years in exile. (2 Kings 14:1-22; 2 Chronicles 25)

AZARIAH   52 Years

Called Uzziah in Chronicles, this king reigned some 50 years, the longest of Judah's kings. As a young man, he took advice from a prophet named Zechariah. He built up the army of Judah and worked on its agriculture and water supplies. Until Azariah, Judah had been a struggling kingdom, with enemy fortifications just five miles from Jerusalem. Under him, the nation achieved true strength. Even so, Azariah gets a short review in the Bible because of his spiritual failings. He did not remove the high places, and he violated the Law of Moses by taking on the work of priests himself. (2 Kings 15:1-17; 2 Chronicles 26)

JEHU	JEHOAHAZ	JEHOASH		JEROBOAM II			
ELISHA (CONTINUED)				JONAH			AMOS

820 B.C.   750 B.C.

| JOASH | | AMAZIAH | | AZARIAH |

ISRAEL

MENAHEM 10 Years

Menahem lasted for ten turbulent years. He gained the throne by murder, and his reign showed a similar ruthlessness. The first of Assyria's three invasions–Israel's "World War I" (see Introduction to 2 Kings)–occurred during Menahem's years, and he frantically tried to buy off the invaders. (2 Kings 15:14-22)

PEKAHIAH 2 Years

Israel was quickly sliding toward anarchy and extermination. Pekahiah survived only two years before a military coup overthrew him. (2 Kings 15:23-26)

PEKAH 20 Years

Pekah turned to international intrigue and conspiracy. He attempted to dethrone the king of Judah in the South. But Judah bought help from Assyria, which promptly invaded Israel for the second time. After occupying all major cities in Israel except the capital Samaria, Assyria began deporting thousands of conquered Israelites to other lands. (2 Kings 15:27-31)

HOSHEA 9 Years

The Bible judges Hoshea as less wicked than some of his predecessors. Nevertheless, Israel's death was certain. Hoshea angered Assyria by turning south to Egypt for aid. The Assyrians attacked, and after a terrible three-year siege, the last stronghold, Samaria, fell to the conquerors. Assyria deported the vast majority of Israel's population, who became the "ten lost tribes of Israel." (2 Kings 17)

JUDAH

AZARIAH (CONTINUED)

JOTHAM 16 Years

After serving as Azariah's proxy king for 15 years (while Azariah was quarantined with leprosy), Jotham took over and continued the practices of his father. He expanded Judah's economic and military strength, but did not pursue religious reforms as fully as he should have. (2 Kings 15:32-38; 2 Chronicles 27)

AHAZ 16 Years

At the very moment Ahaz was being crowned, armies from the North led by King Pekah of Israel were marching into Judah. Ahaz ignored the prophet Isaiah's advice to put his trust in God rather than military alliances. Turning to the mighty empire of Assyria, he purchased aid with treasures from the temple and the king's palace. The strategy worked temporarily: Israel's armies withdrew to defend themselves. But Ahaz opened the doors for later Assyrian invasions of Judah itself. Worse, he made copies of foreign gods and set them up in Jerusalem. Under him, religion in Judah took a precipitous drop. He went so far as to sacrifice his sons in the fire, following the detestable ways of foreign nations. (2 Kings 16; 2 Chronicles 28)

ASSYRIAN INVASION

MENAHEM	PEKAHIAH	PEKAH		HOSHEA	
750 B.C.		HOSEA			715 B.C.
		ISAIAH			▶
		MICAH			▶
	JOTHAM			AHAZ	

ASSYRIAN INVASION

ONLY JUDAH SURVIVES

HEZEKIAH   29 Years

King Hezekiah gets full treatment in both Kings and Chronicles. The first book stresses the political side of his reign while the second reports on his religious reforms. Both were impressive; Hezekiah was one of the best and most important kings of Judah. He immediately stopped idolatry by reopening and cleansing the temple and calling for a period of national repentance. He resurrected the Passover celebration, and worship in Israel reached a peak that had not been seen since the time of David and Solomon. In all this, he listened carefully to advice from the prophet Isaiah. Yet Hezekiah hardly lived in a peaceful era. He faced imminent danger from Assyria and barely survived an invasion and siege. God honored his faithfulness with a miraculous military intervention. In an unprecedented act, he also added 15 years to Hezekiah's life. (2 Kings 18–20; 2 Chronicles 29–32; Isaiah 36–39)

MANASSEH   55 Years

Whatever good Hezekiah had accomplished in his exemplary reign, his son Manasseh undid in 55 years of the worst rule in Judah's history. He reversed Hezekiah's reforms, bringing in all forms of idolatry, including the occult and witchcraft. He killed off prophets, erected idols in God's temple, and sacrificed his own sons on the altar of a heathen god. The Assyrian empire took Manasseh prisoner, leading him away with a hook through his nose. Later he repented, but great damage had been done. After Manasseh, God pronounced a final judgment on the future of Judah. (2 Kings 21:1-18; 2 Chronicles 33:1-20)

715 B.C.

ISAIAH (CONTINUED)

MICAH (CONTINUED)

640 B.C.

HEZEKIAH   **MANASSEH**

ONLY JUDAH SURVIVES

AMON   2 Years

Amon merely continued the practices of his father. He died at the hands of his servants. (2 Kings 21:19-26; 2 Chronicles 33:21-25)

JOSIAH   31 Years

Judah's slide to destruction was interrupted by the amazing rule of its all-time best king. Josiah came to the throne at age eight, but received good counsel from the high priests. In 31 years he carried out the most extensive religious reforms Judah had ever seen. He removed and destroyed the altars, idols, and symbols of ungodly worship from the temple, and destroyed pagan centers throughout the land. In a thrilling sequence of events, he oversaw the rediscovery of the Law of Moses and acted immediately on what it taught. No king equals Josiah for his sincere and devout practices. He even extended his reforms into the decimated regions of Israel in the North.

Josiah had a time of military peace, for during his reign the Assyrian empire was disintegrating. But he unwisely thrust himself into international politics by marching against Egypt. (The prophet Jeremiah had urged against the Egyptian campaign.) Judah would never recover from this fatal mistake, for Josiah died suddenly in battle. His death shocked the nation. After Josiah's death, Egypt installed a puppet king, and no one after him had the ability to rally Judah's religious or political strength. (2 Kings 22:1–23:30; 2 Chronicles 34–35)

JEHOAHAZ   3 Months

The third son of Josiah lasted only three months before being sacked by a pharaoh and carried off in chains. (2 Kings 23:30-34; 2 Chronicles 36:1-4)

640 B.C.			600 B.C.
	ZEPHANIAH		
		JEREMIAH	
	NAHUM		HABAKKUK
AMON		JEHOAHAZ	

JUDAH

JEHOIAKIM 11 Years

Installed by an Egyptian pharaoh, Jehoiakim found himself trapped when Egypt was defeated by a surging Babylon. He quickly shifted allegiance to Nebuchadnezzar of Babylon. One of Judah's worst kings, he stubbornly tried to have the prophet Jeremiah put to death. (Numerous passages in Jeremiah's book make plain his scorn for Jehoiakim.) Finally, after an ill-advised revolt against Nebuchadnezzar, Jehoiakim was captured and killed. (2 Kings 23:36–24:6; 2 Chronicles 36:5-8)

JEHOIACHIN 3 Months

The struggles with Babylon were the "World War II" in Israel's history (see Introduction to 2 Kings). After holding out for three months against Nebuchadnezzar's armies, Jehoiachin surrendered, and was carried away with many other captives, including the prophet Ezekiel. He lived in a Babylonian prison for 40 years. (2 Kings 24:6-17; 25:27-30; 2 Chronicles 36:8-10) Also referred to as Coniah. (Jeremiah 22:24, 28; 37:1)

ZEDEKIAH 11 Years

Zedekiah ruled over Judah during the last 11 years of its existence as an independent state. A weak king, he took bad advice from princes and advisers and often made unwise decisions. He ignored Jeremiah's advice to remain loyal to Babylon and joined an alliance against that empire. As a result, Nebuchadnezzar laid siege to Jerusalem for almost two years, bringing the city to the verge of starvation. At last the Babylonians made a breach in the wall and overran the city. They burned Solomon's temple, the king's palace, and other buildings, and destroyed the walls around Jerusalem. Finally, they took everything of value from the temple. The city was utterly looted. (2 Kings 24:17–25:7; 2 Chronicles 26:11-20)

BABYLONIAN INVASION

Zechariah, Haggai, and Malachi
prophesied later, to the Jewish refugees
who had returned from Babylon.

586 B.C. BABYLONIAN INVASION

640 B.C.	*DANIEL*	525 B.C.
JEREMIAH (CONTINUED)		
	EZEKIEL	
JEHOIAKIM	ZEDEKIAH	

Subject Guide

The Subject Guide is not a "concordance" that shows where the Bible uses a certain word. Rather, it lists major subjects that may be of interest, along with the Bible *passages* (not single verses, usually) that speak to these subjects. Topics of pressing interest or major significance have been highlighted within the list. Although we have tried to be comprehensive, any list of subjects must necessarily be restrictive. The italicized titles in quotes refer to Highlights, Insights, or Introductions on the subject. Page numbers are given in boldface type.

A

AARON – brother of and spokesman for Moses; became the first high priest
character profile, *"Working Together . . . and Apart"* – **p. 183**
with Moses, Exodus 4:10 – 12:50 – **p. 88**
made priest, Exodus 28 – 29 **p. 115**; *"The First High Priest"* – **p. 139**
his role with golden calf, Exodus 32 – **p. 120**
budding of his rod, Numbers 17 – **p. 188**
his death, Numbers 20:23 – 29 – **p. 192**

ABEL – Adam's second son; murdered by his brother Cain
character profile, *"Blood Brothers"* – **p. 29**
his life, Genesis 4:1 – 9 – **p. 29**
example of faith, Hebrews 11:1 – 4 – **p. 1333**
relationship to Christ, Hebrews 12:22 – 24 – **p. 1336**

ABIATHAR – high priest in the days of Saul and David
character profile, *"Outlaw Priest"* – **p. 386**

ABIGAIL – wife of Nabal, became David's wife after Nabal's death
character profile, *"Beauty and Brains"* – **p. 343**

ABSHAI – nephew of David and one of his chief warriors
character profile, *"Bloody Brothers"* – **p. 462**

ABNER – cousin of Saul and commander of his army
character profile, *"On the Wrong Side"* – **p. 353**

ABORTION – death of a fetus through a medical procedure
penalty for harming fetus, Exodus 21:22 – 25 – **p. 108**
unborn life important to God, Psalm 139 – **p. 681**

ABRAHAM – founder of the Jewish nation
character profile, *"Abraham"* – **p. 36**
called by God, Genesis 11:26 – 12:20 – **p. 36**
his life, Genesis 11:26 – 25:11 – **p. 36**
and Melchizedek, Genesis 14:18 – 24 – **p. 39**
covenant with, Genesis 15;17 – **p. 39**
and Hagar, Genesis 16 – **p. 40**
prayed for Sodom and Gomorrah, Genesis 18:16 – 33 – **p. 42**
asked to sacrifice his son, Genesis 22 – **p. 47**
his death, Genesis 25:1 – 11 – **p. 51**
his true offspring are believers, Romans 4 – **p. 1226**; Galatians 3:6 – 29 – **p. 1271**
faith demonstrated by deeds, James 2:20 – 24 – **p. 1340**

ABSALOM – third son of David, by Maacah
character profile, *"All That Glitters"* – **p. 366**
his revenge on Amnon, 2 Samuel 13 – 14 – **p. 363**
in hiding, *"A Refuge with His Family"* – **p. 365**
rebellion against David, 2 Samuel 15:1 – 19:8 – **p. 366**; *"No Way Back"* – **p. 369**

ADAM – the first man
character profile, *"First in Everything"* – **p. 26**
his creation and life, Genesis 1:26 – 5:5 – **p. 25**
his fall into sin, Genesis 3 – **p. 27**
Jesus and the line of Adam, Luke 3:23 – 38 – **p. 1107**
Jesus as second Adam, Romans 5:12 – 21 – **p. 1228**; 1 Corinthians 15:21 – 22,42 – 57 – **p. 1255**

ADOPTION – becoming a child of one who is not your biological parent
Abraham and adoption of an heir, Genesis 15:1 – 6 – **p. 39**; Genesis 16 – **p. 40**
Israel as God's adopted son, Exodus 4:21 – 23 – **p. 89**; Jeremiah 31:9, 16 – 20 – **p. 101**
Believers as God's adopted children, John 1:12 – 13 – **p. 1144**; Romans 8:12 – 25 – **p. 1231**; Galatians 3:26 – 4:7 – **p. 1273**; Ephesians 1:3 – 8 – **p. 1277**

ADULTERY – sexual unfaithfulness of a married person
laws against, Numbers 5:12 – 31 – **p. 173**
David and Bathsheba, 2 Samuel 11 – 12 – **p. 360**
warnings against, Proverbs 5 – **p. 692**; Proverbs 6:20 – 35 – **p. 693**
avoiding, *"A Safeguard Against Lust"* – **p. 186**
Jesus' views on, Matthew 5:27 – 32 – **p. 1037**
effect on the church, 1 Corinthians 5 – **p. 1245**

AFTERLIFE – *see* ETERNAL LIFE, HEAVEN, HELL, RESURRECTION

AGRIPPA – descendent of Herod; king before whom Paul pled his case
character profile, *"Roman Heart"* – **p. 1215**

AHAB – Israel's most wicked king
character profile, *"Worst King Yet"* – **p. 413**
ascended throne, 1 Kings 16:29 – 33 – **p. 405**
contest with Elijah, 1 Kings 18 – **p. 407**
and Naboth's vineyard, 1 Kings 21 – **p. 412**
his death, 1 Kings 22:34 – 38 – **p. 415**

AHASUERUS – king of Persian empire and husband of Esther
character of, *"Ahasuerus: A Wild Man"* – **p. 554**

ALCOHOL – *see* DRINKING ALCOHOL, WINE

Ambition – strong desire for success, honor, or power (*see also* PRIDE, SERVANTHOOD)

competing with God, *"Human Ambition"* – **p. 35**
at the tower of Babel, Genesis 11:1 – 11 – **p. 35**
results of, Matthew 16:21 – 27 – **p. 1053**
of disciples, Mark 9:33 – 37; 10:35 – 45 – **p. 1087**
the antichrist, 2 Thessalonians 2:1 – 4 – **p. 1301**

Assurance of Salvation
—certainty of God's forgiveness and love

sacrifice was made for the sins of the nation (*see also* JUSTIFICATION, SALVATION)
by sacrifice, *"The Reason for Sacrifice"* – **p. 136**
Hebrew ritual of, Leviticus 16 – **p. 150**
Christ as our, Romans 3:21 – 26 – **p. 1225**; 2 Corinthians 5:14 – 21 – **p. 1262**; Hebrews 9 – **p. 1331**; 1 Peter 2:22 – 25 – **p. 1347**; 1 John 1:8 – 2:2 – **p. 1356**

B

BAAL – god of the Phoenicians and Canaanites
worshiped in Israel, 1 Kings 16:29 – 34 – **p. 405**; 2 Kings 17:7 – 23 – **p. 436**; 21:1 – 9 – **p. 443**
defeated by Elijah, 1 Kings 18 – **p. 407**; *"Elijah Rubs It In"* – **p. 409**

BABYLON
as symbol of evil, *"An Evil Queen"* – **p. 784**; *"Apocalyptic Arrogance"* – **p. 867**; *"What Is Babylon?"* – **p. 1383**
and archaeology, *"The Throne Room"* – **p. 939**
fall of, *"Sneak Attack"* – **p. 940**
cruelty of, *"Gambling Prizes"* – **p. 966**
prophecies against, Isaiah 13:1 – 14:23 – **p. 748**; Isaiah 21:1 – 10 – **p. 755**; 47:1 – 15 – **p. 783**; Jeremiah 50:1 – 51:58 – **p. 862**

BACKSLIDING – departure from a life of faith in and obedience to God
displeases God, Psalm 78 – **p. 643**
a serious sin, Hebrews 6:4 – 6 – **p. 1328**; 10:26 – 31 – **p. 1333**
forgiveness for, Revelation 2:4 – 5 – **p. 1369**; Revelation 3:2 – 3,15 – 21 – **p. 1370**
examples of:
Israel at Mount Sinai, Exodus 32 – **p. 120**
Solomon, 1 Kings 11 – **p. 397**
Hymenaeus and Alexander, 1 Timothy 1:19 – 20 – **p. 1306**
in the end times, 2 Timothy 3:1 – 10 – **p. 1313**

BALAAM – man employed by the Moabites to curse the Israelites
character profile, *"Whose Side Is Balaam On?"* – **p. 195**
his loyalty, *"Whose Side Is Balaam On?"* – **p. 195**
stopped by God, Numbers 22 – 24 – **p. 193**
prophecy fulfilled, *"Balaam's Prophecy"* – **p. 197**
death of, Numbers 31:1 – 24 – **p. 203**

BAPTISM – a water ritual, used as a spiritual symbol (*see also* HOLY SPIRIT, JOHN THE BAPTIST)
Jesus' baptism, Matthew 3:13 – 15 – **p. 1035**
as sign of repentance, Matthew 3:1 – 12 – **p. 1035**
as sign of conversion, Matthew 28:16 – 20 – **p. 1071**
in the early church, Acts 2:37 – 41 – **p. 1180**; 8:26 – 39 – **p. 1189**
and the believer's death and resurrection in Christ, Romans 6 – **p. 1228**; Colossians 2:11 – 12 – **p. 1292**
of the Holy Spirit, Acts 1:1 – 8 – **p. 1178**; 1 Corinthians 12:12 – 13 – **p. 1251**

BARABBAS – criminal released by Pilate instead of Jesus
set free, Matthew 27:11 – 26 – **p. 1069**

BARGAINING –
in the middle East, *"Let's Make a Deal"* – **p. 49**; *"Oriental Bargaining"* – **p. 93**

BARNABAS – disciple; name changed from Joseph to one that means "son of encouragement"
character profile, *"The Encourager"* – **p. 1197**

BATHSHEBA – committed adultery with David and later married him (*see also* DAVID, SOLOMON)
character profile, *"Only Following Orders"* – **p. 361**
life of, 2 Samuel 11:1 – 12:25 – **p. 360**
helped Solomon become king, 1 Kings 1:11 – 31 – **p. 383**

Beauty

inner, 1 Samuel 16:1 – 13 – **p. 331**; *"Skin-Deep Beauty"* – **p. 698**; 1 Timothy 2:9 – **p. 1306**; 1 Peter 3:1 – 7 – **p. 1347**
of Bathsheba, 2 Samuel 11 – **p. 360**
of Esther, Esther 2:1 – 18 – **p. 550**
changing standards of, *"Tan Lines"* – **p. 731**

BEGGARS – *see* POOR

BETRAYAL
by a friend, *"Betrayed by a Friend"* – **p. 629**
of Jesus by Judas, Matthew 26:14 – 16,47 – 49 – **p. 1066**

BIBLE
as history, *"Selective History"* – **p. 87**; *"Three Kinds of Bricks"* – **p. 89**; *"Unfair Credit?"* – **p. 434**; *"The Ring of Truth"* – **p. 524**; *"Off at War"* – **p. 551**; *"Is Esther Accurate?"* – **p. 557**; *"Bridge Chapters"* – **p. 770**; *"Dating by Emperors"* – **p. 1104**; *"The Linking Book"* – **p. 1176**; *"In the Reign of . . ."* – **p. 1196**; *"Sailing Log"* – **p. 1218**
compilation of, *"Out of Print"* – **p. 193**; *"Using Other Sources"* – **p. 399**; *"The Five Books"* – **p. 639** *"Belong in the Bible?"* – **p. 1155**; *"Sound Familiar?"* – **p. 628**
in praise of, Psalm 19:7 – 11 – **p. 606**; 119:1 – 176 – **p. 669**
used by Satan, *"Satan and the Bible"* – **p. 652**
languages, *"A Change in Language"* – **p. 933**
literary devices in, *"Well-Turned Phrase"* – **p. 860**; *"Structured Passion"* – **p. 871**; *"A Passion for Punning"* – **p. 986**
translation of, *"Lost in Translation"* – **p. 1084**
importance of, 2 Timothy 3:14 – 17 – **p. 1314**
inspired by God, *"Scripture is God-Breathed"* – **p. 1314**; 2 Peter 1:19 – 21 – **p. 1353**
act on, James 1:19 – 27 – **p. 1340**
interpreting, *"A Book Full of Mysteries"* – **p. 1367**; *"Seals and Scrolls"* – **p. 1373**; *"Old Testament Echoes"* – **p. 1377**

BITTERNESS – lingering resentment or anger
avoid, Ephesians 4:29 – 32 – **p. 1281**
as sin, James 3:13 – 18 – **p. 1341**

BLASPHEMY – bringing reproach against God and his name
a sin against God, Exodus 20:7 – **p. 107**; Leviticus 24:13 – 23 – **p. 159**
Jesus charged with, Matthew 9:1 – 8 – **p. 1042**; Matthew 26:57 – 67 – **p. 1067**
against the Holy Spirit, Mark 3:20 – 30 – **p. 1076**

BLESSINGS
material blessings, Deuteronomy 7:12 – 16 – **p. 219**; Psalm 67 – **p. 634**
spiritual blessings, Psalm 32 – **p. 613**; John 1:14 – 17 – **p. 1144**; Ephesians 1:3 – 14 – **p. 1277**
showers of blessings, Ezekiel 34:26 – 30 – **p. 915**
the Beatitudes, Matthew 5:1 – 11 – **p. 1036**; Luke 6:20 – 22 – **p. 1111**

BLOOD – used to represent the life of a creature, often in sacrifices or rituals of cleansing
instructions to Noah about shedding, Genesis 9:1 – 6 – **p. 33**
role in the covenant, *"Covenant Blood"* – **p. 111**
for purification of priests, Exodus 29 – **p. 117**
in offerings to God, especially for sin, Leviticus 1,3,4 – **p. 132**
the day of atonement, Leviticus 16 – **p. 150**

BLOOD OF CHRIST – shed on the cross as Jesus died
wine as sign of, in the Lord's Supper, Matthew 26:27 – 29 – **p. 1066**; 1 Corinthians 11:23 – 32 – **p. 1251**
as payment for sin, Hebrews 9:11 – 28 – **p. 1331**

redemption through, Ephesians 1:7–8–**p. 1277**; 1 Peter 1:18–19–**p. 1346**

reconciliation through, Ephesians 2:11–18–**p. 1278**

cleansing through, 1 John 1:7–10–**p. 1356**

BOASTING
about God, *"Bragging on God"*–**p. 818**

BODY OF CHRIST
signified by bread in the Lord's Supper, Mark 14:22–24–**p. 1094**

as metaphor for church, Romans 12:3–8–**p. 1235**; 1 Corinthians 12:12–31–**p. 1251**; *"Lessons from the Human Body"*–**p. 1252**

Jesus as the head, Ephesians 1:22–23–**p. 1278**; Colossians 1:18–24–**p. 1291**

completely human, Hebrews 2:14–18–**p. 1326**

now a glorious body, 1 Corinthians 15:35–49–**p. 1255**; Philippians 3:20–21–**p. 1288**

BORN AGAIN – spiritual rebirth or conversion (*see also* CONVERSION, SALVATION)
necessity of, John 3:1–21–**p. 1146**

marked by holiness, Titus 3:4–8–**p. 1318**; 1 Peter 1:13–23–**p. 1346**

C

CAIAPHAS – high priest at the time of Jesus' arrest and crucifixion
character profile, *"Collaborators"*–**p. 1161**

CAIN – first son of Adam and Eve; murdered his brother Abel
character profile, *"Blood Brothers"*–**p. 29**

life of, Genesis 4:1–26–**p. 29**

a warning to believers, 1 John 3:11–13–**p. 1358**

CALEB – one of 12 spies sent by Moses into promised land
report of, Numbers 13:1–14:38–**p. 182**

receives Hebron, Joshua 14:1–15–**p. 266**

CALVARY – *see* GOLGOTHA

CANAAN – land God promised to the Israelites; later called Palestine
trade routes in, *"On the Road"*–**p. 37**

promised to Abraham, Genesis 13:14–17–**p. 38**; Genesis 15:12–21–**p. 39**

promised to Isaac, Genesis 26:1–6–**p. 52**

promised to Jacob, Genesis 28:10–22–**p. 56**

Moses can't go in, Deuteronomy 34:1–12–**p. 248**

Joshua conquers, Joshua 1–12–**p. 252**; *"Two Accounts of Warfare"*–**p. 264**

inhabitants punished, *"Is a War Ever Holy?"*–**p. 263**

inhabitants not eliminated, *"Hints of Failure"*–**p. 268**; *"Missing an Opportunity"*–**p. 269**

CELIBACY – abstaining from marriage
calling to, Matthew 19:4–12–**p. 1056**

advantages of, 1 Corinthians 7:32–40–**p. 1247**

not required, 1 Timothy 4:1–5–**p. 1307**

CHARACTER
revealed, *"Deeper Meanings"*–**p. 699**

CHEATING
by Laban, *"Cheater"*–**p. 58**

by Jacob, *"Misplaced Faith"*–**p. 60**

forbidden, *"Honest Weight"*–**p. 926**

CHILDREN
should honor parents, Exodus 20:12–**p. 107**; Ephesians 6:1–4–**p. 1282**

praising God, *"Children's Power"*–**p. 599**

a gift from God, Psalm 127–**p. 676**

formed by God in the womb, Psalm 139:13–16–**p. 681**

should listen to instruction, Proverbs 1–**p. 689**

suffering of, *"Pity the Children"*–**p. 873**

punishment of, *"Rebel Son"*–**p. 958**

used as an example of humility, Matthew 18:1–4–**p. 1055**

blessed by Jesus, Mark 10:13–16–**p. 1088**

of God through Christ, John 1:12–13–**p. 1144**; Romans 8:12–17–**p. 1231**; Galatians 3:26–4:7–**p. 1273**

CHOIR
David's, *"Bad Father, Good Kids"*–**p. 649**; *"And Now, the Choir . . ."*–**p. 456**

used by Ezra and Nehemiah, *"Victory Party"*–**p. 1260**

heavenly, *"Good News with Bad"*–**p. 1380**

CHRIST – *see* MESSIAH

Christians –name given to followers of Christ

first called, Acts 11:26–**p. 1196**; *"Naming the New Religion"*–**p. 1191**

how to become, Romans 10:9–13–**p. 1233**

marks of, Galatians 5:22–26–**p. 1275**

CHRISTIAN LIVING
over a lifetime, *"A View from Old Age"*–**p. 638**

struggles, *"Inner Struggles"*–**p. 1230**; *"A Positive and a Negative"*–**p. 1249**

questions about, *"Down-to-earth Problems"*–**p. 1236**; *"Weak or Strong?"*–**p. 1237**; *"When Everything Goes Wrong"*–**p. 1248**

and theology, *"Getting Practical"*–**p. 1292**

well-rounded, *"The Search for Wholeness"*–**p. 1293**; *"Words Are Not Enough"*–**p. 1338**

not being idle, *"No Work, No Eat"*–**p. 1302**

training for, *"Athlete in Training"*–**p. 1308**; *"Soldier, Athlete, Farmer"*–**p. 1313**; *"What Is True Faith?"*–**p. 1334**

leaving, *"Can a Believer Fall Away?"*–**p. 1328**

problems with money, *"Conflicts of Rich and Poor"*–**p. 1342**

stages in, *"A Friendly Interruption"*–**p. 1357**

CHURCH – both the local assemblies of Christians and the worldwide community of believers
promised by Christ, Matthew 16:13–20–**p. 1053**

beginnings of, *"Infant Church"*–**p. 1180**

growth of, *"The Linking Book"*–**p. 1176**; *"The Secret to the Early Church"*–**p. 1183**; *"Crossing Racial Barriers"*–**p. 1188**; *"The Danger in Being a Christian"*–**p. 1189**; *"On the Road with the Apostle Paul"*–**p. 1205**

organization of, *"A Cure for Discrimination"*–**p. 1185**; *"The First Church Council"*–**p. 1200**; *"The Hardest Job"*–**p. 1304**; *"Time to Get Organized"*–**p. 1306**

unity of, Romans 12:3–8–**p. 1235**; Ephesians 4:1–14–**p. 1279**

founded on Christ and the apostles, 1 Corinthians 3:1–15–**p. 1243**; Ephesians 2:19–22–**p. 1279**

as body of Christ, 1 Corinthians 12:12–28–**p. 1251**

problems in early, *"When Everything Goes Wrong"*–**p. 1248**; *"Diverse People, Diverse Problems"*–**p. 1316**

locations of early, *"Cities on a Mail Route"*–**p. 1371**

Christ's relationship to, Ephesians 4:7–16–**p. 1280**

Christ's message to seven churches, Revelation 2–3–**p. 1369**

CIRCUMCISION – removal of the foreskin in males; established by God to signify his relationship with the Israelites
sign of covenant, Genesis 17:9–14–**p. 41**

symbolic, *"Uncircumcised Hearts"*–**p. 163**; *"Circumcised Hearts"*–**p. 810**

no longer necessary, Romans 4:4–12–**p. 1226**;
   Galatians 5:1–12–**p. 1274**
linked with baptism, Colossians 2:11–12–**p. 1292**

CITIES OF REFUGE
purpose of, *"Controlling Blood Feuds"*–**p. 208**; *"Cities of
   Refuge"*–**p. 271**

CLEANNESS
laws of clean and unclean, Leviticus 11–15–**p. 142**
cleansing from sin, Psalm 51:1–9–**p. 626**; Hebrews
   10:19–22–**p. 1333**; 1 John 1:5–10–**p. 1356**

COLOSSAE – city in Asia to which Paul wrote the letter
   "Colossians"
Paul's friends in, *"Prominent Names"*–**p. 1294**

Comfort

through silent sharing, *"Keeping Quiet"*–**p. 561**
in grief, Job 2:11–13–**p. 561**; Psalm 23–**p. 608**
in trouble, Psalm 46–**p. 624**; Romans 8:18–39–
   p. 1231
when we sin, Psalm 103–**p. 657**
when afraid, Isaiah 41:8–20–**p. 776**
from God, Isaiah 40:1–11–**p. 773**
from Holy Spirit, John 14:1–4,15–27–**p. 1165**
share with others, 2 Corinthians 1:3–7–**p. 1258**;
   "Mixing Gentleness with Harshness"–**p. 1275**

COMMUNION – *see* LORD'S SUPPER

COMPASSION – to have pity for and show kindness to
   another
of God, Exodus 34:4–7–**p. 122**; Psalm 103:8–12–
   p. 657; Jonah 3–**p. 982**
commanded by God, Micah 6:6–8–**p. 989**; Galatians
   6:1–10–**p. 1275**
of Jesus, Matthew 9:35–38–**p. 1043**; 14:13–14–
   p. 1051; 15:29–39–**p. 1052**; John 11:17–44–
   p. 1160
sign of faith, 1 John 3:11–24–**p. 1358**

COMPLAINING
not condemned by God, *"A Shocking Lack of Piety"*–
   p. 570

CONFESSION – an acknowledgment of the truth
of Christ:
   Peter's, Matthew 16:13–20–**p. 1053**
   Thomas's, John 20:24–31–**p. 1173**
   as Lord, Romans 10:9–13–**p. 1233**; Philippians
      2:9–11–**p. 1286**
   as Son of God, 1 John 4:2–3,13–16–**p. 1358**
of sin:
   Ezra's, Ezra 9–**p. 528**
   David's, Psalm 51–**p. 626**
   Isaiah's, Isaiah 6–**p. 743**
   Daniel's, Daniel 9–**p. 944**
   lost son's, Luke 15:11–32–**p. 1126**
   tax collector's, Luke 18:9–14–**p. 1129**
   to one another, James 5:16–**p. 1343**
   to God, 1 John 1:5–2:2–**p. 1356**

CONFORMITY – to adopt the values and practices of a
   group
to evildoers, Proverbs 4:10–19–**p. 691**
to the world, James 4:1–10,17–**p. 1341**

CONSCIENCE – awareness of one's actions as either
   right or wrong (*see also* CONFESSION,
   FORGIVENESS)
guilty, Psalm 38–**p. 618**
accuses us of sin, Romans 2:12–16–**p. 1224**

be sensitive to others', Romans 14–**p. 1237**;
   1 Corinthians 8–**p. 1248**; 10:23–11:1–**p. 1250**
silencing of, *"Loss of Sensitivity"*–**p. 1281**
cleansed by Christ, Hebrews 10:19–22–**p. 1333**

Conversion –to turn away from sin and
to God through repentance and faith (*see also*
BORN AGAIN, PAUL, SALVATION)

result of God's love, Jeremiah 31:3–14–**p. 841**
of Samaritan woman, John 4:1–30,39–42–**p. 1147**
of an Ethiopian eunuch, Acts 8:26–40–**p. 1189**
of Paul, Acts 9:1–25–**p. 1190**; *"Recruiting from the
   Opposition"*–**p. 1193**
of Lydia, Acts 16:11–15–**p. 1202**
of a jailer, Acts 16:22–34–**p. 1202**
become new through, 2 Corinthians 5:17–19–
   p. 1262
by grace, Ephesians 2:1–10–**p. 1278**

CORINTH
church started, Acts 18:1–17–**p. 1204**
life in, *"The Last Place to Start a Church"*–**p. 1240**;
   "Corinthian Slogans"–**p. 1246**
and Paul, *"A Book of Joy and Sadness"*–**p. 1257**; *"A
   Mysterious Visit"*–**p. 1259**; *"Paul Has Had Enough"*–
   p. 1265

CORNELIUS – first Gentile Christian, a Roman to whom
   Paul preached
character profile, *"Least Likely Convert"*–**p. 1194**

COURAGE
the call to be courageous, Joshua 1–**p. 252**
David's, 1 Samuel 17:26–50–**p. 333**
shown by kings of Judah, *"The Great Reformers"*–**p. 498**
Esther's, *"A Profile of Courage"*–**p. 548**
Daniel's, *"Kidnapped"*–**p. 931**
Daniel's three friends, Daniel 3–**p. 935**
the apostles', Acts 4–**p. 1182**; 5:17–42–**p. 1184**

COVENANT – an agreement between two parties; a
   solemn promise or vow, especially between God
   and people
with Noah, Genesis 9:1–17–**p. 33**
with Abraham, Genesis 15–**p. 39**; 17:1–14–**p. 41**;
   "Promises, Promises"–**p. 48**
with Israelites in Old Testament, *"Book of the Covenant"*–
   p. 105; *"The Covenant"*–**p. 107**; Exodus 19:3–8,24–
   p. 105; *"A Personal Plea"*–**p. 210**; Deuteronomy
   29–**p. 241**
benefits of keeping, *"Healthier, Wealthier, and Wiser"*–
   p. 223
illustrated by Joshua, *"Blessings and Curses"*–**p. 259**
with David, 2 Samuel 7:1–17–**p. 357**
punishment for breaking, *"Day of Reckoning"*–**p. 819**
new, *"A New Covenant"*–**p. 844**; 2 Corinthians 2:12–
   3:18–**p. 1260**; Hebrews 8:7–13–**p. 1331**; 10:1–18–
   p. 1332; *"More Perfect"*–**p. 1331**; *"A Vivid
   Contrast"*–**p. 1336**
with Israelites in New Testament, *"A Crushing Blow to
   Paul"*–**p. 1232**

COVETING – envious desire for something that belongs
   to another (*see also* ENVY, GREED)
commandment on, Exodus 20:17–**p. 107**
Achan's, Joshua 7–**p. 257**
Ahab's, 1 Kings 21:1–14–**p. 412**
result of, James 4:1–10–**p. 1341**

CREATION
account of, Genesis 1–2–**p. 25**; *"God at Work"*–**p. 999**

D

DESERT — see WILDERNESS

DEVIL — see SATAN

DISABILITIES
barriers to those with, *"Barriers to the Disabled"* — **p. 1075**

DISCIPLES
of John the Baptist, *"New Recruits"* — **p. 1082**
calling of, *"Gradual Disciples"* — **p. 1145**
training of, *"Training the 12 Disciples"* — **p. 1086**; *"Baffling Thoughts"* — **p. 1087**
doubting the Resurrection, *"Doubting Thomas"* — **p. 1173**
replacing Judas Iscariot, *"Inner Circle"* — **p. 1089**
transforming of, *"A Change of Heart and Mind"* — **p. 1174**; *"A Man Named 'The Rock' "* — **p. 1348**
make them of all nations, Matthew 28:6 – 20 — **p. 1070**
called Christians, Acts 11:26 — **p. 1196**

DISCIPLESHIP — the act of following and learning from a teacher, especially Jesus
not waiting, *"Burying His Father"* — **p. 1118**
cost of, Luke 14:25 – 34 — **p. 1126**
evidence of, John 15:1 – 17 — **p. 1166**
result of love, John 21:15 – 19 — **p. 1174**

DISCIPLINE — training that molds, instructs, corrects
by parents, Proverbs 23:13 – 23 — **p. 710**; *"How to Raise Children"* — **p. 708**
by God, *"Like Everybody Else"* — **p. 897**; Hebrews 12:1 – 13 — **p. 1335**
by the church, 1 Corinthians 5 — **p. 1245**
by God's word, 2 Timothy 3:14 – 17 — **p. 1314**

DISCOURAGEMENT — (see also COMFORT)
overcoming, Joshua 1:1 – 9 — **p. 252**; Psalm 42 — **p. 621**; 77:1 – 15 — **p. 641**; John 14:1 – 27 — **p. 1165**; 2 Corinthians 4:7 – 12,16 – 18 — **p. 1261**; *"For the Discouraged"* — **p. 1276**
of Job, *"Why Keep on Living?"* — **p. 563**
in life, *"Companion Book"* — **p. 725**

DISCRIMINATION — (see also RACISM)
against the Israelites, *"New Tyrant in Town"* — **p. 86**
on basis of wealth, *"Play No Favorites"* — **p. 1340**
eliminated in Christ, *"The Original Barbarians"* — **p. 1293**; Ephesians 2:11 – 18 — **p. 1278**

DISEASE — (see also HEALING)
cleansing from, *"A Bird Set Free"* — **p. 147**
treatment of, *"Bad Medical Advice"* — **p. 495**

DISOBEDIENCE — (see also OBEDIENCE)
Israel's in entering Canaan, *"Imperfect Timing"* — **p. 185**
warnings against, *"Final Warnings"* — **p. 207**; *"A Scent of Doom"* — **p. 243**

DIVORCE
Mosaic law on, Deuteronomy 24:1 – 4 — **p. 236**
God's view of, *"I Hate Divorce"* — **p. 1022**
Jesus' teaching on, Matthew 19:1 – 12 — **p. 1056**; Mark 10:2 – 12 — **p. 1087**; *"Teaching on Divorce"* — **p. 1088**
a pardonable sin, John 4:4 – 42 — **p. 1147**
Paul's teaching on, 1 Corinthians 7:10 – 16 — **p. 1247**

Doubt *(see also FAITH)*

of Abraham, Genesis 12:10 – 20 — p. 37
of Sarah, Genesis 18:1 – 15 — p. 42
of Moses, Exodus 4:1 – 17 — p. 88
of Gideon, Judges 6 — p. 286
of Peter, Matthew 14:22 – 32 — p. 1051
overcoming, Mark 9:14 – 29 — p. 1086; 11:22 – 25 — p. 1090; James 1:2 – 7 — p. 1339
of John the Baptist, Luke 7:18 – 23 — p. 1113
of Thomas, John 20:24 – 31 — p. 1173

DREAMS — (see also VISIONS)
of Jacob, Genesis 28:10 – 22 — **p. 56**
interpreted by Joseph, Genesis 37 — **p. 67**; 41 — **p. 72**
meaning of, *"A Nightmare"* — **p. 733**; *"A Nation of Dreamers"* — **p. 935**
false prophecy through, Jeremiah 23:25 – 32 — **p. 833**; Ezekiel 13:1 – 9 — **p. 889**
interpreted by Daniel, Daniel 2 — **p. 933**; 4 — **p. 937**
at the birth of Jesus, Matthew 2 — **p. 1034**
of Pilate's wife, Matthew 27:19 — **p. 1069**
in the last days, Acts 2:14 – 21 — **p. 1179**

Drinking Alcohol *(see also WINE)*

warnings about, Proverbs 20:1 — p. 706; 23:29 – 35 — p. 710; Isaiah 5:11 – 12 — p. 742; *"The Dangers of Wine"* — p. 710; Ephesians 5:18 — p. 1281
vow against, *"Teetotalers"* — p. 848
examples of overindulgence
of Noah, Genesis 9:20 — p. 34
of Lot, Genesis 19:32 – 35 — p. 45
of Ahasuerus, Esther 1:10 — p. 550
at the Lord's Supper, 1 Corinthians 11:21 — p. 1251

E

EARTH — (see also ECOLOGY)
created by God, Genesis 1:1 – 25 — **p. 25**; *"Ecology Plus"* — **p. 658**
care for, Genesis 1:26 – 31 — **p. 25**
exhibits God's love, Psalm 33:1 – 11 — **p. 613**
not eternal, *"Outlasting the Universe"* — **p. 657**
ages of, *"Three Worlds"* — **p. 1353**
waits for redemption, Romans 8:18 – 25 — **p. 1231**
destruction of, *"The Fate of the Earth"* — **p. 1354**
new, *"New Earth"* — **p. 801**; 2 Peter 3:3 – 13 — **p. 1353**; Revelation 21:1 – 22:5 — **p. 1386**; *"Eden Regained"* — **p. 1387**

ECOLOGY — keeping a proper balance in nature
God's concern for, *"Respect for Nature"* — **p. 234**
appreciation of, *"Ecology Plus"* — **p. 658**

EDOM — see Esau

EGYPT
Joseph taken there, Genesis 37 — **p. 67**
Israelites moved there, Genesis 39 – 50 — **p. 71**
exodus from, Exodus 1 – 13 — **p. 86**
judgment of, Isaiah 19 — **p. 754**; Jeremiah 42 — **p. 853**; Ezekiel 29 – 30 — **p. 907**
Jesus taken there, Matthew 2:13 – 20 — **p. 1034**

ELDER — a designated leader of the Jewish people and of the church
leaders of the Jewish Council, Acts 5:17 – 42 — **p. 1184**
leaders appointed in churches, Acts 14:21 – 25 — **p. 1199**; Titus 1:5 – 9 — **p. 1317**
Paul's farewell speech to, Acts 20:13 – 38 — **p. 1209**
qualifications for, 1 Timothy 3:1 – 7 — **p. 1306**

ELECTION — God's choosing a people for himself
of Abraham, Genesis 12:1 – 9 — **p. 36**
of Israel, Exodus 19:1 – 6 — **p. 105**; Deuteronomy 10:12 – 22 — **p. 223**; Isaiah 41:8 – 16 — **p. 776**
of Jesus' disciples, John 15:9 – 17 — **p. 1166**
of Jacob, Romans 9:6 – 13 — **p. 1232**
of the church, Ephesians 1:3 – 14 — **p. 1277**; 1 Peter 2:1 – 10 — **p. 1346**
make it sure, 2 Peter 1:3 – 10 — **p. 1352**

Eternal Life −life everlasting with God, which begins at conversion (*see also* BORN AGAIN, CONVERSION, SALVATION, HEAVEN)

life of, Ezra 7 – 10 – **p. 525**; Nehemiah 8 – **p. 539**; 12 – **p. 545**

concern about intermarriage, *"Ezra, a Man of the Heart"* – **p. 526**

F

Faith – trust in and reliance on God

of Abraham, *"Abraham"* – p. 36; Genesis 15:6 – p. 39
Abraham's lack of, *"A Substitute Wife"* – p. 40
simple, *"Keep It Simple"* – p. 244
shown by widow of Zarephath, *"Down to the Last Meal"* – p. 407
shown by Ezra, *"Risk of Faith"* – p. 528
during suffering, *"When Bad Things Happened to a Good Person"* – p. 558; *"Seeing in the Dark"* – p. 593; *"Refiner's Fire"* – p. 1346
living by, *"Beyond Understanding"* – p. 727; *"Whom to Trust?"* – p. 825; Matthew 6:25 – 34 – p. 1039; *"Time to Decide"* – p. 1323
during crisis, *"A Time of Crisis"* – p. 766
lukewarm, *"When Faith Grows Weary"* – p. 1020
necessary for salvation, Romans 3:21 – 5:11 – p. 1225; Galatians 2 – 3 – p. 1271; Ephesians 2:1 – 10 – p. 1278
our part in, *"Working with God"* – p. 1286
heroes of, Hebrews 11 – p. 1333; *"What Is True Faith?"* – p. 1334
shown by deeds, *"Bargain Hunting"* – p. 843; James 2:14 – 26 – p. 1340; *"Words Are Not Enough"* – p. 1338

FAITHFULNESS
of God, Psalm 78 – **p. 643**; Psalm 111 – **p. 665**; Lamentations 3:22 – 32 – **p. 875**
an aspect of the Spirit's fruit, Galatians 5:16 – 26 – **p. 1275**
of Moses, Hebrews 3 – **p. 1326**
expected of Christians, Revelation 2:8 – 11 – **p. 1370**

FALSE PROPHETS
used by God, *"Whose Side Is Balaam On?"* – **p. 195**
tests for, *"Testing Prophets"* – **p. 227**
denounced, *"Doglike Prophets"* – **p. 793**
predicting good, *"Greedy Doctors"* – **p. 814**; *"Whitewash"* – **p. 889**; *"Plenty of Beer"* – **p. 986**
use of dreams, *"Questionable Dreams"* – **p. 833**

FALSE TEACHERS
avoiding, *"Unequal Yokes"* – **p. 1262**
recognizing, *"Battling the Cults"* – **p. 1290**; *"Foolish Questions"* – **p. 1318**; *"A Threat from Within"* – **p. 1351**; *"Who Were the Gnostics?"* – **p. 1359**; *"Undesirable Guests"* – **p. 1361** *"Watch Out"* – **p. 911**
distorting the truth, *"Words That Get Polluted"* – **p. 1355**
Gnostics, *"Pesky Deceivers"* – **p. 1362**
emperor worship, *"Satan's Throne"* – **p. 1370**

FAME
transience of, Isaiah 14:9 – 20 – **p. 751**
unreliability of, Ezekiel 33:30 – 32 – **p. 913**
unimportant, 1 Corinthians 3:1 – 23 – **p. 1243**

Family

established in garden of Eden, Genesis 2:18 – 24 – p. 27
obligations to, *"A Brother's Duty"* – p. 70

quarrels within, *"Family Battles"* – p. 69; *"Family Jealousy"* – p. 182
built by God, Psalm 127 – 128 – p. 676
of God, *"For the Discouraged"* – p. 1276; Ephesians 2:19 – 22 – p. 1279
family relations, Ephesians 5:21 – 6:4 – p. 1281; Colossians 3:18 – 21 – p. 1293

FAMINE
in Egypt and Palestine, *"An Unusual Famine"* – **p. 74**
in Israel, Ruth 1:1 – **p. 308**; 1 Kings 17 – **p. 406**; 2 Kings 6:25 – 8:2 – **p. 425**

FASTING – abstinence from food or drink for a period of time, especially for spiritual reasons
at a time of national crisis, 2 Chronicles 20:1 – 13 – **p. 497**; Esther 4 – **p. 552**; Joel 2:15 – 17 – **p. 965**
true, Isaiah 58 – **p. 794**
proper time for, *"Repent for How Long?"* – **p. 1013**
Jesus' teaching on, Matthew 6:16 – 18 – **p. 1038**
disciples', Acts 13:1 – 3 – **p. 1197**; 14:23 – **p. 1199**

FEAR – reverence and awe for God
commanded, Deuteronomy 6:10 – 25 – **p. 218**; Ecclesiastes 12:8 – 14 – **p. 728**
good, Psalm 33 – **p. 613**
guide to living, *"The Fear of the Lord"* – **p. 694**
the beginning of wisdom, Proverbs 9:10 – 12 – **p. 696**

FEAR – fright or alarm
combating, Psalm 23 – **p. 608**; 56 – **p. 629**; 91 – **p. 652**; Jeremiah 1:4 – 19 – **p. 806**; Luke 12:4 – 12 – **p. 1122**
comfort in, John 14 – **p. 1165**

FELLOWSHIP
expressed in sharing, Acts 2:42 – 47 – **p. 1180**; 4:24 – 35 – **p. 1182**
with the Holy Spirit, 2 Corinthians 13:14 – **p. 1268**
in church, Ephesians 4:17 – 5:21 – **p. 1280**
with God, 1 John 1 – **p. 1356**

FESTIVALS – see JEWISH HOLY DAYS

FLATTERY
deceives, *"Flattering Advice"* – **p. 369**; *"Dangerous Flattery"* – **p. 716**
displeases God, Psalm 12 – **p. 601**

FOOD
provided by God, *"No More Free Lunch"* – **p. 255**
provided by Christ, Matthew 14:13 – 21 – **p. 1051**; John 6 – **p. 1151**
glorify God through, 1 Corinthians 10:23 – 11:1 – **p. 1250**
as god, Philippians 3:19 – **p. 1288**

FOOL – (see also WISDOM)
in biblical terms, *"The Making of a Fool"* – **p. 713**

FOREIGN NATIONS
opposing Judah and Israel, *"Troublesome Neighbors"* – **p. 433**
Israel's alliances with, *"Ahaz's Fateful Decisions"* – **p. 436**; *"The Siege Lifted"* – **p. 849**; *"False Hope"* – **p. 876**; *"The Runaways"* – **p. 900**; *"Unreliable Egypt"* – **p. 908**
praising God, *"Who are God's People?"* – **p. 624**; *"House of Prayer"* – **p. 793**
loved by God, *"God Reaches Out"* – **p. 633**
loss of power of, *"The Decline of Tyre"* – **p. 758**
Cyrus, *"Good Shepherd?"* – **p. 781**
cruelty of, *"Most Ruthless"* – **p. 908**
preaching gospel to, *"To All Nations"* – **p. 1093**
entering the church, *"Earthshaking Change"* – **p. 1195**
salvation of, *"Hope for the Gentiles"* – **p. 821**; *"The Wise Men"* – **p. 1034**
judged by God, *"Just What They Deserved"* – **p. 903**

Forgiveness

human, Genesis 33 – p. 63; 50:15 – 21 – p. 83; Luke 15:17 – 24 – p. 1126; Acts 7:60 – p. 1188
God's, Exodus 34:4 – 7 – p. 122; Psalm 103:8 – 12 – p. 657; Micah 7:18 – 20 – p. 991; *"Nobody Like God"* – p. 991
absolute, *"An End to Guilt"* – p. 863
for sins, Psalm 130 – p. 677
how often, Matthew 18:21 – 35 – p. 1055
through Christ, Mark 2:1 – 11 – p. 1075; Colossians 2:6 – 15 – p. 1292; *"A Modern Peace Child"* – p. 1227
in the church, 2 Corinthians 2:5 – 11 – p. 1260

FREE WILL

Pharaoh's, *"Pharaoh's Hard Heart"* – p. 93
Israel's, *"Free Choice"* – p. 277
David's, *"Satan or the Lord?"* – p. 379

FREEDOM

through obeying, *"Free At Last"* – p. 672
in Christ, John 8:31 – 36 – p. 1156; Galatians 4:21 – 5:26 – p. 1273; *"Legalism"* – p. 1272; *"Paul Fights Back"* – p. 1274
from sin and our human nature, Romans 6 – p. 1228
from law, Romans 8:1 – 17 – p. 1230; Galatians 3:8 – 25 – p. 1272

FRIENDSHIP

acts of, *"Loyal Friends in Death"* – p. 348; *"How to be a Good Friend"* – p. 704
faithfulness in, Proverbs 27:6,10,17 – p. 714
giving advice in, *"A Mixture of True and False"* – p. 565; *"What Not to Say to a Hurting Person"* – p. 564; *"A Wrong Time for Cheer"* – p. 572; *"Battle of Words"* – p. 573; *"A Silent Friend Decides to Speak Up"* – p. 581; *"Kinder, Gentler Friend"* – p. 584
importance of, Ecclesiastes 4:7 – 12 – p. 723
of David and Jonathan, 1 Samuel 20 – p. 336; *"Final Farewell"* – p. 340; *"The Survival of a Family"* – p. 342
of Jesus with Mary, Martha, and Lazarus, John 11:1 – 44 – p. 1159
of Ruth and Naomi, *"A Rare Bond of Love"* – p. 307
with the world, James 4 – p. 1341
with the wrong people, *"Unholy Alliance"* – p. 414

FRUIT OF THE SPIRIT

described, Galatians 5:16 – 26 – p. 1275

FUTURE – (see also SECOND COMING)

seeking omens of, *"The Witch of Endor"* – p. 346; *"Liver-Gazing"* – p. 898
revealed by God, *"Foretelling the Future"* – p. 782; *"A Glimpse of Things to Come"* – p. 798
of the earth, *"Catastrophes to Come?"* – p. 1018
preoccupation with, Matthew 6:25 – 34 – p. 1039; Luke 12:13 – 48 – p. 1122; *"Preparing for the End"* – p. 1298
Jesus' statements about, *"When Will Jesus Return?"* – p. 1064
uncertain, James 4:13 – 17 – p. 1342
of God's kingdom, *"A Happy Ending after All"* – p. 1385

G

GABRIEL – an angel who carried messages from God

with Daniel, Daniel 8, 9 – p. 1343
with Zacharias, Luke 1:5 – 25 – p. 1101
with Mary, Luke 1:26 – 38 – p. 1103

GALILEE – region in northern Palestine

towns given to Hiram, *"Good-for-nothing Towns"* – p. 395
Jesus' ministry there predicted, Isaiah 9:1 – 7 – p. 745; Matthew 4:12 – 17 – p. 1036

Jesus' ministry in, *"Into the Countryside"* – p. 1074
home of Mary and Joseph, Luke 1:26 – p. 1103; 2:39 – p. 1106

GARDEN OF EDEN

God created, Genesis 2:8 – 17 – p. 26
expulsion from, Genesis 3 – p. 27

GENEALOGY

shows God's care, *"Compressed History"* – p. 451
importance to the Israelites, *"A Family Record"* – p. 450; *"Key People"* – p. 456; *"The Source of Genealogies"* – p. 460; *"A People Preserved"* – p. 520; *"Remembering Back"* – p. 642
of Jesus, *"A Bridge from Old to New"* – p. 1031; *"A Gospel for the Gentiles"* – p. 1107

GENTILES – see FOREIGN NATIONS

GIDEON – a warrior and leader of Israel

character profile, *"Unlikely Leaders"* – p. 287
life of, Judges 6 – 8 – p. 286
prepared by God, *"Unlikely Leaders"* – p. 287

GIFTS – special abilities given to believers through the grace of God

stewardship of, Matthew 25:14 – 30 – p. 1064; *"Original Talent"* – p. 1065
use of, Romans 12:3 – 8 – p. 1235; 1 Peter 4:10 – 11 – p. 1349
desire for, 1 Corinthians 12 – 14 – p. 1251; *"Speaking in Tongues"* – p. 1253
God distributes, Ephesians 4:7 – 13 – p. 1280

GIVING

appropriate, *"The Perfect Gift"* – p. 76
for the tabernacle, *"Enthusiastic Givers"* – p. 125
to God, *"Does God Need Our Gifts?"* – p. 626; Malachi 3:6 – 12 – p. 1023
in secret, Matthew 6:1 – 4 – p. 1038
generous, *"Any Poor People?"* – p. 229; 1 Corinthians 16:1 – 4 – p. 1256; 2 Corinthians 8 – 9 – p. 1263; *"Don't Forget the Poor"* – p. 1264; *"Bonuses of Giving"* – p. 1265

GLORY – the grandeur and majesty of God

revealed, Exodus 40:34 – 38 – p. 130; 2 Chronicles 7:1 – 4 – p. 487
of God, Psalm 29 – p. 611; 93 – p. 653; 96 – p. 654
manifested in Jesus, John 1:14 – 18 – p. 1144; John 12:20 – 33 – p. 1162; 2 Corinthians 3 – p. 1260
believers fall short of, Romans 3:10 – 23 – p. 1225

GOD

his creativity, Genesis 1 – 2 – p. 25
encounters with, *"Wrestling with God"* – p. 619; *"God Speaks to Job"* – p. 590; *"A Love Poem to God's Law"* – p. 671; *"Seeing the Unseen God"* – p. 878; *"Drawing Near"* – p. 1329
his name, Exodus 3 – p. 87
self-description, *"Capsule Description"* – p. 122
his holiness, *"A Portable Cathedral"* – p. 124; *"Living with Fire"* – p. 131; *"The Glory of the Lord"* – p. 141; *"A High-Water Mark"* – p. 487; Isaiah 40 – p. 773
his love for his people, *"Freedom Fighters"* – p. 279; *"The New Sodom"* – p. 738; *"The People Who Refuse to Die"* – p. 840
apparent absence of, *"Arms Too Short"* – p. 566; *"Where Is God?"* – p. 577; *"Is God Really Listening?"* – p. 586; *"The Song of the Cross"* – p. 608; *"Wrestling with God"* – p. 619; *"No Happy Ending"* – p. 622
as a shepherd, Psalm 23 – p. 608; *"Good Shepherd"* – p. 1159
knowledge of, *"The Face of God"* – p. 604; *"Walking with God"* – p. 690; *"How to Understand God"* – p. 776; *"Handling Tough Questions"* – p. 1131
always near, *"Near and Nearer"* – p. 674
preparing for, *"Voice in the Wilderness"* – p. 773

arguing with, *"Quarrels with God"* – **p. 782**
appearing in foreign lands, *"Foreign Appearance"* – **p. 880**
his justice, *"God Is Unfair?"* – **p. 895**; *"Atrocities"* – **p. 970**; *"The Problem of Evil"* – **p. 996**
hiding from, *"An Inescapable God"* – **p. 976**; *"Mind Reader"* – **p. 1327**
his plan revealed, *"Not by Chance"* – **p. 1325**

GOLDEN RULE
stated by Jesus, *"Golden Rule"* – **p. 1040**; Luke 6:27 – 36 – **p. 1111**

GOLGOTHA – a place outside Jerusalem where executions occurred
Jesus crucified at, Mark 15:21 – 32 – **p. 1097**; Luke 23:26 – 43 – **p. 1138**

GOSPEL – the "good news"; the message of Christianity
told to Abraham, *"The Gospel to Abraham"* – **p. 43**
written for non-Jews, *"The Fast-paced Gospel"* – **p. 1031**
preaching it, Acts 8:1 – 4 – **p. 1188**; Romans 15:14 – 16 – **p. 1238**
summarized, *"The Gospel in a Nutshell"* – **p. 1146**; *"What It's There For"* – **p. 1228**; Ephesians 2:1 – 10 – **p. 1278**; Colossians 1:3 – 23 – **p. 1291**
not ashamed of, Romans 1:16 – 17 – **p. 1223**
only one, Galatians 1:6 – 9 – **p. 1270**

GOSSIP
as a sin, Romans 1:29 – **p. 1223**; 2 Corinthians 12:20 – **p. 1268**
power of, *"Verbal Dynamite"* – **p. 703**

GOVERNMENT
confronting, Exodus 5 – 14 – **p. 89**; 2 Samuel 12:1 – 14 – **p. 361**; 1 Kings 21 – **p. 412**
of Israel by judges, *"Freedom Fighters"* – **p. 279**
Israel's form of, *"Why Not a King?"* – **p. 320**
of Israel by theocracy, *"Church and State"* – **p. 475**
David's goals for, *"The Company You Keep"* – **p. 656**
qualities needed by, *"Good Government"* – **p. 712**
Judah lacking, *"Total Anarchy"* – **p. 740**
under tyrants, *"In the Hands of Tyrants"* – **p. 947**
disobedience toward, Acts 5:17 – 42 – **p. 1184**
of Israel by Romans, *"Two Rulers"* – **p. 1215**
duty to, Romans 13:1 – 7 – **p. 1236**; Titus 3:1 – 2 – **p. 1318**; 1 Peter 2:13 – 17 – **p. 1347**

GRACE – the undeserved love and salvation God gives
to Jacob, *"A Stairway to Heaven"* – **p. 56**
to Israel, *"Why the Israelites?"* – **p. 219**; *"The Turning Point"* – **p. 912**
parables of, *"Unfair Pay"* – **p. 1057**; Luke 15:11 – 31 – **p. 1126**
through Christ, Romans 5 – **p. 1226**
for salvation, Ephesians 2 – **p. 1278**

GREED
defined, *"Never Enough"* – **p. 724**
futility of, Ecclesiastes 5:8 – 6:12 – **p. 723**
as motive in preaching the gospel, *"Gospel Greed"* – **p. 1189**
evil of, Luke 12:13 – 34 – **p. 1122**; 1 Timothy 6:3 – 10 – **p. 1309**; James 5:1 – 6 – **p. 1342**

GRIEF – see COMFORT, DISCOURAGEMENT, SORROW

GUIDANCE
of the Israelites, *"Unmistakable Guidance"* – **p. 179**
sought by Gideon, *"Putting Out a Fleece"* – **p. 288**
from God's word, Psalm 119 – **p. 669**; 2 Timothy 3:14 – 17 – **p. 1314**
practical, *"Uncommon Sense"* – **p. 687**
from Holy Spirit, John 16:5 – 16 – **p. 1167**

Guilt (see also CONFESSION, BACKSLIDING, FORGIVENESS)

Old Testament guilt offering, Leviticus 5:14 – 6:7 – **p. 136**
overwhelmed by, Psalm 38 – **p. 618**
all guilty before God, Romans 3:10 – 23 – **p. 1225**
acknowledging, Ezra 9 – **p. 528**; Psalm 32 – **p. 613**; 51 – **p. 626**; 1 John 1:7 – 10 – **p. 1356**
relief from, 1 John 1:5 – 2:2 – **p. 1356**

H

HANNAH – mother of Samuel
character profile, *"Deepest Longing"* – **p. 315**
her life, 1 Samuel 1 – 2 – **p. 314**
her prayer for a child, *"Sad, Not Drunk"* – **p. 314**
her life a picture of Israel, *"What Leadership Requires"* – **p. 312**

HAR-MAGEDON – see ARMAGEDDON

HAPPINESS – see JOY

HEALING
prayers for, 2 Samuel 12:15 – 25 – **p. 363**; 1 Kings 17:7 – 24 – **p. 406**; 2 Kings 5 – **p. 384**; 2 Corinthians 12:7 – 10 – **p. 1267**
by Jesus' wounds, *"Healing Wounds"* – **p. 789**
by Jesus, Matthew 8:1 – 17 – **p. 1040**; Mark 5 – **p. 1079**; Luke 4:38 – 41 – **p. 1108**
by disciples, Acts 3:1 – 10 – **p. 1180**; 5:12 – 16 – **p. 1184**; 14:8 – 10 – **p. 1199**; 28:7 – 10 – **p. 1219**
encouraged, James 5:13 – 18 – **p. 1343**

HEART – figuratively, the center of a person; that which gives direction to a person
obeying with your, *"Law of the Heart"* – **p. 238**
God knows, 1 Samuel 16:1 – 13 – **p. 331**
cleansing of, Psalm 51 – **p. 626**
undivided, *"Heart Surgery"* – **p. 649**
life flows from, Proverbs 4:23 – **p. 692**
deceitful, Jeremiah 17:9 – 10 – **p. 825**
leads to action, Matthew 12:33 – 37 – **p. 1046**

Heaven – a place of perfect happiness and eternal communion with God

hints of in Old Testament, *"Life after Death"* – **p. 603**
God rules from, Psalm 99 – **p. 655**; Isaiah 66:1 – 2 – **p. 801**
new, Isaiah 65:17 – 25 – **p. 801**; Revelation 21 – 22 – **p. 1386**
treasures in, Matthew 6:19 – 24 – **p. 1038**
for righteous, Matthew 25:31 – 46 – **p. 1065**
citizenship in, Philippians 3:12 – 4:1 – **p. 1288**
inhabitants of, Hebrews 11 – **p. 1333**
visions of, Revelation 4 – 5 – **p. 1371**; 7 – **p. 1374**

HELL – a place of eternal punishment and sorrow
hints of in Old Testament, Job 24:21 – 26 – **p. 577**; Psalm 49:10 – 15 – **p. 625**; Daniel 12 – **p. 949**
to avoid, Matthew 5:21 – 30 – **p. 1037**; Romans 8:1 – 16 – **p. 1230**
for evildoers, Matthew 13:24 – 30,36 – 43 – **p. 1049**
punishment in, 2 Thessalonians 1:3 – 12 – **p. 1301**; Jude 5 – 13 – **p. 1365**; Revelation 20:11 – 14 – **p. 1386**
keep others from, Jude 17 – 23 – **p. 1365**

HERESIES – *see* FALSE TEACHERS

HEROD – name of a line of rulers of Palestine
character profile, the Herods: *"Lower Authority"* – **p. 1050**
the Great, Matthew 2 – **p. 1034**
Antipas, Matthew 14:1 – 12 – **p. 1050**; *"Guards Without Allies"* – **p. 1196**
Agrippa I, Acts 12:1 – 23 – **p. 1196**

HEZEKIAH – king of Judah for 29 years; reopened the temple his father had closed
character profile, *"Cleaning House"* – **p. 507**
life of, 2 Kings 18 – 20 – **p. 439**; *"King of Contradictions"* – **p. 440**
restores worship, 2 Chronicles 29 – 31 – **p. 507**
crisis with Isaiah, Isaiah 36 – 39 – **p. 770**

HISTORY
God working in, *"God's Hand in History"* – **p. 746**; *"Catastrophes Through God's Eyes"* – **p. 756**; *"Like a Wise Farmer"* – **p. 762**; *"A New Song"* – **p. 774**; *"Ransom for the Captives"* – **p. 778**; *"World at War"* – **p. 857**; *"Kidnapped"* – **p. 931** *"In the Hands of Tyrants"* – **p. 947**; *"The Meaning of a Natural Disaster"* – **p. 962**; *"Light in a Dark Time"* – **p. 984**; *"A Look Behind the Scenes"* – **p. 1379**
as encouragement, *"Why the Cleanup?"* – **p. 453**
interpreting, *"Moral of the Story"* – **p. 461**
prophesied, *"A Prophecy for the World"* – **p. 761**; *"Foretelling the Future"* – **p. 782**; *"New King, New Kingdom"* – **p. 1015**

HOLOCAUST
original meaning of, *"Original Holocaust"* – **p. 132**

HOLY – separated or set apart for God
called to be, Exodus 19:1 – 5 – **p. 105**; Leviticus 11:44 – 45 – **p. 144**; 1 Peter 1:13 – 16 – **p. 1346**; 1 Peter 2:9 – 10 – **p. 1347**
lifestyle, *"National Reminders"* – **p. 177**
God's character, Psalm 99 – **p. 655**; Isaiah 6 – **p. 743**
One of Israel, *"A Key Phrase"* – **p. 749**
all things becoming, *"No More Separation"* – **p. 1019**
imitate God's holiness, Ephesians 4:17 – 5:21 – **p. 1280**

Holy Spirit – the third person of the Trinity; also known as the Counselor who is active in the lives of believers (*see also* FRUIT OF THE SPIRIT)

in the Old Testament, *"The Spirit and Samson"* – **p. 298**; Psalm 51:11 – **p. 627**; Isaiah 11:1 – 5 – **p. 747**; 61:1 – 3 – **p. 796**
his coming prophesied, *"A New Spirit"* – **p. 917**; *"The Spirit Poured Out"* – **p. 966**
anointed Jesus, Luke 3:21 – 22 – **p. 1107**; 4:1 – 27 – **p. 1107**
comfort from, John 14:15 – 31 – **p. 1165**
work of, John 16:5 – 16 – **p. 1167**; *"Branded"* – **p. 1278**
coming to the disciples, Acts 2 – **p. 1178**
in the early church, *"The Secret to the Early Church"* – **p. 1183**
directs the church, Acts 13:1 – 4 – **p. 1197**; 16:6 – 7 – **p. 1201**
filled with, Acts 19:1 – 7 – **p. 1206**; Ephesians 5:18 – **p. 1281**
life through, Romans 8:1 – 17 – **p. 1230**
in Christians, 1 Corinthians 2:6 – 16 – **p. 1243**; 1 Corinthians 3:16 – 17 – **p. 1243**

HOMOSEXUALITY
result of sin, Romans 1:18 – 32 – **p. 1223**

listed as sin, 1 Corinthians 6:9 – 11 – **p. 1246**; 1 Timothy 1:9 – 11 – **p. 1305**

HONESTY
Samuel's, *"Accuse Me!"* – **p. 324**
God desires, Psalm 15 – **p. 602**

HOPE
for the Israelites, *"Hope in a Time of Sorrow"* – **p. 468**; *"Free Again"* – **p. 839**; *"The Turning Point"* – **p. 912**; *"New Hope"* – **p. 960**
in the Lord, Psalm 42 – 43 – **p. 621**; 1 Timothy 6:17 – 19 – **p. 1310**
while waiting for God, *"A Desperate Hope"* – **p. 569**; *"An Outburst of Hope"* – **p. 573**; *"A New Song"* – **p. 774**; *"Hope for the Grieving"* – **p. 875**
because of the past, *"A Time for Hope"* – **p. 481**; *"Remembering Back"* – **p. 642**
for total redemption, *"A Glimpse of Things to Come"* – **p. 798**; *"A Happy Ending After All"* – **p. 1385**
does not disappoint, Romans 5:1 – 11 – **p. 1226**
for resurrection, 1 Corinthians 15 – **p. 1254**
in Christ, Colossians 1:3 – 27 – **p. 1291**; 1 Peter 1:13 – 16 – **p. 1346**

HOSPITALITY
expected, *"A Breach of Hospitality"* – **p. 303**
Jesus' words on, Luke 14:12 – 14 – **p. 1125**
responsibility of, Romans 12:13 – **p. 1235**; 1 Peter 4:9 – **p. 1349**; *"Guidelines for Hospitality"* – **p. 1363**
entertaining angels, Hebrews 13:1 – 3 – **p. 1336**
when not to extend, *"Undesirable Guests"* – **p. 1361**

HUMAN BEINGS
created in God's image, Genesis 1:26 – 31 – **p. 25**
made by God, *"Where We Came From"* – **p. 28**
glory of, Psalm 8 – **p. 599**
intricately made, Psalm 139:13 – 16 – **p. 681**
apart from God, *"Three Problem People"* – **p. 689**; *"Outside the Palace"* – **p. 721**

HUMILITY
of David, *"Rare Trait"* – **p. 469**
living in, Micah 6:6 – 8 – **p. 989**; Colossians 3:12 – 17 – **p. 1293**; 1 Peter 5:5 – 7 – **p. 1350**
like children, Matthew 18:1 – 4 – **p. 1055**
encouraged, *"Luke and the Underdog"* – **p. 1129**; *"The Role of a Servant"* – **p. 1163**; Romans 12:1 – 21 – **p. 1235**; 1 Peter 5:5 – 7 – **p. 1350**
of Christ, 2 Corinthians 8:8 – 9 – **p. 1263**; Philippians 2:1 – 11 – **p. 1286**

HUSBAND
duty to wife, 1 Corinthians 7:1 – 5 – **p. 1246**
love for wife, Ephesians 5:25 – 33 – **p. 1281**; Colossians 3:19 – **p. 1293**

HYPOCRISY
in worshiping God, *"Hypocrites"* – **p. 763**; *"Letting the Inside Match the Outside"* – **p. 1039**
avoid, Matthew 6:1 – 24 – **p. 1038**
described, Matthew 23 – **p. 1061**
condemned, James 1:19 – 2:13 – **p. 1340**; 1 John 3:17 – 19 – **p. 1358**

IDOLATRY – the worship of idols; putting something before God
commandment against, Exodus 20:3 – 6 – **p. 106**
Canaanite, *"Detestable Things"* – **p. 231**
during time of the judges, *"Sad Commentary"* – **p. 302**
attraction of, *"Why All the Fuss about Idols?"* – **p. 437**
Judah's lust for, *"Provoking God"* – **p. 800**
Israel's lust for, *"Smoldering Passion"* – **p. 955**

K

L

instructions concerning, 1 Corinthians 11:17 – 34 – **p. 1250**

LOT – nephew of Abraham who settled in the land near Sodom
character profile, *"Different Pathways"* – **p. 38**
separates from Abram, Genesis 13 – **p. 37**
in Sodom, Genesis 18:16 – 19:38 – **p. 42**

Love

shown to an enemy, *"A Captive's Compassion"* – p. 423; Romans 12:18 – 21 – **p. 1235**
responding to God's, *"God's Great Concern"* – p. 685; *"Spurned"* – p. 1021
between man and woman, *"Whom Should You Marry?"* – p. 707; *"An Intoxicating Love"* – p. 729; *"Let Love Sleep"* – p. 732
proverbs about, *"Love is the Greatest"* – p. 697
symbols of, *"Parable of Love"* – p. 953
power of, *"Love and Death"* – p. 735
expressions of, *"A Brotherly Kiss"* – p. 735
of God for his people, *"Does God Care?"* – p. 778; *"A Lover's Quarrel"* – p. 809; Jeremiah 31:1 – 6 – p. 841
of God for non-Jews, *"Good News with Bad"* – p. 1380
commanded, Mark 12:28 – 34 – p. 1092; *"More Than a Feeling"* – p. 223; John 13:34 – 35 – p. 1164; Romans 12:9 – 21 – p. 1235
described, 1 Corinthians 13 – p. 1252
an aspect of the Spirit's fruit, Galatians 5:13 – 26 – p. 1275
of the world, 1 John 2:15 – 17 – p. 1357
God is, 1 John 4:7 – 21 – p. 1358

LUKE – author of the third Gospel; physician who traveled with Paul
sources, *"Luke the Historian"* – **p. 1102**; *"Jesus' Childhood"* – **p. 1106**
emphasis of, *"A Physician Looks at the Poor"* – **p. 1109**; *"Severe and Gentle Stories"* – **p. 1126**
travel companion of Paul, Acts 16:10 – 17 – **p. 1202**; 20:5 – 21:18 – **p. 1209**; 27:1 – 28:16 – **p. 1217**

LUST – intense desire (*see* SEX)

LYING
by Abraham, *"Abraham's Half-Truth"* – **p. 37**
law against, Exodus 20:16 – **p. 107**
penalty for, Leviticus 6:1 – 7 – **p. 137**
by the Gibeonites, *"Tricked!"* – **p. 260**
by David, *"Disobeying the Law"* – **p. 338**; *"David's Double Game"* – **p. 345**
to David, *"The Traitors' Story"* – **p. 373**
by Peter, Matthew 26:69 – 74 – **p. 1067**
Satan the father of, John 8:44 – **p. 1156**
by Ananias and Sapphira, *"Deadly Deceit"* – **p. 1184**
mark of old nature, Ephesians 4:17 – 5:21 – **p. 1280**

M

MAGIC – *see* ASTROLOGY, WITCHCRAFT

MARK – author of the second Gospel and missionary helper to Paul and Barnabas
character profile, *"Slow Starter"* – **p. 1201**
as author, *"The Anonymous Author?"* – **p. 1095**

MARRIAGE (*see also* DIVORCE, HUSBAND, LOVE, WIFE)
God ordained, Genesis 2:18 – 25 – **p. 27**; *"The First Marriage"* – **p. 27**

with unbelievers, *"Marrying Foreigners"* – **p. 49**; *"Intermarriage"* – **p. 283**; *"The First Sign of Trouble"* – **p. 296**; *"Inconsistent Ethics"* – **p. 489**; *"Corrupt Leaders"* – **p. 529**
for political reasons, *"Political Marriages"* – **p. 427**
importance of, *"Whom Should You Marry?"* – **p. 707**; Matthew 19:1 – 12 – **p. 1056**
joys of, *"An Intoxicating Love"* – **p. 729**
Jewish customs about, *"More Than Engaged"* – **p. 1034**
Jesus' teaching on, *"No-Fault Divorce?"* – **p. 1056**
relationship, Ephesians 5:22 – 33 – **p. 1281**; Colossians 3:18 – 19 – **p. 1293**; 1 Peter 3:1 – 7 – **p. 1347**
Paul's advice on, 1 Corinthians 7 – **p. 1246**

MARTHA AND MARY – sisters of Lazarus; friends of Jesus
character profile, *"Doer and Seeker"* – **p. 1120**
Jesus at home of, Luke 10:38 – 42 – **p. 1120**
at Lazarus's death, John 11 – **p. 1159**
washed Jesus' feet, John 12:1 – 8 – **p. 1161**

MARTYR – one who gives up life for the faith
Stephen as, Acts 7 – **p. 1186**
Paul as, *"A Hint of Trials to Come"* – **p. 1245**; *"A Letter from Death Row"* – **p. 1314**
by Nero, *"Endangered Strangers"* – **p. 1347**
many examples of, Hebrews 11:35 – 40 – **p. 1335**; Revelation 6:9 – 11 – **p. 1373**

MARY – mother of Jesus; wife of Joseph
character profile, *"Saying Yes to God"* – **p. 1104**
Jesus born to, Matthew 1:18 – 2:23 – **p. 1033**; Luke 1:26 – 56 – **p. 1103**; 2 – **p. 1104**
concerned for Jesus, Mark 3:20 – 35 – **p. 1076**; Luke 2:41 – 52 – **p. 1106**
requests Jesus' first miracle, John 2:1 – 11 – **p. 1145**
at crucifixion, John 19:16 – 27 – **p. 1171**

MARY MAGDALENE – a close friend of Jesus
character profile, *"First to See"* – **p. 1173**
present at crucifixion, Mark 15:33 – 41 – **p. 1098**
had been demon-possessed, Luke 8:1 – 3 – **p. 1114**
first one at empty tomb, John 20:1 – 18 – **p. 1172**

MATTHEW – author of the first Gospel; left his work to follow Jesus; also called Levi
transformed, *"Unpopular Profession"* – **p. 1042**
hosted a dinner for Jesus, Mark 2:13 – 17 – **p. 1075**

MEDIATOR – someone who helps bring harmony between two parties
Jesus as, 1 Timothy 2:1 – 6 – **p. 1306**; Hebrews 9:11 – 28 – **p. 1331**

MEDITATION – *see* QUIET TIME

MELCHIZEDEK – priest and king
character profile, *"The Twelfth Man"* – **p. 666**
blessed Abram, Genesis 14:17 – 20 – **p. 39**
pointed to Christ, Psalm 110 – **p. 665**; Hebrews 5:1 – 10 – **p. 1328**; 7 – **p. 1329**; *"Who is Melchizedek?"* – **p. 1329**
as example of leader, *"The Twelfth Man"* – **p. 666**

MEMORIALS
created for future generations, *"Monuments"* – **p. 277**

MEMORIES
giving hope, *"Fond Memories"* – **p. 567**; *"Remembering Back"* – **p. 642**; *"The Good Old Days"* – **p. 747**

Mercy

pleading for, Psalm 4 – p. 597; Luke 18:9 – 14 – p. 1129
of God, Psalm 108:8 – 12 – p. 663; 123 – p. 675; *"Too Merciful a God?"* – p. 983; Luke 1:46 – 79 – p. 1103; Romans 9:15 – 18 – p. 1233

for the merciful, *"A Key Characteristic"* – p. 620;
James 2:12 – 13 – p. 1340

MESSENGERS
in Persia, *"Pony Express"* – p. 552
of good news, *"Lovely Feet"* – p. 789
Paul's, *"Mail Carriers"* – p. 1319

MESSIAH – a king and deliverer expected by the Jewish
people; Christ
precedent for, *"Mystery Man"* – p. 39
promised by God, *"God's Great Promise"* – p. 358; *"Promise
to David"* – p. 678
meaning of, *"The Messiah in the Psalms"* – p. 596
prophecies concerning, Psalm 2 – p. 596; 110 – p. 665;
"The Song of the Cross" – p. 608; *"A Wedding Fit for a
King"* – p. 623; *"The Suffering Servant"* – p. 790; Isaiah
9:1 – 7 – p. 745; 11:1 – 12 – p. 747; 53:1 – 12 – p. 789;
61:1 – 3 – p. 796; Daniel 7:13 – 14 – p. 942; *"Jesus Asks
a Question"* – p. 1134
as a leader, *"The Twelfth Man"* – p. 666
David's son as, *"A Bridge from Old to New"* – p. 1031
Jesus as, Matthew 11:1 – 6 – p. 1044; *"The Killing of a
King"* – p. 1068; *"Short-lived Acceptance"* – p. 1090; *"The
Day of Execution"* – p. 1096; Luke 4:14 – 21 – p. 1107

MICHAEL – the archangel appointed to guard the
Jewish people
with Daniel, Daniel 10 – p. 945; 12:1 – 13 – p. 949
and war in heaven, Revelation 12 – p. 1378

MILITARY – (see also WAR)
serving in, *"Uncommon Military Rules"* – p. 233
trusting in, *"Lessons from the Battlefield"* – p. 511; *"Faith in
God or the Military?"* – p. 750; *"Worshiping the Military"* –
p. 998

MILLENNIUM – Latin word for "thousand years"; used
in connection with a period in the last days
described, Revelation 20:1 – 15 – p. 1385
views of, *"The Millennium"* – p. 1386

MINISTER – see PASTOR

MINISTRY
Paul's style of, *"A Human Letter"* – p. 1260
self-supporting, *"Working for a Living"* – p. 1297

MIRACLES – extraordinary events done through God's
power
ten plagues, *"Day of the Locusts"* – p. 91
limited effect of, *"When God Was Obvious"* – p. 112;
"Miracles Aren't Enough" – p. 1045; *"Don't Tell"* –
p. 1080; *"Sensation-Seekers"* – p. 1121
of Elisha, *"Elisha's Miracles"* – p. 422
after Sermon on the Mount, *"Actions Follow Words"* –
p. 1041
feeding crowds, *"Two Feedings"* – p. 1052; *"Better Bread"* –
p. 1151
not done in Nazareth, *"No Respect at Home"* – p. 1050
done at a distance, *"A Long-distance Miracle"* – p. 1149
lead to belief, John 4:43 – 54 – p. 1149; 20:30 – 31 –
p. 1173; *"John's Reason for Writing"* – p. 1164
done to glorify God, John 11:1 – 44 – p. 1159

MIRIAM – prophetess, sister of Moses and Aaron
character profile, *"Jealous Sister"* – p. 182
led singing/dancing, Exodus 15:19 – 21 – p. 101
disagreed with Moses, Numbers 12 – p. 181

MISSIONS – (see also EVANGELISM)
Israel's role in, *"Catastrophes Through God's Eyes"* – p. 756;
"Israel's Final Destiny" – p. 785
highly praised, Isaiah 52:7 – 10 – p. 788; Romans
10:14 – 15 – p. 1234
command to, Matthew 28:16 – 20 – p. 1071; Luke
24:45 – 52 – p. 1141; Acts 1:1 – 11 – p. 1178

responsibility of every Christian, Acts 8:1 – 6 – p. 1188;
1 Peter 3:15 – 16 – p. 1348
Barnabas and Saul (Paul) sent, Acts 13:1 – 3 – p. 1197
Paul's journeys, Acts 13 – 28 – p. 1197

Money

God owns everything, Deuteronomy 8 – p. 220;
Psalm 24 – p. 609
rules about loans, *"Respect People, Not Money"* –
p. 236
serving, Matthew 6:19 – 34 – p. 1038
stories about, *"Matthew and Money"* – p. 1055
trusting, *"When Money is Useless"* – p. 1122; Psalm
62:10 – p. 632
love of, 1 Timothy 6:3 – 19 – p. 1309; *"Two Familiar
Quotes"* – p. 1309; James 5:1 – 5 – p. 1342

MORDECAI – Benjamite exile who raised Esther, queen
of Persia
character profile, *"Standing Tall"* – p. 552

MOSES – used by God to deliver Israelites from slavery
in Egypt; God gave him the Ten Commandments
character profile, see Introduction to Exodus – p. 84
life of, Exodus 2 – 40 – p. 86; Numbers 1 – 36 – p. 167;
Deuteronomy 1 – 34 – p. 212
birth of, Exodus 2 – p. 86
called by God, Exodus 3 – 4 – p. 87
leads Israelites out of Egypt, Exodus 5 – 15 – p. 89; *"Free at
Last"* – p. 672
received law, Exodus 19 – 31 – p. 105
wilderness wanderings, Numbers 13 – 36 – p. 182
his communication with God, *"The Lord said to Moses . . ."* –
p. 177
punished by God, *"Moses' Sin"* – p. 191; *"Moses Stayed
Out"* – p. 200
final message to Israel, *"A Personal Plea"* – p. 210; *"Dying
Words"* – p. 247
blames Israelites, *"Distributing Blame"* – p. 213
foresees Israel's future, *"A Scent of Doom"* – p. 243; *"Moses
Gets a Preview"* – p. 249
death of, Deuteronomy 34 – p. 248
appears at Jesus' transfiguration, Matthew 17:1 – 13 –
p. 1054
as example of faith, Hebrews 11:24 – 28 – p. 1335

MOTHER
Eve, mother of all living, Genesis 3:20 – 4:25 – p. 29
barren women blessed with children, Genesis 21 – p. 46;
25:21 – 26 – p. 52; 29 – 30 – p. 58; 1 Samuel 1 –
p. 314; Luke 1 – p. 1101
a gift of God, Psalm 127 – 128 – p. 676
responsibilities of, Proverbs 31 – p. 717; 2 Timothy
1:1 – 7 – p. 1312
God compared to, Isaiah 49:15 – p. 786; 66:10 – 13 –
p. 802

MURDER
of Abel by Cain, Genesis 4 – p. 29; 1 John 3:11 – 15 –
p. 1358
law concerning, Genesis 9:5 – 6 – p. 33; *"Reverence for
Life"* – p. 33; Exodus 20:13 – p. 107; Numbers
35:16 – 34 – p. 208
of rivals, *"Married Despots"* – p. 500
Jesus' teaching on, Matthew 5:21 – 26 – p. 1037

MUSIC
used by the prophets, *"Musical Prophets"* – p. 323
organized by David, 1 Chronicles 25 – p. 474
encouraging a new song, Psalm 98 – p. 655
used in worship, *"Call and Response"* – p. 679

PREDESTINATION – doctrine that God has predetermined that all believers are saved through Christ (see also ELECTION, FREE WILL)
Jacob chosen, "Con Man in God's Family?" – **p. 54**
Jews chosen, "Why the Israelites?" – **p. 219**
Eli's sons rejected, "God in Charge" – **p. 316**
God's foreknowledge, Romans 8:28–30 – **p. 1231**
in love, Ephesians 1:3–14 – **p. 1277**

PRIDE – (see also HUMILITY)
of Joseph, "Big Mouth" – **p. 68**
warnings against, Proverbs 8:13 – **p. 694**; 16:5,14 –
    p. 703; 21:4,24 – **p. 707**
God humbles, Isaiah 2:10–22 – **p. 739**
of Jews in Jerusalem, "Smiles Instead of Tears" – **p. 757**
of Antiochus, "Exalted Above the Gods" – **p. 948**
of the complacent, "Unbelievable!" – **p. 997**
avoid, Romans 12 – **p. 1235**
God opposes, James 4:4–6 – **p. 1341**

PRIEST – one designated to perform sacred rites and act as an intermediary between people and God (see also AARON, MELCHIZEDEK)
Old Testament, Exodus 28–29 – **p. 115**; 39:1–31 –
    p. 128; Leviticus 8–10 – **p. 139**
purification of, "The Whole Body" – **p. 117**
regulations for, "Priestly Privileges" – **p. 139**
punished for disobedience, "Fatal Error" – **p. 141**
in politics, "The Priests Take Up Arms" – **p. 502**
false, "Poor Trade" – **p. 954**
Jesus as, Hebrews 4:14–5:10 – **p. 1327**; 7:1–10:18 –
    p. 1329
Christians as, 1 Peter 2:4–12 – **p. 1346**; Revelation 1:6 –
    p. 1369

PRISCILLA – wife of Aquila; co-worker with Paul and instructor of Apollos
character profile, "Power Couple" – **p. 1206**

PRISON
Joseph in, Genesis 39–40 – **p. 71**
visit those in, Matthew 25:31–46 – **p. 1065**
Peter's release from, Acts 12:1–19 – **p. 1196**
Paul in, Acts 16:16–40 – **p. 1202**; 21:27–28:31 – **p. 1211**;
    "Letters from Prison" – **p. 1280**; "A Letter from Death
    Row" – **p. 1314**

PROFANITY
command against, Exodus 20:7 – **p. 107**; Matthew
    5:21–22 – **p. 1037**; Ephesians 4:29–32 – **p. 1281**
dangerous effects of, James 3:1–12 – **p. 1341**

PROMISE – (see also COVENANT)
God's to Abraham, "Promises, Promises" – **p. 48**
waiting for God's, "Shame Forever?" – **p. 651**
Christ's, John 14 – **p. 1165**
believing, Romans 4:13–25 – **p. 1226**
God's, "Unchanged Promises" – **p. 845**; Hebrews
    6:13–20 – **p. 1328**; 7:18–8:13 – **p. 1329**

PROPHECY – an inspired revelation about future events (see also MESSIAH, MILLENNIUM, SECOND COMING)
Abiathar, "Outlaw Priest" – **p. 386**; "Prediction Fulfilled" –
    p. 520; "Out Through the Hole" – **p. 888**; "Alexander the
    Great" – **p. 904**; "Stones Overturned" – **p. 1063**; "Wailing
    Wall" – **p. 1132**; "Speeding Up Death" – **p. 1172**
about Jesus, "Foreshadowing Jesus" – **p. 636**; "A Child Is
    Born" – **p. 745**; "The Suffering Servant" – **p. 790**; "Jesus
    Began Here" – **p. 797**; "Messiah's Birthplace" – **p. 988**;
    "Donkey of Peace" – **p. 1015**; "A Prophecy of Jesus" –
    p. 1018; "Old Testament 101" – **p. 1140**
double meanings, "A Famous Sign" – **p. 744**; "Who Are the
    Shepherds?" – **p. 1017**
illustrated, "A Dramatic Object Lesson" – **p. 755**; "Living
    Parables" – **p. 847**; "Seeing the Unseen God" – **p. 878**

time sequence in, "Shifting Stance in Time" – **p. 767**; "Seeing
    in Two Dimensions" – **p. 989**
change in tone of, "End of the Silence" – **p. 913**
purpose of, "Prophetic Entertainment" – **p. 913**
interpretation of, "Newspaper Prophecy" – **p. 1384**
source is God, 2 Peter 1:19–21 – **p. 1353**

PROPHETS – (see also FALSE PROPHETS)
Moses as, Deuteronomy 18:14–21 – **p. 231**
and kings, "Standing Up to the King" – **p. 400**; "The Prophet
    and Politics" – **p. 425**; "A True or False Prophet?" – **p. 496**
used by God, "The Contest" – **p. 408**
powerful, "Replacing a Legend" – **p. 420**
pain felt by, "God's Reluctant Messenger" – **p. 804**; "A
    Fountain of Tears" – **p. 817**; "The Sad Truth" – **p. 914**
plots against, "Hometown Enemies" – **p. 820**
relationships between, "Favored by God and Kings" –
    p. 944; "Bad News, Good News" – **p. 1011**
rescue of, "Scripture Saves a Life" – **p. 836**; "Close to
    Death" – **p. 850**
sustained by God, "Eat the Scroll" – **p. 881**
parallels in, "Writing to Ezekiel" – **p. 838**; "Jeremiah and
    Ezekiel" – **p. 894**; "Parallel with Isaiah" – **p. 988**
background of, "Royal Blood" – **p. 1002**
Jesus as the final, John 6:14–15 – **p. 1151**; Acts
    3:21–23 – **p. 1181**

PROSTITUTION – sexual intercourse engaged in for money
condemned, Leviticus 19:29 – **p. 153**
warning against, Proverbs 6:20–35 – **p. 693**;
    1 Corinthians 6:12–20 – **p. 1246**

PROVIDENCE OF GOD
for Joseph, "Important Officials" – **p. 72**
for Israelites, "Food Supply" – **p. 102**; "Miracles in the
    Desert" – **p. 241**
in saving Joash, "Preserving the Royal Line" – **p. 431**
in saving the Jews, "A Profile of Courage" – **p. 548**
working through people, "One Safe Jew?" – **p. 553**
in nature, Psalm 104 – **p. 658**; Matthew 10:29–30 –
    p. 1044; Acts 14:14–17 – **p. 1199**
throughout life, "Love Before Birth" – **p. 682**; "I Carried
    You" – **p. 783**
in protecting Christianity, "A Secular View" – **p. 1206**

PUNISHMENT – (see also HELL)
of Lot's wife, "Don't Look Back" – **p. 45**
of God for sin, "A Catastrophe Sent From God" – **p. 44**; "The
    End of Shiloh" – **p. 318**; "An End to Punishment" – **p. 765**;
    "A City in Ruins" – **p. 870**
appropriate, "Punishment by Restitution" – **p. 109**; "An Eye
    for an Eye" – **p. 160**; "Needless Deaths" – **p. 375**
eternal, Matthew 25:31–46, – **p. 1065**; Revelation
    20:11–15, – **p. 1386**

Q

QUIET TIME – a period set aside for prayer, meditation, and Bible study
for renewal, Psalm 1 – **p. 596**; 119:9–48 – **p. 669**
practiced by Jesus, "The Need to Get Away" – **p. 1082**;
    Matthew 14:22–23 – **p. 1051**; Luke 5:15–16 – **p. 1110**;
    6:12–13 – **p. 1111**
to overcome temptation, Mark 14:32–38 – **p. 1094**
for strength, Ephesians 6:10–20 – **p. 1282**
for a sense of peace, Philippians 4:6–9 – **p. 1288**

R

RACHEL – favored wife of Jacob; mother of Joseph and Benjamin
character profile, "Love and Grief" – **p. 61**

life of, Genesis 29:14 – 31:55 – **p. 58**; *"The Women of Genesis"* – **p. 57**
death of, Genesis 35:16 – 20 – **p. 66**

RACISM – belief that one race is superior to others
in Egypt, *"Prejudice"* – **p. 76**
abolished in Christ, *"Forcing a Confrontation"* – **p. 1271**; Galatians 3:26 – 4:7 – **p. 1273**; *"Destroying the Barriers"* – **p. 1279**

RAHAB – a prostitute who helped the Israelites capture Jericho
character profile, *"A Prostitute's Faith"* – **p. 256**
took in spies, Joshua 2:1 – 21 – **p. 252**; Joshua 6:15 – 25 – **p. 256**
ancestor of Christ, *"Rahab's Future"* – **p. 253**
example of faith, James 2:25 – 26 – **p. 1341**

RAHAB – sea monster in mythology
symbol for Egypt, *"Rahab the Monster"* – **p. 788**

RAINBOW
sign of covenant with Noah, Genesis 9:12 – 16 – **p. 34**; *"The Reason for Rainbows"* – **p. 34**

RAPE – sexual intercourse forced on one person by another
at Sodom, Genesis 19:1 – 8 – **p. 43**
of Dinah, Genesis 34 – **p. 65**
penalty for, Deuteronomy 22:25 – 29 – **p. 235**
at Gibeah, Judges 19:16 – 28 – **p. 303**
of Tamar, 2 Samuel 13 – **p. 363**

REBEKAH – wife of Isaac; mother of Esau and Jacob
character profile, *"Forceful Woman"* – **p. 49**
marries Isaac, Genesis 24 – **p. 49**; *"The Women of Genesis"* – **p. 57**
helps Jacob, Genesis 25:19 – 34 – **p. 52**; 27:1 – 28:9 – **p. 53**

REBELLION
against God, *"When God Was Obvious"* – **p. 112**; *"Forty Years of Misery"* – **p. 165**; *"The Worst Rebellion"* – **p. 184**; *"Children of the Desert"* – **p. 213**
at end of the present age, Matthew 24:4 – 25 – **p. 1063**; 2 Thessalonians 2 – **p. 1301**; Revelation 13 – 14 – **p. 1379**

RECONCILIATION – to settle differences; to be in harmony again
of Jacob and Esau, *"Surface Reconciliation"* – **p. 64**
of Joseph and his brothers, *"Family Battles"* – **p. 69**
between people, Matthew 5:23 – 26 – **p. 1037**; Philippians 4:2 – 3 – **p. 1288**
to God, *"Looking for an Arbitrator"* – **p. 567**; 2 Corinthians 5:11 – 6:2 – **p. 1262**; Ephesians 2:11 – 22 – **p. 1278**; Colossians 1:15 – 23 – **p. 1291**

REDEEMER – one who frees or rescues another, especially from sin
Boaz as, *"Expensive Bride"* – **p. 311**
God as, Isaiah 54:1 – 8 – **p. 791**; Luke 1:67 – 69 – **p. 1104**
Christ as, Galatians 3:6 – 14 – **p. 1271**; Colossians 1:13 – 14 – **p. 1291**; Hebrews 9:11 – 14 – **p. 1331**; *"A Modern Peace Child"* – **p. 1227**; 1 Peter 1:17 – 21 – **p. 1346**

REHOBOAM – son of Solomon; first king of Judah
character profile, *"A Fool's Answer"* – **p. 491**
life of, 1 Kings 12 – **p. 399**; 14 – **p. 401**

RELIGION
true, *"Religion at Its Best"* – **p. 794**; *"What God Wants"* – **p. 990**; *"Which One Showed Love?"* – **p. 1119**
mixed, *"How to be Religious Without Pleasing God"* – **p. 956**; *"The New Golden Calf"* – **p. 958**
Paul on Greek religion, Acts 17:22 – 31 – **p. 1204**

combating false, *"Battling the Cults"* – **p. 1290**
pure, James 1:26 – 27 – **p. 1340**

Repentance –to feel sorry for and turn from sins; a common theme of Old Testament prophets

by Israel's kings, *"A Tardy Change of Mind"* – **p. 513**; *"Turnaround"* – **p. 1224**
of the exiles, *"Beginning Again"* – **p. 518**; *"Unprecedented Response"* – **p. 529**
of David, *"David Caught in the Act"* – **p. 627**
temporary, *"A Superficial Change"* – **p. 809**
call to, *"Before It's Too Late"* – **p. 972**
preached by Jesus, Matthew 4:12 – 17 – **p. 1036**; Luke 13:1 – 5 – **p. 1124**
parable concerning, Luke 18:9 – 14 – **p. 1129**
preached by Peter, Acts 2:38 – 41 – **p. 1180**
preached by Paul, Acts 17:22 – 31 – **p. 1204**
described by Paul, 2 Corinthians 7:9 – 10 – **p. 1263**

RESPONSIBILITY
for sin, Ezekiel 18 – **p. 894**
accepting, *"No Excuses"* – **p. 1223**
to love others, 1 John 3:11 – 24 – **p. 1358**

REST
day of, Genesis 2:1 – 3 – **p. 26**; Exodus 20:8 – **p. 107**
for the land, *"Revenge of the Land"* – **p. 163**
year of, *"A Year of Freedom"* – **p. 543**
in God, Psalm 23 – **p. 608**; 62 – **p. 632**
for weary, Matthew 11:25 – 30 – **p. 1045**

RESURRECTION
hinted in Old Testament, *"A Promise of Eternal Life"* – **p. 759**; *"Resurrection"* – **p. 949**; Job 19:23 – 27 – **p. 573**; Ezekiel 37:1 – 14 – **p. 917**; Daniel 12:1 – 2 – **p. 949**
foretold, *"Resurrection!"* – **p. 602**; *"Stubbornly Unconvinced"* – **p. 1128**
of Jesus, Matthew 27:57 – 28:20 – **p. 1070**; *"Final Glimpses of Jesus"* – **p. 1138**; *"More Than a Ghost"* – **p. 1181**
Jesus predicts his own, Mark 8:31 – **p. 1085**; 9:31 – **p. 1087**; 10:33 – 34 – **p. 1088**
of the dead, 1 Corinthians 15 – **p. 1254**; *"The Worst Danger of All"* – **p. 1254**; 1 Thessalonians 4:13 – 18 – **p. 1298**
of the body, *"The Body as a Tent"* – **p. 1261**
as proof of God's power, *"Proven Power"* – **p. 1278**; Ephesians 1:15 – 23 – **p. 1277**
spiritual in Christ, Romans 6:1 – 14 – **p. 1228**; Colossians 2:9 – 15 – **p. 1292**; 3:1 – 17 – **p. 1293**

REVENGE – (*see also* CITIES OF REFUGE)
Joseph not taking, *"Weeping and Terror"* – **p. 78**
of David, *"Paying Back Joab"* – **p. 385**
belongs to God, *"God's Vengeance"* – **p. 246**
on enemies, *"Jehu's Slaughters"* – **p. 430**; do not take, Matthew 5:38 – 47 – **p. 1038**; Romans 12:17 – 21 – **p. 1235**

REVERENCE – (*see also* FEAR)
for God, *"Living With Fire"* – **p. 131**; *"Touch and Die"* – **p. 171**; *"Is God Frightening?"* – **p. 615**

REVELATION – God's disclosure of himself and his truth
in nature, Psalm 19:1 – 6 – **p. 605**; Acts 14:14 – 17 – **p. 1199**; Romans 1:18 – 23 – **p. 1223**
in Jesus Christ, John 1:1 – 18 – **p. 1143**; Hebrews 1 – **p. 1324**

in the Bible, 2 Timothy 3:14-17-**p. 1314**; 2 Peter 1:19-21-**p. 1353**

REWARD
everyone according to deeds, Leviticus 26-**p. 162**; Psalm 62:11-12-**p. 632**; Jeremiah 17:10-**p. 825**; 2 Corinthians 5:1-10-**p. 1261**
for evil, "Short-Run Rewards"-**p. 639**
for serving God, "Why Serve God?"-**p. 1023**
in heaven, Matthew 5:3-12-**p. 1037**; Mark 10:29-31-**p. 1088**; 1 Corinthians 3:10-15-**p. 1243**

RICHES - see MONEY, POOR, WEALTH

RIGHTEOUSNESS - the state of being perfect, without sin
attribute of God, Psalm 7-**p. 598**; Jeremiah 23:1-6-**p. 832**
rewarded by God, "Never Abandoned"-**p. 617**
from God, "Luther's Gateway"-**p. 1223**
by faith, "What God Looks For"-**p. 39**; "The Benefits of Faith"-**p. 613**; "Righteous by Faith"-**p. 998**; Romans 4:6-8-**p. 1226**; Galatians 2:15-21-**p. 1271**; Philippians 3:7-11-**p. 1288**
goal of Christian life, Matthew 6:25-34-**p. 1039**; 1 Timothy 6:11-16-**p. 1309**; 1 Peter 2:24-25-**p. 1347**

ROCK
God as, Deuteronomy 32:1-4-**p. 245**; Psalm 18-**p. 604**; Isaiah 26-**p. 760**
Peter as, Matthew 16:16-20-**p. 1053**; John 1:35-42-**p. 1144**
Christ as, 1 Corinthians 10:1-4-**p. 1249**; 1 Peter 2:1-10-**p. 1346**

ROME - capital of the Roman empire; ruled Palestine during the time of Christ; a church was started here
Paul travels to, "Rome at Last"-**p. 1217**; Acts 27:1-28:31-**p. 1217**
letter (Romans) to church in, "A Most Demanding Audience"-**p. 1221**
treatment of Christians in, "Christians and the Empire"-**p. 1236**

RUTH - Moabite woman who married Boaz and became an ancestor of Jesus
character profile, "Character Counts"-**p. 310**
ethnic background, "The Worst of Times"-**p. 309**
friendship with her mother-in-law, "A Rare Bond of Love"-**p. 307**
in Jesus' genealogy, Matthew 1:5-**p. 1033**

S

SABBATH - a day of worship and rest; traditionally Saturday for Jews
to be kept holy, Exodus 20:8-11-**p. 107**; Ezekiel 20:1-29-**p. 895**
laws concerning, Exodus 31:14-15-**p. 119**; Leviticus 23:1-3-**p. 157**
made for people, Mark 2:23-3:6-**p. 1076**
symbol of eternal rest, Hebrews 4:1-11-**p. 1327**

SACRIFICE - offering of something valuable to God
Cain's and Abel's, Genesis 4:1-5-**p. 29**
Noah's, Genesis 8:20-22-**p. 33**
Abraham's, Genesis 12:1-11-**p. 36**; 22:1-19-**p. 47**
prescribed, Leviticus 1-7-**p. 132**
offered as representative, "The One for the Many"-**p. 134**
types of, "The Reason for Sacrifice"-**p. 136**
choice of, "The Very Best for God"-**p. 157**
Christ as, Isaiah 53-**p. 789**; Hebrews 10-**p. 1332**

our lives as, Romans 12:1-2-**p. 1235**; "A Better Sacrifice"-**p. 619**
of praise, "Sacrifice of Praise"-**p. 1337**

SADDUCEES - a small but powerful Jewish sect in Christ's time; denied life after death
Jesus warns against, Matthew 16:1-12-**p. 1053**
Jesus confronts, Mark 12:18-23-**p. 1091**
opposed early church, Acts 4:1-22-**p. 1182**; 5:17-42-**p. 1184**
opposed Paul, Acts 23:1-11-**p. 1212**

Salvation -deliverance from danger or evil; especially deliverance from all that separates people from God (see also CONVERSION, JUSTIFICATION, REPENTANCE)

available to all, "Who Can Be Saved?"-**p. 792**; Romans 10:1-13-**p. 1233**
marked for, "The Saving Mark"-**p. 886**
Jesus' mission of, Luke 19:1-10-**p. 1130**
through faith, Acts 16:16-34-**p. 1202**
to be completed at end of time, Romans 5:6-11-**p. 1228**
by grace, Ephesians 2:1-10-**p. 1278**; Titus 3:3-8-**p. 1318**

SAMARITAN - an inhabitant of Samaria; a people held in contempt by the Jews
origin of, "Scorched-Earth Policy"-**p. 438**
conflict with returned exiles, Ezra 4-5-**p. 522**; Nehemiah 4-6-**p. 535**
parable of the good, Luke 10:25-37-**p. 1119**
and the Jews, "Bridging Differences"-**p. 1147**
woman with Jesus, John 4:1-42-**p. 1147**

SAMSON - one of the last judges of Israel; a Nazirite known for his physical strength
character profile, "Samson: A Weakness for Women"-**p. 296**
life of, Judges 13-16-**p. 295**
and Delilah, Judges 16-**p. 298**; "Samson: A Weakness for Women"-**p. 296**
death of, "Bring the House Down"-**p. 300**

SAMUEL - last of the judges of Israel
character profile, "Faithful Leadership"-**p. 321**
his early years, 1 Samuel 1:1-3:21-**p. 314**
as a prophet, "Still a Boy"-**p. 317**
leads Israel, 1 Samuel 5:1-8:22-**p. 318**
with Saul, 1 Samuel 9:1-15:35-**p. 321**
anoints David, 1 Samuel 16:1-13-**p. 331**
his death, 1 Samuel 25:1-**p. 342**
man of faith, Hebrews 11:32-**p. 1335**

SANCTIFICATION - act of God by which a believer conforms more and more to the image of Christ (see also HOLY)
Jesus' prayer for, John 17:17-19-**p. 1169**
possible only in Christ, 1 Corinthians 1:1-2-**p. 1242**; 1 Thessalonians 5:16-24-**p. 1299**
by pressing on, Philippians 3:12-4:1-**p. 1288**
Christ's power in, 2 Peter 1:3-11-**p. 1352**

SANHEDRIN - highest Jewish court during Roman times (also referred to as Council)
limits to power, "Appeal for a Death Penalty"-**p. 1097**
Jesus before, Matthew 26:57-68-**p. 1067**; John 18-**p. 1169**
apostles before, Acts 4:1-22-**p. 1182**; 5:17-42-**p. 1184**
Paul before, Acts 23:1-11-**p. 1212**

SARAH – wife of Abraham; gave birth to Isaac in her 90s
character profile, *"Who's Laughing?"* – **p. 42**
life of, Genesis 11:29–12:20 – **p. 36**; 16:1–18:15 – **p. 40**; 21:1–21 – **p. 46**; *"The Women of Genesis"* – **p. 57**
death and burial of, Genesis 23:1–20 – **p. 48**

SATAN – the enemy of God; also called the devil, Beelzebul
tempts Eve, Genesis 3 – **p. 27**
restrained by God, *"The Extent of Satan's Power"* – **p. 560**
torments Job, Job 1–2 – **p. 560**
metaphor for, *"Fall of the Morning Star"* – **p. 751**
our accuser, Zechariah 3 – **p. 1011**
tempts Jesus, Matthew 4:1–11 – **p. 1036**
father of lies, John 8:42–47 – **p. 1156**
resist, *"The Armor of God"* – **p. 1282**; 1 Peter 5:8–11 – **p. 1350**
children of, 1 John 2:28–3:10 – **p. 1357**
war against Christ and the church, Revelation 12 – **p. 1378**
final victory over, Revelation 20 – **p. 1385**

SAUL – the first king of Israel; became extremely jealous of David
character profile, *"Why Saul Was Rejected"* – **p. 330**
early days as king, 1 Samuel 9–15 – **p. 321**
and David, 1 Samuel 16:1–30:31 – **p. 331**
failures of, *"Big Ego"* – **p. 328**; *"Why Saul Was Rejected"* – **p. 330**
as a prophet, *"Out of Control"* – **p. 336**
death of, 1 Samuel 31:1–13 – **p. 348**

SAUL – persecutor of Christians who later was converted and became Paul the missionary (*see also* PAUL)
persecution and conversion of, Acts 9:1–30 – **p. 1190**
name changed to Paul, Acts 13:9 – **p. 1197**

SAVIOR – one who rescues from danger or saves; used in connection with Christ (*see also* SALVATION)
prophecy concerning, Isaiah 59:15–21 – **p. 795**
Jesus as, Acts 4:1–12 – **p. 1182**; 13:13–52 – **p. 1197**

SCAPEGOAT
taking the blame, *"Scapegoat"* – **p. 150**

SECOND COMING – the time when Christ will come again as King
Jesus' teaching on, Matthew 24–25 – **p. 1063**; John 14:1–4 – **p. 1165**; Acts 1:6–8 – **p. 1178**
with resurrection, 1 Corinthians 15:12–28 – **p. 1255**
unexpected, 1 Thessalonians 4:13–5:11 – **p. 1298**
preceded by antichrist, 2 Thessalonians 2 – **p. 1301**
reason for delay of, 2 Peter 3 – **p. 1353**
preoccupation with, *"Preparing for the End"* – **p. 1298**; *"A Patient Who Didn't Follow Orders"* – **p. 1300**; *"A Book Full of Mysteries"* – **p. 1366**
vision of, Revelation 19–20 – **p. 1384**

SECURITY
place of, *"The Hideout"* – **p. 632**
finding, *"Meek Will Inherit"* – **p. 1004**; *"Safe Streets"* – **p. 1014**
in God, Psalm 91 – **p. 652**

SELF-CONTROL
necessary, *"Five Dangerous Responses"* – **p. 715**
an aspect of the Spirit's fruit, Galatians 5:16–26 – **p. 1275**
achieving, *"Athlete in Training"* – **p. 1308**
importance of, *"The Need for Self-Control"* – **p. 1341**

SELFISHNESS – *see* AMBITION

SERMON ON THE MOUNT
words of, Matthew 5–7 – **p. 1036**

SERVANT
servant songs, Isaiah 49:1–6 – **p. 785**; 50:4–9 – **p. 787**; 52:13–53:12 – **p. 789**
Jesus as, Mark 10:35–45 – **p. 1089**; Philippians 2:6–11 – **p. 1286**; 1 Peter 2:18–25 – **p. 1347**
believers as, John 13:1–17 – **p. 1163**; Galatians 5:13–26 – **p. 1275**
Paul as, 1 Corinthians 9:19–23 – **p. 1249**

Sex

God's laws concerning, *"Sex Rules"* – p. 149
in religion, *"Child Sacrifice and Sex"* – p. 152; *"Fertility Gods"* – p. 282; *"Real Prostitution"* – p. 954
joy in, Song of Solomon 1–8 – p. 1239; *"An Intoxicating Love"* – p. 729
leading to trouble, *"Sexual Seduction"* – p. 197; *"Samson: A Weakness for Women"* – p. 296; *"Sin As a Cancer"* – p. 371
adulterous, Proverbs 5 – p. 692; 6:20–7:27 – p. 693
in marriage, Proverbs 5:15–20 – p. 692; 1 Corinthians 7:1–7 – p. 1246
and lust, Matthew 5:27–30 – p. 1037
avoid immoral, 1 Corinthians 6:9–20 – p. 1246; Colossians 3:5–6 – p. 1293
call to purity, 1 Thessalonians 4:1–8 – p. 1297

SHADRACH, MESHACH, AND ABED-NEGO
and Daniel, Daniel 1 – **p. 933**
faith of, *"Whether Rescued or Not"* – **p. 936**
in the fiery furnace, Daniel 3 – **p. 935**

SHAME
consequence of sin, *"Sin and Shame"* – **p. 27**; Ezra 9:6–15 – **p. 528**
Christians need not experience, Psalm 25 – **p. 609**; Psalm 34:1–7 – **p. 615**; Romans 1:16–17 – **p. 1223**; 2 Timothy 1:8–14 – **p. 1312**

SHEOL – *see* DEATH

SHEPHERD
comfort of, Psalm 23 – **p. 608**
God as, Psalm 80:1–4 – **p. 645**; Ezekiel 34 – **p. 913**
bad, Jeremiah 23:1–4 – **p. 832**
parable of, Matthew 18:12–14 – **p. 1055**; Luke 15:3–7 – **p. 1126**
at Jesus' birth, Luke 2:8–20 – **p. 1105**
Jesus as good, John 10:1–21 – **p. 1157**; Hebrews 13:20–21 – **p. 1337**; *"A Modern Shepherd"* – **p. 1158**

SICKNESS – *see* DISEASE, HEALING, PRAYER

SILAS – prophet; co-worker with Paul on his second missionary journey
character profile, *"Singing in Prison"* – **p. 1203**

SIN – (*see also* CONFESSION, EVIL, FORGIVENESS, GUILT)
Adam's and Eve's, Genesis 3 – **p. 27**
unintentional, *"Ignorance Isn't Bliss"* – **p. 134**
against another person, *"Double Jeopardy"* – **p. 137**
far-reaching results, *"Sin As a Cancer"* – **p. 371**
present in everyone, *"Who Seeks God?"* – **p. 602**
confession of, Psalm 32 – **p. 613**; 51 – **p. 626**
symbolized, *"Return to the Void"* – **p. 811**
sexual, *"Two Instances of Evil"* – **p. 957**
God's anger with, Romans 1:18–32 – **p. 1223**; *"More Sin, More Forgiveness?"* – **p. 1228**
dead to, Romans 5:12–6:23 – **p. 1228**
conflict with, Romans 7 – **p. 1229**; *"Inner Struggles"* – **p. 1230**; *"Hidden Dangers"* – **p. 1229**
forgiveness of, 1 John 1:5–2:14 – **p. 1356**

SINAI – name of the mountain where God talked with Moses; also called Mount Horeb
God appeared to Moses at, Exodus 3 – **p. 87**
law given at, Exodus 19 – **p. 105**
worshiping golden calf at, Exodus 32 – **p. 120**
Elijah at, 1 Kings 19:8 – 18 – **p. 410**

SINGING – (see also MUSIC, SONGS)
to the Lord, Ephesians 5:19 – 21 – **p. 1281**; Colossians 3:16 – **p. 1293**

SLAVERY
in Egypt, "Oppressed by Egypt" – **p. 90**
Israel's laws on, "Slave Rights" – **p. 108**
freedom from, Leviticus 25:35 – 55 – **p. 161**; Jeremiah 34:8 – 22 – **p. 846**
to sin, Romans 6:15 – 23 – **p. 1229**; Galatians 4 – **p. 1273**
Paul's advice to slaves, Ephesians 6:5 – 8 – **p. 1282**; Colossians 3:22 – 25 – **p. 1294**; 1 Timothy 6:1 – 2 – **p. 1309**
Paul's advice to slave owner, Ephesians 6:19 – **p. 1282**; Colossians 4:1 – **p. 1294**; "Letter to a Slave Owner" – **p. 1320**
Peter's advice on, 1 Peter 2:18 – 25 – **p. 1347**

SLEEP
peaceful, Psalm 3:5 – **p. 597**
unable to, "Sleepless Nights" – **p. 641**; "Lying in Bed" – **p. 670**

SODOM AND GOMORRAH – cities that God destroyed because of wickedness
Lot saved in, Genesis 18:16 – 19:29 – **p. 42**; "A Catastrophe Sent from God" – **p. 44**
sin of, Ezekiel 16:44 – 52 – **p. 892**

SOLOMON – third and last king of united Israel; son of David and Bathsheba
character profile, see Introduction to 1 Kings – **p. 381**
becomes king, 1 Kings 1:1 – 4:34 – **p. 383**; "A Second Coronation" – **p. 479**
builds temple, 1 Kings 5:1 – 9:9 – **p. 389**
wisdom of, 1 Kings 3:1 – 28 – **p. 387**; 4:29 – 34 – **p. 389**
his wealth, "The Man Who Had Everything" – **p. 349**; "Prosperity under Solomon" – **p. 391**
his personality, "Wise Yet Ruthless" – **p. 387**
God's anger with, 1 Kings 11:1 – 43 – **p. 397**
and his wives, "So Many Women" – **p. 397**
his failures, "Solomon's Peak" – **p. 486**
and the Queen of Sheba, "An Unfounded Rumor" – **p. 489**

SON OF GOD
prophesied, "The Son of God" – **p. 665**
Christ as, Matthew 14:22 – 36 – **p. 1051**
Peter's confession, Matthew 16:13 – 20 – **p. 1053**

SON OF MAN
in Daniel's vision, "A Son of Man" – **p. 943**
Jesus as, "Familiar Title" – **p. 1369**

SONGS
of Moses, Exodus 15:1 – 18 – **p. 100**; "A Story for All Time" – **p. 101**
given to Moses, Deuteronomy 31:19 – 32:43 – **p. 245**; "Mixed Emotions" – **p. 245**
of David, "David's Psalms" – **p. 376**
addressed to God, "Cries from the Heart" – **p. 594**
at the passover, "Psalms of the Last Supper" – **p. 667**
in the New Testament church, Ephesians 5:18 – 20 – **p. 1281**; Colossians 3:15 – 17 – **p. 1293**
in heaven, Revelation 5 – 6 – **p. 1372**

SONS OF GOD
in the Old Testament, "The Sons of God" – **p. 31**; Psalm 82:6 – **p. 647**; "In the Midst of the Rulers'" – **p. 647**

SORROW – (see also COMFORT, DISCOURAGEMENT, GRIEF)
God responds to, Exodus 3:1 – 9 – **p. 87**
symbol of, "Torn Hearts" – **p. 965**
Jesus experiences, Matthew 26:36 – 46 – **p. 1066**

SOUL – the nonphysical element in humans (sometimes called "spirit")
in context of death, Ecclesiastes 12:7 – **p. 728**; Revelation 6:9 – 10 – **p. 1373**
distinguished from spirit, 1 Thessalonians 5:23 – **p. 1299**; Hebrews 4:12 – **p. 1327**
activities of, Deuteronomy 6:1 – 5 – **p. 218**; Psalm 42 – **p. 621**; 103 – **p. 657**; 130 – **p. 677**

SPEECH
power of, "Who Owns Your Lips?" – **p. 601**; "Verbal Dynamite" – **p. 703**
control of, James 3:1 – 12 – **p. 1341**

SPIRIT – see DEMONS, FRUIT OF THE SPIRIT, HOLY SPIRIT

STARVATION
in Jerusalem, "Starving to Death" – **p. 876**

STEALING
command against, Exodus 20:15 – **p. 107**; Ephesians 4:28 – **p. 1281**
laws about, Exodus 22:1 – 15 – **p. 109**; Leviticus 19:11 – 13 – **p. 153**
robbing God, Malachi 3:8 – 10 – **p. 1023**

STEPHEN – the first Christian martyr
character profile, "Dying to Live" – **p. 1186**
chosen as deacon, Acts 6:1 – 7 – **p. 1185**
tried and executed, Acts 6:8 – 8:3 – **p. 1185**

STEWARDSHIP – management and accountability for something that belongs to someone else; especially human stewardship of God's gifts
parable concerning, Matthew 25:14 – 30 – **p. 1064**
faithful, Luke 12:35 – 48 – **p. 1123**; 16:10 – 12 – **p. 1127**
of time, Ephesians 5:15 – 16 – **p. 1281**

SUBMISSION
because of love for Christ, "The Key to Submission" – **p. 1282**
of Christians to each other, Ephesians 5:21 – **p. 1281**
to government, Romans 13:1 – 7 – **p. 1236**; 1 Peter 2:13 – 17 – **p. 1347**

Success

Lot's in Sodom, "A Man of Substance" – **p. 43**
basis for real, "Secret of Success" – **p. 252**
from God, Proverbs 3 – **p. 690**
true, Matthew 5:1 – 12 – **p. 1036**; "God and 'How-to-Succeed' " – **p. 695**
parable concerning, Luke 12:13 – 21 – **p. 1122**
without love, 1 Corinthians 13 – **p. 1252**
from God's perspective, "Not Ashamed" – **p. 1334**

SUFFERING – to endure physical or emotional loss and pain (see also COMFORT, DISCOURAGEMENT, PAIN)
the problem of, Job 1 – 42 – **p. 560**; "When Bad Things Happened to a Good Person" – **p. 558**; "What Not to Say to a Hurting Person" – **p. 564**; "When God Seems Angry" – **p. 571**; "What Job Teaches about Suffering" – **p. 588**; "A Silent Friend Decides to Speak Up" – **p. 581**; "Suffering and Sin" – **p. 1156**
God knows our, Psalm 69 – **p. 636**
God's presence in, Psalm 73 – **p. 639**; "Pain in Redemption" – **p. 842**; "Only Good Things?" – **p. 1231**

without God, *"Total Devastation"* — **p. 964**
with Christ, Romans 8:12 – 17 — **p. 1231**; 2 Corinthians 1:5 – **p. 1258**; 1 Peter 4:12 – 19 — **p. 1349**
compared to eternal glory, *"Worth the Struggle"* — **p. 1231**; 2 Corinthians 4:16 – 18 — **p. 1261**
for Christ, Colossians 1:24 – **p. 1292**; Hebrews 10:32 – 39 – **p. 1333**; Revelation 1 – **p. 1369**
benefits of, *"Waiting It Out"* — **p. 1343**; *"A Word to the Suffering"* — **p. 1344**; *"Radical Shift"* — **p. 1349**
Christ's, 1 Peter 2:13 – 25 – **p. 1347**; *"The Spirits in Prison"* — **p. 1349**
for doing right, 1 Peter 3:8 – 22 – **p. 1347**; 4:12 – 19 – **p. 1349**

SUICIDE — (*see also* JUDAS ISCARIOT, SAUL)
jailer saved from, Acts 16:22 – 36 – **p. 1202**

SWEARING — taking an oath, making a solemn promise (*see also* PROFANITY)
Jesus' teaching on, Matthew 5:33 – 37 – **p. 1037**
of God by himself, Hebrews 6:13 – 15 – **p. 1328**
James's teaching on, James 5:12 – **p. 1343**

SYMBOL
of peace, *"Peace Symbol"* — **p. 33**
of Christ, *"Bronze Snake"* — **p. 192**; *"Last-place Winner"* — **p. 669**; *"Jesus as the Vine"* — **p. 1166**; *"Water, Blood, and Spirit"* — **p. 1360**
of victory, *"Scalps"* — **p. 335**
of humiliation, *"Act of Humiliation"* — **p. 261**; *"Thumbs and Big Toes"* — **p. 281**; *"David's Bad Conscience"* — **p. 340**
of importance, *"The Apple of Your Eye"* — **p. 693**
of evil, *"Gog and Magog"* — **p. 919**
of ineffectiveness, *"Kicking the Oxgoads"* — **p. 1216**
vine and kingdom of God, Psalm 80:8 – 18 – **p. 645**; Isaiah 5:1 – 7 – **p. 741**; John 15:1 – 17 – **p. 1166**
of believers, *"A Play on Words"* — **p. 1346**
in Revelation, *"Strange Creatures"* — **p. 1372**; *"Revelation's Use of Symbols"* — **p. 1376**

T

TABERNACLE — place of worship for Israelites from the time of the desert experience to the completion of the temple when Solomon was king
building instructions, Exodus 25 – 26 – **p. 112**; *"Following Orders"* — **p. 129**
where God dwells, *"A Portable Cathedral"* — **p. 124**
furnishings of, *"Sacred Furniture"* — **p. 126**
during David's reign, *"Two Tabernacles"* — **p. 468**
spiritual, Hebrews 9 – **p. 1331**

TALENTS — *see* GIFTS, STEWARDSHIP

TAXES
Jesus' response to, Matthew 22:15 – 22 – **p. 1061**
Paul's words on, Romans 13:1 – 7 – **p. 1236**

TEMPLE — the Israelite place of worship; the first and most magnificent was built by Solomon
curtain in, *"A Torn Curtain"* — **p. 115**; *"A Temporary Separation"* — **p. 484**; *"A Curtain is Torn"* — **p. 1070**
through many years, *"History of the Temple"* — **p. 390**; *"Between the Temples"* — **p. 516**
limited access, *"Off-limits for People"* — **p. 393**; *"The Temple Destroyed"* — **p. 872**
Solomon's, 1 Kings 5 – 8 – **p. 389**; *"A Man of Blood"* — **p. 472**
God's home, *"Homecoming"* — **p. 648**
opposition to rebuilding, *"Ironic Outcome"* — **p. 524**
rebuilt, Ezra 1 – 6 – **p. 520**; *"The Prophet Who Got Results"* — **p. 1006**; *"Starting Over"* — **p. 1009**; *"Change of Tone"* — **p. 1007**

abuse of, *"A Den of Robbers"* — **p. 815**; *"Detestable Things"* — **p. 885**; *"Drastic Action"* — **p. 1058**; *"Big Business"* — **p. 1090**; John 2:12 – 25 – **p. 1145**
abandoned by God, *"Good-bye, God"* — **p. 887**
Ezekiel's vision of, Ezekiel 40 – 43 – **p. 920**; *"The Turning Point"* — **p. 912**; *"Seeing the New Temple"* — **p. 922**; *"The Glory Returns"* — **p. 924**; *"Taking Measurements"* — **p. 921**
Jesus' body as, John 2:12 – 22 – **p. 1145**
church as, 1 Corinthians 3:16 – 17 – **p. 1243**; 2 Corinthians 6:16 – **p. 1262**; Ephesians 2:18 – 22 – **p. 1279**
heavenly, Hebrews 8:1 – 12 – **p. 1330**; Revelation 21:22 – **p. 1387**

Temptation —something that tests a person's righteousness and strength of character

of Adam and Eve, Genesis 3 – **p. 27**
prayer about, Matthew 6:13 – **p. 1038**
of Jesus, Luke 4:1 – 13 – **p. 1107**; *"Words for the Devil"* — **p. 220**
a way out, 1 Corinthians 10:12 – 13 – **p. 1250**; Hebrews 2:17 – 18 – **p. 1326**; 4:15 – 16 – **p. 1327**
resist, Ephesians 6:10 – 20 – **p. 1282**; *"Bad Models"* — **p. 1365**
origin of, James 1:13 – 18 – **p. 1339**

TEN COMMANDMENTS — the moral laws given to Moses by God
Moses receives, Exodus 19 – 20 – **p. 105**
Moses repeats, Deuteronomy 5 – **p. 217**
Jesus enlarges, Matthew 5 – 7 – **p. 1036**
summary of, Matthew 22:37 – 40 – **p. 1061**; Romans 13:8 – 10 – **p. 1236**

THANKFULNESS
for God's care, Psalm 30 – **p. 611**; 136 – **p. 679**
Paul's, Ephesians 1:15 – 23 – **p. 1277**; Philippians 1:3 – 8 – **p. 1285**; 4:10 – 20 – **p. 1288**; Colossians 1:3 – 7 – **p. 1291**
express, Psalm 100 – **p. 656**; Colossians 3:15 – 17 – **p. 1293**; 1 Thessalonians 5:18 – **p. 1299**

THESSALONICA
Paul's ministry to, *"What Made Paul Successful?"* — **p. 1295**; *"A Patient Who Didn't Follow Orders"* — **p. 1300**

THOMAS — one of the 12 disciples, often called "Doubting Thomas"
character profile, *"Honest Questions"* — **p. 1165**
courage of, John 11:1 – 16 – **p. 1159**
doubt of, John 20:19 – 31 – **p. 1173**

TIME
God's use of, *"God Takes Time"* — **p. 26**
our use of, Ephesians 5:15 – **p. 1281**; Colossians 4:5 – **p. 1294**
for everything, Ecclesiastes 3:1 – 8 – **p. 722**

TIMOTHY — Paul's helper on missionary journeys; while still a young man he took on the responsibilities of guiding the church in Ephesus
character profile, see Introduction to 1 Timothy – **p. 718**
with Paul, Acts 16:1 – 5 – **p. 1201**; 20:1 – 4 – **p. 1208**; Philippians 2:19 – 24 – **p. 1287**; *"The Hardest Job"* — **p. 1304**
sent to Corinth, 1 Corinthians 4:14 – 17 – **p. 1245**
letters to, 1 and 2 Timothy – **p. 1304, 1311**
his calling, *"Timothy's Calling"* — **p. 1306**
successor to Paul, *"Passing the Torch"* — **p. 1311**

TITHE — a tenth of one's income that is given to God
Abraham's, Genesis 14:20 – **p. 39**; Hebrews 7:1 – 10 – **p. 1329**

U

Unity

V

W

Y

Z

The Student Bible, NASB

Notes written and edited by *Philip Yancey* and *Tim Stafford*

Project management and editorial by *Donna Huisjen*

Interior design by *Sharon Wright, Belmont, MI*

Cover design by *Steve Allen, Snellville, GA*

Interior proofreading by *Peachtree Editorial and Proofreading Service, Peachtree City, GA*

Interior typesetting by *Auto-Graphics, Inc., Pomona, CA*

Printing and binding by *R.R. Donnelley & Sons, Crawfordsville, IN*

Map 1: **WORLD OF THE PATRIARCHS**

Caspian Sea

CAUCASUS MTS.

▲ Mt. Ararat

Lake Urmia

Black Sea

Aegean Sea

Troy

Mycenae

Knossos

Caphtor
(Crete)

Kittim
(Cyprus)

The Great Sea

Hattusha

HITTITES

TAURUS MTS.

Carchemish

Aleppo
Ebla

Ugarit

Byblos

PADDAN ARAM
Haran

Tadmor

Mari

Damascus

Hazor

Megiddo
Dothan
Shechem
Bethel
Ai
Beersheba
Gerar
Hebron
Zoar?
Kadesh Barnea

EGYPTIANS

SINAI

Zoan
(Tanis)

On
(Heliopolis)
Succoth

Noph
(Memphis)

Nile R.

Red
Sea

ARABIA

Nineveh

Asshur

Nuzi

BABYLONIANS

Babylon

Nippur
Erech
(Uruk)
Ur

Persian
Gulf

Possible location
of Biblical "Ur of
the Chaldeans,"
where Abraham's
migration began

Possible location of
Sodom and
Gomorrah

→ Abraham's journeys

0   100   200   300 mi.
0 100 200 300 400 km.

© 1986 The Zondervan Corporation

© 1986 The Zondervan Corporation

Map 3: **EXODUS AND CONQUEST OF CANAAN**

Area controlled by ancient Israel
Probable route of wandering in the Sinai
Entry into and conquest of Canaan
× Battle

The Great Sea

Lake Menzaleh

EGYPT
Rameses
GOSHEN
Pithom?
Succoth
DESERT OF SHUR
Great Bitter Lake
On (Heliopolis)
Noph (Memphis)

Besor Br.
Wadi of Egypt

Kedesh
Hazor
Merom BASHAN
Sea of Kinnereth
Mt. Tabor
Edrei ×
Mt. Gilboa
Shechem
Shiloh
Bethel Gilgal? Abel
Gibeon Shittim
Beth Horon Ai AMMON
Jarmuth Jericho Heshbon
Azekah Jerusalem Mt. Nebo
Libnah? Jahaz?
Lachish Hebron Dibon
Eglon? Makkedah?
Debir? MOAB
Beersheba Arnon R.

DESERT OF ZIN
Iye Abarim?
Zered Br.
Oboth?
Punon
Kadesh Barnea

DESERT OF PARAN
Ezion Geber

Marah?
SINAI
Elim?
Dophkah?
DESERT OF SIN
Hazeroth?
Rephidim?
Mt. Sinai (traditional location)

MIDIAN

Nile River

Red Sea

0   25   50   75 mi.
0   25 50 75   100 km.
© 1986 The Zondervan Corporation

Map 4: LAND OF THE TWELVE TRIBES

Cities of refuge
Other cities

Damascus
ARAM
Mt. Hermon
Litani R.
Ijon
Pharpar R.
Tyre
Dan
ASHER
NAPHTALI
Kedesh
Hazor
Acco
Cabul
Merom
EAST
Rimmon
The Great Sea
ZEBULUN
Mt. Tabor
Sea of Kinnereth
Golan
Ashtaroth
Yarmuk R.
Dor
Mt. Moreh
MANASSEH
Edrei
Megiddo
ISSACHAR
Taanach
Jezreel
Beth Shan
Ramoth Gilead
MANASSEH
Jabesh Gilead
Samaria
Tirzah
Mt. Ebal
Jabbok R.
Mahanaim?
Mt. Gerizim
Shechem
Succoth
Aphek
Joppa
Shiloh
Jazer?
DAN
EPHRAIM
GAD
Rabbah
Mizpah
Bethel
AMMON
Gezer
Gibeon
BENJAMIN
Gilgal
Ashdod
Kiriath Jearim
Jericho
Heshbon
Bezer
Ekron
Jerusalem
Mt. Nebo
Ashkelon
Gath
Beth Shemesh
Bethlehem
REUBEN
Eglon?
Lachish
Hebron
Gaza
JUDAH
En Gedi
Salt Sea
Dibon
Gerar
Ziklag
Aroer
Arnon
Beersheba
MOAB
Hormah
SIMEON
Zered Br.
EDOM

0   10   20   30 mi.
0 10 20 30 40 km.

© 1986 The Zondervan Corporation

Map 5: **KINGDOM OF DAVID AND SOLOMON**

Aleppo

Euphrates R.

Tiphsah

HAMATH

Kittim (Cyprus)

Hamath

Qatna

Arvad

Kadesh

Tadmor

The
Great Sea

Gebal
(Byblos)

Berothai

ARAMEAN
DESERT

Litani R.

PHOENICIA

Damascus

Sidon

Mt. Hermon

Tyre

Dan

ARAM

Kedesh

Hazor

Acco

Sea of
Kinnereth

Megiddo

Beth
Shan

Ashtaroth

EASTERN DESERT

Taanach

Mt. Gilboa

Edrei

Ramoth Gilead

Jordan R.

Mahanaim?

Shechem

AMMON

Joppa

Gezer

Rabbah

PHILISTIA

Gibeah

Ashdod

Gath

Medeba

Jerusalem

Gaza

Hebron

Ziklag

Salt
Sea

Beersheba

Kir Hareseth

Tamar

MOAB

Wadi of Egypt

EDOM

Kadesh Barnea

Saul's kingdom

David and Solomon's kingdom

Territory under Solomon's control

SINAI

Ezion Geber

0   20   40   60   80 mi.

0 20 40 60 80 100 km.

Gulf of
Aqaba

© 1986 The Zondervan Corporation

Map 6: PROPHETS IN ISRAEL AND JUDAH

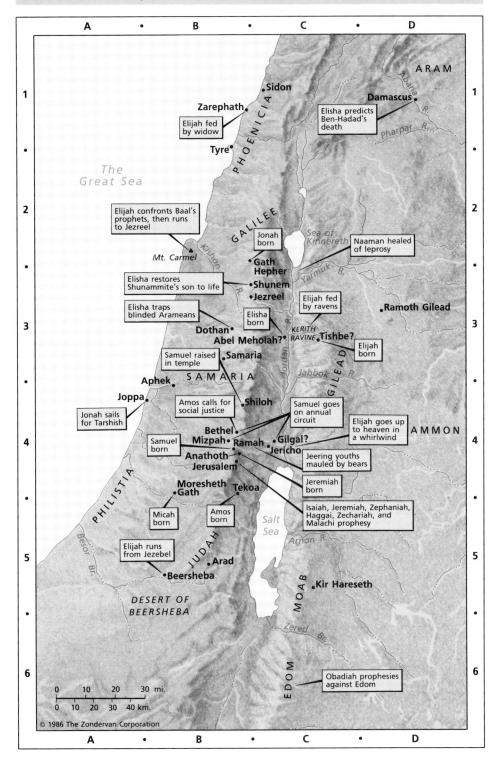

ARAM

Sidon

Zarephath

Elijah fed by widow

Damascus

Elisha predicts Ben-Hadad's death

Pharpar R.

Abana R.

Tyre

PHOENICIA

The Great Sea

Elijah confronts Baal's prophets, then runs to Jezreel

GALILEE

Mt. Carmel

Kishon

Jonah born

Sea of Kinnereth

Naaman healed of leprosy

Gath Hepher

Elisha restores Shunammite's son to life

Shunem

Jezreel

Yarmuk R.

Elijah fed by ravens

Ramoth Gilead

Elisha traps blinded Arameans

Elisha born

KERITH RAVINE

Tishbe?

Elijah born

Dothan

Abel Meholah?

Samuel raised in temple

Samaria

SAMARIA

Jabbok R.

GILEAD

Aphek

Joppa

Jonah sails for Tarshish

Amos calls for social justice

Shiloh

Samuel goes on annual circuit

Elijah goes up to heaven in a whirlwind

AMMON

Bethel

Samuel born

Mizpah

Ramah

Gilgal?

Jericho

Jordan R.

Anathoth

Jerusalem

Jeering youths mauled by bears

Jeremiah born

Moresheth

Gath

Tekoa

Isaiah, Jeremiah, Zephaniah, Haggai, Zechariah, and Malachi prophesy

Micah born

Amos born

Salt Sea

Arnon R.

PHILISTIA

Besor Br.

JUDAH

Elijah runs from Jezebel

Arad

Beersheba

MOAB

Kir Hareseth

DESERT OF BEERSHEBA

Zered Br.

EDOM

Obadiah prophesies against Edom

0 10 20 30 mi.

0 10 20 30 40 km.

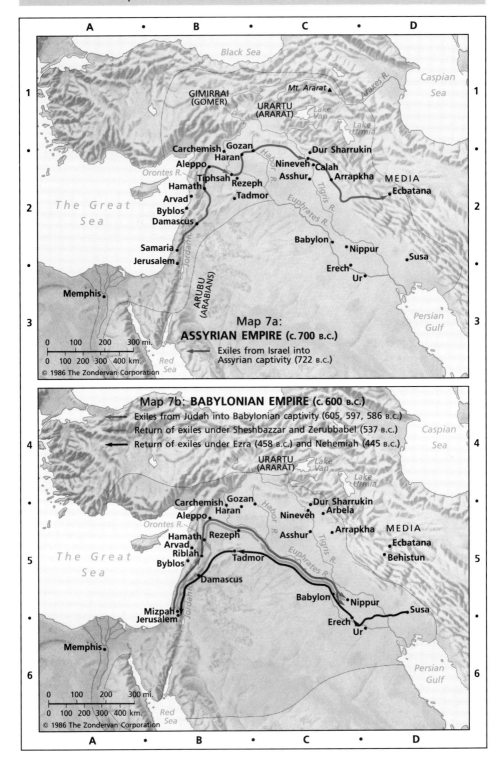

Map 7a:
ASSYRIAN EMPIRE (c. 700 b.c.)

0   100   200   300 mi.

0 100 200 300 400 km.
© 1986 The Zondervan Corporation

Exiles from Israel into
Assyrian captivity (722 b.c.)

Map 7b: **BABYLONIAN EMPIRE (c. 600 b.c.)**

Exiles from Judah into Babylonian captivity (605, 597, 586 b.c.)
Return of exiles under Sheshbazzar and Zerubbabel (537 b.c.)
Return of exiles under Ezra (458 b.c.) and Nehemiah (445 b.c.)

0   100   200   300 mi.

0 100 200 300 400 km.
© 1986 The Zondervan Corporation

Map 8: JERUSALEM IN JESUS' TIME

A • B • C • D

— City walls in Jesus' time
- - - "City of David"
— The "Old City" (surviving walls, built in 16th century)

KIDRON VALLEY

Garden Tomb (alternate site of crucifixion)

Second Wall

Sheep Pool (Bethesda Pool)

Fish Gate

Israel Pool

Antonia Fortress

Sheep Gate

Jesus arrested

Preaching

Gethsemane

Golden Gate

Crucifixion and burial

Inner Court

Altar

Gate Beautiful

Golgotha (traditional site)

TEMPLE

Court of Women

Mt. of Olives

TYROPOEON VALLEY

SECOND QUARTER

Towers' Pool

Court of Men

Court of the Gentiles

Clearing of temple

Gennath Gate

First Wall

Bridge (Wilson's Arch)

Royal Porch

Pinnacle of the Temple (traditional location)

Tower of Phasael

Tower of Hippicus

Stairs (Robinson's Arch)

Huldah Gates

Herod's Palace

Tower of Mariamne

Herod Antipas's Palace

Valley Gate

UPPER CITY

Theater

Serpent's Pool

Jesus before high priests; Peter's denial

TYROPOEON VALLEY

Gihon Spring

KIDRON VALLEY

High Priest's House

ESSENE QUARTER

LOWER CITY
(Possibly part of Jerusalem in Jesus' time)

Hezekiah's Tunnel

Upper Room (traditional site)

Last Supper

Water Gate

Pool of Siloam

Essene Gate

HINNOM VALLEY

0   0.1   0.2 mi.

0   0.1   0.2   0.3 km.

© 1986 The Zondervan Corporation

A • B • C • D

Map 9: JESUS' MINISTRY

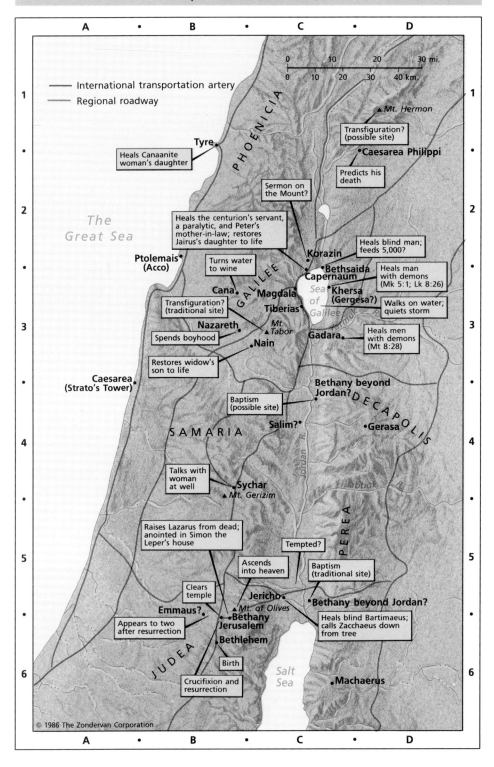

A • B • C • D

1 International transportation artery
  Regional roadway

0   10   20   30 mi.
0 10 20 30 40 km.

PHOENICIA

Mt. Hermon

Transfiguration?
(possible site)

Caesarea Philippi

Tyre

Heals Canaanite
woman's daughter

Predicts his
death

Sermon on
the Mount?

The
Great Sea

Heals the centurion's servant,
a paralytic, and Peter's
mother-in-law; restores
Jairus's daughter to life

Heals blind man;
feeds 5,000?

Korazin

Ptolemais
(Acco)

Turns water
to wine

Bethsaida

Capernaum

Heals man
with demons
(Mk 5:1; Lk 8:26)

GALILEE

Cana

Magdala

Sea
of
Galilee

Khersa
(Gergesa?)

Walks on water;
quiets storm

Transfiguration?
(traditional site)

Tiberias

Nazareth

Mt.
Tabor

Gadara

Heals men
with demons
(Mt 8:28)

Spends boyhood

Nain

Restores widow's
son to life

Caesarea
(Strato's Tower)

Bethany beyond
Jordan?

DECAPOLIS

Baptism
(possible site)

SAMARIA

Salim?

Gerasa

Jordan R.

Talks with
woman
at well

Sychar

Mt. Gerizim

Jabbok R.

PEREA

Raises Lazarus from dead;
anointed in Simon the
Leper's house

Tempted?

Ascends
into heaven

Baptism
(traditional site)

Clears
temple

Jericho

Bethany beyond Jordan?

Emmaus?

Mt. of Olives

Bethany

Heals blind Bartimaeus;
calls Zacchaeus down
from tree

Appears to two
after resurrection

Jerusalem

Bethlehem

JUDEA

Birth

Salt
Sea

Crucifixion and
resurrection

Machaerus

© 1986 The Zondervan Corporation

A • B • C • D

Map 10: APOSTLES' EARLY TRAVELS

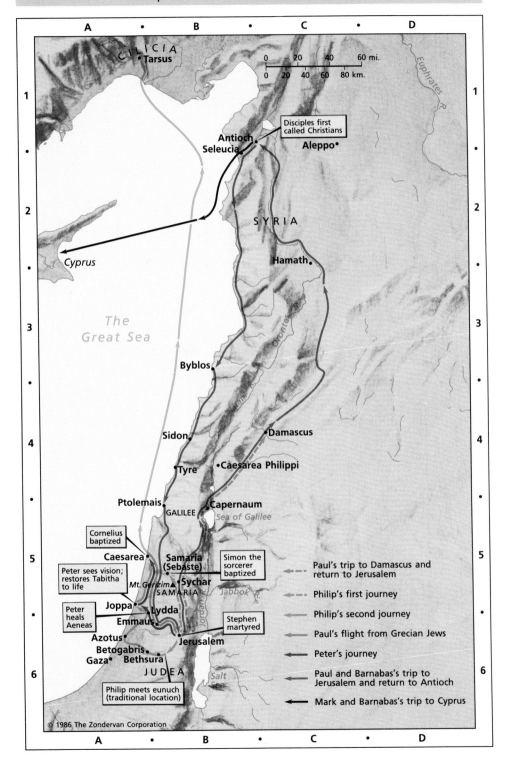

CILICIA
•Tarsus

0   20   40   60 mi.
0 20 40 60 80 km.

Antioch
Seleucia

Disciples first
called Christians

Aleppo•

SYRIA

Cyprus

Hamath•

The
Great Sea

Byblos•

Damascus

Sidon•

Tyre•

•Caesarea Philippi

Ptolemais•

GALILEE •Capernaum
Sea of Galilee

Cornelius
baptized

Caesarea• Samaria
(Sebaste)

Simon the
sorcerer
baptized

Paul's trip to Damascus and
return to Jerusalem

Peter sees vision;
restores Tabitha
to life

Mt. Gerizim▲ •Sychar
SAMARIA

Philip's first journey

Philip's second journey

Peter
heals
Aeneas

Joppa• •Lydda
Emmaus•

Stephen
martyred

Paul's flight from Grecian Jews

Azotus•

Jerusalem•

Peter's journey

Betogabris•
Gaza• •Bethsura

Paul and Barnabas's trip to
Jerusalem and return to Antioch

JUDEA

Mark and Barnabas's trip to Cyprus

Philip meets eunuch
(traditional location)

© 1986 The Zondervan Corporation

A • B • C • D

GALLIA

GERMANIA

DALMATIA

ITALY

Adriatic Sea

Corsica

1

Rome
Forum of Appius
Three Taverns
Puteoli

MACE

Bere

2

Sardinia

Tyrrhenian
Sea

EPIRUS

Rhegium

Ionian
Sea

AC

3

Sicily
Syracuse

NUMIDIA

Malta

AFRICA

4

The

TRIPOLITANIA

5

← First Missionary Journey (A.D. 46–48)

← Second Missionary Journey (A.D. 49–52)

← Third Missionary Journey (A.D. 53–57)

← Trip to Rome (A.D. 59–60)

6

© 1986 The Zondervan Corporation

A • B • C • D

Map 12: THE WORLD TODAY

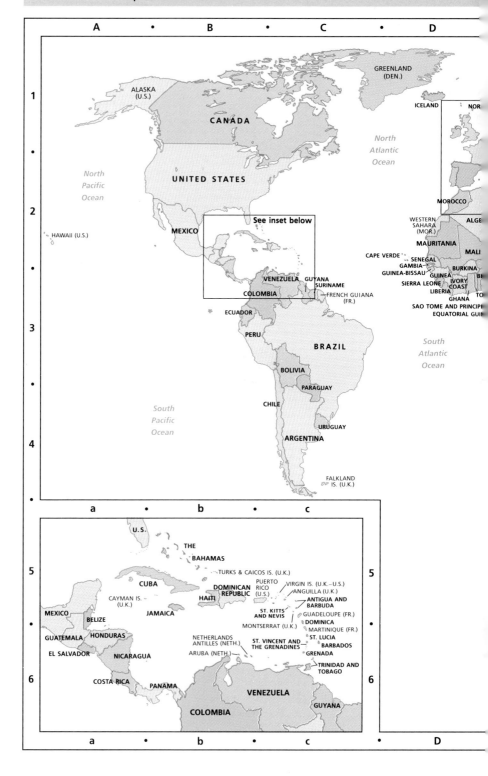